"No other . . .
a pleasure . . .

". . . Excellently organized for the casual traveler who is looking for a mix of recreation and cultural insight."
Washington Post

★ ★ ★ ★ ★ (5-star rating) "Crisply written and remarkably personable. Cleverly organized so you can pluck out the minutest fact in a moment. Satisfyingly thorough."
Réalités

"The information they offer is up-to-date, crisply presented but far from exhaustive, the judgments knowledgeable but not opinionated."   *New York Times*

"The individual volumes are compact, the prose succinct, and the coverage up-to-date and knowledgeable . . . The format is portable and the index admirably detailed."
John Barkham Syndicate

". . . An abundance of excellent directions, diversions, and facts, including perspectives and getting-ready-to-go advice — succinct, detailed, and well organized in an easy-to-follow style."   *Los Angeles Times*

"They contain an amount of information that is truly staggering, besides being surprisingly current."
Detroit News

"These guides address themselves to the needs of the modern traveler demanding precise, qualitative information . . . Upbeat, slick, and well put together."
Dallas Morning News

". . . Attractive to look at, refreshingly easy to read, and generously packed with information."   *Miami Herald*

"These guides are as good as any published, and much better than most."   *Louisville* (Kentucky) *Times*

Stephen Birnbaum Travel Guides

Canada
Caribbean, Bermuda, and the Bahamas
Disneyland
Europe
Europe for Business Travelers
Florida for Free
France
Great Britain
Hawaii
Ireland
Italy
Mexico
South America
Spain and Portugal
United States
USA for Business Travelers
Walt Disney World

CONTRIBUTING EDITORS

Judith Harris Ajello, Duncan Anderson, Melvin Benarde, Gunnar Berj, Patricia Bjaaland, Barbara Bowers, Paolo Braghieri, Mark Brayne, John Buskin, Ron Butler, Ann Campbell-Lord, Linda Carreaga, Rik Cate, Stacey Chanin, Vinod Chhabra, Roger Collis, Charles Cupic, Karen Cure, Stephanie Curtis, Jeff Davidson, Linda Davidson, Martha de la Cal, Claire Devener, Thomas S. Dyman, Bjorn Edlund, Bonnie Edwards, Donna Evleth, Jackie Fierman, Brenda Fine, Ted Folke, Mary Ann Castranova Fusco, Joan Gannij, Fradley Garner, Lois Gelatt, Norman Gelb, Jerry Gerber, Andrew Gillman, Mireille Giuliano, Agnes Gottlieb, Patricia Graves, Petar Hadji-Ristic, Jessica Harris, Elizabeth Healy, Jack Herbert, Marilyn Bruno Herrera, Ritva Hildebrandt, Brian Hill, Connie Hill, Elva Horvath, David Howley, Julian Isherwood, Bruce Johnston, Mark Kalish, Anne Kalosh, Leslie F. Kauffmann, Virginia Kelley, André Leduc, Richard Lee, Alan Levy, Theodora Lurie, Sirrka Makelainen, Thomas C. Marinelli, Carole Martin, J. P. MacBean, Virginia McCune, Erica Meltzer, Diane Melville, Anne Millman, Tamara K. Mitchell, Jack Monet, Cara Morris, Martina Norelli, Ottar Odland, Carol Offen, Pat Patricof, A. E. Pedersen, Clare Pedrick, Samuel Perkins, Susan Pierres, Fred Poe, John Preston, Patricia Tunison Preston, Colin Pringle, Carol Reed, Allen Rokach, Peter Rubie, Margery Safir, Jerrold L. Schecter, Patrick Schultz, George Semmler, Hella Sessoms, Frank Shiell, Janet Steinberg, Janet Stobbart, Phyllis Stoller, Bruce Thorstad, Nancy Patton Van Zant, Betty Vaughn, Florence Vidal, Paul Wade, Richard Walbleigh, Dennis Weber, David Wickers, Mark Williams, Jennifer Wright, Derrick Young, Eleni Ziogas, Sonya Zalubowski, Kristin Zimmerman

DIVERSIONS EDITORS
Jeff Davidson, Linda Davidson

SYMBOLS
Gloria McKeown

MAPS
General Cartography Inc.

COVER
Robert Anthony

A Stephen Birnbaum Travel Guide

Birnbaum's
EUROPE
1990

Stephen Birnbaum
Alexandra Mayes Birnbaum
EDITORS

Lois Spritzer
EXECUTIVE EDITOR

Laura Brengelman
MANAGING EDITOR

Kristin Moehlmann
John Storch
Senior Editors

Catherine J. Langevin
Julie Quick
Associate Editors

Stephen Coleman
Assistant Editor

HOUGHTON MIFFLIN COMPANY / BOSTON   1989

This book is published by special arrangement
with Eric Lasher and Maureen Lasher.

ISBN: 0-395-51149-6 (pbk.)
ISSN: 0749-2561 (Stephen Birnbaum Travel Guides)
ISSN: 0883-2498

Printed in the United States of America

WP 10 9 8 7 6 5 4 3 2 1

Contents

GETTING READY TO GO

All the practical travel data you need to plan your vacation down to the final detail.

When and How to Go

Preparing

On the Road

Sources and Resources

FACTS IN BRIEF

A compilation of pertinent tourist information such as entry requirements and customs, sports, language, currency, clothing requirements, and more for 32 European countries.

THE CITIES

Thorough, qualitative guides to each of the 34 cities most often visited by vacationers and businesspeople. Each section, a comprehensive report of the city's most appealing attractions and amenities, is designed to be used on the spot. Directions and recommendations are immediately accessible because each guide is presented in a consistent form.

DIVERSIONS

A selective guide to 21 active and cerebral vacations including the places to pursue them where your quality of experience is likely to be highest.

DIRECTIONS

Europe's most spectacular routes and roads, most arresting natural wonders, most magnificent châteaux and castles, all organized into over 100 specific driving tours.

A Word from the Editor

There is no record of the specific guidebook that Hannibal and his Carthaginian hordes used to chart the route for their elephant trek through the Alps, but you can be sure that they had the help of at least a rudimentary work describing the basics of European geography. For all we know, it may even have included notes on a reliable inn, where the grog was always warm and spicy. Indeed, guides to Europe have existed literally for centuries, and one might logically ask why another one is necessary amid this plenty.

Our answer is that the nature of European travel — and even the nature of the travelers themselves — has changed dramatically in recent years. As a matter of fact, travel has probably altered and adjusted its rules and regimens more in the last generation than at any time since Marco Polo began all this international marauding. For nearly 2,000 years, travel on the European continent was an extremely elaborate undertaking, one that required extensive, tedious planning. Even as recently as the late 1950s, a person who had actually been to Europe could dine out on his or her experiences for years — assuming he or she didn't bring along all the trip photographs — since such adventures carried considerable cachet and usually were the province of the privileged alone.

With the advent of commercial jet air travel in the late 1950s, however, and of increased-capacity, wide-body aircraft during the mid-1960s, travel to and through Europe became extremely common. In fact, during 3 decades of nearly constant inflation, airfares may be the only commodity in the world that have largely gone down in price. And as a result, international travel is now well within the budgets of mere mortals.

Attitudes as well as costs have changed significantly. Beginning with the so-called flower children of the 1960s, international travel lost much of its aura of mystery. Whereas their parents might have chosen (at least initially) a superficial sampling of Europe — a 14-countries-in-14-days tour, for example — these young people, motivated by wildly inexpensive "youth fares" and the desire to light on that spot on the planet most geographically distant from their parents, simply picked up and settled in some obscure corner of Europe for an indefinite stay. While living as inexpensively as possible, they usually adopted the local language and lifestyle with great gusto and generally immersed themselves in things European.

Thus began the modern explosion of travel to and through Europe. Over the years, the development of inexpensive charter flights and packages fueled and sharpened the new American interest in, and appetite for, more extensive exploration of the Continent.

Now, as we move into the 1990s, those same young people who were in the forefront of the modern travel revolution have undeniably aged. While it may be impolite to point out that they are probably very close to their 40th birthdays (and mostly firmly enmeshed in Establishment activities), their original zeal for travel remains unsated. For them it's hardly news that the way to get to Switzerland is to head for France, hang a left, and then wait for snow-capped mountains to appear. Such experienced and knowledgeable travelers have decided precisely where they want to go and are more often searching for ideas and insights to expand their already sophisticated travel consciousness. And — reverting to their youthful instincts and habits — they are after a deeper understanding and fuller assimilation of the European milieu. Typically, they visit single countries (or even cities) several times, and may actually do so more than once in a single year. The generation that is currently succeeding this pioneering band also has accepted travel as one of life's givens, and serenely sets off on holiday to any part of the globe.

Obviously, any European guidebook must keep pace with, and answer, the real needs of today's travelers. That's why we've tried to create a guide that's specifically organized, written, and edited for this more demanding modern audience, for whom qualitative information is infinitely more desirable than mere quantities of unappraised data. We think that this book, as well as the other guides in our series, represent a new generation of travel guides, ones that are especially responsive to modern needs and interests.

For years, dating back as far as Herr Baedeker, travel guides have tended to be encyclopedic, seemingly much more concerned with demonstrating expertise in geography and history than in any analysis of the sorts of things that genuinely concern a typical tourist. But today, when it is hardly necessary to tell a traveler where London is, it is hard to justify devoting endless guidebook pages to historical perspective. As suggested earlier, it's not impossible that the guidebook reader may have been to Europe nearly as often as the guidebook editor, so it becomes the responsibility of that editor to provide new perceptions and to suggest new directions to make his guide genuinely valuable.

That's exactly what we've tried to do in our series. I think you'll notice a different, more contemporary tone to the text, as well as an organization and focus that are distinctive and more functional. And even a random examination of what follows will demonstrate a substantial departure from the standard guidebook orientation, for we've not only attempted to provide information of a different sort, but we've also tried to present it in a context that makes it particularly accessible.

Needless to say, it's difficult to decide precisely what to include in a guidebook of this size — and what to omit. Early on, we realized that giving up the encyclopedic approach precluded the inclusion of every single route and restaurant, which helped define our overall editorial focus. Similarly, when we discussed the possibility of presenting certain information in other than strict geographical order, we found that the new format enabled us to arrange data in a way that we feel best answers the questions travelers typically ask.

Large numbers of specific questions have provided the real editorial focus for this book. The volume of mail I regularly receive seems to emphasize that modern travelers want very precise information, so we've tried to address these needs and have organized our material in the most responsive way possible. Readers who want to know the best restaurants in Paris or the best beach along the Côte d'Azur will have no trouble whatever extracting that data from this guide.

Travel guides are, above all, reflections of personal taste, and putting one's name on a title page obviously puts one's preferences on the line. But I think I ought to amplify just what "personal" means. I do not believe in the sort of personal guidebook that's a palpable misrepresentation on its face. It is, for example, hardly possible for any single travel writer to visit thousands of restaurants (and nearly as many hotels) in any given year and provide accurate appraisals of each one. And even if it were possible for one human being to survive such an itinerary, it would of necessity have to be done at a dead sprint, and the perceptions derived therefrom would probably be less valid than those of any intelligent individual visiting the same establishments over a period of time. It is, therefore, impossible (especially in an annually revised and updated guidebook *series* such as we offer) to have only one person provide all the data on the entire world.

I also happen to think that such individual orientation is of substantially less value to readers. Visiting a single hotel for just one night or eating one hasty meal in a given restaurant hardly equips anyone to provide appraisals that are of more than passing interest. No amount of doggedly alliterative or oppressively onomatopoeic text can camouflage a technique that is specious on its face. We have, therefore, chosen what I like to describe as the "thee and me" approach to restaurant and hotel appraisal and, to a somewhat more limited degree, to the sites and sights we have included in the other sections of our text. What this really reflects is personal sampling tempered by intelligent counsel from informed local sources, and these additional friends-of-the-editor are almost always residents of the city and/or area about which they have been consulted.

Despite the presence of several editors, a considerable number of writers and researchers, and numerous insightful local correspondents, very precise editing and tailoring keep our text fiercely subjective. So what follows is purposely designed to be the gospel according to Birnbaum, and it represents as much of my own taste and insight as is humanly possible. It is probable, therefore, that if you like your cities distinctive and your mountains uncrowded, prefer small hotels with personality to huge high-rise anonymities, and can't tolerate fresh fish that's been relentlessly overcooked, we're likely to have a long and meaningful relationship. Readers with dissimilar tastes may be less enraptured.

I also should point out something about the person to whom this guidebook is directed. Above all, he or she is a "visitor." This means that such elements as restaurants have been specifically picked to provide the visitor with a representative, enlightening, stimulating, and above all pleasant experience. Since so many extraneous considerations can affect the reception and service accorded a regular restaurant patron, our choices can in no way be construed as a definitive guide to resident dining. We think we've listed all the best places, in various price ranges, but they were chosen with a visitor's viewpoint in mind.

Other evidence of how we've tried to tailor our text to reflect changing travel habits is most apparent in the section we call DIVERSIONS. Where once it was common for travelers to spend a European visit imprisoned by a rigid, cathedral- and museum-seeking itinerary, the emphasis today is more likely to be directed toward pursuing some active pastime or special interest while seeing the surrounding countryside. Such is the amount of perspiration regularly stimulated by today's "leisurely" vacationer that a common by-product of a typical modern holiday is often the need to take another vacation to recover from the first. So we've selected every activity we could reasonably evaluate and organized the material in a way that is especially accessible to activists of either an athletic or cerebral bent. It is no longer necessary, therefore, to wade through a pound or two of extraneous prose just to find the very best golf course or the clearest snorkeling spot within a reasonable radius of your destination.

If there is a single thing that best characterizes the revolution in and evolution of current holiday habits, it is that Americans now consider travel a right rather than a privilege. No longer is a trip to the far corners of the world necessarily a once-in-a-lifetime thing, nor is the idea of visiting exotic, faraway places in the least worrisome. Travel today translates as the enthusiastic desire to sample all of the world's opportunities, to find that elusive quality of experience that is not only enriching but comfortable. For that reason, we've tried to make what follows not only helpful and enlightening, but the sort of welcome companion of which every traveler dreams.

Finally, I should point out that every good travel guide is a living enterprise; that is, no part of this text is cast in bronze. In our annual revisions, we expect to refine, expand, and further hone all our material to serve your travel needs even better. To this end, no contribution is of greater value to us than your personal reaction to what we have written, as well as information reflecting your own experiences while using this book. We earnestly and enthusiastically solicit your comments *and* your opinions and perceptions about places you have recently visited. In this way, we will be able to provide the most current information — including the actual experiences of the travel public — and to make those experiences more readily available to others. So please write to me at 60 E. 42nd St., New York, NY 10165.

I sincerely hope to hear from you.

STEPHEN BIRNBAUM

How to Use This Guide

? A great deal of care has gone into the organization of this guidebook, and we believe it represents a real breakthrough in the presentation of travel material. Our aim has been to create a new, more modern generation of travel books and to make this guide the most useful and practical travel tool available today.

Our text is divided into five basic sections, in order to best present information on every possible aspect of a European vacation. This organization itself should alert you to the vast and varied opportunities available on this continent as well as indicating all the specific, detailed data necessary to plan a trip in Europe. You won't find much of the conventional "quaint villages and beautiful scenery" text in this guide; we've chosen instead to use the available space for more useful and purposeful information. Prospective European itineraries tend to speak for themselves, and with so many diverse travel opportunities, we feel our main job is to explain them and to provide the basic information — how, when, where, how much, and what's best — to allow you to make the most intelligent choices possible.

What follows is a brief summary of our five basic sections and what you can expect to find in each. We believe that you will find both your travel planning and en route enjoyment enhanced by having this book at your side.

GETTING READY TO GO

This mini-encyclopedia of practical travel facts is meant to be a sort of know-it-all companion that provides all the precise information you need to understand how to go about creating a trip to Europe. There are entries on more than two dozen separate topics, including how to travel, what preparations to make before you leave, how to deal with possible emergencies, what to expect in the different countries of Europe, what the trip is likely to cost, and how to avoid prospective problems. The individual entries are specific, realistic, and, where appropriate, cost-oriented.

We expect that you will use this section most in planning your trip, for its ideas and suggestions are intended to facilitate this often confusing time. Entries are intentionally concise, in an effort to get to the meat of the matter with little extraneous prose. This information is further augmented by extensive lists of specific sources from which to obtain even more specialized information, and some suggestions for obtaining travel information on your own.

FACTS IN BRIEF

Here is a compilation of pertinent tourist information, such as entry and customs requirements, languages, currencies, and clothing and climate data on 32 European countries. This section provides easy and immediate access to crucial information to be used at the planning stage as well as on the road.

THE CITIES

Individual reports on the 34 cities most visited by tourists and businesspeople have been researched and written with the help of residents and professional journalists who serve as consultants on their own turf. Useful at the planning stage, THE CITIES is really designed to be used on the spot. Each report offers a short-stay guide within a consistent format: an essay, introducing the city as a historic entity and a contemporary place to live and visit; *At-a-Glance,* a site-by-site survey of the most important (and sometimes most eclectic) sights to see and things to do; *Sources and Resources,* a concise listing of pertinent visitor information, meant to answer myriad potentially pressing questions as they arise — from something as simple as the address of the local tourist office to something more difficult, such as where to find the best nightspot, to see a show, to play tennis, or to get a taxi; and *Best in Town,* our cost-and-quality choices of the best places to eat and sleep on a variety of budgets.

DIVERSIONS

This section is designed to help travelers find the very best locations in which to satisfy their fondest vacation desires, without having to wade through unrelated text. This very selective guide lists the broadest possible range of vacation activities, including all the best places to pursue them.

We start with a list of possibilities that will require some perspiration — sports preferences and other rigorous pursuits — and go on to report on a number of more cerebral and spiritual vacation opportunities. In every case, our suggestion of a particular location — and often our recommendation of a specific resort — is intended to guide you to that special place where the quality of experience is likely to be highest. So whether you opt for golf or tennis, fishing or skiing, Europe's chic-est hotels or most esoteric museums, each entry is the equivalent of a comprehensive checklist of the absolute best.

DIRECTIONS

Here is a series of more than 100 European itineraries, from the greenest counties of Ireland to the most sunlit Greek islands, covering 32 European countries. These itineraries follow Europe's most beautiful routes and roads, past its most spectacular natural wonders, through its most historic cities and countryside. DIRECTIONS is the only section of this book organized geographically, and its itineraries cover the highlights of Great Britain and Ireland and the entire Continent in short, independent segments that describe journeys of 1 to 3 days' duration. Itineraries can be "connected" for longer trips or used individually for short, intensive explorations.

Each entry includes a guide to sightseeing highlights; a qualitative guide to accommodations and food along the road (small inns, pensions, *paradores,* castle hotels, hospitable farms, country hotels, campgrounds, and off-the-main-road discoveries); and suggestions for activities.

Although each of the sections has a distinct format and a unique function, they have all been designed to be used together to provide a complete package of travel information. Sections have been carefully cross-referenced, and you will find that as you finish an entry in one section you are directed to another section and another entry, with complementary information. To use this book to full advantage, take a few minutes to read the table of contents and random entries in each section so you'll have an idea of how it all fits together.

Pick and choose information that you need from different sections. Assume, for example, that you have always wanted to take that typically English vacation, a walking tour through rural England, but you never really knew how to organize it or where to go. Turn first to the hiking section of GETTING READY TO GO as well as the chapters on planning a trip, eating out and hotels in Europe, and climate and clothes. These short, informative entries provide plenty of practical information. For specific information on entering and getting around Britain, shopping, currency, and the like, see FACTS IN BRIEF. But where to go? Turn next to *Great Britain*, DIRECTIONS. Perhaps you choose to walk the 100-odd-mile Cotswold Way. Your trip will certainly begin and end in London, and for a complete rundown on that fabulous city, you should read the London chapter of THE CITIES. Finally, turn to DIVERSIONS to peruse the chapters on sports, hotels, antiques, and other activities in which you are interested to make sure you don't miss anything in the neighborhood.

In other words, the sections of this book are building blocks designed to help put together the best possible trip. Use them selectively as a tool, a source of ideas, a reference work for accurate facts, and a guide to the best buys, the most exciting sites and sights, the most pleasant accommodations and the most delicious food — *the best travel experiences* that you can have.

GETTING READY TO GO

When and How to Go

What's Where

Europe is the world's second smallest continent, encompassing a relatively spare 3.7 million square miles, but with a comparatively dense population of 773 million (an average of 145 people per square mile). It is shaped vaguely like a triangle, bounded by Arctic waters and the Atlantic Ocean on the west, the Mediterranean, Aegean, and Black seas to the south, and an eastern border that follows a somewhat imprecise line through the Soviet Union along the Caucasus Mountains, the Caspian Sea, and then north along the Ural Mountains.

Actually, Europe does not conform to the traditional geographical concept of a continent. It is not a self-contained land area surrounded on all sides by water. It is the western fifth of what is commonly known as Eurasia, the giant landmass that stretches from the Atlantic Ocean to the Japanese islands in the Pacific. In the course of its 3,000 years of recorded history, however, cultural, religious, political, and economic influences — along with a sometimes turbulent intermingling of ethnic groups — have defined Europe as an entity, no matter how diverse its parts or geography.

Its dominant influence in Western civilization is due to its location in the North Temperate Zone and the wealth and diversity of its natural resources. The Continent is divided into northern and southern sections by an immense mountain chain — really a series of mountains and valleys — that includes, west to east, the Pyrenees Mountains, the Rhone Valley, the French-Swiss-Austrian Alps, and the curving Carpathian Mountains, which in Romania recede toward Bucharest and the Black Sea. Below this mountainous demarcation line are countries with generally warmer climates and coasts on the southern seas; north of it are countries of highlands and plains with coasts on the northern seas that separate the main body of the Continent from Scandinavia.

Turmoil has never spared Europe, and this century has been as devastating as any. But time and time again, the resourcefulness of its people and the richness of its natural resources — which have led to successful farmers, miners, and industrial development — have helped it recuperate from the ravages of natural and manmade disaster. And these same strengths gave birth to the amalgam of cultures that forged Western civilization and shaped the world.

What follows is a short survey of the geography of Europe's nations, starting in the far north and moving east and south.

SCANDINAVIA

Scandinavia refers to the segment of Europe consisting of Norway, Sweden, and Denmark — which share close cultural and historical ties and which, today, all have at least titular monarchies — and often includes Iceland, a separate island northwest of mainland Europe. Although Finland is sometimes represented with the Scandinavian countries at the United Nations and the Scandinavian Tourist Board in New York handles Finland, it is not a Scandinavian country. It is included in this section because it, and bordering nations Norway and Sweden, are separated from central Europe by several straits that wind from the Atlantic Ocean into the Baltic Sea and adjacent gulfs. The northernmost part of these countries is in the Arctic Circle, which also touches the northern fringes of Iceland.

ICELAND: This North Atlantic island was settled by Norwegians 10 centuries ago, and its Norwegian character is still strong; Icelanders today speak a language that is basically Old Norse. The 40,000-square-mile island lies east of Greenland, just touching the Arctic Circle; not surprisingly, fishing and the canning and export of fish products are major industries. The population is sparse (200,000) but has a nearly 100% literacy rate, the highest in the world. Summers are damp and cool; the winters are harsh but made habitable by the tempering influence of the Gulf Stream. Features of particular interest to visitors are the natural hot springs flowing beneath the island's surface, providing an abundance of thermal heat.

NORWAY: Scandinavia's northwesternmost country, bordering Sweden, Finland, and a tip of the Soviet Union, Norway has a dramatic fjord-splintered Atlantic coast, lined with sheer and awesome cliffs. The North Cape, the uppermost tip of the country, which reaches deep into the Arctic Circle, is a popular summer cruise destination. Most of the northern region is mountainous, and a quarter of the country is forested. Of necessity, most of the country's 4 million people live in the south, the majority in the coastal region extending from Bergen along the southern Atlantic coast to Oslo, the capital. Some 25,000 Laplanders live in the far north. One of Norway's most important resources is the sea, and the Atlantic Ocean supports much of the country's important fishing industry. These same waters are warmed by the Gulf Stream, which moderates the coastal climate all year.

SWEDEN: Of Europe's three most northerly countries, Sweden lies in the center — between Norway, with which it shares the Scandinavian Peninsula, and Finland, which borders it on the north but is otherwise separated from it by the Baltic Sea. Sweden is one of the world's most prosperous countries and its resources are highly visible: timberlands that cover half the country; mountains of ore along the Norwegian border; and vast northern glacial fields that melt during the summer and send water coursing through the country's carefully dammed rivers and lakes, providing an ample and reliable source of inexpensive power. Highly productive farms and most of the country's 8 million people are in the central and southern regions of the country. Most visited is the historic triangle bounded by the coastal cities of Gothenburg on the west, Malmö, near the southern tip of the country, and Stockholm, the capital, on the Baltic Sea. Sweden is spattered with numerous lakes, rivers, and waterways.

DENMARK: The most southern and also the smallest of the Scandinavian countries covers a total area of 16,600 square miles, extending over several little islands off the coast of north-central Europe and most of the peninsula known appropriately as Jutland, since it actually juts into the straits leading from the North Sea to the Baltic Sea. Because Denmark is made up of flatlands with meager agricultural resources, its people have traditionally depended on trade and conquest for their livelihoods, choices made easy by the country's excellent sea connections. Today it is a highly industrial nation with a population of just over 5 million, famous for chinaware and fine furniture design. A major resource and worldwide attraction is Copenhagen, its capital, known for its convivial and spirited atmosphere. Denmark's possessions include the Faeroe Islands (midway between Scotland and Iceland) and Greenland.

FINLAND: Although Finland shares northern borders with both Norway and Sweden, it shares its longest border with the Soviet Union and is culturally and even topographically distinct from Scandinavia. It covers a relatively flat area of 130,120 square miles. The northern Lapland region, within the Arctic Circle, is composed of treeless plains; the central region of the country is forested; and the coastal areas along its Baltic Sea gulfs are fertile and most populous. Unlike Norway, Denmark, or Sweden, it has no monarchy, and visitors will observe that the country's almost 5 million citizens take fierce pride in their democracy, perhaps because the country was dominated for centuries, first by Sweden and later by Russia, becoming a republic only after World War I. Major cities — Helsinki (the capital), Turku, Tampere — are highly modern, and Helsinki is a popular jumping-off point (notably by cruise ship) for visits to Leningrad and other places in the Soviet Union.

GREAT BRITAIN AND IRELAND

THE UNITED KINGDOM: The islands that make up the United Kingdom, or British Isles, as it sometimes called, lie in the North Atlantic immediately off the northwest coast of France, separated from the Continent by the English Channel, the Strait of Dover, and the North Sea. Dover, on the southwestern tip of England, and Calais, in the northwestern corner of France, are only 25 miles apart. Among the scattering of tiny islands nearby that belong to Great Britain are the Channel Islands, the Isle of Man, and the Orkneys, Hebrides, and Shetlands off the coast of Scotland.

England, Scotland, and Wales are the major entities, together with Northern Ireland, or Ulster, that are now officially referred to as the United Kingdom. The first three countries make up the island nearest the Continent — the largest island in Europe. Northern Ireland is in the northeastern part of the island immediately to the west, the rest of which belongs to the Republic of Ireland, or Eire. In total, the United Kingdom covers some 94,000 square miles and has a population of 56 million. Physically, England dominates, covering well over half the area that extends from the southern coast on the English Channel to Newcastle, at the edge of the Scottish Lowlands. Wales abuts England on the west, projecting into the St. George's Channel, which separates it from Ireland. Scotland forms the northern third of the island. The entire island is characterized by hilly terrain, as distinct from mountainous, although the celebrated Scottish Highlands occasionally rise 3,000 to 4,000 feet above sea level. The island has been able to draw upon its own resources for livestock breeding, mining, energy, and industry, with large oil reserves in the North Sea (shared with Norway). The climate is subject to prevailing southwesterly winds, which account for its frequently cloudy and damp — but essentially mild — weather all year. These generally inviting physical characteristics complement Great Britain's enormous historical, political, and cultural appeal and continue to make it one of the most pleasant countries in the world to visit.

Northern Ireland is primarily an agricultural region with many lakes, although much of the land is actually volcanic. Otherwise, Northern Ireland's geographical and physical characteristics are similar to those of Southern Ireland. Belfast, the capital, is a fairly new city that boomed in the 19th century and was dubbed "the Athens of the North," famed for its linen and shipbuilding industries.

IRISH REPUBLIC: The Republic of Ireland, or Southern Ireland, covers some 27,000 square miles, the lion's share of the island it shares with Northern Ireland; its population is 3.6 million. Highland outcroppings rise to 3,500 feet in places along the country's coasts, but most of Ireland is characterized by fertile plains, scenic lakes, and bays, especially along its Atlantic coastline. The famed River Shannon in the southwest is longer than any river in Great Britain. Ireland is essentially an agricultural country, and the same damp, moist air that tempers Britain's climate is responsible for the renowned green associated with the country by song and legend. Irish Gaelic is the official language, although English is the predominant spoken tongue. Dublin, the capital, is centrally located on the island's east coast, facing the Irish Sea and Wales.

THE BENELUX COUNTRIES

The Benelux countries, so named for the acronym formed by the first letters of BElgium, the NEtherlands, and LUXembourg, form a wedge of lowland terrain in the northwestern corner of continental Europe, between Germany and France and the waters of the North Sea. The three small countries are all monarchies and have a high standard of living.

BELGIUM: Directly north of France, Belgium is heavily industrialized for a country of its modest size (11,781 square miles and just under 10 million people), but it is probably best known as one of Western Europe's major international business and economic centers. Brussels, the capital, is a beautiful city of medieval and Renaissance architecture, with a cosmopolitan atmosphere considerably enhanced by its being the administrative center of the European Economic Community (the EEC, or the Common Market). Because of its geographic position, Belgium has been the battleground in more than its fair share of wars, and large numbers of Europeans and North Americans make pilgrimages to its cemeteries and former battlegrounds, which mark some of the most serious confrontations of World Wars I and II.

THE NETHERLANDS: Much of the Netherlands, or Holland, as it is more commonly known, is actually below sea level, protected from the ravages of the sea by dikes ringing the country's coast. Extending north from Belgium, with an irregular coastline that shelters numerous fishing villages, Holland has had to reclaim much land from the North Sea in order to gain needed farmland (it has an area of 15,700 square miles and a population of 14.6 million). Amsterdam, the capital, is one of the Continent's liveliest cities, with networks of canals lined by historically and architecturally distinctive homes and numerous museums housing works of the Dutch masters and other great European artists.

LUXEMBOURG: Surrounded by Belgium, West Germany, and France, Luxembourg is one of Europe's tiniest independent nations (999 square miles and 400,000 people) and one of its most fortunate. For not only is it a popular tourist destination, but it also makes a comfortable living from forests in the north and iron mines and prosperous farms in the south. The capital, also called Luxembourg, is a walled town built around a 10th-century castle. It is one of the few countries in the world known officially as a grand duchy, a territorial designation bestowed on it by France and dating from the early 19th century, although Luxembourg has long since been independent.

ATLANTIC EUROPE

France and Spain, two of the giants of Europe, have substantial coastlines on both the Atlantic Ocean and the Mediterranean Sea, and act as virtual dikes by separating those two very distinct bodies of water. Sharing Spain's Atlantic coast is Portugal, and thoroughly landlocked high in the Pyrenees Mountains between France and Spain is tiny Andorra. Another tiny country, Gibraltar, sits at the southernmost tip of the Iberian Peninsula, overlooking the straits that connect the Mediterranean to the Atlantic, guarding the entrance to Mediterranean Europe.

FRANCE: Its strategic position between the Atlantic and the Mediterranean has made it the historic crossroads of Europe, witnessing a constant traffic of goods and people. With an area of 211,208 square miles, France is the largest country in Western Europe, a land exceptionally varied and richly productive, with major mountain ranges in the south (the Pyrenees on the border with Spain, the Alps reaching from the Riviera to Switzerland) and a rich basin of farmland in the center. Its famed vineyards grow throughout the country, but are only one item in what may be the most diverse range of agricultural and dairy products on the Continent. France has a population of more than 55.4 million people, more than 2 million of whom live in Paris, the capital.

ANDORRA: Sheep raising and tourism are the mainstays of this small country of 175 square miles (38,000 people) high in the Pyrenees. The major community is Andorra la Vella. The altitude assures snow-capped mountains and chilly evenings year-round, though in the summer months the days can easily reach 80F. (*Please note that although* *temperatures are usually recorded on the Celsius scale in Europe, for purposes of clarity we shall discuss climate and temperature using the more familiar Fahrenheit scale.*)

SPAIN: The second largest country in Western Europe, Spain (194,883 square miles) covers the major portion of the Iberian Peninsula, the Continent's southwesternmost segment of land, and includes the Canary and Balearic islands. Spain shares borders with France (and Andorra), Portugal, which occupies a long rectangle of land separating most of Spain's western border from the ocean, and Gibraltar. The Atlantic Ocean borders the country along the northwest and southwest; the entire eastern coast of the country faces the Mediterranean, and the southern Andalusian region is popular for its warm climate and for "sun and fun" resorts along the extensive coast. Much of the interior of the country consists of relatively arid, high valleys within ranges of mountains that offer limited areas of arable land. Spain has a total population of 38.8 million, and Madrid, at the very center of the country, is one of Europe's largest capitals.

PORTUGAL: This southwestern corner of continental Europe occupies a 35,553-square-mile segment of the Iberian Peninsula, bordered by Spain to the north and east and the Atlantic Ocean to the south and west. Portugal also includes the Azores and the Madeira islands. Much of the northern part of the country is mountainous, notably above the Tagus River, which bisects the country and flows into the Atlantic at Lisbon, the capital. Below the Tagus, Portugal is warm and more agricultural, particularly along the growing resort area of the Algarve, the province that lines the country's southern Atlantic coast. The country has a moist and moderate climate, which is partly responsible for the olives and port wine that are among its most famous products, and for the vivid blooms of its trees and plants. Its population is 10.1 million. In addition to Lisbon and the resort regions, the numerous fishing villages along the coast are popular and colorful tourist attractions.

GIBRALTAR: This 2.25-square-mile piece of land at the southern tip of Spain, creating the passage from the Atlantic into the Mediterranean, is best known for its much-photographed physical landmark, the Rock of Gibraltar. It has served primarily as a military fortress since it became an official British possession in 1713. Gibraltar is a free port.

MEDITERRANEAN EUROPE

The countries listed below — Monaco, Italy (and San Marino, the tiny country in north-central Italy), Malta, Yugoslavia, Albania, and Greece — all have extensive coasts on the Mediterranean or its tributary seas, the Tyrrhenian, Adriatic, Ionian, and Aegean.

MONACO: With an area of 468 acres, this tiny principality within France's Riviera coast, close to the Italian border, is smaller than New York City's Central Park. From the late 19th century until World War II, it developed and sustained a reputation as a winter social center for royalty and wealthy families. Today, however, the visitor profile has a much more diverse social and economic base, although Monte Carlo — the district that encompasses the famed casinos and several elegant turn-of-the-century hotels as well as several luxury hostelries — still caters to a chic, international clientele. Monaco's beautiful setting, overlooking the Mediterranean and rising sharply toward the Maritime Alps of France, which border Monaco on the north, east, and west, contributes to its popularity.

ITALY: Italy is the most central European nation of the Mediterranean, with northern borders on France, Switzerland, Austria, and Yugoslavia. It is a boot-shaped peninsula, the second longest in the world (after Baja California), and covers an area of 116,318 square miles. It is an essentially mountainous country, but several of the most historic port cities of the Western world are along its coastline, including Naples, Genoa, and Venice. The capital, Rome, is midway down the peninsula, a few miles inland from the western coast, and encompasses Vatican City, a sovereign entity within its municipal boundaries. Except for traditional winter weather in the Alpine region of the north and whipping winds along the coasts in colder months, the climate is moderate to very warm throughout the year. Its cities are among the world's most historic. Two major islands — Sicily, at the toe of the peninsula, and Sardinia, west of the mainland across the Tyrrhenian Sea — are part of Italy. The country has a population of 57.2 million.

SAN MARINO: Figuratively, this smallest republic in the world (23 square miles and 23,000 people) could be papered over with the postage stamps that, along with tourism, represent its major industry. San Marino is an enclave within the Apennines, a few miles south of Rimini on Italy's Adriatic coast. The capital, also called San Marino, is the site of a church dating from the 10th century.

MALTA: This speck of an island country 60 miles south of Sicily is actually composed of three islands, of which the largest is also named Malta. It is flat and hot in summer, but its strategic site along the Mediterranean trade routes has subjected it to invading conquerors since the time of the Carthaginians. Its most recent occupants were the British, who maintained it as an important naval base. Malta became an independent republic in 1874. As a tourist destination, it is notable for remnants of fortifications and other structures built during the many centuries of foreign occupancy.

YUGOSLAVIA: The country's long Adriatic coast and the sprinkling of beaches and islands along it have made Yugoslavia a prime vacation spot within the Communist world, equally popular with European and international visitors. The coast stretches from Italy to Albania and also borders Austria, Hungary, Romania, Bulgaria, and Greece. Though much of the country is hilly or mountainous and not especially productive farmland, the northeastern region is flatter and has rich soil. Yugoslavia covers a total area of 99,000 square miles. The coastal region is speckled with fishing villages and resorts. The Danube River runs through Belgrade, the capital, in the west-central part of the country. Its population of 23.2 million includes people of many ethnic backgrounds, but Serbs predominate.

ALBANIA: The recluse among Balkan nations, this is a country of small villages and state farms that even fellow Eastern Europeans find hard to visit. About the size of Maryland — 11,100 square miles, with an estimated population of 3 million — the country has a long Adriatic coast and lies in relation to Yugoslavia and Greece much as Portugal does to Spain. Westerners know it best as the most outspoken of the Eastern European Communist bloc nations, the country that broke relations with the Soviet Union in 1961 to establish close ties with China. After the death of Mao, even these relations cooled, and Albania now trades with Greece, Yugoslavia, Italy, and others. Its post–World War II history, however, is only the most recent warp in a historic tapestry that has been woven by a series of conquering and invading cultures. By AD 800, Albania was under the control of Bulgaria and then, with the rest of the Balkan Peninsula, was swept into the Ottoman Turkish Empire from 1478 until 1912, when for a very brief period (until Italy invaded in 1939) it was first a republic and then a monarchy. Sadly, this rich history is inaccessible to most foreign visitors, for Albania does not welcome Western tourists. We do not, therefore, cover it in this guide.

GREECE: This ancient nation is the land terminus of southeastern Europe. Its mountainous mainland borders Albania, Yugoslavia, Bulgaria, and the small continental portion of Turkey; the seas that surround the country on three sides are the setting for the nation's more than 450 historically celebrated islands, of which the largest and most famous are Crete and Rhodes. Including all its islands, Greece has a total land area of 50,960 square miles and a population of 10 million. The overall climate is moderate, which, as in most coastal Mediterranean spots, gives the country a longer than average tourist season. Once outside Athens, the capital, visitors will see that this is not a prosperous country, since most of the land does not lend itself to agriculture, although half the working population is engaged in farming. Shipping, shipbuilding, and tourism are the most lucrative industries in Greece.

CENTRAL EUROPE

In defining Central Europe, we throw our net as wide as possible to include all those continental European countries east of France and west of the Soviet Union that do not have coasts on the Mediterranean. Included are West Germany, East Germany, and Poland; the landlocked nations of Switzerland, Liechtenstein, Austria, Hungary, and Czechoslovakia; and the Balkan countries of Romania and Bulgaria, both with eastern coastlines on the inland Black Sea. Many of the countries on this list didn't exist as distinct political entities 80 years ago, and we have swept up in one catch countries and cultures that have been in conflict or alliance dozens of times in the past 1,000 years. But ours may not be as arbitrary a distinction as it appears. Most of the countries mentioned here — the exceptions are Romania and Bulgaria — were at one time, in some form, part of the Habsburg Empire, which ruled much of Europe for nearly 700 years. The Habsburgs started as a minor ruling family in Switzerland and Alsace in the 11th century, but from 1278 until 1918 the seat of their power was Austria.

WEST GERMANY: This segment of the nation that was divided after World War II extends south from the North Sea and Denmark into the center of the Continent, covering a total area of 96,000 square miles. Formally known as the Federal Republic of Germany, it borders six other Western European nations — the Netherlands, Belgium, Luxembourg, France, Switzerland, and Austria — as well as East Germany and Czechoslovakia. The most populous country of Europe (60.7 million) outside the Soviet Union, it is also one of the richest, thanks to heavy industrialization, with particular concentration in the Ruhr Valley near the border with the Netherlands and Belgium. Much of the rest of the northern region, however, is a plain devoted to agriculture, and the south of the country is touched by the Bavarian Alps and other mountains in that long chain that bisects the Continent. Southern Germany, a land of considerable charm and beauty, escaped the fate of many of Germany's modern cities, most of which have been rebuilt after heavy damage during World War II. Bonn, the capital, is on the Rhine about midway between the southern and northern boundaries.

EAST GERMANY: Like northern West Germany, East Germany is essentially a plains area. Half the size of West Germany (with a population of 16.7 million), it is nonetheless the most industrially productive of the Eastern European countries outside the Soviet Union. Officially known as the German Democratic Republic, it is bounded by the Baltic Sea on the north, Poland to the east, Czechoslovakia to the south, and West Germany. The people here, like the West Germans, are Teutonic, with more Slavic influence. Having been extensively rebuilt in the past 20 years, East Berlin, the capital, is considerably more modern than other cities in the country.

POLAND: This north-central European state is characterized by relatively even terrain that extends across the northern part of the Continent, although the country's southern border rises into the Carpathian Mountains, which separate it from Czechoslovakia. Poland, bounded by East Germany on the west, the Soviet Union on the east, and the Baltic Sea on the north, covers an area of 120,000 square miles with 37.5 million people. It has firm ethnic and historic roots in central Europe dating from the 9th century, although it went through periods in the 18th century when it virtually disappeared after being divided among the Russian, Prussian, and Austrian empires. Firmly part of the Eastern European bloc today, it is generally more receptive to Western visitors than many of its neighbors. Warsaw, its capital, has survived three attempts to annihilate it, first by the Swedes and the Russians, then the French, and more recently the Nazis. Since World War II, the city has been extensively rebuilt.

CZECHOSLOVAKIA: It's hard not to read something of the labyrinthian history of central Europe in Czechoslovakia, which is surrounded by Poland, Austria, Hungary, the Soviet Union, and East and West Germany. The centuries of wars that carved its shape and decided its borders are the history of Europe. Down its center run the Carpathian Mountains; in the west is its capital, Prague, surrounded by good farm country and lined by mineral-rich mountains; in the east are the Tatra Mountains, a continuation of the Carpathian chain. The country covers a total of 49,000 square miles and has a population of 15.5 million. As a republic, Czechoslovakia is relatively young, having been created at the end of World War I from provinces of the former Austro-Hungarian Empire.

SWITZERLAND: This country is aptly referred to as the crest of Europe, with mountain peaks as high as 15,000 feet above sea level. Surrounded by Italy on the south, France on the west, Germany on the north, and Liechtenstein and Austria on the east, Switzerland is completely landlocked, but its glaciers feed the major rivers of the Continent that flow to the North, Baltic, and Mediterranean seas. Switzerland covers an area of 16,000 square miles. Its deep and fertile valleys are not only scenic, but a source of the nation's important dairy products. The capital, Zurich, is in the north-central part of the country. Its 6.5 million people are for the most part German, French, and Italian, and all three languages are spoken in the country, though the dominant language is Swiss-German, which is spoken by 65% of the natives. Needless to say, most citizens are at least bilingual; English is widely spoken as well. In the eastern canton of Grison, the Latin language of Romansh is still spoken.

LIECHTENSTEIN: Nestled at the eastern border of Switzerland along the Rhine River, Liechtenstein is one of the several small (62 square miles; 28,000 people) principalities of Western Europe that fascinate visitors with their charm and beauty. Despite its size and essentially Alpine topography, it has some farming, though tourism is a far more significant part of the economy. Liechtenstein's principal business, however, is business itself; a carefully maintained tax haven, it attracts a variety of banking and corporate operations to Vaduz, its capital. Today its diplomatic and communications services are provided by Switzerland, but it has a long and proud history that goes back to the 14th century.

AUSTRIA: Like its western neighbor, Switzerland, Austria is totally surrounded by mountains, but the valleys created by its three Alpine ranges extend the length of the country (its total area is 32,375 square miles). Also like Switzerland, Austria is a major ski resort center and has exceptional scenery, both of which give it year-round tourist appeal. Austria's 7.6 million people are predominantly German, and German is the official language, though very small minorities in the country speak Slovenian, Croatian, and Hungarian. This is an accurate reflection of history as well as contemporary geography, for Germany is the country's northwestern neighbor, and it also has borders with Czechoslovakia, Hungary, and Yugoslavia. In many ways, Austria is at the center of the confused history of central Europe; from its capital, Vienna, for more than 600 years it served as the center of power of the Habsburgs, whose dynasty extended from the Netherlands to the Ottoman Empire and gave the Holy Roman Empire the bulk of its emperors.

HUNGARY: One of several fully landlocked nations of central Europe, Hungary lies below southeastern Czechoslovakia and also borders, from west to east, Austria, Yugoslavia, Romania, and a tip of the Soviet Union. Most of Hungary's 36,000 square miles is highly productive agricultural plains, although industry has absorbed most of the working population (total population is about 10.6 million) since the end of World War II. Hungarians are the product of a mixture of races, notably those ethnic groups from what is now the south-central region of the USSR and Turkey who pushed northwest nearly 2,000 years ago. Budapest, the capital, straddles the Danube and is one of Europe's most historic and romantic cities.

ROMANIA: Legendary mountain ranges — the Transylvanian Alps and Carpathians

— forming an arc that divides west and east, are the key physical features of this country. Most of Romania's northern border is along the Ukrainian district of the Soviet Union; the Black Sea is to the east, Bulgaria to the south, and Yugoslavia and Hungary to the west. In total, the country covers 91,700 square miles. Visitors will see pronounced Hungarian and German influences among its 22.8 million people, although the country's history goes back to the time of the Romans. Bucharest, the capital, is a major tourist attraction for foreign visitors as well as the local populace, and the Black Sea resort city of Constanta draws visitors from throughout the eastern part of the Continent.

BULGARIA: Like Romania, its northern neighbor, Bulgaria borders the Black Sea on the east and is physically bisected by a mountain range, the Balkans, which runs east to west through the center of the country. Its other borders are with Turkey, Greece, and Yugoslavia. Covering 43,000 square miles, it has a population of just under 9 million. Primarily a Slavic country, nearly 1,000 years ago it dominated the region from the Black Sea west to the Adriatic. The two world wars in this century depleted many of its resources. Sofia is its capital.

EURASIA

SOVIET UNION: The entire Soviet Union — officially called the Union of Soviet Socialist Republics — has a land area larger than all of the rest of Europe, about 8.65 million square miles, and its European section alone is just about half of Europe's total area. It has a total population of 280 million. Its western boundary extends along the length of the Continent, from the Barents Sea in the north, where it borders the northeastern tip of Norway and Finland, along the Baltic Sea, Poland, Czechoslovakia, Hungary, and Romania to the Black Sea, Caucasus, and Caspian Sea. The Ural Mountains are traditionally considered the dividing line between the European and the eastern (Asian) republics that make up the complete federation of Soviet states. As might be expected for a landmass of this size, the terrain is exceptionally diverse. It ranges from glacial fields within the Arctic Circle to huge forests, a great central plain (incorporating the famed Kirghiz Steppe, a fertile agricultural area), and subtropical pockets along certain coastal areas of the Black and Caspian seas. The Caspian is actually the world's largest landlocked lake. Unlike the rest of Europe, however, the climate of Soviet Europe tends to be more humid and cold, lacking the warmth from the Gulf Stream. The Dnieper River, which empties into the Black Sea, and the Volga River, which is the longest in Europe and extends from the center of the country to the Caspian Sea, are the major waterways of the European part of the USSR. Moscow, the capital, with a population of 8 million, and Leningrad, the former capital, at the easternmost corner of the Baltic Sea, are the major cities.

When to Go

 The decision of exactly when to travel may be imposed by the requirements of a rigid schedule; more likely there will be some choice, and the decision will be made on the basis of precisely what you want to see and do, what activities or events you'd like to attend, and what suits your mood.

There really isn't a "best" time to visit Europe. For North Americans as well as Europeans, the period from mid-May to mid-September has long been — and remains — the peak travel period, traditionally the most popular vacation time. It is important to emphasize, however, that Europe is hardly a single-season destination; more and more vacationers who have a choice are enjoying the substantial advantages of off-season travel. Though many of the lesser tourist attractions may close during the off-season, the major ones remain open and tend to be less crowded — and, throughout Europe, life proceeds at its most natural pace. What's more, travel is generally less expensive.

For some, the most convincing argument in favor of off-season travel is the economic one. Airfares drop and hotel rates go down in the late fall, winter, and early spring. Relatively inexpensive package tours become available, and the independent traveler can go farther on less, too. Europe is not like the Caribbean, where high season and low season are precisely defined and rates drop automatically on a particular date. But many European hotels reduce rates during the off-season, and on the Riviera and at other seaside resorts savings can be as much as 30% to 35%. Although in some areas smaller establishments may close during the off-season in response to reduced demand, there are still plenty of alternatives, and discounts for stays of more than 1 night, particularly over a weekend (when business travelers traditionally go home), are more common.

It should be noted that what the travel industry refers to as shoulder seasons — the 1½ to 2 months preceding and following the peak summer months — are often sought out because they offer reasonably good weather and smaller crowds. But be warned that high-season prices can prevail in many places during these periods, notably in certain popular areas of the Mediterranean — the Greek Islands, several of the more "social" communities of the French Riviera, Spain's Costa del Sol, and Portugal's Algarve. Most major cities in Europe hold at least one international business or industrial show each year (the *Frankfurt Book Fair* each fall is one example, as are the annual fall and spring fashion shows in Paris and Milan), and these are sure to affect the availability of discounts on accommodations. In countries with harvest festivals (mostly wine countries like Spain, Germany, France, and Italy), off-season discounts also may not exist.

In short, Europe's vacation appeal, like many other popular destinations, has become multi-seasonal. But it's a big continent, and the noted exceptions notwithstanding, most travel destinations are decidedly less trafficked and less expensive during the winter.

CLIMATE: Since the travel plans of most North American visitors are traditionally affected by the availability of vacation time and a desire to travel when the weather's best (or at some other specific time, as when a particular sport is most easily played), here is a brief breakdown of appealing destinations by month and/or season.

January, February, March – It's prime ski season, and the central European Alps are the place to be both in terms of challenge and social activity (slopes in Spain, Eastern Europe, and Scandinavia are good destinations for less chic — and less expensive — skiing). During the coldest months, try the southern side of the Alps, which is warmer. Late March and even April skiing can be surprisingly good in the traditional ski centers, which are likely to be less crowded after Easter and offer better service and perhaps even lower prices.

April – Early travelers, particularly Scandinavians on charter flights, head for the Mediterranean, notably Spain's Costa del Sol and the Greek Islands. Tulips, hyacinths, and daffodils are blooming in Holland — until about mid-May. By the way, the guys who wrote "April in Paris" clearly never set foot in the City of Light during damp, dismal, dreary April.

May – The month can be nippy or warm, depending on where you are. If the season isn't too windy or damp, the English countryside can be an attractive destination for a week's drive. Other comfortable spring destinations include Hungary, Italy, and Greece.

June – Most of the Continent has warmed into the 70s, and it is the first full month of Europe's peak season. Take your pick of any place from the Greek Islands (low 80s) to Copenhagen (upper 60s), and don't overlook Iceland, islands in the lower Baltic Sea, and the Scandinavian capitals, which are fairly well protected from the North Atlantic winds.

July and August – It's hot in the Mediterranean, but the best time to visit Scandinavia. This is also the best period for cruises to Norway's North Cape and for visits to Moscow and Leningrad, as well as for tours of Scotland, the Low Countries (Holland, Belgium, Luxembourg), and France. Central Spain can be surprisingly comfortable, since much of it is on an elevated plateau. This is traditional vacation time for Europeans, especially the French, who clear out of Paris in droves in August.

September – North Americans traditionally empty out of the Continent after *Labor Day,* although increasingly greater numbers of visitors are timing their arrivals for the week or two afterward, since the weather remains excellent and many retail establishments on the Continent reopen after summer closings. The Riviera weather is very good, as are resorts on the Black Sea.

October – This is the period for manufacturers' exhibitions, fashion shows, international trade fairs, and food festivals. It's also harvest season throughout much of central Europe, and the fairs and festivals that celebrate these events draw heavy crowds of

AVERAGE TEMPERATURES (in °F)

	January	*April*	*July*	*October*
Albania	35–55	45–65	60–90	50–75
Andorra	40–55	50–70	70–90	45–65
Austria	25–35	40–55	60–75	40–55
Belgium	30–40	40–60	55–75	45–60
Bulgaria	30–45	45–60	65–85	50–70
Czechoslovakia	20–35	40–60	55–80	40–60
Denmark	25–35	35–50	55–70	45–55
Finland	15–30	30–45	55–70	35–50
France	30–45	45–60	60–80	45–60
Germany (East)	25–35	40–55	60–75	45–55
Germany (West)	30–40	40–60	60–80	45–60
Gibralter	40–55	50–70	70–90	45–65
Great Britain	35–45	40–60	50–70	45–60
Greece	40–55	50–70	70–90	45–65
Hungary	20–35	50–70	60–80	35–50
Iceland	30–35	35–45	50–60	35–45
Ireland	35–50	40–60	50–70	40–60
Italy	40–50	50–65	65–80	55–70
Liechtenstein	35–45	40–60	55–75	40–55
Luxembourg	30–40	40–60	55–75	45–55
Malta	50–60	55–70	70–85	65–75
Monaco	45–55	55–60	70–80	60–70
Netherlands	30–40	45–55	60–70	50–60
Norway	20–30	35–50	55–70	35–50
Poland	25–35	35–55	55–75	40–55
Portugal	40–55	35–45	70–90	45–65
Romania	20–35	40–65	60–80	45–65
San Marino	40–50	50–65	65–80	55–70
Soviet Union	below 0	25–50	50–70	20–40
Sweden	20–30	35–45	60–70	40–50
Switzerland	35–45	40–60	55–75	40–55
Yugoslavia	25–35	45–65	60–80	45–65

regional visitors as well as vacationers. The weather tends to be cooler, so pack accordingly.

November and December – Temperatures throughout the Continent are wet and chilly, but not the marrow-freezing cold of the northern US and Canada, except in the northernmost reaches of Europe.

On the preceding page is a chart of seasonal temperature ranges in the countries of Europe. For more climate information, see *Climate and Clothes* (by country) in FACTS IN BRIEF and the individual city reports in THE CITIES.

The European Travel Commission offers an extensive list of events during the entire year for its 23 member countries and islands. For a free copy, send a stamped (45¢), self-addressed business-size envelope (4 x 9½) and $1 for postage, specifying your area of interest, to the European Travel Commission, PO Box 1754, New York, NY 10185 (phone: 212-307-1200).

Traveling by Plane

 The air space between North America and Europe is the most heavily trafficked in the world. It is served by dozens of airlines, almost all of which sell seats at a variety of prices, under widely different terms. You probably will spend more for your airfare than for any other single item in your European travel budget. In order to take advantage of the low fares offered by both scheduled airlines and charter companies, you should know what kinds of flights are available, the rules and regulations pertaining to air travel, and the options for special packages.

SCHEDULED AIRLINES: Among the dozens of airlines serving Europe from the United States, those offering regularly scheduled flights, many on a daily basis, are Aer Lingus, Air France, Air India, Alitalia, American, Austrian Airlines, British Airways, Continental, Delta, Iberia, Icelandair, KLM, Lufthansa, Olympic, Sabena, SAS, Swissair, Pan American, TAP Air, TWA, UTA, and Virgin Atlantic.

Gateways – At present, nonstop flights to Europe depart from Anchorage, Atlanta, Boston, Charlotte, Chicago, Dallas/Ft. Worth, Denver, Detroit, Houston, Los Angeles, Miami, New York, Newark, Orlando, Philadelphia, Pittsburgh, Raleigh, St. Louis, San Francisco, San Diego, Seattle, Tampa, and Washington, DC. Additional direct flights (meaning, usually, that there is no change of flight number between the originating and terminating cities, though there may be one or more stops en route and perhaps a change of plane) depart from some of the above cities and a few others as well. Nonstop or direct, nearly all of these flights land in European capitals.

Tickets – When traveling on one of the many regularly scheduled flights, a full-fare ticket provides maximum travel flexibility (although at considerable expense), because tickets are sold on an open reservation system. This means that there are no advance booking requirements — a prospective passenger can buy a ticket for a flight right up to the minute of takeoff, if seats are available. If your ticket is for a round trip, you can make the return reservation any time you wish, months before you leave or the day before you return. Assuming your passport and any visas are in order, you can stay at your destination for as long as you like. (Tickets are generally good for a year and can be renewed if not used.) You can also cancel your flight at any time without penalty. However, while it is true that this category of ticket can be purchased at the last minute, it is advisable to reserve well in advance during popular travel periods and around holiday times.

No matter what kind of ticket you buy, it is wise to reconfirm that you will be using your return reservations. If you do not call the airline to let them know you will be using the return leg of your reservation, it (or its computer) may assume you are not coming and automatically cancel your seat. Some airlines no longer require reconfirmations; others recommend that you confirm your return flight 48 or 72 hours in advance. Although policies vary from carrier to carrier, reconfirmation is advisable for *all* international flights.

Fares – Airfares are changing so rapidly that even experts find it difficult to keep up with them. This volatile situation is due to a number of factors, including airline deregulation, high labor costs, and vastly increased competition. Before the Airline Deregulation Act of 1978, US airlines had no choice but to set their rates and routes within the guidelines of the Civil Aeronautics Board (CAB), and they could compete for passengers only by offering better service than their competitors. With the loosening of controls (and the elimination of the CAB), airlines are now engaged in a far more intense competition relating to price and schedule, which has opened the door to a wide range of discount fares and promotional offers. Intensifying the competitive atmosphere has been the creation of several new carriers offering fewer frills and far lower prices. These carriers seem to appear and disappear with dismaying regularity. They have, however, served to drive down fares and make older, more entrenched carriers aware that they are in a genuine competition for travelers' dollars.

Perhaps the most common misconception about fares on scheduled airlines is that the cost of the ticket determines how much service will be provided on the flight. This is true only to a certain extent. A far more realistic rule of thumb is that the less you pay for your ticket, the more restrictions and qualifications you're likely to be subject to before getting on the plane (as well as after you get off). These qualifying aspects relate to the months in which you travel, how far in advance you purchase your ticket, the minimum and maximum amount of time you may or must remain abroad, your willingness to make up your mind concerning a return date at the time of booking — and your ability to stick to that decision. It is not uncommon for passengers sitting side by side on the same wide-body jet to have paid fares varying by hundreds of dollars, and all too often the traveler paying more would have been equally willing to accept the terms regulating the far less expensive ticket. The ticket you buy will fall into one of several fare categories currently being offered by scheduled carriers flying between the US and Europe.

In general, the great variety of fares between the US and Europe can be reduced to three basic categories: first class, business or executive class, and tourist, also called economy or coach. In addition, Advance Purchase Excursion (APEX) and "Eurosaver" fares offer savings under certain restrictions.

In a class by itself is the *Concorde,* the supersonic jet developed jointly by France and Great Britain, which cruises at speeds of 1,350 miles an hour (twice the speed of sound) and makes transatlantic crossings in half the time (3¾ hours from New York to Paris) of conventional, subsonic jets. British Airways' *Concorde* flies from Miami, Washington, DC, and New York to London and Paris. Service is "single" class (with champagne and caviar all the way), and the fare is expensive, about 20% more than a first class ticket on a subsonic aircraft. Some discounts have been offered, but time is the real gift of the *Concorde.* For travelers to European destinations other than Paris or London, this "gift" may be more or less valuable as compared to a direct flight when taking connecting flights into account.

A first class ticket is your admission to the special section of the aircraft, with larger seats, more legroom, sleeperette seating on some wide-body aircraft, better food (or more elaborately served food, in any case), free drinks and headsets for movies and music channels, and, above all, personal attention. First class fares are about double those of full-fare economy, although both first class passengers and people paying economy fares are entitled to reserve seats and are sold tickets on an open reservation system. If you're planning to visit several countries in Europe, you may stop in any number of cities en route to your farthest destination, provided that certain set, but generous, maximum permitted mileage limits are respected.

Not too long ago, there were only two classes of air travel, first class and all the rest, usually called economy or tourist. But because passengers paying full economy fares traveled in the same compartment as passengers flying for considerably less on various promotional or discount fares, the airlines introduced special services to compensate those paying the full price. Thus, business class came into being, one of the most successful recent airline innovations. At first, business class passengers were merely curtained off from the other economy passengers. Now a separate cabin, or cabins, usually toward the front of the plane, is the norm. While standards of comfort and service are not as high as in first class, they represent a considerable improvement over conditions in the rear of the plane, with roomier seats, more leg and shoulder space between passengers, and fewer seats abreast. Free liquor and headphones, a choice of meal entrées, and a separate counter for speedier check-in are other inducements. As in first class, you travel on any scheduled flight you wish, you may buy a one-way or round-trip ticket, and the ticket is valid for a year. There are no minimum or maximum stay requirements, no advance booking requirements, and no cancellation penalties, and the fare allows the same unlimited free stopover privileges as first class. Airlines have their own names for their business class service — such as Clipper Class on Pan American, Ambassador Class on TWA, and Le Club on Air France.

The terms of the coach or economy fare may vary slightly from airline to airline, and, in fact, from time to time airlines may be selling more than one type of economy fare. Economy fares sell for substantially less than business fares, the savings effected by limited frills and stopovers. Coach or economy passengers sit more snugly, as many as 10 in a single row on a wide-body jet, behind the first class and business class sections, and receive standard meal service. Alcoholic drinks are not free, nor are the headsets. If there are two economy fares on the books, one (often called "regular economy") may still offer unlimited stopovers. The other, less expensive (often called "special economy"), may limit stopovers to one or two, with a charge (typically $25) for each one. Like first class passengers, however, passengers paying the full coach fare are subject to none of the restrictions that are usually attached to less expensive discount fares. There are no advance booking requirements, no minimum stay requirements, and no cancellation penalties. Tickets are sold on an open reservation system: They can be bought for a flight up to the minute of takeoff, if seats are available, and if the ticket is round-trip, the return reservation can be made any time you wish — months before you leave or the day before you return. Both first class and coach tickets are generally good for a year, after which they can be renewed if not used, and if you ultimately decide not to fly at all, your money will be refunded. The cost of economy and business class tickets does not vary much in the course of the year between the US and Europe, though on some transatlantic routes they vary in price from a basic (low-season) price in effect most of the year to a peak (high-season) price in summer.

Excursions and other discount fares are the airlines' equivalent of a special sale, and usually apply to round-trip bookings. These fares generally differ according to the season and the number of travel days permitted. They are only a bit less flexible than economy tickets and are, therefore, useful for both business travelers and tourists. Most round-trip excursion tickets include strict minimum and maximum stay requirements, and reservations can be changed only within the prescribed time limits, so don't count on extending a ticket beyond the prescribed time of return or staying less time than required. Different airlines may have different regulations concerning the number of stopovers permitted, and sometimes excursion fares are less expensive during midweek. Needless to say, these reduced-rate seats are most limited at busy times such as holidays, when full-fare coach seats sell more quickly than usual. Passengers fortunate enough to get a discount or excursion fare ticket sit with the coach passengers, and, for all intents and purposes, are indistinguishable from them. They receive all the same basic services, even though they have paid anywhere between 30% and 55% less for the trip. Obviously, it's wise to make plans early enough to qualify for the least expensive transportation.

These discount or excursion fares may masquerade under a variety of names and they may vary from city to city, but they invariably have strings attached. In the past, some excursion fares to Europe came unencumbered by advance booking requirements and cancellation penalties, permitted one stopover (but not a free one) in each direction, and had "open jaws," meaning that you could fly to one city and depart from another, arranging and paying for your own transportation between the two. Excursion fares of this type do not, at present, exist on flights between the US and most European destinations, but a newer and less expensive type of excursion, the APEX, or Advance Purchase Excursion, does. As with traditional excursion fares, passengers sit with and receive the same basic services as coach or economy passengers, even though they may have paid up to 50% less for their seats. In return, they are subject to certain restrictions. The ticket is usually good for a minimum of 7 days abroad and a maximum, currently, of 3 months; and, as its name implies, it must be "ticketed" or paid for in its entirety 21 days before departure. The drawback to the APEX is that it penalizes travelers who change their minds — and travel plans. The return reservation must be made at the time of the original ticketing, and if for some reason you change your schedule while abroad, you pay a penalty of $100 or 10% of the ticket value, whichever is greater, as long as you travel within the validity period of your ticket. But, if you change your return to a date less than the minimum stay or more than the maximum stay, the difference between the round-trip APEX fare and the full round-trip coach rate will have to be paid. There is also a penalty of $125 or more for canceling or changing a reservation *before* travel begins — check the specific penalty in effect when you purchase your ticket — so careful planning is imperative. No stopovers are allowed, but it is possible to create an open-jaw effect by buying an APEX on a split-ticket basis, e.g., flying to Paris and returning from Nice (or some other city). The total price would be half the price of an APEX to Paris plus half the price of an APEX to Nice. APEX tickets to Europe are sold at basic and peak rates (peak season is from May through September) and may include surcharges for weekend flights.

There is also a Winter or Super APEX, which may go under different names for different carriers — for instance, Air France calls it the Eurosaver. Similar to the regular APEX fare, it costs slightly less, but is more restrictive. It is available only for off-peak winter travel and is limited to a stay of between 7 and 21 days. Advance purchase is still required (currently, 30 days prior to travel), and ticketing must be completed within 48 hours of reservation. The fare is not refundable except in cases of death or hospitalization.

Another type of fare that is sometimes available is the youth fare. At present, most airlines flying to Europe are using a form of APEX fare as a youth fare for those through age 24. The maximum stay is extended to a year, and the return booking must be left open. Seats can be reserved no more than 3 days before departure, and tickets must be purchased when the reservation is made. The return is booked from Europe in the same manner, no more than 3 days before flight time. There is no cancellation penalty, but the fare is subject to availability, so it may be difficult to book a return during peak travel periods.

Standby fares, at one time the rock-bottom tickets to Europe, have become elusive, but bargain hunters should not hesitate to ask if such fares exist. While the definition of standby varies somewhat from airline to airline, it generally means that you make yourself available to buy a ticket for a flight (usually no sooner than the day of departure), then literally stand by on the chance that a seat will be free. Once aboard, however, you have the same meal service and frills (or lack of them) enjoyed by others in the economy compartment.

Something else to check is the possibility of qualifying for a GIT (group inclusive travel) fare. The requirements vary as to number of travel days, number of stopovers permitted, and number of passengers required for a group. (The last can be as few as two full fares.) The group fare always requires that a specified dollar amount of ground arrangements be purchased, in advance, along with the ticket. The required number of participants varies, the required time abroad varies, and the actual fares also vary, but the cost will be spelled out in brochures distributed by the tour operators handling the ground arrangements. In the past, GIT fares typically were among the least expensive in the fare schedules of the established carriers, and, although very attractive group fares may still appear from time to time, with the advent of discount fares, group fares have all but disappeared from some air routes or their price tags become the equivalent of the other discount fares. Travelers perusing brochures on group package tours to Europe will find that, in almost all cases, the applicable airfare given as a sample (to be added to the price of the land package to obtain the total tour price) is an APEX fare, the same discount fare available to the independent traveler.

Travelers looking for the least expensive possible airfares should, finally, scan the travel pages of their newspapers for announcements of special promotional fares. Most major airlines offer their most attractive special fares to encourage travel in slow seasons and to inaugurate and publicize new routes. Even if none of the above conditions applies, prospective passengers can be fairly sure that the number of discount seats per flight at the lowest price is strictly limited or that the fare offering includes a set expiration date — which means it's absolutely necessary to move fast to enjoy the lowest possible price. Unfortunately, special offers come and go quickly and may not be available precisely when you want to travel.

The leading carriers now also offer a bonus system to frequent travelers. After the first 10,000 miles, for example, you might receive a first class ticket for the coach fare; after another 10,000 miles you might receive a discount on your next ticket purchase. The value of the bonuses continues to increase as you log more miles.

Given the frequency with which the airfare picture changes, it is more than possible that by the time you are ready to fly, the foregoing discussion may be somewhat out of date. That's why it is always wise to comparison shop, and to do a good job of it, it's necessary to read the business and travel sections of your newspaper regularly and to call the airlines that serve your destination from your most convenient gateway. The potential savings are well worth the effort.

Ask about discount or promotional fares and about any conditions that might restrict booking, payment, cancellation, and changes in plans. Check the prices from other cities. A special rate may be offered in a nearby city but not in yours, and it may be enough of a bargain to warrant your leaving from that city. If you have a flexible schedule, investigate standby fares. But remember that, depending on your departure point, they may not work out to be the rock-bottom price. Ask if there is a difference in price for midweek travel versus weekend travel, or if there is a further discount for traveling early in the morning or late at night. Also be sure to investigate package deals, which are offered by virtually every airline. They may include a car rental, accommodations, and/or dining or sightseeing features in addition to the basic airfare; the combined cost of packaged elements is usually considerably less than the cost of the exact same elements when purchased separately.

When you're satisfied that you've found the lowest possible price for which you can conveniently qualify (you may have to call more than once, because different clerks have been known to quote different prices), make your booking. Then, to protect yourself against fare increases, purchase and pay for your ticket as soon as possible after you've received a confirmed reservation. Airlines generally will honor their tickets, even if the operative price at the time of your flight is higher than the price you paid; if fares go up between the time you *reserve* a flight and the time you *pay* for it, you likely will be out of luck. Finally, with excursion or discount fares, it is important to remember that when a reservation clerk says that you must purchase a ticket by a specific date, this is an absolute deadline. Miss it and the airline may automatically cancel your reservation without telling you.

If you don't have the time and patience to investigate personally all possible air departures and connections for a proposed trip, remember that a travel agent can be of inestimable help. A good agent should have all the information on which flights go where and when and which categories of tickets are available on each. Most have computerized reservation links with the major carriers, so that a seat can be reserved and confirmed in minutes. An increasing number of agents also possess fare-comparison computer programs, so they are often very reliable sources of detailed competitive price data. (For more information, see *How to Use a Travel Agent.*)

Low-Fare Airlines – In today's economic climate, increasingly, the stimulus for special fares is the appearance of airlines associated with bargain rates. These tend to be smaller carriers, which can offer more for less because of lower overhead, uncomplicated route networks, and other limitations in their service. On these airlines, all seats on any given flight generally sell for the same price, which is somewhat below the lowest discount fare offered by the larger, more established airlines, even after they cut their fares in response. This gap, too, may disappear in the future, but it is important to note that tickets offered by the smaller airlines specializing in low-cost travel frequently are not subject to the same restrictions as the lowest-priced ticket offered by the more established carriers. They may not require advance purchase or minimum and maximum stays, may involve no cancellation penalties, may be available one-way or round-trip, and may, for all intents and purposes, resemble the competition's high-priced full-fare coach. But never assume this until you know it's so.

London has always been a favorite destination for low-fare airlines. Sadly, more than one of the carriers that flew this route are no longer in existence. At press time, the only airline offering a relatively low fare was Virgin Atlantic (phone: 212-242-1330 in New York City; 800-862-8621 elsewhere), which flies from Newark to London's Gatwick Airport daily year-round, and from Miami to Gatwick at least four times a week. The airline sells tickets in several categories, including business or "upper" class, economy, APEX, and a nonrefundable variation on standby called the Late Saver fare, which must be purchased not more than 7 days prior to travel. At the time of this writing, the Late Saver fare to London was $199 one-way in off-season, rising to $289 one-way during the summer months.

In a class by itself is Icelandair (formerly Icelandic), which has always been a scheduled airline but has long been known as a good source of low-cost flights to Europe (it flies from New York, Boston, Baltimore/Washington, Orlando, and Chicago to Reykjavik, Glasgow, and Luxembourg). In addition, the airline increases the options for its passengers by offering "thru-fares" on connecting flights (aboard Luxembourg's Luxair) to Athens, Frankfurt, Nice, or Paris, coupled with free bus service to many German cities. The airline sells tickets in a variety of categories, from unrestricted economy fares to a sort of standby "3-days-before" fare (which functions just like the youth fares described above but has no age requirement). Travelers should be aware, however, that most Icelandair flights stop in Reykjavik for 45 minutes en route to and from Luxembourg — a minor delay for most, but one that further prolongs the trip for passengers who will wait again in Luxembourg to board connecting flights to their ultimate destinations. For reservations and tickets, contact a travel agent or Icelandair (phone: 212-967-8888 in New York City; 800-223-5500 elsewhere in the US).

Intra-European Fares – The cost of the round trip across the Atlantic is not the only expense to be considered. Flights between European cities, when booked in Europe, can be quite expensive (and best avoided by careful use of stopover rights on the higher priced economy, business class, or first class transatlantic tickets). But discounts have recently been introduced on routes between some European cities

(Dublin and London, and London and Amsterdam, for instance), and other discounts do exist.

Air Inter, France's major domestic airline, for example, offers reduced rates to families, married couples, senior citizens, students, youths, and children of various ages, all of which are available after arrival in Europe. In addition, for foreigners only, the airline offers discounted "Visit France" fares, which must be bought in the US in conjunction with a transatlantic ticket to a European country (both the international flight, which can be aboard any carrier, and the intra-France flight must be issued on the same ticket). Air Inter also offers a discount pass, which permits unlimited travel for any 7-day period within a given month. The pass can be used on all of the airline's routes with the exception of certain peak hour flights, the "red flights" used mostly by business travelers. Further information on ticketing for Air Inter's current airfare packages is available from Air France (Air Inter's general sales agent in the US) or from *Jet Vacations* (phone: 212-247-0999 or 800-JET-0999). See also *Package Tours* for offerings by British Airways.

Other, although perhaps less impressive, discounted transatlantic and intra-European airfare packages may be offered by carriers in other countries. Recent Common Market moves toward airline deregulation are expected to lead gradually to a greater variety of budget fares. In the meantime, however, the high cost of European fares can be avoided by careful use of stopover rights on the higher-priced transatlantic tickets — first class, business class, and full-fare economy. If your ticket doesn't allow stopovers, ask about excursion fares such as PEX and Super PEX — the same as APEX and Super APEX, but without the advance purchase rules and therefore more expensive — APEX for round trips, and Eurobudget for one-way trips. If the restrictions that govern them allow you to use them (frequently the minimum stay requirement means staying over for at least one Saturday night), you may save as much as 35% to 50% off full-fare economy. Note that these fares, which once could be bought only after arrival in Europe, are now sold in the US and can be bought before departure.

It is not easy to inform yourself about stopover possibilities by talking to most airline reservations clerks. More than likely, an inquiry concerning any projected trip will prompt the reply that a particular route is nonstop aboard the carrier in question, thereby precluding stopovers completely, or that the carrier does not fly to all the places you want to visit. It may take additional inquiries, perhaps with the aid of a travel agent, to determine the full range of options regarding stopover privileges. Travelers might be able to squeeze in visits to Lisbon and Madrid on a first class ticket to Nice, for instance; Amsterdam and Brussels can be visited on a ticket to Paris; and Paris might only be the first of many free European stopovers possible on a one-way or round-trip ticket to the Middle East or points beyond. The airline that flies you on the first leg of your trip across the Atlantic issues the ticket, though you may have to use several different airlines in order to complete your travel. First class tickets are valid for a full year, so there's no rush.

Taxes and Other Fees – Travelers who have shopped for the best possible flight at the lowest possible price should be warned that a number of extras will be added to that price and collected by the airline or travel agent who issues the ticket. In addition to the $3 International Air Transportation Tax — a departure tax paid by all passengers flying from the US to a foreign destination — there is now a $10 US Federal Inspection Fee levied on all air and cruise passengers who arrive in the US from outside North America (those arriving from Canada, Mexico, the Caribbean, and US territories are exempt). Payable at the time a round-trip or incoming ticket is purchased, it combines a $5 customs inspection fee and a $5 immigration inspection fee, both instituted in 1986 to finance the hiring of additional inspectors to reduce delays at gateways.

Still another fee is charged by some airlines to cover more stringent security procedures, prompted by recent terrorist incidents. The 8% federal US Transportation Tax, which applies to travel within the US, is already included in advertised fares and in the prices quoted by reservations clerks. It does not apply to passengers flying between US cities en route to a foreign destination, unless the trip includes a stopover of more than 12 hours at a US point. Someone flying from Los Angeles to New York and stopping in New York for more than 12 hours before boarding a flight to Europe, for instance, would pay the 8% tax on the domestic portion of the trip.

Reservations – Those who don't have the time and patience to personally investigate all possible air departures and connections for a proposed trip should consult a travel agent. When making plane reservations through a travel agent, ask the agent to give the airline your home phone number as well as a daytime business number. All too often the agent uses his or her agency number as the official contact for changes in flight plans. During the winter, especially, weather conditions hundreds or even thousands of miles away can wreak havoc with flight schedules. Aircraft are constantly in use, and a plane delayed in the Orient or on the West Coast can miss its scheduled flight from the East Coast the next morning. The airlines are fairly reliable about getting this sort of information to passengers if they can reach them; diligence does little good at 6 PM if the airline has only the agency or an office number.

If you look at the back of your ticket, you'll see the need for reconfirmation of return flights stated explicitly. Some (though increasingly fewer) return reservations from international destinations are automatically canceled after a required reconfirmation period (typically 72 hours) has passed — even if you have a confirmed, fully paid ticket in hand. Reconfirmation is not required on domestic flights, but it is still a good idea, allowing you to make sure in plenty of time that the airline did not slip up in entering your original reservation, or in registering any changes you may have made since, and that it has your seat reservation request in the computer. Every travel agent or airline ticket office should give each passenger a reminder to reconfirm flights, but this seldom happens, so the responsibility rests with the traveler. Don't be lulled into a false sense of security by the "OK" on your ticket next to the number and time of the return flight. That only means that a reservation has been entered; a reconfirmation may still be necessary.

If you plan not to take a reserved flight, by all means inform the airline of your cancellation. Because the problem of "no-shows" is a consistently annoying one for airlines, they are allowed to overbook flights, a practice that often contributes to the threat of denied boarding for a certain number of passengers (see *Getting Bumped,* below). Let the airline know you're not coming and you'll spare everyone some confusion. Bear in mind that only certain kinds of tickets allow the luxury of last-minute changes in flight plans — those sold on an open reservation system (first class and full-fare coach) do, while excursions and other discount fares are often restricted in some way. Even first class and coach passengers should remember that if they do not show up for a flight that is the first of several connecting ones, the airline will cancel all of their reservations unless informed not to do so.

Seating – For most types of tickets, airline seats are usually assigned on a first-come, first-served basis at check-in, although some airlines make it possible to reserve a seat at the time of ticket purchase. Always check in early for your flight, even with advance seat assignments.

Most airlines furnish seating charts, which make choosing a seat much easier, but, in general, there are a few basics to consider. You must decide first whether you prefer the smoking or non-smoking section and a window, aisle, or middle seat.

The amount of legroom provided (as well as chest room, especially when the seat in front of you is in a reclining position) is determined by something called "pitch," a measure of the distance between the back of the seat in front of you and the front of your seat. The amount of pitch is a matter of airline policy, not the type of plane you fly. First class and business class seats have the greatest pitch, a fact that figures prominently in airline advertising. In economy class or coach, the standard pitch ranges from 33 to as little as 31 inches — downright cramped. The number of seats abreast, another factor determining comfort, depends on a combination of airline policy and airplane dimensions. First and business classes have the fewest seats per row. Economy generally has 9 seats per row on a DC-10 or an L-1011, making either one slightly more comfortable than a 747, on which there are normally 10 seats per row. Charter flights on DC-10s and L-1011s, however, often have 10 seats per row and can be noticeably more cramped than 747 charters, on which the seating normally remains at 10 per row.

Airline representatives claim that most aircraft are more stable toward the front and midsection, while seats farthest away from the engines are quietest. Passengers who have long legs and are traveling on a wide-body aircraft might request a seat directly behind a door or emergency exit, since these seats often have greater than average pitch, or a seat in the first row of a given section, since these seats have extra legroom. It is often impossible, however, to see the movie from these seats, which are directly behind the plane's exits. Be aware that the first row of the economy section (called a "bulk-head" seat) on a conventional aircraft (not a widebody) does *not* offer extra legroom, since the fixed partition will not permit passengers to slide their feet under it, and that watching a movie from this first row seat can be difficult and uncomfortable. A window seat protects you from aisle traffic and clumsy serving carts, and also allows you a view, while an aisle seat enables you to get up and stretch your legs without disturbing your fellow travelers. Middle seats are the least desirable, and seats in the last row are the most undesirable of all, since they seldom recline fully. If you wish to avoid children on your flight, remember that families generally do not sit in smoking areas. Once in the air, if you find that you are sitting in an especially noisy section, you are usually free to move to any unoccupied seat — if there is one.

If you have a weight problem, you may face the prospect of a long flight with special trepidation. Center seats in the alignments of wide-body 747s, L1011s, and DC-10s are about 1½ inches wider than those on either side, so larger travelers tend to be more comfortable there.

Simply reserving an airline seat in advance, however, may actually guarantee very little. Most airlines require that passengers arrive at the departure gate at least 30 minutes (sometimes more) ahead of time to hold a seat reservation. United, for example, cancels seat assignments and may not honor reservations of passengers not checked in 20 minutes before the scheduled flight time for flights within the US (except Hawaii), 30 minutes before flights to and from Hawaii, Canada, and Mexico, and 45 minutes to and from all other international destinations. As this is only one airline's policy, it pays to carefully read the fine print on the back of your ticket and plan ahead.

A far better strategy is to visit an airline ticket office (or one of a select group of travel agents) to secure an actual boarding pass for your specific flight. Once this has been issued, airline computers show you as checked in, and you effectively own the seat you have selected (although some carriers may not honor boarding passes of passengers arriving at the gate less than 10 minutes before departure). This is also good — but not foolproof — insurance against getting bumped from an overbooked flight and is, therefore, an especially valuable tactic at peak holiday travel times.

Smoking – The US government has adopted minimum standards to ensure that non-smokers will not be "unreasonably burdened" by passengers who smoke. For a wallet-size guide, which notes in detail the rights of non-smokers according to these regulations, send a stamped, self-addressed envelope to ASH (Action on Smoking and Health), Airline Card, 2013 H St. NW, Washington, DC 20006 (phone: 202-659-4310). The US Department of Transportation has determined that non-smoking sections must be enlarged to accommodate all passengers who wish to sit in a non-smoking section. According to a recently added proviso, however, the airline does not have to shift seating to accommodate non-smokers who arrive late for the flight or travelers flying standby. Cigar and pipe smoking are prohibited on all flights, even in the smoking sections. These rules apply only to domestic flights and to flights by US carriers departing from or returning to the US. They do not apply to flights by foreign carriers into or out of the US.

Flying with Children – On longer flights, the bulkhead seats are usually reserved for families with small children. As a general rule, an infant under 2 years of age (and not occupying a seat) flies to Europe at 10% of whatever fare the accompanying adult is paying. A second infant without a second adult pays the fare applicable to children aged 2 through 11. In most cases this amounts to 50% of an adult economy fare and two-thirds of an adult APEX fare.

Most airlines have complimentary bassinets. Ask about obtaining one when you make your reservation, and when checking in, request a bulkhead or other seat that has enough room in front to use it. On some planes it hooks into a bulkhead wall; on others it is placed on the floor in front of you. Even if you do use a bassinet, babies must be held during takeoff and landing. (For more information on flying with children, see *Hints for Traveling with Children.*)

Meals – If you have specific diet requirements (vegetarian, kosher, low calorie, low sodium, and so on), be sure to let the airlines know well before departure time. There is no extra charge for this option. It is, however, advisable to request special meals when you make your reservations — check-in time is too late. It's also wise to reconfirm that your request for a special meal has made its way into the airline's computer — the time to do this is 24 hours before departure.

Getting Bumped – A special air travel problem is the possibility that an airline will accept more reservations (and sell more tickets) than there are seats on a given flight. This is entirely legal and is done to make up for "no-shows," passengers who don't show up for a flight for which they have made reservations and bought tickets. If the airline has oversold the flight and everyone does show up, there simply aren't enough seats. When this happens, the airline is subject to stringent rules designed to protect travelers.

In such cases, the airline first seeks ticketholders willing to give up their seats voluntarily in return for a negotiable sum of money or some other inducement, such as an offer of upgraded seating on the next flight or a voucher for a free trip at some other time. If there are not enough volunteers, the airline may bump passengers against their wishes. Anyone inconvenienced in this way, however, is entitled to an explanation of the criteria used to determine who does and does not get on the flight, as well as to compensation if the resulting delay exceeds certain limits. If the airline can put the bumped passengers on an alternate flight that gets them to their planned destination within 1 hour of their originally scheduled arrival time, no compensation is owed. If the delay is more than an hour but less than 2 hours on a domestic US flight, they must be paid denied-boarding compensation equivalent to the one-way fare to their destination (but not more than $200). If the delay is more than 2 hours after the original arrival time on a domestic flight or more than 4 hours on an international flight, the compensation must be doubled (not more than $400). The airline may also offer bumped travelers a voucher for a free flight instead of the denied-boarding compensation. The passenger can choose either the money or the voucher, the dollar value of which may be no less than the monetary compensation to which the passenger would be entitled. The voucher is not a substitute for the bumped passenger's original ticket; the airline continues to honor that as well. Keep in mind that the above regulations and policies are for flights leaving the US only; they do *not* apply to charters or to inbound flights from Europe, even on US carriers.

In Europe, each airline is free to determine what compensation it will pay to passengers who are bumped because of overbooking. However, they are required to spell out their policy on the airline ticket. Some European airline policies are similar to the US policy. Passengers involuntarily bumped are generally paid the price of a one-way ticket (up to $200) if the airline can get them to their destination within 4 hours of the original arrival time, and twice that amount (up to $400) if they reach their destination 4 or more hours late. However, don't assume all carriers will be as generous.

To protect yourself as best you can against getting bumped, arrive at the airport early, allowing plenty of time to check in and get to the gate. If the flight is oversold, ask immediately for the written statement explaining the airline's policy on denied-boarding compensation and its boarding priorities. If the airline refuses to give you this information, or if you feel it has not handled the situation properly, file a complaint with both the airline and the appropriate government agency (see *Consumer Protection,* below).

Delays and Cancellations – The above compensation rules also do not apply if the flight is canceled or delayed, or if a smaller aircraft is substituted due to mechanical problems. Each airline has its own policy for assisting passengers whose flights are delayed or canceled or who must wait for another flight because their original one was overbooked. Most airline personnel will make new travel arrangements if necessary. If the delay is longer than 4 hours, the airline may pay for a phone call or telegram, a meal, and in some cases a hotel room and transportation to it.

Deregulation of US airlines has meant that travelers must find out for themselves what they are entitled to receive. A useful booklet, *Fly Rights, A Guide to Air Travel in the US,* is available for $1 from the Superintendent of Documents, US Government Printing Office, Washington, DC 20402-9325 (phone: 202-783-3238). When ordering, specify the booklet's stock number, 050-000-00513-5, and allow 3 to 4 weeks for delivery.

■**Caution:** If you are bumped or miss a flight, be sure to ask the airline to notify other airlines on which you have reservations or connecting flights. When your name is taken off the passenger list of your initial flight, the computer automatically cancels all of your reservations unless *you* take steps to preserve them.

Baggage – Travelers from the US face two different kinds of rules. When you fly on a US airline or on a major international carrier, US baggage regulations will be in effect. Though airline baggage allowances vary slightly, in general all passengers are allowed to carry on board, without charge, one piece of luggage that will fit easily under a seat of the plane or in an overhead bin and whose combined dimensions (length, width, and depth) do not exceed 45 inches. Most airlines will allow you to check this bag in the hold if you prefer not to carry it with you, but a few require that it be carried on and stowed in the cabin. A reasonable amount of reading material, camera equipment, and a handbag are also allowed. In addition, all passengers are allowed to check two bags in the cargo hold: one usually not to exceed 62 inches when length, width, and depth are combined, the other not to exceed 55 inches in combined dimensions. No single bag may weigh more than 70 pounds. Air France, however, permits 88 pounds in first class, 66 pounds in business class, and 50 pounds in economy class; other European carriers' policies may also vary.

Charges for additional, oversize, or overweight bags are usually made at a flat rate, the actual dollar amount varying from carrier to carrier. If you plan to travel with a bike, skis, golf clubs, or other sports gear, be sure to check with the airline beforehand. Most have procedures for handling such baggage, but you will probably have to pay for transport regardless of how much other baggage you have checked.

Airline policies regarding baggage allowances for children vary and are usually based on the percentage of full adult fare paid. Children paying 50% or more of an adult fare on most US carriers are entitled to the same baggage allowance as a full-fare passenger, whereas infants traveling at 10% of an adult fare are entitled to only one piece of baggage, the combined dimensions of which may not exceed 45 inches — 39 inches on

TWA. Particularly for international carriers, it's wise to check ahead; for instance, often there is no luggage allowance for a child traveling on an adult's lap or in a bassinet. (For more information, see *Traveling with Children.*)

On European local or trunk carriers, in general, baggage allowances follow the same guidelines as major carriers. However, especially on regional and local airlines, luggage may be subject to the old weight determination, under which each economy or discount passenger is allowed only a total of 44 pounds of luggage without additional charge. First class or business passengers are allowed a total of 66 pounds.

To reduce the chances of your luggage going astray, remove all airline tags from previous trips, label each bag inside and out — with your business address rather than your home address on the outside, to prevent thieves from knowing whose house might be unguarded. Lock everything and double-check the tag that the airline attaches to make sure that it is coded for your destination: CDG for Charles de Gaulle in Paris or HTH for Heathrow in London, for instance. If your bags are not in the baggage claim area after your flight, or if they're damaged, report the problem to airline personnel immediately. Keep in mind that policies regarding the specific time limit in which you have to make your claim vary from carrier to carrier. Fill out a report form on your lost or damaged luggage and keep a copy of it and your claim check. If you must surrender the check to claim a damaged bag, get a receipt for it to prove that you did, indeed, check your baggage on the flight. If luggage is missing, be sure to give the airline your destination and/or a telephone number where you can be reached. Also take the name and number of the person in charge of recovering lost luggage. Most airlines have emergency funds for passengers stranded away from home without their luggage, but if it turns out your bags are truly lost and not simply delayed, do not then and there sign any paper indicating you'll accept an offered settlement. Since the airline is responsible for the value of your bags within certain statutory limits ($1,250 for a lost bag on a domestic flight; $9.07 per pound on an international flight), you should take some time to assess the extent of your loss (see *Insurance* in this section). It's a good idea to keep records indicating the value of the contents of your luggage. An alternative is to take a Polaroid picture of the most valuable of your packed items just after putting them in your suitcase.

Considering the increased incidence of damage to baggage, it's now more than ever a good idea to keep the sales slips that confirm how much you paid for your bags. These are invaluable in establishing the value of damaged baggage and eliminate any arguments. A better way to protect your precious baggage from the luggage-eating conveyers is to try to carry your gear on board wherever possible.

Be aware that airport security is increasingly an issue all over Europe, and is taken very seriously. Heavily armed police patrol the airports, and unattended luggage of any description may be confiscated and even destroyed. Passengers checking in at an airport may undergo at least two separate inspections of their tickets, passports, and luggage by courteous but serious airline personnel — who ask passengers if their baggage has been out of their possession between packing and the airport or if they have been given gifts or other items to transport — before checked items are accepted into the baggage-handling system. In other words, do not agree to take anything on board for a stranger.

Airline Clubs – US carriers often have clubs for travelers who pay for membership. These clubs are not solely for first class passengers. Membership (which, by law, now requires a fee) entitles the traveler to use the private lounges at airports along their route, to refreshments served in those lounges, and to check-cashing privileges at most of their counters. Extras include special telephone numbers for individual reservations, embossed luggage tags, and a membership card for identification. Two airlines that offer membership in such clubs are: Pan American — the *Clipper Club,* single yearly membership $150, spouse an additional $45, 3-year and lifetime memberships also available — and TWA — the *Ambassador Club,* single yearly membership $150, spouse an additional $25, and lifetime memberships also available. However, these clubs do not have facilities in all airports. Lounge privileges are also offered to first class passengers, and other airlines also offer a variety of special club and lounge facilities in many airports.

CHARTER FLIGHTS: By booking a block of seats on a specially arranged flight, charter operators offer travelers air transportation, often coupled with a hotel room, meals, and other travel services, for a substantial reduction over the full coach or economy fare.

Charters were once the best bargain around, but this is no longer necessarily the case. As a result, charter flights have been discontinued in many areas, but to some popular vacation spots, they can still be a good buy. They are especially attractive to people in smaller cities or out-of-the-way places, because they frequently take off from nearby airports, saving travelers the inconvenience and expense of getting to a major gateway. Where demand persists, charter operators will continue to rent planes or seats from scheduled airlines (or from special charter airlines) and offer flights to the public directly through advertisements or travel agents. You buy the ticket from the operator or the agent, not from the airline owning the plane. With the advent of APEX and various promotional fares on the major airlines and the appearance of low-fare airlines, however, charter flights lost some of their budget-conscious clientele and suffered some lean years, especially on highly competitive routes with a choice of other bargains. At the same time, many of the larger companies running charter programs began to offer both charter flights and discounted scheduled flights (see below). Nevertheless, among the current offerings, charter flights to European cities are common, a sign that they still represent a good value.

Charter travel once required that an individual be a member of a club or other "affinity" group whose main purpose was not travel. But since the approval of "public charters" years ago, operators have had some of the flexibility of scheduled airlines, making charters more competitive. Public charters are open to anyone, whether part of a group or not, and have no advance booking or minimum stay requirements. One-way arrangements are permitted, though charters are almost always round-trip, and it is unlikely that you would be sold a one-way seat on a round-trip flight. Operators can offer air-only charters, selling transportation alone, or they can offer charter packages — the flight plus a combination of land arrangements such as accommodations, meals, tours, or car rental.

From the consumer's standpoint, charters differ from scheduled airlines in two main respects: you generally need to book and pay in advance, and you can't change the itinerary or the departure and return dates once you've booked the flight. In practice, however, these restrictions don't always apply. For instance, it's possible to book a one-way charter in the US, giving you more flexibility in scheduling your return. However, note that American regulations pertaining to charters may be more permissive than the charter laws of other countries. For example, if you want to book a one-way foreign charter back to the US, you may find advance booking rules in force.

Some things to keep in mind about the charter game:

1. It cannot be repeated often enough that if you are forced to cancel your trip, you can lose much (and possibly all) of your money unless you have cancellation insurance, which is a *must* (see *Insurance*). Frequently, if the cancellation is well in advance (often 6 weeks or more), you may forfeit only a $25 or $50 penalty. If you cancel only 2 or 3 weeks before the flight, there may be no refund at all unless you or the operator can supply another passenger.
2. Charter flights may be canceled by the operator up to 10 days before departure for any reason, usually underbooking. Your money is returned in this event, but there may be too little time to make new arrangements.

3. Most charters have little of the flexibility of regularly scheduled flights regarding refunds and the changing of flight dates; if you book a return flight, you must be on it or lose your money.
4. Charter operators are permitted to assess a surcharge, if fuel or other costs warrant it, of up to 10% of the airfare up to 10 days before departure.
5. Because of the economics of charter flights, your plane almost always will be full, so you will be crowded, though not necessarily uncomfortable.

The savings provided by charters varies, depending on their point of departure in the US and the countries to which they are headed (some governments do not allow charters to land at all; others allow them to undercut scheduled fares by a wide margin). As a rule, a charter to any given destination can cost anywhere from $50 to $200 less than an APEX fare on a major carrier, with West Coast charters realizing a greater saving than East Coast charters.

Bookings – If you do take a charter, read the contract's fine print carefully and pay particular attention to the following:

1. Instructions concerning the payment of the deposit and its balance and to whom the check is to be made payable. Ordinarily, checks are made out to an escrow account, which means the charter company can't spend your money until your flight has safely returned. This provides some protection for you. To ensure the safe handling of your money, make out your check to the escrow account, the number of which must appear by law on the brochure, though all too often it is on the back in fine print. Write the details of the charter, including the destination and dates, on the face of the check; on the back, print "For Deposit Only." Your travel agent may prefer that you make out your check to the agency, saying that it will then pay the tour operator the fee minus commission. It is perfectly legal to write the check as we suggest, however, and if your agent objects too vociferously (he or she should trust the tour operator to send the proper commission), consider taking your business elsewhere. If you don't make your check out to the escrow account, you lose the protection of escrow should the trip be canceled. Furthermore, recent bankruptcies in the travel industry have served to point out that even the protection of escrow may not be enough to safeguard a traveler's investment. More and more, insurance is becoming a necessity (see *Insurance*). The charter company should be bonded (usually by an insurance company), and if you want to file a claim against it, the claim should be sent to the bonding agent. The contract will set a time limit within which a claim must be filed.
2. Note specific stipulations and penalties for cancellations. Most charters allow you to cancel up to 45 days in advance, but some cancellation dates are 50 to 60 days before departure.
3. Stipulations regarding cancellation and major changes made by the charterer. US rules say that charter flights may not be canceled within 10 days of departure except when circumstances — such as natural disasters or political upheavals — make it physically impossible to fly. Charterers may make "major changes," however, such as in the date or place of departure or return, but you are entitled to cancel and receive a refund if you don't wish to accept these changes. A price increase of more than 10% at any time up to 10 days before departure is considered a major change; no price increase at all is allowed during the 10 days immediately prior to departure.

DISCOUNTS ON SCHEDULED FLIGHTS: The APEX fare is an example of a promotional fare offered on regularly scheduled transatlantic flights by most major airlines. Promotional fares are often called discount fares because they are lower in price than what used to be the standard airline fare — full-fare economy. Nevertheless, they cost the traveler the same whether they are bought through a travel agent or directly from the airline. Tickets that cost less if bought from some outlet other than the airline do exist, however. While it is likely that the vast majority of travelers flying to Europe in the near future will be doing so on a promotional fare or charter rather than on a "discount" air ticket of this sort, it is still a good idea for cost-conscious consumers to be aware of the latest developments in the budget airfare scene. Note that the following discussion makes clear distinctions among the types of discounts available based on how they reach the consumer; in actual practice, the distinctions are not nearly so precise. One organization may operate part of its business in one fashion and the remainder in another; a second organization may operate all of its business in the same fashion, but outsiders — and sometimes the organization itself — would have difficulty classifying it.

Net Fare Sources – The newest notion for reducing the costs of travel services comes from travel agents who offer individual travelers "net" fares. Defined simply, a net fare is the bare minimum amount at which an airline or tour operator will carry a prospective traveler. It doesn't include the amount that would normally be paid to the travel agent as a commission. Traditionally, such commissions amount to about 10% on domestic fares and from 8% to 20% on international tickets — not counting significant additions to these levels that are payable retroactively when agents sell more than a specific volume of tickets or trips for a single supplier. At press time, at least one travel agency in the US was offering travelers the opportunity to purchase tickets and/or tours for a net price. Instead of making its income from individual commissions, this agency assesses a fixed fee that may or may not be a bargain for travelers; it requires a little arithmetic to determine whether to use the services of a net travel agent or those of one who accepts conventional commissions.

McTravel Travel Services (130 S. Jefferson, Chicago, IL 60606-3691; phone: 800-333-3335 in the US except Illinois; 312-876-1116 in Illinois and Canada) is a formula fee-based agency that rebates its ordinary agency commission to the customer. For domestic flights, an agent will find the lowest retail ticket price, then rebate 8% of that price minus an $8 ticket-writing charge. The rebate percentage for international flights varies from 8% to 20%, depending on the airline selected, and the ticket-writing fee is $20. *McTravel* will rebate on all tickets including max savers, super savers, and senior citizen passes. Available 7 days a week, reservations should be made far enough in advance to allow the tickets to be sent by first class mail, since extra charges accrue for special handling as they do for reservations that require any significant amount of research. It's possible to economize further by making your own reservation, then asking *McTravel* only to write/issue your ticket. For travelers outside the Chicago area, business may be transacted by phone and purchases charged to a credit card.

One of the potential drawbacks of buying from agencies selling travel services at net fares is that your options may be limited. *McTravel* recently lost a court battle with American Airlines, which refused to do business with the discounter. A US District Court in Chicago ruled in the airline's favor, and other carriers are expected to follow suit.

Consolidators and Bucket Shops – Other vendors of travel services can afford to sell tickets to their customers at an even greater discount because the airline has sold the tickets to them at a substantial discount, a practice in which many airlines indulge, albeit discreetly, preferring that the general public not know they are undercutting their own "list" prices. Airlines anticipating a slow season on a particular route sometimes sell off a certain portion of their capacity at a very great discount to a wholesaler, or consolidator. The wholesaler is sometimes a charter operator who resells the seats to the public as though they were charter seats, which is why prospective travelers perusing the brochures of charter operators with large programs frequently see a number of flights designated as "scheduled service." As often as not, however, the consolidator, in turn, sells the seats to an agency specializing in discounting. Airlines can also sell seats directly to such an agency, which thus acts as its own consolidator. The airline offers the seats either at a net wholesale price, but without the volume-purchase requirement that would be difficult for a retail travel agency to fulfill, or at the standard price, but with a commission override large enough (as high as 50%) to allow both a profit and a price reduction to the public.

Travel agencies specializing in discounting were once known as "bucket shops," a term fraught with connotations of unreliability. But in today's highly competitive travel marketplace, more and more conventional travel agencies are selling consolidator-supplied tickets, and the old bucket shops are becoming more respectable, too. Agencies that specialize in discounted tickets are in most large cities and can be found by studying the smaller ads in the travel sections of the Sunday newspapers. They deal largely in transatlantic and other international tickets and, on the whole, do not offer notable reductions on domestic travel, if they sell domestic tickets at all.

Before buying a discounted ticket, whether from a bucket shop or a conventional, full-service travel agency, keep the following considerations in mind: To be in a position to judge how much you'll be saving, first find out the "list" prices of tickets to your destination by calling the major airlines serving the route. Then, do some comparison shopping among agencies, always bearing in mind that the lowest-priced ticket may not provide the most convenient or most comfortable flight (bargain prices are usually available on an airline's less popular routes, so your routing might be roundabout or you may be required to endure a long layover along the way). Also bear in mind that a ticket that may not differ much in price from one available directly from the airline may, however, allow the circumvention of booking restrictions such as the advance-purchase requirement. If your plans are less than final, be sure to find out about any other restrictions, such as penalties for canceling a flight or changing a reservation. Most discount tickets are non-endorsable, meaning they can only be used on the airline that issued them, and they are usually marked "non-refundable" to prevent their being cashed in for a list price refund. (A refund of the price paid for the ticket is often possible, but it is obtained through the outlet from which it was purchased rather than from the airline.)

A great many bucket shops are small businesses operating on a thin margin, so it's a good idea to check the local Better Business Bureau for any complaints registered against the one with which you're dealing before parting with any money. If you still do not feel reassured, consider buying discounted tickets only through a conventional travel agency, which can be expected to have found its own reliable source of consolidator tickets — some of the largest consolidators, in fact, sell only to travel agencies.

A few bucket shops require payment in cash or by certified check or money order, but if credit cards are accepted, use that option, which allows purchasers to protest charges if they do not receive what they paid for. Note, however, if buying from a charter operator selling both scheduled and charter flights, that the scheduled seats are not protected by the regulations — including use of escrow accounts — governing the charter seats. Well-established charter operators, nevertheless, may extend the same protections to their scheduled flights; when this is the case, consumers should be sure that the payment option selected directs their money into the escrow account.

■**Note:** Although rebating and discounting are becoming increasingly common, there is some legal ambiguity concerning them. Strictly speaking, it is legal to discount domestic tickets but not to discount international tickets. On the other hand, the law that prohibits discounting, the Federal Aviation Act of 1958, is consistently ignored these days, in part because consumers benefit from the practice and in part because many illegal arrangements are indistinguishable from legal ones. Since the line separating the two is so fine that even the authorities can't always tell the difference, it is unlikely that most consumers would be able to do so, and, in fact, it is not illegal to *buy* a discount ticket. If the issue of legality bothers you, ask the agency whether any ticket you're about to buy would be permissible under the above-mentioned act.

Other Discount Travel Sources – An excellent source of information on economical travel opportunities is the *Consumer Reports Travel Letter,* published monthly by Consumers Union. It keeps abreast of the scene on a wide variety of fronts, including package tours, rental cars, insurance, and more, but it is especially helpful for its comprehensive coverage of airfares, offering guidance on all the options from scheduled flights on major or low-fare airlines to charters and discount sources. For a year's subscription, send $37 to Consumer Reports Travel Letter, PO Box 2886, Boulder, CO 80322 (phone: 800-525-0643). Another source is *Travel Smart,* a monthly newsletter offering information on a wide variety of trips, with additional discount travel services available to subscribers. For a year's subscription, send $37 to Communications House, 40 Beechdale Rd., Dobbs Ferry, NY 10522 (phone: 914-693-8300 in New York; 800-327-3633 elsewhere in the US).

Still another way to take advantage of bargain airfares is open to those who have a flexible schedule. A number of organizations, usually set up as last-minute travel clubs and functioning on a membership basis, routinely keep in touch with travel suppliers to help them dispose of unsold inventory at discounts of between 15% and 60%. A great deal of the inventory consists of complete tour packages and cruises, but some clubs offer air-only charter seats and, occasionally, seats on scheduled flights. Members pay an annual fee and receive the toll-free number of a telephone hot line to call for information on imminent trips. In some cases, they also receive periodic mailings with information on upcoming trips for which there is more advance notice. Despite the suggestive names of the clubs providing these services, last-minute travel does not necessarily mean than you cannot make plans until literally the last minute. Trips can be announced as little as a few days or as much as 2 months before departure, but the average is from 1 to 4 weeks. It does mean that your choice at any given time is limited to what is offered and, if your heart is set on a particular destination, you might not find what you want, no matter how attractive the bargains. Among these organizations are the following:

Discount Club of America, 61-33 Woodhaven Blvd., Rego Park, NY 11374 (phone: 718-335-9612 or 800-321-9587). Annual fee: $39.

Discount Travel International, Ives Bldg., 114 Forrest Ave., Suite 205, Narberth, PA 19072 (phone: 215-668-2182 in Pennsylvania; 800-824-4000 elsewhere in the US). Annual fee: $45 per household.

Encore Short Notice, 4501 Forbes Blvd., Lanham, MD 20706 (phone: 301-459-8020 or 800-638-0930 for customer service). Annual fee: $36 per family.

Last-Minute Travel Club, 132 Brookline Ave., Boston, MA 02215 (phone: 617-267-9800 or 800-LAST-MIN). Annual fee: $30 per person; $35 per couple or family.

Moment's Notice, 40 E. 49th St., New York, NY 10017 (phone: 212-486-0503). Annual fee: $45 per family.

On Call to Travel, 14335 SW Allen Blvd., Suite 209, Beaverton, OR 97005 (phone: 503-643-7212; members may call collect). Annual fee: $39 per family, first year; $29 yearly thereafter.

Spur-of-the-Moment Tours and Cruises, 10780 Jefferson Blvd., Culver City, CA 90230 (phone: 213-839-2418 in California; 800-343-1991 elsewhere in the US). No fee.

Stand Buys Limited, 311 W. Superior St., Suite 414, Chicago IL 60610 (phone: 800-331-0257 for membership information; 800-848-8402 for customer service; 800-433-9383 for reservations). Annual fee: $45 per family.

Worldwide Discount Travel Club, 1674 Meridian Ave., Miami Beach, FL 33139 (phone: 305-534-2082). Annual fee: $50 per family; $40 per person.

Generic Air Travel – Organizations that apply the same flexible-schedule idea to air travel only and sell tickets at literally the last minute also exist. The service they provide is sometimes known as "generic" air travel, and it operates somewhat like an ordinary airline standby service except that the organizations running it offer seats on not one but several scheduled and charter airlines.

One pioneer of generic flights is *Airhitch* (2901 Broadway, Suite 100, New York, NY 10025; phone: 212-864-2000), which arranges flights to Europe from various US cities at very low prices ($160 or less one-way from the East Coast in 1989, $269 or less from the West Coast, and $229 or less from other points). Precise destinations are not guaranteed, however. Prospective travelers register by paying a fee (applicable toward the fare) and stipulate a range of acceptable departure dates and the place to which they would prefer to fly, along with alternative choices. The Wednesday before the date range begins, they are notified of at least two flights that will be available during the time period, agree on an assignment, and remit the balance of the fare to the company. If they do not accept any of the suggested flights, they lose their deposit; if, through no fault of their own, they do not ultimately get on any agreed-on flight, all of their money is refunded. Return flights are arranged the same way. *Airhitch* cautions that, given the number of variables attached to the flights, they are suitable only for travelers willing to accept approximate destinations, although the time period will be the one specified and, for a majority of travelers, the place of arrival, too. Another of the company's programs, the Target program, offers greater certainty regarding destinations, but for higher prices.

BARTERED TRAVEL SOURCES: Say a company buys advertising space in a newspaper for a hotel. As payment, the hotel gives the company a number of hotel rooms in lieu of cash. This is barter, a common means of exchange among hotels, airlines, car rental companies, cruise lines, tour operators, restaurants, and other service companies. When a bartering company finds itself with excess hotel rooms (or empty airline seats or cruise ship cabin space, and so on) and offers them to the public, considerable savings can be realized.

Bartered-travel clubs can often offer discounts of up to 50% to members who pay an annual fee (approximately $50 at press time) that entitles them to select the flights, cruises, hotels, that the company obtained by barter. Members usually present a voucher, club credit card, or scrip (a dollar-denomination voucher negotiable only for the bartered product) to the hotel, which in turn subtracts the dollar amount from the bartering company's account.

Selling bartered travel is a perfectly legitimate means of retailing. One advantage to club members is that they don't have to wait until the last minute to obtain room or flight reservations. However, hotel rooms and airline seats are usually offered to members on a space-available basis. Ticket vouchers are good only for a particular hotel and cannot be used elsewhere. The same applies to car rentals, cruises, package tours, and restaurants. The following clubs offer bartered travel at a discount to members:

IGT (*In Good Taste*) *Services,* 22 E. 29th St., New York, NY 10016 (phone: 212-725-9600 or 800-444-8872). The annual membership fee of $48 includes $25 credit toward future charges.

The Travel Guild, 18210 Redmond Way, Redmond, WA 98052 (phone: 206-885-1213). Annual membership fee: $48.

Travel World Leisure Club, 225 W. 34th St., Suite 2203, New York, NY 10122 (phone: 212-239-4855 or 800-444-TWLC). Annual membership fee: $50 per family.

CONSUMER PROTECTION: Consumers who feel that they have not been dealt with fairly by an airline should make their complaints known. Begin with the customer service representative at the airport where the problem occurs. If he or she cannot resolve your complaint to your satisfaction, write to the airline's consumer office. In a businesslike, typed letter, explain what reservations you held, what happened, the names of the employees who were involved, and what you expect the airline to do to remedy the situation. Send copies (never the originals) of the tickets, receipts, and other documents that back your claims. Ideally, all correspondence should be sent via certified mail, return receipt requested. This provides proof that your complaint was received.

If you still receive no satisfaction and your complaint is against a US carrier, contact the US Department of Transportation. Passengers with consumer complaints — lost baggage, compensation for getting bumped, smoking and non-smoking rules, deceptive practices by an airline, charter regulations — should write to the Consumer Affairs Division, Room 10405, US Department of Transportation, 400 Seventh St. SW, Washington, DC 20590, or call the office at 202-366-2220. DOT personnel stress, however, that consumers should initially direct their complaints to the airline that provoked them.

Travelers with an unresolved complaint involving a European airline can also contact the US Department of Transportation. DOT personnel will do what they can to help resolve all such complaints, although their influence may be limited.

Consumers with complaints against specific European airlines or other travel-related services can write to the appropriate government agency; the national tourist office (see *Sources and Resources*) should be able to provide this information. Outline the specifics in the native language of the country — French for France, Italian for Italy, and so on — in as much detail as possible. (Keep in mind, if a translator is required, this correspondence could get expensive.) The agency will try to resolve the complaint or, if it is out of its jurisdiction, will refer the matter to the proper authorities, and will notify you in writing (in their own language) about the result of their inquires and/or any action taken.

The Department of Transportation's consumer booklet *Fly-Rights* is a good introduction to regulations governing the airlines. To receive a copy, send $1 to the Consumer Information Center, Department 148V, Pueblo, CO 81002. Make your check or money order payable to: Superintendent of Documents, and specify that you want publication 156-T.

To avoid more serious problems, *always* choose charter flights and tour packages with care. When you consider a charter, ask your travel agent who runs it and carefully check out the company. The Better Business Bureau in the company's home city can report on how many complaints, if any, have been lodged against it in the past. As emphasized above, protect yourself with trip cancellation and interruption insurance, which can help safeguard your investment in the event that you or a traveling companion is unable to make the trip and must cancel too late to receive a full refund from the company providing your travel services. (This is advisable whether you're buying a charter flight alone or a tour package for which the airfare is provided by charter or scheduled flight.) Some travel insurance policies have an additional feature, covering the possibility of default or bankruptcy on the part of the tour operator or airline, charter or scheduled.

Should this type of coverage not be available to you (state insurance regulations vary, there is a wide difference in price, and so on), your best bet is to pay for airline tickets and tour packages with a credit card. The federal Fair Credit Billing Act permits purchasers to refuse payment for credit card charges where services have not been delivered, so the onus of dealing with the receiver for a bankrupt airline falls on the credit card company. Do not rely on another airline to honor the ticket you're holding, since the days when virtually all major carriers subscribed to a default protection program that bound them to do so are long gone. Some airlines may voluntarily step forward to accommodate the stranded passengers of a fellow carrier, but this is now an entirely altruistic act.

Traveling by Ship

 Alas, the days when steamships reigned as the primary means of transatlantic transportation are gone, when Italy, France, Sweden, Germany, Norway, the Netherlands, and England — and the US — had fleets of passenger liners that offered week-plus trips across the North Atlantic. Only one ship (*Cunard*'s *Queen Elizabeth 2*) continues to offer this kind of service between the US and Europe with any degree of regularity; others make the trip at most a few times a year. At the same time, the possibility of booking passage to Europe on a cargo ship is becoming less practical. Fewer and fewer travelers, therefore, set foot on European soil with sea legs developed during an ocean voyage. But due to the growing popularity of trips on the inland waterways of Europe, more and more travelers — particularly repeat travelers — are climbing aboard some kind of waterborne conveyance once they've arrived in Europe and are seeing the country from the banks of a river or the towpath of a canal.

CABINS: The most important factor in determining the price of a cruise is the cabin. Cabin prices are set according to size and location. The size can vary considerably on older ships, less so on newer or more recently modernized ones, and may be entirely uniform on the very newest vessels.

Shipboard accommodations have the same pricing pattern as hotels. Suites, which consist of a sitting room–bedroom combination and occasionally a private small deck that could be compared to a patio, cost the most. Prices for other cabins (interchangeably called staterooms) are usually more expensive on the upper passenger decks, less expensive on lower decks. The outside cabins with portholes facing the water cost more than inside cabins without views and are generally preferred. If the cabin has a bathtub instead of a shower, the price will probably be higher. As in all forms of travel, accommodations are more expensive for single travelers. If you are traveling on your own but want to share a double cabin to reduce the cost, some ship lines will attempt to find someone of the same sex willing to share quarters (see *Hints for Single Travelers*).

FACILITIES AND ACTIVITIES: You may not use your cabin very much. Organized shipboard activities are geared to keep you busy. A standard schedule might consist of swimming, sunbathing, and numerous other outdoor recreations. Evenings are devoted to leisurely dining, lounge shows or movies, bingo and other organized games, gambling, dancing, and a midnight buffet. Your cruise fare includes all of these activities — except the cost of drinks.

All cruise ships have at least one major social lounge, a main dining room, several bars, an entertainment room that may double as a discotheque for late dancing, an exercise room, indoor games facilities, at least one pool, and shopping facilities that can range from a single boutique to an arcade. Still others have gambling casinos and/or slot machines, cardrooms, libraries, children's recreation centers, indoor pools (as well as one or more on open decks), separate movie theaters, and private meeting rooms. Open deck space should be ample, because this is where most passengers spend their days at sea.

Usually there is a social director and staff to organize and coordinate activities. Evening entertainment is provided by professionals. Movies are mostly first-run and drinks are moderate in price (or should be) because a ship is exempt from local taxes when at sea.

To prepare for possible illnesses, travelers should get a prescription from their doctors for pills or stomach pacifiers to counteract motion sickness. All ships with more than 12 passengers have a doctor on board and facilities for handling sickness or medical emergencies.

MEALS: All meals on board are usually included in the basic price of a cruise; they are usually abundant and quite palatable. Evening meals are taken in the main dining room, where tables are assigned according to the passengers' preferences. Tables usually accommodate from two to ten; specify your preference when you book your cruise. If there are two sittings, you can also specify which one you want at the time you book or, at the latest, when you board the ship. Later sittings are usually more leisurely. Breakfast is frequently available in your cabin as well as in the main dining room. For lunch, many passengers prefer the buffet offered on deck, usually at or near the pool, but again, the main dining room is available.

DRESS: Most people pack too much for a cruise on the assumption that daytime wear should be chic and every night is a big event. Comfort is a more realistic criterion.

Daytime wear on most ships is decidedly casual. For warm-weather cruises, women can wear a cover-up over a bathing suit through breakfast, swimming, sunbathing and deck activities, lunch, and early cocktails without any change; for men, shorts (with swim trunks underneath) and a casual shirt will be appropriate on deck or in any public room. (Bare feet and swimsuits are usually inappropriate in the dining room.) For travel in cooler seasons, casual, comfortable clothes, including a variety of layers to adjust for changes in the weather, are appropriate for all daytime activities. (For further information on choosing and packing a basic wardrobe, see *Climate and Clothes* in this section.)

Evening wear for most cruises is dressy-casual. Formal wear is probably not necessary for 1-week cruises, optional for longer ones. There aren't many nights when it's expected. Most ships have a Captain's cocktail party the first or second night out and a farewell dinner near the end of the cruise. Women should feel comfortable in hostess gowns, cocktail dresses, or stylish slacks. (To feel completely secure, you may want to pack one very dressy item.) Jackets and ties are always preferred for men in the evening, but a long-sleeve, open-neck shirt with ascot or scarf is usually an acceptable substitute.

TIPS: Tips are a strictly personal expense, and you *are* expected to tip — in particular, your cabin and dining room stewards. Allow $2.50 a day for each steward (more if you wish), and additional sums for very good service. (*Note:* Tips should be paid by each individual in a cabin, whether there are one, two, or more.) Others who may merit tips are the deck steward who sets up your chair at the pool or elsewhere, the wine steward in the dining room, porters who handle your luggage (tip them individually at the time they assist you), and any others who give you personal service. On some ships you can charge your bar tab to your cabin; throw in the tip when you pay it at the end of the cruise. Smart travelers tip twice during the trip: about midway through the cruise and at the end; even wiser travelers tip a bit at the start of the trip to ensure better service throughout. In all, expect to distribute about 15% of your total fare in tips. Although some cruise lines do have a no-tipping-required policy and you are not penalized by the crew for not tipping, naturally, you aren't penalized for tipping, either. If you can restrain yourself, it is better not to tip on those few ships that discourage it. However, never make the mistake of not tipping on the majority of ships, where it is a common, expected practice.

SHIP SANITATION: The US Public Health Service (PHS) currently inspects all passenger vessels calling at US ports, so very precise information is available on which ships meet its requirements and which do not. The further requirement that ships immediately report any illness that occurs on board adds to the available data.

So the problem for a prospective cruise passenger is to determine whether the ship on which he or she plans to sail has met the official sanitary standard. US regulations require the PHS to publish actual grades for the ships inspected — rather than the old pass or fail designation — so it's now easy to determine any cruise ship's sanitary status. Nearly 4,000 travel agents, public health organizations, and doctors receive a copy of each monthly ship sanitation summary, though a random sampling of travel agents indicated that few had any idea what this ship inspection program is all about. Again, the best advice is to deal with a travel agent who specializes in cruise ships and cruise bookings, for he or she is most likely to have the latest information on the sanitary conditions of all cruise ships. To receive a copy of the most recent summary or a particular inspection report, write to Tom Hunt, Public Health Service, 1015 N. America Way, Room 107, Miami, FL 33132, or call 305-536-4307.

TRANSATLANTIC CROSSINGS: For seagoing enthusiasts, *Cunard*'s *Queen Elizabeth 2* is one of the largest and most comfortable vessels afloat, and it has recently undergone a complete overhaul and refurbishing, from a replacement of its engines to a revitalization and redecoration of passenger quarters. Each year, in addition to a full calendar of Caribbean, Bermudian, and European cruises, plus a round-the-world cruise, the *QE2* schedules approximately a dozen round-trip transatlantic crossings between June and, usually, December.

The *QE2* normally sets its course from New York to Southampton, England (a 5-day trip), and then directly back to the US, although on a few of the crossings it proceeds from Southampton to Cherbourg, France, or to another European port before turning back across the Atlantic. Passengers whose ultimate destination is France spend the night ashore in Southampton and arrive with the ship the next day in Cherbourg; those returning to the US from France embark in Cherbourg and sail directly home. (Similarly, on some crossings, the ship calls at various East Coast US ports in addition to New York, thus giving passengers a choice of where to embark or disembark.) For Europe-bound travelers on crossings *not* scheduled to call at Cherbourg, *Cunard* provides other options: For example, by paying a supplement, these passengers can be transferred by air from Southampton to another European destination.

Transatlantic crossings, however, do not come at bargain prices. Last year, the one-way, per-person cost of passage from New York to either Southampton or Cherbourg ranged from $1,330 (for the least expensive, two-per-cabin, transatlantic class accommodations at the end of the season) to $8,415 (for one of the grandest travel experiences imaginable). *Cunard* brings a voyage aboard a luxury liner within reach of the less affluent traveler, however, by offering an air/sea package in conjunction with British Airways. The one-way ticket to Europe by sea includes an allowance toward return economy class airfare from London to any of 57 North American cities — a free flight home, in essence — provided certain length-of-stay restrictions are respected. The allowance can be applied to an upgraded air ticket if desired, and, if you want to splurge, you can even fly home on a specially reserved British Airways' supersonic *Concorde,* provided you make up the difference between the allowance and the *Concorde* fare (the shortfall at press time was $995). *Cunard* also has various European tour packages applicable to the basic air/sea offer.

Cunard is now also offering a particularly economical round-trip air/sea option for travelers with a flexible schedule. Special "standby" fares are available on some transatlantic crossings between the US and London (20 sailings were offered between April and December 1989) and include airfare on British Airways to a number of US gateways. The package cost (at press time, $999 to $1,099 — depending on dates of travel) includes a berth in a double-occupancy "minimum" room on either the *QE2* or *Cunard*'s *Vistafjord* and a one-way British Airways economy class ticket to or from London and New York, Boston, Philadelphia, Miami, Chicago, Detroit, or Washington, DC. For an additional $100, passengers may fly to or from other British Airways US gateways, including Anchorage, Atlanta, Houston, Los Angeles, Pittsburgh, San

Diego, San Francisco, and Seattle. Although this fare is offered strictly on a space-available basis, confirmations are provided 3 weeks prior to sailing. To qualify for this fare, travelers must submit a written application and a $100 deposit to a travel agent or *Cunard;* full payment is due upon confirmation. For information, check with your travel agent or contact Cunard, 555 Fifth Ave., New York, NY 10017 (phone: 212-661-7777, 800-221-4770, or 800-5-CUNARD).

Another interesting transatlantic crossing possibility for those who have the time is what the industry calls a positioning cruise. This is the sailing of a US- or Caribbean-based vessel from its winter berth to the city in Europe from which it will be offering summer cruise programs. Eastbound positioning cruises take place at particular times in the spring; westbound cruises return in the fall. Since ships do not make the return trip until they need to position themselves for the next cruise season, most lines offering positioning cruises have some sea/air arrangement that allows passengers to fly home economically — though the cruises themselves are not an inexpensive way to travel.

Among the ships that have been offering positioning cruises for a number of years are *Cunard*'s *Vistafjord* and ships of the *Royal Viking Line* and *Royal Cruise Line.* Itineraries and ports of call vary from year to year, and in any given year there may be no positioning cruise allowing passengers to disembark at a specific European port. Typically, the ships sail from Florida or San Juan, Puerto Rico, and cross the Atlantic to any one of a number of European ports where the trip may be broken — Barcelona, Cherbourg, Genoa, Le Havre, Lisbon, Málaga, Piraeus, Southampton, Venice — before proceeding to cruise European waters (i.e., the Mediterranean, the Baltic Sea, the Black Sea, the Norwegian fjords). Passengers can elect to stay aboard for the basic transatlantic segment alone or for both the crossing and the subsequent European cruise. For information, ask your travel agent or contact the following cruise lines directly: Cunard, 555 Fifth Ave., New York, NY 10017 (phone: 212-661-7777, 800-221-4770, or 800-5-CUNARD); Royal Viking Line, 95 Merrick, Coral Gables, FL 33134 (phone: 305-447-9660 or 800-634-8000); Royal Cruise Line, One Maritime Plaza, Suite 1400, San Francisco, CA 94111 (phone: 415-956-7200).

For travelers seeking cruises out of British and continental ports, the opportunities are limitless. Northern European waters are particularly popular in summer, with Copenhagen and Amsterdam major embarkation centers, notably for sailings along Norway's fjord-lined coast as well as to major Baltic ports that include Helsinki, Leningrad, and Stockholm. July is the month of the midnight sun; cruises to witness this phenomenon are available out of Bergen, Norway.

Still other major ports for summer cruises in Europe are Calais and Nice in France; Genoa and Venice in Italy; Mainz, Germany, and Basel, Switzerland, for Rhine boat trips; and of course Piraeus, the famed port city of Athens, from which there are innumerable daily sailings for single-day or week-plus cruises to the Aegean Islands (see *Classic Cruises and Wonderful Waterways,* DIVERSIONS).

FREIGHTERS: These are cargo ships that also take a limited number of passengers (usually about 12) in reasonably comfortable accommodations. The idea of traveling by freighter has long appealed to romantic souls, but there are a number of drawbacks to consider before casting off. Once upon a time, a major advantage of freighter travel was its low cost, but this is no longer the case. Though freighters are usually less expensive than cruise ships, the difference is not as great as it once was, and excursion airfares are certainly even less expensive. Accommodations and recreational facilities vary, but freighters were not designed to amuse passengers, so it is important to appreciate the idea of freighter travel itself. Schedules are erratic, and travelers must fit their timetable to that of the ship. Passengers have found themselves waiting as much as a month for a promised sailing, and because freighters follow their cargo commitments, a scheduled port could be omitted at the last minute or a new one added.

Anyone contemplating taking a freighter from a US port across the Atlantic to a

European port should be aware that at press time, only a few freighter lines were carrying passengers on such crossings. Once a week, *Polish Ocean Lines'* freighters accommodate 6 passengers in 3 double cabins on voyages from 8 to 10 days in length from Port Newark, New Jersey, to Le Havre, Rotterdam, and Bremerhaven. The one-way fare from Newark was $788 per person in 1989, and passengers could also board in Baltimore, Maryland, or Wilmington, North Carolina, for an additional $150; round-trip fares were simply double the one-way fares. For information, contact Gdynia America Line, the general agent for Polish Ocean Lines, at 39 Broadway, 14th Floor, New York, NY 10006 (phone: 212-952-1280). Another line, *Container Ships Reederi,* leaving approximately every 2 weeks, with a capacity of 6 to 9 passengers, sails from Long Beach, California, via the Panama Canal to Le Havre, Rotterdam, and Felixstowe in 23 to 24 days. The one-way, per-person fare is $1,975 to $2,110. For information, contact the line's general agent, *Freighter World Cruises* (address below). *Cast* sails from Montreal, Canada, to Antwerp, Belgium, with a capacity of 12 passengers, taking 16 days eastward (to Europe) and 12 days westward (back to Canada). The one-way fare east ranges from $1,575 to $1,788, the westward fare, from $1,275 to $1,485. Ships depart two or three times a month between April and October. Contact the line's general agent, *Freighter World Cruises* (address below). *Mineral Shipping* sails from Savannah, Georgia, to Rotterdam, Holland, taking several weeks; the one-way fare is $850, round-trip takes 33 days and costs $1,900. It also sails from Savannah to Rotterdam via Jamaica; the one-way ticket is $1,000. The ships sail up to twice monthly year-round and can hold up to 12 passengers. Contact the general agent, *Freighter World Cruises* (address below).

Lykes Lines sails from New Orleans to Rotterdam and Bremerhaven in Holland and Felixstowe in Britain, with a capacity of up to 8 passengers. The trip lasts 12 to 13 days, and ships leave every 8 days year-round. A one-way ticket costs $1,400. Contact Lykes Lines, 300 Poydres, New Orleans, LA 70130 (phone: 504-523-6611). Last, *Mediterranean Shipping Co.* sails from Boston, New York, Baltimore, and Norfolk to Antwerp, Hamburg, Felixstowe, and Le Havre, taking 28 days for the trip. The ships can hold 12 passengers and leave weekly year-round. Prices vary based on departure point and destination, but on average the one-way fare runs between $1,200 and $1,800. Contact Mediterranean Shipping Co., 96 Morton St., New York, NY 10014 (phone: 212-691-3760).

Specialists dealing only (or largely) in freighter travel can help prospective passengers arrange trips. They provide information, schedules, and, when you're ready to sail, booking services. Among these agencies are the following:

Freighter World Cruises: A travel agency specializing in freighters. Publishes *Freighter Space Advisory,* a biweekly newsletter listing space available on sailings worldwide ($27 a year, $25 of which can be credited to the cost of a cruise), and acts as general agent for several freighter lines. 180 S. Lake Ave., Suite 335, Pasadena, CA 91101 (phone: 818-449-3106).

Pearl's Freighter Tips: Pearl Hoffman, an experienced hand in freighter travel, finds sailings for her customers and sends them off with all kinds of information and advice. 175 Great Neck Rd., Suite 306, Great Neck, NY 11021 (phone: 516-487-8351).

TravLTips Cruise and Freighter Travel Association: A freighter travel agency and club ($15 a year) whose members receive the bimonthly *TravLTips* magazine of cruise and freighter travel. PO Box 188, Flushing, NY 11358 (phone: 718-939-2400).

INLAND WATERWAYS: Cruising the canals and rivers of Europe is becoming more and more popular, probably in reaction to the speed of jet travel and the normal rush to do as much as possible in as little time as possible. A cabin cruiser or converted barge averages only about 5 miles an hour, covering in a week of slow floating the same distance a car would travel in a few hours of determined driving. Passengers see only a small section of countryside, but they see it in depth and with an intimacy simply impossible any other way.

There are two ways to cruise the inland waterways: by renting your own self-drive boat or by booking aboard a hotel boat. If you choose to skipper your own diesel-powered cruiser, you will be shown how to handle the craft and told whom to call if you break down. But once you cast off, you and your party — the boats sleep from 2 to 10 people — will be on your own. You help lock-keepers operate the gates and do your own cooking (in addition to village markets, the lock-keepers themselves often have fresh provisions) or eat at cafés and restaurants along the way. The cost of the rental can vary considerably, depending on the size of the boat, the season, and the area. A boat sleeping two comfortably can cost from $550 to $650 per week in spring or fall and jump to $1,100-$1,800 per week at the height of the summer; an 8-berth boat can range anywhere from $1,000 to $8,000 per week. The average rental, however, sleeping 4, works out to about $175 per person per week during the low season and $300 per person per week in the high season. Fuel is not included.

The alternative is to cruise on a hotel boat — usually a converted barge. These can carry anywhere from 6 to 24 guests, occasionally even more, as well as the crew. You can charter the boat and have it all to yourself or join other guests aboard. Cruises usually last from 3 days to a week; accommodations can be simple or quite luxurious. When reading the brochure, note the boat's facilities (most cabins have private washbasins, showers, and toilets, but bathrooms can also be separate and shared) as well as the itinerary and any special emphasis. Many of the European cruises stress food and include tasting excursions to vineyards and wine cellars; others make a point of visiting historic spots.

The travel firms listed below, including the operators of hotel-boat cruises and representatives of self-drive boat suppliers, can provide information or arrange your whole holiday afloat in Europe.

Abercrombie & Kent/Continental Waterways: Runs hotel-boat cruises. 1420 Kensington Rd. Suite 103, Oak Brook, IL 60521 (phone: 312-954-2944 in Illinois; 800-323-7308 elsewhere).

Bargain Boating, Morgantown Travel Service: Books self-drive boats. PO Box 757, Morgantown, WV 26507-0757 (phone: 304-292-8471).

Esplanade Tours: Books hotel-boat cruises. 581 Boylston St., Boston, MA 02116 (phone: 617-266-7465).

Floating Through Europe: Operates hotel-boat cruises. 271 Madison Ave., New York, NY 10016 (phone: 212-685-5600 or 800-221-3140).

The French Experience: Books self-drive boats in the Midi, the Camargue, Aquitaine, the Upper Loire and Nivernais, Burgundy, Alsace and Lorraine, and Brittany. 370 Lexington Ave., Suite 812, New York, NY 10017 (phone: 212-986-3800).

Horizon Cruises: Operates hotel-boat cruises in Burgundy. 16000 Ventura Blvd., Suite 200, Encino, CA 91436 (phone: 818-906-8086 or 800-252-2103 in California; 800-421-0454 elsewhere).

Skipper Travel Services: Books self-drive boats. 210 California Ave., Palo Alto, CA 94306 (phone: 415-321-5658).

■ **A final note on picking a cruise:** A "cruise-only" travel agency can better help you choose a cruise ship and itinerary than a travel agency that does not specialize in cruises. Cruise-only agents are best equipped to tell you about a particular ship's "personality," the kind of person with whom you'll likely be traveling on a particular ship, what dress is acceptable (it varies from ship to ship), and much more. At press time, there were over 275 agencies across the country that belonged to the *National Association of Cruise Only Agencies* (*NACOA*). For a list of the cruise-only agencies in a particular state (requests are limited to three states), send a self-addressed, stamped envelope to NACOA, PO Box 7209, Freeport, NY 11520, or call 816-795-7372.

FERRIES: Numerous ferries link European ports, and nearly all of them carry both passengers and cars — travelers simply drive on and drive off in most cases — and nearly all the routes are in service year-round. Space for cars should be booked as early as possible, especially during the high season, even though most lines schedule more frequent departures during the summer months. Note that long journeys, 8 to 10 hours or more, tend to be scheduled overnight.

Most ferry arrivals and departures are well served by connecting passenger trains or buses, and passengers can buy through train tickets that include the sea portion of the trip. The Paris to London route on through services by train/*Hovercraft*/train, for example, takes an average 5½ hours; from Paris to London on through services by train/ferry/train can take from 7 to 9 hours by day, depending on the route, or about 9½ to 10½ hours overnight.

Touring by Train

Perhaps the most economical, and often the most satisfying, way to see a lot of a foreign country in a relatively short time is by rail. It is certainly the quickest way to travel between two city centers up to 300 miles apart (beyond that, a flight would be quicker, even counting commuting time from airport to city center). But time isn't always the only consideration. Traveling by train is a way to keep moving and to keep seeing at the same time, and with the special discounts available to visitors, it can be an almost irresistible bargain.

Some of the special trains you may encounter in Europe include the *EuroCity* (*EC*) trains, which have ushered in a new phase of European train service. Introduced in 1987, the *EC* network will gradually replace the *Trans-Europe Express* (*TEE*) trains, which have provided the European Economic Community with fast, efficient, not to mention luxurious, service between major cities since the 1950s. *EC*s offer both first and second class service, and supplements must be paid for all departures. The supplement includes the price of a reserved seat, which is obligatory on any *EC* border crossing but not on trips within a country. The *EC* network includes 200 connections within the 12 participating countries: Austria, Belgium, Denmark, France, Italy, Luxembourg, the Netherlands, Norway, Spain, Sweden, Switzerland, and West Germany. The standards for *EC*s are pretty high. Besides being punctual and clean, the trains must connect major cities at high speed with short intermediate stops and have dining facilities and bilingual personnel on board.

If there is no *EC* on a route, the next best train is likely to be an *InterCity* (*IC*) train. There are both national and international *IC* trains. Some, in fact, are former *TEE*s to which second class cars have been added in recent years to help curb high operating costs, a problem aggravated by low ridership. A great many more already existed as part of the rail networks of certain countries (Germany, for instance, has a highly developed *IC* system). Supplements must be paid to ride all continental *IC* trains except the Swiss ones (other exceptions are the *IC* trains of Great Britain, whose railway system has never been integrated with the continental system), while reservations are obligatory only on those crossing borders. Another train of the same high quality is the *Trans-Europ Night* (*TEN*), an overnight train with sleeping quarters. Particularly for summer travel, early reservations are recommended.

France's *TGV*s (*trains à grande vitesse,* "ultra high speed trains") represent the state of the art in train technology. They run fastest (170 mph in commercial operation, though the record is 237.5 mph) on a so-called dedicated track, which has so far been laid between Paris and Lyons. At press time, another high-speed track, from Paris to Le Mans, was scheduled to become operational, and this year a TGV should connect Paris and Bordeaux. But the *TGV* can run at slower speeds on conventional track, so you also can take it on other routes, such as from Paris to Switzerland. *TGV*s carry first and second class passengers, supplements must be paid for rush-hour departures, reservations are obligatory, and from the US, orders must be placed one week in advance by calling 212-582-2110 or any of the *French Rail* offices in the US listed at the end of this section. Amenities aboard the new *TGV*s include a bar car, public telephones, a nursery where parents may leave their children for a few hours, and a private children's area in first class. Facilities for the handicapped are also provided. If ordered in advance, kosher meals are available.

Italy has a high-speed train between Milan and Rome, via Florence and Bologna. In 1991, high-speed trains (or *ICE* trains, for *InterCity Express*) will be running from Hanover to Würzberg, West Germany; and in 1992, they will link Seville and Madrid in Spain. London, Paris, and Brussels are also scheduled to be connected by a high-speed service — via the controversial Channel Tunnel — in 1993, and that network is expected to be extended to Cologne and Amsterdam by 1995.

These trains are but a small part of Europe's highly developed rail service. Hundreds of towns across the Continent are served by "regular" express and local trains. These trains generally have first and second class cars and meal service. (Those that make long overnight trips also offer various sleeping facilities, which must be reserved during peak travel periods.)

ACCOMMODATIONS, FARES, SERVICES: Fares on European trains are based on the quality of accommodations the passenger enjoys. You pay on the basis of traveling first or second class, and on *EC, IC,* some *TGV* trains, and for other expresses such as *Rapidos* in Italy and *Talgos* in Spain, first or second class plus a supplement. Traditionally, seating is arranged in compartments, with three or four passengers on one side facing a like number on the other side, but increasingly, in the newer cars, compartments have been replaced by a central-aisle design.

Tickets can be purchased through travel agents or national railway offices in the US (addresses below) or abroad, as well as at train stations, where domestic and international tickets are usually sold separately and lines can be long. The fare structure differs from country to country, but short hauls are always more expensive on a per-mile basis than longer runs. Most ticket and reservations systems are computerized and efficient. There is a $3 fee for European reservations made in the US (plus a $3 telex fee). Normally, reservations can be made up to 2 months before the travel date; when making a reservation, you can ask for a window seat as well as for a smoking or non-smoking section.

European trains carry two basic kinds of sleeping quarters: "couchettes," the coach seats of a compartment converted to sleeping berths, and "wagons-lits," or sleepers, individual bedrooms that compare favorably with the slumber coaches on transcontinental American trains. First class couchettes (available only in France and Italy) have four berths per compartment; second class has six. The berth is narrow, with a pillow, blanket, and sheet provided. Couchettes cost a standard charge ($14 and $19 per person if bought in the US) added to the basic first or second class fare; wagons-lits are more expensive.

The wide range of dining facilities runs from *prix fixe* menus served in dining cars or at your seat through self-service cafeteria-style cars to vendors hawking their wares through the aisles. In-seat lunch and dinner reservations can be made in advance, but dining car arrangements are made after boarding either by visiting the dining car or through the train steward.

A standardized pictorial code has been fashioned to indicate the many amenities offered at train stations. These include showers as well as restaurants, post and telegraph offices, exchange bureaus, and diaper changing facilities. Most large cities have two or more stations, with service to different parts of the country leaving from different stations, so make sure you know the name of the station for your train.

Baggage can often be checked through to your destination; French and German railways offer door-to-door delivery (which must be arranged locally) in larger towns or cities within the country, although your luggage may not go on the same train you do and may not arrive until the next day. Baggage can be checked overnight at most stations, but it is a good idea to travel as light as possible: Porters are in short supply at most stations, and self-service carts are frequently scarce as well.

Those planning driving routes should be aware that all European railways have some form of auto ferry — called *Motorail* in Britain and *Train-Auto-Couchette* on the Continent — that allows car owners to take to the rails for long distances while their car travels with them on a flatcar. *Note:* The *Train-Auto-Couchette* can only be booked in Europe, and it is quite popular with Europeans, especially in the peak summer months. Your best bet is to make reservations as soon as you get to Europe, the earlier the better.

PASSES: Rail passes are offered by the national railroad companies of most European countries. They allow unlimited train travel within a set time period, and they can save the traveler a considerable amount of money as well as time. The only requirement is that they be validated by an information clerk on the day of your first trip; thereafter, you do not need to stand in line — and lines can be very long in the peak travel season — to buy individual tickets for subsequent trips. The passes are generally meant for foreign tourists only, however, and thus sometimes must be bought before you go.

The Eurailpass, the first and best known of all rail passes, entitles holders to 15 or 21 days or 1, 2, or 3 months of unlimited first class travel. There are four types of passes available, and all offer unlimited first class travel over the rail networks of 17 countries — Austria, Belgium, Denmark, Finland, France, Germany, Greece, Holland, Hungary, Ireland, Italy, Luxembourg, Norway, Portugal, Spain, Sweden, and Switzerland.

With the Eurailpass, you don't pay the supplement ordinarily charged for *EC*s, *IC*s, and other special express trains. The only extras are the nominal reservation fee and sleeper and couchette costs. Eurailpass also includes free travel or substantial reductions on many Danube and Rhine river trips, lake steamers, ferry crossings, auxiliary bus routes as well as scheduled *Europabus* services, and airport to city center rail connections.

The Eurail Youthpass is designed for those under 26 and is good for 1 or 2 months of unlimited second class travel; as with the regular Eurailpass, the holder is exempt from paying supplements. The Eurail Saverpass also resembles the basic Eurailpass, except that it allows 15 days of unlimited first class travel for groups of three or more people traveling together (in peak season); two people traveling together qualify if travel occurs entirely between October 1 and March 31. Another recent addition is the Eurail Flexipass, which can be used for first class travel on any 9 days within a 21-day period. It costs slightly more than the 15-day Eurailpass, and it is a considerable savings over the 21-day pass. On all Eurailpasses, children under 4 travel free and children under 12 for half price.

BritRail passes are issued for either first class or economy travel in England, Wales, and Scotland for periods of 8, 15, or 22 days or 1 month. Children aged 5 through 15 travel for half fare in each of the eight categories. *BritRail* Youth passes, good only in economy accommodations, are sold at four rates to those aged 16 through 25. A senior citizen's pass allows persons 60 and older to travel at special rates in first class. *BritRail* also sells a Rail-Drive package, available for 8 or 15 days. This includes a 4-day car rental within an 8-day period and up to an 8-day car rental within a 15-day period. The car can be picked up and delivered at over 200 locations, including some 100 rail stations and 11 airports throughout Great Britain.

The Eurailpasses and *BritRail* passes must be purchased *before* going abroad from a travel agent or from one of the offices listed below. (*Note* that *BritRail* does not sell Eurailpasses.) A Eurail Aid Office in Europe will replace lost passes when proper documentation is provided; a reissuance fee is charged.

If you're going to tour one country extensively, inquire about national discount plans (before leaving the US in case the plan requires purchase abroad). Many countries issue passes similar to the Eurailpass that allow unlimited travel for defined periods of time over the national transportation network. In addition, there is an endless array of special discount tickets, rail and bike plans, rail and road plans, and other bargains. Most national railroads also offer discounts to those over 60 or 65 and those under 26. Areawide programs also exist: The Benelux Tourail ticket, for instance — which can be purchased only in the Benelux countries — allows unlimited travel in Belgium, the Netherlands, and Luxembourg for 5 days of your choice during a 17-day period from mid-March through mid-September or the last 2 weeks of October and December. The Scandinavian Rail Pass is good for 21 days of first or second class travel on trains throughout Denmark, Finland, Norway, and Sweden and over certain ferry routes as well. It can be bought at any railroad station in Scandinavia. And, for those travelers who want to spend some time in Ireland as well as on the Continent, there is the Irish Republic's own Rambler Ticket.

FURTHER INFORMATION: The *Eurail Traveler's Guide* (which contains a railroad map) and the *Eurail Timetable* are free from Eurailpass (Box 10383, Stamford, CT 06904-2383) and are also available from the Eurail Distribution Centre (Box 300, Succursale R, Montreal, Que. H2S 3K9, Canada). Two other publications may also be of help: The *Eurail Guide* by Marvin Saltzman (available for $10.95 from Eurail Guide Annuals, 27540 Pacific Coast Hwy., Malibu, CA 90265; phone: 213-457-7286), and *Europe by Eurail* by George Wright Ferguson (Globe Pequot Press, PO Box Q, 10 Denlar Dr., Chester, CT 06412; available by mail for $14.95, including postage and handling). Both guides discuss train travel in general, contain information on countries included in the Eurail network (the Saltzman book also discusses Eastern Europe and the rest of the world), and suggest numerous sightseeing excursions by rail from various base cities.

You may also want to buy the *Thomas Cook European Timetable,* a weighty and detailed compendium of European international and national rail services that constitutes the most revered and accurate railway reference in existence. The *Timetable* comes out monthly, but because most European countries switch to summer schedules at the end of May (and back to winter schedules at the end of September), the June edition is the first complete summer schedule (and October the first complete winter schedule). The February through May editions, however, contain increasingly more definitive supplements on upcoming summer schedules, which can be used to plan a trip in advance. The *Thomas Cook European Timetable* is sold by some travel bookstores and by the Forsyth Travel Library, PO Box 2975, Dept. TCT, Shawnee Mission, KS 66201-1375 ($16.95 plus $3 for airmail postage; or call 800-367-7984 or 913-384-0496 and pay by MasterCard or Visa).

Following are addresses for the national railway offices in the US and Canada that sell tickets and passes and make reservations:

BritRail Travel International, 630 Third Ave., New York, NY 10017 (phone: 212-599-5400); 800 S. Hope St., Suite 603, Los Angeles, CA 90017 (phone: 213-624-8787); 2305 Cedar Springs, Cedar Maple Plaza, Suite 210, Dallas, TX

75201 (phone: 214-748-0860); 94 Cumberland St., Toronto, Ont. M5R 1A3, Canada (phone: 416-929-3333); 409 Granvilee St., Vancouver, BC V6C 1T2, Canada (phone: 604-683-6836).

French Rail Inc., 610 Fifth Ave., New York, NY 10020 (phone: 212-582-2110); 2121 Ponce de Leon Blvd., Coral Gables, FL 33134 (phone: 305-445-8648); 11 E. Adams St., Chicago, IL 60603 (phone: 312-427-8691); 9465 Wilshire Blvd., Beverly Hills, CA 90212 (phone: 213-274-6934); 360 Post St., Union Sq., San Francisco, CA 94108 (phone: 415-982-1993). 150 Stanley St., Montreal, Que. H3A 1R3, Canada (phone: 514-288-8255); 55 University Ave., Suite 400, Toronto, Ont. M5J 2H7, Canada; 409 Granville St., Suite 452, Vancouver, BC B6C 1T2, Canada (phone: 604-688-6707).

German Rail, 747 Third Ave., New York, NY 10017 (phone: 212-308-3100); 625 Statler Office Bldg., Boston, MA 02116 (phone: 617-542-0577); 3400 Peachtree Rd. NE, Lenox Towers, Suite 1299, Atlanta, GA 30326 (phone: 404-266-9555); 9575 Higgins Rd., Suite 505, Rosemont, IL 60018 (phone: 312-692-4209); 222 W. Las Colinas, Suite 1050, Irving, TX 75039 (phone: 214-402-8377); 240 Stockton St., Union Sq., San Francisco, CA 94108-5306 (phone: 415-362-6206); 11933 Wilshire Blvd., Los Angeles, CA 90025 (phone: 213-479-2772); The Forum, 425 S. Cherry St., Suite 380, Denver, CO 80222 (phone: 303-320-0239); 1290 Bay St., Toronto, Ont. M5R 2C3, Canada (phone: 416-968-3272).

The Irish Republic. Contact *CIE Tours International,* 122 E. 42nd St., New York, NY 10168 (phone: 212-972-5600 in New York City; 800-CIE-TOUR elsewhere in the US), for bookings and information on the Irish Republic rails.

Northern Ireland Railways. Contact the Northern Ireland Tourist Board, 40 W. 57th St., New York, NY 10019 (phone: 212-765-5144).

Italian State Railways, 666 Fifth Ave., New York, NY 10103 (phone: 212-397-2667); 500 N. Michigan Ave., Suite 1310, Chicago, IL 60611 (phone: 312-644-6651); 6033 W. Century Blvd., Suite 1090, Los Angeles, CA 90045 (phone: 213-338-8620); 2055 Peel St., Montreal, Que. H3A 1V4, Canada (phone: 514-845-9101); 111 Avenue Rd., Suite 808, Toronto, Ont. M5R 3J8, Canada (phone: 416-927-7712).

Swiss Federal Railways, 608 Fifth Ave., New York, NY 10020 (phone: 212-757-5944); 260 Stockton St., San Francisco, CA 94108 (phone: 415-362-2260).

Touring by Car

 Europe is ideally suited for driving tours. Distances between major cities are usually reasonable, and a visitor can use the flexibility of a car to maximum advantage. (See DIRECTIONS for our choices of the most interesting driving itineraries.) Travelers who wish to cover a country from end to end can count on a good system of highways to help them make time, while those choosing to explore only one region will find that the secondary and even lesser roads are generally well surfaced and in good condition. Either way, there is plenty of satisfying scenery en route.

But driving isn't an inexpensive way to travel. Gas prices are far higher in Europe than in North America, and car rentals are seldom available at bargain rates. Keep in mind, however, that driving becomes more economical with more passengers. Because the price of getting wheels abroad will be more than an incidental expense, it is important to investigate every alternative before making a final choice. Many travelers find this expense amply justified when considering that rather than just the means to an end, a well-planned driving route can be an important part of the adventure.

Before setting out, make certain that everything you need is in order. Read about the places you intend to visit and study relevant maps. If at all possible, discuss your trip with someone who has already driven the route to find out about road conditions and available services. If you can't speak to someone personally, try to read about others' experiences. Government tourist offices can be a good source of travel information, although when requesting brochures and maps, be sure to specify the areas you are planning to visit. (See *Tourist Information Offices* for addresses in the US. Also see "Maps" below.)

Driving – A valid driver's license from his or her state of residence enables a US citizen to drive throughout Europe. An International Driving Permit (IDP), which is a translation of the US license in 9 languages, is required in Austria, West Germany, Greece, Hungary, Spain, the USSR, and Bulgaria. Many national tourist boards *strongly* recommend that American drivers obtain an IDP, especially if they plan to do a lot of driving. You can obtain an IDP before you leave from most branches of the *American Automobile Association* (*AAA*). Applicants must be at least 18 years old, and the application must be accompanied by two passport-size photos (some *AAA* branches have a photo machine available), a valid US driver's license, and a fee of $5. The IDP is good for one year and must be accompanied by your US license to be valid.

Liability insurance is also required and is a standard part of any car rental contract. (To be sure of having the appropriate coverage, let the rental staff know in advance about the country borders you plan to cross.) If buying a car and using it abroad, the driver must carry an International Insurance Certificate, known as a Green Card. Your insurance carrier can arrange for a special policy to cover you in Europe, and will automatically issue your Green Card.

Driving is on the right side of the road in most of Europe and the basic rule of the road is "priority to the right"; that is, those coming from the right at intersections have the right of way. Exceptions are priority roads, marked by a sign with a yellow diamond; these have the right of way until the diamond reappears with a black bar and the right of way reverts to those coming from the right. Another exception is the limited form of "priority to the left" that has recently been introduced in Paris. Bound to be confusing, it initially applies only to selected traffic circles. In Great Britain, Ireland, and Malta, driving is on the left side of the road and all rules are reversed. On Swiss mountain passes, traffic going up has priority over traffic coming down.

Use the horn sparingly — only in emergencies and when approaching blind mountain curves. In some cities honking is forbidden; at night, flash your headlights instead. In many European countries, the use of seat belts is compulsory for the driver and front seat passenger (and in France, children under 10 may not sit in the front seat unless the car has no back seat). Zebra stripes and other similar markings on city streets give pedestrians the right of way and cars must stop for them. In many cities, use of the horn is restricted.

Traffic congestion is at its worst on main roads, particularly those radiating from major cities. Look for signs pointing out detours or alternative routes to popular holiday destinations. Service stations, information points, and tourist offices distribute free maps of the alternate routes, which may be the long way around but will probably get you to your goal faster in the end.

Driving in European cities can be a tricky proposition, since many of them do not have street signs at convenient corners but instead identify their byways with plaques attached to the walls of corner buildings. They are often difficult to spot until you've passed them, and since most streets don't run parallel to one another, taking the next turn can lead you astray. Fortunately, most European cities and towns post numerous signs pointing the way to the center of the city, and plotting a course to your destination from there may be far easier. In Italy, look for the signs that read CENTRO CITTÉ; in England, TOWN CENTRE; in France, CENTRE VILLE; in Spain, CENTRO; and in Germany, ZENTRUM or INNENSTADT. Also note that highway signs showing distance from point to point are in kilometers rather than miles (1 mile equals 1.6 kilometers; 1 kilometer equals .62 mile). And speed limits are in kilometers per hour, so think twice before hitting the gas when you see a speed limit of 100. That means 62 miles per hour.

European countries are most zealous in prosecuting offenders of driving laws, especially in the matter of drinking and driving. The Scandinavian countries, those of Eastern Europe, and Great Britain and Ireland routinely administer breath tests and are rigorous in imposing fines and jail sentences. If you've been drinking, do as the natives do and walk home, take a cab, or make sure that a licensed member of your party sticks strictly to seltzer water. Police also have the power to impose on-the-spot fines for other infractions such as speeding, failure to stop at a red light, and failure to wear seat belts.

Roads and Maps – Western Europe's network of highways is as well maintained as any in North America, with a system comparable to the American highway system: expressways, first class roads, and well-surfaced secondary roads (which in outlying areas like Scandinavia's Arctic region may be dirt or gravel but will be carefully maintained, in any case). Three decades ago, a pan-European commission established standards for international European routes, called E roads. Most European maps note E-route numbers together with national route numbers. Single-country maps generally use only a national number. Every European country maintains its own highway system. The pictorial direction signs are standardized under the International Roadsign System and their meanings are indicated by their shapes — triangular signs indicate danger; circular signs give instructions; and rectangular signs are informative.

Except for stretches of free autoroutes (designated by A) near cities, most of the autoroutes in Europe are toll roads, and they are fairly expensive. They save time, gas, and wear and tear on the car, but they are obviously not the roads to take if you want to browse and linger along the way. The other main roads, designated by N, and the secondary, or regional (designated by D), are free, well maintained, and much more picturesque, while minor roads have their own charm. Be aware that in recent years, numerous changes have been taking place in the numbering of European roads. Many N roads have become D roads, some merely changing their prefix from N to D, some changing numbers as well. Another recent development is a new Europe-wide road-numbering system. The European designations, prefaced by an E, appear together with the individual country's numbers; so, for example, autoroute A1 in France could also be called E5, but Germany's A1 would have a different E number. Both designations appear on Michelin's newest maps, but expect discrepancies between the old and new numbers in maps, guidebooks, and brochures for some time to come.

Three particularly good sources of maps, atlases, and travel information are the *American Automobile Association* (*AAA*), Rand McNally, and Kummerley & Frey, whose maps are available in bookstores and map shops around the country. The *AAA* publishes an overall Europe planning map as well as regional maps of Europe that are available to members from the travel agencies in most *AAA* offices. Rand McNally atlases and maps are available in most bookstores or can be bought directly from the following Rand McNally retail stores: 23 E. Madison, Chicago, IL 60602 (phone: 312-332-4627); 150 E. 52nd St., New York, NY 10022 (phone: 212-758-7488); 595 Market St., San Francisco, CA 94105-2803 (phone: 415-777-3131). All Michelin publications — red and green guides as well as road maps (by far the best for tourist tourers) — are available from the US headquarters (Michelin Guides and Maps, PO Box 3305, Spartanburg, SC 29304-3305; phone: 803-599-0850 or 800-423-0485) and are distributed extensively throughout the US. Road maps are also sold at gas stations throughout Europe. Stateside, some free maps can be obtained from the national tourist offices of the countries you plan to visit (see *Tourist Information Offices*).

AAA can also provide members with its 600-page *Travel Guide to Europe* (price varies from branch to branch) and 64-page *Motoring Europe* ($5.95); both are available through local *AAA* offices. Another invaluable guide, *Euroad: The Complete Guide to Motoring in Europe,* is available for $7.80, including postage and handling, from VLE Limited, PO Box 547, Tenafly, NJ 07670 (phone: 201-567-5536).

Automobile Clubs – Most European automobile clubs offer emergency service to any breakdown victim, whether a club member or not. To signal for help, pull over to the side of the road and raise your hood. Motor patrols usually drive small cars painted a uniform color. In northern European countries, they are likely to be yellow. Call boxes are located on many major routes, and numerous countries have a single national number to dial for roadside assistance. Though it isn't necessary to belong to an automobile club to qualify for emergency assistance, service is cheaper, or even free, if you're a member. Due to reciprocal arrangements, *AAA* members are automatically entitled to a number of foreign clubs' services. Join through a US chapter or contact the *AAA* national office at 8111 Gatehouse Rd., Falls Church, VA 22047 (phone: 703-222-6000).

Aside from these options, a driver in distress will have to contact the nearest service center by pay phone. And, although English is spoken widely in Europe, if language is a barrier in explaining your dilemma, the local operator should be able to connect you to an international operator for assistance. Car rental companies also make provisions for breakdowns, emergency service, and assistance; ask for a number to call when you pick up the vehicle.

Gasoline – Petroleum is sold by the liter on the Continent and by the British or "imperial" gallon in the United Kingdom. A liter is slightly more than a quart, and 3.75 liters equal a US gallon. One imperial gallon equals 1.2 US gallons.

Gas prices everywhere rise and fall depending upon the world supply of oil, and the American traveler in Europe is further affected by the prevailing rate of exchange for the dollar. Gas prices are considerably higher in Europe, so check the current prices abroad just before you go, and budget accordingly. Remember that depending on where you're driving, unleaded fuel may be difficult to find. At least until all European gas stations sell unleaded, your best bet is to rent a car that takes leaded gasoline.

Rental cars are usually delivered with a full tank of gas. Remember to fill the tank before you return the car or you will have to pay to refill the tank, and gas is always much more expensive at the rental company's pump than at a service station. This policy may vary for smaller regional companies; ask when picking up the vehicle.

Considering the cost of gas in Europe compared to US prices at the time of this writing, gas economy is of particular concern. The prudent traveler should do some preliminary research, plan an itinerary, and make as many reservations as possible in advance, in order to not waste gas figuring out where to go, stay, or eat. Drive early in the day, when there is less traffic. Then leave your car at the hotel and use local transportation in cities.

Although it may be equally dangerous to drive at a speed much below the posted limit as it is to drive above it (particularly on toll autoroutes — superhighways where the speed limit may be as high as 130 kmh), at 89 kmh (55 mph) a car gets 25% better mileage than at 112 kmh (70 mph). The number of miles per liter or gallon is also increased by driving smoothly. Accelerate gently, anticipate stops, get into high gear quickly, and maintain a steady speed.

RENTING A CAR: Although there are other options, such as leasing or outright purchase, most people who want to drive in Europe simply rent a car through a travel agent or international rental firm before they go or, once they are in Europe, from a local company. Another possibility, also arranged before departure, is to rent the car as part of a larger package. Arrangements of this sort used to be called fly-drive packages, but increasingly you'll also find them described in brochures as self-drive, go-as-you-please, or car tours.

Renting is not inexpensive, but you can economize by determining your own needs and then shopping around among the car rental companies until you find the best deal. As you comparison-shop, keep in mind that rates vary considerably, not only from city to city, but also from location to location within the same city. It might be less expensive to rent a car in the center of a city rather than at the airport. Usually, local companies are less expensive than the national giants. Ask about special rates or promotional deals, such as weekend or weekly rates, bonus coupons for airline tickets, or 24-hour rates that include gas and unlimited mileage.

Requirements – Whether you decide to rent a car in advance from a US rental company with European branches or from a local European company, you should know that renting a car is rarely as simple as signing on the dotted line and roaring off into the night. If you are renting for personal use, you must have a valid driver's license and will have to convince the renting agency that (1) you are personally credit-worthy; and (2) you will bring the car back at the stated time. This will be easy if you have a major credit card (accepted widely in Europe); all large agencies and most local companies accept credit cards in lieu of a cash deposit, as well as for payment of your final bill. If you prefer to pay in cash, leave your credit card imprint as a "deposit," then pay your bill in cash when you return the car.

If you don't have a major credit card, renting a car for personal use becomes more complicated. If you are planning to rent from an international agency with an office near your home, the best thing to do is to call the renting company several days in advance, give them your name, home address, and information on your business or employer; the agency then runs its own credit check on you. This can be time-consuming, so you should try to have it done before you leave home. If you plan to pay for your rental car in cash, it is best to make arrangements in advance — otherwise you must bring along a letter of employment and go to the agency during business hours so that it can call your employer for verification.

In addition to paying the rental fee up front, you will also have to leave a hefty deposit when you pick up the car — either a substantial flat fee or a percentage of the total rental cost. (Each company has a different deposit policy; look around for the best deal.) If you return the car on time, the full deposit will be refunded, otherwise additional charges will be deducted and any unused portion of the deposit refunded.

If you are planning to rent a car once in Europe, *Avis, Hertz,* and other US rental companies *will* usually rent to travelers paying in cash and leaving either a credit card imprint or a substantial amount of cash as a deposit. This is not necessarily standard policy, however, as *Budget,* some other international chains, and many regional Europeans companies *will not* rent to an individual without a credit card. In this case, you may have to call around to find a company that does.

Also keep in mind that although the minimum age to drive a car in Europe is 18 years, the minimum age to rent a car varies with the company. Many firms have a minimum age requirement of 21 years. For others it is 23 or 25 years, and for some models of cars it goes up to 30 years.

No matter which firm you choose, the first factor influencing cost is, naturally, the type and size of car. Rentals are based on a tiered price system, with different sizes of cars — variations of budget, economy, regular, and luxury — often listed as A (the smallest and least expensive) through F, G, or H, and sometimes even higher. The typical A car available in Europe is a two-door subcompact or compact, often a hatchback, seating two or three adults (such as a small Ford, Fiat, Renault, or Peugeot), while the typical F, G, or H luxury car is a four-door sedan seating four or five adults (such as a Mercedes or BMW). The larger the car, the more it costs to rent in the first place and the more gas it consumes, but for some people the greater comfort and extra luggage space of a larger car (in which bags can be safely locked out of sight) may make it worth the additional expense, especially on a long trip. Be warned, too, that relatively few European cars have automatic transmission, and those that do are more likely to be in the F group than the A group. Cars with automatic shift must be specifically requested at the time of booking, and, again, they cost more (anywhere from $5 to $10 a day more than the same model with standard shift) and they consume more gas.

Electing to pay for collision damage waiver (CDW) protection will add considerably to the cost of renting a car. The renter may be responsible for the full value of the vehicle being rented, but you can dispense with the possible obligation to pay even this amount by buying the offered waiver at a cost of about $10 a day. Before making any decisions about optional rental car waivers, check with your own insurance agent and determine whether your personal auto policy covers rented vehicles; if it does, you probably won't need to pay for the waiver. Be aware, too, that increasing numbers of so-called premium credit cards — gold or platinum American Express cards, gold Visas or MasterCards — automatically provide CDW coverage if the car rental is charged to the credit card. However, the specific terms of such coverage differ sharply among individual credit card companies — whose policies may further vary depending on whether rentals are transacted in the US or abroad — so check with the company for information on the amount of coverage provided (also see *Credit and Currency* in this section). Considering that repair costs for a rental car have become a real headache of late, and car rental companies are getting away with steep fees (up to the full retail price of the car) for damage to their property, if you are not otherwise covered it is wise to pay for the insurance offered by the car rental company rather than risk traveling without any coverage.

Overseas, the amount renters may be liable for should damage occur has not risen to the heights it has in the US. Some Europeans car rental agreements include collision damage coverage. In this case, the CDW supplement frees the renter from liability for the deductible amount, which typically ranges from $1,000 to $2,000 at present, but can be more for some luxury car groups. The cost of waiving this liability (as with the full liability waiver), generally $8 to $12 a day in Europe, but several dollars more for luxury cars, is far from negligible, however. Drivers who rent cars in the US are often able to decline the CDW because many personal car insurance policies (subject to their own deductibles) extend to rental cars; unfortunately, such coverage does not usually extend to cars rented beyond the US and Canada. Similarly, the CDW coverage provided by some credit cards if the rental is charged to the card may be limited to cars rented in the US or Canada.

Other costs to be added to the price tag include dropoff charges or one-way service fees. The lowest price quoted by any given company may apply only to a car that is returned to the same location from which it was rented. A slightly higher rate may be charged if the car is to be returned to a different city in the same country, and a considerably higher rate may prevail if the rental begins in one country and ends in another.

A further consideration: Don't forget that car rentals are subject to value-added taxes (VATs), which are *not* included in the quoted prices. If your tour plans include several countries, you should examine your options regarding the pickup and dropoff points. There is a wide variation in this tax rate from country to country: in France the rate is currently 28%; in Belgium it is 25%; in Germany, 14%; in Spain and Luxembourg, 12%; and in Switzerland, no tax is charged. One-way rentals bridging two countries used to be exempt from tax, but that is no longer the case. In general, the tax on one-way rentals is determined by the country in which the car has been rented. However, some agencies that do not maintain their own fleets use a contractor whose country of registration determines the rate of taxation. An example is *Kemwel Car Rental Europe,* whose one-way rentals from all countries except Germany, Italy, and Sweden are taxed at the Danish rate, 22%.

Kemwel's special programs offer savings to the client and allow travel agents to earn commissions on CDW fees and on VATs. The new SuperSaver Plus and UniSaver Plus tariffs offer inclusive rentals in 24 countries throughout Europe and the Middle East. These programs offer full insurance coverage (with a $100 deductible) and all European VATs, plus unlimited mileage. Rates start at $79 and are available in some 35 cities across Europe. Bookings must be reserved and paid for at least 7 days before delivery of the car, and the vehicle must be returned to the *Kemwel* station from which it was originally rented (for address, see below).

Finally, currency fluctuation is another factor to consider. Most brochures quote rental prices in dollars, but these amounts are frequently only guides; that is, they represent the prevailing rate of exchange when the brochure was printed. The rate may be very different when you call to make a reservation and different again when the time comes to ultimately pay the bill (when the amount owed may be paid in cash in foreign currency or as a charge to a credit card, which is recalculated at a still later date's rate of exchange). Some companies guarantee rates in dollars (often for a slight surcharge), but this is an advantage only when the value of the dollar is steadily declining overseas. If the dollar is growing stronger overseas, you may be better off with rates in the local currency.

Renting from the US – Travel agents can arrange foreign rentals for clients, but it is just as easy to do it yourself by calling the international divisions of such familiar car rental firms as *Hertz* (phone: 800-654-3001), *Avis* (phone: 800-331-1084), *Budget* (phone: 800-527-0700), *National* (known in Europe as *Europcar;* phone: 800-227-3876), or *Dollar Rent-a-Car* (known in Europe as *InterRent;* phone: 800-421-6878). All of these companies publish directories listing their foreign locations, and all quote weekly flat rates based on unlimited mileage with the renter paying for gas. Some also offer time and mileage rates (i.e., a basic per-day or per-week charge, plus a charge for each mile, or kilometer, driven), which are generally only to the advantage of those who plan to do very little driving — the basic time and mileage charge for a given period of time is lower than the unlimited mileage charge for a comparable period, but the kilometers add up more quickly than most people expect.

It is also possible to rent a car before you go by contacting any of a number of smaller or less well known US companies that do not operate worldwide but specialize in European auto travel, including leasing and car purchase in addition to car rental, or are actually tour operators with an established European car rental program. These firms, whose names and addresses are listed below, act as agents for a variety of European suppliers, offer unlimited mileage almost exclusively, and frequently manage to undersell their larger competitors by a significant margin. Comparison shopping is always necessary, however, because the company that has the least expensive rentals in one country may not necessarily have the least expensive in another, and even the international giants offer discount plans whose conditions are easy for most travelers to fulfill. *Hertz*'s Affordable Europe, *Avis*'s Supervalue Rates Europe, and similar plans offered by *Budget* and *National* allow discounts of anywhere from 15% to 30% off their usual rates provided that the car is reserved a certain number of days before departure (usually 7, but it can be less), is rented for a minimum period (5 days or, usually, a week), and, in most cases, is returned to the same location that supplied it or to another in the same country.

There are legitimate bargains in car rentals if you shop for them. Call all the familiar car rental names whose toll-free numbers are given above (don't forget to ask about their special discount plans) and then call the smaller companies listed below. In the recent past, the latter have tended to offer significantly lower rates, but it always pays to compare. Begin your comparison shopping early, because the best deals may be booked to capacity quickly and may require payment 14 to 21 days or more before picking up the car.

> *Auto Europe,* PO Box 1097, Camden, ME 04843 (phone: 207-236-8235; 800-223-5555 in the US; 800-458-9503 in Canada).
>
> *Cortell International,* 17310 Red Hill Ave., Irvine, CA 92714 (phone: 800-228-2535).
>
> *Europe by Car,* 1 Rockefeller Plaza, New York, NY 10020, or 9000 Sunset Blvd., Los Angeles, CA 90069 (phone: in New York State, 212-581-3040; in California, 800-252-9401; elsewhere, 800-223-1516).
>
> *Foremost Euro-Car Inc.,* 5430 Van Nuys Blvd., Van Nuys, CA 91401 (phone: in California, 800-272-3299; elsewhere, 800-423-3111).
>
> *Kemwel,* 106 Calvert St., Harrison, NY 10528 (phone: 800-678-0678).

Another economical option is *Wheels International Rent-a-Car.* This company contracts with other car rental agencies worldwide to rent available portions of their fleets at a flat discounted rate. Rentals are for a minimum of 3 days, and full payment must be made in advance. Numerous dropoff alternatives are also available for a minimal additional charge. For information, contact Wheels International Rent-a-Car, Suite 308, 1682 W. 7th Ave., Vancouver, BC V6J 4S6, Canada (phone: 604-731-0441 or 800-663-8888 in the US).

■**Extra Special:** For travelers for whom driving is more than just a means of getting from here to there, *Auto Exclusiv* (2 Frankfurter Strasse, D-6056 Heusenstamm; phone: 06104-3060; North American booking agent, 813-526-6191) rents the very best cars manufactured in Germany. From their headquarters in Heusenstamm, very near the Franfurt airport, they provide top-of-the-line Mercedes, BMWs, and Porsches for a driving tour that has an extra element of excitement — and speed. Prices are hardly inexpensive, but many feel the pleasure of being behind the wheel of a BMW 750iL or a Porsche Carrera is well worth the cost.

Fly/Drive – Airlines, charter companies, car rental companies, and tour operators have been offering fly/drive packages for years, and even though the basic components of the package have changed somewhat — return airfare, a car waiting at the airport, and perhaps a night's lodging in the gateway city all for one price used to be the rule — the idea remains the same. You rent a car *here* for use *there* by booking it along with other arrangements for the trip. These days, the very minimum arrangement possible is the result of a tie-in between a car rental company and an airline, which entitles the customer to a rental car for less than the company's usual rates provided he or she shows proof of having booked a flight on that airline.

Slightly more elaborate fly/drive packages are listed under various names (go-as-you-please, self-drive, or, simply, car tours) in the independent vacations sections of tour catalogues. Their most common ingredients are the rental car plus some sort of hotel voucher plan, with the applicable airfare listed separately. You set off on your trip with a block of prepaid accommodations vouchers, a list of hotels that accept them (usually members of a hotel chain or association), and a reservation for the first night's stay, after which the staff of each hotel books the next one for you or you make advance reservations yourself. Naturally, the greater the number of establishments participating in the scheme, the more freedom you have to range at will during the day's driving and still be near a place to stay for the night. The cost of these combination packages generally varies according to the size of the car and the quality of the hotels; there is usually a surcharge if the car is picked up in one city and dropped off in another. Most airlines also have special rental car rates available when you book their flights, often with a flexible hotel voucher program. For further information on available packages, check with the airline or your travel agent.

Less flexible car tours provide a rental car, a hotel plan, and an itinerary that permits no deviation because the hotels are all reserved in advance. The deluxe car tours packaged by *AutoVenture* (425 Pike St., Suite 502, Seattle, WA 98101; phone: 206-624-6033). whose tours come in either self-drive or chauffeured versions, are of this variety. *Avis* offers less deluxe car tours with set itineraries.

Local Rentals – It has long been common wisdom that the least expensive way to rent a car is to make arrangements in Europe. This is less true today than it used to be. Many medium to large European car rental companies have become the overseas suppliers of stateside companies, such as those mentioned previously, and often the stateside agency, by dint of sheer volume, has been able to negotiate more favorable rates for its US customers than the European firm offers its own. Lower rates may be found by searching out small, strictly local rental companies overseas, whether at less than prime addresses in major cities or in more remote areas. But to find them you must be willing to invest a sufficient amount of vacation time comparing prices on the scene. You must also be prepared to return the car to the location that rented it; dropoff possibilities are likely to be limited. Brochures of some of the smaller companies, often available from tourist board offices in the US, can serve as a useful basis for comparison. Overseas, the local yellow pages is a good place to begin.

Travelers on the Continent intending to rent a car only occasionally, relying mainly on other means of transportation, should be aware of *Mattei,* a French chain with locations throughout France that is also represented in Italy and Spain (for information, call the main office in France at 01-43461150). Also bear in mind that *French Rail Inc.* (*SNCF*) offers a car rental service in conjunction with *Avis* at more than 230 locations in France. The car is reserved at least 24 hours in advance and is waiting for you at the station of your destination, available by the day or longer. Note that the rates are comparable to those charged by *Avis* for cars reserved in Europe: That is, if you know beforehand that you will want the car for more than a few days (for 5 days, for example, the minimum rental period on *Avis*'s discount plan), you will do better to reserve it before leaving the US. A rail-and-drive pass offered by *Hertz,* EurailDrive Escape, is valid in Europe and all the other countries of the Eurail network. (For further information on rail-and-drive packages, see *Touring by Train.*)

Leasing – Anyone planning to be in Europe for 3 weeks or more should compare the cost of renting a car with that of leasing one for the same period. While the money saved by leasing rather than renting for a 23-day (the minimum) or 30-day period may not be great, what is saved over the course of a long-term lease — 45, 60, 90 days, or more, for example — amounts to hundreds, even thousands, of dollars. Part of the saving is due to the fact that leased cars are exempt from the stiff taxes applicable to rented cars. In addition, leasing plans provide for collision insurance with no deductible amount, so there is no need to add the daily cost of collision damage waiver protection offered as an option by rental companies. A further advantage of a car lease — actually a financed purchase/repurchase plan — is that you reserve your car by specific make and model rather than by group only, and it is delivered to you fresh from the factory.

Unfortunately, leasing as described above is offered only in Belgium and France, and the savings it permits can be realized to the fullest only if the cars are picked up and returned in those countries. While leased cars can be delivered to other countries, there is a charge for this service, which can be as high as $250 in the case of some European cities, to which must be added an identical return charge. If you don't intend to keep the car very long, the two charges could nullify the amount saved by leasing rather than renting, so you will have to do some arithmetic. It is possible to lease a car in countries other than Belgium and France, but most of the plans offered are best described as long-term rentals at preferential rates. They differ from true leasing in that you will pay tax and collision damage waiver protection (though it may be included in the quoted price), and the cars are usually late model used cars rather than brand-new.

Among the makes commonly offered on lease plans is *Peugeot* (contact Peugeot Motors of America, 1 Peugeot Plaza, Lyndhurst, NJ 07071). Additionally, some of the firms listed above that arrange car rentals in Europe — *Auto-Europe, Europe by Car, Foremost Euro-Car,* and *Kemwel* — also arrange car leases.

One of the major car leasing companies is *Renault,* offering leases of new cars for 23 days to 6 months. The cars are exempt from tax, all insurance is included, and there is no mileage charge. *Renault* offers the following pickup/dropoff options: free pickup/ dropoff in Paris, Nice, and Calais; free pickup and $85 dropoff fee in Bayonne, Bordeaux, Lyons, Marseilles, Pau, Perpignon, Rennes, Strasbourg, and Toulouse; and charges between $95 and $350 for each pickup or dropoff in Amsterdam, Brussels, Frankfurt, London, Milan, and Zurich and several (even more expensive) locations in Madrid. For further information and reservations, ask your travel agent or contact Renault USA directly at 650 First Ave., New York, NY 10016 (phone: 212-532 1221 in New York State; 800-221-1052 elsewhere).

BUYING A CAR: If your plans include both buying a new car of European make and a driving tour of Europe, it's possible to combine the two ventures and save some money on each. By buying the car abroad and using it during your vacation, you pay quite a bit less for it than the US dealer would charge and at the same time avoid the expense of renting a car during your holiday. There are two basic ways to achieve this desired end, but one, factory delivery, is far simpler than the other, direct import.

Factory delivery means that you place an order for a car in the US, then pick it up in Europe, often literally at the factory gate. It also means that your new car is built to American specifications, complying with all US emission and safety standards. Because of this, only cars made by manufacturers who have established a formal program for such sales to American customers can be bought at the factory. At present, the list includes Audi, BMW, Jaguar, Mercedes, Peugeot, Porsche, Renault, Saab, Volkswagen, and Volvo, among others (whose manufacturers generally restrict their offerings to those models they ordinarily export to the US). The factory delivery price, in US dollars, usually runs about 5% to 15% below the sticker price of the same model at a US dealership and includes the cost of shipping the car home. All contracts except BMW's include US customs duty, but the cost of the incidentals, and the insurance necessary for driving the car around Europe, is extra except for BMW's plan. Occasionally, a car manufacturer will offer a special incentive, such as complimentary airfare.

One of the few disadvantages of factory delivery is that car manufacturers make available only a limited number of cars this way per year, and for certain popular models you may have to get in line early in the season. Another is that you must take your trip when the car is ready, not when you are, although you will usually have 8 to 10 weeks' notice. The actual place of delivery can vary; it is more economical to pick up the car at the factory, but arrangements can be made to have it delivered elsewhere for an extra charge. Cars for factory delivery can usually be ordered either through one of the manufacturer's authorized dealers in the US or through companies — *Europe by Car, Foremost Euro-Car,* and *Kemwel,* among them — that specialize in such transactions.

The other way to buy a car abroad, direct import, is sometimes referred to as "gray market" buying. It is perfectly legal, but not hassle-free. Direct import means that you buy abroad a car that was meant for use abroad, not one built according to US specifications. It can be new or used and may even include — in Great Britain — a steering wheel on the right side of the front seat. The main drawback to direct import is that the process of modification to bring the car into compliance with US standards is expensive and time-consuming; it typically costs an estimated $7,000 in parts and labor and takes about 2 to 6 months. In addition, the same shipping, insurance, and miscellaneous expenses (another $2,000 to $5,000, according to estimates) that may be included in the factory delivery price must be added to the purchase price of the car, and the considerable burden of shepherding it on its journey from showroom to home garage is usually borne by the purchaser. Direct import dealers do exist (they are not the same as your local, factory-authorized foreign car dealer, with whom you are now in competition), but even if you use one, you still need to do a great deal of paperwork yourself.

Once upon a time, the main advantage of the direct import method — besides the fact that it can be used for makes and models not available on factory delivery programs — was that much more money could be saved importing an expensive car. Given today's exchange rates, however, the method's potential greater gain is harder to realize and must be weighed against its greater difficulties. Still, if direct importing interests you, you can obtain a list of those makes and models approved for conversion in this country, and of the converters licensed to bring them up to US specifications, by writing to the Environmental Protection Agency, Manufacturers' Operations Division, EN-340-F, Investigations/Imports Section, 401 M St. SW, Washington, DC 20460, or by calling 202-382-2505.

The regularly revised *Handbook of Vehicle Importation* ($22.95), published by the *Automobile Importers Compliance Association (AICA)*, a trade group of direct importers, modifiers, and others involved in the process, is an invaluable resource for getting a grip on what lies ahead. Order it from AICA, 12030 Sunrise Valley Dr., Suite 201, Reston, VA 22091 (phone: 703-476-1100). If you have special problems getting your car into the US, you might also contact Daniel Kokal, a regulatory consultant with Techlaw, 14500 Avion Pkwy., Suite 300, Chantilly, VA 22021 (phone: 703-818-1000).

Package Tours

 If the mere thought of buying a package for travel to and through Europe conjures up visions of a race through ten countries in as many days in lockstep with a horde of frazzled fellow travelers, remember that packages have come a long way. For one thing, not all packages are necessarily escorted tours, and the one you buy does not have to include any organized touring at all — nor will it necessarily include traveling companions. If it does, however, you'll find that people of all sorts — many just like yourself — are taking advantage of packages today because they are economical and convenient, save the purchaser an immense amount of planning time, and exist in such variety that it's virtually impossible for the Europe-bound traveler not to find one that fits at least the majority of any traveler's preferences. Given the high cost of travel these days, packages have emerged as a good buy.

Aside from the cost-saving advantages, Europe itself is ideally suited to package travel. The reason is that, essentially, Europe is a multiple-country, see-and-do destination as distinct from, say, the Caribbean, where most visitors go to a single island or country for a week or two and unpack everything until they're ready to return home. To be sure, many visitors to Europe do seek out a single city or country for a concentrated visit, booking themselves into a hotel, apartment, home, or villa that serves as a base from which they make regional tours and visits. But for the bulk of North American travelers, Europe remains a destination for cramming in as much travel and sightseeing as possible with the time and money the visitor has available. Hence the popularity — and practicality — of package tours.

There are hundreds of package programs on the market today. In the US, numerous packages to Europe are offered by tour operators or wholesalers, some retail travel agencies, airlines, charter companies, hotels, and even special interest organizations; what goes into them depends on who is organizing them. The most common type, assembled by tour wholesalers and sold through travel agents, can run the gamut from deluxe everything to simple tourist class amenities or even bare necessities. Fly/drive and fly/cruise packages are usually the joint planning efforts of airlines and, respectively, car rental organizations and cruise line operators. Charter flight programs may range from little more than airfare and a minimum of ground arrangements to full-scale tours or vacations. There are also hotel packages, organized by hotel chains or associations of independent hotels and applicable to stays at any combination of member establishments; resort packages, covering arrangements at a specific hotel; and special interest tours, which can be once-only programs organized by particular groups through a retail agency or regular offerings packaged by a tour operator. They can feature food, music or theater festivals, a particular sporting activity or event, a commemorative occasion, even scientific exploration.

In essence, a package is a combination of travel services that can be purchased as a single booking. It may include any or all of the following: transatlantic transportation, local transportation (and/or car rentals), accommodations, some or all meals, sightseeing, entertainment, transfers to and from the hotel at each destination, taxes, tips, escort service, and a variety of incidental features that might be offered as options at additional cost. In other words, a package can be any combination, from a fully escorted tour offered at an all-inclusive price to a simple fly/drive booking allowing you to function totally on your own. Its principal advantage is that it saves money: The cost of the combined arrangements invariably is well below the price that would be paid if all the elements were bought separately, and, particularly if transportation is provided by charter or discount flight, it could even be less than a round-trip economy airline ticket on a regularly scheduled flight. A package tour provides more than economy and convenience: It releases travelers from having to make their own arrangements for each section of the tour.

Lower prices are possible through package travel as a result of high-volume commerce. The tour packager negotiates for services in wholesale quantities — blocks of airline seats or hotel rooms, group meals, dozens of rental cars, busloads of ground transportation, and so on — and they are made available at a lower per-person price because of the quantities purchased for use during a given time period. Most packages, however, are subject to restrictions governing the duration of the trip and require total payment by a given time before departure.

Tour programs generally can be divided into two categories — "escorted" and "independent" — depending on the arrangements offered. An escorted tour means that a guide will accompany the group from the beginning of the tour through to return. On independent tours, there is generally a choice of hotels, meal plans, and sightseeing trips in each city as well as a variety of special excursions. The independent plan is for people who do not want a set itinerary but who prefer confirmed reservations. Whether you choose an escorted or independent tour, always bring along full contact information for your tour operator in case problems arise, although US tour operators may have European affiliates who can give additional assistance or make other arrangements on the spot.

To determine whether a package — or, more specifically, which package — fits your travel plans, start by evaluating your interests and needs, deciding how much and what you want to spend, see, and do. Gather whatever package tour information is available for your time schedule. Be sure that you take the time to read the brochure *carefully* to determine precisely what is included. Keep in mind that travel brochures are written to entice you into signing up for a package tour. Often the language is deceptive and devious. For example, a brochure may quote the lowest prices for a package tour based on facilities that are unavailable during the off-season, undesirable at any season, or just plain nonexistent. Information such as "breakfast included" or taxes (which can add up) are important items. Note, too, that prices quoted in brochures are almost always based on double occupancy. The rate listed is for each of two people sharing a double room, and if you travel alone, the supplement for single accommodations can raise the price considerably (see *Hints for Single Travelers*).

Increasingly, in this age of rapidly rising airfares, the brochure will *not* include the price of the airline ticket in the price of the package, though sample applicable fares from various gateway cities will usually be listed separately as extras to be added to the price of the ground arrangements. Before doing this, get the latest fares from the airline, because the samples will invariably be out of date by the time you read them. If the brochure gives more than one category of sample fares per gateway city — such as an individual tour-basing fare, a group fare, an excursion or other discount ticket, or, in the case of flights to Europe, an APEX, winter, or super APEX — your travel agent or airline tour desk will be able to tell you which one applies to the package you choose, depending on when you travel, how far in advance you book, and other factors. (An individual tour-basing fare is a fare computed as part of a package that includes land arrangements, thereby entitling a carrier to reduce the air portion almost to the absolute minimum. Though it always represents a saving over full-fare coach or economy, lately it has not been as inexpensive as the excursion and other discount fares that are also available to individuals. The group fare is usually the least expensive fare, and it is the tour operator, not you, who makes up the group.) When the brochure does include round-trip transportation in the package price, don't forget to add the round-trip transportation cost from your home to the departure city to come up with the total cost of the package.

Finally, read the general information regarding terms and conditions and the responsibility clause (usually in fine print at the end of the descriptive literature) to determine the precise elements for which the tour operator is — and is not — liable. Here the tour operator frequently expresses the right to change services or schedules as long as equivalent arrangements are offered. This clause also absolves the operator of responsibility for circumstances beyond human control, such as floods or avalanches, or injury to you or your property. In reading, ask the following questions:

1. Does the tour include airfare or other transportation, sightseeing, meals, transfers, taxes, baggage handling, tips, or any other services? Do you want all these services?
2. If the brochure indicates that "some meals" are included, does this mean a welcoming and farewell dinner, two breakfasts, or every evening meal?
3. What classes of hotels are offered? If you will be traveling alone, what is the single supplement?
4. Does the tour itinerary or price vary according to the season?
5. Are the prices guaranteed; that is, if costs increase between the time you book and the time you depart, can surcharges unilaterally be added?
6. Do you get a full refund if you cancel? If not, be sure to obtain cancellation insurance.
7. Can the operator cancel if too few people join?

One of the consumer's biggest problems is finding enough information to judge the reliability of a tour packager, since individuals seldom have direct contact with the firm putting the package together. Usually, a retail travel agent intervenes between customer and tour operator, and much depends on his or her candor and cooperation. So ask a number of questions about the tour you are considering. For example: Has the agent ever used a package provided by this tour operator? How long has the tour operator been in business? Is the tour operator a member of the *United States Tour Operators Association (USTOA)?* (The *USTOA* will provide a list of its members upon request and also offers a useful brochure, *How to Select a Package Tour;* contact the USTOA, 211 E. 51st St., Suite 12B, New York, NY 10022; phone: 212-944-5727. Also check the Better Business Bureau in your area to see if any complaints have been filed against the operator.) Which and how many companies are involved in the package? If air travel is by charter flight, is there an escrow account in which deposits will be held; if so, what is the name of the bank?

This last question is very important. US law requires that tour operators deposit every charter passenger's deposit and subsequent payment in a proper escrow account. Money paid into such an account cannot legally be used except to pay for the costs of a particular package or as a refund if the trip is canceled. To ensure the safe handling of your money, make your check payable to the escrow account — by law, the name of the depository bank appears in the operator-participant contract and is usually found in that mass of minuscule type on the back of the brochure. Write the details of the charter, including the destination and dates, on the face of the check; on the back, print "For Deposit Only." Your travel agent may prefer that you make your check out to the agency, saying that it will then pay the tour operator the fee minus commission. But it is perfectly legal to write your check as we suggest, and if your agent objects too strongly (the agent should have sufficient faith in the tour operator to trust him to send the proper commission), consider taking your business elsewhere. If you don't make your check out to the escrow account, you lose the protection of escrow should the trip be canceled or the tour operator or travel agent fail. Furthermore, recent bankruptcies in the travel industry have served to point out that even the protection of escrow may not be enough to safeguard investment. Increasingly, insurance is becoming a necessity (see *Insurance*), and payment by credit card has become popular since it offers some additional safeguards if the tour operator defaults.

SAMPLE PACKAGES IN EUROPE: Those who may want to add a tour or package arrangement after they are in Europe should know that package tours can be booked at all major capitals and other metropolitan areas. Besides the excitement of adding a vacation within a vacation to your itinerary, these Europe-based packages represent an economical way of getting from one point in Europe to another (and back). The most popular center in which to book while abroad is London. North American travelers find British tours particularly attractive because they're mostly for English-speaking groups and are often accompanied by English-speaking escorts and/or guides. In addition, many British tour operators cater to the budget end of the market. Once upon a time, the smart shopper could pick up a flight from London to Athens and back, plus a week's worth of adequate, if Spartan, accommodations, for less than half the price of an air ticket alone. These days, the bargains are not quite as enticing, though the British still manage to put together a good deal that becomes even better when the exchange rate is favorable to Americans.

The following are some of Britain's major high-volume or economy-minded tour operators. Some have become familiar names in this country recently because they have opened US offices and have begun to market some or all of the tour offerings in their British catalogues directly to the American public, so that booking one of their packages is no different from booking the package of an American tour operator. Almost all of the rest have at least a representative in the US to handle American bookings. Note that most of these offices or representatives prefer to deal with travel agents rather than individuals. Note also that because of the extra costs involved in making arrangements from this end, packages booked here can run 5% to 15% more than if booked in Britain; and if you attempt to book through the British office by mail, your request will most likely be referred to the US representative. Clearly, you will save money by waiting until you are in England to book, but there is no guarantee that the package you want will still be open at the last minute.

Cosmos: In 1989, this firm, the leading budget tour operator, had 43 tours of Europe, including 12 multi-country grand tours, 23 regional tours of the Continent, and 8 of Britain and Ireland. For information or brochures, in the Eastern US, contact Cosmos Tours, 95-25 Queens Blvd., Rego Park, NY 11374 (phone: 800-221-0090); in the Western US including Alaska and Hawaii: 150 S. Los Robles Ave., Pasadena, CA 91101 (phone: 818-449-2019 in California; 800-556-5454 elsewhere in the US). US bookings must be made through a travel agent. The London office is at 180 Vauxhall Bridge Rd., London SW1V 1ED (phone: 828-6751).

Frames Rickards: Reasonably priced coach tours of Europe, Great Britain, and Ireland, including a series of low-cost mini-tours of England, Scotland, and Wales, are available through *Frames*. The company's US agent, *Trophy Tours* (1810 Glenville Dr., Suite 124, Richardson, TX 75081; phone: 800-527-2473), prefers bookings through travel agents. The London office is at 11 Herbrand St., London WC1 N1EX (phone: 837-3111).

Glenton Tours: This long-established company is a specialist in first class but relatively inexpensive motorcoach tours of Great Britain (over 50 itineraries), and it also has one visiting Ireland. The US agent, *European Travel Management* (191 Post Rd. West, Westport, CT 06880; phone: 800-992-7700) prefers booking through travel agents. Head offices in London are at 114 Peckham Rye, London SE15 4JE (phone: 639-9777).

Globus-Gateway: In 1989, *Globus-Gateway* had 79 first class tours of Europe and Britain, including 20 to Britain and Ireland, 54 grand and regional tours of the Continent, and 5 independent city tours of London, Paris, and Amsterdam. Bookings through travel agents only. *Globus-Gateway*'s US and London addresses and phone numbers are the same as those for *Cosmos* (see above).

Thomson Holidays: Great Britain's largest tour operator owns its own airline, Britannia Airways, and its coach tours travel from home turf to Europe and as far afield as the Himalayas. *Thomson* is also known for a broad selection of Mediterranean holiday packages that include round-trip airfare (from Britain) and a week or two or more of villa or apartment rental. Write to Thomson Holidays, Greater London House, Hampstead Rd., London NW1 7SD (phone: 01-387-9321), for information on its tours; bookings may be made through *Portland Holidays* (phone: 01-388-5111) or through travel agencies in Britain.

Trafalgar Tours: This agency offered more than 50 first class motorcoach itineraries of the Continent, Scandinavia, the Soviet Union, and Great Britain and Ireland in 1989, plus a group of budget-conscious CostSaver tours on which savings were realized by scheduling a number of nights in good or select tourist class hotels. Bookings are made through travel agents, but you can contact *Trafalgar Tours* directly at 21 E. 26th St., New York, NY 10010 (phone: in New York City, 212-689-8977; elsewhere, 800-854-0103). In London, the main office is at 15 Grosvenor Pl., London SW1X 7HH (phone: 235-7090).

Not to be discounted is *Thomas Cook,* the best known of all British tour operators. Its name is practically synonymous with the Grand Tour of Europe, but *Cook*'s tours span the world, with itineraries ranging from deluxe to moderate, including some of the budget variety as well. You can book a tour directly through any of its offices in major cities in North America or through any travel agency. Its headquarters are at 45 Berkeley St., Piccadilly, London W1A 1EB (phone: 499-4000).

An example of an escorted, highly structured package is *Olson Travel World*'s 21-day Treasures of France tour, which makes a full circle around the country and includes all meals except two lunches and three dinners at the conclusion of the trip in Paris (where packagers of even the most inclusive tours assume that participants prefer to have a greater amount of free time). For information on this and other European itineraries across the Continent, contact Olson Travel World, 100 N. Sepulveda Blvd., Suite 1010, El Segundo, CA 90245 (phone: 213-615-0711 in California or abroad; 800-421-5785 in California; 800-421-2255 elsewhere in the US).

The following tour operators also offer a wide range of similar packages throughout Europe, including Scandinavia, the Benelux countries, Atlantic, Mediterranean, and Central Europe, as well as Eurasia: *Maupintour* (PO Box 807, Lawrence, KA 66044; phone: 913-843-1211 in Kansas or abroad; 800-255-4266 elsewhere in the US); *Travcoa* (4000 MacArthur Blvd., Suite 650E, Newport Beach, CA 92660; phone: 714-476-2800 abroad; 800-992-2004 in California; 800-992-2003 elsewhere in the US), which offers a lineup of packages, for 17, 19, or 30 days, that include all meals; and *Globus-Gateway* (see above).

British Airways also offers two attractive packages: The London Plus package includes a minimum stay of 3 days in London along with a 3-day stay in a number of European cities, airport transfers between cities, accommodations, and a half-day or more of touring in each city. The Four City Classic package includes 3 days in London and 3 days each in Venice, Florence, and Rome, and air and rail transportation between the cities. Extended-stay options are available for both packages. Note that although these packages may be bought in conjunction with a transatlantic ticket, the airfare is not included in the basic package price.

An equally common type of package to Europe is the fly/drive arrangement, (mentioned above), often described in brochures as a self-drive, go-as-you-please, or car tour. These are independent vacations, geared to travelers who want to cover as much ground as they might on an escorted group sightseeing tour but who prefer to do it on their own. The most flexible plans include no more than a map, a rental car, and a block of as many prepaid hotel vouchers as needed for the length of the stay along with a list of participating hotels. In some cases, only the first night's accommodation is reserved; from then on, travelers book rooms one stop ahead as they create their own itinerary (when the hotels are members of a chain or association, which they usually are, the staff of the last hotel will reserve the next one for you). In other cases, there is a choice of booking en route or booking all the overnight stays in advance. Operators offering these packages usually sell vouchers in more than one price category, and there is the additional option to upgrade accommodations by paying an additional sum directly to the hotel.

Another type of fly/drive arrangement is slightly more restrictive in that the tour packager supplies an itinerary that must be followed day by day, with a specific hotel to be reached each night. Often these plans are more deluxe as well. The car tours packaged by *AutoVenture* (425 Pike St., Suite 502, Seattle, WA 98101; phone: 206-624-6033 in Washington or abroad; 800-426-7502 elsewhere in the US) feature overnight stays in hotels that are elegant converted castles or manor houses or old and distinctive country inns. Any of *AutoVenture*'s itineraries, 6 to 14 days in length, can be bought in either a self-drive or chauffeured version. A similar level of luxury is available on the shorter self-drive or chauffeured tours offered by *David B. Mitchell & Company*, *Relais & Châteaux*'s US representative. For information, contact David B. Mitchell & Company, 200 Madison Ave., New York, NY 10016 (phone: 212-696-1323 or 800-372-1323).

A further possibility for independent travelers is a "stay put" package. Basically, it includes a choice of accommodations (with continental breakfast) in several price ranges, plus any of a number of other features that may not always be needed or wanted but are time-consuming to arrange when they are. Common package features are a half-day sightseeing tour of a city and a boat cruise; others may be anything from a souvenir travel bag to a wine tasting, dinner and a show, or some sort of discount card to be used in shops and restaurants. The packages are usually a week long and are sometimes hosted; that is, a representative of the tour company may be available at a local office or even in the hotel to answer questions, handle problems, and assist in arranging activities and optional excursions. *Jet Vacations* (888 Seventh Ave., New York, NY 10106; phone: 212-247-0999 or 800-JET-0999), a tour operator specializing in travel to Europe, has packages with a wide range of hotel choices among its programs; *American Express Travel Service* (branches throughout the US) also offers European city packages. *The World of Oz* offers a 7-day, 6-night independent holiday package that includes accommodations and a rental car (self-drive or chauffeured). You can spend time at one hotel or travel to a different one each day. Contact World of Oz, 211 E. 43rd St., New York, NY 10017; phone: 212-661-0580 or 800-248-0234.

Special interest tours are a growing sector of the travel industry, and programs focusing on food and wine are prominent among packages of this sort put together for visitors to Europe. One thing to note is that they tend to be quite structured arrangements rather than independent ones, and they are rarely created with the budget traveler in mind. Also note that inclusive as they may be, few food and wine tours include *all* meals in the package price. This is not necessarily a cost-cutting technique on the part of the packager; rather, because of the lavishness of some of the meals, others may be left to the discretion of the participants, not only to allow time for leisure, but also to allow for differing rates of metabolism. Similarly, even on wine tours that spend entire days in practically full-time tasting, unlimited table wine at meals may not always be included in the package price. The brochures are usually clear about what comes with the package and when.

There are also special interest packages catering to travelers particularly interested in the arts. For example, *Dailey-Thorp* (315 W. 57th St., New York, NY 10019; phone: 212-307-1555) offers tours for music and opera lovers, focusing on various European musical events. Other tours also visit major cities each year to enjoy the cultural attractions.

Inland waterway trips on canal or river barges outfitted as hotels are another type of special interest package. Because the pace is slow, these trips frequently appeal to second-time visitors as a way to see a very small section of a country in depth. Hotel barges can carry as few as 6 to 8 or as many as 24 passengers in addition to crews of 3 to 8 people, and while the atmosphere and dress aboard are casual, the accommodations (most have cabins with private bathrooms) and attention paid to food (all meals are usually included, with unlimited table wine common) make many of the cruises quite luxurious. Packages are usually by the week, though shorter and longer ones exist.

Floating through Europe (271 Madison Ave., New York, NY 10016; phone: 212-685-5600; 800-221-3140 outside New York) packages week-long cruise itineraries. *Esplanade Tours* (581 Boylston St., Boston, MA 02116; phone: 617-266-7465 or 800-426-5492) also offers week-long cruises. Both *Abercrombie & Kent/Continental Waterways* (1420 Kensington Rd., Oakbrook, IL 60521; phone: 312-954-2944 in Illinois; 800-323-7308 elsewhere in the US) and *Horizon Cruises* (16000 Ventura Blvd., Suite 408, Encino, CA 91436; phone: 818-906-8086 or 800-252-2103 in California; 800-421-0454 elsewhere in the US) offer a variety of cruises.

Ski packages are foremost among the sports-related packages. The foundation of the package is usually a week or two of hotel or condominium accommodations at a ski resort, and for those choosing the hotel rather than the apartment, the price often includes a meal plan of breakfast and dinner daily. The other features of a ski vacation — round-trip bus, train, or rental car transportation between the airport and the resort, ski passes, baggage handling, taxes and tips — are included in varying combinations according to the packager. If transatlantic transportation is by charter flight (not unusual on ski packages), airfare, too, will be included in the price. Besides *Jet Vacations* (888 Seventh Ave., New York, NY 10106; phone: 212-247-0999 or 800-JET-0999), which offers 1-week ski vacations primarily to French resorts, other ski trip packagers with a number of European destinations, are *Alpine Skiing and Travel* (534 New State Hwy., Raynham, MA 02767; phone: 508-823-7707; 800-551-8822 in Massachusetts; 800-343-9676 elsewhere), *Adventures on Skis* (815 North Rd., Westfield, MA 01085; phone: 413-568-2855 or 800-447-1144 in Massachusetts; 800-628-9655 elsewhere in the US), *Ski Jetaway* (4528 McEver Rd., Oakwood, GA 30566; phone: 404-535-1270 or 800-932-0753 in Georgia; 800-554-4756 elsewhere in the US), and *Steve Lohr's Skiworld and Travel* (206 Central Ave., Jersey City, NJ 07307; phone: 201-798-3900 in New Jersey; 800-223-1306 elsewhere in the US), all with a good selection of resorts. *Club Med,* which operates its own resort villages around the world, has ski resorts in France, Italy, and Switzerland; vacation packages there include lessons at the *Club*'s private ski schools. For membership and details, contact Club Med, 40 W. 57th St., New York, NY 10019 (phone: 800-CLUB MED).

Special interest tours for practitioners and spectators of other sports include many biking and hiking tours of varying levels of difficulty. For the names and addresses of their organizers, see *Camping and Caravanning, Hiking and Biking* in this section. Horseback riding holidays for 1 or 2 weeks are arranged by *FITS Equestrian* (see below). Tennis and golf tours operated in conjunction with canal cruises are organized by *McKinley Wilson International* (PO Box 1623, La Quinta, CA 92253; phone: 619-564-5443). The latest additions to their programs are three Tennis Experience tours. The first, from the last week of May through mid-June, includes center court seats to the French Open International Tennis Championship in Paris; the second is the week-long Luxure Canal Barging and Tennis tour in July, with daily stops at private tennis clubs; and, third, Château Tennis, a weeklong program, run several times between May and October, includes stays at three different châteaux (2 nights at each). The company also arranges independent tours to the French Open. *Jet Vacations* (address above) takes groups to the French Open via *Concorde*.

The Great Balloon Adventure, 1-week or shorter programs run from spring through fall by the *Bombard Society* (6727 Curran St., McLean, VA 22101; phone: 703-448-9407 or 800-862-8537), includes daily flights via hot-air balloon (flown by pilots, not tour participants), sightseeing, hotel accommodations, and meals, many of which are candlelit buffets served after the day's flight. Another way to see Europe from the air is via a helicopter tour through US agent *Hemphill Harris* (16000 Ventura Blvd., Suite 200, Encino, CA 91436; phone: 800-252-2103 in California; 800-421-0454 elsewhere). Offerings range from 1-day jaunts to a 6-day tour.

A staple among special interest packages to Ireland is the golf tour, whose main ingredient is the opportunity to play at some of the most celebrated courses in the world. A fly/drive arrangement is usually involved, with rental car, hotel accommodations for a week or two, often one dinner per day, and some greens fees included. Some packages provide an entire week at one course or a choice of courses, and some combine a golfing holiday in Ireland with a visit to Scottish courses. *BTH Holidays* (185 Madison Ave., New York, NY 10016; phone: 212-684-1820 in New York State; 800-221-1074 elsewhere in the US), *Scottish Golf Holidays* (108 W. Convention Way, Cincinnati, OH 45202; phone: 513-651-0700 in Ohio; 800-222-7977 elsewhere in the US), and *InterGolf* (PO Box 819, Champlain, NY 12919, or 4150 St. Catherine St. W., Suite 390, Montreal, Que. H3Z 2Y5, Canada; phone: 514-933-2771) all have self-drive golf packages and tours by escorted motorcoach; the latter include escorted sightseeing itineraries for non-golfers in the group. *Golf Intercontinental/Marsans* (19 W. 34th St., New York, NY 10001; phone: 212-661-6565 in New York State; 800-223-6114 elsewhere in the US) offers a tour for serious golfers only. *Perry Golf* (5584 Chamblee Dunwoody Rd., Atlanta, GA 30338; phone: 404-394-5400 or 800-344-5257) operates a basic 6-night self-drive package that can be combined with a selection of 3-night "modular tours" to courses in Scotland, as well as with a tour to courses in Northern Ireland. Information about many more golf packages can be obtained from a travel agent or from the appropriate tourist authorities (see *Sources and Resources* for addresses).

Among other sports-oriented packages are those focused on — and guaranteeing entrance in — marathons: *Marathon Tours* (108 Main St., Boston, MA 02129; phone: 617-242-7845), which sends runners off to races around the world, and *Grimes Travel* (250 W. 57th St., New York, NY 10019; phone: 212-307-7797 in New York State; 800-832-7778 elsewhere in the US). Horseback riding holidays are the province of *FITS Equestrian* (2011 Alamo Pintado Rd., Solvang, CA 93463; phone: 805-688-9494), whose choices — not for beginners — include 6 days of riding (nights are spent in hotels) and 8 days polishing skills.

Special interest packages of a non-sporting nature in Ireland include an escorted motorcoach crafts tour offered by *Lynott Tours* (350 Fifth Ave., Suite 2619, New York, NY 10118; phone: 800-537-7575 in New York; 800-221-2474 elsewhere in the US). Participants on the 10-day trip see Waterford crystal, Belleek pottery, and Donegal carpets and tweeds being made; take in Aran knitting demonstrations; talk to quilters and lacemakers; visit a design center; and spend a day at a school where they get the chance to learn something new about their own craft. The Heritage Roots Tours offered by *Celtic International Tours* (161 Central Ave., Albany, NY 12206; phone: 518-463-5511 or 800-833-4373) are for travelers of Irish extraction who wish to know more about their ancestors.

Camping and Caravanning, Hiking and Biking

 CAMPING: Europe welcomes campers, whether alone or with a group, with tents or in recreational vehicles — generally known in Europe as "caravans," a term that technically refers to towable campers as opposed to fully motorized vehicles. Camping is probably the best way to enjoy the countryside. And, fortunately, in Europe campgrounds are plentiful.

Where to Camp – Sites for camping and caravanning are run by government tourist agencies, automobile associations, provinces and municipalities, and private companies. Most are open from Easter through October and they fill quickly at the height of the summer season, so it is a good idea to arrive early in the day if a "pitch" has not been reserved in advance. Caravanning is extremely popular with European vacationers, and many parks cater more to the caravanner than to the tent dweller. In many countries, neither campers nor caravanners are restricted to the official sites. However, using private property means first obtaining the permission of the landowner or tenant — as well as assuming the responsibility of leaving the land exactly as it was found in return for the hospitality. When in difficulty, remember that tourist information offices throughout Europe will gladly direct visitors to sites in the areas they serve.

European campgrounds are well marked and rates are always posted at the entrance. Still, it's best to have a map or check the information available in one of the numerous comprehensive guides to sites across the Continent. It's not always easy to find camping facilities open before June or after September, so a guide that gives this information comes in particularly handy off-season. Directors of campgrounds often have a great deal of information about their region, and some will even arrange local tours or recommend the best restaurants, shops, beaches, or attractions in the immediate area. Campgrounds also provide the atmosphere and opportunity to meet other travelers and exchange useful information. Too much so, sometimes — the popularity of the European campgrounds causes them to be quite crowded during the summer, and campsites are frequently so close together that any attempt at privacy or getting away from it all is sabotaged.

In the US, camping maps, brochures, and lists of sites are distributed by the tourist offices of individual countries, and a variety of useful publications are also available from American and European automobile clubs and other associations. One comprehensive guide, *Camping and Caravanning in Europe* ($14.95), published by the *Automobile Association of Great Britain* (*AA*), lists about 4,000 sites inspected and rated by the *AA* and provides other information of interest to campers. In addition, the *AA*'s *Camping and Caravanning in Britain* ($11.75) lists about 1,000 sites. Both are available from the *AA* (Farnum House, Basingstoke, Hampshire RG21 2EA, England), from the *British Travel Bookshop* (40 W. 57th St., New York, NY 10019; phone: 212-765-0898; when ordering, add a $3 handling charge to the prices above), as well as in other travel bookstores. The *Camping Caravanning France* guide ($11.95), published by Michelin (in French, but with an introduction in English on how to use the book) is readily available at bookstores in France.

The international camping organization *Fédération Internationale de Camping et Caravaning* issues a pass, called a *carnet,* that entitles the bearer to a modest discount at many campgrounds throughout Europe. It is available in the US from the *National Campers and Hikers Association* (4804 Transit Rd., Bldg. 2, Depew, NY 14043; phone: 716-668-6242) for a fee of $23, which includes membership in the organization as well as camping information.

Necessities – For outdoor camping, necessities include a tent with flyscreens (the lighter and easier to carry and assemble the better), a sleeping bag, a foam pad or air mattress, a waterproof ground cloth, first-aid kit (including sunscreen and insect repellent), sewing and toilet kits, backpack stove (building fires is prohibited in many areas, especially during dry periods), fuel for the stove, matches, nested cooking pots and cooking utensils, a canteen, three-quarter ax (well sharpened and sheath-protected), jackknife, and a flashlight with an extra set of batteries.

Keep food simple. Unless backpacking deep into the wilderness, you will probably be close enough to a store to stock up on perishables; staples such as sugar, coffee, and powdered milk can be carried along. Dehydrated food has become quite popular among both hikers and campers, but it can be quite expensive. An economical option for the more enterprising camper is to dry a variety of food at home; camping supply stores and bookstores carry cookbooks covering this simple process. Keep in mind, particularly in wilderness areas, that accessible food will lure scavenging wildlife that may invade tents and vehicles.

As in the US, camping equipment is available for sale or rent throughout Europe, and rentals can be booked in advance through any number of outfitters. The above-mentioned guides to camping and caravanning contain lists of outfitters, and the national tourist offices in the US can supply information on reliable dealers.

Recreational Vehicle Rentals – Recreational vehicles — or RVs, known in Europe as caravans — will appeal most to the kind of person who prefers the flexibility of accommodation — there are countless campgrounds throughout Europe and many provide RV hookups — and enjoys camping with a little extra comfort. An RV undoubtably saves a traveler a great deal of money on lodging and, if cooking appliances are part of the unit, on food as well. However, it is important to remember that renting an RV is a major expense; also, any kind of RV increases gas consumption considerably. Reservations should be made well in advance, as the supply of RVs is limited and the demand great.

Although the term recreational vehicle is applied to all manner of camping vehicles, whether towed or self-propelled, generally the models available for rent in Europe are either towable campers ("caravans") or motorized RVs. The motorized models are usually either vans customized in various ways for camping, often including elevated roofs, or larger, coach-type, fully equipped homes on wheels. Although most motorized models have standard shift, occasionally automatic shift vehicles may be available for an additional charge. Towed vehicles can be hired overseas but are not usually offered by companies in the US.

Make sure that the RV you choose is equipped to deal with the electrical and gas standards of all countries on your itinerary. There are differences, for instance, between the bottled stove gas supplied in Britain and that on the Continent. You should either have a sufficient supply of the type your camper requires or equipment that can use either. When towing a camper, note that nothing towed is automatically covered by the liability insurance of the primary vehicle, and the driver's Green Card must carry an endorsement for the towed vehicle.

Whether driving a camper or towing, it is essential to have some idea of the terrain you'll be encountering en route. Not only are numerous mountain passes closed in winter, but grades are often too steep for certain vehicles to negotiate and some roads are off limits to towed caravans. Car tunnels, or "piggyback" services on trains, usually bypass those summits too difficult to climb, but they also impose dimension limitations and often charge high fees. The *AA* guides cited above provide detailed information on the principal passes and tunnels, as do tourist offices.

Rentals of recreational vehicles can be arranged from the US through several companies, including the following:

Avis Rent-A-Car, 6128 E. 38th St., Tulsa, OK 74135 (phone: 800-331-1084, ext. 7719), has affiliates in France, Holland, and Switzerland; arrangements must be made through the US office.

Connex, 983 Main St., Peekskill, NY 10566 (phone: 800-333-3949).

Cortell International, 17310 Red Hill Ave., Irvine, CA 92714 (phone: 800-228-2535).

Europe by Car, 1 Rockefeller Plaza, New York, NY 10020, or 9000 Sunset Blvd., Los Angeles, CA 90069 (phone: 212-581-3040 in New York State; 800-252-9401 in California; 800-223-1516 elsewhere in the US).

Foremost Euro-Car Inc., 5430 Van Nuys Blvd., Van Nuys, CA 91401 (phone: 800-252-9401 in California; 800-423-3111 in the US).

Another particularly economical option is *Wheels International Rent-a-Car* (Suite 308, 1682 W. 7th Ave., Vancouver BC V6J 4S6, Canada; phone: 604-731-0441 or 800-663-8888 throughout the US). Through contracts with other rental agencies, this company arranges car, minivan, and mobile home rentals at a variety of locations, depending on availability, at a flat discounted rate. Full payment must be made in advance; dropoff alternatives are also available for a minimal additional charge.

Among companies offering RV rentals in Europe are the following:

Autotours, 20 Craven Terrace, London W2, England (phone: 258-0272), offers reasonably priced camping tours of Europe, ranging from 3 to 10 weeks.

FCI Location, Zone Industrielle de Sant-Brendan, Quentin 22800 (phone: 96-74-08-36). Rents motorized RVs on an unlimited-mileage basis; rates vary according to season and include insurance, linens, and other frills.

Trois Soleils, Maison Trois Soleils, 2 Route de Paris, 67117 Ittenheim, France (phone: 88-69-17-17 for reservations; 30-69-06-60 for the Paris branch). Rents motorized RVs as well as some basic campers, through the main office near Strasbourg, however pickup and dropoff locations also include Paris and Montpelier.

A complimentary packet of information on how to operate, maintain, choose, and use a recreational vehicle is available from the *Recreational Vehicle Industry Association* (PO Box 2999, Reston, VA 22090; phone: 703-620-6003). You might also want to subscribe to *Trailer Life,* published by TL Enterprises 29901 Agoura Rd., Agoura, CA 91301 (phone: 818-991-4980); a 1-year subscription costs $11.98. For further information on how to operate, choose, and use an RV, see Richard A. Wolters's *Living on Wheels* (Dutton; currently out of print; check your library).

Organized Trips – Packaged camping tours exist, and they are a good way to have your cake and eat it, too. The problems of advance planning and day-to-day organizing are left to someone else, yet you still reap the benefits that shoestring travel affords. Be aware, however, that these packages are usually geared to the young, with ages 18 to 35 as common limits. Transfer from place to place is by bus or van, as on other sightseeing tours, overnights are in tents, and meal arrangements vary. Often there is a food kitty that covers meals in restaurants or in the camps; sometimes there is a chef, and sometimes the cooking is done by the participants themselves.

The *Specialty Travel Index,* 305 San Anselmo Ave., Suite 217, San Anselmo, CA 94960 (phone: 415-459-4900), is a directory to special interest travel and an invaluable resource. Listings include tour operators specializing in camping, not to mention myriad other interests that combine nicely with a camping trip, such as biking, ballooning, diving, horseback riding, canoeing, motorcycling, and river rafting. It costs $5 per copy, $8 for a year's subscription of two issues.

Among such packages are the camping tours of Europe offered by *Autotours;* a variety of itineraries are available (see above). *Camping Tours of Europe, Ltd.* (2 Guilles Lane, Woodbury, NY 11797; phone: 516-496-7400) also markets the camping tours of British tour operators.

HIKING: If you would rather eliminate all the gear and planning and take to the outdoors unencumbered, park the car and go for a day's hike. Trails abound in Europe, as does specific information on how to find them. Many tourist authorities distribute information sheets on walking and mountaineering, and there are numerous other sources for those intent on getting about on their own.

Marked hiking trails abound in Europe. Germany alone has some 80,000 miles of them in addition to 9,000 Alpine trails. On Britain's Pennine Way, one of the country's official long-distance footpaths and its roughest, you can walk 270 lonely miles up the backbone of England to the Scottish border, a trip recommended only for experienced hikers equipped with maps and compass to steer them through remote moorland and probable bad weather. Less practiced but more gregarious hikers can join the weekend crowds for a short stretch of one of France's easiest *sentiers de grande randonnée,* the Sentier de l'Ile-de-France, a 375-mile route ringing Paris. Equally popular (lodging along the way for July and August is booked months in advance) but much more difficult is the spectacularly scenic Tour du Mont-Blanc, a 100-mile route around the mountain massif taking in three countries — France, Italy, and Switzerland.

Preliminary information on where to hike is available from many tourist offices in the US. The British Tourist Authority's information sheet *Walking* describes national parks, long-distance footpaths, and other walking areas in England, Wales, Scotland, and Northern Ireland. The Irish Tourist Board can supply a general information sheet on walking and rock climbing. The Swiss National Tourist Office recommends *Walking Switzerland — The Swiss Way,* by Marcia and Philip Lieberman ($10.95 from The Mountaineers Books, 306 2nd Ave. W., Seattle, WA 98119; phone: 206-285-2665 or 800-553-4453), and also distributes *Postbus: The Best High-Altitude and Panoramic Walks,* a booklet detailing various scenic routes whose jumping-off points can be reached via the Swiss postbus service. Another useful set of guidebooks is the *Walking Through* series, which covers ten different European cities and is available from VLE Limited, PO Box 547, Tenafly, NJ 07670 (phone: 201-567-5536) for $3 each, or $2.50 each for two or more.

Even those tourist offices that do not have literature on hand (or have little in

English) can direct you to associations in their countries that supply maps, guides, and further information. For long visits, membership in a local club is suggested.

An example of a regional hiking association is the *Fédération Française de la Randonnée Pédestre (FFRP)* (9 Av. Georges-V, 75008 Paris; phone: 47-23-62-32), which offers information (mostly in French) about the vast trail network and maps and guidebooks for specific regions in France. A British company that publishes English translations of the *Topo-Guides* of the *FFRP* and also specializes in maps and other publications for hikers and climbers is the *Robertson MacCarta Shop* (122 King's Cross Rd., London WC1X 9DS, England; phone: 01-278-8278).

Mountaineering clubs are also a particularly good source of trail information suitable for the average hiker. For instance, the *Federation of Mountaineering Clubs of Ireland* (20 Leopardstown Gardens, Blackrock, Co. Dublin; phone: 01-881266) offers information, advice, and a list of general and regional walking and climbing guidebooks for excursions in Ireland that can be ordered through its office or bought at travel bookstores. Those whose hiking enters the realm of mountain climbing can get information from *Club Alpin Français, Commission de Randonnées,* 9 Rue La Boétie, 75008 Paris (phone: 47-42-38-46). The *British Mountaineering Council* (Crawford House, Precinct Centre, Booth St. E., Manchester, M13 9RZ) also furnishes advice on mountaineering and rock climbing and a list of qualified guides.

Serious hikers may want to check at their library for the very comprehensive but out-of-print *On Foot Through Europe: A Trail Guide to France & the Benelux Nations* by Craig Evans, which includes information about guides and guidebooks, weather, lodgings, equipment, useful addresses, long-distance footpaths, cross-country skiing possibilities, national and regional parks, and individual provinces and the resources specific to each.

To make outings safe and pleasant, find out in advance about the trails you plan to hike and be realistic about your own physical limitations. Choose an easy route if you are out of shape. Stick to defined trails unless you are an experience hiker or know the area well. If it is at all wild, let someone know where you are going and when you expect to be back, at least by leaving a note on your car if the hike is impromptu.

All you need for a simple hike are a pair of sturdy shoes and socks; jeans or long pants to keep branches, nettles, and bugs off your legs; a canteen of water; a hat for the sun; and, if you like, a picnic lunch. It is a good idea to dress in layers, so that you can peel off a sweater or two to keep pace with the rising sun and put them back on as the sun goes down. Make sure, too, to wear clothes with pockets or bring a pack to keep your hands free. Some useful and important pocket or pack stuffers include a jackknife, waterproof matches, a map, and a compass. In areas where snakes are common, include a snakebite kit.

Those who prefer to travel as part of an organized group should refer to the January/ February issue of *Sierra Club* magazine for the *Sierra Club*'s annual list of foreign outings. The *Sierra Club* offers a selection of trips each year, usually about 2 weeks in length. In 1989 you could hike through Southern Spain and the Balearic Islands, Wales, Norway, southwestern France, the Austrian Alps and the Italian Dolomites, and the Bavarian Forest in West Germany. Other trips combined hiking with biking (in Ireland and Italy), and there was also a walking tour of Paris. Some are backpacking trips, moving to a new camp each day; others make day hikes from a base camp. Overnights can be in small hotels, inns, or guesthouses, in campgrounds or mountain huts. For information, contact the Sierra Club Outing Dept., 730 Polk St., San Francisco, CA 94109 (phone: 415-776-2211).

American Youth Hostels (see address below) also sponsors foreign hiking trips, though fewer than its foreign biking trips. *AYH*'s 1989 roster included European trips ranging from 15 to 52 days and costing from $1,975 to $3,025. *Mountain Travel,* a company specializing in adventure trips around the world, offers a great variety of trips, from easy walks that can be undertaken by anyone in good health to those that require basic or advanced mountaineering experience. Its trips take in the Alps (including the famous Tour du Mont-Blanc mentioned above) and the Pyrenees as well as the mountains of Britain, Spain, Eastern Europe, Greece, Turkey, and the Soviet Union. Inn-to-inn hiking is an appealing way to see the countryside in the Alps and in the hills of Czechoslovakia. There is also an easy, low-elevation walking tour of the Irish countryside and an expedition to Turkey that includes easy day hikes, boating excursions, and visits to beaches and archaeological sites. All make excellent alternatives for those who aren't in exceptional physical condition. For information, contact Mountain Travel, 6420 Fairmont Ave., El Cerrito, CA 94530 (phone: in California, 415-527-8100; elsewhere, 800-227-2384). Note that *Mountain Travel* also designs special itineraries for independent travelers. *Baumeler Tours* and *Country Cycling Tours* (see "Biking" below) also offer several walking tours.

BIKING: For young or energetic travelers, the bicycle offers a marvelous way of seeing Europe, especially those countries where terrains are especially conducive to easy cycling like the Benelux nations and parts of Scandinavia. Throughout the Continent, secondary roads, which thread through picturesque stretches of countryside, abound. Biking does have its drawbacks: Little baggage can be carried, travel is slow, and cyclists are exposed to the elements. However, should a cyclist need rest or refuge from the weather, there is always a welcoming tavern or comfortable inn around the next bend.

Road Safety – While the car may be the bane of cyclists, cyclists who do not follow the rules of the road strike terror into the hearts of drivers. Follow the same rules and regulations as automobile drivers. Stay to the right side of the road. Ride no more than two abreast — single file where traffic is heavy. Keep three bicycle lengths behind the cycle in front of you. Stay alert to sand, gravel, potholes, and wet or oily surfaces, all of which can make you lose control. Wear bright clothes, and use lights or wear reflective material at dusk or at night, and, above all, even though French cyclists often don't, always wear a helmet.

Choosing, Renting, and Buying a Bike – Although many bicycling enthusiasts choose to take along their own bikes, bicycles can be rented throughout Europe. Long and short rentals are widely available; however, particularly in rural areas, it may pay to check ahead. Cities such as Amsterdam, where biking is a way of life, provide complete cycling services. Certain national railways, including those in Austria, Belgium, France, Germany, the Netherlands, and Switzerland, have bicycles for rent at many train stations, often at a discount for ticketholders. Many also feature "rent it here, leave it there" programs, allowing you to take your bike on the train to another town without returning it to the station from which it was rented. Almost all European trains have facilities for bike transport at nominal fees.

As an alternative to renting, you might consider buying a bicycle in Europe, often for less than you might pay in the US; however, the bicycle may take some getting used to — seats especially need breaking in at first — and it will be subject to a duty by US Customs if its price (or the total of purchases in Europe) exceeds $400. When evaluating this cost, take into account additional charges for shipping. Those planning to buy a bicycle, be it in the US or Europe, should consider a good-quality, lightweight touring bike that has the all-important low gears for hill climbing and riding against the wind. A European bicycle purchased in the US should have proof-of-purchase papers to avoid potential customs problems. Bike shops in major cities that rent bikes sometimes also sell used ones, a particularly economical option that may be even less expensive than a long-term rental.

A bicycle is the correct size for you if you can straddle its center bar with feet flat on the ground and still have an inch or so between your crotch and the bar. (Nowadays, because women's old-fashioned barless bikes are not as strong as men's, most women use men's bicycles.) The seat height is right if your leg is just short of completely extended when you push the pedal to the bottom of its arc.

To be completely comfortable, divide your weight; put about 50% on your saddle and about 25% on your arms and legs. To stop sliding in your seat and for better support, set your saddle level. A firm saddle is better than a soft springy one for a long ride. Experienced cyclists keep the tires fully inflated (pressure requirements vary widely, but are always imprinted on the side of the tire; stay within 5 pounds of the recommended pressure). Do not use top, or tenth, gear all the way; for most riding the middle gears are best. On long rides, remember that until you are very fit, short efforts with rests in between are better than one long haul, and pedal at an even pace.

The happiest biker in a foreign country is the one who arrives best prepared. Bring saddlebags, a handlebar bag, a tool kit that contains a bike wrench, screwdriver, pliers, tire repair kit, cycle oil, and work gloves, a bike repair book, a helmet (a rarity among European cyclists), a rain suit, a water bottle, a flashlight with an extra set of batteries, a small first-aid kit, and muscles that have been limbered up in advance.

Even the smallest towns usually have a bike shop, so it's not difficult to replace or add to gear; however, because tires and tubes are sized to metric dimensions in Europe, when riding your own bike, bring extras from home. Good maps infinitely improve a bike trip, and Michelin and IGN topographical maps, available throughout Europe, provide detailed and clear road references. Seasoned bikers swear that the second day of any trip is always the worst, so keep this in mind and be ready to meet the mental and physical challenges ahead.

Airlines going from the US (or elsewhere) to Europe generally allow bicycles to be checked as baggage; they require that the pedals be removed, handlebars be turned sideways, and the bike be in a shipping carton, which some airlines provide, subject to availability — call ahead to make sure. If buying a shipping carton from a bicycle shop, check the airline's specifications and also ask about storing the carton at the destination airport so you can use it again for the return flight. Although some airlines charge only a nominal fee, if the traveler has already checked two pieces of baggage there may be an additional excess baggage charge of $70 to $80 for the bicycle. As regulations vary from carrier to carrier, be sure to call well before departure to find out the regulations of specific airlines.

A good book to help you plan a trip is *Bicycle Touring in Europe,* by Karen and Gary Hawkins (Pantheon Books; $8.95); it offers information on buying and equipping a touring bike, useful clothing and supplies, and helpful techniques for the long-distance biker. Another book that focuses on Europe is *Bicycling in France;* previously published by Haynes, it's out of print, but check your library. Also useful as a planning aid is *Information and Equipment,* the free store catalogue of the *Metropolitan New York Council of American Youth Hostels (AYH;* 75 Spring St., New York, NY 10012; phone: 212-431-7100). It provides information on equipment and has an excellent bibliography of paperbacks and maps for cyclists, campers, hikers, and travelers touring on skis. The *International Youth Hostel Handbook, Volume One: Europe and the Mediterranean* ($8.95 plus $2 for postage) is a guide to all the hostels of Europe to which members of *AYH* have access; a map of their locations is included. (For information on joining *American Youth Hostels,* see *Hints for Single Travelers.*)

Detailed maps will infinitely improve a biking tour and are available from a number of sources. Bartholomew maps of the National or GT series provide excellent coverage of the United Kingdom. If you cannot find them, write to John Bartholomew & Son Ltd., 12 Duncan St., Edinburgh EH9 1TA, Scotland, for a price list. Detailed Michelin maps (1:200,000) covering Europe and other parts of Europe are available from Michelin Guides and Maps, PO Box 3305, Spartanburg, SC 29304-3305 (phone: 803-599-0850). The *Royal Dutch Touring Club (ANWB),* 220 Wassenaarsewg, 2596 EC, The

Hague, The Netherlands (phone: 70-147-147), publishes a series of detailed maps charting Holland's excellent bike paths. Some of these are also available at the Netherlands Board of Tourism.

Tours – A number of organizations offer bike tours in Europe. Linking up with a bike tour is more expensive than traveling alone, but with experienced leaders, an organized tour often becomes an educational as well as a very social experience that may lead to long-term friendships.

One of the attractions of a bike tour is that shipment of equipment — the bike — is handled by organizers, and the shipping fee is included in the total tour package. Travelers simply deliver the bike to the airport, already disassembled and boxed; shipping boxes can be obtained from most bicycle shops with little difficulty. Bikers not with a tour must make their own arrangements with the airline, and there are no standard procedures (see above). Although some tour organizers will rent bikes, most prefer that participants show up with a bike with which they are already familiar. Another attraction of *some* tours is the existence of a "sag wagon" to carry extra luggage, fatigued cyclists, and their bikes, too, when pedaling another mile is impossible.

Most bike tours are scheduled from May to October, last 1 or 2 weeks, are limited to 20 or 25 people, and provide lodging in inns or hotels, though some use hostels or even tents. Tours vary considerably in style and ambience, so request brochures from several operators in order to make the best decision. When contacting groups, be sure to ask about the maximum number of people on the trip, the maximum number of miles to be traveled each day, and the degree of difficulty of the biking; these particulars should determine which tour you join and can greatly affect your enjoyment of the experience. Planning ahead is essential because trips often fill up 6 months or more in advance.

Among the companies specializing in biking tours to Europe are the following:

Backroads Bicycle Touring, 1516 Fifth St., Berkeley, CA 94710-1713 (phone: 415-527-1555 or 800-533-2573), offers superior food and accommodations on its tours through France, Ireland, and Italy. Tours are geared to beginning and intermediate riders.

Baumeler Tours, 10 Grand Ave., Rockville Center, NY 11570-9861 (phone: 516-766-6160, collect, in New York State; 800-6-ABROAD elsewhere nationwide). Both individual and escorted biking (and hiking) tours are offered in Austria, France, Germany, Italy, the Netherlands, and Switzerland. A van for luggage and bikes is provided; participants may take their own bikes.

Butterfield & Robinson, 70 Bond St., Suite 300, Toronto, Ont. M5B 1X3, Canada (phone: 416-864-1354), offers a number of first class, sophisticated bike trips. Bikes are provided, though you can take your own, and there are many departure dates for each itinerary. This company also offers trips to anyone aged 17 or older; tours are rated at four levels of difficulty.

Country Cycling Tours, 140 W. 83rd St., New York, NY 10024 (phone: 212-874-5151), offers a variety of 14-day itineraries to England, France, Holland, Ireland, and Italy. (Hiking tours are also available.)

Gerhard's Bicycle Odysseys, 4949 SW Macadam, Portland, OR 97201 (phone: 503-223-2402), offers 2-week trips to Europe.

Lucullan Travels Ltd. (402 29th St., Des Moines, IA 50312; phone: 515-243-4089). Organized bike tours emphasize food and wine on itineraries through the vineyards of France. Tour leaders, history professor Julian Archer and his wife, Jane, a professional restaurant reviewer, supply all the commentary on French history, culture, and cuisine. Hot-air balloon launches are a new twist on some of the tours.

Wilderness Travel, 801 Allston Way, Berkeley, CA 94710 (phone: 415-548-0420 or 800-247-6700), an adventure packager known for expeditions in the wild, also offers bicycle trips, with sag wagons a standard feature.

Hundreds of other organizations sponsoring biking tours have sprung up across the Continent in response to the explosion of interest in this form of travel. Among them are: *Euro-bike Tours,* PO Box 40, De Kalb, IL 60115 (phone: 815-758-8851); *Open Roads,* 1601 Summit Dr., Haymarket, VA 22069 (phone: 703-754-4152 or 800-333-2453). The *Sierra Club* also occasionally includes a bike tour in its European offerings. For news about upcoming free-wheeling events, contact the club's Outing Department (address above).

The *American Youth Hostels* and its local chapters or councils also offer a variety of packages. You don't have to be a youngster to take an *AYH* trip; membership is open to all ages (although hostels in Switzerland and Bavaria, Germany, give priority to members age 26 and under, meaning that in summer and on holidays, there will probably not be space available for older travelers), and the catalogue includes a group of trips for adults only. *AYH* tours are for small groups of 9 or 10 participants and tend to be longer than average (up to 5 weeks). Departures are geared to various age groups and levels of skill and frequently feature accommodations in hostels — along with hotels for adult groups and campgrounds for younger groups. The *Metropolitan New York Council of American Youth Hostels* is an affiliate with a particularly broad tour program of its own, and is a good source of camping, hiking, and cycling equipment. For information, contact your local council, the national organization, PO Box 37613, Washington, DC 20013-7613 (phone: 202-783-6161), or The Metropolitan New York Council of the American Youth Hostels, 75 Spring St., New York, NY 10012 (phone: 212-431-7100).

The *International Bicycle Touring Society* (*IBTS*) is a non-profit organization that regularly sponsors low-cost bicycle tours around the US and Canada and overseas led by member volunteers. Participants must be over 21. A sag wagon accompanies the tour group, accommodations are in inns and hotels, and some meals are included. For information, send $2 plus a 39¢ self-addressed stamped envelope to IBTS, PO Box 6979, San Diego, CA 92106-0979 (phone: 619-226-TOUR).

The *League of American Wheelmen* (6707 Whitestone Rd., Suite 209, Baltimore, MD 21207; phone: 301-944-3399) publishes *Tourfinder,* a list of organizations, nonprofit and commercial, that sponsor bicycle tours of the US and abroad; the list is free with membership ($22 individual, $27 family) and can be obtained by non-members who send $4. The *League* can also put you in touch with biking groups in your area. You may also want to investigate the tours of the Continent offered by the *Cyclists' Touring Club* (*CTC*), Britain's largest national association — join early if you want to participate. For information contact CTC, Cotterell House, 69 Meadrow, Godalming, Surrey GU7 3HS, England (phone: 4868-7217).

Preparing

Calculating Costs

$ After years of living relatively high on the hog, travel from North America to Europe dropped off precipitously in 1987 in response, among other considerations, to the relative weakness of the US dollar on the Continent. Many Americans who had enjoyed bargain prices in Europe found that the recent disadvantageous exchange rates really put a crimp in their travel planning. But even though the halcyon days of dollar domination seem over for the present, discount fares and the availability of charter flights can greatly reduce the cost of a European vacation; package tours can even further reduce the price. Europe has always been one of the most popular destinations for both the first-time and the seasoned traveler, and it is certainly one where the competition for American visitors works to inspire surprisingly affordable travel opportunities. Nevertheless, most travelers still have to plan carefully before they go, and prudent marshaling of funds is still necessary.

Estimating the cost of travel expenses in Europe depends on the mode of transportation chosen, what part of the country you plan to visit, how long you will stay there, and, in some cases, what time of the year you plan to travel. In addition to the basics of transportation, hotels, meals, and sightseeing, you have to take into account seasonal price changes, which apply on certain air routings and at popular vacation destinations, as well as inflation, price fluctuations, and the vagaries of currency exchange. So, while the price guidelines in this book will remain useful, costs for both facilities and services may have changed somewhat in the months since publication.

Prices, inflation, and exchange rates are hardly uniform across Europe. Traditionally, northern and central European countries — Scandinavia, the Benelux nations, Germany, Switzerland, Austria — are more expensive and usually have less favorable exchange rates for the dollar than do the Mediterranean and Eastern European countries. In general, all European countries have a saving grace: Though their capitals — like our own major cities — suffer from a relatively high cost of living, travel in the surrounding countryside can be more reasonable, and even inexpensive (depending on your choice of accommodations and means of transport). The dollar normally goes farthest of all in Yugoslavia, Greece, Spain, and Portugal, traditionally the least expensive European countries. Ireland also is still a relatively good buy, whether you plan to stay in Dublin or to ramble around the countryside.

DETERMINING A BUDGET: A realistic appraisal of your travel expenses is the most crucial bit of planning before any trip. It is also, unfortunately, one for which it is most difficult to give precise, practical advice. Travel styles are intensely personal, and personal taste determines cost to a great extent. Will you stay in a hotel every night and eat every meal in a restaurant, or do you want to do some camping and picnicking, thus reducing your daily expenses? Base your calculations on your own travel style, and estimate your expenses from that. If published figures on the cost of travel were always taken as gospel, many trips would not be taken. But in reality, it's possible to economize. On the other hand, don't be lulled into feeling that it is not necessary to do some arithmetic before you go. No matter how generous your budget, without careful planning beforehand — and strict accounting along the way — you will spend more than you anticipated.

When calculating costs, start with the basics, the major expenses being transportation, accommodations, and food. However, don't forget such extras as local transportation, sightseeing, shopping, and miscellaneous items such as laundry, local taxes, and tips. And keep in mind, particularly when calculating the major expenses, that costs vary according to fluctuations in the exchange rate — that is, how much of a given foreign currency the dollar will buy. Package programs can lower the price of a vacation in Europe, because the group rates obtained by the tour packager are usually less expensive than the tariffs charged to someone traveling on a freelance basis, that is, paying for each element — airfare, meals, car rental — separately.

Other expenses, such as the cost of local sightseeing tours, will vary from city to city. Official tourist information offices are plentiful throughout Europe, and most of the better hotels will have someone at the front desk who can provide a rundown on the cost of local tours and full-day excursions. Special discount passes that provide tourists with unlimited travel by the day or the week on regular city transportation are available in many large cities. The local tourist authority (see *Sources and Resources*) or railway office (see *Touring by Train*) can provide information on current discount tickets.

If you spend every night in a moderately priced hotel and eat every meal in a moderately priced restaurant, you can expect to spend around $200 for two people per day. This figure does not include transportation costs, but it does include accommodations (based on two people sharing a room), three meals, some sightseeing, and other modest entertainment costs. The accommodations take into consideration the differences between relatively inexpensive lodgings in rural areas (about $40 to $50 per night for two) and moderate hotels in urban areas (about $80 to $100 per night for two). Meals are all calculated for inexpensive restaurants, and the entertainment normally includes one sightseeing tour and admission to one museum or historic site. These figures are based on averages compiled by travel sources across the country.

You should be able to use these averages to forecast a reasonably accurate picture of your daily travel costs, based on exactly how you want to travel. Savings on the daily allowance can occur while motoring in rural areas; families can take advantage of the wide range of inexpensive accommodations across the Continent. Campgrounds are located throughout Europe and are a particularly inexpensive way to see the countryside.

Picnicking is another excellent way to cut costs, and Europe abounds with well-groomed parks and idyllic pastoral settings. A stop at a delicatessen or market can provide a feast of delicacies or a light meal of fine cheeses and meats, crusty bread, fresh fruit, and perhaps a bottle of wine, at a surprisingly economical price compared to the cost of a restaurant lunch.

In planning your budget, it is also wise to allow a realistic amount for both entertainment and recreation. Are you planning to sightsee and visit museums? Do you intend to spend your days skiing at a popular resort? Is daily tennis a part of your plan? Will your children be disappointed if they don't take a *bateau-mouche* on the Seine or a gondola ride in Venice? If so, charges for these attractions and recreations must be taken into account.

If at any point in the planning process it appears impossible to estimate expenses, consider this suggestion: The easiest way to put a ceiling on the price of all these elements is to consider buying a package tour. A totally planned and escorted tour, with almost all transportation, rooms, meals, sightseeing, local travel, tips, and a dinner show or two included and prepaid, allows you to know beforehand almost exactly what the trip will cost, and the only surprise will be the one you spring on yourself by succumbing to some irresistible, expensive souvenir.

The various types of packages available are discussed in *Package Tours*, in this section, but a few points bear repeating here. Not all packages are package *tours*. There are loosely organized arrangements including nothing more than transatlantic transportation, a stay at a hotel, transfers between hotel and airport, baggage handling, taxes, and tips, which leave the entire matter of how you spend your time and where you eat your meals — and with whom — up to you. Equally common are the hotel-plus-car packages, which take care of accommodations and local transportation. On such independent or hosted "tours," there may be a tour company representative or affiliated travel agent available at a local office to answer questions, or a host may be stationed at a desk in the hotel to arrange optional excursions, but you will never have to travel in a group unless you wish to. More and more, even experienced travelers are being won over by the idea of packaged travel, not only for the convenience and the planning time saved, but above all for the money saved. Whatever elements you choose to include in your package, the organizer has gotten them for you wholesale — and they are prepaid, thus eliminating the dismal prospect of returning to your hotel each night to subtract the day's disbursements from your remaining cash.

The possibility of prepaying certain elements of your trip is an important point to consider even if you intend to be strictly independent, with arrangements entirely of your own making, all bought separately. You may not be able to match the price of the wholesale tour package, but at least you will have introduced an element of predictability into your accounting, thus reducing the risk that some budget-busting expense along the way might put a damper on the rest of your plans. With the independent traveler in mind, what follows are some suggestions of how to pin down the cost of a trip beforehand — but there are two more variables that will influence the cost of your holiday whether you buy a package or do it all yourself. One is timing. If you are willing to travel during the less trafficked off-season months, when airfares are lower, you'll find many hotel rates lower also (except in winter ski resorts). Keep in mind those periods between the traditional high and low seasons, generally referred to as the shoulder months (approximately late March to mid-May and late September to mid-November). Costs are only a little lower than in high season, and although the weather may not be as predictable, you won't be bucking the crowds that in peak months can force a traveler without a hotel reservation into the most expensive hostelry in town. Don't forget, however, to find out what is going on in any place you plan to spend a good deal of your vacation. The availability and possible economy gained by off-season travel are negated if a major conference or other special event is scheduled when you plan to visit.

Another factor influencing the cost of your trip is whether you will be traveling alone or as a couple. The prices quoted for package tours are almost always based on double occupancy of hotel rooms, and the surcharge — or single supplement — for a room by yourself can be quite hefty. When shopping for a hotel room, you'll find that there are many more double rooms than singles. Don't expect a discount if you occupy a double room as a single, and don't expect single rooms to cost less than two-thirds the price of doubles.

Those who want to travel independently but also want to eliminate the element of surprise from their accommodations budgets can take advantage of the hotel voucher scheme that frequently comes as part of a fly/drive package. Travelers receive a block of prepaid vouchers and a list of hotels that accept them as total payment for a night's stay, and for those who may want to upgrade their lodgings from time to time, there is often another set of hotels that accept the same vouchers with payment of a supplement.

TRANSPORTATION: In earlier sections of GETTING READY TO GO we have discussed the comparative costs of different modes of transportation and the myriad special travel rates available through package tours, charter flights, train passes, car rental packages, and other budget deals. See each of the relevant sections for specific information. Transportation is likely to represent the largest item in your travel budget, but the encouraging aspect of this is that you will be able to determine most of these costs before you leave. Most fares will have to be paid in advance, particularly if you take advantage of charter air travel or other special deals.

Airfare is really the easiest cost to pin down, though the range and variety of flights available may be confusing initially. The possibilities are outlined fully in *Traveling by Plane,* in this section. Essentially, the traveler can choose from various types of tickets on scheduled flights, ranging in expense from the luxury of the *Concorde* and first class fares to APEX, discount, and standby tickets or charters.

The most important factors in determining which mode of transportation to choose in touring Europe are the amount of traveling you plan to do and the length of time you will be abroad. If you intend to move about a great deal between cities, a pass allowing unlimited train travel is likely to be the most economical approach. A Eurail-pass is valid throughout much of Europe, is attractively priced, and must be purchased before you leave home. For more information on economical rail options, see *Touring by Train.*

If driving through the countryside is your object, you should look carefully into fly/drive arrangements versus straight rentals and compare the rates offered by some of the smaller US firms specializing in car travel in Europe with the rates offered by the large, familiar car rental names. The latter all have discount plans, provided the car is booked a certain number of days before departure and the rental is for a minimum period of time (see *Touring by Car*). Always look for a flat rate based on unlimited mileage — usually the best deal. Also, when estimating driving costs, don't forget that the price of gas in Europe averages more than double the price you're accustomed to paying in the US, so be sure to take this substantial expense into account.

FOOD: Meals are a more difficult expense to estimate. If you stay in an apartment or are camping out, you will be able to prepare some meals yourself. Depending on where you're staying, groceries can be more expensive than they are at home, but they will certainly cost less than eating out. Restaurant dining — particularly in the better establishments of major tourist cities — is going to hit your purse, wallet, or credit card hardest.

Independent travelers eating all of their meals in restaurants should allow roughly $35 to $60 a day per person for food. This amount includes breakfast, because increasingly the standard breakfast included in the price of accommodations — although in many areas it is posted separately from the price of the room — is continental (coffee and rolls); there is an extra charge for a full breakfast (anything from bacon and eggs to zesty local wurst and potato pancakes). This should also cover taxes and the service charge and perhaps a carafe of wine at dinner — but you won't be splurging. This estimate is based on a fixed menu (at a fixed price) in a moderate, neither-scrimp-nor-splurge restaurant, which can at least include a tasty and occasionally imaginative food selection, but no cocktails before dinner. If ordering à la carte and the pick of the wine list in one of the major cities, be prepared for the tab to rise much higher, and if you're addicted to *haute gastronomie,* the sky is the limit.

All of this is no reason to forgo your trip, however — remember, it's *dining* that is going to hit your wallet hard. Those who are up to a steady diet of fast food can get by on a lot less. And there is some relief out in the countryside, where the breakfast that comes with the bed in typical bed-and-breakfast establishments and small inns can still be a filling one, apt to hold most folks straight through midday, though even travelers on a severe budget are advised not to skip lunch. If you stick to picnic lunches put together from the infinite variety of European delicatessens and markets and finish off the day with a carefully chosen meal in a bistro, *trattoria,* taverna, or pub, you will sacrifice nothing in experience and hold the cost down. Our restaurant selections, chosen to give the best value for money — whether expensive or dirt cheap — are listed in the *Best in Town* sections of THE CITIES and in the *Eating Out* sections of each tour route in DIRECTIONS.

ACCOMMODATIONS: There is a wide choice and a substantial difference in degrees of luxury provided among the expensive, moderate, and inexpensive hotels. Although room costs in Europe cover a very broad spectrum, for purposes of making an estimate, expect to pay in Europe about what you would pay in a major American city for equivalent accommodations. And figure on the high side if you've visiting major tourist centers during high season.

Most expensive — as high as $300 to $500 for a double room — will be the "palace" hotels of Paris and the Riviera. Rates at international hotels with a full complement of business services also tend toward the top of the scale. Generally, the member hotels of international chains in any given city are priced roughly equally. In the larger cities (such as Paris and Rome), this ranges from around $150 up, although similar hotels elsewhere range from about $60 to $80 for a double. There is a big jump from these international class hotels to those in the moderate category in the same city, and prices will be from $20 to as much as $50 less per night.

There is no sacred edict stating that travelers must put up at deluxe hotels in Europe, and, in fact, you might be missing a good deal of the European experience by insisting on international standards and skipping the great small hotels. Especially in Europe, hotels in the first class range usually are available at about one third less than their deluxe counterparts. Second class hotels offer clean, comfortable accommodations, and are often thoroughly charming, and in the even more inexpensive range are hotels that many will find perfectly adequate. In rural areas, there are family-run hotels and inns and bed-and-breakfast establishments that are being used more and more by tourists. In the last of these, you can spend the night in surroundings that may be homey or Spartan but are almost always clean, and where the prices are low. Budget accommodations designed to offer basic (but acceptable) lodging at especially economical prices — a double room may cost as little as $30 to $40 — do exist, and, recognizing the need, travel agents, tour packagers, airlines, and tourist offices are doing what they can to make their whereabouts known.

There are two options for less expensive accommodations for anyone staying for an extended period of time in one place in Europe. One is renting an apartment, called "holiday lets" in Britain. These are available in most European cities and can be arranged through travel agents. The other is a home exchange, in which you and a European family exchange houses for an agreed-upon period of time. Both are discussed in *Accommodations.*

LOCAL TAXES AND SERVICE CHARGES: A sales tax or VAT (value-added tax) is added to both goods and services in many European countries. In Europe, the tax rate ranges from lows of 5.5% and 7% on food to a high of 33.33% on luxury articles. The VAT is buried in the prices charged for hotel rooms and restaurant meals, so you won't even notice it. It is also included in the amount shown on the price tag of purchased goods. There is no escaping the tax on services, but for foreigners, the tax on purchases, typically 18.6%, can frequently be reimbursed. For a full discussion of VAT refunds, see *Shopping.*

A service charge of, usually, 12% to 15% is almost universal on restaurant and hotel bills in Europe. Nevertheless, there are still many situations not covered by the service charge or where an additional gratuity is appropriate. For more on these, see *Tipping.*

■ **A note on our hotel/restaurant cost categories:** There are a great many moderate and inexpensive hotels and restaurants that we have not included in this book. Our *Checking In* and *Eating Out* listings include only those places we think are best in their price range. We have arranged our listings by general price categories: expensive, moderate, and inexpensive. The introductory paragraph of each listing explains just what those categories mean in the context of local prices.

Planning a Trip

123 Travelers fall into two categories: those who make lists and those who do not. Some people prefer to plot the course of their trip to the finest detail, with contingency plans and alternatives at the ready. For others, the joy of a voyage is its spontaneity; exhaustive planning only lessens the thrill of anticipation and the sense of freedom.

However, for most travelers, any week-plus trip to Europe can be too expensive for an "I'll take my chances" type of vacation. Even perennial gypsies and anarchistic wanderers have to take into account the logistics of getting around, and even with minimal baggage, they need to think about packing. Hence at least some planning is crucial. This is not to suggest that you work out your itinerary in minute detail before you go; however, you still have to decide certain basics at the very start: where to go, what to do, and how much to spend. These decisions require a certain amount of forethought, consideration, and planning. So before rigorously planning specific details, you might want to establish your general travel objectives:

1. How much time will you have for the entire trip, and how much of it are you willing to spend getting where you're going?
2. What interests and/or activities do you want to pursue on vacation? Do you want to visit one, a few, or several different places?
3. At what time of year do you want to go?
4. What kind of geography or climate would you prefer?
5. Do you want peace and privacy or lots of action and company?
6. How much money can you spend for the entire vacation?

Obviously, your answers will be determined by your personal tastes and lifestyle. These will condition the degree of comfort you require; whether you will select a tour or opt for total independence; and how much responsibility you want to take for your own arrangements (or whether you want everything arranged for you, with the kinds of services provided in a comprehensive package trip).

With firm answers to these major questions, start reviewing literature on the areas in which you're most interested. Good sources of information are airlines, hotel representatives, and travel agents who specialize in planning and arranging trips (see *How to Use a Travel Agent,* in this section). In addition, European tourist authorities have offices in the US (see *Tourist Information Offices* for addresses). Stop in or write to any of these — all are ready sources for brochures, maps, and other information on European cities and the countryside. Also consult general travel sources such as books and guidebooks. Up-to-date travel information on Europe is plentiful, and you should be able to accumulate everything you want to know, not only about the places you plan to visit, but also about the relevant tour and package options (see *Package Tours*). And if you're visiting Europe for the first time, make a special effort to read up on your destinations' cuisine, history, and culture.

You can now make almost all of your own travel arrangements if you have time to follow through with hotels, airlines, tour operators, and so on. But you'll probably save considerable time and energy if you have a travel agent make them for you. The agent also should be able to advise you of alternate arrangements of which you may not be aware. Only rarely will a travel agent's services cost you any money, and they may even save you some (see *How to Use a Travel Agent*). Well before departure (depending on how far ahead you make your reservations), the agent will deliver a packet that includes all your tickets and hotel confirmations and often a day-by-day outline of where you'll be when, along with a detailed list of all your flights.

Make plans early. During the summer and on American holidays, make hotel reservations at least a month in advance in all major cities. If you are flying at these times, and hope to take advantage of the considerable savings offered through discount fares or charter programs, purchase tickets as early as possible. The more specific your requirements, the farther in advance you should book. Many hotels require deposits before they will guarantee reservations. Be sure you have a receipt for any deposit.

Before your departure, find out what the weather will be like at your destination when you'll be there. Consult *When to Go* for a chart of average temperatures in various countries in Europe and see *How to Pack* for details on what clothes to take. See FACTS IN BRIEF as well as THE CITIES for information on special events that may occur during your stay, as well as other essential details on language, currency, local transportation, and so on.

While making vacation arrangements is fun and exciting, don't forget to prepare for your absence from home. Before you leave, attend to these household matters:

1. Arrange for your mail to be forwarded, held by the post office, or picked up daily at your house. Someone should check your door occasionally to pick up any unexpected deliveries. Piles of mail or packages announce to thieves that no one is home.
2. Cancel all deliveries (newspapers, milk, and so on).
3. Arrange for the lawn to be mowed and plants watered at regular intervals.
4. Arrange for the care of pets.
5. Etch your social security number in a prominent place on all appliances (television sets, radios, cameras, kitchen appliances). This considerably reduces their appeal to thieves and facilitates identification.
6. Leave a house key and your itinerary with a relative or friend. Notify the police, the building manager, or a neighbor that you are leaving and tell them who has your key and itinerary.
7. Empty the refrigerator and lower the thermostat.
8. Immediately before leaving, check that all doors, windows, and garage doors are securely locked.

To discourage thieves further, it is wise to set up several variable timers around the house so that lights and even the television set or a radio go on and off several times in different rooms each night.

Make a list of any valuable items you are carrying with you, including credit card numbers and the serial numbers of your traveler's checks. Put copies in your purse or pocket, and leave other copies at home. Put a label with your name and home address on the inside of your luggage to facilitate identification in case of loss. Put your name and business address — *but never your home address* — on a label on the outside of your luggage.

Review your travel documents. If you are traveling by air, check that your ticket has been filled in correctly. The left side of the ticket should have a list of each stop you will make (even if you are only stopping to change planes), beginning with your departure point. Be sure that the list is correct, and count the number of carbons to see that you have one for each plane you will take. If you have confirmed reservations, be sure that the column marked "status" says "OK" beside each flight. Have in hand vouchers or proof of payment for any reservation for which you've already paid; this includes hotels, transfers to and from the airport, sightseeing tours, car rentals, and special events.

Call to reconfirm your flight 72 hours before departure, both going and returning.

However, this will not prevent you from getting bumped in case the flight is overbooked (see *Traveling by Plane*).

If you are traveling by car, bring your driver's license, proof of insurance, maps, guidebooks, flashlight, an extra set of batteries, first-aid kit, and sunglasses. You may also want to pick up an emergency flasher and a container of water for the radiator.

Finally, you should always bear in mind that despite the most careful plans, things do not always occur on schedule. If you maintain a flexible attitude at all times, shrug cheerfully in the face of postponements and cancellations, you will enjoy yourself a lot more.

How to Use a Travel Agent

 A reliable travel agent remains your best source of service and information for planning a trip abroad, whether you have a specific itinerary and require an agent only to make reservations, or need extensive help in sorting through the maze of airfares, tour offerings, hotel packages, and the scores of other arrangements that may be involved in a trip to the Continent.

You should know what you want from a travel agent so that you can evaluate what you are getting. It is perfectly reasonable to expect your travel agent to be a thoroughly knowledgeable travel specialist, with information about your destination and, even more crucial, a command of current airfares, ground arrangements, and other wrinkles in the travel scene. Most travel agents work through computer reservations systems (CRS) to assess the availability and rates of flights, hotels, and car rental firms, and can book reservations through the CRS. Despite reports of "computer bias," in which a computer may favor one airline over another, the CRS should provide agents with the entire spectrum of flights to a destination and the complete range of fares in considerably less time than it takes to telephone the airlines individually — and at no extra charge to the client.

To make the most intelligent use of a travel agent's time and expertise, you should know something of the economics of the industry. As a client, traditionally you pay nothing for the agent's services; with few exceptions, it's all free, from hotel bookings to advice on package tours. Any money the travel agent makes on the time spent arranging your itinerary — booking hotels, resorts, or flights, or suggesting activities — comes from commissions paid by the suppliers of these services — the airlines, hotels, and so on. These commissions generally run from 8% to 20% of the total cost of the service, although suppliers often reward agencies that sell their services in volume with an increased commission called an override.

Among the few exceptions to the general rule of free service by a travel agency are the agencies beginning to practice *net pricing*. In essence, such travel agencies return all of their commissions and overrides to their customers and make their income instead by charging a flat fee per transaction (thus adding a charge after a reduction has been made). Sometimes, the rebate from the agent arrives later, in the form of a check. Net pricing, however, has become rather controversial since a major airline refused to do business with a leading proponent of net pricing and the courts supported this action (see *Net Fare Sources*).

Net fares and fees are a very recent and not widespread practice, but even a conventional travel agent may sometimes charge a fee for such special services as long-distance telephone or cable costs incurred in making a booking, for reserving a room in a place that does not pay a commission (such as a small, out-of-the-way hotel), or for special attention such as planning a highly personalized itinerary. A fee may also be assessed in instances of deeply discounted airfares. In most instances, however, you'll find that travel agents make their time and experience available to you at no charge, and you do not pay more for an airline ticket, package tour, or other product bought from a travel agent than you would for the same product bought directly from the supplier.

This system implies two things about your relationship with an agent:

1. You will get better service if you arrive at the agent's desk with your basic itinerary already planned. Know roughly where you want to go, what you want to do, and how much you want to spend. Use the agent to make bookings (which pay commissions) and to advise you on facilities, activities, and alternatives within the limits of your basic itinerary. You get the best service when you are requesting commissionable items. Since there are few commissions on camping or driving-camping tours, an agent is unlikely to be very enthusiastic about helping to plan one. (If you have this type of trip in mind, see *Camping and Caravanning, Hiking and Biking,* for other sources of information on campgrounds throughout Europe.) The more vague your plans, the less direction you can expect from most agents. If you walk into an agency and say, "I have two weeks in June; what shall I do?" you will most likely walk out with nothing more than a handful of brochures. So do a little preliminary homework.

2. Be wary. There is always the danger that an incompetent or unethical agent will send you to places offering the best commissions rather than the best facilities for your purposes. The only way to be sure you are getting the best service is to pick a good, reliable travel agent, one who knows where to go for information if he or she is unfamiliar with an area — although most agents are familiar with major destinations throughout Europe.

You should choose a travel agent with the same care with which you would choose a doctor or lawyer. You will be spending a good deal of money on the basis of the agent's judgment, so you have a right to expect that judgment to be mature, informed, and interested. At the moment, unfortunately, there aren't many standards in the travel agent industry to help you gauge competence, and the quality of individual agents varies enormously. At present, only seven states have registration, licensing, or other form of travel agent–related legislation on their books. Rhode Island licenses travel agents; Florida, Hawaii, and Ohio register them; and California, Illinois, and Washington have laws governing the sale of transportation or related services. While state licensing of agents cannot absolutely guarantee competence, it can at least ensure that an agent has met some minimum requirements.

Perhaps the best-prepared agents are those who have completed the CTC Travel Management program offered by the *Institute of Certified Travel Agents* and carry the initials CTC (Certified Travel Counselor) after their names. This indicates a relatively high level of expertise. For a free listing of CTCs in your area, send a self-addressed, stamped, #10 envelope to ICTA, 148 Linden St., Box 82-56, Wellesley, MA 02181 (phone: 617-237-0280).

An agent's membership in the *American Society of Travel Agents* (*ASTA*) can be a useful guideline in making a selection. But keep in mind that *ASTA* is an industry organization, requiring only that its members be licensed in those states where required; be accredited to represent the suppliers whose products they sell, including airline and cruise tickets; and be adherents to its Principles of Professional Conduct and Ethics code. *ASTA* does not guarantee the competence, ethics, or financial soundness of its members, but it does offer some recourse if you feel you have been dealt with unfairly. Complaints may be registered with ASTA, Consumer Affairs Dept., PO Box 23992, Washington, DC 20026-3992 (phone: 703-739-2782). First try to resolve the complaint directly with the supplier. For a list of *ASTA* members in your area, send a self-addressed, stamped, #10 envelope to ASTA, Public Relations Dept., at the address above. There is also the *Association of Retail Travel Agents* (*ARTA*), a smaller but highly respected trade organization similar to *ASTA*. Its member agencies and agents similarly agree to abide by a Code of Ethics, and complaints about a member can be made to ARTA's Grievance Committee, 25 S. Riverside Ave., Croton-on-Hudson, NY 10520 (914-271-HELP).

Agencies listed with the *National Association of Cruise Only Agencies* (*NACOA*) have demonstrated professionalism in the selling of cruises. For a listing of cruise-only agencies in your state (requests are limited to three states), send a self-addressed, stamped envelope to NACOA, PO Box 7209, Freeport, NY 11520. Agencies that belong to a travel consortium, such as *Associated Travel Nationwide* and *Travel Trust International,* have access to preferred rates, as do the huge networks of *American Express* and *Ask Mr. Foster* travel agencies.

A number of banks own travel agencies, too. These provide the same services as other accredited commercial travel bureaus. Anyone can become a client, not only the banks' customers. You can find out more about these agencies, which belong to the *Association of Bank Travel Bureaus,* by asking at your bank or looking in the yellow pages.

Perhaps the best way to find a travel agent is by word of mouth. If the agent (or agency) has done a good job for your friends over a period of time, it probably indicates a certain level of commitment and competence. Always ask not only for the name of the company, but for the name of the specific agent with whom your friends dealt, for it is that individual who will serve you, and quality can vary widely within a single agency. There are some superb travel agents in the business, and they can facilitate vacation or business arrangements greatly.

Once you've made an initial selection from those recommended, be entirely candid with the agent. Budget considerations rank at the top of the list — there's no sense in wasting the agent's (or your) time poring over itineraries you know you can't afford. Similarly, if you like a fair degree of comfort, that fact should not be kept secret from your travel agent, who may assume that you wish to travel on a tight budget when that's not the case.

Entry Requirements and Documents

Most Western European governments (France, Great Britain, Italy, Spain, Greece, and so on) do not require US travelers to obtain visas, though most Eastern European governments *do* (Yugoslavia, Bulgaria, the USSR). However, visas *may* be needed for study, residency, or work.

In general, issuing tourist visas is a routine service provided by the consulates, though it is a good idea to apply well in advance. This is particularly important for travelers who live some distance from the nearest consulate of the country or countries they wish to visit, and are applying by mail. Application must be made at the appropriate consulate within your jurisdiction (see *Tourist Information* for addresses). Two items are necessary to apply for a visa: a valid passport and a completed visa form. (These forms may be obtained through your travel agent or by sending a self-addressed, stamped envelope to the consulate with a written request.) The processing charge is $9 for a 3-month visa, which permits multiple reentries of up to 90 days total, and $15 for a 5-year, multiple-reentry visa. Cash, a money order, or certified check may be used for payment if applying in person; a money order or certified check if applying by mail. Visas are normally issued on the spot; however, if there is a backlog, you may have to return to pick it up a few days later. To avoid frustration and wasted time, it is a good idea to call ahead to check what hours and days visa requests are accepted. Resident aliens of the US should inquire at the nearest consulate to find out what documents are needed to enter Europe; similarly, US citizens intending to remain in Europe for more than 3 months should address themselves to the appropriate consulate.

Vaccination certificates are required only if the traveler is entering from an area of contagion as defined by the World Health Organization. Because smallpox is considered eradicated from the world, only a few countries continue to require visitors to have a smallpox vaccination certificate. You will certainly not need one to travel to Europe or to return to the US.

US passports are now valid for 10 years from the date of issue (5 years for those under age 18). The expired passport itself is not renewable but must be turned in along with your application for a new and valid one (you will get it back, voided, when you receive the new one). Delivery can take as little as 2 weeks or as long as a month, and anyone applying for a passport for the first time should allow at least 4 weeks for delivery — even 6 weeks during the high season, from approximately mid-March to mid-September.

Normal passports contain 24 pages, but frequent travelers can request a 48-page passport at no extra cost. Every individual, regardless of age, must have his or her own passport. Family passports are no longer issued.

Passport renewal can be done by mail, but anyone applying for the first time or anyone under 18 renewing a passport must do so in person at one of the following places:

1. The State Department has passport agencies in Boston, Chicago, Honolulu, Houston, Los Angeles, Miami, New Orleans, New York City, Philadelphia, San Francisco, Seattle, Stamford (CT) Connecticut, and Washington, DC
2. A federal or state courthouse.
3. Any of the 1,000 post offices across the country with designated acceptance facilities.

Application blanks are available at all these offices and must be presented with the following:

1. Proof of US citizenship. This can be a previous passport or one in which you were included. If you are applying for your first passport and you were born in the United States, your official birth certificate is the required proof. If you were born abroad, a Certificate of Naturalization, a Certificate of Citizenship, a Report of Birth Abroad of a Citizen of the United States, or a Certification of Birth is necessary.
2. Two 2-by-2-inch, front-view photographs in color or black and white, with a light, plain background, taken within the previous 6 months. These must be taken by a photographer rather than by a machine.
3. A check or a money order for the $35 passport fee ($20 for travelers under 18) and the $7 execution fee (not required if you are applying for a passport in person at one of the State Department passport agencies or if you are renewing a passport). *Note:* Your best bet is to bring the exact amount; you should have a separate check or money order for each passport. No cash is accepted.
4. Proof of identity. Again, this can be a previous passport, a Certificate of Naturalization or of Citizenship, a driver's license, or a government ID card with a physical description or a photograph. Failing any of these, you should be accompanied by a friend of at least 2 years' standing who will testify to your identity. Credit cards or social security cards do not suffice as proof of identity — but note that since 1988, US citizens *must* supply their social security numbers.

Passports can be renewed by mail on forms obtained at designated locations only if the expired passport was issued no more than 12 years before the date of application for renewal and if it was not issued before the applicant's 16th birthday. Send the completed form with the expired passport, two photos (signed in the center of the back), and $35 (no execution fee required) to the nearest passport agency office.

■**Should you lose your passport abroad:** Report the loss to the nearest US consulate immediately. You can get a 3-month temporary passport directly from the consulate, but you must fill out a "loss of passport" form and follow the same application procedure — and pay the same fees — as you did for the original. It's likely to speed things up if you have a record of your passport number and the place and date of its issue.

■**If you need an emergency passport:** Although a passport application normally takes several weeks to process, it is possible to be issued a passport in a matter of hours. Go directly to your nearest passport office — there is no way, however, to avoid waiting in line — and explain the nature of the emergency, usually as serious as a death in the family; a ticket in hand for a flight the following day will suffice. Should the emergency occur outside of business hours, all is not lost. There's a 24-hour telephone number in Washington, DC (phone: 202-634-3600), that can put you in touch with a State Department duty officer who may be able to expedite your application.

DUTY AND CUSTOMS: As a general rule, the requirements for bringing the majority of items into Europe is that they must be in quantities small enough not to imply commercial import.

Each country has strict regulations regarding the amount of specific goods that may be imported without duty as well as the duty that must be paid if the quantity exceeds these limits. Restrictions generally apply to a broad range of items, including the following: alcoholic beverages, cigarettes, cigars, loose tobacco, perfume and cologne, coffee, tea, and items designated as gifts (valued at a specified amount). When planning a trip to Europe, contact the government tourist authority of each country you plan to visit (for offices in the US, see *Sources and Resources*) for information on procedures, the type and quantity of goods regulated, and duties imposed on overages.

If you are bringing a computer or other electronic equipment for your own use, which you will be taking back to the US, you should register the item with the US Customs Service in order to avoid being asked to pay duties both entering and returning from Europe. (Also see *Customs and Returning to the US,* in this section.) For information on this procedure, as well as for a variety of pamphlets on US customs regulations, contact the local office of the US Customs Service or the central office, PO Box 7407, Washington, DC 20044 (phone: 202-566-8195).

■**One rule to follow:** When passing through customs, it is illegal not to declare dutiable items — penalties range from stiff fines and seizure of the goods to prison terms — so don't try to sneak anything through; it just isn't worth it.

Insurance

It is unfortunate that most decisions to buy travel insurance are impulsive and are usually made without any real consideration of the traveler's existing policies. Too often the result is the purchase of needlessly expensive short-term policies that duplicate existing coverage and reinforce the tendency to buy coverage on a trip-by-trip basis rather than to work out a total and continuing travel insurance package that might well be more effective and economical.

Therefore, the first person with whom you should discuss travel insurance is your own insurance broker, not a travel agent or the clerk behind the airport insurance counter. You may well discover that the insurance you already carry — homeowner's policies and/or accident, health, and life insurance — protects you adequately while you travel and that your real needs are in the more mundane areas of excess value insurance for baggage or trip cancellation insurance.

TYPES OF INSURANCE: To make insurance decisions intelligently, however, you should first understand the basic categories of travel insurance and what they are designed to cover. Then you can decide what you should have in the broader context of your personal insurance needs, and you can choose the most economical way of getting the desired protection: through riders on existing policies; with one-time short-term policies; through a special program put together for the frequent traveler; through coverage that's part of a travel club's benefits; or with a combination policy sold by insurance companies through brokers, automobile clubs, tour operators, and travel agents.

There are seven basic categories of travel insurance:

1. Baggage and personal effects insurance
2. Personal accident and sickness insurance
3. Trip cancellation and interruption insurance
4. Default and/or bankruptcy insurance
5. Flight insurance (to cover death or injury)
6. Automobile insurance (for driving your own or a rented car)
7. Combination policies

Baggage and Personal Effects Insurance – Ask your agent if baggage and personal effects are included in your current homeowner's policy or if you will need a special floater to cover you for the duration of a trip. The object is to protect your bags and their contents in case of damage or theft any time during your travels, not just while you're in flight and covered by the airline's policy. Furthermore, only limited protection is provided by the airline. Baggage liability varies from carrier to carrier, but generally speaking, for domestic flights, luggage is generally insured to $1,250 — that's per passenger, not per bag. For most international flights, including domestic portions of international flights, the airline's liability limit is approximately $20 per kilo or $9.07 per pound (which comes to about $360 per 40-pound suitcase) for checked baggage, and up to $400 per passenger for unchecked baggage. These limits should be specified on your airline ticket, but to be awarded the specified amount, you'll have to provide an itemized list of lost property, and if you're including new and/or expensive items, be prepared for a request that you back up your claim with sales receipts or other proofs of purchase.

If you are carrying goods worth more than the maximum protection offered by the airline, bus, or train company, you should consider excess value insurance. Additional coverage is available from the airlines at an average, currently, of $1 per $100 worth of coverage. This insurance can be purchased at the airline counter when you check in, though you should arrive early to fill out the necessary forms and to avoid holding up other passengers checking in. Major credit card companies, including American Express and Diners Club, also provide coverage for lost or delayed baggage. In some cases, you must enroll in advance to qualify. Check your membership brochure or contact the credit card company for details (see phone numbers listed in *Credit and Currency*). Excess value insurance is also included in certain of the combination travel insurance policies discussed below.

■**A note of warning:** Be sure to read the fine print of any excess value insurance policy; there are often specific exclusions, such as cash, tickets, furs, gold and silver objects, art, and antiques. And remember that insurance companies ordinarily will pay only the depreciated value of the goods rather than their replacement value. The best way to protect the items you're carrying in your luggage is to take photos of your valuables, and keep a record of the serial numbers of such items as cameras, typewriters, radios, and so on. This will establish that you do, indeed, own the objects. If your luggage disappears en route or is damaged, deal with the situation immediately, at the airport or bus station. If an airline loses your luggage, you will be asked to fill out a Property Irregularity Report before you leave the airport. If your property disappears at other transportation centers, tell the local company, but also report it to the police (since the insurance company will check with the police when processing the claim). When traveling by train, if you are sending excess luggage as registered baggage, remember that in many countries only a few trains have provisions for extra cargo; if your baggage has not been checked on your train, it may not be lost, just on the next train!

Personal Accident and Sickness Insurance – This covers you in case of illness during your trip or death in an accident. Most policies insure you for hospital and doctor's expenses, lost income, and so on. In most cases, it is a standard part of existing health insurance policies, though you should check with your broker to be sure that your policy will pay for any medical expenses incurred abroad. If not, take out a separate vacation accident policy or an entire vacation insurance policy that includes health and life coverage.

Trip Cancellation and Interruption Insurance – Although modern public charters have eliminated many of the old advance booking requirements, most charter and package tour passengers still pay for their travel well before departure. The disappointment of having to miss a vacation because of illness or any other reason pales before the awful prospect that not all (and sometimes none) of the money paid in advance might be returned. So cancellation insurance for any package tour is a must. Although cancellation penalties vary (they are listed in the fine print in every tour brochure, and before you purchase a package tour you should know exactly what they are), rarely will a passenger get more than 50% of this money back if forced to cancel within a few weeks of leaving. Therefore, if you book a package tour or charter flight, you should have trip cancellation insurance to guarantee full reimbursement or refund should you, a traveling companion, or a member of your immediate family get sick, forcing you to cancel your trip or *return home early.* The key here is *not* to buy just enough insurance to guarantee full reimbursement for the cost of the package or charter in case of cancellation. The proper amount of coverage should be sufficient to reimburse you for the cost of having to catch up with a tour after its departure or having to travel home at the full economy airfare if you have to forgo the return flight of your charter. There is usually quite a discrepancy between a charter airfare and the amount necessary to travel the same distance on a regularly scheduled flight at full economy fare.

Trip cancellation insurance is available from travel agents and tour operators in two forms: as part of a short-term, all-purpose travel insurance package (sold by the travel agent); or as specific cancellation insurance designed by the tour operator for a specific charter tour. Generally, tour operators' policies are less expensive, but also less inclusive. Cancellation insurance is also available directly from insurance companies or their agents as part of a short-term, all-inclusive travel insurance policy.

Before you decide which policy you want, read each one carefully. (Either can be purchased from a travel agent when you book the charter or package tour.) Be certain that the policy you select includes enough coverage to pay your fare from the farthest destination on your itinerary should you have to miss the charter flight. Also, be sure to check the fine print for stipulations concerning "family members" and "pre-existing medical conditions," as well as allowance for living expenses if you must delay your return due to bodily injury or illness.

Default and/or Bankruptcy Insurance – Although trip cancellation insurance usually protects you if you are unable to complete — or depart on — your trip, a fairly recent innovation is coverage in the event of default and/or bankruptcy on the part of the tour operator, airline, or other travel supplier. In some travel insurance packages, this contingency is included in the trip cancellation portion of the coverage; in others, it is a separate feature. Either way, it is becoming increasingly important. Whereas sophisticated travelers have long known to beware of the possibility of default or bankruptcy when buying a charter flight or tour package, in recent years more than a few respected scheduled airlines have unexpectedly revealed their shaky financial condition, sometimes leaving hordes of stranded ticketholders in their wake. Moreover, the value of escrow protection of a charter passenger's funds has lately been unreliable. While default/bankruptcy insurance will not ordinarily result in reimbursement in time to pay for new arrangements, it can ensure that you will eventually get your money back, and even independent travelers buying no more than an airplane ticket may want to consider it.

Should this type of coverage not be available to you (state insurance regulations vary, there is a wide variation in price, and so on), the best bet is to pay for airline tickets and tour packages with a credit card. The federal Fair Credit Billing Act permits purchasers to refuse payment for credit card charges where services have not been delivered, so the potential onus of dealing with a receiver for a bankrupt airline falls on the credit card company. Do not assume that another airline will automatically honor the ticket you're holding on a bankrupt airline, since the days when virtually all major carriers subscribed to a default protection program are long gone. Some airlines may voluntarily step forward to accommodate stranded passengers, but this is now an entirely altruistic act.

Flight Insurance – US airlines have carefully established limits of liability for the death or injury of passengers. For international flights, they are printed right on the ticket: a maximum of $75,000 in case of death or injury. For domestic flights in the US, the limitation is established by state law, with a few states setting unlimited liability. But remember, these limits of liability are not the same thing as insurance policies; they merely state the *maximum* an airline will pay in the case of death or injury, and every penny of that is usually subject to a legal battle.

This may make you feel that you are not adequately protected, but before you buy last-minute flight insurance from an airport vending machine, consider the purchase in light of your total existing insurance coverage. A careful review of your current policies may reveal that you are already amply covered for accidental death, sometimes up to three times the amount provided for by the flight insurance you're buying in the airport.

Be aware that airport insurance, the kind typically bought at a counter or from a vending machine, is among the most expensive forms of life insurance coverage available, and that even within a single airport, rates for approximately the same coverage vary widely. Often the vending machines are more expensive than coverage sold over the counter, even when policies are with the same national company.

If you buy your plane ticket with an American Express, Carte Blanche, or Diners Club credit card, you are automatically issued life and accident insurance at no extra cost. American Express automatically provides $100,000 in insurance; Carte Blanche provides $150,000, and Diners Club provides $350,000. Additional coverage can be obtained at extremely reasonable prices, but a cardholder must sign up for it in advance. With American Express, $4 per ticket buys an additional $250,000 worth of flight insurance; $6.50 buys $500,000 worth; and $13 provides an added $1 million worth of coverage. Carte Blanche and Diners Club each offer an additional $250,000 worth of insurance for $4; $500,000 for $6.50. Both also provide $1,250 free insurance — over and above what the airline will pay — for checked baggage that's lost or damaged. American Express provides $500 coverage for checked baggage; $1,250 for carry-ons.

Automobile Insurance – Public liability and property damage (third-party) insurance is compulsory in Europe, and whether you drive your own car or a rental you must carry insurance. Car rentals in Europe usually include public liability, property damage, fire, and theft coverage and, sometimes (depending on the car rental company), collision damage coverage with a deductible. In your car rental contract, you'll see that for about $10 to $12 a day, you may buy optional collision damage waiver (CDW) protection. If partial coverage with a deductible is included in the rental contract, CDW will cover the deductible in the event of an accident. If the contract does not include collision damage coverage, you may be liable for as much as the full retail cost of the car, and CDW relieves you of all responsibility for any damage to the rental car. Before agreeing to this coverage, however, check your own auto insurance policy. It may very well cover your entire liability exposure without any additional cost, or you automatically may be covered by the credit card company (American Express, or premium cards from Visa or MasterCard) to which you are charging the cost of your rental.

Your rental contract (with the appropriate insurance box checked off) as well as proof of your personal insurance policy, if applicable, are required as proof of insurance. If you will be driving your own car in Europe, you must carry an International Insurance Certificate (called a Green Card), available through insurance brokers in the US, or take out an special policy for this purpose at customs as you enter the country.

Combination Policies – Short-term insurance policies, which may include any combination or all of the types of insurance discussed above, are available through retail insurance agencies, automobile clubs, and many travel agents. These combination policies are designed to cover you for the duration of a single trip.

Two examples of standard combination policies, providing comprehensive coverage for travelers, are offered by *Wallach & Co.* The first, *HealthCare Global,* is available to men and women up to age 84. The medical insurance, which may be purchased for periods of 10 to 180 days, provides $25,000 medical insurance and $50,000 accidental death benefit. The cost for 10 days is $25; for 75 days and over, it is $1 a day. Combination policies may include additional accidental death coverage and baggage and trip cancellation insurance options. For $3 per day (minimum 10 days, maximum 90 days), another program, *HealthCare Abroad,* offers significantly better coverage in terms of dollar limits, although the age limit is 75. Its basic policy includes $100,000 medical insurance and $25,000 accidental death benefit. As in the first policy, trip cancellation and baggage insurance are also available. For further information, write to Wallach & Co., 243 Church St. NW, Vienna, VA 22180 (phone: 703-281-9500 in Virginia, 800-237-6615 elsewhere in the US).

Other policies of this type include the following:

> *Access America International:* A subsidiary of the Blue Cross/Blue Shield plans of New York and Washington, DC, now available nationwide. Contact Access America, 600 Third Ave., PO Box 807, New York, NY 10163 (phone: 212-490-5345 or 800-284-8300).
>
> *Carefree:* Underwritten by The Hartford. Contact Carefree Travel Insurance, Arm Coverage, PO Box 247, Providence, RI 02901 (phone: 800-645-2424).
>
> *Near:* Part of a benefits package offered by a travel service organization. An added feature is coverage for lost or stolen airline tickets. Contact Near, Inc., 1900 N. MacArthur Blvd., Suite 210, Oklahoma City, OK 73127 (phone: 405-949-2500 or 800-654-6700).

Tele-Trip: Underwritten by the Mutual of Omaha Companies. Contact Tele-Trip Co., PO Box 31685, 3201 Farnam St., Omaha, NE 68131 (phone: 402-345-2400 in Nebraska; 800-228-9792 elsewhere in the US).

Travel Assistance International: Underwritten by Europe Assistance Worldwide Services. Contact Travel Assistance International, 1333 F St. NW, Suite 300, Washington, DC 20005 (phone: 202-347-2025 in Washington; 800-821-2828 elsewhere).

Travel Guard International: Endorsed by the *American Society of Travel Agents* (*ASTA*), underwritten by the Insurance Company of North America, it is available through authorized travel agents, or contact Travel Guard International, 1100 Centerpoint Dr., Stevens Point, WI 54480 (phone: 715-345-0505 in Wisconsin; 800-826-1300 elsewhere).

Travel Insurance PAK: Underwritten by The Travelers. Contact The Travelers Companies, Ticket and Travel Plans, One Tower Sq., Hartford, CT 06183-5040 (phone: 203-277-2319 in Connecticut; 800-243-3174 elsewhere).

WorldCare Travel Assistance Association: Contact this organization at 605 Market St., Suite 1300, San Francisco, CA 94105 (phone: 415-541-4991 or 800-666-4993).

How to Pack

 No one can provide a completely foolproof list of precisely what to pack, so it's best to let common sense, space, and comfort guide you. Keep one maxim in mind: Less is more. You simply won't need as much clothing as you think, and though there is nothing more frustrating than arriving at your destination without just the item that in its absence becomes crucial, you are far more likely to need a forgotten accessory — or a needle and thread or scissors — than a particular piece of clothing.

As with almost anything relating to travel, a little planning can go a long way. There are specific things to consider before you open the first drawer or fold the first pair of underwear:

1. Where are you going (city, country, or both)?
2. How many total days will you be gone?
3. What's the average temperature likely to be during your stay?

The goal is to remain perfectly comfortable, neat, clean, and adequately fashionable wherever you go, but actually to pack as little as possible. The main obstacle to achieving this end is habit: Most of us wake up each morning with an entire wardrobe in our closets, and we assume that our suitcase should offer the same variety and selection. Not so — only our anxiety about being caught short makes us treat a suitcase like a mobile closet. This worry can be eliminated by learning to travel light and by following two firm packing principles:

1. Organize your travel wardrobe around a single color — blue or brown, for example — that allows you to mix, match, and layer clothes. Holding firm to one color scheme will make it easy to eliminate items of clothing that don't harmonize; and by picking clothes for their adaptability and compatibility with your basic color, you will put together the widest selection with the fewest pieces of clothing.
2. Use laundries to renew your wardrobe. Never overpack to ensure a supply of fresh clothing — shirts, blouses, underwear — for each day of a long trip. Businesspeople routinely use hotel laundries to wash and clean clothes. If these are too expensive, there are self-service laundries in most towns of any size.

CLIMATE AND CLOTHES: Exactly what you pack for your trip will be a function of where you are going and when, and the kinds of things you intend to do. As a first step, however, find out about the general weather conditions — temperature, rainfall, seasonal variations — at your destination, as a few degrees can make all the difference between being comfortably attired and very real suffering.

Although most of Europe is farther north than the US — Paris, sitting astride latitude 48°52′ and London 51°30′, are about even with Gaspé, Quebec — the climate is generally milder. Every country in Europe has distinct seasonal changes, but the degree, duration, and drama of the changes vary widely. Residents of the Middle Atlantic states of the US will find that the same wardrobe they would be wearing at home will, with a few adjustments, also be appropriate for most parts of Europe in the same season. However, anyone going to Europe from the late fall through the early spring should take into account that while central heating is prevalent, interiors are not usually heated to the same degree they are in the US. Thus, although there is no need to prepare for sub-zero winters outdoors, most people will probably feel more comfortable wearing heavier clothing indoors than they might at home — for instance, sweaters rather than lightweight shirts and blouses.

More information about the climate in Europe, along with a chart of average low and high temperatures for different countries, is given in *When to Go,* in this section; other sources of information are airlines and travel agents.

Keeping temperature and climate in mind, consider the problem of luggage. Plan on one suitcase per person (and in a pinch, remember that it's always easier to carry two small suitcases than to schlepp one roughly the size of the *QE2*). Standard 26- to 28-inch suitcases can be made to work for 1 week or 1 month, and unless you are going for no more than a weekend, never cram wardrobes for two people into one suitcase.

FASHION: On the whole, Europe is no more formal than North America, so be guided by your own taste. On the Left Bank in Paris, for example, anything goes; on the Right Bank, wear what you would in any cosmopolitan American city. The lucky individual attending an opening night at Milan's *La Scala* opera house should be wearing formal attire (though European students have been attending the opera in blue jeans for years, so don't make yourself crazy), but otherwise a blazer or sport jacket, trousers, and tie will get a man into the finest restaurants anywhere, and sometimes even the tie is not *de rigueur.* For women, a dress or a suit, depending on the season, will do in the same situations. There may be diners at other tables more formally dressed, but you won't be turned away or made to feel self-conscious if you do not match them. By the same token, you won't feel you've overdone it if you choose to turn an evening at an elegant restaurant into something special and dress accordingly.

If you are planning to be on the move — either in a car, bus, train, or plane — consider loose-fitting clothes that do not wrinkle, although the recent trend toward fabrics with a wrinkled look is a boon to travelers. Despite the tendency of designers to use more 100% natural fabrics, synthetics are immensely practical for a trip, and lately have improved immeasurably in appearance. As a general rule, perishable clothes — pure cotton and linen — are hard to keep up and should be left behind. Lightweight wools, manmade fabrics such as jerseys and knits, and drip-dry fabrics that can be rinsed in Woolite or a similar cold-water detergent travel best (although in very hot weather, cotton clothing may be the most comfortable), and prints look fresher longer than solids.

Women should figure on a maximum of five daytime and three late afternoon–evening changes. Whether you are going to be gone for a week or a month, this number should be enough. Again, before packing, lay out every piece of clothing you think you might want to take. Eliminate items that don't mix, match, or interchange within your chosen color scheme. If you can't wear it in at least two distinct incarnations, leave it home.

Men will find that color coordination is crucial. Solid colors coordinate best, and a sport jacket that goes with a pair of pants from a suit and several pairs of slacks provides added options. Hanging bags are best for suits and jackets, and shirts should be chosen that can be used for both daytime and evening wear.

Pack clothes that have a lot of pockets for traveler's checks, documents, and tickets. Then if your bag gets lost or stolen, you will still have the essentials. Men who prefer to keep their pockets free of coins, papers, and keys might consider a shoulder bag, useful for carrying camera equipment as well as daily necessities. And be sure to have comfortable shoes. Pack lightweight sandals for beach and evening wear. It is permissible to wear your most comfortable shoes almost everywhere.

A versatile item of clothing that travelers across the Continent will find indispensable is a raincoat, preferably one with a zip-out lining and a hood. The lining allows you to adapt to temperature changes, and the hood is better suited (and less cumbersome) than an umbrella for fine, misty rain, although a practical alternative is a rain hat that can be rolled up in a pocket or carry-on bag. Also, don't forget to take a warm sweater or jacket. It will not be needed to take the chill off overly air conditioned rooms (air conditioning is not the rule in Europe), but even in a heat wave it will be welcome for exploring caves in Spain or champagne cellars in France.

Finally, prepare for changes in the weather or for atypical temperatures; for instance, if you're going on a day's outing in the mountains, where it is cooler, dress in layers, which means a shirt on top of a T-shirt or lightweight turtleneck, with a sweater or two on top of both, topped by a jacket or windbreaker over all. As the weather changes, you can add or remove clothes as required; and layering adapts well to the ruling principle of dressing according to a single color scheme. Individual items in layers can mix and match, be used together or independently. And finally — since the best touring of castles, churches, and countryside is on foot — pack a comfortable pair of walking shoes.

Your carry-on luggage should contain a survival kit with the basic things you will need in case your luggage gets lost or stolen: a toothbrush, toothpaste, medication, a sweater, nightclothes, and a change of underwear. With all of your essential items at hand at all times, you will be prepared for any unexpected occurrence that separates you from your suitcase. If you have many 1- or 2-night stops, you can live out of your survival case without having to unpack completely each time.

Sundries – If you are traveling in the heat of summer and will be spending a lot of time outdoors, pack special items so you won't spend your entire vacation in a hotel room (or hospital) because of sunburn. Be sure to take a sun hat (to protect hair as well as skin), sunscreen, and tanning lotion, which is available in degrees of sunblock corresponding to the level of your skin's sensitivity. (The quantity of sunscreen is indicated by number: the higher the number, the greater the protection.) A good moisturizer is necessary to help keep your skin from drying out and peeling. The best advice is to take the sun's rays in small doses — no more than 20 minutes at a stretch — increasing the time gradually as your vacation progresses. Also, if you are heading for a ski vacation, do not underestimate the effect of the sun's glare off snowy slopes, especially in higher altitudes — the exposed areas of your face and neck are particularly susceptible to a painful burn.

PACKING: The basic idea of packing is to get everything into the suitcase and out again with as few wrinkles as possible. Simple, casual clothes — shirts, jeans and slacks, permanent press skirts — can be rolled into neat, tight sausages that keep other items in place and leave the clothes themselves amazingly unwrinkled. The rolled clothes can be retrieved, shaken out, and hung up at your destination. However, when you have items that are too bulky or delicate for even careful rolling, the heaviest items should be placed in the bottom of the suitcase, toward the hinges, so that they will not wrinkle more perishable clothes. Candidates for this layer include shoes (stuff them with small items to save space), a toilet kit, handbags (stuff them to help keep their shape), and an alarm clock. Fill out this layer with things that will not wrinkle or will not matter if they do, such as sweaters, socks, a bathing suit, gloves, and underwear.

If you get this first, heavy layer as smooth as possible with the fill-ins, you will have a shelf for the next layer, or the most easily wrinkled items, like slacks, jackets, shirts, dresses, and skirts. These should be buttoned and zipped and laid along the whole length of the suitcase with as little folding as possible. When you do need to make a fold, do it on a crease (as with pants), along a seam in the fabric, or where it will not show, such as shirttails. Alternate each piece of clothing, using one side of the suitcase, then the other, to make the layers as flat as possible. Make the layers even and the total contents of your bag as full and firm as possible to keep things from shifting around during transit. On the top layer put the things you will want at once: nightclothes, an umbrella or raincoat, and a sweater.

With men's two-suiters, follow the same procedure. Then place jackets on hangers, straighten them out, and leave them unbuttoned. If they are too wide for the suitcase, fold them lengthwise down the middle, straighten the shoulders, and fold the sleeves in along the seam.

While packing, it is a good idea to interleave each layer of clothes with plastic cleaning bags, which will help preserve pressed clothes in the suitcase. Unpack your bags as soon as you get to your hotel. Nothing so thoroughly destroys freshly cleaned and pressed clothes as sitting for days in a suitcase. Finally, if something is badly wrinkled and can't be professionally pressed before you must wear it, hang it overnight in a bathroom where the tub has been filled with very hot water; keep the bathroom door closed so that the room becomes something of a steamroom. It really works miracles.

SOME FINAL PACKING HINTS: Some travelers like to have at hand a small bag with the basics for an overnight stay, particularly if they are flying. Always keep necessary medicine, valuable jewelry, and travel or business documents in your purse, briefcase, or carry-on bag, not in the luggage you will check. Tuck a bathing suit into your handbag, too; in case of lost baggage, it's frustrating to be without one. And whether in your overnight bag or checked luggage, cosmetics and any liquids should be packed in plastic bottles or at least wrapped in plastic bags and tied.

Golf clubs and skis may be checked through as luggage (most airlines are accustomed to handling them), but tennis rackets should be carried onto the plane. Some airlines require that bicycles be partially dismantled and packaged (see *Camping and Caravanning, Hiking and Biking*). Check with the airline before departure to see if there is a specific regulation regarding any special equipment or sporting gear you plan to take.

LUGGAGE: If you already own serviceable luggage, do not feel compelled to buy new bags. If, however, you have been looking for an excuse to throw out that old suitcase that saw you through 4 years of college and innumerable weekends, this trip to Europe can be the perfect occasion.

Luggage falls into three categories — hard, soft-sided, and soft — and each has advantages and disadvantages. Hard suitcases have a rigid frame and sides. They provide the most protection from rough handling, but they are also the heaviest. Wheels and pull straps can rectify this problem, but they should be removed before the luggage is checked in or they may well be wrenched off in transit. In addition, hard bags will sometimes pop open, even when locked, so a strap around the suitcase is advised.

Soft-sided suitcases have a rigid frame that has been covered with leather, fabric, or a synthetic material. The weight of the suitcase is greatly reduced, but many of the coverings (except leather, which is also the heaviest) are vulnerable to rips and tears from conveyor machinery. Not surprisingly, the materials that wear better are generally found on more expensive luggage.

The third category, seen more and more frequently, is soft luggage. Lacking any rigid structural element, it comes in a wide variety of shapes and sizes and is easy to carry, especially since it often has a shoulder strap. Most carry-on bags are of this type because they can be squeezed to fit under the plane seat. They are even more vulnerable to damage on conveyor equipment than soft-sided bags, and, as the weak point on these bags is the zipper, be sure to tie some cord or put several straps around the bag for insurance. Also be prepared to find a brand-new set of wrinkles pressed into everything that was carefully ironed before packing.

Whatever type of luggage you choose, remember that it should last for many years. Shop carefully, but be prepared to make a sizable investment. In fact, you might consider putting off the purchase of new luggage until you get to one of Europe's major cities, where fine handcrafted leather goods are found.

It is always a good idea to add an empty, flattened airline bag or similar piece of luggage to your suitcase; you'll find it indispensable as a beach bag or to carry a few items for a day's outing. Keep in mind, too, that you're likely to do some shopping, and save room for those items.

For more information on packing and luggage, send your request with a #10 stamped, self-addressed envelope to Samsonite Travel Advisory Service (PO Box 39609, Dept. 80, Denver, CO 80239) for its free booklet, *Getting a Handle on Luggage*.

Hints for Handicapped Travelers

 From 35 to 50 million people in the US alone have some sort of disability, and at least half this number are physically handicapped. Like everyone else today, they — and the uncounted disabled millions around the world — are on the move. More than ever before, they are demanding facilities they can use comfortably, and they are being heard. The disabled traveler will find that services for the handicapped have improved considerably over the last few years, both in the US and abroad, and though accessibility is far from universal, it is being brought up to more acceptable standards every day.

PLANNING: Good planning is essential: Collect as much information as you can about your specific disability and about facilities for the disabled in the area you're visiting, make your travel arrangements well in advance, and specify to all services involved the exact nature of your condition or restricted mobility — your trip will be much more comfortable if you know that there are accommodations and facilities to suit your needs. The best way to find out if your intended destination can accommodate a handicapped traveler is to write or phone the local tourist authority or hotel and ask specific questions. If you require a corridor of a certain width to maneuver a wheelchair or if you need handles on the bathroom wall for support, ask the hotel manager. A travel agent or the local chapter or national office of the organization that deals with your particular disability — for example, the American Foundation for the Blind or the American Heart Association — will supply the most up-to-date information on the subject. The following sources offer general information on access:

Access to the World, by Louise Weiss, offers sound tips for the disabled traveler abroad. Published by Facts on File, 460 Park Ave. S., New York, NY 10016 (phone: 212-683-2244), it costs $16.95, and can be ordered by phone with a credit card. Henry Holt now publishes this excellent book in paperback; check with your bookstore.

Access Travel: A Guide to the Accessibility of Airport Terminals, published by the Airport Operators Council International, provides information on more than 200 airports worldwide with ratings according to 70 features, including accessibility to bathrooms, corridor width, and parking spaces. For a free copy, write to the Consumer Information Center, Access America, Dept. 571T, Pueblo, CO 81009, or call 202-293-8500 and ask for Item 571T — Access Travel. To help travel agents plan trips for the handicapped, this material is reprinted with additional information on tourist boards, city information offices, and tour operators specializing in travel for the handicapped (see "Tours," below) in the North American edition of the *Official Airline Guides Travel Planner,* issued quarterly by Official Airline Guides, 2000 Clearwater Dr,. Oak Brook, IL 60521 (phone: 312-574-6000).

Access in London (London: Robert Nicholson Publications; $4.95), a detailed accessibility guide to London sites and accommodations, is available at the British Travel Bookshop, 40 W. 57th St., New York, NY 10019 (phone: 212-765-0898).

Air Transportation of Handicapped Persons is a booklet published by the US Department of Transportation and will be sent free upon written request. Ask for "Free Advisory Circular #AC-120-32" from the Distribution Unit, US Dept. of Transportation, Publications Section, M-443-2, Washington, DC 20590.

Comité National Français de Liaison pour la Réadaptation des Handicapés (*CNFLRH*), a French organization affiliated with *Mobility International/USA* (see listing below), is a central source of information to contact both before and during a trip to France (if you visit in person, call for an appointment). The *CNFLRH* also publishes, in French, *Touristes Quand Même!,* a city-by-city listing of services accessible to the handicapped, such as banks, churches, pharmacies, and pools, as well as some tourist sites, medical specialists for the physically disabled — physical therapists, orthopedists, and so on — and sources of wheelchair rental and repair. First issued in 1984 and updated in 1987, it has recently been augmented by a third volume covering Paris alone. *CNFLRH* also offers a list of accessible hotels, one for Paris and another for the rest of the country. To obtain these and other *CNFLRH* publications, which are free (except for a new guide to cinemas and cultural events, *Guide Culturelle*), contact a branch of the French Government Tourist Office, or contact CNFLRH, 38 Bd. Raspail, 75007 Paris (phone: 45-48-90-13).

Handicapped Travel Newsletter, edited by wheelchair-bound Vietnam veteran Michael Quigley, who, undaunted, has traveled to 82 countries around the world and writes regular columns for travel magazines. Issued every 2 months (plus special issues), it is regarded as one of the finest sources of information for the disabled traveler. A subscription is $10 per year; write to Handicapped Travel Newsletter, PO Box 269, Athens, TX 75751.

Information for Individuals with Disabilities (*ICID*), Fort Point Pl., 1st Floor, 27-43 Wormwood St., Boston, MA 02210 (phone: 617-727-5440/1 or 800-462-5015 in Massachusetts only); both voice and TDD (telecommunications device for the deaf). *ICID* provides information and referral services on disability-related issues and will help you research your trip. It also publishes fact sheets on vacation planning, tour operators, travel agents, and travel resources.

The Itinerary is a bimonthly travel magazine for people with disabilities. It includes information on accessibility, tour listings, news of adaptive devices, travel aids, and special services as well as numerous general travel hints. A subscription is $10 a year; write to The Itinerary, PO Box 1084, Bayonne, NJ 07002-1084 (phone: 201-858-3400).

A List of Guidebooks for Handicapped Travelers is a free list of useful publications for the disabled, compiled by the President's Committee on Employment of People with Disabilities, 1111 20th St. NW, Suite 636, Vanguard Bldg., Washington, DC 20036 (published September 1975).

Mobility International/USA (*MIUSA*), the US branch of *Mobility International,* a nonprofit British organization with affiliates in some 35 countries, offers advice and assistance to disabled travelers — including information on accommodations, access guides, and study tours. Its main office is *Mobility International Headquarters* (228 Borough High St., London, SE1 1JX, England; phone: 01-403-5688). Among its affiliates in Europe are *Mobility International Germany* (c/o BAG-C, 5 Eupenerstrasse, D-6500 Mainz, Federal Republic of Germany; phone: 49-61-31-22-5506); *Irish Wheelchair Association* (Aras Chuchulain, Blackheath Dr., Clontars, Dublin 3, Irish Republic; phone: 3531-338241); *Associazone Per l'Assistenza* (29 Via San Barnaba, I-20122 Milano, Italy; phone: 39-25-51-2009); *Mobility International Switzerland* (Postfach 129, 71 Feldeggstrasse, CH-8032 Zurich, Switzerland; phone: 41-13-83-0497); *Trivsel and Tryghed* (4 Driftskontoret Sydskraenten, DK-4400, Kalundborg, Denmark; phone: 03-50-9611). Among its publications are a quarterly newsletter and a comprehensive sourcebook, *World of Options: A Guide to International Education Exchange, Community Service, and Travel for Persons with Disabilities.* Individual membership is $20 a year; subscription to the newsletter alone is $10 annually. For more information, contact MIUSA, PO Box 3551, Eugene, OR 97403; phone: 503-343-1284, voice and TTD (telecommunications device for the deaf).

National Rehabilitation Information Center, 8455 Colesville Rd., Suite 935, Silver Spring, MD 20910 (phone: 301-588-9284). A general information and referral service.

Paralyzed Veterans of America (*PVA*) is a national organization that offers information and advocacy services for veterans with spinal cord injuries. *PVA* also sponsors *Access to the Skies,* a program that coordinates the efforts of the national and international air travel industry in providing airport and airplane access for the handicapped. Members also receive several helpful publications as well as regular notification of conferences on subjects of interest to the handicapped traveler. For information, contact PVA/ATTS Program, 801 18th St. NW, Washington, DC 20006 (phone: 202-USA-1300).

Royal Association for Disability and Rehabilitation (*RADAR*), 25 Mortimer St., London W1N 8AB, England (phone: 011-44-1-637-5400), offers a number of publications for the handicapped, including a comprehensive guide, *Holidays and Travel Abroad for the Disabled,* which covers all of Europe and provides helpful advice to the disabled traveler abroad. Available by writing to *RADAR,* the price, including airmail postage, is £3 (approximately $4.50); *RADAR* requires payment in pounds sterling, so this should be sent via an international money order (available at the post office).

Society for the Advancement of Travel for the Handicapped (*SATH*), 26 Court St., Penthouse, Brooklyn, NY 11242 (phone: 718-858-5483). To keep abreast of developments in travel for the handicapped as they occur, you may want to join *SATH,* a non-profit organization whose members include travel agents, tour operators, and other travel suppliers as well as consumers. Membership costs $40 ($25 for students and travelers who are 65 and older), and the fee is tax deductible. *SATH* publishes a quarterly newsletter, an excellent booklet, *Travel Tips for the Handicapped,* and provides information on travel agents or tour operators in the US and overseas who have experience (or an interest) in travel for the handicapped. *SATH* also offers a free 48-page guide, *The United States Welcomes Handicapped Visitors,* which covers domestic transportation and accommodations, as well as travel insurance, customs regulations, and other useful hints for the handicapped traveler abroad. Send a self-addressed, #10 envelope to *SATH* at the address above; include $1 for postage.

Travel Information Service at Moss Rehabilitation Hospital is a service designed to help physically handicapped people plan trips. It cannot make travel arrangements but, for a nominal fee per package, it will supply information from its files on as many as three cities, countries, or special interests. Write to the Travel Information Service, Moss Rehabilitation Hospital, 12th St. and Tabor Rd., Philadelphia, PA 19141 (phone: 215-456-9600).

TravelAbility, by Lois Reamy, is a vast database with information on tours for the handicapped, coping with public transport, and finding accommodations, special equipment, and travel agents, and includes a helpful step-by-step planning guide. Although geared mainly to travel in the US, it is full of information useful to handicapped travelers anywhere. Published by Macmillan, *TravelAbility* is currently out of print but may be available at your library.

A number of organizations throughout Europe provide, not only information for the disabled traveler, but in some cases an escort who will meet the traveler at the airport. You will need to write well in advance, however, to take advantage of current offerings. Among these organizations are the following:

Air Service for the Disabled, Langenhagen GM BH 3000, Hanover 42, Flughafen, Postfach 420280, West Germany. Information and escort facilities for disabled travelers.

Holiday Guides for the Handicapped through Switzerland, Postfach 129, CH-8032, Zurich, Switzerland. Information and potential guide services.

The National Institute of Social Services, Ministry of Labour, Health and Social Security, 52 Maria De Gusman, Madrid 3, Spain. Information and escort services.

Paris Airport Authority, 1 World Trade Center, Suite 2555, New York, NY 10048. Information and escort services.

Swedish Central Committee for Rehabilitation, Box 303, S-161, 26 Bromma, Sweden. Information and escort services.

Other good sources of information are the tourist offices of the particular countries you plan to visit. Many publish brochures specifically for the handicapped (although not always in English) and often include a clippings service on articles about disabled travel that will also be sent on request. The Danish Tourist Board's *Access in Denmark — A Tourist Guide for the Disabled* and the Netherlands Board of Tourism's *Holiday in Holland for the Handicapped* are two particularly comprehensive publications, both available in English. The Swedish National Tourist Office and the Irish Tourist Board publish guides to accessible accommodations and restaurants and may also be able to provide assistance with escorts, while the accommodations guide published by the Norwegian Tourist Board notes which hotels are accessible for travelers in wheelchairs. The British Tourist Authority also carries pamphlets on disabled access in Great Britain. For the US addresses of these and other government tourist authorities, see *National Tourist Offices in the US.*

In the Republic of Ireland, the *National Rehabilitation Board* (25 Clyde Rd., Dublin 4, Ireland; phone: 01-685181 or 689618) is the central source of information on facilities for the handicapped, and the *Union of Voluntary Organisations for the Handicapped* (29 Eaton Sq., Monkstown, Co. Dublin; phone: 01-809251 or 803142) will provide addresses and phone numbers of local volunteer organizations serving the handicapped. In Northern Ireland, the *Northern Ireland Council for the Handicapped* (Northern Ireland Council of Social Service, 2 Annadale Ave., Belfast BT7 3JH, Northern Ireland, UK; phone: 232-640011) is the central source of information for the handicapped, and in conjunction with the Northern Ireland Tourist Board, publishes and distributes the free booklet *The Disabled Tourist in Northern Ireland: Things to See, Places to Stay,* which provides useful information on everything from access for wheelchair visitors to overnight accommodations and facilities for the hearing-impaired and for visually handicapped people.

For accommodation slanted to the disabled traveler, visitors to London should try the *Ramada* hotel (Berners St., London W1A 3BE (phone: 01-636-1629); the *London Tara* hotel (Scarsdale Pl., Wrights Lane, Kensington, London W8 5SR), which offers discounts for disabled travelers booking well in advance through the charity-registered *Visitors Club* (10 Gloucester Dr., Finsbury Park, London N4 2LP; phone: 01-800-8696). *John Grooms* (10 Gloucester Dr., Finsbury Park, London N4 2LP; phone: 01-802-7272) offers apartments ("flats") that are fully accessible to wheelchair users and sleeps up to 6 people. The rents are from £122 (Sterling) to £135 (approximately $183 to $210) per week. They also have bungalows from £62 to £194 ($93 to $290) per week; chalets from £62 to £144 ($93 to $220); and caravans (fully motorized RVs or towed campers) from £62 to £139 ($93 to $212). (*Note:* Although the *Visitors Club* and *John Grooms* share the same mailing address, they are separate organizations.)

For accommodations elsewhere in Great Britain, try *Swallow* hotels (Seaburn Terrace, Sunderland, Tyne and Wear, SR6 8BB; phone: 091-529-4545; in the US call Thomas McFerran at 800-444-1545), with some 35 properties. Also worth mentioning is the *Alison Park* hotel (3 Temple Rd., Buxton, Derbyshire SK17 9BA; phone: 0298-22473), an ideal base for touring the Peak District. For self-contained holiday cottage rental, try *Cressbrook Hall Cottages* (Cressbrook, Derbyshire SK17 8SY; phone: 0298-871289), also in the Peak District near Buxton. *Country Holidays* (Spring Mill, Stonybank Rd., Earby (nr. Colne), Lancashire, BB8 6RW; phone: 0282-445340), with 4,000 rental properties stretching from the Scottish Highlands to Land's End in Cornwall, also offers a free brochure for disabled travelers covering facilities in England.

Other services for the handicapped in Great Britain include: *Triscope* (63 Esmond Rd., London W4 1JE; phone: 01-994-9294), a telephone-based information and referral service (not a booking agent) that can help with transportation options for specific journeys in either London or the rest of the country, which may also be able to recommend outlets leasing small family vehicles adapted to take a wheelchair. *Carelink* and *Airbus* are weekday minibus services adapted to take wheelchairs that connect with main line *BritRail* stations and Heathrow airport; for information, contact London Regional Transport Unit for Disabled Passengers, 55 Broadway, London SW1H 0BD (phone: 01-227-3312). *Artsline* (5 Crowndale Rd., London NW1 1TU; phone: 01-388-2227) offers free telephone advice on disabled access, programs, and facilities at London theaters and art venues (the agency does not make bookings); a monthly magazine and cassette tape are also available. And for general information, there's *Holiday Care Service* (2 Old Bank Chambers, Station Rd., Horley, Surrey RH6 9HW; phone: 0293-774535), a first-rate, free advisory service on accommodations, transportation, and holiday packages throughout Europe for disabled visitors.

Regularly revised hotel and restaurant guides using the symbol of access (a person in a wheelchair; see the symbol at the beginning of this chapter) to point out accommodations suitable for wheelchair-bound guests include *Egon Ronay's Lucas Guide* and the *Michelin Red Guide to Great Britain and Ireland,* both of which sell for $17.95 in general and travel bookstores. The Irish Tourist Board (in the Republic) also uses the symbol in its annual *Guide to Hotels and Guesthouses,* but its *Accommodation and Restaurant Guide for Disabled Persons,* available free from US offices, is an access guide and is much more useful.

The *Canadian Rehabilitation Council for the Disabled* publishes two useful books by Cinnie Noble. The first, *Handi-Travel: A Resource Book for Disabled and Elderly Travelers* ($14.45 Canadian or $12.95 US postpaid), is a comprehensive travel guide full of practical tips for those with disabilities affecting mobility, hearing, or sight. The *Handicapped Traveler* ($12.95; plus $2 for shipping and handling, 50¢ each additional copy), though written for travel agents, also provides a wealth of useful information for the disabled traveler. To order these books, and for other useful information, contact the Canadian Rehabilitation Council for the Disabled, 1 Yonge St., Suite 2110, Toronto, Ont. M5E 1E5, Canada (phone: 416-862-0340).

A few more basic resources to look for are *Travel for the Disabled* by Helen Hecker ($9.95) and, by the same author, *The Directory of Travel Agencies for the Disabled* ($12.95). *Wheelchair Vagabond* by John G. Nelson is another useful guidebook for those confined to a wheelchair (softcover, $9.95; hardcover, $14.95). All three are published by Twin Peaks Press, PO Box 129, Vancouver, WA 98666; to order call 800-637-CALM. Additionally, *The Physically Disabled Traveler's Guide* by Rod W. Durgin and Norene Lindsay is helpful and informative; it's available from Resource Directories (3361 Executive Pkwy., Suite 302, Toledo, OH 43606; phone: 419-536-5353) for $9.95, plus $2 for postage and handling.

Also check the library for Mary Meister Walzer's *A Travel Guide for the Disabled: Western Europe* (Van Nostrand Reinhold), which gives access ratings to a fair number of hotels along with information on the accessibility of some sightseeing attractions, restaurants, theaters, stores, and more.

It should be noted that almost all of the material published with disabled travelers in mind deals with the wheelchair-bound traveler, for whom architectural barriers are of prime concern. For travelers with diabetes, the pamphlet *Ticket to Safe Travel* is available for 50¢ from the New York Diabetes Association, 505 Eighth Ave., 21st Floor, New York, NY 10018 (phone: 212-947-9707). Another, *Travel for the Patient with Chronic Obstructive Pulmonary Disease,* is available for $2 from Dr. Harold Silver, 1601 18th St. NW, Washington, DC 20009 (phone: 202-667-0134). For blind travelers, *Seeing Eye Dogs as Air Travelers* can be obtained free from the Seeing Eye, Box 375, Washington Valley Rd., Morristown, NJ 07960 (phone: 201-539-4425).

Travelers who depend on Seeing Eye dogs should check with the airline they plan to fly and the authorities of the countries they plan to visit well in advance. In general, the rules that apply to bringing any dog into the country apply without exception to Seeing Eye dogs. Some countries require only that you bring a valid health certificate issued by a qualified veterinarian stating that your dog is fully vaccinated and in good health; others require a lengthy quarantine period, while still others prohibit the importation of any animal. Most countries require a rabies vaccination certificate guaranteeing that the animal does not have rabies. The animal must be vaccinated within a specified period, usually not less than 15 to 30 days or more than 11 months before departure. In addition, often this certificate must be certified and stamped by the US Department of Agriculture (USDA). For the location of the nearest USDA office providing this service as well as for other useful information, contact the US Department of Agriculture, APHIS, Federal Center Bldg., Hyattsville, MD 20782; phone: 301-962-7726. For the specific requirements of the countries you plan to visit, contact the appropriate tourist board offices in the US (see *Tourist Information Offices* for addresses).

Note: Any dog brought into the British Isles, including Northern Ireland and the Irish Republic, must spend 6 months in quarantine. Dogs brought into Finland and Sweden require a 4-month quarantine period. So blind travelers to these countries should consider other alternatives, such as traveling with a companion.

PLANE: Advise the airline that you are handicapped when you book your flight. The Federal Aviation Administration (FAA) has ruled that US airlines must accept disabled and handicapped passengers as long as the airline has advance notice and the passenger represents no insurmountable problem in the emergency evacuation procedures. As a matter of course, US airlines were pretty good about helping handicapped passengers even before the ruling, although each airline has somewhat different procedures. European airlines are also generally good about accommodating the disabled traveler, but, again, policies vary from carrier to carrier. Ask for specifics when you book your flight.

Disabled passengers should always make reservations well in advance and should provide the airline with all relevant details of their condition at that time. These details include information on mobility, toilet and special oxygen needs, and requirements for airline-supplied equipment, such as a wheelchair or portable oxygen. Be sure that the person you speak to understands fully the degree of your disability — the more details provided, the more effective the help the airline can give you. On the day before the flight, call back to make sure that all arrangements have been taken care of, and on the day of the flight, arrive early so that you can board before the rest of the passengers. Carry a medical certificate with you, stating your specific disability or the need to carry particular medicine. (Some airlines require the certificate; you should find out the regulations of the airline you'll be flying well beforehand.)

Because most airports have jetways (corridors connecting the terminal with the door of the plane), a disabled passenger can usually be taken as far as the plane, and sometimes right onto it, in a wheelchair. If not, a narrow boarding chair may be used to take you to your seat. Your own wheelchair, which will be folded and put in the baggage compartment, should be tagged as escort luggage to assure that it's available at planeside upon landing rather than in the baggage claim area. Travel is not quite as simple if your wheelchair is battery-operated: Unless it has non-spillable batteries, it might not be accepted on board, and you will have to check with the airline ahead of time to find out how the batteries and the chair should be packaged for the flight. Usually people in wheelchairs are asked to wait until other passengers have disembarked. If you are making a tight connection, be sure to tell the attendant.

Passengers who use oxygen may not use their personal supply in the cabin, though it may be carried on the plane as cargo when properly packed and labeled. If you will need oxygen during the flight, the airline will supply it to you (there is a charge) provided you have given advance notice — 24 hours to a few days, depending on the carrier.

Several airlines now have booklets describing procedures for accommodating the handicapped on their flights and including other information. For example, United Airlines has a list of travel tips for the handicapped; contact United Airlines, Consumer Affairs Dept., PO Box 66100, Chicago, IL 60666 (phone: 312-952-6796).

Useful information on every stage of air travel from planning to arrival is provided in the free booklet *Incapacitated Passengers Air Travel Guide.* To receive a copy, write to Senior Manager, Passenger Services, International Air Transport Association, 2000 Peel St., Montreal, Que. H3A 2R4, Canada (phone: 514-844-6311). For an access guide to over 200 airports worldwide, write for *Access Travel: A Guide to the Accessibility of Airport Terminals,* published by the Airport Operators Council International (see listing above). *Air Transportation of Handicapped Persons* is another useful booklet and explains the general guidelines that govern air carrier policies. It is also available free upon written request. Ask for "Free Advisory Circular #AC-120-32" from the Distribution Unit, US Department of Transportation, Publications Section, M-443-2, Washington, DC 20590; for speedy service, enclose a self-addressed mailing label with your request.

SHIP: Cunard's *Queen Elizabeth 2* is considered the best-equipped ship for the handicapped — all but the top deck is accessible. The *QE2* crosses the Atlantic regularly from June through December between New York and its home port of Southampton, England, sometimes calling at Cherbourg, France, and occasionally at other European ports. (For further information, see *Traveling by Ship.*)

GROUND TRANSPORTATION: Perhaps the simplest solution to getting around is to travel with an able-bodied companion who can drive. If you are accustomed to driving your own hand-controlled car and are determined to rent one, you may have to do some extensive research, as it is difficult to find rental cars fitted with hand controls in Europe. If agencies do provide hand-control cars, they are apt to be few and in high demand. The best course is to contact the major car rental agencies listed in *Touring by Car* well before your departure, but be forewarned, you may still be out of luck. Other sources for information on vehicles adapted for the handicapped are the organizations discussed above.

Another quite expensive option is to hire a chauffeured auto. Other alternatives include taking taxis or using local public transportation; however, your mobility may be limited in rural areas.

BUS AND TRAIN: Bus travel, which in many countries may be limited except in metropolitan areas, is not recommended for travelers who are totally wheelchair-bound unless they have someone along who can lift them on and off or they are members of a group tour designed for the handicapped and are using a specially outfitted bus. If you have some mobility, however, you'll find local personnel usually quite happy to help you board and exit.

Train travel for the wheelchair-bound is well organized in Europe and becoming more so every day. All *TGV* trains, for example — France's very high speed trains, which happen to be the fastest trains in the world — have doors at platform level so that passengers can roll on and off, and spaces have been set aside where they can stay in their wheelchairs. A booklet describing *SNCF* (*Société Nationale des Chemins de Fer Français,* or *French Rail Inc.*) services for the handicapped can be picked up in major railroad stations in France, primarily in Paris. Unfortunately, it is issued in French only.

Other trains in Europe are not as well adapted to wheelchairs, but timetables for each route often specify which departures are accessible. And on trains that cannot accommodate wheelchairs, depending on the type of train, wheelchair passengers can sometimes travel in the guard's van (the baggage car). Arrangements are usually made in advance through the area manager. For further information on this option, general accessibility, and for timetables, contact the country's rail service representatives in the US (addresses are listed in *Touring by Train*) or ask for information at regional rail offices abroad.

TOURS: Programs designed for the physically impaired are run by specialists who have researched hotels, restaurants, and sites to be sure they present no insurmountable obstacles. The following travel agencies and tour operators specialize in making group and individual arrangements for travelers with physical or other disabilities. All of them have experience in travel to Europe and many of them have specific experience in travel to France. Because of the requirements of handicapped travel, however, the same packages may not be offered regularly.

Access: The Foundation for Accessibility by the Disabled, PO Box 356, Malvern, NY 11565 (phone: 516-887-568). Referral service that acts as an intermediary with tour operators and agents worldwide. Also provides information on accessibility at various locations.

Accessible Tours/Directions Unlimited, 720 N. Bedford Rd., Bedford Hills, NY 10507 (phone: 914-241-1700 in New York State; 800-533-5343 elsewhere). Arranges group or individual tours for disabled persons traveling with able-bodied friends or family members. Accepts the solo traveler if completely self-sufficient.

Evergreen Travel Service/Wings on Wheels Tours, 19505L 44th Ave. W., Lynnwood, WA 98036 (phone: 206-776-1184; 800-562-9298 in Washington State; 800-435-2288 elsewhere). The oldest company in the world offering worldwide tours and cruises for the disabled (Wings on Wheels) and sight impaired/blind (White Cane Tours). Most programs are first class or deluxe, and include escort by the owner or his family.

Flying Wheels Travel, 143 W. Bridge St., Box 382, Owatonna, MN 55060 (phone: 507-451-5005 or 800-533-0363). Handles both tours and individual arrangements.

The Guided Tour, 555 Ashbourne Rd., Elkins Park, PA 19117 (phone: 215-782-1370). Arranges tours for people with developmental and learning disabilities, and sponsors separate tours for members of the same population who are also physically disabled or who simply need a slower pace.

InterpreTours, Ask Mr. Foster Travel Service, 16660 Ventura Blvd., Encino, CA 91436 (phone: 818-788-4118 for voice; 818-788-5328 for TDD — telecommunications device for the deaf). Arranges independent travel, cruises, and tours for the deaf, with an interpreter as tour guide.

Mobility Tours, 84 E. 10th St., 2nd Floor, New York, NY 10003 (phone: 212-353-0240). Associated with *SATH,* this agency arranges tours for both physically and developmentally disabled people.

Sprout, 204 W. 20th St., New York, NY 10011 (phone: 212-431-1265). Arranges travel programs for mildly and moderately disabled adults, 18 years of age and over.

Travel Horizons Unlimited, 11 E. 44th St., New York, NY 10017 (phone: 212-687-5121). Travel agent and registered nurse Mary Ann Hamm designs individual trips for travelers requiring all types of kidney dialysis and handles arrangements for the dialysis.

Whole Person Tours, PO Box 1084, Bayonne, NJ 07002-1084 (phone: 201-858-3400). Handicapped owner Bob Zywicki travels the world with his wheelchair, and offers a number of escorted tours (many by himself) for the disabled. A catalogue of foreign and domestic programs designed for travelers with disabilities is available for $2. *Whole Person Tours* also publishes *The Itinerary,* a bimonthly newsletter for disabled travelers (a 1-year subscription costs $10).

Another special guiding service is offered by Oxford historian William Forrester, who became London's first fully qualified and registered guide in a wheelchair. He escorts travelers for entire holidays, or just helps in planning an independent tour suited to each traveler's particular interests and mobility starting at £80 (Sterling). Contact William Forrester, 1 Belvedere Close, Manor Rd., Guildford, Surrey GU2 6NP (phone: 0483-575401).

Hints for Single Travelers

Just about the last trip in human history on which the participants were neatly paired was the voyage of Noah's Ark. Ever since, passenger lists and tour groups have reflected the same kind of asymmetry that occurs in real life, as countless individuals set forth to see the world unaccompanied (or unencumbered, depending on your outlook) by spouse, lover, friend, or relative.

There are some things to be said for traveling alone. There is the pleasure of privacy, though a solitary traveler must be self-reliant, independent, and responsible. Unfortunately, traveling alone can also turn a traveler into a second class citizen.

The truth is that the travel industry is not very fair to people who vacation by themselves. People traveling alone almost invariably end up paying more than individuals traveling in pairs. Most travel bargains, including package tours, accommodations, resort packages, and cruises, are based on *double-occupancy* rates. This means that the per-person price is offered on the basis of two people traveling together and sharing a double room (which means they will each spend a good deal more on meals and extras). The single traveler will have to pay a surcharge, called a single supplement, for exactly the same package. In extreme cases, this can add as much as 30% to 55% to the basic per-person rate. As far as the travel industry is concerned, single travel has not yet come into its own.

Don't despair, however. Throughout Europe, there are scores of smaller hotels and other hostelries where, in addition to a more cozy atmosphere, prices are still quite reasonable for the single traveler. There are, after all, countless thousands of individuals who *do* travel alone. Inevitably, their greatest obstacle is the single supplement charge, which prevents them from cashing in on travel bargains available to anyone traveling as part of a pair.

The obvious, most effective alternative is to find a traveling companion. Even special "singles' tours" that promise no supplements are based on people sharing double rooms. Perhaps the most recent innovation along these lines is the creation of organizations that "introduce" single travelers to one another, somewhat like a dating service. If you are interested in finding another single traveler to help share the cost, consider contacting the agencies listed below. Some charge fees, others are free, but the basic service is the same: to match the unattached person with a compatible travel mate. Among the better established of these agencies are the following:

Cosmos: This agency, specializing in budget motorcoach tours of Europe, offers a guaranteed-share plan whereby singles who wish to share rooms (and avoid paying the single supplement) are matched by the tour escort with like-minded individuals of the same sex and charged the basic tour price. Those wishing to stay on their own pay a single supplement. Contact *Cosmos* at one of their three North American branches: 95-25 Queens Blvd., Rego Park, NY 11374 (phone: 800-221-0090 from the eastern US); 150 S. Los Robles Ave., Pasadena, CA 91101 (phone: 818-449-0919 or 800-556-5454 from the western US); 1801 Eglinton Ave. W., Suite 104, Toronto, Ont. M6E 2H8, Canada (phone: 416-787-1281).

Grand Circle Travel: Arranges escorted cruise/air packages for "mature" travelers, including singles. Membership, which is automatic when you book a trip through *Grand Circle,* includes a free subscription to its quarterly magazine, discount certificates on future trips, and other extras. Contact Grand Circle Travel, 347 Congress St., Boston, MA 02210 (phone: 617-350-7500; 800-221-2610 in the US).

Jane's International: This service puts potential traveling companions in touch with one another. No age limit, no fee. For information, contact Jane's International, 2603 Bath Ave., Brooklyn, NY 11214 (phone: 718-266-2045).

Saga International Holidays: An organization for seniors over 60, including singles. Members receive the club magazine, which includes a classified section aimed at helping lone travelers find suitable companions. A 3-year membership costs $5. Contact Saga International Holidays, 120 Boylston St., Boston MA 02116 (phone: 617-451-6808 or one of the following nationwide numbers: for reservations, 800-343-0273; for customer service, 800-441-6662; for brochures, 800-248-2234).

Singleworld, which organizes its own packages and also books singles on the cruises and tours of other operators, arranges shared accommodations if requested, charging a one-time surcharge that is much less than the single supplement would be. *Singleworld* is actually a club joined through travel agents for a yearly fee of $20, paid at the time of booking. About two-thirds of this agency's clientele are under 35, and about half this number are women, but *Singleworld* organizes tours and cruises with departures categorized by age group. 401 Theodore Fremd Ave., Rye, NY 10580 (phone: 914-967-3334 or 800-223-6490 in the continental US).

Travel Companion Exchange: Every 8 weeks this group publishes a directory of singles looking for travel companions and provides members with full-page profiles of likely partners. Members fill out a lengthy questionnaire to establish a personal profile and write a small listing much like an ad in a personal column. This listing is circulated to other members, who can request a copy of the complete questionnaire and then go on to make contact to plan a joint vacation.

It is wise to join as far ahead of your scheduled vacation as possible so that there's enough time to determine the suitability of prospective companions. Membership fees range from $3 to $11 per month (with a 6-month minimum), depending on the level of service required. PO Box 833, Amityville, NY 11701 (phone: 516-454-0880).

Travel Mates International: Will search for and arrange shares on existing package tours for men and women of any age. It will also organize group tours for its own clients. Annual membership fee is $15. 49 W. 44th St., New York, NY 10036 (phone: 212-221-6565).

A special guidebook for solo travelers, prepared by Eleanor Adams Baxel, offers information on how to avoid paying supplementary charges, how to pick the right travel agent, how to calculate costs, and much more. Entitled *A Guide for Solo Travel Abroad,* it was published by the Berkshire Traveller Press but is now out of print, so look for it in your library.

The single traveler who is particularly interested in getting to know Europeans better than chance encounters in train stations would allow may be interested in two very different possibilities. One is *Club Med,* an organization that heartily welcomes singles. Of its more than 100 activity-oriented resorts in countries around the world, most are in Europe, and the majority of guests at its European resorts are European. For details, contact Club Med, 3 E. 54th St., New York, NY 10022 (phone: 800-CLUB-MED), or one of the two *Club Med* boutiques (in San Francisco, 415-982-4200; in New York, 212-750-1687).

WOMEN AND STUDENTS: Two specific groups of single travelers deserve special mention: women and students. Countless women travel by themselves in Europe, and such an adventure need not be feared. You will generally find people courteous and welcoming, but remember that crime is a worldwide problem. (In fact, many European cities are generally regarded as safer than American cities — for everyone, including single women.) Keep a careful eye on your belongings while on the beach or lounging in a park; lock your car and hotel doors; deposit your valuables in the hotel's safe; and don't hitchhike.

One lingering inhibition many female travelers still harbor is that of eating alone in public places. The trick here is to relax and enjoy your meal and surroundings; while you may run across the occasional unenlightened waiter, dining solo is no longer uncommon. A book offering lively, helpful advice on female solo travel is *The Traveling Woman,* by Dena Kaye. Though out of print, it may be found in your library.

A large number of single travelers, needless to say, are students. Travel *is* education. Travel broadens a person's knowledge and deepens his or her perception of the world in a way no media or "armchair" experience ever can. In addition, to study a country's language, art, culture, or history in one of its own schools is to enjoy the highest form of liberal education.

There are many benefits for students abroad, and to begin to discover them, consult the *Council on International Educational Exchange* (*CIEE*) at 205 E. 42nd St., New York, NY 10017 (phone: 212-661-1414), and 312 Sutter St., San Francisco, CA 94108 (phone: 415-421-3473). *CIEE,* which administers a variety of work, study, and travel programs for students, is the US sponsor of the International Student Identity Card (ISIC). Reductions on trains, airfare, and entry fees to most museums and other exhibitions are only some of the advantages of the card. To apply for it, write to *CIEE* at one of the above addresses and mark the letter "Attn. Student ID." Application requires a $10 fee, a passport-size photograph, and proof that you are a matriculating student (either a transcript or a letter or bill from your school registrar with the school's official seal; high school and junior high students can use their report cards). There is no maximum age limit, but you must be at least 12 years old. The *ID Discount Guide,* which gives details of the discounts country by country, is free with membership. Another card of value in Europe and also available through *CIEE* is the Federation of International Youth Travel Organizations (FIYTO) card. This provides many of the benefits of the ISIC card and will give you entrée to certain "youth hotels" throughout Europe. Cardholders, in this case, need not be students, merely under age 26. To apply, send $10 with a passport-size photo and proof of birth date.

CIEE also sponsors charter flights to Europe that are open to students and non-students of any age. Flights between New York and Brussels, Geneva, London, Madrid, Nice, Paris, Rome, and Zurich (with budget-priced add-ons available from Seattle, San Francisco, Los Angeles, San Diego, Las Vegas, Salt Lake City, Denver, St. Louis, El Paso, Minneapolis, and 10 other US cities) leave at least twice weekly in high season, less frequently at other times. Regularly scheduled direct flights are also offered from Boston to Brussels and Paris and from Chicago to Brussels.

Another company that specializes in travel for 18- to 30-year-olds is *STI* (8619 Reseda Blvd., Suite 103, Northridge, CA 91324; phone: 800-637-7687 in California; 800-225-2780 elsewhere). It offers multi-country escorted tours of 2 weeks to 52 days, several including 2 or 3 days in Paris. *Contiki Holidays* (1432 E. Katella Ave., Anaheim, CA 92805; phone: 714-937-0611) specializes in vacations for 18- to 35-year-olds; accommodations are in "Contiki Villages," with cabins or tents, and "Contiki Clubs," and itineraries include special stopovers in châteaux.

Youth fares on transatlantic flights are currently offered by most of the scheduled airlines flying to Europe. Although it may change, at press time the youth fare was almost the same as the standard APEX fare, and there are substantial drawbacks: a 14-day minimum stay, no stopovers, notification of availability and payment in full 24 hours before the flight, and the return can only be left open if this is arranged before the trip, and is again subject to 24-hour notice of availability. This last restriction means that if you must be home by a certain date, you are better off with a different type of ticket. Discount fares vary from carrier to carrier, and some offer discounts to students and youths. To find out about current discounts, contact the individual airlines. Also see *Traveling by Plane* in this section for more information on economical flight alternatives.

One version of the Eurailpass is restricted to travelers (including non-students) under 26 years of age. The Eurail Youthpass entitles the bearer to either 1 or 2 months of unlimited second class rail travel in 17 countries. In addition, it is honored on many European steamers and ferries and on railroad connections between the airport and the center of town in various cities. The pass also entitles the bearer to reduced rates on some bus lines in several countries. The Eurail Youthpass can be purchased only by those living outside Europe or North Africa, and it must be purchased before departure. Contact the offices of the *German Federal Railroad, Swiss Federal Railways,* or *French Rail Inc.* (For addresses in the US, see *Touring by Train.*)

Students and singles in general should also keep in mind that youth hostels exist in many cities throughout Europe. They are always inexpensive, generally clean and well situated, and are a sure place to meet other people traveling alone. They are run by the hosteling associations of some 60-plus countries that make up the *International Youth Hostel Federation (IYHF);* membership in one of the national associations affords access to the hostels of the rest. To join the American affiliate, *American Youth Hostels (AYH),* write to the national office at PO Box 37613, Washington, DC 20013-7613 (phone: 202-783-6161), or contact the AYH council nearest you. Membership in *AYH* costs $20 for people between the ages of 18 and 54; $10 for anyone outside those limits. (If joining by mail, add $1 for the cost of handling and postage.) The *AYH Handbook,* which lists hostels in the US, comes with your *AYH* card; the *International Handbooks,* which list hostels worldwide (*Volume I* covers Europe and the Mediterranean), must be purchased ($8.95 plus $2 for postage). Those who go abroad without an *AYH* card can get an *International Youth Hostel Federation* guest card (for the equivalent of about $18) by contacting one of the national *IYH* associations in Europe. These associations also publish handbooks to hostels in their areas. In addition, the tourist boards also publish information sheets on hostels and on hosteling package holidays.

Many private houses and farms throughout the countryside make a pleasant home base and offer a chance to meet local people. The United States Servas Committee, a non-profit organization designed to promote world peace, keeps a list of hosts worldwide who are willing to take visitors into their homes as guests for a 2-night stay. (See "Home Stays," *Accommodations.*) On many farms, travelers will get a room and a hearty breakfast for as little as $10 a day. Again, publications on such programs in individual countries are also available from tourist authorities.

And there's always camping. Virtually any area of the countryside throughout Europe has a place to pitch a tent and enjoy the scenery. There are numerous national parks, and, with permission, it's often possible to camp on private acres of farmland. Many of the campsites have showers, laundry rooms, public phones, eating facilities, and shops. (For more information, see *Camping and Caravanning, Hiking and Biking.*)

STUDYING ABROAD: Opportunities for study in Europe range from summer or academic-year courses in a language and civilization of a country designed specifically for foreigners (including those whose school days are well behind them) to long-term university attendance by those intending to take a degree.

An organization specializing in travel as an educational experience is the *American Institute for Foreign Study* (*AIFS*). Approximately a third of the participants in its 100-some programs around the world — tours, academic year, and summer programs — choose to study in France. *AIFS* caters primarily to bona fide high school or college students, but its non-credit international learning and continuing education programs are open to independent travelers of all ages. (Approximately 30% of *AIFS* students are over 25.) Contact AIFS at 102 Greenwich Ave., Greenwich, CT 06830 (phone: 203-869-9090 or 203-863-6087 for summer programs).

Elderhostel is a network of schools, colleges, and universities that sponsor week-long study programs for people over 60 years of age on campuses throughout the US and Europe. Some of its programs are offered in cooperation with the *Experiment in International Living* (below) and involve home stays. Contact *Elderhostel,* 80 Boylston St., Suite 400, Boston, MA 02116 (phone: 617-426-7788). The University of New Hampshire, the original sponsor of *Elderhostel,* has its own program for travelers over 50; contact Interhostel, University of New Hampshire, Division of Continuing Education, 6 Garrison Ave., Durham, NH 03824 (phone: 603-862-1147 weekdays, 1:30 to 4 PM Eastern Standard Time). For more details about both programs, see *Hints for Older Travelers.*

Experiment in International Living, which sponsors home-stay educational travel. The organization aims its programs at high school or college students, but it can also arrange home stays of 1 to 4 weeks for adults in more than 40 countries. Kipling Rd., Box E-10, Brattleboro, VT 05301-0676 (phone: 802-257-7751 or 800-345-2929).

Institute of International Education (*IIE*), an information resource center that annually publishes several reference books on study abroad, including *Academic Year Abroad* ($19.95), *Vacation Study Abroad* ($19.95), and *Study in the United Kingdom and Ireland* ($14.95). Prices include book-rate postage; first class postage is $4 extra. All volumes are available from IIE headquarters, 809 UN Plaza, New York, NY 10017 (phone: 212-883-8200).

National Association of Secondary School Principals (*NASSP*), an association of administrators, teachers, and state education officials. It sponsors *School Part-*

nership International, a program in which secondary schools in the US are linked with partner schools abroad for an annual short-term exchange of students and faculty. Contact NASSP, 1904 Association Dr., Reston, VA 22091 (phone: 703-860-0200).

WORKING ABROAD: Jobs for foreigners in Europe are not easy to come by and in general do not pay well enough to cover all the expenses of a trip. They do provide an invaluable learning experience, however, while helping to make a trip more affordable. Work permits can be obtained through the *Council on International Exchange* (address above) only by students over 18 who are working toward a degree and who are enrolled in a US college or university. The permit allows them to work for 3 months at any time of year, but the students must find their own jobs. (Jobs as bilingual hotel, restaurant, and office workers are among those most commonly found.)

Hints for Older Travelers

 Special package deals and more free time are just two factors that have given Americans over age 65 a chance to see the world at affordable prices. Senior citizens make up an ever-growing segment of the travel population, and the trend among them is to travel more frequently and for longer periods of time. No longer limited by 3-week vacations or the business week, older travelers can take advantage of off-season, off-peak travel, which is both less expensive and more pleasant than traveling at prime time in high season. In addition, overseas, as in the US, discounts are frequently available.

PLANNING: When planning a vacation, prepare your itinerary with one eye on your own physical condition and the other on a topographical map. Keep in mind variations in climate, terrain, and altitudes, which may pose some danger for anyone with heart or breathing problems.

An excellent book to read before embarking on any trip, domestic or foreign, is Rosalind Massow's *Travel Easy: The Practical Guide for People Over 50,* available for $8.95 (plus $1.75 postage and handling per order, not per book) from AARP Books, c/o Scott, Foresman, 1865 Miner St., Des Plaines, IL 60016 (phone: 800-238-2300). It discusses a host of subjects, from choosing a destination to getting set for departure, with chapters on transportation options, tours, cruises, avoiding health problems, and handling dental emergencies en route. Another book, *The International Health Guide for Senior Citizens,* covers such topics as trip preparations, food and water precautions, adjusting to weather and climate conditions, finding a doctor, motion sickness, and jet lag. The book also discusses specific health and travel problems, and includes a list of resource organizations that can provide medical assistance for travelers; it is available for $4.95 postpaid from Pilot Books, 103 Cooper St., Babylon, NY 11702 (phone: 516-422-2225). A third book on health for older travelers, Rosalind Massow's excellent *Now It's Your Turn to Travel,* has a chapter on medical problems. Published by Collier Books, it is out of print but available in libraries. Also, see *Medical and Legal Aid,* in this section. Other excellent books for budget-conscious older travelers are: *The Discount Guide for Travelers Over 55* by Caroline and Walter Weintz (Dutton; $7.95) and *The Senior Citizen's Guide to Budget Travel in Europe* ($3.95 plus $1 for postage and handling, from Pilot Books, 103 Cooper St., Babylon, NY 11702; phone: 516-422-2225).

Travel Tips for Senior Citizens (State Department publication 8970), a booklet with general advice, is available for $1 from the Superintendent of Documents, US Government Printing Office, Washington, DC 20402 (phone: 202-783-3238). The booklet *101*

Tips for the Mature Traveler is available free from Grand Circle Travel, 347 Congress St., Suite 3A, Boston, MA 02210 (phone: 617-350-7500 or 800-221-2610).

If you are traveling in the fall, winter, or spring, bear in mind that you will not always find central heating in public places in Europe and that even if your hotel has it, it may not warm your room up to the temperature you're accustomed to at home. Bear in mind also that even in summer you will need something warm for the evening in many areas throughout the Continent, and there are areas where rainwear year-round is a good idea, too. However, remember that one secret to happy traveling is to *pack lightly.* (For further hints on what to bring and how to pack it, see *How to Pack,* in this section.)

HEALTH: Health facilities in Europe are generally excellent; however, an inability to speak the language can pose a serious problem, not in receiving treatment at large hospitals, where many doctors and other staff members will speak English, but in getting help elsewhere or in getting to the place where help is available. A number of organizations exist to help travelers avoid or deal with a medical emergency overseas. For further information on these services, see *Medical and Legal Aid and Consular Services.*

A pre-trip medical and dental checkup are strongly recommended, particularly for older travelers. In addition, be sure to take along any prescription medication you need, enough to last *without a new prescription* for the duration of your trip; pack all medications with a note from your doctor for the benefit of airport authorities. It is also wise to bring a few common non-prescription over-the-counter medications with you: aspirin and something for stomach upset may come in handy. If you have specific medical problems, bring prescriptions and a "medical file" composed of the following:

1. A summary of medical history and current diagnosis.
2. A list of drugs to which you are allergic.
3. Your most recent electrocardiogram, if you have heart problems.
4. Your doctor's name, address, and telephone number

■**A word of caution:** Don't overdo it. Allow time for some relaxing each day to refresh yourself for the next scheduled sightseeing event. Traveling across time zones can be exhausting, and adjusting to major climatic changes can make you feel dizzy and drained. Plan on spending at least one full day resting before you start touring. If you're part of a group tour, be sure to check the itinerary thoroughly. Some package deals sound wonderful because they include all the places you've ever dreamed of visiting. In fact, they can become so hectic and tiring that you'll be reaching for a pillow instead of a camera.

DISCOUNTS AND PACKAGES: Since guidelines change from place to place, it's a good idea to inquire in advance about discounts for transportation, hotels, concerts, movies, museums, and other activities. The tourist authorities of the countries you plan to visit can give the most up-to-date information about discounts and programs for older travelers in Europe (see *Tourist Information Offices*).

Many US hotel and motel chains, airlines, car rental companies, bus lines, and other travel suppliers offer discounts to older travelers. Some of these discounts, however, are extended only to bona fide members of certain senior citizens organizations. Because the same organizations frequently offer package tours to both domestic and international destinations, the benefits of membership are twofold: Those who join can take advantage of discounts as individual travelers and also reap the savings that group travel affords. In addition, because the age requirements for some of these organizations are quite low (or nonexistent), the benefits can begin to accrue early. Among the organizations dedicated to helping you see the world are the following:

American Association of Retired Persons (AARP): The largest and best known of these organizations. Membership is open to anyone 50 or over, whether retired or not. *AARP* offers travel programs, designed exclusively for senior citizens, that cover the globe and include a broad range of escorted tours, hosted tours, and cruises, including regional tours of rural areas of Europe, extended vacations in European cities, and resorts with accommodations in apartments. Dues are $5 a year, or $12.50 for 3 years, and include spouse. For membership information, contact AARP at 1909 K St. NW, Washington, DC 20049 (phone: 202-347-8800); for travel information and reservations, contact AARP Travel Service, PO Box 29233, Los Angeles, CA 90009 (phone: 213-322-7323 or 800-227-7737).

Mature Outlook: This organization has replaced the *National Association of Mature People.* Through its *Travel Alert,* last-minute tours, cruises, and other vacation packages are available to members at special savings. Hotel and car rental discounts and travel accident insurance are also available. Membership is open to anyone 50 years of age or older, costs $9.95 a year, and includes its bimonthly newsletter and magazine as well as information on package tours. Contact the Customer Service Center, 6001 N. Clark St., Chicago, IL 60660 (phone: 800-336-6330).

National Council of Senior Citizens: Here, too, the emphasis is always on keeping costs low. The roster of tours offered is different each year and the travel service will also book individual tours for members. Although most members are over 50, membership is open to anyone, regardless of age, for an annual fee of $12 per person or $16 per couple. Lifetime membership costs $150. For information, contact the National Council of Senior Citizens, 925 15th St. NW, Washington, DC 20005 (phone: 202-347-8800).

Certain travel agencies and tour operators specialize in group travel for older travelers, among them are the following:

Gadabout Tours: Offers escorted tours to many North American destinations but also has tours to Europe. See a travel agent or contact Gadabout Tours, 700 E. Tahquitz, Palm Springs, CA 92262 (phone: 619-325-5556 or 800-521-7309 in California; 800-952-5068 elsewhere).

Grand Circle Travel: Caters exclusively to the over-50 traveler and packages a large variety of escorted tours, cruises, and extended vacations. *Grand Circle* also publishes a quarterly magazine (with a column for the single traveler) and a helpful free booklet entitled *101 Tips for the Mature Traveler Abroad.* Contact Grand Circle Travel, 347 Congress St., Suite 3A, Boston, MA 02210 (phone: 617-350-7500 or 800-221-2610).

Grandtravel: An agency that specializes in trips for older people and their grandchildren (aunts and uncles are welcome, too), it helps bring the generations together through travel. Ten itineraries that coincide with school vacations emphasize historic and natural sites. Transportation, accommodations, and activities are thoughtfully arranged to meet the needs of the young and the young-at-heart. Contact Grandtravel, Suite 706, 6900 Wisconsin Ave., Chevy Chase, MD 20815 (phone: 301-986-0790 in Maryland; 800-247-7551 elsewhere in the US).

Insight International Tours: Packages tours for the mature traveler that emphasize heritage. Bookings must be made through a travel agent. For details, contact Insight International Tours, 17310 Redhill Ave., Suite 330, Irvine, CA 92714 (phone: 714-261-5373 or 800-792-7209 in California; 800-582-8380 elsewhere).

Saga International Holidays: A subsidiary of a British company specializing in the older traveler, *Saga* offers a broad selection of escorted coach tours, cruises, apartment-stay holidays, and combinations thereof for people age 60 and over or those 50 to 59 traveling with someone 60 or older. Members of the Saga Holiday Club receive the club magazine, which also contains a column aimed at helping lone travelers find suitable traveling companions (see *Hints for Single Travelers*). A 3-year membership in the club costs $5. Contact Saga International Holidays, 120 Boylston St., Boston MA 02116 (phone: 617-451-6808 or one of the following nationwide numbers: for reservations, 800-343-0273; for customer service, 800-441-6662; for brochure requests, 800-248-2234).

Many travel agencies, particularly the larger ones, are delighted to make presentations to help a group select destinations. A local chamber of commerce should be able to provide the names of such agencies. Once a time and place are determined, an organization member or travel agent can obtain group quotations for transportation, accommodations, meal plans, and sightseeing. Groups of 40 or more usually get the best breaks.

Another choice open to older travelers is a trip that includes an educational element. *Interhostel,* a program sponsored by the Division of Continuing Education of the University of New Hampshire, sends travelers back to school at cooperating institutions in 33 countries on 4 continents. Participants attend lectures on the history, economy, politics, and cultural life of the country they are visiting, go on field trips, and take part in activities meant to introduce them to their foreign contemporaries. Trips are for 2 weeks, accommodations are on campus in university residence halls or off campus in modest hotels (double occupancy). Groups are limited to 35 to 40 participants who are at least 50 years old (or at least 40 if a participating spouse is at least 50), physically active, and not in need of special diets. For further information or to receive the three free seasonal catalogues, contact Interhostel, UNH Division of Continuing Education, 6 Garrison Ave., Durham, NH 03824 (phone: 603-862-1147 weekdays, 1 to 4 PM).

Similar to *Interhostel* is *Elderhostel,* a nonprofit organization offering educational programs at a huge number of schools in the US and Canada as well as at cooperating institutions overseas. Most international programs run for 3 weeks and feature a special topic each week at a different location. Accommodations are in residence halls, and meals are taken in student cafeterias. Travel to the overseas programs is by designated scheduled flights, and arrangements to remain abroad at the end of the program are possible. Age and health qualifications for participation are similar to those for Interhostelers — Elderhostelers must be at least 60 years old (younger if a spouse or companion qualifies), in good health, and not in need of special diets. For information, write to Elderhostel, 80 Boylston St., Suite 400, Boston, MA 02116 (phone: 617-426-7788).

Hints for Traveling with Children

What better way to be receptive to the experiences you will encounter than to take along the young, wide-eyed members of your family? Their company does not have to be a burden or their presence an excessive expense. The current generation of discounts for children and family package deals can make a trip together quite reasonable.

A family trip will be an investment in your children's future, making geography and history come alive to them and leaving a sure memory that will be among the fondest you will share with them someday. Their insights will be refreshing to you; their impulses may take you to unexpected places with unexpected dividends. The experience will be invaluable to them at any age.

PLANNING: It is necessary to take some extra time beforehand to prepare children for travel. Here are several hints for making a trip with children easy and fun.

1. Children, like everyone else, will derive more pleasure from a trip if they know something about the country before they arrive. Begin their education about a month before you leave. Using maps and travel magazines and books, give children a clear idea of where you are going and how far away it is. Part of the excitement of the journey will be associating the tiny dots on the map with the very real places they will soon visit. You can show them pictures of streets and scenes in which they will stand. Don't shirk history lessons, but don't burden them with dates. Make history light, anecdotal, pertinent, but most of all, fun. If you simply make materials available and keep your destination and your plans a topic of everyday conversation, your children will absorb more than you realize.

2. Children should help to plan the itinerary, and where you go and what you do should reflect some of their ideas. If they already know something about the sites they'll visit, they'll have the excitement of recognition when they arrive and the illumination of seeing how something is or is not the way they expected it to be.

3. Learn the languages of the countries you will be visiting with your children — a few basics like "hello," "good-bye," and "thanks a lot." You need no other motive than a perfectly selfish one: Thus armed, your children will delight the Europeans and help break the ice wherever you go.

4. Familiarize the children with foreign currencies (see FACTS IN BRIEF). Give them an allowance for the trip and be sure they understand just how far it will or won't go.

5. Give children specific responsibilities: The job of carrying their own flight bags and looking after their personal things, along with some other light chores, will give them a stake in the journey. Tell them how they can be helpful when you are checking in or out of hotels.

6. Give each child a diary or scrapbook to take along. Filling these with impressions, observations, and mementos will pass the time on trains and planes and help them assimilate their experiences.

No matter what the reading level of your children, there are books to prepare them for a trip. The very youngest may enjoy *Babar Loses His Crown* (Random House), in which Babar the elephant sightsees in Paris. Miroslav Sasek's travel series for children (Macmillan) includes *This Is Greece* and *This Is Ireland,* geared to readers in grades 3 to 6. The delightful *Artstart* series by Ernest Raboff (Doubleday), designed to introduce children ages 5 to 12 to famous artists and their works, may help to lengthen their attention span in museums; Piero Ventura's beautifully illustrated *Great Painters* (Putnam) is an excellent introduction to Italian, Flemish, English, and French painting for older children (ages 12 and up). David Macaulay's *Cathedral: The Story of Its Construction* (Houghton Mifflin; kindergarten through grade 5), in which line drawings explain the process to those who cannot read the text, may stimulate an interest in medieval architecture; *Castle* is by the same author. James Giblin's *Walls: Defenses Throughout History* (Little, Brown) discusses the walled city of Carcassonne, Hadrian's Wall in England, and the great defensive walls of World Wars I and II, among others, and will appeal to teenage readers.

And, for parents, *Travel with Your Children* publishes a newsletter, *Family Travel Times,* that focuses on the child traveler and offers helpful hints. Membership is $35 a year. For a sample copy of the newsletter, send $1 to Travel with Your Children, 80 Eighth Ave., New York, NY 10011 (phone: 212-206-0688). If your trip passes through Paris, pick up a copy of *Kids Extra!,* an English-language quarterly that suggests museums and restaurants suited to children and gives ideas for day trips from Paris as well as listing helpful hints and resources.

PACKING: Choose your children's clothes much as you would your own. Select a basic color (perhaps different for each child) and coordinate everything with it. Plan their wardrobes with layering in mind — shirts and sweaters that can be taken off and put back on as the temperature varies. Take only drip-dry, wrinkle-resistant items that the children can manage themselves and comfortable shoes — sneakers and sandals. Younger children will need more changes, but keep it to a minimum. No one likes to carry added luggage (remember that *you* will have to manage most of it!).

Take as many handy snacks as you can squeeze into the corners of your suitcases — things like dried fruit and nut mixes, hard candies, peanut butter, and crackers — and moist towelettes for cleaning. Don't worry if your supply of nibbles is quickly depleted. Airports and train stations are well stocked with such items.

Pack a special medical kit including children's aspirin or acetaminophen, an antihistamine or decongestant, Dramamine, and diarrhea medication. Do not feel you must pack a vacation's worth of Pampers. Disposable diapers — called "nappies" in the British Isles, *les couches* in France, *pañales desechables* in Spain, *pannolini di carta* in Italy, and *wegwerswindel* (pronounced "vekvervindel") in Germany — are available in most drugstores and supermarkets throughout Europe. A selection of baby foods is also available in most supermarkets, but in case you cannot find the instant formula to which your child is accustomed, bring along a supply in the 8-ounce "ready-to-feed" cans. Disposable nursers are expensive but handy. If you breast-feed your baby, there is no reason you can't enjoy your trip; just be sure you get enough rest and liquids.

Good toys to take for infants are the same sorts of things they like at home — well-made, bright huggables and chewables; for small children, a favorite doll or stuffed animal for comfort, spelling and counting games, and tying, braiding, and lacing activities; for older children, playing cards, travel board games with magnetic pieces, and hand-held electronic games. Softcover books and art materials (crayons, markers, paper, scissors, glue sticks, and stickers) ward off boredom for children of most ages, as do radio-cassette players with headphones. Take along a variety of musical and storytelling cassettes, extra batteries, and maybe even an extra set of headphones so that two children can listen. *Advice:* Avoid toys that are noisy, breakable, or spillable, those that require a large play area, and those that have lots of little pieces that can be scattered and lost. When traveling, coordinate activities with attention spans; dole out playthings one at a time so you don't run out of diversions before you get where you're going. Children become restless during long waiting periods, and a game plus a small snack — such as a box of raisins or crackers — will help keep them quiet. It is also a good idea to carry tissues, Band-Aids, a pocket medicine kit (described above), and moistened washclothes.

GETTING THERE AND GETTING AROUND: Begin early to investigate all available discount and charter flights, as well as any package deals and special rates offered by the major airlines. Booking is sometimes required up to 2 months in advance. You may well find that charter plans offer no reductions for children, or not enough to offset the risk of last-minute delays or other inconveniences to which charters are subject. The major scheduled airlines, on the other hand, almost invariably provide hefty discounts for children (for specific information on fares and in-flight accommodations for children, also see *Traveling by Plane*).

PLANE: When you make your reservations, let the airlines know that you are traveling with a child. As a general rule, a child under 2 years of age flies to Europe at 10% of the fare paid by the accompanying adult as long as the child is kept on the adult's lap. However, particularly on longer flights, this may not be comfortable. (Don't despair, though. If there are empty seats around you, no one will object to your putting your child down. Armrests on airplanes are generally removable.) A second child under 2 without a second accompanying adult flies to Europe at the same fare applicable to children from 2 through 11, which is usually half an adult economy fare and two-thirds an adult APEX fare.

If traveling with an infant, request a bulkhead seat and ask to be given a bassinet. Request seats on the aisle if you have a toddler or if you think you will need to use the bathroom frequently. (Try to discourage children from being in the aisle when meals are served.) Carry onto the plane all you will need to care for and occupy your children during the flight — diapers, formula, "lovies," books, sweaters, and so on. (Never check as baggage any item essential to a child's well-being, such as prescription medicine.) Dress your baby simply, with a minimum of buttons and snaps, because the only place you may have to change a diaper is at your seat. The flight attendant can warm a bottle for you.

Just as you would request a vegetarian or kosher meal, you are entitled to ask for a hot dog or hamburger in lieu of the airline's regular dinner if you give at least 24 hours' notice. Some, but not all, airlines have baby food aboard. While you should bring along toys from home, you can also ask about children's diversions. Some carriers, such as Pan American, United, and Delta, have terrific free packages of games, coloring books, and puzzles.

When the plane takes off and lands, make sure your baby is nursing or has a bottle, pacifier, or thumb in its mouth. This sucking will make the child swallow and help to clear stopped ears. A piece of hard candy will do the same thing for an older child.

Avoid night flights. Since you probably won't sleep nearly as well as your kids, you risk an impossible first day at your destination, groggily taking care of your rested, energetic children. Nap time is, however, a good time to travel, especially for babies, and try to travel during off-hours, when there are apt to be extra seats. If you do have to take a long night flight, keep in mind that when you disembark, you will probably be tired and not really ready for sightseeing. The best thing to do is to head for your hotel, shower, have a snack, and take a nap. If your children are too excited to sleep, give them some toys to play with while you rest.

■**Note:** Newborn babies, whose lungs may not be able to adjust to the altitude, should not be taken aboard an airplane. And some airlines may refuse to allow a pregnant woman aboard in her 8th or 9th month for fear that something could go wrong with an in-flight birth. Check with the airline ahead of time and carry a letter from your doctor stating that you are fit to travel and indicating the estimated date of birth.

SHIP AND TRAIN: By ship, children under 12 usually travel at a considerably reduced fare. If you plan to travel by train when abroad, note that on some European railways, children under 4 travel free provided they do not occupy a seat; children under 4 occupying a seat and from ages 4 through 11 also often travel at a lower fare. The Eurailpass is good for unlimited train travel throughout Europe. It must be bought in the US, so plan before you leave.

ACCOMMODATIONS AND MEALS: Often a cot will be placed in a hotel room at little or no extra charge. If you wish to sleep in separate rooms, special rates are sometimes available for families in adjoining rooms; some places do not charge for children under a certain age. In many of the larger chain hotels, the staffs are more used to noisy or slightly misbehaving children. These hotels are also likely to have swimming pools or gamerooms — both popular with most young travelers. Write to the hotel in advance to discuss how old your children are, how long you plan to stay, and to ask for suggestions on sleeping arrangements.

You might want to look into accommodations along the way that will add to the color of your trip. For instance, the many country inns, farmhouses, and cottages throughout Europe can be a delightful experience for the whole family and provide a view of European life different from that gained in a conventional hotel. And don't forget castles and châteaus, many of which double as hotels. Children will love them. Camping facilities are often in beautiful, out-of-the-way spots and are generally good, well equipped, and less expensive than any hotel. (See *Accommodations* and *Camping and Caravanning, Hiking and Biking.*)

For the times you will want to be without the children — for an evening's entertainment or a particularly rigorous stint of sightseeing — it is possible to arrange for a baby sitter at the hotel desk. Whether the sitter is hired directly or through an agency, ask for and check references.

As far as food goes, don't deny yourself or your children the delights of a new cuisine. Encourage them to try new things and don't forget about picnics. There's nothing lovelier than stopping in your tracks at a beautiful view and eating lunch as you muse on the surroundings.

THINGS TO REMEMBER: If you are spending your vacation traveling, rather than visiting one spot or engaging in one activity, pace the days with children in mind; break the trip into half-day segments, with running around or "doing" time built in; keep travel time on the road to a maximum of 4 or 5 hours a day. First and foremost, don't forget that a child's attention span is far shorter than an adult's. Children don't have to see every museum or all of any museum to learn something from their trip; watching, playing with, and talking to other children can be equally enlightening experiences. Also, remember the places that children the world over love to visit: zoos, country fairs and small amusement parks, beaches and nature trails. Let your children lead the way sometimes — their perspective is different from yours, and they may help you see things you would never have noticed on your own.

Staying Healthy

The surest way to return home in good health is to be prepared for medical problems that might occur on vacation. Below we've outlined some things you need to think about before you go.

Obviously, your state of health is crucial to the success of a vacation. There's nothing like an injury or illness, whether serious or relatively minor, to dampen or destroy a holiday. And health problems always seem more debilitating when you are away. However, most problems can be prevented or greatly alleviated with intelligent foresight and attention to precautionary details.

Older travelers or anyone suffering from a chronic medical condition, such as diabetes, high blood pressure, cardiopulmonary disease, asthma, or ear, eye, or sinus trouble, should consult a physician before leaving home. A checkup is advisable. A dental checkup is not a bad idea, either.

People with conditions requiring special consideration when traveling should consider seeing, in addition to their regular physician, a specialist in travel medicine. For a referral in a particular community, contact the nearest medical school or ask a local doctor to recommend such a specialist. The *American Society of Tropical Medicine and Hygiene* publishes a directory of more than 70 travel doctors across the country. Send a 9-by-12-inch self-addressed, stamped envelope ($1.05 postage) to Dr. Leonard Marcus, Tufts University, 200 W. Boro Rd., North Grafton, MA 01536.

FIRST AID: Put together a compact, personal medical kit including Band-Aids, first-aid cream, antiseptic, nose drops, insect repellent, aspirin, an extra pair of prescription glasses, sunglasses, or contact lenses (and a copy of your prescription for glasses or lenses), over-the-counter remedies for diarrhea, indigestion, and motion sickness, a thermometer, and a supply of those prescription medicines you take regularly. In a corner of your kit, keep a list of all the drugs you have brought and their purpose as well as duplicate copies of your doctor's prescriptions (or a note from your doctor). These copies could come in handy if you are ever questioned by police or airport authorities about any drugs you are carrying and in case you need to refill any prescriptions in the event of loss. It is also a good idea to ask your doctor to prepare a medical identification card that includes such information as your blood type, your social security number, any allergies or chronic health problems you have, and your medical insurance information. Considering the essential contents of this kit, keep it with you, rather than in your luggage.

SUNBURN: Depending on when and where you're vacationing, the burning power of the sun can be phenomenal and can quickly cause severe sunburn or sunstroke. To protect yourself, wear sunglasses, take along a broad-brimmed hat and cover-up, and use a sunscreen lotion. When choosing a sunscreen, look for one that has a PABA (para-amino-benzoic acid) base. PABA blocks out most of the harmful ultraviolet rays of the sun.

Some tips on tanning:

1. Allow only 20 minutes or so the first day; increase your exposure gradually.
2. You are most likely to get a painful burn when the sun is the strongest, between 10 AM and 2 PM.
3. When judging if you've had enough sun, remember that time in the water (in terms of exposure to ultraviolet rays) is the same as time lying on the beach.
4. A beach umbrella or other cover doesn't keep all the rays of the sun from reaching you. If you are sensitive to light, be especially careful.
5. As many ultraviolet rays reach you on cloudy days as on sunny days. Even if you don't feel hot, you are still exposed to rays.

If, despite these precautions, you find yourself with a painful sunburn, take a cooling bath, apply a first-aid spray or the liquid of an aloe plant, and stay out of the sun. If you develop a more serious burn and experience chills, fever, nausea, headaches, or dizziness, consult a doctor at once.

WATER SAFETY: Europe is famous for its beaches, but it's important to remember that the sea, especially the wild Atlantic and the Mediterranean, can be treacherous. A few precautions are necessary. Beware of the undertow, that current of water running back down the beach after a wave has washed ashore; it can knock you off your feet and into the surf. Even more dangerous is the riptide, a strong current of water running against the tide, which can pull you out toward sea. If this happens, don't panic or try to fight the current, because it will only exhaust you; instead, ride it out while waiting for it to subside, which usually happens not too far from shore, or try swimming away parallel to the beach.

INSECTS AND OTHER PESTS: Mosquitoes, horseflies, and other biting insects can be troublesome, so as we have said, be sure to pack a repellent. If you are bitten by a snake, call a doctor immediately. Insects such as cockroaches and water bugs thrive in warm weather, but pose no serious health threat.

FOOD AND WATER: Water is clean and potable throughout most of Europe. Still, travelers may want to do as the Europeans do and drink bottled water, at least at the beginning of the trip. This is not because there is something wrong with the water, but because any new microbes to which the digestive tract has not had time to become accustomed may cause mild stomach or intestinal upsets. Particularly in rural areas, the water supply may not be thoroughly purified and residents either have developed immunities to the natural bacteria or boil it for drinking. You should also avoid drinking water from streams or freshwater pools. In campgrounds, water is usually indicated as drinkable or for washing only — if you're not sure, ask.

Milk is pasteurized throughout Europe, and milk products (cheese, yogurt, ice cream, and so on) are safe to eat, as are fresh produce, meat, poultry, and fish. Because of Mediterranean pollution, however, fish and shellfish should be eaten cooked.

Following all these precautions will not guarantee an illness-free trip, but should minimize the risk. As a final hedge against economic if not physical problems, make sure your health insurance will cover all eventualities while you are away. If not, there are policies designed specifically for travel. Many are worth investigating. As with all insurance, they seem like a waste of money until you need them. For further information, also see *Insurance* and *Medical and Legal Aid and Consular Services,* in this section.

HELPFUL PUBLICATIONS: Practically every phase of health care — before, during, and after a trip — is covered in *The New Traveler's Health Guide* by Drs. Patrick J. Doyle and James E. Banta. It is available for $4.95, plus $2 postage and handling, from Acropolis Books Ltd., 2400 17th St. NW, Washington, DC 20009-9964 (phone: 800-451-7771).

For more information regarding preventive health care for travelers, contact *IAMAT* (*International Association for Medical Assistance to Travelers*), 417 Center St., Lewiston, NY 14092 (phone: 716-754-4883) or write to the US Government Printing Office, Washington, DC 20402, for the US Public Health Service's booklet *Health Information for International Travel* (HEW Publication CDC-86-8280; enclose check or money order for $4.75 payable to Superintendent of Documents).

On the Road

Credit and Currency

 It may seem hard to believe, but one of the greatest (and least understood) costs of travel is money itself. If that sounds simplistic, consider the fact that you can lose as much as 30% of your dollars' value simply by changing money at the wrong place or in the wrong form. So your one single objective in relation to the care and retention of your travel funds is to make them stretch as far as possible. When you do spend money, it should be on things that expand and enhance your travel experience, so that no buying power is lost due to carelessness or lack of knowledge. This requires more than merely ferreting out the best airfare or the most charming budget hotel. It means being canny about the management of money itself. Herewith, a primer on making money go as far as possible overseas. (For a country-by-country listing of foreign currencies throughout Europe, see FACTS IN BRIEF.)

FOREIGN EXCHANGE: Rule number one is as simple as it is inflexible: Exchange your money only at banks, where dollars always buy the greatest amount of foreign currency. Unless someone holds a gun to your head, never (repeat: *never*) exchange dollars for foreign currency at hotels, restaurants, or retail shops, where you are sure to lose a significant amount of your dollars' buying power.

Rule number two: Estimate your needs carefully; if you overbuy you lose twice — buying and selling back. Every time you exchange money, someone is making a profit, and rest assured it isn't you. In countries with foreign exchange restrictions (most Eastern European countries), you may be forced to turn in local currency when you leave (and in extreme cases, without the opportunity to sell it back). And even in countries with no such restrictions, you will have to declare and pay taxes on anything over a specified amount. Use up foreign notes before leaving, saving just enough for airport departure taxes (which often must be paid in local currency), other last-minute incidentals, and tips.

Rule number three: Don't buy money on the black market. The exchange rate may be better, but it is a common practice to pass off counterfeit bills to unsuspecting foreigners who aren't familiar with the local currency. It's usually a sucker's game, and you are almost always the sucker; it can also land you in jail.

Rule number four: Learn the local currency quickly and keep aware of daily fluctuations in the exchange rate. These are listed in the English-language *International Herald Tribune* daily for the preceding day, as well as in every major newspaper in Europe. Banks post their daily exchange rates, which might vary by a few cents from a neighboring bank's posted rate. Rates change to some degree every day. For rough calculations, it is quick and safe to use round figures, but for purchases and actual currency exchanges, carry a small pocket calculator that helps you compute the exact rate. Inexpensive calculators specifically designed to quickly convert currency amounts for travelers are widely available.

TIP PACKS: It's not a bad idea to buy a *small* amount of coins and banknotes before your departure. But note the emphasis on "small," because exchange rates for these "tip packs" are uniformly terrible. Still, their advantages are threefold: You become familiar with the currency (really the only way to guard against being cheated during your first few hours in a new country); you are guaranteed some money should you arrive when a bank or exchange counter isn't open or available; and you don't have to depend on hotel desks, porters, or taxi drivers to change your money. A "tip pack" is the only foreign currency you should buy before you leave.

TRAVELER'S CHECKS: It's wise to carry traveler's checks on the road instead of (or in addition to) cash, since it's possible to replace them if they are stolen or lost; travelers can usually receive partial or full replacement funds the same day if they have their purchase receipt and proper identification. Issued in various denominations and available in both US dollars and foreign currencies, with adequate proof of identification (credit cards, driver's license, passport), traveler's checks are as good as cash in most hotels, restaurants, stores, and banks; listed below are types of traveler's checks readily recognized and convertible in Europe. However, don't assume that restaurants, smaller shops, or other establishments in small towns are going to be able to change checks of large denominations. Worldwide, more and more establishments are beginning to restrict the amount of traveler's checks they will accept or cash, so it is wise to purchase at least some of your checks in small denominations — say, $20 or the equivalent in the local currency. Also, don't expect to change them into US currency except at banks and international airports.

Every type of traveler's check is legal tender in banks around the world, and each company guarantees full replacement if checks are lost or stolen. After that the similarity ends. Some charge a fee for purchase, others are free; you can buy traveler's checks at almost any bank, and some are available by mail. Most important, each traveler's check issuer differs slightly in its refund policy — the amount refunded immediately, the accessibility of refund locations, and the availability of a 24-hour refund service.

We cannot overemphasize the importance of knowing how to replace lost or stolen checks. All of the traveler's check companies have agents around the world, both in their own name and at other associated agencies (usually, but not necessarily, banks), where refunds can be obtained during business hours. Most of them also have 24-hour toll-free telephone lines, and some will even provide emergency funds to tide you over on a Sunday.

Be sure to make a photocopy of the refund instructions that will be given to you by the issuing institution at the time of purchase. To avoid complications should you need to redeem lost checks, keep the purchase receipt and an accurate list, by serial number, of the checks that have been spent or cashed. You may want to incorporate this information in an "emergency packet," also including your passport number and date of issue, the numbers of the credit cards you are carrying, and any other bits of information you can't bear to be without. Always keep these records separate from the checks and original records themselves (you may want to give them to a traveling companion to hold).

Although most people understand the necessity of carrying travel funds in the form of traveler's checks as protection against loss or theft, an equally good reason is that traveler's checks invariably get a better rate of exchange than cash — usually by at least 1%. The reasons are technical, but it is a fact of travel life that should not be ignored.

That 1% won't do you much good, however, if you have already spent it buying your traveler's checks. Several of the major traveler's check companies charge 1% for the privilege of using their checks; others don't, but the issuing institution (i.e., the particular bank at which you purchase them) may itself charge a fee. Thomas Cook checks issued in US currency are free if you make your travel arrangements through its travel agency, for example; and if you purchase traveler's checks at a bank in which you or your company maintains significant accounts (especially commercial accounts of some size), the bank might absorb the 1% fee as a courtesy. American Express traveler's checks are available without charge to members of the *Automobile Association of America* (*AAA*) if obtained at an *AAA* office.

American Express, Citicorp, Thomas Cook, MasterCard, and Visa all offer traveler's checks, but not at all locations. Call the service numbers listed below to find a participating branch near you. Note, however, that the exchange rates are usually far less favorable than those available from banks abroad, so it is generally better to carry the bulk of your travel funds overseas in US dollar traveler's checks. Here is a list of the major companies whose traveler's checks are accepted in Europe and the numbers to call in case loss or theft makes replacement necessary:

American Express: To report lost or stolen checks in the continental US, call 800-221-7282. From Europe, American Express advises travelers to call 44-273571-600 in Brighton, England; another (slower) option is to call 801-968-8300, collect; or contact the nearest American Express office. (As we went to press, American Express had just announced a 3-hour replacement of lost or stolen traveler's checks.)

Bank of America: To report lost or stolen checks in the US, call 800-227-3460, in Europe, 19-0590-2122; elsewhere worldwide, 415-624-5400 or 415-622-3800, collect.

Citicorp: To report lost or stolen checks in the US, call 800-645-6556; from Europe and elsewhere worldwide, call 813-623-1709, collect.

MasterCard: To report lost or stolen checks in the US, call 800-223-9920. In Europe call the New York office, 212-974-5696, collect, and they will direct you to the nearest branch of MasterCard or Wagons-Lits, their European agent.

Thomas Cook MasterCard: To report lost or stolen checks in the US, call 800-223-9920. In Europe call the New York office, 212-974-5696, collect, and they will direct you to the nearest branch of Thomas Cook or Wagons-Lits, their European agent.

Visa: To report lost or stolen checks in the continental US, 800-227-6811; from Europe, 415-574-7111, collect. From Europe, you can also call this London number collect: 01-937-8091.

CREDIT CARDS: There are two different kinds of credit cards available to consumers in the US, and travelers must decide which kind best serves their interests — although they often elect to carry both. "Convenience" or "travel and entertainment" cards — American Express, Diners Club, and Carte Blanche — are widely accepted. They cost the cardholder a basic annual membership fee ($35 to $50 is typical for these three), but put no strict limit on the amount that may be charged on the card in any month. However, the entire amount charged must be paid in full at the end of each billing period (usually a month), so the cardholder is not actually extended any long-term credit.

"Bank cards" are also rarely issued free these days (with the exception of Sears' Discover Card), and certain services they provide (check cashing, for example) can carry an extra charge. But this category comprises *real* credit cards, in the sense that the cardholder has the privilege of paying a small amount (1/36 is typical) of the total outstanding balance in each billing period. For this privilege, the cardholder is charged a high annual interest rate (currently three to four times the going bank passbook savings rate) on the balance owed. Many banks now charge interest from the purchase date, not from the first billing date (as they used to do); consider this when you are calculating the actual cost of a purchase. In addition, a maximum is set on the total amount the cardholder can charge, which represents the limit of credit the card company is willing to extend. The major bank cards are Visa and MasterCard, with Discover growing rapidly.

Getting any credit card will involve a fairly extensive credit check; to pass, you will need a job (at which you have worked for at least a year), a minimum salary, and a good credit rating.

Note that some establishments you may encounter during the course of your travels may not honor any credit cards and some may not honor all cards, so there is a practical reason to carry more than one when you travel. Also keep in mind that some major US credit cards may be issued under different names in Europe. In Europe, MasterCard goes under the name Eurocard and Visa is often called Carte Bleue — wherever the equivalents are accepted, MasterCard and Visa may be used. The following is a list of credit cards that enjoy wide domestic and international acceptance:

American Express: Emergency personal check cashing at American Express or representatives' offices (up to $200 cash in local currency, $800 in traveler's checks); emergency personal check cashing for guests at participating hotels (up to $250), and, for holders of airline tickets, at participating airlines in the US (up to $250). Extended payment plan for cruises, tours, and railway and airline tickets, as well as other pre-paid travel arrangements. $100,000 free travel accident insurance on plane, train, bus, and ship if ticket was charged to card; up to $1 million additional low-cost flight insurance available. Contact American Express Card, PO Box 39, Church St. Station, New York, NY 10008 (phone: 212-477-5700 in New York; 800-528-4800 elsewhere in the US).

Carte Blanche: Extended payment plan for air travel (up to $2,000). $150,000 free travel accident insurance on plane, train, and ship if ticket was charged to card, plus $1,250 checked or carry-on baggage insurance and $25,000 rental car insurance. Contact Carte Blanche, PO Box 17326, Denver, CO 80217 (phone: 800-525-9135 in the US; 303-790-2433 abroad, cardholders may call collect).

Diners Club: Emergency personal check cashing at participating Citibank branches and other designated banks worldwide (up to $1,000 in a 14-day period); emergency personal check cashing for guests at participating hotels (up to $250 per stay). Qualified card members are eligible for extended payment plan. $350,000 free travel accident insurance on plane, train, and ship if ticket was charged to your card, plus $1,250 checked and carry-on baggage insurance and $25,000 rental car insurance. Medical, legal, and travel assistance available worldwide (phone: 800-356-3448 in the US; collect from outside the US, 214-680-6480). Contact Diners Club, PO Box 17326, Denver, CO 80217 (phone: 800-525-9135 in the US; 303-790-2433, collect, for customer service; 303-790-8632, collect 24 hours, for lost or stolen cards).

Discover Card: Created by Sears, Roebuck and Co., it provides the holder with cash advance at more than 500 locations in the US and offers a revolving credit line for purchases at a wide range of service establishments. Other deposit, lending, and investment services are also available. For information, call 800-858-5588 in the US (if you can't reach this number by dialing directly, dial for an operator who will be able to place the call).

MasterCard: Cash advance at participating banks worldwide, and a revolving credit line for purchases at a wide range of service establishments. Interest charge on unpaid balance and other details are set by issuing bank. Check with your bank for information. MasterCard also offers a 24-hour emergency lost card service (phone: 800-336-8472 in the US; outside the US, 415-574-7700, collect).

Visa: Cash advance at participating banks worldwide, and a revolving credit line for purchases at a wide range of service establishments provided by issuer. Interest charge on unpaid balance and other details are set by issuing bank. Check with your bank for information. Visa also offers a 24-hour emergency lost card service (phone: 800-336-8472 in the US; outside the US, 415-574-7700, collect).

One of the thorniest problems relating to the use of credit cards abroad concerns the rate of exchange at which a purchase is charged. Be aware that the exchange rate in effect on the date that you make a foreign purchase or pay for a foreign service has nothing at all to do with the rate of exchange at which your purchase is billed to you when you get the invoice months later in the US. The amount American Express (and other convenience cards) charges is ultimately a function of the exchange rate in effect on the day your charge is received at an American Express service center, and there is a 1-year limit on the time a shop or hotel can take to forward its charge slips. The rate at which Visa and other bank cards process an item is a function of the rate at which the hotel's or shop's bank processed it.

The principle at work in this credit card–exchange rate roulette is simple but very hard to predict. You make a purchase at a particular dollar versus local currency exchange rate. If the dollar gets stronger in the time between purchase and billing, your purchase actually costs you less than you anticipated. If the dollar drops in value during the interim, you pay more than you thought you would. There isn't much you can do about these vagaries except to follow one very broad, very clumsy rule of thumb: If the dollar is doing well at the time of purchase, its value increasing against the local currency, use your credit card on the assumption it will still be doing well when billing takes place. If the dollar is doing badly, assume it will continue to do badly and pay with traveler's checks. If you get too badly stuck, the best recourse is to complain, loudly. Be aware, too, that most credit card companies charge an unannounced, un-itemized 1% fee for converting foreign currency charges to US dollars.

No matter what you are using — traveler's checks, credit cards, or cash — plan ahead. Also, carry your travel funds carefully. You might consider carrying them (cash and traveler's checks) in more than one place. Never put money in a back pocket or an open purse. Money should be kept in a buttoned front pocket, in a money purse pinned inside your shirt or blouse, or in one of the convenient money belts or leg pouches sold by many travel shops. It may be quaint and old-fashioned, but it's safe.

SENDING MONEY ABROAD: If you have used up your traveler's checks, cashed as many emergency personal checks as your credit card allows, drawn on your cash advance line to the fullest extent, and still need money, have it sent abroad via the *Western Union Telegraph Company.* A friend or relative can go, cash in hand, to any of *Western Union*'s 9,000 offices in the US, where, for a *minimum* charge of $11 (it rises with the amount of the transaction) plus a $22 international bank fee, the funds will be transferred to *Western Union*'s correspondent bank or the main post office branch in the country you're visiting. When the money arrives in Europe, you will not be notified; you must go to the bank or post office to inquire. The funds will be turned over in local currency, based on the rate of exchange in effect on the day of receipt. For a higher fee, the US party to this transaction may use a MasterCard or Visa card to send up to $2,000 by phone by dialing *Western Union*'s toll-free number (800-325-4176) anywhere in the US. Allow 2 to 5 business days for delivery (faster than any other form of international bank transfer, a method usually so cumbersome and time-consuming that it is of little use to the average traveler).

If you are literally down to your last centime, the nearest US consulate (see *Medical and Legal Aid and Consular Services*) will let you call home collect to set these matters in motion.

Accommodations

 From elegant, centuries-old castle resorts to modern, functional high-rises and modest, inexpensive inns, it's easy to be comfortable and well cared for on almost any budget in Europe. Admittedly, the Mediterranean coast is full of deluxe establishments providing expensive services to people with money to burn, but, fortunately, affordable alternatives have always been available, particularly in the countryside.

On the whole, deluxe and first class accommodations in Europe, especially in the large metropolitan centers (London, Paris, and so on), are just as expensive as the same types of accommodations in the US (see *Calculating Costs,* in this section). When the dollar is strong, such top-of-the-line establishments are within the range of a great number of travelers who previously would not have been able to afford them. But lately, the rate of exchange has rendered princely accommodations very pricey. Once upon a time, such things as the superiority of New World plumbing made many of the numerous less expensive alternatives unacceptable for North Americans. Today, the gap has closed considerably, and in most countries the majority of hostelries catering to the tourist trade are likely to be at least adequate in their basic facilities. When shopping around, also keep in mind that although for all accommodations in Europe, the price quoted must include the minimum 10% value added tax (VAT), an additional service charge, usually of 10%, 12½%, or 15%, is often added to hotel and guesthouse bills.

Our accommodations choices are included in the *Best in Town* sections of THE CITIES and in the *Best en Route* sections of each tour route in DIRECTIONS. They have been selected for a variety of traveling budgets, but the lists are not comprehensive; with some diligent searching, before you leave and en route, you can turn up an equal number of "special places" that are uniquely yours. Also consult the numerous brochures and booklets available free from European tourist offices in the US (see *Tourist Information Offices* for addresses).

RESERVATIONS: To the extent that you are able to settle on a precise itinerary beforehand, it is best to make advance reservations for accommodations in any major European city or resort area, even if you are traveling during the off-season — to be sure of finding space in the hotel of your choice, several months before arrival is not too soon to make the booking. Hotel rooms in the larger provincial cities should also be reserved ahead year-round. Because many of them are also important convention centers, even off-season travelers may find hotel space scarce and Full signs everywhere if a large convention is in town. Also keep in mind that larger hotels are the ones most frequently booked as 2- and 3-day stopover centers for the thousands of tour groups ranging the Continent.

During the peak travel season — May to October — visitors should expect to pay a premium for traveling in Europe. However, not even a willingness to pay for top accommodations will guarantee a room if you don't have reservations. This also can be the case in smaller cities, villages, and throughout the countryside (especially in areas near major summer destinations), where the number of rooms and limited facilities, not the price, is likely to be the qualifying factor. It is wise to make reservations as far in advance as possible for popular tourist areas throughout Europe, and this advice becomes particularly compelling during July and August, when Europeans themselves take to the road, packing vacation spots and coastal resorts.

All the hotel entries in the *Best in Town* sections of THE CITIES chapters include phone numbers for reservations; however, the simplest approach may be to leave it all to a travel agent, who will provide this service at no charge if the hotels in question pay commissions. The regional hotel guides distributed by government tourist offices often use a symbol to show which establishments pay such a commission — the larger and more expensive ones invariably do, and more and more budget hotels are beginning to follow suit. If the one you pick doesn't, the travel agent may charge a fee to cover costs or you may have to make the reservation yourself.

Reserving a room yourself is not difficult if you intend to stay mainly in hotels that are members of chains or associations, whether European ones with US representatives or American ones with hotels overseas. Most international hotel chains list their toll-free (800) reservation numbers in the white pages of the telephone directory, and any hotel within a chain can assure reservations for you at sister facilities. Naturally, the more links in the chain, the more likely that an entire stay can be booked with a minimum number of letters or phone calls to one central reservations system. If booking with primarily European establishments, either a travel agent or the particular European government tourist office will be able to tell you who in the US represents the chain or a particular hotel. (The US phone numbers of a few of the chains and associations in Europe are given in the discussion of hotels below.)

Hotels that are not represented in the US will have to be contacted directly. If you choose to write rather than telephone, it's a good idea to enclose at least two International Reply Coupons (sold at post offices) to facilitate a response and to leave plenty of time for the answer. Give full details of your requirements and several alternate dates, if possible. You will probably be asked to send a deposit for one night's lodging, payable by foreign draft; in return, be sure to get written confirmation of the reservation.

If the hotel you want has no rooms available on your chosen dates, take heart. The advice to make reservations early is always woven into every travel article; making a *late* reservation may be almost as good advice. It's not at all unusual for hotel rooms, totally unavailable as far as 6 months in advance, to suddenly become available 6 days — or even 6 hours — before your arrival. Cancellations tend to occur closer to rather than farther from a designated date, and somewhat flexible travelers recognize that there will almost always be some cancellation on the day they plan to arrive. Though not all travelers would face the prospect of arriving in a strange city without a reservation with equal sangfroid, there are services that help book empty rooms for those who risk it. Generally, information on these services is available at the airport information desk or from the local tourist board office.

OVERBOOKING: The worldwide travel boom has brought with it some abuses that are pretty much standard operating procedure in any industry facing demand that frequently outstrips supply. Anticipating a certain percentage of no-shows, hotels routinely overbook rooms. When cancellations don't occur and everybody with a reservation arrives as promised, it's not impossible to find yourself with a valid reservation for which no room exists.

There's no sure way to avoid all the pitfalls of overbooking, but you can minimize the risks. Always carry evidence of your confirmed reservation. This should be a direct communication from the hotel — to you or your travel agent — and should specify the exact dates and duration of your accommodations and the price. The weakest form of confirmation is the voucher slip a travel agent routinely issues, since it carries no official indication that the hotel itself has verified your reservation.

Even better is the increasing opportunity to guarantee hotel reservations by giving the hotel (or its reservation system) your credit card number and agreeing that the hotel is authorized to charge you for that room no matter what. It's still possible to cancel if you do so before 6 PM of the day of your reservation (before 4 PM in some areas), but when you do cancel under this arrangement, make sure you get a cancellation number to protect you from being billed erroneously.

If all these precautions fail and you are left standing at the reservation desk with a reservation the hotel clerk won't honor, you have a last resort: Complain as long and as loudly as necessary to get satisfaction! The person who makes the most noise usually gets the last room in the house. It might as well be you.

What if you can't get reservations in the first place? This is a problem that often confronts businesspeople who can't plan months ahead. The word from savvy travelers is that a bit of currency (perhaps attached discreetly to a business card) often increases your chances with recalcitrant desk clerks. There are less venal ways of improving your odds, however. If you are making reservations for business, ask an associate at your destination to make reservations for you.

There is a good reason to do this above and beyond the very real point that a resident' has the broadest knowledge of local hotels. Often a hotel will appear sold out on its computer when in fact a few rooms are available. The proliferation of computerized reservations has made it unwise for a hotel to indicate that it suddenly has five rooms available (from cancellations) when there might be 30 or 40 travel agents lined up in the computer waiting for them. That small a number of vacancies is much more likely to be held by the hotel for its own sale, so a local associate is an invaluable conduit to these otherwise inaccessible rooms.

Hotels and Guesthouses: One way to select the type of hotel that fits your finances and personal needs is to become familiar with the official hotel grading system used in the countries you plan to visit. Not all European governments grade hotels, but most do. Many use a system of five categories, assigning a letter or a certain number of stars to each according to specific criteria, such as the number of rooms, the percentage of rooms with private bathrooms, and the presence of other amenities. Behind these grades may be found anything from a luxurious, turreted castle redolent of European history to a large, modern, and functional high-rise or a simple, family-run hostelry. While the results of these assessments may not tally with your own judgments, and while the five-star (deluxe) or one-star (plain but comfortable) hotels of one country may not measure up to those of another, by knowing the rating in advance you'll have a reasonable idea of the type of accommodations to expect — and their price. The national tourist offices of countries that grade hotels should be able to furnish you with a general price range for each category in their system.

Guesthouses, called "pensions" on the Continent, are often rated on a scale similar to the one used for hotels. Though it is sometimes difficult to distinguish between some of the smaller, family-run hotels and the guesthouses, the latter are almost always family enterprises and tend to be more informal and personal in their hospitality. The official dividing line is the meal service: The hotel dining room is open to non-guests. Guesthouses cater exclusively to their guests, and in some cases will serve breakfast only (generally a full one, which is included in the room price), though usually a partial- or full-board plan by the day or the week will be available. Guesthouses, too, can vary in atmosphere from old, converted Georgian residences to brand-new, built-for-the-purpose premises. Bathroom facilities vary considerably: in a top-graded hotel, most rooms will likely have private bathrooms; in a top-graded guesthouse, some rooms with private bath may be available; in either hotel or guesthouse where a private bath is lacking, the room will often have hot and cold running water.

A great many hotels in Europe are members of chains or hotel associations. Some of the well-known non-European names with properties in Europe, particularly in major cities, are: *Hilton International* (phone: 800-445-8667), with 80 properties, including three- to five-star hotels; *Holiday Inn* (phone: 800-465-4329), with 74 European establishments; *Inter-Continental* (phone: 800-327-0200), with 50 four- to five-star hotels; and *Best Western,* a group of about 1,460 independent three- to four-star "L" hotels in 31 countries linked to *Best Western International* (for a directory, the *Best Western International Atlas & Hotel Guide: Europe & Israel,* call 800-274-6835 or 800-528-1234).

Among the larger European chains, whose names may be less familiar but many of whom nevertheless have a US office that will provide information and take reservations, is *Pullman International,* a group of approximately 125 hotels in Europe subdivided into *Pullman* (deluxe and first class rated hotels), the *Altéa* (first class and superior rated hotels, but in secondary cities)*,* and the *Arcade* (primo and budget hotels). *Pullman*'s US representative can be reached at 200 W. 57th St., New York, NY 10019 (phone: 212-757-6500 or 800-223-9862). Reservations for all *Pullman* properties can also be made through *Utell International,* 10605 Burt Circle, Omaha, NE 68114 (phone: 800-44-UTELL). *Mercure,* with approximately 100 three-star hotels throughout Europe, *Novotel,* with approximately 238 three-star hotels, *Sofitel,* with about 55 four-star hotels, and *Ibis,* with about 250 budget hotels, are all represented by *Resinter Reservations,* 2 Overhill Rd., Scarsdale, NY 10583 (phone: 800-221-4542).

Other European hotel associations include names such as *Minotels Europe,* (phone: 800-336-4668), with 600 tourist class establishments in 20 countries, and *Trusthouse Forte* (phone: 800-225-5843), with 230 three- to five-star hotels throughout Europe.

SPECIAL PLACES: Among the most interesting accommodations in Europe are those truly distinctive and frequently historic facilities whose ambience and style reflect something special of the country they are in. Examples of these are the country inns, manor houses, and bed-and-breakfast establishments of Britain and Ireland; the famed *relais* of France; converted castles in Germany; the architecturally distinctive *paradores* of Spain; the resort health spas of southeastern Europe; and Italy's *pensiones,* virtually a cultural institution within that country, although this style of accommodation has long been available throughout the Continent. Many of these unique hostelries are included in the individual reports in THE CITIES and in "Best en Route" in DIRECTIONS.

British Castles and Country House Hotels – Found throughout the British Isles and neighboring islands, these inns specialize in the traditional atmosphere, service, and hospitality of the great English country estates. Many once were country homes, manor houses, or castles, and a number are noteworthy for architectural features, gardens or parklands, riverside or lake settings, or locations in dell, dale, and mountain. The real attraction, however, is the history associated with so many of them and their antique decors. Most have modern facilities (television sets, private baths) along with traditional features such as fireplaces and sitting rooms. They are much sought out by the British themselves as weekend retreats. Weekend reservations are a must; midweek reservations are strongly recommended during high season. Prices range roughly from $40 to $125 and up per person, including breakfast. For information, contact the British Tourist Authority.

Relais & Châteaux – Most members of this association are in France, but the group does extend to many other countries. Some properties are actually ancient castles or palaces — dating back more than 1,000 years — which have been converted to hotels. Others — the *relais* — are old inns, manor houses, even converted mills, convents, and monasteries. A few well-known city and resort establishments are included, such as the *Crillon* in Paris and the *Marbella Club* in Spain, but most are in quiet country surroundings, graced with parks and flowering gardens. *Relais & Châteaux* hotels are often expensive, but no more than you would pay for deluxe, authentically elegant accommodations and service anywhere in the world (and many are not all that costly). All have good restaurants (another group of association members, *Relais Gourmands,* is composed of especially fine restaurants), and the properties themselves adhere to uniformly high standards. The *Relais* catalogue ($5) is available in travel bookstores or by mail from David B. Mitchell & Company, 200 Madison Ave., New York, NY 10016 (phone: 212-696-1323 or 800-372-1323).

Gast im Schloss – Germany's contribution to high style and historic accommodations is this association of hotels and restaurants in castles, mansions, and historic buildings. Most of these properties have exceptionally picturesque settings and surroundings — on hills overlooking the Rhine, alongside lakes, or in densely wooded parks and parklands. Though stylish and often grand, there is nonetheless a prevailing sense of informality in most of the hotels. All have modern facilities and many offer numerous activities — tennis, riding, hunting, fishing, swimming, golf — either on the property or nearby. Prices are moderate to expensive, the atmosphere friendly and hospitable, and many of the properties present the romantic appeal of dinner before an open fireplace and a room in a castle turret. Special itineraries have been designed for motorists who want to visit several hotels in the association. An illustrated *Gast im Schloss* booklet is available from the German National Tourist Office.

Paradores and Pousadas – Since 1928 the Spanish government has been renovating abandoned castles, old inns, and historic structures — and raising some modern buildings — to create its excellent system of *paradores*. Guests can stay in Moorish castles or splendidly ornate hunting chalets completely fitted out with modern facilities, and yet prices are often very reasonable. Within the Spanish system of grading hotels, *paradores* range from three- to four-star establishments, with prices for a double room in 1989 ranging from approximately $85 to $135. Tax, tip, and breakfast are included in such figures, which vary little from low to high season. Portugal has a similar network of state-run inns called *pousadas*. Some are newly built; others are converted historic buildings, palaces, and monasteries; all have modern conveniences. Rates for a room for two range from about $60 to $110, may be somewhat lower during the off-season and at the higher end of the scale during high season, and include tax, tips, and breakfast. For further information, contact the Spanish and Portuguese National Tourist Offices, or Marketing Ahead, 433 Fifth Ave., New York, NY 10016 (phone: 212-686-9213).

Pensiones – Italy's contribution to continental accommodations happily remains part of the entire European travel scene. *Pensiones* (the anglicized spelling is *pensions*) are ideal for the visitor wishing to spend some time getting to know a city. Their chief attractions are family-style quarters for a limited number of visitors, home meals for those who wish to dine in-house, and more reasonable prices than one would pay at a hotel. In other words, *pensiones* offer a more personal type of living — and economy — for those who are traveling on their own. Whatever may be sacrificed in the way of front desk and other services at regular hotels is usually compensated for at *pensiones* by an element of charm. The prices of these establishments in Italy last year ranged from about $35 to $75 (including taxes, without meals) for a double room with private bath, although it must be pointed out that few of the cheaper establishments have private baths. The more expensive *pensiones* serve two or three meals a day and some — as in seaside resorts in summer — require that you take one or more of them. The cheaper may serve only breakfast. A list of *pensiones* in the main tourist centers is available directly from the Italian Government Travel Office.

Bed and Breakfast – Bed-and-breakfast establishments (commonly known as B&Bs) provide exactly what the name implies. Though any hotel or guesthouse does the same, it is unusual for a bed-and-breakfast establishment to offer the extra services found in the other establishments, and consequently the bed-and-breakfast route is often the least expensive way to go.

Beyond these two fundamentals, nothing else is predictable about going the bed-and-breakfast route. The bed may be in an extra room in a family home, in an apartment with separate entrance, or in a free-standing cottage elsewhere on the property. You may have a patio, garden, and pool at your door, or only the bare necessities. Accommodations range from private homes and lovely mansions to small inns and guesthouses. A private bath isn't always offered, so check before you reserve. The best rule of thumb is to find out as much as you can before you book to avoid disappointment.

In the United Kingdom, where they are a staple of the low-cost lodging scene, they are found wherever there are extra rooms to let in a private home and a host or hostess willing to attend to the details of this homespun form of hospitality. They are also increasingly common elsewhere in Europe in both metropolitan and rural areas.

Travelers interested in B&B accommodations should contact the *European Experience,* 370 Lexington Ave., New York, NY 10017 (phone: 212-986-3800). Two other US B&B reservation services also listing B&Bs in Europe are *Travellers B&B Reservation Service,* PO Box 492, Mercer Island, WA 98040 (phone: 206-232-2345), handling reservations for B&Bs in Great Britain only, although the service also offers personal itinerary planning, and *Bed & Breakfast in Arizona,* PO Box 8628, Scottsdale, AZ 85252 (phone: 602-952-0134 or 995-2831, or 800-822-8885 in Arizona only), which books stays at B&Bs in Austria, Germany, Italy, Switzerland, and Great Britain.

Another useful source of information on B&B establishments overseas is the annual brochure published by the *Bed & Breakfast Reservations Services Worldwide, Inc.* (a trade association), which provides a list of its members for $3. To order the most recent edition, write to Bed & Breakfast Reservations Services Worldwide, Inc., PO Box 14797, Dept. 174, Baton Rouge, LA 70898, or call 504-346-1928.

Farmhouses – In the country, city people rediscover the sounds of songbirds and the smell of grass. Suburbanites get the chance to poke around an area where the nearest neighbor lives miles away. Parents can say to their children, "No, milk does not start out in a carton," and then prove it. Youngsters can see people who live differently, think differently, and have different values. But even if there were no lessons to be learned, a stay at a farm would be a decidedly pleasant way to pass a couple of weeks, so it's no wonder that all over Europe there are hundreds of farms welcoming guests.

Farm families in Europe often put up guests on a bed-and-breakfast basis — for a night or two or by the week, with weekly half-board plans available. Travelers can pick a traditional or a modern farm, a dairy farm over a sheep farm, one with ponies to ride, or one near a river for fishing. If the peace and quiet and the coziness of the welcome are appealing, a farmhouse can be an ideal base from which to explore a region by car or by foot and an especially good idea for those traveling with children.

Apartments, Homes, and Cottages – An alternative to hotels for the visitor content to stay in one spot for a week or more is to rent a house or an apartment (usually called a "flat" overseas). Known to Europeans as a "holiday let" or a "self-catering holiday," a vacation in a furnished rental has both the advantages and disadvantages of living "at home" abroad. It is certainly less expensive than staying in a first class hotel for the same period of time (though luxury rentals are available, too); it has the comforts of home, including a kitchen, which means saving on food; and it gives a sense of the country that a large hotel often cannot. On the other hand, a certain amount of housework is involved because if you don't eat out, you have to cook, and though some holiday lets come with a cleaning person, most don't.

A number of tourist boards issue region-by-region guides to cottages, castles, houses, bungalows, chalets, and flats for rent that meet some range of minimum standards. In addition, companies in the US arrange rentals in Europe. They handle bookings and confirmation paperwork, generally for a fee included in the rental price. Among such agencies are the following:

At Home Abroad: Offerings in Western Europe include castles, a fishing lodge, and elegant country houses. Photographs of properties can be requested by mail for a $50 registration fee. 405 E. 56th St., Apt. 6H, New York, NY 10022 (phone: 212-421-9165).

Country Homes and Castles: The specialty is large properties, as its name suggests. 4092 N. Ivy Rd., Atlanta, GA 30342 (phone: 404-231-5837), and 900 Wilshire Blvd., Suite 830, Los Angeles, CA 90017 (phone: 213-629-4861).

Eastone Overseas Accommodations: Cottages, houses, and apartments. 198 Southampton Drive, Jupiter, FL 33458 (phone: 407-575-6991/2).

Rent a Vacation Everywhere (RAVE): Modern condominium apartments, cottages, and castles throughout Europe, particularly France and Italy. 328 Main St. E., Suite 526, Rochester, NY 14604 (phone: 716-454-6440).

Villas International (formerly *Interchange*): Some 5,000 rentals include a good selection of simple cottages, some windmills, apartments, châteaux, and an assortment of other gracious properties. 71 W. 23rd St., New York, NY 10010 (phone: 212-929-7585 in New York State; 800-221-2260 elsewhere in the US).

HOME EXCHANGES: Another alternative for families who are content to stay in one place during their vacation is a home exchange: The Smith family from Chicago moves into the home of the Jimenez family in Madrid, while the Jimenez family enjoys a stay in the Smiths' home. The home exchange is an exceptionally inexpensive way to ensure comfortable, reasonable living quarters with amenities that no hotel could possibly offer, often including a car. Moreover, it allows you to live in a new community in a way that few tourists ever do: For a little while, at least, you will become something of a resident.

Several companies publish directories of individuals and families willing to trade homes with others for a specific period of time. In some cases, you must be willing to list your own home in the directory; in others, you can subscribe without appearing in it. Most listings are for straight exchanges only, but each of the directories also has a number of listings placed by people interested in either exchanging or renting (for instance, if they own a second home). Other types of arrangements include exchanges of hospitality while owners are in residence or youth exchanges, where your teenager is put up as a guest in return for your putting up their teenager at a later date. A few house-sitting opportunities also are available. In most cases, arrangements for the actual exchange take place directly between the you and the foreign host. There is no guarantee that you will find a listing in the area in which you are interested, but each of the organizations given below includes European homes among its hundreds or even thousands of foreign listings.

International Home Exchange Service/Intervac US: The $35 fee includes copies of the three directories published yearly and an option to list your home in one of them; a black-and-white photo may be included with the listing for an additional $8.50. A 20% discount is given to travelers over 65. Box 3975, San Francisco, CA 94119 (phone: 415-435-3497).

InterService Home Exchange, Inc.: An affiliate of *Intervac International,* this service publishes three directories annually which include more than 6,000 exchanges in over 300 countries worldwide. For $35, interested home-swappers are listed in and receive a copy of the February, March, and May directories; a black-and-white photo of your home may be included for an additional $10. Box 387, Glen Echo, MD 20812 (phone: 301-229-7567).

Loan-A-Home: Specializes in long-term (4 months or more — excluding July and August) housing arrangements worldwide for students and professors, businesspeople, and retirees, although its two annual directories (with supplements) carry a small list of short-term rentals and/or exchanges. $30 for a copy of one directory and one supplement; $40 for a copy of two directories and two supplements. 2 Park Lane, 6E, Mt. Vernon, NY 10552 (phone: 914-664-7640).

Vacation Exchange Club: Some 6,000 listings, about half of which are foreign. For $24.70, the subscriber receives two directories, one in late winter, one in the spring, and is listed in one. For $16, the subscriber receives both directories but no listing. 12006 111th Ave., Suite 12, Youngtown, AZ 85363 (phone: 602-972-2186).

World Wide Exchange: The $45 annual membership fee includes one listing (for house, yacht, or motorhome) and three guides. 1344 Pacific Ave., Suite 103, Santa Cruz, CA 95060 (phone: 408-425-0531).

Home Exchange International, with offices in New York, Los Angeles, London, Paris, and Milan, functions differently in that it publishes no directory and shepherds the exchange process most of the way. Interested parties supply *HEI* with photographs of themselves and their homes, information on the type of home they want and where, and a registration fee of $40. The company then works with its other offices to propose a few possibilities, and only when a match is made do the parties exchange names, addresses, and phone numbers. For this service, *HEI* charges a closing fee, which ranges from $150 to $450 for domestic or international switches from 2 weeks to 3 months and from $275 to $525 for switches longer than 3 months. Contact Home Exchange International, 185 Park Row, PO Box 878, New York, NY 10038-0272 (phone: 212-349-5340), or 22458 Ventura Blvd., Woodland Hills, CA 91364 (phone: 818-992-8990).

HOME STAYS: If the idea of actually staying in a private home as the guest of a foreign family appeals to you, check with the United States Servas Committee, which maintains a list of hosts throughout the world willing to throw open their doors to foreigners, entirely free of charge. The aim of this non-profit cultural program is to promote international understanding and peace, and every effort is made to discourage freeloaders. Servas will send you an application form and the name of the nearest of some 200 interviewers around the US for you to contact. After the interview, if you're approved, you'll receive documentation certifying you as a Servas traveler. There is a membership fee of $45 for an individual and there is also a deposit of $15 to receive the host list, refunded on its return. The list gives the name, address, age, occupation, and other particulars of the hosts, including languages spoken. From then on, it is up to you to write to them directly, and Servas makes no guarantee that you will be accommodated. If you are, you'll normally stay 2 nights.

Servas stresses that you should choose only people you really want to meet and that for this brief period you should be interested mainly in your hosts, not in sightseeing. It also suggests that one way to show your appreciation once you've returned home is to become a host yourself. The minimum age of a Servas traveler is 18 (however, children under 18 may accompany their parents), and though quite a few are young people who've just finished college, there are travelers (and hosts) in all age ranges and occupations. Contact Servas at 11 John St., Room 706, New York, NY 10038 (phone: 212-267-0252).

Another organization arranging home stays is *In the English Manner,* which specializes in home stays with British families, but also has a few Irish families who open their homes to guests. Prospective hosts have been visited by the company to assure that only those genuinely interested in meeting foreigners and making their stay a memorable experience participate. Hosts, in fact, are probably better screened than guests, who need merely supply the company with family members' names and ages, occupations, special interests, and other pertinent data, such as allergies. The company then selects a few possible hosts and lets the client make the final decision. There is a minimum stay of 3 nights, which can be divided among three different families if desired, but no maximum stay except what is mutually agreeable to both hosts and guests. The entire cost of the stay is paid in advance. Meals that guests decide upon in advance are also pre-paid; meals and other extras decided upon during the stay are paid in cash on departure (to avoid embarrassment, the company advises clients beforehand what the hosts charge). The program is not for budget travelers, since the cost ranges from $100 to over $200 per night per couple, with an average of $160 to $170 per night. But the homes are not ordinary; they include several country houses, some larger stately homes, and a castle. Single rates are available, and there are reductions for children. Contact

In the English Manner, PO Box 936, Alamo, CA 95407 (phone: 415-935-7065 in California; 800-422-0799 elsewhere). For other local organizations and services offering home exchanges, contact the local tourist authority.

Dining Out

For the North American abroad, no aspect of going native is as easy as exploring the local cuisine and the rites of table according to the custom of the country. A nation, a region, or even a town can make an irrefutably individual declaration in the very way it brings together the products of its farms and gardens. Wherever you go, stick to what is indigenous; nine times out of ten the best cooking will be that closest to "home" — wherever you happen to be. Often your most personal view of a people will be at a table. By sticking to the native traditions, you will discover an intimate aspect of a nation's character and pride.

There is no better example of this than the food of Britain. The unjustly maligned British cuisine can be excellent if you stick to what the country does best: roasted meats (beef and mutton), grilled chops (pork, lamb, and veal), and meat pies and puddings. Perhaps the best of British cooking comes at breakfast and teatime. As antidote to the cold wet mornings, your bed-and-breakfast may (and should) begin with eggs, bacon, grilled sausages, maybe a grilled kidney and tomato, kippers (smoked herring filets), and, of course, toast, tea, and marmalade. Teatime brings a comforting procession of tea cakes and sandwiches of countless description, crumpets, scones, and Sally Lunns (sweet tea cakes served hot, named for a woman in Bath who first created the recipe 200 years ago), served with dollops of fresh cream and black currant jam. Somerset Maugham reckoned that the only way to survive in England (he lived out his days on the Côte d'Azur) was to have breakfast and tea three times a day. Do not forget that a ready source of satisfying and inexpensive sustenance is the Ploughman's Lunch served in pubs, consisting of (real) English Cheddar cheese, York ham, dark bread, and beer.

In non-English-speaking countries, you will often have the frustrating experience of being presented with a menu that might be written in Martian, for all the information it gives you. An excellent pocket-size guide available in bookstores is the Berlitz *European Menu Reader,* which will help you decode menus in 14 European languages. It also deals with the differences in American and British terminology.

Moving across the water, to speak of *a* Scandinavian cuisine as though there were only one would offend Danes, Swedes, Finns, and Norwegians alike. However, some elements are shared by these countries: dill, sour cream, herring, and aquavit. Along with the dozen-odd recipes for herring — smoked, pickled, creamed — there are the pickled and smoked versions of salmon from Sweden and Norway. The Finns have over 10,000 lakes, so their catch comes equally from fresh and salt water. The lobsterlike freshwater crayfish is particularly prized. Denmark is blessed with an intensive dairy industry and concomitantly fine local blue Tybo (with and without caraway) and Jarlsberg cheese. You can try them all, if you like, on the national munchie, the Danish open-face sandwich. The Swedish smorgasbord should be experienced at least once if only to know how to do it properly: Begin with herring, change plates for the salmon, and so on right through the Swedish meatballs. In Norway, head straight for the salmon and the boiled cod with buttered potatoes — the fewer adornments, the better.

The Nordic influence has pervaded northern Germany, where herring is also a staple. Like British cooking, that of Germany is hearty and straightforward. The German people retain an affection for the cakes, tarts, and other confections that accompany afternoon coffee at the *Konditorei* (pastry shop). Their two staffs of life — and this is true from the Rhine nearly to the Volga — are potatoes and beer. The potatoes are usually boiled, garnished with parsley and butter, and served with the sauerbraten and roast pork and countless boiled and grilled wursts. As for the beers, the Germans are only outdone by the British in their available variety of brews. Though it is less true now than in the past, nearly all towns of any size have breweries. Sauerkraut is not ubiquitous, as it is far more important in southern Germany than northern. Excellent breads of a dozen types — dark, light, rye, *Vollkorn* (whole grain), *Bauernbrot* (peasant bread) — make excellent sandwiches.

Eastern European dishes are characterized by the superb food of Hungary. *Gulyas* (goulash) has put Hungarian cuisine in the global spotlight, but you'll find the real thing only here in Hungary. Familiar as it may be, it probably will not be what you expect if you have eaten it outside its native land. Here it is served as a soup (a very thick one) containing meat (usually beef or pork), onions, sour cream, and lots of paprika. *Halázlé* (Hungarian bouillabaisse), although indigenous to Lake Balaton, has become a favorite in Budapest as well. A clear soup, usually made with *fogas* (pike perch) or bream, it is seasoned with onions and an ocean of spices — one of them paprika, naturally. *Kolozsuári rakotikáposzia* translates as "layered cabbage," but the dish loses something in the translation. Between the layers of cabbage, you'll find eggs and sausages and an acre of sour cream. Crisp pork chops top off everything. Don't be intimidated by the idea that paprika dishes might be too incendiary. Any restaurant in town can temper its cooking to your taste.

The natural gastronomic foil to this Slavic richness, and one central Europeans themselves flock to, is the sun-baked cooking of the Mediterranean. This cuisine of the sun and sea crosses national boundaries from Málaga, Spain, to Athens, Greece, and derives its appeal from an array of flavorful ingredients simply prepared and presented. Olive oil, garlic, tomato, basil, anchovies, wild thyme, and fish and shellfish of every description are the staples. *Pissaladière niçoise,* the tart of onion, tomatoes, olives, and anchovies, is only slightly less famous than the Marseilles fish soup (it's more than that) of saffron, garlic, tomato, and seafood, called bouillabaisse. Not surprisingly, Mediterranean fish soups come with many names: In Barcelona they call it *zarazuela;* in Southern France the generic name is *bourride;* in Italy, depending where you are, it's called *buridda, zuppa di pesce,* or *cacciuco.* Greece and Yugoslavia have a profusion of fish and shellfish dishes — oysters, mussels, and shrimp especially — usually simply grilled or fried or done up into stews and soups. Their lamb and goat dishes retain the same seaborne tang, roasted or grilled with garlic and oil.

There is more to the kitchens of Spain, France, and Italy than the Mediterranean Sea. The best and easiest entrée into the amenities of Spanish life would be a visit to a *tapas* bar, where the dozens of appetizers (*tapas*), ranging from bits of sausage and cheese to stewed game birds and pickled vegetables, are downed with slices of the dry-cured ham called *serrano* and *copitas* full of *fino* (dry) sherry. Spanish cooking at its best is a matter of fresh ingredients simply prepared; two examples are the garlic soup of central Spain and *gazpacho,* made from the early ripening tomatoes, peppers, and other vegetables. The expensive golden spice, saffron, though not exactly a staple, appears with rice in the national chicken and rice dish *arroz con pollo* and in the traditional dish of shellfish and chicken on a bed of saffron rice known as *paella.*

Of all the countries of Europe, Italy is perhaps the most compartmentalized when it comes to food. Dishes and ingredients we regard as the Italian national heritage are often restricted to a single region. *Pesto,* the pungent paste made of basil, garlic, pine nuts, Parmesan, and olive oil, is found in Genoa and not in Venice. The Milanese favorite *risotto alla milanese* (rice cooked with saffron and Parmesan) and minestrone are not native to Naples, which in turn is home to spaghetti with a fish and tomato sauce and delicious fish-garnished pizza. Two rules to remember are that from Tuscany south, olive oil is used increasingly instead of butter, and Tuscany is the heart of the country for the purest, and some would say best, Italian cooking. The best place to sample it is outside the larger cities in one of the small town inns called *bucas.* Here the Tuscan staples of beans, beef, and Chianti will be given their best showing. Venice has made the word *scampi* universally recognized as shrimp broiled in butter. More strictly Venetian is the luxurious combination of oysters and caviar — the caviar from sturgeon fished from the Po River. Wherever you go in Italy, keep in mind that the *caffès* serve more than just coffee: Chocolate truffles and small pastries make for a pleasant way to kill an hour and watch the world go by.

Which brings us at last to France. All that pertains to eating and drinking in the land of the Gauls is a matter of great concern, and any visit to the country, however short, will be enriched immensely by your getting into the spirit of the place. Though it is less true than it used to be, France remains a country of regional cooking, and savvy travelers will explore the specialties wherever they go. Burgundy (Bourgogne), stretching from Lyons north, is home to the wine-rich beef stew *boeuf bourguignon,* a boggling array of sausages and pâtés, which go perfectly with cool Beaujolais and Pouilly-Fuissé, and delectably tender roast chickens from Bresse. In the southwest between Bordeaux and Périgueux, roast duck, preserved goose, and the fattened liver of each — *foie gras* — are local prizes, and farther south in Bayonne they make a raw cured ham, *jambon de Bayonne.* Following the specialties of the region is important not only because they are what the local chefs know and make best, but also because in partaking of the *plats,* you will deepen your understanding of the local differences in character and attitude. They might make a terrific *cassoulet* — the bean and meat casserole famous in Toulouse — in some restaurant in Colmar in the Alsatian wine country, but why dilute your Alsatian experience with that hearty southern dish when you could have *choucroute garnie,* the native rendition of sauerkraut, sausages, and pieces of smoked ham and pork? By experiencing at first hand, so to speak, the Alsatian synthesis of French finesse with hearty German ingredients, you will have made a big step toward understanding the makeup of that beautiful region on the Rhine. When in the Mediterranean Pyrenees, your appreciation of the rugged country and the bluff, resilient people can only be increased when eating a leg of mountain lamb, roast partridge in cabbage, or the redoubtable wild boar stew *civet de sanglier.*

There is one type of French cooking that is, in a sense, national, and this is *haute cuisine* as practiced in the best and most expensive restaurants of the country. Whether of the rich and elaborate *cuisine classique* or the lighter, more fantasy-inspired *cuisine nouvelle* variety, the best practitioners of this cooking, because of the expense and artistry involved, transcend the limits of their region. No matter how slim your budget, you should try to indulge yourself at least once at one of France's best *haute cuisine* temples. Think of it as an experience that will live far beyond the few pleasant hours you spend at table.

But aside from a few comparatively rare gastronomic highs in France and Italy, where great and elaborate dining is part of the national temper, your best meals will be found in the bistros, *trattorias, tavernas,* and pubs of Europe, wherever the fare is simple and catered to local tastes. Seeking these places out will do much to enhance your enjoyment of a European trip, for it is by an accumulation of these intimacies that you look into a nation's heart. For our list of Europe's finest restaurants, see "The Shrines of European Gastronomy," DIVERSIONS.

Time Zones and Business Hours

 TIME ZONES: The countries of Europe fall into three time zones. Greenwich Mean Time — measured from Greenwich, England, at longitude 0°0′ — is the base from which all other time zones are measured. Areas in zones west of Greenwich have earlier times and are called Greenwich Minus; those to the east have later times and are called Greenwich Plus. For example, New York City is 5 zones west, or 5 hours earlier, than Greenwich (so it is Greenwich Minus 5);

when it is noon in Greenwich, it is 7 AM in New York. Greenwich Mean Time includes Ireland, Great Britain, and Portugal. All other Western European countries, including Spain, Czechoslovakia, East Germany, Hungary, and Yugoslavia, fall into Central European Time, and are an hour later than Greenwich Mean Time (Greenwich Plus 1). When it is noon in Greenwich it is 1 PM in East Berlin. The remaining Eastern European countries, as well as Greece, Turkey, Finland, and western Russia, are Greenwich Plus 2; Moscow is Greenwich Plus 3.

Almost all European nations move their clocks an hour ahead in late spring and an hour back in the fall, corresponding to daylight saving time in the US, although the date of the change tends to be earlier by a couple of weeks than the date we have adopted in the US. For 2 weeks in the spring, then, the time difference between the US and most European countries is one hour greater than usual; in the fall for a two-week period, there is one hour less differential.

European timetables use a 24-hour clock to denote arrival and departure times, which means that hours are denoted sequentially from 1 AM. A train leaving at 6 AM will be noted as leaving at 6:00; but a train leaving at 6 PM will be noted as leaving at 18:00. Midnight is 24:00.

PUBLIC HOLIDAYS: Holidays also vary within countries, but if generalization can be attempted it is that (1) all businesses close down for a national day once a year and (2) religious holidays are more widely celebrated in Europe than in the US. *Easter* is often a 4-day celebration — *Good Friday* through *Easter Monday* — and *Ascension Day, Whitmonday* or *Pentecost, The Assumption, All Saints' Day, Christmas Day,* and the following day (December 26, called *Boxing Day* in the United Kingdom) are all observed. For information on holidays throughout Europe, see *Special Events* in FACTS IN BRIEF and THE CITIES.

BUSINESS HOURS: Travelers who are used to the American workday may be surprised to find that the Europeans follow a more eccentric schedule. Businesses open on weekdays between 8 and 9 AM and, in the northern European countries, continue through the day until 4 or 5 PM. The central and southern European countries tend to close for a 2- to 2½-hour lunch break (although the trend is currently moving toward shorter, 1-hour breaks) and therefore close later in the evening — between 5:30 and 7. There are variations, of course. For instance, offices in Yugoslavia open at 7 AM or even earlier and remain open to 2:30 PM or so, although stores and other types of businesses keep more familiar hours.

Banks close an hour or two earlier than businesses as a rule but tend to open on weekdays at about the same time. If it's vital to you, check in advance because there are some exceptions: In West Germany, for example, banks are open from 9 AM to 12:30 PM, and then open again from 1:30 or 2:30 to 3:30 or 4:30 PM (and some, but not all, are open Saturday mornings until noon); in Italy, they close at 1:30 PM and do not reopen; and in other countries there may be branches open late one evening during the week and for some period of time on Saturdays.

Small food stores such as butcher shops and bakeries may open at 9 AM, close for lunch around 12:30 or 1 PM, reopen at 3:30 or 4 PM, and close between 7 and 8 PM. They and other small shops close on Monday mornings and sometimes for the whole day, but if open Sunday, close by 1 or 2PM.

Mail, Telephone, and Electricity

MAIL: The equivalent of US general delivery is called *Poste Restante* throughout Europe and is probably the best way for travelers to have mail sent if they do not have a definite address. As there are often several post offices in major cities, it is important that the address and/or specific name of the office be indicated (not just the name of the city), and travelers should be sure to call at the correct office when inquiring after mail.

If you are an American Express customer (a cardholder, a carrier of American Express traveler's checks, or traveling on an *American Express Travel Service* tour), you can have mail sent to its offices in cities on your routes; letters are held free of charge — registered mail and packages are not accepted. You must be able to show an American Express card, traveler's checks, or a voucher proving you are on one of the company's tours to avoid paying for mail privileges. Those who aren't clients must pay a nominal charge each time they ask if they have received mail, whether they actually have a letter or not. There is also a forwarding fee, for clients and non-clients alike. Mail should be addressed to you, care of American Express, and should be marked "Client Mail Service." Additional information on its mail service and addresses of American Express offices in Europe are contained in the pamphlet *Services and Offices*, available from any US branch of American Express.

US embassies and consulates abroad do not accept mail for tourists. They will, however, help out in emergencies, if you need to receive important business documents or personal papers, for example. It is best to inform them either by separate letter or cable, or by phone if you are in the country already, that you will be using their address for this purpose.

TELEPHONE: Direct dialing within the country, between nations, and overseas is the rule rather than the exception in Europe. A lot of digits are involved once a caller starts dialing beyond national borders, but avoiding operator-assisted calls can cut costs considerably and bring rates into a reasonable range — except for calls made through hotel switchboards. One of the most unpleasant surprises travelers encounter is the amount they find tacked on to their hotel bill for telephone calls, because foreign hotels routinely add surcharges that can be the equivalent of a daily room rate. It's not at all uncommon to find 300% or 400% added to the actual telephone charges.

Until recently, the only recourse against this unconscionable overcharging was to call collect when phoning from abroad or to use a telephone credit card (available through a simple procedure from any local US phone company). Now, *American Telephone and Telegraph* (*AT&T*) offers USA Direct, a service that connects users, via a toll-free number, with an *AT&T* operator in the US, who will then put a call through at the standard international rate. (It's possible to dial USA Direct from Northern Ireland; the service is not available in the Republic.) For a brochure and wallet card listing toll-free numbers by country, contact International Information Service, AT&T Communications, 635 Grant St., Pittsburgh, PA 15219 (phone: 800-874-4000). International Telecharge offers a similar service, *Diplomat* (formerly, *Quick Call USA*), 108 S. Akard, Dallas, TX 75252 (phone: 800-234-4840).

AT&T has also put together Teleplan, an agreement among certain hoteliers that sets a limit on surcharges for calls made by guests from their rooms. Teleplan is currently in effect in selected hotels throughout Europe. Teleplan agreements stipulate a flat amount for credit card or collect calls (currently between $1 and $10) and a flat percentage (between 20% and 100%) on calls paid for at the hotel. For further information, contact *AT&T*'s International Information Service (see above).

Until Teleplan becomes universal, it's wise to ask the surcharge rate *before* calling from a hotel. If the rate is high, it's best to use a telephone credit card or one of the direct-dial services listed above, place the call collect, or place the call and ask the party to call right back. If none of these choices is possible, make international calls from the local post office or special telephone center to avoid surcharges.

Making connections in Europe can sometimes be hit or miss — all exchanges are not always in operation on the same day. If the number dialed does not go through, try later or the next day. So be warned: Those who have to make an important call — to make a hotel reservation in another city, for instance — should do so a few days ahead.

ELECTRICITY: The US runs on 110-volt, 60-cycle alternating current; Europe runs on 220- or 240-volt, 50-cycle alternating current. The large difference between US and European voltage means that without a converter, the motor of a US appliance used overseas would run at twice the speed at which it's meant to operate and would quickly burn out. Travelers can solve the problem by buying a lightweight converter to transform foreign voltage into the domestic kind (there are two types of converters, depending on the wattage of the appliance) or by buying dual-voltage appliances that convert from one to the other at the flick of a switch (hair dryers of this sort are common). The difference between the 50- and 60-cycle currents will cause no problem — the appliance will simply run more slowly — but it will still be necessary to deal with differing socket configurations before plugging in.

Sets of plugs for use worldwide can be bought at hardware stores or from the *Franzus Company,* 53 W. 23rd St., New York, NY 10010 (phone: 212-463-9593). *Franzus* also publishes a useful brochure, *Foreign Electricity Is No Deep Dark Secret,* which provides information about converters and adapter plugs for electrical appliances to be used abroad but made for use in the US. For a free copy, send a stamped, self-addressed envelope to *Franzus* at the above address; a catalogue of other travel accessories is available on request.

Medical and Legal Aid and Consular Services

MEDICAL AID ABROAD: You will discover, in the event of an emergency, that most tourist facilities — transportation companies, hotels, and resorts — are equipped to handle the situation quickly and efficiently. Most towns and cities of any size have a public hospital, and even the tiniest hamlet has a medical clinic or private physician nearby. The level of medical care available in Europe is generally excellent, providing the same basic specialties and services that are available in the US. All hospitals are prepared for emergency cases, and many hospitals also have walk-in clinics designed to serve people who do not really need emergency service, but who have no place to go for immediate medical attention.

Before you go, be sure to check with your insurance company about the applicability of your policy while you're abroad; many policies do not apply, and others are not accepted in Europe. Older travelers should know that Medicare does not make payments outside the US, and for the most part, free public health services (in those countries that have them — Great Britain, for example) do not provide free medical or dental care to visitors, except in (and only in) a few instances. If your medical policy does not protect you while you're traveling, there are comprehensive combination policies specifically designed to fill the gap. For a discussion of medical insurance and a list of inclusive combination policies, see *Insurance* elsewhere in this section.

If a bona fide emergency occurs, the fastest way to receive attention may be to take a taxi to the emergency room of the nearest hospital. An alternative is to dial the local emergency number used to summon the police, fire trucks, and ambulances. If you don't know this number, simply dial for the operator and ask for someone who speaks English — in some areas, this may mean you'll need to reach an international operator — or have someone make the call for you. Since ambulance dispatchers are accustomed to taking calls from doctors only, state immediately that you are a foreign tourist and then the nature of your problem and your location.

If a doctor is needed for something less than an emergency, there are several ways to find one. Ask at the hotel or check the local post office, where neighborhood physicians may be listed (though they often aren't). Dialing the emergency number will also help find a doctor. Callers will often be given the name of a general practitioner, since private doctors, usually specialists, may see patients upon referral only. For the seriously ill or injured traveler, however, it is best to see a private doctor. It's usually possible to find one without a referral through the US consulate (see address and phone number below) or directly through a hospital, especially if you are in an emergency situation. If you are already at the hospital, you may see the specialist there, or you may make an appointment to be seen at his or her office.

In addition, though general practitioners deliver primary care, there is no violation of protocol in approaching a specialist directly. Call the appropriate department of a teaching hospital or the US Embassy (address and phone number below), which also maintains a list of doctors. Remember that if you are hospitalized, you will have to pay, even in an emergency.

If you are staying in a hotel or motel, ask for help in reaching a doctor or other emergency services, or for the house physician, who may visit you in your room or ask you to visit an office. (This service is apt to be expensive, especially if the doctor makes a "house" call to your room.)

Emergency dental care is also available throughout Europe (again, see the front page of the local telephone directory), although travelers are strongly advised to have a dental checkup some weeks before the trip to allow time for any necessary work to be done. *A word of caution about foreign dentists in general:* In many countries, the tendency may be to extract a tooth as soon as it gives the least bit of trouble.

There should be no problem finding a 24-hour drugstore (called a "chemist" in Great Britain; *pharmacie* in France; *farmacie* in Italy for drugs only and *profumerie* for cosmetics and toiletries; and *farmacia* in Spain) in any major city. In the case of minor complaints, some pharmacists may do some prescribing and are not averse to filling a foreign prescription; however, do not count on this. Although many do, in Scandinavia, Holland, Great Britain, Ireland, and a few other countries, you may need a local doctor to rewrite the prescription. Nevertheless, to make most effective use of the drugstore, it's a good idea to ask your doctor for the generic names of any drugs you use so that you can ask for their equivalents should you need a refill. Americans will also notice that some drugs sold only by prescription in the US are sold over the counter in Europe. Though this can be very handy, be aware that common cold medicines and aspirin that contain codeine or other controlled substances will not be allowed back into the US.

Emergency assistance is also available from the various medical programs designed for travelers who have chronic ailments or whose illness requires them to return home. The *Medic Alert Foundation* sells identification emblems that specify that the wearer has a health condition that may not be readily apparent to a casual observer. A heart condition, diabetes, epilepsy, or severe allergy is the sort of thing that these emblems were developed to communicate, conditions that can result in tragic errors if not recognized when emergency treatment is necessary and when you may be unable to speak for yourself. In addition to the identification emblems, the foundation maintains a computerized central file from which your complete medical history is available 24 hours a day by telephone (the phone number is clearly inscribed on the ID badge). The one-time membership is tax deductible and ranges from $25 to $45, and is based on the type of metal from which the emblem is made, the choices ranging from stainless steel to 10K gold-filled. For information, contact the Medic Alert Foundation, Turlock, CA 95381-1009 (phone: 209-668-3333 or 800-ID-ALERT).

International SOS Assistance also offers a program to cover medical emergencies while traveling. Members are provided with telephone access — 24 hours a day, 365 days a year — to a worldwide, monitored, multilingual network of medical centers. A phone call brings assistance ranging from a telephone consultation to transportation home by ambulance or aircraft, and in some cases transportation of a family member to wherever you are hospitalized. The service can be purchased for a week ($15), a week plus additional days ($15, plus $2 for each additional day), a month ($45), or a year ($195). For information, contact International SOS Assistance, PO Box 11568, Philadelphia, PA 19116 (phone: 215-244-1500 or 800-523-8930).

The *International Association for Medical Assistance to Travellers* (*IAMAT*) provides its members with a directory of affiliated medical centers in over 140 countries (500 cities) to call for a list of participating doctors. A non-profit organization, *IAMAT* appreciates donations; for $25, a set of worldwide climate charts detailing weather and sanitary conditions will be included. To join, write well in advance of your trip (processing takes about 3 weeks) to IAMAT, 417 Center St., Lewiston, NY 14092 (phone: 716-754-4883).

The *International Health Care Service* provides information about health conditions in various countries, advice on immunizations recommended, and treatment if necessary. A pre-travel counseling and immunization package costs $175; a post-travel screening, $75, plus lab work. Appointments are necessary. The service also publishes *The International Health Care Travelers Guide,* available for $4.50 with a self-addressed envelope. Contact the International Health Care Service, New York Hospital–Cornell Medical Center, 440 E. 69th St., New York, NY 10021 (phone: 212-472-4284).

Those who return home ill with a condition they suspect is travel related and beyond the experience of their regular physician should consider seeing a specialist in travel medicine. For information on finding such a specialist in your area, see *Staying Healthy,* in this section.

For a thorough description of the medical services in Europe's larger cities, see *Traveling Healthy,* by Sheilah M. Hillman and Robert S. Hillman, MD. Unfortunately out of print, it may be found in the library.

LEGAL AID ABROAD: It is often far more alarming to be arrested abroad than at home for an infringement of the law. Not only are you alone among strangers, but the punishment can be worse. Granted, the US consulate can advise you of your rights and provide a list of lawyers, but it cannot interfere with local due process. The best advice is to be honest and law-abiding. If you get a traffic ticket, pay it. If you are approached by drug hawkers, ignore them. The penalties for possession of hashish, marijuana, cocaine, and other narcotics are generally more severe than in the US.

CONSULAR SERVICES: There is one crucial place to keep in mind when outside the US, namely, the American Services section of the US consulate. If you are injured or become seriously ill, the consulate will direct you to medical assistance and notify your relatives. If, while abroad, you become involved in a dispute that could lead to legal action, the consulate, once again, is the place to turn. And in case of natural disasters or civil unrest, consulates around the world handle the evacuation of US citizens if such a procedure is necessary. Keep in mind, though, that nowhere does the consulate act as an arbitrator or ombudsman on an American citizen's behalf. The consul has no power, authorized or otherwise, to subvert, alter, or contravene the legal processes, however unfair, of the country in which he or she serves. Nor can a consul oil the machinery of a foreign bureaucracy or provide legal advice. The consul's responsibilities do include providing a list of lawyers and information on local sources of legal aid, informing relatives in the US, and organizing and administrating any defense monies sent from home. If a case is tried unfairly or the punishment seems unusually severe, the consul can make a formal complaint to the authorities. In a case of what is called "legitimate and proven poverty" — of an American stranded abroad without funds — the consul will contact sources of money, such as family or friends in the US, and, as a last resort, arrange for repatriation at government expense, although this is a loan, which must be repaid.

Do not expect the consulate to help you with trivial difficulties such as canceled reservations or lost baggage. The consulate is primarily concerned with the day-to-day administration of services such as issuing passports and visas; providing notarial services; the distribution of VA, social security, and civil service benefits to resident Americans; depositions; extradition cases; and reports to Washington of births and deaths of US citizens.

A list of US embassies and consulates in Europe follows. The first address listed is always that of the US Embassy; those that follow are of consulates in cities other than the one in which the embassy is located. Mailing addresses may differ, so check first.

Austria: 16 Boltzmanngasse, Vienna (phone: 01-222-315511); A-5020 Giselakai 51, Salzburg (662-28-601)

Belgium: 27 Bd. du Régent, B-1000 Brussels (phone: 02-513-3830); Rubens Center, 5 Nationalestraat, B-2000 Antwerp (phone: 03-225-0071)

Bulgaria: 1A Stamboliski Blvd., Sofia (phone: 02-884801)

Czechoslovakia: 15 Trziste, 12548 Prague 1 (phone: 02-536641 through 49)

Denmark: 24 Dag Hammarskjölds Alle, 2100 Copenhagen (phone: 01-423144)

Finland: 14A Itainen Puistotie, 00140 Helsinki (phone: 0-171931)

France: 2 Av. Gabriel, 75382 Paris Cedex 08 (phone: 01-42-96-12-02 or 42-61-80-75); 22 Cours du Maréchal-Foch, 33080 Bordeaux Cedex (phone: 56-52-65-95); 7 Quai Général-Sarrail, 69454 Lyons Cedex 3 (phone: 78-24-68-49); 12 Blvd. Paul-Peytral, 13286 Marseilles Cedex (phone: 91-54-92-00); 15 Av. d'Alsace, 67082 Strasbourg Cedex (phone: 88-35-31-04)

East Germany: 4-5 Neustaedtische Kirchstrasse, 1080 Berlin (phone: 02-220-2741).

West Germany: Deichmanns Rue, 5300 Bonn 2 (phone: 0228-3391); 170 Clayallee, D-1000 Berlin 33 (Dahlem) (phone: 30-83-240-87); 21 Siesmayerstrasse, 6000 Frankfurt Am Main (phone: 69-753-05-01 or -04-01); 27/28 Alsterufer, 2000 Hamburg 36 (phone: 040-411-71-01); 5 Königinstrasse, 8000 Munich 22 (phone: 089-2-30-11); 7 Urbanstrasse, 7000 Stuttgart (phone: 0711-21-02-21)

Greece: 91 Vasilissis Sophias Blvd., 10160 Athens (phone: 01-721-29-51); 59 Leoforos Nikis, GR-546-22 Thessaloniki (phone: 31-266-121)

Hungary: 12 V. Szabadsag Ter., Budapest (phone: 01-126450)

Iceland: 21 Laufasvegue, Reykjavik (phone: 01-29100)

Ireland: 42 Elgin Rd., Dublin 4 (phone: 01-688-777)

Italy: 119/A Via Veneto, 00187 Rome (phone: 646741); Banca d'America e d'Italia Bldg., 6 Piazza Portello, 09794 Genoa (phone: 010-28-27-41 through 5); 2/10 Via Principe Amedeo, 20121 Milan (phone: 02-652841 through 5); Piazza della Repubblica, 80122 Naples (phone: 081-66-09-66); 1 Via Vaccarini, 90143 Palermo (phone: 091-34-35-32); 38 Lungarno Amerigo Vespucci, Florence (phone: 055-29-82-76).

Luxembourg: 22 Bd. Emmanuel-Servais, Luxembourg 2535 (phone: 460123 through 7)

Netherlands: 102 Lange Voorhout, The Hague (phone: 170-62-49-11); Museumplein 19, Amsterdam (phone: 120-64-56-61)

Norway: 18 Drammensveien, Oslo 2 (phone: 02-448550)

Poland: 29/31 Aleje Ujazdowskle, Warsaw (phone: 22-283-041 through 9)

Portugal: Av. das Forcas Armadas, 1600 Lisbon (phone: 01-726-6600)

Romania: 7-9 Strada Tudor Arghezi, Bucharest (phone: 0-104040)

Spain: 75 Serrano, Madrid (phone: 1-276-3400 or -3600); 33 Via Layetana, Barcelona (phone: 3-219-9550)

Sweden: 101 Strandvagen, S-115-27 Stockholm (phone: 08-783-5300)

Switzerland: 93 Jubilaeumstrasse, 3005 Bern (phone: 031-43-70-11); 11 Route de Pregny, 1292 Chambesy, Geneva (phone: 22-99-02-11); 141 Zolliikerstrasse, 8008 Zurich (01-552566)

United Kingdom: 24/31 Grosvenor Sq. W., London W1A 1AE (phone: 01-499-9000); Queen's House, 14 Queen St., Belfast BT1 6EQ (phone: 232-228239); 3 Regent Terr., Edinburgh EH7 5BW (phone: 031-556-8315)

USSR: 19/21/23 Ulitsa Chaikovskogo, Moscow (phone: 096-252-2451 through -2459); 15 Ulitsa Petra Lavrova, Box L, Leningrad (phone: 812-274-8235)

Yugoslavia: 50 Kneza Milosa, Belgrade (phone: 011-645-655); 2 Brace Kavurica, Zagreb (041-444-800)

If your itinerary includes any country not on the above list, its national tourist office will tell you which consulate or embassy abroad is charged with responsibility for Americans there.

The US State Department operates a Citizens Emergency Center, which offers a number of services to American travelers abroad and their families at home. In addition to giving callers up-to-date information on trouble spots, the center will contact authorities abroad in an attempt to locate a traveler or deliver an urgent message. In case of death, illness, arrest, destitution, or repatriation of an American citizen on foreign soil, it will relay information to relatives here if the consulate is unable to do so. Travel advisory information is available 24 hours a day to people with touch-tone phones by calling 202-647-5225. Callers with rotary phones can call this number from 8:15 AM to 10 PM (Eastern Standard Time) on weekdays; 9 AM to 3 PM Saturdays. For emergency calls, from 8:15 AM to 10 PM weekdays, and 9 AM to 3 PM Saturdays, call 202-647-5225. For emergency calls only, at all other times, call 202-634-3600 and ask for the Duty Officer.

Drinking and Drug Laws

DRINKING: It is more than likely that some of the warmest memories of a trip to Europe will be moments of conviviality shared over a drink in a neighborhood pub, a *Weinstube,* or a sunlit café. As in the US, national taxes on alcohol affect the price of liquor in Europe. Mixed drinks are somewhat more expensive than at home. Local wine, beer, and other liquor are reasonably priced, so take this opportunity to savor them at the source.

With the exception of European beer, which at around 5% has a slightly higher alcoholic content than that of North America, European beverages are no stronger than those found in the US: Wines and champagne contain a standard 12% alcohol; fortified wines such as sherry, port, and the aperitifs have anywhere between 12% and 18%; and brandies and hard liquor between 40% and 50% (80 to 100 proof). The potency of such famed liquors as Russian vodka, Scandinavian aquavit, and Yugoslavian *slivovitz* derives from the fact that they are often taken fast and neat rather than that they have high alcoholic content.

Europe offers a wide variety of alcoholic drinks, and you should taste as many as you can. A short survey of some of the favorites:

Austria – Here the classic drink combination (especially in summer) is a shot of schnapps followed by a chaser of beer. Schnapps is a general term for a wide range of liquors, distilled from grain at about 80 proof. Enjoyed in a *Gasthaus,* schnapps is served straight up.

Britain – Scotch whisky and English ale are the favorites in England's pubs. Whisky may be tempered with a little water (never ice), and ale comes at room temperature, except when it is called lager, which is usually chilled.

Bulgaria – A bar is a *bar* (same spelling), and the favorite drink is a small, chilled glass of *slivovitz,* a flavorful spirit made from plums.

France – Wine by the glass or carafe is the trademark of Parisian cafés, where the house choice (*vin maison*) is usually reasonably priced and palatable.

Germany – The size of many German waistlines testifies to the overriding popularity of *Bier*, served by the *viertel liter* (one-quarter liter) in a *Taverne* or *Bier Keller* (beer cellar).

Greece – High-proof *ouzo* is the drink of choice. The best is made from grapes, tasting faintly of licorice (it's flavored with anise), and is served on the rocks or with water in a *kafenio* (coffeehouse). Another widely imbibed favorite is *retsina,* a traditional resin-flavored wine.

Ireland – Guinness stout, a dark, syrupy ale with a thick, creamy head and a pronounced bitterness from hops, is the favorite in local pubs.

Italy – Along with wine, the popular drink at a local *caffè* is Campari, usually served on the rocks with soda and a twist.

Poland – Polish vodka, traditionally served neat and slightly chilled in a liqueur glass, is distilled from grain. Available in *bars* (same spelling), it often comes with a grind of fresh pepper or a twist of lemon.

Scandinavia – Without a doubt, the regional drink is aquavit, a flavored neutral spirit, sometimes derived from potatoes, sometimes from grain. Served icy cold in a tulip-shape glass, occasionally with a side of beer, aquavit is almost always imbibed with meals. In fancy restaurants, the bottle is brought to the table encased in a jacket of ice.

Spain – In addition to a glass of red wine (*a tinto*), the *gente* enjoy a wide range of excellent sherries. Most people will order a glass of sherry (*a fino*), served in a small glass to be sipped leisurely in an outdoor *café* or *bar* (same spelling).

Switzerland – On the French side, drinking habits run along Gallic lines; that is, wine is preferred. On the German side, a cup of coffee with schnapps or a mug of beer is popular.

Yugoslavia – Once again, the taste is for plums, and *slivovitz,* served in a *gostina* (bar), is considered the national drink.

National taxes on alcohol in the Common Market countries affect the prices of liquor there, not — as used to be the case — the fact that they are manufactured in other countries. Any alcoholic beverage is expensive in Denmark because it is highly taxed. In France, if a drink costs a lot, it's because the café prices it that way. Gin is as cheap in Italy as in Great Britain. However, in Austria, not a Common Market country, taxes make imported liquor exorbitant, so it is best to drink whatever alcoholic beverage is produced locally.

Whiskey and gin are not indigenous to the Continent, and as a general rule, mixed drinks are expensive. If you like a drop before dinner, a good way to save money is to buy a bottle of your favorite brand at the airport before leaving the US and enjoy it in your hotel before setting forth. European countries allow a quart or more of hard liquor and at least one bottle of wine to be brought in duty-free.

A warning: When setting off for an evening including some serious drinking, visitors should leave their cars behind and make alternate plans for getting back to the hotel. Aside from the obvious danger in which you place yourself and others on the road, there are strict laws against drunk driving throughout Europe, and they are zealously enforced — confiscation of the driver's license, high fines, and even imprisonment are common penalties.

DRUGS: Illegal narcotics are as prevalent in Europe as in the US, but don't be deluded into believing that this easy access denotes a casual attitude on the part of law enforcement authorities. The moderate legal and social acceptance that marijuana has gained in the US has no counterpart in Europe.

The best advice we can offer is: Don't carry, use, buy, or sell illegal drugs. The dangers are clear enough when indulging in your own home; if you take drugs while traveling, you may not only endanger your own life but also put your fellow travelers in jeopardy. And if you get caught, you may end up spending your hard-earned vacation funds on bail and attorney's fees — and end up in jail.

Those who carry medicines that contain a controlled drug should be sure to have a current doctor's prescription with them. There isn't much that the American consulate can do for drug offenders beyond providing a list of lawyers. Having broken a local law, an offender puts his or her fate in the hands of the local authorities.

Ironically, travelers can get into almost as much trouble coming through US customs with over-the-counter drugs picked up abroad that contain substances that are controlled in the US. Cold medicines, pain relievers, and the like often have codeine or codeine derivatives that are illegal except by prescription in the US. Throw them out before leaving for home.

Tipping

 Throughout Europe, you will find the custom of including some kind of service charge as part of a meal more common than in North America. If *service compris* (or *incluso* or *eingeschlossen*) is printed on the menu, followed by a percentage figure, you will know that that percentage of your bill will be automatically added as a service charge (in some cases, it is already calculated in the menu prices). Unfortunately, not every restaurant notes that the charge is added, but you should feel no embarrassment about asking a waiter at the time the bill is presented. *Service compris* generally ranges from 15% to 20%. If it isn't added, a 15% tip — just as in the US — is usually a safe figure, although one should never hesitate to penalize poor service or reward excellent and efficient attention by leaving less or more. If the tip has been added, no further gratuity is expected — though it's a common practice in Europe for diners to leave a few extra coins on the table. The emphasis is on *few*, and the equivalent of $1 is usually quite adequate.

Although it's not necessary to tip the maître d' of most restaurants — unless he has been especially helpful in providing a table or arranging a special party — when tipping is appropriate, the least amount should be the local equivalent of $5. In the finest restaurants, where a multiplicity of servers are present, plan to tip 5% to the captain in addition to the standard 15% for the waiter. The sommelier (wine waiter) is entitled to a gratuity of approximately $2 per bottle of wine.

In allocating gratuities at a restaurant, pay particular attention to what has become the standard credit card charge form, which now includes separate places for indicating gratuities for waiters and/or captains. If these separate boxes do not appear on the charge slip presented, simply ask the waiter or captain how these separate tips should be indicated. Be aware, too, of the increasingly common, devious practice of placing the amount of an entire restaurant bill (in which service has already been included) in the top box of a charge slip, leaving the "tip" box and "total" ominously empty. Don't be intimidated: Leave the "tip" box blank and just repeat the total amount under "total" before signing.

There is virtually no tipping in pubs in the Great Britain — unless you care to offer the barman an occasional drink — not a bad policy to follow in other countries. It is not uncommon, however, to leave a few coins for a barmaid; and for those served at a table in a bar or cocktail lounge, a small gratuity, $1, is usual for the server.

As in restaurants, visitors will normally find a service charge of 10% to 15% included in their final hotel bill at most hotels. No additional gratuities are required — or expected — beyond this billed service charge. It is unlikely, however, that a service charge will be added to bills in small guesthouses or modest bed-and-breakfast establishments. In these cases, guests should let their instincts be their guide; no tipping is expected by members of the family who own the house, but it is a nice gesture to leave something for others — such as a dining room waiter or a maid — who may have been helpful. A gratuity of $1 per night is adequate in most cases.

If a hotel does not automatically add a service charge, it is perfectly proper for guests to ask to have an extra 10% to 15% added to their bill, to be distributed among those who served them. This may be an especially convenient solution in a large hotel, where it's difficult to determine just who out of a horde of attendants actually performed particular services. For those who prefer to distribute tips themselves, a chambermaid generally is tipped at the rate of $1 per day. Tip the concierge or hall porter for specific services only, with the amount of such gratuities dependent on the level of service provided. Doormen and/or porters are generally tipped at the rate of $1 per bag for carrying luggage, along with a small additional amount if a doorman helps with a cab or car. Other miscellaneous tips to hotel staff depend entirely on the service rendered.

Once upon a time, taxi drivers in Europe would give one a rather odd look if presented with a tip for a fare, but times have changed, and 10%–15% of the amount on the meter is now a standard gratuity. Porters in airports expect to be compensated at the rate of about $1 per bag, as do porters who carry bags in railway or bus stations.

Theater ushers are not tipped, though it is common practice to purchase a program from the person who shows you to your seat. Sightseeing tour guides are usually tipped; members of a group may discuss a total amount among themselves and contribute equally to the gratuity.

Shopping

Browsing through the department stores, street markets, small shops, and craft centers of Europe will undoubtedly be one of the highlights of a trip. Visitors from the US may not be quite as enthusiastic about prices as they might have been a few years ago, but there is still plenty of value left for the money and enough quality and craftsmanship to make many an item irresistible. To help steer visitors toward the best, several sections of this book are devoted to shopping. In THE CITIES, individual city reports include a listing of specific stores, boutiques, and markets, as well as descriptions of special shopping streets where they exist. And sections in DIVERSIONS describe not only where to find antiques and other collectibles, but also — for those who have yet to experience this stimulating form of acquisition — how to buy them at auctions.

WHAT TO BUY: In Europe, crafts are thriving. Products in traditional and modern styles and combinations of the two are found in craft centers, workshops, and stores throughout the Continent. Details are in the information sheets available from the various tourist authorities' offices in the US (see *Tourist Information Offices*).

HOW TO SHOP ABROAD: The goods are enticing, but even so, top-quality goods are not necessarily less expensive in a fashionable boutique in the capital of the country from which they came than they are in an equally fashionable US store. To be sure, visitors should do some homework before going and should arrive prepared with a list of the goods they want — as specific as possible, with brands or labels — and the cost of each in the US. In some cases, visitors will find it less expensive to buy abroad, but frequently they will find it is not, and knowing the difference is crucial to a successful shopping trip. On arrival, it is still necessary to comparison shop as much as time permits, bearing in mind that articles can be less costly the closer the buyer gets to the point of manufacture, and least expensive of all in the factory that makes the item — if it sells to the public. Visitors will get a better price at small factories and shops, for example, than in the major cities and towns.

DUTY-FREE SHOPS: If common sense says that it is always less expensive to buy goods in an airport duty-free shop than to buy them at home or in the streets of a foreign city, travelers should best be aware of some basic facts. Duty-free, first of all, does not mean that the goods travelers buy will be free of duty when they return to the US. Rather, it means that the shop has paid no import tax acquiring goods of foreign make because the goods are not to be used in the country, which is why duty-free goods are available only in the restricted, passengers-only area of international airports or are delivered to departing passengers on the plane. In a duty-free store, travelers save money only on goods of foreign make because they are the only items on which import tax would be charged in any other store. There is usually no saving on locally made items, although in countries that impose VAT taxes (see below) that are refundable to foreigners, the prices in airport duty-free shops are also minus this tax, sparing travelers the often cumbersome procedures they otherwise have to follow to obtain a VAT refund. Beyond this, there is little reason to delay buying local souvenirs until reaching the airport. In fact, because airport duty-free shops usually pay high rents, the locally made goods sold there may well be more expensive than they would be in a downtown store. The real bargains are foreign goods, but — let the buyer beware — not all foreign goods are automatically less expensive in an airport duty-free shop. Spirits, smoking materials, and perfumes are fairly standard bargains, but when buying cameras, watches, clothing, chocolates and other foods, and luxury items, be sure to know what they cost elsewhere. Terrific savings do exist (they are the reason for such shops, after all), but so do overpriced items that an unwary shopper might find equally tempting.

Two of Europe's best known duty-free shops are at Europe's Shannon Airport, the oldest, and at Amsterdam's Schiphol Airport, the largest. You can get a catalogue of the Amsterdam shop — useful for price comparisons — through KLM Royal Dutch Airlines offices or by writing to the Amsterdam Airport Shopping Centre, PO Box 7501, 1118 ZG Schiphol Airport, Holland. Shannon Airport also operates a mail-order service that can be used long after you've left Europe; pick up the catalogue as you pass through Shannon or request it from Shannon Development, 757 Third Ave., 19th Floor, New York, NY 10017 (phone: 212-371-5550).

VALUE ADDED TAX: Commonly abbreviated VAT, this is a tax levied by various European countries and added to the purchase price of most merchandise. The standard VAT rate in Europe is 10% or 25%, with the higher rate applying to luxury goods such as watches, jewelry, furs, glass, and cameras (food and transportation exempt). The tax is intended for residents (and is already included in the price tag), but visitors are required to pay it, too, unless they have purchases shipped directly to an address abroad by the store. If visitors pay the tax and take purchases with them, however, they are entitled to a refund under a variety of retail export schemes that have been in operation for several years. In the past, returning travelers have complained of delays in receiving the refunds and of difficulties in converting checks written in foreign currency into dollars, but new services have recently been introduced that greatly streamline the refund procedure.

One such service, offered in the Irish Republic, is a new system called Cashback. To obtain a refund, visitors must shop only in stores participating in the scheme (look for the Cashback sign in over 1,000 shops nationwide, including major department stores). When leaving the country, visitors should have all of their Cashback vouchers from all stores stamped by customs (customs officials may ask to see the merchandise, so it's a good idea not to pack it in the bottom of a suitcase). Refund checks are sent out within 21 days of receipt of the vouchers, and refunds by credit card generally appear on the cardholder's statement within one month of receipt.

Those who happen to do their shopping in a store that is not part of the Cashback scheme should not despair. It is necessary to show the salesperson a passport and ask for a VAT relief form, which will be filled out on the premises. At departure, have the form validated at the customs desk and mail it back to the *store* (stores generally supply stamped, self-addressed envelopes for this purpose). Note that stores are under no obligation to perform this service, and those that do may require a minimum purchase below which they refuse to process the forms. They will also deduct a small charge from the refund for doing so.

Throughout the United Kingdom another new streamlined service — called Tourist Tax Free Shopping (TTFS) — has made its debut and has gained wide acceptance among stores in Great Britain. Where it is offered — participating stores display a TTFS sign — refunds come from a central source. They are sent out within 5 days of receipt of the vouchers and may come in the form of a dollar check, a foreign currency check, or a credit to a credit card account, as preferred, but on-the-spot cash refunds are not possible.

A VAT refund by dollar check or by credit to a credit card account is relatively hassle-free, but those who receive a check in a foreign currency will probably find that their US banks will assess a fee, as much as $15 or more, for converting it into US dollars. Far less costly is the alternative of sending the foreign currency check (after endorsing it) to *Ruesch International,* 1140 19th St. NW, Suite 320, Washington, DC 20036 (phone: 800-424-2923), which will convert it to a dollar check for a flat $2 fee (which will be deducted from the dollar check). *Ruesch* also has offices at 1888 Century Park E., Suite 1960, Los Angeles, CA 90067 (phone: 213-284-3235), and 730 Fifth Ave., Suite 900, New York, NY 10019 (phone: 212-333-8641).

Customs and Returning to the US

 The duty-fee allowance for US citizens returning from abroad is $400, provided your purchases accompany you and are for personal use. A flat 10% duty based on the "fair retail value in country of acquisition" is assessed on the next $1,000 worth of merchandise brought in for personal use or gifts. Amounts over $1,400 are dutiable at a variety of rates. The average rate for typical tourist purchases is about 12%, but you can find out rates on specific items by consulting *Tariff Schedules of the United States* in a library or at any US Customs Service office.

Families traveling together may make a joint declaration to customs, a procedure that permits one member to exceed his or her duty-free exemption to the extent that another falls short. Families may also pool purchases dutiable under the flat rate. A family of three, for example, would be eligible for up to a total of $3,000 at the 10% flat duty rate (after each member had used up his or her $400 duty-free exemption) rather than three separate $1,000 allowances. This grouping of purchases is extremely useful when considering the duty on a high-tariff item, such as jewelry or a fur coat. Individuals are allowed 1 carton of cigarettes (200) and 1 liter of alcohol if over 21. Alcohol above this allowance is liable for both duty and an Internal Revenue tax. Antiques, if they are 100 or more years old and you have proof from the seller of that fact, are duty free, as are paintings and drawings if done entirely by hand.

Personal exemptions can be used once every 30 days; in order to be eligible, an individual must have been out of the country for more than 48 hours. If any portion of the exemption has been used once within any 30-day period or if your trip is less than 48 hours long, the duty-free allowance is cut to $25. The allotment for individual "unsolicited" gifts mailed from abroad (no more than one per day per recipient) has been raised to $50 retail value per gift. These gifts do not have to be declared and are not included in your duty-free exemption.

Tourists have long been forbidden to bring into the US foreign-made US trademarked articles purchased abroad (if the trademark is recorded with customs) without written permission. It's now possible to enter with one such item in your possession as long as it's for personal use.

Clearing customs is a simple procedure. Forms are distributed by airline or ship personnel before arrival. If your purchases total no more than the duty-free $400 limit, you need only fill out the identification part of the form and make an oral declaration to the customs inspector. If entering with more than $400 worth of goods, you must submit a written declaration. It is illegal not to declare dutiable items; not to do so, in fact, constitutes smuggling, and the penalty can be anything from stiff fines and seizure of the goods to prison sentences. It simply isn't worth doing. Nor should you go along with the suggestions of foreign merchants who offer to help you secure a bargain by deceiving customs officials in any way. Such transactions are frequently a setup, using the foreign merchant as an agent of US customs. Another agent of US customs is TECS, the Treasury Enforcement Communications System, a computer that stores all kinds of pertinent information on returning citizens. There is a basic rule to buying goods abroad, and it should never be broken. If you can't afford the duty on something, don't buy it. Your list or verbal declaration should include all items purchased abroad as well as gifts received abroad, purchases made at the behest of others, the value of repairs, and anything brought in for resale in the US.

Do not include in the list items that do not accompany you, i.e., purchases that you have mailed or had shipped home. These are dutiable in any case, even if for your own use and even if the items that accompany your return from the same trip do not exhaust your $400 duty-free exemption. In fact, it is a good idea, if you have accumulated too much while abroad, to mail home any personal effects (made and bought in the US) that you no longer need rather than your foreign purchases. These personal effects pass through customs as "American goods returned" and are not subject to duty. If you cannot avoid shipping home your foreign purchases, however, the US Customs Service suggests that the package be clearly marked "Not for Sale" and that a copy of the bill of sale be included. The customs examiner will usually accept this as indicative of the article's fair retail value, but if he or she believes it to be falsified or feels the goods have been seriously undervalued, a higher retail value may be assigned. Remember, the examiner is empowered to impose a duty based on his or her assessment of the value of the goods. The duty owed is collected by the US Postal Service when the package is delivered. More information on mailing packages home from abroad is contained in the US Customs Service pamphlet *International Mail Imports* (see below for where to write for this and other useful brochures).

Gold, gold medals, bullion, and up to $10,000 in currency or negotiable instruments may be brought into the US without being declared. Sums over $10,000 must be declared in writing. Drugs are totally illegal with the exception of medication prescribed by a physician. It's a good idea to travel with no more than you actually need of any medication and to have the prescription on hand in case any question arises either abroad or when reentering the US.

Customs implements the rigorous Department of Agriculture regulations concerning the importation of vegetable matter, seeds, bulbs, and the like. Living vegetable matter may not be imported without a permit, and everything must be inspected, permit or not. Processed foods and baked goods are usually okay. Regulations on meat products generally depend on the country of origin and manner of processing. As a rule, commercially canned meat, hermetically sealed and cooked in the can so that it can be stored without refrigeration, is permitted, but not all canned meat fulfills this requirement. Be careful in buying pâté, for instance. Goose liver pâté in itself is acceptable, but the pork fat that is often part of it, either as an ingredient or a rind, is not. Even canned pâtés may not be admitted for this reason. (The imported ones you see in US stores have been prepared and packaged according to US regulations.)

Customs also enforces federal laws that prohibit the entry of articles made from the furs or hides of animals on the endangered species list. Beware of shoes, bags, and belts made of crocodile and certain kinds of lizard, and if you're shopping for big-ticket items, beware of fur coats made from the spotted cats. All can be found in Europe, but they will be confiscated upon your return, and there will be no refund. For information about animals on the endangered species list, contact the Department of the Interior, US Fish and Wildlife Service, Office of Management Authority, PO Box 27329, Washington, DC 20038-7329 (phone: 202-343-5634), and ask for the free publication *Facts About Federal Wildlife Laws.*

Customs agents are businesslike, efficient, and not unkind. During the peak season, clearance can take time, but this is generally because of the strain imposed by a number of jumbo jets disgorging their passengers at the same time, not because of unwarranted zealousness on the part of the customs people. Efforts to streamline procedures include the Citizens' Bypass Program, which allows Americans whose purchases are under $400 to go to the "green line," where they simply show their passports to the customs inspector. This, in effect, completely eliminates the old obligatory inspection, although inspectors still retain the right to search any luggage they choose, so don't do anything foolish and illegal.

The US Customs Service publishes a series of free pamphlets with customs information. It includes *Know Before You Go,* a basic discussion of customs requirements pertaining to all travelers; *International Mail Imports; Travelers' Tips on Bringing Food, Plant, and Animal Products into the United States; Importing a Car; GSP and the Traveler; Pocket Hints; Currency Reporting; Pets, Wildlife, US Customs; Customs Hints for Visitors (Nonresidents);* and *Trademark Information for Travelers.* For the entire series or individual pamphlets, write to the US Customs Service, PO Box 7407, Washington, DC 20044, or contact any of the seven regional offices, in Boston, Chicago, Houston, Los Angeles, Miami, New Orleans, and New York. The Customs Service has a tape-recorded message whereby callers using Touch-tone phones can get more information on various topics; the number is 202-566-8195. These pamphlets provide great briefing material, but if you still have questions when you're in Europe, you can contact the customs representative at the US Embassy in the particular country you're visiting.

Sources and Resources

Tourist Information Offices

European tourist authorities are generally the best sources of travel and entry information, and the literature offered is usually free. When requesting brochures and maps, specify the areas you plan to visit, and state your interests regarding hotels, restaurants, special events, tourist attractions, guided tours, and sports facilities. Remember that different countries have different entry requirements, so if your plans include several countries, contact the tourism office of each one. For more foreign entry information, see *Entry Requirements and Documents,* in this section, as well as FACTS IN BRIEF.

The best places for tourist information in each European city are listed in the individual city reports in THE CITIES. Below is a list of European tourist authorities in the US.

Andorra: Sindicat d'Iniciativa de les Vales d'Andorra, 1923 W. Irving Park Rd., Chicago, IL 60613 (phone: 312-472-7660).

Austria: Austrian National Tourist Office, 500 Fifth Ave., Suite 2009, New York, NY 10110 (phone: 212-944-6880); 11601 Wilshire Blvd., Suite 2480, Los Angeles, CA 90025 (phone: 213-477-3332); 500 N. Michigan Ave., Suite 544, Chicago, IL 60611 (phone: 312-644-5556); 4800 San Felipe St., Suite 500, Houston, TX 77056 (phone: 713-850-9999).

Belgium: Belgian National Tourist Office, 745 Fifth Ave., New York, NY 10151 (phone: 212-758-8130).

Bulgaria: Balkan Holidays/USA/Ltd., 161 E. 86th St., New York, NY 10028 (phone: 212-722-1110).

Czechoslovakia: Čedok, Czechoslovak Travel Bureau, 10 E. 40th St., Suite 1902, New York, NY 10016 (phone: 212-689-9720). Embassy of Czechoslovakia, 3900 Linnean Ave. NW, Washington, DC 20008 (phone: 202-363-6308).

Denmark: Danish Tourist Board, 655 Third Ave., New York, NY 10017 (phone: 212-949-2333); 150 N. Michigan Ave, Suite 2110, Chicago, IL 60601 (phone: 312-726-1120); 8929 Wilshire Blvd., Suite 300, Beverly Hills, CA 90211 (phone: 213-854-1549).

Finland: Finnish Tourist Board, 655 Third Ave., New York, NY 10017 (phone: 212-949-2333); 1900 Ave. of the Stars, Suite 1070, Los Angeles, CA 90067 (phone: 213-277-5226).

France: French Government Tourist Office, 610 Fifth Ave., New York, NY 10020-2452 (for mail inquiries only); 628 Fifth Ave., New York, NY 10020 (phone: 212-757-1125); 9454 Wilshire Blvd., Suite 303, Beverly Hills, CA 90212-2967 (phone: 213-271-6665); One Hallidie Plaza, San Francisco, CA 94102 (phone: 415-986-4161); 645 N. Michigan Ave., Chicago, IL 60611-2836 (phone: 312-337-6301); 2305 Cedar Springs Rd., Suite 205, Dallas, TX 75201 (phone: 214-720-4010).

East Germany: Embassy of the German Democratic Republic, 1717 Massachusetts Ave. NW, Washington, DC 20036 (phone: 202-232-3134); Koch Travel Bureau, 157 E. 86th St., New York, NY 10028 (phone: 212-369-3800).

West Germany: German National Tourist Office, 747 Third Ave., 33rd Floor, New York, NY 10017 (phone: 212-308-3300); 444 S. Flower St., Suite 2230, Los Angeles, CA 90071 (phone: 213-688-7332).

Gibraltar: Gibraltar Information Bureau, 710 The Madison Offices, 1155 15th Street NW, Washington, DC 20005 (phone: 202-452-1108).

Great Britain: British Tourist Authority, 40 W. 57th St., New York, NY 10019 (phone: 212-581-4700); 350 S. Figueroa St., Suite 450, Los Angeles, CA 90071 (phone: 213-628-3525); John Hancock Center, Suite 3320, 875 N. Michigan Ave., Chicago, IL 60611 (phone: 312-787-0490); Cedar Maple Plaza, 2305 Cedar Springs Rd., Suite 210, Dallas, TX 75201-1814 (phone: 214-720-4040).

Greece: Greek National Tourist Organization, Olympic Tower, 5th Floor, 645 Fifth Ave., New York, NY 10022 (phone: 212-421-5777); 611 W. Sixth St., Suite 1998, Los Angeles, CA 90017 (phone: 213-626-6696); 168 N. Michigan Ave., Chicago, IL 60601 (phone: 312-782-1084).

Hungary: Hungarian Travel Bureau (IBUSZ), 1 Parker Plaza, Suite 1104, Ft. Lee, NJ 07024 (phone: 201-592-8585 or 212-582-7412).

Iceland: Iceland Tourist Board, 655 Third Ave., New York, NY 10017 (phone: 212-949-2333).

Irish Republic: Irish Tourist Board, 757 Third Ave., New York, NY 10017 (phone: 212-418-0800).

Northern Ireland: Northern Ireland Tourist Board, 40 W. 57th St., New York, NY 10019 (phone: 212-765-5144).

Italy: Italian Government Travel Office, 630 Fifth Ave., Suite 1565, New York, NY 10111 (phone: 212-245-4822); 500 N. Michigan Ave., Chicago, IL 60611 (phone: 312-644-0990); 360 Post St., San Francisco, CA 94108 (phone: 415-392-5266).

Liechtenstein: Swiss National Tourist Office, 608 Fifth Ave., New York, NY 10020 (phone: 212-757-5944); 150 N. Michigan Ave., Suite 2930, Chicago, IL 60601 (phone: 312-630-5840); 260 Stockton St., San Francisco, CA 94108 (phone: 415-362-2260).

Luxembourg: Luxembourg National Tourist Office, 801 Second Ave., New York, NY 10017 (phone: 212-370-9850).

Malta: Malta Tourist Information Office, c/o Consulate of Malta, 249 E. 35th St., New York, NY 10016 (phone: 212-725-2345); 2017 Connecticut Ave. NW, Washington, DC 20008 (phone: 202-462-3611).

Monaco: Monaco Government Tourist and Convention Bureau, 845 Third Ave., New York, NY 10022 (phone: 212-759-5227); 407 S. Dearborn St., Chicago, IL 60605 (phone: 312-939-7863).

Netherlands: Netherlands Board of Tourism, 355 Lexington Ave., New York, NY 10017 (phone: 212-370-7367); 225 N. Michigan Ave., Suite 326, Chicago, IL 60601 (phone: 312-819-0300); 90 New Montgomery St., Suite 305, San Francisco, CA 94105 (phone: 415-543-6772).

Norway: Norwegian Tourist Board, 655 Third Ave., New York, NY 10017 (phone: 212-949-2333); 150 N. Michigan Ave., Suite 2110, Chicago, IL 60601 (phone: 312-726-1120); 8929 Wilshire Blvd., Suite 300, Beverly Hills, CA 90211 (phone: 213-854-1549).

Poland: Polish National Tourist Office, 333 N. Michigan Ave., Chicago, IL 60601 (phone: 312-236-9013); Orbis Polish Travel Agency, 500 Fifth Ave., Suite 300, New York, NY 10110 (phone: 212-391-0844).

Portugal: Portuguese National Tourist Office, 590 Fifth Ave., New York, NY 10036-4704 (phone: 212-354-4403).

Romania: Romanian National Tourist Office, 573 Third Ave., New York, NY 10016 (phone: 212-697-6971).

San Marino: San Marino Government Tourist Office, 1685 E. Big Beaver Rd., Troy, MI 48083 (phone: 313-528-1190, Wednesdays and Saturdays from 11 AM to 2 PM only).

Spain: Spanish National Tourist Office, 665 Fifth Ave., New York, NY 10022 (phone: 212-759-8822); 845 N. Michigan Ave., Chicago, IL 60611 (phone: 312-642-1992); San Vicente Plaza Bldg., 8383 Wilshire Blvd., Beverly Hills, CA 90211 (phone: 213-658-7188).

Sweden: Swedish Tourist Board, 655 Third Ave., New York, NY 10017 (phone: 212-949-2333); 150 N. Michigan Ave., Suite 2110, Chicago, IL 60601 (phone: 312-726-1120); 8929 Wilshire Blvd., Suite 300, Beverly Hills, CA 90211 (phone: 213-854-1549).

Switzerland: Swiss National Tourist Office, 608 Fifth Ave., New York, NY 10020 (phone: 212-757-5944); 150 N. Michigan Ave., Suite 2930, Chicago, IL 60601 (phone: 312-630-5840; 260 Stockton St., San Francisco, CA 94108 (phone: 415-362-2260).

USSR: Intourist Travel Information Office, 630 Fifth Ave., New York, NY 10111 (phone: 212-757-3884).

Yugoslavia: Yugoslav National Tourist Office, 630 Fifth Ave., Suite 280, New York, NY 10111 (phone: 212-757-2801).

Theater and Special Event Tickets

The various tourist authorities can also supply information on the many special events and festivals that take place in Europe, though they cannot in all cases provide the actual program or detailed information on ticket prices. In more than one section of this book you will come across mention of events to spark your interest — everything from music festivals and special theater seasons to sporting championships — along with addresses to write for descriptive brochures, reservations, or tickets. Since many of these occasions are sometimes fully booked well in advance, if there is something you would surely not want to miss, you should think about making your reservation well before you go. If you do write, remember that any request from the US should be accompanied by an International Reply Coupon to ensure a response (send two of them for an airmail response). Tickets can usually be paid for by an international money order or by foreign draft. These international coupons, money orders, and drafts are available at US post offices and banks.

Books and Magazines

Throughout GETTING READY TO GO, numerous books and brochures have been recommended as good sources of further information on a variety of topics. In many cases, these have been publications of the various tourist authorities and are available free through their offices both here and abroad. Others may be found in the travel section of any good general bookstore.

The following stores and/or mail-order houses also specialize in travel, but not in travel to any particular country or continent. They offer books on Europe along with guides to the rest of the world and, in some cases, even an old Baedeker guidebook or two.

Book Passage, 51 Tamal Vista, Corte Madera, CA 94925 (phone: 415-927-0960 in California; 800-321-9785 elsewhere in the US). Travel guides and maps to all areas of the world. A free catalogue is available.

The Complete Traveller, 199 Madison Ave., New York, NY 10016 (phone: 212-685-9007). Travel guides and maps. A catalogue is available for $2.

Forsyth Travel Library, PO Box 2975, 9154 W. 57th St., Shawnee Mission, KS 66201-1375 (phone: 913-384-0496 or 800-367-7984). Travel guides and maps, old and new, to all parts of the world. Ask for the Europe-only catalogue or the more extensive, worldwide catalogue.

Gourmet Guides, 2801 Leavenworth St., San Francisco, CA 94133 (phone: 415-771-3671). Travel guides and maps, along with cookbooks. Mail-order lists available on request.

Phileas Fogg's Books and Maps, Stanford Shopping Center, Palo Alto, CA 94304 (phone: 415-327-1754). Travel guides, maps, and language aids.

The Travel Suppliers, 727 N. Placentia Ave., Fullerton, CA 92631 (phone: 714-528-2502). Books and maps, plus travel paraphernalia from money belts and pouches to voltage and currency converters. Catalogue available.

Traveller's Bookstore, 22 W. 52nd St. (lobby), New York, NY 10019 (phone: 212-664-0995). Comprehensive collection of travel guides and maps. A catalogue is available for $2.

Wayfarer Books, PO Box 1121, Davenport, IA 52805 (phone: 319-355-3902). Travel guides and maps. Mail order only; call or write for a catalogue.

In addition, the *Librairie de France/Libreria Hispanica* (French and Spanish Book Corporation), which specializes in language dictionaries and French and Spanish fiction and nonfiction, carries some French-language guidebooks published in France. Of the company's two shops in New York, the one at 610 Fifth Ave., New York, NY 10020 (phone: 212-581-8810), has the greater selection of travel material; the other store is at 115 Fifth Ave., New York, NY 10003 (212-673-7400).

A subscription to the *International Herald Tribune* is also a good idea. This English-language newspaper is written and edited mostly in Paris and is *the* newspaper read regularly and avidly by Americans abroad to keep up with world news, US news, sports, the stock market (US and foreign), fluctuations in the exchange rate, and an assortment of help wanted ads, real estate listings, and personals, pan-European in scope. Issued 6 days a week, it is available the same day at newsstands throughout the US and in cities worldwide, including London, Frankfurt, Paris, Marseilles, The Hague, Zurich, and Rome. Home delivery is also widely available. To subscribe, write or call the Subscription Manager, International Herald Tribune, 850 Third Ave., 10th Floor, New York, NY 10022 (phone: 212-752-3890 or 800-882-2884).

Before or after your trip, you may want to subscribe to various publications devoted exclusively to a particular European city or country. For information on such publications, contact the appropriate tourist authority or see "Local Coverage" in THE CITIES.

Weights and Measures

When you are traveling in Europe, you'll find that just about every quantity, whether it is distance, weight, or capacity, will be in an unfamiliar figure. In fact, this is true for travel almost everywhere in the world, since the US is one of the last countries to make its way to the metric system. It may happen soon in the US, and your trip to Europe may familiarize you with what will one day be the weights and measures at your grocery store.

There are some specific things to keep in mind during your trip. Fruits and vegetables at a market are generally recorded in kilos (kilograms), as is your luggage at the airport and your body weight. (This latter is particularly pleasing to people of large build, who instead of weighing 220 pounds hit the scales at a mere 100 kilos.) A kilo is 2.2 pounds and 1 pound is .45 kilos. Body temperature is usually measured in degrees Centigrade or Celsius rather than Fahrenheit — a normal body temperature is 37C, not 98.6F, and freezing is 0C rather than 32F — although in Great Britain, the Irish Republic, and elsewhere on the Continent, the Fahrenheit scale may still be in use. Gasoline stations sell gas by the liter (approximately four to a gallon) although in the United Kingdom gas may still be sold by the British or "Imperial" gallon, which is 20% larger than the US gallon. Tire pressure gauges are in kilograms per square centimeter rather than pounds per square inch. Highway signs are written in kilometers rather than miles (1 mile equals 1.6 kilometers; 1 kilometer equals .62 mile). And speed limits are in kilometers per hour, so think twice before hitting the gas when you see a speed limit of 100. That means 62 miles per hour.

The tables and conversion factors listed below should give you all the information you will need to understand any transaction, road sign, or map you encounter on your travels.

APPROXIMATE EQUIVALENTS		
Metric Unit	**Abbreviation**	**US Equivalent**
LENGTH		
meter	m	39.37 inches
kilometer	km	.62 mile
millimeter	mm	.04 inch
CAPACITY		
liter	l	1.057 quarts
WEIGHT		
gram	g	.035 ounce
kilogram	kg	2.2 pounds
metric ton	MT	1.1 tons
ENERGY		
kilowatt	kw	1.34 horsepower

CONVERSION TABLES
METRIC TO US MEASUREMENTS

Multiply:	by:	to convert to:
LENGTH		
millimeters	.04	inches
meters	3.3	feet
meters	1.1	yards
kilometers	.6	miles
CAPACITY		
liters	2.11	pints (liquid)
liters	1.06	quarts (liquid)
liters	.26	gallons (liquid)
WEIGHT		
grams	.04	ounces (avoir.)
kilograms	2.2	pounds (avoir.)

US TO METRIC MEASUREMENTS

LENGTH		
inches	25.0	millimeters
feet	.3	meters
yards	.9	meters
miles	1.6	kilometers
CAPACITY		
pints	.47	liters
quarts	.95	liters
gallons	3.8	liters
WEIGHT		
ounces	28.0	grams
pounds	.45	kilograms

TEMPERATURE

$$°F = (°C \times 9/5) + 32 \qquad °C = (°F - 32) \times 5/9$$

Camera and Equipment

Vacations are everybody's favorite time for taking pictures. After all, most of us want to remember the places we visit — and show them off to others — through spectacular photographs. Here are a few suggestions to help you get the best results from your picture-taking.

BEFORE THE TRIP: If you're taking out your camera after a long period in mothballs or have just bought a new one, check it thoroughly before you leave to prevent unexpected breakdowns and disappointing pictures.

1. Shoot at least one test roll, using the kind of film you plan to take along with you. Use all the shutter speeds and f-stops on your camera, and vary the focus to make sure everything is in order. Do this well before departure so that there will be time to have the film developed and to make repairs if necessary. If you're in a rush, most large cities have custom labs that can process film in as little as an hour. Repairs, unfortunately, take longer.

2. Clean the camera thoroughly, inside and out. Dust and dirt can jam mechanisms, scratch film, and mar photographs. Remove surface dust from the lenses and camera body with a soft camel's-hair brush. Next, use at least two layers of crumpled lens tissue and your breath to clean lenses and filters. Don't rub hard and don't use water, saliva, or compressed air on lenses or filters because they are easily damaged. Persistent stains can be removed by using a Q-tip moistened with liquid lens cleaner. Anything that doesn't come off easily needs professional attention. Once your lenses are clean, protect them from dirt and damage with inexpensive skylight or ultraviolet filters.

3. Check the batteries for the light meter, and take along extras just in case they wear out during the trip.

EQUIPMENT TO TAKE ALONG: Keep your gear light and compact. Items that are too heavy or bulky to be carried comfortably on a full-day excursion will likely stay in your hotel room.

1. Most single lens reflex (SLR) cameras come with a 50mm, or "normal," lens, a general purpose lens that frames subjects within an approximately average angle of view. This is good for street scenes taken at a distance of 25 feet or more and for full-length portraits shot at 8 to 12 feet. You can expand your photographic options with a wide-angle lens, such as a 35mm, 28mm, or 24mm. These give a broader than normal angle of view and greater than normal "depth of field," that is, sharp focus from foreground to background. They are especially handy for panoramas, cityscapes, and for large buildings or statuary from which you can't step back. For extreme closeups, a macro-lens is best, but a screw-on magnifying lens is an inexpensive alternative. Telephoto lenses, 65mm to 1000mm, are good for shooting details from a distance (as in animal photography), but since they tend to be heavy and bulky, unless you anticipate a frequent need for them, omit them from vacation photography equipment. A zoom, which is a big lens but relatively light, has a variable angle of view so it gives a range of options. Try a 35mm to 80mm; beware of inexpensive models that give poor quality photographs. Protect all lenses with skylight or ultraviolet filters, which should be removed for cleaning only. A polarizing filter helps to eliminate glare and reflection and to achieve fully saturated colors in very bright sunlight. Take

along a couple of extra lens caps (they're the first things to get lost) or buy an inexpensive lens cap "leash."

2. Travel photographs work best in color. Good slide films are Kodachrome 64 and Fujichrome 50, both moderate- to slow-speed films that provide saturated colors and work well in most outdoor lighting situations. For very bright conditions, try slower film like Kodachrome 25. If the weather is cloudy or you're indoors with only natural light, use a faster film, such as Kodachrome or Ektachrome 200 or 400. These can be "pushed" to higher speeds. There are even faster films on the market for low-light situations. The result may be pictures with whiter, colder tones and a grainier image, but high-speed films open up picture possibilities that slower films cannot.

Films tend to render color in slightly different ways. Kodachrome brings out reds and oranges. Fujichrome is noted for its yellows, greens, and whites. Agfachrome mutes bright tones, producing fine browns, yellows, and whites. Anticipate what you are likely to see, and take along whichever types of film will enhance your results. You might test films as you test your camera (see above).

If you prefer film that develops into prints rather than slides, try Kodacolor 100 or 400 for most lighting situations. Vericolor is a professional film that gives excellent results, especially in skin tones, but it suffers shifts in color when subjected to temperature extremes; take it along for people photography *if* you're sure you can protect it from heat and cold. All lens and filter information applies equally to print and slide films.

How much film should you take? If you are serious about your photography, pack one roll of film (36 exposures) for each day of your trip. Film is especially expensive abroad, and any leftovers can be bartered away or brought home and safely stored in your refrigerator. Processing is also generally more expensive away from home — and not always as good. If you are concerned about airport security X-rays damaging your undeveloped film (X-rays do not affect processed film), store it in lead-lined bags sold in camera shops. This possibility is not as much of a threat as it used to be, however. In the US, incidents of X-ray damage to unprocessed film (exposed or unexposed) are minimal because low-dosage X-ray equipment is used virtually everywhere. As a rule of thumb, photo industry sources say that film with speeds up to ASA 400 can go through security machinery in the US five times without any noticeable effect. Overseas, the situation varies from country to country, but at least in Western Europe the trend is also toward equipment that delivers less and less radiation. While it is doubtful that one exposure would ruin your pictures, if you're traveling without a protective bag, you may want to ask to have your photo equipment inspected by hand, especially on a prolonged trip with repeated security checks. (Naturally, this is possible only if you're carrying your film and camera on board with you; it's a good idea anyway, because it helps to preclude loss or theft or the possibility at some airports that checked baggage will be X-rayed more heavily than hand baggage.) In the US, Federal Aviation Administration regulations require that if you request a hand inspection, you get it, but overseas the response may depend on the humor of the inspector. One type of film that should never be subjected to X-rays, even in the US, is the new, very high speed film with an ASA rating of 1000. If you are taking some of this overseas, note that there are lead-lined bags made especially for it. Finally, the walk-through metal detector devices at airports do not affect film, though the film cartridges will set them off.

3. A small battery-powered electronic flash unit, or "strobe," is handy for very dim light or at night, but only if the subject is at a distance of 15 feet or less. Flash units cannot illuminate an entire scene, and many museums do not permit flash photography, so take such a unit only if you know you will need it. If your camera

does not have a hot-shoe, you will need a PC cord to synchronize the flash with your shutter. Be sure to take along extra batteries.

4. Invest in a broad camera strap if you now have a thin one. It will make carrying the camera much more comfortable. For safety and ease of use, keep the camera strapped around your neck (not on your shoulder) whenever it is out of its bag.

5. A sturdy canvas or leather camera bag, preferably with padded pockets — not an airline bag — will keep equipment clean, organized, and easy to find.

6. For cleaning, bring along a camel's-hair brush that retracts into a rubber squeeze bulb. Also, take plenty of lens tissue and plastic bags to protect equipment from dust.

SOME TIPS: For better pictures, remember the following pointers:

1. *Get close.* Move in to get your subject to fill the frame.
2. *Vary your angle.* Shoot from above or below — look for unusual perspectives.
3. *Pay attention to backgrounds.* Keep it simple or blur it out.
4. *Look for details.* Not just a whole building, but a decorative element; not just an entire street scene, but a single remarkable face.
5. *Don't be lazy.* Always carry your camera gear with you, loaded and ready for those unexpected memorable moments.

FACTS IN BRIEF

Facts in Brief

The tourist authority addresses listed below are for information within each country. For US addresses of national tourist authorities, see *Tourist Information Offices*, GETTING READY TO GO.

Andorra

TOURIST INFORMATION: The center for assistance is the Sindicat d'Iniciativa de les Valles d'Andorra, c/o Dr. Vilanova, Andorra la Vella (phone: 20214).

ENTRY REQUIREMENTS: Andorra has none, but France and Spain have checkpoints on their sides of the border and will request a valid US passport. If you plan to arrive or leave via the French border, note that, due to a recent change in policy, you no longer need a visa for crossing into or out of France.

CLIMATE AND CLOTHES: All 175 square miles of Andorra are tucked into a few folds high up in the eastern Pyrenees between Spain and France. The altitude assures snow-capped mountains and chilly evenings the year round, but the temperature on June, July, and August days can easily reach 80F (25C) before plunging at nightfall, so pack cottons as well as heavy sweaters.

MONEY: The French franc, which equals 100 centimes, and Spanish peseta, which equals 100 centimos, are both legal tender.

LANGUAGE: Catalan, spoken in neighboring Spain, is the official tongue, but French and Spanish are equally common. Shopkeepers and hoteliers speak English.

GETTING THERE/GETTING AROUND: Trains – Andorra is one of the few countries in Europe without an inch of train track on its territory. The nearest station in Spain is at Puigcerda, from which bus connections are available to Seu d' Urgell and Andorra la Vella. If you're traveling from Madrid, take the train to Lleida, then connect with a bus to Seu d'Urgell and Andorra.

From France, the French railway stops at Ax-les-Thermes, Hospitalet-près-l'Andorre, and La Tour de Carol. From these towns, bus connections are available to Andorra la Vella.

Buses – Seasonal bus service between La Tour de Carol, France, and the main centers in Andorra is provided by *Autos Víuda Pujol Huguet.* There are also daily buses from Barcelona, Spain. Microbuses serve the principal Andorran villages from Andorra la Vella.

Cars – Winter snows can close the main French Rte. 20 to Andorra. The alternate, all-weather route is Spain's Rte. C1313 from Puigcerda to Seu d'Urgell, where it connects with Rte. C145 to Andorra.

SPECIAL EVENTS: The *Feste de Andorra la Vella* is the first Saturday, Sunday, and Monday in August.

SHOPPING: On weekends, the roads leading through Andorra la Vella are as clogged with shoppers as Macy's aisles during Christmas. Tax-free merchandise (often a euphemism for smuggled goods) is the goal, and cars bulging with purchases can barely pass one another on the narrow thoroughfare. Cigarettes, sheepskin jackets, liquor, Parisian fashions, gasoline, canned goods, and perfume are just a few of the bargains that lure the shopper. Most stores are open 7 days a week.

TIPPING: Sometimes restaurants and hotels include service charges, sometimes not. From 10% to 15% is the expected tip.

Austria

TOURIST INFORMATION: Literature can be obtained from the Austrian National Tourist Office (Oesterreichische Fremdenverkehrswerbung), 1 Margarethen Strasse, A-1040 Vienna (phone: 222-588660). Regional information is provided by state tourist offices found in the capital cities of the nine states and called either *Landesfremden-verkehrsverband* or *Fremdenverkehrsverband.*

ENTRY REQUIREMENTS: US citizens with valid US passports need no visas for visits of 3 months or less.

CLIMATE AND CLOTHES: Mountains cover over 70% of the country and altitude rather than latitude determines temperature. Be prepared for summer showers. On the whole, the climate is moderate with summer daytime averages in the 70s F (20C) and nights cooling to the 50s F (10C). Winter days are in the 30s F (0 degrees C) and 40s F (5C). Comfortable sporting gear is standard. For Vienna, you'll want something chic for a gala evening on the town.

MONEY: The Austrian Schilling (AS internationally, S in Austria) is divided into 100 Groschen.

LANGUAGE: German (*hochdeutsch*) is the written language and is taught in the schools, but numerous and pronounced regional dialects exist. English is taught as the second language and is understood in major tourist areas.

GETTING THERE/GETTING AROUND: Airlines – Austrian Airlines, Pan American, Romanian Air (TAROM), and Royal Jordanian Airlines (ALIA) have nonstop service to Vienna from New York, but TAROM is not recommended because of its poor service. (Royal Jordanian also offers direct flights from Los Angeles.) Austrian Airlines, as well as many other European airlines, connect most major European cities with Vienna and other Austrian destinations. TWA has service to Vienna via Frankfurt. Austrian Airlines offers daily domestic service from Vienna to Graz, Klagenfurt, Linz, and Salzburg; Tyrolean Airways has daily service to Innsbruck and Frankfurt.

Trains – *Austrian Federal Railways* (*OeBB*) offers the Austrian Network Pass, which provides unlimited travel on trains in Austria for 1 month. This pass can be purchased at all Austrian railroad stations. Senior citizen discounts of 50% are available to travelers over 60 (women) and 65 (men) on trains, the postal buses, and buses operated by the *Federal Railways* (not local transit). An application form may be picked up at the railroad stations throughout Austria as well as those in Frankfurt, Munich, and Zurich. Also available at Austrian rail stations is the Rabbit Card, which allows 4 days of unlimited train travel. It must be used within 10 days from the date of purchase.

Cars – European makes can be rented from the usual array of international and local firms in all major Austrian cities. The tax rate on rental cars is 21% unless the car is kept 22 days or longer, in which case the tax rate is 33%. The *Austrian Federal Railways,* in cooperation with *Avis* and *Inter-Rent,* offers car rentals for pickup at certain stations, including Vienna, Graz, and Salzburg. The reservation must be made at least two hours prior to arrival at the station where the car will be picked up. Reservations may be made at any railroad station, *OeBB*-appointed travel agencies, or with the conductor on express trains; maximium rental period is 3 days. Road condition information in English can be obtained daily from 6 AM to 10 PM in Vienna by phoning 72997 and from other areas by dialing 02-227-2997.

SPECIAL EVENTS: Austria's most famous musical festivals are the *International Music Festival of Vienna,* May and June, reservations from the *Austrian Travel Agency*

(7 Friedrichstrasse, A-1010 Vienna; phone: 158-8000); the *Carinthian Summer Festival* in Ossiach and Villach, June through August, reservations are available from 76 Gumpendorfer Str., A-1060 Vienna (phone: 568198) or A-9570 Ossiach (phone: 43510 or 43502); the *Bregenz Festival on Lake Constance* in July and August, for reservations contact Kartenbüro, Postfach 119, A-6901 Bregenz (phone: 557-422-8110); and the *Salzburg Festival,* also in July and August, reservations procedure varies according to event. To ensure that you get the tickets you want to these and other festivals, contact the Austrian National Tourist Office in the US for full details on how to order tickets well before your departure.

SHOPPING: Dirndls, lederhosen, alpine hats with a rakish feather or enameled emblem, and fabric printed with folkloric patterns are all evocative of provincial Austria and can be purchased regionally at *Heimatwerk* shops, which generally have the best selection of local artisans' work. Other specialties include the ubiquitous enamelware, Loden cloth coats and jackets, well-designed sweaters, Viennese petit-point articles, precious jewelry, porcelain, and glassware. Sleek Austrian skiwear is a bargain only for those already paying top dollar.

Stores are open between 8 AM and 6 PM; some close for 2 hours at noon for lunch. Most are closed Saturday afternoons, and all day Sundays. To obtain a VAT refund, ask the Austrian National Tourist Office for a copy of the booklet *Tax Refunds for Shopping in Austria.* The procedure is complicated.

TIPPING: Service charges run between 10% and 15% on restaurant and hotel bills, with the higher percentage included in luxury establishment bills. Leave a small amount of change for the waiter or the maid. Porters and bellmen should receive 10 schillings per bag, doormen about 5, and taxi drivers 10% of the fare.

Belgium

TOURIST INFORMATION: Town Hall, Grand Place, 1000 Bruxelles (Brussels), is the address for Tourist Information Brussels (TIB), (phone: 513-8940); tourist information for the city and country: 61 Rue Marché aux Herbes (phone: 513-9090). Tourist offices in all other cities are called either Syndicat d'Initiative or Dienst voor Toerisme.

ENTRY REQUIREMENTS: A valid US passport is good for visits of 3 months or less by US citizens.

CLIMATE AND CLOTHES: The sea is the predominant influence on the weather and the gently undulating hills that cover a good part of the country's interior don't stop the prevailing westerlies. In the Ardennes, morning fogs near the shore turn into evening mists. The climate is temperate with few extremes. Temperatures reach 70F (21C) in summer and drop to the low 40s (near 0 degrees C) in winter. Dress is cosmopolitan and French in style. Bikinis are much in evidence on Belgium's west coast beaches, but none are St.-Tropez style, and whatever swimming attire you wear you must keep on.

MONEY: The Belgian franc (BF) equals 100 centimes.

LANGUAGE: French is spoken by inhabitants of the Walloon area south of Brussels — about 32% of the population. Brussels itself is primarily French-speaking but lies in Flanders, where the official language is Flemish, an accented version of Dutch. German is the third national language but is spoken by less than 1% of the inhabitants. English is widely understood.

GETTING THERE/GETTING AROUND: Airlines – Sabena flies nonstop from Anchorage, Atlanta, Boston, Chicago, New York, Montreal, and Toronto to Brussels. From New York to Brussels, Pan American flies direct via London, and TWA, nonstop.

Trains – Belgium's rail network is said to be the world's most comprehensive. The

Société Nationale Chemin de Fer Belge (*SNCB*) offers several reduced-fare plans and also the Benelux Tourrail Pass, good for 5 days of travel in a 17-day period on the Belgian, Dutch, and Luxembourg railways.

Bus – *Europabus* is a network of tourist bus services operated by the European railways. Both scheduled services and tours are offered. Contact *Europa,* 50 L'Epervier, Pl. de Brouckere, 1000 Brussels (phone: 217-0025), or *Debock,* 105 Rue Marché aux Herbes, 1000 Brussels (phone: 02-217-0025).

Cars – Motoring information as well as breakdown service is provided by the *Touring Club de Belgique,* 44 Rue de la Loi, 1040 Brussels (phone: 233-2211), and the *Royal Automobile Club de Belgique,* which also has an SOS breakdown number (phone: 736-5959). The small yellow cars of the touring *secours* (literally, "help") patrol offer assistance to motorists in need.

SPECIAL EVENTS: Belgian folkloric pageants and processions are famed and numerous. *Carnival* in Binche climaxes on *Shrove Tuesday* with costumed and ostrich-plumed "Gilles" pummeling the crowds with oranges. *Ascension Thursday* in May is celebrated in Bruges by the famed *Procession of the Holy Blood;* also in May, the *Cat Festival* of Iper features costumes, floats, and the tossing of plush cats from the town's belfry.

SHOPPING: Chocolate is a Belgian specialty. *Godiva* (owned by the US *Campbell Soup Company*) has its own stores in Belgium, but is by no means the only source for fine chocolates. The true devotee should also seek out the *Neuhaus, Corne de la Toison d'Or,* and *Wittamer* brands.

Pewter, manufactured by *Les Potstainiers Hugo* in Huy and *Meestertingieters* in Tongeren, and *Val St. Lambert* crystal are good buys. Belgian linen and laces are justifiably famous.

The beautifully balanced sporting guns of the *Fabrique Nationale* in Herstal, among the aristocracy of shotguns, can be specially ordered with scenes hand etched by local craftsmen.

Larger Belgian stores are open from 9:15 AM to 6 PM. Smaller shops that close for lunch usually remain open until 8 PM.

TIPPING: A 16% service charge is added to most restaurant bills and is also included on taxi meters.

Bulgaria

TOURIST INFORMATION: Balkantourist, the state travel agency, has headquarters at 1 Vitoša Blvd. in Sofia (phone: 43331). Local tourist information offices throughout the country provide maps and other materials and assistance. For more information on travel to Bulgaria and the rest of Central and Eastern Europe, contact *Balkan Holidays/USA/Ltd.,* 161 E. 86th St., New York, NY 10028 (phone: 212-722-1110).

ENTRY REQUIREMENTS: US citizens require a visa to enter the country unless they are traveling with a tour group or with a group of six or more and possess a voucher indicating they have prepaid for tourist services. People entering on business or without prearranged accommodations must obtain visas from the Bulgarian embassy or consulate before leaving the US. When applying for a business visa, you must present a "letter of invitation" from the company you are visiting. Both tourist and business visas cost $15 and are available within 7 business days of filling out the appropriate forms. Contact the Bulgarian Embassy, 1621 22nd St. NW, Washington, DC 20008 (phone: 202-387-7969).

CLIMATE AND CLOTHES: The Balkan Mountains (highest range is the Rila Dagh, at more than 9,000 feet) crisscross the country to reach straight to the edge of the Black

Sea and its golden beaches. Summers are dry but not oppressively hot (80s F, high 20s C) and winters cold, dry, and relatively windless with temperatures in the 30s F (around 0 degrees C). Informality is the keynote in summer dress. Jackets and ties (and warm coats) are best for fall and winter in Sofia, the capital.

MONEY: The lev equals 100 stotinki. *Note:* The exchange rate is 200% higher for tourists (with voucher).

LANGUAGE: Bulgarian, a South Slavic tongue, is similar to Russian and uses the Cyrillic alphabet. You can just navigate the tourist circuit with English (Russian is the second language) and should consider the use of English-speaking guides if you wish to communicate in the countryside.

GETTING THERE/GETTING AROUND: Airlines – There's no direct US-Bulgaria service, but Balkanair and other international carriers connect Sofia to all European capitals. Within Bulgaria, Balkanair flies between major cities at reasonable rates.

Bus – Tours run by *Balkantourist* are accompanied by multilingual guides, alleviate the language problem, and are suggested for sightseeing.

Trains – The *BDG* (*Bulgarian State Railway*) service between Sofia and Varna on the Black Sea is frequent and efficient, but most other trains are locals and crowded. There is also service between Sofia and other major capitals, such as Istanbul and Vienna.

Cars – Probably the best bet for the tourist, with rentals of Russian Lada, Mercedes-Benzes, Volkswagens, and Toyotas available through *Shipka,* the touring agency of the *Bulgarian Motorists Union,* 6 Sveta Sofia St., Sofia (phone: 879921), or through *Balkantourist,* 1 Vitoša Blvd., Sofia (phone: 43331). Free emergency assistance is provided by road aid cars that patrol the highways or can be called (phone: 146).

SPECIAL EVENTS: Bulgaria is the world's leading exporter of attar of roses and one of the biggest festivals occurs the first Sunday in June celebrating the harvest of the huge rose crop, which covers a 20-mile swath in the Kazanlŭk area.

Slunchev Bryag, best known as Sunny Beach, on Bulgaria's Riviera hosts a pop music festival called *Golden Orpheus* in early June, which brings entertainers and groups from all over the world. In a more serious vein, Sofia's continuous musical weeks in May and June concentrate on the classical, and Plovdiv has chamber music concerts throughout the month of June. Humor is the focus of Gabrovo's biannual (odd years only) comedic extravaganza, which brings tourists from all over the world to this centrally located town for 10 days in mid-May.

SHOPPING: Attar of roses in hand-carved wooden containers is the most popular Bulgarian souvenir, but larger purchases could include leather goods or the rugs made in Kotel (in general, a center for crafts), which come in a variety of colorful designs, or those of Chiprovtsi. The *Bulgarian Artists Union* runs shops around the country featuring products of the membership, and the state-run foreign currency *Corecom* stores are a good source for other Bulgarian products including silks and sheepskin coats. Normal store hours are 8:30 AM to 7 PM Mondays through Saturdays, with a 2-hour break at midday. In small towns, stores may close early on Saturdays.

TIPPING: In theory tips are not accepted; in practice they are. About 10% of a restaurant bill.

Czechoslovakia

TOURIST INFORMATION: *Cedok*'s blue sign with the white bird in flight signifies general tourist services at some 150 locations throughout the country. Its main office is at 18 Na Příkopě, Prague (phone: 212-7111), and its accommodations service is at 5 Panská, Prague. Larger cities also have tourist information centers.

ENTRY REQUIREMENTS: US tourists require a visa good for visits of up to 30 days. Czechoslovak consulates and embassies abroad issue visas within 24 hours upon receipt of an application, two passport photos, and a fee of $16. In order to obtain a visa, proof of prepaid land arrangements or *Cedok* vouchers amounting to $18 per person per day must be submitted. This foreign exchange requirement can be handled at the border.

CLIMATE AND CLOTHES: Czechoslovakia is really three contiguous areas snaking across central Europe, and temperatures are about the same in all three — Bohemia, Moravia, and Slovakia. Average temperatures are around 70F (21C) in summer, and the low 20s F (a little below 0 degrees C) in winter, although mountains are chillier in both seasons.

Dress is casual but conservative. Evenings at luxury resorts such as Karlovy Vary (Carlsbad) and Mariánské Lázně (Marienbad) call for reasonably dressy clothes.

MONEY: One koruna (Kčs.) consists of 100 halers. It is illegal to import or export Czechoslovak currency.

LANGUAGE: Czech is spoken by about two thirds of the population — those living in the Czech Socialist Republic — a combination of the Bohemian and Moravian countries. Slovak, the native language of the rest of the population, is spoken in the eastern Slovak Socialist Republic. Both languages are Slavic and very similar. Those engaged in tourism speak English.

GETTING THERE/GETTING AROUND: Airlines – CSA, the Czechoslovak airline, flies the New York–Prague route with Ilyusin 62s nonstop in summer and from Montreal year-round. Pan American flies to Prague via Frankfurt. Prague is the hub from which domestic flights on CSA radiate to 13 airports, including Brno, Bratislava, Košice, Ostrava, Piešťany (for spas), and Poprad in the Tatras (for skiing and mountaineering).

Bus – Next to the airlines, express bus service to East Germany, Austria, Poland, Russia, Yugoslavia, and Hungary, as well as domestic service aboard *CSAD* coaches, is probably the fastest way of traveling in Czechoslovakia.

Trains – There's frequent service aboard trains of the *Ceskoslovenské Státní Dráhy* (*CSD*) and various European expresses stop at Prague, Bratislava, and Brno.

Cars – Rentals are available from *Pragocar,* with outlets in the major cities. The Yellow Angels in four-wheel-drive vehicles of the *Ustredni Automotoklub* provide emergency service for motorists. Gas coupons are sold at frontier crossings, at the automobile club office in Prague at 29 Opletalova (phone: 223544), and at Zivnostenska Bank, 20 Na Příkopě, Prague.

SPECIAL EVENTS: Fine international performances are part of Prague's annual spring music festival, *Prague Spring* (*Pražské Jaro*), beginning May 12, the anniversary of the Czech composer Bedřich Smetana's death, and continuing through June 1. Two colorful folk festivals offer grand displays of typical costumes, music, and dances of the republic's two states, the *Moravian Fete* held in Strážnice in June, and the *Slovakian Festival* in Východná in July.

SHOPPING: Antiques are a lure, and the small shops in Prague delight the collector and window-shopper alike. However, antiques must be purchased at *Tuzex*-approved shops to be eligible for export. State-supported *Tuzex* shops sell a wide range of crafts and tourist goods, such as Bohemian glass and porcelain and fine quality records, for foreign currency. Modern applied arts are sold at *Art Centrum* in Prague and special folk art outlets for hand-painted Easter eggs, straw Christmas ornaments, jewelry, woven linens, and the like, are found in many towns. Long store hours facilitate shopping. Shops are open Mondays through Fridays from 8 or 9 AM to 6 PM, Saturdays from 9 AM to 1 PM.

TIPPING: Restaurant bills don't include service charges, and at least 10% should be added; taxi drivers also expect 10% tips; 5 korunas should be given to porters and doormen.

Denmark

TOURIST INFORMATION: The central office of Denmark's Turistråd, across the street from Copenhagen's Town Hall at 22 Hans Christian Andersens Blvd., Copenhagen V (phone: 111325), has maps, brochures, and literature on touring the entire country as well as Greenland and the Faeroe Islands; regional tourist offices in Denmark's major cities are equally well stocked. Innumerable local *turistbureaus* are distinguished by the international tourist logo, a green sign carrying a lowercase *i.*

ENTRY REQUIREMENTS: A valid US passport is good for visits of 3 months or less.

CLIMATE AND CLOTHES: Thanks to the Gulf Stream, winters are relatively mild with daytime temperatures averaging 34F (about 0 degrees C) in February, the coldest month. The changeable summer weather often includes rainstorms and the long summer nights can be chilly but summer days average about 70F (21C). The casual Danish lifestyle is reflected in an equally casual attitude about clothes.

MONEY: The Danish krone (DKr) equals 100 øre.

LANGUAGE: Danish, but English has been compulsory in secondary schools since World War II and is spoken and understood throughout the country.

GETTING THERE/GETTING AROUND: Airlines – SAS flies nonstop to Copenhagen from Anchorage, Chicago, Los Angeles, New York, and Seattle. Northwest flies nonstop to Copenhagen from Boston. Icelandair has regularly scheduled flights from New York to Copenhagen (with a stop in Reykjavik); TWA flies nonstop and direct from New York to Stockholm and to Copenhagen. Danair's domestic flights leave Copenhagen's Kastrup Airport for Bornholm, Funen, and nine airports in Jutland and the Faeroe Islands. SAS has service to Greenland from Copenhagen. In the winter, cheap charters carry sun-starved Scandinavians to warmer Mediterranean shores such as Greece, Israel, and Mallorca.

Trains – The modern *Intercity* and *L* (*Lyntog*) expresses cover the country at great speeds, navigating the crossing between Zealand and Funen aboard huge, handsome ferries. At other junctions, you leave the train, cross by boat, and board another train to continue. The Danish State Railway, *Dansk Statsbaner* (*DSB*), is one of the sponsors of the Scandinavian Rail Pass and also honors the Eurailpass, Eurail Youthpass, and Eurail Saverpass.

Ferries – The *DSB* ferries are an integral part of the highway and rail system and, though they have been supplemented by bridges, they are still an essential part of the major crossing between Funen and Zealand, called the Store Baelt (Great Belt).

SPECIAL EVENTS: In July and August, Odense re-creates local boy Hans Christian Andersen's fairy tales. Frederikssund's *Viking Festival* in June and July is a fine historical pageant. An array of first class cultural events is held all summer long at Copenhagen's *Tivoli* amusement park, open from May to mid-September.

SHOPPING: Shopping in Copenhagen is a trip in itself. *Bing & Grøndahl* and *Royal Copenhagen* porcelain, *Holmegaard* glass, *Georg Jensen* silver, and furs from *A. C. Bang* and *Birgir Christensen* are but a few of the products that make the dedicated shopper shiver with delight. Some better buys are *Bornholm* ceramics, handmade woolens from Tönder and the Faeroe Islands, and *Lego* toys. Herring, ham, and the national drink, aquavit, can always cheer you up when you contemplate your empty wallet back home. Denmark has a stiff value added (MOMS) tax of about 18%, but most of it can be saved by shopping at stores that display the Tax Free sign (minimum purchase per shop for this service is DKr. 1,200).

In general, stores are open weekdays between 9 AM and 5:30 PM and on Saturday mornings.

TIPPING: Railway porters and washroom attendants receive tips, but otherwise they are not expected unless a special service has been provided. Service charges are always included in restaurant, hotel, and taxi bills.

Finland

TOURIST INFORMATION: The Finnish Tourist Board (MEK) has a regional office in Rovaniemi and is based in Helsinki, with a tourist information office at 26 Unioninkatu, 00130 Helsinki (phone: 144511). All cities and towns have city tourist offices (Matkailutoimisto), identified by the lowercase *i* on a green background.

ENTRY REQUIREMENTS: A valid US passport is required for visits of 3 months or less by US citizens.

CLIMATE AND CLOTHES: In the south, snow covers the country from December to mid-April, when it begins melting. Winter comes earlier to the north, around the end of October, and stays later, until mid-May. Midday temperatures in Helsinki average 72F (22C) in July, the warmest month, and 20F (−7C) in February, the coldest. At Ivalo, to the far north, warm July days average 66F (18C) and cool February days, 7F (−13C).

Informal dress is frowned upon in the better restaurants, where jackets and ties are expected. In general, the tenor is slightly more conservative than in other Scandinavian countries.

MONEY: The Finnish markka (FIM) equals 100 pennis.

LANGUAGE: Finland's two official tongues are Finnish, spoken by 93% of the Finnish people, which like Hungarian and Estonian is a Finno-Ugric language; and Swedish, an Indo-European language spoken by about 6.2% of the people. Lappish, also Finno-Ugric, is the native speech of about 2,000 citizens. English is found in the major tourist centers and is the country's most widely spoken foreign language.

GETTING THERE/GETTING AROUND: Airlines – Only Finnair flights link New York, Seattle, and Los Angeles with Helsinki nonstop. Pan American flies to Helsinki from New York, with a stop in Stockholm, and SAS flies from New York to Helsinki via Copenhagen and Stockholm. Domestically, they serve 21 cities at some of the cheapest fares in Europe. Finnair offers a Holiday Ticket good for 15 days of unlimited domestic air travel, as well as family and senior citizen discounts.

Trains – *Valtionrautatiet* (*VR*) provides excellent equipment and relatively inexpensive service and offers a selection of discount tourist plans including the Finnrail Pass, for various periods of unlimited travel; the Tourist Ticket, which includes bus, boat, air, and train travel, valid for a year; and the Scandinavian Rail Pass and Eurailpass.

Cars – The 519-mile trip between Helsinki and Rovaniemi, the capital of Lapland on the Arctic Circle, takes about 12 hours by car over well-maintained, year-round roads. Car rentals are readily available in Helsinki.

Ferries, Ships, and Other Transport – The series of interconnecting lakes in western, central, and southeastern Finland seems to take up more room than the landmass there. A varied fleet, from hydrofoils to small lake steamers, provides service in this unique area. The railroad's northern terminus is Kemijarvi, just above the Arctic Circle. As a result, buses are the primary surface transport as well as being a major means of transit in the northern region of Lapland. Contact *Oy Matkahuolto Ab,* 3 Simonkatu , 00100 Helsinki (phone: 642744), for overseas bus depots, reservations, and ticket sales in Finland.

SPECIAL EVENTS: All Finland is a festival between June and September, with many diverse cultural events. Music is the theme of most, with the performing arts celebrated in Helsinki throughout the summer.

In late February the *Salpausselkä Skiing Championships* feature cross-country ski races at Lahti. The beginning of March brings the *Kuopio Skating Marathon* in Kuopio. Also in Feburary is the 75-km *Finlandia Ski Race* between Hämeenlinna and Lahti. Reindeer roundups in Lapland are in progress from October to January.

SHOPPING: The Finnish genius for modern design has made *Marimekko* fabrics, *Arabia* ceramics, and *Iittala* glassware international household names. *Lapponia* jewelry, fusing gold and silver in stylized replicas of natural forms, is highly regarded, as is the *Aarikka* line of wooden jewelry. Multicolored patterned rya rugs come from Finland as do the orange-handled scissors made by *Fiskars,* which also makes a fine line of steel cutlery. Traditional decorated *Puukko* sheath knives make perfect presents for outdoor people. For an overall view of Finnish products, stop at Helsinki's *Design Center,* 19 Kasarminkatu.

The Finnish 16% sales tax (VAT) can be avoided (via a refund in the mail) by having stores send purchases to your departure point or directly home. Or you can save between 11% and 13% — to be refunded at your point of departure — and take the package with you, sealed, under the new tax-free program. Summer shopping hours are generally 8:30 AM to 5 PM Mondays through Thursdays, until 8 PM on Fridays, and 9 AM to 3 PM on Saturdays.

TIPPING: Restaurants add a 14% service charge during the week and 15% on Sundays and holidays, but you can leave a bit extra for the waiter, and make sure to tip about 3 Fmks to the restaurant doorman. Hotel bills also include the service. Porters receive 3 Fmks but others, including cab drivers, don't expect tips.

France

TOURIST INFORMATION: The main Office of Tourism is at 127 Champs-Elysées, 75008 Paris (phone: 472-08898 for information in English; 472-36172 in French), with branches at the major train stations, such as the Gare du Nord, Gare de l'Est, Gare de Lyon, and Gare d'Austerlitz, and at major airports throughout France. Local Syndicats d'Initiative (SI) supply literature in cities and towns. Regional information is available in Paris from the more than 20 provincial tourist bureaus, called collectively Maisons de Province à Paris, scattered around the city.

ENTRY REQUIREMENTS: A visa is no longer required to enter France; the only requirement is a valid US passport.

CLIMATE AND CLOTHES: It's generally fair and warm in the summertime, particularly in the south. Winters are mild, with overall daytime averages in the 40s F (about 5C), rising to highs of around 55F (12C) in January and February along the Riviera.

The celebrated French sense of style is best illustrated by the manner of dress. Visitors will certainly not feel ill at ease dressed casually and comfortably, but you may find a visit to Paris the perfect opportunity to practice a little Parisian chic.

MONEY: The French franc (F) equals 100 centimes.

LANGUAGE: French is spoken with verve and pride and, while you can normally get by in English, use whatever French words and phrases you know. Residents of Paris have a reputation for dealing coldly with non-French speakers. This is only partially justified, and in the provinces visitors will find few who speak English but an enormous amount of cordiality and patience.

GETTING THERE/GETTING AROUND: Airlines – Air France has daily *Concorde* flights between New York and Paris. *Concorde* flights take 3 hours 45 minutes from New York to Paris. Tickets cost about 20% more than subsonic first class fares. Air

France flies nonstop to Paris from Anchorage, Boston, Chicago, Houston, Los Angeles, Miami, New York, Philadelphia, San Francisco, and Washington, DC, and from New York to Nice; TWA flies nonstop from Boston, Los Angeles, New York, St. Louis, and Washington, DC; Pan American flies nonstop from New York, Miami, and Washington, DC, to Paris, and from New York to Nice. Delta flies nonstop from Atlanta; American has nonstops from Chicago, New York, Dallas/Ft. Worth, and Raleigh/Durham; Continental flies nonstop from Newark to Paris, and UTA from San Francisco. Air Inter, the national domestic carrier, serves all of France, including Corsica.

Trains – With over 22,000 miles of track, France has the largest rail network on the Continent, and, with crack Corail and turbotrains and the *TGV* (*train à grande vitesse*), the fastest trains. Although the *TGV* has set records, in commercial operation its speed is 168 mph. It cuts the trip from Paris to Lyons to 2 hours, and there are numerous round-trips daily. The new *Atlantique* line offers service between Paris and both Le-Mans and Tours.

The France Railpass offers unlimited travel over the entire *Société Nationale des Chemins de Fer Français* (*SNCF*) or *French Rail Inc.* railway system. Available for either first- or second class travel, for periods of 4 or 9 non-consecutive days within 15 days (for the 4-day pass) or one month (for the 9-day pass), it must be purchased before going abroad, either from a travel agent or from *French Rail Inc.* offices in the US. Bonuses include round-trip transfer from the Paris airports to downtown, a Metropass, and various discounts. For train information in English in Paris, call 438-05050; elsewhere, add the city code: 1. For information, contact French Rail Inc., 610 Fifth Ave., New York, NY 10020 (phone: 212-582-2110).

Cars – French toll roads, *autoroutes,* are well patrolled, and breakdown service is readily available. Emergency call boxes are being installed on other routes.

SPECIAL EVENTS: The *Festival d' Avignon,* a theater festival held annually in July and August, has no peer in France. Some wonderful, purely musical festivals take place each summer, among them the Strasbourg *International Music Festival* in early June, the *International Festival of Lyric Art and Music* in mid-July in Aix-en-Provence, and the *Berlioz Festival* in September in Lyon.

Famous sporting events include the *Le Mans* 24-hour race in mid-June and the *Tour de France,* the world's premier bicycle race, the first 3 weeks in July. The *Air Show* at Le Bourget takes place in June of odd-numbered years and the *Auto Show* in Paris in October of even years.

Dijon's *Gastronomic Fair* in early November is followed by the *Three Days of Glory* in Clos-de-Vougeot, Beaune, and Meursault nearby. The *Cannes Film Festival* is held annually in May.

SHOPPING: Boutiques, no matter how beautiful, are pricey. You will do much better in wholesale outlets or stores that carry seconds, discontinued lines, and overstocks. The savings are significant. Decent prices on housewares can be found in large Parisian department stores or their branches, as well as at the usually less expensive *Prisunic* and *Monoprix* chains.

For the ultimate in bric-a-brac shopping stop at any hamlet, no matter how small, on market day. Regional products include faience pottery from Quimper and Vallauris and porcelain from Limoges, as well as truffles from Périgord, mustards from Dijon, and herbs from Provence, also the home of lovely printed fabrics, exemplified by the Souleido cottons.

Most department stores are open Mondays through Saturdays from 9:30 AM to 6:30 PM, with one or two late-night closings. Boutiques close on Mondays as well as Sundays.

TIPPING: Hotel and restaurant bills include a 12% to 15% service charge. The doorman should receive 5F per piece, for help with suitcases; the room service waiter

10F; the chambermaid should get 10F per day. Taxi drivers are rarely tipped by the French but may expect it from an American; 15% will suffice.

East Germany

TOURIST INFORMATION: The *Reisebüro der DDR* (Travel Agency of the German Democratic Republic) is charged with all tourist matters. The central office in East Berlin is at 1026 Alexanderplatz 5 (phone: 215-4170 or 215-4171). There are *Reisebüro* offices throughout the country and at all international border crossings as well. Most cities also have their own information bureaus.

ENTRY REQUIREMENTS: In order to obtain a visa you need the dates and itinerary for your visit and must then obtain prepaid hotel reservations for each night. Necessary application forms may be had directly from the *Reisebüro* in East Berlin, from US travel agents, *Reisebüro*-appointed agencies in Western Europe, and *Reisebüro* offices in Eastern Europe, but you are strongly advised to obtain all your documents before leaving the US. *Koch Travel Bureau,* 157 E. 86th St., New York, NY 10028 (phone: 212-369-3800), can answer questions and handle the arrangements. The cost is determined by the telex fee ($25), the confirmation fee ($28), and the handling charges ($20 per person for the entire itinerary). Once the visa has been processed (which can take 8 to 10 weeks), the GDR issues a visa entitlement certificate that entitles the holder to the required visa — which costs $9 — either at the border or from the embassy in Washington, DC. (Since you'll have to wait in line at the border anyway, it is preferable to obtain your visa there.) If you plan to stay with friends or relatives rather than in a hotel, a provisional visa ($45; $60 for express handling) will be required; allow 2 to 3 months for handling. Transit visas can be obtained directly at the border. Day passes for visits to East Berlin (visits must end at midnight) are issued in West Berlin at Checkpoint Charlie or for pedestrians only at the Bahnhof Friedrichstrasse. These cost about 30 DM (West German marks).

CLIMATE AND CLOTHES: The primarily flat topography stretches as far south as Leipzig, where the foothills of the Thuringian Mountains begin. Climatic changes can be abrupt as a result of the combination of the moist northern Baltic maritime climate with that of the mountains to the south and west. The average temperature in July is 62F (16C), although it can rise as high as 85F (29C). The January average is 20F (-6C) but it can plunge to 0 degrees F (-18C). Casual, informal dress is fine.

MONEY: The ostmark (OM internationally, M mark, in East Germany) consists of 100 pfennigs. There's no limit to the amount of foreign currency that can be brought in, but it must be declared upon entering. It's illegal to import or export ostmarks. West German marks (deutsch marks) are cheerfully accepted, as are dollars.

LANGUAGE: *Hochdeutsch,* High German, is the official language, but *Platt* (or low) *Deutsch* is spoken in the north and the Saxon dialect is common in the south. About 300,000 Sorbs (Wends) live in Lusatia and speak a Slavic tongue. Many engaged in tourism speak English.

GETTING THERE/GETTING AROUND: Airlines – Pan American flies nonstop from New York to West Berlin's Tegel Airport; KLM and SAS both have connections from New York to East Berlin's Schönefeld Airport — KLM through Amsterdam; SAS via Stockholm; Interflug, the GDR line, has flights from Amsterdam and Copenhagen to East Berlin.

Trains – *Deutsche Reichsbahn* (*DR*) trains run frequently and many have automobile transport facilities, particularly useful if you're making connections with the car and passenger ferries crossing the Baltic between Warnemünde and Gedser, Denmark, or Sassnitz and Trelleborg, Sweden.

Cars – Travel in locally available rental cars, or your own, is unrestricted although you must have prearranged overnight accommodations that must be honored. A valid driver's license is required and GDR insurance must be purchased even if you have a Green Card. It may be purchased at the border and is payable in West German marks. Autobahns are toll roads, unless you are in transit to and from West Germany. You can pay for gas in foreign currency or, better yet, with discount gas coupons purchased at branches of the GDR State Bank at the border.

SPECIAL EVENTS: Leipzig's industrial fairs originated over 800 years ago and are held semiannually in the spring and fall. Hotel space is limited and reservations should be made 6 months in advance. If there is no space in Leipzig, you may be luckier in Halle, 20 minutes away.

The cultural scene is lively year-round. Advance ticket reservations can be made with US travel agents or *Reisebüro* offices for performances of popular attractions such as operas at the *Deutsche Staatsoper* in East Berlin and the Semperoper in Dresden, for plays by the Brecht-created *Berliner Ensemble,* and for concerts in Leipzig.

SHOPPING: Porcelain manufacturing began in Meissen and you can buy the products as well as tour the plant, *Staatliche Porzellan-Fabrik,* there. Craft articles include stoneware, hand-carved wood products, and embroidery. Goose-down bedding has traditionally kept the population warm and can do the same for you if you care to carry some home. Stores are generally open 10 AM to 7 PM weekdays (until 8 PM Thursdays) in Berlin, and from 9 AM to 6 PM weekdays outside Berlin. On Saturdays, only large stores are open, and only in the morning. Intershops are open 9 AM to 5 or 6 PM.

TIPPING: Not officially encouraged, but accepted; a tip of 10%, or a minimum of 3 OMs for small services, is the norm. Tips in deutsche marks or dollars are preferred.

West Germany

TOURIST INFORMATION: The German National Tourist Board (Deutsche Zentrale für Tourismus, DZT) is at 69 Beethovenstrasse, D-6000 Frankfurt am Main (phone: 069-75720). A small charge is usually made for regional publications, available at local tour offices, called *Verkehrsverein* or *Verkehrsant,* found in train stations, city halls, tourist kiosks, and storefronts throughout the country.

ENTRY REQUIREMENTS: No visa is necessary for periods of 3 months or less for US citizens with valid US passports.

CLIMATE AND CLOTHES: Generally moderate temperatures prevail from the shores of the North Sea south over the forests and river valleys to the slopes of the Bavarian Alps. Summer days average a comfortable 70F (21C), but be prepared for chilly evenings that sometimes dip to the low to mid-50s F (about 10C).

Dress is conservative in the cities, though not forbiddingly so. Ties for men are absolutely required only in the casinos and better restaurants; jackets will suffice in most first class establishments. There are some nude beaches; except for these, keep your suit on.

MONEY: The deutsche mark (DM) equals 100 pfennigs.

LANGUAGE: High German is the written language and the one that's commonly spoken, albeit with different accents, throughout the country. Regional dialects, Bavarian for one, are on the wane but are still found in small towns and rural areas.

English, mandatory in German schools since World War II, is common among the younger generations and is the second language of the country today.

GETTING THERE/GETTING AROUND: Airlines – Lufthansa regularly schedules nonstop flights to Frankfurt from New York, Chicago, Miami, Atlanta, Boston, Dallas, Los Angeles, San Francisco, Washington, DC, and San Juan; to Munich from New

York; and to Düsseldorf from Chicago, New York, Los Angeles, and Miami. Direct service is available from Chicago and Los Angeles to Munich via Düsseldorf; Philadelphia to Frankfurt via New York or Montreal; and to Frankfurt from Houston via Atlanta. There are also numerous connecting flights to Berlin, Nuremberg, and other major cities. Pan American now offers nonstop service to Frankfurt, Hamburg, and Munich and direct flights to West Berlin and Stuttgart, all from New York. TWA flies nonstop to Frankfurt from New York and St. Louis, and Delta has nonstop service from Atlanta to Munich and Frankfurt. Northwest has nonstop service from Boston and Detroit to Frankfurt.

Trains – The Germanrail Pass is good for 4, 9, or 16 days of unlimited travel over the *Deutsche Bundesbahn*'s (*DB*) 15,000-mile rail network. Included with all but the 4-day pass is a discount for travel to West Berlin. The Pass can be obtained in the US and in West Germany, but it is available only to those whose permanent residence is outside West Germany and West Berlin. *DB* also sells youth tickets and offers discounts to senior citizens. (Eurailpasses are valid on the *DB.*)

Cars – The exceptionally large range of models available for rent runs the gamut from VWs to a selection of motor homes. Money-saving rentals of 30 days or more, called leases, are good values.

Cruises – Advance reservations are essential for the exceedingly popular 2-, 3-, 4-, and 5-day Rhine cruises run by the *Koln-Düsseldorfer German Rhine Line* (*K-D*), Frankenwerft 15,5000 Cologne, West Germany. Book in the US through *Rhine Cruise Agency,* 170 Hamilton Ave., White Plains, NY 10601 (phone: 914-948-3600; in the western US, 800-858-8587; in the eastern US, 800-346-6525).

SPECIAL EVENTS: The *Richard Wagner Opera Festival* in Bayreuth takes place in July and August every year. The prudent will order direct from Bayreuth at least a year in advance. (The deadline is November 15 of the year preceding the concert date.) Write: Festspielleitung Bayreuth, Postfach 100262, 8580 Bayreuth. The German National Tourist Office's *Calendar of Events* is insurance against missing any of the fairs, folk festivals, concerts, and the like, that take place throughout the country each year.

SHOPPING: You can save something like $2,000 to $6,000 on the US purchase price of any Mercedes diesel model if you order it in advance from a US dealer or overseas delivery specialist to be picked up in Germany. Making a more modest dent in your wallet are excellent German steel cutlery, goose-down comforters, Rosenthal china and glassware, cameras, optical goods, and toys (wooden ones for the younger set or, for the more sophisticated, multicomponent structural types such as *Fischer technik*).

Inquire locally about rebates on the German 14% VAT sales tax. Stores are open weekdays from 9 AM to 6 PM with some closing for lunch. They follow the same hours the first Saturday of every month but close at 2 PM the other three Saturdays.

TIPPING: A 10% to 12% service charge is customarily included in restaurant checks. Superior service may warrant something in addition. Porters receive 1 deutsche mark a bag. Taxi drivers should get about 15% of the fare.

Gibraltar

TOURIST INFORMATION: The Gibraltar Government Tourist Office is at Cathedral Square (phone: 350-76400) on the Rock; write for literature to Cathedral Square, PO Box 303, Gibraltar.

ENTRY REQUIREMENTS: US citizens can enter this British colony with a valid US passport and can stay for up to 3 months.

CLIMATE AND CLOTHES: Hot summer temperatures in the high 80s and low 90s (mid-20s to low 30s C) are kept comfortable both by southeasterly sea breezes and by dips in the Mediterranean. Lightweight, light-colored clothes are pro forma. The rainy season is during the cooler — mid-60s to low 70s (16C to 22C) — winter months.

MONEY: The pound sterling (£) equals 100 pence. Gibraltar prints its own bank notes, which can only be used locally; the British pound sterling is also valid.

LANGUAGE: Gibraltar residents are British subjects and English is the official language, but Spanish is commonly spoken.

GETTING THERE/GETTING AROUND: GB Airways, British Airways, and Air Europe fly from London in 2½ hours. GB Airways also operates frequently scheduled 20-minute flights to Tangiers. There is catamaran service to Tangiers. Entry from Spain presents no problem: The border is open 24 hours daily and visitors may easily walk or drive across.

On the Rock, touring is done on foot or by minibus, taxi, or rental car. Driving is on the right.

SPECIAL EVENTS: A self-governing British colony, Gibraltar celebrates a few anniversaries like the *Battle of Trafalgar Day,* in October, and *Remembrance Day,* in November. The Changing of the Guard takes place at 11 every Tuesday morning outside the governor's residence. The main religious festival in this predominantly Catholic colony is *Holy Week,* when outdoor processions and special services are held. Deep-sea and pier fishing competitions take place year-round, and shark angling competitions are held twice yearly.

SHOPPING: Gibraltar has very good shopping for tourists, with duty-free facilities at the air terminal and at a few shops. Also, there is no VAT. It's a bargain bonanza for British products such as whiskey, woolens, and linens, as well as such international goods as gold jewelry, pearls, leather goods, fishing tackle, sporting goods, and watches. North African mementos including camel saddles and djellabas can be picked up at one of the raffish bazaars that coexist with the more stately boutiques. Cigarettes, tobacco and, yes, Havana cigars are very nicely priced.

Normal shopping hours are 9 AM to 1 PM and 3 to 7 PM weekdays and 9 AM to 1 PM on Saturdays. However, whenever a cruise ship is in port the stores are open.

TIPPING: Most restaurant bills include service. If not, 10% to 15% is expected.

Great Britain

TOURIST INFORMATION: Over 700 Tourist Information Centres (TICs) provide accommodations listings as well as literature throughout England, Wales, Scotland, and Northern Ireland. The central London office is the British Travel Centre, 12 Regent St., Piccadilly Circus, London SW1Y 4PQ (phone: 730-3400).

ENTRY REQUIREMENTS: A valid US passport is the only requirement for stays of 3 months or less by US citizens.

CLIMATE AND CLOTHES: Daily temperatures average in the low 60s F (about 16C) in summer and hover around 40F (6C) in December, January, and February. Winter is wetter than summer, with 15 or 16 rainy days a month as opposed to summer's 12 or 13. The seasons are well defined though not as extreme as those in our northeastern states. Dress accordingly. A finely tuned sense of fashion is terrific in London but not necessary in the country. Bring a folding umbrella.

MONEY: The pound sterling (£) is divided into 100 pence.

LANGUAGE: English is the national language, but Welsh is widely spoken in Wales, as is Gaelic in the Outer Islands in Scotland. Regional dialects are often heard in Scotland, Yorkshire, and Cornwall.

GETTING THERE/GETTING AROUND: Airlines – British Airways flies to London from Anchorage, Atlanta, Boston, Chicago, Dallas, Detroit, Houston, Los Angeles, Miami (*Concorde* and subsonic service), New York (*Concorde* and subsonic service), Philadelphia, Pittsburgh, Orlando, San Juan, San Francisco, Seattle, Tampa, and Washington, DC (*Concorde* and subsonic service). US carriers with nonstop service to London are Pan American out of Chicago, Detroit, Miami, New York, San Francisco, Seattle, and Washington, DC; Delta, from Atlanta; TWA from Boston, Chicago, Los Angeles, New York, and St. Louis; American from Dallas/Ft. Worth; Northwest from Boston and Minneapolis; and Continental from Newark, Houston, Denver, and Miami. TWA also flies to London on a connecting flight out of Philadelphia. Additional service is provided by Virgin Atlantic Airways, Air India, and Air New Zealand.

At least 10 domestic airlines serve the major cities and islands. British Airways runs many shuttle flights daily between Glasgow, Edinburgh, Belfast, Manchester, and London.

Trains – *BritRail*'s 125 intercity trains offer superb service, and *BR*'s numerous bargain plans for travelers couldn't be more tempting: BritRail pass, BritRail Youth pass for those under 26; and the Senior Citizen Pass, available for reduced-rate first class travel for those 60 or over.

Cars – Yes, they still drive on the left-hand side of the road. If you're a member of the *AAA* in the US, you might be entitled to reciprocal membership privileges with the *RAC* or *AA*, two British automobile clubs.

SPECIAL EVENTS: A mind-boggling array greets the visitor, with the theater perhaps the first goal of most. The *Royal Shakespeare Company* performances begin in Stratford in late March or early April and continue through January. The *National Theatre* on London's South Bank has performances year-round. The *Edinburgh Festival,* Scotland's all-cultural bash, which coincides with the *Military Tattoo,* runs for 3 weeks in August. Opera at Glyndebourne, East Sussex, from the end of May to mid-August is an elegant, dressy occasion.

Dates for some of the more famous sporting events? June for the *Derby* in Epsom, Surrey, and the *Royal Ascot* races in Ascot, Berkshire; late June to early July for the *All England Lawn Tennis Championships* (better known as *Wimbledon*) in London, and for the *Henley Regatta* in Henley-on-Thames; July for the *British Grand Prix* and early August for *Cowes' Sailing Week,* on the Isle of Wight; and every 2 years (even-numbered) in September for the *Farnborough Air Show* in Hampshire.

The *Queen's Official Birthday* is saluted by mounted guards "Trooping the Color" in London, the second Saturday in June.

SHOPPING: There are still a few antiques left, in spite of the shiploads consigned to US dealers, and it's fun to hunt for them. In London try Tower Bridge Rd. (New Caledonian Market) — a dealer's market — very early Friday mornings. However, you don't have to look far to find new and unused china from quality suppliers such as *Minton, Royal Doulton, Aynsley,* and *Wedgwood.*

Harris tweeds, *Liberty* prints in cotton and silk, and ancestral tartans are sold by the yard and are made up into fashionable clothes. *Burberry* and *Jaeger* are good labels, and there are less expensive durable sport clothes at *Marks & Spencer* stores around the country. Main sale months are January and July.

Sales tax (VAT) is 15%. Most stores will arrange to refund VAT to foreign buyers who take the goods out of the country.

Shops open weekdays and Saturdays from 9 AM to 5:30 PM. Hours may differ in small towns, where shops sometimes close at noon one day a week, and in London, where most shops open and close later.

TIPPING: Service charges of between 10% and 15% are usually included in hotel bills but make sure. Otherwise the tipping standard is between 10% and 15% in restaurants and taxis, and 50 pence per bag for bellmen and porters.

Greece

TOURIST INFORMATION: The National Tourist Organization of Greece (EOT in Greek) has its main office at 2 Amerikis St. in Athens (phone: 322-3111). There are ten regional branches and four bureaus at frontier crossings. In most cities and towns, special tourist police provide information as well as assistance.

ENTRY REQUIREMENTS: A valid US passport is good for visits of up to 3 months.

CLIMATE AND CLOTHES: The country boasts more than 3,000 hours of sunshine a year. Hot summers, with averages in the low 90s F (about 30C), are mitigated somewhat by the *meltemia* breezes. Winters are mostly mild; January averages about 52F (12C) in Athens and ten degrees less to the north.

Lightweight white and pastel clothes are appropriate summerwear. Pack something dressy for the captain's dinner if planning a cruise; ties are required for men only for admittance to one of the country's three gambling casinos.

MONEY: The drachma (Dr) is divided into 100 lepta.

LANGUAGE: Greek; English is spoken on the tourist circuit.

GETTING THERE/GETTING AROUND: Airlines – Olympic Airlines and TWA have nonstop service from New York to Athens. Domestic flights radiate from Olympic's Hellinikon Airport near Athens to about 20 cities and islands at the season's height.

Trains – Three international expresses reach Athens through Belgrade. However, because Yugoslavia is not included in the *Eurail* system, those with Eurailpasses enter Greece via ferry from Brindisi, Italy. The *Hellenic State Railway* (*OSE*) uses buses as well as trains to offer frequent service throughout the country. These routes are supplemented by privately run bus companies.

Cars – The *Automobile and Touring Club* (*ELPA*) mans road patrols and highway stations as well as an emergency number (phone: 104) good within a 60-kilometer range of major cities.

SPECIAL EVENTS: The annual *Athens Festival* is held every day in the Odeon, built by Herod Atticus in AD 161, from June through September. Superb Greek dramas are presented outdoors at Epidaurus on weekends from the end of June until the end of September. Schedules and tickets for both are available from the Athens Festival Box Office, 4 Stadiou St., Athens (phone: 322-1459 or 322-3111, ext. 240), which also sells tickets to the daily sound-and-light shows in English at the Acropolis from April through October.

SHOPPING: To educate yourself in the range and variety of crafts produced in Greece before making a purchase, visit one of the *EOMMEX* (National Organization of Hellenic Handicrafts) showrooms in Athens and 13 other major Greek cities. Unfortunately they display but don't sell handmade wares. There's also a permanent exhibit of ceramics at Maroussi, where Greek pottery is sold as well as displayed.

Caftans, shirts, and dresses made from striped and textured *sedoni* cotton, which was originally used as sheeting, as well as from the heavier grades of colored cloth are widely available. Traditional fishermen's clothes, including lacy wool undershirts and navy blue hats, are trendy additions to a wardrobe. Two small items in great favor with the incurably anxious are worry beads and evil eyes.

During the summer, gift and craft shops are open daily except Sundays from 8 AM to 9 PM. Regular stores are open Mondays, Wednesdays, and Saturdays from 8 AM to 2:30 PM and Tuesdays, Thursdays, and Fridays from 8 AM to 1:30 PM and 5 to 8 PM.

TIPPING: The minimum tip for a small service is 10 drachmas. Service charges are included in most bills, but it is customary to add 5% to 10%.

Hungary

TOURIST INFORMATION: Branches of *IBUSZ,* the state travel company, are found in all major cities. The central office is at 5 Felszabadulás tér, 1364 Budapest 5 (phone: 186866). *IBUSZ* also has a 24-hour accommodations service at 3 Petöfi tér, 1052 in Budapest (phone: 184842). Tourist offices in smaller cities and towns are called *Idegenforgalmi Hivatal.*

ENTRY REQUIREMENTS: Tourist visas good for 30 days (and valid only for 6 months from the date of issue) are required and must be applied for with two passport photos and a valid US passport. They're obtained from Hungarian consulates abroad as well as at highway border crossings, on the Vienna-Budapest hydrofoil, and at the Budapest airport, but are not available on trains.

CLIMATE AND CLOTHES: Hungary is a small — 35,910-square-mile — nation bisected by the Danube River. Lake Balaton to the west is Europe's second largest lake and a good place to cool off during the typically hot summers, with temperatures averaging 86F (30C). Winters are cold (about 30F, −1C) and dry. Hungarians take pains to look their best. Casual, tacky dress usually indicates a tourist.

MONEY: The forint (Ft) equals 100 fillér.

LANGUAGE: Hungarian, a Finno-Ugric tongue, is the native language of 95% of the population. German is the second language (a heritage of the Austro-Hungarian Empire) but English is becoming increasingly common.

GETTING THERE/GETTING AROUND: Airlines – Malev, the Hungarian national airline, flies nonstop from New York to Budapest. Other flights to Budapest are offered from New York by KLM, via Amsterdam; Lufthansa, via Munich and Düsseldorf; SAS, via Copenhagen; British Airways, via London; Air France, via Paris (with a change of airport); Finnair, via Helsinki; and Pan American, via Frankfurt. Malev has service between Ferihegy Airport, Budapest, and 40 major cities in Europe and the Middle East.

Trains – Budapest is a transfer point for some 25 international expresses, including the *Nord Orient Express* and the *Wiener Walzer.* Nationally, the *MÁV* (*Magyar Állam-vasutak*) diesel or electric express trains run often and are comfortable. Hungary is a member of the *Eurail* network. From the US, *Eurail* information for Hungary can be obtained through French, Italian, Swiss, or German railroads.

Cars – International firms and *IBUSZ* rent European models. Some words of caution: The law against driving after drinking is carefully enforced: You are breaking the law if found driving with *any* alcohol in the blood.

SPECIAL EVENTS: Feasts and gaiety are traditional when the wine harvest begins in the fall. Important vineyard areas include Tokay; the Badacsony mountain slopes near Balaton; Eger (where the red "Bulls' Blood" is made); Sopron; and parts of the Puszta. Fall also starts the season at Budapest's opera house, the *Academy of Music.* During the summer you can hear music of native sons Franz Liszt, Béla Bartók, or Franz Lehár in Budapest's Margaret Island open-air theater. And the *Budapest Spring Festival* is held in late March.

SHOPPING: Embroidery patterns and techniques, startling in their color and complexity, vary from region to region, and those of the Kalocsa, Mezökövesd, Pálóc, and Sárköz areas are highly regarded. Painted and carved wooden vessels and objects originally made by shepherds are still fashioned today, also true of peasant earthenware.

Village potters produce local as well as more modern styles. Sándor Kántor working today in Karcag exemplifies this trend. *Folkart and Handicraft Cooperatives* around the country sell these products for forints or they can be bought with foreign exchange from Intertourist shops.

Stores are open weekdays from 8 AM to 5 PM; Thursdays they often stay open until 7 or 8 PM. On Saturdays, stores are open half-days, from 8 AM to 1 PM.

TIPPING: Add 15% to restaurant bills; 20 forints is the usual small tip for taxi drivers, porters, and hairdressers.

Iceland

TOURIST INFORMATION: The Iceland Tourist Board's head office is at 3 Laugarvegur, Reykjavik (phone: 27488).

ENTRY REQUIREMENTS: US citizens need only a valid passport for visits of 3 months or less.

CLIMATE AND CLOTHES: While far more temperate in winter than might be expected — 31F (0 degrees C) is the average January temperature in Reykjavík — summers are cool, with July averages in the low 60s F (10C).

Daylight is continuous from mid-May through August but gradually lessens until there are only 3 or 4 hours of daylight in each 24-hour period from November through January. Careful attention is paid to fashion. Jeans are fine for Saturday night disco-ing but won't do for dinner in the more staid restaurants.

MONEY: The Icelandic krona (IKr) equals 100 aurar.

LANGUAGE: Modern Icelandic hasn't changed much from the Old Norse spoken by the ancient Vikings who colonized the island 1,100 years ago. Danish is the second language, and English is compulsory in high school and is widely spoken, particularly by the younger generation.

GETTING THERE/GETTING AROUND: Airlines – Icelandair has nonstop service from New York to Keflavík Airport, about 45 minutes from the capital. Reykjavik is the hub of Icelandair's domestic flights to 16 cities in the nation. These flights, by the way, cost very little more than bus service to the same destinations.

Trains – There are no trains in Iceland.

Buses – BSI (*Bifreidastod Island,* or *Iceland Coach Company*) is the umbrella group for most of the national bus companies and is headquartered at the *Umferdarmidstodin* (bus station) in Reykjavík (phone: 22300). There's a total of about 8,000 miles of road, about 4,500 of which are covered by the coaches. In 1974 the road encircling the island known as the ring route was completed, although parts of it remain unpaved. Coach passes for this road, as well as passes good for unlimited travel anywhere in the country, are available from *BSI.*

Cars – There are plenty of car rental firms, with most supplying VW beetles and four-wheel-drive wagons. Be advised that most roads are unpaved and surfaced in dirt or crushed volcanic matter.

SPECIAL EVENTS: June 17 heralds the widely celebrated *National Day.* In early August, the Westman Islands (a small group of islands south of Iceland) holds a summer festival featuring bonfires and open-air entertainment. One of the most famous events is the biennial *Reykjavik Arts Festival* (being held in June 1990), featuring top artists in opera, ballet, and theater, as well as famous sculptors and painters from around the world.

SHOPPING: The fluffy, earth-colored *Lopi* wool blankets, outerwear, and accessories are synonymous with Iceland. Sheep are also the source of the shearling coats, jackets, and hats made here.

Several fine potters hand-throw earthenware containers in natural colors. Crushed lava is a common addition to highly glazed ceramic pieces popular as souvenirs.

The *Icemart* shop at Keflavik Airport sells all of these products.

Stores are open weekdays from 9 AM to 6 PM and some, but not all, from 10 AM to noon on Saturdays.

TIPPING: Service charges are added to most bills and extra tips are not expected.

Ireland

TOURIST INFORMATION: The lowercase *i* identifies tourist information offices in some 70 locations around the country. The Irish Tourist Board (Bord Failte) publications are also available on a regional basis and in Dublin at 14 Upper O'Connell St., Dublin 1 (phone: 747733).

ENTRY REQUIREMENTS: US citizens require only a valid passport.

CLIMATE AND CLOTHES: Summer highs are in the mid-60s F (around 18C) and winter averages in the 40s F (around 4C). This is partially explained by the chilling east winds. Make sure you have a warm wool sweater or jacket even in summer. Tweeds are worn year-round and lend a conservative cast to what is essentially a casual mode of dress.

MONEY: The Irish pound (IR£) equals 100 pence. Be aware that the Irish pound (punt) and the British pound are no longer tied to one another and are not interchangeable. Each has its own value in relation to world currencies, and the Irish pound has lately been trading at a level roughly 10% less than its British counterpart.

LANGUAGE: Though Irish, or Gaelic, is the national language, English is spoken more widely today except in those few areas where Gaelic is still dominant, primarily on the West Coast.

GETTING THERE/GETTING AROUND: Airlines – Aer Lingus flies nonstop from Boston and New York into Ireland's Shannon International Airport, always continuing to Dublin, and also provides domestic service between Dublin and Cork; Pan American flies nonstop to Shannon from New York; Delta, from Atlanta. Aer Arann schedules flights between Galway and the Aran Islands in Galway Bay, and Ryan Air now flies from London to Dublin and Waterford.

Trains – *Córas Iompair Éireann* (*CIE*), the national transport company, with its supertrain intercity service, manages railroads as well as bus routes. Rambler tickets good for 8 or 15 days are an inexpensive way to cover Erin and the 15-day Overlander ticket includes travel in Northern Ireland. Both tickets can be used for either bus or train travel.

Cars – Mobile homes as well as cars can be rented here and the Irish Tourist Board has mapped out a number of scenic tours for the motorist.

Ferries – Car- and passenger-carrying ferries connect Great Britain with Ireland. The ferries run between Holyhead and Dun Laoghaire; Holyhead and Dublin; Liverpool and Dublin; and Fishguard and Rosslare, and between Cork and Swansea. Between Britain and Ireland, the operators are the *B&I Line* (in the US, book through *Lynott Tours,* phone: 212-760-0101 in New York; 800-221-2474 elsewhere), *Sealink Ferries* (in the US, book through *Britrail,* phone: 212-599-5400), and *P&O European Ferries* (in the US, phone: 800-221-3254). The *Irish Ferries'* ships sail between Rosslare and Le Havre, Rosslare and Cherbourg, and Cork and Le Havre (book through *CIE Tours,* phone: in the US, 800-243-7687; in New York, 212-697-3914). *Brittany Ferries* operate between Cork and Roscoff, France (in the US, book through *P&O European Ferries,* phone: 800-221-3254).

SPECIAL EVENTS: The Royal Dublin Society organizes the *Dublin Horse Show* in

August, an outstanding sporting and social event, as well as the *Spring Show and Industries Fair* in May, a trade and livestock exhibition. Traditional Irish ballads are celebrated, at a different site each year, in the *Fleadh Cheoil na h-Éireann,* Ireland's premier cultural festival, in August. Other major festivals are the *Rose of Tralee Festival* in late August at Tralee and the *Cork International Choral and Folk Dance Festival* in April. Rarely performed 18th- and 19th-century operas are presented at the *Wexford Opera Festival,* a must if you're near Wexford in late October. Also in late October is the *Guinness Jazz Festival* in Cork, drawing talented musicians from around the world. St. Patrick gets his due during a week of celebrations throughout the country in mid-March. New plays by Irish authors feature in the *Dublin Theatre Festival,* held from late September to October.

September culminates both of Ireland's most popular spectator sport seasons in Dublin with the *All Ireland Hurling Finals* followed by the *All Ireland Football Finals.*

SHOPPING: Crafts are thriving in Ireland. Products in the traditional and modern international styles and combinations of the two are found in craft centers, workshops, and stores throughout the country. Details are in the *Irish Crafts* information sheet from Irish Tourist Board offices in the US. The traditional and highly prized white wool Aran sweaters and hats, earthenware in modern but natural shapes, and exceedingly well executed jewelry in contemporary styles are typical of the work currently being done.

Pearly *Belleek* china, luminous *Waterford* crystal, and Irish lace endow any table with elegance. Irish smoked salmon goes well in such a setting.

Irish sales tax (VAT) is charged at varying rates — from 10% to 25% in the Irish Republic, and 15% in Northern Ireland. Avoid it by having products shipped directly home, or reclaim the VAT by having your invoice stamped at customs.

Stores are open between 9 AM and 5:30 PM daily except Sundays, with one early closing day in rural areas — usually either Mondays or Wednesdays. Some stores in Dublin are closed Mondays.

TIPPING: Check to make sure the customary 10% to 15% service charge is added to restaurant and hotel bills. If so, no further tip is necessary. Taxi drivers get 10% to 15% and porters about 50 pence per bag.

Italy

TOURIST INFORMATION: Publications and assistance are provided on a region-by-region basis by various Assessorati e Aziende Regionali del Turismo (ART) offices; in provinces by the Enti Provinciali per il Turismo (EPT); and in towns and resort areas from assorted Aziende Autonome di Soggiorno e Turismo (AAST) offices.

ENTRY REQUIREMENTS: US citizens require only a valid US passport for visits of 3 months or less.

CLIMATE AND CLOTHES: Hot summers get hotter the farther south you go (high 80s F or about 30C), but are mitigated by shore breezes along Italy's 5,000-mile coastline. Northern Alpine areas are exceedingly cold in winter as are the Apennines, but temperatures are in the relatively mild 40s F (around 7C) and even warmer along the Italian Riviera and the Amalfi and Sicilian coasts. Residents of Milan, Italy's fashion capital, dress chicly, though they are more conservative than Romans, who follow every fashion fad. Florence, too, is a fashion center. Stylishly casual resort wear is perfect for the beach areas and jeans are fine for the hill country.

MONEY: The Italian currency unit is the lira (often abbreviated *Lit.*); the plural of lira is lire.

LANGUAGE: Italian is universally spoken but Italy's original city-states each had their own dialect and literature and in some places these dialects — Sardinian, Sicilian, Neapolitan, Venetian, and Milanese — are still spoken.

GETTING THERE/GETTING AROUND: Airlines – Alitalia flies nonstop from Chicago, Los Angeles, and New York to Milan. To Rome, there's nonstop service from New York and direct service, via Milan, from Chicago and Los Angeles. There is also summertime direct service from Boston to both Milan (nonstop) and Rome (direct, via Milan) and from New York to Palermo via Rome. Pan American has nonstop service from New York to Milan and Rome; TWA flies from Boston (via New York), Chicago (via New York), and New York (nonstop) to both Milan and Rome, and offers summer nonstops from Boston to Rome. Service within Italy is provided by Alitalia and ATI.

Trains – Kilometer for kilometer, among the least expensive in Europe. Travel is fastest on *rapidi* (including *TEE* and *IC* trains), which connect major cities; *espressi* are the next fastest. A high-speed line now links Rome and Florence, as well as Rome and Milan.

Cars – Italy's toll roads are excellent, but be prepared for the speed of traffic.

SPECIAL EVENTS: Summer outdoor performances of Italian operas are held in July and August in Rome's *Terme di Caracalla;* from mid-July through mid-August in Verona's *Arena;* and in July at the *Arena Sferisterio* in Macerata. The regular opera season at such notable houses as *La Scala* in Milan, *San Carlo* in Naples, and the *Opera* in Rome runs from December to June. Two festivals of note that feature concerts, ballet, opera, and drama are Spoleto's *Festival of Two Worlds,* between mid-June and mid-July, and Florence's *Maggio Musicale Fiorentino* in May and June.

Colorful pageants that feature medieval costumes include Gubbio's *Race of the Candles* on May 15; Siena's *Il Palio,* a horse race in medieval garb, held on July 2 and August 16; Venice's *Il Redentore,* a gondola procession and race the third Sunday in July; and Marostica's *Living Chess Game,* every other September (in even-numbered years).

SHOPPING: Italian leather goods, textiles, jewelry, and ceramics are fine buys. Most elegantly hand-stitched sheets, carefully worked boots, stunningly designed silk ties and scarves, and subtly knit fabrics fill the boutiques of Rome and Milan. *Upim, Standa, Coin,* and *Rinascente* chain stores are great for locally made finds from bras to ceramics. Florence is known especially for handicrafts. Baskets from the straw market in Florence are terrific to tote your purchases around in, including perhaps rolls of the gorgeous Florentine papers, appropriate for lining drawers or covering notebooks.

Store hours are generally from 9 AM to 1 PM and 3:30 or 4 to 7:30 or 8 PM; stores in northern Italy have shorter hours and earlier closing times.

TIPPING: Keep a handful of lire notes ready. In spite of 15% to 18% service charges at your hotel and 15% usually added to restaurant bills, you'll be expected to give about 1,000 to 1,500 lire or more to chambermaids for each night you stay, and at least 1,500 lire to bellhops for each bag they take, and so on. Waiters and wine stewards get an extra 10% of the bill. Taxi drivers receive 15% of the meter, hairdressers 15% of the bill. Even service station attendants expect about 1,000 or more lire for cleaning windshields and giving directions. Theater ushers are tipped 1,000 lire.

Liechtenstein

TOURIST INFORMATION: Locally available at the Liechtenstein Tourist Office, 37 Städtle, 9490 Vaduz, Principality of Liechtenstein (phone: 075-21443).

ENTRY REQUIREMENTS: If entering from Switzerland, there are no border formalities whatsoever. US citizens can visit the country as tourists for up to 3 months with a valid US passport.

CLIMATE AND CLOTHES: This tiny country is a land of mountains and valleys. The eastern two thirds of its 61 square miles are covered by mountains of moderate height; these drop to the beautiful and fertile Rhine Valley in the west, and the entire country, like its neighbors Switzerland and Austria, is cooled and made temperate by the *Föhn,* the famous south wind of this section of central Europe. Travelers will feel perfectly comfortable in informal clothes throughout Liechtenstein.

MONEY: The Swiss franc (sfr) is made up of 100 centimes.

LANGUAGE: Liechtenstein's official language is German, but many citizens speak a dialect similar to that of southwestern Germany and Alsace, and accents vary from village to village. Most people involved in any way with tourists speak English.

GETTING THERE/GETTING AROUND: There are no flights into this tiny country simply because it has no airport. After flying into Zurich, Switzerland, you travel by train to Sargans or Buchs, Switzerland. The rail line between Zurich and Vienna passes through Liechtenstein, but not Vaduz, the capital. Express trains make stops at Buchs and at Feldkirch, Austria, with postal buses providing the link between these stations and Vaduz.

SPECIAL EVENTS: The prince's birthday in August is celebrated as a national holiday. The first Sunday of Lent signals *Bonfire Sunday* with the lighting of fires and torches followed by traditional pancake suppers.

SHOPPING: Beautiful postage stamps and prestamped postcards are collector's items, inexpensive souvenirs, and also a leading local industry. Swiss watches, optical goods, and music boxes are reasonably priced. Shops are open weekdays from 8 AM to noon and from 1:30 to 6:30 PM, with Saturday closings at around 4 PM.

TIPPING: A 15% service charge is included in all hotel and restaurant bills.

Luxembourg

TOURIST INFORMATION: The Office National du Tourisme (ONT), with general information on the country, is at 77 Rue d'Anvers, PO Box 1001, L-1010 Luxembourg City (phone: 400808). The Syndicat d'Initiative in most towns provides local information. It is based at the Place d'Armes (phone: 22809). ONT and Syndicat offices are identified by the national information logo of a blue knight on a white background.

ENTRY REQUIREMENTS: US citizens can stay in Luxembourg for up to 3 months with a valid US passport.

CLIMATE AND CLOTHES: Hilly and forested in the north, Luxembourg has a storybook look, with pastoral farms stretching in the south along the banks of the Moselle River, which separates the country from neighboring Germany. Temperatures are moderate: summer days in the low 70s F (20s C) and winter days in the 40s F (around 5C). Dress for the weather, not for society, and carry a wool sweater or jacket in the summer in the Ardennes and sturdy shoes for hiking in the mountains.

MONEY: The Luxembourg franc (Lux. F.) equals 100 centimes. Belgian and Luxembourg francs can be used interchangeably, but the Luxembourg franc is not widely accepted outside the country. Change francs for other currencies before leaving.

LANGUAGE: It's a trilingual country: French is the official language, but German is spoken by most people, and Letzeburgesch, a Low German dialect, by all. English, compulsory in high school, is understood everywhere.

GETTING THERE/GETTING AROUND: Airlines – Icelandair provides direct service (via Reykjavik) from New York, and Orlando. Findel Airport is just outside Luxembourg City.

Trains – The *Chemin de Fer Luxembourgeois* (*CFL*) offers a number of reduced-fare plans, including weekend excursion rates, flat-fee 1-day, 5-day, and 1-month network passes, and senior citizen half-fare tickets. The Benelux Tourrail Pass, good for any 5 days of travel in a 17-day period in Belgium, Luxembourg, and the Netherlands, is available at railway stations.

Cars – Luxembourg car rental fleets probably have the cheapest rates on the Continent for periods of a week or more. If you pick up and deliver your car there, you will probably pay less than the rate for the same car rented in Belgium and dropped off in Paris.

SPECIAL EVENTS: The *Octave,* an annual pilgrimage to Our Lady of Luxembourg, takes place the fifth Sunday after Easter in both Luxembourg City and Diekirch, with the royal family of Luxembourg participating in the closing procession; the *St. Willibrord's Dancing Procession* is held on Whitsun Tuesday about a month later in Echternach. *Remembrance Day* honors General George Patton, Jr., early each July in Ettelbrück; and Grevenmacher holds its *Grape and Wine Festival* (one of the many towns along the Moselle to do so) in mid-September.

SHOPPING: The beautiful porcelains and crystal of *Villeroy and Boch* are produced in Septfontaines, where the factory store is open to visitors. A regional specialty is the earthenware pottery of Nospelt, northwest of Luxembourg City, where there's a 2-week exhibit of local work each August. They are sold locally in leading shops.

Stores are open Tuesdays through Saturdays from 8:30 AM to noon and from 2 to 6 PM; Mondays from 2 to 6 PM; closed Sundays. VAT varies between 7% and 12% and can be avoided by having purchases sent directly to the airport for collection before boarding the plane. Some stores will reimburse the VAT if the customer returns with an invoice cleared by customs authorities.

TIPPING: A 15% service charge is included in hotel, restaurant, and bar bills. Porters and bellmen receive about 20 francs per bag and taxi drivers 15% of the meter charge.

The Maltese Islands

TOURIST INFORMATION: The Malta National Tourist Office is in Valletta (phone: 22444), on the main island of Malta.

ENTRY REQUIREMENTS: US citizens require a valid US passport for visits of up to 3 months.

CLIMATE AND CLOTHES: Vibrantly clear and sunny weather makes Malta very appealing to tourists. What rain there is falls between November and February, also the period of highest winds. Temperatures climb into the 90s F (30s C) in the heat of the Mediterranean summer, but otherwise hover in the 70s F (20s C). A holiday mood prevails throughout the country and informality is the keynote, though bikinis, fine for the beach, should not be worn off the sands.

MONEY: The Maltese lira (LM) is divided into 100 cents.

LANGUAGE: Maltese is a Semitic language derived from Phoenician, and uses the Latin alphabet instead of the Arabic in its printed form. It is influenced by Italian (Sicily is only 60 miles to the north) and English (Malta was a British colony for some 160 years). Today, both Italian and English are spoken by almost all inhabitants.

GETTING THERE/GETTING AROUND: Airlines – Air Malta has nonstop daily flights from London and Rome (twice daily during the summer) to Luqa Airport outside Valletta. Other destinations served twice weekly or weekly include Copenhagen, Paris, Lyons, Frankfurt, Zurich, Amsterdam, Munich, and Cairo. The islands of Malta and Gozo are linked by frequent car and passenger ferries. The third Maltese island, Comino, less than a square mile in area, has only one hotel, no cars, and is connected by scheduled boat service to the island of Malta.

Cars – A variety of cars can be rented in Malta as well as in Rabat, the capital of the island of Gozo. Driving on the left-hand side of the road is a custom inherited from the British.

SPECIAL EVENTS: Two-day *festas,* honoring the patron saint of different Maltese villages, provide plenty of local color and gaiety in this exceedingly Catholic republic. They're concentrated in the summer months and feature processions of saints' images through village streets, accompanied by bands, marchers, and a lot of fireworks. Valletta's *Carnival* is celebrated by the whole country on the second weekend in May with a float parade and enormous papier-mâché characters as well as much merrymaking.

SHOPPING: An overview of the country's typical handcrafts can be obtained from a visit to the *Centru Snajja Maltim* (Malta Crafts Center) opposite St. John's Cathedral in Valletta. However, you shouldn't miss the *Crafts Village,* at Ta Qali near Mdina, where you can see the products being made as well as purchase them on the spot. The heavy lacework is in the traditional mode. Decorative glass is manufactured here and so are Persian-style rugs. Maltese gold and silver filigree jewelry is beautiful. Stores open at 9 AM and close at 7 PM (8 PM on Saturdays) with a 3- to 4-hour lunch break.

TIPPING: The norm is 10%. Sometimes it is included in restaurant bills.

Monaco

TOURIST INFORMATION: The National Office of Tourism is at 2a Bd. des Moulins, Monte Carlo, 98030 Monaco (phone: 933-08701).

ENTRY REQUIREMENTS: There is no frontier between France and Monaco, and French immigration regulations apply. If you plan to arrive or leave via France, note that, due to a recent change in policy you no longer need a visa for crossing into or out of France.

CLIMATE AND CLOTHES: Monaco claims 305 days of sun every year, with averages for water temperature and air temperature about the same: in the high 70s F (20s C) in summer, dropping to the mid-50s F (around 10C) in winter. For clothes, what goes on the French Riviera is appropriate here but topless is allowed only at the Beach Club. Casual dress suffices in the casino's American Room, but coat and tie are required in the other rooms. You can always dress up more if you wish.

MONEY: The French franc (F), made up of 100 centimes, is the most popular currency. French bank notes are legal tender here, but Monégasque coins bearing Prince Rainier's likeness are circulated domestically and can be exchanged for French francs in France.

LANGUAGE: French is spoken, but the singular Monégasque dialect, a mixture of Italian and Niçois, is officially encouraged and mandatory in grade school. English is also taught in the schools and is spoken in hotels, restaurants, and at the casinos.

GETTING THERE/GETTING AROUND: With the exception of a few local bus routes, Monaco relies on France for transportation and other services.

Airlines – Pan American and Air France fly nonstop from New York to Nice. British Airways provides service from New York to Nice via London; Sabena via Brussels; and Iberia by way of Madrid. Heli Air, Monaco's helicopters, connect Monte Carlo with the airport as well as with other destinations on the Riviera. There's also bus service between the airport and Monaco.

Trains – The *Gare de Monaco/Monte Carlo* is on the *SNCF*'s (*Société Nationale des Chemins de Fer Français*) Riviera line. Several international trains make stops there such as the overnight *Train Bleu* from Paris. *SNCF*'s *Métrazur* shuttles along the Côte d'Azur between Cannes and Menton, stopping at Monaco every 30 minutes. Both the Eurailpass and *SNCF*'s France Railpass include Monaco.

Cars – The principality is easily reached from Autoroute A8 or from the scenic Route de la Moyenne Corniche. The *Automobile Club of Monaco,* 23 Bd. Albert-I, Monte Carlo (phone: 303220), provides information for motorists as well as details on the Grand Prix.

SPECIAL EVENTS: April is the month for the *International Tennis World Championships.* The *Grand Prix de Monaco* is generally held in May, when futuristic Formula 1 racing cars take to the Belle Epoque streets of Monte Carlo. Several nights in late July and early August are enlivened by the *International Fireworks Festival;* the elegant *Monégasque Red Cross Gala* is held on the first Friday in August. January brings sports cars in abundance for the *Monte Carlo Rallye,* and the *International Circus Festival* comes in February.

SHOPPING: All the international names in perfume, jewelry, and clothes are carried by the chic shops surrounding the casino. Local embroidery, ceramics, and other handcrafted products are sold at *Boutique du Rocher,* the proceeds of which go to charity. Monégasque stamps are highly prized by collectors.

TIPPING: All bills — hotel, restaurant, and taxi — include a 15% service charge. Tips are not expected, but if you consider the service extraordinary, they are accepted.

The Netherlands

TOURIST INFORMATION: The ubiquitous VVV (Vereniging voor Vreemdelingen Verkeer) is based at 9-15 Rokin, Amsterdam (phone: 551-2512). But for touring information, go to the VVV at 10 Stationsplaein, Amsterdam (phone: 266444). Offices, easily identified throughout the country by a triangular logo of three Vs, provide lists of accommodations as well as information services.

ENTRY REQUIREMENTS: US citizens require only a valid US passport for stays up to 3 months.

MONEY: The guilder (also called florin; both are abbreviated Fl.) is made up of 100 cents.

CLIMATE AND CLOTHES: The influence of the surrounding North Sea results in a temperate, if damp, climate. June through September are the warmest months, with daytime highs around 70F (21C), and July through November is the rainiest time. Winter lows are in the 30s F (around 0 degrees C). Dress is casual.

LANGUAGE: The national language is Dutch, but English is spoken by many people.

GETTING THERE/GETTING AROUND: Airlines – KLM flies to Amsterdam's Schiphol Airport nonstop from Atlanta, Chicago, Houston, Los Angeles, New York, and Orlando. Domestically, KLM's City Hoppers connect Amsterdam and Eindhoven, Enschede, Groningen, Rotterdam, and Maastricht as well as other Dutch and some Belgian cities.

Trains – Service is extensive and frequent. The claim is made that all towns in Holland have trains in both directions at least once an hour. Discount plans offered by the *Nederlandse Spoorwegen* (*NS*) include 3- and 7-day Rail Ranger Passes. (Note that the 3-day pass can only be obtained at the US branches of the Netherlands Board of Tourism.) The *NS* also sells the Benelux Tourrail pass for any 5 days of travel in a 17-day period in the three-country area.

Cars – Emergency road service is provided by the yellow cars of the *Royal Dutch Touring Club*'s (*ANWB*) Wegenwacht service.

Cruises – Rhine River trips of 2 days or more begin in Amsterdam and Rotterdam. Two-, three-, and four-country cruises are available, with stops in France, Germany, and Switzerland. Schedules and reservation information are available from *K-D Rhine* headquarters, 15 Frankenwerft, 5000 Cologne, Germany; or *Rhine Cruise Agency,* 170

Hamilton Ave., White Plains, NY 10601 (phone: 914-948-3600; or in the western US, 800-858-8587; in the eastern US, 800-346-6525). VVV has details on local boat trips.

SPECIAL EVENTS: Bulbs flower in awesome profusion at the famed *Keukenhof* (kitchen garden) in Lisse from the end of March through the third week of May, with crocuses, daffodils, tulips, and hyacinths. The equally colorful displays of commercial bulb growers are free for the looking in areas east, north, and south of Amsterdam.

Famous cheese markets are held at Alkmaar on Fridays from May through September and at Gouda on Thursdays from mid-June through August. They start at 9:30 or 10 AM and continue for most of the day; check with local hotel or tourist offices for exact hours. The second Saturday in May is *Windmill Day,* with some 400 mills testing their sails; in July and August, 17 mills near Kinderdijk are in operation from 2:30 to 5:30 PM on Saturdays. *The Holland Festival,* the nation's cultural bash, is held throughout June, with various cities holding events. Available by mail from the Chicago office of the Netherlands Board of Tourism or through KLM packages are two travel bonus programs. The Holland Leisure Card ($12) is good for discounts on car, train, and plane travel; on selected accommodations; on canal cruises; on shopping at selected stores and diamond polishers; and on admissions to major tourist attractions. The Holland Leisure Card-Plus ($25) features free access to more than 375 museums as well as all the discounts offered with the Holland Leisure Card.

SHOPPING: Amsterdam is one of the world's diamond cutting centers, but before you purchase, a few words of caution: Not only have diamond prices skyrocketed because of speculation in recent years, but there is often a dramatic difference between Dutch and US appraisals of the same diamond, with US estimates of value often lower than Dutch. Less controversial purchases? Dröste chocolates, with the ever-popular sectioned apple, make a nice small gift. Equally delicious and long-lasting are the whole (unsectioned) Edam and Gouda cheeses. Art prints are reasonable here and Dutch reproductions are of high quality. Blue Delftware is produced by *Porceleyne Fles* in Delft. A softer hued blue porcelain is made in Makkum in Friesland. Check the *Vroom en Dreesman* (V en D) chain of stores throughout the country for locally manufactured goods in a wide range of prices. Shops are generally open from 8:30 or 9 AM to 5:30 or 6 PM. They're closed Sundays and another half day during the week, usually Monday mornings or Wednesday afternoons.

TIPPING: A 15% service charge is included in hotel and restaurant bills. The porters at train stations get 65 (Dutch) cents per bag by law; bellmen expect less. A guilder is the usual tip for small services.

Norway

TOURIST INFORMATION: The central organization is the Norwegian Tourist Board, Havnelageret, 1 Langkaia, 0150, Oslo 1 (phone: 427044). Regional tourist offices called Reiselivsrad (TTKs) are in major towns, and tourist information offices are in smaller towns and villages.

ENTRY REQUIREMENTS: US citizens require a valid US passport for stays of up to 3 months.

CLIMATE AND CLOTHES: Above the Arctic Circle in Kirkenes near the Russian border, round-the-clock days in summer and long winter nights average in the mid-50s F (10C) and mid-teens F (−0 degrees C to −10C) respectively. Oslo's southern summer temperatures average in the low 70s F (about 20C). The fjords are warm enough for summer swimming. Plan on some pretty dresses and spiffy jackets for the 14-day North Cape cruises but otherwise dress is casual and comfortable.

MONEY: The Norwegian krone (NOK) equals 100 øre.

LANGUAGE: Norwegian is the national language. English is commonplace among the younger generation and those in the tourist industry. However, don't expect to chat with northern farmers and fishermen unless you speak Norwegian.

GETTING THERE/GETTING AROUND: Airlines – SAS has direct service from New York to Oslo and from Chicago to Oslo via Copenhagen. Flights are also available from New York on Pan American via London and on Icelandair via Reykjavik. TWA has nonstop service from New York to Oslo. Plane travel is common in this long, narrow land, and three lines, Widerøe's Flyveselskap, Braathen's SAFE, and SAS, cover the routes.

Trains – The routes are well engineered and magnificently scenic with modern equipment and a notably comfortable second class. The Oslo-Bergen trip across the Hardanger plateau is particularly breathtaking. *Norges Statsbaners (NSB)* participates in the Scandinavian Railpass and has discounts for senior citizens and families.

Cars – The Arctic Highway runs 1,564 miles from Oslo to Kirkenes but is hardly an expressway. Hard-surface, winding roads are fine for exploring but not for covering a lot of ground in a short time. Snow closes certain passes in winter, making May through September prime driving time.

Cruises – Ships provide three kinds of coastal travel: among one or several fjords on an areawide basis; coastal trips with steamers calling at various ports between Bergen and Kirkenes; and 14-day North Cape cruises. Inquire locally about the first, with the *Bergen Line* for information on the second, and either *Royal Viking Lines* or *Norwegian American Cruises* for North Cape cruise schedules.

SPECIAL EVENTS: The century-old *Holmenkollen Ski Festival* outside Oslo at the beginning of March attracts top talent and underscores Norway's role as the cradle of modern skiing. Other leading cross-country races include downtown Oslo's *Monolith* in January and Lillehammer's *Birkebeiner* in March. Jazz is a mania for many in Scandinavia and for none more so than the Norwegians, who hold four international festivals annually: in Bergen late May to early June; at Kongsberg in early July; Molde the end of July; and Voss in March. Classical music, together with ballet, opera, and drama, makes up the *Bergen International Festival,* which runs from late May to early June. The Nobel Peace Prize is presented in Oslo in December.

SHOPPING: The colorful, intricately patterned hand-knit Norwegian sweaters never wear out. Wood-handled, stainless steel Norwegian cutlery is exceptionally stylish, as are blond bentwood chairs of impeccable design. Sports equipment is well known and well made: Rods, spools, hand-tied flies, and *O. Mustad & Son* hooks for the fisherman; *Bonna, Epoke, Skilom,* and *Asnes* cross-country skis, and *Rottefella* bindings for cross-country skiers. Stores are generally open weekdays from 8:30 AM to 5 PM (Thursday nights until 7 PM) and Saturdays until 2 PM.

TIPPING: Between 2 and 3 NOK is the usual small tip for bellmen, porters, chambermaids (per night), and cloakroom personnel. A 15% service charge is usually added to restaurant bills.

Poland

TOURIST INFORMATION: Informacja Turystyczna (IT) centers are everywhere: hotels, at the frontier, along highways and at airports, railway stations, and seaports. *Orbis,* the national travel bureau, has its headquarters at 16 ul. Bracka, Warsaw (phone: 260271).

ENTRY REQUIREMENTS: A regular visa, issued for periods of up to 90 days (or a transit visa good for 2 days) must be obtained from a consular office before reaching Poland (allow 2 weeks for processing). Applying for the visa necessitates a valid passport, two photos, and a visa fee of $20. Details from the Polish National Tourist Office, 333 N. Michigan Ave., Chicago, IL 60601 (phone: 312-236-9013).

CLIMATE AND CLOTHES: Autumn, normally crisp and sunny, is a long, lovely season, especially in the forests and hills that cover about a third of the country. Snow covers the Carpathian Mountains by mid-December and lasts until April. Winter temperatures hover around 26F (−3C), while summers are warm and dry, with an average temperature of 68F (20C). Blue jeans are okay for daytime touring and shopping, but evenings at the theater and best restaurants call for dresses and ties.

MONEY: The zloty (Zl) is made up of 100 groszy. No import or export of Polish currency is allowed. Unused zlotys must be left at the border, where a receipt for the amount is issued. When you return to the US, the New York Orbis office, upon presentation of this receipt, will make a refund in dollars, covering the amount of the unused zlotys. There is a mandatory exchange of $15 for each day that a pleasure, professional, and/or business traveler remains in Poland; $7 per day if you are of Polish origin and visiting relatives or are between the ages of 16 and 21. There is an exemption for those days you are on a tour or have prepaid for a hotel.

LANGUAGE: Polish, Slavic in origin, is the official language, but German and English are also spoken.

GETTING THERE/GETTING AROUND: Airlines – LOT and Pan American fly nonstop to Warsaw, and Pan American to Cracow (via Frankfurt and Prague) from New York. Within Poland, LOT's reasonably priced flights connect Warsaw with 10 cities and also Cracow and Katowice to Gdansk, Poznau, and Szczecin.

Trains – The *Polskie Koleje Panstwowe* or *PKP*'s Polrailpass for 8, 15, 21, or 30 days of unlimited rail travel is a bargain. The modern expresses providing frequent intercity service are the best-equipped trains.

Cars – Both self-drive and chauffered Fiats and Fords are rented by *Orbis Rent-a-Car,* at Hotel Forum, ul. 27 Nowogrodzka, Warsaw (phone: 293875). *PZM (the Polish Automobile and Motorcycle Federation)* is the organization to contact for routings, reservations, and emergency assistance. *PZM* border offices as well as those in cities sell gas coupons for foreign exchange, which save 20% over zloty prices. The address for its Foreign Touring Office is ul. 19 Sandomierska, 02-567 Warsaw (phone: 495642).

SPECIAL EVENTS: The *Chopin Piano Competition* is held every 4 years in Warsaw (the next is scheduled for fall 1990). If you can't make it, there are spring and summer Chopin concerts in Warsaw's lovely Lazienki Park and a month devoted to his music at the Duszniki Spa each August. More music? Warsaw hosts an internationally famous *Modern Music Festival* each September, and in August organists from all over the world come to Oliwa on the Baltic to give concerts on the cathedral's superb organ. Warsaw's *Jazz Jamboree* is an October event drawing fans from everywhere.

The *Poster Biennale* — a competition of graphic art posters depicting various events, people, and places, held in Warsaw's largest art galleries in June of even years — is one of the most prestigious contests of its kind. *CEPELIA,* the national folk art cooperative, has an enormous display and sale of regionally made products in Warsaw each June.

In March, Zakopane, a resort in the Tatra Mountains, holds the most important Nordic and Alpine ski races of the season. And in May all attention is focused on the big, international *Berlin-Warsaw-Prague Bicycle Race.*

SHOPPING: State-run shops include *DESA,* which specializes in fine arts and quality merchandise such as crystal and Wloclawkek pottery, and *CEPELIA,* the craft co-op with the best regional wares, including Baltic amber beads and jewelry, kilim-style flat weave rugs, sheepskin outerwear — especially those decorated with Zakopane embroidery — and Silesian lace.

Shops are usually open weekdays from 11 AM to 7 PM, while major department stores are open from 10 AM to 8 PM. Many shops are closed on Saturdays. Those that do open generally conduct business until 5 PM.

TIPPING: The usual tip is 10% of hotel, restaurant, hairdresser, and taxi bills. Service charges are not included in most bills.

Portugal

TOURIST INFORMATION: Portugal's main tourist information agency, Instituto de Promocao Turistica, is at 51 Rua Alexandra Herculano, 2nd Floor, Lisbon (phone: 681174). Postos do Turismo, Tourist Posts, provide tourist information at offices throughout the country. The main branches are at the Palácio Foz on the Praça dos Restauradores (phone: 363314), at the airport, and at Santa Apolonia train station in Lisbon. For immediate information by telephone (in English), call 369450.

ENTRY REQUIREMENTS: US citizens need only a valid US passport for stays of up to 60 days.

CLIMATE AND CLOTHES: Lacking in extremes, the weather is mostly sunny and mild, ranging between 50 and 75F (10 to 24C) year-round on the mainland and in the Azores. Madeira, off the African coast to the southwest, is a bit warmer and attracts sun and sand lovers in all seasons, but the tourist trade peaks December through April. Resort wear, including long skirts for evenings, is de rigueur here in the winter just as it is during the summer season in the Algarve.

MONEY: The escudo is abbreviated with a dollar sign, which takes the place of the decimal point in our currency (for example, 8$50), and equals 100 centavos.

LANGUAGE: Portuguese, though English is spoken in major tourist areas.

GETTING THERE/GETTING AROUND: Airlines – TAP–Air Portugal and TWA both fly nonstop from New York to Lisbon. TAP flies nonstop from Boston to Ponta Delgada in the Azores, and some other flights stop there. Domestically, TAP has jet service to Oporto and Faro, Terceira, and San Miguel in the Azores, and Funchal and Porto Santo in Madeira. Scheduled five-passenger Beechcrafts fly to Bragança, Faro, and Vila Real.

Trains – Because the track gauge is an unusually wide 9 inches (in Spain as well), the cars on the efficient and modern *CP* (*Companhia dos Caminhos de Ferro Portugueses*) are wider and extremely comfortable. The *CP*'s electric trains make frequent runs from Lisbon to Sintra and Cascais. Reservations are suggested on the express trains to Pôrto and the Algarve, the *International Sud-Expresso* to Paris, and the twice-daily trains to Madrid.

The *CP* sells economical Tourist Tickets good for unlimited travel for periods of 5, 10, or 15 days and has other discount plans for groups. Senior citizen discount is 50%.

Cars – Services for the stranded motorist include call boxes, a frequent sight along major routes. Emergency numbers are 02-316732 in the north, 01-7386121 in the south; operators can speak English. Members of *AAA* will receive faster assistance. If someone is injured, call 115 anywhere in Portugal.

SPECIAL EVENTS: The streets erupt with color and pageantry during celebrations commemorating various saints. Tradition calls for folk dancing, fireworks, processions, and bullfights. Of particular note is the *Festa do Santo Antonio* held in mid-June in Lisbon's Moorish Alfama section and the *Festa do São Silvestre* on New Year's Eve in Madeira, where elaborate fireworks are set off from barges in the harbor. A running of the bulls is part of the festivities at Villa Franca de Xira in July. And for local color nearer Lisbon, Mercês, just outside Sintra, holds a fair annually at the end of October featuring food and crafts.

SHOPPING: Hand-painted *azulejos* were once used as ballast for ships crossing the

Atlantic — they now weigh down suitcases on international jets. Tiles in myriad designs are made by *Sant'Anna, Viúva Lamego,* and *Sacavem* in or near Lisbon. *Vista Alegre* makes exquisite porcelain in both antique and modern designs. Craftsmen's skills are considered a precious resource in Portugal, where apprentices are carefully nurtured in order to retain this shopper's paradise for tin and copperware, wrought-iron products, the hand-stitched rugs called Arraiolos, and filigree in silver and gold.

White port wine, difficult to find in the US, as well as red port and fine old Madeiras are elegant and warming souvenirs.

Stores are open from 9 AM to 1 PM and 3 to 7 PM weekdays and 9 AM to 1 PM on Saturdays. Shopping center hours are from 10 AM to 9 PM daily.

TIPPING: Tips in the 10% to 15% range are expected even though a 10% service charge is normally included on hotel and restaurant bills. Porters and bellmen should receive from 20$00 to 25$00 per bag.

Romania

TOURIST INFORMATION: Carpati, the national tourist office, embraces all phases of travel and is in Bucharest at 7 Magheru Blvd. (phone: 145160). In towns where there is no Carpati office, county tourist offices (Oficiul Judetean de Turism) provide travel assistance.

ENTRY REQUIREMENTS: Tourist visas, good for visits of up to 60 days, cost $16 and require a valid US passport for documentation. They're available at Romanian diplomatic offices in the US (Romanian Consular Office, 1607 23rd St. NW, Washington, DC 20008: phone: 202-232-4748 or 232-4749), at the border, or at Otopeni Airport in Bucharest. If accommodations are not arranged in advance, you will be required to change $10 for each day of your visit, and you will not be able to refund this amount when you leave the country. This guarantees a minimum expenditure of $10; amounts over that will be refunded when you leave.

CLIMATE AND CLOTHES: The mode of dress reflects the atmosphere: It's relaxed and casual. Black Sea bathing resorts are informal — suitable for summer heat — and daytime temperatures average around 82F (28C) in July and August. Carpathian ski resorts, usually blanketed in 3 feet of snow during the high season (December to March), have temperatures in the mid to upper 30s F (around 0 degrees C). Overall, the four seasons are clearly defined and the climate is similar to New York's.

MONEY: The leu (L) equals 100 bani. Romanian currency is not convertible, and it is illegal to enter or leave the country with it.

LANGUAGE: Romanian, a Romance language derived directly from Latin, shows some Slavic influences. French, the second language until after World War II, is not spoken much now; English is becoming more common.

GETTING THERE/GETTING AROUND: Airlines – TAROM, Romanian Air Transport, has direct flights from New York to Bucharest via Vienna and Luxembourg; Pan American also flies direct from New York. Other major airlines have connecting flights from Europe. Domestically, TAROM has one or more flights a day between Bucharest and 14 destinations.

Trains – *Caile Ferate Române* (*CFR*), the *Romanian Railway Company,* with diesel and electrically equipped trains, accepts Interail passes but not Eurail. International expresses connect Romania with both Eastern and other European countries.

Cars – Carpati, the national tourist office, and its branches in the major cities offer car rentals (limited to the nationally produced Dacia 1300 and 2000 and the Oltcit-Club), accommodations, itineraries, and road assistance. The national tourist office also sells discount gas coupons at border crossings.

Cruises – The Danube (Dunărea) River enters the Black Sea from southern Romania, forming a natural boundary with Yugoslavia and Bulgaria. River cruises from Vienna to the Black Sea and the Danube Delta, and shorter trips between Romanian towns are run by *NAVROM.*

SPECIAL EVENTS: Centuries-old folk customs are very much alive today and festivals are colorful displays of dances, costumes, and folk art. Carpati publishes a calendar with histories of major celebrations. Most noteworthy are the *Simbra Oilor* at Oas (the first Sunday in May), marking the return of the sheep to the pasture; the *Girls Fair* at Mount Gaina, originally more of a mating game for singles than a fair, has grown into a major folk festival on the third Sunday in July; and the *Hora de la Prislop,* with a galaxy of dances and costumes, the second Sunday in August at Mount Prislop.

SHOPPING: Given the continuing strength of folkloric traditions it's not surprising that crafts are carefully nurtured and products highly prized. Pottery is produced at over 200 locations: the black pottery of Marginea in Bukovina, the Corund near Moldavia, the Vama in Oas, and particularly the pottery of the Oltenia provinces. Potters fairs provide grand selections from a variety of craftsmen and regions. Rugs run the gamut from the flatwoven or *scoarta* style exemplified by Moldavian and Banat rugs to Persian hand-knotted, high-pile rugs. Glass paintings from the 18th and 19th centuries have inspired a modern generation of glass painters. The best examples of Romanian art can be viewed and purchased at government-sponsored *Galeriile de Arta* boutiques. Keep an eye out for silk dresses in subdued, abstract patterns hand-painted by leading artists, a scarce but stunning find. *COMTURIST* shops sell a wide range of products for foreign exchange, including caviar from sturgeon caught in the Danube Delta.

Smaller shops have shorter hours of 9 AM to 1 PM and again from 4 PM to 8 PM; department stores stay open from 9 AM to 6 PM; food markets from 7 AM to 6 PM. Stores are closed on Sundays.

TIPPING: Though not expected, tips are accepted for special services.

San Marino

TOURIST INFORMATION: The Government Tourist Board is near the walls of the city at the Palazzo del Turismo, Cont. Omagnano, Republic of San Marino 47031 (via Italy) (phone: 992101). It's crucial to write "via Italy" on the envelope to avoid mail being sent to California.

ENTRY REQUIREMENTS: There are no border formalities between San Marino and Italy; your valid US passport is all that is required for 3 months or less.

CLIMATE: Summer days average around 82F (28C) in spite of the republic's setting on craggy peaks high above the Romagna plain. Relatively mild winters in the 40s F (4 to 9C) are chilled by the constant presence of the somewhat unsettling *garbino* wind blowing from the south.

MONEY: The Italian lira (Lit) circulates in San Marino, but some local coins and medallions are minted as souvenirs.

LANGUAGE: The Sammarinese dialect is commonly used but Italian is the official tongue. English is spoken by about 30% of the population.

GETTING THERE/GETTING AROUND: Airlines – Rimini, Italy, 14 miles (22 km) to the east, has the nearest airport and is the closest stop for trains and express buses. Local buses make frequent connections between Rimini and San Marino.

Cars – Take the Rimini exit off autostrada A14 and proceed about 11 miles (18 km) west. Drive right up Monte Titano to the capital or leave your car below and take the cable car (*funivia*) or the shuttle buses to the ramparts.

SPECIAL EVENTS: September 3 celebrates the day of the country's patron saint, Saint Marino, with a crossbow contest among members of the Crossbowmen's Corps, who dress in traditional Renaissance costumes.

Two captain's regents rule San Marino for periods of only 6 months at a time and their investiture ceremonies, every April 1 and October 1, are elaborate affairs with costumed guards and foreign representatives in attendance.

Every other summer the *International Art Biennale* takes place in San Marino, and an international grand prix is held annually near San Marino, in April.

SHOPPING: San Marino stamps are a major source of revenue and have considerable value among collectors. Both modern and traditional ceramic pieces are popular and unique souvenirs. And even this minuscule land produces its own wine — a tasty Muscatel (*Moscato*).

TIPPING: Service charges are usually added but check to make sure. Tips of between 1,000 and 2,000 lira should be given for small services.

The Soviet Union

TOURIST INFORMATION: *Intourist,* the USSR Company for Foreign Travel, arranges all trips to the USSR through its appointed travel agents in the US. The head office is 16 Marx Prospekt, Moscow 103009 (phone: 203-6962). Intourist has branches in most cities.

ENTRY REQUIREMENTS: Visas are required, and there are three kinds: tourist, "ordinary" (for business or family visits), and transit. All need advance planning. Once your trip has been confirmed by Intourist in Moscow, your travel agent must file an application with a consular office in the US a minimum of 14 days before your arrival in the USSR. An itinerary complete with dates must be submitted along with a $15 processing fee and other documents. Intourist offices furnish procedural details. Contact Intourist at 630 Fifth Ave., Suite 868, New York, NY 10111 (phone: 212-757-3884).

CLIMATE AND CLOTHES: Make no mistake, it's warm in summer and very, very cold in winter, but Moscow is at least dry, crisp, and often sunny even when your breath steams the air. This guide deals exclusively with the European portion of the USSR, where winter temperatures average 20F (−7C), usually lower, and summers rarely get above the 70s F (20s C). Boots, warm socks, heavy coats, and lined gloves are essential in winter. You'll also want something festive for the inevitable farewell gala if you're part of a group tour.

MONEY: 1 rouble (Rbl.) is made up of 100 kopecks. Roubles cannot be taken into or out of the Soviet Union. When initially exchanging currency, a customs certificate is issued that must be presented to exchange roubles for dollars. Money can be exchanged only through outlets of the State Bank of the USSR. When you leave the country, any remaining Russian currency can be changed into dollars at the bank of the last border point — provided that you have bank receipts of previous transactions. Major credit cards are widely accepted.

LANGUAGE: More than 100 ethnic groups live in the Soviet Union's 15 republics. Russian, an East Slavic language, is the official tongue. Intourist personnel and workers in the hotel and restaurant industries speak English.

GETTING THERE/GETTING AROUND: Precious little flexibility in travel arrangements is allowed. Predetermined itineraries are required, and routes and modes of transportation are restricted. Once you arrive, it's possible to extend your stay, provided the hotel has rooms available.

Airlines – Aeroflot flies to Moscow from Montreal, Washington, DC, and New York; all flights include a stopover in Canada except for one nonstop flight from New York. Pan American also flies nonstop to Moscow, with some flights continuing to Leningrad. Planes are clearly a boon for travel in the world's largest country — 6,800 miles east to west and 2,800 miles north to south. Aeroflot has thousands of domestic flights to cities in all the republics at reasonable rates.

Trains – The Moscow-Leningrad route is quickly traveled on the Soviet railway's *Sovyetskaya Zheleznaya Doroga (SZD)*, while the *Trans-Siberian Railroad* covers 6,250 miles of the USSR, going through over 65 towns and villages. The entire *Trans-Siberian* trip — from Moscow to Nakhodka — takes about 8 days. Overall, the trains aren't terribly fast, but most are comfortable. Passage is arranged through *Intourist*.

Cars – You can drive a rental car or your own automobile into the Soviet Union at certain border points and may also rent Russian makes from Intourist in certain cities. The restricted driving routes in the country are determined and fully arranged through *Intourist,* which also provides the necessary papers for car touring and insurance. One word to the wise motorist: Obey Russian rules of the road — they're strictly enforced.

SPECIAL EVENTS: Among a number of government-sponsored cultural events, Moscow's *Russian Winter Festival* from Christmas Day through the first week in January offers the repertoire of the country's finest ballet, opera, symphonic, and theatrical companies; the spectacular Moscow circus with its dancing bears; and horse-pulled sleigh (*troika*) rides. Other folk and classical music festivals include *Kiev Spring* in May, and *White Nights* in Leningrad in June.

SHOPPING: Fine performances by Soviet virtuosos and orchestras are captured on the technically excellent *Meloydia* records. Good opera glasses make appropriate gifts for the culturally inclined and fur hats and lined gloves for those living in cold climes.

Caviar's not only an antidote to Socialist austerity but a luxurious memento. Exquisitely painted and lacquered *palekh* boxes, reputedly a dying art, represent the height of refinement and are lovely souvenirs. Purchases can be made with foreign currency at the *Beryozka* shops in major hotels or with roubles at stores such as *GUM, Detsky Mir* (Child's World), and *Melodia.*

Shopping hours for department stores are from 8 AM to 9 PM, and in smaller shops from 11 AM to 2 PM and from 3 to 8 PM; most shops are closed Sundays.

TIPPING: Tipping is not officially sanctioned.

Spain

TOURIST INFORMATION: Oficinas de Información y Turismo are found in all major cities, train stations, and airports. In addition to dispensing literature and giving travel assistance, they sell inexpensive tourist insurance policies covering medical expenses, accidents, and baggage theft.

ENTRY REQUIREMENTS: A valid US passport is good for visits of 6 months or less.

CLIMATE AND CLOTHES: Surrounded by the sea, the Iberian Peninsula is dominated by the vast interior central plateau where river valleys have formed lateral depressions interspersed with mountain ranges. In Spain, the result of this diversity is a varied climate: Coolest and most humid along the north Mar Cantábrico coast, with winters averaging 26F (-3C) and summer temperatures of around 77F (25C); dry and arid in the central regions; tremendously hot during summers in Andalusia to the south (up to 95F, 35C); and year-round temperate (66F, 19C), sunny days abound on the Costa del Sol and in the Balearic and Canary islands.

The fashionable Spanish dress with enviable panache, so in leading cities wear your most chic clothing. Generally, casual clothes, suitable for the climate, are acceptable tourist attire, and in the resorts, most anything goes.

MONEY: The peseta (Pta) is the unit of currency.

LANGUAGE: Castilian Spanish is the official tongue, but other regional languages are: Catalán (Catalonia), Basque (Basque country which, in Basque, is *Euskadi*), Gallego (Galicia), Valenciano (Levant provinces), and Mallorquín (the Balearic Islands). English is understood in principal resorts, hotels, restaurants, and shops but not too far off the tourist track.

GETTING THERE/GETTING AROUND: Airlines – Iberia Airlines of Spain operates nonstops to Madrid from Chicago, Los Angeles, Miami, and New York as well as nonstops between New York and Barcelona, and direct service between New York and Málaga via Barcelona or Madrid. Other airlines serving Spain are TWA with nonstops from New York to Madrid, and connecting flights from Los Angeles, and Pan American from New York to Madrid. Aeroméxico has nonstop service from Miami. Early morning arrival schedules enable easy connections to cities throughout mainland Spain, the Canary and Balearic Islands. Iberia's economical Visit Spain AirPass, which must be purchased in conjunction with an Iberia transatlantic flight, offers unlimited travel throughout Spain and the Balearic Islands in a 60-day period on Iberia and Aviaco, Spain's domestic carrier. Iberia's "air bridge" (*Puente Aereo*) shuttle has flights between Madrid and Barcelona departing every 30 minutes throughout the day.

Trains – It is possible to take high-speed, air conditioned trains like the *Talgo* to Paris, Marseilles, Geneva, and Rome without changing at the borders. *RENFE's* (*Spanish National Railways*) best equipment is usually found on the longer distance runs between major cities and are widely recommended. However, some second class trains can be slower, more crowded, and often poorly equipped. Buses are best for short hauls and excursions. Rail passes for 8, 15, or 22 days of travel are sold through *Donna Brunstad Associates,* 431 Post Rd. E., Suite 671, Westport, CT 06880 (phone: 203-454-8916), and at any RENFE offices and stations in Spain.

Cars – Rental rates are particularly reasonable and one-way Iberian rentals that allow pickup in Spain and dropoff in Portugal (or vice versa) are useful for touring. VAT on car rentals was recently reduced to 12%.

SPECIAL EVENTS: All cities and towns in Spain hold fairs or fiestas (*ferias*), some more colorful and exciting than others. Undoubtedly the three most famous are: Valencia's *Fallas de San José* in mid-March, when groups of huge figures (*ninots*) are composed into satirical groups (*fallas*), paraded, and finally set on fire; the *Feria de Sevilla* in late April, with the citizenry parading on horseback in elegant regional dress to the accompaniment of music and flamenco dancing; and the *Feria de San Fermín* in Pamplona the second week of July, with the historic running of the bulls.

The most splendid Holy Week (*Semana Santa*) observances take place in Andalusia, with particularly notable processions in Seville and Málaga. The sherry wine harvest is celebrated in Jerez de la Frontera in mid-September.

SHOPPING: Leather goods, from supple suede gloves and elegant calf handbags to wineskins that require careful curing (*botas*), are excellent purchases, with perhaps the best selection found in Madrid. Designer clothes, including those of Pertegaz and Balenciaga, are the height of fashion. Costume jewelry is imaginative, and the black and white pearls labeled Perlas Majórica are world famous.

Other exceptional buys are shoes, from classic calf pumps to provincial cloth espadrilles; porcelain by *Lladró* and pottery by regional craftsmen; and wool rugs using technologies translated from tapestry makers or simple cotton-rag throws. Spanish sherry is unequaled and *fino* is a fine buy, as are brandies. Saffron is a tasty addition to your Spanish recipes.

Shops are usually open from 9:30 AM to 1 PM and from 4:30 to 8 PM on weekdays and are closed Saturday afternoons and Sundays. Department stores now stay open through the traditional 3-hour siesta, and most are open all day Saturday, from 9:30 AM to 7:30 or 8 PM.

TIPPING: Though service charges of 15% are included in restaurant bills, extra tips of between 5% and 10%, depending on the attention you receive, are expected. Taxi drivers receive 5% of the meter and, in most cases, 50 to 100 pesetas is enough for porters, bellmen, and per night for chambermaids.

Sweden

TOURIST INFORMATION: The identifying logo of the over 200 Turistbyrå is the international lowercase white *i* against a green background. Regional information is provided by the Swedish Tourist Board, Sverigehuset, Hammgatan, Stockholm (phone: 789-2000).

ENTRY REQUIREMENTS: For visits of 3 months or less, a valid US passport is all that is necessary.

CLIMATE AND CLOTHES: July and August temperatures range in the low to mid 60s F (about 18C) around the sea-level cities of Malmö, Gothenburg, and Stockholm. January and February, the coolest months, average 26F (− 3C) in Stockholm, slightly warmer in the south. The well-styled, yet comfortable and functional, clothing of the Swedes mirror their refined sense of design and informal, outdoor orientation. Casual dress is fine in summer but in fall and winter, you'll want a more cosmopolitan look.

MONEY: The Swedish krona (SEK) equals 100 øre.

LANGUAGE: Swedish, but people with a firm command of English are common.

GETTING THERE/GETTING AROUND: Sweden is about 1,000 miles long from top to toe. Transportation on clean, modern equipment with an enviable on-time record makes all areas, from Malmö in the south to beyond the Arctic Circle, easily accessible.

Airlines – SAS flies nonstop from New York to Stockholm and direct from Chicago to Stockholm and from New York to Gothenburg (via Copenhagen). In addition, there are connecting flights to Stockholm via Copenhagen from Los Angeles and Seattle. Pan American has nonstop service to Stockholm from New York; TWA has direct service via Oslo. Thirty-two cities in Sweden are connected by the domestic airline, Linjeflyg.

Trains – *Staten Järnvägar (SJ)* diesel and electric trains are comfortable and fast. Service in the north is augmented by postal buses that carry passengers to outlying areas. The *SJ* network is part of the Scandinavian Railpass, good for 21 days of unlimited travel in first or second class on all trains, the *Helsingør-Malmö* ferry, and also for 50% discounts on other specified ferry runs.

Cars – Most major US car rental firms are represented in Sweden. For a motoring map with suggested itineraries, contact the Swedish Tourist Board, 655 Third Ave., New York, NY 10017 (phone: 212-949-2333).

SPECIAL EVENTS: Midsummer is greeted with great gaiety the weekend closest to the summer solstice in late June. Maypoles, garlands, flower-decked houses, dancing, and special midsummer dishes typify this most popular festival. *Santa Lucia's Day,* December 13, ushers in Christmas with young girls and women wearing crowns of candles and distributing traditional pastries at dawn.

The rococo *Drottningholm Court Theater* outside Stockholm presents primarily 18th-century operas, ballets, and classical music mid-May to mid-September.

SHOPPING: The famed crystal of *Orrefors* and *Kosta Boda* can be bought in Stockholm or you can visit the glass district near Växjo, where 36 of the nation's 44 glassworks are concentrated. Seconds are sold at shops adjoining the factories.

Swedish cotton and woolen fabrics are used to advantage by designers such as *Katja*. If you're thinking mink, it's a good buy here.

Beautifully designed kitchenware and utensils, in a variety of materials, are quality items, as is furniture. Avoid the 23% VAT (called MOMS) by having the store send merchandise directly to your home. Also, many stores throughout Sweden participate in the Scandinavian Taxfree program. An export receipt is issued at the time of purchase and is then presented at designated airport and ferry terminals for a partial VAT refund.

Shops are generally open weekdays between 10 AM and 6 PM and on Saturdays from 10 AM until anywhere between 1 and 4 PM.

TIPPING: A 13% service charge is automatically tacked on to restaurant tabs and hotels add 15%. Taxi drivers expect a 15% tip.

Switzerland

TOURIST INFORMATION: The headquarters of the Swiss National Tourist Office (Schweizerische Verkehrszentrale) is at Bellariastrasse 38, CH-8027 Zurich (phone: 01-202-3737). All but the tiniest Swiss towns have efficient and well-prepared tourist offices, and regional centers have region-wide information.

ENTRY REQUIREMENTS: A valid US passport. No visa is required for visits of less than 3 months.

CLIMATE AND CLOTHES: Famous for its snow-capped mountains — at 15,217 feet the Dufourspitze on Monte Rosa is the highest — Switzerland also boasts a sun belt along Lake Maggiore (890 feet above sea level) complete with palm trees. These contrasts indicate not only a variety of climates but also abrupt changes in the weather. However, normal summer daytime highs average in the mid-70s F (24C).

The citizen's dress is generally conservative in color and style. However, you'll be at ease if you dress according to the activities you pursue.

MONEY: The Swiss franc (SFr) is made up of 100 centimes (French) or rappen (German).

LANGUAGE: There are at least four. German, used by 65% of the population; French by 19%, Italian by 12%, and Romansh, derived from Latin, by less than 1%. Swiss dialects, called collectively Schweizerdeutsch, vary from region to region. English is widely understood.

GETTING THERE/GETTING AROUND: The transportation network is beautifully integrated and famed for the punctuality of its moving parts. The key to its workings is the *Official Timetable* available for $8 from the Swiss National Tourist Office (SNTO) branches in the US or abroad. Note that anyone driving on the superhighways in Switzerland must buy a special car sticker, now used in lieu of tolls. Cars rented in Switzerland usually have these stickers; if you're driving into the country, they can be purchased for 30 SFr. ($22) at border crossings.

Airlines – Swissair has daily nonstop service to Zurich and Geneva from New York. There are also nonstop flights from Atlanta, Boston, and Chicago to Zurich and a direct flight from Chicago to Geneva via Zurich. Pan American and TWA fly nonstop to Zurich from New York, and American flies nonstop from Chicago to Zurich, and from New York to Geneva via Zurich.

Trains – This small country has 2,000 miles of electrified track covering its terrain. The *SBB* (*Schweizerische Bundesbahnen*) offers the Swiss Pass, allowing unlimited trips on trains, boats, and postal buses and a discount of 20% on mountain railways and cable cars. The Pass also includes free transportation, within 24 cities, on the public transportation system. Other transportation bargains include Half-Fare Cards for the general public. For information on all discount cards, contact any of the SNTO branches in the US before you go.

Cars – Road service and information are provided by the *Automobile Club de Suisse,* Wasserwerkgasse 39, 3000 Bern 13 (phone: 031-224722), and the *Touring Club Suisse,* 9 Rue Pierre-Fatio, 1211 Geneva 3 (phone: 022-371-2812). For breakdown service, phone 140, and for road conditions, 163 from anywhere in the country. The national Swiss number for information in English is 111.

SPECIAL EVENTS: The list of Swiss festivals goes on and on whether your interest lies in music, history, industry, or sports. World-renowned occasions, such as Geneva's 10-day *International Motor Show* in March and the *Lucerne Music Festival* of musical events in August are most enjoyable, but don't overlook the patriotic and folkloric observances that give a clear sense of Swiss culture. The major national event of this kind is celebrated all around Switzerland on August 1, when fireworks light the sky to commemorate the founding of the Swiss Confederation. A complete roster of special events is available at SNTO offices.

SHOPPING: Switzerland is synonymous with watches and the wondrous array awaiting your choice is overwhelming. The watchmaker's sweetest rival in Switzerland is the chocolatier. Be sure to try many a connoisseur's favorite — *Lindt.* Not surprisingly, quality music boxes, precision tools, optical goods, and drafting sets are good buys. Multibladed and multipurpose red *Swiss Army* knives are universally popular.

Caran d'Ache pastels, crayons, colored pencils, and pens are treasured by children as well as professional artists. Also art books, most notably the *Skira* series — an exemplary collection — are published here.

Stores in the major cities are open from 8 AM to 6:30 PM on weekdays except on Monday mornings, when they are often closed. Stores close at 4 PM on Saturdays and all day on Sundays. In smaller towns, closing for an hour and a half at noon is common.

TIPPING: A 15% service charge is added to hotel, restaurant, and bar bills as well as automatically included in taxi fares, so that only porters and bellmen require tipping, about one franc per bag.

Yugoslavia

TOURIST INFORMATION: Major cities have Tourist Information Offices, identified by the internationally recognized green sign with the white *i.* The two main Tourist Information Centers of Belgrade are at the railway station and in the subway at Terazije Street next to the Albania building (phone: 635343 or 635622). The Tourist Association of Belgrade can be reached at 339696 or 327834. In small towns, the words *Turist Biro* and *Drustvo* denote information locations.

ENTRY REQUIREMENTS: Visas good for visits of up to 90 days can be obtained at all Yugoslavian border points, embassies, and consulates abroad. A valid US passport is the only document needed for a visa, which will be issued within 24 hours, free of charge. There are consulates in Chicago, Cleveland, New York, Pittsburgh, San Francisco, and Washington, DC.

CLIMATE AND CLOTHES: Swimming is comfortable along the Adriatic coast from May through October, when water temperatures hit the mid-60s F (about 18C) (at least from Dubrovnik south). They rise to the mid-70s F (24C) in summer, when air temperatures hit the low 80s F (28C). Inland summers are hot; winters in the mountains are cold, with snows beginning in December and lingering through April.

Dressing or undressing is your choice on the many nude beaches found along the

Istrian Peninsula. Zagreb requires the most conservative clothes and Dubrovnik and Sveti Stefan are scenes of the more chic lóoks.

MONEY: The dinar (Din) equals 100 paras.

LANGUAGE: Serbo-Croatian is the official language in four of the six republics: Croatia, Bosnia-Herzegovina, Montenegro, and Serbia. Although all citizens speak the same language, it has two written versions: The Serbs, affiliated with the Eastern Orthodox Church, use the Cyrillic alphabet and the Croats, mostly Roman Catholics, use a modified Latin version. Macedonian and Slovenian are the languages of Macedonia and Slovenia. More and more students are choosing English as their second language and it is frequently spoken by the young as well as those associated with the tourist industry.

GETTING THERE/GETTING AROUND: The *Jugoslovenski Zeljeznice* (*JZ*) rail line runs inland from north to south, with occasional spurs east to cities along the coast. Planes, the Adriatic Highway, and the sea are the best ways to get to and between points on the Istrian and Dalmatian coasts and islands and to the southern Adriatic coast.

Airlines – Pan American flies to Belgrade via Frankfurt and Zagreb. JAT (Jugoslovenske Aerotransport), or Yugoslav Airlines, flies nonstop from New York to Belgrade, Dubrovnik, Ljubljana, and Zagreb. Those cities are also served from Chicago via New York. JAT also has service from Los Angeles. The extensive domestic service is rated a bargain by European standards.

Trains – The jewel in the *JZ*'s crown is the 325-mile line between Belgrade and Bar on the Montenegro coast. It's an engineering tour de force — 254 tunnels and 234 bridges had to be built in order to complete the line. The fastest, most comfortably equipped are the business trains (*Poslovni voz*).

Cars – Probably the best way to view the scenic Adriatic coast. Rentals are readily available and gas coupons — available at border crossings — save 5% over regular prices but only if your car has foreign plates. If a breakdown occurs, call 987, an emergency number manned by the SPI (local automobile club).

SPECIAL EVENTS: Summer here is a festival of culture and folklore. The most elaborate event is the *Dubrovnik Summer Festival,* an artistic extravaganza in mid-July through August, with performances set in historic locales and parks. Others include: Zagreb's *International Review of Original Folklore* in July, with over 80 groups the world over plus Yugoslavian troupes competing in a stunning exhibition of regional dances and costumes; Split's *Melodies of the Adriatic* festival in early July; and Korcula's celebration featuring the *Moreska Sword Dance,* Thursdays from May through September.

SHOPPING: Yugoslavia is well known for primitive art. The works of leading artists are widely reproduced and internationally acclaimed. The delicate, colorful, and detailed paintings on glass are exquisite. Check the major cities for exhibitions and dealers.

Many stores specialize in the fine native handcrafts, such as embroidery, sweaters, leatherware, woodcarvings, ceramics, and the bright and cheerfully colored Bosnian and Serbian rugs.

The town of Samobor near Zagreb lends its name to the country's finest crystal.

Shops are open from 7 AM to noon and 2 or 3 to 7 or 8 PM on weekdays; Saturdays, from 8 AM to 3 PM. Stores are closed Sundays.

TIPPING: Discretionary at hotels and restaurants, as service charges of 10% to 15% are put on the bills, but it's best to give a few dinars extra. Porters receive 50 dinars per bag.

THE
CITIES

AMSTERDAM

More than any other major city in Europe, Amsterdam seems to have been designed with people in mind. It is a city built to human scale, refreshingly free of high-rise monuments to corporate egotism. It does not overawe or oppress. Its small streets, graceful canals, and narrow buildings invite exploration. Even its mansions — the elegant 17th-century houses built on the canals by earlier generations of the great and wealthy — are grand without being grandiose.

Emerging from Amsterdam's Central Station to face a welter of taxis, trams, bicycles, boats and bridges, commuters and traffic, one might not believe that it is a soothing city. But cross the traffic and follow any of the canals that lace the city like the concentric tiers of a football stadium, and you will discover its serenity. The four largest and most historic canals — Singel, Herengracht, Keizersgracht, and Prinsengracht — pass near almost everything worth seeing at some point in their grand perambulation around the city.

These canals and the buildings that line them were the heart of Holland's thriving trade for centuries, and as you walk your eye will begin to pick out the details that distinguish the city's singular traditional architecture — unique gables and spires atop the attenuated and tipsy houses that delineate 17th- and 18th-century Amsterdam from the modern city. The finest old houses, built by rich traders, are along Herengracht (aptly, "Gentlemen's Canal"). On Singel, at the Munt, is the flower market, with flower-burdened boats and barges moored along the canal. And a few blocks from where Singel leaves the port are two cat boats, filled with Amsterdam's stray cats. And most canals are picturesquely dotted with houseboats. Walking the canals is not only unavoidable in Amsterdam, it is one of the chief joys of city life. And being a sensible lot, when Amsterdammers are in a hurry, they prefer to navigate the narrow canal streets by bicycle. Where cars get stuck for hours behind vans and trucks, bikes whiz through. (Of a population of 700,000, some 600,000 people have bicycles, and any visitor can join them for the price of a rental and the willpower to ignore hectic traffic.)

Amsterdam has plenty of historical structures — more than 7,000 on the protected list — but few monuments as such. And though its beautiful 17th-century central area has been preserved largely intact, and the city must rank among the world's tops in museums per capita — 44 at last count — it is no architectural mausoleum. You will find that most of these protected 17th- and 18th-century buildings are carrying on business pretty much as usual today. They house small firms, families, cluttered shops, cafés, prostitutes — or all of them together. This is the genius of Amsterdam. In a word, the city has spirit.

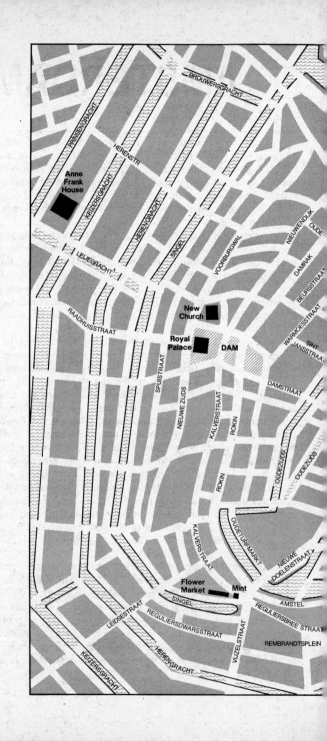

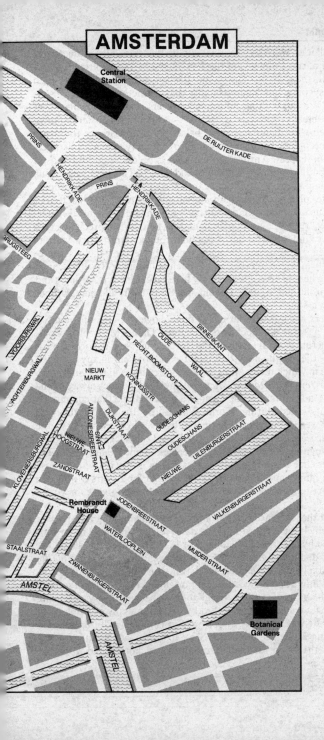

AMSTERDAM

Central
Station

DE RUIJTER KADE

PRINS

HENDRIKKADE

PRINS

HENDRIKKADE

BRUGSTEEG

BINNENKANT

VOORBURGWAL

OUDE

RECHT BOOMSTOOT

WAAL

ACHTERBURGWAL

NIEUW
MARKT

KONINGSSTR

DIJKSTRAAT

OUDESCHANS

KLOVENIERSBURGWAL

ANTONIESBREESTRAAT

SINT

OUDESCHANS

UILENBURGERSTRAAT

NIEUWE
HOOGSTRAAT

NIEUWE

ZANDSTRAAT

Rembrandt
House

JODENBREESTRAAT

VALKENBURGERSTRAAT

STAALSTRAAT

WATERLOOPLEIN

MUIDER STRAAT

ZWANENBURGERSTRAAT

AMSTEL

AMSTEL

Botanical
Gardens

The Dutch call it *gezelligheid,* a special quality that translates inadequately as "coziness." It means intimacy, of the sort offered by the traditional, dark-walled cafés with their shaded lamps and Persian-carpeted tables, but also openness, the easygoing, informal sociability that characterizes so many Amsterdammers. It is a quality that informs all aspects of life in the city, from dress — which almost everywhere is eclectic — to politics. Amsterdammers are not concerned with dictating beliefs, behavior, or appearance to others.

This casual acceptance of different standards, the city's famed tolerance, is firmly rooted in its past. Amsterdam has always been first and foremost a mercantile city, built on middle class values and money. This has by no means proved a bad thing, and the city has always exerted an influence disproportionate to its size, placing Amsterdam among the ten most-popular tourist destinations in Europe, and making it Europe's fourth largest financial center.

The city's early "regent" class of merchants was unique in appreciating that intolerance of any kind is bad for business, and throughout its history Amsterdam has displayed a truly admirable reluctance to persecute whichever heretics were currently in vogue. As the great French philosopher René Descartes put it while living here in 1631, "Everybody here except me is in business and so absorbed by profit making that I could spend my entire life here without being noticed by a soul."

Amsterdammers are not without convictions, however. One of the city's few monuments, a statue of a dockworker at Jonas Daniël Meijerplein, commemorates the heroic general strike of 1941 protesting Nazi deportations of the city's Jews — the only demonstration of its kind to occur in any occupied country, and one in which many of the strikers were shot. On the same *plein,* or square, is the *Jewish Historical Museum,* and just a block away is the Homomonument, a sculpture in the form of a pink triangle that commemorates homosexuals killed during World War II. By the end of the war, Amsterdammers were hiding nearly as many fugitives in their homes as the Germans had succeeded in rounding up for forced labor camps. The most famous of these fugitives, of course, was 14-year-old Anne Frank, who documented her experience so unforgettably for posterity in her diary; the house where the Frank family and friends were sequestered for 2 years is now one of the major tourist sights in Amsterdam — a heartrending visit for young and old alike.

But it is fitting that the earliest known document mentioning Amsterdam by name, from which the city traditionally dates its founding, had to do with commerce. Issued by the Count of Holland in 1275 and on view today at the city archives, the document granted the inhabitants around the "dam on the Amstel" exemption from toll charges on the transport of locally made goods.

In spite of this important concession, that original dam, the site of today's Dam Square in the heart of the city, could not have seemed a very promising location to its first occupants. Surrounded by the flat, marshy swampland of the river estuary, it was regularly swept by storms that blew in unimpeded from the bordering Zuiderzee (Southern Sea). It was so lacking in resources of any kind that the wood for the community's first houses had to be imported.

But, as the Dutch like to boast, while God made the world, they made the Netherlands, and today the Zuiderzee is gone, walled out by a massive, 19-mile dike completed in 1932 and supporting Highway E-10, which now links the provinces of North Holland and Friesland. In the sea's place is the reclaimed Flevoland polder and the immense freshwater Ijsselmeer. And the uninviting landscape has disappeared beneath the capital itself, most of whose buildings are supported by an estimated 5 million wooden piles driven deep into the soggy ground.

Amsterdam's convenient central location for trade was virtually its only natural resource, and Amsterdammers, who soon became known for their acute (and frequently ruthless) business practices, were quick to take advantage of the fact. By the dawn of the 16th century, the early settlement had grown into a thriving city of about 12,000. This original city center, still referred to locally as the *walletjes* for the early walls surrounding it, is better known nowadays as the famous red-light district, with prostitutes, porno shops, and sex clubs incongruously housed in a picturesque quarter of preserved 17th- and 18th-century homes and warehouses, second-hand bookstores, boutiques, and Chinese restaurants.

Amsterdam reached the peak of its fortune during the Golden Age of the 17th century, when it became the center of a worldwide maritime empire and the base of the country's emergence as a major world power in spite of (in fact, largely because of) an almost perpetual state of war. With characteristic aplomb, the city carried on a highly profitable trade with both its enemies and allies, even going so far at one point as to insure enemy ships against destruction by Dutch forces. It also offered sanctuary to a stream of skilled refugees from other cities — again to its own considerable profit — and it was during this period that work was completed on the rapidly expanding city's crowning glory: the elegant network of canals ringing it, along which the great and newly rich constructed magnificent homes. Today Amsterdam has more canals than Venice — 165 — containing more than 60 miles of waterways and spanned by some 1,000 bridges.

The period following the Golden Age was one of decline for both the city and the country. By the dawn of the 19th century, Holland was a French province under Napoleon. After the emperor's defeat, it became a Dutch monarchy for the first time in 1815 under King Willem I. World War I bypassed the country, and by the time it was invaded by Nazi forces in World War II, Holland had become one of the most backward nations in Europe.

Today it is one of the most progressive, and much of the credit for this must go to Amsterdam. For this great and unique city, which even the Dutch themselves don't really understand and tend to dismiss as "difficult," has never lost its sense of pride or determined independence. Today, thanks largely to its opportunistic burghers and the liberal traditions they helped to establish, Amsterdam remains a city, more than anything else, of possibilities. It is open, *gezellig*, vibrant, amoral, fascinating, and — above all — alive. Certainly it is a city to be seen but, even more, a city to settle into, if only for a few days.

AMSTERDAM AT-A-GLANCE

SEEING THE CITY: During summer months, the towers of two of Amsterdam's most historic churches offer the best views of the old city center areas. The Oude Kerk (Old Church), which dates from the early 14th century, is in the heart of the *walletjes* district in the oldest part of the city at Oudekerksplein; open daily except Sundays from 10 AM to 4 PM (phone: 258284). The Westerkerk (Western Church), Rembrandt's burial place, was completed in 1631 and is amid Amsterdam's Golden Age canals in the most beautiful part of the city at the Westermarkt. Boasting the city's tallest church tower, at more than 250 feet, it can usually be visited from 2 to 5 PM on Tuesdays, Wednesdays, Fridays, and Saturdays from June 1 until September 15 (phone: 842705).

At the harbor next to Central Station is the modern Harbor Building housing the *MartInn* restaurant, from which you can enjoy a panoramic view of the harbor and canals in comfort. Open weekdays for lunch and dinner until 9:30 PM. Reservations necessary. 7 De Ruiterkade (phone: 256277). For a spectacular view of Amsterdam's newer southern fringe area, visit the elegant *Ciel Bleu* French restaurant atop the 23-story luxury *Okura* hotel. Open daily from 6:30 PM to 1 AM. Reservations advised. 175 Ferdinand Bolstraat (phone: 787111). Another place to see the rooftops and canal configurations is the coffee shop on the 6th floor of the *Metz* department store, 455 Keizersgracht (phone: 248810). Open during regular store hours: 10 AM to 6 PM daily; Mondays from 1 PM, Thursdays to 9 PM, Saturdays from 10 AM.

Taking a boat tour of Amsterdam's canals has become a virtual tourist cliché, but it's still the best way to make a first acquaintance with the city. Several operators along the Rokin, the Damrak, and the Nassaukade run the tours, which last about an hour. The best tour is run by *Kooij,* near the Dam on the Rokin at the intersection with Spui. Tours depart every few minutes (phone: 233810). At ground level, six do-it-yourself walking tours from the VVV, the tourist office (opposite Central Station; phone: 266444), make it easy and fun to explore on foot.

SPECIAL PLACES: The major sights of Amsterdam are grouped conveniently around a few principal areas, all within walking distance of one another. The city's central landmark and natural focal point is Dam Square, or simply, the Dam. At the end of the Damrak — a short street leading from the harbor and Central Station — the busy square is dominated by the distinctive war memorial constructed there in 1956. In good weather, the steps ringing the monument are a sea of young people — residents and tourists — resting, singing, making plans; but sadly, pickpockets and drug dealers seem to have taken over the park. The open plaza of the square opposite the monument often attracts a variety of spontaneous and organized activities, festivals, and jazz concerts, and free puppet shows are staged there on one or two afternoons a week during the summer.

Royal Palace – Hailed as the "eighth wonder of the world" after its completion in 1662 because of the 13,659 wooden piles holding it up. Its regal interior, decorated by the leading artists of the time, can be viewed daily during the summer from 12:30 to 4 PM and on Wednesdays in winter at 1:45 PM by arrangement. Don't expect to see the Queen unless she is receiving official visitors that day; she lives in the Royal Palace in The Hague. Admission charge. On Dam Square, opposite the war memorial across the plaza (phone: 248698).

New Church (Nieuwe Kerk) – An imposing late Gothic church dating from around 1500 and the traditional place of inauguration of new monarchs. Following 2 decades of restoration, the church reopened in time for the installation of Queen Beatrix in 1980 and now features concerts and exhibitions. On Dam Square, next to the Royal Palace. Open weekdays 11 AM to 4 PM, Sundays noon to 5 PM, with an organ concert at 3 PM; closed January and February (phone: 268168).

The Three Bottles (De Drie Fleschjes) – A historic, cask-lined tasting house unchanged since it first opened for business in 1650. Make sure you sample some of the traditional "old Holland" liqueurs (the best-known brands are Bols and Hoppe) that are its specialty. Open daily except Sundays from noon to 8:30 PM. Behind the Nieuwe Kerk at 16 Gravenstraat (phone: 248443).

Wynand Fockink – Another atmosphere-saturated tasting house notable for its 1679 interior, collection of hand-painted mugs, and illustrated bottles immortalizing all of Amsterdam's mayors since 1800 (irreverently known as turkeys). Sample the mellow, aged gin (*oude jenever*) or taste a liqueur or two. Seeing one of these splendid establishments should not stop you from visiting the other as well. Each is special in its own way and they're well within crawling distance of each other. Open daily except Sundays from 11 AM to 8 PM. Directly behind the Dam monument at 31 Pijlsteeg (phone: 243989).

Canals – More than any other, Amsterdam is a city to stroll through. Not to be missed is its most beautiful section — the concentric rings of canals known as the Singel (Moat), Herengracht (Gentlemen's Canal), Keizersgracht (Emperor's Canal), and Prinsengracht (Prince's Canal). To see what the elegant homes lining the canals originally looked like, visit the *Willet-Holthuysen Museum,* open daily from 11 AM to 5 PM. Admission charge. 605 Herengracht (phone: 264290).

Anne Frank House – A short way west of the Dam and just around the corner from the Westerkerk is the house containing the secret annex where the Frank family and their friends hid from the Nazis for 2 years. No matter how prepared you are, you will be shocked by the size and vulnerability of the quarters that housed 14-year-old Anne, her parents and sister, their friends the Van Daans and their teenage son Peter, and a dentist named Dussel. You'll go in behind a bookcase that disguised the entrance to the upstairs hideout and see the simple artifacts, photos, and newspaper clippings that speak so mutely and eloquently of tragic times.

Anne's father, Otto Frank (who was the lone survivor of the Gestapo raid in August 1944 that sent the whole group to extermination camps), found Anne's diary, which has become one of the great cultural documents of this century.

Downstairs is an excellent video show and exhibition on the city and its Jews during the war, a tale of heroism and cowardice. A visit to Anne's house is an excellent way to introduce young people to the horrors of the Holocaust. Open daily from 9 AM to 5 PM, Sundays from 10 AM, and to 7 PM from June through August. Admission charge. 263 Prinsengracht (phone: 264533).

Jordaan – Amsterdam's colorful working class district. Devote a day to simply exploring the maze of narrow streets and alleys with their innumerable small boutiques and arts and crafts shops sprinkled among the more traditional businesses . . . and several nights to experiencing the Jordaaners themselves in their characteristic neighborhood cafés — unlike any others in Amsterdam (see *Nightclubs and Nightlife*). The major part of the Jordaan is bordered by the Rozengracht, Lijnbaansgracht, Brouwersgracht, and Prinsengracht, with the most interesting shops concentrated on the 2e Anjeliersdwarsstraat, 2e Tuindwarsstraat, and 2e Egelantiersdwarsstraat. Try to catch the Monday market on the Noordermarkt.

Walletjes – Immediately to the east of the Dam is the picturesque old-city center named for the medieval walls that once surrounded it. This attractive area includes a number of purely historic sites, described in the entries that follow, and is worth a daytime walk. Ironically, perhaps, the area is now best known as the red-light district, a European capital of public sex. And it really is public; everything is out in the open, with no effort at concealment. (Once Paris was the world's sex capital; now it looks tame in comparison with once-puritanical cities like Copenhagen and Amsterdam). Almost 1,000 "girls," many of them extremely attractive, line OZ Voorburgwal, the Oudezijds Achterburgwal, and the small neighboring streets, standing in windows with real red lights, on the streets, and even riding bicycles. There are live sex shows and sex shops all along OZ Voorburgwal. As in any city's "Times Square" area, watch out for pickpockets and street criminals.

The Zeedijk, the old sailors' quarter, is being restored to its 17th-century grandeur, with the *Golden Tulip Barbizon Palace* hotel (see *Checking In*) and smart shops as its focal points. Amsterdam's Chinese community celebrates both New Year's Eve and the Chinese New Year with a huge display of fireworks on the bridge by the Zeedijk.

Amstelkring Museum – The 17th century was a period of repression of Catholics, and at least 26 clandestine churches were built in city attics by 1681. This one, nicknamed "Our Dear Lord in the Attic" and extending through the joined attics of three houses, is equipped with everything from organ to baroque altar. The entry house was set up in 1663 and has one of the few completely preserved classical 17th-century living rooms still existing in Amsterdam. Open daily from 10 AM to 5 PM, Sundays from 1 PM. Guided tours by appointment. Admission charge. In the heart of the *walletjes* district at 40 Oude Zijds Voorburgwal (phone: 246604).

Waag (Weigh-House) – Part of a gate and a fragment of the old city walls dating from 1488, the Waag was later converted into a weighing house. Anatomy lessons were given here from 1619 until 1939, an early one of which was the subject of Rembrandt's famous painting *The Anatomy Lesson of Dr. Tulp.*

Schreierstoren (Weepers' Tower) – Dating from 1569, this is another fragment of the original city walls. Henry Hudson departed from here on his voyage to the New World in 1609. Tradition has it that the tower got its name from the sailors' wives who used to see off their husbands from here. Between the *walletjes* district and Central Station at the corners of Prins Hendrikkade and Geldersekade.

Flea Market – This is Amsterdam's famous open-air secondhand market. A major part of the fun used to be haggling over the price of treasures unearthed from the random mounds, but a surfeit of affluent visitors has spoiled the dealers somewhat, and these days there are few treasures to be found. The market has returned to the original Waterlooplein location (for which it was originally named). Open daily except Sundays from 10 AM to 4 PM.

Rembrandt House – The house where Rembrandt lived and worked from about 1639 to 1658 is fully restored and furnished much as it must have appeared to him. Virtually all of his 250 etchings are on display here. Open daily from 10 AM to 5 PM, Sundays from 1 PM. Admission charge. Near the flea market at 4-6 Jodenbreestraat (phone: 249486).

Munt (Mint) – A short street called the Rokin leads to the Munt. Although named for the coining use it was put to after the French occupation, this monument, which dates from 1490, is interesting as another piece of the original city walls.

Rembrandtsplein – Turning left at the Munt takes you into the Reguliersbreestraat, which leads directly into the concentration of piano bars, nightclubs, and casinos around the Rembrandtsplein. Once the city's butter market, Rembrandtsplein is now a pedestrian-only precinct and a leading center of nightlife, known particularly for striptease clubs and topless bars. If you enter the Rembrandtsplein from Amstelstraat, a street on your right, called Engelse Pelgrimsteeg, is where some of the English Pilgrims lived before leaving for the New World.

Try to catch a film at the *Tuschinski,* just before the square. This ornate Art Deco theater is worth seeing regardless of what's playing. 26 Reguliersbreestraat (phone: 262633).

Begijnhof – The best known of the 75 *hofjes* (enclosed courtyards) still scattered around Amsterdam and unobtrusively concealed behind ordinary doors in the walls of residential buildings. Founded in 1346 as a cloister, it is now, like the other *hofjes,* an idyllic inner-city residential block for the elderly, but anyone may take advantage of the oasis of tranquillity provided by the courtyard. The Begijnhof also contains Amsterdam's English church as well as its oldest surviving house at #34, built in about 1470 (not open to the public except for concerts). The easy-to-miss entrance is on a short street called Spui, leading from the Rokin.

Leidseplein – One of the city's major centers of nightlife; in the summer its open terrace is also a favorite daytime gathering place for dedicated people watchers and beer drinkers; in winter, its open-air ice skating rink is popular. Next door is the *Stadsschouwburg,* a leading municipal theater. 26 Leidseplein (phone: 242311).

Vondel Park – Amsterdam's beautiful main park, with 120 acres of woodland, waterways, grassy fields, and one of the best jogging tracks in town. In summer, it is transformed into just the kind of colorful human zoo Amsterdam would be expected to produce, with a number of open-air events presented on an almost daily basis (see *Special Events*). Bordered by Constantijn Huygensstraat, Overtoom, Amstelveenseweg, Koninginneweg/Willemsparkweg.

Rijksmuseum – This world-famous museum is probably best known for Rembrandt's *Night Watch,* but it also has the world's greatest collection of Dutch masters and other painters from the 15th to the 19th century. Open Tuesdays through Saturdays from 10 AM to 5 PM, Sundays from 1 PM. Admission charge. 42 Stadhouderskade (phone: 732121).

Stedelijk Museum – Amsterdam's museum of modern art, with paintings and sculptures dating from the mid-19th century as well as changing exhibitions of contemporary international artists. Open from 11 AM to 5 PM daily. Admission charge. 13 Paulus Potterstraat (phone: 573-2911).

Van Gogh Museum – Grouped with the *Rijksmuseum* and the *Stedelijk* along Amsterdam's appropriately named Museumplein, this newest of the city's big three museums opened in 1972. Its ultramodern facilities feature an unrivaled collection of 200 paintings and 400 drawings by the famous Dutch artist. To commemorate the 100th anniversary of Van Gogh's death, the museum will display an additional 120 paintings on loan from collections around the world in a special exhibition from March 30 through July 29, 1990. On Sundays from 2 to 4 PM, adults can take art lessons, complete with live models. Open weekdays (except Mondays) from 10 AM to 5 PM, Sundays from 1 PM (during the centenary exhibition, 9 AM to 9 PM). 7 Paulus Potterstraat (phone: 764881).

RAI – Amsterdam's modern congress and exhibition center has a regularly changing schedule of major international trade fairs and expositions. 8 Europaplein, reachable by train from Schiphol Airport (phone: 541-1411).

Albert Cuyp Market – Amsterdam's largest and most colorful street market, with rows of stalls selling food, flowers, clothing, books, and practically everything else imaginable. It extends for blocks along the street for which it is named, starting at the Ferdinand Bolstraat, not far from the Museumplein. Closed Sundays; not to be missed whether or not you buy.

Aviodome Museum – A perfect way to fill in waiting time at Schiphol Airport, with exhibits on everything to do with flight, from a model of the first flying reptile of 150 million years ago to a replica of the Wright Brothers' plane, a mockup of a modern jet cabin, and a half-scale model of the Apollo Moon Lander. Open 10 AM to 5 PM; closed Mondays. Admission charge. Schiphol International Airport, about 6 miles (9.6 km) from Amsterdam on Highway E-10 to The Hague (phone: 173640).

Scheepvaart (Maritime) Museum – This collection pays tribute to the country's

3 centuries of globe-girdling exploits. Displays include ship models, nautical paintings, and charts. Open Tuesdays through Fridays from 10 AM to 5 PM; Sundays from 1 to 5 PM. Admission charge. 1 Kattenburgerplein (phone: 523-2311).

World Trade Center – This colossal complex of offices, shops, and exhibition halls caters to the international businesses that are the lifeblood of the city. 1 Strawinskylaan; take the train from Schiphol Airport (phone: 575-9111).

Jewish Historical Museum – In new quarters since 1987, at the former German Synagogue Neie Shoel, its extensive collection focuses on the customs and festivals of Jewish people in the Netherlands. Open daily from 11 AM to 5 PM; Sundays, 1 to 5 PM. 204 Jonas Daniël Meyerplein (phone: 269945).

Muziektheater – A 1,600-seat, very contemporary complex, overlooking the Amstel River, it combines the functions of Amsterdam's City Hall (Stadhuis) and Opera House. The home of the *Netherlands Opera Company* and the *National Ballet*. 3 Amstel (phone: 255455).

■**EXTRA SPECIAL:** Most of the attractions around the world that require rising before dawn are usually not worth it. A notable exception is the morning flower auctions held in Aalsmeer, just outside Amsterdam. Both the place and the activity are unique.

The flower auctions are held in a building said to be the largest under a single roof on this planet — occupying an area greater than 50 football fields. Acres and acres of freshly cut, fragrant roses set beside equal acreage of tulips, carnations, and other blossoms. There are cut flowers as far as the eye can see: a scene that overwhelms the senses.

Operations at Aalsmeer begin before dawn, with the six auction rooms going into action around 7 AM. The bidding "clocks" involve hundreds of bidders who occupy the steep grandstands above the constant parade of carts full of blooms to be bid upon. More than 4,000 flower growers are part of this immense cooperative, and it's a sight that is both beautiful and aromatic.

The auction is open weekdays from 7:30 to 11:30 AM. Any hotel in Amsterdam can help arrange transportation. There are other notable auction houses in Amsterdam, including *Christie's* and *Sotheby's* (see *Auctions in Europe,* DIVERSIONS).

SOURCES AND RESOURCES

 TOURIST INFORMATION: For brochures, general information, and inexpensive maps showing all the major sights, lists of many of the city's hotels and restaurants, and similar materials, go to the city tourist offices (VVV) in the Old Dutch Coffee House opposite the Central Station or at 106 Leidseplein. Open weekdays and Saturdays from 9 AM to 8:30 PM, Sundays from 10 AM to 5:30 PM (phone: 266444).

Before leaving home, pick up the Dutch Leisure Card, which provides discounts on car, train, and plane travel as well as breaks on shopping and attractions in the Netherlands. For details, contact the Netherlands Board of Tourism, Information Dept., 355 Lexington Ave., New York, NY 10017 (phone: 212-370-7367).

The most detailed commercial map (which includes the entire public transport system) is the *Falkplan,* available at any newsstand.

The US Consulate is at 19 Museumplein (phone: 664-5661).

Local Coverage – The best guide to what's on is the weekly *Amsterdam This Week,* free from the VVV. Current films, which are shown in their original language, are also listed. Don't take the bar, club, and restaurant listings as definitive, however, since the establishments pay to be included. *This Week* and the *Amsterdam Times* also contain listings of museums and other sights as well as general information and useful tips.

The English-language monthly magazine *Holland Herald* covers activities of interest to visitors throughout the country and runs features on restaurants, shopping, special attractions, and Dutch life in general. It is available on KLM flights and at local KLM offices.

Most of Amsterdam's bookshops have books in English on various aspects of the city and the rest of the Netherlands. For the best selection, try *Scheltema Holkema Vermeulen,* 16-18 Koningsplein (phone: 267212); *Athenaeum,* 14 Spui (phone: 226248); or any of the *AKO* establishments around town. *Premsela,* 78 Van Baerlestraat, (phone: 662-4266), and *Art Book,* 645 Prinsengracht (phone: 259337), have stunning art volumes, as do many of the major museums. The *American Book Discount,* 185 Kalverstraat (phone: 255537), is devoted solely to British, American, and Dutch publications in English. *Van Gennep,* 283 Spuisstraat (phone: 247033), specializes in remaindered art, jazz, and literature books, and *Book Traffic,* 50 Leliegracht (phone: 204690), has a variety of secondhand books in Dutch and English.

Food – *Amsterdam This Week* has restaurant listings, although, as noted above, the establishments pay to be included.

Telephone – The area code for Amsterdam is 020.

CLIMATE AND CLOTHES: In Holland, they say you can often experience four seasons in one day. Amsterdam winters tend to be mild, with the minimum average temperature in the coldest months of January and February at about 31F (0 Celsius). The sunniest month is June, and peak average temperature throughout the summer is about 70F (21C). You can dress lightly, but bring along an extra jacket. Useful accessories are an umbrella — if you can keep it from blowing away — and a wool scarf to brace against the wind year-round.

GETTING AROUND: Airport – Schiphol Airport, which handles both domestic and international carriers, is about a 25-minute ride from the center of Amsterdam; taxi fare to downtown should run about 50 to 55 Dutch florins (about $25 to $27.50). Schiphol Line trains leave every 15 minutes for the Amsterdam South railway terminals at the World Trade Center and the RAI Congress Hall (both close to the city center), the terminal by the Fashion Trade Center, and Central Station; cost is about 4.40 florins ($2.20) one way. KLM provides bus service from the airport to several central hotels for about 12 florins ($6) each way. Buses leave every 30 minutes.

Bicycle – If you have nerves of steel, do as the Dutch do and rent a bike, but make sure you leave it securely locked! One source is *Rent-a-Bike* at Central Station, 33 Stationsplein (phone: 248391). Deposit required.

Boat – A boat tour of the canals is the best way to get the feel of the city. In addition to the glass-topped sightseeing boats already mentioned under *Special Places,* water taxis accommodating up to 8 people can be hired or flagged down year-round for transportation or sightseeing (at a flat group rate of about 95 florins/$47.50 an hour, or by the meter at about 25 florins/$12.50 for 15 minutes; phone: 750909). Canal bikes (pedal boats) for 2 to 4 persons can be rented opposite the *Rijksmuseum,* next to the *Anne Frank House,* and at various spots around town, April to October (phone: 265574).

Bus, Train, and Tram – Central Railway Station, 1 Stationsplein, at the end of Damrak, is also the hub for the city's local trams and buses. For train information, call 202266; for buses and trams, 272727. Most hotels have free copies of the *City Transport Welcome Folder,* which lists all pertinent information in English.

The workhorse of Amsterdam's exemplary public transportation system is its network of frequently running trams (streetcars), supplemented by bus routes and a metro (subway) line. The city is divided into tariff zones. Buy a day card (*dagkaart*) from the driver for 8.85 florins (about $4.45) or a multiple "strip card" at any tobacco shop or the bus office at Central Station, which can be used for short trips during the week. Tell the driver your destination, and he will stamp the appropriate strip for that zone. Most places in the city center require two strips. Cards can also be purchased at reduced prices from the GVB (city transport) office in front of Central Station, where simplified maps of the system are available as well. All cards are good for unlimited transfers within the same zone for 1 hour after being stamped. If transferring, you can enter trams by the rear door. Persons over 65 and under 10 travel at half-fare. After the normal system shuts down (around midnight), the night bus network (*nachtbus*), covering the main routes through the city, is in service. Since the trams run on an honor system, tram police often board unannounced and ask to see tickets. The fine is 27 florins ($13.50) if you're caught without one.

Car Rental – *Avis, Buget,* and *Hertz* and many smaller firms are well represented at Schiphol Airport and in the city, but driving in Amsterdam is no way to have a happy holiday. If you do, here are some basic survival tips: (1) Trams have absolute right-of-way and enjoy exercising it; (2) all other traffic coming from the right usually has priority and the Dutch regard yielding as a matter of dent before dishonor; (3) stay out of marked cycle lanes and watch out for kamikaze cyclists; (4) taxis are allowed to drive on tram tracks; and (5) keep a good book handy to spare your blood pressure. Rules of the road are contained in the *Welcome to Holland* brochure, published by the National Tourist Office and available from most VVVs.

Taxi – Service is expensive, and taxis don't normally cruise, although you can sometimes flag down an empty one. The best place to get one is at one of the many taxi stands around the center of town.

SPECIAL EVENTS: In Amsterdam, 1990 is the year of van Gogh. The official celebration begins on March 30, the date of the master's birth, and continues through July 29, the date of his death. The *Van Gogh Museum* has launched a comprehensive exhibition of 120 paintings from museums and private collections around the world which van Gogh himself felt were his most important works. Among them will be several examples of his *Sunflowers* canvases. Museum hours during this period will be from 9 AM to 9 PM daily. Art and antiques share the spotlight during *Amsterdam Art Weeks,* from early to late March. The *Queen's Birthday,* April 30, is a time of uninhibited celebration throughout the land. In Amsterdam, festivities include street fairs with live music and ethnic food stands on the Dam, a citywide "yard sale" of secondhand goods, and a fireworks display. During June, the annual *Holland Festival* is a day-and-night cultural extravaganza crammed with dance, music, and theater performances by top Dutch and foreign companies; July is the month for showcasing young talent with the *Summer Festival.* Throughout the summer, various music, mime, dance, theater, and special children's programs for all tastes are presented free on many days of the week in the Vondel Park. *Sail Amsterdam,* a major event that occurs every 5 years, begins on August 8 with a parade of classic tall ships, which sail from Ijmuiden to Amsterdam's harbor. This year, a replica of the *Amsterdam,* an 18th-century tall ship that was sunk by the British on its maiden voyage, will be seen for the first time as it leads the parade. The *Uitmarkt* is a free performing arts festival held at various locations the last weekend of August; simultaneously, all concert and theater organizations offer special low prices to introduce the new season. At the beginning of September, the world's largest floral procession departs from Aalsmeer, site of the world's biggest flower auction (see *Extra Special*), winding its way to Dam Square by late afternoon. In mid-September, Jordaaners celebrate their own district and way of life with markets, fairs, cabarets, and other festivities during the 2-week *Jordaan Festival.* In mid-November, thousands line the streets as St. Nicholas, the original Santa Claus, makes his grand entry into Amsterdam. The parade begins by Central Station, heads down the Dam, and loops around town.

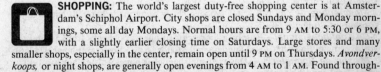

MUSEUMS: Amsterdam has about 50 altogether. Additional museums of interest not mentioned under *Special Places* include the following.

Allard-Pierson Museum – An archaeological collection spanning several thousand years of classical culture. 127 Oude Turfmarkt (phone: 525-2556).

Amsterdam Historical Museum – In a former orphanage dating from 1414, with changing exhibitions as well as permanent displays about the history of Amsterdam. Open daily from 11 AM to 5 PM. 92 Kalverstraat (phone: 255822).

Biblical Museum – Devoted to the origins of the history of the "book of books," it also includes archaeology exhibits in two 17th-century canal houses. Admission charge. 366 Herengracht (phone: 247949).

Fodor Museum – Contemporary Dutch artists and photographers. 609 Keizersgracht (phone: 249919).

't Kromhout – Exhibition and demonstration of 19th-century shipbuilding. 147 Hoogte Kadijk (phone: 276777).

Madame Tussaud's Waxworks Museum – An affiliate of the London branch, it displays wax models of famous people. Open daily from 10 AM to 6 PM; 9 AM to 7 PM in July and August (Sundays from 10 AM). Admission charge. 156 Kalverstraat (phone: 229949).

Netherlands Film Museum – Continuing exhibits on the history of film. 3 Vondelpark (phone: 831646).

Netherlands Technology Museum – Modern technology, from physics to computers. Admission charge. 129 Tolstraat (phone: 646-6021).

Theater Museum – A collection of historical objects relating to Dutch theater. 168 Herengracht (phone: 235104).

Tropen (Royal Tropical) Museum – A showcase for culture and developments in the Third World. 2 Linneausstraat (phone: 568-8200).

Additional monuments include the *Noorderkerk* (Northern Church), from 1623, at the Noordermarkt; *Zuiderkerk* (Southern Church), 1611, Zandstraat; *Portuguese Synagogue,* dating from 1675, at Jones Daniël Meijerplein; and *Montelbaanstoren,* a city wall fragment dating from 1512, at the corner of Oude Schans and Oude Waal.

SHOPPING: The world's largest duty-free shopping center is at Amsterdam's Schiphol Airport. City shops are closed Sundays and Monday mornings, some all day Mondays. Normal hours are from 9 AM to 5:30 or 6 PM, with a slightly earlier closing time on Saturdays. Large stores and many smaller shops, especially in the center, remain open until 9 PM on Thursdays. *Avondverkoops,* or night shops, are generally open evenings from 4 AM to 1 AM. Found throughout the city, they sell fresh fruits and vegetables, prepared foods, wines, and staples. One of the best is *Sterk,* across from the *Musiektheater* on the Waterlooplein.

Amsterdam's finest stores (including haute couture houses) are along the P. C. Hooftstraat, adjacent Van Baerlestraat, and on the Beethovenstraat. The Leidsestraat, between the Spui and Leidseplein, and the pedestrian-only Kalverstraat, from the Dam to the Munt, are other busy shopping districts. Some of the best shops can also be found on the small side streets connecting the canals — Herenstraat, Prinsenstraat, Runstraat, Huidenstraat — and along the Utrechtstraat.

Amsterdam has had a long history as a center of the diamond industry, and a number of old firms are happy to show visitors around their works. Whether you can afford to buy diamonds or not, you may want to see how the precious gems are polished to perfection. Contact *Amsterdam Diamond Centre,* 1-5 Rokin (phone: 245787); *Gassan Diamond House,* 17-23 Nieuwe Achtergracht (phone: 225333); *Coster Diamonds* at 2-4 Paulus Potterstraat (phone: 762222); *Herman Schipper,* 3 Heiligeweg (phone: 236572); *Holshuysen-Stoeltie,* 13-17 Wagenstraat (phone: 237601); and *Van Moppes Diamonds,* 2-6 Albert Cuypstraat (phone: 761242). Pick up an introductory brochure about diamonds from the city tourist office.

Other good buys besides diamonds are famous Delftware, handicrafts, tulip bulbs, and antiques (watch out, however, for abundant fake diamonds or fake antiques; to be safe, stick to recommended merchants). The greatest concentration of antiques shops is to be found along the Nieuwe Spiegelstraat, Spiegelgracht, and adjacent streets near the Rijksmuseum. There is also an indoor antiques market at 38 Looiersgracht, between the Leidseplein and Jordaan, open Mondays through Thursdays and Saturdays from 11 AM to 5 PM (phone: 249038). Stamps and coins are featured every Wednesday and Saturday afternoon on the Nieuwe Zijds Voorburgwal between the Dam and the Spui, and old books are on offer daily (except Sundays) at the historic Oudemanhuispoort, between Oude Zijds Achterburgwal and Kloveniersburgwal. At the Noordermarkt, a bird market and *boerenmkt* (farmer's market) take place Saturdays until 3 PM, and a popular flea market and textiles sale take place Mondays until 1 PM. For other Amsterdam markets and the Jordaan, see *Special Places.*

The following shops are especially recommended:

Authentic Ship Models – A fascinating array of wooden model ships and maritime antiques. A variety of "do-it-yourself" model kits featuring windmills and da Vinci machinery as well as ships. 191 Bloemstraat (phone: 246601).

De Bijenkorf (The Beehive) – Amsterdam's renowned emporium concentrates on the finest in contemporary fashions and furnishings. At the Dam (phone: 218080).

Bonebakker – This is the place for diamonds; the oldest and most respected gem merchant in the Netherlands, founded in 1792. Although the premises are elegant, prices aren't a bit higher than anywhere else. 88-90 Rokin (phone: 232294).

Christopher Clarke – An English designer who creates unique earrings and accessories in a shop that looks like a jewelry box. 4 Molsteeg (phone: 200017).

Decorativa – For plants and flowers. At the flower market, 544 Singel (phone: 251774), or 27 Herenstraat (phone: 248377).

Focke & Meltzer – Headquarters for famous European china and crystal since 1823. 65 P. C. Hooftstraat (phone: 664-2311) and 124 Rokin (phone: 231944).

Hajenius – "Everything for the smoker" since 1826, including custom-rolled cigars. 92-96 Rokin (phone: 237494).

Klompenboer – You can watch wooden shoes being made here. 20 Nieuw Zijds Voorburgwal (phone: 230632).

De Kookboekhandel – Run by a food critic, it offers cookbooks from around the world, many in English. Closed Sundays and Mondays. 26 Runstraat (phone: 224768).

Maison de Bonneterie – This elegant, chandelier-hung Amsterdam institution, dating from the 19th century, specializes in quality fashion. 183 Kalverstraat (phone: 262162).

Metz – Designer clothes and decorative items plus an excellent selection of imports. The 6th-floor coffee shop offers a panorama of 17th-century rooftops. 455 Keizersgracht (phone: 248810).

Porceleyne Fles – Good for Delft blue. 12 Muntplein at the base of the Munt (phone: 232271).

Tesselschade – Handmade dolls and typical crafts. 33 Leidseplein (phone: 236665).

Vroom and Dreesman – Amsterdam's second department store, carrying a wide range of goods. 201 Kalverstraat (phone: 220171) and other locations.

Wijs and Zoon – For gift tulip bulb packages. Opposite the flower boats at 508 Singel (phone: 221261).

SPORTS AND FITNESS: Sports facilities in the city are much in demand and largely restricted to members. Those listed here are open to members *and* the general public alike, but call first to make sure there's a place for you. Additional facilities outside Amsterdam are included in *The Netherlands*, DIRECTIONS.

Boating – *'t Kompas Loosdrecht*, in Loosdrecht, outside Amsterdam, has sailing equipment (phone: 02158-1431). *Robinson*, at 6 Dorpsstraat, Landsmeer (phone: 02809-1346), has rowing equipment.

Bowling – *Knijn*, 3 Scheldeplein (phone: 664-2211).

Cycling – There are special paths for exploring the Amsterdamse Bos woodland park south of the city, where bikes can also be rented (phone: 445473).

Fishing – At the *Bosbaan* in the Amsterdamse Bos, but you have to go through the formality of getting a license first, obtainable from any post office (phone: 431414).

Fitness Centers – The *Sonesta Splash Club*, 1 Kattengat (phone: 271044), and the *Marriott Health Club*, 21 Stadhouderskade (phone: 835151), are both open to the public and offer sauna, whirlpool baths, Turkish bath, and massage. The *Sonesta* also has workout equipment and aerobic exercise classes, and the *Americain* has a gym and a sauna. The *Hôtel de l'Europe* has a health club and a pool.

Golf – The *Amsterdam Golf Club* is at 4 Zwarte Laantje (phone: 943650).

Horseback Riding – *Amsterdamse Manege*, 25 Nieuwe Kalfjeslaan, Amsterdam (phone: 431342), has indoor and ring riding only. Horses can be rented at *Boszicht Manege*, 25 Bosrandweg (phone: 413054).

Jogging – Try Vondel Park in the city center (entrance at Stadhouderskade and Vossiusstraat); or run along the Amstel River or in the Bos (wood) on the southern edge of town (take tram #12 to the river; bus #65 to the Bos).

Skating – *Jaap Eden Rink*, from November to February, 64 Radioweg (phone: 949894) or Leidseplein. Dutch artificial ice rinks are open only in the winter months. You can skate on the canals in winter when they freeze over.

Soccer – Amsterdam is, of course, the home of the world-famous *Ajax* soccer team. It's easier to get tickets to heaven than to home games, but if you're feeling blessed, you can always try at *Olympic Stadium*, 20 Stadionplein (phone: 711115).

Swimming – The *Hôtel de l'Europe* has the newest pool in town. 2-8 Niewe Doelenstraat (phone: 234836). The *Marnixbad* is a public pool at 5 Marnixplein (phone: 254843).

Tennis and Squash – *Park Tennis* has courts at 10 Stadionstraat (phone: 662-8767). Indoor and outdoor courts are available at *Gold Star*, 20 Karel Lotsslaan (phone: 445483). Squash courts are at *Squash City*, near Centraal Station at 6 Ketelmakerstraat (phone: 267883).

THEATER: The *Mickery*, 12 Herenmarkt (phone: 234968), produces foreign avant-garde drama — usually in English. The group runs a club at 117 Rozengracht (phone: 276181), which is popular with theater people. There are several resident English-language companies presenting contemporary plays in Amsterdam. The best are *ESTA*, which performs at the *Centrum Bellevue Theater*, 90 Leidsekade (phone: 247248), and the *American Repertory Theater*, 4 Kerkstraat (phone: 259495). The *Shaffy Theater*, 324 Keizersgracht (phone: 231311), hosts dance programs and, on occasion, English groups on tour. The *Carré*, 115-125 Amstel (phone: 225225), frequently has top international performers and groups. Current schedules are listed for all of these in the *This Week* guide, and the VVV will also accept bookings (in person only).

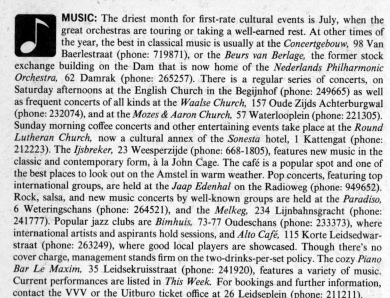

MUSIC: The driest month for first-rate cultural events is July, when the great orchestras are touring or taking a well-earned rest. At other times of the year, the best in classical music is usually at the *Concertgebouw,* 98 Van Baerlestraat (phone: 719871), or the *Beurs van Berlage,* the former stock exchange building on the Dam that is now home of the *Nederlands Philharmonic Orchestra,* 62 Damrak (phone: 265257). There is a regular series of concerts, on Saturday afternoons at the English Church in the Begijnhof (phone: 249665) as well as frequent concerts of all kinds at the *Waalse Church,* 157 Oude Zijds Achterburgwal (phone: 232074), and at the *Mozes & Aaron Church,* 57 Waterlooplein (phone: 221305). Sunday morning coffee concerts and other entertaining events take place at the *Round Lutheran Church,* now a cultural annex of the *Sonesta* hotel, 1 Kattengat (phone: 212223). The *Ijsbreker,* 23 Weesperzijde (phone: 668-1805), features new music in the classic and contemporary form, à la John Cage. The café is a popular spot and one of the best places to look out on the Amstel in warm weather. Pop concerts, featuring top international groups, are held at the *Jaap Edenhal* on the Radioweg (phone: 949652). Rock, salsa, and new music concerts by well-known groups are held at the *Paradiso,* 6 Weteringschans (phone: 264521), and the *Melkeg,* 234 Lijnbahnsgracht (phone: 241777). Popular jazz clubs are *Bimhuis,* 73-77 Oudeschans (phone: 233373), where international artists and aspirants hold sessions, and *Alto Café,* 115 Korte Leidsedwarstraat (phone: 263249), where good local players are showcased. Though there's no cover charge, management stands firm on the two-drinks-per-set policy. The cozy *Piano Bar Le Maxim,* 35 Leidsekruisstraat (phone: 241920), features a variety of music. Current performances are listed in *This Week.* For bookings and further information, contact the VVV or the Uitburo ticket office at 26 Leidseplein (phone: 211211).

NIGHTCLUBS AND NIGHTLIFE: The greatest concentration of cafés, nightclubs, and discotheques is around the Leidseplein, Rembrandtsplein, and adjoining Thorbeckeplein, and many keep going until 3AM or later. Popular discos are *Mazzo,* 114 Rozengracht (phone: 267500); *Chic,* 133 Rozengracht (phone: 221031); *Roxy,* 465 Singel (phone: 200354); and *Juliana's,* at the *Hilton International,* 138 Apollolaan (phone: 737313). There is generally a $5 to $20 cover charge, and at *Juliana's,* a dress code. The *Hilton* also has a gambling casino, open daily from 2 PM to 3 AM.

The center of erotic activity is the famous red-light district immediately east of the Damrak, bordered by the Warmoestraat, Zeedijk, and Damstraat as far as the Kloveniersburgwal. Rows of prostitutes are on display here behind street-level windows, and there are many hard-core sex clubs, films, porno shops, and the like. Most famous of the sex clubs is the 3-story *Casa Rosso,* 108 Oude Zijds Voorburgwal (phone: 262221). The most exclusive, which caters to the rich and famous, is not in the district at all. This is *Yab-Yum,* 295 Singel (phone: 249503). Another of the well-established clubs outside the district is *Bayadera,* 18 Westeinde (phone: 251123).

What really distinguishes Amsterdam's nightlife is its unique cafés (highly recommended is *Amsterdam Pub Guide* by Ben ten Holter). A full listing of the best would fill this volume, but the representative sample that follows will get you started well. For other recommended places, see the jazz cafés listed under *Music* and those serving food under *Eating Out. Hoppe,* dating from 1670, is the most famous and most "in" of the traditional "brown" (small, dark, Old World, intimate, lively, convivial) cafés, 18-20 Spui (phone: 237849); *Gollem,* a minuscule place especially famed among those in the know for its wide variety of Belgian Trappist beers, 4 Raamsteg (phone: 266645); *Papeneiland,* tracing its ancestry back to a coffin-maker who sold drinks at the beginning of the 17th century, claims to be the oldest café in Amsterdam. It is distinguished by a tunnel entrance in its cellar that formerly led under the canal and was used by 17th-century Catholics as a secret way of getting together for worship (2 Prinsengracht; phone: 241989). *De Klepel* has a loyal clientele that has come to play chess for the past 20 years. Light lunches and snacks are served; chamber music and jazz sessions are held on alternate Sundays from 5 to 8 PM (22 Prinsenstraat; phone: 238244). *Café de Prins* is one of the better "eet cafés" in the city. Across from the *Anne Frank House,* it is especially good for dinner or Sunday brunch (124 Prinsengracht; phone: 249382). *Nol* is a typical Jordaan café that comes alive nightly in a special "Old Amsterdam" way, complete with animated sing-alongs. Not to be missed if you enjoy people uninhibitedly enjoying themselves, 109 Westerstraat (phone: 245380). For drinks mixed with music, visit *De Twee Zwaantjes,* where for several generations the local brew has been served accompanied by a song (114 Prinsengracht; phone: 252729). Note that most Amsterdam cafés normally close at 1 AM on weekdays, an hour later on weekends. Many serve an important function as congenial daytime gathering places as well, and quite a few start the day (with excellent coffee, if you prefer), but not until 10 or 11 AM. There are also some "night cafés" that are open from 10 PM to 3 or 4 AM. *Faith's Corner,* in the Jordaan at 90 Lindengracht (phone: 248864), is one of the best.

BEST IN TOWN

CHECKING IN: Visitors arriving without a hotel reservation (not recommended), should go to the VVV, which, for a nominal fee (a little over a dollar), will almost always be able to find a room in one of Amsterdam's more than 200 hotels. Reservations can be made through the Netherlands Reservation Centre (NRC), PO Box 404, Leidschendam 2260 AK (phone: 070-202500). Note that while the larger hotels and restaurants accept major international credit cards (primarily American Express, Diners Club, MasterCard, and Visa), plastic payment is not widely accepted in Holland. (It is becoming more prevalent, however, and businesses displaying the Eurocard logo also accept MasterCard and Visa.)

Rates in most hotels vary according to the time of year and the size of individual rooms. In general, Amsterdam hotels are not inexpensive. Expect to pay $150 or more for a double room in those places listed as expensive, $80 to $100 for those we have rated moderate, and under $60 for inexpensive accommodations. All telephone numbers are in the 020 area code unless otherwise indicated.

The big international hostelries add a charge for the breakfast of your choice, but the more traditional Dutch hotels still include it as part of the basic room rate. It may be either continental (coffee and rolls) or Dutch (heartier, with bread, cheese, and soft-boiled egg).

Americain (or American) – It is difficult to explain precisely what makes this landmark hotel, built in 1882, so special, but its ornate Art Nouveau café-restaurant, protected as a historical monument, is certainly part of the answer. Both Dutch and visiting celebrities find their way here eventually — as does everyone else in Amsterdam. A glass of beer, served by black-suited waiters, costs about the same as anywhere else in town and the clientele ranges from jeans-clad students to the jet set. More than any other hotel, this one captures the indefinable essence of the city. It features a fitness center with a sauna. 28 Leidseplein (phone: 234813). Expensive.

Amstel Inter-Continental – The grand dame of Amsterdam hotels since it opened in 1866 on the beautiful river of the same name. Celebrities and royalty stay here, and so should you if you want to find out what Old World opulence and service are really all about. The intimate *La Rive* restaurant with a view offers continental fare; the menu changes seasonally. It has 111 rooms. 1 Professor Tulpplein (phone: 226060). Expensive.

Apollo – The English country house atmosphere of this 217-room hostelry is enhanced by its lobby, which faces the water. Its special feature is a waterside bar and outdoor terrace with panoramic views of five canals. There's also a non-smoking floor, laundry and dry cleaning services, valet, and free use of bicycles. British management. 2 Apollolaan (phone: 735922). Expensive.

Golden Tulip Barbizon Palace – Close to the Central Station and the picturesque inner harbor, this brand-new 268-room luxury hotel combines some of the city's most historic façades with an ultramodern interior. 59-72 Prins Hendrikskade, at Zeedijk (phone: 556-4564). Expensive.

Grand Hotel Krasnapolsky – Over the years, the "Kras" has grown from a unique coffee shop begun by a Polish immigrant to an Amsterdam institution, and the complete renovation of its 330 rooms has not destroyed its character or its atmosphere. The only hotel actually on the Dam, at #9 (phone: 554-9111). Expensive.

Hilton International – This modern, commercial, 274-room canalside hotel is decorated with original Dutch paintings. Its bar, disco, and casino offer evening entertainment. 138 Apollolaan (phone: 780780). Expensive.

Holiday Inn Crowne Plaza – The first deluxe European property opened by the ubiquitous American chain began operations in 1987 with 270 rooms. Right in the city center. Amenities include a health club, swimming pool, 2 saunas, whirlpool bath, several restaurants, a lobby bar, and typical Dutch café. 5 Nieuwe Zijds Voorburgwal (phone: 200500 or 275511). Expensive.

Hôtel de l'Europe – An honorable alternative to the *Amstel,* this elegant, 180-room hotel traces its origins to a fortress built in 1481 to defend the city. It was completely rebuilt in 1895 and has retained the grandeur of that extravagant period. Features include a health club and a pool. 2-8 Nieuwe Doelenstraat (phone: 234836). Expensive.

Okura – A 23-story hotel with 768 beds, owned and operated by a Japanese concern. The *Ciel Bleu Penthouse* features fine French food to accompany a panoramic view. There are 2 coffee shops, a sauna, and shopping arcade. At 175 Ferdinand Bolstraat (phone: 787111). Expensive.

Pulitzer – An attractive mix of old and new, with 241 rooms and 8 apartments built into a group of 2 dozen connected historic canal houses. The rooms are modern but by no means uniform, since their layout has been determined by the original architecture. The original roof beams have also been retained. 315-331 Prinsengracht (phone: 228333). Expensive.

SAS Royal – Opening in the spring of 1990 in the heart of Amsterdam, this 5-story hotel with a Scandinavian touch has 250 rooms and 15 apartments, plus a restaurant, café, and bar. The presidential suite has its own sauna. Operated by SAS Airlines, the hotel has an SAS check-in counter. Between the Dam and the opera house, just 5 minutes from the Rokin, 13 Russland. Expensive.

Ambassade – A pleasant, old-fashioned, traditional Dutch hotel whose 43 rooms, all with baths and TV sets, are in a historic canal house furnished with antiques. 341 Herengracht (phone: 262333). Moderate.

Canal House – It has 27 newly renovated, cozy and comfortable rooms, most overlooking the canal, set in a homey, antiques-furnished 17th-century merchant's house. All rooms have private baths and phones and come with Dutch breakfast. Elevator available. 148 Keizersgracht (phone: 225182). Moderate.

Jan Luyken – In the heart of the concert and museum quarter, this first class 63-room hotel combines modern amenities with traditional Dutch hospitality. 54-58 Jan Luykenstraat (phone: 764111). Moderate.

Toren – Centrally located near the historic Jordaan quarter and minutes from the *Anne Frank House,* it features comfortable, clean rooms and a bar/restaurant. Rates include breakfast. 164 Keizersgracht (phone: 020-226352). Moderate.

Wiechmann – Owned by a former Oklahoman, a Mr. Boddy, this 30-room hotel (only 12 rooms have bath or shower) is friendly, comfortable, and reasonable. It has a bar and a breakfast room; no elevator. 328-330 Prinsengracht (phone: 263321). Moderate.

Esperance – This small (6-room) family hotel is between the *Rijksmuseum* and the Heineken Brewery. Room rates include breakfast. 49 Stadhovderskade (phone: 714049). Inexpensive.

Groenendael – Smack in the city center, this place offers clean, simple rooms hung with art by local artists. The lounge, with a stereo and TV set, provides a congenial atmosphere. Room rates include breakfast. 15 Nieuwendijk (phone: 244822). Inexpensive.

Mikado – Enlarged and modernized, this small hotel overlooking the Amstel River has 26 unusually spacious rooms, each with private bath and telephone. The friendly personal touches for which it was known in its previous, smaller incarnation, remain, however. Breakfast is included. 107-111 Amstel (phone: 237068). Inexpensive.

Wijnnobel – Small (12 rooms; none with bath or shower), with no phones or elevators, this hotel features prewar European atmosphere, a hospitable host, and breakfast served in rooms. There is a small gold sign outside, a marble entrance, and formidable stairs (non-climbers, beware!). 9 Vossiusstraat (phone: 662-2298). Inexpensive.

 EATING OUT: Amsterdam is justly famed for its restaurants — more than 200 specializing in foreign food alone — and especially renowned for its Indonesian import, *rijsttafel* (rice table). Don't miss the chance to experience this multi-course (up to 20) extravaganza.

In a traditional *rijsttafel* — the ceremonial Indonesian feast adopted by Dutch colonials — a large dish of rice is surrounded by up to 20 smaller dishes of meat and chicken with a variety of sauces, prawns, meat kebabs (or *satés*) in peanut sauce, fried bananas, cucumber in sour sauce — and many, many others, some spicy and some bland. It is a treat. If you want lighter fare, try *bami goreng,* stir-fried noodles with strips of vegetables and meat, or *nasi goreng,* a plate of rice with vegetables and meat. All are served in Amsterdam's ubiquitous Indonesian restaurants, and some can be modified for vegetarians.

Traditional Dutch foods and drinks should also be sampled. You probably are already familiar with Gouda and Edam, the popular Dutch cheeses. Vendors in the many open-air stalls around the city also hawk salted raw herring, a Dutch favorite, for about $2.

Meals in Holland are designed to stick to your ribs and to warm you in winter. Especially good in cold weather (if you need an excuse) is classic Dutch split-pea soup, or *erwtensoep.* Also good are *capucijners,* an indigenous Dutch bean; Dutch beef stew (*hutspot*); and kale with potatoes and sausage (*boerenkool met rookworst*).

Dutch beer is almost uniformly excellent. Gin is the native liquor, *jenever* in Dutch; *oude jenever* is aged gin, milder and mellower; *jonge jenever* is stronger and plainer in taste.

For the best in inexpensive eating, try one of our recommended cafés ($20 or less for two) or a traditional *broodjeswinkel* (sandwich shop, not to be confused with modern junk-food snack bars).

At the restaurants we have rated as expensive, be prepared to part with $90 or more for a complete dinner for two, including wine, drinks, and coffee. You can get away with considerably less, however, if you choose carefully from the varied menus. Places in the moderate category range between $50 and $75 for everything; at those listed as inexpensive, expect to pay about $35 (with the simplest about half that).

Note that any restaurant displaying the blue Tourist Menu sign (there are several in Amsterdam) must provide a three-course meal for the fixed price of about $10 to $12 (not including drinks). In Amsterdam, service charges and local taxes are usually included in the bill. Reservations are always necessary unless otherwise stated. Credit cards are accepted only where specifically mentioned. All telephone numbers are in the 020 area code.

Beddington's – Jeanne Beddington has been called a chef's chef because of her innovative cuisine. The room has clean modern lines and does not upstage the food in this "power" dining spot. Closed weekends. Reservations necessary. 6-8 Roelof Hartstraat (phone: 765201). Expensive.

Christophe – An intimate, decidedly chic restaurant that recently earned one Michelin star. Some of the city's other chefs often eat here. Closed Sundays. 46 Leliegracht (phone: 020-250807). Expensive.

De Kersentuin (Cherry Orchard) – Quintessential nouvelle cuisine (with many ingredients flown in daily from France) served in the lush surroundings of a room out of a Chekhov play. Food, service, and decor are among the most distinctive in town. One Michelin star. Open weekdays for lunch, daily except Sundays for dinner. Reservations advised. Major credit cards. In the *Garden* hotel, 7 Dijssel-hofplantsoen (phone: 664-2121). Expensive.

De Trechter – Call for a reservation the minute you arrive in town and perhaps you will be lucky enough to get one of the half dozen tables at this haute cuisine French restaurant with one Michelin star. Every dish is cooked to order — and to perfection. Dinner only; closed Sundays and Mondays. 63 Hobbemakade (phone: 711263). Expensive.

Brasserie von Baerle – Down the street from the *Concertgebouw,* it is a true brasserie in terms of its eclectic menu, which features creative pizza and more elaborate fare. This is where the movers and shakers come for lunch and dinner; Sunday brunch also draws a crowd. Closed Saturdays. 158 Van Baerlestraat (phone: 791532). Expensive to moderate.

Silveren Spiegel – Picturesque and charming are the only words to describe this intimate, antiques-furnished restaurant set in two very crooked houses dating from 1614. The food is international; the service, excellent; the wine list, impressive. Open weekdays for lunch; daily except Sundays for dinner. Major credit cards. 4 Kattengat (phone: 246589). Expensive to moderate.

D'Vijff Vlieghen (Five Flies) – It's a bit of an adventure just finding this place. The main door doesn't open, so you must enter by way of a side street, called D'Viff Vlieghen. Once inside, you are transported to the 17th century by a series of delightful dining rooms built in that era, complete with real Rembrandt drawings on the walls. Try the typical Dutch dishes using fresh, local ingredients. Up a steep set of stairs is an intimate *jenever* bar. Open daily for dinner. 294 Spuistraat (phone: 248369). Expensive to moderate.

Brasserie 404 – A pleasant, informal place specializing in fish dishes and the best soups in town. Closed Sundays. No reservations. 404 Singel (phone: 233522). Moderate.

Café Luxembourg – On the historic Spui square, this unique café features appetizers supplied by top restaurants in the city and good wines by the glass. Open daily. 22 Spui (phone: 206264). Moderate.

Entrecôte – True to its name, this elegant restaurant on Amsterdam's stylish shopping street serves fine beef and veal, which comes with a salad and crispy *pommes* *frites.* Dinner only; closed Sundays and Mondays. 70 P. C. Hooftstraat (phone: 737776). Moderate.

Entre Sol – Between Central Station and the Red Light district, it features authentic Flemish cuisine and attracts a loyal clientele. Open Wednesdays to Sundays for dinner only. 29 Geldersekade (phone: 237912). Moderate.

Oesterbar – This is the place for serious fish eaters: nothing fancy, just remarkably fresh fish and shellfish of all kinds, cooked simply, but to perfection. Solo diners can enjoy a meal seated at the counter near the ovens or at the one near the fish tanks. If you prefer eating at a conventional table, reserve one downstairs. Open daily. 10 Leidseplein (phone: 232988). Moderate.

Provençal – French lunch and dinner specialties, premium service, and a pleasant atmosphere. Open weekdays for lunch, daily for dinner. Opposite the *Rijksmuseum* near the Speigelgracht, at 91 Weteringscans (phone: 239619). Moderate.

De Blauwe Hollandeer – It features authentic cooking just as any Dutch grandmother makes, from a typical *hutsput* (a stew made with leeks, carrots, potatoes, and beef) to the classic mashed potatoes and endives. Open daily for dinner. In the Leidseplein district, 28 Leidsekruistraat (phone: 233014). Moderate to inexpensive.

Café Descartes – An authentic French restaurant hidden in the Maison Descartes, it seats 25-30 patrons in the 17th-century building's original kitchen. Soups, salads, and house specialties such as *coq au vin,* rabbit stew, and cassoulet are offered at café prices. Lunch and dinner menu changes daily. Closed weekends. Next to the French consulate at 2 Vijzelgracht (phone: 221913). Moderate to inexpensive.

Koh-I-Noor – This Indian restaurant serves tasty curries and tandoori specialties. The service is good; the atmosphere, authentic. Open daily for dinner. Two locations: 29 Westermkt, opposite the Westertoren (phone: 233133), and 18 Rokin, opposite Dam Square (phone: 272118). Moderate to inexpensive.

Lonny's – Here is elegant dining, reasonably priced. Lonny is one of the city's veteran chefs. Take-out available. Open daily for dinner. 48 Rozengracht (phone: 238950). Moderate to inexpensive.

Sea Palace – Amsterdam's only multilevel floating restaurant captures the flavor of the Far East with Pekinese and Shanghai specialties served in a reconstructed Chinese pagoda overlooking the inner harbor. Dim sum is featured on Sundays. Open daily. Reservations advised. 8 Oosterdokskade (phone: 264777). Moderate to inexpensive.

Sluizer – The good, solid fish served in this Old World restaurant with marble-topped tables and fringed lampshades makes it popular with Amsterdammers and visitors alike. The restaurant next door shares the same name and offers a menu with meat dishes. In warm weather, patrons can dine on the terrace in a secluded garden. Open daily. No reservations. 45 Utrechtsestraat (phone: 263557). Moderate to inexpensive.

Baguette – Just a bridge away from the Rembrandtsplein, this *croissanterie-potagerie* specializes in sandwiches and soups in the French style. Open daily. 534 Herengracht (phone: 250853). Inexpensive.

Broodje van Kootje – The most famous of Amsterdam's traditional sandwich shops. The food is varied, wholesome, and inexpensive. Recommended for a quick lunch or snack. For breakfast, try an *uitsmijter* — the Dutch version of ham and eggs. Open daily from 9:30 AM to 1:30 AM. 20 Leidseplein (phone: 232046), 12 Rembrandtsplein (phone: 236513), and 28 Spui (phone: 237451). Inexpensive.

Ouede is Oude – Opened in 1986, this café/bar has a neighborhood ambience, with walls covered with works by local artists. The recently expanded dinner menu now includes fish and vetetarian dishes as well as the old standbys: steaks with homemade sauces and Indonesian saté. Vagabond the cat greets all visitors. Open daily for breakfast, lunch, and dinner to 1 AM (2 AM Fridays and Saturdays). 9 Oude Leliestraat (phone: 246700). Inexpensive.

Pancake Corner – Plate-size pancakes are served with a variety of toppings. Also worth a try is the kettle of mussels, served with salad and *pommes frites.* Open daily for lunch and dinner. Across from the Leidseplein, 51 Kleine Gartmanplantsoen (phone: 276303). Inexpensive.

Poentjak Pas – The place serves one of the best *rijstaffels* in the city, as well as other Indonesian dishes. Also try the omelette with vegetables or the spicy string beans. Open daily (except Mondays) for dinner only. 366 Nassaukade, by the Leidseplein (phone: 180906). Inexpensive.

Pompadour – A plush environment in which to sample handmade chocolates by the piece and creamy pastries made daily. Open daily except Sundays. 12 Huidenstraat (phone: 239554). Inexpensive.

Rondo – This tiny, unadorned, but very popular spot next to the Flower Market offers a bargain brunch with fresh bagels on Sunday mornings and simple fare and homemade desserts at other times. Closed Sundays. No reservations. 6 Reguliersdwarsstraat (phone: 259046). Inexpensive.

Vennington – On a pleasant shopping street between the Prinsengracht and the Keizersgracht, this neighborhood café attracts an interesting crowd for breakfasts and late lunches. Closed Sundays. 2 Prinsenstraat (phone: 259398). Inexpensive.

ATHENS

Athens is the site of the greatest achievements of the classical age of Greece. Its architectural, social, artistic, and political triumphs have become a universal legacy. Against its ancient standards are measured the cultural, intellectual, and spiritual development of all Western civilizations.

In Athens the units of this measure are everywhere apparent. Drive down a wide thoroughfare and you pass the Temple of the Olympian Zeus, masterfully carved Corinthian columns still intact, honoring the highest of Greek gods. Turn a corner in Monastiraki, the flea market, and you come upon the Agora, the ancient marketplace crowned by the Theseion, one of the best-preserved Doric temples, sacred to blacksmiths, who worked here 2,000 years ago; follow the Panathenaic Way, the grand ceremonial path of Ancient Athens, and like centuries of Athenians before you, you approach the Acropolis, the crown of Greek culture high on a rock above Athens.

For more than 2,000 years the Acropolis has dominated the city — first as a spiritual center and fortress; later as the site of the Parthenon, a temple honoring Athena, the patron goddess of Athens; still later as the locus of churches, mosques, and even harems as it was transformed by different conquerors. Today, stripped of the many statues that once lined the way, with drums and columns strewn about, the Acropolis remains, even in ruins, majestic and monumental.

The setting inspires contemplation, its starkness somehow appropriate. Bared to its essentials, you can only imagine the golden age of Greece (in the middle of the 5th century BC) when Pericles had the Parthenon built — every column curving slightly inward in order to appear perfectly straight at a distance — when the dramas of Aeschylus and Sophocles were performed for the first time in the Theater of Dionysus below; when democracy first brought all citizens together to decide their common fate on the Pnyx hill to the west.

The Acropolis commands an excellent view of the surrounding Attic plain and overlapping layers of Western civilization. Immediately below the walls lies the Agora; adjacent is the Plaka district, the 19th-century area frequented by Lord Byron when he lived in Athens. In the distance to the north rises Mt. Parnes, the highest mountain in Attica, and Mt. Pentelikon, where Pentelic marble is quarried. Between the mountains spreads the Mesogheia Valley, where grapes for resinated wine (*retsina*) are harvested. To the south lies the Saronic Gulf; slightly west of there a smokestack marks the offshore island of Salamis, where the Greeks defeated the Persians in the famous naval battle of 480 BC.

To the east lies the modern city, spread out around the Acropolis almost like an afterthought. Planned by German architects for King Otto in 1840, Athens was designed to accommodate a maximum of 200,000 people. Today

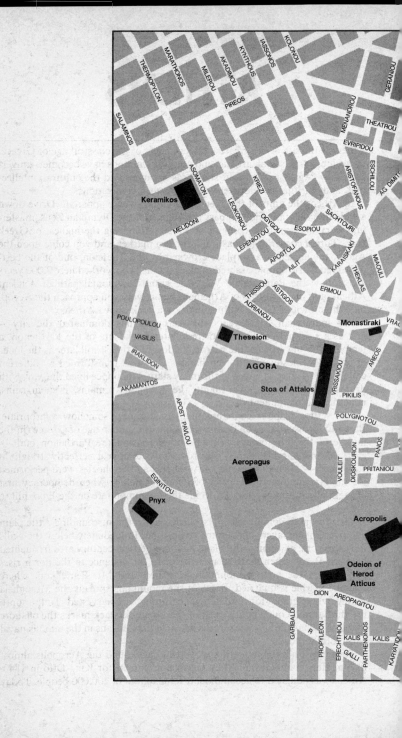

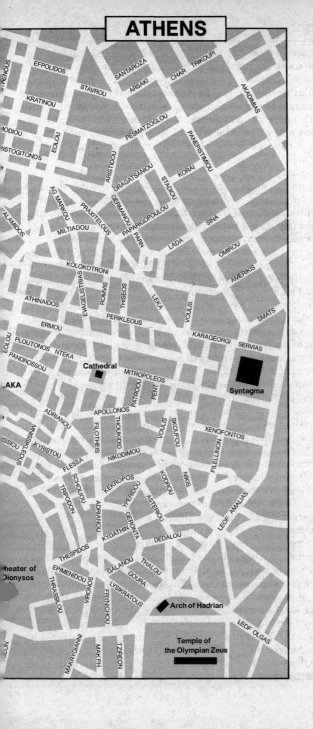

ATHENS

some 3.6 million people inhabit Greater Athens, which extends past the port of Piraeus. Most roads are narrow and inadequate for the ever-increasing number of automobiles. Traffic is horrendous, with streets congested during seemingly interminable rush hours. The indefatigable breeze blowing in from the sea doesn't manage to keep the air fresh, for Athens is blanketed, winter and summer, with a hazy cloud of pollution. To combat both the traffic and pollution problems, only half of Athens's vehicles are permitted into the city's center on any given day (odd license-plate numbers on odd days, even numbers on even days). In addition, many narrow downtown streets are being converted to pedestrian walkways.

These intransigently modern problems have not been able to dim the city's splendid natural advantages. Athens's perfect Mediterranean climate — the sun shines brilliantly most of the year and the air is dry even in midsummer — endows the city with a relaxed atmosphere and outlook.

Athenians embrace their environment with relish. The cream-colored, terraced marble apartments built into the hills are sunny and airy. Athenians take to the beaches lining the coasts year-round for sun, sea, and vigorous, noisy games. As early as April, a few leathery-looking old men paddle around in the water — and are joined by everyone else quite comfortably from May to October. In Syntagma and Kolonaki Squares, residents spend hours over cups of coffee — the thick, muddy Greek variety — discussing life and politics or just people watching. Athenian workers break in the afternoons for a few hours, return to work, and head out to dinner quite late, about 10 PM. Even on weeknights, *tavernas* — informal restaurants — are full past midnight. In many *bouzoukia* — nightclubs in which traditional bouzouki music is played — the entertainment does not really start until midnight. Despite the big-city veneer, people take their time.

Travelers will find this both engaging and perplexing. The lifestyle is quite pleasant, but it takes its toll on the economy. Greece has mastered a few industries — its shipping fleet is the largest in the world, and tourism has been a well-organized business — but still Greece is one of the least productive of the major countries in Europe. A member of the European Economic Community (EEC) only since January 1, 1981, Greece entered as its tenth and poorest member. Greek economic analysts hoped that this action would boost the economy. But Greek industries and workers, previously sheltered by import restrictions, now face stiffer competition from Common Market countries, and the government is balking continually at conforming to standing EEC regulations, many of which favor the northern European members. However, some benefits are beginning to roll in, and Greece stands to obtain billions of dollars worth of agricultural and regional development subsidies.

The most populous and advanced city in Greece, Athens is caught between the incongruities of a valiant past and a problematic present. The dilemma is in part historic. After the classical age of Greece, Athens was conquered and dominated by foreign powers. Though the early rulers were relatively benign, Athens lost the freedom and democratic structure that nurtured its greatest cultural achievements. First conquered by the Macedonians and later by the Romans, Athens remained an important seat of learning until the Edict of Justinian closed the schools of philosophy in AD 529. Under Byzantine rule, many temples were modified to Christian use, and Athens became just another provincial city. After the fall of Constantinople in 1453, the Ottomans seized the city and ruled for almost 400 years, during which time the most sacred sites of the Acropolis were damaged and desecrated.

Athens became the capital of a liberated Greece after the conclusion of the War of Independence in 1829. The country suffered heavy loss of life during the Nazi occupation of 1941–45 and again during the Greek Civil War of 1946. It was ruled as a monarchy until 1967, when King Constantine fled after failing to topple the military dictatorship established earlier in the year. Papadopoulos and his junta endured for 7 long, bitter years; a civilian government was finally restored in 1974 and the monarchy abolished by plebiscite in favor of a republic. With the election of Andreas Papandreou in 1981, Greece had its first Socialist government. But by the late 1980s, the administration was troubled by economic woes and scandals. As we went to press, elections slated for June 1989 were expected to return a conservative, pro-Western regime to power.

Athens has, in a sense, gone full circle. Though its ancient history is very ancient indeed, as a modern democracy Athens is entirely new, with an almost burdensome history and a future still unmade. Perhaps this split in its history has created the ambivalent nature of modern Athens — a city somewhat overshadowed by the glories of its past. Greece in general — and Athens in particular — has had more than its share of contemporary problems, many of them a by-product of the geographic fact of being very near the center of the world's most virulent and violent conflicts. But the determined government is urgently seeking solutions that are consistent with the Greek view of the globe, and while they still remain to be found, the will to search continues strong.

ATHENS AT-A-GLANCE

SEEING THE CITY: Lycabettus, the city's highest hill, opens up a panorama of Athens — Syntagma Square and the National Gardens, the Acropolis and its surrounding hills, and in the distance, the Saronic Gulf. The 912-foot summit is crowned by the tiny 19th-century chapel of St. George, visible from other parts of the city and worth a closer look. A café halfway up and a restaurant at the top provide unsurpassed views, refreshments, and meals. Approaches to the summit include roads, a funicular, and footpaths that afford ever-expanding views of Athens. Open daily (the funicular operates from 8 AM to midnight). Entrance at Ploutarchou and Aristipou in Kolonaki (no phone). Accessible by bus #023 from Kaningos and Kolonaki Squares.

SPECIAL PLACES: Most of the interesting sights of Athens are within easy walking distance of one another. Archaeological sites are concentrated around the Acropolis. The narrow, winding streets of the immediately adjacent areas of the Plaka district and Monastiraki lend themselves to walking. Syntagma Square, the center of modern Athens, is a 20-minute walk or short cab ride away.

The Acropolis – Dominating the Athenian landscape, this monument of Western civilization is unsurpassed in its beauty, architectural splendor, and historical importance. Situated on a massive 512-foot limestone rock, 300 feet above the general level of the city, this naturally strategic location has been inhabited since Neolithic times. In about 1500 BC, a Mycenean ruler crowned the height with a citadel; during the same period, the first in a series of a temples honoring Athena, the goddess of the city, was built — a tradition that continued over the centuries. In 480 BC, the Persians sacked the city and destroyed the Acropolis. Some 35 years later, Pericles, the renowned Athenian statesman, conceived a plan to rebuild the Acropolis on a grand scale as the true capital of Greek civilization. Under the direction of the architects Iktinos and Kallikrates, structures were erected that endure today. The Propylea, the monumental entrance on the west, was constructed between 449 and 444 BC. Though the roof was destroyed by a Venetian cannon volley in 1687, the rows of columns — Doric on the outside (without bases) and Ionic on the inside (with bases and more elaborate capitals) — still line the way. On the south side of the Propylea stands the temple of the Wingless Victory, Athena Nike, built between 425 and 422 BC in monolithic Ionic columns. On the north side of the entrance is a Roman tower built in the 1st century AD as a votive offering by Agrippa, nephew of Emperor Augustus.

Beyond the Propylea, on the highest part of the hill, stands the Parthenon, the main temple of the Acropolis, built between 447 and 432 BC of white Pentelic marble. This is the virgin Athena's most sacred temple, and everything about it is a celebration of perfect order, from its Doric columns to the *metopes* — friezes with reliefs of mythological battles — that decorate it. The Greek government is waging a feisty campaign against the *British Museum* in London to get it to return many missing *metopes*, taken by Lord Elgin nearly 200 years ago and now called the Elgin marbles. From a distance the columns appear perfectly parallel and straight, an illusion that is sustained only by a minor miracle of engineering, the turning of each column slightly inward to create an image of perfect harmony. To the north is the Erechtheion, a temple honoring both Athena and Poseidon, god of the sea, who in ancient times lost out to Athena in the battle for the worship of the Athenians. The Ionic structure contains several architectural novelties, including the Karyatids, sculptures of lovely maidens that support a porch and stylized sculptural decor of little friezes of palm flowers between the capitals and columns that influenced the later Corinthian style. Because of environmental damage, five of the six original Karyatids have been replaced by copies. Four of the originals can now be seen at the *Acropolis Museum.* Athena is the patron of Athens because she gave mankind the gift of the olive, and her olive tree stands at the west side of the temple; a saltwater spring to represent Poseidon is said to have sprung inside the temple in ancient times. Close inspection of the supporting wall directly north of the Erechtheion reveals several drums that survive from the first Acropolis; their purpose is to keep alive the memory of the catastrophic sack of Athens by the Persians.

Over the years, the Acropolis has undergone many alterations at the hands of conquerors. The Parthenon and the Erechtheion were converted into churches during the Byzantine era. During the Turkish occupation, the Parthenon was used as a mosque and the Erechtheion as a harem.

Even today, air pollution and the high sulfur content of rainwater are turning the marble to soft gypsum. The work of reconstruction is under way. Rehabilitation of the Erechtheion was recently completed; the limestone Acropolis rock base is being stabilized; architects began a 10-year renovation of the Parthenon in 1983 and will soon follow with reconstruction of the Propylea. Despite hardships, the Acropolis has endured thousands of years as one of the highest accomplishments of Western civilization.

The *Acropolis Museum* houses most of the works of art discovered in the Acropolis since excavation began in 1835. Highlights of the collection include fragments of the Parthenon frieze and numerous sculptures — the *Kritian Boy,* the *Calf Bearer,* the *Rider and the Running Hound,* and the *Kourai* maidens. Open weekdays from 8 AM to 5 PM, weekends from 8:30 AM to 3 PM. Admission charge. Entrance on Areopagitou St. (phone: 321-0219). From Syntagma Square, take bus #230 from Amalias Ave. and Othonos St.

Pnyx – This hill on the west side of the Acropolis, which now serves as the theater for the sound and light show, is the true cradle of Athenian democracy. Here, in classical times, Athenians assembled to decide issues. All free male citizens were summoned to the hill. Officers carrying ropes covered with fresh paint would round up those who didn't come and mark them so that they could be identified and fined. No such penalties are incurred today for those who don't attend the sound and light show. The script delivers a dramatized history of the Acropolis in ridiculously over-blown language. But the view of the Acropolis is spectacular. Shows in English are held nightly at 9 PM from April 1 to October 31. Admission charge. Entrance on Areopagitou St. opposite the Acropolis.

Areopagus – The highest court of ancient Athens convened on this hill below the Acropolis. According to Aeschylus, Orestes was tried here for the murder of his mother, Klytemnestra. The jury split and Athena broke the tie by throwing her support behind Orestes. Legend has it that he had been chased by the Furies — mythological creatures with women's heads and birds' bodies. In AD 51, St. Paul delivered his Sermon of the Unknown God from this site. Open daily. No admission charge. Just below the west slope of the Acropolis.

Mouseion Hill – In 1687, a Venetian cannon fired from this hill severely damaged the Parthenon. At the top, there's a monument of Philopappos, a prominent Athenian of the 2nd century AD. Open daily. No admission charge. Areopagitou west of the Acropolis.

Agora (Stoa of Attalos) – The commercial and public center of ancient Athens spreads out below the Acropolis, which was the town's spiritual and military center. Situated at the junction of the three main roads of the time — from Piraeus, the Mesogheia Valley, and the mountains — the Agora was the main marketplace. Leaders, philosophers, and common people gathered here to discuss current events and metaphysics. During the classical age of Greece, Sophocles taught here, and the plays of Aeschylus were performed in the theater. Much of what remains — columns, statues — is in ruins, but you can re-create the scene imaginatively. You needn't work too hard on the reconstructed *Stoa of Attalos*. Originally built in the 2nd century BC by Attalos II, King of Pergamon, the marble-colonnaded structure was rebuilt with funds from private American donors. Once an arcade of shops, the *Stoa* is now a museum housing artifacts excavated from the site, including early plans for the building and the Acropolis and a collection of marble statues and sculptures. The Theseion, or Temple of Hephaistos and Athena, sits atop the highest point of the Agora. These two were patron saints of the blacksmiths and coppersmiths, past and present, who worked nearby. Built between 444 and 442 BC, the Theseion is one of the best preserved Doric temples in existence. In the 7th century AD, the temple was adapted to Christian use as a church sacred to St. George. Most of the ruins are scattered between the *Stoa* and the Theseion. Open daily; museum open Tuesdays through Sundays from 8:30 AM to 3 PM. Admission charge. Entrance on Adrianou (phone: 321-0185).

Keramikos – The cemetery of ancient Athens has some original graves in place, including the Memorial of Dexilos, honoring a knight killed in action at Corinth in the 4th century BC. Other graves are in the *Oberlaender Museum*, just beside the cemetery entrance. Open Tuesdays through Sundays from 8:30 AM to 3 PM. Admission charge. 148 Ermou St., below Monastiraki (phone: 346-3552).

Theater of Dionysos – Built in the 4th century BC, this is the oldest of the Greek theaters. The plays of Sophocles, Euripides, Aristophanes, and Aeschylus were first performed here. Open daily. Admission charge. Dionisiou Areopagitou St., on the slope of the Acropolis (phone: 322-4625).

Odeion of Herod Atticus – Athens's other ancient theater was built in AD 160 by a rich Athenian philosopher. The structure illustrates the Roman influence on later Greek architecture. This theater is now the setting of the annual, summer-long *Athens Festival,* which features opera, ballet, and concerts performed by first-rate companies from Europe and the US. Open daily. No admission charge. On the southern slope of the Acropolis (phone: 922-6330).

Temple of the Olympian Zeus – Honoring Zeus, the supreme god of heaven and earth, this massive temple was built over a 700-year period beginning in the 6th century BC. The temple was the largest constructed in the elaborate Corinthian style. Only 14 columns remain intact; one is fallen — all are beautifully carved. Open daily except Mondays from 8:30 AM to 3 PM. Admission charge. Vasilissis Olgas and Amalias (phone: 922-6330).

Arch of Hadrian – Roman Emperor Hadrian had this arch built in AD 132 to demarcate the city he built from the earlier city, which was said to have been erected by the mythological King Theseus. Open daily. No admission charge. Vasilissis Olgas and Amalias. (phone: 922-6330).

Olympic Stadium – On the site of the ancient Panathenean Stadium, this white marble structure was the stadium for the first modern Olympic games in 1896. Open daily. No admission charge. Vasileos Konstantinou and Agras.

The Plaka District – Hugging the north and northeast slopes of the Acropolis, this section of 19th-century Athens retains its essential nature. The narrow, winding streets are lined with restored 1- and 2-story houses, shops selling popular Greek art, and lively *tavernas.* One of the best places to go for dinner and evening entertainment is *Xynos,* 4 Angelou Geronda (phone: 322-1065). (For a full description of this and other Plaka district restaurants, see *Eating Out.*) At the west side of the Plaka district are the Roman Agora and the unusual Tower of the Winds Monument. Dating from the 1st century BC, this marble octagonal structure has eight reliefs, each personifying a wind blowing from a different direction. Open daily. No admission charge. Between Ermou and the north slope of the Acropolis.

Monastiraki – Traditions of leatherworking and metalsmithing first carried on in the adjacent Agora continue here today. Numerous shops carry a wide variety of items, including antiques, jewelry, leather goods, copper, and bronze. You can see coppersmiths work in the back of their shops. Sometimes you can bargain for goods. For more information, see *Shopping.* Open daily. No admission charge. Off Monastiraki Square, on and around Ifestou.

Greek Orthodox Cathedral – This has been the headquarters of the Greek Orthodox Church since 1864. The structure is actually composed of stones from 72 demolished cathedrals, and the interior is impressively ornate. Note the lovely 12th-century Byzantine church immediately to the south. Open daily. Mitropoleos, between Syntagma and Monastiraki.

Syntagma Square – The center of modern Athens, this is prime territory for watching the world go by. Sitting at one of the cafés, you can watch foreign businesspeople rushing in and out of the luxurious *NJV Meridien* and *Grande Bretagne* hotels, office workers heading home, and a special breed of Greek men called *kamaki* (harpooners) trying to pick up female tourists. The House of Parliament and Memorial to the Unknown Soldier flank the east side of the square. Twenty minutes before every hour, *evzones,* soldiers in traditional dress, perform the Changing of the Guard ceremony; Sundays at 11 AM the entire regiment comes out in full regalia. No admission charge. Between Arageorgi Servias and Othonos.

National Gardens – These shady gardens provide pleasant relief from the summer sun. Queen Amalia, wife of King Otto, had them designed some 140 years ago. Peacocks and waterfowl are at home here, and nightingales sing in the spring. Open daily. No admission charge. Entrances on Amalias, Vasilissis Sofias, and Irodou Attikou.

Benaki Museum – Just a short walk from Syntagma, this collection from the private holdings of Antonios Benakis has an eclectic display — costumes, ceramics, furniture, and arms. Some of the highlights are Lord Byron's writing desk, Moslem wood carvings, and delicate Byzantine miniatures. Open daily from 8:30 AM to 2 PM. Admission charge. 1 Koumbari at Vasilissis Sofias (phone: 361-1617).

National Archaeological Museum – One of the world's greatest museums, this institution houses a treasure of art spanning 2,500 years of ancient Greek civilization. The scope and breadth of the collection are staggering — rooms and rooms of Greek vases, statues, and sculpture. Some of the highlights are the Death Mask of Agamemnon; a statue of Anavissos Kouros, the finest of the tradition of *kouroi,* beautiful youths represented nude in a rigid stance with their left feet slightly forward and their arms at their sides; the bronze statue of Poseidon, god of the sea, discovered at Cape Artemisium in 1928; the statue of the Youth from Marathon; and the sculpture of the bronze Jockey and Horse of Artemisium. Open Mondays from 11 AM to 5 PM, Tuesdays through Fridays from 8 AM to 5 PM, and weekends from 8:30 AM to 3 PM. Admission charge. 44 Patission between Tositsa and Irakliou (phone: 821-7717).

■**EXTRA SPECIAL:** When you've had your fill of the city, head for Sounion and the Temple of Poseidon, 40 miles (64 km) south of Athens along the southwest coast. Though the road is somewhat congested in the summer, the route follows the Saronic Gulf, and the view is Greece at its most elemental — sun, rock, and sea. The closer you get to Sounion, the better it gets, as the road winds around steep cliffs overlooking spectacular vistas.

High on a cliff above the sea stands the Temple of Poseidon. Only 15 Doric columns remain, but the temple of the sea god is beautiful in all its starkness. The setting, the ever-changing light, the crashing waves, inspired no less a personage than Byron to engrave his name in the marble. Later he wrote in *Don Juan,* "Place me on Sunium's marble steep/Where nothing save the waves and I/May hear our mutual murmurs sweep . . ." Open daily from 10 AM to sunset. Admission charge (phone: 029-239363).

En route you can stop off for a swim in the little town of Vouliagmeni, home of the *Astir Palace,* one of Europe's great resorts. Built on a hill above Vouliagmeni Beach, the hotel has a marble terrace with a spectacular view, luxury bungalows on the beach, and a variety of fine restaurants.

SOURCES AND RESOURCES

TOURIST INFORMATION: The National Tourist Organization of Greece (NTOG; its Greek acronym is EOT) provides all manner of information — free maps, brochures, and pamphlets — and supervises tourist services, from the classification of hotels and restaurants to the operation of public beaches; 2 Amerikis St., near Syntagma Square (phone: 322-2545 or 322-3111 (-19), ext. 342). The NTOG also runs an information desk at Hellinikon, Athens's international airport. Another source of tourist information and aid is the Tourist Police, a branch of the Metropolitan Police that helps travelers find accommodations. For information 24 hours a day in several languages, call the special number — 171. The headquarters of the Tourist Police is at 7 Syngrou (phone: 923-9224); other offices are at Larissa Railway Station (phone: 821-3574) and Hellinikon Airport (phone: 981-9730).

The US Embassy and Consulate is at 91 Vasilissis Sophias (phone: 721-2951 or 721-8401).

Local Coverage – The *Athens News* is the only local English-language daily, but most leading foreign newspapers and magazines, including the *International Herald Tribune,* are available at hotels and Syntagma or Kolonaki news kiosks. The *Athenian* is a monthly magazine in English with articles on contemporary Greece and thorough listings of entertainment events, points of interest, and restaurants. *This Week in Athens,* distributed by the NTOG, is a weekly pamphlet with information on current activities as well as general information. *Greece's Weekly,* a newsmagazine, focuses on national and international politics.

For additional English-language guides to Athens and Greece, try *Eleftheroudakis Books,* 4 Nikis St. (phone: 322-1231 or 322-9388), or *Compendium Bookshop,* 28 Nikis St.

Food – Check the Restaurants and Entertainment sections of the *Athenian* or the *Athens News.*

Telephone – The area code for Athens is 01.

 CLIMATE AND CLOTHES: Athens has an almost ideal climate — plenty of sunshine and dry air most of the year. In summer, Athens is at its most basic — rocky hills, sun-drenched streets, and long beaches. Even during July and August when the temperatures exceed 90F (32C) cool evening breezes make the heat bearable. During May, June, September, and October, days are somewhat cooler, with temperatures ranging from 60F to 80F (between 16C and 31C). The beaches are less crowded and the water is still warm enough for swimming. In spring, the hills come to life with gentle hues of green and colorful wild flowers. Winters are mild, with temperatures in the 40s and 50s F (between 5C and 13C), damper air, and more rain than any other season.

If you're visiting during the summer, lightweight clothes are essential — shorts, loose shifts, cotton suits. Summer evenings are cooler and call for sweaters or light jackets. For the spring and fall, a light jacket or coat is advisable. You can use a winter coat during the cold months, but another good way to counter the penetrating dampness is by wearing a few layers of sweaters. Seeing the city any time of year makes demands on your feet — bring comfortable walking shoes.

 GETTING AROUND: Airport – Athen's airport is about 6½ miles (11 km) from Syntagma Square in the center of the city, about a half-hour drive. Taxi fare should run about 300 to 400 drachmas ($2 to $2.60). Airport buses from both the West (for Olympic Airways) and East (foreign airlines) terminals will take you to Syntagma Square for less than 100 drachmas (about 65¢). From Athens, take express buses A and O from Syntagma Square or Omonia Square, or buses #133, #122, and #167 to the West terminal; express buses A and O to the East terminal leave from Syntagma Square and Omonia Square every 20 minutes from 6 AM to midnight, while bus #121 leaves every 40 minutes from Vasilissis Olgas Ave.

Bus – There are some 40 bus and trolley routes serving central Athens and the outlying areas. Buses and electric trolleys run from 5 AM to 12 or 12:30 AM. They afford a convenient, inexpensive, and fairly comfortable way to get around, provided you avoid them during rush hours: 7 to 9 AM, 2 to 3 PM, 5 to 6 PM, and 8 to 10 PM. The fare is 30 drachmas (about 20¢) to any point in the Athens-Piraeus area, provided there is no transfer. Bus routes are outlined on the NTOG map of Athens, but you can always check with the NTOG or Tourist Police (phone: 171) for information.

Car Rental – All major car rental companies have offices in Athens. A valid international driver's license is required for Americans. Some of the most reliable agencies are: *Avis,* 48 Amalias (phone: 322-4951); *Budget,* 8 Syngrou (phone: 821-4771); *Hellascars,* 7 Stadiou (phone: 923-5352); and *Hertz,* 12 Syngrou (phone: 922-0102).

Subway – Until Athens builds two proposed subway lines, the city's only line passes through central Athens, linking Piraeus, the major port, with the suburb of Kifissia. The line goes underground only downtown and emerges outside town. The fare is 30 drachmas (20¢), no matter how far you go. Trains run frequently between 5:30 AM and midnight.

Taxi – Cab fares in Athens are inexpensive when compared to those in other major European cities. Most cabs are individually owned, but rates are standardized, so if you want to avoid being taken for a ride, ask the hotel desk or tourist office how much your trip usually costs. You can pick up a cab at stands near the main squares, major hotels, or railway stations, or hail one in the street, though it's difficult to find one during rush hours. To hail one, you must clearly shout your destination (hotel or area) and stand on a street with traffic going in that direction. Sharing a cab is a common practice, but you pay your full fare even if you share. Extra fare is charged for luggage. To call for a taxi, phone 321-4058.

Tours – Various companies offer sightseeing tours of Athens by air conditioned bus as well as half- and full-day excursions to attractions within a few hours of the city — Cape Sounion, Delphi, Corinth, Mycenae, Epidaurus, and so on. Two of the best companies are *Chat Tours,* 4 Stadiou (phone: 323-6582, 322-3137), and *Key Tours,* 2 Ermou (phone: 323-2520, 323-3756). If you would like to hire a government-trained guide, contact the NTOG, a travel agent such as American Express, or the hotel concierge.

Train – Stathmos Larissis, the main train station (phone: 522-2491), is a short cab ride from downtown that costs about 240 drachmas (about $1.60). For information about trains to the Peloponnesus, which leave from the station on Pelopos St. (behind the main station), call 362-4402.

 SPECIAL EVENTS: On *Good Friday,* one of the most solemn religious holidays (usually in April), an impressive candlelight *Epitaph Procession* leads from the Greek Orthodox Cathedral on Mitropoleos to Syntagma Square and back. The *Athens Festival* is an international arts festival presenting a full summer of theater, music, opera, and ballet performed by renowned artists from Greece, Europe, and the US. Most of the events are held in the Herod Atticus Odeion, a Roman amphitheater built in AD 160 at the foot of the rock of the Acropolis — a setting that enhances the contemporary entertainment by creating links with the rich artistic heritage of Greece. Tickets are available at 4 Stadiou in the arcade (phone: 322-3111, ext. 240, or 322-1459), or at the theater just before the performance. The *Athens Wine Festival* offers a good time for both Athenians and tourists from mid-July to early September. Held in a lovely pine-wooded park at Daphni, 7 miles (11 km) from Athens, admission entitles you to unlimited access to wine produced in all different regions of Greece. Inexpensive drinking glasses are for sale that make nice souvenirs. A few concessions and *tavernas* provide snacks and meals — barbecued chicken and souvlaki. Groups perform traditional and popular music and dances that get pretty merry as the night wears on. The *Athens Open International Marathon,* usually held the fourth Sunday in October, follows the route of Pheidippidis from near the Tomb of Marathon to Olympic Stadium, site of the first modern Olympics in 1896.

 MUSEUMS: For a complete description of the *National Archaeological Museum,* the *Acropolis Museum,* the *Benaki Museum,* and the *Agora Museum (Stoa of Attalos)* see *Special Places.* Other interesting museums include the following.

Byzantine Museum – Religious art and icons dating from the period of Byzantine occupation, from the 3rd to 15th century. 22 Vasilissis Sofias (phone: 721-1027).

Goulandris Natural History Museum – Greece's plant and animal life, geology, and paleontology. 13 Levidou in Kifissia (phone: 808-6405).

Jewish Museum of Greece – Judeo-Greek and Sephardic religions and folk art are represented. 36 Amalias (phone: 323-1577).

Kanellopoulos Museum – A private collection of pre- and post-Christian art and artifacts. Theorias and Panos in the Plaka district (phone: 321-2313).

Museum of Greek Folk Art – Traditional arts and crafts, including embroidery, carved wooden objects, and paintings. 17 Kydathinaion in the Plaka district (phone: 321-3018).

Museum of the Cyclades – Two thousand years of the Bronze Age Cycladic civilization, whose simple geometric lines and austere marble shapes have a strong influence on 20th-century sculpture. 4 Neofitou Douka in Kolonaki (phone: 724-9706).

National History and Ethnological Museum – Portraits, arms, and mementos of the heroes of the 1821 War of Independence, plus Lord Byron's sword and helmet. 13 Stadiou on Kolokotronis Square, in the former Parliament House (phone: 323-7617).

War Museum – Weapons, uniforms, regimental flags, medals, and more. Vasilissis Sofias and Rizari (phone: 729-0543).

SHOPPING: Goods from all over Greece are available in stores in Athens. Specialties include gold and silver jewelry, embroidered shirts and dresses, fabrics, *flokati* rugs of fluffy sheep wool, pottery, onyx, marble, alabaster, and leather goods. These are available in the main shopping area downtown around Syntagma, Omonia, and Kolonaki Squares as well as in Monastiraki, the flea market, where shopping sometimes involves bargaining. The best pottery is available in Maroussi at shops along Kifissias Blvd.

Before you buy handicrafts, visit the *National Organization of Hellenic Handicrafts,* 9 Mitropoleos (phone: 322-1017), where items are exhibited to give some standard notions of quality and price. Except for carpets, goods are not for sale.

Another thing to keep in mind is where the regional specialties originate. Some of the best jewelry comes from Ioannina; interesting ceramics from Sifnos and Skopelos; and highly original embroidery from Skyros, Crete, Lefkas, and Rhodes. The Thessaly and Epirus regions specialize in *flokati* rugs.

Downtown stores are usually open Mondays, Wednesdays, and Saturdays from 8 AM to 2:30 PM; Tuesdays, Thursdays, and Fridays from 8 AM to 1:30 PM and from 5 to 8 PM. Shops around Monastiraki remain open on Sundays from 8 AM to 12:30 PM.

Benaki Museum – This is the place to pick up prints and jewelry with reproductions of themes and designs in the museum's collection. A wide variety of items — from matchbooks, scarves, and tablecloths to needlepoint kits — is also available. 1 Koumbari at the corner of Vasilissis Sofias (phone: 361-1617).

Greek Women's Institution – Exquisite embroideries and handwoven fabrics from the islands are on sale here, along with reproductions of old embroidery patterns from the *Benaki Museum* collection. 13 Voukourestiou (phone: 362-4038).

Lalaounis – This internationally known jeweler does original and traditional Greek designs in gold and silver. Voukourestiou (phone: 361-1371) and Panepistimiou (phone: 362-4354).

Lyceum of Greek Women – Woven fabrics, embroidery, bedspreads, rugs, curtains, and pillowcases are sold along with ceramics and jewelry. 17 Dimokritou (phone: 363-7698).

Monastiraki – A flea market section that is a bargainer's heaven, where you can find just about anything for any price, depending on your bargaining skills. Myriad small stalls carry everything from first class junk to quality copper, brass, antique jewelry, icons, old books, and leather goods, sandals and embroidered shirts and dresses. Open daily, but Sunday is really a field day, with an open-air bazaar from 8 AM to noon. Off Monastiraki Square, on and around Ifestou.

National Welfare Organization – This nonprofit organization runs four shops that carry a wide variety of crafts, from moderately priced copper and woven products to embroideries, jewelry, and rugs. 6 Ypatias (phone: 322-2146), 135 Vassilissis Sofias (phone: 646-0603 or 646-0921), and 24 Voukourestiou (phone: 361-1443).

Parthenis – A new star among Greek designers, he is the first to export Greek women's fashions successfully on a large scale to the US and Europe. His designs are avant-garde and medium-priced. Dimokritou and Tsakalof in Kolonaki (phone: 363-0020 or 363-3158) and Nikis near the Plaka district.

Periptero – These small kiosks at street corners carry an eclectic assortment of goods — newspapers, chocolate, pens, pencils, film, cosmetics, books, dolls, and pharmaceutical items. For 7 drachmas (about 2¢) you can use the telephone.

XEN – The *YWCA* store has a small but attractive collection of handmade embroideries. 11 Amerikis (phone: 362-4231).

Zolotas – An internationally renowned jeweler who does both original and traditional designs in silver and gold. 10 Panepistimiou (phone: 361-3782).

SPORTS AND FITNESS: The Mediterranean climate, a long coastline, and well-organized beaches combine to make Athens good territory for those who enjoy sports.

Fitness Centers – *Caravel Executive Club,* in the *Caravel* hotel, 2 Vas. Alexandrou Ave. (phone: 729-0721), has a gym, jogging track, and sauna; *Nautilus Gym,* 30 Ioan. Metaxa, Glyfada (phone: 894-2111), is a small coed health studio.

Golf – At the 18-hole *Glyfada Golf Club,* 8 miles (13 km) from the center of Athens (phone: 894-6820), you can challenge 72 par on a gradually sloping course in the foothills of Mt. Hymettus, overlooking the Saronic Gulf. The 6,808-yard course has well-maintained fairways lined with pine trees. Clubs and carts are available for rent and a city bus links the course with downtown.

Horseback Riding – The *Tatoi Riding Club* welcomes travelers to its four open-air tracks (Varimbombi; phone: 801-4513). Slightly less expensive, and open to visitors, is the *Athens Riding Club,* Gerakas, Aghia Paraskevi (phone: 661-1088).

Jogging – The National Garden, next to the Parliament Building in the center of town, is honeycombed with dirt tracks.

Sailing – Quite popular, particularly in Piraeus, where many residents maintain private boats in Mikrolimano, the small harbor, or in the larger Zea Marina. Many sailing regattas are held throughout the year. For information: Sailing Clubs Federation, 15A Xenofontos (phone: 323-6813 or 323-5560).

Swimming – The beaches to the north and south of Athens are some of the cleanest you'll find so close to any major city. Within an hour's bus or cab ride from downtown, you can swim and sunbathe at attractive beaches that have lovely natural settings and complete facilities — changing rooms, refreshment stands, playgrounds, canoe and paddleboat rentals, and tennis, basketball, and volleyball courts. The NTOG operates a large, clean beach 25 miles (40 km) to the north at Porto Rafti (phone: 0299-72572). There are two good NTOG beaches to the south, both 10 miles (16 km) from downtown at Voula (phone: 895-3248 and 895-9590); Vouliagmeni, 16 miles (26 km) from the center (phone: 896-0906), a long and popular beach jutting out between sea and bay; and Varkiza, 24 miles (38 km) from town, where bungalows are available (phone: 897-2102). Glyfada, 10 miles (16 km) from Athens, is a fashionable resort area with good beaches. Beaches are open year-round, though most people swim between May and October. There's a small admission charge at the NTOG beaches. Bear in mind that because of Greece's lack of treatment plants for sewage and industrial waste, the farther from the city, the cleaner the water.

Tennis – The NTOG beaches listed above have outdoor tennis courts; only the court at Varkiza is open daily year-round. No equipment is provided and a modest fee is charged. The courts at the *Agios Kosmas Athletic Center* in Attica (phone: 981-2112) are open to non-members.

Water Skiing – Several training centers in Vouliagmeni provide instruction for beginners and equipment for those with experience: *Naval Club,* Vouliagmeni Bay (phone: 896-2416); *Lypiterakou School,* Akti Vouliagmeni Beach (phone: 896-0743); and *G. Kasidokosta School,* Astir Vouliagmeni Beach (phone: 896-0820).

 THEATER: Athens has a fairly active theater scene, but plays are presented almost exclusively in Greek. The state theatrical company, the *National Theater* in Athens, 20 Agiou Constantinou (phone: 522-6947 or 522-5501), performs modern and classical plays as well as works by foreign playwrights (translated into Greek). During the summer, the company performs in the ancient *Epidauros* theater as part of the *Athens Festival.*

Language is no barrier to appreciating the folk dances performed by the renowned *Dora Stratou Dance Company* of Athens. Performances are held nightly from early May until the end of September at the theater on Philopappou Hill (phone: 8 AM to 2 PM, 324-4395; after 5:30 PM, 921-4650).

 MUSIC: The *Athens State Orchestra* gives classical concerts during the winter and spring, and *Lyriki Skini,* the National Opera Company, performs operas with foreign guest stars during the winter and spring at the *Olympia Theater,* 59 Akadimias (phone: 361-2461). During the summer, both groups participate in the *Athens Festival. Parnassos Hall,* 8 Agiou Georgiou Karits (phone: 323-8745), has regular recitals throughout the year which offer a look at Greek musical culture. For traditional Greek bouzouki music, see *Nightclubs and Nightlife.*

 NIGHTCLUBS AND NIGHTLIFE: Athens has an active nightlife. Athenians tend to dine late, so very often things don't get rolling until after 10 PM. Whether you're interested in a simple evening sitting around a café or more elaborate dining and entertainment (which can get rather costly), you'll find numerous places to go and plenty of company. Bars and other night spots close at 2 AM weekdays, 3 AM Sundays.

The most celebrated of Greek social institutions are the *tavernas* — restaurant-cafés that come in all sizes and styles, with or without entertainment. In summer, the dining is alfresco beneath the stars and wandering vines. The emphasis is on eating, but there's often a variety of entertainment: clubs featuring local singers or groups that generally perform folk songs and popular music (the Plaka district is one of the most lively, with a profusion of *tavernas* and *boîtes*). Among the most popular *tavernas* are *Xynos,* 4 Angelou Geronda in the Plaka district (phone: 322-1065), which features guitarists performing Greek songs; *Myrtia,* 35 Markou Moussourou in Pangrati (phone: 701-2276); and *Epistrefe,* in Nea Kifissias, west of the National Rd. (phone: 246-8166), for bouzouki and balalaika music. Best bets for *boîtes* are concentrated in the Plaka district: *Apanemia,* 4 Tholou (phone: 324-8580); *Diagonios,* 111 Andrianou (phone: 323-3644); *Esperides,* 6 Tholou (phone: 322-5482); and *Zoom,* 37 Kydathineon (phone: 322-5920).

If you're interested in a frenetic nightlife scene, try *bouzoukia* (establishments where the emphasis is on traditional bouzouki music) or nightclubs. As the volume of the music increases, so does the pace: People burst balloons, toss flowers, throw plates, and break into impromptu dances as the level of energy becomes almost as high as the tab for drinks, dinner, entertainment, and broken plates. For classic bouzouki by renowned composers and singers and *rembetika* — the Greek version of blues — try *Harama,* Endos Skopeftiriou in Kesariani (phone: 766-4869). Reservations are necessary. Though the doors open at about 10 PM, the excitement really starts around midnight and keeps building. Two excellent *bouzouki* clubs in Glyfada are *Neraida* and *Deliua.*

For a more subdued evening, you can spend hours over coffee, drinks, and pastry at *Dionysos Zonar*'s and *Floka,* two well-known cafés off Syntagma, on Panepistimiou.

Or sip drinks at *Ratka,* a fashionable Kolonaki bar, 22 Haritos (phone: 729-0746). Popular tavernas in the Plaka district include *To Terani,* at the intersection of Ragkava Tripodon and Epixarmov Sts., and *Kafe Plaka,* Tripodon at Flessa and Lysion Sts.

If you're interested in trying your luck, the *Mont Parnes Casino,* 22 miles (35 km) from Athens (phone: 322-9412) in the *Mont Parnes* hotel, operates games of chance — baccarat, chemin de fer, blackjack, and roulette. There's also a club for dining and dancing. You may drive to the top of the mountain or leave your car at the parking lot and reach the hotel entrance by cable car.

Saturday night fever is a fundamental part of Athens nightlife. Among the classiest discos are *Barbarella,* 253 Syngrou (phone: 942-5601); *Can Can Disco,* Kifissou and Petrou Ralli (544-4460); *Papagayo,* 37 P. Ioakim (phone: 724-0736); and *Make Up,* beginning of Panepistimiou, in an arcade just west of Voukourestiou (phone: 364-2160). Make reservations. Less exclusive but still hot is *Athens, Athens,* 253 Syngrou Ave., in Nea Smyrni (phone: 942-5602).

BEST IN TOWN

CHECKING IN: Athens has a wide variety of hotels. The chic *Athenaeum Inter-Continental* and the renowned *Grande Bretagne* top the list, which also includes the *Athens Hilton International* and *Ledra Marriott* as well as less plush but no less pleasant accommodations. The NTOG is in the process of changing over to a star ratings system, but in the meantime it divides hotels into five categories — Deluxe, A, B, C, and D. Listed below are our choices for the best hotels in all categories, from the most posh to least expensive (though still comfortable) rooms. Hotel prices in Greece compare very favorably to those elsewhere in Europe. In all categories, Greek hotels generally offer good value; many moderately priced and inexpensive hotels have lots of class — swimming pools and rooftop sundecks, gardens, or bars with panoramic views of the city. In peak season, expect to pay $130 to $250 a night for a double room in the expensive category (deluxe hotels); around $50 to $100 in the moderate; and $40 or less for inexpensive lodging. A number of hotels lower their rates by as much as 20% off-season, from November through March. Rates often include continental breakfasts; half-board is compulsory at many hotels on the islands. All telephone numbers are in the 01 area code unless otherwise indicated.

Astir Palace – Opened in 1983, this property faces the House of Parliament and is within an easy walk of the smart shops of Kolonaki. One of the most tastefully decorated hotels in Athens, it caters mainly to a well-heeled business clientele. The 79 beautiful rooms, all air conditioned, look onto a small sunken garden studded with ruins of ancient Athens that were uncovered during the excavation. The hotel also has a restaurant and a coffee shop. Syntagma Sq. (phone: 364-3112). Expensive.

Athenaeum Inter-Continental – A luxury hotel that's a study in space and light: A massive glass atrium fills the huge, beige marble lobby with light, and picture windows illuminate separate living and sleeping areas in all 597 rooms. Furnishings are modern and comfortable. French and continental food is served at *La Rôtisserie;* across the way, the *Café Pergola,* which opens onto a terrace with a free-form swimming pool, serves the best Sunday brunch in Athens. Other amenities include a pub, tea lounge, and disco. 89-93 Syngrou Ave. (phone: 902-3666). Expensive.

Athens Hilton International – Something of a landmark, if not of Greek history, then of luxury, comfort, and services. At the *Byzantine Café,* homesick Americans can buy real American milkshakes for more than American prices; *Ta Nissia*

Taverna serves excellent Greek specialties (see *Eating Out*), and there's also a bar. During the warmest months, an international set hangs out around the large outdoor swimming pool, the best in Athens. The 473 air conditioned rooms are modern and nicely appointed, with views of the Acropolis or the mountains to the north. 46 Vasilissis Sofias (phone: 722-0201). Expensive.

Grande Bretagne – A grand old hotel, built in 1826 and currently undergoing a major overhaul, retains its old-fashioned elegance. The lobby and public rooms are spacious, with marble floors, Oriental carpets, valuable paintings, and mahogany armchairs. Right on Syntagma Square in the heart of the city, with 394 rooms and 25 palatial suites (some with Acropolis views), the hotel is still the scene of state receptions and its guest list includes the most prominent personalities of the last 150 years. Among the facilities are an elegant dining room, an American-style bar and a restaurant and coffee shop. The hotel is air conditioned throughout. 1 Vas. Georgiou Ave., on Syntagma Sq. (phone: 323-0251). Expensive.

Ledra Marriott – Attractive, with a marble lobby and fresh flowers throughout its public spaces, it also boasts notably attentive service. The 258 rooms are quite large, and each has a marble bath, 3 telephones, mini-bar, and movies on the color TV sets. Athens's only Polynesian restaurant, the *Kona Kai,* is here, as are the *Ledra Grill,* serving continental cuisine, and the family-style *Zephyron.* The hotel's rooftop pool (and whirlpool bath) offers a splendid view of the Acropolis. 115 Syngrou Ave. (phone: 934-7711). Expensive.

NJV Meridien – One of the newest additions to Syntagma Square, this 182-room property is a marvel of French sophistication, modern efficiency, and exquisite taste. Marble, mirrors, and leather are the hallmarks of the elegant public spaces. Superior rooms have balconies overlooking the square. Facilities include 2 restaurants, a bar, shops, air conditioning, satellite TV, and mini-bars. Syntagma Sq. (phone: 255-3019). Expensive.

St. George Lycabettus – At the foot of Lycabettus stands another fashionable hotel, complete with black marble floors, a rooftop pool, and 154 plush, air conditioned rooms — brass trimmings, thick carpets, and balconies with beautiful views. Plushest of all are the corner suites that have air conditioning, balconies on two sides, and lots of space. There's an attractive restaurant serving international cuisine, a grill, bar, beauty parlor, and sauna. 2 Kleomenous (phone: 729-0711). Expensive to moderate.

Athens Gate – Overlooking the Arch of Hadrian and the Temple of the Olympian Zeus, this modern, brightly furnished hotel offers excellent value. The 106 rooms have balconies, private baths, and good views. The rooftop sundeck commands a panoramic view of Athens — from the Parliament, Lycabettus, the Olympic Stadium, and the Acropolis to the Saronic Gulf in the distance. The *Athenian Restaurant* serves traditional Greek dishes and international specialties, too. There's also a well-appointed bar done in marble, leather, and chrome. 10 Syngrou (phone: 923-8302). Moderate.

Attika Palace – This modern 8-story hotel in the heart of town is a convenient and comfortable place to stay. Though the lobby is small, the 78 rooms are large, airy, and nicely furnished, with private baths, air conditioning, and telephones. Many have balconies, and the rooms on the top two floors have sweeping views of the city and the Acropolis. Spacious hallways and lounges, restaurant and bar. 6 Karageorgi Servias, off Syntagma Sq. (phone: 322-3007). Moderate.

Divani Zafolia-Alexandras – This hotel near the Archaeological Museum has a neo-Byzantine decor, a much-frequented swimming pool, and a roof garden. The 192 rooms have private baths, balconies, and air conditioning. The *Grand Byzantine* is a large bar, and the restaurant serves international cuisine. Underground garage. 87-89 Alexandras (phone: 644-9012). Moderate.

Electra – Another first-rate hotel in the center of the city, the 110 rooms are simply and comfortably furnished and air conditioned. The bar is good for a quick drink or a more leisurely cocktail after a day's sightseeing. The restaurant serves both Greek and international specialties. Service is first rate. 5 Ermou, just off Syntagma Sq. (phone: 322-3223). Moderate.

Park – This luxurious hotel is in a quiet section of town convenient to the *National Archaeological Museum.* The building is topped off with a swimming pool and a roof garden bar that offer good views of the Acropolis and Lycabettus Hill. The 146 air conditioned rooms are fully equipped with radios and TV sets, private baths, and refrigerator bars. The *Latina,* one of 2 restaurants, serves Italian specialties; snacks are available 24 hours a day at the coffee shop. Boutiques, shops, and a bank. 10 Alexandras (phone: 883-2712). Moderate.

Titania – Between the city's two main squares, Syntagma and Omonia, this 398-room hotel is stylish both inside and out. Atop the 8-story structure are a bar and terrace with stunning views. Rooms are done in bright colors and contemporary designs. All have air conditioning, phones, and bathrooms. Other facilities include a 24-hour coffee shop, a restaurant, and a piano bar. 52 Panepistimiou (phone: 360-9612). Moderate.

Athenian Inn – Very little traffic passes by this exceptionally clean and attractive pension on a side street in the chic Kolonaki quarter. The 28 rooms, as well as the small bar and dining room, are outfitted with the dark rustic furniture and fabrics of the Greek countryside. 22 Haritos (phone: 723-9552). Moderate to inexpensive.

Ermeion – Right in the center of Athenian life, this hotel is 5 minutes from central Syntagma Square and the flea market at Monastiraki. Friendly proprietors run this clean, 29-room property. 66 Ermou (phone: 321-2753). Inexpensive.

Museum – This hotel near the *National Archaeological Museum* has 58 clean and comfortable rooms, a large lobby, a bar, and a recreation room. 16 Bouboulinas and Tossitsa (phone: 360-5612). Inexpensive.

Nefeli – In the shadow of the Acropolis, this attractive hotel has 18 simply furnished rooms with private baths and telephones. Other facilities include a coffee shop and roof garden facing the Acropolis. 16a Iperidou in the Plaka district (phone: 322-8044). Inexpensive.

Niki – Another excellent value, this small hotel near Syntagma Square has 24 clean, standard rooms. 27 Nikis (phone: 322-0913). Inexpensive.

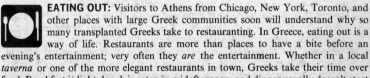 **EATING OUT:** Visitors to Athens from Chicago, New York, Toronto, and other places with large Greek communities soon will understand why so many transplanted Greeks take to restauranting. In Greece, eating out is a way of life. Restaurants are more than places to have a bite before an evening's entertainment; very often they *are* the entertainment. Whether in a local *taverna* or one of the more elegant restaurants in town, Greeks take their time over food. Breakfast is light; lunch is eaten in midafternoon; and dinner usually doesn't start until 9 PM, when the *tavernas* begin to open. Then the parade of Greek food begins: appetizers — *horiatikosalata* (tomato, cucumber, olives, and feta cheese salad), *taramosalata* (a fish roe spread), *plaki* (a bean dish), *melitsanosalata* (eggplant salad), *dolmadakia* (grape leaves stuffed with meat, rice, and onions, served with a lemon sauce). Next is the entrée: There's a choice of grilled meats — baby lamb or beef, veal, or chicken — and a wide assortment of seafood — octopus, squid, red snapper, lobster, or *youvetsi* (a casserole). *Retsina,* a resinated wine, either white or red, traditionally accompanies *taverna* meals, although locally brewed beers have become popular. Greeks indulge their love for rich pastries and thick, strong coffee at cafés. What makes all this even more attractive is the relatively modest tab. Expect to pay around $30 and

up for a dinner for two in the places listed as expensive; $20 or less in those listed as moderate; and $10 and under in the inexpensive category. Prices include drinks and tips. Many restaurants are open only for dinner, so telephone beforehand. All telephone numbers are in the 01 area code unless otherwise indicated.

L'Abreuvoir – The oldest French restaurant in Athens, it is also one of the best, serving marvelously light soufflés, snails, and tender swordfish steak. In summer, dine in the garden under mulberry trees. It is the perfect spot for a secluded lunch for two. Open daily. Reservations necessary at night only. 51 Xenokratous, Kolonaki (phone: 722-9061). Expensive.

Bayazzo – Owned by a German chef named Klaus, who once cooked for the Shah of Iran, this is the only restaurant serving nouvelle cuisine in Athens. It is also, by far, the most elegant (with a little theater of mechanized, antique china clowns), the best, and the most expensive. But it's worth every drachma. Imagine a "dialogue of veal with mushrooms and green apple" or a cocotte of "swordfish in disguise" topped with puff pastry. The desserts are truly sinful and deserve a visit just for themselves. Dinner only; closed Sundays and Christmas. Reservations advised. 35 Ploutarhou St. at Dinokratou, Kolonaki (phone: 729-1420). Expensive.

Gerofinikas – Run by Greeks from Istanbul, the specialties here are Greek and Turkish. A wide variety of *mezedakia* and seafood specialties are on display in the showcase up front. Old favorites are shrimp wrapped in smoked salmon, extraordinarily light *taramosalata,* smoked trout, a wide assortment of salads, and such entrées as lobster thermidor, swordfish on a skewer, and grilled meats. Don't pass up dessert — strawberries with cream or *ekmek kadayifi* (Turkish bread pudding). Service is good, and dining is leisurely. Open daily for lunch and dinner. Reservations advised. 10 Pindarou (phone: 362-2719, 363-6710). Expensive.

Nautilus – A restaurateur and a chef from the island of Mykonos have made a hit among locals with their new restaurant in Ambelokipi, east of Lycabettus. The building itself is exquisitely decorated with brass, mahogany, linen, and candlelight; there's even Big Band music to dine by. The food will satisfy any gourmand from start to finish: beef-stuffed artichokes, prawns, and prosciutto as appetizers; lobster, bouillabaisse, and swordfish entrées; and desserts such as banana fritters and chocolate mousse. Open daily for dinner. Reservations advised. 6 Fthiotidos St. at Kifissias Ave. (phone: 693-0089). Expensive.

Ta Nissia – Spacious and elegant, with all the trimmings — high redwood ceiling, marble floors, and brass ornaments with traditional designs. The atmosphere is quite pleasant, complete with wandering troubadours singing Greek songs. The food maintains a high style from the *mezedakia* (delicious hors d'oeuvres), through the main course — leg of lamb, and roast suckling pig prepared in its own juices — to the rich desserts. Open daily. Reservations advised. 46 Vasilissis Sofias, in the *Hilton* (phone: 722-0201). Expensive.

Dionyssos – The two restaurants by this name have similar menus and different, though equally splendid, views — one offers a panorama from the top of Lycabettus; the other, the Acropolis. Such views make the visit worthwhile, but the varied menu is usually only mediocre. The waiters at both are multilingual. Open daily. No reservations needed. Dionisiou Areopagitou, just opposite the Acropolis (phone: 923-1936), and Mt. Lycabettus, accessible by the funicular that starts at the top of Ploutarchou, above Kolonaki Sq. (phone: 722-6374). Expensive to moderate.

Mikrolimano – This is a little port in Piraeus that harbors a row of seafood restaurants. Fishermen get up at 3 AM to catch the sweet and succulent daily fare, such as *garides* (prawns), *octapodi* (octopus), *astako* (crawfish, lobster, or langouste), *barbounia* (red mullet), and *garides yiovetsi* (a shrimp, cheese, wine, and tomato casserole that most of the restaurants along the port claim to have invented). The usual procedure here is to go into a restaurant and make your selection straight from the refrigerator. In summer, you would then saunter back outside and dine beside the small yachts, right on the quay where musicians and flower vendors stroll. Because of the decrease in catches of late, however, most restaurants have turned to using frozen fish — often without admitting it. Check first with a sniff, or a look at the eyes for brightness.

A few good restaurants right on the small port are *Kuyu and Kaplanis* (phone: 411-1623) for red snapper baked with shrimp, mushrooms, and whiskey; *Zorba No. 1* (phone: 412-3315) for a stunning variety of *mezedakia, kasemburek* (pastries filled with cheese and tomatoes), shellfish in delicate sauces, and stuffed eggplant; and *The Black Goat* for its great selection of fresh, fresh fish (this last is a popular yachtsmen's rendezvous (phone: 427626). No reservations needed at any of the Mickrolimano fish tavernas. Expensive to moderate.

Myrtia – If you want a spirited Greek atmosphere, head for the hill behind the Olympic Stadium. Here serenading guitarists play all the popular Greek tunes, some of which you may recognize. The menu is fixed: plate after plate of *mezedakia,* meat, salad, potatoes, and fruit. Excellent food and service and a warm ambience have long attracted Greece's best-known celebrities. Closed Sundays. Reservations advised. 35 Markou Mousouri (phone: 701-2276 or 751-1686). Expensive to moderate.

Act I – Right in the center of town, this cozy restaurant/cocktail lounge is reminiscent of a New York piano bar. Evenings, a pianist plays old American favorites as well as contemporary Greek hits. The food is plentiful and good, including Greek and American specialties. 18 Akademias (phone: 360-2492). Moderate.

Ellinikon – This sophisticated little place, one of the many trendy café-restaurants on Kolonaki Sq., is said to be "where the elite meet." Indeed, fashionable young men and women, as well as visiting executives from the US and around the Continent, are the usual clientele. The restaurant serves a variety of continental and local dishes, the best of which are blanketed with a rich egg and lemon sauce spiked with wine. The pastries are also quite good. Open daily. No reservations needed. 19-20 Kolonaki Sq. (phone: 361-5866). Moderate.

Hermion – Just south of the Greek Orthodox cathedral on Mitropoleos, this stylish tavern is tucked away in an appealing cul-de-sac. The food is always fresh, imaginative, and light on the oil. Be sure to try the eggplant croquettes. Open daily. No reservations needed. 15 Pandrossou, off Kapnikareas near the Adrianou St. square (phone: 324-6725 or 324-7148). Moderate.

Lotofagos – A homey restaurant that is actually a cottage in Kifissia, one of Athens's most prosperous suburbs. Surrounded by a fireplace, copper pots, and earthenware, diners order from a menu that includes chicken with mangoes, spaghetti primavera, and fresh salad vegetables. The key is always left in the door so that customers can enter like one of the family. Closed Tuesdays and Wednesdays. Reservations advised. 4 Aghias Lavras, Kifissia (phone: 801-3201). Moderate.

Stagecoach – This American steakhouse (which doubles as a café) is renowned in Athens as a center of expatriate life. Its huge mahogany bar is frequented by many a homesick traveler, and its restaurant offers hearty American fare such as steaks, giant hamburgers, and perked coffee. Closed Sundays. Reservations taken. 14 Voukourestiou, near Syntagma (phone: 363-5145). Moderate.

Ta Kalamia – One of the most famous tavernas in Greece (its name translates as "bamboo"), moved from polluted central Athens to a breezy northern suburb. The first course here, a mixture of wonderful *mezedakia,* is followed by a variety of imaginative meat dishes. In summer, dine alfresco in a garden lined with live bamboo. Open daily. No reservations necessary. Aghiou Georgiou and 26 Aiskilou, Halandri (phone: 681-0529). Moderate.

Zafiris – Off the beaten track in the Plaka district, this little restaurant serves fine game dishes and attracts the likes of Greek presidents, present and past. Open daily. Reservations advised. 4 Thespidos, in the Plaka district (phone: 322-5460). Moderate.

Tou Georgou – Georgos, the owner, likes to greet his guests personally and might even take your order. With a winning smile, he races downstairs, as fast as his rather hefty frame allows, to prepare "catastrophe cheese pies" (so good they're a catastrophe for your figure), bonfilet in pepper sauce, or any other of his famous concoctions. Open nightly. No reservations necessary. 46 Vrilissou, Polygono, on the northern Athens mountain road (phone: 644-7298). Moderate to inexpensive.

Xynos – Though much of the rest of the Plaka district has become highly commercialized, this old, well-known *taverna* retains a fair measure of authenticity. The place is always lively with guitarists playing popular Greek songs and plenty of good retsina to go around. Food is typically Greek and good — veal *hasapi,* lamb *yiouvetsi,* Greek salads, shish kebab, and spicy appetizers. During the summer, the action takes place in the garden; in winter, inside where the walls are lined with amusing murals of Greek life. Closed Sundays. Reservations suggested. 4 Angelou Gerondos (phone: 322-1065). Moderate to inexpensive.

Apotsos – This cozy indoor *ouzerie* is popular with writers, professors, models, and actors who enjoy the simple but tasty Greek dishes and the low prices. The atmosphere is casual and cluttered, and the *taverna*'s walls a collage of old signs, photographs, and other memorabilia. Closed Sundays. No reservations necessary. In an arcade at 10 Panepistimiou, just west of Voukourestiou (phone: 363-7046). Inexpensive.

Bouillabaisse – One of the best *tavernas* in Athens in which to enjoy the famous French fish soup that gave this restaurant its name. There's also a variety of other well-prepared seafood. Attentive waiters serve meals on a large pebbled terrace overhung with trailing vine leaves. Open daily. 28 Zisimopoulou, Amphithea, just behind the Athens Planetarium (phone: 941-9082). Inexpensive.

O Platanos – One of the oldest *tavernas* in the Plaka district, this place is off a small street away from the hectic crowd. It is simply decorated, but has a large and well-prepared selection of Greek foods and unbeatable prices. Closed Sundays. 4 Diogenous (phone: 322-0666). Inexpensive.

Socrates' Prison – The owners of this unpretentious *taverna* — a former prison — claim it really was the site of Socrates' internment. Good food, house wine, and boisterous conversation make it a jolly spot. Reservations not necessary. Open daily. 20 Mitseon, across from *Herod Atticus* theater (phone: 922-3434). Inexpensive.

■**Note:** If you're interested in a unique gastronomic experience, head a few miles east out of Athens on the road that leads up Mt. Hymettus. You'll come to Kareas, a small town on the mountain, which is inhabited chiefly by Romanian refugees. They have set up several restaurants along the road serving unusual dishes — *stiphado* (hare stew with small onions in tomato sauce) and grilled meats including baby lamb and goat. As you eat, you can enjoy the cool mountain air, which provides welcome relief on hot summer days, and an excellent view of Athens.

BARCELONA

Seeing a circle of men and women move in simple, slow steps to the music of flute and drum in a sun-drenched square on a Sunday afternoon provides an almost visceral understanding of Barcelona and its people. This regional dance, the *sardana* — once described by a poet as a dance "of people going forth holding hands" — is indicative of the sense of community and passion for music that is typical of Barcelona.

The *sardana* appears to begin spontaneously. People walking back from mass or a Sunday stroll begin to linger in the cathedral square. Seemingly from nowhere, a band gathers and begins to play what sounds like rhythmic dirges. The people set aside purses, prayer books, and hymnals, then join hands to form large circles. Slowly, the circles revolve as the dancers step out the intricately counted measures on tiptoe, and are soon caught up in the intensity of the music. They hold their hands high; some close their eyes. The music continues in melodic tones. Then, almost abruptly, the *sardana* is over. The dancers nod to their neighbors, gather their belongings, and continue on their way home.

You will have seen the soul of Barcelona, witnessed the strong communal feeling that tempers the legendary Catalonian individualism. There has always been strong regional identity and pride here. After the death of Francisco Franco in 1975, the native Catalan language, no longer suppressed, quickly regained its dominant place in the region. Streets and place names were changed back to Catalan from Castilian, and with the democratic constitution of King Juan Carlos, the Region of Catalonia — encompassing the provinces of Barcelona, Gerona, Lérida, and Tarragona — was designated one of the country's 17 *comunidades autónomas* (autonomous communities).

Across the Pyrenees from France, south of the Costa Brava (literally, "wild coast") along the Mediterranean Sea, Barcelona's history and language link it as much to France as to Spain. Catalan, the lilting language of the region, is derived from the French *langue d'oc,* or Provençal, and is spoken in French Catalonia as well.

The history of Barcelona dates to 218 BC, when Hamilcar Barça, a Carthaginian, founded Barcino. The city flourished under both the Romans and the Visigoths before being overrun by the Moors. The powerful Counts of Barcelona were able to drive the Moors from the lands to the south in the 10th century, and by 1100 Barcelona had dominion over all of Catalonia.

At one point, it was said that "every fish in the Mediterranean wore the red and yellow stripes of the kingdom led by Catalonia." Barcelona was a major Mediterranean power, a force whose might and power can be felt even today in the medieval streets of the city's old Gothic quarter, the Barri Gòtic. During the 1400s, it rivaled Genoa and Venice in Mediterranean trade. But although Columbus sailed from Barcelona on his historic voyage, the discov-

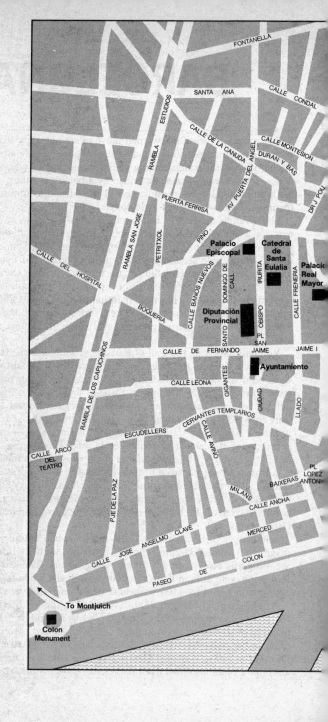

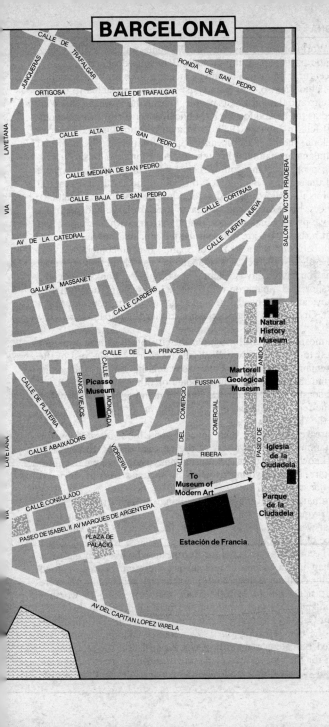

ery of the New World proved disastrous for Catalonia, and as Seville, Cádiz, and other Atlantic ports rose in importance, Barcelona declined.

Early in this century, Barcelona became a meeting place for artists, including Joan Miró, Pablo Picasso, and Juan Gris, who were attracted to the life and color of the city and the spirit of its people. During the Spanish Civil War, Barcelona served as the capital for the Republican government from November 1937 until it fell, in January 1939, to Franco's Nationalists.

Today, Barcelona, the most European of Spanish cities, is big, rich, and commercial. Catalans are famous throughout Spain for their business acumen, and young people seeking commercial advancement are drawn here from all parts of the country. Barcelona is the publishing and literary capital of Spain, as well as its major port and second largest city (pop. 1,755,000). Government offices, boulevards, and fountains here are large and pompous exhibitions of civic pride; Catalans walk the city streets with a swagger and a confidence that boasts, "We are different, better educated, more culturally aware, and much better off than the rest of Spain." It is no coincidence that Barcelona has the highest literacy rate in Spain and can claim to be the only city where the patron saint's day is celebrated with gifts of books to friends. "There's a bookshop and a bank on every block," they claim, and bellhops and shoeshine boys are often buried in books that on closer inspection turn out to be French, German, or English classics, rather than Spanish mystery novels.

The seaport atmosphere is felt throughout the city, but it is most apparent in the area closest to the waterfront. With all the charms of the rest of the city, the harbor remains a focal point: a place to watch the comings and goings of cruise ships and tankers; to hire motorboats or other pleasure craft for cruises along the coast; to photograph the 200-foot monument to Christopher Columbus and the replica of his caravel, *Santa María;* or merely to be part of the bustle of the docks.

Barcelonans are renowned for their love of good food, attested by the profusion of restaurants and the variety of the regional dishes. But most of all, Catalans are known for their love of music. Many people belong to choral societies and choirs, and the young usually join societies to learn regional dances, such as the *sardana.*

If you are fortunate some evening to be walking through the Barri Gòtic at dusk and hear voices softly singing a medieval madrigal as though the spirits of the past were alive, pause and savor the moment: You will have found the essence of Barcelona.

Barcelona has become a favored spot for Europeans who like their big cities to have more than just a cathedral and an art museum. Scores of good restaurants and chic designer fashion boutiques (the city police uniforms were designed by couturier Antonio Miró!) attract visitors seeking to worship Gaudí and his contemporaries for providing the finest modernist architecture in Europe. Recent Catalan prosperity has restored the ancient, revamped the old, and forged the new. Hosting the 1992 Summer Olympic Games has merely accelerated Barcelona's already speedy facelift.

In preparation for the games, Barcelona will spend over $100 million on the construction of 12 new hotels, and is building a new, $150-million terminal at El Prat Airport, capable of handling over 12 million passengers a year. The technologically advanced terminal will be completed by June 1991. These and other multibillion-dollar projects, however, are designed not solely for the Olympics but will be permanent assets, expanding the city's tourism and sports facilities for the 21st century. It is a concept referred to locally as "Post Olympica," providing a sense of the city's confidence in its future.

BARCELONA AT-A-GLANCE

SEEING THE CITY: There are excellent panoramic views of Barcelona, its harbor, the foothills of the Pyrenees, and the Mediterranean from the top of Tibidabo, a 1,745-foot mountain on the northwest edge of the city. The heights on the mountain can be reached by car or by funicular at the end of Carrer Balmes.

SPECIAL PLACES: The old medieval heart of Barcelona, the Barri Gòtic, is crisscrossed by alleyways weaving among ancient palaces, churches, and medieval apartment blocks. Most of the city's chief buildings and monuments of historic interest and artistic value are in this area. When the walls of this old city were pulled down during the 19th century, Barcelona expanded into the Eixample (literally "enlargement"), a grid pattern of wide streets and boulevards. La Diagonal and Gran Vía de les Corts Catalanes, modern Barcelona's major streets, cut across this chessboard. To the southeast is Montjuïc, a sports and recreation area (site of the Olympic complex) that also contains five museums and Poble Espanyol (Spanish Village), an amalgamation of native architectural styles, complete with full-size replicas of domestic and municipal buildings from every region of the country.

BARRI GÒTIC

Catedral de Santa Eulalia – Begun in 1298, the cathedral was built on the site of a 4th-century Christian church that was damaged by Almanzor in the late 10th century. The present structure is an excellent example of Mediterranean Gothic architecture. The two octagonal towers over the transepts are most impressive. The interior is laid out in classic Catalan Gothic form, with three aisles neatly engineered to produce an overall effect of grandeur and uplift. The smoke from a million penitents' candles adds to the interior darkness. The enclosed choir is dedicated to the Knights of the Golden Fleece. Holy Roman Emperor Charles V included the Kings of Denmark, Poland, Hungary, France, Portugal, and England in this "club," and Henry VIII had a stall on the emperor's right in the top row. Near the sanctuary is the tomb of the cathedral's founder, Ramón Berenguer, and his wife. The chapel of San Raimundo contains the Gothic tomb of St. Raymond of Peñafort, which was retrieved from the site's earlier church. The chapel of St. Benedict houses the lifelike Altarpiece of the Transfiguration, by the great 15th-century Catalan artist Bernat Martorell. The small museum contains various religious treasures, a beautiful 14th-century Italian altar, and the 15th-century *La Pietat,* painted by Bartolomé Bermejo. Open daily, 7:30 AM to 1:30 PM and 2 to 7:30 PM. Admission charge. Carrer de Santa Llúcia.

Palau de la Generalitat (Statehouse) – This ceremonious 15th-century Gothic structure was the seat of the ancient Catalonian parliament and now houses the executive branch of Catalonia's autonomous government. The chapel of St. George has splendid 17th-century vaulting, with a dome and hanging capitals, and a 15th-century statue of the saint. The three-aisled, 16th-century Salón de San Jorge (St. George

Room) features interesting vaults, a transept, and a dome by Pere Blai. It is in this room that most important decisions of state have been handed down over the centuries. Open Sundays, 10 AM to 1 PM. Expanded hours are expected by 1990. Plaça de Sant Jaume.

Ajuntament de Barcelona (Town Hall) – Like the Palau de la Generalitat across the square, the Ajuntament is one of the finest examples of Gothic civil architecture in the Spanish Mediterranean style. The highlights of this 14th- to 19th-century political center are the Saló del Consell de Cent (Chamber of the Council of One Hundred) and the Saló de Sesion (Session Chamber), both restored to their original glory. Open Mondays through Saturdays, 9:30 AM to 1:30 PM and 4:30 to 7:30 PM; holidays, 9:30 AM to 1:30 PM. Closed mid-December through mid-January. Plaça de Sant Jaume.

Palau Reial (Great Royal Palace) – The former palace of the Counts of Barcelona, who later became the Kings of Aragon. Built in the 14th century, it contained one large room, the Saló del Tinell, a magnificent banquet hall with a paneled ceiling supported by six arches. Legend has it that on his return from the New World, Christopher Columbus was presented to King Ferdinand and Queen Isabella here. The museum contains several exhibition rooms, but its main feature is a stylized painting of the Catholic monarchs sitting on the palace's great steps, surrounded by the heroic Columbus and the American Indians he brought home on his return voyage. Open Tuesdays through Saturdays, 10 AM to 1:30 PM and 3 to 7 PM; Sundays, 10 AM to 2 PM. Small admission fee. Plaça del Reí.

Museu d'Historia de la Ciutat (Museum of City History) – Connected to the Palau Reial, the museum features the history of Barcelona from Carthaginian trading port to Olympic city. Begin a tour in the basement rooms, which contain the excavated remains of a nearby Roman settlement, including houses, waterworks, statues, and ceramics. The museum's upper floors contain numerous sculptures, household items, weapons, mosaics, paintings, and holy relics. Open Tuesdays through Saturdays, 9 AM to 2 PM and 3:30 to 8:30 PM; Sundays, 9 AM to 2 PM; and Mondays, 3:30 to 8:30 PM. Small admission fee. Plaça del Reí (phone: 221-0144).

MONTJUÏC

Called the "Hill of the Jews" (there once was a Jewish cemetery here), this is the city's playground. Buildings to house exhibitions for the 1929 World's Fair still scale the slopes of Montaña de Montjuïc, a huge fortress hill overlooking the sea.

Poble Espanyol (Spanish Village) – Built for the 1929 World's Fair, the Poble Espanyol is a five-acre exhibition of Spanish art and architecture in the form of a traditional village. The model village displays architecture from every region of Spain, and most re-create actual structures. Full-scale replicas include a Plaza Mayor, a Calle de la Conquista, and a Plaza de la Iglesia. A walk through the simulated streets and plazas emphasize the wide diversity of native Spanish architecture. The display also features traditional artisans at work; their carvings, pottery, glass, leather, and metal-works are sold in the village's 35 shops. Open daily, 9 AM to 8 PM. Closed some holidays. Small admission fee. Avenida Marqués de Comillas, Parque de Montjuïc.

Museu d'Art de Catalunya (Museum of Catalonian Art) – Also built for the 1929 World's Fair, in an imitation Renaissance-baroque style, the museum houses a superb collection of Romanesque and Gothic art and artifacts from small Catalonian churches, including frescoes, wood carvings, ceramics, and everyday utensils of medieval life. Often referred to as "the Prado of Romanesque art," the museum also contains a splendid collection of medieval paintings, Visigoth and early Christian stonework, beautiful 12th- to 14th-century frescoes and triptychs, and canvases by Velázquez, Zurbarán, and El Greco. Open Tuesdays through Sundays, 9:30 AM to 2 PM. Parque de Montjuïc (phone: 223-1824).

Fundació Miró (Joan Miró Foundation) – Montjuïc's newest museum (1975) is a light, airy tribute to Catalonia's surrealist master, who was also an outstanding sculptor and weaver, as his *Tapis de la Fundació* demonstrates. Numerous sculptures of brightly painted bronze are displayed on terraces off the museum's upper level. A stroll through the galleries illustrates the artist's various styles and mediums. This is most evident in his *Self Portrait,* which is, in effect, two pictures on one canvas. Drawing from a reflection in a convex mirror, the artist's eyes resemble starlike forms that are repeated elsewhere on the canvas, giving the picture a peculiar hypnotic quality. The museum holds frequent special exhibitions, and also features a library and well-stocked art bookstore. Open Tuesdays through Saturdays, 11 AM to 8 PM; Sundays and holidays, 11 AM to 2:30 PM. Small admission fee. Parque de Montjuïc (phone: 319-1908).

Museo Arqueològic (Archaeological Museum) – Exhibitions include relics found in the excavation of the Greco-Roman city of nearby Empúries, various jewels and miniatures, and other remnants of Spain's prehistoric cultures, as well as a fine collection of Greek, Carthaginian, and Roman statues and mosaics. Open Tuesdays through Saturdays, 9:30 AM to 1 PM and 4 to 7 PM; Sundays, 9:30 AM to 1 PM; and holidays, 10 AM to 2 PM. Small admission fee. Carrer de Lérida (phone: 233-2149).

Olympic Ring – Montjuïc has been designated the principal site for the July 29 to August 9, 1992, Summer Olympics. The sports facilities in the *Anella Olímpica* will include the main, 70,000-seat *Olympic Stadium,* where the opening and closing ceremonies, as well as the track and field events, will be held; a new 17,000-seat domed *Olympic Hall,* smaller stadiums and sports halls, indoor and outdoor swimming pools, and practice fields, all within walking distance of one another. The numerous bicycle and jogging paths are popular exercise sites; at times it seems that everyone in the city is in training for the Olympics.

EIXAMPLE

Barcelona's well-planned "enlargement," implemented in 1859 after the city's medieval walls were torn down. This area is considered by many to be Barcelona's special pride because of its late-19th- and early-20th-century architecture, unparalleled in all of Europe. Many of Gaudí's most interesting works are here. Now the city's financial center, the attractive, tree-lined boulevards still make for a pleasant stroll. Each *fanalsbanc* (lamppost and mosaic bench) on the Passeig de Gràcia dates from 1900.

La Sagrada Familia (Church of the Holy Family) – Antonio Gaudí was a leader in the Art Nouveau movement in architecture, and although he was killed in a tram accident in 1926 before he could complete his most famous and controversial work, his La Sagrada Familia, in the Plaça de la Sagrada Familia, is one of Spain's most extraordinary buildings. Begun in 1884, the church was originally designed by Francisco del Villar in the neo-Gothic style. When Gaudí was commissioned to take over the project in 1891, he changed the designs considerably. The famous east façade, carved to suggest molten stone, has four tall spires and a porch filled with sculptures illustrating Nativity scenes. Notice the Virgin Mary, Joseph, and the infant Christ, painted in appropriate hues, above the main portal. Only this side of the church was completed when Gaudí died in 1926, and although he left no plans, work still continues on the structure. Few expect its completion before the mid-21st century. Open daily, June through August, 8 AM to 9 PM; September through May, 9 AM to 7 PM. Small admission fee.

Casa Leí Morera – One of three buildings on Passeig de Gràcia between Calle de Aragò and Consell de Cent (called *la manzana de la discordia,* or "the block of disagreement"), built during the peak of the Catalan modernist movement. The upper floors of the building, designed by Domenech i Montaner in 1905, are lined with flowers and winged lions, while the elaborate interior (now a tourist office) features exotically paneled walls, floors, and ceilings. 35 Passeig de Gràcia.

Casa Amatller and Casa Batlló – Making up the remainder of the "block of disagreement," the former was designed in a cubical pattern with a Dutch gable look by Puig i Cadafalch in 1900; it contrasts greatly with its neighbor, Casa Batlló, typically

Gaudí (1905) with mask-shaped balconies, swelling wooden doors, delicate tiles, and sensuous curves in stone and iron. Passeig de Gràcia. (To view the latter, obtain a letter of permission from Catadra Gaudí, 7 Avenida Pedralbes; phone: 204-5250.)

Casa Milá – Popularly known as La Pedrera, it is regarded as the classic example of Gaudí's modernist architecture, with its almost sculptural attempt to distance itself from the harsh, square lines of the turn-of-the-century apartment blocks. Notice the intricate ironwork around the balconies, and the diversity of the front gate's egg-shaped windowpanes. The famous roof terrace features more strange formations covering the chimneys and ventilators. Rooftop tours are conducted hourly, weekdays, 10 AM to 1 PM and 4 to 5 PM; Saturdays, 10 AM to noon; and alternating Sundays, 11 AM to noon.

Parc Güell – Originally planned as a real estate development by Gaudí and his friend, Count Eusebio Güell, a noted Barcelona industrialist and civic leader. Only two houses were completed, however, and in 1926, the city purchased the property. Today, the gingerbread-type houses are surrounded by a raised plaza that is, in fact, the roof for what would have been the development's marketplace. Supported by 96 mock-classical columns, the roof is edged with an undulating bench and is covered with a quilt mosaic of broken glass and tiles. One of the houses, Casa-Museu Gaudí, contains drawings, models, furniture, and other items belonging to the noted architect. Open daily, May through September, 8 AM to 9 PM; October through November, 9 AM to 7 PM; and December through April, 9 AM to 6 PM. Admission fee. Calle Larrad.

OTHER BARCELONA ATTRACTIONS

Las Ramblas – This is the city's favorite and liveliest promenade, brimming with activity. Comprising five avenues that run from the harbor to Plaça Catalunya and beyond, Las Ramblas was originally a drainage channel. Along the tree-lined pedestrian esplanade, Catalans gather to read a favorite newspaper or magazine at a sidewalk café, shop at the book, bird, and flower stands, or merely chat and stroll with friends. Look for the sidewalk mosaic by Miró at the Plaça de Boquería; stroll to the nearby Mercat de Sant Josep (St. Joseph's market, better known as the Boquería); and be sure to visit the *Gran Teatre del Liceu*, 61 Rambla, one of the world's great opera houses. Don't be fooled by its drab exterior, as it has one of the world's largest and most majestic auditoriums. Tours are conducted September through June on weekdays, 11:30 AM to 12:15 PM. Small admission fee. Also see Gaudí's first major work, the Palau Güell, at 3 Nou de la Rambla, now the *Museu de les Arts de L'Espectacle* (theater museum).

Museu Picasso – Housed in the beautiful 15th-century Palau Agüilar that is of nearly as much interest as the master's works. A lovely Gothic-Renaissance courtyard opens to the roof, surrounded by tiers of galleries with arcades of pointed arches and slender columns. Lithographs and early works from the artist's years in Málaga and Barcelona (1889-1905) make up most of the collection, but there are a few special pieces. One is the large exhibition of 44 bizarre variations of *Las Meninas*, the famous Velázquez painting in Madrid's *Prado*. Also notice examples of Picasso's warm and unpretentious ceramic work, which includes brightly painted plates and jugs. Open Tuesdays through Saturdays, 9 AM to 2 PM and 4 to 8:30 PM; Sundays and holidays, 9 AM to 2 PM; and Mondays, 4 to 8:30 PM. Small admission fee. 15 Montcada (phone: 319-6902).

The Waterfront – Barcelona's historic seagoing tradition has earned it a reputation as the largest city on the Mediterranean shore; today it remains a compulsory port of call for the major international cruise ship lines. The towering Monument a Colom (Columbus Monument), erected in 1886, is the tallest monument to the noted explorer in the world. Take the elevator to the top floor for an extraordinary view of the city and the sea. Open July through October, Tuesdays through Sundays, 9 AM to 9 PM;

and November through June, Tuesdays through Sundays, 10:30 AM to 2 PM and 3:30 to 6:30 PM. Small admission fee.

Nearby, the 13th-century Reials Drassanes (medieval shipyards) stand as testimony to Catalan industrial architecture during the Middle Ages. From these yards were launched the ships that carried the red and yellow Catalan flag to the "far corners" of the world, as it was known, years before Columbus's bold discovery. The *Museu Marítim* (Maritime Museum), 1 Puerto de la Pau (phone: 318-3245), now occupies the yards and displays old maps and compasses and a full-size reproduction of the galley *Real,* Don Juan de Austria's victorious flagship in the Battle of Lepanto in 1571. There are also models of ancient fishing boats, freighters, and interesting ship figureheads. Open Tuesdays through Saturdays, 10 AM to 2 PM and 4 to 7 PM; Sundays and holidays, 10 AM to 3 PM. The small admission fee also includes a tour of the full-size replica of the *Santa María,* the caravel on which Columbus sailed to America, which is in the nearby harbor. Open daily, 9 AM to 2 PM and 3 to 7 PM.

■**EXTRA SPECIAL:** The Montserrat Sierra lies 40 miles (64.4 km) northwest of Barcelona in the geographical and spiritual heart of Catalonia. The many legends that surround Montserrat, which inspired Wagner's opera *Parsifal,* are undoubtedly rooted in the strangely unreal appearance of these impressive mountain peaks. Tucked within is the Benedictine monastery whose Marian shrine has attracted pilgrims for over 700 years. *La Moreneta (The Black Madonna),* a polychrome statue of the Virgin Mary, represents the spiritual life of the province and is central to Catalan unity. Legend has it that St. Luke carved the statue and presented it to St. Peter in Barcelona in AD 50. Actually, the tall, slim carving dates from the 12th century. It sits impassively above the main altar of the monastery in a small chamber, accepting pilgrims' reverential kisses on her outstretched right hand, which holds a sphere of the world. Take the #2 funicular from near the monastery, then walk another half hour from the top to reach San Jerónimo Belvedere, the isolated hermitages of Sant Geroni, Sant Miquel, and Sant Joan, and La Santa Cova, the cave where the statue of the Madonna was found. At 4,061 feet above sea level, the views, which stretch from the Pyrenees to the Balearic Islands, are breathtaking as well as vertiginous.

SOURCES AND RESOURCES

TOURIST INFORMATION: Brochures, maps, and general information are available from the Patronat Municipal de Turisme de Barcelona (Barcelona Tourist Bureau), open weekdays, 9 AM to 2:30 PM and 3:30 to 5:30 PM, 35 Passeig de Gràcia (phone: 215-4477). There are also tourist offices at 658 Gran Vía de les Corts Catalanes (phone: 301-7443), Sants central train station (phone: 410-2594), the Porta de la Pau Colon (Columbus Statue; phone: 302-5224), Plaça Sant Jaume (phone: 318-2525), Poble Espanyol, Montjuïc (phone: 325-7866), and El Prat Airport (phone: 325-5829).

The US Consulate is at 33 Vía Layetana (phone: 319-9550).

Local Coverage – The best city map is published by Distrimapas (about $3), available at bookstores and newsstands throughout the city, and the tourist offices provide good free maps and brochures. There is no English-language paper published in Barcelona, but the weekly *Guía del Ocio* and monthly *Vivir en Barcelona* provide comprehensive lists of museums, nightspots, restaurants, and other attractions; the latter also carries an English-language section with tourist information.

Telephone – The area code for Barcelona is 93.

CLIMATE AND CLOTHES: Although Barcelona is a Mediterranean port, it can get a bit cold in winter. Temperatures range from a low of 44F in January to a high of 83F in August. Barcelona is a formal city. If you are planning to attend the opera, for instance, be aware that virtually all of the audience will be in formal dress. For daytime, casual attire will suffice.

 GETTING AROUND: Airport – Barcelona's airport, El Prat, handles both domestic and international flights, and is about 30 minutes from downtown by taxi; the fare ranges from $15 to $20. Trains run between the airport and Estació Central Sants, connecting with the *Metro* lines, every 20 minutes; the trip takes 15 minutes and the fare is approximately $1. Iberia's shuttle (*Puente Aereo*) has flights to and from Madrid every hour throughout the day.

Bus – More than 50 bus lines crisscross the city. The Barcelona Singular combined ticket (approximately $4.25 per day, $8.50 for 3 days) offers unlimited use of the #100 bus line, which links the main streets, the Tramvia Blau (blue tram) to Tibidabo, and the funicular and cable car on Montjuïc. *Casacas Rojas* (Red Jackets) on the #100 serve as city guides and will answer questions.

Car Rental – Cars are useful for day trips from Barcelona, but usually are more trouble than they are worth for touring in the city. All the major international and local car rental firms have offices at the airport.

Taxi – Taxis can be hailed while they cruise the streets, or ordered by telephone. During the day, *Lliure* or *Libre* in the window indicates that a cab is available; at night, a green light shines on the roof. Fares are moderate, and the city is divided into various fare zones.

Train – The main railway stations are Estació Central Sants, Avenida de Roma (phone: 322-4142), Estació de França, on Marqués de la Argentera (phone: 319-3200), and Estació Passeig de Gràcia, on Passeig de Gràcia-Aragó (phone: 216-0636). For fare and schedule information, contact *Spanish National Railways* (*RENFE*), 13 Passeig de Gràcia (phone: 322-4142).

Subway – A *Metro* sign indicates an entrance to Barcelona's modern, clean subway system. A *Pase Temporal* for 1, 3, or 5 days offers unlimited subway and bus travel on the 5 lines that serve the city.

 SPECIAL EVENTS: Religious holidays and saints' days are the occasion of numerous festivities in Barcelona. April 23 is the *Day of Sant Jordi* (St. George), patron saint of Catalonia. Flower stands overflow with roses, and bookstalls on Las Ramblas are bustling, because this is the day for lovers, and its gifts are a flower and a book. Bonfires, fireworks, dancing, and revelry mark the nights before the feast days of *Sant Joan* (St. John) and *St. Peter* (June 23 and 28, respectively). On Thursdays from June through September, the Guardia Urbana (city police) don scarlet tunics and white plumed helmets for a riding exhibition at 9 PM at the Pista Hipica "La Fuxarda," Montjuïc. The *Feast of Our Lady of Mercy,* honoring the city's patron saint, is celebrated the last week in September with folk dancing, fireworks displays, and general gaiety that includes teams of men forming *castellers* (human pyramids).

 MUSEUMS: Barcelonans love museums and exhibitions, and the city has several important museums in addition to those previously listed in *Special Places.*

Museu d'Art Modern (Museum of Modern Art) – Paintings and sculptures by Catalan artists little known outside the region, as well as 19th-century romantic and neo-classic paintings. Parc de la Ciutadella (phone: 319-5728).

Museu d'Automats (Museum of Automation) – Mechanical dolls and animals. Parc del Tibidabo (phone: 211-7942).

Museu d'Calzado (Shoemakers' Museum) – 1st-century slave sandals, 3rd-century shepherd's footware, and a collection of famous people's shoes. Plaça Sant Felip Neri.

Museu d'Etnològic (Ethnological Museum) – Specimens gathered by expeditions to Spanish-influenced cultures abroad. Passeig de Santa Madrona, Parque de Montjuïc (phone: 224-6402).

Museu del Futbol Club Barcelona (Barcelona Soccer Museum) – Trophies and videos highlighting the famous local soccer club's illustrious history. Camp Nou Stadium (phone: 330-9411).

Museu de Geolgia "Martorell" (Martorell Geological Museum) – A history of the region's geology. Parc de la ·Ciutadella (phone: 319-6895).

Museu Frederic Marés (Federico Marés Museum) – Romanesque and Gothic ceramics and paintings, including medieval wooden religious statuary, Roman busts, and Spanish stone figures. 10 Carrer del Comtes de Barcelona (phone: 310-5800).

Museu d'Militar (Military Museum) – Military uniforms, toy soldiers, models of forts, and a collection of 17th- to 19th-century guns. Parque de Montjuïc.

Museu de la Música – Old and antique musical instruments. 373 Diagonal.

Museu Picasso (Picasso Museum) – Collection reflecting Picasso's early sketches and posters from around 1900, as well as some of his later works. 15 Carrer de Montcada (phone: 319-6310).

 SHOPPING: Barcelona has been a textile center for centuries. Fashion-conscious Barcelonans believe that their city has more in common with Paris than Madrid, providing them with contemporary chic right at home. The avenues of Passeig de Gràcia and Rambla de Catalunya are lined with elegant shops featuring leatherware, furs, accessories, and jewelry for men and women, as well as boutiques carrying Spain's *moda joven* (youth fashion). Barcelona's three modern shopping centers are *Boulevard Rosa,* 55 Passeig de Gràcia; *Halley,* 62 Passeig de Gràcia; and *Via Wagner,* at Plaza Wagner. Stores are open daily from 9 AM to 8 PM, although some smaller shops may close between 1:30 and 4 PM. All are closed Sundays.

Adolfo Domínguez – The famous Galician designer for men. 89 Passeig de Gràcia.

Bd Ediciones de Diseño – Specializing in furniture and household objects designed by local artists and architects, as well as the latest in high tech and executive "toys." 291 Mayorca.

Jean Pierre Bua – Features the classic (but exciting) styles of noted designer Roser Marcé. 467 La Diagonal.

Centre Permanent D'Artesania – Beautiful wicker baskets, clay bowls, and other souvenirs smartly crafted by Catalan artisans. 55 Passeig de Gràcia.

Corte Inglés – A major branch of Spain's largest and most expensive department store chain, where everything from Lladró porcelains to Spanish leather gloves can be found. Plaça de Catalunya.

Loewe – A branch of Spain's best-known and most expensive purveyor of fine leather goods. 35 Passeig de Gràcia.

La Manual Alpargatera – The finest handmade leather shoes in Barcelona, featuring the *espardenyas* (espadrille) used for dancing the *sardana.* 2 Calle Aviñó.

Poble Espanyol – These 35 stores feature pottery, carvings, glassware, leather goods, and other typical folk crafts are made by traditional artisans from every region of Spain. Parque de Montjuïc.

Tema – A selection by Spanish designers Manuel Pina, Jesus del Pozo, and Jorge Gonsalves (a favorite of Queen Sofia). 10 Ferran Agulló.

Markets are very popular in Barcelona. The Els Encants antiques market is held every Monday, Wednesday, Friday, and Saturday in the Plaça de les Glóries; the Gothic antique market takes place every Thursday (except holidays) in the Plaça Nova; coins and postage stamps are traded and sold in the Plaça Reial, Sundays 10 AM to 2

PM; and the coin and book market at Ronda Sant Antoni takes place every Sunday from 10 AM to 2 PM.

SPORTS AND FITNESS: Barcelona is busy preparing for its role as host to the Summer Olympic Games in 1992; the sports-minded city already boasts many major facilities, including the 120,000-seat *Camp Nou* soccer stadium, the largest in Europe.

Bullfighting – Catalans claim they abhor bullfighting, and in fact most of the spectators' faces are those of tourists. It's usually possible, however, to catch a bullfight on Sundays between 5 and 6 PM at the *Plaça Monumental* and *Les Arenes* bullrings, at either end of the Gran Via de les Cortes Catalanes. Tickets can be bought at the rings or from the advance ticket office at 24 Muntaner.

Fitness Centers – Barcelona has a number of municipal sports centers that charge minimal admission for visitors. A favorite is the Piscina Bernardo Picornell, at *Club Natació Montjuïc,* with an outdoor Olympic-size pool for summer swimming and sunning, and an indoor pool open year-round (phone: 325-9281). Others include *Esportiu Can Carelleu* (phone: 203-7874), *Gimnas Municipal Montjuïc* (phone: 223-0266), and *Tenis Pompeia* (phone: 224-7926).

Golf – There are several golf courses in Barcelona and its environs, including the *Real Club de Golf "El Prat,"* near the airport (phone: 318-9190), *Club de Golf San Cugat,* San Cugat del Vallés (phone: 674-8400), and *Club de Golf Vallromanas,* 59 Via Augusta (phone: 568-0362).

Jogging – Parc de la Ciutadella, near the center of town, has a good track. The paths surrounding Montjuïc are also popular jogging spots.

Soccer – *Futbol Club (F.C.) Barcelona* represents the spirit of Catalonia, especially when the opponent is longtime rival *Real Madrid.* More than 125,000 fans regularly attend home games, played at *Camp Nou Stadium. Espanyol de Sarrià,* the other, less popular, "major league" club in town, plays at *Sarrià Stadium.*

Swimming – Take a dip in the waters that will host the Olympic swimming events at *Piscina Picornell,* on Montjuïc, near the main stadium (phone: 325-9281).

Tennis – Courts may be available at the *Barcelona Royal Tennis Club,* 5 Bosch I Gimpera (phone: 203-7758); and *Turó,* 673 La Diagonal (phone: 203-8958).

THEATER: Barcelona has a lively theater life, with everything from satirical reviews to musical theater. Most work is performed in Spanish or Catalan. Two popular theaters are *Apolo,* 59 Paral-el (phone: 241-4006), and *Victória,* 67 Paral-el (phone: 241-3985). Comedy/drama theaters include *Teatre Lliure,* 2 Leopoldo Alas (phone: 218-9251); *Teatre Romea,* 5 Hospitalet (phone: 317-7189); and *Teatre Polirama,* 115 Estudis (phone: 317-7599).

MUSIC: Musical groups offer recitals and concerts all year long. The opera season opens in November at the *Gran Teatro Liceo,* 1 San Pablo (phone: 318-9122). The *Municipal Orchestra* and visiting orchestras perform at the *Palau de la Música,* a dazzling 1908 landmark of Catalan modernism, 1 Amadeo Vives (phone: 301-1104). Every October, Barcelona hosts the *International Festival of Music,* featuring classical concerts at the *Palau de la Música* and elsewhere in the city.

NIGHTCLUBS AND NIGHTLIFE: Barcelona has plenty of action, but beware, since the city also has its share of muggers and purse snatchers. Be on the lookout for criminals on motorcycles and minibikes, who snatch purses from pedestrians and from cars parked or stopped at traffic signals. The city's pubs, bars, and cafés start to fill up between 10 and 11 PM, but they merely serve as a warm-up for the clubs and discotheques, which open at kick into high gear at 1 or 2 AM. A Las Vegas–style nightclub, *Scala Barcelona,* presents elaborate dinner shows and dancing, 47 Paseo de San Juan (phone: 232-6363). The *Gran Casino de Barcelona,* 26 miles (41.8 km) from the city, offers dining and gambling in a 19th-century chateau setting (phone: 893-3666). For flamenco try *El Cordobés,* 35 Rambles Capuchinos (phone: 317-6653); *Andalucia,* 27 Ramblas; and *El Patio Andaluz,* 242 Aribau (phone: 209-3375). Shows are continuous from 10 PM to 3 AM, but really get going after midnight, when the performers and the audiences are warmed up. Popular discotheques include *Bikini,* which features rock and Latin beats, 517 La Diagonal (phone: 230-5134); the *Up and Down,* with loud music downstairs and a restaurant and a more "sophisticated" club upstairs, 179 Numancia (phone: 204-8809); and *Studio 54,* a weekends-only favorite, boasting lots of elbow room and the best light show in town, 64 Paral-el (phone: 329-5454). For hot jazz, try the live jams at *La Cova del Drac,* 30 Tusset (phone: 216-5642).

BEST IN TOWN

CHECKING IN: Barcelona has always been short on hotel space; not surprisingly, the drive now is on to double the number of beds available in time for the 1992 Summer Olympics. In an already noisy city, the sounds of construction are an added intrusion. When making reservations, ask for a quiet room. By 1992, 5,000 new hotel rooms will have been added to the city's present 14,100-room hotel capacity, not only to accommodate Olympic visitors, but also to serve as permanent expansions of the city's tourism infrastructure to meet the demands of the 21st century. Additionally, in anticipation of the estimated half-million visitors expected to attend the Olympics, some of the world's most luxurious cruise ships will dock in Barcelona's harbor during the games to serve as overflow accommodations.

Expect to pay between $110 and $160 a night for a double room at one of Barcelona's expensive hotels; $55 to $100 at one that is moderately priced; and less than $50 at an inexpensive hotel. All telephone numbers are in the 93 area code unless otherwise indicated.

Avenida Palace – Polished brass and fancy carpets lend a tasteful, Old World atmosphere to this deluxe property. The fair-size, 229 rooms are air conditioned, cheerful, and quiet, with color TV sets and mini-bars. The public areas are adorned with sedate paintings, careful reproductions, and interesting antiques. The staff is carefully trained and attentive. 605 Gran Vía de les Corts Catalanes (phone: 301-9600). Expensive.

Condes de Barcelona – In the striking Art Nouveau Casa Batlló, which was refurbished in 1986 and converted into a luxury hotel. The 100 air conditioned rooms and suites feature all the amenities, and the location in the heart of the Eixample is ideal. The small lobby also leads to the excellent *Brasserie Condal* restaurant. 75 Passeig de Gràcia (phone: 215-0616). Expensive.

Gran Derby – The only one of its kind in Barcelona. All 39 rooms are air conditioned suites and duplexes, complete with a sitting room, color TV set, bar, and refrigerator. The very fashionable decor of black and white marble and the helpful staff make up for the somewhat inconvenient location. 28 Loreto (phone: 322-3215). Expensive.

Gran Sarriá – Near the Plaça Francesc Macià, it has been recently renovated and is a favorite of businesspeople. All 314 rooms are air conditioned with king-size beds. The *elite* floor features its own concierge for quicker and more personal service. 50 Avenida de Sarriá (phone: 410-6060). Expensive.

Majestic – A Barcelona classic, recently restored and refurbished, its 360 rooms are air conditioned and feature a range of amenities including color TV sets, in-room English-language movies, built-in hair dryers, and mini-bars. There is also a gymnasium, sauna, and rooftop swimming pool. Its central location is amid Gaudí's Art Nouveau buildings, fine restaurants, and shops. 70 Passeig de Gràcia (phone: 215-4512). Expensive.

Princesa Sofía – Part of the European HUSA chain, its 514 rooms are decorated in contemporary style, with large, tiled bathrooms, direct-dial telephones, color TV sets, and mini-bars. Fully air conditioned, the hotel features an indoor swimming pool, gym, sauna, and restaurants. Plaça de Pius XII (phone: 330-7111). Expensive.

Ramada Renaissance – Previously the grand old *Manila,* it has been completely refurbished and luxuriously modernized. Ideally placed near the Gothic quarter, it has 2 restaurants; the Renaissance Club rooms on the top 4 floors are extra-luxurious, featuring Minitel computer terminals and free breakfast. 111 Ramblas (phone: 318-6200). Expensive.

Ritz – Built in 1919, this deluxe aristocrat, where Barcelona society celebrates, sports a brand-new face and lives up to its reputation for superb service in an elegant, charming atmosphere. A favorite meeting place — especially during afternoon tea, which is served in the lounge with a string quartet softly playing — the hotel is the choice of many international celebrities. All 314 rooms are air conditioned and feature high ceilings and marble skirting boards. There is also a fine restaurant. 668 Gran Via de les Corts Catalanes (phone: 318-5200). Expensive.

Colón – An old favorite facing the cathedral in the Barri Gòtic, it has been recently refurbished, although the lovely old marble bathrooms remain. Clean, pleasantly decorated, with 161 air conditioned, high-ceilinged rooms. Rooms on the 6th floor have large, open terraces. 7 Avenida de la Catedral (phone: 301-1404). Moderate.

Derby – Sister to the *Gran Derby,* this elegant establishment features a novel decor highlighted by hushed colors, diffused lighting, and impressive wood trim and ornamentation. The 116 air conditioned rooms have private baths; those on the top floor have large terraces. The intimate piano bar adds an extra special touch. 21 Loreto (phone: 322-3215). Moderate.

Gala Placidia – Particularly suitable for families on long visits, its 28 suites have sitting rooms with fireplaces, dining areas, and refrigerators, as well as small bedrooms. 112 Vía Augusta (phone: 217-8200). Moderate.

Gran Calderón – Another long-time Barcelona favorite with the business crowd, recent renovations have given it a bright new image. The generously proportioned 244 rooms are air conditioned, and most have been equipped with the gadgets frequent business travelers expect. The rooftop swimming pool, sauna, and sun terrace command a splendid view of the city. 26 Rambla de Catalunya (phone: 301-0000). Moderate.

Regente – The gem of Barcelona's smaller establishments, on a quiet, tree-lined extension of Las Ramblas. All 78 rooms are comfortable, smartly decorated, with private baths and color TV sets. Door handles, wall panels, windows, and other fixtures are of the Art Nouveau sentiment. Breakfast is included in the rate, and there is also a rooftop pool, private garage, and a cozy bar. 76 Rambla de Catalunya (phone: 215-2570). Moderate.

Rialto – In the heart of the Barri Gòtic, this simple but stylish hotel is part of the Gargallo group, specializing in small, centrally located accommodations. All 112 rooms are air conditioned. 42 Ferrán (phone: 318-5212). Inexpensive.

 EATING OUT: Catalans eat late. Lunch is typically served from 1 to 3:30 PM in most restaurants, and dinner, between 8:30 and 11 PM. Check for the daily special — *menú del día,* usually a three-course meal with bread and wine — which restaurants are required by law to offer at a set price.

Catalans take pride in their cuisine, which is more sophisticated and French-oriented than that of the rest of Spain. Try the soup of lobster, crayfish, squid, mussels, and whitefish of various types called *zarzuela.* The most basic Catalan dish is *escudella i carn d'olla,* a hearty stew of sausage, beans, meatballs, and spices. The ubiquitous caramel custard, *crema catalana,* made with eggs, milk, sugar, and cinnamon, usually tops off the meal. Expect to pay $60 or more for a dinner for two in restaurants classified as expensive, $30 to $50 in the moderate range, and under $25 in the inexpensive places. All telephone numbers are in the 93 area code unless otherwise indicated.

Agut d'Avignon – A favorite for both lunch and dinner, this beautiful multi-level restaurant in the Gothic quarter has whitewashed walls, oak plank floors, and antique furnishings. Its traditional Catalan food — especially the duck with figs — is excellent. Winner of the International Personality of the Year Award in Gastronomy, owner-hostess Mercedes Giralt lends her considerable charm to it all. Closed August, Sundays, and Holy Week. Reservations essential. 3 Trinidad (phone: 302-6043). Expensive.

Ama Lur – Only a tiny plaque and a doorbell mark the entrance. After being "buzzed in," climb the stairs to the tall mahogany doors, and enter the drawing room with plush sofas and carved pillars. Once in the equally stunning dining room, begin with the cold melon soup, followed by one of the many veal or *merluza* (hake) specialties. Closed August, Sundays, holidays, and Holy Week. 275 Mallorca (phone: 215-3024). Expensive.

El Dorado Petit – In an elite neighborhood, this award-winning restaurant combines local and French dishes in a "new Catalan" style and elegance. For starters, try the shrimp salad vinaigrette, or the cold cod salad with cilantro and thyme. Entrées include *bacalao* wrapped in bell peppers, scallops in leek julienne, and goose liver and duck liver pâtés. Among the dessert specialties are exquisite homemade ice creams and sherbets. There is also a walk-through wine cellar. Closed Sundays and the first 2 weeks in August. 51 Dolors Monserdá (phone: 204-5506). Expensive.

Florián – Rosa Grau cooks while her husband, Javier, minds the front, where pictures line the walls. Pasta with sea urchin sauce, ravioli stuffed with four cheeses, and red mullet with black olives are examples of Rosa's flair with local products. Closed Sundays, Holy Week, 2 weeks in August, and Christmas. 20 Bertran i Serra (phone: 212-4627). Expensive.

Jaume de Provença – Innovative chef Jaume Bargues reacts well to what's available at the market. Frequent specialties include crab lasagna, sea bass stuffed with fresh salmon, and pig's trotters with roquefort cheese sauce. 88 Provença (phone: 230-0029). Expensive.

Neichel – When the taste buds crave something French, this luxurious and elegant restaurant is the place to visit. Revel in selections that might include rare slices of duck breast lavished with juniper and wild raspberries, lobster salad garnished with quail eggs and truffle strips, or a wonderful seafood platter of *merluza,* mollusks, and freshwater crab in two tasty sauces. Closed August, Sundays, holidays, Christmas week, and Holy Week. 16 bis Avenida Pedralbes (phone: 203-8408). Expensive.

Quo Vadis – Muted paneling, soft lights, and harmonious decor provide a pleasing ambience at this top establishment. Service is solicitous and the highly original international cuisine is excellent. Closed Sundays. Reservations essential. 7 Carmen (phone: 302-4072). Expensive.

Reno – Another impressive kitchen that uses local recipes in a classical way, *Reno*'s specialties include sole with freshwater crayfish, hake with anchovy sauce, and roast duck with honey and sherry vinegar. The *Menu Reno* offers a sample of the house's most popular dishes. 27 Tuset (phone: 200-9129). Expensive.

Azulete – Imaginative international cuisine is served here, and the house, with its gardens and fountain, is a delight. The dining room of this former mansion is actually a glass-enclosed garden. Tables are arranged around a decorative pool, surrounded by lush vegetation. Specialties include tiny medallions of pork, crowned with disks of mushroom purée, and broiled *lubina* (sea bass) with fresh dill. For dessert, try figs with strawberry-scented honey. Closed Sundays and November. 281 Via Augusta (phone: 203-5943). Expensive to moderate.

Arcs de Sant Gervasi – One of Barcelona's newer favorites, in the effervescent neighborhood near the Plaça Francese Maciá. Try the gratin of eggplant, ham, and tiny shrimp, or the rare slices of duck with zucchini mousse and pear slices. 103 Santoló (phone: 201-9277). Moderate.

Brasserie Flo – The atmosphere is Parisian; the meat dishes, especially the barbecue, are outstanding. A favorite place for café society, in jeans or tuxedo, and open late for the after-theater crowd. 10 Jonqueres (phone: 317-8037). Moderate.

Bota del Racó – Gigantic portions of savory Catalan specialties in a rustic atmosphere. Always crowded, but worth the (usually short) wait. Try the *parrilladas* (assorted grilled meat or fish). Closed Mondays. 232 Virgen de Montserrat (phone: 256-6002). Moderate.

Caracoles – At first glance, this looks like a tourist trap, but the good solid Catalan cooking is most impressive. Try *los caracoles* (snails); the langostinos are also fresh and delicious. Open daily. Reservations needed (but even so, you'll have to wait during rush hours). 14 Escudillers (phone: 302-3185). Moderate.

Casa Isidro – The morning market determines the selection of standard-setting Catalan dishes in this Barcelona landmark that was a favorite of Joan Miró. There is also an intelligently stocked wine cellar. Make reservations *at least* 2 days in advance! Closed Sundays, holidays, Christmas week, and Holy Week. 12 Las Flores (phone: 241-1139). Moderate.

Dorada – On an average day, this popular eatery serves 1,200 meals! The dining room is fitted with nautical relics, which suits the mostly seafood menu, which is more national than regional. Among the favorites are Galician scallops and *zarzuela* (seafood stew). Service is deft, and despite the crowds, never rushed. Closed Sundays. 44 Traversa de Gracià (phone: 200-6322). Moderate.

Señor Parellada – Near the *Museu Picasso,* this refined and ambitious restaurant serves traditional Catalan cuisine at very reasonable prices. Try the *escalivada,* a cold salad of red peppers, onions, eggplant, and thin slices of cod; or breast of duck with tarragon vinegar. Closed Sundays and holidays. 37 Carrer Platería (phone: 315-4010). Moderate.

Siete Puertas – A Barcelona favorite ever since it opened in 1936, it still retains its original decor and charm. Catalan cuisine including great seafood and homemade deserts are served in abundant proportions, and the large dining rooms are packed on weekends. 14 Passeig Isabel II, at the Barceloneta peninsula, near the waterfront (phone: 319-3033). Moderate.

Can Costa – Barceloneta, the peninsula protecting the port from the sea, is noted for its narrow streets, colorful atmosphere, and a plethora of wonderful seafood restaurants, such as this find. The freshest fish is served picnic-style at this delightful establishment. Open daily. Barceloneta (phone: 315-1903). Inexpensive.

Egipte – Very popular and unabashedly Bohemian, it's nestled behind the Boquería Market. That's why the food tastes so fresh. 12 Calle Jerusalem (phone: 317-7480). Inexpensive.

Els Quarte Gats – The third incarnation of the popular *Barri Gòtic* café. The original, which opened in 1897, was associated with the Belle Epoque Modernista movement, where Picasso had his first show. Dine on unpretentious Catalan dishes in a pleasant atmosphere, surrounded by the works of Tápies, Clavé, Miró, and other important Catalan painters. Closed holidays. 3 Carrer de Montsió (phone: 302-4140). Inexpensive.

Les Corts Catalanes – A wonderful vegetarian delicatessen, one block from the Passieg de Gràcia, serving everything from vegetable lasagna to cheese or spinach *empanadas* (pot pies). 603 Gran Via de les Corts Catalanes (phone: 301-0376). Inexpensive.

 TAPAS BARS: Barcelona has numerous *tapas* bars, the most colorful of which are on the avenues of Las Ramblas and in the area surrounding the *Picasso Museum.* Some of the popular choices include *Alt Heidelberg,* 5 Ronda Universitat; *Ideal Cocktail Bar,* 89 Aribau; *Pañol* and *Ramonet,* both in the Barceloneta port area; *Cervecería,* at the top of Las Ramblas; *Bodega La Plata,* 28 Calle Mercad; *Alba,* 168 Paris; and *Casa Tejada,* 3 Tenor Viñas.

EAST BERLIN

Most foreign visitors coming here for the first time find the short trip through the Berlin Wall an adventure full of the Cold War drama as portrayed in Len Deighton's *Funeral in Berlin* and John le Carré's *The Spy Who Came In from the Cold.* Once past the border formalities, however, the feeling of excitement gives way to the intriguing observation that East Berlin, though full of surprises, has little similarity to Cold War fictional fantasies. For this is a vigorous, multifaceted city, and if some of it lives in the past, it is more likely to be the past of bygone Prussian history than the cloak-and-dagger drama of Iron Curtain conflicts.

Strangely enough, it was The Wall, that sad reminder of Europe's political division, that brought about the condition of normalcy one finds everywhere in this metropolis of 1.1 million people. After World War II, East Germany was slowly bleeding to death. Thousands were escaping daily to the West, using the relatively unguarded route from East to West Berlin. Since The Wall went up in 1961, however, escape has become not only all but impossible but gradually unnecessary as well, as more and more East Germans become more and more content with their lives in this Communist country of which East Berlin has been the capital since 1949.

Though the ugly barbed wire is still very much of a raw wound on both sides of The Wall, the Iron Curtain is no longer as savagely impenetrable as it once was, with 1-day visas to visit East Berlin readily available to Westerners of all nationalities. Whatever the rights and wrongs of the division of Germany and Berlin, people in central Europe, and especially Berlin, have had to make their peace with a state of affairs that is in the hands of statesmen in far-off Moscow and Washington. And nowhere has this process of coping with the immutable laws of history affected people's lives more than in East Berlin. The effects can be seen and felt in every nook and cranny, but most especially in East Berliners' determined conviction that this is their home.

They are proud of what they have accomplished since 1945, when the ruins of war were the only sights to be seen in a city virtually bombed flat by the Allies. To some extent, this pride is justified, in view of the material achievements of the past decades. There is little visible poverty in East Germany, no unemployment, and everyone seems to have enough to eat. The people of East Germany are also proud of their industrial state, whose production ranks about tenth in the world. They boast greater productivity per capita than the USSR; a higher per capita income than Italy, Ireland, and socialist Eastern Europe; and oddly enough, more television sets per capita than France. Most observers attribute East Germany's progress to a combination of party discipline and the traditional German habit of hard work.

On the other hand, there is a notable shortage of luxury articles. West German radio and television transmit daily reminders of the capitalist world's wealth and cultural vitality, and this impression is reinforced by the constant stream of visitors from across The Wall. Since 1972, West Berliners have been making extensive use of the 45 days a year allotted them for visiting relatives and friends in East Berlin. As a result, jeans and rock music are as popular here as they are in Los Angeles or Munich, and the authorities in East Germany actually encourage non-Communist appetites. The West continues to fascinate people here, and Western currency (*valuta*) is much coveted, though little of this fascination is political.

In many respects, East Germany is a nation in the middle; besides being the westernmost country in the Communist bloc, it is also just about in the middle of Europe, where Eastern Europe meets Western. East Germany is bounded by Czechoslovakia on the south and the Baltic Sea on the north. Berlin is actually closer to Poland on the east than to West Germany on the west.

Recently spruced up for the tourist trade, East Berlin is still hardly a match for West Berlin, but it is no longer so shockingly shabby by contrast. Compared to West Berlin, there are far fewer people in the streets and fewer speak English, nightlife isn't much to rave about, and clothes aren't nearly as trendy. Yet East Berlin encompasses the oldest sections of Berlin, and it is a city in which those interested can glimpse a very different kind of social system at work.

The two cities — modern Communist Berlin and ancient Berlin — are curiously intermixed. On the site of the modern Palast der Republik, where East Germany's parliament meets, the Hohenzollerns built a palace and ruled first as electors of Brandenburg (from the early 15th century), then as kings of Prussia, and finally as German emperors. They made their small capital an architectural jewel, lining the main street — Unter den Linden — with magnificent baroque palaces. Although the war destroyed or severely damaged every one of these historical monuments, the Communist regime has spared no efforts in restoring most of them to their former splendor.

The old Prussian military flair is still one of the striking characteristics of East Berlin. The changing of the guard on Unter den Linden, replete with goose-stepping soldiers, lively martial music, and the pageantry of flags and banners, is a clear reminder that East Germany sees itself as the successor to what it calls the "benign" features of Prussia's heritage.

East Berlin, however, does not only dwell on past glory. The Communist authorities here have also gone about turning much of their new capital into a showcase modeled on Moscow. Nowhere is this more evident than in the Karl-Marx-Allee. Formerly Frankfurter Allee and Stalin Allee ("Rue de Debâcle" is the nickname wry East Berliners have given this example of early postwar reconstruction), this wide boulevard, with its typically Eastern European postwar architecture, represents the remodeling of the city in the "spirit of Communism." However, more recent architecture — at Alexanderplatz, for example — is more graceful and much more pleasing to the eye.

Despite widespread Western influence in matters of consumption and culture, the strong hand of the Soviet Union and its Communist allies is omnipresent. For 20 years, Walter Ulbricht, East Germany's Communist leader until 1971, ran a tight ship. No doubt about it: This is the capital of a linchpin

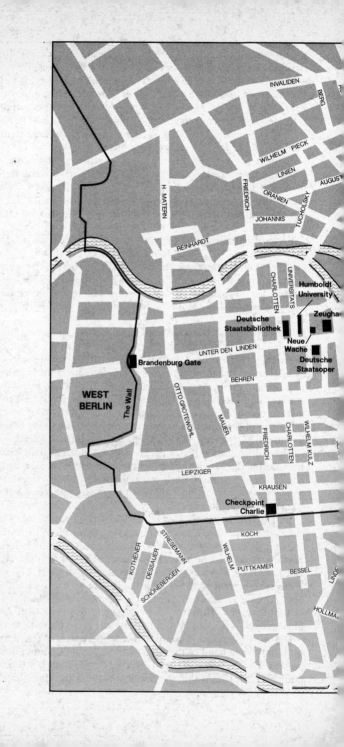

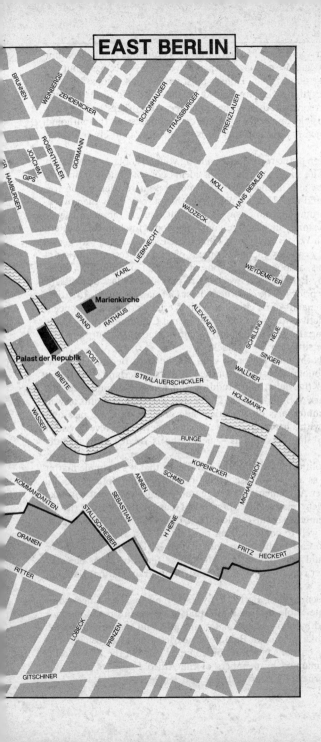

EAST BERLIN

Eastern bloc country, and one of Eastern Europe's economic giants. Communist banners and slogans are no longer as pervasive as they once were, but free enterprise is almost nonexistent. Hotels, most restaurants, shops, theaters, and just about everything else are owned by the state. Uniformed police, soldiers, and other representatives of the "first German workers' and farmers' state" are highly visible, and serve to reinforce the impression that although East Berlin may tolerate jeans and rock, it is nonetheless a closely controlled society.

There is opposition to the regime, even among young people, but it is rarely open or obvious. The small number of dissidents consist almost entirely of churchgoers, artists, and intellectuals, who most resent restrictions on free speech, assembly, and travel to the West. Another sore point is the government's policy regarding consumerism. A point at issue is the countrywide chain of *Intershop* stores, in which anyone may come to shop for Western goods, but only with Western currency. Only those East Germans with access to Western currency can buy the luxury items offered to Western tourists at a discount. (For this, among other reasons, it is not uncommon for visitors to be approached by East Berliners wanting to purchase dollars or deutsche marks.) Because its priorities lie elsewhere, East Germany is unable to satisfy all the consumer demands of its citizens. With Western propaganda concentrating on the restrictive situation in East Berlin and Communist propaganda significantly ignoring it, the truth is hard to know. One of the purposes of a visit is to judge the situation for yourself.

But that is hardly the only reason to visit. Unlike West Berlin, which has had to substitute economic prosperity for the loss of its hinterland, East Berlin is closely linked to the quiet, lake-studded, and forested countryside surrounding it, the Mark of Brandenburg. The people, although not quite as well dressed as their counterparts on the other side of The Wall, are pleasant, polite, and infused with a heartening sense of camaraderie. Wherever a visitor goes — museums, restaurants, hotels — he or she is treated with friendly courtesy.

The Cold War political division of the city means that it's a simple matter to use West Berlin as a base for discovering this fascinating "other" Berlin. And the Four Power Agreement of 1971 guarantees that your visit will take place in an atmosphere relatively free of political tension. (Since 1974, the US has maintained an embassy in this world capital.) John le Carré notwithstanding, you would do well to come in from the cold to East Berlin.

You can travel to East Berlin either with a West Berlin sightseeing bus or on your own. Should you choose the latter, take the subway or elevated S-Bahn to the border control point at the East Berlin train station, Bahnhof Friedrichstrasse.

Another way to enter East Berlin is by car or by foot via Checkpoint Charlie, an elaborate "hole in The Wall" that has been in operation since 1961. It can be used by non-German nationals only, and the formalities for visitors are exactly like the ones at Bahnhof Friedrichstrasse (see below). The one difference is the customs check if you come by car. On the West Berlin side of The Wall, manned by members of the Allied Forces, Checkpoint Charlie is at the corner of Friedrichstrasse and Kochstrasse.

To visit East Berlin, you will need a valid US passport and 5 deutsche marks for a day's visa, and you will have to exchange at least 25 deutsche marks to get in — at the manipulated rate of one deutsche mark for one East German mark — but you can exchange any amount above that minimum. Remember that you are never allowed to leave East Germany with East German marks in your pocket; you have to exchange money at the border control point when entering East Berlin; and you are required to spend at least the minimum amount before leaving. (Anything above the minimum amount can be changed back to Western currency at the border.) No Western printed matter is allowed into East Berlin, and there are strict rules regarding the amount and kinds of Western goods you can bring with you as gifts.

■ **SPECIAL NOTE:** You must leave East Berlin by midnight unless you get a special entry visa. Information and application forms are available from the Reisebüro in East Berlin (the East German government's official travel agency; see *Sources and Resources*), from US travel agents, the East German Embassy in Washington, Reisebüro-appointed agencies in Western Europe, and Reisebüro offices in Eastern Europe. Processing can take up to 8 weeks. Once the application is processed, the government issues a Visa Entitlement Certificate, which allows you to obtain a visa at the border or from the embassy in Washington. (Transit visas are issued at the border if you present a visa for the next country.) Savvy travelers anxious to see other parts of East Germany stay at an East Berlin hotel, where visas are often issued (with the help of the hotel concierge) in a single day.

EAST BERLIN AT-A-GLANCE

SEEING THE CITY: The slender spire of the Fernsehturm (television tower) climbs to a height of 1,209 feet above the city and The Wall. Built in 1969, it is Europe's second tallest tower. A revolving sphere at 655 feet is decked out with studio and transmission facilities as well as with a restaurant and café, from which there is a magnificent view of both Berlins. Open daily. Between Alexanderplatz and Marx-Engels-Platz (phone: 212-3333).

SPECIAL PLACES: Most of the city has been laid out in a grid pattern, making it easy to get around. Orient yourself on the important downtown streets: Friedrichstrasse runs north to south, Unter den Linden and Karl-Marx-Allee, east to west. The center of the city is on an island in the Spree River. Most of downtown is negotiable by foot. For outlying areas, use the U-Bahn (subway), buses, streetcars, or S-Bahn (aboveground trains). See *Getting Around.*

DOWNTOWN

Unter den Linden – Some 1,500 yards long and almost 70 yards wide, this avenue is in the very heart of East Berlin. Originally laid out to connect the royal palace with the hunting preserve, the Tiergarten, it got its name from the rows of linden trees that were planted on both sides and in the center of the wide boulevard. In the 18th and 19th centuries, a number of magnificent structures were built along the boulevard. Although many were bombed in the last war, the government has faithfully restored those that survived.

Zeughaus (Arsenal) – Built between 1695 and 1706, this lovely baroque structure is the oldest on Unter den Linden. Set on the Spree, it overlooks historic Museum Island (Museumsinsel). Originally an arsenal (hence the name), the building now houses the *Museum für Deutsche Geschichte* (Museum of German History), which is devoted to a Marxist view of German history. Closed Fridays. 2 Unter den Linden (phone: 200-0591).

Neue Wache (The New Guard House) – Built in 1818, this has been a monument to the victims of fascism and militarism since 1960. It is guarded by members of the People's Army, and there is a colorful ceremonial changing of the guard every Wednesday at 2:30 PM. 4 Unter den Linden.

Humboldt University – Erected in the mid-18th century, it became Friedrich Wilhelm University in 1810. Since 1949, this, the largest university in East Germany, has been known by its present name. Famous teachers included Hegel, Max Planck, and Einstein; Marx and Engels were students here. 6 Unter den Linden.

Deutsche Staatsbibliothek (German State Library) – Built in the early 20th century, the library occupies the site of the former Prussian State Library; the latter's stock of books that remained in East Berlin during the war has been stored here. The rest are at the Staatsbibliothek in West Berlin. 8 Unter den Linden.

Brandenburger Tor (Brandenburg Gate) – There is very little of historical interest between the Deutsche Staatsbibliothek and this massive Berlin landmark at the western end of Unter den Linden. The Brandenburg Gate has been inaccessible to cars and pedestrians since August 1961, when The Wall was erected only a few yards away. The closest you can get to the gate on this side of The Wall is the corner of Otto-Grotewohl-Strasse (formerly Wilhelmstrasse), about 100 yards away. This late-18th-century triumphal arch is brilliantly lit at night. Pariser Platz.

Altes Palais (Old Palace) – On the south side of Unter den Linden, the first historic structure one sees is the Old Palace. Built in 1836, it was the residence of Emperor William I during the last 50 years of his life. It is now used by Humboldt University. 9 Unter den Linden.

Alte Bibliothek (Old Library) – The Prussian State Library was here until 1914. Built in the late 18th century, it is now part of Humboldt University. Set back from Unter den Linden, on Bebelplatz. (Formerly Opernplatz, made famous during the Nazi burning of books in 1933.)

St. Hedwigs Kathedrale – This Roman Catholic cathedral dates from the late 18th century and was built according to plans laid down by Frederick the Great (who was by all appearances impressed by the Pantheon in Rome). Gutted in the war, it has been just as carefully restored as most other Unter den Linden landmarks. Bebelplatz.

Deutsche Staatsoper (The German State Opera) – The opera house was built in 1743 and burned down 100 years later. Rebuilt, it was twice destroyed by bombs during the last war. Almost 1,500 people can attend performances here (for ticket information see "Music," *Sources and Resources*). 7 Unter den Linden.

Palais Unter den Linden – Originally built in the 17th century, it was known as the Kronprinzenpalais until 1945. The rebuilt façade, however, is modeled on the one added in 1857. Two German emperors were born here, and during the Weimar Republic, it was used as a museum of contemporary art; today the government maintains it as an official guest house. 1 Unter den Linden.

Palast der Republik – Past Unter den Linden, on the island in the Spree, this was the site of the former royal palace, severely damaged during the war. The Hohenzollerns resided here from 1451 to 1918. Dismantled in 1950, it is now a multipurpose building, housing, among other things, the East German parliament, theaters, and restaurants and cafés. The architecture is extremely modern. Marx-Engels-Platz.

Staatsratsgebäude – The East German government, the State Council, meets in this modern structure. The centerpiece is one of the portals from the former royal palace. South side of Marx-Engels-Platz.

Museumsinsel – On the north side of Marx-Engels-Platz, surrounded on three sides by the Spree River, is one of the world's largest and most magnificent museum complexes. The buildings date to the 19th and early 20th centuries. The *Altes Museum* accommodates contemporary paintings and the *Cabinet of Engravings,* containing 135,000 prints by German and foreign masters (15th to 18th century); among the latter treasures are Botticelli's illustrations of scenes from Dante's *Divine Comedy.* Across the street is the *National Gallery,* which houses 19th- and early-20th-century art. Behind this is the *Pergamon Museum,* whose collection of antique art is one of the most important in the world. Its showpieces are the huge Pergamon Altar and the remarkable Roman Market Gate of Miletus, both 2nd century BC. The entrance gate to the ancient city of Babylonia and the procession street are also overwhelming sights. In this building are also the *Far Eastern Collection,* the *Museum of Ethnography,* the *Near Eastern Museum,* and the *Islamic Museum.*

At the northernmost tip of this island of museums is the *Bode Museum,* once the famed *Kaiser Friedrich Museum.* It now houses the *Egyptian Museum,* the *Early Christian and Byzantine Collection,* the *Picture Gallery,* the *Sculpture Collection,* the *Cabinet of Coins* and the *Museum of Pre- and Proto-History.* Among the treasures here are such masterpieces of German sculpture as the 12th-century Naumburg Crucifix and the Winged Altarpiece from Minden Cathedral (15th century).

Except for the *Near Eastern Museum* and part of the antique collection, both at the *Pergamon Museum,* the *Museumsinsel* is closed Mondays and Tuesdays.

Marienkirche (St. Mary's Church) – Just past the *Museumsinsel,* in the shadows of the Fernsehturm, is St. Mary's, Berlin's second oldest church. First erected in 1240, it is a pleasant combination of Gothic and neo-classical styles. Karl-Liebknecht-Str.

Nicolai Quarter – A charming 16th-century neighborhood, destroyed by bombs in World War II and later rebuilt, it's perfect for a leisurely stroll through narrow streets, replete with gas lanterns and several period taverns, as well as for a visit to the city's oldest church, Nikolaikirche (ca. 1230) or to the Ephraim Palais (1766). Between the Spree and City Hall (Rathaus).

Jüdischer Friedhof Weissensee (Jewish Cemetery) – In the Weissensee district, this is said to be the largest Jewish cemetery in Europe. Recently restored by the East German government, it contains thousands of graves, all marked by large, ornate tombstones in late-19th- and early-20th-century style. Male visitors must wear hats. Closed Fridays after 2 PM and on Saturdays. 45 Herbert-Baum-Str.

SUBURBS

Sowjetisches Ehrenmal – Within the confines of verdant Treptower Park, not far from the left bank of the Spree, is this huge Soviet War Memorial. Dedicated in 1949, it honors more than 5,000 Soviet soldiers who fell in the battle for Berlin in 1945. Much of the material used came from the ruins of Hitler's Reich Chancellery. Open daily. Entrance from Puschkinallee and Am Treptower Park.

Tierpark – East Berlin's zoo was opened in 1955 on the grounds of Friedrichsfelde Palace. The animals are shown as far as possible in herds or family groups, in spacious enclosures that blend with the landscape. Open daily. 125 Am Tierpark (phone: 510-0111).

■**EXTRA SPECIAL:** Much of East Berlin's area is water; the Spree River and its tributaries flow through the city for a total of 20 miles before joining the Havel in West Berlin. The extensive forests in the outlying areas to the south combine with the waterways to form a vacationer's paradise. You might enjoy a scenic boat ride with the Weisse Flotte, a fleet of 60 white excursion ships that ply these waters every day from March to September (phone: 27120). Boats depart eight times a day from the piers on the Spree at the Treptower Park S-Bahn station. (This trip is mostly for Berliners, so English is rarely spoken on board.)

You can get on and off these boats as often as you wish. Along the way you might want to stop off at these sights: the Müggelturm, a 98-foot-high tower near Berlin's largest lake; the Rathaus of Köpenick; and the Mecklenburger Dorf in Köpenick, a replica of a North German village of the last century, featuring typical snacks and beverages at very reasonable prices.

The sights may be approached by land (subway, streetcar, S-Bahn, or bus) as well as by water (closed Mondays and Tuesdays).

SOURCES AND RESOURCES

 TOURIST INFORMATION: General information, brochures, and maps can be obtained at the Fernsehturm. Open daily. Between Alexanderplatz and Marx-Engels-Platz (phone: 212-4675). The best detailed map, *Berlin Stadtatlas,* is available at bookstores in West Berlin only. The East German Travel Agency (Reisebüro) maintains a special Tourist Service Bureau for foreign visitors on the first floor of its skyscraper at 5 Alexanderplatz (phone: 215-4402). Open daily.

The US Embassy is at 4-5 Neustädtische Kirchstrasse (phone: 220-2741).

Local Coverage – A monthly calendar of events, entitled *Wohin in Berlin,* is available at the Fernsehturm, at the main hotels, and at most newsstands in East Berlin; it is in German only. Information in English can be obtained both at the Fernsehturm and at the Tourist Service Bureau on Alexanderplatz. Listings of cultural events can also be requested from the tourist office in West Berlin. East Germany's largest bookstore, *Das Internationale Buch,* is at Spandauer Str. and Karl-Liebknecht-Str., above the *Gastmahl des Meeres* restaurant (phone: 210-9431).

Food – There is no food guide to East Berlin. We suggest that you buy a helpful volume (in German) entitled *Berlin von 7 bis 7;* available in West Berlin only, it contains listings for East Berlin.

Telephone – The area code for East Berlin is 02. All telephone numbers in East Berlin can also be reached from West Berlin by first dialing the area code 0372.

 CLIMATE AND CLOTHES: The weather is very similar to that in the northeastern US, although it is not as hot in summer or as cold in winter. The temperature is rarely above 70F (19C) or below freezing. Rain can fall at any time of the year.

You'll find dress to be more conservative in East Berlin than in West Berlin. Many restaurants require that men wear a necktie, and some have a selection of ties from which patrons may choose.

 GETTING AROUND: Airport – Schöenfeld Airport handles international flights only (there are no domestic flights in East Germany). It is 45 minutes from downtown by taxi with a fare of 30 East German marks (about $4); it takes an hour to travel by S-Bahn. For information about buses to the airport from West Berlin, phone 301-8028.

Car Rental – The major American firms are represented. You can get information at the East German Travel Agency (see above).

Subway, Bus, and Train – Equipped with the same kinds of yellow cars as in West Berlin, East Berlin's two subway (U-Bahn) lines will get you to many places in the city. There is a good network of buses and streetcars, as well as an extensive interurban railroad system, the S-Bahn, which reaches most parts of the city and beyond. East Germans are not without a sense of humor; the streetcars — made in Czechoslovakia, but too heavy for the East Berlin cobblestone track beds — are called "Dubček's

Revenge," referring to the former Czech leader and the dislodged cobblestones. Keep in mind that you may not leave the city limits if you only have a day's visa. Maps are available at the Fernsehturm or at the East German Travel Agency (see above).

The main railway station is Hauptbahnhof, at the corner of Am Hauptbahnhof and Strasse der Pariser Kommune (phone: 49531 for schedule and fare information on local trains; 49541 for international trains).

Taxi – Do not hail taxis in the streets. There are taxi stands all over town. To call a taxi in the downtown area, dial 3644 or 3646.

SPECIAL EVENTS: Every autumn, the city puts on an ambitious theater and music festival. Another venerable traditional event, and one that appeals to people of all ages, is the annual *Christmas Fair,* held on the open area between Alexanderplatz and Jannowitz Brücke from the end of November to a week before Christmas.

MUSEUMS: In addition to the Zeughaus and the museums in the *Museum-sinsel* complex, described in *Special Places,* there is one additional institution worth a visit: *Märkisches Museum,* 5 Am Köllnischen Park (phone: 270-0514), which surveys Berlin's history and is one of the best of its kind in Europe (closed Mondays and Tuesdays).

SHOPPING: The opportunities are limited. Most stores belong to the state chains and offer items whose quality often leaves much to be desired. However, Western goods at low prices can be had at the *Intershop* stores at the *Grand, Metropol, Palast, Unter den Linden, Berolina,* and *Stadt Berlin* hotels as well as at Schöenefeld Airport. You must pay in Western currency at the *Intershops.*

Keep in mind that the West Berlin customs authorities will not allow you to bring back more than 200 cigarettes or one bottle of liquor if you have spent only a day in East Berlin. The *Intershops* and the following recommended stores accept Diners Club and American Express credit cards, except for *Haus des Kindes:*

Glas/Porzellan – Crystal and china. 62 Karl-Marx-Allee.

Haus des Kindes – Department store for children's clothing and toys. South side of Strausberger Platz.

Das Internationale Buch – East Germany's largest bookstore. Spandauer-Str. corner of Karl-Liebknecht-Str.

Pelzmoden – Furs. 37-39 Unter den Linden.

Uhren/Schmuck – Watches and jewelry. 14 Unter den Linden.

SPORTS AND FITNESS: Fitness Centers – East Berlin has virtually no fitness centers; the only ones available are at the *Grand, Metropol,* and *Palast* hotels (see *Best in Town*) and are open only to registered guests.

Jogging – A good, central park for running is Friedrichshain Volkspark, between Friedenstrasse and Am Friedrichshain. Bus #57 travels there from the *Grand, Metropol,* and *Palast* hotels.

THEATER: Berlin's noble theater tradition continues unabated under the postwar East German regime. The classical repertoire holds sway at the *Deutsches Theater,* 13a Schumannstr. (phone: 287-1225), and — at the same address — at the intimate *Kammerspiele,* which was founded in 1906 by Max Reinhardt (phone: 287-1226). Another small stage, the *Maxim Gorki Theater,* also performs plays from the classical repertoire as well as dramas by the Russian playwright. For Brecht fans, a visit to the *Berliner Ensemble* — which the German dramatist founded in 1948 — is a must, at Bertolt-Brecht-Platz (phone: 282-3160). Genuine, albeit slightly muted, political and social satire can be enjoyed at the *Distel,* whose shows are performed at two small theaters at 101 Friedrichstr. (phone: 207-1291) and 9 Degnerstr. (phone: 376-5174). Tickets to all theater performances in the city can be bought directly at the box offices; they can also be ordered at the ground-floor theater and concert ticket counter of the theaters' visitors service at the *Palast* hotel (closed Sundays), Spandauer Str. (phone: 212-5258/5902).

MUSIC: Some of the world's best opera performances are heard at the 18th-century *Deutsche Staatsoper,* 7 Unter den Linden (phone: 207-1362). No less renowned, the *Komische Oper,* at 55-57 Behrenstr. (phone: 229-2555), is much more modern in its approach to opera. Some of the world's best orchestras perform in two concert halls in the newly restored *Schauspielhaus* (built in 1820), Platz der Akademie (phone: 227-2129 or 227-2122). International pop and folk music stars perform at the theater in Palast der Republik, Marx-Engels-Pl. (phone: 238-2354). If you are lucky enough to get tickets, you can also enjoy some of Europe's best pop and rock music in East Berlin, performed by such East German groups as the *Puhdys,* at the new *Friedrichstadtpalast,* 107 Friedrichstr. (phone: 283-6474). Tickets are available at box offices or at the government travel agency.

NIGHTCLUBS AND NIGHTLIFE: For obvious reasons, East Berlin's nightlife is nothing to write home about. There are two relatively lively night spots, each featuring dancing to live music as well as stage shows. There is a cover charge at the *Moskva-Bar,* 34 Karl-Marx-Allee (phone: 279-4052). At the *Lindencorso,* you can not only dance to live music in the *Konzertcafé,* you can also enjoy interesting musical shows and revues in the 1st-floor *Nachtbar Havanna* (cover charge; closed Tuesdays and Wednesdays), 17 Unter den Linden (phone: 220-2461). If it is just a quiet time you want, with drinks and snacks, two interesting pub-like places in historic settings can be recommended: *Raabediele* (open daily), in Ermeler Haus, 10-12 Märkisches Ufer (phone: 275-5103); and *Zur letzten Instanz* (closed weekends), 16-17 Waisenstr. (phone: 212-5528). After dark, singles gather at the *Pinguin Bar,* 39 Rosa-Luxemburg-Str. (phone: 282-7432), for dancing.

BEST IN TOWN

CHECKING IN: Compared to most Western European cities, East Berlin offers a small selection of comfortable hotel accommodations. The widespread destruction of World War II is largely to blame for this situation as well as the fact that the authorities have given higher priority to other problems, like housing and industry. Nevertheless, increased prosperity in the entire Eastern bloc and the country's need for foreign exchange — especially from the West — have inspired a recent spate of hotel construction. Our offerings, though meager, include a number of those hotels.

Remember: You will need a special entry visa (valid for more than a day) if you want to stay overnight in East Berlin. For information on this and for listings of more modest, although much less comfortable accommodation, consult the government travel agency (see *Sources and Resources*).

The hotels in our listings have a bath or shower in every room, and the rooms are all equipped with telephones. Each hotel has a restaurant on the premises, and those in the expensive category have an *Intershop* (see *Shopping*). All can provide access for guests in wheelchairs. Reservations must be made in advance. Hotel rates are high for visitors from the West; in fact, they are double the price charged to guests from Eastern bloc countries. For a double room in those hotels we have classed as expensive, expect to pay $150 and up; $70 to $145 in the moderate category; under $70 in the inexpensive class. Payment must be made in Western currency or by credit card. All telephone numbers are in the 02 area code unless otherwise indicated.

Grand – Right in the historic downtown area, this hotel offers authentic luxury and comfort. The 350 well-appointed rooms, the spacious lobby, and the 14 restaurants and cafés all seem so "Western" that it's hard to avoid a little disorientation at this elegant premises in the middle of a workers' state. Many Europeans stay here happily when West Berlin hotels are full. 158-164 Friedrichstr. (phone: 20920). Expensive.

Metropol – This handsome 340-room high-rise was built in the mid-1970s by a Swedish firm and is without doubt one of the best hotels in town. Extras are a sauna and a garage. Both accommodations and service are bound to appeal to those used to Western European luxury hotels. 150-153 Friedrichstr. (phone: 22040). Expensive.

Palast – A 600-room hotel that provides first class service, luxurious accommodations, and a good view of the city. Its restaurants serve a variety of cuisines from Asian to French. 5 Karl Liebknecht Str. (phone: 2410). Expensive.

Berolina – Pleasantly set back from bustling Karl-Marx-Allee, this 300-plus-room hotel offers first class service and comfort. Restaurant and cozy grill/bar on the premises. 31 Karl-Marx-Allee (phone: 210-9541). Moderate.

Stadt Berlin – In the middle of East Berlin's downtown area, its 994 rooms make it the largest in the city. Right behind the hotel is Alexanderplatz; closed off to automobile traffic, the square is ringed by restaurants, stores, the Fernsehturm, and other public buildings. It has a sauna and a garage. Alexanderplatz (phone: 2190). Moderate.

Hospiz am Bahnhof Friedrichstrasse – Near the rail entry to East Berlin, this clean, well-run hospice has no frills, but its 110 rooms are comfortable and reasonably priced. 8 Albrechtstr. (phone: 284030). Inexpensive.

 EATING OUT: Continuing an old Berlin tradition, East Germany's capital offers a large number of good restaurants. Most of them are in the downtown area, and the food ranges from native German to continental to ethnic (chiefly Eastern European). In general, though, restaurants here are inferior to those of West Berlin.

Prices are quite reasonable. A dinner for two, with drinks and wine, costs about $30 or more at restaurants in the expensive category; between $20 and $30 in the moderate range; and less than $20 at places classified as inexpensive. Tips are included in the bill. All telephone numbers are in the 02 area code unless otherwise indicated.

Zur Goldenen Gans – The "Golden Goose" is the pride of the *Grand* hotel. The food and decor are Thuringian, with such specialties as roast goose and grilled sausages with bacon-laden potato salad. Native East German red wines are featured. It is one of the rare spots in the *Grand* that accept East German marks, so this is a good place to spend the currency you were forced to buy at the border. Open daily. Reservations necessary. 158-164 Friedrichstr. (phone: 20920). Expensive.

Panorama – A fitting name for a restaurant on the 37th floor of the *Stadt Berlin* hotel. The food almost equals the marvelous view. Try the daily specialties. Open daily. Reservations necessary. Alexanderplatz (phone: 2190). Expensive.

Ganymed – On the Spree, near Bahnhof Friedrichstrasse (handy if you arrive by subway or S-Bahn). As at many restaurants here, there is background music. The atmosphere is comfortable and intimate. Continental food and good wines. Open daily; supper only on Mondays. Reservations advised. 5 Schiffbauerdamm (phone: 282-9540). Expensive to moderate.

Metropol – This hotel dining room, tastefully decorated, features rustic Gemütlichkeit. The food is continental and of the best standard. Open daily. Reservations advised. 150-153 Friedrichstr. (phone: 22040). Expensive to moderate.

Stockinger – Simply furnished, but still one of the city's finest restaurants. Along with traditional German fare, the menu features several exotic Oriental dishes. The big hit, though, is the 2-ounce can of Molossol caviar for under $30. Closed Sundays and Mondays. Reservations advised. 61 Schönhauser Allee (phone: 448-3110). Expensive to moderate.

Fernsehturm – Europe's second largest tower (described in *Seeing the City*) has a revolving café-restaurant from which, at a height of 655 feet, you get a breathtaking all-around view of East and West Berlin. The food is also good. There is a $3 admission charge, and you have to be finished within an hour. Open daily. Reservations advised from 10 AM to 2 PM. Between Alexanderplatz and Marx-Engels-Platz (phone: 212-3333). Moderate.

Moskva – Worth a visit just to sample its Russian specialties. Open daily. Reservations advised. 34 Karl-Marx-Allee (phone: 270-0341). Moderate.

Offenbach Stuben – This intimate, cozy restaurant is one of the few eateries here that is privately run. The German and continental cuisine are fine, as are the beverages. Closed Sundays and Mondays. Reservations advised. 8 Stubbenkammerstr. (phone: 448-4106). Moderate.

Palast der Republik – On the site of the former Prussian royal palace the authorities put up this huge multipurpose building in the mid-1970s (see *Special Places*). Three large restaurants offer good continental food. The *Spree* is closed Mondays; the *Palast* is closed Tuesdays; and the *Linden* closes Wednesdays. Reservations advised. No credit cards. Marx-Engels-Platz (phone: 238-2364). Moderate.

Zum Stilbruch – Once a traditional Berlin tavern, now a small and cozy restaurant. The continental dishes are well prepared and efficiently served at prices that prevailed in West Germany 25 years ago. The specialties are the Eastern European dishes (upon request). Closed weekends. Reservations advised. 84 Florastr. (phone: 483-0494). Moderate.

Gastmahl des Meeres – Fish is the only dish served in this conveniently located restaurant in city center. East Germany's largest bookstore, *Das Internationale Buch* (see *Sources and Resources*) is right above the ground-floor dining room. Slightly more expensive is *Rendezvous für Feinschmecker,* the fancy grill one floor below street level where fish also reigns supreme. Open daily. No reservations necessary. Spandauer Str., at the corner of Karl-Liebknecht-Str. (phone: 212-3286). Moderate to inexpensive.

Ermeler Haus – If you prefer to avoid the hustle and bustle of the immediate downtown area, this is for you. The baroque structure, built in 1703, is one of the few historic buildings left, aside from those on Unter den Linden. The interior is all rococo, as is the restaurant, which offers good continental dishes in intimate surroundings. Open daily. Reservations advised. 10-12 Märkisches Ufer (phone: 275-5103). Inexpensive.

Möwe – Across the Spree from Bahnhof Friedrichstrasse and down the road a bit is this intimate, tastefully appointed grill-restaurant. *Möwe,* German for dove, is the symbol of the local artists' association, whose club this is. It is, however, open to the public. This pleasant place is frequented by an intelligent, wide-awake crowd. The kitchen is praiseworthy: continental cuisine, with a nod to the East. Closed Mondays. No reservations necessary. No credit cards. 18 Hermann-Matern-Str. (phone: 282-5741). Inexpensive.

Müggelsee-Perle – Recently rated as one of East Germany's top restaurants. The fish, fowl, and game dishes are best; also try the Berlin pea soup. On the shore of East Berlin's largest lake, Grosser Müggelsee, the restaurant is accessible by excursion ship (see *Extra Special*) as well as by bus and car. Open daily. Reservations not needed. Am Grossen Müggelsee (phone: 657-3044). Inexpensive.

WEST BERLIN

The first fact of life in West Berlin is location — not geography, but location. West Berlin is smack in the heart of East Germany — 110 miles from the West German border, and the same distance from the Baltic Sea in the north and Czechoslovakia to the south. It is only 52 miles from the Polish border at the Oder River. West Berlin is closer to Warsaw than it is to Munich. The city has had only 4 decades to get used to the sobering reality that after 300 years it is no longer the political center of Germany. West Berlin — the cultural center and wellspring of German life — is very far from the rest of West Germany.

In 1963, when John F. Kennedy told thousands of cheering Germans that he, too, was a Berliner, he made a political statement of rare depth and resonance. Not only did it sum up the current state of the Cold War — very frigid, indeed, since the building of the Berlin Wall 2 years earlier — but its unspoken promise of a worldwide community of sympathy for the plight of West Berliners managed to touch and soothe the profound anxiety of the city and its residents. For 15 years, West Berliners had lived in an isolation made more desolate by the overpowering cultural and historic importance of their city before World War II. Long gone was the imperial Berlin that ruled Germany until World War I; gone was the devil-may-care Berlin of the 1920s and early 1930s so admirably captured by Christopher Isherwood in its mad gaiety and decadence; gone even were the days of terrible power of the Third Reich. Berlin was a capital city without a country. And then in 1961 the city was irreversibly truncated, and West Berliners saw the few treasured historic buildings that had survived the war disappear behind the blank and pitiless concrete face of The Wall. As The Wall went up, they lost family, friends, city, and heritage overnight. This radical surgery left a wake of shock, an anger that had hardly begun to dissipate when President Kennedy visited in 1963. It also left a stubborn determination to remain free, which more than any other emotion from that dark period still drives the city today.

The division of Berlin, now a fact of life for West Berlin's 1.9 million and East Berlin's 1.1 million people, began in 1944, when the US, Great Britain, and the Soviet Union, meeting in London, divided not only the city, but all of Germany, into occupied zones.

Because no written Soviet guarantee of access from West Germany existed, the Western Allies were unable to prevent Moscow from launching a land blockade on West Berlin in 1948. It took a whole year of a massive Allied airlift to force the Soviets to back down. West Berlin had been saved from slow starvation, but 70 Allied airmen and 8 German workers died trying to keep West Berlin's lifeline open. The city divided along Cold War political lines into two separate municipal entities. Soviet threats against West Berlin, which continued throughout the 1950s, culminated in the overnight building of The Wall by the East German Communist regime on August 13, 1961. The concrete barrier effectively sealed off the 185 square miles of West Berlin from the 156 square miles of East Berlin. That ugly 9-foot-high symbol of what ails Europe's body politic kept the people of West Berlin separated from East Berlin. Nevertheless, thousands of Berliners on either side of the dividing line continued to maintain bonds of blood and friendship.

This effort was made easier in 1971 when the three Western Allies met with the Soviet Union and produced the Four Power Agreement on Berlin to reduce East-West tension over the city. Since then, access to West Berlin from West Germany has been assured, and both halves of the city have settled down to a relatively normal existence. Nevertheless, West Berlin continues to be the only city in Europe under military occupation. In the Western sectors, sovereignty is still exercised by the Americans, the British, and the French; and the 13,000 Allied troops here are a visible reminder for the West Berliners that Western guarantees enable them to live and work in freedom. Although they have the last word, the occupying powers have delegated civil authority in the city to the West Berliners and have allowed West Berlin to enter into close legal, monetary, and economic ties with West Germany. Political democracy is now deeply entrenched in West Berlin.

World War II and its aftermath gave the heart of the old city to East Berlin, and the new, truncated West Berlin, rising from the ashes of the war, has had to create its own urban essence. That it has succeeded in this massive enterprise is an understatement.

Since the war devastated Berlin, construction of new buildings has greatly changed the appearance of the city. A small part of the architecture of the past — the majestic Charlottenburg and Bellevue palaces, for example — has managed to survive war and change. But Tegel Airport, as well as numerous hospitals, schools, factories, businesses, and housing projects, have all been built in a kind of anonymous contemporary style — many of the buildings are high-rises — and at a pace that continues unabated. In 1987, the city's International Building Exhibition, a massive program that entailed the reconstruction and renovation of many war-struck districts in West Berlin, was completed. The glitz and the glitter of Kurfürstendamm, West Berlin's prestigious international thoroughfare, have become its trademark.

But what makes West Berlin an outstanding place in which to live and to visit is its culture. Continuing its prewar role, the city remains a cultural center of the very first order. It has 19 theaters, and one company, the *Schaubühne,* is said by critics to be one of the world's best German-speaking troupes. Also of international rank are the famed *Berlin Philharmonic Orchestra* and numerous museums like the great *Dahlem Museum,* the *National Gallery,* and the *Bauhaus Museum.* There is a kind of creative ferment here and a cult of quality that has attracted many writers, artists, composers, architects, and actors. As confirmation of the city's stature, the EEC chose West Berlin to be its cultural capital for 1988.

West Berlin is not only a cultural but an educational center, and one of the finest in Europe. The Free University and the Technical University, where many young Germans study, enjoy excellent reputations. Despite the great

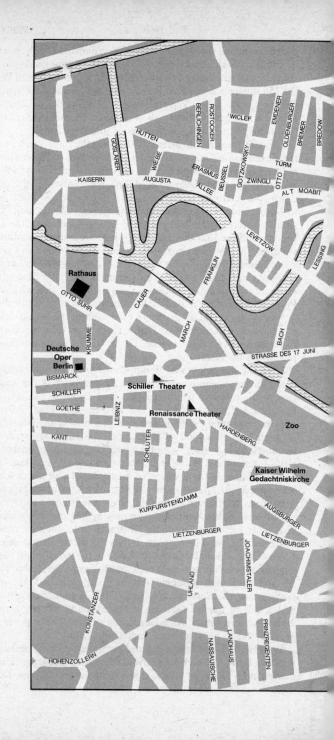

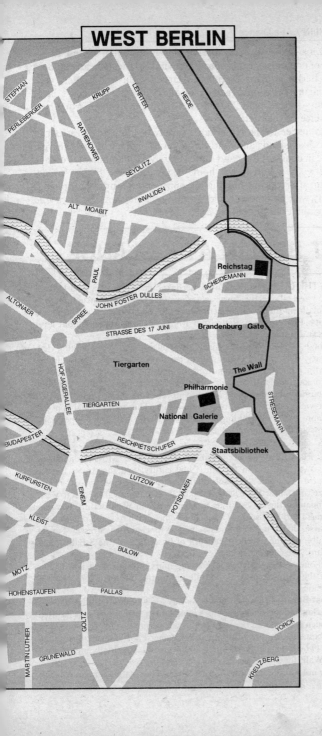

WEST BERLIN

many older citizens living in West Berlin, this is a city of — and for — the young, a city of pop music, experimental movies and theaters, and student hangouts. West Berlin is West Germany's largest industrial center, with headquarters of many firms such as Borsig and Siemens. The city's large foreign population — more than 250,000 non-Germans live and work here — adds special spice to the melting pot.

It is hard to do justice to the remarkable variety of life here. West Berlin is for people who like islands and who thrive on exchanges of high energy. Things seem to be in constant flux, and there is rarely a dull moment. Perhaps Christopher Isherwood would feel at home in this new and highly sophisticated West Berlin after all. The indomitable spirit of the courageous, pugnacious, and worldly wise Berliners would certainly remind him of the city he wrote about more than half a century ago.

WEST BERLIN AT-A-GLANCE

SEEING THE CITY: The Funkturm, Berlin's radio tower, is a steel-latticed tower 453 feet above the town. An elevator ascends the structure to a viewing platform that, weather permitting, offers a good view of Germany's largest city. Platform open daily from 10 AM to 11:30 PM; restaurant level open 10 AM to 11 PM. Messedamm (phone: 30381).

Although not as high, the top floor of Europa-Center offers a more breathtaking view of this fascinating city, since it is in the middle of the downtown area. The building, a business center with numerous shops and restaurants, was erected in 1965 and is grouped around two courtyards. Its 22-story tower is 270 feet high. On the top floor are the *I-Punkt* restaurant and a café and a nightclub. The roof terrace commands an extensive panoramic view, especially impressive after dark. The sparkling lights of the broad Kurfürstendamm give you an inkling of what West Berlin is all about. Open daily until midnight. Breitscheidpl. (phone: 261-1014 and 262-7670).

SPECIAL PLACES: West Berlin is easy to get around. Most of the downtown area was laid out in the late 19th century, and the streets form a sensible grid. You can see much of that part of the city by foot, if you familiarize yourself with the main thoroughfares. Running from east to west, these are Kurfürstendamm (the closest thing to Main Street in West Berlin), Hardenbergstrasse, Kantstrasse and Strasse des 17 Juni. The chief north to south connections are Potsdamer Strasse, Joachimstaler Strasse, and Wilmersdorfer Strasse. To get beyond the city center, use the excellent network of buses, trains (the S-Bahn), and subways (the U-Bahn). See *Getting Around.*

Various operators offer a wide range of sightseeing tours through West Berlin. For times and places of the daily departures, consult the tourist office (see *Sources and Resources*) or your hotel.

The Wall and East Berlin – The Wall snakes its way for 30 miles right through the center of Greater Berlin, and it is one of the city's main tourist attractions, as is its often artistic graffiti. Wooden pedestals on the West Berlin side permit you to get a good view of East Berlin. The best sites for doing this are at Potsdamer Platz and across from the Brandenburg Gate. (The latter landmark, now 200 years old, is actually on the East Berlin side of The Wall; for a detailed description, see *East Berlin.*)

You will probably not want to miss East Berlin, which is fascinating for two reasons:

It offers Westerners easy access to a firsthand experience of life in Eastern Europe, and it holds the older, historic section of Berlin.

Many West Berlin visitors travel to East Berlin on a West Berlin sightseeing bus. For information, consult the tourist office (see *Sources and Resources*). To go on your own, either take the subway or S-Bahn to the border control point at the East Berlin train station, Bahnhof Friedrichstrasse, or drive or walk to Checkpoint Charlie, manned by members of the Allied Forces, at the corner of Friedrichstrasse and Kochstrasse. Checkpoint Charlie can only be used by non-German nationals, and the formalities are exactly like the ones you have to go through at Bahnhof Friedrichstrasse.

In order to get in to East Berlin for 1 day (you must return by midnight), you will need a passport, and 5 deutsche marks for a 1-day visa. You must also exchange at least 25 deutsche marks into East German marks at the rate of one for one, and you must spend at least this amount in East Berlin. If you wish, you can exchange and spend more than the 25 marks, but you are not allowed to cross the border with East German currency. (Any extra currency can be converted back to deutsche marks at the border.) No Western printed matter is allowed and there are strict rules about what and how much you can bring into East Berlin as gifts. For a detailed report on the city, see *East Berlin*.

Kaiser Wilhelm Gedächtniskirche – This huge neo-Romanesque church was built toward the end of the 19th century, but it was almost completely destroyed by Allied bombing during World War II and has been only partially rebuilt. Its hexagonal bell tower and the octagonal church are new. The old west tower, 207 feet tall, was preserved in its ruined state. Partially new, partially old, partially preserved, and partially destroyed, it has become a symbol of the city and Berliners consider it the focal point. Breitscheidpl.

Zoo – One block north of the Gedächtniskirche is West Berlin's zoo. When Berlin's zoological gardens were laid out in 1841, the site was well outside the city; today, it is smack in the heart of West Berlin. This was Germany's first zoo, and it still has more species than any other zoo in the world. Open daily. Admission charge. 8 Hardenbergpl. (phone: 261-1101).

Aquarium – Next door to the zoo, with the most comprehensive collection in the world. The prewar building has been completely renovated, but it still has the tropical hall in which you can watch large numbers of alligators and crocodiles in their own environment; your vantage point is a bridge a mere 10 feet or so above the bloodthirsty creatures. Open daily. Admission charge. 32 Budapester Str. (phone: 261-1101).

Tiergarten – This beautiful public park — far more extensive than the zoological gardens, which are at its western fringe — was originally the royal hunting preserve. It is now one of the world's largest and most beautifully landscaped urban parks and is dotted with charming lakes and ponds. The Tiergarten extends from the zoo to the Wall at the Brandenburg Gate, about 2 miles (3 km) away.

Congress Hall – A gift of the American people in 1957, this ultramodern structure stands in the Tiergarten, on the banks of the Spree. Always controversial because of its bold design, it suffered a major setback in 1980, when the roof collapsed, but it was repaired and the building reopened in 1987. In addition to exhibition halls and conference rooms, it has a charming riverside restaurant. Nearby is a new, 140-foot-tall carillon, whose 68 bells resound daily at noon and 6 PM.

Reichstag – At the eastern edge of the Tiergarten, just north of the Brandenburg Gate, is Germany's former parliament building, built in the late 19th century in Italian High Renaissance style. Gutted by fire by Hitler's supporters in 1933, it has been rebuilt and is now used for political conclaves. The Wall runs right beside the building; there is a good view of East Berlin and the Brandenburg Gate. A permanent display is devoted to recent German history. Closed Mondays. No admission charge. Pl. der Republik (phone: 397-7141).

Philharmonie – The home of the world-renowned *Berlin Philharmonic Orchestra* is just a few blocks south of the Reichstag, at the southern fringe of the Tiergarten. The building's asymmetrical architecture has been controversial ever since it was completed in 1963. The concert hall can accommodate an audience of 2,200, seated in "terraces" surrounding the stage. Group visits are permitted daily at 9 AM provided no concert or rehearsal is in progress. The *Chamber Music Hall,* a near-mirror image of the *Philharmonie,* is next door. No admission charge. Matthäikirchpl. (phone: 261-4383).

Museum of Musical Instruments – This museum holds an intriguing collection of European instruments that date from the 16th century. Music lovers will particularly enjoy such rarities as Frederick the Great's flute and Edvard Grieg's piano. Closed Mondays. No admission charge. 1 Tiergartenstr. (phone: 254810).

Museum of Arts and Crafts – Next door to the *Philharmonie,* in the city's developing cultural center, is this imposing new museum that houses a unique collection of German artifacts from the past 900 years. Closed Mondays. No admission charge. 6 Tiergartenstr. (phone: 266-2911).

New National Galerie – Designed by Ludwig Mies van der Rohe, this striking building houses West Berlin's collections of late-19th- and 20th-century art. Jazz concerts are held during the summer months in the sculpture garden. Closed Mondays. No admission charge. 50 Potsdamer Str. (phone: 266-2666).

Staatsbibliothek – Directly opposite the *National Gallery* is the new State Library, West Berlin's successor to the Prussian State Library in East Berlin. This starkly modern structure was opened in 1978. Its collection of more than 3 million volumes makes it one of the world's largest. Exhibitions and lectures are also presented. Closed Sundays. No admission charge. 33 Potsdamer Str. (phone: 2661).

War Memorial – Plaques and impressive statuary are grouped in the courtyard of this building near the Tiergarten and *National Gallery,* which housed the German Armed Forces Supreme Command during World War II, to honor the German officers who were shot here for the ill-fated uprising against Hitler on July 20, 1944. There is a historical documentary center on the 2nd floor. Open daily. No admission charge. 14 Stauffenbergstr. (phone: 260-42202). Also interesting is the Plötzensee Memorial, Hüttigpfad.

Prinz Albrecht Galände (Topography of Terror) – On this site next to The Wall was the headquarters of Nazi terror: the Gestapo and the SS. It now houses a moving and informative documentary exhibition devoted to the victims of the Hitler regime. Open daily, except Mondays, from 10 AM to 6 PM. No admission charge. 110 Stresemannstr. (phone: 254-86703).

Museum of Transport and Technology – Across the Landwehr Canal and a bit east is this growing showplace, which houses a very interesting collection devoted to the historic development of the railroad, the automobile, the bicycle, and the airplane. Closed Mondays. No admission charge. 9 Trebbiner Str. (phone: 254840).

Rathaus Schöneberg – More than a mile due south is West Berlin's city hall, which also functions as the seat of government for the borough of Schöneberg. There is a good panoramic view from the top of the spireless tower, which contains a replica of the American Liberty Bell, presented to the Berliners by General Lucius Clay in 1950. On June 26, 1963, President John F. Kennedy made his "Ich bin ein Berliner" speech to a gathering of over 450,000 citizens from the balcony here. The tower can be ascended Wednesdays, Saturdays, and Sundays from April to September. No admission charge. John-F.-Kennedy-Pl. (phone: 7831).

Schloss Charlottenburg – A few miles to the northwest is this truly majestic palace, the best example of royal Prussian architecture in Berlin. Begun in 1695, it took 100 years to build. The historic royal chambers, completely restored since the massive destruction of the last war, are open daily, except Mondays, for a small fee. The palace also houses the *Pre-Historic Museum* and the Romantic gallery of early-19th-century art (closed Fridays; no admission charge). The beautifully laid out park behind the palace is one of the nicest areas in the city. Luisenpl. (phone: 320911).

International Congress Center and Fairgrounds – About a mile and a half (2 km) southwest of the palace is West Berlin's most modern structure, the recently opened ICC, as it is called. Across the street from this looming building, and connected to it by a covered pedestrian walkway, are the rambling fairgrounds, the site of the year-round fairs and exhibitions, which include international *Green Week* (an agricultural exhibition) and the German radio and TV exhibition. On the fairgrounds is the Funk-turm or radio tower (see *Seeing the City*). Masurenallee and Messedamm (phone: 30381).

Olympic Stadium – Another 2 miles (3.2 km) to the west, this huge sports arena casts its shadow over the low-lying houses of a pleasant residential area. It was built for the 1936 Olympic Games, and if you look hard, you can still make out the "royal" box, from which Hitler and his cohorts took in the spectacle. It is open daily to the public when no sports events are on. No admission charge except for the ascent by elevator to the top of the adjacent bell tower. Olympischer Pl. (phone: 304-0676).

Spandau Citadel – Even farther west, on the Havel River, is the historic Spandau Citadel. The oldest edifice on the grounds, the Julius Tower, dates from the 14th century. The citadel, which had served as a fortification, a prison, and the royal treasury, is now a local history museum. The Nazi war criminals were not housed here but at the prison in Wilhelmstrasse, in the middle of Spandau. The citadel is open to the public, for an admission charge, except Mondays. Am Juliusturm (phone: 33911).

Museum Center in Dahlem – To the south, in the fashionable and lovely section of Dahlem, is West Berlin's largest museum complex. Its extensive buildings accommodate several institutions, and you can spend at least a full day going through them: the *Painting Gallery,* an important collection of European painting from the Middle Ages to the 18th century, with good pieces of fanciful rococo art; the *Sculpture Department,* with Byzantine and European sculpture from the 3rd to the 18th century; the *Ethnographic Museum,* with one of the world's most complete collections; *Museums of Islamic, Indian, and Far Eastern Art;* and the *Department of Prints and Engravings.* All are closed Mondays; no admission charge. 8 Lansstr. (phone: 83011).

Botanical Gardens – No more than half a mile to the east are the largest botanical gardens in Germany and one of the world's most significant collections of flora. Of special interest in the 104-acre gardens are the geographical gardens, where plants from various parts of the world flourish in carefully maintained native environments. There is a fascinating botanic display at the museum, next to the entrance of the gardens. The gardens are open daily; the museum closes Mondays. Admission charge to both museum and gardens. 6 Königin-Luise-Str. (phone: 830060).

■**EXTRA SPECIAL:** Largely unknown to most tourists, who rarely leave the downtown area, the western sections of West Berlin are mostly forests and waterways. The Havel River, Tegeler See, and Wannsee, as well as the Grunewald, Tegel, and Spandau forests, make up at least one-fourth of West Berlin's total area. To see it all, board one of the 70 ships that make daily trips on the Havel. Boats leave eight times a day from Easter until the end of September. There are many Havel ship lines; the largest is Stern and Kreisschiffahrt, 60 Sachtleben Str. (phone: 810-0040).

Along the way, get off at any number of points and explore to your heart's content, then reboard a boat. Stopping-off points include Grunewald Tower, formerly Kaiser Wilhelm Tower, dating from the 19th century and affording a good view from the top; Lindwerder Island, with restaurants offering snacks of beer, coffee, and cake; and Pfaueninsel (Peacock Island), a beautiful example of an 18th-century formal garden with small pavilions, ponds, and a château dating from 1796 that is open to the public. All stops on this trip are well provisioned with restaurants and beer gardens. (The only catch is that since these boats are mostly for Berliners and rarely cater to foreign visitors, English is usually not spoken by the guides).

SOURCES AND RESOURCES

 TOURIST INFORMATION: The tourist office (Verkehrsamt) will supply you with all sorts of free information in English about West Berlin. This includes a general tourist map and numerous brochures. For the best detailed local map, go to a bookstore and ask for *Berlin Stadtatlas,* which costs the equivalent of $6. The tourist office is in the large complex of shops and restaurants at Europa-Center, at the foot of Kurfürstendamm (phone: 21234). It also maintains branches at Tegel Airport and on the ground floor of Europa-Center (entrance on Budapesterstr.), both open daily until 10:30 PM. Another source of information is *Dial Berlin,* a private tourism consortium that has a telephone hot line in the US (800-237-5469).

The US Consulate is at 170 Clayallee (phone: 832-4087).

Local Coverage – There is no newspaper in English, but a monthly calendar of events called *Berlin Programm* is available at the tourist office and at newsstands; some of the information is in English.

Food – *Berlin Programm* has limited restaurant listings (in German). The tourist office can provide dining information in English.

Telephone – The area code for West Berlin is 030.

 CLIMATE AND CLOTHES: Although Berlin is farther north than any city in the US (except those of Alaska), its climate is very temperate. Though more temperate in both summer and winter, you will find weather conditions here very similar to those prevailing in the northeastern US. Temperatures rarely go above 70F (21C) and seldom slip below freezing. Rain can fall at any time of the year. Berlin's air tends to be fresher and less damp than West Germany's because of the lake-studded woodlands surrounding the city, but smog does set in at times. Even when dining out, dress is casual, and a good pair of walking shoes is essential.

 GETTING AROUND: Airport – Tegel Airport handles all domestic and international flights and is a 20- to 30-minute ride from downtown. Taxi fare to the center of the city should run about 20 deutsche marks (about $11). The #9 bus provides service from the airport to downtown and leaves from just outside Gate 8 every 15 minutes between 5:30 AM and midnight.

Car Rental – The major American firms are represented as well as several European companies. Information can be obtained at any hotel.

Subway and Bus – Berlin has one of the world's most efficient public transportation systems. The subway, or U-Bahn, with its snappy little yellow cars, has been a fact of life here since 1902, and its 8 lines serve almost every part of the city. The U-Bahn is fast, clean, convenient, and one of the cheapest in Germany. The 100-year-old S-Bahn "el," with three lines, was taken over by West Berlin's public transit authority in 1984. A ticket ($1.40) is valid for a trip from one end of the city to the other, and you can transfer as often as you wish within the U-Bahn system, the elevated S-Bahn, and to any of the 84 bus lines that ply West Berlin's streets. A carnet, valid for five rides, is available. The West Berlin Transport Authority also sells a ticket valid for 24 hours on all U-Bahn, S-Bahn, and bus lines, which costs $5. A 6-day tourist ticket, which costs $15, is also available.

Taxi – Taxis can be hailed in the streets, and there are cabstands all over town and at the major hotels. Fares are posted near the stands. (To call a cab, dial 6902 or 261026.)

 SPECIAL EVENTS: *Green Week,* an annual agricultural fair, takes place at the fairgrounds toward the end of January. The *Berlin Film Festival,* another annual fixture, is in February. A *Festival of German Drama* is performed every May, and once a year in September the city puts on its ambitious *Festival of the Arts.* A *Jazz Festival* attracts international soloists to West Berlin every year during the first week of November.

 MUSEUMS: The *Prussian State Museums* in Dahlem, at Charlottenburg Palace, and near the Tiergarten are described in *Special Places.* West Berlin also has two unusual art collections, each of them dating from the late 18th century. Directly opposite Charlottenburg Palace is the *Egyptian Museum,* whose priceless treasures include the world-renowned bust of Queen Nefertiti and the magnificent Kalabsha Gate. Closed Fridays. No admission charge. 70 Schlossstr. (phone: 320911). The *Museum of Local Art and History* is in a beautiful 18th-century rococo building, once the Prussian Supreme Court, which has been lovingly restored. Visit the beer cellar, which features traditional Berlin snacks and beverages. Closed Mondays. Admission charge. 14 Lindenstr. (phone: 25860).

 SHOPPING: West Berlin, this capitalist jewel in a Communist setting, has an abundance of interesting shops. There is hardly anything you cannot buy here, and some of the items offered for sale are truly unique. If you just want to browse before making up your mind, go through Europa-Center, at the foot of Kurfürstendamm in the middle of the downtown area. This city within a city has scores of small shops and boutiques offering a variety of typical German specialties. German cameras, including those by Leica, Rollei, and Zeiss, are available here, but it is necessary to do very careful comparison shopping. The same brands are often less expensive in the US. Optical goods such as binoculars, telescopes, and microscopes are also German specialties, and there are good buys in china and porcelain; great names in the latter are Meissen, Rosenthal, and KPM (State Porcelain Manufactory). Women's and men's fashions, toys, cutlery, and clocks are good buys, too. Although you might want to do some exploring on your own, here is a small sample of recommended stores:

Antiquitäten Döbler – Porcelain, crystal, and pewter. 8 Keithstr. (phone: 211-9344).

Dürlich – Antique furniture. 5 Keithstr. (phone: 243660).

Gronert – Antiques. 10 Keithstr. (phone: 241585).

J. A. Henckels – Cutlery. 33 Kurfürstendamm (phone: 881-3315).

Horn's – The latest in women's fashions. 213 Kurfürstendamm (phone: 881-4055).

Jil Sander Boutique – Chic women's wear. 48 Kurfürstendamm (phone: 883-3730).

Ka De We – Germany's largest and best-stocked department store, with simply everything, including an enormous food shop with a score of lunch counters (6th floor). 21-24 Tauentzienstr. (phone: 21210).

Marga Schoeller – English and American books. 33 Knesebeckstr. (phone: 881-1112).

Staatliche Porzellan Manufaktur Berlin (*KPM*) – Beautiful china. The factory is at 1 Wegelystrasse, the salesroom at 205 Kurfürstendamm (phone: 390090).

Vom Winde Verweht (*Gone with the Wind*) – An Anglo-American kite emporium featuring fascinating European kites at low prices. 81 Eisenacher Str. (phone: 784-7769 or 795-4700).

SPORTS AND FITNESS: Bicycling – You can rent a bicycle by the hour for a jaunt through the expansive Grunewald forest from *F. Damrau,* Schmetterlingspl. (phone: 811-5829; call before 9 AM).

 Fitness Center – *Sportscenter Gerstenberger,* 19-21 Körnerstr. (phone: 261-2937).

Golf – The *Golf und Landclub,* Berlin-Wannsee, has a 9-hole golf course. Stölpchen-weg (phone: 805-5075).

Ice Hockey – From November through April, you can see professional games at the *Eissporthalle.* Jafféstr. (phone: 30381).

Ice Skating – In the winter, there are various public rinks in the city. Consult the tourist office for sites and hours.

Jogging – Best is the central Tiergarten park. Farther out, runners prefer Grune-wald forest.

Soccer – *Hertha* and *Blau-Weiss,* West Berlin's entries in the West German profes-sional soccer leagues, play Saturdays at the *Olympic Stadium.* Olympischer Pl. (phone: 304-0676).

Swimming – Aquatic sports can be enjoyed at a number of indoor and outdoor pools; each of West Berlin's 12 boroughs has at least one public facility. There is a sandy beach lining crystal water at Glienicker See, a lake at the westernmost fringe of the city.

Tennis – In addition to several private clubs, the city has a number of public courts. For locations and hours of admission, consult the tourist office.

Trotting Races – Every Wednesday and Sunday there is racing at the trotting course in *Mariendorf.* 222 Mariendorfer Damm (phone: 74011).

THEATER: Theater in West Berlin, still Germany's theatrical metropolis, is an all-German affair. For a look at the classical repertoire, go to the *Schiller Theater,* 110 Bismarckstr. (phone: 319-5236). What is probably one of the most important German-language theaters in the world is a three-stage complex, *Schaubühne am Lehniner Platz,* 153 Kurfürstendamm (phone: 890023). Other prominent theaters are: *Renaissance Theater,* 6 Hardenbergstr. (phone: 312-4202); *Freie Volksbühne,* Schaperstr. 24 (phone: 881-3742); *Theater am Kurfürsten-damm,* 206 Kurfürstendamm (phone: 882-3789); *Komödie,* 206 Kurfürstendamm (phone: 882-7893); *Tribüne,* 18-20 Otto-Suhr-Allee (phone: 341-2600). One of Europe's most successful children's theaters is *Grips,* 22 Altonaer Str. (phone: 391-4004). Con-sult the monthly calendar of events, *Berlin Programm,* for complete listings of all performances.

MUSIC: West Berlin is one of the world's musical centers, with perform-ances of everything from classical to pop and rock. The *Berlin Philharmonic Orchestra,* conducted by Herbert von Karajan, performs at the *Philharmo-nie,* 1 Matthäikirchpl. (phone: 254880). The *Radio Symphony Orchestra* gives most of its concerts at one of West Berlin's two broadcasting stations, *Sender Freies Berlin,* at 8-14 Masurenallee (for tickets, dial 302-7242). Concerts and recitals of classical music can be heard at the *Hochschule der Künste* (College of Arts), 1 Fasanenstr. (phone: 318-52374). One of the world's leading opera houses, the *Deutsche Oper,* has daily performances (once a week ballet is scheduled), 34-37 Bismarckstr. (phone: 341-0249). Operettas and musicals are launched at *Theater des Westens,* 12 Kantstr. (phone: 312-1022). Pop concerts, many by visiting international stars, are performed at the *Philharmonie* (above) and at the *Deutschlandhalle,* Messedamm (phone: 30381). For the latest in jazz and rock music, attend one of the concerts that are frequently given at *Quartier Latin,* 96 Potsdamer Str. (phone: 261-3707). For the latest listings, consult the *Berlin Programm.*

NIGHTCLUBS AND NIGHTLIFE: For live music and dancing, try some of these popular places: *Loretta,* 89 Lietzenburger Str. (phone: 882-7863); *Salsa,* 13 Wielandstr. (phone: 324-1642); *Habel's Bierhaus,* 12 Theodor-Heuss-Pl. (phone: 301-7092). It is not only the young crowd that likes to dance at these clubs: *Café Keese,* 108 Bismarckstr. (phone: 312-9111); *Big Apple,* 13 Bundesalle (phone: 881-2887); *Buccaneer,* 32 Rankestr. (phone: 245057); *Bristol-Bar,* in the *Kempinski* hotel, 27 Kurfürstendamm (phone: 881091). Discotheques hit this city with a big splash in the late 1970s and they are still jumping. For the youngsters, *Dschungel,* is really "in" at 53 Nürnberger Str. (phone: 246698). The following discos, however, are popular with people from all age groups: *Empire,* 30 Hauptstr. (phone: 784-8565); *Far Out,* 156 Fürstendamm (phone: 320-0701); *Abraxas,* 134 Kantstr. (phone: 312-9493); *Pool,* 19 Motzstr. (phone: 247529); *Annabell's,* 64 Fasanenstr. (phone: 883-5220); *Metropol,* 5 Nollendorfpl. (phone: 216-4122); *VIP-Club,* top of the Europa-Center, Breitscheidpl. (phone: 261-2452); and *Big Eden,* 202 Kurfürstendamm (phone: 323-5849). A gay club featuring music, dancing, and an occasional show is *Bi Ba Bo,* 5 Pfalzburger Str. (phone: 883-2685).

Talking about shows, one cannot forget West Berlin's cabarets. Both *Stachelsch-weine,* Europa-Center (phone: 261-4795), and *Wühlmäuse,* Lietzenburgerstr. corner of Nürnberger Str. (phone: 213-7047), put on interesting performances, devoted chiefly to literary and political satire. Nightclubs featuring transvestite shows have long been a German specialty. If you like this sort of thing — and even if you do not — you will be pleasantly surprised; visit *La Cage,* 24 Welser Str. (phone: 248950), or *Chez Nous,* 14 Marburger Str. (phone: 213-1810). Jazz buffs have two very popular clubs at their disposal, each of them featuring live music: *Quasimodo,* 12A Kantstr. (phone: 312-8086), and *Flöz,* 37 Nassauische Str. (phone: 861-1000). Folk music from Ireland reigns supreme at the *Irish Harp Pub,* 15 Giesebrechtstr. (phone: 883-6687), and at *Go In,* 17 Bleibtreustr. (phone: 881-7218).

West Berlin is known for its multitude of small, intimate, pub-like bars, which offer no more than excellent drinks, a few snacks, and lots of *Gemütlichkeit* (congeniality). Three of them are worthy of mention: *Die Kleine Weltlaterne,* which caters to an arty crowd, 22 Nestorstr. (phone: 892-6585); *Lutter & Wegener,* a wine cellar of note, 55 Schlüterstr. (phone: 881-3440); and *Zwiebelfisch,* a favorite haunt for journalists and students, 7-8 Savignypl. (phone: 317363). If gambling is one of your sins, visit the city's one and only licensed gambling casino, on the ground floor at the Budapester Str. side of Europa-Center, for roulette, baccarat, and blackjack. It's open daily from 3 PM to 3 AM (phone: 261-1501).

BEST IN TOWN

CHECKING IN: Visitors can choose from one of the best assortments of hotels in all of Germany. Since there always seems to be something happening in this scintillating city, overnight accommodations are often hard to find and it is advisable to make advance reservations — either directly with the hotel of your choice or through the city's efficient tourist office (see *Sources and Resources*); *Dial Berlin* can also help here (see *Sources and Resources*). Our selection includes some of the luxury hotels, as well as establishments that can be classified as moderate and inexpensive. Many of the latter are exciting little houses, noted for their charm. A word of caution: Hotel accommodations are extremely expensive in West Germany, and West Berlin follows suit. Should you prefer more modest, although somewhat less comfortable rooms, the Tourist Office is the place to turn to. The hotels in our selection have a bath or a shower in every room, and in almost every case the rooms have telephones. For a double room in those hotels we have classed as expensive, expect to pay $110 and up; from $65 to $110 in the moderate category; under $65 in the inexpensive class. All telephone numbers are in the 030 area code unless otherwise indicated.

Am Zoo – When Thomas Wolfe came to Berlin in the early 1930s, he stayed at this 145-room hotel, one of the traditional downtown establishments. Breakfast is included. 25 Kurfürstendamm (phone: 883091). Expensive.

Berlin Excelsior – Another luxury hotel, just off Kurfürstendamm in the center of town, the *Excelsior* is planned for conventions as well as pleasure; thus it offers typing and secretarial services in addition to the usual amenities. All 325 rooms have refrigerators, and public rooms include a breakfast room, restaurant, bar, and banquet room. 14 Hardenbergstr. (phone: 31991). Expensive.

Bristol Kempinski – As West Berlin's most traditional hostelry, this newly renovated 358-room hotel has a motto of noblesse oblige. Formerly on Unter den Linden, now in East Berlin, it is the classiest hotel in West Berlin. Its present location in the middle of West Berlin's golden mile — the Kurfürstendamm — makes it ideal for sightseeing. It also boasts a renowned restaurant (see *Eating Out*), *The Grill*, and the *Bristol Bar*. Breakfast is extra. 27 Kurfürstendamm (phone: 884340). Expensive.

Grand Hotel Esplanade – With 385 rooms, plus 17 suites, this luxury hotel is idyllically set on a canal — but it's downtown West Berlin, not Amsterdam, that's just around the corner. The rooms, service, and other amenities are well above standard, and several restaurants are on the premises. 15 Lützowufer (phone: 261011). Expensive.

Inter-Continental – The *Hilton,* as this building was known for 20 years (until the end of 1978), was a trademark in West Berlin. *Inter-Continental* has now assumed the management of this 600-room establishment, and it continues to offer luxurious accommodations in an area a bit removed from West Berlin's hustle and bustle. Although only a stone's throw from the center of activities, it overlooks the Tiergarten and has several restaurants (especially good is *Zum Hugenotten*) as well as a popular ballroom. Breakfast is extra. 2 Budapester Str. (phone: 26020). Expensive.

Palace – Just behind the Gedächtniskirche and within the orb of the Europa Center. In addition to a large number of apartments, this imposing downtown hotel has 160 well-appointed rooms as well as such amenities as a swimming pool and a sauna. 42 Budapester Str. (phone: 269111). Expensive.

Penta – With 425 rooms, this hotel is one of West Berlin's largest and most modern. On the premises are such amenities as a restaurant, bar, beer cellar, swimming pool, sauna, solarium, and an underground garage. Centrally located at 65 Nürnberger Str. (phone: 210070). Expensive.

Schweizerhof – This 441-room establishment is opposite the *Inter-Continental* and is managed by that chain. The ongoing motif is Swiss, as the name implies, and the service is excellent. There is a restaurant; breakfast is extra. 21-31 Budapester Str. (phone: 26960). Expensive.

Seehof – Only 2½ miles (4 km) down the road from the downtown area, on the Lietzensee lake. The 80-room hotel overlooks a small park. 11 Lietzensee Ufer (phone: 320020). Expensive.

Steigenberger – One of West Germany's largest hotel chains recently opened this comfortable establishment with 400 rooms, several restaurants and bars, a swimming pool, sauna, and shopping arcade. Downtown, facing lovely Los Angeles Platz (phone: 21080). Expensive.

Gehrhus – This charming 34-room hotel looks like the palace it was in 1912; its very first guest was Kaiser Wilhelm. The romantic atmosphere is heightened by the quiet location, 20 minutes from downtown West Berlin. Breakfast is included. 4-10 Brahmsstr. (phone: 826-2081). Expensive to moderate.

Am Studio – A modern hotel offering a magnificent view of the city from each of its 78 rooms. 80 Kaiserdamm (phone: 302081). Moderate.

Börse – This 38-room hotel is right in the middle of town, so don't expect too much peace and quiet. But here you are surrounded by shops, cafés, restaurants, theaters, and movie houses. 34 Kurfürstendamm (phone: 881-3021). Moderate.

Novotel – Next to Tegel Airport, this 187-room hotel provides efficiency without any sacrifice of comfort. Sauna, solarium, and swimming pool on the premises. 202 Kurt-Schumacher Damm (phone: 41060). Moderate.

Plaza – Just around the corner from Kurfürstendamm is this 131-room alternative to more expensive accommodations. 63 Knesebeckstr. (phone: 884130). Moderate.

Econtel – Midway between the airport and downtown and near the opera house and Charlottenburg Palace, this hotel puts its accent on comfort rather than luxury, but it doesn't sacrifice modern facilities. 24-26 Sömmeringstr. (phone: 344001). Inexpensive.

Sachsenhof – This well-run 65-room hotel is right in the middle of Christopher Isherwood's Berlin. He lived around the corner in 17 Nollendorfstrasse. 7 Motzstr. (phone: 216-2074). Inexpensive.

 EATING OUT: German food is hearty and can be very good or, at its worst, as heavy as lead. Main courses usually consist of roasted or stewed meat with boiled potatoes or dumplings (called *Knödel,* which are very heavy) and sauerkraut, cabbage or other vegetables, like string beans. Wiener schnitzel and sauerbraten are well-known specialties.

Like other Continentals, Germans like rolls for breakfast, occasionally the sweet, cruller-like pastries called *Krapfen* and *Berliner Pfannkuchen.* Then at mid-morning they often have a snack of sausages and bread called *Brotzeit* or "breadtime."

Sausages are the specialty in Germany at any time of day or night; they are made from pork, veal, and game. The frankfurter, which originated in Vienna, is longer, slimmer, and better than the American variety. *Weisswurst* is white sausage made mostly of veal; *Bratwurst* is pork sausage; a *Regensburger* is a spicy pork sausage.

Interesting appetizers are herring, which is very popular and comes in many varieties, and *Hase im Topf,* a delicious rabbit pâté. Soups are popular and very substantial: *Leberknödelsuppe* (liver dumpling soup), *Erbsensuppe* (pea soup), and *Kohlsuppe* (cabbage soup) are just a few. *Schwarzbrot,* or dark bread, is very tasty, especially Westphalian pumpernickel.

For a typical Berlin treat, try a *Konditorei,* a little shop that offers excellent cakes and pastries with coffee or tea. Special desserts are *Schwarzwälder Kirschtorte,* a Black Forest cherry cake with whipped cream; *Baumkuchen,* a towering cake with icing; *Gugelhupf,* a marvelous coffee cake; *Käsekuchen,* or cheesecake; special *Berliner Pfannkuchen* or cruller; and many others.

What's more, Germans are justifiably famous for their beer and wine. In South Germany, light beer (*helles*) and dark (*dunkles*) come in many sizes and varieties. Most beers come from Munich, but you might want to try *Berliner Weisse* in the summer, a whitish beer made from wheat and often served *mit Schuss,* or raspberry juice. North Germans drink *pilsener* beer. *Bierkeller* (beer restaurants) serve food as well as beer.

Germany produces a lot of wine, some of it very good. You may be disappointed in *Liebfraumilch,* which is not a place name (it means "Milk of Our Lady") and thus not reliable. Best bets are the Moselles — light, pleasant, and often cheap — like *Wehlener Sonnenuhr, Piesporter,* or *Zeltinger.* Rhine wines, of course, are famous — some of the best are *Niersteiner, Oppenheimer,* and *Schloss Johannisberger.* Baden wines are equally renowned, especially *Weissherbst,* a rosé.

Expect to pay $60 or more at restaurants in the expensive category; between $30 and $60 in the moderate range; and less than $30 at places classed as inexpensive. Prices are for a dinner for two, not including drinks and wine. Tips are included in the bill. All telephone numbers are in the 030 area code unless otherwise indicated.

Bamberger Reiter – Here is creative nouvelle Austro-French cuisine served in a cozy atmosphere. The menu is composed of two fixed "tastings," one of five courses, the other of seven (don't despair; portions are modest). There is also a wide selection of French and German wines. The garden at the front is very pleasant in spring and summer. Dinner only; closed Sundays and Mondays. 7 Regensburger Str. (there are two such streets in West Berlin; this is the one on the corner of Bamberger St.; phone: 244282). Expensive.

Berlin – One of the best hotel restaurants in town, with continental dishes served in elegant surroundings. You can dine either in the restaurant or in the smaller grill room. Lunch is cheaper than dinner. Grill room closed Sundays. Reservations advised. 62 Kurfürstenstr. (phone: 26050). Expensive.

Chalet Corniche – A special place is this beautiful former country mansion in the Grunewald section, on the western fringe of the city. Not only does the impressive architecture (the house was built around a big old tree) give you the feeling of *bonhomie,* but the view through the tall windows onto wide lawns and a beautiful lake is as soul-satisfying as the cuisine. We recommend the veal steaks and the seafood specialties. Open daily. Reservations advised. 56 Königsallee (phone: 892-8597). Expensive.

Frühsammer's Restaurant An der Rehwiese – For inspired continental cuisine, this is the place — well worth the sojourn to the suburbs. Closed Sundays. Reservations advised. 101 Matterhornstr. (phone: 803-2720). Expensive.

Rockendorf's – Although a bit off the beaten track, this restaurant is well worth the trip. It's in a turn-of-the-century villa in the suburb of Waidmannslust. Nostalgia is trump here, as well as imaginatively prepared continental dishes and a very good choice of wines. Closed Sundays, Mondays, and 3 weeks in August. Reservations advised. 1 Düsterhauptstr. (phone: 402-3099). Expensive.

Alt-Luxemburg – The nouvelle cuisine at this cozy bistro near the city center has attracted its share of well-deserved attention. The seafood specialties, in particular, are worthy of serious consideration. Closed Sundays, Mondays, and 3 weeks in July. Reservations advised. 70 Pestalozzistr. (phone: 323-8730). Expensive to moderate.

Conti Fischstuben – As the name implies, this is for lovers of seafood. A small restaurant in the *Ambassador* with an exclusive flair. Closed Sundays. Reservations advised. 42 Bayreuther Str. (phone: 2190-2362). Expensive to moderate.

Daitokai – This genuine Japanese haunt is close to the Kurfürstendamm. The food is good, the service friendly, and you can sit on the floor in Japanese style. Closed Mondays. No reservations. Europa-Center (phone: 261-8099). Expensive to moderate.

Kardell – Specialties are leg of lamb, game, steaks, and fish. Herr Kardell, the owner, still runs the place with obsessive detail. Open daily; supper only Saturdays. Reservations advised. 24 Gervinusstr. (phone: 324-1066). Expensive to moderate.

Kempinski Grill – The candlight glow, creamy decor, and piano music are all serenely old-fashioned. The menu features lobster (a Berlin obsession) in salad, soup, and sauce. Grilled fish and steaks are also recommended. Round off the evening with a stop at the *Kempinski* hotel's soothing *Bristol Bar.* Closed Sundays.

Reservations advised. 27 Kurfürstendamm (phone: 884340). Expensive to moderate.

Paris-Moskau – Not far from the Reichstag, in a somewhat undistinguished neighborhood, is this distinguished restaurant. Its three dining rooms are in a charming 2-story house, all done in white. In addition to excellent continental cuisine and drinks served by a young, dedicated team, it features a very pleasant atmosphere, heightened by an artistic decor and two terraces. Open daily. Reservations advised. 141 Alt-Moabit (phone: 394-2081). Expensive to moderate.

Anselmo – A must for devotees of Italian cuisine. This intimate restaurant features an imaginative and well-run kitchen, rustic decor, and a pleasant atmosphere. Closed Mondays. Reservations advised. 17 Damaschkestr. (phone: 323-3094). Moderate.

Ax-Bax – The beautiful people often hang out in this nicely designed bar that has no identifying sign on the door. In addition to the drinks and glitter, it also has good food. Open daily from 7:30 PM; closed Saturdays. 34 Leibnizstr. (phone: 313-8594). Moderate.

Blockhaus Nikolskoe – For fans of German history and good continental food, this restaurant, high above the wide Havel River, looks like a Russian dacha. It was built in log cabin fashion in 1819 by Prussian King Friedrich Wilhelm III for his daughter, Charlotte, and her husband, Grand Duke Nicholas (later Russian Czar Nicholas I). Closed Thursdays and in the winter after 7 PM. Reservations advised. It is in a forested area, with no street address; ask directions when you make reservations (phone: 805-2914). Moderate.

Exil – This out-of-the-way place is well worth the trip. On a canal in Kreuzberg, it features well-prepared Viennese dishes. You can dine at the bower-like terrace, weather permitting. The service is also charmingly Viennese. Dinner only; closed Mondays. Reservations advised. 44a Paul-Lincke-Ufer (phone: 612-7037). Moderate.

Florian – A finely tuned crew maintains this admirable restaurant. The menu emphasizes French, Austrian, and Bohemian cuisines, and the wines and the service are as good as the food. The neighborhood is "in" and so *Florian* is frequented by artists, film people, and the so-called New Wave set. Supper only. Closed December 24-31. Reservations advised. 52 Grolmanstr. (phone: 313-9184). Moderate.

Fofi's – A Greek-style bistro that has become a magnet for the "in" crowd, and indeed, the attractions here are the Greek cuisine and the clientele. Open daily for supper; closed December 24. Reservations advised. 70 Fasanenstr. — look for the *"estiatorio"* sign (phone: 881-8785).

Hongkong – The kitchen staff here knows how to make the tantalizing most of basic Cantonese cooking, with an extensive menu and excellent service to go with a convenient location. Open daily. Reservations advised. 210 Kurfürstendamm (phone: 881-5756). Moderate.

I-Punkt – The international menu is adequate, but most people come here for the spectacular view. On the 20th floor of the Europa-Center complex, the restaurant offers one of the best panoramic views of West Berlin. Especially impressive after dark (described in *Seeing the City*). Open daily. Reservations not necessary. Europa-Center at Breitscheidpl. (phone: 261-1014). Moderate.

Mundart – This new restaurant in Kreuzberg, a former working class district that has gone arty, features French cuisine, though the imaginative chef, Jacques, is no disciple of nouvelle. The decor, service, and excellent wines are also highly commendable. Dinner only; closed Mondays and July. Reservations advised. 33-34 Muskauer Str. (phone: 612-2061). Moderate.

November – On the south bank of the Lanwehrkanal, oppposite the *National Gallery,* this bistro-like, intimate restaurant is a favorite of writers, artists, and others belonging to the cultural scene. The sophisticated ambience is in charming contrast to the up-market tone of the cuisine offered by an extremely obliging staff. Try the leg of lamb or game dishes. Open daily for supper only. Reservations advised. 65 Schoeneberger Ufer (phone: 261-3882). Moderate.

Paris-Bar – A traditional bistro that is a magnet for students and artists drawn by the French cuisine as well as the paintings on the walls. Closed Sundays. Reservations advised. 152 Kantstr. (phone: 313-8052). Moderate.

Im Reichstag – One wing of this late-19th-century building, formerly the seat of the German parliament (see *Special Places*), has been set aside as a restaurant. Solid German food in a historic setting. Closed Mondays. Reservations advised. Platz der Republik (phone: 397-7172). Moderate.

Schipkapass – A rustically decorated Czech restaurant, featuring those two mainstays of every good Bohemian kitchen: Prague ham and Pilsner beer. You can feast on the large portions. Open daily for supper. Reservations advised. 185 Hohenzollerndamm (phone: 871941). Moderate.

El Bodegón – This lively Spanish *finca,* featuring a wide range of Iberian dishes, is much frequented by students, musicians, and artists. The atmosphere is genuinely Spanish, including guitar music, chiefly flamenco. Open daily, supper only. Reservations not necessary. 61 Schlüterstr. (phone: 312-4497). Inexpensive.

Brasserie – You will find a true French bistro here. The decor, food, and wine are typical of the Gallic provinces. There is also a small enclosed terrace. Open daily. Reservations not necessary. 3 Wittenbergpl. (phone: 245786). Inexpensive.

Café Möhring – This traditional German *Konditorei* has three locations on the city's busy Kurfürstendamm. Here you can enjoy rich cakes, light Danish pastry, and other wonders from their own bakery to go along with your coffee or tea. Light hot meals are also available. Open daily; closes at noon on December 24. 163, 213, and 234 Kurfürstendamm (phone: 892-5075, 881-2075, and 882-3844). Inexpensive.

Einstein – The high-ceilinged and mirrored dining room in this turn-of-the-century villa is a perfect setting for an afternoon's Viennese coffee and pastry. Open daily until 2 AM. No reservations. 58 Kurfürstenstr. (phone: 261-5096). Inexpensive.

Hardtke – Two traditional restaurants with traditionally hearty German food such as fresh *Leberwurst* and *Blutwurst.* All meat dishes come from its own butcher shops. Rustic, friendly atmosphere. Open daily. Reservations accepted. 27 and 27B Meinekestr. (phone: 881-9827). Inexpensive.

Hollandstüb'l – Dutch cuisine, with the accent on dishes from the East Indies (*nasi goreng, rijsttafel,* and so on). The decor is a holdover from the 1920s, when this was one of Berlin's more popular restaurants. Open daily. No reservations. 11 Martin-Luther-Str. (phone: 248593). Inexpensive.

Litfass – Not far from the Kurfürstendamm and the famous *Schaubühne* theater is this unpretentious Portuguese restaurant. Among the specialties are shark steaks and potted chicken in garlic sauce. Open daily. No reservations. 49 Sybelstr. (phone: 323-2215). Inexpensive.

Häagen-Dazs – A refreshing taste from home, its name notwithstanding. The same good ice cream (you won't have any trouble translating from the German *eiscrem*); ask for one *kugel* (scoop) or two *kugeln.* 224 Kurfürstendamm. Inexpensive.

BRUSSELS

As the headquarters of NATO, the Common Market, the Benelux Union, and the European Atomic Energy Community, Brussels is not only the capital of Belgium and of the Belgian province of Brabant, it is in many ways the capital of all Europe. Three distinct sets of ambassadors reside in the city: one for Belgium, one for NATO, and one for the Common Market. It is a common joke that if someone were to yell "Fire!" in a Brussels theater, half the audience would run out to safety, and the other half would call their home governments for instructions.

Brussels is a fast-paced modern city of 977,000 people (including suburbs), rivaling New York City in its often ruthless destruction of the old in favor of the new. There are skyscrapers, traffic problems, and broad avenues with underpasses and overpasses. Much of the city is starkly modern; what is not modern is frankly medieval, and of that, happily, much remains.

The Grand' Place, the magnificent square that justly is the city's pride and joy, was a prosperous marketplace in the Middle Ages, when it was known as the Grote Markt. Splendid old baroque guild houses, with façades ornately decorated in gold, line the square, its noble 15th-century Gothic Hôtel de Ville in the southwest facing the palatial 18th-century *Maison du Roi,* now the municipal museum. Nearby, the still narrow and cobbled streets bear quaint medieval names reminiscent of the market that was held there: Bread Street, Pepper Street, Street of the Herb Market, and Little Street of the Butchers. Besides produce, goods such as lace, tapestries, jewelry, crystal, and leather are, as they have always been, the staples of the city's trade. The heart of the city is enclosed by a rough hexagon of boulevards that run along its 14th-century ramparts. Within this belt of ancient streets lies almost all of historic Brussels. Much of the history of the city — and to some degree, the very history of all Europe — can be traced in its growth from Grote Markt to Common Market.

Brussels lies just northeast of the geographic center of Belgium, surrounded by vast forests. Sitting on the crucial intersection of a north-south river (the Senne River now runs underground through the city) and an east-west land route (between Bruges and Cologne), Brussels's destiny as a marketplace was inevitable. Today's city, which celebrated its millennium in 1979, traces its origins to the earliest known written records of the area, which date from 979; but on the eastern edge of town, near the Common Market headquarters, excavations have uncovered Stone Age burial mounds that reveal that a thriving community was on the spot in 5000 BC. The historic town was known as Bruocsella, a bustling Christian community in the 7th century that within 200 years had become an established market for produce from the Senne River valley. The city's character as a center of trade and business was already established. By 1288 Brussels was important enough to be the object of a

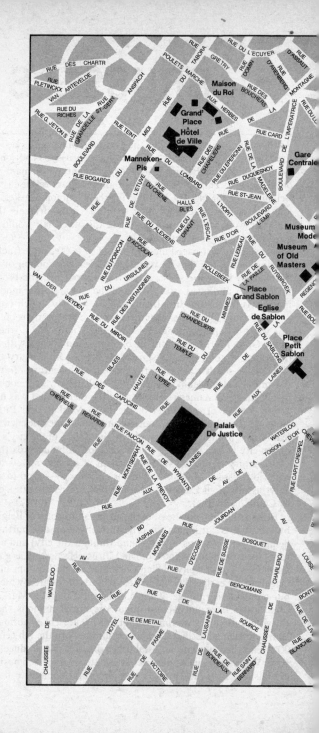

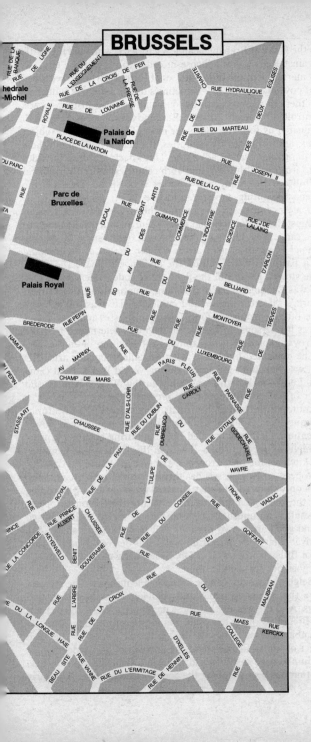

BRUSSELS

pitched battle by the Duke of Brabant, Jean le Victorieux, who won the battle of Woeringen against Renalt the Bellicose in order to protect the city. As nobles of the city married into the ruling houses of Europe, Brussels seesawed between the great powers of Europe — sometimes in one sphere of influence, sometimes in another. In the course of its long and troubled history, it was allied with or controlled by Spain, Austria, Burgundy, France, and Holland.

Although dominated by foreign powers for most of its history and subject to wars, rebellions, and invasions for centuries, the canny Belgian burghers learned early on to prosper even in adversity. This knack of riding the tides of history came to fruition in the 15th and 16th centuries under the political domination of Philip of Burgundy and Charles V of Spain. This was the golden age of Flemish painting, tapestry, and lace.

Finally in 1830, after centuries of foreign rule, the people of Brussels began the revolution against the Hollanders that made them an independent nation. It happened in a strange way: During a performance of an opera, *La Muette de Portici* by Daniel François Auber, at the *Théâtre Royal de la Monnaie* (Mint Theater), a patriotic song aroused the audience to leave the opera house, take to the streets, and begin the fight. After independence, the first King of Belgium was Leopold of Saksen-Koburg, a naturalized Englishman and Queen Victoria's "dearest uncle" and confidant. He was followed by Leopold II, who is often remembered for his many mistresses and for the fact that the Congo was his personal property, but who was determined to make Brussels a truly royal capital. Town planning, not painting or music, fascinated him and he dedicated himself to what he called "outside art." His nephew, Albert I, was Belgium's great hero during World War I. Next came the controversial Leopold III, who was king during World War II and abdicated in favor of his son, Baudouin, the present king.

Brussels has known little tranquillity in its long history. For centuries Spain, Austria, France, and Holland made Belgium an arena for their power politics; in this century, Germany invaded Belgium during both world wars and used it as a highway for its armies. Twice in this century the Germans have set up field kitchens for their troops in the Grand' Place.

Like many European cities, Brussels has thrived despite such vicissitudes. Its people have not only endured, but have amassed great fortunes while doing it, and garnered the sophistication and taste to use their money to best advantage. The result is an unusually rich tapestry of a city, well endowed with good food and good art.— two passions that most Belgians share. The food of Brussels rivals that of France, from which it is derived. And it is said that if a resident of Brussels loses wife or job, he neither gets drunk nor calls out his rival. He goes out for a good dinner.

A clue to the Belgian character can be found in Flemish art. The greatest Belgian artists are the Breughels, elder and younger; Hans Memling; and Peter Paul Rubens. And the worlds that these men portrayed — the peasant simplicity of the Breughels' lusty canvases, the mysticism of Memling, and Rubens's deft combination of things of the spirit and things of the flesh — reflect an aspect of life in Brussels and the attitude of its residents.

Although Belgium's place in the world is firmly established, a domestic problem remains that has been plaguing the country for centuries. The early tribes that settled Belgium were Latin and Germanic, and the country today is a mixture — not a blend — of the two heritages. Linguistically and culturally, the two have never fused. The bitterness between the two factions has led to a series of political crises that continue to this day. The Walloons, French-speaking Belgians, live in Belgium's four southwestern provinces; the Flemish, who speak Flemish (or Nederlands), a form of Dutch, are in the north and northeast. The government, a democratic republic, is an uneasy coalition between the two groups. Brussels sits in Brabant, the central province, and, as a compromise, every street sign here is in both languages, just as every official speech or decree has to be in French and Flemish. One solution for people is to speak the ubiquitous third language, a good British English.

This 1,000-year-old cosmopolitan and international city is a delightful and restorative place to visit, with its variety of excellent restaurants, the wealth of great Flemish paintings in its *Museum of Old Masters,* and the exquisite and ubiquitous Art Nouveau architecture. Brussels is, above all, an art-loving city, and it hosts nearly 100 museums and a number of gracious parks. The ebullient creativity of the Bruxellois is evident everywhere, even in the subways: In a city where riders are treated daily to views of works by such leading Belgian artists as Paul Delvaux, it should come as no surprise that this is also the comic-strip capital of the world. Whatever else you do, you will find yourself returning again and again to the Grand' Place. Some people prefer it in the early morning, when it is given over to a vast flower market and the sun drenches the colors splashed across the cobblestones. Others prefer it at night, when floodlights lace the centuries-old buildings with gold. Day or night, taken in from the comfort of one of the cafés that ring it, the Grand' Place is a sight one never forgets.

BRUSSELS AT-A-GLANCE

SEEING THE CITY: The Palais de Justice, at Place Poelaert, is on a hill from which you can see the city, especially the older section of town. The Palais was one of the largest monuments built in Europe during the 19th century.

SPECIAL PLACES: Most of the interesting sights in town are situated within the inner circle of boulevards that enclose the central sections of town; a great majority lie in the rather small area between the Grand' Place and Parc de Bruxelles and can easily be covered on foot.

IN TOWN

Grand' Place – Reputed to be Europe's most beautiful square and an irresistible magnet to everyone, Grand' Place is the historic heart of Brussels. It doesn't matter whether you see it for the first time by day or by night. Just wander around it and get the feel of the place. Then go back a second time for your serious sightseeing. And don't miss the bird market and the flower market, both on Sunday mornings.

It is hard to believe that this beautiful square was destroyed by Louis XIV's armies in 1695 during a 35-hour bombardment. Most of the square, including the spire of the town hall, burned down, but within 3 years the people of Brussels had rebuilt it all.

In the square are the guild houses, the King's House (see below), and the town hall, unquestionably the most beautiful building in Brussels. Its spire is topped by a statue of St. Michael, patron saint of Brussels. Construction was begun in the 15th century and its style is pure Gothic. Inside is an excellent collection of tapestries. The building is considered a symbol of the city's freedom and it is rated as one of Europe's finest examples of 15th-century architecture. Closed Saturdays and Mondays. Admission charge (phone: 512-7554).

The other buildings around the square are guildhalls built between 1696 and 1698, after the originals were destroyed in the 1695 bombardment. Among the guilds represented are the bakers, coopers, archers, boatmen, haberdashers, butchers, and brewers.

Wander through the narrow, medieval streets leading off the Grand' Place. Their names are straight out of the Middle Ages: Street of the Herring, Stove Street, Pepper Street, Butter Street, Street of the Cheese Market — all dating from when this area was one vast marketplace.

Maison du Roi (King's House) – This historic building, on the site of a 13th-century bread market, was rebuilt in the 1870s. It houses the *Musée Communal* (Municipal Museum of the City of Brussels), which has exhibitions on the history and archaeology of the city. There are also examples of the applied arts of Brussels, such as tapestries, lace, and goldsmiths' work, and here are displayed the clothing and uniforms for the *Manneken-Pis* (see below). Closed weekend afternoons and Mondays. Admission charge. Grand' Place (phone: 511-2742).

Maison des Brasseurs (Brewery Museum) – Set in the building of the ancient brewers' guild, right in the Grand' Place, is a collection of old beer-making equipment. Next door is a charming drinking house where you can taste the various beers. Closed Saturday afternoons, Sundays, and the week between Christmas and New Year's. Admission charge. 10 Grand' Place (phone: 511-4987).

Manneken-Pis – Southwest of the Grand' Place is the small bronze 17th-century statue by Jerôme Duquesnoy. This impudent little boy making water is considered symbolic of the city's irreverent spirit. There are many guesses as to its origin, but all that anybody knows for sure is that it has been here since 1619. Periodically, he is stolen and then returned safely. His dazzling wardrobe, which he sometimes wears, is on display at the King's House. He has over 396 suits of clothing, given to him by everybody from Louis XV of France to the Boy Scouts of America and the Allied Armies of World War II. Rue de l'Etuve, just off the Grand' Place.

Galeries St.-Hubert – Built in 1847, just north of the Grand' Place, this is the oldest arcade in Europe and has been a fashionable promenade since it was built. There are elegant shops and restaurants here, and the surrounding streets, such as the quaint and narrow Petite Rue des Bouchers, are known for their many fine restaurants. Rue du Marché-aux-Herbes.

Parc de Bruxelles (Brussels Park) – Near the fine arts complex, this historic park was originally the hunting ground of the Dukes of Brabant. It was laid out in the formal French manner during the 18th century, when it was a fashionable promenade. In 1830, the park was the scene of heavy fighting between Dutch troops and patriots. The Palais du Roi, the office of the sovereign, overlooks the park just east of the Place Royale. The Rue Ducale boasts a row of aristocratic mansions. Byron lived in #51 when he composed the Waterloo stanzas of *Childe Harold.*

Royal Square – Between the palace and the fine arts complex is this elegantly proportioned neo-classical square, built during the 18th century. The statue of Charles of Lorraine was removed by anti-Royalists during the French Revolution and replaced by one of Godfrey of Bouillon, leader of the first Crusade.

Musée d'Art Ancien (Museum of Old Masters) – This is a very large collection of paintings, mostly Flemish, from the 14th to the 17th century. Included are the works of Rubens, the Breughels, and Van Dyck, among others. Closed Mondays and public holidays. No admission charge. 3 Rue de la Régence (phone: 513-9630).

Museum of Modern Art – Next to the *Musée d'Art Ancien,* this new building — with underground levels — is a dramatic showcase for an extensive collection of art from 1880 to the present. This museum contains what is probably the most extensive collection of works by Belgium's greatest modern artists — among them Paul Delvaux, James Ensor, and René Magritte. When taken together, the two-museum complex (known as the *Royal Museums of Fine Arts*), comprises one of Europe's most impressive art museums. Closed Mondays and public holidays. 1 Pl. Royale (phone: 513-9630).

Church of Notre-Dame-des-Victoires — du-Sablon – Right near the fine arts complex, this 15th-century church is an outstanding example of late Gothic architecture. According to tradition, a Brussels woman had a vision that she should bring a statue of the Virgin Mary from Antwerp to Brussels; when she did so, her boat was guided by angels. She presented the statue to the crossbowmen, and their chapel became a popular place for pilgrimage. So many people crowded the chapel that in 1400 work began on the present church. Pl. du Petit Sablon.

Grand Sablon Square – Below the church, the heart of the antiques center of Brussels is the scene of a book and antiques market on weekends. The streets of this bustling area are lined with art galleries, antiques shops, cafés, restaurants, and the city's most esteemed bakery, *Wittamer.* Just off the square is the Romanesque church of Notre-Dame-de-la-Chapelle, burial place of painter Pieter Brueghel the Elder and the philosopher Spinoza.

Petit Sablon Square – This square is dotted with 48 small bronze statues representing the medieval trade guilds. A formal garden slopes down the square from the church above and contains statues of the counts of Egmont and Hoorn, two of Brussels's martyrs of independence. In 1568 these great Flemish (Catholic) noblemen were beheaded in the Grand' Place for protesting to Philip II of Spain about persecution of Protestants. Egmont's courage was celebrated in a play by Goethe and an overture by Beethoven. Nearby, his home, the 16th-century Egmont Palace, is now the scene of many international receptions. Off the Place du Petit Sablon is the Rue des Six Jeunes Hommes, which has some lovely old houses.

St. Michael's Cathedral – Sitting majestically on top of a hill near the center of town, the national cathedral of Belgium is one of the oldest buildings in Brussels. Begun in the 13th century, it's in typical Belgian Gothic style. Its 16th-century stained glass windows were donated by Emperor Charles V. The baroque pulpit and the mausoleums are also worthy of note. Bd. de l'Impératrice at Place Ste. Gudule.

Colonne du Congrès (Congress Column) – Near the cathedral, the column was built in 1850 to honor the national congress that promulgated the Belgian constitution, after the 1830 revolution. On top of the column is a statue of King Leopold I. In front is the eternal flame that burns in memory of the unknown soldiers from both world wars. From the esplanade there is a good view of the entire city. Rue Royale, north of St. Michael's Cathedral at Place du Congrès.

Royal Museum of Art and History – In the Parc du Cinquantenaire at the eastern end of town, this is one of the largest museums of its kind. Its exhibits include ancient civilizations, particularly Egyptian and Greco-Roman, Belgian history and folklore, and the useful and decorative arts in Europe. Closed Mondays and certain holidays. No admission charge. 10 Parc du Cinquantenaire (phone: 733-9610).

Art Nouveau in Brussels – Surprisingly few foreigners are aware that Brussels is home to more important examples of buildings designed in the graciously curvilinear, turn-of-the-century architectural style known as Art Nouveau than any other city in the world. In addition to the museum/workshop of *Victor Horta,* one of Art Nouveau's foremost proponents (25 Rue Américaine), a number of period buildings still stand in Brussels. The *Hôtel Solvay* (224 Av. Louise), *Maison Stoclet* (281 Av. de Tervuren), and *Hôtel Tassel* (6 Rue Paul-Emile Janson, now the Mexican Embassy) are probably the most famous of the private residences. Among the public Art Nouveau buildings worth visiting are two hotels — the *Pullman Astoria* (103 Rue Royale) and the *Métropole* (31 Pl. de Brouckère) — a restaurant, *De Ultième Hallucinatie* (316 Rue Royale), and the *Falstaff Café* (25-27 Rue Henri-Maus). Excellent specialized tours can be arranged through ARAU (phone: 513-4761).

OUT OF TOWN

Since Belgium is such a small country (only 11,750 square miles), even its major cities of Bruges, Antwerp, and Ghent are within a short distance of Brussels.

Maison d'Erasme (Erasmus's House) – In the southwestern suburb of Anderlecht, this was not, in fact, Erasmus's house, but the home of a friend where the "Prince of Humanists" stayed in about 1521. Nevertheless, this is a beautiful patrician residence, immensely evocative of the personality of the man. Rooms are richly furnished in 16th-century style; there's a library and a quiet walled garden as well as documents to illustrate the life and work of Erasmus. The house also includes a small but excellent collection of Renaissance paintings, including Hans Holbein's portrait of Erasmus and works by Roger van der Weyden and Hieronymus Bosch. Closed Tuesdays and Fridays. Admission charge. 31 Rue du Chapitre, Anderlecht (phone: 521-1383).

Church of St. Pierre and St. Guidon – Also in Anderlecht, at Place de la Vaillance (phone: 521-8415), not far from Erasmus's House, you might want to look at the 15th-century Gothic Church of St. Pierre and St. Guidon with its ancient crypt and Renaissance wall paintings. Just north of the church on the Rue du Chapelain is a small, interesting Flemish convent (*béguinage*), founded in 1252 and restored in 1956 to its original appearance, with the mother superior's room, kitchen, courtyard, and so on. 4 Rue du Chapelain, Anderlecht.

Atomium – The Parc du Centenaire, in a northern suburb of Brussels, was the site of the 1958 World's Fair. The symbol of the fair is the Atomium, which represents the molecule of a crystal of iron magnified 65 billion times. There's an elevator to a restaurant at the top and escalators to various spheres that contain exhibitions — most of them now dated — on the peaceful uses of atomic energy. There is also a vast group of exhibition halls dating from the 1935 and 1958 World's Fairs. Opened just recently on the site is the Bruparck, comprised of the Oceadium, an indoor, aquatic amusement park; Kinepolis, with 23 movie theaters under one roof; the Village, whose cafés, restaurants, shops, and playground all evoke Brussels of the past; and Mini-Europe, with 400 models (scaled 1:25) of the Old World's most famous landmarks. Open daily. Admission charge. Heysel, Laeken (phone 478-6161).

Waterloo – On the night before the battle, the Duchess of Richmond gave a huge ball on Brussels's Rue Royale that was immortalized in Lord Byron's *Childe Harold's Pilgrimage* and Thackeray's novel *Vanity Fair.* The site of the famous battle is only 12 miles (19 km) south of the city and is accessible by public bus and by coach excursions. If you climb the lion monument (Butte du Lion), you can see a somewhat obstructed view of the battlefield itself. There is a museum of battle nearby. Open daily. Admission charge. 90 Chemin des Vertes Bornes (phone: 384-3139).

A better sense of the battle can be gained from a visit to another museum in the town of Waterloo, which is 1.8 miles (3 km) north of the battlefield and was once Wellington's headquarters. *Wellington Museum* (closed the week between Christmas and New Year's). Admission charge. 147 Chaussée de Bruxelles (phone: 354-5954).

Villers-la-Ville – About 15 miles (24 km) south of Waterloo are the awe-inspiring ruins of a 12th-century Cistercian abbey, complete with dining hall and brewery. Closed October through mid-March. Admission charge (phone: 071-879555).

Beersel Castle – This early-14th-century château-fort is 10 miles (16 km) south of Brussels. The brick building, with three towers and set in the middle of a moat, has no furnishings but does have the obligatory drawbridge, lookout tower, and torture room. Visitors (especially those with small children) should be careful around the castle since there are lots of open windows and few safety rails. Open daily from March to mid-November, weekends only the rest of the year; closed in January. Admission charge.

Gaasbeek Castle – This historic 13th-century castle (many times restored) is 6 miles (10 km) southwest of Brussels. Though its exterior, with seven round towers, is medieval, its interior contains Renaissance furnishings and valuable tapestries, furniture, and objets d'art. There's a 100-acre park. The view from the terrace in the garden was painted by Pieter Breughel the Elder. Closed Mondays from April through October, Fridays in July and August. No admission charge.

■**EXTRA SPECIAL:** Take a 1¼-hour train ride to Bruges (in Flemish, Brugge), often called Die Scone, "the beautiful." This is one of Europe's best-preserved medieval cities, a place of rare charm: narrow cobbled streets with picturesque canals spanned by more than 50 bridges. The maze of winding streets makes driving difficult, but most of the places in-town can be reached on foot.

Everything centers around the Grote Markt, or main square; you can enjoy a 40-minute tour of the city by the canal boats that are anchored just southeast of the Grote Markt or rent a horse-drawn carriage right in the square. Also on the Grote Markt is the tourist office. Don't miss the famous belfry, very tall — 353 feet — with a carillon of 49 bells. Concerts are held year-round.

Bruges is famous as a lacemaking center, and the finest examples of the art are exhibited in the *Gruuthuse Museum,* a 15th-century palace with fine furniture and a superb collection of old Flemish lace. Other outstanding places are the *Groeninge Museum,* containing a great many fine examples of Flemish art; the graceful 13th-century Gothic cathedral; and the *Memling Museum* at St. Jans Hospital, containing the oldest pharmacy in the world as well as many important works of the great 15th-century painter.

Bruges has many other sights, not least of which are the streets themselves, narrow and winding and lined with gabled houses. You can see the town in one rather strenuous day or, if you choose, stay overnight at one of the charming hotels, such as the *Duc de Bourgogne* at 12 Huidenvettersplein (phone: 050-332038).

SOURCES AND RESOURCES

 TOURIST INFORMATION: Basic information about Brussels is available in the US from the Belgian National Tourist Office, 745 Fifth Ave., New York, NY 10151 (212-758-8130). In Brussels, be sure to visit the main office at 61 Rue Marché-aux-Herbes (phone: 512-3030) for excellent maps and leaflets, calendars of tourist events, and aid of any sort, or the Brussels Tourist Office in the Hôtel de Ville, Grand' Place (phone: 513-8940). At the airport, contact a multilingual hostess in the baggage area, or phone 722-3000.

The American Embassy is at 27 Bd. du Régent (phone: 513-3830).

Local Coverage – The best English-language publication is *The Bulletin,* a weekly in a newsmagazine format. It's available at local newsstands.

Food – The tourist office puts out a booklet, *Gourmet Restaurants,* available for a small fee. It includes a gastronomic rating of more than 100 restaurants as decided by "five of the best food critics in Brussels."

Telephone – The area code for Brussels is 02.

CLIMATE AND CLOTHES: Brussels has a temperate climate, much like that of the northeast corner of the US. But the stormy North Sea is not far away, so rain and wind often batter the capital. Take a raincoat or umbrella, just to be safe. Summer weather is variable, with mean temperatures in the 70s F (21-26C); winter temperatures are rarely below freezing and hover around 40F (4C).

Dress as you would in any world capital. Dress up for dinner at the more fashionable restaurants. *Note:* Women should avoid wearing shorts, especially short shorts. These are rarely seen on streets or in shops and will invite unwelcome stares.

 GETTING AROUND: Airport – Brussels National Airport at Zaventem is a 20-minute drive from downtown. Taxi fare should run about 1,000 Belgian francs (about $26). Greater Brussels taxis (*Autolux,* phone: 720-3604; *Taxis Oranges,* phone: 513-6200) are more economical than those parked at the airport. An efficient train service links the airport directly with center city; it operates every 20 to 30 minutes from 5:39 AM to 11:46 PM. City buses marked BZ or 358 run from Zaventem to the North Station.

Bus, Tram, and Métro – A clear, detailed map is available at the tourist office. Rides are inexpensive, and you can buy a five- or ten-ride card at a savings. There is a special 1-day unlimited ticket for about $4.

Car Rental – *Avis* is at 145 Rue Américaine (phone: 537-1280) and *Hertz* is at 8 Bd. Lemonnier (phone: 513-2886). Offices of major rental agencies are also found at Zaventem airport.

Taxi – Taxis are plentiful but quite expensive. The tip is included in the fare. You can order a cab from *Taxis Verts* (Green Taxis) by calling 511-2244, or pick one up at a taxi stand.

 SPECIAL EVENTS: Every spring, usually in May, the *Royal Palace Greenhouses* are opened to the public. In Laeken, just a few miles north of downtown Brussels, the indoor gardens feature exotic flowering trees and plants, many of them native to Zaire, once the Belgian colony called the Congo. Call the tourist office for exact dates and hours (phone: 512-3030).

Starting officially on June 27, but actually in late May with a series of preliminary park concerts dubbed "kiosks à musique," is the annual *Festival Musical d'Eté.*

The *Ommegang* pageant takes place in the Grand' Place on the first Thursday in July at 9 PM. It is a centuries-old spectacle commemorating the miraculous arrival of a statue of the Virgin Mary in the Sablon church. The word *ommegang* means "to walk around," which is done much as it was in the 16th century for Charles V and his court. The oldest and noblest families take part in the procession, representing their ancestors who took part in the original pageant. This colorful, splendid tradition is one of Belgium's most popular attractions. Tickets for bleacher seats go fast; see the tourist office.

During August, September, and early October, Brussels is part of the *Festival of Flanders,* one of Europe's major music festivals, featuring internationally known orchestras, soloists, operas, and dance companies — and tickets are reasonably priced. For information write the Festival of Flanders, 18 Eugène Flageyplein, Brussels 1050 (phone: 648-1484). Not to be outdone, Wallonia has its own music festival beginning in June. Contact the Festival of Wallonia, 175 Rue des Brasseurs, Namur 5000 (phone: 081-223034) for details. There's also a month-long fair in summer (mid-July to mid-August) on the Boulevard du Midi, featuring rides and local foods.

In August, when the royal couple take their holiday, the ornate sitting rooms and splendid ballroom of the Royal Palace are open for inspection by one and all. No admission charge. Place des Palais.

Every other year in September and October since 1969, Brussels has produced its own international arts festival in which the events focus on a specific nation. Art exhibitions; music, dance, and theater performances; film screenings; and literary conferences all attract the top names in their respective fields. *Europalia* in 1989 was devoted to the arts of Japan, and in 1991 will focus on Portugal.

 MUSEUMS: Besides those mentioned in *Special Places,* some of the more interesting museums include the following.

Autoworld – A spectacular collection of vintage cars, opened in 1986. Featured are curious old Peugeots and Model-T Fords, along with the Cadillacs of FDR and JFK. Open daily. Admission charge. Esplanade du Cinquantenaire, Etterbeek (phone: 736-4165).

Chinese Pavilion – A first-rate collection of 17th- and 18th-century Chinese and Japanese porcelains. Closed Mondays and public holidays. No admission charge. 44 Av. Van Praet Laeken (phone: 268-1608).

Horta Museum – The home and studio of the Art Nouveau architect Victor Horta. Open daily except Mondays and public holidays, from 2 to 5:30 PM. Admission charge. 25 Rue Américaine (phone: 537-1692).

Museum of Fine Arts of Ixelles – Splendid Dürers, Toulouse-Lautrec posters, and works of French and Belgian Impressionists. Closed Mondays, weekday mornings, and public holidays. No admission charge to the permanent collection. 71 Rue Jean-Van-Volsem, Ixelles (phone: 511-9084).

Museum of Musical Instruments – Housing 5,000 instruments from the Bronze Age to the present. Open Sunday mornings; Tuesday, Thursday, and Saturday afternoons; and Wednesday evenings. 17 Pl. du Petit Sablon (phone: 512-0848).

Museum of Natural Science – Noteworthy for its collection of well-preserved dinosaur skeletons, unearthed in western Belgium in 1878. Open daily. No admission charge. 29 Rue Vautier, Ixelles (648-0475).

Royal Library – More than 3 million volumes as well as coins, maps, and splendid illuminated manuscripts. Closed Sundays, holidays, and the last week of August. No admission charge. Mont des Arts (phone: 519-5311).

Royal Museum of Central Africa – The brainchild of colonialist King Leopold II, it has an interesting art gallery and a panorama of African life. A formal French garden sits behind the museum. Open daily. No admission charge. 13 Leuvensesteenweg, Tervuren (phone: 767-5401).

 SHOPPING: Brussels is not a city for bargain hunters, but you will get top quality for the price you pay. In Brussels, or any other Belgian city, look for Val St. Lambert, one of the world's finest crystals. Pewter and linen are also excellent values. Leather goods and women's clothing are terribly chic and equally *cher.* All the top couturiers are represented here, from Dior and Armani to Valentino and Olivier Strelli.

Lace is the product you will see most often, especially in the souvenir shops around the Grand' Place. Some of the little old ladies who made Brussels lace world famous are still working, but alas, much of the lace is now machine-made in Hong Kong. This lace is usually used on cocktail napkins and placemats, which make small, inexpensive, and easily portable gifts. Look carefully at tags to know what you are buying.

Belgian carpets are usually of a very high standard. In most cases, they are mechanically produced and offer a wide variety of styles and materials. Copies of Oriental designs are said to be the biggest sellers now — even in the Middle East. To ensure quality, look for the "T" mark on the carpet backing.

Antiques are usually of excellent quality. Try the Saturday and Sunday market at the Place du Grand Sablon. You will usually see some lovely things there, even if you are only "just looking." There is also a book market at the same place.

Although there are fine shops all over the city, there are two main shopping districts. The more modestly priced is the one in the area including the Boulevard Adolphe-Max, the Boulevard Anspach, Rue Neuve, Rue Marché-aux-Herbes, and Galeries St.-Hubert. The other, uptown, where the chic boutiques are located, is the Avenue Louise, Avenue de la Toison d'Or, and the Boulevard de Waterloo. The newly renovated Les Jardins du Sablons, at 36 Pl. du Sablon and 6 Rue des Minimes, houses 36 shops and a tearoom under its skylit cupola. Anderlecht, a suburb of Brussels, has one of the largest covered suburban shopping centers in Europe.

A good place to get a sampling of everything is at *L'Innovation* (also known as *Inno*), Brussels's finest department store (111 Rue Neuve).

Art et Sélection – Famous Val St. Lambert crystal. 83 Rue Marché-aux-Herbes.

Biot-Believre – Linen tablecloths and the like, hand embroidered on request. 8 Rue de Naples.

CBRS – The best of Belgian carpets from a variety of manufacturers. 431 Bd. Emile-Bockstael.

Corné Toison d'Or – Belgian chocolates for the connoisseur. 12 Av. de la Toison d'Or, 24-26 Galerie du Roi, and several other locations.

Delvaux – The Gucci of Brussels, this is *the* place for leather goods. 31 Galerie de la Reine, 22-24 Bd. Adolphe-Max, and 24a Av. de la Toison d'Or.

Dujardin – A Belgian institution, this unique store sells fashionable, well-made clothing for children. 8-10 Av. Louise.

Madymous – Official distributor of Huy pewter, considered Belgium's best. Look for the Huy hallmark (the town's castle mark) to be sure. 42b-c-d Rue du Noyer.

Manufacture Belge de Dentelles – Lace and lacemaking. 6-8 Galerie de la Reine.

Nina Meert – A boutique for dresses, blouses, and lingerie made of Belgian lace and linen. 5 Rue de Florence.

Textilux Center – A large selection of Brussels tapestries in traditional and modern designs. 41 Rue du Lombard, near the *Mannekin-Pis.*

Wittamer – Delectable chocolates and pastries. 12-13 Pl. au Grand Sablon.

 SPORTS AND FITNESS: Fitness Centers – The facilities at the *Brussels Hilton,* 38 Bd. de Waterloo (phone: 513-8877), and the *Brussels Sheraton,* 3 Pl. Rogier (phone: 219-3400), can be used for a fee. The *Woluwé* sports center, near Forêt de Soignes at 87 Av. Mounier (phone: 762-8522), has an Olympic-size swimming pool and also charges admission.

Golf – The *Royale Golf Club de Belgique* (Royal Golf Club of Belgium), Château de Ravenstein, Tervuren (phone: 767-5801), is the diplomats' club. The clubhouse is in one of the buildings belonging to the Ravenstein Château property. The facilities are excellent and only 7 miles (11 km) from downtown Brussels.

Horseback Riding – Try *Royal Etrier Belge,* 19 Chaussée du Vert Chasseur (phone: 374-2860), or contact the *Fédération Royale Belge des Sports Equestries,* 38 Av. Hamoir (phone: 374-4734).

Jogging – Best is Brussels Park, opposite the Royal Palace and bordered by Rue Royal. More expansive is Cinquantenaire Park (take the Métro to Schuman and you'll spot the park just ahead). About a mile away on Avenue de Tervuren is the hilly Woluwé Park (tram #44 from Montgomery Métro station). Farther afield is the Forêt de Soignes (Royal Forest), just outside the city (take tram #44 and signal the driver to stop as the woodland comes into sight). Because of the traffic, jogging is not recommended on the streets of Brussels. Real enthusiasts will enjoy the annual 20-km race held in June at the Cinquantenaire Park.

Soccer – Known as *football,* this is the most popular spectator sport. Major games are played at *Heysel Stadium,* 135 Av. du Marathon (phone: 513-3977).

Swimming – At *Bains de Bruxelles,* 28 Rue du Chevreuil (phone: 511-2468); *Ca-*

lypso, 60 Av. L. Wiener, Boitsfort (phone: 673-3929); and *Poséidon,* 2 Av. des Vaillants, Woluwé-St.-Lambert (phone: 771-6655).

   Tennis – Try the *Brussels Lawn Tennis Club,* 890 Chaussée de Waterloo (phone: 374-9259).

 THEATER: The marionette theater, *de Toone,* is a must. Popular plays are performed by puppets in Brussels slang nightly except Sundays, at 21 Petite Rue des Bouchers (phone: 217-2753). Most modern plays are in French or Flemish, though occasionally there is some amateur theater in English. Brussels has more than 17 theaters staging a variety of plays; check the daily newspapers for schedules.

 MUSIC: One of the world's most prestigious music competitions is the *Concours Reine Elisabeth,* named for the grandmother of the present king. It takes place in May and is usually covered by TV and radio.

   The *Théâtre Royal de la Monnaie,* Pl. de la Monnaie (phone: 218-1202), has been renovated in splendid fashion. The *Monnaie* is the home of opera and ballet in Brussels, but it is also an important part of its history. The original building dated from the late 17th century and was built on the site of the old mint (hence the name). The present building dates from 1817. In 1830, at a performance of Auber's opera *La Muette de Portici* at the *Monnaie,* one of the patriotic songs ("Sacred love of the fatherland, give us courage and pride") so inflamed the audience that they streamed out of the opera house and unleashed the rebellion that led ultimately to Belgium's independence. Recitals and concerts by world-famous musicians are given throughout the year, usually in the *Palais des Beaux-Arts,* 23 Rue Ravenstein (phone: 512-5045). Sunday morning concerts, usually by string quartets, are offered at the *Astoria* hotel, 103 Rue Royale. Call 513-0965 (*La Boîte à Musique*).

 NIGHTCLUBS AND NIGHTLIFE: As in most large cities, the nightclubs are often tourist traps, so be prepared to spend a lot of money if you go to them. *En Plein Ciel,* 38 Bd. de Waterloo (phone: 513-8877), the rooftop restaurant of the *Hilton* hotel, has a small dance floor. The atmosphere is pleasant; the view, on a starry night, impressive. Reservations are necessary. *Le Mozart,* at 541 Chaussée d'Alsemberg (phone: 344-0809), is a pub that serves jazz as well as food until 4 AM. You can have dinner up until 6 AM at *Safir,* the classic all-night spot at 23 Petite Rue des Bouchers (phone: 511-8478). Reservations are not necessary. Live jazz late into the night in a requisite smoky atmosphere is the Saturday-night staple at *Bierodrome,* 21 Pl. Fernand-Cocq. Pol (phone: 512-0456), the owner, is a fixture on the local jazz scene. Popular discos include *Le Crocodile Club,* at the *Royal Windsor* hotel, 5 Rue Duquesnoy (phone: 511-4215); *Le Garage,* 16-18 Rue Duquesnoy (phone: 512-6622), for trendy but blaring New Wave; and Brussels's most outrageous disco, *Le Mirano Continental* at 38 Chaussée de Louvain (phone: 217-3756).

   Brussels also has some superb café-bistros, including *'T Spinnekopke,* 1 Pl. du Jardin aux Fleurs (phone: 511-8695), and *De Ultième Hallucinatie,* 316 Rue Royale (phone: 217-0614), an Art Nouveau marvel where fine food is served. For a pleasant nightcap, try *Au Roi d'Espagne* in the Grand' Place (phone: 513-0807) or *Au Bon Vieux Temps,* 12 Rue Marché-aux-Herbes (phone: 217-2626). The *Café Métropole* has an Art Nouveau interior and a outdoor café heated for year-round dining (phone: 219-2384). Reservations are not necessary. The *Falstaff Bistro,* near the Grand' Place at 17-23 Rue Maus (phone: 511-8789), has turn-of-the-century decor and a lively clientele. Beer lovers might stop by *La Houblonnière,* 4 Pl. de Londres (phone: 511-1423), *La Lunette,* 3 Pl. de la Monnaie (218-0378), or *Le Jugement Dernier,* 165 Chaussée de Haecht (phone: 217-9597), where scores of Belgian beers are available for sampling.

BEST IN TOWN

 CHECKING IN: A double room and bath in an expensive Brussels hotel usually runs from $145 to $200 and more; a moderately priced hotel charges between $80 and $125; an inexpensive hotel can be $50 to $80. Rates include a 16% service charge and VAT. Significantly lower rates prevail on weekends and during July and August. All telephone numbers are in the 02 area code unless otherwise indicated.

Amigo – Gracious and comfortable, in an ideal location, only 1 street away from the Grand' Place. It has the charm (but not the noise) of the square and an aristocratic interior with velvet upholstery and silk wainscoting. There's a garage, a restaurant, a bar, and 183 spacious rooms and suites. Best are the 6th-floor apartments with terraces. 1-3 Rue de l'Amigo (phone: 511-5910). Expensive.

Arcade Stéphanie – Close to one of the best shopping districts in Brussels, this 142-room hotel is convenient for shoppers, but its front rooms can be noisy. Children under 12 free in adult's room. 91-93 Av. Louise (phone: 539-0240). Expensive.

Brussels Sheraton – Brussels's largest hotel (540 rooms) has several dining rooms, including one serving haute cuisine, and a coffee shop. It's a sleek, modern, 31-story affair with a handsome lobby, well-appointed, good-size rooms, a discotheque, a fitness center, and a pool. 3 Pl. Rogier (phone: 219-3400). Expensive.

Hilton International Brussels – This skyscraper hotel is one of the city's largest (369 rooms), near the Avenue Louise shopping area, and is where the international business set hangs out. All rooms have TV sets and air conditioning; duplexes have balconies and full kitchens. The roof garden restaurant affords a superb view of the city, and there is an authentic French restaurant, an English pub, and a bar-discotheque patronized by locals. 38 Bd. de Waterloo (phone: 513-8877). Expensive.

Holiday Inn Brussels Airport – Like any other member of the chain, this large (228-room) hotel is clean, convenient, and standardized. It has tennis courts, a pool, and a sauna. Courtesy buses run to the airport and into town. 7 Holiday St., near the airport in Diegem (phone: 720-5865). Expensive.

Jollyhotel Atlanta – Recently redone, this hotel takes its name from the heyday of *Gone With the Wind.* There is a new rooftop restaurant, *La Veranda,* with a good view of the city. The hotel is downtown, and some of the 244 rooms can be noisy. 7 Bd. Adolphe-Max (phone: 217-0120). Expensive.

Pullman Astoria – A smaller hotel (113 rooms) with a lovely staircase and quiet, comfortable rooms, this hostelry is a souvenir of the Belle Epoque. The bar is decorated to represent a Pullman compartment. 103 Rue Royale (phone: 217-6290). Expensive.

Regency – One of the more gracious of the newer hotels, with 320 rooms, many deluxe suites, a stylish restaurant, meeting facilities, and a 24-hour coffee shop. Unfortunately, the neighborhood is not the safest. 250 Rue Royale (phone: 217-1234). Expensive.

Royal Windsor – In the Grand' Place area, this 300-room hotel is Tudor style and its restaurants offer a variety of menus. Its atmosphere is British; its ambience modern and quite pleasant, with soundproofed rooms, TV sets, various room sizes, interesting paneling, and handwoven fabrics. Underground parking garage. 5-7 Rue Duquesnoy (phone: 511-4215). Expensive.

Métropole – The city's last remaining 19th-century hotel has 410 rooms decorated in styles ranging from Art Deco to modern. The lobby, café, and restaurant have recently been restored but still retain last century's charm. 31 Pl. de Brouckère (phone: 217-2300). Expensive to moderate.

Palace – Recently renovated, this 360-room hotel was built in 1910 and overlooks the Botanical Gardens. 3 Rue Gineste (phone: 217-6200). Expensive to moderate.

City Garden – Modern, spacious, and comfortable, this 96-room residential hotel offers kitchenettes and proximity to the Métro and Common Market headquarters. 59 Rue Joseph II (phone: 230-0945). Moderate.

La Légende – This small (32-room) hotel is centrally located in the city, a short walk from the *Manneken-Pis.* 33 Rue de l'Etuve (phone: 512-8290). Inexpensive.

Noga – Although close to the interesting Rue Neuve shopping district, this small hotel is very quiet. 38 Rue du Béguinage (phone: 218-6763). Inexpensive.

 EATING OUT: Brussels's pride in good food extends from the most fashionable to the simplest restaurants, from the most elaborate haute cuisine to simply prepared fresh produce. A good restaurant in Brussels goes to exceptional lengths to please a patron who enjoys good food. If you order pâté, for example, you won't get by without sampling several varieties, while the restaurateur beams at every sign of pleasure that you show. Belgium's cooks are some of the best in the world, and Belgian food, once a stepchild of French cuisine, has developed its own specialties. These include the inevitable Brussels sprouts; asparagus from Malines; red cabbage prepared *à la flamande* (with apple); *carbonnades flamandes,* or beef braised in beer; blood and white sausage called *boudin; waterzooi de volaille,* or chicken in a vegetable and cream soup; *anguilles au vert,* or eels, served with herbs; and mussels served in a variety of ways. Belgian pastries are excellent, especially *pain à la grecque,* a very light, sweet rusk; *gaufres,* or waffles; and tarts made with custard, sugar, or rice. And don't miss *pralines,* the famous Belgian chocolate with a variety of fillings. Bruxellois, the people of Brussels, will tell you that their chocolate is the best in the world — and they may be right. Beer is special here, too, including, among others, Faro, Gueuze-Lambiek, Kriek-Lambiek, and Trappiste.

There are about 1,700 restaurants in the city, and the best rate as virtual national monuments. It's all too easy to spend a small fortune for a good meal, but it's not absolutely necessary. It is unusual to have a bad meal anywhere. A dinner for two, including wine (and remember, most wine is imported), in an expensive restaurant averages $160 to $200; in a moderately priced restaurant, it comes to between $80 and $125; and in an inexpensive one, $75 or less. Unless otherwise noted, Brussels's restaurants take major credit cards. All telephone numbers are in the 02 area code unless otherwise indicated.

Barbizon – This recently renovated, charming villa is in the midst of the Forêt de Soignes and serves such specialties as aspic-coated lobster, smoked salmon and asparagus, and duck and endive salad. Closed Tuesdays and Wednesdays. 95 Welriekendedreef (phone: 657-0462). Expensive.

Bernard – You may initially believe that you have wandered into a grocery store by mistake, but go up one flight to the small dining room where the tables are tucked nose to nose. It looks unpretentious, but it caters mostly to knowledgeable Belgian gastronomes. Closed Sundays, holidays, Monday evenings, and July. Reservations necessary. 93 Rue de Namur (phone: 512-8821). Expensive.

Bruneau – One of Brussels's finest restaurants, boasting three Michelin stars, *Bruneau* serves excellent French cuisine against a pleasant background approaching Art Deco style. Try the *menu de dégustation,* which includes wines chosen to perfectly complement this sampling of the house specialties. Closed Tuesday nights and Wednesdays. 73-75 Av. Broustin (phone: 427-6978). Expensive.

Comme Chez Soi – From the outside, this small townhouse looks inconsequential;

inside is one of the best restaurants in Belgium, and one of the few outside France to earn three Michelin stars. Try the mussels, fish, venison, foie gras, and pastries. Closed Sundays, Mondays, the week of Christmas, and August. Reservations necessary. 23 Pl. Rouppe (phone: 512-2921). Expensive.

La Cravache d'Or – Reopened in October 1988 after extensive renovation, this small, elegant restaurant offers a varied repertoire of foods from land and sea. Open daily. Reservations necessary. 10 Pl. Albert-Leemans (phone: 538-3746). Expensive.

De Bijgaarden – Imaginative cuisine combines with superb management at this impeccable suburban restaurant. *Pheasant Smitane* and *sole Hôtellerie* share the menu with other creative house specialties. Closed Sundays. 20 Isidoor Van Beveren Straat, Groot Bijgaarden (phone: 466-4485). Expensive.

Au Duc d'Arenberg – A 17th-century house with white walls and lots of paintings is the setting for this cheerful restaurant, best known for duck and Normandy crêpes. Closed Sundays and the last week of December. Reservations advised. 9 Pl. du Petit Sablon (phone: 511-1475). Expensive.

L'Ecailler du Palais Royal – Unpretentious from the outside, this is a superb seafood restaurant in a 16th-century guild house in the Grand Sablon. Try turbot, lobster, and oysters in season. Closed Sundays, public holidays, and August. Reservations necessary. 18-20 Rue Bodenbroek (phone: 511-9950). Expensive.

La Maison du Cygne – Making its home in an exquisite 16th-century building, this elegant restaurant is especially proud of such creations as lobster cassoulet, pheasant with chicory, and milk-fed lamb. Closed Saturday lunch, Sundays, and 1 week in August. Reservations advised. 2 Rue Charles Buls, Grand' Place (phone: 511-8244). Expensive.

Les Quatre Saisons – The *Royal Windsor* hotel's award-winning French restaurant is as elegant in ambience as it is in cuisine. Try the duck liver braised in vinegar and mangos, the *salade de Mesclun,* or the sole and crayfish in a lobster and saffron sauce. Open daily for lunch and dinner. Reservations advised. 5 Rue Duquesnoy (phone: 511-4215). Expensive.

Romeyer – The most recent Belgian restaurant to earn a third Michelin star, it's actually a country lodge in the Forêt de Soignes, just a few miles outside the city. Specialties include lobster sausage and stuffed crayfish. Closed Sunday evenings, Mondays, and February and August. Reservations necessary. 109 Steenweg op Groenendaal, Hoeilaart (phone: 657-0581). Expensive.

Villa Lorraine – Probably the country's most famous restaurant. The setting is a lovely villa just outside the city limits; the service is impeccable, the decor sumptuous, the food the sort of French-style stuff of which dreams are made. Try the hot lobster pâté or the sole. Closed Sundays and most of July. Reservations necessary. 75 Av. du Vivier d'Oie (phone: 374-3163). Expensive.

Les Années Folles – A tiny, friendly bistro with a menu that has often been imitated. A reasonably priced fixed menu is always available. Duck breast salad and veal escalope with Calvados are recommended. Closed Saturday lunch and Sundays. 17 Rue Haute (phone: 513-5858). Moderate.

Aux Armes de Bruxelles – This is one of the traditional Brussels restaurants on one of the narrow little streets leading off the Grand' Place. Its specialty is fish. Closed Mondays and the second half of June. Reservations advised. 13 Rue des Bouchers (phone: 511-5598). Moderate.

Auberge de Boendael – Although this restaurant isn't downtown, it's definitely worth the ride for its delicious meat and fish specialties that are grilled over a wood fire. Try to save room for a dessert of homemade coffee ice cream (*café glacé*) and sorbets. Closed weekends. Reservations necessary. 12 Sq. du Vieux Tilleul (phone: 672-7055). Moderate.

Café Henry – A popular tavern with a restaurant in the back that's informal and inviting. Try the steaks or the lamb chops. Dixieland jazz on weekend nights. 8 Bd. de Waterloo (phone: 512-1090). Moderate.

Maison du Boeuf – In the *Brussels Hilton,* overlooking the gardens of the Egmont Palace, this restaurant specializes in shellfish as well as beef. Open daily. Reservations advised. 38 Bd. de Waterloo (phone: 513-8877). Moderate.

L'Ogenblik – A small restaurant with the feel of a Paris bistro. All the waiters wear floor-length aprons, and the menu changes daily to offer astonishing variety. The house specialty, bouillabaisse, is chock full of half a dozen kinds of seafood. Closed Sundays. 1 Galerie des Princes (phone: 511-6151). Moderate.

Chez Jean – Usually packed with regulars, this simple establishment just off the Grand' Place serves tasty Belgian fare. Daily specials are scrawled in soap on wall mirrors. Closed Sundays and Mondays. Reservations advised. 6 Rue Chapeliers (phone: 511-9815). Moderate to inexpensive.

'T Kelderke – A congenial and rustic bistro that serves hearty Belgian fare such as rabbit stewed in beer and *waterzooi.* Closed Saturdays for lunch. 15 Grand' Place (phone: 513-7344). Inexpensive.

St.-Pierre – A modest little place tucked away off the Grand' Place. The service is good and the quality of the food reliable. Open daily for lunch and dinner. 76 Marché aux Herbes (phone: 511-8291). Inexpensive.

Au Vieux Saint-Martin – A favorite place for artists, it is bright and cheerful, with newspapers and magazines to read if you are dining alone. The menu is simple, with Belgian specialties. Open daily. No reservations or credit cards. 38 Pl. du Grand Sablon (phone: 512-6476). Inexpensive.

Le Vimar – Tucked into the corner of a busy square near Common Market headquarters, this small restaurant has long been a favorite of the Bruxellois. Seafood is the specialty: Try the turbot with leeks, mussels in white wine sauce, or seafood casserole. Closed late July to mid-August. Reservations advised. 70 Pl. Jourdan (phone: 231-0949). Inexpensive.

Vincent – On one of the narrow, cobblestone streets near the Grand' Place, this is the place to go for Belgian specialties. *Moules à l'escargot* (mussels cooked in a butter and garlic sauce) is a tasty starter; steaks are a good main course. Closed August. Reservations advised. 8 Rue des Dominicains (phone: 511-2302). Inexpensive.

BUDAPEST

The Danube, central Europe's great river — which flows for 1,770 miles from the Black Forest to the Black Sea, through Ulm, Regensburg, Linz, and Vienna — is particularly wide and beautiful when it reaches Budapest. Arriving from Vienna on the hydrofoil — a 4½-hour trip around the Danube Bend — visitors see Budapest at its most splendid. Buda and Pest, two of the city's three parts (along with smaller Óbuda), each face that mighty river, forming the physical and spiritual center of the Hungarian capital.

Sprawling over the rolling hills of Buda and the almost endless plain of Pest, the two halves of the city form strophe and antistrophe around the Danube. Buda rises and falls along its hills in a swelling reprise of medieval cobblestone streets and ancient buildings, crowned by the neo-Gothic tower of Matthias Church. The streets of Pest — the governmental and commercial center of the city — run in rings and radials around grand squares of monumental buildings and dramatic statues and memorials. Buda and Pest have been united only since 1873, and one has the feeling that the marriage has not yet settled into comfortable middle age. From the river, an observer clearly sees the two buildings that best characterize Budapest's two halves: Matthias Church in Buda, where generations of Hungarian kings were crowned; and Pest's neo-Gothic Parliament, towering like a huge wedding cake on the banks of the river. It is as if both parts of the city relate to the Danube more comfortably than to each other.

So beautiful is this city of 2 million people — one-fifth of the country's population — that visitors might not suspect that Budapest, like other European cities, has a history of recurrent invasion, destruction, and reconstruction that only intensified in this century, including a siege and heavy bombing in World War II in which 33,000 buildings and all the city's bridges were demolished. Witnesses to the revolutionary uprising in 1956 report that Budapest's citizens — who justly adore their city — took to the streets with tears of helplessness streaming down their cheeks as Soviet tanks smashed across the boulevards.

The Hungarian nation was founded by Árpád, a semi-legendary chief of the Magyars, who brought his people from the Urals in the 9th century. Before this time, Budapest had been a Roman town of considerable size called Aquincum. The Magyar cities of Buda and Pest grew as trade and craft centers, thriving especially under Hungary's first king, St. Stephen (who reigned from 997 to 1038). A bloody invasion in 1241, by the Mongols, destroyed both Buda and Pest. The cities were rebuilt and became more and more splendid until the Ottoman Turks arrived in the 16th century, bringing 150 years of decay, poverty, and captivity to Buda. The country fell into the Habsburg Empire in 1686 and stayed there — despite a liberal revolt in March 1948, which czarist troops brutally suppressed the following year, at

Vienna's request — until the end of World War I. Under the bitterly re-
sented Trianon Peace Treaty (1920), Hungary lost a third of its territory to
the new states of Czechoslovakia, Romania, and Yugoslavia. A former admiral in the imperial navy, Miklós Horthy, set up an oppressive right-wing
regime that later allied itself with Nazi Germany. Then Germany occupied
Hungary from 1944 until the country's liberation by the Soviet Red Army
in April 1945. Another oppressive regime followed, this time Communist.
In recent years, however, Hungary's people have enjoyed a relatively liberal
atmosphere, although the government retains strict alliance to the Soviet
bloc.

Today's Budapest is not a place where a tourist is likely to encounter any
of the rigors of dialectical materialism. On the contrary, this is a city that
loves good living. In the absence of an aristocratic elite, Hungary worships
its artists, writers, and musicians. Rock 'n' roll, jeans, provocative T-shirts in
various languages, a tradition of satire, Western magazines, fads, and foods
— all are evident on the streets of Budapest, and visitors from other Communist countries are said to be amazed and titillated by the permissiveness of city
life. Budapest's rich and diverse cultural life includes 22 theaters (where
admission, thanks to government subsidies, is often the equivalent of only
50¢), two opera houses, an operetta theater, three concert halls, a puppet
theater, and more than 20 museums. Bookstores and Gypsy violinists seem
to be everywhere. And meeting at a café is still part of the social and intellectual life.

Hungarian cuisine has absorbed Turkish, French, Italian, Slavic, and other
influences into a deliciously unique blend. The wines of Hungary, like the
world-famous Tokay, are very popular and very good, and Hungarian pastries
rank among the best in the world. There is a popular saying in Budapest that
goes something like, "If only we could afford to live as well as we do —
how well we would live." It is an aphorism that seems ill suited to a Communist country, but it fits life in Budapest like a glove. Its slightly irreverent
humor is characteristic of a city that has listened to tales sweeping down the
river for centuries, and where living well is in part pleasure and part duty,
a tribute to centuries of the good life provided by Budapest and its psychic
source, the ancient, untroubled Danube.

BUDAPEST AT-A-GLANCE

SEEING THE CITY: The best view of Budapest is from the top of Gellért
Hill (Gellért hegy) on the Buda side, which can be climbed from Gellért
Square (Gellért tér). From the balustrades of a stone fort built in 1850 you
will enjoy a panorama of the Danube with its bridges — Margaret Bridge
to Margaret Island in the middle of the Danube, the recreational center of the city; the
historic Chain Bridge to Castle Hill on the Buda side, the oldest part of town; and the
Elizabeth Bridge that connects Buda with the Inner City on the Pest side, the busy
downtown commercial and shopping center.

In front of the fort, or Citadella, is the gigantic Liberation Monument, a statue of
a woman holding an olive branch, which is sometimes called Budapest's Statue of

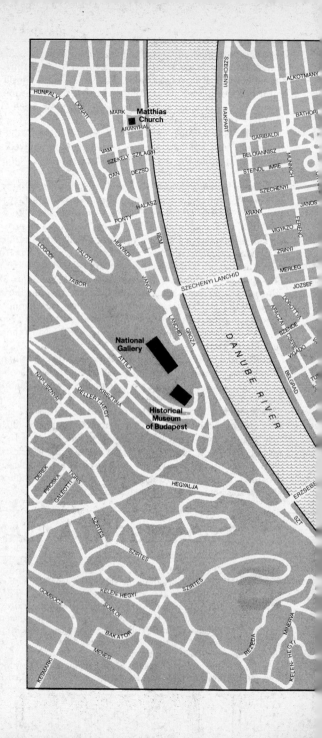

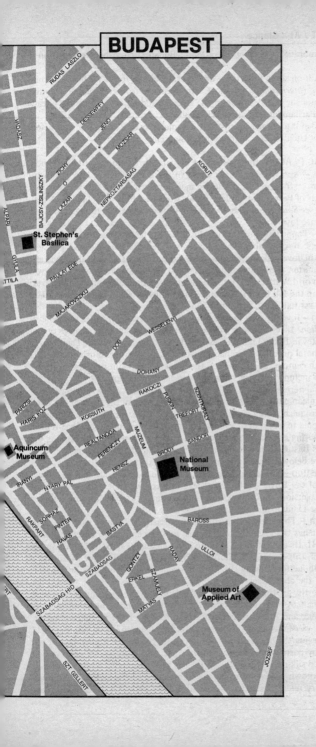

Liberty; it commemorates the Soviet liberation of Budapest from Nazi occupation in 1945.

Since Buda is built on seven hills, there are several views of the city. One of the best is from the *Hilton International,* in the Castle District, from where the Danube, Margaret Island, and the flat Pest side of the river, including the spectacular façade of the Hungarian Parliament, are all clearly visible.

Budapest is divided into numerous districts designated by a Roman numeral before the street address. "Utca" means "street" in Hungarian.

SPECIAL PLACES: Budapest, once actually three cities — Buda, Obuda, and Pest — sprawls along both banks of the Danube River and·is difficult to explore on foot because of the distances involved. To make matters worse, the streets of Pest run in circles; Buda's streets are hilly and cobbled. A map is strongly advised (see *Sources and Resources*). Public transportation, though crowded, is good, and fares are low.

Castle District – Topped by monuments, this hill is the heart of medieval Budapest, with cobbled streets, narrow alleys, and lovely squares. Its baroque and classical buildings, painted in lovely pastel shades, now house famous restaurants, writers' houses, a student quarter, and many landmarks of old Budapest. Much of the area was badly damaged in World War II, and restorations include a funicular railway (Budavári Sikló) that climbs up the hill from the Danube. The railway leaves from Clark Adám tér, 7:30 AM to 10 PM daily; the trip takes 50 seconds.

Budapest Hilton – It is not even faintly ironic that the first sight to see in medieval Budapest is the *Hilton.* It took 10 years to build, primarily because it occupies one of the most historic sites in Buda, high on Castle Hill, looking down on the Danube. As excavation for the hotel proceeded, archaeologists kept uncovering ruins and artifacts dating from the 13th century, and in the end the hotel elected — in response to strong local pressure — to include many of these ruins in its own design.

As a result, its modern stone and glass façade includes the walls and tower of a 13th-century Dominican church and a Jesuit monastery. Part of the front of the hotel is a 17th-century baroque building, once a Jesuit college. Inside, the thoroughly modern decor has been adapted to incorporate Gothic columns, Roman milestones, bas-reliefs, and shards found during excavation. Reflected in a rosy glass wall of the hotel is the famous Fishermen's Bastion, a neo-Romanesque series of arches and towers overlooking the Danube (see below). The Matthias Church is next door.

Fishermen's Bastion – So named because the fishermen of the city had to protect this northern side of the Royal Castle from siege in medieval times, the bastion is a turn-of-the-century version of Romanesque ramparts and turrets affording another vantage point of the Danube and the city.

Matthias Church – This neo-Gothic edifice atop Castle Hill dates from the 13th century, although it has been rebuilt many times, most recently after severe damage during World War II. Its correct name is Church of Our Lady. With its Gothic spires and colored tile roof, this coronation church of Hungarian kings has one of Europe's most memorable silhouettes. During the Turkish occupation of Hungary in the 16th and 17th centuries, the church served as a mosque.

Especially noteworthy are the baroque gilt and splendor of the nave and the baroque and Renaissance chalices and vestments in the treasury. Sunday morning mass is celebrated with music, and there are frequent organ recitals. I, 2 Szentháromság tér.

Café Ruszwurm – Just down the block from Matthias Church is this fabulous 1827 pastry shop, still serving the best baked goods in central Europe. With displays of old utensils once used by pastry cooks, 19th-century signs, and Biedermeier cherrywood furniture with striped silk upholstery, *Ruszwurm* has been designated a historic monument. Its pastries, known all over Europe, are miraculously light and rich. You can hardly go wrong: Try *rétes,* or strudel; vanilla slices; or *Ruszwurm* cake, a chocolate cake filled with chocolate cream and seasoned with orange peel and rum. I, 7 Szentháromság tér (phone: 755284).

Royal Palace – Reduced to rubble by bombs in 1944–45, the palace has been carefully rebuilt to incorporate all the styles of its historic past. That was not its first reconstruction. When bombed out, it existed primarily as an 18th-century building with some baroque touches; before that it had been destroyed and rebuilt several times since it was first constructed as a castle. It now houses the *Historical Museum of Budapest* and the *National Gallery*. I, 2 Szent György tér.

Historical Museum of Budapest – In Wing E (the southern wing) of the Royal Palace, the museum contains archaeological remains of the ancient town and the history of the construction of the palace. It displays splendid furniture, sculpture, ceramics, glass, and china; the halls, dating from the 15th century, have Renaissance doorcases carved in red marble. I, 2 Szent György tér (phone: 560727).

Hungarian National Gallery – Newly housed in the Royal Palace, this museum displays the works of the greatest Hungarian artists of the 19th and 20th centuries. English-language guides are available. I, 17 Dísz tér, Wings B, C, and D.

Aquincum Museum – One of the most significant excavations of a Roman urban area outside Italy, Aquincum (meaning "ample waters") in its heyday had almost 100,000 inhabitants. Its streets, homes, temple, and amphitheater have been unearthed 4 miles upstream of the city center on the western bank of the Danube. The museum on the site has mosaics, jewelry, glass, and inscribed stones. III, 139 Szentendrei út (phone: 687650).

Margaret Island (Margitsziget) – This resort and recreation island lies right in the middle of the river, accessible from both banks by the Margaret Bridge (Margit híd). Cars and trains enter from Árpád Bridge to the north; on summer weekends, a bus runs between the southern end of the island and the hotels near Árpád Bridge. The whole island is a park, with a sports stadium, a large municipal swimming pool, a rose garden, a fountain, several hotels, restaurants, and spas. During the summer months, when theaters close, the performances move to outdoor quarters here; you can see plays, concerts, films, and sports events. For specific programs, inquire at the national tourist office, *IBUSZ* (see *Sources and Resources*).

Inner City Parish Church (Belvárosi Templom) – This is the oldest building in Pest, begun in the 12th century. It shows evidence of many styles of construction, including a Romanesque arch, a Gothic chancel, a Muslim prayer niche, and a Roman wall. V, 15 Március (March 15) Square.

St. Stephen's Basilica – With its large dome and two tall spires, the basilica (officially known as St. Stephen's Parish Church) dominates the flat landscape of Pest. Built in the 19th century, its murals and altarpieces are by leading Hungarian painters and sculptors. V, Bajcsy-Zsilinszky út.

Hungarian National Museum – This oldest and most important museum in Budapest houses the greatest historical and archaeological collections of the country. The first collections were bequeathed to the museum in 1802, and the buildings were erected between 1837 and 1847. One of the prehistoric exhibitions displays the most ancient remnant of European man, the skull from Vértesszölös. There are also Roman ceramics, Avar gold and silver work, and the famous Hungarian Crown of St. Stephen and other historic crown jewels. Among the gold objects are a chiseled Byzantine crown (called the Crown of Monomachos) and the gold baton of Franz Liszt. There is also an exhibition of minerals. VIII, 14-16 Múzeum körút (phone: 134400).

Museum of Applied Arts – Another one of the great museums of Budapest; its most important collections are European and Hungarian ceramics, the work of goldsmiths and silversmiths from the 15th to 17th century, Italian Renaissance textiles, Turkish carpets, and Flemish tapestries from the 17th century. IX, 33-37 Üllői út (phone: 175222).

Parliament – Mirrored in the Danube, these impressive buildings on the Pest side are reminiscent of London's Houses of Parliament. Finished in 1902, they were built over a period of 20 years. A maze of 10 courtyards, 29 staircases, and 88 statues, Parliament is a favorite haunt for lovers after dark. Along Széchenyi rakpart and backed by Kossuth Lajos tér.

People's Republic Road (Népköztársaság Utja) – This noble avenue, which extends from near the Basilica to Heroes' Square, has known many names that reflect Budapest's stormy past, among them Stalin Avenue and, in 1956, Avenue of Hungarian Youth. It is lined with palaces on both sides, many of which were designed by the architect Miklós Ybl in the 1870s and 1880s; among these buildings are the *State Opera House* and several theaters. Number 60 once housed the Gestapo, the Communist secret police.

Heroes' Square (Hősök Tere) – At the end of Népköztársaság is a large square marked with the Millennial Monument, which was begun in 1896 to celebrate Hungary's thousand years. A semicircular colonnade displays a pantheon of Hungarian historical figures. On this square are the *Museum of Fine Arts* and the *Art Gallery.*

Museum of Fine Arts – Here is the greatest collection of its kind in the country. The building is at the entrance of Városliget (City Park), on the left as you face the Millennial Monument. More than 100,000 works of art are housed in this neo-classical structure. Among the masterpieces are seven paintings by El Greco and five by Goya. The Italian and Dutch sections have many world-famous paintings, including the *Madonna Esterházy* by Raphael and the *Sermon of St. John the Baptist* by Pieter Breughel, the Elder. The museum also has permanent exhibitions of Egyptian antiquities, Greco-Roman antiquities, and modern European painting and sculpture. XIV, 41 Dózsa György út (phone: 429759).

City Park (Városliget) – This large park just behind Heroes' Square contains an artificial lake; a public spa, Széchenyi Baths; a zoo; a botanical garden; an amusement park; and Vajdahunyad Castle, a conglomeration of Hungarian architectural styles.

Café Gerbeaud (Cukrászda) – In the heart of Pest, facing a beautifully restored square bustling with tourist and street entertainers, the *Gerbeaud* is no mere pastry shop; it is an institution. As in Vienna, the coffeehouses of Budapest have traditionally served as social and literary centers, and this one, with its decadent pastries and leisured atmosphere reminiscent of days gone by, is the best in town. V, 7 Vörösmarty tér (phone: 186823).

Korona – Another pastry shop, convenient for strollers in the Castle District, *Korona* is also a gathering place for literary types, featuring poetry readings and other literary events, often in foreign languages. I, 16 Disz tér (phone: 756139).

Óbuda – The Fő tér, or Main Square, of this district is an island of charming old houses and taverns in a sea of housing estates. Concerts and exhibitions are held in the Zichy Palace at #3, but the numerous surrounding restaurants — many with outdoor seating — are an even bigger attraction.

Imre Varga Collection – Portrait monuments by the internationally famous sculptor Imre Varga are scattered throughout his native Hungary. Samples of his work are on permanent exhibition here, and sometimes the artist himself is on hand. III, 7 Laktanya u.

Spas – Hungary is famous for its thermal spas. Budapest spas — there are some 20 in the city today — date from the Roman era and from the Turks, who built several baths in the city in the 16th century, among them the Rudas (I, 9 Döbrenti tér; dating from 1566 and completely renovated in 1987) and Király (I, 84 Fő u) spas in Buda, both still functioning. Although these spas treat people who are suffering from respiratory, rheumatic, and circulatory ailments, they are restorative for almost anyone, especially anyone suffering from obesity or simple fatigue. Treatments include drinking cures (mineral waters), baths in lukewarm or very hot mineral pools, mud packs, and massages, all directed by specialists under the direction of doctors. However, there is a large caveat about Budapest spas: They are not all hygienic. For this reason the spas around Hungary's Lake Balaton are more famous and more widely patronized by Westerners. If you are interested in Budapest spas, try the *Thermál Hotel Margitsziget* or its new neighbor, the *Ramada Grand* hotel, on Margaret Island, or contact the tourist office, IBUSZ, for help in making a judicious selection (see *Sources and Resources*).

■ **EXTRA SPECIAL:** A boat trip on the beautiful Danube is an experience you will not soon forget. From May to September, IBUSZ offers several day tours to the Danube Bend area, about 31 miles (50 km) north of Budapest, where the Danube makes a hairpin turn that changes its west-east course to a north-south course. This is an area rich in scenery, with limestone hills and volcanic mountains, and in history, with river communities that date from Roman times. Tours depart Wednesdays and Saturdays at 8:30 AM from the Vigadó tér landing dock; cost is $23. For further information, inquire at IBUSZ (phone: 181223; see *Sources and Resources*). From the beginning of April through October, there are daily hydrofoil trips between Budapest and Vienna; for information, contact MAHART, V, Belgrád rakpart (phone: 181953 or 181706).

SOURCES AND RESOURCES

TOURIST INFORMATION: For general information, brochures, and maps, contact IBUSZ (the Hungarian travel bureau), V, 5 Felszabadulás tér (phone: 186866), or 3 Petőfi tér (phone: 185707), open 24 hours; or the Budapest Tourist Office, V, 5 Roosevelt tér (phone: 173555). Or contact Tourinform, V, 2 Sütő utca (phone: 179800), open from 8 AM to 8 PM. Of the many travel agencies offering sightseeing tours of the country, *IPV Tourisme* offers particularly imaginative packages with an accent on Hungarian culture and history, 22 Angol u., Budapest H-1149 (phone: 633406). English-language guidebooks to Budapest and elsewhere in Hungary are sold in the city's hotel shops and in bookstores. City maps, booklets on Budapest attractions, and other information are available from the US office of IBUSZ, 1 Parker Plaza, Suite 1104, Ft. Lee, NJ 07024 (phone: 201-592-8585 or 800-367-7878).

The US Embassy is at V, 12 Szabadság tér (phone: 126450).

Local Coverage – A comprehensive free monthly bulletin in German and English, *Programme in Hungary,* is available at hotel desks. An illustrated daily paper in English and German, the *Daily News,* is available at newsstands and hotels. Major international papers, such as the London *Times* and the *International Herald Tribune,* are available at some newspaper stores in the center.

Food – *Budapest: A Critical Guide* by Andràs Török, published in Budapest by Park/Officina Nova and available only in Hungary, is the best source of restaurant information, along with an excellent discussion of the city's architecture. *Programme in Hungary* lists a few restaurants, but not in detail.

Telephone – The area code for Budapest is 01.

CLIMATE AND CLOTHES: The wooded Buda hills protect the city against extremes of heat and cold, but summers can be hot and humid. In summer the average temperature is about 72F (22C); in winter it is about 34F (1C). Dress in Hungary tends to be more informal than in the US. Men usually wear open-necked shirts, except in theaters and good restaurants, where they usually wear ties and dark suits.

GETTING AROUND: Airport – Ferihegy Airport handles all international flights (there is no domestic service in Hungary). A new, second terminal handles MALÉV (the Hungarian national carrier) flights. The drive from the airport to downtown Budapest is about a half-hour and a taxi ride should cost approximately 150 forint (Fts; about $3). The airport bus service to the International Bus Station on Engels Square is much less. It runs every half hour and takes 30 minutes to reach Bus Terminal 1 (Fts. 20; 30¢) and 40 minutes to Terminal 2 (Fts. 30; 50¢). For information on air travel, contact MALÉV, V, 2 Roosevelt tér (phone: 189033), or V, 2 Dorottya utca (phone: 184333 or 185913). For airport information, call 579123.

Bus, Tram, and Subway – Public transportation is efficient and very cheap. Tickets are sold at tobacco shops, kiosks, and ticket offices, but not on the vehicles. Each ticket, valid for one trip, must be punched in the machines inside the vehicles. Yellow tickets are good on the Metro (subway), trams, and trolleybuses; blue tickets are good for bus transportation only.

Bus Tours – You might wish to get acquainted with Budapest by taking the 3-hour tour of the city offered daily by *IBUSZ*, VII, 3/C Tanács krt. (phone: 423140), for tour information; or contact the branch offices listed above or the Budapest Tourist Office). A new, 4-hour *IBUSZ* tour conducted Wednesdays at 2 PM from Engels Square offers a look at the city's cultural life, with art studio and museum visits and concerts ($15).

Car Rental – *IBUSZ-Avis*, V, 8 Martinelli tér (phone: 186222, 184158, or 184240), and V, 5 Türr Istbán u. (phone: 179299); *Főtaxi-Hertz*, VII, 24 Kertész u. (phone: 116116); *Budget*, 43 Ferenc krt. (phone: 131466). There are branches of *Budget, Avis,* and *Hertz* at the airport.

Motorboat – The *Dunatúra* water taxi service offers individualized Danube tours from May through September. They can be booked through hotels or at the boat dock at Petőfi Square.

Taxi – There are taxi stands throughout the city; rates are cheap and a 10%-15% tip is customary. The two state-run taxi companies are *Főotaxi* (phone: 222222) and *Volántaxi* (phone: 666666). There are also several private taxi services; their rates will vary.

Train – The main office of the Hungarian State Railways (MÁV), VI, 35 Népköztársaság útja (phone: 228049), handles tickets, reservations, and general train information. Major stations are the Eastern (Keleti), Baross tér (phone: 136835), for eastbound and most international trains; and the Western (Nyugati), Marx tér (phone: 490115) for trains headed west. A fast, dependable EuroCity train — the *Léhar* — now runs between Budapest and Vienna in under 3 hours.

SPECIAL EVENTS: The *Budapest Spring Festival,* 10 days in March, is the highlight of the cultural season and features concerts, folk dance, and other performances. In 1986, Hungary became the host country for the annual *Formula 1 Grand Prix* on the Hungaroring at Mogyoród, about a half-hour's drive from Budapest. This international auto race takes place in August. Tickets are available at the Forma-1 GT-1PV box office, V, 2 Vigadó tér (phone: 175067). *Budapest Music Weeks,* in early fall, include international competitions for various types of musicians and many concerts. For information about this and other special events, contact IBUSZ (see above).

Besides *Christmas, Boxing Day* (December 26), *New Year's Day,* and *Easter Monday,* Hungarians celebrate political anniversaries on April 4 (*Liberation from the Nazis*), May 1 (*Labor Day*), and August 20 (*St. Stephen's Day,* for the first King of Hungary; now *Constitution Day*). In 1989 a new national holiday was declared: March 15, marking the beginning of the Hungarian Revolution of 1848, a date sacred to Hungarian patriots. In addition to official celebrations, peaceful marches and demonstrations organized by opposition groups are the order of the day; motorists take note.

MUSEUMS: Several museums provide an introduction to Hungary's rich religious heritage: *Collections of Ecclesiastical Treasures* at the Matthias Church (I, Szentháromság tér) and at St. Stephen's Basilica (V, Szent István tér); the *National Evangelical Museum* (V, 4 Deak tér); and the recently opened *Bible Museum* (IX, 28 Ráday u.). In addition to these museums and the museums listed in *Special Places,* you may wish to visit the following.

Béla Bartók Memorial House – Concerts are presented here on occasion. II, 29 Csalán út.

Ethnographic Museum – A glimpse into the country's past. V, 12 Kossuth tér.

Ferenc (Franz) Liszt Museum – Set up in Liszt's apartment in the old Academy of Music; a site for piano recitals. VI, 35 Vörösmarty u.

Museum of Hungarian Commerce and Catering – I, 4 Fortuna utca.

Musical History Museum – Historical instruments. An exhibition called Béla Bartók's Workshop traces the composer's creative process. A concert series is presented here. I, 7 Táncsics Mihály utca.

Museum of Postage Stamps – An extensive collection that includes some very rare stamps. VII, 47 Hársfa utca.

Semmelweis Museum of the History of Medicine – A fascinating look at the development of European and Hungarian medicine from Roman times to the present. Dr. Ignác Semmelweis, the man responsible for the cure for childbed fever, was born in the building that now houses the museum. I, 1-3 Apród utca.

SHOPPING: Most shops are state owned. As in other Communist countries, high-quality consumer goods are not generally available to Hungarians. Thus the items in a Budapest department store would appear shabby by Western standards. However, the *Intertourist, Utastourist,* and *Konsumtourist* shops sell a considerably better array of gifts for foreign currency only. Here you can find colorful pottery, Herend and Alföldi porcelain, Matyó and Kalocsa embroideries, which can be used for wall hangings or even framed as folk art. The country is famous for its peasant blouses, dolls in regional costumes, and embroidered sheepskin jackets. There are also herdsmen's carvings on wood and horn. There are *Intertourist Shops* in all the major hotels and on Kigyó utca in Pest. Budapest also has shops and cooperatives devoted exclusively to folk art: these include the beautifully remodeled *Folk Art Center* at V, 14 Váci utca; V, 12 Régiposta út; V, 2 Kossuth Lajos utca; and XIII, 26 Szent István krt.

A big bargain in Budapest is custom-made clothing, both suits for men and dresses for women. The workmanship and style are excellent, but it is best to bring your own material, as there is little good fabric around. Ask your hotel porter for the nearest tailor or dressmaker or try the *Klára Rotschild Salon,* V, 12 Váci utca (phone: 184090).

At any grocery store you can buy an authentic, inexpensive, and very portable souvenir — a packet of Hungarian paprika, the real stuff, not the red dust generally sprinkled on as a decorative touch in the US. Or buy a bottle of Hungarian wine at one of the many delicatessens. One of the ethnographic prints sold at *Photography Gallery,* 7 Váci utca, also makes a good souvenir.

Helia D Studio – An array of cosmetics that make great gifts. English-speaking staff. V, 19-21 Váci utca.

Herbária – A wonderful selection of herbal teas, spices, and natural cosmetics. V, 4 Tolbuhin krt.

Luca Folklor Shop – A tiny treasure trove of gift items. Open daily. V, 7-9 Régiposta utca.

National Center of Museums Shop – Reproductions of museum objects. V, 7 József Nádor tér.

Rózsavölgyi – Hungarian classical and folk music. V, 5 Martinelli tér.

Zsuzsa Lőrincz – Genuine folk costumes and pottery, mostly from Transylvania. V, 14 Régiposta utca.

 SPORTS AND FITNESS: Boating – By arrangement with IBUSZ (see above), you can rent a sailboat, sailing dinghy, motorboat, small hydrofoil, and even water skis by the hour or by the day. It is the very best way to enjoy the Danube.

Fishing – Licenses are issued by the National Federation of Hungarian Anglers (MOHOSZ), V, 6 Október utca (phone: 325315); and at the fishing information bureau at II, 1 Bem József utca.

Fitness Centers – The facilities at both the *Forum* (12-14 Apáczai Csere János utca, phone: 178088), and the *Atrium Hyatt* (2 Roosevelt tér, phone: 383000), are open to non-guests for a small fee. Budapest is renowned for its medicinal baths; among the best are the *Gellért* (XI, 4 Kelenhegyi út), and the *Lukács* (II, 25-29 Frankel Leó út).

Golf – Minibuses transport guests to a 9-hole course set amid oak and acacia trees on an island in the Danube, just north of the city limits (Kisoroszi, Szentendrei-sziget; for information phone the *Hilton* at 751000 or 751230). The *Vörös Csillag* (Red Star) hotel, XII, 21 Rege út (phone: 750416), has a mini-golf course.

Greyhound Racing – On the Danube embankment, just outside Budapest, there are races from May to September. Inquire at IBUSZ for details (see above).

Horse Racing – There are trotting races at the track at VIII, 9 Kerepesi út, and flat racing at the track at X, 9 Albertirsai út.

Horseback Riding – A very popular pastime in this land of horsemen. There are schools and stables in and around Budapest, including the *Petneházy Riding School,* II, 5 Feketefej utca (phone: 164267). Information on riding tours is provided by IBUSZ (see above), or *Pegazus Tours,* V, 5 Károlyi Mihály u. (phone: 171552).

Jogging – Margitsziget (Margaret Island), in the center of the city in the Danube River, is the best place to run. The island is roughly 2 miles long and ½ mile wide, and most of it is given over to sports facilities. Either take a cab to the island's *Thermál* hotel and choose a path from there, or jog over on the pedestrian-only Margaret Bridge. Running is also pleasant along the foothills near the *Budapest* hotel, II, 47-49 Szilágy Erzsébet fasor. For information on jogging, call the Futapest Club, XIII, 14/6 Fürst Sándor u. (phone: 328739).

Skating – There is a large outdoor ice skating rink in City Park, near Vajdahunyad Castle (XIV, Népstadion út). Skating competitions and other athletic events take place at the recently built *Budapest Sports Hall,* XIV, 1-3 Istvánmezei út (phone: 636430).

Skiing – The Buda hills right in and around Budapest, accessible by bus and funicular, have several slopes, the most popular of which is the Szabadsághegy.

Soccer – As in many European countries, soccer (called football) is the most popular spectator sport. The largest city stadium is the *People's Stadium* (*Népstadion*) near City Park in Pest, seating 96,000 spectators. XIV, 3-5 Istvánmezei út (phone: 636430). Information on games and other sports events is available from the ticket bureau at VI, 6 Népköztársaság útja (phone: 124234).

Swimming – Budapest has many indoor and outdoor pools. People swim in the Danube, but it is not too clean (though not nearly as dirty as, say, the Hudson River in New York) and sometimes has strong currents. The largest public facility — both indoor and outdoor — is the *National Swimming Pool* on Margaret Island. In addition, many hotels have pools, both ordinary and thermal. The stately *Gellért,* for example, has an outdoor pool with artificial waves, in a park setting, XI, 1 Szt. Gellért tér. In the Városliget (City Park), the turn-of-the-century *Széchenyi Baths* include 3 large outdoor pools, also open in winter, XIV, 11 Állatkerti krt.

Tennis – There are tennis courts near *Dózsa Stadium* on Margaret Island; at *FTC Sporttelep* (Sports Grounds) at 129 Üllői út; and on Szabadság Hill, near the *Olympia* hotel, 40 Eötvös út. The *Flamenco* hotel has an indoor court, XI, 7 Tas vezér utca (phone: 252250), and the *Novotel Budapest,* XII, 63-67 Alkotás utca, also has courts.

 THEATER: In Budapest everyone goes to the numerous theaters that are subsidized by the state and are very cheap. Most performances are, of course, in Hungarian, but you might enjoy seeing a Shakespearean or some other familiar play in Hungarian. If not, the *Municipal Operetta Theater* at VI, 19 Nagymező utca in Pest, has performances of Kálmán, Lehár, Romberg, and other great operetta composers whose works need no translation. The *Main Puppet Theater,* at VI, 69Népköztársaság útja, presents everything from the *Three Little Pigs* to *The Miraculous Mandarin* for children and revues and satires for adults. The *Municipal Grand Circus* is at XIV, 7 Állatkerti körút, in the City Park (phone: 428300; weekdays only).

For tickets and more details see the current *Programme in Hungary,* contact *IBUSZ* (see above), or call the *Central Booking Agency for Theaters,* VI, 18 Népköztársaság útja (phone: 120000).

 MUSIC: Budapest has a rich musical life; this city of Bartók and Kodály has two opera houses, several symphony orchestras, and a great many chamber groups. The renovated *Hungarian State Opera House,* VI, 22 Népköztársaság útja (phone: 530170), and the *Erkel Theater,* VIII, 30 Köztársaság tér (phone: 330540), offer operas and ballets. Concerts are given at the *Academy of Music* at VI, 8 Liszt Ferenc tér (phone: 420179), and at the *Pest Concert Hall* (Vigadó), V, 1 Vigadó tér (phone: 189167 or 189903), facing the Danube. The Matthias Church also has concerts. There is a Concert Ticket Office at V, 1 Vörösmarty tér (phone: 176222). On Sundays at 11 AM concerts are held at the *Ethnographic Museum,* V, 12 Kossuth tér, sometimes featuring children's folk dancing.

In the summer, the music goes outdoors to Margaret Island. For tickets and information contact *IBUSZ* or the *Central Booking Agency* (see *Theater*).

 NIGHTCLUBS AND NIGHTLIFE: Though much more lively than that of other Eastern European cities, Budapest's nightlife is somewhat limited. There are great cabarets in such hotels as the *Bellevue* in the *Duna Inter-Continental* and the *Troubadour* in the *Budapest Hilton* (see *Checking In*). Others worth a visit are the *Maxim Varieté,* VII, 3 Akácfa utca; *Moulin Rouge,* VI, 17 Nagymező utca; *Casanova,* I, 4 Batthyány tér; and the nightclub program of the *Lidó* (V, 5 Szabadsajtó út), a famous café at the turn of the century and now a restaurant with entertainment. All stay open until at least 4 AM, most until 5 AM. After that, there is always a Turkish bath or a sauna.

In the hotels, try the *Béke Orfeum,* at the *Béke,* VI, 97 Lenin krt., and *Horoszkóp,* at the *Buda-Penta,* I, 41-43 Krisztina krt., which appeals to a younger crowd. Western visitors can try their luck at the *Hilton*'s elegant *Casino,* using hard currency; open daily from 5 PM (phone: 751000). The two other casinos in Hungary are at the *Thermál* hotel in Hévíz and in the western town of Sopron, on the Austrian border.

For a unique evening out, you might want to see some Hungarian folk dancing. The national dance, the *csárdás,* created in the mid-19th century, is still done at village weddings and festivities and at the *Municipal Cultural Center* at XI, 47 Fehérvári út. Also, the *Korona Pastry Shop* in the Buda Castle District at 16 Disz tér, has become a popular evening spot for Hungarians and foreign visitors who like poetry, prose, and music. A selection from the best Hungarian contemporary and classical literature is occasionally presented in foreign languages.

BEST IN TOWN

 CHECKING IN: Although new hotels are constantly being built, there is often a shortage of hotel rooms in Budapest, especially during the summer. It is advisable to make reservations well in advance, either through your own travel agent or through *IBUSZ* (see *Sources and Resources*).

Hotel prices in Budapest, however, are quite reasonable compared with those of other European capitals. We have listed as expensive hotels that charge from $100 to $165 and up for a double; $45 to $100 as moderate; and $20 to $40 as inexpensive. Note that *IBUSZ* rents rooms in private homes (usually with shared bath) from $12 per day. All telephone numbers are in the 01 area code unless otherwise indicated.

Atrium Hyatt – A central courtyard densely lined with hanging greenery is the focus of this 357-room luxury hotel. It has a top-floor VIP Regency Club, a swimming pool, and a health club. Its *Old Timer* restaurant has international cuisine, the *Tokaj* has Hungarian fare and Gypsy music, the *Atrium Terrace* is its coffee shop, and the rustic *Clark Brasserie* is very popular for snacks accompanied by draft beer (see *Eating Out*). V, 2 Roosevelt tér (phone: 383000). Expensive.

Béke Radisson – A reconstructed old hotel with a turn-of-the-century ambience, evident particularly in the beautiful *Zsolnay Café*. VI, 97 Lenin krt. (phone: 323300). Expensive.

Budapest Hilton International – This 323-room hotel sits on a hill in Buda's Castle District, behind the Fishermen's Bastion, overlooking the Danube, adjacent to the Matthias Church. The hotel includes ruins of a 13th-century church of the Dominican Order (where concerts are presented on warm summer evenings) and a Jesuit monastery. A walkway with a glass wall allows guests to see the restored cloisters. There's a restaurant called *Halászbástya* (see *Eating Out*); a wine cellar dubbed *Dr. Faust,* a coffee shop with rustic decor; a 2-level espresso bar with an outdoor terrace; the colorful *Kalocsa* restaurant; and the *Codex Bar,* which occupies the site of the country's first printing workshop, opened in the 15th century. I, 1-3 Hess András tér (phone: 751000). Expensive.

Duna Inter-Continental – This deluxe 350-room hotel is on Pest's riverside Corso, a traditional promenade between the Chain and Elizabeth bridges. All rooms have a view of Buda Castle on the opposite bank. A recent renovation endowed this already well-accoutered hotel with a pool, fitness center, squash court, solarium, and sauna. Among the restaurants: the peasant-inn-style *Csárda,* the *Rendezvous,* and the *Bellevue,* in addition to the *Intermezzo* terrace café, the *Tokaj* wine cellar, and a nightclub. V, 4 Apáczai Csere János utca (phone: 175122). Expensive.

Forum – A first class, 408-room property next to the *Hyatt,* featuring wonderful river views, an efficient staff, and a lavish breakfast buffet. It boasts a swimming pool and a health club with a bar. For dining, choose between the elegant *Silhouette* restaurant and the informal *Forum Grill* (open from 6 AM to 2 AM). For pastries and coffee, stop by the *Viennese Café.* V, 12-14 Apáczai Csere János utca (phone: 178088). Expensive.

Ramada Grand Hotel Margitsziget – A recently renovated spa dating from the 19th century, connected to the *Thermál* hotel by an underground passage. XIII, Margaret Island (phone: 111000). Expensive.

Thermál Hotel Margitsziget – This 340-room luxury spa hotel has health facilities with diagnostic and treatment centers and equipment for hydrotherapy and physiotherapy. It has a swimming pool, solarium, sauna, and fitness rooms, and offers special inclusive packages with spa treatments and diet plans. XIII, Margaret Island (phone: 311100). Expensive.

Gellért – This 240-room Old World hotel is on the Buda side of the Danube near Liberation Memorial Park, at the foot of Gellért Hill. It has a swimming pool with medicinal waters, a thermal bath, and sun terrace. The hotel is famous for its Hungarian cuisine, and there is a restaurant with Gypsy music, an espresso bar, a beer hall, and a nightclub. XI, 1 Szt. Gellért tér (phone: 460700). Expensive to moderate.

Nemzeti – Restored a few years ago to its 1880s grandeur, this 76-room hotel has an elegant restaurant with Gypsy music and a beer hall. 4 József krt. (phone: 339160). Expensive to moderate.

Astoria – Another renovated old hotel, this one has a marvelous café. V, 19 Kossuth Lajos u. (phone: 173411). Moderate.

Buda-Penta – Near the Southern Railway Station and Underground Terminal in Buda, it has 392 rooms plus 7 apartments, all with air conditioning, plus a swimming pool and health club, a restaurant, coffee shop, beer hall, and nightclub. I, 41-43 Krisztina körút (phone: 566333). Moderate.

Erzsébet – An attractive modern property on the site of a much older one. The *János Beer Cellar* has kept the furnishings of its popular predecessor. V, 11-15 Károlyi Mihály u. (phone: 382111). Moderate.

Grand Hotel Hungaria – Opposite the Eastern Railway Station stands a bustling new hotel — the biggest in the country — with a restaurant, beer hall, wine cellar, Jugendstil (Art Nouveau) café, and nightclub. VII, Rákóczi út (phone: 229050). Moderate.

Novotel Budapest – A quick drive from the city center, with 324 rooms, a small pool, tennis courts, restaurants, and bars. The Budapest Convention Center is next door. XII, 63-67 Alkotás utca (phone: 869588). Moderate.

Taverna – The main pedestrian shopping street in Pest boasts a well-designed new hotel with 224 rooms, a restaurant, beer hall, pastry shop, fast-food eatery, and champagne bar. V, 20 Váci utca (phone: 383522). Moderate.

Olympia – Somewhat on the outskirts of town in the residential Buda hills, this pleasant hotel has a swimming pool, health club, tennis court, and restaurants. There's also a nightclub with floor shows. XII, 40 Eötvös utca (phone: 568011). Inexpensive.

 EATING OUT: The justly celebrated cuisine of Hungary dates from ancient times. The most celebrated ingredient is paprika, the red pepper that comes in different strengths and is used copiously, most notably in *paprikás csirke* (paprika chicken) and in sauces. (Don't worry about paprika dishes being too hot; any restaurant will be glad to spice to your taste.) Another culinary characteristic is the use of pork drippings, which in concert with the ubiquitous sour creams, makes meals so conspicuously caloric here. Various Hungarian dishes have become world famous, particularly goulash (*gulyás*), which will not be what you expect if you have eaten it outside Hungary. Here it is a very thick soup with meat (usually beef or pork), onions, sour cream, and paprika. If you like fish, try Hungarian bouillabaisse (*halászlé*), a clear soup made with *fogas* (a unique pike-perch caught only in Lake Balaton) or bream, seasoned with onions and many spices including paprika. *Kolozsvári rakott káposzta,* or layered cabbage, includes eggs and sausage, heaps of sour cream, and crisp pork chops.

Hungarian rye bread is superb, and a biscuit called *pogácsa,* a flaky pastry strewn with bits of crackling pork, is delicious. Hungarian pastries are absolutely fabulous; Budapest is the place to let that diet go. You might start with *rétes* (strudel) or *dobos torta,* the famous many-layered cake — but the sky is the limit. Filled with apricot preserves and *lekvár* (prune preserves), walnuts, hazelnuts, crushed poppy seeds, and chocolate, they are all sinfully delectable.

Hungarian wines are wonderful, especially Tokay, which is often sweet; Tokaji

Szamorodni and Tokaji Aszú are famous dessert wines made from hand-picked, shriveled, "noble rot" grapes. A popular choice with meals is Egri Bikavér (Bull's Blood), a heavy red wine. Leányka is a delicious white wine.

Hungarians love to linger over small cups of strong coffee, called *eszpresszó,* or over *dupla,* which is strong double mocha brew. These are available everywhere — in pastry shops, cafés, and the *Mackó* shops, whose symbol is a bear cub.

Budapest has over 2,000 restaurants, cafés, pastry shops, wine and beer cellars, and taverns. A few of the highlights are listed below. There is an important distinction to be made among eating establishments in Budapest: Whenever possible, try to determine if a restaurant is private or state-run. The food at private establishments is generally of a higher quality and the service is better. The concierge at your hotel should be able to help in this regard. For a dinner for two with wine, expect to pay $50 to $60 in restaurants listed as expensive; $20 to $30 in those categorized as moderate; and $10 to $20 in inexpensive places. All telephone numbers are in the 01 area code unless otherwise indicated.

Alabárdos – In one of the most beautiful Gothic buildings in the Castle District. Try the house specialty, meat flambé served with great ceremony on a sword. Closed Sundays. I, 2 Országház utca (phone: 560851). Expensive.

Halászbástya – Next to the *Hilton,* inside one of the towers of the Fishermen's Bastion (see *Special Places*), with a fabulous view of the Parliament building and the town. Hungarian food and Gypsy music are featured. Open daily. I, Fishermen's Bastion (phone: 561446). Expensive.

Hungária – For that big night on the town, this evocative eatery (known as the *New York Café* before World War II) wins the laurels. A Budapest institution since 1894, it is palatial in every respect. The Art Nouveau decor, gilt columns, frosted glass globes, and glittering mirrors will probably remind you more of an opera house or a royal palace than a restaurant. If opulence and its concomitant ambience is what you sèek, by all means visit. However, if food is your primary interest, a downturn in its near-legendary gastronomic reputation may dissuade you. Among the specialties well worth trying are *kengurufarokleves* (kangaroo tail soup), *crêpes à la Hortobágy* (crêpes stuffed with meat and served with a paprika sauce), *sertésborda magyarovári módra* (pork cutlet with mushrooms, ham, and cheese), and a dessert called *omlette surprise* (parfait in sponge cake baked in a froth of egg white). The *Hungária* is not only a top restaurant but a coffeehouse, café, and nightclub. Don't be put off by the incongruous, Soviet-style chandeliers. Open daily. VII, 9-11 Lenin körút (phone: 223849). Expensive.

Gundel – Perhaps the most famous chef in Budapest's history was Károly Gundel, and his restaurant still evokes an era of grand style in Budapest. Come for the crêpe filled with hazelnuts and cream and covered by a bittersweet chocolate sauce. Your mouth throws a party for your entire body! Open daily. XIV, 2 Állatkerti út, in the Városliget (phone: 221002). Expensive.

Légrádi Testvérek (Légrádi Brothers) – Make reservations at least a week in advance (only 30 persons, maximum) for this outstanding private restaurant. Traditional Hungarian specialties are prepared at the table. Dinner only, weekdays. V, 23 Magyar utca (phone: 186804) Expensive.

Vén Buda (Old Buda) – A fairly recent arrival on the culinary scene, but already a firmly established favorite. Closed weekends. II, 22 Erőd u. (phone: 153396). Expensive.

Kárpátia – Traditional Hungarian specialties are served under vaulted ceilings with musical interludes in the evenings. Open daily. V, 4-8 Károlyi Mihály u. (phone: 170303). Expensive to moderate.

Borkóstoló (Gresham Wine Bar) – Near the Houses of Parliament, here you can taste fine Hungarian wines such as Tokay, which is often sweet; Egri Bikavér (bull's blood), a marvelous dry red wine believed to have medicinal value; and Leányka, a good white wine. Closed Sundays. V, Mérleg utca (phone: 172502). Moderate.

Mátyás Pince – Tourists are not the only people drawn to this romantic beer cellar in central Pest, where the real commodities are copious quantities of wine and even richer servings of Gypsy music and old Budapest spirit. If you actually get hungry, its fish dishes are well known around the city. Open daily. V, 7 Március 15 tér (phone: 181693). Moderate.

Ménes Csárda – This small, cozy establishment with an equestrian decor became an instant hit after it opened in 1982. It serves unusual Hungarian specialties — often prepared at your table — in attractive ceramic dishes made for the restaurant by a local artist. Try the stuffed filet of pork with *tápióbicskei hozzávaló* and the cherry or cottage cheese (*túrós*) strudel. Good, light wines are available. While you dine, a Gypsy cimbalom player performs. Open daily. V, 15 Apáczai Csere János utca (phone: 170803). Expensive.

Vadrózsa – In a private villa with a shady garden, this restaurant features charcoal-broiled specialties such as goose liver and pike-perch, plus other tempting dishes. Very friendly service. Closed Mondays. II, 12 Pentelei Molnár utca (phone: 351118). Expensive to moderate.

Vasmacska – The interior of this restaurant evokes the atmosphere of an officers' wardroom on a ship. The house specialty is a hearty bean dish with different kinds of smoked meat. Downstairs is a less expensive beer hall. III, 3-5 Laktanya utca (phone: 887123). Expensive to moderate.

Aranybárány Borozó – The new Golden Lamb Wine Bar specializes, naturally, in lamb dishes, served in a cellar decorated with shepherd motifs. Open daily. V, 4 Marmincad u. (phone: 172703). Moderate.

Aranymókus Kertvendéglő (Golden Squirrel Garden) – Traditional game dishes (but no squirrel). A short taxi ride from the center. Closed Mondays. XII, 25 Istenhegyi út (phone: 556728 or 559594). Moderate.

Hanna – A kosher restaurant, open only for lunch. Closed Saturdays. VII, 35 Dob u. (phone: 421072). Moderate.

Kiskakukk – An extensive year-round menu of game dishes, served in noisy, plain surroundings. Open daily. XIII, 12 Pozsonyi út (phone: 321732). Moderate.

Kispipa – A brasserie atmosphere — bright lights, red tablecloths, and friendly chatter by diners who all seem to know each other — prevails at this private eatery. It features an extensive menu of Hungarian specialties and is a 5-minute taxi ride from the major hotels in Pest. Closed Sundays. Reservations necessary. 38 Akácfa u. (phone: 422587). Moderate.

Régi Országház – This old inn on the north side of the castle in Buda offers many rooms with different decors, a wine cellar, Gypsy music, and jazz. Open daily. I, 17 Országház utca (phone: 750650). Moderate.

Sipos Halászkert – Known as the *New Sipos* — to distinguish it from the almost-demolished original *Régi Sipos Halászkert* (Old Sipos), at 46 Lajos utca (phone: 686480) — this is a case of new quarters for an old standby — a fish restaurant with a tradition that began half a century ago. There is music and a garden. On the recently restored Fő Square in the Óbuda district (phone: 888745). Moderate.

Százéves (100-éves) – The restaurant is actually more than a half century older than the 100 years its name indicates. In a lovely baroque town palace in the center of the city, its atmosphere is intimate and the food enjoyable. Service can be slow at lunchtime, when it's very crowded. Open daily. V, 2 Pesti Barnabás utca (phone: 183608). Moderate.

Apostolok – This old brasserie is centrally located and very popular, especially for lunch. Open daily. V, 4-6 Kígyó utca (phone: 183704). Moderate to inexpensive.

Dunakorzó – Near the riverside cluster of deluxe hotels. Undistinguished decor but known among hearty eaters for its heaping portions of solid Hungarian fare. Open daily. V, 3 Vigadó tér (phone: 186362). Moderate to inexpensive.

Kisbuda – A charming place, with good Hungarian food, a cozy interior, and a large garden. Closed Sunday dinner. Frankel Leó utca (phone: 152244). Moderate to inexpensive.

Pest-Buda – Operating in the same building in the Castle District since 1880, when it had a local carriage trade and attracted visitors from as far away as Vienna. It is not suited for big functions or balls, but rather is a place for family suppers, with romantic, vaulted dining rooms and period furnishings. Try the Wiener schnitzel. Open daily. I, 3 Fortuna utca (phone: 569849). Moderate to inexpensive.

Pilvax – This old café-restaurant in the heart of the inner city of Pest is noted for its chicken broth, pastries, and cakes. Gypsy music accompanies the meal. V, 1-3 Pilvax köz (phone: 175902). Moderate to inexpensive.

Alföldi – This is where Hungarians come for Sunday lunch; it's noisy and offers simple, traditional fare. V, 4 Kecskeméti u. (phone: 174404). Inexpensive.

Clark Brasserie (Söröző) – Stop here for a glass of beer or wine and a fast light meal, such as a bowl of mushroom soup (*vargánya leves*). The cabbage strudel (*káposztás rétes*) is a must. A new specialty is the Nomad Roast — a sirloin and veal roast grilled on a slab of stone at the table (for two people). V, 15 Apáczai Csere János utca (phone: 170803). Inexpensive.

COPENHAGEN

In the early mornings of 1848 in Copenhagen's old waterfront district, Nyhavn, a tall, top-hatted figure could often be seen emerging from the elegant portals of #67B. A few books underneath his arm, the figure would walk in the direction of the docks, with the apparent intention of inspecting the wooden sailing ships moored there. However, he had other things on his mind.

The figure was Hans Christian Andersen, Denmark's beloved raconteur of fairy tales and the country's most famous citizen. A poor shoemaker's son who allegorized the remarkable tale of his own life in *The Ugly Duckling,* Andersen often found inspiration during these morning walks around Nyhavn, where he lived for some 20 years. The stately old merchants' townhouses, the shabby sailors' bars, the tattoo parlors, and all the other assorted arcana of dockside life — so much of which is the same today — must have provided good soil for his fertile imagination. Once, when questioned about his literary methods, he replied, "It came without incentive — while I was walking on the street the thought came to me."

Thus it is no surprise to discover that Andersen's first literary success, a fantastic tale in the E. T. A. Hoffmann tradition, bore the title *A Walk from Holmen's Canal to the East Point of the Island of Amager in the Years 1828 and 1829.*

During that same period, a mere 10 blocks away from Andersen, one might find that dour theologian and progenitor of existentialism, Søren Kierkegaard, out taking *his* morning constitutional. Kierkegaard and Andersen were literary contemporaries, and although they had about as much in common as Hamlet and Victor Borge, their writings bear witness to the fact that they both loved their walks in Copenhagen.

The largest city in Scandinavia, with a population of about 1.5 million, Copenhagen is on the northeastern shore of Zealand, the largest of Denmark's approximately 500 islands. Here the Danes have somehow managed to synthesize the urban sophistication of a large continental city with the friendly charm of a small village. And Copenhagen remains a pedestrian's paradise. Swanky Strøget (the Strolling Street) is Europe's oldest and longest "walking street." The backbone of the city, Strøget links Kongens Nytorv, the largest square in the harbor, with Rådhuspladsen, the largest square in the downtown area. You can find just about anything you could want on Strøget — with its modern department stores, tiny boutiques, ice cream stands, bars, theaters, sex shops, street musicians, park benches, and infinite opportunities for idle conversation — just about anything, that is, except cars and automotive pollution.

This congenial and idyllic atmosphere might lead the casual observer to believe that Copenhagen has been lucky enough to occupy some turgid back-

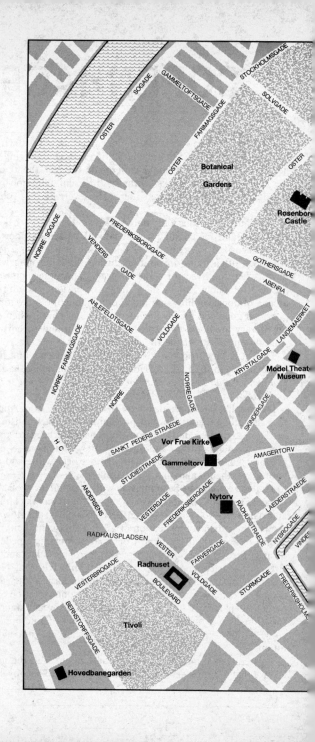

COPENHAGEN

VOLDGADE

DELFINGADE

ELSDYRSGADE

SUENSONSGADE

GRONNINGEN

HAREGADE

RIGENSGADE

ESPLANADEN

FREDERICIAGADE

ADELGADE

Museum of
Decorative Art

KRONPRINSESSEGADE

BORGERGADE

STORE KONGENSGADE

DRONNINGENS TVAERGADE

BREDGADE

Amalienborg
Castle

ADELGADE

BORGERGEADE

AMALIENGADE

NY ØSTERGADE

BREMERHOLM

PILESTRAEDE

KONGENS
NYTORV

NYHAVN

NYHAVN

ØSTERGADE

KØBMAGERGADE

NIKOLAJGADE

HEIBERGSGADE

HERLUF TROLLES GADE

PEDER

ADMIRALGADE

KAN

NIELS JUELS GADE

TORDENSKJOLDGADE

HOLBERGSGADE

SKRAMS

HAVNEGADE

HOLMENS

VED STRANDEN

Thorvaldsen
Museum

Christiansborg
Castle

KNIPPELS BRO

BRYGGE

CHRISTIANS

INDERHAVNEN

water of history, far from the dynamic fury of world events. On the contrary, Copenhagen has had a rich and dramatic history, a history of which the Danes are justly proud. Because of its strategic location on the Øresund, a narrow seaway connecting the North and the Baltic seas (and separating Denmark from Sweden), Copenhagen has been besieged by the Swedes, leveled by the English, and occupied by the Germans.

According to Danish tradition, København (literally, "Merchants' Harbor") was founded in 1167 by a Bishop Absalon during the reign of Valdemar the Great. Absalon built a fortress on the island of Slotsholmen to protect the port, and the ruins of this fortress are still visible in the cellars of the parliament building Christiansborg.

In 1416, King Erik of Pomerania made Copenhagen the capital of Denmark, but it was not until the reign of Christian IV (1588-1648) and the Danish Renaissance that Copenhagen acquired some of the features one associates with it today. Christian IV was a great builder, and many of his contributions still stand — the Stock Exchange, Rosenborg Castle, the Round Tower, Kongens Have Park, and the residential districts of Nyboder and Christianshavn.

Disaster struck Copenhagen during the following century: The great fire of 1728 destroyed two-fifths of the houses in the city. Wood and straw thatch buildings were particularly combustible, and the narrow streets and alleys made firefighting all but impossible. A second great fire in 1795 reduced another fifth of the city to ashes.

Efforts at reconstruction were delayed by war. In 1801, the Danes found themselves confronted by a large English fleet under the command of Lord Nelson. Legend has it that the Danes hoisted a cease-fire flag after a heavy bombardment, whereupon Nelson raised his telescope to his blind eye and ordered the attack intensified. The subsequent Danish resistance was a highwater mark in the patriotic lore of Copenhagen. The English retired, only to send a larger fleet in 1807 to finish the job. A fierce rocket assault left most of Copenhagen in flames, and the city capitulated — for the first time in modern history.

Displaying their remarkable recuperative powers, the Danes quickly rebuilt the city. The Danish golden age of the mid-19th century followed, a time in which social progress, as evidenced by the parliamentary constitution of 1849, was accompanied by a flourishing of the arts. Many of the buildings one sees today are remnants of the Danish golden age. Fittingly, the old ramparts were removed during this era and replaced with a lush and verdant belt of parks.

Denmark lost its border provinces to Prussia in a war in 1864 but managed to steer clear of any other major conflicts until the 5-year German occupation during World War II. From April 9, 1940, to May 5, 1945, the heroic resistance of the Danish people to the Nazis was nearly unanimous. When the Danish merchant fleet was ordered by the Germans to make for a neutral port at the time of the occupation, more than 90% of the seamen (about 5,000 men) chose to answer the appeal of London radio to sail to an Allied port and join the war. Of the 5,000, 600 died and 60% of the ships were sunk. Back in Copenhagen, the underground press flourished and isolated incidents of resistance were numerous, reaching a climax on August 29, 1943, when the

Danish government unanimously and unqualifiedly said no to German ultimatums. Open resistance began: sabotage by underground groups, arms supplies, intelligence activities, and, most dramatically, escape routes for Jews and other war victims. About 7,000 persons were successfully evacuated to Sweden, and only 450 arrested and taken to Germany. The Danes paid a price for their courageous actions: Their resistance was met with violent Nazi countermeasures such as arrests, deportations, executions, and random shootings. Yet the Danes remained so active in resisting Hitler that Denmark was generally recognized as a de facto ally.

Postwar Copenhagen is a unique blend of historical charm and modern efficiency. Enlightened social reform and respect for aesthetic and sentimental values make Copenhagen one of the most delightful cities in Europe. The brutal new skyscrapers that loom over the horizon of many European cities have been exiled to the suburbs here, and one is hard pressed to find any symptoms of urban blight.

Denmark is a highly advanced country politically and socially. Its government, which resembles England's, is a constitutional monarchy with Queen Margrethe II on the throne and a parliament of 179 members called the Folketing. Widely known as a nation that provides for its citizens, Denmark has a comprehensive social security system and national health insurance. Its standard of living was rated the best in the world in a recent survey by the University of Pennsylvania. But its cost of living is higher than that of the US or West Germany. In recent years, Denmark has run up a colossal foreign debt, with annual net interest payments hitting the 25 billion kroner mark. This is due in large part to a slump in exports and dependence on foreign oil. This deficit was accompanied by high unemployment (about 10%) and inflation. In an effort to deal with these problems, the government instituted wage and price controls and gave several more twists to the tax screw, simultaneously freezing total expenditure in real terms. Taxes today are among the world's highest.

Aside from its political prominence as the capital of Denmark, Copenhagen is also the site of a major shipyard and design center, and is the home of the Carlsberg and Tuborg breweries, which produce one of Denmark's leading exports — beer.

The Danish people enjoy a reputation for being masters of recreational pursuits; in fact, Copenhagen is known among more reserved Scandinavians as a den of sex, drugs, and rock 'n' roll — in short, a nordic Shangri-La. This reputation is not entirely unjustified, as Copenhagen is a place to have a good time, sinful or otherwise.

Ever since the Vikings left their women responsible for the farms when they went out on plundering raids, Danes have had an unusually liberal attitude toward sex. In 1967, Denmark became the first country in the world to abolish all restrictions on the sale of pornographic literature to adults. After an initial boom, the sales of pornography actually went down, as did the number of sex crimes. Male tourists who expect Danish women to be especially promiscuous may be disappointed; there is probably no great difference in promiscuity from country to country in Europe.

Whatever your pleasure, whether it be pornography or the *Royal Danish*

Ballet, you will find much to enjoy in Copenhagen. A statue of the town's symbol, the *Little Mermaid,* perches petite and green on the waterfront to greet all visitors. Commissioned by Carlsberg magnate Carl Jacobsen in 1913, the statue was completed in 1915 and has survived the repeated humiliations of being doused in red paint, then in blue paint, and even decapitated. The *Mermaid* was erected by the Danes to express their gratitude to Hans Christian Andersen for his love of fantasy and of his fellow man.

In Andersen's tale, a mermaid falls hopelessly in love with a mortal prince who, alas, loves another. Begging to have feet so she can walk like a human, the mermaid suffers great physical pain whenever she takes a step as well as emotional anguish when she finds that her prince's romantic instincts are otherwise inclined. In the end she must pay the penalty of dissolving into an incorporeal spirit whose function is to help mortals navigate in perilous waters.

The spirits of the mermaid, the snow queen, the nightingale, and the ugly duckling seem to haunt the picture book streets of the Copenhagen that Hans Christian Andersen loved so dearly. And no wonder. Even today, in spite of its dominant role as Denmark's political and commercial center, Copenhagen's skyline is still much the same as it was in his day — a fairy tale conglomeration of ancient church steeples, spiraling golden towers, massive domes, and staircased gables.

COPENHAGEN AT-A-GLANCE

SEEING THE CITY: There are no World Trade Centers or Eiffel Towers in Copenhagen, but a far more authentic alternative exists in the Round Tower. Built in 1642 by the monarch Christian IV as an observatory, it offers a panorama of the spires and steeples of the old town of Copenhagen. Peter the Great of Russia reportedly led a carriage containing the Czarina Catherine to the top of the Round Tower in the 18th century, but today's visitors will unfortunately have to climb the 687-foot spiral walkway. Be advised, however, that the observatory on the roof is open only in clear weather. Open daily; admission charge. The Round Tower (Rundetårn) is on Købmagergade.

Several of Copenhagen's churches also provide views of the city, including the bizarre baroque tower of Vor Frelsers Kirke on Prinsessegade, which is also open to visitors. Here the spiral stairway is on the outside of the tower, so bring a sweater if it's chilly.

A spectacular view of Copenhagen is afforded by the *Top of Town* restaurant on the 25th floor of the *Scandinavia* hotel, 70 Amager Blvd.

SPECIAL PLACES: Copenhagen is a pedestrian's paradise, and it is relatively easy to get oriented after finding Strøget, the "strolling" street, which is made up of five connecting pedestrian streets, none of them named Strøget. (From Rådhuspladsen, the names are Frederiksberggade, Nygode, Vimmelskaftet, Smagertorv, and Østergade.) The medieval street plan of the old town is irregular, however, and once you leave the downtown area and familiar landmarks, it is possible to get lost. Danes are generally very helpful, and, as nearly everyone seems to speak English, it is very difficult to get hopelessly lost. In addition to the tourist office, banks and many stores give away city maps with street guides, both in English.

DOWNTOWN

Slotsholmen Island and Christiansborg Palace – In the central part of Copenhagen it is possible to visit the island where Absalon built his fortress in 1167, founding the city. The best way to get there is to walk from Rådhuspladsen down Vester Voldgade, left on Stormgade, and across the bridge leading into Porthusgade, where you will be confronted with *Thorvaldsen's Museum* to your left and, to your right, Christiansborg Palace, with the seat of the Danish parliament on one side and royal reception rooms on the other. Bertil Thorvaldsen was the most famous Danish sculptor; in 1838 he donated all of his work to the city of his birth, and in turn, the city built the museum to house his variations on classical themes. The museum is open daily, except Mondays, from 10 AM to 5 PM year-round; no admission charge. English-language guided tours are available at 4 PM on Sundays and Wednesdays from June through September.

Christiansborg was completed in 1740, burned in 1794, rebuilt in 1828, and burned down once more. The present palace, in a mixed baroque/rococo design by Thorvald Jorgenson, was built from 1906 to 1928 (although the buildings around the riding ground remain from the 1740s). Guided English-language tours of the royal reception rooms take place at 11 AM and 1 and 3 PM daily (except Mondays) in summer, at 2 PM (except Mondays and Saturdays) in winter. Underneath the palace, ruins of Absalon's fortress and its successor, Copenhaven Castle, are open from 9:30 AM to 4 PM daily (closed Saturdays in winter).

Copenhagen's Cathedral (Vor Frue Kirke) – Using Rådhuspladsen as a starting point, you reach the old section of Copenhagen by taking a left down Vester Voldgade and then taking a right on Studiestraede. Up ahead you will see Vor Frue Kirke, Copenhagen's neo-classic cathedral, which was completed in 1829. Open daily.

Gammeltorv – If you take a right on Nørregade in front of the cathedral, you will enter the oldest part of the city — the marketplace of Gammeltorv, which the fortress on Slotsholmen was built to defend in 1167. In addition to being the first marketplace in Copenhagen, Gammeltorv has been the site of jousting tournaments and public executions and is still a center for social activity. Nytorv was added in 1606 as an extension of Gammeltorv. *Caritas* ("Charity"), the city's oldest fountain, donated by King Christian IV in 1609, is here.

Model Theater Museum (Dukketeatermuseet) – At the end of Skindergade, the street that runs through the Latin Quarter, Copenhagen's university area, this museum has a historical collection of toy theaters. Open Mondays, Wednesdays, and Fridays from 12:30 to 5:30 PM. 52 Købmagergade.

Botanical Gardens (Botanisk Have) – A park and greenhouses sport both tropical and subtropical plants; in the summer, the "wildlife" on view includes topless sunbathers. Open daily. No admission charge. Entrance at Gothersgade and Sølvgade. 128 Gothersgade.

Rosenborg Castle (Rosenborg Slot) – This Renaissance castle was built by Christian IV over the 11-year period from 1606 to 1617. Its fine interiors contain the crown jewels and treasures of the Danish royal family from the 15th to the 19th century. Open daily from May until late October; Tuesdays, Fridays, and Sundays in winter. No admission charge. 4A Oster Voldgade.

Amalienborg Palace – The residence of the Danish royal family since 1794, Amalienborg is another spectacular example of Danish rococo, with four identical palaces set perfectly against the harbor background. Unfortunately, it can be seen only from the outside. When the royal family is in residence, however, there is plenty of pomp for all to see during the daily Changing of the Guard. The Royal Guard leaves the Rosenborg Castle at 11:30 AM and marches through the streets, to arrive at the Amalienborg Palace at noon.

The Harbor – The harbor area, or Nyhavn, favorite haunt for sailors from around the world and home of Hans Christian Andersen for many years, is a fascinating area where you can run into all manner of characters ranging from sleek fashion models walking their Afghan hounds to the proverbial drunken sailors who may have just been decorated at Tattoo Jack's. For an interesting tour, start at the *Royal Theater* at Kongens Nytorv, then follow the left-hand side of Nyhavn Canal toward the water. En route you can look at the sturdy fishing boats and sailing ships. The right-hand side of Nyhavn, also known as the Charlottenborg side, has been an elegant residential area for many years. It was here, in #67, that Andersen lived between 1845 and 1864 and wrote his famous fairy tales. In recent years, a number of good, small restaurants have emerged on both sides of Nyhavn; the sailors' bars here — *Cap Horn,* the *Brooklyn,* and others — may seem exotic, but are generally no bargain, and seem to survive by enticing inebriated Swedes on their way to the ferry back to Sweden.

Museum of Decorative Art (Kunstindustrimuseet) – Founded in 1890, the museum contains European and Oriental applied art from the Middle Ages to modern times, including a fine collection of contemporary decorative art. Open daily, except Mondays, from 1 to 4 PM. No admission charge on weekdays except during July and August. 68 Bredgade.

Resistance Museum (Frihedsmuseet) – In Churchill Park just outside the entrance to Kastellet — or the citadel, Copenhagen's old harbor fortifications that are open from 6 AM to sundown — the *Frihedsmuseet* contains relics from the resistance movement during the German occupation of 1940–45. Closed Mondays. No admission charge. Churchill Park at Langelinie.

Langelinie Pavilion and Promenade – One of the loveliest spots in Copenhagen is just opposite the citadel, overlooking the harbor — the Langelinie *Pavilion* and Promenade. The *Pavilion* is an elegant (and pricey) restaurant where you can gaze at the moonlit waters and dine and dance until the wee hours. Should you want a breath of fresh air, you can always suggest a walk along the promenade to take a look at *Den Lille Havfrue* (*Little Mermaid*), erected in 1913 thanks to a grant from Carlsberg Brewery magnate Carl Jacobsen.

Carlsberg Brewery – In case you're wondering how they make the stuff that everybody seems to be drinking, you will be happy to learn that guests are welcome at the Carlsberg Brewery, a 20-minute walk from Rådhuspladsen, or take the #6 bus. Danes take their beer as seriously as the Irish take Guinness stout, and be advised that Elephant Beer, the world-famous Danish brew by Carlsberg, is about twice as strong as regular American beer (or even the Elephant Beer marketed in the US). Closed weekends; free tours conducted on weekdays at 11 AM and 2:30 PM. 140 Ny Carlsberg-vej (phone: 31-211221; for groups of 10 or more, ask for ext. 1312).

Tuborg Brewery – Tuborg, which can be reached by bus #1, also welcomes visitors on weekdays. Free tours at 10 AM and 12:30 and 2:30 PM comprise an hour of walking and a half-hour of quaffing. 54 Strandvejen (phone: 31-293311, ext. 2212).

Tivoli – On the south side of Rådhuspladsen you will find the fabled Tivoli, Copenhagen's favorite summer recreation facility. Built in 1843 on top of old city ramparts, Tivoli is a dazzling hybrid of gardens (160,000 flowers), lakes, theaters, dance halls, and restaurants, illuminated at night by over 100,000 colored lights. Whether you are looking for a first class restaurant such as *Belle Terasse* or *Divan I and II* or the tawdry company of a one-armed bandit, Tivoli has it all.

The season starts runs from late April to mid-September, from 10 AM to midnight daily. Internationally known artists perform on an outdoor stage every night. The concert hall features nightly concerts with orchestras and soloists, often free of charge. Other entertainment includes the *Tivoli Boy Guard* marching band, the *Pantomime Theater,* children's theater, promenade concerts every night around the gardens, and amusement park facilities. Especially recommended are the fireworks at 11:45 PM Wednesdays, Fridays, Saturdays, and holidays. Vesterbrogade, near Town Hall Square.

Lake Pavilion (Søpavilion) – A 10-minute walk from Town Hall Square, the old pavilion on Lake Peblinge offers live music, cabaret, art shows, and international food and drink year-round. Søpavillion has much the same magic as Tivoli's 19th-century *Pantomime Theater* — the same architect designed both. Three picture-perfect lakes draw sailors in summer, skaters in winter, and joggers doing laps in all seasons. Go even if just for coffee and the view. Open daily from noon until 2 AM. Admission charge for shows. 24 Gyldenløvesgade (phone: 33-151224).

Tycho Brahe Planetarium – Named for the famous 16th-century Danish astronomer, this planetarium, opened in late 1989, is one of Europe's largest. It contains: a 275-seat theater, a restaurant, library, and exhibitions on astronomy and space exploration. Guided tours will be available in English. Open daily from 10 AM to 10 PM, Sundays from noon. Admission charge. 10 Gl. Kongevej (phone: 33-121224).

Christiania – The dreams of the 1960s may have died sometime in the early 70s, and the media would have us believe that the Age of Love has become the Age of Punk; however, the news has not yet reached Copenhagen. Christiania, a sprawling section of Copenhagen that covers about 10 square blocks in the Christianshavn district, can easily be found by walking toward the towering golden spire of the aforementioned Vor Frelser Kirke. The casual visitor will be assaulted by a helter-skelter patchwork of theatrical spectacles, conceptual art pieces, strung-out hippies, stray children and dogs, psychedelic paintings, and, yes, whatever you want to smoke, if such is your bent. Although this community has been the subject of hot debate in Copenhagen, its very existence is symptomatic of the Danes' civic tolerance.

OUTSIDE THE CITY

Dragør – Dragør is an enchanting fishing village south of Copenhagen that dates from the 16th century and is still in vintage condition. Its streets are paved with cobblestones, and 65 of its quaint, old, red-roofed houses are protected historical sites, making an address here both fashionable and expensive. On the tip of the island of Amager, Dragør 5s about a 30-minute ride from Rådhuspladsen on bus #30 or #33, and worth the trip if you want to see a village straight from the pages of Hans Christian Andersen.

The oldest house in the village is the home of the *Dragør Museum,* open in summer only, daily except Mondays. Two old inns, the *Dragør Kro* and the *Café Beghuset,* offer bars for relaxing and restaurants that serve Danish and French specialties. Both are open daily, year-round, with a small admission charge. The most pleasant way to get here is by boat; there are ferry connections from Dragør to the town of Limhamn in Sweden.

Open-Air Museum (Frilandsmuseet) – This is a half-hour ride outside the city on the #84 or #384 bus, or by S train to Sorgenfri station, and is an elaborate tribute to the joys of being down on the farm in the Danish countryside. (Just more proof that the Danes are incurable romantics.) Old houses from the various regions of Denmark have been dismantled and moved here, piece by piece, and efforts have even been made to re-create the ecological environment of each kind of farm. Interiors have also been re-created, and during the summer the visitor can watch sheep being sheared, wool being carded, garments being spun, and other examples of agrarian toil. There is a modern restaurant, but if you have not had your fill of pastoral splendor, there are also picnic tables and benches. The *Open-Air Museum* is open all year, though only Sundays in winter. (A winter visit will make it easy for you to understand why so many Danes live in Copenhagen.) Admission charge. 100 Kongevejen, Sorgenfri, Kgs. Lyngby.

Elsinore (Helsingør) – About a 45-minute train ride north of Copenhagen lies the site of Hamlet's famous castle, Helsingør. In case you had been looking forward to roaming the ramparts in search of the ghost, you may be disappointed to learn that the present castle, Kronborg, is not the original but was built in the 16th and 17th centuries. The Danes insist that Hamlet did exist, however, and refer the curious to the medieval Danish historian Saxo Grammaticus's epic work, *Gesta Danorum*, for further details. Some rooms, including the King's and Queen's apartments, are open daily for an admission charge. Also on the Kronborg grounds is the *Mercantile and Maritime Museum*. Perhaps the best thing about the castle is the magnificent view of the sound from the ramparts. Occasionally, visiting theatrical groups perform *Hamlet* in the courtyard. The eastern outskirts of Helsingør are not far from the ferry docks.

Louisiana Modern Art Museum – In the town of Humlebaek, 22 miles (about 35 km) north of Copenhagen, in a park overlooking the sea, the *Louisiana* has the most important collection of modern Danish art in Europe as well as works by Andy Warhol and other internationally renowned artists. Originally the private collection of art patron Knud W. Jensen, the *Louisiana* was opened to the public in 1958. If you like well-displayed modern art and beautiful scenery — another plus is the lovely views afforded by the museum's picture windows — stop en route to Helsingør. Open daily. Admission charge for adults. All-inclusive tickets for transportation and museum admission are sold at the Central Station. Take the train to Humlebaek or the #188 bus from Klampenborg station. 13 Gammel Strandvej, Humlebaek.

Roskilde – About 19 miles (30 km) west of Copenhagen is an ancient city that was the capital of Denmark until the 15th century. During the 13th century it was one of the premier cities in Europe and, prior to that, it was the site of the first Danish church (a short-lived wooden affair erected by Harald Bluetooth in 980), Roskilde is a treasure trove of Viking artifacts and other items of archaeological interest. Roskilde Cathedral was built in the 1170s by Bishop Absalon on top of Harald's church, and aside from being the first Gothic cathedral in Denmark, it is the burial place of 38 Danish kings and queens. The tour in the cathedral will lead you from one spectacular marble sarcophagus to another. The cathedral, or Domkirke, is open daily for a small admission charge; it is closed during religious services. Take the train to Roskilde or bus #123 (phone: 42-352700).

A relic of heathen culture, the *Vikingeskibshallen* (Viking Ship Museum) contains five reconstructed Viking ships that were sunk off Roskilde around AD 1000. Aside from this magnificent bit of salvage work, the museum offers detailed descriptions of Viking seafaring techniques and life on board ship. When seeing the boats, it is somewhat awe inspiring to remember that they sailed these things across the Atlantic to Greenland and Newfoundland. Open daily. Standengen, Roskilde (phone: 42-356555).

Oldtidsbyen – In Lejre, 7 miles (about 11 km) west of Roskilde, the Oldtidsbyen is a reconstruction of an old Iron Age village. Run by the Historical Archaeological Research Center, the Oldtidsbyen was created with grants from the Carlsberg Foundation and the government for the purpose of studying Iron Age life. Open daily May through September. Admission charge.

Bornholm – Should the summer be extremely warm or should you just be suffering from a stiff dose of the urban blues, why not follow the example of the Danes and beat a retreat to Bornholm, a beautiful island in the Baltic between Denmark and Sweden. An overnight ferry trip from Copenhagen, Bornholm is the secret summer paradise for the nature-loving Danes and Swedes, and offers over 200 Viking burial mounds, 40 rune stones, and 4 round churches from the early Middle Ages. There are also several spectacular beaches. If interested, write to the Bornholm Tourist Office, 4 Munch Petersvej, Rønne DK-3700 (phone: 53-950810).

■ **EXTRA SPECIAL:** About 23 miles (36 km) north of Copenhagen, at Hillerød, lies the impressive Frederiksborg Castle — a building that many consider to be Europe's most beautiful Renaissance castle. Built on the grounds of an old manor by Christian IV, between 1600 and 1620, most of the structure was gutted by fire in 1859. It was then reconstructed from the original drawings, thanks chiefly to funding from the Carlsberg Foundation. Since 1878, the castle has been the *National Historical Museum,* in which collections of Danish artifacts, including costumes, armor, artwork, and furniture, are arranged in the rooms as though they were still the sites for daily life of an earlier time. Particularly noteworthy is the chapel — one of the few rooms untouched by the fire. Since it continues to be used as the chapel of the Danish Orders of Chivalry, its walls are lined with the crests of heads of state, industry, and the arts. The altar is made of silver and ornately carved ebony; the organ (ca. 1600) has its original pipes and is still played. The throne room includes a throne "elevator," which permitted the King to make rather dramatic appearances as he emerged through the floor. Castle grounds and museum are open daily. Admission charge. From Copenhagen, take the S-train to Hillerød.

SOURCES AND RESOURCES

TOURIST INFORMATION: For general information, brochures, and maps, contact the Danish National Tourist Office, 655 Third Ave., New York, NY 10017 (phone: 212-949-2333). In Copenhagen, contact Danish Tourist Information at 22 H. C. Andersen Blvd. (phone: 33-111325); or the Tourist Association of Copenhagen, in the Magasin du Nord department store, Kongens Nytorv (phone: 33-114433). Students may wish to consult the Youth Information Center, 13 Rädhusstrade (phone: 33-156518). For assistance in finding accommodations, a room service, Use-It, is at Kiosk P in Copenhagen's main rail station (see "Getting Around," below).

The US Embassy is at 24 Dag Hammarskjöld Allée (phone: 31-423144).

Local Coverage – The Copenhagen Tourist Office should be able to keep you abreast of events of interest. *Copenhagen This Week,* available at hotels and the tourist offices, is also helpful. Unfortunately, there are no English-language newspapers in Copenhagen. If you miss news from home, buy the traveler's daily blessing, the *International Herald Tribune* (about $2), or listen to the 8:10 AM English news on Radio Denmark, Program I.

Food – The Danish Tourist Board and Copenhagen Tourist Office publish a brochure, *Copenhagen,* which lists and advertises several restaurants. Eating places are also listed in *Copenhagen This Week.*

Telephone – The area codes for Copenhagen are 31 through 49.

CLIMATE AND CLOTHES: Thanks to the Gulf Stream, Denmark has a rather mild, if somewhat undramatic, climate. The average daytime temperature from June to August is 70F (20C). Due to its northerly latitude, Copenhagen gets sunshine long into the evenings during the summer months, but once the sun goes down, it does get chilly, so bring sweaters. In recent years there has also been a good deal of rain and fog in the summer, so bring raincoats as well. The winters have much less sun but have an average temperature just above 32F (0C) and snow is infrequent. Hence you will not need Arctic gear, only warm winter clothes.

As far as dress is concerned, the Danes do not stand on ceremony, and informal attire is acceptable in most theaters and restaurants. Men should bring a tie and jacket if they are planning to dine at the more exclusive restaurants.

GETTING AROUND: Airport – The completely remodeled Kastrup International, with its upgraded restaurants, boutiques, and other attractions, has been christened "Europe's most beautiful airport." It handles both international and domestic flights and is a 20-minute taxi ride from the center of town (an average fare is 110 Danish kroner (about $16). Bus service operates every 20 minutes on the hour between the airport and Copenhagen's main railway station. Fare: 24 DKr. (about $3.50).

Bicycle – If you want your own means of transport, why not follow the example of the Danes and get a bicycle? Nearly all streets have separate lanes for bicycle traffic, and except for the worst winter months, it is often easier to ride a bicycle than drive a car on Copenhagen's narrow streets. Bicycles can be rented at *Københavns Cyklebørs,* 159 Gothersgade (phone: 33-140717), for about $7 a day with a deposit of $17.

Bus – As mentioned previously, Copenhagen is small enough to be seen on foot, but the bus system offers a cheap and efficient alternative if your feet are weary from the cobblestones. The city bus system (HT/Copenhagen Transport) is excellent and is supplemented by electric S-trains to the suburbs. Local buses and S-trains start running at 5 AM (6 on Sundays), and the last regular departures from downtown are at about 1 AM. All buses and railways in Copenhagen and environs are in a collective fare system. This means within defined zones, tickets are good for a full hour's travel by bus or train with unlimited transfers. Buy your tickets from bus drivers or at train stations. Discount tickets, good for ten trips, can be bought at stations, HT ticket offices, or from bus drivers. You stamp your ticket yourself by running it through the automatic machine at the front of the bus, where you board; when taking the train, you will see the machine on the platform. This is important, as an invalid or unstamped ticket can cost you up to $15, and they are checked now and again.

The Copenhagen Card, available for 1, 2, or 3 days, provides unlimited travel by bus or train in the metropolitan area, substantial reductions on fares for crossings to Sweden, and free admission to more than 40 museums. The card can be purchased at hotels, major railway stations, travel agencies, and the tourist information office; it costs DKr. 80 (about $11), DKr. 140 ($20), or DKr. 180 ($26).

Car Rental – To rent a car, you must be at least 20, although some firms require 25. Reputable companies include *Avis,* 1 Kampmannsgade (phone: 33-152299), *Hertz,* 3 Ved Vesterport (phone: 01-127700), *Europcar,* 70 Gammel Kongevej (phone: 31-246677), and *Inter Rent* at 6 Jernbanegade (phone: 33-116200).

Taxi – Taxis are expensive but fast, and can be hailed on the streets. They are available when the green light is on, and the tip is included in the fare. To call a taxi, phone 31-353535.

Train – The city's main railway station is Hovedbanegaarden, on Vesterbrogade (phone: 33-141701, for fares and schedules).

SPECIAL EVENTS: The advent of spring in Copenhagen is heralded by the opening of *Bakken,* Scandinavia's oldest (500 years old) festive amusement park in the Deer Park north of Copenhagen (April 1) and in Tivoli (May 1). The century-old *Benneweis Circus,* Jernbanegade (phone: 33-142192), begins its season on or about May 8 and ends about October 20. Each summer Copenhagen holds an international festival in June. The theme alternates between the *Festival of Fools* (focusing on theater) and the *Copenhagen Carnival,* the largest pre-Lenten celebration in northern Europe. Then there's the swinging *Copenhagen Jazz Festival* in midsummer.

MUSEUMS: In addition to those mentioned in *Special Places,* Copenhagen boasts a number of other well-organized museums, the most notable of which are the following.

Copenhagen's City Museum and the Søren Kierkegaard Collection (Københavns Bymuseum og Søren Kierkegaard-Samlingen) – The city's 800 years in pictures and mementos; also Søren Kierkegaard curios. 59 Vesterbrogade.

Danish Film Museum (Det Danske Filmmuseum) – 4 Store Søndervoldstraede.

Geological Museum (Geologisk Museum) – Meteorites, fossils, and minerals. 5-7 Øster Voldgade.

National Museum (Nationalmuseet) – Prehistoric Denmark from the Ice Age to the Vikings. 12 Frederiksholms Kanal.

New Carlsberg Glyptotek – Egyptian, Greek, Etruscan, and Roman art; also 19th-century French and Danish works. Dantes Plads.

Stock Exchange (Børsen) – Built in 1624. Børsgade.

Toy Museum (Legetøjsmuseet) – Toys from generations ago, with films daily at 11 AM and 2 PM. 13 Teglgårdstraede.

Royal Museum of Fine Arts (Statens Museum for Kunst) – Danish and European works of art, including a Matisse collection. Sølvgade at Øster Voldgade.

Zoological Museum – Animal life through exhibitions, models, and dioramas. 15 Universitetsparken.

SHOPPING: With all its perambulating pedways, Copenhagen is ideal for the consumer. Keep in mind that the 22% sales tax in Denmark is included in the price. To avoid this tax, have the goods delivered to you at the airport, or present the sales slips and article(s) at the customs counter there for the 22% refund. If you have the items shipped directly to the US, make a note of the store's name and address, keep your receipt, and insure all goods against damage.

Denmark is world famous for beautifully designed wares for the home — furniture, of course; sterling silver by *Georg Jensen* and others; and porcelain by *Bing & Grøndahl* and *Royal Copenhagen.* Also, Copenhagen is northern Europe's main fur trading center. It might be wise to check the prices of these items before you leave home, as savings may not be substantial in Denmark.

Another Danish claim to fame is pastry, though in Denmark the doughy, sticky pastry we know as danish bears little resemblance to the crispy, buttery concoctions Danes call Vienna bread. Follow your taste buds into the nearest bake shop for a whiff of those *kanelstaenger, snegle, tebirkes, borgmesterstaenger,* and their caloric ilk. In the core of the old town, Copenhagen's oldest active bakery, *Hos Kurt Lorenz* (29 Skt. Pedersstr.) — which traces its owner-family history back to 1652 — has them all. Also on the culinary front, at *J. Chr. Andersen's Eftf.* (32 Købmagergade) you'll find from 450 to 500 different kinds of cheese, many of them homemade — or at least home-aged. If you fancy chocolate made of Gran Marnier cheese, this is the place. Purchases can be vacuum-packed for the trip home.

You might wish to stroll down Strøget, the most famous of the city's shopping streets, three-quarters of a mile long. Strøget is not one but actually five connecting streets, none of them named Strøget (see *Special Places*). This stretch abounds in department stores and specialty shops. And take a look at the side streets as well.

Other pedestrian streets are Fiolstraede and Købmagergade in the old Latin Quarter, once the student quarter and now more cosmopolitan, the place to go for antiques and rare books as well as boutiques and specialty shops.

A. C. Bang – A fine place for furs. 27 Østergade.

Bing & Grøndahl – World-famous porcelain. 4 Amagertorv.

Bang and Olufsen – Superb TV sets and sound equipment. 3 Ostergade.

Anthon Berg – Irresistible Danish chocolates, many filled with marzipan or liqueurs. 1 Ostergade.

Birger Christensen – Also for furs. 38 Østergade.

Boghallen – For English-language paperbacks and the latest hardcovers. Also Denmark's largest selection of travel books. 37 Rådhuspladsen.

C. Danel – Furniture. 124 Gammel Kongevej.

Dansk Kunst Håndvaerk – An exciting boutique offering the work of 60 craftspeople in glass, ceramics, textiles, jewelry, and knitwear. 1 Amagertorv.

Hans Hansen Silver – Similar quality and lower prices than *Georg Jensen.* 16 Amagertorv.

Illum – Large department store with selections of all typical Danish wares; also a fine restaurant. 52 Østergade.

Illums Bolighus – World-renowned furnishings center of modern design. 10 Amagertorv.

Georg Jensen Silver – Needs no introduction. 40 Østergade.

Den Kongelige Porcelainsfabrik – Royal Copenhagen Porcelain Factory, next door to Bing & Grøndahl. 6 Amagertorv.

Magasin du Nord – Largest and best-known department store; every variety of Danish merchandise well displayed. 13 Kongens Nytorv.

A. Michelsen – High-quality silver. 40 Bredgade.

Paustian – Avant-garde furniture in a prize-winning building. On Copenhagen's northernmost harborfront, 2 Kalkbraenderiløbskaj (take the S-train east to Nordhavn and walk).

Rosenthal Studio Haus A/S – Porcelain. 21 Frederiksberggade.

SPORTS AND FITNESS: Copenhagen does not have the variety of sports facilities found in many American cities, but the few sports popular in Denmark are *very* popular.

Bicycle Racing – Due to the Danish mania for bicycles, this is one of Denmark's biggest international sports. *Ordrup Cykelbane* is open 1 day a week; contact *Brøndbt Stadion* for information (phone: 32-455841; Brannersvej and Charlottenlund are open from May to September, usually Tuesdays and Sundays. In addition, every year around the last weekend in January the exciting Copenhagen Six-Day International Cycle Race is held.

Fitness Centers – *Form & Figur,* 25 Amagertorv (phone: 33-143202), accepts non-members on 'a temporary basis (3-month minimum), as do *Copenhagen Squash Club,* Vestersøhus, Vestersøgade (phone: 33-118638), and *Københavns Boldklub* (tennis club), Peter Bangsvej (phone: 31-714180).

Horse Racing – Not many horses in Denmark, but the Danes enjoy gambling. Klampenborg Galopbane, Klampenborgvej, Klampenborg. Races are on Saturdays between mid-April and mid-December.

Jogging – The parks, Kongens Have and Faelledparken, as well as Central Lakes (Søerne), are all good spots, 10 minutes from Town Hall Square.

Soccer – Known in Denmark as *fodbold,* there are matches every weekend from April to June and August to November. The Danish national team also plays World Cup matches in Copenhagen at Idraetsparken, Østerbro.

Swimming – The coast north of Copenhagen has many beaches, and the water is relatively warm in the latter part of the summer. In the northern suburb of Klampenborg, Bellevue Strandpark, a city beach, is very popular. South of Copenhagen, Køge Bay Strandpark is an area of beaches, marinas, and dunes. Topless, if not nude, bathing is the norm in Denmark, especially for the young. There are also a number of excellent Olympic-size public pools, both indoor and outdoor. Between May 15 and August 31, try Bavnehøj Friluftsbad, 90 Enghavevej (phone: 31-214900). For year-round indoor swimming, try Kildeskovshallen, 25 Adolfsver, Gentofte (phone: 31-682822).

 THEATER: Because the arts in Denmark are government subsidized, tickets are an incredible bargain. From September through May, the famous *Det Kongelieg Tester* (Royal Theater) at Kongens Nytorv is worth a visit. The *Danish National Theater* and national opera company perform here, in Danish, as does the *Royal Danish Ballet,* one of the world's foremost companies. There are two stages: the Old Stage (Gamle Scene) and the New Stage (Nye Scene). For all bookings, phone: 33-141002. In the summer there are lighter diversions, like cabarets at Tivoli, beer hall entertainment at Bakken, and international acts at the *Benneweis Circus.* The *Mermaid Theatre,* 27 Skt. Pedersstr. (phone: 33-114303), is Scandinavia's only permanent English-language stage, presenting Scandinavian plays in summer and British and American works in winter. A cabaret in the style of an old English musical is presented during Christmastime.

 MUSIC: Besides opera at the *Royal Theater* (see above) there are classical music concerts, performed by the *Radio Symphony Orchestra* in *Radio Concert Hall* and *Zealand Symphony Hall* in Tivoli. Students of the *Royal Danish Academy of Music* give regular concerts, usually free, at 1 Niels Brocksgade. During the winter season there are also modern music concerts at *New Carlsberg Glyptotek* (see *Museums*) and *Louisiana Museum* (see *Special Places*). Excellent jazz and big-name guest stars are often available at *Montmartre,* the northern European jazz capital, 41 Nørregade (phone: 33-127836). The world's best rock bands often give extraordinary performances in Copenhagen, as the audiences tend to be very responsive, at *Falkonér Teatret,* Falkonér Allé (phone: 31-868501). If you want to make bookings for musical or theatrical events and you can't make it to the theater, these ticket agents may help: *Saga Ticket Center,* 25 Vesterbrøgade (phone: 31-238800); *Wilhelm Hansen,* 9-11 Gothersgade (phone: 33-155457).

 NIGHTCLUBS AND NIGHTLIFE: Popular traditional night spots with food, live music, and dancing are the *Scandinavia* hotel's *After 8,* 70 Amager Blvd. (phone: 31-112334), and *Nautilus,* 24-28 Toldbodgade (phone: 33-118282), in the *Copenhagen Admiral. La Brasserie,* in the *Hotel d'Angleterre,* 34 Kongens Nytorv (phone: 31-238800), is a trendy new spot to see and be seen.

More informal are *Den Røde Pimpernel,* 7 Hans Christian Andersen Blvd. (phone: 33-122032), and the lively *HongKong,* 7 Nyhavn (phone: 33-129272). If you like discotheques, there are several alternatives, but nothing that measures up to New York's finest. Most of them require specific dress, and their pretensions of exclusivity often extend to asking you to buy a phony membership card at the door. The best of the lot are *Annabel's,* 16 Lille Kongensgade and 12-14 *On the Rox,* Pilestraede.

The music cafés are a much better deal, and are much friendlier. The best are, in addition to the aforementioned *Montmartre, Daddy's Dance Hall* (rock and punk), 9 Axeltorv (phone: 33-114679), and *La Fontaine,* 11 Kompagnistraede (phone: 33-116098). This place specializes in jazz, but is perhaps best known for being the place *everyone* goes to for morning coffee after a night on the town. Another late-night bar-restaurant-café, just behind the *Royal Theater,* is *Brønnum,* Kongens Nytorv (phone: 33-930365), from midnight to 5 AM. *Yow,* 12 Larsbjørnstraede (phone: 33-139005), is the "in" spot for sandwiches, salads, and drinks from 11 AM to 1 AM. For folk music and a younger crowd, try *Vognhjulet,* 67 Thorsgade (phone: 31-831570).

BEST IN TOWN

 CHECKING IN: There are a few large luxury hotels in Copenhagen, and they are not only a bit expensive by American standards, but too often the service is indifferent. Depending on the season, prices range from $120 to $260 for a double room with shower and bath at a luxury hotel to $60 to $70 for the same facilities at a less pretentious establishment. When booking rooms, check whether breakfast is included and whether you will have a shower or a bath. Also, look for off-season discounts. Expect to pay $120 or more for a double in those hotels we classify as expensive; between $70 and $115 for hotels in our moderate category; and under $70 in the inexpensive range. Remember to book in advance, if possible, during summer months. Also, be forewarned that many of the less-expensive establishments are closed during the Christmas-New Year's holidays. All telephone numbers are in the 33 through 49 area codes unless otherwise indicated.

d'Angleterre – Built in 1775 and renovated most recently in 1987 by its Swedish owners, this 126-room hostelry is the oldest and most fashionable in town. The old-fashioned paneled rooms and the location near Nyhavn give something of the sensation of being on a very classy ocean liner. There's a good, reasonably priced French restaurant, an "in" eatery, *La Brasserie,* and a bar called *The Bar.* 34 Kongens Nytorv (phone: 33-120095). Expensive.

Copenhagen Admiral – In an old warehouse on the waterfront near *d'Angleterre* and a good deal less expensive, the *Admiral* is one of the largest and newest hotels in Copenhagen. In the evening, the congenial *Nautilus* nightclub opens downstairs. 24 Toldbodgade (phone: 33-118282). Expensive.

Grand – A few blocks away from Tivoli and Rådhuspladsen and right near the Central Railway Station, newly renovated and expanded, this 142-room hotel is conveniently located, with a wide variety of room sizes. 9 Vesterbrogade (phone: 31-313600). Expensive.

Plaza – If finely wrought antique furnishings, mahogany paneling, and luxurious comfort appeal to you, consider reserving one of the 96 rooms here. Because of the unusually high quality of accoutrements and service, you need to make reservations months well ahead of your intended arrival. 4 Bernstorffsgade (phone: 33-149262). Expensive.

Scandinavia – This 542-room modern skyscraper run by SAS is the largest in town. Like the *Sheraton Copenhagen,* it caters basically to the needs and tastes of businesspeople on the move. On the 25th floor is the *Top of Town* restaurant, which affords spectacular views of the city, while downstairs is *After 8.* 70 Amager Blvd. (phone: 33-112324). Expensive.

Sheraton Copenhagen – An alternative to the above, with 470 rooms, a pleasant view of the city, and the *King's Court Bar.* 6 Vester Søgade (phone: 33-143535). Expensive.

Avenue – A 72-room property in western Copenhagen, about 20 blocks from Rådhuspladsen. Closed between December 23 and January 1. Room and board available. 29 Åboulevarden (phone: 35-373111). Moderate.

Cosmopole – Just a block south of Tivoli, with 245 beds and a wide variety of rooms and pension rates, this spot is a good bargain for the single tourist. 11 Colbjørnsensgade (phone: 31-213333). Moderate.

Østerport – Though this long, low hotel alongside the railroad tracks looks rather odd, it provides comfortable accommodations and a good smørgasbørd lunch. 5 Oslo Plads (phone: 33-112266). Moderate.

Viking – An honorable old salt's hotel near Nyhavn, this 91-room property provides an address in the heart of the city's harbor section. 65 Bredgade (phone: 33-124550). Moderate to inexpensive.

Absalon – A clean little hotel in the harbor for those on a limited budget. The 260 rooms rent for a wide variety of prices. 19 Helgolandsgade (phone: 31-242211). Inexpensive.

Ibsens – Here is a decent alternative to the *Absalon,* a 46-room hotel on a quiet side street near the Botanical Gardens. 25 Vendersgade (phone: 33-131913). Inexpensive.

 EATING OUT: The Danes enjoy good food as well as good beer and "snaps" (aquavit), and there are a number of classy old restaurants with capital continental cuisine — especially French. There are also many small taverns, or *kro,* with Danish specialties like open-face sandwiches or *smørrebrød.* Increasingly popular are the little croissant shops that are popping up all over the city. An inexpensive croissant sandwich at lunch is a good way to stretch the budget in order to afford a splurge at dinner.

A Dane will never refuse a snaps with herring — and there are plenty of other reasons to indulge as well. Snaps is usually imbibed icy cold, by the glass or the bottle, and is often chased by one of the many wonderful Danish beers. The best snaps are Aalborg's Jubileum and Harald Jensen.

The proper way to toast is to raise your glass to eye level, say *"Skål,"* and look your companions in the eye. Toss back the entire shot — if you're hardy enough — and, before returning the glass to the table, hold it at eye level again. Aquavit may also be drunk in the form of "punch" (heated and sweetened with a sugar cube) or in coffee.

Reservations are not usually a problem, but it is always wise to call. Be advised that liquor is heavily taxed and likely to be about twice as expensive as at home — your bill in general may seem a bit high, but remember that the 15% service charge is included in the price. So check before leaving a tip. Expect to pay at least $60 for a meal for two at a restaurant in our expensive category; $40 to $60 in the moderate range; and $30 to $40 in any restaurant listed as inexpensive. Prices don't include wine and drinks. All telephone numbers are in the 31 through 49 area codes, unless otherwise indicated.

Baron of Beef/Flora Danica – A fine French-Danish restaurant right behind Tivoli in the *Plaza* hotel. Danish food especially recommended for samples of local specialties. Closed Christmas Eve to New Year's. 4 Bernstorffsgade (phone: 33-149262). Expensive.

Belle Terrasse – The most elegant restaurant in Tivoli. Lush gardens, live music, very romantic ambience. An experience, though an expensive one. Reservations necessary. Closed September through April. Tivoli (phone: 33-121136). Expensive.

La Cocotte – Good French cuisine and wines characterize this restaurant, tucked away at the rear of the *Richmond* hotel. Closed Sundays and major holidays. 33 Vester Farimagsgade (phone: 31-140407). Expensive.

Egoisten – A traditional restaurant with an enduring reputation for its haute cuisine. Closed weekends. 12 Hovedvagtsg. (phone: 33-127971). Expensive.

Els – The murals date from the mid-19th century, when the restaurant was a coffeehouse. The menu is nouvelle-inspired Danish and French. Closed December 24-25 and December 31-January 1. 3 Store Strandstraede (phone: 33-141341). Expensive.

Imperial – One of the city's best. The house specialty is salmon and carved beef, which virtually melts in the mouth. Although expensive, the prix fixe includes all you can eat. Closed Christmas. In the *Imperial* hotel, 9 Vester Farimagsgade (phone: 33-128000). Expensive.

Langelinie Pavillonen – In the harbor north of Amalienborg Castle, with a magnificent view of the waterfront. Music, dancing . . . and the *Little Mermaid*. The food is overpriced and ordinary, but worth it for the setting. Open daily for dinner only, except from December 22–31; no music on Sundays. Langelinie (phone: 33-121214). Expensive.

Copenhagen Corner – Ask for a window table for a good view of pedestrian traffic past Rådhuspladsen (City Hall Square). The food seems to be slipping lately, but the surroundings are still pleasant and it is always packed. Closed December 24–25 and January 1. Rådhuspladsen (phone: 33-914545). Expensive to moderate.

La Brasserie – The *d'Angleterre* hotel's trendy new eatery has a varied menu including enticing hot and cold hors d'oeuvres, "quick meals," and complete dinners like fish, pheasant, and pork tenderloin. Open daily. 34 Kongens Nytorv (phone: 33-320122). Moderate.

Chico's Cantina – Mexican, with an international flavor. Run by former Canadian hockey star Dwight Watson. A very popular spot so be sure to make reservations. Open daily from noon to midnight; closed December 24 and 31 and January 1. 2 Borgergade (phone: 33-114108). Moderate.

Dahua – Chinese food in Copenhagen is not bad, and this is among the best. Closed Christmas Eve. 8 Gammel Torv (phone: 33-157855). Moderate.

Fiskehusets – Across the canal from Christiansborg, the best seafood restaurant in Copenhagen. Closed Sundays and from December 20–January 7. 38 Gammel Strand (phone: 33-158915). Moderate.

Påfuglen – If you want to dine in Tivoli for more reasonable rates, try this family-style place. Closed September to May. Tivoli (phone: 33-129540). Moderate.

Wessels Kro – Want to partake of the famous Danish *store kolde bord* ("the great cold table")? There's a wide assortment of Danish hams and other cold cuts at this quaint old tavern. Closed New Year's Eve. 7 Svaertegade (phone: 33-126793). Moderate.

Peder Oxe – This popular meeting place has a little something for everybody's tastes, but the specialties are meat dishes and serve-yourself salads. It's very "in," so book ahead. Closed Christmas Eve. 11 Gråbrødre Torv (phone: 33-110077). Moderate to inexpensive.

Cranks – Related to the original in London, this is one vegetarian buffet that even a died-in-the-wool carnivore will enjoy. Popular dishes include eggplant parmesan and meatless moussaka. Closed Sundays and major holidays. 12-14 Grönnegade, Pistolstr. (phone: 33-151690). Inexpensive.

Mongolian Barbecue – Among the best in the latest crop of its kind, this restaurant offers all you can eat from a choice of lamb, chicken, pork, and beef, for about $16. Open for dinner only; closed Christmas. Downstairs at 66 St. Kongensgade (phone: 33-146466). Inexpensive.

Parnas – A crazy place with live piano bar and hash with béarnaise sauce. Friendly artists' bar otherwise. Open from noon until 3 AM; closed Sundays, Christmas Eve, and New Year's Eve. 16 Lille Kongensgade (phone: 33-114910). Inexpensive.

DUBLIN

Dublin is a friendly city steeped in a history often troubled, sometimes splendid; a city of wide Georgian streets, elegant squares, magnificent doorways; a city of memorable sunsets that bathe the 18th-century red brick façades until the houses seem to glow with their own fire and the windows seem made of gold; a city of ancient churches and cathedrals thrusting their hallowed spires and towers against the skyline; a city where the English language acquires a unique dimension and where the dark, creamy-headed Guinness stout flows abundantly in companionable pubs. This is a city like no other European capital, set like a jewel in the sweep of Dublin Bay. Behind, to the south, rise the Dublin hills and the Wicklow Mountains. Through the city the river Liffey — James Joyce's Anna Livia Plurabelle — wends its leisurely way to the sea, spanned as it passes through Dublin by 11 bridges.

Once there was only one bridge. Indeed, it was not so much a bridge as a mere ford in the river, and it stood approximately where the Father Matthew Bridge stands today. It was built by the first Celtic inhabitants of what is now Dublin. When they came here, we cannot be sure; what is certain is that, by AD 140, they were well established on this site. The Celts themselves probably referred to the spot by a name that endures to this day — the official Gaelic *Baile Átha Cliath* (town of the ford of the hurdles).

It was not, however, until the coming of the Vikings in the 9th century that Dublin as we now know it began to take shape. The old Celtic settlement had at no time been a place of national importance; its significance was as a ford of the Liffey en route to the ancient royal capital of Tara. In AD 837, 65 Viking longboats sailed into Dublin Harbor and up the mouth of the River Liffey. These early Viking settlers established themselves a little downstream from the old Celtic settlement, on a spot where the Poddle, which now flows underground, entered the Liffey, causing it to form a dark pool, or *dubh linn*. The Vikings referred to their settlement by these two Gaelic words, and the anglicized version became the city's modern English name. Dublin rapidly became the focal point of the Viking invasion of Ireland. Then, as the Vikings began to see that trading was ultimately more profitable than plunder, and as they began to settle and intermarry in their new homeland, Dublin became a major center for their extensive European trade. Not long after their arrival, they were converted to Christianity and in 1034 erected a cathedral, which became the nucleus of modern Christ Church. The cathedral stood in the center of Viking Dublin and allows us to place the ancient city accurately.

Just over 3 centuries after the coming of the Vikings, new invaders swept Ireland. In 1169 the first contingent of Normans landed on the beach of

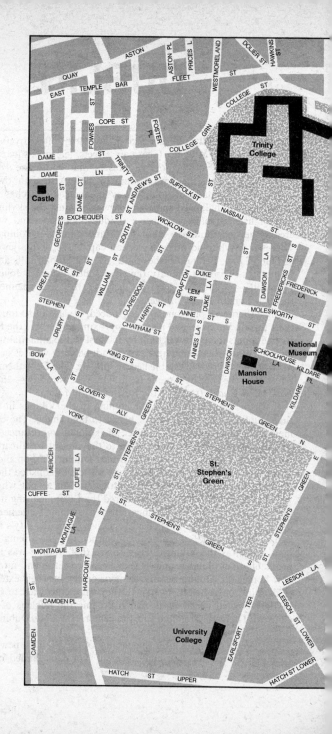

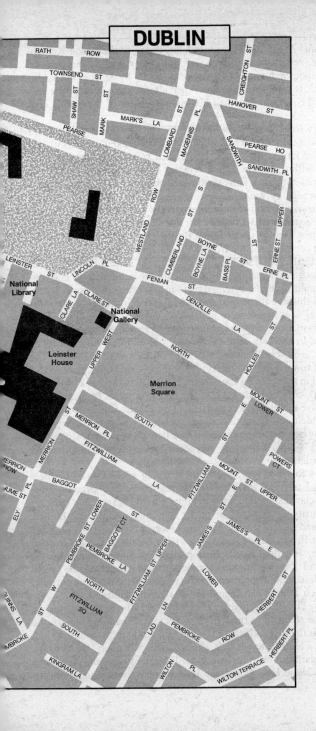

DUBLIN

Bannow, in County Wexford. Two years later, the powerful baron Richard Gilbert de Clare, otherwise known as Strongbow, arrived at the gates of Dublin with a thousand men. The city was taken by storm; its Viking king and inhabitants were forced to flee. Thereafter Dublin became the center of the English conquest, as it had become the center of the Viking conquest.

Not long afterward, the city was fortified by Dublin Castle, built not far from the old Viking cathedral. The cathedral had been taken over by Strongbow and a new and larger edifice had been erected in its place. The city walls were built along with the castle. (Their remains can be seen at St. Audeon's Arch, below Christ Church.) Thus medieval Dublin began to take shape, a small area surrounded by walls.

In shape and in size Dublin did not alter greatly until the arrival of a new viceroy, or king's representative, in 1662 heralded Dublin's rise to a definitive national importance. Dublin, under James Butler, Duke of Ormonde, became and remained the central arena for Ireland's social, political, and cultural life.

Butler, believing that the stability of a government should be reflected in public works, began municipal improvements almost immediately. The solitary, medieval Dublin Bridge was joined by four new bridges across the river; Phoenix Park (to this day the largest enclosed urban park in the world) was walled and several new streets were built.

Dublin's importance as a city and as a seaport increased enormously in the late 17th century. In the 18th century, however, Dublin truly flourished, as it became one of the most brilliant and sparkling capitals in all of Europe. The strong movement toward parliamentary independence that took place at this time was reflected in the splendid Parliament House (now the Bank of Ireland in College Green), commenced in 1729, the first in a series of great public buildings. Extensive rebuilding was carried out on Dublin Castle and Trinity College. The Wide Streets Commission was set up. It was as if the city were proudly preparing for the unprecedented position of importance it would occupy when, in 1782, parliamentary independence was conceded to Ireland by the British Parliament.

Great buildings followed one another in dizzying succession — Leinster House, the Royal Exchange, the Mansion House, the Four Courts, the Custom House. Irish classical architecture, in all its gravity, beauty, and balance, reached full maturity. It flowered in public buildings and private houses, spacious squares and elegant streets. This was Georgian Dublin (various King Georges sat on the British throne in the period): the Dublin of Henry Grattan, Oliver Goldsmith, Jonathan Swift, Bishop Berkeley and Edmund Burke, David Garrick and Peg Woffington. Handel himself conducted the world première of his *Messiah* in this glittering city, whose center was concentrated in the area between Dublin Castle and the Parliament House.

Architecturally, Dublin reached its zenith in the 18th century. Later, its brilliance would be sculpted in the written word rather than in stone. In the 19th century, with the dismantling of the Parliament, Dublin's political and social life suffered a blow from which it was not to recover easily. By contrast, its literary life began to flower, for two great literary movements were born in Dublin — the Gaelic League and the Irish literary renaissance. Between them, the two movements revived and romanticized the early legends and history of Ireland. The literary renaissance — spearheaded by William Butler Yeats, Lady Augusta Gregory, Douglas Hyde, and John Millington Synge, to name but a few — placed a splendid and indelible mark on 20th-century English literature. (Equally renowned are Irish or Ireland-born writers not directly associated with the Irish literary renaissance, such as Samuel Beckett, who was born in Dublin in 1906 and won the Nobel Prize for literature in 1969; George Bernard Shaw, who wrote in England but was born in Dublin; and the Irish playwright Brendan Behan.) The movement found its greatest expression in the creation of the Abbey Theatre, associated forever with the brilliant plays of Sean O'Casey. For many years the Abbey was the most famous theater in the world. The Gaelic League had more popular appeal; with its dream of the restoration of the Gaelic language and the reestablishment of a separate Irish cultural nation, it provided a great deal of the inspiration for the Easter Rebellion of 1916.

This uprising, concentrated in Dublin, sparked the 5-year War of Independence, which culminated in the Anglo-Irish Treaty of 1921 (whereby Ireland gained the status of free state). The signing of the treaty was followed by civil war in 1922–23, during which many buildings that had escaped damage in 1916 suffered badly. Today, happily, all the heirlooms of the 18th century have been restored to their original grandeur.

Dublin today, with a population of 1 million, is far larger than it has been at any other stage of its history. Nevertheless, it is still an eminently walkable city. The crossroads of medieval and 18th-century Dublin remain the center of interest. Within a half-mile radius of the Bank of Ireland on College Green lie the cathedrals, the museums, Dublin Castle, the great Georgian public buildings, the parks, and the shops. All are neatly enclosed by the Royal Canal to the north and the Grand Canal to the south.

Thanks to the *Dublin Millennium* celebrations in 1988, the downtown area of the city now enjoys a number of permanent enhancements, including 10 new sculptures by modern Irish craftspersons. The most notable pieces include a freestanding "liberty bell" in St. Patrick's Cathedral Park, a replica of a Viking ship on Essex Quay, and a double arch on a traffic island in Merrion Row, near St. Stephen's Green. In the heart of the city on O'Connell Street there is also an elaborate new fountain, with 40 spouts, and designed to represent the course of the River Liffey. The river itself is represented by a larger-than-life sculpture of a reclining female nude, *Anna Livia*.

A major urban improvement is the rejuvenation of Grafton Street as a pedestrian shopping area, with brick walkways, benches, and plants. The shops along Grafton and nearby have also perked up, with smart new façades and signs.

Besides sightseeing, a visitor should sample Dublin's abundant cultural offerings, especially its theaters. But the true focal point of Dubliners' social life is the pub, and it is there one must go to find it. Dublin can be a comfortable, "down home" place to visit, so slow down and enjoy it. It has an endearing earthiness, a quality that inspired James Joyce to refer to his native city in off-color, though affectionate, terms as "strumpet city in the sunset" and "dear, dirty Dublin."

DUBLIN AT-A-GLANCE

SEEING THE CITY: Views of this essentially flat city are best from a number of restaurants in the surrounding hills; particularly nice is *Killakee House* in Rathfarnham (phone: 932645 or 932917). Or see Dublin from afar from the neighboring Wicklow Mountains.

SPECIAL PLACES: Central Dublin is very compact. Since traffic can move slowly, by far the best way to see the city is on foot. A *CIE (Córas Iompair Éireann, National Transport Company)* sightseeing tour lasts for about 3 hours and is an excellent and enjoyable way of getting one's bearings. Tours leave from the central bus station, Store St. (phone: 787777 or 746301). *Gray Line,* 3 Clanwilliam Ter., also operates tours (phone: 619666). Then, making full use of Dublin's splendid, signposted *Tourist Trail,* the determined sightseer should set off on foot to see and experience as much of Dublin as time allows.

SOUTH DOWNTOWN

Merrion Square – This is the loveliest of Dublin's Georgian squares, a study in balance and elegance that evokes the graciousness of a vanished age. Note particularly the variety of fanlights on doorways. At No. 1, the young Oscar Wilde lived with his celebrated parents, the surgeon Sir William Wills Wilde and poetess Speranza; No. 42 was the home of Sir Jonah Barrington, 18th-century barrister and raconteur; at No. 58 lived Daniel O'Connell, the "Liberator" who won Catholic emancipation in 1829; No. 70 was the home of tragic Sheridan Le Fanu, author of sinister tales such as *Uncle Silas* and *Through a Glass Darkly* (after his wife's death in 1858, he shut himself up there, appearing only after nightfall to walk in the shadows of Merrion Square); at No. 82 lived William Butler Yeats, poet and Nobel Prize winner. Today, the only house in the square used as a private dwelling is No. 71, where well-known couturière Sybil Connolly has her home and studio.

Leinster House – When young Lord Kildare, Earl of Leinster, chose to build a mansion here in 1745, all of fashionable Dublin protested, for at that time the north side of the city was the fashionable side. Undaunted, he went ahead with his plan, asserting prophetically, "Where I go, fashion will follow." The house Lord Kildare built is said to resemble the White House, whose architect, James Hoban of Carlow, studied in Dublin after the completion of Leinster House. The building was purchased in the 19th century by the Royal Dublin Society, and in 1921 the Parliament of the new Irish Free State chose the building as its meeting place. Leinster House continues to be the meeting place of the Dáil (House of Representatives) and Seanad (Senate). When the Dáil is in session, visitors may watch from the visitors' gallery. Apply for tickets at the main gate. Kildare St., Merrion Sq. (phone: 789911).

National Museum – When Leinster House belonged to the Royal Dublin Society, it became the nucleus of a complex of cultural buildings — the *National Gallery,* the National Library, the *Museum of Natural History,* and the *National Museum.* These are all worth visiting, but the *National Museum* specially should not be missed. Its collection of gold objects dating from the Bronze Age to early Christian times is almost without parallel in Western Europe. No admission charge. Kildare St. (phone: 765521).

Genealogical Office and Heraldic Museum – Formerly in Dublin Castle, this is the domain of Ireland's chief herald, the ideal starting point for an ancestry hunt. 2 Kildare St. (phone: 608670).

St. Stephen's Green – Not far from Merrion Square lies St. Stephen's Green, the loveliest of Dublin's many public parks. Its 22 acres contain gardens, a waterfall, and an ornamental lake. In summer, it's an excellent place to sit and watch working Dublin take its lunch; bands play on the bandstand in July and August.

Mansion House – Dublin preceded London in building a Mansion House for its lord mayor in 1715. In the Round Room, the Declaration of Irish Independence was adopted in 1919, and the Anglo-Irish Treaty of 1921 was signed there. The Round Room is usually open to visitors. Dawson St. (phone: 762852).

Trinity College – Dawson Street descends to meet Trinity College, the oldest university in Ireland, founded by Elizabeth I of England on the site of the 12th-century Monastery of All Hallows. Alumni of the college include Oliver Goldsmith, Edmund Burke, Jonathan Swift, Bishop Berkeley (pronounced "*bark*-lee," who also lent his name to Berkeley in California), William Congreve, Thomas Moore, Sheridan Le Fanu, Oscar Wilde, and J. P. Donleavy, to name but a few. No trace of the original Elizabethan structure remains; the oldest surviving part of the college dates from 1700. The Long Room, Trinity's famous library, is the longest single-chamber library in existence. It contains a priceless collection of 800,000 volumes and 3,000 ancient manuscripts and papyri. The library's chief treasure is the *Book of Kells,* an 8th-century manuscript transcription of the four gospels described as the "most beautiful book in the world." Closed Saturday afternoons and Sundays. Admission charge April to October. College Green (phone: 772941).

Parliament House – Facing Trinity College is the monumental Parliament House, now the Bank of Ireland. Built in 1729 and regarded as one of the finest examples of the architecture of its period, this was the first of the great series of 18th-century public buildings in Dublin. As its name implies, it was erected to house the Irish Parliament in the century that saw the birth of Home Rule. College Green (phone: 776801).

Dublin Castle – Dame Street leads westward from College Green toward the older part of the city, where the early Viking and Norman settlers established themselves. Castles have gone up and down on the site of the present castle. A Celtic *rath* was almost certainly followed by a wooden Viking fortress, and this in turn was supplanted by the great stone castle erected by John of England in the 13th century. The castle was for 400 years the center of English rule in Ireland; for much of this time it had as grim a reputation as the Tower of London. Although the present building is essentially 18th century, one of the four towers that flanked the original moated castle survives as the Record Tower. The 15th-century Bedford Tower was the state prison; the Georgian State Apartments, formerly the residence of the English viceroys, were beautifully restored between 1950 and 1963 and are now used for state functions. St. Patrick's Hall in the State Apartments was the scene of the inauguration of Ireland's first president, Douglas Hyde; here, too, President John F. Kennedy was made a freeman of Dublin.

The Bedford Tower, the Chapel Royal, and the State Apartments can be visited for an admission charge. Dublin Castle (phone: 777129).

Christ Church Cathedral – Not far from Dublin Castle, the massive shape of Christ Church Cathedral crowns the hill on which the ancient city stood. Founded in 1038 by Viking King Sitric Silkenbeard of Dublin, Christ Church was demolished in the 12th century and rebuilt by the Norman Richard Gilbert de Clare (Strongbow), who is buried within its walls. The cruciform building has been much restored through the centuries, but the beautiful pointed nave and the wonderful stonework remain virtually unchanged. These walls have witnessed many dramatic scenes in the course of Irish history. Christ Church today is the Church of Ireland (Protestant) cathedral for the diocese of Dublin. The vaulted crypt remains one of the largest in Ireland. In front of this cathedral Dubliners traditionally gather to ring in the New Year. The cathedral and crypt are open. Christ Church Pl. (phone: 778099).

St. Audeon's Arch and the City Walls – The 13th-century church of St. Audeon is Dublin's oldest parish church. It was founded by early Norman settlers, who gave it the name St. Ouen, or Audeon, after the patron saint of their native Rouen. Close to the church is a flight of steps leading down to St. Audeon's Arch, the sole surviving gateway of the medieval city walls. Open daily (phone: 791855).

St. Patrick's Cathedral – Christ Church stood within the old walled city. One of its 12th-century archbishops, John Comyn, felt that while he remained under municipal jurisdiction he could not achieve the temporal power for which he thirsted. Accordingly, he left the city walls and built a fine palace within a stone's throw of Christ Church. Today St. Patrick's is the national cathedral of the Church of Ireland. By the 19th century both cathedrals were in a state of considerable disrepair. Henry Roe, a distiller, came to the aid of Christ Church, restoring it at his own expense; Sir Benjamin Lee Guinness of the famous brewing family came to the assistance of St. Patrick's — hence the saying in Dublin that "Christ Church was restored with glasses, St. Patrick's with pints!" Crane St. off Thomas.

The early English interior of St. Patrick's is very beautiful; the nave is the longest in Ireland. The cathedral's particular fascination, however, lies in its wealth of monuments, especially the Geraldine Door, the Cork Memorial, and the monument to Dame St. Leger. The greatest interest of all, though, is in the long association with St. Patrick's of Jonathan Swift, author of *Gulliver's Travels* and dean of the cathedral for 32 years. Within these walls he is buried, beside his loving Stella. On a slab near the entrance is carved the epitaph he composed for himself, which Yeats described as the greatest epitaph in literature: "He lies where furious indignation can no longer rend his heart." Open to visitors. St. Patrick's Cathedral (phone: 754817).

Guinness Brewery – Founded in 1759 by Arthur Guinness with a mere £100, Guinness's today is the largest exporting stout brewery in the world. The former Guinness Hop Store, on Crane St. adjacent to the main brewery, was once the storage building for the ingredients for the world-famous dark stout, and the aroma remains. Now it is a public hall showcasing traveling displays, art shows, technological works, and contemporary arts. The Visitors Centre shows an audiovisual presentation about the making of the famous brew, complete with free samples. Also of note are the *Guinness Museum* and the *Cooper's Museum*. Admission charge for the rotating exhibitions (phone: 756701 or 536700).

Royal Hospital – One of Ireland's oldest public buildings, this 17th-century treasure was restored for IR£20 million and reopened in 1985 on its 300th anniversary. Originally built as a home for aged veterans, it is now Ireland's official *National Centre for Culture and the Arts*. Displays range from *National Museum* pieces to traveling art exhibitions from as far away as China. The restoration of the Grand Hall/dining room has been rated as one of Europe's finest achievements of the century. Also used for public concerts, recitals, and lectures (check the Dublin newspapers). Surrounding the building are 50 acres of grounds, including an 18th-century formal garden, a courtyard, a sculpture park, and Bully's Acre, the resting place of many 11th-century Irish chieftains. Closed Mondays. Admission charge. Kilmainham (phone: 718666 or 719147).

NORTH DOWNTOWN

Four Courts – Almost across the river from Guinness's lies the stately Four Courts of Justice, dating from the apogee of the 18th century. The building was begun by Thomas Cooley and completed by James Gandon, the greatest of all the Georgian architects. Court sittings (Supreme and High) are open to the public. No admission charge. Inns Quay (phone: 725555).

St. Michan's Church – Not far from the Four Courts is St. Michan's, a 17th-century church built on the site of a 10th-century Viking church. The 18th-century organ is

said to have been played by Handel when he was in Dublin for the first public performance of *Messiah.*

Of more immediate interest, perhaps, is the extraordinary crypt, with its remarkable
preservative atmosphere: Bodies have lain here for centuries without decomposing, and
you can, if you feel so inclined, shake the hand of an 8-foot-tall Crusader! Open
weekdays and Saturday mornings. Admission charge. Church St. (phone: 724154).

Moore Street – Near the historic General Post Office (2 blocks west of Henry Street)
is Moore Street. Here, among the fruit and flower sellers, the true voice of Dublin is
audible — lively, warm, voluble, speaking an English that is straight Sean O'Casey.

Municipal Gallery of Modern Art – Beyond the Garden of Remembrance (a memorial to those who died for Irish freedom), on the north side of Parnell Square, is
Charlemont House. Lord Charlemont, for whom the house was designed by Sir William Chambers in 1764, was a great patron of the arts; it is fitting that his house became,
in recent times, the *Municipal Gallery of Modern Art.* The gallery should not be missed;
it has an outstanding collection of Impressionist paintings, and the works of more
recent artists such as Picasso, Utrillo, and Bonnard are well represented, to say nothing
of such prominent Irish painters as Sir William Orpen, John B. Yeats (the poet's
father), and Jack Yeats (the poet's brother). Closed Mondays. Parnell Sq. (phone:
741903).

Abbey Theatre – Alas, the original *Abbey Theatre,* founded by Yeats and Lady
Gregory on the site of the old city morgue, is no more. In 1951, at the close of a
performance of O'Casey's *Plough and the Stars* — a play that ends with Dublin blazing
in the aftermath of rebellion — the theater itself caught fire and was burned to the
ground. The new Abbey, designed by Michael Scott, one of the country's foremost
architects, opened in 1966 on the site of the original building. The lobby, which can
be seen daily except Sundays, contains interesting portraits of those connected with the
theater's early successes. Performances nightly except Sundays. Abbey St. (phone:
744505 or 787222).

Custom House – This masterpiece of Georgian architecture adorns the north bank
of the Liffey, to the east of O'Connell St. It was the *chef d'oeuvre* of James Gandon
and is one of the finest buildings of its kind in Europe. Now occupied by government
offices and closed to the public, it should nonetheless be seen at close range: The carved
riverheads that form the keystones of the arches and entrances are splendid. Custom
House Quay (phone: 742961).

SUBURBS

Phoenix Park – Northwest of the city center, Phoenix Park is the largest enclosed
urban park in the world. Within its walls are the residences of the President of the
Republic and the US Ambassador. The park covers 1,760 acres, beautifully planted
with a great variety of trees. Among the attractions are the lovely People's Gardens,
a herd of fallow deer, the horse-race course, and the Zoological Gardens. Dublin Zoo
is said to be the most beautiful zoo in Europe; it also has a most impressive collection
of animals and holds several records for lion breeding. The park and zoo are open daily.
Admission charge for the zoo (phone: 213021 or 771425).

Chester Beatty Library – Founded by an American-born, naturalized British resident in Ireland, this library is considered to be the most valuable and representative
private collection of Oriental manuscripts and miniatures in the world. The "copper
millionaire with a heart of gold," Chester Beatty willed his marvelous library to the
people of Dublin. Open Tuesdays through Saturdays. 20 Shrewsbury Rd., Ballsbridge
(phone: 692386).

Malahide Castle – In a north city suburb of Dublin, Malahide Castle has only
recently been opened to the public. For 8 centuries this was the home of the Talbots

of Malahide. Magnificently furnished in mostly 18th-century style with part of the very valuable National Portrait Collection on view, it is well worth a visit. A very elaborate model railway is also on display. Admission charge. Malahide, Co. Dublin (phone: 452337 or 452655).

Newbridge House and Park – Built in 1740, this country mansion is full of memorabilia of the Cobbe family, including original hand-carved furniture collected through the years, portraits, memoirs, daybooks, a museum of world travels, and an extensive doll collection. Downstairs, visitors can view a kitchen and laundry room from 1760, complete with ancient implements. The wooded grounds (365 acres) have picnic areas and walking trails. Five miles north of Dublin Airport and 12 miles from the city center, Newbridge can be comfortably combined with an excursion to nearby Malahide Castle. Open 10 AM to 5 PM weekdays, 2 to 6 PM Sundays, June through October; 2 to 5 PM Wednesdays and Sundays, November through March. Admission charge. Off the Dublin–Belfast road, N1, at Donabate, Co. Dublin (phone: 436534 or 436535).

■ **EXTRA SPECIAL:** The beautiful Boyne Valley is one of Ireland's most storied and evocative sites, and it makes an easy and interesting day trip. Leave Dublin by the Navan road, passing through Dunshaughlin (which takes its name from a church founded by St. Seachnall, a companion of St. Patrick). Six miles south of Navan, signposted to the left, is the Hill of Tara. Although only some grassy mounds and earthworks recall a splendid past, it is impossible to remain unmoved by the site's history: This is Royal Tara, where High Kings of Ireland were crowned on the Lia Fail (Stone of Destiny) before time began. And it was here, at the tribes' great triennial Feis of Tara, that laws were enacted and revised. Now, as Moore writes in his immortal song, "No more to chiefs and ladies bright / The harp of Tara swells / The chord alone that breaks at night / Its tale of ruin tells."

Returning to the Navan road, you will pass the striking ruins of 16th-century Athlumney Castle on the east bank of the Boyne, about 1½ miles from Navan. Continue through Donaghmore, with its remains of a 12th-century church and a round tower. Nearby, below the Boyne Bridge, lies Log na Ri (Hollow of the King), where people once swam their herds of cattle ceremoniously across the river to protect them from the "little people" and from natural disasters.

The village of Slane lies on one of the loveliest stretches of the Boyne. There are some delightful Georgian houses, but the history of this small town goes back far beyond the 18th century. On the hill that overlooks Slane, St. Patrick lit the paschal fire on Holy Saturday, AD 433, and drew upon himself the wrath of the high king's druids. Patrick emerged victorious from the ensuing confrontation, and Christianity began its reign in Ireland. On the slopes of the hill are the remains of an ancient earthen fort and the ruins of a 16th-century church. Apart from archaeological interest, the climb up Slane Hill is well worth the effort — rewarding the energetic with fine views across the tranquil Boyne Valley to Trim and Drogheda. Just outside the town lies the estate of Slane Castle, a 19th-century castellated mansion in which the present occupant, Lord Mountcharles, has opened a fine restaurant (phone: 041-24207).

Downstream from Slane is Brugh na Boinne (the Palace of the Boyne), a vast necropolis more than 4,000 years old. Here, beneath a chain of tumuli, kings of Ireland were laid to rest in passage graves of remarkable complexity. The tumuli of Dowth, Knowth, and Newgrange in particular are of major interest, both for their extent and the amazing diversity of their sculptured ornamentation. Newgrange is one of the finest passage graves in all of Western Europe, and it has been opened to the public. A permanent archaeological exhibition and guided tours are available. Closed Mondays (phone: 041-24274).

Farther down the Boyne Valley is Drogheda, an ancient town that has witnessed many dramatic scenes in the course of Irish history, most of which involve the contention of Royalists and Puritans for the English throne. Oliver Cromwell burned the city to the ground during a vicious siege in the 1640s, and James II was defeated by William of Orange on July 12, 1690. Reminders of Drogheda's past include the 13th-century St. Laurence's Gate, the only survivors of the original ten gates in this once-walled city; the ruins of 13th-century St. Mary's Abbey; the Norman motte-and-bailey of Millmount and the fine Millmount Museum; and St. Peter's Church, where the head of St. Oliver Plunkett, martyred archbishop of Armagh, is enshrined.

Five miles north of Drogheda is Monasterboice, an ancient monastic settlement noteworthy for one of the most perfect high crosses in Ireland — the intricately carved 10th-century Cross of Muiredach. Southwest of Monasterboice are the impressive ruins of Mellifont Abbey. Dating from 1142, this was the first Cistercian foundation in Ireland and heralded a whole new style of ecclesiastical architecture. Note especially the remains of the gate house and the octagonal lavabo.

Return to Dublin via N1.

SOURCES AND RESOURCES

TOURIST INFORMATION: For information, brochures, and maps before departure, contact the Irish Tourist Board, 757 Third Ave., New York, NY 10017 (phone: 212-418-0800). For on-the-spot information and assistance, call the Dublin Tourist Board at Dublin Airport (phone: 376387) or 14 O'Connell St. (phone: 747733). The tourist board personnel offer advice on all aspects of a stay in Ireland and can make theater bookings and hotel reservations anywhere in the country. Two useful guides, *Dining in Ireland* and *The Dublin Guide,* are available at the tourist board and at most bookstores.

Tourist Trail, published by the Dublin Tourist Board and available at its offices, is an excellent walking guide to Dublin. Another invaluable publication is *Dublin: Official Guide.* The best city map is the Ordnance Survey Dublin Map; less detailed but generally adequate maps are also available.

The US Embassy is at 42 Elgin Rd., Ballsbridge (phone: 68-87-77).

Local Coverage – *In Dublin,* published fortnightly, covers every conceivable activity in Dublin, including theater, cinema, music, exhibitions, sports, and cabarets. *What's On in Dublin* and *Tourism News* are published monthly by the Dublin Tourist Board and are available at its offices. Large daily newspapers are the *Irish Times,* the *Irish Independent,* and the *Irish Press;* evening papers are the *Evening Herald* and the *Evening Press.*

Telephone – The area code for Dublin and immediate vicinity is 01.

CLIMATE AND CLOTHES: Although Ireland is farther north than most of the US — Dublin, sitting astride latitude 53°20', is as far north as Goose Bay, Labrador — the climate is generally much milder. The Gulf Stream, which warms the coasts, brings moderate temperatures year-round, with few sub-zero winters or blistering hot summers. Winter temperatures rarely dip below 40F (5C) and summer temperatures usually rise no higher than 70F (21C). The stereotype about Irish weather being wet is true: It rains often throughout the year, and even on fairly clear days, the air feels damp.

The temperate climate makes packing rather simple, if not altogether lightweight.

A versatile item of clothing travelers will find indispensable is a raincoat, preferably with a zip-out lining and a hood. The removable lining affords adaptability to temperature changes, and the hood is better suited (and less cumbersome) than an umbrella for the fine, misty rain. Other appropriate apparel includes a warm wool sweater or jacket, even in summer (tweeds are worn year-round). And finally — since the best touring of castles, churches, and countryside is on foot — pack a comfortable pair of walking shoes. Generally speaking, a typical fall wardrobe in the northern tier of the US will probably have everything that's needed for the trip.

GETTING AROUND: Airport – Dublin Airport is north of the city at Collinstown. In normal traffic, a trip from the airport to downtown takes 35 to 40 minutes, with an average taxi fare of $10. *CIE (Córas Iompair Éireann, National Transport Company)* operates bus service (see below), timed to meet all flights, between the airport and the central bus station.

Bus and Train – *Bus Éireann,* a division of *CIE,* operates rail and bus service not only in Dublin but nationwide. Cross-city bus routes are extensive. The fare is collected after the passenger is seated (exact fare is not required). Although Dublin has no subway, a new commuter rail system, *Dublin Area Rapid Transit (DART),* runs from central Dublin along the bay as far north as Howth and as far south as Bray. It is swift, dependable, and safe at all hours.

Day tours from Dublin are operated by *Bus Éireann* from the central bus station, Store St. (phone: 746301 or 787777). A wide range of tours is available. Guided walking tours of various parts of the city are also available; check with the tourist board for times and meeting points.

All information regarding bus and rail travel throughout the republic can be obtained by calling 787777. Official *Bus Éireann* and *Irish Rail* timetables are available at newsstands.

Car Rental – Many Dublin firms offer excellent self-drive opportunities. *Dan Dooley,* 42 Westland Row (phone: 772733; at the airport 428355), and *Murray's,* Baggot Street Bridge (phone: 681777; at the airport 378179), are both dependable. More information and brochures are available from the tourist board.

Taxi – There are taxi stands throughout the city, especially near main hotels, and cabs can also be hailed in the streets. Your first conversation with a Dublin cab driver will assure you that you are in fact in Ireland. Among the companies that operate a 24-hour radio service are *Blue Cabs* (phone: 761111), *Co-op Taxis* (phone: 766666), and *National Radio Cabs* (phone: 772222).

SPECIAL EVENTS: Outstanding annual events include *St. Patrick's Day,* March 17, with a parade and many other festivities; an *Irish Music Festival (Feis Cheoil)* in May; the *Festival in Great Irish Houses* in June, featuring concerts by international celebrities in Georgian mansions near Dublin; *Bloomsday,* June 16, when James Joyce aficionados gather from around the world to follow the circuitous path through Dublin that takes Leopold Bloom from morning until late at night in *Ulysses;* the *Horse Show,* the principal sporting and social event of the year, in August; the *Dublin Theatre Festival* in September and October, featuring new plays by Irish authors; and the *Dublin Marathon,* the last Monday in October. For details about these and other events, inquire at the tourist board (see "Tourist Information," above).

MUSEUMS: The *National Museum,* the *Heraldic Museum,* and the Royal Hospital are described in "Special Places." Dublin is also the home of the *Dublin Civic Museum,* S. William St.; the *National Wax Museum,* off Parnell Sq.; and the *Irish Jewish Museum,* 3/4 Walworth Rd., off Victoria St.

The *Museum of Childhood* is a private collection of antique dolls and toys. Admission charge. The Palms, 20 Palmerstown Park, Rathmines (phone: 973223).

 SHOPPING: Neatly balanced on both banks of the Liffey, Dublin has two downtown shopping areas: one around O'Connell and Henry streets, the other centered in Grafton Street and its environs (stores on the south side are more elegant). Powerscourt Town House Centre, just off Grafton Street, has a number of clothing, antiques, and craft shops in a courtyard built around a pretty townhouse. Good buys are the chunky Aran sweaters, Donegal tweed, Waterford and Galway crystal, and Belleek china. *Brown Thomas* and *Switzer's* are the main department stores on Grafton Street; *Arnott's, Roche's,* and *Clery's* are fine stores in the O'Connell and Henry streets area. The two newest shopping complexes are the Royal Hibernian Way on Dawson Street and St. Stephen's Green Shopping Centre on the green. Other recommended shops include the following:

Laura Ashley – Fashion and fabrics for the home, women, and children. 60 Grafton St. (phone: 795433).

Best of Irish – A wide range of Irish goods — crystal, china, hand-knit goods, jewelry, linens, and tweeds — can be found here. Open daily. Next to the *Westbury* hotel, on Harry St., off Grafton St. (phone: 791233).

Bewley's Café Ltd. – A Dublin landmark, it's an emporium of coffees and teas of all nations, with a tempting candy selection as well. Sampling is encouraged. There are 5 shops in the Dublin area, but only the one on Grafton Street has waitress service. 78/79 Grafton St. (phone: 776761).

Blarney Woolen Mills – A branch of the Cork-based family enterprise, this huge new shop is known for its very competitive prices. It stocks all the visitor favorites, from tweeds and hand-knits to crystal, china, pottery, and souvenirs. (*Blarney* has taken over the former *Kilkenny Shop.*) 21/23 St. (phone: 710068).

Cleo Ltd. – For more than 50 years, one of Dublin's most fashionable sources for hand-knit and handwoven cloaks, caps, suits, coats, and shawls. 18 Kildare St. (phone: 761421).

Sybil Connolly – Ireland's reigning couturière; her romantic ball gowns of finely pleated Irish linen are indeed special. 71 Merrion Sq. (phone: 767281).

Paul Costelloe – Designer of ready-to-wear for women. 73 Cork St. (phone: 538874).

Pat Crowley – Silky, seductive blouses and dresses. 14 Duke St. (phone: 710219).

Eason & Son Ltd. – Jam-packed with tomes and paperbacks, maps, records, and stationery. 40/42 Lower O'Connell St. (phone: 733811).

Patrick Flood – Silver and gold jewelry in traditional Irish designs. Unit 14C, 1st floor, Powerscourt Town House Centre (phone: 770615).

Fred Hanna – Bookseller to Trinity College. New and used books; excellent books and maps on Ireland. 28/29 Nassau St. (phone: 771255).

Heraldic Artists – A good source for family crests, flags, scrolls, and genealogy tomes. 3 Nassau St. (phone: 762391).

House of Ireland – Top-quality Irish and European goods — from Aynsley, Lladro, Spode, Wedgwood, Waterford, and Hummel crystal and china to hand-knits, kilts, linens, and shillelaghs. 37/38 Nassau St. and 6465 Dawson St. (phone: 714543).

H. Johnston Ltd. – Traditional blackthorn walking sticks. 11 Wicklow St. (phone: 771249).

Kapp and Peterson – Tobacco and hand-carved pipes for men and women. 55 Grafton St. (phone: 714652).

Kevin & Howlin Ltd. – Men's ready-to-wear and made-to-measure clothing. The store now carries some women's tweeds. 31 Nassau St. (phone: 770257).

Mullins of Dublin – Coats of arms emblazoned on parchments, plaques, and even doorknockers. 36 Upper O'Connell St. (phone: 741133).

Fergus O'Farrell – For more than 25 years, this has been a showcase for top-quality Irish crafts — from woodcarvings and brass door knockers to beaten copper art; also handmade candles, stationery, and prints from 19th-century woodcuts. 62 Dawson St. (phone: 770862).

Sheepskin Shop – Just the spot to stock up on high-quality sheepskin and lambskin suits and coats. The shop also has a varied selection of leather trousers, suits, and jackets. 20 Wicklow St. (phone: 719585).

Tower Design Craft Centre – Once a sugar refinery, this renovated 1862 tower houses the workshops of more than 30 innovative craftspeople, with work ranging from heraldic jewelry, Irish oak woodcarvings, and hand-cut crystal to Chez Nous Irish chocolates, stained glass, toys, and fishing tackle. Self-service restaurant. Ideal for a rainy day. Pearse St. (phone: 775655).

Waltons Musical Instrument Galleries – Bagpipes and Irish harps as well as records. 2/5 N Frederick St. (phone: 747805).

SPORTS AND FITNESS: Bicycling – Irish Raleigh Industries operates *Rent-a-Bike* at a number of city firms (phone: 261333). Two downtown shops offering bicycle rentals are *Pedal Power*, 65 Mespil Rd. (phone: 687923), and *McDonald's*, 38 Wexford St. (phone: 752586). Charges average $3.50 per day or $18 per week.

Gaelic Games – Football and hurling are two fast, enthralling field sports; important matches are played at *Croke Park*. For details, see the calendar of events in *In Dublin* or call Croke Park (phone: 743111).

Golf – More than 30 golf courses are within easy reach of Dublin; visitors are welcome at all clubs on weekdays, but gaining admission can be more difficult on weekends. Two of the finest courses in the world, *Portmarnock* (phone: 323082) and *Royal Dublin* (phone: 336346), are just north of the city and should not be missed.

Greyhound Racing – An exciting spectator sport, racing can be seen regularly at two tracks, *Shelbourne Park Stadium* and *Harold's Cross Stadium*, each an 8-minute ride from the city center. Details in *In Dublin* or at the tourist board.

Horse Racing – *Phoenix Park* is the site of races in the city, but the course is straight, not circular, which makes for frustrating viewing. You can see the start, the middle, or the end, but you won't see the whole race. Better is the well-known racecourse *Curragh*, about a mile outside the town of Kildare in County Kildare, less than an hour's drive from Dublin. Six miles south of the city, Leopardstown has a modern racecourse.

Horseback Riding – A list of riding establishments close to Dublin is available at the tourist board.

Tennis – Ireland has a first-rate international facility — the *Kilternan Tennis Centre* — about a 15-minute taxi ride from the city center. With 4 indoor and 4 outdoor courts, it is open daily from 7 AM to midnight, year-round. Equipment rental at *Pro Shop Kilternan* (phone: 953729 or 955559). There are a few public courts, generally outdoors, in and around Dublin, where visitors can play for a small fee. The most central is Herbert Park, Ballsbridge (phone: 684364).

THEATER: For complete program listings see the publications listed in *Tourist Information*, above. There are eight main theaters in the city center; smaller theater troupes perform in the universities, in suburban theaters, and occasionally in pubs and hotels. The main theaters are the *Abbey* and the *Peacock*, both at Lower Abbey St. (phone: 744505 or 787222); the *Gate* (the theater of Michael MacLiammoir and Hilton Edwards), Cavendish Row (phone: 744045); the *Gaiety*, S. King St. (phone: 771717), mostly for revues, musicals, and opera; the

Olympia, Dame St. (phone: 778962), for everything from revues to straight plays; the *Eblana,* Store St. (phone: 746707), a small theater offering mostly modern comedy; the *Focus,* Pembroke Pl. (phone: 763071), for Russian and Scandinavian works; and the *Project Arts Centre,* 39 E. Essex St. (phone: 712321), very avant-garde.

For children, the *Lambert Mews Puppet Theatre* in the suburb of Monkstown will prove irresistible. Clifden La., Monkstown (phone: 800974).

It is always advisable to reserve in advance for theater in Dublin. You can make bookings at theaters; the tourist board; the information desks of *Switzer's* and *Brown Thomas* stores, Grafton St.; and the *Ticket Bureau,* 4 Westbury Mall, off Grafton St. (phone: 794455). Most of the theaters accept telephone reservations and credit cards.

 MUSIC: The *National Concert Hall,* Earlsfort Ter., off St. Stephen's Green (phone: 711888), is the center of Dublin's active musical life and the home of the *RTE (Radio Telefis Éireann) Symphony Orchestra. RTE* performances are held regularly, as are a variety of other concerts. For a schedule, phone the concert hall or check local publications. In April and September the *Dublin Grand Opera Society* holds its spring and winter seasons at the *Gaiety Theatre.* Traditional Irish music is a must. Sessions (*seisiún*) are held at many places around the city by an organization called *Comhaltas Ceoltóirí Éireann* (phone: 800295); ballad sessions are held nightly except Sundays in the *Abbey Tavern,* Howth, 10 miles north of the city on the coast (phone: 322006 or 390307). Many pubs offer music informally — *O'Donoghue's* in Merrion Row is one of the most famous (and least comfortable). Try also *Toner's* and the *Baggot Inn,* both on Lower Baggot St.; *Kitty O'Shea's,* Upper Grand Canal St.; or *Foley's,* Merrion Row. Many other pubs are listed in *In Dublin.*

 NIGHTCLUBS AND NIGHTLIFE: There is little in the way of large-scale cabaret-cum-dancing in Dublin; swinging Dublin tends to congregate on the discotheque scene. Premises range from the large, lively places where an escort is not necessarily required to small, intimate clubs. Most discotheques have only wine licenses.

Among the more established discotheques on a rapidly changing scene are the large and lively *Annabel's* in the *Burlington* hotel, *Raffles* in the *Sachs, Blinkers* at Leopardstown racecourse, and *Rumours* on O'Connell St. Smaller, more intimate clubs are mainly to be found in the Leeson St. area: *Blonds, Samantha's, Styx,* and *Buck's* are a few. The most famous traditional cabaret in Dublin is the established *Jurys Cabaret,* nightly except Mondays (phone: 605000). Also good are the *Braemor Rooms,* Churchtown (phone: 988664); *Doyle's Irish Cabaret* at the *Burlington* (phone: 605222); and the *Clontarf Castle* dinner show (phone: 332271).

BEST IN TOWN

CHECKING IN: Since the late 1970s, with the opening of the 5-star *Berkeley Court* and the *Westbury* and the refurbishment of the *Shelbourne* and *Jurys,* Dublin's hotels have risen remarkably in quality, but they are still not at the top of world class standards. Expect to pay more than $200 for a double room in hotels classified as very expensive; $110 to $190 for those classified as expensive; $70 to $100 in those listed as moderate; and less than $70 for an inexpensive room. A room with Irish breakfast for two in a private home in a residential neighborhood will cost $45 or less.

Note: The tourist board offers a list of hotels it has inspected and graded; it also offers a computerized reservation service all over Ireland (see *Tourist Information,* above). All telephone numbers are in the 01 area code unless otherwise indicated.

Shelbourne – This venerable hotel, a nice mixture of the dignified and the lively, is now more polished than ever after a $5-million facelift. Some rooms are truly splendid, particularly the front rooms on the 2nd floor. Many are supremely comfortable, if compact. But the sense of history in the creaky-floored hallways, the glittering function rooms, and the varied clientele — from socialites to literati — make this establishment especially appealing. The *Horseshoe Bar* is one of the livelier fixtures of Dublin pub life, while the *Aisling* restaurant, with its 1826 plasterwork and trio of Waterford crystal chandeliers, is a showcase for modern Irish cuisine. 27 St. Stephen's Green (phone: 766471). Very expensive.

Berkeley Court – The flagship of the P. V. Doyle Group and the first Irish member of the Leading Hotels of the World group. Close to the city in the leafy suburb of Ballsbridge, the hotel combines graciousness with modern efficiency. Contemporary and antique furnishings harmonize, and the service is exceptionally warm. There are 220 rooms, 6 suites with Jacuzzis, an excellent dining room, a conservatory-style coffee shop, a health center with indoor pool and saunas, and a shopping arcade. Lansdowne Rd. (phone: 601711). Expensive.

Bloom's – Centrally located, this intimate hotel (a member of the Quality Inn group) has a high commitment to service. Its 86 rooms have color TV sets, air conditioning, trouser-pressers, free mixers and ice, and direct-dial telephones. Every corridor has an ice cabinet and a shoeshine. Fine dining is offered in the *Blazes Boylan Grill Room,* and there are two lively bars, *Bogie's* and *Yesterday's.* Anglesea St. (phone: 715622). Expensive.

Burlington – Ireland's largest hotel, with 500 rooms, was completely refurbished in 1987. Restaurants include an international dining room, the *Sussex,* and the cozy *Diplomat* for beef and seafood. Trendy *Mespil Bar,* with its cheery hanging plants, globe lights and brass, has a popular lunch buffet. A musical revue is performed at *Doyle's Irish Cabaret* on summer evenings, and there's year-round entertainment in *Annabel's* lounge. Leeson St. (phone: 605222). Expensive.

Gresham – Once considered one of the grandest of Dublin hotels, the *Gresham* has changed ownership a number of times and has come to rest in the Ryan Holdings Group. Though you could hardly call it grand these days, this 179-room hotel once attracted many a luminary. Upper O'Connell St. (phone: 746881). Expensive.

Jurys – In Ballsbridge opposite the American Embassy, this modern complex has a multi-story, skylit lobby area and a dome-shaped central atrium. The main hotel offers 290 rooms, each with well-equipped bathroom. In early 1989, 100 extra large rooms and suites were added in a separate but connected 8-story wing. Known as the *Towers,* this section is a first for Ireland — featuring computer-key-accessible rooms, each with a bay window, mini-bar, three telephone lines, well-lit work area, satellite TV, marble and tile bathroom (equipped with hair dryer, heated towel rack, terrycloth robe, and basket of amenities), walk-in closet, and either king- or queen-size beds. All the *Towers'* rooms are decorated with designer fabrics and specially styled furnishings, such as rocking recliner chairs. Two floors are designated as non-smoking. The *Towers* has its own hospitality lounge, separate elevators, and entrance. Both sections of the hotel share an array of services including 2 restaurants, a 23-hour coffee shop, two bars, an indoor/outdoor swimming pool, and health center. For entertainment, there is *Jurys Cabaret,* Ireland's longest running variety show. Northumberland Rd. (phone: 605000; FAX: 605540). Main hotel, expensive; Towers, very expensive.

Westbury – The newest luxury addition to the Doyle Group, this hotel is the fashionable centerpiece of a chic new mall of shops and restaurants. The management emphasizes elegance, and the 150 rooms have canopied beds and an abundance of mahogany and brass furnishings. Private suites with Jacuzzis are also available. The most noteworthy of its restaurants is the grand *Russell Room.* Grafton St. (phone: 791122). Expensive.

Russell Court – Two former Georgian houses have been transformed into this convenient new hotel less than a block from St. Stephen's Green. The decor in the public areas is Art Deco, and the 22 modern bedrooms, all with bath, have light woods and pastel tones. Facilities include a restaurant, lounge, and nightclub. 21-23 Harcourt St. (phone: 784991). Expensive to moderate.

Ariel House – A homey guesthouse with 15 rooms and a restaurant with a wine license. One block from the DART station for easy commuting to the city center. Room rates include full breakfast. 52 Lansdowne Rd. (phone: 685512). Moderate.

Montrose – Similar to but larger than the *Tara Tower,* near the National Radio and Television studios and across the road from the new Belfield campus of University College, Dublin. About 10 minutes' drive from the city center, on a well-serviced bus route. Its 190 bedrooms are comfortable, and it has a good restaurant. Amenities include a grill, bars, health center, hairdressing salon, and souvenir shop. Stillorgan Rd. (phone: 693311). Moderate.

Skylon – Midway between downtown and the Dublin Airport, this modern northside hostelry has 100 rooms all done in a colorful Irish motif. The hotel also features a restaurant/grill that stays open until midnight. Upper Drumcondra Rd. (phone: 379121). Moderate.

Tara Tower – Ten minutes' drive from the city center, on a well-serviced bus route, this modern hotel is comfortable and very reasonably priced. The 100 bedrooms have radio, television sets, and telephone, and many overlook Dublin Bay. The lobby is small, but the hotel's good restaurant/grill is open until midnight. Merrion Rd. (phone: 694666). Moderate.

Anglesea Townhouse – Near the American Embassy, this Edwardian residence is the home of Helen Kirrane, who spoils her guests with hearty breakfasts of fresh fish, homemade breads and scones, fresh juices, baked fruits, and warm cereals. Heirlooms and family antiques add to the ambience of this jewel of a bed-and-breakfast guesthouse. All 7 rooms have private bath-shower, TV sets, and direct-dial telephones. 63 Anglesea Rd., Ballsbridge (phone: 683877). Inexpensive.

Egan's House – Another comfortable guesthouse, offering 23 rooms, all with private baths. There is also a small restaurant. 7 Iona Park (phone: 303611). Inexpensive.

Iona House – A guesthouse with 14 rooms, 12 with private baths, and a restaurant/ coffee shop serving breakfast to late snacks. 5 Iona Park (phone: 306217). Inexpensive.

Mount Herbert – Close to the city center, this well-run, family-owned property has 88 rooms (77 with private baths), a new health facility, and a fairly good restaurant. No bar (wine license only) but a very pleasant atmosphere. 7 Herbert Rd. (phone: 684321). Inexpensive.

 EATING OUT: Where food is concerned, Ireland, first and foremost an agricultural country, has outstanding raw materials. But truly distinctive and innovative Irish cuisine really does not exist. Traditional dishes such as Irish stew, Dublin coddle, and bacon and cabbage are served, but this kind of dish is a *rara avis* on the menu of most better restaurants, being looked down upon as too common to prepare for discriminating diners.

Where the serving of its enviable agricultural produce is concerned, Ireland's top restaurants can compare with the best anywhere. Dublin offers a wide range of first class restaurants, a somewhat more restricted range of moderately priced establishments, and a number of fast-service, inexpensive eating places.

Dinner for two, excluding drinks, will cost $100 and up in expensive restaurants; $50 to $95 in moderate places; and under $50 in inexpensive ones. Reservations are always recommended, especially at expensive and moderate establishments. Unless noted otherwise, most are closed Sundays and holidays. All telephone numbers are in the 01 area code unless otherwise indicated.

Berkeley Court – One of the best hotel restaurants, this is in an elegant, lavishly appointed room; its prizewinning chef produces highly satisfactory cuisine. Open daily. Lansdowne Rd. (phone: 601711). Expensive.

Celtic Mews – In an old Georgian mews with a warm, welcoming atmosphere, this is one of Dublin's original fine dining spots. Entrées range from pheasant and lobster to classic Irish stew. Dinner only. 109A Lower Baggot St. (phone: 760796). Expensive.

Le Coq Hardi – Run by owner/chef John Howard, twice Gold Medal winner in the prestigious Hotelympia/Salon Culinaire contest, this is a gracious Georgian establishment. Its extensive à la carte menu offers many house specialties such as Howard's renowned *caneton à l'orange.* Reservations necessary. Major credit cards. 35 Pembroke Rd., Ballsbridge (phone: 689070). Expensive.

Ernie's – Master seafood chef Ernie Evans earned a far-reaching reputation at the *Towers* hotel on the Ring of Kerry. Still specializing in *fruits de mer,* he now works magic on such dishes as Valencia scallops, garlic prawns, and fresh salmon. Dinner only; closed Sundays and Mondays. Mulberry Gardens, Donnybrook (phone: 693300). Expensive.

Grey Door – Open since 1978, this restaurant has achieved an enviable reputation for fine Russian and Finnish cuisine. The wine list is good and the more adventurous imbiber can sample such rarities as Russian champagne. The setting behind this elegant doorway in the heart of Georgian Dublin is intimate, rather like dining in a private home. 23 Upper Pembroke St. (phone: 763286). Expensive.

King Sitric – This superb small restaurant, right on the bay, serves perfectly cooked fish and excellent wines in a tastefully restored old house. It also specializes in game birds such as grouse and snipe. The service is very good. East Pier, Howth (phone: 325235). Expensive.

Locks – A French provincial eatery on the banks of the Grand Canal near Portobello Bridge. Only the freshest produce is used for such dishes as wild salmon and breast of pigeon. 1 Windsor Ter., Portobello (phone: 752025). Expensive.

Lord Edward – Strictly for seafood lovers (no meat on the menu), it is in a tall Victorian building opposite historic Christ Church Cathedral, in the older part of the city. The seafood is prepared and served in the classic French style. Reservations necessary. 23 Christ Church Pl. (phone: 542420). Expensive.

Old Dublin – This cozy eatery has rose-colored linens and walls and roaring fireplaces. Specialties on the menu include Scandinavian-style fish, which owner Eamonn Walsh learned to love while in Finland. For meat eaters there's filet à la Novgorod — chateaubriand sliced and served on sauerkraut alongside fried kasha, spicy mushrooms, caviar, and sour cream. There is also a good wine list. Open weekdays for lunch and dinner; Saturdays for dinner only; closed holidays. 91 Francis St. (phone: 542028 or 542346). Expensive.

Patrick Guilbaud – A trendy place for nouvelle cuisine that draws an equally stylish crowd. Specialties include breast of duck in cider sauce, veal kidneys and sweetbreads, lamb's tongue and brill, and bacon in curry sauce. 46 James Pl., off Baggot St. (phone: 764192). Expensive.

White's on the Green – An elegantly appointed gathering place for media stars, celebrities, and expense-account diners, it has the air of a Georgian garden. Dublin's newest "in" spot features *cuisine moderne* and the finest service traditions. Menu ranges from veal sweetbreads with fennel and celery to roast wild salmon or *panaché* of lamb with fresh tarragon. 119 St. Stephen's Green (phone: 751975). Expensive.

Coffers – Around the corner from *Bloom's* hotel, this small, comfortable restaurant specializes in steaks — varying from a plain filet to a pork steak cooked in fresh apples and Pernod. It features a special pre-theater dinner daily except Sundays. 6 Cope St. (phone: 715900 or 715740). Moderate.

Gallery 22 – A pleasant, gardenlike atmosphere pervades this restaurant near the *Shelbourne*. The innovative menu includes seafood pancakes, rack of lamb, sea trout, and filet steak with vermouth sauce. A pre-theater dinner is offered. 22 St. Stephen's Green (phone: 686169). Moderate.

La Grenouille – A French-style bistro next to the Powerscourt Town House Centre. Each dish on the limited menu is cooked to order. Choices range from rack of lamb or poulet in blue cheese sauce to steak and duck, all served with an array of fresh vegetables. Open daily for dinner, a rarity in Dublin. 64 S William St. (phone: 779157). Moderate.

Osprey's – Around the corner from *Jurys* and the American Embassy, this cozy candlelit restaurant has two small dining rooms, each with a fireplace. Flambé cooking is a specialty here, as are such international dishes as beef Wellington, salmon *en croûte,* chicken Madeira, weiner schnitzel, and Dover sole. 41/43 Shelbourne Rd. (phone: 608087). Moderate.

Rudyards – On 3 floors of a tall, narrow house in Crown Alley, it offers a combination of mildly exotic continental dishes, from spinach-stuffed pancakes to navarin of lamb, pasta, and tomato pie and beef in orange sauce. Reservations not necessary. 15 Crown Alley, off Dame St. (phone: 710846). Moderate to inexpensive.

Shannons – Dubliners looking for a good restaurant have put this place on the top of their list. It is bright and airy, with many plants, flowers, wide windows, and an open kitchen. The menu features the freshest of Irish seafoods, produce, and prime meats; unique combination dishes include breast of chicken layered with salmon and a fan of trout with turbot. Service is first rate. Dinner nightly; lunch only on Sundays. The Grove, Stillorgan (phone: 887963). Moderate.

Unicorn – Established in 1939, this small Italian bistro is a favorite with Irish politicians and literati. All pastas and sauces are made by owners Renato and Nina Sidoli. Open from 10AM to 6PM except Sundays. Merrion Ct., off Merrion Row (phone: 762182 or 688552). Moderate to inexpensive.

Bad Ass Café – One of the newest, brightest, and liveliest spots to hit town in some time. Famed as much for its (loud) rock music and videos as for its great pizza. Steaks are another specialty. 9/11 Crown Alley, behind the Central Bank on Dame St. (phone: 712596). Inexpensive.

Beshoff – Owned by a family long known as purveyors of fresh fish, this is a classy version of the traditional Dublin fish-and-chip shop, with a black-and-white marble decor. The menu features chips (French fries) with salmon, shark, squid, turbot, or prawns, as well as the humble cod. Open daily, noon to midnight. 14 Westmoreland St. (phone: 778781) and 5/6 Upper O'Connell St. (phone: 743223). Inexpensive.

Captain America's – Specializes in "genuine American hamburgers," Tex-Mex, and barbecue dishes, served with American beer and rock music. Open daily. Grafton Ct., 1st floor, Grafton St. (phone: 715266). Inexpensive.

Casper & Giumbini's Drink and Food Emporium – A lively restaurant with some traditional Irish dishes, such as Irish stew (not always easy to come by in Irish restaurants). There's also an exotic range of cocktails and a selection of international beers. Brunch served Saturdays and Sundays. 6 Wicklow St. (phone: 794347). Inexpensive.

SHARING A PINT: Until you have been in a pub, you have not experienced Dublin. Here Dubliners come to pursue two serious occupations: drinking and conversation. Many pubs are ugly and modern, complete with Muzak and plastic, but plenty of traditional pubs remain — noisy, companionable places for the pursuit of friendly ghosts of bygone Dublin in an unhurried atmosphere. Some favorites are the *Horseshoe Bar* in the *Shelbourne* hotel, St. Stephen's Green (phone: 766471), favored by the uppity, horsey set; the *Bailey,* 2 Duke St. (phone: 773055), a literary pub that actually displays the door of nearby 7 Eccles St., where Joyce's Molly and Leopold Bloom lived; *O'Donoghue's,* off St. Stephen's Green, for Irish ballads; the *Palace Bar* on Fleet St., a traditional haunt of journalists and literati; *Mulligans* of Poolbeg St., renowned for the quality of its pint, appreciated equally by the dock workers and students (from nearby Trinity College), who form its main clientele; the *Stag's Head,* Dame Ct. (a great haunt of the legal profession), which serves hearty hot lunches at reasonable prices; *Neary's,* Chatham St., which offers delicacies like smoked salmon and oysters in season; the *Brazen Head,* Bridge St., and *Davy Byrne's,* 21 Duke St., for plain drinking and gab; *Doheny and Nesbitts* on Merrion Row, which is always known simply as Nesbitts — try the bar, not the modernized upstairs lounge; and last, but very far from least, the utterly delightful *Ryans,* Parkgate St., with its shining mirrors, courteous barmen, and snugs where guests can drink quietly.

WINE BARS: A popular addition to the Dublin scene are wine bars, which generally offer light meals and good wines at moderate prices.

Kilmartin's – Originally owned by a turf accountant (a bookie), this bar retains both its name and its racing decor under new owners. Run by two young women, both cordon bleu chefs, Kilmartin's specializes in poached salmon and crispy duck. The house wine is particularly good. 19 Upper Baggot St. (phone: 686674).

Mitchell's – In the cellar (where else!) of *Mitchell's Wine Merchants,* this is where swinging Dubliners lunch. The menu is somewhat limited, but the helpings are large, the cooking quite good, and the desserts mouth-watering. Alas, it's not open in the evenings. Get there before 12:30 PM, or you'll find yourself in for a long wait at lunchtime (which you can while away by sampling some of Mitchell's splendid wines). 21 Kildare St. (phone: 680367).

Shrimp's – Tiny but charmingly decorated, it is not the place to air your most intimate thoughts. The food, however, is tempting and you can choose from a good range of wines. 1 Anne's La. (phone: 713143).

Timmerman's – Arched ceilings, old church pews, and empty wine barrels dominate the decor of this unique spot. The menu is simple — quiche, lasagna, steaks, corned beef, and a variety of fruit and vegetable salads. A popular choice to accompany wine is a platter of 15 different Irish cheeses. Music in the evenings. Powerscourt Town House Centre, 59 S. William St. (phone: 717425 or 794186).

EDINBURGH

Other beautiful and famous urban centers such as Rome or San Francisco may share the distinction of being built on hills, but Edinburgh, a stark and in some ways still medieval city whose streets have often flowed with blood, alone can claim to be built on extinct volcanoes.

Astride one of these, high above the houses where Edinburgh's 440,000 inhabitants dwell, looms Edinburgh Castle, a portentous fairy tale structure that often makes visitors gasp the first time they see it. It seems almost supernatural, with ancient stonemasonry rising out of volcanic rock as if there were no dividing line between the two.

From the 7th century on, there was a fortress where Edinburgh Castle now stands, and as life in the Middle Ages became more civilized, life within the fortress spilled onto the long sloping ridge — carved by glaciers ages after the volcanic era — that runs down from Edinburgh Castle to the foot of Arthur's Seat, another extinct volcano, crowning Edinburgh's central park. The ridge, with its clusters of high stone and wood tenements, its one thin, snakelike public street, its cathedral, and its tollbooth, was (and still is) the securing knot at the center of Scotland's legal, commercial, and artistic fiber.

Walking around central Edinburgh today is sheer joy. There's very little need for a map; it's hard to get lost. Every time you reach a hilltop, there's a glorious vista of the sweeping fusion of earth, sky, and sea, and every glance up an alley reveals fantastic steeples, jagged, smoking, chimney-potted skylines, or beauteous rotund domes. The city lights its most imposing public buildings at night, and they are legion, spread out over a series of precipices and valleys. Nature provides incredible sunsets, the product of Scotland's unique slowly fading evening light (the "gloaming") and rapid change in the evening temperature. Legend and romance are at every hand. Somebody famous lived in almost every residence.

At the head of the legend and romance brigade are the arch Presbyterian John Knox and Mary, Queen of Scots, who together dominated life in the Edinburgh of the late 16th century. (Not that they dominated it together. When Mary arrived in Edinburgh in the autumn of 1561 as Scotland's very young and very Catholic new queen, Knox described the event in his diary as God having fouled the air with black fog and seeping rain.) The political and religious strife attendant upon Mary's reign is notorious, as are her two marriages and the three deaths associated with them, the last of these her own (she was beheaded by her cousin Queen Elizabeth I of England, to whom she had fled for asylum). Mary lived in Holyrood Palace, by the abbey at the base of Arthur's Seat. John Knox lived up the ridge from her near St. Giles's Cathedral, within the city gates. Both residences still stand and are open to the public today.

Their Edinburgh reached its full flower around the end of the 17th century, when the tenements along the ridge had grown 15 (or more) tottering stories high and housed uncounted numbers of people, all of whom threw their

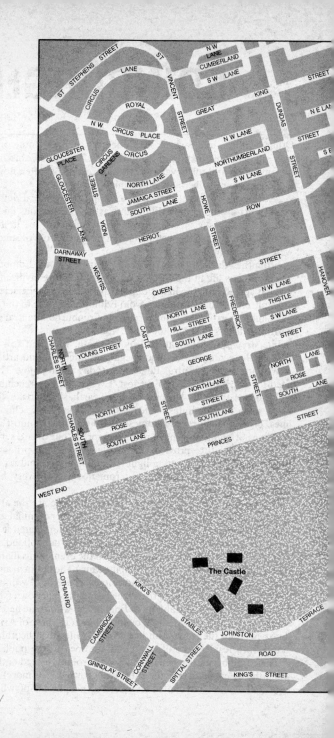

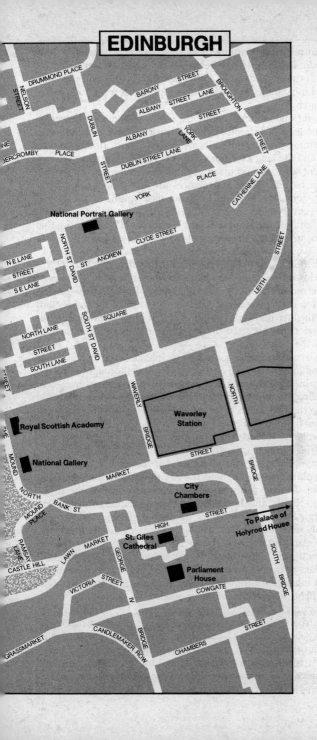

garbage into the central street, warning those below with nothing more than the terse cry *"Gardez-loo!"* Buildings frequently collapsed. Water could be had only from one of the city's six wells, called *pennywells* (their sites are still marked today), and inhabitants would line up with buckets from 3 AM on to be sure of some water.

These cramped and malodorous conditions, plus a plethora of alehouses and a police force made up of decrepit Highlanders back from European wars, no doubt had something to do with the locals' favorite sport, rioting on fete days, parade days, and the king's birthday. Riots occasioned by more serious events were frequent also and occurred regularly in every age up to the Victorian and even beyond. Famous instances are the assassination of a wealthy councillor, John MacMorran, by dissatisfied youths at the Royal High School (16th century); "Cleanse the Causeway," a battle in the streets between two noble families, the Douglases and Hamiltons (17th century); the Jenny Geddes affair, in which a Presbyterian fishwife caused pandemonium by throwing a stool at a dean who was reading the new Episcopal service book in St. Giles's Cathedral — the first event in the British Civil War (17th century); the Porteous Riots, immortalized by Sir Walter Scott in *The Heart of Midlothian* (18th century); and the trial of William Burke, whose sale of his victims' corpses to the University of Edinburgh's medical luminaries did so much to further the international reputation of that great institution (19th century). Religious riots have scarred the city's history repeatedly, although the last one was in the 1930s.

Obviously this wizened medieval town had to spread out somehow, and luckily, in the second half of the 18th century, its by now thoroughly Protestant God sent it an increase in trade and prosperity. City fathers erected a wealth of new buildings on another ridge to the north — known as the New Town, connected to the Old Town by bridges. The classically proportioned beauty of New Town buildings, many of which were designed by the world-renowned British architect Robert Adam, is a testament to what is generally regarded as Edinburgh's golden age, part of the so-called Scottish Enlightenment. It was a great age not only for architects but for writers, publishers, philosophers, and politicians. Throughout the city, taverns became the sites of ongoing seminars. Among many other well-known people of the time, David Hume, Adam Smith, and James Boswell were Edinburgh men.

Today's Edinburgh has lost some of its traditional vibrancy and color, though it is certainly safer and cleaner. The near stranglehold the Presbyterian Church of Scotland attained on the social institutions during Queen Victoria's reign meant that industriousness, temperance, and respectability — all the middle class virtues — took supreme command of the city. About 60% of the present inhabitants are white-collar workers, an unusually high proportion, which helps keep the local flavor staid.

Nonetheless, signs are that things are livening up. Since 1979, an avalanche of flashy pubs, nightspots, and restaurants has shattered the city's sober air. Edinburgh has always been favored by geography, situated as it is on the Firth of Forth, an inlet in the North Sea, and surrounded by woods, rolling hills, and lochs (lakes). It is not only a national capital but a port whose chief exports include whisky, coal, and machinery; a large brewing center; and a center for nuclear and electronics research.

And though the idea of a Scottish Assembly at Edinburgh — favored by a majority of Scottish voters — was set aside on a technicality a few years ago, a groundswell of agitation for Scotland's greater control of its own affairs remains. Who can say whether Edinburgh's second golden age is at hand? Perhaps not all its volcanoes are extinct.

Certainly the smell of sulfur has been ominously in the air, as the ancient capital has been made a battleground for the local repercussions of Thatcherism's bitter conflicts. Increased government pressure on the BBC has resulted in the shelving of plans for a National Broadcasting Centre for Scotland, and the transfer of news and current affairs to Glasgow. Labour party victories in local government elections have been offset by government privatization of Edinburgh city transport, which has led to at least temporary transport chaos, if not actual Streetcar Wars. The *Edinburgh Festival* (see *Extra Special*) has been caught in the crossfire, weakened by government slashing of arts budgets and local Labour Council charges of elitism. In fact, the *Festival* has continued to maintain high standards and has reached out to embrace populism, increased internationalism, and the avant-garde. It would seem that, despite continuing pressure, the theater pageant is reviving, rejuvenated.

If anything, occasional disasters heighten the innumerable triumphs of what is undoubtedly the world's greatest arts festival. The low-budget *Film Festival* can't be Cannes, but its stature increases steadily. Unfortunately, mismanagement, anti-apartheid boycotts, and underfunding made the Commonwealth Games of 1986 a financial disaster, and Edinburgh's complacency has been additionally jolted by a growing preference for Glasgow as the site of future sporting events. The old Glasgow taunt that Edinburgh is "fur coat and nae knickers" has all too much relevance in a cold financial climate. The capital has had to look to its laurels, which means, among other things, that tourists are currently taken far less for granted.

EDINBURGH AT-A-GLANCE

SEEING THE CITY: Edinburgh has many wonderful views; on a clear day, there are striking panoramas from the top of any of its extinct volcanoes. To the north lies the sparkling Firth of Forth and, beyond it, the ancient kingdom of Fife. To the south are the lovely Pentland Hills and surrounding plowed farmlands. Look eastward, where the giant Bass Rock, off the coast of Berwickshire, meets your eye. Look westward to see across the whole nation to Ben Lomond, nearly on the west coast of Scotland! If you have a car, drive up Arthur's Seat (the road begins just by Holyrood Palace), park at Dunsapie Loch, and walk to the uppermost height (a steep and furzy climb — wear flat shoes and watch out for falling sheep). If you have no car, see the city from Edinburgh Castle.

SPECIAL PLACES: The "Royal Mile" is the oldest part of the city, the road that runs downhill from Edinburgh Castle to Holyrood Palace. It comprises four contiguous streets: Castle Hill, the Lawnmarket, High Street, and the Canongate. Since the entire citizenry of Edinburgh lived and worked for centuries either on or just off these four streets, the Royal Mile is practically groaning with objects and sites of historic fascination: 16th- and 17th-century houses, well preserved, with their adjacent courtyards and closes; residences of famous writers and distinguished thinkers; St. Giles's Cathedral, the High Kirk of Edinburgh, with its 17th-century spire in the shape of the Scottish crown; excellent museums; the classical City Chambers; and the building where Scotland's Parliament met from 1639 until union with England's in 1707.

THE ROYAL MILE

Edinburgh Castle – The oldest building in Edinburgh is part of the castle structure, a tiny ethereal chapel built by Queen Margaret, the wife of the Malcolm who features in *Macbeth*. King James VI of Scotland (later James I of England) was born here. The Scottish Regalia, including Sceptre and Crown, are on display. These disappeared after the union of Scotland with England and were found, over 100 years later, by Sir Walter Scott (who was leading a government commission appointed to look for them) in an old locked box. Emotion ran so high that his daughter, who was present on the occasion, fainted when he lifted the lid. Also in the castle is the Scottish National War Memorial, honoring Scots who died in the two world wars (phone: 225-9846).

Outlook Tower Visitor Centre – A short distance east of the castle, climb up 98 steps, walk outside, and find yourself face to face with church spires. The camera obscura, actually a periscope, throws a revolving image of nearby streets and buildings onto a circular table, while one of the tower's denizens gives an excellent historical talk. Downstairs is a very good book shop carrying everything from Lady Antonia Fraser's best-selling biography of Mary, Queen of Scots, to gleaming coffee table volumes about one of the national obsessions, Scotch whisky. Open daily on weekdays from 10 AM to 5 PM, weekends to 4 PM. Admission charge. Castle Hill (phone: 226-3709).

Parliament House – Built from 1632 to 1640, after Charles I suggested that it replace the Collegiate buildings of St. Giles's Cathedral, this historic sanctum once housed Scotland's Parliament and is today the country's supreme court. Until 1982, tourists could enter only by written request. Its showpiece is the Great Hall, with a fine hammer-beam roof and walls laden with portraits by Raeburn and other famous Scottish artists. Also of interest is the Signet Library, a splendid example of interior decoration, with an exquisite ceiling. Written permission of the librarian is required to visit, however. Closed Saturdays through Mondays. Admission charge for library. Upper High St. (phone: 225-2595).

St. Giles's Cathedral – A church of some sort has stood here for over 1,000 years. The medieval building here was named for the Athenian saint Egidius (Giles). St. Giles's has often been showered by flying religious fur, especially at the time of the Reformation. In 1559–60 soldiers were put on guard at the church and many of its treasures hidden in private Catholic homes; Protestant nobles nonetheless ravaged the altars. Later, English troops came to their aid and stripped St. Giles's from top to bottom. It was at this stage that John Knox, a prime mover in this sequence of events, was made minister of St. Giles's. His unmarked grave is believed to be under Parliament Square, just outside St. Giles's. Open Mondays through Saturdays, 9 AM to 5 PM, (7 PM in summer); Sundays, open afternoons only. Upper High St. (phone: 225-4363).

Mercat Cross, or Market Cross – Near the east door of St. Giles's stands a monument restored in 1885 by W. E. Gladstone, prime minister of Britain off and on from 1868 to 1894. Here was the crossroads at which proclamations were read out and public hangings took place, until well into the 19th century. It was also the commercial focal point of old Edinburgh, the place being so thick with butchers, bakers, merchants, burgesses, lawyers, tinkers, tailors, farmers, drovers, and fishmongers that the town council issued ordinances requiring each trade to occupy its own separate neighboring street or close (hence the names you see on the entrances to the closes as you go down the Royal Mile: Fleshmarket Close, Advocates' Close, and so on). City tradesmen never obeyed these ordinances, however, and the Mercat Cross remained as colorful as ever until the city began to spread out in the second half of the 18th century. High St., by St. Giles's.

Advocates' Close and Anchor Close – These are typical of the many narrow alleys that gave access to the inns and taverns that were so much a part of Edinburgh's 18th-century cultural life. Doors to these places (taverns no longer) were topped by stone architraves dating from the 16th century and bearing inscriptions like "Blissit Be God of Al His Gifts" or "Spes Altera Vitae" (these two examples are still in Advocates' Close today). In Anchor Close was Douglas's, where the poet Robert Burns habitually drank. Entrances of both closes are from High St.

John Knox's House – Legend says that Scotland's fieriest preacher of all time lived here, but historians say no. However, legend has won, and this attractive 15th-century dwelling was preserved when most of its neighbors were razed during the widening of High Street in 1849. Open October through March, 10 AM to 4 PM; 10 AM to 5 PM the rest of the year. Closed Sundays. Admission charge. 45 High St. (phone: 556-6961).

Acheson House – When King Charles I was crowned at Edinburgh in 1633, Sir Archibald Acheson, baronet, was his secretary of state. Acheson built this house, a small courtyard mansion, the only one of its kind in Edinburgh, in the same year. It was the height of elegance in its day, yet 100 years later it had become a popular brothel and 200 years after that was inhabited by 14 families, though it had been built to house one. It was bought and restored by the Marquess of Bute in 1935, whereupon, despite its history, it was leased to the Canongate Kirk for a manse! Today it houses the *Scottish Craft Centre,* where you can buy all sorts of attractive handmade items. Closed Sundays. No admission charge. 140 the Canongate (phone: 556-8136).

Canongate Kirkyard – Opposite Acheson House. Pause long enough to read the long list — mounted on a plaque — of notables buried there. The Canongate.

Brass Rubbing Centre – Visitors may rub any of the brasses or stones on show. Materials are provided for a fee that probably won't come to more than about $8. The brass commemorating Robert Bruce, King of Scotland from 1306 to 1329, is very impressive. In addition to being nice souvenirs, your own finished products make beautiful gifts. Closed Sundays, except from 2 to 5 PM during the *Edinburgh Festival.* In Trinity Apse, Chalmers Close, off High St. (phone: 556-4364).

Holyrood Palace – A royal retreat since the beginning of the 16th century, the palace is where Queen Elizabeth II stays when she is in residence in Edinburgh. It is made of stone, a huge, imposing round-towered edifice befitting kings and queens. Most of what you see of it now was built by Charles II from 1671, but it is chiefly associated with Mary, Queen of Scots, who lived in it well before that for 6 contentious, sensational years. The old part, still extant, contains her bedroom and the supper room in which David Riccio, her secretary, was brutally murdered before her very eyes by a gang of armed men that included her jealous husband, her cousin Lord Darnley. By the side of the palace, within its spacious grounds, are the picturesque ruins of Holyrood Abbey and the lodge known as Queen Mary's Bath House, where she reputedly bathed in red wine. A guide will take you through it all, sparing no gory details. Closed Sundays from November through March and when the queen is in town. Admission charge. At the bottom of the Canongate (phone: 556-7371).

Scotch Whiskey Heritage Centre – Just next door to the entrance to the Edinburgh Castle, this new tourist attraction features an hour-long tour, in an electric barrel car, showing the role of whiskey in Scotland's turbulent past. The sounds and even the smells of the distilling industry are tantalizingly reproduced. You will emerge knowing exactly how to make whiskey. 358 Castlehill (phone: 220-0441).

Scottish Poetry Library – For anyone who visits Britain to explore America's literary ancestry, an hour or two browsing here should bring rich pleasure. An extensive collection of books, magazines, and tapes with Scottish works in English, Scots, and Gaelic is housed in this 18th-century building in a courtyard off the Royal Mile. The building was formerly owned by Edinburgh's most famous burglar, Deacon William Brodie, a respectable town councillor by day and a criminal by night, who was hanged in 1788. 14 High St. No admission charge (phone: 557-2876).

BEYOND THE ROYAL MILE

Princes Street Gardens – Princes Street is modern Edinburgh's Main Street, its Broadway, and its Fifth Avenue. The gardens stretch nearly the street's whole length on the south side, where the old Nor' Loch, which was used in medieval times as the castle moat, once stood. The city spends thousands of pounds every year to keep the gardens opulent with flowers. In summer months (June–September) there are concerts, children's shows, variety acts, and do-it-yourself Scottish country dancing (to professional bands) here. Gates close at dusk. Princes St.

National Gallery Scotland – Smack in the middle of Princes Street Gardens, on a manmade embankment called the Mound, is this exquisite museum, opened in 1859. It contains paintings by British and European masters from the 14th century to Cézanne. Open daily except Sunday mornings. The Mound (phone: 556-8921).

Scott Monument – Sir Walter Scott is certainly one of Edinburgh's favorite sons — his face even decorates all Bank of Scotland notes, even though he was the most famous bankrupt in Scottish history. The elaborate 200-foot Gothic monument on the east end of Princes Street Gardens helps make Edinburgh's skyline the ornamental marvel it is. Its 287 steps take you to the summit. (Don't attempt it if you suffer vertigo.) Closed Sundays. Admission charge. Princes St. (phone: 225-2424, ext. 6596).

New Town – To the north of Princes Street lies the largest neo-classical townscape in Europe, built between the 1760s and 1830s. Assiduous conservation means that little has changed externally in these streets, squares, and crescents. Three of the more interesting ones are Charlotte Square (designed by Robert Adam), Moray Place, and Ann Street. The New Town Conservation Centre, 13A Dundas St. (phone: 557-5222), conducts personalized tours Mondays through Fridays; call ahead to arrange a time. The Centre also offers exibitions, a reference library, and various publications.

Georgian House – On the most gracious square in the elegant New Town, the National Trust for Scotland has furnished a house in period style and opened it to the public. The kitchen is a wonderland of utilitarian objects that would have belonged to a typical high class late-18th-century ménage. Fascinating audio-visual sessions on the history and topography of the New Town come with the admission price. Open daily April through October; weekends only in November; closed December through March. 7 Charlotte Sq. (phone: 225-2160).

Edinburgh Zoo – Opposite the Pentland Hills, away from the city center, en route to the western suburb of Corstorphine, is a zoo with a view and the world's most famous penguins, the largest colony in captivity. Every afternoon at 2:30, from April through September, they perform their delightful Penguin Parade through the park grounds. Open daily. Admission charge. Corstorphine Rd., Murrayfield (phone: 334-9171).

Grassmarket – This ancient street is flanked by many cozy eateries, elegant shops, and seedy-looking flophouses. The West Bow, off the street's east end, has some intriguing boutiques. Leading from the Grassmarket is Cowgate, with the 16th-century Magdalen Chapel (phone the Scottish Reformation Society to see it: 220-1450).

Dean Village – This 800-year-old grain milling town on the Water of Leith is over 100 feet below the level of much of the rest of the city and a good place to soak up local color. In summer the woodland walk along the river is popping with bohemians who live in the next village, Stockbridge. End of Bell's Brae (turn left off

Queensferry St. onto Bell's Brae as you approach Dean Bridge from the west end of Princes St.).

Water of Leith Walkway – The Walkway extends from the outlying district of Colinton, on the southwest side of the city, near the Water of Leith's source, to the mouth of the Water of Leith at Edinburgh's chief seaport, a distance of over 10 miles. The Stockbridge section of the Walkway, including the woodland path from Dean Village, features St. Bernard's Well, so named to honor 12th-century St. Bernard of Clairvaux, said to have restored himself to health with the Well's healing waters after a frosty reception by the Scottish court when he tried to raise a Scottish army for the Second Crusade. The Well is encased in an impressive Doric rotunda featuring a marble statue of Hygeia, Goddess of Health.

Greyfriars Kirk – This historic Presbyterian church, dedicated on Christmas 1620, was the site of a pre-Reformation Franciscan friary. It is also where Presbyterians declared their opposition to the prescribed Episcopalianism of Charles I by signing the National Covenant in blood in 1638. Open from March through September. George IV Bridge (phone: 225-8839).

Edinburgh Crystal Visitors Centre – Cut-glass items sell like hotcakes in the Edinburgh shops, and here's a chance to see how they are made. Operating in a town about 12 miles (19 km) south of Edinburgh, the *Centre* offers guided tours on weekdays; guests can see the glass blown, sheared and cut. There is also a factory shop on two floors, along with a restaurant. Children under 10 are not allowed. At Eastfield near Penicuik; take Straiton Rd. south from town (phone: 0968-75128).

■ **EXTRA SPECIAL:** The *Edinburgh International Festival* is held every year during the last 3 weeks of August. It features the best-known, most highly regarded performers in opera, music, theater, and dance. Each year brings different orchestras, soloists, theater and opera companies — all are usually topnotch.

Accompanying the festival proper is the phenomenal *Edinburgh Festival Fringe,* an orgy of over 1,000 productions by amateur and lesser-known professional companies from Europe, Great Britain, and the US who come to Edinburgh at their own expense to strike a blow for art and for themselves. The *Edinburgh Military Tattoo,* a spectacular concert in full Highland dress by the massed pipe bands of Her Majesty's Scottish regiments, blasts forth most nights during the festival on the Castle Esplanade.

Coinciding with the first 2 weeks of the *International Festival* is the *Edinburgh International Film Festival.* Entries are screened at 88 Lothian Road, where the rest of the year *Filmhouse* (phone: 228-2688) offers a varied diet of classics and art movies in bijou surroundings with outstanding restaurant and bar facilities. The *Edinburgh International Jazz Festival* convenes during the second week of the festival. Pick up the succession of lively concerts at the Edinburgh Festival Club, in the Edinburgh University Staff Club, 9/15 Chambers St. (phone: 226-5639).

Those interested are advised to reserve tickets — and hotel space — as far in advance as possible, especially for the most popular attractions such as the *Tattoo.* A detailed *Festival* brochure is available at the British Tourist Authority in the US (see *Sources and Resources*) by May or June. Book reservations through a travel agent or write directly to the individual events. For the International Festival, it's the Festival Box Office, 21 Market St., Edinburgh EH1 1BW (phone: 226-4001); for the Tattoo, the Ticket Centre, 31-33 Waverly Bridge, Edinburgh EH1 1QB (phone: 225-3732); and the Edinburgh Festival Fringe Society, 180 High St. (phone: 226-5257 or 226-5259; reservations, 226-5138). The Film and Jazz festivals are more informal and easier to get tickets for once you're in Edinburgh.

SOURCES AND RESOURCES

 TOURIST INFORMATION: The City of Edinburgh Tourist Centre, Waverley Market, 3 Princes St., Edinburgh EH2 2QP (phone: 557-1700), offers information, maps, and leaflets, and stocks all City of Edinburgh publications. On sale there is the *Edinburgh Official Guide,* updated annually. In it is a reasonable working map of downtown areas, with places of interest marked. A good, more detailed map is the Edinburgh number of the *Geographia Street Atlas and Index* series, on sale at most local bookshops. The pamphlets on Edinburgh history and legend at the *Camera Obscura* bookshop (see *Special Places*) will add greatly to your appreciation of what you see of the city. Each costs about $3. For a selection of other publications of local interest, also check the Ticket Centre, Waverley Bridge (phone: 225-1188), open weekdays 10 AM to 4:30 PM; Saturdays, to 12:30 PM; during high summer, open later and on the weekends.

The US Consulate is at 3 Regent Terr. (phone: 556-8315).

The Tourist Centre also has leaflets on guided walking tours in Edinburgh, including tours of the Royal Mile, the New Town, Leith, and a Robert Louis Stevenson trail. Among the assortment is a small foray into the dark side of Edinburgh's history entitled *Ghosts, Ghouls, Gallows.*

For information concerning travel in other parts of Scotland, drop by the new Scottish Travel Centre in St. Andrews Square (phone: 557-5522)

Local Coverage – The *Scotsman,* morning daily; the *Edinburgh Evening News,* evening daily; *What's On,* published monthly by the city, listing forthcoming happenings; another *What's On,* a free, privately owned monthly, available in most hotel lobbies; and *The List,* a comprehensive Glasgow and Edinburgh events guide (phone: 558-1191). Also see the *Festival Times* during the Edinburgh Festival.

Food – See *Restaurants in Edinburgh,* sold by the Tourist Board.

Telephone – The area code for Edinburgh is 031.

 CLIMATE AND CLOTHES: A day with no rain is a rarity, even in summer. When the wind blows, put millstones in your shoes. Mists are not unknown either. Temperatures usually don't go below freezing in winter or over 70F (21C) in summer. A raincoat with a zip-in wool lining that fits over everything you own is part of a recommended survival kit.

 GETTING AROUND: Airport – Edinburgh Airport is about a half-hour from the center of town; the average taxi fare is $11. An "Airlink" bus, #100, travels from the airport to Waverley Bridge, making stops en route at the *Caledonian* hotel and at Haymarket and Murrayfield (phone: 226-5087). The tourist desk at Edinburgh Airport (phone: 333-2167) will provide information.

Bus – *Lothian Region Transport* headquarters is at 14 Queen St. (phone: 554-4494), parallel to Princes St., 2 blocks away. Route maps are no longer available because routes are subject to change every 3 months. The Ticket Centre at Waverley Bridge also houses a City Transport Information Bureau, where details on each current bus route (except for St. Andrew Square Bus Station) can be obtained (phone: 226-5087). Passengers can reach most places from Princes St.; exact fare required. The Tourist Board office can provide information on bus tours of the city and countryside. Longer-distance buses go from St. Andrew Square Bus Station, St. Andrew Sq. (phone: 556-8464).

Car Rental – All major national firms are represented at the airport and in town.

Taxi – There are cabstands at St. Andrew Square Bus Station and in Waverley Station, off Princes St. To call a cab, phone *City Cabs* (phone: 228-1211), *Central Radio Taxis* (phone: 229-2468), or *Radiocabs* (phone: 225-6736 or 225-9000).

Train – The main railway station is Waverley Station at Princes St. and Waverley Bridge (phone: 556-2451). All trains *not* bound for London also stop at Haymarket Station, about 3 blocks west of Princes St. To catch a train here, add about 4 minutes to departure time from Waverley Station.

SPECIAL EVENTS: The *Edinburgh International Festival* and the concurrent *Edinburgh Festival Fringe,* the *Edinburgh Military Tatoo,* the *Edinburgh International Film Festival,* and the *Edinburgh International Jazz Festival* are held every year during the last 3 weeks in August. (For details, see *Extra Special.*) The *Edinburgh Folk Festival* occurs in early spring. For details, contact the Folk Festival office, 16A Fleshmarket Close (phone: 220-0464).

MUSEUMS: The city runs two museums of local history: *Huntly House,* the Canongate (phone: 225-2424, ext. 6689), and the *Lady Stair's House* (a Burns, Scott, and Stevenson museum), Lawnmarket (phone: 225-2424, ext. 6593). The *National Gallery of Scotland,* one of the three Scottish national galleries, is described in *Special Places.* Other museums include the following:

Central Library – An outstanding collection of maps, prints, photographs, books, and newspapers. The Reference, Scotland, and Edinburgh rooms are invaluable. George IV Bridge (phone: 225-5584).

City Art Centre – A particular pride and joy of the City of Edinburgh, this beautifully converted former fruit warehouse now houses Scottish paintings and sculpture, temporary exhibitions of fine arts, and a popular café. Opposite the *Fruitmarket Gallery* at 2-4 Market St. (phone: 225-2424, ext. 6650).

DeMarco Gallery – Headquarters for avant-garde art. 17-21 Blackfriars St. (phone: 557-0707).

Edinburgh Wax Museum – With every notorious Scot from Macbeth to Billy Connolly, and a particularly effective gruesome Chamber of Horrors that makes Mme. Tussaud's look like a high school prom. Admission charge. 142 High St. (phone: 226-4445).

Fruitmarket Gallery – Near the railway station, with a changing program of avant-garde exhibitions from various countries. 29 Market St. (phone: 225-2383).

Holography Gallery – This exhibition above the *Wax Museum*'s knickknack shop has the finest range of holography in North Britain. 140 High St. (phone: 220-1566).

Lauriston Castle – A fine 16th-century tower enlarged to become a historic home; good art and furniture collections. Open weekends only, 2 to 4 PM; guided tours only. Admission charge. Off Cramond Rd. S. (phone: 336-2060 or 225-2424, ext. 6689).

National Library of Scotland – Exhibits on Scotland's literati through the ages. Temporary admission to the reading room may be obtained by serious inquirers. George IV Bridge (phone: 226-4531).

Museum of Childhood – Antique toys, games, dolls, and costumes, all beautifully explained and arranged. 38 High St. (phone: 225-2424, ext. 6646).

National Library of Scotland – Exhibitions on Scotland's literati through the ages. George IV Bridge (phone: 226-4531).

The People's Story – The story of the working class of Edinburgh through the centuries, including sections on the development of trade unions, health, welfare, and leisure. In the Canongate Tollbooth, 163 Canongate (phone: 225-2424, ext. 6679).

Royal Scottish Museum – A museum of natural history, science, and technology, great for kids. Chambers St. (phone: 225-7534).

Russell Collection of Harpischords and Clavichords – A feast for lovers of early keyboard music. Housed in *St. Cecilia's Hall,* a restored 18th-century concert hall, the collection is owned by Edinburgh University. A faculty member lead tours at 2 PM on Wednesdays and Saturdays and at 10:30 AM daily except Sundays during the *Edinburgh Festival.* Admission charge. Corner of Cowgate and Niddry Sts. (phone: 667-1011, ext. 4577).

Scottish National Gallery of Modern Art – Matisse to Picasso. Belford Rd. (phone: 556-8921).

Scottish National Portrait Gallery – Features paintings of Mary Queen of Scots, Robert Burns, Sir Walter Scott, and more. 1 Queen St. (phone: 556-8921).

SHOPPING: Princes Street is Edinburgh's main shopping street, chock-a-block with a variety of stores. In addition, at the east end of Princes Street is Waverley Market, a large, modern shopping mall with Waverley Station at its base and the Tourist Office on the roof. Open daily until 6 PM, except Thursdays until 7 PM. The best buy is in Scottish tartans and woolens. Also worth a look are antiques — particularly Victoriana — in the area around St. Stephen's Street in Stockbridge. Bone china and Scottish crystal are attractive, and don't miss the shortbread, which is on sale everywhere. We especially recommend the following shops:

Debenham's – A branch of the London firm, with clothes, accessories, cosmetics, and more. 109-112 Princes St. (phone: 225-1320).

Edinburgh Woollen Mill – A good, inexpensive alternative to the *Scotch House* 62 Princes St. (phone: 225-4966); 453 Lawnmarket (phone: 225-1525); and 139 Princes St. (phone: 226-3840).

Jenner's Department Store – Sells everything, especially bone china and Scottish crystal. A particularly good selection of fine food items, ideal for packing fancy picnics. Princes and St. David's Sts. (phone: 225-2442).

Pitlochry Knitwear – Bargains in Scottish products, especially sweaters, kilts, and ladies' suits. 28 North Bridge (phone: 225-3893).

James Pringle's Woolen Mill – If it's made of wool, it's probably sold here! Low prices for top-quality goods is the policy of this factory outlet, which also provides free taxi service from your hotel to their door. 70-74 Bangor Rd. (phone: 553-5161).

Scotch House – Classy, expensive woolens such as kilts, sweaters, tweeds, scarves, shawls, and mohairs. 60 Princes St. (phone: 556-1252).

Whisky Shop – This connoisseurs' paradise claims to have the largest selection of whiskies anywhere in the world. Waverly Market (phone: 558-1588).

Also worth visiting is St. Mary's Street. Leading off the Royal Mile, it's rapidly becoming famous for shops selling secondhand clothes, jewelry, and objets d'art.

SPORTS AND FITNESS: Fitness Center – *Meadowbank Sports Centre,* 139 London Rd. (phone: 661-5351), has a large gym with weights and exercise equipment, a 400-meter track, and classes in archery, boxing, fencing, and judo.

Golf – Scotland's national mania. A letter from your home club president or pro should get you into any of the city's 22 courses (you'll usually need it only for the posh, private ones like *Royal Burgess, Bruntsfield,* both in suburban Barnton, and *Muirfield* — home of the world's oldest group of players, the Honourable Company of Edinburgh Golfers — in nearby Gullane). Clubs can be rented. Full details on public courses are listed in the *Edinburgh Official Guide,* in the map *Golf Courses of Scotland,* and in the free leaflet *Golf Courses in Scotland,* all available at the tourist office.

Jogging – A good bet is *Holyrood Park,* near the huge stone palace at the foot of Canongate. An especially popular run is around Arthur's Seat, an extinct volcano in the center of the park.

Skiing – *Hillend Ski Center* on the Pentland Hills is the largest artificial slope in

Great Britain. Equipment for hire. Open daily, 9:30 AM to 9 PM; weekends May through August, 9:30 AM to 5 PM (phone: 445-4433).

Swimming – Have a dip in the luxurious *Royal Commonwealth Pool,* built for the 1970 Commonwealth Games. Open weekdays, 9 AM to 9 PM, weekends, 10 AM to 4 PM. Dalkeith Rd. (phone: 667-7211). For other sports, consult the *Edinburgh Official Guide* and the Edinburgh Tourist Centre's *What's On.*

THEATER: The *King's,* 2 Leven St. (phone: 229-1201), and the *Royal Lyceum,* Grindlay St. (phone: 229-9697), are Edinburgh's two main venues. The *King's* presents everything from occasional touring productions of the finest of London's *National Theatre* to unfunny, patronizing junk. On the other hand, the *Royal Lyceum* has been gaining an increasingly high reputation for presenting interesting productions, primarily of established plays. The *Playhouse,* 20 Greenside Pl. (phone: 557-2590), is a converted cinema where musical productions are staged. The *Traverse,* 112 West Bow (phone: 226-2633), is a small theater which has become internationally known for its productions of avant-garde theater pieces and for presenting the work of new playwrights from all over the world. The *Netherbow,* 43 High St. (phone: 556-9579), and *Theatre Workshop,* 34 Hamilton Pl. (phone: 225-7942), mount small-scale, artistic productions. Schedules are in the dailies and in *The List.*

MUSIC: Classical music is the city's overriding passion. Highbrow musical events are held at *Usher Hall,* Lothian Rd. (phone: 228-1155), where the *Scottish National Orchestra* holds performances on Friday nights at 7:30. The *Scottish Opera Company,* which has excellent standards, has seasons at the *King's,* and also at the *Playhouse* (see *Theater* for addresses), where other famous names in both classical and nonclassical music give concerts. For chamber music and occasional jazz, try *Queen's Hall,* Clerk St. (phone: 668-3456). At *St. Mary's Cathedral,* Palmerston Pl. (phone: 225-6293), evensong is sung on weekday afternoons at 5:15 by a trained choir with boy sopranos. Also, countless amateur groups swell the city's halls and churches. Details are available in the dailies and in *The List.*

NIGHTCLUBS AND NIGHTLIFE: Edinburgh isn't exactly Las Vegas; it isn't even Philadelphia. Discos here are usually filled with a very young crowd, but you could risk the following if you're under thirty: *Zenatec,* 56 Fountainbridge (phone: 229-7733); *Cinderellas Rockerfellas,* 99 St. Stephen St. (phone: 556-0266); and *Outer Limits* (teenagers leave at 11 PM so others can roll up to an after-hours bar), W. Tollcross (phone: 228-3252). *Amphitheatre,* in a deconsecrated movie theater, is officially a nightclub and, as we go to press, *the* place to go; it's on the Lothian Rd. between *Usher Hall* and Princes St. (phone: 229-7670). Jazz and folk music can be heard at bars and hotels around the city; check the *Evening News'* Nightlife page or *What's On* magazine.

BEST IN TOWN

CHECKING IN: In Scotland, it is practically impossible to get a room without an accompanying kippers-to-nuts Big Scottish Breakfast (you pay for it whether you eat it or not). Expect to shell out $155 and up for a double with breakfast in the hotels listed below as expensive; $90 to $155 for those in the moderate category; between $55 and $90 for the cheapies-but-goodies in the inexpensive range. Unless otherwise noted, hotels accept all major credit cards. Should you find it impossible to get into any of our selected hotels, the City of Edinburgh District Council at the airport and in town at the Tourist Centre, Waverley Market, 3 Princes St. (phone: 557-1700), has an accommodations service covering all of Edinburgh and the surrounding district. All telephone numbers are in the 031 area code unless otherwise indicated.

Caledonian – A large, Edwardian, former railroad hotel with 254 rooms, 2 dining rooms, and 3 bars. Recently completely refurbished, it boasts great views of Edinburgh Castle. The new decoration is very engaging, and the rooms have been made infinitely more appealing. Celebrities love it. Phones in rooms. West end of Princes St. (phone: 225-2433). Expensive.

Carlton Highland – This building has been remarkably transformed from an old department store into a grand and sophisticated Victorian hotel. Recently opened with 207 rooms, 2 dining rooms, and a bar. North Bridge, off Princes St. (phone: 556-7277). Expensive.

Dalhousie Castle – Originally built during the 12th century and enlarged ever since (Queen Victoria once stayed here). Now it's a luxury country house hotel with 24 rooms. About 8 miles (13 km) south of Edinburgh (phone: 087-520153). Expensive.

Edinburgh Sheraton – This honey-colored hotel, just off Princes Street, seems architecturally incongruous in the neighborhood, but it can't be beat for its range of modern amenities: 263 very well equipped rooms, a health club and gym, sauna and whirlpool bath, swimming pool, parking, bar, and restaurant. 1 Festival Sq. (phone: 229-9131). Expensive.

George – In the New Town, between Charlotte and St. Andrew Squares, it's known for its gracious comfort. It has 195 bedrooms, 2 dining rooms, and a long bar. Phones in rooms. 19-21 George St. (phone: 225-1251). Expensive.

Hilton National – A flashy, contemporary property away from the center of things but with a beautiful view of the Water of Leith and close to Dean Village and the *Museum of Modern Art.* There are 146 rooms and 2 restaurants. 69 Belford Rd. (phone: 332-2545). Expensive.

King James Thistle – An oasis of charm and friendliness in St. James Centre (otherwise known as Edinburgh's leading eyesore). Guests are treated graciously by the staff of this 147-room hotel; the *St. Jacques* restaurant offers Scots food prepared *à la France.* Top of Leith Walk at Princes St. (phone: 556-0111). Expensive.

Ladbroke Dragonara – A flashy, contemporary property away from the center of things but with a beautiful view of the Water of Leith and close to Dean Village and the *Museum of Modern Art.* There are 146 rooms (with phones) and 2 restaurants. 69 Belford Rd. (phone: 332-2545). Expensive.

Post House – An ultramodern, all-conveniences affair, this is a good place to be if you have a car (it's beside the zoo, outside the city center). Its low-priced coffeehouse is less stuffily British than almost anywhere else. Breakfast optional. All 208 rooms have phones. Corstorphine Rd. (phone: 334-0390). Expensive.

Royal Scot – This 252-room modern structure is the epitome of the faultless airport hotel. Direct access to M8 for Glasgow. 111 Glasgow Rd. (phone: 334-9191). Expensive.

Howard – Its flower-filled window boxes are the last word in winsomeness. It has 25 rooms, with phones (and, surprisingly for a hotel this size, private baths). 32-36 Great King St. (phone: 557-3500). Expensive to moderate.

Braid Hills – Muriel Spark fans will remember that this is where Miss Jean Brodie, by then past her prime, took tea. An old, established, family-run, 68-room hotel in the southern suburbs toward the Pentland Hills. 134 Braid Rd. (phone: 447-8888). Moderate.

Donmaree – This sweet little family hotel, in a respectable suburb, has 17 rooms. 21 Mayfield Gardens (phone: 667-3641). Moderate to inexpensive.

Galloway Guest House – Not as well equipped as the *Donmaree* (none of the 10 rooms has a phone), but more centrally located, just off the panoramic Dean Bridge, and the room rate includes breakfast. Dinner served off-season only, but guests have limited access to the kitchen. No credit cards. 22 Dean Park Crescent (phone: 332-3672). Inexpensive.

 EATING OUT: Reports on Scottish food vary from calling it a joke to claiming it is at least superior to English cooking. Still, visitors might want to try some of the following specialties: cock-a-leekie soup (chicken and leek), salmon, haddock, trout, and Aberdeen Angus beef. Skip any offering of haggis (spicy intestines) except on a purely experimental basis. Scones originated in Scotland, and shortbread shouldn't be missed. Restaurants usually keep the city's formal hours (lunch until 2:30, dinner anywhere from 6 on). Expect to pay $45 and up for dinner for two, excluding wine and tips, in establishments listed as very expensive; $30 to $45 for expensive; $30 to $50 in moderate establishments; and under $30 in inexpensive places. All telephone numbers are in the 031 area code unless otherwise indicated.

Pompadour – The fascinating lunch menu here is a steadily unfurling history of Scots cooking; dinners feature French cuisine. In the *Caledonian* hotel, Princes St. (phone: 225-2433). Very expensive.

L'Auberge – A discreet, indeed positively diplomatic, restaurant that serves French fare, most notably fish and game. Open daily. 56 St. Mary's St. between Cowgate and Canongate (phone: 556-5888). Expensive.

Beehive Inn – Among the fittings in this Old Town restaurant is a cell door from the very old town jail. Steaks and fish are served from an open charcoal grill and are followed by luscious desserts. Closed Sundays. Major credit cards. 18 Grassmarket (phone: 225-7171). Expensive.

Cosmo's – Edinburgh's link to Rome. Everybody who works here is fiercely Italian, as is the menu. Fabulous seafood and veal; the cocktail bar is made of imported Italian marble. Closed Sundays and Mondays. Reservations necessary. Major credit cards. 58A Castle St. (phone: 226-6743). Expensive.

Howtowdie – White tablecloths and glass cases full of taxidermists' birds set the tone at this Highland-style establishment long famed for its ritzy image and traditional Scottish cooking. Closed Sundays, October to April. Reservations necessary. 27A Stafford St. (phone: 225-6291). Expensive.

Merchant's – A trendy French restaurant with white tablecloths, silver, crystal, and waitresses wearing trousers; there's also a green parrot that sleeps at lunchtime and can be pacified at dinner with a monkey-nut. Closed Sundays. 17 Merchant St. (phone: 225-4009). Expensive.

Prestonfield House – A 300-year-old country estate within its own peacock-laden park grounds. Candlelit dinners in rooms with tapestries, paintings, and blazing open fires. French cooking. Reservations necessary. Major credit cards. Off Priestfield Rd. (phone: 667-8000). Expensive.

Arches – The dining room adjoining this bustling university-area bar has very good lunches and elegant dinners. Open daily. 66-67 South Bridge (phone: 556-0200). Moderate.

Blake's – An upmarket establishment (formerly *Nimmo's*) serving à la carte seafood, steaks, and rack of lamb. There's also a charming wine bar. Closed Saturdays for lunch. Reservations advised. 101 Shandwick Pl. (phone: 229-6119). Moderate.

Shamiana – Tandoori (Indian) food at its finest. Everything is cooked from scratch with delicate spices. Pale pink tablecloths, bone china, waitresses in saris, give the place a rarefied air. Open daily from 6 to 11:30 PM; lunch weekdays from 12 to 2 PM. Reservations necessary. Major credit cards. 14A Brougham St. (phone: 228-2265). Moderate.

Skipper's Bistro – A jolly waterfront seafood restaurant in Leith, justly famous for its imaginative preparations and the freshness of its ingredients. Reservations necessary. Closed Sundays. 1A Dock Pl., Leith (phone: 554-1018). Moderate.

Stockbridge Steak House – Offering steaks but also stressing other examples of Scottish and Irish cuisine. 42 St. Stephen St. (phone: 226-5877). Moderate.

Helios Fountain – Among other specialties featured at this trendy café is a selection of vegetarian pies and goulashes invented each morning by the hip proprietors in time for lunch. It's a great spot for eavesdropping on intellectual conversations or for watching people browse over the books and jewelry-making materials also sold here. Open from 10 AM to 6 PM; closed Sundays. 7 Grassmarket (phone: 229-7884). Inexpensive.

Henderson's Salad Table – This cafeteria-style vegetarian's heaven-on-earth may keep diners standing in line for as long as 15 minutes, but it's worth it. Piles of salads, hot pots, opulent desserts available continuously day and evening. Closed Sundays. 94 Hanover St. (phone: 225-2131). Inexpensive.

SHARING A PINT: Until recently, boozing was restricted to puritanical hours. But now it's possible to imbibe from 11 AM to 11 PM, and a few places have opened up where the taps keep flowing until the wee hours. Among the best pubs: the *Abbotsford,* 3 Rose St. (phone: 225-5276), is a haunt of Scotland's "Makars" (playwrights and poets) and journalists; *Bennet's,* Leven St. (phone: 229-5143), is a noisy but atmospheric theater-district pub with a Victorian hangover; the *Beau Brummel,* 99 Hanover St. (phone: 225-4680), is a neo-Regency plush artifact in mid-city; and the *Tilted Wig,* 3 Cumberland St. (phone: 556-1824), facetiously known as the Wilted Twig, is notable for its uncompromising trendiness and has a clientele of bar-hogging English smoothies, whom you can scatter at a stroke by standing in the doorway shouting, "Nigel, your MG's on fire!" For enjoyable courtyard drinking facilities, join the crowd of university students at the *Pear Tree,* 36 W. Nicolson St., off Buccleuch St. (phone: 667-7796). For folk music, try the *Fiddler's Arms,* 9-11 Grassmarket (phone: 229-2665).

Rutherford's, Drummond St., off South Bridge opposite Old College, was much frequented by Robert Louis Stevenson and Arthur Conan Doyle when they were university students in the 1870s, although they never knowingly met. *Stewart's,* across the road, is a fine working-class pub, and if the private back room is free, you and your friends can occupy it for an old-fashioned disputatious Scottish inquiry into philosophy — see Scott's *Guy Mannering. Preservation Hall,* 9 Victoria St. (phone: 226-3816), opposite the *Bookfare* bookshop, is large, commodious, ornamented with fine epigraphs against drink, and offers rock and jazz music evenings. *Mather's,* 25 Broughton St. (phone: 556-6754), is the ecumenical watering hole for left-wing labor, nationalist, and sexual politicos. Opulent barges sometimes carry licenses in tourist season on the Leith waterfront. Find out at the *Waterfront Wine Bar,* 1C Dock Pl., Leith (phone: 554-7427). Also try *The Malt Shovel,* 57 Shore, Leith (phone: 554-8784). Both offer bar lunches.

FLORENCE

Florence, city of the arts, jewel of the Renaissance, symbol of the Tuscan pride in grace and refinement, is for many an acquired taste. Rome has romance, Venice intrigue, and Naples a poignant gaiety; Florence may seem too austere, too serious, too severe. The elegance that is Florence does not seize you immediately — not like the splashing fountains of Rome, the noisy laughter and song of Naples, the pastel chandeliers peeking out of patrician palaces along Venice's Grand Canal.

Next to the mellow tangerine hues of Rome, the pinks of Venice, and the orgy of color that is Naples, Florence is a study in neutral shades: blacks and whites, beiges and browns, a splattering of dark green. Its people seem less spontaneous and exuberant than Romans or Neapolitans, more hard-working and reserved, with a sort of innate sense of dignity and pride.

Florentine palaces are more like fortresses, at first glance rather forbidding and uninviting to the visitor; the city's somber streets are lined with solid, direct architecture; its civic sculpture is noble and restrained. But this is only a superficial view of Florence. Step into the palaces and you will be awed by the beauty of fine details as well as by some of the world's greatest art treasures. Look at the fine Florentine crafts in gold and leather and exquisite fabrics in the elegant but classically serious shops. It won't take long before you will understand why the culture and art of Florence have attracted people from around the world through the centuries, and why it is as much a favorite of artists, students, and expatriates today as it was at its apogee under the Medicis in the 15th century.

Florence was the home of Cimabue and Giotto, the fathers of Italian painting; of Brunelleschi, Donatello, and Masaccio, who paved the way for the Renaissance; of the Della Robbias, Botticelli, Leonardo da Vinci, and Michelangelo; of Dante Alighieri, Petrarch, and Boccaccio; of Machiavelli and Galileo. Art, science, and life found their finest, most powerful expression in Florence, and records of this splendid past fill the city's many galleries, museums, churches, and palaces, demanding attention.

Florence — *Firenze* in Italian — probably originated as an Etruscan center, but it was only under the Romans in the 1st century BC that it became a true city. Like so many other cities of its time, Roman Florence grew up along the fertile banks of a river, in this case the Arno, amid the rolling green hills of Tuscany. Its Latin name, *Florentia* ("flowering"), probably referred to the city's florid growth, although some ancient historians attributed it to Florinus, the Roman general who besieged the nearby Etruscan hill town of Fiesole in 63 BC.

During the Roman rule, Florence became a thriving military and trading center, with its share of temples, baths, a town hall, and an amphitheater, but few architectural monuments of that epoch have survived. After the fall of

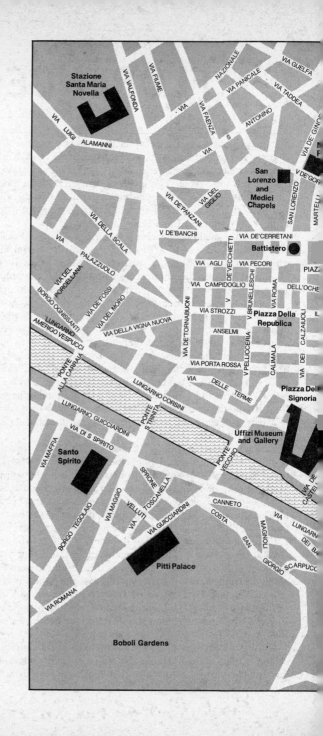

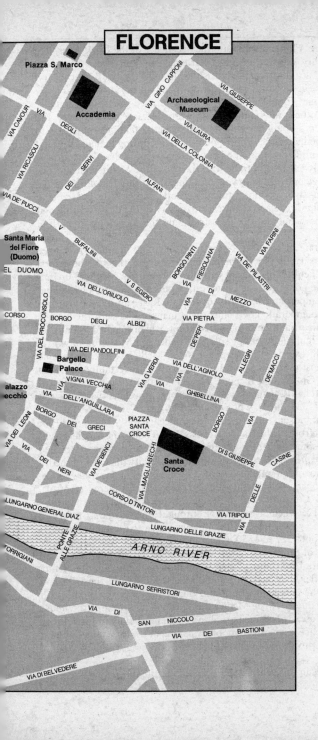

FLORENCE

Piazza S. Marco

Accademia

VIA GINO CAPPONI

VIA GIUSEPPE

Archaeological Museum

VIA CAVOUR

VIA

DEGLI

VIA RICASOLI

DEI

SERVI

VIA DE' PUCCI

VIA LAURA

VIA DELLA COLONNA

ALFANI

Santa Maria del Fiore (Duomo)

EL DUOMO

V BUFALINI

VIA DELL'ORIUOLO

V S EGIDIO

BORGO PINTI

VIA FIESOLANA

VIA DE PILASTRI

VIA FARINI

VIA

DI

MEZZO

CORSO

VIA DEL PROCONSOLO

BORGO

DEGLI

ALBIZI

VIA PIETRA

DE' PEPI

VIA DEI PANDOLFINI

Bargello Palace

VIA G.VERDI

VIA DELL'AGNOLO

ALLEGRI

DE MACCI

VIGNA VECCHIA

VIA

alazzo ecchio

VIA

DELL'ANGUILLARA

GHIBELLINA

BORGO

VIA

BORGO

DEI

LEONI

DEI

GRECI

PIAZZA SANTA CROCE

VIA. MAGLIABECHI

VIA DE BENCI

Santa Croce

DI S GIUSEPPE

CASINE

VIA

DEI

NERI

CORSO D TINTORI

DELLE

VIA TRIPOLI

VIA

LUNGARNO GENERAL DIAZ

LUNGARNO DELLE GRAZIE

PONTE ALLE GRAZIE

TORRIGIANI

ARNO RIVER

LUNGARNO SERRISTORI

VIA

DI

SAN

NICCOLO

VIA

DEI

BASTIONI

VIA DI BELVEDERE

the Roman Empire, Florence sank into the decadence of the Dark Ages, and despite a temporary reprieve during Charlemagne's 8th- and 9th-century European empire, it did not really flourish again until the late 11th century. It was then that the great guilds were developed and the florin-based currency began to appear, and Florence became a powerful, self-governing republic.

In the 12th century, interfamily feuds were widespread, and over 150 square stone towers — built for defense by influential families right next to their houses — dominated the city's skyline. Even so, during that and the next century, the Florentine population of about 60,000 (twice that of London at the time) was busily engaged in trade with the rest of the Mediterranean. The amazing building boom that followed, bringing about the demolition of the fortified houses in favor of more gracious public and private *palazzi* and magnificent churches, reflected the great prosperity of the city's trading and banking families, its wool and silk industries, and the enormous strength of the florin.

As a free city-state or *comune,* Florence managed to maintain a balance between the authority of the Germanic emperors and that of the popes, overcoming the difficulties of internal struggles between the burgher Guelphs (who supported the pope) and the aristocratic Ghibellines (who were behind the Holy Roman Emperor). Eventually, by the late 13th century, the Guelphs won power and a democratic government was inaugurated with the famous Ordinances of Justice. So began Florence's ascent, which spanned 3 centuries and reached its height and greatest splendor under the Medici family.

Owing in large measure to the patronage of the Medicis, Florence became the liveliest and most creative city in Europe. While this certainly pertained during the time of Giovanni di Bicci de' Medici (1360–1429) and his illustrious dynasty of merchants, bankers, and art patrons, as well as that of his son Cosimo the Elder (1389–1464), who continued to gather artists around him, it was Cosimo's grandson Lorenzo the Magnificent (1449–1492) who put Florence in the forefront of the Italian Renaissance. Today, the Medici might be thought of as something of a political machine, since they controlled — through their wealth and personal power alone — a city that was, in theory at least, still a democratic republic governed by members of the trade guilds. Their *de facto* rule was not uncontested, however. They suffered reversals, such as the Pazzi Conspiracy in 1478, and twice they were expelled — from 1494 to 1512, when a revolution brought the religious reformer Savonarola briefly to power (and an attempt was made to reestablish democracy), and again from 1527 to 1530, when another republic was set up, only to fall to the troops of Emperor Charles V and lead to the Medici restoration.

Finally, in the late 16th century, their glory days behind them, the Medici gained an official title. They became grand dukes (Cosimo I was the first), and Florence became the capital of the grand duchy of Tuscany. In the 18th century, the grand duchy of the Medici was succeeded by that of the house of Lorraine, until Tuscany became part of the kingdom of Italy in 1860. From 1865 to 1871, Florence reigned as temporary capital of the kingdom, but with the capital's transfer to Rome, the history of Florence merges with that of the rest of Italy.

Two catastrophes in this century have caused inestimable damage to Florence's art treasures. In 1944, all the beloved bridges crossing the Arno — except for the Ponte Vecchio — were blown up by the Nazis. Reconstruction began as soon as the Germans retreated. Then, 2 decades later, in November 1966, the Arno burst its banks, covering the historic center with a muddy slime. Over 1,400 works of art, 2 million valuable books, and countless homes were damaged by floodwaters that reached depths of 23 feet. The people of Florence, with help from all over the world, rose to the challenge. Before the floodwaters had receded, they began the painstaking chore of rescuing their treasures from 600,000 tons of mud, oil, and debris.

Today, the city of Florence — with a population of more than half a million — is still a vital force in the arts, in culture, and in science, as well as an industrial, commercial, and university center and a leader in the fields of handicrafts and fashion. Note, indeed, how the Florentines dress, their fine attention to detail and the remarkable sense of style that turns an ordinary outfit into something personal and very special. And note the almost challenging local swagger. Then realize that these are people who wake up every morning to the marvels of Michelangelo, who literally live in a textbook of the 15th-century Renaissance. Their artistic and cultural heritage is unsurpassed, truly unique in the world. No doubt you'll agree, they have every reason to be proud.

FLORENCE AT-A-GLANCE

SEEING THE CITY: The picture-postcard view of Florence is the one from Piazzale Michelangelo, on the far side of the Arno. From here, more than 300 feet above sea level, the eye embraces the entire city and neighboring hill towns as far as Pistoia, but it is the foreground that rivets the attention. The Arno, with all its bridges, from Ponte San Niccolò to Ponte della Vittoria, the Palazzo Vecchio, with its tower and crenelations, the *Uffizi,* the flank of Santa Croce, numerous spires and domes — all are in the picture. And looming over the whole, like a whale washed ashore in the land of Lilliput, is the massive Duomo, with its bell tower and giant red cupola. The *piazzale* is reached by a splendid tree-lined avenue, called the Viale dei Colli, which begins at Ponte San Niccolò and winds up to the enormous square under the name of Viale Michelangelo. It then proceeds beyond the square as far as the Porta Romana under the names of Viale Galileo and Viale Machiavelli. From the bridge to the Roman Gate is a scenic 4-mile walk, but it's also possible to trace the same route aboard bus #13 from the station. Another extraordinary view, of Florence and the entire Arno Valley, can be enjoyed from the lookout terrace just before the Church of St. Francis, perched on a hill studded with cypress trees and sumptuous villas in neighboring Fiesole (see *Special Places*).

SPECIAL PLACES: The Arno is a good orientation point for first-time visitors to Florence. Most of the city sits on the north, or right, bank of the river, including its principal squares: Piazza del Duomo, the religious heart of Florence; Piazza della Repubblica, its bustling commercial center; and Piazza della Signoria, the ancient political center and today a favorite meeting place because of its outdoor cafés. The most elegant shopping street, Via Tornabuoni, runs from the Arno to Piazza Antinori. The other side of the river is known as the Oltrarno, literally, "beyond the Arno." Sights here include the *Pitti Palace* and

Boboli Gardens, the churches of Santo Spirito and Santa Maria del Carmine, and Piazzale Michelangelo.

THE CATHEDRAL (DUOMO) COMPLEX

Il Duomo (The Cathedral) – The Cathedral of Santa Maria del Fiore was begun in 1296 by the Sienese architect Arnolfo di Cambio and took 173 years to complete. Dominating a large double square, it is the fourth longest church in the world (after St. Peter's in Rome, St. Paul's in London, and the church of Milan) and is said to be capable of holding over 20,000 people. The gigantic project was financed by the Florentine republic and the Clothmakers Guild in an age of faith when every city-state aspired to claim the biggest and most important cathedral as its own. Besides religious services, the Duomo has served as the site of major civic ceremonies and many noteworthy historical events, such as the Pazzi Conspiracy, when Giuliano de' Medici was assassinated in 1478. The original façade, never completed, was destroyed in the 16th century and replaced in the late 19th century. Whereas the exterior walls are encased in colorful marble (white from Carrara, green from Prato, and pink from Siena), the interior seems plain and cold by comparison, a brownish-gray sandstone called *pietra forte* and soberly decorated in keeping with the Florentine character. Most of the original statuary that adorned the Duomo, including, most recently, Michelangelo's unfinished *Pietà,* has been moved to the *Museo dell'Opera del Duomo* (see below). The remains of the ancient church of Santa Reparata, the original cathedral of Florence, which came to light under the Duomo during the extensive excavation after the 1966 flood, are very interesting (take the staircase near the entrance on the right side of the nave). The crypt is particularly haunting.

The public competition for the design of the dome was won by a Florentine, Filippo Brunelleschi, who had marveled at the great engineering feat of ancient Rome, the dome of the Pantheon. The Renaissance architect's mighty cupola, built between 1420 and 1436, the first since antiquity, subsequently inspired Michelangelo as he faced the important task of designing the dome of St. Peter's in Rome. Brunelleschi's dome surpasses both the Pantheon and St. Peter's, although today it is seriously cracked and monitored by computer. Over 371 feet high and 148 feet across, it has double walls between which a 463-step staircase leads to a lantern at the top (also a Brunelleschi design). Restorations have been under way for more than a decade and, due to the necessity of scaffolding — not to mention the huge green canvas drape — there is little available light for viewing the dome's immense fresco (begun by Vasari). Still, the 40-minute climb up and down is well worth the effort for the breathtaking panorama from the top and for a true sense of the awesome size of this artistic and technical masterpiece. No, Virginia, there is no elevator.

Il Campanile (Bell Tower) – The graceful free-standing belfry of the Duomo, one of the most unusual in Italy, was begun by Giotto in 1334 (when he was 67) and eventually completed by Francesco Talenti. The bas-reliefs adorning the base are copies of originals by Giotto and Luca della Robbia that have been removed to the *Duomo Museum,* as have the statues of the Prophets (done by various artists, including Donatello) that stood in the niches. The 414-stair climb to the top leads to a terrace with another bird's-eye view of Florence. There's no elevator.

Il Battistero (The Baptistry) – The baptistry, dedicated to St. John the Baptist, the patron saint of Florence, is a unique treasure, the origins of which are lost in time. The octagonal building may date to the 4th century, contemporary with the Church of Santa Reparata, while the exterior of white and green marble dates to the 12th century and is typical of the Tuscan Romanesque style, with an Oriental influence. To this day, the baptistry is still used for baptisms, and many a famous Florentine (such as Dante Alighieri) has been baptized here. On the *Feast of St. John* (June 24), the relics of the saint are displayed in the building and candles are lit in his honor (see *Special Events*).

The interior is covered with magnificent Byzantine mosaics by 13th- and 14th-century Florentine and Venetian masters, but it is the three gilded bronze doorways that are the main tourist attraction. The *south door,* by Andrea Pisano, is the oldest, dating from the early 14th century. In the Gothic style, it has 28 panels with reliefs of the life of St. John the Baptist and the cardinal and theological virtues. The *north door* (1403–1424), in late Gothic style, was the result of a competition in which the unanimous winner was Lorenzo Ghiberti (Brunelleschi was among the competitors). It, too, is divided into 28 panels depicting scenes from the life of Christ, the Evangelists, and the Doctors of the Church. Ghiberti's east door, however, facing the cathedral, is his masterpiece. In full Renaissance style, it was defined by Michelangelo as worthy of being the "gate of paradise." Begun in 1425 and completed in 1452, when Ghiberti was 74 years old, it consists of 10 panels illustrating Old Testament stories and medallions containing self-portraits of Ghiberti and his adopted son, Vittorio (who designed the frame), as well as portraits of their principal contemporaries.

There are admission charges to visit the cathedral dome (closed Sundays and holidays), the crypt, and the bell tower (both closed Sunday and holiday afternoons). Piazza del Duomo.

Museo dell'Opera del Duomo (Duomo Museum) – Masterpieces from the cathedral, the baptistry, and the bell tower are here, especially sculpture: Michelangelo's unfinished *Pietà* (third of his four), Donatello's *Mary Magdalene,* the famous choir lofts (*cantorie*) by Luca della Robbia and Donatello, the precious silver altar frontal from the baptistry, fragments from the original cathedral façade, even the original wooden scale model of Brunelleschi's dome. Closed Sunday afternoons; admission charge. 9 Piazza del Duomo.

ELSEWHERE DOWNTOWN

Galleria degli Uffizi (Uffizi Museum and Gallery) – Italy's most important art museum is in a Renaissance palace built on the site of an 11th-century church (San Piero Scheraggio), the remains of which are incorporated in the palazzo and may still be seen. The splendor of this museum derives not only from the great works it contains but also from the 16th-century building itself, which was commissioned by Cosimo I and designed by Vasari (completed by Buontalenti) to house the Medicis' administrative offices, or *uffizi.* In 1581, Francesco I began converting the top floor into an art museum destined to become one of the world's greatest. The three corridors, with light streaming through their great windows, are a spectacle in themselves, and the collection they contain is so vast — the most important Italian and European paintings of the 13th through the 18th century — that we suggest taking along a good guide or guidebook (Luciano Berti's is excellent) and comfortable shoes. Remember also to allow more time for a visit here than you think you'll need. At the top of the monumental staircase (there is also an elevator) on the second floor is the Prints and Drawings Collection; the museum proper (painting and sculpture) is on the third floor. Fifteen rooms are devoted to Florentine and Tuscan masterpieces, including the work of Cimabue, Giotto, Fra Filippo Lippi, Paolo Uccello, Fra Angelico, Da Vinci, and Michelangelo, not to mention such other non-Florentine masters as Raphael, Titian, Tintoretto, Caravaggio, Rubens, Van Dyck, and Rembrandt. The Botticelli Room contains the master's *Birth of Venus* and his restored *Allegoria della Primavera* (Allegory of Spring) as well as other allegorical and mythological works that make this the most important Botticelli collection in the world.

For diehards, there is an important collection of self-portraits lining the Corridoio Vasariano (Vasari Corridor) that may be visited by special arrangement. The portraits include those of Raphael, Rubens, Van Dyck, Velázquez, Bernini, Canova, Corot, Fattori, and Chagall. Even without the portraits, the half-mile walk would be fascinating. The corridor is actually a raised passageway built in the 1560s to allow members of the Medici court to move from their old palace and offices (Palazzo Vecchio and Uffizi) to their new palace (Palazzo Pitti) without having to resort to the streets. It crosses the river on the tops of shops on the Ponte Vecchio and affords splendid views of the Arno, the Church of Santa Felicità, and the Boboli Gardens. Closed Mondays and Sunday and holiday afternoons; admission charge. To visit the Vasari Corridor, write well in advance to the Uffizi (there's no extra fee). 6 Loggiato degli Uffizi (phone: 218341).

Palazzo della Signoria or Palazzo Vecchio (Old Palace) – This fortress-like palace, built by Arnolfo di Cambio between 1298 and 1314 as the seat of Florence's new democratic government of *priori,* or guild leaders, began as Florence's Town Hall and is still just that. From 1540 to 1550, it was temporarily the residence of the Medicis as they progressed from their ancestral home, the Medici-Riccardi Palace, to their new home in the Palazzo Pitti. Although in a rather severe Gothic style, it is at once powerful and graceful, with a lofty tower 308 feet high. Beyond its rusticated façade is an elaborately ornate courtyard highlighted by Verrocchio's delightful fountain of a bronze cherub holding a dolphin (1476). The medieval austerity of the exterior also contrasts with the sumptuous apartments inside. The massive Salone dei Cinquecento (Salon of the Five Hundred) on the first floor, built in 1496 for Savonarola's short-lived republican Council of Five Hundred, is decorated with frescoes by Vasari. Also, don't miss Vasari's *studiolo,* Francesco de' Medici's gem of a study, with magnificent armadio doors painted by artists of the schools of Bronzino and Vasari. On the third floor is a new exhibition of 140 works of art removed from Italy by the Nazis and recovered by Rodolfo Siviero, the famed Italian art sleuth. Closed Saturdays and Sunday and holiday afternoons; admission charge. Piazza della Signoria (phone: 27681).

Loggia dei Lanzi or Loggia della Signoria – Built between 1379 and 1 for the election and proclamation of public officials and other ceremonies, it took its name in the 16th century from Cosimo I's Germano-Swiss mercenary soldiers (known in Italian as *lanzichenecchi*), who were stationed here. Today the *loggia* is a delightful open-air museum with masterpieces of sculpture from various periods under its arches. Particularly noteworthy are Cellini's *Perseus* and Giambologna's *Rape of the Sabines.* Piazza della Signoria.

Ponte Vecchio – The "old bridge" is indeed Florence's oldest and the only one to survive the Nazi destruction in 1944, although the houses at either end were blown up by the Germans. Built on the site of a Roman crossing, the first stone version was swept away in a flood in 1333 and rebuilt in 1345 as it is now, with rows of shops lining both sides (the backs of which, supported on brackets, overhang the Arno). They were occupied by butchers until Cosimo I assigned them to gold- and silversmiths in the late 16th century.

Palazzo Pitti e Galleria Palatina (Pitti Palace and Palatine Gallery) – On the side of the Arno opposite the *Uffizi,* and a few blocks from the riverbank, is a rugged, austere, 15th-century palace built to the plans of Brunelleschi, originally for the Pitti family. When it was bought by Cosimo I and his wife, Eleonora of Toledo, in the 16th century, it was enlarged and became the seat of the Medici grand dukes and later of the Savoy royal family until 1871. The enormous building now houses several museums: The *Galleria Palatina,* upstairs on the first floor and one of the must-sees, is devoted to 16th- and 17th-century art — works by Raphael (11 in all), Rubens, Murillo, Andrea del Sarto, Fra Filippo Lippi, Titian, Veronese, and Tintoretto, to name a few (there are over 650) — arranged in no apparent order. The gallery, in fact, still resembles a sumptuous apartment in a palace more than a museum. Priceless masterpieces seem to hang at random in elaborately decorated rooms filled with tapestries, frescoes, and gilded stuccoes. The Appartamenti Monumentali (Royal Apartments), in another wing of the same floor and once inhabited in turn by the Medici, Lorraine, and

Savoy families, reopened in 1989 after 2 years of restoration work. The *Museo degli Argenti* (Silver Museum), occupying 16 rooms on the ground floor and another must-see, is filled not only with silverware but also with gold, jewels, cameos, tapestries, furniture, crystal, and ivory of the Medicis. Still another museum, the *Galleria d'Arte Moderna,* on the second floor, houses mainly 19th-century Tuscan works. There is also a *Coach and Carriage Museum* (temporarily closed). An entrance on the left side of the palace leads to the Boboli Gardens, which extend for acres and are open until dusk. A delightful example of a 16th-century Italian garden, they were laid out for Eleonora of Toledo and are studded with cypress trees, unusual statuary, grottoes, and fountains — plus the *Museo delle Porcellane* (Porcelain Museum) and the fairly new *Galleria del Costume* (Costume Gallery) in the Palazzina della Meridiana.

The *Palatine Gallery* (phone: 210323), the *Gallery of Modern Art* (phone: 287096), the *Silver Museum* (phone: 212557), and the *Costume Gallery* (phone: 212557) are open daily except Mondays. One admission charge covers the *Palatine Gallery,* the *Silver Museum,* and the Royal Apartments. The *Gallery of Modern Art* charges a separate admission. No admission charge to the Boboli Gardens (phone: 213440), *Porcelain Museum,* and *Costume Gallery.* Piazza dei Pitti (phone: 213440).

Palazzo del Bargello e Museo Nazionale (Bargello Palace and National Museum) – The *Bargello* is to sculpture what the *Uffizi* is to painting, yet for some reason it is visited far less frequently by tourists. The building, the *Palazzo del Podestà,* is one of the finest and best-preserved examples of Florence's 13th- and 14th-century medieval architecture. Inside, the entire school of Florentine and Tuscan sculpture is represented: Donatello, Verrocchio, Cellini, Michelangelo, the Della Robbias, and others. Closed Mondays; admission charge. 4 Via del Proconsolo (phone: 210801).

Santa Croce (Church of the Holy Cross) – Italy's largest and best-known Franciscan church, Santa Croce was begun late in the 13th century and was enriched over the centuries with numerous works of art as well as tombs of many famous Italians, including Michelangelo, Machiavelli, Rossini, and Galileo (there is a funeral monument to Dante here, but he is buried in Ravenna). Under Santa Croce are the remains of an earlier chapel founded by St. Francis of Assisi in 1228. The church is particularly noteworthy for a wooden crucifix by Donatello, for chapels with frescoes by Taddeo and Agnolo Gaddi, and above all for the fresco cycles by Giotto in the Bardi and Peruzzi chapels. Go outside the church and turn left to visit the 14th-century cloister and the 15th-century Pazzi Chapel, a Renaissance gem by Brunelleschi, designed at the height of his career. During the 1966 flood, the waters reached the top of the cloister's arches and damage here was particularly severe. Piazza Santa Croce.

Galleria dell'Accademia (Academy of Fine Arts Gallery) – Michelangelo's original *David* was brought here from Piazza della Signoria (where one of many first-rate copies takes its place) in 1873. Since then, millions of visitors have come just to see this monumental sculpture (about a million a year now) carved from a single block of Carrara marble and, in the same room, the four unfinished *Slaves* that Michelangelo meant to adorn Pope Julius II's unrealized tomb for St. Peter's in Rome. In the summer, lines form down the street and the doors often close when it gets too crowded. Unfortunately, many visitors ignore the rich collection of Florentine paintings — from 13th-century Primitives to 16th-century Mannerists — and the five new rooms opened in 1985 to display works that had never before been shown to the public. These include 14th- and 15th-century works and an extraordinary collection of Russian icons brought to Florence by the Lorraines when they succeeded the Medicis during the first half of the 18th century. Closed Mondays; admission charge. 60 Via Ricasoli (phone: 214375).

Convento di San Marco (Museum of St. Mark) – Vasari described this monastery as a perfect example of monastic architecture. It was built in the 15th century by the Medici architect Michelozzo (who actually rebuilt a more ancient Dominican monastery) and its walls — as well as more than 40 monks' cells — were frescoed by Fra

Angelico (and his assistants), who lived here as a monk from 1438 to 1445. Now a Fra Angelico museum, it contains panel paintings brought from various churches and galleries in addition to the painter's wonderful *Crucifixion* (in the chapter house across the cloister) and his exquisite *Annunciation* (at the top of the stairs leading to the dormitory). In addition to the cells decorated by Fra Angelico, see the one used by the reforming martyr Savonarola. There are also paintings by Fra Bartolomeo (see his portrait of Savonarola), Ghirlandaio, Paolo Uccello, and others. Closed Mondays, admission charge. 1 Piazza San Marco (phone: 210741).

Piazza della Santissima Annunziata (Square of the Most Holy Annunciation) – This square best preserves the essence of the Florentine Renaissance spirit. It has porticoes on three sides, a 16th-century palace (by Ammannati) on the fourth, plus an early-17th-century equestrian statue of Ferdinando I de' Medici by Giambologna in the middle. Most interesting is the portico on the east side, that of the Spedale degli Innocenti (Hospital of the Innocents), built in the early 15th century by Brunelleschi as a home for orphans and abandoned children, one of Florence's oldest charity institutions and the world's first foundling hospital. Except for the two imitations at either end, the ceramic tondos of swaddled babies are by Andrea della Robbia. Inside, the *Galleria dello Spedale degli Innocenti* (closed Wednesdays; admission charge) contains works by Ghirlandaio and others.

The Chiesa della Santissima Annunziata (Church of the Most Holy Annunciation), on the north side of the square, is much loved by Florentine brides, who traditionally leave their bouquets at one of its altars after the wedding ceremony. The church was founded in the 13th century, but rebuilt in the 15th century by Michelozzo. The left door of the church portico leads into the Chiostro dei Morti (Cloister of the Dead), which contains the *Madonna del Sacco,* a famous fresco by Andrea del Sarto. The middle door leads into the church via the Chiostrino dei Voti (Little Cloister of the Vows), with frescoes by several famous artists of the 16th century, including Del Sarto, Pontormo, and Rosso Fiorentino. Of the numerous artworks in the church itself, Andrea del Castagno's fresco of the Trinity, over the altar of the second chapel on the left, is one of the most prized.

Chiesa di San Lorenzo (Church of St. Lawrence) – This 15th-century Renaissance building was designed by Brunelleschi as the Medici parish church. A later façade, by Michelangelo, was never completed. Make your way to the Sagrestia Vecchia (Old Sacristy), the earliest part of the church and one of Brunelleschi's most notable early creations, remarkable for the purity and harmony of the overall conception. It contains, besides decorations by Donatello, the tombs of several Medicis, including Giovanni di Bicci. Be sure to go outside and through a doorway to the left of the façade to the Chiostro di San Lorenzo and to the Biblioteca Mediceo-Laurenziana (Laurentian Library; closed Sundays and holidays), a Michelangelo masterpiece designed to hold the Medici collection of manuscripts — 10,000 precious volumes. Piazza San Lorenzo.

Cappelle Medicee (Medici Chapels) – Once part of San Lorenzo, these famous Medici funerary chapels now have a separate entrance. The first of the chapels, the Cappella dei Principi (Chapel of the Princes), where Cosimo I and the other grand dukes of Tuscany lie, is the later of the two, and it is a family burial vault supreme: The elaborate baroque interior took all of the 17th and 18th centuries to complete. Note the fine examples of Florentine mosaic, fine inlay done with semiprecious stones. But the real attraction here is the other chapel, the Sagrestia Nuova (New Sacristy), a companion piece to the Sagrestia Vecchia (see above). This magnificent show is by Michelangelo, who was commissioned by Cardinal Giulio de' Medici (later Pope Clement VII) and Pope Leo X (another Medici) to design both the interior — Michelangelo's first architectural job — and the statuary as a fitting resting place for members of their family. Michelangelo worked on it from 1521 to 1533 and left two of the projected tombs incomplete, but those he finished — the tomb of Lorenzo II, duke of Urbino, with the figures of Dawn and Dusk, and the tomb of Giuliano, Duke of Nemours, with the figures of Night and Day, are extraordinary. (Lorenzo il Magnifico and his brother Giuliano, the latter murdered in the Duomo, are buried in the tomb opposite the altar, which bears a splendid *Madonna with Child* by Michelangelo.) Don't miss the feeling of this room as a whole; with its square plan and imposing dome (especially its unusual trapezoidal windows), one almost has a sensation of soaring upward! Closed Mondays. Admission charge. Piazza Madonna degli Aldobrandini (phone: 213206).

Palazzo Medici-Riccardi (Medici-Riccardi Palace) – Not far from San Lorenzo is the palace where the Medici family lived until 1540, when they moved to the Palazzo Vecchio. When Cosimo the Elder decided to build a mansion for the family, he first asked Brunelleschi to design it but rejected the architect's plans as too luxurious and likely to create excessive envy. So Michelozzo was the master responsible for what was to be the first authentic Renaissance mansion — as well as a barometer of the proper lifestyle for a Florentine banker. Be sure to visit the tiny chapel to see Benozzo Gozzoli's wonderful fresco of the Three Kings on their way to Bethlehem. Closed Wednesdays. 1 Via Cavour (phone: 2760).

Santa Maria Novella – Designed by two Dominican monks in the late 13th century and largely completed by the mid-14th century (except for the façade, which was designed by Leon Battista Alberti and finished in the late 15th century), this church figures in Boccaccio's *Decameron* as the place where his protagonists discuss the plague of 1348, the Black Death. Michelangelo, at the age of 13, was sent here to study painting under Ghirlandaio, whose frescoes adorn the otherwise gloomy interior, as do others by Masaccio, Filippino Lippi, and followers of Giotto. See the Gondi and Strozzi chapels and the great Chiostro Verde (Green Cloister), so called for the predominance of green in the decoration by Paolo Uccello and his school. Piazza Santa Maria Novella.

Orsanmichele – This solid, square 14th-century structure once housed wheat for emergency use on its upper floors, while the ground floor was a church, and the whole was adopted by the city's artisans and guilds and used as an oratory — an unusual combination. Outside, the 14 statues in the niches representing patron saints of the guilds were sculpted by the best Florentine artists of the 14th to 16th centuries. The interior is dominated by a huge 14th-century tabernacle of colored marble by Andrea Orcagna. On St. Anne's Day, July 26, the building is decorated with flags of the guilds to commemorate the expulsion of the tyrannical Duke of Athens from Florence on July 26, 1343. Via dei Calzaiuoli.

Sinagoga (Synagogue) – Built in the late 19th century by the Florentine Jewish community in the Sephardic-Moorish style, this is one of the world's most beautiful synagogues. It was severely damaged during the 1966 floods but was lovingly and accurately restored. Visits are permitted from 9 AM until half an hour before rites. Ring the bell at the smaller of the two gates, and an English-speaking woman will take you around. 4 Via Farini (phone: 245252).

Mercato Nuovo (Straw Market) – This covered market near Piazza della Signoria dates from the 16th century. It holds an amazing assortment of handbags, sun hats, and placemats in traditional Florentine straw and raffia, wonderful embroidery work, typical gilt-pattern wooden articles, and other souvenirs. The symbol of the market is the *Porcellino,* an imposing and slightly daunting bronze statue of a wild boar. Rub its shiny nose and toss a coin into the fountain to ensure a return visit. Piazza del Mercato Nuovo.

ENVIRONS

San Miniato al Monte – Near Piazzale Michelangelo, this lovely church beloved by the Florentines dominates the hill of the same name and looks out over a broad panorama of Florence and the surrounding hills — a romantic setting that makes it a particular favorite for weddings. One of the best examples of Tuscan Romanesque architecture and design in the city, it was built from the 11th to the 13th century on the spot where St. Miniato, martyred in the 3rd century, is reputed to have placed his severed head after carrying it up from Florence. The façade is in the typical green and white marble of the Florentine Romanesque style, as is the pulpit inside, and the geometric patterns on the inlaid floor are Oriental. Art treasures include Michelozzo's Crucifix Chapel, with terra-cotta decorations by Luca della Robbia; Spinello Aretino's frescoes in the sacristy; and the Chapel of the Cardinal of Portugal, a Renaissance addition that contains works by Baldovinetti, Antonio and Piero del Pollaiolo, and Luca della Robbia. The monks of San Miniato repeat vespers in Gregorian chant every day from 4:45 to 5:30 PM. By all means stop by the adjoining cemetery, a wonderful collection of Italian funerary art (the English painter Henry Savage Landor and Carlo Lorenzini, author of *Pinocchio,* are buried here). The fortifications surrounding the church were designed by Michelangelo against the imperial troops of Charles V.

Fiesole – This beautiful village on a hill overlooking Florence and the Arno was an ancient Etruscan settlement and, later, a Roman city. The Duomo, begun in the 11th century and radically restored in the 19th, is on the main square, Piazza Mino da Fiesole, and just off the square is the *Teatro Romano,* built about 80 BC, where classical plays are sometimes performed, especially during the summer festival (*L'Estate Fiesolana*), which is devoted primarily to music. Take the picturesque Via San Francesco leading out of the square and walk up to the Church of St. Francis, passing the public gardens along the way and stopping at the terrace to enjoy the splendid view of Florence. The church, built in the 14th and 15th centuries, contains some very charming cloisters, especially the tiny Choistrino di San Bernardino. Fiesole is 5 miles north of Florence and can be reached by bus #7 from the railway station or Piazza San Marco.

■**EXTRA SPECIAL:** Scattered about the Florentine countryside are a number of stately villas of the historic aristocracy of Florence, three of which are associated with the Medici family. On the road to Sesto Fiorentino, about 5 miles north of the city, are the 16th-century *Villa della Petraia* (originally a castle of the Brunelleschi family, rebuilt in 1575 for a Medici cardinal by Buontalenti) and, just down the hill, the 15th-century *Villa di Castello,* which was taken over by the Medicis in 1477. Both have lovely gardens and fountains by Tribolo. The *Villa Medici at Poggio a Caiano,* at the foot of Monte Albano, about 10 miles (16 km) northwest of Florence, was rebuilt for Lorenzo the Magnificent by Giuliano da Sangallo from 1480 to 1485. The gardens of all three villas are usually open daily except Mondays; the interiors of the Petraia and Poggio a Caiano villas may also be visited (but hours and policies change; call 451208 for information regarding the former, 877012 for the latter). *Agriturist* runs organized excursions to the villas as well as to country estates in the neighboring wine-growing region. For information, contact Agriturist, 3 Piazza San Direnze (phone: 287838).

SOURCES AND RESOURCES

TOURIST INFORMATION: The tourist information office of the *Azienda Autonoma di Turismo* (open weekdays from 9 AM to 1 PM), 15 Via Tornabuoni (phone: 216544, 217459), will provide general information, brochures, and maps of the city and the surrounding area, as will the *Ente Provinciale per il Turismo,* 16 Via Alessandro Manzoni (phone: 247-8141). There's also a tourist information booth just outside the train station as well as a new office on Via

Cavour, open until 7 PM nightly. For information on Tuscany, contact the Regional Tourist Office, 26 Via di Novoli. Helpful for younger travelers is the *Student Travel Service (STS)*, 18r Via Zannetti (phone: 268396, 292067).

The US Consulate is at 38 Lungarno Amerigo Vespucci (phone: 298276).

Numerous maps and pocket-size guidebooks to Florence, such as the *Storti Guides,* are published in Italy and are available at newsstands throughout the city. Excellent guides available in bookstores are by Luciano Berti and by Rolando and Piero Fusi. Background reading before your trip might include Mary McCarthy's classic *The Stones of Florence* (Harcourt), a discussion of the history and character of the city as seen through its art, and Christopher Hibbert's *The House of Medici: Its Rise and Fall* (Morrow), a study of the city's most influential family.

As an introduction to Florence, take in *The Florence Experience,* a 45-minute super-wide-screen multivision presentation with commentary in six languages simultaneously. It not only introduces the history and culture of the city, but it provides the only opportunity to see many of the flood-damaged paintings currently being restored. Shown daily in the summer from 9 AM to 4:45 PM, on the hour. Cinema Edison, Piazza della Repubblica.

Local Coverage – Check the brochure *Florence Concierge Information,* available at most hotels, or pick up a copy of *Florence Today* at the tourist information office. Florence's daily newspapers are *La Nazione* and *Città.*

Telephone – The area code for Florence is 055.

CLIMATE AND CLOTHES: Florence's climate can be rather severe: cold and damp in winter and stifling in summer. Spring and fall are the best times to visit, particularly when it doesn't happen to rain. The hottest time is from mid-June to mid-September, when temperatures range from 60F (15C) to 90F (32C). Temperatures rarely drop below freezing in winter — the range is 36F (2C) to 52F (11C) from December through mid-March, but the cold is often gripping. Heavy overcoats are advisable, and an umbrella is a necessity.

GETTING AROUND: Most visitors find Florence one of the easiest of European cities to navigate. Although it is fairly large, the scale is rather intimate, and it's easy to get just about anywhere on foot. Almost all the major sites are on the north side, or right bank, of the river, but most of those on the Oltrarno side ("beyond the Arno") are within easy walking distance of the center. Visitors are sometimes confused by the numbers on Florentine buildings, for houses are numbered according to a double system. Black (*nero*) numbers indicate dwellings, while red (*rosso*) numbers — indicated by an "r" after the number in street addresses — are commercial buildings (shops and such). The black and the red have little relationship to each other, so you may find a black 68 next to a red 5.

Airport – Florence has no international airport; the closest one is Pisa's Galileo Galilei Airport (phone: 050-28088/47196/29329), a 1-hour train ride from the city, but too often closed due to nearly ubiquitous early morning fog. Travelers destined for flights from Pisa's airport can check bags through to their final destination from Florence's train station, where a Pisa airport check-in counter has been set up on Quai 5. It's far safer, though, to take the train to Rome or even to Milan and fly out of Italy from there. From Florence's main train station, the minibus operated by Auto Alberghi (phone: 261624) stops at most of the city's hotels for a fee.

Florence does have a domestic aiport, Peretola Civic Airport, 11 Via Del Termine (phone: 370123), with some flights to Milan, Venice, Turin, and Trieste. Recently, service to this airport has been expanded, with scheduled flights arriving from Rome, Paris, Nice, London, and Frankfurt. Peretola is a 10-minute drive from downtown; taxi fare into the city will run about $6 to $7.50.

Buses – ATAF is the city bus company, running about 40 city and suburban routes. Bus routes are listed in the yellow pages of the telephone directory. Tickets — which should be purchased before boarding — can be bought at tobacco counters, in bars, and at some newsstands; they cost about 50¢ and can be used more than once, with a 1½-hour time limit. Children under 1 meter (39 inches) tall ride free. As there are no ticket collectors (only automatic stamping machines), many passengers do not buy tickets, but anybody caught without one by the occasional controller is fined on the spot. The back door of the bus is for boarding, the middle for disembarking; the front door is only for season ticketholders. At rush hour, buses are impossibly crowded and it's sometimes difficult to get off at the desired stop. Walking is often faster and more enjoyable, but pedestrians are cautioned to watch out for buses and taxis in special lanes permitting them to travel the wrong way on many one-way streets.

Bicycles, Mopeds, and Motorbikes – *Ciao & Basta,* 24 Costa dei Magnoli (phone: 293357 or 263985), rents bicycles; *Bici-Città* (phone: 499319 or 296335) will furnish two free bikes for 2 hours upon presentation of a *SCAF* car park coupon, and has three locations: Fortezza da Basso, Piazza Pitti, and Stazione Centrale on Via Alamanni (by the stairway). Motorbikes are available from *Program,* 135r Borgo Ognissanti (phone: 282916), and *Sabra,* 8 Via Artisti (phone: 576256 or 579609), which also rents mopeds. Ride carefully!

Car Rental – *Avis,* 128r Borgo Ognissanti (phone: 298826 or 213629); *Eurodrive,* 48r Via della Scala (phone: 298817); *Europcar,* 53 Borgo Ognissanti (phone: 294130); *Garage S. Lucia,* 9r Via Orti Oricellari (phone: 216583); *Hertz,* 33 Via Maso Finiguerra (phone: 282260); *InterRent Autonoleggio,* 1r Via il Prato (phone: 218665); *Italy by Car* (*Budget*), 134r Borgo Ognissanti (phone: 293021); *Maggiore,* 11 Via Maso Finiguerra (phone: 210238); and *Program,* 135r Borgo Ognissanti (phone: 262724).

Taxi – You can hail a cruising taxi (it's available if the light on top is lit) or pick one up at one of the numerous cabstands around the city. You can call for a taxi by dialing 4798 or 4390. Cabs are metered, but there are extra charges for night rides, luggage, station pickups, and the like. It is customary to leave a small tip. A general rule is to round off the fare to the nearest 500 or 1,000 lire (40¢ or 75¢).

Train – Stazione Centrale Santa Maria Novella, the city's main railway station (phone: 278785), is near the church of the same name, at Piazza Stazione.

 SPECIAL EVENTS: Florence is bathed in medieval splendor each year for festivities surrounding the *Festa di San Giovanni Battista* (Feast of St. John the Baptist), June 24. Part of the tradition for the past several hundred years has been the *Calcio in Costume,* which consists of more than 500 men wearing colorful 16th-century costumes — with modern T-shirts — and playing a very rough game of soccer. Actually, because there are four teams, representing the old rival neighborhoods of San Giovanni, Santo Spirito, Santa Croce, and Santa Maria Novella (distinguishable by their green, white, blue, and red costumes, respectively), three games are played, two preliminaries and a final. One is usually scheduled on June 24 and the other two within a week or two before or after that date. The game, which resembles wrestling, rugby, and soccer, with the round leather ball thrown more often than kicked, originated in the Roman *arpasto,* played on sandy ground by soldiers training for war. It evolved through the Middle Ages and the Renaissance (in 1530 there was a most famous match played by the Florentines in defiance of the imperial troops of Charles V who were besieging the city), lapsed for about a century and a half, and then was revived in 1930. Also revived was the preliminary parade of Florentine guild officials, followed by the four teams led by their resident noblemen on horseback (the best known of whom is the Marchese Emilio Pucci di Barsento, the fashion designer). Because the game and its 8,000 or so spectators constitute some danger to the fountains and statuary of Florence's historic *piazze,* it was moved at one point to the Boboli Gardens, only to be banned there, too. It may be back soon — on Piazza Santa Croce.

Among the other folkloric events is the centuries-old ceremony called the *Scoppio del Carro,* literally "bursting the cart," which takes place traditionally on Easter Sunday in celebration of a Christian victory in one of the Crusades and culminates in a great fireworks display. A large cart drawn by white oxen is brought to Piazza del Duomo and connected to the main altar of the cathedral by a metal wire. At the stroke of noon, when the bells announce the Resurrection of Christ, the cardinal archbishop of Florence sets off a dove-shaped rocket that runs along the wire to the cart filled with firecrackers. When the cart explodes, the Florentine spectators jump with joy, taking the event and the flight of the "dove" as a good omen for the future. Occasionally the dove doesn't make it and sighs of something worse than disappointment fill the square, as this is considered a bad omen indeed. On *Ascension Day* each May, Florentines celebrate the *Festa del Grillo* by going to the Cascine, a park along the Arno at the edge of the center, and buying crickets in cages, only to set them free. The *Festa delle Rificolone,* September 7, is celebrated with a procession along the Arno and across the Ponte San Niccolò with colorful paper lanterns and torches.

The *Biennale Dell'Antiquariato,* an important international antiques fair, is held every 2 years in the fall here at the Palazzo Strozzi.

MUSEUMS: Since museums are possibly the city's top attraction, quite a few have already been described under *Special Places.* A few more of the 70 or so museums in the city are listed here, along with additional churches and palaces whose artwork makes them, in effect, museums, too. The tourist information office (phone: 217459) or the Superintendent of Museums and Galleries (phone: 218314) can provide information about hours.

Badia Fiorentina – The church of a former Benedictine abbey (*badia*), with a part-Romanesque, part-Gothic *campanile,* it was founded in the 10th century, enlarged in the 13th, and rebuilt in the 17th. Opposite the Bargello. Via del Proconsolo.

Casa Buonarroti – The small house Michelangelo bought for his next of kin, containing some of the master's early works, as well as works done in his honor by some of the foremost artists of the 16th and 17th centuries. Closed Tuesdays. 70 Via Ghibellina.

Casa di Dante – A small museum in what is believed to have been Dante's house, it documents his life, times, and work. Closed Wednesdays. 1 Via Santa Margherita.

Casa Guidi – Robert and Elizabeth Barrett Browning lived on the first floor of this 15th-century palazzo at the corner of the Pitti Palace from shortly after their secret marriage in 1846 until Elizabeth's death in 1861. Now called the Browning Institute, it is an unfinished museum and a memorial to both poets. 8 Piazza San Felice.

Cenacolo di Sant'Apollonia – The refectory of a former convent, containing Andrea del Castagno's remarkable fresco of the Last Supper (ca. 1450). Closed Mondays. 1 Via XXVII Aprile.

Museo di Antropologia ed Etnologia (Museum of Anthropology and Ethnology) – First of its genre in Italy, continually enlarged, now with more than 30 rooms and a vast collection divided by race, continent, and culture. Open by appointment Wednesdays and Fridays. 12 Via del Proconsolo (phone: 296449).

Museo Bardini – Sculpture, tapestries, bronzes, furniture, and paintings. Closed Wednesdays. 1 Piazza dei Mozzi.

Museo Firenze Com'Era (Florence "As It Was" Museum) – Collection of mainly 19th-century maps, paintings, documents, and photos illustrating aspects of the city over the centuries. There is also a permanent exhibition of works by the 20th-century artist Ottone Rosai. Closed Thursdays. 24 Via dell'Oriuolo.

Museo della Fondazione Horne (Horne Museum) – A jewel of a museum —

paintings, drawings, sculptures, furniture, ceramics, coins, and unusual old household utensils, the collection of an Englishman, Herbert Percy Horne, bequeathed to the city in 1916 and set up in his 15th-century *palazzetto*. Closed Sundays. 6 Via de' Benci.

Museo Stibbert – Vast collection (about 50,000 pieces) of art objects, antiques, arms from all over the world, and other curiosities left by the English collector Stibbert, with his villa and gardens. 26 Via Federico Stibbert.

Museo di Storia della Scienza (Museum of the History of Science) – Scientific instruments, including Galileo's telescopes, and odd items documenting the development of modern science from the Renaissance to the 20th century. Closed Sundays. 1 Piazza de'Giudici.

Museo degli Strumenti Musicali Antichi (Museum of Antique Musical Instruments) – Collection of musical instruments begun by Ferdinando de' Medici in the 17th century. 80 Via degli Alfani.

Ognissanti (Church of All Saints) – Built in the 13th century and rebuilt in the 17th, it contains extraordinary frescoes by Ghirlandaio and Botticelli and is the burial place of the latter as well as of the family of Amerigo Vespucci. Piazza d'Ognissanti.

Palazzo Davanzati – A well-preserved 14th-century palace with 15th-century furniture, tapestries, and ceramics, also known as the *Museo della Casa Fiorentina Antica* or the *Florentine House Museum.* 13 Via Porta Rossa.

Palazzo Strozzi – This masterpiece of Renaissance architecture is the scene of a biennial international antiques show, held in the fall. Piazza Strozzi.

Santi Apostoli (Church of the Holy Apostles) – Built in the 11th century, redecorated in the 15th and 16th centuries, and restored in the 1930s, it holds the flints said to have been brought back from Jerusalem during the Crusades and still used to light the Holy Fire in the Duomo for the *Scoppio del Carro* at Easter (see *Special Events*).

Santa Maria del Carmine – Dating from the second half of the 13th century, this Carmelite church was mostly destroyed in a fire in 1771, but the Corsini and Brancacci chapels were spared. The latter contains the Masaccio frescoes that inspired Renaissance painters from Fra Angelico to Raphael. Piazza del Carmine.

Santo Spirito (Church of the Holy Spirit) – One of Brunelleschi's last works, and a gem, notable as one of the finest examples of a Renaissance church as well as for some two dozen chapels with masterpieces by Donatello, Ghirlandaio, Filippino Lippi, Sansovino, and others. Piazza Santo Spirito.

Santa Trinità (Church of the Holy Trinity) – One of the oldest churches in Florence, built in the 11th century with a 16th-century façade. See the Ghirlandaio frescoes in the Sassetti Chapel — one shows the church with its original Romanesque façade. Piazza Santa Trinità.

SHOPPING: Shopping is absolutely wonderful in Florence, arguably Italy's most fashionable city. For clothing, the smartest streets are Via Tornabuoni, Via della Vigna Nuova, Via Calzaiuoli, and Via Roma. The shops lining the Ponte Vecchio have been selling beautiful gold and silver jewelry since 1593. Antiques, leather goods, and handmade lingerie are other specialties of Florentine shops. As of this writing, Florentine store hours are unpredictable. Check with your concierge before setting out for a shopping spree. Traditional winter store hours are: 9 AM to 1 PM and 3:30 to 7:30 PM Tuesdays through Saturdays (3:30 to 7:30 PM on Mondays). The summer finds these stores closed on Saturday afternoons rather than on Monday mornings, and the evening closing hour is extended by a half hour to 8. Food shops traditionally close on Wednesdays.

Alex – The best in designer clothes for women — Gianni Versace, Yamamoto, Byblos, Claude Montana, Basile, Thierry Mugler. 19r and 5r Via della Vigna Nuova.

Antico Setificio Fiorentino – Fabulous fabrics, all hand-loomed. 97r Via della Vigna Nuova.

Antognoni Sport – Unisex activewear. 55-59r Via Porta Rossa.

Beltrami – A chain of elegant, expensive leatherwear shops: shoes, bags, jackets, pants, and other items. 31r, 44r, and 202r Via Calzaiuoli; 1r Via dei Pecori; 11r Via Calimala; and 28 Via Tornabuoni.

Benetton – Colorful, reasonably priced sportswear for the young at heart. 66-68r Via Por Santa Maria and 2r Via Calimala (among other locations).

Bijoux Cascio – Moderately priced jewelry, particularly in gold; the designs are the shop's own. 32r Via Tornabuoni (among other locations).

BM – An English-language bookstore. 4r Borgo Ognissanti.

Bottega Veneta – Part of the worldwide chain, with exquisite leather goods. 3-4r Piazza Ognissanti.

Mario Buccellati – Fine jewelry and table silver in traditional Florentine designs. 71r Via Tornabuoni.

Loretta Caponi – Exquisite handmade lingerie and linens by this second-generation shop that designs for Nina Ricci and Dior. 38-40r Borgo Ognissanti.

Cellerini – High-quality bags and suitcases made by a craftsman in a workshop above the store. 9 Via del Sole.

Cirri – Lovely linens. 38-40r Via Por Santa Maria.

David – Leather bags, luggage, shoes, clothes. 11-13r Via Roma.

Feltrinelli – Art books. 12-20r Via Cavour.

Ferragamo – The famous shoemaker's headquarters in Italy, with the widest selection of styles and colors. 12-16r Via Tornabuoni.

Gants – Gloves of the highest quality; they make their own. 78r Via Porta Rossa.

Gerard – Way-out, punk, and exotic fashions for men and women. 18-20r Via Vaccherreccia.

Gherardini – A century-old leather shop, also selling sunglasses and perfumes, run by an old Florentine family (the subject of the *Mona Lisa* was a Gherardini). 57r Via della Vigna Nuova (among other locations).

Giannini – Stationers with class; the finest of Florentine paper products. 37r Piazza Pitti.

Gori Boutique – Santa Croce Leather School products, as well as articles by Italy's top-name designers. 13r Piazza Santa Croce.

Gucci – The parent store of Italy's best known leather and fashion purveyor. Less expensive than in the US, but hardly inexpensive. 57-73-75r Via Tornabuoni.

Happy Jack – Fine men's boutique; alterations done quickly. 7-13r Via della Vigna Nuova.

Libreria Franco Maria Ricci – Fine books selected by the publishers of *FMR* magazine. 41r Via delle Belle Donne.

Libreria Salimbeni – Specializes in art books. 14r Via Matteo Palmieri.

Lily of Florence – Shoes in American sizes. 2r Via Guicciardini.

Madova – Italy's most competent glovemaker. 1r Via Guicciardini.

Melli – Antique jewelry, ivory, silver, clocks. 48 Ponte Vecchio.

Mercato Nuovo (Straw Market) – The covered market, with all sorts of items made of straw, wood, and leather. Piazza del Mercato Nuovo.

Mercato di San Lorenzo – An open-air market selling everything from used clothing to hot tripe sandwiches. Mohair sweaters are a good buy, as are handbags. Piazza San Lorenzo.

Mujer – Original fashions for the adventurous woman. 6r Via Vaccherreccia.

Neuber – British and Italian wools. 32r Via Strozzi.

Emilio Paoli – Straw market with class — locally produced gift articles and imports. 26r Via della Vigna Nuova.

Papiro – *Papier à cuve*, or marbled paper, a method of hand-decoration invented in the 17th century; lovely stationery. 55 Via Cavour (among other locations).

Parson – Trendy women's boutique. 16-18r Via Tosinghi.

La Pelle – Leather clothes made to order in two stores. 11-13r and 11-14r Via Guicciardini.

Pineider – Italy's most famous stationers. 13r Piazza della Signoria and 76r Via Tornabuoni.

Pratesi – Elegant linens. 8-10 Lungarno Amerigo Vespucci.

Primi Mesi – Embroidered crib and carriage sets; maternity, infants, and toddlers wear. 23r Via dei Cimatori.

Principe – A small but elegant department store. 21-29r Piazza Strozzi.

Emilio Pucci Boutique – Pucci fashions. Palazzo Pucci, 6 Via de' Pucci.

Renard – Leather, suede, and sheepskin clothing. 21-23r Via dei Martelli.

Santa Croce Leather School – Top-quality leather goods (gloves, boxes, wallets, handbags, garments, and shoes) from the school and shop inside the monastery of Santa Croce. 16 Piazza Santa Croce or (through the garden) Via San Giuseppe 5r.

Schwicker – Quality gifts by Florentine artisans. 40r Piazza Pitti .

Seeber – English-language bookshop. 70 Via Tornabuoni.

Stefanel – Colorful sportswear. Via Borgo San Lorenzo.

Tanino Crisci – The most stylish shoe shop (for men and women) in town. 43-45 Via Tornabuoni.

Ugo Poggi – Florentine handicrafts in silver, china, glass. 26r Via degli Strozzi.

Ungaro Parallèle – High fashion for women. 30r Via della Vigna Nuova.

UPIM – A large, moderately priced department store. Piazza della Repubblica.

Mario Valentino – Designer shoes and bags. 67r Via Tornabuoni.

Valmar – Tapestry items perfect for everything from upholstery to women's belts. 53r Via Porta Rossa.

Zanobetti – Classic clothing and leather goods for men and women. 20-22r Via Calimala.

SPORTS AND FITNESS: Check with your concierge to find out which sports facilities are currently open to the public. Most are private clubs, but a day visit can often be arranged for a fee.

Fitness Centers – *Indoor Club,* 15 Via Bardazzi (phone: 430275); *Sauna Finlandese,* 108 Via Cavour (phone: 587246); *Tropos,* 20a Via Orcagna (phone: 671581).

Golf – There is a good 18-hole course (closed Mondays) at *Golf dell'Ugolino* in nearby Impruneta, 3 Via Chiantigiana (phone: 205-1009).

Horseback Riding – For information, call *Piazzale Cascine* (phone: 360056).

Jogging – The best place to run is the Cascine, a very long, narrow park along the Arno west of the center. To get there, follow the river to Ponte della Vittoria.

Soccer – See the *Florentina* in action from September to May at the *Stadio Comunale,* designed by Pier Luigi Nervi. 4/6 Viale Manfredo Fanti (phone: 572625).

Squash – Courts can be reserved at the *Centro Squasch Firenze,* 24-29 Viale Piombino (phone: 710055).

Swimming – Swimmers will do best to stay at one of the following hotels: *Crest, Croce di Malta, Jolly Carlton, Kraft, Minerva, Park Palace, Villa Belvedere, Villa Medici,* or *Villa sull'Arno* or, outside the city, at the *Grand Hotel Villa Cora, Villa La Massa, Villa San Michele,* or the *Villa Villoresi.* There are also a few indoor and outdoor public pools, including *Piscina Costoli,* Viale Paoli (phone: 655744); and *Piscina Le Pavoniere,* an outdoor pool in a pleasant park, at Viale Degli Olmi (phone: 367506).

Tennis – Play tennis at the semi-public *Circolo Tennis alle Cascine,* 1 Viale Visarno (phone: 356651); at *Assi-Giglio-Rosso,* 64 Viale Michelangelo (phone: 681-2686 or 687858); and at *Il Poggetto,* 24/B Via Michele Mercati (phone: 460127).

THEATER: If you'd like to see a play in Italian, the principal theaters in Florence are the *Teatro della Pergola,* 32 Via della Pergola (phone: 247-9651); the *Teatro Niccolini,* 5 Via Ricasoli (phone: 213282); and *Tenda Città di Firenze,* Via de Nicola (phone: 650-4112). A relatively new addition to the city's theater scene, *Teatro Variety,* 47 Via del Madonnone (phone: 660632), offers singers and humorous contemporary pieces. Films in English are shown frequently at the *Cinema Astro,* Piazza San Simone near Santa Croce (phone: 222388).

MUSIC: Opera begins earlier in Florence than in most Italian cities. The season at the *Teatro Comunale,* Corso Italia (phone: 277-9313), the principal opera house and concert hall, runs from October to early January, with ballet in July. The annual *Maggio Musicale Fiorentino* festival, which attracts some of the world's finest musicians and singers, is also held here in May and June. The *Teatro della Pergola* (see *Theater*) is the scene of Saturday afternoon concerts from autumn through spring. Open-air concerts are held in the cloisters of the *Badia Fiesolana* (in Fiesole) and of the *Ospedale degli Innocenti* on summer evenings, and occasionally in other historic monuments such as the recently restored and reopened Church of *Santo Stefano al Ponte Vecchio,* now the seat of the *Regional Tuscan Orchestra.*

NIGHTCLUBS AND NIGHTLIFE: A Florentine evening usually begins with an *aperitivo* at one of the cafés on Piazza della Signoria or Piazza della Repubblica, at *Harry's Bar,* 22r Lungarno Amerigo Vespucci (phone: 296700), or at the bar in the *Excelsior* hotel (see *Checking In*). Because nightspots come and go so quickly — and since most are closed at least one night of the week — it is always a good idea to check with your concierge before going out. Discos and piano bars are among the most popular forms of evening entertainment, and tops among the former are *Tenax,* 46 Via Pratese (phone: 373050) and *Jackie-O',* 24/A Via dell'Erta Canina (phone: 234-0854) (phone: 216146 or 217345). Other discos include the recently renovated *Yab Yum,* 5r Via Sassetti (phone: 282018); *Full-Up,* 21r Via della Vigna Vecchia (phone: 293006); and *Plegine,* 26r Piazza Santa Maria Novella. *Chapeau* is a new disco/piano bar, 57-59r Via Verdi (phone: 298738). For the very young crowd, dancing happens at *Space Electronic,* 37 Via Palazzuolo (phone: 293082), and under the summer stars at *Central Park,* Parco Cascine, 13 Via Fosso Macinante (phone: 356723). If a quieter evening is called for, there are numerous lovely piano bars from which to choose, such as the elegant *Loggia Tornaquinci,* nestled atop a 16th-century Medici building at 6r Via Tornabuoni (phone: 219148). Others include the *Caffè,* 9 Piazza Pitti (phone: 296241); and *Oberon,* 12r Via dell'Erta Canina (phone: 216516). The elegant *Oliviero,* 51r Via della Terme (phone: 287643), is a restaurant with piano bar, the place for a romantic evening. There are also piano bars at some of the hotels, such as the *Anglo-American,* the *Londra,* the *Majestic,* and the *Savoy. Il Salotto* is a new "private" club open to everyone. Situated in a 15th-century palazzo at 33 Borgo Pinti, it's not surprising that it boasts a clientele of Florentine nobility, artists, and wealthy merchants. Popular for drinks is the *Caffè Strozzi,* 16-19 Piazza Strozzi (phone: 212574), with outdoor tables for good people watching. But the ancient *Caffè Rivoire,* a chocolate shop, bakery, and coffeehouse on Piazza della Signoria, is still the city's traditional meeting place. Three other local favorites are *Gilli,* a Belle Epoque café with a lively outdoor terrace on 39r Piazza della Repubblica (phone: 296310); *Giacosa,* 83 Via Tornabuoni (phone: 296226), where the elite meet over truffle-paste sandwiches; and *Procacci,* a café/bar serving white truffle-paste sandwiches and other elegant snacks to a chic local crowd at 33 Via Tornabuoni.

BEST IN TOWN

CHECKING IN: Florence is well organized for visitors, with more than 400 hotels to accommodate more than 20,000 travelers. Still, somehow, it's hard to find a room in high season. The hotel count above and the list below include former *pensioni,* something like boarding houses, but now officially designated as "hotels." A few still require that some meals be taken, a feature that is specified for those that do. (Half-board means you must take breakfast and either lunch or dinner at the establishment.) At an expensive hotel, plan on spending from $175 to more than $400 a night for a double room. Moderate-priced establishments cost between $80 and $175; inexpensive lodging ranges from $50 to $80. All telephone numbers are in the 055 area code unless otherwise indicated.

Excelsior – Beside the Arno, just a short walk from the city center, traditional in both style and service. Part of the reliably luxurious and efficient CIGA chain. The excellent terrace restaurant, *Il Cestello,* has a splendid view when the stained glass windows are opened. The 205-room hotel is a favorite of Florentines and their guests. 3 Piazza Ognissanti (phone: 264201). Expensive.

Grand Hotel Villa Cora – A neo-classical villa built during the period when Florence was the capital of Italy. The name comes from one of the many former owners, an ambassador. As a private villa, it hosted Napoleon's widow, Eugénie, as well as Tchaikovsky's patron, the Baroness Von Meck. It offers spacious rooms and suites (56 rooms) decorated in the original style, grand public rooms, and a magnificent garden with heated pool, all about 2 miles (3.2 km) from the chaotic city center. On the other side of the Boboli Gardens. 18 Viale Machiavelli (phone: 229-8451). Expensive.

Regency Umbria – A small (31-room) patrician villa set in a quiet residential area and decorated with exquisite taste. Like its sister in Rome (the *Lord Byron*), it offers calm and privacy, discreetly displaying its Relais et Châteaux crest at the entrance. There is a charming garden and an excellent restaurant. 3 Piazza Massimo d'Azeglio (phone: 245247). Expensive.

Savoy – A classic gem in the heart of Florence, with most of its 100 rooms decorated in Venetian style. It also has a popular piano bar. 7 Piazza della Repubblica (phone: 283313). Expensive.

Torre di Bellosguardo – The majestic, cypress-framed site on a hill overlooking Florence's terra cotta roofs makes this handsome deluxe hostelry a special place to stay. A sunny veranda, lush gardens, and swimming pool, as well as beamed-ceiling rooms, each individually decorated with antiques, add to the charm. 2 Via Roti Michelozzi (phone: 229-8145). Expensive.

Villa Medici – A reconstruction of the 18th-century Sonnino de Renzis Palace, halfway between the railroad station and the River Arno. Many of the 110 charming, spacious rooms have balconies affording panoramic views. The grand public rooms, tranquil gardens, and elegant service are all worthy of a hotel of this class. The swimming pool is a bow to contemporary tastes. 42 Via del Prato (phone: 261331). Expensive.

Villa San Michele – Dramatically set about 5 miles (8 km) from Florence, on the slopes below Fiesole. Originally an ancient monastery, built by the Davanzati family in the late 15th century and designed in part by Michelangelo, it became a private villa during Napoleon's day and was transformed into one of Tuscany's most romantic hotels in the 1950s. (Brigitte Bardot honeymooned here in the 1960s.) Restored to its former glory and recently under new management, it now has 28 rooms (most with Jacuzzis), intimate dining indoors or in the open-air *loggia,* fragrant gardens with splendid views, a pool, and limousine service into the city. Half-board required. Open from March to mid-November. 4 Via Doccia, Fiesole (phone: 59451). Expensive.

Fenice Palace – Recently reopened after extensive renovation and restoration, the 67 guestrooms occupy 4 floors in a 19th-century palazzo near the Duomo. The accommodations offer considerable comfort and some magnificent views of the city's major monuments. 10 Via Martelli (phone: 263942). Expensive to moderate.

Grand Hotel Minerva – The 107 rooms here are large and comfortably furnished, all with private modern baths. The staff is pleasant, and the hotel is near the train station, convenient to shopping and the major museums. 16 Piazza Santa Maria Novella (phone: 284555). Expensive to moderate.

Tornabuoni Beacci – This delightful former *pensione* occupies the top floors of a 14th-century palace on Florence's most elegant street. It's traditional yet cheerful and sunny, provides excellent service, and has a charming terrace. Guests are required to take breakfast and another meal (half-board) during high season. 3 Via Tornabuoni (phone: 212645). Expensive to moderate.

Anglo-American – Between the train station and the river, very near the *Teatro Comunale,* with 118 recently refurbished rooms. 9 Via Garibaldi (phone: 282114). Moderate.

Grand Hotel Baglioni – A traditional hotel in refined Tuscan taste: parquet floors, solid furnishings, handsome carpets, sober — even somber — atmosphere and service, with nearly 200 rooms. It's near the railway station and only a short walk from the best shopping. The roof garden restaurant has an enviable view of the historic city. 6 Piazza dell'Unità Italiana (phone: 218441). Moderate.

Hotel de la Ville – Dark, quiet, and somber, the perfect hotel for light sleepers. Its double doors and storm windows provide a peaceful oasis in the center of Florence, just off the elegant Via Tornabuoni. 87 rooms. 1 Piazza Antinori (phone: 261805). Moderate.

Jolly Carlton – Large and modern, this 167-room member of the efficient Jolly chain has a pool and a wonderful view from the terrace. It's near the Cascine park. 4/A Piazza Vittorio Veneto (phone: 2770). Moderate.

Kraft – This modern 66-room hotel in a nice area near the Teatro Comunale has a roof-garden restaurant sporting umbrella pines and a cypress tree as well as a splendid panorama and a rooftop swimming pool. 2 Via Solferino (phone: 284273). Moderate.

Lungarno – Comfortable, functional, and cheerful. Set between the Ponte Vecchio and the Ponte Santa Trinità on the Oltrarno side of town, with about 70 modern rooms, the best of which have terraces and balconies overlooking the Arno. 14 Borgo San Jacopo (phone: 264211). Moderate.

Mona Lisa – On a tiny side street, this hotel in an old renovated building offers Old World charm and style with modern comforts. 27 Borgo Pinti (phone: 247-9751). Moderate.

Villa Villoresi – About 5 miles (8 km) from the center of Florence, it's another noble home away from home. It dates to the 12th century, but for the last 200 years it has been the property of the Villoresi family, who turned it into a hotel in the 1960s. With only 28 rooms, they manage to impart a sense of family as well as history. Bedroom walls have frescoes and meals are good. There is a pool in the garden among the olive trees. 2 Via Ciampi, Località Colonnata, Sesto Fiorentino (phone: 448-9032). Moderate to inexpensive.

Balestri – A clean, no-frills stopping place overlooking the Arno. It has 50 rooms, no restaurant. 7 Piazza Mentana (phone: 214743). Inexpensive.

Bencistà – This 15th-century villa, an inn among the olive trees near Fiesole, is a beautiful bargain for those whose shoestrings do not stretch as far as the *Villa San Michele*. Half-board is required. No phones in the rooms. Open mid-March to November. 4 Via Benedetto da Maiano, between Fiesole and San Domenico (phone: 59163). Inexpensive.

Continental – In an ideal, albeit sometimes noisy, spot overlooking the Ponte Vecchio, this is as efficient as its sister hotel across the river, the *Lungarno,* which you can see from the terrace. No restaurant. 2 Lungarno Acciaiuoli (phone: 282392). Inexpensive.

Pendini – An old-style, family-run hotel for over 100 years, in a building far older but recently renovated. 2 Via degli Strozzi (phone: 211170). Inexpensive.

Porta Rossa – One of Florence's oldest hotels (14th century, with a 13th-century tower) and perhaps in need of a little sprucing up. Balzac and Stendhal, they say, slept here. It has Renaissance public rooms (good for meetings in the commercial center of the city) and a terrace overlooking the Ponte Vecchio. 19 Via Porta Rossa (phone: 287551). Inexpensive.

Quisisana Ponte Vecchio – Between the Ponte Vecchio and the Uffizi, with a view of the former from a charming terrace. 4 Lungarno Archibusieri (phone: 216692). Inexpensive.

La Residenza – A small hotel, recently renovated, with a lovely terrace on Florence's best shopping street. Half-board is required during high season. 8 Via Tornabuoni (phone: 284197). Inexpensive.

Silla – The large flowered terrace overlooks the river and a park on the Oltrarno side of town. A quiet, charming, and friendly place with 3 large newer rooms on the third floor. No restaurant; usually closed in December. 5 Via dei Renai (phone: 234-2889). Inexpensive.

 EATING OUT: Back in the 16th century, Catherine de' Medici married King Henry II of France, and her cousin Maria de' Medici married Henry IV. The girls took to the French court — along with their trousseaus — their cooks and their recipes for creams, sauces, pastries, and ice creams. As an Elizabethan poet once said, "Tuscany provided creams and cakes and lively Florentine women to sweeten the taste and minds of the French."

Following their departure, the fanciness went out of Florentine food, and French cooking began to shine. But today, Florentine cooking, while simpler and more straightforward than it was during the Renaissance, is still at the top of the list of Italy's many varied regional dishes. No small contributing factor to this culinary art is the quality of the ingredients. Tuscany boasts excellent olive oil and wine, exquisite fruits and vegetables, good game in season, fresh fish from its coast, as well as salami, sausages, and every kind of meat. A *bistecca alla fiorentina,* thick and juicy on the bone and traditionally accompanied by new potatoes or white beans drenched in pure golden olive oil, is a meal fit for the fussiest of kings. Diners can roughly gauge the price of a restaurant before entering by the cost per kilo (2.2 pounds) of its Florentine steak on the menu displayed outside. Fortunately, one steak is usually more than enough for two persons, and it is not considered a gaffe to order one steak for two or more.

Mealtimes in Florence are earlier than in Rome, beginning by 12:30 or 1 PM for lunch, 7:30 or 8 PM for dinner. Many of the typical mom 'n' pop restaurants are small, popular, and crowded. If you don't book, be prepared to wait and eventually share a table (single guests are often seated at a communal table — a respectable way of meeting residents). Also unlike Rome, you won't be encouraged to linger over your dessert wine if there are people waiting for your table. Food, like most everything else in Florentine life, is taken seriously; do your business and socializing elsewhere. A full meal for two including the house wine or the low-priced (but excellent) local Chianti at an expensive restaurant will cost between $80 and $150. Expect to pay between $50 and $80 at a moderate restaurant and under $50 at an inexpensive one. One final note: Many of the *trattorie* and smaller eating establishments do not accept credit cards, so if you're planning to pay with plastic, call ahead and inquire. All telephone numbers are in the 055 area code unless otherwise indicated.

Enoteca Pinchiorri – In the 15th-century Ciofi-Iacometti Palace, with a delightful courtyard for dining alfresco, this is possibly Italy's best restaurant and certainly the place for that grand dinner in Florence. The four chefs prepare exquisite traditional and nouvelle dishes with a Franco-Italian flavor, perhaps a mosaic of sweet and sour fish, sweetbread salad with shrimp sauce, ricotta and salami pie, or medallions of veal with capers and lime. The wine collection (60,000 bottles) is outstanding, understandably so, since the restaurant actually began as a wine showroom. Closed Sundays, Mondays at lunch, and August. Reservations necessary. 87 Via Ghibellina (phone: 242757). Very expensive.

Il Barrino – Originally opened by renowned singer Gino Paoli, this tiny, luxurious restaurant has changed hands often and has lost some of its glamour, but it continues to offer an interesting, although brief, menu and has the advantage of staying open later than most. Dinner only; closed Sundays and August. Reservations necessary. 2r Via de' Biffi (phone: 215180). Expensive.

Campidoglio – White tablecloths and elegant service set this attractive restaurant apart from most Florentine *trattorie,* and the excellent Italian fare makes it worth the tab. 8r Via Campidoglio (phone: 287770). Expensive.

Il Cenacolo – Relatively new, "The Last Supper" is the latest rage in refined restaurants. The ambience is ultra-cool, with a lovely garden for alfresco dining in fine weather. The cuisine is both traditional and new, featuring some old Florentine recipes with an innovative flair and a light touch for today's health-conscious patrons. There is also a bar in which to drown your sorrows after you settle the tab. Closed Sundays all day and Mondays at lunch. Reservations necessary. 34 Via Borgognissanti (phone: 219493). Expensive.

Harry's Bar – No relation to the famed eatery in Venice, but Americans tend to flock here just the same. Italian specialties are best, though it's also the place to find a hamburger and French fries. Closed Sundays and mid-December to mid-January. Reservations advised. 22r Lungarno Amerigo Vespucci (phone: 296700). Expensive.

Sabatini – Once Florence's top restaurant, but thoroughly outclassed in recent years. It's still quiet, dignified, and noted for its traditional cuisine, but the quality has slipped. Some may find the standard menu far less interesting than those of less expensive *trattorie.* Closed Mondays. Reservations advised. 9/A Via Panzani (phone: 211559 or 282802). Expensive.

Cantinetta Antinori – Not quite a restaurant, but a typically rustic yet fashionably chic *cantina,* with food designed to accompany the Antinori wines. Perfect for a light lunch of salami or *finocchiona* with bread, *crostini* (chicken liver canapés), soup, or a modest hot dish such as tripe or *bollito* (mixed boiled meats). Closed weekends and August. 3 Piazza Antinori (phone: 292234). Expensive to moderate.

Cibreo – Also named after a historic Florentine dish, one so good it is said to have given Catherine de' Medici near fatal indigestion from overeating. Although the menu offers interesting old Tuscan dishes, it does not limit itself to the traditional Florentine fare it does so well. Genoese minestrone, eggplant Parmesan from the south, polenta from the Veneto, plus savory appetizers such as walnut and pecorino cheese salad, soups, seafood with an unusual twist (mussel terrine, squid stew), and homemade desserts are all available, as are good wines. In summer, there's alfresco dining. Closed Sundays and from late July to mid-September. Reservations necessary. 118r Via de' Macci (phone: 234-1100). Expensive to moderate.

Coco Lezzone – Another Florentine favorite, serving authentic local food using the best ingredients and no pretenses. Try the *pappa al pomodoro,* a thick soup made of fresh tomatoes, herbs, and bread. This restaurant is crowded and hurried; don't expect to linger. Closed Sundays, Saturdays in the summer and Tuesdays in the winter, the last week in July, and August. 26r Via del Parioncino (phone: 287178). Expensive to moderate.

Da Noi – Currently *di moda* (in fashion), this small restaurant offers a menu that's extremely imaginative yet traditional. Try the *crespelle* (crêpes) stuffed with spinach and ricotta cheese in a sweet pepper sauce, or fresh fish prepared with sage and rosemary or with tarragon. Delicious desserts. Closed Mondays and August. Reservations advised. 46r Via Fiesolana (phone: 242917). Expensive to moderate.

Taverna del Bronzino – Rustic yet elegant, set in a 16th-century palazzo furnished with antiques and a garden for alfresco dining in season. *Crostini ai funghi porcini* (wild mushroom canapés), *tortelloni al cedro,* and renowned Florentine beef with green peppers are specialties. Closed Sundays. Reservations advised. 25-27r Via delle Ruote (phone: 495220). Expensive to moderate.

La Vecchia Cucina – New and out of the way, but with a *nuova cucina* worth trying when you've had your fill of wonderfully traditional Tuscan food. The innovative menu of a half-dozen first and second courses and three desserts is recited by the owner (tricky if you don't speak Italian), and it changes every week. Interesting wine list. Closed Sundays and August. Reservations advised. 1r Viale Edmondo De Amicis (phone: 660143). Expensive to moderate.

Cammillo – An appealing, bustling spot near the Ponte S. Trinita, offering authentic dishes such as tripe *alla fiorentina* and, in season, pasta with white truffles. Closed Wednesdays and Thursdays. 57r Borgo San Jacopo (phone: 212427). Moderate.

La Carabaccia – Named after an antique Florentine dish (none other than onion soup) loved by the Medicis, the menu changes daily according to what's good at the market. Five starters and five main courses are generally offered, occasionally featuring parts of an animal you never thought you could eat (don't ask!). Very popular, informal, and unrushed. Closed Sundays, Mondays at lunch, and August. Reservations advised. 190r Via Palazzuolo (phone: 214782). Moderate.

Le Cave – A delightful stop in Fiesole and sheer magic in early summer and fall, when it's great to lunch under the linden trees and gaze out over the splendid valley. Indoors is warm, cozy, and rustic, as is the country-style cuisine, beginning with excellent prosciutto, *finocchiona,* and other local salami, chicken and truffle croquettes, canapés of mozzarella and mushrooms, *crespelle* or ravioli, and the house specialty, *gallina al mattone,* spring chicken grilled on an open fire and seriously seasoned with black pepper and the purest of virgin olive oils. Closed Thursdays, Sunday evenings, and August. 16 Via delle Cave 16, Località Maiano, Fiesole (phone: 59133). Moderate.

Cinghaile Bianco – Cozy and hospitable, this *trattoria* serves great pasta and other tasty Florentine specialties at reasonable prices. 43r Borgo San Jacopo (phone: 215706). Moderate.

Da Ganino (Ex-Mario) – Long a Florentine favorite, this typically tiny Tuscan *trattoria* changed hands a few years ago and has surpassed its former glory. Now run by a family of enthusiastic non-restaurateurs, it has been spruced up a bit, but is still small and cozy in the winter, with al fresco dining on the small square in fine weather. Here is some of the best Florentine cuisine, including fresh mushrooms and truffles in season and a justifiably famous cheesecake. Closed Sundays, 3 weeks in August, and Christmas. Reservations advised. 4r Piazza dei Cimatori (phone: 214125). Moderate.

Garga – The unusual specialties of this former butcher shop include *zuppa di cavoli neri* (soup of a bitter green local vegetable), *risotto* of leeks and bacon, and *gnocchetti verdi* (pasta of spinach and ricotta) — all exquisitely prepared. Absolutely tiny, but terrific. Closed Sundays. Reservations necessary. 9 Via del Moro (phone: 298898 or 218094). Moderate.

Il Latini – This popular eatery, in the former stables of the historic Palazzo Rucellai, serves such solid and abundant fare as hearty Tuscan soups, unpretentious meat platters, grilled fish, fresh vegetables, and traditional desserts. Not for romantic evenings, here you sit at long communal tables and the food keeps arriving. Good value. Closed Mondays and at lunch on Tuesdays. 6r Via Palchetti (phone: 210916). Moderate.

La Loggia – On the most spectacular site in Florence, with a view over the entire city, it's run by some former *Sabatini* waiters who, by employing traditional Tuscan cuisine and efficient service despite the crowds, have transformed a once-mediocre restaurant into a Florentine favorite. The panorama from the terrace makes it especially pleasant during the summer. Closed Wednesdays. Reservations advised. 1 Piazzale Michelangelo (phone: 287032 or 2342832). Moderate.

Pierot – The specialty is seafood, especially on Tuesdays and Fridays. The menu is long and ever changing, depending on the availability of ingredients, but if you spot the traditional squid and beet dish called *inzimino di calamari e bietoline,* try it; ditto the chestnut ice cream for dessert. Open later than most. Closed Sundays and the last 3 weeks of July. Reservations advised. 25r Piazza Taddeo Gaddi (phone: 702100). Moderate.

La Sostanza – Popularly called Troia, literally a hog (also a woman of easy virtue), this is one of Florence's oldest and most cherished *trattorie,* serving some of the best steaks in town. If you haven't had a *bistecca alla fiorentina* with Tuscan beans, get here early. The place is picturesquely plain and tiny, the turnover as fast as the service (which can be rude if you try to linger). Communal tables. Closed Saturday evenings, Sundays, and August. 25r Via del Porcellana (phone: 212691). Moderate.

Tredici Gobbi – Once known for Hungarian cooking, which still simmmers on the back burner, Tuscan specialties have come to the fore. Closed Sunday evenings, Mondays, and August. 9r Via del Porcellana (phone: 298769). Moderate.

Antico Fattore – In the shadow of the Uffizi, it's famous for its *ribollita,* a vegetable soup so thick with broccoli, bread, and white beans a spoon stands up in it. The rest of the menu is equally hearty peasant fare. Closed Sundays, Mondays, and mid-July to early August. 1r Via Lambertesca (phone: 261215). Moderate to inexpensive.

Angiolino – Very good potluck and very economical. This is on the Pitti side of the river and the ambience is cozy. Closed Sundays and Mondays. 36r Via di Santo Spirito (phone: 298976). Inexpensive.

Fagioli – A cheery, rustic ambience and a full bar. Enjoy the *passato di fagioli con pasta,* a thick soup of white beans and pasta. Closed weekends and August. 47r Corso Tintori (phone: 244285). Inexpensive.

Le Mossacce – Still largely frequented by habitués, it's filled with long paper-covered tables and serves good country cooking. Try the *ribollita,* a thick and hearty vegetable soup. Closed Saturday nights, Sundays, and August. 55r Via del Proconsolo (phone: 294361). Inexpensive.

Vecchia Bettola – A typical Tuscan *trattoria* with quality home-style cooking and marble tabletops. Closed Mondays and Tuesdays. 32-34r Viale Ariosto (phone: 224158). Inexpensive.

Note: When the urge for something delectably *dolce* becomes irresistible, we head for one of our two overwhelming favorites. *Vivoli,* 7 Via Isola della Stinche, serves the best *gelati* in town, in flavors from chocolate to grapefruit, fresh strawberry to tea. *Rivoire,* on the Piazza della Signoria (a combination coffeehouse/candy shop), sells a confection of creamed chocolate that you literally eat with a spoon. It's sold in individual boxes — with spoon attached!

FRANKFURT

Trade and traffic have formed Frankfurt's destiny since its earliest existence as a community, more than 1,200 years ago. Its location on the Main River at the heart of the European continent made it the crossroads of prehistoric trade routes linking northern Europe with the Mediterranean areas, and Eastern with Western Europe. The city grew, spreading out to meet the imperial forest of Dreieich in the south and the wooded Taunus Mountains encircling the broad plain formed by the Main as it flows toward the Rhine. Frankfurt today is a bustling commercial city with a genuine international flair. It is also a city with many parks and museums. Look behind the imposing glass and steel of modern Frankfurt and you will find lovingly restored landmarks that highlight the city's long history.

The Celts were here first, but were forced west across the Rhine by migrating German tribes. Romans had settled along the Main by the 1st century AD, but they fled the Saxon tribes, who, in turn, were driven out by the Franks in 496. The little settlement on the Main became the site of the Franks' ford — where Saxons from south of the river could cross over to trade.

Ludwig the German, first ruler of the German Empire and a grandson of Charlemagne, made Frankfurt his capital, and from 1356 to 1792 Frankfurt was where the Holy Roman emperors were elected. Frankfurt was granted the right to mint money in the 16th century, and since that time finance and trade have been synonymous with it. The Rothschild financial dynasty started here with Meyer Amschel Rothschild (1743–1812); his sons who succeeded him were known as "the five Frankfurters."

Frankfurt also claims Germany's greatest poet, Johann Wolfgang von Goethe, as its own. Goethe was born here in 1749. St. Paul's Church, where Germany's first National Assembly met in 1848, has become a symbol of German liberalism.

In this century, Frankfurt once again earned a reputation as a center of liberalism, as pockets of opposition to the Nazis were centered here. Although a massive Allied air attack during World War II destroyed much of the city, Frankfurt was quick to rebuild after the war and never really stopped. The city has made a conscious attempt to relieve the coldness of modern skyscrapers with attractive pedestrian precincts for shopping and strolling or simply relaxing in an outdoor café. The city's parks and forest and neighboring green belts are much used by Frankfurt's urban population.

Around 600,000 people live in Frankfurt proper, but the greater Frankfurt area, extending across the fertile Main valley and up into the Taunus Mountains, has a population of more than a million. Frankfurt's citizens work in its financial center and in the chemical, electronics, machine tool, and printing industries. They are cosmopolitan and used to sampling the world's best goods as the result of the role Frankfurt plays as an international trade center.

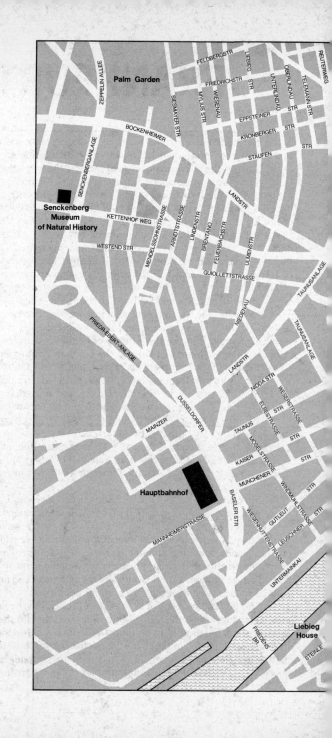

Frankfurt has become a city of superlatives: There are more skyscrapers here than in any other West German city, the fastest trains, the most cars per capita, the most banks, and the largest airport. Recently, however, Frankfurters have expressed fears that all the efficiency, the money making, and the slightly smug air of success may have an adverse effect on the casual approach to life that exists here more than in some other German cities. This is, after all, the city that shuts down for an afternoon each spring so that its citizens can walk in the woods. A city whose mascot is that bumbling little kid, Struwwelpeter, is in danger of becoming Manhattan on the Main — "Mainhattan," as the Frankfurters sarcastically call it.

FRANKFURT AT-A-GLANCE

 SEEING THE CITY: You get a sweeping view of the Main valley, the Taunus Mountains, and the city from the glass-enclosed observation deck of the 1,086-foot television tower near Rosa Luxemburgstrasse in the Ginnheim section of northwest Frankfurt. There is a cafeteria and a revolving restaurant in the tower — the tallest structure in West Germany. Admission charge for the observation platform. Open daily, March through September.

SPECIAL PLACES: Central Frankfurt is on the right bank of a bend in the Main. Most of the commercial and historic areas are in a small area ringed by a series of green parks that follow the old city walls. Across the Main is a district called Sachsenhausen. Both these areas are ideal for exploring on foot. But you can also see Frankfurt on weekends by riding the *Ebbelwei Express,* gaily painted streetcars that begin circle tours of the city every 40 minutes. With your ride you'll get music, and you can buy some of Frankfurt's famous apple wine (*Apfelwein*) to sip along the way. Hop aboard at any of the 18 *Ebbelwei Express* stops, including those in the Theaterplatz, at the main railroad station, or at the intersection of Gartenstrasse and Schweizerstrasse in Sachsenhausen. It costs about $2.50 for an hour's ride; call 136-82425 for information.

DOWNTOWN

Hauptwache – This beautifully reconstructed baroque building, once a sentry house dating from 1730, and the little square over which it presides are considered the heart of Frankfurt. There is a lovely outdoor café in which you can enjoy coffee and cake while you get your bearings. Just in front of the café is an escalator leading from the street to a huge underground shopping mall. Before leaving the square, though, you may want to visit St. Katharine's Church (Katharinenkirche), where the poet Goethe was christened and confirmed. An der Hauptwache.

Goethe's House and Museum – A few blocks southwest of the Hauptwache is the boyhood home of Frankfurt's favorite son. Faithfully reconstructed after the war and furnished with many original possessions of the poet's family, the house offers a fascinating peek at 18th-century life in a wealthy, commercial city. In an adjoining museum, you can see documents on Goethe's life and work as well as pictures and sculpture by well-known artists of his era. Open daily. Admission charge. 23 Grosser Hirschgraben (phone: 282824).

Römerberg – South of the Hauptwache, on a broad square with a statue of Justice, are three adjoining burghers' houses that have served as Frankfurt's city hall since 1405. The three gabled façades and the row of seven medieval houses across the street are the symbol of this city. History comes alive in the Imperial Hall (Kaisersaal) where banquets were held to celebrate the coronations of the Holy Roman Emperors. East of Römerberg Platz is the Cathedral of St. Bartholomew (the Dom), built between the 13th and 15th centuries on a Carolingian foundation dating from 852. The cathedral's outstanding feature is a 15th-century dome and lantern tower. Between Römerbery and the cathedral is the *Kunsthalle,* a series of exhibition halls.

Alt-Sachsenhausen – A few steps from Römerberg, near where the ancient Franks forded the river, the Eiserner Steg footbridge leads across the river into another old section of the city. (*Sachsenhausen* means "Saxons' houses.") Here you can enjoy the jumble of half-timbered houses and rough cobbled streets with their inviting pubs and restaurants, and the charming little squares and pretty fountains that are particularly lively meeting places at night and on weekends.

Palmengarten (Palm Garden) – One of Europe's most famous botanical gardens, these 55 acres of trees, meadows, ponds, gardens, and footpaths offer a welcome sanctuary from the bustling city. Over 12,000 varieties of plants grow in the park and thousands of orchids and cacti are displayed in its conservatories. A traditional Sunday afternoon entertainment in Frankfurt is a stroll through the flower gardens, perhaps, pausing to listen to one of the concerts, followed by an elaborate ice cream sundae on the flower-bedecked terrace of the *Palmengarten* restaurant Open daily. Admission charge. Entrance at Palmengartenstr. (phone: 212-3939).

Zoologischer Garten (Frankfurt Zoo) – This is one of Europe's oldest zoos, but nonetheless one of its most up to date. Founded in 1858, the zoo is noted for its beautifully landscaped open-air enclosures and for its success in breeding rare species. Open daily. Admission charge. 16 Alfred-Brehm-Pl. (phone: 212-3731).

Frankfurter Wertpapierbörse (Frankfurt Stock Exchange) – Frankfurt is one of the most important financial centers in the world. Nearly 400 German and overseas banks have headquarters or subsidiaries in the city. Although open to the public less than an hour on any given day, no tour of the financial district would be complete without a visit to the spectators' gallery to watch the activity on the floor. Open weekdays, 11:30 AM to 12:15 PM. No admission charge. Börsenpl. (phone: 219-7382).

Städelsches Kunstinstitut und Städtische Galerie (Städel Museum Institute of Art and Municipal Gallery) – Famous works of Flemish Primitives and German masters of the 16th century are on display in the 2nd-floor picture gallery. Open daily except Mondays, 10 AM to 5 PM. Admission charge. 63 Schaumainkai (phone: 617092).

Alte Oper (Old Opera House) – A victim of wartime bombing, this 100-year-old landmark was finally rebuilt in 1981. Although no opera is performed here, the ultramodern complex of rooms and halls is now used for concerts and conferences. The façade and the vestibule (now a café) were fully restored. Opernplatz (phone: 134-0400).

SUBURBS

Deutsches Ledermuseum (Leather Museum) – Exhibitions of the history of shoes and handbags are displayed in a wonderfully fragrant museum in Offenbach just 5 miles (8 km) southeast of Frankfurt. Open daily. Admission charge. 86 Frankfurterstr., in Offenbach (phone: 813020).

■ **EXTRA SPECIAL:** The charming old town of Marburg an der Lahn, remarkable for its university, its castle, and the first Gothic church ever built in Germany (between 1235 and 1285), is 59 miles (94 km) north of Frankfurt in the Hesse region. The church is dedicated to St. Elizabeth of Hungary, who lived and performed good works here. The university is a center for Protestant theology. On the market square in the old quarter of town, you can see several old half-timbered houses dating from the mid-16th century. As you wander the twisting alleys of the old quarter, you may meet country people in traditional costume, particularly if your visit coincides with market days, Wednesdays and Saturdays.

SOURCES AND RESOURCES

TOURIST INFORMATION: For information, maps, brochures, hotel and restaurant listings, plus special sightseeing tours and tickets to local events, see the Frankfurt Tourist Association (Frankfurter Verkehrsamt). It has information bureaus on the north side of the main train station, opposite track 23 (phone: 212-8849 or 212-8850), and on level B of the Hauptwache underground mall (phone: 212-8708). The office at the train station is open daily; the one at Hauptwache closes on Sundays.

Frankfurt Guide of the City, by Franz Lerner, is the best guide published in English. It is filled with city history and interesting facts as well as a variety of walking tours. It is available at bookstores and some newsstands.

The US Consulate is at 21 Siesmayerstr. (phone: 283401).

Local Coverage – *Seven,* an English-language weekly that carries a calendar of events throughout Germany, is available at newsstands.

Food – *Seven* also has restaurant listings.

Telephone – The area code for Frankfurt is 069.

CLIMATE AND CLOTHES: Frankfurt's climate is similar to San Francisco's — seldom very hot or very cold. However, it is often overcast and frequently foggy and rainy, so a raincoat is recommended in all seasons. Late spring and fall are apt to be the most pleasant times to visit. There is very little air conditioning — so some visitors may find it uncomfortable during the occasional summer week when temperatures climb into the 80s F (around 26C-32C).

GETTING AROUND: Frankfurt has a clean, efficient, and quiet rapid transit system of buses, streetcars, subways, and trains. The trip from the Rhine-Main Airport to Frankfurt's main railway station takes only 12 minutes by train. Use the same kind of ticket for the entire system. Buy tickets from automatic dispensers before boarding or purchase a special 1-day, cut-rate ticket at the tourist information bureaus. Maps and timetables are conveniently posted throughout the system.

Airport – Frankfurt's Rhine-Main Airport handles both domestic and international flights. It's about a 20-minute drive from the airport to downtown, and a taxi will cost 30-35 deutsche marks (about $16-$19). The S-14 and S-15 lines of the S-Bahn interurban train system speed their way to downtown Frankfurt in just 11 minutes (look for signs to the S-Bahn, and take the trains headed for Hauptbahnhof).

Buses and Streetcars – City buses (*Stadtbus*) and streetcars (*Strassenbahn*) transport passengers inexpensively to all parts of the city and to many suburbs.

Car Rental – All major international firms are represented. But if driving a special German vehicle — Porsche, BMW, Mercedes — on the autobahn at top speed is one reason you're visiting Germany, get in touch with *Auto Exclusiv.* They rent ultra-high performance vehicles (booking in North America, call 813-526-6292).

Subways and Trains – The subway system, called the *U-Bahn,* and the new fast trains, *S-Bahn,* to outlying areas get you where you want to go quickly and comfortably. The main stops are at Hauptwache and the railway station.

Taxi – There are stands near major hotels, stations, and at some intersections. Most public telephone booths have a taxi call-number posted. But taxis are expensive.

SPECIAL EVENTS: Frankfurt is at its busiest during the more than a dozen trade fairs that draw some 1.2 million visitors to the city each year. The biggest of these are the *International Frankfurt Fairs* held in spring and fall and the *Book Fair* in October. Most of these events are held at the fairgrounds (*Messegelände*), a huge exhibition center near the main railway station. The tradition of trade fairs in Frankfurt dates back 800 years. There are also numerous public fairs, such as the *Main Fair,* in August, in the streets between the river and St. Paul's Church; and *Dippemess,* a big country fair held in April and again in September, with colorful stalls of crockery the main attraction. One other very special local holiday deserves mention: *Wäldchestag.* On the Tuesday following Whitmonday, most Frankfurters leave the city to walk in the neighboring woods, eat sausages and drink beer, and dance in the Forest House (*Oberforsthaus*).

 MUSEUMS: In addition to those mentioned in *Special Places,* Frankfurt has a number of interesting museums (most of which charge no admission). They are all closed Mondays.

   Bundespostmuseum (Postal Museum) – Exhibits relating to the history of the post office and the telephone company, including a large collection of stamps. 53 Schaumainkai (phone: 60601).

   Film Museum – 41 Schaumainkai (phone: 212-8830).

   Historisches Museum (History Museum) – Frankfurt over the years. 19 Saalgasse am Römerberg (phone: 212-5599).

   Jüdisches Museum (Jewish Museum) – Jewish life in Germany, through exhibitions, seminars, readings, and films. 14-15 Untermainkai (phone: 212-5000).

   Liebieghaus (Liebieg House) – Ancient and modern sculpture. 71 Schaumainkai (phone: 638907).

   Museum für Kunsthandwerk (Museum of Arts and Crafts) – 30,000 European and Asian handicrafts. 17 Schaumainkai (phone: 212-4037).

   Museum für Völkerkunde (Museum of Ethnology) – Changing exhibitions, with emphasis on Third World countries. 29 Schaumainkai (phone: 212-5391).

   Naturmuseum Senckenberg (Senckenberg Museum of Natural History) – Animals, plants, fossils, and geological items, including an impressive collection of dinosaurs and prehistoric whales. 25 Senckenberganlange. The exception, it is open daily (phone: 75421).

   Schirn Kunsthalle – Modern art. Am Römerberg (phone: 15450).

 SHOPPING: As befits Europe's major transportation hub, Frankfurt is filled with goods from all over the world. It is said that more money passes through the cash registers of the well-stocked department stores on the Zeil than on any other street in Europe. The best-known department stores are *Kaufhof,* 116 Zeil, and *Hertie,* 90 Zeil. There are several pedestrian streets besides the Zeil, including Grosse Bockenheimerstrasse, with its chic boutiques and elegant apparel shops. Incidentally, this street is known locally as Fressgasse (a rough English equivalent is "Gluttony Alley") because it is lined with so many restaurants, wine bars, and delicatessens. The best buys are the well-known German cutlery, expensive but superbly made leather clothing, and Frankfurt's distinctive blue and gray pottery.

   Bellak – The best in German handicrafts. 20 Goethestr.

   Leder-Stoll – Expensive leather goods. 68 Schweizer Str. and 50 Schäfergasse.

   Lorey – Hummel, Meissen, and Rosenthal figurines. 16 Schillerstr.

   Rosenthal am Kaiserplatz – Porcelain. 10 Friedensstr.

SPORTS AND FITNESS: One out of every six Frankfurt residents belongs to some type of sports club, and walking and jogging along the river or the marked paths in the city forest and in the nearby Taunus Mountains have reached epidemic proportion. Physical fitness is even sponsored by the state government, which maintains *Trimm Dich* facilities ("keep yourself trim"), a 1.5-mile (2.5-km) illustrated course of exercises and jogging in the city forest. Frankfurt is a major soccer city, with professional matches held in the *Wald Stadium,* Mörfelder

Landstr. (phone: 670-8011). There's also a 6-day bicycle race each year at the *Festhalle* at the fairgrounds.

Bicycling – Besides the 6-day race, numerous cycling events are scheduled during summer months, and there are paths in the city parks and the forest.

Fitness Center – The *United Sporting Club,* 150A Mainzer Landstr. (phone: 735050), is open to non-members.

Golf – The 18-hole course at *Frankfurter Golfclub* is just west of *Wald Stadium.* 41 Golf Str. (phone: 666-2317/8).

Horse Racing – Flat races and steeplechase races are held at *Racecourse Frankfurt-South* in suburban Niederrad, Schwarzwaldstr. (phone: 677018).

Ice Skating – You can skate or just watch other people at various rinks, including one at the *Wald Stadium.*

Jogging – About a mile from the city center in Grüneburgpark; take the subway to Holzhausenstr. or bus #36 to Grüneburg Weg. Better yet, try Stadtwald, south of the Main River and 4 miles from downtown; take the S-Bahn's S-8 line to Oberrad.

Soccer – *Eintracht* is Frankfurt's professional club. You can join the enthusiastic supporters at *Wald Stadium* nearly every other weekend during the season (for tickets, phone: 678040).

Swimming – Several hotels have swimming pools, and there are numerous indoor and outdoor pools throughout the city. *Stadtbad Mitte,* 4-8 Hochstr., has warm and cold pools as well as saunas (phone: 212-5238).

Tennis – Exhibition matches are played at *Wald Stadium* and the *Festhalle.* It is difficult for visitors to get court time at parks and clubs because of local demand.

 THEATER: Frankfurt has 20 theaters, but performances generally are in German, so they may be of limited interest unless you know the language. *The City Theater* is in temporary quarters: the large stage in Bockenheimer Warte (phone: 256-2434) and the small stage in Hofstriz (phone: 256-2395). The *Fritz Rémond-Theater* is at the Frankfurt Zoo, 16 Alfred Brehm Pl. (phone: 435166), and often produces current British and American hits in German. Drama is offered at the *Theater am Turm* (*TAT*), 2 Eschersheimer Landstr. (phone: 154-5110), and you'll find light comedy the specialty at *Die Kömodie,* Theaterpl. (phone: 284580).

 MUSIC: Whatever your taste in music, from opera and jazz to punk, you'll hear it in Frankfurt. Following a fire in 1988, the *City Opera* has had to perform on the stage of the theater in the *Städtische Buhnen* arts complex on Theaterplatz (phone: 236061). There are frequent choral, symphony, and chamber music concerts at *Hessischer-Rundfunk,* 8 Bertramstr. (phone: 1551), at the huge *Jahrhunderthalle* in suburban Höchst (phone: 360-1211), and at the *Old Opera House,* Opernplatz (phone: 134-0400). Jazz lovers will love Frankfurt, which is purported to have more than 100 daily performances, ranging from traditional New Orleans to modern jazz. *Der Jazzkeller,* 18a Kleine Bockenheimerstr. (phone: 288537), is the best-known club, but you should also try *Jazz-Kneipe,* 70 Berlinerstr. (phone: 287173); *Sinkkasten Arts Club,* 5 Brönnerstr. (phone: 280385); *Jazzhaus,* 12 Kleine Bockenheimerstr. (phone: 287194); and *Jazz-Life Podium,* 22 Kleine Rittergasse (phone: 626346).

 NIGHTCLUBS AND NIGHTLIFE: All of the city's big hotels offer music and dancing, and discotheques are cropping up all over the city. *Why Not,* on Hauptwache Pl., doesn't really get going until after midnight, then stays open until 4 AM. *Tangente,* 87 Bockenheimer Landstr. (phone: 745773), features a pub upstairs and a disco in the cellar. One of the trendiest discos is *Dorian Gray,* at the airport, modeled after New York's late Studio 54. Then there's *Roxanne,*

1-3 Grosse Friedberger Str. (phone: 294340), a dance club that attracts devotees of all ages. *Blue Infinitum* in the *Plaza* hotel, 2-10 Hamburger Allee (phone: 770721), features floor shows as well as dancing, as do *St. John's Inn,* 20 Grosser Hirschgraben, and *Vogue,* 14 Junghofstr. Pub-hopping in Sachsenhausen gets merrier and merrier as the night wears on. Look for the traditional green wreath hanging over the door to identify taverns that serve Frankfurt's special apple wine. Among the most authentic are *Zum Fichtekraenzi,* 5 Wallstr. (phone: 612778); *Zum Gemalten Hause,* 67 Schweizerstr. (phone: 614559); and *Apfelweinwirtschaft Wagner,* 71 Schweizerstr. (phone: 612565).

BEST IN TOWN

 CHECKING IN: Although Frankfurt has a total of 200 hotels and pensions, with over 14,000 beds, only the most confident traveler comes here without a reservation. Space is always tight, and empty hotel rooms are nearly nonexistent during the big trade fairs, when, incidentally, the highest prices normally prevail. At an expensive hotel, expect to pay from $100 to more than $200 a night for a double room. Moderate hotels charge from $50 to $100; anything below must be considered inexpensive. Virtually all hotels in Frankfurt, regardless of price, share the German virtue of cleanliness. All telephone numbers are in the 069 area code unless otherwise indicated.

Canadian Pacific Frankfurt Plaza – Frankfurt's newest luxury hotel — the tallest in West Germany — is near the fairgrounds, but its decor is more sophisticated than you might expect from a hotel that caters to conventioneers. There is a bakery on the premises, a small disco, and a seductive piano bar, *Die Biblio Theke.* 2-10 Hamburger Allee (phone: 79550). Expensive.

Frankfurt Inter-Continental – One of Europe's largest, with American-style hotel service. It has a swimming pool, sauna, and solarium, a glittering nightclub, and several restaurants, including one on the roof with an enchanting view of the Main and Frankfurt's skyline. Ask for a room on the river side. 43 Wilhelm-Leuschnerstr. (phone: 26050). Expensive.

Frankfurt-Sheraton – Walk right in from the airport's central terminal. A recent extension has made this one of West Germany's largest hotels, with 820 rooms. In addition to the usual amenities, there is a comfortable restaurant, *Papillon,* with an extensive menu and good wine list. The *Red Baron* nightclub is a popular late night spot. Central terminal, Rhine-Main Airport (phone: 69770). Expensive.

Frankfurter Hof – In the tradition of grand European hotels; it was refurbished and restored to its prewar charm after serving as headquarters for the Allied occupation forces. It's easy to find an attractive spot here where a waiter will bring a drink, a newspaper, or a message. International movers and shakers from the political and financial worlds dine in the *Restaurant Français* (see *Eating Out*). The less expensive *Grill* has an extensive menu and offers excellent service. 17 Kaiserpl. (phone: 21502). Expensive.

Parkhotel Frankfurt – Typical of small European-style luxury hotels, including what many Frankfurters consider "the best table in town" in its restaurant, *La Truffe* (see *Eating Out*). Conveniently near the main train station. 26 Wiesenhüttenpl. (phone: 26970). Expensive.

Admiral – In a nice location near the zoo, this 67-room hotel offers good service and reasonable rates. 25 Hölderlinstr. (phone: 448021). Moderate.

Haus Hübner – This small hotel is in a pleasant neighborhood not far from the main train station. 23 Westendstr. (phone: 746044). Moderate.

Hotel am Dom – Although in the historic downtown area, this smallish hostelry is an oasis of quiet. 3 Kannengiessergasse (phone: 282141). Moderate.

Motel Frankfurt – A rarity in Germany is a motel in the city center. This one, with 66 rooms, is convenient and offers good service and reasonable rates. 204 Escher-sheimer Landstr. (phone: 568011). Moderate.

Hotel am Holzhausenpark – The charm of this small hotel is its location on a quiet street facing a small park north of the city center. Seven languages are spoken here, making it a favorite of international visitors. 62 Holzhausenstr. (phone: 590801). Moderate.

Mozart – This charming 35-room hotel is next to the US military headquarters. Note that the quieter rooms are in the back. 17 Parkstr. (phone: 550831). Moderate.

Diana – With 24 rooms, this small hostelry is near the city center. No frills, but standard comfort. Breakfast extra. 83 Westendstr. (phone: 747007). Moderate to inexpensive.

Maingau – In Sachsenhausen, on the south bank of the Main River, this is a particularly reasonably priced hotel. 38-40 Schifferstr. (phone: 617001). Moderate to inexpensive.

Weisses Haus – This small, pleasant hotel is conveniently located just off the city center. No frills here, but there is a restaurant on the premises and the rooms certainly live up to German standards for comfort and cleanliness. 18 Jahnstr. (phone: 554605). Inexpensive.

 EATING OUT: Though Frankfurt is not noted for its culinary arts, local specialties are prepared just as well in restaurants as in private homes. The large population of foreign-born residents inspires a wide spectrum of European and Asian cuisine. Lunch is often the main daily meal, and in most places it is served between 11 AM and 3 PM. Restaurants then close until about 5:30 PM. Except in big hotel restaurants, it is difficult to just drop in anywhere for a late lunch. However, there is a late afternoon *Kaffee* ritual, at which Frankfurters fortify themselves with coffee and pastry or a snack at a *Konditorei*. A local specialty that is a perfect nosh with beer or wine is *Handkäs mit Musik:* soft Limburger cheese mixed with vinegar, oil, a bit of onion, and a few caraway seeds.' And whether the frankfurter originated here or not, you can still buy the best franks in Frankfurt, on the freshest rolls, from a cart right outside the *Kaufhof* department store. You'll pay $50 or more for two, not including drinks or extras, at restaurants in the expensive category; $30 to $50, in the moderate range; and under $30 at inexpensive places. All telephone numbers are in the 069 area code unless otherwise indicated.

Erno's Bistro – A French bistro with checkered tablecloths and superior cooking. It's apt to be crowded, but worth the wait for a table. Closed weekends and mid-June to mid-July. 15 Liebigstr. (phone: 721997). Expensive.

Humperdinck – Not your typical Hansel and Gretel atmosphere nor your typical German fare. Instead, this establishment in the fashionable Westend district concocts wonderful nouvelle cuisine dishes, with an emphasis on seafood and lamb. Closed Saturdays until 7 PM, Sundays, and during the summer school vacation. Reservations advised. 95 Grüneburgweg (phone: 722122). Expensive.

Français – Game and French cuisine and excellent service have made this dining room at the *Frankfurter Hof* a particular favorite of people used to eating the best. Closed Sundays and holidays. Reservations advised. 17 Kaiserpl. (phone: 21502). Expensive.

La Truffe – Recently redone, this restaurant in the *Park* hotel is decorated in almost as classically elegant a fashion as its traditional French cuisine. Try the truffle dishes, the delicious cheeses, and the fine wines. Closed for Saturday lunches,

Sundays, and mid-July to mid-August. Reservations advised. 36 Wiesenhüttenpl. (phone: 269-8830). Expensive.

Le Midi – A relatively new, intimate place serving excellent French fare at reasonable prices. Closed weekends and during the summer school holidays. Reservations advised. 47 Liebigstr. (phone: 721438). Expensive to moderate.

Rôtisserie – This elegant restaurant in the *Inter-Continental* hotel is a first class eating establishment, especially when game is in season. Closed Sundays. Reservations advised. 43 Wilhelm Leuschnerstr. (phone: 230561). Expensive to moderate.

Alte Brückenmühle – On the Sachsenhausen side of the river, this cozy eatery's decor is in the traditional, old German style. The menu features the choicest cuts of veal, beef, pork, poultry, game, and fish — all prepared in accordance with old Frankfurt recipes. Lunch specials are especially reasonable in price. Closed for lunch on Saturdays. 10 Wallstr. (phone: 612543). Moderate.

Börsenkeller – In the financial district, serving delicious roast pork and other local specialties in a large rustic room decorated with wood tables, wrought-iron lamps, and candles. Closed Sundays. Reservations advised for midday. 11 Schillerstr. (phone: 281115). Moderate.

Dippegucker – Decorated in typical Frankfurt style, with hanging brass lamps and bright tablecloths, this restaurant is popular with families for Sunday afternoon dinner. Hearty portions of good German food, including Frankfurt's famous smoked pork chops with sauerkraut, *Rippchen mit Kraut,* are served here. Closed Christmas Eve. Reservations advised. 40 Eschenheimer Anlage (phone: 551965). Moderate.

Frankfurter Stubb – German specialties are beautifully prepared in this well-appointed cellar restaurant at the *Frankfurter Hof.* When white asparagus (*Spargel*) from the Schwetzinger area south of Frankfurt is in season, in May, it is presented here in an imaginative array of dishes, served with wine chosen to complement its delicate flavor. Closed Sundays. 33 Bethmannstr. (phone: 21502). Moderate.

Gargantua – Despite its name, this charming restaurant is intimate. The crowd it attracts is one that prefers first class continental cuisine at reasonable prices, and it often takes on a counterculture flavor. Closed Sundays, Mondays, and July; no lunch on weekends. Reservations advised. 3 Friesengasse (phone: 776442). Moderate.

Knoblauch – The name means garlic in German, an ingredient used with a deft hand in the fragrant, hearty, delicious French food. A warm, noisy, cheerful place, it is actually a pub-restaurant and art gallery. Closed Saturdays and Sundays. 39 Staufenstr. (phone: 722828). Moderate.

Altes Zollhaus – Travelers who could not make it through the Frankfurt city gates in time found refuge for the night in this former customs house, dating from the 18th century. Now one of Frankfurt's newest restaurants, it specializes in local dishes. Closed Mondays. Reservations advised. 531 Friedberger Landstr. (phone: 472707). Inexpensive.

Künstlerkeller – In the cellar of a former Carmelite monastery dating from the 13th century. Hearty food, and the convivial patrons will make you feel both comfortable and welcome. Be sure to ask the hostess for her wine recommendations. Closed Mondays. No reservations. 2 Seckbächer Gasse (phone: 292242). Inexpensive.

GENEVA

Probably the most international of all cities, Geneva is where world leaders have often gathered in order to negotiate agreements and dream of peace. It is the birthplace and headquarters of the International Red Cross, founded in 1863 by Henri Dunant, a native son. The Geneva Convention, binding nations to care for all sick and wounded in war, was signed here in 1864. Home to the defunct League of Nations, center of the European United Nations, Geneva has hosted Big Four foreign ministers' conferences in 1954 and 1959 and has been the site of the nuclear disarmament talks.

Geneva's international role is a historical one, certainly due in part to its central location at one of Europe's crossroads. Near the French border and not far from Italy, where the Rhone River flows into its 45-mile-long lake, called Lake Geneva in English and Lac Léman in French, the city has had a very long and distinguished history. "Gen-eva," a Ligurian word that is the same as "Genoa," means "emerging from the waters." Waters were important in the city's history, since Geneva was the site of the only bridge across the Rhone for many centuries, a bridge that had been built and rebuilt many times even before the Romans took the city from the Celts in 58 BC.

Because of its strategic location, Geneva was also the site of many feuds and wars, from the rivalry between its prince bishop and the Duke of Savoy during the 15th century to Napoleon's occupation from 1798 to 1815. The year 1815 marked Geneva's entry into the Swiss Confederation to protect its long-fought-for independence and peace.

During the Middle Ages, Geneva, as host to a series of international fairs, took up its international vocation. The Protestant Reformation left a deeper mark on Geneva than on any other city, since John Calvin himself chose it as his headquarters, earning for Geneva the title of "the Rome of the Protestants." Here Calvin preached and prayed but also acted as a dictatorial ruler, building new ramparts, creating his own laws, and even burning his enemy, Miguel Serveto, at the stake for his incompatible religious opinions. Calvin's most influential move was the founding of the University of Geneva in 1559: For 2 centuries thereafter, Geneva became the schoolmaster for all of Protestant Europe. So austere and rigid was the tone of this Calvinist city that many of its own citizens, the most famous of whom was Jean-Jacques Rousseau, opted to flee. The great 18th-century philosopher never returned to his birthplace after his books were burned there.

Other celebrities found Geneva more congenial, notably Rousseau's great rival Voltaire and that great Swiss writer and personality Madame de Staël. And virtually all the romantics flocked to the city and its surrounding lake: Chateaubriand, Byron, Dostoyevsky, Goethe, and Victor Hugo were just a few.

Today, with more than 160,000 inhabitants, Geneva is rather small for a major city. Human in scale, its sights can easily be seen on foot. Its two most characteristic landmarks are the Jet d'Eau, said to be the tallest fountain in the world, rising to a height of between 400 and 500 feet from May to October; and the Flower Clock in the Jardin Anglais, with its face made of flowers and its hands keeping perfect time — as befits a city that is the home of the leading watchmakers of the world.

Whether you want to buy a watch; walk along the quais, particularly the Quai du Mont-Blanc with its panoramic view of the Alps; visit this capital of the Reformation with its old town clustered in narrow streets around the Cathedral of St. Pierre; or, as many do, use Geneva as a base for exploring the Alps or the lake — Geneva, the international city, will warmly extend toward you its traditional hospitality.

GENEVA AT-A-GLANCE

SEEING THE CITY: The best view of the town and its surroundings is from the North Tower of Cathédrale St.-Pierre; on a clear day it is well worth the 153 steps and the admission charge; the panorama of city, lake, Alps, and Jura Mountains is spectacular. Another superb view — and the one most often photographed — is from the Quai du Mont-Blanc near the bridge; on the sailboat-dotted lake you can see the famous Jet d'Eau, pride of Geneva, with the Alps as background.

SPECIAL PLACES: The old town, built on a hill around its famous Reformation Cathedral, was important in medieval times as the site of international fairs. The few streets in the immediate vicinity of the Bourg de Four are easily explored on foot. Just stroll down the narrow, cobblestone streets, discovering delightful corners like Place Bourg de Four, the former market square, have coffee or snacks in one of the cafés, and browse in the antiques stores. In summer there are regular walks in the old town with English-speaking guides; ask at the tourist office (see *Sources and Resources*) for details.

Carouge – Within the city limits is a little old town where time stands still and people live their quiet lives independent of busy Geneva, between its low houses, shady squares, fountains, and pubs. Enchanting! Carouge is becoming more and more popular after dark, though, when its cafés and small theaters fill up.

DOWNTOWN

Cathédrale St.-Pierre – Built in the 12th to 13th century on the site of earlier churches, Cathédrale St.-Pierre was reconstructed later; John Calvin preached here, and his chair can be seen in the austere interior. The archaeological excavations under the church, which date from the 4th century AD, were opened to the public in 1986. Open daily; closed at lunchtime. Grand Rue Hôtel de Ville.

Calvin Auditorium – Next door to Cathédrale St.-Pierre is a Gothic church where John Knox used to preach; it was restored in 1959 for John Calvin's 450th anniversary. Grand Rue Hôtel de Ville.

Maison Tavel – A few steps from Calvin Auditorium is the oldest house in Geneva, already in existence by 1303. Inside, the *Museum of Old Geneva,* opened in late 1986, features a collection of historic engravings as well as changing exhibitions on Old Geneva. Grand Rue Hôtel de Ville.

Old Arsenal – Across the street from the Maison Tavel is the arsenal dating from

GENEVA

LAKE GENEVA

PROMENADE DU LAC

Jardin Anglais

GENERAL GUISAN

QUAI GUSTAVE ADOR

GUSTAVE ADOR

RUE DU ROVERAY

To Parc de la Grange

QUAI DU LAC

RUE DU LAC

RUE MUZY

R.DE LA SCIE

RUE VERSONNEX

RUE DES EAUX-VIVES

RUE DU TRENTE-ET-UN-DÉCEMBRE

RUE DE LA BLANVALET

RUE DE MONCHOISY

RUE DU NANT

RUE DU RHONE

RUE D'ITALIE

DE RIVE

RUE

RUE PIERRE FATIO

ROND-POINT DE RIVE

BD HELVETIQUE

RUE DES GLACIS DE RIVE

AV DE FRONTENEX

DU PARC

FLA VALLÉE

RUE

DALCROZE

RUE AMI LULLIN

FERDINAND HODLER

RUE ADRIEN LACHENAL

RUE ST-LAURENT

RUE DE LA TERRASSIERE

DE VILLEREUSE

Museum of Art and History

Museum of Old Musical Instruments

BOULEVARD

RUE LEFORT

RUE CHARLES

RUE DE MONNETIER

RUE MONT- DE-SION

GALLAND

BOULEVARD DES TRANCHEES

RTE DE MALAGNOU

RUE -TOR

the days of Napoleon. (Its cannons were seized by the Austrians in 1814.) On the wall are three modern mosaics by Cingria. Grand Rue Hôtel de Ville.

Hôtel de Ville – Geneva's town hall, where the Geneva Convention was signed in 1864 in the Alabama Court. (The room where the signing took place may be visited by applying to the guardian.) Its oldest part is Baudet Tower, erected in 1455. Grand Rue Hôtel de Ville.

St. Germain Church – On the site of an early Christian basilica, with beautiful modern stained glass windows, it is an example of 15th-century Gothic architecture. Grand Rue Hôtel de Ville.

Reformation Monument – Under the ramparts that used to surround the town, in a pleasant park belonging to the university, is a long, plain wall, erected in 1917, with statues of the main Reformation leaders — Calvin, Knox, Farel, de Bèze — flanked by other, less prominent personages; bas-reliefs and tablets tell the story of Calvin, one of the world leaders of the Protestant Reformation. Promenade des Bastions.

Promenade on the Quais – Both sides of the lake are interesting. You might start at Quai du Mont-Blanc (see *Seeing the City*). Here are several top hotels, a landing pier, and a monument to the Duke of Brunswick who left his fortune to the town about 100 years ago (with the condition that he get a monument like the Scaligeri in Verona); see the panoramic table on the quai, a map of nearby and distant peaks that are especially beautiful in the afternoon when the sun sets on the Alps. If you go north, the quai ends at the Botanical Garden, in a succession of beautifully manicured city parks. However, following the river westward from the Pont (Bridge) du Mont-Blanc is the Quai des Bergues, with the charming, small Rousseau Island just off it. This is a wonderful place for a rest, under large trees and the statue of Geneva's famous son.

On the opposite side of the bridge (Pont du Mont-Blanc) is the Jardin Anglais (English Garden), with a huge clock whose face is composed of flowers, the hands giving the exact time — typically Genevois.

Parc de la Grange – From the Jardin Anglais, the Quai Gustave-Ador eventually runs into the delightful Parc de la Grange, with one of the finest rose gardens in Europe (overpowering in June) and the even larger Parc des Eaux-Vives.

Palais des Nations – The former League of Nations palace, as big as Versailles, now houses the European section of the UN as well as a small museum of diplomatic history and a *Philatelic Museum*. Several impressive halls in the palace were decorated by European and African artists. There are daily guided tours. Closed at the end of December for 14 days. Admission charge. Av. de la Paix (phone: 734-6011). In surrounding buildings are other international offices, such as the World Health Organization (phone: 791-2111) and the International Red Cross (phone: 734-6001). Especially striking is the new building of the International Labor Office. This impressive structure has a luxurious marble interior and artistic decorations from all over the world (phone: 799-6111). Group visits to the above three organizations can be arranged by special request.

Museum of Art and History – The important archaeological section features medieval furniture, sculpture, an armory, and an excellent fine arts collection; one of the most interesting paintings is Conrad Witz's *Miraculous Fishing*, painted in 1444 for an altar of the cathedral with a background depicting medieval Geneva. Closed Monday mornings. No admission charge. 2 Rue Charles-Galland (phone: 290011).

Musée de l'Horlogerie (Watch Museum) – This is an exquisite collection of watches, clocks, and enamelworks from the 16th century on, with emphasis on artisans from Geneva, which is a worldwide watchmaking center. The setting is a charming townhouse and park, now owned by the city. Closed Monday mornings. No admission charge. 15 Rte. de Malagnou (phone: 736-7412).

Ariana Museum – One of three great museums in Europe that specialize in porcelain and pottery — mainly European but also some Chinese and Japanese — it is in a large villa near the UN. Closed October to March or April (it varies) and Mondays. No admission charge. 10 Av. de la Paix (phone: 734-2950).

Baur Collections – In the home of the original owner, with a small garden, this is a private collection of superb Chinese and Japanese ceramics. Open afternoons only; closed Mondays. Admission charge. 8 Rue Munier-Romilly (phone: 461729).

Barbier-Mueller Museum – This outstanding private collection of Primitive art has twice-yearly exhibits of African, Indonesian, Pacific, and pre-Columbian items. Open afternoons only; closed Sundays and Mondays. Admission charge. 4 Rue de l'Ecole de Chimie (phone: 200253).

Musée d'Instruments Anciens de Musique (Museum of Old Musical Instruments) – This private collection was bought by the city, but its former owner is still the curator. All the instruments, however old, can still be played, and on occasion visiting musicians do just that. Open Tuesdays, Thursdays, and Fridays; check opening hours. Admission charge. Next to the Russian church at 23 Rue Lefort (phone: 469565).

Musée de l'Histoire des Sciences (Museum of the History of Science) – A collection of instruments and souvenirs mainly of Swiss scientists (mathematical, medical, astronomical, physics, and other items) is in a lovely setting. Closed in the morning and from November to April. No admission charge. Villa Bartholoni, 128 Rue de Lausanne (phone: 731-6985).

Institut et Musée Voltaire – The beautiful residence of Voltaire, with his furniture, art objects, manuscripts, correspondence, and works, is open every weekday afternoon. No admission charge. 25 Rue des Délices (phone: 447133).

Musée Internationale de la Croix-Rouge (International Red Cross Museum) – Geneva's newest museum opened late in 1988 and displays documents of the Red Cross over the course of its history, since 1863. Closed Tuesdays. Admission charge. 17 Av. de la Paix (phone: 734-5248).

Jean-Jacques Rousseau Museum – The manuscripts, letters, pictures, and death mask of Rousseau can be seen here daily, except for Saturday afternoons and Sundays. No admission charge. The Public and University Library, Salle Lullin, Promenade des Bastions (phone: 208266).

OUT OF TOWN

Bodmerian Library – In the bewitching setting of the luxurious villa of Zurich millionaire Martin Bodmer, in the suburb of Cologny (about 2 mi/3 km from Geneva), with a panoramic view of the lake and the town, this is a unique private collection of rare manuscripts, first editions, and incunabula; the villa also houses a research institute. The exhibitions of the collection change occasionally. Open Thursday afternoons. Admission charge. Chemin du Guignard, Cologny (phone: 736-2370).

Château de Penthes – This 18th-century private château is in a lovely park and features views of the Alps and lake. It houses the *Museum of Swiss Expatriates,* where documents from the Middle Ages to the 1980s are found. The *Geneva Military Museum* is in an adjoining pavilion; a second pavilion has a pleasant coffee shop. Closed Mondays. Admission charge. 18 Chemin de l'Impératrice, Pregny-Chambésy, about a mile (1.6 km) outside the city (phone: 734-9021).

Boat Ride on the Lake and the Rhone – Beautiful Lake Geneva (Lac Léman), 45 miles long with Geneva on its western end, Lausanne in the middle, and Vevey and Montreux to the east, has been popular with nature lovers at least since the days of Rousseau. Its southern shore is in France; the northern shore in Switzerland is the more famous part. The romantics loved Lake Geneva, particularly the area around Vevey and Montreux, and the list of greats who've lived here is formidable: Byron, Goethe, Victor Hugo, and Balzac are just a few.

The Castle of Chillon — celebrated by Byron in "The Prisoner of Chillon" in 1816 — can be visited by boat. This 9th-century castle held François Bonivard prisoner; he was chained to a pillar for 4 years (1532–36) for delivering Protestant sermons.

A trip on the lake is a must, with its vineyards, châteaux, and old towns. Cruises of varying lengths are offered several times a day by three different companies — except in winter. There are also daily trips down the unspoiled, wooded shores of the Rhone. For details, inquire at the tourist office (see *Sources and Resources*) or at Navigation Mouettes Genevoises (phone: 732-2944).

Château de Coppet – About 6 miles (9.6 km) from Geneva, on the lake, in the charming little town of Coppet, is the castle and park of the famous Madame de Staël, the meeting place of some of the greatest minds of the 18th and early 19th centuries. Madame de Staël led a complicated and unconventional life, which is described in her famous autobiography; she was separated from her husband for the love of the novelist Benjamin Constant. She wrote several successful novels and a study of German Romanticism that so enraged Napoleon that he destroyed an entire edition as "un-French," and she was forced to flee to England and Russia. Closed November to February and Mondays. Admission charge (phone: 761028).

■**EXTRA SPECIAL:** Mt. Salève, the "house mountain" of Geneva, is only about 4 miles (6 km) away in France. Salève's peak is 4,000 feet high; in fall and winter, when the city is often deep in fog, Salève towers above it all.

Go by car or by the #8 bus from Geneva to Veyrier, where the cable car affords a magnificent view at any time of the Valley of the Arve, Geneva, and Mont-Blanc. There are scores of walks, including the steep Pas de l'Echelle from Veyrier to Monnetier, a picturesque village with a number of good restaurants. If you wish, you can continue to Rocher-de-Faverges.

In warm weather — for the more daring or just for spectators — Mt. Salève is a center for hang gliding.

SOURCES AND RESOURCES

TOURIST INFORMATION: For general information, brochures, and maps, contact the Office du Tourisme, at Gare Cornavin (the main train station, phone: 738-5200). In the US, contact the Swiss National Tourist Office, 608 Fifth Ave., New York, NY 10020 (phone: 212-757-5944).

The US Consulate is at 11 Route de Pregny in the northern suburb of Chambésy, on the western shore of Lake Geneva (phone: 990211).

Local Coverage – *This Week in Geneva,* a bilingual publication, is helpful for practical information, cultural programs, and advertisements; it also contains a concise "guided tour" of the city. (You can also get it separately in a pamphlet without advertising.)

There are no local newspapers in English, but the daily *International Herald Tribune* is available for world news.

Food – Restaurants are advertised in *This Week in Geneva.*

Telephone – The area code for Geneva is 022.

CLIMATE AND CLOTHES: The temperature in Geneva is never very hot or very cold; the average in summer is 65F (18C), 34F in winter (1C). When the cold north wind called the *bise* blows, it goes through your bones, sunshine or not; it also clears the air of fog, dust, and germs.

Rain rarely lasts long, but in winter, fog can persist for days. Bring a raincoat and a sweater in any season, and a scarf or a hat for that *bise*. People dress fashionably in Geneva, as in New York or any cosmopolitan city. The Swiss tend to be on the conservative side. Jackets and ties are required for men in some restaurants.

GETTING AROUND: Airport – Cointrin Airport (phone: 993111 for flight information) handles both domestic and international traffic. It's about a 15-minute drive from downtown, and taxi fare will run from 25 to 35 Swiss francs (about $15 to $22). There is also bus service to and from Gare Cornavin, the main railroad station.

Bus – There are many buses and they run frequently. You must buy a ticket from a vending machine at all stops. (You cannot buy it on the bus, and you are fined if found without one.) Information booklets with bus routes are available for a small fee. On #1 at Cornavin (the railroad station) you can take a circular sightseeing tour, returning as #11 to the same spot.

Car Rental – All major firms are represented at the airport and in the city. (The rates are among the highest in Europe.) *Avis* has offices at 44 Rue Lausanne (phone: 731-9000) and the airport (phone: 798-2300); *Budget* at 37 Rue Lausanne (phone: 732-5252) and the airport (phone: 798-2253); *Bucher* at 4 Rue Fendt (phone: 734-6210); and *Autolocation Leman* at 6 Rue Amat (phone: 732-0143).

Taxi – Taxis are more expensive than in the US, but the tip is included in the fare. They can be hailed all over the city; the light on top indicates availability.

Train – The main train station is Gare Cornavin, at Pl. Cornavin (phone: 731-6450).

SPECIAL EVENTS: The *International Motor Show,* for 10 days in early March, is one of the most important in Europe, keeping all Geneva excited and its hotels packed. The *First of August,* Independence Day, is a national holiday commemorating the founding of the Swiss Confederation, with bonfires on the hills. *Fête de Genève* is a long weekend in mid-August, with fairs and processions, culminating in magnificent fireworks on the lake. The *Watch and Jewelry Show* (Montres et Bijoux), with a display of the latest products, is in October of odd-numbered years. The *Escalade,* on or around December 13, the most typically Genevois celebration, commemorates the city's 1602 victory over the Savoyard enemy with a colorful evening torchlight pageant in the darkened streets, with medieval costumes and all-night partying.

MUSEUMS: In addition to the museums described in *Special Places,* the following are also interesting.

Musée d'Etnographie – A rich worldwide collection. 65-67 Bd. Carl-Vogt (phone: 281218).

Musée d'Histoire Naturelle – The most modern natural history display in Europe. 1 Rte. de Malagnou (phone: 359130).

Musée Rath – Its watch and jewelry exhibition is one of Switzerland's finest. Pl. Neuve (phone: 285616).

Museum of the Reformation – A monument to the most important figures of the Reformation. Public and University Library, Salle Lullin. Promenade des Bastions (phone: 208266).

Petit Palais – Modern art from 1890 to the present, especially Renoir and Picasso. 2 Terr. St.-Victor (phone: 461433).

SHOPPING: The main shopping area, offering the best and most expensive stores, is around Rue du Rhone and its parallel and side streets. Other shopping streets are *les rues basses,* literally "downhill streets": A few are Rue du Marché, Rue de la Confédération, and Rue de Rive. Also, many new (and expensive) boutiques and gift shops have recently opened up in the small streets around Place du Bourg-de-Four in Old Town.

Geneva's version of New York City's Trump Tower, Confédération Centre, opened in 1986. It features several levels of shops, from designer boutiques to cafés, in an attractive Art Nouveau decor. Rue de la Confédération.

Geneva's best buys are watches — the most famous in the world — jewelry, toys, clothes, and the nearly ubiquitous Swiss Army knives. There is a flea market on Wednesdays and Saturdays on the Plain de Plainpalais and a flower and vegetable market on Saturday mornings on the streets of *les rues basses*.

To sample everything, try Geneva's best-known department stores, *Placette* at Rue Grenus and *Grand Passage* at 50 Rue du Rhone.

A la Bonbonnière – Geneva's best chocolates. 11 Rue de Rive.

Aux Mille Cadeaux – Lovely gifts, music boxes, cuckoo clocks. 11 Rue Céard.

Bon Génie – Fashion. Pl. du Molard.

Bucherer – Watches and jewelry. 26 Quai Général-Guisan.

Buchs Antiques – Antiques. Grand Rue.

Au Chalet Suisse – Lace blouses and tablecloths; hand-embroidered accessories. 18 Quai de Général-Guisan.

Collet – Jewelry. 8 Pl. du Molard.

Davidoff – The original home of these famous cigars. 2 Rue de Rive.

Galerie Catherine van Notten – Swiss paintings. 17 Grand Rue.

Gübelin – More fine watches and jewelry. 1 Pl. du Molard.

Hermès – Fine fashion in expensive ties, leathergoods, scarves, and saddlery. 43 Rue du Rhone.

Librarie des Amateurs – English, German, and French classic books. 15 Grand Rue.

Ludwig Miller – Original jewelry designs. Rue de Chandronniers.

Naville – The biggest international bookstore in Geneva has four branches. 5 Rue de la Confédération and 5-7 Rue Lévrier are the most central.

Patek Philippe – The famous watches and jewelry. 22 Quai du Général-Guisan.

Piaget – More timepieces and jewelry. 40 Rue du Rhone.

Salome – Art Deco and contemporary furnishings and accessories. 5 Rue de Chandronniers.

Schmitt – An antiques shop in the old town specializing in English pieces. 3 Rue de l'Hôtel de Ville.

Soleido – Patterned fabrics from Provence. Rue de la Cité and Grand Rue.

Spengler – An excellent big store with reasonably priced clothes for men, women, and children (not designer names). 26 Bd. Georges-Favon.

Sturzenegger – Fine Swiss embroidery and linens. 3 Rue du Rhone.

Tabbah – Pricey jewelry and other trifles. 25-27 Rue du Rhone.

Uniprix – The *Woolworth's* of Geneva. 4 Rue Croix-d'Or.

Van Cleef & Arpels – A branch of the world-famous jeweler. 12 Quai de Général-Guisan.

SPORTS AND FITNESS: Fitness Center – *John Valentine Fitness Club,* 12 Rue Gautier (phone: 732-8050) offers a 1-day pass.

Golf – The 18-hole *Golf Club of Geneva* (phone: 327701), in a magnificent setting in Cologny, is private but accepts guests who write or call in advance. Open March to December. Geneva has no public courses.

Ice Skating – Indoor and outdoor skating is offered only in winter, at *Vernets* skating rink at Quai des Vernets.

Jogging – Best for running are Parc Mont Repos, Parc Bertrand, Parc des Eaux-Vives, and the quais on both sides of the lake.

Sailing – The most obvious sport in Geneva; rentals are all along the quais, especially Quais Mont-Blanc, Wilson, and Gustave-Ador.

Skiing – There are excellent runs, very crowded on weekends, within 1 hour of Geneva in the marvelous resorts of Haute Savoie in France. The best known are Chamonix and Megève, about an hour away; the new resort, Flaine, is even closer. The closest good skiing in Switzerland is in Champéry or on the Glacier of Les Diablerets, about 1½ hours away.

Soccer – Called football in Europe, soccer is very popular. Games are in different stadiums, including *Stade des Charmilles*.

Swimming – Beaches on the lake are open in summer, like the Geneva Beach on Quay Gustave-Ador and Pâquis Beach on the Quai du Mont-Blanc (and two beaches on the Rte. de Lausanne). The indoor pool of Les Vernets is in the suburb of Acacias, 4-6 Rue Hans-Wilsdorf.

Tennis – There are several clubs; courts must be reserved in advance. Try the *Geneva Tennis Club* at Parc des Eaux-Vives (phone: 735-5350).

 THEATER: The major theaters are the *Théâtre de Carouge,* Rue Joseph-Girard, and *Le Caveau,* Av. Ste.-Clotilde. Performances are in French except for some visiting companies. International shows are presented at the *Grand Casino* at the *Hilton* hotel, 19 Quai du Mont-Blanc.

 MUSIC: Operas are performed in the *Grand Théâtre* from October to May (not daily), with one production per month and greatly varying quality. The opera is at Pl. Neuve (phone: 212311). There are also excellent popular and classical concerts. The *Orchestre de la Suisse Romande* gives regular performances with many renowned guest artists. Tickets are somewhat difficult to get. Most performances are at *Victoria Hall,* Rue Hornung (phone: 288121). There are also frequent concerts and recitals in churches, and open-air concerts in season.

 NIGHTCLUBS AND NIGHTLIFE: Geneva has the most active nightlife in Switzerland (which does not mean all that much) — enjoyed mainly by visiting and resident foreigners. The best are the private clubs. *Griffins,* Bd. Helvétique (phone: 735-1218), is a favorite and has good food. Among a dozen places with shows, the most popular and international are *Ba-Ta-Clan,* the best-known striptease spot at 15 Rue de la Fontaine (phone: 296498); or *Pussy Cat Saloon,* another striptease spot (in the same building as *Club 58*), at 15 Glacis de Rive (phone: 735-1515); *Maxim's,* with music hall show and dining run by Bob Azzam, 2 Rue Thalberg (phone: 732-9900); and *La Garçonnière,* which offers a transvestite show at 22 Pl. Bémont at Cité (phone: 282161). Several of the good hotel restaurants have dance floors (*Richemond,* Jardin Brunswick). *Régine's,* a member of the chic, international discotheque chain, is attached to the *Hilton's Grand Casino* at 19 Quai du Mont-Blanc (phone: 731-5735). At the *Hilton* and other Swiss casinos, only minimum bets are allowed, so most gamblers go to Divonne in France, 12½ miles (20 km) away.

BEST IN TOWN

 CHECKING IN: There are many hotels, but the small, charming, inexpensive ones with atmosphere are almost nonexistent; the rule is either old-time luxury or functional modern. Most hotels are clustered around the main railroad station, only a few minutes from the lake. All the hotels listed here have telephones in rooms; most also have radios. Reservations are highly advised. The range for a double with a bath and/or shower in the expensive category is $200 and up; moderate, $100 to $175; inexpensive, $50 to $85. In the outskirts you will find more moderate rates. All telephone numbers are in the 022 area code unless otherwise indicated.

Les Armures – In a 17th-century building in the old town, this is considered by many the most charming hotel in Geneva. There are 24 rooms and 4 suites. Decor is rustic-elegant: beamed ceilings, vaulted doors. Its popular restaurant is the oldest in Geneva (see *Eating Out*). Major credit cards. 1 Rue du Puits-St.-Pierre (phone: 289172). Expensive.

Beau-Rivage – Has retained its Old World charm in spite of recent renovations; there are 120 rooms, some with superb lakefront views. Its famous restaurant is called *Chat Botté*. Major credit cards. 13 Quai du Mont-Blanc (phone: 731-0221). Expensive.

Des Bergues – A grand, splendidly renovated property in a choice location, downtown near the lake. It has 109 rooms, 8 suites, the elegant *Amphitryon* restaurant, and room service from 6 AM to midnight. 33 Quai des Bergues (phone: 731-5050). Expensive.

Hôtel de la Cigogne – The newest and most unusual hotel in the city center, 100 yards from the lake, it was built in 1903 as a bordello and recently renovated. The decor of each of its 50 rooms is different, and some are furnished with collectors' items, such as the beds of one-time visitors Cary Grant and Barbara Hutton. 17 Pl. Longemalle (phone: 214242). Expensive.

Geneva Penta – Equidistant from the airport and downtown, this new property has 320 rooms, and a fitness center with sauna. 75-77 Av. Louis-Casai (phone: 798-4700). Expensive.

NOGA Hilton International – This sleek, modern hostelry with 300 rooms, right on Lake Geneva, is currently the most expensive in the city. Guests can enjoy a sauna, heated pool, boutiques, nightclub, discotheque, and numerous restaurants (among them *Le Cygne*, one of the best in town). Parking available. 19 Quai du Mont-Blanc (phone: 731-9811). Expensive.

Du Rhône – A favorite of vacationers and businesspeople alike, this modern hotel has 350 cheerful rooms, most with a view, 2 restaurants, and a terrace. The 5th floor is reserved for non-smokers. The famous wine cellar houses 200,000 bottles of mostly French and Swiss wines. The hotel is headquarters for the the International Wine Academy and frequently hosts the Trophée des Barmen, an international wine-tasting competition. Quai Turretini (phone: 731-9831). Expensive.

Le Richemond – Still the most prestigious hotel in town, abounding with understated elegance; its rooms are generally full. The restaurant, *Le Gentilhomme*, is one of the best in town, with dance music at night. Major credit cards. Jardin Brunswick (phone: 731-1400). Expensive.

Amat-Carlton – A very comfortable, modern property with pleasant, spacious rooms with balconies. Apartments with kitchens for longer stays (10-day minimum) are available. Major credit cards. 22 Rue Amat (phone: 731-6850). Moderate.

Du Midi – In an excellent location, this pleasant, modern hotel has 80 comfortable rooms, some with river views; cafés and restaurants. Major credit cards. Pl. Chevelu (phone: 731-7800). Moderate.

La Tourelle – About 10 minutes from the center of town (direct bus service) in luxurious, residential Vésenaz, featuring 24 attractive, comfortable rooms in a villa with a garden and a view of the lake. Closed December and January. American Express, Diners Club (discouraged). 26 Rte. d'Hermance, Genève-Vésenaz (phone: 752-1628). Moderate to inexpensive.

Des Tourelles – (No connection with *La Tourelle*.) This is a very modest, family-type, centrally located hotel with 24 rooms *without* private showers (or toilets), but they are available on every floor. The place is pleasant and sunny and offers a view of the river. No credit cards. 2 Bd. James-Fazy (phone: 732-4423). Inexpensive.

Le Grenil – Connected with the YMCA, this modern hotel is not far from the city center, with a snack restaurant; an excellent value. Most of its 50 rooms have showers and private toilets. Major credit cards. 7 Av. Ste.-Clotilde (phone: 283055). Inexpensive.

Lido – A "best buy," this is an excellently run 32-room, no-frills hotel in a central location. Major credit cards. 8 Rue Chantepoulet (phone: 731-5530). Inexpensive.

 EATING OUT: Geneva has more than 1,100 eating establishments in all categories. Strangely, there are not as many different cuisines as one might expect — French cooking dominates all other varieties, with Italian second. Definitely try the French-Swiss cheese dishes, like fondue and *raclette* (delicious cheese, melted on an open fire in individual portions, eaten with tiny potatoes) served in special inexpensive pubs. Also, try the excellent lake fish, like *perche* (perch) and, if available, the rare *omble chevalier* (grayling), found only in Lac Léman. When ordering, ask for the *carte,* as *menu* applies only to the daily set meal. Tips are included in bills, but it is customary to add a bit. Our price range is for a three-course dinner for two, without drinks, wine, or coffee. Count on $100 to $150 and up for expensive places, $65 to $90 for moderate, and $40 to $50 for an inexpensive meal. Set lunch menus are considerably less expensive in many restaurants. All telephone numbers are in the 022 area code unless otherwise indicated.

Le Béarn – This small, elegant restaurant is among the best in town, serving fresh, imaginative dishes and delicious warm desserts. Closed Saturdays at lunchtime, Sundays, and mid-July through mid-August. Some credit cards. 4 Quai de la Poste (phone: 210028). Expensive.

Girardet – *Extra special:* In Crissier, a tiny town only 36 miles (60 km) from Geneva (just outside Lausanne), superbly talented chef Fredy Girardet has created a restaurant that is simply the best in Europe. Be sure to write for dinner reservations, but no more than 2 months ahead; call for lunch weeks ahead. If you splurge only once during your European stay, do it here. Closed Sundays, Mondays, parts of August, Christmas. No credit cards. 1 Rte. d'Yverdon, Crissier (phone: 021-634-0505). Expensive.

La Perle du Lac – On the lake, in Parc Mon Repos; in summer you can dine outside with the ravishing view; in winter it is intimate, elegant, and candlelit. A less expensive café adjoins the restaurant. Closed Mondays. Some credit cards. 128 Rue de Lausanne (phone: 731-7935). Expensive.

Tse Fung – In *Hôtel la Réserve* at the city limits, this is one of the best Chinese restaurants in Europe. Open daily. Credit cards. 301 Rte. Romelles, 1293 Bellevue (phone: 774-1736). Expensive.

Chez Valentino – A lively Italian place with fabulous hors d'oeuvres featuring a flower-filled terrace in spring and summer, 3 miles (5 km) from city center. Closed Mondays and Tuesdays at lunch and August. Some credit cards. 63 Rte. de Thonon, Vésenaz (phone: 752-1440). Expensive to moderate.

L'Olivier de Provence – Cozy, elegant French restaurant in the charming setting of Carouge. In summer it has a big, tree-shaded garden. Closed Sundays. Credit cards. 13 Rue Jacques-Dalphin (phone: 420450). Expensive to moderate.

Auberge de la Mère Royaume – A cozy, paneled "old Geneva style" place with French specialties. Closed Saturday lunch and Sundays. Credit cards. 9 Rue des Corps-Saints (phone: 732-7008). Moderate.

Hostellerie de la Vendée – With a functional, sober interior, but outstanding service and food, frequented by chic local clientele; it offers seasonal specialties. On the outskirts of town. Closed Sundays. Credit cards. 28 Chemin de la Vendée, Petit Lancy (phone: 792-0411). Moderate.

Edelweiss – A Swiss chalet with folk music and regional specialties. Open daily. 2 Pl. Navigation (phone: 731-4940). Moderate.

Les Armures – The oldest restaurant in Geneva, this is a good place for *raclette,* fondue, or even pizza, in *Les Armures* hotel in the heart of the old town. It has atmosphere. Closed Sundays, Monday lunch. Credit cards. 1 Rue du Puits-St.-Pierre (phone: 283442). Moderate to inexpensive.

Cave Valaisanne et Chalet Suisse – This cozy, friendly restaurant serves an excellent fondue as well as other good cheese dishes. Open daily. Credit cards. 23 Bd. Georges-Favon (phone: 281236). Moderate to inexpensive.

Café des Beaux-Arts – A modest but very lively bistro that is very popular with residents (cheese-potato au gratin a specialty). Closed Mondays and the second Sunday of the month. No credit cards. 32 Rue de Carouge (phone: 291501). Inexpensive.

Café du Centre – This pleasant *brasserie* is on historic Place du Molard, with a huge variety of dishes served till well after midnight. (The more expensive restaurant is upstairs.) Open daily. No credit cards. 5 Pl. du Molard (phone: 218586). Inexpensive.

Palais de Justice – An unassuming little place with lots of local color, on the romantic square of the old town. Closed Sundays and Monday lunch. No credit cards. 8 Pl. Bourg-de-Four (phone: 204254). Inexpensive.

HELSINKI

On the southern coast of Finland lies Helsinki, the Daughter of the Baltic, a city almost as close to Russia geographically and culturally as to Scandinavia. Helsinki overlooks the Gulf of Finland on the Baltic Sea; across the gulf lie the Soviet republics of Estonia and Latvia, and at the far eastern end of the gulf is Leningrad.

Midway between Stockholm to the west and Leningrad to the east, Helsinki reflects both Eastern and Western influences. The Eastern presence in Finland dates back to the 1st century AD, when nomadic Finnish-speaking fishermen and hunters migrated to the area from Eastern Europe, forcing the Lapps, the original inhabitants, to move north to Lapland. Even the Finnish language is most closely related, not to the Scandinavian languages, as one might imagine, but to Estonian.

Hemmed in by Sweden and Russia — Finland shares a 335-mile border with Sweden on the west, a 788-mile border with the Soviet Union on the east — it is no wonder that Finland became the buffer and the buffeted in wars between the two great rival powers. From the 13th century, when Finland was conquered by the Swedes, through the 19th century, when Russia took over — and until the Finnish nation declared its independence in 1917 — Finland suffered in the recurring wars between the two countries.

In 1812, shortly after the Russians conquered Finland in the Napoleonic Wars, Czar Alexander I moved the capital to Helsinki from Turku, a city on the west coast. In 1828, the university was moved from Turku, and Helsinki became an intellectual as well as a political center.

Around the same time, in 1808, the city was ravaged by a fire that totally demolished its crowded wooden buildings. When subsequently rebuilt as the nation's capital, Helsinki was well planned and deliberately spacious. Carefully charted by Johan Albrecht Ehrenström and executed by the noted architect Carl Ludvig Engel, the reconstruction was completed by 1840. The neo-classical buildings in the old center of town date from this period. Because of a 5-year renovation program begun in 1984, many of them now house new shops, restaurants, and cafés.

The skyline of this pollution-free city is accented by the imposing dome of the Lutheran cathedral (1840) and the onion-shaped domes of the Russian Orthodox church (1868). Helsinki's gleaming pastel buildings, many of which were designed by distinguished architects and built of local pale granite, have earned it the title of White City of the North. But this is a place to see interesting modern architecture as well; the Finnish nation, world renowned for its achievements in modern design, has produced such notables as Eliel Saarinen and Alvar Aalto, and many striking examples of their work can be seen here. Surely the most dramatic of Helsinki's many fine specimens of modern architecture is Temppeliaukio Church, blasted from solid rock, de-

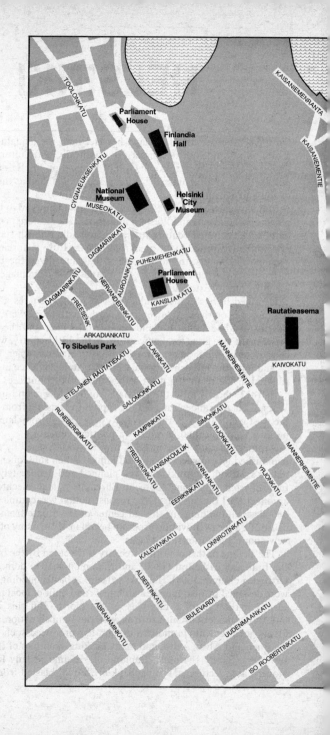

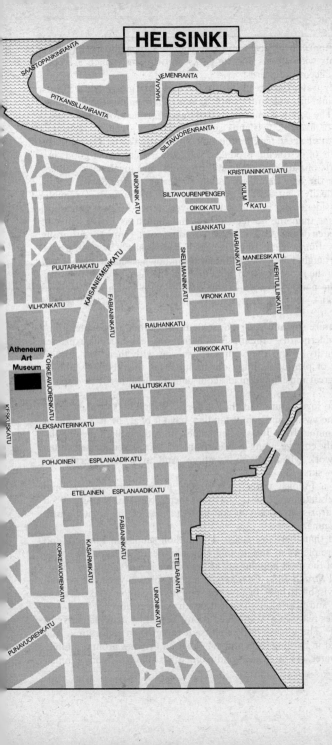

HELSINKI

SÄÄSTÖPANKINRANTA

PITKÄNSILLANRANTA

HAKANIEMENRANTA

SILTAVUORENRANTA

UNIONINKATU

KRISTIANINKATUATU

SILTAVOURENPENGER

KULMA KATU

OIKOKATU

LIISANKATU

MARIANKATU

MANEESIKATU

SNELLMANINKATU

MERITULLINKATU

PUUTARHAKATU

KAISANIEMENKATU

FABIANINKATU

VILHONKATU

VIRONKATU

RAUHANKATU

KIRKKOKATU

Atheneum Art Museum

KORKEAVUORENKATU

HALLITUSKATU

KESKUSKATU

ALEKSANTERINKATU

POHJOINEN ESPLANAADIKATU

ETELÄINEN ESPLANAADIKATU

FABIANINKATU

KORKEAVUORENKATU

KASARMIKATU

UNIONINKATU

ETELÄRANTA

PUNAVUORENKATU

signed by two Finnish brothers, Timo and Tuomo Suomalainen. Helsinki is also noted for its wide streets and its parks and squares, which are often graced by magnificent sculptures.

Surrounded by water on three sides (to the north are green fields, forests, and lakes), Helsinki has a natural seaport that is kept open most of the winter by icebreakers. The port was once protected by the fortifications on Suomenlinna, a group of five rocky islands south of the city's center. Helsinki's harbor, the nation's largest, handles the bulk of the nation's maritime activity. Finland's imports of petroleum products, vehicles, and consumer goods just exceed its exports of paper, wood, metal products, and machinery.

Today, as the the only capitalist nation bordering on the Soviet Union, Finland is fanatically neutral. The government is a parliamentary republic headed by a president who is elected for a 6-year term. Finland's standard of living is higher than the Soviet Union's and almost as high as that of neighboring Sweden or the US. Like other Scandinavians, Finns are culturally advanced. Many Finns speak English, which has replaced Swedish as the second language taught in schools. Illiteracy is unknown, social welfare is well provided, and all the proceeds from gambling are allocated to public charity. Some 60% of the nation's people live in cities — with half a million, over 10%, in Helsinki — making their living from manufacturing and service industries.

Though by nature shy and reserved, sometimes a brooding people, Finns are passionate underneath — the music of native son Jean Sibelius expresses this hidden intensity — and they can surprise you with their wry humor. They are lovers of pleasure (dining out as much as their budgets allow), appreciators of great music, and mad about dancing, whether it be disco or cheek to cheek.

The Finns also love nature and the outdoors. With 188,000 lakes in the country, everyone swims and many families have a boat, be it a canoe or luxury yacht. Summer, from June to September, finds the bulk of the population at the family cottage along a waterfront of lake, river, or sea, often commuting to work when not on vacation. And in winter everyone — young and old — skis.

Cleanliness is a Finnish virtue. The streets, homes, shops, hotels, and restaurants of Helsinki are spotless. The Finns themselves are a well-scrubbed people, hardly surprising when you consider that one of the great Finnish pastimes is the sauna.

It is estimated that there are nearly 1½ million saunas in Finland, and certainly there are plenty in and around Helsinki; nearly every hotel has at least one. Four of the most popular are at the *Palace, Kalastajatorppa, Inter-Continental,* and *Strand Inter-Continental* hotels; since anyone can go and many do, it is advisable to book in advance. You may wish to partake of some "sauna sausage" and beer after the event, as the natives do.

The sauna takes place in a wood-lined room, heated by a special stove to about 176F-212F. The intense heat is pleasant rather than suffocating. The saunas users, clad in bathing suits and robes, sit on benches around a table, sipping bottled water, chatting, and conducting other affairs — many Finnish business deals are transacted in this relaxed atmosphere. Water is thrown on a layer of stones on the stove in order to produce *löyly,* or steam, which causes perspiration. Light whisking with birch twigs acts to increase the body's circulation. Ideally the sauna user cools off with a dip in a lake, sea, or swimming pool. In winter, many Finns take a dip in a hole in the ice, which they call *avanto.*

Would-be polar bear or not, you will surely experience a euphoric sense of total relaxation and well-being after the sauna. Don't miss it.

HELSINKI AT-A-GLANCE

 SEEING THE CITY: From the steps of Helsinki's majestic cathedral, an observer's eyes can span the old part of the city and in a sweeping glance draw a capsule understanding of the city's history. In front of the church is the spacious Senate Square, designed during the early 19th century in neo-classical style to form a homogeneous whole. The Sederholm residence, built in 1755–57, is the oldest building in the city. On the west side of the square, always in harmony with the design, is Helsinki University; on the east side is the Government Building. Nearby is Esplanadi Park (Esplanadipuisto), center of Helsinki's business activities. Beginning at the Market Place, the tree-lined avenue, with a wide promenade for strollers and ample room for traffic on either side, ends several blocks north at Mannerheimintie (Mannerheim Street).

A tourist soon realizes that the Finns' dedication to nature is no myth. There is no crowding in Helsinki. As many as 240 parks, of all sizes, dot the city's landscape, leaving almost 30% of the metropolitan area open. Throughout Helsinki, the working people, the retired, the students, and the newcomers, too, find squares, triangles, and parks of all kinds to stop at for a rest.

On a summer walking tour in this part of town, it's fun to take time out at the *Kappeli* restaurant, a charming old dining place at the edge of Esplanadi Park, for lunch or coffee in the afternoon. In a tranquil setting, foreign visitors soon fall into the casual, lighthearted mood of the Finns, many of whom gravitate there at lunch hour to enjoy the leisure of drinking beer outdoors and listening to a potpourri of music played by modern and traditional bands in the gazebo-like bandstand in the park or to watch folk dances.

 SPECIAL PLACES: Trams and buses run frequently in all directions (see *Sources and Resources*), but most foreign visitors prefer to explore the city by foot. Fortunately, downtown Helsinki is rather compact. Chances are you will be staying in a hotel that is centrally located, so you will be within walking distance of many of the city's attractions.

DOWNTOWN

Finlandia Hall – Either as part of a sightseeing tour or, even better, to attend a performance, you should not miss this $9-million marble edifice, the last architectural triumph of the country's great Alvar Aalto, world acclaimed for his simple yet elegant design. The sleek, white concert and congress hall is set in Hesperia Park on Mannerheimintie, almost directly across from the *National Museum.* You can't miss it. Check at your hotel desk for a free copy of *Helsinki This Week* to learn the program schedule. 4 Karamzininkatu (phone: 40241).

Sibelius Monument – Dedicated in 1967 to Finland's revered composer, Jean Sibelius, this monument is a giant sculpture of tubular steel pipes. To the side of this impressive work, which dwarfs visitors, the sculptress Eila Hiltunen molded a head of the composer. Lighted at night, the bold monument is a gripping sight. Sibelius Park.

Cathedral – The cornerstone of Carl Ludwig Engel's Lutheran cathedral was laid in 1830, and the cathedral was consecrated in 1852. Today it remains a parish church, but it is also the scene of national festive services. Open daily from 9 AM to 7 PM, Sundays from noon. Senate Square.

Uspensky Cathedral – This classic example of Byzantine-Slavic brick architecture was completed in 1868 and restored for its 100th anniversary. Open Wednesdays from 2 to 6 PM and Thursdays from 9 AM to 1 PM. 1 Kanavakatu.

Temppeliaukio Church – Known as the Rock Church, this unique house of worship was designed by two brothers, Timo and Tuomo Suomalainen. Carved out of solid rock, it is topped with a copper dome that spans 70 feet. It occupies most of a block and from the street or air only the dome is visible. The interior is pink and gray granite with vertical glass strips cut into the ceiling that allow light to enter in dramatic shafts. Breathtakingly beautiful in its simplicity. Open daily. 3 Lutherinkatu (phone: 494698).

Parliament House – Visitors are welcome except when Parliament is in recess. You can join a guided tour at certain hours or attend plenary sessions in the galleries. No admission charge. 30 Mannerheimintie (phone: 4321).

National Museum – Founded in 1893, this large museum also includes an extensive library. The government-owned building was designed in 1910 by the noted Finnish architects Saarinen, Gesellius, and Lindgren. Collections include archaeological, historical, and ethnological displays. There are 19,000 archaeological items from the Stone, Bronze, and Iron Ages in Scandinavia and the Soviet Union; 80,000 historical items include Finnish interiors, costumes, textiles, weapons, metals, and coins; Finnish, Ugric, and Lapp ethnic collections include 15,300 items on hunting, textiles, folk art, and furniture. 34 Mannerheimintie (phone: 40251).

Art Museum of the Ateneum – Paintings, sculptures, drawings, and etchings — mostly modern Finnish but also foreign and classical. Open daily. No admission charge Saturdays. 3 Kansakoulukatu (phone: 694-5933).

Seurasaari – This charming park and open-air museum provides a representative picture of early Finland, complete with farm and manor houses that were transported from all over the country and reassembled here. You might want to picnic outdoors. The museum, which sits on an island, offers some entertainment in the summer, mostly folk dancers in colorful native garb. Bus #24 will take you there, and you enter by a footbridge. Open daily, May 2 to August 30. No admission charge Wednesdays. Seurasaari Island (phone: 484712).

Helsinki Zoo – In 1988, this largest of Finland's zoos marked its 100th birthday. Most animals are housed in their natural environment on Korkeasaari Island near the city. Besides northern animals, the collection includes llamas, bison, bears, and lions, and a number of endangered species, among them the rare snow leopard. Weather permitting, guests can have lunch in an open-air café and gaze out to sea toward Helsinki's skyline and South Harbor. In the summer, ferry service is available from the shore of Market Square, and motorboat service brings visitors here from the shore of Hakaniemi Square. The zoo is also accessible overland via Mustikkamaa bus #16 from Erottaja to Kulosaari, from where there is a 1-mile walk through Mustikkamaa Island, across the pedestrian bridge to Korkeasaari. Open daily (phone: 170077).

Suomenlinna Sveaborg – An intriguing island, one of a group of five rocky islands to the south of the city center, only a 15-minute boat ride from South Harbor. This 18th-century fortification, reputed to be the largest sea fortress in the world, is well worth a visit. Built in 1748, when Finland was part of Sweden, the fortress was planned and directed by Marshal Augustin Ehrensvärd. Called the Gibraltar of the North, the fortress capitulated to the Russians in 1808 and defended itself successfully against an Anglo-French fleet in 1855, during the Crimean War.

A visitor can explore the fortifications of Susisaari (Wolf Island) and Kustaanmiekka (Gustav's Sword) with their forts and casements, parks and walks.

Nearby, on the island of Susisaari, the *Ehrensvärd Museum* exhibits Suomenlinna's history. The *Armfelt Museum* on the island of Kustaanmiekka shows the life of the 19th-century Finnish gentry; also on Kustaanmiekka are the *Coast Defense Artillery Museum* and the submarine *Vesikko*.

The islands also have art exhibitions and a restaurant open in the summer.

The ferry from Market Square to Suomenlinna leaves hourly on the half-hour and takes about 15 minutes. In summer, tours start at the information kiosk (phone: 668154).

Senate Square – In order to appreciate Helsinki's rich history, a visit to the complex of neo-classical buildings built between 1818 and 1852 is a must: The cathedral, government palace, city administration, and university buildings are now surrounded by modern shops and cafés.

Stadium Tower – The *Olympic Stadium* with its 236-foot-high tower was designed by Yrjö Lindegren and Toivo Jäntti. In front is Wäinö Aaltonen's statue of gold medal runner Paavo Nurmi. 3 Eteläïnen Stadionintie (phone: 440363).

Botanical Gardens of the University – Established in 1833, this lush park holds Finland's largest botanical collection. There is a variety of trees, shrubs, and grasses common to Finland; the greenhouses showcase exotic tropical plants. 44 Unioninkatu (phone: 631150).

Presidential Palace – Once the Heidenstrauch mansion, the imposing palace was designed by Pehr Granstedt and completed in 1814. It served as the czar's residence when he visited Finland and became the Presidential Palace when Finland gained independence. Closed to the public. 1 Pohjoisesplanadi.

Kauppatori Market Square – At the foot of Esplanade at South Harbor is the open-air marketplace, one of the most visited spots in Helsinki. Open daily except Sundays, it is filled with brightly colored stalls, manned by old and young alike, that sell everything from fresh flowers and vegetables and fruit to trinkets and freshly caught fish. Bustling and bursting with color, it's a place to see and a place to mingle with the Finns. Browse or buy, but be sure to stop long enough to taste the freshly brewed coffee and munch on the delicate Finnish pastries. From May 15 to August 30, the evening market is open 3:30 to 8 PM Mondays through Fridays.

Linnanmäki – Helsinki's answer to Copenhagen's Tivoli is patronized by Finns from all parts of the country as well as residents and tourists. It's more than an amusement park; only 30% of its visitors are children. Founded in the mid-1940s, the park includes 25 different rides, an indoor and an open-air theater, restaurants, two small cafés, a dancing pavilion, and assorted kiosks. Special rides are the gigantic Big Dipper and a carousel built in 1892 with hand-carved animals. The *Peacock Theater* seats 906 indoors and features internationally known comedians, clowns, acrobats, musicians, and marionettes. The open-air auditorium offers similar entertainments plus high-wire acrobatic acts.

A special aspect of Linnanmäki is that its proceeds, often exceeding $250,000 a year, are donated to various children's charities, hence the title "the park with the heart." Open daily except Mondays, May through August. Admission charge; rides extra.

SUBURBS

Tapiola – Called the Garden City of Finland, it's a utopian suburb designed in the 1950s to emphasize the quality of living in harmony with the surrounding nature. Tapiola, taken from the Finnish national epic *Kalevala,* was an imaginary place where the fabled people lived. It was built step by step by a group of private non-profit organizations, and it still is not considered complete. About 17,000 people share the 670 acres, which include their own newspapers, clubs, shopping centers, a marina, a sports arena, libraries, and an outdoor glassed-in swimming pool. Within a short distance of Tapiola is another interesting architectural sight, the Technical University in Otaniemi, designed by Alvar Aalto. Don't miss Dipoli, the campus clubhouse.

You might want to check with the Helsinki City Tourist Office (see *Sources and Resources*) for a sightseeing tour. Tapiola is a short but expensive cab ride from downtown Helsinki, or take a bus marked Tapiola from the bus station.

■ **EXTRA SPECIAL:** Since Finland is a country of 188,000 lakes and 180,000 islands, it would be sheer folly to make it to this land and not experience some part of the visit on water. Get another perspective on the capital from a boat. There are leisurely paced sightseeing and lunch cruises and Archipelago tours that depart daily from Market Square from June 1 to August 31, taking you past innumerable little islands and around peninsulas. You can choose between a ride that lasts 1¼ hours or one that runs for 5 hours, including lunch. You'll enjoy this respite on a warm summer day.

SOURCES AND RESOURCES

TOURIST INFORMATION: For general information, brochures, and maps, contact the Finland Tourist Board, 655 Third Ave., New York, NY 10017 (phone: 212-370-5540), or the Helsinki City Tourist Office, 19 Pohjoises-planadi (phone: 169-3757 and 174088). "Helsinki Today" (phone: 058) gives recorded programs of events in the city.

The US Embassy is at 14 Itainen Puistotie (phone: 171931).

Local Coverage – No English-language newspapers are published in Helsinki. The *International Herald Tribune* is available at the better hotels, newsstands, and the airport. *Academic Book Store,* 39 Pohjoiseplenadi, carries a large selection of newspapers and magazines in many languages.

Food – A little red book, *Where to Eat in Helsinki,* gives restaurants from one to five stars; it's published by the Gastronomic Society of Finland and is available at the *Academic Book Store.* Also indispensable is *Food from Finland,* a Finnish cookbook that contains recipes and text written in English by Anna-Maija and Juha Tanttu.

Telephone – The area code for Helsinki is 0.

CLIMATE AND CLOTHES: Weather in Helsinki can be cold and gray in winter. The cold is no different from that of the US Great Lakes area in winter. A heavy coat and sweater (wool dresses and/or a suit, for women), a pair of lined boots, and good wool- or silk-lined gloves will see you through the outdoors in fine shape. Don't worry about the heating indoors; hotels and restaurants are more than comfortable.

Casual clothes are in order, but ties and jackets are required for men in most hotel dining rooms. Women can use a couple of cocktail dresses. In summer or winter, pants suits are popular here.

For hot weather, lightweight cotton or drip-dry clothes are ideal. Bring a bathing suit or two; add a sweater and a raincoat, to play safe. The thermometer in summer can rise from a coolish 50F to 60F (10C to 16C) to the hot 90s (about 30C to 32C). At this time of year, tourists are treated to a bonus — almost 19 hours of daylight.

A note on the midnight sun and the winter darkness: The area of northern Finland that lies within the Arctic Circle has 2 months of midnight sun (June and July) and

2 of winter darkness (December and January). In southern Finland (which includes Helsinki), midsummer offers about 5 hours of nocturnal twilight.

 GETTING AROUND: Airport – Helsinki-Vantaa Airport, 12 miles north of the city, handles both domestic and international traffic. Taxi fare from the airport to downtown runs about $25. Finnair buses travel between the airport and the air terminal adjoining the *Inter-Continental* hotel, at 21 Töölönkatu (phone: 818-7770), or from the new city terminal at the central train station, 3 Asema Aukio (phone: 818-7980). The buses run two to five times every hour and cost about $5 one way.

Taxi – Cabstands, clearly marked "Taksi," are at every few corners, with plenty of cabs waiting their turns. Cabs are plentiful but not cheap; the meters start at about $2.55 (no tipping). You can hail a cab when the sign is illuminated.

Tram and Bus – Trams 3T and 3B, which can be boarded anywhere along their route, offer a tour of the business and residential areas of the capital, with a taped commentary in English during the summer months. In addition, a 24-hour tourist ticket, available at the Helsinki City Tourist Office, entitles you to unlimited travel on trams and buses for about $10. The Helsinki Card ($15 to $24) provides unlimited travel on trams, buses, subways (linking the city center and the eastern suburbs), and ferries, as well as free admission to 40 museums, discount theater and concert tickets, and special weekend discounts at hotels. It can be purchased at the airport, the Helsinki City Tourist Office, or *Stockmann's* department store. Tram, bus, and metro tickets are priced at 6 Finnish marks (about $1.50). Phone the bus station for information: 602122.

Train – The city's main train station is Rautatieasema, 13 Vilhonkatu (phone: 7071 or 659411). With its splendid Art Nouveau architecture and good restaurants, the station is a destination in itself.

Car Rental – Besides *Avis, Budget,* and *Hertz,* there are *InterRent, Europcar,* and others. Car rental desks are found at the airport and in many hotel lobbies.

 SPECIAL EVENTS: More than a decade ago, Finland introduced over 800 summer festivals, produced and presented in various sections of the country. The idea was to attract foreign visitors and to familiarize them with the Finnish people and their achievements and, at the same time, to entertain them with local professional talent and international luminaries. The events run from symphonic concerts and opera performances given in a 15th-century castle courtyard to rock, folk, jazz, and pop music; to art exhibits; to seminars on world problems — cultural fare for everyone, including the small fry. For information, contact *Finland Festivals,* 3A Vuorikatu, 17th floor (phone: 607386).

The *Finland Festival* chain of dozens of programs generally starts in mid-June and runs till mid-August. These are followed by the big *Helsinki Festival,* which includes as many as 100 presentations between late August and early September. For complete program information, contact *Helsinki Festival,* Unioninkatu 28 (phone: 659688).

Visitors might also like to catch the *Changing of the Guard* at the Main Guard Post, behind the President's Palace every day at 1 PM.

 MUSEUMS: In addition to the museums described in *Special Places,* the following are noteworthy.

Ainola – Once the home of composer Jean Sibelius. Järvenpää (phone: 287322).

City Museum – The history of the city from its founding to the present. 2 Karamzin-katu (phone: 169-3444).

Gallen-Kallela – The castle-like studio-home of Finland's national painter Akseli Gallen-Kallela. Closed Mondays. Espoo (phone: 513388); reachable by tram #4 to

Munkkiniemi, then either walk about a mile to Espoo or take bus #33 (weekdays only).

Hvitträsk – The former studio and residence of architects and designers Eliel Saarinen, Armas Lindgren, and Herman Gesellius now serves as a cultural center and is open year-round. Bus #166 from platform 62 at the central bus station will get you there in 40 minutes. The restaurant serves excellent seasonal Finnish cuisine (phone: 297-6033) and the gift shop sells unique handicrafts. Luoma, Kirkkonummi (phone: 90-297-5779).

Urho Kekkonen Museum (Tamminiemi) – The home of Urho Kekkonen, Finland's late president, from 1956 to 1986, it opened as a museum in 1987. Adjacent to the *Seurasaari Open-Air Museum* (phone: 480684).

Mannerheim Museum – Originally the home of Finland's great war hero and president Marshal Mannerheim. 14 Kalliolinnantie (phone: 635443).

Museum of Applied Arts – Finnish industrial design and native handicrafts. 23 Korkeavuorenkatu (phone: 174455).

Museum of Finnish Architecture – Archives and exhibitions of Finnish architecture, past and present. 24 Kasarmikatu (phone: 661918).

Photographic Museum of Finland – Exhibitions of work by Finnish and international photographers. 6 Keskuskatu (phone: 658544).

 SHOPPING: Shopping can be fun and profitable in Finland. You'll run into some of the best buys in Europe if you're interested in textiles, ceramics, glassware, jewelry, handicrafts, furs, and leather goods. Jewelry includes gold items fashioned after centuries-old ornaments as well as bold modern designs in silver and wood. Famed rya rugs woven in fine wools are bargains. Furs are great in Finland, and the most famous designers create astonishing — and expensive — works of art from mink, fox, and lynx, among others. *Marimekko and Vuokko* clothes and fabrics, *Arabia* glass and pottery, and *Aarikka* wooden toys are also exceptional items. *Note:* Before you go shopping, visit the *Finnish Design Center* at 19 Kasarmikatu (phone: 626388), a permanent exhibition of Finnish handicrafts and industrial design.

The main shopping area in Helsinki is in the vicinity of the large hotels, particularly along Aleksanterinkatu and Esplanadi Park and their side streets.

Special tip: Department stores and finer shops will provide an 11% refund receipt for sales tax for both cash and credit card purchases by foreign visitors; it can be cashed at the airport or on board ships sailing between Finland and Sweden.

Aarikka – Toys and other design articles in wood and silver. The *i-shop* next door has glass, crystal, giftware, and kitchen utensils. 27 Pohjoisesplanadi (phone: 652277).

Academic Book Store – One of the world's largest bookstores, designed by Aalto. Visit the *Café Aalto* between book buying. 39 Pohjoisesplanadi.

Agora – A shopping patio surrounded by elegant boutiques filled with jewelry, crystal, sculpture, furs, fashions, and Finland's only genuine tearoom. 30 Unioninkatu.

Arabia – Ceramics, crystal, and exquisite china. 25 Pohjoisesplanadi (phone: 170055). Visit its gallery at 135 Hämeentie.

Artek – Aalto furniture, lamps, textiles, and assorted design products. 3 Keskuskatu.

Forum – A modern shopping plaza packed with boutiques and shops displaying novelty items. Its 4 floors also offer restaurants, cafés, and a delicatessen. 20 Mannerheimintie.

Kalevala-Koru – Extensive selection of traditional folk jewelry in gold, silver, and bronze. 25 Unioninkatu (phone: 171520).

Marimekko – Fabric and clothing. 31 Pohjoisesplanadi (phone: 177944).

Old Harbor (Wanha Satama) – Two historic warehouses built in 1897 have been restored and now house boutiques, restaurants, and crafts exhibitions. Near the Presidential Palace.

Senate Center – A complex of bazaars, art galleries, shops, restaurants, and cafés in the revived old town Empire buildings. Handicrafts, fashions, furs, and articles for the home. 28 Aleksanterinkatu.

Stockmann's – The leading department store. 52 Aleksanterinkatu.

Studio Tarja Niskanen – High-style, top-quality furs by one of Finland's premier designers. 33 Pohjoisesplanadi (phone: 642577).

Vuokko – Bold new fashions. 25 Pohjoisesplanadi (phone: 750144).

SPORTS AND FITNESS: Because of its climate, Finland is a paradise for all varieties of winter sports. Lovers of nature and the outdoors, Finns go in for boating and bicycling as well as skiing.

Bicycling – Finland is big on bicycling. There are prescribed routes, but you can plan out your own by using maps. Those around Helsinki and other cities run partly on special bicycle lanes. There are also some old country roads in good cycling condition. Check with the Helsinki City Tourist Office for details, including where to rent a bike.

Boating – There are many yachting clubs on the islands right outside Helsinki. A boat can be rented, but the reefy waters are rather tricky. Check with the Yachting Association or the Motor Boat Association, both at 12 Radiokatu (phone: 1581). The *Nautic Center,* 9 Itälahdenkatu (phone: 670271), rents boats with or without a crew.

Bowling – For information about the 79 bowling alleys in Finland, contact the Finnish Bowling Federation, 3 Ruusulankatu (phone: 409133).

Fitness Centers – *Nautilus Sports Center,* 17B Salomonkatu (phone: 694-5833); *Forum Gym,* 23B Yrjönkatu (phone: 602702).

Golf – The best part of golfing in this country in summer is that you can tee off as late as 10 PM, in daylight, and finish 18 holes later in daytime because there are almost 24 hours of light. For course information, contact the Finnish Golf Union, 12 Radiokatu (phone: 1581). The *Hesperia* hotel has a golf simulator (phone: 43101).

Jogging – Finns are health oriented and are on the jogging kick, too. Americans dedicated to the daily ritual will find paths close to *Olympic Stadium* and in the Kaivopuisto park in the southern part of the city or around Hesperia Park near the city center.

Horseback Riding – You won't have trouble finding a horse to ride. Check with the Finnish Equestrian Federation, 12 Radiokatu (phone: 158-2315).

Hunting – Finland's big game is moose. Three- to four-day packages, including tests at shooting areas, licenses, insurance, comfortable accommodations, and full board are available to those who want to join in the sport. The season runs from late October to December. Contact the Fishing and Hunting Department, 3A Hallituskatu, Helsinki 00170 (phone: 1601).

Saunas – Most hotels have their own saunas; it's best to book them in advance. Public saunas usually do not accept reservations. Contact the Helsinki City Tourist Office for further information.

Skiing – Skiing is to Finns as baseball is to Americans. In Finland skiing means mostly cross-country skiing, for which its terrain is ideal. All over the country there are marked and often illuminated ski trails of varying lengths and difficulty. There are also numerous downhill slopes with ski lifts. The peak season for skiing in south and central Finland is from January to March; in Lapland it runs from late autumn through May. (A bonus for skiers in May is a deep suntan, which is produced by 14 to 16 hours of sunshine.)

Ski equipment can be rented at *Stadion Retkeilymaja,* at 3B Pohjois Stadionintie (phone: 496071), and all ski centers.

You can — and many Finns do this on weekends — just put on your skis and follow tracks on the Gulf of Finland to the islands. There are ski tracks all around Helsinki.

Or you may prefer a weekend or week-long ski package at one of the many winter sports centers all over Finland. Resorts offer cross-country skiing, of course, as well as ski lifts, downhill slopes, marked and illuminated ski trails, keep-fit rooms, guided excursions, saunas, evening entertainment, and ski instruction. Two popular areas near Helsinki are Messilä (65 mi/100 km) near the site of international skiing competitions in February, and Hyvinkää (about 40 mi/64 km).

Further information about skiing is available from the local sports association, *Suomen Latu,* 7 Fabianinkatu (phone: 170101); the Helsinki City Tourist Office (see above); or from any travel agent in Helsinki.

Veteran skiers may enter the *Finlandia Ski Race* (cross-country) in early March or any of a number of ski races. Inquire at the Finland National Tourist Office.

Soccer – In summer there are games between Finland and other countries. Check *Helsinki This Week* for schedules.

Squash – For information on the 600 squash courts throughout Finland, contact the Finnish Squash Racquets Association, 12 Radiokatu (phone: 158-2495).

Tennis – Tennis is popular in Scandinavia. Helsinki alone has 31 clubs. It's best to bring your own racket. For booking a court and other information, call the Finnish Tennis Association, 12 Radiokatu (phone: 1581).

Winter Sports and Activities – A unique experience in Lapland is a reindeer safari, often complete with a Lapp guide; participants travel by reindeer sledge across the fells and spend the night in a modern log cabin. For information about such winter tours, contact the Finland Travel Bureau Ltd., 10A Kaivokatu, 00100 Helsinki (phone: 18261).

 THEATER: The top three theaters in town are the *Finnish National Theater* (Kansallisteatteri) at Asema-aukio (railway station plaza) (phone: 171826); *City Theater* (Kaupunginteatteri) 5 Eläintarhantie (phone: 394-0300 or 394-0400), and the *Swedish Theater* (Svenska Teatern) Erottaja (phone: 171244). You may not understand Swedish or Finnish, which are the languages of practically all productions, but you might want to take in one performance just for fun. In summer there are only open-air performances.

 MUSIC: There's always an excellent choice of concerts by symphony orchestras, chamber groups, and jazz artists. Many name performers from Europe, the US, and other countries can be seen, so don't be surprised if you find a group of Japanese instrumentalists playing one concert and the *New York Philharmonic* at another. Major concert halls include: *Finlandia Hall,* 4 Karamzininkatu; *House of Culture* (Kulttuuritalo), 4 Sturenkatu; *Sibelius Academy,* 9 P. Rautatiekatu; *House of Nobility* (Ritarihuone), 3 Aleksanterinkatu; and *Finnish National Opera,* 23-27 Bulevardi (phone: 129255). (Operas are sung in their original languages.) *Musiikki-Fazer,* 11 Aleksanterinkatu (phone: 56011), is the main agency for concert and opera tickets. A new opera house is currently under construction on Mannerheimintie at the edge of Hesperia Park.

 NIGHTLIFE AND NIGHTCLUBS: Finns are nightlifers, especially the under-50 segment of the population, who are endowed with limitless endurance. The disco has won points in this city, and the proof is in the crowds that flock to "nightclubs," as discos are called here, at various locales around the city. Two of the liveliest are the *Old Baker's,* 12 Mannerheimintie (phone: 605607), and the *Fizz,* next door at 10 Mannerheimintie (phone: 641717). For more elegant surroundings, try the discos at the *Hesperia, Inter-Continental,* and *Strand Inter-Continental* hotels, all open to 3 AM. Roulette, which is restricted to a limit of 25¢ per chip, is popular here. You'll find roulette wheels in many hotels and nightspots.

BEST IN TOWN

CHECKING IN: Most of the city's accommodations are centrally located, modern, and equipped with all the amenities that make for a comfortable stay (and all of the hotels listed below have at least one sauna). Although there is something of a hotel boom going on in Helsinki, reservations should still be made in advance, especially during the peak of the summer season. For those traveling to Finland in summer, seasonal discount accommodations coupons, called Finncheques, are available. These coupons reduce hotel rates considerably and are good at any of 160 hotels across the country; a full breakfast is also included. Finncheques can be purchased in the US from Holiday Tours of America, 40 E. 49th St., New York, NY 10017 (212-832-9072 or 800-223-0567). For travelers on a budget who want a glimpse of Finnish life, the Finland Tourist Board and local travel agencies can arrange farm holidays.

Expect to pay $125 and up a night for a double room in a hotel in the expensive category; $80 to $120 in the moderate category; and $75 and under in the inexpensive category. Credit cards are accepted everywhere. All telephone numbers are in the 0 area code unless otherwise indicated.

Hesperia – This luxury hotel is across the street from Hesperia Park and a stone's throw from *Finlandia Hall.* Its good location, fine service, outstanding Russian and French style grill room, boutiques, disco, sauna, and swimming pool make it a popular choice. There's also roulette in the lobby for those who follow the sportin' life. Suites available. 50 Mannerheimintie (phone: 43101). Expensive.

Inter-Continental – With 555 rooms, this is Scandinavia's largest hotel. Thirty luxury suites are available. The sauna on the top floor offers a chance to look out over the city from the adjoining terrace. Roulette may be played in the *Baltic Lounge* on the main floor or on the 9th-floor lounge with a panoramic view. Elegant seafood dishes are served at *Galateia,* also on the 9th floor (see *Eating Out*). Take time to saunter through the shopping arcade in the lobby. 46-48 Mannerheimintie (phone: 441331 or 40551). Expensive.

Kalastajatorppa – In the perfect setting of a park, bordered by the blue waters of the Gulf of Finland, "Fisherman's Cottage," as the hotel's name translates, is a spacious and ultramodern hotel with 235 rooms outside the city center. Its newest annex is designed so that windows from double rooms overlook the sea. Several handsome suites are available. This latest addition to the hotel connects to the older section via a whitewashed rock tunnel, brilliantly lighted for walking. A romantic formal garden invites a stroll between dancing sessions in the main dining room or *Red Room* disco. Lots of activity in this hotel, including tennis courts, a private beach, and two indoor pools. 1 Kalastajatorpantie (phone: 488011). Expensive.

Marski – In the center of town, across from *Stockmann's* department store. Check in on the main floor of the hotel, which is in an office building. Hotel rooms begin on the 3rd floor. It's a little more like a business traveler's hotel but equipped with most desired facilities, including 2 saunas. The *Fizz* bar behind the reception desk is popular for cocktails in the late afternoon and for disco dancing at night. 10 Mannerheimintie (phone: 68061). Expensive.

Palace – This gracious hotel is near the South Harbor and the Market Place. An older hotel with only 59 rooms, it has been beautifully renovated; the accommodations are most comfortable and the service fine. The Italian *La Vista* restaurant on the 2nd floor and the *Gourmet* dining room on the 9th floor serve excellent fare (see *Eating Out*), and the *American Bar* on the top floor is a delight. In summer you can take your drinks and lunch on the terrace and enjoy the wide expanse of sea, watching ships come and go. Three saunas. 10 Eteläranta (phone: 171114). Expensive.

Ramada Presidentti – A luxurious establishment that's centrally located with 500 rooms. It has a good steakhouse and several other restaurants. Room service to 1 AM. Sauna and swimming pool. 4 Eteläinen Rautatienkatu (phone: 6911). Expensive.

Strand Inter-Continental – Elegant and intimate, this 200-room hotel opened in 1989 on the waterfront near the old city center. The top floor has 4 saunas, each with its own terrace, and a swimming pool; also restaurants. 4 John Stenberginranta (phone: 39351).

Socis-Seurahuone – Across from the railway station, this hotel has traditional Old World charm and has been beautifully renovated. It also has a good restaurant, a classic Art Deco café and pub, and 118 rooms with modern conveniences. 12 Kaivokatu (phone: 170441). Expensive to moderate.

Aurora – In the heart of Helsinki, this small, dependable hotel has a restaurant, bar, swimming pool, and sauna. 50 Helsinginkatu (phone: 717400). Moderate.

Klaus Kurki – Frequented mostly by businesspeople, this has comfortable rooms, a quiet bar, a pleasant restaurant, and an unpretentious wine cellar serving quick, moderately priced lunches. 2-4 Bulevardi (phone: 602322). Moderate.

Rivoli Jardin – A charming and cozy hotel with 54 rooms, it is well run and centrally located. Bar, café, and winter garden. Fitness room and sauna. Snacks are available through room service (until midnight), but there's no full-service restaurant. 40 Kasarminkatu (phone: 177880). Moderate.

Torni – In the heart of town, known for its different restaurants, ranging from Balkan to Spanish. The small bar on the 13th floor has a spectacular view of the city and the sea. *Torni* has 155 rooms with modern conveniences. 26 Yrjönkatu (phone: 644611). Moderate.

Hospiz – This *YMCA* hotel near the center of town has 163 rooms and a restaurant (no liquor license); good for a family on a budget. 17 Vuorikatu (phone: 170481). Moderate to inexpensive.

Anna – A quiet, comfortable place, it has 58 rooms. 1 Annankatu (phone: 648011). Inexpensive.

Marttahotelli – Near the business district, this 45-room hotel run by the Finnish Housewives' Association is quiet and has a restaurant without a liquor license. 24 Uudenmaankatu (phone: 646211). Inexpensive.

■**Note:** During June, July, and August, the university's student quarters are for rent. They offer more modest accommodations and services than ordinary hotels but are quite comfortable and reasonably priced. For general hotel bookings in Finland contact the *Hotel Booking Center,* Railway Station, 00100 Helsinki (phone: 171133), or the Finland Travel Association, 25 Mikonkatu (phone: 170868).

EATING OUT: Although Finnish cuisine shows marked Eastern (Russian) and Western (French and Swedish) influences, there are some dishes that are uniquely Finnish. You will see Swedish smorgasbord with Finnish variations (called *voileipäpöytä* by the Finns), especially for lunch. Fish dishes are popular in Finland, especially salmon, whitefish, and Baltic herring. Not to be missed are the delicious little native crayfish, which taste like American lobster but are even better; they are in season from about July 20 until September.

You also might want to try reindeer meat, which is served in many forms — as steaks, chops, and stews, for example — but especially tasty is reindeer tongue, served smoked or in a Madeira sauce. *Vorshmack* is a hearty dish that blends herring, mutton, beef, and onions, and is served with sour cream and a baked potato. Fried Baltic herring is also quite tasty.

Another typical dish is *karjalanpiirakka,* a pastry dough of rye flour (rye bread is big in Finland), filled with rice or potato; also *kalakukko,* a fish and pork pie.

The national dessert is Finnish crêpes, called *ohukainen.* Also delicious are fresh berries, especially strawberries and cloudberries (yellowish raspberries), and the chewy Lapp cheese, which is served warm with a berry sauce.

Finns drink their own high-quality beer and vodka (often served, as the Russians do, ice cold with hors d'oeuvres); also brandy, Scotch, and Campari. Try Finnish after-dinner liqueurs made with berries, particularly *mesimarja* (from brambleberries), *lakka* (from cloudberries), and *karpalo* (from cranberries).

There are many small, upbeat restaurants in Helsinki, not to mention cafeterias, snack bars, hamburger joints, and pizzerias for eating on the run. But Helsinki still lacks any good American-style restaurants that serve a variety of salads, juicy steaks, and baked potatoes.

Dress is informal, but in the evening jackets and ties are required for men. Women can wear casual or cocktail dresses. If you feel like dressing up, by all means do. You won't be alone.

Note: There are a number of charming, strictly summer restaurants in Helsinki that are near water or on small islands; great for dinner and dancing. The *Walhalla* on the island fortress of Suomenlinna is one of the most charming. Check the reception desk at your hotel or get a list from the Helsinki City Tourist Office.

Remember, there is no tipping in restaurants; a service charge is included in your bill. However, leaving a small additional gratuity is a common practice. The obligatory cloakroom fee to restaurant doormen is usually clearly indicated; if not, it is about $1.

Restaurant prices are comparable to those in other European countries; expect to pay $90 to $150 for dinner for two with one drink at an expensive restaurant; $50 to $85 is moderate; $25 to $45 is inexpensive (with beer). Due to government regulation of alcoholic beverages, prices are very high except at *Alko,* the state liquor stores found through Finland. Finally, if you want to look up an eating place in the phone book, the Finnish word for restaurant is *ravintola.* All telephone numbers are in the 0 area code.

Alexander Nevski – A Russian restaurant in the same complex — and around the corner from — *Havis Amanda.* Closed Sundays. 17 Pohtoisesplanadi (phone: 639610). Expensive.

George – A sophisticated restaurant in the heart of Helsinki known for consistently high standards. The decor is timeless and unpretentious. Closed Sundays. 17 Kalevankatu (phone: 647662). Expensive.

Havis Amanda – Cellar restaurant with charming atmosphere. Table d'hôte menu and à la carte. Specializes in seafood and enjoys a reputation for excellence. Luscious desserts. Closed Sundays. 23 Unioninkatu (phone: 666882). Expensive.

Hesperia Russian Room – Reviving culinary traditions from the time of the czars, this dining room in the *Hesperia* hotel offers exciting taste experiences and old-time Russian atmosphere. The menu offers traditional Russian dishes as well as international ones prepared à la Russe. Open daily. 50 Mannerheimintu (phone: 43101). Expensive.

Galateia – The *Inter-Continental*'s elegant seafood restaurant, on the 9th floor, with a panoramic city view and a luminous interior. 46-48 Mannerheimintie (phone: 441331). Expensive.

Gourmet – One of the *Palace* hotel's two restaurants, it is considered among the city's best — in fact, the chef, Eero Mäkelä, has earned a Michelin star for the restaurant, the only one in Helsinki. The highlight is international and Finnish cuisine. Closed weekends. Reservations necessary. 10 Eteläranta (phone: 171114). Expensive.

Pamir – Finnish fish and game dishes served in a tranquil setting, with muted colors and Saarinen furniture. In summer there's waterfront terrace dining. Closed Sundays. In the *Strand Inter-Continental,* 4 John Steinberginranta (phone: 39351). Expensive.

Savoy – In the center of town at the top of an office building designed by Alvar Aalto. One of the better patronized dining places for intimate luncheons. Continental, international menus, Finnish specialties, and a good *vorschmack.* Closed weekends. 14 Eteläesplanadi (phone: 176571). Expensive.

Svenska Klubben – After entering a pleasant, castle-like hall, surrounded by beautifully decorated rooms and salons, diners will be delighted by the cuisine and distinguished service. 6 Maurinkatu (phone: 628706). Expensive.

Bellevue – Not too far from Market Square near the Russian Orthodox church, this humble establishment is considered one of the best of several Russian restaurants in Helsinki. Closed in January and February. 3 Rahapajankatu (phone: 179560). Expensive to moderate.

Kappeli – This large establishment has several dining rooms, a coffeehouse, and a beer cellar, with outdoor service in summer. Its atmosphere is part of its attraction. Near the colorful Market Square. A lively concert from the bandstand across the adjoining park accompanies your lunch. Dancing at night. Open daily. Reservations advised. Esplanadipuisto (Esplanadi Park) (phone: 179242). Expensive to moderate.

Kosmos – A slice of Finnish bohemian life — the patrons are painters, poets, and philosophers — with a versatile bistro menu. The beefy men at the door act as bouncers and check coats; local protocol dictates that you tip them 4 marks (about $1). Reservations necessary. 3 Kalevankatu (phone: 607717). Expensive to moderate.

Piekka – Both the cuisine and the atmosphere are authentically Finnish. The menu features rich soups, fresh fish and game according to season, and tasty desserts of local berries and cheeses. 68 Mannerheimtie (phone: 445738). Expensive to moderate.

Säkkipilli and **The Old Baker's** – A busy downtown spot with two restaurants, a pub, and a disco. Closed weekends. Corner of 2 Kalevankatu and 12 Mannerheimintie (phone: 605607). *Säkkipilli,* expensive; *Old Baker's,* moderate.

Bulevardia – A bohemian bastion. The drinks and the people watching are a little more exciting than the food, which is tasty and not too pricey. Open daily. 34 Bulevardi (phone: 645243). Moderate.

Katariina – A new addition to the dining scene, it combines the French and Finnish cuisines in innovative ways. Good wines by the glass, unusual for Finland. Closed Sundays. 22-24 Aleksanterinkatu (phone: 656722). Moderate.

Troikka – Whoever once proclaimed that you can find better Russian food in Helsinki than in Moscow or Leningrad must have dined here. Antique icons, tapestries, and balalaika music create an ambience fit for a czar. Closed weekends. 3 Caloniukesenkatu (phone: 445229). Moderate.

Wellamo – Locals come here for hearty soups and daily specials of the season according to the whim of the proprietress. The art on the walls is for sale and changes monthly. Closed Mondays. 9 Vyokatu (phone: 663139). Moderate.

Happy Days – A coffee shop in the center of town. Open daily. 2 Pohjoisesplanadi (phone: 624023). Moderate to inexpensive.

Kasvisravintola – Basic vegetarian restaurant, with a health food shop on the premises. Open daily. 3 Korkeavuorenkatu (phone: 179212). Moderate to inexpensive.

Aurora – Tearoom, serving light fare in a cozy atmosphere. Open daily. 50 Helsinginkatu (phone: 717400). Inexpensive.

Le Buffet – Drop in during a day of shopping to relax and enjoy seafood, fresh salads, or just a snack. Closed Sundays. Forum shopping center, 20 Mannerheimintie (phone: 694-1319). Inexpensive.

Café Ekberg – A Helsinki institution for breakfast, lunch, or simply tea, with a no-frills ambience. The baked goods are made daily on the premises. Closed Sundays. 9 Bulevardi (phone: 605269). Inexpensive.

Elite – Striking Functionalist decor was restored with loving care to create this restaurant frequented by artists and writers. Order local specialties like Baltic herring or *vorschmack,* or just try the soup and salad bar. Open daily. Excellent house wines. 22 Et. Hesperiankatu (phone: 495542). Inexpensive.

Fazer – One of several tearooms/sweetshops run by the famed chocolate manufacturer, which also serves light meals and the best ice cream in town. Closed Sundays. 3 Kluuvikatu (phone: 666597). Inexpensive.

Ursula – A café alongside the Kaivopuisto shore with a harbor view (phone: 652-817). Open daily. Inexpensive.

Wanhan Kahuila – This student hangout is a good place to quaff a beer and have a chat. Terrace dining in summer. Open daily. 3 Mannerheimtie (phone: 667376). Inexpensive.

LENINGRAD

Imperial Russia: music, art, theater, ballet, literary salons, glittering court life. This city was the center of the lavish, reckless social milieu immortalized by Pushkin, Dostoyevsky, Tolstoy, and Turgenev. Almost inevitably, it was also the Cradle of the Revolution: Bloody Sunday, the storming of the Winter Palace, and Lenin's triumphant return from exile. Leningrad is relatively young for a European city of such rich cultural and political heritage — less than 285 years old — but what happened here has changed the course of world history.

In a city of such great beauty, where virtually every downtown building displays a plaque noting its historical significance, it is sometimes difficult to focus on the people who live here and the life of the city today. But Leningrad is also a city where a visitor is immediately comfortable. When the days lengthen and dusk comes late, it is hard to resist walking among the people strolling arm in arm in the streets or relaxing in the parks in the fading light that casts its strange glimmer over the city. These glorious White Nights of summer are a consequence of Leningrad's location on the Gulf of Finland at about the same latitude as Helsinki. Leningrad is built on a series of islands, 403 miles northwest of Moscow. Although its climate is less harsh than the capital's, the harbor is frozen 3 or 4 months of the year.

The hundreds of islands near the mouth of the Neva River, at a point where the Baltic Sea penetrates deepest into its eastern shore, were disputed for centuries by a succession of Finns, Swedes, and Russians. The Neva was an important early trade artery between Europe and Asia. In 1703, after defeating Sweden, Peter the Great built a fortress here to ensure against future invasions. Within 9 years, Peter had built a new city, his "window on Europe," and had moved the capital from Moscow.

St. Petersburg — Petrograd — as the new capital was originally called, was designed from the first to rival the beauty of Western Europe's finest cities. It developed in well-planned stages, acquiring an elegant façade as government buildings, cathedrals, and private residences of the nobility took their places along the Neva and the Fontanka and Moika rivers. Many of the most beautiful palaces were built in the last half of the 18th century under the direction of Catherine the Great's favorite French and Italian architects. As the excessive indulgence of the gentry increased, the lives of the czars' subjects became even more intolerable. Serfs were in semislavery. In St. Petersburg itself, overcrowded hovels where workers lived in miserable poverty surrounded the beautiful palaces, the lovely parks, and the great squares and avenues. This incredible contrast between the lifestyle of the nobility and the daily oppression of the workers was impossible to ignore. Change was inevitable.

On January 9, 1905, thousands of workers marched with their wives and children to the Winter Palace to petition Czar Nicholas II to intervene on behalf of better working conditions. The czar's troops opened fire at close range. The resulting massacre, known in Russian history as Bloody Sunday, was the spark that ignited the Revolution of 1905. Nicholas made some concessions that allowed him to survive the popular uprising, but only for a time. His inability to rule, further economic hardship brought on by World War I, and continued revolutionary activity brought down the whole structure of czardom in March 1917. A new era in Russian history began in November of that year when a Soviet government replaced the provisional government. It also meant a new era for this city: The capital was moved back to Moscow.

The city was renamed Leningrad in 1924 after the death of Lenin. Although its political importance diminished when Moscow became the seat of government, the city continued to grow as an industrial and commercial center until World War II. Almost 700,000 Russians lost their lives and some 10,000 buildings were destroyed during the 900-day German siege of Leningrad. But the city emerged from the war determined to restore its former beauty, and today Leningrad remains the most European of Soviet cities. The canals, rivers, and low buildings remind one of Venice, and Nevsky Prospekt has much of the air of the great boulevards of Paris. The parallels are reinforced by the 18th- and 19th-century baroque and neo-classical architecture that dominates the central city. The Sheremetyev Palace, Count Orlov's Marble Palace, Prince Potemkin's Taurida Palace, and, of course, the Winter Palace are among the noble homes restored and used today as museums, offices, meeting houses — lacking the grandeur of their original state yet eminently more functional.

Even Leningrad's present modernization plan is designed to preserve the beauty of the city's past. New construction in the downtown area must be completed within existing façades. No skyscrapers are permitted to mar the horizon; glass and concrete structures are prohibited in central Leningrad. Modern building is allowed beyond the city center, however, and numerous large apartment complexes have been built to house the city's 4.5 million people. Most of the industrial expansion — from the shipbuilding industry to factories producing hydrogenerators — has taken place in outlying areas.

Leningrad has an extraordinarily rich cultural heritage, with direct links to the most fundamental changes in Russian political history. It is a city that speaks most eloquently of its past.

LENINGRAD AT-A-GLANCE

SEEING THE CITY: There is no one vantage point that will provide a good view of the entire city. Peter the Great's decree that no structure should be taller than the spires of the Cathedral of Saints Peter and Paul (about 400 feet), along with the fact that the city is built on marshland, has created a relatively low skyline. However, if you stand beside the Neva opposite the Peter and Paul Fortress, you can get a sense of where and how the city began. At the Admiral Building, where the city's three major avenues converge, you can grasp Leningrad's

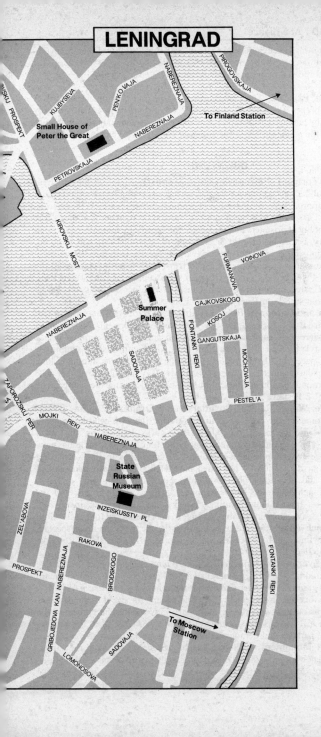

layout and planning. In Palace Square, the site of czarist splendor and bloody revolution, you can get in touch with the city's history; on Nevsky Prospekt at Griboyedov Canal, you can feel the contemporary pulse of the city.

 SPECIAL PLACES: The major sites of Leningrad are spread out over a number of the 101 islands that interconnect to form the city, but all are easily reached by public transportation. You can visit them on your own or arrange tours of the major sites with the *Intourist* travel service bureau (see *Sources and Resources*).

DOWNTOWN

Peter and Paul Fortress (Petropavlovskaya Krepost) – Before Peter the Great chose this site to build a new capital for Russia, he had ordered a fortress built to bar the Swedish fleet's approach. As St. Petersburg became secure from attack, the fortress, established in May 1703, came to be used more as a prison for opponents of the czarist regime. The list of political prisoners included Peter the Great's own son, the Czarevich Alexei; Dostoyevsky, before his exile to Siberia; and the anarchist Mikhail Bakunin. The Cathedral of Saints Peter and Paul (Petropavlovsky Sobor), with its tall, extremely slender golden spire, stands in the center of the fortress. It is the burial place of all the Russian czars from Peter I to Alexander III, with the exception of Peter II. In 1924, the *Peter and Paul Fortress* became a museum. Closed Wednesdays. Admission charge. Reached from Revolutsii Sq. on Peter and Paul Fortress Island.

Summer Palace and Garden of Peter I (Letny Sad; Dvorets-Musei Petra I) – Across the Neva from the fortress, on the Kutuzov Embankment (Nabereznaya Kutuzova), is a 30-acre park, laid out in 1704, and an unpretentious summer palace built in the Dutch style for Peter the Great. The park, filled with classical sculptures, is a favorite open space with Leningraders, particularly during the summer's long White Nights. The palace is open daily except Tuesdays, May through November. The park is open year-round, although the sculpture is covered during the winter. The park's entrance is at 2 Pestelya St.

State Hermitage; Winter Palace (Gosudarstvenni Ermitazh; Zimnniy Dvoryets) – Built as a home for the czars and czarinas during the 18th-century reigns of Elizabeth and Catherine the Great, the *Winter Palace* was designed by the Italian architect Rastrelli. The grandiose baroque palace and four adjacent buildings now house the Hermitage collection, one of the finest art collections in the world. The splendor of the room decorations — patterned parquet floors, molded and painted ceilings, furniture, and decorative objects of malachite, lapis lazuli, and jasper — dazzle the eye as much as the da Vincis, Raphaels, Titians, Rembrandts, and the Impressionist and post-Impressionist paintings. When you think you have already seen every richness and extravagance imaginable, arrange to take the special tour of the Gold Treasure Room, which holds the exquisite jewels of Catherine the Great and a spectacular collection of Scythian gold. Closed Mondays. Admission charge. 36 Dvortsovaya Nab. (phone: 219-8601 or 212-9545).

Palace Square (Dvortsovaya Pl.) – Between the *Winter Palace* and the great curve of the Admiralty Building, the former general staff headquarters, is the central square of the city. The red granite Alexander Column in the center was erected in 1832 as a monument to the victory over Napoleon in 1812. This square, the site of Bloody Sunday in 1905, is closely associated with the revolutionary movement. The climax of the October Revolution in 1917 was the storming of the *Winter Palace* from this square. Each year there are parades and demonstrations here to mark the event.

Peter the Great Monument – The famous bronze statue of Peter the Great, designed by the French sculptor E. M. Falconet, stands in the center of the grassy Decemberists Square (Dekabristov Pl.) to the west of the Admiralty Building. The statue, commissioned by Catherine the Great, depicts Peter astride a horse whose hoofs are trampling a writhing snake (said to be a symbolic representation of Sweden).

St. Isaac's Cathedral Museum (Isaakievsky Sobor) – Leningrad's largest church — and one of the world's largest domed structures — stands to the south of December-ists Square. The cathedral is filled with mosaic and painted ceiling murals, decorated with 14 kinds of minerals and semiprecious stones. Malachite and lapis lazuli columns form a part of the massive gilded iconostasis before the altar. A Foucault pendulum that moves 13° each hour is suspended from the central dome. Closed Tuesdays. Isaakievskaya Sq.

Alexander Nevsky Monastery (Aleksandr Nevskaya Lavra) – The monastery's Trinity Cathedral (Troitsky Sobor) was built in 1722 to house the remains of St. Alexander Nevsky, which had been brought here from Vladimir. In 1922, the silver sarcophagus containing the saint's ashes was moved to the Hermitage. The monastery also has ten other churches, four cemeteries (known as necropolises), a seminary, and the *Museum of Urban Sculpture*. The 18th-century necropolis includes the graves of Peter I's sister and Mikhail Lomonosov, the scientist who founded Moscow University. The 19th-century necropolis includes the graves of Dostoyevsky, Tchaikovsky, Moussorgsky, Rimsky-Korsakov, and Borodin. You must buy a ticket to enter these cemeteries, but you may visit the interesting modern necropolis opposite the cathedral without charge. Note its unusual grave markers, such as the propeller of the plane in which a pilot met his death and a miniature oil rig for three oilfield workers. The *Museum of Urban Sculpture* has models and site photographs of most of the city's monuments. Closed Thursdays. Admission charge. Near the Aleksandra Nevskovo Metro stop. 1 Aleksandra Nevskovo Sq.

Russian State Museum (Gosudarstvenni Russky Musei) – Next to the *Tretyakov Gallery* in Moscow, this is the largest collection of Russian art in the world. There are some 300,000 examples of Russian painting, sculpture, decorative arts, and folk arts in this museum in the former Mikhailovsky Palace. Closed Tuesdays. Admission charge. 4/2 Inzhenernaya St. (phone: 314-3448).

Ethnographical Museum of the Peoples of the USSR (Gosudarstvenni Musei Etnografii Narodov USSR) – In a wing of the *Russian State Museum* but with its own entrance, this museum houses a beautiful collection of clothing, household goods, and folk articles associated with the daily life and customs of the peoples of the 15 republics that make up the USSR. Closed Mondays. Admission charge. 4/1 Inzhenernaya St. (phone: 210-3888).

Church of the Blood of the Savior (Khram Spasa na Krovi) – Built in the Old Russian style similar to St. Basil's in Moscow, this church was erected at the end of the 19th century on the spot where Alexander II was assassinated. The exterior is covered with mosaics. Open daily. Just north of the Russian State Museum. 1 Griboyedova Kan. Nab.

Bridges of Leningrad – From the ironwork of the large, impressive Kirov Bridge over the Neva to the multitude of small bridges connecting the islands, these structures are a natural museum of the city. The stone turrets and chains of the Lomonosov Bridge over the Fontanka are an example of the earliest bridges. This heavy style soon gave way to light, airy ironwork decorated with lions, gilded griffins, sphinxes, and other delightful creatures. There are hundreds of these bridges, large and small, and they create one of the unifying aspects of the city. The most famous, perhaps, is the Anich-kov, which spans the Fontanka River at Nevsky Prospekt and has four sculptures by Peter Klodt.

Smolny Monastery and Institute – The cathedral and convent of the monastery were built in the 18th century by Czarina Elizabeth, and the institute was founded during the reign of Catherine II as a school for young ladies of the nobility. The room at the institute where Lenin later lived and worked is now a museum. Tours of the interiors are available by special arrangement, but the park may be visited at any time. Along the Neva between Smolnovo St. and Smolny Prospekt, about 7 blocks east of the Cernysevskaya Metro stop.

Piskarevskoye Memorial Cemetery – An eternal flame and small museum are at the entrance of these memorial grounds commemorating the 900-day siege of Leningrad during World War II. Some 500,000 of those who died before the ring of the blockade was broken in 1943 were buried in mass graves here. The museum contains photographs and documents about the heroism of the city's residents during the blockade. North of the Smolny Monastery, across the Neva in the northeast sector of the city. Piskarevsky Prospekt.

Lenin Monument at the Finland Station – Lenin arrived at the Finland Station after 10 years in exile, and it was here, on April 3, 1917, that he spoke to workers from the turret of an armored car. In 1926, a statue of Lenin standing on an armored car was erected in a square in front of the railway station to commemorate the event and to mark the ninth anniversary of the revolution. Near the Lenina Sq. Metro stop. Lenina Sq.

Cruiser *Aurora* (Creiser *Avrora*) – A blank shot fired from this cruiser signaled the beginning of the October Revolution. Now the cruiser is permanently moored in the Neva, opposite the *Leningrad* hotel (see *Checking In*). Closed Fridays. Admission charge. Petrogradskaya Nab.

ENVIRONS

Pushkin – Once known as the Czar's Village, this town is the site of the Yekaterinsky Palace, named for Peter the Great's wife, Catherine I. Built during the reigns of Elizabeth and Catherine II in a 1,482-acre park, the palace has a stunning aqua façade, decorated with gold and white ornaments. Part of the palace is now a museum, with exhibitions of furniture, china, and the palace's history. There's also a museum with manuscripts, rare books, and the personal belongings of Alexander Pushkin, who studied at the school for the nobility attached to the palace. The village was renamed for the poet in 1937, on the 100th anniversary of his death. The museums are closed on Tuesdays. Train service is available from the Vitebsky Station in Leningrad, with buses and taxis available at the station here. Fourteen miles (22 km) south of Leningrad along Moscow Prospekt.

Pavlovsk – One of the most beautifully restored palaces in the Soviet Union is less than 2 miles (3 km) from Pushkin. Originally hunting grounds that belonged to the Czar's Village, the palace grounds constitute one of the largest landscaped parks in Europe. The land and palace were a gift from Catherine II to her son Paul in 1777. You enter the 1,500-acre park on a road from Pushkin through cast-iron gates and over a wooden bridge. The palace is closed Fridays. Fifteen miles (24 km) south of Leningrad along Moscow Prospekt.

■**EXTRA SPECIAL:** On the southern shore of the Gulf of Finland, Peter the Great built Petrodvorets, the Grand Palace, which he hoped would rival Versailles. He personally drafted the layout of the 300-acre park and gave detailed instructions on the design of the spectacular system of fountains that cascade through the park and gardens. The buildings were badly damaged during World War II but have been restored carefully, according to the original plans. Some 129 of the fountains in the system that begins on the Ropshinskiye Heights 13 miles (21 km) away are working today. The most impressive of these is the Samson Fountain, directly in front of the Grand Palace, which portrays Samson ripping open the jaws of a lion as a spray of water rises from the lion's mouth. Petrodvorets is about 20 miles (32 km) southwest of the city. It can be reached by leaving the city along Stacek Prospekt or, in summer, by hydrofoil down the Neva into the gulf.

SOURCES AND RESOURCES

TOURIST INFORMATION: It is best to buy comprehensive guides to Leningrad before you leave the US. Two of the most useful are *The Complete Guide to the Soviet Union,* by Victor and Jennifer Louis (St. Martin's Press; $9.95), and the *Blue Guide to Leningrad and Moscow* (W. W. Norton; $18.95). A good guide to the city and its museums is *Next Time You Go to Russia,* by Charles A. Ward (Scribners; $8.95). *Leningrad: Art and Architecture,* by V. Schwartz (Moscow: Progress Publishers), is especially good and may be obtained in the US through stores that import Russian publications. *Leningrad, Its Monuments and Architectural Complexes* (Leningrad: Aurora Art Publishers) is a beautifully illustrated book sold in *Beriozka* stores (see *Shopping*) in Leningrad.

Although good transportation and city maps are available in hotels at news or book kiosks for very reasonable prices, it is helpful to take along a *Falkplan* map for Leningrad (Hamburg: Falk-Verlag; $6.95), available in the US. This pocket map is designed to be used in sections and includes a street name index and gazetteer for monuments, museums, hotels, and theaters. *Intourist* deals with all adult foreign travel in the USSR and provides English-speaking guides (3 St. Isaac's Sq.). Although you will have an English-speaking guide with you during tour activities, it would be helpful to learn the Russian (Cyrillic) alphabet and the sound for each of its characters. Many Russian words have English or French cognates, so once you sound out the words, life can become much simpler. Especially helpful is the Berlitz book *Russian for Travellers* ($1.95).

Local Coverage – You can buy the *Moscow News,* an English-language weekly newspaper, or you may find the *International Herald Tribune,* English daily newspapers, and some weekly magazines on sale in *Intourist* hotels occasionally.

The American Consulate General is at 15 Ulitsa Petra Lavrova St. (phone: 274-8235).

Telephone – Leningrad cannot be dialed direct from the US. Calls must go through an international operator.

Phone books are nearly impossible to find in Leningrad, but you can get directory assistance from the hotel desk or service bureau. Telephones in hotel rooms are connected to the city system. To use a public pay phone, deposit a 2-kopek coin in the pay slot before lifting the receiver, then dial when you hear a continuous buzzing sound. For long-distance calls, book them at least an hour ahead of time through the service bureau in your hotel.

CLIMATE AND CLOTHES: Leningrad is near the Gulf of Finland and the Baltic Sea and, although farther north, tends to be warmer than Moscow. The temperatures average 16F to 19F (-9C to -7C) during January and in the mid-60s F (16C-18C) during July, with about 6 to 13 days of precipitation per month. During the late spring and summer, the days are very long, but in December, when the canals and rivers are frozen over and the cold is intense, the short days make life something of an endurance test. Even so, this winter weather does not daunt the Walrus Club, whose members swim in the Neva beside the Peter and Paul Fortress in an area cleared of ice just for them. The river is frozen from mid-November to April.

If you travel during these cold months, a fur hat, heavy coat, boots, gloves, and scarves are essential, but tour buses and building interiors are well heated, so tourists normally are not unduly distressed by the cold. In Russia, one must check one's coat at restaurants, museums, and theaters, so a heavy loop or chain should be sewn into the collar. (The check rooms have only coat hooks, no hangers.)

In warmer weather, a raincoat with a removable lining or a sweater and raincoat will suffice. Winter is a good 6 months long, so it can still be quite cool in early fall and late spring. Even in the summertime a sweater is welcome for evenings. A travel umbrella is essential in this city.

 GETTING AROUND: Leningrad has a small but exceedingly good subway system, called the Metro, which is supplemented by a network of bus, trolley, and tram routes that enable you to move about the city with relative ease. Fares on each are less than a dime. Good, inexpensive, transportation maps are generally available in the hotels.

Airport – Leningrad Airport is 30 to 45 minutes from downtown by taxi; the fare is 5 to 6 rubles ($3-$4). Transportation from the airport to downtown can also be arranged in advance through *Intourist* (see *Sources and Resources*).

Boats – In summer, hydrofoils and excursion boats ply the Neva River, the canals, and the smaller rivers. The fare usually ranges from 25¢ to 75¢, depending on the length of the trip.

Bus, Trolley, and Tram – These vehicles all have self-service cash boxes and require exact change. You deposit your fare when you get on, and get a ticket by turning a knob on the side of the cash box. If it is crowded, you will be expected to pass your money to whoever is standing next to the cash box. If you happen to be standing near the cash box during the rush hour, you may end up feeling just like a native after dispensing 15 or 20 tickets.

Car Rentals – Rentals can be made with or without a chauffeur, through *Intourist*. They must be paid for in Western currency or with a credit card.

Metro – Since Leningrad is built on marshy land, the stations for the 25-mile Metro are exceptionally deep. In fact, some escalator rides from the surface take 2 minutes — and escalators here move much more rapidly than they do in the US. Be warned: Stand to the right on down escalators; the left lane is for "runners." Coming up, however, you can stand on either side.

Taxi – Taxis are available at taxi stands or through hotel service bureaus, but they are expensive compared to other forms of transportation. Taxis and taxi stands can be recognized by a green "T" and a checkered pattern.

Train – The two main railway stations are Moscow Station, at Ploshchad Vosstania, and Finland Station, just north of Lenin Sq.

 SPECIAL EVENTS: *Leningrad Spring,* March 31–April 7, is a week of festivities celebrating the end of winter. The major annual arts festival in Leningrad is called *White Nights,* and is held June 21–29, when days here are so long that there is only a brief period of dusk each night. During the festival, there are performances by the *Kirov Opera and Ballet* (see *Theater*), the *Maly Theater Opera and Ballet,* and by various top Soviet singers and musicians. Here, as in Moscow, major celebrations are held on *International Labor Day,* May 1; *Victory Day,* May 9; *Constitution Day,* October 7; and *Revolution Day,* November 7.

 MUSEUMS: Leningrad is a major art center; many of the best-known museums are listed in *Special Places.* In addition, you may enjoy visiting — either individually or with an *Intourist* guided tour — some of the following:

Brodsky House Museum (Musei-Kvartirna I. I. Brodskovo) – The home of the portraitist of Lenin. 3 Iskusstv Sq. (phone: 211-2000).

Central Naval Museum (Tsentralny Voenno-Morskoi Musei) – A collection of ship models begun by Peter the Great in 1709, and more. 4 Pushkinskaya Sq. (phone: 218-2502).

House Museum of Peter I (Musei "Domik Petra I") – The dwelling used by Peter the Great while the Peter and Paul Fortress was being constructed. 2 Petrovskaya Nab. (phone: 238-9070).

Leningrad Branch of the Central Lenin Museum (Leningradsky Filial Tsentralnovo Muzeya V. I. Lenina) – Originally the Smolny nunnery, it was built in Russian baroque style by Rastrelli in 1764 and houses historical exhibitions. 5/1 Khalturina St. (phone: 315-9195).

Museum of History of Religion and Atheism of the USSR (Gosudarstvenni Musei Istorii Religii i Ateizma) – In the Cathedral of Our Lady of Kazan, it is worth visiting for the architecture. 2 Kazanskaya Sq. (phone: 311-0495).

Peter the Great Museum of Anthropology and Ethnography (Musei Antropologii i Etnografii im. Petra Velikovo) – An exhibition of rarities, curiosities, and oddities of nature, started by Peter the Great. 3 Universitetskaya Nab. (phone: 218-1412).

Pushkin Apartment Museum (Musei Kvartira A. S. Pushkina) – The house where Pushkin lived during the last months of his life. 12 R. Moiki Nab. (phone: 223282).

State Museum of the History of Leningrad (Gosudarstvenni Musei Istorii Leningrada) – Founded in 1918, it depicts the city's history through exhibits, art works, and models. 44 Krasnovo Flota Nab. (phone: 212-7798).

Zoological Museum (Zoologichesky Musei) – Over 100,000 exhibits in this former warehouse next to the stock exchange. Notable are the mammoths preserved in permafrost. 1 Universitetskaya Nab. (phone: 218-0112). Also of interest may be the Zoological Park at 1 Park Lenina (phone: 232-4828).

 SHOPPING: For foreigners, the best buys will usually be found at the government-run hard-currency shops known as *Beriozka* (literally, "little birch tree"). These shops sell just about anything Russia is noted for: furs, amber, jewelry, silver, balalaikas, vodka, caviar, wooden toys, and samovars. There are *Beriozkas* in most hotels and at two downtown locations: 9 Nevsky Prospekt and 26 Gertsena St. Payment in these shops must be made in foreign currency or with traveler's checks or credit cards.

You can also shop where the Russians do, using Soviet currency. If you do, select the item you want and take it to a clerk, who will give you a sales slip, which you take to the cash desk, the *Kacca.* When you pay, you'll receive a receipt, which you return to the clerk, who will give you your merchandise, already wrapped.

Soviet department stores are usually open from 9 AM to 6 PM; food stores, however, may remain open later.

Dom Knigi – The largest bookstore in Leningrad, with posters, reproductions, and postcards on the second floor. The building itself is of interest because it was the Russian headquarters of the Singer Sewing Machine Co. early in this century; it has some wonderful Art Nouveau details as well as distinctive metalwork sculpture on its roof. 28 Nevsky Prospekt.

Gostiny Dvor – A huge, sprawling department store. Leningrad's answer to Moscow's *GUM.* 35 Nevsky Prospekt.

 SPORTS: Hundreds of sporting events are held each year in Leningrad's two major sports arenas: *Kirov Stadium,* Morskoi Prospekt, and *Yubileini Sports Palace,* Dobrolyubova Prospekt 18. Leningraders are particularly fond of soccer and ice hockey. Schedules for current matches and events and tickets are available through your hotel service bureau.

THEATER: Your hotel service bureau will have tickets and information on performance schedules. For popular companies, such as the renowned *Kirov Ballet,* tickets will cost from $25 to $40. Performances begin early; usually 7 PM for the theater and 7:30 PM for the circus and puppet shows. During intermission, be sure to try the theater buffet, which includes open-faced salami and sturgeon sandwiches, cakes, cookies, soft drinks, and other snacks. Besides the *Kirov Academic Theater of Opera and Ballet* (Akademichesky Teatr Operi i Baleta im S. M. Kirova), 1 Teatralnaya Sq., the major theaters in Leningrad include the *Maly Theater of Opera and Ballet* (Akademichesky Mali Teatr Operi i Baleta), Iskusstv Sq.; *Bolshoi Puppet Theater* (Bolshoi Teatr Kukol), 10 Nekrasova St.; *Leningrad State Circus* (Leningradsky Gosudarstvenni Tsirk), 3 R. Fontanki Nab.; *Pushkin Academic Drama Theater* (Akademichesky Teatr Drami im. A. S. Pushkina), 2 Ostrovskovo Sq.; *Gorky Academic Bolshoi Drama Theater* (Akademichesky BolshoiDramatichesky Teatr im. M. Gorkovo), 65 R. Fontanki Nab.; *Academic Theater of Comedy* (Akademichesky Teatr Komedii), 56 Nevsky Prospekt; and *Theater of Musical Comedy* (Teatr Muzikalnoi Komedii), 13 Rakova St.

MUSIC: Tickets and performance schedules for concerts can be obtained through your hotel service bureaus. Concerts usually begin at 7:30 PM. The major concert halls are the *Leningrad Philharmonia* (Leningradskaya Philarmoniya), 2 Brodskovo St., and *Glinka State Academic Chorus Kapella* (Gosudarstvennaya Akademicheskaya Khorovaya Kapella im. M. I. Glinki), 20 R. Moiki Nab.

NIGHTCLUBS AND NIGHTLIFE: There are no nightclubs of the Western type, but at restaurants, dancing is as much a part of the evening as the meal. Most nighttime activity here centers on one of the many theater or concert hall performances. There are late night, foreign-currency bars on the 10th floor of the *Leningrad* hotel, on the lower floor of the *Moskva,* and in the *Astoria, Pribaltiskaya,* and *Evropeiskaya* (see *Checking In*). There are also several buffets in the *Moskva* and *Leningrad* that stay open late, serving both food and drink. In terms of big-city nightlife, this may be scant fare, but considering the range and quality of early evening entertainment, most visitors find it a more than acceptable tradeoff.

BEST IN TOWN

CHECKING IN: Hotel accommodations in the Soviet Union are handled somewhat differently than in Western Europe. Before entering Russia, every visitor must have confirmed and paid hotel reservations, arranged through *Intourist,* by a travel agent, or by Pan American World Airways. You must apply for a visa listing all proposed stops and their duration, and once approved, deviations from your itinerary must be negotiated with a local *Intourist* representative. Visa applications also can be handled by your travel agency. Changes in your program can be requested at the *Intourist* service bureau in your hotel after you arrive, but do not count on the requests being approved. Usually, you will not be told the hotel to which you have been assigned until you arrive in the city. Accommodations can be purchased in any available class, but in Leningrad deluxe suite, deluxe, and first class are usually the only available rates unless you are traveling with a group. The top rate is about $240 for double occupancy in a deluxe suite. A deluxe room runs close to $150, and a first class double will cost $100. Rates for travelers requesting single rooms are about twice the rate for double occupancy. No meals are included in the advance payment plan. The hotels have banks, *Beriozkas,* postcard and stamp kiosks, service bureaus, beauty parlors, barber shops, and newsstands to serve most tourists' needs.

Astoria – Some people call this the most civilized hotel in Russia. Built in 1912 in the heart of downtown Leningrad, this fine old hotel has only 260 rooms and is currently undergoing restoration. It is noted for its restaurant and late-night bar. This is where Hitler planned to hold his victory banquet after his armies captured Leningrad; the invitation is framed and hangs in the lobby. 39 Gertsena St. (phone: 219-1100). Deluxe.

Evropeiskaya – One of Leningrad's small but grand old hotels, this one has not been kept up as well as the *Astoria,* but it still has charm. Off Nevsky Prospekt, it has 268 rooms, a good restaurant, and a late-night bar. Next door is the *Sadko,* one of Leningrad's best restaurants (see *Eating Out*). 1/7 Brodskovo St. (phone: 211-1949). Deluxe.

Leningrad – Completed in 1970, this fine hotel overlooks the Neva River and has accommodations for 1,300 guests. Clean lines and lots of light reveal the Finnish source of the building plans. It has a good restaurant, a late-night bar on the 10th floor, and buffets on every other floor. 5/2 Pirogovskaya Nab. (phone: 542-9123). Deluxe.

Moskva – A mammoth in the typical Russian style. Even though it was opened in 1977, it is not as modern in appearance or facilities as the *Leningrad.* Still, the staff is noted for its helpfulness and it is ideally located for connections with public transportation. The hotel has a restaurant and bar, as well as buffets in the central portion of the building on each floor. 2 Alexandra Nevskovo Sq. (phone: 274-2051). Deluxe.

Pribaltiiskaya – The latest, and the best, of the city's new hotels, with 2,400 rooms, including a number of 3-room suites. Overlooking the Gulf of Finland, it is far from the city's center, but has several good restaurants, cafés, and bars, which makes eating and evening pursuits somewhat more convenient. 14 Korables-troitelei St. (phone: 356-0158). Deluxe.

Sovetskaya – A city-owned hotel sometimes used by *Intourist* to handle overflow bookings, this place is large and comfortable and has the largest *Beriozka* in the city. However, it is somewhat less conveniently located in the southwestern part of the city. 43 Lermontovsky Prospekt (phone: 259-2656). First class.

 EATING OUT: The food situation throughout the Soviet Union is poor. The prices are high at restaurants in *Intourist* hotels and at special hard currency bars and — except in the very best hotels — the ingredients are often of mediocre or poor quality. Do sample the street cuisine, however. Venders sell tasty meat-, mushroom-, or cabbage-filled fried pastries (*pirozhki*), and ice cream (*morozhenoye*) here is delicious. Try some *Kvass,* a drink made from fermented black bread and sold from small tanks on the sidewalks. Flavored mineral water is sold from automatic dispensers. Here they use community glasses instead of paper cups, but you can wash the glass by pressing down on the spigot in the machine. Put the clean glass under the spout, drop in your coins, and return the glass to the washing spot when you've finished your drink.

You should not drink tap water or the water served at your restaurant table because a parasite, called *giardia lamblia,* is believed to be prevalent in the Leningrad water system. It can cause violent intestinal illness that can require hospitalization if not properly treated. There is an incubation period of about 2 weeks; therefore, this illness should not be confused with the usual travelers' maladies. You can avoid this parasite by taking minimal precautions; cooked food, tea, coffee, bottled water, and soft drinks are quite safe.

Meals at major restaurants in Leningrad can be booked in advance through your hotel service bureau. You will receive a prix fixe menu, obviating the need to speak Russian. Dinner prices range from $30 to $50 for two. Any drinks ordered in addition to the vodka and wine included in the prix fixe dinner must be paid for in Soviet currency. Most of the Leningrad hotels have dining rooms with live bands, dancing and, occasionally, a floor show. Reservations for hotel restaurants also should be made in advance with your hotel service bureau. There are also many cafés in Leningrad, providing a good opportunity to mix with local residents. The service bureaus won't make reservations for these cafés, so arrive early in case there's a wait. Payment in the cafés must be in Soviet currency. Finally, as in other Soviet cities, private or cooperative cafés and restaurants have become popular; the service bureau at your hotel will provide addresses and phone numbers for the best of these.

Baku – An Azerbaijani restaurant with an upstairs room for dancing. Reservations necessary. Sadovaya St. between Rakova St. and Nevsky Prospekt.

Fregat – One of Leningrad's newer restaurants, specializing in Old Russian dishes, including recipes that date back to the time of Peter the Great. Good atmosphere. 39/14 Bolshoi Prospekt, Vasilyevski Ostrov (phone: 213-4923).

Kavkazky – Specializing in Caucasian dishes, such as the shish kebab, known as Caucasian *shashlik*. 25 Nevsky Prospekt.

Kronwerk – An old sailboat moored by the Peter and Paul Fortress has been turned into a restaurant with a floor show at night. Here the atmosphere is more important than the food. Reservations necessary. 3 Myniskaya Nab. (phone: 232-8620).

Neva Café – A popular restaurant that can seat 1,000 people. Also at this address is the *Sever Café*, famous for tortes and other desserts. *Intourist* will not make reservations here, so go early to secure a table. 44 Nevsky Prospekt.

Sadko – One of the best restaurants in Leningrad with traditional Russian fare, such as beef Stroganoff, skewered meatballs (called *Lyulya Kebab*), and blinis (crêpes stuffed with caviar, smoked salmon, or other delicacies). A balalaika orchestra, singers, and, occasionally, folk dancers, provide entertainment. Next to the *Evropeiskaya* (see *Checking In*). Brodskovo St. and Nevsky Prospekt.

LISBON

Lisbon is a bit like the heroine of an old movie who faces the gravest of perils in every reel — but emerges in the end, still beautiful. During its more than 2,000 years of history, the city has undergone devastating earthquakes, plagues, fires, floods, invasions by barbarians, sackings, revolutions, and, more recently, the incursion of ugly urban development and pollution. But Lisbon remains beautiful, if a trifle faded and disheveled. At certain times of the day, the sun casts a golden reflection so intense that the broad expanse of estuary facing the city seems literally to live up to its popular name, Mar da Palha, or "Sea of Straw." And as the sun moves across the sky, the pastel buildings, tree-lined boulevards, cobblestone streets, and mosaic sidewalks of this city built in tiers on seven hills are bathed again and again in new perspectives of light.

Legend says that Lisbon was founded by Ulysses, who gave it the name Olisipo. Less romantic historians say that the ancient name was Phoenician in origin and that the city grew up gradually as a port town on the estuary of the Tagus, where traders from many lands drew their boats to shore to sell their wares — or perhaps to raid. Gradually, safety-conscious inhabitants moved to the top of the hill where the old St. George's Castle stands today, and then, little by little, occupied the surrounding hills.

Over the centuries, many people came and went: Celts, Phoenicians, Carthaginians, Romans, Visigoths, and Moors, until the 12th century, when the city was taken by the Christian Portuguese. As Portugal built its vast empire during the 15th and 16th centuries, citizens from many diverse lands came to live in Lisbon. And when, after decades of dictatorship ended in 1974 and the country dissolved the remnants of its empire, a new wave of immigrants arrived from Angola, Mozambique, Timor, and the Cape Verde Islands.

More than 1.6 million people live in Lisbon and its environs today, and yet, in some ways, this westernmost capital of Europe is still a small town. The *lisboetas,* accustomed to foreigners, are tolerant of their visitors' ways, their dress, and their inability to speak Portuguese. They can usually give directions in English. Sometimes they will even drop what they are doing and take a visitor where he or she wants to go.

Lisbon has known moments of glory. The Romans, who arrived in 205 BC, made it, after Mérida in Spain, the most important city on the Iberian peninsula, a place with baths, a theater, a 6-mile-long aqueduct (not the one standing today), and Roman roads stretching in all directions. In their turn, the Moors, whose stay lasted from 714 to 1147, gathered their most brilliant thinkers, scientists, and writers at Aschbouna — as they renamed the city — and made it a renowned center of learning. Lisbon began to come into its own as Portuguese, however, only after its recapture from the Moors during the 12th century (Dom Afonso Henriques, Portugal's first king, and an army

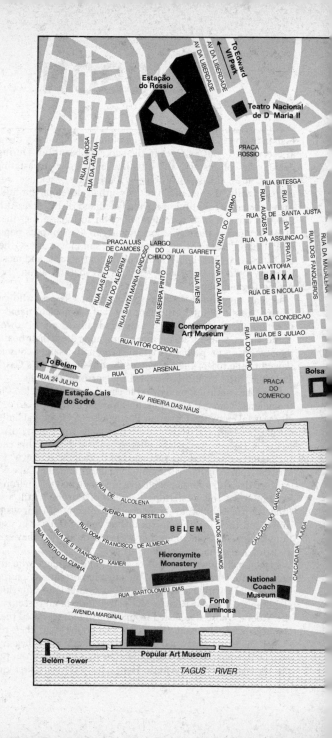

of crusaders from northern Europe besieged the castle for 17 weeks to accomplish that), and after King Afonso III's transfer of the court from Coimbra in 1260. By the 14th century, Lisbon had nearly 4 miles of walls, with 77 towers and 38 entranceways.

The city's greatest glory came during the 15th and 16th centuries. At a time when the world's seas were uncharted and darkness and superstition ruled men's imaginations, Lisbon was sending forth Portuguese caravels into the unknown, and her explorers were bringing the world's riches back from Africa, India, Brazil, and China. The Age of Discovery, as it is called, was ushered in by Prince Henry the Navigator (1394–1460), the son of King João I and his English wife, Philippa of Lancaster. During the early 15th century, Prince Henry established a school of navigation at Sagres, in southwest Portugal, and from there ships sailing under his authority explored the coast of Africa, making great strides in the study of geography, map-making, and shipbuilding. His contributions to the advancement of exploration led, at the end of the century, not only to the epochal voyage of Christopher Columbus, but also to the voyages of Bartholomeu Dias, who rounded the Cape of Good Hope in 1488, and of Vasco da Gama, who sailed out from Lisbon in 1497 and returned 2 years later after reaching the Indies. Portugal's so-called Spice Age had begun.

Trade with India, and later with Brazil — discovered by Pedro Alvares Cabral in 1500 — made Lisbon immensely rich. By the 16th century, the city was a great commercial and maritime power, the "Queen of the Tagus," ruling from one of the best harbors in Europe. Churches and palaces were built. In 1502, King Manuel I, wishing to erect a memorial to Portugal's explorers, began construction of one of Lisbon's greatest monuments, the Jerónimos Monastery in Belém, the Lisbon suburb from which Vasco da Gama had set sail. The ropes, anchors, and seaweed carved on this building (and on others of the period) are typical of the uniquely Portuguese decorative style that came to be known as Manueline.

But all was not joyful. Persecution of Jews began during the late 15th century, and the Inquisition was introduced during the early 16th century, to endure some 200 years. Thousands died in the *autos-da-fé* in Praça do Comércio, or were tortured in the Palace of the Inquisition in the Rossio. In 1580, Philip II of Spain annexed the country and became Philip I of Portugal; Spanish rule lasted until 1640, when the Spanish governor of Lisbon was deposed by a group of Portuguese noblemen. Lisbon then revived its profitable trade with the rest of the world, and a spate of new building began. This time, given the discovery of gold in Brazil during the late 17th century, the characteristic decorative element of the period was richly gilded baroque woodwork — it was from the Portuguese word *barroco,* meaning "rough pearl," that the style got its name. The reign of João V (1706–50) was known for its magnificence.

Then, on All Saints' Day morning, November 1, 1755, while most of Lisbon was at mass, one of the worst earthquakes ever known shook the city like a straw in the wind. Within minutes, two-thirds of Lisbon was in ruins. A 40-foot tidal wave rose on the Tagus and slammed into the city. Fires, begun by tapers lighted in the churches for the feast day and fanned by a violent windstorm, burned what the quake had left intact. As many as 40,000 people perished — causing philosophers, among them Voltaire, to conclude that this was not, after all, the most perfect of all worlds.

Prime Minister Marquês de Pombal quickly and efficiently set out to rebuild Lisbon on the rubble covering the valley floor between two of its hills. The stately plan of the city's classical squares and boulevards was traced out, and the straight lines and 18th-century proportions of the quarter called the Baixa — lower town — grew up in place of the previous medieval jumble. The Baixa's parallel streets are lined with nearly uniform, 5-story buildings.

Pombal is best remembered for this accomplishment, not for the reign of terror that he instituted against his enemies that made Lisbon a city of fear. Political turmoil marked the rest of the 18th century and the 19th. In 1908, King Carlos I and his son were assassinated in Praça do Comércio. In 1910, the monarchy fell when King Manuel II was forced to abdicate. The royal family went into exile and a republic was proclaimed. But the country endured the tight reins of the dictatorship of António de Oliveira Salazar, a professor of finance from Coimbra University, from 1932 to 1968. He put the country's finances in order and kept Portugal out of World War II, but during the nearly half century he and his successor, Marcello Caetano, remained in power, Portugal was gradually turned into a police state.

On the 25th of April, 1974, a group of young officers staged a coup in Lisbon and helped set up a democratically elected government. It was a revolution in which few lives were lost, but it altered the face of the capital. As the streets became the scene of demonstrations by newly formed labor unions and political parties, once-pristine buildings and monuments were spray-painted with slogans, and mosaic sidewalks that used to be scoured daily became grubby. Up to this time, Lisbon had been the capital of the world's last colonial empire, but with the breakup of the empire following the revolution, nearly a million refugees poured into the city. The government housed some in hotels; others lived in shanties. Their crated belongings lined the banks of the Tagus.

Within a few years, the situation stabilized. The refugees were miraculously absorbed into the life of the city and helped make Lisbon a more dynamic place. The city's beauty began to reemerge from under the posters and slogans and grime. Many of the old buildings — the greater part of Lisbon's stock is from the late 18th and 19th centuries, with much plain, utilitarian architecture added during this century — are molding away from neglect. But some of the more important ones are getting a face wash and repairs. Post-modern buildings, in glass and bright colors, mostly the work of architect Tomás Taveira, also have appeared.

Portugal joined the European Economic Community (Common Market) in 1986, bringing in new investment funds and products for Lisbon's shelves. Anyone who knows the city but has been away for a while will find that Lisbon today is not the same as it was even a very few years ago. Many of the streets in the Baixa are being closed to traffic and turned into pedestrian malls paved with cobblestones. Musicians entertain the strollers, and sidewalk artists offer inexpensive portraits. Artisans offer jewelry, leatherwork, embroidery, and other wares from little stalls. There are many attractive open-air cafés and restaurants. Hotels have been renovated and more new accommodations for visitors seem to be added each year. The delights of Lisbon are again apparent; maybe that's why tourism is flourishing.

LISBON AT-A-GLANCE

SEEING THE CITY: A city built on hills frequently surprises visitors with lovely views that emerge without warning around unexpected corners. Lisbon is such a place. It has 17 natural balconies — called *miradouros* — from which to view the city. Foremost of these is the hilltop on which the ruins of St. George's Castle stand. All of the squares are laid out beneath: Praça do Comércio by the banks of the Tagus; the Rossio with its fountains and flower stalls; Praça da Figueira, the bustling market square; Praça dos Restauradores with its monument to Portugal's independence; the circular Praça Marquês de Pombal at the end of the broad Avenida da Liberdade; and beyond that, the lovely Parque Eduardo VII. On a clear day, it is possible to see the castles of Sintra far to the west. On the opposite hill across the city in the Bairro Alto, from the terrace on Rua de São Pedro de Alcântara, there is a picture-postcard view of the castle, with the Alfama district spread down the slopes below its walls.

Another breathtaking view is from the bridge across the Tagus, known since the 1974 revolution as Ponte 25 de Abril, but previously named for Salazar, who built it in the 1960s. The third longest suspension bridge in the world, it is particularly spectacular at night, when its cables, the ships in the river, and the city are all brightly lit. On the other side, there is a marvelous panorama of the Tagus estuary from the top of the statue of Cristo Rei (Christ the King), a gift to Portugal from Brazil. (There is a small entrance fee, and an elevator takes visitors up.) Those without a car can cross the river by ferry from Praça do Comércio and take a bus from Cacilhas to the statue.

SPECIAL PLACES: In ancient times, and later under the Moors, Lisbon was contained within walls that surrounded the hill where St. George's Castle now stands. Today, that area is the Alfama, the oldest part of the city, where traces of the picturesque Judiaria (Jewish Quarter) and Mouraria (Moorish Quarter) can still be seen, along with Roman remains. The Alfama has been destroyed several times by earthquakes, but it was always rebuilt along the same plan, its tortuous, narrow streets spiraling down from the top of the hill to the Baixa below. The Baixa, to the west of the Alfama, is the main shopping and commercial district of Lisbon. Built after the earthquake in a grid fashion, it stretches northward from Praça do Comércio by the river to the top of the Rossio, one of the city's main squares, and includes such aptly named streets as Rua do Ouro (Gold Street) and Rua da Prata (Silver Street), lined with gold and silver shops, fine jewelers, and banks. Up the hill west of the Rossio is the part of the Baixa known locally as the Chiado — not much more than 10 square blocks. This is also a popular shopping district dotted with coffeehouses and outdoor cafés, but a disastrous fire in September 1988 destroyed a great number of the shops — including two of Europe's oldest department stores — and other landmarks. They have not yet been rebuilt.

Higher up is the Bairro Alto, or "high quarter," above and to the west of Praça dos Restauradores and the Rossio. At one time the wealthy (and later a seedy) residential district, it has been taken over by the avant-garde and become the center of nightlife in downtown Lisbon, with fine restaurants, typical *tascas* (taverns or small eating places), and *fado* houses, where sad Portuguese folk songs are performed. West of the Bairro Alto are the Madragoa and Lapa districts, residential areas where restaurants, government buildings, embassies, and several museums and art galleries can also be found. Modern Lisbon, with museums, the zoo, and new quarters, stretches to the north and east of the downtown area.

The Belém quarter is along the riverbank west of all of the above. Because it suffered very little in the 1755 earthquake, many of its fine palaces and monuments are still standing. Belém is also home to several museums, as well as many restaurants.

ST. GEORGE'S CASTLE AND THE ALFAMA

Castelo de São Jorge (St. George's Castle) – Built on one of Lisbon's highest hills, this castle with ten towers is considered the cradle of the city. An Iron Age *castro,* or fortified hilltop town, was probably located here, succeeded by Roman fortifications (Roman walls and other remains are being excavated), a fortress built by the Visigoths during the 5th century, and later, a Moorish fortified town. The present castle was built during the 12th century, though it has been much altered since. Within the grounds are lovely gardens where peacocks roam free, the remains of an Arabic palace where the Kings of Portugal lived from the 14th to the 16th century, and a good restaurant. From the terrace on the south side, from the towers, and from the walk around the ramparts, the views of Lisbon are extensive. Open daily from 9 AM to 7 PM (6 PM in winter). Rua Costa do Castelo.

Alfama – This old quarter slopes downhill from St. George's Castle. A cobbled labyrinth with some streets so narrow that pedestrians must walk in single file, it is one of the most colorful spots in Europe. Its streets are overhung with balconies ablaze with scarlet geraniums and lined with little taverns decorated with strings of peppers, garlic, and cheese. By day, caged canaries on the balconies sing in the sun; at night, wrought-iron lamps light the scene; and on washdays, the buildings are strung with clotheslines and drying laundry. Although some medieval mansions and Moorish buildings exist, most of the houses date from the late 18th century, after the earthquake. The best times to see the Alfama are in the morning when the markets are open, late in the afternoon when the streets and squares are alive with people, or on a moonlit evening. The quarter stretches north to south from the castle to the banks of the Tagus and east to west from the cathedral to the vicinity of the church of São Vicente de Fora.

Sé (Cathedral) – Lisbon's oldest church, built just after the Christian reconquest of the 12th century, suffered much earthquake damage in 1755, but was rebuilt during the 18th century and restored during this one. It is a typical fortress-church of solid, massive construction, with battlements and towers. The plain façade is Romanesque, but the burial chapel, the ambulatory, and the cloister are pure Gothic. The cathedral's imposing baroque organ is notable, and there is a museum displaying religious vestments and ecclesiastical gold. Open from 10 AM to 5 PM; closed Mondays. Admission charge. Largo da Sé (phone: 867652).

Nossa Senhora da Conceição Velha – Built during the early 16th century on the site of Lisbon's ancient synagogue, this was completely devastated in the 1755 earthquake, but its original Manueline portal survived. The beautiful doorway, richly carved with limestone figures, was retained for the new church — which, however, has little of note inside. Rua da Alfândega.

Casa dos Bicos (House of Pointed Stones) – When it was built during the 16th century, this house belonged to the family of Afonso de Albuquerque, a famous Portuguese viceroy to India. The earthquake reduced the 4-story structure to only several feet of foundations, but it has been completely rebuilt. The façade is covered with pyramidal stones, similar to the Casa de los Picos in Segovia, Spain, and the Palazzo dei Diamanti in Ferrara, Italy. The house is now used as an art gallery and is open to the public only when there are special exhibitions. Rua dos Bacalhoeiros (phone: 877330).

Museu-Escola de Artes Decorativas (Museum-School of Decorative Arts) –

Housed in a 17th-century palace that survived the earthquake, this contains collections of Portuguese porcelain, silver, crystal, paintings, tapestries, and furniture, mostly of the 17th and 18th centuries. They're arranged not museum style but much more beguilingly as the furnishings of an aristocratic Lisboan home of yesteryear. The objects were once the property of Dr. Ricardo Espírito Santo Silva, who set up a foundation both to create a museum and to preserve the skills and tools of traditional Portuguese craftsmanship. The foundation runs a school and workshops for the reproduction and restoration of antiques — furniture, books, fabrics, and so on — adjacent to the museum, which visitors may tour. An appointment is required for the workshops (phone: 872429 or 872173). The museum is open Tuesdays through Saturdays from 10 AM to 1 PM and from 2:30 to 5 PM. Admission charge. 2 Largo das Portas do Sol (phone: 862184).

Igreja de São Vicente de Fora (Church of St. Vincent Outside the Walls) – The church, a remnant of an old monastery, was built during the late 16th and early 17th century by Filippo Terzi and sports a Mannerist façade. It is notable for the cloister, lavishly lined with 18th-century *azulejos.* Beyond, set up in the old monastery refectory, is the Panteão Real (Royal Pantheon), the mausoleum of the Bragança family, which ruled Portugal from 1640 to 1910. Most of the Bragança kings and queens, including Portugal's last monarchs, are buried here. Open from 10 AM to 5 PM; closed Mondays. Admission charge. Praça de São Vicente (phone: 876470).

Museu Militar (Military Museum) – In an 18th-century arsenal near the river and the Santa Apolónia train station, it contains cannons, guns, swords, armor, and uniforms, as well as paintings, sculptures, coin collections, and other mementos of Portugal's wars. One room is dedicated to the discoveries of Vasco da Gama. Open from 10 AM to 4 PM, Sundays from 11 AM to 5 PM; closed Mondays. Admission charge. Largo dos Caminhos de Ferros (phone: 867135).

Igreja de Santa Engrácia – Begun during the 17th century and not completed until 1966, when it was also restored, this church gave rise to a Portuguese expression, *"obras de Santa Engrácia,"* used to describe a seemingly never-ending task. The grandiose structure, with a baroque façade and an interior richly decorated in marble, now serves as the Panteão Nacional (National Pantheon), containing the tombs of Portuguese presidents and other famous figures, as well as memorials to some — Henry the Navigator, Luis de Camões, Vasco da Gama, and others — who are not buried here. Open from 10 AM to 5 PM; closed Mondays. Admission charge. Campo de Santa Clara (phone: 871529).

Igreja da Madre de Deus (Church of the Mother of God) – The convent complex here was founded in 1501, but what is seen today was built during the 18th century. The church is resplendent with ornate gilded baroque woodwork, oil paintings, Dutch tiles, and Portuguese *azulejos;* the adjoining cloisters, one Renaissance, one Manueline, are also decorated with *azulejos.* The *Museu Nacional do Azulejo,* is installed here, too, displaying Portuguese and foreign tiles from the 15th century to the present, including some in singerie style, showing monkeys dressed and acting like people. Open from 10 AM to 5 PM; closed Mondays. Admission charge. Rua da Madre de Deus (phone: 847747).

BAIXA

Praça do Comércio – This impressive riverside square, laid out after the earthquake by Prime Minister Marqués de Pombal, is edged on three sides by arcaded neo-classic buildings. It's also known as Terreiro do Paço (Palace Square), after the royal palace that stood here in pre-earthquake days, and, to the English, as Black Horse Square, after the bronze equestrian statue of King José I, a design by the 18th-century sculptor Joaquim Machado de Castro, standing in the middle. The triumphal arch on the north side of the square, leading to Rua Augusta and the rest of the Baixa, was finished during the late 19th century. The square was the scene of the assassination of King Carlos I and his son in 1908.

Elevador de Santa Justa (Santa Justa Elevator) – This iron structure reminiscent of the Eiffel Tower — and often erroneously attributed to Eiffel — was designed by Raoul Mesnier, a Portuguese engineer of French descent, and erected in 1898. It not only spares visitors' feet the climb from Rua do Ouro to Largo do Carmo in the Chiado, but also provides a panoramic view of the city from the top.

Igreja do Carmo (Carmo Church) – Built during the 14th century, this was an imposing, majestic structure that overlooked the city until it was largely destroyed by the 1755 earthquake. The shell, with Gothic arches and a Gothic doorway, remains, and is floodlit at night. The ruins have been turned into the *Museu Arqueológico do Carmo,* containing prehistoric, Roman, Visigoth, and medieval artifacts, medieval sculpture, *azulejos,* and inscriptions. Open from 10 AM to 1 PM and from 2 to 5 PM (July through September, 10 AM to 6 PM); closed Sundays. Admission charge. Largo do Carmo (phone: 346-0473).

Rossio – Officially called Praça de Dom Pedro IV, after the 18th-century king who is the subject of the statue in the center, this is the heart of the city and the northern limit of the Baixa. As early as the 13th century, this was the city's marketplace, but like Praça do Comércio and the rest of the Baixa, it was destroyed by the earthquake of 1755; the square was then newly laid out by Pombal. On the north side is the 19th-century *Teatro Nacional de Dona Maria II,* standing on the site of a one-time royal palace, that during the 16th century, became the seat of the Inquisition. The square is much cheerier now, graced with many flower stalls, fountains, and open-air cafés.

BAIRRO ALTO

Solar do Vinho de Porto – This comfortable bar run by the Port Wine Institute is the next best thing to a trip to Portugal's northern capital. It's stocked with all types and vintages of Porto — the official name for port wine — which visitors can order by the glass. There are about 160 different kinds, so go early or, better, often. Open daily from 10 AM to 11:30 PM. 45 Rua de São Pedro de Alcântara (phone: 366444 or 323307).

Igreja de São Roque (Church of St. Rock) – This 16th-century church has a flat wooden ceiling painted to look like a vaulted one, but it's best known for the baroque Capela de São João Baptista, the fourth chapel on the left. The chapel was commissioned during the mid-18th century by King João V, designed in Rome and assembled there, blessed by the Pope — and then dismantled, to be delivered to Portugal aboard three ships and rebuilt at its present address. The lapis lazuli, porphyry, marble, alabaster, ivory, and other precious and semiprecious building materials cost the king dearly, but the workmanship was impeccable, as can be seen in the *Baptism of Christ,* which looks like an oil painting but is actually an exquisitely fine mosaic. The *Museu de São Roque* adjoining the church contains paintings and liturgical objects and richly embroidered vestments. Open from 10 AM to 5 PM; closed Mondays. Admission charge. Largo Trindade Coelho (phone: 346-0361).

NORTHERN AND WESTERN LISBON

Parque Eduard VII (Edward VII Park) – Downtown Lisbon's largest green space is this formally landscaped park at one end of Avenida da Liberdade, just beyond Praça Marquês de Pombal. From the top of the park, the view extends over the lower town to the Tagus. In the northwest corner is the charming Estufa Fria (Cold Greenhouse), where lush tropical plants grow in abundance among streams, pools, and waterfalls. A slatted roof protects them from the extremes of summer and winter. The greenhouse is open daily from 9 AM to 6 PM (5 PM in winter). Admission charge (phone: 682278).

Museu Calouste Gulbenkian (Gulbenkian Museum) – When the Armenian oil tycoon Calouste Sarkis Gulbenkian died in 1955, he left most of his estate and his enormous art collection to Portugal, the country to which he had fled during World War II and where he spent the last years of his life. The result was the Calouste Gulbenkian Foundation, a modern building that houses not only this museum, but also auditoriums, a library, and exhibition space. Don't miss the museum, a repository of 50 years of astute collecting — 3,000 pieces including works Gulbenkian bought from the *Hermitage Museum* in the 1920s, when the Soviet Union needed foreign currency. The treasures include fine European paintings, sculpture, 18th-century French furniture, Chinese vases, Japanese lacquerwork, Greek and Roman coins, medieval ivories, illuminated manuscripts, Middle Eastern textiles and ceramics, and more. There is also a marvelous collection of small Egyptian pieces and a superb collection of Art Nouveau jewelry by René Lalique. Open from 10 AM to 5 PM (July through October, its hours on Wednesdays and Saturdays are from 2 to 7:30 PM). Admission charge. 45 Avenida de Berna (phone: 734309).

Centro de Arte Moderna (Modern Art Center) – In the gardens behind the *Gulbenkian Museum,* with an impressive collection of 19th- and 20th-century Portuguese and foreign paintings and sculpture, including paintings by António Almeida Negreiros. A cafeteria overlooks the gardens. The hours are the same as those of the *Gulbenkian Museum.* Admission charge. Rua Dr. Nicolau de Bettencourt (phone: 734309).

Jardim Zoológico (Zoo) – The zoo, set in a 65-acre park, is home to some 2,000 animals, including an elephant who rings a bell for money. Other distractions include pony rides for children, rowboats, and a small train. Open from 9 AM to 8 PM daily from April through October (closes at 6 PM the rest of the year). Admission charge. Parque das Larangeiras (phone: 726-8041).

Palácio dos Marqueses da Fronteira – West of the zoo, on the edge of the Parque Florestal de Monsanto, is an interesting palace built during the second half of the 17th century and originally used by its aristocratic owners as a hunting lodge. It's notable for the great number of *azulejos* that cover its walls — both inside and outside in the formal gardens — many of them depicting historical events. The palace is still privately owned but open to visitors on Mondays and Wednesdays from 10 AM to noon and on Saturdays from 3 to 6:30 PM. Admission charge. 1 Largo de São Domingos de Benfica (phone: 782023).

Aqueduto das Aguas Livres – Built during the first half of the 18th century to bring water from Caneças (11 miles northwest of Lisbon) to a reservoir near the present Amoreiras complex, the Aguas Livres Aqueduct miraculously survived the 1755 earthquake and still supplies the city with drinking water. It consists of 109 stone arches, some of them underground, but an impressive stretch of it (with one arch 214 feet high) runs through the Parque Florestal de Monsanto and the Campolide section of town, and can be seen from the road (N7) that leads to Estoril and Sintra. With special permission, it is possible to visit the inside of the aqueduct, with its towers, fountains, and statuary; inquire at the tourist office.

Basílica da Estrela (Basilica of the Star) – Built by Queen Maria I between 1779 and 1790, it fulfilled a vow she had made while petitioning God to grant her a son. The dome is one of Lisbon's landmarks; the tomb of the founder is inside. This church reflects the style of the school of sculpture founded at Mafra by the Italian sculptor Alessandro Giusti, one of whose Portuguese pupils, Joaquim Machado de Castro, was responsible for the manger figures here. Open daily. Praça da Estrela.

Museu Nacional de Arte Antiga (National Museum of Ancient Art) – One of the most important of Lisbon's museums, this is housed partly in a 17th-century palace that once belonged to Pombal (and partly in an adjacent 20th-century building and a chapel belonging to an old convent that no longer survives). Although it contains numerous foreign works, such as a celebrated Bosch triptych, *The Temptation of St. Anthony,* and Dürer's *St. Jerome* (to name only two), the museum is most notable for its paintings of the Portuguese school, especially primitives of the 15th and 16th centuries. The prize in this group — perhaps the most famous painting in Portugal — is the polyptych of the *Adoration of St. Vincent,* a masterpiece by Nuno Gonçalves, the most important Portuguese painter of the 15th century. The six-panel polyptych is precious not only for its artistic merit (and because it's the only Gonçalves painting still extant), but also because it constitutes a document of Portuguese society of the time. Also in the museum are sculptures, Portuguese, European, and Oriental ceramics; objects in silver and gold; and jewelry, furniture, and tapestries. A tea garden overlooking the river is open in summer. Open from 10 AM to 1 PM and from 2:30 to 5 PM; closed Mondays. Admission charge. 95 Rua das Janelas Verdes (phone: 672725).

BELEM

Mosteiro dos Jerónimos (Hieronymite Monastery) – One of Lisbon's great landmarks, this white marble monastery was founded in 1502 by King Manuel I to give thanks for the successful return of Vasco da Gama's fleet from the Indies and in general to commemorate all the great voyages of Portugal's explorers during the Age of Discovery. Because Vasco da Gama had sailed from Belém in 1497, to return 2 years later, the site of a small mariners' chapel here seemed a fitting one for the memorial, about which it is said that it was "built by pepper," since it was paid for by riches brought by the spice trade. The sea motifs — seashells, ropes, anchors, and other symbols — that are carved throughout in great profusion are the characteristic decorative elements of the Manueline style of architecture, a uniquely Portuguese style that represented a transition from Gothic to Renaissance and eventually took its name from Dom Manuel. The monastery is considered the country's finest example of Manueline architecture: The two portals, the extremely slender columns and characteristic network vaulting of the church, and the richly sculpted 2-story cloister are exceptionally beautiful. King Manuel I and several other monarchs are buried in the church, as is Vasco da Gama. The long galleries to the west of the monastery, neo-Manueline from the 19th century, contain the *Museu Nacional de Arqueologia e Etnologia* (open for temporary exhibitions). Other annexes house the *Museu da Marinha* (see below) and the *Planetario Calouste Gulbenkian,* which has sessions several days a week (times are posted outside). The monastery is open from 10 AM to 6:30 PM, July through September (to 5 PM the rest of the year); closed Mondays. Admission charge. Praça do Império (phone: 617020).

Museu da Marinha (Naval Museum) – In a modern extension to the west of the Jerónimos Monastery, this museum contains models of boats from all eras of Portuguese history, including the caravels of the Age of Discovery, warships, trading ships, seaplanes, and examples of traditional fishing boats from various regions. One pavilion houses ceremonial boats, of which the late-18th-century galley built for the wedding of Crown Prince João and a Spanish princess is the star. Open from 10 AM to 5 PM; closed Mondays. Admission charge. Praça do Império (phone: 612541).

Museu Nacional dos Coches (National Coach Museum) – Probably the finest coach collection in the world, in a building that was once the riding school of the Palácio de Belém, formerly a royal palace and now the presidential palace. The collection contains coaches ranging from the 16th through the 19th centuries and although some are simple (such as the one that carried Philip III of Spain when he came to claim the throne as King Philip II of Portugal), most are beautifully carved and gilded works of art suitable for transporting royal personages or their emissaries (note the 18th-century coaches of the Portuguese ambassador to the Holy See). Open from 10 AM to 1 PM and from 2:30 to 6:30 PM (closes at 5:30 PM from October through May); closed Mondays. Admission charge. Praça Afonso de Albuquerque (phone: 638022).

Padrão dos Descobrimentos (Monument to the Discoveries) – On the river in front of the monastery, this is a modern monument, put up in 1960 to commemorate the 500th anniversary of the death of Prince Henry the Navigator. It's shaped like the prow of a Portuguese caravel, with the prince as a figurehead leading a sculptured frieze of the personages of the time seaward.

Torre de Belém (Tower of Belém) – This quadrangular, 5-story tower, which looks like a huge chess piece, stands on the banks of the Tagus, west of the Monument to the Discoveries. The Portuguese consider it a symbol of their brave past, and its image is often used on official papers. Built during the 16th century to protect the river from pirates (because land has been reclaimed from the river since then, the tower was at one time farther out, surrounded by water), it later functioned as a prison. This is another example of Manueline architecture, richly decorated with sea motifs, statues, stone tracery, and Moorish balconies. Inside is a permanent exhibition of 15th- and 16th-century armaments and navigational instruments. Visitors may climb to the top for a view of the Tagus from the outside terrace. Open from 10 AM to 6:30 PM (to 5 PM from October through May). Admission charge. Off Avenida Marginal (phone: 616892).

Palácio Nacional da Ajuda – In the hills behind Belém, this former royal palace was built during the early 19th century and is full of furniture, paintings, sculpture, and objets d'art left much as they were when royalty still occupied the premises. The widow of King Luis, Maria Pia of Savoy, who died in 1911, was its last royal inhabitant, but the palace is still used occasionally by the government for state dinners. Open from 10 AM to 5 PM; closed Mondays. Admission charge. Largo da Ajuda (phone: 637095).

ENVIRONS

Estoril – This seaside suburb about 15 miles (25 km) west of Lisbon became internationally famous during World War II when both Allied and Axis spies were tripping over each other, notably at the *Palácio* hotel. Since Portugal was neutral, there was a gentlemen's agreement: Allied diplomats could play golf at the local clubs on certain days, Axis diplomats on others. Immediately after the war, Estoril became the home of numerous members of Europe's exiled royalty, giving it a touch of glamour. The crowned heads are gone now, but Estoril, with its bars and cafés and gambling casino, is still a glamorous place. Its large turn-of-the-century mansions, hidden away behind spacious lawns and gardens flanking winding, hilly streets and wide avenues, lend it a definitely Old World air. The Parque do Estoril, a lovely garden of stately palm trees and purple-red bougainvillea, faces the seaside esplanade and the beach. The modern, elegant Casino Estoril sits at the top of the park. The residential district of Monte Estoril is west of the park, tending to merge with Cascais. Estoril can be easily reached by train from Lisbon's Cais do Sodré station or via the beach highway (Estrada Marginal).

Cascais – Once a simple fishing village whose picturesque, brightly painted boats headed out to sea each morning, Cascais (pronounced Cash-ka-*ish*) has evolved during this century into a beach resort and home to thousands of European — especially British — expatriates and, like Estoril, deposed royalty and dictators. Today, the fast-growing town, just west of Estoril, makes its living largely from tourism, although fishermen remain and the sight of fish being auctioned off at the market (on weekday evenings) by the beach is worth seeing. Cascais has few monuments to detain sightseers: There is one important church, the Manueline Nossa Senhora da Assunção, notable for its 18th-century *azulejos* and for its paintings by Josefa de Obidos; the Citadel, a 17th-century military building; and the *Museu-Biblioteca Condes de Castro Guimarães,* with paintings, sculpture, furniture, and objets d'art set up in an old mansion (closed Tuesdays). It has plenty of other distractions, however. The bullfights held on summer Sundays at the Monumental de Cascais attract many visitors. Water sports and sailing are available from its beaches; there are also riding stables, tennis courts, and golf courses in the vicinity. The town (and the coast around it) are famous for their seafood restaurants, many of which overlook the bay and the sea. There is no dearth of nightlife, either, as Cascais is full of bars and discos. Along the coast west of town is the Boca do Inferno (Mouth of Hell), a set of rocky cliffs full of caves and smaller cavities through which the sea storms and rages — an awesome sight. Farther along the coast road, 5½ miles (9 km) from Cascais, is Praia do Guincho, an immense stretch of sand between two promontories where the wind howls (*guincho* means "shriek"), the sea is rough, and the undertow dangerous; it is popular with brave surfers. Still farther along is a headland, Cabo da Roca, the westernmost point of Europe, where there is a lighthouse. Cascais can be reached by train from Lisbon's Cais do Sodré station.

Queluz – This town 7 miles (12 km) northwest of Lisbon is known for its lovely pink rococo Palácio Nacional, where official guests of the Portuguese government are usually housed. The palace was begun in 1747 by the Infante Dom Pedro, who became Pedro III, consort of Queen Maria I, an unfortunate queen who lived here after going mad following Pedro's death and that of her oldest son. Designed by Mateus Vicente de Oliveira, a pupil of the architect of the Mafra Monastery, the royal residence took decades to finish and has been restored after being partially destroyed by fire in this century. Its rooms are filled with Portuguese furnishings and tapestries, Italian glassware and marble, Dutch tiles, Chinese screens, Austrian porcelain, and other exquisite antiques; its gardens are laid out to resemble those of Versailles (Queen Maria had been engaged to Louis XV), with fountains, statuary, and *azulejos*. Among the more striking rooms are the Throne Room, the Hall of Mirrors, the Hall of the Ambassadors, the Music Salon, and the Queen's Dressing Room. Chamber music concerts and other cultural events take place here during the summer. The palace is open from 10 AM to 1 PM and from 2 to 5 PM; closed Tuesdays. Admission charge (phone: 435-0039). Queluz can be reached by train from Lisbon's Rossio station.

■**EXTRA SPECIAL:** The beauty of Sintra, a town on the north slope of the Serra de Sintra 17 miles (28 km) northwest of Lisbon, has been sung through the ages, most notably by Portugal's most famous poet, Camoës, in *The Lusiads,* and by Lord Byron, who called it a "glorious Eden" in *Childe Harold.* The town has an enchanting setting, swathed in towering trees, dense ferns, and plants and flowers of every description brought by the Portuguese from all corners of their once far-flung empire — all kept green by water gushing from the rocks in springs and little waterfalls tumbling everywhere down the mountain. Mists from the nearby Atlantic often envelop its heights and lend it an ethereal and unreal air (as well as give it a pleasant climate in summer while, on occasion, obscuring its majestic views). Among the oldest towns in Portugal, it was occupied by the Moors, who built two castles, one of them winding around the side of the mountain from pinnacle to pinnacle and the other in the center of the present town. After Sintra was taken from the Moors during the 12th century, it became a favorite summer residence of the Portuguese monarchs. Over the centuries, they built the imposing National Palace in town on the site of one of the Moorish castles and the whimsical, Disneyland-like Pena Palace on the very peak of the mountain, where it can be seen from as far away as Lisbon and the Arrábida Peninsula.

Sintra is very crowded in summer and on weekends. It can be reached by car on N117 and N249 or by train from the Rossio station. Those who come by train can take a taxi to visit the palaces that are some distance from the center; otherwise, the tourist office at Praça da República (phone: 923-1157) provides maps for those who want to walk. There are also horse-drawn carriages that take visitors sightseeing around town. Good restaurants and hotels abound, as do excellent shops selling handicrafts, especially rugs, porcelain, and straw goods. The Feira de Sintra, a market that takes place on the second and fourth Sundays of every month, sells everything imaginable. During the *Sintra Music Festival,* held from mid-June to mid-July, concerts take place in the palaces and other public buildings.

The Palácio Nacional de Sintra, in the main square, was built on the foundations of a Moorish palace by King João I during the late 14th century and added to by King Manuel I during the early 16th century. Later, it received still further additions, making the enormous structure a survey of styles from Moorish through Mudejar, Gothic, Manueline, and Renaissance to baroque. Outside, besides the twin conical chimneys that dominate the town, the most notable feature of the palace is the characteristic Manueline windows. Inside, its most important feature is the *azulejos* facing its walls throughout, some of the finest to be seen in the country. One of the most interesting rooms is the Sala dos Brasoẽs (Hall of the Coats of Arms), built during Manuel's reign; its ceiling is an octagonal wooden cupola whose painted panels show the coats of arms of the king, his 8 children, and the 72 noble families of Portugal at the time. (The blue and white wall tiles depicting hunting scenes are from the 18th century.) In the Sala das Pêgas (Hall of the Magpies), the ceiling is decorated with 136 magpies — painted, so the story goes, on the orders of João I after his wife, Philippa of Lancaster, caught him kissing one of the ladies-in-waiting. (There were 136 ladies-in-waiting at court, and the idea was to put an end to gossip among them.) The largest room is the Sala dos Cisnes (Hall of Swans), so named because of the ceramic swans decorating it and the painted ones on the ceiling. The palace is open from 10 AM to 1 PM and from 2 to 5 PM; closed Wednesdays. Admission charge (phone: 923-4118).

The Palácio Nacional da Pena, standing on the highest peak above Sintra, is reached up a spectacular road of hairpin curves through beautiful parks and woods. After religious orders were expelled from Portugal in 1832, Ferdinand of Saxe-Coburg-Gotha, consort of Queen Maria II, bought a small 16th-century monastery that stood on this spot and commissioned a German architect, Baron Eschwege, to create a new medieval palace around it. Inspired by the Bavarian castles in his own country, the architect combined their styles with Moorish, Gothic, and Manueline elements to create a fantastic building complete with gold-topped domes, turrets, crenellated walls, parapets, and a drawbridge. The cloister and chapel of the monastery were preserved; the latter has a black alabaster and marble altarpiece executed during the 16th century by Nicolas Chanterene, although its stained glass windows are 19th-century German. The rooms of the palace proper are filled with furniture and ornaments of many different periods and are particularly noteworthy because they have been left much as they were when last occupied by the royal family, which fled into exile in 1910. The views from the palace verandahs are spectacular, and the Parque da Pena surrounding it, planted during the 19th century, is also impressive, containing plants and trees from all over the world. The palace is open from 9 AM to 6 PM (to 5 PM in winter); closed Mondays. Admission charge (phone: 923-0227).

Still another of Sintra's palaces, the Palácio dos Seteais, has been turned into a luxury hotel (see *Checking In*), but there are other sights to see, including the Castelos dos Mouros, or Moorish Castle, off the same road that leads to the Pena Palace, about halfway up the mountain. It was originally built by the Moors during the 8th or 9th century and was restored after the Christian reconquest of the 12th century and later by King Fernando I. It has five rather dilapidated towers, a keep, and long walls that undulate over a great part of the mountain. Elsewhere is the Quinta de Monserrate, a palace and park built by a 19th-century Englishman, Sir Francis Cook, about 2 miles (3 km) from Sintra via N375. The palace is an odd-looking, three-domed structure, but it is the wonderful gardens, landscaped on a steep slope, that are the prime attraction (open daily from 9 AM to sunset). Another sight is the Convento dos Capuchos, 4 miles (6.5 km) from town via

N247-3. Built in the 16th century, it is a peculiar place in that the monks' cells are carved out of rock and lined with cork to keep out the damp. (Ring the bell and the caretaker opens the door.)

SOURCES AND RESOURCES

 TOURIST INFORMATION: Maps, brochures, shopping guides, listings of monthly events, and other information can be obtained from any of the Postos de Turismo (Tourist Posts) run by the Direcção-Geral do Turismo (Directorate General for Tourism), which is based at 86 Avenida António Augusto de Aguiar. A tourist post is at the same address (phone: 575091), but perhaps the most convenient one in downtown Lisbon is the one at Palácio Foz in Praça dos Restauradores (phone: 346-3624). Other branches are at Lisbon Airport (phone: 885974), at the Santa Apolónia train station (phone: 867848), and at the Alcântara boat dock (phone: 600756). English-speaking staff is available to answer questions and help make hotel reservations. It is possible to hire English-speaking guides through the tourist offices or by calling the guides union, the Sindicato Nacional da Atividade Turistica, Tradutores e Intérpretes (phone: 323298).

The US Embassy is on Avenida das Forças Armadas (phone: 726-6600).

Local Coverage – The leading daily is the *Diario de Noticias,* a morning paper. *Seminario* and *Expresso* are two of the most prestigious weekly papers. English-language newspapers and magazines are on sale at most newsstands.

Telephone – The area code for Lisbon is 01.

 CLIMATE AND CLOTHES: The weather is unpredictable, but it is seldom too hot or too cold, with temperatures ranging from 59F to 82F in summer and from 48F to 59F in winter. April in Portugal is usually one of the rainiest months. It is almost invariably cool after the sun goes down, so even in summer a sweater will come in handy. Almost any kind of attire is acceptable, but be sure to bring a pair of comfortable walking shoes for Lisbon's cobblestone streets.

 GETTING AROUND: Although various sections of the city, such as the Alfama, are ideal for strolling, remember that Lisbon is built on seven hills; visitors will probably want to ride from one section to another. Parking is problematic, so public transportation and taxis are the best bet.

Airport – Lisbon's airport for both domestic and international flights, Portela de Sacavém (phone: 802060), is only 5 miles northeast of the center, a 15- to 30-minute drive, depending on traffic. Taxi fare to most hotels should come to $5 or less. The Linha Verde (Green Line) express bus runs between the airport and the Santa Apolónia train station, stopping at major downtown points. TAP Air Portugal's local address is 3A Praça Marquês de Pombal (phone: 544080 or 575020). For information on TAP's subsidiary, Linhas Aéreas Regionais (LAR), which has flights to many cities as well as to Madeira and the Azores, phone 887119 or 896102.

Boat – Ferryboats, carrying both passengers and cars, cross the Tagus every few minutes from the Praça do Comércio and Cais do Sodré for Cacilhas, Barreiro, and other points. There is also a river service to Cascais. Short cruises on the Tagus take place from April through October.

Bus – City buses and trams are run by CARRIS (Lisbon Transport Company). Maps and other information can be obtained at the window at the side of the Santa Justa Elevator, just off Rua do Carmo. Bus and tram fares vary according to the zone; the basic fare is 90 escudos (60 ¢). Tourist passes for 7 days of unlimited travel by bus, tram, subway, ferryboat, and the Santa Justa Elevator can be bought at the Praça dos Restauradores and Praça Marquês de Pombal subway stations and at the Santa Justa Elevator. Lisbon's trams are not only vintage vehicles and picturesque in themselves, but many go through the more historic parts of the city, providing a cheap way to take a tour. Long-distance bus service is provided by Rodoviária Nacional, the state-owned bus company, whose terminal is at Casal de Ribeiro (phone: 545439).

Car Rental – Most major firms have offices in Lisbon and at the airport. *Avis* is at 12C Avenida Praia da Vitória (phone: 561177); the airport (phone: 894836); the Santa Apolónia train station (phone: 876887); and the *Alfa* (phone: 726-3360), *Penta* (phone: 726-5629), *Ritz* (phone: 691521), and *Sheraton* (phone: 575757) hotels. *Hertz* is at 10 Avenida 5 de Outubro (phone: 579077), 10 Avenida Visconde Seabra (phone: 772944), and the *Novotel* hotel, 1642 Avenida José Malhoa (phone: 726-7221). *Budget* has offices at 33 Avenida Fontes Pereira de Melo (phone: 560015), 124 Rua do Arsenal (phone: 320913 or 320861), and the airport (phone: 801785 or 801738).

Elevator – The Elevador de Santa Justa takes passengers from Rua do Ouro in the Baixa to Largo do Carmo in the Chiado. The Portuguese also refer to several streetcars that travel a steep route as "elevators," among them the Gloria Elevator, running from the west side of Praça dos Restauradores to the Bairro Alto.

Subway – The underground system serving Lisbon is called the *Metropolitano*. A large "M" aboveground designates the stations — Rossio and Restauradores are the most central ones. The fare is 35 escudos (25 ¢) to any point. (The unlimited-travel tourist pass is valid underground.) Beware of pickpockets.

Taxi – Cabs are metered and inexpensive — a ride to almost any part of the city will cost less than $5. For trips outside Lisbon, a set rate per kilometer is charged beyond the city limits. Taxis can be hailed on the street or picked up at cabstands conveniently scattered around town. (Note that by law passengers must get in and out on the sidewalk side, not the street side.) To call a cab, phone 732756, 825061, or 659151.

Train – Frequent, fast electric trains connecting Lisbon with Belém, Estoril, and Cascais leave from the Estação Cais do Sodré (phone: 370181) by the river near Praça do Comércio. Trains to Queluz and Sintra operate from the Estação do Rossio (phone: 877092), just off the Rossio. (The recently cleaned façade of this 19th-century neo-Manueline building, with its elaborate carvings and statues, is a charmer.) Trains for most of the rest of Portugal and elsewhere in Europe leave from Estação Santa Apolónia (phone: 876025), along the river east of the Alfama district. The station for trains to the Algarve is Estaçao Sul e Sueste (phone: 877179), on the east side of Praça do Comércio. These southbound trains actually leave from Barreiro, on the south bank of the Tagus, but tickets include the price of the ferry ride from the station. Trains between Lisbon, Porto, and Faro have air conditioned coaches with bar and restaurant service.

 SPECIAL EVENTS: In ancient times, the *Festas dos Santos Populares* (Feasts of the Popular Saints), held in June, were celebrations of the summer solstice, but they are now Christian rites in honor of Santo António (St. Anthony), São João (St. John), and São Pedro (St. Peter). The *Feast of St. Anthony,* June 13 and the night before, is a bit like New Year's Eve and New Year's Day. Although most people associate St. Anthony (of Padua) with Italy, he was actually born in the Alfama in Lisbon, and people here make much ado about it. The old quarter comes alive on the eve: Dances are held in streets festooned with colored lanterns, and throughout the night gallons of good, rough wine are drunk to wash down mountains of sardines roasted on open barbecues. The saint is a powerful matchmaker, so this is the night when the city's young girls hope to meet their future husbands. Street stalls sell little pots of a spicy-smelling green herb called *manjerico,* each pot holding a message of advice or consolation for lovers. In the Baixa, neighborhood associations bedecked in traditional costumes parade down Avenida da Liberdade, each attempting to outdo the display of the others. For the *Feast of St. John,* on June 23 and 24, people make bonfires sprinkled with scented herbs and thistles and jump over them to show their daring, an ancient rite connected with fertility. The final celebration is the *Feast of St. Peter,* on June 29. In little towns around Lisbon, such as Montijo, there is a running of the bulls and a blessing of ships on this day.

 MUSEUMS: In addition to those discussed in *Special Places,* Lisbon also has the following museums that may be of interest. Note that most museums are closed on Mondays, and that many that ordinarily impose an admission charge are free on Sundays.

Museu de Arte Popular (Folk Art Museum) – Furniture, paintings, ceramics, baskets, and other items illustrating the handicrafts, customs, and life of the various Portuguese regions. Closed Mondays. Avenida Brasília, Belém (phone: 611282).

Museu da Cidade (City Museum) – Maps, engravings, and other objects telling the story of Lisbon, set up in an 18th-century palace. Closed Mondays. 245 Campo Grande (phone: 759-1617).

Museu Nacional do Teatro (National Theater Museum) – Costumes, scenery, drawings, programs, posters, and other theatrical memorabilia. Closed Mondays. 10-12 Estrada do Lumiar (phone: 759-1102).

Museu Nacional do Traje (National Costume Museum) – Changing exhibitions of Portuguese and foreign costumes, accessories, and fabric, in a lovely old suburban house about a mile north of the City Museum. Closed Mondays. 5 Largo São João Baptista, Parque de Monteiro-Mor, Lumiar (phone: 759-0318).

Museu Rafael Bordalo Pinheiro – Devoted to the works of the 19th-century caricaturist, ceramist, and painter of the same name. Closed Mondays. 382 Campo Grande (phone: 759-0816).

 SHOPPING: The Baixa, between the Rossio and the river, is the most important shopping area in Lisbon. That includes the Chiado, where many fashionable shops are still located, even though some of the most famous ones, along with two department stores, burned down when fire ravaged much of this historic shopping district in 1988. Shops in the downtown area are open Mondays through Fridays from 9 AM to 1 PM and from 3 to 5 PM, Saturdays from 9 AM to 1 PM; many *centros comerciais* (shopping centers) stay open until midnight. The most famous, with sophisticated shops of all kinds — more than 300 of them — is the *Centro Comercial das Amoreiras,* a post-modern complex on Avenida Engenheiro Duarte Pacheco with huge towers in pinks and greens and glass, designed by architect Tomás Taveira. At the other extreme is the *Feira da Ladra,* or Thieves' Market, a flea market held Tuesdays and Saturdays on Largo de Santa Clara at the edge of the Alfama. Among the best buys in Lisbon are gold, silver, and jewelry — relatively inexpensive craftsmanship and the guaranteed content of the gold and silver make many pieces a bargain. There has been a Renaissance in painting, tapestry making, and ceramics, with the accompanying opening of many new galleries. A revival in tile making, often in reproduction of 17th- and 18th-century designs, has also taken place, and many of the stores selling these wares will pack and ship. Rugs from Arraiolos and lace from Madeira, beautiful glass and crystal, copperware, fishermen's sweaters, and baskets are other good buys, along with fashionable clothing, shoes, and leather goods. Note that many of the shops below have branches in the Amoreiras Shopping Center.

Artesanato Arameiro – A wide variety of regional handicrafts — lace, rugs, ceramics, copperware, and filigree. 62 Praça dos Restauradores (phone: 320238).

Atlantis – Crystal tableware from Alcobaça. Centro Comercial das Amoreiras (phone: 693670).

Augustus – Elegant clothes for women. Centro Comercial das Amoreiras (phone: 693479).

Casa dos Bordados da Madeira – Embroidery and lace from Madeira and a wide selection of other Portuguese handicrafts. 135 Rua Primeiro de Dezembro (phone: 321447).

Casa Quintão – Beautiful handmade Arraiolos rugs that are works of art. 30 Rua Ivens (phone: 365837).

Charles – A very wide selection of shoes. 105 Rua do Carmo (phone: 320700).

Charlot – A very fashionable boutique with designer labels from Portugal, Italy, and France. 28 Rua Barata Salgueiro (phone: 573665).

Diadema – Lovely gold and silver jewelry. 166 Rua do Ouro (phone: 321362).

Fábrica de Cerâmica Viúva Lamego – Makes and sells reproductions of old tiles; its bird and animal motifs are famous, but it also makes high-quality modern designs. 25 Largo do Intendente Pina Manique (phone: 521401).

Fábrica de Loiça de Sacavém – Fine porcelain in traditional and modern patterns. 57 Avenida da Liberdade (phone: 323902).

Galeria Comicos – A good new gallery showing avant-garde paintings. 1B Rua Tenente Raul Cascais (phone: 677794).

Galeria 111 – The longest established of Lisbon's art galleries, selling the best of contemporary Portuguese artists. 111 Campo Grande (phone: 767406).

Helio – Top-quality shoes for men and women. 93 Rua do Carmo (phone: 322725).

Joalharia Mergulhão – One of the oldest jewelers in the city. 162 Rua de São Paulo (phone: 346-0013).

Livraria Bertrand – An enormous selection of books. Corner of Rua Garrett and Rua Anchieta (phone: 320081).

Livraria Buchholz – A large stock of foreign books as well as Portuguese ones. 4 Rua do Duque de Palmela (phone: 547358).

Madeira Gobelins – Embroidery, woven tapestries, and carpets from Madeira. 40 Rua Castilho (phone: 563708).

Madeira House – Lisbon's oldest shop dealing in genuine Madeira embroidery and lace, it also sells less expensive embroidered linens. 131 Rua Augusta (phone: 320557).

New York – A classy shop with the latest in women's clothes. 206 Rua do Ouro (phone: 321764).

Ourivesaria Pimenta – Fine jewelry, watches, and silver. 257 Rua Augusta (phone: 324564).

Porfirios – For young and trendy dressers. 63 Rua da Vitória (phone: 368274).

Rosa & Teixeira – A highly ranked tailor selling his own lines for men and women. 204 Avenida da Liberdade (phone: 542063).

Ana Salazar – Clothes by Ana Salazar, Portugal's most famous avant-garde designer for women. 87 Rua do Carmo (phone: 372289).

Sant'Anna – Reproductions of 17th- and 18th-century tiles, made in the shop's own factory. 95 Rua do Alecrim (phone: 322537). The factory, at 96 Calçada da Boa Hora, can be visited, but call first (phone: 638292).

Vista Alegre – The makers of Portugal's finest porcelain. 52 Rua Ivens (phone: 328612) and 18 Largo do Chiado (phone: 361401).

 SPORTS AND FITNESS: Bullfighting – Portuguese bullfighting, quite different from the Spanish version, is more a spectacle of horsemanship than a fight. Bulls are never killed in the ring here, and the fighting is done mostly on horseback, with the *cavaleiros* wearing magnificent 18th-century costumes as they ride against the bulls. After the horseman finishes with a mock kill, the *forcados* — eight young men dressed in brown pants, white shirts, cummerbunds, and tasseled caps — jump over the barrier and line up to wrestle the bull: the most popular part of the bullfight. Their leader taunts the bull to charge and when it does, the leader grabs it around the neck and they all wrestle it to the ground. Although there is a bullfight at Easter, the season begins in earnest in June and generally runs through September, with contests usually held on Thursdays, Sundays, and holidays. The most important fights take place in Lisbon at the *Praça de Touros do Campo Pequeno* (Campo Pequeno Bullring), a mosque-like structure with minarets all around its walls, on Avenida da República (phone: 732093), and at the *Monumental de Cascais.*

Fishing – Boats for deep-sea fishing can be rented from local fishermen at Sesimbra, a fishing village 27 miles (43 km) south of Lisbon, or at Cascais.

Fitness Centers – *Health Club Soleil,* a chain, is in the *Sheraton* hotel, 1 Rua Latino Coelho (phone: 553353); the *Palácio* in Estoril (phone: 268-8184); the *Estoril-Sol* in Cascais (phone: 286-8005); and at *Squash Soleil,* Centro Comercial das Amoreiras, Avenida Engenheiro Duarte Pacheco (phone: 692907).

Golf – The *Clube de Golf do Estoril* (phone: 268-0176), on Avenida da República in Estoril, has 27 holes; caddies and clubs can be rented, and lessons by professionals are available. Also in the Estoril-Cascais area are the *Estoril-Sol Golf Club* (phone: 923-2461), Estrada da Lagoa Azul, with 9 holes belonging to the *Estoril-Sol* hotel; and the *Clube de Golfe da Marinha* (phone: 289881 or 289901), an 18-hole Robert Trent Jones course in the Quinta da Marinha tourist development at Cascais. The British *Lisbon Sports Club* (phone: 431-0077) has an 18-hole course at Casal da Carregueira, on the Belas-Sabugo road, approximately 15½ miles (25 km) northwest of Lisbon. The *Clube de Campo de Lisboa* (Lisbon Country Club), Quinta da Aroeira, Fonte da Telha (phone: 226-1802 or 226-1358), has 18 holes on the coast, 9½ miles (15 km) south of Lisbon.

Horseback Riding – Equestrians can be accommodated at the *Clube de Campo de Lisboa* (phone: 226-1802 or 226-1060) south of Lisbon; at the *Clube da Marinha* (phone: 289282) at Cascais; at the *Pony Club Cascais,* Quinta da Bicuda (284-3233); and at the *Clube de Campo Dom Carlos I* (phone: 285-1403), Estrada Areia, Praia do Guincho.

Jogging – Attractive as it may seem, jogging in Lisbon's central Parque Eduardo VII is not recommended, especially alone or at night. Instead, run along the riverside between the Ponte 25 de Abril and Belém. Another good place is the fitness circuit in the *Estadio Nacional* (National Stadium) area on the outskirts of the city on the way to Estoril, where the track winds through pleasant pine woods. (But do not jog alone.) The park in Estoril and the seafront in Cascais are also good.

Soccer – This is Portugal's most popular sport by far, and it's ruled by a triumvirate of three top clubs: *Sporting* and *Benfica,* from Lisbon, and *Porto,* from the northern capital of Porto. Any game in which one of these teams takes part should be worth watching, as the rivalries are very intense. (Note that the crowds are not unruly here and there has been no hooliganism, as in some other parts of Europe.) The season runs from August until the end of June, and matches are played on Sundays at various stadiums; tickets can be obtained with the help of the hotel desk.

Swimming – The entire coast west of the city and south of it across the river is banded with sandy beaches, and many hotels have private swimming pools. However, water pollution has become a problem on some of the beaches between Lisbon and Estoril, so check first about possible health hazards. (Don't go in the water unless the blue safety flag is flying.) In Estoril, the *Tamariz* restaurant, on the beach, has changing rooms.

Tennis – Courts are available at Estoril's *Clube de Tênis,* Avenida Amaral (phone: 268-6669); at the *Clube de Campo Dom Carlos I,* Estrada Areia, Praia do Guincho (phone: 285-2362); and at the *Lisbon Sports Club* (phone: 431-0077), Casal da Carregueira, 15½ miles (25 km) northwest of Lisbon near Belas.

THEATER: Classic and contemporary plays are presented year-round except during July at the *Teatro Nacional de Dona Maria II,* Praça Dom Pedro IV (phone: 371078). Performances take place in Portuguese, of course. The *revista,* or revue, a popular Lisbon tradition embracing topical sketches, satire, music, and dancing reminiscent of old-fashioned vaudeville, can make for a lively evening even for those who don't understand the language. The best revues are presented in small theaters in the rather ramshackle Parque Mayer theater district, just off Avenida da Liberdade.

 MUSIC: Lisbon's opera house, the *Teatro Nacional de São Carlos* (phone: 368408 or 368664), is at 9 Rua Serpa Pinto, near the Chiado district downtown. Built during the 18th century, it is one of Europe's prettiest, with an apricot-colored interior set off by touches of green and gold. The season runs from mid-December until May. Various ballet companies also perform at the opera house, but the Gulbenkian Foundation sponsors what is one of the best ballet companies in Europe at the moment, performing both classical and modern dance. Performances take place at the auditorium of the Gulbenkian Foundation building at 45 Avenida de Berna (phone: 779131). Symphony and chamber music concerts can also be heard here and at the *Teatro Municipal de São Luis,* Rua António Maria Cardoso (phone: 327172).

 NIGHTCLUBS AND NIGHTLIFE: Lisbon's popular *fado* houses — restaurants with *fado* music — are scattered throughout the old Alfama and Bairro Alto districts. *Fado,* which means "fate" or "destiny," is the name given to the anecdotal, satirical, sentimental, or occasionally happy songs performed, usually by a woman swathed in black (the *fadista*), to the accompaniment of one or more 12-stringed guitars. Although *fado* has become commercialized and many restaurants beef up their shows with folk dancing and popular music, a visitor may be lucky enough to be on hand some night when the singers and the musicians are in the mood to revive the real thing. Do not make a sound during the singing — neither the singers nor the spectators permit it. Some particularly good spots are *Senhor Vinho,* 18 Rua do Meio à Lapa (phone: 672681), where the *fado* is pure; *O Faia,* 54 Rua da Barroca (phone: 321923), one of the best known; *Adega Machado,* 91 Rua do Norte (phone: 360095), fun because it offers spirited folk dancing; *Lisboa à Noite,* 69 Rua das Gáveas (phone: 368557); and *A Severa,* 51-61 Rua das Gáveas (phone: 364006). All are in the Bairro Alto, except *Senhor Vinho,* which is in the Lapa district west of the Bairro Alto. Those who are not dining should go after 10 PM. Reservations are essential.

The newest, biggest, and hottest nightspot in town (Spanish Royalty attended the opening) is the *Bairro Alto,* 48-52 Travessa dos Inglesinhos (phone: 322717), with dancing to a live band every night, plus a show — anything from Spanish flamenco to a circus act.

The top discotheques are sometimes difficult to get into for all but regular customers (they're often frequented by local socialites), and many impose an expensive cover charge. Some of the best are *Banana Power,* 52 Rua Cascais (phone 631815), in the Alcântara dock area west of the center toward Belém; the *Fragil Bar,* 128 Rua da Atalaia (phone: 369578), in the Bairro Alto; *Ad Lib,* 18 Rua Barata Salgueiro (phone: 561717); *Stones,* 1 Rua do Olival (phone: 664545); *Whispers,* 35 Avenida Fontes Pereira de Melo (phone: 575489); *Trumps,* 104-B Rua da Imprensa Nacional (phone: 671059), which has a huge dance floor; and *Springfellows,* Avenida Oscar Monteiro Torres, which is very fancy and on three floors. *Procópio,* 21-21A Avenida Alto São Francisco (phone: 652851), is a bar with live music after 11PM; *Loucuras,* 37 Avenida Pedro Alvares Cabral (phone: 681117), also offers live music. African music —

especially from Cape Verde — is heard all over town. *Clave di Nos,* 100 Rua do Norte (phone: 368420), a restaurant with good food, has a good Cape Verdian band.

Bars to try in Estoril include the *Founder's Inn,* 11D Rua Dom Afonso Henriques (phone: 268-2221); *Ray's Bar,* 25 Avenida Saboia (phone: 269-0106), west of the center in Monte Estoril; and the *English Bar,* Estrada Marginal, Monte Estoril (phone: 268-0413). In Estoril, however, don't miss a night at the world-famous *Casino Estoril* (phone: 268-4521), a shiny new building in the Parque Estoril. It's open every day (to those over 21 endowed with a passport) from 3 PM to 3 AM, and has all the classic European and American games: roulette, baccarat, chemin de fer, blackjack, French bank, slot machines, bingo. The roulette stakes are higher than in Portugal's other casinos, and the slot machines sometimes spit out jackpots of more than $200,000. But gambling is only one of the attractions. The glittering restaurant-nightclub resembles the *Lido* in Paris, with balconies and a main floor seating 800 and the only really international show in the country.

Cascais has a spirited nightlife, with many bars and cafés such as the *John Bull,* an English-style pub at 32 Praça Costa Pinto (phone: 283319); *Tren Velho,* a converted train coach sitting beside the station at Avenida Duquesa de Palmela (phone: 286-7355); *Bar 21,* an attractive cocktail lounge at 1A Travessa da Misericórdia (phone: 286-7518 or 286-4462), and *Cutty Sark,* 6 Travessa da Ressureição. The list of popular discos includes *Coconuts,* 7 Boca do Inferno (phone: 284-4109), with an outdoor terrace by the sea; *Julianas,* 10 Avenida 25 de Abril (phone: 286-4052); and the very snooty *Van Gogo,* 9 Travessa da Alfarrobeira (phone: 283378). For *fado* in Cascais, try *Forte Dom Rodrigo,* Estrada de Birre (phone: 285-1373), or *Picadeiro Maria d'Almeida,* Quinta da Guia, Torre (phone: 289982).

BEST IN TOWN

 CHECKING IN: A visitor's primary decision will be whether to stay right in Lisbon, to commute (with thousands of *lisboetas*) from Estoril or Cascais via the clean, inexpensive trains that run into the city about every 20 minutes, or even to stay in Sintra. Whichever your choice, a double room with bath will cost from $80 to $130 a night in a hotel in the expensive category, from $50 to $70 in the moderate range, and $30 to $40 in the inexpensive range. Reservations are necessary. All telephone numbers are in the 01 area code unless otherwise indicated.

LISBON

Alfa – A very modern 350-room luxury high-rise near the zoo and the *Gulbenkian Museum.* It has 3 restaurants (one with a panoramic view), a swimming pool, sauna, shops, and a hairdresser. Avenida Columbano Bordalo Pinheiro (phone: 726-2121 or 726-4516). Expensive.

Altis – This 9-story ultra-modern hotel of steel, glass, and concrete has 305 rooms, a nice view from its rooftop grill, and a heated indoor swimming pool. It's about halfway between the Rossio train station and Parque Eduardo VII. 11 Rua Castilho (phone: 522496). Expensive.

Avenida Palace – Built in 1894 in the grand hotel style, it has become a landmark, with its rather faded elegance evoking another era. It's near Praça dos Restauradores and has 100 recently refurbished rooms and suites, a good restaurant, and a bar. 123 Rua Primeiro de Dezembro (phone: 366104). Expensive.

Diplomático – Well situated near Parque Eduardo VII, it has 90 rooms equipped with air conditioning, mini-bars, and TV sets, plus a restaurant, bar, and private parking. 74 Rua Castilho (phone: 562041). Expensive.

Fénix – Right on Praça Marquês de Pombal, it has 122 air conditioned rooms and a well-known restaurant, the *Bodegón* (see *Eating Out*), with a nicely appointed bar. 8 Praça Marquês de Pombal (phone: 535121). Expensive.

Lisboa Sheraton – One of the best of the chain in Europe, this 400-room high-rise offers comfortable accommodations, marble bathrooms, and elegant public areas and lounges. All rooms are air conditioned, and there is a heated, open-air swimming pool, plus several restaurants (including the 29th-floor *Panorama*), bars, shops, and a health club. It's a bit away from the city center, a few blocks north of Praça Marquês de Pombal. 1 Rua Latino Coelho (phone: 575757). Expensive.

Meridien – A sparkling addition to Lisbon's complement of modern luxury hotels, it overlooks Parque Eduardo VII. The decor runs to chrome, marble, and splashing fountains, and the restaurants feature French cooking, hardly unusual in a hotel run by a subsidiary of Air France. 149 Rua Castilho (phone: 690900). Expensive.

Penta – This large, modern hotel is a short cab ride from the center of town, beyond the *Gulbenkian Museum*. It has restaurants and bars, a disco, shops, a swimming pool on the grounds, and a shuttle service to the city center and the airport; the 592 rooms are fully equipped, with private baths, balconies, color TV sets, video, radio, and direct-dial telephones. 1600 Avenida dos Combatentes (phone: 740141). Expensive.

Plaza – Centrally located off Avenida da Liberdade and decorated in Art Nouveau style; there are 100 air conditioned rooms, in addition to the well-known *Condestable* restaurant and the *Eduardian Bar,* a popular meeting place. 7 Travessa do Salitre (phone: 346-3922). Expensive.

Ritz Inter-Continental – On a hill overlooking Parque Eduardo VII, this luxury hotel is contemporary on the outside (built in the 1950s), but traditional within. The appointments are dazzling — silks, satins, and suedes — and some of its 260 rooms and 40 suites are furnished with reproductions of antiques. It has large public rooms and a lovely piano bar overlooking the park, fine shops, a tearoom, coffee shop, disco, and beauty parlor, as well as the *Grill Room* (see *Eating Out*), one of the most fashionable restaurants in Lisbon. Bedrooms are air conditioned, soundproofed, and equipped with mini-bars, TV sets, radio, and in-house movies; some have balconies overlooking the park. 88 Rua Rodrigo da Fonseca (phone: 692020). Expensive.

Tivoli – Well situated, with 350 rooms and suites. Because it's so convenient, right on the main avenue downtown, the lobby is a popular meeting place for businesspeople as well as tourists (and the excellent bar just off the lobby is a favorite of local journalists). Restaurant and a popular rooftop grill room. 185 Avenida da Liberdade (phone: 530181). Expensive.

Flórida – Near Praça Marquês de Pombal, it has 120 air conditioned rooms with all the facilities (bath, telephones, TV sets, radio); no restaurant, but there's a bar, a gift shop, and a hairdresser. 32 Avenida Duque de Palmela (phone: 576145). Expensive to moderate.

Príncipe Real – A small downtown hotel, off Avenida da Liberdade. There are 24 rooms, a restaurant, and a bar. 53 Rua da Alegria (phone: 346-0116). Expensive to moderate.

Rex – Modern, with 70 rooms, on the edge of Parque Eduardo VII, near the more prestigious *Ritz* and *Meridien* hotels. All rooms have air conditioning, TV sets, and radio; half have balconies overlooking the park. There are 2 restaurants (one with a panoramic view) and a bar. 169 Rua Castilho (phone: 682161). Expensive to moderate.

Dom Carlos – Comfortable and recently remodeled, it's at Praça Marquês de Pombal. The 73 rooms are air conditioned and equipped with private baths, TV sets, and mini-bars. No restaurant, but there is a breakfast room and a bar. 121 Avenida Duque de Loulé (phone: 539071). Moderate.

Eduardo VII – Not far from Praça Marquês de Pombal, it has 110 air conditioned rooms with private baths and other conveniences. The hotel also has an excellent rooftop restaurant with a view of the city. 5 Avenida Fontes Pereira de Melo (phone: 530141). Moderate.

Flamingo – Small, conveniently located, with 39 rooms — some of them air conditioned. All have soundproofing, TV sets, and mini-bars. The hotel also has a good restaurant and a bar. 41 Rua Castilho (phone: 532191). Moderate.

Príncipe – Northeast of Parque Eduardo VII, it has 70 air conditioned rooms with bath, TV sets, and telephone, plus a restaurant and bar. 201 Avenida Duque de Avila (phone: 536151). Moderate.

Tivoli Jardim – On a quieter street behind its sister, the *Tivoli,* and therefore, a much quieter hotel. New and modern, it has 120 rooms with bath (many with balconies), a restaurant, bar, snack bar, and car park. The service is first rate. 7-9 Rua Júlio César Machado (phone: 539971). Moderate.

York House – One of the most attractive places to stay in Lisbon, although it is some distance west of the heart of the city, close to the *Museu Nacional de Arte Antiga.* Housed in a 16th-century building that was once a convent, this lovely, antiques-filled *pensão* — with a restaurant and a nice bar with tables in the garden — is a particular favorite of British visitors, writers, and embassy personnel. It's easily missed, since there is no sign outside: Enter the grounds by a gate and go up a staircase to a garden cloister. An annex to this small hostelry is in a townhouse down the street, making a total of 58 rooms, 39 with bath. 32 Rua das Janelas Verdes (phone: 662435). Moderate.

Dom Manuel – A modern and efficient small hotel (64 rooms with bath), just around the corner from the *Gulbenkian Museum.* The rooms are small, but comfortably appointed, with air conditioning, TV sets, and video. There is a breakfast room and a bar, but no restaurant. 189 Avenida Duque de Avila (phone: 576160). Moderate to inexpensive.

Miraparque – In a quiet location facing Parque Eduardo VII, it has 100 rooms with bath, a restaurant, and a bar. 12 Avenida Sidónio Pais (phone: 578070). Moderate to inexpensive.

Imperador – A *pensão* of 45 rooms with bath, northeast of Parque Eduardo VII. Third floor, 55 Avenida 5 de Outubro (phone: 574657). Inexpensive.

Insulana – In the Baixa, this *albergaria* (inn) has 32 rooms with bath. Third floor, 52 Rua Assunção (phone: 323131 or 328013). Inexpensive.

Senhora do Monte – Like the *York House,* this is an insider's inn. Small, in the old Graça quarter northeast of St. George's Castle, it has good views of Lisbon from some of its 27 rooms (all with bath). It's not the best place for access, but old hands swear by it. 39 Calçada do Monte (phone: 862846). Inexpensive.

Torre – This modern, attractive little place is a 15-minute taxi ride from the center, but convenient for sightseeing in Belém, where's it's right beside one of Lisbon's best known sights — the Jerónimos Monastery. There are 50 rooms with bath, a bar, and a restaurant. 8 Rua dos Jerónimos (phone: 637332). Inexpensive.

ESTORIL

Atlántico – In the pleasant residential district of Monte Estoril, this is a modern hotel on the sea (or rather, nearly on the sea, since the electric train tracks run between it and the beach). There are 175 air conditioned rooms (some with balconies overlooking the Atlantic), a terrace with a large saltwater swimming pool, an excellent restaurant, bar, nightclub, and billiards room. Estrada Marginal, Monte Estoril (phone: 268-5170). Expensive.

Lennox Country Club – A hillside *estalagem* (inn) standing in a garden setting overlooking the coast. There are 32 rooms with bath, some in the main building, which was once a private home, and some in modern additions, plus a very good restaurant with excellent service, a kidney-shaped, heated outdoor swimming pool, and a tennis court. The inn emphasizes golf — golfing memorabilia decorate it, there is a putting green, and free transportation is provided to courses in the area, as well as to area riding stables. 5 Rua Engenheiro Alvaro Pedro de Sousa (phone: 268-0424). Expensive.

Palácio – Imagine Allied and Axis spies peeping around pillars during World War II and the jewels of exiled royalty glinting in the light of crystal chandeliers; that's the essence of this gracious, Old World hotel by the park. The public rooms are majestic, the staff the sort that seems to remember everyone who has ever stayed here, and the 200 rooms and suites, with traditional and contemporary furnishings, are air conditioned. In addition to the dining room, there is the adjoining, superlative *Four Seasons Grill* (see *Eating Out*). A heated swimming pool and cabanas are in the lovely gardens behind the hotel; the beach on the Atlantic is a 5-minute walk away. Temporary membership in the nearby Estoril Golf Club is available (hotel guests don't pay green fees); there are tennis courts next door. Parque Estoril (phone: 268-0400). Expensive.

Cibra – Modern and freshly renovated, it has 90 rooms with bath, a bar, a rooftop restaurant, and a swimming pool. It's also close to the beach. Estrada Marginal, Monte Estoril (phone: 268-1811). Expensive to moderate.

Grande – On a hill overlooking the sea in Monte Estoril, this is a modern establishment with 73 rooms with bath (some with balconies), a bar, restaurant, and covered swimming pool. Avenida Sabóia, Monte Estoril (phone: 268-4609). Expensive to moderate.

Anka Estoril – This modern hotel, recently remodeled, is near the park in front of the *Palácio*. It has 91 air conditioned rooms, some with balconies, a panoramic restaurant on the 7th floor, a bar, and a swimming pool. Estrada Marginal (phone: 268-1811). Expensive to moderate.

Alvorada – Another modern hostelry, near the casino, with 51 rooms, each with private bath and a balcony. There's no swimming pool, but there is a solarium on top, and the hotel is only 200 yards from the beach. Breakfast room and bar; no restaurant. 3 Rua de Lisboa (phone: 268-0070). Moderate.

Founder's Inn – British-owned and also known as the *Estalagem do Fundador*, it has 14 pleasant rooms with bath, each furnished differently. The restaurant serves excellent English cooking; there's also a bar, with music, that's a local nightspot. A freshwater pool is on the grounds, which are on a hillside, set back from the beachfront. 11 Rua Dom Afonso Henriques (phone: 268-2221). Moderate.

Inglaterra – A charming, turn-of-the-century private home turned hotel, set in gardens near the *Palácio*. Inside, the 45 rooms with bath are spare and contemporary, rather than old-fashioned in style; there's a bar, restaurant, and swimming pool. 1 Rua do Porto (phone: 268-4461). Moderate.

Lido – A very comfortable, modern hotel in a quiet spot on a hillside away from the beach, but not far from the casino and park. The 62 rooms and suites all have private baths and balconies, telephones, and radios; the hotel has a restaurant, bar, a large swimming pool, a solarium, and a terrace with a view of the ocean. 12 Rua do Alentejo (phone: 268-4098). Moderate.

Pica-Pau – A good *pensão* in a nice old white-painted villa with a red tile roof, near the *Lido* and the *Founder's Inn*. The 48 rooms with bath are completely modern; there is a bar, a restaurant, and a swimming pool. 48 Rua Dom Afonso Henriques (phone: 268-0556). Moderate to inexpensive.

Smart – Another *pensão*, in a very large old house that's been recently remodeled.

It has 16 rooms, most with TV sets and private baths (the rest have washbasins), a breakfast room (no restaurant), and a garden with palm trees. It's not far from the beach. 3 Rua José Viana (phone: 268-2164). Inexpensive.

CASCAIS

Albatroz – A luxury hotel perched on rocks at the water's edge. The location is choice, which is not hard to understand since the core of this hotel was built during the 19th century as a villa for the royal family. After its transformation, royalty continued to patronize it as paying guests, as did movie stars and other VIPs. Between the original building and a newer balconied addition, there are 40 rooms with bath. An excellent restaurant (see *Eating Out*) and bar, both surrounded by windows overlooking the sea, and a swimming pool with plenty of room for sunbathing are further attractions. 100 Rua Frederico Arouca (phone: 282821). Expensive.

Baia – Right on the beach, in the heart of town, where the local fishermen tie up their painted boats. There are 85 rooms in this modern hotel, most with balconies; restaurant and terrace bar. Avenida Marginal (phone: 281033). Expensive.

Cidadela – Near the center of town, with 140 rooms and some apartments, each with its own seaview balcony. The hotel has a good restaurant, a bar, and a swimming pool set amid attractive gardens. Avenida 25 de Abril (phone: 282921). Expensive.

Estoril-Sol – The biggest hotel on the coast, with 347 rooms and suites. It's east of town, between the center of Cascais and Monte Estoril, and is separated from the water only by the electric train tracks (an underground passage leads directly to the beach). The *Estoril-Sol* is rife with facilities: an Olympic-sized swimming pool, a children's pool, 5 bars, a large, panoramic rooftop restaurant, a disco, shops, a health club, sauna, squash courts, a bowling alley, and its own 9-hole golf course in lovely surroundings nearby. Parque Palmela (phone: 282831). Expensive.

Farol – A charming *estalagem* (inn) in a building that was once the private house of an aristocratic family. It's by the sea, just west of the center along the road to Boca do Inferno and Praia do Guincho. It has 20 rooms with bath, a swimming pool, tennis court, bar, snack bar, and a restaurant that overlooks the water. 7 Estrada da Boca do Inferno (phone: 280173). Expensive.

Guincho – The waves crash on three sides of this restored 17th-century fortress that looks out to sea from a rocky promontory 5½ miles (9 km) northwest of Cascais. The site is spectacular, with beach on both sides, although walking on the beach is recommended more than going in the water, due to the treacherous undertow here, near the westernmost point of continental Europe. The 36 rooms and suites of this elegant hotel all have private baths, old brick-vaulted ceilings, telephones, mini-bars, and TV sets, and some have balconies. There is a bar and a panoramic restaurant (see *Eating Out*). Praia do Guincho (phone: 285-0491). Expensive.

Dom Carlos – This *pensão* in the center of Cascais occupies a restored house built in 1640, and the breakfast room and chapel maintain the decorations of that period. There are 18 rooms with bath, a TV salon, and a garden with trees. 8 Rua Latino Coelho (phone: 286-8463). Moderate.

Equador – All the rooms in this very attractive new apartment-hotel are equipped with a kitchenette, bath, balcony, telephone, and radio. Set back and above the city center (but within walking distance), it has a restaurant, bar, swimming pools, a mini-market, sauna, solarium, disco, and gameroom. There are 117 units. Alto da Pampilheira (phone: 284-0890). Moderate.

Nau – The location is convenient — in front of the train station and only 150 yards or so from the beach. This modern hotel has 56 rooms with baths and balconies, plus a TV room, a bar, and a restaurant with a terrace. 14 Rua Dra. Iracy Doyle (phone: 282861). Moderate.

Nossa Senhora das Preces – An *estalagem* (inn) close to the Boca do Inferno. It has 15 rooms, each with a private bath and telephone, 4 with terraces overlooking the sea. Swimming pool, tennis court, and bar, but no restaurant. 43 Rua Visconde da Gandarinha (phone: 284-0376). Moderate.

Valbom – An *albergaria* (inn) in the center of Cascais, near the train station, it's better looking inside than from the outside. There are 40 rooms with private bath; bar, but no restaurant (breakfast is served). 14 Avenida Valbom (phone: 285801). Inexpensive.

SINTRA

Palácio dos Seteais – One of the loveliest and most romantic hotels in Europe. Built at the end of the 18th century for the Dutch consul in Lisbon, it was sold to the 5th Marquês de Marialva and was often visited by royalty. Marble gleams underfoot and murals line the walls of the public rooms; the 18 guestrooms are beautifully decorated with antiques, handwoven rugs, and tapestries. Just outside Sintra, the hotel has a bar and a well-known restaurant overlooking spacious gardens, a formal, windowed salon with views of the Sintra valley, and a swimming pool and tennis courts. 8 Rua Barbosa do Bocage (phone: 923-3200). Expensive.

Tivoli Sintra – The best in town, this is off the main square of Sintra, right by the National Palace. The modern building has all the modern conveniences, along with traditional Portuguese touches in the decor. There are 75 air conditioned rooms with private baths, balconies, TV sets, and telephones. A highly regarded restaurant with a view (see *Eating Out*), lounges, bars, a hairdresser, and a garage are among the facilities. Praça da República (phone: 923-3505). Expensive.

Central – Short on rooms (only 11, all with private bath), it's long on charm, and on the main square, in front of the palace. There is a tearoom, a bar, and a pleasant restaurant with a terrace for lunch in the summer. 35 Praça da República (phone: 923-0963). Moderate.

Raposa – A small *pensão* near the center in a restored 200-year-old house. The 9 rooms (6 with private bath) are decorated in period style. Bar and tearoom, but no restaurant. 3 Rua Dr. Alfredo Costa (phone: 923-0465). Inexpensive.

Sintra – In São Pedro de Sintra, a 10-minute walk from downtown. This *pensáo* has 13 rooms (10 with private bath), a swimming pool, TV room, and a breakfast room (no restaurant). Travessa dos Avelares, São Pedro de Sintra (phone: 923-0738). Inexpensive.

Portugal's Turismo de Habitação, or Manor Houses program — a network of elegant old aristocratic estates, country homes, and other such privately owned properties taking in small numbers of paying guests — is most active in the rural north, but travelers interested in this type of accommodation do have some choices in the Lisbon area. Among them is the charming *Casal São Roque,* by the sea in Estoril. Built at the beginning of the century and furnished accordingly, it has 6 rooms for guests, 4 with private baths; the hosts will serve meals upon request. Contact *Casal São Roque,* Avenida Marginal, 2765 Estoril (phone: 268-0217). In the center of Cascais, there's the *Casa da Pérgola,* set in lovely gardens, offering a luxurious suite and 5 bedrooms with private bath. Contact Casa da Pérgola, 13 Avenida Valbom, 2736 Cascais (phone: 284-0040).

Sintra has three properties. The *Quinta de São Thiago* is an imposing noble house several centuries old, surrounded by vast lawns with a swimming pool, near the *Palácio dos Seteais.* There are 7 double bedrooms, luxuriously furnished with antiques; the owners (an Englishman and his Spanish wife) serve meals on request. Contact *Quinta de São Thiago,* 2710 Sintra (phone: 923-2923). The *Quinta da Capella* is another impressive old noble house surrounded by gardens, beyond Seteais and the Quinta de Monserrate. One suite and 4 beautifully furnished bedrooms with private baths — or 2 independent apartments — are available. Contact *Quinta da Capella,* Estrada de Monserrate, 2710 Sintra (phone: 923-0210). Finally, the *Vila das Rosas* is a large, white 19th-century house with a red tile roof on the northern outskirts of Sintra; 4 double rooms with bath, a suite of 3 rooms with bath, and a cottage in the garden are available. In summer, breakfast is served in the cool wine cellar; other meals are served on request. Contact *Vila das Rosas,* 2-4 Rua António Cunha, 2710 Sintra (phone: 923-4216). The *Quinta de São Thiago* and the *Quinta da Capella* are in the expensive price category; the remaining three are moderate. Reservations for all of the above can also be made through Turihab, Praça da República, 4990 Ponte de Lima (phone: 058-942335) or through the Direcção-Geral do Turismo, Turismo de Habitação, 51 Rua Alexandre Herculano, 1200 Lisbon (phone: 681713).

 EATING OUT: Portuguese food offers a surprising variety of tastes. Over the centuries, this seagoing nation's cuisine has come under the influence of far-flung countries in Asia, Africa, and the Americas, as well as neighboring Spain and nearby France. Lisbon's restaurants reflect this heritage (and all its regional permutations). Fish and seafood abound and are usually fresh and delicious. Those who want to splurge should order steamed lobster or grilled prawns, or dishes such as *arroz de marisco* (rice with shellfish). Stuffed crab and boiled sea spider (eaten by cracking it open with a wooden mallet) are flavorful, and codfish is a great local favorite — it's said the Portuguese have as many ways to prepare it as there are days in the year, one of the best being *bacalhau à Gomes de Sá,* named for a Porto restaurant owner. The best restaurants serve delicious smoked swordfish, sliced very thin, with lemon and capers, but for something uniquely Portuguese, sample the charcoal-grilled sardines sold in the street. Lisbon's meat is best grilled, but typical dishes such as *cozido à portuguesa* (a stew of boiled vegetables, sausages, and different types of meats, popular in the north) and *iscas à portuguesa* (thin slices of calf's liver marinated in wine, garlic, and bay leaves, and cooked in a shallow earthenware dish) are worth trying. Desserts, mostly based on eggs, sugar, and almonds, tend to be too sweet for some palates, but there are good cheeses — *queijo da Serra,* from northeastern Portugal, and *Serpa,* from the Alentejo, among the best. Wines from all over the country appear on the city's wine lists. The rule is to choose those that are more than 5 years old (except for northern *vinhos verdes,* which should be less than 2 years old, but which are not often found in Lisbon). Pungent, fruity Bairrada wines, mellow, woody Dão wines, and flowery Douro wines are all good. Bucelas is an excellent white from a small demarcated zone north of Lisbon.

Dinner for two, with a local wine, averages from $50 to $70 at restaurants listed below as expensive, from $30 to $50 at moderate establishments, and from $20 to $30 at inexpensive restaurants. Customary dining time is no earlier than 7:30 PM, but many restaurants close their kitchens at 11 PM. Lunch is served between noon and 2:30 PM. All telephone numbers are in the 01 area code unless otherwise indicated.

LISBON

Aviz – One of the best restaurants in town. When the old *Aviz* hotel — where the multimillionaire Calouste Gulbenkian spent the final days of his life in Lisbon — was torn down, Chef Alberto Rapetti and some of his staff opened this restaurant just off Largo do Chiado, bringing with them all the elegance and flair that had made the old hostelry an international favorite. The decor is very Belle Epoque, the food excellent, and the service flawless. Closed Saturdays at lunch and on Sundays. Reservations advised. 12B Rua Serpa Pinto (phone: 328391). Expensive.

Bodegón – A worthy hotel restaurant, in the cellar of the *Fénix* hotel, with a comfortable adjoining bar. There is a Spanish theme to the decor, and good Spanish — and international — dishes on the menu. Open daily. 8 Praça Marquês de Pombal (phone: 535121). Expensive.

Casa da Comida – A discreetly elegant restaurant in a converted house, with tables set around a charming enclosed garden and an adjoining period bar. The food is delicious and beautifully presented. Closed Saturdays at lunch and Sundays. Reservations advised. 1 Travessa das Amoreiras (phone: 685386). Expensive.

Chester – Although this attractive little restaurant near the *Ritz* specializes in steaks, it also has shellfish live in tanks for the choosing and the fish is always fresh. Reservations advised. Closed Sundays. 87 Rua Rodrigo da Fonseca (phone: 657347). Expensive.

Clara – Very elegant, spacious restaurant serving excellent regional Portuguese and international food — one of Lisbon's best. It's in an old house with gardens that are illuminated at night. Closed Sundays. 49 Campo dos Mártires de Pátria (phone: 570434). Expensive.

Escorial – A famous restaurant in a district, near Praça dos Restauradores, that's noted for the seafood served. Elegantly decorated, with a nice bar, and known for good service, it also serves excellent international cuisine. Closed only on the 1st of May — Labor Day in Europe. 47 Rua das Portas de Santo Antão (phone: 346-3758). Expensive.

Gambrinus – Famous for fish and seafood, with numerous small dining rooms that fan out from the open blue-tiled kitchen. In the heart of the city, it is usually jammed with businesspeople at lunchtime. Reservations necessary. Open daily. 25 Rua das Portas de Santo Antão (phone: 321466). Expensive.

Michel – The owner, a well-known cook on television in Portugal, specializes in nouvelle cuisine, Portuguese style, although traditional French dishes are also served. Handsomely decorated, this is in the Alfama, just below St. George's Castle. Closed Saturdays at lunch and Sundays. 5 Largo de Santa Cruz do Castelo (phone: 864358). Expensive.

Ritz Grill Room – The restaurant of the *Ritz* hotel prepares unusually good food and is a fashionable gathering place for Lisbon businesspeople. Open daily. Reservations advised. 88 Rua Rodrigo da Fonseca (phone: 692020). Expensive.

Tágide – A beautiful staircase leads from the small dining room on the 1st floor to a 2nd-floor dining area where picture windows afford a great view of the Tagus, a must for visitors who want to see the city and eat well at the same time. Portuguese and international dishes share the menu; the service is pleasant and impeccable. Closed Sundays. 18 Largo da Biblioteca Pública (phone: 320720). Expensive.

Tavares – Lisbon's oldest restaurant began as a café in 1784 and became a luxurious restaurant in 1861. After celebrating its 200th birthday, this city landmark had its gold leaf walls redone, its mirrors replated, its armchairs reupholstered, and more, so the light from its crystal chandeliers shines on a scene that's as opulent as ever, the haunt of businesspeople, government officials, and the like, and the perfect setting for excellent food and fine wine. Closed Saturdays at lunch and Sundays. Reservations advised. 37 Rua da Misericórdia (phone: 321112). Expensive.

Conventual – The menu is based on old Portuguese convent and monastery recipes, some of which go back to the 17th century, and objects from churches decorate the premises. Typical dishes include *bacalhau com coentros* (cod with coriander) and *ensopada de borrego* (lamb stew). Closed Saturdays at lunch and Sundays. Reservations advised. 44 Praça das Flores (phone: 609196). Expensive to moderate.

Restaurante 33 – Good food and a pleasant atmosphere prevail in this well appointed restaurant behind an elegant clapboard façade, not far from the *Ritz*.

Closed Sundays. 33 Rua Alexandre Herculano (phone: 546079). Expensive to moderate.

Sua Excelência – In the Madragoa quarter, near the embassy residences. Knock on the door to gain entry and the attentive owner will read out the entire menu in English, if so desired. He serves a very good *açorda* (a sort of "dry" soup, or stew, a combination of seafood, bread, eggs, and coriander) and Mozambique prawns with a peppery sauce. Closed Tuesday evenings, Wednesdays, and the month of September. 42 Rua do Conde (phone: 603614). Expensive to moderate.

Caseiro – A good restaurant among the many near the Jerónimos Monastery in Belém. It is typically Portuguese, specializing in regional dishes and seafood, and attractively decorated. Closed Mondays. 5 Rua de Belém (phone: 638803). Moderate.

Espelho d'Agua – In Belém, right on the river facing the Monument to the Discoveries, this has a panoramic view from the air conditioned dining room and bar. Typical Portuguese dishes are served. Closed Sundays. Avenida de Brasília (phone: 617373). Moderate.

Faz Figura – Overlooking the Tagus in the Alfama quarter, its wood paneling and leather chairs give it the atmosphere of an exclusive club, but there is also a verandah where diners can sit and watch the ships on the river. Fish and seafood, Portuguese and international dishes, are all available. Closed Sundays. 15B Rua do Paraíso (phone: 868981). Moderate.

Gondola – A long-established Italian restaurant near the *Gulbenkian Museum* and a favorite with visitors. There's a lovely vine-covered garden for summer dining. Closed Saturday evenings and Sundays. 64 Avenida de Berna (phone: 770426). Moderate.

Laçerda – Also near the *Gulbenkian Museum,* this small place used to be a butcher shop and is still devoted to meat (choose a cut from the hook by the door). Photos of celebrities who have dined here decorate the walls, and strings of garlic and onions hang from the ceiling. Closed Sundays. 36 Avenida de Berna (phone: 774057). Moderate.

Pap'Açorda – The entrance to this Bairro Alto bakery-turned-restaurant is through an old paneled bar. Inside, there is a very attractive enclosed garden banked with green plants. The mixed fish grilled on a skewer is very good, but the specialty of the house is the porridgy seafood-bread-eggs-and-coriander mixture known as *açorda*. Book in advance. Closed Saturdays at lunch and Sundays. 57 Rua da Atalaia (phone: 346-4811). Moderate.

Varina da Madragoa – An old tavern turned into a blue-and-white tiled restaurant, near Parliament. Good Portuguese food, including excellent *bacalhau,* or codfish. Open daily. 36 Rua das Madres (phone: 665533). Moderate.

Bomjardim – Considered tops in preparing *frango na brasa,* chicken that's charcoal-broiled on a rotating spit and, if it's desired, accompanied by a fiery chili sauce (*piri piri*). This is one of Lisbon's most popular — and least expensive — culinary delights. There are 2 *Bomjardim* restaurants facing each other just off Praça dos Restauradores. Noisy and crowded at lunchtime; open daily. 10-11 Travessa de Santo Antão (phone: 327424). Inexpensive.

Bota Alta – Exceptionally good Portuguese cooking is served in a cheery bistro atmosphere. It's in the midst of the Bairro Alto nightlife and usually very busy. Closed Sundays. 35-37 Travessa da Queimada (phone: 327959). Inexpensive.

Porto d'Abrigo – Although not imposing in appearance, this tiny eatery is one of Lisbon's culinary landmarks. Famous for its Portuguese specialties, it's usually very crowded at lunchtime. Reservations advised. Closed Sundays. 16 Rua dos Remolares (phone: 346-0875). Inexpensive.

Xico Carreira – In the picturesque, rather shabby theater district off Avenida da

Liberdade, it's off the beaten track for most people and full of local color. A former bullfighter owns it; posters and mementos of the sport decorate it. Try the *bife a cortador* (big grilled steaks) or the *cozido transmontano* (boiled dinner of vegetables, sausages, and meats). Crowded at lunchtime. Closed Sundays. Parque Mayer (phone: 346-3805). Inexpensive.

ESTORIL

Casino Estoril – The glittering, balcony-lined restaurant here is known for its international show — at 11:30 every night, with stars such as Julio Iglesias and Dionne Warwick — but it's no less recommendable for food and service, both excellent. It has a long menu of Portuguese and international dishes. Open daily. Parque Estoril (phone: 268-4521). Expensive.

Choupana – On a cliff overlooking the sea a bit over a mile (2 km) east of Estoril, this specializes in seafood, but has a varied menu of other dishes as well. The dining room is large, panoramic, and air conditioned. Later at night, there is a show and music until all hours. Open daily. Estrada Marginal, São João do Estoril (phone: 268-3099). Expensive.

Four Seasons Grill – A very elegant restaurant for the finest dining in Estoril. The long menu of Portuguese and international dishes changes four times a year, according to the seasons, and when it does, so does the china, the decor, and the waiters' uniforms. This is run by the *Palácio* hotel, which is next door, and can be entered using either its own street entrance or the hotel lobby. Open daily. Parque Estoril (phone: 268-0400). Expensive.

English Bar – A brown and white building overlooking the water, with windows all around. It's cozily decorated in the English manner (and has a popular bar), but serves very good Portuguese and international dishes. Closed Sundays. Estrada Marginal, Monte Estoril (phone: 269-0413). Expensive to moderate.

A Maré – By the sea with a lovely panoramic view and a varied menu. There is a large air conditioned dining room and, in summer, an outside barbecue. Open daily. Estrada Marginal, Monte Estoril (phone: 268-5570). Expensive to moderate.

Ferra Mulinhas – Portuguese and Hungarian cooking. It's open only for dinner and is closed Tuesdays. 5A Rua Viveiro (phone: 268-0005). Moderate.

Garrafão – A fish and seafood restaurant with its own vivarium, on the outskirts of Estoril. Closed Thursdays. Amoreira (phone: 268-4195). Inexpensive.

CASCAIS

Albatroz – This outstanding restaurant is the dining room of the hotel of the same name, which is set on rocks at the edge of the sea. It's known for a varied menu of well-prepared dishes, including good seafood, and the picture windows that surround it make it exceedingly fine for its views as well. Open daily. 100 Rua Frederico Arouca (phone: 282821). Expensive.

Baluarte – By the sea, with 2 air conditioned dining rooms featuring splendid views. It specializes in seafood, but also has a long menu of other Portuguese and international dishes. Open daily. 1 Avenida Marechal Carmona (phone: 286-7198). Expensive.

Hotel do Guincho – The restaurant here, in a clifftop hotel that was once a fortress guarding continental Europe's westernmost extremity, is surrounded by windows looking onto the crashing Atlantic. The location alone makes it a wonderful lunch or dinner spot for those on a day's outing along the coast, but the excellence of the food — with emphasis on seafood — and of the service would recommend it even without the view. 5½ miles (9 km) northwest of Cascais. Open daily. Praia do Guincho (phone: 285-0491). Expensive.

João Padeiro – From its beginnings a number of years ago as a simple eatery, this has become one of the most renowned seafood restaurants in Cascais. Old stone grinding wheels and pieces from windmills decorate the 3 dining rooms most attractively. Closed Tuesdays. 12 Rua Visconde da Luz (phone: 280232). Expensive.

Muchaxo – In an *estalagem* by the same name, this is one of the most famous seafood restaurants on the Lisbon coast. The inn is by the sea, so there is a marvelous view over the water. Open daily. Praia do Guincho (phone: 285-0221). Expensive.

Pescador – A charming restaurant near the fish market, it is decorated with a fishermen's motif. Fish and seafood are very good here. Open daily. 10B Rua das Flores (phone: 282054). Expensive to moderate.

Visconde da Luz – Set in a park in the center of town, there are 2 dining rooms serving very good seafood and other Portuguese dishes. Closed Mondays. Jardim Visconde da Luz (phone: 286-6848). Expensive to moderate.

O Batel – Nicely decorated in a rustic fashion, this is another good seafood restaurant, near the fish market. Open daily. 4 Travessa das Flores (phone: 280215). Moderate.

Beira Mar – One of the longest established of the seafood restaurants near the fish market. Decorated with blue and white tiles, it serves international fare in addition to good seafood. Open daily. 6 Rua das Flores (phone: 280152). Moderate.

Burladero – By the bullring, it is large, air conditioned, and specializes in grilled meats. Closed for lunch on Wednesdays and Thursdays. Praça de Touros (phone: 286-8751). Moderate.

Duke of Wellington – A downtown, English-style pub, with a small restaurant serving very good French and English dishes. Open daily. 32 Rua Frederico Arouca (phone: 280394). Moderate.

John Bull – Another well-known English pub with a good little restaurant attached. International fare. Open daily. 31 Praça Costa Pinto (phone: 283319). Moderate.

O Pipas – A smart seafood restaurant in the center of town, near the fish market, it consists of a small air conditioned dining room decorated with wine barrels and hanging garlic and sausages. Open daily. 1B Rua das Flores (phone: 286-4501). Moderate.

A Taverna de Gil Vicente – A cozy little restaurant with a fireplace, it features international cooking. 22 Rua dos Navegantes (phone: 282032). Moderate.

Galegos – A simple place near the center of town that serves Portuguese and northern Spanish dishes. Open daily. 3 Avenida Valbom (phone: 282586). Inexpensive.

Lavagante – This plain restaurant has 2 air conditioned dining rooms serving seafood and Portuguese dishes. It also has its own vivarium. Closed Mondays. 59 Rua Poço Novo (phone: 284-0154). Inexpensive.

QUELUZ

Cozinha Velha – The name means Old Kitchen, and this is the former royal kitchen of the National Palace at Queluz, now turned into a restaurant with considerable atmosphere. It has high stone arches, a 15-foot-long marble worktable, a walk-in fireplace, enormous spits, and walls lined with copper pots and utensils, many of them originals. Excellent food, combined with the splendor of the setting, make this an experience to remember. Air conditioned; open daily. Palácio Nacional de Queluz (phone: 950740). Expensive.

Poço – A large restaurant with 3 air conditioned dining rooms serving good Portuguese food. Closed Mondays. 33 Avenida da República (phone: 957737). Inexpensive.

SINTRA

Monserrate – The floor-to-ceiling windows of this air conditioned hotel restaurant afford a panoramic view of the valley below Sintra. The menu features international dishes. Open daily. *Tivoli Sintra* hotel, Praça da República (phone: 923-3505). Expensive.

Palácio dos Seteais – An 18th-century palace makes a lovely setting for lunch on a sunny day, especially a leisurely Sunday, and especially when the restaurant has an adjoining garden terrace on which to indulge in after-dinner coffee. This very elegant restaurant, serving well-prepared Portuguese and international dishes, is outside Sintra, in the hotel of the same name. Open daily. 8 Rua Barbosa do Bocage (phone: 923-3200). Expensive.

Dos Arcos – Typical Portuguese dishes are served in an attractive setting that includes a waterfall. In an old part of town, a 10-minute walk from downtown. Open daily. 4 Rua Serpa Pinto, São Pedro de Sintra (phone: 923-0264). Moderate.

Cantinho de São Pedro – This rustic restaurant, also in São Pedro de Sintra, has 2 large dining rooms and a wine cellar. Try it for seafood, game, or one of the many French dishes on the menu. Closed Mondays and Thursday evenings. 18 Praça Dom Fernando II, São Pedro de Sintra (phone: 923-0267). Moderate.

Galeria Real – Above a gallery of antique shops in São Pedro de Sintra, this is a lovely dining room, filled with antiques. The menu features Portuguese and French food. Open daily. Rua Tude de Sousa, São Pedro de Sintra (phone: 923-1661). Moderate.

Solar de São Pedro – Two large dining rooms with fireplaces and a menu of French and Portuguese selections keep this place busy. Closed Tuesday evenings and Wednesdays. 12 Praça Dom Fernando II, São Pedro de Sintra (phone: 923-1860). Moderate.

Adega do Saloio – The rustic decor, the strings of onions and garlic hanging from the ceiling, the fireplaces, and the open kitchen tell visitors that this "countryman's winery" is aptly named. Meat, fish, and seafood grilled on the spit are the specialties. At the entrance to Sintra from Lisbon or Estoril. Closed Tuesdays. Chão de Meninos (phone: 923-1422). Moderate to inexpensive.

Portelinho – Small, air conditioned, with a bar, it serves a variety of Portuguese regional dishes at reasonable prices. Open daily. 66-70 Avenida Movimento das Forças Armadas (phone: 923-3857). Inexpensive.

LONDON

British author and journalist V. S. Pritchett noted that the essence of London was contained in the very sound of its name: Lon-don, a weighty word, solid, monumental, dignified, even ponderous. London is a shapeless city without a center; it sprawls anarchically over 620 square miles and brims over with a variety of neighborhoods and people. One of its sharpest observers, Daniel Defoe, portrayed London in the 18th century much as it could be described today: "It is . . . stretched out in buildings, straggling, confused . . . out of all shape, uncompact and unequal; neither long nor broad, round or square."

London can best be understood not as one city but as a conglomeration of villages that were incorporated whole, one by one, as the monster expanded — Chelsea, Battersea, Paddington, and Hampstead are just a few. Fortunately, all of its important parks and squares have remained inviolate, but not without a struggle, for London's merchant class — its backbone and its pride — often resisted and defeated town planners, ever since Parliament turned down Sir Christopher Wren's splendid plan to rebuild after the fire of 1666. It was royalty and aristocracy that created and preserved the parks — St. James's Park, Hyde Park, Kensington Gardens, Regent's Park, and Kew Gardens were all royal parks — and their enthusiasm became contagious. The passionate regard of Londoners for their green spots has been one of the city's saving graces as it grew so helplessly and recklessly, more in the spirit of commerce than of urban planning.

Today's London — though marred by soulless high-rise intruders of glass and concrete — boasts more greenery than any metropolis could reasonably hope to retain in these philistine times. Aside from its many garden squares and the meticulously tended plots of so many Londoners' homes, the city is punctuated by a series of large parks and commons; besides those already mentioned, there are Wimbledon Common, Richmond Deer Park, Primrose Hill, Hampstead Heath — the list goes on and on. And to make even more certain that citification does not intrude too far into London life, a green belt, almost 100 square miles of forest and grassland, virtually encircles the city and, to the chagrin and impatience of developers, is meticulously preserved by law.

London's other natural resource, the River Thames, has not been so fortunate. As any glance at a map will show, London follows the serpentine meanderings of the Thames, England's principal river. Nearly everything of interest in London is on or near the Thames, for London is London because it is a natural port. The river has always been London's mainstay, for centuries its only east-west road, and it has justifiably been said that "every drop of the Thames is liquid history." At the site of the Naval College in Greenwich, for example, there once stood a royal palace where Henry VIII and

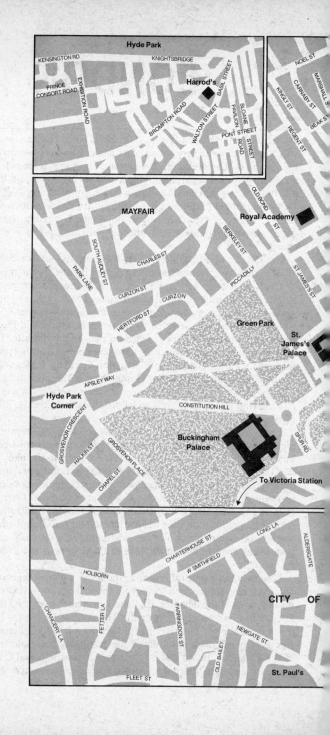

Elizabeth I were born, and where tournaments, pageants, and banquets were held.

A great river port and a city of gardens, London is also a city of stately squares and monuments, of royalty with its pomp and ceremony, a cosmopolitan city of the first rank. Until World War II, it was the capital of the mammoth and far-flung British Empire upon which, it was said, the sun never set. For many centuries, a powerful Britannia ruled a considerable section of the globe — the largest since Roman times — and the English language spread from the inconsiderable British Isles to become the dominant language all over the world, from North America to India.

If the British Empire has contracted drastically, it has done so gracefully, among memories of its greatest days. And if once-subject peoples hated their oppressor, they still love London, and many have chosen to live there. London is still the center of the Commonwealth of independent nations that were once British colonies, and its cosmopolitan atmosphere owes a great deal to the ubiquity of former colonials. Their presence is felt in the substantial Indian-Pakistani community in the Southall district of West London; in the strong Caribbean flavor in Brixton; in Chinatown in and around Gerrard Street — a hop, skip, and a jump from Piccadilly Circus; in the Cypriot groceries and bakeries of Camden Town; and in the majestic mosque on the fringe of Regent's Park.

A tantalizing diversity of accents flavors the English language here — accents from Australia and Barbados, Bangladesh and Nigeria, Canada and Malaysia, Kenya and South Africa, Sri Lanka and Ireland, Hong Kong and the US. And then the various inflections of Britain itself are also to be heard in the streets of London — the lilt and rasp of cockney, Oxford, Somerset, Yorkshire, the Scottish Highlands, and the Welsh mining towns.

London's somewhat onomatopoeic name derives from the Celtic term *Llyn-din*, meaning "river place," but little is known of London before it was renamed *Londinium* by the Romans in AD 43. The rather fantastical 12th-century historian Geoffrey of Monmouth may have originated the myth widespread in Shakespeare's day — that London was founded by Brute, a direct descendant of Aeneas in 1108 BC, who named it Troynovant, New Troy, or Trenovant. Even in medieval times, London had grandiose notions of its own importance — a prideful self-image that has been amply justified by history. Nevertheless, yet another chunk of Roman London has recently been uncovered by archaeologists from the *British Museum*. While excavating the foundation of the 15th-century Guildhall chapel, they found Roman works more than 1 meter wide that have been identified as Roman London's missing amphitheater. The site should be open to visitors early in 1990 (phone: 660-3699).

The city was sufficiently prominent for the Norman invader William the Conqueror to make it his capital in 1066. During the Middle Ages, the expansion of trade, population growth, and the energetic activities of its guilds of merchants and craftsmen promoted London's prosperity. Indisputably, London's golden age was the English Renaissance, the 16th century, the time of Queen Elizabeth I, Shakespeare, and Drake's defeat of the Spanish Armada. Most of the Tudor buildings of London were wiped out in the great fire of 1666. Christopher Wren, the architect of genius, undertook to rebuild many buildings and churches, the most outstanding of which is St. Paul's Cathedral. The 18th century, a highly sophisticated age, saw the building of noble homes and stately squares, many of them part of a grand expansion program developed by the prince regent's chief architect, John Nash. One of the best examples of his work is the terrace of largely crown-owned Regency houses surrounding Regent's Park. In the early 19th century, interest continued in homes and squares; and only in the Victorian age, the height of the Empire, were public buildings like the Houses of Parliament redesigned, this time in grand and fanciful neo-Gothic style.

London has seen whole catalogues of heroes and villains, crises and conflagrations, come and go, sometimes swallowed whole in the passage of time, sometimes leaving relics. Still on elegant display is stately Hampton Court Palace, the most magnificent of England's palaces, where Henry VIII lived now and again with five of his six wives. There is a spot downtown — in front of the Banqueting House on Whitehall — where another king, Charles I, was beheaded by his subjects, who were calmly committing dreaded regicide 150 years before the presumably more emotional and explosive French across the English Channel even contemplated such a gesture.

London has lived through the unbounded permissiveness of the flamboyantly royal Restoration period (1660-85), when even King Charles II frequented brothels and didn't care who knew it, and it has survived the stern moral puritanism of the Victorian era, when it was downright rude to refer to the *breast* of chicken or a piano *leg*. And most recently, London stood up with exemplary courage under the devastating effects of the Nazi bombings, which destroyed a great many buildings and killed thousands of people.

Many of our images of London, taken from old movies, actually mirror its realities: Big Ben rises above the Houses of Parliament, somberly striking the hour; ramrod-straight scarlet-uniformed soldiers half hide their faces in towering black bearskin hats; waiters at the Bank of England still sport the kinds of top hats and tailcoats their predecessors wore for a century; lawyers in court still don wigs and black robes. A few images, however, are outdated: The bowler hat has been slipping steadily out of fashion for years, and rigidly enforced environmental regulations have made London's once-famous pea soup fog a thing of the past.

London's nearly infinite variety of urban moods includes the sturdy edifices lining Whitehall, center of the British government, with Trafalgar Square at its head and Parliament at its foot; the elegant shopping areas of Knightsbridge, Bond Street, Kensington, and the Burlington Arcade; suburban chic in Barnes and Blackheath; handsome squares in Bloomsbury; melancholy mystery in Victoria and Waterloo train stations with their spy-movie atmosphere; the vitality of East End street markets; and the riparian tranquillity of Thames-side towpaths in Putney and along Hammersmith Mall.

The British have a talent that amounts to a genius for government — for democracy and political tolerance — a talent that has been developing ever since the Magna Carta was signed in 1215 and one that makes London's ambience easy and relaxed for individualists of all sorts. It is no wonder that the eccentric and inveterate Londoner of the city's 18th-century heyday, Dr.

Samuel Johnson, once declared, "When a man is tired of London, he is tired of life, for there is in London all that life can afford."

Johnson's opinion, though somewhat overblown, was essentially shared by one of several modern American writers who chose to live in London. Disillusioned with New York, Boston, and Paris, Henry James decided in favor of London in 1881. Somehow he concluded that London was a place eminently suited to human life: "It is not a pleasant place; it is not agreeable, or cheerful, or easy, or exempt from reproach. It is only magnificent. You can draw up a tremendous list of reasons why it should be unsupportable. The fogs, the smoke, the dirt, the darkness, the wet, the distances, the ugliness, the brutal size of the place, the horrible numerosity of society . . . but . . . London is on the whole the most possible form of life."

LONDON AT-A-GLANCE

SEEING THE CITY: London has, for the most part, resisted the temptation to build high. Aside from a handful of modest gestures toward skyscraping, there aren't many towering structures to obscure panoramic overviews of the city from its higher vantage points, which include:

London Hilton International – There were discreet noises of disapproval from Buckingham Palace when it was realized that the view from the roof bar of the *Hilton* included not only the palace grounds but, with high-powered binoculars, the inside of some of the royal chambers as well. In fact, the view over Mayfair, Hyde Park, and Westminster is breathtaking. Park La. (phone: 493-8000).

Westminster Cathedral – Not to be confused with Westminster Abbey. The top of the bell tower of London's Roman Catholic cathedral looks down on a broad expanse of the inner city. An elevator takes visitors up for a token charge (from April to September). Off Victoria St. near the station, at Ashley Pl., SW1.

Hampstead Heath – Climb to the top of Parliament Hill, on the southern rim of this "wilderness" in north London. On a clear day, the view south from the Heath makes the city look like a vast village.

South Bank Arts Center – On the south bank of Waterloo Bridge is the bunker-like complex of cultural buildings, including the Royal Festival Hall, the *National Theatre,* the *National Film Theatre,* the *Hayward Gallery,* and other cultural attractions. For a view of London, look across the Thames — upriver to the Houses of Parliament, downriver to St. Paul's Cathedral.

Tower Bridge Walkway – The upper part of one of London's famous landmarks is open to visitors. In addition to the viewing gallery, there is an exhibition on the history of London's bridges and a museum that includes the bridge's Victorian steam pumping engines. Open November through March, 10 AM to 4:45 PM; April through October, 10 AM to 6:30 PM. Admission charge. Tower Hill Underground Station.

St. Paul's Cathedral – The reward for climbing the 600 steps into the dome of this cathedral — the largest in the world after St. Peter's in Rome — is a panoramic view of London.

Docklands – This development is so huge, it includes its own railroad, plus apartment, commercial, and office buildings seemingly without end. As we went to press, the landscape still contained a forest of construction cranes, but even now it's a wonderful place to explore. The Docklands Light Railway, a high-tech, overhead train, runs from Tower Hill to Greenwich, speeding over the fast-changing and fascinating terrain. If food shopping is on your agenda, visiting the Docklands will put to rest forever the image of British homemakers buying the family's food in tiny neighborhood greengrocers and small butcher shops. There's a market here called the *Super Store*, a British interpretation of a California supermarket, and the *Billingsgate Market*, originally on Lower Thames St., has moved here. It's where some of London's premier chefs pick out their produce and fresh fish early in the morning, and it's the best place to pick up a side of smoked Scottish salmon to cart home.

SPECIAL PLACES/ATTRACTIONS: Surveying London from the steps of St. Paul's Cathedral at the turn of the 19th century, a visiting Prussian general commented to his English host: "What a place to plunder!" Even those who are less rapacious will appreciate the extraordinary wealth of sights London displays for visitors to inspect. Though some are dispersed in various corners of this vast city, most are clustered reasonably close together in or near the inner districts of Westminster, the City, and Kensington. Twenty Photospot locations — places to stand to get the best photographs of famous sights — have been indicated throughout Westminster with blue and white signs fixed to lampposts.

WESTMINSTER

Changing of the Guard – An American who lived in London once said, "There's just no better way to convince yourself that you're in London!" This famous ceremony takes place daily from April to mid-August (alternate days in winter) promptly at 11:30 AM in the Buckingham Palace forecourt, at 11:15 AM at St. James's Palace, and at 11:30 AM at the Tower of London. (In very wet weather, it may be canceled.)

Horse Guards – If you haven't had enough, you can see a new guard of 12 members of the Household Cavalry troop in with trumpet and standard, daily at 11 AM, 10 on Sundays, on the west side of Whitehall. Incidentally, they come from stables not far from Hyde Park and make a daily parade along the south roadway of Hyde Park, past Buckingham Palace, and then on to Trafalgar Square to turn into Whitehall. Their progress is as much fun to watch as the actual ceremony.

Buckingham Palace – The royal standard flies from the roof when the monarch is in residence at her London home. Although George III bought the palace in 1762, sovereigns officially still live in St. James's Palace around the corner in Pall Mall; Buckingham Palace did not become the actual principal regal dwelling until 1837, when Queen Victoria moved in. The palace, unfortunately, is open only to invited guests (the *Queen's Gallery* and Royal Mews are open to the public; see below). The queen's summer garden parties are held on the palace lawns. The interior contains magnificently decorated apartments, a superb picture gallery, and a throne room (66 feet long), where foreign ambassadors are received and knights are knighted. The palace grounds contain the largest private garden in London (40 acres). And the gate that originally was built for the entrance, too narrow for the coaches of George IV, now marks the Hyde Park end of Oxford Street and is known as Marble Arch. Buckingham Palace Rd.

State Visits – If you aren't going to be in London for the queen's official birthday in June, you might want to see her greet a foreign dignitary in full regalia. This happens quite frequently and is announced in the royal calendar in *The Times*. The queen meets her guest at Victoria Station, and they ride to Buckingham Palace in a procession of horse-drawn coaches, followed by the colorful Horse Guards. Meanwhile, at Hyde Park Corner, the cannoneers on horseback perform elaborate maneuvers before their salute thunders through the whole city.

Queen's Gallery – Treasures from the royal art collection are on display in this room of the palace only. Exhibitions change about once a year. Open Tuesdays through Saturdays from 10:30 AM to 5 PM, Sundays from 2 to 5 PM. Admission charge. Buckingham Palace Rd., SW1.

Royal Academy – In a building that resembles a cross between a mausoleum, a railroad station, and a funeral parlor are the works of *the* established, leading, fashionable painters of the past. It's also where some of the major exhibitions to visit London are mounted. Admission charge. Burlington House, Piccadilly, W1 (phone: 439-7438).

Royal Mews – The mews is a palace alley where the magnificent bridal coach, other state coaches, and the horses that draw them are stabled. The public is admitted on Wednesdays and Thursdays from 2 to 4 PM. Admission charge. Buckingham Palace Rd. SW1.

St. James's Park – Parks are everywhere in London and Londoners love them. This is one of the nicest, where at lunch hour on a sunny day you can see the impeccably dressed London businessmen lounging on the grass, their shoes and shirts off. With its sizable lake (designed by John Nash) inhabited by pelicans and other wild fowl, St. James's was originally a royal deer park, drained under Henry VIII in 1532 and laid out as a pleasure ground for Charles II.

The Mall – The wide avenue parallel to Pall Mall and lined with lime trees and Regency buildings leads from Trafalgar Square to Buckingham Palace. This is the principal ceremonial route used by Queen Elizabeth and her escort of Household Cavalry for the State Opening of Parliament (October/November) and the *Trooping the Colour* (see *Special Events*). It is closed to traffic on Sunday afternoons.

Trafalgar Square – One of London's most heavily trafficked squares is built around the towering Nelson's Column — a 145-foot monument that honors Lord Nelson, victor at the naval Battle of Trafalgar in 1805. At the base of the monument are four huge bronze lions and two fountains. Flanked by handsome buildings, including the *National Gallery* and the 18th-century church of St. Martin in the Fields, the square is a favorite gathering place for political demonstrations, tourists, and pigeons.

Piccadilly Circus – Downtown London finds its center here in the heart of the theater district and on the edge of Soho. This is the London equivalent of Times Square — lots of it is just as tacky — and at the center of the busy "circus," or traffic circle, is the restored statue of Eros (moved about 40 feet from its original perch), which actually was designed in 1893 as *The Angel of Christian Charity,* a memorial to the charitable Earl of Shaftesbury — the archer and his bow were meant as a pun on his name. The Trocadero, a recently converted 3-story shopping and entertainment complex featuring the *International Village Restaurant,* has lent Piccadilly a new level of bustle. Popular exhibitions include the *Guinness World Records* display and the London Experience, for a look at the city's history. Separate admission charges.

National Gallery – One of the world's great art museums, this is an inexhaustible feast for art lovers. In the vast collection on display are works by such masters as Uccello, Leonardo da Vinci, Titian, Rembrandt, Rubens, Cranach, Gainsborough, El Greco, Renoir, Cézanne, and Van Gogh. Open daily, 10 AM to 6 PM; Sundays, 2 to 6 PM. Trafalgar Sq., WC2 (phone: 839-3321).

National Portrait Gallery – Right behind the *National Gallery* sits this delightful museum. Nearly every English celebrity from the last 500 years is pictured here, with the earliest personalities at the top and the 20th-century notables at the bottom. Open: weekdays, 10 AM to 5 PM; Saturdays, 10 AM to 6 PM; Sundays, 2 to 6 PM. 2 St. Martin's Pl., WC2 (phone: 930-1552).

Whitehall – A broad boulevard stretching from Trafalgar Square to Parliament Square, lined most of the way by government ministries and such historic buildings as the Banqueting House (completed in 1622, with a ceiling painted by Rubens) and the Horse Guards (whose central archway is ceremonially guarded by mounted troopers).

Detective novel fans may be interested to know that from 1890 to 1967, Scotland Yard occupied the Norman Shaw Building at the Trafalgar end of Whitehall; it now houses offices for members of Parliament. The Yard has moved to Victoria Street near St. James's Park.

Downing Street – Off Whitehall, a street of small, unpretentious Georgian houses includes the official residences of the most important figures in the British government, the Prime Minister at #10 and the Chancellor of the Exchequer (Britain's secretary of the treasury) at #11.

Cabinet War Rooms – Constructed to resemble its wartime appearance, this underground complex of 20 rooms was Winston Churchill's auxiliary command post during World War II, which he used most often during the German Luftwaffe's blitz on London. Of special note are the map room, with maps pinpointing the positions of Allied and German troops in the final stages of the war, and the cabinet room, where the prime minister met with his staff. Open daily. Admission charge. Beneath the government building on Great George St., SW1 (phone: 930-6961).

Westminster Abbey – It's easy to get lost among the endlessly fascinating tombs and plaques and not even notice the Abbey's splendid architecture, so do look at the structure itself and don't miss the cloisters, which display its Gothic design to advantage. Note also the fine Tudor chapel of Henry VII, with its tall windows and lovely fan-tracery vaulting, and the 13th-century chapel of St. Edward the Confessor, containing England's Coronation Chair and Scotland's ancient coronation Stone of Scone.

Ever since William the Conqueror was crowned here in 1066, the Abbey has been the traditional place where English monarchs are crowned, married, and buried. You don't have to be an Anglophile to be moved by the numerous tombs and memorials with their fascinating inscriptions — here are honored (not necessarily buried) kings and queens, soldiers, statesmen, and many other prominent English men and women. Poets' Corner, in the south transept, contains the tombs of Chaucer, Ben Jonson, Tennyson, Browning, and many others — plus memorials to nearly every English poet of note, and to some Americans such as Longfellow and T. S. Eliot.

The Abbey is itself a lesson in English history. A church has stood on this site since at least AD 170; in the 8th century, it was a Benedictine monastery. The current early–English Gothic edifice, begun in the 13th century, took almost 300 years to build.

Guided tours are offered six times a day except Sundays. Admission charge to the royal chapels and Poet's Corner. Broad Sanctuary, SW1, between Victoria and Millbank (phone: 222-5152).

Houses of Parliament – The imposing neo-Gothic, mid-19th-century buildings of the Palace of Westminster, as it is sometimes called, look especially splendid from the opposite side of the river. There are separate chambers for the House of Commons and the House of Lords, and visitors are admitted to the Strangers' Galleries of both houses by lining up at St. Stephen's Entrance, opposite Westminster Abbey. Big Ben, the world-famous 13½-ton bell in the clock tower of the palace, which is illuminated when Parliament is in session, still strikes the hours. The buildings themselves are closed to the public, although Westminster Hall, with its magnificent hammer-beam roof, can be seen by special arrangement with a member of Parliament. The gold and scarlet House of Lords is also well worth seeing. St. Margaret St., SW1 (phone: 219-3000).

Tate Gallery – London's fine art museum includes an impressive collection of British paintings from the 16th century to the dawn of the 20th century, as well as modern British and international art. Best of all are masterpieces by Turner, Constable, Hogarth, and Blake. The Turner collection is housed in the ultra-modern Clore Gallery extension. Millbank, SW1 (phone: 821-1313).

Soho – This area of London is full of character; lively, bustling, and noisy by day; indiscreetly enticing by night. Its name comes from the ancient hunting cry used centuries ago when the area was parkland. The hunting, in a way, still goes on, particularly by undercover detectives. Soho lacks the sophistication and glamor of its counterparts in Europe but it's not all sleazy, either. The striptease clubs vie for customers with the numerous restaurants serving moderately priced food (mostly Italian and Chinese). Soho offers a diversity of entertainments: Shaftesbury Avenue is lined with theaters and movie houses. Gerrard Street abounds with Chinese restaurants, and it is the place to go for Chinese New Year celebrations. London's liveliest fruit and vegetable market is on Berwick Street (if you shop here, never touch the produce, as the vendors will get furious). Frith Street is a favorite Italian haunt, the best place for a foaming cappuccino and a view of Italian TV at the *Bar Italia.* Old Compton Street has several good delicatessens, perfect places to buy a picnic lunch to take to Soho Square.

Covent Garden – Tucked away behind The Strand, Covent Garden was the site of London's main fruit, vegetable, and flower market for over 300 years. The area was immortalized in Shaw's *Pygmalion* and the musical *My Fair Lady* by the scene in which young Eliza Doolittle sells flowers to the ladies and gents emerging from the *Royal Opera House.* The *Opera House* is still there, but the market moved south of the river in 1974 and the Garden has since undergone extensive redevelopment. The central market building has been converted into London's first permanent late-night shopping center with emphasis on all-British goods. In the former flower market is the *London Transport Museum,* whose exhibitions include a replica of the first horse-drawn bus and a steam locomotive built in 1866. Boutiques selling quality clothes for men and women are springing up all over, along with discos, wine bars, and brasserie-style restaurants. On weekends the whole area is packed with young people. One nice touch: Just to remind everyone of the Old Covent Garden, there are about 40 of the original wrought-iron trading stands from which the home-produced wares of English craftsmen and women are sold.

Bloomsbury – Well-designed squares — Bloomsbury Square, Bedford Square, Russell Square, and others — surrounded by pretty, terraced houses form this aristocratic district. Within its confines are the *British Museum* and the Centre of the University of London. The Bloomsbury group of writers and artists included Virginia Woolf, her husband Leonard Woolf, her sister Vanessa Bell and her husband Clive Bell, Lytton Strachey, E. M. Forster, Roger Fry, and John Maynard Keynes. Living nearby and peripheral to this central group were D. H. Lawrence, Bertrand Russell, and others. Unfortunately, none of the original buildings in Bloomsbury Square has survived, but the garden is still there, and nearby Bedford Square remains complete. Virginia Woolf lived at 46 Gordon Square before her marriage.

British Museum – One of the world's largest museums offers a dazzling array of permanent exhibitions — including the legendary Elgin Marbles (from the Parthenon) and the Rosetta Stone. In 1985 seven new sculpture galleries were opened, exhibiting some 1,500 Greek and Roman treasures. This magnificent collection includes two of the seven wonders of the ancient world: the Mausoleum of Halicarnassus and the Temple of Artemus at Ephesus. There is an equally impressive parade of temporary displays. The Egyptian and Mesopotamian galleries are especially stunning. The manuscript room of the British Library, within the museum, displays the original Magna Carta, together with the signatures of a great many famous authors — Shakespeare, Dickens, Austen, and Joyce among them — and numerous original manuscripts, including *Alice in Wonderland.* The British Library has an enormous collection, since every book published in Britain must be sent there. If you wish to use the library, consult a copy of its catalogue, stocked by major world libraries. Send in your requests with call numbers; many books often take 2 days to arrive from storage or other branches. The library also has a remarkable, gigantic Reading Room where many of the world's great books — Marx's *Das Kapital,* for example — were written (access is limited; you must call or write to the museum's British Library Reference Division for permission). Open Mondays through Saturdays, 10 AM to 5 PM; Sundays, 2:30 to 6 PM. Great Russell St. WC1 (phone: museum, 636-1555; library, 636-1544).

Oxford, Regent, Bond and Kensington High Streets – London's main shopping streets include large department and specialty stores (*Selfridges, Debenhams, John*

Lewis, Liberty, D. H. Evans), chain stores offering good value in clothes (*Marks & Spencer, C & A, British Home Stores, Littlewoods*), and scores of popular clothing chains (the *Gap, Laura Ashley, Benetton, Principles*).

Burlington Arcade – A charming covered shopping promenade dating from the Regency period (early 19th century), the arcade contains elegant, expensive shops selling cashmere sweaters (we recently saw some here that were 10-ply!), antique jewelry, and other expensive items. One entrance is on Piccadilly (the street, not the circus), the other near Old Bond St., W1.

Hyde Park – London's most famous patch of greenery (361 acres) is particularly well known for its Speakers' Corner at Marble Arch, where crowds gather on Sunday afternoons to hear impromptu diatribes and debates. Among the park's other attractions are sculptures by Henry Moore; an extensive bridle path; a cycle path; the Serpentine lake, where boats for rowing and sailing can be rented and where there's swimming in the summer; a bird sanctuary; and vast expanses of lawn.

Madame Tussaud's – The popularity of this wax museum (recently voted Britain's favorite indoor attraction) is undiminished by the persistent criticism that its effigies are a little bland, and visitors are quite likely to find themselves innocently addressing a waxwork attendant — or murderer. Madame moved to London from Paris in 1802, when she was 74, crossing the Channel with her waxwork effigies of heads that had rolled during the French Revolution. The current museum includes many modern and historical personalities and the gory Chamber of Horrors, with its murderers and hangmen. Open daily, 10 AM to 5:30 PM; in July and August, 10 AM to 6 PM. Admission charge. Marylebone Rd., NW1 (phone: 935-6861).

London Planetarium – During 30-minute shows, visitors travel through space and time under a huge starlit dome. Interesting commentary accompanies the show. Guests can save money by purchasing a combination ticket to the planetarium and *Madame Tussaud's* — both at the same address, Marylebone Rd., NW1. There is also a Laserium show at 6 PM. Closed Mondays (phone: 486-1121).

THE CITY

The difference between London and the City of London can be confusing to a visitor. They are, in fact, two distinctly different entities, one within the other. The City of London, usually called only the City, covers the original Roman London. It is now the "square mile" financial and commercial center of the great metropolis. With a Lord Mayor (who only serves in a ceremonial capacity), a police force, and rapidly growing new developments, it is the core of Greater London. The governing council, the London Residuary Body, administers 32 boroughs including the City.

St. Paul's Cathedral – The cathedral church of the London Anglican diocese stands atop Ludgate Hill and is the largest church in London. This Renaissance masterpiece by Sir Christopher Wren took 35 years to build (1675-1710). Its domed exterior is majestic and its sparse decorations are gold and mosaic. The interior contains particularly splendid choir stalls, screens, and, inside the spectacular dome, the "whispering gallery," with its strange acoustics. Nelson and Wellington are buried below the main floor, and there is a fine statue of John Donne, metaphysical poet and dean of St. Paul's from 1621 to 1631 — he stands looking quite alive on an urn in an up-ended coffin which, typically, he bought during his lifetime and kept in his house. Wren himself was buried here in 1723, with his epitaph inscribed beneath the dome in Latin: "If you seek his monument, look around you."

A gorgeous monument it remains; though damaged by bombs during World War II, it became a rallying point for the flagging spirits of wartime Londoners. More recently, St. Paul's raised British spirits as the site for the wedding of Prince Charles and Lady Diana Spencer in July 1981. The Golden Gallery at the top of the dome, 542 steps from the ground, offers an excellent view of the city. St. Paul's Churchyard, EC4.

Old Bailey – This is the colloquial name for London's Central Criminal Court, on the site of the notorious Newgate Prison. Visitors are admitted to the court, on a space-available basis, to audit the proceedings and to see lawyers and judges clad in wigs and robes. Old Bailey, EC4 (phone: 248-3277).

Museum of London – Exhibits and displays depict London history from the Roman occupation to modern times. Opened in 1976, this museum in the Barbican area includes Roman remains, Anglo-Saxon artifacts, Renaissance musical instruments, a cell from old Newgate prison, Victorian shops and offices, an audio-visual re-creation of the 1666 Great Fire, and the Lord Mayor's golden stagecoach. Closed Mondays. Open Tuesdays through Saturdays, 10 AM to 6 PM; Sundays, 2 to 6 PM. 150 London Wall, EC2 (phone: 600-3699).

Barbican Centre for Arts and Conferences – Served by underground stations Barbican, St. Paul's, and Moorgate, the Barbican, which opened in 1982, includes 6,000 apartments, the Guildhall School of Music and Drama, and the restored St. Giles's Church (1390). The *Barbican* also features the 2,026-seat *Barbican Hall,* which doubles as a conference site (with simultaneous translation system), and *Concert Hall* (*London Symphony Orchestra*); the 1,166-seat *Barbican Theatre* (the *Royal Shakespeare Company*'s London stage); a 200-seat studio theater; sculpture courtyard; art exhibition galleries; seminar rooms; 3 cinemas; 2 exhibition halls; a municipal lending library; and restaurants and bars. Silk St. EC2 (phone: for guided tours and general information, 638-4141; recorded information, 628-2295; credit card bookings, 638-8891 or 628-8795; *Royal Shakespeare Company* performances, 628-3351.

Bank of England – Banker to the British government, holder of the country's gold reserves in its vaults, controller of Britain's banking and monetary affairs, "the Old Lady of Threadneedle Street" is the most famous bank in the world. Bathed in tradition as well as the mechanics of modern high finance, its porters and messengers wear traditional livery. Visits by appointment only. Threadneedle St., EC2 (phone: 601-4444).

Mansion House – The official residence of the Lord Mayor of London, containing his private apartments, built in the 18th century in Renaissance style. Permission to view the house may be obtained by writing, well in advance of your visit, to the Public Relations Office, City of London, Guildhall, London EC2P 2EJ. Mansion House St., EC4 (phone: 626-2500).

Lloyd's – A new, strikingly dramatic, futuristic building now houses the world's most important seller of international maritime and high-risk insurance. The exhibition and gallery overlooking the trading floor is open to visitors (advance booking required for groups) on weekdays from 10 AM to 4 PM. Corner of Lime and Leadenhall Sts. (phone: 623-7100, ext. 3733).

Stock Exchange – The second largest exchange in the world can be seen from the viewing gallery on weekdays from 9:45 AM to 3:15 PM. Old Broad St., EC2 (phone: 588-2355).

The Monument – A fluted Doric column, topped by a flaming urn, was designed by Sir Christopher Wren to commemorate the Great Fire of London (1666) and stands 202 feet tall. (It was allegedly 202 feet from the bakery on Pudding Lane where the fire began.) The view from the top is partially obstructed by new buildings. Closed Sundays in winter. Admission charge. Monument St., EC3 (phone: 626-2717).

Tower of London – Originally conceived as a fortress to keep "fierce" Londoners at bay and to guard the river approaches, it has served as a palace, a prison, a mint, and an observatory as well. Today the main points of interest are the Crown Jewels; the White Tower (the oldest building), with its exhibition of ancient arms, armor, and torture implements; St. John's Chapel, the oldest church in London; the Bloody Tower, where the two little princes disappeared in 1483 and Sir Walter Raleigh languished from 1603 to 1615; an exhibition of old military weapons; Tower Green, where two of Henry VIII's queens — and many others — were beheaded; and Traitors' Gate, through which boats bearing prisoners entered the castle. The yeoman warders ("Beefeaters") still wear historic uniforms. They also give excellent recitals of that segment of English history that was played out within the tower walls. You can see the wonderful Ceremony of the Keys here every night at 9:30 PM; reserve tickets several months ahead. Closed Sundays in winter. Admission charge. Send a stamped, self-addressed envelope to Resident Governor Constable's Office, HM Tower of London, EC3N 4AB (phone: 709-0765).

Fleet Street – Most native and foreign newspapers and press associations once had offices here — in the center of London's active newspaper world — and some still do, despite the growing exodus to more technologically advanced plants elsewhere. The street also boasts two 17th-century pubs, the *Cock Tavern* (#22) and the *Cheshire Cheese* (just off Fleet St. at 5 Little Essex St.), where Dr. Samuel Johnson held court for the literary giants of his day.

Johnson's House – Johnson lived in nearby Gough Square, where he wrote his famous *Dictionary;* the house is now a museum of Johnsoniana. Admission charge. 17 Gough Sq., EC4 (phone: 353-3745).

Inns of Court – Quaint and quiet precincts house the ancient buildings, grounds, and gardens that mark the traditional center of Britain's legal profession. Only the four Inns of Court — Gray's, Lincoln's, and the Inner and Middle Temple — have the right to call would-be barristers to the bar to practice law. Especially charming is the still-Dickensian Lincoln's Inn, where young Dickens worked as an office boy. In its great hall the writer later set his fictional case of Jarndyce v. Jarndyce in *Bleak House.* John Donne once preached in the Lincoln's Inn chapel, designed by Inigo Jones. Both hall and chapel can be seen on weekdays if you apply at the Gatehouse in Chancery Lane WC2 (phone: 405-1393). Also lovely are the gardens of Lincoln's Inn Fields, laid out in 1618 by Inigo Jones. The neo-Gothic Royal Courts of Justice in the Strand, better known as the Law Courts, are home to the High Court and the Court of Appeal of England and Wales, which pass judgment on Britain's most important civil cases. The courts, unlike the Old Bailey, are closed to the public, but the vaulted, cathedral-like great hall is open to all.

OTHER LONDON ATTRACTIONS

Regent's Park – The sprawling 472-acre park just north of the city center has beautiful gardens, vast lawns, a pond with paddleboats, and one of the finest zoos in the world. Crescents of elegant terraced homes border the park. Admission charge.

Camden Passage – This quaint pedestrian alleyway lined with antiques and specialty shops has an open-air market — pushcarts selling curios and antiques — on Tuesdays, Wednesday mornings, and Saturdays. Just off Upper St. in Islington, north of the city, N1.

Hampstead Heath – The North London bucolic paradise of wild heathland, meadows, and wooded dells is the highest point in London. Kenwood House, an 18th-century estate on the heath, is home to the Iveagh Bequest, a collection of art (Gainsborough, Rembrandt, Turner, and others) assembled by the first Earl of Iveagh. Lakeside concerts, both classical and jazz, are held on the grounds in summer (for details, call 734-1877).

Kew Gardens – Here are the Royal Botanic Gardens, with tens of thousands of trees and other plants (though the freak hurricane of October 1987 severely damaged hundreds of prize specimens and several sections of the gardens are still closed to the public). The gardens' primary purpose is to serve the science of botany by researching, cultivating, experimenting, and identifying plants. There are shaded walks, floral displays, and magnificent Victorian glass greenhouses — especially the Temperate House, with some 3,000 different plants, including a 60-foot Chilean wine palm. Open daily. Admission charge.

Portobello Road – This area is famous for its antiques shops, junk shops, and outdoor pushcarts; it is one of the largest street markets in the world. The pushcarts are out only on Fridays and Saturdays, which are the best and most crowded days for the market. Less well known is Bermondsey Market, Long Lane at Tower Bridge Rd., SE1, on Fridays from 7 AM on; this is where the antiques on Portobello Road or Camden Passage were probably purchased.

Victoria and Albert Museum – Born of the 1851 Exhibition, the museum contains a vast collection of fine and applied arts (probably the largest collection of the latter in the world) — an amalgam of the great, the odd, and the ugly. Especially delightful are the English period rooms. There are superb collections of paintings, prints, ceramics, metalwork, costumes, and armor in the museum, which also contains English miniatures and famous Raphael cartoons. The museum's new Henry Cole Wing (named after its founder) houses a broad selection of changing exhibitions as well as an interesting permanent display of printmaking techniques. Jazz concerts and fashion shows are held in the Italianate Pirelli Garden at the heart of the museum. Closed Fridays. Entry donation suggested. Cromwell Rd., SW7 (phone: 589-6371).

Greenwich – This Thames-side borough is traditionally associated with British seapower, especially when Britain "ruled the waves"; it includes such notable sights as the *National Maritime Museum* on Romney Rd. (phone: 858-4422), containing superb exhibits on Britain's illustrious nautical past; the Old Royal Observatory, with astronomical instruments; *Cutty Sark,* a superbly preserved 19th-century clipper ship that's open to visitors; Royal Naval College, with beautiful painted hall and chapel; and Greenwich Park, 200 acres of greenery sloping down toward the river.

Richmond Park – The largest urban park in Britain is one of the few with herds of deer roaming free. (Hunting them is illegal, though this was once a royal hunting preserve established by Charles I.) It also has large oaks and rhododendron gardens. From nearby Richmond Hill there is a magnificent view of the Thames Valley.

Manor Houses – Six beautifully maintained historic homes are in Greater London. Notable for their architecture, antiques, grounds, and, in the case of Kenwood, an 18th-century art collection, these homes are all accessible by bus and subway: Kenwood House (Hampstead tube stop; open daily), Ham House (Richmond tube stop; closed Mondays; admission charge), Chiswick (Turnham Green or Chiswick Park tube stop; open daily; admission charge), Syon House (Gunnersbury tube stop; open daily; admission charge). Osterley Park House (Osterley tube stop; closed Mondays; admission charge), and Apsley House, home of the Duke of Wellington (149 Piccadilly; open Tuesdays through Sundays from 11 AM to 5 PM; admission charge).

Hampton Court – On the Thames, this sumptuous palace and gardens are in London's southwest corner. Begun by Cardinal Wolsey in 1515, the palace was appropriated by Henry VIII and was a royal residence for 2 centuries. Its attractions include a picture gallery, tapestries, state apartments, Tudor kitchens, the original tennis court, a moat, a great vine (2 centuries old), gardens, and a maze. You can get there by bus, by train, or, best of all, in summer take the boat from Westminster Pier. Open daily. Admission charge. Hampton, Middlesex (phone: 977-8441).

Freud Museum – This house was the North London home of the seminal psychiatrist after he left Vienna in 1938. His antiquities collection, library, desk, and famous couch are all on display. Open 10 AM to 5 PM daily, 1 to 5 PM Sundays. 20 Maresfield Gardens, NW3.

Highgate Cemetery – The awe-inspiring grave of Karl Marx in the new cemetery (open until 3:45 PM in winter, dusk in summer) attracts countless visitors, who can then stroll past the overgrown gravestones and catacombs of the not-so-famous in the old cemetery across the road (open until 3 PM in winter, dusk in summer). Entrance to the latter is by guided tour only (hourly). No admission charge. Highgate Hill, NW3.

Thames Flood Barrier – A massive and intriguing defense structure across the river at Woolwich Reach near Greenwich. Boats regularly leave Barrier Gardens Pier (or the riverside promenade nearby) for visits up close. The public is not allowed on the barrier itself, but audio-visual displays at the Visitor Centre, on the river's south bank just downstream, explain its background and illustrate the risk to London of exceptionally high tides. Open weekdays from 10 AM to 5 PM, weekends to 5:30 PM. Admission charge. Accessible from London by road, by river (from Westminster Pier to Barrier Gardens Pier), and by rail (to Charlton Station). 1 Unity Way, Woolwich (phone: 854-1373). While on the south bank, make a day of it with lunch at *Tides,* near the flood defense system.

■**EXTRA SPECIAL:** Windsor Castle is the largest inhabited castle in the world. The queen's official residence, it was built by William the Conqueror in 1066 after his victory at the Battle of Hastings. Among the sovereigns buried here are Queen Victoria and her consort, Albert. Windsor looks like a fairy tale castle in a child's picturebook: The huge Norman edifice looms majestically above the town; visitors feel awed and enchanted as they climb up the curving cobblestone street from the train station, past pubs and shops, toward Henry VIII's Gateway. The castle precincts are open daily, and there's a regular Changing of the Guard. The State Apartments, which can be toured when they're not in use, are splendidly decorated with paintings, tapestries, furniture, and rugs. There is also an exhibition of drawings by Leonardo da Vinci, Michelangelo, and Raphael, and a room displaying Queen Mary's dollhouse. Separate admission charges. For information, call 075-386-8286.

The castle is bordered by 4,800 acres of parkland on one side and the town on the other. While the town still has a certain charm, heavy tourism is beginning to have a deleterious effect. Across the river is Eton — considered by some to be the more attractive town — which is famous as the home of the exclusive boys' school founded by Henry IV in 1440.

The train from Paddington stops right in the center of Windsor (travel time is 39 minutes); there's also a Green Line coach from Victoria (1½ hours).

Don't miss taking one of the many boat trips along the Thames to places like Marlow, Cookham, or Henley (where the first rowing regatta in the world was held in 1839). The Royal Windsor Safari Park is also southwest of London. Once a royal hunting ground, it's now a drive-through zoo, whose residents include baboons, camels, rhinos, cheetahs, and Bengal tigers. Be warned: In summer the park is very popular and traffic is bumper to bumper. An alternative would be to take the safari bus. Open daily. Admission charge.

For a spectacular side trip out of London, there is nothing quite like Oxford and Stratford-on-Avon, Shakespeare's birthplace — both of which can be seen in a 1-day organized bus tour. Otherwise you can choose one; the regular bus from Victoria Coach Station to Stratford (90 mi/144 km) travels via Oxford (65 mi/105 km), so you can catch a glimpse of the ancient colleges if you try hard.

Shakespeare's birthplace is still an Elizabethan town, and even if there's no time to see a play at the *Shakespeare Memorial Theatre,* the Tudor houses, with their overhung gables and traditional straw roofs, are a very pleasant sight. The poet's birthplace is a must, as is the grave at charming Holy Trinity Church. The Great Garden of New Place, said to contain every flower that Shakespeare mentioned in his plays, and Anne Hathaway's Cottage, are both enjoyable.

Oxford is England's oldest university town; its fine Gothic buildings have cloistered many famous Englishmen. Most of the great colleges are on High Street (the

High) or Broad Street (the Broad). See Queen's College, Christ Church, Trinity College, the Bodleian Library, and the marvelous *Ashmolean Museum of Art;* be sure to look in a bookstore too — and *Blackwell's* on Broad Street is one of the finest in the world. Students usually guide the university tours.

Another highly recommended day trip, less ambitious than Stratford and Oxford, is Cambridge, only 1 hour and 20 minutes from London by train. Cambridge is even more delightful than Oxford because the town takes full advantage of the River Cam. So don't fail to walk along "the Backs" — the back lawns of several colleges, leading down to the river; or better yet, rent a canoe or a punt, a flat-bottomed boat that is propelled by a long pole. (It's easier than it sounds.) The town has two parallel main streets that change their names every 2 blocks; one is a shopping street and the other is lined with colleges. Don't miss *Heffer's* on Trinity Street; it's the biggest branch of the best bookstore in Cambridge. Stroll through the famous colleges — King's, Trinity, Queens, Jesus, Magdalene, and Clare. King's College Chapel is a 15th-century Gothic structure that is a real beauty. Also see at least one garden and one dining hall.

The last of the notable attractions in the area, 5 miles (8 km) to the southwest of London, are the Savill and Valley gardens — 35 acres of flowering shrubs, rare flowers, and woodland. Open daily. Admission charge.

SOURCES AND RESOURCES

TOURIST INFORMATION: In the US, contact the British Tourist Authority, 40 W. 57th St., New York, NY 10019 (phone: 212-581-4700). The London Visitor and Convention Bureau is the best source of information for attractions and events once you get to London. Its Tourist Information Centre on the forecourt of Victoria British Rail Station is open Mondays through Saturdays, 9 AM to 7 PM; Sundays, 9 AM to 5 PM. Many leaflets and brochures on the city's landmarks and events are available; staff people are also on hand to answer questions on what to do, how, and when. Other branches are at the tube station at Heathrow Airport Terminals 1, 2, and 3, *Harrods* and *Selfridges* stores, and the Tower of London (Easter to October only). A Telephone Information Service is offered daily except Sundays, 9 AM to 6 PM (phone: 730-3488).

The British Travel Centre books travel tickets, reserves accommodations and theater tickets, and sells guidebooks. It offers a free information service, including an information hotline covering the whole of Britain. Open 9 AM to 6:30 PM, daily except Sundays. 4 Lower Regent St. (phone: 730-3400).

Among the most comprehensive and useful guidebooks to London are the *Blue Guide to London* (Benn); *London Round the Clock* (CPC Guidebooks); and *Londonwalks* (Holt, Rinehart & Winston). *Naked London* (Queen Anne Press) lists the city's more unusual, less visited sights for dedicated sleuths. The annual *Good Food Guide* ($16.95) and *Egon Ronay's* hotel and restaurant guide ($19.95) are available in most bookstores (prices slightly lower in Great Britain). For detailed information on 200 London museums, including maps, consult the *London Museums and Collections Guide* (CPC Guidebooks; $12). The *Shell Guide to the History of London* (Michael Joseph) bristles with exciting, accurate details on the city. *London: Louise Nicholson's Definitive Guide* (Bodley Head) comes surprisingly close to the claims of the title. Susie Elms's *The London Theatre Scene* (Frank Cook) gives fair coverage of an essential aspect of the city.

London A-Z and *Nicholson's Street Finder,* inexpensive pocket-size books of street maps (available in bookstores and from most "newsagents"), are very useful for finding

London addresses. Also helpful are maps of the subway system and bus routes and the *London Regional Transport Visitors Guide* — all available free from the London Transport information centers at several stations, including Victoria, Piccadilly, Charing Cross, Oxford Circus, and Heathrow Central, and at the ticket booths of many other stations (phone: 222-1234 for information).

The US Embassy is at 24/31 Grosvenor Sq. W. (phone: 499-9000).

Local Coverage – Of London's several newspapers, the *Times* the *Sunday Times,* the *Observer* (Sundays only), the *Guardian,* the *Independent,* and the *Daily Telegraph* are the most useful for visitors. Also helpful are the weekly magazines *City Limits, Time Out,* and *New Statesman.* The *Evening Standard* is the paper most read by Londoners. For business news, read the *Financial Times* and the *Weekly Economist.*

Telephone – The area code for London is 01.

CLIMATE AND CLOTHES: Conventional wisdom has it that Britain doesn't have climate — it only has weather. The weather in London is often unreliable and unpredictable, with beautiful sun-drenched mornings regularly turning into dreary afternoons — and vice versa. The televised weather reports aren't much help — with their lugubrious references to possible "sunny intervals." Still, legends about incessant rain in London are exaggerated (though having a raincoat or umbrella is advisable). In fact, London has less rain than Rome, which is known as a sunny city. It's just that the rain is spread out over more days. The British capital is very much a city of the temperate zone. With occasional exceptions, summers tend to be moderately warm, with few days having temperatures above 75F (24C), and winters moderately cold, with few days dropping below 30F (− 1C). Spring and autumn tend to be most comfortable, with little more than a sweater or light overcoat required (and a raincoat ready for contingencies). In this age of informality, no place still requires formal evening dress, though nightclubs and a few haute cuisine restaurants may insist that men wear jackets and ties and women be appropriately attired.

GETTING AROUND: Airports – London's two main airports are Heathrow, which opened its $20 million Terminal 4 in April 1986, and Gatwick, both of which handle international and domestic traffic. Heathrow is 15 miles and about 50 minutes from downtown; a taxi into town will cost about $30-$40 unless you share: Two passengers to the West Central district, for example, pay about $15; three pay $12 each; four, $11 each; and five (the maximum), $10 each. (When sharing, the cab meter is turned off and passengers agree beforehand on the order of destinations. There's a shared-cab rank at Terminal 1, and they're also available at London's 200 taxi stands.) The trip downtown can easily be made on the London underground (subway) from two stations at Heathrow: One serves terminals 1, 2, and 3; the other serves Terminal 4. Piccadilly Line trains leave every 4 to 10 minutes and operate between 5 AM (6:45 on Sundays) and 11:30 PM; the trip takes about 45 minutes. Stops are convenient to most of London's main hotel areas, and the line feeds into the rest of the London underground network. Airbus A1 and scheduled bus #767 run between Heathrow and Victoria (one of the city's main and most central railway stations); airbus A2 goes from the airport to Paddington (another major rail station); and airbus A3 connects with a third mainline station, Euston.

Gatwick Airport is 29 miles and 40 minutes from downtown; a taxi into the city will cost about $45. Gatwick is not connected to the underground system, but it does have its own rail station, with express trains leaving for Victoria Station every 15 minutes from 6 AM to 10 PM during the day and hourly through the rest of the night. The journey takes about 30 minutes and is by far the best transportation alternative between airport and town. Green Line bus 777 travels between Gatwick Airport and Victoria Station (phone: 668-7261 for information) and costs about $5.50 for the 70-minute trip.

If you prefer the royal treatment, phone *Friends in London;* they'll meet you at the airport in a Rolls-Royce, whisk you to your hotel with champagne to sip on the way, and spend up to an hour answering questions about London. The service costs about $120 to $182, depending on the airport. Phone 240-9670; in the US, contact Wilson and Lake Tours International, 1 Appian Way, Suite 704-8, South San Francisco, CA 94080 (phone: 415-589-0352).

Boat – The *Riverbus,* a high-speed riverboat service run by the Thames Line, links east London to west between Greenland Pier and Chelsea Harbour. It runs at approximately 15-minute intervals, weekdays from 7 AM to 10 PM, weekends from 10 AM to 6 PM, calling at 8 piers (phone: 941-6513).

For a leisurely view of London from the Thames, tour boats leave roughly every half hour from Westminster Pier at the foot of Westminster Bridge and from Charing Cross Pier on Victoria Embankment; they sail (summers only) upriver to Kew or downriver to the Tower of London, Greenwich, and the massive Thames flood barrier. An inclusive ticket covering a round-trip boat ride from central London to Greenwich and entry to the *National Maritime Museum,* the Old Royal Observatory, and the *Cutty Sark* clipper is available for about $10 from the British Travel Centre, the Victoria Tourist Information Centre, and at Charing Cross, Westminster, and Tower piers. A journey along Regent's Canal through north London is offered (summers only) by *Jason's Trip,* opposite 60 Blomfield Rd., Little Venice, W9 (phone: 286-3428). For further information about these and other boat trips, contact the London Visitor and Convention Bureau's River Boat Information Service (phone: 730-4812).

Bus and Underground – The London public transport system gets sluggish now and then but is normally reasonably efficient. Its subway, called the underground or tube, and its bus lines cover the city pretty well, though buses suffer from traffic congestion, and the underground is notoriously thin south of the Thames. The tops of London's famous red double-decker buses do, however, offer some delightful views of the city and its people. The underground is easy to understand and to use, with clear directions and poster maps in all stations. Pick up free bus and underground maps from tourist offices or underground ticket booths. The fares on both trains and buses are set according to length of the journey. On most buses, conductors take payment after you tell them where you're going; some require that you pay as you enter. Underground tickets are bought on entering a station. Retain your ticket; you'll have to surrender it when you get off (or have to pay again), and bus inspectors make spot checks to see that no one's stealing a ride. There are also Red Arrow express buses, which link all the mainline British Rail stations, but you'll have to check stops before you get on. With just a few exceptions, public transport comes to a halt around midnight; it varies according to underground line and bus route. If you're going to be traveling late, check available facilities. For 24-hour travel information, phone 222-1234.

A London Transport Visitor Travelcard can be purchased in the US from travel agents and *BritRail Travel International* offices in New York, Dallas, and Los Angeles, or in London from *London Regional Transport* travel information centers. The card provides unlimited travel on virtually all of London's bus and underground networks and costs about $4 for 1 day (available only in London), $12 for 3 days, $16 for 4 days, and $26 for 7 days. If purchased in the US, a book of discount vouchers for many of the city's sights is included; for purchase in London, a passport-size photo must be provided.

The underground links Heathrow, London's main airport, with central London. The Piccadilly Line zips from Piccadilly Circus to the airport in about 40 minutes. (The underground does not connect with Gatwick Airport, but there are trains to Victoria Station every 15 minutes from 6 AM to 10 PM during the day and hourly through the rest of the night. The ride takes about 30 minutes.) Buses also link Heathrow with the city. For bus and underground information, call 222-1234.

One of the least expensive and most comprehensive ways to tour the city is to take *London Transport*'s 2-hour unconducted bus tour, which leaves every hour from four sites: Marble Arch, Piccadilly Circus, Baker Street tube station, and Victoria Station (phone: 222-1234). Other guided bus tours are offered by *American Express* (phone: 930-4411), *Frames* (phone: 837-6311), *Harrods* (phone: 581-3603), and *Thomas Cook* (phone: 499-4000).

From June through October, a Tourist Trail ticket serves the three daily coach routes from London to Edinburgh (via Oxford, Stratford, Chester, and Windemere), London to Edinburgh (via Cambridge, Lincoln, York, and Durham), and London to York (via Stratford and Lincoln). The ticket allows unlimited travel on the luxury coaches for 15 days and costs $115, with a discount for holders of Britexpress coach passes. Tickets are available at Victoria Coach Station (phone: 730-0202).

Car Rental – Several agencies, including *Hertz,* at 35 Edgware Rd., W2 (phone: 402-4242), and *Avis,* 35 Headford Pl., SW1 (phone: 245-9862), are represented in London. *Swan National,* 305 Chiswick High Rd., W4 (phone: 995-4665), and *Thrifty,* 67 Brent St., NW4 (phone: 202-0093), are less expensive, or try *Guy Salmon Car Rentals,* 7-23 Bryanston St., Marble Arch (phone: 408-1255), or *Godfrey Davis,* Davis House, Wilton Rd., SW1 (phone: 834-8484). In addition, *Budget Rent-A-Car* has four reservation desks at Heathrow Airport terminals (phone: 759-2216 or 759-0069). And for riding in style, call *Avis Luxury Car Services* (phone: 235-3235) for chauffeur-driven Rolls-Royces and Daimlers.

Helicopter Flights – See London from the air. Sightseeing tours are available for about $230 (plus VAT) per hour. The standard flight includes an aerial tour of the major London sites; special views available on request. Make a reservation with *Cabair Air Taxis Ltd.,* Elstree Aerodrome, Borehamwood, Hertfordshire, WC6 (phone: 953-4411).

Taxi – Those fine old London cabs are gradually being supplemented with more "practical" models. It is one of life's great tragedies. Although dashboard computers in cabs are becoming increasingly more common, too, London cabbies seem generally pleased with the new system; the computers allow communication between driver and dispatcher so that the cab's home office knows who's empty and who's closest to a prospective fare. Riders will be happy to know that the computer also allows drivers to check on possible traffic problems and to obtain basic route instructions. Whether you end up in a computerized or "regular" cab, taxi fares in London are increasingly expensive (though you don't mind the price so much if you're riding in the big, old, comfortable vehicles), and a 15% tip is customary. Tell a London cabby where you're going *before* entering the cab. When it rains or late at night, an empty cab (identifiable by the glow of the roof light) is often very difficult to find, so it is wise to carry the telephone number of one or more of the cab companies that respond to calls by phone. There are also many "minicab" companies that do not respond when hailed on the street, nor do they use meters. They operate on a fixed fare basis between their home base and your destination, and you have to call their central office to book one. Hotel porters or reception desks usually can make arrangements to have such a car pick you up at a specified time and place. Be aware that taxi rates are higher after 8 PM (and sometimes even higher after midnight) and on weekends and holidays.

Several firms and taxi drivers offer guided tours of London; details are available at information centers. You can arrange for the personal services of a member of London's Guild of Guides by phoning the London Visitor and Convention Bureau's Guide Dept. (phone: 730-3450).

Train – London has 11 principal train stations, each the starting point for trains to a particular region, with occasional overlapping of routes. The ones you are most likely to encounter include King's Cross (phone: 278-2477), the departure point for Northeast England and eastern Scotland, including Edinburgh; St. Pancras (phone: 387-8537), for trains going north as far as Sheffield; Euston (phone: 387-7070), serving the Midlands, North Wales, including Holyhead and ferries for Dun Laoghaire, Ireland, Northwest England, and western Scotland, including Glasgow; Paddington (phone: 262-6767), for the West Country and South Wales, including Fishguard and ferries for Rosslare, Ireland; Victoria (phone: 928-5100), for Gatwick Airport and, along with Charing Cross Station (phone: 928-5100), for departures to Southeast England; and Liverpool St. Station (phone: 283-7171), for departures to East Anglia and to Harwich for ferries to the Continent and Scandinavia. All of these stations are connected via London's underground.

BritRail's Travelpak transportation program is intended for travelers who wish to venture out of London. It includes round-trip journeys from Gatwick or Heathrow airports to central London; the London Explorer; and a 4-day *BritRail* pass for unlimited train travel within Britain. Maps and timetables are also included. *BritRail* Travelpaks must be obtained before leaving the US from any North American *BritRail* office. Write BritRail, 630 Third Ave., New York, NY 10017 (phone: 212-599-5400).

Walking Tours – A trained guide can show you Shakespeare's London or that of Dickens or Jack the Ripper — many different themes are offered. These reasonably priced tours last up to 2 hours, generally in the afternoon or evening. *City Walks* offers a Sherlock Holmes Trail of Mystery and Whodunit Tour departing from the Baker St. Underground Station at the Baker St. exit on Tuesdays and Saturdays at 10:30 AM (phone: 937-4281). *Citisights* (phone: 739-2372) start from the *Museum of London,* London Wall. *Streets of London* (phone: 882-3414) start from various underground stations. *Londoner Pub Walks* (phone: 883-2656) start from Temple underground station (Dist. and Circle) on Fridays at 7:30 PM. *London Walks* (phone: 882-2763) provides tours from a variety of points.

 SPECIAL EVENTS: Dates vary marginally from year to year and should be checked — together with details — with the London Visitor and Convention Bureau. In late March/early April, the Oxford and Cambridge rowing "eights" race through the waters from Putney to Mortlake, an important competition for the two universities, whose respective teams practice for months beforehand. In early June you can enjoy the annual *Trooping the Colour,* England's most elaborate display of pageantry — a Horse Guards' parade, with military music and much pomp and circumstance — all in celebration of the queen's official birthday. You can see some of the parade without a ticket, but for the ceremony you must book before March 1 by writing to the Brigade Major, Headquarters, Household Division, Horseguards, Whitehall SW1 (do not send money). The world-famous *Chelsea Flower Show* takes place in late May. Late June heralds the *Wimbledon Lawn Tennis Championship* — the world's most prestigious — complete with a member of the royal family presenting the prizes. The *Henley Royal Regatta,* in early July (at Henley-on-Thames, a 1-hour train ride from London), is an international rowing competition and one of the big social events of the year. Watch from the towpath (free) or from within the Regatta enclosure ($3-$5). The *Royal Tournament,* a military pageant, takes place at Earls Court for 3 weeks in July. October or November is the time for the *State Opening of Parliament; Guy Fawkes Day* is on November 5, when fireworks and bonfires mark the anniversary of the plot to blow up both houses of Parliament and King James I in 1605; and on the second Saturday in November, an inaugural procession for the new lord mayor, who rides in a golden carriage, followed by floats and bands.

 MUSEUMS: Many of London's museums and galleries have no admission charge; others charge $1.50 to $3. A number of the museums are described in *Special Places.* Others of note include:

    Bethnal Green Museum of Childhood – Impressive collection of more than 4,000 toys, including dolls and dollhouses, games, and puppets. Cambridge Heath Rd., E2 (phone: 980-3204).

Courtauld Institute Galleries – A remarkable collection of French Impressionist and post-Impressionist paintings. Somerset House, the Strand (phone: 935-9242).

Dickens's House – Manuscripts of early works, first editions, and personal memorabilia. 48 Doughty St., WC1 (phone: 405-2127).

Dulwich College Picture Gallery – Works by European masters in one of England's most beautiful art galleries. The college itself boasts such famous alumni as P. G. Wodehouse and Raymond Chandler. College Rd., SE21 (phone: 693-5254).

Institute of Contemporary Arts – Exhibitions of up-to-date British art, film, theater, manifesto. Closed Mondays. Nash House, Duke of York Steps. The Mall, SW1 (phone: 930-3647).

Jewish Museum – Art and antiques illustrating Jewish history. Woburn House, Upper Woburn Pl., WC1 (phone: 388-4525).

London Toy and Model Museum – This charming Victorian building houses a fine collection of model trains and mechanical toys. October House, 23 Craven Hill, W2 (phone: 262-7905).

Museum of Mankind – Ethnographic exhibitions. 6 Burlington Gardens, W1 (phone: 437-2224).

Musical Museum – One of Europe's most comprehensive collections of pianos and mechanical musical instruments, all in good working condition. 368 High St., Brentford, Middlesex (phone: 560-8108).

Natural History Museum – Exhibitions of native wildlife, plants, fossils, and minerals. Cromwell Rd., SW7 (phone: 589-6323).

Science Museum – The development of science and industry, including an Exploration of Space exhibition. Exhibition Rd., SW7 (phone: 589-3456).

Sir John Soane's Museum – Its collection includes Hogarth's series *The Rake's Progress*. 13 Lincoln's Inn Fields, WC2 (phone: 405-2107).

Space Adventure – Aims to offer all the sights, sounds, and sensations of space travel. What is claimed to be Europe's — perhaps even the world's — largest flight simulator re-creates the movements of space travel, complemented by audiovisual effects. Step inside and experience countdown, launch, G-forces, interplanetary travel, reentry, and landing. Open daily. 92-94 Tooley St. (phone: 378-1405).

Theatre Museum – Britain's newest collection of theatrical material has been given its own home. Everything from circus to pop, grand opera to mime, straight theater to Punch and Judy and pantomime is here, as well as an excellent informal café/ restaurant on the main floor. 1E Tavistock St., WC2 (phone: 836-7891).

Wallace Collection – Sir Richard Wallace's fine collection of European paintings, sculpture, and armor. Hertford House, Manchester Sq., W1 (phone: 935-0687).

Whitechapel Art Gallery – An East End haven for modern art, including works by Moore, Hepworth, and Hockney. Includes exhibitions of contemporary British artists, along with Third World and ethnic minority artists. 80 Whitechapel High St., E7 (phone: 377-0107).

 SHOPPING: Stores are generally open from 9 AM to 5:30 or 6 PM, daily except Sundays, but Covent Garden stays open until 7 PM, and the shops in the West End stay open until about 7:30 PM on Thursdays. Although London is traditionally one of the most expensive cities in the world, savvy shoppers can still find good buys. The current lure, however, is more for fine British workmanship and style than very low prices.

The favorite items on any shopping list in London are cashmere and Shetland knitwear; fabric (tweeds, blends, men's suitings); riding gear; custom-made men's suits, shirts, shoes, and hats; shotguns; china and crystal; umbrellas; antiques; sporting goods;

and English food specialties (jams, marmalade, various blended teas, Stilton cheese, shortbread, and others). Books published by British houses, once a fine buy, are now far higher in price, and you probably will do better to buy the US editions. For secondhand books, though, London still hides treasures. The Charing Cross Road is a good place to start, and even pricey establishments may have basements with long out-of-print paperbacks in good condition along with unfashionable Victoriana at very low prices. See Sheppard's *Directory of Second-Hand and Antiquarian Bookshops of the British Isles* for tips. But as all bargain hunters know, there is no substitute for your own voyages of discovery.

Devoted bargain hunters recognize that the best time to buy British is during the semiannual sales that usually occur from Boxing Day (December 26) through the early part of the New Year and again in early July. The Christmas/New Year's sales offer by far the best bargains in the city, and the crowds can be the equal of the low prices. Many stores remain open on New Year's Day to accommodate the bargain hunters. The best-publicized single sale is that held by *Harrods* for 3 weeks beginning the first Friday in January — opening day is an event in itself.

Be sure to take your passport when you shop, and always inquire about the VAT refund application forms when you make a purchase of over $25. The VAT (Value Added Tax) is a 15% surcharge payable at the sales counter, but foreign customers usually will be reimbursed for it at home. For purchases at any of the 10,000 shops displaying the London Tax Free Shopping logo, retailers issue vouchers that will be stamped by Customs when you leave the country and then posted to LTFS (21-24 Cockspur St., SW1); a refund is issued in local currency in as few as 4 days.

Though scattered about the city, the most appealing shops tend to center in the West End area, particularly along Bond, Oxford, South Molton, Regent, and Jermyn streets and Piccadilly. Other good areas are Kings Road, Kensington High Street, and Kensington Church Street, along with Knightsbridge and Covent Garden.

This is a city of markets; we have already described Portobello Road and Camden Passage in *Special Places*. Also worthy of note is Camden Lock Market (Camden High St. NW1) on weekends for far-out clothes, leather items, antiques, and trinkets. The restored Jubilee Market on the south side of Covent Garden piazza is one of the largest indoor markets in the country. It features antiques and a flea market on Mondays; housewares, clothing, and jewelry Tuesdays through Fridays; and crafts on weekends. Or get up early on a Sunday morning and head for the East End to sample a typically English transport café ("caff") breakfast at *Fred's* (40 Aberfeldy St., E1) before tackling the very famous Petticoat Lane for food, inexpensive clothes, crockery, and even the proverbial kitchen sink.

The following stores are only a sampling of London's treasure houses.

Anderson and Sheppard – Reputable "made-to-measure" tailor for men's clothes. 30 Savile Row, W1.

Antiquarius – A good place for antiques. 135-141 King's Rd., SW3.

Aquascutum – Raincoats and jackets for men and women. 100 Regent St., W1.

Laura Ashley – A relatively inexpensive women's boutique specializing in romantic styled skirts, dresses, and blouses. 183 Sloane St., SW1; plus other branches on Hampstead High St., Harriet St., and Fulham Rd.

Asprey & Company – Fine jewelry, silver, and luggage. 165-169 New Bond St., W1.

Bates – A gentlemen's hatter, and our favorite. Check out the eight-part caps. 21A Jermyn St., SW1.

W. Bill Ltd. – Shetland sweaters, knit ties, argyle socks, club mufflers, gloves. 28 Old Bond St., W1.

Body Shop – More than 150 different beauty products (perfumes, soaps, hair and skin care products — famous for not having been tested on animals), from the worldwide chain that started in Brighton. 32 Great Marlborough St., W1.

Browns – Beautiful but expensive women's clothes, at 23-27 S. Molton St. W1; and a cosmetics branch on Hampstead High St., NW3.

Burberrys – Superb but expensive men's and women's raincoats and traditional clothes, and home of the now nearly ubiquitous plaid that began life as a raincoat lining. 18 Haymarket, SW1.

Cavendish Rare Books – Specializes in travel books and adventure accounts from long, long ago. Princes Arcade, W1.

Church & Co. – Superior men's shoes. 58-59 Burlington Arcade, W1; Old Bond St.

Conran's – Terence Conran has transformed the beautiful Michelin Building into a larger, more exclusive and expensive version of his well-known *Habitat* stores. However, the export of larger furniture and furnishings is probably better arranged through a New York branch. 77 Fulham Rd., SW3.

Jasper Conran – Top British designer clothes from Terence Conran's son. 37 Beauchamp Pl., SW3.

Crocodile – Chic and expensive women's clothes. 57 Beauchamp Pl., SW3.

Justin De Blank – Excellent specialty foods, especially cheese and take-out dishes. 42 Elizabeth St., SW1.

Dillon's – A good bookstore, London's most scholastic, partly owned by London University. 1 Malet St., WC1.

Emmanuel – Creative designers of Princess Diana's wedding dress and other clothing for members of the aristocracy. 10 Beauchamp Pl., SW3.

Feathers – French and Italian designer clothing for women. 40 Hans Crescent, SW1.

Fortnum and Mason – Boasts designer originals (usually of the rather dowdy variety), an appealing soda fountain-cum-restaurant, and one of the most elegant grocery departments in the world (where the staff wears striped morning trousers and swallow-tail coats). 181 Piccadilly, W1.

Foyle's – London's largest bookstore. 119 Charing Cross Rd., WC2.

Thomas Goode and Company – London's best china and glass shop first opened in 1827. Even if you don't plan to buy anything, you may want to look at their beautiful 1876 showroom. 19 S. Audley St., W1.

Grays Market – The hundreds of stalls here and at the annex down the street sell everything from antique playing cards to 16th-century furniture. 1-7 Davies Mews, W1 and 58 Davies St., W1.

Habitat – Up-to-the-minute designs with realistic prices for furniture and household goods. 156 Tottenham Court Rd., W1, and 206 King's Rd., SW3.

Halcyon Days – The best place to find authentic Battersea boxes — both antique and new. 14 Brook St., W1.

Hamley's – The largest toy shop in the world. 200 Regent St., W1.

Harrods – The ultimate department store, although it does tend to be quite expensive. It has everything, even a mortuary and a bank, and what it doesn't stock it will get for you. The "food halls" particularly fascinate visitors, and traditional British merchandise is available in abundance. For those interested in trendy styles, it has the *Way In* boutique. Its annual January sale is legendary. Or splurge on a $320 tour of London in the store's vintage Rolls-Royce, the "Flying Lady." 87-135 Brompton Rd., Knightsbridge, SW1.

Douglas Hayward – A reputable made-to-order tailor. 95 Mount St., W1.

Heal's – Furniture and fabrics in the best modern designs. (It also has a popular lunch-meeting restaurant.) 196 Tottenham Court Rd., W1.

Jaeger – Tailored (and expensive) men's and women's clothes. 204 Regent St., W1.

Herbert Johnson – Men's hats. 13 Old Burlington St., W1.

Peter Jones – Another good, well-stocked department store, offering moderately priced, tasteful goods. Sloane Sq., SW1.

John Keil – Lovely, expensive antiques. 25 Mount St., W1.

Kent & Curwen – The place to buy authentic cricket caps, Henley club ties, and all sorts of similarly preppy raiment. 39 St. James's St., SW1 and 6 Royal Arcade, W1.

Kilkenny – All things Irish, including Paul Costelloe linen shirts and tweeds, hand knits, rugs, pottery, and Waterford crystal. 150 New Bond St., W1.

John Lewis – Another good department store, "never knowingly undersold" and particularly noted for its fabrics and household goods. 278 Oxford St., W1.

Liberty – Famous for print fabrics. Scarves and ties a specialty. 210 Regent St., W1.

Lillywhites – The whole gamut of sporting goods. Piccadilly Circus, SW1.

John Lobb – World-famous for custom-made shoes that will last 10 years or more, with proper care. 9 St. James's St., SW1.

James Lock and Company – The royal hatters. They fitted a crown for the queen's coronation, and they'll happily fit you for your first bowler. 6 St. James's St., SW1.

Lord's – Tops in ties. 66/70 Burlington Arcade, W1.

Marks & Spencer – Locally nicknamed "Marks & Sparks," this chain specializes in clothes for the whole family, made to high standards and sold at very reasonable prices. Its linens and sweaters (especially cashmere and Shetland) are among the best buys in Britain. 458 Oxford St., W1 (and many branches).

Moss Bros. – Men's formal attire (including dress tartans) and high-quality riding clothes for sale and hire. Bedford St., WC2.

Harvey Nichols – Lady Di's favorite luxury department store, specializing in women's haute couture. Knightsbridge, SW1.

Partridge Ltd. – Fine (but expensive) antiques. 144 New Bond St., W1.

Paul Smith – Britain's number one men's designer has two adjacent shops in Covent Garden. 43-44 Floral St., WC2.

James Purdey and Sons – The place to go for custom-made shotguns and other shooting gear. 57 S. Audley St., W1.

Reject China Shop – Good buys in slightly (invisible) irregular, name-brand china. Glassware, crystal, and flatware, too. For a fee, the shop will ship your purchases back home. 33-35 Beauchamp Pl., SW3, or 134 Regent St., W1.

Peter Robinson Top Shop – Young, trendy, moderately priced women's clothing. 216 Oxford St., W1.

Scotch House – Famous for Scottish cashmeres, sweaters, tartans — a wide selection of well-known labels. 2 Brompton Rd., SW1 and many branches.

Selfridges – This famous department store offers somewhat less variety than *Harrods*, but it has just about everything too — only a little less expensive. The extensive china and crystal department carries most patterns available. Oxford St., W1.

David Shilling – His one-off (a tad eccentric) hat creations always create a stir at Ascot. 44 Chiltern St., W1.

Shirin – The best designer cashmeres in town. 51 Beauchamp Pl., SW3.

Simpson's – Standard garments for men and women. 203 Eagle Pl., W1.

James Smith and Sons – The oldest umbrella shop in Europe. 53 New Oxford St., WC1.

Smythson of Bond Street – The world's best place to buy diaries, note pads, and calendars, many in Florentine marbled paper; also exotic ledgers in which to record odd data. 54 New Bond St., W1.

Sotheby Parke Bernet – The world's oldest art auctioneer, interesting to look at even if you don't plan to buy. They auction books, porcelain, furniture, jewelry, and works of art; at times, even such odd items as vintage cars and wines. Viewing hours are between 9:30 AM and 4:30 PM on weekdays, Bloomfield Pl., W1 (phone: 493-8080).

Swaine, Adeney, Brigg, and Sons – Riding gear and their famous pure silk umbrellas. 185 Piccadilly, W1.

Turnbull and Asser – Men's shirts made to order. 71-72 Jermyn St., SW1.

Twinings – Tea — and nothing but — in bags, balls, and bulk. 216 Strand.

Waterstone's – Look for the maroon canopy of this huge chain of bookstores, whose instant success is due mainly to enterprising, well-informed staff and late, late hours (it's open till midnight in Edinburgh, for example). There are many branches, including ones on Hampstead High St., Old Brompton Rd., Charing Cross Rd., and High St., Kensington.

Wedgwood – Porcelain. 266 and 270 Regent St., W1.

Westaway and Westaway – Cashmere and Shetland wool kilts, sweaters, scarves, and blankets. 65 Great Russell St. and 29 Bloomsbury, WC1.

SPORTS AND FITNESS: Soccer (called football hereabouts) and cricket are the most popular spectator pastimes, but London offers a wide variety of other sports.

Cricket – The season runs from mid-April to early September. The best places to watch it are at *Lord's Cricket Ground,* St. John's Wood Rd. NW8 (phone: 289-1615), and *The Oval,* Kennington, SE11 (phone: 582-6660).

Fishing – Several public ponds right in London are accessible to the angler. A permit is required from the Royal Parks Department, the Storeyard, Hyde Park, W2 (phone: 262-5484). The department can also provide information on where to fish.

Fitness Centers – *David Morgan Health Club,* 3 Hanover Sq., W1 (phone: 639-3353); *Pineapple Dance Studios,* 7 Langley St., WC2 (phone: 836-4004); and several branches around town.

Golf – Aside from private clubs, for which membership is required, there are several municipal courses, some of which rent clubs. Try *Pickett's Lock Center,* Pickett's Lock La., N9 (phone: 803-3611), *Addington Court,* Featherbed La., Addington, Croydon (phone: 657-0281), and *Beckenham Place Park,* Beckenham, Kent (phone: 650-2292). *Wentworth, Virginia Water, Surrey (phone: Wentworth 2201), and Sunningdale,* Ridgemount Rd., Sunningdale, Berkshire (phone: Ascot 21681), are the best courses within driving distance of London, and a letter from your home club pro or president (plus a polite phone call) may gain access to their courses.

Greyhound Racing – *Empire Stadium,* Empire Way, Wembley (phone: 902-1234), and others. There are evening races, so check the afternoon newspapers for details.

Horse Racing – Nine major racecourses are within easy reach of London, including *Epsom,* where the Derby (pronounced Darby) is run, and *Ascot,* where the Royal Ascot takes place — both in June. The flat racing season is from March to November; steeplechasing, August to June. Call the *Jockey Club,* 42 Portman Sq., W1 (phone: 486-4921), for information.

Horseback Riding – Try *Bathurst Riding Stables,* 63 Bathurst Mews, W2 (phone: 723-2813), and *Ross Nye's Riding Establishment,* 8 Bathurst Mews, W2 (phone: 262-3791).

Ice Skating – There is the *Queen's Ice Skating Club,* 17 Queensway, W2 (phone: 229-0172), and *Silver Blades Ice Rink,* 386 Streatham High Rd., SW16 (phone: 769-7861). Skates are for rent at both rinks.

Jogging – Most pleasant for running are Hyde Park, bordered by Kensington Rd., Park La., and Bayswater Rd.; Hampstead Heath, North London; and Regent's Park, bordered by Prince Albert Rd., Albany St., Marylebone Rd., and Park Rd.

Rugby – An autumn-through-spring spectacle at *Rugby Football Ground,* Whitton Rd., Twickenham (phone: 892-8161).

Soccer – The big sport in Britain. The local football season is autumn to spring and the most popular clubs are *Arsenal,* Highbury Stadium, Avenell Rd., N5 (phone: 359-0131); *Chelsea,* Stamford Bridge, Fulham Rd., SW6 (phone: 381-0111); *West Ham United,* Boleyn Ground, Green St., E13 (phone: 470-1325). As a spectator, be careful at games. Violence and overcrowding have been a major problem in recent years.

Swimming – Several excellent indoor public pools include: *Swiss Cottage Center,*

Adelaide Rd., NW3 (phone: 586-5989); *Putney Swimming Baths,* 376 Upper Richmond Rd., SW15 (phone: 789-1124); and *The Oasis,* 167 High Holborn,, WC1 (phone: 836-9555). There is outdoor swimming in the Hyde Park Serpentine, and Hampstead Heath, in the summer.

Tennis – Aside from private clubs, more than 50 London public parks have tennis courts available to all. Get information from the London Visitor and Convention Bureau (phone: 730-3488).

 THEATER: London remains the theater capital of the world, with about 50 theaters regularly putting on plays in and around its West End theater district and a vigorous collection of "fringe" theaters in various parts of town. Best known, and most accomplished, are the two main repertory theater companies — the *National Theatre Company* at the *National Theatre,* South Bank, SE1 (phone: 928-2252), and the *Royal Shakespeare Company (RSC)* at the *Barbican Centre,* The Barbican, EC2 (phone: 628-8795); from time to time, both present dazzling versions of classics and new plays, although they sometimes trade on their reputations — the *National* mistaking dreariness for realism, and the *RSC,* staidness for reliability. (For dependable critical reviews, consult the *Observer*'s Michael Ratcliffe and the *Guardian*'s Michael Billington.) Shakespeare's plays are also performed in summer at the open-air theater in Regents Park, NW1 (phone: 935-5756).

In the West End, presentations include both first class and second-rate drama and comedy, a fair sprinkling of farce (for which the British have a particular fondness), and the best of imports from the American stage. Visitors from the US often find attending theater in London easier — and somewhat less expensive — than it is at home. Except for the small handful of runaway box office successes, tickets are usually available for all performances. In most cases, you can reserve by telephone, but tickets must be picked up well before curtain time. *The West End Theatre Society* operates a half-price ticket kiosk in Leicester Square. It posts a list of shows for which remaining seats may be purchased at half-price on the day of the performance. Ticket agencies that offer tickets to all shows, charging a small commission, include *Keith Prowse & Co.* (phone: 437-8976), *Dial-A-Ticket* (phone: 930-8331/2), and *Ace Tickets* (phone: 223-8173).

The quality of London's fringe theater varies from accomplished and imaginative to amateurish. Theaters in pubs are at the *King's Head* in Islington, 115 Upper St., N1 (phone: 226-1916), and at the *Bush,* in the *Bush* hotel, Shepherd's Bush Green (phone: 743-3388). The *Riverside Studios* in Hammersmith, Crisp Rd., W6 (phone: 748-3354), the *Tricycle Theatre* at 269 Kilburn High Rd., NW6 (phone: 328-8626), and the *New End Theatre* in Hampstead, 27 New End, NW3 (phone: 435-6054), have established reputations for the excellence of their productions, which often move on to the West End and sometimes even directly to Broadway. Also keep an eye on the *Donmar Warehouse* for major transfers from the *Edinburgh Festival Fringe* (an enormous collection of amateur films) or for exciting avant-garde companies such as *Cheek by Jowl;* 41 Earlham St., Covent Garden (phone: 836-3028). Lunchtime fringe theater presentations offer an alternative to sightseeing on rainy days.

A visit to *St. Martin's* is now tantamount to seeing a major London landmark, as it houses Agatha Christie's *The Mousetrap,* transferred from the *Ambassador* next door; there's a fresh cast each year, and it's been running since 1952 — the longest run ever in nightly theater. The play is an exciting, tantalizing, and mildly frightening mystery-thriller. If you tell whodunit, you are ruined socially. West St., Cambridge Circus (phone: 836-1443).

Check *Time Out* or *City Limits* for comprehensive lists, plot summaries, and theater phone numbers. Daily papers list West End performances.

Show tours to London are very popular in season; see your travel agent for package deals. If you want to reserve specific tickets before you arrive in London, there are agencies in the US that keep a listing of what's on in London. For a service charge of about $5 per ticket, they will sell you the best seats only. Contact *Edwards & Edwards,* One Times Square Plaza, New York, NY 10036 (phone: 212-944-0290 or 800-223-6108) or *Keith Prowse & Co.,* 234 W. 44th St., New York, NY 10036 (phone: 212-398-1430 or 800-223-4446).

CINEMA: London may not be the equal of Paris as a movie metropolis, but many say it's stronger when it comes to very good, little-known films, often from the US or Commonwealth countries. British film is startling in both similarities and contrasts to that of the US. In Great Britain, Chaplin, Hitchcock, and Laughton are regarded as English. The *British Film Institute* (21 Stephen St., Soho; phone: 255-1444) has an incomparable British and international film library; it also administers the National Film Archive, contains first class documentation and filmographic material, and publishes the monthly *Film Bulletin* and quarterly *Sight and Sound* as well as running the *London Film Festival* (November) in the *National Film Theatre* (*NFT*) on the South Bank near Waterloo Station and Bridge (phone: 928-3232). Membership is required at the *NFT* (about 65¢ a day or $15.70 for a year), but it's well worth it for its two cinemas; wide variety of old and new British, US, and international movies; good bookshop, and eating facilities. The success of the *London Film Festival* in past years testifies to the high caliber of London's critics, who include the *Evening Standard*'s Alexander Walker, the *Guardian*'s Derek Malcolm, the *Financial Times*'s Nigel Andrews and, above all, the *Observer*'s Philip French; the *Film Festival* appoints one of them as its *supremo* of the year.

As with the theater, there are big divisions between West End and fringe (or independent) cinema. The West End strives for probable box office smash hits, so watch out for long lines at Friday openings and head for early showings, some of which begin not long after noon. Monday admission prices are lower. For sheer luxury, the *Curzon Mayfair* on Mayfair's Curzon St. in the West End is unbeatable for both low budget and commercial films (phone: 499-3737). The most exciting film fare usually is found in independents, and sometimes you must travel to remote parts of London to see outstanding work in an almost empty cinema; check what's showing in places like *Everyman* at Hampstead (phone: 435-1525), the *Museum of London* at London Wall near Barbican (phone: 600-3699), the luxurious, comfortable *Barbican Cinema* (phone: 638-8891), *Screen* on Baker St. (phone: 935-2772), *Screen on the Green* at Islington (phone: 226-3520), and *Screen on the Hill* at Hempstead (phone: 435-3366). All feature late-night showings and children's screenings on Saturdays (as do the *Barbican* and *NFT*). In some cases you may have to pay moderate club fees. Most British cinemas now ban smoking in the auditorium. Telephone the theaters for show times.

Next to the *National Film Theatre* is the new *Museum of the Moving Image* that, among other sites, shows fine movies sidestepped by the big distributors. The museum has more than 50 exhibitions and 1,000 clips from various old and recent films and TV shows. There's also a good bit of movie memorabilia, including Charlie Chaplin's hat and cane. Closed Mondays. Open Tuesdays through Saturdays, 10 AM to 8 PM; Sundays, 10 AM to 6 PM. Admission charge (phone: 928-3535).

MUSIC: Few cities offer a greater variety of musical performances — both classical music and the many varieties of popular music. For classical music, the focus of attention is the *South Banks Arts Center* with its three concert halls — *Royal Festival Hall, Queen Elizabeth Hall,* and the *Purcell Room* — (phone: 928-3191 for all three); the *Barbican Hall,* home of the *London Symphony Orchestra* (phone: 628-8795); and the *Royal Albert Hall,* Kensington Gore, SW7 (phone: 589-8212). The latter is the home of the *Henry Wood Promenade Concerts,*

or more simply, the *Proms,* an 8-week series of orchestral concerts that have been a popular feature of the London summer scene (July to September) for decades. Tickets are inexpensive, because the Proms came into being to give students and other people who are not affluent an opportunity to dress up and be part of a grand musical event. The performances are tops (some broadcast live by the BBC), and the SRO audience is large and enthusiastic. *Wigmore Hall,* Wigmore St., W1 (phone: 935-2141), is best known for recitals of chamber music and performances by some of the world's most accomplished instrumental and vocal soloists. Concerts are also often held in the dignified, splendid setting of St. John's Church, Smith Sq., SW1 (phone: 222-1061). The *London Symphony Orchestra* performs at *Barbican Centre,* The Barbican, EC2. During the summer, outdoor concerts are given at Kenwood, Crystal Palace, and Holland Park, and bands play in many of London's parks.

Operas at *Covent Garden Royal Opera House,* Floral St., WC2 (phone: 240-1066), are internationally famous. The *English National Opera Company* offers its performances at the *London Coliseum,* St. Martin's La., WC2 (phone: 836-3161). The best of London's ballet performances are presented at *Covent Garden,* the *Coliseum,* and *Sadler's Wells,* Roseberry Ave., EC1 (phone: 837-1672), as well as *The Place,* 17 Duke Rd.,* WC1 (phone: 387-0161), home of the *London Contemporary Dance Theatre* and the *London School of Contemporary Dance.* Details about all performances are listed in the arts sections of the Sunday newspapers.

Although superstar musicians and vocalists usually appear in the city's larger halls, good live popular music can be heard in London's music pubs. Among the best of them are the *Dublin Castle,* 94 Parkway, NW1 (phone: 485-1773); *King's Head,* 4 Fulham High St., SW6 (phone: 736-1413); *Kensington,* 54 Russell Gardens, Holland Rd., W14 (phone: 603-3245); and *Hope and Anchor,* 207 Upper St., N1 (phone: 359-4510).

 NIGHTCLUBS AND NIGHTLIFE: It used to be that they virtually rolled up the sidewalks in London at 11 PM. Now there's a very lively and often wild nightlife, including nightclubs, jazz clubs, historical feast entertainments, and gambling casinos. Some wind up around midnight; most go on until well into the early morning hours. In Covent Garden and still-trendy-after-all-these-years Chelsea, particularly along King's and Fulham roads, are fashionable pubs, wine bars, and restaurants. Two nightclubs with floor shows are the *London Room,* Drury La., WC2 (phone: 831-8863) and *Omar Khayyam,* 177 Regent St., W1 (phone: 734-7675). There is dancing at both. There's a show but no dancing at *Madisons,* Camden Lock, Chalk Farm Rd., NW1 (phone: 485-6044). The best jazz clubs are *Ronnie Scott's,* 47 Frith St., W1 (phone: 439-0747), and *The 100 Club,* 100 Oxford St., W1 (phone: 636-0933). For jazz and a slice, try *Pizza Express,* 10 Dean St., W1 (phone: 437-9595), with live music nightly except Mondays. *Dingwalls,* Camden Lock, Chalk Farm Rd., NW1 (phone: 267-4967) and the *Town and Country Club,* 9 Highgate Rd., NW5 (phone: 267-3334), have a continually changing program of much-acclaimed performers of rock music.

For a special treat, London offers the *medieval banquet,* complete with traditional meals served by costumed waiters and waitresses. Menus resemble those of traditional Elizabethan feasts, and there is period music, horseplay, occasional mock sword fights, Shakespearean playlets, and other light entertainment. Try *Tudor Rooms,* 17 Swallow St., W1 (phone: 240-3978); *Beefeater,* St. Katherine Dock, E1 (phone: 408-1001); and *Shakespeare's Tavern,* Blackfriars La., EC4 (phone: 408-1001).

The disco scene changes rapidly, and many places — such as expensive and exclusive *Annabel's,* 44 Berkeley Sq., W1 (phone: 629-3558) — are open only to members. Clubs of the moment include: the *Hippodrome,* Charing Cross Rd., WC2 (phone: 437-4311); *Stringfellows,* 16-19 Upper St. Martin's La., WC2 (phone: 240-5534); *Legend's,* 29 Old Burlington St., W1 (phone: 437-9933); *Crazy Larry's,* Lots Rd., SW10 (phone: 352-

3518); *Xenon,* 196 Piccadilly, W1 (phone: 734-9344); *Tramp,* 40 Jermyn St., SW1 (phone: 734-0565), where the chic social set meets to disco (members only); and *Limelight,* at 136 Shaftesbury Ave., W1 (phone: 434-0572). A smart addition to the West London night scene is the *Broadway Boulevard* club in Ealing, particularly convenient for guests at the Heathrow hotels (phone: 840-0616).

Female impersonators regularly perform at the *Union Tavern,* 146 Camberwell New Rd., SE5 (phone: 735-3605); *Jongleurs Cabaret Club* at the *Coronet,* Lavender Gardens SW11 (phone: 585-0955); and *Black Cap,* 171 Camden High St., NW1 (phone: 485-1742). Phone for details.

BEST IN TOWN

CHECKING IN: Visitors arriving in London between early spring and mid-autumn without hotel reservations are in for an unpleasant adventure. For many years now, there has been a glaring shortage of hotel rooms in the British capital during the prime tourist season, which each year seems to begin earlier and end later. (For a small fee, the Tourist Information Centre at Victoria Station Forecourt, or at the underground station in Heathrow, will try to help you find a room.) This fact, plus years of general inflation and the difficulty of finding suitable hotel staff are largely responsible for often excessive hotel charges, generally out of keeping with other costs in Britain. As a rule, expensive hotels do not include any meals in their prices; moderate and inexpensive hotels generally include continental breakfasts. Prices — with bath, English breakfast, VAT, and a 10% service charge sometimes included — are $130 to $250 and up for a double room in an expensive hotel; $85 to $120 in moderate; and $60 to $80, inexpensive. All telephone numbers are in the 01 area code unless otherwise indicated.

As an alternative to conventional hotel accommodations, it's easy to stay in one of 500 private homes and apartments through a program called *Your Home in London.* These vary from a single in a bed-and-breakfast establishment for $30 a night to a 2-bedroom apartment in central London for $140 a night. For information, in the US phone 301-269-6232. If you are particularly interested in service flats (apartments with close to traditional hotel services — mostly daily maid service), contact *Eastone Overseas Accommodations,* 6682 141st Lane N., Palm Beach Gardens, FL 33418 (phone: 407-575-6991), or *Hometours International,* 1170 Broadway, New York, NY 10001 (phone: 212-689-0851 or 800-367-4668). Service flats range from the very elegant to the very modest at a bed-and-breakfast establishment.

Blakes – A row of Victorian townhouses has been transformed into this 55-room, refurbished hotel, where many employees wear warrior-like uniforms. There's black antique furniture on the lower level; the upper floors are decorated in pale gray and pastels. The bathrooms are made of marble, and there are black and red silk sheets in many rooms. Facilities include a first rate restaurant, a glass-enclosed courtyard, FAX machine, laundry service, and 24-hour room service. 33 Roland Gardens, SW7 (phone: 370-6701). Expensive.

Basil Street – A relic with a reputation for graceful, old-fashioned service and beautiful antique furnishings to match. It draws a faithful international clientele who, if they can reserve one of its 94 rooms, prefer staying here to patronizing any of the impersonal, newer hotels. It has a women's health club and is just down the street from *Harrods.* 8 Basil St., SW3 (phone: 581-3311). Expensive.

Beaufort – A tranquil and very elegant hotel comprised of two Victorian houses in Beaufort Gardens, the heart of fashionable Knightsbridge. It offers 28 comfortable and attractively decorated rooms, each with a plenitude of facilities: stereo/cassette player; TV set; direct-dial phone; hair dryer; magazines and books; a decanter of brandy; and even a teddy bear for the youngsters. Breakfast is brought on a tray each morning. Convenient to restaurants and shops (*Harrods* is just around the corner). 33 Beaufort Gardens, SW3 1PP (phone: 584-5252). Expensive.

Berkeley – Remarkably understated, this 150-room hotel manages to preserve its impeccably high standards while keeping a low profile. Soft-spoken service complements the tastefully lavish, traditional English decor. There are also a health club and a new gymnasium. Wilton Pl., SW1 (phone: 235-6000). Expensive.

Britannia – Mahogany furniture, velvet armchairs, rooms painted in colors you might choose at home — all very tasteful and solid, despite the anonymity of the spacious foyer with the pretentious chandeliers. This is where the American Embassy — also on the square — often puts up visiting middle-ranking State Department officials. Now part of the Inter-Continental chain. Grosvenor Sq., W1 (phone: 629-9400). Expensive.

Brown's – As English as you can get, retaining pleasing, quaint, Victorian charm, and not at all marred by heavy, sturdy furniture or the somewhat hushed atmosphere. Strong on service. If it's an English tea you're after, this is the place (tie and jacket required). Dover St., W1 (phone: 493-6020). Expensive.

Cadogan Thistle – Very comfortable, older, 69-room place, redolent of Edwardian England. Oscar Wilde was arrested here, and Lillie Langtry, who was having an affair with the Prince of Wales (later Edward VII), lived next door. The furniture and decor are original, but modern conveniences are offered as well. 75 Sloane St., SW1 (phone: 235-7141). Expensive.

Cavendish – Famous as the *Bentinck,* the hotel run by Louisa Trotter (in real life, Rosa Lewis) in the TV series "The Duchess of Duke Street," this modern replacement offers one of the most attractive locations in central London, near Piccadilly. Its 253 rooms are comfortable, though hardly elegant. Jermyn St., SW1 (phone: 930-2111). Expensive.

Chesterfield – In the heart of Mayfair and near Hyde Park, this small, recently rebuilt Georgian mansion has a certain exclusive elegance. Its 113 bedrooms are thoroughly modernized and well equipped. Amenities include a restaurant, a wood-paneled library, and a small bar that opens onto a flower-filled patio. 35 Charles St., W1 (phone: 491-2622). Expensive.

Churchill – Once inside, a turn-of-the-century mood is reflected in the discreet decor. This is a well-run, efficient place, with a pleasant restaurant and a snack room that serves the best bacon and eggs in London. Very popular with Americans. Portman Sq., W1 (phone: 486-5800). Expensive.

Claridges – This plush 209-room outpost for visiting royalty, heads of state, and other distinguished and/or affluent foreigners is an Art Deco treasure. The line of chauffered limousines outside the main entrance sometimes makes traffic seem impenetrable. Wrought-iron balconies and a sweeping foyer staircase help provide a stately setting for one of London's most elegant hostelries. Liveried footmen serve afternoon tea. Brook St., W1 (phone: 629-8860). Expensive.

Connaught – A touch too sober for high livers; a trifle too formal for the rough-and-ready crowd. But there aren't many hotels left in the world that can rival it for welcome, elegance, and comfort — particularly in its luxurious suites. Unfortunately, though, the restaurant's food is losing its once high reputation. Carlos Pl., W1 (phone: 499-7070). Expensive.

Dorchester – Closed while undergoing an ambitious £70-million renovation, this Mayfair classic is scheduled to reopen in the spring of 1990 — more luxurious than ever. Park La., W1 (phone: 629-8888). Expensive.

Dorset Square – Set in a lovely garden (formerly Thomas Lord's cricket grounds) in the heart of London, this Georgian country house is one of the city's most elegant and charming hotels. Guests can choose from the 37 rooms in the main hotel or truly treat themselves by staying in one of the suites across the way. The suites include sitting and drawing rooms and are elegantly furnished with marble bathrooms, working fireplaces, and antiques. The Royal Suite features a grand piano. 39/40 Dorset Sq., NW1 6QN (phone: 723-7874)

Draycott – The 26 rooms here are each distinctively decorated. While there's no restaurant, there is a breakfast room and 24-hour room service. Staying here is like living in a fashionable London townhouse. 24-26 Cadogan Gardens, SW3 (phone: 730-6466). Expensive.

Drury Lane Moat House – Near the theater district and fashionable Covent Garden, this 153-room hotel is ultra-modern, with a cool, sophisticated decor. There's an elegant bar, and lunch is served on the terrace. 10 Drury La., High Holborn, WC2 (phone: 836-6666). Expensive.

Dukes – Despite its modest size (only 39 rooms and 18 suites), this is an establishment where nobility and prestige shine through. The exterior is an exquisite Edwardian façade, there's a peaceful, flower-filled courtyard; and some suites are named for former dukes. A virtual total reconstruction has produced accommodations of great taste and warmth, and the snug location, down a quiet cul-de-sac, does its best to seem authentically British. Piccadilly, Buckingham Palace, Trafalgar Square, Hyde Park Corner, and the shops of Bond Street and the Burlington Arcade are all within walking distance. 35 St. James's Pl., SW1A (phone: 491-4840 or 800-223-5581). Expensive.

Fenja – In this new first class Victorian townhouse, each of the 13 bedrooms is named for a writer or artist with associations nearby (Jane Austen, Hilaire Belloc, Henry James, John Singer Sargent). There are private bath/showers with luxury fittings, crystal decanters filled with liquor, and terrycloth bathrobes. Room service is also available 24 hours a day. 69 Cadogan Gardens, SW3 (phone: 589-7333). Expensive.

Forty-Seven Park Street – One of our most cherished secrets, these "service flats" are a favorite of folks who are staying for more than a few days; the accommodations are small apartments perfect for extended visits. Breakfast alone is worth crossing the Atlantic, since "room service" here is provided by the elegant *Le Gavroche* restaurant, which flourishes downstairs. Owned by the Roux Brothers, who also own the restaurant (and the *Wayside Inn* out in Bray), the furnishings are luxurious in the best English taste. The setting, roughly between Hyde Park and Grosvenor Square, is also ideal. 47 Park St. (phone: 491-7282). Expensive.

Gatwick Hilton International – Part of the airport's expansion program, this 552-room hotel provides much-needed accommodations for the ever-increasing number of visitors using the Gatwick gateway. Connected to the terminal by an enclosed walkway; facilities include many services for business travelers: bars, health club, 24-hour room service, and more. Gatwick Airport (phone: 0293-518080). Expensive.

Grosvenor House – This 472-room grande dame facing Hyde Park has a health club, a swimming pool, some interesting shops, the much-lauded *Pavilion* restaurant, the *Park Lounge,* which serves traditional afternoon teas, and the exclusive *Crown Club* on the top floor for members only — usually businesspeople who require special services — with rooms, suites, a lounge, and complimentary extras. Park La., W1 (phone: 499-6363). Expensive.

Halcyon – A $15-million restoration brought back to glamour the two Belle Epoque mansions that are the foundations of this property. Some of the rooms feature four-poster beds and Jacuzzis, plus all modern conveniences. Its *Kingfisher* restaurant is among London's best. 81 Holland Park, W11 (phone: 727-7288). Expensive.

Hilton International Kensington – A bit out of the way, this modern hotel offers a great deal of comfort at prices below those of most Hiltons. Services include a restaurant, piano lounge, a Japanese restaurant, and a lavish brunch on Sundays. Rooms are well designed and well maintained. 179-199 Holland Park Ave. (phone: 603-3355). Expensive.

Hyde Park – The only hotel in Hyde Park — it held apartments in Victorian times — played host to Rudolph Valentino in the 1920s and George VI and Queen Elizabeth in 1948. Today it continues to offer some of the finest accommodations in London. The spacious bedrooms are furnished with lovely antique furniture, modern bathrooms, and mini-bars. Some rooms also have spectacular views of the park. Marble stairs, chandeliers, and beautiful plants are all part of the elegant decor. Visit the *Park Room* overlooking Hyde Park for delicious meals, including breakfast and afternoon tea. There is also a grill room, drawing room, and business lounge, which provides international communication services. 66 Knightsbridge, SW1 Y7LA (phone: 235-2000). Expensive.

Inn on the Park – Don't be deceived by the modern exterior; everything is traditional (and wonderful) within. A fine example of the superb service routinely offered by members of the Four Seasons chain, the rooms are comfortable, tastefully furnished, and spacious. The breakfast buffet is delightful; the restaurant, first rate. Hamilton Pl., Piccadilly, W1 (phone: 499-0888). Expensive.

Inter-Continental – Smack-dab in the middle of the West End, right on Hyde Park Corner, with windows overlooking the route of the Royal Horse Guards as they go cantering off for the Changing of the Guard each morning. Its 490 well-proportioned rooms have refrigerated bars. Modern and comfortable, particularly the Art Deco *Le Soufflé* restaurant, but the location's the main allure. 1 Hamilton Pl., Hyde Park Corner, W1 (phone: 409-3131). Expensive.

London Hilton International – Right off Hyde Park Corner, near shopping and theater, this contemporary high-rise offers comfortable accommodations (445 rooms) and spectacular views of the park and the city. Special attention to execcutives includes a multilingual switchboard, secretarial staff, office equipment, and private dining rooms. There's every conceivable service plus 3 restaurants — the *Roof,* with a view; the *Polynesian;* and the new *British Harvest,* serving organically grown traditional British produce — a disco, and a snack bar. 22 Park La., W1 (phone: 493-8000). Expensive.

London Marriott – Close to the American Embassy and West End shopping, Marriott's recent refurbishment has transformed this modern hotel. It's bright and busy, and it has everything — lounge, bar, two restaurants, shops, 227 very comfortable rooms, and good service. Grosvenor Sq., W1 (phone: 493-1232). Expensive.

Londonderry – This deluxe hotel overlooks Hyde Park; it recently reopened after an extensive tasteful refurbishment. Its 3 penthouse suites and 150 rooms feature a French Mediterranean decor, a theme echoed in both the *Isle de France* restaurant and adjoining bar. Park La., W1 (phone: 493-7292). Expensive.

Mayfair Holiday Inn – Renovation hasn't damaged the hotel's all-pervading Regency style, unusual for this chain. Sitting in London's highly prestigious property belt, it has 192 rooms, the à la carte *Berkeley* restaurant, and an evening pianist in the *Dauphin* cocktail bar. 3 Berkeley St., W1 (phone: 493-8282). Expensive.

Le Meridien – Formerly the *New Piccadilly,* between the Royal Academy and Piccadilly Circus, this hotel recently underwent a £16-million refurbishment, though the rooms remain mostly modest in size and rather dark. A lofty, Edwardian marble entrance hall leads to the 284 rooms and 24 suites. The *Terrace* restaurant, on the second floor, seats 140 under a glass roof, and the space beneath the hotel has been transformed into the biggest health club in Europe. There is also a less formal restaurant, a bar, and a cocktail lounge. Piccadilly, W1 (phone: 734-8000). Expensive.

Montcalm – A smaller, elegant hotel with a lovely façade, a warm-toned and understated interior, and topnotch service. Its 114 rooms have all the usual comforts, and many of its 6 suites are especially luxurious. There's a bar, and in *Les Célébrités* restaurant, chef Gary Houiellbecq brings to bear all the skills he employed at the acclaimed *Compleat Angler* in Marlow. Great Cumberland Pl., W1 (phone: 402-4288). Expensive.

Mountbatten – The life and times of Earl Mountbatten of Burma is the theme throughout this refurbished, wonderfully eccentric hotel's public rooms, all with exhibitions of various mementos from India. All 127 rooms feature Italian marble bathrooms, satellite color TV, and in-house movies, while 7 suites have whirlpool baths. Monmouth St., Covent Garden, WC2 (phone: 836-4300). Expensive.

Park Lane – If you don't mind the noise of the city streets, the site of this hotel, in the heart of the West End, is appealing. Some of the 324 rooms have views of Green Park across the street. Piccadilly, W1 (phone: 499-6321). Expensive.

Ritz – The fellow who was heard to mutter snootily "Nobody stays at the *Ritz* anymore" was off-base, especially since the recent renovation restored much of the old luster and certainly got the "bugs" out. With 130 rooms, it now ranks among London's finest stopping places, and it's hard to find another hotel in London with more elegant surroundings. Tea is a particularly pleasant experience; the dining room is equally splendid, with its stately interior columns, opulent ceiling frescoes, and the view of Green Park. There was a time when the quality of the cuisine wasn't quite equal to the decor, but that has largely changed. Piccadilly, W1 (phone: 493-8181). Expensive.

Royal Court – Clean, comfortable, and recently refurbished, the hotel has a courteous, helpful staff, at the head of London's fashionable Chelsea shopping and residential district and within quick, easy reach of the rest of the action in town. Sloane Sq., SW1 (phone: 730-9191). Expensive.

Royal Horseguards Thistle – This 262-room hotel overlooks the Thames with views of the South Bank. Recently modernized, it is a good base for those interested in the changing of the Buckingham Palace guard, Westminster Abbey, and the Houses of Parliament. Riverside rooms have balconies and there's a pleasant terrace. 2 Whitehall Ct., SW1 (phone: 839-3400). Expensive.

St. James's Club – For about $480 ($320 per year thereafter) and an introduction by a member, you can join this exclusive residential club in the heart of London (though you don't need to bother for your first stay). Guests have full use of club suites. Some of the best food in the city is served in the downstairs dining room. 7 Park Pl., SW1 (phone: 629-7688). Expensive.

Savoy – A favorite of film and theater performers, some of whom check in for months. Still one of London's top addresses, it's a 200-room hotel with armies of chambermaids and porters to keep things running. The reputation of its famous *Savoy Grill* has been restored through a beautiful resuscitation of the decor and a revitalization of the kitchen. The Thames Suites are the most beautiful accommodations in the entire city. The Strand, WC2 (phone: 836-4343). Expensive.

Selfridges – Just behind the department store of the same name, modern in both furnishings and tone, with a refreshing, unaffected courtesy. Convenient for shopping. Orchard St., W1 (phone: 408-2080). Expensive.

Stafford – In a surprisingly quiet side street close to the city center, this is where many American television and newspaper organizations often lodge visiting correspondents to give them efficient, friendly, British small-hotel management at its best. Owned by Cunard, which has refurbished the 62 rooms in smashing style. 16 St. James's Pl., SW1 (phone: 493-0111). Expensive.

White House – A very big hotel, converted from apartments, in a quiet spot near Regents Park. Modernized and efficiently run, its facilities include a coffee shop and wine bar. Albany St., NW1 (phone: 387-1200). Expensive.

White's – What used to be three 19th-century merchant bankers' private homes have been transformed into one of London's most charming small hotels. It has personality that the larger ones lack — a cobbled forecourt, a glass-and-iron-covered entryway, even a paneled writing room where tea is served in the afternoon. Choose a room at the front, overlooking Hyde Park, and take breakfast on the balcony. Lancaster Gate, W2 (phone: 262-2711). Expensive.

Abbey Court – In the Notting Hill Gate area near Portobello Market, this elegant hotel has 24 rooms of various sizes, each with private bath, TV set, hair dryer, and trouser press. The flowers in the common areas are especially lovely. Breakfast is served in the room, and 24-hour room service is also available. No restaurant. 20 Pembridge Gardens, W2 (phone: 221-7518). Expensive to moderate.

Alexander – This South Kensington hotel in an agreeable off-Brompton retreat — a peaceful place to escape from the world — was recently tastefully refurbished. Its elegant, unpretentious decor includes fine fabrics, tile bathrooms for each of the 40 rooms, and some four-poster beds. In-house movies are offered along with 24-hour room service and a garden for fine weather. 9 Sumner Place, SW7 (phone: 581-1591). Expensive to moderate.

Number Sixteen – In four adjoining townhouses, this delightfully comfortable hotel puts the accent on personal service. The 32 rooms feature fresh flowers and full bath/showers. Continental breakfast is served in all rooms, some of which have terraces leading to the conservatory and garden. There is a small bar. Children under 12 are not welcome. 16 Sumner Pl., SW7 (phone: 589-5232). Expensive to moderate.

Capital – Recently refurbished, with an excellent French restaurant, an intimate lounge, and a lively bar. All 60 rooms have air conditioning, color TV sets, and radios. 22 Basil St., Knightsbridge, SW3 (phone: 589-5171). Moderate.

Durrants – This elegant Regency-style hotel has a splendid location behind the Wallace Collection and is only a few minutes' walk from the shopping on Oxford Street. It has been family-run for over 50 years and all the 95 rooms have retained their character while being kept comfortably up to date. George St., W1 (phone: 935-8131). Moderate.

Ebury Court – A small hotel with smallish but cozy rooms and an intimate atmosphere (the owners dine with guests in the restaurant). Its faithful clientele testifies to its comfort, suitability, and "country house in London" touches. Hard to beat — all things considered — in a town where hotel prices tend to be unreasonable. Fewer than half of the 39 rooms have a bath or shower. 26 Ebury St., SW1 (phone: 730-8147). Moderate.

Embassy House – Over a million dollars has just been spent on renovating this Edwardian building on a wide tree-lined street in Kensington. It is very near the *Albert Hall* and all the main museums and an easy walk from *Harrods* and Hyde Park. There are 68 rooms, and although the decor is modern, there are elaborate high ceilings and elegant staircases. There's also a restaurant and bar. 31 Queens Gate, SW7 (phone: 584-7222). Moderate.

Harewood – This small, modern hotel is well maintained by a pleasant and efficient staff. Some of its 93 rooms have private terraces. Restaurant and wine bar. Harewood Row, NW1 (phone: 262-2707). Moderate.

Pastoria – In the very center of the West End, near all theaters, this pleasant, comfortable little hotel has 52 rooms, most with baths and TV sets; it has a bar and a restaurant. St. Martin's St., WC2 (phone: 930-8641). Moderate.

Ramada Inn – Completely refurbished, redecorated, and generally upgraded, all 510 rooms have private bath and in-house movies. There's also a comfortable Victorian pub. Lillie Rd., SW6 (phone: 385-1255). Moderate.

Wilbraham – A charming, authentic, 52-room bed-and-breakfast establishment, just around the corner from *Harrods* and Sloane Square. 1 Wilbraham Pl., SW3 (phone: 730-8296). Moderate.

Claverley – Named the Best "Bed and Breakfast Hotel" in 1987 by the British Tourist Authority, this establishment in the middle of London has 36 rooms, 30 of which have private baths; some rooms have four-poster beds. All bedrooms have floral decor, and each has a heated towel rack in the bathroom. In the reading room, guests can help themselves to newspapers, coffee, tea, and cookies. A fine British breakfast is served in the morning. 13 Beaufort Gardens, SW3 (phone: 589-8541). Moderate to inexpensive.

Blanford – This pleasant bed-and-breakfast establishment has 33 rooms decorated in pastel greens and pinks, each with a color TV set and direct dial telephone. A British breakfast is served in the morning, and complimentary newspapers are available. 80 Chiltern St, W1M 1PS (phone: 486-3103). Inexpensive.

Delmere – Nearly 200 years old, this lovely hotel was designed by architect Samuel Pepys Cockerell, the student of Benjamin H. Latrobe, who designed the south wing of the Capitol in Washington, D.C. The hotel has 40 rooms equipped with private showers or baths, hair dryers, and the makings for tea and coffee. There is also a bar and a restaurant, *Le Sous Sol,* where food is grilled on stones — hot slabs of Matterhorn rock. The staff, mostly from Holland, is very friendly. Paddington Station, where trains leave for Bath and South Wales, is a mere 5-minute walk away. 130 Sussex Gardens, Hyde Park, W2 1UB (phone: 706-3344).

Diplomat – Small, with no restaurant and only 24 rooms — all with baths — it is nonetheless comfortable, friendly, and affordable. In Belgravia at 2 Chesham St., SW1 (phone: 235-1544). Inexpensive.

La Place – A fine bed-and-breakfast establishment with 24 rooms, including private baths, TV sets, and king-size or two double beds; some rooms also have mini-bars. British breakfast is served in the morning. 17 Nottingham Pl., W1M 3FB (phone: 486-2323). Inexpensive.

Observatory House – This bed-and-breakfast establishment was once owned by Count Dangerville of France, and many members of royalty have slept here since then, including the exiled King of Yugoslavia. In 1988 the hotel was renovated in Victorian decor, and all 27 rooms have a private shower, color TV set, telephone, trouser press, and tea and coffee supplies. Some rooms are for non-smokers only. 37 Hornton St., Kensington, W8 7NR (phone: 937-1577). Inexpensive.

Winchester – Near Victoria Station, this bed-and-breakfast establishment is in an old townhouse with a Victorian façade; the interior was completely refurbished with, among other facilities, modern bathrooms and new furniture. The 18 bedrooms include showers, color TV sets, and radios. Guests are treated to an English breakfast in the morning. 17 Belgrave Rd., Victoria, SW1 (phone: 878-2972). Inexpensive.

YMCA – This relatively new "Y" could be the best and most comfortable low-cost hotel in the middle of London. The 168 adequate, tidy rooms are complemented by a series of facilities not often found in hotels — including squash courts, a gym, billiard room, swimming pool, and sauna. Close to the *British Museum* and Oxford Street shopping district. Men and women of all ages are welcome, and triple rooms are available. 112 Great Russell St., WC1 (phone: 636-8616). Inexpensive.

 EATING OUT: Few London restaurants were ever known for the excellence of their cuisine — and some visitors of times past might call that a charitable understatement. But there's been a notable transformation in recent years. While restaurants offering really good English cooking — and not simply "chips with everything" — are still not easy to find (some are listed below), there has been a veritable explosion of good foreign restaurants in town (some of which are also noted below).

A meal for two will cost about $150 at a restaurant listed as very expensive; $100, expensive; $50 to $75 is moderate; and $30 and under inexpensive. Prices do not include wine, tips, or drinks. Most London restaurants have adopted the continental habit of adding a service charge to the bill, so make certain you're not tipping twice. Reservations are necessary in all restaurants below. All telephone numbers are in the 01 area code unless otherwise indicated.

Le Gavroche – Probably the best French restaurant in London and, according to *Guide Michelin,* one of the best in the entire country, with three stars to its credit (only one other establishment in Britain has received such a high rating). The food is classic French; many of the dishes by those chefs extraordinaire, the Roux brothers, qualify as genuine masterpieces. Reserve well in advance. Closed weekends. 43 Upper Brook St., W1 (phone: 408-0881). Very expensive.

L'Arlequin – A tiny establishment that offers unusual and innovative Gallic cooking by proprietor Christian Delteil, who reputedly makes the best sorbets in London. Closed weekends. 123 Queenstown Rd., SW8 (phone: 622-0555). Expensive.

Bibendum – On the 2nd floor of the former Michelin building, renovated by Sir Terence Conran of the *Habitat* chain of stores. Chef Simon Hopkinson's good taste ranges beyond the classic French dishes. Michelin House, 81 Fulham Rd., SW3 (phone: 581-5817). Expensive.

Le Bistroquet – A chic, French-ish brasserie. Ceiling fans rotate and spiky-haired waiters and waitresses whiz between tables as fish dishes cooked in parchment are cut open, filling the air with the scent of capers and fresh fennel. Open daily. 273-275 Camden High St., NW1 (phone: 485-9607). Expensive.

Capital Hotel Restaurant – The elegant, comfortable, small dining room in this hotel near *Harrods* offers well-chosen, admirably prepared French dishes. It is considered by some discriminating Londoners to be the best place in town to eat. Shuns the aren't-you-lucky-to-get-a-table attitude flaunted by some other better London restaurants. 22-24 Basil St., SW3 (phone: 589-5171). Expensive.

Cavaliers' – Sue and David Cavaliers' restaurant, south of the river in upwardly mobile Battersea, serves French fare prepared by an accomplished British chef. Closed Sundays and Mondays. 129 Queenstown Rd., SW8 (phone: 720-6960). Expensive.

Connaught – Very dignified and proper, this restaurant, with one Michelin star, has a fine reputation for both its cuisine and elegant service. Frankly, these guys carry stuffy to sometimes excessive lengths, but it's hard not to appreciate the masterful culinary performance. The setting — lots of rich paneling and crystal chandeliers — matches the distinction of the menu. Closed weekends. At the *Connaught* hotel, Carlos Pl., W1 (phone: 499-7070). Expensive.

Gay Hussar – Among the best Hungarian restaurants this side of Budapest, its substantial menu offers a varied selection: chicken ragout soup, goulash, roast pork, and lots more. The food here is extremely filling as well as delicious. Informal atmosphere, with a regular clientele drawn from London's newspaper and publishing world. Closed Sundays. Make reservations early. 2 Greek St., W1 (phone: 437-0973). Expensive.

Guinea Grill – This unimposing restaurant substitutes displays of its fresh food — steaks, chops, fresh vegetables — for a menu. It's as good as it looks, cooked with care. Closed Sundays. 26 Bruton Pl., W1 (phone: 629-5613). Expensive.

Hilaire – Once serving only superb French food, this spot now also offers impressive English dishes, imaginatively prepared and charmingly served. Closed Saturdays for lunch and Sundays. 68 Old Brompton Rd. (phone: 584-8993). Expensive.

Leith's – A fine continental restaurant in an out-of-the-way Victorian building northwest of Kensington Gardens, this spot serves very good entrées, hors d'oeuvres, and desserts as part of a fine *prix fixe* dinner. An excellent vegetarian menu is also available, and its wine selection is very good. Open daily for dinner. 92 Kensington Park Rd., W11 (phone: 229-4481). Expensive.

Lichfield's – Fish and game are the chef's specialties here: Try ballantine of quail, for example, set on a bed of apples and bathed in Calvados sauce. As an alternative to the train, take a boat to Richmond from Westminster Pier, lunch at *Lichfield's*, and walk it off on Richmond Green. Open Tuesdays, Fridays, and Sundays for lunch; Tuesdays through Saturdays for dinner. 13 Lichfield Terrace, Sheen Rd., Richmond (phone: 940-5236). Expensive.

Poons – This Cantonese restaurant has built a reputation for good, authentic cooking and specializes in top-quality fish dishes and wind-dried food. You can even watch the chefs at work through a glass partition. Closed Sundays. 41 King St., WC2 (phone: 240-1743), and 4 Leicester St. WC2 (phone: 437-1528). Expensive.

Rue St. Jacques – Lavishly decorated with huge gold-framed mirrors. The food here is marked by rich cream sauces. A delicous vegetarian main course is also available. Pricey, but well worth it. The formality stretches to jacket-and-tie requirement and a doorman who provides parking service. Closed Saturdays for lunch and Sundays for dinner. 5 Charlotte St., W1 (phone: 637-0222). Expensive.

Savoy Grill – Renowned as a celebrity-watching ground, but actually inhabited mostly by a male, business clientele. Although the menu features some classic French dishes, the English grills and roasts are its specialty. The lovely, newly restored decor resembles a luxurious ship's dining room (first class, natch) of 50 years ago. Perfect for after theater. Closed Sundays. At the *Savoy* hotel, The Strand, WC2 (phone: 836-4343). Expensive.

Tante Claire – Run by chef Pierre Koffman and his wife, Annie, this newly expanded establishment has been awarded two Michelin stars as well as many other honors. While fish dishes are the chef's specialty, everything — especially the duck, calf's liver, and *pied de cochon farci aux morilles* (pig's foot stuffed with foie gras and mushrooms) — is excellent. The *prix fixe* lunch is a remarkably good value at around $20. Closed weekends. 68 Royal Hospital Rd., SW3 (phone: 352-6045). Expensive.

Wilton's – Good food, skillfully prepared, elegantly served in a plush, rather formal Victorian setting. Game, fish, oxtail, steak and kidney pie — what the best of English cooking can be all about. Closed Sundays and 3 weeks in July/August. 55 Jermyn St., SW1 (phone: 629-9955). Expensive.

Langan's Brasserie – Still trendy after all these years, and still a popular haunt for celebrities. Ask for a downstairs table and take your time studying the lengthy menu. Reservations necessary. 1 Stratton St., W1 (phone: 491-8822)). Expensive to moderate. *Langan's Bistro* serves slightly simpler and less expensive dishes prepared in the same style. Both closed weekends for lunch. 26 Devonshire St., W1 (phone: 935-4531). Moderate.

Bloom's – A large restaurant specializing in Jewish food, *Bloom's* has a bright and bustling atmosphere, a bit like the dining room of a large hotel, with waiters who almost — but not quite — throw the food at you. The popular take-out counter serves up the best hot salt beef (like corned beef) sandwiches in town. House wine is Israeli. Closed Friday evenings and Saturdays. 130 Golders Green Rd., NW11 (phone: 455-1338), and 90 Whitechapel High St. E1 (phone: 247-6001). Moderate.

Bombay Brasserie – At lunchtime there is an Indian buffet; at dinner, classic cooking from the Bombay region. Parsi dishes, rarely found outside of India itself, are also included. And the setting is lovely, with lots of banana plants, wicker chairs, and ceiling fans. Popular with both the American and British show-biz colonies. Open daily. Courtfield Close, Courtfield Rd., SW7 (phone: 370-4040). Moderate.

Camden Brasserie – The daily specials are posted on a board outside this restaurant in an increasingly fashionable part of town. Among the selections are meats and fish grilled over an open fire. 216 Camden High St., NW1 (phone: 482-2114). Moderate.

Chuen Cheng Ku – At this huge restaurant in the heart of Chinatown, the overwhelming majority of the clientele is Chinese. The specialty here is dim sum, served daily until 6 PM. Also try the pork with chili and salt, duck webs, steamed lobster with ginger, and shark fin soup. 17 Wardour St., W1 (phone: 734-3281). Moderate.

Hungry Horse – This is the place to discover what a properly made English meat pie and Yorkshire pudding should taste like, as well as other English goodies. Don't be put off by having to pass under an archway and climb down a flight of stairs to get there — if anything, the inside looks a touch too tidy. Closed Sundays for dinner. 196 Fulham Rd., SW10 (phone: 352-7757). Moderate.

123 – One block from the Japanese Embassy, this is where the staff eats, a sure sign of quality. But be warned that there are two menus, one in English, the other in Japanese, and they are vastly different. The latter offers a far more extensive array of sashimi. Ask the waiter to translate. Closed weekends. 27 Davies St., W1 (phone: 409-0750). Moderate.

Porters – A very English eatery in Covent Garden, famous for its home-cooked pies — steak, mushroom, and vegetable are a specialty. The kitchen, bar, and basement are even more spacious since the restaurant was completely redecorated. Open daily. 17 Henrietta St., WC2 (phone: 836-6466). Moderate.

Le Routier – The English equivalent of a truck stop, with an interesting location overlooking the craft workshops and canal at Camden Lock. Inside you'll find a brasserie atmosphere, with specialties of the day chalked up on a blackboard. Very popular for lunch on weekends. Open daily. Commercial Pl., Chalk Farm Rd., NW1 (phone: 485-0360). Another branch, closed weekends, is at Foley St., W1 (phone: 631-3962). Moderate.

La Ruelle – Just off Kensington High Street, this small French restaurant recently introduced an imaginative selection of vegetarian dishes to its classic menu. Closed weekends. 14 Wright's La., W8 (phone: 937-8525). Moderate.

Shezan – A quiet, brick and tile restaurant just below street level that prepares some very fine Pakistani food. Specialties include marinated-in-yogurt *murg tikka Lahori* (chicken cooked in *tandoori*, or clay ovens) and *kabab kabli* (minced spiced beef). An enthusiastic staff will explain the intricacies of tandoori cooking, help with your order, and lavish excellent service upon you. Closed Sundays. 16 Cheval Pl., SW7 (phone: 589-7918). Moderate.

Sweetings – A special London experience, this traditional fish restaurant is one of the great lunchtime attractions in London's financial district. You may have to sit at a counter with your lobster, brill, or haddock — but it will be fresh and perfectly prepared. Weekday lunchtime only; no reservations, so expect a wait. 39 Queen Victoria St., EC4 (phone: 248-3062). Moderate.

Tate Gallery Restaurant – Who would expect one of London's better restaurants to be in a fine art museum? But there it is — a genuine culinary outpost (leaning toward French cuisine) with a very good wine list. Not just another meal between the masterpieces. Lunch only. Closed Sundays. Tate Gallery. Millbank, SW 1 (phone: 834-6754). Moderate.

La Trattoria dei Pescatori – A busy atmosphere pervades this restaurant, whose decor includes a boat, terra cotta tiles, copper pans, and chunky ceiling beams. The menu is enormous, with trout, halibut, salmon, shrimp, turbot, and lobster appearing in several guises. A typical specialty is *misto dei crostacei alla crema* — Mediterranean prawns, scallops, shrimp, and mussels sautéed with onions and herbs, simmered in fish stock and Asti, with a touch of cream. Closed Sundays. 57 Charlotte St., W1 (phone: 580-3289). Moderate.

Treasure of China – In a landmark Georgian building, this restaurant is a leader in original Peking and Szechuan cuisine. Owners Tony Low and Roger Norman offer a selective daily menu as well as superb banquets celebrating Chinese festivals. Open daily. 10 Nelson Rd., SE10 (phone: 858-9884). Moderate.

Tuttons – One of the few restaurants in London that serves food all day, it's a very popular and lively brasserie in a former Covent Garden warehouse and a handy snack spot for theatergoers. Open from 10 AM to 11:30 PM Sundays through Thursdays; 10 AM to midnight Fridays and Saturdays. 11 Russell St., WC2 (phone: 836-1167). Moderate.

Wheeler's – One of the chain of London seafood restaurants with the same name, this is the original and the best of the lot. It's an old-fashioned, narrow establishment, on three floors, which specializes in the many ways of preparing Dover sole, most of them delicious. The oyster bar on the ground floor is our favorite perch. Closed Sundays. Duke of York St. at Apple Tree Yard (phone: 930-2460). Moderate.

Chiang Mai – Thai restaurants are a rarity in London. This one is easy to spot since it's the only eatery in Soho (and probably the whole of Britain) with a carved wooden elephant poised on the sidewalk. The menu offers such dishes as coconut chicken and galanga soup. Those unfamiliar with Thai cooking should inquire about the spiciness of individual dishes before ordering. Closed Sundays. 48 Frith St., W1 (phone: 437-7444). Moderate to inexpensive.

HQ – An unusual (for London) Créole-style menu is the main attraction at this new restaurant/wine bar in trendy Camden Lock. Its location above the art and craft shops affords guests good views of the canal and weekend street performers. Open daily. Commercial Pl. (phone: 485-6044). Moderate to inexpensive.

Kettner's – As you check your coat, you have to make your choice — a bottle of champagne at the bar (25 labels in stock), a humble but tasty salad in the brasserie-style café, or a pizza in the beautifully furnished dining room reminiscent of an Edwardian hotel. Open daily. 29 Romilly St., Soho, W1 (phone: 437-6437).

Khyber – A wide selection of Indian Punjabi specialties as well as tasty vegetarian dishes are served here. Try the *pannir,* mild cheese cooked with peas, meat, and spices, and the *aloa gobi,* a cauliflower dish. Open daily. 56 Westbourne Grove, W2 (phone: 727-4385). Moderate to inexpensive.

Last Days of the Raj – This popular restaurant on the eastern fringe of Covent Garden serves dishes from India's Punjabi region. Punjabi cuisine is rather mild, and one of its specialties is meat prepared *tandoori* style — marinated in yogurt and spices, then baked in a special tray oven. Some kind of tandoori cooking is usually on the menu in addition to other specials, which change every few months. The exotic mango-based cocktails are powerful, and the service is extremely friendly. Be sure to dine at the Drury Lane *Raj,* as other restaurants are now trading on the original restaurant's good name. Closed Sundays. 22 Drury La., WC2 (phone: 836-1628). Moderate to inexpensive.

Smolensky's Balloon – This American-owned cocktail bar/restaurant with a 1930s piano-bar atmosphere is guaranteed to make you feel homesick. Steaks and fries figure largely on the menu, offset by some interesting vegetarian dishes. Open daily, noon to 11:45 PM, Sundays noon to 10:30 PM. 1 Dover St., W1 (phone: 491-1199). Moderate to inexpensive.

Bangkok – Known for its *saté* — small tender slices of beef marinated in a curry and soy sauce and served with a palate-destroying hot peanut sauce. From your butcher block table you can watch your meal being prepared by chefs in the windowed kitchen. Closed Sundays. 9 Bute St., SW7 (phone: 584-8529). Inexpensive.

Café Maxim's – In the same building as *Maxim's de Paris,* it aims to combine the atmosphere of a brasserie with the already familiar *Maxim's* style. Live jazz in the evenings. Closed Saturdays at lunch and Sundays. Clareville House, Panton St., SW1 (phone: 839-4809). Inexpensive.

Calabash – West African cuisine gives this restaurant a unique position on London's restaurant map, especially since it's in the bubbling Covent Garden district. The service is accommodating and helpful and the food is both good and different. Closed Sundays. Downstairs at London's "Africa Centre," 38 King St., WC2 (phone: 836-1976). Inexpensive.

La Capannina – Homemade pasta is offered by this unpretentious, friendly Italian restaurant, typical of those that flourish in Soho. Closed Saturdays for lunch and Sundays. 24 Romilly St., W1 (phone: 437-2473). Inexpensive.

Chicago Pizza Pie Factory – A little while ago, an American advertising executive turned his back on the ad world to bring London deep-dish pizza Windy City style, along with Budweiser beer and chocolate cheesecake. Londoners beat a path to his door and haven't yet stopped clamoring to get in. Open daily. 17 Hanover Sq., W1 (phone: 629-2669). Inexpensive.

Cosmoba – A small and friendly family-run Italian restaurant that is basic in every respect — except for its food. Tucked down a tiny alleyway and always packed with regulars. Closed Sundays. 9 Cosmo Pl., WC1 (phone: 837-0904). Inexpensive.

Cranks – There are four branches of this self-service vegetarian restaurant. All are popular and serve good homemade desserts as well as salads, quiches, and other hot food. Drop in for coffee or afternoon tea. 8 Marshall St., W1 (phone: 437-9431), open for dinner daily except Sundays; 11 The Market, Covent Garden, WC1 (phone: 379-6508), open daily; Tottenham St., W1 (phone: 631-3912), closed Sundays; and Unit 11, Adelaide St., WC2 (phone: 631-3192), closed Sundays. Inexpensive.

Dumpling Inn – This Peking-style restaurant serves excellent Oriental dumplings, and most of the other dishes are equally good. Try the fried seaweed; it's got lots of vitamins and tastes terrific. The service, though efficient, is a little brisk. Open daily. 15A Gerrard St., W1 (phone: 437-2567). Inexpensive.

Geales' – This place serves up truly English — and fresh — fish and chips in a setting that looks like a 1930s tearoom. Go early, because *Geales'* is no secret. Closed Sundays and the last 3 weeks in August. 2 Farmer St., W8 (phone: 727-7969). Inexpensive.

Hard Rock Café – This is the original. An American-style eating emporium with a loud jukebox and good burgers. It's always crowded, and the lines stretch well out into the street. As much a T-shirt vendor (at the shop around the corner) these days as a restaurant. Open daily. 150 Old Park La., W1 (phone: 629-0382). Inexpensive.

Kalamaras Taverna – A small, friendly eatery with authentic Greek food prepared under the watchful eye of the Greek owner. The menu here is more varied than that in most of the other Greek/Cypriot restaurants in London. Bouzouki music is sometimes played in the evenings. Closed Sundays. 66 and 76 Inverness Mews, W2, off Queensway (phone: 727-5082 or 727-9122). Inexpensive.

My Old Dutch – This authentic Dutch pancake house serves endless varieties of sweet and savory pancakes on genuine blue Delft plates. Loud music. Open daily. 132 High Holborn, WC1 (phone: 242-5200). Inexpensive.

Oodles – A "country food" restaurant with branches on four of London's busiest streets. Wholesome quiches, spicy curries, and unusual salads are served under ceilings hung with (fake) country flowers and branches. Closed Sundays. 42 New Oxford St. WC1 (phone: 580-9521); 31 Cathedral Pl. EC1 (phone: 248-2550); 113 High Holborn WC1 (phone: 405-3838); and 128 Edgeware Rd., W2 (phone: 723-7548). Inexpensive.

Standard – Possibly the best Indian restaurant value in London, so it tends to get crowded quickly. There are no reservations, so dine early to beat the rush. Open daily. 23 Westbourne Grove, W2 (phone: 727-4818). Inexpensive.

Widow Applebaum – Not an authentic New York Jewish delicatessen, but this place serves pretty good herring, cold cuts, chopped liver, potato salad, dill pickles, and apple pie. Closed Sundays. 46 S Molton St., W1 (phone: 629-4649). Inexpensive.

SHARING A PINT: There are several thousand pubs in London, the vast majority of which are owned by the six big brewers. Most of these pubs have two bars: the "public," which is for the working man who wants to get on with the business of drinking, and the "saloon" or "lounge," which makes an attempt at providing comfort and may serve good food and wine as well as beer. Liquor at the latter may cost more. Among the means by which pubs are appraised is the brand and variety of draft brews that spew forth from their taps. The extraordinary variety can easily perplex the uninitiated. There's ale: bitter, mild, stout; and lager, whose varying tastes provide a perfect excuse to linger longer in pubs you find particularly convivial. Eating in a crowded pub is not always easy because the limited number of tables are barely large enough to hold all the empty beer glasses, let alone food. Pub food is hearty but not especially imaginative: a ploughman's lunch, which is a hunk of bread and cheese plus pickle; cottage pie, which is ground meat with mashed potato on top baked in the oven; sausages; and sandwiches. The number (and quality) of pubs serving fancier food is increasing, since British law has recently expanded opening hours for pubs offering food. The law used to require pubs to close for several hours from late afternoon to early evening; now most open at 10:30 or 11 AM and remain open all day.

Here are the names of pubs where we like to raise a pint or two: *Dirty Dick's,* 202 Bishopsgate, EC 2, is offbeat but popular, with fake bats and spiders hanging from the ceilings, sawdust on the floor, and good bar snacks; *Sherlock Holmes,* 10 Northumberland St. (phone: 930-2644) is the pub that Holmes's creator, Arthur Conan Doyle, used to frequent when it was still the *Northumberland Arms,* and which he mentioned in *Hound of the Baskervilles;* a glass-enclosed replica of Holmes's Baker Street study is there, along with Holmes memorabilia. *The Audley,* 41 Mount St., W1, is our favorite luncheon stop in the high-rent district, with fine sandwiches and salad plates in an atypically hygienic environment. Other fine spots include *The Antelope,* 22 Eaton Terrace, SW1, where the Bellamys (or even Hudson, their butler) might have sipped a lager on the way home to nearby 165 Eaton Place; *The Grenadier,* 18 Wilton Row, SW1, perhaps the poshest pub site in town, just off Belgravia Square; *Admiral Codrington,* 17 Mossop St., SW3, is large and Victorian, with brass beer pumps, engraved mirrors, and good food; *Dickens Inn* by the Tower, St. Katherine's Way, E1, is a converted warehouse overlooking a colorful yacht marina and serving shellfish snacks; *George Inn,* 77 Borough High St., SE1, dates from 1676 and retains the original gallery for viewing Shakespearean plays in the summer; *The Flask,* 77 Highgate West Hill, N6, serves drinks at three paneled bars and on its outside patio; *The Lamb,* 94 Lambs Conduit St., WC1, is also paneled and hung with photos of past music hall performers; *Museum Tavern,* 49 Great Russell St., WC1, is across the road from the *British Museum* and decorated with hanging flower baskets; *Princess Louise,* 208 High Holborn, WC1, has live music, cabaret, and a wine bar upstairs with good food; *Bull and Bush,* North End Way, NW3, owes its fame to the Edwardian music hall song "Down at the Old Bull and Bush." Former customers include Thomas Gainsborough and Charles Dickens. It has an outdoor bar and barbecue for balmy summer evenings. *Prospect of Whitby,* 57 Wapping Wall, E1, the oldest riverside pub in London, was once the haunt of thieves and smugglers (now it draws jazz lovers. *Ye Olde Cheshire Cheese,* 5 Little Essex St., EC4 (just off Fleet

St.), is a 17th-century pub with paneled walls and sawdust floors popular with the Fleet Street set.

 WINE BARS: An innovation on the London scene, they serve wine by the glass or bottle, accompanied by such light fare as quiche and salad, and occasionally full meals. Prices tend to be lower in wine bars than in restaurants, and tables can often be reserved in advance. Here's a selection of the finest: *Boos,* 1 Glentworth St., NW1, combines rustic decor with simple homemade food; *Cork and Bottle,* 44-46 Cranbourn St., WC2, is patronized by the London wine trade and has a classical guitarist providing background music; *Draycott's,* 114 Draycott Ave., SW3, has tables outside and is frequented by the smart London set; *Ebury Wine Bar,* 139 Ebury St., SW1, in the heart of Belgravia, serves good food (try the English pudding) and offers live music nightly; *Le Bistroquet,* 273-275 Camden High St., NW1, is one of London's trendiest spots, popular with the city's yuppies; *Shampers,* 4 Kingly St., W1, is near the famous *Liberty* department store and sometimes has a classical guitarist in the evenings; *Bar des Amis,* 11-14 Hanover Pl., WC2, is a crowded watering hole in fashionable Covent Garden; *Crawford's,* 10-11 Crawford St., W1, is a lively basement bar serving full cold buffet lunches and suppers; *Penny's Place,* 6 King St., WC2, can be too crowded for comfort, but always has good wines, food, and music; *Julie's,* 137 Portland Rd., W11, has become a landmark for aging flower children of the '60s; *El Vino,* 47 Fleet St., EC4, *the* haunt for journalists, is most famous for refusing to serve women at the bar.

MADRID

When King Philip II proclaimed Madrid the capital of Spain and all her colonies in 1561, he said that he chose it because of the "healthy air and brilliant skies" and because, "Like the body's heart, it is located in the center of the Peninsula." Philip was right. Madrid's air is delightfully dry and invigorating. Its "Velázquez skies" that so inspired the court painter are dramatically bright, with more than 3,000 hours of sunshine annually. As a result of Philip's proclamation, what had been an insignificant Castilian town of 17,000 suddenly burst into being as the cosmopolitan nucleus of the Spanish Empire — upon which, in those days, the sun never set. One of Europe's youngest capitals, Madrid grew fast, as if making up for lost time. A comment by a Spanish poet in 1644 continued to be true until just a few decades ago: "Each day, new houses are being built, and those that used to be on the outskirts are now in the middle of the town."

The city has blossomed into today's glamorous metropolis of 4.3 million that thrives on its own vitality. More than ever, it is ebullient, outgoing, fun-loving, proud, stylish, and creative, with a nightlife that doesn't stop; a city intensely lived in and adored by its melting pot of inhabitants. Throughout Madrid's history, a great proportion of its residents have been born elsewhere in Spain, a country of various and diverse cultures. Yet soon after their arrival, they feel "adopted" and become as genuinely *madrileño* as native sons and daughters.

According to a saying as meaningful to *madrileños* as the Cibeles Fountain, "the next best place after Madrid is heaven, but with a peephole for looking down at it." The city has a way of enticing foreigners as well. Visitors invariably feel at home in Madrid — much more so, of course, if they speak Spanish. Another popular saying, often seen on bumper stickers, boasts that Madrid is *"el pórtico al cielo"* ("the gateway to heaven"). The city is, in fact, the highest capital in Europe — 2,135 feet above the sea level of the Mediterranean at Alicante, affirmed by a plaque at Puerta del Sol.

Despite its high-tech, high fashion, streamlined skyscrapers up the Castellana, and its being declared the Cultural Capital of Europe for the year 1992 by the European Economic Community (EEC), Madrid still endearingly refers to itself as a "town," or *villa*. Its official name during the 16th century was the "Very Noble, Loyal, Heroic, Imperial, and Distinguished Village and Court of Madrid, Capital of Spain," or, simply, "Villa." The city hall, for example, is Casa de la Villa, the modern concert-theater-exhibition center is Centro Cultural del la Villa, and the summer-long program of concerts, fairs, and entertainment is called *"Veranos en la Villa."* *Madrileños* love to be out on the streets, where walking or strolling is an activity in itself, rather than just a means of getting somewhere. And they enjoy crowding together. In spring, summer, and fall, thousands of outdoor *terrazas* (cafés), set up on

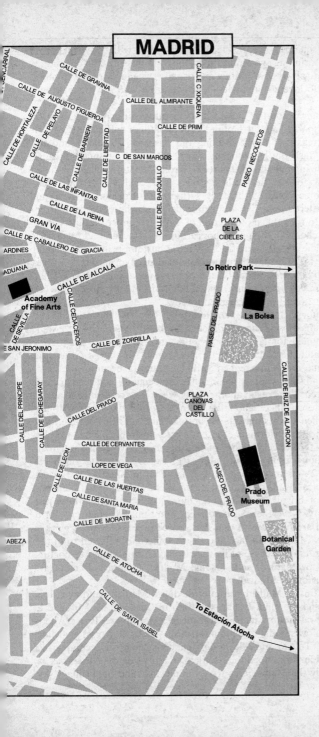

sidewalks and in squares and parks, teem day and night with convivial people chatting, eating, drinking, gossiping (locals love to gossip), and looking at each other. There's always eye contact and usually a friendly or witty greeting — *madrileños* also love a quick wit — even to those who are just buying a newspaper.

La movida, Madrid's on-the-move, artistic-creative surge of the late 1970s and early 1980s, sparked a rebirth of indoor and outdoor café society. Stylish *madrileños* congregate at *terrazas* along the Paseo de Recoletos and the Castellana from dusk until practically dawn. Crowded late-night Spanish style pubs specializing in high-decibel rock 'n' roll or soothing classical music line Calle Huertas, one of the liveliest streets in the old part of town that, amazingly, is also occupied by the early 17th-century Convent of the Trinitarias, where cloistered nuns live and embroider, and where Miguel de Cervantes is buried. In the typical old section of Lavapiés, entire families gather to eat, drink, and chat with their neighbors at simple restaurants adorned with sidewalk tables. The *tertulia,* an age-old Madrid custom, brings experts and devotees together for informal discussions about their favorite subjects. Visitors will surely find *tertulias* about theater or literature at the *Café Gijón,* art at the *Círculo de Bellas Artes* lounge, and bullfighting and breeding at the bar of the *Wellington* hotel, to name a random few.

When it's time for the midday *aperitivo* around 1 PM (when stores, offices, and many museums close), thousands of *tapas* bars, *tabernas,* and swank cafés become jammed for a couple of hours until lunchtime, when they suddenly empty and the restaurants fill up. Around 4 or 5 PM (when the stores, offices, and museums reopen), the restaurants become vacant — it's customary to go somewhere else for coffee or cognac — and the bars and cafés are reactivated. They reach another peak when it's *aperitivo* time again, around 8 PM (as stores, offices, and museums close for the day), before dinner around 10 PM, when the restaurants fill up once more. Then it's time for a movie, concert, theater performance, jazz at a café, or simply a *paseo* (stroll).

Madrid boasts the longest nights of any Spanish city, even though in midsummer the sun doesn't set until almost 11 PM. Discotheques don't get started until 1 or 2 AM, and at many, the action continues until 7 AM. Then it's time for a typical Madrid breakfast of thick hot chocolate with *churros* (sticks or loops of crispy fried dough), elbow to elbow with others just beginning their day. Nevertheless, *madrileños* don't mistake their city for a vacation spot and are fully aware that it is indeed a place for hard work.

There are many Madrids. In fact, the city is sometimes referred to in the plural — *los madriles* — because of its various facets. In addition to nocturnal Madrid, daytime Madrid, and seasonal Madrid, there are different architectural and historical Madrids.

Not much remains of Madrid Antiguo (medieval Madrid), and even less is known, but legends abound. In 852, the Emir of Córdoba, Muhammad I, chose the strategic ravine-top site above the meager Manzanares River (where the Royal Palace now stands) to build a fortified Alcázar (fortress) guarding the route between Toledo and Alcalá de Henares against the reconquering Christians. The Moors described their settlement alongside the Alcázar as "a village bordered by the Manzanares River on one side and the brilliant sky on the other." They called it Magerit (later mispronounced as Madrid by Castilians), meaning delicious and "plentiful flowing water," from the nearby Sierra de Guadarrama. (This water from the Lozoya River continues to supply the city, and is also the brand name of a bottled mineral water).

Magerit began to grow, and walls were continually built to enclose the town, keeping up with its random expansion. Fragments of these old walls, as well as sections of underground passageways to the Alcázar, have been uncovered as recently as the 1970s — a major site can be seen at Cuesta de la Vega. A few well-preserved remnants of medieval Magerit still stand today: the house and tower of the Lujanes family and the adjacent Periodicals Library building, both at Plaza de la Villa; the Moorish Quarter (La Morería); and the towers of the church of San Nicolás de los Servitas and the church of San Pedro.

In 1083, King Alfonso VI and his Christian troops reconquered Madrid and took up residence in the Alcázar. Then the *madrileño* melting pot expanded with the subsequent influx of Christians into what then became medieval Christian Madrid, and more walls were built to surround it.

Madrid really began to take shape when King Philip II of the Habsburg House of Austria raised its rank to capital of Spain, moving the throne and court there from Toledo. During his reign and those of his successors during the 16th and 17th centuries, what is known as Madrid de los Austrias, or the Madrid of the Habsburgs, was built. This is the charming and picturesque section of Old Madrid, the hub of which is the Plaza Mayor. The establishment of the capital drew multitudes from all parts of Spain. Following the Court, nobility and gentry built their mansions, and the clergy founded churches, convents, monasteries, and hospitals. Merchants, artisans, and innkeepers set up shop, and laborers, adventurers, and bandits rounded out the mixture. Habsburg Madrid grew into a labyrinth of meandering narrow cobblestone streets and tiny squares, lined with severe buildings of stone, brick, and masonry topped by roofs that blended into a burnt-red "sea of tiles." With the Spanish Empire at its apogee, the *siglo do oro* (golden age) of Renaissance literature flourished in Habsburg Madrid; streets, squares, and statues bear the names of Cervantes, Lope de Vega, Tirso de Molina, Quevedo, and Calderón de la Barca, all of whom lived here.

The city continued fanning out southward, creating the delightful *barrios* (neighborhoods) such as Lavapiés and Embajadores, lively with *tabernas, mesones* (inns), vendors, organ-grinders, and artisans. The authentically typical and uniquely *madrileño* personality of these barrios and their colorful people are defined by the word *castizo* — the inspiration of many 18th- and 19th-century *zarzuelas* (traditional Spanish musical dramas), for example *La Verbena de la Paloma,* which are presented outdoors during the summer at La Corrala, in the heart of Madrid Castizo at Plaza Agustín Lara. (Lara, a Mexican composer who had never been to Madrid, wrote the city's unofficial anthem, "Madrid, Madrid, Madrid.") Those who visit Madrid during the first half of August should be sure to stroll around these *barrios castizos* to see *madrileños* of all ages, bedecked in traditional costumes, dancing the graceful *chotis* in the streets and enjoying the *verbenas* (fairs).

When the Habsburg dynasty died out at the end of the 17th century, King

Philip V, grandson of France's King Louis XIV, was the chief claimant to the throne of Spain. After a war of succession, he established the Bourbon dynasty as the legitimate heir to the kingdom. The Bourbon monarchs began a new century and era in Madrid, known as Madrid de los Borbones. They wanted a splendid new European capital worthy of their neo-classic French models. When the Alcázar burned down, Philip V commissioned top architects (Spaniard Ventura Rodríguez and Italian Francesco Sabatini) to create in its place a grandiose palace comparable to Versailles. To the east of old Habsburg Madrid, systematic expansion with wide avenues and large squares, laid out in geometric configuration, transformed Madrid into a model city of the Enlightenment — the Madrid of the Bourbons. The city's urban renewal, embellishment, and social progress culminated with the reign of *madrileno* King Charles III, "the Construction King of the Enlightenment," known affectionately as the "King-Mayor." Charles commissioned Juan de Villanueva to design the neo-classic *Natural Science Museum,* which later became the *Prado Museum,* and the adjacent Botanical Gardens. The exquisite tree-lined Paseo del Prado, with its Neptuno, Apolo, and Cibeles fountains by Ventura Rodríguez, and the monumental Puerta de Alcalá (then marking the eastern end of the city) are among the legacies of Charles III.

The steady progress of the city and the country foundered, however, in 1808, when Napoleon was encouraged to invade Spain because of the weakness of Carlos IV, the next Bourbon king. The French invasion of Madrid was successful, following the bloody executions of resisting Spanish patriots on the night of May 2, a tragedy immortalized by Goya in his famous paintings now in the *Prado.* At the Plaza de la Lealtad on Paseo del Prado, a memorial obelisk with an eternal flame commemorates *el dos de mayo.*

Napoleon forced the crowning of his brother, Joseph Bonaparte, as King of Spain. "Pepe Botella" (Bottle Joe), as he was called (either for his drinking habits or for having put a tax on liquor), in his quest for open space for ongoing urban renewal, tore down picturesque chunks of Habsburg Madrid, including much of the Retiro Park Palace and a church in the small Plaza de Ramales that contained the grave of Velázquez. But the Spanish War of Independence led to the expulsion of the French and the return to the throne of a Bourbon king, Fernando VII, in 1813.

In the last third of the 19th century, Romantic Madrid spread farther northward. Aristocratic palatial mansions graced the elegant Barrio de Salamanca, where today some of Madrid's finest shops and boutiques line Calles Serrano and Velázquez. Paseo del Prado extended north to become Paseo de Recoletos and, farther north, Paseo de la Castellana. By the early 20th century, a transportation problem arose: There was no street connecting the new outlying districts of Salamanca and Argüellas. The solution was to chop through part of Old Madrid and construct a new thoroughfare, the Gran Vía.

The instability of the monarchy during the early 20th century led to further political upheaval. Alfonso XIII finally abdicated in 1931 to avoid a civil war. But the Socialist Republican government's decentralization plan and reform measures aroused strenuous right-wing opposition, which resulted in insurrection and, in 1936, the Spanish Civil War. Madrid, which remained aligned with the Republican government, was blown to pieces at the hands of Generalissimo Francisco Franco's Nationalist forces. During the nearly 40 years of Franco's dictatorship, Madrid's spirit and creativity were stifled. Franco's death in 1975, the restoration of the monarchy, and the institution of a representative, democratic government brought about a dramatic multifaceted surge of activity ranging from construction to culture. As if making up for those 40 years of lost time, *madrileños,* with their newfound affluence and freedom of expression, have made their city one of Europe's most energetic and trend setting, in art, fashion, music, and theater. In the mid-1980s, the late mayor Enrique Tierno Galván inspired an amazing revival of *madrileño* affection for its own traditions and lore, and fomented the arts and the *movida madrileña.* He was so revered that after his death in 1986, a *zarzuela* was written about him.

With its new symphonic *Auditorio Nacional,* the revitalized *Opera House,* the *Queen Sofía Art Center,* and the expanding *Prado Museum,* Madrid is fast becoming a major cultural power. The city continues to spread outward, absorbing surrounding towns in order to meet the needs of a growing populace. This is an exciting time to visit and savor its new vitality. While the city attempts to redefine itself and refocus its vision toward the future, it is at the same time preserving the best of its proud past — people can still hear organ-grinders in the streets of Old Madrid. The city will certainly live up to its EEC designation as 1992's European Cultural Capital of the Year.

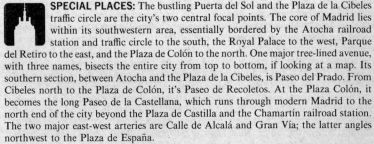

MADRID AT-A-GLANCE

SEEING THE CITY: For a wonderfully romantic view of Madrid, watch the sun set from the 25th-floor roof garden and pool of the *Plaza* hotel. The sharp "Velázquez sky," portrayed in the artist's famous paintings, is usually tinted with a golden hue. Looking over the "sea of tile" rooftops, visitors will see a fine view of the Royal Palace and, to the north, the distant Sierra de Guadarrama. The hotel's terrace and pool are open daily during the summer months. Admission charge. 2 Plaza de España (phone: 247-1200).

SPECIAL PLACES: The bustling Puerta del Sol and the Plaza de la Cibeles traffic circle are the city's two central focal points. The core of Madrid lies within its southwestern area, essentially bordered by the Atocha railroad station and traffic circle to the south, the Royal Palace to the west, Parque del Retiro to the east, and the Plaza de Colón to the north. One major tree-lined avenue, with three names, bisects the entire city from top to bottom, if looking at a map. Its southern section, between Atocha and the Plaza de la Cibeles, is Paseo del Prado. From Cibeles north to the Plaza de Colón, it's Paseo de Recoletos. At the Plaza Colón, it becomes the long Paseo de la Castellana, which runs through modern Madrid to the north end of the city beyond the Plaza de Castilla and the Chamartín railroad station. The two major east-west arteries are Calle de Alcalá and Gran Vía; the latter angles northwest to the Plaza de España.

For a basic overview, take a half-day motorcoach tour of the city with *Julía Tours,* 38 Calle Capitán Haya (phone: 270-4300); *Pullmantur,* 8 Plaza de Oriente (phone: 241-1805); or *Trapsatur,* 23 Calle San Bernardo (phone: 241-6320). Their brochures indicating departure points and times are distributed at the reception desks of most hotels. The best way to see Madrid, however, is by walking; in fact, many picturesque areas can be seen only on foot. In the center of the city, things are much closer than they seem from the inside of a motorcoach or taxi. A good stroll, for starters, is from Puerta del Sol to the Plaza Mayor, then downhill to the Plaza de Oriente. Good maps of the city are provided free of charge at the tourist offices. Keep in mind that most museums close on Mondays, some at midday, and smaller ones during the entire month of August.

Plaza Mayor – Oddly enough, this grandiose main square, which is closed to vehicular traffic, is easily missed if you don't aim for it and enter through one of the nine arched entryways. Built during the 17th century by order of King Philip III, it is the quintessence of Habsburg Madrid — cobblestones, tile roofs, and imposing austere buildings. Initially, the square shared the irregularity of the surrounding architectural chaos. Its perfectly rectangular shape and flat surface are a result of the redesign project by Juan Gómez de Mora, who was commissioned by Philip III to "straighten it out." The plaza became the stage for a wide variety of 17th- and 18th-century spectacles and special occasions — audiences of over 50,000 crammed the square to witness hangings, burnings, and decapitations of heretics, as well as canonizations of saints (such as St. Teresa and St. Isidro, Madrid's patron saint), jousting tournaments, theater (including plays by Lope de Vega), circuses, and even bullfights. The 447 balconies of the surrounding buildings served as spectator "boxes" — not for the tenants, but rather for royalty and aristocrats. Today, the Plaza Mayor is still lively, but with tamer entertainment — *la tuna,* or strolling student minstrels, amateur musicians, artists, and on-the-spot portrait painters selling their works, summer concerts and ballets, and outdoor cafés for watching it all. Myriad shops, many over a century old and all worth browsing through, line the arcades around the plaza. On Sunday mornings, philatelists and numismatists set up shop in the arcades, to the delight of stamp and coin collectors. Visitors can easily lose their sense of direction inside this vast enclosure; it's helpful to know that the bronze equestrian statue of Philip III in the center is facing east (toward the *Prado Museum*). The legendary Arco de Cuchilleros entrance is at the southwest corner.

Puerta del Sol – This vast oblong plaza is the bustling nerve center of modern Madrid life. Ten streets converge here, including the arteries of Alcalá, San Jerónimo, Mayor, and Arenal. Its name, "Gate of the Sun" in English, comes from a long-disappeared medieval city wall carved with a sunburst. On the south side, the 18th-century Comunidad government building, originally the Central Post Office, is topped by a clock tower. At midnight on New Year's Eve, thousands gather to hear the clock strike and swallow one grape at each stroke to ensure 12 months of good fortune during the new year. Near the curb in front of the building's main entrance, a famous yet inconspicuous emblem in the sidewalk marks the "kilometer zero" central point from which all Spanish highways radiate and from which their distance is measured. Directly across the plaza, at the entrance to one of the two pedestrian streets, stands the venerated bronze statue of the *Oso y el Madroño* (the bear and the madrona berry tree), the symbol and coat of arms of Madrid since the 13th century.

Museo Nacional del Prado (Prado Museum) – One of the world's supreme art museums, the *Prado* is a treasure house of over 4,000 universal masterpieces, most of which were acquired over the centuries by art-loving Spanish monarchs. The wealth of Spanish paintings includes famous works by El Greco (including *Adoration of the Shepherds*), Zurbarán, Velázquez (including *The Spinners* and *Maids of Honor*), Murillo, Ribera (including *Martyrdom of St. Bartholomew*), and Goya (including *Naked Maja* and *Maja Clothed*). On the ground floor, a special section is devoted to the tapestry cartoons designed by Goya for the palace-monastery at San Lorenzo del El Escorial (see *Extra Special*) and to his extraordinary *Disasters of War* etchings, which represent his thoughts and comments on Spain's War of Independence. Visitors will also find Goya's stunning *Second of May* and *Third of May* canvases. Vast rooms are devoted to Italians Fra Angelico, Botticelli, Raphael, Correggio, Caravaggio, Titian, Tintoretto, and Veronese. Other rooms display paintings by Flemish and German masters such as Rubens, van der Weyden, Hieronymus Bosch (including *The Garden of Earthly Delights*), Memling, Dürer, and Van Dyck. From the Dutch are works by Rembrandt, Metsu, and Hobbema. French art is represented by Poussin, Lorrain, and Watteau, and the English by Reynolds, Gainsborough, and Lawrence.

The neo-classic *Prado* building was originally a natural science museum, conceived by Carlos III, the Enlightenment "King-Mayor," who ordered its construction by architect Juan de Villanueva. In 1819, King Ferdinand VII converted it into a museum to house the royal art collection. A bronze statue of Velázquez stands before the main façade; a statue of Goya at the north façade, and one of Murillo at the south side. In addition to the main *Prado,* or Villanueva building, the museum also has two annexes. Just up a hill from the Goya statue is the Casón del Buen Retiro, which resembles a small Greek temple. It was once the stately ballroom of the 17th-century Royal Retiro Palace complex, which was destroyed during the French occupation of Madrid. Up the stairs is the *Museum of 19th-Century Spanish Painting.* At its other side, facing Parque del Retiro, a separate entrance leads to a section devoted to Picasso's monumental *Guernica,* which portrays the horrors of the Spanish Civil War and the devastating bombardment of that Basque town. Still in the planning stages is the removal of the *Guernica,* and the drawings related to it, from the Casón del Buen Retiro to the *Queen Sofía Art Center,* which is devoted to contemporary art. Diagonally across the Plaza Cánovas del Castillo (Neptune Fountain) is the other annex, the splendid Villahermosa Palace. Its spacious interior is presently being redesigned to house the recently acquired Thyssen-Bornemisza Collection, considered the most important private art collection in the world. The project is scheduled for completion in 1991.

The *Prado* has had a steadily increasing inventory of possessions, which long ago outgrew the museum's walls. The main building has recently undergone a major refurbishment program, opening some two dozen remodeled rooms to display works previously in storage or on loan to other Spanish museums. Expansion plans for additional exhibit space include the acquisition in the mid-1990s of the nearby 17th-century Salón de Reinos building, which currently houses the *Museo del Ejército* (Army Museum).

The *Prado* collection is so vast that it is impossible to savor its wonders in a single visit. If time is limited, it is best to select a few galleries of special interest, or enlist the services of the extremely knowledgeable government-licensed free-lance guides at the main entrance. The guides are more readily available in the early morning, and their fee is approximately $15 per hour. Reproductions from the *Prado's* collection, postcards, and fine arts books are sold at the shop inside the museum. There is also a bar-restaurant on the premises, open during museum hours. The *Prado* is open Tuesdays through Saturdays, 9 AM to 6:45 PM; Sundays, 10 AM to 1:45 PM. Closed holidays. The $4 admission charge grants access to the main building and the annexes. Paseo del Prado (phone: 468-0950 or 239-8023).

Palacio Real (Royal Palace) – The Moors chose this strategic site overlooking the Manzanares River to build their Alcázar, or castle-fortress. After the Reconquest during the 11th century, the Christian leaders renovated and moved into the Alcázar. Philip II made it the royal residence upon proclaiming Madrid the capital of Spain in 1561. During the reign of Philip V, Spain's first Bourbon monarch, the Alcázar was destroyed by fire on Christmas Eve, 1734. The king then commissioned top Spanish and Italian architects to construct a glorious new palace in the neo-classic style on the very same rugged steep site. It took 26 years to build the colossus of granite and white limestone, with walls 13 feet thick, over 2,000 rooms, 23 courtyards, and magnificently opulent interiors. "King-Mayor" Charles III finally became the first royal resident. The east façade faces the grand Plaza de Oriente; at the north side are the formal Sabatini

Gardens; and down the slopes on the west side is the Campo del Moro — 20 acres of forest, manicured gardens, and fountains, and now a public park. The main entrance is on the south side, through the tall iron gates leading into an immense courtyard called the Plaza de la Armería (armory), a setting for the pageantry of royal occasions. The imposing structure at the courtyard's south end is just a façade — so far. Under construction for over a century, it will eventually become Madrid's Catedral de la Almudena, honoring the patroness of the city. Upon completion, it will be the oldest *new* cathedral in the world!

There is a choice of tours by section, and all tours alternate with English-speaking National Patrimony guides. The palace is open Mondays through Saturdays, 9:30 AM to 12:45 PM and 1:30 to 5:45 PM; Sundays and holidays, 9:30 AM to 1:30 PM (closed during royal occasions, which are not always announced in advance). Admission charge. Plaza de Oriente (phone: 248-7404).

Plaza de Oriente – To the disappointment of Asian tourists, its name in Spanish just means East (*oriente*) Square, so named simply because it faces the east façade on the Royal Palace. Across the plaza from the palace is the *Teatro Real* (Royal Theater), which, after a major 2-year revamping of its interior, is scheduled to reopen in 1991 as one of Europe's finest opera houses. In the center of the plaza stands the 9-ton bronze equestrian statue of King Philip IV, based on a drawing by Velázquez. Philip's horse is rearing, supported solely by its hind legs, posing an equilibrium problem for sculptor Pedro Tacca. He consulted none other than the illustrious Galileo, whose solution was to make the front end of the statue hollow and the rear end solid.

Centro de Arte Reina Sofía (Queen Sofía Art Center) – This gargantuan 18th-century building was originally Madrid's Hospital General de San Carlos until 1965. Following a tremendous 6-year reconstruction project, the building reopened in 1986 as a museum devoted to contemporary art, named in honor of the present Queen of Spain. A long-term program of continuous expansion within its own vast space is intended to position the center among the world's leading contemporary art galleries. In the planning stages is the permanent hanging here of Picasso's *Guernica,* now in the *Prado*'s Casón del Buen Retiro annex. Important works from other contemporary art collections in Madrid are also being consolidated here. In addition to major scheduled exhibitions of internationally known contemporary artists, there are extensive research facilities, seminars, and workshops. Open Wednesdays through Mondays, 10 AM to 9 PM. Admission charge. 52 Calle Santa Isabel (phone: 467-5062).

Plaza de la Cibeles – Dominating Madrid's favorite traffic circle is the fountain and statue of the Greek fertility goddess Cibeles, astride her chariot drawn by two rather friendly looking lions. A Madrid custom requires that visitors "say hello to La Cibeles" upon arrival in town. Almost drowning out the vision of the Cibeles Fountain with its massiveness, the wedding-cake turn-of-the-century Palacio de Comunicaciones (now the city's post office) on the plaza is so imposing that *madrileños* often refer to it as "Our Lady of Communications." Both Cibeles and the monumental arches of the Puerta de Alcalá (Alcalá Gate) up the street at the Plaza de la Independencia are 18th-century endowments of the Bourbon "King-Mayor" Charles III. On the southwest side of the Plaza de la Cibeles is the Banco de España; on the northwest side, the Palacio de Buenavista, which houses the Ministry of Defense.

Parque del Retiro (Retreat Park) – During the early 17th century, it was a royal retreat and the grounds of both a royal palace complex and a porcelain factory, then on the outskirts of town. Now Madrid's public park, right in the city, the Retiro covers 300 peaceful acres of forest, manicured gardens, statuary, fountains, picnic grounds, and cafés. It is a delightful place for strolling, jogging, a horse-and-carriage ride, or a boat ride around the lake, which is overlooked by the huge curved-shaped monument to King Alfonso VII. Art exhibitions are held at the park's Palacio de Cristal, a 19th-century jewel of glass and wrought iron, and at the Palacio de Velázquez, named for its architect, not for the painter. During the summer, at 10 PM and midnight, classical and flamenco concerts are staged in the Cecilio Rodríguez Gardens (Menéndez Pelayo entrance), and the outdoor cinema (entrance on Alfonso XIII) features Spanish and foreign (including US) films. The park's loveliest entrance is through the wrought-iron gates at the Plaza de la Independencia, also referred to as the Puerta de Alcalá.

Plaza de la Villa – One of Madrid's most charming squares, its architectural diversity makes it especially interesting. Dominating the west side, the 17th-century neoclassic Casa de la Villa, also called the Ayuntamiento (City Hall), was designed by Juan Gómez de Mora, the same architect who planned the Plaza Mayor. Adding to the *madrileño* atmosphere, its carillon chimes the hour with *zarzuela* melodies and plays 20-minute concerts every evening. Along the back of the square is the 16th-century Plateresque Casa de Cisneros palace, built by the nephew and heir of the cardinal regent of the same name. On the west side are the old Periodicals Library, with a large *mudejar* doorway, and the massive medieval Lujanes Tower, one of the oldest in Madrid and full of legends (one of its prisoners was King François I of France). Separating these two structures, the tiny Calle de Codo (Elbow Street) angles down to the tranquil Plaza del Cordón, which is surrounded by historic noble mansions. The bronze statue in the center of the Plaza de la Villa honors Admiral Alvaro de Bazán, who fought — as did Cervantes — against the Turks in the Battle of Lepanto in 1571. The City Hall's splendid museum collection is open to the public every Monday (except holidays), from 5 to 7 PM, with free tours escorted by guides from the Madrid Tourist Board. Plaza de la Villa (phone: 542-5512).

Museo de la Real Academia de Bellas Artes de San Fernando (Museum of the San Fernando Royal Academy of Fine Arts) – Housed in a splendid 18th-century palace just east of the Puerta del Sol, the academy's permanent collection comprises some 1,500 paintings and over 800 sculptures. There are works by El Greco, Velázquez, Zurbarán, Murillo, Goya, and Sorolla, to name a few, as well as by Italian and Flemish masters. The only painting of George Washington in Spain is here; the portrait commemorates the Treaty of Friendship between Spain and the US. Closed to the public for 12 years, the museum reopened in 1986 and is gradually regaining the international renown it deserves. The museum also hosts prestigious scheduled exhibitions throughout the year. Open Tuesdays through Saturdays, 9 AM to 7 PM; Sundays and Mondays, 9 AM to 2 PM; during the summer, 9 AM to 2 PM daily. Admission charge. 13 Calle de Alcalá (phone: 532-1546).

Convento de las Descalzas Reales – Behind its stark stone façade is an awesomely opulent interior filled with an astonishing wealth of artistic treasures and ornamentation bestowed by kings and noblemen. In 1559, Princess Juana of Austria, sister of Philip II, opened this convent of the Royal Barefoot Carmelite Nuns. It welcomed disconsolate empresses, queens, princesses, and *infantas,* including Juana's sister María, Empress of Germany. The grandiose stairway is a breathtaking example of *barroco madrileño,* every centimeter lavishly decorated with frescoes and carved wood. Art treasures include works by El Greco, Zurbarán, Titian, and Sáncho Coello, as well as Rubens tapestries. From the windows of the upper floor is a lovely view over the tranquil rooftop garden, where the cloistered nuns still grow their vegetables just as they have for centuries. They're unaffected by the bustling Gran Vía just 1 block north, and the gigantic *El Corte Inglés* department store practically alongside. Visitors are escorted by resident guides of the National Patrimony, who provide explanatory tours in Spanish. Tours in English should be arranged through the *Office of Museums* (phone: 248-7404). The convent was declared European Museum of the Year in 1988 by the EEC. Hours vary according to season, and they are limited because the cloistered nuns both maintain and use the museum sections in their daily life. Generally, however, the convent museum is open Tuesdays through Saturdays, 10 AM to 1:30 PM. The small admission charge includes the tour. Plaza de las Descalzas Reales (phone: 522-0687).

Convento de la Encarnación (Convent of the Incarnation) – Built by order of Queen Margarita of Austria, wife of King Philip III, this Augustinian convent was blessed in 1616. Designed in the severe classical style by Juan Gómez de Mora, its façade gives no clue of the bounteous religious and secular art treasures inside. The dazzling reliquary room displays some 1,500 religious relics contained in priceless gold and silver urns and jeweled cases. Among them, a legendary vial contains the blood of St. Pantaleón, which is said to liquefy every year on his birthday, July 27. Set back in the center of the façade is the contrasting neo-classic 18th-century church designed by Ventura Rodríguez. A statue of Lope de Vega graces the convent's peaceful front garden. Like the Descalzas Reales, it is an active cloistered convent, and individuals and groups must be escorted by resident guides; English tours can be arranged through the Office of Museums (phone: 248-7404). Open Tuesdays through Saturdays, 10 AM to 1:30 PM. Admission charge. Plaza de la Encarnación (phone: 247-0510).

Museo Municipal – Devoted to the history of Madrid, this fine museum will enhance any visitor's awareness of the city's evolution, culture, and personality. It is filled with art, furnishings, porcelains, photographs, engravings, and meticulously detailed maps and models of the city and its parts during the 17th, 18th, and 19th centuries. The building, declared a National Monument in 1919, was originally an 18th-century hospital, and its elaborately ornate Churrigueresque entrance is in itself a worthwhile sight. Open Tuesdays through Saturdays, 10 AM to 2 PM and 5 to 9 PM; Sundays, 10 AM to 2:30 PM. Admission charge. 78 Calle Fuencarral (phone: 521-6656).

Mercado Puerta de Toledo – In 1988, Madrid's old Central Fish Market (*mercado*) was rebuilt and opened as this sparkling cultural and shopping showcase of Spain's fine handicrafts, art, antiques, jewelry, fashion, interior design, and gastronomy. It is also the setting for concerts, recitals, and art and photography exhibitions. Scheduled video projections include a "bird's-eye view" of Madrid past and present. At the courtyard entrance is a functional Monument to Time: a giant sculptured combination sundial and lunar clock, considered the world's largest. The Mercado is adjacent to the Puerta de Toledo, one of the ancient city gates, dominated by a 19th-century neo-classic triumphal arch. Joseph Bonaparte initiated construction of the arch; ironically, its completion celebrated the ousting of the French in the War of Independence, and the "welcome back" of Bourbon King Ferdinand VII. Open daily and nightly. 1 Ronda de Toledo (phone: 266-7200).

Jardín Botánico (Botanical Garden) – With its entrance facing the south façade on the *Prado Museum,* the garden was designed in 1774 by the same architect as the museum building, Juan de Villanueva. Twenty manicured acres contain some 30,000 species of plants and flowers from Spain and throughout the world. Charles III commissioned the project as part of his urban refurbishment program. By his order, therapeutic and medicinal plants and herbs were distributed free in the small Plaza de Murillo, which has a bronze statue of the 17th-century painter and the "Four Fountains" of mythological triton cherubs playing with dolphins. Open daily, 10 AM to 7 PM (later in summer). Admission charge. On Paseo del Prado at 2 Plaza de Murillo (phone: 468-2025).

Real Fábrica de Tapices (Royal Tapestry Factory) – Established in the early 18th century, this factory-museum continues to use authentic traditional techniques in producing handmade Spanish tapestries and rugs. In addition to seeing the permanent collection, visit the workshops and watch master craftsmen at work, weaving tapestries from cartoons by Goya and other artists, and knotting luxuriant rugs. They also do intricate restoration work. Rugs and tapestries can be purchased by special order, and can even be custom made from a design provided by the customer. Open weekdays, 9:30 AM to 12:30 PM. Closed August. Admission charge. 3 Calle Fuenterrabía (phone: 551-3400).

Museo del Ejército (Army Museum) – Everything imaginable related to battle

throughout Spain's history is here in an amazing array of over 27,000 items —
uniforms, armor, cannons, swords (including one belonging to El Cid), stupendous
collections of miniature soldiers, and portraits of heroines and heroes (such as Cervantes, when he lost his hand in the Battle of Lepanto). Downstairs, a curious collection
of damaged carriages and automobiles whose illustrious passengers were assassinated
en route recounts Madrid's turbulent political history. It's all chock-a-block within the
vast and lavishly Baroque interior of one of the two surviving buildings of the 17th-
century Royal Retiro Palace complex (the other is the adjacent Casón del Buen Retiro,
which the museum's pleasant bar overlooks). Whatever your interests, this is well worth
seeing — while it lasts. Plans have been laid for the ever-expanding *Prado Museum* to
take over this palatial building, and for the collection to be moved in the mid-1990s
to a new venue at the Ministry of Defense complex in the Moncloa district. Open
Tuesdays through Sundays, 10 AM to 2 PM. Admission charge. 1 Calle Méndez Núñez
(phone: 522-0628).

Museo Arqueológico Nacional (National Archaeological Museum) – The feature piece among the Iberian and classical antiquities is the enigmatic *Dama de Elche,*
a dramatic Iberian bust of a priestess, or perhaps an aristocrat, estimated to have been
sculpted during the 4th century BC. Also on display are basket weavings and funeral
objects of early Iberians, as well as Neolithic, Celtic, ancient Greek, Roman, and
Visigothic artifacts and handicrafts. In the garden at the entrance is an underground
replica of the famous Altamira Cave and its prehistoric paintings. The Biblioteca
Nacional (National Library) is in the same building, with its entrance on the Castellana
side (see below). Open Tuesdays through Sundays, 9:30 AM to 1:30 PM. Admission
charge. 13 Calle Serrano (phone: 403-6607).

Biblioteca Nacional (National Library) – With over 4 million volumes, this is one
of the world's richest libraries, truly a researcher's paradise. The library was inaugurated in 1892 to commemorate the 4th Centennial of the Discovery of America. Statues
of Cervantes, Lope de Vega, and other illustrious Spaniards of letters stand at the
classical columned entrance. Scheduled and seasonal exhibits of publications and
graphics are held in the ground floor galleries. Open Tuesdays through Saturdays, 10
AM to 9 PM; Sundays and holidays, 10 AM to 2 PM. The admission charge includes
entrance to the *National Archaeological Museum* at the opposite side of the same
building. 20 Paseo de Recoletos (phone: 275-6800).

Casa de Campo – Once the private royal hunting grounds, this 4,300-acre forested
public park on the right bank of the Manzanares River is a playground for *madrileños*
and visitors alike. It has a zoo (complete with a panda), picnic and fair grounds
(important trade fairs and conventions are held here), and a giant amusement park,
Parque de Atracciones, with rides and entertainment at an outdoor theater rife with
a spirited carnival atmosphere. Other highlights include a concert stadium, an all-
encompassing sports complex, a small lake, and the bullpens of La Venta de Batán (for
bullfight practice and previews of the bulls). The park is easily reached by bus, metro,
taxi, or *teleférico* (cable car), which runs from Paseo del Pintor Rosales in the Parque
del Oeste, near the Plaza de España. The zoo is open daily, April through September;
weekends and holidays only, October through March. Admission charge. Casa de
Campo (phone: 463-2900).

Basílica de San Francisco el Grande – A few blocks south of the Royal Palace,
this neo-classic church is one of the largest and most richly decorated in Madrid.
Another project of King Charles III, it was designed by the city's finest 18th-century
architects. Six side chapels (the first on the left was painted by Goya) line its circular
interior, which is topped by a cupola 108 feet in diameter. The museum inside the
church contains a wealth of religious art. Open Tuesdays through Saturdays, 11 AM
to 1 PM and 4 to 7 PM. Closed holidays. Admission charge. Plaza de San Francisco
(phone: 265-3800).

■**EXTRA SPECIAL:** Some 30 miles (48 km) northwest of Madrid, the colossal monastery-palace of San Lorenzo del El Escorial symbolizes the grandeur of the Spanish Empire during its 16th-century golden age. King Philip II ordered its construction on a foothill of the Sierra de Guadarrama to commemorate Spain's victory over France at St. Quentin, Flanders, and also to serve as a pantheon for his father, Holy Roman Emperor Charles V, and himself. It took more than 1,500 workmen 21 years to complete this extraordinary, austere monument designed by Juan de Herrera. The gray granite edifice, with hundreds of rooms and thousands of windows, is a sight never to be forgotten. The guided tour includes visits to the royal apartments, the museums (with paintings by Titian, Ribera, Velázquez, Tintoretto, Dürer, Lucas Jordan, and others), the royal pantheon with its tombs of Spanish monarchs, the library (with 40,000 priceless volumes and 4,700 manuscripts), and the basilica. To reach the castle-monastery by car, take the N-VI national highway to Guadarrama, then head south on C600; or take the more scenic, country route C505. There is frequent train and bus service between Madrid and the contiguous town of San Lorenzo del El Escorial, which is charming and well worth seeing. Open Tuesdays through Sundays, 10 AM to 1 PM and 3 to 6 PM. Admission charge (phone: 890-5903).

Nearby, to the north, is the *Valley of the Fallen* (Valle de los Caídos), a spectacular memorial to those who died in the Spanish Civil War. A huge basilica containing the tombs of soldiers from both sides has been hollowed into a mountain. Generalissimo Francisco Franco, who ordered the monument's construction, is also buried here. A granite cross stands 500 feet in the air atop the mountain peak. Open daily, 10 AM to 6 PM. Small parking fee (phone: 890-5611).

SOURCES AND RESOURCES

 TOURIST INFORMATION: All Madrid hotels distribute street maps and magazines listing current events. Information, maps, and brochures can be obtained from the following Tourist Information offices. City of Madrid: 3 Plaza Mayor (phone: 266-5477). City and Province (Comunidad) of Madrid: 2 Duque de Medinaceli, near the *Palace* hotel (phone: 429-4951); Madrid and all Spain: Torre de Madrid, Plaza de España, 1 Calle Princesa (phone: 241-2325). There are also offices at Barajas Airport and the Chamartín train station.

The US Consulate is at 75 Calle Serrano (phone: 276-3400 or 3600).

Local Coverage – *ABC* and *El País* are Madrid's most popular Spanish-language daily newspapers, covering local, national, and international events. A slick English-language magazine, *Spanish Quarterly,* carries tourist information, schedules of events, and articles on fashion and cultural events. Madrid's *Guía del Ocio,* in Spanish, is the most complete weekly guide for food, entertainment, culture, and sports.

Telephone – The area code for Madrid is 91.

 CLIMATE AND CLOTHES: From June through September, the average daily temperature in Madrid is 75F (24C), but days can be very hot and dry, and evenings cool. In January, the average daily temperature dips to 40F (4C), making warm clothes a necessity.

GETTING AROUND: Airport – Aeropuerto de Barajas, about 10 miles (16 km) from downtown Madrid, handles both international and domestic flights. It is about a 20-minute taxi ride from the center of the city, depending on traffic; the fare will run about $15. (Note that taxis charge an additional

$1.50 for picking up passengers at the airport as well as another 25¢ per bag. There is also a 50¢ surcharge for all rides at night (11:30 PM to 6 AM) and all day on Sundays and holidays. Public buses depart for the airport every 15 minutes from a terminal under the Plaza de Colón on the Castellana; the buses are yellow and are marked "Aeropuerto". There is no train service to the airport.

Bus – Excellent, inexpensive bus service is available in Madrid. Signs clearly marking the routes are at each bus stop. "Bonobus" passes are good for ten discounted rides. Microbuses cost a bit more — though still less than 60¢ — and have upholstered seats and air conditioning.

Car Rental – All major international and Spanish firms are represented. Agencies in the city include *América,* 23 Calle Cartagena (phone: 246-7919); *Atesa,* 59 Gran Vía (phone: 247-0202) and 25 Calle Princesa (phone: 241-5004); *Avis,* 60 Gran Vía (phone: 247-2048) and 57 Paseo de la Castellana (phone: 441-0579); *Europcar,* 29 Calle Orense (phone: 445-9930) and 12 Calle García de Paredes (phone: 448-8706); *Hertz,* 88 Gran Vía (phone: 242-1000) and 46 Calle Doctor Fleming (phone: 457-1772); and *Ital,* 31 Calle Princesa (phone: 241-9403).

Subway – Madrid's Metro is efficient and clean. Stops along all ten subway lines are clearly marked, and color-coded Metro maps are easy to read. Metro tickets purchased from booths or machines are put into electronic turnstiles in order to enter. Do not discard the ticket until the end of the ride. Discounted ten-ride tickets are also available.

Taxi – Metered cabs are either black or white with a diagonal red line. If a cab is available it will have a windshield sign that says *libre* or an illuminated green light on its roof. Fares are moderate.

Train – The two major stations of the Spanish National Railway (RENFE) are Charmartín at the north end of Madrid and Atocha at the south end. Both service long-run trains as well as commuter trains to surrounding areas. West of the Plaza de España, a third station, Principe Pío (also called Estación del Norte), services some lines to northern Spain. RENFE's main city ticket office is at 44 Calle de Alcalá (phone: 429-0518 for information; 429-8228 for reservations).

From May to October, RENFE operates a series of special weekend tourist trains offering 1-day excursions to nearby places of interest, or 2-day packages including hotel accommodations to more distant destinations. Museum entrance fees, guided tours, motorcoach sightseeing, and, in some cases, meals are included. Each train has the theme name of its destination. The Saturday and Sunday one-day excursion trains head for Aranjuez (*Tren de la Fresa,* or "Strawberry Train"); Toledo (*Ciudad de Toledo*); Avila (*Murallas de Avila*); Sigüenza (*Doncel de Sigüenza*); and the Piedra River and Monastery in Aragon (*Monasterio de Piedra*). The cost is approximately $15-$20, with discounts for children. Weekend trains, leaving Saturday morning and returning Sunday night, make trips to Cáceres (*Ciudad Monumental de Cáceres*); Burgos (*Tierras del Cid*); Cuenca (*Ciudad Encantada de Cuenca*); Valladolid (*Cuna del Descubrimiento*); Salamanca (*Plaza Mayor de Salamanca*); Soria (*Camino de Soria*); Zamora (*Románico de Zamora*); and Palencia (*Camino de Santiago Palentino*). Prices range from approximately $60 to $120, depending on the train and choice of hotel. Reservations should be booked in advance, at RENFE offices or travel agencies throughout Madrid. This innovative tourist train concept has been so successful that new destinations are added every season.

 SPECIAL EVENTS: Madrid marks Spain's national holidays in its own special and exuberant ways, and, in addition, celebrates its own holidays, fairs, and festivals around the calendar. On the eve of the Epiphany, January 6, children delight at the *Cabalgata de los Reyes,* the procession of the gift-giving Three Wise Men through the city streets. At the end of January, the *Feria Internacional de Turismo* (*FITUR*), a major 4-day trade and consumer tourism fair, is held at Casa de Campo. *Madrileños* go all out, as only they can, for *Carnival* frolic, frocks, and parades in February, ending on *Ash Wednesday* with the allegorical *Entierro de la Sardina* (Burial of the Sardine). The *International Festival of Theater and Film* is held in April. On the *Second of May,* at 2 Plaza de Mayo in the Malasaña district, processions and events commemorate Madrid's uprising against the massacring French, which Goya portrayed so dramatically. Most *madrileño* of all are the *Fiestas de San Isidro* — 10 days of nonstop street fairs, festivals, concerts, special daily bullfights, and more, all celebrating the *Day of St. Isidro,* Madrid's patron saint, on May 15. Goya depicted the age-old tradition of picnics and merrymaking at the Meadows of San Isidro alongside the Manzanares River. On June 13, the *Verbena de San Antonio* takes place at the shrine of San Antonio de la Florida, with outdoor singing and dancing, and traditional drinking from the fountain. It's also customary to throw pins into the holy water; young "spinsters" dip in, and their chances for acquiring a mate depend on the number of pins that stick in their hands. Madrid is extra-lively during the summer, despite the mass exodus of summer vacationers. During July, August, and early September, the City Government of Madrid presents *Veranos en la Villa* (Summers in the "Village"), 2-plus months of countless cultural events featuring international superstars and local talent — ballets, symphonies, operas, jazz, rock, pop, salsa, *zarzuelas,* films, and exhibitions — in open-air and theater settings throughout the city. Fitting in neatly to all this, and linked together, is a continuum of three colorful *verbenas* celebrating the dates of three of Madrid's most popular saints: San Cayetano (August 3), San Lorenzo (August 5), and La Virgen de la Paloma (August 15). In the *castizo* (authentically typical) neighborhoods of Old Madrid (Lavapiés, Embajadores, and Puerta de Toledo) *madrileños,* from toddlers to great-grandparents, dress in the traditional attire of *chulos* and *chulapas* reminiscent of 19th-century zarzuelas. They gather at lively street fairs to eat, drink, and dance the *chotis* and *pasodoble,* enjoying musical groups, folk music performances, organ grinders, processions, *limonada* (not lemonade, but a kind of white-wine sangria), and their own innate ebullience. The world-class *Madrid International Jazz Festival* is held in late October and/or early November. From October through December, the *Fiesta de Otoño* (Autumn Festival), also organized by the city government, presents an abundance of concerts and performances by top international and Spanish companies at Madrid theaters and concert halls. November 9 celebrates the day of Madrid's patroness, La Virgen de la Almudena. During the Christmas–New Year season, the city is bedecked with festive lights, and the Plaza Mayor fills with countless stands selling Christmas decorations, figurines for Nativity scenes, candies, wreaths, and Christmas trees. On *New Year's Eve,* throngs gather at the Puerta del Sol to swallow one grape at each stroke of the clock at midnight, wishing for 12 months of good luck in the new year. As if all of this weren't enough, each barrio expresses its individual personality with its own *fiestas* and *festivales* throughout the year.

MUSEUMS: Many museums are described in *Special Places.* Included in the following list of additional museums are churches that should not to be overlooked, because of their artistic value. Keep in mind that museum hours may vary during summer; a morning visit is also recommended, since many museums close in the early afternoon.

Basílica de San Miguel – An unusual 18th-century church with an air of Italian baroque in its convex façade and graceful interior. 4 Calle de San Justo.

Casa-Museo de Lope de Vega (Lope de Vega's House and Museum) – The home and garden of Spain's great golden age dramatist. Open Tuesdays and Thursdays, 10 AM to 2 PM. Closed summers. Admission charge. 11 Calle Cervantes (phone: 239-4605).

Catedral de San Isidro – This imposing 17th-century church was designated Cathedral of Madrid in 1885, a status considered temporary at the time, awaiting completion of the Catedral de la Almudena, which has been under construction for over a century. On the altar sit the entombed remains of St. Isidro, patron saint of Madrid, and those of his wife, Santa María de la Cabeza. 37 Calle Toledo.

Círculo de Bellas Artes (Fine Arts Circle) – Several galleries of this art, design, and photography center exhibit works by students and prominent masters. 42 Calle de Alcalá (phone: 531-8505).

Estudio y Museo Sorolla (Sorolla Studio and Museum) – The house in which the Valencian impressionist "Painter of Light," Joaquín Sorolla, lived, worked, and died in 1923. Contents include a collection of his works; the studio and library remain intact. Open Tuesdays through Sundays, 10 AM to 3 PM. Admission charge. 37 Calle General Martínez Campos (phone: 410-1584).

Fundación Casa de Alba (House of Alba Foundation) – Within the magnificent 18th-century Palacio de Liria, the former residence of the Duchess of Alba, is her family's priceless private collection of art, tapestries, archives, and furnishings. Admission (free) must be requested well in advance, by writing to Fundación Casa de Alba, 20 Calle Princesa, 28008 Madrid (phone: 247-5302).

Iglesia y Convento de San Jerónimo el Real (Church and Convent of San Jerónimo) – This giant Gothic temple, which overlooks the *Prado,* was built by order of King Ferdinand and Queen Isabella in 1503. Closed for massive renovation, the church and convent are not scheduled to reopen until the mid-1990s. 19 Calle Ruiz de Alarcón.

Museo de América (Americas Museum) – Pre-Columbian artifacts and American and Philippine crafts, including a Maya Palenque calendar, Columbian clay figurines, and folk art that preceded and followed the arrival of the conquistadors. Open Tuesdays through Sundays, 10 AM to 7 PM. Admission charge. 6 Avenida Reyes Católicos (phone: 243-9437).

Museo Cerralbo – The palatial 19th-century mansion of the Marquis of Cerralbo houses an important collection of art, antiques, ceramics, tapestries, and ancient artifacts. Outstanding among the paintings are works by El Greco, Ribera, Velázquez, Zurbarán, Ribera, and Van Dyck. Open Tuesdays through Sundays, 10 AM to 2 PM and 4 to 6 PM. Closed Mondays and August. Admission charge. 17 Calle Ventura Rodríguez (phone: 247-3647).

Museo de Escultura Abstracta al Aire Libre (Outdoor Museum of Abstract Sculpture) – Contemporary Spanish sculptures permanently placed on a pedestrian area on the Castellana, under the Calles Eduardo Dato–Juan Bravo overpass. Open continuously.

Museo Español de Arte Contemporáneo (Spanish Contemporary Art Museum) – "Contemporary" is defined here as the mid-19th century onward, including the 1960s abstractionists such as Antonio Tapies. Works by Eduardo Vicente, Picasso, Juan de Echevarría, Solana, and Rosales represent every major modern art movement in "contemporary" Spain. Open Tuesdays through Saturdays, 10 AM to 6 PM; Sundays and holidays, 10 AM to 3 PM. Admission charge. 2 Avenida Juan de Herrera, Ciudad Universitaria (phone: 449-7150).

Museo de Figuras de Cera (Wax Museum) – A gallery of 400 historic world personages, including celebrity bullfighters and such Spanish notables as the fictional Don Quixote and Sancho Panza. Open daily, 10:30 AM to 1:30 PM and 4 to 8 PM. Admission charge. Centro Colón (phone: 419-2282).

Museo Lázaro Galdiano – Named for its founder, who donated his eminent and comprehensive collection of art, jewelry, ivories, and enamels. Open Tuesdays through Sundays, 10 AM to 2 PM. Closed Mondays and August. 122 Calle Serrano (phone: 261-6084).

Museo Nacional de Artes Decorativas (National Museum of Decorative Arts) – Four floors of furniture, porcelains, jewelry, collections of Spanish tiles and fans, a full Valencian kitchen, and handicrafts from the 16th through 19th centuries.

Open Tuesdays through Fridays, 10 AM to 3 PM; weekends, 10 AM to 2 PM. Closed Mondays and summers. Admission charge. 12 Calle Montálban (phone: 521-3440).

Museo Nacional Ferroviario (National Railroad Museum) – Madrid's first train station, Estación de las Delicias, is now a museum complete with intact antique trains, royal cars, and other predecessors of the modern railroad. From May through October, the restored 19th-century "Strawberry Train" (Tren de la Fresa), departs here on one-day excursions to Aranjuez. Open Tuesdays through Saturdays, 10 AM to 5 PM; Sundays and holidays, 10 AM to 2 PM. Admission charge. 61 Paseo de las Delicias (phone: 227-3121).

Museo Naval (Maritime Museum) – Models of ships and ports, nautical instruments, and maps, including Juan de la Cosa's historic *mapa mundi,* the first map to include the New World, drawn in 1500. Open Tuesdays through Sundays, 10:30 AM to 1:30 PM. Closed Mondays and August. Just off Paseo del Prado at 2 Calle Montálban (phone: 521-0419).

Museo Panteón de Goya (Pantheon of Goya, also called Ermita de San Antonio) – Goya painted the magnificent religious frescoes on the dome and walls of this small 18th-century church, which was to become his tomb. Open Tuesdays through Fridays, 10 AM to 1:30 PM and 4 to 7 PM; weekends and holidays, 10 AM to 1:30 PM. No admission charge. Glorieta de San Antonio de la Florida (phone: 542-0722).

Museo Romántico (Romantic Museum) – Paintings, furniture, and decor of 19th-century Madrid, housed in an 18th-century mansion. Open Tuesdays through Saturdays, 10 AM to 6 PM; Sundays, 10 AM to 2 PM. Admission charge. Closed August. 13 Calle San Mateo (phone: 448-1071).

Museo Taurino (Bullfighting Museum) – An important collection of historical bullfight memorabilia including photographs, archives, celebrity bullfighters' "suits of lights," and even taxidermic trophies of ears, tails, and whole bulls. Open weekdays, 9 AM to 3 PM; during bullfighting season (March through October), open Sundays, closed Mondays. Admission charge. Plaza de Toros Monumental de las Ventas, 237 Calle de Alcalá (phone: 255-1857).

Templo de Debod – A gift from the Egyptian government in the 1970s, this 2,500-year-old Egyptian temple was shipped to Madrid in 1,359 cases and reassembled, towering over a reflecting pool. Theater and music performances are held here in summer. Open daily, 10 AM to 1 PM; holidays, 10 AM to 3 PM. No admission charge. Parque del Oeste.

SHOPPING: Madrid's 54,000 stores and shops offer everything imaginable, from high fashion to flamenco guitars. Handicrafts, artisanry, fine leather goods, embroidery, ceramics, Lladró porcelains, art, and antiques are among the enticing buys available throughout the city. Everything goes on sale twice a year — after Christmas, which in Spain means about January 7, and during the summer. The big summer sales (*rebajas*) begin in July, and prices are reduced even more during the first 3 weeks of August. Shops generally open at 9:30 AM, close from 1:30 to 4:30 PM for lunch and siesta, and close for the night at 8 PM. Spain's two major department store chains have their flagship stores as well as several branches in Madrid. *El Corte Inglés,* 3 Calle Preciados (phone: 232-8100), and *Galerías Preciados,* Plaza de Callao (phone: 522-4771), do not close in the afternoon and are particularly helpful to tourists, even providing interpreters for customers while they shop.

Four affiliated stores specializing in fine china, porcelain (especially Lladró) and Majórica pearls line the Gran Vía: *Souvenirs,* 11 Gran Vía, near Alcalá (phone: 521-5119); *Vinvinda,* 44 Gran Vía, near Plaza de Callao (phone: 213-0514); *Regalos A.R.,* 46 Gran Vía (phone: 522-6869); and *La Galette,* 67 Gran Vía, near Plaza de España (phone: 248-8938). Window shopping is a favorite pastime along Calle Serrano, with its elegant boutiques, shops, and galleries, and the Plaza Mayor area is full of unusual shopping opportunities.

In Spain, the value added tax (VAT) is 12%, considerably less than in some other European cities.

Antigua Casa Talavera – An overwhelming array of authentic regional handcrafted ceramics and dinnerware from all over Spain form an overwhelming display in this small family-owned shop just off the Gran Vía, near Plaza de Santo Domingo. 2 Calle Isabela la Católica (phone: 247-3417).

Artespaña – Government run, with a wide range of handicrafts and home furnishings from all over Spain. Among several branches is one at 3 Plaza de las Cortes (phone: 429-1251).

Ascot – An excellent women's boutique selling haute couture and ready-to-wear garments by María Teresa de Vega, a favorite designer among Madrid's beautiful people. Two branches, 88 Calle Serrano and La Morleja.

El Aventurero – A small bookstore specializing in guidebooks, maps, and books on the art of bullfighting and art photography, with an ample selection in English. Just off Plaza Mayor, 15 Calle Toledo (phone: 266-4457).

Elena Benarroch – Exceptionally stylish women's furs designed with an interesting mixture of modernity and elegance. 18-24 Calle Monte Esquinza.

Canalejas – Top-quality men's shirtmakers in the classic European fit. 20 Carrera de San Jerónimo (phone: 521-8075).

Joaquín Berao – Fine jewelry by the imaginative young Spanish designer, featuring limited-edition earrings, bracelets, rings, and pendants in ultra-modern designs of gold, silver, bronze, and titanium. 13 Calle Conde de Xiquena.

Casa de Diego – Founded in 1858, this classic store manufacturers hand-painted fans, and frames for displaying them, and well as crafted canes and umbrellas. Two locations: 12 Puerta del Sol (phone: 522-6643), and 4 Calle Mesonero Romanos (phone: 531-0223).

Celso García – A first-rate store for men's and women's fashions and accessories, with several branches: 52 Calle Serrano (phone: 431-6760), 83 Paseo de la Castellana (phone: 455-4100), 11 Puerta del Sol (phone: 222-8337), and 62 Calle Alberto Aguilera (phone: 243-0405).

Cortefiel – Leading men's and women's fashions and accessories are carried at their stores at 40 Calle Serrano (phone: 431-3342). Outlets at 178 Paseo de la Castellana (phone: 259-5713) and 27 Gran Vía (phone: 247-1701) specialize in men's fashions only, while the shops at 146 Paseo de la Castellana (phone: 250-3638) and 13 Calle Precaidos (phone: 222-6567) cater exclusively to women.

El Corte Inglés Record Department – The latest in Spanish classical, pop, and flamenco music on record, tape, and compact disc, as well as a complete selection of every other type of recorded music. They even carry Sevillana dance lessons on video cassette. Across from the main store at 3 Calle Preciados (phone: 232-8100).

Cuesta de Moyano – A string of 33 bookstalls along the south side of the Botanical Gardens. Browse here for new, used, and out-of-print finds of everything imaginable in publishing. Calle de Claudio Moyano (no phone).

Discos Sol – For the collector, this unique store carries a valuable inventory of Spanish classical, popular, Sevillanas, and flamenco records spanning generations and available nowhere else. 1 Calle Espoz y Mina, 2nd floor (phone: 531-3828).

Adolfo Domínguez – The boutique of the innovative Spanish celebrity designer whose daring women's fashions set the trend "wrinkles (in the fabric, that is) are beautiful." 4 Calle Ortega y Gasset (phone: 276-0084).

Gil, Sucesor de Anatolín Quevedo – Spanish and international celebrities purchase work-of-art shawls, *mantillas,* and embroidery at this generations-old establishment. 2 Carrera de San Jerónimo (phone: 521-2549).

Gritos de Madrid – A good ceramics shop owned by master craftsman Eduardo Fernández and featuring his works. He is responsible for the restoration of Madrid's interesting hand-illustrated tile street signs. 6 Plaza Mayor (phone: 265-9154).

Loewe – Fine leather fashions for men and women, as well as accessories and luggage. Several locations: 8 Gran Vía, 26 Calle Serrano, and in the *Palace* hotel; a new shop at 34 Calle Serrano carries men's fashions exclusively.

Mercado Puerta de Toledo – A shopping showcase of the finest in Spanish handicrafts, art, fashion, antiques, jewelry, interior design, and gastronomy in over 150 shops, boutiques, and galleries. Simple computer terminals point out what and where everything is in this sparkling new complex, all under one roof (see *Special Places*). 1 Ronda de Toledo (phone: 266-7200).

El Rastro – Madrid's legendary Sunday morning and holiday open-air flea market, where hundreds of stands offer everything from canaries to museum-quality antiques. It spreads for countless blocks in the old section of the city, starting at Plaza de Cascorro and fanning south to Ronda de Toledo. Browse for copper, brass, ironwork, embroidery, china, or tiles. Bargaining (preferably in Spanish) is customary, so don't pay the first price asked, and guard any wallets or purses.

Seseña – Always in style in Spain, capes are becoming the "in" thing for evening-wear everywhere, and this store, founded in 1901, manufactures a fine line for men and women. 23 Calle Cruz (phone: 531-6840).

Zurro – Gloves made to order. 16 Calle Preciados and 4 Calle Carmen.

 SPORTS AND FITNESS: Basketball – Madrid plays host to much of the finest basketball in Europe. The city is represented by such teams as *Real Madrid* and *Estudiantes* and is also the home of the Spanish National and Olympic squads. The most important games are played at the *Palacio de Deportes,* 99 Calle Jorge Juan (phone: 401-9100), and at the *Polideportivo Magariños,* 127 Calle Serrano (phone: 262-4022).

Bullfighting – Although not universally appreciated, bullfighting is the most renowned sport of Spain — Spaniards insist it is an art — and the largest bullfighting ring in Madrid is *Plaza de Toros Monumental de las Ventas,* which seats 22,300 people. There is also a smaller ring, *Plaza de Toros de Carabanchel,* near the Metro stop Vista Alegre. The season runs from May 15 through September. Tickets may be purchased the day of the event at a counter at 3 Calle Victoria (near the Puerta del Sol), at the bullring, or through a hotel concierge.

Fishing – There are fishing reserves along the Lozoya, Madarquillos, Jarama, and Cofio rivers not far from Madrid. They are mostly populated by trout, carp, black bass, pike, and barbel. The Santillana reservoir is particularly good for pike. For season and license information, contact the *Dirección General del Medio Rural,* 39 Calle Jorge Juan (phone: 435-5121).

Fitness Centers – Madrid boasts 27 municipal gymnasiums; for information on the one nearest your hotel, call 464-9050.

Golf – Madrid boasts several excellent private golf courses, such as *Nuevo Club de Golf de Madrid,* Las Matas, Carretera de la Coruña (phone: 630-0820); *Club de Campo Villa de Madrid,* Carretera de Castilla (phone: 207-0395); and *Real Club de la Puerta de Hierro,* Avenida Miraflores, Ciudad Puerta de Hierro (phone: 216-1635). Hotels can provide information regarding private entry into these clubs, and the *Federación España de Golf* (phone: 455-2682) has details on most of the area's facilities. Six miles (9.6 km) north of Madrid, on the Burgos Highway, is the Jack Nicklaus–designed *Club de Golf la Moraleja,* 50 Calle Marqués Viuda de Aldana (phone: 650-0700).

Horse Racing – The *Hipódromo de la Zarzuela,* La Coruña Highway, 4 miles (7 km) north of the city, features Sunday afternoon races during spring and fall meetings. Buses for the track leave from Calle Princesa and Hilarión Eslava (phone: 207-0140).

Jogging – Parque del Retiro and Casa de Campo both have jogging tracks.

Skiing – *Puerto de Navacerrada,* a mountain resort just 38 miles (61 km) north of Madrid, has 12 ski runs and 6 lifts (phone: 852-1435).

Soccer – Madrid is a legendary name in the world of soccer. *Real Madrid,* one of Spain's most popular teams, plays its home games at the *Estadio Santiago Bernabéu,* 1 Calle Concha Espina (phone: 250-0600), while its rival, *Atlético de Madrid,* takes the field at the *Estadio Vicente Calderón,* 6 Paseo Virgen del Puerto (phone: 266-4707).

Swimming – Madrid has 150 public swimming pools, including *Stella,* 231 Calle Arturo Soria.

Tennis – There are hundreds of public and private tennis courts in town. Among the city's tennis facilities are *Club de Campo,* Carretera de Castilla (phone: 207-0395), featuring 35 courts; and *Club de Tenis Chamartín,* 2 Calle Federico Salmón (phone: 250-5965), with 28 courts.

 THEATER: Theater productions are in Spanish only, but ballets, operas, and zarzuelas, or operettas, have universal appeal and are inexpensive. Check local listings for the *Teatro de la Zarzuela,* 4 Calle Jovellanos (phone: 429-8216), and the *Centro Cultural de la Villa,* Plaza de Colón (phone: 275-6080).

 MUSIC: Bolero and fandango are the typically Castilian dances and flamenco is Andalusian, but it is the latter most tourists want to see, so there are numerous excellent flamenco *tablaos* (cabarets) in Madrid. Some of the best are *Corral de la Morería,* 17 Calle Morería (phone: 265-1137); *Café de Chinitas,* 7 Calle Torija (phone: 248-5135); *Torres Bermejas,* 11 Calle Mesonero Romanos (phone: 232-3322); and, about 5 miles (8 km) outside Madrid on the Carretera Burgos, *Venta del Gato,* 214 Avenida de Burgos (phone: 776-6060). *Café Central,* 10 Plaza del Angel (phone: 468-0844), offers live music nightly (jazz, classical, salsa, or folk) as well as late dinner. Classical music concerts are held weekends at the *Teatro Real,* Plaza de Oriente (phone: 248-1405), and there are free recitals on certain weekdays at *Fundación Juan March,* 77 Calle Castelló (phone: 435-4240), and *Sala Fénix,* 33 Paseo de la Castellana (phone: 419-8216).

 NIGHTCLUBS AND NIGHTLIFE: Nightlife in Madrid can continue all night. Cover charges at cabarets and nightclubs include one drink, dancing, and floor shows that are becoming more risqué by the night. Top choices include *Scala-Meliá Castilla,* 43 Calle Capitán Haya (phone: 450-4400), and *Florida Park,* in the Parque del Retiro (phone: 273-7804). For a night of gambling, dining, dancing, and entertainment, the *Casino Gran Madrid* has it all; it's 20 minutes from downtown at Torrelodones, with free transportation from 6 Plaza de España (phone: 859-0312). The latest dance rage in Madrid is the *sevillanas. Madrileños* have adopted the delightful dance music of their Andalusian cousins as their own and, by popular demand, *sevillanas* music plays at many discos; dozens of *salas rocieras* — new nightclubs dedicated to dancing and watching *sevillanas* — attract teens, married couples, and diplomats alike. Among the best is *Villa Rosa,* Plaza de Santa Ana (phone: 437-8905), which features star performers in its floor shows. *La Maestranza,* near the Plaza de Castilla (at 16 Calle Mauricio Legendre; phone: 315-9059) also serves outstanding Andalusian cuisine. Discotheques and *boítes* usually run two sessions a night, at 7 and 11 PM. Among the more popular are *Pachá,* 11 Calle Barceló (phone: 446-0137); *Boccaccio,* 16 Calle Marqués de la Ensenada (phone: 419-1008); and *Joy Eslava,* 11 Calle Arenal (phone: 266-3733). Striptease shows are the attraction at *Alazán,* 24 Paseo de la Castellana (phone: 435-8948). The tavern *Cervecería Alemana,* an old Hemingway hangout, 6 Plaza de Santa Ana (phone: 429-7033), remains a favorite nightspot. *Madrileños* love to *pasear,* or stroll along the streets, and from April through October thousands of *terrazas* — outdoor cafés lining plazas, parks, and avenues — are jumping with nocturnal activity. Late revelers usually cap the evening with thick hot chocolate and *churros,* a greasy and delicious fried dough, at *Chocolatería de San Ginés* (in the alley behind San Ginés church), open from 1 AM until the morning rush hour.

BEST IN TOWN

CHECKING IN: Modern Madrid boasts over 50,000 hotel rooms, with accommodations ranging from the city's luxury hotels (*Ritz* and *Villa Magna*), to countless *hostales* and *pensiones.* Although finding a place to stay in the city is generally never a problem, reservations are nonetheless recommended, especially between May and September and during such events as national and local festivals, expositions, conventions, and the like. Expect to pay $450 or more a night for a double room in a hotel listed as very expensive, from $170 to $300 in an establishment listed as expensive, from $65 to $160 in a moderately priced hotel, and $50 or less in an inexpensive hotel. Double rooms in *pensiones* and *residencias,* without private baths, are available for less than $20 a night. All telephone numbers are in the 91 area code unless otherwise indicated.

Ritz – The sheer epitome of elegance, luxury, and Belle Epoque grace, this classic and impeccably maintained jewel opened in 1910 at the behest of King Alfonso XIII. No two of the 156 air conditioned rooms and suites are alike, but all are sumptuously decorated with paintings, antiques, and tailored handwoven carpeting from the Royal Tapestry Factory. Jacket-and-tie attire is appropriate for men in the bar and the exquisite *Ritz* restaurant, one of Madrid's finest (see *Eating Out*). The casual *Ritz Garden Terrace* also offers delightful dining, cocktails, and *tapas.* 5 Plaza de la Lealtad (phone: 521-2857). Very expensive.

Villa Magna – A modern yet stately building of glass and marble set amid landscaped gardens in the heart of aristocratic Madrid. A multi-million dollar remodeling project in 1989 has added unequaled luxury, luster, and technology. The 194 spacious, air conditioned rooms provide the epitome of luxury. Supreme personal service enhances the hotel's atmosphere of casual elegance. Delightful for relaxing and socializing, the new *Champagne Bar* boasts Europe's finest selection, with 252 French and Spanish vintages, and the *Villa Magna* restaurant is celebrated for its imaginative specialties (see *Eating Out*). Richly decorated private salons accommodate meetings and banquets. 22 Paseo de la Castellana (phone: 261-4900). Very expensive.

Barajas – The raison d'être of this 230-room hotel is its proximity to Madrid's Barajas International Airport. All rooms are air conditioned and have color TV sets. Guests can enjoy the garden swimming pool, bar, restaurant, and health club. Half-day rates are available for meetings or jet-lag therapy. Free transportation is provided to and from the airport terminals. 305 Avenida Logroño (phone: 747-7700). Expensive.

Castellana Inter-Continental – Opened in the early 1950s as the *Castellana Hilton,* this has been a traditional favorite of Americans traveling to Madrid for business or pleasure. Its 310 air conditioned rooms have been refurbished with modern deluxe accoutrements and nicely decorated in pleasant pastels. Next to the stately marble-pillared lobby is a health club, several boutiques, and the *Continentes* restaurant and *La Ronda* piano bar. 49 Paseo de la Castellana (phone: 410-0200). Expensive.

Eurobuilding – An extremely well designed modern hotel complex off the northern section of the Castellana near the convention center and *Estadio Santiago Bernabéu.* Within the complex, in addition to the 421-room hotel building, the *Euro-*

building 2 tower comprises 154 apartment-style units. All rooms and apartments are air conditioned. There are also 2 swimming pools, a health club, a hair salon, stores, and 4 restaurants. 23 Calle Padre Damián (phone: 457-1700). Expensive.

Holiday Inn Madrid – This modern and busy establishment is typical of the US Holiday Inn chain, with 344 air conditioned rooms, a swimming pool, health club, gymnasium, shopping arcade, and restaurants. A perfect place for anyone who wants to be near the Azca shopping and commercial complex, the convention center, *Estadio Santiago Bernabéu,* and the Castellana. 4 Plaza Carlos Trías Bertrán (phone: 456-7014). Expensive.

Meliá Castilla – Nearly 1,000 air conditioned rooms in a modern high-rise just off the Castellana in northern Madrid's business section. Facilities and meeting rooms cater primarily to executive travelers. There is also a swimming pool, gymnasium, sauna, shopping arcade, several restaurants and bars, and *Scala Meliá Castilla,* a Las Vegas–style nightclub. 43 Calle Capitán Haya (phone: 571-2211). Expensive.

Meliá Madrid – Ideally located near the Plaza de España and extremely well run. The 266 air conditioned rooms in this gleaming white, modern hotel are tastefully decorated in various styles, and feature color TV sets. The dining room, grill, bar, and *Bong Bing* discotheque are popular meeting places. There is also a gymnasium, sauna, and conference facilities complete with state-of-the-art audiovisual equipment. 27 Calle Princesa (phone: 241-8200). Expensive.

Miguel Angel – Conveniently located on the Paseo de la Castellana, this 304-room hotel combines ultramodern luxuries with classic decor; 17th-, 18th-, and 19th-century paintings, tapestries, and furniture decorate the lobby and suites. Most rooms have balconies, and all offer color TV sets, which feature movies in English. Facilities include an indoor swimming pool, health club, gymnasium, sauna, and Jacuzzi. Guests can enjoy fine food at the *Florencia* restaurant; afternoon tea and cocktails at the *Bar Farnesio,* and dinner, dancing, and live entertainment at the *Boite Zacarías* restaurant. 31 Calle Miguel Angel (phone: 442-8199). Expensive.

Monte Real – In a tranquil residential district about 20 minutes from the city center, this luxurious establishment is near the *Real Club de la Puerta de Hierro.* All 77 rooms are air conditioned and have color TV sets. Facilities include a swimming pool, sauna, lovely gardens, a restaurant, and a bar. 17 Calle Arroyo del Fresno, Puerta de Hierro (phone: 216-2140). Expensive.

Palace – Inaugurated in 1920, this aristocratic Madrid landmark was, like the *Ritz,* built by personal order of King Alfonso XIII. Its Old World Belle Epoque elegance and decor are faithfully maintained, while the utmost of modern facilities makes for true luxury in the spacious 518 air conditioned rooms and suites. In the heart of the city, the hotel overlooks the Neptune Fountain and the Paseo del Prado. Regular guests include star bullfighters, musicians, politicians, artists, and executives. The lobby, topped by an impressive glass cupola, is a popular meeting place. Its walls and ceilings have recently been embellished with trompe l'oeil painting. 7 Plaza de las Cortes (phone: 429-7551). Expensive.

Villa Real – Madrid's newest hotel (opened in April 1989), its design and atmosphere embody Old World grace; marble, bronze, and handcrafted wood, works of fine art and antique furnishings create a seignorial interior decor. All 115 luxurious rooms and suites are air conditioned and feature satellite TV sets, mini-bars, and 3 or more high-tech telephones. Elegantly furnished top-floor duplexes feature 2 bathrooms — one has a sauna, the other a Jacuzzi. Their large private balconies overlook the Parliament Palace, the Neptune Fountain, and the *Prado Museum*'s Villahermosa Palace. There is 24-hour room service, and the staff is friendly, personal, and perfectionist. The hotel's choice setting — between Paseo del Prado and Puerta del Sol — couldn't be more ideal. 10-11 Plaza de la Cortes (phone: 420-3767). Expensive.

Wellington – An aristocrat among hotels, in the fashionable Salamanca district near Parque del Retiro. The owner raised brave bulls; a stuffed triumphant one, named Cucharito, resides in the lounge amid the antique tapestries. Bullfighters, breeders, and aficionados stay and congregate here. All of the spacious 258 rooms are air conditioned and feature color TV sets. In summer, the outdoor swimming pool and the garden with its restaurant, bar, and health club are lively gathering spots. 8 Calle Velázquez (phone: 275-4400). Expensive.

Tryp Fénix – This Madrid aristocrat has been refurbished and reborn and is once again considered among the city's finest. All 216 rooms are air conditioned and have all the modern conveniences. Ideally situated on the tree-lined Castellana at Plaza de Colón, it features up-to-the-minute amenities surrounded by an air of sparkling elegance. 2 Calle Hermosilla (phone: 431-6700). Expensive to moderate.

Alcalá – Right on the north edge of Parque del Retiro and the Plaza de la Independencia, in the genteel Salamanca district, this hotel is within easy walking distance of fine shops and restaurants on Calle Serrano, as well as the *Prado* and other museums. All 153 air conditioned rooms feature color TV sets. Its restaurant features enticing Basque specialties. 66 Calle de Alcalá (phone: 435-1060). Moderate.

Arosa – Although its on the bustling Gran Vía, it has the charm, peaceful mood, and personalized service of a small luxury establishment. The 126 air conditioned rooms, no two exactly alike, are tastefully decorated; luxurious bathrooms feature built-in hair dryers, fabulous showers in the bathtubs, and other treats, such as soothing bath salts. The atmosphere is delightful in the bar, lounge, and restaurant. Doormen at the small, elegant side-street entrance know guests by name. 21 Calle de la Salud (phone: 232-1600). Moderate.

Carlton – A complete renovation has enhanced the comforts of this establishment. In a unique spot — the southern part of central Madrid — it is near the Atocha train station complex, as well as within easy walking distance of the *Queen Sofia Art Center* and, a little farther north, the Botanical Gardens and the *Prado*. All of the 133 air conditioned rooms have color TV sets. 26 Paseo de las Delicias (phone: 239-7100). Moderate.

Charmatín – The single adventure of this 378-room hotel is the fact that it is set in the modern Chamartín train station complex at the north end of the city. All rooms are air conditioned, with color TV sets, and offer excellent views. Estación de Chamartín (phone: 733-7011). Moderate.

Emperador – Right on the Gran Vía. All 232 rooms are air conditioned and feature color TV sets. Unusual among the many hotels in the immediate area, it boasts a rooftop garden with a swimming pool and excellent views of the city. 53 Gran Vía (phone: 413-6511). Moderate.

Escultor – Near the Castellana in a quiet residential area, its 82 air conditioned, apartment-style units offer separate sitting rooms with color TV sets, complete kitchens, and mini-bars. 5 Calle Miguel Angel (phone: 410-4203). Moderate.

Mayorazgo – Excellent service and 200 well-appointed, comfortable, air conditioned rooms just a step from the central Gran Vía. The decor provides a retreat to a pleasant Castilian past. 3 Calle Flor Baja (phone: 247-2600). Moderate.

Plaza – Within the gigantic Edificio España landmark building of the early 1950s, this hotel with 306 rooms (all air conditioned) is usually swarming with tour groups. The 26th-floor swimming pool and terrace restaurant offer marvelous panoramic views of the city. 2 Plaza de España (phone: 247-1200). Moderate.

Pullman – Contemporary couches and antique desks in the lobby are set off by scenes of English fox hunting and horse racing. The 99 rooms are brightly decorated and air conditioned, and have color TV sets and mini-bars. There is also a full-service restaurant and bar. On a quiet street just off the Plaza de España. 1 Calle Tutor (phone: 241-9880). Moderate.

Serrano – Small and tasteful, refined and immaculate, on a quiet street between the Castellana and the boutique-lined Calle Serrano. Its marble-floored lobby is richly decorated with antiques, including a large 17th-century tapestry, comfortable furnishings, and huge arrangements of fresh flowers. All 34 rooms are air conditioned and have color TV sets. No restaurant, but snacks and sandwiches are available at the bar. 8 Calle Marqués de Villamejor (phone: 435-5200). Moderate.

Suecia – Hemingway lived here, and guests who happen to stay in his suite (the number is not disclosed), might receive a complimentary book from the management (which is Swiss — hence the name). Recent expansion has added deluxe modern rooms and suites within the same building, but the original ones are well maintained and very comfortable. All 67 rooms, old and new, are air conditioned and have color TV sets. A great advantage is the location — on a quiet street just west of Paseo del Prado, around the corner from Calle de Alcalá. Smoked salmon and smorgasbord are main attractions in the *Bellman* restaurant. 4 Calle Marqués de Casa Riera (phone: 531-6900). Moderate.

Carlos V – Conveniently located, with 67 rooms, in the busy pedestrian area between the Gran Vía and Puerta del Sol, near the Convento de las Descalzas Reales and *El Corte Inglés* department store. 5 Calle Maestro Vitoria (phone: 531-4100). Moderate to inexpensive.

Don Diego – A well-kept *pension* near the Parque del Retiro in Madrid's prestigious Salamanca district. The 58 rooms feature lovely leather and wood furniture and large closets; several have ample balconies. There is a comfortable TV lounge and a bar that serves good sandwiches and breakfast. 45 Calle Velázquez (phone: 435-0760). Moderate to inexpensive.

Puerta Toledo – Away from major hotel clusters, it is on the fringe of picturesque Old Madrid, facing the Triumphal Arch of the Puerta de Toledo and near the new Mercado Puerta de Toledo. Its 160 rooms are air conditioned, comfortable, and well maintained. 4 Calle Glorieta Puerta de Toledo (phone: 474-7100). Moderate to inexpensive.

Tryp Victoria – The large bay windows of this venerated vintage landmark overlook the charming Plaza Santa Ana in the heart of Old Madrid. Since the early 1920s, it has been a favorite of *madrileño* intellectuals and bullfighters who gather for drinks, stimulating *tertulias,* and banquets. Most of the 110 rooms are small singles, all with private baths. With its recent acquisition by the Tryp hotel chain, a well-deserved refurbishment is anticipated. 7 Plaza del Angel (phone: 531-4500). Moderate to inexpensive.

Jamic – A small *pension* centrally located across the street from the *Palace* hotel and near the *Prado.* 4 Plaza de las Cortes (phone: 429-0068). Inexpensive.

Lisboa – This excellently run residential *hostel* has 23 rooms, all with private baths and telephones, plus maid service, a TV lounge, and an elevator. The location is terrific: just off the Plaza Santa Ana in charming Old Madrid, yet a short walk to the *Palace,* the *Ritz,* and the *Prado.* English is spoken and credit cards accepted. Fine restaurants of all price ranges line the street. 17 Calle Ventura de la Vega (phone: 429-9894). Inexpensive.

 EATING OUT: *Madrileños* eat the main meal of their day during the work break from 2 to 4 PM. An early-evening snack (*merienda*) such as wine, *tapas, chocolate con churros,* or coffee and sweets takes the edge off appetites until a light supper is eaten after 10 PM. For those who can't adjust to the Spanish schedule, there are always *cafeterías* and snack bars, and many restaurants start serving dinner at about 8:30 PM to accommodate non-Spaniards. Very expensive restaurants will charge $150 or more for a dinner for two with wine; similar fare will cost $75 to $130 at expensively priced restaurants, between $30 and $70 at moderate eateries, and $25 or less at inexpensive ones. Most restaurants offer a set menu (*menú*

del día), with a complete meal for a lower price. Some restaurants include the 6% Value Added Tax in their menu prices. Check beforehand whether the menu says *IVA incluido* or *IVA no incluido*. All telephone numbers are in the 91 area code unless otherwise indicated.

Horcher – Operated for generations by the Horcher family, this is one of Madrid's most elegant place for continental cuisine, with an Austro-Hungarian flair. Dining here is an experience in luxury and indulgence that should include such delicacies as *chuletas de ternasco a la Castiliana* (baby lamb chops), endive salad (with truffles), and crêpes Sir Holten for dessert. Diners might even try the classic goulash. Reservations are necessary for lunch and dinner. Closed Sundays. 6 Calle Alfonso XII (phone: 522-0731). Very expensive.

Jockey – A Madrid classic, intimate and elegant, and a recipient of the National Gastronomic Award. The continental cuisine is superb, as are traditional dishes such as *cocido madrileño,* a savory stew, the broth of which is served as a side dish. Other specialties include *perdiz Española* (partridge), *lomo de lubina* (pork loin with sea bass), and *mousse de anguila* (eel mousse). Closed Sundays and August. 6 Calle Amador de los Ríos (phone: 419-1003). Very expensive.

Ritz – The sumptuous restaurant of the luxurious *Ritz* hotel, serving French cuisine befitting the Limoges dinnerware and Louis XV silver service. Chamber music adds to the regal ecstasy. Open daily for breakfast, lunch, and dinner. 5 Plaza de la Lealtad (phone: 521-2857). Very expensive.

Villa Magna – The recent remodeling of Madrid's superlative *Villa Magna* hotel has placed its restaurant among the city's finest. Its new prizewinning chef, Cristóbal Blanco, designs such nouvelle delicacies as grilled scallops with caviar in basil sauce, served on precious china especially designed by Paloma Picasso. The *Champagne Bar* features 252 French and Spanish vintages. The only question here is whether dinner is worth the astronomical $600 price tag per table setting! Also open for breakfast and lunch. 22 Paseo de la Castellana (phone: 261-4900). Very expensive.

Zalacaín – Considered by many to be the finest restaurant in all of Spain, and even the world, it celebrates Basque, French, and highly imaginative haute cuisines, with an emphasis on seafood. The service here *is* perfection. Daily specials are also served. Luxuriously decorated, its tables shimmer with gleaming glasses, polished silverware, and fresh flower arrangements. Reservations are required. Closed Saturdays for lunch, Sundays, August, Easter Week, Holy Week, and holidays. 4 Calle Alvarez de Baena (phone: 261-4840). Very expensive.

Cabo Mayor – The owner and chef are both recipients of the National Gastronmy Award, and for good reason: Their fresh seafood from the province of Santander is imaginatively prepared, and the vegetable dishes are superlative. Nautical trappings of boat hulls and squared portholes belie the marked sophistication of the inspired kitchen. Try the tender medallions of monkfish showered with baby eels and bracketed with tiny clams in an aromatic saffron sauce, *lomo de merluza* (loin of pork with hake), or *cigalas y langostinos con verduras al jerez sibarita* (crayfish and prawns with green vegetables in sherry sauce). Closed Sundays, the last 2 weeks of August, Christmas Week, New Year's Week, and Easter Week. 37 Calle Juan Ramón Jiménez (phone: 250-8776). Expensive.

El Cenador del Prado – This restaurant is favored by aficionados of nouvelle cuisine. The artistic decor is that of an elegant conservatory. Try *patatas a la importancia con almejas* (potatoes with clams), *crema de melón a la hierbabuena* (melon cream with mint), or *pato al vinagre de frambuesas* (duck with raspberry vinegar). Reservations advised. Closed Saturdays and Sunday for lunch. 4 Calle del Prado (phone: 429-1561). Expensive.

La Dorada – Fresh seafood of every imaginable variety is flown in daily from the

Mediterranean to this mammoth establishment, whose Andalusian fare is best enjoyed by making reservations for one of the private dining rooms. Reservations are necessary, as this place is always crowded. Closed Sundays and August. 64-66 Calle Orense (phone: 270-2002). Expensive.

Fortuny – Relatively new on Madrid's restaurant scene, it soon established its place among the preferred, with outstanding international haute cuisine. In an aristocratic 19th-century mansion, it offers private dining rooms for banquets or intimacy. There is also an outdoor terrace with an artificial waterfall for summer dining. Closed Sundays and holidays. 34 Calle Fortuny (phone: 308-3268). Expensive.

La Gamella – American owner-chef-host Richard Stephens, also an instructor at Madrid's famed Alambique School of Gastronomy, dedicates his creative flair to New Spanish cuisine. Using choice ingredients, he offers adventures in taste with dishes such as slices of cured duck breast in Belgian endives with walnut oil for starters, turbot in wild mushroom sauce with a fresh tomato coulis, and irresistible desserts, complimented with a fine wine list. At its new location facing Parque del Retiro, in the aristocratic building in which philosopher José Ortega y Gasset was born in 1883, this intimate restaurant is decorated with *colorista* design and art. A private dining room downstairs seats 10. Closed Saturdays for lunch. 4 Calle Alfonso XII (phone: 532-4509). Expensive.

Gure-Etxea – This is the best Basque cuisine in Madrid, with specialties such as *porrusalda* (leek and potato soup with cod), and a variety of fish dishes. The atmosphere is pleasant and the service welcoming. Reservations advised. Closed Sundays and August. 12 Plaza de la Paja (phone: 265-6149). Expensive.

O'Pazo – The morning catch from the Cantabrian Sea — lobster, hake, turbot, endemic sea bass, and varieties of shellfish — is flown in wriggling fresh and prepared with loving care to delight the clientele, who fill the place for both lunch and dinner. Closed Sundays and August. 20 Calle Reina Mercedes (phone: 253-2333). Expensive.

Platerías – Its intimate low-key elegance in the heart of Old Madrid creates a pleasant atmosphere for enjoying authentic Spanish dishes, such as *callos madrileños* (succulent tripe, Madrid style), *chipirones* (cuttlefish in its own ink), and remarkable vegetable plates. Reservations advised. Closed Sundays. 11 Plaza de Santa Ana (phone: 429-7048). Expensive.

Principe de Viana – Fine seasonal Basque-Navarran specialties are served in a relaxed, elegant atmosphere. Closed Saturdays for lunch, Sundays, and August 15-September 1. 5 Calle Manuel de Falla (phone: 259-1448). Expensive.

La Trianera – Another favorite of seafood lovers. The owner prizes his flown-in catch and serves fish and shellfish as nature intended. No fishing village in the world can compete with the grilled sole served here. Reservations advised. Closed Sundays and August. 60 Calle Lagasca (phone: 276-8035). Expensive.

Café de Oriente – Here, anything from *tapas* to haute French cuisine can be enjoyed in a delightful *madrileño* atmosphere. It is an ideal place for afternoon tea or cocktails at a sidewalk table overlooking the square and the Royal Palace or inside the delightful café; for fine Castilian dining downstairs in the vaulted 17th-century Sala Capitular de San Gil; or for superb French-Basque cuisine in the restaurant or one of the private dining rooms frequented by royalty and diplomats. Closed Mondays for lunch, Sundays, and August. 2 Plaza de Oriente (phone: 247-1564). Expensive to moderate.

Antigua Casa Sobrino de Botín – Also known as *Casa Botín,* this is one of Madrid's oldest restaurants — founded in 1725. It is famous for its Castilian-style roast suckling pig and baby lamb, one of which is usually featured on the *menú del día.* Lunch and dinner seem to fall into two "shifts," with the early-eating tourists first, followed by *madrileños,* whose normal dining hours are after 2 and 9 PM, respectively. 17 Calle Cuchilleros (phone: 266-4217). Moderate.

Café Gijón – This 100-year-old Madrid institution is a traditional meeting and greeting place for intellectuals and artists, who gather here to enjoy good food and conversation. During the summer, its sidewalk café is one of the city's liveliest. 21 Paseo de Recoletos (phone: 532-5425). Moderate.

Casa Lucio – Owner Lucio Blázquez has made this casual restaurant an institution among the elite who enjoy fine Spanish food, especially seafood. Its location in Old Madrid adds to the flavor. Reservations advised. Closed Saturdays for lunch and August. 35 Calle Cava Baja (phone: 265-3252). Moderate.

Casa Paco – The steaks served in this old tavern are excellent. Other specialties include cured ham and typical *madrilenian* dishes. Closed Sundays and August. 11 Calle Puerta Cerrada (phone: 266-3166). Moderate.

La Chata – This totally typical *mesón* bears the nickname of Madrid's adored Infanta Isabel (the only child of Queen Isabella II). The regal woman is depicted on the wonderful hand-painted tile façade by artist Eduardo Fernández. The morsels at the *tapas* bar are delicious, and the small restaurant specializes in roast suckling pig and lamb dishes. 24 Calle Cava Baja (phone: 266-1458). Moderate.

El Cuchi – The Spanish link of Mexico's famous *Carlos 'n' Charlie's* chain, with specialties of both worlds served by a gregarious staff. It's casual, and jammed with humorous paraphernalia. One of its claims to fame: "Hemingway never ate here." 3 Calle Cuchilleros (phone: 255-4424). Moderate.

Los Galayos – A typical tavern serving fine Castillian roast suckling pig and lamb, with a *tapas* bar and an outdoor café right alongside the Plaza Mayor. 1 Plaza Mayor (phone: 265-6222). Moderate.

La Galette – Outstanding vegetarian and non-vegetarian dishes and Viennese pastries are served in a delightful atmosphere. Good location in the elegant Salamanca district. Its popularity makes reservations essential. Closed Sundays. 11 Conde de Aranda (phone: 276-0641). Moderate.

El Ingenuo – Named for the ingenuous Don Quixote, this unpretentious, family-run restaurant is decorated with Quixote and Sancho Panza memorabilia, and its menu delights diners who fall into either category of physique. The seafood is impeccably fresh since it is flown in from the Bay of Biscay, and the pork, lamb, and beef are all locally farm-grown. Just off the Plaza de España at 19 Calle Leganitos (phone: 241-9133). Moderate.

La Maestranza – Andalusian in its cooking, atmosphere, and decor, with great sevillanas music groups playing for professional dancers and the customers who know this Andalusian folk dance, which has become Madrid's latest rage. Closed Sundays. 16 Calle Mauricio Legendre (phone: 315-9059). Moderate.

El Mentidero de la Villa – Inventive French cuisine by Japanese chef Ken Sato, in a delightful modern art decor. Specialties include *rollo de primavera con puerros y gambas* (spring rolls with leeks and shrimp) and *pato con manzana* (duck with apple). Closed Sundays. 6 Calle Santo Tomé (phone: 419-5506). Moderate.

La Mesa Redonda – A small eatery on one of Old Madrid's most charming little streets. Its American owners serve the best *Thanksgiving* dinner in town. Other specialties include beef bourguignon and stews. Dinner only; closed Sundays. 17 Calle Nuncio (phone: 265-0289). Moderate.

Posada de la Villa – Although its 3-story building is relatively new, this authentic eatery dates back to 1642, when it was originally a *posada* (inn) for out-of-towners. It has retained its tradition of hospitality and still offers fine typical dishes such as *cocido madrileño* and roasted pig and lamb. Closed Sunday evenings. 9 Calle Cava Baja (phone: 266-1860). Moderate.

La Quinta del Sordo – The façade on this award-winning restaurant is adorned with fine hand-painted tile mosaics. Its name means "house of the deaf man," referring to the place where Goya lived in Madrid. Reproductions of Goya art and memorabilia add to the decor. An array of fine Castilian dishes offers memorable dining in a pleasant atmosphere. Closed Sunday evenings. 10 Calle Sacramento (phone: 248-1852). Moderate.

Riazor – An unpretentious turn-of-the-century establishment with a cordial atmosphere, fine traditional fare, and a cornucopia of hot and cold *tapas* served with verve at the bar. The upstairs dining room has panels adjustable to fit a size range of banquet parties. 1 short block south of Plaza Mayor at 19 Calle Toledo (phone: 266-5466). Moderate.

Taberna del Alabardero – A Madrid classic, just around the corner from the Opera House, this was the tavern of the Royal Palace guards (*alabardero* means halberdier, or a soldier armed with a combination pike and ax). There is a wonderful *tapas* bar, and succulent Spanish and Basque dishes are served in cozy dining rooms reminiscent of 19th-century Madrid. 6 Calle Felipe V (phone: 241-5192). Moderate.

Foster's Hollywood – It's a *restaurante americano,* complete with a variety of hamburgers and barbecued spare ribs. Far from a *yanqui* fast-food joint, it's a small chain of pleasant restaurants with good service and atmosphere. Several branches: 1 Calle Magallanes (phone: 488-9165); in the Chamartín district at 3 Calle Apolonio Morales (phone: 457-7911); across from the *María Guerrero Theater* at 1 Calle Tamayo y Baus (phone: 231-5115); 16 Calle del Cristo (phone: 638-6791); 14-16 Avenida de Brasil (phone: 455-1688); 80 Calle Velázquez (phone: 435-6128); and 100 Calle Guzmán el Bueno (phone: 234-4923). Inexpensive.

El Granero de Lavapiés – Good vegetarian food in one of Madrid's most typical neighborhoods. 10 Calle Argumosa (phone: 467-7611). Inexpensive.

La Salsería – Befitting its name, this small bar with an outdoor café specializes in sauces — 15 kinds, served in the holes of a conveniently held artist's palette, in the center of which are ruffled fried potatoes for dipping. Try *spaghetti a la Siciliana* as well. Across the traffic circle from Mercado Puerta de Toledo. Closed Mondays. 2 Calle Ronda de Toledo (phone: 266-0890). Inexpensive.

Mesón Museo del Jamón – Any restaurant with 4,000 hams dangling from its ceiling and draping its walls deserves the name "Ham Museum," and there are four such pork paradises in central Madrid. Fine hams from the regions of Jabugo, Murcia, Salamanca, and Extremadura are served in various ways, including sandwiches, at the stand-up bars and at dining tables. Also featured are an array of cheeses, a great deli, and roast chicken. Any dish can also be prepared to take out. 6 Carrera San Jerónimo (phone: 521-0340); 72 Gran Vía (phone: 241-2023); 44 Paseo del Prado (phone: 230-4385); 54 Calle Atocha (phone: 227-0716). Inexpensive.

Taberna de Antonio Sánchez – Genuinely typical of Old Madrid, it has been a venerated favorite ever since it was founded by a legendary bullfighter more than 150 years ago. The small, unpretentious dining rooms are charming, and the realm of wonderful food — seafood, Spanish cuisine, salads, and desserts — is served with care. Closed Sunday evenings. 13 Calle Mesón de Paredes (phone: 239-7826). Inexpensive.

 TAPAS BARS: *El tapeo* (enjoying *tapas*) is a way of life in Spain, especially in Madrid, where there are literally thousands of places to do so. Practically every bar (not to be confused with pubs or *bares americanos,* which are for drinks only) serves *tapas,* as do *tabernas, mesones, tascas, cervecerías,* and even *cafeterías.* Many establishments specializing in *tapas* also have a few tables or even dining rooms in addition to their stand-up bar. Toothpicks and fingers are the most common utensils; a few slices of bread are usually optional; and shrimp, langostino, mussel and clam shells, olive pits, napkins, and almost everything else are dropped on the floor, which is swept and scoured after each surge (from 1 to 3 and 7 to 9 PM, more or less — usually more).

A *chato* (glass of wine) or a *caña* (draft beer) is customarily served with a free *tapita*. For those who prefer a larger portion, ask for a *ración,* which can be a small meal in itself. Never pay until completely finished; the bartender will probably remember everything you consumed, even if you don't. He'll deliver your change on a saucer; leave a few *duros* (5-peseta coins) as a tip, and always say *gracias* and *adios* when you depart. *Tapas* bar hopping is at its best in the central and old sections of Madrid. One of the city's best *tapas* bars is *La Trucha,* just off Plaza de Santa Ana at 5 Calle Manuel de Falla (phone: 259-1448). Everything from bull tails to succulent red pimentos and *trucha* (trout) is served with gusto. *Bocaito,* 6 Calle Libertad (phone: 232-1219), offers a limitless selection of outstanding treats, while *La Mi Venta,* 7 Plaza Marina Española (phone: 248-5091) specializes in select hams and *raciones.* Other favorites include *Casa Labra,* 12 Calle Tetuán (phone: 532-1405), specializing in fluff-fried *bacalao* (cod); *Mejillonería El Pasaje,* 3 Pasaje de Matheu (phone: 521-5155), featuring mussels exclusively; *Cervecería Alemana,* 6 Plaza Santa Ana (phone: 429-7033); *Monje Cervecería,* 21 Calle Arenal (phone: 248-3598); *El Oso y el Madroño,* 4 Calle de la Bolsa (phone: 232-1377); *La Torre del Oro,* 25 Plaza Mayor (phone: 266-5016); *El Shotis,* 11 Calle Cava Baja (phone: 265-3230); and *Valle del Tietar,* 5 Calle Ciudad Rodrigo (phone: 248-0511).

MARSEILLES

Some cities pass through a chrysalis stage as important ports before they emerge into greatness as commercial centers or industrial powers. Not so Marseilles. As it has been for 25 centuries, since before the Greeks controlled the wine-dark seas of the Mediterranean, modern Marseilles is above all else a port city. In 600 BC, Phocaean Greeks from Asia Minor founded the city, calling it Massalia, and then, as now, it acted as port of entry for goods, people, ideas, and most of all, history. (A commemorative block near Marseilles's thriving Vieux Port proclaims with perfect accuracy and stunning lack of modesty: "They founded Marseilles, from which civilization reached the West.")

With a population just brushing 1 million, Marseilles is among France's largest cities. But that may say more about the importance of the Mediterranean to France than of France's influence on Marseilles. Landlocked Paris, so gay in springtime and so gray in winter, is another country, 500 miles away, every mile of which must be traveled on land. It is a journey that traditional Marseillais, otherwise so effusive and warm, are reluctant to make. Marseilles and its people face steadfastly toward the sea, from which they have always drawn such strength.

When the city provisioned the Crusaders and welcomed back their booty, it was trading with Africa, the Near East, and the Far East. Today the names have changed, but France's major port does business with the same countries, and a lot more besides. Marseillais have as much in common with Italians and Greeks — fellow Mediterraneans — as they do with Parisians.

Unlike Paris, which has become predictable and bourgeois by comparison, Marseilles is France's connection to the sensuous, boisterous world of the Mediterranean. Sailors from all over the world roam the Canebière, the famous street leading up from the Vieux Port (old port) in search of women, excitement, or perhaps a little bit of smuggling on the side on their next tour of duty. And frequently violence still erupts, as it did in the gangland murder at the *Bar du Téléphone* not too many years ago. The milieu of the French underworld endures as a presence, for Marseilles remains, as both Interpol and Hollywood would have it, "the French connection." Even though many of the drug middlemen have moved on to Amsterdam or Berlin, Gene Hackman would still recognize the place. But an odd question lingers: Do we consider port cities wicked because of Marseilles, or do we feel such thrilling wickedness in Marseilles because it is so much the port city of our dreams?

As in all great port cities, numerous foreigners and immigrants have settled in Marseilles — particularly industrial workers from the island of Corsica and a large number of North Africans. Often poor, many Algerians, Tunisians, and Moroccans live in slums around the Porte d'Aix and the Rue Ste.-Barbe, where shops sell inexpensive North African items, but where few people feel

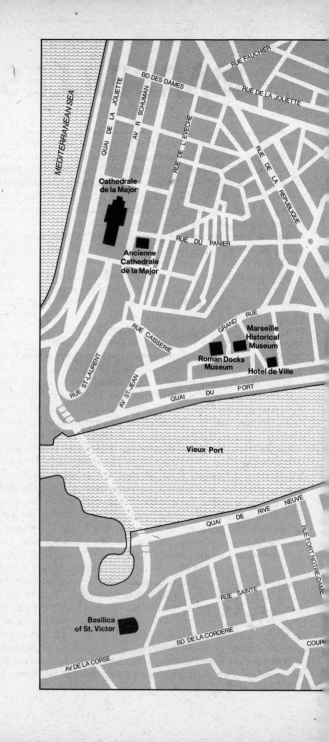

comfortable wandering after dark. The area is perfectly safe in the daytime, however, and it's worth a visit for the colors and smells alone.

Life is lived boisterously in the Marseilles streets, particularly in the area around the Vieux Port, which is now a harbor for pleasure boats and for sidewalk restaurants offering bouillabaisse. Although the Germans dynamited much of the picturesque but seedy old quarter during World War II (because it was a center for the Resistance), some reminders of Marseilles's tradition still survive.

From the beginning, the city prospered at the hands of the Greek traders, declined under Roman rule, and was revived by the Crusaders, whom Marseilles supplied with food and weapons. Devastated by the great plague in 1720, in which 50,000 of its citizens perished, Marseilles rose again to support the French Revolution with enthusiasm. In 1792, 500 volunteers marched to Paris, singing a new war song composed at Strasbourg by a young officer named Rouget de Lisle. All the way to Paris, the Marseillais sang the new song with Mediterranean exuberance. Practice improved their performance, so that when the troops reached Paris, their expert chorus electrified all listeners. The song caught on and became France's stirring national anthem, named not for the city but for those staunch choristers, "La Marseillaise."

One hundred years later, the opening of the Suez Canal virtually assured the continued maritime success of Marseilles, and commercial traffic abandoned the small Vieux Port for a new one directly to the north. The new port was also destroyed during World War II, but it was rebuilt and expanded. Flat, nondescript, and soulless buildings have risen on the once vibrant site of the old quarter. Ironically, every new groundbreaking brings the possibility of unearthing still more traces of earlier civilizations, like the Roman docks discovered in the 1940s or the Greek ramparts found in 1967. Medieval churches now stand side by side with steel and glass apartment buildings. The ongoing excavations at the Centre Bourse are open to visitors.

Many visitors to Marseilles are heading off to the Côte d'Azur and are in the city only to change trains at the newly rebuilt Gare St.-Charles or planes at the modern Aéroport de Marignane. But there's sufficient reason to linger. Step into a café on the Vieux Port as the burning Mediterranean sun starts to sink in the sky and order a milky white *pastis,* an anise-flavored apéritif. (Or duck into the less seedy *La Samaritaine* at Bd. de la République.) Around you are spectacular white limestone hills and in front, a harbor filled with the cries and accents of far-off lands. Drink it all in, along with your *pastis.* Who knows? You may, like the American writer M. F. K. Fisher, fall in love with Marseilles and stay longer, soaking in its rich Mediterranean atmosphere and exploring its abundant historic remains.

MARSEILLES AT-A-GLANCE

SEEING THE CITY: Take the #60 bus up to this hilly city's most imposing height, a 531-foot limestone bluff crowned by the Basilica of Notre-Dame-de-la-Garde, known to the Provençal as La Bonne Mère. There's an extraordinary view — particularly at sunset — from the terrace: The boats on the Vieux Port, the white rocky islands, and the densely built city stretch out below. The half-Roman, half-Byzantine basilica itself, topped by a huge gilded statue of the Virgin, is far less of a draw than its view, but inside it does have interesting hand-painted offerings to the Virgin as thanks for curing various ailments. Pl. du Colonel Eden.

SPECIAL PLACES: If you walk down the Gare St.-Charles's monumental staircase and continue on the Boulevard d'Athènes, you'll come to a busy central shopping street, the Canebière. Visitors are sometimes disappointed at the modern, occasionally tacky appearance of this celebrated boulevard that runs into the Vieux Port. During the Middle Ages there were hemp fields here, or *chénevières* (hence the name Canebière); the broad plane-tree-lined concourse is still the key artery — and essential reference point — of Marseilles. During December, it becomes the backdrop for the colorful *santons* fair, where folk art takes center stage in the form of clay figures, some 2 to 3 feet tall, representing both the Christmas story and Provençal life in centuries past.

IN THE CITY

Vieux Port – Follow the Canebière down to the Quai des Belges and you'll arrive at the Vieux Port. Today a harbor for small fishing boats and yachts, it's far more picturesque than the burgeoning new port to the north. Its entrance is framed by the 17th-century forts of St. Jean and St. Nicholas (a Foreign Legion base). Terraced restaurants featuring bouillabaisse (at staggering prices) overlook the animated marina. A fresh-fish market does a lively business every morning. This is the heart of Marseilles. It is still possible to ferry from one side of the Vieux Port to the other, as in Pagnol's films. Ferries make the trip every 2 or 3 minutes from 7 AM to 7 PM daily.

Musée des Beaux-Arts – In the 19th-century Palais de Longchamp — noteworthy in its own right for impressive fountains and gardens (and even a zoo) — the museum offers a considerable display of art. Paintings from the Italian, Flemish, Dutch, and French (David, Courbet, Ingres) schools share the palace's left wing with works by Marseilles natives Honoré Daumier and Pierre Puget and by other Provençal artists. On the first floor is a charming children's museum. The right wing of the palace contains a natural history museum. Open daily from 10 AM to 5 PM. Admission charge. Pl. Bernex (phone: 91-62-21-17).

Musée Grobet-Labadié – Near the Longchamp Palace, this 19th-century showplace is furnished opulently, exactly as it was when the musician Louis Grobet lived there. Stop by before or after visiting the *Fine Arts Museum.* Closed Tuesday and Wednesday mornings. 140 Bd. Longchamp (phone: 91-62-21-82 or 91-08-96-04).

Outdoor Markets – Wander through the city's raucous market areas and take in their vivid sights and smells. They're particularly alive in the mornings on the Quai des Belges, where the fishermen and their wives sell their catch directly. Also, note the food market on Rue Longue des Capucins (at Rue Vacon, near the Canebière); the flea markets near the Porte d'Aix (that is, the triumphal arch in Pl. Jules-Guesde at the end of Rue d'Aix); the daily book market on Le Cours Julien; and Rue St.-Barbe in the Algerian quarter (but avoid this racially troubled area after dark).

Le Cours Julien – This unique public square has splashing fountains, interesting boutiques, bookstores, restaurants, and an innovative art gallery (see *Shopping*). It will take an hour to explore the whole plaza, but allow yourself the pleasure of real contact with the youth, vigor, and creativity of Marseilles. To get here, walk north from the Old Port, up the Canebière, then East onto Bd. Garibaldi, which crosses Le Cours Julien.

Musée des Docks Romains – An unexpected benefit came from the Germans' 1943 bombing of the old quarter. Fascinating remains of long-buried Roman docks and statuary were unearthed in the course of rebuilding the area, and the museum incorporates the original setting plus objects retrieved offshore. Open daily from 10 AM to 5 PM. Admission charge. 28 Pl. Vivaux (phone: 91-91-24-62).

Musée d'Histoire de Marseille – Excavations of the ancient Greek port and ramparts are now a museum. The open-air archaeological dig features the remains of a boat excavated on the site. Closed Sundays and Mondays. Admission charge. Square Belsunce (phone: 91-90-42-22).

Le Panier – From the Quai du Port, the narrow streets climb toward what little remains of Old Marseilles. Reminiscent of Paris's Montmartre (and likewise beginning to suffer the same "renewal" fate), the Panier quarter is a maze of tiny streets reverberating with the exuberant sounds of daily life in a Provençal neighborhood. It is not lacking for art galleries or interesting bistros. Behind the Hôtel de Ville, climb the steps to the left of Notre-Dame des Accoules' bell tower, the remains of a 12th-century church.

Galeries de la Vieille Charité – It mounts exhibitions on old and new Marseilles. Open daily from 10 AM to 5 PM. 2 Rue de la Charité (phone: 91-56-28-38).

Cathédrales de la Major – Reminiscent of Moslem mosques, the cathedrals' domes and cupolas dominate the Quai de la Tourette. The sadly battered Ancienne (Old) Major was built in the 12th century in pure Romanesque style on the ruins of the Roman Temple of Diana. The huge, ostentatious cathedral next to it was built in the 19th century in a Romanesque-Byzantine style. Pl. de la Major.

Basilique St.-Victor – The present fortified Gothic church dates from the 11th to the 14th century, but the real interest lies below, in its crypt, which is actually an ancient basilica founded in the 5th century in honor of the 3rd-century martyr St. Victor. This basilica contains a chapel and the tomb of two 3rd-century martyrs in addition to pagan and early Christian catacombs. The church also hosts concerts; call for the program. Crypt closed Sundays. Admission charge. Pl. St.-Victor (phone: 91-33-25-86).

Cité Radieuse – Designed by the renowned Le Corbusier, the 17-story housing development — or *unité d'habitation* — was avant garde for its time (1947–52) and is still a landmark in modern functional architecture. There is a moderately priced hotel with a number of shops on the premises. 280 Bd. Michelet.

Parc Borély – This is a lovely stretch of greenery where you can take some sun by the lake, rent a bicycle, or visit three museums on the premises: the *Château Borély,* the *Archaeological Museum* in the château, or the *Lapidary Museum* in an adjoining annex (see below for details about each museum). There's also a quaint racetrack on the same site. The park itself closes after dark. Promenade de la Plage and Av. Clot-Bey.

Château Borély – Built by a rich businessman between 1767 and 1778, it contains fine 18th-century salons (closed Tuesdays and Wednesday mornings; admission charge). Opened in March 1989 in the château, the *Musée de la Mode* is Marseilles's newest museum. Open daily from 10 AM to 5 PM. Av. Clot Bey, Parc Borély (phone: 91-73-21-60).

Musée d'Archéologie – This museum, in the *Château Borély,* has Egyptian, Greek, and Roman pieces, including ceramics, bronzes, and antique glass. Parc Borély (phone: 91-73-21-60).

Musée Lapidaire – In a structure next to the *Château Borély,* this museum contains Greek, Roman, and Christian art, including sarcophagi and marine antiquities; outdoors there's an archaeological garden. Parc Borély (phone: 91-73-21-60).

OUT OF TOWN

Promenade de la Corniche – This scenic coast road that winds for some 3 miles (5 km) south of the Vieux Port passes in its course Marseilles's most spectacular homes and a breathtaking view of the sea and the islands, including the Château d'If and the

Frioul Islands (see below). Also known as the Corniche Président-J.-F.-Kennedy, it passes a picture-postcard fishing port, Vallon des Auffes, and lovely rocky coves before it becomes the promenade de la Plage (with Parc Borély) and continues toward Cassis, a beautiful fishing town, now also a summer resort, that was celebrated by Derain, Vlaminck, Matisse, and Dufy. Cassis is 14 miles (22 km) from Marseilles. Beautiful, sandy Prado Beach is also along the Corniche road; watch for signs. Pick up Corniche Président-J.-F.-Kennedy at Rue des Catalans.

Château d'If – Set on a rocky island, this beautiful castle was built in the 16th century for defense and then turned into a state prison, whose most famous "guest" was Alexander Dumas's Count of Monte Cristo. Inside some cells are carvings by Huguenot prisoners. Open daily. Admission charge. The château can be reached by boats that leave about every 15 minutes for a 20-minute ride from the Quai des Belges (phone: 91-55-50-09).

Château Gombert – This village just outside the city limits claims the *Musée des Arts et Traditions Populaires du Terroir Marseillais* (Museum of Popular Art and Traditions), 5 Pl. des Héros (phone: 91-68-14-38). Among its exhibitions are pottery, pewter, and glass displays. Open only on Saturday, Sunday, and Monday afternoons. In summer the town holds a festival of Provençal folklore. Follow the Autoroute north toward Lyons and exit at La Rose.

Allauch – On a cliff with a church on top and windmills all around, it offers a good view of Marseilles and the harbor and is known for *suce-miel*, a type of lollipop made of honey, and *croquants aux amandes*, almond biscuits. To get here, take Boulevard de la Libération out of Marseilles and follow signs north to St. Barnabé/Allauch.

Frioul Islands – These islands southwest of Marseilles have sparkling creeks that provide an idyllic retreat from the city's sometimes torrid atmosphere. Boats leave for the islands from the Quai des Belges every 15 minutes. Les Armateurs Côtiers (phone: 91-55-50-09).

■ **EXTRA SPECIAL:** For unsurpassed and unspoiled natural beauty, don't leave the region without seeing its spectacular *calanques* along the coast between Marseilles and Cassis. The *calanques* are crystal-clear narrow creeks running between stark white limestone cliffs that soar up to 650 feet, much like small fjords. They can be approached only by foot (about 1½ hours each way) or by boat, thereby ensuring a minimum number of tourists. The closest *calanques* — Sormiou and Morgiou — can be reached from Roy d'Espagne (take bus #44) and Les Baumettes (#22), respectively. For information on organized hiking ventures, visit *Les Excursionnistes Marseillais,* 16 Rue de la Rotonde, Tuesdays through Saturdays from 6 to 8 PM. Otherwise, leave by boat from Quai des Belges (phone: 91-84-75-52).

SOURCES AND RESOURCES

TOURIST INFORMATION: The English-speaking staff of the Office du Tourisme, 4 La Canebière (phone: 91-54-91-11), provides hotel reservations, maps, guides, and advice; also ask for *La Charte de la Bouillabaisse,* which gives the real recipe for this much maligned and poorly imitated fish soup and provides a list of those restaurants serving the authentic concoction. A second tourist office is at Gare St.-Charles (phone: 91-50-59-18).

For a closer look at Marseilles, read *A Considerable Town,* by the American M. F. K. Fisher; it's a charming and personal account of a city she loves.

A good street-indexed map is the *Carte et Plan Fréjet,* available at major bookstores along the Canebière. They also carry general English-language guidebooks, but no local English publications exist. Also, pick up a copy of *Trimestre,* a quarterly listing of what's happening.

Guided tours of Marseilles are available in English from *Valadou,* 73 La Canebière (phone: 91-91-90-02), for $7 to $8.

Local Coverage – If you read French, pick up *Le Mois à Marseille* or *Poche Soir* for current events. The local newspapers, *Le Méridional* and *Le Provençal,* are available at any newsstand.

Telephone – The area code for Marseilles is 91; it must be used, even when dialing within the city. The area code for the airport is 42. When calling a number in Marseilles from the Paris region (including Ile de France), dial 16, then the eight-digit number. When calling a number in Marseilles from outside Paris, dial only the eight-digit number. When calling Marseilles from the US, dial only the country code 33 and the eight-digit number.

 CLIMATE AND CLOTHES: The Mediterranean climate is dry and joyously sunny 300 days a year, with warm summer temperatures in the high 80s F (30C-32C) and mild winter temperatures that rarely go below 40F (4C). It rains in spring and fall in brief but heavy downpours. The city can be windy, with the capricious *mistral* whipping down the Rhone at up to 65 miles an hour and lasting anywhere from a few hours to a few days.

 GETTING AROUND: Airport – Marseilles-Marignane Airport is about 18 miles northwest of the city (phone: 42-89-90-10 or, in Marseilles, 91-54-92-92). International and domestic terminals are adjacent in the main airport concourse. For a taxi into town, 24 hours a day, call 42-78-24-44; the 20-to 30-minute ride will cost about 200F ($33). There are buses every 15 minutes in both directions from 6 AM to 8 PM and according to flight schedules; the approximate time to Gare St.-Charles, the main train station, is 30 minutes, and the fare is about 32F ($5). For information on regular bus service to the airport from Marseilles, call 91-50-59-34.

Boat – Boats leave for the Frioul Islands (see *Special Places*) from the Quai des Belges every 15 minutes. Les Armateurs Côtiers (phone: 91-55-50-09).

Bus and Métro – Marseilles's attractive subway system is coordinated with the buses, allowing easy — and free — transfers between systems. The métro goes in only two directions, so it's difficult to get lost. Buy a *carnet* of six tickets instead of the single ticket. The métro shuts down each night at 12:30 AM and most buses stop running even earlier. For information, phone 91-91-92-10. For information about regular bus service to Marignane Airport, phone 91-50-59-34.

Car Rental – Major international firms are represented.

Ferry – For ferries to Corsica, inquire at SNCM, 61 Bd. des Dames (phone: 91-56-32-00).

Taxi – There are cabstands around the city, or call *Taxi Tupp* (phone: 91-05-80-80); *Marseille Taxi* (phone: 91-02-20-20); or *Taxi 2000* (phone: 91-49-20-00).

Train – Marseilles's train station is Gare St.-Charles (phone: 91-08-50-50 for information, 91-08-84-12 for reservations). The extension of the Paris-Lyons high-speed TGV line to Valence (expected to be completed by 1993) will cut travel time between Paris and Marseilles to just over 3 hours; until then, it takes about 4½ hours.

 SPECIAL EVENTS: From late June through mid-August, the *Théâtre aux Etoiles* presents outdoor theater, concerts, and ballet at *Palais du Pharo,* the palace and gardens set panoramically above the harbor entrance at Bd. Charles-Livon (for information, phone the tourist office: 91-54-91-11).

There's also an *International Folklore Festival* in early July at the Château Gombert, Pl. des Héros, as well as a live crèche at Christmas. The best events during the rest of the year are the *Santons Fair,* during which the traditional hand-painted clay statuettes fill Christmas crèches all over the city (December 1–January 6); *La Fête de Mai,* when the Cours Julien and Place Carli are closed to cars and open to circus acts, theater troupes, and singers (late May); and the *Garlic Fair,* when mounds of garlic cover the sidewalks of Cour Belsunce (June 15–July 15).

MUSEUMS: Besides those described in *Special Places,* there are two other notable Marseilles museums.

Musée Cantini – Provençal ceramics and often outstanding contemporary art exhibitions. Open daily from 10 AM to 5 PM. Admission charge. 19 Rue Grignan (phone: 91-54-77-75).

Musée du Vieux Marseille – A folklore museum set up in a 16th-century house, the Maison Diamantée (Diamond House), so called for the shape of its stone facing and best known for its *santon* collection (see *Shopping*). Open daily. Admission charge. Rue de la Prison (phone: 91-55-10-19).

SHOPPING: Major department stores, elegant couturier and gift shops, and enough shoe shops to make a centipede happy are clustered in the frenetic area around the Canebière (Rue de Rome, Rue Paradis, and Rue St.-Ferréol). The flashy and trendy Centre Bourse shopping center is north of the Canebière. Less expensive shops, usually selling North African items, are in the vicinity of the Porte d'Aix (Arc de Triomphe).

Typical Marseillais souvenirs include clay *santons,* which can be found in tourist shops or at numerous booths set up for the Christmas *Santons Fair* on the Canebière. The word *santon* is derived from the Italian *santibelli,* "the beautiful saints." These small, naively modeled and brightly colored figurines represent both biblical figures and traditional characters of Provence life such as the Gypsy, the shepherd, and the milkmaid.

Or try some *navettes* (half-bread, half-cake loaves that stay fresh for months) from a remarkable 200-year-old bakery, *Le Four des Navettes,* 136 Rue Sainte (phone: 91-33-32-12).

Les Arcenaulx, a bookstore and publishing house, sells new and old editions and has a tearoom, a restaurant, and an antiques shop at 25 Cours Estienne d'Orves (phone: 91-54-39-37). *Parenthèses,* a bookstore and publisher of books on jazz, is a storehouse of books on music, the arts, and architecture, at 72 Cours Julien (phone: 91-48-74-44). *Galerie Roger Pailhas,* an art gallery that promotes the work of international artists, including some of Marseilles's most original ones, is at 61 Cours Julien (phone: 91-42-18-01).

SPORTS AND FITNESS: Professional sports include auto racing, basketball, horse racing, ice hockey, rugby, and soccer. Inquire at the tourist office.

Fishing – Notably for gilt-head and mackerel: off the Corniche, in the *calanques,* the Frioul Islands, and in nearby fishing villages.

Golf – The nearest 18-hole course is 14 miles (22 km) away at the *Golf Club Aix-Marseille,* Domaine de Riquetti, Les Milles, Aix-en-Provence (phone: 42-24-20-41).

Horseback Riding – Inquire at the *Centre Equestre de la Ville de Marseille,* 33 Carthage (phone: 91-73-72-94).

Jogging – Take bus #21 to Domaine de Luminy, about 4 miles (6 km) from the city center. Or try Parc Borély, 3 miles (5 km) south of the city by the Promenade de la Corniche.

Sailing – Contact *Centre Nautique Roucas-Blanc,* Plage du Roucas-Blanc (phone: 91-22-72-49).

Swimming – *Piscine Luminy,* Rte. Léon-Lachamp (phone: 91-41-26-59).

Tennis and Squash – Try the courts at *Tennis Municipaux,* Allée Ray-Grassi (phone: 91-77-83-89), or *Tennis Didier* (phone: 91-26-16-05). Both *Set-Squash Marseille,* 265 Av. de Mazargues (phone: 91-71-94-71), and *Prado Squash,* 26 bis Bd. Michelet (phone: 91-22-03-45), provide facilities for tennis as well as squash.

Water Sports – For information, call or visit the *Fédération des Sociétés Nautiques des Bouches du Rhône,* 10 Av. de la Corse (phone: 91-54-34-88).

THEATER: Theater has been booming in Marseilles, with more than 10 new stages opening in the past few years. In addition to the summertime *Théâtre aux Etoiles* (phone: 91-31-04-99), there's a surprisingly good choice of theater activity year-round. The choices range from the intimate *Centre Culturel* (theater and music), 33 Cours Julien (phone: 91-47-09-64), to the *Café-Thèâtre Jérémie* (food and informal amateur productions); *Café-Théâtre du Vieux Panier,* 52 Rue St.-Françoise (phone: 91-91-00-74), and the *Théâtre de Poche,* 2 Av. Maréchal-Foch (phone: 91-72-41-27), to the more ambitious new national theater, *La Criée,* 30 Quai de Rive Neuve, where reservations are necessary (phone: 91-54-74-54 or 91-54-70-54), and *Théâtre Axel Toursky,* 22 Av. Edouard-Vaillant (phone: 91-02-58-35). An especially interesting program is offered by the *Théâtre du Gyptis,* 136 Rue Loubon (phone: 91-08-10-18). The *Théâtre Massalia,* 60 Rue Grignan (phone: 91-55-66-06), has been converted into a unique marionette theater featuring performances by marionette companies from all over Europe. For experimental theater, visit *Théâtre de Poche,* 70 Av. A. Zenatti (phone: 91-72-42-27), and *Théâtre de Lenche,* 4 Pl. de Lenche (phone: 91-91-55-56 or 91-91-52-22). (*Note:* Those who don't speak French will endure no handicap while enjoying operettas or mime performances, which are presented frequently.) For theater information and tickets, visit the office of the FNAC at Centre Bourse.

MUSIC: The Marseillais know good opera and ballet as well as they know bouillabaisse. The sometimes outstanding *Opéra de Marseille,* Pl. Ernest-Reyer (phone: 91-55-14-99), and the recently launched *Théâtre de Recherche de Marseille (TRM),* Espace Massalia, 60 Rue Grignan (phone: 91-55-66-06), both have devoted followings. In addition, the *Opéra de Marseille* is the home of the *Compagnie Roland Petit,* France's well-known ballet company. Chamber music and organ recitals are frequent at major churches and occasionally outdoors on the Vieux Port. Popular music doesn't fare nearly as well. There are occasional acts at *Théâtre Axel Toursky,* 22 Av. Edouard-Vaillant (phone: 91-02-58-35).

NIGHTCLUBS AND NIGHTLIFE: Marseilles does not suffer from inactivity after dark, with action ranging from the sedate to the frenetic. In the former category, visitors will find soothing piano bars such as *Le Beauvau* in the *Beauvau* hotel, 9 Rue Beauvau (phone: 91-54-91-00), whose barman really knows his trade; and *Le Garbo,* 9 Quai de Rive Neuve (phone: 91-33-34-20), whose evocative decor recalls the period and style of its namesake. There's traditional Andalusian dancing at *Le Sangria,* 145 Bd. Rabattau (phone: 91-79-64-35). The most "in" night spots include *Bunny's Club,* 2 Rue Corneille (phone: 91-54-09-02), with a packed dance floor and an excellent sound system; *Abbaye de la Commanderie,* 20 Rue Corneille (phone: 91-33-45-56), a cabaret that draws its neighbor's overflow with a *sympathique* evening of nonstop songs; and *London Club,* 73 Corniche Kennedy (phone: 91-52-64-04), a friendly nightclub/disco. At the moment, the young set favors *Le Rock*

A Billy, 5 Rue Molière (phone: 91-54-70-36), so called because the bodies of old cars provide the atmosphere (if one can call it that); and the famous, as well as the would-bes, congregate at *Le Juke,* 6 Rue Lully (phone: 91-33-14-88). Unique *Espace Julien,* 33 Cours Julien (phone: 91-47-09-64), offers jazz occasionally and an open cabaret where anyone can perform; it's also a learning center for everything from musical instruments to dance to gymnastics.

BEST IN TOWN

 CHECKING IN: Marseilles traditionally has had a meager selection of good hotels. With a recent spurt of hotel construction, there's now an overabundance of ultramodern luxury rooms, but no improvement in the lower price ranges. Expect to pay $65 or more for a double room (including breakfast) in expensive hotels; $40 to $65 for moderate; and under $40 for an inexpensive one.

Altea – Formerly the *Frantel,* this is one of the city's newest hotels in the center, just a 5-minute walk from the Old Port. It belongs to a major French chain but distinguishes itself by its taste, pleasant piano bar, and an outstanding restaurant, *L'Oursinade* (see *Eating Out*). The 200 rooms have all the luxury hotel amenities. Rue Neuve-St.-Martin (phone: 91-91-91-29). Expensive.

Pullman Beauvau – Next to the tourist office and just down the street from the *Opéra,* this is one of Marseilles's four-star hotels. Most of its 72 rooms face the Vieux Port. 4 Rue Beauvau (phone: 91-54-91-00). Expensive.

Concorde Palm Beach – A supermodern hotel by the sea, with an outdoor pool and a good restaurant, *La Réserve.* 2 Promenade de la Plage (phone: 91-76-20-00). Expensive.

Le Petit Nice – This small (18 rooms and suites in 2 buildings), gracious hotel, built in the 19th century as a private villa, has a shaded garden and a superb two-star Michelin restaurant (see *Eating Out*) to recommend it, all looking out over the Mediterranean from a magnificent position on the Corniche. The restaurant is closed Mondays and at lunch on winter Tuesdays; the hotel is closed in January and the first week in February. 160 Corniche Président-J.-F.-Kennedy (phone: 91-59-25-92). Expensive.

Sofitel Vieux Port – A magnificent modern hotel with a splendid view from its perch above the entrance to the Old Port, near the Palais du Pharo. It has some 200 rooms, air conditioning, a heated outdoor pool, a cozy bar, and a fine restaurant, *Les Trois Forts* (see *Eating Out*). 36 Bd. Charles-Livon (phone: 91-52-90-19). Expensive.

Astoria – One of a number of small, old Marseilles hotels that have been renovated in recent years, this turn-of-the-century relic now has a bright, skylit lobby filled with plants and rooms with contemporary furnishings. 10 Bd. Garibaldi (phone: 91-33-33-50). Moderate.

Bompard – In a quiet park on a hill not far from the sea, only a 5-minute drive (on the coastal road) from the bustle of the Vieux Port. Some of its 40-plus rooms — in the main building or surrounding bungalows — have kitchenettes. No restaurant. 2 Rue des Flots-Bleus (phone: 91-52-10-93). Moderate.

Grand Hôtel Noailles – Still the classic Marseilles hotel, this stylish old building has undergone a recent renovation, after losing 90 of its 160 rooms to office space. It now features steel and plexiglas decor, with luxury appointments and direct-dial phones in many rooms. 66 La Canebière (phone: 91-54-91-48). Moderate.

Le Corbusier – There are only 24 rooms, and each gives the experience of living in a city apartment. 280 Bd. Michelet (phone: 91-77-18-15). Moderate to inexpensive.

Esterel – This small, comfortable, quiet hotel is convenient to the *métro* and shopping. Rooms are air conditioned and have color TV sets. No restaurant. 124 Rue Paradis (phone: 91-37-13-90). Inexpensive.

Grand Hôtel de Genève – Old, now modernized, in a quiet pedestrian precinct just behind the Old Port. No restaurant. 3 bis Rue Reine-Elizabeth (phone: 91-90-51-42). Inexpensive.

Urbis – Part of a nationwide chain, this modern hotel contains 148 rooms, a restaurant, bar, and conference facilities. Close to the Vieux Port and a street above the Cours d'Estienne d'Orves. 46 Rue Sainte (phone: 91-54-73-73). Inexpensive.

EATING OUT: What it has traditionally lacked in hotels, Marseilles has always made up for in restaurants; they are among France's finest, and that is saying a lot. Besides classic French cuisine, be sure to try Provençal (from Provence — the southern region of France that straddles the Rhone River) specialties. The city is virtually synonymous with bouillabaisse, a dish not to be missed. In its classical form, this soup is based on Mediterranean rockfish (called *rouget*), but other fish and shellfish are usually added, particularly lobster and crab. The seasoning (cayenne, garlic, tomatoes, herbs) is very special, but the star ingredient is saffron, which gives bouillabaisse its golden color. It is often served with *rouille,* a relish made of red pepper, garlic, and fish broth, as well as with *aïoli,* a delicious olive-oil-based garlic mayonnaise. Another dish common on menus in Marseilles is *bourride,* a fish stew that some prefer to bouillabaisse.

Other regional specialties include *anchoïade,* anchovies and olive oil mashed into a paste that accompanies raw vegetables; *poutargue,* fish eggs grated in oil, then pressed and dried to become a sort of white caviar; *navettes,* flat biscuits flavored with orange-flower water; and *fougasses,* flat, salty breads in leaf designs, flavored with walnuts, olives, bacon, or cheese.

You may also wish to sample *pastis,* the anise-flavored apéritif that tastes something like licorice. Usually colorless, *pastis* is served diluted with ice water, which turns it cloudy white. Also try wines from Provence, particularly the dry, pleasant rosé.

Expect to pay $70 and considerably higher in the expensive category (for two without wine); from $45 to $70 in the moderate range; and under $45 in the inexpensive category. These prices include a service charge.

Calypso – This outstanding restaurant offers a classic sea view and Marseilles's best bouillabaisse. No meat or vegetables here, just impeccably served seafood. But the quality and quantity leave nothing to be desired. Its twin and peer — *Michel* — is across the street. Closed Sundays, Mondays, and August. Reservations necessary. 3 Rue des Catalans (phone: 91-52-64-00). Expensive.

Chez Brun (Aux Mets de Provence) – At this venerable family-run restaurant, you'll eat in the *ancienne* style. Up to 20 dishes of the true Provençal cuisine, which means fish and olive-spiced specialties. Closed Sundays, Mondays, and holidays. Reservations necessary. 18 Quai du Rive Neuve; on the 2nd floor; the entrance is hard to find, so watch closely! (phone: 91-33-35-38). Expensive.

Michel (Les Catalans) – Across the street from the *Calypso*. The menu is short, the prices are right, and the seafood is succulent, rating one Michelin star. Don't miss the bouillabaisse. Closed Tuesdays, Wednesdays, and July. 6 Rue des Catalans (phone: 91-52-64-22 or 91-52-30-63). Expensive.

Miramar – Touted by locals as one of the best sources on the quay of the old port for authentic bouillabaisse, this modern restaurant also serves a wide variety of other fish dishes and regional specialties. Closed Sundays and August. 12 Quai du Port (phone: 91-91-10-40). Expensive.

Le Petit Nice – A two-star Michelin establishment that deserves a third rosette. Our favorite dining spot in Marseilles; the view alone is worth the price of admission. The tomato tart appetizer is the most beautiful single menu item we've ever had on our *plats,* and the lobster ragoût is equally impressive. Closed Mondays and at lunch during the winter. Reservations necessary. 160 Corniche Président-J.-F.-Kennedy (phone: 91-59-25-92). Expensive.

New York – For seafood again, try this restaurant in the old harbor area. Especially good are the fish terrine and the *bourride.* The owner fell in love with New York when he was a sailor — thus the name. Closed Sundays. 7 Quai des Belges (phone: 91-33-60-98 or 91-33-91-79). Expensive to moderate.

L'Oursinade – In the *Altéa* hotel, this serves very fine Provençal cuisine in an atmosphere of understated elegance. Closed Sundays and late July through August. Rue Neuve-St.-Martin (phone: 91-56-05-02). Expensive to moderate.

Les Trois Forts – You'll find a panoramic view of the Old Port here, and such inventive dishes as lamb's liver braised with melon and honey. Sofitel Vieux Port, 36 Bd. Charles-Livon (phone: 91-52-90-19). Expensive to moderate.

L'Avant-Scène – The cuisine here runs to fairly light French, and the place is actually a café/art gallery/theater/magazine shop all rolled into one. The theater is downstairs, and there's a fashion designer's atelier upstairs. Open nightly from 8 PM to 2 AM. 59 Cours Julien (phone: 91-42-19-29). Moderate.

Chez Caruso – This is where the locals go when they crave some delicious Italian food. Closed Sunday nights, Mondays, and from mid-October through mid-November. 158 Quai du Port (phone: 91-90-94-04). Moderate.

Chez Fonfon – In an old fishing club, it's heavy on local color and boat scenes, real bouillabaisse, and other fish dishes. 140 Vallen des Auffes (phone: 91-52-14-38). Moderate.

Cousin, Cousine – Interesting nouvelle cuisine is served here, along with good local wines. Try the hot oysters with broccoli and pheasant in wine sauce. Closed weekends. 102 Cours Julien (phone: 91-48-14-50). Moderate.

Au Pescadou – On entering you'll immediately be dazzled by the spectacular array of fresh oysters, clams, mussels and other seafood delicacies. With ingredients like these, only the simplest preparation is needed. Closed July and August. Reservations advised. Closed Sundays and Mondays. 19 Pl. Castellane (phone: 91-78-36-01). Moderate.

Les Platanes (Restaurant des Abattoirs) – By the slaughterhouse, at the city's northern extreme, this immense old café is where the butchers themselves eat. Choose from beef, pork, veal, and a great selection of sausages. Lunch only; closed weekends. Reservations advised. 7 Av. Journet (phone: 91-60-93-17). Moderate.

Texas Fiesta – Run by a Frenchman who used to live in Houston, this lively spot serves up Tex-Mex food, margaritas, American beer, and, on Tuesday nights, country music. Open daily. 70 Cours Julien (phone: 91-48-49-24). Moderate.

Aux Baguettes d'Or – Just behind the *Opéra,* it offers authentic Vietnamese cuisine and friendly service, and is sometimes frequented by singers after performances. Closed Wednesdays. 65 Rue Francis-Davso (phone: 91-54-20-39). Moderate to inexpensive.

Dmitri – Hungarian and Russian specialties are the order of the day. Closed Sundays and Mondays. 6 Rue Meolan (phone: 91-54-09-68). Inexpensive.

La Kahenas – This Tunisian restaurant offers daily specials, mint tea, pastries, and is crowded at lunch. Closed Sundays. 2 Rue de la République (phone: 91-90-61-93). Inexpensive.

Tarte Julie – Every pie imaginable, sweet or salty, is here, along with pizzas and salads. Closed Sundays. 14 Av. du Prado (phone: 91-37-23-45). Inexpensive.

Le Tonneau – This colorful, tiny place is right off the Canebière. Its copious, family-style meals of rabbit or *fricassé de volaille* are often served in front of the TV set. Closed weekends and 3 weeks in August. Reservations not necessary. 9 Rue Beauvau (phone: 91-33-63-92). Inexpensive.

BARS AND CAFÉS: At 5 PM the old Marseillais (barely a woman in sight) gather for *pastis* and tall tales at *Les Cafés du Panier,* just outside Marseilles at Rue St.-Françoise (phone: 91-91-00-74). Facing the Vieux Port is *Le Petit Pernod,* 30 Rue des Trois Mages (phone: 91-48-43-07), where the bourgeoise congregate. *Place Thiars,* 38A Pl. Thiars (phone: 91-33-07-25), is an artists' haunt that becomes even more popular in the summer, when it attracts tourists and theater people to its alfresco dining. The barman really knows his stuff at *Le Beauvau,* 9 Rue Beauvau (phone: 91-54-91-00). Expect a lovely evening at *Le Garbo,* 9 Quai de Rive-Neuve (phone: 91-33-34-20), whose decor recalls the 1930s (call in advance to make sure the piano player is scheduled the night you plan to attend).

MILAN

Milan is the financial and commercial hub of Italy and one of the most important business centers in the world. At first glance, it is a city of cold, uninspired skyscrapers, a city whose energizing force is money. Even the museum devoted to Leonardo da Vinci here testifies as much to his scientific and technical genius as to his artistic spirit. The people of Milan are industrious, sophisticated, chic, serious — not inclined to watch the world pass by from a sunny café table.

Although with nearly 2 million people Milan is a distant second in size to Rome, many Milanese think of their city as Italy's real capital; it is arguably more powerful than Rome. There are more than 400 banks in Milan. As a silk market, it rivals Lyons. Its *International Trade Fair* each spring draws hundreds of thousands of businesspeople from all over the world, as do its autumn and spring showings of luxury fashions. Milan boasts the prestigious Luigi Bocconi Commercial University, whose graduates include successful economists, bankers, and company presidents. The city is also the center of Italian publishing and in more recent years has won acclaim as the focal point of a new dynamism in both international design and fashion.

Still, Milan's economic preoccupation is tempered by an appreciation of less mundane pursuits. It is the *La Scala* opera house, with its perfect acoustics and grand traditions, not the Milan Stock Exchange (Borsa Valori), that is the pride of the city. The opening of the opera season each December is an important event for all of Italy, when newspapers print even the menus for the traditional midnight supper parties in the tony restaurants.

The very heart of Milan is its Gothic Duomo; the spires of Milan's magnificent cathedral seem to soar in defiance of the less ethereal buildings around it, though many of them often boast lovely *fin de siècle* architectural details and delightful, secret courtyard gardens. At the same time, Milan is the gateway to the Lombardy lake region, to ski resorts along the Swiss border to the North, and to the mist-veiled charm of the broad Po River — with its rice paddies, fishermen, and even a school of *naïf* painters — to the South.

So it is unfortunate that many visitors who look for the Italy of sunny skies, outdoor cafés, and quaint villages may hurry through Milan. The early-19th-century French writer Stendahl lived here for 4 decades; when he died in 1842, there were instructions for his tombstone to read: "Arrigo [Henry] Beyle [his real surname], Milanese — Lived, Wrote, Loved." Stendahl's enthusiasm for Milan, which in 1800 was one of Europe's wealthiest and most luxurious cities, was boundless: "For me this city is the most beautiful place on earth," he once wrote. The Milanese themselves passionately ascribe to this view and will point with pride to the city's best-known monuments as well as to other symbols of its illustrious past, such as the 16 Corinthian columns outside the 4th-century San Lorenzo Basilica, the remains of the 16th-century

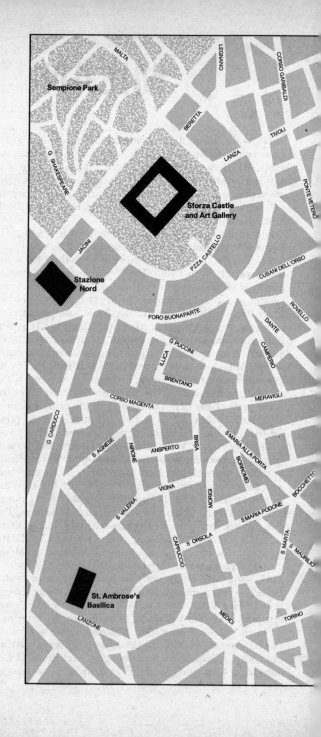

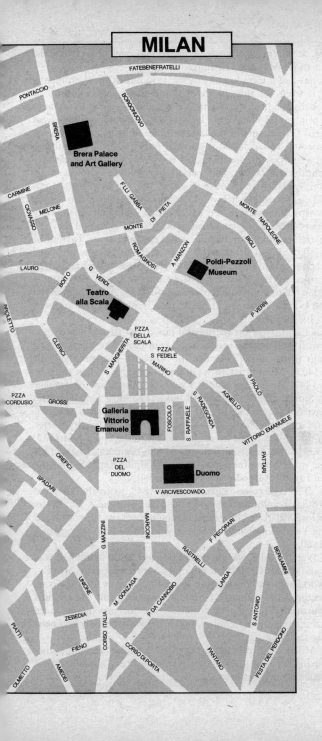

MILAN

FATEBENEFRATELLI

PONTACCIO

BORGONUOVO

BRERA

**Brera Palace
and Art Gallery**

CARMINE

CIOVASSO

MELONE

F.LLI GABBA

DI PIETA

MONTE

MONTE NAPOLEONE

LAURO

BOITO

G. VERDI

ROMAGNOSI

A. MANZON

BIGLI

**Poldi-Pezzoli
Museum**

**Teatro
alla Scala**

P. VERRI

RIOLETTO

CLERICI

S. MARGHERITA

PZZA
DELLA
SCALA

PZZA
S FEDELE

MARINO

S PAOLO

PZZA
CORDUSIO

GROSSI

**Galleria
Vittorio
Emanuele**

FOSCOLO

S RADEGONDA

S RAFFAELE

AGNELLO

VITTORIO EMANUELE

OREFICI

PZZA
DEL
DUOMO

Duomo

PATTARI

SPADARI

V ARCIVESCOVADO

G MAZZINI

MARCONI

F PECORARI

RASTRELLI

BERGAMINI

UNIONE

M GONZAGA

P DA CANNOBIO

LARGA

ZEBEDIA

S ANTONIO

PIATTI

FIENO

CORSO ITALIA

CORSO DI PORTA

PANTANO

FESTA DEL PERDONO

OLMETTO

AMEDEI

Spanish ramparts, or the traces of *navigli* (canals) that once crisscrossed the city and linked it to other regions of Italy.

Indeed, Milan has had a tumultuous history. Invading armies continually descended upon it from the time it was a Celtic settlement called Mediolanum. The Romans subdued the city in 222 BC, and it eventually grew to rival Rome for primacy of the West. In AD 313, Constantine the Great officially recognized Christianity in the famous Edict of Milan, and with the coming of Christianity, Milan found a spiritual father in Bishop Ambrose (later proclaimed a saint), who accomplished the seemingly impossible task of conciliating church and state. This period was followed, however, by barbarian invasions by Huns and Goths. Then, in 568, the Lombards (Lungobardi), who had originated in northwest Germany, pushed their way southward to cross the Alps and invade the Po Valley towns, including Milan. They ruled for more than 2 centuries, giving their name to the region, and they left their imprint on the art and architecture, language, and laws. Tyrranical Frankish rulers followed, but around the year 1000 the Milanese bishops wrested temporal power from them, and Milan became one of the first Italian city-states to be ruled by the church. Constant wars followed, and after a 9-month siege Milan fell to Frederick Barbarossa. In 1176, all the cities in the area united in the Lombard League to defeat the German invader and win recognition of its independence.

This ushered in a century of prosperity and power, as local family dynasties, beginnining with the Torriani, assumed power in 1260. The Visconti then seized power from them in 1277. Under the Visconti, particularly Gian Galeazzo (1345–1402), Milan grew in wealth and splendor. When the Visconti died out in 1447, Milan experienced 3 years of republican government before Francesco Sforza proclaimed himself duke. The most famous of the Sforzas was Ludovico il Moro (1451–1508), who brought Leonardo da Vinci, Donato Bramante, and other artists to Milan to enhance the city. After Ludovico's death, Milan fell to the invading French, to the Spanish in 1535, and, then, in 1713, to the Austrian Empire. At the beginning of the 19th century, Napoleon made Milan the capital of the Cisalpine Republic, but the tyrannic Austrian rulers returned when Napoleon fell.

The succession of foreign rulers began to ebb in 1848, when the Milanese staged a glorious 5-day revolution, known as the *Cinque Giornate*. But it was nearly 10 years before Milan was liberated and could throw its support to the Piedmontese King Victor Emmanuel of Savoy, who would become king of a unified Italy in 1860.

During World War II, Milan was the site of bitter partisan fighting; it was bombed 15 times and many of its historic buildings were damaged extensively. But restoration work and new construction began immediately after the war. Bomb damage required the complete rebuilding of about half the region's factories, which proved a blessing in disguise since the new plants were extremely modern manufacturing entities, making them especially competitive and spawning the boom of the 1950s and 1960s.

Contemporary Milan is surrounded by a massive, smoke-belching industrial belt — producing auto parts, chemicals, manmade fibers, appliances and rubber. The consequent smog has been somewhat reduced in recent years, but still remains a problem, as do polluted waterways. On the positive side, modern Milan is a virtual maze of four-lane highways connecting it with the other northern industrial cities — Genoa, Turin, Venice, and Brescia — and, by the Autostrada del Sole, to Rome and southern Italy.

The center of Italy's publishing and advertising industry and private TV networks, Milan specializes in innovative industrial design and avant-garde graphics. Its textile design and fashions are on a par with those of Paris. The city itself is prosperous and elegant; its people enjoy a high standard of living and a stimulating cultural and intellectual life. Whether you come on business, to attend the opera, to patronize the elegant Milanese fashion houses, or to admire the city's art treasures, you will find Milan's sophistication equal to that of London or Paris or New York, but always uncompromisingly Italian.

MILAN AT-A-GLANCE

SEEING THE CITY: For a grand view of Milan, the surrounding Lombard plain, the Alps, and the Apennines, climb the 166 steps, or take an elevator, to the roof of the cathedral (see *Special Places*). From here, more stairs take you to the topmost gallery at the base of the cathedral's central spire, 354 feet from the ground. The stairway to the roof is entered from the south transept near the Medici tomb; the elevator is entered from outside the church, on the north side (toward the *Rinascente* department store); an elevator on the south side is sometimes also in operation. Both are open daily and charge admission. There is also a 350-foot viewing tower in Sempione Park (see *Special Places*).

SPECIAL PLACES: The huge Piazza del Duomo (Cathedral Square), with its perennial pigeons and ever-present pensioners, is one of the city's few pedestrian oases and the heart of this bustling metropolis. Leading north from Piazza del Duomo to Piazza della Scala is the elegant glass-domed arcade, the Galleria Vittorio Emanuele. Built in the last century under the direction of architect Giuseppe Mengoni, who later committed suicide, it has for decades been considered the *salotto,* or salon, of Milan for its exclusive shops, bookstores, cafés, and restaurants.

Some of the city's tourist attractions are too far from the center to reach comfortably on foot, but ATM, the local bus and tram system, connects these sites efficiently, as does the relatively new and clean subway system.

DOWNTOWN

Il Duomo (Cathedral) – The most magnificent Milanese monument is the recently restored white marble cathedral, with 135 spires and more than 2,200 sculptures decorating its exterior. From the roof, reached by an elevator or a 166-step climb, you can study the details of its pinnacles and flying buttresses. The interior of the cathedral, divided into five main aisles by an imposing stand of 58 columns, contains another 2,000 sculptures. The cathedral is considered the finest example of Gothic architecture in northern Italy, although its own architectural peculiarities — it was begun in 1386 but not completed until 1813 — prevent it from being pure Gothic. Only St. Peter's in Rome is larger. Piazza del Duomo.

Teatro alla Scala (La Scala) – The most famous opera house in the world was built between 1776 and 1778 on the site of the church of Santa Maria della Scala. It was here that works by Donizetti, Rossini, Bellini, and Verdi were first acclaimed and where Arturo Toscanini conducted and was artistic director for many years. The neo-classic building, damaged extensively during World War II, was reopened in 1946. Its acoustics are perfect. Traditionally, *La Scala*'s season begins on December 7, the feast day of Milan's patron saint, St. Ambrose, and lasts until the end of May. The box office (phone: 807041/42/43/44) is open daily, 10 AM to 1 PM and 3:30 to 5:30 PM (until 9:30 PM on the day of a performance); closed Mondays. Agencies do not exist, so opera tickets are difficult to obtain, but the theater can be visited by appointment (phone: 887-9377). The adjacent *Museo della Scala* (Scala Museum) houses a rich collection of manuscripts, costumes, and other memorabilia from the theater's history. Open daily. Admission charge. The theater and museum are north of Piazza del Duomo, through the Galleria Vittorio Emanuele, on Piazza della Scala (phone: 805-3418).

Museo Poldi Pezzoli (Poldi-Pezzoli Museum) – The Milanese nobleman Gian Giacomo Poldi-Pezzoli bequeathed his home and exquisite private art collection to the city in 1879. It includes some prime examples of Renaissance to 17th-century paintings and sculpture, Oriental porcelains, Persian carpets, and tapestries. There are also a Botticelli portrait of the Madonna, paintings by Giovanni Battista Tiepolo, Pollaiolo and Fra Bartolomeo, as well as Giovanni Bellini's *Pietà*. Open from 9:30 AM to 12:30 PM and 2:30 to 5:30 PM except Mondays. Admission charge. A short walk from La Scala. 12 Via Manzoni (phone: 794889).

Palazzo e Pinacoteca di Brera (Brera Palace and Art Gallery) – One of the most important state-owned galleries in Italy, and Milan's finest, is housed in the 17th-century Brera Palace. Its 38 rooms contain a broad representation of Italian painting, with particularly good examples from the Venetian and Lombard schools, including such masterpieces as Andrea Mantegna's *Dead Christ*, Raphael's *Wedding Feast of the Virgin*, and Caravaggio's *Dinner at Emmaus*. The palace also has an important library (founded in 1770) of incunabula and manuscripts, plus a collection of all books printed in the Milanese province since 1788. In the courtyard is a monumental statue of Napoleon I, depicted as a conquering Caesar. The art gallery is closed Mondays. Admission charge except Sundays. The library is closed Sundays. A few blocks north of *La Scala*. 28 Via Brera (phone: 808387).

Castello Sforzesco e Museo d'Arte Antica (Sforza Castle and Museum of Antique Art) – In the mid-15th century, Duke Francesco Sforza built this large, square brick castle on the site of a castle of the Visconti that had been destroyed. It became a fortress after the fall of the Sforzas and was damaged repeatedly in sieges before restoration began in the 19th century. Further damaged during World War II, it has been repaired, and today houses the *Museo d'Arte Antica* (Museum of Antique Art) whose treasures include the unfinished *Rondanini Pietà*, the last work of Michelangelo. The museum is entered from the courtyard of the residential part of the castle, the Corte Ducale. Closed Mondays and at lunchtime. West of the Brera. Piazza Castello (phone: 6236, ext. 3940).

The castle also houses an art library and a collection of rare manuscripts. Well-publicized temporary exhibitions are often set up in other rooms. Beyond the castle is the beautiful 116-acre Parco Sempione (Sempione Park), with an aquarium, sports arena, and neo-classic Arco della Pace (Arch of Peace), a triumphal arch with statues and bas-relief. The arch, on the model of Septimius Severus at Rome, marks the beginning of the historic Corso Sempione (Simplon Road) through the Alps to France, which was built by order of Napoleon.

Basilica e Museo di Sant'Ambrogio (St. Ambrose's Basilica and Museum) – The basilica was founded in the 4th century by Bishop Ambrose (later St. Ambrose), who baptized St. Augustine here. The bas-relief on the doorway dates from the time of St. Ambrose, and the two bronze doors are from the 9th century. The basilica was enlarged in the 11th century, and its superb atrium was added in the 12th century. Two other early Christian saints — Gervase and Protasius — are buried with St. Ambrose in the crypt. The ceiling of the apse is decorated with 10th-century mosaics. Above the portico is the *Museo di Sant'Ambrogio* (Museum of St. Ambrose), where you can see a 12th-century cross, a missal of Gian Galeazzo Visconti, and other religious treasures. The museum is closed Tuesdays. Admission charge. South of the Sforza Castle. 15 Piazza Sant'Ambrogio (phone: 872059).

Santa Maria delle Grazie (The Church of St. Mary of Grace) – The interior of this recently restored brick and terra cotta church, representing a period of transition from the Gothic to the Renaissance, is decorated with some fine 15th-century frescoes. But the church, though beautiful in itself, is usually visited because Leonardo da Vinci's *The Last Supper* is on a wall of the refectory of the former Dominican convent next to it. *The Last Supper* was painted in tempera, which is not particularly durable, and though it has been restored several times, it has suffered considerable deterioration. Another attempt to restore the painting to its original grandeur should be completed (if funds are found) within the next few years; meanwhile, the refectory remains open to visitors. Admission charge. A few blocks northwest of Sant'Ambrogio. Piazza Santa Maria delle Grazie.

ENVIRONS

Certosa di Pavia (Carthusian Monastery) – Gian Galeazzo Visconti founded this monastery in 1396 as a family mausoleum. With its façade of multicolored marble sculpture and its interior heavily decorated with frescoes, baroque grillwork, and other ornamentation, the monastery is one of the most remarkable buildings in Italy. It is conveniently reached from Milan by coach excursion or by road. Closed Mondays. No admission charge, but donations are welcome. Sixteen miles (25.5 km) from Milan, just off the Milan-Pavia Road (phone: 925613 for information on guided tours).

Pavia – On the banks of the Ticino, this city was the capital of the Lombard kingdom and later a free commune, until it fell to the Visconti in 1359. The famous University of Pavia was officially founded in the same century, although its origins go back to the 9th century. The 15th-century Duomo (with a 19th-century façade, however) is flanked by an 11th-century tower and backed by the 16th-century Broletto (Town Hall). An admirable church (Leonardo da Vinci and Bramante helped with the plans), it is nevertheless a relative newcomer — not far away is the Romanesque Basilica di San Michele, a 12th-century rebuilding of the 7th-century church where Charlemagne and Frederick Barbarossa were crowned Lombard kings. Still another Romanesque church, San Pietro in Ciel d'Oro, holds the tomb of St. Augustine. Pavia's main street, the Strada Nuova, is lined with elegant shops and ends at the river, which is crossed by a postwar reconstruction of a 14th-century covered bridge. Five miles (8 km) south of the Certosa di Pavia.

Monza – The world-famous Monza *Autodromo* is the scene of the Italian *Grand Prix Formula One* race early in September each year. Visitors can drive around the course, with its well-known seven corners (admission charge). The Autodromo is in a splendid park that was once part of the Villa Reale (Royal Villa) and now has golf courses, a racecourse, and a swimming pool, as well as the auto track. The cathedral at Monza is also worth a visit. Built in the 13th and 14th centuries, it has a façade of white, green, and black marble, notable for its harmonious proportions and decorations. Monza is easily reached by bus or train; by road, it is 7 miles (11 km) northeast of Milan on SS 36.

■**EXTRA SPECIAL:** Until the early part of this century, Milan was crisscrossed by canals (*navigli*). Today only two remain, and their environs (it's a fair walk; from the Piazza del Duomo take Via Torino and Corso di Porta Ticinese) are perhaps the most picturesque in Milan. A stroll through this quarter provides a marked contrast to the rest of this modern, bustling city. On the last Sunday of every month, there is a huge and fascinating antiques market along the *navigli.*

SOURCES AND RESOURCES

 TOURIST INFORMATION: General tourist information is available at the Palazzo del Turismo of the Provincial Tourist Board (Ente Provinciale per il Turismo, or EPT), conveniently located at one side of the Piazza del Duomo, 1 Via Marconi (phone: 809662 or 870016), and at the central train terminal (phone: 669-0432 or 669-0532)). The EPT will make hotel reservations within Milan and provide information on other regions of Italy.

The US Consulate is at 32 Piazza della Repubblica (phone: 652841).

Local Coverage – The tourist board can provide copies of *Tutta Milano,* a useful guide in English, which includes activities, facts, phone numbers, and listings of restaurants and discos. The monthly *Night & Day Milano,* distributed by many hotels, has bulletins on special events, and *Viva Milano,* a weekly entertainment newspaper in Italian, provides up-to-date information on shops, fairs, restaurants, and discos. Other publications, such as the monthly *Milano Mese* and *Un Ospite di Milano* (*A Guest in Milano*), produced by the Hotel Concierges Association, are often available in hotels.

The Milan Trade Fair Center is at 1 Largo Domodossola (phone: 49971). During fair events, an office is set up at Linate Airport (phone: 738-2431).

Food – *La Guida d'Italia* has a comprehensive list of restaurants and wine shops in Milan and throughout Italy. It is published by L'Espresso and is sold on newsstands.

Telephone – The area code for Milan is 02.

 CLIMATE AND CLOTHES: Milan temperatures are generally moderate, although the city occasionally suffers extremes of heat or cold. Summer can be hot and airless, with temperatures as high as 85F (29C); winter can be cold, wet, and foggy, with temperatures below 10F (-12C) and occasional snow. Boots and an umbrella are a must if you visit during fall or winter. The Milanese are fashion conscious, so there are many places where running shoes and jeans are out of place. You may also want to bring something special for evenings. Opening night at *La Scala* is strictly formal; after that informal dress is acceptable.

 GETTING AROUND: Much of the center of Milan has been closed to traffic, so it is far more convenient for visitors to use public transportation. Inexpensive day tickets that allow unlimited travel on the public transportation system can be purchased at the ATM Ufficio Abbonamenti at the Piazza del Duomo subway station, at the Stazione Centrale, and at the EPT on Via Marconi.

Airports – Malpensa Airport is about 28 miles and less than an hour's drive from the center of Milan; a taxi ride into town can cost as much as $70. Buses to Malpensa leave from Stazione Centrale (the main railway station), on the east side of the Galleria delle Carrozze, 2½ hours before every flight and cost about $5.50 (phone: 669-0836 for schedules). They also stop at the east entrance of Porta Garibaldi Station en route.

Linate Airport handles domestic traffic, as well as some international — but not intercontinental — flights. Linate is 5 miles and 15 minutes (longer if traffic is heavy) from downtown Milan; taxi fare into the center of the city is about $14.50. Bus #73 leaves for the airport from Corso Europa, Piazza San Babila, and Porta Garibaldi Station every 20 minutes between 5:40 AM and 8:40 PM, stops at the Stazione Centrale, and costs about 50¢ (phone: 748-52200 or 748-52207).

Although there is no regular transportation between Malpensa and Linate airports, Alitalia occasionally provides group transfers when two connecting Alitalia flights are involved.

Bus and Tram – The local bus and tram service, ATM, efficiently connects various points of this sprawling city. Tickets are sold at tobacconists and newsstands throughout the city and must be purchased in advance. They can be used for the subway as well.

Car Rental – Most international firms are represented. *Avis, Europcar, Hertz,* and *Maggiore* all have counters at both Malpensa and Linate airports and at several locations in the city. Central reservations numbers are *Avis* (phone: 6981); *Europcar* (phone: 607-1053); *Hertz* (phone: 20483); *Maggiore* (phone: 524-3846). *Budget* is at Via Vittor Pisani 13 (phone: 670-3151) and at Malpensa (phone: 868221) and Linate (phone: 738-5639). *InterRent* is at Corso Como 4 (phone: 657-0477 or 659-9417) and at Malpensa (phone: 868124) and Linate (phone: 733585). *Avis, Hertz,* and *Maggiore* also have branches at the train station.

Subway – The efficient, clean *Metropolitana Milanese (MM)* has two lines, and a third is near completion. The most useful for tourists is line 1, which runs south from near the main railway station, through Piazza del Duomo, and west beyond Piazza Santa Maria delle Grazie. Tickets are sold at coin-operated machines in each station and at many tobacconists.

Taxi – Taxis can be hailed while cruising, picked up at a cabstand, or called by radio taxi (phone: 8388, 8585, 6767, or 5251). Meters begin at about $3 plus arrival and waiting time if the cab is called by phone. Do not be surprised if the driver asks for a surcharge after 10 PM or on Sundays or holidays. There is an additional small charge for baggage.

Train – Milan's main train station is Stazione Centrale, Piazzale Duca d'Aosta (phone: 67500). Several smaller stations serve local commuter lines. The largest of these is Porta Garibaldi, the departure point for trains to Turin, Pavia, Monza, Bergamo, and other points (phone: 655-2078). Visitors going on to Rome might try the new nonstop trains leaving Milan daily at 7:50 AM and 6:55 PM. During the 5-hour trip, hostesses provide newspapers, interpreter services, and a free meal in the dining car. The cost is about $75, and tickets must be booked in advance.

SPECIAL EVENTS: The annual *International Trade Fair* held in late April since the 1920s has put Milan squarely on the international business map. Although this is the city's biggest, there are various other trade fairs and exhibitions (including the showings of designer collections, the twice yearly fashion fair, and the September furniture fair) almost every month except July and August, making advance hotel reservations essential. Information and a year-round calander of events can be obtained from the main Trade Fair office, 1 Largo Domodossola (phone: 49971). In July and August, the city sponsors a variety of outdoor cultural events; sometimes restaurants join in by serving regional specialties in the parks. The opening of the opera season at *La Scala,* which takes place each year on December 7, is the city's major cultural event.

MUSEUMS: In addition to those listed in *Special Places,* there are several other museums in Milan worth a visit.

Basilica di San Lorenzo Maggiore – This 4th-century church is the oldest in the West. 39 Corso di Porta Ticinese.

Biblioteca e Pinacoteca Ambrosiana (Ambrosiana Library and Art Gallery) – 2 Piazza Pio XI (phone: 800146).

Galleria d'Arte Moderna (Modern Art Gallery) – Villa Comunale, 16 Via Palestro (phone: 702819).

Museo e Casa di Manzoni (Manzoni Museum and House) – The former home of Alessandro Manzoni, author of the 19th-century classic *I Promessi Sposi* (*The Betrothed*). 1 Via Morone (phone: 871019).

Museo del Risorgimento Nazionale (National Museum of the Risorgimento) – 23 Via Borgonuovo (phone: 869-3549).

Museo della Scienza e della Tecnica Leonardo da Vinci (Leonardo da Vinci Museum of Science and Technology) – 21 Via San Vittore (phone: 462709).

Musea di Storia Contemporanea (Museum of Contemporary History) – 6 Via Sant' Andrea (phone: 706245).

Museo di Milano (Museum of Milan) – 6 Via Sant' Andrea (phone: 706245).

Palazzo Reale (Royal Palace) – A beautiful 18th-century building that houses the *Museum of Contemporary Art* and prestigious temporary exhibitions. Piazza del Duomo (phone: 6236).

Milan also has scores of art galleries with interesting shows. They are generally open from 10:30 AM to 1 PM and 4 to 8 PM except Mondays. The following offer an excellent selection of contemporary and early-20th-century Italian art:

Ala Salvatore – 2 Piazza Umanitoria (phone: 540-0612).

Arte Centro – 11 Via Brera (phone: 865888).

Centro Annunciata – 44 Via Manzoni (phone: 796026).

Cinque Fiori – 5 Via Fiori (phone: 871017).

Galleria Philippe Daverio – 6/a Via Montenapoleone (phone: 798695).

Toselli – 9 Via del Carmine (phone: 805-0434).

SHOPPING: With the explosion of Italian design and fashion over the last 10 years, Milan has become an international style center full of enticing, if expensive, shops, including showrooms and boutiques of many of Italy's major contemporary clothing designers. It is also a center for antiques and home furnishings. The main shopping area comprises the streets near Piazza del Duomo and *La Scala,* particularly the elegant Via Montenapoleone, Via della Spiga, and Via Sant'Andrea. Here you'll find the boutiques of top Italian designers (*Giorgio Armani* at 9 Via Sant'Andrea, *Gianni Versace* at 4 and 25 Via della Spiga; *Enrico Coveri* at Via San Pietro all'Orto; *Missoni* at 1 Via Montenapoleone; *Ferragamo* at Via Montenapoleone, and *Krizia,* 23 Via della Spiga), most of whom are based in Milan. Boutiques offering modern fashions and antique clothes are also scattered throughout the old Brera quarter — Milan's Left Bank — and around St. Ambrose's Basilica. Early in December, a flea market near the basilica features a wide selection of clothes, antiques, old books, and knickknacks. Shop hours generally are from 9 AM to 12:30 PM and 3:30 to 7:30 PM. Most shops are closed on Monday mornings.

Accademia – Fine menswear and accessories. 11 Via Solferino.

Arflex – Armchairs and chaises that are produced by top designers and are among the best known in Italy. 28 Via Durini.

Arte Antica – One of the city's best-known antiques stores, with French porcelain, clocks, and furniture. 11 Via Sant'Andrea.

L'Artisan Parfumeur – A new shop specializing in perfumes and home scents. 3 Via Francesco Sforza.

Beltrami – Shoes, handbags, and accessories in the finest leathers. 19 Via Montenapoleone.

Guanti Berni – Beautiful leather gloves for men and women. Via Sant'Andrea.

Brigatti – Considered Milan's finest men's sportswear shop. Also has a ski boutique for the entire family. 15 Corso Venezia.

Mario Buccellati – Jeweler famed for his finely chased, engraved gold. 4 Via Montenapoleone.

Calderoni – Exquisite jewelry and silver. 8 Via Montenapoleone.

Carrano – Stylish women's shoes. 21 Via Sant'Andrea.

Centenari – Fine old prints and paintings. 92 Galleria Vittorio Emanuele II.

Cittone Oggi – One of Milan's most elegant and stylish furniture stores. 4 Via Bigli.

Cose – Chic and trendy women's clothing. 8 Via della Spiga.

Tanino Crisci – The best in finely crafted men's and women's footwear. 3 Via Montenapoleone.

Decomania – Art Deco objects and furniture. 5/9 Via Fiori Chiari.

Dispensa Gualtiero Marchesi – The maestro of Italian nouvelle cooking has just opened this shop selling culinary items from pâté to placemats. 6 Via San Giovanni sul Muro.

Erreuno – Elegant fashions from Armani's boutique collection for women. 15 Via della Spiga.

Fendi – High-fashion furs designed by Karl Lagerfeld. 16 Via Sant' Andrea.

Fontanna – Furniture and designs by the avant-garde Memphis Milano School. 3 Via Montenapoleone.

Frette – Luxurious linens for bed and bath. 29 Via Manzoni.

Galtrucco – Shimmering silks from Lake Como, by the meter or ready to wear. 27 Via Montenapoleone.

Franco and Aldo Lorenzi – Elegant travel and smoking accessories for men. 9 Via Montenapoleone.

Mastro Geppetto – Dolls, toys, models, plus a life-size Pinocchio. 14 Corso Matteotti.

Gio Moretti – Clothing labels for the whole family. 4, 6, and 9 Via della Spiga.

Orsi – A small but highly regarded antiques shop, with lovely 17th- and 18th-century furniture. 14 Via Bagutta.

Shara Pagano – Simply smashing costume jewelry, belts, and bags. 7 Via della Spiga.

Peck – This fancy food store should not be missed, especially by those eager for the best in dried porcini mushrooms, truffles, and other Italian specialties. 9 Via Spadari.

Provera – Top-quality wines sold in a 1920s' shop that specializes in wines from the North. Sold by the bottle or the glass; there are a few tables for tasting. 7 Corso Magenta.

Rubinacci – Top French designers and the store's own elegant line of women's fashions. 10 Via Sant'Andrea.

Mila Schön – Milan's own very high fashion designer's principal showroom. 2 Via Montenapoleone. Her boutique is nearby at #6.

Vittorio Siniscalchi – One of Milan's best custom shirtmakers for men. 8 Via Gesu.

Stationery – The city's best-stocked stationery store, with interesting gadgets and office accessories. 3 Via Solferino.

Alberto Subert – Fine Italian and imported antiques. 22 Via della Spiga.

T & J Vestor – Missoni's madras tablecloth and napkin sets. 38 Via Manzoni.

DISCOUNT SHOPS

If you're one of those — like us — who tries to make every lira go a long, long way, here are some select discount outlets where fine Italian goods and fashions are often found at far less than the prices in fancier shops.

Emporio – Discounted classic, spirited clothing from previous and current seasons; *not* part of *Armani's Emporio.* 11 Via Prini, near Corso Sempione.

Misul – Women's clothes in luxurious fabrics, often sold at far less than retail prices. Call for an appointment. 3 Via San Calocero.

Niki – Elegant women's clothes at half the usual price. 78 Viale Montenero.

Il Salvagente – Armani, Valentino, and other famous designer clothes for men, women, and children; in a warehouse-like store offering excellent discounts. 16 Via Fratelli Bronzetti.

SPORTS AND FITNESS: For general information, contact the *Ripartizione Sport-Turismo* (Municipal Sports and Tourism Department), 2 Via Marconi (phone: 865294). *Pronto Sport* (phone: 801466) provides up-to-date information on sporting events.

Bicycling – Rentals by the hour, day, or month at *Vittorio Comizzoli,* 60 Via Washington (phone: 498-4694).

Fitness Centers – *Skorpion Center,* 24 Corso Vittorio Emanuele (phone: 781424 or 796098); *Club Francesco Conti,* 7 Via de Toqueville (phone: 657-0294).

Golf – There are several golf courses in the Milan area, the largest and most accessible of which is the 27-hole course at the *Golf Club Milano* in the park at nearby Monza (phone: 303081).

Horseback Riding – There are two riding stables in Milan: the *Centro Ippico Lombardo,* 21 Via Fetonte (phone: 408-4270) and the *Centro Ippico Milanese,* 20 Via Macconago (phone: 539-2013). For more information, get in touch with the Milan branch of ANTE, the national equestrian society, 44B Via Piranesi (phone: 738-4615).

Horse Racing – Thoroughbred and trotting races are run at the internationally famous *Ippodromo San Siro* (phone: 452-1854), on the eastern outskirts of Milan.

Ice Skating – There is a rink in operation from September through May at the Palazzo del Ghiaccio, 14 Via Piranesi (phone: 7398). Skates can be rented at *Saini,* 136 Via Corelli (phone: 738-0841).

Jogging – Try Parco Sempione or the Giardini Pubblici (Public Gardens).

Soccer – From September to May, both *Inter* and *Milan* play at *Stadio Comunale Giuseppe Meazza,* 5 Via Piccolomini (phone: 454123 or 408-4123).

Squash – Courts are available at the *Giambellino Squash Club,* 5 Via Giambellino (phone: 422-5979).

Swimming – Public indoor pools include *Cozzi,* 35 Viale Tunisia; *Mincio,* 13 Via Mincio, and *Solari,* 11 Via Montevideo. Open-air pools include *Lido,* 15 Piazzale Lotto, near the *San Siro Stadium; Romano,* 35 Via Ponzio; and *Piscina Olimpica* in the park at Monza.

Tennis – Public courts should be booked well ahead of time. Some of the main courts are at *Bonacossa,* 74 Via Mecenate (phone: 506-1277); *Centro Polisportivo,* 48 Via Valvassori Peroni (phone: 236-6254); *Lido di Milano,* 15 Piazzale Lotto (phone: 391667), and *Ripamonti,* 4 Via Iseo (phone: 645-9253).

THEATER: You can take in classical Italian theater productions, including ones by world-famous director Giorgio Strehler, at the *Piccolo Teatro,* 2 Via Rovello (phone: 877663); the *Manzoni,* 40 Via Manzoni (phone: 790543); the *Salone Pier Lombardo,* 14 Via Pierlombardo (phone: 584410); or the *Teatro Lirico,* 14 Via Larga (phone: 866418). For avant-garde and experimental theater, try the *Carcano,* 63 Corso di Porto Romana (phone: 551-81377); the *Centro Ricerca Teatro,* 7 Via Ulisse Dini (phone: 846-6592 or 846-5693); or the *Frigoriferia Suburbana,* 8 Via Donatello .

MUSIC: The renowned *La Scala* (see *Special Places*) is an obvious must for any opera fan, but there are also ballets and concerts held here; Piazza della Scala (phone: 807041). Concerts also are held at the *Auditorium Angelicum,* 2 Piazza Sant'Angelo (phone: 632748), and the *Conservatorio di Musica,* 12 Via Conservatorio (phone: 701755). Tickets to the *Angelicum* are sold at Via Gustavo Favo 4 or at *Ricordi Music Shop,* 2 Via Berchet.

NIGHTCLUBS AND NIGHTLIFE: Milan has a variety of nightclubs offering both dinner and dancing. The most popular of these include *Charley Max,* 2 Via Marconi (phone: 871416); *Caffè Roma,* 4 Via Ancona (phone: 876960); and *Nepentha,* 1 Piazza Diaz (phone: 804837). Top discos include *American Disaster,* 48 Via Boscovich (phone: 225728); *Good Mood,* 29 Via Turati (phone: 669349); *Plastic* (a favorite with the young, avant-garde crowd), 120 Via Umbria (no phone); and *Odissea,* 3 Via Besenzanica (phone: 407-5653). Live music, including jazz, can be heard regularly at numerous clubs, among them *Capolinea,* 119 Via Ludovico il Moro (phone: 428602); *Ca'Bianca,* a music and cabaret spot near the Naviglio Grande canal, 117 Via Ludovico il Moro; and *Le Scimmie,* 49 Via Ascanio Sforza (phone: 839-1874). The latter also has rock or blues as does *Live Music,* 4 Via Ciaia (phone: 668-8738). Milanese folk tunes and ballads are performed at *Osteria Amici Miei,* 14 Via Nicola d'Apulia (phone: 285-0001).

Milan has many cozy piano bars that are ideal for a late drink and snack. Try *Golden Memory,* 22 Via Lazzaro Papi (phone: 548-4209); *Gershwin's,* Via Corrado il Salico 10 (phone: 849-7722); or the elegant *Momus,* Via Fiori Chiari 8 (phone: 896227). There are striptease shows at *Teatrino,* 3 Corsia dei Servi (phone: 793716), *Maschere,* 7 Via Borgogna (phone: 705584), *Venua,* 1 Via Giardino (phone: 805-0330); and *Smeraldo,* Piazza 25 Aprile (phone: 662768).

BEST IN TOWN

CHECKING IN: As an international business center, Milan offers a wide range of accommodations for the visitor, from traditional, old-fashioned hotels to efficient, modern, commercial ones. Very expensive hotels here will cost $300 or more a night for a double room; expensive hotels will cost from $250 to $300 a night; moderate hotels charge $100 to $250 for a double; and inexpensive hotels will charge between $70 and $100. Unless otherwise noted, all Milan hotels accept major credit cards. All telephone numbers are in the 02 area code unless otherwise indicated.

Pierre Milano – Recently opened in the city center, this luxurious 47-room hotel is slightly off the beaten track, but it is, nevertheless, a favorite of the VIP business crowd. There is an American bar on the premises, but no restaurant. 32 Via de Amicis (phone: 805-6221). Very expensive.

Excelsior Gallia – Built by the Gallia family in the early 1930s and recently restructured and redecorated in the grand style, this luxury hotel with 241 rooms and 12 suites is spacious, efficient, and friendly. Its restaurant ranks among the city's very finest (see *Eating Out*). Near the central train station. 9 Piazza Duca D'Aosta (phone: 6277). Expensive.

Grand Hotel Duomo – Much favored by the movers and shakers of Italian commerce. Bilevel rooms provide a businesslike sitting room, while touches of marble and Oriental carpets add swank to the contemporary decor. In the heart of town, just off Piazza del Duomo, but on a pedestrian street that ensures quiet. 1 Via San Raffaele (phone: 8833). Expensive.

Milano Hilton International – An attractive hotel in the new commercial center facing the main railway station, about a mile north of the center and the cathedral, it is tastefully decorated in a mixture of Italian provincial and modern styles. There is also a colorful, moderately priced Italian restaurant and a discotheque. The service is first rate. 12 Via Galvani (phone: 6983). Expensive.

Palace – Recently transformed by a $2.5-million renovation, each floor has a different color scheme and the rooms have been decorated in ultramodern style. The smaller new wing is more conventional than the renovated old wing. Dining on the roof garden or in the famous and attractive *Casanova Grill*, with its refined decor. 20 Piazza della Repubblica (phone: 6336). Expensive.

Principe di Savoia – A classic deluxe hotel, with marble baths, antiques, thick rugs, air conditioning, and attractive dining and drinking facilities. There are kitchenette apartments with balconies in the new wing. The location is excellent: just north of the cathedral on a fashionable street away from the busy main road, yet within walking distance of Milan's boutique-lined Via Montenapoleone. 17 Piazza della Repubblica (phone: 6230). Expensive.

Executive – Next to the old airport bus terminal, about a mile from downtown Milan, this American-style hotel has a pleasant staff, deluxe rooms, a good restaurant and bar, saunas, and a swimming pool. 45 Via Don Luigi Sturzo (phone: 6294). Expensive to moderate.

Jolly President – This centrally located deluxe hotel has 235 comfortable rooms and a restaurant. 10 Largo Augusto (phone: 7746). Expensive to moderate.

Europeo – Not far from the center of town, this fine hotel has its own peaceful garden, all the modern conveniences, and very good service. 38 Via Canonica (phone: 331-4926). Moderate.

Lord Internazionale – A tiny, reasonably priced hotel on a busy little shopping street near the cathedral. Rooms are quite small, but okay for short stays. There is no restaurant, but the management is pleasant and accommodating. 11 Via Spadari (phone: 865616). Moderate.

Manin – This small, first class hostelry is about a half mile from *La Scala*. Some of the rooms have been renovated in a modern style; the older rooms are not impressive but are spacious and comfortable. There's also a very good restaurant and bar. 7 Via Manin (phone: 659-6511). Moderate.

Nasco – A new, American-style hotel, it's an excellent choice when downtown hotels are full. 40 Via Spallanzani (phone: 204-3841). Moderate.

Manzoni – Small, pleasant and quiet, it's right in the city's center. No restaurant, but room service provides snacks. There's a shopping mall nearby. 20 Via Santo Spirito (phone: 705700 or 705697). Moderate to inexpensive.

Antica Locanda Solferino – Delightful tiny hotel, with only 11 rooms, in the old Brera quarter a few blocks north of *La Scala*. This was once a tavern and retains much of the Old World *fin-de-siècle* charm in its furniture and decor. No credit cards. Book far in advance. 2 Via Castelfidardo (phone: 657-1203). Inexpensive.

Centro – A small budget hotel in the heart of downtown Milan. 46 Via Broletto (phone: 875232). Inexpensive.

 EATING OUT: It is a time of special grace for dining out in Milan. Its restaurants today are among the world's finest. Milanese food, like much of northern fare, differs from other Italian food in that butter is used more often than olive oil. Look for special dishes made with the fabulous Italian white truffles, *tartufi bianchi,* from the neighboring Piedmont region, when they are in season between September and Christmas. Rice from the region's own plantations is used as a food base, with saffron-perfumed *risotto alla milanese* the favorite provender — best eaten with a steaming *ossobuco* (veal shank). The Milanese also love fresh fish and know how to prepare it. In September, try delicious white peaches. Expect to pay $100 or more for dinner for two at one of Milan's expensive restaurants — among the most expensive in Italy; $55 to $80 at a moderately priced restaurant; and $30 to $50 at an inexpensive one. Prices don't include drinks, wine, or tips. It is a good idea to have reservations at any Milanese restaurant and to check whether it accepts credit cards. All telephone numbers are in the 02 area code unless otherwise indicated.

Gaultiero Marchesi – Owned by Italy's most eminent chef, this restaurant provides an elegant setting for an Italian nouvelle cuisine that the forces of Michelin consider the best in Italy. Fortunately, success has not dimmed its luster, and today it is better than ever. Closed Sundays, Mondays for lunch, and August. Reservations necessary. 9 Via Bonvesin della Riva (phone: 741246). Very expensive.

El Toulà – One of Milan's finest restaurants, created by the noted restaurateur Alfredo Beltrame and situated behind *La Scala.* Try the pasta specialty, *manicaretti.* Closed Sundays; from June to August, closed Saturdays as well. 6 Piazza Paolo Ferrari (phone: 870302). Very expensive.

Calajunco – The Aeolian islands inspired this fine Sicilian restaurant's menu, which includes zucchini blossom–stuffed ravioli with squid sauce and, for an antipasto, seashell "plates" brimming with linguini in a mixed shellfish sauce. The unique fish sausage is also worth trying. Closed Sundays and some holidays. 5 Via Stoppani (phone: 204-6003). Expensive.

Gallia's – Some of Milan's hotels provide fine dining, and here is one of the best. At the *Excelsior Gallia,* diners can savor traditional dishes, such as the delicious *tournedos Rossini,* in an elegant setting. Piazza Duca d'Aosta (phone: 6277). Expensive.

Giannino – So famous that some people reserve 6 months in advance, this is a beloved bastion of traditional Italian fare, including homemade pasta and pastries. The fish is also excellent. Elegant private dining rooms can be provided by arrangement. Closed Sundays and August. 8 Via Amatore Sciesa (phone: 545-2948). Expensive.

Saint Andrews – This elegant downtown dining place with dark paneled walls and plush upholstery is a favorite of Milanese executives. Closed Sundays and August. 23 Via Sant'Andrea (phone: 793132). Expensive.

Savini – Everything here, from the service to the decor, including the crystal chandeliers and red silk lampshades, is classic and exquisite. While the food does not always merit the steep bill, the traditional Northern Italian dishes are better choices than the more continental cuisine. Private rooms are available. Closed Sundays and August. Reservations advised. 11 Galleria Vittorio Emanuele (phone: 805-8343). Expensive.

La Scaletta – The Italian *nuova cucina* at this outstanding, elegantly appointed 2-room restaurant is so popular among Milanese diners that reservations are necessary. Try the *risotto alle fragole* (strawberry risotto). Closed Sundays, Mondays, Christmas, New Year's, and August. No credit cards. 3 Piazza Stazione Porta Genova (phone: 835-0290). Expensive.

Stendhal – Named for the French author (who lived in the area), the menu offers Brera's finest dining. It's everything a fancy restaurant should be: intimate, candlelit, beautiful. And the food is memorable — from fresh *porcini* mushrooms to delectable desserts. Closed Saturday lunch and Sundays. Via San Marco near Via Ancona (phone: 653917 or 655-5587).

Aimo and Nadia – A husband and wife team from Tuscany run this small restaurant in an unprepossessing area of Milan, but the food is anything but anonymous. *Ovoli* (mushrooms) and Alba truffles abound, but the real culinary triumphs are the zucchini blossoms stuffed with seafood and cheese; the desserts are also luscious. Closed Sundays and August. American Express only. 6 Via Montecuccoli (phone: 416886). Expensive to moderate.

Biffi Scala – A favorite place for late-night suppers, particularly after the opera, although the name is more glamorous than the food. Reservations necessary. Piazza della Scala (phone: 876332). Expensive to moderate.

Boeucc – Artists dine next to financiers in this traditional downtown restaurant. In the local dialect, the name means "hole-in-the-wall," but the clientele, service, traditional menu (here's the place for the real Milanese, saffron-perfumed risotto), and vast wine list give a lie to the name. Closed Saturdays. 2 Piazza Belgioioso (phone: 790224). Expensive to moderate.

Don Lisander – On summer evenings, downtown diners can enjoy the courtyard garden at this reliable old favorite. It offers a sampler menu of impeccably prepared traditional Italian dishes year-round. Closed Saturday evenings and Sundays. 12A Via Manzoni (phone: 790130). Expensive to moderate.

Gran San Bernardo da Alfredo – Alfredo Valli serves some of the best regional cooking in town in this large and friendly restaurant. Try the *risotto alla Milanese,* the veal cutlet, or the classic Lombardy stew of pork, sausages, carrots, and white wine, *casseoeula,* served with cornbread, or *polenta.* Closed weekends and August. 14 Via Borgese (phone: 331-9000). Expensive to moderate.

Il Porto – The specialties at this family-run restaurant are fresh fish and friendly service. Closed Sundays and August. Reservations necessary. Piazzale Cantore (phone: 832-1481). Expensive to moderate.

Alfio – It has a central location, an enclosed winter garden, and very good antipasti, risotto, and fish and meat dishes. Closed Saturdays and August. 31 Via Senato (phone: 780731). Moderate.

Bice – Years ago, Tuscan-bred Bice Mungai opened a tiny shop in which she served staples from home, such as *la ribollita* (vegetable soup made with purple cabbage). From such beginnings come today's wide menu of both meat and fish specialties, including *risotto al pesce* (risotto with fish). In season, wild mushrooms, stuffed pheasant, and truffle toppings are also served. Closed Mondays in August and 10 days at Christmas. 23 Via Borgospesso (phone: 702572). Moderate.

La Brisa – In the heart of the city, though hidden away, with a garden and a first class kitchen. Popular with financiers and artists. Closed for lunch on weekends. 15 Via Brisa (phone: 872001). Moderate.

Canovianio – Right in the Duomo's shadow, highly accessible creative cuisine is served in a stunning interior. Closed Sundays. 6 Via Hoepli (phone: 805-8472). Moderate.

Cavallini – With a garden for summer dining, this cosmopolitan *trattoria* reflects decades of sober culinary industry. Fresh fish is served daily, and the *tortellini in brodo* (small stuffed pasta in broth) is outstanding. Closed Sundays, during mid-August, and some holidays. 2 Via Mauro Macchi (phone: 669-3174). Moderate.

Le Colline Pisane – This lively Tuscan *trattoria* serves fine food in pleasant surroundings. Closed Sundays and August. Reservations advised. 5 Largo La Fobba (phone: 659-9136). Moderate.

Decio Carugati – The food critic and author Decio himself is the host here. His creative, adventurous culinary compositions and fine wines are widely admired. Closed Sundays. 2 Via Corsica at the corner of Via Vigevano (phone: 832-3970). Moderate.

Al Garibaldi – An unpretentious eatery catering to Milan's young professional crowd. The kitchen dispenses topnotch inventive food with great professionalism. Closed Fridays, Christmas, and August. 7 Viale Montegrappa (phone: 659-8006). Moderate.

Gli Orti di Leonardo – The Milanese have quickly beat a path to the door of this newcomer, where fish hors d'oeuvres are served and followed by "little risotti," made with surprising ingredients. A rich choice of wines is available. 6/8 Via Aristide de Togni (phone: 498-3476). Moderate.

Malatesta Il Punto – Quail eggs with truffles, eel pâté with pine nuts, and Chinese fondu for two are among the specialties of this popular restaurant, one of several in Milan offering a fixed price sampler menu (*menù degustazione*). Closed Sundays and part of August. 29 Via Bianca di Savoia (phone: 546-1079). Moderate.

Il Mazzetto Guarnito – With just 7 tables, this place offers the maximum of personal attention as well as a chance to sample the wizardry of its young chef. Closed Saturdays and Sunday at lunch. 55 Corso Garibaldi (phone: 879925). Moderate.

Osteria del Vecchio Canneto – It's definitely the place to try for wonderful fish. Sample the baked clams au gratin, the mixed fish grill, and the fine Abruzzi wine. Closed Sundays and August. 56 Via Solferino (phone: 659-8498). Moderate.

Osteria di Porta Cicca – In one of the oldest parts of the city, with only 11 tables, be prepared for truly innovative dining. Favorites are *tagliolini* with zucchini blossoms and chunks of salmon, and poppy-seed-coated salmon steaks served with a whipped horseradish cream. Closed Sundays and Mondays, except the last Sunday of the month, and September to May. 51 Ripa di Porta Ticinese (phone: 832-4451). Moderate.

La Pantera – Near Milan University, this Tuscan-style restaurant is run with loving care by Tina Lucchesi and her family. The *involtini* (stuffed veal slices), *farro* (a staple grain eaten by the ancient Romans), chickpeas in olive oil, and *la ribollita* (hearty vegetable soup) are among the specialties. Reservations advised. Closed Tuesdays. 12 Via Festa del Perdono (phone: 805-7374). Moderate.

Peck – An offshoot of *Peck,* the elegant food emporium. In addition to a pleasant bar, there is a restaurant, which probably has the best wine list in town. Closed Sundays and August. 4 Via Victor Hugo (phone: 876774). Moderate.

Rigolo – A large, friendly place that's a favorite of local journalists and businesspeople, this restaurant serves Tuscan specialties (such as thick, grilled steaks) and a superb selection of homemade desserts. Closed Mondays and August. 11 Via Solferino (phone: 805-9768). Moderate.

Il Sole – A favorite with Milanese, thanks to its relaxed atmosphere. Try the ricotta-based *gnocchetti* (little dumplings) in herb butter and homemade *tagliatelle* in a yellow bell pepper cream sauce. Dinner only. Closed Mondays. 5 Via Curtatone (phone: 5518-8500). Moderate.

L'Ulmet – Milanese adore this restaurant for its successful combination of traditional and creative Italian fare. Built on ancient Roman foundations, its roof incorporates a 1,600-year-old plinth. Wild game is served in season. For dessert, try the crêpes with honey and pine nuts. Closed Sundays and Monday lunches. At the corner of Via Disciplini and Via Olmetto (phone: 805-9260). Moderate.

Il Verdi – *The* place for lunch these days. The menu offers a choice of 24 salads, ranging from the seafaring *Innamorata* with trout, octopus, and potatoes to a mango, corn, and bamboo-based Orientale. There is a full regular menu as well, and the restaurant is also open for dinner. Closed Saturday lunch and Sundays. No reservations. 5 Piazza Mirabello (phone: 651412). Moderate.

La Vittoria – Opened in 1905, this friendly *ristorante* has kept pace with the times. It offers an ever-changing menu, and the selection of olive oils makes salad dressings an adventure. Closed Saturday lunch and Sundays. 6 Via Anfiteatro (phone: 860726). Moderate.

Il Brigadino – The menu includes a variety of creative dishes, including fruit-based *rissotti.* A *prix fixe* lunch makes this a popular spot with fashion models and photographers. Closed Sundays. 14 Via Savona (phone: 835-4812). Moderate to inexpensive.

Giardino – Near the banks of the Naviglio River, this restaurant in the 19th-century courtyard spreads out under surrounding trees in summer and is enlivened by passing musicians. The food is simple but delicious and the atmosphere is reminiscent of a 19th-century Milanese tavern or *Osteria.* Closed Tuesdays. 36 Alzaia Naviglio Grande (phone: 839-9321). Moderate to inexpensive.

El Pouliereu – Summer diners delight in the century-old trees in the garden here, and in winter guests savor the mixed boiled meats. Fish, game, and other hearty, well-prepared dishes are also served. Closed Wednesdays and in mid-August. 337 Via Rapiamonti (phone: 569-0954). Moderate to inexpensive.

San Fermo – The main lure is a wide selection of fixed price lunches as well as its signature *insalatone*. Closed Sunday and Monday lunch. 1 Via San Fermo della Battaglia (phone: 655-1784). Moderate to inexpensive.

Al Materel – It's rustic Lombardy at its best, with old family recipes, homemade pasta, and, in season, wild game and wild mushrooms. Closed Tuesdays. Via Solera Montegazza (phone: 654204). Inexpensive.

Osteria del Binari – Elegant but economical, serving an impressive choice of traditional dishes from several Italian regions. The salami and cheeses win high marks. Closed Sundays and mid-August. 1 Via Tortona (phone: 839-9428). Inexpensive.

La Topia – Run by a multi-ethnic couple, the menu includes specialties from the Liguria region (near Genoa), Yugoslavia, and the French countryside. This spot is a summertime favorite. Dinner only. Closed Sundays. 46 Via Argelati (phone: 837-3469). Inexpensive.

Quattro Mori – Near the Sforza Castle, this elegant, family-run restaurant serves traditional Milanese food. It has a garden. Closed Sundays and August. Via San Giovanni sul Muro 2 (phone: 870617). Moderate to inexpensive.

Along with its fine restaurants, Milan now boasts some of Italy's best *paninerie* (sandwich shops), which offer a variety of hot and cold sandwiches of sometimes unusual combinations. Try *Bar Magenta* at 13 Via Carducci (phone: 805-3808) or *Paninomania* at Corso Porta Romana (phone: 576827). For Milan's best coffee, visit *Marches*, Via Meravighi; customers must stand at the bar, but they linger over hand-dipped chocolates and the Milanese Christmas specialty, the *panettone* (fruitcake).

MOSCOW

For many Westerners, Moscow is so closely associated with Soviet hegemony that it seems as much a political philosophy as a place. Visitors to Moscow, the city, however, are exposed to a feast of sights, a rich selection of cultural activities, and contact with warm, generous, and responsive people.

Moscow has always been on the periphery of Europe. Situated on the Moskva River deep in the northwestern region of what is the world's largest state in area (the Soviet Union encompasses 8.65 million square miles), it was impervious to outside cultural and economic influences for centuries. The original Moscow architecture, for example, developed in the 15th century when imported Byzantine traditions were forced into conformity with the native arts of northwestern Russia. The bulbous domes that are a characteristic feature of Russian churches are apparently a native Russian form.

A bit of history helps explain the city better. There is archaeological evidence that people occupied this area along the Moskva as early as the Neolithic period, but the first mention of the tiny village of Moscow is found in Russian chronicles of 1147. Yuri Dolgoruky, a Prince of Suzdal, had established a small wooden fortress on a hill overlooking the river, in the same vicinity as the present Kremlin. (The word *kremlin* is a transliteration of the old Russian word for fortress.) At first merely a stop on the river trade route between the Baltic Sea and the Black Sea, Moscow became the capital of the principality in the 13th century and was the center of power in the northern area when Mongol Tartars overran the Russian lands.

The present brick walls of the Kremlin were firmly in place by the late 15th century, but they could not prevent the town growing up outside the fortress from being destroyed by the Crimean Tartars in 1571 and again by the Poles in the 17th century. Following these troubled times, Moscow began to expand and establish itself as a powerful city under a long line of Romanov czars. The most famous Romanov was Peter I, called Peter the Great, who was much enamored of Holland and Western Europe. In 1714, Peter the Great moved the capital from Moscow to a new city he was building on the Gulf of Finland to reflect the taste and culture of the West.

Although the capital was moved to St. Petersburg (now Leningrad), Moscow remained an important center of the Orthodox Church and, as they had done since the reign of Ivan the Terrible, Russian czars continued to return to the Assumption (Uspensky) Cathedral in the Kremlin for their coronations. During the 18th and 19th centuries, Moscow established its university and its major theaters and continued to expand its boundaries. As the city spread out from the Kremlin complex, the ring of fortress monasteries and convents that had served as Moscow's protective perimeter became an integral part of the city itself. A contemporary city map reflects this gradual expansion in ever-widening rings from the Kremlin–Red Square center.

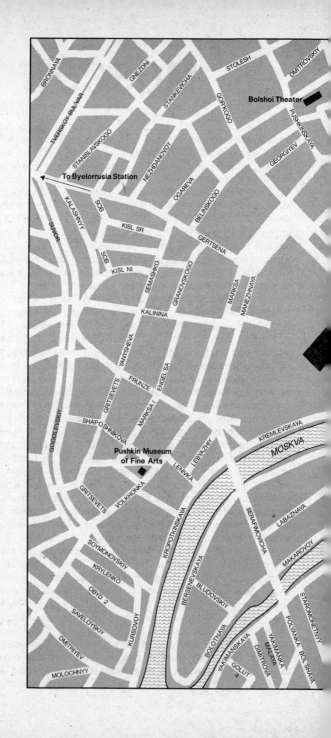

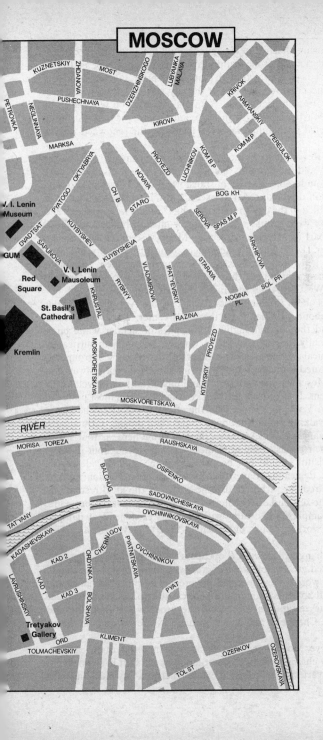

In his zeal to ensure that his new capital would have no rival, Peter the Great had decreed that no stone buildings be erected anywhere in Russia except in St. Petersburg. So, even though Napoleon's armies failed to conquer Moscow in 1812, nearly three-quarters of the city was destroyed in the fires in the wake of the French occupation. A special commission was set up by Alexander I to reconstruct Moscow in 1825, and several magnificent buildings were constructed in the imperial style, including the renowned *Bolshoi Theater.*

After the 1917 Revolution, the new Bolshevik government returned the capital to Moscow, and the Kremlin once again was the seat of power. Since then, Moscow has undergone a series of transformations. Between 1926 and 1939, the population doubled; today it exceeds 8 million. New offices, and later skyscrapers, filled in the city's modern skyline. Streets were widened and old areas of the city were razed to make way for modern hotels and offices. In 1935, the first part of Moscow's extensive Metro system was completed. During World War II, 75 Nazi divisions massed against the city but were unable to conquer it. Moscow handed the German armies their first major defeat as the Russian people bore the brunt of the most ferocious German attacks while the Western Allies organized their strategy with the US.

Moscow today is about three-quarters the size of Los Angeles. A circular bypass highway, about 16 miles from the city's center, marks its present boundaries. Beyond the circular highway are miles of slender white birch trees and, occasionally, one of the quaint wooden houses with intricately carved façades typical of this area. The generally flat country surrounding Moscow has facilitated the construction and maintenance of a railway network that makes Moscow a manufacturing and industrial hub as well as the center of government. It is, indeed, the heart of the USSR, its most powerful and important city. You can comprehend the ethnic diversity of the Soviet Union merely by walking along Moscow's streets. Ukrainians, Lithuanians, Caucasians, Georgians, central Asians — they all come here, as tourists, to shop or to bring their goods to sell at farmers' markets throughout the city.

The first-time visitor should not be put off by the stoic façade of the Muscovite's public demeanor. Eavesdrop on a wedding reception in your hotel or visit the circus or racetrack or dine at one of the local restaurants and you will find the zest and exuberance with which Russians celebrate life. The bureaucratic complexity of dealing with everyday existence may dampen enthusiasm during working hours, but when it's time to play, Russian spirits revive rapidly.

And things are changing. *Glasnost* ("openness") and *perestroika* ("restructuring") have created greater tolerance of creative activity that is reflected in the theater, the art world, television, and the press. The effort to change and renew the moribund Soviet economic and political system has yet to produce very many concrete results, but observing the process is stimulating and thought provoking. Change — and a new openness — are certainly in the air — and tangible.

To the Western eye, Moscow may always be more imposing than beautiful. Its appearance may change with new construction or the shift in seasons, but its character never varies: It is a city that exudes energy, a city pulsating with power, and any visitor leaves feeling that he or she has gained new insight into the Soviet psyche.

MOSCOW AT-A-GLANCE

 SEEING THE CITY: The lookout point in front of Moscow State University in Lenin Hills affords the best panorama of the city. Below you is the Moskva River and the Luzhniki sports complex, while in the distance you can see the gold and silver domes of Novodevichy Convent and the Kremlin complex (see *Special Places*) and seven look-alike skyscrapers. The university is near the Leninskie Gory Metro stop. There's a fine view of Red Square and the Kremlin from the *Rossia* restaurant on the top floor of the 21-story tower wing of the *Rossia* hotel. 6 Razina St. (phone: 298-1153).

 SPECIAL PLACES: Moscow grew up in concentric rings around the Kremlin, and much of what is of interest to the visitor is within the area bounded by the Boulevard Ring, Bulvarnoye Koltso. However, there is also much to explore in the area between the Boulevard Ring and the more outlying Garden Ring, Sadovoye Koltso, which roughly duplicates an old earthen wall that was demolished early in the last century. Gorky Street (Gorkovo St.), which runs from Revolution Square (Revolyutsii Sq.) northwest to Byelorusskaya Square (Belorusskovo Vokzala Sq.) and the railway terminus for trains from Western Europe, is considered Moscow's main street. Near the Kremlin, Arbat Street, which runs for less than a mile, is closed to vehicles. It has become a meeting place for amateur and professional musicians and artists who paint portraits, strum guitars, and attract crowds of young people and the curious, particularly on weekends. There are open-air food shops, street clowns, and pantomime performers in good weather. The Arbat's new atmosphere is an outgrowth of *glasnost,* and not to be missed.

INSIDE THE KREMLIN

Kremlin Complex – Kremlins, or fortresses, can be found in a number of old Russian towns. None, however, is as well known as the Moscow Kremlin, which occupies 69 acres overlooking the Moskva and is the seat of the Soviet government. The entire complex is surrounded by a red fortress wall studded with towers. Atop five of these towers are gigantic red stars that are lighted at night. Buried in the Kremlin walls are the ashes of various Russian heroes and two Americans — John Reed, whose book, *Ten Days That Shook the World,* is an eyewitness account of the Russian Revolution, and William ("Big Bill") Haywood, founder of the International Workers of the World (IWW), forerunner of the American Communist party. There are guided tours of the Kremlin complex, or you can walk through the grounds on your own. Open daily.

Cathedral Square – The central square in the Kremlin takes its name from the three principal cathedrals situated here. The largest one, Assumption (Uspensky) Cathedral, with its white limestone walls and five gilded domes, was built around 1475. This was the private cathedral of the czars, many of whom were crowned here, but when Napoleon occupied Moscow his men used it for a stable and burned some of its icons for firewood. Annunciation (Blagoveshchensky) Cathedral had three cupolas when it was built in early-Moscow style between 1484 and 1489. But when six new domes were added during reconstruction after a fire in the 16th century, it became known as the "golden-domed" cathedral. The five domes of Archangel Michael (Arkhangelsky) Cathedral, built between 1505 and 1509, are painted silver. All the czars from Ivan Kalita to Peter the Great, except for Boris Godunov, are buried here. Also on the square is the Palace of Facets (Granovitaya Palata), the oldest public building in Moscow, dating from 1473 to 1491; the Belltower of Ivan the Great, and several other early cathedrals. A kiosk sells tickets for the major cathedrals, which now function only as museums, not as religious institutions. Closed Thursdays.

Grand Kremlin Palace – Once the residence of the imperial family in Moscow, the palace today is a government building where the Supreme Soviets of the USSR and of the Russian Federation meet. Built from 1838 to 1849, the yellow-and-white-walled palace appears from the outside to have three floors. Actually, there are only two; the second floor has two tiers of windows. Not open to the general public except by special tour.

Armory (Oruzheinaya Palata) – The luxury of court life in czarist Russia is manifest in the halls of this museum next to the Grand Kremlin Palace. Wonderful treasures of gold and silver, Fabergé eggs, royal carriages, ball gowns, and other royal regalia are preserved here. If you are lucky, you may be able to join one of the very small tour groups admitted to the Diamond Fund (Almaznyi Fond USSR), open daily except Thursdays. This section of the armory holds Catherine II's diamond-encrusted crown, her scepter with its Orlov diamond, and her golden orb as well as other precious gems. Advance arrangement for this tour must be made through *Intourist* (see *Sources and Resources*).

OUTSIDE THE KREMLIN

Red Square (Krasnaya Ploshchad) – This enormous square — 2,280 feet long and 426 feet wide — is the heart of Moscow and the Soviet Union. It is bounded on the west by the Kremlin wall and the Lenin Mausoleum, on the south by St. Basil's Cathedral, on the east by the mammoth department store, *GUM,* and on the north by the *State History Museum.* The chief festivals — *May Day* on May 1 and *Revolution Memorial Day* on November 7 — take place amid much flag waving in this square.

V.I. Lenin Mausoleum (Mausolei V.I. Lenin) – The body of V. I. Lenin, the Russian revolutionary and founder of Bolshevism, is displayed in its glass sarcophagus in this huge red and black, stepped mausoleum in front of the Kremlin wall. An impressive changing of the guard ceremony takes place in front of the mausoleum every hour. New guards goose-step out of the Kremlin through the main gate at 2 minutes before the hour and replace the old guards in front of the tomb as the clock in the Kremlin's Spassky Tower chimes the hour. Incredible numbers of people pass through the mausoleum each week to view Lenin's body. Closed Mondays and Fridays. On Red Square.

St. Basil's Cathedral (Pokrovsky Sobor) – St. Basil's is to Moscow what the Eiffel Tower is to Paris and the Statue of Liberty is to New York — a symbol uniquely expressive of the city. The gay colors and fanciful patterns of the cupolas of the cathedral's nine chapels have fascinated visitors since St. Basil's was built at the bidding of Ivan the Terrible in the mid-16th century to celebrate the liberation of the Russian state from the Tartar yoke. Legend has it that terrible Ivan had the architects blinded when it was finished, so that they could never build a finer church. Take time to go inside and wander through the narrow passages to the tiny but extensively frescoed chapels. St. Basil's no longer has a religious function; it is a museum. Closed Tuesdays and the first Monday of the month. Admission charge. On Red Square.

GUM – One of the best-known — and largest (but poorly stocked) — department stores in the world, *GUM* (an acronym, pronounced *goom*) was built in the late 19th century as an arcade for nearly 1,000 small shops. It is said that some 350,000 shoppers wander through the three levels of this government-operated store each day. Closed Sundays; open 8 AM to 9 PM. On Red Square.

Central V. I. Lenin Museum (Tsentralny Musei V. I. Lenin) – Photographs of early revolutionary leaders and documents relating to Lenin's rise to power are housed in this red brick parliament (Duma) building on Revolution Square, just north of Red

Square. Among the thousands of exhibits in the museum's 22 halls are many of Lenin's manuscripts, letters, and personal belongings, including a 1920 Rolls-Royce. Closed Mondays. Admission charge. 4 Revolution Sq. (phone: 925-4808).

Central Market (Tsentralny Rynok) – Flowers and produce are available year-round at this open-air market. Farmers from the southern republics come to Moscow weekly to sell their goods in the free enterprise markets here and elsewhere around the city — great places to see Muscovites with their defenses down. A few blocks west of the Kolkhoznaya Metro stop. 15 Tsvetnoi Prospekt.

Metro – Moscow's subway system is one of the city's most interesting museums in addition to being a clean, efficient means of transportation. Each of its more than 100 stations has its own aesthetic scheme: stained glass windows, mosaics set with gold, crystal chandeliers, marble and stainless steel columns, bronze statues. The first line of the Metro was opened in 1935; the newer the station, the less ornate it is likely to be. Some of the station platforms, reached by fast escalators, are as much as 300 feet underground. For a single, very small fare (5 kopeks; about 3¢) you can ride the entire system, getting off at every station for a look. Since trains arrive every 2 to 4 minutes, you can cover much of the system in a short time. The most central station is at Revolution Square. Open daily, 6 AM to 1 AM.

New Maiden Convent (Novodevichy Monastyr) – Founded in 1524 to commemorate the liberation of Smolensk, this richly endowed convent was part of a ring of fortress-monasteries and convents that formed a protective circle around the Kremlin. Boris Godunov was proclaimed czar from this convent; Peter I's sister, Sophia, was imprisoned here when she encouraged rebellion against him; noble families sent their unmarried daughters and widowed, or unwanted, wives to live here. There is a functioning Russian Orthodox church here, but the convent's *Smolensk Cathedral* now serves as a museum of Russian applied arts from the 16th and 17th centuries. Chekhov, Gogol, Prokofiev, Stanislavski, Khrushchev, and other famous Russians are buried in a cemetery to the south of the convent. Closed Tuesdays and the first Monday of the month. Near the Sportivnaya Metro station. Also reached by trolleys #11 and #15 or buses #108 and #132. Between Novodevichy Proyed and Bolshaya Pirogovskaya.

Moscow State University – South of the convent, across the Moskva, the monumental Moscow State University towers above the city from its 415-acre site in Lenin Hills. Statistics offer the best summary of the world's largest university. The new buildings put up during the late Stalinist period between 1949 and 1953 contain 45,000 rooms connected by some 90 miles of corridors. The main building is 787 feet tall and its façade is 1,470 feet long. The university was founded in 1755 by Russian scientist Mikhail Lomonosov and officially bears his name. Near the Universitet and Leninskije Gory Metro stops. Also reached by bus and trolley. Universitetskij Prospekt.

Pushkin Museum of Fine Arts (Gosudarstvenni Musei Izobrazitelnikh Iskusstv im. A. S. Pushkina) – Originally built as an educational museum, the *Pushkin* still has a large study collection of plaster casts of world sculpture. However, its most important works are in its rich collection of ancient Oriental and Renaissance art and its collection of 19th- and early-20th-century French paintings, including the work of Paul Cézanne, Claude Monet, and Pierre Auguste Renoir. Closed Mondays, open 10:30 AM to 8 PM. Admission charge. A few blocks southwest of the Kremlin's Borovitsky Tower, near the Kropotkinskaya Metro stop. 12 Volkhonka St. (phone: 203-9578).

Moscow Circus – The Moscow circus is noted for its music, lights, breathtaking aerial feats, special animal acts, and spectacular finales, but it is perhaps best known for its clowns. The role of the clowns in the Russian circus is central to the entire evening. The master clown is seen between each act, filling time with silly skits and riotous routines while equipment is being rearranged. Performances start at 7:30 PM, and tickets can be arranged through *Intourist*. 17 Vernadskovo Prospekt, Lenin Hills.

USSR Exhibition of Economic Achievements (Vistavka Dostizheny Narodnogno Khozyaistva SSSR-VDNKh) – This is sort of the Smithsonian Institution of the

Soviet Union. All aspects of Soviet life — agriculture, industry, culture, and science — are detailed by the exhibits at this 553-acre park and pavilion site in northwest Moscow. The park, which has a zoo and a circus, is a popular place for Muscovites to spend a free day. In winter there is skiing, skating, and riding in a *troika,* the Russian horse-drawn sleigh. Outside the main entrance is an impressive monument to the Soviet space effort, a gleaming rocket trail in titanium called *Conquerors of Space.* The famous sculpture *The Worker and the Collective Farm Woman,* created by Vera Mukhina for the Paris Fair of 1937, stands at the North Gates entrance. The various buildings have different hours and closing days. The VDNKH Metro stop is just beside the main entrance. Mira Prospekt.

ENVIRONS

Kolomenskoye Estate-Museum – Established as a country estate for the ruling family in the 14th century, Kolomenskoye is on a hill beside the Moskva River about 10 miles (16 km) southeast of the Kremlin. The first stone church in the Russian "tent roof" style was erected here by Ivan Kalita in 1532, and several churches and buildings from the 16th and 17th century can also be seen here. The museum has interesting exhibitions of door locks and keys, ceramic tiles and stones, and carved-wood architectural details (closed Mondays and Tuesdays; admission charge). The buildings can be seen from the main road, but the entrance is from a dirt road off the Kashirskoye Chaussée (Highway).

Kuskovo Estate – One of the best collections of 18th-century Russian art can be found in the palace of this estate that once belonged to the Sheremetiev family, one of the oldest Russian noble families. The palace has pine-log walls faced with painted boards and was built by serf craftsmen. Since 1932, it has been known as the *State Museum of Ceramics,* with collections of Russian porcelain, glass, china, and majolica. A 70-acre formal French garden completes the ensemble. Closed Tuesdays. Admission charge. The estate is about 6 miles (10 km) from central Moscow, along the Ryazanskoye Highway.

Arkhangelskoye Estate – The museum in the palace on this estate contains a collection of European painting and sculpture, but a visit is recommended primarily because of the grounds and the pleasant setting beside the Moskva. The park is in the French style, with statues and monuments lining the avenues. The museum is closed Mondays and Tuesdays. Admission charge. Arkhangelskoye is 10 miles (16 km) from Moscow and can be reached by taking Leningradsky Prospekt to the Volokolamskoye Highway and then taking the left fork onto Petrovo-Dalniye Highway.

■**EXTRA SPECIAL:** There are two old cities northeast of Moscow that hold special attraction for the visitor. Arrangements to visit them are best made well in advance through *Intourist.*

Zagorsk: This little town on the Koshura and Glimitza rivers is the center of the handmade toy industry. Its *Toy Museum* (136 Krasnoi Armiyi Prospekt) has a wonderful collection of toys from the Bronze Age to the present. The reason most visitors come here, however, is to see the Trinity Monastery of St. Sergius (Troitskio-Sergievskaya Lavra), one of the most important surviving medieval monasteries in the Soviet Union. Founded by St. Sergius in 1340, the monastery has important historical significance as well as importance as a center of art and learning. During the Time of Troubles, it withstood a 16-month siege by Polish troops. Today it is the center for Russian Orthodoxy and a major pilgrimage site.

The monastery's Trinity Cathedral (Troitsky Sobor), built between 1422 and 1427, holds the tomb of St. Sergius and many beautiful icons. Assumption (Uspensky) Cathedral is best known for its stunning blue domes decorated with gold stars. Boris Godunov and members of his family are buried in tombs beside this cathedral. In the museum housed in other monastery buildings you can see rich collections of Russian ecclesiastical art, portraits, rare fabrics, and Russian handicrafts; closed Fridays. Zagorsk is about 45 miles (72 km) from central Moscow. Follow Mira Prospekt onto the Jaroslavskoje Highway, which will take you to Zagorsk.

Suzdal: A settlement since at least the 10th century, Suzdal has become a museum-city of ancient monasteries, churches, and convents and secular buildings spanning the centuries. Inside the walls of the Suzdal Kremlin beside the River Kamenka, you'll find the Nativity of the Virgin (Rozhdestvensky) Cathedral, built between 1222 and 1225. Its star-studded blue domes are similar to those at the Assumption Cathedral in Zagorsk. The *Suzdal Local Museum* is in the Archbishop's Palace near the cathedral and features collections of early Russian icons, clothing, and jewelry. Recently, representative 18th- and 19th-century buildings have been brought to Suzdal from various regions of the country and installed in the open-air *Museum of Wooden Architecture* beside the river.

Suzdal is 22 miles (35 km) due north of Vladimir, another ancient city worth a visit. You may want to make a 2-day excursion from Moscow and use Vladimir as a base for your trip to Suzdal. If you leave Moscow by Entusiastov Prospekt, it runs into Gorkovskoye Highway, which will take you to Vladimir, 114 miles (182 km) to the northeast. If you plan to go directly to Suzdal, drive north along the Klasma River out of Vladimir. There also are frequent trains from Moscow's Kursk railway station to Vladimir.

SOURCES AND RESOURCES

TOURIST INFORMATION: *Intourist* is the largest travel agency in the Soviet Union. It owns hotels and restaurants and deals with all types of foreign travel. In Moscow, the *Intourist* office is at 16 Marx Prospekt (phone: 203-6962). There are two other travel agencies in the Soviet Union: the *Tourist Council of the Trade Unions,* which organizes visits by trade union delegations, and *Sputnik,* 4 Lebyazhny Pereulok (phone: 223-9512), which organizes group tours for young people. *Intourist* provides English-speaking guides for general and specific sightseeing, but for your own enjoyment, take the time to learn the Russian (Cyrillic) alphabet and the sound of each of its characters. When you sound out the signs you see, you will recognize many English and French cognates.

The US Embassy is at 19/21/23 Chaikovskovo St. (phone: 252-2451/9).

Although good transportation and city maps are available at hotel kiosks in Moscow, comprehensive travel guides in English should be purchased before you leave the US. One of the most useful general guides is *The Complete Guide to the Soviet Union,* by Victor and Jennifer Louis (St. Martin's Press; $9.95). *The Blue Guide*'s look at Moscow and Leningrad (Benn; $17.95) is another good travel handbook. A good guide to Moscow and its museums is *Next Time You Go to Russia,* by Charles A. Ward (Scribners; $8.95).

The *Falkplan City Map of Moscow* (Hamburg: Falk-Verlag; $6.95) is a valuable backup for local maps and is available in bookstores throughout the US. It is an excellent, handy pocket map with a street name index, public transportation routes, and lists of hotels, museums, and theaters.

Local Coverage – An English edition of the weekly paper *Moscow News* is usually available at hotels. The *International Herald Tribune* and some Western European and North American dailies and weeklies can sometimes be purchased at kiosks and hard currency shops, although not on a regular basis. If you are desperate for news of the world, stop by the American Embassy for an update. Otherwise, bring along a short-wave radio or be content with blissful ignorance.

Telephone – Moscow cannot be dialed direct from the US. Calls must go through an international operator.

A word about telephones: Telephone directories seem to be one of Russia's rarest commodities, but you can get assistance at your hotel's desk or service bureau. The service bureau can book long-distance calls for you, but it is advisable to arrange the call at least an hour before you wish to make connections. To use the pay phones, deposit a 2-kopek coin in the slot before lifting the receiver. Dial when you hear a continuous buzzing sound.

CLIMATE AND CLOTHES: The harshness of the Moscow winter has sent shivers from the pages of a hundred Russian novels. Snow begins to fall as early as October, and by December the city is usually covered with snow and ice. So it's true that winter can be excruciating for the uninitiated — it defeated Napoleon, after all — but it is also true that the overcast winter half-days give way each spring to a glory of lilacs and tulips and that summer in this city is wonderfully mild. Temperatures can range from zero degrees F (-18C) in January to about 70F (21C) in July. Boots, a heavy coat, scarf, warm hat, and gloves are essential in winter. Layered clothing is the best approach, since the interiors of buildings are well heated. It rains an average of 8 to 12 days a month, so bring a travel umbrella.

One need not dress up in Moscow, but on the other hand, shorts are in poor taste and blue jeans are inappropriate for evenings out. You are expected to check your coat when entering any public building or restaurant. (It is simply not considered "cultured," *neh kulturno,* to take your coat with you.) All garments are hung on hooks, so it is a good idea to sew a chain or heavy loop into your coat collar in order to prevent damage — and dark looks from the cloakroom attendant.

It is preferable to pack clothes made of washable fabrics. Laundry service is available in hotels, but it is often slow, and dry cleaning is of questionable quality at best.

GETTING AROUND: Moscow has a very efficient and exceptionally inexpensive public transportation system. From late spring through early fall, you might also take one of the low-priced boats that cruise along the Moskva River, stopping in different parts of the city.

Airports – Sheremetjevo Airport, which services international flights, is about 40 minutes from downtown by taxi; the fare is about 10 rubles (about $6). Vnukovo Airport, mainly for domestic flights, is also 40 minutes from downtown by cab, with a fare of 10 Rbls (about $6).

Bus, Tram, and Trolley – These transport lines operate from 6 AM to 1:30 AM and cost only 5 kopeks — less than a dime. Bus tickets can be obtained from the driver in units of 10 (50 kopeks) or from a hotel newsstand. Riders punch their own tickets and retain them until the end of the ride. (There are periodic inspections to enforce the honor system of paying the fare.) Maps showing the routes for all lines are available at hotel kiosks.

Car Rental – Automobiles, with or without chauffeurs, may be rented through *Intourist* (phone: 215-6191) for use in the city. Rentals must be paid for in foreign currency or with a credit card.

Metro – The subway has several interconnected lines. One runs in a rough circle; the others radiate out to different parts of the city. Trains arrive and depart at the various stations frequently and operate from 6 AM to 1 AM.

Taxi – Taxi fare is uniform for the entire country: 20 kopeks (approximately 12¢) per kilometer. Normally, they can only be found at cabstands — marked with a "T" and a checkered pattern similar to the one on taxi doors — or at hotels. They can be ordered in advance, however, through your hotel service bureau or, if you speak

Russian, by calling 927-0040 or 225-0000. It is best to order a taxi at least an hour in advance. If you are on the street and taxis do not stop, try raising two fingers, which means that you will pay twice the fare on the meter — a standard practice in Moscow. Also, American cigarettes are highly prized by most Moscow taxi drivers.

Train – Moscow supports over a dozen train stations. Check at any *Intourist* hotel for information about locations, fares, and schedules.

SPECIAL EVENTS: Because pictures of the ceremonies in Red Square are transmitted around the world, the *International Labor Day* celebration, with its parades and demonstrations every May 1, and the anniversary of the *1917 Russian Revolution,* celebrated November 7, are probably the best-known events in Moscow. There are also two major festivals of the arts: *Russian Winter Festival,* December 25 to January 5, and *Moscow Stars Festival of Folk and Classical Dance,* May 5-13. *International Women's Day,* March 8, commemorates the Second International Conference of Socialist Women, which took place in Copenhagen in 1910. April 22 is *Lenin's birthday.*

MUSEUMS: Besides those mentioned in *Special Places,* Moscow has numerous museums devoted to Russian art and folk craft, the work of famous writers and composers who lived here, and various aspects of Russian history.

Central Exhibition Hall, *or* **"Manege" (Tsentralni Vistavochni Sal)** – Art exhibitions in the former stables of the czars. 50-letiya Oktyabrya Sq. (phone: 202-9304).

Chekhov Museum – Exhibitions concerning Russia's greatest playwright. 6 Sadovaya-Kudrinskaya St. (phone: 291-6154).

Darwin Museum – In a merchant's house that was built in the early 20th century, a zoological collection. 1 Malaya Pirogovskaya St. (phone: 246-6470).

Doestoyevsky Apartment-Museum – Memorabilia of the great author. 2 Doestoyskovo St. (phone: 281-1085).

Glinka State Central Museum of Musical Culture (Gosudarstvenni Tsentralni Musei Musikalnoi Kulturi im. M. I. Glinki) – Compositions by Russian composers, along with 1,500 instruments. 4 Georgievsky Pereulok (phone: 292-6669).

Gorky Museum – The writer's life in letters, manuscripts, and pictures. 25A Vorovskovo St. (phone: 290-0535).

Lenin Funeral Train Pavilion-Museum – Near the Paveletsky Station. 1 Lenina Sq. (phone: 235-2898).

Museum of Folk Art (Musei Narodnovo Iskusstva) – Folk arts, such as embroidery, enamelwork, and woodcarvings. 7 Stanislavskovo St. (phone: 290-2114).

Museum of the Revolution (Tsentralni Musei Revolyutsii SSSR) – Documents the 1905 revolution; the revolt of February 1917; and the Great October Socialist Revolution. 21 Gorkovo St. (phone: 299-5217).

Andrei Rublev Museum of Old Russian Art – In Moscow's oldest cathedral, a good collection of restored icons. 10 Pryamikova Sq. (phone: 278-1429).

State History Museum – Moscow's oldest museum. 1/2 Red Square (phone: 228-8452).

State Museum of Oriental Art (Gosudarstvenni Musei Iskusstv Narodov Vostoka) – Crafts of the Soviet Far East, plus Chinese, Indian, and Japanese arts. 16 Obukha St. (phone: 227-3411).

Leo Tolstoy Home (Filial Museya L. H. Tolstovo) – The restored home of the writer, who lived here from 1882 to 1909. 21 Leva Tolstovo St. (phone: 246-6112).

Leo Tolstoy Museum (Gosudarstvenni Literaturni Musei L. H. Tolstovo) – In the former Lopukhin mansion, it contains manuscripts and other memorabilia. 11 Kropokinskaya St. (phone: 202-2190).

SHOPPING: There are wonderful things to buy here: amber, furs, samovars, lacquer boxes, balalaikas, caviar, vodka, and that ultimate Russian souvenir, Matryoshka dolls, a family of gaily painted wooden dolls hidden one inside the other. Tourists usually can find the widest variety of goods and the best prices at the special government stores, *Beriozkas.* These stores only accept foreign currency, traveler's checks, or credit cards. Most *Intourist* hotels have such shops, although they vary in size and variety of stock. The largest is in the *Rossia* hotel.

Soviet department stores are usually open from 9 AM to 6 PM; food stores, however, may remain open later. If you decide instead to use Russian currency and shop where the Muscovites do, here are some suggestions:

Arbat Street – Outdoor offerings of paintings and portrait sketches and a collection of stores with antiques, posters, and books. Worth a visit to buy or browse and to taste the atmosphere of *glasnost.*

Detsky Mir – The name translates to "Children's World," and this shop is particularly noted for its wonderful toys. 2 Marksa Prospekt.

Dom Knigi – Beautiful souvenir books about Moscow and the Soviet Union and colorful Russian posters and postcards can be purchased at this House of Books. 26 Kalinina Prospekt.

GUM – Moscow's huge, government-run department store (see *Special Places*). On Red Square.

Izmailovo Park – An outdoor art market on Sundays in good weather offers a wide range of contemporary paintings by both rank amateurs and accomplished artists. Arts, crafts, and jewelry are also for sale, and the people watching is often more exciting than the art on display.

Melodia – As its name suggests, this is the place to buy records of some of those marvelous Russian folk songs you've been hearing since you arrived. 40 Kalinina Prospekt.

 SPORTS AND FITNESS: Muscovites are avid sports fans, particularly of ice hockey, soccer, and horse racing. Attending such events is a good way to see Soviet citizens at leisure, enjoying themselves with exuberance and spirit. Schedules and tickets are available through the *Intourist* service bureaus. In addition to the new Olympic sports complex, there is a major sports facility across the Moskva River from Moscow State University: Luzhniki Park. The *Central Lenin Stadium,* Luzhniki, seats 103,000 people and is used for soccer matches and track and field meets as well as for various international competitions. This stadium was the scene of the opening and closing of the 1980 Olympic Games and the principal athletic center for the games. A totally new sports complex, built near Mir Prospekt for the Olympics, has the largest indoor stadium in Europe.

Horse Racing – Harness and thoroughbred racing with low-stake pari-mutuel betting takes place each Wednesday, Saturday, and Sunday at the *Hippodrome Racecourse,* 22 Begovaya St. Post time is 5 PM, with an additional program at 1 PM on Sundays. In winter, there are also exciting *troika* races held on the snow or ice.

Ice Hockey – The most popular ice hockey teams in Moscow are *Spartak, Dinamo, TSSKA,* and the *Red Army.* Ticket and schedule information is available from *Intourist.*

Soccer – This sport is a passion with many Muscovites. The *Dynamo Stadium,* 36 Leningradskii Prospekt, holds 60,000 people and was built for one of Moscow's powerhouse teams, but the main events are held at the *Central Lenin Stadium* in Luzhniki.

Swimming – The water for the *Moskva Open-Air Swimming Pool,* 37 Kropotkinskaya Nab., is heated so the pool can be used all year. In winter, when the steam gathers over the pool, it may look like something from Dante's *Inferno,* but this steam layer protects the swimmers from the cold. There also are other pools and several bathing beaches in Moscow. Swimming competitions take place at the *Palace of Water Sports,*

27 Mironovskaya. The *Cosmos* hotel, 150 Pr. Mira (phone: 217-0785/6), has an indoor pool and a sauna.

 THEATER: *Intourist* service bureaus can provide schedules and tickets, but don't expect to get tickets for popular companies, such as the *Bolshoi Ballet,* unless you book well ahead of time. Moscovites used to look forward to a special treat at theater performances: the buffet during intermissions. These included caviar, sandwiches, chocolates, or delectable Russian ice cream, but the food shortages these days make for disappointing fare. The most famous theater here is the *Bolshoi Theater* (Gosudarstvenni Akademichesky Bolshoi Teatr Soyuza SSR), 2 Sverdlova Sq. The *Bolshoi Opera* and the *Bolshoi Ballet* also perform at the 6,000-seat *Palace of Congresses Theater* inside the Kremlin complex. (Enter through Kutafia-Troitsky Gate on Prospekt Marksa at Prospekt Kalinina.) Other major theaters here are: *Maly Theater,* 1/6 Sverdlova Sq., which stages Russian classics; *Moscow Drama and Comedy Theater,* known also as *Taganka,* 76 Chkalova St., considered this city's most avant-garde theater; *State Central Puppet Theater,* 26 Spartakovskaya St.; *Stanislavsky and Nemirovich-Danchenko Academic Musical Theater,* 17 Pushkinskaya St., which presents ballets as well as musical events.

 MUSIC: Ticket and schedule information is available from *Intourist.* The three most important concert halls for music lovers in Moscow are the *Moscow State Conservatoire,* 13 Gertsena St.; the *Tchaikovsky Concert Hall,* 20 Sadovaya Bolskaya St. in Mayakovsky Sq.; and the *Hall of Columns* in the Trade Unions House, 1 Pushkinskaya St. Opera is performed at the *Bolshoi Theater* and the *Stanislavsky and Nemirovich-Danchenko Academic Musical Theater* (see *Theater*). For something a bit lighter, try the *Moscow Operetta Theater,* 6 Pushkinskaya St.

 NIGHTCLUBS AND NIGHTLIFE: Nightlife in Western terms really doesn't exist here. Some restaurants do have dancing each night, and some foreign-currency bars stay open for late drinkers. Brand new is the modest-by-Western standards casino at the *Savoy* hotel (3 Zhdanova), the first in the USSR. Gamblers play with chips drawn on credit cards or non-ruble currency, and winnings are paid in checks drawn on a Finnish bank, cashable outside the country. With the rich selection of theater, ballet, opera, music, the circus, and sports from which to choose, evenings need never be boring. And at any hour of the night, a walk in floodlit Red Square is a very special experience.

BEST IN TOWN

 CHECKING IN: Whether traveling with a group or as an individual, visitors must have paid reservations for accommodations before entering the Soviet Union. These reservations can be made through *Intourist* or through a travel agent. It's possible to request a particular hotel when you make your reservation, but normally you will not be advised of your assigned hotel until you arrive. There are three types of tourist accommodation: deluxe suite, deluxe, and first class. Double occupancy in a deluxe suite (available in hotels given a deluxe rating) costs as much as $240; in deluxe rooms, $150; and in first class (available in hotels given a first class rating), about $100. No meals are included in these prices.

   Cosmos – Recently built, this large and comfortable hotel is near the Soviet Economic Achievements Exhibit, which is rather far from the city's center. Fortunately for its guests, a number of restaurants and bars are found on the premises. 150 Pr. Mira (phone: 217-0785). Deluxe.

Intourist – Completed in 1970, this 22-story hotel is on Gorky Street, a short walk from Red Square. Rooms are quite comfortable and you leave your room key at the front desk rather than with the floor matron, which is the typical procedure at hotels in Moscow. There's a floor show and dancing in the *Stars Sky* restaurant on the ground floor and a late-night, foreign-currency bar on a lower level. The *Intourist* Central Excursion Bureau is right next door. 3 Gorkovo St. (phone: 203-4008). Deluxe.

Metropol – As we went to press, this hotel was under reconstruction, with reopening scheduled for 1990. The façade of this beautiful turn-of-the-century hotel is decorated with a marvelous majolica relief that reproduces Mikhail Vrubel's *Dream Princess*. It is close to the *Bolshoi* and *Maly* theaters on Sverdlova Sq. (see *Theaters*) and has a friendly outdoor café during warm weather. The public rooms here are elegantly appointed, and its restaurants — particularly the *Russian Tea Room* (Russkaya Chainaya) — serve very good food. 1/4 Prospekt Marksa (phone: 225-6673 and 225-6212). Deluxe.

Mezhdunarodnaya I and II – Perhaps Moscow's best modern hotel, it was built specifically to receive foreign business travelers. In addition to numerous restaurants and bars, visitors can take advantage of a health center, swimming pool, saunas, and a bowling alley. *Intourist* does not provide reservations here, but many Western travel agencies do. 12 Krasnopresnenskaya Nab. (phone: 253-2382 or 253-7708). Deluxe.

Savoy – Moscow's first real nod toward Western-style luxury is the recent $17 million renovation of the former *Berlin* hotel, now the number one stopping place for visitors with hard currency: no rubles accepted, and credit cards are preferred vs. cash. There are 86 tiled baths, room service, 24-hour news from CNN, in-house translators, a restaurant and bar, and the first gambling casino in the USSR. 3 Zhdanova (No phone available at press time. Telex: 871-411-620; Fax: 230-2186). Deluxe.

National – A deluxe rating for this fine old hotel could be granted solely on the view of the Kremlin it offers. Opened in 1903, it provides elegant surroundings, an excellent restaurant on the ground floor, and a late-night, hard-currency bar on the second floor. 14/1 Prospekt Marksa (phone: 203-6083 and 203-5568). Deluxe to first class.

Rossia – This is Europe's largest hotel, capable of accommodating 6,000 guests. It is so large that it has four separate wings, each with its own entrance and dining facility. On the top floor of the 21-story tower wing, the *Rossia* restaurant provides a great view of the Kremlin and Red Square (see *Seeing the City*). The south wing has its own 3,000-seat concert hall and two cinemas. On the corner of the east wing is the entrance to an enormous foreign-currency *Beriozka* shop (see *Shopping*). Near St. Basil's Cathedral, the *Rossia* was completed in 1967 for the 50th anniversary of the Revolution. North Wing, 6 Razina St. (phone: 298-5401); East Wing, 1 Moskvoretskaya Nab. (phone: 298-1173). Deluxe to first class.

Ukraina – One of the seven look-alike skyscrapers built during the late Stalinist period (Moscow State University is the largest), the *Ukraina* is a large hotel on the banks of the Moskva. It is some distance from the center of the city, however. Kutuzovsky Prospekt (phone: 243-3030). Deluxe to first class.

EATING OUT: You may book *prix fixe* menu meals through the *Intourist* service bureaus for many Moscow restaurants. Payment to the service bureau usually is in foreign currency and may range from $20 to $40 per person. However, this includes appetizers, entrée, dessert, vodka, wines, fruit drinks, and coffee, as well as music and dancing. A relatively new dining option exists in the form of private or cooperative restaurants and cafés (ask about them at the service bureau in your hotel). If you go to the cafés or restaurants on your own, you must pay in Russian currency, although credit cards are accepted in all *Intourist*-sponsored restaurants and some co-op cafés. These restaurants will not fall into any fine dining category, but they do offer a wide variety of national foods from the various regions and republics of the Soviet Union. If you like black caviar (called *ikra*), indulge yourself. If you like vegetables, you'll be disappointed; even in summer, vegetables are puny compared to any available in the West. In fact, it won't take long to figure out that Moscow is a center of cholesterol, with fatty sausages, salami, sour cream, butter, and eggs on menus in the better hotels — and that's just breakfast.

Aragvi – This bustling Georgian restaurant, once the closest thing to luxury dining in Moscow, is no longer so exalted. But with its music and clientele heavily weighted on the tourist side, it is still popular. Georgian food is highly seasoned; specialties include a spicy meat soup called *kharcho;* skewered roast Georgian mutton, *shashlik po kharski;* and roast chicken pressed between scalding stones, *tsiplyata tabaka.* Reservations necessary. 6 Gorkovo St. (phone: 229-3762).

Arbat – Seats 2,000 people. Almost always filled with tourists, this restaurant offers a floor show as well as music and dancing. Kalinina Prospekt (phone: 291-1403).

Baku – Azerbaijan cuisine and music. The cuisine is similar to Turkish food. Try meatballs in vine leaves (*dolma*) or the sour milk and meat soup, *dovta.* 24 Gorkovo St. (phone: 299-8506).

Kropotkinskaya 36 – Inaugurated in 1986, this is both the first and one of the best of the coöperative restaurants. The food is good, as is the atmosphere, particularly in the basement room. Reservations necessary. 36 Kropotkinskaya St. (phone: 201-7500).

National – Good food and an excellent view of the Kremlin. On the ground floor of one of Moscow's fine old hotels, the *National* (see *Checking In*). A late-night bar on the second floor serves whiskey and other drinks for hard currency. 1 Gorkovo St. (phone: 203-5595).

Pekin – The Chinese food served here is cooked under the supervision of chefs from China. Also featured are music and dancing. 1 Sadovaya Bolshaya (phone: 209-1865).

Slavyansky Bazar – Traditional Slav cuisine and music. Originally opened in 1870, this has always been a favorite dining spot of writers and musicians. 25-vo, 17 Oktyabrya St. (phone: 221-1872).

Tsentralnyi – Traditional Russian food, such as beef Stroganoff and skewered mutton and onions, *shashlik.* Originally opened in 1865 as *Filippov's.* 10 Gorkovo St. (phone: 229-7235).

Uzbekistan – Uzbek cuisine and music. Sample the large meat-filled dumplings, *muntyi,* or the soup made of minced meat, eggs, and dumplings. 29 Neglinnaya St. (phone: 294-6053).

■**Mezhdunarodnaya Hotel Complex:** Several good restaurants, cafés, and bars can be found at the complex, also known as the International Trade Center (12 Krasnopresnenskaya Nab.). Although some do not accept rubles, all require reservations. Three of the better ones are the *Continental,* with European atmosphere, soft music, and good food (phone: 253-9798); the *Russky,* for Russian cuisine and a Gypsy show in the evenings (phone: 253-2373); and *Sakura,* for authentic Japanese cuisine (foreign currency only; phone: 253-2824).

MUNICH

To many people, Bavaria is a place apart from the rest of West Germany; gayer, more rosy-cheeked, less Teutonic. And Munich, the principal city of this southern region in the lap of the Bavarian Alps, is one of the jolliest cities in all Europe. It is, of course, renowned for two of the wildest, noisiest, fun-filled festivals anywhere. During *Oktoberfest* each year (held in September, oddly enough), hundreds of thousands of Germans and tourists celebrate the wedding of Crown Prince Ludwig to Princess Therese von Sachsen-Hildburghausen. The fact that the wedding took place in 1810 doesn't deter the crowd's enthusiasm one bit. Then, less than 4 months later, *Müncheners* go on another binge, called *Fasching*. Traditionally, all sorts of bizarre behavior is acceptable — and usually takes place — during this carnival season, preceding Lenten abstinence.

Even when there is no formal festival taking place, this is the beer capital of the world. Germans guzzle more beer than the people of any other country: 150 liters per person per year. But the Bavarians do even better, downing 250 liters apiece annually.

The thing that makes Munich so special, however, is that it is able to combine this earnest lust for life with modern sophistication. There is a pleasing blend of elegance and rustic charm, the naughty and the nice, here. Bavarian beer gardens and folk art coexist with Paris fashion, grand opera, and astrophysics, giving rise to such nicknames as "Village of a Million," and "Metropolis with a Heart."

As a cultural center, Munich has produced the largest number of German Nobel Prize winners; it is the home of the respected *Bavarian State Opera,* more than 60 legitimate theaters and cabarets, and important scientific institutes; and it is the largest university city in Germany, with more than 100,000 students in residence.

Statistics show that only one in three of Munich's 1.3 million citizens was born here, and one in ten is foreign-born. There is little wonder, though, that a cosmopolitan center that manages to retain a strong Alpine village flavor is so attractive to outsiders.

During the past 830 years, Munich has grown up along the banks of the Isar River, which flows down from the Bavarian Alps through forest and farmland before cutting a determined path through the eastern part of the city on its way to meet the Danube. On very clear days, the Alps, some 50 miles away, provide a stunning backdrop for the city.

Munich takes its name from the monks, *Munichen* in High German, who founded a Benedictine monastery in this area in the 9th century. The city itself was established beside the Isar River in 1158 by Henry the Lion, Duke of Saxony, who had been ceded part of Bavaria by Emperor Friedrich Barbarossa. But in 1180 Barbarossa replaced Duke Henry with the Palatine Count Otto von Wittelsbach. From that time, the House of Wittelsbach was closely linked to Bavaria's and Munich's fortunes until the monarchy was replaced by a republic after World War I.

Toward the middle of the 19th century, Bavarian King Ludwig I put much of his energy into making Munich the most beautiful city in Europe. It was during his reign that many of the city's great buildings were erected and Ludwigstrasse was built. However, the king was forced to abdicate in 1848 when the scandal of his liaison with the Spanish dancer Lola Montez lent fuel to a revolutionary movement. His 18-year-old grandson, Ludwig II, became king in 1864 and carried out an even more grandiose building scheme. He ordered the construction of three extravagant castles and commissioned an array of phantasmagoria ranging from a boat in the shape of a huge shell to furniture, porcelain, and robes. Often called the Dream King, Ludwig II was much loved by his subjects, but court doctors declared him to be in an "advanced stage of mental disorder" and he was stripped of his powers shortly before he died by drowning at the age of 40.

After Germany's defeat in World War I, Munich was the center of the Nazi movement. Adolf Hitler and his National Socialists made an abortive attempt to seize power here in 1923 during the infamous Beer Garden Putsch. In 1938, Mussolini, Chamberlain, and Daladier met here with Hitler and agreed to let Germany annex the Sudetenland.

Much of the city was destroyed in bombing raids during World War II, but unlike some of its sister cities, Munich eschewed the modern and reconstructed its past. Except for the space-age architecture of the suburban Olympic Village, built for the 1972 summer games, and the new Gasteig Cultural Center, Munich looks like a typical old European city. In some cases, original plans were used in the reconstruction or restoration of Munich landmarks. Today the city's public buildings reflect the many styles in which they were built over the centuries: late Gothic, Venetian Renaissance, neo-classical, rococo, and baroque. Church spires and bell towers, rather than high-rise office buildings, dominate the skyline.

Modern Munich is many things: an Old World city, a center of culture and sophistication, a city of gaiety, an intellectual center, and, with all its beer, *Wurst,* and *Gemütlichkeit,* a carnival of life.

MUNICH AT-A-GLANCE

 SEEING THE CITY: An exceptional view of Munich and the Bavarian Alps is available from the television tower (Olympiaturm) just northwest of the city at Olympic Village. The 943-foot tower was erected to facilitate televising the 1972 Summer Olympics. A $2 elevator ride will take you to the tower terrace at 623 feet, with its impressive panorama of the city. There is also a dining room, the *Tower* restaurant, which revolves for a 360° view.

 SPECIAL PLACES: Marienplatz, with its tall white column of the Virgin, the city's patron, is the heart of Munich. Many of the streets leading from it have been closed to traffic and turned into a pedestrian zone called *Fussgängerbereich.* About 8 blocks west of Marienplatz is the central square, Karlsplatz, known locally as Stachus, where buses, trams, and subways to all parts

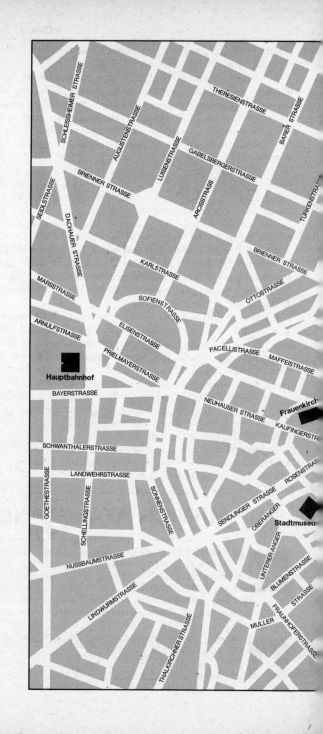

of the city arrive and depart. Visitors are often confused because street names change abruptly in central Munich for no apparent reason. You can always get back to the center again, though, because there are numerous signs pointing the way and the spires and towers of landmark churches stand out above the lower red-roofed buildings that constitute the heart of Munich. The Isar River cuts through the city's eastern section, and a walk north along its banks will lead to a huge, lovely park, the English Garden. On the west side of the park lies the Schwabing district. Munich has a superbly integrated system of buses, trams, and subways to help you enjoy the city.

DOWNTOWN

Schwabing – At the turn of the century, it had a reputation as an artistic and intellectual center. Today this district to the north of the University of Munich is known to most visitors as the place "where the action is" in Munich. By day Schwabing resembles any other German residential district, but about six in the evening people swarm into its streets looking for a good time. The sidewalks along Leopoldstrasse, Schwabing's main street, and on Amalienstrasse and Türkenstrasse take on a festive air. You'll see a confusion of sights: painters displaying their art, street musicians, poets offering their latest verses, barbers giving haircuts on the sidewalk, palm readers, quick-sketch artists. You can buy sandals, copper jewelry, ceramics, beads, belts — just about anything, in fact, including genuine and bogus antiques. Schwabing has more than 200 restaurants, with Greek, Yugoslavian, Italian, and Bavarian the most popular. There are countless discotheques, jazz *Kellers,* cafés, and boutiques.

Alte Pinakothek (Old Pinakothek) – One of the world's great art galleries, this huge Renaissance building contains large and important collections of Dutch and Flemish painting from the 14th to the 18th century. The museum was built from 1826 to 1836 to house paintings gathered by the Dukes of Wittelsbach. Ludwig I made numerous other acquisitions that enhanced the museum's reputation. Among its treasures are important works by Albrecht Dürer and Peter Paul Rubens. Closed Mondays. Admission charge. 27 Barer Str. (phone: 238-05216).

Deutsches Museum (German Museum) – Considered the largest technical museum in the world, the *German Museum* is on an island in the Isar River southeast of the city center. Included in its massive displays are the original 139-foot U-boat built in 1906, locomotives from the Bavarian State Railway, a collection of antique pianos and organs, a Messerschmitt 267 jet fighter from 1944, a planetarium, salt and coal mining exhibits in actual caverns, the aeronautical and space center, and much, much more. Unfortunately, detailed descriptions are only available in German, but it's still very much worth a visit. Open daily. Admission charge. Reached by subway or by walking across one of several bridges connecting the island with the city. Isar Island (phone: 21791).

Gasteig Cultural Center – High on the right bank of the Isar River, just 400 yards from the *German Museum,* is Munich's newest attraction. It unites under one roof a philharmonic hall, two smaller concert halls, the Richard Strauss music conservatory, and the municipal library. The $130-million building has an ultramodern design, a sharp contrast to the surrounding neighborhood. 5 Rosenheimer Str. (phone: 418-1614).

Englischer Garten (English Garden) – This 18th-century garden, one of the oldest landscaped parks on the Continent, is a favorite meeting place. It has lakes, pavilions, riding trails, a site frequented by nude sunbathers, a Japanese teahouse, and Chinesischer Turm (Chinese Tower). At the base of the tower is the city's largest beer garden, where the favorite pastime is quenching one's thirst with a liter of beer while enjoying the passing scene. If you want to splurge, a pleasant carriage ride through the park will cost about $12 for a half-hour. The park is northeast of the city's center, between Schwabing and the Isar River.

Frauenkirche (Cathedral of Our Lady) – The onion domes atop two 325-feet symmetrical towers have made this late Gothic cathedral Munich's most distinctive landmark. Its dull red brick façade was damaged extensively during air raids in 1944, but it has been rebuilt. The cathedral contains a rich depository of religious works of art, relics, sacred tombs, and the mausoleum of Emperor Ludwig IV. An elevator inside the south tower goes to the top of one of the towers, from which there is a good view of the city. 1 Frauenpl.

Residenz (Palace) – Although damaged during World War II, the royal palace has regained much of its glory. Built for the Dukes of Wittelsbach, the palace has been extended over the centuries to form a complex of buildings with seven inner courts. There are state rooms and royal suites in Renaissance, rococo, and neo-classical styles and displays of royal treasures. Closed Mondays. Admission charge. Entrance at 3 Max-Joseph-Pl. (phone: 224641).

Bayerisches Nationalmuseum (Bavarian National Museum) – The vast array of art and historical memorabilia from the Middle Ages to the 19th century on display here should give you an excellent introduction to Bavarian culture. The museum has what may be the most extensive collection of arts and crafts in the world. Along with its tapestries and wood carvings, the museum is best known for its unique Krippenschau Collection of Christmas crèches (nativity scenes). Closed Mondays. Admission charge. 3 Prinzregentenstr. (phone: 21681).

Hofbräuhaus – This immense beer hall is a dance palace, a restaurant, and a national monument to the good life. In the beer garden, you'll be part of a scene people around the world associate with Munich: cheerful fräuleins carrying as many as 10 steins of beer at once, waitresses and waiters in peasant costumes moving through a noisy crowd selling pretzels stacked on long sticks, or white radishes cut into fancy spirals — both suitably salty to help you work up a thirst. It's not expensive, and is a must on any visitor's sightseeing agenda. 9 Am Platzl (phone: 221676).

Neues Rathaus (New City Hall) – Munich's new city hall dominates Marienplatz. Each day throngs of people peer up at its famous carillon (Glockenspiel), waiting to see the mechanical knights and their squires joust while the carillon signals to the city that it is 11 AM. It is a delightful diversion, not to be missed. Marienpl.

Viktualienmarkt (Victuals Market) – A few blocks south of Marienplatz, farmers, butchers, bakers, and other purveyors of food specialties set out their wares in an open-air market Mondays through Saturdays. It's the perfect place to browse, take pictures, and buy a snack or picnic fixings. Viktualienmarkt.

SUBURBS

Olympiapark (Olympic Village) – Built for the 1972 Olympic Games, also the scene of the terrorist kidnapping (and later massacre) of Israeli athletes. The modern sports complex includes swimming pools, tracks, and gymnasiums. The park also has an 80,000-seat stadium — under an extraordinary skinlike roof — and an artificial lake. The housing built for Olympic athletes and officials is now a major residential suburb. Guided tours are available, and you can even swim in one of the pools that Mark Spitz made famous in his successful pursuit of seven gold medals. Admission charge. It can be reached easily by bus or subway. Oberwiesenfeld (phone: 306-13479 or 306-13424).

Schloss Nymphenburg (Nymphenburg Palace and Park) – Just west of the city limits stands a splendid 495-acre park with lakes and hunting lodges and Nymphenburg Palace, once the residence of the Bavarian kings. The great hall of the palace is decorated with frescoes by Johann Baptist Zimmermann, and a museum (*Marstallmuseum*) in the south wing of the palace houses state carriages and sleighs. The *Nymphenburg China Factory,* with showrooms open to the public, is on the north crescent of the grounds. Concerts are presented on the grounds during summer months, and it is a particularly lovely spot to visit when the rhododendron are in bloom from May through June. Closed Mondays. Admission charge. Entrance from Menzingerstr. (phone: 179081).

Tierpark Hellabrunn (Hellabrunn Zoo) – Europe's largest zoo, Hellabrunn keeps its extensive collection of animals in a 173-acre natural setting of forestland and rivers. The zoo is famous for breeding rare animals and for its anthropoid ape section. Open daily; guided tours on Wednesdays. Small admission charge. There is regular bus service from Marienpl. Four miles (6 km) south of Munich at 6 Siebenbrunnerstr. (phone: 661021).

Dachau – The name has evoked nothing but horror since this first Nazi concentration camp was built in 1933. Some 200,000 prisoners and deportees were received here. The number who died or disappeared is uncertain, although it is estimated that 32,000 may have perished. The magnitude of the atrocities committed is compounded by the natural beauty of the area: Dachau itself is a charming terraced town near a misty heath. The old administration building is now used as a museum where photos, memorabilia, and exhibitions document what transpired here. A film about the camp is shown twice daily (at 11:30 AM and 3:30 PM) in English. This is not a place for the fainthearted. Closed Mondays, December 24, and the afternoons of December 31 and Shrove Tuesday. No admission charge. Dachau, 14 miles (22 km) northwest of Munich, can be reached by Petershausen commuter train (S-2) from the main railway station. There is a direct bus (#722) from the station to the camp (phone: 08131-1741 or 08131-84566).

■**EXTRA SPECIAL:** It's said that over 650 kinds of beer are brewed in Bavaria, including those made privately. Munich is the home of six of Germany's major producers; one of them, *Spaten* (which alone makes nine different labels), will arrange tours upon request. During a half-hour walk through the plant, accompanied by an English-speaking guide, guests learn the various steps of beer-making — from germination of the barley to bottling the brew. The tour is an essential preliminary to enlightened imbibing. 46 Marsstr. (phone: 5122 for reservations).

SOURCES AND RESOURCES

TOURIST INFORMATION: The Munich Tourist Office has information counters at the main railway station, Hauptbahnhof, Bayerstr. entrance 2 (phone: 239-1256), and at the Arrivals Hall of Riem Airport (phone: 907256). Both are open daily until late evening. For information in English on museums and other sights, call the tourist office at 239162 or 239172.

The tourist office publishes an official monthly program, *München,* that lists theater, museum, and concert schedules, special exhibitions, hotels, camping facilities, and other useful information, but it is only published in German. However, many hotels provide literature in English focusing on Munich's activities and entertainment programs.

The US Consulate is at 5 Königinstr. (phone: 23011).

Local Coverage – The twice weekly *Munich Times* is an English-language newspaper.

Food – The *Munich Times* has restaurant listings, as does the tourist office's *München,* in German.

Telephone – The area code for Munich is 089.

CLIMATE AND CLOTHES: Because of the proximity to the shifting air currents of the Alps, Munich's weather can be unpredictable. Except for sunny September, come prepared for extremes. You'll need solid shoes, rain boots, warm underwear, a windbreaker, and a hat or cap. Temperatures can range from a high of 74F (23C) in July to a chilly 26F (−3C) in January. Munich is a very fashion-conscious city, so you'll probably want to dress up for evening unless your nights on the town are going to be in informal Schwabing.

GETTING AROUND: Munich has an integrated rapid transit system, and the tickets that you buy from the blue dispensers at stations, streetcar stops, and on those vehicles bearing a white and green "K" sign can be used on buses, streetcars, subways, and local trains. You can cancel the tickets yourself in automatic canceling machines at the barriers of stations and in streetcars and buses bearing a yellow and black "E." There is a reduced-rate ticket for about $4 that permits unlimited transport in a 24-hour period. These special tickets are sold at the tourist offices and all ticket offices.

Airport – Munich-Riem Airport handles both domestic and international traffic. It's about a 30-minute drive to downtown Munich, and a taxi will cost from 25 to 30 deutsche marks ($14-$16). The airport's bus service to the city center leaves from in front of the main terminal; in the other direction, buses leave every 20 minutes from Munich's main train station (Hauptbahnhof), at Bahnhofplatz. For flight information, call 921-12127.

Bus and Streetcar – The Karlsplatz is the main junction for Munich's streetcars, and the East Railway Station (Ostbahnhof) across the Isar from central Munich is the terminal for many of the city's blue and white buses.

Car Rental – There are international and local rental firms in downtown Munich and at the airport. If you do drive, you should know that in some areas of Munich traffic-light poles contain two sets of lights: one on top for cars and a bottom set for bicycles. Munich also employs "motorbike" women, easily recognized by their light blue jumpsuits, who patrol the highways to aid lost or stranded motorists. Fluent in several languages, these women carry maps, tourist information, and other helpful material.

Subway and Train – Munich's subway is called the U-Bahn. It crosses the city in a north-south direction and has its central stops at Marienplatz and Hauptbahnhof. Like most European underground rail systems, the U-Bahn is clean, modern, and efficient. The S-Bahn, which connects with the U-Bahn at Marienplatz and Hauptbahnhof, is the interurban express line. It runs underground across the city in an east-west direction. Outside the city, it branches out over the whole federal railway network. For information on S-Bahn trains, call 557575. For information on trains to other part of the country, call 592991 or 593321 (schedules) and 554141 (fares).

Taxi – Munich's taxis are expensive. It will cost you nearly $3 just to have the driver flip down the arm of the meter. Taxis can be hailed on the street, or you can get one radio-dispatched by dialing 21611.

SPECIAL EVENTS: Munich is famous the world over for *Oktoberfest,* celebrated from late September through the first Sunday in October, and the pre-Lenten carnival, *Fasching,* which engulfs the entire city during the month preceding *Ash Wednesday* each February or March. *Oktoberfest* is 16 riotous days of beer drinking, sausage eating, and merrymaking at Theresa's Meadow, a fairgrounds where local breweries set up gaily decorated beer-garden buildings, brass bands oom-pah-pah continuously, and oxen are roasted on open spits. Unbelievable quantities of beer are drunk: Some 750,000 kegs are tapped. *Fasching,*

which has been celebrated in Munich since the 14th century, hints more of indulgence in forbidden pleasures of the flesh (there is a traditional agreement that husbands and wives overlook one another's indiscretions during *Fasching*), but it, too, is characterized by lots of drinking and endless fun-seeking. The nonstop street reveling is all the more colorful for the outlandish costumes the celebrants don for fancy balls and an enormous parade through the city.

MUSEUMS: Besides those mentioned in *Special Places,* notable museums in Munich include the following.

Antikensammlungen – Classical art, including Joseph Loeb's collection of Etruscan gold and silver. 1 Königspl. (phone: 598359).

BMW-Museum – Cars, motorcycles, and airplane engines of the Bavaria Motor Works. 130 Petuelring (phone: 389-53307).

Münchner Stadtmuseum (City Museum) – Munich's history since the Middle Ages. 1 St.-Jakobs-Pl. (phone: 233-2370).

Städtische Galerie im Lenbachhaus (Gallery in Lenbachhaus) – Kandinsky and the Blue Rider School. 33 Luisenstr. (phone: 521041).

Glyptothek – Greek and Roman sculpture. 3 Königspl.(phone: 286100).

Kunsthalle – Gallery used for temporary, visiting exhibitions. 15 Theatinerstr. (phone: 224412).

Museum in Stuck-Villa – Turn-of-the-century art. 60 Prinzregentenstr. (phone: 470-7086).

Neue Pinakothek – 19th- and early-20th-century art. 29 Barerstr. (phone: 238-05195).

Staatsgalerie Moderner Kunst (State Museum of Modern Art) – 20th-century sculpture and painting. 1 Prinzregentenstr. (phone: 292710).

Valentin Museum – Dedicated to one of Munich's legendary entertainers, Karl Valentin. Gate Tower, Isartorpl. (phone: 223266).

SHOPPING: Munich is such an elegant shopping city that some visitors confess to losing all sense of proportion once turned loose in the pedestrian zone. Shops tempt you with Bavarian beer steins, wonderful antiques, marvelous German porcelain, and items of German steel as well as Parisian fashions. Munich's most elegant shops can be found along Maximilianstrasse and Briennerstrasse and the small streets between Marienplatz and Odeonsplatz. Most of the antiques shops are concentrated in Neuturmstrasse, near Marienplatz. The city's leading department stores are *Kaufhof* on Marienplatz and *Karstadt,* near Karlsplatz. Most stores are open from 9 AM to 6 PM on weekdays, but close at 2 PM on Saturdays.

Alois Dallmayr – A world-famous fancy food store. 14-15 Dienerstr.

Anglia English Bookstore – The biggest selection of English-language paperbacks in southern Germany. 3 Schellingstr.

Auer Dult – A wonderful flea market for secondhand goods, antiques, and curiosities. Set up three times a year — usually in April, July, and October. Mariahilfpl., across the Isar in the southeastern district of Au.

Beck – Famous for textiles, women's wear, and Bavarian handicrafts. Marienpl.

Biebl – Solingen carving sets and other items made of this renowned German steel. 25 Karlspl.

Dieter Stange-Erlenbach Pelze – Famed for its timeless and fashionable furs — for him and for her. 21 Maximilianstr.

Dirndlkönigin – An interesting display of Bavarian handicrafts, including the best selection of Bavarian folk costumes in Munich. 18 Residenzstr.

Kunstring – New and antique dinnerware. 4 Briennerstr. (phone: 281532).

Loden-Frey – Men's and women's loden coats in great variety. 7-9 Maffeistr.

Ludwig Mory – A huge and varied stock of interesting beer steins. In the new city hall. 8 Marienpl.

Maendler – High fashion for women. 7 Theatinerstr. (phone: 220437).

Moderne Creation München (MCM) – The latest in chic fashion accessories. 11 Nicolaistr.

Moshammer's – Clothing for men. 14 Maximilianstr. (phone: 226924).

Nymphenburger Crystalworks – Nymphenburger dinnerware, the "service of Bavarian kings." 1 Odeonspl. (phone: 282428).

Pini – The city's largest store for cameras and allied equipment. Am Stachus (Karlspl.).

Rosenthal – Home of the marvelous china, crystal, and cutlery. 8 Theatinerstr.

Staatliche Porzellan Manufaktur – The main distributor of Nymphenburg porcelain. Odeonspl.

Wallach Haus – Bavarian furniture, dirndls, and peasant dresses. 3 Residenzstr.

Walter – Leather clothing for men and women. 9 Amalienstr.

Wesely – Wax art candles typical of this region. 1 Rindermarkt.

 SPORTS AND FITNESS: The excellent facilities built for the 1972 Summer Olympics are used by a variety of professional teams in Munich, providing visitors with an opportunity to see everything from European soccer and basketball to ice hockey and track and field events. Sports schedules are listed in the monthly tourist office program, *München.* If you are a swimmer, you might enjoy using the *Olympic Swimming Hall* in Olympic Village. It's open to the public daily. The *Sportstudio,* 16 Hansastr. (phone: 573479), is a fitness center open to nonmembers. For jogging, try the English Garden, which stretches north from Prinzregentenstr. and is easily accessible from downtown. Cycling enthusiasts can rent bicycles at the entrance to the English Garden, at the corner of Königinstr. and Veterinärstr. (phone: 397016).

 THEATER: Munich has been known for centuries as a theater city. You can see everything from Greek tragedy to classical ballet to modern experimental drama in the numerous theaters here. The chief theaters are the *Opera House, National Theater,* Max-Joseph-Pl. (phone: 221316); the *Cuvilliés Theater* in the Royal Palace, 1 Residenzstr. (phone: 221316); *Theater in Marstall,* Marstallpl. (phone: 221316); *Residenz Theater,* 1 Max-Joseph-Pl. (phone: 225754); *Prinzregententheater,* 12 Prinzregentenpl. (phone: 225754); *Münchner Kammerspiele* in Schauspielhaus, 26 Maximilianstr. (phone: 237-21328); the *Münchner Marionettentheater* (Munich Puppet Theater), 29a Blumenstr. at Sendlinger-Tor-Pl. (phone: 265712); and the *Münchner Theater für Kinder* (Munich Theater for Children), 46 Dachauer Str. (phone: 595454 and 593858).

 MUSIC: The first opera was performed in Munich in 1650, and the names of Wagner, Mozart, and Richard Strauss (Strauss was born in Munich) are closely linked with the *Bavarian State Opera,* which performs in the *National Theater.* Tickets are on sale at 11 Maximilianstr. (phone: 221316). Opera also can be heard at the *Staatstheater an Gärtnerplatz,* 3 Gärtnerpl. (phone: 201-6767). Hardly a day passes without a classical music concert at one of the halls at the *Gasteig Cultural Center* (phone: 418-1614; see *Special Places*); jazz can be heard at clubs such as *Allotria,* 33 Türkenstr. (phone: 285858); *Unterfahrt,* 96 Kirchenstr. (phone: 448-2794); *Jenny's Place,* 50 Georgenstr. (phone: 271-9354); and *Schwabinger Podium,* 1 Wagnerstr. (phone: 399482). For rock and pop, try *Alabama-Halle,* 418 Schleissheimer Str. (phone: 351-3085).

NIGHTCLUBS AND NIGHTLIFE: Nightlife and Schwabing are almost interchangeable terms. You can dance over an aquarium filled with sharks at *Aquarius* in the *Holiday Inn* (see *Checking In*), 194 Leopoldstr. (phone: 340971), disco at *Cadillac,* 1 Theklastr. (phone: 266974), or rock the night away at the club in the *Bayerischer Hof* (see *Checking In*), 2-6 Promenade pl. (phone: 212-0994). Music and other entertainment is offered at *Clip,* 25 Leopoldstr. (phone: 394578, and *Domicile,* at 19 Leopoldstr. (phone: 399451), offers jazz and rock. One of the oldest Schwabing dance spots is *P-1,* 1 Prinzregentenstr. (phone: 294252). There's always an interesting program of live music on tap at *MUH,* 19 Innere Wiener Str. (phone: 448-9833). A relatively new disco that appeals to "smart" Muenchners is *Bubbles,* 25 Oscar-von-Miller-Ring (phone: 281182). At *Harry's New York Bar,* you can gawk at the celebrities while imbibing one of 500 different drinks; 9 Falkenturmstr. (phone: 222760). Biting humor and satire are the offerings at the literary cabaret, *Lach und Schiessgesellschaft,* Ursulastr. (phone: 391997); and don't miss Gisela's vocal renditions at her bistro, *Schwabinger Gisela,* 38 Herzog-Heinrich-Str. (phone: 534901). *Waldwirtschaft Grosshesselohe* offers great Bavarian beer as well as live jazz music at 3 Georg-Kalb-Str. (phone: 795088).

If you prefer gambling, take the *Garmisch Casino's Blitz Bus* or one of the other buses the casinos run to bring players from Munich to the Garmisch area at the foot of the Alps, 54 miles (87 km) away. The buses leave from the north side of the main railway station at 5 PM on weekdays and at 2 PM Sundays. They leave Garmisch at 11 PM for the return to Munich. The trip takes about 1 hour and 35 minutes each way.

BEST IN TOWN

CHECKING IN: Except during *Oktoberfest* and *Fasching,* there is plenty of hotel space in Munich, but prices are high any time of the year. Top hotels will cost a minimum of $100 a night for a double, and most of their rooms are much higher; moderate-priced hotels charge between $50 and $100 a night; and anything below $50 must be considered inexpensive. And just so you don't forget, make reservations ahead if you're coming for *Oktoberfest* or *Fasching.* Munich also has many delightful, inexpensive pensions. They don't have all the conveniences of a modern hotel, but they do have *Gemütlichkeit,* and that warmth and geniality is one of the best reasons to visit Munich. All telephone numbers are in the 089 area code unless otherwise indicated.

Bayerischer Hof-Palais Montgelas – Long considered Munich's landmark hotel, this 442-room property has managed to regain its repuatation for excellent service and high standards. The hotel has always had a top-drawer clientele, including Ludwig I, who favored it because the royal palace didn't have bathtubs. More recent facilities include a *Trader Vic's* restaurant and a rooftop pool. 2-6 Promenadepl. (phone: 21200). Expensive.

Continental – A favorite of those who know the city well, it's close to the center of town and known affectionately as the *Conti.* Filled with flowers and priceless antiques, it has just been completely renovated. The hotel is part of a group of buildings known as the Kunstblock, the center of the Munich art and antiques market. 5 Max-Joseph-Str. (phone: 551570). Expensive.

Four Seasons (Vier Jahreszeiten) – Only a few blocks from the glittering *National State Opera,* this is one of the great hotels of Europe, exuding opulence and elegance right through to its ultramodern wing and rooftop swimming pool. Its restaurant is wonderful (see *Eating Out*). Owned by Inter-Continental. 17 Maximilianstr. (phone: 230390). Expensive.

Holiday Inn Munich – A 360-room hotel on Schwabing's main thoroughfare, the home of the *Yellow Submarine* (see *Nightclubs and Nightlife*). 194 Leopoldstr. (phone: 340971). Expensive.

Königshof – Despite its central location, this traditional and comfortable establishment is quiet. It also boasts one of Munich's best hotel restaurants, which has a great view of busy Karlsplatz. 25 Karlsplatz (phone: 551360). Expensive.

Munich Hilton International – Close to the picturesque English Garden, this 500-room hostelry is designed to meet the particular needs of the international business traveler. There are several restaurants, a pool, a sauna, a shopping arcade, and a massive underground garage. 7 Am Tucherpark (phone: 38450). Expensive.

Munich Sheraton – East of the center of town, this 650-room hotel is clearly geared to the convention trade. There is a 1,200-seat meeting hall with sophisticated sound and translating units. 6 Arabellastr. (phone: 92640). Expensive.

Penta – Part of a European chain and designed to cut down on rapidly soaring hotel prices, it caters to a predominantly business clientele. Guests carry their own baggage to their rooms. A unit in each room dispenses drinks, snacks, and even continental breakfast (eliminating the need for room service). There is an extensive shopping arcade and restaurant complex under the hotel, which is near the *German Museum.* 3 Hochstr. (phone: 448-5555). Expensive.

Platzl – On the site of an old historic mill, this 170-bed hotel has modern conveniences. It is in the old city center, across the street from the *Hofbräuhaus* (see *Special Places*). 8-9 Münzstr. (phone: 237030). Expensive.

Biederstein – Charming, probably Munich's quietest hotel. It's on the fringe of Schwabing, next to the English Garden park. 18 Keferstr. (phone: 395072). Moderate.

Daniel – Plain, but clean and comfortable quarters; and a great location near the train station, subway, and within walking distance of most shopping. A good value. 5 Sonnenstr. (phone: 554945). Moderate.

Intercity – In the main railway station building, but surprisingly quiet and comfortable. 2 Bahnhofpl. (phone: 558571). Moderate.

Leopold – This 80-room hotel, on the fringe of Schwabing, is in an old 19th-century house. The new back wing is quieter and faces a garden. 119 Leopoldstr. (phone: 367061). Moderate.

Lettl – Centrally located, with breakfast included in the tariff. When reserving, ask for a room in the new wing. 53 Amalienstr. (phone: 283026). Moderate.

Uhland – A charming little hotel in a lovely old building on a street near Theresa's Meadow. 1 Uhlandstr. (phone: 539277). Moderate.

Mariahilf – A particular favorite with English tourists, this pension is in a quiet sector of the city across the Isar from central Munich. 83 Lilienstr. (phone: 484834). Inexpensive.

Mariandl – This charming pension near Theresa's Meadow has not only 25 quiet rooms but also a restaurant famed for its evenings of free classical music. 51 Goethestr. (phone: 534108). Inexpensive.

Theresia – In Schwabing, very close to the museums, is this well-run establishment. 51 Luisenstr. (phone: 521250 and 535158). Inexpensive.

 EATING OUT: Bavarian cuisine is hearty and heavy, and most of it seems created to make you consume inordinate amounts of beer. Liver dumplings, *Leberknödel,* is the most famous of more than four score Bavarian dumplings. *Leberkäse* translates as liver cheese but is neither; it's a baked pâté of beef and bacon. Pork sausages and sauerkraut, *Schweinswürstl mit Kraut,* is another unforgettable local dish. Munich is the sausage (*Wurst*) capital of the world. *Weisswurst,* a veal-based white sausage, is sold throughout the city by street vendors as well as in beer gardens. It's best at about 11 AM. You'll also want to taste some of the local pretzels and salt rolls and sticks sold under such names as *Brez'n, Römische,* and *Salzstangerl.* Another specialty here is the large, tasty white radish, *Radi,* cut in spirals and sold with plenty of salt. If all of this makes you very thirsty, order *ein Mass Bier;* that's a liter. Otherwise, a half liter, *eine Halbe,* should suffice. If Bavarian food is too much for you every day, you can choose from a wide variety of other ethnic foods, especially in the conglomeration of foreign restaurants in Schwabing, some of them the best in Germany.

Like everything else in Munich, dining out can be very expensive. Even beer hall fare, once the staple of budget-minded students, can add up quickly to $15, $20, or more. At expensive restaurants expect to pay a minimum of $60 for a meal for two; $30 to $50 should be considered in the moderate price range; and anything below that, inexpensive. Unless otherwise noted, make reservations. All telephone numbers are in the 089 area code unless otherwise indicated.

Aubergine – This was Munich's and West Germany's first Michelin three-star restaurant. Chef Eckart Witzigmann insists on only the freshest ingredients, and his menu is sprinkled with dishes like venison with wild berries and lobster fricassee. Closed Sundays, Mondays, 2 weeks in August, and from December 24 to January 1. 5 Maximianspl. (phone: 598171). Expensive.

Boettner – A tiny wine restaurant in a high-ceilinged, paneled room behind a caviar-lobster shop. It has only about ten tables and is always crowded. The specialty here is lobster. 8 Theatinerstr. (phone: 221210). Expensive.

Käferschenke – This started out as a corner grocery store, worked itself up to one of Europe's largest delicatessens and Germany's biggest catering service, and now includes a popular restaurant upstairs over the sprawling store. You can get anything from homemade head cheese (*Presskopf*), to bass from the Mediterranean. Closed Sundays. 73 Prinzregentenstr. (phone: 41681). Expensive.

Sabitzer – A favorite of Munich's beautiful people, decorated all in white with turn-of-the-century art hung on the walls, this fine, small restaurant serves nouvelle cuisine. Closed Saturday afternoons and Sundays. Reservations advised. 21 Reitmorstr. (phone: 298584). Expensive.

Tantris – This three-star Michelin restaurant in Schwabing serves some of the best of modern, light French cuisine outside France. Closed Sundays as well as Saturday and Monday afternoons; also closed for 3 weeks after Pentecost. 7 Johann-Fichte-Str. (phone: 362061 or 362062). Expensive.

Vier Jahreszeiten (Four Seasons) – In the *Four Seasons* hotel, this restaurant is quiet and ultra elegant, and its delicious Bavarian cuisine is among the finest in Germany. If you try the *Auszug aus schwarzen Trüffeln* (essence of black truffles), you're sure to agree. Closed Saturday lunch, Mondays, and August. 17 Maximilianstr. (phone: 230390). Expensive.

Bistro Terrine – The latest culinary vogue in Munich is the bistro, and this one is in the middle of swinging Schwabing. Its continental cuisine is complemented by the heady Mediterranean atmosphere. Closed Sundays and holidays. 89 Amalienstr. (phone: 281780). Moderate.

Goldene Stadt – Bohemian dishes are served in the four adjoining dining rooms here. A photomural of a bridge over the Moldau in central Prague dominates the main dining room. Closed Sundays. 44 Oberanger (phone: 264382). Moderate.

Halali – Not far from Schwabing, this unusually reasonably priced restaurant serves quality nouvelle cuisine fare with a hearty Bavarian touch. Closed Saturday lunch and Sundays. 22 Schönfeldstr. (phone: 285909). Moderate.

Mifune – Ever since actor Toshiro Mifune opened this restaurant, it's been a must for lovers of Japanese food. Closed Sundays. 136 Ismaninger Str. (phone: 987572). Moderate.

Spatenhaus – This is a fine example of a typical Bavarian *Gaststätte* (inn), with its whitewashed walls, pine tables and chairs, and many cozy niches. A delicious dinner here might include roast duck, suckling pig, or hare with mushrooms in cream sauce; dessert could be the flaky apple strudel or crisp apple fritters. No reservations. 12 Residenzstr. (phone: 227841/2). Moderate.

Spöckmeier – This popular *Gasthaus* — which some say serves the best veal sausages in town — has two dining rooms: The vast, whitewashed and raftered hall downstairs bustles with shoppers and sightseers, and the smaller, paneled room upstairs hums with the quiet conversation of elegant drinkers. Closed Sundays in the summer. No reservations. 9 Rosenstr., just off Marienpl. (phone: 268088). Moderate.

Weisses Bräuhaus – Perhaps the most traditional of Munich's restaurants, this inn has been serving hearty food and wheat beer at the same site for over 400 years. A best bet is the roast pork with dumplings. No reservations. 10 Tal (phone: 299875). Moderate.

Zum Alten Markt – Just a stone's throw from the colorful Viktualienmarkt, this new downtown restaurant is a must for lovers of good but reasonably priced continental fare with an emphasis on fish and veal dishes. Closed Sundays. Reservations advised. 3 Dreifaltigkeitsplatz (phone: 299995). Moderate.

Bratwurst-Herzl – Around the corner from the Viktualienmarkt (see *Special Places*), this is one of the last truly Bavarian establishments in swinging Munich. Open for lunch only, but be seated by 11 AM, since this is very popular with Munichers. Closed Sundays. No reservations. 3 Heiliggeiststr. (phone: 226219). Inexpensive.

Donisl – A visit here is a Munich must: This centuries-old beer hall is where many Muenchners come for their daily beer and sausage ration, especially in the late morning. Next to city hall, the Neues Rathaus. Open daily. No reservations. 1 Weinstr., at Marienpl. (phone: 220184). Inexpensive.

Pfälzer Weinprobierstube – This tradition-laden wine cellar, in the former royal Residenz (see *Special Places*), features vintages from the Palatinate (Pfälz). The hearty food is also from that former Bavarian region. Open daily. No reservations. 1 Residenzstr. (phone: 225628). Inexpensive.

Weinstadl – Wine reigns supreme here, as does Munich *Gemütlichkeit*. It is in one of the city's oldest and most beautiful private buildings, built in the Gothic style in 1550. Open from 4 PM to midnight; closed Sundays. No reservations. 5 Burgstr. (phone: 221047). Inexpensive.

NAPLES

Naples, Gothic and baroque under an azure sky, intellectual capital of the Mezzogiorno, and Italy's third most populated city, with nearly 1.5 million inhabitants, has often been described as one of the world's most beautiful seaports. Indeed, the magnificent Bay of Naples has long been lauded by its many illustrious visitors for its gently curving shoreline and palm-lined seaside avenues, its mild climate, sunny beaches, and romantic islands.

But Naples has always had a darker side. The brooding Mt. Vesuvius, "its terror and its pride," ever hovering over the city, buried neighboring Pompeii and Herculaneum when it erupted in AD 79. And the eerie Phlegrean Fields (Campi Flegrei), a steaming volcanic area just north of here whose violent beauty inspired both Homer and Virgil, was regarded by the ancients as the entrance to the underworld. More recently, the earthquake that devastated southern Italy in November 1980 took a tragic toll even in Naples, adding yet another major problem to the city's permanent ills of unemployment, crime, and disease.

For some visitors today, Naples is a disappointment. The old quarter is among the most densely populated areas in the world; infant mortality and unemployment rates here are the highest in Italy — almost a third of the city's labor force is unemployed, and another estimated 40,000 persons derive their livelihood from smuggling. When a cholera outbreak in 1973 revealed that Naples had no sewers and was living on a beautiful but poisoned bay, "See Naples and die," once a popular saying beckoning visitors to the seductive charms of the city, suddenly acquired a morbid and foreboding significance. But the poor of Naples survive with a surprising stoicism, and the people themselves are one of the city's attractions, laughing off their many problems, helping each other with an extraordinary sense of warmth and humanity — they are a people incapable of hatred, of any kind of discrimination, yet strongly emotional, sensitive, full of fantasy. Just remember the best movies of the postwar school of Italian neo-realism, directed by Roberto Rossellini, Vittorio De Sica, and Francesco Rosi, or the theatrical masterpieces of the famed Eduardo De Filippo, the voluptuous figure of Sophia Loren representing the Neapolitan woman — madonna, mother, and *puttana* (whore) all in one.

Watch them live: Naples is like a theater of life. Stroll along Via Caracciolo and see the fishermen pulling in their nets, oblivious to the traffic behind them; buy lemons and oranges or sulfur water from men and women who transact their business across 17th-century marble tabletops; give in to the importuning of pizza vendors hawking their wares; or, when the jostling of the small, crowded streets becomes too much to bear, retire to a table in the elegant Galleria Umberto I or to the old *Caffè Gambrinus* on Via Chiaia and watch well-dressed Neapolitans socialize over an afternoon coffee or *aperitivo.*

Naples is also famous for its music, its festivals, its colorful arts. Neapolitan popular songs are, short of operatic arias, the best-known tunes to have come out of Italy; anyone who can strum a guitar or a mandolin knows at least one, and nearly everyone can sing along, at least the refrain. In the 17th and 18th centuries, the works of a Neapolitan school of composers — Alessandro Scarlatti was its leader — were just as well known; Pergolesi, Paisiello, and Cimarosa drew capacity crowds. The city's opera house, *Teatro San Carlo,* built in 1737, remains one of the world's finest. A Neapolitan school of painting, characterized by realism and warm colors, flourished in the 18th and 19th centuries. In the 18th century, too, the famous Capodimonte porcelain factory was turning out highly elaborate pieces for members of the royal court, while less exalted folk artists were raising the making of nativity scenes, or Christmas cribs, into an art. The shepherds and angels of many an *ignoto Napoletano* (unknown Neapolitan) live on in museums.

The city that was to spawn so much natural talent was founded as a Greek colony, probably in the 7th century BC, and was first called Parthenope, later Neapolis. Little remains of its earliest period. Then, along with the rest of the Italian peninsula, it became part of the great Roman Empire, and its intensely green countryside and sunny shores were soon studded with palatial villas of wealthy Romans who chose to spend the winters in Naples's milder climate.

But the tranquillity of the Roman period came to an end with the fall of the empire, and Naples sank into the abyss of the Dark Ages, as did all of Italy. The city came into its own again under the French rulers of the House of Anjou, who made it the capital of their Angevin kingdom of southern Italy in the 13th century and continued its progress under the Catalonian rulers of the House of Aragon, who took over in 1442. Then, in 1503, Naples (with Sicily) became a part of Spain, ruled for more than two centuries by Spanish viceroys who exploited the Italian provinces for the benefit of the Spanish treasury; so heavily taxed were the commoners (nobles and clergy were exempt) that in 1647 they rose up, led by Masaniello, but the revolution was crushed. After a short period under Austrian rule, it was the turn of the Bourbons, who arrived in 1734 and established the Kingdom of the Two Sicilies, with Naples as the capital. Its ancient dignity restored, Naples became one of Europe's major cities, attracting leaders in art, music, and literature until the unification of Italy in 1860. Economic and political problems gradually diminished its prestige, however, and damage from World War II dealt a severe blow to an already sick economy.

Today, thanks to a busy port, Naples is an important industrial and commercial center. It is a city both wise and violent, religious and pagan, magical and dirty, old and new. It attracts thieves, tourists, artists, and lovers of beauty with a contagious gaiety and exuberant, if chaotic, vitality. Its wealth of historical monuments; proximity to the Amalfi Coast, Capri, and the archaeological treasures of Pompeii and Herculaneum; and the magnificent — if somewhat tarnished — splendors of the romantic Bay of Naples, make it one of the world's great cities and a perennial tourist attraction.

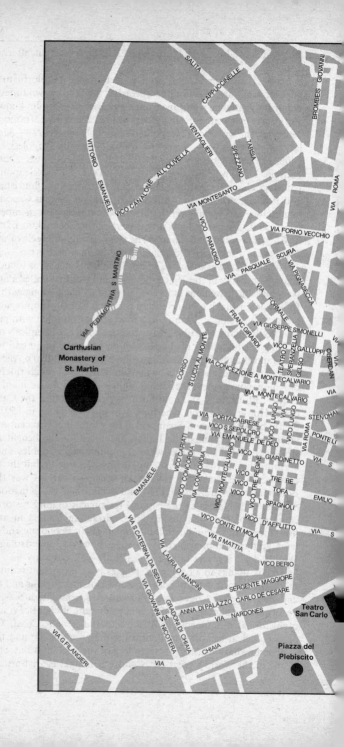

NAPLES AT-A-GLANCE

SEEING THE CITY: Panoramic views of Naples and the bay are at every turn. Within the city, the outstanding view is from Room 25 of the *Certosa di San Martino* (Carthusian Monastery of St. Martin), now a museum. Depending on the weather and the visibility, however, the most spectacular view is from Mt. Vesuvius, some 15 miles (18 km) southeast of Naples. For more information on both these vantage points, see *Special Places,* below.

SPECIAL PLACES: To make sightseeing easier, think of Naples as divided into the following sections: In the area roughly between Piazza Municipio and Piazza del Plebiscito, there are monumental buildings and relatively wide-open spaces. The old quarter is near narrow Spacca-Napoli Street (the classic photos of streets strung with washing are taken here) and the historic center is to the northeast. Farther inland is Naples on the hills, the Vomero being the principal hill and an elegant residential district. To the west of the Piazza del Plebiscito area is Naples by the bay. Where the workaday port ends, a lovely promenade begins along the shore before the port of Santa Lucia and extends as far as another port area, Mergellina. Most museums in Naples are open 9 AM to 2 PM Tuesdays through Saturdays, and 9 AM to 1 PM Sundays and holidays.

DOWNTOWN

Castel Nuovo (New Castle) – This landmark on the Neapolitan waterfront, also called the Castel Angioino (Angevin Castle) or Maschio Angioino, was built in the late 13th century by Charles I of Anjou, who modeled it on the castle at Angers. In the mid-15th century, Alphonse I of Aragon made substantial alterations. The triumphal arch sandwiched between two towers at the entry celebrates his entrance into Naples in 1443 and is an early example of Renaissance art in Naples. Inside the courtyard, the doorway to the Chapel of St. Barbara (or the Palatine Chapel), the only part of the castle remaining from Angevin times, is noteworthy, but the castle proper is not open to visitors. Piazza Municipio.

Palazzo Reale (Royal Palace) – Built in the early 17th century by Domenico Fontana for the Spanish viceroys, later enlarged and restored, this became the home of the Bourbon Kings of Naples and was then inhabited from time to time by the Kings of Italy. The niches on the façade contain statues of eight famous kings of the various dynasties that ruled Naples, including Charles I of Anjou, Alphonse I of Aragon, and Victor Emmanuel II of Italy. The palace is now a museum whose rooms contain original Bourbon furnishings, paintings, statues, and porcelain. Closed Mondays. Admission charge. Piazza del Plebiscito (phone: 413888).

Piazza del Plebiscito – This vast semicircle cut off on one side by the Palazzo Reale is the center of public life in Naples. Directly opposite the palace is the Church of San Francesco di Paola, a copy of the Pantheon in Rome, built by order of Ferdinand I of Bourbon in the late 18th century. Equestrian statues in the center of the square are of Ferdinand (by Canova) and Charles III of Bourbon.

Teatro San Carlo – Italy's second most famous opera house is just off Piazza del Plebiscito and 40 years older than *La Scala.* Built under Charles of Bourbon in 1737 and inaugurated on the feast day of St. Charles Borromeo (whence its name), it was destroyed by fire in 1816 and thoroughly rebuilt in neo-classic style within 6 months, with Ionic columns, niches, and bas-reliefs on the outside and a fresco of Apollo and the Muses on the ceiling of the sumptuous auditorium — which seats 3,000 and has perfect acoustics. *San Carlo* audiences were the first ever to hear Bellini's *La Sonnambula,* Donizetti's *Lucia di Lammermoor,* and many other great works. Those not attending a performance can tour the theater in the morning, by prior arrangement. Closed Mondays. Via San Carlo (phone: 797-2370).

Galleria Umberto I – Across the street from *San Carlo,* this is the perfect place to sit down for a *caffè* or an ice cream. The Victorian arcade of glass and steel, topped with a cupola, was built from 1887 to 1890, and is younger than the one in Milan.

Chiesa di Sant'Anna dei Lombardi (Church of St. Anne of the Lombards) – This church was built in the 15th century and rebuilt in the 17th century. It is best known for its Renaissance sculptures, particularly for the eight life-size terra cotta figures of the *Pietà* (1492) by Guido Mazzoni — extremely realistic and rather eerie when seen from the main part of the church (it's in a chapel to the right at the far end). Via Monteoliveto.

Chiesa di Santa Chiara (Church of St. Clare) – The church of the Poor Clares was built by order of Sancia of Majorca, wife of Robert I of Anjou, in the early 14th century. From the beginning, it was the church of the Neapolitan nobility. By the 18th century, it was covered with baroque decoration, but following serious damage in World War II, it has been rebuilt in its original Provençal-Gothic style. Be sure to see the 14th-century tomb of Robert of Anjou behind the altar and then go out to see the adjoining Chiostro delle Clarisse (Cloister of the Poor Clares). This unique 18th-century cloister is a lovely bower of greenery and flowers studded with columns and lined with seats entirely covered with majolica tiles — a colorful, welcome surprise. Via Benedetto Croce.

Chiesa del Gesù Nuovo – Just across the square from Santa Chiara on land surrounding the Palazzo Sanseverino. The interior of this late-16th-century church is full of baroque marblework and painting. The unusual façade was originally built in the 15th century for the palace. Piazza del Gesù Nuovo.

Chiesa di San Lorenzo Maggiore (Church of St. Lawrence Major) – One of the most important medieval churches in Naples, it was begun in the late 13th century by French architects, who did the polygonal Gothic apse, and was finished in the next century by local architects. Boccaccio fell in love with Fiammetta in this church in 1334 and Petrarch, who was living in the adjoining monastery, came here to pray during a terrible storm in 1345. Piazza San Gaetano.

Duomo (Cathedral) – The cathedral of Naples is dedicated to the city's patron saint, San Gennaro. It was built by the Angevins (in the late 13th and early 14th centuries) on the site of a previous basilica dedicated to Santa Stefania, which in its turn had been built on the foundations of a Roman temple dedicated to Apollo. It also incorporates a smaller basilica dating from the 5th century and dedicated to Santa Restituta. Rebuilt several times, the Duomo's 19th-century façade still sports 15th-century doorways. It contains the famous Chapel of San Gennaro (third chapel on the right), a triumph of 17th-century baroque art built in fulfillment of a vow made by Neapolitans for the passing of a plague. (The Latin inscription notes that the chapel is consecrated to the saint for his having saved the city not only from plague but also from hunger, war, and the fires of Vesuvius, by virtue of his miraculous blood.) Two vials of San Gennaro's dried blood are stored in a reliquary in the chapel, and twice a year, in May and September, all of Naples — or as many people as the church and the street in front can hold — gathers to await the miracle of the liquefaction of the blood (see *Special Events*). If the miracle happens, all is well with the city. Via del Duomo.

Museo Archeologico Nazionale (National Archaeological Museum) – One of the most important museums in the world dedicated to Greco-Roman antiquity. Among its precious artworks are sculptures collected by Pope Paul III of the Farnese family during 16th-century excavations of the ruins of Rome, including two huge statues found at the Baths of Caracalla: the *Farnese Hercules,* a Greek copy of a bronze original by Lysippus, and the *Farnese Bull,* a Roman copy of a Hellenistic bronze, carved from a single block of marble. The museum is also the repository of art and artifacts removed from Pompeii and Herculaneum since the 18th century. Most impressive of these are the exquisite mosaics from Pompeii and the bronzes from the Villa dei Papiri at Herculaneum, especially the water carriers (or dancers) and the two athletes. Other items removed from Pompeii and Herculaneum include silverware and glassware, combs, mirrors, and other toiletry articles, some furniture, and foodstuffs, such as carbonized bread, olives, grapes, onions, figs, and dates. Two other important collections to see in this 16th-century palace — which was first a barracks and then the seat of the university until the Bourbon King of Naples turned it into a museum in 1777 — are the Santangelo collection of ancient coins and the Borgia collection of Egyptian and Etruscan art. Closed Mondays. Admission charge for those between the ages of 18 and 60. Piazza Museo (phone: 440166).

Catacombe di San Gennaro (Catacombs of St. Januarius) – The remains of San Gennaro lay in these catacombs from the 5th to the 9th century. On two levels, they date from the 2nd century and probably began as the tomb of a noble family that was later donated to the Christian community as a burial place. They are important for their early Christian wall paintings. Guided visits take place on weekend mornings. Admission charge. Off Via di Capodimonte, past the church of the Madre del Buon Consiglio.

Museo e Gallerie Nazionali di Capodimonte (Capodimonte Museum and Picture Gallery) – One of Italy's best collections of paintings from the 14th through the 16th century is displayed in the grandiose 18th-century palace of a former royal estate on the hills in the northeastern part of the city. A Simone Martini panel (1317) of Robert of Anjou being crowned King of Naples is one of the museum's treasures; other masters represented are Bellini, Masaccio, Botticelli, Correggio, and Titian, among whose portraits of the Farnese family is a well-known one of Pope Paul III. The royal apartments on the first floor include a marvelous parlor, the Salottino di Maria Amalia, completely built and decorated in Capodimonte ceramics (some of which were shattered in the 1980 earthquake). In the park surrounding the palace a wedding party is often having pictures taken — it's one of the Neapolitans' favorite backgrounds. Closed Mondays. Admission charge for those between the ages of 18 and 60. Parco di Capodimonte (phone: 741-0881).

Certosa di San Martino (Carthusian Monastery and National Museum of St. Martin) – Now a museum, this enormous monastery founded by the Angevin dynasty is beautifully situated on the Vomero Hill, next to an Angevin fortress, the Castel Sant'Elmo. The monastery was renovated in the 16th and 17th centuries (in the latter period by Cosimo Fanzago), so it is today a monument to the baroque. The church immediately to the left as you enter is lavishly done in baroque inlay of variously colored marbles and stones (see, too, the rooms behind the altar, including the one to the left with the intricate inlay of wood). In the museum the marvelous view from the belvedere of room 25 is said to have inspired the saying "See Naples and die." The museum contains a collection of 19th-century Neapolitan painting, a naval section, a collection of memorabilia from the kingdom of Naples, and some striking 18th- and 19th-century *presepi,* or nativity scenes. The most famous is the Presepe Cuciniello, a room-size installation with countless figures and particularly graceful angels. Another *presepe* fits in an eggshell. Closed Mondays. Admission charge. Via Tito Angelini (phone: 377005).

Porto di Santa Lucia e il Lungomare (Santa Lucia Port and the Waterfront) – One of the best-known Neapolitan songs has immortalized this tiny port abob with picturesque fishing and pleasure boats. It is formed by a jetty that leads out from the mainland to a small island entirely occupied by the Borgo Marinaro, a so-called fishing village now populated largely with restaurants, and the Castel dell'Ovo (Egg Castle, not to be confused with the *Castel Nuovo,* described above). The fortress dates from the 12th century, but monks lived here even earlier, and in Roman times a patrician villa occupied the site. Santa Lucia is the focal point of seaside Naples: Via Nazario Sauro approaches it from the east; Via Partenope passes in front of it; and Via Caracciolo leads away from it to the west. The three together constitute Naples's *lungomare,* a broad promenade along the water that is *the* place in Naples to take the early evening *passeggiata* (stroll) and watch the sun go down. For at least half a mile of its length, Via Caracciolo is backed by the greenery of the Villa Comunale, or public park, which is stuffed with life — young lovers hugging, kids playing ball, grandparents taking the air with the grandchildren, fathers renting miniature cars for mere toddlers who are learning to become Neapolitan drivers. Ice cream is consumed by all.

ENVIRONS

Campi-Flegrei (Phlegrean Fields) – Hot springs and sulfurous gases rise from this dark, violent volcanic area that extends west of Naples from Capo Posillipo to Capo Miseno, along the Gulf of Pozzuoli. Its name comes from the Greek, meaning "burning," and it is an area as rich in archaeological remains as in geophysical phenomena. The remains of the Greek colony of Cuma, founded in the 8th century BC, are about 12 miles (20 km) west of Naples (closed Mondays; admission charge), as are remains of Roman baths at Baia (closed Mondays; admission charge). In Sophia Loren's hometown, Pozzuoli (8 mi/13 km west), the third largest amphitheater in Italy, built when the town was a major port in Roman times, can be visited (closed Mondays; admission charge). Also in Pozzuoli is a Roman temple, partially submerged in water, that reveals the effects of bradyseism, or "slow earthquake," to which the whole area is subject; less or more of the pillars is visible as the earth rises and falls. Lakes — such as Lago d'Averno and Lago Miseno — have formed in the craters of extinct volcanoes in the Campi Flegrei, but the Solfatara crater just north of Pozzuoli is merely dormant (its last eruption was in the 12th century). Full of steaming fumaroles and containing the remains of a Roman spa, it is open daily (admission charge). Pozzuoli is the last stop of the *metropolitana* from Piazza Garibaldi in Naples; Baia and Cuma are stops of the Ferrovia Cumana suburban train line leaving from Piazza Montesanto.

Vesuvio (Mount Vesuvius) – This still-active volcano about 15 miles (24 km) southeast of Naples last erupted in 1944 and has averaged one eruption every 35 years over the past 300. Its most famous eruption was the one that buried Pompeii and Herculaneum in AD 79 (see *Campania and the Amalfi Coast* in DIRECTIONS). That explosion came from Monte Somma, 3,713 feet high, one of the volcano's two present summits; some 200 years later, another summit, Monte Nuovo, 4,189 feet high, formed, and this is the one that is now called Mount Vesuvius. There is no longer a chair lift to the top of Monte Nuovo, but the ascent can still be made on foot in the company of the obligatory guide, who leads small groups along the path that follows the edge of the crater, from which there are views down into the enormous cavity or out toward the sea and the surrounding towns. All that is visible of Vesuvius's cataclysmic power, however, are the vapors rising from fumaroles, and the guide occasionally descends a bit into the crater for a better look at these vents. To reach Vesuvius by public transportation, take the Circumvesuviana railway (Napoli–Barra–Torre del Greco–Torre Annunziata line) from Stazione Circumvesuviana on Corso Garibaldi (it is reached by means of the down escalator from the main train station in Naples). Get off at Herculaneum (Ercolano) or Pugliano, then take a bus to the *stazione inferiore,* where a guide may be hired. Don't bother going on an overcast day.

■**EXTRA SPECIAL:** No stay in Naples is complete without a sunny drive up the famed promontory of Posillipo, a few miles southwest of the center, perhaps culminating in an alfresco lunch at Marechiaro overlooking the southern end of the Bay of Naples. The road from Mergellina climbs past villas and fragrant gardens, becoming Via Nuova di Posillipo, which was begun by order of Murat, King of Naples, and completed in 1830. Don't miss the view of Cape Posillipo (from Via Ferdinando Russo just past Piazza Salvatore di Giacomo) before continuing up Via Nuova di Posillipo to the winding Via Salvatore di Giacomo, which ends at Marechiaro, a most picturesque fishing village built high above the sea. It was made famous by a song of the same name written by Salvatore di Giacomo, the first line of which is inscribed in the wall of an old house overlooking the water, marking the window celebrated in the song. On the way down, stop at the Parco della Rimembranza for spectacular views of the Bay of Naples on one side and the Bay of Pozzuoli on the other.

SOURCES AND RESOURCES

TOURIST INFORMATION: For general information, brochures, and maps of Naples and its environs, contact the Ente Provinciale per il Turismo (EPT), 10/A Via Partenope (phone: 406289); branches or booths are at the Stazione Centrale, the Stazione di Mergellina, and at the Aeroporto di Capodichino. The Azienda Autonoma di Turismo di Napoli, or local tourist office, is based in the Palazzo Reale at Piazza del Plebiscito (phone: 418744), but it has branches, including one at Piazza del Gesù Nuovo and one at the Castel dell'Ovo. The *Associazione Alberghi per la Gioventù* (Association of Youth Hostels) is at 9 Via del Chiostro (phone: 551-3151).

The US Consulate is at Piazza della Repubblica (phone: 660966).

Local Coverage – Among its other brochures, the AAST puts out an interesting one entitled *Naples — The Old City: A Stratified Multiple Itinerary Map* that traces four itineraries through the historic center (roughly the area between Piazza del Gesù Nuovo and the Duomo), each route corresponding to a period in Neapolitan art: medieval, Renaissance, baroque, and rococo. The office also publishes a useful booklet, *Qui Napoli,* which is distributed monthly to the better hotels. Listings are in Italian and English. Another good monthly guide is *Napoli Top,* available in bars, hotels and at newsstands. The Neapolitans' daily newspaper is *Il Mattino.*

Telephone – The area code for Naples is 081.

CLIMATE AND CLOTHES: June and September are the best months to visit Naples. Summer is hot, with average highs of 84F (29C). Winters, though milder than in more northerly parts of Italy, can be rainy. Temperatures stay well above freezing. Light summer clothes are in order from May through September. Women may want a light wrap for evenings (and for covering bare shoulders when visiting churches). A raincoat or light overcoat is often handy in winter.

GETTING AROUND: Many of the major sights are easily accessible by foot. For others, such as the Parco di Capodimonte and sights on the Vomero, alternate means of transportation are desirable. Do everything you can to avoid driving in the city: Neapolitan traffic jams belong in the *Guinness Book of World Records.*

Airport – Capodichino Airport serves mostly domestic and some international flights. A taxi ride from downtown takes anywhere from 15 to 45 minutes, depending on the traffic, and costs about $22; from the airport to downtown, the fare is double the meter. Night and holiday rides cost extra, as does baggage; ask to see the *tabella* (fare table). There is no special airport bus, but bus #14 from the main train station, Stazione Centrale, stops at the airport. The trip takes 30 minutes to an hour depending on traffic. Tickets cost about 50¢ and must be purchased in advance at a tobacco shop or newsstand.

Boats – Ferries and hydrofoils for Capri, Ischia, and Procida leave from the Molo Beverello, in front of Piazza Municipio and the Castel Nuovo, or from Mergellina's Porto Sannazaro.

Bus and Tram – Main routes and schedules are listed in the supplement to the telephone directory, *Tutto Città.* Tickets cost 600 lire (about 50¢) and must be bought in advance at a tobacco shop or newsstand.

Car Rental – Major international firms are on Via Partenope: *Avis,* 32 Via Partenope (phone: 407333); *Europcar,* 38 Via Partenope (phone: 401454); *Hertz,* 29 Via Partenope (phone: 400400); *InterRent,* 14 Via Partenope (phone: 422332). In addition, most of these companies have branches elsewhere in the city, including the railway station at Piazza Garibaldi and Capodichino Airport. *Maggiore* is at 92 Via Cervantes (phone: 321900) and the railway station. Only a few gas stations are open at night. Check with your hotel or see the listings in *Qui Napoli* or *Napoli Top.*

Funicular – Four funicular lines connect lower-lying parts of Naples to neighborhoods on the hills. Of the three that go to the Vomero, the Funicolare Centrale, from Via Toledo to Piazza Fuga, and the Funicolare di Montesanto, from Piazza Montesanto to Via Morghen, are useful for visiting the Certosa di San Martino. The fourth funicular connects the Mergellina area to the Posillipo area.

Subway – The *metropolitana* runs from Napoli Gianturco to Pozzuoli Solfatara, making useful stops at the Stazione Centrale, Piazza Cavour (near the *National Archaeological Museum*), Piazza Montesanto and Piazza Amedeo (near funiculars), Mergellina, Campi Flegrei, and elsewhere en route.

Taxi – Taxis can be hailed while they cruise or may be picked up at any cabstand. For a radio-dispatched taxi call 364444 or 364340. Do not use unmetered taxis, and before you get in, verify that your driver can make change at the end of the ride.

Train – Naples's main train station is Stazione Centrale, Piazza Garibaldi (phone: 553-4188). Trains to Herculaneum, Pompeii, and Sorrento, operated by the suburban railway, Ferrovia Circemvesuviana, leave from the nearby Stazione Circumvesuviana, Corso Garibaldi (phone: 779-2444), reached by the down escalator from Stazione Centrale. Trains to Campi Flegrei points, operated by the another suburban railway, Ferrovia Cumana, leave from Piazza Montesanto (phone: 551-3328).

 SPECIAL EVENTS: Twice a year (on the Saturday before the first Sunday in May and on September 19), Neapolitans crowd into the Duomo of San Gennaro and pray for the *Miracle,* the liquefying of the dried blood of their patron saint that is kept in two vials in a chapel of the church. The miracle is supposed to have first occurred on the hands of a bishop transporting the body after San Gennaro's martyrdom in Pozzuoli on September 19, 305, and it has been happening regularly since the first recorded recurrence in 1389 — regularly, but not *always.* The event is something of a mass fortune telling, because when it fails, some disaster is expected to befall the city — in the past it might have been plague, in the future it could be Vesuvius. The miracle lets Naples know that the saint is still with them, and nowhere is the atmosphere more alive with anticipation than in the chapel downstairs, where San Gennaro's bones are kept and the people plead for a sign. Other important festivals celebrate the feast of *Santa Maria del Carmine* on July 16, and the *Madonna di Piedigrotta,* which lasts several days in early September.

 MUSEUMS: In addition to those mentioned in *Special Places,* a number of other museums and churches are impressive.

Aquarium – One of the oldest, if not *the* oldest, in Europe (1872), housing some 200 species of Mediterranean marine life, all collected from the Bay of Naples. Villa Comunale (phone: 583-3111).

Cappella Sansevero (Sansevero Chapel) – The funerary chapel of the Sangro family, containing the *Veiled Christ* by Giuseppe Sammartino and many other 18th-century sculptures. 19 Via Francesco De Sanctis.

Chiesa di San Domenico Maggiore (Church of St. Dominic Major) – A 13th-century church, frequently restored, containing the famous crucifix of St. Thomas Aquinas (who lived and taught in the adjoining monastery) and paintings by Titian, Luca Giordano, Solimena, Simone Martini, and others. Piazza San Domenico.

Chiesa di San Gregorio Armeno (Church of St. Gregory of Armenia) – A baroque church worth a visit for its famous nativity scene. Via San Gregorio Armeno.

Chiesa di San Paolo Maggiore (Church of St. Paul Major) – A church of the late 16th century, wonderfully Neapolitan baroque in style, with paintings by Stanzione, Solimena, and Paolo de Matteis. Piazza San Gaetano.

Chiesa di Santa Maria del Carmine (Church of Santa Maria del Carmine) – Built in the 12th century and substantially reconstructed between 1283 and 1300, this church is home to a venerated image of the Madonna. An adjacent tower is the scene of a mock burning and other celebrations on the saint's day, July 16 (see *Special Events*). Piazza del Carmine.

Museo Civico Filangieri (Filangieri Civic Museum) – Arms, furniture, porcelain, costumes, and paintings, housed in the 15th-century Palazzo Cuomo. Open weekdays 9AM to 2PM; Sundays and holidays 9AM to 1PM. Admission charge. 288 Via Duomo (phone: 203175).

Museo Duca di Martina (Duke of Martina Museum) – Ivories, enamels, china, and majolica, European and Oriental, are displayed in the Villa Floridiana, a small neo-classical palace in the Vomero section, with splendid gardens and a panoramic view of the bay. Closed Mondays. Admission charge. Via Cimarosa (phone: 377315).

Museo Principe Aragona Pignatelli Cortes (Prince of Aragon Pignatelli Cortes Museum) – A collection of 19th-century furniture and china, plus a coach museum in the park's pavilion, with French and English carriages. Riviera di Chiaia (phone: 669675).

SHOPPING: For shopping purposes, Naples is commonly divided into a *zona elegante* (elegant zone) and a *zona commerciale* (commercial zone). The most fashionable shopping area, the *zona elegante,* is centered around Piazza dei Martiri, along Via Calabritto, Via Filangieri, Via dei Mille, and Via Chiaia. The latter leads to the more commercial zone between Piazza Trieste e Trento and Piazza Dante along Via Roma (also called Via Toledo after the viceroy who opened it in 1536) and toward the main railroad station along Corso Umberto I. Ceramics and porcelains have been sold here since the Bourbon kings founded the Capodimonte school and factory in the 18th century. Although original Capodimonte pieces are collectors' items and Capodimonte-style figurines are produced by companies all over Italy, the production of more traditional ceramics, in popular folk styles, continues to thrive in Naples and the vicinity. Another important product of the area is coral, much of which, it is said, is now imported from Southeast Asia but handcrafted nevertheless in nearby Torre del Greco, where there are several large factories and showrooms (*Giovanni Apa,* in Torre del Greco, just off the Naples-Pompeii Highway, is one source of coral and cameos). Neapolitan street markets are very colorful (always beware of pickpockets and *scippatori,* who speed by on motorbikes, grabbing bags and gold chains from shoulders and necks as they go). Among the markets are *Resina,* for new or used clothing and fabrics; *Spacca-Napoli,* for books and silver objects; *Antignano,* for fabrics, household goods, and food; and, at Christmas, *San Liborio,* for traditional Neapolitan nativity figures. Antiques shops are found mostly in the area around Piazza dei Martiri and Via Santa Maria di Costantinopoli.

Baracca e Burattini – Opposite the entrance to the archaeological museum, an artisan shop selling masks, marionettes, and lovely dolls. 2 Piazza del Museo.

Berisio – Antique books. 28 Via Port'Alba.

Chiurazzi – Bronze reproductions of sculptures in the archaeological museum, in all sizes. 271 Via ai Ponti Rossi.

Coin – A good department store. 10 Via Scarlatti.

Ospedale delle Bambole – Handcrafted dolls. 81 Via San Biagio dei Librai.

La Rinascente – Another good department store. 343 Via Roma.

Il Sagittario – Curious leather goods (masks, sculptures). 10/A Via Santa Chiara.

La Soffitta – Hand-painted ceramics. 12 Via Benedetto Croce.

 SPORTS AND FITNESS: Most sports facilities belong to private clubs, so check with the concierge of your hotel about which may be currently open to the public.

Fitness Centers – *Athletic Club* (men) and *Silhouette* (women), 21 Via Fiorentini (phone: 313160 or 313342).

Jogging – One good place to run is the *lungomare* (seafront promenade) along Via Caracciolo and Via Partenope from the port of Santa Lucia to the Mergellina. The Villa Comunale, the park behind Via Caracciolo, is another good spot.

Soccer – From September to May, *Napoli* plays at the *Stadio San Paolo,* Piazzale Vincenzo Tecchio, Fuorigrotta (phone: 615623 or 619205). Its capacity is 100,000 fierce fans.

Swimming – The polluted Bay of Naples is not the best spot for water sports, but there are fine seaside resorts on the nearby islands and along the Amalfi Coast.

Tennis – There are public courts at several tennis clubs, including the *Sporting Club Virgilio,* 6 Via Tito Lucrezio Caro (phone: 769-5261); the *Tennis Club Vomero,* 8 Via Rossini (phone: 658912); and the *Tennis Club Napoli,* Villa Comunale, Via Caracciolo (phone: 384801).

 THEATER: Even those who speak Italian probably won't readily understand the Neapolitan dialect, but just for color and sheer vitality, take in a performance by the renowned *Repertory Group of Eduardo de Filippo* at the *Teatro San Ferdinando,* Piazza Teatro San Ferdinando (phone: 444500). A fine place to sample Neapolitan music and folklore is the *Circolo della Stampa* (reserve seats through your concierge). Other theatrical groups perform at the *Politeama,* Via Monte di Dio (phone: 401643); *Cilea,* Via San Domenico, at Corso Europa (phone: 656265); *Sannazaro,* 157 Via Chiaia (phone: 411723); and *Bracco,* 40 Via Tarsia (phone: 347005).

 MUSIC: The season at the *Teatro San Carlo,* Via San Carlo (box office closed Mondays; phone: 797-2370 or 797-2111), one of the finest opera houses in the world, generally runs from December through most of June. Then, from mid-September through mid-November, the theater is the scene of a series of symphonic concerts, the *Concerti d'Autunno* (Autumn Concerts). The *Associazione Alessandro Scarlatti* performs at Piazza dei Martiri 58 (phone: 406011). Still more symphony and chamber concerts, by groups such as the *Accademia Musicale Napoletana* and others, are scheduled frequently at the *Auditorium RAI-TV,* Via Guglielmo Marconi (phone: 610122); in the church or cloisters of Santa Chiara, Via Benedetto Croce (phone: 207697 or 320582); and in numerous other churches about town. In the summer, concerts are also held in the gardens at Capodimonte.

NIGHTCLUBS AND NIGHTLIFE: Like most port towns, Naples has a number of seedy bars and rip-off joints to be avoided. *Harry's Bar,* behind the *Excelsior* at 11 Via Lucilio (phone: 407810), is the spot for a quiet drink or a late dinner in an elegant setting. *Il Gabbiano,* also near the principal hotels at 26 Via Partenope, is a piano bar that serves late snacks (phone: 411666). The newest and most elegant nightclub in town is the *Virgilio,* 6 Via Tito Lucrezio Caro (phone: 769-5261), up on the exquisite Posillipo Hill, one of the poshest areas in Naples. Another swanky nightspot is *Rosolino,* 5-7 Via Nazario Sauro (phone: 415873), which is also a piano bar and restaurant. Worth looking into are *Chez Moi,* Parco Margherita 13; *Boomerang* on Via Giotto; *My Way,* Via Cappella Vecchia; *Casablanca* at 101 Via Petrarca; and *Villa Scipione,* 4 Via Scipione Capece.

BEST IN TOWN

 CHECKING IN: An expensive hotel in Naples will charge from $130 to $200 a night for a double room, with the *Excelsior* starting at about $160 and going up to more than $300; moderately priced hotels range from $90 to $130; and in the inexpensive category you'll be charged $40 to $90. All telephone numbers are in the 081 area code unless otherwise indicated.

Excelsior – Naples's only truly deluxe hotel, part of the reliable CIGA chain, it dominates the port of Santa Lucia, with terraced seaside rooms overlooking the 12th-century Castel dell'Ovo, the old fishing village of Borgo Marinaro, and the whole bay. The *Casanova Grill* takes some prizes, too (see *Eating Out*). There are 138 air conditioned rooms and a garage nearby. 48 Via Partenope (phone: 417111). Very expensive.

Britannique – Offering Swiss management and efficiency, it's hospitable and very clean. Most of the 86 rooms in this old converted villa are large, and since it's set on a hillside up and back from the waterfront, most of them have attractive views. 133 Corso Vittorio Emanuele (phone: 660933). Expensive.

Miramare – Also conveniently located, with the added attraction of the waterfront, this hotel is reputable, comfortable, and small (26 rooms). It has recently been renovated and upgraded. Although it has no restaurant, there is a lovely breakfast terrace, and it is very near *La Cantinella* (see *Eating Out*). 24 Via Nazario Sauro (phone: 416675). Expensive.

Royal – Another hotel on the Santa Lucia waterfront, this one is Naples's biggest (300 rooms). It's modern and busy, and it has a rooftop pool, garage, and air conditioning. 38 Via Partenope (phone: 400244). Expensive.

Vesuvio – Close to the *Excelsior,* Naples's second hotel also faces the picturesque port of Santa Lucia. It has 174 rooms, good baths, a decor ranging from period style to modern, a garage, and air conditioning. 45 Via Partenope (phone: 417044). Expensive.

Paradiso – The breathtaking panoramic view of the entire Bay of Naples, seen from the front bedrooms and the roof terrace, make this hotel particularly appealing. 11 Via Catullo (phone 660233). Expensive to moderate.

Mediterraneo – This recently renovated hotel has a convenient location in the commercial center of town, behind Piazza Municipio, but it's not very romantic. Garage and air conditioning; more than 250 rooms. Via Nuova Ponte di Tappia (phone: 551-2240). Moderate.

San Germano – A few miles drive from the center of Naples, it's in rather nondescript surroundings at the crossroads for the *Ippodromo di Agnano* racecourse. The new management has given a facelift to this efficient hotel with some 100 pleasant rooms (each with TV set and air conditioning), a lovely garden, swimming pool, tennis courts, and a garage. 41 Via Beccadelli (phone: 7605422). Moderate.

Le Fontane al Mare – Nicely located and a very good value, this hotel has 21 rooms, but no restaurant. 14 Via N. Tommaseo (phone: 416354). Inexpensive.

Rex – A reliable family-style hotel in the Santa Lucia quarter, with 40 rooms but no restaurant. 12 Via Palepoli (phone: 416388). Inexpensive.

EATING OUT: While Italian food is not all pasta and pizza, both originated in Naples and are a staple of Southern Italy. Here pasta is almost always eaten as a first course at lunch, while it is usually replaced at the evening meal by a light broth or soup (if the evening meal itself hasn't been replaced altogether by a pizza, which is generally served only in the evenings). Naples is the home of *spaghetti c'a pummarola* (*spaghetti al pomodoro* in proper Italian), born of the mating of pasta with the tomato not too long after the latter arrived in Italy from South America in the 16th century. It is still the most popular pasta dish, easily prepared, vividly colorful, fragrant with additions of basil or parsley, oregano, and garlic, and topped with tangy Parmesan cheese. Other Neapolitan favorites are *vermicelli con le vongole* (pasta with clams, with or without tomatoes, in a garlic and olive oil sauce), or *con zucchine* (with zucchini, garlic, and oil), and *pasta e fagioli* (a very thick white bean soup with short pasta).

As Naples is seafood country, the best main course here is simple fresh fish grilled and seasoned with olive oil and lemon. But if you're watching your budget, be careful. Most quality fish is sold by weight at restaurants, and you'd do well to avoid those whose prices are listed on the menu *al kilo* (per kilogram), which can turn an otherwise modest bill into a major monetary setback. Exceptions to this rule are lesser fish such as *alici* (anchovies), which, when fresh, can be tastefully prepared in oil, garlic, and parsley, and *fritto misto,* a mixture of fried shrimp, squid, and small local fish. One piece of advice: Don't eat raw seafood that may have come from the polluted Bay of Naples. Local meat, not of very good quality, is usually served drowned in a tomato (*pizzaiola*) or other sauce. Dinner for two with a house wine will run from $75 to well over $100 at a restaurant listed as expensive, from $50 to $75 at a moderate one, and from $20 to $50 at an inexpensive place. All telephone numbers are in the 081 area code unless otherwise indicated.

La Cantinella – A favorite of Neapolitans, visiting dignitaries, and tourists staying nearby along the picturesque port of Santa Lucia. Fresh fish, as everywhere, is at a premium, but local clams and mussels mated with a hint of garlic, parsley, and *pummarola* or tomato and lavished on a steaming plate of linguine constitute one of the great pleasures of Southern Italian life, within reach of everyone's pocket. The service is friendly and efficient. Closed Sundays. 23 Via Nazario Sauro (phone: 404884 or 405375). Expensive.

Casanova Grill – A delightfully intimate restaurant for such a grand hotel as the *Excelsior,* it offers a wide selection of enticing antipasti, plenty of fresh fish, Neapolitan specialties such as pasta with seafood, a remarkable fish soup, and roast baby lamb with rosemary and garlic — all prepared and served with care and refinement. 48 Via Partenope (phone: 417111). Expensive.

Giuseppone a Mare – Traditionally one of Naples's best fish restaurants, with incomparable views from Cape Posillipo, it seems to have its ups and downs in quality, service, and price. Still, it's worth trying if you're in the Posillipo area. Closed Sundays and from Christmas through New Year's. 13 Via Ferdinando Russo, Capo Posillipo (phone: 769-6002). Expensive.

Rosolino – An elegant supper club, piano bar, and nightclub in the Santa Lucia quarter, just a skip and a jump from the *Excelsior* and *Vesuvio* hotels. The restaurant is open at lunch, too; closed Sundays. Reservations necessary at dinner. 5-7 Via Nazario Sauro (phone: 415873). Expensive.

La Sacrestia – Dine alfresco here on delicious Neapolitan dishes such as homemade pasta stuffed with ricotta cheese, *scazzette di Fra' Leopoldo,* or any of the fresh fish dishes. On a hillside beyond Mergellina that affords splendid views from the terrace, it is closed Wednesdays (Sundays in July and August). 116 Via Orazio (phone: 664186). Expensive.

La Fazenda – Very Neapolitan, serving homemade garlic bread, wonderful pasta dishes, fresh fish, home-raised chickens, and exquisite desserts. In the Posillipo area, the surroundings are rustic, with spectacular views of the bay and flowers everywhere. Closed Sundays and 2 weeks in August. Calata Marechiaro 58 (phone: 769-7420). Expensive to moderate.

Amici Miei – Traditional Neapolitan cuisine is served in a traditionally elegant ambience in one of the elegant residential zones of Naples, near the *Politeama Theater*. Closed Mondays and August. 78 Via Monte di Dio (phone: 405727). Moderate.

Ciro a Santa Brigida – In the center of town, this has been one of the best and busiest of Naples' *trattorie-pizzerie* since the 1920s. Sample the great variety of fresh fish or pasta such as *lasagna imbottita* and *maccheroni alla siciliana*. This is also a good place for *pastiera,* a typical Neapolitan dessert made of ricotta cheese and wheat. Closed Sundays. 71 Via Santa Brigida (phone: 324072). Moderate.

Don Salvatore – It has been said that "Mergellina without Don Salvatore would be like Naples without Vesuvius." It's a longtime Neapolitan favorite where everything is good, from antipasto to pasta, fish, meat, and pizza (served evenings only). Closed Wednesdays. 5 Via Mergellina (phone: 681817). Moderate.

Dora – The ambience here is that of a small fishing boat and the fish served is first class. Try the *linguine all'aragosta* (pasta with crayfish). Closed Sundays and August. 30 Via Ferdinando Palasciano, Riviera di Chiaia (phone: 684149). Moderate.

Il Gallo Nero – Elegant dining in an antiques-filled 19th-century villa or on a terrace with a splendid view of Mergellina. Classic favorites as well as sensible innovations are on the menu, plus fresh fish and imaginative meat dishes. Open evenings only, except Sundays, when it's open for lunch only; closed Mondays and August. 466 Via Tasso (phone: 643012). Moderate.

La Bersagliera – In good weather, the Borgo Marinaro facing the Castel dell'Ovo can't be beat for local color. And this is the only one of these portside restaurants that makes it: Sometimes a dose of sun in a spectacular setting is worth more than a flawless meal. Specialties include good varied *antipasti,* fresh octopus salad, and a surprisingly inexpensive mixed grill of seafood that includes a tender and tasty fresh squid — a dish certainly worth a repeat visit. Naples' famous *scugnizzi* (streetwise waifs) ask for pieces of bread as they pass by between swims in the polluted bay. Closed Tuesdays. 10 Borgo Marinaro, Santa Lucia (phone: 415692). Moderate to inexpensive.

Osteria al Canterbury – Like many Neapolitan eating places, this one keeps its doors locked to ward off holdups. But don't be put off — inside, the atmosphere is warm and welcoming, with red-and-white checkered tablecloths and walls lined with wine bottles. Try the *maccheroni di casa Canterbury* (homemade pasta topped with mozzarella, eggplant, and a tomatoey meat sauce). The set lunchtime menu is particularly inexpensive. Closed Sundays. 6 Via Ascensione a Chiajà (phone: 413584). Moderate to inexpensive.

Pizzeria Bellini – This is one of the city's oldest *pizzerie.* Besides a vast assortment of pizza (the most famous, with fresh basil and tomato), there are pasta, fish, and meat dishes. Closed Wednesdays. 80 Via Santa Maria di Costantinopoli (phone: 459774). Moderate to inexpensive.

Il Pulcinella – A genuine family-style restaurant, cozy, friendly, and delicious. Closed Mondays and from July to September — but it's really a winter ambience anyway. 4 Vico Ischitella (phone: 764-2216). Moderate to inexpensive.

Gorizia – One of the Vomero's older *pizzerie,* now a full restaurant with traditional

Neapolitan cuisine. The pizzas are still noteworthy (evenings only). Closed Wednesdays and August. 29 Via Bernini (phone: 242248). Inexpensive.

Vini e Cucina – The food is delicious — real home cooking, Neapolitan style — and so this little Mergellina restaurant is increasingly popular and often impossibly crowded. Closed Sundays. 762 Corso Vittorio Emanuele (no phone). Inexpensive.

NICE

Those who remember the halcyon days of ornate villas, swaying palms, and languid luxury under an azure sky may shake their heads sadly at the Côte d'Azur of today: a symphony in cement, a real estate speculator's orgy of high-rise apartment blocks, pillbox hotels, and honky-tonk pizza parlors. Its once-quaint little marinas are linked by a permanent shoreline traffic jam, and some of its renowned beaches now look more like a horde of people dangling their feet from the edge of a freeway.

But Nice, somehow, has managed to keep its head above the concrete and retain its special flavor — a mixture of Marseilles, the *Mardi Gras,* and the Mediterranean. Even in the dead of winter, there is always something faintly festive about Nice: Perhaps it's all that city strung along all that sea. And at the first shine of sun, the café tables come out, the awnings unfurl, and strollers in sandals are back clacking along the Promenade des Anglais. In the summer, the population of 400,000 burgeons with holiday-makers from Paris, Piccadilly, and Peoria — though no longer from St. Petersburg — and an empty or moderately priced hotel room is harder to find than a winning lottery ticket. And a lot more scarce than a movie star.

The Greeks founded the city in 350 BC as a little market town and auxiliary port. The stolid Romans, too, discovered the pleasures of the Riviera, and the remains of their lavish colonization are evident today in the Arena and the Baths on the hill at Cimiez — the city's elegant residential section. In the 14th century, the House of Savoy wrested the growing city from the counts of Provence and retained almost unbroken possession of it for close to 500 years. Napoleon lived for a time at number 6 on what is today the Rue Bonaparte, later on Rue St.-François-de-Paule by the opera house. In 1860, the head of the House of Savoy and King of newly unified Italy, Victor Emmanuel II, ceded the region to France in return for military support against an Austrian invasion. Giuseppe Garibaldi, the Italian patriot, was born here, as was Masséna, the general Wellington admired most after Napoleon. In modern times, the beauty and climate of Nice have made it the amusement park of the European aristocracy, an off-season refuge from harsh northern climes and irritating revolutions.

The city, between Cannes and Monte Carlo, is one big easy-to-scan color postcard: the lapis lazuli of the Bay of Angels (Baie des Anges), the activity of the Vieux Port, and the timelessness of the towering Castle (Château) — the name given to the hill with the ruins of an old fortress that looms over the harbor. Along the bay runs the fabled Promenade des Anglais, a broad seafront avenue that resembles a mile-long outdoor café. At one end of the promenade is the city's pulse, Place Masséna: semitropical gardens set against crimson buildings and cool graceful arcades. Avenue Jean-Médecin is Main Street, bisecting the city with a straight line from Place Masséna to the railroad station. The old city, La Vieille Ville, is a little piano-shaped quarter — all narrow and cobbled and noisy, and pungently southern — that huddles in the shadow of the Château. La Vieille Ville's boundaries are the Quai des Etats-Unis and the Boulevard Jean-Jaurès beside the Paillon River, which is covered in parts by esplanades and divides the old town from modern Nice to the west.

Nice's heritage is culturally rich. Rodin, Modigliani, and Toulouse-Lautrec are among the numerous artists who have converged on the city since the 19th century. Matisse spent the last years of his life close to Nice, and for many years Chagall lived nearby; their works can be seen in the city's *Musée Matisse* and *Musée National Marc Chagall.* Music lovers flock to the renowned *Opéra de Nice,* and a variety of concerts are performed all year long throughout the city. And if you prefer fun and frolicking to art and music, Nice offers that too — not just with its usual festivities, but with a big bang during *Carnival.*

NICE AT-A-GLANCE

SEEING THE CITY: The long azure sweep of the bay, the compact jumble of red tile roofs in La Vieille Ville, the foothills of Provence, and the Maritime Alps rising sharply just outside the city are best seen from a viewing platform at the summit of the 300-foot Château. It can be reached by an elevator — or a 300-step climb — at the end of the Quai des Etats-Unis, where the quay joins the Rue des Ponchettes. Now there is a train from the Promenade des Anglais that goes through La Vieille Ville en route to the hills of the Château; from there, an exceptional panorama of Nice's port and the Bay of Angels unfolds before you. For information and reservations, call *Les Trains Touristiques* (phone: 93-71-44-77).

SPECIAL PLACES: Nice is a city to be seen casually, to be ambled through under a morning or late-afternoon sun, especially in and around the old city and the renowned flower market, Le Marché aux Fleurs. Let your discoveries be guided by casual occurrences: the purchase of a peach in an open market, a cold glass of Corsican white wine at a portside café, the scent of thyme wafting from the flower market.

IN THE CITY

Promenade des Anglais – If you only have an hour in Nice, spend it strolling along this promenade from the Place Masséna to the *Négresco* hotel (see *Checking In*). Ornate hotels grace one side, and a narrow, crowded strip of pebbled beach separates you from the brilliant blue of the bay. The promenade takes its name from the city's English colony, which constructed the path that was the predecessor of this one. You can lunch in your bathing suit on several excellent private beaches along the Promenade des Anglais. Prices are moderate and carafe wines are good.

La Vieille Ville (Old City) – Old Nice is a tight labyrinth of winding streets and alleys, steep ascents between medieval buildings, and balconies festooned with rainbows of drying laundry. The character of the city as it grew down the slopes of the Château from the 14th to the 18th century is in striking contrast to the city of expansive patrician promenades that developed in more modern times. Of late, it has shown indications of evolving into Nice's artists' quarter. Explore the Rue Rossetti, the Rue de la Boucherie, or the Rue du Collet. Crowd your way through the teeming street

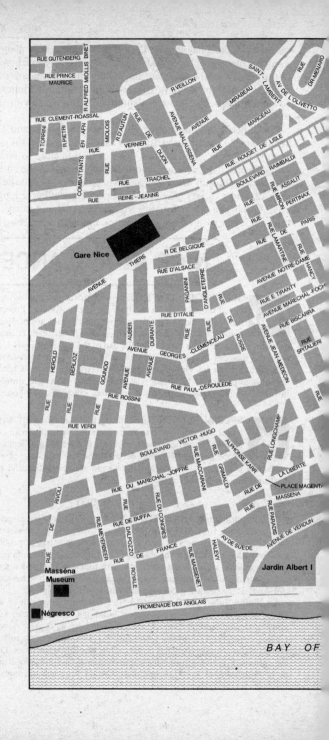

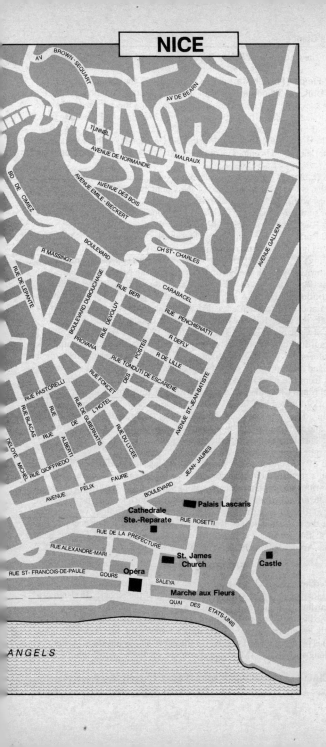

markets. Stop in at the Cathedral of Sainte Réparate and the 17th-century Church of St. James.

Le Marché aux Fleurs (Flower Market) – On the edge of the old city, just behind the Quai des Etats-Unis, you'll find the wholesale flower market that offers one of Nice's most colorful spectacles. The varieties of blossoms are dazzling, the aromas heady, and there are a few well-placed cafés, where you can see, sniff, and sip, all at the same time. Closed Mondays and Sunday afternoons. Cours Saleya.

Le Marché de la Brocante (Antiques Market) – On Mondays, the huge square where the flower market is held becomes an antiques and bric-a-brac market of unusual allure. Cours Saleya.

Palais Lascaris (Lascaris Palace) – A splendid private palace of the 17th century in Genoese style, this is the former residence of the Count Lascaris-Ventimiglia. It is noted for its ceilings with frescoes, its decorative woodwork, and its regal staircase. Closed Mondays in summer; Mondays, Tuesdays, and some public holidays in winter; and November. 15 Rue Droite (phone: 93-62-05-54).

Vieux Port (Old Port) – To the east of the Château, the harbor of Nice is an artful array of multicolored boats, from one-man dinghies and kayaks to the white steamers that make the crossing to Corsica. Excursion boats leave from the port and putter along to nearby Riviera towns. To reach the port, go out around the base of the Château at the far end of Quai des Etats-Unis or take Rue Cassini south from Place Garibaldi.

Cathédrale Orthodoxe Russe – A reminder of the days when the royal Romanovs roamed the Riviera and the promenade bustled with grand dukes, ballerinas, and an occasional Bolshevik, the cathedral was built in the Belle Epoque of the 19th century, under the auspices of Czar Nicholas himself. Built from 1903 to 1914, it is considered one of the most beautiful churches of its style outside of Russia. The church supports a bouquet of ornate onion domes in the ancient Russian style. Inside are a rich collection of icons and an impressive, carved iconostasis — the traditional screen that separates the altar from the nave in an Orthodox church. Bd. du Tzarewitch.

Musée National Marc Chagall – On a wooded hill in Cimiez in 1972, this modern museum houses works donated by Chagall, including the 17 canvases that make up his *Biblical Message.* In addition to the many fine paintings, the museum has sculptures, mosaics, sketches, and lithographs, all by Chagall. In summer, a tearoom is set up in the garden. Closed Tuesdays. Admission charge except Wednesdays. Av. du Dr. Menard and Bd. de Cimiez (phone: 93-81-75-75).

Musée Matisse et d'Archéologie – Henri Matisse had his studio in the Cimiez section of Nice, and a representative collection of his work — canvases, drawings, and sculpture done at various stages of his career — along with some of the artist's personal effects and his private art collection, has up to now shared quarters with the collection of artifacts found at the Roman site of Cimiez. A separate building was recently completed to house the archaeological collection, and Matisse's work now occupies the villa. His tomb is at the north end of a nearby cemetery, where Raoul Dufy is also buried. 164 Av. des Arènes (phone: 93-81-59-57).

ENVIRONS

Eze Village – Perched on a rock spike 1,550 feet above the sea, this unusual village — once a medieval fortress — offers a splendid panorama of the Riviera. It also has a tropical garden (Jardin Exotique) and a church with a beautiful 15th-century font. Nietzsche is supposed to have first worked out his masterpiece, *Thus Spake Zarathustra,* here. The walk from the Lower (Inferieure) Corniche up the Nietzsche Pass (Sentier Nietzsche) is picturesque and well worth the effort. Eze is less than 7 miles (11 km) from Nice, along the Middle (Moyenne) Corniche on the way to Monte Carlo.

■**EXTRA SPECIAL:** The Chapelle du Rosaire (Rosary Chapel), designed and decorated by Matisse (who thought it his masterpiece), is the main reason so many people have rediscovered Vence, a picturesque old market town some 13½ miles (22 km) northwest of Nice. The stunning stained glass windows, the murals, and the church vestments created by Matisse may bring you here, but you'll also enjoy the setting — on a rock promontory, sheltered by the last foothills of the Alps — and the charm of the old town, enclosed in elliptical walls and entered through five arched gateways. Restricted access and the small dimensions of the chapel can result in its being crowded, however, especially when a tour bus is visiting. The chapel, on Av. Henri-Matisse, is open Tuesdays and Thursdays from 10 to 11:30 AM and 2:30 to 5:30 PM; other days by appointment (phone: 93-58-03-26). For those who are interested in the town itself, a stop at the tourist office in the central plaza (Pl. du Grand Jardin; phone: 93-58-06-38) will provide ample ideas about what to see and how to get there.

SOURCES AND RESOURCES

 TOURIST INFORMATION: The Nice Office de Tourisme–Syndicat d'Initiative, whose hostesses speak English, has three branches: next to the railway station on Av. Thiers (phone: 93-87-07-07), 5 Av. Gustave (phone: 93-87-60-60), and at the Acropolis, 1 Esplanade Kennedy (phone: 93-92-82-82). There's also a welcome desk near the airport.

Local Coverage – The daily newspaper of the area is *Nice-Matin.* A free weekly directory of activities on the Riviera, *Sept Jours–Sept Nuits,* is distributed in the lobbies of most hotels. Also pick up the weekly *Semaine des Spectacles.* All are in French, but they're easy to decipher. *Riviera,* a glossy, expensive weekly, is an English-language Niçois publication that covers social life on the Côte d'Azur.

Telephone – The area code for Nice is 93; it must be used, even when dialing within the city. When calling a number in Nice from the Paris region (including Ile de France), dial 16, then the eight-digit number. When calling a number in Nice from outside Paris, dial only the eight-digit number. When calling Nice from the US, dial only the country code 33 and the eight-digit number.

 CLIMATE AND CLOTHES: Hot summer days in Nice are tempered by fresh breezes off the bay, and winter months are mild. The average temperature in January is 48F (9C). But there is a lot more rain than the tourist officials like to admit (Nice averages 66 days of rain a year), and sudden bouts of the whipping *mistral* — cold gusts of wind from the northwest — in spring. So bring something warm and something waterproof, even if you are coming to soak up the sun. Dress is casual just about everywhere, though you'll want something special for the evenings at the more elegant restaurants.

 GETTING AROUND: It's a good thing that central Nice is compact and easily accessible by foot, because traffic becomes ludicrous during the tourist seasons. Many areas have become pedestrian zones, such as Rue Masséna and some of its cross streets, as well as numerous streets in the Vieille Ville. If you want to move faster, rent a motorbike, moped, scooter, or bicycle from *Nicea Location Rent,* 29 Rue Paganini (phone: 93-16-10-30).

Airport – Nice–Côte d'Azur Airport (phone: 93-21-30-12 or 93-21-30-30), about 4 miles (6.4 km) west of the city, handles both domestic and international traffic. The approximately 10-minute taxi ride into town costs about 80F (about $13). The airport shuttle is part of the municipal bus network, Transports Urbains de Nice (24 Rue Hôtel des Postes; phone: 93-62-08-08). Leaving about every 20 minutes, it makes runs to the airport from 6 AM to 8 PM and continues to bring passengers into town from the airport until 11 PM. The shuttle leaves Nice from Av. Félix-Faure next to the information office at the Gare Routière; some of the buses into Nice go directly to the train station.

There is also a shuttle service from the Nice airport to Menton, which stops at the coastal resorts along the way — Villefranche, Beaulieu, Eze, Cap d'Ail, Monaco, Monte Carlo, and Roquebrune. Leaving approximately every hour from 7 AM to 8 PM, depending on the season, the trip takes about 1½ hours each way and costs 57F ($10) one way, 100F ($17) round-trip (phone: 93-21-30-83). In addition, helicopter service to Monaco is available. For details, call *Héli-Air Monaco* (phone: 93-21-34-62 at the airport, 93-30-80-88 at the Héliport de Fontvieille in Monaco).

Boats – *Gallus* boats cruise along the Riviera. Apply to SATAM, 22 Rue Bottéro (phone: 93-55-33-33). For ferries to Corsica, inquire at SNCM, 3 Av. Gustave (phone: 93-96-47-10).

Bus – You can hop on a bus for outlying districts, such as Cimiez, at the Place Masséna. The central station for the urban bus network is at 10 Av. Félix-Faure, Traverse Flandres Dunkerque (phone: 93-62-08-08). Nearby, the main station for regional buses is the Gare Routière, Bd. Jean-Jaurès and Promenade Paillon (phone: 93-85-61-81).

Car Rental – Major international firms are represented, both downtown and at the airport: *Avis* (phone: 93-80-63-52 and 93-87-90-11); *Budget* (phone: 93-16-24-16 and 93-21-36-50); *Europcar* (phone: 93-88-64-04 and 93-21-36-44); and *Hertz* (phone: 93-87-11-87 and 93-21-36-72).

Taxi – Cabs are expensive, so watch the meter and remember streets often are clogged with traffic at certain hours. There are usually plenty of cabs at designated stands, and they can also be hailed in the streets; or phone a taxi at 93-52-32-32 or 93-88-89-93.

Train – The Gare SNCF is on Av. Thiers (phone: 93-87-50-50). Another station, Gare de Provence, 33 Av. Malausséna (phone: 93-88-28-56), belongs to the Chemins de Fer de Provence (Provence Railways), a narrow-gauge railway that operates on a scenic route between Nice and Digne, approximately 100 miles (160 km) to the north-west.

SPECIAL EVENTS: The Nice event par excellence is *Carnival,* which begins 3 weekends before Lent and ends when His Majesty, King Carnival, is burned in effigy on *Shrove Tuesday.* The festivities include myriad parades and floats, marching bands and majorettes, fireworks and flowers, giant papier-mâché heads and masked balls. The *Fête des Mais* is a month of Sundays in May, with special merriment in the gardens of the Roman Arena at Cimiez. In July, the 10-day *Grande Parade du Jazz,* also in the Cimiez gardens, is the biggest jazz festival in Europe. To find out more about special events in Nice, contact *Comité des Fêtes,* 5 Promenade des Anglais (phone: 93-87-16-28).

MUSEUMS: The Chagall and Matisse museums described in *Special Places* are the most impressive in Nice, but there are several others of interest. For more museum information, pick up *Museums of Nice,* an illustrated guide in English, available at the tourist office.

Musée d'Histoire Naturelle or Musée Barla (Natural History Museum) – Exhibitions on marine life, paleontology, and mineralogy. 3 Cours Saleya (phone: 93-85-18-44).

Musée International d'Art Naïf Anatole Jakovsky (Anatole Jakovsky International Museum of Naive Art) – Jakovsky's collection of almost 600 paintings documenting naive art from the 18th century to the present, representing some 27 countries. Closed in November. Château Ste.-Hélène, Av. Val-Marie (phone: 93-71-78-33).

Musée Jules Chéret – Nice's municipal art museum, with works by Fragonard,

Renoir, Degas, Picasso. This is one of the few authentic buildings remaining from La Belle Epoque. 33 Av. des Baumettes (phone: 93-44-50-72).

Musée Masséna – Memorabilia of Napoleon's trusted marshal and exhibitions on the history of Nice. 65 Rue de France (phone: 93-88-11-34).

Musée Naval – From its perch atop the Tour Bellanda (a former residence of Berlioz), this museum overlooks spectacular grounds. It houses the expected — ship models, arms, navigation instruments — and the not so expected, such as models of the port at various times in its history. Tour Bellanda, Parc du Château (phone: 93-80-47-61).

Musée de Terra Amata – Artifacts from this excavated prehistoric site that is about 400,000 years old. 25 Bd. Carnot (phone: 93-55-59-93).

SHOPPING: Street market shopping in the Vieille Ville is the least expensive and the most fun. Rue Masséna, Place Magenta, and Rue Paradis are the pedestrian zone of shops and cafés, with Rue Paradis noted for its elegant shops. There's also a flea market on Boulevard Risso every day except Sunday.

Alziari – Oils, spices, rustic wooden kitchenware, and olive oil soap. 14 Rue St.-François-de-Paule (phone: 93-85-76-92).

Comtesse du Barry – French food delicacies of every description; 57 varieties of foie gras. 5 Rue Halévy (phone: 93-88-49-16).

Confiserie du Vieux Nice – A sweets factory with Provence specialties such as candied fruits and flowers. Watch the stuff being made downstairs, then buy it upstairs. 14 Quai Papacino and Rue Robilante (phone: 93-55-43-50).

Galeries Lafayettes – Part of a nationwide chain of department stores that has a VAT rebate for tourists and an English-speaking staff. 6 Av. Jean-Médecin (phone: 93-85-40-21).

Nice-Etoile – A new shopping mall with an art gallery on the 2nd floor. 24 Av. Jean-Médecin.

Riviera Bookshop – A wide choice of books in English. 10 Rue Chauvain (phone: 93-85-84-61).

La Tour des Antiquaires – A complex of 22 antiques galleries. 7 Promenade des Anglais.

Vogade – For chocolate lovers. 1 Pl. Masséna (phone: 93-87-89-41).

Louis Vuitton – Handbags, luggage, and other items with the status LVs. English spoken, prices high. Check erratic seasonal opening hours. 2 Av. de Suède (phone: 93-87-87-47).

SPORTS AND FITNESS: Boating – Various kinds of small boats are available for hire in the Vieux Port. Windsurfing craft, *planches à voile,* can be rented at bathing establishments along the promenade.

Bowling – At 5 Esplanade Kennedy (phone: 93-55-33-11); open from 11 AM to 2 AM.

Fitness Center – The *Centre Profil* at the *Méridien* hotel, 1 Promenade des Anglais (phone: 93-82-25-25), has an American instructor and is open to the public.

Golf – The most spectacular course is at Mont-Agel in the hills above Monte Carlo. There are also good courses at Biot and Valbonne.

Horse Racing – Thoroughbred racing takes place at the *Hippodrome de Côte d'Azur* in nearby Cagnes-sur-Mer.

Horseback Riding – Horses can be rented at *Club Hippique de Nice,* 368 Rte. de Grenoble (phone: 93-29-81-10); *Centre Regional de Randonnées et de Tourisme Equestre,* Rte. de Sain Cézaire, 06460 St.-Vallier-de-Thiey (phone: 93-42-62-98); and *Relais Equestre de la Ferme,* Rte. Nationale 98, 83400 Hyères (phone: 94-66-41-78).

Jogging – The wide sidewalk on the sea side of the Promenade des Anglais is good for early morning jogging. The Parc de Vaugrenier, 5 miles (8 km) west of Nice on N7, has a jogging track equipped with exercise stations.

Skiing – From November to April, you can ski on the slopes at Valberg, Isola, Esteng d'Entraunes, Auron, and Gréolières-les-Neiges in the Alps, only an hour or two away.

Swimming – The Ruhl Plage is the most central of Nice bathing beaches. Castel Plage is set right into the rock of Pointe de Rauba Capeù below the Château. In winter, you can swim at *Piscine Municipale J. Médecin,* 178 Rue de France (phone: 93-86-24-01); or try *Piscine Jean Bouin* in the *Palais des Sports,* next to the Acropolis, near the Palais de l'Exposition (phone: 93-13-13-13).

Tennis – Contact the *Nice Lawn Tennis Club,* Parc Imperial (phone: 93-96-17-70), or the *Ligue de la Côte d'Azur,* 5 Av. Suzanne-Lenglen (phone: 93-96-92-90). Squash is played at *Club Vauban,* 18 Rue Mal Vauban (phone: 93-29-09-78).

THEATER: In summer, all of Nice's best theatrical experiences take place outdoors: cabarets, concerts, theater, and folkloric shows at *Théâtre de Verdure,* in the Albert I Garden just off Place Masséna (phone: 93-87-77-39 or 93-82-38-68), and at the Roman Arena in Cimiez. Check with the tourist office for more information. *Théâtre du Vieux Nice,* 4 Rue St.-Joseph (phone: 93-62-00-03), is a music hall with operettas and dancing. The *Nouveau Théâtre de Nice,* Esplanade des Victoires (phone: 93-56-86-86), presents a season of plays in French from October through April. For modern theater, try the *Théâtre de l'Alphabet,* 69 Rue Roquebillière (phone: 93-89-52-01).

MUSIC: In addition to musical performances outdoors in summer, there is an opera season at the *Théâtre de l'Opéra,* Quai des Etats-Unis, from November through April. The box office is at 4 Rue St.-François-de-Paule (phone: 93-80-59-83 for information; 93-85-67-31 for reservations). The *Nice Philharmonic Orchestra* plays a musical spring and a musical autumn at the opera house. Jazz can be heard year-round at Cimiez's *Centre Culturel et Sportif Municipal,* 49 Av. de la Marne (phone: 93-81-09-09).

NIGHTCLUBS AND NIGHTLIFE: Probably the best-known nightspot in Nice is the recently reopened *Casino Ruhl,* on the ground floor of the *Méridien* hotel, 1 Promenade des Anglais (phone: 93-87-95-87). Smaller than its counterparts in Monte Carlo, it has a full complement of *jeux,* not to mention a Las Vegas–style cabaret and a disco called the *Jok' Club.* Another disco, perhaps the hottest in town, attracting a young crowd, is *La Camargue,* 5 Pl. Charles-Felix (phone: 93-85-74-10). *Le Sphinx,* 29 Rue de Préfecture (phone: 93-62-28-62), hosts a cool crowd, features video clips, and serves breakfast from 5 AM on weekends. The *Cheap American Restaurant* advertises an "American ambience" and food, with jazz musicians performing informal jams; it is at 5 Rue Barillerie (phone: 93-80-46-76). The *Casino Club,* 2 Rue Sacha-Guitry (formerly the Rue St.-Michel; phone: 93-80-55-77), offers machine games and roulette, starting at 3 PM. Gambling enthusiasts can also go to Cannes, 20 miles (32 km) southwest, or Monte Carlo, 13 miles (21 km) northeast.

BEST IN TOWN

CHECKING IN: Nice's hotels can be divided into those along the Promenade des Anglais, with a view of the bay — and the traffic — and those set back on quieter streets. At an expensive hotel expect to pay $100 or more per night for a double; $60 to $100 at a moderately priced hotel; less than $60 a night is inexpensive. However, expect prices to leap upward by one-half in summer, and perhaps even double on the most expensive end. Do not show up in the summer high season without a reservation unless you want to become an expert in Riviera hotel lobbies. Be aware, though, that Nice has a good supply of furnished rooms for visitors who plan to stay a week or more; a brochure is available upon request from the Syndicat d'Initiative.

Grand Hôtel Aston – This property is recommended not only because it is in the center of town, but also because it faces the fountains in the Place Masséna. 12 Av. Félix-Faure (phone: 93-80-62-50). Expensive.

Beach Regency – A deluxe, modern, fully air conditioned, 322-room hotel. The management has established a very fine restaurant, *Le Rendez Vous,* and such lively activities as *thés dansants* (tea dances) and festive buffet lunches on Sundays. And there's still a swimming pool on the roof as well as a good terrace restaurant overlooking the bay. The location is a bit away from the center, toward the airport, but the street address is still right. 223 Promenade des Anglais (phone: 93-83-91-51). Expensive.

Elysée Palace – Opened in 1988, this elegant hostelry boasts all the amenities desired by travelers on holiday or business. It's 100 feet from the sea yet is near the center of town, with 150 rooms and suites. Facilities include a rooftop swimming pool with a bar, a fitness room and sauna, a garage, 2 conference rooms, and an excellent restaurant. Outside, the hotel's signature is a 250-ton granite statue of a woman by Sacha Sosno. 33 Rue François-I (phone: 93-80-11-10). Expensive.

Holiday Inn – This hotel is opposite the airport, with a regular free shuttle. Air conditioned throughout, it has modern luxury appointments, a pool, sauna, and solarium. Nice Airport, 179 Bd. René-Cassin (phone: 93-83-91-92). Expensive.

Méridien – Above the *Ruhl Casino* near the Albert I Garden, this shiny, modern, somewhat impersonal hotel has lots of glass and escalators, and is luxurious in a more streamlined way than the Victorian dowager hotels that gave the Riviera its reputation. There's a good restaurant, piano bar, and health club, as well as an underground parking lot that offers access to the pedestrian zone. 1 Promenade des Anglais (phone: 93-82-25-25). Expensive.

Négresco – One of those Côte d'Azur landmarks where everyone should stay at least once before the revolution comes. A great wedding cake hotel overlooking the promenade, with elaborately appointed rooms, a fine restaurant called *Chantecler* (see *Eating Out*), and staff in 18th-century raiment. In the central atrium, a ton of Baccarat crystal is suspended over what is allegedly the largest Aubusson carpet in the world. The building itself has been designated a national monument. 37 Promenade des Anglais (phone: 93-88-39-51). Expensive.

Plaza Concorde – A traditional palace, it is beautifully restored and in the center of town facing the Albert I Garden and the sea. The view from the rooftop terrace is magnificent. 12 Av. de Verdun (phone: 93-87-80-41). Expensive.

Splendid-Sofitel – This 100-year-old hotel has been run by the same family for three generations, though it's been modernized, with TV sets and air conditioning. Only 500 yards from the sea, but it, too, has a pool as well as a sauna on the premises. 50 Bd. Victor-Hugo (phone: 93-88-69-54). Expensive.

Pullman – In the center of town, this deluxe hotel is a 5-minute walk from Place Masséna. The rooms are air conditioned and soundproof. Among the hotel's attractions are a Polynesian bar, pool and sauna, exotic interior gardens, and a great view from the rooftop terrace. 28 Av. Notre-Dame (phone: 93-80-30-24). Expensive to moderate.

Westminster Concorde – An old hotel in the grand tradition, facing the sea. All the rooms have mini-bars and color TV sets, and there's a good restaurant, bar, and disco. 27 Promenade des Anglais (phone: 93-88-29-44). Expensive to moderate.

Albert I – One of the best situated hotels in Nice, it is 50 yards from the beach and Place Masséna and a 2-minute walk from the pedestrian zone. Good views of the sea and the gardens. 4 Av. des Phocéens (phone: 93-85-74-01 or 93-85-70-02). Moderate.

Grand Hôtel de Florence – A small, new hotel, central yet quiet, and air conditioned. No restaurant. 3 Rue Paul-Déroulède (phone: 93-88-46-87). Moderate.

Napoléon – This typical, gracious Niçois building is on a quiet corner a few streets back from the beachfront, near the pedestrian zone. The owner is also the manager and the atmosphere is warm and welcoming. Bar, but no restaurant. 6 Rue Grimaldi (phone: 93-87-70-07). Moderate.

La Pérouse – A charming small hotel at the far end of the Quai des Etats-Unis, with a view of the entire bay. It offers gardens, pool, sauna. One drawback: traffic noise on an uphill curve outside. No restaurant. 11 Quai Rauba-Capeù (phone: 93-62-34-63). Moderate.

West End – Here is traditional elegance of a somewhat British flavor. A faithful clientele seems to have been coming back each year since the Crimean War. There are 101 rooms in this seafront location, but no restaurant. 31 Promenade des Anglais (phone: 93-88-79-91). Moderate.

Brice – This old hotel is 4 blocks from the Promenade des Anglais, in a delightful flower garden with orange and palm trees. 44 Rue Maréchal-Joffre (phone: 93-88-14-44). Moderate to inexpensive.

New York – An old white building with tropical flora in its entrance court, on a side street off the busy Avenue Jean-Médecin. Centrally located and recently remodeled despite its elderly-looking exterior. 44 Av. Maréchal-Foch (phone: 93-92-04-19). Moderate to inexpensive.

Résidencehôtel Ulys – Among the finest and most economical choices of Nice's many apartment hotels. The 88 studio and 1-bedroom apartments are clean, modern, and fully equipped with kitchens, and many have balconies overlooking the sea. Maid service by the day or week. 179 Promenade des Anglais (phone: 93-96-26-30). Moderate to inexpensive.

Berne – A small, comfortable, completely renovated hotel directly opposite the train station. No restaurant, but there's a pleasant cafeteria decorated in a rustic style. 1 Av. Thiers (phone: 93-88-25-08). Inexpensive.

Georges – Only 18 rooms, but each is comfortable, clean, well cared for, and looks as if it's been decorated with surplus *Négresco* furnishings. Rooms are understandably hard to come by in the summer, but it's well worth the necessary advance planning. 3 Rue Henri-Cordier (phone: 93-86-23-41). Inexpensive.

Impérial – In a garden with palm trees and exotic plants, this quiet hotel is a bit out of town but close to the Exhibition Center and Congress Hall. Restaurant on the premises. Closed November through January. 8 Bd. Carabacel (phone: 93-62-21-40). Inexpensive.

Primotel Suisse – A small hotel in the traditional style, close to the old town. Its restaurant offers a panoramic view of the Bay of Angels. 15 Quai Rauba-Capeò (phone: 93-62-33-00). Inexpensive.

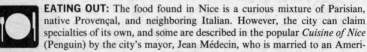 **EATING OUT:** The food found in Nice is a curious mixture of Parisian, native Provençal, and neighboring Italian. However, the city can claim specialties of its own, and some are described in the popular *Cuisine of Nice* (Penguin) by the city's mayor, Jean Médecin, who is married to an American. Specialties include *pissaladière*, a kind of pizza topped with black olives, onions, and anchovies; *stocaficada*, a ragoût of stockfish, served with potatoes, tomatoes, peppers, and zucchini; *gnocchi à la niçoise*, a kind of potato dumpling; and *pain bagnat*, a loaf of French bread split down the middle, soaked in olive oil, and garnished with

tomatoes, radishes, peppers, onion, hard-boiled egg, black olives, and parsley. *Soupe au pistou* is a vegetable bean soup with garlic, basil, and herbs. *Socca,* a popular dish in bars of the old town and port, is an enormous pancake made from chickpea flour and olive oil, baked like pizza or fried in oil. It is usually washed down with a solid red wine or a little glass of *pointu* (chilled rosé).

Nice has the distinction of being the only major city in France, apart from Bordeaux, which grows its own Appellation Contrôlée wines within the city limits. These are the Bellet reds, whites, and rosés, which must be tried during your stay here. At expensive restaurants, expect to pay $100 or more for two for dinner; $50 to $100 at moderately priced restaurants; and a minimum of $50 at inexpensive restaurants. Prices don't include drinks or wine; usually a service charge is included.

L'Ane Rouge – Fine seafood specialties include oysters in champagne, lobster, *bourride* (fish stew) — or try the sweetbreads. One Michelin star; fancy. Closed mid-July to September, Saturday evenings, and Sundays. 7 Quai des Deux-Emmanuel (phone: 93-89-49-63). Expensive.

Chantecler – Since chef Jacques Maximin left, the expensive, elegant fare is certainly less thrilling, though such specialties as *gourmandise de foie gras,* a luxurious pâté, a fish fantasy called *charlotte de St.-Pierre,* and inventive dishes like lobster ravioli are still consistent. The *menu dégustation* features tiny, elegant portions of a dozen different dishes. Closed in November. Reservations at this two-star restaurant are a must in summer. 37 Promenade des Anglais (phone: 93-88-39-51). Expensive.

Château de la Chèvre d'Or – For a special treat, drive east out of Nice on the Moyenne Corniche to the perched village of Eze (see *Special Places*), where you will find this excellent restaurant in a restored medieval manor house with a garden. (It's also a hotel.) Dine on lobster mousse or rack of lamb, while enjoying a spectacular panorama of the sea. Closed from November 15 to February 15 and on Wednesdays from October to Easter. Reservations necessary. Moyenne Corniche, Eze (phone: 93-41-12-12). Expensive.

Coco Beach – A large fish restaurant, a few yards from the sea, that is popular with residents who appreciate good food. Renowned for its bouillabaisse, lobster, and grilled fish of all kinds. Closed Mondays and Sunday evenings and mid-November to mid-December. 2 Av. Jean-Lorrain (phone: 93-89-39-26). Expensive.

Colombe d'Or – This gallery-restaurant in a small hotel (with pool) just outside the gates of the old town in St.-Paul-de-Vence is most noted for its collection of post-Impressionist art. (It was here that the late Simone Signoret met Yves Montand and married him in the presence of the hotel owner.) Matisse and other artists sometimes paid their bills during the 1920s and '30s with the paintings that now decorate the walls. The restaurant specializes in grills and roasts, and there is a lovely view from its terrace in summer. Closed early November to mid-December and a week or two in mid-January. Reservations advised. About 14 miles (22 km) northwest of Nice in St.-Paul-de-Vence (phone: 93-32-80-02). Expensive.

Le Moulin de Mougins – One of the most extraordinary dining experiences on the Côte d'Azur thrives in Roger Vergé's converted 16th-century mill in the charming market town of Mougins. The cuisine has justifiably earned three Michelin stars, and among the specialties to be enjoyed are braised slivers of Provençal duck in honey and lemon sauce, escalope of fresh salmon, lobster *fricassée,* pâté of sole, and for dessert, cold wild strawberry soufflé. Closed Mondays, Thursdays at lunch, mid-November to mid-December, and mid-February to mid-March. Reservations necessary. About 20 miles (32 km) west of Nice in Mougins (phone: 93-75-78-24). Expensive.

La Poularde (Chez Lucullus) – Very elegant French dining in the solid bourgeois tradition with plenty of rich cream sauces; turn-of-the-century decor with lots of wrought iron. Try the veal kidneys flambéed in champagne, the grilled lobster, or the roast lamb. Closed Wednesdays and mid-July to mid-August. Reserve, even a few days ahead. 9 Rue Gustave-Deloye (phone: 93-85-22-90). Expensive.

Chez Don Camillo – A tranquil, intimate place, this restaurant offers an appetizing taste of Italy (in case you're not going to make it across the border), but with a Niçois accent. Closed Sundays and early to mid-July. Reservations necessary. 5 Rue des Ponchettes (phone: 93-85-67-95). Expensive to moderate.

Le Jardin Gourmand – Another good fish address, better known for the chef's preparation of vegetables. Closed Sundays. 15 Rue Biscarra (phone: 93-62-48-00). Expensive to moderate.

Rôtisserie de St.-Pancrace – Dine on prawn stew, quenelles of salmon, roast pigeon, or ravioli stuffed with foie gras, among other dishes that have earned the restaurant its Michelin star. A lovely view from the garden terrace. Closed Mondays except in July and August and from early January to early February. In the village of St.-Pancrace, about 5 miles (8 km) north of Nice on D914 (phone: 93-84-43-69). Expensive to moderate.

La Toque Blanche – This 10-table restaurant offers magnificent fish dishes and has a *prix fixe* lunch weekdays. Closed Sunday evenings, Mondays, and mid-July through mid-August. 10 Rue de la Buffa (phone: 93-88-38-18). Expensive to moderate.

Albert's Bar – An American-style bar and grill with a decor reminiscent of the thirties, it offers such traditional French dishes as *blanquette de veau* (veal stew) along with Slavic specialties such as blinis with salmon. Closed Sundays and August. 1 Rue Maurice-Jaubert (phone: 93-53-37-72). Moderate.

Auberge de Bellet – This beautifully decorated restaurant is the ideal place to sample the range of local Bellet wines. Accompany them with braised chicken with mint or the *fricassée* of fish with herb butter. In summer you can eat outdoors in the shaded garden. Closed Tuesdays. A mile to the west of St.-Pancrace in the village of St.-Romans-de-Bellet (phone: 93-37-83-84). Moderate.

Bông Laï – For a change of pace, this Vietnamese-Chinese restaurant is quite good, especially the lacquered duck and the fish in ginger — even the chop suey. Closed Mondays, Tuesdays, and the last 3 weeks of December. 14 Rue Alsace-Lorraine (phone: 93-88-75-36). Moderate.

Le Champagne – The emphasis is on fish, delicately prepared with fine sauces, served in a comfortable setting. 12 Av. Félix-Faure (phone: 93-80-62-52). Moderate.

Au Chapon Fin – This charming place in the old quarter has a limited menu of delicious, regional food. Closed Sundays, holidays, mid- to late June, 2 weeks at Christmas. 1 Rue du Moulin (phone: 93-80-56-92). Moderate.

Chez les Pêcheurs – The specialties of this seafood restaurant in the Old Port include fish pâté and grilled deep sea bass (*loup de mer*). Closed Wednesdays, for lunch in summer, and November. 18 Quai Docks (phone: 93-89-59-61). Moderate.

Au Ciel d'Azur – Elegant dining where you'd least expect it — on the second floor of the airport. Very good fish, especially the sole, and luscious desserts. And if you find yourself at the airport with time to kill but little appetite, the restaurant's adjoining bar is a comfortable refuge from the crowded self-service restaurant-bar on the 3rd floor. Aéroport de Nice (phone: 93-21-36-36). Moderate.

Michel – This restaurant, also called *Le Grand Pavois,* has very good seafood dishes, especially the fish soup, stuffed mussels, and the sole meunière. Closed Mondays and July. 11 Rue Meyerbeer (phone: 93-88-77-42). Moderate.

Au Passage – A Vietnamese restaurant with French cooking, too. Excellent sauces; simple atmosphere. 11 bis Bd. Raimbaldi (phone: 93-80-23-15). Moderate.

L'Univers "Cesar" – A great place for pasta, which is served in all shapes and styles (even flambéed) and with proper ceremony by Cesar himself. Deep-sea bass (*loup* *de mer*) with cèpes and artichokes is another specialty of the house. The Niçois seem to come for the festive atmosphere as much as for the food, and at times it can be a bit of a circus. You might even bump into Jean-Claude Killy or some other French celebrity. Open daily until 2 AM. 54 Bd. Jean-Jaurès (phone: 93-62-32-22). Moderate.

La Coquille – A popular, unpretentious seafood restaurant that displays its wares on the street and also prepares food to take out. Good for oysters. Closed Mondays. 36 Cours Saleya (phone: 93-85-58-82). Moderate to inexpensive.

Rendez-Vous des Sportifs – A cheery family-run restaurant specializing in Niçois cuisine. Here you can sample the whole range of regional specialties, including *pissaladière,* stockfish, and *aubergine* (eggplant) fried in olive oil. Closed Sundays. 120 Bd. de la Madeleine (phone: 93-86-21-39). Moderate to inexpensive.

Ruhl Plage – The best of the beach restaurants along the Promenade des Anglais serves good grilled fish, salads, and carafe wines. A pool for children and all kinds of water sports facilities make it a popular summer lunch spot with the Niçois. Open from March through November, or as long as the weather stays warm. Opposite the *Casino Ruhl,* which is at 1 Promenade des Anglais (phone: 93-87-09-70). Moderate to inexpensive.

Biererie Chez Nino – You may find yourself the only out-of-towner in this old bistro tucked away in a tiny street near the train station. The place features a hundred different beers (both bottled and draft) from 22 countries, and its friendly owner will help you choose the right one to accompany your meal. Good grills and stockfish. The pictures on display are painted by local artists and there's a guitarist singing songs by Jacques Brel and other *chansonniers.* The clientele is a democratic mix of business suits and leather jackets. Closed Sundays and August. 50 Rue Trachel (phone: 93-88-07-71). Inexpensive.

La Méranda – Simple and plain but highly recommended by the Niçois, this tiny, crowded place near the flower market is run by a husband and wife team. Service is a bit slow, as each dish is prepared to order. Tripes niçoises and pâtés *au pistou* are splendid choices. Closed February, August, Saturday evenings, Sundays, and Mondays. 4 Rue de la Terrasse (no phone). Inexpensive.

La Nissarda – In an attractive setting, just a 10-minute walk from Place Masséna, serving many local specialties. Closed Wednesdays and for 2 weeks in July. 17 Rue Gubernatis (phone: 93-85-26-29). Inexpensive.

La Pizza – The best pizza this side of Ventimiglia (and possibly Milan), and good pasta, too. Young folks congregate en masse here until midnight. In the heart of the pedestrian zone, at 34 Rue Masséna (phone: 93-87-70-29). Inexpensive.

A la Ribote – The crazy-quilt menu lists oysters, fish, paëlla, and couscous, along with a daily special. Closed Saturdays. 5 Av. de Bellet, Pl. de Caserne des Pompiers Magnan (phone: 93-86-56-26). Inexpensive.

Rive Gauche – A small, friendly bistro with an Art Deco interior. Good food, like calves' liver and duck, and an excellent value. Closed Saturdays, Sundays, and August. 27 Rue Ribotti (phone: 93-62-16-72). Inexpensive.

Taverne du Château – Good Niçois cooking in a lively family place in Old Nice. 42 Rue Droite (phone: 93-62-37-73). Inexpensive.

 BARS AND CAFÉS: The *Scotch Tea House,* 4 Av. de Suede, is very British and proper (phone: 93-16-03-55). *Café de France,* at 64 Rue de France, is a landmark where old and young Niçois alike, as well as out-of-towners, drink coffee or beer or dine from a light menu (phone: 93-88-50-81). An older crowd frequents *Le Mississippi,* 5 Promenade des Anglais (phone: 93-82-06-61). At water's edge is *Le Queenie,* 19 Promenade des Anglais, a café with a bamboo and glass decor (phone: 93-88-52-50). *Bar L'Hermitage* (also called *Bar des Oiseaux*) 5 Rue

St. Vincent, is a colorful place where, legend has it, the owner carries a bird on her shoulder; ask for a *piconbière,* the house specialty (phone: 93-80-27-33). *Le Valentino,* 3 Promenade des Anglais, features live music in decor centered on black lacquered wood (phone: 93-87-09-27); and there's an exotic African ambience at *Le Pam-Pam Massena,* 1 Rue Desboutin (phone: 93-80-21-60). *Le Musting,* 19 Rue Droite, is a *cave* with a very young clientele, a dance floor, and a billiard table (phone: 93-80-56-27). Late-night places include *Bar-Tabac des Fleurs,* 13 Cours Saleya, a bar near the Marché des Fleurs that *opens* at 4 AM and *Le Frog,* on Rue Milton-Robbins, where you can drink and listen to live music after the restaurant closes (closed Sundays; phone: 93-85-85-65). *Le Cheap,* 4 Rue de la Barillerie, features spare ribs, some French food, and good cocktails, and a great lineup of sounds from rock to jazz and soul (closed Sundays; phone: 93-80-46-76).

OSLO

The capital of Norway sits at the head of a 60-mile fjord on the country's southeastern coast, framed by a vast expanse of lakeland, woods, and moors, where fir-treed hills rise 2,000 feet. The oldest of the Scandinavian capitals, Oslo is enormous: 15 square miles, only a tenth of which is urban and town districts. The rest is a marvelous outdoor playground for Oslo's approximately 450,500 residents and its visitors from around the world.

Oslo today is a jumble of architectural styles, but each year more modern concrete and glass buildings replace old wooden structures. Along with its attempts at modernization in this century, the city of Oslo has made a conscious effort to integrate art into the daily lives of its citizens. Frescoes and wood carvings decorate public and private buildings, and sculpture is an integral part of public squares and parks. In spring and summer, all this colorful art, the small malls and shopping streets, and outdoor cafés give the center of the city the feeling of a medieval festival.

People are believed to have lived at the head of the Oslo fjord 7,000 years ago. But the history of Oslo as we know it dates from 1048, when the Viking King Harald, called "Harald Hard Rule," built a commercial town in what is now east Oslo.

During the reign of Harald's successor, Olav Kyrre (1066–93), Oslo became an ecclesiastical center, its principal cathedral named after the city's patron saint, St. Hallvard. The foundation stones are all that remain today of this once mighty cathedral that served as the burial place of so many Viking kings.

Medieval Oslo reached its zenith during the reign of King Haakon V Magnusson (1299–1319), who built the majestic Akershus Castle and Fortress and decreed Oslo the capital of Norway. After Haakon's death the city went into decline. Many of its people were killed by the Black Death in 1349, and when Norway united with Denmark, Oslo lost its importance as a capital. Several times the city was devastated by fire, and in 1624 all of its wooden buildings succumbed to flames.

King Christian IV, who ruled Norway and Denmark at the time, ordered a new capital built somewhat farther west, behind the walls of Akershus. He named it Christiania, a name that was used until 1925, when the ancient name of Oslo was restored. The streets laid out by Christian IV are still the main streets of central Oslo. And a few of the stone and half-timbered buildings from this era can be seen today.

In 1814, during the Napoleonic wars, Norway and Denmark were separated and there followed a 90-year union with Sweden. Oslo's main street, the hub of the city today, is named for the first of the Swedish-Norwegian kings, Karl Johan. After the union with Sweden was dissolved in 1905, the Norwegian capital entered a period of expansion, interrupted only by World War

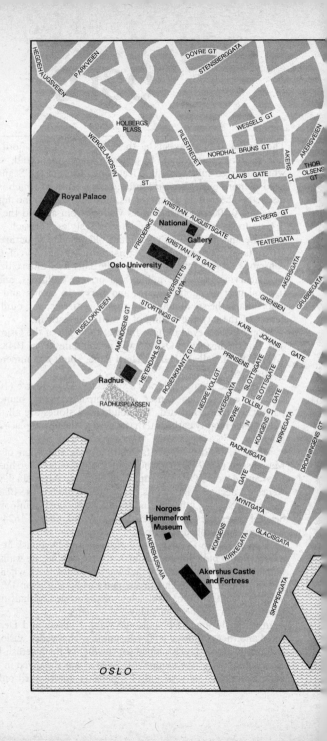

I and the German Occupation during World War II. Since 1917, Oslo has been Norway's most important maritime city as well. Its harbor has more than 8 miles of quays, and the world's largest tourist ships can dock in Oslo.

Norway is a constitutional monarchy with a parliamentary government whose current prime minister is a woman, Gro Harlem Brundtland. She presides over an 18-member cabinet that includes 8 women, giving Norway the distinction of having the highest proportion of women in top government posts in the world. As head of the World Commission of Environment and Development, Brundtland has drawn global attention to her country's commitment to environmental issues. The king, Olav V, lives in the Royal Palace at one end of Karl Johans Gate and the parliament meets in the century-old National Assembly building (Stortingsbygningen) a few blocks away.

Like virtually all Norwegians, the king is an avid cross-country skier and can occasionally be seen heading for one of the thousands of trails within the city limits. Oslo residents often ski at night after work, and many of the city's most festive events are connected with skiing and other winter sports.

Ski jumping originated near Oslo in 1879. The Holmenkollen Ski Jump, which can be seen from most parts of Oslo, has been a landmark since it was built for the 1952 Winter Olympics. The jumping tower itself is 184 feet high and its summit is 1,350 feet above the fjord overlooking Oslo. It is the combination of such manmade sights with an extraordinary natural beauty that makes Oslo a very special place to visit.

OSLO AT-A-GLANCE

SEEING THE CITY: Spectacular views of the city and the Oslo fjord are available from several vantage points in the hilly, wooded area, Oslomarka, on the east, north, and west of the city. Perhaps the best panorama is from Tryvannstårnet, a 390-foot observation tower atop the 1,600-foot-high Tryvann Hill on the outskirts of Oslo. It is reached by taking the Holmenkollen suburban rail line to Voksenkollen. The *Summit 21 Lounge & Bar* on the top of the *Scandinavia* hotel offers a fine view of the city from downtown; it serves a buffet lunch in the afternoon and is a bar from 3 PM to 12:30 AM. 30 Holbergs Gate (phone: 113000). The *Panorama Bar,* crowning the new 35-story *Oslo Plaza* hotel (opening March 1990) in the Vaterland development, provides a stunning vista. If you're feeling brave, ride the external glass elevator to the top.

SPECIAL PLACES: In Oslo the special places are not the museum and tourist sites but the different parts of the city that reflect its past. The once-controversial Vigeland Sculpture Park is a must for any visitor. History and architecture buffs will enjoy walking along Oslo Harbor's bustling Rådhus Gate, whose buildings were among Oslo's finest private and public residences in the 17th and 18th centuries. Pause on the summit of nearby Akershus Fortress, dating from medieval times. For a feeling of Victorian Oslo, meander along the streets directly behind the Royal Palace. They house the city's embassies and consulates, and the area is one of Oslo's most charming urban residential districts. The Homansbyen area is a protected historical enclave. In the latter half of the last century, the district's well-heeled residents tried to outdo each other by building houses grander and more unusual than those of their neighbors. The result is a not unpleasant mix of architectural styles; today, most of the homes remain single-family residences.

Travel out to Bygdøy peninsula for a glimpse of the good and easy life of many of modern Oslo's inhabitants with their expensive homes and swimming beaches side-by-side with Viking and polar ship museums. The peninsula, which juts into the fjord southwest of the harbor, can be reached by bus or, in summer, by one of the ferries that leave from near city hall. And by all means, take the tram up to Holmenkollen to experience the Oslo of the outdoor enthusiast — miles and miles of untouched forest and the widest network of ski trails in the world, over 1,300 miles worth. The Holmenkollen area is also the latest fashionable address, each new home bigger and more luxurious than its predecessor.

DOWNTOWN

Vaterland – A city within a city, this new development features a 9,000-seat hall for musical and sporting events, several eateries, a movie theater, an art gallery, designer boutiques, two luxurious hotels including the pricey *Oslo Plaza,* and a bus terminal. By 1991, it will house Norway's most extensive conference facilities and a new train station.

Oslo Harbor – Stroll along this busy, modern waterfront and you will see graceful white cruise ships that ply the fjords, small ferries, and private boats. Don't miss the chance to snack on tasty, tiny shrimp sold by fishermen who catch them at sea and cook them aboard their boats as they head back to the pier in front of city hall.

Oslo City Hall (Rådhus) – A spacious square with fountains and sculpture separates this outstanding landmark from the harbor. City Hall, although boxy, is lavishly embellished with contemporary Norwegian sculpture, wood carvings, paintings, and tapestries. The Oslo Tourist Board is at the rear of the building facing the harbor. Guided tours available. Open daily. No admission charge. Rådhusplassen (phone: 410090).

Aker Brygge – Oslo's first "Fisherman's Wharf" opened in 1986 and has been a favorite waterfront gathering point for residents and visitors ever since. It features lots of little shops, boutiques, a theater, fast-food stands, ice cream parlors, bakeries, delicatessens, wine bars, and restaurants offering fare from Mexico, China, and other lands. Open year-round, with jazz concerts presented outside in summer.

Oslo Cathedral (Domkirken) – Although both its exterior and interior have been restored since the cathedral was first built in the late 17th century, the altarpiece and pulpit are original, dating from 1699. Of particular interest are the bronze doors by Dagfinn Werenskiold, the stained glass windows by Emanuel Vigeland, and the ceiling decorations by Hugo Lous Mohr. Closed Saturdays from September to May. Regular services are held on Sundays at 11 AM and 7:30 PM. Stortorvet (phone: 412793). The old stables that were built around the cathedral have been converted to small shops. You can browse for antiques or watch silversmiths, weavers, potters, and other artists and craftsmen at work.

Ruin Park (Minneparken) – The foundation stones of St. Hallvard Cathedral can be seen in this park with a number of archaeological excavations from medieval Oslo. At the park's edge is Ladegård, a private residence built in 1725 on the ruins of the bishop's palace dating from 1200. Oslo Gate at Bispegata. It's best reached by taxi or by tram #9.

Oslo's Markets – Three large, colorful outdoor markets are favorite spots for picture taking. Garden and greenhouse plants are sold in Stortorvet Square, near the cathedral; vegetables, fruits, and flowers are on sale in Grønland Torg and Youngstorget. Open daily except Sundays until mid-afternoon.

Akershus Castle and Fortress (Akershus Festning og Slott) – Built originally by King Haakon V about 1300, this is one of the most important relics of medieval

Norway. It was rebuilt in Renaissance style under King Christian IV in the 17th century. It has been restored and is used now by the government for state occasions and festivities. Buildings are open daily, May 2 to September 15. Sunday afternoon concerts in the chapel. Admission charge. Admission to the grounds, which are open all year, is free. Entrance from Rådhus Gate, a short stroll from city hall.

Norwegian Resistance Museum (Norges Hjemmefront Museum) – This stirring museum, on the grounds of Akershus Fortress, contains materials and memorabilia from the German occupation of Norway (1940-45) during World War II. Open daily. Admission charge. Akershus (phone: 403138).

Gamle Aker Church (Gamle Aker Kirke) – Built in 1100, this is by far the oldest building in Oslo and the oldest stone church in Scandinavia still in use as a parish church. Open Tuesday and Thursdays afternoons or by appointment. Guided tours from mid-May through August. Sunday services at 11 AM. No admission charge. 26 Akersbakken (phone: 461168).

Royal Palace (Slottet) – The residence of King Olav V is not open to the public, but you can visit the grounds. Get there in time for the changing of the guard each day at 1:30 PM. A brass band plays weekdays when the king is in residence, marked by the flying of his standard from the palace roof. At the west end of Karl Johans Gate.

Vigeland Sculpture Park (Vigelandsanlegget) – A world of people and animals sculpted in granite, iron, and bronze by Gustav Vigeland inhabit a lovely 80-acre park in the western section of Oslo. In 1921, the city of Oslo offered the brilliant, egocentric Norwegian sculptor a free hand in carving his masterwork in Frogner Park, a depiction of the whole cycle of human life. He was given a studio, workmen, assistants, and all the funds he needed — the cost ran into the millions by the time the job was finished in 1943. Vigeland takes on birth, growth, joy, suffering, and death in the 650-piece collection of huge, writhing, nude figures in metal and stone. Once considered controversial, the only thing controversial in the park today is its topless sunbathers. On the grounds there's also a statue of Abraham Lincoln, presented to Norway by the people of North Dakota on July 4, 1914. The park has a swimming pool, tennis courts, and a sports arena, and is a favorite spot for Oslo's residents summer and winter. In summer, there are two restaurants in addition to the year-round cafeteria. Open day and night all year. No admission charge. Frogner.

Vigeland Museum (Vigeland Museet) – Just across the road from the southern end of Vigeland Park is Vigeland's former residence and studio. It contains 1,650 sculptures, 420 woodcuts, hundreds of plates for woodcuts, and some 11,000 sketches by the eminent Norwegian artist. During the summer, concerts are held in the museum's courtyard. Closed Mondays. No admission charge. 32 Nobels Gate (phone: 442306).

Munch Museum (Munch Museet) – Edvard Munch, the Norwegian expressionist painter and graphic artist who died in 1944, bequeathed all his art to the city of Oslo. This light, airy, spacious museum was built in the eastern section of the city to house the almost 1,100 oil paintings, 4,500 drawings, 15,000 prints, and notes, letters, sketches, and other materials in the collection. Closed Mondays. Admission charge only from May 15 to September 5. 53 Tøyen Gate (phone: 673774).

National Gallery (Nasjonalgalleriet) – Norway's principal art collection. The emphasis is on Norwegian artists, but there is a representative sample of international artists, particularly the French Impressionists. Munch's much-reproduced *Madonna* is here. Open daily. No admission charge. 13 Universitets Gate (phone: 200404).

Museum of Modern Art (Sammtidsmuseet) – Inaugurated in 1989, this new branch of the *National Gallery* is devoted to modern paintings and photography. The collection will be updated annually in order always to include works from the last 40 years; older acquisitions will revert to the National Gallery. At Bankplassen, downtown.

Oslo University (Universitas Osloensis) – The main attraction for tourists at the university's downtown campus is the old festival hall, called the Aula, with its Munch paintings. This is where the award ceremony for the Nobel Peace Prize usually takes place (it's the only Nobel Prize awarded here; the others are presented in Stockholm). Open weekday afternoons in July. During the winter, admittance is upon request (phone: 330070, ext. 756). No admission charge. Karl Johans Gate.

Natural History Museum (De Naturhistoriske Museer) – Visitors with children will especially enjoy this excellent museum, with displays and reproductions of Norwegian flora and fauna. Exhibitions are informative and interesting. Open every afternoon except Mondays. No admission charge. A short stroll from the *Munch Museum* through Oslo's Botanical Gardens, 1 Sars Gate, Tøyen (phone: 686960).

THE PENINSULA

Viking Ship House (Vikingskiphuset) – Three longships, the *Gokstad ship,* the *Tune ship,* and the *Oseberg ship,* from AD 800–900, will take you back to the days when Vikings roamed the seas. The upswept prow of the *Oseberg ship,* with a stunning pattern of carved animals, is an excellent example of the workmanship and beauty that characterized these ships. The museum also has collections of utensils, gold and silver jewelry, and accoutrements from the Viking period. Open daily. Admission charge. 35 Huk Aveny (phone: 438379).

Norwegian Folk Museum (Norsk Folkemuseum) – Some 150 wooden buildings from all over Norway have been placed in a picturesque park near the *Viking Ship House* to provide a representative picture of Norway's past. One of the museum's treasures is a unique hand-hewn, wooden stave church from 1200. You can also see the last apartment of Norwegian playwright Henrik Ibsen and a group of buildings from Sami (Lapp) communities in Norway's extreme north. Buildings open daily from March to November; park open year-round. Admission charge. 10 Museumveien (phone: 437020).

Kon-Tiki Museum (Kon-Tiki Museet) – The balsa raft *Kon-Tiki,* used by Thor Heyerdahl and his crew on their 1947 voyage across the Pacific Ocean from Peru to Polynesia, is preserved here along with Easter Island statues and an underwater display. Also on display is the papyrus boat *Ra II,* on which Heyerdahl traveled across the Atlantic Ocean from North Africa to Barbados in 1970. Open daily. Admission charge. Bygdøy (phone: 438050).

Norwegian Maritime Museum (Norsk Sjøfartsmuseum) – Norway's long maritime traditions are recalled by the collections inside this museum, a short walk from the *Kon-Tiki.* Outside the building, you can see Roald Amundsen's Polar ship, *Gjøa,* the first vessel to navigate a northwest passage in 1903–6. Guided tours. Open daily. Admission charge. Bygdøy (phone: 438240).

Fram Museum (Polarskipet Fram) – The third ship museum in the area houses the *Fram,* built for Fridtjof Nansen's Polar Expedition of 1893–96 and also used by Amundsen on his expedition to the South Pole in 1910–12. Open Sundays only in November, closed December to April 15; otherwise open daily. Admission charge. Bygdøy (phone: 438370).

SUBURBS

Ski Museum (Skimuseet) – The world's oldest ski museum is inside the takeoff structure on the giant Holmenkollen ski-jumping hill. The collection outlines the history of skiing from the well-preserved tip of a ski found in a bog and believed to be some 2,500 years old to skis used in early Polar expeditions as well as modern equipment. Admission charge. A 20-minute ride by the Holmenkollen railway from central Oslo and a 10-minute walk from the Holmenkollen Station. Holmenkollen (phone: 141690).

Frogneseteren – A 20- to 30-minute walk up the hill from the *Ski Museum* will take you 1,460 feet above sea level to a panoramic view of Oslo and the fjord. You can also stop in at the cozy lodge and restaurant here (see *Eating Out*). If you have the stamina, another 20 minutes of uphill walking (or go there directly by getting off at the Voksenkollen station on the Holmenkollen railway) will lead you to the 390-foot Tryvannstårnet, the highest lookout tower in Scandinavia. Admission charge.

Emanuel Vigeland Museum – This small, two-room, churchlike museum was built and decorated by Emanuel Vigeland, Gustav's younger brother. The main chamber's principal fresco, entitled *Vita,* has earned it the distinction of being Oslo's most controversial museum. Call for hours. No admission charge. A 7-minute walk from the Slemdal stop on the Holmenkollen tram line (phone: 149342).

Children's Art Museum – A very moving museum containing 70,000 children's drawings, paintings, ceramics, and sculpture from all over the world, in a former private home with a lovely garden. Open workshop and musical activities for children, but also wonderful for adults to visit. Closed Mondays and Thursdays. 4 Lille Frøens vei (Frøen stop on the Holmenkollen tram line; phone: 468573).

Sonja Henie–Niels Onstad Art Center (Sonja Henie–Niels Onstads Kunstsenter) – The art center, 7 miles (11 km) west of Oslo near Fornebu Airport, was opened in 1968. It houses the permanent collection of 20th-century art donated by the international skating star and her husband. Included are works by Picasso, Miró, Villon, and Munch. Exhibitions and other events illustrating current trends and ideas in film, music, architecture, literature, and the applied arts are scheduled regularly. One room features Sonja Henie's trophies and prizes; otherwise the museum is dedicated to art. Open daily; during the summer old Sonja Henie movies are shown on Sunday evenings. Admission charge. Reached by bus from central Oslo. Høvikodden, 1311 Høvik (phone: 543050).

Ekeberg Park – There's a fine view of Oslo and the fjord from the 685-foot hill in this lovely park just southeast of the city. It was on this hill that the oldest works of art in Oslo, Stone Age carvings some 3,000 years old, were found in 1915. These rock carvings can be seen between the Merchant Navy Academy here and Kongsveien. The park is easily reached by the Ljabru tram. For a unique experience, the Oslo Travel Association (see *Sources and Resources*) may be able to arrange a torchlit sleigh ride through the Ekeberg woods.

Tusenfryd – The name of Oslo's new amusement park means "A Thousand Delights." It has a roller coaster, clowns, music, miniature golf, movie theaters, restaurants, and other things to delight children of all ages. Admission charge. Dyreparken in east Oslo (phone: 09-946363).

■**EXTRA SPECIAL:** In the ancient fortress town of Fredrikstad, 60 miles (96 km) south of Oslo, you can watch craftsmen and designers at work in their quaint workshops, weaving and printing textiles, blowing glass, making silver jewelry, pottery, and furniture. *Plus Organization* operates a permanent exhibition and salesroom for the arts and crafts produced there.

One hour north of Oslo, in the small Norwegian town of Jevnaker, lies Norway's most famous crystal factory, *Hadeland Glassverks.* The factory offers tours of its glass-blowing plant year-round and special tours in English during the summer. A permanent glass museum and a "firsts" and "seconds" shop make a visit especially rewarding. There's also a smaller glass factory, *Randsfjord,* just minutes away. The drive alone is worth the trip on a clear day, as it offers a peek into many cross sections of rural Norway — a crystal blue lake nestled in a picture-perfect valley, apple orchards, and farmlands.

The tourist board can arrange individually tailored full- and half-day Land Rover safaris in the Oslo forests ($65 for 4 hours, $110 for 8 hours; meals and equipment included; discount available with the Oslo Card). Rambling, canoeing, and fishing are the diversions in the summer and skiing and snowshoe tours are the winter features. Contact the tourist office at least 1 day ahead.

SOURCES AND RESOURCES

 TOURIST INFORMATION: The Oslo Tourist Board provides free information and maps and arranges tours and guide service at its tourist office in city hall (phone: 427170). Open daily except during the winter, when it is closed Sundays.

The association publishes *Oslo This Week* (on a monthly basis, oddly enough); you'll want to check it for special attractions. It's available at most hotels, travel agencies, and at the tourist office.

The US Embassy is at 18 Drammensveien (phone: 448550).

Local Coverage – Oslo doesn't have an English-language newspaper, but American and British periodicals as well as the *International Herald Tribune* are widely available. Look for them at Narvesen kiosks. *Aftenposten,* one of Norway's most important newspapers, carries a summary of the day's news in English during the summer. Radio listeners can tune in to 93 FM on Sunday mornings for "Norway Today," an English broadcast with international news and features. Many large hotels have equipped all rooms with 24-hour English-text television, which provides international news and local information. Some have also introduced Cable News Network (CNN).

Food – Both *Oslo This Week* and *Oslo Guide '90* have dining information.

Telephone – The area code for Oslo is 02.

 CLIMATE AND CLOTHES: From April to September, the nights are very short in Oslo. Since the sun shines 24 hours a day during midsummer above the Arctic Circle, some visitors may want to bring a sleeping mask or some other device to prevent the brightness from disturbing their rest. Summers are short but pleasant, although it can be quite rainy along the coast. Medium-weight clothing and a light raincoat are most practical during the summer. The Gulf Stream keeps Norway's climate temperate, but it is seldom hot. Temperatures range from about 15F (−10C) in January to just about 75F (25C) in July. Be sure to bring boots, gloves, and other warm gear in winter.

 GETTING AROUND: Airport – The recently renovated Fornebu Airport, which handles domestic and international flights, is a 20-minute trip from downtown. Taxi fare runs from 75 to 95 Norwegian kronen ($11-$14). At a third of the taxi price, bus service operates between the airport and the Vaterland development, Sentralbanestrasjonen railway station, the Parliament, *Scandinavia* hotel, and the *National Theater* on Stortings Gate (phone: 424991).

Gardermoen Airport, 51 km (32 miles) north of the city, handles charter flights as well as all nonstop transatlantic flights. The trip downtown takes almost an hour, and taxi fare can run up to $100. Bus service between the airport and downtown Oslo is available for 50 Norwegian kronen (about $7).

International traffic may eventually be discontinued to Gardermoen, Fornebu, or both. After decades of political squabbling, Norway is constructing a new main airport at Hurum, a virgin site southwest of Oslo. The project, expected to cost $2 billion, involves building roads and a bridge link over the fjord to the capital. Completion is scheduled for the mid-1990s.

Bus, Tram, and Train – The new main bus terminal is at Vaterland. Most of the buses running through the city center stop at Wessels Plass and by the University Square or at the *National Theater.* For information about timetables and fares, call 417030.

Oslo has two railway stations. Vestbanen, at 2-4 Enga, is for all local traffic west of the station as well as for travel to the cities of Kristiansand and Stavanger. Sentralbanestasjonen, in the Jernbanetorvet railway square at the end of Karl Johans Gate, handles all local stops not served by Vestbanen and trains to Bergen, Aandalsnes, Trondheim, Røros, and Bodø. It has just been completely renovated and offers a bank, accommodations center, restaurants, cafés, and shops. The National Theater station and the new, main Stortinga subway station handle local trains to Skien, Moss, Eidsvoll, and other destinations, and are connected by an underground tunnel to the main downtown tram station, National Theater. For all train information, phone 421919.

Car Rental – Major American and European firms are represented.

Ferry and Local Boats – Boats and ferries leave from various piers along the harbor. For information on timetables, call the tourist office at 427170.

Taxi – You can call a taxi by dialing 388090, or find one at any taxi stand. Taxi stands are listed in part 1A of the telephone directory under the heading *Drosjer.* You can also hail a taxi on the street, but drivers are not allowed to pick up passengers near a taxi stand. To order a taxi, you must call at least an hour before you need it (phone: 388080).

Underground (T-Banen) and Suburban Tram lines – The National Theater and the new Stortinga stations are the central stops for most electrified trams and the subway to the forested park areas on the outskirts of Oslo. If you're planning to be in the city for 1 month, check with Oslo Sporveiers office in Kirkeristen (by the cathedral at Dronningens Gate 27) about its universal card, to be used for travel on various buses, trams, the underground, and even some ferries. You'll need a photograph for the card, which costs about $34 (phone: 417030).

Note: Short-term travel discounts are also available. A 24-hour Tourist Ticket costs about $5 and offers unlimited travel within a 24-hour period on local buses, trams, subways, suburban railways, and even local ferries. It is sold at all Narvesen kiosks (those marked with a large blue and white "N"), Innkvartering at 5 Oslo, the Oslo Tourist Board, main subway stations, post offices, and ticket offices. The first time the card is used it is stamped with the date and time. Another option is a *flerreisekort,* a card offering a 15% discount per prepaid trip. Cards may be purchased for 4 or 14 trips at Narvesen kiosks or from any conductor. Oslo also offers an extensive Oslo Card, which includes unlimited free travel on the city's trains, buses, underground, and boats; special prices at car rental firms; half price on trains to and from the capital; and admission to museums. It is valid for 1, 2, or 3 days. Single tickets may be purchased for about $1.50 per trip. Complete information is available at the tourist office or Oslo Sporveiers office.

Warning: Public transportation in Oslo operates on an honor system, with occasional spot checks. Travel without a valid ticket results in an on-the-spot fine of about $13. If you are using a discount card, be sure to validate it in the special machines on the waiting platforms and in the trams themselves.

 SPECIAL EVENTS: In January, the *Monolith Meet,* a major cross-country ski race, takes place in the Vigeland Sculpture Park. The sporting calendar for January and February features a number of international speed-skating events, which often include the European or World Championships. The annual *Holmenkollen Ski Festival,* which attracts the cream of the world's cross-country skiers and ski jumpers, takes place in early March. *Holmenkollen Day* is the last Sunday of the festival, when up to 100,000 spectators make their way to the Holmenkollen Ski Jump to watch a special jumping competition. Easter is a special time of year for Norwegians, and most towns and cities are deserted over the long holiday weekend as the entire population takes off for its last fling on the slopes — something a traveler should keep in mind. A few major hotels and restaurants may remain open, but the majority are closed. *Constitution Day,* May 17, is Norway's biggest holiday. One of the few days each year when national dress is worn, it is a photographer's delight. The children's parade up Karl Johans Gate to the Royal Palace is the highlight of the day, indeed, of any visit to Norway. Reservations must be made very far in advance. Tourists in June will be treated to one of Norway's favorite events: Midsummer Night's Eve, or *Sankthansaften,* on June 23. Bonfires are lit everywhere on this festive evening, and a trip along the coastline, or out on Oslo fjord, is a special treat. Summer visitors have the opportunity to attend the famous *Bislet Games,* world class track and field events at *Bislet Stadium* that attract top international athletes. July is the main summer vacation month in Norway, and Oslo is pitiably void of Norwegians during these weeks. *Note:* On July 4, celebrations of American *Independence Day* are held, usually in Vigeland Park. Check with the Oslo Tourist Board for details.

 MUSEUMS: In addition to those listed in *Special Places,* other notable Oslo museums are the following.
   Historical Museum (Historisk Museum) – The university collection of antiquities. 2 Fredriks Gate (phone: 416300).
   Museum of Applied Art (Kunstindustrimuseet) – Applied art from the Middle Ages to the present. 1 St. Olavs Gate (phone: 203578).
   Norwegian Customs Museum (Norsk Tollmuseum) – The Customs House, depicted in exhibitions and models. 1A Tollbugt. (phone: 414960).
   Norwegian Science and Industry Museum (Norsk Teknisk Museum) – Science and technology, including many working models. 141 Kjelsåsveien, Etterstad (phone: 222550).
   Post Museum (Postmuseet) – Three centuries of communications. 15 Dronningens Gate (phone: 408062).

 SHOPPING: Like other Scandinavian cities, Oslo is not a haven for bargain hunters. Prices are high, but you can get good value for your dollar if you concentrate on typically Norwegian items: arts and crafts, pewter, enameled silver, ski sweaters, and, if you are buying furs, Norwegian blue fox and black saga mink. Department stores like *Steen & Strøm* (23 Kongensgt.) carry many of the same items as specialty shops do, but at lower prices. Several exhibition and sales centers have a wide range of Norwegian products on display, so you can get a good idea of what is available. Shops generally are open 9 AM to 5 PM on weekdays (department stores from 10 AM to 6 PM), but close at 1 or 2 PM on Saturdays and remain open until 6 or 7 PM on Thursdays. The city has recently relaxed its laws on opening hours, so you may find some shops open even later.

Oslo has three main shopping districts that are of interest to visitors. The first is downtown Oslo, from Karl Johans Gate past the *Grand* hotel, passing the famous *William Schmidt & Co.,* a stylish and expensive, old gift shop with classic sweaters and other gift items (41 Karl Johans Gate), and the main sales shop of Norway's favorite chocolate manufacturer, *Freia* (#31). Turn left and wander up Lille Grensen shopping street until you emerge at Grensen. Turn right. Two blocks up on the left is one of Oslo's most tempting stores, *Glasmagasinet,* renowned for having the city's best selection of crystal and tableware (10 Stortorvet). Behind is *Husfliden,* Norway's home arts and crafts shop (4 Møllergaten). This is the place to buy homespun fabrics, handwoven and handsewn clothing and household linens, hand-knit winter sportswear, sealskin slippers, and woodcarvings. All the items represent the best of traditional Norwegian crafts, perfect for small gifts and better quality souvenir items.

Beyond *Husfliden* lies the arts and crafts center *Brukskunstsentret i Basarhallene,* behind the Oslo Cathedral. A number of craftspeople have small shops in the arcade. Return via Karl Johans Gate, past two fine jewelry stores, *David Andersen* (20 Karl Johans Gate) and *J. Tostrup* (#25). The former is particularly known for its fine enameled silver, while the latter is the capital's oldest silversmith. Farther on, past the small boulevard park and on the other side of the street, is *Norway Designs A/S* (28 Stortings Gate), with its beautiful displays of clothing, crystal, and fine-quality arts and crafts.

Most people visiting Oslo have a Norwegian sweater on their shopping list, and almost every shop in town tries to fill the need. One, however, prides itself on having the largest selection: *The Oslo Sweater Shop,* in the shopping arcade of the *Scandinavia* hotel (5 Tullinsgt.). If it's fur you crave, be sure to shop around before making a major purchase. Unfortunately, not every fur in Norway is of high quality. After some looking, you'll be better able to distinguish the best from the ordinary. In Norway, quality is almost always proportional to price. Two of the best places to buy fur are *A. C. Bang* (27 Østergade) and *Karsten Philip Pelse* (43 Vimmelskaftet).

Another popular shopping district is Victoria Terrasse, called Vika by residents. Built just before the turn of the century, this plaza was named after England's Queen Victoria. Its government buildings, exclusive shops, and colorful boutiques make it a popular strolling area. This small shopping district is rather elite and attractive and just a few minutes' walk from downtown Oslo, south of the Royal Palace.

The third shopping district is along Bogstadveien street, linking the northernmost corner of the grounds of the Royal Palace with Majorstua, a major transportation crossroads north of downtown. Its attractive shops and boutiques make the street a favorite with Oslo's well-to-do, and its site slightly off the beaten track means few (or no) tourist items and a more authentic atmosphere. Begin a morning by walking and shopping along this street, have an inexpensive lunch in one of the many salad bars, and then take the tram up to Holmenkollen and Frognerseteren (see *Suburbs*) to complete a full Oslo day.

 SPORTS AND FITNESS: Oslo considers itself the world skiing capital, but the city provides a natural playground for sports enthusiasts of all stripes.

Boating – Sailing or boating on the Oslo fjord can be a delightful experience. *Sun Yachting Scandinavia A.S.* rents 25- to 40-foot motorboats and sailboats, bareboat or with a crew. They can also help arrange longer vacations along the coastline (including Lofoten). 43 Akersgaten (phone: 331270). Smaller boats, sailboats, and canoes can be rented by the hour, day, or week. Inquire at the Oslo Tourist Board (phone: 424170) for current listings.

Camping – Three campsites are close to the city. *Ekeberg Camping* at Ekebergsletta is next to Oslo's largest natural park and less than 2.5 miles (4 km) from the center of town. It has a riding school, a children's wading pool, a recreation and sports ground, a kiosk, and a shop and is open from June through August (phone: 198568). *Bogstad Camping,* near Bogstad Lake about 6 miles (9.6 km) from the city, is open all year and has winter-insulated cabins for rent. It also has shops, a cafeteria, a post office (open only during summer), a gas station, and other conveniences (phone: 507680). *Stubljan Camping* at Hvervenbukta is a third choice (phone: 612706), open June through August.

Curling – There are several curling clubs in Oslo, and members of foreign clubs are welcome to use their rinks. For information apply to *Oslo Curlingkrets,* attn: Ellen Storvik (phone: 486902).

Cycling – It is possible to enjoy cycling in the Oslomarka area without being unduly bothered by auto traffic. Suggested cycle tours of the area can be obtained from the *Norwegian Cycling Association,* 20 Majorstuvn. (phone: 442731). Many local tourist offices and hotels rent bicycles for about $10 a day, as does *Den Rustne Eike,* behind the Royal Palace at 32 Oscars Gate (phone: 441880), but be prepared to pay a hefty refundable deposit.

Fishing – There is good trout fishing in the hills north of Oslo. A fishing license is available at local sports stores, but first a national permit must be purchased at the post office for $5. Pimpling, or ice fishing, is popular in the Oslomarka area and on the Oslo fjord whenever the ice is safe. You can't rent equipment, but if you have your own, you are in for a wonderful time. On the fjord ice, you'll find marked trails to follow.

Fitness Centers – *Friskoteket A/S,* 9A Bogstadveien (phone: 460090), has weights and exercise equipment, squash, a sauna, and a physical therapist on staff. *High Energy,* 10 Osterhausgaten (phone: 360600) is an American-style gym. For a low-impact workout or Tae Kwon Do, try *Fitness Network* at 39 Maridalsvn. (phone: 297016). Larger hotels, like the *SAS Scandinavia,* have facilities on the premises.

Golf – The best-known links are the *Bogstad Golf Course,* near Bogstad Lake and the Bogstad camping grounds (phone: 240567). To play, visitors must show membership in an established golf club and pay greens fees; equipment may be rented.

Hiking – In summer, there is a network of about 1,860 miles of paths for hikers in the Oslo area. July and August are the best months for mountain walking. Midtstuen and Frognerseteren stations on the Holmenkollen Railway are good starting points. *Den Norske Turistforening (DNT),* at 28 Stortings Gate, publishes excellent maps covering the mountain areas with suggested tour routes. If you'd prefer to hike with a group, *DNT* can organize conducted tours with guides and reasonably priced lodging in mountain huts.

Ice Skating – The skating season lasts from December until mid-March. Oslo prepares and maintains outdoor rinks in some 150 locations. There is also an artificial frozen rink open to the public at *Valle Hovin* from mid-October to mid-March. Admission to the rinks is free, but there is a small fee for the use of changing rooms. Ice hockey, speed skating, and figure skating competitions are held frequently at the *Bislett, Frogner,* and *Jordal Amfi* stadiums and the Oslo Spectrum, a 9,000-seat arena in the Vaterland development. Details of such events are listed in *Oslo This Week.*

Jogging – A good choice is Frognerparken, 5 to 10 minutes from downtown. For a more rural setting, try any of the paths at Holmenkollen (Holmenkollen tram to Frognerseteren stop). Many paths are clearly marked with destination and distance. Nordmarka, about 20 minutes north of Oslo, is a wilderness area ideally suited for joggers who wish to escape the crowds.

Skiing – Skiing is the national pastime in Norway, and the Oslo municipality maintains more than 1,300 miles of ski trails through the surrounding woods and hills of Oslomarka. These are primarily for cross-country skiing, but hills for ski jumping and alpine skiing are available, too. Most alpine hills are lighted for night skiing, which can be particularly exhilarating. There are even a few ski trails specifically for the blind. The best part is that all of the best spots are only a short ride by bus or suburban railway from downtown Oslo. The Sognsvann railway line goes to Lake Sognsvann, a popular starting point for ski tourers. Buses leave the capital about every hour for Skansebakken in the Sørkedalen district and Skar in the Maridalen district, two other convenient starting points for ski tourers. There are also buses to such slalom centers as Kirkerudbakken in neighboring Baerum and Ingierkollen at Kolbotn. *Tomm Murstad's* ski school at Øvreseter, near the Vaxenkollen terminal of the Holmenkollen railway, is one of several that rent equipment and provide instruction in cross-country and slalom during the winter months (phone: 144665 or 143510; ask for Elisabet Torkildsen). Information on skiing and related activities in the Oslo area is available from the *Ski Association,* 5 Kongev. (phone: 141690).

Swimming – Besides several beaches on the Bygdøy peninsula where you can swim in the Oslo fjord, there are a number of public swimming pools, including an outdoor pool at Vigeland Park (see *Special Places*). The Vigeland Park pool has a wonderful, spacious lawn surrounding it and a slide complex that is a child's fantasy. Nudist bathing beaches are on the northeast side of Svartkulp, a small lake north of Oslo; outside the city on the south side of Langøyene in Oslo Harbor, reached by ferry from the Oslo docks; and on the south side of Bygdøy, near Huk. Three public baths and swimming pools near the center of the city are *Tøyenbadet,* 90 Helgesens Gate (phone: 671889), *Bislet bad,* 60 Pilestredet (phone: 464176), and *Vestkantbadet,* 1 Sommerogaten (phone: 440726). All have saunas.

Windsurfing – It's the craze in Norway, too. The most popular area is around Bygdøy peninsula. Rent equipment from *Sea-Sport Windsurfing Center,* 60A Bygdøy Allé (phone: 447928).

THEATER: Programs are published in the daily press and in *Oslo This Week.* Most performances start at 7:30 PM and are in Norwegian. You can see an Ibsen play at the *National Theater* (Nationaltheatret), Norway's principal theater, 15 Stortings Gate in Studenterlunden Park (phone: 412710). *Amfiscenen,* the experimental stage of the *National Theater,* is in the same building (phone: 410475), but up five flights of stairs. The *Puppet Theater* (Dukketeatret), in the same building as the *Oslo City Museum,* is a delight not only for children, 67 Frognerveien (phone: 421188, 420743); *Det Norske Teatret,* 8 Kristian IV's Gate (phone: 424617), produces foreign plays and musicals in the Norwegian language known as *ny norsk* or new Norwegian; *Oslo nye teater* features classic and modern comedy, 10 Rosenkrantz Gate (phone: 421188); *Chat Noir* presents cabaret acts, Roald Amundsensgt. (no phone), and *ABC-teatret* is the place for light comedy and cabaret (classics in summer), 1 St. Olavsplass (phone: 112166). Fine dining and revues are tastefully combined at Mølla, 21 Sagveien (phone: 375450). Internationally famous shows such as *La Cage aux Folles* are usually performed at *Château Neuf,* 7 Slemdalsvn. (phone: 693154 or 605424). Those in search of English-language productions must watch for special guest appearances by visiting groups. During the tourist season, there are occasional shows in English. All films shown in Norway are screened in their original language and subtitled in Norwegian. It may be tricky figuring out a movie's original title, however; newspaper listings sometimes carry the Norwegian title, usually followed by the country of origin.

MUSIC: Music has deep roots in Oslo's cultural life. The *Royal Guard's* band plays outside the Royal Palace whenever King Olav V is in residence between October 1 and June 24, at the changing of the guard at 1:30 PM, and museums and libraries arrange public concerts regularly. *The Oslo Philharmonic Orchestra* gives numerous concerts during the autumn and winter season. Many of the concerts are held in the university's festival hall or at the *Oslo Concert Hall* (Oslo Konserthus), 14 Munkedamsveien (phone: 209333); in July and August, the concert hall's *Lille Sal* is the site of Norwegian folk dancing on Mondays and Thursdays at 9 PM. *Den Norske Opera* hosts ballets as well as operas at 23C Storgt., Youngstorget (phone: for advance sales, 429475 or 427724). Oslo's newest concert hall, *Byhallen* at Vaterland, hosts both rock concerts and classical events. *Note:* Tickets for most concert and theater performances can also be obtained at the *Ticket Center* (Billet Sentralen), 35 Karl Johans Gate (phone: 427677).

NIGHTCLUBS AND NIGHTLIFE: Oslo nightlife has blossomed in recent years, and the capital is losing its former sleepy reputation. Wine bars, discos, and supper clubs — offering fine dining at one level and live dance bands or cabaret shows at another — abound. *Humla* (26 Universitetsgt., phone: 424420), is a popular supper club where even visitors over 40 won't feel out of place; at the same address (and phone number) is *Barock,* a trendy restaurant and disco.

The discos *Bonanza* at the *Grand* hotel, *El Toro* in the *Bristol,* and the *Frascati Dancing Bar* at 20 Stortingsgt. cater to more mature crowds, while *Galaxy* in the *Scandinavia* hotel and *Creml* just off Karl Johans Gate are popular with the younger set. *Smuget* (on Kirkeveien, near Karl Johans Gate) is a 3-level establishment with an eatery, a disco, and a live jazz/blues/rock section. Yuppies gather for wine, beer, or dinner at *Josefina Vertshus,* 16 Josefina Gate (phone: 603126), a pub housed in an old villa in historic Homansbyen. There are a number of good jazz clubs. Try *Jazz Alive* at 2B Observatoriegt. (phone: 440745), or ask at your hotel for current clubs and night spots. The largest gay club is the *Metropol,* 8 Akers Gate (phone: 421767). Two pleasant café–wine bars are *Fru Blom's* at 41B Karl Johans Gate (serving vintage wines by the glass, pâtés, cheeses, and other tasty snacks) and *Café Sjakk Matt* at 5 Haakon VIIs Gate. After an evening zipping down the floodlit Trysvannskleiva ski run, skiers gather around the blazing log fire at the lakeside *Trysvannstua Lodge* (phone: 144134). On summer evenings, the places to see and be seen are the outdoor cafés at Studenterlunden, just off Karl Johans Gate. The *Panorama Bar,* 35 floors up at the *Oslo Plaza* hotel in Vaterland, is sure to become a popular place (opening in March 1990).

BEST IN TOWN

CHECKING IN: Oslo has a more than adequate number of good modern hotels, but reservations must be made early if you plan to visit during the busiest ski periods (February, March, or Easter), May 17, or at the height of the summer tourist season. If you do arrive without a place to stay, *Innkvartering,* the accommodations center at Oslo S (Central Station), makes room reservations at hotels, pensions, and private homes for a small fee and a refundable deposit. In general, however, no advance bookings are made, and you must show up at the center in person on the day you require the room. (It is worth writing at least 3 weeks ahead to Innkvartering, Oslo S, 1 Jernbanatorget, 0154 Oslo 1.) For a double room with bath, expect to pay about $150 to $225 a night at expensive hotels; from $90 to $150 for those in the moderate range. Anything under $90 a night falls into the inexpensive category. For budget travelers, some simple pensions, two youth hostels, and many of Oslo's best hotels offer special weekend rates year-round. All telephone numbers are in the 02 area code unless otherwise indicated.

Ambassadeur – This charming, small hotel in the west end of the city is popular with diplomats and has suites and demi-suites. The *Spisestuen* restaurant, open for lunch and dinner, serves "nouvelle Norwegian" cuisine. 15 Camilla Collettsvei (phone: 441835). Expensive.

Bristol – A very traditional European stopping place, set right in the center of town. It offers pleasant, large rooms, an inviting lobby bar, a disco with a Spanish atmosphere, and a popular grill room. 7 Kristian IV's Gate (phone: 415840). Expensive.

Continental – This centrally located, first-rate hotel has 2 restaurants worth noting: *Annen Etage,* one of Oslo's best, and *Theatercaféen,* one of the city's most popular old-fashioned cafés (see *Eating Out*). Recent guests have reported, however, that the service is not up to par. 24/26 Stortings Gate (phone: 419060). Expensive.

Grand – Oslo's most prestigious hotel: dignified, traditional, and offering excellent service. It has spacious rooms, 3 bars, 5 elegant restaurants, pool and exercise facilities, and a perfect downtown location. If money is no object, book the Tower Suite or the Nobel Suite, which houses each year's Nobel Peace Prize winner. Also 25 junior suites. 31 Karl Johans Gate (phone: 429390). Expensive.

Holmenkollen Park Hotel Rica – Storybook style, timber-beamed, with comfortable (but small) rooms, also distinguished by an excellent view of Oslo from its lovely setting on Holmenkollen Hill on the outskirts of the city. A huge fireplace dominates its public salon; some rooms have terraces, and its attractive restaurant features Norwegian specialties (try the salmon). Reached by car or the Holmenkollen suburban tram line. 26 Kongeveien, Holmenkollåsen (phone: 146090). Expensive.

KNA Park Avenue Hotellet – Not far from the Royal Palace, west of the city center, formerly owned by the *Royal Norwegian Automobile Club*. Recently remodeled, it also has a good restaurant and bar. 68 Parkveien (phone: 446970). Expensive.

Nobel – Convenience is a keynote here. Small, centrally located, and near the *Grand* hotel. 33 Karl Johans Gate (phone: 427480). Expensive.

Oslo Plaza – With 712 luxurious rooms and suites, it's by far the country's largest hotel. The 35-story glass structure towers over Oslo, with the *Panorama Bar* on the very top. Opening early 1990. Vaterland (phone: 423660). Expensive.

Sara Hotel Christiania – Its mood and decor inspired by the 300-year history of Christiania (Oslo), this 539-room property features 90 suites, including the sumptuous 2-story King's Suite. A restaurant, café, and bar are housed in the marble and brass atrium. Opening early 1990. Vaterland (phone: 429410). Expensive.

Sara Hotel Oslo – This major Oslo hotel is near the east railroad station. The main attractions are its convenience and pleasant restaurant, *Oslo Haven*. The sumptuous buffet breakfasts are a bonus. 3 B. Gunnerus Gate (phone: 429410). Expensive.

SAS Scandinavia – A large, high-rise hotel near the Royal Palace, many rooms have lovely views of the city and the fjord. Facilities include a health club and swimming pool, 5 restaurants (see *Eating Out*) and bars, the most notable of which is the *Summit Bar* on the 21st floor. 30 Holbergs Gate (phone: 113000). Expensive.

Sheraton – This hotel, with 245 rooms and suites, is about 20 minutes from the city center, overlooking the Oslo fjord. Don't let the spartan exterior put you off; the elegant interiors won't. The *Atrium* garden café is airy and pleasant, while the *L'Orchidée* restaurant is Art Deco in style. Try the chef's daily special. Sauna and fitness center. 184 Sandviksveien (phone: 545700). Expensive.

Triangel Apartments – Just around the corner from the *Triangel* hotel, these 41 new units have kitchenettes and are available for daily or long-term rental. Special rates are offered for monthly leasing. 38 Pilestredet (phone: 208855). Expensive to moderate.

Gabelshus – A quiet, established hotel with a loyal clientele, the atmosphere of a stately home, and an impeccable restaurant. A 15-minute walk from the city center. 16 Gabels Gate (phone: 552260). Moderate.

Stefanhotellet – This clean, modest hotel, operated by the local Mission society, has a renowned restaurant (see *Eating Out*), but no liquor, wine, or beer is served on the premises. 1 Rosenkrantz Gate (phone: 429250). Moderate.

Triangel – Modest, modernized, operated by the Mission Society (no alcohol on premises). Centrally located. 1 Holbergs Plass (phone: 208855). Moderate.

Vika Atrium – A new hotel a stone's throw from the harbor, Aker Brygge, and City Hall, with 72 rooms and a restaurant open for breakfast, lunch, and dinner. It's not luxurious, but has high standards, and the location can't be beat. 45 Monkedamsveien (phone: 331220). Moderate.

Munch – All the conveniences of a hotel in a far higher price range, but no restaurant. 5 Munchs Gate (phone: 424275). Moderate to inexpensive.

Hall Hotell-Pension – This small west end establishment caters to visitors who stay for several weeks or even months. No private bathrooms. 21 Fritzners Gate (phone: 557726). Inexpensive.

EATING OUT: As you might expect, Norwegian cuisine centers on a wide range of fish and seafood specialties in addition to game. Norwegian trout and salmon are not to be missed, but you will also find delicious meals of cod, haddock, and coalfish. *Gravlax* is one type of smoked salmon to sample, but if it is too hard on your pocketbook, try another Norwegian delicacy: warm smoked mackerel. Sample the beer: *brigg* and *lettøl* are the weakest, lager is called *pils,* and *export* or *Gold* is the strongest. *Akevitt* (the Norwegian spelling of *aquavit*), which is made from potatoes and herbs and spices, accompanies special meals (with a beer chaser). Both reindeer and moose steaks are excellent, especially in the fall during the hunting season. Breakfast can vary from the simple continental — coffee, rolls, butter, and marmalade — to the traditional Norwegian *koldtbord* — a buffet with everything from assorted herring dishes to salmon and paper-thin slices of roast beef.

Dining out in Oslo is expensive. Most visitors sample at least one *koldtbord* lunch, almost all of which include some hot dishes. A dinner at an expensive restaurant will cost $50 or more per person; moderately priced establishments charge about $20 for a meal; and those in the inexpensive category charge less than $20. It's the price of beer and wine that can skyrocket the cost of a dinner for two into a $100 to $200 tab. Credit cards are welcomed at large restaurants, but smaller ones generally don't accept them. Many restaurants close during the Christmas and Easter holidays. All telephone numbers are in the 02 area code unless otherwise indicated.

Best bet for a quick and inexpensive lunch is a *konditori,* or bakery tearoom, where the Norwegians tend to eat. Enticingly fresh noontime selections include sandwiches, cakes, coffee, and tea, to be enjoyed at small tables or counters. Or take them along to eat in a park.

For a large selection of restaurants offering a choice of different sorts of food in varying price categories, stroll around Aker Brygge at the harbor or the new Vaterland development.

Annen Etage – Elegant and traditional Norwegian-European restaurant featuring French and Norwegian cuisine, on the second floor of the *Continental* hotel. Piano music. Reservations advised. Open weekdays for lunch and dinner and Sundays for early dinner (closed Saturdays). 24/26 Stortings Gate (phone: 419060). Expensive.

Bagatelle – The only Oslo restaurant to have a star in the Michelin guide. Fine nouvelle cuisine and a distinguished wine cellar. The menu is set; diners need only choose the number of courses: 5 or 7. Open Tuesdays through Fridays for lunch, and daily for dinner except Sundays. Closed July. Reservations necessary. 3-5 Bygdøy allé (phone: 446397). Expensive.

Etoile – On the sixth floor of the *Grand* hotel, with a glass roof and a beautiful view of the city, this first class kitchen serves French and Norwegian food. Open daily, noon to midnight. Lunch table from noon to 2:30 PM. 31 Karl Johans Gate (phone: 429390). Expensive.

Frascati – This popular old meeting and dining spot in downtown Oslo is open daily except Sundays from 3:30 PM to 4 AM. Live music and a disco nightly. 20 Stortings Gate (phone: 416876). Expensive.

Holberg – An excellent grill restaurant with an international à la carte menu. It holds special gastronomical weeks in autumn and spring. Its decorations are from the Holberg époque by Bjorn Winblad. In the *Scandinavia* hotel. Open daily at 5 PM. 30 Holbergs Gate (phone: 113000). Expensive.

La Mer – Perhaps the best fish and seafood restaurant in Oslo. Call 2 days ahead and order the house special, *bouillabaisse.* Open daily except Sundays at 4 PM. 31 Pilestredet (phone: 203445). Expensive.

Mølla – This fine fish and game restaurant is in an old textile mill on the banks of the River Akerselva, which was the setting for Oskar Braaten's novels about factory workers' lives in the beginning of the century. After dinner, there's a dancing bar and musical revues are presented. Open daily except Sundays at 3 PM. Reservations advised. 21 Sagveien (phone: 375450). Expensive.

Najaden – This first class restaurant with a very pleasant atmosphere is in the *Maritime Museum*. It offers a special tourist's lunch with assorted herrings, hot dishes, and cheeses. Open daily. 37 Bygdøynesv., Bydøy peninsula (phone: 438180). Expensive.

Tre Kokker – Intimate and elegant, decorated with modern Norwegian art. The traditional Norwegian menu specializes in fish and game, and the food is excellent. The three chefs ("tre kokker") work in full view of diners. Open weekdays from 4 PM, Saturdays for dinner. Reservations necessary. 30 Drammensveien (phone: 442650). Expensive.

Blom – Charmingly decorated with the shields of members of the Norwegian Society of Artists (can you find Charlie Chaplin's and Liv Ullmann's?). The art and antiques on its walls are alone worth a visit. It specializes in fish and game, and has a popular open-sandwich buffet at lunchtime. Closed Sundays. 39/41 Karl Johans Gate (phone: 427300). Expensive to moderate.

Bygdøystuene – Formerly the *Folk Museum Restaurant,* it has a classic interior and menu. In summer it becomes a charming open-air restaurant. Open daily. Bygdøy peninsula (phone: 440080). Expensive to moderate.

De Fem Stuer – Another of the city's top places for a fine lunch from a buffet that is one of the city's best. The decor is attractive, the view over the city and its environs outstanding. Open daily. Reservations advised. In the romantic *Holmenkollen Park* hotel, 26 Kongeveien, Holmenkollåsen (phone: 146090). Expensive to moderate.

Norberto – One of Oslo's best restaurants, much acclaimed by visiting food editors and critics. The specials are moderately priced — if everyone at the table orders the same thing. Open daily for dinner. 85 Sognsv. (phone: 230485). Expensive to moderate.

Theatercaféen – This unrivaled Oslo favorite, much frequented by artists, is in the *Continental* hotel. The orchestra favors waltzes, but there is no dancing. A place to see and be seen. Window tables are the most fashionable. Open daily. Dinner reservations advised. 24/26 Stortings Gate (phone: 419060). Expensive to moderate.

Café Sjakk Matt – One of Oslo's most popular cafés, it's open midday for lunch and serves small snacks after 3 PM. Open daily. 5 Haakon VII's Gate, near Vika (phone: 834156). Moderate.

Grand Café – This busy restaurant in the *Grand* hotel has large murals of life in Old Christiania at the turn of the century, when it was Ibsen's destination twice daily. Music after 7 PM. Jazz brunch on Sundays. Open daily until 11:30 PM. 31 Karl Johans Gate (phone: 429390). Moderate.

Håndverkeran Bar and Grill – A meeting place for artists and journalists, who flock to its special sandwich buffet from 11 AM to 2 PM each day. Masculine atmosphere. Closed Sundays. 7 Rosenkrantz Gate (phone: 418358). Moderate.

Stefanhotellet – The top-floor restaurant in one of the Mission hotels. Serves excellent Norwegian food and an interesting selection of nonalcoholic wines. Open daily for dinner; lunch on Sundays. 1 Rosenkrantz Gate (phone: 429250). Moderate.

Tostrupkjelleren – The best of Oslo's basement restaurants, a meeting place for politicians, journalists, and businesspeople that serves international cuisines. Open for lunch and dinner daily except Sundays. 25 Karl Johans Gate (phone: 421470). Moderate.

Frognerseteren Kafé – Both à la carte restaurant and cafeteria, this establishment at Holmenkollen has the feel of a ski lodge. Try the fresh salmon or the "wild" stew of elk, reindeer, and berries. In summer, crowds gather on the terrace overlooking Oslofjord to soak up the sun while enjoying apple cake served with mounds of fresh whipped cream. Open for lunch and dinner. 200 Holmenkollen (phone: 143736). Restaurant, moderate; cafeteria, inexpensive.

Holmenkollen – The kitchen features Norwegian dishes, the dining room features a spectacular view of the city and fjord. Try the large lunch buffet. Open daily. Reached by the Holmenkollen line. 119 Holmenkollveien, Holmenkollåsen (phone: 146226). Inexpensive.

Peppe's Pizza – Launched in 1969 by an American-Norwegian couple, the thin-crust pizza became an overnight success. Decorated in a farmhouse motif — cozy, dark, filled with antiques — there are four branches in Oslo, including one in the city center at 4 Stortingsgt. (phone: 425418), open daily. A large pizza weighs in at about 2.2 pounds, serves 3 to 4, and costs from $16 to $24. Inexpensive.

PARIS

It was Victor Hugo, the great French poet and novelist, who captured the true spirit of his native city when he called it "the heir of Rome, the mundane pilgrim's home away from home." If Rome, for all its earthly exuberance, never lets the visitor forget that it is the spiritual home of the West, Paris — with its supreme joie de vivre and its passion for eating, drinking, and dressing well — belongs unabashedly to the material world.

Like a magnet, Paris has always attracted visitors and exiles from all corners of the earth. At the same time, it remains not so much an international city as a very French one, and a provincial one at that. Paris has its own argot, and each neighborhood retains its peculiar character, so that the great capital is still very much a city of 20 villages.

But parochialism aside — and forgetting about the consummate haughtiness of Parisians (someone once remarked that Parisians don't even like themselves) — the main attraction of the City of Light is its beauty. When you speak of the ultimate European city, it must be Paris, if only for the view from the Place de la Concorde or the Tuileries toward the Arc de Triomphe, or similarly striking sights beside the Seine. Here is the fashion capital of the world and the center of gastronomic invention and execution. Here the men all seem to swagger with the insouciance of privilege, and even the humblest shopgirl dresses with the care of a haute couture mannequin. Paris is the reason "foreign" means "French" to so many travelers.

Paris is in the north-central part of France, in the rich agricultural area of the Seine River valley. With a population of nearly 2 million people, it is France's largest city, an industrial and commercial center, and an important river port. Roughly elliptical in shape, the city has more than doubled in size in the last century. Its limits now are the ring of mid-19th-century fortifications that once were well beyond its boundaries. At its western edge is the vast Bois de Boulogne and to the east the Bois de Vincennes — two enormous parks. Curving through Paris, the Seine divides the city into its northern Right Bank (Rive Droite) and southern Left Bank (Rive Gauche). The Right Bank extends from the Bois de Boulogne on the far west, through Place Charles-de-Gaulle (l'Etoile), which surrounds the Arc de Triomphe, and farther east to the Tuileries Gardens and the fabulous *Louvre*. North of the *Louvre* is the area of the Grands Boulevards, centers of business and fashion; farther north is the district of Montmartre, built on a hill and crowned by the domed Eglise du Sacré-Coeur, an area that has attracted great artists (and many of markedly less greatness) since the days of Monet and Renoir.

The Left Bank sweeps from the Eiffel Tower on the west through the Latin Quarter, with its university and bohemian and intellectual community. South of the Latin Quarter is Montparnasse, once inhabited jointly by artists and intellectuals and laborers, now a large urban renewal project that includes a suburban-style shopping center around the Tour Montparnasse.

In the middle of the Seine are two islands, the Ile de la Cité and the Ile St.-Louis, the oldest parts of Paris. It was on the Ile de la Cité (in the 3rd century BC) that Celtic fishermen known as Parisii first built a settlement they named Lutetia, "place surrounded by water." Caesar conquered the city for Rome in 52 BC, and, in about AD 300, Paris was invaded by Germanic tribes, the strongest of which were the Franks. In 451, when Attila the Hun threatened to overrun Paris, a holy woman named Geneviève promised to defend the city by praying. She succeeded — the enemy decided to spare the capital — and Geneviève became the patron saint of Paris. Clovis I, the first Christian King of the Franks, made Paris his capital in the 6th century. Relentless Norman sieges, famine, and plague curtailed the city's development, but at the end of the 10th century peace and prosperity came with the triumph of Hugh Capet over the Carolingians. Capet ascended the throne, the first of a long line of Capétian kings, and Paris became the "central jewel of the French crown," a great cultural center and seat of learning.

The Capétian monarchs contributed much to the growth of the city over the next few centuries. A defensive wall was begun in 1180 by Philip Augustus to protect the expanding Right Bank business and trading center as well as the intellectual quarter around the newly formed university on the Left Bank. He then built a new royal palace, the *Louvre,* just outside these ramparts, but he never lived there. Medieval Paris was a splendid city, a leader in the arts and in the intellectual life of Europe. The Sorbonne attracted such outstanding scholars as Alexander of Hales, Giovanni di Fidanza (St. Bonaventure), Albertus Magnus, and Thomas Aquinas.

The Ile de la Cité remained a warren of narrow streets and wood and plaster houses, but the banks of the Seine continued to be built up in both directions. Renaissance kings, patrons of the arts, added their own architectural and aesthetic embellishments to the flourishing city. Major streets were laid out; some of Paris's most charming squares were constructed; the Pont Neuf, the first stone bridge spanning the Seine, was completed; and Le Nôtre, the royal gardener, introduced proportion, harmony, and beauty with his extraordinary Tuileries.

Louis XIV, who was responsible for many of the most notable Parisian landmarks, including Les Invalides, moved the court to Versailles in the late 17th century. Paris nevertheless continued to blossom, and it was under the Sun King's rule that France and Paris first won international prestige. Visitors were drawn to the city, luxury trades were begun, and the Panthéon, Champ-de-Mars parade ground, and Ecole Militaire were built. In 1785, at age 16, Napoleon Bonaparte graduated from this military school with the notation in his report: "Will go far if circumstances permit!"

French history reflects the conflict between the two extremes of the French character, both equally strong: a tradition of aristocracy and a penchant for revolution. To the French aristocracy we owe magnificent palaces like the *Louvre,* the Luxembourg Palace, and Versailles, with their formal gardens. At the same time, the people of Paris have always been noisily rebellious and independent: from 1358, when the mob rebelled against the Dauphin, to the

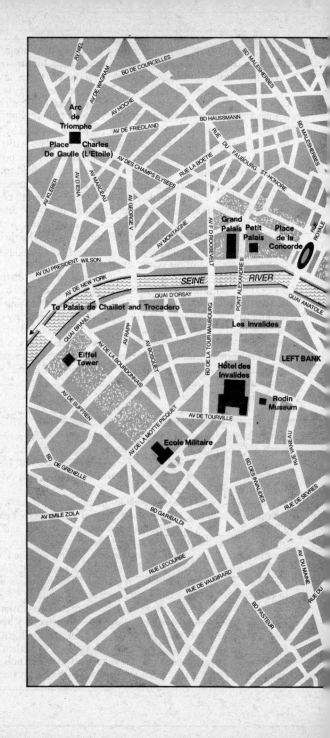

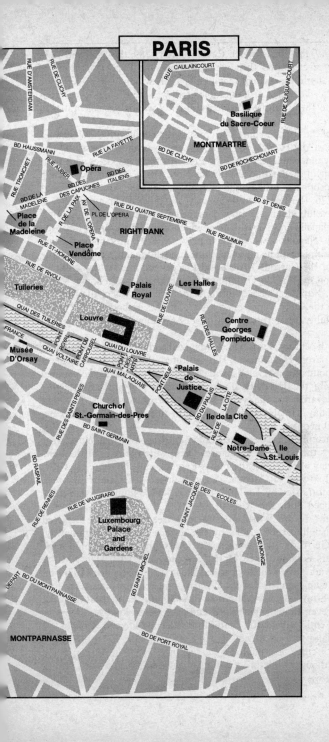

PARIS

RUE D'AMSTERDAM
RUE DE CLICHY
RUE CAULAINCOURT
RUE DE CLIGNANCOURT

Basilique
du Sacré-Coeur

MONTMARTRE

BD HAUSSMANN
RUE LA FAYETTE
BD DE CLICHY
BD DE ROCHECHOUART

RUE TRONCHET
RUE AUBER
Opéra
BD DES
ITALIENS

BD DE LA
MADELEINE
BD DES
DES CAPUCINES
BD ST DENIS

Place
de la
Madeleine

RUE DE LA PAIX
AV. DE L'OPERA
PL DE L'OPERA
RUE DU QUATRE SEPTEMBRE

RIGHT BANK
RUE REAUMUR

Place
Vendôme

RUE ST-HONORE

RUE DE RIVOLI

Tuileries

Palais
Royal
Les Halles

RUE DE LOUVRE

QUAI DES TUILERIES
Louvre
Centre
Georges
Pompidou

FRANCE
QUAI DU LOUVRE
RUE DES HALLES

Musée
D'Orsay
QUAI VOLTAIRE
QUAI MALAQUAIS
PONT ROYAL
PONT DU CARROUSEL
PONT DES ARTS
PONT NEUF

Palais
de
Justice

BD DU PALAIS
LA CITE

Church of
St.-Germain-des-Pres
Ile de la Cite

RUE DES SAINTS PERES
BD SAINT GERMAIN
RUE DE LA CITE

Notre-Dame
Ile
St.-Louis

BD RASPAIL

RUE DE RENNES

RUE DE VAUGIRARD
RUE DES ECOLES

R SAINT JACQUES

Luxembourg
Palace
and
Gardens

RUE MONGE

DEPART
BD DU MONTPARNASSE

BD SAINT MICHEL

MONTPARNASSE
BD DE PORT ROYAL

Fronde in 1648–49, the great French Revolution of 1789, the 1830 and 1848 revolutions that reverberated throughout Europe, the Paris Commune of 1870–71, and finally to the student rebellion of 1968, which nearly overthrew the Fifth Republic. The most profound one of all was the French Revolution at the close of the 18th century, the bicentennial of which was celebrated in grand style in 1989.

The excesses of the French court, the consummate luxury of the Versailles of Louis XIV, cost the French people dearly in taxes and oppression. The Parisians, fiercely independent, forced the French king to his knees with their dramatic storming of the Bastille in 1789. Inspired by the ideas of the French and English philosophers of the Enlightenment, just like the American founding fathers in 1776, the French subsequently overthrew their monarchy.

During the Revolution, unruly mobs damaged many of the city's buildings, including Ste.-Chapelle and Notre-Dame, which were not restored until the mid-19th century. Napoleon, who came to power in 1799, was too busy being a conqueror to complete all he planned, though he did manage to restore the *Louvre,* construct the Carrousel Arch and Place Vendôme victory column, and begin work on the Arc de Triomphe and the Madeleine. Though something of a tyrant, Napoleon's conquests spread the new ideas of the Revolution — including the Code Napoléon, a system of laws embodying the ideals of "Liberty, Equality, Fraternity" — to places as far away as Canada and Moscow.

Later in the 19th century, Paris was reorganized and modernized by a great urban planner, Baron Haussmann. He instituted the brilliant system of squares as focal points for marvelous, wide boulevards and roads; he planned the Place de l'Opéra, the Bois de Boulogne and Bois de Vincennes, the railway stations, the boulevards, and the system of 20 *arrondissements* (districts) that make up Paris today. He also destroyed most of the center of the old Cité, displacing 25,000 people.

During the peaceful lull between the Franco-Prussian War and World War I, the city of Paris thrived as never before. These were the days of the Belle Epoque, the heyday of Maxim's, the Folies-Bergère, and the can-can, whose spirit is captured so well in Offenbach's heady music for *Gaité Parisienne.* Montmartre, immortalized by Toulouse-Lautrec, was so uninhibited that the foreign press dubbed Paris the "City of Sin."

In the 2 decades before World War II, this free-spirited city attracted politically and socially exiled artists by the dozens: Picasso, Hemingway, Fitzgerald, and Gertrude Stein were just a few. Only in Paris could such avant-garde writers as James Joyce, D. H. Lawrence, and, later, Henry Miller find publishers. And Paris, which witnessed the first Impressionist exhibition in 1874 — introducing Monet, Renoir, Pissarro, and Seurat — heard the first performance of Stravinsky's revolutionary *Sacre du Printemps* (Rite of Spring) in 1913, even though the baffled audience jeered loudly.

As the quintessentially beautiful center of intellectual life and home of the arts, Paris can claim to have earned its City of Light title. Even though it, like other modern cities, is troubled by a rise in crime — at *Maxim's,* for instance, a precautionary bulletproof window has been installed — its beauty and libertarian atmosphere remain. Its supreme talent for civilized living has made the city beloved by the French and foreigners alike. After all, these are the people who made food preparation a fine art, and, despite the unfortunate presence of fast-food vendors on the Champs-Elysées, the French passion for haute cuisine remains unrivaled. And as the undisputed capital of fashion, male and female, Paris continues to be the best-dressed city in the world, and Rue du Faubourg-St.-Honoré remains the standard by which all other shopping streets are measured.

However avant-garde in dress, Parisians are a conservative lot when it comes to any changes in the appearance of their beloved city. When the Eiffel Tower was built in 1889, Guy de Maupassant commented, "I spend all my afternoons on the Eiffel Tower; it's the only place in Paris from which you can't see it." So today's Parisians grumble about the ultramodern *Centre Georges Pompidou,* a focus for every type of modern art: theater, music, dance, circus, painting, sculpture, photography, and film, and about Le Forum, a sunken glass structure filled with boutiques in what was once Les Halles, the bawdy produce market. They also don't seem especially thrilled by I. M. Pei's glass pyramids that form the new entrance to the *Louvre.*

Parisians accept innovations reluctantly because they want their city to remain as it has always been. They love their remarkable heritage inordinately, and perhaps it is this love, together with the irrepressible sense of good living, that has made Paris so eternally attractive to others.

PARIS AT-A-GLANCE

SEEING THE CITY: It's impossible to single out just one perfect Paris panorama; they exist in profusion. The most popular is the bird's-eye view from the top of the Eiffel Tower on the Left Bank; there are three places to have snacks and drinks and enjoy a view (on a clear day) of more than 50 miles. The tower is open daily, 10 AM to 11 PM; admission charge (Champ-de-Mars; phone: 45-50-34-56). From the top of the towers of Notre-Dame, eager spectators enjoy close-ups of the cathedral's Gothic spires and flying buttresses, along with a magnificent view of the Cité and the rest of Paris. Start climbing the steps at the foot of the north tower on Rue du Cloítre Notre-Dame, 4e. Admission charge (phone: 43-25-42-92). On the Right Bank there's a stunning view from the terrace of Sacré-Coeur. The observatory on Tour Montparnasse also offers a striking panorama, as does the landing at the top of the escalator at the *Centre Georges Pompidou.*

The most satisfying view, if not the highest, is from the top of the Arc de Triomphe. The arch is the center of Place Charles-de-Gaulle, once Place de l'Etoile (Square of the Star), so called because it is the center of a "star" whose radiating points are the 12 broad avenues, including the Champs-Elysées, planned and built by Baron Haussmann in the mid-19th century. Open daily, 10 AM to 5:30 PM. Admission charge (phone: 43-80-31-31).

For the truly extravagant, there are helicopter tours that start at $80 per person from the Héliport de Paris at the foot of the *Sofitel* hotel. *Héli-France,* 4 Av. de la Porte de Sèvres, 15e (phone: 45-57-53-67), offers tours daily for a minimum of 4 people, and *Héli-Cap* (phone: 45-57-75-51) offers tours weekdays for a minimum of 4 people.

SPECIAL PLACES: Getting around this sprawling metropolis isn't difficult once you understand the layout of the 20 *arrondissements*. We suggest that visitors orient themselves by taking one of the many excellent sightseeing tours offered by *Cityrama,* 4 Pl. des Pyramides, 1er (phone: 42-60-30-14), or *Paris Vision,* 214 Rue de Rivoli, 1er (phone: 42-60-31-25). Their bubble-topped double-decker buses are equipped with earphones for simultaneous commentary in English and several other languages. Reserve through any travel agent or your hotel's concierge.

Once you have a better idea of the basic layout of the city, buy a copy of *Paris Indispensable* or *Plan de Paris par Arrondissement* at any bookshop or newsstand. These little life-savers list streets alphabetically and indicate the nearest métro station on individual maps and an overall plan. Now you're ready to set out by foot (the most rewarding) or by métro (the fastest and surest) to discover Paris for yourself.

LA RIVE DROITE (THE RIGHT BANK)

Arc de Triomphe and Place de l'Etoile – This monumental arch (165 feet high, 148 feet wide) was built between 1806 and 1836 to commemorate Napoleon's victories. It underwent a major clean-up and restoration last year for the bicentennial of the French Revolution. Note the frieze and its 6-foot-high figures, the 10 impressive sculptures (especially Rude's *La Marseillaise* on the right as you face the Champs-Elysées), and the arches inscribed with the names of Bonaparte's victories as well as those of Empire heroes. Beneath the arch is the French Tomb of the Unknown Soldier and its Eternal Flame, which is rekindled each day at 6:30 PM. An elevator (or 284 steps) carries visitors to the top for a magnificent view of the city and the 12 avenues radiating from l'Etoile. Admission charge. Pl. Charles-de-Gaulle (phone: 43-80-31-31).

Champs-Elysées – Paris's legendary promenade, the "Elysian fields," was swampland until 1616. It has come to be synonymous with everything glamorous in the city, though the "Golden Arches" and shlocky shops have replaced much of the glitter. It stretches for more than 2 miles between the Place de la Concorde and the Place Charles-de-Gaulle (l'Etoile). The very broad avenue, lined with rows of plane and horse chestnut trees, shops, cafés, and cinemas, is perfect for a stroll, window shopping, and people watching.

The area from the Place de la Concorde to the Rond-Point Champs-Elysées is a charming park, where Parisians often bring their children. On the north side of the gardens is the Palais de l'Elysée, the official home of the president of the French Republic. Ceremonial events, such as the *Bastille Day Parade* (July 14), frequently take place along the Champs-Elysées.

Grand Palais – Off the Champs-Elysées, on opposite sides of Avenue Winston-Churchill, are the elaborate turn-of-the-century *Grand Palais* and *Petit Palais* (Large Palace and Small Palace), built of glass and stone for the 1900 World Exposition. With its stone columns, mosaic frieze, and flat glass dome, the *Grand Palais* contains a large exhibition area and the *Palais de la Découverte,* the Paris science museum, and the *Planetarium.* Closed Tuesdays; open Wednesdays until 10 PM. Av. Franklin-Roosevelt, 8e (phone: 42-89-54-10).

Petit Palais – Built contemporaneously with the *Grand Palais,* this is now the *Paris Musée des Beaux-Arts,* containing exhibitions of the city's history as well as a variety of fine and applied arts. Closed Mondays. Admission charge. Av. Winston-Churchill, 8e (phone: 42-65-12-73).

Place de la Concorde – This square, surely one of the most magnificent in the world, is grandly situated in the midst of equally grand landmarks: the *Louvre* and the Tuileries on one side, the Champs-Elysées and the Arc de Triomphe on another, the Seine and the Napoleonic Palais Bourbon on a third, and the pillared façade of the Madeleine on the fourth. Designed by Gabriel for Louis XV, the elegant square was where his unfortunate successor, Louis XVI, lost his head to the guillotine, as did Marie Antoinette, Robespierre, Charlotte Corday, and others. It was first named for Louis XV, then called Place de la Révolution by the triumphant revolutionaries. Ornamenting the square, the eight colossal statues representing important French provincial capitals were recently polished and blasted clean for the 1989 bicentennial celebration. The 3,300-year-old, 75-foot-high obelisk was a gift from Egypt in 1829.

Jardin des Tuileries – Carefully laid out in patterned geometric shapes, with clipped shrubbery and formal flower beds, statues, and fountains, this is one of the finest examples of French garden design (in contrast to an informal English garden, exemplified by the Bois de Boulogne). Along the Seine, between the Place de la Concorde and the *Louvre.*

Rue de Rivoli – This charming old street has perfume shops, souvenir stores, boutiques, bookstores, cafés, and such hotels as the *Meurice* and the *Inter-Continental* under its 19th-century arcades. The section facing the Tuileries, from the Place de la Concorde to the *Louvre,* is an especially good place to explore on rainy days.

In the *Orangerie,* a museum across the gardens, is a series of large paintings of water lilies by Monet called the *Nymphéas* and the collection of Jean Walter and Paul Guillaume, with works by Cézanne, Renoir, Matisse, Picasso, and others. Open 10 AM to 4:30 PM; closed Tuesdays. Admission charge. Pl. de la Concorde and Quai des Tuileries, 1er (phone: 42-97-48-16).

Louvre – Built on the site of a medieval fortress on the banks of the Seine, this palace was the home of the French kings in the 16th and 17th centuries, until Louis XIV moved the court to Versailles in 1682. In 1793, it became a museum and is now one of the world's greatest art repositories. It's easy to spend a couple of days here, savoring treasures like the *Venus de Milo, Winged Victory,* the *Mona Lisa,* and the French crown jewels — just a few of the 200,000 pieces in six different collections.

Nor is the outside of this huge edifice to be overlooked. Note especially the Cour Carrée (the courtyard of the old *Louvre*), the southwest corner of which, dating from the mid-1550s, is the oldest part of the palace and a beautiful example of the Renaissance style that François I had so recently introduced from Italy. Note, too, the Colonnade, which forms the eastern front of the Cour Carrée, facing the Place du Louvre; fully classical in style, it dates from the late 1660s, not too long before the Sun King left for Versailles. Newer wings of the *Louvre* embrace the palace gardens, in the midst of which stands the Arc de Triomphe du Carrousel, erected by Napoleon. From here, the vista across the Tuileries and the Place de la Concorde and on up the Champs-Elysées to the Arc de Triomphe is one of the most beautiful in Paris — which says a lot. The new glass pyramids — designed by I. M. Pei and opened in 1989 — sit center stage in the *Louvre*'s grand interior courtyard; the largest one serves as the museum's main entrance. The controversial structures, completely at odds with their surroundings, are the first step of a major expansion; when completed, the *Louvre*'s underground galleries, shops, and exhibition space will connect the North and South Wings, increasing museum space by almost 80%.

Good guided tours in English, covering the highlights of the *Louvre,* are frequently available, although not every day, so be sure to check in advance. Open from 9:45 AM to 6:30 PM; closed Tuesdays. Admission charge except Sundays. Pl. du Louvre, 1er (phone: 42-60-39-26).

Place Vendôme – Just north of the Tuileries is an aristocrat of a square, one of the loveliest in Paris, the octagonal Place Vendôme, designed by Mansart in the 17th century. Its arcades contain world-famous jewelers, perfumers, and banks, the *Ritz* hotel, and the Ministry of Justice. The 144-foot column in the center is covered with bronze from the 1,200 cannons captured at Austerlitz by Napoleon in 1805. Just off Place Vendôme is the famous Rue du Faubourg-St.-Honoré, one of the oldest streets in Paris, which now holds elegant shops selling the world's most expensive made-to-order items. To the north is the Rue de la Paix, noted for its jewelers.

Opéra – Charles Garnier's imposing rococo edifice stands in its own busy square, its façade decorated with sculpture, including Carpeaux's *The Dance*. The ornate interior has an impressive grand staircase, a beautiful foyer, lavish marble from every quarry in France, and Chagall's controversially decorated dome. Until recently, the opera house could only be seen by attending a performances (September–June); now, however, visitors may explore its magnificent interior and enjoy its special exhibitions daily from 11 AM to 4:30 PM. Pl. de l'Opéra, 9e (phone: 47-42-57-50).

L'Opéra Bastille – In sharp contrast to Garnier's *Opéra* is the curved glass façade of 20th-century architect Carlos Ott's new Paris opera house. Set against the historic landscape of the Bastille quarter, this futuristic building houses over 30 acres of multi-purpose theaters, shops, and an urban promenade. Inaugurated for the bicentennial of the revolution on July 14, 1989, the opera house's first regular performances begin in January 1990. Pl. de la Bastille, 11e (phone: 43-42-92-92).

La Madeleine – Starting in 1764, the Church of St. Mary Magdalene was built and razed twice before the present structure was commissioned by Napoleon in 1806 to honor his armies. The church is based on a Greek temple design, its 65-foot-high Corinthian columns supporting the sculptured frieze. From its portals, the view extends down Rue Royale to Place de la Concorde and over to the dome of Les Invalides. Nearby are some of Paris's most tantalizing food shops. Open from 7:30 AM to 7 PM as well as during concerts (held 4 PM Sundays) and other frequent musical events. Pl. de la Madeleine, 8e (phone: 42-65-52-17).

Sacré-Coeur and Montmartre – Built on the highest of Paris's seven hills, the white-domed Basilica of Sacré-Coeur provides an extraordinary view from its steps, especially at dawn or sunset. The area around the church was the artists' quarter of late-19th- and early-20th-century Paris. The more garish aspects of Montmartre's notoriously frivolous 1890s nightlife, particularly the dancers and personalities at the *Moulin Rouge,* were immortalized by the paintings of Henri de Toulouse-Lautrec. And if the streets look familiar, chances are you've seen them in the paintings of Utrillo; they still look the same. The Place du Tertre is still charming, though often filled with tourists and overly eager, mostly undertalented artists. Go early to see it as it was when Braque, Dufy, Modigliani, Picasso, Rousseau, and Utrillo lived here. Montmartre has the last of Paris's vineyards — and still contains old houses, narrow alleys, steep stairways, and carefree cafés enough to provide a full day's entertainment; at night, this is one of the centers of Paris life. Spare yourself most of the climb to Sacré-Coeur by taking the funicular from Place St.-Pierre. Butte Montmartre, 18e.

Les Halles – Just northeast of the *Louvre,* this 80-acre area, formerly the Central Market, "the Belly of Paris," was razed in 1969. Gone are the picturesque early morning fruit and vegetable vendors, butchers in blood-spattered aprons, truckers bringing the freshest produce from all over France. Their places have been usurped by trendy shops and galleries of youthful entrepreneurs and artisans, small restaurants with lots of charm, the world's largest subway station, acres of trellised gardens and playgrounds, and Le Forum, a vast complex of boutiques, ranging from the super-chic designer ready-to-wear to more ordinary shops, as well as concert space and movie theaters. Touch-sensitive locator devices, which help visitors find products and services, are strategically placed. A few echoes of the earthy past remain, however, and you can still dine at *Au Pied de Cochon, Pharamond,* and *L'Escargot Montorgueil,* or have a drink with the workmen (before noon) at one of the old brasseries.

Le Centre National d'Art et de Culture Georges Pompidou (Le Centre Georges Pompidou) – Better known as "the Beaubourg," after the plateau on which it is built, this stark, 6-level creation of steel and glass, with its exterior escalators and blue, white, and red pipes, created a stir the moment its construction began. Outside, a computerized digital clock ticks off the seconds remaining until the 21st century. This wildly popular museum brings together all the contemporary art forms — painting, sculpture, the plastic arts, industrial design, music, literature, cinema, and theater — under one roof, and that roof offers one of the most exciting views of Paris. The old houses and cobbled, tree-shaded streets and squares vie for attention with galleries, boutiques, and the spectacle provided by jugglers, mimes, acrobats, and magicians in the plaza out front. The scene in the courtyard often rivals the exhibits inside. Open weekdays from noon to 10 PM; 10 AM to 10 PM weekends. Closed Tuesdays; no admission charge on Sundays except for special exhibitions. Rue Rambuteau, at the corner of Rue St.-Martin, 4e (phone: 42-77-12-33).

Le Marais – Northeast of the *Louvre,* a marshland until the 16th century, this district became the height of residential fashion during the 17th century. But as the aristocracy moved on, it fell into disrepair. Recently, after a long period of neglect, it has been enjoying a complete facelift. Spurred on by the opening of the *Picasso Museum* in the Hôtel du Salé, preservationists have lovingly restored more than a hundred of the magnificent old mansions to their former grandeur. They are now museums of exquisite beauty, with muraled walls and ceilings, and their courtyards are the sites of dramatic and musical presentations during the summer *Festival du Marais.* Among the houses to note are the Palais de Soubise, now the National Archives, and the Hôtels d'Aumont, de Clisson, de Rohan, de Sens, and de Sully (*hôtel* in this sense means private residence or townhouse). The Caisse Nationale des Monuments, housed in the last one, can provide maps of the area as well as fascinating and detailed tours. It also offers lectures on Saturdays and Sundays. 62 Rue St.-Antoine, 4e (phone: 42-74-22-22).

Place des Vosges – In the Marais district, the oldest square in Paris — and also one of the most beautiful — was completed in 1612 by order of Henri IV, with its houses elegantly "built to a like symmetry." Though many of the houses have been rebuilt inside, their original façades remain, and the newly restored square is one of Paris's enduring delights. Corneille, Racine, and Mme. de Sévigné lived here. At #6 is the *Maison de Victor Hugo,* once the poet's home, and now a museum. Closed Mondays. Admission charge (4e; phone: 42-72-10-16).

Musée Carnavalet (Carnavalet Museum) – Also in the Marais, this was once the home of Mme. de Sévigné, a noted 17th-century letter writer, and now its beautifully arranged exhibits cover the history of Paris from the days of Henri IV to the present. Its recent expansion through the *lycée* next door and into the neighboring *Le Peletier* hotel doubled the exhibition space, making it the largest museum in the world devoted to the history of a single capital city. The expansion, done primarily to house a permanent major exhibition on the French Revolution, was part of Paris's celebration of the bicentennial of the revolution in 1989. Watch for concerts and special exhibitions here. Closed Mondays. No admission charge on Sundays. 23 Rue de Sévigné, 3e (phone: 42-72-21-13).

Musée Picasso (Picasso Museum) – This long-awaited museum, which contains a large part of the artist's private collection, is now open at the Hôtel du Salé. To tell the truth, the building is at least as interesting as the artwork it houses — too many recent works, too few early ones — but a visit is worthwhile just to see Picasso's collection of works by other artists (the Cézannes are best). Closed Tuesdays; half-price on Sundays. 5 Rue de Thorigny, 3e (phone: 42-71-25-21).

Cimetière Père Lachaise (Père Lachaise Cemetery) – For those who like cemeteries, this one is a beauty. In a wooded park, it's the final resting place of many illustrious personalities. A map is available at the gate to help you find the tombs of Balzac, Sarah Bernhardt, Chopin, Colette, Corot, Delacroix, Héloise and Abelard, La Fontaine, Modigliani, Musset, Edith Piaf, Rossini, and Oscar Wilde, among others. Note, too, the legions of resident cats. Bd. de Ménilmontant at Rue de la Roquette, 20e (phone: 43-70-70-33).

La Villette – The City of Sciences and Industry, a celebration of technology, stands in its own park on the edge of the capital and houses a planetarium, the spherical Géode cinema, lots of hands-on displays, and a half-dozen exhibitions at any given time. Restaurants and snack bars. Closed Mondays. 30 Av. Cotentin Cariou, 20e (phone: 42-40-60-00 or 40-05-06-07).

Bois de Boulogne – Originally part of the Forest of Rouvre, on the western edge of Paris, this 2,140-acre park was planned along English lines by Napoleon. Ride a horse or a bike, row a boat, shoot skeet, go bowling, smell roses, picnic on the grass, see horse races at Auteuil and Longchamp, visit a zoo, see a play, walk to a waterfall — and there's lots more.

Bois de Vincennes – As a counterpart to the Bois de Boulogne, a park, a palace, and a zoological garden were laid out on 2,300 acres during Napoleon III's time. Visit the 14th-century château and its lovely chapel; the large and lovely floral garden; and the zoo, with animals in their natural habitat. It's at the southeast edge of Paris (métro: Château de Vincennes).

Palais de Chaillot – Built for the Paris Exposition of 1937 — on the site of the old Palais du Trocadéro left over from the Exposition of 1878 — its terraces have excellent views across gardens and fountains to the Eiffel Tower on the Left Bank. Two wings house a theater, an aquarium, and four museums — *du Cinéma* (phone: 45-53-74-39), *de l'Homme* (Anthropology; phone: 45-53-70-60), *de la Marine* (Maritime; phone: 45-53-31-70), *des Monuments Français* (monument reproductions; phone: 47-27-97-27). Closed Tuesdays and major holidays. Pl. du Trocadéro, 16e.

LA RIVE GAUCHE (THE LEFT BANK)

Tour Eiffel (Eiffel Tower) – It is impossible to imagine the Paris skyline without this mighty symbol, yet what has been called Gustav Eiffel's folly was never meant to be permanent. Originally built for the Universal Exposition of 1889, it was due to be torn down in 1909, but it was saved because of the development of the wireless — the first transatlantic wireless telephones were operated from the tower in 1916. Its centennial was celebrated with great fanfare in 1989. Extensive renovations have taken place, and a post office, three restaurants (*Jules Verne* is the best), and a few boutiques have opened up on the first-floor landing. On a really good day, it's possible to see for 50 miles. Open daily. Admission charge. Champ-de-Mars, 7e (phone: 45-50-34-56).

Chaillot to UNESCO – From the Eiffel Tower, it is possible to look out over a group of Paris's 20th-century buildings and gardens on both sides of the Seine, including the Palais de Chaillot, the Trocadéro and Champ-de-Mars gardens, and the UNESCO buildings. Also part of the area (but not of the same century) is the huge Ecole Militaire, an impressive example of 18th-century French architecture on Avenue de la Motte-Picquet. The Y-shaped building just beyond it, facing Place de Fontenoy, is the main UNESCO building, dating from 1958. It has frescoes by Picasso, Henry Moore's *Reclining Silhouette*, a mobile by Calder, murals by Miró, and Japanese gardens by Noguchi.

Les Invalides – Built by Louis XIV as a refuge for disabled soldiers, this vast classical building has more than 10 miles of corridors and a golden dome by Mansart. For yet another splendid Parisian view, approach the building from the Alexandre III bridge. Besides being a masterpiece of the age of Louis XIV (17th century), the Church of St. Louis, part of the complex, contains the impressive red and green granite Tomb of Napoleon (admission charge). Also at Les Invalides is the *Musée de l'Armée,* one of the world's richest museums, displaying arms and armor together with mementos of French military history. Av. de Tourville, Pl. Vauban, 7e (phone: 45-51-92-84).

Musée d'Orsay (Orsay Museum) – This imposing former railway station has been transformed (by the Milanese architect Gae Aulenti, among others) into one of the shining examples of modern curating. Its eclectic collection includes not only the

Impressionist paintings decanted from cramped quarters in the *Jeu de Paume,* but also less consecrated academic work and a panorama of the 19th century's achievements in sculpture, photography, and the applied arts. Closed Mondays. Admission charge; reduced on Sundays. 1 Rue de Bellechasse, 7e (phone: 45-49-11-11).

Musée Rodin (Rodin Museum) – The famous statue *The Thinker* is in the garden of this splendid 18th-century residence. The chapel and the mansion also contain Rodin sculpture. Closed Tuesdays. Admission charge. 77 Rue de Varenne, 7e (phone: 47-05-01-34).

Montparnasse – Just south of the Luxembourg Gardens, in the early 20th century there arose an artists' colony of avant-garde painters, writers, and Russian political exiles. Here Hemingway, Picasso, and Scott and Zelda sipped and supped in places like *La Closerie des Lilas, La Coupole, Le Dôme, Le Select,* and *La Rotonde.* The cafés, small restaurants, and winding streets still exist in the shadow of a new shopping center.

Tour Montparnasse – This giant new complex now dominates Montparnasse. The fastest elevator in Europe whisks Parisians and tourists alike up 59 stories for a view *down* over the Eiffel Tower, from 9:30 AM to 9:30 PM daily for a fee. The shopping center here boasts all the famous names, and the surrounding office buildings are the headquarters of some of France's largest companies. 33 Av. du Maine, 15e, and Bd. de Vaugirard, 14e (phone: 45-38-32-32).

Palais et Jardin du Luxembourg (Luxembourg Palace and Garden) – In what were once the southern suburbs, the Luxembourg Palace and Garden were built for Marie de Médicis in 1612. A prison during the Revolution, the Renaissance palace now houses the French Senate. The classic, formal gardens, with lovely statues and the famous Médicis fountain, are popular with students meeting under the chestnut trees and with neighborhood children playing around the artificial lake. 15 Rue de Vaugirard, 6e.

Mosquée de Paris (Paris Mosque) – One of the most beautiful structures of its kind in the non-Muslim — or even in the Muslim — world, it is dominated by a 130-foot-high minaret in gleaming white marble. Shoes are taken off before entering the pebble-lined gardens full of flowers and dwarf trees. Inside, the Hall of Prayer, with its lush Oriental carpets, may be visited daily except Fridays, from 10 AM to noon and 2 to 4 PM. Admission charge. Next door is a restaurant and a patio for sipping Turkish coffee and tasting Oriental sweets. Pl. du Puits-de-l'Ermite, 5e (phone: 45-35-97-33).

Panthéon – This 18th-century "nonreligious Temple of Fame dedicated to all the gods" has an impressive interior, with murals depicting the life of St.-Geneviève, patron saint of Paris. It contains the tombs of Victor Hugo, the Resistance leader Jean Moulin, Rousseau, Voltaire, and Emile Zola. Open daily from 10 AM to noon and 2 to 5 PM. Admission charge. Pl. du Panthéon, 5e (phone: 43-54-34-51).

Quartier Latin (Latin Quarter) – Extending from the Luxembourg Gardens and the Panthéon to the Seine, this famous neighborhood still maintains its unique atmosphere. A focal point for Sorbonne students since the Middle Ages, it's a mad jumble of narrow streets, old churches, and academic buildings. Boulevard St.-Michel and Boulevard St.-Germain are its main arteries, both lined with cafés, bookstores, and boutiques of every imaginable kind. There are also some charming old side streets, such as the Rue de la Huchette, near Place St.-Michel. And don't miss the famous *bouquinistes* (bookstalls) along the Seine, around the Place St.-Michel on the Quai des Grands-Augustins and the Quai St.-Michel.

Eglise St.-Germain-des-Prés (Church of St.-Germain-des-Prés) – Probably the oldest church in Paris, it once belonged to an abbey of the same name. The original basilica (AD 558) was destroyed and rebuilt many times. The Romanesque steeple and its massive tower date from 1014. Inside, the choir and sanctuary are as they were in the 12th century, and the marble shafts used in the slender columns are 14 centuries old. Pl. St.-Germain-des-Prés, 6e (phone: 43-25-41-71).

Surrounding the church is the *quartier* of Paris's "fashionable" intellectuals and artists, with art galleries, boutiques, and renowned people-watchers' cafés such as the *Flore* (Sartre's favorite) and *Aux Deux Magots* (a Hemingway haunt).

Musée de Cluny (Cluny Museum) – One of the last remaining examples of medieval domestic architecture in Paris. The 15th-century residence of the abbots of Cluny later became the home of Mary Tudor and is now a museum of medieval arts and crafts, including the celebrated *Lady and the Unicorn* tapestry. Closed Tuesdays. Admission charge. 6 Pl. Paul-Painlevé, 5e (phone: 43-25-62-00).

Eglise St.-Sévérin (Church of St. Séverin) – This church still retains its beautiful Flamboyant Gothic ambulatory, considered a masterpiece of its kind, and lovely old stained glass windows dating from the 15th and 16th centuries. The small garden and the restored charnel house are also of interest. 3 Rue des Prêtres, 5e (phone: 43-25-96-63).

Eglise St.-Julien-le-Pauvre (Church of St. Julien le Pauvre) – One of the smallest and oldest churches (12th to 13th century) in Paris offers a superb view of Notre-Dame from its charming Place René-Viviani. 1 Rue St.-Julien-le-Pauvre, 5e (no phone).

THE ISLANDS

Ile de la Cité – The birthplace of Paris, settled by Gallic fishermen about 250 BC, this island in the Seine is so rich in historical monuments that an entire day could be spent here and on the neighboring Ile St.-Louis. A walk all around the islands, along the lovely, tree-shaded quais on both banks of the Seine, opens up one breathtaking view of Notre-Dame Cathedral after another.

Cathédrale de Notre-Dame de Paris (Cathedral of Our Lady) – It is said that the Druids once worshiped on this consecrated ground. The Romans built their temple, and many Christian churches followed. In 1163, the foundations were laid for the present cathedral, one of the world's finest examples of Gothic architecture, grand in size and proportion. Henri VI and Napoleon were crowned here. Take a guided tour (offered in English at noon Tuesdays and in French at noon weekdays, 2:30 PM Saturdays, and 2 PM Sundays) or quietly explore on your own, but be sure to climb the 225-foot towers for a marvelous view of the city and try to see the splendid stained glass rose windows at sunset. Pl. du Parvis, 4e (phone: 43-26-07-39).

Palais de Justice and Sainte-Chapelle – This complex recalls centuries of history; it was the first seat of the Roman military government, then the headquarters of the early kings, and finally the law courts. In the 13th century, St.-Louis (Louis IX) built a new palace and added Sainte-Chapelle to house the Sacred Crown of Thorns and other holy relics. Built in less than 3 years, the chapel, with its 15 splendid stained glass windows and 247-foot spire, is one of the jewels of Paris. Open daily from 10 AM to 4:30 PM. Admission charge. 4 Bd. du Palais, 1er (phone: 43-54-30-09).

Conciergerie – This remnant of the Old Royal Palace was used as a prison during the Revolution. Here Marie Antoinette, the Duke of Orléans, Mme. du Barry, and many others of lesser fame awaited the guillotine. It was extensively restored during the celebration of the bicentennial of the French Revolution, and the great arch-filled hall is especially striking. Open daily. Admission charge. 4 Bd. du Palais, 1er (phone: 43-54-30-06).

Ile St.-Louis – Walk across the footbridge at the back of Notre-Dame and you're in a charming, tranquil village. This "enchanted isle" has managed to keep its provincial charm despite its central location. Follow the main street, Rue St.-Louis-en-l'Ile, down the middle of the island, past courtyards, balconies, old doors, curious stairways, the Eglise St.-Louis, and discreet plaques bearing the names of illustrious former residents (Mme. Curie, Voltaire, Baudelaire, Gautier, and Daumier, for example); then take the quai back along the edge.

■**EXTRA SPECIAL:** Versailles, by far the most magnificent of all the French châteaux, is 13 miles (21 km) southwest of Paris, accessible by train or bus. Louis XIV, called the Sun King because of the splendor of his court, took a small château used by Louis III, enlarged it, and really outdid himself. The vast, intricate formal gardens, designed by the great Le Nôtre, cover 250 acres and include 600 fountains, for which a river had to be diverted. At one time, the palace itself housed 6,000 people, and the court numbered 20,000. Louis kept his nobles in constant competition over his favors, hoping to distract them from any opposition to his rule. It's impossible to see all of Versailles in one day, but don't miss the Hall of Mirrors, the Royal Apartments, and the Chapel. Also on the grounds are the Grand Trianon, a smaller palace often visited by Louis XIV, and the Petit Trianon, a favorite of Marie-Antoinette, who also liked Le Hameau (the hamlet), a model farm where she and her companions played at being peasants. More than 20 additional rooms — the apartments of the dauphin and dauphine — are now open to visitors Thursdays through Sundays; gardens open daily from 9:45 AM to 5 PM; the château and Trianons closed Mondays and holidays. Guided tours in English are available from 10 AM to 3:30 PM. Admission charge (phone: 30-84-74-00). A spectacular illumination and display of the great fountains takes place on Sunday evenings during the summer. For more information, contact the Versailles Tourist Office, 7 Rue des Reservoirs (phone: 39-50-36-22).

SOURCES AND RESOURCES

TOURIST INFORMATION: For information in the US, contact the French Government Tourist Office, 610 Fifth Ave., New York, NY 10020 (phone: 212-757-1125). In Paris, the Office de Tourisme de Paris, 127 Champs-Elysées, 8e (phone: 47-23-61-72), open daily from 9 AM to 8 PM, is the place to go for information, brochures, maps, or hotel reservations. Other offices include those at major train stations, such as the Gare du Nord (phone: 45-26-94-82) and the Gare de Lyon (phone: 43-43-33-24).

Local Coverage – *Paris Selection* is the official tourist office magazine in French and English. It lists events, sights, "Paris by Night" tours, places to hear jazz, some hotels, restaurants, shopping, and other information. Far more complete are three weekly guides, *L'Officiel des Spectacles, Paris 7,* and *Une Semaine à Paris–Pariscope.* All are in simple French and are available at newsstands. Most major newsstands carry *Passion,* a tabloid in English that comes out ten times a year, listing cultural events and giving a youthful, lively, American perspective on Paris.

Telephone – In 1986, the entire French telephone system was overhauled, giving each subscriber a basic eight-digit number. All phone numbers in Paris now begin with the prefix 4 (incorporated into the numbers given here); in the area surrounding Paris, they are preceded by either 3 or 6. When calling a number in the Paris region (including Ile-de-France) from Paris, dial only the eight-digit number. When calling a number in Paris from outside the Paris region, dial 16, then 1, then the eight-digit number. When calling Paris from the US, dial the country code 33, the city code 1, and the eight-digit number.

The pay phones on Paris street corners don't use tokens anymore. Phone cards are available in 40- and 120-franc denominations at post offices and tobacco shops. Before dialing from a pay phone, put the card into the slot on the phone and close the hood. When the franc value remaining on the card is displayed, you can dial your call.

CLIMATE AND CLOTHES: Paris has about the same weather as our Middle Atlantic states, though it's usually not warmer than 75F (24C) or colder than 30F (−1C). It rains frequently year-round, so a raincoat and folding umbrella are absolute musts. Air conditioning is still rather rare, and thermostats are usually set relatively low in winter. Whoever wrote about the glories of April in Paris clearly never spent a spring in Paris's chilly gray damp.

 GETTING AROUND: Airports − Charles de Gaulle Airport, Roissy, 16 miles (25 km) northeast of Paris, has two terminals: Aérogare 1, for foreign airlines, and Aérogare 2, for Air France flights. The two terminals are connected by a free shuttle bus. Air France airport buses (phone: 42-99-20-18), open to passengers of all airlines for 36F (about $6), leave for the Palais des Congrès (métro station: Porte Maillot) every 12 minutes from 5:40 AM to 11 PM and take between 30 and 50 minutes, depending on traffic. City bus #350 between the airport and the Gare du Nord train station is also available, but it is generally slow, taking up to an hour. Roissy-Rail runs between the aiport and the Gare du Nord every 15 minutes and takes about 35 minutes. (A shuttle bus connects the airport to Roissy station, and from there to the Gare du Nord is by train.) Taxis into town cost 160F (about $26) or more for most destinations.

Orly Airport, 10 miles (16 km) south of Paris, has two terminals; Orly Ouest, mainly for domestic flights and flights to Geneva, and Orly Sud, for international flights. The two terminals are connected by a free shuttle bus. Air France buses (phone: 43-23-97-10) leave for a terminus on the Esplanade des Invalides (métro station: Invalides) every 12 minutes and take from 30 to 45 minutes, depending on traffic. City bus #215, which links the airport to Denfert-Rochereau, in southern Paris, takes about a half-hour. Orly-Rail, a combination shuttle bus to Orly station and train to various stops in the city such as Luxembourg, St.-Michel, and Invalides, runs every 15 or 30 minutes depending on the time of day and takes 35 to 50 minutes, according to the stop. A taxi into town costs 80F (about $13) and up.

Buses linking Charles de Gaulle and Orly airports run roughly every half-hour and take from 50 to 75 minutes.

Boat − See Paris from the Seine by day and by night for about 25 francs (about $4). Modern, glass-enclosed river ramblers provide a constantly changing picture of the city. Contact *Bateaux-Mouches,* Pont d'Alma, 7e (phone: 42-25-96-10); *Vedettes Paris–Tour Eiffel,* Pont d'Iéna, 7e (phone: 47-05-50-00); and *Vedettes Pont-Neuf,* Square Vert-Galant, 1er (phone: 46-33-98-38). On May 1, 1989, "bus-boat" service on the Seine was inaugurated. *Les Bateaux Parisiens* departs from the Hôtel de Ville (city hall) every 45 minutes from 10 AM to 8 PM daily, with stops at Nôtre-Dame, the *Louvre,* and the *Musée d'Orsay.* As we went to press, fare was set at 7 to 20 francs ($1-$3). The seasonal operation runs through September.

Bus − Generally operates from 6:30 AM to 9:30 PM. Slow but good for sightseeing. Métro tickets are valid on all city-run buses. Lines are numbered, and both stops and buses have signs indicating routes. One or two tickets may be required, depending on the distance traveled. The RATP, which operates both the métro and bus system, has also designated certain lines as being of particular interest to tourists. A panel on the front of the bus indicates in English and German "This bus is good for sightseeing." RATP has a tourist office at Pl. de la Madeleine, next to the flower market (phone: 42-65-31-18 or 43-46-14-14), which organizes bus trips in Paris and the region.

Car Rental − Book when making your plane reservation, or contact: *Avis* (phone: 45-50-32-31), *Budget* (phone: 46-68-55-55), *Europcar* (phone: 45-00-08-06), *Hertz* (phone: 47-88-51-51), or *Mattei* (phone: 43-46-11-50).

Métro − Operating from 5:30 AM to about 1 AM, it is safe, clean, quiet, easy to use, and, since the Paris rapid transit authority (RATP) began to sponsor cultural events and art exhibits in some subway stops in an effort to cut down on crime and make commuting more enjoyable, entertaining as well. The events have been so popular that so far they've been offered in about 200 of Paris's 368 métro stations.

The different lines are identified by the names of their terminals at either end. Every station has clear directional maps, some with push-button devices that light up the proper route after a destination button is pushed. Keep your ticket (you may need it to leave) and don't cheat; there are spot checks. Those caught in first class with a second class ticket are subject to an immediate fine, except from 6 PM until 9 AM, when anyone is allowed in a first class car.

A 10-ticket book (*carnet*) is available at a reduced rate. The Paris-Sésame card, a tourist ticket that entitles the bearer to 2, 4, or 7 consecutive days of unlimited first class travel on the métro and on city-run buses, may be purchased in France upon presentation of your passport at 44 subway stations and 4 regional express stations or at any of the 6 French National Railroads stations. In the US, the card is available from *Marketing Challengers International,* 10 E. 21st St., New York, NY 10010 (phone: 212-529-8484).

SITU – Handy streetside bus and subway directions are now available in some métro stations from SITU (Système d'Information des Trajets Urbains), a computer that prints out the fastest routing onto a wallet-size piece of paper complete with the estimated length of trip. The RATP (the rapid transit authority) service is free and augments the lighted wall maps that guide métro riders. High-traffic spots such as the Châtelet métro station, outside the Gare Montparnasse and on the Boulevard St.-Germain, now sport SITU machines, with more on the way.

Taxi – Taxis can be found at stands at main intersections, outside railway stations and official buildings, and in the streets. A taxi is free if the entire TAXI sign is illuminated (with a white light); the small light *beside* the roof light signifies availability after dark. But be aware that Parisian cab drivers are notoriously selective about whom they will pick up and how many passengers they will allow in their cab — a foursome inevitably has trouble. You can also call *Taxi Bleu* (phone: 42-02-42-02) and *Radio Taxi* (phone: 47-39-33-33). The meter starts running from the time the cab is dispatched, and a tip of about 15% is customary. Fares increase at night.

Train – Paris has six main train stations, each one serving a different area of the country. The general information number is 45-82-50-50; for telephone reservations, 45-65-60-60. North: Gare du Nord, 18 Rue de Dunkerque (phone: 42-80-63-63); East: Gare de l'Est, Pl. du 11-Novembre (phone: 42-03-96-31); Southeast: Gare de Lyon, 20 Bd. Diderot (phone: 40-19-60-00); Southwest: Gare d'Austerlitz, 51 Quai d'Austerlitz (phone: 45-84-14-19); West: Gare Montparnasse, 17 Bd. de Vaugirard (phone: 40-48-10-00); West and Northwest: Gare St.-Lazare, 20 Rue de Rome (phone: 42-85-88-00). The TGV (*train à grande vitesse*), the world's fastest train, has cut 2 hours off the usual 4-hour ride between Paris and Lyons; it similarly shortens traveling time to Marseilles, the Côte d'Azur, and Switzerland. It leaves from the Gare de Lyon; reservations are necessary. As we went to press, a new TGV line from Paris to Tours was scheduled to open soon.

 SPECIAL EVENTS: After the Christmas season, Paris prepares for the January fashion shows, when press and buyers come to town to pass judgment on the spring and summer haute couture collections. (The general public can see what the designers have wrought after the professionals leave.) More buyers come to town in February and March for the ready-to-wear shows (fall and winter clothes), open to the trade only. March is the month of the first *Foire à la Ferraille et aux Jambons* of the year. This fair of regional food products held concurrently with an antiques flea market (not items of the best quality, but not junk, either) is repeated in September. The running of the *Prix du Président de la République,* the first big horse race of the year, takes place at Auteuil on the last Sunday of the month. From late April to early May is the *Foire de Paris,* the capital's big international trade fair. In mid-May there's the *Paris Marathon;* in late May (through early June), the *French Open Tennis Championships.* Odd years only, the *Paris International Air Show* is an early June attraction at Le Bourget Airport. Horse races crowd the calendar in June — there's not only the *Prix de Diane* at Chantilly, but also the *Grande Semaine* at Longchamp, Auteuil, and St.-Cloud. And in the middle of June, the *Festival du Marais* begins a month's worth of music and dance performances in the courtyards of the Marais district's old townhouses. *Bastille Day,* July 14, is celebrated with music and fireworks, parades, and dancing till dawn in every neighborhood. Meanwhile, the *Tour de France* is under way; the cyclists arrive in Paris for the finish of the 3-week race later in July. Also in July, press and buyers arrive to view the fall and winter haute couture collections, but the ready-to-wear shows (spring and summer clothes) wait until September and October, because August for Parisians is vacation time. Practically the whole country takes a holiday then, and in the capital, the classical concerts of the *Festival Estival* (from mid-July to mid-September) are among the few distractions. When they finish, the *Festival d'Automne,* a celebration of the contemporary in music, dance, and theater, takes over (it goes until December). The *Foire à la Ferraille et aux Jambons* returns in September, but in the even years it's eclipsed by the *Biennale des Antiquaires,* a major antiques event from late September to early October. Also in even years in early October is the *Paris Motor Show.* Every year on the first Sunday of October, the last big horse race of the season, the *Prix de l'Arc de Triomphe,* is run at Longchamp; and every year in early October, Paris holds the *Fête des Vendanges à Montmartre* to celebrate the harvest of the city's last remaining vineyard. On November 11, ceremonies at the Arc de Triomphe and a parade mark *Armistice Day.* An *International Cat Show* and a *Horse and Pony Show* come in early December; then comes Christmas, which is celebrated most movingly with a Christmas Eve midnight mass at Notre-Dame. At midnight a week later, the New Year bows in to spontaneous street revelry in the Latin Quarter and along the Champs-Elysées.

 MUSEUMS: Many Paris museums (*musées*) are free or offer reduced admission fees on Sundays. "La Carte," a pass that can be used at over 60 museums and monuments in the city, is available at métro stations and at major museums (or in the US from *Marketing Challengers International,* 10 E. 21st St., New York, NY 10010; phone: 212-529-8484). Prices are the equivalent of $10 for a 1-day pass, $20 for a 3-day pass, and $30 for a 5-day pass. Museums of interest not described in *Special Places* include the following.

Archaeological Crypt of Notre Dame – Under the square in front of the cathedral. There are foundations of 3rd-century Roman structures and remains of walls and floor plans from later periods. Open daily, 10 AM to 4:30 PM. Parvis de Notre-Dame, 4e (phone: 43-29-83-51).

Catacombs – Dating from the Gallo-Roman era and containing the remains of Danton, Robespierre, and many others. Bring a flashlight. Closed Mondays. 2 Pl. Denfert-Rochereau, 14e (phone: 43-22-47-63).

Egouts (Sewers of Paris) – Underground city of tunnels, a very popular afternoon tour on Mondays, Wednesdays, and the last Saturday of the month, except on holidays and the days preceding and following them. 93 Quai d'Orsay, 16e (phone: 47-05-10-29).

Maison de Balzac – The house where he lived, with a garden leading to one of the prettiest little alleys in Paris. Closed Mondays. 47 Rue Raynouard, 16e (phone: 42-24-56-38).

Manufacture des Gobelins – The famous tapestry factory, in operation since the 15th century. Guided tours of the workshops take place Tuesdays, Wednesdays, and Thursdays from 2:15 to 3:15 PM. 42 Av. des Gobelins, 13e (phone: 43-37-12-60).

Musée de l'Affiche et de la Publicité – Three centuries of French posters and exhibitions on advertising history are housed in a building with an awesome Art Nouveau interior courtyard. Unfortunately, only a small portion of the entire collection can be shown at any one time. Exhibits change every few months. A good place to buy reprints of historic posters. Closed Tuesdays. 18 Rue de Paradis, 10e (phone: 42-46-13-09).

Musée des Antiquités Nationales – Archaeological specimens from prehistoric through Merovingian times, including an impressive Gallo-Roman collection. Open daily, except Tuesdays, from 9 AM to noon and 1:30 to 5:15 PM. Pl. du Château, St.-Germain-en-Laye (phone: 34-51-53-65).

Musée des Arts Africains et Océaniens – One of the world's finest collections of African and Oceanic art. Closed Tuesdays. 293 Av. Daumesnil, 12e (phone: 43-43-14-54).

Musée des Arts Décoratifs – Furniture and applied arts from the Middle Ages to the present, Oriental carpets, and Dubuffet paintings and drawings. Galerie Art Nouveau–Art Deco features Jeanne Lanvin's bedroom and bath. Closed Mondays and Tuesdays. 107 Rue de Rivoli, 1er (phone: 42-60-32-14).

Musée Cernuschi – Art of China. Closed Mondays and holidays. 7 Av. Velásquez, 8e (phone: 45-63-50-75).

Musée Cognacq-Jay – Art, snuffboxes, and watches from the 17th and 18th centuries. Closed Mondays. 25 Bd. des Capucines, 2e (phone: 42-61-94-54).

Musée des Collections Historiques de la Préfecture de Police – On the second floor of the modern police precinct building in the 5th *arrondissement,* just off the Boulevard St.-Germain, are the arrest orders for Charlotte Corday, among others, and collections of contemporary engravings and guillotine blades. Open weekdays, 9 AM to 5 PM, Fridays to 4:30 PM. 1 bis Rue des Carmes, 5e (phone: 43-29-21-57).

Musée Eugène-Delacroix – Studio and garden of the great painter; exhibits change yearly. Closed Tuesdays. 6 Rue de Furstemberg, 6e (phone: 43-54-04-87).

Musée Grévin – Waxworks of French history from Charlemagne to the present day. 10 Bd. Montmartre, 9e (phone: 47-70-85-05). A branch devoted to La Belle Epoque is in the Forum shopping complex at Les Halles. Open daily (phone: 42-61-28-50).

Musée Guimet – The *Louvre*'s Far East collection. Closed Tuesdays. 6 Pl. d'Iéna, 16e (phone: 47-23-61-65).

Musée Jacquemart-André – 18th-century French decorative art and European Renaissance treasures, as well as frequent special exhibitions. Closed Mondays. 158 Bd. Haussmann, 8e (phone: 45-62-39-94).

Musée Marmottan – Superb Monets, though several were stolen in a daring 1985 robbery and have yet to be recovered. Closed Mondays. 2 Rue Louis-Boilly, 16e (phone: 42-24-07-02).

Musée de la Mode et du Costume – A panorama of French contributions to fashion in the elegant Palais Calliéra. Closed Mondays. 10 Av. Pierre-I-de-Serbie, 16e (phone: 47-20-85-23).

Musée de la Monnaie – More than 2,000 coins and 450 medallions, plus historic coinage machines. Open daily, except Mondays, from 1 to 6 PM. Admission charge. 11 Quai de Conti, 6e (phone: 40-46-56-66).

Musée Gustave Moreau – A collection of the works of the early symbolist. Closed Tuesdays. 14 Rue de la Rochefoucauld, 9e (phone: 48-74-38-50).

Musée Nissim de Camondo – A former manor house filled with beautiful furnishings and art objects from the 18th century. Closed Mondays, Tuesdays, and holidays. 63 Rue de Monceau, 8e (phone: 45-63-26-32).

Musée de Sèvres – Just outside Paris, next door to the Sèvres factory, one of the world's finest collections of porcelain. Closed Tuesdays. 4 Grand-Rue, Sèvres (phone: 45-34-99-05).

Musée du Vin – In a former 13th-century abbey, the museum was established in 1981. The history and making of wine is traced through displays, artifacts, and a series of wax figure tableaux. Open daily, except Mondays, from noon to 6 PM. Admission charge includes a glass of wine. 5-7 Sq. Charles-Dickens, 16e. Métro: Passy (phone: 45-25-63-26).

Pavillon des Arts – An exhibition space in the mushroom-shaped buildings overlooking the Les Halles Forum complex. Presentations range from ancient to modern, paintings to sculpture. Closed Mondays and holidays. 101 Rue Rambuteau, 1er (phone: 42-33-82-50).

 GALLERIES: Few artists live in Montparnasse nowadays, as the center of the Paris art scene has shifted from the narrow streets of the Quartier Latin, which set the pace in the 1950s, to the Right Bank around the Centre Georges Pompidou. Here are some galleries of note:

Artcurial – Early moderns, such as Braque and Sonia Delaunay, as well as sculpture and prints, with a fine art bookshop. 9 Av. Matignon, 8e (phone: 42-99-16-16).

Beaubourg – Well-known names in the Paris art scene, including Niki de Saint-Phalle, César, Tinguely, Klossowski. 23 Rue du Renard, 4e (phone: 42-71-20-50).

Claude Bernard – Francis Bacon, David Hockney, and Raymond Mason are among the artists exhibited here. 5 Rue des Beaux-Arts, 6e (phone: 43-26-97-07).

Isy Brachot – Master surrealists, American hyper-realists, and new realists. 35 Rue Guénégaud, 6e (phone: 43-54-22-40).

Caroline Corre – Exhibitions by contemporary artists, specializing in unique artists' books. 14 Rue Guénégaud, 6e (phone: 43-54-57-67).

Agathe Gaillard – Contemporary photography, including Cartier-Bresson and the like. 3 Rue du Pont-Louis-Philippe, 4e (phone: 42-77-38-24).

Maeght-Lelong – The great moderns on display include Chagall, Tapies, Bacon, Moore, Miró. 13-14 Rue de Téhéran, 8e (phone: 45-63-13-19).

Daniel Malingue – Works by the Impressionists as well as notable Parisian artists from the 1930s to the 1950s — Foujita, Fautrier, and so forth. 26 Av. Matignon, 8e (phone: 42-66-60-33).

Nikki Diana Marquardt – Spacious new gallery of contemporary work recently opened by an enterprising dealer from the Bronx. 9 Pl. des Vosges, 4e (phone: 42-78-21-00).

Hervé Odermatt Cazeau – Early moderns — among them Picasso, Léger, Pissarro — and antiques. 85 bis Rue du Faubourg-St.-Honoré, 8e (phone: 42-66-92-58).

Darthea Speyer – Run by a former American Embassy attaché, now an art dealer. Contemporary painting. 6 Rue Jacques-Callot, 6e (phone: 43-54-78-41).

Virginia Zabriskie – Early and contemporary photography by Atget, Brassaï, Diane Arbus. Also painting and, occasionally, sculpture. 37 Rue Quincampoix, 4e (phone: 42-72-35-47).

 SHOPPING: From new wave fashions to classic haute couture, Paris starts the trends and sets the styles the world copies. Prices are generally high, but more than a few people are willing to pay for the quality of the products, not to mention the cachet of a Paris label, which enhances the appeal of many things besides clothing. Perfumes, cosmetics, jewelry, leather goods and accessories, wine and liqueurs, porcelain, and art are among the many other things for which Paris is famous.

The big department stores are excellent places to get an idea of what's available. They include *Galeries Lafayette,* 40 Bd. Haussmann, 9e (phone: 42-82-50-00), and branches; *Au Printemps,* 64 Bd. Haussmann, 9e (phone: 42-85-50-00); *Aux Trois-Quartiers,* 17 Bd. de la Madeleine, 1er (phone: 42-60-39-30); *La Samaritaine,* 19 Rue de la Monnaie,

1er (phone: 45-08-33-33); *Le Bazar de l'Hôtel de Ville,* 52 Rue de Rivoli, 4e (phone: 42-74-90-00); and *Au Bon Marché,* 22 Rue de Sèvres, 7e (phone: 45-49-21-22). Two major shopping centers — Porte Maillot, Pl. de la Porte Maillot, and Maine Montparnasse, at the intersection of Bd. Montparnasse and Rue de Rennes — are also worth a visit.

There are several shopping neighborhoods, and they tend to be specialized. Haute couture can be found in the streets around the Champs-Elysées: Av. George-V, Av. Montaigne, Rue François-I, and Rue du Faubourg-St.-Honoré; famous designers are also represented in department stores. Boutiques are especially numerous on Av. Victor-Hugo, Rue de Passy, Bd. des Capucines, in the St.-Germain-des-Prés area, in the neighborhood of the Opéra, in the Forum des Halles shopping center, and around the Place des Victoires. The Rue d'Alésia has several blocks devoted solely to discount shops.

The Rue de Paradis is lined with crystal and china shops — all at discount prices — and St.-Germain-des-Prés has more than its share of art galleries. The best and most expensive antiques dealers are along the Faubourg-St.-Honoré on the Right Bank. On the Left Bank there's Le Carré Rive Gauche, an association of more than 100 antiques shops in the area bordered by Quai Voltaire, Rue de l'Université, Rue des Sts.-Pères, and Rue du Bac. Antiques and curio collectors should explore Paris's several flea markets, which include the Marché d'Aligre, at the Place d'Aligre; Montreuil, near the Porte de Montreuil; Vanves, near the Porte de Vanves; and the largest and the best known, Puces de St.-Ouen, near the Porte de Clignancourt.

A few more tips: Sales take place during the first weeks in January and in late June and July. Any shop labeled *dégriffé* (the word means, literally, without the label) offers discounts on brand-name clothing, often last season's styles. Discount shops are also known as "stock" shops. The French value-added tax (VAT; typically 18.6% and as high as 33.33% on luxury articles) can be refunded on most purchases made by foreigners provided a minimum of 1,200F ($200) is spent in one store. Forms must be filled out and the refund is usually mailed to your home. Large department stores and the so-called duty-free shops have facilitated the procedure, but refunds can be obtained from any store willing to cooperate. If the refund is not exactly equal to the tax — 15% to 25% refunds are common — it's because stores may retain some of it as reimbursement for their extra expense in handling the paperwork.

Here is a sampling of the wealth of shops in Paris, many of which have more than one location in the city:

Agnès B – Supremely wearable, trendy, casual clothes. 3 and 6 Rue du Jour, 1er; 13 Rue Michelet, 6e; 25 Av. Pierre-I-de-Serbie, 16e; and 81 Rue d' Assas, 6e.

Azzedine Alaïa – The Tunisian designer who brought the body back. 17 Rue du Parc-Royal, 3e.

Laura Ashley – The English designer's familiar floral prints. 94 Rue des Rennes, 6e; and 261 Rue St.-Honoré, 1er.

Baccarat – For high-quality porcelain and crystal. 30 bis Rue du Paradis; 10e.

La Bagagerie – Perhaps the best bag and belt boutique in the world. 74 Rue de Passy, 16e, and 41 Rue du Four, 6e.

Au Bain Marie – Simply the most beautiful shop in Paris for kitchenware and tabletop accessories. 10 Rue Boissy-d'Anglas, 8e.

Pierre Balmain – Couturier boutique for women's fashions. 44 Rue François-I, 8e, and other locations.

Beauté Divine – Antique perfume bottles, Art Deco bathroom accessories, glove stretchers, nail buffers, mustache cups. A browser's delight. 40 Rue St.-Sulpice, 6e.

Dorothée Bis – One of the oldest and most successful Paris boutiques, definitely a trendsetter. 33 Rue de Sèvres, 6e.

Brentano's – This bookstore stocks British and American novels, critiques on the

American arts, and a variety of books on technical and business subjects — in English. 37 Av. de l'Opéra, 2e.

Cacharel – Fashionable ready-to-wear clothes in great prints. 34 Rue Tronchet, 8e, and other branches.

Cadolle – Founded in 1889 by the woman credited with inventing the brassiere, it still sells corsets as well as other items of frilly, pretty lingerie. 14 Rue Cambon, 1er.

Pierre Cardin – A famous designer's own boutique. 83 Rue du Faubourg-St.-Honoré, 8e; 27 Av. Victor-Hugo, 16e; and other locations.

Carel – Beautiful shoes. 12 Rond-Point des Champs-Elysées, 8e, and other locations.

Carita – Paris's most extensive — and friendliest — beauty/hair salon. 11 Rue Faubourg-St.-Honoré, 8e.

Cartier – Fabulous jewelry. 13 Rue de la Paix, 2e, and other branches.

Céline – A popular women's boutique. 24 Rue François-I, 8e; for shoes it's 3 Av. Victor-Hugo, 16e.

Cerruti – For women's clothing, 15 Pl. de la Madeleine, 8e; for men's, 27 Rue Royale, 8e.

Chanel – Classic women's fashions, inspired by the late, legendary Coco Chanel, now executed by Karl Lagerfeld. 42 Av. Montaigne, 8e, and 31 Rue Cambon, 1er.

Charvet – Paris's answer to Savile Row. An all-in-one men's shop, where shirts are the house specialty — they stock more than 4,000. Ties, too. 28 Pl. Vendôme, 1er.

La Chaume – Stem for stem, the most beautiful flower shop in Paris. Buy a bouquet for an *amie* or for *vous même*. 10 Rue Royale, 8e.

Chloé – Designs for women. 3 Rue de Gribeauval and 60 Rue du Faubourg-St.-Honoré, 8e.

Christofle – The internationally famous silversmith. 12 Rue Royale, 8e.

Courrèges – Another bastion of haute couture with its own boutique. 40 Rue François-I, 8e, and 46 Rue du Faubourg-St.-Honoré, 8e.

E. Dehillerin – An enormous selection of professional cookware. 18-20 Rue Coquillière, 1er.

Christian Dior – One of the most famous couture names in the world. 28 Av. Montaigne, 8e; Miss Dior and Baby Dior for children are also at this location.

Hôtel Drouot – Paris's huge auction house operates daily except Sundays. Good buys. 9 Rue Drouot, 9e.

Les Drugstores Publicis – A uniquely French version of the American drugstore, with an amazing variety of goods — perfume, books, records, foreign newspapers, magazines, film, cigarettes, food, and more, all wildly overpriced. 149 Bd. St.-Germain, 6e, 133 Av. des Champs-Elysées, 8e, and 1 Av. Matignon, 8e.

Erès – Avant-garde sportswear for men and women. 2 Rue Tronchet, 8e.

Fabrice – Trendy, fine costume jewelry. 33 and 54 Rue Bonaparte, 6e.

Fauchon – *The* place to buy fine food and wine of every variety, from *oeufs en gêlée* to condiments and candy. 28 Pl. de la Madeleine, 8e.

Louis Féraud – Couturier fashions for women at 88 Rue du Faubourg-St.-Honoré, and men at #62, 8e, and other locations.

Fouquet – Beautiful displays of chocolates, fresh fruit candies, herbs, condiments, and jams. 22 Rue Francois-I, 8e, and other branches.

Freddy – A popular shop for gifts, offering perfumes, gloves, ties, scarves, and other items at good prices. 10 Rue Auber, 9e.

Maud Frizon – Sophisticated, imaginative shoes. 79-83 Rue des Sts.-Pères, 6e.

La Gaminerie – Reasonably priced, good sportswear; outstanding window displays. 137 Bd. St.-Germain, 6e.

Monique Germain – Unique hand-painted silk clothing at affordable prices: cocktail dresses, bridal wear, padded patchwork jackets. 59 Bd. Raspail, 6e.

Givenchy – Beautifully tailored clothing by the master couturier. 3 Av. George-V,

8e; *Nouvelle Boutique,* 66 Av. Victor-Hugo, 16e; and *Givenchy Gentleman,* 29 Av. George-V, 8e.

Guerlain – For fine perfume and cosmetics. 2 Pl. Vendôme, 1er; 68 Champs-Elysées, 8e; 29 Rue de Sèvres, 6e; and 93 Rue de Passy, 16e.

Daniel Hechter – Sportswear and casual clothing for men and women. 12 Rue du Faubourg-St.-Honoré, 8e, and other locations.

Hermès – For the very best ties, scarves, handbags, shoes, saddles, and accessories, though the prices may send you into cardiac arrest. 24 Rue du Faubourg-St.-Honoré, 8e.

IGN (French National Geographic Institute) – All manner of maps — ancient and modern, foreign and domestic, esoteric and mundane — are sold here. 107 Rue La Boétie, 8e.

Charles Jourdan – Sleek, high-fashion shoes. 5 Bd. de la Madeleine, 8e, is one of many outlets.

Kenzo – Avant-garde fashions by the Japanese designer. 3 Pl. des Victoires, 1er.

Lalique – The famous crystal. 11 Rue Royale, 8e.

Lancôme – Cosmetics. 29 Rue du Faubourg-St.-Honoré, 8e.

Lanvin – Another fabulous designer, with several spacious, colorful boutiques under one roof. 15, 17, and 22 Rue du Faubourg-St.-Honoré, 8e.

Ted Lapidus – A compromise between haute couture and excellent ready-to-wear. 23 Rue du Faubourg-St.-Honoré, 8e; 35 Rue François-I, 8e; and other branches.

Guy Laroche – Classic and conservative couture. 30 Rue du Faubourg-St.-Honoré, 8e, and 29 Av. Montaigne, 8e.

Marché aux Puces – Paris's famous Flea Market, with 3,000 dealers in antiques and secondhand items. Open Saturdays, Sundays, and Mondays. Bargaining is a must. Porte de Clignancourt, 18e.

Missoni – Innovative, original Italian knitwear. 43 Rue du Bac, 7e.

Morabito – Magnificent handbags and luggage at steep prices. 1 Pl. Vendôme, 1er.

Hanae Mori – The grande dame of Japanese designers in Paris. 17 Av. Montaigne, 8e; 62 Rue Faubourg-St.-Honoré, 8e.

Le Must de Cartier – Actually two boutiques, on either side of the *Ritz* hotel, offer such Cartier items as lighters and watches at prices that, though not low, are almost reasonable when you deduct the 25% VAT tax. 7 and 23 Pl. Vendôme, 1er.

Au Nain Bleu – The city's greatest toy store. 408 Rue St.-Honoré, 8e.

Marie Papier – Handsome marbled stationery and writing accessories. 26 Rue Vavin, 6e.

Le Petit Faune – A marvelous place to buy children's things. 33 Rue Jacob, 6e, and other locations.

Porthault – Terribly expensive, but elegantly exquisite bed and table linens. 18 Av. Montaigne, 8e.

Nina Ricci – Women's fashions, as well as the famous perfume. 17 Rue François-I, 8e, and 39 Av. Montaigne, 8e.

Sonia Rykiel – Stunning sportswear and knits. 6 Rue de Grenelle, 6e.

Yves Saint Laurent – The world-renowned designer, considered one of the most famous names in high fashion. 38 Rue du Faubourg-St.-Honoré, 8e, and 5 Av. Marceau, 8e, and other locations.

Jean-Louis Scherrer – A top designer, whose clothes are favored by the Parisian chic. 51-53 Av. Montaigne, 8e.

Shakespeare and Company – This legendary English-language bookstore, opposite Notre-Dame, is something of a tourist attraction in itself. 37 Rue de la Bûcherie, 5e.

W. H. Smith and Sons – The largest (and best) Parisian bookstore for reading material in English. It sells the Sunday *New York Times,* in addition to many British and American magazines and books. 248 Rue de Rivoli, 1er.

Per Spook – One of Paris's best young designers. 18 Av. George-V, 8e, and elsewhere.

Souleiado – Vibrant, traditional Provençal fabrics made into scarves, shawls, totes, and tableware. 78 Rue de Seine, 6e, and Forum des Halles, 1er.

Chantal Thomass – Ultra-feminine fashions, 5 Rue du Vieux-Colombier, 6e; sexy lingerie, 11 Rue Madame, 6e, and other locations.

Toraya – First foreign branch of this purveyor of Japanese *pâtisseries*. 10 Rue St.-Florentin, 1er.

Torrente – Women's fashions. 9 Rue du Faubourg-St.-Honoré, 8e.

Emmanuel Ungaro – Couturier boutique for women. 2 Av. Montaigne, 8e.

Van Cleef & Arpels – One of the world's great jewelers. 22 Pl. Vendôme, 1er.

Victoire – Ready-to-wear, with attractive accessories. 12 Pl. des Victoires, 1er.

Louis Vuitton – High-quality luggage and handbags. 78 bis Av. Marceau, 8e, and the new shop at St. Av. Montaigne, 8e.

BEST DISCOUNT SHOPS

If you're one of those — like us — who believes that the eighth deadly sin is buying retail, you'll treasure these inexpensive outlets.

Bab's – High fashion at low — or at least reasonable — prices. 29 Av. Marceau, 16e, and 89 bis Av. des Ternes, 17e.

Dorothée Bis Stock – Ms. Bis's well-known designs at about 40% off. 74 Rue d'Alésia, 14e.

Boétie 104 – Good buys on men's and women's shoes. 104 Rue La Boétie, 8e.

Boutique Stock – A vast selection of big-name knits at less than wholesale. 26, 30, 51, and 5 bis Rue St.-Placide, 6e; and 92 and 96 Rue d'Alésia, 14e.

Cacharel Stock – Surprisingly current Cacharel fashions at about a 40% discount. 114 Rue d'Alésia, 14e.

Pierre Cardin Stock – Terrific buys on the famed designer's men's clothing. 11 Bd. Sebastopol, 2e.

Catherine – One of the most hospitable of the perfume and cosmetics shops. A 40% discount (including VAT) is given on all purchases if the total exceeds 1,200F (about $200). 6 Rue Castiglione, 1er.

Emmanuelle Khanh – The designer's clothes at a substantial discount. 6 Rue Pierre-Lescot, 1er.

Lady Soldes – Prime fashion labels at less than normal prices. 221 Rue du Faubourg-St.-Honoré, 8e.

Lanvin Soldes Trois – Lanvin fashions at about half their retail cost. 3 Rue de Vienne, 8e.

Anna Lowe – Saint Laurent's stylings, among others, at a discount. 35 Av. Matignon, 8e.

Mendès – Less than wholesale prices on haute couture, especially Saint Laurent and Lanvin. 65 Rue Montmartre, 2e.

MicMac Stock – Sportswear for less. 13 Rue Laugier, 17e.

Miss Griffes – The very best of haute couture in small sizes (10 and under) at small prices. Alterations. 19 Rue de Penthièvre, 8e.

Mod Soldes – Names like Laroche and Lapidus at sale prices. 20 Rue Petit Champs, 1er.

Reciproque – Billed as the largest *"depot-vent"* in Paris, this outlet features names like Chanel, Alaia, Lanvin, and Scherrer. Several hundred square yards of display area are arranged by designer and size. 95 Rue de la Pompe, 16e; men's clothing and accessories, 101 Rue de la Pompe, 16e.

Jean-Louis Scherrer – Haute couture labels by Scherrer and others at about half their original prices. 29 Av. Ledru-Rollin, 12e.

Stock 2 – Features Daniel Hechter at discount for men, women, and children. 92 Rue d'Alésia, 14e.

■ **Note**: For a modest price ($5-$40), you can also take home a bit of the *Louvre*. The museum's 200-year-old Department of Calcography houses a collection of 16,000 engraved copper plates — renderings of monuments, battles, coronations, Egyptian pyramids, and portraits — dating from the 17th century. Prints made from these engravings come reproduced on thick vellum, embossed with the *Louvre*'s imprint. The Calcography Department (open daily, except Tuesdays, from 2 to 5 PM), is 1 flight up from the Porte Barbet de Jouy entrance on the Seine side of the *Louvre*.

 SPORTS AND FITNESS: Biking – Rentals are available in the Bois de Boulogne and the Bois de Vincennes, or contact the *Fédération Française de Cyclo-tourisme*, 8 Rue Jean-Marie-Jégo, 13e (phone: 45-80-30-21); *Bicy-Club de France*, 8 Pl. de la Porte Champerret, 17e (phone: 47-66-55-92); or *Paris-Vélo*, 2 Rue du Fer à Moulin, 5e (phone: 43-37-59-22). The world-famous Tour de France bicycle race takes place in July and ends in Paris.

Fitness Centers – The *Garden Gym*, 65 Av. des Champs-Elysées, 8e, (phone: 42-25-87-20), and 123 Av. Charles-de-Gaulle, Neuilly (phone: 47-47-62-62), is open daily to non-members for a fee.

Golf – For general information, contact the *Fédération Française du Golf*, 69 Av. Victor-Hugo, 16e (phone: 45-00-43-72). It is usually possible to play on any course during the week by simply paying a greens fee. Weekends may be more difficult. *Ozoir-la-Ferrière*, Château des Agneaux, 15 miles (24 km) away (phone: 60-28-20-79), welcomes Americans (closed Tuesdays); and *St.-Germain-en-Laye*, 12½ miles (19 km) away (phone: 34-51-75-90), accepts non-members on weekdays only. The *Racing Club de France*, La Boulie, Versailles (phone: 39-50-59-41), and *St.-Nom-la-Bretèche*, in the suburb of the same name (phone: 34-62-54-00), accept guests of members only. It's best to call at least 2 days in advance to schedule a time.

Horse Racing – Of the eight tracks in and around Paris, two major ones are in the Bois de Boulogne: *Longchamp* (phone: 42-24-13-29) for flat races and *Auteuil* (phone: 47-23-54-12 or 47-23-54-32) for steeplechase. *St.-Cloud* (phone: 43-59-20-70), a few miles west of Paris, and *Chantilly* (phone: 42-66-92-02), about 25 miles (40 km) north of the city, are both for flat racing. *Vincennes*, Bois de Vincennes (phone: 47-42-07-70), is the trotting track. Important races take place from spring through fall, but the *Grande Semaine* (Big Week) comes in late June, when nine major races — beginning with the *Grand Steeplechase de Paris* at *Auteuil* and including the *Grand Prix de Paris* at *Longchamp* — are scheduled.

Jogging – The streets and sidewalks of Paris may be ideal for lovers, but they're not meant for runners. There are, however, a number of places where you can jog happily; one of the most pleasant is the 2,500-acre Bois de Boulogne. Four more central parks are the Jardin du Luxembourg (reachable by métro: Luxembourg), the Champ-de-Mars gardens (just behind the Eiffel Tower; métro: Iéna), Parc Monceau (métro: Monceau), and the Jardin des Tuileries (métro: Tuileries, Louvre, or Concorde).

Soccer – There are matches from early August to mid-June at Parc des Princes, Av. du Parc-des-Princes, 16e (phone: 42-88-02-76).

Swimming – At the heart of Paris, rather unsuitably near the National Assembly, lies the *Piscine Deligny*, notorious in the summer for its acres of topless women bathers and, on the 3rd-floor deck, nude sunbathers of both sexes. The pool is set in a floating barge on the Seine beside the Concorde bridge; it is, says the sign, filled with fresh water. Open May to September. 25 Quai Anatole-France, 7e (phone: 45-51-72-15). Other pools include *Piscine des Halles,* 10 Pl. de la Rotonde, 4e (phone: 42-36-98-44); *Pontoise,* 19 Rue de Pontoise, 5e (phone: 43-54-82-45); *Butte-aux-Cailles,* 5 Pl. Paul-Verlaine, 13e (phone: 45-89-60-05); *Keller,* 14 Rue de l'Ingénieur-Robert-Keller, 15e (phone: 45-77-12-12); *Jean-Taris,* 16 Rue Thouin, 5e (phone: 43-25-54-03); *Tour Montparnasse,* beneath the tower at 66 Bd. de Montparnasse, 15e (phone: 45-38-65-19); *Molitor,* 2 Av. de Porte Molitor, 16e (phone: 46-51-02-73); *Neuilly,* 50 Rue Pauline-Borghèse, Neuilly (phone: 47-22-69-59).

Tennis – For general information, call *Ligue Régionale de Paris,* 74 Rue de Rome, 17e (phone: 45-22-22-08), or the *Fédération Française de Tennis, Roland Garros Stadium,* 16e (phone: 47-43-48-00).

THEATER: The most complete listings of theatrical performances, operas, concerts, and movies are found in the *Officiel des Spectacles* and *Une Semaine à Paris–Pariscope* (see *Tourist Information,* above). The season is generally from September to June. Tickets are less expensive than in New York and are obtained at each box office, through brokers (*American Express* and *Thomas Cook* act in that capacity and are good), your hotel's trusty concierge, or with the new high-tech Billetels that were installed in 1988 at the *Galeries Lafayette,* the *Centre Georges Pompidou,* and other locations. Insert a credit card into a slot on the Billetel and choose from over 100 upcoming theater events and concerts. The device will spew out a display of dates, seats, and prices, from which you can order your tickets — they will be printed on the spot and charged to your credit card. Half-price, day-of-performance theater tickets are available at the kiosks at the Châtelet-les Halles, 1er (Tuesdays–Saturdays 12:45 to 7 PM); and at 15 Place de la Madeleine, 8e (Tuesdays-Saturdays, 12:30 to 8 PM; Sundays, 12:30 to 4 PM). The curtain usually goes up at 8:30 PM.

For those who speak French: Performances of classical plays by Molière, Racine, and Corneille take place at the *Comédie-Française,* Pl. du Théâtre, 1er (phone: 40-15-00-15). Two other national theaters are *Théâtre de L'Odéon,* 1 Pl. Paul-Claudel, 6e (phone: 43-25-70-32), and *Théâtre National de Chaillot,* Pl. du Trocadéro, 16e (phone: 47-27-81-15). Last, but not least, the *Théâtre du Soleil,* in an old cartridge factory, La Cartoucherie de Vincennes, on the outskirts of Paris in the Bois de Vincennes, 12e (phone: 43-74-24-08), offers colorful productions ranging from contemporary political works to Shakespeare.

It's not really necessary to speak the language to enjoy the opera, dance, or musical comedy at *L'Opéra,* Pl. de l'Opéra, 9e (phone: 40-17-33-33 or 40-17-34-10); the new *L'Opéra Bastille,* Pl. de la Bastille, 11e (phone: 43-42-92-92); *Salle Favart–Opéra Comique,* 5 Rue Favart, 9e (phone: 42-96-12-20); or *Théâtre Musical de Paris,* 1 Pl. du Châtelet, 1er (phone: 42-61-19-83). Theater tickets can be reserved through *SOS-Théâtre,* 73 Champs-Elysées, 8e (phone: 42-25-67-07).

For those who consider French their second language, Paris's many café-theaters offer amusing songs, sketches, satires, and takeoffs on topical trends and events. Among them are *Café de la Gare,* 41 Rue du Temple, 4e (phone: 42-78-52-51), and *Café d'Edgar,* 58 Bd. Edgar-Quinet, 14e (phone: 43-22-11-02).

CINEMA: With no less than 200 movie houses, Paris is a real treat for film buffs. No other metropolis offers such a cinematographic feast — current French chic, recent imports from across the Atlantic, grainy 1930s classics, and the latest and most select of Third World and Eastern European offerings. In any given week, there are up to 200 different movies shown, generally in their original versions with French subtitles.

Film distribution is erratic, to say the least, so the French often get their *Indiana Jones* and *Beverly Hills Cop* flicks up to a year late. But the system works both ways: Many of the front-runners at Cannes first hit the screens here, which gives you a jump on friends back home.

Both *Pariscope* and the *Officiel de Spectacles,* which come out on Wednesday, the day the programs change, contain the full selection each week. *Pariscope* has thought of almost every possible way to classify films, sorting them into new releases and revivals, broad categories (for instance, the *drame psychologique* label means it will be heavier than a *comédie dramatique*), location by *arrondissement,* late-night showings, and so on.

Films shown with their original-language sound tracks are called VO, (*version originale*); it's worth watching out for that crucial "VO" tag, otherwise you may find yourself wincing at a French-dubbed version, called VF, (*version française*). Broadly speaking, the undubbed variety of film flourishes on the Champs-Elysées and on the Left Bank, and it's also a safe bet to avoid the mostly French-patronized houses of les Grands Boulevards.

The timetables aren't always reliable, so it's worth checking by telephone — if you can decipher the recorded messages that spell out exactly when the five or so showings a day begin. A *séance* (sitting) generally begins with advertisements (often imaginatively made by out-of-work French film directors), and the movie proper begins up to 20 minutes later.

There's more room in the big movie houses on the Champs-Elysées, but the cozier Latin Quarter establishments tend to specialize in the unusual and avant-garde — often the only showing such films will ever get. For the ultimate in high tech, the *Géode* offers a B-Max hemispherical screen, cupped inside a reflecting geodesic dome, at the La Villette Sciences and Industry complex. The program is, however, limited to a single scientifically oriented film at any given time, whereas the *Forum Horizon,* in the new underground section of Les Halles, offers a choice of four first-run movies and claims to have one of the city's best sound systems. Some more out-of-the-way venues like the *Olympique Entrepôt* and the *Lucernaire* at Montparnasse are social centers in themselves, incorporating restaurants and/or other theaters.

Paris's cinemathèque — at the *Palais de Chaillot* — runs a packed schedule of reruns at rates lower than those of the commercial cinemas. The recently opened *Videothèque de Paris,* in the Forum les Halles, is the world's first public video library. Visitors can select individual showings or attend regularly scheduled theater screenings of films and television programs chronicling Paris's history (phone: 40-26-34-30).

Then there are two period pieces almost worth a visit in themselves. *Le Ranelagh,* at 5 Rue des Vignes, 16e (phone: 42-88-64-44), has an exquisite 19th-century interior where films and live theater are performed. *La Pagode,* at 57 bis Rue de Babylone, 7e (phone: 47-05-12-15), with flying cranes, cherry blossoms, and a tearoom, is built around a Japanese temple that was shipped over to Paris by the proprietor of a department store in the 1920s.

MUSIC: The *Orchestre de Paris,* under the direction of Daniel Barenboim, is based at the *Salle Pleyel* — the *Carnegie Hall* of Paris, 252 Rue du Faubourg-St.-Honoré, 8e (phone: 45-63-88-73). Other classical recitals are held at the *Salle Gaveau,* 45 Rue La Boétie (phone: 49-53-05-07), at the *Théâtre des Champs-Elysées,* 15 Av. Montaigne, 8e (phone: 47-23-47-77), and at the *Palais des Congrès,* Porte Maillot (phone: 46-40-22-22). The *Orchestre Philharmonic* performs at a variety of places, including the *Grand Auditorium* at *Maison de la Radio,* 116 Av. du Président-J.-F.-Kennedy (phone: 42-30-15-16 or 42-30-18-18). Special concerts are frequently held in Paris's many places of worship, with moving music at High Mass on Sundays. The *Palais des Congrès* and the *Olympia,* 28 Bd. des Capucines (phone: 47-42-82-45), are the places to see well-known international pop and rock artists. Innovative contemporary music — much of it created by computer — is the province of the *Institut de Recherche et de Coopération Acoustique Musique* (IRCAM), whose musicians can be heard in various auditoriums of the *Centre Georges Pompidou,* 31 Rue St.-Merri (phone: 42-77-12-33).

NIGHTCLUBS AND NIGHTLIFE: Organized "Paris by Night" group tours (*Cityrama, Paris Vision,* and other operators offer them; see *Special Places*) include at least one "Spectacle" — beautiful girls in minimal, yet elaborate, costumes, with lavish sets and effects and sophisticated striptease. Most music halls offer a package (starting as high as $90 per person), with dinner, dancing, and a half-bottle of champagne. It is possible to go to these places on your own, save money by skipping dinner and the champagne (both usually way below par), and take a seat at the bar to see the show. The most famous extravaganzas occur nightly at *Alcazar,* 62 Rue Mazarine, 6e (phone: 43-29-02-20); *Crazy Horse Saloon,* 12 Av. George-V, 8e (phone: 47-23-32-32); *Folies-Bergère,* 32 Rue Richer, 9e (phone: 42-46-77-11); *Lido (Cabaret Normandie),* 116 bis Champs-Elysées, 8e (phone: 45-63-11-61); *Moulin Rouge,* Pl. Blanche, 18e (phone: 46-06-00-19); and *Paradis Latin,* 28 Rue du Cardinal-Lemoine, 5e (phone: 43-25-28-28). An amusing evening can also be spent at smaller cabaret shows like *René Cousinier* (*La Branlette*), 4 Impasse Marie-Blanche, 18e (phone: 46-06-49-46); *Au Lapin Agile,* 22 Rue des Saules, 18e (phone: 46-06-85-87); and *Michou,* 80 Rue des Martyrs, 18e (phone: 46-06-16-04). Reserve all a few days in advance.

Discotheque or private club, there's one big difference. Fashionable "in" spots like *Le Palace,* 8 Rue Faubourg-Montmartre, 9e (phone: 42-46-10-87); *Régine's,* 49 Rue de Ponthieu, 8e (phone: 43-59-21-60); *Chez Castel,* 15 Rue Princesse, 6e (members only; phone: 43-26-90-22); *Olivia Valère,* 40 Rue de Colisée, 8e (members only; phone: 42-25-11-68); and *Elysées Matignon,* 2 Av. Matignon, 8e (phone: 42-25-73-13), super-screen potential guests. No reason is given for accepting some and turning others away; go here with a regular or look as if you'd fit in with the crowd. Go early and on a weeknight — when your chances of getting past the gatekeeper are at least 50-50. Don't despair if you're refused; the following places are just as much fun and usually more hospitable: *Les Bains,* 7 Rue du Bourg-l'Abbé, 3e (phone: 48-87-01-80); *L'Aventure,* 4 Av. Victor-Hugo, 16e (phone: 45-01-66-79); and *L'Ecume des Nuits, Méridien* hotel, 81 Bd. Gouvion-St.-Cyr, 17e (phone: 47-58-12-30).

Some pleasant, popular bars for a nightcap include: *Bar de la Closerie des Lilas,* 171 Bd. Montparnasse, 6e (phone: 43-26-70-50); *Harry's New York Bar,* 5 Rue Daunou, 2e (phone: 42-61-71-14); *Fouquet's,* 99 Champs-Elysées, 8e (phone: 47-23-70-60); *Ascot Bar,* 66 Rue Pierre-Charron, 8e (phone: 43-59-28-15); *Bar Anglais,* Plaza-Athénée Hôtel, 25 Av. Montaigne, 8e (phone: 47-23-78-33); and *Pub Winston Churchill,* 5 Rue de Presbourg, 16e (phone: 45-00-75-35).

Jazz buffs have a large choice with *Caveau de la Huchette,* 5 Rue de la Huchette, 5e (phone: 43-26-65-05); *Le Bilboquet,* 13 Rue St.-Benoit, 6e (phone: 45-48-81-84); *New Morning,* 7–9 Rue des Petites Ecuries, 10e (phone: 45-23-51-41); *Slow Club,* 130 Rue de Rivoli, 1er (phone: 42-33-84-30); and *Le Petit Journal,* 71 Bd. St.-Michel, 6e (phone: 43-26-28-59).

Enghien-les-Bains, 8 miles (13 km) away, is the only casino in the Paris vicinity (3 Av. de Ceinture, Enghien-les-Bains; phone: 34-12-90-00). Open from 3 PM to about 4 AM, it can easily be reached by train from the Gare du Nord.

BEST IN TOWN

CHECKING IN: Paris offers a broad choice of accommodations, from luxurious palaces with every service to more humble budget hotels. However, they are all strictly controlled by the government and must post their rates, so you can be sure that the price you are being charged is correct. Below is a selection from all categories; in general, expect to spend $300 and up per night for a double room in the "palace" hotels, which we've listed as very expensive; from $170 to $300 in expensive; $70 to $170 in moderate; and $70 or less in inexpensive.

Except for July, August, and December, the least crowded months, hotel rooms are usually at a premium in Paris. To reserve your first choice, we advise making reservations at least a month in advance, even farther ahead for the smaller, less expensive places. Watch for the dates of special events, when hotels are even more crowded than usual. An alternative to the hotel options listed here are the apartment rentals offered by *Paris Accueil/Paris Sejour* (see *Accommodations and Reservations,* GETTING READY TO GO).

Street addresses of the hotels below are followed by their *arrondissement* number.

Bristol – A palace with a special, almost intimate cachet. Service is impeccable, as are the 188 spacious, quiet rooms and huge, marble baths. The beautiful little restaurant and comfortable lobby cocktail lounge are additional pleasures. A new wing includes a heated swimming pool on the 6th-floor terrace. 112 Rue du Faubourg-St.-Honoré, 8e (phone: 42-66-91-45; in the US, 800-999-1802). Very expensive.

Crillon – No sign out front, just discreet gold "C's" on the doors. Recently renovated and refurbished, the *Crillon* is currently the only "palace" hotel in Paris still owned by a Frenchman. The rooms on the Place de la Concorde side, though rather noisy, have the view of views; rooms facing the courtyards are just as nice and much more tranquil. The popular bar and 2 elegant restaurants, *L'Obélisque* and *Les Ambassadeurs* (which rates two Michelin stars), are often frequented by journalists and US and British embassy personnel. 10 Pl. de la Concorde, 8e (phone: 42-65-24-24). Very expensive.

George V – This nonpareil pick of movie moguls and international tycoons has 288 elegantly traditional or handsome contemporary rooms and 63 suites: some, facing the lovely courtyard, have their own balconies; those on the upper floors, a nice view. The recent roof-to-cellar refurbishing has spruced things up splendidly. And there are now 2 restaurants, *Les Princes* and a grill, as well as a tearoom. One of the liveliest and chic-est bars in the city is here, with a bartender who mixes a mean martini. The patio is a summer delight. 31 Av. George-V, 8e (phone: 47-23-54-00). Very expensive.

Meurice – Refined Louis XV and XVI elegance and a wide range of services are offered at prices slightly below those of the other "palaces." The hotel, re-acquired in 1988 by the CIGA chain, has 187 rooms and especially nice suites, a popular bar, a restaurant, *Le Meurice,* and the chandeliered *Pompadour* tearoom. The location and hospitality couldn't be better, and a restoration of the first-floor public room is in process. 228 Rue de Rivoli, 1er (phone: 42-60-38-60). Very expensive.

Plaza-Athénée – Once one of the legendary hotels, this favorite of the sophisticated seeking serene surroundings and superior service has 218 rooms, many in need of a facelift. Although some grumbling has been reported, the *Relais* tables are still much in demand at lunch and late supper, and the two-star *Régence,* summer patio, tea tables, and downstairs English bar are still places to see and be seen. 25 Av. Montaigne, 8e (phone: 47-23-78-33). Very expensive.

Résidence Maxim's – Pierre Cardin's luxurious venture is near the Elysée Palace. No expense has been spared here to create sybaritic splendor. The 39 suites range in style from sleek modern to Belle Epoque, with original Art Nouveau pieces from Cardin's own collections, and every bathroom has been individually redesigned. *Le Caviarteria,* its restaurant, is already making a name in the city, and has a pleasant terrace in summer; *La Tonnelle* serves tea and breakfast, and doubles as a tea salon; and the bar, *Le Maximin,* is open late. 42 Av. Gabriel, 8e (phone: 45-61-96-33). Very expensive.

Ritz – Optimum comfort, privacy, and personal service are offered here, in one of the world's most gracious and distinguished hotels. A recent restoration and expansion includes a new health club (with pool, sauna, and squash courts), an extensive business center, and the Ritz Escoffier Ecole de Cuisine. The latest addition is the *Ritz Club,* a nightclub and discotheque on the lower level, which opened in 1989 to hotel guests and club members only. The 162 redecorated rooms still preserve their antique treasures. This turn-of-the-century monument is *the* place to splurge, the bars are fashionable meeting places, and the two-star *Ritz-Espadon* restaurant carries on the tradition of the legendary *Escoffier.* 15 Pl. Vendôme, 1er (phone: 42-60-38-30). Very expensive.

Royal Monceau – Newly renovated, in impeccable taste, this elegant property not far from the Arc de Triomphe has 3 restaurants — one with an attractive garden setting — as well as 2 bars, a fitness center, pool, Jacuzzi, and beauty salon. 37 Av. Hoche, 8e (phone: 45-61-98-00). Very expensive.

San Régis – Tastefully renovated under new ownership, with each room individually rethought. This is an elegant place to feel at home in comfortable surroundings. 12 Rue Jean-Goujon, 8e (phone: 43-59-41-90). Very expensive to expensive.

Westminster – Between the Opéra and the *Ritz,* it was at one time quite prestigious, but declined somewhat before its recent renovation. The paneling, marble fireplaces, and parquet floors of its traditional decor remain; air conditioning has been installed, and a new restaurant, *Le Céladon,* and cocktail lounge replace the old grill and bar. Some of the 101 rooms and apartments overlook the street, some an inner courtyard. 13 Rue de la Paix, 2e (phone: 42-61-57-46). Very expensive to expensive.

Grand – This has long been a favorite of Americans abroad, with its "meeting place of the world," the *Café de la Paix.* It has 530 newly modernized rooms and 10 luxurious new suites, plus cheerful bars and restaurants — and a prime spot (next to the *Opéra*). Now part of the Inter-Continental chain. 2 Rue Scribe, 9e (phone: 42-68-12-13). Expensive.

Holiday Inn Place de la République – In the heart of town, in a 120-year-old edifice that evokes the grandeur of the Second Empire — its façade is unlike any *Holiday Inn* you've seen before. Of the 333 pleasantly decorated rooms, those facing the courtyard are preferable to those facing the square. Restaurant, piano bar, and air conditioning. 10 Pl. de la République, 11e (phone: 43-55-44-34). Expensive.

L'Hôtel – Still considered chic, this small Left Bank hotel is favored by experienced international travelers, though the 27 tiny rooms are showing wear and tear. The attractive restaurant, complete with waterfall, is flanked by a piano bar, and the location can't be beat. 13 Rue des Beaux-Arts, 6e (phone: 43-25-27-22). Expensive.

Inter-Continental – The 500 rooms and suites have been restored to re-create turn-of-the-century elegance with modern conveniences. The top-floor Louis XVI "garret" rooms are cozy and look out over the Tuileries. There's an American-style coffee shop, a grill, popular bar, and *L'Estrela* nightclub. This hotel is very popular and packed with tour groups. 3 Rue de Castiglione, 1er (phone: 42-60-37-80). Expensive.

Lancaster – Recent visitors have been heard to complain about this small, 57-room townhouse. However, there are still flowers everywhere, a cozy bar, and a restaurant with courtyard service in summer. Run by London's Savoy group. 7 Rue de Berri, 8e (phone: 43-59-90-43). Expensive.

Méridien – Air France's well-run, 1,027-room, modern American-style hotel has all the expected French flair. Rooms are on the small side but tastefully decorated, quiet, and with good views. There are 4 attractive restaurants, a shopping arcade, lively bars, and a chic nightclub, *L'Ecume des Nuits.* 81 Bd. Gouvion-St.-Cyr, 17e (phone: 47-58-12-30). Expensive.

Méridien Montparnasse – With 952 rooms, this ultramodern giant is in the heart of Montparnasse. It has a futuristic lobby, efficient service, a coffee shop, bars, and the *Montparnasse 25* restaurant, with a view, and in summer a garden restaurant. 19 Rue du Commandant-René-Mouchotte, 14e (phone: 43-20-15-51). Expensive.

Paris Hilton International – Its 474 modern rooms are only a few steps from the Eiffel Tower. Those facing the river have the best view. The glass-walled rendezvous *Le Toit de Paris* has dancing and a glittering nighttime view; *Le Western* serves T-bone steaks, apple pie à la mode, and brownies (mostly to French diners). The coffee shop is a magnet for homesick Americans. 18 Av. de Suffren, 15e (phone: 42-73-92-00). Expensive.

Pavillon de la Reine – Supreme location for the Marais's only luxury hotel, owned by the management of the *Relais Christine* and similarly appointed. It's 49 spacious rooms look out on a garden or courtyard. The setting on the Place des Vosges is regal, and the *Picasso Museum* is only a couple of minutes away on foot. 28 Pl. des Vosges, 3e (phone: 42-77-96-40). Expensive.

Pullman St.-Jacques – This four-star hotel has 797 up-to-date rooms, a nice shopping arcade, a cinema, 4 restaurants (one Japanese, one Chinese, one French, and an informal coffee shop), and the lively *Bar Tahonga*. A bit out of the way, but the métro is close by. 17 Bd. St.-Jacques, 14e (phone: 45-89-89-80). Expensive.

Raphael – A very spacious, stately place, with a Turner in the lobby downstairs and paneling painted with sphinxes in the generous rooms. Less well known among the top Paris hotels, but favored by film folk and the like. 17 Av. Kléber, 16e (phone: 45-02-16-00). Expensive.

Relais Christine – Thorough renovation turned this 16th-century cloister into a lovely small hotel with modern fixtures and lots of old-fashioned charm. 3 Rue Christine, 6e (phone: 43-26-71-80). Expensive.

Résidence du Roy – If you feel like cooking for yourself within easy reach of the Champs-Elysées, this establishment offers self-contained studios, suites, and duplexes, complete with kitchen facilities. Management could be better, however. 8 Rue François-I, 8e (phone: 42-89-59-59). Expensive.

Abbaye St.-Germain – On a quiet street, this small, delightful hotel was once a convent. The lobby has exposed stone arches, and the elegant public and private rooms are furnished with antiques, tastefully selected fabrics, and marble baths. There's a lovely garden and a bar, but recently there have been some complaints about the service. 10 Rue Cassette, 6e (phone: 45-44-38-11). Moderate.

Angleterre – Its 29 classic, clean, unpretentious rooms are in what was once the British Embassy, now a national monument. 44 Rue Jacob, 6e (phone: 42-60-34-72). Moderate.

Danube – The rooms, with their four-poster bamboo beds, are comfortable, and some of them overlook an attractive courtyard typical of the Left Bank. 58 Rue Jacob, 6e (phone: 42-60-34-70). Moderate.

Deux Iles – This beautifully redecorated 17th-century house is on the historic Ile St.-Louis. It has a tropical garden and the decor is in bamboo, rattan, and braided rope. The rooms have French provincial fabrics and Louis XIV ceramic tiles in the bathrooms. But there's one drawback: the rooms aren't very large. 59 Rue St.-Louis-en-l'Ile, 4e (phone: 43-26-13-35). Moderate.

Grand Hôtel Taranne – Anybody anxious to get into the Left Bank scene should love it here, for the 35 rooms are literally on top of the *Brasserie Lipp*. Each room is unique: #4 has exposed beams, a TV set, and a mini-bar; #3 has a Louis XIII–style bed; #17, the oddest, has lights and a disco ball. 153 Bd. St.-Germain, 6e (phone: 42-22-21-65). Moderate.

Grand Hôtel de l'Univers – This modern hotel is tucked away on a quiet street, but St.-Germain-des-Prés and the Latin Quarter are only 2 steps away. No restaurant. 6 Rue Grégoire-de-Tours, 6e (phone: 43-29-37-00). Moderate.

Jeu de Paume – The architect owner of this former *jeu de paume* (tennis court) has artfully married old and new in this newest addition to the exclusive Ile St.-Louis hotels. High-tech lighting, modern artwork, and a sleek glass elevator are set against ancient ceiling beams and warm limestone brick hearths. There's a country feeling here. Rooms are comfortable and reasonably priced. 54 Rue St.-Louis-en-l'Ile, 4e (phone: 43-26-14-18). Moderate.

Lord Byron – On a quiet street off the Champs-Elysées, it has a pleasant courtyard and 30 comfortable, homey rooms. The staff is friendly and speaks good English, and a family atmosphere prevails. 5 Rue de Chateaubriand, 8e (phone: 43-59-89-98). Moderate.

Lutèce – Here are 23 luxurious rooms (one split-level) on the charming Ile St.-Louis. Positively ravishing, with exquisite toile fabrics and wallpaper and raw wood beams. 65 Rue St.-Louis-en-l'Ile, 4e (phone: 43-26-23-52). Moderate.

Madison – Offers 55 large, bright rooms, some with balconies, all recently redecorated by new management. 143 Bd. St.-Germain, 6e (phone: 43-29-72-50). Moderate.

Odéon – Small, modernized, and charming, it's in the heart of the St.-Germain area on the Left Bank. No restaurant. 3 Rue de l'Odéon, 6e (phone: 43-25-90-67). Moderate.

Regent's Garden – On a quiet street near the Etoile, it has 40 spacious rooms, some with large marble fireplaces. The property is now run by young hoteliers who make you feel you are in your own home. A country atmosphere pervades. There's also a garden and parking. 6 Rue Pierre-Demours, 17e (phone: 45-74-07-30). Moderate.

Résidence Charles-Dullin – In a sleepy corner of Montmartre, near the leafy square of the Théâtre de l'Atelier, this residential hotel charges nightly, weekly, and monthly rates. The apartments have kitchens, and some overlook a peaceful garden. 10 Pl. Charles-Dullin, 18e (phone: 42-57-14-55). Moderate.

Ste.-Beuve – A stylish hotel cheerfully managed in Montparnasse, with rooms and lobby designed by David Hicks. 9 Rue Ste.-Beuve, 6e (phone: 45-48-20-07). Moderate.

St.-Louis – On magical Ile St.-Louis, practically in the shadow of Nôtre Dame, this small hotel will make the first-time visitor fall in love with the city forever. The 21 rooms aren't large, but they're pretty, and the 3 fifth-floor rooms under the eaves are enchanting, with tiny balconies overlooking Parisian rooftops. No TV sets, but baths are clean and modern, and there's a charming breakfast room and a warm welcome. 75 Rue St.-Louis-en-Ile, 4e (phone: 46-34-04-80). Moderate.

St.-Simon – If you're in search of things past, this may be one of the best places in town. In 2 big townhouses in a beautiful, quiet backwater off the Boulevard St.-Germain, this elegant little hotel veritably reeks of Proust. Just a 5-minute walk from the spectacular new *Musée d'Orsay*. 14 Rue de St.-Simon, 7e (phone: 45-48-35-66). Moderate.

Tuileries – With a good location in a "real" neighborhood in the heart of the city, it has a well-tended look and attractive carved wood bedsteads. 10 Rue St.-Hyacinthe, 1er (phone: 42-61-04-17 or 42-61-06-94). Moderate.

L'Université – Its 28 charmingly renovated rooms of all shapes and sizes are in a former 18th-century mansion. 22 Rue de l'Université, 7e (phone: 42-61-09-39). Moderate.

Vendôme – This older "house" has 36 immaculate high-ceilinged rooms with brass beds, and the location couldn't be better. There is a small restaurant with a limited menu, and a bar. 1 Pl. Vendôme, 1er (phone: 42-60-32-84). Moderate.

La Villa – The old *Isly* hotel has been reborn with post-modern decor in its 35 rooms with bath. The location can't be beat, and there's even a jazz club in the cellar. 29 Rue Jacob, 6e (phone: 43-26-60-00). Moderate.

West End – A friendly, 60-room hotel on the Right Bank. The front desk keeps a close, concerned watch on comings and goings, which some may find reassuring. 7 Rue Clément-Marot, 8e (phone: 47-20-30-78). Moderate.

Chomel – Spruced up and newly renovated, this establishment is near the *Au Bon Marché* department store. 15 Rue Chomel, 7e (phone: 45-48-55-52). Moderate to inexpensive.

Celestins – This tiny hotel sits on a quiet residential street on the edge of the newly chic Marais (Paris's oldest neighborhood), a short walk from the Place des Vosges, the *Louvre,* the quais along the Seine, and the Bastille nightclubs. Dating from the 18th century, when it belonged to the Celestin Convent, it has 14 small rooms, which still have their original dark wood walls and ceiling beams. Number 18, the nicest, has an extra couch; number 20 has a skylight in the bathroom. Historical status has barred installation of an elevator, however. 1 Rue Charles-V, 4e (phone: 48-87-87-04). Moderate to inexpensive.

Ferrandi – Popular with international businessmen, this no-frills hotel is done up in browns and blues, with a winding wood staircase and a quiet lounge. 92 Rue du Cherche-Midi, 6e (phone: 42-22-97-40). Moderate to inexpensive.

Parc St.-Severin – An interesting new property in the heart of the 5th *arrondissement* on the Left Bank, it has a total of 27 rooms, including a top-floor penthouse with a wraparound balcony. The decor is modern but understated, and the overall ambience is appealing even though the neighborhood is less than the quietest in Paris. 22 Rue de la Parcheminerie, 5e (phone: 43-54-32-17). Moderate to inexpensive.

St.-Merry – A stone's throw from the *Centre Georges Pompidou* arts complex, this mock-medieval establishment may be the most bizarre hotel in Paris. It not only backs onto the Eglise St.-Merry, but it has a communion rail as a banister and ancient oaken confessionals as broom closets. The rooms, hung with dark, demonic oil portraits, have church pews for benches, and some rooms are even spliced by a flying buttress. In dubious taste, perhaps, but there's nothing else like it. 78 Rue de la Verrerie, 4e (phone: 42-78-14-15). Moderate to inexpensive.

St.-Thomas-d'Aquin – Built in the 1880s, this unpretentious hotel is a simple, functional base from which to explore a shopper's paradise of new wave designer boutiques and tiny restaurants. The 21 rooms are clean and neat, and baths are modern (though tubs are half-size). Breakfast included. 3 Rue d'Pré-aux-Clercs, 7e (phone: 42-61-01-22). Moderate to inexpensive.

Ambassade – In the center of the 16th arrondissement, which many consider the heart and soul of Paris, this hotel is equidistant from the Arc de Triomphe, the Place du Trocadero, the Eiffel Tower, the Bois de Boulogne, and the designer shops on Av. Victor-Hugo. It has 38 pleasant rooms, each with wicker bedstead, pastel wallpaper, TV set, and clock-radio; many of the baths have been redone in beige marble. The ground-floor breakfast room doubles as a bar in the afternoon. 79 Rue Lauriston, 16e (phone: 45-53-41-15). Inexpensive.

Amélie – Centrally located, this comfortable hotel was renovated in 1985 and now has 15 rooms, each with a color TV set, direct-dial telephone, and mini-bar. Breakfast is included in the room rate, which makes this one of Paris's better values. 5 Rue Amélie, 7e (phone: 45-51-74-75). Inexpensive.

D'Argenson – The upper-middle class residential district in which this hotel is located is off the typical tourist track but convenient to major department stores on the Bd. Haussmann and a 15-minute walk from the *Opéra*. The showplace rooms — numbers 23, 33, 43, and 53 — feature fireplaces and brand-new bathrooms. Breakfast included. 15 Rue d'Argenson, 8e (phone: 42-65-16-87). Inexpensive.

Bretonnerie – This restored 17th-century townhouse takes itself seriously, with petit point, dark wood furnishings, and several attic rooms with beams that overlook the narrow streets of the newly fashionable Marais area. 22 Rue Ste.-Croix-de-la-Bretonnerie, 4e (phone: 48-87-77-63). Inexpensive.

Ceramic – Close to the Champs-Elysées, the Faubourg St.-Honoré, and the métro, this 53-room establishment with an Art Nouveau façade has been designated a national historic treasure. Request a room facing the street, particularly number 412 — enormous, with a crystal chandelier and wide bay windows. Room rates include breakfast. 34 Av. de Wagram, 17e (phone: 42-27-20-30). Inexpensive.

Delavigne – A good value and location (just down the street from the *Odéon* theater), this refurbished hotel has an enlightened manager who says he isn't interested in simply handing out keys, but enjoys introducing foreigners to Paris. 1 Rue Casimir-Delavigne, 6e (phone: 43-29-31-50). Inexpensive.

Deux Continents – A cozy red sitting room looks invitingly onto the street here, in this 40-room establishment on the Left Bank. 25 Rue Jacob, 6e (phone: 43-26-72-46). Inexpensive.

Esmeralda – Some of the rooms here look directly at Notre-Dame over the gardens of St.-Julien-le-Pauvre, one of Paris's most ancient churches. The oak beams and furniture round out the medieval atmosphere. Small and friendly, especially popular with the theatrical crowd. 4 Rue St.-Julien-le-Pauvre, 5e (phone: 43-54-19-20). Inexpensive.

Family – A longtime favorite with Americans — you're treated just like part of the family. Although it changed owners about a year ago, the staff is the same. It has 25 small but comfortable rooms, recently renovated. 35 Rue Cambon, 1er (phone: 42-61-54-84). Inexpensive.

Grandes Ecoles – This is just the sort of place that shouldn't appear in a guidebook (even the proprietress says so) and that people recommend only to the right friends. Insulated from the street by a delightful courtyard and its garden, it is a simple 19th-century private house with plain comforts, but it's long on atmosphere. There aren't many like it in Paris. 75 Rue Cardinal-Lemoine, 5e (phone: 43-26-79-23). Inexpensive.

Le Jardin des Plantes – In addition to a magnificent setting across from the Parisian Botanical Gardens, near the Sorbonne, there are 33 airy, spotless rooms and baths, each with its own floral motif. The owner, a psychologist, has anticipated the traveler's every need: All rooms have mini-bars, TV sets, and hair dryers; some have alcoves large enough for extra beds for children; iron, ironing board, and sauna are available in the basement. Breakfast can be enjoyed in the sunny ground-floor coffee bar or on the fifth-floor terrace and rose garden. Art exhibits and classical music concerts are held on Sundays in the vaulted cellar. 5 Rue Linné, 5e (phone: 47-07-06-20). Inexpensive.

Jeanne d'Arc – This little place on a quiet street in the Marais doesn't get top marks for decor and its facilities are simple, but somehow its appeal has spread from Minnesota to Melbourne. It's well placed at the colorful end of the Rue de Rivoli, and the management is friendly and speaks English. 3 Rue Jarente, 4e (phone: 48-87-62-11). Inexpensive.

Lenox – Between the busy St.-Germain area and the boutiques nearby, it's small and very tastefully done, with a small bar. Popular with the fashion crowd. 9 Rue de l'Université, 7e (phone: 42-96-10-95). Inexpensive.

London Palace – In the heart of the business district, with 50 rooms, each with a color TV set and direct-dial telephone. 32 Bd. des Italiens, 9e (phone: 48-24-54-64). Inexpensive.

Prima Lepic – A 38-room hotel in Montmartre, a busy neighborhood of winding little streets that evoke the romance of *la vie bohème,* Utrillo, Picasso, Toulouse-Lautrec and the *Moulin Rouge.* Recently renovated by cheerful young owners, rooms sport pretty floral wallpapers and one-of-a-kind furnishings — a wicker chair, a mirrored armoire, a 1930s lamp. Number 56, on the top floor, looks out over Paris, and travelers with a child should make special note of room #2, which connects to another room. There's an elevator, and the public spaces are charming. 29 Rue Lepic, 18e (phone: 46-06-44-64). Inexpensive.

Prince Albert – Despite its unprepossessing aura of faded glory, this has its site to recommend it: just off the quiet and unspoiled Marché St.-Honoré and a hop, skip, and jump from the Tuileries gardens. 5 Rue St.-Hyacinthe, 1er (phone: 42-61-58-36). Inexpensive.

St.-André-des-Arts – A rambling old favorite among the chic and hip whose purses are slim but whose tastes are discerning. 66 Rue St.-André-des-Arts, 6e (phone: 43-26-96-16). Inexpensive.

Sévigné – Recently moved up a notch in the government's classification system, an elevator and new bathrooms have been installed. If it's a little noisy (right on the Rue de Rivoli), the warm welcome and handy location make up for it. 2 Rue Malher, 4e (phone: 42-72-76-17). Inexpensive.

Solférino – A cozy place with Oriental rugs scattered about. The 34 tiny rooms have floral wallpaper, and there's a plant-filled breakfast and sitting room. 91 Rue de Lille, 7e (phone: 47-05-85-54). Inexpensive.

Le Vieux Marais – Near the *Centre Georges Pompidou* this is one of the few agreeable hotels in the Marais area, with brightly sprigged walls in the cheerful, if not very large, rooms. The breakfast room has an impressive wall-size engraving of the Place des Vosges, not far away. 8 Rue du Plâtre, 4e (phone: 42-78-47-22). Inexpensive.

Welcome – Overlooking the Bd. St.-Germain, it's simple but comfortable. 66 Rue de Seine, 6e (phone: 46-34-24-80). Inexpensive.

Chancelier Boucherat – A plain, friendly establishment with no airs and with a clientele that returns. Near the Place de la République. 110 Rue de Turenne, 3e (phone: 42-72-86-83). Very inexpensive.

Du Globe – A tiny, charming hotel on a quiet street in the heart of the St.-Germain area. 15 Rue des Quatre Vents, 6e (phone: 43-26-35-50). Very inexpensive.

Henri IV – No one could call this modern — the fittings obviously haven't been changed for decades, and there's only a bidet and basin in the room, since the bathrooms are down the hall. But the *Henri IV* has a reputation and a history, not least because it is the only hotel on the Place Dauphine on the Ile de la Cité — the real core of Paris. Prices are breathtakingly low. 25 Pl. Dauphine, 1er (phone: 43-54-44-53). Very inexpensive.

 EATING OUT: Paris considers itself the culinary capital of the world, and you will never forget food for long here. Whether you grab just a fresh croissant and café au lait for breakfast or splurge on an epicurean fantasy for dinner, this is the city in which to indulge all your gastronomic dreams. Remember, too, that there is no such thing as "French" food; rather, Paris provides the perfect mosaic in which to try regional delights from Provence, Alsace, Normandy, Brittany, and many other delicious places.

Restaurants classed as very expensive charge $250 and way up for two; expensive is $150 to $200; moderate, $100 to $150; inexpensive, less than $100; and very inexpensive, $50 or less. A service charge of 15% is added to the bill, but most people leave a small additional tip for good service. Street addresses of the restaurants below are followed by their *arrondissement* number.

Note: To save frustration and embarrassment, always *reconfirm* dinner reservations before noon on the appointed day. It may come as a surprise to discover that many of the elite Paris restaurants close over the weekend; also note that many Paris restaurants are closed for part or all of July or August. It's best to check ahead in order to avoid disappointment at the restaurant of your choice, and it's also worth remembering that many offer special lunch menus at considerably lower prices. Here is a small sampling of the best restaurants that Paris has to offer:

L'Ambroisie – This quietly elegant establishment, in new quarters beneath the arcade of historic Place des Vosges, is the showcase for chef Bernard Paucaud's equally elegant cuisine. The menu is limited to only a few entrées, such as duck with foie gras, skate and sliced green cabbage in sherry vinegar sauce, veal sweetbreads with shallots and parsley on ultra-fresh pasta, delicately battered chicken thighs in a piquant sauce, and oxtail in a savory sauce, but the quality has earned the place three Michelin stars. Closed Sundays and Monday lunch, August, and holidays. 9 Pl. des Vosges, 4e (phone: 42-78-51-45). Very expensive.

Le Grand Véfour – Founded in 1760, this sedately elegant Empire-style establishment — with paintings on the mirrors — is known for refined menus and perfect service. It's famous for toast Rothschild (shrimp in crayfish sauce set in a brioche) and pigeon Aristide Briand (boned roast pigeon stuffed with foie gras and truffles). Closed Saturdays at lunch, Sundays, and August. 17 Rue Beaujolais, 1er (phone: 42-96-56-27). Very expensive.

Jamin – Due to the culinary talents of owner-chef Joel Robuchon, named 1987 "chef of the year" by *Le Chef* magazine, this is now one of the city's finest restaurants — with a three-star ranking by Michelin — and one of the most difficult to get into. Robuchon calls his cuisine "moderne," similar to but not always as light as nouvelle. The dining room is very small, so reserve far in advance. Waiting time is almost 8 weeks. Closed weekends and July. 32 Rue de Longchamp, 16e (phone: 47-27-12-27). Very expensive.

Lasserre – The ultimate in luxury, with a magical ceiling that opens periodically during dinner to reveal the nighttime sky. Equally sublime is the food, served in the *style Lasserre* — that is, vermeil dessert settings, plates rimmed in gold, and extravagant garnishes with each dish. The classic menu is heavy on foie gras, caviar, truffles, and rich sauces. Michelin downgraded the food to two stars a few years ago, but we think it's still topnotch. Closed Sundays, Monday lunch, and August. 17 Av. Franklin-D.-Roosevelt, 8e (phone: 43-59-53-43). Very expensive.

Lucas-Carton – Once proprietor of the Michelin three-star restaurant called *L'Archestrate,* chef Alain Senderens dropped that name when he moved to larger, more elegant quarters in a historic building that boasts a gorgeous Belle Epoque interior. Senderens enjoys the reputation as one of France's most innovative culinary talents, combining many tenets of nouvelle cuisine with Oriental and African influences. Closed weekends and most of August. 9 Pl. de la Madeleine, 8e (phone: 42-65-22-90). Very expensive.

Maxim's – A legend for its Belle Epoque decor and atmosphere. It's good for celebrations, but it's hard to feel comfortable if you aren't known here. Now owned by fashion designer Pierre Cardin, it has been entirely refurbished, and there is a bar in the 1st-floor salons. This is one of the few places in Paris where you are expected to dress formally — on Friday evenings. There's an orchestra for dancing from 9:30 PM until 2 AM. Closed Sundays. 3 Rue Royale, 8e (phone: 42-65-27-94). Very expensive.

Olympe – Owner and chef Dominique Nahmias is the first female chef to be awarded three toques — very high honors — by Gault & Millau. Her nouvelle cuisine is painstakingly prepared and simply glorious; an excellent wine list adds to the meal's enjoyment. Closed Saturdays at lunch, Sundays, Mondays, and August. 8 Rue Nicolas-Charlet, 15e (phone: 47-34-86-08). Very expensive.

Le Taillevent – Full of tradition, Louis XVI furnishings, 18th-century porcelain dinner service — all in a 19th-century mansion — this epicurean haven offers no-nonsense *cuisine classique,* which is currently the best in Paris. Try terrine of truffled sweetbreads, seafood sausage, duck in cider, and especially chef Claude Deligne's soufflés in original flavors like Alsatian pear and cinnamon chocolate. Three stars in the *Guide Michelin.* Closed weekends and August. Americans often have difficulty reserving here, and it's best to try at least 60 days ahead. 15 Rue Lamennais, 8e (phone: 45-61-12-90). Very expensive.

La Tour d'Argent – Another of the five Parisian restaurants to be awarded three stars by the *Guide Michelin* and probably the best known — though recent visits have not been up to the standards of years past. The spectacular view of Notre-Dame and the Ile St.-Louis competes with the food for the attention of a very touristy clientele. Pressed duck — prepared before you — is the specialty, but the 15 other varieties of duck are equally interesting. A single main dish here can cost $100, and to be quite frank, it just ain't worth it. Closed Mondays. 15 Quai de la Tournelle, 5e (phone: 43-54-23-31). Very expensive.

L'Ami Louis – This is the archetypal Parisian bistro, rather unattractive physically but with huge portions of food that we rate as marvelous. Though the original Louis is gone, his heirs have maintained the rough welcome and informal ambience. Specialties include foie gras, roast chicken, spring lamb, ham, and Burgundy wines. A favorite among Americans, this is the place to sample authentic French fries. Closed Mondays, Tuesdays, and July and August. 32 Rue de Vertbois, 3e (phone: 48-87-77-48). Expensive.

Apicius – Jean-Pierre Vigato's highly original recipes have won him a reputation as one of Paris's finest chefs. Favorites include such delicacies as sweet-and-sour foie gras, *rougets* (a Mediterranean fish) with olive oil and potato purée, and a *panaché* of five mouth-watering chocolate desserts. Closed weekends and August. 122 Av. de Villiers, 17e (phone: 43-80-19-66). Expensive.

Le Carré des Feuillants – Alain Dutournier of *Le Trou Gascon* has now set up shop right in midtown. The cuisine is still Gascon-inspired, but Dutournier is allowing his imagination more license, with, for example, such creations as frogs' legs with watercress sauce and salmon served with braised cabbage and bacon. Michelin has awarded him two stars. Closed Saturdays for lunch and Sundays. 14 Rue de Castiglione, 1er (phone: 42-86-82-82). Expensive.

Castel – You might be able to get a reservation at this, one of the few private clubs in Paris, if you ask for help from the concierge at one of the town's grand hotels. The Belle Epoque interior is breathtaking, the cooking fine, and there's a disco in the basement. Specialties include lobster and chicken with cucumbers. Closed Sundays. 15 Rue Princesse, 6e (phone: 43-26-90-22). Expensive.

Chiberta – Elegant and modern, the acclaimed cooking of Jean Michel Bédier is basically nouvelle cuisine. Try *bavarois de saumon au coulis de tomates frais* (salmon mousse with fresh tomato sauce) and *marbré de rouget au fenouil* (red mullet with fennel). Closed weekends and August. 3 Rue Arsène-Houssaye, 8e (phone: 45-63-77-90). Expensive.

Le Divellec – This bright and airy place serves some exquisitely fresh seafood. Try the sea bass, the *rouget,* and the sautéed turbot. The latter is served with "black pasta" — thick strips of pasta flavored with squid ink — an unusual and delicious concoction. Closed Sundays and Mondays and August. 107 Rue de l'Université, 7e (phone: 45-51-91-96). Expensive.

Dodin-Bouffant – Popular because it was set up by the gifted and imaginative

Jacques Manière, who is no longer there, it still offers excellent seafood and inventive dishes. Open late. Closed Sundays, 2 weeks at Christmastime, and August. 25 Rue Frédéric-Sauton, 5e (phone: 43-25-25-14). Expensive.

Drouant – Founded in 1880, this classic favorite recently reopened after an extensive face-lift, with an ambitious new chef and menu. Open daily. 18 Rue Gaillon, 2e (phone: 42-65-15-16). Expensive.

Duquesnoy – One of Paris's most promising young chefs, Jean-Paul Duquesnoy, is in his element in ravishing new quarters. Warm carved woods and tasteful decor set the stage for specialties that include a new potato and caviar salad, terrine of leeks and *langoustine*, and a chocolate-mousse-and-pistachio-filled *mille-feuille*. Two Michelin stars. Closed Saturday lunch and Sundays. 6 Av. Bosquet, 7e (phone: 47-05-96-78). Expensive.

L'Escargot Montorgueil – Kouiquette Terrail has given new life to this ornamental monument from the 1800s. Snails five different ways, but also delicious fish, pheasant, beef, soufflés, and excellent wine values. Closed Monday evenings. 38 Rue Montorgueil, 1er (phone: 42-36-83-51). Expensive.

Faugeron – Among the finest nouvelle restaurants, awarded two stars by Michelin, it rates even higher with us. Superb cuisine, lovely service, and one of Paris's prettiest table settings in what was once an old school. Closed weekends and August. 52 Rue de Longchamp, 16e (phone: 47-04-24-53). Expensive.

Jacques Cagna – This talented chef always provides an interesting menu at his charming premises on the Left Bank, very near the Seine. Closed August, Christmas week, two Saturdays a month, and Sundays. 14 Rue des Grands-Augustins, 6e (phone: 43-26-49-39). Expensive.

Lamazère – This is truffle heaven, the menu a triumph of rich products from the southwest of France. The owner is a magician in the real sense of the word, as well as with food. The elegant bar and salons are open late. Closed Sundays and August. 23 Rue de Ponthieu, 8e (phone: 43-59-66-66). Expensive.

Ledoyen – This grand dowager of Paris restaurants received a major facelift recently when the capital's nightlife queen, Régine, took it over. Its new look and menus ordained by staff chef Jacques Maximin have received generally favorable reviews, particularly from high-powered businesspeople. Closed Sundays and August. Carré des Champs-Elysées, 8e (phone: 42-66-54-77). Expensive.

La Maison Blanche – Decidedly "in," this restaurant is fashionably elegant, and its talented young chef, José Lampréia, prepares an inventive, contemporary version of soul-satisfying *cuisine bourgeoise*. Closed Saturday lunch, Sundays and Mondays, the first 2 weeks of September, and from Christmas to New Year's Day. 82 Bd. Lefebvre, 15e (phone: 48-28-38-83). Expensive.

Le Petit Montmorency – In his new location near the Champs-Elysées, chef Daniel Bouché still presents one of the most exciting and unusual menus in Paris. Very, very popular. Closed weekends and August. 5 Rue Rabelais, 8e (phone: 42-25-11-19). Expensive.

Le Pré Catelan – It's the large restaurant right in the middle of the Bois de Boulogne, and believe it or not, the food is very good. Ingredients are fresh and sauces are light. Specialties include four or five new dishes daily. Closed Sunday evenings, Mondays, and the first 2 weeks of February. Rte. de Suresnes, Bois de Boulogne, 16e (phone: 45-24-55-58). Expensive.

Prunier Traktir – The best of everything that comes from the sea; the *marmite dieppoise* alone is worth the trip. Closed Mondays. 16 Av. Victor-Hugo, 16e (phone: 45-00-89-12). Expensive.

Quai des Ormes – Elegant dining on the Seine, with an English-speaking staff. In summer, try to sit on the 1st-floor terrace overlooking Notre-Dame. Closed weekends and August. 72 Quai de l'Hôtel-de-Ville, 4e (phone: 42-74-72-22). Expensive.

Régine's – The food is actually good in this beautifully decorated nightclub, which is frequented by Parisians as well as the chic international set. Ask your hotel manager to get you in because it's nominally a private club. Try the foie gras (made on the premises) and the goose. Closed Sundays. 49 Rue de Ponthieu, 8e (phone: 43-59-21-60). Expensive.

Relais Louis XIII – Old-style decor and new cuisine in one of Paris's prettiest houses. Closed Sundays, Monday lunch, and August. 8 Rue des Grands-Augustins, 6e (phone: 43-26-75-96) Expensive.

Restaurant d'Hubert – This fine chef has set up shop in trendy, new surroundings and serves inventive nouvelle cuisine, including such dishes as a lobster and peach salad and a combination of sweetbreads and *langoustines* in sauce flavored with truffles. Closed Saturdays for lunch and Sundays. 25 Rue de Richelieu, 1er (phone: 42-96-08-47). Expensive.

Vivarois – Claude Peyrot is one of France's finest chefs. Specialties in his small, elegant eating place include curried oysters au gratin, turbot, and an assortment of desserts. Closed weekends and August. 192 Av. Victor-Hugo, 16e (phone: 45-04-04-31). Expensive.

Auberge des Deux Signes – This place was once the cellars of the priory of St.-Julien-le-Pauvre; try to get an upstairs table overlooking the gardens. Auvergnat cooking *à la nouvelle cuisine.* Closed Sundays. 46 Rue Galande, 5e (phone: 43-25-46-56). Expensive to moderate.

Brasserie Lorraine – Bustling and convivial until late at night, this place pulls in the neighborhood's bourgeoisie for animated evenings over the foie gras salads. Pl. des Ternes, 8e (phone: 42-27-80-04). Expensive to moderate.

La Cantine des Gourmets – This restaurant specializes in light, inventive creations of high quality. Closed Sundays. 113 Av. Bourdonnais, 7e (phone: 47-05-47-96). Expensive to moderate.

La Coquille – A classic bistro, where the service is unpretentious and warm, and the food consistently good. From October to May, the house specialty is coquilles St.-Jacques, a version that consists of scallops roasted with butter, shallots, and parsley. Closed Sundays, Mondays, holidays, and August. 6 Rue du Débarcadère, 17e (phone: 45-74-25-95). Expensive to moderate.

Le Duc – The atmosphere is warm and comfortable, and Paul Minchelli is incomparably inventive with fish and shellfish (cooked and raw). Quality and variety are the rule here, with such specialties as curried oysters, tuna tartar, coquilles St.-Jacques *cru,* and an extraordinary seafood platter. Closed Saturdays, Sundays, and Mondays. 243 Bd. Raspail, 14e (phone: 43-22-59-59 or 43-20-96-30). Expensive to moderate.

Morot-Gaudry – On the top floor of a 1920s building with a great view of the Eiffel Tower, especially from the flowered terrace. Among the inventive dishes are calf's liver with raspberry vinegar, compote of chicken with leeks, and rice cake with ginger. Closed weekends. 6 Rue de la Cavalerie, 15e (phone: 45-67-06-85). Expensive to moderate.

Pavillon des Princes – Under the direction of Pascal Bonichon, this restaurant produces delicious duck sausage salad with avocado, coquilles St.-Jacques with fresh pasta, and lamb nuggets with cabbage and tomatoes. Open daily. On the edge of the Bois de Boulogne. 69 Av. de la Porte d'Auteuil, 16e (phone: 47-43-15-15). Expensive to moderate.

Au Quai d'Orsay – Fashionable, sophisticated, very French, very intimate, and recently redecorated. Traditional copious bourgeois cooking and good Beaujolais. Closed Sundays. 49 Quai d'Orsay, 7e (phone: 45-51-58-58). Expensive to moderate.

Le Trou Gascon – Alain Dutournier created the inspired and unusual cuisine that features southwestern French specialties and a vast choice of regional wines and Armagnacs. He has moved on to a more elegant neighborhood, but his wife holds down the fort here. Closed weekends. 40 Rue Taine, 12e (phone: 43-44-34-26). Expensive to moderate.

Allard – A very popular bistro with hearty country cooking and excellent Burgundy wines. Snails, turbot, and beef bourguignon are the prime lures. Spring, when the new turnips arrive, is a special time here. Don't miss the chocolate charlotte for dessert. Closed weekends and August. 41 Rue St.-André-des-Arts, 6e (phone: 43-26-48-23). Moderate.

Ambassade d'Auvergne – This restaurant's young chef creates delicious, unusual, classic Auvergnat dishes with a modern touch (try the lentil salad). Recently redecorated, it is also known for seasonal specialties and wonderful cakes. 22 Rue du Grenier-St.-Lazare, 3e (phone: 42-72-31-22). Moderate.

L'Aquitaine – This is the seafood branch of the *Restaurant du Marché* (below). Unusual seafood dishes are prepared by Christiane Massia, and there's a delightful summer terrace. Closed Sundays and Mondays. 54 Rue de Dantzig, 15e (phone: 48-28-67-38). Moderate.

Astier – An honest-to-goodness neighborhood hangout that is always packed, because the clientele knows they can rely on it for the staples of bourgeois cooking, lovingly prepared. Closed weekends and August. 44 Rue Jean-Pierre-Timbaud, 11e (phone: 43-57-16-35). Moderate.

La Barrière Poquelin – The excellent cooking *à la nouvelle cuisine* includes a splendid foie gras salad. Closed Saturdays for lunch, Sundays, and the 3 weeks in August. 17 Rue Molière, 1er (phone: 42-96-22-19). Moderate.

Bistro 121 – A hearty menu and excellent wines are offered in a modern setting that's always chic and crowded. Try *poisson cru mariné au citron vert* (seafood marinated in lime juice) and chocolate charlotte for dessert. Closed Sunday evenings, Mondays, and mid-July to mid-August. 121 Rue de la Convention, 15e (phone: 45-57-52-90). Moderate.

Le Bistrot de Paris – Michel Oliver offers informality, original and classic bistro fare, and a good wine list, which attract a crowd. Closed Saturdays for lunch and Sundays. 33 Rue de Lille, 7e (phone: 42-61-16-83). Moderate.

Le Boeuf sur le Toit – In the building that once housed a restaurant of the same name, a haunt of Jean Cocteau and other Paris artists in the 1940s, this eatery off the Champs-Elysées is managed by the Flo Group, well known for good value in atmospheric surroundings. Piano bar until 2 AM. 34 Rue du Colisée, 8e (phone: 43-59-83-80). Moderate.

Bofinger – For magnificent Belle Epoque decor, this is the place; it's one of Paris's oldest brasseries and it is beautiful, even if the food is occasionally disappointing. Order onion soup and *choucroute* and you won't be unhappy. Open daily. 5 Rue de la Bastille, 4e (phone: 42-72-87-82). Moderate.

Cactus Bleu – High tech, trendy, and lighted by aqua-neon, this newcomer draws a chic young crowd to Paris's up and coming Bastille quarter for "Cal-Mex" food and margaritas at the bar. 8 Rue de Lappe, 11e (phone: 43-38-30-20). Moderate.

Café de la Jatte – Only those in the know venture this far down the Seine for dinner. This leafy island, l'Ile de la Jatte, was ripe for a smart renovation, and this huge, high-ceilinged dining room, with half-moon-shaped windows and a pink floor, is now full of the chic-est local clientele. The fare is healthy and simple: generous salads and roast chicken along with more nouvelle items. 60 Av. Vital-Bouhot, Neuilly, a 15-minute drive from central Paris (phone: 47-45-04-20). Moderate.

Chez Benoît – A pretty but unpretentious bistro with wonderful old-fashioned Lyonnaise cooking and exquisite wines. Just about at the top of the bistro list, rated one Michelin star. Closed weekends and August. 20 Rue St.-Martin, 4e (phone: 42-72-25-76). Moderate.

Chez Georges – This narrow, old-fashioned bistro — with a whole platoon of matronly waitresses in starched aprons — is a bastion of traditional French cooking. Closed Sundays and holidays. 1 Rue du Mail, 2e (phone: 42-60-07-11). Moderate.

Chez Josephine and **La Rôtisserie Chez Dumonet** – Two restaurants share the same building and management. *Josephine* is an old-time bistro with traditional cuisine and an excellent wine cellar; the *Rôtisserie* is lively and more modern, with steaks and grills over an open fire. *Josephine* is closed weekends and July; the *Rôtisserie,* Mondays, Tuesdays, and August. 117 Rue du Cherche-Midi, 6e (phone: 45-48-52-40). Moderate.

Chez Pauline – The perfect bistro — the tiny, paneled downstairs room is brightened by large mirrors and fresh flowers; the service plates look like Florentine marble. Try the oysters in a watercress sauce, an assortment of seafood with a saffron sauce, and save room for dessert; *mille-feuille* of orange with raspberry sauce is sublime. Lunch is the prime time here; even at dinner, try to reserve a downstairs table. Closed weekends, July, and December 24–January 2. 5 Rue Villedo, 1er (phone: 42-96-20-70). Moderate.

Chez Pierre Vedel – Truly original cuisine. Closed weekends, from mid-July to mid-August, and at Christmastime. 19 Rue Duranton, 15e (phone: 45-58-43-17). Moderate.

Chez Toutoune – This modest place specializing in Provençal dishes has become very popular for two good reasons: The food is tasty and the prices are fairly reasonable. The five-course, *prix fixe* menu features a rather short but very interesting selection of appetizers, entrées, and desserts. Closed Sundays and mid-August to mid-September. 5 Rue de Pontoise, 5e (phone: 43-26-56-81). Moderate.

La Coupole – This big, brassy brasserie, once the haunt of Hemingway, Josephine Baker, and Picasso, recently underwent a major facelift by its new owner, the Flo Group. The atmosphere is still great, the food still mediocre. Open daily until 2 AM. Closed August. 102 Bd. du Montparnasse, 14e (phone: 43-20-14-20). Moderate.

Le Dômarais – This used to be the *Crédit Municipal,* or state pawnshop, and its elegant cupola now houses a sophisticated restaurant serving such inventions as Camembert fondue, grilled Bayonne ham, and a *petit salé* of duck. Closed Saturdays for lunch and Mondays. 53 bis Rue des Francs Bourgeois, 4e (phone: 42-74-54-17). Moderate.

L'Escargot Montorgueil – The polished paneling, the brass fittings, and the spiral staircase at this beautiful place dating from 1830 only add to the pleasure of a meal, which might include snails in any of half a dozen styles or duck with orange sauce. Closed Monday lunch. 38 Rue Montorgueil, 28e (phone: 42-36-83-51). Moderate.

La Ferme St.-Simon – Among our favorites for wholesome *cuisine d'autrefois* (old-fashioned cooking). Nothing very chi-chi here, just well-prepared, authentic dishes — the kinds you'd expect from a traditional Left Bank restaurant. Leave room for dessert; the owner was once a top assistant to Gaston Lenôtre. A perfect place for lunch. Reservations advised. Closed Saturday lunch, Sundays, and August. 6 Rue de St.-Simon, 7e (phone: 45-48-35-74). Moderate.

Au Gamin de Paris – Combines the coziness of a classic bistro with the chic of a historic Marais building and serves well-prepared, imaginative food. Open daily. 51 Rue Vieille du Temple, 4e (phone: 42-78-97-24). Moderate.

Jo Goldenberg – This is the best-known eating house in the Marais's quaint Jewish quarter, with good chopped liver and cheesecake and a range of Eastern European

Jewish specialties. It's also a fine place to sip mint tea at the counter in the middle of a busy day. Open daily. 7 Rue des Rosiers, 4e (phone: 48-87-20-16 or 48-87-70-39). Moderate.

Julien – Belle Epoque decor with all the flourishes. Reliable, if uninspired, meals are served in a bustling atmosphere until 1:30 AM. Open daily. 16 Rue du Faubourg-St.-Denis, 10e (phone: 47-70-12-06). Moderate.

Restaurant du Marché – Cuisine Landaise, which means solid, country-style cooking — foie gras, *confits d'oie,* and fine wines from the Landes region in the southwest of France, near Bordeaux. An amazing choice of herb teas and a pretty terrace for summer dining. 59 Rue de Dantzig, 15e (phone: 45-32-26-88). Moderate.

La Marée – Unobtrusive on the outside, there is great comfort within — also the freshest of fish, the best restaurant wine values in Paris, and fabulous desserts. Closed weekends, holidays, and August. 1 Rue Daru, 8e (phone: 47-63-52-42). Moderate.

Le Moulin du Village – Light and airy, especially in summer, when tables are put out on the cobbles of Cité Berryer, a tiny pedestrian alley very near the Madeleine, just off the Rue Royale. Cuisine is nouvelle and wines good. Steven Spurrier, the well-known British wine merchant, recently sold the place and his neighboring *Blue Fox* wine bar to another Englishman, the owner of *Willi's* and other popular wine bars. Closed Sundays. 25 Rue Royale, 8e (phone: 42-65-08-47). Moderate.

Le Muniche – St.-Germain's best brasserie is a bustling place with a rather extensive menu, and it's popular until 3 AM. 25 Rue de Buci, 6e (phone: 46-33-62-09). Moderate.

La Petite Chaise – Founded in 1680, it occupies two stories of a 17th-century stone house on the Left Bank. The intimate (and slightly run down) atmosphere of the home of an ancient aunt characterizes this place, with brocaded walls, brass chandeliers, and antique oils contributing to the period decor. The trout you see swimming in a tank are also on the menu, as are specialties like shellfish crêpes and veal Pojarsky, in which the meat is combined with minced chicken. Always open. 36 Rue de Grenelle, 7e (phone: 42-22-13-35). Moderate.

Pierre Traiteur – A delightful place with admirable bourgeois cooking and lovely Chinon and Saumur wines. Closed weekends and August. 10 Rue de Richelieu, 1er (phone: 42-96-09-17). Moderate.

Le Récamier – The so-called garden is actually a courtyard between a couple of high-rise buildings, but as the sun goes down, it's a very congenial place to dine in good weather. Martin Cantegrit is a perfect host, and the menu features first-rate fish dishes (try the turbot, if possible). The apple tart for dessert is special (order it warm), and the wine list is one of the most fairly priced on the Left Bank. Reservations advised. Closed Sundays. 4 Rue Récamier, 7e (phone: 45-48-86-58). Moderate.

Le Soufflé – On the street just behind the Rue Rivoli, not far from Place Vendôme, this is the place to enjoy an orgy of soufflés. We suggest crayfish soufflé for an appetizer, cheese soufflé as a main course, and chocolate soufflé for dessert. Closed Sundays. 36 Rue du Mont-Thabor, 1er (phone: 42-60-27-19). Moderate.

Tan-Dinh – The perfect pause from a constant diet of French specialties, it recently lost its Michelin star, but its Vietnamese specialties remain simply superb. Shrimp rolls, Vietnamese ravioli, and minced filet of beef are only three examples of the marvelous menu (ask for the version in English). Remarkable wine list. No credit cards. Reservations advised. Closed Sundays and August. 60 Rue de Verneuil, 7e (phone: 45-44-04-84). Moderate.

Le Train Bleu – Fine food, good wine, and Baroque decor so gorgeous it's been made a national monument. And it's in a train station. Gare de Lyon, 20 Bd. Diderot, 12e (phone: 43-43-09-06). Moderate.

Ty-Coz – Breton cuisine features fish, cider, and crêpes; no meat, no cheese. Closed Sundays and Mondays. 35 Rue St.-Georges, 9e (phone: 48-78-34-61). Moderate.

Le Zeyer – After a hard morning discount-shopping on the nearby Rue d'Alésia, here's a good neighborhood place for mussels *marinière,* grilled lotte with sorrel, or platters of shellfish. Open daily. 234 Av. du Maine, 14e (phone: 45-40-43-88). Moderate.

Androuët – There's a great cheese emporium on the main floor and, upstairs, a unique restaurant where cheese is the base of every dish. In recent years the quality has slid somewhat, but it is still a unique experience. Closed Sundays. 41 Rue Amsterdam, 8e (phone: 48-74-26-93). Moderate to inexpensive.

Brasserie Lipp – This famous café is fashionable for a late supper of *choucroute* and Alsatian beer and for people-watching inside and out, but be aware that you are likely to be dispatched to second-floor "Siberia." The food's just as good there, however. Closed 15 days at Christmas. 155 Bd. St.-Germain, 6e (phone: 45-48-53-91). Moderate to inexpensive.

Chez La Vieille – Adrienne's cooking is simple, savory, and very popular. For lunch only. Closed weekends. 37 Rue de l'Arbre-Sec, 1er (phone: 42-60-15-78). Moderate to inexpensive.

Clos de la Tour – This popular restaurant has "bistro moderne" decor. Closed Saturdays at lunch, Sundays, and August. 22 Rue Falguière, 15e (phone: 43-22-34-73). Moderate to inexpensive.

Coup de Coeur – With a two-level design reminiscent of Manhattan's stark Upper West Side eating establishments, this restaurant features inventive cuisine, eager waiters, and an interesting wine list. Closed Sundays. 19 Rue St.-Augustin, 2e (phone: 47-03-45-70). Moderate to inexpensive.

L'Epicurien – There are just 55 seats here, in three little rooms around a garden. Closed Saturday lunch and Sundays. 11 Rue de Nesle, 6e (phone: 43-29-55-78). Moderate to inexpensive.

Joe Allen's – Just like Joe Allen's on West 46th Street in New York City, it has good T-bone steaks, hamburgers, chili, and apple pie. Open till 1 AM. Reserve after 8 PM. 30 Rue Pierre-Lescot, 1er (phone: 42-36-70-13). Moderate to inexpensive.

Les Noces de Jeannette – Under new management, this place now offers inventive cuisine at reasonable prices. Closed Sunday evenings. 14 Rue Favart, 2e (phone: 42-96-36-89). Moderate to inexpensive.

Le Petit Niçois – This tiny bistro, serving delicious bouillabaisse, is a favorite of French TV news crews who broadcast from a nearby building. A few good specials vary from night to night. Closed Sundays and Monday lunch. 10 Rue Amélie, 7e (phone: 45-51-83-65). Moderate to inexpensive.

Au Petit Riche – Genuine 1900s decor, subtle Touraine cooking, and inexpensive Vouvray, Chinon, and Bourgueil wines. Closed Sundays and August. 25 Rue Le Peletier, 9e (phone: 47-70-68-68). Moderate to inexpensive.

Le Pharamond – Serves only the best Norman food in a beautiful Belle Epoque, timbered townhouse recently declared a historic monument by the French government. Famous for *tripes à la mode de Caen* and *pommes soufflés,* since 1862. Closed Sundays, Monday lunch, and July. 24 Rue de la Grande-Truanderie, 1er (phone: 42-33-06-72). Moderate to inexpensive.

Au Pied de Cochon – No more *choucroute* on the menu (sob!). Crowded and colorful 24 hours a day, its customers enjoy shellfish, pigs' feet, and great crocks of onion soup, all in the old Les Halles area. Unfortunately, the food and service aren't what they used to be, and a garish redecoration has mangled most of the old atmosphere. 6 Rue Coquillière, 1er (phone: 42-36-11-75). Moderate to inexpensive.

L'Amanguier – This series of garden restaurants serves an appetizing brand of nouvelle cuisine. Stick to a main course, which comes with a choice of appetizers, and the price is suprisingly low, but the desserts and the cocktails are tempting. 51 Rue du Théâtre, 15e (phone: 45-77-04-01); 110 Rue de Richelieu, 2e (phone: 42-96-37-79); 43 Av. des Ternes, 17e (phone: 43-80-19-28); and 12 Av. de Madrid, Neuilly (phone: 47-45-79-73). Inexpensive.

Atelier Maître Albert – Unlike most other restaurants on the Left Bank, this one is pleasantly roomy, with a log fire in winter and an honest prix fixe menu year-round. Notre-Dame looms up in front of you as you walk out the door and onto the quai. Closed Sundays. 1 Rue Maître-Albert, 5e (phone: 46-33-13-78). Inexpensive.

Aux Bigorneaux – A souvenir of the old Les Halles, this place is frequented by arty types and journalists. Especially recommended are the *foie gras frais maison,* the chicory salad, the steak au poivre, the Réserve Maison wine, and the sumptuous desserts. Reservations advised. Closed Mondays. 12 Rue Mondétour, 1er (phone: 45-08-49-33). Inexpensive.

Brasserie Flo – One of the last of the brasseries of the 1900s, now owned by the enterprising Flo Group. Hidden in a hard-to-find courtyard, it's excellent for oysters, foie gras, wild boar, and Alsatian specialties. Open daily and late. 7 Cour des Petites-Ecuries, 10e (phone: 47-70-13-59). Inexpensive.

Chez Fernand – A nondescript hole in the wall that produces surprisingly tasty dishes. *Pot au feu,* steak with shallots, and fish pâté are all first rate, but the real lure is the huge tube of chocolate mousse served for dessert — a chocoholic's fantasy come true. Open evenings only. 13 Rue Guirsade, 6e (phone: 43-54-61-47). Inexpensive.

Chez Jenny – A roisterous Alsatian brasserie, where the waitresses still wear white lace collars and dirndls. There are oysters year-round, though perhaps more in keeping with the place's character are the huge platters of *choucroute* (sauerkraut and assorted pork meats) accompanied by good Riesling wine. Open daily. 39 Bd. du Temple, 3e (phone: 42-74-75-75). Inexpensive.

Chez Maître Paul – Offers quality Franc Comtoise cooking (that means excellent chicken) and good Bourgueil and Jura wines. Closed Sundays, Mondays, August, and Christmas week. 12 Rue Monsieur-le-Prince, 6e (phone: 43-54-74-59). Inexpensive.

Chez Marianne – A friendly Jewish delicatessen and restaurant; the falafels make nourishing fuel for any exploration of the Marais. Closed Fridays. 2 Rue des Hospitalières-St.-Gervais, 4e (phone: 42-72-18-86). Inexpensive.

Chez Yvette – This excellent, small, bourgeois restaurant has good home cooking, lots of choices, and great desserts. Closed weekends and August. 46 bis Bd. Montparnasse, 6e (phone: 42-22-45-54). Inexpensive.

Chicago Meatpackers – If homesickness strikes, head to this new spot for hamburgers or chili; finish your American food fix with pie — apple, mud, or pecan — or chocolate chip cheese cake. 9 Rue Coquillière. Inexpensive.

Gérard – This bistro serves up a hearty *pot-au-feu* and other country favorites. Closed Saturday lunch and Sundays. 4 Rue du Mail, 2e (phone: 42-96-24-36). Inexpensive.

Au Gourmet-de-l'Isle – Remarkable for its location, ambience, quality, and prices. Closed Mondays, Thursdays, and August. 42 Rue St.-Louis-en-l'Ile, 4e (phone: 43-26-79-27). Inexpensive.

Le Jardin de la Mouffe – There's a choice of hors d'oeuvres, entrées, and desserts, plus a cheese course and half a carafe of wine and a pretty garden view. Closed Sundays and Mondays. 75 Rue Mouffetard, 5e (phone: 47-07-19-29). Inexpensive.

Lunchtime – One of the few restaurants in Paris that satisfies the desire for a light lunch, serving crispy mixed salads made with the freshest greens and a wide range of sandwiches, including blue cheese with cream, curried chicken with currants, and American standbys such as roast beef. The desserts are homemade and delicious. Lunch only. Closed Saturdays, Sundays, holidays, and August. 156 bis Av. Charles-de-Gaulle, Neuilly (phone: 46-24-08-99). Inexpensive.

Le Mange Tout – Very good traditional country cooking made from the freshest of produce from the restaurant's own farms is dished out in a modern (but cozy) setting. Closed Sundays, Monday lunch, 2 weeks in February, and mid-August to mid-September. 30 Rue Lacépède, 5e (phone: 45-35-53-93). Inexpensive.

Paul – Once a secret bistro, it is now known by the whole world. There's good solid fare here, and the premises are always packed. Closed Mondays, Tuesdays, and August. 15 Pl. Dauphine, 1er (phone: 43-54-21-48). Inexpensive.

Le Petit Prince – Dark and candlelit, with a mirrored interior, this old favorite of the gay crowd is a good bargain. The menu includes such dishes as snails with sorrel sauce and leg of lamb with red currant sauce. Open daily for dinner only. 12 Rue de Lanneau, 5e (phone: 43-54-77-26). Inexpensive.

Petit Zinc – This is a popular late (3 AM) spot for fish, oysters, foie gras, and an ample, reasonably priced wine list. 25 Rue de Buci, 6e (phone: 43-54-79-34). Inexpensive.

Polidor – The regulars here keep their napkins in numbered pigeonholes, and the place's history includes frequent patronage by such starving artists as Paul Verlaine, James Joyce, Ernest Hemingway, and, more recently, Jean-Paul Belmondo. The College of Pataphysics, founded by Raymond Queneau and Ionesco, still meets here regularly for the good family-style food. Ask to see the house scrapbook. Closed Sundays, Mondays, and August. 41 Rue Monsieur-le-Prince, 6e (phone: 43-26-95-34). Inexpensive.

Le Procope – One of Paris's oldest restaurants, where the food is reasonably good and the atmosphere couldn't be more Parisian. 13 Rue de l'Ancienne-Comédie, 6e (phone: 43-26-99-20). Inexpensive.

Relais de Venise – There's always a crowd waiting outside this place near the Porte Maillot, better known as *L'Entrecôte*. The *prix fixe* menu includes free second helpings of steak with pepper sauce and French fries. Fancy strawberry desserts cost extra. Open daily. No reservations. 271 Bd. Pereire, 17e (phone: 45-74-27-97). Inexpensive.

Robert et Louise – A family bistro, with warm paneled decor and a very high standard for ingredients and cooking. Try the *boeuf bourguignon* or the open-fire–grilled *côte de boeuf*. Also good are the *fromage blanc* and the wine *en pichet*. Closed Sundays, holidays, and August. 64 Rue Vieille-du-Temple, 3e (phone: 42-78-55-89). Inexpensive.

Le Roi du Pot-au-Feu – A very good place to sample this delicious peasant dish. Closed Sundays. 34 Rue Vignon, 9e (phone: 47-42-37-10).

La Route du Beaujolais – It's a barnlike workers' bistro on the Left Bank, serving Lyonnaise specialties and Beaujolais wines. Don't miss the *charcuterie* and the fresh bread here, and try the *tarte tatin* (caramelized apple tart) for dessert. Closed Sundays. 17 Rue de Lourmel, 15e (phone: 45-79-31-63). Inexpensive.

Le Trumilou – The formidable proprietress sets the tone of this robust establishment, which serves huge, steaming portions of boar, pheasant, and venison in season under a frieze of some excruciatingly bad rustic oils. Closed Mondays. 94 Quai de l'Hôtel-de-Ville, 5e (phone: 42-77-63-98). Inexpensive.

Vagenende – An Art Nouveau spot with fantasy decor that has changed little since it opened in 1898. It features adequate, filling meals at low prices. Open daily until 1 AM. 142 Bd. St.-Germain, 6e (phone: 43-26-68-18). Inexpensive.

Assiette au Boeuf – Steaks, salad, and *pommes frites,* with music in the evening. No reservations. Open daily until 1 AM. 123 Champs-Elysées, 8e (phone: 47-20-01-13). Very inexpensive.

Bistro de la Gare – Michel Oliver offers a choice of three appetizers and three main courses with *pommes frites.* Excellent for a quick lunch. No reservations. Open daily at 10 branches, including 73 Champs-Elysées, 8e (phone: 43-59-67-83); 59 Bd. Montparnasse, 6e (phone: 45-48-38-01); 38 Bd. des Italiens, 9e (phone: 42-24-49-61). Very inexpensive.

Chartier – Huge, turn-of-the-century place with lots of down-to-earth food for the money. 7 Rue du Faubourg-Montmartre, 9e (phone: 47-70-86-29). Very inexpensive.

Drouot – The younger member of the Chartier family, but less known, and with more berets and fewer tourists. The waiters and waitresses, clad in black and white, look as if they emerged from a Renoir painting, although the decor is 1920s, with brass hat stands. The simple food is a bargain. To avoid a long wait for a table, arrive before 9 PM. 103 Rue de Richelieu, 2e (phone: 42-96-68-23). Very inexpensive.

L'Etoile Verte – Not much to look at, but always full, it serves fresh and generous helpings of standard French classics — quenelles, seafood timbales, and so forth — at rock-bottom prices. Open daily. 13 Rue Brey, 17e (phone: 43-80-69-34). Very inexpensive.

L'Olympic Bar – Crowded at all hours, this popular hangout is open for meals at lunch only. Blue-collar workers, students, executives, fashionable women, and others eat and drink with pinball noise as a background. The decor is nothing to speak of, but the food is good, the portions huge, and the price is right. Closed Sundays and sometimes for Saturday lunch. 77 Rue St.-Dominique, 7e (phone: 45-51-59-20). Very inexpensive.

Le Petit Gavroche – A hole-in-the-wall bistro-cum-restaurant with a lively clientele, an inexpensive and classic menu, and the feeling that nothing has changed in years. 15 Rue Ste.-Croix-de-la-Bretonnerie, 4e (phone: 48-87-74-26). Very inexpensive.

Le Petit St.-Benoît – This is French cooking at its simplest, in a plain little restaurant with tiled floors and curly hat stands. Open weekdays. 4 Rue St.-Benoît, 6e (phone: 42-60-27-92). Very inexpensive.

Au Pied de Fouet – This former coach house has had its habitués, including celebrities as diverse as Graham Greene, Le Corbusier, and Georges Pompidou. Service is fast and friendly, and it's a place to order the daily special. Desserts, such as *charlotte au chocolat,* are marvelous. Arrive early; it closes at 9 PM. Closed Saturday evenings, Sundays, 2 weeks at Christmas and Easter, and August. 45 Rue de Babylone, 7e (phone: 47-05-12-27). Very inexpensive.

Le Tourtour – Enter through the 1920s gallery boutique and you're in a cozy room serving a full menu until 1 AM. Specialties include beef with mustard sauce and Berthillon sherbets. Closed Sundays. There's also a theater next door with two or three shows nightly except on Sundays and Mondays. 20 Rue Quincampoix, 4e (phone: 48-87-82-48). Very inexpensive.

■**EXTRA SPECIAL:** Although we've noted the existence of *Fauchon* in *Shopping,* we would be remiss in omitting it from the restaurant listings. Actually two spectacular stores stocking elegant edibles, *Fauchon* is considered so much a bastion of the privileged that one of its stores was bombed by radicals in 1978. But both shops are now thankfully back in full working order, which is a blessing for every abdomen in town.

One *Fauchon* shop specializes in the most beautiful fruits and vegetables available anywhere, plus pâtés, terrines, and as many other incomparable carry-out items as even the most jaded gourmet's palate could conceive. If you're planning any sort of picnic, this is the place to pack your hamper.

But it's across the narrow street in the far corner of the Place de la Madeleine that all of Paris congregates for nonpareil pastries, coffee, and an occasional snack or drink. Chocolate *opéra* cakes and macaroons in many hues, as well as *mille feuilles* and other custardy concoctions, are sold by the slice and can be eaten standing at one of the narrow ledges right in the store. If you need a sugar surge during the course of your Paris meanderings, this is the place to take your high-caloric break.

For chocoholics: The very best hot chocolate in Paris (if not the universe) is served at *Angelina's* on the Rue Rivoli, 1er. The best chocolate ice cream in the City of Light is at *Berthillon's* (31 Rue St.-Louis-en-l'Ile, 4e) on the Ile St.-Louis and the new site near the Porte Maillot métro in the Palais de Congrès. The best (and most generous) servings of chocolate mousse are offered at *Chez Fernand,* 13 Rue Guirsade, 6e, on the Left Bank.

 WINE BARS AND CAFÉS: Choosing a place to drink is not a pressing problem in Paris. Following is a selection of watering holes to suit a variety of tastes and thirsts. Prices tend to be higher than in the United States, with a *café crème* or a glass of red wine costing $3 or more in the more expensive establishments. The moderate ones charge $2 to $3 for the same, and you pay less than $2 in the inexpensive spots.

Café Costes – Paris's latest word in Postmodernism, something of a revolution on the scene. It has an impressive marble stairway, a clock inspired by Fritz Lang's film *Metropolis,* some wild high tech restrooms, and a fashionable complement of lounge lizards. Open daily. Sq. des Innocents, 1er (phone: 45-08-54-39). Expensive.

Fouquet's – All the cafés on the Champs-Elysées are overpriced and most are nasty, so it may be worth paying the inflated tab for a coffee at this one, which at least has more style than all the rest — as well as a large corner for outdoor tables in summer. Always open. 99 Champs-Elysées, 8e (phone: 47-23-70-60). Expensive.

Harry's Bar – The son of the original Harry, who opened this celebrated establishment in 1911, is still at the helm here. And the memories of past patrons like Ernest Hemingway, Gertrude Stein, and George Gershwin are almost as tangible as the university flags and banners that hang from the paneled walls. Open 10:30 AM to 4 AM every day but Christmas. 5 Rue Daunou, 2e (phone: 42-61-71-14). Expensive.

Willi's – An enterprising Englishman set up this smart little wine bar, a pleasant walk through the Palais Royal gardens and only minutes from the *Louvre.* The wine selection — a list of 150 — is one of the best in Paris, with an emphasis on Côtes du Rhone. The chef creates some appetizing salads as well as a *plat du jour.* Closed Sundays. 13 Rue des Petits-Champs, 1er (phone: 42-61-05-09). Expensive to moderate.

Blue Fox – On a cobbled market street behind the Madeleine, this wine bar has a list of about 20 reasonably priced wines by the glass that changes every 2 weeks. And there's good *charcuterie* to go with them. Closed Saturday evenings and Sundays. Cité Berryer, 25 Rue Royale, 8e (phone: 42-65-08-47 or 42-65-10-72). Moderate.

L'Ecluse – This unassuming bistro looking onto the Seine has fathered five others, more sophisticated, in the Rue François-I, at the Madeleine, at the *Opera,* in Les Halles, and in Neuilly. Its red velvet benches and wooden tables — not to mention its Bordeaux and its fresh, homemade foie gras — remain unchanged. Open daily. 15 Quai des Grands-Augustins, 6e (phone: 46-33-58-74), and several other places in Paris. Moderate.

Le Pain et Le Vin – An imaginative wine bar with daily hot luncheon specials. It's operated by four Parisian chefs, including Alain Dutournier of the *Carré des Feuilliants* and *Au Trou Gascon.* Closed Wednesday evenings. Several locations, including 1 Rue d'Armaille, 17e (phone: 47-63-88-29). Moderate.

Le Petit Bacchus – A wine bar specializing in unusual regional wines, displayed in crowded rows. You can buy wine by the bottle to take home or on a picnic, or sample them at the counter with cheese and *charcuterie.* Closed Sundays and Mondays. 13 Rue du Cherche-Midi, 6e (phone: 45-44-01-07). Moderate.

Taverne Henri IV – A selection of nearly 20 wines are offered by the glass, along with generous servings of simple food such as open sandwiches of ham, cheese, sausage, or a terrine of wild boar. You can also order cold food combinations by the platter. Closed weekends. 13 Pl. du Pont-Neuf, 1er (phone: 43-54-27-90). Moderate.

Zimmer – Centrally located and with new moldings and chandeliers, this is the place to stop off for a drink before or after a show at one of the nearby theaters. 1 Pl. du Châtelet, 4e (phone: 42-36-74-04). Moderate.

Jacques Melac – An old-fashioned wine bar run by a young, extravagantly mustachioed man from the Auvergne who bottles and sells his own rustic wines. Closed Sundays and Mondays. 42 Rue Léon-Frot, 11e (phone: 43-70-59-27). Inexpensive.

Au Duc de Richelieu – Specializes in the wines of Beaujolais, Chiroubles, Juliénas, St.-Amour, and so on. A cozy atmosphere and lots of wine-tasting certificates on the walls. Closed Sundays and August. 110 Rue de Richelieu, 2e (phone: 42-96-38-38). Inexpensive.

La Palette – This Left Bank hideaway on a quiet square, with outdoor tables during the summer, stays lively with a young crowd until 2 AM every morning except in August. Perhaps the monocled gentlemen on the 1930s tiles and the oils hung on the walls paid the bills of never-to-be-successful painters. Closed Sundays, holidays, and August. 43 Rue de Seine, 6e (phone: 43-26-68-15). Inexpensive.

Le Rubis – A tiny corner bar with an old-fashioned atmosphere and a big selection of wines — about 30 in all. With your glass of wine try the pork *rillettes,* a savory meat paste made on the premises. Closed on weekends and 2 weeks in August. 10 Rue du Marché-St.-Honoré, 1er (phone: 42-61-03-34). Inexpensive.

Au Sauvignon – The no-nonsense couple in blue overalls who run this tiny corner bar look as if they just stepped in from the country. They seem to be in perpetual motion, pouring the white Sauvignon and carving up chunky sandwiches from the famous *Poilane* bakery not far away. Closed Sundays, 2 weeks in January, Easter, and August. 80 Rue des Sts.-Pères, 7e (phone: 45-48-49-02). Inexpensive.

La Tartine – One of the old, authentic bistros, with a colorful local clientele and a good selection of wine by the glass. Closed Tuesdays and Wednesday mornings. 24 Rue de Rivoli, 4e (phone: 42-72-76-85). Inexpensive.

PRAGUE

Goethe once called Prague "the most precious stone in the stone crown of the world." The beauty of Prague has remained legendary ever since the Middle Ages. If you wish to step back in time, you can choose no better country than Czechoslovakia and no better city than Prague, its thousand-year-old capital.

The historical center of this city is the largest protected urban area in the world, for two reasons. First, Czechoslovakia escaped the heavy bombings of World War II, emerging almost unscathed physically. Second, almost half the 3,507 buildings now standing on Prague's original medieval ground plan are under landmark protection. The task of halting their decay — and restoring them to their former grandeur — is a dauntingly costly one, which can only be attacked piecemeal. Over the last couple of years, a good deal of scaffolding has come down to reveal breathtakingly beautiful façades.

In the center of Bohemia, Czechoslovakia's westernmost province, Prague is a sumptuous blend of nature and architecture. Like Rome, it is built on seven hills and is divided by a river, the Vltava (called the Moldau in German), which is spanned by 15 bridges. The city, everywhere dotted with parks, waterways, and gardens, overwhelms the visitor with its architecture. As in many European cities and towns, you can see layers of architectural periods and styles — Romanesque, Gothic, baroque, neo-classical, Art Nouveau, and modern. The Old Town is itself a course in the architecture of the last 500 years.

But Prague is best known for its distinguished examples of the Gothic and baroque styles. Gothic spires are literally everywhere in Prague, particularly in the Old Town, which boasts the Týn Church, 1365, with its Gothic exterior, complete with twin towers and flying buttresses (and, typically, a baroque interior), and the inspiring early Gothic Old-New Synagogue, majestically tall, with fluted pillars, pointed arches, and delicate stone embellishments.

Prague's baroque heritage includes the Wallenstein Palace, built by Italian architects between 1624 and 1630. It is an early baroque ensemble harmonizing sculptures, paintings, fountains, gardens, and a *sala terrena.* In an exuberant mood, Bohemia's rich 17th-century merchants and nobles invited Italian and German architects — notably the great Kryštof Dienzenhofer and his son, Kilián Ignaz — to decorate the capital in magnificent baroque style. First father, then son, supervised the building of the Church of St. Nicholas, a masterpiece complete with typically baroque features such as great curving forms, painted ceilings, and elaborate decorative effects.

Prague's history can be read not only in its buildings but also on the map of the city. The earliest settlements, first recorded in the 9th century, were at the foot of two ancient castles perched high on the tops of hills — Vyšehrad on the right bank of the Vltava and Hradčany on the left; these

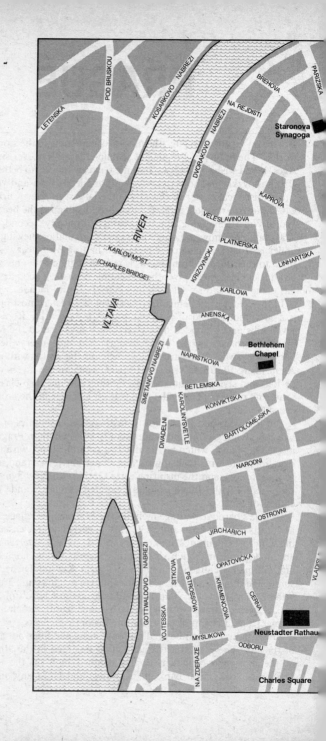

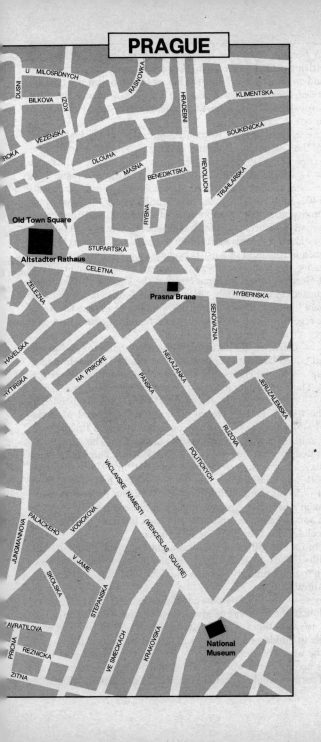

PRAGUE

U MILOSRDNYCH

DUSNI

BILKOVA

KOZI

KLIMENTSKA

RASNOVKA

HRADEBNI

VEZENSKA

ROKA

SOUKENICKA

DLOUHA

MASNA

BENEDIKTSKA

REVOLUCNI

TRUHLARSKA

RYBNA

Old Town Square

STUPARTSKA

Altstadter Rathaus

CELETNA

ZELEZNA

Prasna Brana

HYBERNSKA

SENOVAZNA

HAVELSKA

HYTIRSKA

NA PRIKOPE

PANSKA

NEKAZANKA

JERUZALEMSKA

RUZOVA

POLITICKYCH

VACLAVSKE NAMESTI (WENCESLAS SQUARE)

JUNGMANNOVA

PALACKEHO

VODICKOVA

V JAME

SKOLSKA

STEPANSKA

VE SMECKACH

KRAKOVSKA

National Museum

AVRATILOVA

PRICNA

REZNICKA

ZITNA

strongholds later became residences of the Bohemian kings. On the right bank, a small settlement then formed a market center, which developed into the Old Town, and on the opposite bank, the Lesser Quarter grew up. Finally, Charles IV founded the New Town near the Old Town during the 14th century. The five royal towns of Prague, each retaining its distinct personality, officially became one in 1784.

Prague, first the seat of the Holy Roman Empire, then of the Habsburgs, was the capital of the kingdom of Bohemia, coming into its full glory during the reign of Charles IV (1346–78). Charles, a man of culture and vision, founded the New Town, built Charles University, reconstructed Prague Castle in the Gothic style, and initiated the construction of St. Vitus Cathedral.

Beginning in 1402, John Huss preached his "fighting words" — advocating the reform of church abuses and the supremacy of Czech national aspirations in the face of German influences — from Prague's Bethlehem Chapel until he was burned at the stake in 1415; his martyrdom triggered the religious Hussite wars. In 1526, when Ferdinand I of Austria became king, the long oppression of the Czechs under the Habsburgs began. Vienna's efforts to reintroduce Catholicism and Germanization by force inspired the Czechs to passionate resistance — climaxed by the famous "defenestration" of two government officials: They were literally thrown out of the windows of Prague Castle in 1618, sparking a revolt by the Czech nobility and thereby Central Europe's devastating Thirty Years' War.

After the Czechs' defeat at the Battle of White Mountain (1620), foreign nobles confiscated Czech lands, and Germanization reached its height under the Austrian Empress Maria Theresa in 1749, when German was made the official language. The Czech national spirit, however oppressed, was never vanquished; by 1918 the Republic of Czechoslovakia was born. Independence was tragically short-lived: Hitler's troops occupied Bohemia and Moravia from 1939 until 1945, when the Czechs rose up against them in Prague, and held out bravely until the Soviet Army arrived 4 days later. (The Americans had already liberated western Bohemia, including Pilsen.) The Communist state of Czechoslavakia was the result of a čoup d'état in 1948.

Prague is a subtle and complex city, unfolding itself leaf by leaf, and then only to the most observant and curious visitors. To know Prague a visitor must amble through it slowly — discovering a palace here, a tower there, a decorative touch somewhere else, and now and then lingering at one of its numerous wine cellars and beer halls for refreshment.

Don't look here for the glitter of Parisian nightlife or the hurlyburly of London's Piccadilly Circus. Instead, stop, look, and listen to Prague, because the city has much to tell, primarily through the rich blend of its architecture and its lovely natural setting.

Those who choose to stroll through the cobblestone streets, full of shadows at night, will follow in the footsteps of Mozart, Rilke, and Apollinaire, all of whom lived here, to say nothing of Franz Kafka, who was born here and who resided for a while in Golden Lane, a crooked little street behind the forbidding Castle. In the words of another lover of Prague, the French poet Paul Valéry, "There is no city in the world in which magnificent wholes and valuable details and corners would be better combined, more happily situated."

PRAGUE AT-A-GLANCE

 SEEING THE CITY: To catch the drama of Prague, visit the *Golden Prague* restaurant, on the eighth floor of the *Prague Inter-Continental* hotel (see *Best in Town,* "Checking In"), for a spectacular view of Prague Castle, particularly beautiful at sunset when the castle is a black silhouette and the last rays of the sun splash red and gold into the Vltava River. You'll know at once why this city is called Golden Prague. A view in the opposite direction opens out when traveling up Petřín Hill in the funicular (now open after decades of disuse).

 SPECIAL PLACES: Any exploration should begin with a half-day tour of the city by motorcoach, with multilingual guide, offered by *Cedok,* the national tourist office. Buses leave from the *Cedok* branch office at 6 Bílkova, opposite the *Inter-Continental* (phone: 231-8255 or 231-9744). From then on, put on your walking shoes, and, as we said, take in the city at a slow pace.

Historical Prague was originally five independent towns, and each of these five districts — New Town, Old Town, Lesser Town, Hradčany, and Vyšehrad — retains its individual character.

NEW TOWN (NOVÉ MĚSTO)

Prague's New Town dates from 1348, when it was established by King Charles IV. Wenceslas Square, with its profusion of shops, hotels, and restaurants, is the center of the modern city of Prague and a logical starting point for seeing the city.

Wenceslas Square (Václavské náměstí) – St. Václav ("Good King Wenceslas"), seated on his horse, guards this square, which is really a boulevard. Dominated by the *National Museum,* Wenceslas Square is the central thoroughfare of the city, lined with Art Nouveau hotels, restaurants, cafés, and shops.

National Museum (Národní muzeum) – The imposing neo-Renaissance façade and the interior decorations of this building express the spirit of late-19th-century Czech nationalism in which it was built. Inside are paintings on Czech historical themes, fossils, stamps, and archaeological items. One of the few museums open Mondays (closed Tuesdays instead). 68 Václavské náměstí.

Flek's Inn (U Fleků) – Stop in and see one of Prague's most famous old pubs. No one knows quite how old it is, but it was in existence in 1499. Huge, with music and singing guests, *U Fleků* specializes in strong, dark beer. 11 Křemencova (phone: 292436).

The Chalice (U Kalicha) – Another famous beer hall, which is disappointingly modern in character (but full of literary allusions), where the Good Soldier Švejk consumed his Pilsners. 14 Na bojišti (phone: 290701).

Slavia Café – Opposite the *National Theater* along the embankment, this is a gathering place for artists and intellectuals. 1 Národní (phone: 265616).

Charles Square (Karlovo náměstí) – Now a park surrounded by old buildings, the New Town's oldest square was the center around which the town was proudly planned by Charles IV in 1348. Charles Square remains Prague's largest square. On the north side is the oldest building in the New Town, the New Town Hall (Novoměstská radnice), site of its government from 1398 to 1784. On the south side of Charles Square, at #40, is an 18th-century baroque building known as Faust's House. Ever since the 14th century, houses on this site have been associated with alchemy and other occult practices. (The origin of the Faust legend is uncertain; it is sometimes said to have arisen from the strange adventures of a 16th-century English alchemist named Edward Kelley.)

Dvořák Museum – Once a summer residence called Villa Amerika (in the early 18th century), this lovely baroque building was designed by the noted architect K. I. Dienzenhofer. Fittingly, the building now houses mementos of the Czech composer of the great *New World Symphony* (which uses American folk tunes), Antonín Dvořák. In the sculpture garden in back of the house, Dvořák's music is performed during the summer. Closed Mondays. 20 Ke Karlovu, not far from Charles Square.

OLD TOWN (STARÉ MĚSTO)

Walk here just before dusk, when the winding, narrow, cobblestone streets seem to merge into dim Gothic arcades. The Old Town, which contains most of the oldest buildings in Prague, dates from 1120. A great many medieval exteriors have been preserved in this area.

Powder Tower (Prašna brana) – This gate to the Old Town, once used to store gunpowder, was first built in 1475, then rebuilt in the late 19th century. Here the Czech kings departed for the coronation route long ago. If you climb its 186 steps, the view is delightful. Na příkopě.

Celetná Street (Celetná ulice) – Recently renovated baroque townhouses line this curving street, once part of the royal coronation route. Today, the visitor can follow it from the Powder Tower to Old Town Square, seeing the Carolinum, a 14th-century building that was part of the original university founded by King Charles IV (9 Celetná) along the way. Nearby, at 11 Železná, is the *Tyl Theater,* where Mozart's masterpiece, *Don Giovanni,* had its world première in 1787 and where scenes from the 1984 film *Amadeus* were shot. (It is presently being renovated.)

Old Town Square (Staroměstské náměstí) – The center of Prague's Old Town, this important square was given a facelift in time for the 1988 celebration of the 40th anniversary of the Communist takeover. The monument to John Huss was erected in 1915, 500 years after the religious reformer was burned at the stake. Every hour on the hour, crowds gather to watch the astronomical clock built in 1490 on the Old Town Hall as its mechanical figures of Christ, the 12 apostles, and allegorical *memento mori* figures perform their solemn march. The Town Hall itself was founded in 1338 and rebuilt many times; the many treasures within include a dungeon and a well in the cellar and a 15th-century council chamber still used by Prague's city government, decorated by 60 imaginative coats of arms belonging to the guilds of Prague. Guided tours are given hourly, following the clock's ritual.

On the east side of the square is the Church of Our Lady at Týn, dating from 1365, with its twin Gothic spires. Once the property of the Hussites and later of the Jesuits, this beautiful church combines a Gothic exterior with a baroque interior. Tycho de Brahe, the Danish astronomer, was buried here in 1601. A pretty little café, *U Týna,* is at 15 Staromětské mámestí. Nearby is the recently opened *House of the Bell* (Dům u Zvonu), a Gothic structure that serves as a municipal art exhibition hall, where concerts are performed.

This is "Kafka territory:" A bust of the writer commemorates the site of his birth in 1883, at 5 U radnice. He grew up in the graffiti-decorated house next to the Old Town Hall, and his father ran a shop on the ground floor of the rococo Goltz-Kinský Palace on the Old Town Square.

The Jewish Quarter – Walk north from the Old Town Hall on Pařížská street and turn left on Červená to see the Old-New Synagogue (Staronová synagoga), the oldest surviving synagogue in Europe (1270). One of Prague's most beautiful examples of the early Gothic style, it is truly inspiring, with its fluted pillars and sculptural decorations.

Jewish traders founded the Prague ghetto as early as the 9th century, and it became a center of Jewish culture by the 17th century. Visit the Old Jewish Cemetery of the 15th to 18th centuries, with its 12,000 tombstones, several layers deep. It belongs to the *State Jewish Museum* along with several former synagogues that now house exhibitions of religious articles and Hebrew manuscripts. In the restored Pinkas Synagogue, 3 Široká, the names of 77,700 Jewish men, women, and children murdered by the Nazis are painted on the interior walls.

Convent of the Blessed Agnes – New exhibition halls were recently opened in a partly reconstructed Gothic convent for a collection of 19th-century Czech paintings. 17 U milosrdných.

Bethlehem Chapel (Betlémská kaple) – Here on the southern edge of the Old Town, the church reformer John Huss preached his revolutionary ideas from 1402 until his martyrdom in 1415. To the Czechs, Huss has become a symbol of freedom from oppression and is revered as a national hero. The present chapel is a painstaking reconstruction of the original Gothic building, and the wooden threshold of the pulpit, once trod by Huss himself, is now protected under glass. 5 Betlémské náměstí.

Charles Bridge – One of the oldest and most beautiful bridges in Europe was built of stone in 1357 by Charles IV, between the Old Town and the Lesser Town. It is lined on both sides by fine statues of the baroque period (1683–1714). The Lesser Town end has two towers; the higher one may be climbed for a spectacular view. The bridge is a favorite strolling place day or night, and it offers views of the castle, the Vltava River, and the lovely island of Kampa with its chestnut trees.

LESSER TOWN (MALÁ STRANA)

Sometimes called Little Town, this is Prague's baroque soul, founded in 1257 as the second of the royal towns (after the Old Town). During the 17th and 18th centuries, foreign noblemen and the Catholic Church engaged some outstanding architects and artists to embellish what is the city's most picturesque quarter. Full of old palaces — including the magnificent Wallenstein Palace, where concerts are held during the summer — Lesser Town is a maze of little, crooked, cobblestone lanes full of old churches, museums, inns, wine cellars, and charming little parks. It is best just to wander around the town and discover its nooks and crannies for yourself.

Lesser Town Square (Malostranské náměstí) – Surrounded by 16th-century houses with arcades, the square — like the entire Lesser Town — is dominated by the Jesuit church of St. Nicholas. Designed by famous 18th-century architects, the Dienzenhofers and Anselm Lurago, this is the finest baroque building in Prague.

Wallenstein Palace (Valdštejnský palác) – Northwest of St. Nicholas's Church is the magnificent baroque palace begun in 1624 by Italian architects for the great Habsburg general Albrecht Wallenstein. Unfortunately, the frescoes inside can't be seen because the building also houses the Ministry of Culture, but the public concerts in the garden are an experience that should not be missed. Valdštejnské náměstí.

Neruda Street (Nerudova ulice) – Leading from the Lesser Town to the castle and lined on both sides by baroque façades is one of the most beautiful streets in the Lesser Town. Many townhouses on this street have preserved the old signs used before numbers were introduced: red eagle, three violins, golden goblet, and other quaint names.

HRADČANY

Near the castle of the same name, which was probably begun in the 9th century, there grew up the Prague town of Hradčany, officially founded in 1320.

Prague Castle (Hradčany) – Today the seat of the government, this castle has been a Slav stronghold, residence of the Kings of Bohemia, and the seat of the president of the Republic; it is the history of the Czech nation in stone. With three walled and dizzyingly complex courtyards, the castle is best grasped with the help of a *Cedok* tour (see *Sources and Resources*). Perhaps most interesting is the interior of the vaulted, Gothic Vladislav Hall, where jousting tournaments once took place.

St. Vitus's Cathedral (Katedrála sv. Vita) – Dominating the castle is this Gothic mausoleum of the Czech kings and repository for the Czech crown jewels. (The jewels, however, are rarely shown to the public.)

Golden Lane (Zlatá ulička) – Just north of the castle, one of Prague's most charming cobblestone streets with little houses and shops is famous as the legendary street of alchemists who tried to turn lead into gold. Franz Kafka lived at #24 in 1917; it is now a bookstore.

National Gallery – European Old Master paintings adorn the museum in the baroque Šternberk Palace on Castle Square. 15 Hradčanské náměstí.

St. George's Convent – An extensive collection of Czech Gothic art, which is superbly installed in the first convent founded in Bohemia. Jiřské náměstí.

The Loretto – So named because it was built in 1626 on the model of a pilgrimage church in Loretto, Italy. It is famous for the 1694 carillon in its clock tower and for the "Loretto treasury," a collection of extremely valuable 16th- to 18th-century jewelry and religious applied arts. Loretánské náměstí.

Strahov Monastery (Strahovský klášter) – West of the castle, high above the green slopes of Petřín Hill, is a gigantic monastery, which once rivaled the castle itself in magnificence and whose garden provides a lovely view of Prague. Today, Strahov houses the *Museum of Czech Literature;* two baroque library halls may also be seen. Pohořelec.

VYŠEHRAD

High up on cliffs that rise above the Vltava on the side opposite Hradčany, this fortress and the town around it were probably founded in the 9th century. However, no one knows how old Vyšehrad really is; it may be much older.

Vyšehrad Fortress – Walk around the grounds, which include a park, the 11th-century Rotunda of St. Martin, and the Church of St. Peter and St. Paul.

Vyšehrad Cemetery – When you are in Vyšehrad, don't miss the burial place of the country's greats: Antonín Dvořák, Karel Čapek, Jan Kubelik, Jan Neruda, and Bedřich Smetana are just a few.

■**EXTRA SPECIAL:** Kutná Hora, 42 miles (67 km) southeast of Prague, is a former silver mining town, which boomed in the 13th century, when its rich deposits were used to help create the splendor of the Bohemian court. Here coins — including the thaler — were minted by craftsmen imported from Florence. The Vlašský Dvůr, a 13th-century palace where the craftsmen worked, a fine coin museum, a church whose vault is lined entirely with human skulls, and the unusual Gothic roof of St. Barbara's Church are all here.

To see Český Šternberk, a 13th-century hilltop castle, as well, take *Cedok*'s 1-day bus excursion — "Pearls of Czech Gothic Art" — on Thursdays.

SOURCES AND RESOURCES

TOURIST INFORMATION: For general information, brochures, maps, and tour bookings, contact *Cedok,* 18 Na příkopě, Prague 1 (phone: 212-7111), or Prague Information Service, 20 Na příkopě (phone: 544444). The latter can arrange for private guides at its 4 Panská office (phone: 223411 or 224311). In New York, contact *Cedok,* Czechoslovak Travel Bureau, 10 E. 40th St., New York, NY 10016 (phone: 212-689-9720).

The US Embassy is at 15 Třžistě (phone: 536641).

Note: In Prague there are a number of black market money-changers who offer roughly three times the official exchange rate. However tempting they may seem, stay away; if you are caught, the penalty is prison.

Local Coverage – You won't find any English-language newspapers in Prague, though a few select hotels carry German-language publications.

Food – Your best bet is to consult *Cedok.*

Telephone – The area code for Prague is 02.

 CLIMATE AND CLOTHES: Prague has cold, damp winters and warm summers, with clearly defined spring and autumn seasons. The average winter temperature is 30F (−1C); the average summer temperature, 70F (21C). Wear comfortable clothes, not too dressy, and good walking shoes.

 GETTING AROUND: Airport – Praha-Ruzyně Airport, about 40 minutes from downtown by taxi, handles both domestic and international flights. Cab fare is about 100 koruna (Kčs.; about $3). Bus service connecting the airport and downtown leaves from Revoluční třída downtown and costs 6 Kčs. (about 20¢); for more information, check with the CSA counter at the airport. Shuttle bus service connecting the airport and major hotels costs $5 (payable in US currency only); more information can be obtained from the *Cedok* counter at the airport.

Bus and Tram – Public transportation is inexpensive and good; for 1 crown (10¢) you can buy a ticket at any newsstand or tobacco shop — not on the bus or tram. The ticket is punched once you are aboard. *Cedok*'s half-day motorcoach tour is a good introduction to the city and costs about $9.

Car Rental – At *Pragocar,* Nové Město, 42 Štěpánská (phone: 235-2825 or 235-2809); or at Ruzyně Airport (phone: 367807).

Metro – Built in cooperation with the Russians and still expanding, the subway system is fast, safe, and clean. The same 1-crown ticket used for buses and trams can be purchased in metro stations.

Taxi – Reasonably priced taxis can be called at major hotels.

Train – The main train station is Praha Hlavní Nádraží, on Vítězného února (phone: 216-11111).

 SPECIAL EVENTS: *Prague Spring* (Pražské Jaro), held every mid-May to early June since 1946, offers concerts, including internationally known soloists, orchestras, chamber ensembles, and operas. Tickets are about $5. Inquire at *Cedok* for further information (see above).

 MUSEUMS: In addition to the museums mentioned in *Special Places,* there are the *Bedřich Smetana Museum,* 1 Novotného lavka, Staré Město; and the *Bertramka,* 169 Mozartova, a 17th-century mansion in the Smíchov district, where Mozart stayed, now the *Mozart Museum.* Music lovers should stop by the *Museum of Musical Instruments,* which is the second largest collection of antique instruments in the world, at 2 Lázeňská, Malá Strana. A new history exhibition, the *Museum of the Nation's Past,* opened in 1987 in the Lobkovic Palace, Jiřská St., behind Prague Castle; its emphasis is on the baroque period.

 SHOPPING: The best buys, both in Czech wares and foreign imports, can be had at the *Tuzex* chain of shops, which accepts payment in hard — i.e., Western — currency only. Branches in leading hotels specialize in typical Czech items, particularly Bohemian glass and crystal and Czech crafts such as embroidered clothing, woodcarvings, and peasant pottery. *Tuzex* will mail purchased goods anywhere. Main shops are at 13 Rytířská and 18 Železná.

Bohemian glass and crystal are world famous. Especially recommended is *Moser,* 12 Na příkopě (which also has a *Tuzex* section on its elegant premises). Also convenient is the *Bohemia* shop at 2 Pařížská, on Old Town Square. Two doors away is a *Bižuterie* aglitter with rhinestone tiaras and beaded necklaces.

Crafts can be bought in the Wenceslas Square area at *Slovenská Jizba,* 40 Wenceslas Square, and *Krásná Jizba,* 36 Národní třída; and at Christmastime, gingerbread tree ornaments are baked and sold at *Ceská Jizba,* 12 Karlova. Contemporary artworks are sold at *Galerie Centrum,* 6 ul. 28 října, and *Galerie Platýz,* 37 Národní třída. For good recordings of Czech composers such as Smetana and Dvořák, browse through the new record shop in the Underground station at náměstí Republiky.

SPORTS AND FITNESS: Fitness Centers – The *Forum Praha* hotel, Kongresová ul. (phone: 410111), has a modern penthouse fitness center with gym, pool, squash courts, saunas, and solarium; in the hotel's pub is a bowling alley. The *Inter-Continental* hotel, nám. Curieových (phone: 231-1812), has exercise equipment and a sauna. The *Panorama* hotel has a pool, sauna, and a solarium, at 7 Milevská (phone: 416-1111). *Plavecký Stadión,* 74 Podolská, a 20-minute drive south of Prague in Podolí (phone: 439152), has an Olympic-size pool, steam room, and sauna.

Jogging – A good place is the Stromovka park, a 15-minute walk or 5-minute ride northeast from downtown.

Mini-Golf – At both the *International* hotel, 1 nám. Družby, Prague 6-Dejvice (phone: 321051), and the *Forum Praha* hotel, Kongresova ul. (phone: 410111).

Soccer – Games are played at *Sparta Stadium,* 97 Obránců míru, Letná. *Cedok* has tickets, 6 Bílkova, near the *Inter-Continental.*

Tennis – There are indoor and outdoor courts at Klamovka, Prague 5-Košíře (phone: 521333), and elsewhere. Book court time through *Cedok,* 18 Na příkopě, Prague 1 (phone: 2127111).

THEATER: Don't miss going to *Laterna Magika,* 40 Národní (phone: 260033), a unique theater experience devised by the Czechs. It's not necessary to know Czech to enjoy this review, which includes dance, music, and film. It costs about $3. Also popular with foreigners are the pantomime productions at the *Na zábradlí theater,* 5 Anenské nám. (phone: 236-0409). Other theaters include the *National Theater,* 2 Národni (phone: 205364), for the classics (in Czech), and its recently completed, architecturally controversial, offshoot next door, the *New Stage* (phone: 206260); and the *Smetana Theater,* 8 Vítězného února (phone: 269746).

MUSIC: Prague is a city that Mozart loved, where *Don Giovanni* had its world première; here Dvořák and Smetana lived and composed their music. Prague is still a very musical city. Concerts can be heard at the House of Artists, *Dvořák Hall,* náměstí Krasnoarmejců (phone: 231-9164); Municipal House, *Smetana Hall,* 5 náměstí Republiky (phone: 232-5858); and Palace of Culture, *Congress Hall,* 65 ul. 5 května (phone: 417-1111). Operas are performed at the *National* and *Smetana* theaters (see *Theater*).

During *Prague Spring,* concerts take place in various churches throughout the city. For specific information inquire at *Cedok* (see above).

NIGHTCLUBS AND NIGHTLIFE: Prague is not a big nightclub town, but there are a few interesting after-dark places with live music and dancing. For dancing try *Alfa,* 28 Václavské náměstí (phone: 223220), or *Jalta,* 45 Václavské náměstí (phone: 264683); *Est-Bar,* 19 Washingtonova (phone:

222552), has dancing and entertainment; *International Club,* 1 náměstí Družby (phone: 321051), dancing; *Lucerna,* 61 Štěpánská (phone: 246153), and *Revue Alhambra* at the *Ambassador Hotel,* 5 Václavské náměstí (phone: 220467) have entertainment. Those with a penchant for *gambling* can now indulge themselves at Prague's first roulette casino in the *Forum Praha* hotel, Kongresová ul. (phone: 410111).

BEST IN TOWN

 CHECKING IN: *Cedok* operates a vast network called Interhotels, which includes most of the best hotels in Czechoslovakia. One intriguing Prague option is called a "botel" (*boat* plus *hotel*), several of which are anchored in the Vltava River. For all hotels, advance bookings are highly recommended, as there remains a shortage of space in Prague. Interhotels are rated Deluxe, First Class (A), and Second Class (B); our categories of expensive, moderate, and inexpensive are roughly parallel. *Cedok* accepts bookings for non-deluxe hotels only on a half-board basis (meal vouchers can be used outside the hotel). Expect to pay from $70 to $120 for a double room in an expensive hotel; $40 to $70 for moderate; and $20 to $40 for inexpensive. All telephone numbers are in the 02 area code unless otherwise indicated.

Alcron – A longtime favorite among journalists and diplomats, with 140 rooms and plenty of Old World charm, plus a restaurant offering French and Czech specialties. Decorated with crystal chandeliers and rose carpeting. There are 2 other restaurants, a beer restaurant, and a lounge café. Off Wenceslas Square at 40 Štěpánská (phone: 235-9216). Expensive.

At the Three Ostriches (Ú tři pštrosů) – At the Lesser Town end of the Charles Bridge, this pretty 16th-century house is now Prague's most exclusive hotel, with a charming restaurant. Its 18 rooms must be reserved at least a month in advance. 12 Dražického náměstí (phone: 536151). Expensive.

Esplanade – An Old World establishment with a friendly, family atmosphere and an excellent restaurant. 19 Washingtonova (phone: 226056). Expensive.

Forum Praha – Opened in 1988, opposite the *Palace of Culture* conference center/concert hall, this is the most ambitious hotel in the country. It is a massive skyscraper with 492 doubles and 39 suites (including a "Presidential" suite), all of which have color TV sets featuring in-house movies and an international cable channel. Only 5 minutes from downtown via taxi or subway. Other amenities include a fitness center, bowling alley, gift shops, luxury restaurant, nightclub, café, and the first casino in Prague. Kongresová ul. (phone: 410111). Expensive.

International – This comfortable Soviet-style hotel is 15 minutes by subway from the center of Prague. In summer, Czech "beer party" and Slovak "wine party" entertainment programs are offered, which include dinner and folk songs and dances. Tickets also available at *Cedok.* 1 náměstí Družby (phone: 321051). Expensive.

Jalta – A favorite of Americans, with 88 rooms, each with its own bath. The service staff is friendly and helpful, and the *Jalta Club* has live music for dancing. 45 Václavské náměstí (phone: 265541). Expensive.

Palace Praha – A completely reconstructed old hotel, formerly shabby, now deluxe, with Art Nouveau decor. There are 125 rooms and suites, a French restaurant, sauna, and conference facilities. In the heart of Prague, near the Old Town. 12 Panská (phone: not available at press time). Expensive.

Prague Inter-Continental – This 11-story modern hotel on the edge of the Old Town is sophisticated and convenient. With 398 rooms, it offers superb views of the castle and the Old Town. 5 Náměstí Curieových (phone: 231-1812; reservations, 231-9756). Expensive.

Ambassador – Exudes a somewhat faded Old World charm, with 115 rooms, a good restaurant, the *Pasáž Café,* and the *Embassy Bar.* Many of its rooms are furnished in Louis XIV style, with beautiful Czech crystal chandeliers. 5 Václavské náměstí (phone: 214-3111). Expensive to moderate.

Panorama – A large hotel with a pool and saunas, four subway stops from the center of town. 7 Milevská (phone: 416-1111). Expensive to moderate.

Paříž – This lovely *Jugendstil* (Art Nouveau) hotel reopened in 1986 after long years of renovation. It has a café and a good restaurant decorated with blue mosaic tiles, serving Czech specialties. 1 U Obecního domu (phone: 231-6612). Moderate.

Flora – A good example of a second class hotel that is clean and a good value; however, less than half of the 203 rooms have a toilet and bath. With an attractive lobby and a very pleasant wine restaurant, it is 15 minutes from downtown by tram. 121 Vinohradská (phone: 274241). Inexpensive.

■**Note:** Three "botels" (built as hotels) are anchored in the Vltava River, with staterooms and bars; all are shipshape, lots of fun, and inexpensive. Each of them has about 80 rooms that are charming, though understandably somewhat cramped. They are: *Admirál,* Hořejší nábřeží (phone: 548685); *Albatros,* Nábřeží L. Svobody (phone: 231-3634); and *Racek,* Dvorecká louka (phone: 425793).

 EATING OUT: Prague has thousands of eating places — outdoor cafés, wine cellars, pubs, and international restaurants. Most require advance reservations; most are reasonable in price and accept major credit cards. Czech cuisine is hearty and good, although it is weak on produce and fresh vegetables rarely appear on the menu. Specialties include *knedlíky* (dumplings), both plain and filled with fruit or meat; baked pork with sauerkraut; *svíčková,* a beef marinated in spicy cream sauce; *uzené maso,* or smoked pork with potato dumplings and spinach; and roast goose or duck.

Wines from southern Moravia are the best; sample Tři Grácie in red, rosé, or white. For moderate to inexpensive eating, try the beer halls (*pivnicy*) and wine cellars (*vinárny*) all over town.

Restaurant prices in Prague are generally quite reasonable; we have rated a dinner for two at $30 and up as expensive; $20 to $30 as moderate; and $10 to $20 as inexpensive. All telephone numbers are in the 02 area code unless otherwise indicated.

At the Swans (U labutí) – This wine restaurant offers Czech specialties and atmosphere, with its old-fashioned nooks, vaulted ceilings, and window casings dating from the 14th century. Open daily for dinner. 11 Hradčanské náměstí (phone: 539476). Expensive.

Chinese Restaurant (Čínská Restaurace) – Run by a Czech, this place serves some surprisingly good Chinese food in an atmosphere that is authentically Oriental. There are intimate booths for quiet dining. Closed Sundays. 19 Vodičkova (phone: 262697). Expensive.

Diplomatic Club – A luxury establishment that caters to foreign visitors, it is complemented with a bar and a video room. Closed weekends. Reservations necessary. 21 Karlova (phone: 261878 or 265701). Expensive.

Hanavský Pavilón – Try the *svíčková* in this *Jugendstil* (Art Nouveau) restaurant; there is also a disco club. Open daily. Letná Park (phone: 325792). Expensive.

Opera Grill – Most agree that this is Prague's finest restaurant, notwithstanding its recent move (still convenient to the *National Theater*). The food is excellent, and so is the wine cellar. After dinner, a specialty is brandy served in a giant crystal snifter. Closed weekends. Reservations necessary. 35 Karolíny Světlé, in the Old Town (phone: 265508). Expensive.

St. Klara (Svatá Klára) – Three hundred years ago Count Václav Vojtěch spent his evenings in his wine cellar a few steps below his baroque château. Today, foreign diplomats and others in the know frequent this *vinárna* (wine restaurant). It's cozier now than in the count's days, with its fireplace, fine service, accomplished cuisine, and selection of Moravian wines. Specialties range from fondue bourguignon to *palacinky flambé,* a classic Czech dessert. Open weekdays for dinner. Reservations necessary. Zoo Troja (phone: 841213). Expensive.

At the Spider (U pavouka) – When the dining room is full, as it usually is, ask to be seated in the elegantly appointed cocktail area. In the courtyard of 17 Celetná (phone: 231-8714). Expensive to moderate.

Nabozízek – The funicular from Ujezd Street in Malá Strana brings diners to this pleasant restaurant with a terrace for good food and a gorgeous view. Petín Park (phone: 539705). Expensive to moderate.

At the Golden Stag (U zlatého jelena) – This small, intimate wine cellar has vaulted ceilings, tile floors, and wooden tables. Open daily. 11 Celetná (phone: 268595). Moderate.

At the Golden Well (U zlaté studny) – Hearty fare is served at this stone-walled wine cellar with intimate niches for shadowy dining à deux. The building itself is famous for its gorgeous façade sculpture dating from 1714. 2 Karlova (phone: 263302). Expensive.

At the Green Frog (U zelené žáby) – A favorite wine cellar with Americans, this place is more than 8 centuries old. The house specialty is grilled meat with sauerkraut. 8 U Radnice (phone: 262815). Moderate.

At the Painters' (U malířů) – Reservations are a must at this wine tavern, which is better known for its picturesque painted decor than for its food. Closed Sundays. 11 Maltézské nám. (phone: 531883). Moderate.

At the Red Wheel (U červenéhokola) – In an open-air courtyard, it may take some effort to find this small restaurant — and even more to get in, since it is always booked up — but it is well worth the trouble. Closed Fridays. 2 Anežská (phone: 231-8941). Moderate.

At the 7 Angels (U sedmi andělů) – Furnished in a spare and elegant style — with a baroque accent. Try the *síp Amoruv* ("arrow of love"), a specialty platter of grilled meats. Closed Mondays. 20 Jilská (phone: 266355). Moderate.

Municipal House (Obecní dům) – On the left as one enters is an ornate *Jugendstil* café and on the right an equally flamboyant restaurant, recently renovated and very convenient for lunch in the shopping area. Náměstí Republiky (phone: 231-0616). Moderate.

Paroplavba – A fish restaurant that specializes in trout, prepared in six different ways. Closed Mondays. On the B. Engels Embankment, below street level (phone: 294964). Moderate.

Pezinocká Vinárna – This is a beautifully designed Slovak wine restaurant with Gypsy music. In the new House of Slovak Culture, 4 Purkyňova (phone: 291996). Moderate.

Praha Expo '58 – Winner of the 1958 Brussels World's Fair medal, this restaurant, in the Letenské Sády park, between the Šverma and Hlávka bridges, offers diners a splendid view of the Vltava River and of the city. The food is excellent, particularly the pastries, which are a house specialty. Letenské sady (phone: 374546). Moderate.

U Golema – A good place to lunch before or after touring the *Jewish Museum.* Elegantly simple decor. Try the veal with apple slices. 8 Maislova (phone: 231-0372). Moderate.

Moskva – A newly reconstructed Russian .tearoom-restaurant, above a Russian fast-food eatery called *Arbat*. Open daily. In the pedestrian zone, at 29 Na příkopě (phone: 262774). Moderate.

Vikárka – In the shadow of St. Vitus's Cathedral at Prague Castle, this small pub originally prepared meals only for church dignitaries. Now it is a favorite with Czechs and visitors. The restaurant specialty is called Bishop's Hat, a veal and cheese dish. 6 Vikářská (phone: 535150). Moderate.

At the Red Lobster (U červenéhoraka) – A small, pretty place for lunch or dinner. Open daily. 30 Karlova (phone: 265538). Inexpensive.

At the Town Hall (U Radnice) – Under the arcades just southeast of Old Town Square, this typical beer cellar caters to businesspeople at lunch and dinner. It serves one of the best duck dinners in town. Open daily. 2 Malé náměstí (phone: 262822). Inexpensive.

Evropa Café – The pastries are only so-so, but the decor is a *Jugendstil* feast for the eyes. In the *Evropa* hotel, 29 Václavské náměstí (phone: 263720). Inexpensive.

U sv. Tomáše – Prague's oldest beer hall is huge, with vaulted ceilings. Populated by young students, the place offers plain wooden tables and huge steins of beer. The best dish is a plate of pork, sauerkraut, and dumplings. Open daily. 12 Letenská (phone: 530064). Inexpensive.

ROME

If you're traveling from the north, you'll quickly understand why *Italia meridionale,* or southern Italy, begins in Rome: ancient stone ruins basking in the southern sun, baroque swirls teasing the senses at every turn, religious art exploding with color and Catholic sensuality — celebrating life with the conspicuous joie de vivre (here known as *gioia di vivere*) of southern Europe. Rome reaches out to your senses, blinding you with colors, beckoning you to stay. Its appeal is gripping and obviously romantic, inspiring throughout history many an illustrious northern visitor — such as Goethe, Keats, Byron, and Shelley — though today these romantic souls might be repelled by the insufferable noise, the screaming traffic, the exasperating strikes, political demonstrations, and general chaos of modern Rome. Yet despite the familiar symptoms of contemporary blight, Rome remains the Eternal City, ancient capital of the Western world, and center of Christianity for nearly 2,000 years.

Rome lies roughly in the center of the region of Lazio (Latium), just below the knee of boot-shaped Italy, between the Tyrrhenian Sea to the west and the Apennine Mountains to the east. The Tiber River gently curves through the city, with ancient Rome on its left bank, Vatican City and Trastevere (*tras* means across; *tevere,* Tiber) on its right. The original seven hills of Rome are all on the left bank, as is its modern center — the shopping areas that surround Piazza di Spagna (the so-called Spanish Steps), Piazza del Popolo, Via del Corso, Via del Tritone, and the legendary Via Veneto, celebrated in Fellini's film *La Dolce Vita.*

The 3rd-century Aurelian Walls still surround ancient Rome as well as most of papal and modern Rome. The city is unique because its fine buildings span so many centuries of history. There are ancient Roman remains, the most famous of which are the Colosseum and the Forum; buildings from the early Christian period such as the Castel Sant'Angelo; and a wealth of dazzling Renaissance and baroque architecture — from St. Peter's itself to Piazza del Campidoglio, the square designed by Michelangelo. The city abounds in churches, palaces, parks, *piazze,* statues, and fountains — all of which sparkle in the golden light and clear blue sky of the region.

Even Rome's beginnings are shrouded in a romantic legend that attributes the city's birth to Romulus and Remus, twin sons of the war god Mars and Rhea, a Vestal Virgin, who encountered Mars in a forest one day. The babies, left to die on the shore of the Tiber River at the foot of the Palatine Hill, were rescued and suckled through infancy by an old she-wolf and grew up to lead a band of adventurers and outlaws. Romulus, the stronger leader of the two, is said to have founded Rome in 753 BC, killing his brother to become its first king.

But earlier traces of habitation have been found on the Palatine Hill — one of the original seven hills — the site of Roma Quadrata, a primitive Rome

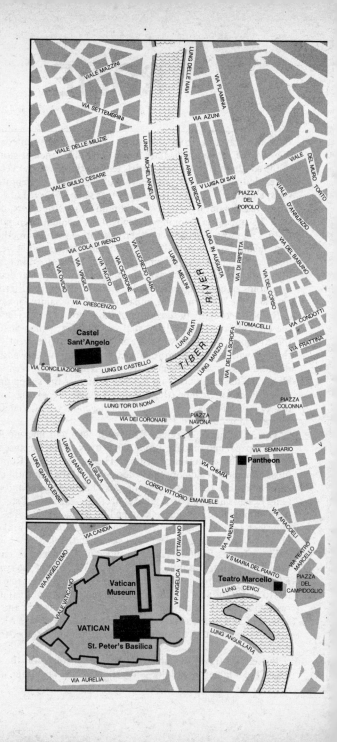

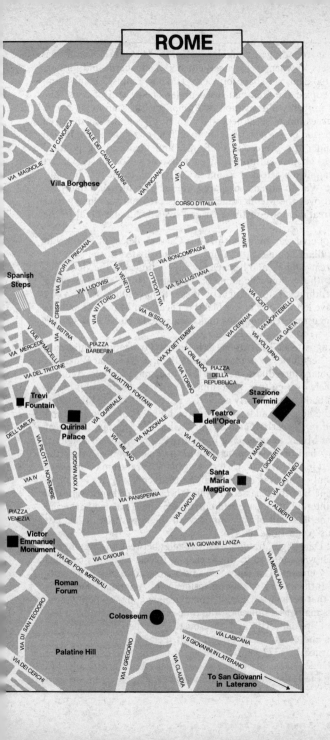

squared off by a surrounding rectangular wall. More likely, the traditional founding date refers to when the first settlements of shepherds and farmers on the Palatine took on the shape of a city and the Latins, Sabines, and Etruscans who peopled the area had fused under one system of laws. The name *Roma* was probably a derivation of *Ruma,* an Etruscan noble name.

Following a succession of seven legendary kings, a republic was declared in 509 BC, and a period of expansion began. By 270 BC or so, the entire Italian peninsula was under the protection of Rome, and the resulting political unification brought about a cultural unity as well, a new Roman style in art and literature. Hannibal's defeat at Zama in 201 BC, an event that brought the Second Punic War to an end, prepared the way for further expansion: Rome's dominion over the Mediterranean and its eventual supremacy over Alexander the Great's empire in the East and over Spain and Gaul in the West.

A long period of civil war ended with Julius Caesar's defeat of Pompey in 48 BC, but the brilliant conqueror of Gaul was assassinated in the Senate 4 years later. His great-nephew and heir, Octavian, continued in the victorious vein, becoming, with the honorific name of Augustus, Rome's first emperor and one of its best administrators. Augustus is said to have found Rome a city of brick and to have left it a city of marble; the Theater of Marcellus and the Mausoleum of Augustus are among his many fine constructions that survive today.

The reign of Augustus (27 BC–AD 14) saw Roman civilization at its peak, and it ushered in 2 centuries of peace known as the Pax Romana. Wherever they went, the Romans introduced brilliant feats of engineering and architecture, as well as their own culture, government, and law. Persecution of the Christians, which had begun as early as Nero's reign — he blamed the burning of Rome on the new sect and executed large numbers of them in AD 64 — came to an end in the early fourth century, when Constantine the Great issued the Edict of Milan, guaranteeing freedom of worship for all religions. But Rome by now had become top-heavy with its own administration; the empire was divided in 395, with an eastern section in Byzantium (Constantinople, now Istanbul). This was the beginning of the end.

Rome's grandeur had long passed by the 5th century, when a series of economic crises, internal decadence and corruption, and repeated barbarian invasions led to the final fall of the empire with the deposition of her last emperor, Romulus Augustulus, in 476.

Thus began the Dark Ages, fraught with struggles between the empire and the Church, which was centered in the papacy at Rome. Struggles between empire and papacy ensued. The Holy See, under Pope Clement V, actually fled Rome in the 14th century, taking up residence in Avignon, France, for 70 years. During that period, the city of Rome declined, and its population, which had been as many as a million at the time of Augustus, shrank to less than 50,000. The Capitoline Hill and once-bustling Roman Forum became pastures for goats and cows. Sheep grazed in St. Peter's.

The popes returned in 1377, and Rome again became the capital of the Catholic world. Under papal patronage it was soon reborn artistically and culturally. During the 15th century, restoration of St. Peter's began, prior to its complete reconstruction; the Vatican complex was built; and new palaces, churches, and well-planned streets changed the face of the city. Powerful popes commissioned artists and architects to beautify Rome, and their genius created sumptuous palaces, splendid villas, and squares adorned with fountains and obelisks, until a second city grew out of the ruins of ancient Rome to match its former splendor. The 17th century brought the birth of baroque Rome, with its dominating. figure, architect, sculptor, and painter Gian Lorenzo Bernini, whose masterpieces perhaps still best symbolize the spirit of this magnificent and undeniably theatrical city.

The comfortable security of the popes was shaken by the arrival of Napoleon Bonaparte in 1798. He soon set up a republic of Rome, deporting Pope Pius VI briefly to France, and in 1805 he was crowned King of Italy, proclaiming Rome a sort of second capital of the French Empire. In 1809, Napoleon declared the papal territories a part of France and in return was excommunicated by Pope Pius VII, who was deported to Fontainebleau. By 1815, the Napoleonic regime had collapsed, the papal kingdom was reconciled with France, and the pope was back in Rome, but the sparks of nationalistic passion had already been ignited in Italian hearts.

Friction between papal neutralism and patriotic fervor drove Pope Pius IX out of Rome to Gaeta in 1848. In 1849, Rome was again proclaimed a republic under the leadership of patriot Giuseppe Mazzini. Twice the French tried to restore the temporal power of the pope in Rome, meeting strong resistance from Republican forces led by Garibaldi. Finally, in 1870, the Italians entered Rome through a breach in the Aurelian Walls at Porta Pia and incorporated the city into the kingdom of Italy. That act dissolved the pontifical state and made Italian unity complete. A year later, Rome became the capital of the kingdom.

Mussolini's march on Rome in 1922 began the infamous Fascist regime that lasted until his downfall some 20 years later. The city was then occupied by the Germans until its liberation in 1944 by the Allies. In 1946, a referendum was held and Italy was declared a republic — just as it had been nearly 2½ millennia earlier.

Today, Rome is still the capital of Italy and of the Catholic Church, as well as the home of some 4 million people (up from 260,000 inhabitants in 1870). Many Romans are employed in tourism-related industries and in government — in a city often strangled by bureaucratic problems. Besides filmmaking (in its cinematic heyday, Rome was called "Hollywood on the Tiber") and a certain amount of printing, there is some small-scale production of foodstuffs, pharmaceuticals, building materials, plastics, glass, clothing, and handmade crafts.

Yet, for a society with significant problems — insufficient housing, impossible traffic, a soaring cost of living, and worrisome pollution — today's Romans still enjoy a relaxed way of life, as they have done for centuries. Perhaps nowhere north of Naples is the *arte di arrangiarsi* — the art of making do, or surviving with style — learned with such skill and practiced with such a timeless sense of resignation.

The *dolce vita* nightlife, more a figment of Fellini's imagination than a reality for any more than a handful of rich and/or famous Romans, has become somewhat subdued, but an unmistakable air of conviviality still prevails.

Not even soaring prices have limited the traditional Roman pastime of lingering lunches and late-night dinners at the city's 5,000 or so restaurants and *trattorie*. A sunny day at any time of the year still fills the cobblestone squares with diners at open-air eateries. They are usually engaged in animated conversation over their robust Roman food and inexpensive carafe wine from the Castelli (the surrounding hill towns such as Frascati). Most visitors are pleased to "do as the Romans do." No sense worrying about high prices and pollution if the inhabitants don't.

Roma, Non Basta Una Vita (*Rome, A Lifetime Is Not Enough*), by the late Italian author and journalist Silvio Negro, hints, with justification, at the impossibility of ever knowing everything about this city. For visitors who harbor the illusion of having seen all the ruins, churches, and monuments of Rome's glorious past, it may be time to begin discovering her countless hidden treasures, best done by walking the back streets and alleyways of the historic center (which is now, for the most part, a "pedestrian island").

If you feel suffocated by city life, try a day or two in the neighboring countryside. The surrounding Lazio region, sandwiched between the Tyrrhenian Sea and the Apennine Mountains, offers seaside resorts, rolling hills topped by medieval towns, picturesque lakes, rivers, and green meadows studded with umbrella pines, cypress trees, and wildflowers. Take an organized excursion to the Villa d'Este and Hadrian's Villa in Tivoli; to the Castelli Romani, or Roman hill towns, where the pope has his summer home; or to the excavations of Ostia Antica, the ancient port of Rome.

But take time to sit back and enjoy Rome. Visit the Forum and the Colosseum by day, and return at night when the ruins are bathed in gentler light to meditate over the rise and fall of ancient Rome. Watch the play of water in the Trevi Fountain or any of Rome's nearly 1,000 other fountains of every size and shape. See the ancient Roman Theater of Marcellus, which has been a Roman amphitheater, a medieval fort, a Renaissance palace, and which now contains apartments. Enjoy the superb cooking of the Lazio region. Ride a bicycle or jog in the Villa Borghese. Sip an *aperitivo* on the famed Via Veneto or at one of the many *caffès* that suddenly appear in unexpected corners of the historic city center.

Locally it is believed that on the last day of the world, while all the rest of humankind broods and repents, the Romans will throw a great farewell party, a gastronomic feast to end them all, with wine flowing from the city's many fountains. With the apocalypse not yet at hand, and despite the agonies besetting the country at large, the Eternal City remains eternally inviting.

ROME AT-A-GLANCE

SEEING THE CITY: Enjoy the magnificent view of all of Rome and the surrounding hill towns from Piazzale Garibaldi at the top of the Giancolo (Janiculum hill). It's best at sunset. Another panorama is visible from the top of St. Peter's dome. For a view of Rome dominated by St. Peter's, go to the terrace of the Pincio, next to the Villa Borghese, above Piazza del Popolo. And the most unusual view is of the dome of St. Peter's as seen in miniature through the keyhole of the gate to the priory of the Knights of Malta, on Piazza dei Cavalieri di Malta at the end of Via di Santa Sabina, on the Aventine hill. The picturesque piazza was designed by engraver Piranesi, a surrealist in spirit though he lived in the 18th century. For a real treat, a bird's eye view of Rome is available via helicopter. Leaving from the Centro Sperimentale d'Aviazione at Urbe Airport, 825 Via Saleria (phone: 812-3017), the $80 fee yields 20 minutes of breathtaking spectacle. (Minimum of five passengers; reserve several days in advance.)

 SPECIAL PLACES: Rome cannot be seen in a day, 3 days, a week, or even a year. If your time is limited to a few days, an organized bus tour is your best bet. (A quick and interesting one covers some 45 major sights in 3 hours. It leaves Piazza dei Cinquecento at 3:30 PM and, in winter, at 2:30 PM and costs about $5. Check the ATAC booth in the square for bus No. 110; it operates daily in season, weekends only out of season.) Then, when you've seen where your interests lie, grab your most comfortable walking shoes and a map. Most of historic Rome, which is also the city's center today, is within the 3rd-century Aurelian Walls and is delightfully walkable.

For practical purposes, the "must sees" below are divided into ancient, papal, and modern Rome, but elements of two or all three categories are often found in one site — such as a sleek modern furniture shop in a Renaissance palace built with stones from the Colosseum. A further heading focuses on the palaces, fountains, splendid piazzas, and streets of Rome. The ancient center of the city is very close to Piazza Venezia, the heart of the modern city, and most of the sights of ancient Rome are around the Capitoline, Palatine, and Aventine hills. They can be seen on foot — though they were not built — in one day. Much of papal Rome is centered in the Vatican, but since all of Rome is a religious center, some of its many fascinating and beautiful churches are included under this heading. (For other churches, and for museums not mentioned below, see "Museums" in *Sources and Resources.*)

Virtually all the museums, monuments, and archaeological sites run by the state or city are closed on Sunday afternoons and Mondays. Opening and closing hours change often (some are closed indefinitely because of strikes, personnel shortages, or restorations — it is estimated that only a third of Italy's artworks are exhibited), so check with your hotel or the tourist office before starting out. Where possible, we have listed hours that seem relatively reliable.

Warning: Pickpockets work all around the city, but are especially numerous on buses and at the most popular tourist spots, even though plainclothes police scour these areas. Watch out especially for Gypsy children who will beg or ask for a light while accomplices make straight for your wallet or purse. Carry your shoulder bag on the arm *away* from passing vehicular traffic to avoid bag snatchers on motor scooters. Avoid carrying your passport and any significant amount of money around with you, and be sure to store valuables in a hotel safe-deposit box.

ANCIENT ROME

Colosseo (Colosseum) – It's said that when the Colosseum falls, Rome will fall — and the world will follow. This symbol of the eternity of Rome, the grandest and most celebrated of all its monuments, was completed in AD 80, and it is a logical starting point for a visitor to ancient Rome. See it in daylight, and return to see it by moonlight. The enormous arena, ⅓ mile in circumference and 137 feet high, once accommodated 50,000 spectators. To provide shade in the summer, a special detachment of sailors stretched a great awning over the top. There were 80 entrances (progressively numbered, except for the four main ones), allowing the crowds to quickly claim their marble seats. Underneath were subterranean passages where animals and other apparatus were hidden from view. In the arena itself, Christians were thrown to lions, wild beasts destroyed one another, and gladiators fought to the death. Gladiatorial combats lasted until 404, when Onorius put an end to them (possibly after a monk had thrown himself into the arena in protest and was killed by the angry crowd); animal combats were stopped toward the middle of the 6th century.

The Colosseum was abused by later generations. It was a fort in the Middle Ages; something of a quarry during the Renaissance, when its marble and travertine were used in the construction of St. Peter's and other buildings; and in the 18th century it even became a manure depot for the production of saltpeter. Yet it remains a symbol of the grandeur of Rome. Open daily. Admission charge for the upper level. Piazzale del Colosseo.

Palatino (Palatine Hill) – Adjacent to the Colosseum and the Roman Forum, the Palatine is where Rome began. Its Latin name is the source of the word *palace*. In fact, great men — Cicero, Crassus, Marc Antony — lived on this regal hill, and the emperors of Rome — Augustus, Tiberius, Caligula, Nero, Domitian, Septimius Severus — built their palaces here, turning the hill into an imperial preserve. A 12th-century author called the spot the "palace of the Monarchy of the Earth, wherein is the capital seat of the whole world." In ruins by the Middle Ages, the ancient structures were incorporated into the sumptuous Villa Farnese in the 16th century, and the Farnese Gardens were laid out, the first botanical gardens in the world.

The Palatine is a lovely spot for a walk or a picnic. See especially the so-called House of Livia (actually of her husband, Augustus), with its remarkable frescoes; Domitian's Palace of the Flavians, built by his favorite architect, Rabirius; the impressive stadium; the view from the terrace of the Palace of Septimius Severus; and the remains of the Farnese Gardens at the top with another superb panorama of the nearby Forums. Closed Tuesdays; admission charge includes the Roman Forum. Enter at Via di San Gregorio or by way of the Roman Forum on Via dei Fori Imperiali.

Foro Romano (Roman Forum) – Adjoining the Palatine Hill is the Roman Forum, a mass of ruins overgrown with weeds and trees that was the commercial, civil, and religious center of ancient Rome. Its large ceremonial buildings included three triumphal arches, two public halls, half a dozen temples, and numerous monuments and statues. Set in what was once a marshy valley at the foot of the Capitoline Hill, the Forum was abandoned after the barbarian invasions and had become a cattle pasture by the Renaissance. When excavations began during the last century, it was under 20 feet of dirt.

Highlights of the Forum include the triumphal Arch of Septimius Severus, built by that emperor in AD 203; the Arch of Titus (AD 81), adorned with scenes depicting the victories of Titus, especially his conquest of Jerusalem and the spoils of Solomon's Temple; the ten magnificent marble columns — with a 16th-century baroque façade — of the Temple of Antoninus and Faustina; the eight columns of the Temple of Saturn (497 BC), site of the Saturnalia, the precursor of our Mardi Gras; three splendid Corinthian columns of the Temple of Castor and Pollux (484 BC); the Temple of Vesta and the nearby House of the Vestal Virgins, where highly esteemed virgins guarded the sacred flame of Vesta and their virginity — under the threat of being buried alive if they lost the latter. The once imposing Basilica of Maxentius (Basilica di Massenzio), otherwise known as the Basilica of Constantine, because it was begun by one and finished by the other, still has imposing proportions: 328 by 249 feet. Only the north aisle and three huge arches remain of this former law court and exchange.

As this is one of the most bewildering archaeological sites, a guide is extremely useful, especially for short-term visitors. A detailed plan and portable sound guide are available at the entrance. Open from 9 AM to 3 PM. Closed Tuesdays. Admission charge includes the Palatine Hill. Entrance on Via dei Fori Imperiali, opposite Via Cavour.

Fori Imperiali (Imperial Forums) – Next to the Roman Forum and now divided in two by Via dei Fori Imperiali is the civic center begun by Caesar to meet the demands of the expanding city when the Roman Forum became too congested. It was completed by Augustus, with further additions by later emperors. Abandoned in the Middle Ages, the Imperial Forums were revived by Mussolini, who constructed Via dei Fori Imperiali in 1932.

Two of the major sights are Trajan's Forum and Trajan's Market. Trajan's Forum, although not open to visitors, can be seen from the sidewalk surrounding it. It is memorable for the formidable 138-foot-high Trajan's Column, composed of 19 blocks of marble, now beautifully restored. The column is decorated with a spiral frieze depicting the Roman army under Trajan during the campaign against the Dacians — some 2,500 figures climbing toward the top where, since 1588, a statue of St. Peter has stood instead of the original one of Trajan. The Market (entered at 94 Via IV Novembre) is a 3-story construction with about 150 shops and commercial exchanges. Admission charge for Trajan's Market (closed Sunday afternoons and Mondays). Via dei Fori Imperiali.

Carcere Mamertino (Mamertine Prison) – Just off Via dei Fori Imperiali between the Roman Forum and the Campidoglio is the prison where Vercingetorix died and where, according to legend, St. Peter was imprisoned by Nero and used a miraculous spring to baptize his fellow inmates. From 509 to 27 BC it was a state prison where many were tortured and slaughtered. Much later, the prison became a chapel consecrated to St. Peter (called *San Pietro in Carcere*). To Charles Dickens it was a "ponderous, obdurate old prison . . . hideous and fearsome to behold." The gloomy dungeons below, made of enormous blocks of stone, may be the oldest structures in Rome. Via San Pietro in Carcere off Via dei Fori Imperiali.

Circo Massimo (Circus Maximus) – A few ruins dot the open grassy valley that once was the site of the great 4th-century BC arena. Originally ⅓ of a mile long and big enough to accommodate 250,000 spectators, the horseshoe shape of this racetrack served as a pattern for the other circuses that later arose in the Roman world. Today, the obelisks that decorated a long central shelf can be seen in Rome's Piazza del Laterano and Piazza del Popolo. The medieval tower that still stands is one of the few remains of the great fortresses built by the Frangipane family. Behind the Palatine Hill.

Pantheon – This, the best preserved of Roman buildings, was founded in 27 BC by Agrippa, who probably dedicated it to the seven planetary divinities, and rebuilt by Hadrian in AD 125. It became a Christian church in 606 and contains the tombs of Raphael and the first two Kings of Italy. The building is remarkable for its round plan combined with a Greek-style rectangular porch of 16 Corinthian columns (3 were replaced in the Renaissance), for the ingenuity evident in the construction of the dome, and for its balanced proportions (the diameter of the interior and the height of the dome are the same). Closed Mondays. Piazza della Rotonda.

Terme di Caracalla (Baths of Caracalla) – These ruins are in the southern part of the city, near the beginning of the Appia Antica. Built in the 3rd century, they accommodated 1,600 bathers, but all that's left are sun-baked walls and some wall paintings. The vast scale makes a picturesque ruin, however, and Shelley composed *Prometheus Unbound* here. In summer, a stage and bleachers go up and the baths become the site of the Rome Opera's outdoor opera season — although because of protests by archaeologists, the future of opera at Caracalla is in question. Closed Mondays. Enter on Viale delle Terme di Caracalla, just short of Piazzale Numa Pompilio.

Porta San Sebastiano (St. Sebastian Gate) – This majestic opening in the 3rd-century Aurelian Walls (which encircle the city of Rome for 12 miles, with 383 defense towers) marks the beginning of the Appia Antica. It was, in fact, originally called the Porta Appia, and was rebuilt in the 5th century and restored again in the 6th century. Every Sunday morning, guided tours walk along the walls from Porta San Sebastiano to Porta Latina, affording good views of the Baths of Caracalla, the Appia Antica, and the Alban hills in the distance. The *Museo delle Mura* (Museum of the Walls), incorporated into the two medieval towers of the gate, contains local archaeological finds. Open Tuesdays through Saturdays from 9 AM to 1:30 PM; Tuesdays, Thursdays, and Saturdays from 4 to 7 PM; and Sundays from 9 AM to 1 PM. 18 Porta San Sebastiano.

Via Appia Antica (Appian Way) – Portions of this famous 2,300-year-old road are still paved with the well-laid stones of the Romans. By 190 BC the Appian Way extended all the way from Rome to Capua, Benevento, and Brindisi on Italy's southeastern coast. Although its most famous sights are the Catacombs (see below), many other interesting ruins are scattered along the first 10 miles (16 km) of the route, which were used as a graveyard by patrician families because Roman law forbade burial (but not cremation) within the walls. Among the sights worth seeing is the Domine Quo Vadis chapel, about ½ mile beyond Porta San Sebastiano. It was built in the mid-9th century on the site where St. Peter, fleeing from Nero, had a vision of Christ. St. Peter said "Domine quo vadis?" ("Lord, whither goest thou?"). Christ replied that he was going back to Rome to be crucified again because Peter had abandoned the Christians in a moment of danger. Peter then returned to Rome to face his own martyrdom. Also see the Tomb of Cecilia Metella, daughter of a Roman general, a very picturesque ruin not quite 2 miles (3 km) from Porta San Sebastiano.

Catacombe di San Callisto (Catacombs of St. Calixtus) – Of all the catacombs in Rome, these are the most famous. Catacombs are burial places in the form of galleries, or tunnels — miles of them, arranged in as many as five tiers — carved underground. Marble or terra-cotta slabs mark the openings where the bodies were laid to rest. Early Christians hid, prayed, and were buried in them from the 1st through the 4th centuries. After Christianity became the official religion of Rome, they were no longer necessary, but they remained places of pilgrimage because they contain the remains of so many early martyrs. St. Cecilia, St. Eusebius, and many martyred popes are buried here. Take a guided bus tour or a public bus. At the catacombs, guides, who are often priests, conduct regular tours in several languages. Closed Wednesdays. Admission charge. 110 Via Appia Antica.

Terme di Diocleziano (Baths of Diocletian) – West of the center of Rome, not far from the train station, are the largest baths in the empire, built in AD 305 to hold 3,000 people. The site now houses both the *Church of Santa Maria degli Angeli,* adapted by Michelangelo from the hall of the tepidarium of the baths, and the *Museo Nazionale Romano* (National Museum of Rome). The museum, one of the great archaeological museums of the world, contains numerous objects from ancient Rome — paintings, statuary, stuccowork, bronzes, objects of art, and even a mummy of a young girl. Admission to the museum, which is closed Mondays. The church is on Piazza della Repubblica; museum entrance is on Piazza dei Cinquecento.

Castel Sant'Angelo – Dramatically facing the 2nd-century Ponte Sant'Angelo (St. Angelo Bridge — lined with statues of angels, including two originals by Bernini), this imposing monument was built by Hadrian in AD 139 as a burial place for himself and his family, but it has undergone many alterations, including the addition of the square wall with bastions at each corner named after the four evangelists. Later, as a fortress and prison, it saw a lot of history, especially in the 16th century. Some of the victims of the Borgias met their end here, popes took refuge here from antipapal forces (an underground passage connects it to the Vatican), and Benvenuto Cellini spent time as a prisoner on the premises. The last act of Puccini's opera *Tosca* takes place here. It is now a museum containing relics, works of art, ancient weapons, a prison cell, and a recently restored, 300-year-old papal bathtub. Closed Mondays. Admission charge. Lungotevere Castello.

Teatro di Marcello (Theater of Marcellus) – Begun by Caesar, completed by Augustus, and named after the latter's nephew, this was the first stone theater in Rome and was said to have been the model for the Colosseum. It seated from 10,000 to 14,000 spectators and was in use for over 300 years. During the Middle Ages, what remained of the edifice became a fortress, and during the 16th century, the Savelli family transformed it into a palace, which later passed to the powerful Orsini family. The sumptuous apartments at the top are still inhabited by the Orsinis, whose device of a bear (*orso*) appears on the gateway in Via di Monte Savello, where the theater's stage once stood. Via del Teatro di Marcello. The palace can be visited only with a permit from City Hall: *Comune di Roma,* Ripartizione X, 29 Via del Portico d'Ottavia.

Largo Argentina – Just west of Piazza Venezia are the remains of four Roman temples, which, still unidentified, are among the oldest relics in Rome. It was at this site that Julius Caesar was actually assassinated (the Senate was temporarily meeting here because of fire damage to the Forum). The area is also the home of Rome's largest stray cat colony. Corso Vittorio Emanuele II.

Piramide di Caio Cestio (Pyramid of Caius Cestius) – In the southern part of the city, near the Protestant Cemetery, is Rome's only pyramid. Completely covered with white marble, 121 feet high, it has a burial chamber inside decorated with frescoes and inscriptions. (Note: the interior can be visited only with special permission from the *Sovrintendenza Comunale ai Musei,* Monumenti, 3 Piazza Caffarelli.) Piazzale Ostiense.

PAPAL ROME

Città del Vaticano (Vatican City) – The Vatican City State, the world's second smallest country (the smallest is also in Rome, the Sovereign Military Order of Malta, on Via Condotti), fits into a land area of less than 1 square mile within the city of Rome. Headquarters of the Roman Catholic Church, the Vatican has been an independent state under the sovereignty of the pope since the Lateran Treaties were concluded in 1929. The Vatican has its own printing press and newspaper (*Osservatore Romano*), its own currency, railway, and radio station, as well as its own post office and postage stamps (thriving right now, with the surrounding Italian post offices functioning so badly, so do all your mailing from here! Vatican stamps may be used in Rome but not elsewhere in Italy, while Italian stamps may *not* be used in Vatican mailboxes). Its extraterritorial rights cover the other major basilicas (Santa Maria Maggiore, San Giovanni in Laterano, and San Paolo Fuori le Mura), the pope's summer home at Castel Gandolfo, and a few other buildings. The Vatican is governed politically by the pope and protected by an army of Swiss Guards whose uniforms were designed by Michelangelo.

General audiences are held by the pope every Wednesday on St. Peter's Square (at 10 AM during the summer; 11 AM in winter); in bad weather they are held in the Sala Udienza Paolo VI. Special audiences can be arranged for groups of 25 to 50 persons. Given John Paul II's propensity for travel, however, it is a good idea to check on his whereabouts before trekking off to the Vatican to see him. From March to October, guided tours are offered of the Vatican Gardens (Fridays; $6.50), the gardens and basilica (Tuesdays and Saturdays; $7), and the gardens and Sistine Chapel (Mondays and Thursdays; about $13). During the winter, tours of the gardens are on Tuesdays, Thursdays, and Saturdays. Behind-the-scenes tours have recently been offered to places within the Vatican that are usually closed to the public (such as the mosaic school, radio station, and railway terminal). Tours leave at 10 AM; it is advisable to purchase tickets in advance and to book an English-speaking guide. Buy the tickets at the *Vatican Tourist Information Office* on the left side of St. Peter's Square, facing the church.

Piazza San Pietro (St. Peter's Square) – This 17th-century architectural masterpiece was created by Gian Lorenzo Bernini, the originator of the baroque style in Rome. The vast, open area is elliptical, with two semicircular colonnades, each four deep in Doric columns, framing the façade of St. Peter's Basilica. The colonnades are surmounted with statues of saints. An 83½-foot obelisk, brought from Heliopolis to Rome by Caligula, marks the center of the square and is flanked by two fountains that are still fed by the nearly 4-century-old Acqua Paola aqueduct. Find the circular paving stone between the obelisk and one of the fountains and turn toward a colonnade: From that vantage point it will appear to be only a single row of columns.

Basilica di San Pietro (St. Peter's Basilica) – The first church here was built by Constantine on the site where St. Peter was martyred and subsequently buried. Some 11 centuries later it was the worse for wear, so renovation and then total reconstruction were undertaken. Michelangelo deserves a great deal of the credit for the existing church, but not all of it: Bramante began the plans in the early 16th century, with the dome of the Pantheon in mind; Michelangelo finished them in mid-century, thinking of Brunelleschi's dome in Florence. Giacomo della Porta took over the project at Michelangelo's death, actually raising the dome by the end of the century. In the early 17th century, Carlo Maderno made some modifications to the structure and completed the façade, and by the middle of the century Bernini was working on his colonnades. The vast dome of St. Peter's is visible from nearly everywhere in the city, just as the entire city is visible from the summit of the dome. For a fee, a visitor may go up into the dome by elevator, then take a staircase to the top for a panoramic view of Rome or a bird's-eye view of the pope's backyard.

The door farthest to the right of the portico is the Holy Door, opened and closed by the pope at the beginning and end of each Jubilee Year, usually only four times a century. The door farthest to the left is by the modern Italian sculptor Giacomo Manzù and dates from the 1960s. Among the treasures and masterpieces inside the basilica are the famous *Pietà* by Michelangelo (now encased in bulletproof glass since its mutilation and restoration several years ago); the *Baldacchino* by Bernini, a colossal baroque amalgam of architecture and decorative sculpture weighing 46 tons; and the 13th-century statue of St. Peter by Arnolfo Di Cambio, his toes kissed smooth by the faithful. The interior of St. Peter's is gigantic and so overloaded with decoration that it takes some time to get a sense of the whole. Piazza San Pietro.

Musei Vaticani (Vatican Museums) – The Vatican's museum complex houses one of the most impressive collections in the world, embracing works of art of every epoch. It also contains some masterpieces created on the spot, foremost of which is the extraordinary Sistine Chapel, with Michelangelo's frescoes of the *Creation* on the ceiling (painted from 1508 to 1512) and his *Last Judgment* on the altar wall (1534 to 1541). The highly controversial restoration (sponsored by Japan's largest TV network) took 8 years, and the removal of centuries of soot revealed unexpected vibrancy in Michelangelo's use of color. A new lighting system was installed in the chapel and footnotes are being added to art histories.

While Michelangelo was painting the Sistine Chapel ceiling for Pope Julius II, the 25-year-old Raphael was working on the Stanza della Segnatura, one of the magnificent Raphael Rooms commissioned by the same pope, which would occupy the painter until his death. Also part of the Vatican museum complex are the *Pio-Clementino Museum of Greco-Roman Antiquities,* which houses such marvelous statues as *Laocoön and His Sons* and the *Apollo Belvedere;* the *Gregorian Etruscan Museum;* the *Pinacoteca* or Picture Gallery; the Library; and the new Gregorian Profane, Pio-Cristiano, and Missionary-Ethnological sectors. Open 9 AM to 2 PM (longer in summer); closed Sundays except the last Sunday of the month, when the complex is open at no charge; other times there is an admission charge. Entrance on Viale Vaticano (phone: 698-3333).

San Giovanni in Laterano (Church of St. John Lateran) – Founded by Pope Melchiades in the 4th century, this is the cathedral of Rome, the pope's parish church, in effect. It suffered barbarian vandalism, an earthquake, and several fires across the centuries; its interior was largely rebuilt in the 17th century by Borromini, who maintained the 16th-century wooden ceiling (the principal façade belongs to the 18th century). Older sections are the lovely cloisters, dating from the 13th century, and the baptistry, from the time of Constantine. The adjoining Lateran Palace was built in the 15th century on the site of an earlier one that had been the home of the popes from Constantine's day to the Avignon Captivity and that had been destroyed by fire. In front of the palace and church are the Scala Santa (Holy Stairs), traditionally believed to have come from the palace of Pontius Pilate in Jerusalem and to have been climbed by Christ at the time of the Passion. The 28 marble steps, climbed by worshipers on their knees, lead to the Sancta Sanctorum, once the popes' private chapel (not open to the public, but visible through the grating). Both the chapel and the stairs were part of the earlier Lateran Palace but survived the fire. Also in the piazza is the oldest obelisk in Rome. Piazza di San Giovanni in Laterano.

Santa Maria Maggiore (Church of St. Mary Major) – A 5th-century church, rebuilt in the 13th century, with an 18th-century façade and the tallest campanile in Rome. It has particularly interesting 5th-century mosaics and a ceiling that was, according to tradition, gilded with the first gold to arrive from the New World. Piazza di Santa Maria Maggiore.

PIAZZAS, PALACES, AND OTHER SIGHTS

Piazza del Campidoglio – The Capitoline was the smallest of the original seven hills, but since it was the political and religious center of ancient Rome, it was also the most important. When the need arose in the 16th century for some modern city planning, the task was given to someone worthy of the setting. Thus, the harmonious square seen today, with its delicate, elliptical, star-patterned pavement centered on a magnificent 2nd-century bronze equestrian statue of Marcus Aurelius (removed for restoration), is the design of none other than Michelangelo. The piazza is flanked by palaces on three sides: Palazzo Nuovo and Palazzo dei Conservatori, facing each other and together making up the *Musei Capitolini* (Capitoline Museums), and the Palazzo Senatorio, between the two, which houses officials of the municipal government. The *Capitoline Museums* are famous for an especially valuable collection of antique sculptures, including the *Capitoline Venus,* the *Dying Gaul,* a bronze statue (known as the *Spinario*) of a boy removing a thorn from his foot, and the *Capitoline Wolf,* an Etruscan bronze to which Romulus and Remus were added during the Renaissance. The museums are closed Sunday afternoons and Mondays. Admission charge.

Piazza di Spagna (Spanish Steps) – One of the most picturesque settings of 18th-century Rome was named after a palace that housed the Spanish Embassy to the Holy See. The famous Spanish Steps were actually built by the French to connect the French quarter above with the Spanish area below. One of Rome's fine French churches, Trinità dei Monti, hovers over the 138 steps at the top, as does an ancient obelisk placed there by Pius VI in 1789. At the bottom of the steps — which in the spring are covered with hundreds of pots of azaleas — is the Barcaccia fountain, depicting a sinking barge, inspired by the Tiber's flooding in 1589. Modern art historians disagree on whether this fountain, the oldest architectural feature of the square, was designed by Pietro Bernini or his son, the famous Gian Lorenzo Bernini.

Over the years, the steps have become a haunt of large crowds of young visitors, and all manner of crafts sales, caricature sketchers, and musicians contribute to the throng. The house where John Keats spent the last 3 months of his life and died, in February 1821, is next to the Spanish Steps at #26. It is now the *Keats-Shelley Memorial House,* a museum dedicated to the English Romantic poets, especially Keats, Shelley, Byron, and Leigh Hunt, with a library of more than 9,000 volumes of their works. The exterior is currently under restoration. Closed weekends. Admission charge.

Via Condotti – A sort of Fifth Avenue of Rome, lined with the city's most exclusive shops, including *Gucci, Bulgari,* and *Ferragamo.* Only a few blocks long, it begins at the foot of the Spanish Steps, ends at Via del Corso, and is a favorite street for window shopping and the ritual evening *passeggiata,* or promenade, since it is — like much of the area — closed to traffic. Via Condotti's name derives from the water conduits built under it by Gregory XIII in the 16th century.

One of Via Condotti's landmarks is the famous *Caffè Greco,* at #86, long a hangout for Romans and foreigners. Among its habitués were Goethe, Byron, Liszt, Buffalo Bill, Mark Twain, Oscar Wilde, and the Italian painter Giorgio de Chirico. The place is full of busts, statues, and varied mementos of its clientele, and the somber waiters still dress in tails. Another landmark, at #68, is the smallest sovereign state in the world, consisting of one historic palazzo. If you peek into its charming courtyard, you'll see cars with number plates bearing the letters SMOM (the Sovereign Military Order of Malta). Besides its own licenses, the order, founded during the Crusades, also issues a few passports and has its own diplomatic service and small merchant fleet.

Piazza del Popolo – This semicircular square at the foot of the Pincio was designed in neo-classical style by Valadier between 1816 and 1820. At its center is the second oldest obelisk in Rome, dating from the 13th century BC. Twin-domed churches (Santa Maria di Montesanto and Santa Maria dei Miracoli) face a ceremonial gate where the Via Flaminia enters Rome. Next to the gate is the remarkable early Renaissance church of Santa Maria del Popolo, an artistic treasure containing two paintings by Caravaggio, sculptures by Bernini, and frescoes by Pinturicchio, among others. The piazza's two open-air cafés, *Rosati* and *Canova,* are favorite meeting places.

Piazza Navona – This harmonious ensemble of Roman baroque is today a favorite haunt of Romans and tourists alike. It is also one of Rome's most historic squares, built on the site of Domitian's stadium. In the center is Bernini's fine *Fontana dei Quattro Fiumi* (Fountain of the Four Rivers), the huge figures representing the Nile, Ganges, Danube, and Plata. On the west side of the square is the church of Sant'Agnese in Agone, much of it the work of a Bernini assistant, Borromini. There was little love lost between the two men, and according to a popular local legend, the hand of the Plata figure is raised in self-defense, just in case the façade of the church falls down, while the Nile figure hides under a veil to avoid seeing Borromini's mistakes. However, since the fountain was completed a year before the church was begun, the story doesn't hold water. From the 17th to the mid-19th century, the square would be flooded on August weekends, and the aristocrats of the city would cool off by splashing through the water in their carriages. Nowadays, during the Christmas season, until Epiphany, it is lined with booths selling sweets, toys, and nativity figures.

Piazza Farnese – This square is dominated by Palazzo Farnese, the most beautiful 16th-century palace in Rome. Commissioned by Cardinal Alessandro Farnese (later Pope Paul III), it was begun in 1514 by Sangallo the Younger, continued by Michelangelo, and completed by Della Porta in 1589. Opera fans will know it as the location of Scarpia's apartment in the second act of Puccini's *Tosca.* Today it is occupied by the French Embassy and can be visited only with special permission. The two fountains on the square incorporate bathtubs of Egyptian granite brought from the Baths of Caracalla.

Piazza Campo dei Fiori – Very near Piazza Farnese, one of Rome's most colorful squares is the scene of a general market every morning. In the center — surrounded by delicious cheeses, salamis, ripe fruit and vegetables, and *fiori* (flowers) of every kind — is a statue of the philosopher Giordano Bruno, who was burned at the stake here for heresy in 1600. Watch your wallet — this is a hangout for thieves.

Piazza Mattei – A delightful clearing on the edge of the ancient Jewish ghetto, this small square's famous *Fontana delle Tartarughe* (Fountain of the Tortoises), sculpted in 1585 by Taddeo Landini, is one of Rome's most delightful. Four naked boys lean against the base and toss life-size bronze tortoises into a marble bowl above. The water moves in several directions, creating a magical effect in the tiny square.

Piazza del Quirinale – The Quirinal Palace was built by the popes in the late 16th to early 17th century as a summer residence, became the royal palace after the unification of Italy, and is now the official residence of the president of Italy. The so-called *Monte Cavallo* (Horse Tamers') *Fountain* is composed of two groups of statues depicting Castor and Pollux with their horses and a granite basin from the Forum once used as a cattle trough. The obelisk in the center is from the Mausoleum of Augustus. The square affords a marvelous view of Rome and St. Peter's.

Fontana di Trevi (Trevi Fountain) – Designed by Nicola Salvi and completed in 1762, the Trevi Fountain took 30 years to build and is the last important monumental baroque work in Rome. Incongruously situated in a tiny square tucked away amidst narrow, cobblestoned streets, the magnificent fountain is quite striking when you suddenly come upon it at the turn of a corner. Extensive restoration work is under way on the fountain, but you can see the colossal Oceanus in stone that rides a chariot drawn by seahorses and is surrounded by a fantasy of gods, tritons, and horses. According to legend, you will return to Rome if you throw a coin over your left shoulder into the fountain. Young Roman men like to congregate in the small square on summer evenings, trying to pick up foreign girls. Some prefer to pick your pocket — so be careful. Piazza di Trevi.

Piazza Barberini – At the foot of Via Veneto, this square in northern Rome has two of Bernini's famous fountains: the *Triton Fountain* in travertine, representing a triton sitting upon a scallop shell supported by four dolphins and blowing a conch; and the *Fountain of the Bees* on the corner of the Veneto, with three Barberini bees (of that family's crest) on the edge of a pool spurting thin jets of water into the basin below.

Villa Borghese (Borghese Gardens) – In the northern section of the city, this is Rome's most magnificent park, with hills, lakes, villas, and vistas. It is the former estate of Cardinal Scipione Borghese, designed for him in the 17th century and enlarged in the 18th century. Two museums are here: the recently reopened *Galleria Borghese,* housed in the cardinal's small palace and noted for its Caravaggios, its Bernini sculptures, and Antonio Canova's statue of the reclining *Pauline Borghese;* and the *Galleria Nazionale d'Arte Moderna,* with its Italian modern works. The Villa Borghese is a wonderful place to sit in the shade of an umbrella pine on a hot summer day. Enter through the Porta Pinciana, at the top of Via Veneto, or walk up to the Pincio from Piazza del Popolo. The main entrance is at Piazzale Flaminio, just outside the Porta del Popolo.

Cimitero Protestante (Protestant Cemetery) – In the southern part of the city, behind the pyramid of Caius Cestius, the Protestant Cemetery is principally a foreign enclave that harbors the remains of many adopted non-Catholics who chose to live and die in Rome: Keats, Shelley, Trelawny, Goethe's bastard son, and the Italian Communist leader Gramsci. There is nothing sad here — no pathos, no morbid sense of death — and few gardens are so delightful on a spring morning. 6 Via Caio Cestio.

Synagogue – Along the Lungotevere Cenci, in the former Ghetto, it also houses a permanent exhibition of ritual objects from the 16th to the 19th century, plus documents of recent history. Open daily except Saturdays and on Jewish holidays. Via Lungotevere Cenci.

MODERN ROME

Monumento a Vittorio Emanuele II (Monument to Victor Emmanuel II) – Sometimes called the Vittoriano, this most conspicuous landmark of questionable taste was completed in 1911 to celebrate the unification of Italy. Built of white Brescian marble and overwhelming the Capitoline Hill, it is often derided by Romans as the "wedding cake" or the "typewriter." It contains Italy's Tomb of the Unknown Soldier from World War I, and from the top you can see the network of modern boulevards built by Mussolini to open out the site of ancient Rome: Via dei Fori Imperiali, Via di San Gregorio, Via del Teatro di Marcello, and Via Nazionale — a busy and somewhat chaotic shopping street leading to the railroad station. Turn your back to the monument and note the 15th-century Palazzo Venezia to your left. It was from the small balcony of this building, his official residence, that Mussolini made his speeches. Piazza Venezia.

Via Vittorio Veneto – Popularly known as Via Veneto, this wide, café-lined street winds from a gate in the ancient Roman wall, the Porta Pinciana, down past the American Embassy to Piazza Barberini. The portion around Via Boncompagni is elegant, but the street also attracts a mixed crowd — from down-and-out actors and decadent Roman nobility to seedy gigolos and male prostitutes. Well-to-do Americans still stay in the fine hotels. The entire area, including the adjacent Via Bissolati with its many foreign airline offices, is well patrolled by police.

Porta Portese – Rome's flea market takes place on the edge of Trastevere on Sundays from dawn to about 1 or 2 PM. It's a colorful, chaotic happening. Genuine antiques are few and far between, quickly scooped up before most people are out of bed. Still, you'll find some interesting junk, secondhand clothes, shoes, jeans, items brought by East European immigrants, pop records, used tires and car parts, black market cigarettes — everything from Sicilian puppets to old postcards, sheet music, and broken bidets. Some say that if your wallet is stolen at the entrance, you'll find it for sale near the exit. Via Portuense.

OUT OF TOWN

Esposizione Universale di Roma (EUR) – Mussolini's ultramodern quarter was designed southwest of the center for an international exhibition that was supposed to take place in 1942 but never did. It's now a fashionable garden suburb and the site of international congresses and trade shows as well as of some remarkable sports installations built for the Olympic Games of 1960, including the Palazzo dello Sport, with a dome by Pier Luigi Nervi. The *Museo della Civiltà Romana* (Museum of Roman Civilization) is worth seeing for its thorough reconstruction of ancient Rome at the time of Constantine. Closed Mondays. Admission charge. 10 Piazza Giovanni Agnelli (phone: 592-6135).

Ostia Antica – This immense excavation site about 15 miles (24 km) southwest of Rome was once the great trading port of ancient Rome, much closer to the mouth of the Tiber than it is today. Fairly recently uncovered, the ruins are picturesquely surrounded with pines and cypresses. They have not had much chance to crumble, and they reveal a great deal about the building methods of the Romans and the management of a far-flung empire.

A visit takes about half a day. Among the chief sites are the Piazzale delle Corporazioni (Corporations' Square), once 70 commercial offices, with mottoes and emblems in mosaics revealing that the merchants were shipwrights, caulkers, ropemakers, furriers, and shipowners from all over the ancient world; the capitolium and forum, baths, apartment blocks, and several private houses, especially the House of Cupid and Psyche; and the restored theater, used in the summer to present classical plays in Italian translation. Recent excavations have brought evidence of the town's Jewish community. Take the Decumanus Maximus to the end, turn left, and a few hundred yards away, on what was once the seashore, a synagogue stands, a moving testimonial to the Jewish presence in Rome in earliest times. A local museum traces the development of Ostia Antica and displays some outstanding statues, busts, and frescoes. Closed Mondays. Admission charge. To reach Ostia Antica, take the *metropolitana* (not all trains, however) from Stazione Termini, a train from Stazione Ostiense, an ACOTRAL bus from Via Giolitti, or a car.

The Lido di Ostia or Lido di Roma is 2½ miles (4 km) southwest of Ostia. It's the most popular, most polluted, and most crowded seaside resort close to the city. Although there are more pleasant beaches both north and south of Rome, pollution has been so bad in recent years that swimming has been banned at many of them.

Castelli Romani – Rome's "castles" are actually 13 hill towns set in the lovely Alban Hills region southeast of Rome, an area where popes and powerful families of the past built fortresses, palaces, and other retreats. The mountains, the volcanic lakes of Nemi and Albano, chestnut groves, olive trees, and vines producing the famous Castelli wine continuè to make the area a favorite destination of Romans who want to get away from the city on a fine day. Particularly charming are Frascati, known for its villas and its wines; Grottaferrata, famous for its fortified monastery, which can be visited; beautiful Lake Nemi, with its vivid blue waters and wooded surroundings, where Diana was worshiped; and Monte Cavo, a mountain whose summit can be reached by a toll road and which offers a panorama of the Castelli from a height of 3,124 feet. The Castelli Romani are best seen on an organized tour or by car. (For more information and a suggested itinerary, see Lazio in DIRECTIONS.)

■**EXTRA SPECIAL:** Fountain fans should not miss Tivoli, a charming town perched on a hill and on a tributary of the Tiber (the Aniene) about 20 miles (32 km) east of Rome. It's famous for its villas, gardens, and, above all, cascading waters — all immortalized by Fragonard's 18th-century landscapes. Called *Tibur* by the ancient Romans, it was even then a resort for wealthy citizens, who bathed in its thermal waters, which remain therepeutic to this day.

The *Villa d'Este,* built for a cardinal in the 16th century, is the prime attraction — or, rather, its terraced gardens are. They contain some 500 fountains, large and small, including the jets of water lining the famous Avenue of the Hundred Fountains and the huge Organ Fountain, so named because it once worked a hydraulic organ. The villa and gardens are open to the public daily (admission charge); on summer nights the fountains are beautifully illuminated, and there's a sound-and-light show. Nearby, the *Villa Gregoriana,* built by Pope Gregory XVI in the 19th century, has sloping gardens and lovely cascades (which are best on Sundays, since most of the water is used for industrial purposes on other days), but it is definitely to be seen only after you have seen the *Villa d'Este.* It, too, is open daily; admission charge.

Only 4 miles (6½ km) southwest of Tivoli is *Villa Adriana* (Hadrian's Villa), the most sumptuous of the villas left from ancient Roman times. It was built from AD 125 to 134 by the Emperor Hadrian, whose pleasure was to strew the grounds with replicas of famous buildings he had seen elsewhere in his empire. Extensively excavated and surrounded by greenery, the ruins of the villa include the *Maritime Theater,* built on an island and surrounded by a canal; the Golden Square in front of the remains of the palace; and the Terrace of Tempe, with a view of the valley of the same name. There are statues, fountains, cypress-lined avenues, pools, lakes, and canals. Closed Mondays; admission charge. You can see Tivoli with a guided tour or take an ACOTRAL bus from Via Gaeta or a train from Stazione Termini. *Villa Adriana* can also be reached by bus from Via Gaeta, but note that while one bus, leaving every hour, stops first at *Villa Adriana* and then at Tivoli, the other, goes directly to Tivoli and entails getting off at a cross-roads and walking about a half-mile to *Villa Adriana.*

SOURCES AND RESOURCES

TOURIST INFORMATION: The Ente Provinciale per il Turismo (EPT) for Rome and Lazio, headquartered at 11 Via Parigi (phone: 461851), has its main information office at 5 Via Parigi (phone: 463748), with branches at Stazione Termini and in the customs area at Leonardo da Vinci Airport at Fiumicino. There are also branches at the Feronia "Punto Blu" and Frascati Est service areas of the A1 and A2 highways, respectively, for those arriving by car. All branches stock various booklets, maps, and hotel listings, all free. Ask for the monthly listing of events, *Carnet.*

The US Embassy and consulate are at 119/A and 121 Via Vittorio Veneto respectively (phone: 46741).

For some good background material about Rome, see Georgina Masson's *Companion Guide to Rome* and Eleanor Clark's *Rome and a Villa,* both useful and amusing. A locally published book on the city's hidden treasures, *In Rome They Say,* by Margherita Naval, is also good reading; 30 walks through the city are described and mapped in *The Heart of Rome.* There are several English-language bookstores in the Spanish Steps area: the *Lion Bookshop,* 181 Via del Babuino, *Anglo-American Book Company,* 57 Via della Vite, and the *Bookshelf,* 23 Via Due Macelli (in the Tritone Gallery). The *Economy Book Center,* 136 Via Torino, is particularly good for paperbacks.

Local Coverage – The *International Herald Tribune,* now also printed in Rome, is available at most newsstands each morning; it often lists major events in Italy in its Saturday "Weekend" section. *A Guest in Rome* is published by the Golden Key Association of Concierges. Available at newsstands are *Going Places and Doing Things,* complete with maps, museum listings, and such; and *This Week in Rome. La Repubblica* and *Il Messaggero* are the two local daily newspapers that list local events; the former has an interesting Saturday supplement called "TrovaRoma" that lists the week's events, shows, theater, new movies, and more. *Wanted in Rome* is a useful handout found in American shops and schools.

Food – *La Guida d'Italia* is a comprehensive guide to restaurants and wine shops in Rome and throughout Italy. In Italian, it is published by L'Espresso and available at newsstands.

Telephone – The area code for Rome is 06.

 CLIMATE AND CLOTHES: Generally, it should be hot from mid-June through September, and only very light clothing is needed. Average temperatures in July and August hover around 82F (27C), but a heavy sirocco wind from the African deserts often brings the maximum above 100F (38C). (Don't always expect air conditioning.) Fortunately, Romans are quite informal, except for very special occasions, and men rarely wear jackets or ties in the summer. Women should be careful when visiting churches, where immodest dress (bare shoulders included) is frowned upon if not downright forbidden. A refreshing breeze often offers relief on summer evenings, making a light wrap advisable. Winters are moderate, with temperatures averaging 47F (8C) from December through February. Although snow is very rare and it seldom drops below freezing, the *tramontana* wind from the north can be very chilling (definitely overcoat weather); winter rains can be heavy.

 GETTING AROUND: Airports – Leonardo da Vinci Airport in Fiumicino (phone: 60121), about 21 miles from downtown Rome, handles both international and domestic traffic. Check in at least a half-hour before flights and allow waiting time in line, or you risk losing your reservation. In only moderate traffic, taxi travel time to the city is about 45 minutes and will cost about $40, with additional costs for baggage, night — after 10 PM — and holiday trips). ACOTRAL buses run between the airport and the city air terminal on the Via Giolitti side of Stazione Termini, the central railway station. Buses leave every 15 minutes and cost about $3.50; ticket desks are clearly marked at both locations. ACOTRAL buses leave the airport every 30 minutes for the town of Cinecittà, where you can pick up the subway to Rome. Ciampino Airport handles mostly charter traffic (phone: 4694). Scheduled to open in 1990, metro service between Fiumicino and the Piranide station will carry passengers to and from Rome. Urbe Airport, is for private planes; it's a

15-minutes taxi ride from the center, and public transport (by bus) is also available from Piazza Vescorio; 825 Via Salaria (phone: 812-0524).

Bicycle and Moped – Pollution and insufferable traffic jams have made bicycling a popular alternative to driving for many Romàns. *Collalti* rents bikes at 82 Via del Pellegrino (phone: 654-1084); *Roma Rent* is at Via Vespasiano (corner of Via Germanico; phone: 310941). Others will be found at Piazza San Silvestro, above the Piazza del Popolo at the Pincio, and at Viale della Pineta and Viale dei Bambini in the Villa Borghese Gardens. To rent a moped, scooter or motorbike, try *Scoot-a-long,* 304 Via Cavour (phone: 678-0206), and *Motonoleggio,* 66 Via della Purificazione, near Piazza Barberini (phone: 465485). By law, helmets must be worn while riding scooters or motorbikes.

Boat – From April through October, weather permitting, the *Tiber I* carries 150 passengers on evening cruises along the river from Ponte Palatino (near Porta Portese) for guided stargazing. For information and reservations, phone *Tourvisa* at 445-0284 or 445-4284 or the *Associazione Amici del Tevere* (Friends of the Tiber Society) at 637-0268.

Bus – ATAC (Azienda Tramvie e Autobus Comune di Roma), the city bus company, is the rather weak backbone of Rome's public transportation system. Buses — and a few tram lines — run sporadically throughout the city, exasperating potential passengers on rainy days when traffic is at a standstill, and particularly during August when the number of buses in use is greatly reduced while drivers are on vacation. Most central routes are extremely crowded, getting off where you'd like is sometimes impossible, pickpockets are rampant, and some lines discontinue service after 9 PM, midnight, or 1 AM. Tickets, which currently cost about 50¢, must be purchased before boarding and are available at certain newsstands, tobacco shops, and bars. (Be aware that these outlets frequently exhaust their ticket supply, and the fine for riding without a ticket is about $7.50.) Remember to get on the bus via the back doors, stamp your ticket in the machine, and exit via the middle doors (the front doors are used only by *abbonati,* season ticketholders). Visitors can save money by buying half- or full-day tickets at the ATAC information booth in Piazza dei Cinquecento or at principal bus stations, such as those at Piazza San Silvestro and Piazza Risorgimento. Tourists will appreciate the new, tiny, electric-powered #119, which loops through downtown Rome between Piazza del Popolo and close to Piazza Navona, passing the Spanish Steps. Weekly tourist tickets and route maps are sold at the ATAC information booth and at the Ufficio Abbonamenti of ATAC at Largo Giovanni Montemartini. For ATAC information, phone 4695. Bus service to points out of town is run by ACOTRAL (including buses to Leonardo da Vinci Airport at Fiumicino). For ACOTRAL information, phone 57531. The Rome telephone directory's *TuttoCittà* supplement lists every street in the city and contains detailed maps of each zone as well as zip codes, bus routes, and taxi stands.

Car Rental – Major car rental firms such as *Avis,* 38/A Via Sardegna (phone: 470-1228 in Rome, 167-863063 toll-free in Italy); *Budget,* 24 Via Sistina (phone: 461905); *Europcar,* 7 Via Lombardia (phone: 688-8042); and *Hertz,* 28 Via Sallustiana (phone: 547991); as well as several reliable Italian companies such as *Maggiore,* 8/A Via Po (phone: 851620), have offices in the city and at the airport and railway stations. Note that gas stations close at lunch and at 7 PM in winter, 7:30 PM in summer. Most are closed Sundays. Self-service stations operate with 10,000-lire ($7.50) notes.

Horse-Drawn Carriages – Rome's *carrozzelle* accommodate up to five passengers and are available at major city squares (Piazza San Pietro, di Spagna, Venezia, and Navona), in front of the Colosseum, near the Trevi Fountain, on Via Veneto, and in the Villa Borghese. They can be hired by the half hour, hour, half day, or full day. Arrange the price with the driver before boarding — one hour currently costs about $40 minimum.

Subway – The *metropolitana,* Rome's subway, consists of two lines. Linea A runs roughly east-west, from an area close to the Vatican, across the Tiber, through the historic center (Piazza di Spagna, Piazza Barberini, Stazione Termini), and over to the eastern edge of the city just past Cinecittà. Linea B, which is partly an underground and partly a surface railroad, runs north-south, from Stazione Termini to the Colosseum and down to the southern suburb of EUR. The fare is about 50¢, and tickets are sold at certain newsstands, tobacco shops, and bars, as well as at most stations. Subway entrances are marked by a large red M.

Taxi – Cabs can be hailed or found at numerous stands, which are listed in the yellow pages with their phone numbers. The *Radio Taxi* telephone numbers are 3570, 3875, 4994, and 8433. Taxi rates are increasing regularly, and drivers are obliged to show you, if asked, the current list of added charges. After 10 PM, a night charge is added, and there are surcharges for holidays and for suitcases.

Train – Rome's main train station is Stazione Termini (phone: 4775 for information; 110 for reservations). There are several suburban stations, but the visitor is unlikely to use them except for Stazione Ostiense, from where trains depart for Ostia Antica and the Lido di Ostia.

 SPECIAL EVENTS: The events of the church calendar — too numerous to mention here — are extra special in Rome. For *Natale,* or Christmas, decorations go up around the city, churches display their sometimes movable, elaborate *presepi* (nativity scenes), and a colorful toy and candy fair begins in Piazza Navona. The season, including the fair, lasts until *Epiphany,* January 6, when children receive gifts from a witch known as the Befana to add to those Babbo Natale (Father Christmas) or the Bambino Gesù (Baby Jesus) brought them at Christmas. The intervening *Capodanno,* New Year's, is celebrated with a bang here as in much of the rest of Italy — firecrackers snap, crackle, and pop from early evening, and at midnight all manner of old, discarded objects come flying out of open windows. (Don't be on the street!) During the *Settimana Santa* (Holy Week), the city swarms with visitors. Religious ceremonies abound, particularly on Good Friday, when pilgrims, on their knees, climb the Scala Santa at St. John Lateran and the pope conducts the famous *Via Crucis* (Way of the Cross) procession between the Colosseum and the Palatine Hill. At noon on Easter Sunday, he pronounces the *Urbi et Orbi* blessing in St. Peter's Square. The day after Easter is *Pasquetta* (Little Easter), when Romans usually go out to the country for a picnic or an extended lunch in a rustic *trattoria.* The arrival of spring is celebrated in April with a colorful display of potted azaleas covering the Spanish Steps, and in May a picturesque street nearby, Via Margutta, is filled with an exhibition of paintings by artists of varied talents. (The Via Margutta art fair is repeated in the fall.) In May, too, Villa Borghese's lush Piazza di Siena becomes the site of the *International Horse Show,* and soon after that is the *International Tennis Championship* at Foro Italico. An antiques show also takes place in spring and fall along the charming Via dei Coronari (near Piazza Navona), and there's an *International Rose Show* at the delightful Roseto di Valle Murcia on the Aventine Hill. In late May or June the vast *Fiera di Roma,* a national industrial exhibition, takes place at the fairgrounds along Via Cristoforo Colombo. In mid-July the *Festa di Noiantri* is celebrated in one of Rome's oldest quarters, Trastevere. This is a great pagan feast, involving plenty of eating, music, and fireworks — as filmed by Fellini in his surrealistic/realistic *Roma.*

There are also innumerable characteristic *feste* or *sagre* (the latter meaning "consecrations," usually of some local food or beverage at the height of its season) in the many hill towns surrounding Rome. The *Sagra dell'Uva* (consecration of the grape) is the first Sunday in October at Marino celebrates the new vintage with grapes sold from stalls set up in the quaint old streets and wine instead of water gushing out of the fountain in the main square! Also worth seeing is the *Infiorata* at Genzano di Roma.

On a Sunday in mid-June, a brightly colored carpet of beautifully arranged flowers is laid along the entire Via Livia. Both towns are about 15 miles (24 km) south of Rome in the *Castelli Romani* (see "Out of Town" in *Special Places*).

 MUSEUMS: Many museums are described in *Special Places*. Included in the following list of additional museums are churches that should be seen because of their artistic value. Most museums are closed on Mondays and some charge no admission on Sundays. Always check the hours before setting out.

Galleria Colonna – The Colonna family collection of mainly 17th-century Italian paintings. Open Saturdays only, from 9 AM to 1 PM. Palazzo Colonna, 17 Via della Pilotta.

Galleria Doria Pamphili – The private collection of the Doria family, Italian and foreign paintings from the 15th to the 17th century. Open Tuesdays, Fridays, Saturdays, and Sundays, 10 AM to 1 PM. Palazzo Doria, 1/A Piazza del Collegio Romano.

Galleria Nazionale d'Arte Antica (National Gallery of Ancient Art) – Paintings by Italian artists from the 13th to the 18th century, plus some Dutch and Flemish works. Palazzo Barberini, 13 Via delle Quattro Fontane.

Galleria Spada – Renaissance art and Roman marble work from the 2nd and 3rd centuries. Open Tuesdays and Saturdays, 9 AM to 2 PM. Palazzo Spada, 13 Piazza Capo di Ferro.

Museo Nazionale d'Arte Orientale (National Museum of Oriental Art) – Pottery, bronzes, stone, and wooden sculpture from the Middle and Far East. 248 Via Merulana.

Museo di Palazzo Venezia (Palazzo Venezia Museum) – Tapestries, paintings, sculpture, and varied objects. 3 Piazza Venezia.

Museo di Roma (Museum of Rome) – Paintings, sculptures, and other objects illustrating the history of Rome from the Middle Ages to the present. 10 Piazza San Pantaleo.

Sant'Agostino (St. Augustine) – A 15th-century church containing the *Madonna of the Pilgrims* by Caravaggio and the *Prophet Isaiah* by Raphael. Piazza di Sant'Agostino.

Sant'Andrea al Quirinale (St. Andrew at the Quirinale) – A baroque church by Bernini, to be compared with Borromini's church on the same street. Via del Quirinale.

San Carlo alle Quattro Fontane (St. Charles at the Four Fountains) – A small baroque church by Borromini, it was designed to fit into one of the pilasters of St. Peter's. Via del Quirinale, corner Via delle Quattro Fontane.

San Clemente – An early Christian basilica with frescoes and a remarkable mosaic. Piazza di San Clemente.

San Luigi dei Francesi (St. Louis of the French) – The French national church, built in the 16th century and containing three Caravaggios. Piazza San Luigi dei Francesi.

Santa Maria d'Aracoeli (St. Mary of the Altar of Heaven) – A Romanesque-Gothic church with frescoes by Pinturicchio and a 14th-century staircase built in thanksgiving for the lifting of a plague. Piazza d'Aracoeli.

Santa Maria in Cosmedin – A Romanesque church known for the *Bocca della Verità* (Mouth of Truth) in its portico — a Roman drain cover in the shape of a face whose mouth, according to legend, will bite off the hand of anyone who has told a lie. Piazza della Bocca della Verità.

Santa Maria sopra Minerva (St. Mary over Minerva) – Built over a Roman temple, with (unusual for Rome) a Gothic interior and frescoes by Filippino Lippi. Piazza della Minerva.

Santa Maria in Trastevere – An ancient church, the first in Rome dedicated to the Virgin, with 12th- and 13th-century mosaics. Piazza Santa Maria in Trastevere.

Santa Maria della Vittoria (St. Mary of the Victory) – Baroque to the core, especially in Bernini's Cornaro Chapel. Via XX Settembre.

San Pietro in Vincoli (St. Peter in Chains) – Erected in the 5th century to preserve St. Peter's chains, this church contains Michelangelo's magnificent statue of Moses. Piazza di San Pietro in Vincoli.

Santa Sabina – A simple 5th-century basilica, with its original cypress doors and a 13th-century cloister and bell tower. Piazza Pietro d'Illiria.

Villa Giulia – A remarkable, beautifully displayed Etruscan collection in a 16th-century villa by Vignola. 9 Piazzale di Villa Giulia.

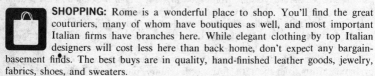

SHOPPING: Rome is a wonderful place to shop. You'll find the great couturiers, many of whom have boutiques as well, and most important Italian firms have branches here. While elegant clothing by top Italian designers will cost less here than back home, don't expect any bargain-basement finds. The best buys are in quality, hand-finished leather goods, jewelry, fabrics, shoes, and sweaters.

The chicest shopping area is around the bottom of the Spanish Steps, beginning with the elegant Via Condotti, which runs east to west and is lined with Rome's most exclusive shops, such as *Gucci, Bulgari, Beltrami,* and *Ferragamo.* Via del Babuino, which connects the Spanish Steps to Piazza del Popolo, has traditionally been better known for its antiques shops, but is coming into its own as a high-fashion street, as is nearby Via Bocca di Leone, where there are such designers' boutiques as *Valentino, Ungaro, Versace, Trussardi,* and *Yves Saint Laurent.* Running parallel to Via Condotti are several more streets, most closed to traffic, with fashionable boutiques, such as Via Borgognona (*Fendi, Versace, Missoni, Laura Biagiotti,* and *Testa*), Via delle Carrozze, Via Frattina (for men's fashions at *Testa,* women's at *Max Mara,* as well as costume jewelry, lingerie, and some ceramics), Via Vittoria, and Via della Croce (known particularly for its delicious but pricey delicatessens such as *Ercoli,* or *Fior Fiore* for cheese, bread, and cookies). All of these streets end at Via del Corso, the main street of Rome, which runs north to south and is lined with shops tending to resemble each other more and more with their offerings of the latest fashions in shoes, handbags, and sportswear, particularly along the stretch between Piazza del Popolo and Largo Chigi, where Via del Tritone begins. There are some fine shops along Via del Tritone, Via Sistina, and in the Via Veneto area.

On the other side of the river toward the Vatican are two popular shopping streets that are slightly less expensive, Via Cola di Rienzo and Via Ottaviano. Also somewhat less expensive is Via Nazionale, near the railroad station. For inexpensive new and secondhand clothes, visit the daily market on Via Sannio, near San Giovanni, and the flea market on Sunday mornings at Porta Portese. For old prints and odds and ends, try the market at Piazza della Fontanella Borghese every morning except Sunday; antiques can be found along Via del Babuino, Via dei Coronari, Via del Boverno Vecchio, Via del Governo Vecchio, Via Margutta, and Via Giulia.

The following are but a few recommended shops in Rome:

Giorgio Armani – High fashion for men and women. 102 and 139 Via del Babuino.

Bertè – Old and new toys. 107-111 Piazza Navona.

Laura Biagiotti – Elegant women's wear. 43 Via Borgognona, corner of Via Belsiana.

Bises – A place for fine fabrics. 93 Via del Gesù. Bises' *Boutique Uomo,* for men, is at 1-3-5 Corso Vittorio Emanuele.

Bomba e De Clercq – Exclusive sweaters and blouses with handcrafted details. 39 Via dell'Oca, behind Piazza del Popolo.

Borsalino – World-renowned hats. 157/B Via IV Novembre.

Buccellati – A fine jeweler with a unique way of working with gold. A store for connoisseurs. 31 Via Condotti.

Bulgari – One of the world's most famous high-style jewelers, offering fabulous creations in gold, silver, platinum, and precious stones. 10 Via Condotti.

Capodarte – The latest styles in shoes and boots — many with matching bags — and some stylish fashions for women. 14/A Via Sistina.

Davide Cenci – Classic elegance for men and women. 4-7 Campomarzio.

Cerruti 1881 – Favorite fashions for Italian yuppies. 20 Piazza San Lorenzo in Lucina.

Cesari – Household linens including, tablecloths and placemats, lingerie and beachwear. 1 Via Barberini.

Croff Centro Casa – Household supplies and gifts, some of Italian design and some imports. 197 Via Cola di Rienzo, 137 Via Tomacelli, and 52 Via XX Settembre.

Discount System – Rome's only high-fashion discount store, featuring clothing, shoes, and leather goods up to 50% off retail. 35 Via Viminale.

Fendi – Canvas and leather bags, baggage and clothing. 39 Via Borgognona; shoes and purse accessories, 4/E Via Borgognona and 55/A Largo Goldoni.

Ferragamo – For high-style women's shoes. 66 Via Condotti.

Gianfranco Ferré – High fashion for women. 6 Via Borgognona.

Filippo – An avant-garde boutique for men and women. 7 bis Via Borgognona and 6 Via Condotti.

Fiorucci – Famed, funky sportswear and shoes. 12 Via Genova, 19 Via della Farnesina, 236 Via Nazionale, 27 Via della Maddalena, and elsewhere.

Fornari – Fine silver and other gifts. 71-72 Via Frattina.

Maud Frizon – Original shoes for women, with corresponding prices. 38 Via Borgognona.

Nazareno Gabrielli – Leather goods. 3-5 Via Sant'Andrea delle Fratte and 29 Via Borgognona.

Galtrucco – All kinds of fabrics, especially silks. 23 Via del Tritone.

Genny – Ever-popular boutique for women. 27 Piazza di Spagna.

Gucci – Be ready to wait in line for men's and women's shoes, luggage, handbags, and other leather goods. 8 Via Condotti.

Krizia – Elegant women's boutique. 11/B Piazza di Spagna.

Laurent – Good buys in leatherwear. 3 Via Frattina.

Lio Bazaar – Amusing women's shoes. 35 Via Borgognona.

Lion Bookshop – The city's oldest English-language bookstore, chock full of volumes on Rome's history, travel, and food. 181 Via del Babuino.

Maccalè – Yet another fine boutique for women. 69 Via della Croce.

Bruno Magli – Top-quality shoes and boots of classical elegance. 70 Via Veneto, 1 Via del Gambero, and 237 Via Cola di Rienzo.

Mail – English and western saddlery and other riding gear. 154 Via Germanico.

Miranda – Colorful women's woven shawls and jackets. 220 Via delle Carrozze.

Missoni – High-fashion knitwear. Via Borgognona 38/B. *Missoni Uomo,* for men, is at 78 Piazza di Spagna.

Ai Monasteri – Products ranging from bath oils to honey and liqueurs from more than 20 monasteries. 72 Corso del Rinascimento.

Moriondo & Gariglio – Delicious hand-dipped chocolates and violets crystallized in sugar. 2 Via della Pilotta.

Myricae – Hand-painted ceramics and such, made by Italian craftsmen from Sardinia to Deruta. 36 Via Frattina.

Naj Oleari – Famed cotton fabrics and accessories from bags to lampshades. 25A Via di San Giacomo.

Ottica Scientifica – Eyeglasses and contact lenses fitted by one of Rome's best and most scrupulous optometrists; camera supplies and electronic equipment also. 19 Via delle Convertite, near Piazza San Silvestro.

Carlo Palazzi – Creative, high-quality fashions for men. 7/C Via Borgognona.

Perla – Avant-garde look for young women. 88 Piazza di Spagna.

Petochi – A treasure trove of fine jewelry and old and new tea services. 72 Piazza di Spagna.

Pineider – Italy's famed stationer. 68-69 Via Due Macelli and Piazza Cardelli.

Polidori – Exclusive menswear and tailoring at 84 Via Condotti and 4C Via Borgognona; finest pure silks and other fabrics at 4A Via Borgognona.

Ramirez – Latest shoe fashions at reasonable prices. 73 Via del Corso, 81 Via Frattina, and Via Cola di Rienzo.

Franco Maria Ricci – Sumptuously printed books by a discriminating publisher, sold in an elegant setting. 4D Via Borgognona.

Rinascente – One of the few department stores, offering good buys on gloves, scarves, and small gifts. Piazza Colonna and Piazza Fiume.

Sabatini – Best buys on film and camera equipment, catering to the professional photographer. 166/A Via Germanico (downstairs).

Raphael Salato – For famous-maker Italian men's and women's shoes. 104 and 149 Via Veneto; 34 Piazza di Spagna.

Sansone – Italy's largest selection of Italian and imported luggage, trunks, and travel bags, as well as wallets, purses, knapsacks, etc. Repairs and custom designs. 4 Via XX Settembre.

Schostal – Since 1870, traditional supplier of stockings (in silk, linen, cotton, etc.) and other undergarments for men and women. Moderate prices. 158 Via del Corso.

Al Sogno Giocattoli – Toys, including huge stuffed animals in amusing window displays. 53 Piazza Navona.

Stefanel – Lively, youthful sportswear at a dozen branches, the most central of which are 148 Via del Corso, 31-32 Via Frattina, 41 Via Tritone, 227 Via Nazionale, and 191-193 Via Cola di Rienzo.

Testa – For offbeat, resort, and casual clothes for men. 13 Via Borgognona, 104-106 Via Frattina.

Trimani – Rome's oldest wine shop. Its marble decorations are a national monument. 20 Via Goito.

Valentino – Bold, high-fashion clothes for men and women. 13 Via Condotti for men, 15-18 Via Bocca di Leone for women; haute couture salon at 24 Via Gregoriana.

Mario Valentino – Fine shoes and leather goods. 58 and 84 Via Frattina.

Gianni Versace – The Milanese designer's Rome outlets. 41 Via Borgognona and 29 Via Bocca di Leone.

Vertecchi – Rome's most important stationer and artists' supplier, also selling gifts and design products. 38 and 70 Via della Croce, 18 Via Pietro da Cortona, and 12/F Via Attilio Regolo.

SPORTS AND FITNESS: Auto Racing – The *Autodromo di Roma* (Valle Lunga racetrack), Campagnano di Roma, Via Cassia, Km 34 (phone: 904-1027). Take a bus from Via Lepanto.

Fitness Centers – *Aldrovandi Health Center,* Aldrovandi Hotel, 15 Via Ulisse Aldrovandi (phone: 841091); *American Aerobic Association,* 5 Via Giovanni Amendola (phone: 475-4496), run by a former Jane Fonda Workshop instructor. Most others, like the huge new one beneath the Villa Borghese, are by membership only.

Golf – Both the *Circolo del Golf Roma,* 3 Via dell'Acqua Santa (phone: 783407), about 8 miles (12 km) from the center, and the *Olgiata Golf Club,* 15 Largo Olgiata (phone: 378-9141), about 12 miles (19 km), have 18-hole courses and extend guest privileges to members of foreign clubs. The former is open to guests Tuesdays through Saturdays; the latter, Tuesdays to Fridays. The 9-hole *Golf Club Fioranello* is at Via Appia Nuova, Santa Maria delle Mole (phone: 608291).

Horse Racing – Trotting races take place at the *Ippodromo Tor di Valle,* Via del Mare, km 9 (phone: 656-4129). Flat races take place at the *Ippodromo delle Capannelle,* 1255 Via Appia, Km 12 (phone: 799-3143) in the spring and fall.

Horseback Riding – For lessons at various levels of proficiency, rentals by the hour (sometimes a subscription for several hours is required), or guided rides in the country, contact the *Circolo Ippico Appia Antica,* Via Appia Nuova, km 16.5 (phone: 600197); *Società Ippica Romana,* 30 Via dei Monti della Farnesina (phone: 396-6386); *Scuola d'Equitazione Le Piane,* Campagnano (phone: 904-2478 or 904-1925), or *Circolo Buttero Fontana Nuova,* near Sacrofano, outside Rome (phone: 903-6040). For weekend or weeklong riding vacations, contact *Agriturist* (phone: 651-2342) or *Turismo Verde* (phone: 576850 or 576874).

Jogging – There are two tracks at the *Galoppatoio* in the Villa Borghese; enter at the top of Via Veneto or from Piazza del Popolo. *Villa Glori* has a 1,180-meter track which is illuminated at night; *Villa Pamphili* has three tracks, as does *Villa Ada,* and *Villa Torlonia* has one pretty track flanked by palm and acacia trees; at *Acqua Acetosa* there is also a dressing room open until 5 PM; and the Baths of Caracalla provide another good running spot (between the road and the Terme).

Soccer – Two highly competitive teams, *Roma* and *Lazio,* play on Sundays from September to May at the *Olympic Stadium,* Foro Italico (phone: 36851).

Swimming – The pools at the *Cavalieri Hilton,* 101 Via Cadlolo (phone: 3151), and the *Aldrovandi,* 15 Via Ulisse Aldrovandi (phone: 841091), are open to non-guests for a fee. Public pools include the *Piscina Olimpica* at Foro Italico (phone: 360-8591, 360-1498) and the *Piscina delle Rose* at EUR (phone: 592-6717). Swimming in the sea near Rome has become dangerous due to very high levels of pollution; signs prohibiting swimming speckle many nearby beaches. The beach nearest Rome is at Ostia, and it's among the most polluted, very crowded, and strung from end to end with bathing establishments charging admission for entry and use of changing rooms. There are stretches of free beach at Castel Fusano and Castel Porziano, southeast of Ostia; the first is reachable by subway from Stazione Termini (not all trains). Fregene, farther north along the coast, is very popular with fashionable (and mostly topless) Romans. There's also swimming at Lake Bracciano, about 20 miles (32 km) north of Rome.

Tennis – Most courts belong to private clubs. Those at the *Cavalieri Hilton,* 101 Via Cadlolo (phone: 3151), and at the *Sheraton Roma,* viale del Pattinaggio (phone: 5453), are open to non-guests for a fee. There are public courts occasionally available at the *Foro Italico* (phone: 361-9021).

Windsurfing – Windsurf boards and lessons are available at *Castel Porziano* (*primo cancello,* or first gate); at the *Stabilimento La Baia* (phone: 646-1647) and the *Miraggio Sporting Club* (phone: 646-1802) in Fregene; and at the *Centro Surf Bracciano* (phone: 902-4568) at Lake Bracciano.

 THEATER: During the theater season, approximately October through May, check *A Guest in Rome, La Repubblica*'s Saturday insert "TrovaRoma," or *This Week in Rome* for listings. Most theater in Italian consists of revivals of the classics (including Goldoni's and Pirandello's works and English and French classics in translation) and some avant-garde works. The principal theaters are the *Teatro Eliseo,* 183 Via Nazionale (phone: 462114), the *Teatro Argentina,* 52 Largo Argentina (phone: 654-4601), and the *Teatro Quirino,* 1 Via Minghetti (phone: 679-4585). A season of classical drama (in Italian, and sometimes in Greek) is held in July each year in the open-air *Teatro Romano di Ostia Antica* (phone: 565-1913). The *Teatro Sistina,* 129 Via Sistina (phone: 475-6841), is Rome's best music hall, offering top class, often imported, musical entertainment on Monday nights, when the regular rep is resting (in the fall, they usually run top-name Brazilian entertainment Monday nights). The charming, turn-of-the-century cabaret theater *Salone Margarita* offers late-night shows and Sunday afternoon concerts, 75 Via Due Macelli (phone: 679-1439). For films in English, check the newspapers for *Cinema Pasquino*, Vicolo del Piede (phone: 580-3622) in Trastevere.

 MUSIC: Again, for current schedules, check *A Guest in Rome* or *This Week in Rome*. The regular opera season at the *Teatro dell'Opera*, 1 Piazza Beniamino Gigli, corner Via Firenze (phone: 461755 or 463641), runs from December through May. During July and August there is a summer opera season at the *Baths of Caracalla*, although given the wear and tear on the ruins, its future is in doubt. (Tickets are on sale at the *Teatro dell'Opera* box office or, on the day of performance, at *Caracalla*.) The *Rome Ballet* Company also performs at the *Teatro dell'Opera*. Rome's *RAI* symphony orchestra, one of four orchestras run by Radiotelevisione Italiana, the state television network, holds its concert season at the *Auditorio del Foro Italico*, 1 Piazza Lauro de Bosis (phone: 474-4776), from October to June. At roughly the same time, the venerable *Accademia Nazionale di Santa Cecilia* gives first class concerts with international guest artists, either at the *Auditorio Santa Cecilia*, 4 Via della Conciliazione (phone: 654-1044), or at the smaller *Sala Concerti* (Concert Hall), 18 Via dei Greci (box office at 6 Via Vittoria; phone: 679-0389). In July and August, there's an outdoor season at the Campidoglio and ballet in the *Orti Botanici* (Botanical Gardens) on the street of the same name. Between October and May, the *Accademia Filarmonica Romana* sponsors a series of concerts at the *Teatro Olimpico*, 17 Piazza Gentile da Fabriano (phone: 396-2635 or 393304) — its summer season is held in the garden at the academy headquarters, 118 Via Flaminia (phone: 360-1752) — and the *Istituzione Universitaria dei Concerti* holds concerts at the *Auditorium San Leone Magno*, 38 Via Bolzano (phone: 853216), and at the university's *Aula Magna*, 1 Piazzale Aldo Moro (phone: 361-0051). From November to April, there are concerts at the *Auditorio del Gonfalone*, 32 Via del Gonfalone (phone: 687-5952), and around Rome by the *Coro Polifonico Romano*. Still other musical groups use the *Teatro Ghione*, 37 Via delle Fornaci (phone: 637-2294). Finally, there are concerts in many, many churches throughout the year, and music festivals — classical, jazz, pop, and folk — outdoors in the parks and *piazze* during the summer. For jazz and other modern music in clubs, see *Nightclubs and Nightlife* below.

 NIGHTCLUBS AND NIGHTLIFE: Nightspots are born and die so quickly, slip into and out of fashion so easily, that it is best to inquire at your hotel about what is currently popular. A new and successful formula is to involve spectators in after-dinner shows at restaurants (around 11 or 11:30 PM). In most places, a cover charge buys an expensive (about $20) first drink, or *consumazione*, after which the drink prices drop. One such place, with a 1940s ambience, is *Gilda*, 97 Via Mario de' Fiore (phone: 678-4838 or 679-7396), with live music, a pricey restaurant, and a young clientele. Another popular nightspot cum restaurant is *Talent Scout*, 29 Via Alberico II (phone: 654-7137). Also fashionable are the *Open Gate*, 22 Via San Nicola da Tolentino (phone: 475-0464), *Hysteria*, 3 Via Giovannelli (phone: 864587), and *Jackie O'*, 11 Via Boncompagni (phone: 461401). Both *Jackie O'* and *Open Gate* are also restaurants, but be prepared to spend. *Bella Blu*, 21 Via Luciani (phone: 360-8840), is an elegant cocktail bar and restaurant. The *Acropolis* (formerly *Much More*), 52 Via Luciani (phone: 870504) has an all-night restaurant and is currently Rome's most "in" spot for the gilded younger set. *Vicolo delle Stelle*, 22 Via Cesare Beccaria (phone: 361-1240), plays disco and funk music until 6 AM. *Piper '80*, 9 Via Tagliamento (phone: 854459), features a different event (video, breakdance, fashion shows, etc.) every evening. *Executive Club*, 11/A Via San Saba (phone: 578-2022), admits women for free on Wednesdays and Sundays and is preferred by the younger set, mostly punks and teenagers. *La Makumba*, 19 Via degli Olimpionici (phone: 396-4392), jumps with African, Caribbean, and Latin rhythms. *Atmosphere*, 11/A Via Romagnosi (phone: 361-1231), has a piano bar and disco. A special summer treat is the *Apollonia*, near the Via Appia Antica at 41 Via Tor Carbone (phone: 799-0680), where you can dine, dance, and swim in the pool. Mainly for gays are the *St. James*, 37/A Via Campania (phone: 493706), *Angelo Azzurro*, Via Cardinale Merry del Val (phone: 580-0472), and *L'Alibi*, 44 Via di Monte Testaccio (phone: 574-3448). Of these, the *St. James*, the first gay place in Rome, is the most traditional, a jacket-and-tie atmosphere. You may be asked to pay a "membership fee" in some Rome clubs or may be refused entry altogether if the doorman doesn't like your looks.

Other clubs include *Il Veleno*, 27 Via Sardegna (phone: 493583), decorated in mock ancient Roman style with marble-like columns and a restaurant; *Fonclea*, 82/A Via Crescenzio (phone: 653-0302), also a beer hall with board games and a restaurant; *Club 84*, 84 Via Emilia (phone: 474-2205); *L'Incontro*, a disco (often featuring Brazilian music) and piano bar at 25 Via della Penna (phone: 361-0934); the *Cavalieri Hilton*'s *La Pergola* roof garden, 101 Via Cadlolo (phone: 3151); and *New Life*, 8 Via XX Settembre (phone: 474-0997). Check with your hotel about new nightspots such as the *Black Out, Magic Fly, Ti Odio, Revolution, Olimpo, New Scarabocchio, Ebrite*, and *Amnesty Club*. The *Hostaria dell'Orso* has a disco upstairs (*La Cabala*), and a quiet comfy piano bar (*Blue Bar*) with guitarists on the main floor. At *L'Arciliuto*, an intimate musical salon and bar in what is reputed to be Raphael's old studio on Piazza Montevecchio, a pianist accompanies the owner-guitarist-lutist-music historian, whose repertoire includes ancient madrigals, classic Neapolitan love songs, and current Broadway hits. *Notorious* is an elegant disco/club and restaurant at 22 Via San Nicola da Tolentino (phone: 474-6888) with a late-night show including a drag performance by manager Claudio Belfiore. There are several other bars with music but no dancing, such as the yuppie, over-rated *Hemingway*, 10 Piazza delle Coppelle, near the Pantheon (phone: 654-4135), which has tables outdoors in good weather (closed Saturday afternoons); *Le Nane*, 21 Via Paolo Mercuri (phone: 654-5132); *Birdland*, 33 Passeggiata di Ripetta (phone: 678-6312); *Aldebaran*, 54 Via Galvani; *La Privé*, Via della Penna, behind Piazza del Popolo; the *Tartarughino*, 2 Via della Scrofa, and *Al Piccolo*, 48 Via Emilia, both of which also have restaurants; *Cappello a Cilindro*, 47 Via del Vantaggio; and several hotels and cafés in the Via Veneto area, such as the *Eden* hotel's *Roof Garden Bar*, the *White Elephant, George's*, and the *Aldrovandi* hotel across the park. *Manuia*, in Trastevere, 54-56 Vicolo del Cinque (phone: 581-7016), is a garden restaurant and bar that traditionally has live Brazilian music.

For an open-air nightcap, bars at both the Piazza del Pantheon and the Piazza Navona are popular. Tourists, prostitutes, and gigolos stake their claims to various vantage points along Via Veneto. For a late snack, there are plenty of places, some with music, poetry readings, video, or other attractions. Most popular are *Le Cornacchie*, 53 Piazza Rondanini, *La Poeteca*, 47 Vicolo dei Soldati, *Chef du Village*, 125-127 Via del Governo Vecchio (which recently has become more of an exotic restaurant), and *Dito al Naso*, 4 Via del Fiume. Open until around midnight are *Il Calice*, 20 Via dei Delfini, and *Il Calisé*, 14-16 Via Col di Lana. Others are *Gamela Vini*, 35 Via Frangipani, *Cul de Sac*, on Piazza Pasquino, *Tabasco*, 52 Piazza Capranica, *Coffee Shop No Stop*, in Parioli at 43 Piazza Euclide, and *Camarillo*, 30 Via Properzio, which also has live music, as does *Alfellini*, 5 Via Francesca Carletti (phone: 578-3595).

Folk music can be heard at the *Folkstudio*, 3 Via Gaetano Sacchi in Trastevere (phone: 589-2374), *El Trauco*, 5 Via Fonte dell'Olio (phone: 589-5928), and *Le Cabanon* (see *Eating Out*). Jazz is the thing at *Music Inn*, Largo dei Fiorentini 3 (phone: 654-4934), *Mississippi Jazz Club*, 17 Borgo Angelico (phone: 654-5652), *Saint Louis*

Music City, 13/A Via del Cardello (phone: 474-5076), *Tusitala,* 13/A Via dei Neofiti (phone: 678-3237), the excellent *Alexanderplatz,* 9 Via Ostia (phone: 359-9398), *Blue Lab Music Club,* 3 Vicolo del Fico (phone: 687-9075), *Big Mama,* 18 Vicolo San Francesco a Ripa (phone: 582551), the *Billie Holiday Jazz Club,* 43 Via degli Orti di Trastevere (phone: 581-6121), and *Corto Maltese Jazz,* in Ostia at Via Stiepovic (phone: 569-8794). For jazz and rock, check out *Sottosopra,* 68 Via Panisperna (phone: 589-1431), the *Café Caruso,* at the Testaccio, 36 Via di Montetestaccio, and *Grigio Notte,* 30/B Via dei Fienaroli (phone: 581-3249). Roman music can be heard at the supper clubs *Fantasie di Trastevere,* 6 Via di Santa Dorotea (phone: 589-2986), *Da Meo Patacca,* 30 Piazza dei Mercanti (phone: 581-6198), and *Da Ciceruacchio,* 1 Via del Porto (phone: 580-6046), all in the heart of Trastevere. If you're curious about cabaret in Italian, go to *Il Bagaglino* at *Salone Margherita,* 75 Via Due Macelli (phone: 679-1439), or *Il Puff,* 4 Via Gigi Zanazzo (phone: 581-0721). The city's English-speaking community frequents the *Fiddler's Elbow,* near Santa Maria Maggiore; the *Little Bar,* 54/A Via Gregoriana; and *Bandiera Gialla,* 41 Via della Purificazione, where Americans studying in Rome meet every Friday night (phone: 465951).

BEST IN TOWN

CHECKING IN: Of the more than 500 hotels in Rome, the following are recommended either for some special charm, location, or bargain price in their category. Those without restaurants are noted, although all serve breakfast if desired, and all have heating and telephones in the rooms unless otherwise stated. Expect to pay from $175 to over $450 for a double room with bath in the hotels listed as expensive, from $100 to $170 in the moderate category, and under $100 (as low as $45) in the inexpensive category. All telephone numbers are in the 06 area code unless otherwise indicated.

Ambasciatori Palace – Across the street from the US Embassy, this recently refurbished hotel has 145 generally spacious rooms, old-fashioned amenities, and a very convenient location. 70 Via Veneto (phone: 610241). Expensive.

Cavalieri Hilton International – Far from the historic center of Rome at the top of a lovely hill (Monte Mario) overlooking much of the city, with shuttle buses to Via Veneto and Piazza di Spagna running hourly during shopping hours only. But the swimming pool is especially desirable in summer, and the rooftop restaurant, *La Pergola,* has been gathering high praise from food critics. A resort property with year-round swimming, tennis, sauna, and other diversions, it has 387 newly refurbished rooms. 101 Via Cadlolo (phone: 3151). Expensive.

Eden – Among the most elegant in Rome, this hotel has excellent service, an intimate roof garden restaurant, and a panoramic bar. There are 116 air conditioned rooms with TV sets. 49 Via Ludovisi (phone: 474-3551). Expensive.

Excelsior – Big, bustling, but efficient, it dominates Via Veneto, next to the US Embassy. It's a favorite with Americans, and the bar is a popular meeting place. There are 383 rooms in this member of the CIGA chain. 125 Via Vittorio Veneto (phone: 4708). Expensive.

Grand – The pride of the CIGA chain in Rome and traditionally the capital's most dignified hotel, it is truly grand — formal, well run, and elegant in style and service. It has 175 rooms and a central (if not exactly prime) location between the railroad station and Via Veneto areas. High tea is also served with harp music and fine food. 3 Via Vittorio Emanuele Orlando (phone: 4709). Expensive.

Hassler — Villa Medici – At the top of the Spanish Steps and within easy striking distance of the best shopping in Rome, favored by a loyal clientele. Guestrooms could stand some refurbishing, and the public rooms have seen better days. Each of the 108 rooms is individually decorated, and manager Albert Wirth is an attentive host. The roof garden restaurant has good food and splendid views. 6 Piazza Trinità dei Monti (phone: 768-2651). Expensive.

Lord Byron – A small (47 rooms) first-rate hotel in the fashionable Parioli residential district, this was once a private villa, and it maintains the atmosphere of a private club. It has a celebrated restaurant, *Relais Le Jardin* (see *Eating Out*). 5 Via Giuseppe de Notaris (phone: 360-9541). Expensive.

Sheraton Roma – Rome's largest hotel (587 rooms) opened in the early 1980s and sprawls over the modern suburb of EUR, an area that was originally developed by Mussolini for a world's fair and is connected to the center of town by bus and subway. The hotel has full 24-hour room service (rare in Italy), a piano bar, swimming pool, tennis courts, sauna. Viale del Pattinaggio (phone: 5453). Expensive.

Aldrovandi – This quiet 139-room hotel in a fashionable residential area next to the Villa Borghese, and not far from Via Veneto, has a delightful park with a swimming pool and a full-facility health club. Its restaurant, *Relais le Piscine,* is next door (although it has a different street address), 6 Via Mangili. The hotel is at 15 Via Ulisse Aldrovandi (phone: 841091). Moderate.

Anglo-Americano – Just off Piazza Barberini, it has 115 rooms, and the back ones look out on the garden of Palazzo Barberini. 12 Via delle Quattro Fontane (phone: 472941). Moderate.

Atlas – On a street made famous during World War II, with 45 recently renovated rooms and a flowered roof garden, in a a central location. 3 Via Rasella (phone: 475-7739). Moderate.

Cardinal – On Renaissance Rome's stateliest street, this restored 66-room palace (attributed to Bramante) is convenient for exploring some of the city's hidden treasures, but less so for shopping in the city center. No restaurant. 62 Via Giulia (phone: 654-2719). Moderate.

Cicerone – This is in the residential and commercial area of Prati on the Vatican side of the river, but convenient nevertheless because it's just across from Piazza del Popolo and the Spanish Steps. It has modern and spacious public areas, 237 well-appointed rooms, friendly, attentive service, and a large garage. 55/C Via Cicerone (phone: 3576). Moderate.

Eliseo – Just off Via Veneto, this has traditional furnishings (with a slightly French air) in the public rooms and in some of the 50 guestrooms; others are super modern. A roof restaurant looks out over the tops of the umbrella pines in the Villa Borghese. 30 Via di Porta Pinciana (phone: 460556). Moderate.

Flora – At the top of Via Veneto, right next to the Villa Borghese, the 174 rooms are traditional, reliable, and not without charm. 191 Via Vittorio Veneto (phone: 497281). Moderate.

Forum – Built around a medieval tower in the middle of the Imperial Forums, this charming 79-room hotel is a bit out of the way but worth any inconvenience for the spectacular view of ancient Rome from its roof garden. The food here is less spectacular. 25 Via Tor de' Conti (phone: 679-2446). Moderate.

D'Inghilterra – Extremely popular with knowledgeable travelers, its 102 rooms have numbered Anatole France and Ernest Hemingway among their many illustrious guests. Particularly attractive are the new, small suites on the fifth floor, some with their own flowered terraces. It's very near the Spanish Steps and right in the middle of the central shopping area. There is no restaurant, but its ever-crowded bar is a cozy haven for Roman patricians. 14 Via Bocca di Leone (phone: 672161). Moderate.

Locarno – Near the Piazza del Popolo and the Spanish Steps, this Belle Epoque hotel often attracts artists, writers, and intellectuals. The 35 rooms have Victorian furniture, and many are large enough to include couches and desks. During winter, a fire burns in the lounge, and in the summer drinks and breakfast are served on the terrace. 22 Via della Penna (phone: 361-0841/2/3 or 360-1641). Moderate.

Nazionale – Another old favorite (of Sartre and de Beauvoir, among others), the 76 rooms here are very central, next to the Chamber of Deputies, between Via del Corso and the Pantheon. 131 Piazza Montecitorio (phone: 678-9251). Moderate.

Parco dei Principi – This modern hotel is on the edge of Villa Borghese in the Parioli residential district, not far from Via Veneto. It has 203 rooms and a small swimming pool in a lovely garden. 5 Via Gerolamo Frescobaldi (phone: 841071). Moderate.

Raphael – Behind Piazza Navona, it's a favorite of Italian politicians (it's near the Senate and the Chamber of Deputies), with 83 recently renovated but smallish rooms. 2 Largo Febo (phone: 650881). Moderate.

La Residenza – An exceptional bargain on a quiet street just behind Via Veneto. With only 27 recently renovated and luxurious rooms, it feels much more like a private villa than a hotel. Book well in advance. Full American breakfast, but no restaurant per se. 22 Via Emilia (phone: 460789). Moderate.

Sitea – Gianni de Luca and his Scottish wife, Shirley, have bestowed the coziness of a private home on their 40-room, 5-floor hotel opposite the *Grand*. Rooms have high ceilings, crystal chandeliers, and hand-painted Florentine dressers. Other amenities: sitting rooms and a sun-drenched penthouse bar. 90 Via Vittorio Emanuele Orlando (phone: 475-1560). Moderate.

Teatro di Pompeo – History, literally, is at the root of this hotel, as its foundation was originally laid in 55 BC and is said to have supported the Theater of Pompey, where Julius Caesar met his untimely end. The hotel is on a quiet street, and the 12 rooms have hand-painted tiles and beamed ceilings. 8 Largo del Pallaro (phone: 654-5531 or 687-2812). Moderate.

Villa Florence – A charming 19th-century patrician villa in a residential area a few minutes' drive from the Via Veneto. The comfortable, modern rooms have TV sets, radio, and mini-bar, and are complemented by touches of ancient Rome in the public areas. Parking facilities and nice gardens. 28 Via Nomentana (phone: 858138 or 864461). Moderate.

Gregoriana – On the street of the same name — high fashion's headquarters in Rome — this tiny (19 rooms) gem attracts the fashionable. Its decor is reminiscent of Art Deco, with room letters (rather than numbers) by 1930s fashion illustrator Erté. No restaurant, though a continental breakfast is included. 18 Via Gregoriana (phone: 679-4269 or 679-7988). Inexpensive.

Degli Aranci – This small, quiet hotel in the Parioli residential district has 48 rooms, a bar, and a lovely garden restaurant. 11 Via Barnaba Oriani (phone: 870202; 805250). Inexpensive.

Campo dé Fiori – Near the Campo dé Fiori square — a market area since the 1500s — the Renaissance palaces, the giant Palazza Cancelleria, and the Palazzo Farnese (French Embassy), which was partly designed by Michelangelo, this hotel is one of the coziest (and narrowest) in the area. The rustic rooms are small and sparsely decorated, but the exposed brick walls, hand-painted bathroom ceilings, and detailed architecture make up for the lack of space. For guests willing to climb six flights, there's a wonderful view of the city from the roof garden. No restaurant or bar. 6 Via del Biscione (phone: 654-0865 or 687-4886).

Columbus – In a restored 15th-century palace right in front of St. Peter's, this 107-room hotel offers antique furniture, paintings, and a garden — a lot of atmosphere for the price. 33 Via della Conciliazione (phone: 656-5435). Inexpensive.

Coronet – Guests won't find luxurious accommodations at this pensione, but it is in a peaceful area just a few blocks from the Piazza Venezia (the center of Rome), and its neighbor is the Palazza Doria, a palace which is still the home of the family who built it. Some rooms have a private bath. No restaurant. 5 Piazza Grazioli (phone: 679-2341). Inexpensive.

Dinesen – Off Via Veneto and next to the Villa Borghese, the 20 rooms in this charming hotel with a 19th-century air are a real bargain. Breakfast is included. No restaurant. 18 Via di Porta Pinciana (phone: 475-4501 or 460932). Inexpensive.

Fabrello White – For the traveler who's seeking basic, affordable accommodations, this pensione is a good bet. The 33 rooms — some with a private bath, some without — have a wide range of decor. Some have terrace views of the river, some have ornamental fireplaces, others have a turn-of-the-century dormitory look. Guests can't be picky, but the management tries very hard to please everyone. On the right bank of the Tiber, it's a 10-minute walk to the Spanish Steps shopping area. 11 Via Vittoria Colonna (phone: 360-4446/7). Inexpensive.

Fontana – A recently restored 13th-century monastery next to the Trevi Fountain, with cell-like rooms — though 10 of the 30 rooms have great views of the fabulous fountain — and a lovely rooftop bar. 96 Piazza di Trevi (phone: 678-6113). Inexpensive.

King – The 61 rooms in this well-positioned, immaculate hotel are reasonably priced. No restaurant, though breakfast is served. 131 Via Sistina (phone: 474-1515). Inexpensive.

Margutta – Try for the two rooms on the roof (#50 and #51), complete with fireplaces and surrounded by a terrace. This 21-room hotel is near Piazza del Popolo. No restaurant. 34 Via Laurina (phone: 679-8440). Inexpensive.

Sant'Anselmo – In a small villa on the Aventine Hill, this beflowered bargain has 26 rooms, a family atmosphere, but no restaurant. (Nearby are 4 other villas — with this one, totaling about 120 rooms — each with similar accommodations and prices, and all run by the same management.) Reservations necessary well in advance. 2 Piazza di Sant'Anselmo (phone: 574-3547). Inexpensive.

Scalinata di Spagna – Tiny but spectacularly placed overlooking the Spanish Steps, it's opposite the pricey *Hassler.* No restaurant and no phones in the 14 rooms. 17 Piazza Trinità dei Monti (phone: 679-3006). Inexpensive.

 EATING OUT: The ancient Romans were the originators of the first fully developed cuisine of the Western world. Drawing on an abundance of fine, natural ingredients from the fertile Roman countryside and influenced by Greece and Asia Minor, they evolved a gastronomic tradition still felt in the kitchens of Europe today.

While the lavish and exotic banquets of exaggerated proportions described in detail by Roman writers such as Petronius and Pliny no doubt existed, they were relatively infrequent and probably more a vulgar show of *nouveaux riches* than typical examples of local custom. The old nobility, then as now, must have found such conspicuous consumption in poor taste, and in fact, the beginnings of genuine Roman gastronomic traditions were more likely among the humble masses, whose specialties included such staples as lentils and chickpeas, still regularly offered in Roman *trattorie.* Even the ancient Romans' beloved sauce of rotted fish, *garum,* is echoed in the olive oil, anchovy bit, and garlic sauce that anoints the quintessential Roman salad green, crisp and curly *puntarelle.*

Unfortunately, today's authentically Roman kitchens are dwindling in number. One by one, the old-fashioned, inexpensive mamma-papa *trattorie* are becoming Chinese restaurants, of which Rome now boasts 140, none of them superior. In addition, fast-food joints have arrived with a vengeance. Rome's traditional fare is further threatened by the standardized fad menus, which include such vogues as *rughetta* (rugola), tucked everywhere and often cooked to little effect. Watch out, too, for the new handy way to deal with leftover *carpaccio* (raw slivers of beef), sautéed *stracci* ("rags"). The trendy dessert is currently *tiramisù*, a Tyrolean calorie bomb of mascarpone cheese, liqueur, and coffee. The very ease of its preparation, with no cooking involved, is elbowing out better and more interesting desserts.

The bright side is that a new generation of well-trained cooks is bringing back forgotten regional dishes and devising new versions of old standbys. These relative youngsters call their fare "creative cuisine," the fruit of their labors, and are well worth seeking out. The decreasing number of authentic Roman kitchens makes the survivors all the more precious, and it means that while a careful diner may test the new, he or she will seek out and cherish the authentic old.

Real Roman cooking is quite like the real Roman people — robust and hearty, imbued with a total disregard for tomorrow. There's no room in the popular Roman philosophy of *carpe diem* for thoughts of cholesterol or calories or preoccupations with heartburn, hangovers, or garlic-laden breath. These considerations disappear before a steaming dish of fragrant *spaghetti alla matriciana* (tomato, special bacon, and tangy *pecorino* — ewe's milk cheese), deep-fried *filetti di baccalà* (salt cod fillet), or *coda alla vaccinara* (oxtail stewed in tomato, onion and celery) — all accompanied by the abundant wines of the surrounding hill towns, the Castelli Romani.

Since Rome is close to the sea, its restaurants offer abundant fresh fish — particularly on Tuesdays and Fridays — but it is costly. All restaurants are required to identify frozen fish as well as other frozen ingredients. Don't hesitate to try the *antipasta marinara* (a mixture of seafoods in a light sauce of olive oil, lemon, parsley, and garlic), the *spaghetti alle vongole* (spaghetti with clam sauce — the clam shells come as well), and as a main course, trout from the nearby lakes or rock fish from the Mediterranean.

Veal is typically Roman, served as *saltimbocca alla romana* (literally, "hop-into-the-mouth," flavored with ham, sage, and Marsala wine) or roasted with the fresh rosemary that grows in every garden. *Abbacchio al forno* is milk-fed baby lamb roasted with garlic and rosemary, and *abbacchio brodettato* is cooked in a sauce of egg yolks and lemon juice. *Abbacchio scottadito* ("finger burning") are tiny grilled lamb chops. On festive occasions, suckling pig (*porchetta*) appears on the menu; it is stuffed with herbs, roasted, and thickly sliced. Its street-stand version is eaten between thick slabs of country bread. Watch, too, for such Roman specialties as *tripa* (tripe flavored with mint, Parmesan cheese, and tomato sauce), *coniglio* (rabbit), *capretto* (kid), *coratella* (lamb's heart), *animelle* (sweetbreads), and, in season, *cinghiale* (wild boar). Wild boar dried sausages are popular as an antipasto course, along with salamis; the local Roman salami is prepared with tasty fennel seeds.

Pasta dishes include the incredibly simple *spaghetti alla carbonara* (with egg, salt pork, and *pecorino* cheese). *Penne all'arrabbiata* are short pasta in a tomato and garlic sauce "rabid" with hot peppers. The familiar *fettuccine all'Alfredo* depends upon the quality of the homemade strips of egg pasta in a rich sauce of cream, butter, and Parmesan.

Fresh, seasonal vegetables, which are often treated as a separate course, provide the base for many a savory antipasto, accompany the main dish, and are even munched raw — for instance, *finocchio al pinzimonio* (fennel dipped into the purest of olive oil seasoned with salt and pepper) — after a particularly heavy meal to "clean the palate." Several local greens are unknown to visitors, such as *agretti, bieta, cicoria,* and *broccolo romano* — the last two often boiled briefly, then sautéed with olive oil, garlic, and hot red peppers. Salad ingredients include the red *radicchio,* wild aromatic herbs, and the juicy tomatoes so cherished during the sultry summer months when they are served with ultra-aromatic basil — the sun's special gift to Mediterranean terraces and gardens. Tomatoes are also stuffed with rice and roasted; yellow, red, and green sweet peppers, eggplant, mushrooms, green and broad beans, and zucchini are favorite vegetables for antipasto; while asparagus and artichokes are especially prized in season. The latter is stuffed with mint and garlic and is stewed with olive oil seasoning *alla romana,* or opened out like a flower and deep-fried *alla giudia* (Jewish style).

After such a meal, Romans normally have fresh fruit for dessert, although there is no shortage of sweet desserts (such as *montebianco, zuppa inglese,* and, of course, *gelato* (ice cream). For a final *digestivo,* bottles brought to the table may include *Sambuca Romana* (it has an aniseed base), *grappa* (made from the third and fourth grape pressings and normally over 60 proof!), and some sort of *amaro* (which means bitter, but is more often quite sweet). Fancier restaurants suggest whiskey or chilled Russian or Polish vodka. Whew!

A full meal, including house wine, may run $25 for two in a modest restaurant, while the same fare may cost twice that amount if the restaurant is even marginally fashionable. Most dining is à la carte, although a *menu turistico* is offered at some unpretentious *trattorie* for very reasonable prices. Less expensive are the quick service, often cafeteria-style, *rosticcerie* and *tavole calde* (literally "hot tables"). Most café-bars serve sandwiches as well as that delicious and filling health snack, *frullato di frutta* (a mixture of frothy blended fruit and milk), which is as inviting as a swim on a hot summer day. Be careful when ordering fresh fish or Florentine steaks *al kilo* — by weight — as this may swell a bill way out of proportion, even at average-priced restaurants. Dinner for two (with wine) costs from $100 to over $250 in restaurants below classed as expensive; $60 to $100 is moderate; and below $60 is inexpensive. All telephone numbers are in the 06 area code unless otherwise indicated.

Relais Le Jardin – This is a rare oasis of quiet and refinement in an increasingly chaotic city. The ambience is sheer elegance, the result of a combination of antiques and top modern Italian design — not to mention the white-gloved gentlemen who serve with perfect professionalism. The menu — light nouvelle cuisine, Italian style — includes such dishes as flan of watercress with scallops, pasta with quail and wild porcini mushrooms, and fresh sturgeon with white wine and mussels, and the fanciful wine list offers poetic descriptions along with an invitation to re-create the true art of living. Since this is one of Rome's most expensive restaurants, one comes expecting perfection — and usually finds it. Closed Sundays. Reservations necessary. *Lord Byron* hotel, 5 Via Giuseppe De Notaris (phone: 360-9541). Very expensive.

Ai Tre Scalini – The magazine *Tutto Turismo* named this Rome's top restaurant. Owners Roanna Dupre and Matteo Cicala change the menu frequently, but you'll be lucky if you find the fish soup or the fish-stuffed ravioli. The decor is simple; it's the food and wines that are special. Only 7 tables, 30 diners in all, so reservations are necessary. Closed Mondays. 16 Via dei Santi Quattro (phone: 732695). Very expensive.

Alberto Ciarla – Alberto, long an impassioned diver and spearfisherman, is another restaurateur who knows where to find fresh fish. Following a visit to the Far East, he now also offers several raw fish dishes and is constantly trying new recipes to adorn his top-quality ingredients. Ciarla is rated one of Rome's finest chefs; the 1989 *L'Espresso* guide gave him its highest marks, three chef's hats. His herb sauces are a welcome change from the more usual ways of preparing Italy's favorite food. For meat lovers, the "Alter Ego" menu offers a pâté of wild pigeon, baby lamb, and game — including venison — in season. In good weather, there's alfresco dining on a little piece of a Trastevere street. Dinner only; closed Sundays. Reservations advised. 40 Piazza San Cosimato (phone: 581-8668). Expensive.

Bacaro – A tiny, exclusive gastronomic refuge with a total seating capacity of 16. Innovative food is accompanied by an intelligent selection of wines (let them choose the wines for each course). The unwritten menu changes daily but usually includes *originalissimi* homemade pasta dishes such as *tonarelli neri con salsa di* *gamberi* (black pasta, from squid ink, with shrimp sauce). A sampler menu — *menù degustazione* — is offered by chef Francesca Dolcetti. Tables outdoors in season. Dinner only; closed Sundays. Reservations necessary. 27 Via degli Spagnoli (phone: 658-4110). Expensive.

Le Cabanon – French and Tunisian food are served in an intimate ambience accompanied by Mediterranean melodies sung by the well-traveled owner, Enzo Rallo. South American or Francophilice singers ably fill in the gaps. The usual onion soup and *escargots,* as well as a delicious Tunisian *brik à l'oeuf* (a pastry concealing a challengingly dripping egg within), *couscous,* and *merguez* sausages are among the choices. Open evenings only, and until late. Reservations necessary. Closed Sundays and August. 4 Vicolo della Luce (phone: 581-8106). Expensive.

Il Cardinale – In a restored bicycle shop off the stately Via Giulia, decorated in a somewhat precious turn-of-the-century style, this popular evening spot specializes in refined Roman Jewish dishes. Light starters include salmon or Gorgonzola mousse, salads of artichokes and pecorino cheese, or mushrooms, arugula, and grana cheese. More substantial fare includes pasta with broccoli or artichoke sauces, grilled eels, a sweetbread casserole with mushrooms, and *aliciotti con l'indivia* (an anchovy and endive dish) as well as good *soufflé alla francese.* Closed Sundays and August. Reservations necessary. 6 Via delle Carceri (phone: 656-9336). Expensive.

Er Cucurucú – Delightful gardens overlooking the Tiber provide one of Rome's most pleasant summer settings for dining al fresco, while inside it's cozy and rustic. The *antipasti* are good, and so are the meats grilled on an open fire. Ask for *bruschetta con pomodori* (toasted country bread smothered in fresh tomatoes and oregano), and a *spiedino misto,* a sort of shish kebab bearing great chunks of veal, pork, and sausage, all interspersed with onions and peppers and grilled for all noses to savor. Closed Mondays. 10 Via Capoprati (phone: 354434 or 382592). Expensive.

Girarrosto Toscano – Old fashioned and serious, it's a fine eatery for lovers of classic Tuscan fare. The sizzling Florentine steaks are grilled to perfection. The rest is perfect, too, but this is not always a restful place. Closed Wednesdays and 2 weeks between late July and early August. Reservations necessary. 29 Via Campania (phone: 493759). Expensive.

Papà Giovanni – It's small and intimate, with paintings and wine bottles lining the walls, and the bar is very well stocked — sip a Kir as an *aperitivo* while choosing from over 700 wines. The highly praised fare is basically refined Roman, with truffles a seasonal specialty. Try *panzerotti al tartufo* (small ravioli with truffles). The interesting menu varies, so ask your waiter for current specialties. Closed Sundays and August. Reservations necessary. 4 Via dei Sediari (phone: 656-5308). Expensive.

Passetto – For the best of classical Roman cuisine; this Belle Epoque restaurant is a beloved local institution. In addition to the excellent antipasto, try the *filetto con carciofi* (steak with artichokes) and *porcini* mushrooms with asparagus, if they're in season. 13-14 Via Zanardelli (phone: 654-3696). Expensive.

Il Pianeta Terra – This Planet Earth comes close to paradise. A young couple, half Tuscan and half Sicilian, has created an elegant, traditional, yet adventurous dining place in the heart of Rome. Starters such as ravioli stuffed with sea bass in a pistachio sauce or pasta with clams and broccoli lead to exciting main courses, such as the pigeon stuffed with artichokes or with oysters and clams, and to delicate desserts such as carrot cake with chocolate and almonds. The wine list is intelligently chosen. Dinner only; closed Mondays and from mid-July through August. Reservations necessary. 94-95 Via Arco del Monte (phone: 656-9893 or 679-9828). Expensive.

Pino e Dino – Although Pino and Dino have gone, a new management continues their menu of exciting regional dishes, from the robust *pasta e broccoli alla cala-brese* (for women diners it's served with a delicate rose) to *capretto abruzzese arrosto* (roast Abruzzi kid). The restaurant is on one of Rome's more picturesque squares, but a summer meal *all'aperto* is only slightly more enticing here than a cozy winter meal indoors surrounded by wine bottles and artisan products from all over Italy. Closed Mondays and most of August. 22 Piazza di Montevecchio (phone: 656-1319). Expensive.

Quinzi e Gabrieli – Seafood is a very serious subject here. It is prepared as naturally as possible for a maximum of 22 diners. In season, the oyster bar is popular. Closed Sundays. Near the Pantheon, at 5 Via delle Coppelle (phone: 687-9389). Expensive.

La Rosetta – One of Rome's most famed fish restaurants, the ever-crowded ex-*Carmelo* is small, disguised as a fishing boat with smells of salt water and sun and just a hint of garlic. The chef grills, fries, boils, or bakes to perfection any — or a mixture of all — of the fish and seafood available. A favorite specialty is *pappardelle al pescatore* (wide noodles in a piquant tomato sauce with mussels, clams, and parsley) or Sicilian-style *pasta con le sarde,* flavored with wild fennel. Closed Sundays, Mondays at lunchtime, and August. Reservations necessary. 9 Via della Rosetta (phone: 656-1002). Expensive.

San Luigi – Another addition to the Roman scene, off the beaten track on the Vatican side of the river. Softly lit and cozy, refined yet homey, this is a family affair: Giuliana, *la mamma,* brought from her Neapolitan home some patrician and peasant recipes, a creative gastronomic streak, and a few sons and others to keep it *"in famiglia."* Currently considered one of Rome's top restaurants, it has an innovative menu that changes constantly. Dinner only; closed Sundays and August. Reservations advised. 10 Via Mocenigo (phone: 302-9704). Expensive.

Specchio delle Mie Brame – One of the quality restaurants of the *nouvelle vague.* The result is grand on occasion; the downstairs bar has charm and yuppies galore. Open until 2AM for dinner only. Closed Sundays. 5 Via degli Specchi (phone: 686-1566). Expensive.

El Toulà – One of Rome's best for more than 2 decades. The decor is elegant: softly lit warm browns and beiges, antique paintings, fresh flowers, and deep chairs. The cuisine is international, but the regional (Venetian) dishes outshine all others — and the simpler the better. Try the *risotto nero di seppie* (a rice dish black with cuttlefish ink), *radicchio di Treviso ai ferri* (red lettuce, grilled), and *gigot alla menta* (roast lamb with mint sauce). There's an impressive wine list. Closed Sundays and August. Reservations necessary. 29/B Via della Lupa (phone: 678-1196). Expensive.

Il Veliero – After Carmelo turned over his very successful fish restaurant *La Rosetta* to his son, he founded this sibling. Fish is flown to Rome daily from the owner's native Sicily, and the chef prepares both classic and nouvelle dishes. Near the Campo de Fiori outdoor market. Closed Mondays. 32 Via Monserrato (phone: 654-2636). Expensive.

Alvaro al Circo Massimo – Let Alvaro suggest what's best that day and you'll not go wrong, whether it's fresh fish, game such as *fagiano* (pheasant) or *faraona* (guinea hen), or mushrooms (try grilled porcini). The ambience is rustic indoors, and there are tables outdoors during the summer. Closed Mondays. Reservations are generally not necessary. 53 Via dei Cerchi (phone: 678-6112). Expensive to moderate.

Il Canto del Riso – There are two, actually — summer and winter. In warmer days it's a gussied-up river barge lurking under the Ponte Cavour, while in winter the restaurant makes its home in a historic building in old Rome. The name means "the Rice Song," and a northern connection (Veneto/Friuli) explains the preponderance of rice dishes: *risotto ai capasanti* (rice with scallops) is only one of more than a dozen rice starters. Another fine first course is the sautéed mussels and clams, aptly followed by swordfish flown in from Sicily (in season). (One note of caution: Both restaurants have a penchant for dreadful, loud music.) Closed Sunday nights, Mondays, and in bad weather. Reservations necessary. Summer: Walk down to the river from Lungotevere Mellini, on the Vatican side (phone: 361-0430); winter: 21 Cordonata (phone: 678-6227) Expensive to moderate.

La Majella – On a delightful square colorfully illuminated in the summer for outdoor dining, this efficient organization with delicious food owes its fame and popularity to owner/manager Signor Antonio. The pope (while still a cardinal) was among his clientele, and the menu is nearly as long as the Bible. Fresh seafood is the major attraction. Closed Sundays and a week in August. Reservations advised. 45 Piazza Sant'Apollinare (phone: 656-4174). Expensive to moderate.

Osteria dell'Antiquario – This small eatery on a picturesque little square along the antiques-shop-lined Via dei Coronari prides itself on genuine Roman fare, well prepared with the finest seasonal ingredients. Alfresco dining in fine weather. Closed Sundays. Reservations advised. 27 Piazza San Simeone (phone: 687-9694). Expensive to moderate.

Piccolo Mondo – Not exactly a "find," this cheerful and busy restaurant behind Via Veneto has been popular with Italians and foreigners alike for years. Among the many varied *antipasti* displayed at the entrance are exquisite *mozzarellini alla panna* (small balls of fresh buffalo's milk cheese swimming in cream), as well as eggplant and peppers prepared in several tempting ways. There are sidewalk tables in good weather. Closed Sundays and most of August. Reservations advised. 39 Via Aurora (phone: 485680 and 475-4595). Expensive to moderate.

Piperno – A summer dinner outdoors on this quiet Renaissance *piazzetta,* next to the Palazzo Cenci — which still reeks "of ancient evil and nameless crimes" — is sheer magic. Indoors it is modern and less magical, and the classic Roman-Jewish cooking can be a bit heavy. The great specialty is *fritto vegetariano* (zucchini flowers, mozzarella cheese, salt cod, rice and potato balls, and artichokes — the latter *alla giudia,* or "Jewish style" — all individually deep fried, the artichokes golden brown, crisp and crackling). Closed Sunday nights, Mondays, and August. Reservations necessary. 9 Monte de' Cenci (phone: 654-0629). Expensive to moderate.

Taverna Flavia – It's been fashionable with members of the film world, journalists, and politicians for over 30 years. Owner Mimmo keeps their autographed pictures hanging on the walls — one entire room is devoted to Elizabeth Taylor — and the *Sardi's* style survives, despite the crash of "Hollywood on the Tiber" long ago. The address is just around the corner from the *Grand* hotel, and it's open quite late. Good pasta dishes and fine grilled fish. Closed Saturday lunch, all day Sundays, and August. Reservations necessary. 9-11 Via Flavia (phone: 474-5214). Expensive to moderate.

Vecchia Roma – The setting is truly out of a midsummer night's dream on magical Piazza Campitelli on the fringe of Rome's Jewish quarter. The menu is traditional, the ingredients fresh, the salads pleasing. Closed Wednesdays and 2 weeks in August. Reservations advised. 18 Piazza Campitelli (phone: 656-4604). Expensive to moderate.

Andrea – Tops for the Via Veneto area. In season, fettuccine with artichoke sauce; always on the menu, ricotta-stuffed fresh ravioli. Pleasant service, a serviceable house wine, and sweeties to sweeten the bill. Closed Sundays. 26 Via Sardegna (phone: 493707). Moderate.

Dal Bolognese – Strategically set next to the popular *Caffè Rosati* on Piazza del Popolo and with a menu nearly as long as the list of celebrities who frequent this fashionable eatery, it's run by two brothers from Bologna. Star-gazers will still enjoy such specialties as homemade *tortelloni* (pasta twists stuffed with ricotta cheese) and the *bollito misto* (boiled beef, tongue, chicken, pig's trotter). There are tables outdoors in good weather. Closed Mondays and most of August. Reservations necessary. 1 Piazza del Popolo (phone: 361-1426). Moderate.

La Campana – This unprepossessing place, among Rome's oldest restaurants, is favored by everyone from local folk to the stars and staff of RAI, Italian radio-television. Waiters help decipher the menu, which tempts most with *carciofi alla romana* (fresh artichokes in garlic and oil), *tonnarelli alla chitarra* (homemade pasta in an egg and cheese sauce), and ricotta-filled ravioli with butter and fresh sage. Closed Mondays and August. Vicolo della Campana 18 (phone: 687-5273 or 656-7820). Moderate.

Cecchino dal 1887 – Among the most Roman of all dining places, it's known for oxtail, tripe, brains with artichokes, and *spaghetti con pajatta* (spaghetti in a tomato sauce with lamb's intestines). If offal is too offputting, try the *bucatini all'amatriciana* (a hearty pasta dish with bacon). 30 Via Monte Testaccio (phone: 574-6318 or 574-3816). Moderate.

Le Colline Emiliane – With Tuscan inspiration and truffle toppings, an eatery like this is becoming a rarity. Service is prompt, decor simple, and the *maccheroncini al funghetto* delicious. It has a well-deserved reputation for consistency over the years. Closed Fridays. Near Via Veneto. 22 Via degli Avignonesi (phone: 481-7538). Moderate.

Il Drappo – Drapes softly frame the two small rooms of this *ristorantino* run by the brother-sister team of Paolo and Valentina Tolu from Sardinia. They offer delicate dishes based on robust island fare, but add fragrance with wild fennel, myrtle, and herbs. The innovative menu, recited by Paolo and artfully prepared by Valentina, always begins with mixed *antipasti* including *carta di musica* (hors d'oeuvres on crisp Sardinian wafers). Closed Sundays and 2 weeks in August. Reservations necessary. 9 Vicolo del Malpasso (phone: 687-7365). Moderate.

Da Luciano – Another restaurant in Rome's Jewish ghetto (one of the oldest in the world), with outdoor tables on one of the city's most colorful streets. *Luciano's* serves authentic old Roman Jewish (kosher) dishes such as pasta with broccoli, red mullet with grapes and pine nuts, and an amazingly light, breaded, and deep-fried mixture of vegetables (onions, potatoes, zucchini flowers, and so forth). Plans are under way to provide after-dinner music — live, classical, or jazz — at the end of the long narrow dining room. Closed Friday evenings and for Saturday lunch. Via Portico d'Ottavia (phone: 656-1613). Moderate.

Al Moro – Not far from the Trevi Fountain, this is a quiet, dignified place. Traditional seasonal dishes such as pasta with truffles are a must. 13 Vicola delle Bollette (phone: 678-3495). Moderate.

Nino – A reliable place, frequented by artists, actors, and aristocrats, and near the Spanish Steps, it is truly Tuscan. The cuisine is composed of the best ingredients, ably yet simply prepared, and the service is serious, if not exactly heartwarming. Specialties: *zuppa di fagioli alla Francovich* (thick Tuscan white bean soup with garlic), *bistecca alla fiorentina* (thick succulent T-bone steak), and for dessert *castagnaccio* (semisweet chestnut cake). Closed Sundays. Reservations advised. 11 Via Borgognona (phone: 679-5676). Moderate.

Al Pompiere – Visiting firemen and travelers adore this bright, traditional restaurant near the Campo de' Fiori, whose name means "The Fireman." Pleasant decor and a menu that includes deep-fried artichokes and mozzarella-stuffed zucchini blossoms. Closed Sundays. 38 Via Santa Maria Calderari (phone: 686-8377). Moderate.

Pierluigi – The fish is fresh, the piazza is charming, the price is a bargain, and in summer, the dining is alfresco. Reservations, therefore, are necessary at this popular *trattoria* in the heart of old Rome. Closed Mondays. 144 Piazza de' Ricci (phone: 686-1302). Moderate.

Settimio all'Arancio – Simple but good, right in the heart of downtown Rome, near the old Jewish ghetto. It's always crowded. Particularly noteworthy is the *fusili con melanzane* (pasta with eggplant). 50 Via dell'Arancio (phone: 687-6119). Moderate.

Shangri Là-Corsetti – In EUR, it's much favored by American businessmen who like the fresh fish. The public pool alongside can be agreeable despite the loud, loud music. 141 Viale Algeria (phone: 591-6441). Moderate.

Sora Cecilia – Founded in 1898, this modest *trattoria* offers homemade *agnolotti* (large ravioli) and good *penne all'arabiata* (pasta with a peppery tomato sauce). 27 Via Poli (phone: 678-9096). Moderate.

Il Falchetto – Conveniently set off Via del Corso, with a few tables outdoors in fine weather, this might seem a tourist haven. But knowledgeable Romans fill the small rooms even in the gray days of winter. One of the pasta specialties to try is *paglia e fieno al salmone* (green and yellow noodles with a creamy smoked salmon sauce). The imaginative game, veal, and fish dishes are also delicious. Closed Fridays. 12-14 Via Montecatini (phone: 679-1160). Moderate to inexpensive.

Isola del Sole – A converted houseboat on the Tiber offers a variation on the theme of alfresco dining — with lunches under a welcome winter sun, or candlelit dining with the summer stars as backdrop. Try pasta with eggplant and ricotta, ravioli stuffed with *porcini* mushrooms, or *carpaccio* (thin slices of raw beef seasoned with olive oil, lemon, and flaked Parmesan cheese). Extra-special chocolate mousse. A second barge has been added to house a bar and late-night pastry shop with music. Closed Mondays. Reservations advised (for best service, get there when they open at 8:30 PM). Between Ponte Matteotti and the Metropolitana train bridge; walk down to the river from Lungotevere Arnaldo da Brescia (phone: 360-1400). Moderate to inexpensive.

Mario – A Tuscan favorite, with the usual Tuscan specialties such as Francovich soup, Florentine steaks, and delicious game in season, all prepared with admirable care and dedication by Mario himself, but served by only three overworked waiters. Closed Sundays and August. Via della Vite 55 (phone: 678-3818). Moderate to inexpensive.

Otello alla Concordia – A delightful *trattoria* in the middle of the Piazza di Spagna shopping area, with certain tables reserved for habitués and a colorful courtyard for fine weather dining. The menu is Roman, and it changes daily, depending a great deal on the season. Closed Sundays, Christmas week, and the first week in January. No reservations. 81 Via della Croce (phone: 679-1178). Moderate to inexpensive.

Taverna della Scala – This recently refurbished *trattoria,* with outdoor tables during fine weather, serves typical Roman cuisine and, at night, pizza. *Fettuccine* with *funghi porcini* is excellent, and the roast suckling pig is lean, moist, and tender. Closed Tuesdays. 19 Piazza della Scala (phone: 589-0100). Moderate to inexpensive.

Il Barroccio – *Pane rùstico,* crusty country-style bread, is made here every day, and that's reason enough to visit. On a side street not far from the Pantheon, this is a prime place to try crostini in all its infinite permutations, and if you want to sample Roman-style pizza, do it here. Visa accepted. 13 Via dei Pastini (phone: 679-3797). Inexpensive.

I Canoisti – Newest of the river restaurants, "The Canoeists" brought their chef from the Via Veneto's famed *Café de Paris.* Set on the banks of the Tiber, beneath the Duca d'Aosta Bridge, it has alfresco dining in summer and a rustic barge for indoor meals during inclement weather. Specialties include *fettuccini* with tuna and wild *porcini* mushrooms, breast of chicken with almonds, and petits fours of *tartufini* and *cremini.* Closed Tuesdays. Via Capoprati (phone: 390247). Inexpensive.

La Carbonara – Tucked into a corner of the square in which Rome's most appealing morning food market has been held for centuries, this is where *spaghetti alla carbonara* (the sauce is eggs and bacon) is said to have been invented. That's reason enough to appear here at noontime, after surveying all the other menu items in their wild state on the stalls outside. The unpretentious atmosphere serves as a perfect environment for determined gluttony. American Express accepted. 23 Campo dei Fiori (phone: 656-4783). Inexpensive.

Checco er Carettiere – In the Trastevere area — the Greenwich Village of Rome — this eatery has a large and friendly interior, with a dining room that's paneled and pleasantly noisy. A guitarist strolls among the tables, a flower girl proffers blossoms, and a fledgling artist opens her portfolio to display sketches of surrounding landmarks. What's more, the food's super. An antipasto made entirely of seafood is a specialty, and there's a unique mixture of tomatoes and potatoes. American Express and Visa accepted. 10/13 Via Benedetta (phone: 581-7018). Inexpensive.

Costanza – For those who prize a bit of history with their supper, this group of vaulted dining rooms includes a 2,000-year-old entryway to the ancient Theater of Pompeii. The location is a tiny piazza that's reached by navigating a narrow alley, so it's wise to make a dry run in daylight if you plan to come after dark. Don't miss the chance to watch the chef in action at the grill; the daily specials created thereon are usually the best choices. American Express and Visa accepted. 63 Piazza Paradiso (phone: 656-1717 or 654-1002). Inexpensive.

Ettore Lo Sgobbone – A *trattoria* popular with newspaper and TV journalists, noted for its unpretentious northern home-style cooking. Pasta and rice (*risotto*) courses are excellent: Try the simple *tonnarelli al pomodoro e basilico* (pasta with fresh tomato and basil sauce) or *risotto nero di seppie* (rice cooked with cuttlefish and its ink). Reservations advised for the few tables outdoors on the rather dreary, typically working class street. Closed Tuesdays. 8-10 Via dei Podesti (phone: 390798). Inexpensive.

La Fiorentina – This favorite Roman pizzeria, with its wood-burning oven and grill, is in residential Prati on the Vatican side of the river. It serves pizza even at lunchtime, a rarity in Italy. Tables on the street in good weather. Closed Wednesdays all day, Thursdays at lunch. 22 Via Andrea Doria (phone: 312310). Inexpensive.

Da Fortunato – The formal name of this popular eating place, barely a block from the Pantheon, is *Ristorante del Pantheon,* and it's a favorite among young, chic Rome residents. Paper-thin proscuitto is served by waiters familiar with, and friendly to, Americans, and it's almost impossible to dine here without witnessing some intense family drama being played out at an adjacent table. The *cotoletta alla Milanese* (breaded veal chop) and spinach with oil and lemon are among the specialties, as is the fish risotto. No credit cards. 55 Via del Pantheon (phone: 679-2788). Inexpensive.

Da Giggetto – In Rome's Jewish ghetto, this is the place to sample the fried artichokes that most Roman menus identify as "Jewish style," as well as zucchini flowers stuffed with mozzarella and *crostini* (fried bread offered with an assortment of toppings). There are a number of small dining rooms, all served by fiercely indifferent waiters. But don't take the lack of attention personally; they ignore everybody. The food is first-rate and the experience absolutely authentic. No credit cards. 21A Via del Portico d'Ottavia (phone: 656-1105). Inexpensive.

Da Giulio – Another bargain for budget-minded travelers, on a tiny street off Via Giulia in a historic building. A few tables line the sunless street in the summer, and inside is most pleasant — if a bit noisy — with an original vaulted ceiling and paintings by local artists. Roman family-style cooking. Closed Sundays. No reservations. 19 Via della Barchetta. Inexpensive.

Grotte Teatro di Pompeo – One of several places in this tiny, packed neighborhood that claims to be the place where Julius Caesar met his untimely end. On any chilly day, the *zuppa di verdura* (vegetable soup) can keep one's inner self warm, and the *fettuccini verdi alla Gorgonzola* (green noodles in a rich cheese sauce) is a wonderful pasta choice. The interior isn't impressive — this used to be one of central Rome's favorite pizzerias — but the unprepossessing premises don't bother guests. This is the perfect place for budget-minded visitors to try *osso buco con funghi* (veal shank with wild mushrooms) and *saltimbocca alla Romana* (small pieces of veal with prosciutto). Visa accepted. 63 Piazza Paradiso (phone: 656-1717 or 654-1002). Inexpensive.

Le Maschere – For a taste of Calabria's Costa Viola, fragrant with garlic and devilish with red peppers, try this rustic and charming 17th- century cellar behind *Largo Argentina*. The fare is not for fragile stomachs: *antipasti* of tangy salamis, marinated anchovies, and stuffed, pickled, or highly seasoned vegetables of every sort; pasta with broccoli or eggplant, or the traditional *struncatura* (handmade whole-wheat pasta with anchovies, garlic, and breadcrumbs); fresh swordfish harpooned off the Calabrian coast, *stoccafisso* (salt cod stew with potatoes), or meats grilled on an open fire; pizzas, southern sweets, 100-proof fresh fruit salad, and *tuma* (Calabrian sheep's milk cheese). Dinner only. Closed Tuesdays and part of August. 29 Via Monte della Farina (phone: 687-9444). Inexpensive.

Al Piedone – Tiny and unpretentious, this spot is much favored by newsmen and politicos from nearby Parliament. Try the rigatoni with broccoli, sausage, and bacon, or the Puglia-style *orecchietti* (pasta) with hot red pepper, broccoli, and anchovies. The roast veal stuffed with almonds, pine nuts, and raisins is truly special. Closed Sundays. 28 Via del Piè di Marco (phone: 679-8628). Inexpensive.

Polese – This is a bargain any time of the year, either outside under the trees of the spacious square or inside the intimate rooms of the Borgia palace. A great summer starter is *bresaola con rughetta* (cured beef with arugula, seasoned with olive oil, lemon, and freshly grated black pepper), and the *pasta al pesto* is fine year-round. Closed Tuesdays. Reservations taken reluctantly (come and wait your turn). 40 Piazza Sforza Cesarini (phone: 656-1709). Inexpensive.

La Sacrestia – Lots of places claim the best pizza in town, but here it is, fresh from the wood-burning oven. Good pasta, good draft beer, ever-crowded and cheery, with kitsch decor. Near the Pantheon. Closed Wednesdays. 89 Via del Seminario (phone: 679-7581). Inexpensive.

Su Recreu – Finding this spot isn't easy, but the food is worth the expedition. The large buffet antipasto is a "take all you want" affair, and there are about a dozen hot and cold choices. The authentic mozzarella (made with buffalo milk) is marvelous, as is anything cooked on the large wood fire right at the entrance. The owners come from Sardinia, and often *carta da musica* (hot, crisp, Sardinian bread) is on the menu. No credit cards. 17 Via de Buon Consiglo; one block off the Via Cavour, not far from the Forum and the Via del Colosseo (phone: 679-0363 or 679-4918). Inexpensive.

La Tavernetta – It looks like a take-out pasta shop, but there are actually four narrow dining rooms set one above the other. This is a tiny, tidy spot, barely a block from the Spanish Steps (toward the Piazza Barberini), where the homemade pasta is pretty near perfect. Major credit cards. 147 Via Sistina (phone: 679-3124). Inexpensive.

Tullio – Up a narrow hill, just a few yards from the juncture of the Via Veneto and the Piazza Barberini is this eatery that serves superb *carciofi all Romana* (fried artichokes) and fettuccine with truffles. It's a custom to place a straw-covered bottle of Chianti on the table — diners pay only for what is drunk — and if you're not planning to visit Florence, this is a good place to try a steak grilled in Florentine style. Major credit cards. 26 Via di San Nicola da Tolentino (phone: 475-8564 or 474-5560). Inexpensive.

La Villetta al Piramide – Near the Protestant Cemetery and the marble pyramid, this cheery, large *trattoria* is run by owner-cook Ada Mercuri Olivetti, who once took first prize over 4,000 other Roman cooks for her spaghetti all'Amatriciana, made with special bacon, tomato, and cheese. She serves other wholesome, hearty dishes, including vegetable antipasti. Closed Wednesdays. 53 Viale Piramide Cestia (phone: 574-0204). Inexpensive.

For lighter meals, Rome's many *caffès* are also well worth trying. The most fashionable spots for the lunch or pre-dinner *aperitivo* are the *Caffè Greco* or the *Baretto* on Via Condotti, *Rosati* or *Canova* on Piazza del Popolo, and *Harry's Bar, Carpano,* the *Café de Paris, Doney's,* or others on Via Veneto. Best for light lunches are *Canova* and *Café de Paris. Babington's* at Piazza di Spagna is an English tearoom which serves expensive snacks and lucious cakes. Currently *alla moda* also is the little *Bar della Pace* on Piazza della Pace behind Piazza Navona, which is frequented by vendors from the nearby market in the morning and pre-lunch period, and then later in the day (until 3 AM) by all types, from artists and filmmakers to punks and politicians who, when the little marble tables fill up, rest their drinks and their bottoms on cars parked in the square.

At the tiny, busy Piazza Sant'Eustachio, the *Bar Eustachio* serves what is reputed to be the best coffee in town (but this is more an Italian-style espresso bar where a quick coffee is downed while standing, more a shot of caffeine than cause for lingering). Then, on summer evenings, the after-dinner crowd often moves toward one of the many *gelaterie* in Rome, some of which are much more than ice cream parlors, since they serve exotic long drinks and *semifreddi* (like the famous *tartufo* (double chocolate truffle) at Piazza Navona's *Tre Scalini*), and a few have lovely gardens and even live music. *Selarum,* 12 Via dei Fienaroli, and *Fassi,* 45 Corso d'Italia, have both gardens and music. Perhaps the best-known *gelateria,* however, is the very crowded *Giolitti,* 40 Via Uffici del Vicario, not far from Piazza Colonna; it boasts a tearoom (closed Mondays). Others are the sleek, high-tech *Gelateria della Palma* (which is also a piano bar), at the corner of Via della Maddalena and Via delle Coppelle; and *Fiocco di Neve,* 51 Via del Pantheon (all near the Pantheon); *Gelofestival,* 29 Viale Trastevere, in Trastevere; and *Biançaneve,* 1 Piazza Pasquale Paoli, where Corso Vittorio Emanuele II meets the Lungotevere dei Fiorentini. Favorites in the fashionable Parioli residential district are *Gelateria Duse* (also called *Giovanni*), 1 Via Eleonora Duse, and *Bar San Filippo,* 8 Via San Filippo, both specializing in *semifreddi; Bar Gelateria Cile,* 1-2 Piazza Santiago del Cile; the nearby *Giardino Ferranti,* 29 Via Giovanni Pacini; and the *Casina delle Muse* at Piazzale della Muse, for a fabulous *granita di caffè con panna* (coffee ice with cream).

SALZBURG

For music lovers, Salzburg is mostly Mozart. But even those who are not enthralled by classical music are captivated by the charm of this almost picture-perfect small city in the mountains of west-central Austria.

Salzburg is a city of four distinct seasons and moods. Spring brings blossoms to the orchards, music to the theaters and churches, and wildflowers to the meadows within sight of the heart of the city. Summer is the exuberance of the renowned *Salzburg Music Festival,* lazy days sailing on lakes, hours spent nursing a glass of wine or iced chocolate in a terrace café. In fall, the foliage show can rival New England's, and the city seems to return to its birthright as the masses of tourists evaporate. Winter is, for some, the best season — almost romantically silent and personal as the snowflakes waft through wrought-iron shop signs onto twisting, cobbled streets.

The visitor is blessed with an astonishingly small area to get to know. Familiarity of place comes rapidly. The Old City — a maze of unsquared corners, labyrinthine lanes, curious steeples, and surprisingly spacious squares — is nestled between Monk's Mountain (Mönchsberg) and the Salzach River, which divides the city. On the right bank, modern Salzburg spreads east. The city's environs are breathtaking: azure glacial lakes, stunning châteaux, charming, timeless villages, and, always, the Alps.

An ancient Celtic settlement and then a Roman trading center, Salzburg was by AD 798 the seat of an archbishopric. The Salzburg archbishops also held the title of princes of the Holy Roman Empire and were the leading ecclesiastics of the German-speaking world. They built a beautiful city, but some ruled with extreme intolerance, expelling Jews and persecuting Protestants. After Salzburg was secularized in 1803, it became part of Bavaria for a time, but was returned to Austria in 1818.

The economy here was long based on the salt from the mines of the region, hence the name of the city and province. Today, industry, farming, and the development of resorts and spas, as well as tourism, contribute to a comfortable standard of living for the more than 400,000 people of the province.

Although Wolfgang Amadeus Mozart was born here and it was here that his remarkable prodigy was first acknowledged, he was not really appreciated in Salzburg during his brief lifetime. Mozart left Salzburg for good at the age of 25, after breaking with Archbishop Hieronymus Colloredo, one of the last of the long line of autocratic archbishops who ruled Salzburg for nearly 1,000 years. Today, however, the apartment in which he was born (in 1756) and the house in which he and his family later lived are landmarks. There is a square bearing his name with a statue of the composer at its center. A music academy, the *Mozarteum,* honors him, and in its garden is a wooden pavilion in which Mozart is said to have worked on his last opera, *The Magic Flute.* The garden pavilion was brought here from Mozart's Vienna home a century ago.

The *Salzburg Festival,* which draws thousands of visitors to the area in late July and August each year, is often dominated by his music. And there is a special *Mozart Week* festival during the last week in January.

Salzburg escaped serious damage during World War II while Austria was annexed to Germany. However, the *Salzburg Festival* — though it continued through 1943 — declined in significance because many musicians could not or would not participate. Following the Allied victory in Europe, the festival was revived and continues to be one of the most important musical events in Europe. But whether you visit for the sounds of music or *caffè mit schlag,* Salzburg will enchant you.

SALZBURG AT-A-GLANCE

SEEING THE CITY: The almost fairy tale quality of Salzburg envelops you immediately as you approach the city from the east: the copper domes and belfries of the Old City outlined against a backdrop of mountains, the mighty fortress-castle (Festung Hohensalzburg) silhouetted against the sky. The terraces and the watch tower of the fort afford fine panoramas of the city and the Salzburg Alps to the south. It is reached by funicular (for a small charge) from Festungsgasse, near St. Peter's Churchyard at the foot of the mountain.

SPECIAL PLACES: The Old City lies on the left bank of the Salzach River, girded by Hohensalzburg and the orchard-laden Monk's Mountain (Mönchsberg). The modern city, on the right bank, is bordered on the south by another mountain, Kapuzinerberg.

Hohensalzburg – The castle and fortress 400 feet above the city, atop a block of Dolomite rock, was begun in 1077 and completed in 1681. It was the stronghold, and sometime residence, of the archbishops of Salzburg. The castle's staterooms retain original decorations of Gothic wood carving, coffered ceilings, and intricate ironwork. Of particular interest are the huge porcelain stove (c. 1501) in the Gilded Room and the hand-operated barrel organ dating from 1502. Guided tours. Open daily. Admission charge. From March through October and Christmas to mid-January it can be reached by funicular from Festungsgasse near St. Peter's Churchyard.

The Old City – Beneath Hohensalzburg, crowded between the mountains and the river, are the colorful, narrow streets of the Old City. The main thoroughfare, Getreidegasse, is lined with quaint shops and charming 5- and 6-story houses. In the old patrician house at #9 is the third-floor apartment in which Mozart was born (*Mozarts-Geburtshaus*) and where he composed nearly all his early works. It is now a museum (open daily; admission charge). Getreidegasse leads into Judengasse, in the middle of what once was the Jewish ghetto. It, too, has shops adorned with medieval wrought-iron signs and picturesque buildings. The two streets meet near the Old Market Square (Alter Markt), with its colorful flower stalls, 16th-century fountain, and 18th-century pharmacy.

The Cathedral (Dom) – This fine early baroque cathedral with its two symmetrical towers, fine marble façade, and massive bronze doors was consecrated in 1628. When fire destroyed the previous late Romanesque cathedral in 1598, Archbishop Wolf Dietrich wanted to build a new one larger than St. Peter's church in Rome. But he was condemned for misconduct (he had 12 children by Salome Alt, his mistress) and died imprisoned in Hohensalzburg. His successors built a more modest, though quite beautiful, version. Note the Romanesque baptismal font where Mozart was baptized in 1756.

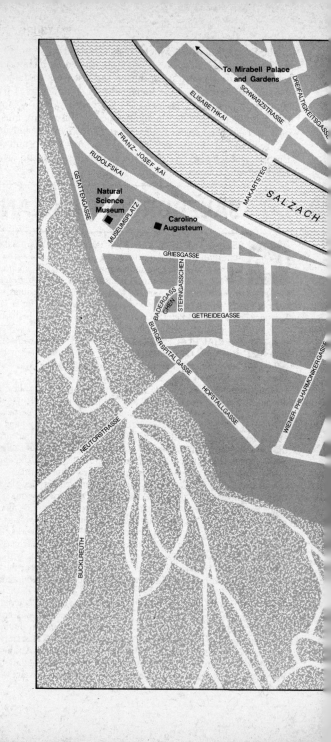

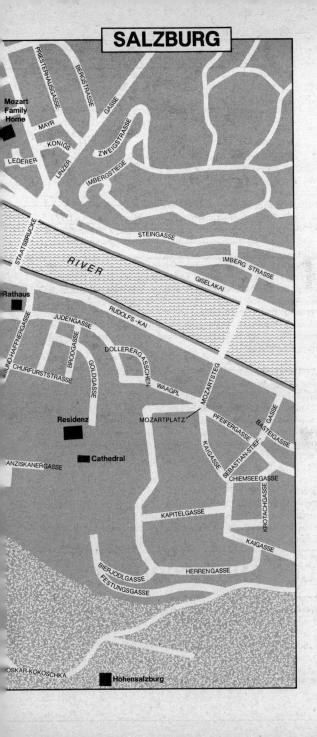

The cathedral's treasure is on view in the museum, which is open daily from May to October. Admission charge for the museum. Dompl.

Residenz – The series of buildings on the north side of the Domplatz once comprised the ecclesiastical palace of the prince-archbishops. There are 15 staterooms, decorated with fine frescoes and paintings, on the third floor, and a gallery of European painting from the 16th through 19th century that includes the work of Rembrandt, Rubens, Breughel, and others. Young Mozart often played for guests of the prince-archbishop in the Conference Hall. Across the large square in front of the Residenz is an 18th-century carillon, or *Glockenspiel*, with 35 bells, played each day at 6 AM, 11 AM, and 7 PM. The Residenz is closed Sundays. Guided tours, except when events are in progress. Admission charge. 1 Residenzpl.

Mirabell Palace and Gardens – Archbishop Wolf Dietrich built a lovely palace on the right bank of the Salzach for his paramour, Salome Alt, in 1606. It was later rebuilt and remodeled after being destroyed by fire in 1818. The grand ceremonial staircase, decorated with marble angels, is of particular interest, and the Marble Hall is a favorite place for weddings. Candlelit chamber music concerts are held here. The gardens, laid out in the early 18th century, are adorned with statues and marble vases, flowers of great variety, and small pools. East of Schwarzstr.

Hellbrunn Palace (Schloss Hellbrunn) – Once the summer residence of Archbishop Marcus Sitticus, this 17th-century castle is known primarily for its trick fountains, which spray unsuspecting visitors with water, and its theater of more than 100 mechanical figures that are set in motion by a clockwork movement to the music of an organ. Also on the grounds are a zoo (Alpenzoo) and the *Salzburg Folklore Museum* in the Monatsschlösschen. The palace is open daily, April through October; the zoo is open all year. Admission charge. At the end of Hellbrunnerstr., off Alpenstr., 3 miles (5 km) south of downtown Salzburg.

■**EXTRA SPECIAL:** The fantastic ice formations that have developed at the entrance to the caves of the World of the Ice Giants (Eisriesenwelt) are world renowned. The caves open at 5,459 feet on the western cliffs of the Hochkogel, some 30 miles (48 km) south of Salzburg. They may be visited from May through early October; detailed information is available from the state tourist information office in Mozartpl. (see *Sources and Resources*). You'll need warm clothes and sturdy shoes. If you drive there, stop at Hallein and visit the Dürnnberg salt mines, which have been worked since Neolithic times, and the lovely Golling Waterfalls near the village of Golling. Leave Salzburg on Route 311 for Hallein, Golling, and the village of Werfen. It is best to take the Werfen taxibus service to the cable car station for the caves.

American Express and several bus companies run a daily *Sound of Music Tour* of the film's locations, covering some 65 miles in 3 hours with the Rodgers and Hammerstein score playing on the bus's sound system. It's corny but still fun. Information: American Express, 5 Mozartpl. (phone: 842501).

SOURCES AND RESOURCES

TOURIST INFORMATION: The City of Salzburg Visitors' Bureau (Stadt-verkehrsbüro), which can provide you with maps, brochures, and various information, has its main office at 7 Auerspergstr. (phone: 80720). There are several branches, including one at 5 Mozartpl., in the Old City, and another in the main railway station. The tourist office for the province of Salzburg (Landestourismus) is at 1 Mozartpl. (phone: 80420 or 843264).

The US Consulate is at 51 Giselakai (phone: 28601).

Local Coverage – The *International Herald Tribune* and other major English-language newspapers can be purchased at newsstands downtown.

Food – *Restaurant Guide,* published by the tourist office, contains listings.

Telephone – The area code for Salzburg is 0662.

CLIMATE AND CLOTHES: Even in the coldest month, January, temperatures in Salzburg don't go much below 14F (−10C). July is the warmest month; temperatures reach about 85F (29C). September is the most consistently pleasant month. Tweeds, knits, and woolens are apropos for the cooler months, and many visitors buy locally made Loden coats and folkwear. For important events during the *Salzburg Festival,* dress is quite formal.

GETTING AROUND: Just about everything of interest to the visitor is within easy walking distance of the Residenzplatz. The entire Old City and the Getreidegasse are pedestrian zones.

Airport – Salzburg Airport, which handles both international and domestic traffic, is a 10-minute drive from downtown; taxi fare should run about 150 Austrian schillings (about $12). City bus line #77 connects the airport with Salzburg's main train station on Südtirolerplatz (phone: 20551, for bus information).

Bus – There is quick, comfortable bus service. Buses stop running at 11 PM.

Car Rental – Major international firms are represented.

Taxi – There are taxi stands at key spots throughout the city, and you may book one in advance by calling 76111. Fares, even though cabs are metered, can be high.

Train – Salzburg's main train station, the Hauptbahnhof, is on Südtirolerplatz (phone: 1717 for information).

SPECIAL EVENTS: Programs for the *Salzburg Festival* are announced at the beginning of the year. Ticket requests must be addressed to: Ticket Office of the Salzburg Festival, Festspielhaus, Salzburg A-5010, Austria. It is often impossible to secure tickets to major events once the festival has begun. However, tickets may be available for chamber music concerts and outdoor performances.

Information about programs and tickets for the *Mozart Week* music festival, during the last week in January, and the *Easter Festival* and Whitsun concerts, long under the direction of Herbert von Karajan, also is available from the New York office of the Austrian National Tourist Office.

MUSEUMS: In addition to those already mentioned in *Special Places,* Salzburg has several museums of interest.

Baroque Museum (Salzburger Barockmuseum) – Kurt Rossacher's collection of paintings and sculpture from the baroque era. Mirabell Gardens Orangerie (phone: 77432).

Burg Museum – Exhibitions about the city's development. Hohensalzburg (phone: 8042-2123).

Carolino Augusteum – Named for Franz I's fourth wife, it contains artifacts from the Iron Age, Roman-era relics, Gothic sculpture, miniatures, furniture, musical instruments, paintings, and more. 6 Museumspl. (phone: 843145).

Mozart Family Home (Mozarts Wohnhaus) – The composer's family lived here from 1773 to 1787. 8 Makartpl. (phone: 71776).

Natural Science Museum (Haus der Natur) – Dioramas that illustrate the earth's history, and exhibitions that trace man's relationship with nature. 5 Museumspl. (phone: 842653).

Toy Museum – In St. Blaise's Church, Bürgerspital (phone: 847560).

SHOPPING: Loden coats and *Lederhosen,* antiques, and handmade sweaters are good buys in Salzburg. Most department stores are open from 9 AM to 6 PM.

Peter B. Burges – Antique small furnishings — reputedly the Aga Khan's favorite. 31 Gstättengasse.

Jahn-Markl – *Lederhosen* and leather garments. 3 Residenzpl.

Lanz – Home of the internationally known line of cotton prints, dirndls, and other sporty women's clothes. 4 Schwarzstr.

Salzburger Heimatwerk – Handmade peasant crafts of the region. 9 Residenzpl.

Slezak – Quality leather handbags and briefcases, gloves, sweaters, and souvenirs. 8 Makartpl.

Street Markets – Fruits and vegetables are on sale at the *Grünmarkt* at Universitätsplatz and Wiener Philharmonikergasse every morning but Sunday (Saturday is liveliest) and on weekday afternoons. On Thursday mornings flowers and crafts, as well as a wide variety of edibles, are sold at the *Schrannenmarkt* near St. Andrew's Church.

SPORTS AND FITNESS: Fitness Centers – *Jogger's Gym,* 15a Augustinergasse (phone: 845033), has a sauna, massage, solarium, exercise equipment, and an English-speaking physical trainer. The *Paracelsus Kurhaus,* 2 Auerspergstr. (phone: 73200), is a medical spa that, in addition to peat mud and brine treatments by prescription, offers massage, breathing exercises, underwater gymnastics, and an indoor swimming pool with a solarium and sun terrace.

Golf – A 9-hole course is available at the *Klesheim Golf Country Club,* Klesheim, on the western outskirts of the city (phone: 850851).

Jogging – Any of Salzburg's many parks is pleasant, but runners can exercise while sightseeing by circling the Mönchsberg, the mountain on which the castle is perched, or by following Hellbrunner Allee, the wide boulevard that leads to Hellbrunn Palace. There are fitness runs, ranging from a mile at *Naturpark Aigen* to the slightly more than 3-mile *Gaisberg Circular Run.* On both sides of the Salzach River are fitness trails where you pause every few yards to perform some diagrammed physical feat. On the commercial side of the river, the Fitnessparcour starts and ends at Schloss Aigen; it's just short of a mile long. On the scenic side, another course (about a half mile) starts just across a manmade lake from Schloss Leopoldskron, which served as Baron von Trapp's home in the film *The Sound of Music.*

Swimming – An indoor pool is at the *Kurhaus* in the Mirabell Gardens and there are outdoor pools in several parks. Bathing caps are a must for everyone.

Tennis – Courts are available at *Tennisklub Salzburg,* 3 Ignaz Rieder Kai (phone: 22403), or the *Tenniscentrum,* Kasern, in the suburb of Lengfelden (phone: 50550).

THEATER: The performance of *Everyman* (Jedermann), the morality play by Hugo von Hofmannsthal, each year in the forecourt of the cathedral is one of the few non-Mozart traditions connected with the *Salzburg Festival.* The famous *Salzburg Marionette Theater* (Salzburger Marionetten Theater), 24 Schwarzstr. (phone: 72406), gives performances of operas and operettas. The season runs from Easter through September; events also take place at Christmastime.

MUSIC: Salzburg is a city of music even in non-festival months. The *Landestheater,* 22 Schwarzstr. (phone: 74086), schedules musicals, operettas, and operas as well as its regular diet of classical and contemporary drama from September through mid-June. There are organ concerts and other music at the *Mozarteum,* 26 Schwarzstr. (phone: 73155), chamber music in the Residenz and Mirabell palaces, and more music in churches and parks throughout the year.

NIGHTCLUBS AND NIGHTLIFE: Three pillars of Salzburg's "Bermuda Triangle" — where one can be swallowed up in a maze of bars, discos, and night-owl cafés — are the *Sonderbar,* 3 Steingasse (phone: 73662), *Seitensprung,* 5 Steingasse, and *Bazillus,* 2a Imbergstr. (phone: 71631). If space to boogie is a priority, try *Friesacher Stadl,* 57 Anif (phone: 06246-2411), in the suburb of Anif. And there is folk dancing at the *Sternbräu* beer garden, 23 Getreidegasse (phone: 842140), every Friday night. If you see posters advertising that the *Salzburger Stierwascher* folkloric group is playing in town, be sure to go. You could gamble the night away at the elegant *Salzburg Casino* on Mönchsberg (phone: 845-6560).

BEST IN TOWN

 CHECKING IN: Salzburg has a rich range of accommodations, but it must be stressed that reservations should be made months in advance for the festival season. There is a hotel "finding service" at the railway station at 5 Mozartplatz and on the main entrance roads (look for the green and white "i" for information). The price of a double room with breakfast in an expensive hotel will range from $125 to $200 a night; in a moderately priced hotel, from $75 to $125; and in an inexpensive one, from $45 to $75. The highest rates apply during the *Salzburg Festival.* All telephone numbers are in the 0662 area code unless otherwise indicated.

Goldener Hirsch – A group of 800-year-old patrician houses have been joined to create a country inn ambience in the heart of the Old City. Rooms vary in size; many have antique furnishings or native folk art hangings. The dining room serves some of the best food in the city (see *Eating Out*). Major credit cards. 37 Getreidegasse (phone: 848511). Expensive.

Österreichischer Hof – Across the Salzach River from the Old City near the *Mozarteum,* this traditional hotel has an impressive skylighted central court. Rooms vary, but many have high ceilings, and all are large, comfortable, and cheerful. Try to reserve a room overlooking the river. Excellent food (see *Eating Out*). Major credit cards. 5-7 Schwarzstr. (phone: 72541). Expensive.

Sheraton – Opened in 1984, this hotel chain's Austrian base is perfectly situated downtown, beside the Paracelsus Kurhaus spa, the Mirabell Gardens, and the Salzburg Conference Center. Major credit cards. 4 Auerspergstrasse (phone: 793210). Expensive.

Kasererbräu – The rooms — some baroque or Biedermeier, others contemporary — are in a 13th-century house in the center of Old Salzburg. Major credit cards. 33 Kaigasse (phone: 842406). Moderate.

Pitter – A rambling, cozy, family-run downtown hotel with 5 restaurants, of which the *Rainer Stube* is most favored by natives in the know. Major credit cards. 6-8 Rainerstrasse (phone: 785710). Moderate.

Weisse Taube – In the center of the city, this is a small hotel with rafters, wrought iron, and all amenities. 9 Kaigasse (phone: 842404). Moderate.

Cottage – Large but cozy, this hotel is near the way up to the Gaisberg, a mountain that affords good skiing and panoramic views of Salzburg, Berchtesgaden, and the Austrian and Bavarian Alps. Major credit cards. 12 Joseph-Messnerstr. (phone: 24571). Moderate to inexpensive.

Elefant – This ancient inn in the heart of the Old City is well kept and friendly. Folk art embellishes a basic simplicity. Major credit cards. 4 Sigmund-Haffnergasse (phone: 843397). Inexpensive.

EATING OUT: Besides the breaded veal cutlet, called wiener schnitzel, typical Austrian fare includes dumplings, *Knödel* and *Nockerl;* spicy stew, *Gulasch;* and, naturally, plenty of pastries. But the city's most famous dessert is an extravagant soufflé, called *Salzburger Nockerln,* that's like an immense, baked mousse, usually served with a dollop of raspberry or other fruit jam. Dinner for two with beer or house wine at an expensive restaurant will cost between $75 and $95; from $45 to $75 at a moderately priced restaurant; and from $25 to $45 at an inexpensive one. Although a 10% tip is included in most menu prices, an extra 5% gratuity is expected if service has been adequate. All telephone numbers are in the 0662 area code unless otherwise indicated.

Goldener Hirsch – The most discriminating palate will find satisfaction at this fine restaurant in one of Salzburg's most attractive hotels. Its exciting and inventive kitchen prepares both continental dishes and Austrian specialties. As for dessert, it is noted for its excellent *Salzburger Nockerln.* Open daily. 37 Getreidegasse (phone: 848511). Expensive.

Winkler – The food is getting better all the time, but the view from Mönchsberg makes it even more worthwhile. Reached by lift from the foot of the mountain at Gstättengasse. Closed Mondays. 32 Mönchsberg (phone: 841-2150). Expensive.

Österreichischer Hof – Some of the best dishes in Salzburg are prepared in the kitchen of this fine hotel restaurant. Specialties include pike in crayfish sauce, *Hechtspatzen in Krebsensauce,* and venison pie, *Wildpastete.* Open daily. 5-7 Schwarzstr. (phone: 72541). Expensive to moderate.

Alt Salzburg – The elegant red and gold interior of this excellent restaurant merely adds to its cozy ambience. Closed Sundays except during summer festivals. Major credit cards. 2 Bürgerspitalgasse (phone: 841476). Moderate.

Purzelbaum – A very fashionable and good restaurant, centrally located, is housed in one of the city's oldest inns and has a charming little garden for summer dining. Closed Sundays. Major credit cards. 7 Zugallistr. (phone: 848843). Moderate.

Festungsrestaurant – Good food and a view from the fortress-castle are available here. Open daily. Festung Hohensalzburg (phone: 841780). Moderate to inexpensive.

Stiftskellerei St. Peter – A wine cellar in the 16th century, this popular spot serves local peasant dishes, such as *Bauernschmaus:* smoked pork, sausage, sauerkraut, and dumplings. The wine is from the abbey's own vineyards. In the summer, dine in the lovely courtyard. Closed Mondays. Next to St. Peter's Church (phone: 841-2680). Moderate to inexpensive.

Stieglkeller – This beer garden, seat of the Stiegl brewery, is a beloved institution for natives as well as tourists, and folklore shows are presented between June and September. Closed October through April. 10 Festungsgasse (phone: 842681). Inexpensive.

In addition to the restaurants listed above, Salzburg has numerous old-fashioned cafés that serve snacks and pastry. Especially recommended are *Café Bazar, Café Glockenspiel, Café Mozartkugel,* and *Café Tomaselli,* all of which are centrally located and fall into either the moderate or inexpensive categories. Also, you might indulge in fanciful pastries and ice cream creations at one of Salzburg's delightful *Konditoreien,* such as *Schatz,* 3 Getreidegasse (phone: 842792), *Bazar,* 3 Schwarzstr. (phone: 74278), and *Tomaselli* (phone: 844488), or *Fuerst* (phone: 843759) in the Alter Markt.

STOCKHOLM

After the trauma caused by the assassination of Prime Minister Olof Palme in 1986, Stockholm has returned to its familiar role as a model city. Despite some concern over sporadic outbreaks of teenage violence and waves of graffiti, this is still a place where the streets are relatively safe and even downtown waterways are stocked with fish and clean enough for swimming. Here the visitor finds that rare phenomenon among big cities: one that improves with age.

Sweden's 700-year-old capital is quite simply one of the most beautiful cities in the world. From the winding, cobbled streets of its medieval district to the granite, marble, and glass of its modern downtown commercial and shopping complexes, it exudes a serene majesty. While Venice crumbles and city administrations around the world struggle with the ubiquitous demons of traffic, pollution, and crime, Stockholm grows stronger in its quiet way.

Stockholm was founded in the 13th century on a small, strategically located island on Sweden's east coast where the waters of Lake Mälaren join the Baltic Sea. As Stockholm grew, the original Old Town (Gamla Stan) became known as the City between the Bridges. Through the centuries, the number of bridges it was between proliferated as the city spread across wide bays, broad channels, and narrow waterways until today its population of 666,000 is spread over 14 islands. Stockholm's harbor opens into an archipelago of 24,000 islands, skerries, and islets. It is the Baltic's largest port, and yet it has no bawdy, tawdry waterfront quarter to act as a breeding ground of poverty and vice. And its encircling bracelets of water have freed Stockholm from the ugly collar of drab suburbs that blight so many of Europe's cities.

Not so many years ago, Stockholm was looked upon as a beautiful, romantic city, but sadly provincial by continental standards. Today Stockholm stands as the showpiece of Sweden's democratic socialism: a clean, well-planned metropolis as sophisticated, subtle, and savvy as any, whose people enjoy a high standard of living. Remote from the power blocks and conurbations of central Europe, Stockholm has been content to pursue a slow, steady plan of development. Sweden's geographic and political isolation helped spare it the ravages of World War II, and public officials with a sense of aesthetics guided the city's growth to ensure a pleasing harmony of line and tone. The result has been a comfortable marriage of modern — and supermodern — architecture and restored historic façades. Once one of Europe's poor countries, its economy dominated by agriculture, Sweden has been transformed over the past 100 years into a modern welfare state. It is a constitutional monarchy with a parliamentary government system. Yet despite the obvious social equality of its citizens, the sober elegance of some of Stockholm's older districts still manages to convey an overall impression of bourgeois complacency.

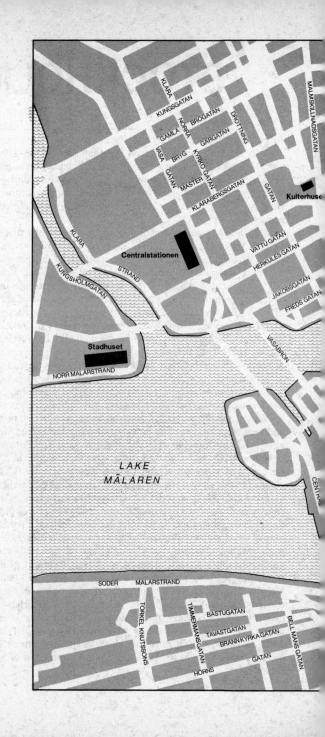

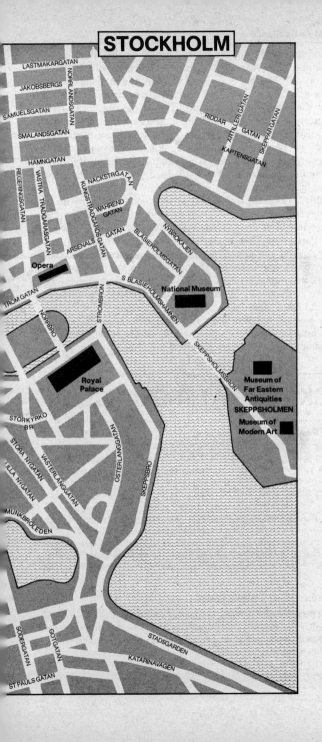

There is one exception to the city's ultra-low profile on the international scene. In mid-December each year, the red carpet is taken out of mothballs, the silverware and crystal chandeliers are given a polish, and preparations are made to receive the annual crop of Nobel Prize winners (the Peace Prize is presented in Oslo; the others in Stockholm). This is the one local event guaranteed to set teletype machines chattering in news agencies around the world. With its ancient streets and contemporary consciousness, Stockholm is a fitting place for such pomp and circumstance. Visitors who wonder how strict the formalities are at the traditional Nobel banquet are merely informed that all who seek admittance — right down to the hard-bitten press photographers — must wear full evening dress.

Yet the city's stuffy, elder statesman pose is quickly contradicted by manifestations of bustling commercialism and progressive liberal thought. Turning the next corner may delight or shock. Cabinet ministers have been known to ride the subway to Parliament. Palace guards wear shoulder-length hair, and the prime minister donned a sequinned jacket to open a disco for the city's young set. One has come to expect the unexpected. Even so, the mood of calm can be shaken by the occasional incident. Zealous internal revenue investigators once triggered a public outcry by seizing the distinguished film director Ingmar Bergman and taking him "downtown for questioning" in a manner as dramatic as the plots of his own films. If nothing this exciting happens during your visit, however, there is still a wealth of historical buildings, museums, and monuments, not to mention uninhibited nightlife, to occupy your time.

STOCKHOLM AT-A-GLANCE

SEEING THE CITY: The very best aerial view of Stockholm is from planes circling the city before landing; if you can't have that, ascend to the the observation gallery atop the 419-foot Kaknäs TV tower on the eastern edge of town. A bird's-eye view is the only way to comprehend fully the idyllic setting of the city. A mosaic of wooded islands and winding waterways enhanced by twisting copper spires and turreted roofs stretches almost as far as the eye can see.

SPECIAL PLACES: Sightseeing tours by bus run regularly from March through November (only on weekends and some weekdays the rest of the year), but most of central Stockholm can be explored on foot. The narrow lanes and charming squares of the Old Town especially reward the casual stroller. Sightseeing barges provide a fascinating "under the bridges" perspective on the city.

DOWNTOWN

Wasa Dockyard (Wasavarvet) – When the man-of-war *Wasa* was launched in 1628, she was intended as the flagship of the Royal Swedish Navy. But she foundered on the way out of Stockholm's harbor on her maiden voyage. This tragic — and embarrassing — mishap was but a dim memory when the wreck was rediscovered in 1956. During the next 5 years, a salvaging operation raised the remarkably well preserved warship and some 24,000 historic items aboard her from the harbor bottom. The *Wasa* and her fittings are now housed in a special museum complex. A short film detailing the salvage operation precedes regular guided tours in English. Open daily. Admisson charge. Djurgården (phone: 666-4900).

Skansen – This folklore center and summer meeting place for people of all ages is within walking distance of the *Wasa Museum*. Opened in 1891, Skansen was the prototype for outdoor museums now found throughout the world. More than 150 buildings of historic interest, brought here from various regions of Sweden, reflect the daily lives of rural and urban Swedes through the ages. In summer, craftsmen demonstrate glass blowing, weaving, and other traditional skills. Skansen's hilltop setting also houses a zoo; and concerts, open-air dancing, and shows here enliven the Stockholm summer scene. The grounds are not fully open during the winter, but a traditional Christmas market is held at Skansen on three Sundays during Yuletide. Grounds open daily in summer until 11:30 PM, buildings close earlier. Admission charge. Djurgården (phone: 663-0500).

Stockholm Medieval Museum (Medeltidsmuseet) – At Strömparterren Norrbro, this museum explores the development of Stockholm from 1250 to 1550. Closed Mondays (phone: 206168).

Old Town (Gamla Stan) – Birger Jarl founded the city of Stockholm on the central island of Gamla Stan in 1252. This Old Town district, a warren of small buildings jumbled together in crooked rows, is unmistakably medieval in character. Narrow lanes open onto market squares where merchants have traded since the 13th century. Even today, this remains one of the liveliest districts of the city. Careful and continuous renovation has preserved the buildings that now house about 300 small shops, restaurants, nightclubs, artists' studios, and boutiques. South of Stockholm's modern center; reachable by several short bridges.

Royal Palace (Stockholms Slott) – The royal family has now taken up residence at Drottningholm Palace (see below) to provide a greener environment for the children. Parts of the Royal Palace and the Royal Treasury with the crown jewels are open to the public, official engagements permitting. The palace, with its baroque and rococo furnishings and exquisite collections of tapestry and chinaware, was built in the late 17th and early 18th centuries. There is a small shop in one of the wings, where "royal" souvenirs can be purchased. A colorful changing of the guard ceremony takes place each midday in summer; 1 PM Sundays. Open until midafternoon; closed Mondays. Admission charge. At the foot of Norrbro Bridge, on Gamla Stan (phone: 118551).

Stockholm Cathedral (Storkyrkan) – A short walk from the Royal Palace, through the Old Town, takes you to Stockholm Cathedral, built in the 13th century and rebuilt between 1736 and 1742. Its ornate interior includes a masterful wood sculpture, *Saint George and the Dragon* by Bernt Nötke, dating from 1479. Behind the Royal Palace on Trångsund.

City Hall (Stadshuset) – The colonnaded red brick façade of this seat of Stockholm government is a masterpiece of architectural understatement. The building, dedicated in 1923, contains a spectacular Golden Hall, whose walls are covered with mosaics depicting Swedish history, made up of nearly 18 million gilded tiles. Guided tours are offered daily at 10 AM, and there are additional tours at noon on weekends. The 320-foot City Hall tower (open from May to mid-September, 10 AM to 3 PM) offers an impressive panorama of the city. Admission charge. 1 Hantverkargatan (phone: 785-9060).

Postal Museum (Postmuseum) – A large and outstanding collection of postage stamps is housed in Gamla Stan in this lovely old building with an interesting history connected with the postal services. There is an authetic 19th-century mail coach, which has been modernized and extended. The prides of the collection are two rare 1847

Mauritius stamps and a quarter-sheet of 4-Skilling banco. Don't bother making an offer, they're priceless. Closed Mondays. No admission charge. 6 Lilla Nygatan (phone: 781-1755).

Museum of Far Eastern Antiquities (Östasiatiska Museet) – Surprisingly, Sweden has a long tradition in sinological studies. The Chinese exhibition here includes Stone Age ceramics from 2000 BC; a rich collection of jade pieces; carvings in wood, ivory, and horn; Chinese lacquer; and interesting everyday paraphernalia such as mirrors and dress hooks. The museum also has collections of fine arts and handicrafts from Japan, Korea, and India. Closed Mondays. Admission charge. Skeppsholmen (phone: 666-4250).

Östermalms Saluhall – This large old covered market is where Stockholm's gourmets buy fresh meat, fish, and delicatessen goods. Steeped in atmosphere and rich in lively characters, the market offers visitors a taste of typical Swedish market trading from the past. Here, too, are salad bars and health food counters. Ask at *Lisa Elmquist's* for her recipe for dill-cured salmon (*gravlax*). A few blocks east of the city center on Östermalmstorg.

Kungsträdgården – This broad, tree-lined avenue-cum-park with its dancing fountains in summer and ice skating during the winter months is an ideal place to engage in the pleasures of people watching. In the summer, there is often a show at the bandstand. Kungsträdgardsgatan.

Stockholm's Steamers – By the City Hall and opposite the *Grand* hotel one can catch sight of smart white steamships bobbing at their moorings. These genuine turn-of-the-century steam vessels are lovingly preserved and still contribute to the heavy summer traffic out to the archipelago. There is a powerful, romantic attachment to the islands they serve that stretch from Stockholm's doorstep right out to sea. You will not have touched the heart of the city until you have made the steamer trip out to an island paradise, such as the yachting center, Sandhamn. Several steamer operators offer frequent trips of varying lengths to the islands. Throughout the summer, daily ferry service to Sandhamn is run by *Strommakanal AB,* 30 Skeppsbron (phone: 233375 for schedule information, 241100 for steamer rental). Local tourist offices have information on other schedules.

Waldemarsudde – This beautiful retreat in an exquisite setting was the home of the late Prince Eugen, an accomplished artist. His fine collection of paintings and sculpture is on exhibit here. Closed Mondays. Admission charge. Djurgården (phone: 662-1833).

House of Culture (Kulturhuset) – A modern center where exhibitions of art, handicraft, and design are featured and information is available on urban planning, history, culture, and Swedish social policies. Tourists may find its library and foreign newspapers particularly useful. There is a lunch restaurant on the top floor which overlooks the square. Closed Mondays. 3 Sergelstorg (phone: 700-0100).

Museum of Modern Art (Moderna Museet) – Interesting special exhibitions of the work of contemporary artists complement the permanent collection of 20th-century art. Open from 11 AM to 9 PM; weekends until 5 PM; closed Mondays. Admission charge. Skeppsholmen (phone: 666-4250).

SUBURBS

Millesgården – Many of the finest works of sculptor Carl Milles are displayed in the terraced garden of his former home on fashionable Lidingö Island overlooking central Stockholm. The waterside residence also contains the sculptor's rich art collection, including some of the classical Greek and Roman statues that influenced his own work. Open from 11 AM to 3 PM, Tuesdays to Fridays year-round, except from June to mid-August, when the hours are 5 to 7 PM, Tuesdays through Thursdays. Admission charge. Reached by subway to Ropsten, where buses leave frequently for Millesgården. 2 Carl Milles väg, on Lidingö (phone: 765-0553).

Drottningholm Palace – This 17th-century palace was built for dowager Queen Hedvig Eleonora on the island of Lovön just 5 miles (8 km) west of Stockholm. The French-style palace and its beautiful gardens suffer from the inevitable comparison with Versailles but deserve recognition in their own right. The Chinese Pavilion, a small, rococo summer house in the park, also is open to visitors. The palace and grounds are reached by road or by steamer that departs from Klara Mälarstrand near City Hall. Visitors also can take the subway to Brommaplan and then change to Mälaröbuses, which stop here. Palace open daily May through September; Chinese Pavilion open daily April to mid-October. Admission charge. Lovön (phone: 759-0310).

Drottningholm Court Theater (Drottningholms Slottsteater) – On the palace grounds, this superb rococo building fully deserves separate mention as one of the most perfectly preserved 18th-century theaters anywhere. During summer months, the theater's original stage sets and machinery are used for performances of period operas and ballets. But the 350-seat auditorium and theater museum are worthy of a visit at any time. Guided tours are available. Open May through September. Admission charge. Lovön (phone: 759-0406).

■**EXTRA SPECIAL:** The university and cathedral city of Uppsala lies less than 40 miles (64 km) north of Stockholm and offers much of historic interest to make the trip worthwhile. In addition to the medieval cathedral and fine 17th-century castle, the famous silver Bible *Codex Argenteus* is housed in the university library; Swedish botanist Carolus Linnaeus is honored with a museum at his former home; and there are burial mounds that represent the only Viking remains in this part of Sweden. Soak up the atmosphere as you down Viking mead, brewed from hops and honey and served in traditional ornamental horns at the pub near the mounds.

On the way to Uppsala, a short detour will take you to the oldest town in Sweden, Sigtuna. This small community was once immensely important, serving as the capital of the nation for over a century.

SOURCES AND RESOURCES

TOURIST INFORMATION: For general tourist information, call at Sweden House, Kungsträdgården (phone: 789-2000), where the Swedish Tourist Board and the Stockholm Information Service provide maps and literature. The $12-a-day Stockholm Card (half price for children under 18) — good for a free sightseeing tour, unlimited use of public transportation, and admission to most museums — can be bought at Sweden House and several other locations, including Pressbyrån newsstands. Call *Frida,* an automatic information service (phone: 221840), for a summary of the day's events in English. Most hotels supply copies of *Stockholm This Week,* a free review of current activities in the city. During the winter, ask for the *Stimulating Stockholm* program.

A useful address for businesspeople is *Industrihuset,* 19 Storgatan, headquarters for the Swedish Trade Council (phone: 783-8500) and numerous other Swedish industrial organizations and export bodies.

The US Embassy is at 101 Strandvagen (phone: 783-5300).

Local Coverage – There are no English-language newspapers published in Sweden, though the *International Herald Tribune* and British papers are available at Gallerian (a shopping arcade) and at newsstands. National dailies sometimes produce English-language sections for tourist in summer.

Food – Consult the restaurant listings in *Stockholm This Week.*

Telephone – The area code for Stockholm is 08.

CLIMATE AND CLOTHES: Bear in mind that Stockholm shares the same latitude as lower Alaska, and the summer climate will seem surprisingly mild. June, July, and August usually are the warmest months, with a good chance of sunshine and temperatures averaging about 70F (21C) during the daytime. You'll need a sweater or jacket for cool summer evenings from May through September. During May and June, there is only a short period of darkness each night at this latitude, resulting in long, gloriously romantic evenings. Winter usually sets in sometime during November. Thereafter, temperatures fall well below zero and heavy snowfall can be expected on and off until March or April. The good news is the low humidity, which makes for a dry, crisp, and, in some ways, pleasant cold. Woolen underwear, a heavy topcoat, warm gloves, and sensible footwear are recommended. Rubber overshoes are useful and can be purchased locally.

GETTING AROUND: Airports – Arlanda International Airport, which serves both domestic and international flights, is a 30- to 45-minute trip from downtown. The average taxi fare is 230 to 250 Swedish kronen (about $37-$41); *SAS Limousine* (797-3700) charges Skr. 185 (about $30) per person to and from downtown, Skr. 240 (about $39) to and from the southern suburbs (discounted for more than one passenger to the same address). The new City Terminal, next to the Central Station, has regular airport bus service, with an intermediate stop at Jarva Krog. A free bus service is operated between domestic and international terminals at the airport.

Bromma Airport, which serves a few local airlines as well as charter flights, is a 15-minute trip from downtown. The average taxi fare is Skr. 80. (about $13). There is no bus service to the airport.

Subway, Bus, and Train – The Stockholm subway, with entrances marked by *tunnelbana* signs, is clean (except for graffiti), efficient, extensive, and by far the quickest means of intracity transportation. The newer stations have been designed by leading artists. The Kungsträdgården station downtown, for instance, has stone statues and miniature waterfalls. Some residents avoid the subway at night because of intermittent disturbances by homeward-bound revelers (harsh drinking-and-driving laws keep them off the roads). Note that considerable fare reductions are often in effect during the summer. Check with the tourist office or where you purchase your tickets.

All parts of the city are linked by bus routes, but during morning and evening rush hours progress can be slow despite special bus-only traffic lanes. Special tourist discount tickets (including the Stockholm Card; see above) for subways, buses, and streetcars can be purchased at major bus and subway stations as well as at Pressbyrån (Press Agency).

Central Station, the main railway (commuter and international trains), bus, and subway station, is at Vasagatan (phone: 248040 for information and reservations).

Taxi – Taxis are rather expensive but plentiful, except during rush hours and inclement weather. They can be hailed in the street — an illuminated roof sign indicates they are available — but the surest way is to call the central booking number, 150000 (phone: 320000 in suburban areas), or book in advance by calling 150400, where you may ask for a Tourist-Taxi with a bilingual driver. Several cab companies are now taking advantage of a new ruling allowing them to open their own exchanges; one is *Top Cab* (phone: 200000).

Car Rental – Major firms are represented at Stockholm-Arlanda Airport and at downtown locations.

Ferry Service – Small ferryboats operate regular services between Räntmästartrappan by the Old Town and Allmänna Gränd on Djurgården, and in summer between Nybroplan downtown and Allmänna Gränd. Cheap and great fun.

SPECIAL EVENTS: *Walpurgis Night,* April 30, heralds the arrival of spring and is celebrated with bonfires in public places. *Labor Day,* May 1, is an occasion for parades and political speeches. *Midsummer* is a charming festival (originally pagan and very ancient) occurring in the third or fourth week of June, when pagan rites are celebrated with folk dances, raising the Maypole, and general merrymaking. The month of July sees *Summer Stockholm,* a festival of athletic contests, music, and drama. The Nobel festivities take place annually in December, but access is difficult to everything but the public lectures of the prizewinners. On *St. Lucia's* feast day, December 13, Swedish children traditionally wake their parents in the early morning hours to serve them saffron buns and coffee. Some of Stockholm's major hotels celebrate the day by sending blond *Lucia* maidens, wearing wreaths of candles on their heads, to serve the traditional breakfast to guests in their rooms. There are also special evening festivities at Skansen (see *Special Places*).

 MUSEUMS: Stockholm has over 50 museums, art galleries, and historic buildings. Most museums are closed Mondays. Those of note not listed in *Special Places* include the following.

Hallwyl Museum – Collections of weapons, paintings, and Chinese porcelain. 4 Hamngatan (phone: 666-4499).

House of Nobility – In this historic, 17th-century building, exhibitions pertain to the knight order in Sweden. Riddarhustorget (phone: 100857).

Museum of National Antiquities and the Royal Coin Cabinet (Historiska Museet and Kungliga Myntkabinettet) – Thirty rooms and 10,000 years of history. The second floor houses the coin collection. 13-17 Narvavägen (phone: 783-9400).

National Maritime Museum (Sjöhistoriska Museet) – Exhibitions deal with the Swedish navy and merchant marine in a building designed by Ragnar Östberg. Djurgårdsbrunnsvägen (phone: 666-4900).

National Museum of Fine Arts (Nationalmuseum) – Opened in 1794, it contains works by Breughel, El Greco, Rembrandt, Rubens, and Swedish artists. Södra Blasieholmshamnen (phone: 666-4250).

National Museum of Science and Technology – 7 Museivägen (phone: 663-1085).

Nordiska Museet – Over a million objects illustrate life in Sweden since the 16th century. Djurgården (phone: 666-4600). Closed Fridays.

Riddarholm Church – Founded in the 13th century, this pantheon contains the tombs of Swedish kings and other famous Swedes. Riddarholmen, across the bridge from the Old Town (phone: 789-8500).

Royal Army Museum (Armémuseum) – Arms and artillery from the 16th century to the present. 13 Riddargatan (phone: 661-7602 or 660-3853).

Strindberg Museum – Sweden's most famous playwright lived here before his death in 1912. 85 Drottninggatan (phone: 113789).

Swedish Museum of Natural History – Frescati (phone: 666-4040).

Thiel Gallery – The private collection of Ernest Thiel; especially noteworthy are the late-19th-century paintings by Swedish artists. On Djurgården (phone: 662-5884).

SHOPPING: Shopping is a major pastime of affluent Swedes, which is reflected in the heavy concentration of richly stocked department stores, trendy boutiques, and exclusive shops. Stockholm's main shopping district is the area around Sergelstorg Square, Hamngatan, Kungsgatan, and the market square, Hötorget, and adjoining streets. Adjoining Hötorget is the department store *PUB,* where visitors can buy anything from souvenirs to mink coats. *Nordiska Kompaniet* (just called *NK* in Sweden), 18-20 Hamngatan, is the largest department store in Scandinavia and offers a good selection of knitwear. The department stores usually have a shopping service with English-speaking clerks. Two large indoor shopping arcades downtown, Sturegalleriet, at Stureplan, and Gallerian, accessible from Hamngatan and Regeringsgatan, save a tourist from getting a blue nose from window shopping outdoors in the depth of winter. Best buys are Swedish glass, textiles, ceramics, stainless steel housewares, furs, and Swedish crafts. Try the Old Town for antiques. Shopping hours are generally 9 AM to 6 PM weekdays and to 3 PM Saturdays. Some shops stay open an hour later during winter months.

Casselryds – Elegant crystal and porcelain at favorable prices. A 25-minute drive south from downtown, but free limousine service to and from your hotel can be arranged (phone: 710-5116). 5 Storholmsgatan, Skårholmen. *Casselryds* also has a small showroom centrally located at 11 Hamngaten.

Duka Aveny – Stock of over 1,700 different glasses. 41 Kungsgatan.

Georg Jensen Silver AB – Specializes in silverware, glassware, and porcelain. 13 Birger Jarlsgatan.

Hasselblads Foto – Home of the Swedish camera that American astronauts used in their space explorations. 16 Hamngatan, 71 Sveavägen, and 21 Sergelgatan.

Läns Hemslöjden – Center for Swedish handicrafts and souvenirs. 14 Drottninggatan.

Carl Malmsten – The largest exponent of Swedish modern furniture. 5B Strandvägen.

Nordkalottshoppen – Genuine handicrafts from Lappland. 48 Norrbackagatan.

Svensk Hemslöjd – More handicrafts, run by the Swedish Handicraft Society. 44 Sveavägen.

Svenskt Tenn – Outstanding pewter designs and fabrics for the home. 5A Strandvägen.

 SPORTS AND FITNESS: Stockholm has several soccer and ice hockey teams in the premier division of the league, and these are the major spectator sports. Schedules and ticket information are available from the tourist offices (see *Sources and Resources.*)

Basketball – Swedish basketball has had quite a lift from imported American players in recent years. Stockholm's top teams are *Solna* and *Alvik*. Games are played at various stadiums.

Fitness Center – *World Class Hälsostudion,* 68 Luntmakargatan (phone: 345410), offers weights and exercise equipment, Jacuzzi, sunbeds, and massage.

Golf – There are some fine 18-hole courses in the Stockholm region, *Drottningholm* (phone: 759-0085), *Lidingö* (phone: 765-7911), and *Djursholm* (phone: 755-1477) being among the finest. During the Swedish vacation month, July, foreign visitors may play these courses as guests, provided they show a membership card from their home club and evidence of their official handicap.

Ice Hockey – Swedish teams are very competitive internationally and players are known for their good skating ability. Stockholm's top teams *AIK* and *Djurgården* play at the new *Globe Arena,* Johanneshov, during the winter season, November through March.

Jogging – Djurgarden Park, an island virtually free of buildings save museums, is a 10-minute walk from the center of town.

Soccer – The season is split into spring and autumn. *AIK* and *Djurgården* play at *Råsunda Football Stadium,* Solna, and *Hammarby* plays at *Söder Stadium.* A giant, new indoor arena called *The Globe* is near *Söder Stadium.*

Tennis – Future Bjorn Borgs and lesser mortals can keep up their game at the *Royal Tennis Hall,* 75 Lidingovagen (phone: 670350). The tennis hall also has squash courts.

Trotting – A popular spectator sport with gambling permitted. *Solvalla Stadium* has regular meetings during most of the year.

THEATER: Few visitors would wish to sit through Strindberg in the original or hear *West Side Story* in Swedish, but those who do will find the current program at the *Royal Dramatic Theatre* (Dramaten), Nybroplan (phone: 667-0680), and other theaters in *Stockholm This Week.* The regular theater and opera season runs from the end of August to the middle of June.

MUSIC: The *Royal Opera House* (Operan), just off Gustav Adolphs Torg, offers fine performances during the season, with local talent and prominent international singers (phone: 248240 for reservations, 203515 for other information). In summer there are performances at *Drottningholm Court Theater* (see *At-a-Glance*). During the season there are also frequent concerts at the *Concert Hall* (Konserthuset) (phone: 102110), *Berwald Hall* (Berwaldhallen), and *House of Culture* (Kulturhuset). In summer, there are outdoor concerts in several city parks and at Skansen. Church recitals take place at the cathedral, Engelbrekts Church, Adolf Fredriks Church, Gustav Vasa Church, and St. Jacobs. Tickets and information can be obtained at a booth in Gallerian. Last-minute tickets are sold at the kiosk on Norrmalmstorg.

NIGHTCLUBS AND NIGHTLIFE: Top discos are *Atlantic,* 3 Teatergatan (phone: 218907), *Café Opera,* Operahuset (phone: 110026), *Valentino,* 24 Birger Jarlsgatan (phone: 142780), and *Melody,* 27 Birger Jarlsgatan (phone: 212100). These are the places to be seen; known habitués include royalty, pop stars, and international tennis aces. Otherwise the plethora of discos is a fast-changing scene. The palatial rooms of the classic nightspot in downtown Berzelli Park, *Berns,* have opened again after painstaking restoration (phone: 614-0550/55/60). *Bacchi Wapen,* 5 Järntorgsgatan in the Old Town (phone: 116671), is a nightclub with a cabaret featuring racy shows for tired executives and male striptease for ladies only (pick the right night!). *Dixie Queen* is an elegant riverboat berthed at Nybroviken/Strandvägen for gourmet dining and nightclubbing (phone: 674500). *Hamburger Börs,* an exclusive nightclub that once tried to book Sammy Davis, Jr., and got the reply: "Mr. Davis doesn't play hamburger joints," has been renamed *Börsen,* and Davis is among the many top artists who have performed here (6 Jakobsgatan; phone: 101600).

BEST IN TOWN

CHECKING IN: Stockholm hotels have a high rate of occupancy all year round, so it's wise to arrange reservations well in advance of arrival. If you do arrive without a hotel reservation, *Hotellcentralen,* on the lower floor at the central railway station, is the official accommodation agency (phone: 240880, but note that the only reservation that can be made over the phone is for the Stockholm Package described below, with 1 week advance notice). Those visiting from mid-June through August and on weekends should ask about the special rates offered by most hotels. From June 9 through August 13, the Stockholm Package offers bargain rates of $35 to $68 — breakfast included — in first class hotels, with the Stockholm Card (see *Sources and Resources*). Rates quoted are per person in double rooms. The package is sold by travel agents in Sweden and *Hotellcentralen.* A double at one of the hotels listed below as expensive can cost $190 and up, $100 to $175 at those classed as moderate. Although we don't list an inexpensive category, numerous pensions and youth hostels are available. (Contact *Sweden House,* Kungsträdgården, 789-2000; or, in the US, *American Youth Hostels,* listed in GETTING READY TO GO, "Hints for Single Travelers.") All telephone numbers are in the 08 area code unless otherwise indicated.

Diplomat – Small, sophisticated rooms, individually furnished in classic style. The hotel is centrally located at the edge of the fashionable diplomatic quarter in a building of historic significance and great character. It has 131 rooms with telephones, a cocktail bar, and the elegant *Tea House*. 7C Strandvägen (phone: 663-5800). Expensive.

Grand – Although newly renovated, this hotel remains steeped in European tradition and good old-fashioned luxury. Opposite the Royal Palace, it is the most exclusive hotel in town. If you are coming to collect a Nobel Prize, don't settle for anything less; there are 315 rooms, 2 restaurants, a winter garden, and bar. Every room has a telephone. 8 Södra Blasieholmen (phone: 221020). Expensive.

Park – In a quiet spot but still close to the center of things, this hotel is modern, exclusive, and not so large that it fails to offer attentive service. Totally renovated during 1988, all 202 rooms have telephones, and a brasserie, piano bar, and first class restaurant are on the premises. 43 Karlavägen (phone: 229620). Expensive.

Reisen – An interesting old building in the Old Town, with modern facilities and a fine view of the harbor. The hotel has 113 rooms with telephones, a grill room, piano bar, sauna, and pool in its medieval vaults. 12-14 Skeppsbron (phone: 223260). Expensive.

Royal Viking – The special features of this modern, 340-room hotel include 3 duplex suites with whirlpool bath and sauna, a glass-roofed winter garden with arcades and restaurants, and the *Sky Bar* on the top floor, with a lovely view. Near the Central Station. 1 Vasagatan (phone: 141000). Expensive.

Sergel Plaza – In the heart of the city's business and shopping district and its elegant appointments, which include 18th-century artwork and antiques, this recently built 406-room hotel has much to recommend it. Along with a formal restaurant, lobby bar, and piano bar with nightly entertainment, it has a beauty salon offering sauna, massage, solarium, and whirlpool baths. 9 Brunkebergstorg (phone: 226600). Expensive.

Sheraton-Stockholm – Large, modern, very much an American-owned, international-style hotel with an excellent location on the waterfront overlooking the Old Town. Its impressive lobby is always busy. The main restaurant, *Premiere,* has an extraordinarily rich ambience for such a newcomer. The 475 rooms, of which 51 are in the top-floor executive Towers section, all have telephones. 6 Tegelbacken (phone: 142600). Expensive.

Strand – A delightful, old-fashioned waterfront hotel, newly renovated. High-ceilinged rooms (137) combine old Swedish furniture with new Italian textiles and lighting; bathrooms are stunning. Besides the dining room, there's the atrium *Piazza* lounge and restaurant, fancifully done up as the courtyard of an Italian *palazzo*. 9 Nybrokajen (phone: 222900). Expensive.

Continental – In an excellent central location, with modern apartments. There are 250 rooms with telephone, a cafeteria, restaurant, bars, and bistro. 4 Klara Vattu-gränd (phone: 244020). Expensive to moderate.

Adlon – Centrally located but small and unpretentious. Only 62 rooms, all with telephone; breakfast only is served in the dining room. 42 Vasagatan (phone: 245400). Moderate.

Flamingo – A pleasant, recently renovated, 128-room hotel in a suburb that is 10 minutes from downtown by subway. 11 Hotellgatan, Solna (phone: 830800). Moderate.

 EATING OUT: Swedish food was made famous by the smorgasbord, a seemingly endless array of delicacies from smoked salmon and dozens of varieties of herring to lingonberry jam and honey. If it's on the menu, you might want to try another Swedish specialty: elk steak accompanied by red currant or rowanberry jelly. *Surströmming,* fermented Baltic herring, has as many detractors as fans. If you'd like to sample some in the traditional way, eat it on a slice of *norrland* bread with Swedish *mandel* potatoes and, perhaps, a glass of *snaps* to wash it down. Recent years have seen a great expansion of inexpensive, mass-production pizzerias, kebab and hamburger restaurants, and self-service cafeterias in Stockholm. But this new food culture has done little to harm the more established (and expensive) restaurants. A three-course dinner for two, with wine and service, can run $150 and up at an expensive restaurant, $75 to $100 at a moderately priced place, $50 or less at an inexpensive one. It's possible to enjoy a good lunch at a modest price at restaurants all over Stockholm, while dining out in the evening tends to be more demanding on the wallet. One tip to help cut costs: Look for the words *Dagens rätt* on the menu. That means "today's special." All telephone numbers are in the 08 area code unless otherwise indicated.

Erik's – The fish and seafood dishes are well prepared at this converted barge, with an oyster bar on its bridge. Closed Sundays. Reservations advised. 17 Kajplats, Strandvägen (phone: 660-6060). Expensive.

Erik's – That's right — same name, different restaurant. This one is on dry land, in the Old Town. At least one columnist regards it as the best in Stockholm. It is an expensive and discreet haunt of those who love good food and have the means to enjoy it. Closed Sundays. 17 Osterlånggatan (phone: 238500). Expensive.

L'Escargot – Traditional French cuisine in an elegant setting, with a brasserie downstairs and fine dining one floor up. Known for excellent service as well as an extensive wine list. Try the snails with Roquefort sauce — one of the house specialties. Brasserie open daily for lunch and dinner; dining room open daily except Sundays for dinner only. Reservations advised. 8 Scheelegatan (phone: 530577). Expensive.

Operakällaren – An institution in Sweden and a restaurant with a truly international reputation, it prepares the state banquets at the Royal Palace. Its kitchen sets the standard by which other restaurants all over the country are judged. It has palatial rooms with high ceilings and carved oak paneling hung with fine art, a baroque grill room, and a magnificent smorgasbord. *Operabaren* and *Café Opera,* in the same building, are meeting places for Stockholm intellectuals. Open daily. Reservations necessary. Operahuset. Main dining room (phone: 242700 or 111125), *Café Opera* (phone: 242707 or 110026), *Operabaren* (phone: 107935). Expensive.

Ulriksdals Inn – In the park of Ulriksdals Palace, it features a fine smorgasbord as well as French and international fare. Open daily for lunch and dinner; closes Sundays at 6:30 PM. Slottspark, Solna (phone: 850815). Expensive.

Propaganda – A lively restaurant in recently renovated rooms dating from the turn of the century, it serves French and Swedish cuisine. Open daily. 20 Birger Jarlsgatan (phone: 240100). Expensive to moderate.

Aurora – An intimate hideaway. Closed Sundays. Reservations advised. 11 Munkbron (phone: 219359). Expensive to moderate.

La Brochette – Delightfully and authentically French: All the head chefs are French. The traditional but varied menu offers well-prepared food served in an inviting but constantly crowded dining room. It offers a good selection of wines. Closed Sundays. Reservations advised. 27 Storgatan (phone: 662-2000). Expensive to moderate.

Finsmakaren – A modest little restaurant 15 minutes by taxi from downtown. The fine food and friendly service draw praise from all quarters. Closed weekends and July. Reservations advised. 9 Råsundavägen, Solna (phone: 276771). Expensive to moderate.

Latona – Swedish specialties in a medieval setting. Open daily. Reservations advised. 79 Västerlånggatan (phone: 113260). Expensive to moderate.

Mälardrottningen – Once heiress Barbara Hutton's luxurious yacht, now an unusual 59-room hotel with several exclusive restaurants and a cocktail bar on the bridge. Open weekdays for lunch, daily for dinner. Reservations necessary. Moored at Riddarholmen (phone: 243600). Expensive to moderate.

Martini – Centrally located, this restaurant is fashionable and serves continental cuisine. Closed Sundays. Reservations necessary. 4 Norrmalmstorg (phone: 200420). Expensive to moderate.

Nils Emil's – The elegant decor and small size of this congenial restaurant conspire with the superb food to make dining here an intoxicatingly intimate experience. Closed Sundays. Reservations advised. 122 Folkungagatan (phone: 407209). Expensive to moderate.

Stortorgskällaren – Near the Royal Palace. Veranda dining in summertime. Open daily. Reservations advised. 7 Stortorget (phone: 105533). Expensive to moderate.

Wärdshuset Godthem – A hundred-year-old inn in the Djurgården park. Good, varied menu, pleasant view across the bay, intoxicating atmosphere, and welcoming staff make this more a journey into 19th-century hospitality than just dining out. Open daily. 9 Rosendalsvägen (phone: 661-0722). Expensive to moderate.

Capri – One of the best of the wave of pizzerias that swept to popularity in Stockholm during the '70s. Mock grotto interior contrasts with the genuine Italian cooking. Friendly and informal. Open daily. 15 Nybrogatan (phone: 662-3132). Moderate.

La Familia – The name tells you that this neighborhood restaurant is run by a family of Italians. Well-prepared pasta dishes are served in a friendly atmosphere. Open for lunch weekdays and for dinner daily except Mondays. 45 Alströmergaten (phone: 506310). Moderate.

Gässlingen – This small restaurant is somewhat off the main tourist beat but worth the detour if you want to eat well and mingle with the locals — without denting a modest travel budget. Homey interior and a varied menu with a broad price range. Closed weekends. No reservations. 93 Brännkyrkagatan (phone: 669-5495). Moderate to inexpensive.

Coco and Carmen – This lunch restaurant opened on the former premises of a bakery whose original ovens are preserved as a curiosity. The very tasteful interior has authentic 1920s furnishings. Serves reasonably priced light dishes such as cheese pie, toast *skagen,* soups, salads, and herring. Caters to a very genteel public but leans more toward friendliness than stuffiness. Closed weekends. Reservations advised. 7 Banergatan (phone: 660-9954). Inexpensive.

Restaurants of the Old Town – There are several cellar restaurants in the narrow lanes of the Old Town in centuries-old vaults, where every nook and cranny seem to have a story of its own. The proprietors are, for the most part, lively individuals whose feeling for haute cuisine is equaled only by their love of the Old Town and its medieval history. The food is excellent and the menus normally include delicacies from the traditional Swedish kitchen, perhaps raw spiced salmon or snow grouse.

Which one is best? Everyone has a favorite, but here are our two: *Diana* – Unconventional, mixed clientele. Closed Sundays. Reservations advised. 2 Brunnsgränd (phone: 107310). Expensive to moderate. *Fem Små Hus* – Five interconnected buildings form a honeycomb of vaults, arches, and alcoves. Ideal setting for intimate dining. Open daily. Reservations advised. 10 Nygränd (phone: 100482). Expensive to moderate.

VENICE

Venice is one of the world's most photic — and photographic — cities. As the sun sets, it burnishes the old buildings with a splendid, rosy glow that is reflected, then refracted, in the waters of the canals. The city is luminously beautiful, both in radiant, peak-season August and in bleak, wet November. And it is painfully beautiful when suddenly, on some late-winter morning, the rain trickles to a halt, the cloud curtains part, and trapezoids of sunlight reheat the ancient stones. Then there is an ineffable sense of renewal as the café tables are set up again in St. Mark's Square, and pigeons and waiters alike swoop out from the dark arcades while an orchestra begins another airy melody. Little wonder that, long before photography, Romantic painting flourished here.

Venice is 117 islets separated by 150 canals and joined by 400 bridges on Italy's northeastern Adriatic coast. A 3-mile bridge reaches across the Laguna Veneta (Venetian Lagoon), connecting it to the mainland near the small town of Mestre. The city is protected from the force of the Adriatic Sea by the natural breakwater of the Lido, a long, narrow sandbar that is one of the most fashionable resorts on the Adriatic.

The lagoon city began as a place of refuge from the violent barbarian invasions of the 5th century; mainland inhabitants fled to the isolated islands. As communities grew up, the islands became connected to one another, and Venice developed into a powerful, flourishing city-state. During the Crusades, this little maritime republic came to dominate the entire Mediterranean, and the winged Venetian lion, symbol of St. Mark, the city's protector, stood guard over a network of palaces from the Strait of Gibraltar to the Bosporus. This was the city of Marco Polo.

Renaissance Venice was the focal point for the great trade routes from the Middle East, and the markets beside the city's Ponte di Rialto (Rialto Bridge) were a pulse of European commerce. The doges — the city's rulers — celebrated their mastery of the Mediterranean with an annual ceremony of marriage to the sea, and the golden ducats that overflowed the city's coffers financed some of the world's most spectacular art and architecture. The Venetian school of painting, which produced magnificent colorists, began with Giorgione and achieved its apogee in the 16th century with Titian Vecellio, Paolo Veronese, and Jacopo Tintoretto. The proud, thousand-year Venetian independence ended with the Treaty of Campoformio in 1797, when Napoleon traded the territory to Austria. In 1866, after nearly 70 years of Bonaparte and Habsburg domination, the city was joined to newly unified Italy.

Today, Venice proper has a population of nearly 132,000 — 400,000 including the metropolitan area. The millions of tourists who swarm through its narrow streets and tiny squares make up Venice's chief industry —

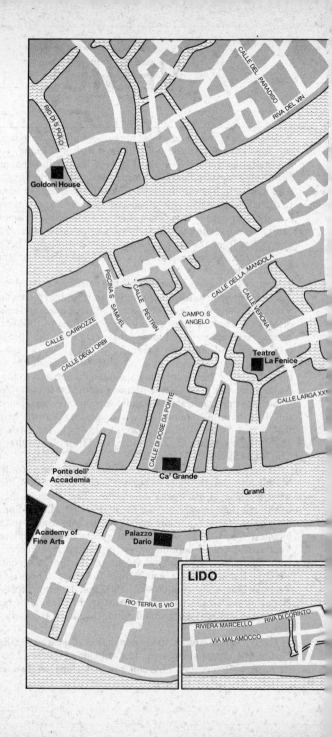

and they leave behind well over $100 million a year. A gaudy party atmosphere reigns from Easter to October, with a midsummer explosion sometimes as crass as it is colorful: the landing stages jammed and listing with tour groups, long lines waiting for frozen custard by the Doge's Palace, and the big Lido ferries packed with sun-scorched day-trippers. Hawkers and hustlers populate every corner. In its way the scene is as vibrant, insistent, chaotic, and vulgar as anything from the days of the international market on the Ponte di Rialto.

And yet, even on *Ferragosto* weekend, Italy's state holiday in mid-August, it's still possible to turn deliberately from the main thoroughfare and string together a few random rights and lefts to find yourself in a haven of quiet back alleys, on a tiny bridge across a deserted canal, in the middle of a silent, sun-baked *piazzetta,* with a fruit stall, a splashing fountain — and not a tourist in sight.

Venice in winter is a totally different experience: placid, gray, and startlingly visual. Suddenly, there is no one between you and the noble palaces, the soaring churches, the dark canals. Only the mysterious masked merriment of *Carnevale* (February 17-27 in 1990) interrupts the chilly repose of the time when Venice is most emphatically a community of Venetians.

Not everyone loves Venice. D. H. Lawrence called it "an abhorrent, green, slippery city," and it does have a dark, decadent quality, sometimes a damp depressiveness. (An inscription on a sundial says, "I count only the happy hours.") But few cities have attracted so many illustrious admirers. Shakespeare set one of his best-known plays, *The Merchant of Venice,* here. Galileo Galilei used the bell tower in St. Mark's Square to test his telescope. Richard Wagner composed here. Lord Byron and Henry James wrote here. It's not hard to feel the ghosts of these and others who, as James said, "have seemed to find [here] something that no other place could give."

VENICE AT-A-GLANCE

SEEING THE CITY: The traditional vantage point from which to admire Venice is the summit of the 324-foot red *campanile* (bell tower) in St. Mark's Square. The view on all sides is breathtaking — from the red-shingled rooftops and countless domes of the city to the distant islands that dot the wide lagoon. There's an elevator to the top or, for the heartier, a ramp. Open daily. Admission charge.

For a bird's-eye view of St. Mark's Square itself (and the rest of the lagoon city), take a short boat ride to the Isola San Giorgio (#5 ferryboat from the Riva degli Schiavoni — one stop) and ride the elevator to the top of the church tower. The church itself, a masterpiece by Andrea Palladio, contains two major works by Tintoretto. It also has beautiful carved wooden choir stalls depicting the life of St. Benedict. Open daily. Admission charge.

SPECIAL PLACES: St. Mark's Square is the center of life in Venice; from here sightseers can board steamers to the Lido and other islands as well as to the various quarters of the city. The Corso della Gente is not a street, but a phrase Venetians use to describe the "flow of people" that roughly parallels the Grand Canal, snaking through the heart of the city from the bridge (Ponte degli

Scalzi) near the Santa Lucia Railway Station to St. Mark's Square. You can follow it instinctively without once asking for directions.

DOWNTOWN

Piazza San Marco (St. Mark's Square) – Napoleon called this huge marble square the finest drawing room in Europe. Bells chime, flocks of pigeons crisscross the sky, violins play, couples embrace in the sunset — while the visitor takes it all in from a congenial café. A mere turn of the head allows you to admire St. Mark's Basilica, the Doge's Palace, the 9th-century bell tower, the clock tower where giant bronze Moors have struck the hours for 5 centuries, the old law courts, and the old library, which now houses the archaeological museum. In the *piazzetta,* through which the square opens onto the Grand Canal, there are two granite columns — one topped by the Lion of St. Mark, the other by a statue of St. Theodore.

Basilica di San Marco (St. Mark's Basilica) – This masterpiece of Venetian-Byzantine architecture was built in 830 to shelter the tomb of St. Mark, whose bones had been smuggled out of Alexandria. When first built, it was not a cathedral but a chapel for the doges. The present basilica was constructed during the 11th century, but the phenomenal decoration of the interior and exterior continued well into the 16th century. The basilica has a large dome and four smaller ones; its imposing façade of variegated marble and sculpture has five large doorways. The four famous bronze horses that have adorned the central doorway since 1207, when they were brought here after the sack of Constantinople, were removed in 1980 for restoration. Plaster replicas have taken their place in the doorway, and the originals are now on permanent display in the basilica's museum. Inside, the walls are encrusted with precious art, rare marbles, and magnificent mosaics. Behind the high altar in the chancel is the famous gold altarpiece, the *Pala d'Oro,* and the basilica's treasury includes rare relics as well as Byzantine goldwork and enamels. Open daily. Admission charge for the chancel and treasury. Piazza San Marco.

Palazzo Ducale (Doge's Palace) – Next to the basilica is the pink and white palace with an unusual double *loggia* that served as the residence of the doges and the seat of government. The finest room in the palace is the Grand Council Chamber, containing paintings by Tintoretto and Veronese. You may also visit the doge's apartments and the armory. The palace is connected to the old prisons by the famous Ponte dei Sospiri (Bridge of Sighs), whose name comes from the lamentations of prisoners supposedly taken across the bridge to be executed. Open daily. Admission charge. St. Mark's Square (phone: 522-4951).

Grand Canal – Lined with some 200 marble palaces built between the 12th and the 18th century, the Grand Canal has been called the finest street with the finest houses in the world. On the right (east bank) are the Palazzo Vendramin-Calergi, where Wagner died, now the winter home of the *Municipal Casino;* the Ca' d'Oro (Golden House), so called because its ornate façade once was entirely gilded; the Palazzo Mocenigo, where Lord Byron lived; and *Palazzo Grassi,* an art museum recently bought and refurbished by the Agnelli family of Fiat fame. On the left (west bank) are the *Palazzo Pesaro,* which houses the modern art gallery, and the *Ca' Rezzonico,* an architectural jewel that contains the civic museum of 18th-century art. A good way to see all of these beautiful *palazzi* is to take a slow boat ride over the entire 2-mile length of the Grand Canal with the #1 line.

Chiesa di Santa Maria della Salute – Dedicated to the Madonna for delivering Venice from a plague, this 17th-century baroque church is just across the Grand Canal from St. Mark's Square. Its octagonal shape and white Istrian limestone façade are easily recognizable in innumerable paintings of Venetian scenes and panoramas. Inside are paintings of the New Testament by Titian and Tintoretto, Campo della Salute, Dorsoduro.

Chiesa del Redentore (Church of the Redeemer) – A must for architectural enthusiasts, this 16th-century church is known for its perfect proportions and remarkable harmony both inside and out. It was built by Andrea Palladio on a point of the Giudecca Island, a short ferry ride (take a #5) from St. Mark's by way of Isola San Giorgio. The yearly *Feast of the Redeemer* (the third Sunday in July; see *Special Events*) used to be attended by the doge, who reached the church across a bridge of boats. Campo Redentore. 1 Sola della Guidecca, Dorsoduro.

Galleria dell'Accademia (Gallery of Fine Arts) – Brief but frequent visits are the best way to savor the rich contents of this great art gallery. Of particular interest are Veronese's *Supper in the House of Levi,* Titian's *Presentation of the Virgin,* Tintoretto's *Transport of the Body of St. Mark,* and Giorgione's *Tempesta.* The paintings of Venice by Antonio Canaletto, Francesco Guardi, and Gentile Bellini are the academy's most Venetian selections, both by subject and artist, and meld all impressions of the city. Closed Mondays. Admission charge except Sundays. Campo della Carità, Dorsoduro.

Museo del Settecento Veneziano (Museum of Eighteenth-Century Venice) – Built in the 17th century, *Ca' Rezzonico* — the palace that has housed the museum since 1936 — has a magnificent exterior that is best observed from the Grand Canal (in turn, its windows afford superb views of the canal). A splendid backdrop for some of the most sumptuous treasures of 18th-century Venetian art, the palace itself is known for its grandiose decor and its frescoes by Giandomenico Tiepolo and his son Giambattista. Closed Fridays. Admission charge. Ca' Rezzonico Dorsoduro (phone: 522-4543).

Scuola Grande di San Rocco (Great School of San Rocco) – The Venetian *scuola* was not a school, but something of a cross between a trade guild and a religious brotherhood that supplied wealthy patronage for the arts. San Rocco contains a rich collection of Tintorettos — some 56 canvases depicting stories from the Old and New Testaments. Open daily. Admission charge. Campo San Rocco, San Polo.

Chiesa di Santa Maria Gloriosa dei Frari (St. Mary's Church) – Known simply as *Frari,* this church is considered by many to be the most splendid in Venice after St. Mark's. It contains three unquestioned masterpieces: the *Assumption* and the *Madonna of Ca' Pesaro,* both by Titian, and Giovanni Bellini's triptych on the sacristy altar. An excellent way to appreciate its beauty is to attend an early morning mass before the tourists come. Open daily. Next to the *Scuola Grande di San Rocco.* Campo dei Frari, San Polo.

Chiesa di Santa Maria del Carmelo (Church of Our Lady of Mount Carmel) – Also known as the Chiesa dei Carmini (Church of the Carmelites), this 14th-century Gothic church with a 17th-century campanile — crowned by a statue of the Virgin — still has original gilded wooden ornamentation in its nave. Also worthy of attention are the church walls, which are lined with many 17th- and 18th-century paintings. The cloister adjacent to the church (see the next entry) now belongs to the State Institute of Art. Open daily. Campo Santa Margherita, Dorsoduro.

Scuola Grande dei Carmini (Great School of the Carmelites) – Next to the Carmelite Church, this gracious 17th-century palace contains the most extensive collection of works by Giambattista Tiepolo anywhere in Venice. Paintings and frescoes adorn the interior. Closed Sundays. Admission charge. Campo Santa Margherita, Dorsoduro.

Scuola San Giorgio degli Schiavoni (School of St. George of the Slavonians) – This small building, beyond St. Mark's Square in a part of the city most visitors do not tour, contains one of the city's most overlooked treasures: the frieze of paintings by Vittore Carpaccio depicting stories of St. George, St. Jerome, and St. Tryphon. Closed Mondays. Admission charge. Calle dei Furlani, Castello.

ENVIRONS

The Lido – For most of the 20th century, this shoestring island — across the lagoon from Venice proper — has been one of the world's most extravagant resorts. Indeed, the word *lido* has come to mean, in much of the world's lexicon, any fashionable, luxuriously equipped beach resort. There has always been a touch of decadence to the Venetian Lido with its elegant rambling hotels, sumptuous villas, swank casino, and world-weary, wealthy clientele. Thomas Mann used the Lido's posh *Grand Hotel des Bains* (see *Checking In*) as a background for his haunting novella *Death in Venice*. Today, thousands of cabins and cabanas line the Lido's fine sandy beaches, and purists assert that the old resort has gone to seed. But the tourists still come by the thousands — some drawn by the tinsel of an international film festival, others by the trendiness of a pop music celebration, but most lured by the legendary Lido ambience. There are buses on the island, which can be reached by frequent boat service from Riva degli Schiavoni. There is also a car ferry from Piazzale Roma.

Murano – This island has been the home of Venetian glassmaking since the 13th century. Visitors can watch the glass blowing and molding processes at one of the island factories but should be aware of the high-pressure tactics used to sell the glass. The island's *Museo Vetrario* (Glassworks Museum), 8 Fondamenta Giustinian, has one of the world's best collections of Venetian glass. Closed Tuesdays. Admission charge except Sundays. Murano is 15 minutes by *vaporetto* (steamer) from Fondamenta Nuove.

Burano – The colorful homes, small boats, and nets and tackle of the fishermen who live here add charm to this little island, best known as a center of lacemaking, still practiced by some island women. Burano is 30 minutes by steamer from Fondamenta Nuove.

Torcello – This was one of the most prosperous colonies on the lagoon in the 5th and 6th centuries, but as Venice grew, Torcello declined. The main square is now overgrown with grass. Most of the cathedral, as it appears today, dates from the 7th to 13th centuries. It has several fine Byzantine mosaics and an interesting iconostasis. The island is 45 minutes by steamer from Fondamenta Nuove.

■**EXTRA SPECIAL:** West of Venice the so-called Brenta Riviera was where many wealthy Venetian merchants built luxury summer residences in the 16th century, many designed by Andrea Palladio or Andrea Sansovino. During the 17th and 18th centuries a luxurious barge, *Il Burchiello,* made a daily trip along the lazy Brenta, which links Venice and Padua. Today's tourist can enjoy the same cruise, from March through April, by motorized boat from Pontile Giardinetto near St. Mark's Square. The excursion, which includes lunch in Oriago and a bus return from Padua, takes a full day. The boat leaves from Venice to Padua on Tuesdays, Thursdays, and Saturdays, and it returns from Padua to Venice on Sundays, Wednesdays, and Fridays. Apply at Compagnia Italiana Turismo (CIT), open year-round, St. Mark's Square (phone: 528-5480), for information. (It is also possible to tour the area by car on a road that roughly parallels the canal.)

South of Venice is the seaside town of *Chioggia,* once a major stronghold of the Venetian Republic. Now little more than a fishing port, it retains tantalizing traces of its past glory. The 13th-century Church of San Domenico displays works by Carpaccio and Tintoretto; the highly decorated baroque altar contrasts with its simpler surroundings. There are numerous other small churches in Chioggia, some in a poor state of repair, but all with significant works of Venetian art. The *duomo,* or cathedral and bishopric, which stands at the end of Corso del Popolo, is a grandiose 17th-century building reconstructed on the ruins of the original 12th-century church. Inside are paintings that recount some of the history and sacred legends of Chioggia. Around the corner is the celebrated Piazza Vescovile. Bordered by plane trees and an ornamented balustrade, it has been a favorite subject for painters through the ages. Chioggia can be reached by boat, passing several other lagoon islands on the way, or by bus from the train station of Piazzale Roma. On the waterfront is an excellent, inexpensive restaurant, *El Gato,* which specializes in lagoon fish, served with fresh salads and local wines.

SOURCES AND RESOURCES

TOURIST INFORMATION: A free pocket-sized map of Venice, listing the various boat routes around the city, is available from the Azienda di Promozione Turistica (APT), 4421 Calle Rimedio, Castello (phone: 522-6110) or the APT Santa Lucia train station. Both provide tour guides for small groups. The *Associazione Guide Turistiche,* 5267 Calle delle Bande, Castello (phone: 520-9038), has a list of multilingual tour guides whose fixed rates are approved by the local tourist board.

The nearest US Consulate is in Milan, at 1 Largo Donegani (phone: 02-652841).

Local Coverage – The weeklies *Un Ospite a Venezia* (*A Guest in Venice*) and *Venezia Per Conoscere La Città* are useful multilingual booklets published weekly and available at newsstands; both list up-to-date museum schedules, special events, entertainment programs, and other activities. *The Companion Guide to Venice* by Hugh Honour (London: Collins; $6.95) is a sensitive, well-written guide to the city; it is available in many bookstores.

Telephone – The area code for Venice is 041.

CLIMATE AND CLOTHES: The lightest clothes you have will be appropriate for Venice in summer. Temperatures in July can reach 90F (32C). Although there is rarely extreme cold in winter — 40F (4C) is considered a very chilly January — precipitation ranges from fine mist to torrential downpour and the winds off the lagoon can be more chilling than Alpine snow. You'll need woolens and sweaters to wear under wind and rain gear, and, if the high water (*acqua alta*) comes up over the canal banks, you'll want high rubber boots for slogging around.

GETTING AROUND: Losing yourself in Venice is inevitable — and recommended. However, major confusion can be avoided by knowing a few facts. Since 1711, Venice has been divided into six *sestieri* or wards, namely San Marco, Castello, Canerreggio, San Polo, Dorsoduro, and Santa Croce. "Downtown" Venice — the largest of the six — is San Marco. The *sestieri* are used as points of reference and are part of a location's address. All locations have two: One is the official mailing address and the other is a specific street address. A store's mailing address, for instance, could be 2250 San Marco, while its mailing address is 2250 Calle dei Fuseri.

There are no cars in Venice. After crossing the Ponte della Libertà, visitors leave their cars in the lots and garages at Piazzale Roma. An even better idea for those arriving by car — to avoid the terrible congestion of the high season — is to park in Mestre and catch the train to Venice, a journey of only 10 minutes or so. An added advantage of this strategy is that the sight of Venice has a far greater impact when one steps out of the train terminal into the midst of the city's beauty.

Airport – Marco Polo airport (phone: 661111) serves both domestic and international flights. It is 8 miles from the city and is reachable by *motoscafo* (motorboat) service, which leaves from St. Mark's Square and costs about $8 per person. A private motorboat taxi (*taxi acquei*) for up to four people is about $60, including bags. *ATVO* bus service from the parking area of Piazzale Roma (across the Grand Canal from the Santa Lucia train station) costs about $3 per person. Ask for time schedules at Compagnia Italiana Turismo, St. Mark's Square, or at the tourist office in Piazzale Roma. Also consult the weekly booklet *Un Ospite a Venezia* (*A Guest in Venice*), available at newsstands.

Bus and Train – The bus station (phone: 528-87886) is at Piazzale Roma; the train station, Stazione Santa Lucia (phone: 715555), is across the Grand Canal from the bus station.

Gondola – An hour's tour of the city in one of these sleek, black boats can cost you as much as $50, but for 15¢ you can get a short sample by taking a canal ferry, called a *traghetto,* across the Grand Canal at various points some distance from the bridges. If it's the gondoliers' barcaroles you've been waiting to hear, you can enjoy them for free by leaning over one of the bridges as they pass by in the evening.

Motoscafi* and *Vaporetti – The little steamers that make up the municipal transit system are inexpensive and fun. The *motoscafi* are express boats, making only a few important stops. The *vaporetti* are much slower; #1 chugs leisurely along the whole length of the Grand Canal, and #5 meanders for more than an hour through interesting parts of the city. Tickets cost between $1.50 and $2.50. If you're in a rush to get to the station or elsewhere, you can ask your hotel to call a taxi *acquei* (motorboat). Although they're almost as expensive as gondolas, they're faster (phone: 5222303).

 SPECIAL EVENTS: In mid to late February (February 17-27 in 1990), Venetians celebrate *Carnevale,* a 10-day pre-Lenten fete that includes outdoor masked balls, 24-hour street theater, and pop music. Later in the year, on the night between the third Saturday and Sunday in July, illuminated gondolas glide along the canals while musicians play from barges on the lagoon and fireworks paint the sky. This is the *Festa del Redentore* (Feast of the Redeemer), one of the most special celebrations of the year in Venice. No one goes to bed before dawn. On the first Sunday in September, gondola races and a procession of decorated barges filled with Venetians in Renaissance dress highlight the *Regata Storica* (Historic Regatta) on the Grand Canal. The annual *International Film Festival* is held on the Lido in late August and early September, and in even-numbered years the important *Esposizione Internazionale d'Arte Moderna* (International Exposition of Modern Art), better known as *Biennale d'Arts,* takes place in a small park beyond the Riva dei Sette Martiri from June through October.

 MUSEUMS: Besides those mentioned in *Special Places,* Venice has a number of museums of special interest (most are closed on Mondays):

Civico Museo Correr (Correr Civic Museum) – A collection of historical curios from the Venetian Republic. Also, a picture gallery with works from the 13th to the 18th century, along with prints, sketches, and ceramics. Piazza San Marco.

Galleria Giorgio Franchetti (Franchetti Gallery) – Bronze sculpture from the 12th through the 16th century as well as an important collection of Renaissance paintings from Venice and Tuscany. Ca' D'Oro, 3932 Cannareggio (phone: 523-8790, 522-2349).

Museo Archeologico (Archaeological Museum) – Ancient Greek and Roman statues, Greek and Etruscan vases, Egyptian and Assyrian jewels and antiques. Piazza San Marco (phone: 225978).

Museo d'Arte Moderna (International Gallery of Modern Art) – 19th- and 20th-century works from Italian and foreign artists such as Boccioni, Hayez, Casorati, Klimt, Rodin, Chagall, and Kandinsky. Ca' Pesaro, Santa Croce.

Museo Guggenheim (Guggenheim Museum) – A modern art collection from the Solomon Guggenheim Foundation of New York, including works from the cubist, abstract, surrealist, and expressionist movements. Artists represented include Picasso, Braque, Max Ernst, and Jackson Pollock. Closed November through April. Palazzo Venier dei Leoni, 701 San Giorgio, Dorsoduro (phone: 706288).

Palazzo Grassi (also called Palazzo Fiat) – Splendidly restored, important artistic expositions of international themes. Canal Grande at Campo San Samuele, San Marco.

SHOPPING: Venetian glass is a seductive item, but not all of it is of high quality. Do a bit of comparison shopping first, and if you can, visit the museum and factories on Murano (see *Special Places*). Also consider the inexpensive necklaces of colorful Venetian glass beads. Other items worth purchasing are the traditional handmade paper *Carnevale* masks, which are currently enjoying a renaissance. Two of the best mask workshops are at 2008/A Piazza San Paolo and at 1077/A Calle de l'Ogio o de la Rughetta (midway between the Rialto and St. Mark's Square). In addition, there are many fine jewelry stores on the Ponte di Rialto.

The *Mercato di Rialto,* near the Rialto Bridge, is one of the city's most colorful outdoor food markets. It is fascinating to wander here, even if you aren't shopping. During the Middle Ages, this area was the Wall Street of Europe, since Venice was queen of the seas and, therefore, queen of trade. In those days, spices, silver, and silks from the overland Eastern trade route were all sold here, and banks surrounded the area. Now it is more the staples of life that are sold from the small stalls — fruits and vegetables, coffee and cheeses, fresh game and seafood. The sounds and smells are pure Venice.

Venice's main shopping district is the area directly surrounding St. Mark's Square or in the adjacent Merceria. While most shops are open in the mornings from 9 AM to 1 PM, they close for a long lunch, reopen around 3:30 PM, and remain open until 7 or 7:30. Most Venetian merchants accept major American credit cards.

Barozzi – Antique furniture, mainly Venetian. 2052 Via XXII Marzo, San Marco.

Domini – Fine silverware and china. 659-664 Calle Larga San Marco, San Marco.

Al Duca d'Aosta – Sports clothes, accessories, formerly for men only, but women's wear is now available across the street. 4946 Merceria del Capitello, San Marco (phone: 985988).

Elysée – Elegant footwear. 4485 Calle Goldoni.

Fendi – Chic clothing and leather goods. 1474 Salizzada San San Moisè (phone: 520-5733).

Jesurum & Co. – Exquisite lace and other handmade needlework. Ponte Canonica and Piazza San Marco.

Libreria Antiquaria La Fenice – Old books and prints. Campo San Fantin and 1850 Piazza San Marco, San Marco.

Mondo Novo – Papier-mâché masks — alligators, camels, and mummies — for *Carnevale.* Campo Santa Margherita, Dorsoduro (phone: 528-7344).

Nardi – Beautiful jewelry in the Venetian tradition. 69 Piazza San Marco, San Marco (phone: 522-5733).

Piazzesi – Notebooks, boxes, albums, and other gift articles crafted from handmade marbled papers in classic Italian style. 2511 Campiello Della Feltrina, San Marco (phone: 522-1202).

Salviati – A 100-year-old firm with the highest traditions of craftsmanship in Venetian glass. 195 San Gregorio, Dorsoduro (largest collection); 78 Piazza San Marco, San Marco, and the glassworks museum in Murano.

V. Trois – An exclusive representative of luxurious Fortuny fabrics. 2666 Campo San Maurizio, San Marco (phone: 522-2905).

SPORTS AND FITNESS: The visitor to Venice gets plenty of exercise climbing up and down its hundreds of bridges. For more organized sports, one must move to the open spaces of the Lido.

Fitness Center – *Palestra Europ,* 6661/V Castello (phone: 520-7475), is the only fitness center in Venice open to visitors.

Golf – The *Golf Club Lido di Venezia* is a championship course at the far western end of the Lido (phone: 731333). It's reached by the #11 boat from Riva degli Schiavoni or by the C bus from Santa Maria Elisabetta, the main Lido dock.

Jogging – Just east of St. Mark's Square, the Riva degli Schiavoni runs southeast along the water toward the Riva dei Sette Martiri and the Giardini Pubblici (public gardens) — a good 20-minute jog. Runners may also jog on the Lido beach.

Soccer – From September to May, *Venezia* plays at *Stadio Comunale P. L. Penzo*, S. Elena (phone: 528-7418).

Swimming – The northern end of the Lido has municipal beaches, all of which charge admission. Other beaches are the domain of the great luxury hotels of the Lido, but cabanas are available for an entrance fee. There is also a public pool at *Piscina Comunale Sacca Fisola,* Guidecca (phone: 528-5430)

Tennis – The *Tennis Club,* 41/D Lungomare Marconi (phone: 526-0335), has 7 courts (2 covered; 2 lighted). Visitors can also play at the *Henkell Club,* Via Malamocco (phone: 526-0122), or the *Tennis Club Lido,* Via Sandro Gallo 163 (phone: 526-0945).

Yachting – The *Ciga Yacht Club* hires out sailing boats or gives lessons to enthusiasts through the *Excelsior Palace* hotel (see *Checking In*) on the Lido (phone: 526-0201).

 THEATER: Music, rather than drama, is the performing art of Venice. However, the *Teatro Verde,* on the little island of San Giorgio Maggiore just across from Piazza San Marco, is a lovely outdoor amphitheater that looks out over the lagoon. It's a marvelous place to spend a summer evening, even if you're watching a classic theater piece done in an incomprehensible Venetian dialect (open to the public only during performances). Another pleasant theater for traditional and contemporary productions is *Teatro Goldoni,* 4650/B Calle Goldoni, San Marco (phone: 520-5422). *Teatro Ridotto,* a delightful little rococo theater, hosts dance performances as well as drama. It's just off San Marco, at Calle Vallaresso (phone: 522-2939).

 MUSIC: Venice is a city with a rich musical tradition and a full calendar of musical events — as you will see from the wall posters that announce forthcoming concerts. *Teatro La Fenice,* 1977 Campo San Fantin (phone: 521-0161), which dates from the late 17th century, is the city's main auditorium. A first night at the *Fenice,* site of world premières of opera classics by such composers as Verdi and Rossini, is a highlight of the social season. Its gold and pink plush interior is pure Venetian; tours are permitted when rehearsals are not in progress. In summer, open-air concerts are held in the courtyard of the Doge's Palace, and there are concerts in various churches (where the acoustics are fabulous). If possible, attend a performance by either of the city's stellar chamber music groups: the *Solisti Veneti* or the *Sestetto a Fiati di Venezia* (Venice Wind Sextet). In winter, too, you can attend concerts in churches and in the ornate salons of palaces such as the 17th-century Palazzo Labia (now the Venice office of Italian state radio and television). Many church concerts are free, though contributions are welcome. Look for posters advertising these musical events along the main route between the Rialto and St. Mark's.

 NIGHTLIFE: *Martini Scala Piano Bar,* 1983 San Marco (phone: 522-4121), is Venice's chic-est nightspot and open until 3 AM. Next to the *Teatro La Fenice,* which supplies it with a glossy, after-theater crowd, is a pleasant outdoor terrace and good food (see *Eating Out*). *Linea D'Ombra* is a lively jazz club, Fondamento Zattere, Dorsoduro (phone: 528-5295). As long as the weather holds, the city's best nightlife is the nonstop show in Piazza San Marco. Take up residence in one of the cafés, listen to the schmaltzy orchestra, and watch the world go by. Popular places for rock and disco are the *Acropolis* on the Lido at Lungomare Marconi (phone: 536-0466) and *El Souk Disco,* 1056/A Accademia (phone: 520-0371).

For gambling enthusiasts, the *Municipal Casino* at the Lido (phone: 526-0626) is open from April through September — its winter home is the elegant *Palazzo Vendramin-Calergi* on the Grand Canal (phone: 710211), open from October through March.

BEST IN TOWN

 CHECKING IN: Your first decision is whether to stay out at the Lido or right in the center of town. But even if you stay in the center, it's easy to use the frequent ferry service (from Riva degli Schiavoni) any time you feel the urge to swim or play a game of tennis. Expensive hotels here will charge from $250 to $500 per night for a double; moderately priced hotels, $100 to $250; and inexpensive ones, $50 to $100. Many hotels offer significant discounts in winter. All telephone numbers are in the 041 area code unless otherwise indicated.

Bauer Grünwald and Grand Hotel – Visiting royalty often stays in the poshest suites in this Grand Canal hotel near St. Mark's Square. Its roof garden, piano bar, and fine restaurant offer some of the loveliest vantage points from which to admire the city. 1459 Campo San Moisè, San Marco (phone: 523-1520). Expensive.

Cipriani – On the serene Isola Giudecca, this charming hotel has a peaceful, luxuriant garden, a swimming pool, and stunning views of the lagoon. Very formal, very capable service that's a throwback to a more elegant, opulent age. A 24-hour deluxe motorboat shuttle service transports guests to and from St. Mark's Square in 5 minutes. Fine restaurant. Open March through November. 10 Giudecca, Dorsoduro (phone: 520-7744; FAX: 520-3930). Expensive.

Danieli – One of Venice's oldest and most romantic hotels (and one of the biggest) was once the residence of a 14th-century doge. It has a modern annex that is less evocative but is still a favorite for wealthy honeymooners. 4196 Riva Schiavoni, San Marco (phone: 522-6480; FAX: 520-0208). Expensive.

Europe and Regina – With a terrace overlooking the Grand Canal, this gracious hotel offers a fine view of the Chiesa di Santa Maria della Salute. 2159 Calle Larga XXII Marzo, San Marco (phone: 520-0477; FAX: 523-1533). Expensive.

Excelsior Palace – This luxurious modern hotel, recently refurbished in a Hispano-Moorish style, made the Lido famous. It has its own fine restaurant, beach, tennis courts, horseback riding, and golf course. Open April through October. 40 Lungomare Marconi, Lido (phone: 526-0201). Expensive.

Grand Hotel des Bains – On the Lido, this luxurious and gracefully old-fashioned hotel is where Visconti filmed much of *Death in Venice*. Its painstaking renovations were completed last year. Although not as grand as it once was, it has spacious rooms and bathrooms. The stately porticoed hotel is across the road from the private beach. Open April through October. 17 Lungomare Marconi, Lido (phone: 765921; FAX: 526-0113). Expensive.

Gritti Palace – There are those — Ernest Hemingway was one — who would rather stay in this one-of-a-kind crown jewel than anywhere else in Europe. Once the Renaissance residence of a Venetian doge who died in 1538, it is one of the world's most celebrated hotels — famous for excellent service, a classic dining room, and a beautiful dining terrace on the canal. 2467 Campo Santa Maria del Giglio, San Marco (phone: 794611). Expensive.

Londra Palace – This charming hotel on a popular promenade offers wonderful views of the Bacino di San Marco and the Byzantine Chiesa di San Zaccaria. All 69 rooms have modern bathrooms, and many have private balconies. Other amenities include a very good restaurant and an elegant bar, which stays open late by Venetian standards. 4171 Riva degli Schiavoni, San Marco (phone: 520-0533). Expensive.

Monaco and Grand Canal – The intimate seclusion of this elegant yet homey hotel is just a minute's walk from St. Mark's Square. Constructed from three 18th-century family houses, it has its own flowered terrace and acclaimed restaurant on the Grand Canal. San Marco 1325 (phone: 520-0211; FAX: 520-0501). Expensive to moderate.

Ala – Across a small square from the *Gritti*, this hotel has many of the more expensive hotel's advantages at about one-third the cost. The atmosphere is gracious and traditional, with 85 rooms. It's about equidistant from Piazza San Marco and the Galleria dell'Accademia (see *Special Places*). 2494 Campo Santa Maria del Giglio, San Marco (phone: 520-8333). Moderate.

Bonvecchiati – This comfortable, 86-room hotel near St. Mark's Square is tastefully decorated and boasts an impressive collection of contemporary art. A bar and lovely terrace restaurant overlook a lively canal. 4488 Calle Goldoni, San Marco (phone: 528-5017). Moderate.

La Fenice et des Artistes – Beside the *Teatro La Fenice* (see *Theater*), this hotel is popular with performers and musicians. It consists of four buildings around a pretty garden and has comfortable, well-appointed rooms. One of the city's most popular restaurants, *Taverna La Fenice* (see *Eating Out*), is downstairs. 1937/A Campo San Fantin, San Marco (phone: 523-2333; FAX: 520-3721). Moderate.

Do Pozzi – A small, attractive hotel just a block away from St. Mark's Square, it has a pleasant atmosphere and a lively canalside restaurant, *Da Raffaele*. Breakfast is served in a charming courtyard. 2373 Calle Larga XXII Marzo, San Marco (phone: 707855; 520-6390). Moderate.

Pullman Park – On the outskirts of the Papodopoli gardens, this hotel is a short walk from Piazzale Roma, the first stop for everyone en route from the airport by bus or car. Rooms are furnished in 18th-century Venetian style. It has easy access to the main *vaporetto* lines to all parts of Venice. 245 Santa Croce (phone: 528-5394; FAX: 523-0043). Moderate.

Flora – This small jewel of a hotel has a lovely patio and garden. The atmosphere is tranquil and gracious. Just around the corner from Piazza San Marco. Closed November through January. 2283/A Calle Larga XXII Marzo, San Marco (phone: 520-5708 or 520-5844). Moderate.

Kette – Tucked in a quiet spot between *La Fenice* and St. Mark's Square, this especially charming and efficient hostelry is within strolling distance of several Grand Canal palazzi, and it has its own private dock for gondolas. 2053 Piscina San Moisè, San Marco (phone: 522-8964 or 522-2730). Moderate.

Quattro Fontane – Transformed from a villa built last century, this quiet hotel with excellent service offers the peace of an English country garden. It still has the air of a family dwelling, with antique furniture of various origins and a pleasant alfresco restaurant. Closed most of October through the end of April. Via Quattro Fontane, Lido (phone: 526-0227). Moderate.

Santa Chiara – This 26-room hotel on the Grand Canal — with beamed ceilings and antique furniture — is particularly convenient for guests arriving by car (Piazzale Roma is around the corner). Private garage space. Easy access to the main *vaporetto* stops. 548 Santa Croce (phone: 706955). Moderate.

Torino – Tucked in a corner near fancier hotels, close to Piazza San Marco, this comfortable place is within easy reach of *La Fenice*. 2356 Calle delle Ostreghe, San Marco (phone: 520-5222). Moderate.

Pensione Accademia – In the 17th-century *Villa Maravegie*, this tranquil, rather stately, family-run establishment is near the Galleria dell'Accademia. It has a lovely garden where breakfast is served, with a view down a small canal to the Grand Canal. With wide vestibules, high ceilings, and the ambience of a private home from another era. Reservations advised. 1058 Fondamento Maravegie, Dorsoduro (phone: 523-7846). Inexpensive.

La Residenza – This delightful 14th-century building is little more than a stone's throw from the busy Riva degli Schiavoni. Closed mid-January to mid-February and mid-November to mid-December. 3608 Campo Bandiera e Moro, San Marco (phone: 528-5315). Inexpensive.

 EATING OUT: One of life's great pleasures is dining out in Venice in good weather — alongside a canal, on one of the wide, sunny squares, or in a little garden shaded by vine leaves. But in winter the crowded tables and warm interiors offer refuge from the misty, melancholy streets. Prices for dinner for two, with wine, range from $80 to $110 at an expensive restaurant; $55 to $75 at a moderate one; and $35 to $45 at an inexpensive place. Don't plan to linger too late; most restaurants take their last orders at about 10:30 PM or earlier. All telephone numbers are in the 041 area code unless otherwise indicated.

Club del Doge – Part of the *Gritti Palace* hotel on the Grand Canal, this is the place for a vast selection of traditional Venetian dishes served in deluxe surroundings. In good weather, diners are served on a canalside terrace. Reservations advised. 2467 Campo Santa Maria del Giglio, San Marco (phone: 794611). Very expensive.

Antico Martini – One of Venice's classiest restaurants, across the square from *La Fenice* (see *Theater*), is closed on Tuesdays and at lunch Wednesdays. The *cocktail di crostacei* (seafood cocktail) and the *filetto di San Pietro alla Betty* (St. Peter's filet with seafood) are dishes of national repute. Reservations necessary. 1983 Campo San Fantin, San Marco (phone: 522-4121). Expensive.

Caffè Florian – Open since 1720, this beautiful, slightly frayed *caffè* looks out on the entire Piazza San Marco scene. It's the perfect site from which to watch the world go by while sipping coffee and nibbling a sandwich or sweet confection. Closed Wednesdays, October through June and the last 2 weeks in November. 57 Piazza San Marco (phone: 528-5338). Expensive.

La Caravella – In the *Saturna* hotel, a dignified 14th-century palazzo owned by the the Pisani family who gave Venice many doges, this restaurant has a typically Venetian atmosphere. The chef's specialties include *bigoli in salsa*. Closed Wednesdays in winter. Reservations advised. 2397 Via XXII Marzo, San Marco (phone: 520-8901). Expensive.

Harry's Bar – The original establishment to carry this moniker and long a Venetian landmark, it is also the city's only restaurant to be awarded two Michelin stars. This popular spot is crowded with tourists in summer, but it makes an elegant, international rendezvous in the off-season. The food is splendid 11 months a year, though it may be a bit overpriced. The *Bellini* cocktail was born here. Closed Mondays and January. Reservations advised (as well as appropriate attire; even the famous have been turned away for wearing shorts). Near the San Marco motorboat station. 1323 Calle Vallaresso, San Marco (phone: 523-6797). Expensive.

Locanda Cipriani – The almost pastoral tranquillity of the garden makes this a perfect place for a leisurely lunch. The restaurant, under the same management as *Harry's Bar*, sits on an ancient piazza on the sleepy island of Torcello (see *Special Places*). You can get lunch and transportation in one fare by taking the motor launch that leaves from the dock adjacent to *Harry's Bar* at noon and brings diners back after lunch. There are also 6 bedrooms for guests who book well in advance. Open daily, except Tuesdays, March 15 through October. Reservations advised in summer. Piazza Torcello, Torcello (phone: 730757). Expensive.

La Colomba – Sooner or later, everyone drops in at this favorite Venetian hangout. Large and crowded, the restaurant has a lovely outside terrace, a creative array of seafood specialties, and a renowned collection of modern art on the walls. Try *cartoccio Colomba,* Adriatic fish baked in a paper bag. Closed Wednesdays from November through June. 1665 Piscina di Frezzeria, San Marco (phone: 522-1175). Expensive to moderate.

Al Graspo de Ua – This colorful, popular restaurant attracted the likes of President Reagan and others during the 1987 summit. In a 19th-century blacksmith's shop, it offers great Venetian food, fresh fish, and a good selection of wines. Closed Mondays and Tuesdays. 5094 Calle Bombaseri (phone: 522-3647). Expensive to moderate.

Malamocco – A favorite of after-theater crowds, it has elegant 18th-century decor and a pretty garden for outdoor eating. Specialties include *carpaccio* (slices of fine raw beef dressed with oil and lemon) and *pesce al cartoccio* (fish roasted in paper). Closed Thursdays. 4650 Campiello del Vin (phone: 522-7438). Expensive to moderate.

Antica Bessetta – Venetian home cooking is hard to beat, and here it is at its best in the vegetable and pasta dishes as well as in the more sophisticated fish specialties. Closed Tuesdays, Wednesdays, and mid-July to mid-August. 1395 Calle Salvio. Moderate.

Caffè Orientale – In a particularly delightful spot near the Chiesa Dei Frari and on the Rio Marin, this relatively new restaurant is adapted both for working Venetians' and foot-weary tourists' lunches. The menu (be prepared for Venetian dialect) includes Adriatic fish specialties. A bargain. Closed Mondays and January. 2426 Calle Dell' Olio, San Polo (phone: 719804). Moderate.

Al Giglio – Set in a charming piazza with an alfresco terrace, this intimate restaurant offers very good fish and meat dishes in an atmosphere of calm and elegance. Closed Wednesdays. Reservations advised. Near Piazza San Marco, 2477 Campo Santa Maria del Giglio (phone: 528-9456). Moderate.

Da Ivo – Both Florentine and Venetian specialties are found at this *trattoria* frequented by more locals than tourists. Try the *pappardelle alla marinara* for the pasta course and the thick *bistecca alla Florentina.* Closed Sundays and the last 3 weeks of January. 1809 Calle dei Fuseri, San Marco (phone: 528-5004). Moderate.

Lavena Caffè – One of the Piazza San Marco's historical *caffès,* it is said that Richard Wagner found his inspiration here. Specializes in light food, but don't miss the "Lavena's Cup" ice cream extravaganza. An orchestra plays until midnight from early March through mid-November. Closed Tuesdays, October through June. 1720 Diazza San Marco. Moderate.

Noemi – Salmon mousse, *risotto nero,* and shrimp pâté are the specialties at this well-known, cozy, family-run restaurant. There are also 15 pleasant and moderately priced bedrooms upstairs. Closed Sundays, Monday mornings, and January 5 to February 15. 909-912 Calle dei Fabbri, San Marco (phone: 522-5238). Moderate.

Osteria da Fiore – Fresh seafood only — accompanied by fresh vegetable specialties such as mushrooms, artichokes, and *radicchio* — is served in this former hostelry. Closed Sundays, Mondays, and the last 3 weeks of August. 2202 Calle del Scaletèr, San Polo (phone: 721308). Moderate.

Taverna La Fenice – This elegant restaurant, popular with performers, musicians, and theatergoers, is part of the hotel *La Fenice et des Artistes* (see *Checking In*). Its food and decor are characteristically Venetian, and it stays open for after-theater diners. Closed Sundays, Monday mornings, and January 7 to February 14. Reservations advised. 1938 Campo De La Fenice, San Marco (phone: 522-3856). Moderate.

Trattoria Do Forni – Open all year in the *Montecarlo* hotel, it has a lovely garden. Fish of various sorts are a specialty here, on a menu that's extensive and varied.

A favorite dining spot for Venetians. Closed Thursdays. 468 Calle Specchieri, San Marco (phone: 523-2148). Moderate.

Da Valentino – On the Lido, this small restaurant with garden and terrace serves Venetian fish and meat specialties, including game in season. Homemade desserts and good local wines are an integral part of any meal here. Seating is limited, so book in advance. Closed Mondays and October through mid-November. 81 San Gallo (phone: 526-0128). Moderate.

Alla Madonna – This is a brightly lit, lively restaurant on a little side street near the Ponte di Rialto. It has a fixed menu daily featuring Venetian specialties. Closed Wednesdays, the first week in August, and December 24 to January 31. 594 Calle della Madonna (phone: 522-3824). Moderate to inexpensive.

Al Theatro – An after-show meeting place for performers, musicians, and hungry roulette players, this popular *rosticceria* serves everything from a late-night pizza to a five-course meal. Next to *La Fenice*. Closed Mondays. 1916 Campo San Fantin, San Marco (phone: 523-7214). Inexpensive.

Antica Locanda Montin – Simple decor, simple Venetian food, and some of the city's most interesting people are found in this out-of-the-way restaurant, usually referred to simply by its last name. It's popular with artists and journalists and has a cool, attractive arbor. Closed Tuesday evenings and Wednesdays. 1147 Fondamenta Eremite — also known as Fondamenta di Borga (phone: 27151). Inexpensive.

Osteria Ca' d'Oro alla Vedova – This attractive restaurant has a particularly well stocked wine cellar to accompany its Venetian fish and vegetable dishes and Veneto cheeses. Cannaregio, 3912 Strada Nova (phone: 528-5324). Inexpensive.

VIENNA

For more than 600 years, Vienna was the glittering capital of the Habsburg Empire. Its magnificent palaces and ballrooms are now active with tourists and special events when not housing ministries and other organizations, but the city lives on in a mood of genteel nostalgia. Although a quarter of its 1.5 million people are over 60, Vienna is experiencing a rejuvenation and is gaining an international character as it emerges as an East-West crossroads. Even with an influx of foreigners, however, the Viennese traditions of formality and hand kissing live on within an active social life that centers around the ubiquitous coffeehouses and a flourishing musical scene.

Vienna does not let you forget that it is the city of Mozart, Beethoven, Schubert, Haydn, Brahms, Johann Strauss, and so many other musical giants. Its major opera house, operetta theater, *Philharmonic* and *Symphony* orchestras, and *Vienna Boys' Choir* are as remarkable in quality as in popularity. And the richness of its cultural life is matched only by the richness of its divine pastries, strudel, and the legendary *Sachertorte.* Most endearing of all, perhaps, is the civilized indolence that is cultivated in the coffeehouses, where people read, converse, receive mail and telephone calls, or merely relax and slowly sip coffee.

Situated in the northeast corner of Austria, only 33 miles west of Bratislava, Czechoslovakia, and a few hours' drive from Budapest, Vienna has a distinctly middle European flavor that sets it apart from such Western cities as Paris, Brussels, and Geneva. It's even a bit provincial. Women still wear the traditional gray and green hunting hat with a long, imperious feather, while men will occasionally sport capes, knickers, and green-trimmed Sunday-best uniforms. The mountains and the countryside never seem very far away. They aren't; the Vienna Woods begin at the city's western edge and are very much a part of the city life.

Downtown Vienna is not on the Danube; that river runs through its northeastern quarter, though the Danube Canal, diverted from the river, does touch the inner city. Vienna is easy to grasp geographically if you think of it from the inside out. Begin with the Stephansdom, the great cathedral that towers over the heart of the inner city. Its square, the Stephansplatz, is at the intersection of Graben and Kärntnerstrasse, and if you stand there, all Vienna will eventually pass by. Surrounding the cathedral, the Innere Stadt (Inner City) is a wobbly circle bounded on three sides by the Ringstrasse and on a fourth by the Danube Canal. The Ringstrasse changes names nine times, but all the versions end with the syllable "ring," which accurately describes its shape; it follows the outline of the old city walls. Inside the Ring, the narrow winding streets seem in perfect harmony with the Old World charm and *Gemütlichkeit* (companionable coziness) for which Vienna is famous. The Hofburg, the old imperial winter palace, still sprawls impressively in the heart

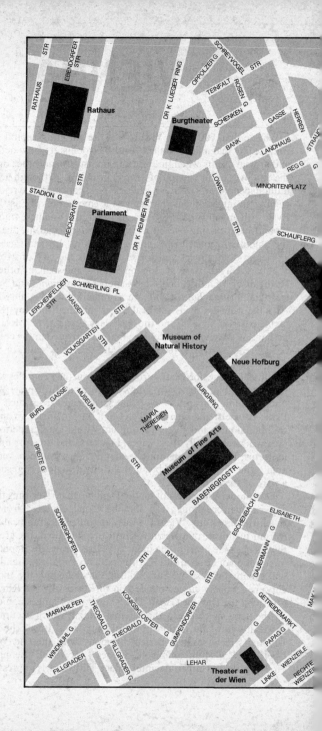

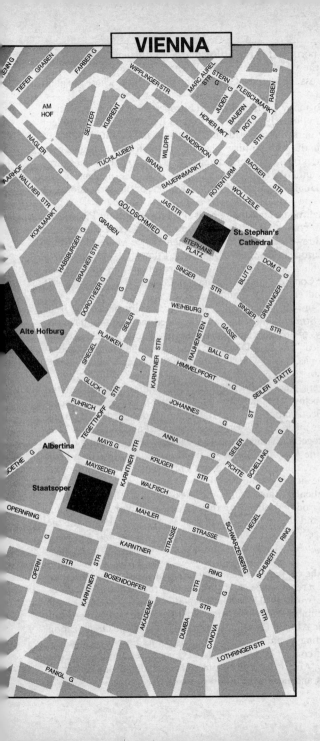

of the city. To the northwest is the little suburb of Grinzing, with its many wine taverns, and the vast expanse of the Wienerwald, the Vienna Woods. And to the east, across the Danube Canal, is the Prater park, where the giant Ferris wheel turns.

Vienna — like so many of the cities of Europe — started as a Roman legionnaires' camp in the early years of the Roman Empire. It had a turbulent and violent history until the powerful and commercially oriented Dukes of Babenberg arrived in the 10th century. The city's modern history begins with the accession of the great Habsburg dynasty in 1278, and the Habsburgs dominated Vienna until the end of World War I. As the nucleus of the flourishing Austro-Hungarian Empire, Vienna was one of the cornerstones of Europe.

In 1814, in the ballrooms and dining halls of the Schönbrunn Palace, the Congress of Vienna, composed of the most powerful rulers of Europe and dominated by the shrewd negotiations of Austrian Prince Metternich, redesigned the map of Europe in the wake of Napoleon's downfall. Meetings were held in leisurely Viennese style, accompanied by receptions and balls, so that it was said that "the Congress doesn't advance, it dances." Beethoven himself conducted a gala concert for the dignitaries.

A few years later, in 1820, a new dance, the waltz, was introduced by Josef Lanner and Johann Strauss senior. The waltz reached the height of its popularity during the days of Strauss's son, Johann Strauss junior, "the king of the waltz," who composed "The Blue Danube," "Tales from the Vienna Woods," and numerous other pieces, and who shuttled the 300 musicians in his employ from one ballroom to another.

Vienna's golden era coincided with that of the waltz and spanned the 68-year reign of the beloved Franz Joseph I (1848–1916). The emperor undertook to transform Vienna much as Baron Haussmann redesigned Paris during the same period. The medieval city walls were removed and the Ring boulevards constructed, together with trees, parks, gardens, buildings, and monuments. The *Opera,* the *Fine Arts Museum,* the *Burgtheater,* the Town Hall, and the Parliament were part of Franz Joseph's plan. And while the emperor was transforming the city, Sigmund Freud, an outwardly conventional Viennese doctor, was patiently transforming our ideas about the human mind.

Vienna began a period of decline with the end of World War I, the dissolution of the empire, and the ruinous depression. World War II brought the Nazis, drastic damage by Allied bombings, and a decade-long four-way division of the city by the Allied powers — a division that ended with the State Treaty of 1955.

Modern Vienna, the capital of a democratic republic, has recovered sufficiently to experience a renaissance of its 19th-century role as Europe's boardroom. Officially the world's "Third United Nations City," Vienna is the headquarters for a number of UN agencies, like the Industrial Development Organization and the Atomic Energy Agency; the home of the Organization of Petroleum Exporting Countries; and — because of its East-West straddle — a natural point of contact between the NATO countries and those of the Warsaw Pact. Today, Austria carefully protects its neutrality by law, allowing no military alliances and no foreign military bases.

The period of postwar peace has brought about a resurgence of music and coffeehouses, the two basic ingredients of contemporary Viennese social life. The musical life of the city seems to involve everyone: Kiosks are plastered with notices of a cornucopia of concerts; the sounds of music being practiced seem to float from nearby open windows; many of the people in the street are carrying instrument cases. The great events of the social season revolve around the *Opera* and the *Philharmonic,* and people in dinner jackets and long gowns who glide past you in the early evening are inevitably going to *hear* something. But it is perhaps typical of Vienna that the finest places in the *Opera House* are the ten rows of standing room, dead center on a raised platform at the back of the orchestra. The houses of all of Vienna's great composers are carefully preserved and reverently visited. And a visit from Leonard Bernstein arouses far more passion than one from the US president.

Pastry eating is a national ritual that seems to be almost as important as Sunday morning mass. The windows of the city's bakeries and *Konditoreien* overflow with strudel, *Sachertorte,* cheesecakes, and nut horns, and the whipped cream flows like water. At teatime — and every other time — Viennese families stand with high seriousness before the glass pastry altars choosing, after long reflection, the afternoon's 2,000 calories. When in Vienna, gorge as the Viennese do: If you start early and fit your last pastry in by five, you should still have room for dinner — and a little evening pastry.

Or if you are sated with pastries, just sit in a café, order coffee or wine, and drink in the spectacle of old Vienna. Though it is a city haunted by the ghosts of the vanished Habsburg rulers, it is also blessed with their legacy of cultural brilliance, architectural splendor, and leisured living.

VIENNA AT-A-GLANCE

SEEING THE CITY: The Donauturm — the Danube Tower — is an 846-foot-high column that was, in fact, built for seeing the city. Opened in 1964, across the river from the main city, it has two high-speed elevators that whisk you to the observation platform and the two revolving restaurants at the summit. From the tower you look over the green expanse of the Danube Park below, and the adjacent United Nations City, and across the river to the spires and domes of the Innere Stadt, and to the Wienerwald beyond. On a clear day, the horizon sweeps from the Alps to the plains of Hungary. Open from 9 AM until midnight, with winter times an hour shorter at each end. The last elevator leaves an hour before closing. Wien XXII, Donaupark (phone: 235368).

For a more accessible view from an enchanting public garden across a Vienna that still resembles a Canaletto cityscape, stand on the terrace of the Upper Belvedere Palace. The entrance is from 27 Prinz-Eugen-Strasse, near the Südbahnhof railway station.

SPECIAL PLACES: The Inner City (Innere Stadt), encircled by the Danube Canal and the Ring boulevards, spans about 1 square mile and is best explored on foot. Its main street is the Kärntnerstrasse-Rotenturmstrasse, and its heart is the Stephansplatz, the cathedral square.

DOWNTOWN

St. Stephen's Cathedral (Stephansdom) – The most important Gothic structure in Austria, its soaring, ornate spire is a trademark of Vienna. Though called the Dom, its roof is actually a dramatically sloped wedge whose intricately patterned inlay gleams in the sun. The scene of some great events in Austrian history, the Stephansdom was the site of the famous double marriage of 1515 between the Habsburgs and the Bohemian and Hungarian dynasties, a union that laid the foundations of the Austrian Empire. You can climb the staircase to the south tower or go down to the catacombs for a fee. An elevator will take you up the north tower to the cathedral's giant bell, the Pummerin, and another good view of Vienna. Noteworthy are the Romanesque west door, called the Giants' Doorway, the carved wood altarpiece in the left apsidal chapel, and the 15th-century red marble tomb of Friedrich III. 1 Stephanspl.

Spanish Riding School – The history of this most unique of Viennese institutions goes back some 400 years, when the first Spanish horses were brought to Austria under the aegis of Emperor Maximilian II. The imperial stud originated at Lipizza near Trieste; today its stunning white thoroughbred Lipizzaners are raised at Piber in southeastern Austria. The Riding School holds about 50 performances a year in Vienna on most Sundays at 10:45 AM and Wednesdays at 7 PM from March to June and September to December. Tickets are in fierce demand for the 600 seats and 275 standing places, and the rule of thumb for Sunday performances is to write *6 months ahead* to Spanische Reitschule, Hofburg, Vienna A-1010, Austria (don't send any money; you pay when you pick them up). Or buy a ticket from a local travel agent for a 20% fee; try *Wagons-Lits Cook,* 2A Kärntner Ring, Vienna A-1010 (phone: 657631), or *Austrian Travel Agency,* 3-5 Opernring, Vienna A-1010 (phone: 588000). Tickets for Wednesday night performances and for a shorter program on Saturday mornings are available only through agencies.

Second best are the training sessions, usually held Tuesday through Saturday mornings from 10 AM to noon. There is a fee, but no advance reservations are taken — you stand in line in the Josefsplatz. The traditionally uniformed riders lead the majestic white stallions through their paces to the strains of classic Viennese music in a great baroque hall that is like an equestrian ballroom. The all-white building was designed in 1735 by the master Viennese architect Josef Fischer von Erlach. 1 Michaelerpl. (phone: 533-90310).

Imperial Stables (Stallburg) – A glassed-in passageway separates the riding school from the stables, which are seldom, if ever, open to the public, but the adjacent New Stallburg painting gallery houses some fine French Impressionists. 2 Reitschulgasse.

The Hofburg – This was the winter residence of the Habsburgs, and, in fact, you will be inside it while you visit the Riding School and the Imperial Stables. It is an extensive architectural complex whose buildings range from early Gothic to turn of the century. The oldest part is the 13th-century Swiss Court (the Schweizerhof), with the Imperial Chapel (the Burgkapelle), where Haydn and Schubert were choirboys and Mozart a young music master. Today, the chapel is the site of the Sunday morning masses sung by the *Vienna Boys' Choir.* You should also visit the sumptuous Imperial Apartments and the Treasury, which contains the fabulous crown jewels. 1 Michaelerpl. (phone: Apartments, 587-5554, ext. 515; Treasury, 533-7931).

Albertina – Near the Hofburg, the *Albertina* — whose name derives from its founder Duke Albert of Sachsen-Teschen — houses the world's greatest collection of graphic arts: etchings, engravings, color prints, sketches, woodcuts. The highlight is a complete collection of Albrecht Dürer's etchings, which are only a fraction, however, of the more than 1 million items in the *Albertina.* Whatever is not on display can be studied in portfolios in the *Albertina*'s library. Closed Sundays in July and August. 1 Augustinerstr. (phone: 534830).

Museum of Fine Arts (Kunsthistorisches Museum) – One of the most dramatic experiences of painting in Europe is the roomful of Pieter Breughels (the Elder), which represents more than half the known body of work of this strange genius. *Children's Games, The Ascent to Calvary, Hunters in the Snow, Peasant Wedding, The Country Dance, Battle Between Carnival and Lent* — they're all here. Unlike the usual quick peek at an isolated world-famed canvas, this room provides a unified perception of the vision of a great creative mind; it's like reading Joyce's *Ulysses* or listening to Beethoven's *Ninth*. The vision is dark, ironic, disturbing, almost satanic; the paintings are simply superb. Here too are some of Rubens's finest works — including the great Ildefonso Altar painting, the portrait of his second wife, Helène Fourment, and a splendid self-portrait that is one of his last paintings. The museum also has works of Velázquez, Titian, Rembrandt, Holbein, Van Dyck, Giorgione, Cranach, and Raphael, as well as a Cellini salt cellar that is a Renaissance gold masterpiece. Closed Mondays. Certain collections are open Tuesday and Friday evenings from 7 until 9. 1 Maria-Theresienpl. (phone: 934541).

Viennese Cafés – If you only had an hour to see all of Vienna, you might get the best cross section of the city in one of its traditional cafés, sipping one of the ten-odd varieties of coffee you can order, munching a piece of *Apfelstrudel,* leafing through one of the newspapers the house provides, clipped onto a kind of short browsing pole. The Viennese café is a cross between living room, office, club, and enclosed street corner — where habitués lounge by the hour. *Jause* — the Viennese version of 5 o'clock tea — is generally the liveliest café hour.

Some of the city's most pleasant traditional cafés include *Tirolerhof,* corner of Führichgasse and Tegetthoffstr.; *Landtmann,* 4 Dr.-Karl-Lueger-Ring; *Hummel,* 66 Josefstädterstr.; and *Hawelka,* 6 Dorotheergasse.

More pastry-oriented cafés or *Konditoreien* include *Demel,* 14 Kohlmarkt; *Lehmann,* 12 Graben; *Heiner,* 21 Kärntnerstr. and 9 Wollzeile; *Sluka,* 8 Rathausplatz; and *Bürgerhof,* 127 Gentzgasse.

Some of the most enjoyable coffeehouses include *Café Rathaus,* 5 Landesgerichtsstrasse; *Sperl,* 11 Gumpendorfer Strasse; *Café Grünwald,* 10 Bauernmarkt; *Café Central,* 14 Herrengasse; *Café Museum,* 6 Friedrichstrasse; and *Alte Backstube,* 34 Lange Gasse.

Cafés that regularly offer music to munch pastries by include: *Café Schwarzenberg,* 17 Kärntner Ring; *Hotel Imperial* café, 16 Kärntner Ring; and *Café Prückel,* 24 Stubenring.

BEYOND THE CENTER

Schönbrunn – West of the center of town, this vast palace was the summer residence of the Habsburgs, inevitably compared with the Bourbons' little country place in Versailles, which was built at almost exactly the same time. The palace itself has 1,441 rooms; the grounds are vast, and the sights various. There are the royal apartments and gala rooms, the delightful rococo palace theater (which was the stage for Max Reinhardt's world-famed acting school), the dazzling collection of imperial carriages, the beautifully groomed baroque park and gardens, the Pheasant Walk, the Tyrolean Garden, the Imperial Chapel, and the Gloriette — a colonnaded structure on the panoramic hill where the palace was originally meant to stand.

Also at Schönbrunn is the oldest zoo in Europe, once the imperial menagerie, with several thousand exotic animals centered around the graceful pavilion where the Empress Maria Theresa used to take her morning coffee. The palace itself is open daily and on summer evenings. During the summer, evening tours are frequently combined with concerts. The park and the zoo are open throughout the year; the Gloriette only from May through October. Schönbrunner-Schloss-Str. (phone: 833646).

Prater and Riesenrad – For a change of pace, visit this immense green space, northeast of the center of town. The Prater was once the private game preserve of the Habsburg princes, but as early as 1766 the Emperor Joseph II opened the gardens to the public. Ideal for strolling or bicycling, the Prater's Hauptallée is a 3-mile-long boulevard, flanked by lovely chestnut trees and leading to the Lusthaus, once the imperial hunting lodge. In summer, veer left at the Lusthaus onto Aspernallee or Schwarzenstockallee and wend your way to *Gustav Lindmayer's Fischrestaurant* (phone: 218-9580; closed Mondays), where you can sit on the banks of the Danube and enjoy a bowl of *Fischbeuschl* soup or a Pilsener while barges and hydrofoils pass by.

At the entrance to the Prater amusement park stands the Riesenrad, the giant Ferris wheel, almost as much a symbol of Vienna as the Stephansdom spire. A landmark since the end of the 19th century, its great iron superstructure survived World War II, despite the bombs and fire that consumed most of the Prater. Only half as many of the bright red cars were replaced after the war, but the Riesenrad turns as ever. The panorama of Vienna is stunning as you swing to the top of the wheel's orbit — and *Third Man* devotees will remember Joseph Cotten and a menacing Orson Welles standing precariously by the open car door. Open April to November.

Grinzing – The place is a charming little suburb not quite half an hour north of downtown Vienna, but the name really stands for a whole aspect of Viennese life. Grinzing is where the Viennese go in the evening, in the summer, on Sunday afternoon — for food, wine, and merriment, and perhaps to remind themselves of the simple, hearty country pleasures that are at the root of so much of Austrian life. The food is the traditional *Brathendl* and *Backhendl* — tender young grilled and fried chicken; the wine is the *Heurigen*, which really means "from this year." In fact, *Heurigen* is the general name for the rustic taverns that dot Vienna's outskirts and specialize in the new wine, with old wooden tables and aging musicians. In the warm season, there is a place to sit out under an arbor; in the winter there may be a crackling fire. Many of the Viennese arrive with elaborate box lunches from home or from richly stocked delicatessens. It is wise to take the #38 tram to and from Grinzing instead of driving.

■**EXTRA SPECIAL:** The Wienerwald, the Vienna woods of the Johann Strauss waltzes, is a vast, unspoiled forest to the west and south of the city. The nearer edges are popular for Sunday outings, the deeper recesses fine for serious hiking or bike riding. (Bikes can be rented.) There are numerous well-marked trails.

At Mayerling in the Vienna Woods, on a snowy night in 1889, Crown Prince Rudolf — the only son of the Emperor Franz Joseph — and his lover, the Baroness Mary Vetsera, committed double suicide in a hunting lodge. The emperor, who had refused to allow the dissolution of his son's unhappy marriage, had the fatal bedroom torn down and a chapel built in its place.

A day's excursion can also take you to the ancient Cistercian monastery at Heiligenkreuz, through the lovely wooded Helenental and Europe's largest underground lake, the Seegrotte, to the vineyards of Perchtoldsdorf and Gumpoldskirchen and past one of the Prince of Liechtenstein's Austrian castles. Rent a car, take a sightseeing tour offered by *Vienna Sightseeing Tours* (*Wiener Rundfahrten*) 4/11 Stelzhamergasse, Vienna A-1030 (phone: 724683), or take trolley #38 to Grinzing and continue by bus 38A to Kahlenberg and explore the many hiking trails in the woods.

Or take the #43 tram from downtown to Neuwaldegg and a 1½-hour hike (one-third of it uphill) to the *Sofienalpe* hotel, 13 Sofienalpenstr. (phone: 462432), where you can stay the night or just dine on wild boar and *Millirahmstrudel*, a cottage cheese pastry served hot with vanilla sauce.

SOURCES AND RESOURCES

 TOURIST INFORMATION: The Vienna City Tourist Office, in the underground passage by the opera (Opernpassage), is open daily (phone: 431608) and issues a free monthly program of all events of note in the city. A calendar of events is posted in every hotel and in other places throughout the city. Be sure to pick up a list of museum hours, as these are often subject to change. Freytag and Berndt publishes a good map of Vienna, which includes a brief guide to the city in English. The *Falk Plan* is a gorgeous, intricate, fold-out map that comes in two sizes. These maps are available at many of the city's bookstores.

The US Embassy is at 16 Bolzmanngasse (phone: 315511).

Local Coverage – *Vienna Life, Falter,* and *Wiener,* which list everything going on, are available at the *Shakespeare & Co.* bookstore (2 Sterngasse) and other outlets. Or tune in to Blue Danube Radio — in English, with news, pop music, and a list of events — at 102.5 on the dial between 7 and 9 AM, noon and 2 PM, and 6 and 8 PM.

Food – *Restaurant Guide,* published by the tourist office, contains listings, as does the monthly *Hallo Wien.*

Telephone – The area code for Vienna is 01.

 CLIMATE AND CLOTHES: Perched 561 feet above sea level, Vienna is warm and sunny in summer. Temperatures average about 77F (25C). Winters are rainy, raw, gusty, and snowy, but temperatures average above freezing, 34F–37F (1C–3C). If you go to Vienna in the winter, be sure to take appropriate footwear against the cold and wet. As for dress, Vienna is a surprisingly formal city, with classic dressiness still pretty much the rule at theaters, concerts, or restaurants. Take something reasonably elegant along, or you may feel uncomfortable.

 GETTING AROUND: Airport – Vienna Airport handles international and domestic flights. It is 20 minutes from downtown by taxi or bus, and taxi fare is about 270 Austrian schillings (about $21). Airport buses cost about 50 schillings ($4) and run to and from the City Air Terminal in the *Wien Hilton International* every 20 minutes during the day; at night they run according to flight schedules. There is also hourly bus service during the day from Vienna Airport to the Südbahnhof and Westbahnhof rail terminals (phone: 565-01717 or 565-05404, for more information). An hourly train runs from the airport to Wien-Mitte, a subway and rail station beneath the City Air Terminal in the *Hilton,* and Wien-Nord, a subway and rail station at the northernmost tip of the Prater; the trip takes a half-hour and costs about 25 schillings (about $2).

Boat – Between April and October, the *Danube Steamship Company* (DDSG) provides sightseeing boat trips along the canal. Boats depart frequently for 1- to 2½-hour excursions from Schwedenbrücke on the canal. They also offer Hungarian-operated hydrofoil trips to Budapest (a 4½-hour trip; it's almost as fast as the train and much more scenic) as well as 10-hour excursions on a pleasure boat called the *Tancsics,* around the Danube Bend and past (but not into) Bratislava, Czechoslovakia, and Rajka, Hungary. For information, call 217100.

Car Rental – *Hertz* is at 17 Kärntner Ring (phone: 512-8677); *Avis* at 33 Weyringergasse (phone: 505-5839); and *Inter-Rent Austria* at 7 Schubertring (phone: 756717).

Fiaker – A horse-drawn carriage, as Viennese as the Habsburgs, is a favorite mode of transportation to weddings and carnival balls or just for trundling about the old city. The public transport map marks Fiaker stands, and three reliable coachmen are Martin

Stelzel, 32 Gumpendorferstr. (phone: 566587); Rudi Glück, 16/VIIGestettengasse (phone: 722-9804); and Johann Paukner, 13/8 Mohsgasse (phone: 787918).

Shuttle Service – *Mazur Shuttle* is a minibus service that will drop you off or pick you up at your hotel. Make arrangements through the airline, the desk at the airport, or at your hotel (phone: 7770-2901).

Subway, Bus, and Train – Three efficient subway lines penetrate the heart of the Innere Stadt. Pleasant and quaintly Viennese are the lumbering red and white streetcars that weave through the city. For a few cents, the public transport office, in the underground passage by the *Opera,* will sell you a beautiful multilingual transport map that marks all the routes of the U-Bahn, Stadtbahn, Schnellbahn, tram, and bus, and explains the mysteries of tickets, passes, stamping machines, and the like. Buy tickets at any tobacconist's (Tabak Trafik) at reduced prices or from the conductor or machine. Tourists can buy discount full-day tickets, good for unlimited riding on all public transport, at tobacconists' counters in the airport and rail stations.

Taxi – You can call radio taxis by phoning any of these numbers: 3130; 4369; 60160; 9101.

 SPECIAL EVENTS: The Viennese special event par excellence is *Fasching,* which loosely describes the carnival period from the New Year until Ash Wednesday — the beginning of Lent. For some 2 months, the city bursts into organized merriment with a series of *Fasching* balls ranging from white-tie-and-champagne affairs like the *New Year's Eve Emperor's Ball* in the Hofburg to the *Vienna Plumbers Guild Ball* at a large hotel. The season's highlight is always the *Opera Ball,* which is held in the *Opera House* in February or March with the Austrian president on hand. Other old favorites: the *Wiener Philharmoniker Ball,* held in the *Musikverein* concert hall; the *Vienna Physicians Ball; Huntsmen's Ball of the Green Cross;* and the *Fool's Night of the Vienna Men's Choir.* The names are those of the sponsoring society, but they are all open to the general public, as is the *Champagne Ball* — begun in November 1986 — which now marks the opening of the European ball season. A complete schedule and ticket information are available from the Vienna Tourist Board, 5 Kinderspitalgasse (phone: 431608).

The *Wiener Festwochen* is an orgy of music and theater, five festival weeks that generally run from mid-May to late June and attract internationally known musicians and theater groups. There is a garnish of side events: exhibitions, conferences, song festivals, and the like. For information and tickets: Büro der Wiener Festwochen, 11 Lehargasse (phone: 586-1676).

■**EXTRA SPECIAL:** The Ultimate New Year's Eve. If you've spent all your life hating New Year's Eve, there's a spectacular way to get over the grudge — spend it in Vienna. It requires substantial planning (and even more money) to motivate the concierge at your hotel to produce hard-to-get tickets to otherwise sold-out performances, but it's an event you will not soon forget.

A perfect New Year's celebration should begin with the annual exuberant performance of *Die Fledermaus* at the *Staatsoper* or *Volksoper* (see *Theater*). From there, move on to the *Imperial Ball* at the Hofburg Winter Palace for a glimpse of the old Imperial Ballroom (it's not worth staying, since the party has become too commercial). Then it's on to the *Hotel-Palais Schwarzenberg,* where 150 guests are entertained royally in the old palace ballroom and drinks are served in a small room notable for the two immense Rubenses on the walls. The Gobelin tapestries aren't exactly shabby, either. At midnight, the fireworks display rivals a Fourth of July extravaganza, and there's something special about dancing in the New Year to the strains of "The Blue Danube Waltz" (rather than "Auld Lang Syne"). At about 2 AM, a Tyrolean oompah band marches through the palace trumpeting away and all the guests march behind. Not bad.

Don't stay up too late, however, because the festivities begin again early on New Year's Day. At 11 AM in the *Musikverein,* the *Vienna Philharmonic* rouses celebrants from any morning lethargy with a program of Strauss (father and son) waltzes and polkas that just about takes the roof off the hall. The flowers come from Holland, but the music is pure Vienna. If you can't get tickets for the performance, the next best thing is to buy a ticket for the sumptuous buffet brunch in the Johann Strauss Ballroom of the *Inter-Continental* hotel (28 Johannesgasse). Fill your plate with food and your glass with champagne, then take them into the adjoining room, where the concert is televised on a larger-than-life screen.

Otherwise, New Year's lunch is at *Demel's* (for those who can get in), though any other coffeehouse will do. The late afternoon is for napping, and the New Year's climax is that evening, after a dinner of *Tafelspitz* at the *Sacher* hotel, when the *Vienna Symphony* performs Beethoven's "Ninth" in the *Konzerthaus* (see *Music*). Hearing the hundreds of voices sing the last movement, "Ode to Joy," is quite an experience.

MUSEUMS: Besides those mentioned in *Special Places,* the following museums are also interesting:

Austrian Gallery of 19th- and 20th-Century Art (Österreichische Galerie des 19 und 20 Jahrhunderts) – *Jugendstil* (Art Nouveau) painters and Austrian Expressionists, such as Oskar Kokoschka, Gustav Klimt, and others. 27 Upper Belvedere, Prinz-Eugen-Str. (phone: 784-1580).

Clock Museum of the City of Vienna (Uhrenmuseum der Stadt Wien) – Opened in 1921, it has over 900 timepieces. 2 Schulhof (phone: 533-2265).

Sigmund Freud Museum – Freud's personal collection of books and photos, plus the famous couch, in the house in which he lived from 1891 to 1938. 19 Berggasse (phone: 311596).

Historical Museum of the City of Vienna (Historisches Musumder Stadt Wien) – Three floors of exhibitions on the city's history and culture. 4 Karlspl. (phone: 505-87470).

Künstlerhaus (House of Artists) – Art exhibitions. 5 Karlsplatz (phone: 5879-6630).

Mozart Memorial – The composer's home from 1784 to 1787. 5 Domgasse (phone: 513-6294).

Museum of Baroque Art and the Museum of Austrian Medieval Art (Österreichisches Barockmuseum and Österreichisches Museum mittelalterlicher Kunst) – Lower Belvedere, 6a Rennweg (phone: 784-1580).

New Hofburg Collections of Weapons and Ancient Musical Instruments and Ephesus Museum of Archeology – All at Heldenpl. (phone: 930620 or 934541).

Picture Gallery of the Academy of Fine Arts – 3 Schillerpl. (phone: 588160).

Schubert Museum – The composer's birthplace. 54 Nussdorfer Str. (phone: 345-9924).

Secession – Exhibitions in what was the meeting place and gallery of *Jugendstil* artists, who seceded from the traditionalists in 1897. 12 Friedrichstr. (phone: 587-5307).

Johann Strauss Museum – 54 Praterstr. (phone: 240121).

SHOPPING: The center for shopping is the area around Kärntnerstrasse, Graben, and Kohlmarkt; most department stores are on Mariahilferstrasse. Some good buys are antiques, knitwear, glassware, crystal, porcelain, petitpoint, musical instruments and scores, fur hats, riding gear, and, of course, *Lederhosen* (leather pants), *Loden* coats, and *Sachertorte* (chocolate cake).

The *Dorotheum* is the oldest auction house in Europe. Founded in 1707 by the Emperor Joseph I as a pawnshop for the poor, the *Dorotheum* is a city landmark and part of Viennese social life, even if you aren't interested in antiques. (You can pay a *Sensal,* a licensed bidder — who is absolutely honest — to bid for you at a small fee.) The Dorotheergasse, along with its surrounding streets, is one of Europe's finest streets for antiques. 11 Dorotheergasse (phone: 515600).

The *Naschmarkt,* an outdoor fruit and vegetable market, is not to be missed. It's held daily except Sundays south of the Opera Quarter, between Linke and Rechte Wienzeile. The *Flohmarkt,* a flea market, is held every Saturday near the Naschmarkt.

Note: You can avoid most of the 10% to 32% VAT if you are going to take your purchases out of Austria. Fill out a tax refund slip in the shop. The slip has to be stamped by the customs inspector when you leave Austria. You can bring it to the *Austrian Automobile-Motorcycle & Touring Club (ÖAMTC)* border stations or the Austrian Credit Institute (ÖCI) counters at airports, or mail the slip and sales receipt, along with the address of your bank and your account number, either to the shop or to ÖAMTC Mehrwertsteuerverrechnung, 1-3 Schubertring, Vienna 1010. Eventually you will receive a refund for the amount of the VAT.

W. F. Adlmüller – The highest fashion (and the most imaginative) in Vienna, for women and men. 41 Kärntnerstr. (phone: 526650).

Lobmeyr – Crystal. 26 Kärntnerstrasse (phone: 512-0508).

Loden Plankl – A very reputable, if expensive, place for dirndls, *Lederhosen,* and other regional wear. 6 Michaelerpl. (phone: 533-8032).

Österreichische Werkstätten – Austrian handicrafts. 6 Karntnerstr. (phone: 512-2418).

Polak – Riding gear. 17 Arnsteing (phone: 831238).

Resi Hammerer – This is *the* place for haute couture *Loden* and sports apparel for ladies. 29-31 Kärntnerstr. (phone: 526952).

Rosenthal-Studio – China and silver — and a beautiful wall mosaic outside. 16 Kärntnerstr. (phone: 523994).

Sacher – This has been the official chocolate cake (*Sachertorte*) outlet since 1832. You can eat one or have one of six different sizes shipped to the pastry lover of your choice. Kärntnerstr., around the corner from the main entrance of the hotel (phone: 51456).

Smejkal – One of the best of many places in Vienna that specialize in petit-point embroidery. In the underground Opernpassage and at 9 Kohlmarkt.

Susi – Traditional Austrian clothing, including capes and hand-embroidered sweaters. 58 Währingerstr. (phone: 344-0992).

F. and J. Votruba – A century-old dynasty that deals in musical items, including instruments, scores, records, and anything you can think of. 4 Lerchenfelder Gürtel (phone: 936-8675).

SPORTS AND FITNESS: Bicycling – Both the Prater and large tracts of the Vienna Woods are delightful for riding. Bicycles can be rented from *Radfahrverein Prater,* 8 Vivariumstr. (phone: 266644).

Fitness Center – *Vienna International Fitness Centre,* 7 Nibelungengasse (phone: 587-3710), is run by an American, John Harris, and has 20 Nautilus machines, exercise bicycles, aerobics classes, sauna, steambath, Jacuzzi, solarium, and massage.

Golf – *Vienna Golfclub,* 65a Freudenau (phone: 218-0564).

Horse Racing – Year-round at the beautiful *Freudenau* (for flat racing and steeplechase racing) or *Krieau* (harness racing) tracks, both in the Prater.

Horseback Riding – If you want to be a participant rather than a spectator, this is the city in which to do it. Two good riding centers are the *Wiener Reitinstitut,* 17 Barmherzigengasse (phone: 713-5111), and *Reiter Zentrum Kreuttal,* 9 miles (15 km) north of the city, with a nice restaurant and guestrooms. A-2112 Ritzendorf 1 (phone: 02263-6561).

Jogging – Stadtpark, which separates the *Inter-Continental* from the *Hilton,* Volksgarten, and Burggarten are all good central parks. Farther out, but still within the city limits, are the Prater and the Lainzer Tiergarten. The latter — a 5,300-acre nature preserve — is closed Mondays and Tuesdays.

Tennis – The *Floridsdorfer Tennis Club* has 15 courts, an indoor hall, and no fee. 5 Lorettopl. (phone: 381283). There's also *Vereinigte Tennisanlagen,* pleasantly situated in the Prater, with its own restaurant at Prater Hauptallée (phone: 246384); and *Reifen Tree,* Wien-Liesing, 370 Breitenfurterstr. (phone: 869574).

Walking – Virtually the Austrian national sport; there is a several-hundred-kilometer circuit of walking and hiking trails in the Vienna Woods, excellently marked and serviced by numerous inexpensive inns.

 THEATER: Two famous old theaters are worth a visit, even if you have only a rudimentary knowledge of German: the beautiful *Theater in der Josefstadt,* 26 Josefstädterstr. (phone: 425127); and the musical house *Theater an der Wien,* which played host to the world premières of classics like Beethoven's "Fidelio" and Lehar's "The Merry Widow," 6 Linke Wienzeile (phone: 58830). Tickets for all Vienna productions are also available from the many agencies around town, but you will pay a 21.6% markup.

Vienna also has an English theater, which has been going strong since 1963 and is now housed in a lovely neo-baroque building at 12 Josefsgasse (phone: 421260 or 428284). Its perennial attraction, Ruth Brinkmann as Ruth Draper, is a must.

 MUSIC: The great Viennese musical experience is a concert by the *Wiener Philharmoniker,* whose headquarters are at the *Musikverein,* 3 Dumbastr. (phone: 658190). Daytime box office at 6 Karlspl. The other major concert hall, with three separate auditoriums, is the *Konzerthaus,* 20 Lothringerstr. (phone: 721211). Also on any "must" list of Vienna musical experiences is the *Vienna Boys' Choir* (Wiener Sängerknaben). There is singing at mass in the Burgkapelle of the Hofburg most Sunday and religious holiday mornings at 9:15, though not in July or August. Tickets can be obtained by writing in advance to *Verwaltung der Hofmusikkapelle,* Hofburg, Schweizerhof, Vienna A-1010; what's left is sold every Friday afternoon from 5 PM on (get there at least an hour before) at the Burgkapelle for the following Sunday morning.

The *Staatsoper,* 2 Opernring, is one of the three or four most important opera houses in the world. During the course of a long season (September through June), most of the great names in today's opera world make an appearance. In addition to the opera, there are three other state theaters: the *Burgtheater,* 2 Dr. Karl Lueger-Ring, which features classical repertory; the *Volksoper,* 78 Währingerstr., which specializes in light opera, Viennese operetta, and musicals; and the *Akademietheater,* 1 Lisztstr., which performs modern plays, using the *Burgtheater* company. Tickets for all four theaters are available from 15 days to 2 months ahead: write to Bundestheaterverband, 1 Goethegasse, Vienna A-1010. Starting the week preceding a performance, you can buy tickets at the central state theater box office: Bundestheaterkasse, 3 Hanuschgasse — in a courtyard just behind the opera house (phone for all state theaters: 514440).

Devoted music lovers might enjoy a visit to the old Bösendorfer Piano building, 4 Canovagasse, back to back with the *Musikverein;* and, in summer, a tour of the homes of the great composers — Beethoven, Schubert, Mozart, Haydn, Strauss — who lived and worked in Vienna, organized by *Cityrama,* 1 Börsegasse (phone: 534130), or by other major travel agencies.

 NIGHTCLUBS AND NIGHTLIFE: The most traditional Viennese night on the town is at one of the *Heurigen* in Grinzing: lots of new wine to wash down dinner and a good dose of *Schrammelmusik* — Viennese folk music. Moored near the Mary Bridge (Marienbrücke) on the Danube Canal is the old riverboat called the *Johann Strauss;* a string orchestra provides music for dancing from 4 to 6 and 8:30 to 10:45 PM daily (phone: 639367). Cobenzlgasse is the main street of Heurigen-dom: try the *Altes Presshaus* at #15, *Gertrude Marchart* at #17, the *Grinzinger Hauermandl* at #20, the *Grinzinger Weinbottich* at #28, or *Bach-Hengl,* a block away, at 9 Sandgasse. An "in" bar with music and a lively, classy crowd is the *Eden-Bar,* 2 Liliengasse (phone: 512-7450), open until 4 AM. The reigning discos are the *Queen Anne,* 12 Johannesgasse (phone: 512-0203), and the *Take Five,* 3a Annagasse (phone: 523276). For floor shows, try *Renz,* 50 Zirkusgasse (phone: 243135), near the Prater, or the *Casanova Erotic Revue Bar Theater,* 6-8 Dorotheerg. (phone: 512-9845 or 512-9869). Vienna is one of the few major European cities with legal gambling. The *Casino Cercle Wien* is in the Palais Esterhazy, 41 Kärntnerstr. (phone: 524836). In nearby Baden-bei-Wien, the casino is bigger, flashier, and cash-ier.

BEST IN TOWN

CHECKING IN: The nicest place to stay in Vienna is in the Innere Stadt — or just on the edge of it. Don't be put off by first impressions; many of the quaint hotels appear older than they do quaint — but they do have a particular Viennese charm. A double room with bath and breakfast costs from about $200 to $300 in hotels listed as expensive; $100 to $200 is moderate; and below $75 is inexpensive. All telephone numbers are in the 01 area code unless otherwise indicated.

Bristol – It's just across the street from the *Opera House,* overlooking the Ring, and the 128 rooms are large and beautifully furnished. Lots of polished wood, black tile bathrooms with twin sinks, instant room service — and one of the great hotel bars of Europe. Major credit cards. 1 Kärntner Ring (phone: 515160). Expensive.

Imperial – This regal building, built in 1869 as a private palace for the Duke of Württemberg, served as the Russian headquarters after World War II. It's more palatial in feeling and style than the *Bristol* and *Sacher;* its 160 rooms are superb and its service sublime. Wagner lived here for months during the productions of his operas around the corner. The hotel's restaurant has made a glorious comeback. Major credit cards. 16 Kärntner Ring (phone: 501100). Expensive.

Im Palais Schwarzenberg – Incomparably situated in its own manicured garden park in the center of Vienna, the rooms are set in a section of the old palace and exude an incomparable aura of dignity and Old World character. The only hotel in Vienna that's a member of the Relais & Châteaux. The kitchen is one of the most elegant in the city and the service is first rate. 9 Schwarzenbergpl. (phone: 784515). Expensive.

Plaza Wien – Vienna's newest hotel is also one of its most attractive. Opened in 1988 on central Schottenring, this is a very "European" *Hilton,* with large yet cozy rooms that feature bathrobes, hair dryers, fresh fruit, and the *International Herald Tribune* delivered every morning. The sixth floor is a designated non-smoking area. The cheery, bright *Le Jardin* restaurant serves continental, American, or Viennese breakfasts, lunches, and Sunday brunches. The Italian *La Scala* is best for dinner by candlelight — its famous chef Werner Matt has the ambition to turn it into Vienna's best restaurant. Major credit cards. 11 Schottenring (phone: 313900). Expensive.

Sacher – Over 100 years old, it's really a symbol of Vienna and a favorite of music lovers, listeners, and performers. Elegance, tradition, and the past are all in the air, in the ornate rococo decor, and in the faithful and distinguished clientele. The 121 rooms are modest but comfortable, and the service is impeccable. The concierge here is fabled for producing tickets (albeit sometimes at staggering prices) to Vienna's most noteworthy musical events. The hotel's restaurant is a center of Viennese social life (see *Eating Out*), and the elegant coffeehouse made the *Sachertorte* legendary. The *Opera House* is a 10-second walk away. Major credit cards. 2 Philharmonikerstr. (phone: 51456). Expensive.

Vienna Inter-Continental – Built in 1964 at one end of the elegant Stadtpark, this imposing member of the worldwide chain has become a landmark where the Viennese love to eat, meet, dance, and gossip. Among its many virtues are imaginative and excellent Austrian and international cuisine in its *Four Seasons* restaurant and a special floor for non-smokers. 498 rooms. Major credit cards. 28 Johannesgasse (phone: 71122). Expensive.

Vienna Marriott – Glassy and modern, this American-style hotel on the Ring, opposite the Stadtpark, is an attractive oasis of openness in a city of fairly forbidding hotel lobbies. With a waterfall to sip drinks by, a swimming pool, whirlpool bath, sauna, and ice machines on every floor, modern conveniences abound. Of the 304 rooms, 22 are reserved for non-smokers. Major credit cards. 12a Parkring (phone: 515180). Expensive.

Wien Hilton International – Built directly across the Stadtpark, this high-rise quickly earned a loyal following for its turn-of-the-century *Klimt Bar;* the folksy, traditional *Vindobona Cellar; Park Café,* with good food and drink and a view; and *Rôtisserie Prinz-Eugen,* a fine restaurant that was the first in Vienna to win a Michelin star. 620 rooms. Major credit cards. Am Stadtpark (phone: 752652). Expensive.

Astoria – The hotel lies in the pedestrian haven behind the *Vienna State Opera.* There's a lively international atmosphere in the lobby, but the upstairs restaurant attracts a local crowd that enjoys the four-course Opera Menu (which can be taken in installments before and after performances). 110 rooms. Major credit cards. 32-34 Kärntnerstr. (phone: 51577). Expensive to moderate.

Mailbergerhof – Tucked quietly into a courtyard in the Annagasse with an unimposing entrance and a first-floor reception room, this is nevertheless a favorite of music and theater people, particularly for longer stays in one of its 6 lovely apartment suites. 46 rooms. American Express. 7 Annagasse (phone: 512-0641). Expensive to moderate.

SAS Palais – This Belle Epoque palace on the Ring has been lovingly restored by the Scandinavian Airlines System to create a luxury hotel with a fine French restaurant, *La Siècle.* Its many jet-age amenities include airline check-in, a Royal Club, and a Business Club. Major credit cards. Parkring and Weihburggasse (phone: 515170). Expensive to moderate.

Biedermeier im Sünnhof – A charming hotel complex in beautifully restored houses, complete with restaurants and shops on the premises. Major credit cards. 28 Landstrasser Hauptstr. (phone: 755575). Moderate.

Graben – On a little dark street just off the Graben, but right in the middle of artistic and antiquarian Vienna. The building is a little drab, but just across the street is the city's liveliest hangout, the *Café Hawelka,* and the best sandwiches in Vienna are next door at *Tržesniewski.* 46 rooms. Major credit cards. 3 Dorotheergasse (phone: 512-1531). Moderate.

Kaiserin Elisabeth – In a building that dates from the 14th century, just off the Kärntnerstrasse, this 77-room hotel is on the same street as several of Vienna's better restaurants, so you're always sure of a good dinner — come snow or high water. Major credit cards. 3 Weihburggasse (phone: 51526). Moderate.

König von Ungarn – In one form or another, this fine old house has been in the hotel business since 1764. After its most recent renovation in 1977, it blossomed forth with a glass-roofed atrium and a 3-story, century-old, indoor tree around which coffee and cocktails are served. The *King of Hungary* restaurant serves international cuisine. 32 rooms. 10 Schulerstr. (phone: 526520). Moderate.

Römischer Kaiser – This handsome, baroque national trust building was erected in 1684 as the private palace of the imperial chancellor, then served as a military academy. It has been a hotel since the turn of the century. There is a charming little café on the front doorstep. 26 rooms. Major credit cards. 16 Annagasse (phone: 512-7751). Moderate.

Stephansplatz – Just 5 paces across the pedestrian mall to the main portal of the Stephanskirche, this may be the best location in town. It's also perched above a subway station that has a medieval chapel within; though the hotel's architecture is modern and without character, you are in the heart of Vienna, and the first-floor café is the heart of the heart. 72 rooms. Major credit cards. 9 Stephanspl. (phone: 534050). Moderate.

Pension Wiener – When Sam and Helen Thau retired, they sold their posh *Hôtel de France* on the Ring and opened this small hostelry atop a well-located, but quiet, downtown office building. If you like to take your Viennese *Gemütlichkeit* with a little Jewish mothering and all modern conveniences, this is the place. No credit cards. 16 Seilergasse (phone: 512-2809). Moderate to inexpensive.

Wandl – In the heart of Vienna, behind baroque St. Peter's church (which has a famous crèche every Christmas), this pleasant, modest hotel has been family owned for generations. No credit cards. 9 Petersplatz (phone: 534550). Moderate to inexpensive.

Schweizerhof – Just behind a marvelous clock on which statues of Vienna's greats — from Marcus Aurelius to Josef Haydn — march at midday, this 57-room hotel is very much a slice of old Vienna, with something rather pleasantly faded about its stylishness. Major credit cards. 22 Bauernmarkt (phone: 533-1931). Inexpensive.

 EATING OUT: Viennese cooking ranks among the best in Europe. Don't eat for a week before; you won't be able to for a week after. Make sure, at some point, to have a stand-up sausage in the street (the safest and best *Würstelstand* is outside the main Creditanstalt-Bankverein, 6 Schotteng.) and to fit in at least one *Beisel,* one *Heurigen,* and one coffeehouse. A *Beisel* is like a bistro, a cozy inexpensive neighborhood restaurant, open all hours. A *Heurigen* is a tavern that specializes in wine of new vintage, sometimes has entertainment, and often offers food. It can be recognized by a tuft of greenery hanging over the door. And coffeehouses are a way of life in Vienna, a place to sit, read newspapers, converse, receive guests and mail, and make phone calls.

The highlights of Viennese cuisine include the *Wiener schnitzel,* ideally a lightly breaded veal cutlet. Hungarian goulash (*Rindsgulasch*) is also popular, as is *Tafelspitz,* or boiled beef with vegetables and horseradish sauce. Desserts in Vienna are positively sinful, especially baked ones such as *Strudel, Sachertorte,* and *Linzertorte,* a tart of raspberry jam and almonds. And there are always mounds of *Schlag* (whipped cream). Coffee is special in Vienna and it comes in many varieties, especially *Mokka,* which is black; *Brauner,* coffee with milk; *Melange* or *Milchkaffee,* frothing with hot milk; and *Einspänner,* with whipped cream in a glass.

A meal for two will cost from $70 to $140 or more in restaurants classed as expensive; $40 to $65 is moderate; and below $30 is inexpensive. Although a 10% tip is included in most menu prices, an extra 5% gratuity is expected if service has been adequate. All telephone numbers are in the 01 area code unless otherwise indicated.

Korso – Possibly the best food in Vienna is served in this lovely restaurant fitted out with Art Nouveau decor. Closed Saturdays at lunch. Major credit cards. 2 Mahlerstr. (phone: 51516). Expensive.

Im Palais Schwarzenberg – Overlooking the formal gardens of the palace-hotel of the same name, this elegant restaurant is a reflection of the establishment's status as Vienna's only member of the Relais & Châteaux group. The menu is French-flavored more than typically Viennese, and the service is merely perfect. A fine respite from an excess of *Schnitzels* and *schlag.* Open daily. 9 Schwarzenbergpl. (phone: 784515). Expensive.

Sacher – There are those who would rather dine here than at any other place in Europe. It's superbly elegant, and it reeks of tradition. Dinner here before or after the opera is the quintessence of Vienna. Ordering *Tafelspitz* and wearing a tie are mandatory, and will put the waiter on your side from the start. Open daily. Reservations necessary well in advance. 4 Philharmonikerstr. (phone: 51456). Expensive.

Zu den Drei Husaren – *The Three Hussars* has beautiful, typically Viennese decor in the old style, an abundance of plush velour and drapery. It's famous for the incredibly huge procession of hors d'oeuvres that is wheeled by your table (note that the charge is by the piece). If necessary, skip the main course in order to leave room for the special dessert, *Husaren Pfannkuchen.* Open only for dinner; closed Sundays and often from mid-July to mid-August. Reservations necessary. 4 Weih-burggasse (phone: 512-1092). Expensive.

Zimmermann – This *Heuriger,* or tavern serving new wine, is absolutely charming. Its several cozy rooms surround a flower-filled courtyard and both the food and atmosphere are top-notch. Former chancellor Bruno Kreisky lives nearby and is a frequent guest. Closed Sundays. Major credit cards. 5 Armbrustgasse (phone: 372211). Moderate.

Zum Weissen Rauchfangkehrer – A homey place — rustic furnishings, wooden benches, lovely hanging iron lamps, painted glass — on a street of elegant restaurants. The food is good, and for dessert take a deep breath and ask the waiter for *Brandteigschokoladecremekrapfen.* Your reward for saying that 31-letter mouthful will be one of the best chocolate cream puffs ever, preferably in the *klavierzimmer* ("piano room"). Open daily. Reservations necessary. 4 Weihburggasse (phone: 523471). Moderate.

Figlmüller – A Viennese incarnation of a pre-war Broadway eatery with waiters to match, who serve up platters overflowing with lusciously thin, tender pork schnitzels in a bustling but friendly atmosphere. A good place to sample traditional Viennese food and *Gemütlichkeit.* Closed Saturday nights, Sundays, and August. Downtown: 5 Wollzeile (phone: 526177). In warm weather, try *Figlmüller*'s garden restaurant in Grinzing: 55 Grinzingerstr. (phone: 324257 or 323015). Moderate to inexpensive.

Griechenbeisl – Vienna's oldest pub: It's touristy, but oozes with charm. Viennese music is featured in the evenings. Open daily. 11 Fleischmarkt (phone: 533-1977). Moderate to inexpensive.

Toni Wagner's Glacisbeisel – Inside the walls of the former imperial stables (now a trade fairgrounds), this *Beisel* near the *English Theater* boasts imaginative soups and good schnitzels. During summer, you can eat in a garden built into the ramparts. Open for lunch weekdays, for dinner daily; closed Sundays. 1 Messepl. (phone: 961658). Inexpensive.

Tržesniewski – A must of musts. This isn't a proper restaurant, but is instead an ever-thronged sandwich bar, offering endless varieties of miniature open sandwiches from great bins of assorted Viennese goodies. Dark bread, draft beer, and *Apfelsaft,* apple cider. Open weekdays until 7:30 PM; closed Saturday afternoons and Sundays. No reservations. 1 Dorotheergasse (phone: 523291). Inexpensive.

WARSAW

Warsaw, like its people, is a pleasant surprise, but it takes a little effort to get to know each. On first impression, the capital seems as gray and forbidding as the poured concrete buildings with which the Poles quickly rebuilt their city after it was reduced to smoking rubble during World War II. The skyline, dominated by the Stalinesque Palace of Culture and Science, seems as no-nonsense and functional as the 1.7 million inhabitants who go about their business each day in the Polish capital.

A closer look will reveal the statuary of nymphs and satyrs in the 18th-century Saxon Gardens, where cavalrymen once exercised their horses, and the elegance of the neo-classic Lazienki Palace and baths, where Polish kings entertained their guests. The smiles of strolling couples, the glee of children feeding ducks, and the seemingly ubiquitous little kiosks selling flowers all combine to create an atmosphere both pleasant and inviting. Varsovians — as the residents of Warsaw are called — take the time to beautify their lives in small ways.

Just a little farther is the true heart of the city, the Old Town. Dating from the 14th century, it is a mixture of Renaissance and baroque buildings around a central marketplace. After the Nazi destruction of World War II, every detail, from the wrought-iron shop signs to the widening medieval streets, was lovingly restored through the joint efforts of the Polish government, the work of volunteers, and donations from Poles from all over the world, particularly in the US. To some, the obvious newness of the buildings gives too much of a feeling of a Hollywood set. But to the Poles, the new Old Town is a symbol of their determination to keep their heritage.

The Poles have had to work hard to preserve their past and their identity as a people. Three times in Warsaw's 900-year history there have been attempts to annihilate the city. Throughout the 17th and 18th centuries, the city was occupied repeatedly by Swedes and Russians. The Swedes razed the city in the 17th century, and it was sacked in the 18th century during the suppression of an insurrection. Poland ceased to exist as a nation when it was partitioned in 1795 and Warsaw was given to Prussia. Napoleon captured the city in 1806 and formed the Duchy of Warsaw, but in 1813 it was retaken by the Russians. Poland was not restored as a nation until after World War I.

Then came the German occupation of World War II and the creation of the Warsaw ghetto. German and Polish Jews were shipped to Warsaw while Hitler's Nazis were pondering the details of the "Final Solution." In 1942 and 1943 almost half a million died of starvation or were executed. The Jews of the ghetto had inspired the world in 1943 by rising up in a fierce, if losing, battle against the Germans. The following year, all the underground groups united in a 63-day battle against the Nazis, which is remembered as the Warsaw Uprising. When it failed, the Nazis began the systematic destruction of the city. Hitler issued an order that not one stone of the city be left standing.

More than 200,000 people were killed here; most of those who survived were deported.

Warsaw and its people were devastated by the war. And the city remembers. War plaques and monuments are everywhere; the *Historical Museum of the City of Warsaw* shows visitors captured Nazi film, documenting the destruction of the city. Today there is a new Warsaw, incorporating the past and looking with hope toward the future. After the war, the Polish Communist government took advantage of the rebuilding opportunity to move industrial and warehouse facilities to the outskirts. Park areas were tripled in size and streets were widened.

The Vistula (Wisła) River splits the city, with the downtown area on the left, higher bank, and the Praga housing suburb on the right. The symbol of Warsaw is Syrena, a winged mermaid armed with a sword and shield, whose statue guards the city from the Kościuszko embankment. For Varsovians, she personifies the city's proud motto: "Defies the Storm." Given the recent emergence of Solidarity as the leading vote-getter in the 1989 general election, it might indicate that such defiance has proved quite effective.

WARSAW AT-A-GLANCE

SEEING THE CITY: For a general sense of Warsaw's postwar reconstruction and continuing modernization, take the elevator to the 30th-floor terrace of the Palace of Culture and Science, Pl. Defilad. From here, on a bright, clear day, you can see beyond the outskirts of the city, which are marked by heavy industry, modern buildings, and new housing estates. There is a small charge for the elevator.

SPECIAL PLACES: The Old Town is just north of the Slasko-Dabrowski Bridge (Most Śląsko-Dąbrowski). Most sights and activities of interest to tourists are to be found between this area and Łazienkowski Park south of Pl. Na Rozdroźu.

Royal Castle – Warsaw's most important historical monument, its Royal Castle, built between the 14th and 18th centuries, was blown up by the Nazis in their campaign to wipe Poland off the face of the map. Now the painstaking effort to rebuild this important symbol of the continuity of Polish history is finished, and its imposing silhouette forms an impressive background to King Sigismund's Column in the middle of Zamkowy Square. The Royal Castle rejoins the ranks of the most beautiful palaces in Europe. Adjacent to Pl. Zamkowy.

Old Town (Stare Miasto) – Sigismund III Column, the oldest monument in Warsaw (1644), stands in the center of Zamkowy Square adjoining the Royal Castle grounds and at the edge of the Old Town. Nearby is the baroque, tin-roofed Pod Blacha Palace, noted for its attic crowned with a richly ornamented cartouche bearing coats-of-arms. The Old Town Market Square is the most beautiful square in Warsaw — enclosed by re-created baroque houses, filled with flowers, and alive with little shops and café life. Nearby is St. John's Cathedral, where Jozef Cardinal Glemp delivers the homily to the deeply religious, Roman Catholic Poles. Old walls that once fortified the city and the Barbican, a sort of tower house of the mid-16th century, have been reconstructed and add to the atmosphere of the district. West of the Vistula, north of the Śląsko-Dąbrowski Bridge.

World War II Monuments – So extensive was the heroic resistance to the Nazis that even the churches and cemeteries of Warsaw were scenes of fierce fighting. The city's

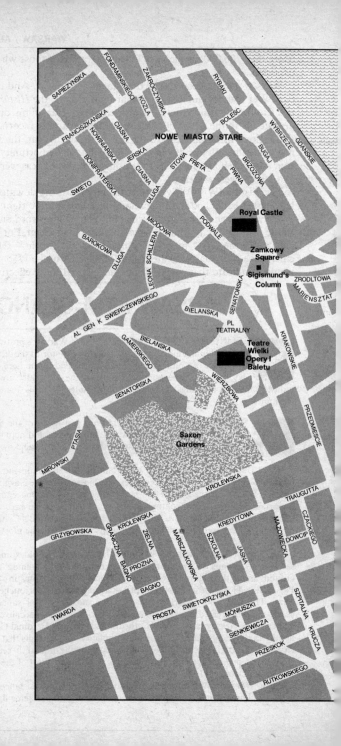

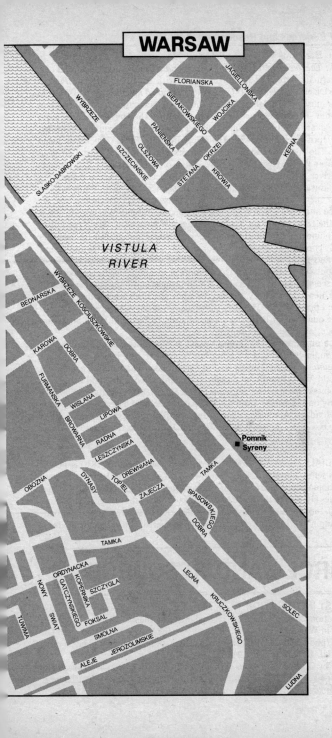

Monument to the Heroes of Warsaw — Warsaw Nike — stands in Pl. Teatralny in front of the *Wielki Theater* (see "Music" in *Sources and Resources*). It is sort of a new version of the mermaid Syrena, a fighting goddess with sword raised. The *Pawiak Prison,* 24/26 Ul. Dzielna, where 35,000 Poles were executed and another 65,000 were detained, is now a museum. The ghetto where the Jewish population was walled up in 1941 was not rebuilt. It is remembered by a Monument to the Heroes of the Ghetto on a small grassy square at Zamenhofa and Anielewicza streets and exhibits connected with the Ghetto Uprising at the Jewish Historical Institute, 79 al. Świerczewskiego (phone: 271843). The former Gestapo headquarters and prison on Armii Wojska Polskiego Street near Pl. Na Rozdroźu is now a Mausoleum to Struggle and Martyr- dom. Across the river in Praga is a Monument to Brotherhood-in-Arms, celebrating Polish friendship toward the Soviet Union, whose soldiers liberated Warsaw. The monument is near the crossing of Targowa and Świerczewskiego streets.

Łazienki Palace and Park – The splendid Palace on the Water in Warsaw's loveliest park was built in the 18th century for Stanisław August Poniatowski, last of the Polish kings. The Nazis plundered its collections and devastated the palace, but the interiors have been carefully copied and restored. There are some 18 other buildings and monu- ments in the spacious park, including the White House, once the residence in exile of the future King Louis XVIII of France. The monument to Chopin at the southern end of the park is the scene of Sunday afternoon Chopin concerts. At the southern end of the gardens is the new conservatory, a place to enjoy the town's best cup of coffee, chocolate cake, and piano music. The Belweder Palace, official residence of the Presi- dent of the State Council, is in Belweder Park, adjacent to Łazienki Park. Southeast of Pl. Na Rozdroźu, along al. Ujazdowskie.

Wilanów Palace and Park – This Polish version of Versailles was built in the late 17th century as a summer residence for King Jan Sobieski III and is now a branch of the *National Museum.* Baroque terraces lead to a small lake. The baroque palace was restored after World War II and contains furniture, china, portraits, and other me- mentoes of the Sobieski family. The *Museum of the Polish Poster* (Museum Plakatu) is in a new building on the palace grounds. The palace is closed Tuesdays; the poster museum, closed Mondays. Admission charge. Just south of the city, less than 6 miles (9 km) from the city center. Reached by express bus B or bus #180 from Ul. Mars- załkowska.

■**EXTRA SPECIAL:** The manor house where Chopin was born in 1810 is now a museum. It is set in a lovely park in Żelazowa Wola, some 33 miles (53 km) west of the city. Chopin concerts are held on Sundays during the summer at the Chopin home. Six miles (10 km) to the north of Żelazowa Wola, in the village of Brochów, there is a mid-16th-century Renaissance fortified church where Chopin was bap- tized. The Chopin family birth certificates are in the parish church. Leave Warsaw by Route 1.

SOURCES AND RESOURCES

TOURIST INFORMATION: Maps and information are available at Tourist Information Centers, which can be recognized by their "IT" signs. The main centers in Warsaw are at 1/13 Pl. Zamkowy (phone: 270000), and at 16 Ul. Bracka (phone: 260271); another such center is open 24 hours a day, 7 days a week, at 16/22 Ul. Krucza (phone: 217823).

This Is Warsaw, by Olgierd Budrewicz with photos by Jan Styczyński, is an excellent, often witty, pocket-size guide in English (Wag Art Publishers; about $1.50). There is also *A Guide to Warsaw and Environs* (Sport I Turystyka Publishers; under $1), which is more readily available in Poland. The city map (*Plan Miasta*) is a detailed plan of Warsaw that, although in Polish, is extremely useful. It is published by PPWK and costs about $1.50, but is rather difficult to find in Warsaw's bookstores.

The US Embassy is at 29/31 Aleje Ujazdowskie (phone: 283041 through -49).

Local Coverage – The *Warsaw Voice* is a new English-language newspaper. The *International Herald Tribune* is available in the larger hotels.

Food – Your best bet is to consult the tourist information centers for dining recommendations.

Telephone – The area code for Warsaw is 022.

 CLIMATE AND CLOTHES: Warsaw winters can be bitter. Snowfall was so heavy during the winter of 1978–79 that the city was immobilized for several weeks. Temperatures are usually below freezing during January and February, and even in summer they normally don't go much above 75F (24C). Rainwear is essential during most of the year. Be aware, too, that the city is very windy, especially during the winter.

 GETTING AROUND: The Old Town, the Vistula embankment, and the whole route of Krakowskie Przedmieście, Nowy Świat, and al. Ujazdowskie streets are best seen on foot. But Poland's capital is a very big city, so at some point you will probably want to use municipal transportation.

Airports – Warsaw's domestic and international airports — collectively known as Okęcie — are placed together, connected by a 5-minute shuttle bus ride. Okęcie is a 20-minute cab ride from downtown; the fare is about $5-$6. Bus service provided by the Polish airline LOT travels between the airport and the LOT office on Waryńskiego Street. Fare is about 50¢.

Bus and Tram – Avoid them if possible during rush hours, but they are the cheapest way to get around. Route signs are at each stop. Buy your ticket before boarding at a nearby tobacco or newspaper kiosk, called a *Ruch,* then cancel it in a special machine on the coach. It's a good idea to buy extra tickets since *Ruchs* are often closed.

Car Rental – The government-run *Orbis Rent-a-Car* at the *Forum* hotel, 24-26 Ul. Nowogrodzka (phone: 293875), arranges for self-drive or chauffeur-driven car rentals. Arrangements also can be made at major hotels and the airport or before arrival through *Avis, Europcar,* and *Hertz.*

Taxi – Cabs may be hailed on the street, and rates are quite inexpensive. To order a taxi by phone, call 919. Make sure the driver turns on the meter at the onset of the ride.

Train – The main train station is at the corner of Emilii Plater and Aleje Jerozalimskie, in the center of town (phone: 200361 for local train schedules and information, 257554 for international trains). A "PolRailPass" is available in Poland at Orbis travel agencies; payment must be made in foreign currency.

 SPECIAL EVENTS: The holidays most important to the predominantly Catholic Poles tend to be religious, such as *Christmas, Easter,* and the *Feast of Corpus Christi.* In addition, an *International Book Fair* is held here each May, and there is an *International Poster Biennale* in June of even-numbered years. The *"Warsaw Autumn" International Festival of Modern Music* is an important September event, and the *Jazz Jamboree* held in late October is the oldest jazz festival in central and Eastern Europe.

 MUSEUMS: In addition to those described in *Special Places,* Warsaw has a number of other interesting museums. All are closed Mondays.

Archaeological Museum – Tools and other relics of prehistoric Baltic peoples. 5 Ul. Długa (phone: 313221).

Chopin's Drawing Room – Period furnishings. In the former Raczyński Palace (also once known as the Czapski Palace, now the *Academy of Fine Arts*). 5 Ul. Krakowskie Przedmieście.

Maria Skłodowska-Curie Museum and House – The chemist's home before she moved to Paris. 16 Ul. Freta (phone: 318092).

Ethnographic Museum – Peasant life, folk art, and costumes. 1 Ul. Kredytowa (phone: 277641).

Historical Museum of the City of Warsaw – Pictures and exhibitions of Warsaw through the centuries. 48 Old Town Market Sq. (phone: 310251).

National Museum – Poland's greatest art collection. 3 Ul. Jerozolimskie (phone: 211031).

SHOPPING: Shops in Warsaw generally are open from 11 AM to 7 PM, but department stores open earlier and close later. Avoid the crowds by shopping before 3 PM. Leather, linen, and folk art ranging from wonderful woodcarvings to handsome handwoven rugs are good buys here. (There are restrictions on the quantity and types of items you can take out of Poland; check with authorities before your trip.)

On February 1, 1989, the government introduced exit custom duties on all items bought in the country. The tax is from 100% to 300% of the value of the goods, except on those goods purchased in special shops that deal only in foreign currency, and must be paid upon leaving Poland. You should always keep receipts of the items, along with receipts proving that the zlotys were exchanged at official rates.

Art – Stylized folk art and works of modern art. 17 Ul. Krakowskie Przedmieście.

Cepelia – Government shops that sell souvenirs and folk art. 2 and 5 Pl. Konstytucji, 8/10 Old Town Market Square, 23/31 Ul. Krucza, 99/101 Ul. Marszałkowska, and many others.

Desa – Government shops specializing in old and contemporary Polish art. For posters, etchings, and woodcuts, the shop is at 30 Ul. Rutkowskiego; for coins and medals, 17 Ul. Nowotki; and for antique jewelry, 48 Ul. Nowy Świat.

Orno – Handmade artistic silverwork. 83 Ul. Marszałkowska, 52 Ul. Nowy Świat, and 13 Ul. Świętojańska.

Persian Market (*Perski Rynek*) – Each Sunday between 9 AM and 3 PM at this flea market, you can buy anything from antiques to homemade tripe soup to German war medals. Take bus A to the end of the line, then follow the crowd. Ul. Jana Kasprowicza at Ul. Przytyk.

Pewex – A chain of hard-currency stores scattered throughout the city that sell local goods and hard-to-get imports such as chocolate, coffee, and liquor (vodka is very inexpensive here).

Rozyckiego Market (*Bazar Rozyckiego*) – Capitalism runs rampant daily here. Everything from fur coats and Western clothing to smuggled Russian caviar — all at negotiable prices — is for sale. Also available are homemade foods sold by the many elderly women who cater to both buyers and sellers from their sidewalk stands. At Ul. Targowa, two tram stops (N. 9, 13) from Pl. Zamkowy.

Supersam – A huge supermarket where shortages are often apparent. Near Pl. Unii Lubelskiej and Ul. Warynskiego.

SPORTS AND FITNESS: Horse Racing – The *Suzewiec Race Course*, on the southern extremity of the city, is one of the largest in Europe. Races are held on Wednesdays, Saturdays, and Sundays in summer.

Soccer – *Legia*, the best and most popular Warsaw team, plays its matches at various stadiums around the country.

Swimming – In summer there is swimming at the *Legia* pool on Ul. Łazienkowska or the indoor pool at the Palace of Culture and Science, 6 Pl. Defilad. There are no public beaches, and you cannot swim in the river.

 THEATER: Advance booking for theater or cinema tickets can be made through the Tourist Information Center, 1/13 Pl. Zamkowy (phone: 270000), or the *SPATIF* ticket office, 25 Al. Jerozolimskie (phone: 285995). The city's foremost drama theaters include *Polski,* 2 Ul. Karasia (phone: 267992); *Dramatyczny,* in the Palace of Culture and Science, Pl. Defilad (phone: 200211); and *Ateneum,* 2 Ul. St. Jaracza (phone: 267330 or 262421). There are several children's theaters in Warsaw, including the *Lalka* puppet theater in the Palace of Culture and Science (phone: 200211).

 MUSIC: Opera and ballet are performed at *Warsaw's Grand Theater of Opera and Ballet* (Teatr Wielki Opery I Baletu), Pl. Teatralny (phone: 263287). The prestigious international *Chopin Piano Competitions* are held every 5 years at the *Filharmonia,* 20 Ul. Sienkiewicza (phone: 275712), and there are operettas staged at the *Operetka,* 49 Ul. Nowogrodzka (phone: 280360).

 NIGHTCLUBS AND NIGHTLIFE: You'll need a fairly sophisticated knowledge of Polish to appreciate the humor at one of Warsaw's popular satirical cafés, but you might try one for the atmosphere.

For jazz, try *Akwarium,* a modern glass nightspot on Ul. Emilii Plater, near the Palace of Culture and Science. One of the city's best private clubs is *SARP,* 13 Foksal, which is run by the association of Polish architects and artists. However, you must be taken there by a member.

BEST IN TOWN

CHECKING IN: Since Warsaw is home to less than a dozen hotels, booking well in advance is strongly advised, especially during the summer. Expect to pay from $70 to $105 a night for a double in one of Warsaw's expensive hotels; from $50 to $70 in the moderate range. Prices include breakfast.

Another housing option is the bed-and-breakfast type of accommodation, but in Warsaw, such places lack the breakfast. What they do provide, however, is an opportunity for a rare glimpse into the lives of the ordinary Poles. Bookings and information are available through *Syrena* offices at 17 Ul. Krucza (phone: 287540 or 217864). All telephone numbers are in the 022 area code unless otherwise indicated.

Victoria Inter-Continental – Warsaw's best hotel is close to the *Wielki Theater* and Saxon Gardens. Its 370 rooms are pleasantly decorated, and the *Canaletto* restaurant specializes in Polish dishes. Swimming pool. Major credit cards. 11 Ul. Królewska (phone: 279051 or 279271). Expensive.

Orbis-Europejski – The 279 rooms — including singles and doubles, with and without bath, and suites — are functionally modern in this grand 4-story hotel building, over 100 years old. A café looks out on the Saxon Gardens and the Monument to the Unknown Soldier. Major credit cards. 13 Ul. Krakowskie Przedmieście (phone: 265051). Expensive to moderate.

Orbis Forum – The Inter-Continental chain's second hotel in Warsaw is bigger, but not as nice. Its 751 rooms are of modest size and sparsely decorated. It has a central location, however, near the Palace of Culture and Science. Major credit cards. 24/26 Ul. Nowogrodzka (phone: 210271 or 280364). Expensive to moderate.

Orbis-Grand – The more than 410 rooms here are rather plain, but the midtown location is a plus. It has a rooftop café with glass-enclosed terrace and a swimming pool. On the eighth floor is a disco, making seventh-floor rooms places to be avoided, due to the noise. 28 Ul. Krucza (phone: 294051). Moderate.

Orbis-Solec – Somewhat away from the center, but nicely situated on the bank of the Vistula, this hotel has 147 rooms with showers and toilets. The decor is minimal motel-modern. 1 Ul. Zagórna (phone: 259241). Moderate.

 EATING OUT: Food shortages are a fact of life in Poland. The best victuals usually go to the first class hotels, so local restaurants with character may not always have the ingredients they need. They serve dinner relatively early, and by 10:30 PM most of the kitchens are already dark. Dinner for two, even with wine, at an expensive restaurant will be reasonable — $25 to $35 and up; a moderately priced restaurant will charge $15 to $25; and an inexpensive restaurant will serve meals from a dollar or two per person. All telephone numbers are in the 022 area code unless otherwise indicated.

Bazyliszek – Easily Warsaw's premier restaurant, best known for its wild game. It's on the second floor over a snack bar and has an Old Warsaw ambience. The decor features hussars' armor and wooden beams. A horse and carriage is usually outside to take you for a romantic ride through the city after dinner. Open daily. 7/9 Old Town Market Sq. (phone: 311841). Expensive.

Zajazd Napoleonski – In a neighborhood not meant for strolling, this is a small, private hotel and restaurant. The uniformed, white-gloved staff serves superb food with great style. Dinner for two with wine will run $50 to $60. Open daily. 83 Ul. Ptowiecka (phone: 153454 or 153068). Expensive.

Cristal-Budapeszt – Cristal and Budapeszt are two separate rooms in this popular Hungarian restaurant. The Budapeszt Room has a folk motif and Gypsy orchestra; the Cristal has a modern Polish discotheque atmosphere. In either room, start with *zupa gulaszowa:* meat and vegetables in a delicious paprika-seasoned broth, served in steaming cauldrons. Open daily. 21/25 Marszałkowska (phone: 253433). Moderate.

Wilanow – Traditional Polish cuisine in a modern ambience. Open daily. 27 Ul. Wiertnicza (phone: 421852). Moderate.

Karczma Slupska – Traditional Kashubian — northern Polish — cuisine is served in a quaint regional restaurant with embroidered curtains and an unusual bar. The seats at the bar are carousel horses that move up and down, controlled from behind the bar. Among the specialties are the nut soup and boar pâté. 125 Czerniakowska (phone: 414552). Moderate to inexpensive.

Dzik – You'll recognize this restaurant by the mounted head of a wild boar, or *dzik,* outside over the front door. The specialty here, naturally enough, is wild game. There are a number of rather threadbare stuffed animal heads mounted on the wall. Customers here tend to get a bit rowdy as the evening progresses. 42 Nowogrodzka (phone: 219728). Inexpensive.

Staropolska – Near the university, this restaurant is a mainstay among academic types. Although the menu is limited, it has one of the best cold buffets in Warsaw, with veal in aspic and steak tartare. Also sample the broth with hard-boiled egg and sausage, called *zurek staropolski.* Old *Beatles* tapes or European disco music plays continuously. 8 Krakowskie Przedmieście (phone: 269070). Inexpensive.

Trojka – This ground-floor restaurant at the Palace of Culture and Science offers a selection of typical Russian food. In the evenings, entertainment is provided by a Russian orchestra. Pl. Defilad (phone: 200211). Inexpensive.

ZURICH

Zurich is Switzerland's largest city, and the country's hundreds of years of peace and democracy have enabled it to develop into a great industrial and financial center, city of the fabled "gnomes" of the international money market. Indeed, banks dominate the Bahnhofstrasse, the famous shopping street, almost as much as the elegant shops do — and vaults of gold are literally buried beneath its pavement. C. G. Jung, one of Zurich's most celebrated residents, once said, "The relation of Zurich to the world is not spiritual but commercial."

Be careful in Zurich if you are on a tight budget; this is one of Europe's most expensive cities. With more than 360,000 residents, Zurich is Switzerland's richest city. Land prices are so high that the number of citizens who can afford to live in town declines steadily, and a constant migration to the suburbs decreases the population each year.

At the foot of Lake Zurich and offering a panoramic view of the Alps on clear days, Zurich is also one of the most beautiful cities in Europe. It is in northern Switzerland, not far from the West German border, on the spot where the Limmat River flows *out* of (not into) Lake Zurich. Its modern social center is concentrated on both banks of the river, its broad shopping street running parallel to the river from the main railroad station to the lake. Old Zurich is close by; the picturesque quay on the right side of the river is lined with 16th- and 17th-century guild houses, now converted into homes, shops, and restaurants. And the town's oldest quarter surrounds its two medieval churches, the Grossmünster on the right bank and the Fraumünster on the left, with narrow, winding streets, old houses with typical oriel windows, and interesting wrought-iron signs.

Zurich, which celebrated its 2,000th anniversary in 1986, derives its name from the Latin *Turicum,* which is derived from the Celtic *dur,* meaning "water." The first signs of habitation (6000 BC) were found near the site of the present opera house; the later Celtic settlement was colonized by the Romans in the 1st century BC, becoming a customs outpost; after the fall of the Roman Empire, the barbarian tribe of the Allemans settled here, giving many of the people the Germanic physical and psychological traits that are still recognizable today. At the crossing of two important trade routes, one from France to Eastern Europe and the other from Germany to Italy, Zurich was a busy commercial town from its earliest days. The city expanded continuously, becoming a powerful city-state; always fiercely independent in spirit, it joined the Swiss Confederation in the 14th century. During the Protestant Reformation in the 16th century, the Grossmünster Cathedral became the pulpit of the zealous and controversial Protestant reformer Ulrich Zwingli.

The majority of Zurich's people speak the Schwyzerdütsch dialect that you

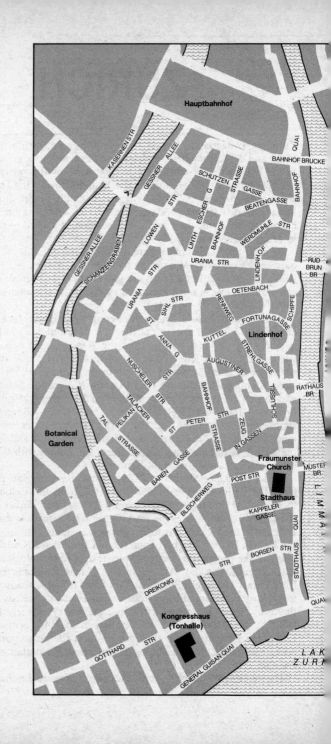

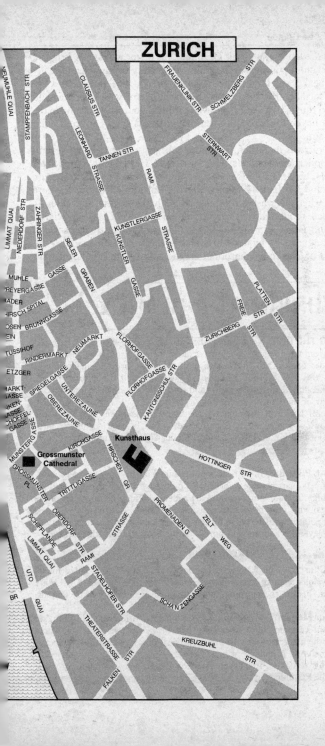

ZURICH

won't understand even if you speak German. Yet many will speak English, and tiny Switzerland has always been a country of many languages and many cultures; 70% speak Swiss German, 20% speak French, 9% Italian, and 1% Romansh. The social spirit of the Swiss has been one of wise tolerance and cooperation, and the justly celebrated Swiss political neutrality has made the city of Zurich a haven for such 20th-century greats as James Joyce, Lenin, and Thomas Mann.

Paradoxically, it was in Zurich, the most bourgeois of cities, that several revolutionary modern movements were nurtured: Here Lenin pored over Marx and Engels, wrote his famous essay, "Imperialism, The Highest State of Capitalism," and left in 1917 to organize the Bolshevik Revolution; here James Joyce — when he wasn't romping through the streets and cafés — wrote that ultimate modern novel, *Ulysses;* and in the noisy *Cabaret Voltaire,* Tristan Tzara and Hans Arp formulated the ideas of the outrageous Dada movement, a vanguard of modern art. Harry Lime notwithstanding, the peaceful comfort of Zurich has harbored creations far more significant than the cuckoo clock.

ZURICH AT-A-GLANCE

 SEEING THE CITY: No question, the most enchanting view of the city and lake is from Quai Bridge, where river and lake join. From here you can see both sides of the Old Town, with church towers, bridges, and medieval façades: this is a beautiful sight in daylight or at night. If you turn around, you can see the lake, dotted with sailboats — and on a Föhn (warm Alpine wind) day a picture-book view of the Alps.

To see the general layout of the city, try the Sonnenbergterasse, in front of the *Sonnenberg* hotel on Zurichberg, on the eastern edge of town, or have a drink or a meal at the *Sonnenberg* restaurant, at 98 Aurorastr. (phone: 470047), or try the terrace of the University *in* town.

 SPECIAL PLACES: On both sides of the Limmat, the old town has cobblestone streets, narrow lanes, corners decorated by fountains, small antique shops, high fashion boutiques, and art galleries. Watch for the dates of the buildings, which are hewn into the stone doorways.

A good starting point is Münsterhof, a former pig market where recent excavations uncovered several layers of housing and burial, dating back to the 12th century.

DOWNTOWN

Fraumünster Church – This 12th-century church at Münsterhof is noted for its chapel, with marvelous stained glass windows created in 1970 and 1978 by Marc Chagall. Try to see them in the morning light. The organ here is also justly famous. Münster Platz.

Guildhouse "Zur Meisen" – A splendid rococo building with a wrought-iron gate houses the excellent ceramic collection of the *Historical Museum,* which is worth visiting if only for the marvelous view from its stuccoed rooms. No admission charge. Closed daily at lunch and Mondays. Münster Platz.

Lindenhof – This romantic, tree-covered lookout point, a few climbing crooked alleys away from the Fraumünster, was a fort in Celtic and Roman times; a Freemason lodge stands there now. Lindenhof offers a lovely view of the old town and is a favorite spot for lovers after dark.

St. Peterhofstatt – Another small, charming square surrounded by old buildings.

Grossmünster (Cathedral) – According to legend, this church was founded by Charlemagne, whose horse bowed down on the spot where the city's patron saints, martyrs Felix and Regula, died after walking from the river carrying their cut-off heads. This was the parish church of Ulrich Zwingli, one of the Reformation's most revered leaders, who converted Zurich to Protestantism in the mid-16th century. Its towers became a landmark of Zurich; the inside is rather cold and austere. 4 Zwingliplatz.

Nägelihof – A delightful, small enclave, off 42 Limmatquai, this recently reconstructed square features cafés, amusing shops, two movie theaters, and a most unusual view of the Grossmünster towers.

Bahnhofstrasse – "The most beautiful shopping street in the world," and certainly one of the most expensive, Bahnhofstrasse was built on a site that was an ancient moat about 100 years ago. Running from the lake to the main railway station, it's a shopper's and stroller's paradise — with rows of banks, shops, cafés for people watching — graced in summer with the intoxicating scent of linden trees and around Christmas with magnificent illuminations. There is a colorful flower and vegetable market at its lake end every Tuesday and Friday morning and a flea market every Saturday in summer.

Schweizerisches Landesmuseum (Swiss National Museum) – The largest and most complete collection of Swiss history is in a pseudo-castle behind the railroad station. Especially interesting are the prehistoric finds, the reconstructed Celtic tomb, Carolingian frescoes, and the treasury and some old paintings of Zurich. A brochure is available in English. Closed Mondays. No admission charge. 2 Museumstr. (phone: 221-1010).

Museum Rietberg – One of the most important collections of non-European art in Europe is set in the enchanting Wesendonck Villa, outside of the city center. Here Richard Wagner was often a guest, and his love affair with the hostess inspired *Tristan and Isolde*. The villa is surrounded by a magnificent private park, so bring a sandwich and you can spend a delightful day wandering in and out of the museum. The backbone of this collection is the donation of Baron von der Heydt, who had his world-famous treasures in 24 different museums before the *Rietberg* opened in 1952. Art items are mainly Indian, Southeast Asian, Chinese, Japanese, and African. The guidebook in English is recommended. Closed Mondays. Admission charge except Wednesday evenings and Sundays. 15 Gablerstr. (phone: 202-4528).

Kunsthaus (Fine Arts Museum) – In 1976, the building was rebuilt in "open museum" style, without rigidly dividing floors, walls, and stairs. The permanent exhibition includes an excellent collection of art from the Middle Ages until today, with emphasis on 19th- and 20th-century European works by Monet, Munch, Giacometti, Rodin, Chagall, and others. Closed Monday mornings. Admission charge except Sundays and Wednesday afternoons. 1 Heimpl. (phone: 251-6755).

Boat Trip on the Lake – Don't miss this on a beautiful sunny day. Daily cruises vary in length from 1½ to 4 hours; the long one that includes Rapperswil is best. Boats depart from Bürkliplatz, at the lake end of Bahnhofstr. In summer there are special lunch cruises. For information call Zurichsee Schiffahrtsgesellschaft (phone: 482-1033) or the Zurich Tourist Office (phone: 211-4000).

Wohnmuseum – Two charming private houses from the 17th and 18th centuries display period interiors with interesting furniture; in the basement there is a collection of dolls made by the famous Swiss artist Sacha Morgenthaler. Closed at lunch hour in winter and Mondays. No admission charge. 22 Bärengasse (phone: 211-1716).

E. G. Bührle Collection – This is an extremely important private art collection, mainly from the 19th century, which includes French Impressionist paintings, medieval sculptures, and other items. The collection is in the private villa of the industrialist Emil

Bührle, who died in 1956. Open on Tuesday and Friday afternoons only. Admission charge. 172 Zollikerstr. (phone: 550086).

Beyer's Watch & Clock Museum – The oldest watch shop in Switzerland. Inside is the private collection of the Beyer family — rare and interesting items dating from 1400 BC to the present. Closed weekends. No admission charge. 31 Bahnhofstr. (221-1080).

Botanical Garden – Rare plants from all over the world and a good cafeteria with a large terrace. The gardens could be combined with a visit to the nearby Bührle villa. Open daily. No admission charge. 107 Zollikerstr. (phone: 385-4411).

Zurich Toy Museum – The exhibits here are from the antiques collection of the same Franz Carl Weber who owns the famous toy shop (see *Shopping*). Closed mornings and Sundays. No admission charge. 15 Fortunagasse (phone: 211-9305).

OUT OF TOWN

Schaffhausen-Rhinefall and Stein am Rhein – Schaffhausen, 35 miles (56 km) north, is a wonderfully preserved medieval town, with a most photogenic fortress and the Rhinefall, Europe's largest waterfall (no match for Niagara); the best view is from Neuhausen, on the terrace of the *Bellevue* hotel. (Try their wine and fish while admiring the view.) Open daily (phone: 053-222121). Stein am Rhein, 13 miles (21 km) farther east, is a delight with its intricately painted housefronts and a museum in a former monastery. (You have to share it with loads of other tourists, though.) If possible, return through the gentle wine country around Stammheim, with villages of half-timbered houses, vineyards, and orchards.

St. Gallen and Appenzell – About 70 miles (112 km) northeast is St. Gallen, a Swiss textile center, with a spectacular abbey-library in its cathedral (100,000 volumes of rare books and manuscripts). From here it is only a short drive into the country's most genuinely rural region, the Appenzell. (Its capital has the same name.) The region has farms, pastures, folk art (embroidery and wood carvings), and lovely painted houses; around the Säntis (mountain) there is some high Alpine scenery, including a cable car that climbs to a 7,500-foot peak. Return via the picturesque road to Wattwil, with a stop in Rapperswil on the lake; then follow the shore to Zurich. This trip offers a good cross-section of the "real" but not so well known Switzerland.

■ **EXTRA SPECIAL:** Zurich is a perfect base for dozens of short and long excursions, easily accessible also by public transportation (or organized tours).

An excellent half-day trip would be to Einsiedeln, about 25 miles (40 km) southeast of Zurich, which offers Alpine scenery (splendid walks in summer, skiing in winter), and a world-famous baroque abbey, which is magnificent.

A cable car in Weglosen, only 10 minutes farther by car, takes you into the "real" mountains.

SOURCES AND RESOURCES

 TOURIST INFORMATION: For general information, brochures, and maps, contact Verkehrsverein Zürich, Hauptbahnhof (phone: 211-4000). In the US, contact the Swiss National Tourist Office, 608 Fifth Ave., New York NY 10020 (phone: 212-757-5944). For business travelers, a good address to know is that of the Swiss-American Chamber of Commerce, 41 Talacker (phone: 211-2454).

The best pocket guidebook in English is *Travel Guide Zürich,* published by Polyglot, available at any local bookstore. (You can order it in the US, but be sure to get the latest edition.)

The *Zürich News,* which comes out every Friday, has a detailed listing of events for the coming week plus a 2-week forecast. It is available at all hotels and at the tourist office. *The Shopping Guide Zürich* is a monthly publication available at hotels and selected shops.

The US Consulate is at 141 Zollikerstr. (phone: 552566).

Local Coverage – There is no English-language newspaper, but for world news the best is the daily (except Sundays) *International Herald Tribune.*

Food – Consult the *Zürich News* for a rundown of restaurants in the city.

Telephone – The area code for Zurich is 01.

 CLIMATE AND CLOTHES: Good weather cannot be taken for granted, but if it's good, it's intoxicatingly so. Zurich weather is Atlantic influenced, with the moderating effect of the Alps; long rainy periods are possible, mainly in spring and summer — weather is best generally in the fall. Föhn wind brings magnificent days with deep blue skies and high temperatures in winter; it can bring rain in summer. Winter is quite mild, around freezing; summer temperature is seldom over 80F (26C).

A warm sweater and a raincoat are necessary in any season. Dress styles are similar to those in New York City; people dress fashionably, although the Swiss tend to be more conservative and more careful about color coordination. Jackets and ties are right for some restaurants.

 GETTING AROUND: Airport – Kloten Airport, about 10 minutes from the center of town by train and 20 minutes by car, handles both domestic and international flights: Terminal A handles flights within Europe; Terminal B handles all the others. Trains to the airport leave every 20 minutes from the Hauptbahnhof, Zurich's main train station; the stop is called Kloten Airport (Flughafen). Cab fare from the city to the airport is about 40 Swiss francs (about $25).

Bus – The supermodern blue streetcars (VBZ) are best. Automatic machines at every stop issue tickets for exact change. (You cannot pay on the tram and you are fined if found without a ticket.) The same applies to buses. If you intend to use them a lot, it is best to get a 1-day or a season ticket. An informative multilingual brochure, giving all the details, including rates and routes, is available at information booths marked "VBZ" in the underground Shopville at the main railroad station, at Paradepl. and Bellevuepl., or at the Zurich Tourist Office.

The in-season city tours by a golden tram, "Goldtimer," on Wednesdays, Fridays, and Sundays are lots of fun.

Bikes – Available for rent at most railroad stations, bikes provide a somewhat cheaper (and certainly delightful) means of getting where you're going. They can be taken onto passenger trains for a small fee and returned at any station.

Car Rental – All major firms are represented at the airport and in the city. *Avis* has offices at 17 Gartenhofstr. (phone: 242-2040); *Budget,* 33 Lindenstr. (phone: 471717); *Europcar,* 53 Josefstr. (phone: 271-5656; for reservations outside Switzerland, 432-7240); and *Avag,* a local firm whose rates are sometimes lower, 123 Sihlfeldstr. (phone: 242-8866).

Taxi – Among the most expensive in the world (tip included in the fare), taxis can be flagged down; the light on top indicates availability. To call a cab: 271-1111 or 241-4100.

Train – The main train station is Hauptbahnhof, at Bahnhofpl. (phone: 211-5010 for information).

SPECIAL EVENTS: The *Zurich Carnival* (Fasnacht) is celebrated with masked processions and costume balls at the end of February or early March. The most typical and colorful event of all, the *Sechseläuten,* generally on the third Monday in April, celebrates the burning of winter on Bellevueplatz (a giant snowman is stuffed with firecrackers) as the 6 o'clock bells ring. This ceremony is preceded by a picturesque procession of medieval guilds in traditional costumes and carriages. These are members of fraternities, whose membership is inherited by the males in the best Zurich families.

There is also the yearly *June Festival,* with top musical and theatrical events. The first of August is a national holiday, commemorating the founding of the Swiss Confederation; it is celebrated with fireworks and bonfires.

MUSEUMS: Most Zurich museums are described in *Special Places.* Also noteworthy is the *Museum Bellerive,* at 3 Höschgasse (phone: 251-4377), annexed to the *Museum of Applied Arts,* in a charming villa on a lake with excellent temporary exhibitions. The university has several interesting collections, among them the *Ethnological Museum* (non-European), at 40 Pelikanstr. (phone: 221-3191), and the *Medicinhistorical Collection,* including items ranging from primitive instruments and techniques to present-day ones, at 71 Rämistr. (phone: 257-2298). In 1987, the *Foundation for Constructive & Concrete Art,* 317 Seefeldstr. (phone: 533808), opened to present high-quality, international exhibits. The *Museum of Applied Arts,* 60 Austellungstr. (phone: 271-6700), and *Helmhaus,* 31 Limmatquai (phone: 251-6177), have interesting temporary exhibitions.

SHOPPING: It is hard to know where to begin in this shopper's paradise, with some of the best (and most expensive) merchandise in the world. The major hunting ground for shoppers is the ultra-elegant Bahnhofstrasse and its side streets (Storchengasse, In Gassen, and Rennweg).

The best buys in Switzerland are watches, which can be purchased here even though most are made in Geneva. Other interesting items are Swiss chocolates, embroidery and linens, optical instruments, and the wonderful (and inescapable) Swiss Army knives. *Jelmoli* and *Globus,* both at Bahnhofstr., are the two best-known department stores (the former with more solid quality and larger choice, the latter more "with it" and with lower prices); you can sample all Swiss wares here. General shopping hours are 9 AM to 6:30 PM during the week (to 9 PM on Thursdays), and 9 AM to 4 PM on Saturdays.

The old town is full of fashion boutiques, art galleries, and antiques shops, and there is more casual shopping along Limmatquai. In rainy weather, you might want to try Shopville under the main railroad station.

Albrecht-Schlapfer – Lovely eiderdowns and linens. 10 Lintheschergasse.

Bally – Famous for shoes. 66 Bahnhofstr.

Bernhard Ilg – Jewelry. 128 Limmatquai.

Paul Binder – More jewelry. 4 Storchengasse.

Bucherer – Fine watches and jewelry. 50 Bahnhofstr.

Café Schober – Cakes, cookies, chocolates, and homemade marmalades. 4 Napfgasse.

Fioramis – Interior design. 30 Kirchgasse.

Grieder – Women's specialty shop. 30 Bahnhofstr.

Gübelin – Watches and jewelry. 36 Bahnhofstr.

Hannes B – Upscale menswear. Eingang Limmatseite.

Haus Zum Engel – Antiques. 24 Kirchgasse.

Heimatwerk – Top-quality Swiss handicrafts. 2 Bahnhofstr.

Keinath – Fine, old silver and antiques. 19 Wühre (near *Storchen* hotel).

Koch – Optical instruments. 11 Bahnhofstr.

Margot Witte Mathys – Antiques and women's hats. 24 Münstergasse.

Medieval Art & View – Books on music, art, and food of the Middle Ages. 71 Rämistr.

Meister Zur Meisen – Crystal, silver, and jewels. 20 Münsterhof.

Metro – Art Deco objects. 19 Oberdorfstr.

Musik Hug – Musical instruments, including Alp horns and wooden spoons called *loffeli.* 26-28 Limmatquai.

Operissimo – Everything to do with the opera — records, books, antiquarian items, opera glasses, etc. 15 Färberstr.

Pastorini – Creative and educational toys in a traditonal family enterpirse. 3 Weinplatz.

Payot – Books in English. 9 Bahnhofstr.

Rosenfeld – Discounted watches, music boxes, and Swiss Army knives. 33 Strehlgasse.

Spitzenhaus – Handmade lace and embroidered organdy. 14 Börsenstr.

Sprüngli – This place is 100 years old, and famous for chocolates and pastry. There is also a café here (see *Eating Out*). Bahnhofstr. at Paradepl.

Sturzenegger – Fine Swiss embroidery and linen. 48 Bahnhofstr.

Teehaus Wühre – Enchanting small tea shop with a wide selection of its own blends. 15 Wühre.

Teuscher – Great chocolates. 9 Storchengasse. The company also has its own tea and coffee shop called *Schober,* on 4 Napfgasse (phone: 251-8060).

Travel Book Shop – Books about all aspects of travel — many in English that are unavailable elsewhere. Informed staff. 20 Rindermarkt.

Vogt – An antiques store in the old town that specializes in folk art. 13 Neumarkt.

WZ – Antique furnishings. 38 Kirchgasse.

F. C. Weber – Toys and (yes) cuckoo clocks. 62 Bahnhofstr.

SPORTS AND FITNESS: Fitness Centers – Both the *Atmos Fitness Club,* in the *Zürich* hotel, 42 Neumühlequai (phone: 363-4040), and the *Town Squash Luxor Fitness Centre,* 35 Glärnischstr. (phone: 202-3838), offer one-time visits.

Golf – There are no public courses; the *Dolder Golf Club* accepts visitors. 66 Kurhausstr. (phone: 475045).

Hiking – Dozens of marked trails are on the outskirts of town.

Jogging – Run along Lake Zurich, on either side of Bellevue Bridge, or in Dolder Forest.

Sailing and Rowing – Boat rental is along Utoquai.

Skating – The ice rink at Dolder is open only in winter.

Skiing – From December to March skiing is good; there are accessible runs within an hour from Zurich; equipment rental is possible.

Soccer – Several national and international matches are played at *Hardturm* and *Letzigrund* stadiums.

Swimming – Two good beaches are right on the lake (best is Tiefenbrunnen, popular with topless bathers), and there's an attractive pool at Dolder in the Zurichberg forest. In winter, one indoor public pool (Hallenbad) is open in town.

THEATER: There are two main theaters: *Schauspielhaus,* 34 Rämistr. (phone: 202-2222), produces plays in classical German and *Theater am Neumarkt,* 5 Neumarkt (phone: 251-1818), performs avant-garde works. There are twice yearly productions of the *British Comedy Club* and also of guest companies — mainly during *June Festival.* (See listings in local publications.) Movies are all in the original language with subtitles.

MUSIC: There is a variety to choose from. Top-quality operas, ballets, and operettas are presented at the *Opernhaus,* 1 Schillerstr. (phone: 251-6922). Regular classical concerts of the *Tonhalle Orchester* and visiting orchestras are given at the *Tonhalle,* 7 Claridenstr. (phone: 201-1580). There are also frequent concerts and recitals in several churches, mainly Fraumünster, Grossmünster, and St. Peter. Much less choice is available in jazz, rock, pop, and folk. The central ticket office for most cultural events is at Billetzentrale, Werdmühlepl. (phone: 221-2283); closed weekends.

NIGHTCLUBS AND NIGHTLIFE: The latest most public establishments can stay open is 2 AM (a few private clubs excepted, but outsiders cannot get in). *Diagonal* discotheque is the best, and if you are the guest of the *Baur au Lac* hotel, you can get a temporary membership. The *Joker-Club,* 5 Gotthardstr. (phone: 202-2262), is the best place for live music and dancing; it often offers top shows as well. *Roxy,* 11 Beatengasse (phone: 211-5457), and *Xenox,* 43 Dufourstr. (phone: 251-9422), are very fashionable with young people. *Kindli,* 1 Pfalzgasse (phone: 211-4182), is *the* folklore show in town — very touristy, but fun. The *Birdwatcher's Club,* 16 Schützengasse (phone: 211-5058), is a smart, semiprivate club that opens at 5 PM and becomes a lively disco by 9. For striptease with live music, try *The Red House,* 17 Marktgasse (phone: 252-1530); the *King's Club,* 1 Talstr., also offers good shows (mainly striptease) and dancing to disco music (phone: 211-2333).

BEST IN TOWN

CHECKING IN: The following are our top choices from an inventory of over 90 hotels. During the week, reservations are necessary. Continental breakfast or buffet is included everywhere, whether it is taken or not. All hotels listed have telephones in rooms; most also have radios.

Be warned that prices in Swiss cities are expensive, even higher than in Germany or the US, but not as high as in Austria and much of Italy). The range for a double room with a shower or bath in the expensive category is $200 and up; in the moderate category, $120 to $180; in the inexpensive category, $65 to $80 (slightly less without a private bath). Several smaller hotels offer winter reductions. All telephone numbers are in the 01 area code unless otherwise indicated.

Baur au Lac – The most prestigious hotel in the city center, it offers understated Old World luxury, beautiful grounds, and a celebrity-dotted guest list; its 170 rooms are always full. It's set in its own gardens facing the lake and features adjacent parking. The *Grill Room* is a fashionable restaurant. 1 Talstr. (phone: 221-1650). Expensive.

Dolder Grand – A famous luxury hotel in the Zurichberg forest, built in fairy tale castle style, with a fabulous view, 200 antique and modern rooms, free transportation into town, and a first class restaurant. 65 Kurhausstr. (phone: 251-6231). Expensive.

Carlton Elite – This long established, traditional but modern hotel on mid-Bahnhofstrasse could not be more central to banks and shopping. It has Zurich's first pub, plus an excellent Italian restaurant. A few of the top-floor rooms have private roof gardens; split-level suites also. 41 Bahnhofstr. (phone: 211-6560). Expensive to moderate.

Central Plaza – Completely reconstructed, this centrally located hotel is bright and cheery, with pastel decor and palm trees. Several popular restaurant and bars create a lively ambience. 1 Central (phone: 251-5555). Expensive to moderate.

St. Gotthard – This first class hotel has a terrific location on the upper end of the elegant Bahnhofstr. (and near the railway station), as well as 140 modern rooms, a very good seafood restaurant, and a restored Art Nouveau café that serves snacks. 87 Bahnhofstr. (phone: 211-5500). Expensive to moderate.

Splügenschloss – A few steps from the lake, this charming hotel in a turn-of-the-century building has 55 cozy rooms and suites, all luxuriously furnished, some with balconies. There's a pleasant restaurant and bar, plus a meeting room for up to 30 persons. Member of Relais & Châteaux. 2 Splügenstr. (phone: 201-0800). Expensive to moderate.

Zum Storchen – Zurich's oldest (built in the 14th century) and most romantically situated hotel, in the heart of Old Town on the Limmat River. Rooms, except for the corner ones, tend to be small and spartan, but those with a river view are much in demand (and require reservations far in advance). There's also a nice restaurant with a fireplace, and dining on the terrace in summer. 2 Weinplatz (phone: 211-5510). Expensive to moderate.

Zurich – A modern high-rise, right behind the main railroad station on the riverbank. Rooms on the higher floors afford fabulous views of the city and the Alps. Indoor swimming pool, bowling alley, and fitness club are features. 42 Neumühlequai (phone: 363-6363). Expensive to moderate.

Eos – Opened in 1988, this Art Nouveau villa in the green, exclusive residential area of the Zurichberg has a romantic little garden and 24 rooms, each with its own ambience. 17 Carmenstr. (phone: 471060). Moderate.

Florhof – A lovely old patrician building — renovation, unfortunately, destroyed the atmosphere-filled coziness. Good restaurant. 4 Florhofgasse (phone: 474470). Moderate.

Helmhaus – An excellent value — superbly run, central location in a historic building, with 24 modern, cheerful rooms. No restaurant. 30 Schiffländepl. (phone: 251-8810). Moderate.

Kindli – Although its exterior is 500 years old, inside is a modern, tastefully furnished hotel with but 22 rooms (each with a TV set). Its restaurant is where the well-known folklore show is presented (see *Nightclubs and Nightlife*). 1 Pfalzgasse (phone: 211-5917). Moderate.

Nova Park – This hotel has an off-center location and caters mostly to business travelers. Its fitness club has everything from a Turkish bath to massage to a swimming pool. Headquarters of the Backgammon Club of Switzerland. Several restaurants, bars, and a discotheque. 420 Badenerstr. (phone: 491-2222). Moderate.

Opera – Next to the opera house (best of the 67 modern rooms are on the top floor), with a pleasant, large lobby/sitting room. No restaurant. 5 Dufourstr. (phone: 251-9090). Moderate.

Tiefenau – Private atmosphere in this quiet, 150-year-old townhouse with garden is special: all recently restored 27 rooms are bed/sitting rooms, most furnished with antiques, some very large; lovely sitting and dining rooms. Near the *Fine Arts Museum*. 8-10 Steinwiesstr. (phone: 251-2409). Moderate.

Limmathof – This perfectly located, rather modest hotel is near the railroad station, with 55 no-frills (but pleasant) modern rooms. No credit cards. 142 Limmatquai (phone: 474220). Inexpensive.

 EATING OUT: More than 1,000 restaurant choices flourish here in all varieties and price ranges. A service charge is included in all bills, but it is customary to leave a small tip anyway. It is rare to see plain water on the table, and as the only beverage ordered, it is certainly frowned on. One

American woman reports being threatened by a Swiss waiter who warned that if she drank only water with her fondue, all manner of ills would strike her digestion. (Incidentally, most restaurants serve wine by the glass at reasonable prices.)

Switzerland is a country where the culinary traditions of Germany, Italy, and France meet, but there are specialties that are particularly Swiss. The people of Zurich — known for their interest in good food — like minced veal or calf's liver with cream (*geschnetzeltes Kalbsfleisch*) or roasted calf liver with bacon (*Leberspiessli*). Also local in Zurich is *Kalbsbratwurst,* a delicious veal sausage.

If you like cheese, try fondue, the national dish made with a combination of several Swiss cheeses and wine. Also try the crisp hash-brown potato "pancake" called *Rösti.* Desserts feature fresh cream and delicious Swiss chocolate; try *Zuger Kirschtorte,* a cake soaked in Kirsch, a cherry brandy. Visit at least one of the many tearooms for which Zurich is famous; they serve tea or coffee with a choice of pastries.

Like hotel prices, restaurant costs can also be stiff. Many places have less expensive luncheon menus. Our price range is for a three-course dinner for two without drinks, wine, or coffee. Count $85 and up as expensive; $60 to $80 as moderate; about $45 and under as inexpensive. In the better restaurants, reservations will be necessary. All telephone numbers are in the 01 area code unless otherwise indicated.

Chez Max – In the suburb of Zollikon, this is one of the best restaurants in Switzerland; Max Kehl, its owner-chef, creates culinary masterpieces that are never heavy on the stomach (only on the memory and the pocketbook). Closed Sundays and Mondays. Reservations necessary for dinner. Major credit cards. 53 Seestr., Zollikon (phone: 391-8877). Expensive.

Kronenhalle – This is the best known place in Zurich, where "everybody" goes, from local artists to visiting celebrities; walls are covered with original Picassos, Mirós, and other works from the private collection of the owner. International food with Swiss specialties. Try the chocolate mousse. Open daily. Reservations necessary. Major credit cards. 4 Rämistr. (phone: 251-0256 or 251-6669). Expensive.

Flühgasse – In an enchanting 16th-century inn, the food served here is among the best in Zurich. The emphasis is on light Swiss dishes. Closed Saturdays and Sundays. Major credit cards. 214 Zollikerstr. (phone: 531215). Expensive to moderate.

Zunfthaus zum Rüden – One of the most spectacular medieval guild houses with a Gothic interior and a fabulous view on the Limmat offers delicious food. Open daily except Sundays in summer. Reservations advised. Major credit cards. 42 Limmatquai (phone: 261-9566). Expensive to moderate.

California – This offbeat restaurant has menus in English, California wines, and American food with an international touch. Informal, friendly atmosphere, and small garden. Open daily; Saturdays and Sundays from 6 PM only. Major credit cards. 125 Asylstr. (phone: 535680). Moderate.

Mövenpick – Whether you want a good hamburger, some homemade cakes, or a full meal, the smart snack shop/restaurants in this chain are almost always open. 4 Paradepl. (phone: 221-3252) and 1 Zeltweg (phone: 690444), among other branches (including the airport). Moderate.

Oepfelchammer – This place has the *most* enchanting, cozy atmosphere. In this historic house, a special student fraternity room accepts anybody for a glass of wine at one long wooden table. The small restaurant has excellent "Old Zurich" specialties and other dishes; good open wines. Closed Sundays. Reservations necessary. Diners Card. 12 Rindermarkt (phone: 251-2336). Moderate.

Sprüngli – For a tasty breakfast, snack lunch, or afternoon hot chocolate, this is a most famous and elegant café and candy shop. Closed for dinner and Sundays. No credit cards in the café (accepted in shop). Bahnhofstr. at Paradepl. (phone: 211-0795). Moderate.

Wolfbach – Excellent, small restaurant, specializing in freshwater fish. Closed Sundays. Most major credit cards. 35 Wolfbachsrt., near the *Fine Arts Museum* (phone: 252-5180). Moderate.

Belcanto – In the city's *Opera House,* this restaurant is open every day (from morning to midnight) and offers a menu ranging from light snacks to full meals. Interesting cultural ambience (especially before the opera); outdoor terrace. Open daily. Theater Platz (phone: 251-6951). Moderate to inexpensive.

Blue Duck (Blaue Ente) – In an old grain mill, this is Zurich's liveliest and trendiest restaurant. The reasonable menu is devoted to adding fantasy to the meal. Open daily. Reservations necessary. Major credit cards. 223 Seefeldstr. (phone: 557706). Moderate to inexpensive.

Pinte Vaudoise – Swiss cheese specialties, like fondue and *raclette,* are offered in a cozy, paneled tavern. Closed Sundays. No credit cards. 4 Kruggasse (phone: 252-6009). Moderate to inexpensive.

Tres Kilos – The first and only Mexican restaurant in Zurich is extremely popular with locals. Very lively and noisy with a young, chic crowd. Open daily. Reservations necessary. No credit cards. 175 Dufoursrt. (phone: 550233). Moderate to inexpensive.

Gleich – A vegetarian's delight, with dishes of great imagination and quality, this place is famous for homemade fruit tarts and special juices. No alcohol. Closed Saturday afternoons and Sundays. No credit cards. 9 Seefeldstr. (phone: 251-3203). Inexpensive.

Hiltl Vegi – The oldest vegetarian restaurant in town serves delicious salads, Indian curries, and other imaginative dishes. There are 55 varieties of fresh tea in the upstairs restaurant's daily afternoon "tea buffet." Open daily. No credit cards. 28 Sihlstrt. (phone: 221-3870). Inexpensive.

Kropf – An Art Nouveau beer hall, almost an institution, with good-and-plenty Swiss/German/Austrian food, frequented by all classes. Pleasant terrace in summer. Closed Sundays. American Express. 16 Gassen (near Paradelpl.) (phone: 221-1805). Inexpensive.

Select – The most popular meeting place for artists, students, and chess players; serves good food and snacks (good hamburgers and outstanding ice cream). No alcohol. Sidewalk tables. Open daily. No credit cards. 16 Limmatquai (phone: 252-4372). Inexpensive.

Schober – A delight of gilded, picture-postcard charm, this is the oldest café in town. Cold snacks and marvelous sweets are available to eat there or to take with you. Open daily, closed evenings. No credit cards. 4 Napfgasse (phone: 251-8060). Inexpensive.

DIVERSIONS

Introduction

If you made a random selection of passengers on any transatlantic flight and asked what they considered to be the most desirable things to see and do in Europe, the answers would vary enormously. The sportsman — his thoughts lingering affectionately on a favorite rod stored carefully in the hold — might select salmon fishing in Ireland or Scotland; the culture maven would more likely lean toward the most extravagant collections of art and architecture in the world; the gastronome would favor the restaurants of Alfred Giradet, Alain Senderens, and Michel Guérard; the hedonist, the beaches lining the Mediterranean from Gibraltar to Turkey; the mountaineer, the Alps; and the rest of the passengers, a wide combination of all these things and, perhaps, if it is a return visit, the guestroom of a favorite château in the Loire Valley or the view from a particular hill in southern Italy or a mountain in the Peloponnese.

What best characterizes Europe is not only its diversity but also its density. Three quarters of a continent and some 2,000 miles lie between America's highest mountains and the great urban cultural centers of the East Coast; but Basel, Switzerland, tucked between Germany's Black Forest and the foothills of the Alps, has one of Europe's finest small museums and is less than half a day's drive from Strasbourg, France, and the exquisite villages of Alsace. The number of activities that can be enjoyed within a day of Basel is simply staggering. And Basel is just one medium-size city near the center of Europe.

The unparalleled proximity of Europe's great cities and its historic countryside offers a variety of experience that couldn't be better suited to contemporary travelers. Certainly North Americans would travel to Europe under almost any conditions; to some degree the majority of us have an ancestral tie to Europe, and every trip carries with it something of a small celebratory homecoming. But today travelers are uniquely willing to take advantage of the enormous range of activities Europe offers, and of the fact that museum and mountain, ski slope and opera house, are virtually cheek by jowl.

But the sheer wealth of European attractions poses a challenge. Combining the right setting with the right activity is an art even back home, and facing a continent of 33 nations, an equal number of major cities, and hundreds of regions, districts, and areas, all with distinct cultural features, can cause even the savviest traveler some trepidation.

The pertinent question is: Where is the quality of experience highest? In the following pages we suggest the best places in Europe to pursue 21 different activities — from tennis, golf, and fishing to the abundant wildernesses of this most civilized of continents, the most accomplished theatrical and operatic performances, and we even assist in ferreting out auctions, flea markets, antiques shops, and Europe's finest shopping streets. Each section represents a distillation of the best in Europe, a selective guide to Europe at its most intriguing, calculated to make your visit an unparalleled experience.

For the Body

Europe's Unparalleled Ski Scene

 Skiing is one of the most memorable activities any downhiller can enjoy during a European vacation. In the first place, no other mountains in the world are quite like the Alps and their surrounding ranges. America has peaks as high, but the valleys in Europe are generally lower, so that the ski runs in Europe tend to be longer and more diverse. And most of the prime European ski resort towns and villages possess an atmosphere that simply can't be found elsewhere.

Europe's ski centers come in all sizes and shapes. There are giants like St.-Moritz, Kitzbühel, and Chamonix, which offer vast assortments of runs and lifts, multilingual instructors, and facilities for a score of other winter sports, including — increasingly — cross-country skiing (now often called ski touring), plus well-equipped shops, fine hotels, lively nightlife, and all the other accoutrements required by the glossy good life of Europe's leisure classes.

Then there are the small resorts, with only a handful of lifts — but runs that go on and on, and an atmosphere that is less chaotic and more *gemütlich* (comfortable and cozy) than that of the majors. A good many of these smaller areas (and larger ones as well) have teamed up with similar sites nearby and installed a couple of extra lifts that enable guests to ski from one area to the other. These resort combinations often offer the ski facilities of far bigger areas, but with the pleasant, intimate après-ski life found only in small villages. It is also not unknown — as at Zermatt — literally to ski from one European country to another and then back again.

Almost everywhere in Europe, it's now possible to arrange for powder tours. There is, for example, helicopter skiing in many parts of Switzerland; the tours around Lauterbrunnen and Zermatt are especially beautiful. And a number of mountain tours are accessible via the various ski lifts. A cable car carries skiers to the top of the Aiguille du Midi, near Chamonix, in the French Alps, to begin the endless run down the glacier known as the Vallée Blanche — full of crevasses and melted-snow pools, surrounded by high peaks. The Jungfraujochbahn, the railroad that ascends Switzerland's highest mountain, the Jungfrau, leads to the start of a number of runs that will take you to the Concordiaplatz, where four glaciers cross. Best of all, there's no need to be a super-expert (just a strong intermediate whose knees will not go wobbly crossing a crevasse on a snow bridge scarcely wider than a pair of skis). Good skiers can tackle the Haute Route from Chamonix to Zermatt, overnighting on the way in mountain huts. (Information: Hochalpine Bergsteigerschule, Zermatt CH-39920, Switzerland; phone: 028-673456.) By the way, these excursions are mainly spring flings.

In summer, skiing continues on the tip-tilted glaciers — among others — at Corvatsch, in the Upper Engadine above the towns of St.-Moritz and Silvaplana, and at Les Diablerets in the Suisse Romande above the town of Gstaad.

The list of ski resorts that follows includes some of the best of the Continent's offerings in all departments.

But first, some general hints for enjoying skiing in Europe:

If you possibly can, avoid skiing in Europe at Christmastime. Not only are the lift lines miserably long, but the weather conditions are also unreliable enough so that you might well end up learning how to make parallel turns on grass and mud. If you have no choice about when to go, at least try to get your skiing in before December 26, while European families are still sitting around their Christmas trees. Late January usually offers the best combination of good snow, slightly longer sunny days, off-peak prices, and manageable crowds.

Try, also, to hold out for a half-pension arrangement with your hotel. European skiers take lunch seriously, so there is lots of fine, uncrowded skiing possible while they are indulging in a long midday meal.

In virtually all the ski centers on our roster, the choice of hotels is large, and even the most modest little *gasthaus* usually offers cozy pine-paneled rooms, fluffy eiderdowns, and handsome Tyrolean furniture. We've included a few favorites in each price range: Expensive (E), Moderate (M), Inexpensive (I) — or, at least, more moderate. Each town, no matter how tiny, has a tourist office that can provide up-to-date information about hotel availability, unusual tours, ski schools, and so on. Take their reports of snow conditions with a grain of salt, however.

KITZBÜHEL, Austria: Don't be put off by the comparatively low altitude (2,642 feet). The region is a famous snow bowl that often has better ski conditions than resorts with twice its base elevation. The movie star of Austrian skiing, Kitzbühel is colorful, animated, international. The town is a kind of Tyrolean showpiece, with white peaks rising behind brightly painted buildings. Cable cars and chair lifts connect its ski areas with those of four neighboring towns to provide fantastic skiing possibilities. If you prefer less glitter, lodge a little way down the road in charming St. Johann-in-Tyrol, convenient to all Kitzbühel's facilities. Lodgings: *Klausner* (M); *Gasthof Eggerwirt* (I); *Weisses Rössl* (E).

OBERGURGL, Austria: One of the highest villages in the Alps, the town is far less known as a ski resort than as a mountaineering center. At the end of the 31-mile (50-km) Ötztal Road (off the main Innsbruck highway), it has a pleasant Shangri-La quality. The 6,232-foot base elevation means both more sunlight and higher wind, and visitors return to the flatland a healthy-looking bronze. Evening pleasures are simpler than at the more cosmopolitan centers, but a day on the Gaisberg–Hohe Mut will send you to bed by 9:15 anyway. Lodgings: *Hochfirst* (E); *Enzian* (M); *Gasthof Gamper* (I).

ST. ANTON-AM-ARLBERG, Austria: Halfway between Innsbruck and Zurich on the main Arlberg road, St. Anton is a rather ordinary, heavily trafficked town. But the mountains above, rising from a 4,264-foot base, offer a vast network of lifts and superb skiing, ideal for vigorous skiers who like to spend most of the day on the slopes (as most St. Anton skiers do). The village is not the best for non-skiers. St. Christoph, about 4 miles (6.5 km) away near the top of the Arlberg Pass, is small, cheerful, and convenient to the high-altitude beginners' slopes. Lodgings: *Schwarzer Adler* (E); *Tannenhof* (M); *Fremdenheim Fallesin* (I).

ZÜRS-LECH, Austria: Lech, a friendly, sunny mountain village on the shores of the River Lech, and Zürs, which grew up as a sort of hotel colony when skiing boomed in the Vorarlberg, share excellent, lift-linked slopes and broad snowfields that make intermediates look like experts. There's a wonderful run all the way down to St. Anton and the chance to make the return trip in a bright yellow Austrian postal bus. With a base elevation of 4,756 feet, this is a good area to try in early winter, when the rest of the countryside is still patched with green and brown. Lodgings: *Gasthof Post,* Lech (E); *Zürserhof,* Zürs (E); *Central,* Lech (M); *Ulli,* Zürs (M); *Pension Kirchblick,* Lech (I); *Gasthof Schweizerhaus,* Zürs (I).

STARÝ SMOKOVEC, Czechoslovakia: Eastern Europe's best skiing is found in the heart of the High Tatras, in a national park in a region full of deep woods, frozen lakes, and craggy peaks. For skiing, there are jumps and slalom runs and long, gentle cross-country trails. The base elevation is 3,280 feet, and compared to the big centers of capitalist decadence in the West, the mood is pastoral and low key; you won't feel out of place in last season's stretch pants. Lodgings: the fine old *Grand Hotel Starýy Smokovec* (E); and at Novy Smokovec, the *Parkhotel* (M) and the *Bystrina* (I).

CHAMONIX, France: The presence of towering Mont-Blanc, the highest mountain in Europe, has made Chamonix, with a base elevation of 3,280 feet, the most famous resort in the French Alps (which are now connected to Courmayeur in Italy by the Tunnel du Mont-Blanc). The snowscapes amid the spires and glaciers of a whole range of 13,000-foot mountains are spectacular, and the *téléphérique* ride to the Aiguille du Midi is one of the great European experiences — with or without skis. The expert skiing is unexcelled anywhere, though even competent intermediates can make the magical 12.4-mile glacier run down the Vallée Blanche from the Aiguille. The lively nightlife, the fine French cuisine, and the busy gambling casino all make the resort a delight for non-skiers; the clientele is definitely sporty. Lodgings: *Mont-Blanc* (E); *Richemond* (M); *Roma* (I).

VAL-D'ISÈRE, France: Once a mountain resort and hunting village of the Duke of Savoy, this town built around a quaint 16th-century church lies on the Col de l'Iseran, the highest pass in the Alps; the base elevation is 6,068 feet. France's top skiers come here in preference to more chic centers like Mégève and Chamonix, and most of the evening talk at the town's modern, comfortable ski hotels is about trails and boots and bindings. The ski school has a fine reputation for serious, systematic instruction, and when the snow is deep or conditions are icy, the big runs are best left to the experts. Val-d'Isère is an ideal place for a long stay devoted to real improvement in the sport. Lodgings: *Christiania* (E); *Santons* (M); *Bellevue* (I).

VALLOIRE, France: A great deal of lift building and trail making has taken Valloire dramatically out of the "Sleepy Alpine hamlet" class — the base elevation is now 4,592 feet. But it's still less international and far less congested than many centers with comparable facilities. Just near the Galibier Pass, the old part of the village centers around a large, friendly ice-skating rink and an old church. There is a fine cross-country run through the Col du Mt. Tabor to the Italian town of Bardonecchia. Lodgings: *Rapin* (E); *Les Carrettes* (M); *Centre* (I).

GARMISCH-PARTENKIRCHEN, Germany: Americans first got to know this Alpine ski resort back in the days when it was chiefly the US military that occupied the powdery slopes and a few dollars bought all the snow you could ski. The town itself is large, modern, and busy, and offers a whole range of winter sports activities, including curling and bobsledding. High above is the 9,840-foot Zugspitze, Germany's tallest mountain, whose peak, miraculously, is accessible by cog railway and cable car. There is a fine assortment of lifts and trails for every grade of skier, and the facilities are scrupulously maintained by a large local staff. Lodgings: *Wittelsbach* (E); *Bellevue* (M); *Edelweiss* (I); or, glamorously perched at 8,692 feet on the Zugspitzplatt, just under the summit, the *Schneefernerhaus* (E).

REIT IM WINKL, Germany: A picturesque Bavarian town in the middle of a wide-open valley, with a base elevation of 2,296 feet, this is not the kind of place you're likely to see represented on bumper stickers and ski parka patches. Yet, with some two dozen tows and chair lifts fanned out on a cluster of broad plateaus and mild peaks under 6,560 feet, it's ideal for beginners and intermediates; the ski circus between Winklmoos-Alm, Dürnbachhorn, and Kammerköhr-Steinplatte is immensely satisfying and only of medium difficulty. There is a 2.5-mile toboggan trail, with a smaller version for children, and a fleet of horse-drawn sleighs for drives in the country, *Dr. Zhivago* style — that is, with fur blankets wrapped around your knees. Evenings, sausage and sauerkraut are piled into small mountains on your dinner plate at any of the nearby restaurants. Lodgings: *Unterwirt* (**E**); *Altenburger Hof* (**M**); *Edelweiss* (**I**).

CORTINA D'AMPEZZO, Italy: The country's number one ski resort, which attracts a stylish, predominantly Italian crowd, held Italy's first Winter Olympics back in 1956 and subsequently boomed, so that it is now one of the best-equipped ski towns in the Alps. One of its special pleasures is ice skating in the huge open shell of its *Olympic Stadium,* which you can have to yourself on virtually any early January morning. But whatever your sport, you're always surrounded here by the toothy spikes of the Dolomites. A lift network that links a series of high passes provides access to a great deal of terrain without ever doubling back, and a powerful sun is always there — even in February and March — to remind you that Venice and the Mediterranean are only a few hours away. Lodgings: *Cristallo* (**E**); *Concordia Parc* (**M**); *Menardi* (**I**).

LIVIGNO, Italy: The characteristic wooden houses of this curious, little-known village are strung out along about 7.5 miles of a valley near the Italian and Swiss frontiers. Not so long ago, cross-country skiers had these broad snowfields, the pretty lake, the gentle landscape, and the limitless horizons almost all to themselves. Now there's downhill skiing as well. The region's development has been enthusiastic but not excessive, and the area offers several hostelries and a number of attractive slopes with a base elevation of 6,068 feet. Lodgings: *Du Lac* (**E**); *Palú* (**M**); *Alpina* (**I**).

SESTRIERE, Italy: Like Courchevel in France, this development of the Fiat company was built — expressly as a ski resort — on once-empty snowfields, so there's little of the cozy sense found in older ski towns. Nonetheless, there's a great deal of life here in season, along with superb high-altitude runs — rising from a base of about 6,560 feet — for every level of skier (it's possible to ski here for a week without ever repeating a run); a fine ski school (though a number of the instructors speak only rudimentary English); and lots of sun, evenly distributed between the slopes and the large terraces with deck chairs and umbrella tables. Sestriere is a marvelous place on weekdays, but impossible on weekends in high season, when big tour buses arrive by the score from Torino (Turin), about 56 miles (90 km) away. Lodgings: *Cristallo* (**E**); *Belvedere* (**M**), a local landmark; *Olimpic* (**I**).

KLOSTERS, Switzerland: Davos, some 7.5 miles (12 km) away by road, is one of the Alps' finest ski centers, but it's a big, citified, not always attractive spot. By far the nicest place to stay in the region is the charming animated village of Klosters, which is connected to Davos by the ski lifts of the great Parsenn area. The Parsenn snowfields, with a base elevation of about 4,000 feet, are wonderfully varied, and while there are a number of areas that are rewarding for beginners, the area is also rich in challenging runs that are so long they make you feel as if you're crossing all of Switzerland. The Klosters Valley gets early shade — but its brisk nightlife starts just after twilight and seems to keep going until the tows open in the morning. Not a village of cowbells and milkmaids, Klosters is cosmopolitan, expensive — and great fun. Lodgings: *Vereina* (**E**); *Sporthotel Kurhaus* (**M**); *Pension Soldanella* (**I**).

MÜRREN, Switzerland: Famous in the annals of ski racing as the site of the great Alpine-Kandahar course and the founding place of the Kandahar Ski Club, this sunny, romantic village, on a kind of balcony overhanging the Lauterbrunnen Valley, is little known among vacationing skiers and can still be a discovery even to Alpine veterans. Some of the toughest, most exciting slopes in Switzerland, as well as countless simpler trails, rise above the 5,412-foot base; many runs end up within a few minutes' walk of the hotels. There's a spectacular revolving restaurant on the peak of the Schilthorn. Lodgings: *Mürren* (**E**); *Sporthotel-Edelweiss* (**M**); *Alpina* (**I**).

ST.-MORITZ, Switzerland: Possessed of such a long-standing, far-reaching reputation for being elegant, expensive, and sophisticated that a number of serious skiers spend years avoiding it — and years regretting their boycott when they finally do break down and go. The sheiks and the furs and the Lamborghinis are all there, but so are some of the finest, most exciting, best-maintained ski runs in Europe. It would take several days to ski them all just once. There is not just something for everybody — there's everything for everybody. The base elevation is 6,068 feet. The town has grown into a small ski city, and you can easily pick up a mink or a Matisse along with your boot wax. Make sure to have coffee and pastry at *Hanselmann*. Lodgings: *The Palace* (**E**) or *Suvretta House* (**E**), if you can afford it; *Neues Post* (**M**); *Languard* (**I**).

WENGEN, Switzerland: Like Zermatt, Wengen, in the middle of the Bernese Oberland, is car-free (with the nearest garages and parking lots a 15-minute train ride away at Lauterbrunnen). The town, which extends along a sheltered plateau at the foot of the imposing Jungfrau at 4,264 feet, shares a vast ski terrain with nearby Scheidegg and Grindelwald. There is a choice of mountain railways (including the renowned Jungfraujochbahn), which offer newer, higher ski trails at every stop. And the unparalleled Jungfrau Glacier runs are open from the middle of February until the end of May. In addition to all this skiing, there is a great deal of hockey, skating, curling, and just plain walking on well-packed, breathtakingly scenic snowy mountain paths. Lodgings: *Regina* (**E**); *Bellevue* (**M**); *Schweizerheim* (**I**).

ZERMATT, Switzerland: On a car-choked continent, the no-autos-at-all policy in Zermatt, at 5,248 feet, is especially delightful. And despite the town's heavy international traffic, it maintains a rustic village flavor. Zermatt also has that unique Alpine monument, the Matterhorn, looming above and a dazzling fishnet of cog railways, cable cars, gondolas, T-bars, and pommel lifts that serve an enormous variety of runs across snowfields and through the trees. And when you've done all that, there's a famous run over the Theodule Pass to Breuil-Cervinia in Italy. In addition, there's fine springtime skiing and regular town-to-glacier helicopter service. All in all, Zermatt probably offers Europe's most complete skiing experience. Lodgings: *Monte Rosa* (**E**); *Alpenblick* (**M**); *Chesa Valese* (**I**).

Tennis

 Most American passions eventually sweep Europe as well, and tennis is no exception. The number of courts, players, clubs, and sleek designer outfits has soared in the last decade, so that tennis is now as much the sport of European butchers and bakers as it once was of barons. However, the groundswell started from a far narrower base than in America, and the sport still has a long way to go. Facilities aren't as extensive as in the US, instruction isn't as expert, and there is still a shortage of high-powered accessories like videotape units, ball machines, and the like. And the organized tennis vacation is still a comparative rarity. Still, the rapid rise of tennis champions all across the Continent is causing the number of players and facilities to increase exponentially.

Tennis etiquette is, however, still pretty primitive, particularly in the Mediterranean countries. If you were brought up in a world of tennis whites, "sorry, partner," and "take two, please," you may be put off by the noise level both on and off the courts, and by the general lack of reverence for the game. Nonetheless, a tennis match is still a fine, rapid way to escape the standard tourist circuit and get into local life. Travel with your tennis gear — and be sure to bring it all, so that your day need not be marred by the exorbitant cost of a Swiss T-shirt or a pair of German socks. Many clubs welcome brief visits by foreigners, so you may suddenly find yourself with a circle of Dutch or Danish friends. Like French in the gambling casino, English is the lingua franca of the tennis court, particularly among the well-to-do.

Synthetic court surfaces are still uncommon in Europe, so it's relatively easy to enjoy the pleasures of English grass courts and well-kept red clay ones — and often in spectacularly beautiful settings.

A cultural parenthesis: When Europeans kick back stray balls, it's not out of rudeness or impatience but because of their early soccer training.

Here are some good places to try a little serving and volleying on European tennis courts:

COPENHAGEN, Denmark: Ever since the success of Bjorn Börg, tennis has taken a great leap forward all over Scandinavia. The climate in Copenhagen in spring and summer is delightful for court capers, and a number of clubs offer temporary membership to visiting foreigners, including: *Boldklubben af 1893,* 10 Per Henrik Lings Allé (phone: 381890); 37 *Hellerup Idraetsklub,* Hartmannsvej, Hellerup (phone: 621428); and 147 *Kjøbenhavns Boldklub,* Peter Bangsvej (phone: 714180). You can get additional information about facilities, tournaments, and the like from the courteous *Dansk Tennis Vorbund, Brøndby Stadion,* 20 Idraettens Hus, Glostrup, Copenhagen 2600, Denmark (phone: 32-455555).

BEDFORD, England: *Woodlands Tennis Centre* has a beautiful rural facility in Milton Ernest, one of the unspoiled villages along the River Ouse near Bedford. This tennis school offers courses for young people and adults at every level, from beginner to expert. Accommodations are either in the historic 17th-century center itself, with local families, or in a nearby hotel. Although summer is prime time, the school also runs weekend courses during the off-season. Fishing, boating, horseback riding, cycling, and squash are easily arranged. Information: Tennis Coaching International, Woodlands Tennis Centre, Milton Ernest, Bedford, England (phone: 02302-2914).

BODMIN, England: *Tennisville Holidays* in Cornwall is very British and very family oriented, with a cheerful atmosphere and excellent coaching. Courses are usually a week, but many guests stay longer. Both private and group instruction. Open from Easter to September, with simple but companionable accommodations. Housing with families available for kids — who can stay on their own while parents travel. Information: Tennisville, Sunny Banks Farm, Fletchers Bridge, Bodmin, Cornwall PL30 4AN, England (phone: 0208-75048).

HAILSHAM, England: *Windmill Hill Place Residential Tennis Centre* is 50 miles (80 km) from London and 10 minutes from the sea, near the resort town of Eastbourne. There are 8 grass, 6 all-weather, and 4 indoor courts amid 20 acres of wooded grounds, and the main residence is an elegant Georgian mansion. Weekend and week-long sessions year-round. Information: Windmill Hill Place Tennis Resort, Windmill Hill, Hailsham, East Sussex BN27 4RZ, England (phone: 0323-832552).

L'ALPE D'HUEZ (ISÈRE), France: A number of French towns, particularly in the mountain districts, organize summer tennis courses (*stages de tennis*) — week-long tennis holidays that package room and board along with intensive tennis instruction and court time. This one is among the best, with 5 businesslike weekdays devoted to physical preparation and 5 hours daily to instruction and training. Offered mid-July to mid-August. Information: Stage de Tennis, Office de Tourisme, Maison de l'Alpe, L'Alpe d'Huez 38750, France (phone: 76-80-35-41); or Club des Sports, L' Alpe d' Huez 38750, France (phone: 76-80-34-42).

CAP D'AGDE, France: The *Club Pierre Barthès* is one of Europe's most dazzling complexes. Its 62 courts (6 covered and 16 lighted) are just a forehand away from one of the Mediterranean's choicest beaches. A lovely colony of guest villas and apartments and a small hotel. Open year-round; book well in advance, especially for summer. Information: Club Pierre Barthès, BP 547, Cap d'Agde 34305, France (phone: 67-26-00-06).

LA BAULE, France: Nestled in the lush but carefully groomed grounds of one of Brittany's star beach resorts, the *Tennis Country Club* at La Baule provides 29 courts, as well as accommodations in nearby luxury hotels. Amenities include video analysis of your game, sauna, and a heated saltwater pool. It's pleasant to play 4 hours of tennis each day and spend the remaining 20 windsurfing, golfing, or discoing. Information: Tennis Country Club, 113 Av. de Lattre de Tassigny, La Baule Cedex 44504, France (phone: 40-60-23-44).

CARGÈSE, France: One of the very best spots to play tennis in Europe is at one of the many "vacation villages" of the *Club Med. Le Club,* as it's known in its native France, offers facilities that are extensive, instruction that is first rate, and settings that are consistently attractive and maintained with ecological fervor. The *Cargèse Club Med,* on the Gulf of Chioni in Corsica, is a fine place to mix tennis and the sea. There are 10 courts with the green Corsican hills on one side and a rocky bay and wide, blond beach on the other. Accommodation is in very comfortable separate bungalows. And the *Club* organizes various excursions around the most inviting parts of Corsica. Open from mid-May to mid-September. Information: Club Med, Cargèse 20130, France; or contact the Club's New York office at 3 E. 54th St., New York, NY 10022 (phone: 800-CLUB-MED).

POMPADOUR, France: The super-efficient *Club Med* operation virtually guarantees a successful vacation, and this verdant paradise is no exception. There are 19 covered tennis courts, so even a rainy week in October won't dampen a tennis buff's dream holiday. And for those who need to rest their backhand, horseback riding along tree-lined paths, a 9-hole pitch and putt golf course, a heated swimming pool, and a pony club for children are also available. Information: Club Med, Domaine de Noaiiles, Arnac-Pompadour 19230, France; or in the US (see above).

VITTEL, France: This *Club Med* village — in the green French countryside — is the best of them all for tennis: There are 25 courts (17 clay), frequent tournaments, and instruction at all levels — and you'll never have any trouble finding partners on short notice. Accommodation is available in several of the gracious old spa hotels that went up here in the days when taking the waters was an indispensable interlude for the Parisian upper classes. Open May through September. Information: Club Med, Vittel 88000, France; or in the US (see *Cargèse, France*).

BADEN-BADEN, Germany: The main tennis club of Germany's most elegant spa has 9 carefully groomed courts in the middle of the lush Lichtentalerallée promenade. Giant ancient trees surround you and fine stately hotels like the *Brenner's Park* are just a hard forehand away. Information: *Tennis Club Rot-Weiss,* 5 Sekretariat, Lichtentalerallée, Baden-Baden D-7570, Germany (phone: 07221-24141) — and this is only one of several clubs in town. The Visitors' Bureau offers special all-inclusive tennis weeks, including instruction. General information: 8 Baden-Baden Verkehrsverein, Augustaplatz, Baden-Baden D-7570, Germany (phone: 07221-275200).

BERNKASTEL-KUES and OBERLAHR, Germany: A highly professional setup split among three handsome resort hotels, *Hans Pötter's Tennis School* has videotape recorders, backboards, ball machines, and indoor and outdoor courts which are open for both day and night play through the year. You can sign up for special intensive weekend courses, or for more leisurely vacation weeks which will leave you time for excursions in the hill and lake country of the Rhine River valley. The *Mosel* has a brand-new 4-court *halle* that opens like a convertible, and there are 4 more at the *Westerwald Treff.* Information: Tennisschule Potter, Westerwald Treff, Oberlahr 5231, Germany (phone: 02685-870); Mosel Hotelpark, Bernkastel-Kues 5550, Germany (phone: 06531-2011); or the *Waldbrunnen,* 7 Brunnenstrasse, Windhagen-Rederscheid 5469, Germany (phone: 02645-150).

ATHENS, Greece: Athens is one of those enviable Mediterranean capitals where the weather is good for tennis all year long; though it's sometimes breezy and sometimes hot, it's always worth bringing your gear. Play and instruction are pleasantly inexpensive by US standards, and a strong American player is often treated as a kind of visiting apostle in Greek clubs. Courts and clubs to sample include the *Athens Tennis Club,* 2 Vas. Olgas Ave. (phone: 01-923-2872); *Attic Tennis Club,* Dafni and Kalliga St., Filothei (phone: 01-682-5649); *Kifissia Athletic Club,* 45 Tatoiou Rd., Strofyli, Kifissia (phone: 01-807-0100); and the *Glyfada Tennis Club,* Diadochou Pavlou Ave., Glyfada (phone: 01-895-3012). More detailed information is available from the Greek Tennis Federation, 89 Patission St., Athens 104 (phone: 01-821-0478).

CORFU, Greece: Of the myriad Greek islands, this is the one where tennis has made the deepest inroads. *Club Med* has a seaside village at Ipsos with 15 courts that start to function in early May and attract a large assortment of first class vacation players. Accommodation is in simple but charming thatched huts, with communal dining areas. The sea is all around, and water skiing is also popular. Information: Club Med, Corfu, Ipsos-Corfu, Greece, or contact *Club Med* in New York (see *Cargèse, France*). Another spot where you'll find good players is the *Corfu Tennis Club* (4 Romanou St., Corfu, Greece; phone: 37021). The club, which has been around since 1896, retains its gracious, tennis-is-all-that-counts air. Good courts are also available at the *Hilton International* hotel, the *Roda Beach,* and the *Nissaki.*

CAPO RIZZUTO, Italy: Following the French *Club Med* model of sports-oriented vacation villages, the 9 Italian Valtur complexes have cornered the market in the peninsula's glamorous locations. They guarantee luxurious accommodations and provide the same round-the-clock relaxing frenzy as their Gallic counterparts. Near Cefalu, on the northern coast of Sicily, is *Pollina,* with 8 tennis courts, 4 of them lighted so you can water-ski all day and save tennis for a nightcap. *Capo Rizzuto,* on the Ionian coast of Calabria, has 8 courts, 5 lighted, and special tennis weeks with top coaches in June and July. Both are open from May through September. Information: Valtur Vacanze, 42 Via Milano, Rome 00184, Italy (phone: 06-482-1000).

ROME, Italy: The town has been tennis mad ever since Italy won its Davis Cup, and there are some 50 clubs and centers, with a preponderance of clay courts. Among those that welcome transient players are the *Circolo Tennis Belle Arti,* 158 Via Flaminia (phone: 360-6529); the *Circolo Tennis della Stampa,* Piazza Mancini at the Duca d'Aosta Bridge (phone: 396-0792); and the *Oasi di Pace,* 2 Via degli Eugenii, Appia Antica (phone: 799-4550). For complete information and a list of every court in town contact the Federazione Italiana Tennis, 70 Viale Tiziano, Rome 00100, Italy (phone: 36851).

MONTE CARLO, Monaco: The *Monte Carlo Country Club* (actually on French soil) has 23 splendid clay and synthetic courts, set into the rich surrounding greenery like precious stones. You'll also find a panoramic view of the bay and skilled multilingual instructors. Four courts are lighted; and from mid-April to mid-September, you can sign up for special 5-day courses. Two squash courts are available as well. Information: Monte Carlo Country Club, BP 342, Monte Carlo, Monaco (phone: 93-78-20-45).

VALE DO LOBO, Portugal: The *Roger Taylor Tennis Center,* run by Britain's former top star, is in the middle of an enticing resort area on the sunny Algarve coast. There are 12 courts (6 lighted; 2 covered) and a 5-hour daily clinic that starts off with seaside jogging. Superb golf and swimming are also available. Guest accommodations are in *Vale do Lobo* villas or the luxurious *Dona Filipa* hotel. The complex is only 9 miles (15 km) from Faro Airport. Information and reservations through the London office: Roger Taylor Tennis Center, Urbanizaçao de Luxo, 8100 Vale do Lobo, Algarve, Portugal (phone: 94779); or Roger Taylor Tennis Holidays Ltd., 85 High St., Wimbledon, London SW19 5EG (phone: 947-9727).

MARBELLA, Spain: Lew Hoad — remember Hoad and Rosewall? — runs one of the best-known tennis schools in Europe here on the heavily developed Costa del Sol, with courses and programs for all kinds of players. You can lodge in apartments near the school, or, some 15 miles (24 km) away, at the deluxe *Los Monteros* hotel complex by the sea, whose spacious grounds are full of lawns, swimming pools, palm trees, and tropical foliage. There are also 10 additional tennis courts here along with 5 squash courts. Information: Lew Hoad's Campo de Tenis, Apartado 111, Fuengirola, Marbella (Málaga), Spain (phone: 474858). The area is also home to one of the biggest tennis operations of the *Club Med,* with 16 courts, 4 of them lighted, and accommodations in a large, comfortable hotel about 6 miles (9.5 km) from the beach. Shuttle service is provided. Open year-round. Information: Club Med, Don Miguel, Marbella (Málaga), Spain; or contact the Club's New York office (see under *Cargèse, France*).

GSTAAD, Switzerland: The dowager *Palace* hotel, the tennis hot spot in Switzerland, features the Roy Emerson Tennis Weeks in June and July as its main offering, back to back with the Swiss Championships. Emerson is not just a big name, his instruction is as exciting as his demonstrations. The prices are high, but the hotel and the tennis facilities are all spectacular — so if you can afford it, by all means go. Information: Palace Hotel, Gstaad 3780, Switzerland (phone: 030-83131). A number of other Swiss resort towns organize special tennis weeks in summer and offer packages that include rooms, meals, instruction, and unlimited play. Among those that combine the best facilities with the most attractive settings are the *Derby* hotel, Davos Dorf CH 7260, Switzerland (phone: 083-61166); and the *Tennisschule Laax, Sporthotel Signina,* Laax (GR) 7032, Switzerland (phone: 081-390151). Similar packages are also available in the snazzy towns of Ascona and St. Moritz. For details, contact the Verkehrsbüro at 6612 Via B. Papio, Ascona, Switzerland (phone: 093-355544) or at St. Moritz 7500, Switzerland (phone: 082-33147).

THE GREAT EUROPEAN TOURNAMENTS

WIMBLEDON, Wimbledon, England: Still a magnet to players good enough to compete for much bigger cash prizes elsewhere, this tourney, held in late June and early July, is an experience even if you've never held a racket. Grass courts, strawberry teas, and the legendary Centre Court are all high points, and the world class matches going on quietly on all the outlying lawns end up being merely side shows. Good seats for late-round matches are completely sold out months in advance, as are a good many seats throughout the tourney; and there are long lines for the tickets that are available. However, patience is generally rewarded. Centre Court and Court Number One seats are allocated by lottery. Send a stamped, self-addressed envelope with your request for an allocation form in October; you should receive it early in the new year. Information: All-England Lawn Tennis Club, Church Rd., Wimbledon, London, SW19 5AE (phone: 946-2244). Tickets are available in the US as part of the tours offered by *Keith Prowse & Co.,* 234 W. 44th St., New York, NY 10036 (phone: 212-398-1430; 800-223-4446 outside New York); Abbey Box Office, 1775 Broadway, Suite 530, New York, NY 10019 (phone: 212-265-7800); or *Traveltix International,* 400 Madison Ave., Suite 411, New York, NY 10017 (phone: 212-688-3700).

FRENCH OPEN, Paris, France: Held at *Roland Garros Stadium,* generally in early June, this tournament's traditions go back to the great days of La Coste, Borotra, and Lenglen. It is a good notch above Rome in prestige and professionalism. Information: Le Secrétaire Général, Fédération Française de Tennis, Stade Roland Garros, 2 Av. Gordon-Bennett, Paris 75016, France (phone: 47-43-48-00).

ITALIAN INTERNATIONAL CHAMPIONSHIPS, Rome, Italy: Generally held in late May, this event, also known as the Italian Open, has a pleasant Tiber-side setting among the cypresses, but the noisy, soccer-style crowds deter some world class players from participating. For exact dates and ticket information, contact the Federazione Italiana Tennis, 70 Viale Tiziano, Rome, Italy (phone: 396-2300).

Great Golf Courses

There is a fair amount of controversy between the Scots and the Dutch as to who actually invented the game of golf, but there's little doubt as to who has been most instrumental in advancing it around the world. Golf is now almost universally conceded to be a game of primarily British origin, and the expansion of the number of places to play around the globe follows a track that almost exactly mirrors the expansion of the British Empire. And even where the Britons did not actually annex territory, their vacation preferences clearly affected the construction of golf courses, as evidenced by the courses that exist in such exotic Eastern European spots as Karlovy Vary and Mariánské Lázně. Non-Czechs know them better as the historic spas of Carlsbad and Marienbad, the favorite haunts of the Hanoverian Kings of England, who were returning to visit their then-German homelands.

It will come as no surprise that the finest courses in Europe are found in England, Scotland, and Ireland, but what *is* surprising is the fact that these courses are almost always hospitable to visiting golfers. (See also "Scotland's Fabled Golf Courses," DIRECTIONS.) For the few private clubs among the best in Europe, it's always a wise idea to carry your home club membership card and a letter from your own club president or golf professional asking for hospitality. Europeans put great store in interclub reciprocity and will almost always honor such an official request.

Herewith, the best and most accessible golf courses in Europe:

ROYAL ANTWERP, Kapellenbos, Belgium: As its majestic name implies, this has long been a favorite of Belgian kings. The oldest club in Belgium, it was founded and laid out in 1888 by British immigrants. Set among beautiful pine and silver birch woods, this generally level course makes gauging distances a formidable challenge. The several long par 4's will force even a seasoned golfer to use a long iron to the green. Information: Royal Antwerp Golf Club, 2 George Capianlei, 2080 Kapellenbos, LE2 Antwerpen, Belgium (phone: 03-6668456).

SUNNINGDALE, Sunningdale, England: While the Old Course is considered the championship layout here, the New is probably the harder of the two. When you play them, you will discover that the decision on difficulty is an arbitrary one at best. Fairways and greens are meticulously maintained, and this is perhaps the finest single set of courses in England. Private but persuasible. Information: Sunningdale Golf Club, Ridgemount Rd., Sunningdale, Berkshire, England (phone: 0990-21681).

WENTWORTH, Virginia Water, England: The East Course at Wentworth is generally considered the prettiest of the three courses and can do wonders for a shaky backswing. (There's also a par 3 layout here.) But it's the West Course that is sometimes not so affectionately called the "Burma Road." For a high-handicap player, the West is not unlike putting an innocent head into the mouth of an unfriendly lion. Again, Wentworth is a private club that's likely to offer access to traveling players on weekdays upon presentation of your own club membership card and a letter from your club president. Information: Wentworth Golf Club, Virginia Water, Surrey, England (phone: 09904-2201).

CHANTILLY, Chantilly, France: Known for food and lace, Chantilly is also famous for Chateau de Chantilly, the home of French kings, and the elegant Golf Club de

Chantilly, only 5 minutes from the historic castle. With its Old World charm and aristocratic ambience, this British-designed course winds through an impressive forest just 25 miles (40 km) north of Paris. Information: Golf Club de Chantilly, 60500 Vineuil-Saint Firmin, Chantilly, France (phone: 44-57-04-43).

ZUR VAHR, Bremen, West Germany: On 220 acres of the thickly forested Garlstedter Heath, this course is full of tall, dense pine groves that surround players from tee to green, necessitating long, accurate drives and little need for bunkers, which number only 24. Rated as one of the finest championship courses in Europe by professionals. Information: Zur Vahr Golf Club, 15 Deliusweg, Bremen 33, West Germany (phone: 421-236657).

BALLYBUNION, Ballybunion, Republic of Ireland: No less an authority than Herbert Warren Wind calls the original layout here one of the ten toughest courses in the world, and you will have no reason to disagree. The course is laid out at the point where the Shannon River estuary meets the Atlantic Ocean, and you should be not the least concerned that the out-of-bounds area beside the 14th hole is a graveyard. A Robert Trent Jones 18-hole course has been added, but it is the old track that is the real attraction. Information: Ballybunion Golf Club, County Kerry, Republic of Ireland (phone: 068-27146).

KILLARNEY GOLF AND FISHING CLUB, Killarney, Republic of Ireland: There are now two courses here beside the legendary lakes, and it's the older course that is the stronger. The scenery is startling in this fabled spot, and it may take an act of will to keep your head down, though it may not be worth the effort. The sight of the lakes framing the purple mountains is a once-in-a-lifetime experience. Information: Killarney Golf and Fishing Club, Mahoney's Point, Killarney, County Kerry, Republic of Ireland (phone: 064-31034).

PORTMARNOCK, Portmarnock, Republic of Ireland: This fabled layout (just outside Dublin) is perhaps the best single course in the Republic. The short flag sticks, which are set on springs to let them swing freely in the breeze, tell you something about the wind hazards here, though again the quality of the course is superb. Be prepared for soaring scores but a bracing outing. Information: Portmarnock Golf Club, Portmarnock, County Dublin, Republic of Ireland (phone: 323082).

ROYAL DUBLIN, Dollymount, Republic of Ireland: The "other" Dublin area golfing magnet that, though second to Portmarnock, still deserves a place among the Continent's best. Again, the winds blow here and the rough grows to a size not normally known in the New World. Information: Royal Dublin Golf Club, Dollymount, Dublin 3, Republic of Ireland (phone: 337153).

LAHINCH, Lahinch, Republic of Ireland: This extraordinary course has been known to inflict players with every plague save famine and flood. It has one short par 5 that has been lengthened a bit by putting something that looks like the Great Wall of China in the middle of the fairway, and to add a little extra spice to your round, there's a 145-yard par 3 that's completely blind. Would you like to guess how they managed that? Our pick for the best in the west of Ireland. Information: Lahinch Golf Club, Lahinch, County Clare, Republic of Ireland (phone: 065-81003).

ROYAL PORTRUSH, Portrush, Northern Ireland: Though the troubles in Northern Ireland persist, the golf remains above the internecine disputes. The *Dunluce Course* is the championship layout here and is named after the striking old castle that is perched on the white cliffs above the fairways. Information: Royal Portrush Golf Club, Dunluce Rd., Portrush BT56 8 JQ, Northern Ireland (phone: 0265-822311).

ROYAL COUNTY DOWN, Newcastle, Northern Ireland: This is "where the Mountains of Mourne meet the sea." They played the British Amateur championship here several years ago, and there are hazards in certain places that can prove rather startling to weak-kneed players. The minutes of the founding club meeting in 1889 reported that "the Secretaries were empowered to employ Tom Morris to lay out the course at a cost not to exceed £4." God alone only knows how old Tom hacked this course out of the rough sandhills for that price, but he sure made a beauty. Information: Royal County Down Golf Club, Newcastle, County Down, Northern Ireland (phone: 03967-23314).

KENNEMER, Zandvoort, The Netherlands: Rated among the best golf courses on the Continent, this club offers the delightful surprise of rolling sand dunes, an unusual element in a country that is otherwise flat. Excellent, challenging play for the accomplished golfer. Information: Kennemer Golf and Country Club, 78-80 Kennemerweg, 2042 XT Zandvoort, The Netherlands (phone: 02507-12836).

PENINA GOLF CLUB, Algarve, Portugal: Designed by Henry Cotton, who was three times the British Open champion, the course has managed to overcome the disadvantage of being set on very flat terrain. Literally hundreds of thousands of trees and shrubs were planted to provide a frame for the golf holes, and this former rice field is now a fine test of golfing skill. The large *Penina Golf* hotel adjoins the golf course. Information: Penina Golf Club, Monte de Alvor, PO Box 146, Penina, Portimao, Algarve 8502, Portugal (phone: 082-22051).

QUINTA DO LAGO, Algarve, Portugal: Now ranked among the top ten courses in the world, this relative newcomer — and recent site of the Portuguese Open — basks under 300 days of sunshine a year. Even while most northern European courses are damp and dreary, the 27 holes here normally can be played in shirtsleeves in December. Designed by Bill Mitchell, the late American architect, Quinta do Lago spreads along the Algarve coast over undulating land fringed by umbrella pines. Another new course nearby, San Lorenzo, promises to be even more demanding — and serene. In the estuary beside its 6th and 7th holes, Portuguese women digging for seafood may be the only distractions of the day. Information: Quinta do Lago Golf Club, Almancil, Loulé 1800, Portugal.

MUIRFIELD, Gullane, East Lothian, Scotland: Home of the Honourable Company of Edinburgh Golfers and the oldest golf club in existence, Muirfield has provided challenging play to generations of golfers since 1744 and, as befitting a world class course, has been the scene of countless British Open tournaments. This may be the hardest course in Scotland to get to play; be sure to write well in advance asking for access. Information: Muirfield Golf Club, Gullane, Eath Lothian, Scotland (phone: 620-842123).

OLD COURSE, St. Andrews, Fife, Scotland: This is the prime magnet that draws all of the world's golfers, for this course dates, they say, from the 15th century. Its aura is only slightly diminished by the bathers and strollers who consistently cross the 1st and 18th fairways — it's the shortest route to the beach — though once out on the course, its extreme difficulty and careful design become more readily apparent. There are four other courses on the same site — the Eden, Jubilee, and New (which was opened in 1894) are best — but it's the Old that you *must* play. Plan your play date here carefully, because there's no golfing on the Old Course on Sunday, and applications for tee times on most days must be made months in advance. A "fiver" to the starter can, however, work wonders. Information: Links Management Committee, Golf Pl., St. Andrews, Fife, Scotland (phone: 0334-75757).

GLENEAGLES, Auchterarder, Scotland: The Scots tend to denigrate this superb quartet of courses because they do not conform to the treasured linksland tradition. But visiting golfers will fall prey to no such prejudice, and the King's Course in particular is an absolute joy to play. It's also consistently in the best condition of any Scottish course and the extraordinary hotel here is reason enough for a visit. The month of June will allow play while gorse and broom are in bloom. Information:

Gleneagles Hotel Golf Course, Auchterarder, Perthshire, Scotland (phone: 07646-3543).

CARNOUSTIE, Carnoustie, Scotland: Just 5 miles (8 km) from St. Andrews is this site of a half dozen British Open golf tournaments. If the Championship Course (the better of the two tracks here) is the least impressive of the championship Scottish courses at first glance, it takes only one round of play to appreciate its true value. It encompasses the very essence of what's best about playing golf in Scotland, and the back 9 in particular — with the famous 14th hole called "Spectacles" and the three backbreaking finishing holes — will leave you with memories (not necessarily pleasant) that you will not soon forget. Now that the course is off the Open rota (too few accommodations), access is easier. Information: Carnoustie Golf Club, Links Parade, Carnoustie, Tayside DD7 7JE, Scotland (phone: 0241-53249).

ROYAL TROON, Troon, Scotland: Laid out along the beach, with the outgoing 9 heading virtually straight down the strand and the closing 9 paralleling it only a few yards inland, the prime distractions include the fact that the course lies directly below the flight path into Prestwick Airport and that there's a railroad track beside most of the back 9. So it sometimes seems as though players are about to be sucked up into the jet wash or run over by the 3:45 from Glasgow. Another classic British Open layout (and site of the 1989 tournament), it is one of the few private clubs in Scotland that is open to visitors; playing privileges are usually made available to members of clubs in the US who can produce a respectable certificate of handicap. Women are allowed to play the Championship links only on Mondays, Wednesdays, and Fridays. Information: Royal Troon Golf Club, Craigend Rd., Troon, Ayrshire, Scotland (phone: 0292-311555).

TURNBERRY, Turnberry, Scotland: The two courses here, the Ailsa and the Arran, are quite close in quality, but it's the Ailsa on which the British Open was played in 1977 and again in 1986. The wind blows in from the sea, and it sometimes takes an act of courage just to stand up on the craggy tees and hit out into the teeth of what occasionally seems like a gale. The beautiful *Turnberry* hotel — now being completely refurbished by new Japanese owners — provides some respite from the elements, but the golfing challenge is the real lure here. Information: Turnberry Hotel and Golf Courses, Turnberry, Ayrshire, Scotland (phone: 0655-31000).

LA MANGA CAMPO DE GOLF, Los Belones, Spain: The home of the Spanish Open, it's the "most superbly maintained" course in the world, according to Gary Player. The two 18-hole championship layouts offer tantalizing views of the Mediterranean from nearly every tee, and the sights and scenery provide a sort of ancillary hazard. Information: La Manga Campo de Golf, Los Belones, Cartagena, Murcia 30385, Spain (phone: 0968-569111).

TORREQUEBRADA, Benalmadena, Spain: Originally planned as a recreation center and golf course for vacationing German physicians, it's now a hotel, casino, and golf course open to the public, with a championship course designed by well-known Spanish golfer Pepe Gancedo. With the beautiful, sunny Costa del Sol as its backdrop, the course, though not long, is one of the most dramatic in Europe. About 15 miles (24 km) from Malaga. Information: Torrequebrada, PO Box 67, Carretera de Cadiz, KM 220, Benalmadena, Costa del Sol, Spain (phone: 52-446000).

FALSTERBO, Falsterbo, Sweden: Some 300 miles (480 km) from Stockholm and only 30 miles (48 km) from Copenhagen, it was founded in 1909 as a 9-hole course and expanded to 18 holes in 1930, making it one of the first full-fledged golf courses in Sweden. The exciting layout provides a fresh challenge with each wind change, and the naturally beautiful setting on a peninsula affords golfers stunning views across the sound to Denmark and along the Swedish shoreline. Information: Falsterbo Golf Club, Box 71, F-23011 Falsterbo, Sweden (phone: 40-470078 or 40-472722).

European Beaches:
Sun and Sand on Six Seas

 When you look down on a teeming Riviera beach in the middle of July, it's hard to believe that it wasn't so many decades ago that the great Riviera hotels closed down for the season with the first searing rays of the midsummer sun. Nothing can turn back the clock, however, or dismantle the seafront condominiums and cement-block hotels, or banish the sun-seeking Scandinavian hordes.

But Europe has many beaches of great natural beauty, whatever their manmade garnish: beaches that offer a vast assortment of marine pleasures, beaches where the people are more fun to watch than the fish ever were.

Some caveats: The crowds during the first 3 weeks of August, when Europe's entire population seems bent on cramming in vacation, are too much of a good thing (late June and early September are the ideal times).

Also, though you will find surf far tamer here than in America, you will also find far less in the way of skilled lifeguard protection. And though the waves are gentle, the sun is fierce: Take it in carefully measured doses and keep smearing on that fancy French suntan goo.

KNOKKE, Belgium: The North Sea has a wintry sound to it, and, indeed, the water is briskly unlike that of the bathtubby Mediterranean. Nonetheless, the broad beaches along the Royal Road that is the Belgian coastline are beautifully kept and ideal for summer vacationing. Knokke, in the corner by the Dutch border, is the most complete of resorts: You'll find fine cuisine, ample sports facilities, gracious garden-rimmed villas, a gambling casino, and the country's most inviting hotel, *La Réserve* — lapped about by the sea, the swimming pool, and little Victoria Lake. But there are simpler pleasures as well, among them less-developed southerly beaches such as Blankenberge and Wenduine. You can walk along the dikes and the great empty dunes, go on pony rides and ride the traditional sail carts on the beach, or take in any number of the colorful folk festivals that take place all along the coast. And, in case of a cloudy day, there is a varied choice of easy excursions: the fish market at Zeebrugge, the bird reserve at Het Zwin, the lovely old village of Damme, and beautiful, canal-crossed Bruges.

LE CAP D'AGDE, France: The ancient Greeks used to anchor their ships off this jutting promontory. And a lot of modern French prefer its wide sandy beaches and deep calm coves to the overbuilt, overrun, overpriced Côte d'Azur. Unlike the Riviera, the development of this coastline from St.-Cyprien to Port Camargue has been carefully controlled to retain its natural beauty. There are good facilities for boating and for tennis (at the *Club Pierre Barthès*) and hills nearby that offer many wonderful walks. And the surrounding region is one of France's most attractive and least visited: You can day-trip to the walled towns of Carcassonne and Aigues-Mortes, the Roman theater at Nîmes, and the horse farms of Camargue; and, at Béziers, take in bloodless bullfights.

PORTO-VECCHIO, Corsica, France: According to our First Law of Beaches, islands have the best ones, and the best of these are the least accessible. Witness Porto-Vecchio. A 5.5-mile-long bay that gives its name to the small fishing port at its head, Porto-Vecchio plunges into the eastern coast of Corsica, just opposite the side where most boats and planes arriving from the French mainland discharge their passengers. The beaches predicted by the First Law are here in force — fine-sand strands like La

Marine, Golfo di Sogno, St.-Cyprien, Pinarello, and Palombaggia, which flank the port town. The vegetation is subtropical; umbrella pines and conifers peculiar to the area line the coast. Other local specialties are lobsters and nudism. For information about the latter, contact: Syndicat d'Initiative, Porto-Vecchio, Place Hôtel de Ville, Corsica 20210, France (phone: 95-70-09-58). For off-beach entertainment, you can fly or sail to Bonifacio, a medieval fortress town at the southern tip of the island that is still entered by drawbridge. And from there, it's only 7.5 miles by ferry to Sardinia.

THASSOS, Greece: A Greek island, but not one of *the* Greek islands, Thassos lies in the northernmost part of the country, about an hour's ferry ride off the coast of Macedonia. Cooler than its sunbaked southern cousins, Thassos is also heavily wooded and its landscape is a study in greens — the silvery sage of the olive groves, the dark greens of the towering firs. Makriamos, a few kilometers south of Limenas, the principal town, is the island's best beach, but if you drive the circular shore road, you'll find a dozen more: Skala Panagia, Kinira, Skala Marion, Skala Sotiros, Skala Rahoniou, and others. The quiet bays of Arhangelos and Agios Ioanis are also idyllic. The tree-covered ruins of the acropolis of ancient Thassos will remind you you're in Greece. Should there be a cloudy day, you can take the ferry back to Kavala and amble around the Byzantine fortress and the Imaret, a center of the country's Moslem culture.

GULF OF MIRABELLO, Crete, Greece: Crete's choicest beaches are on either side of the town of Agios Nikolaos, which lies at the head of this deep bay (Kólpos Mirampelou in Greek) on the far eastern end of the island. Along with the beaches are some of the island's choicest beach hotels: the *Minos Beach,* the *Mirabello,* the *Elounda Beach,* the *Elounda Gulf Villas;* their most attractive accommodations are in Cretan-style bungalows right on the beachfront. Agios Nikolaos is full of animated taverns and fish restaurants, mainly along the docks and on the banks of Voulismeni, a tiny volcanic lake. Between sunbaths, you can hire a little boat to go out to the islet of Spinalonga, where you can explore a charming Venetian castle; drive or stroll to the village of Kritsa to have an ouzo, a game of backgammon, and a look at the frescoes in its 13th-century church.

FORTE DEI MARMI, Italy: The Italian Riviera della Versilia is really like a gigantic seaside café, and the chief amusement is watching the passing (or sprawling) parade: the phalanxes of multicolored umbrellas, deck chairs, and sentry-box cabins; the fleets of pedalboats; the sippers of Campari, builders of sand castles, players of volleyball, and scantily clad waders — out more to be seen than to enjoy the warm surf. The whole expanse between the Lido di Camaiore and the bustling resort town of Viareggio is really one long marina. Patrician families from Rome, Florence, and Milan have been coming here every summer for a century, though in recent years, many of their pined and palmed seafront villas have been transformed into small hotels. Never expect romantic solitude, and remember that all of Italy vacations in mid-August.

COSTA SMERALDA, Sardinia, Italy: In the space of only a few years, $200 million and the Aga Khan transformed a rocky, primitive wasteland between the port of Olbia and La Maddalena at Sardinia's tip into the country's most glamorous beach complex. The boulders are still there and the water is a cloudless cobalt blue, but scattered from cove to cove are four elegant hotels, cleverly designed so that they seem to have grown out of the rocks: the *Romazzino,* the *Cervo,* the *Pitrizza,* the *Cala di Volpe.* The crowd can get very fancy, particularly when the yacht fleet is in — but the sun-and-sea life is superbly simple. There are boat and air connections from several mainland cities, but remember to reserve well in advance for a midsummer visit.

LIDO, Venice, Italy: Just a reminder that while you are visiting one of the most beautiful cities in the world you can also swim, sunbathe, and eat shrimp along the Lido, a long, skinny island bordered on one side by the sea and on the other by the Venetian lagoon, just a short boat ride from downtown Venice. There is golf, tennis, riding, boating, and plenty of beach life on the wide strands (some of them public, and some — immaculately groomed — the private reserves of the great seafront hotels). When you've had enough of the sun, you can go for a stroll along the Venetian canals or sip an *aperitivo* in Piazza San Marco.

PRAIA DE ROCHA, Portugal: Some of Europe's finest beaches are along a 62-mile stretch of Portuguese coastline, between Faro and the Sagres promontory in the country's southernmost province, the Algarve. The strands face south toward Africa, and both the air and the water stay temperate most of the year. The heavy development that the area has undergone in recent years has taken its toll on the coast's raw natural beauty, but, in exchange, has provided it with an array of fine shorefront hotels: the *Algarve* at Praia de Rocha, the *Golf da Penina* at Penina, and the *Alvor Praia* at Prainha, to name just a few. Praia de Rocha has a beige yellow beach set against craggy red cliffs that erosion has sculpted into strange, exotic shapes: Rock spires, arches, and hollows make a kind of natural labyrinth on the sand. In the old fortress of St. Catherine, there is a good seafood restaurant (grilled sardines and *vinho verde* are local specialties) and stunning lookout point; the nearby port of Portimâo gets a steady traffic of colorful fishing craft. The golf links at Penina offer three separate courses, with a total of 36 holes, on 360 acres that roll across the foothills of the Monchiquo Mountains.

MAMAIA, Romania: The Black Sea is one of those bodies of water that Americans learn about in geography class, but never consider for swimming. Yet the Romanian and Bulgarian Black Sea coasts are to Eastern Europe what the Riviera is to France. Dr. Ana Aslan's discovery of the supposed wonder drug Gerovital has attracted a score of health-cure seekers to Romania. But there's still an immense gap between Techirghiol and St.-Tropez. Mamaia, a 5-mile strip of beach and rich vegetation between the Black Sea and Lake Siutghiol, offers a wide choice of hotels that — though the architecture is uniformly Moscow Modern — boast rooms and facilities fully as satisfactory as those of their Western counterparts. The crowd is international (with a preponderance of Eastern Europeans), and the nightlife and sports facilities are as abundant and varied as in the West — but prices are quite reasonable, and there's a refreshing plenitude of rustic Romanian restaurants serving wines and meals you'd never in an eon encounter in the Hamptons.

FORMENTOR, Majorca, Spain: First find the Balearic Islands, three and a half clumps of land about 100 miles off the eastern coast of Spain. The largest clump is Majorca; the thin tongue of land that runs off the top is Cape Formentor. Though honky-tonk Palma de Mallorca, its urbanized beaches, and its tour-bus traffic jams may mar the idyllic green countryside, the almond groves and wild flowers and the high shoreline cliffs that you see as you make the 40-mile (64-km) drive north from the capital to Formentor will give you entirely different feelings. Formentor's beaches — and those of Cala de San Vincente — are superb, and so is the *Formentor* hotel, surrounded by pine woods and looking majestically toward the sea, the bay, the mountains, the rust-colored bluffs. The cape ends with a dramatically positioned lighthouse. Not far away is the village of Puerto de Pollensa, where you can ingest a bowl of seafood stew and an *ensaimada* (the Majorcan pastry specialty), take a boat ride on the bay, and have a look at the hilltop Notre Dame de Puig.

KUŞADASI, Turkey: About 60 miles (96 km) south of Izmir, this lovely old town founded in the 17th century by Genoese traders occupies the site of an ancient Greek settlement on a sandy peninsula across the protected bay from the Greek island of Samos. The little beaches all around the town and along the road to Selçuk are among the prettiest in the Aegean, and the area is famous for the variety of wild birds and flowers that soften the glare of sand, sun, and whitewashed houses. Near the port is *Öküz Mehmet Paşa,* an old traders' inn transformed into a luxury hotel and restaurant (information from *Ninotour,* Kuşadasi). Just keep saying *karides, çipura, barbunya,* and *trança şiş,* and the waiters will keep bringing you the four freshest fish in Turkey.

A 15-minute drive away is Ephesus, the ruins of the Ionian city that was the capital of all Asia Minor — one of the Mediterranean's most enthralling archaeological sites. The skin diving around Kuşadasi is particularly rewarding: The water is crystalline, and there are as many brightly colored fish in the sea as there are birds in the air and flowers on land.

DUBROVNIK, Yugoslavia: Far down the Dalmatian coast, not far from the Albanian border, this walled and turreted city is one of Europe's best preserved and most captivating — and it would be worth a visit even if it were in the middle of a desert. Instead, it juts out dramatically into the gleaming blue Adriatic. Inside the medieval walls is a collection of fine Renaissance palaces and churches, many dating from the great period of Venetian domination of the sea. The feeling of antiquity is heightened by the absence of cars and there's a wide flagstone main promenade that teems with life in summer, especially in July and August during a 6-week music festival. Out on both sides of the town are the beaches — long and bright, some of sand and others of scrubbed white pebbles; just across from the port is the tiny island of Lokrum, a wooded national park with fine swimming and skin diving and, hidden among the pines, a splendid outdoor restaurant installed in an ancient structure that began its life as a monastery. Big ferries, tiny dinghies, and just about any other kind of boat you can name putter up and down the coast in season, and you have a choice of a variety of maritime excursions from an hour's fishing offshore to a weekend cruise to Venice.

CLUB MED: *Club Med* isn't really a club at all, but a chain of over a hundred vacation villages sited strategically on some of the most pleasurable parts of the planet. The idea started in France, and the head office is in Paris — but the clientele is, by now, thoroughly international. Guests are usually on the young side and interested in active vacations. There's always a variety of sports to enjoy, everything from judo to water skiing, and a *Club Med* vacation can be an exceptionally good deal for those who take advantage of the activities, because there's no extra charge. But the *Club*'s settings are protected and beautifully landscaped and friendly (like a summer camp for big kids) and the outside world is kept at a distance, so you can enjoy yourself just as much if you do nothing more active than snooze in the sun. Accommodation at the *Club*'s beach and seaside villages is usually in attractive, functional bungalows, and there are communal dining facilities. Some of the best *Clubs* for beach life include Pakostane in Yugoslavia, Corfu in Greece, and Foça in Turkey. You can get a complete list and information from the US office: Club Med, 3 E. 54th St., New York, NY 10022 (phone: 800-CLUB-MED).

The European Mountain Experience

 Maybe Europe's mountains will look like its beaches in another decade, with vacationers climbing shoulder to shoulder past little men hawking alpenstocks and chocolate bars on each peak. But at least for now, the mountain country — often no more than a morning's drive from subways and stock exchanges — is still a wilderness paradise and has something to offer both pick-and-crampon types bound to scale the murderous North Wall of the Eiger and weekend enthusiasts accustomed to nothing more strenuous than strolls in the Vienna Woods.

There is a sense of good fellowship in the mountains: While beach people more often than not resent each other's territorial encroachment, mountain people share a sense of physical accomplishment that makes the trails and the Alpine huts very friendly places to be.

Though mountains are mountains — dangerous if you don't know what you're about — the Alps are for the most part as accommodating as the Continent itself. Europeans are great hikers, and there are miles and miles of well-marked trails. Most good European mountain areas are also liberally scattered with huts and refuges where climbers can get meals that, at the end of a day on the trail, taste better than a banquet at *Maxim's* and bunk on a mattress that feels as good as any at the *Ritz*. When the sun goes down, there's usually plenty of mulled wine and lusty singing. Many hikers spend weeks just trekking from one hut to the next. Some areas, especially in Teutonic countries, are so geared to entertaining hikers that they hand out small cards listing all the main huts, each of which is provided with a rubber stamp so that you can brand your card in the appropriate space. The goal is to end up with a stamp after the name of every hut on the card.

Whether you go out walking for a week or just a day, there are some precautions to observe. You don't have to outfit yourself for the conquest of Everest on your first stroll, but stout boots will certainly enhance the experience and a knapsack will come in handy. In it you should stuff a pocket flashlight and — no matter how hot the sun and cloudless the sky when you embark — a lightweight rain parka and a sweater. Alpine weather is enormously capricious and you can easily experience four seasons in a day. If you'll be out longer than that, you may want to bring a good long book. (Picking an area where excursions to the valleys are a possibility is a good idea if you're easily daunted by rain.)

And don't fail to buy a good map before you set out; take it to the local tourist office to find out about the relative hazards and pleasures of the local trails. Never start out knowing nothing.

Here we've assembled a list of areas that will provide you with the most satisfying mountain experiences. Each item is keyed according to the activities you can enjoy there: Rambling (**R**), on walking paths that are easy enough to be pleasurable to children and beginning hikers; Trudging (**T**), on longer and steeper trails that will challenge intermediate hikers and adults; and Dangling (**D**), rope-and-crampon mountain goat stuff, suitable for trained climbers.

GROSSGLOCKNER and GROSSVENEDIGER, Austria: Austria's two star peaks both rise out of craggy ranges that offer a mountaineer's paradise of challenging climbs. The graves in the little mountain cemetery in the churchyard of Kals are grisly reminders of the perils of the Glockner, the tougher of the two. Experts can commence the ascent to its peak and to Grossvenediger's summit from a number of well-placed refuges throughout the area. For everyone else, there are *hütte*-to-*hütte* hikes that last several days and cover some of the Alps' most dramatic terrain. For information: Tiroler Fremdenverkehrswerbung, 6 Bozner Platz, Innsbruck A-6010, Austria (phone: 5222-20777); or Fremdenverkehrsbüro, 90 Postfach, Lienz 9900, Austria (phone: 485-24747). A good way to make either climb is under the auspices of the *Hochgebirgsschule Tyrol,* an Innsbruck climbing school and guide operation. To find out more, contact Hochgebirgsschule Tyrol, 3 Kaiser Josef-strasse, A-6020 Innsbruck, Innrain 67 (phone: 522-228900). **T, D**

OBERGURGL, Austria: On a wide, sunny plain at 6,560 feet in the middle of the Ötztaler Alps, this town — one of the highest in Europe — offers a choice of accommodations that range from luxury hotels to simple wooden chalets, and the surrounding mountains are dotted with *hüttes* — refuges where hikers can find simple food and shelter. A great ring of glaciers and towering peaks and an abundance of high Alpine flora make for startling scenery, which can be seen from afar along easy trails a half hour from town, or conquered if you have the inclination and the skill. Obergurgl is a ski resort in winter; the town of Vent, on the other side of the Ramolkogl, is quieter and far less developed. It is also the jumping-off point for the ascent of the 12,464-foot Wildspitze. For information about instruction and guided climbs: Hochgebirgsschule Obergurgl, Haus Schönblick, Obergurgl 53, Tyrol A-6456, Austria (phone: 525-6251). **R, T**

HIGH TATRAS, Czechoslovakia: Like most of Eastern Europe, this magnificent mountain district is generally overlooked by Americans, though the resort areas are less developed and less expensive than their Western cousins. There is also a century-old tradition of climbing and a well-maintained network of huts and hotels. Starý Smokovec (3,280 feet), Strbske Pleso (4,428 feet), and Tatranská Lomnica (2,788 feet) are the main starting points for area excursions. The hotel at Popradské Pleso (4,920 feet) is right by the lake, and is a fine springboard for trips into the popular Pic Rysy group. The *Sliezsky Dom,* a comfortable, modern hotel at 5,576 feet, has easy access to the Gerlachovský Stít and the whole Tatra range. Among the best high *chata* (mountain huts) are the *Zbojnícka,* the *Terryho,* the *Iames Pod Solískom,* and the *Pod Rysmi,* which at 7,380 feet is the highest *chata* in Czechoslovakia. Information: Čedok, 18 Na Příkopě, Prague 111 35, Czechoslovakia (phone: 212-7111); or Čedok, Room 1902, 10 E. 40th St., New York, NY 10016 (phone: 212-689-9720). **R, T**

CUMBRIA and LANCASHIRE, England: From April through October, fell-walking and rock-climbing are favorite sports among the crags and crests of the Lake District counties, but it's certainly more Albion than Alpine. Centers for guided jaunts, rock-climbing courses, wildlife observation, and bird-watching are *Footpath Holidays,* 4 Holly Walk, Andover, Hampshire SP10 3PJ, England (phone: 0264-52689); *English Wanderer,* 13 Wellington Court, Spencers Wood, Reading RG7 1BN, England (phone: 0734-882515). For more information on walking in Britain: British Tourist Authority, Thames Tower, Black's Road, Hammersmith, London W6 9EL (phone: 730-3488). **R, T**

MONT-BLANC, France and Italy: Though the highest mountain in the Alps is now pierced by a two-country tunnel that eliminates the need to climb over its majestic summit, it still provides some of the most challenging mountaineering in Europe. Chamonix — a classy ski resort town that attracts everyone from sun-deck loungers to helmeted, pick-toting rock climbers — is the principal center on the French side; the *Compagnie des Guides* (Maison de la Montagne, 190 Pl. de l'Eglise, Chamonix 74400, France; phone: 50-53-00-88) is the best source of information and assistance. Courmayeur, on the Italian side, is less developed: It basks in a great natural amphitheater bisected by the Dora River and sprinkled with picture-postcard Alpine hamlets. For details: Azienda di Soggiorno, Piazzale Monte Bianco, Courmayeur, Italy (phone: 842060). If the taming of Mont-Blanc by tunnel and cable car takes the romance out of the mountain for you, try going farther afield in the Valle d'Aosta to lesser-known centers like Paquier, Valtournenches, Cogne, and Valsavaranche in the Gran Paradiso National Park. For information on the whole area: Ufficio Informazioni Turistiche della Valle d'Aosta, 8 Piazza E Chanoux, Aosta, Italy (phone: 0165-35655). **R, T, D**

DOLOMITES, Italy: The hard hiking in this vast range south of the Brenner Pass — long a favorite region of expert and experienced climbers — has remained largely uncharted. Yet its jagged peaks, rising like giant rusty pink fangs above smooth snow meadows, are one of the most awesome natural sights in Europe, and if you ever cross the Sella, the Falzarego, the Pordoi, and the Pellegrino passes under a full moon, the rest of your life may seem anticlimactic. Cortina d'Ampezzo — a former site of the Winter Olympics and now a favorite summer resort of affluent Italians from the flatlands — is the classiest of a number of towns that are perfect places to begin mountain rambles; Corvara, Ortisei, and Canazei are equally beautiful and just as well placed. And because a large chunk of the Dolomites once belonged to Austria, the atmosphere — as well as the language — in all these towns is far more likely to be Teutonic than Latin. The Marmolada and the Gruppo Sella are the major peaks, but there are dozens more. For information: Azienda di Promozione Turistica, 21 Via Pesaro, Bellino, Italy (phone: 0437-940083); Azienda di Soggiorno e Turismo, 8 Piazza Walther, Bolzano, Italy (phone: 0471-975656); Azienda Autonoma per il Turismo, 4 Via Alfieri, Trento, Italy (phone: 0461-983880). **R, T, D**

MATTERHORN and MONTE ROSA, Switzerland: The car-free town of Zermatt, accessible only by railway, offers access to a dozen peaks of the "4,000 Club" —

a sobriquet that refers to those mountain peaks over 4,000 meters (13,120 feet) high — representing five of the six highest mountains in Europe. If you don't want to be bothered with the Andes or the Himalayas this year, this area of the Swiss Alps will provide nine lives' worth of advanced climbing. The *High Alpine School,* which runs summer courses for experts, can also supply guides — advisable on these treacherous trails no matter how many times you have hopped up Mt. McKinley. Information: Hochalpine Bergsteigerschule Zermatt and Bergführerverein, Zermatt 3920, Switzerland (phone: 028-673456); and Verkehrsverein, Zermatt 3920, Switzerland (phone: 028-661181). **D**

PONTRESINA, Switzerland: The Swiss take even their strolling seriously, and scores of footpaths are scrupulously marked by destination and estimated hiking time. That is especially true in the glorious Engadine Valley — one of those places that has everything for everybody. The 4.3-mile walk from Alp Languard to Muottas Muragl is a novice's dream: High but level, it offers spectacular vistas of the Engadine lakes and the whole Bernina Range. The area is also supplied with Alpine gardens and a game reserve, a choice of chair lifts and railways so that you can start your tour up high, plus huts with panoramic views, where you can savor three-star lunches. For experts, there's plenty of ice and rock climbing on the Piz Palu; and some of the most exciting climbing in Switzerland is on the 13,120-foot Piz Bernina. The fine *Mountain School* has a large team of expert guides and offers a variety of courses for aspiring mountaineers. Information: Schweizer Bergsteigerschule, Chesa Hotel Engadinerhof, Pontresina CH-7504, Switzerland (phone: 082-66444); and Kur und Verkehrsverein, Pontresina CH-7504, Switzerland (phone: 082-66488). **R, T, D**

STRADA ALTA LEVENTINA, Switzerland: Much to the delight of Alpine hikers, the Swiss government (which is never neutral about nature) has recently refurbished the old St. Gotthard High Road, a medieval mule track and pilgrim's way. The whole trail, which runs 27.9 miles, makes a comfortable 3-day excursion, and there's plenty of fine food and comfortable shelter along the way. You start from Airolo, 3,772 feet, and on the first day travel via Brugnasco, Cresta, and Lurengo to Osco. The second day, you pass through Targuel, Rossura, Sorsello, Gianón, and Anzonico; and on the third day through Segno, Sobrio, Diganengo, and Pollegio Biasca. Just follow the red and white signs. Information: Ente Turistico di Leventina, Faido 6760, Switzerland (phone: 094-381616); or Swiss National Tourist Office, 608 Fifth Ave., New York, NY 10020 (phone: 212-757-5944). **R**

Going for Game: Hunting and Fishing

With the growth of the environmental movement in Europe, fishing and hunting aren't the wide-open free-for-alls that they were as recently as a decade ago. Nevertheless, the possibilities for pursuing these sports are rich and extensive. From the Scottish Highlands to Poland's Mazur Lakes, from the Tatra Mountains of Czechoslovakia to the coasts of Brittany, there is an abundance of wildlife — often in spectacular settings.

THE HUNT

In the last 10 years, seasons have been shortened and are more rigorously observed. At the same time license costs have risen sharply: In Greece, for example, a 15-day hunting permit that cost $25 not long ago now sells for over $150 In some countries — Germany, Belgium, and Holland among them — you can hunt only as the guest of the owner of a private game reserve. (Foreigners may make contact through sporting magazines and clubs, but hired hospitality has a hefty price tag.)

Here are some of your best bets for unparalleled European hunting adventures.

ŽIDLOCHOVICE, Southern Moravia, Czechoslovakia: This Eastern European country, practically one giant game reserve, offers some of the finest hunting in Europe; the pheasant preserve at Židlochovice, near Brno, is one of its unique and richest areas, attracting hunters from all over the Continent by the hundreds every autumn. Northern Moravia also has two excellent reserves in the Jeseniky and Beskydy districts. Either way, you must go in one of the groups organized by Čedok, the national travel bureau. For information: Čedok-Lovy, 18 Na Příkopě, Prague, Czechoslovakia; or Čedok, 10 E. 40th St., New York, NY 10016 (phone: 212-689-9720). Prague, incidentally, has a number of specialty shops where you can buy excellent hunting equipment.

WEST COUNTRY, England: When the English say "hunting" they mean on horseback, with hounds; it is an activity as British as taking high tea. Two hotels in Devon specialize in arranging hunting holidays: the *Crown,* Exford, Somerset, England (phone: 064-383-5545), and the *Arundell Arms,* Lifton, Devon, England (phone: 0566-84666). You will surely need to be a proficient horseman to keep up with the Tallyho-Joneses. For information on hunting and shooting in Britain, contact: British Tourist Authority, 40 W. 57th St., New York, NY 10019 (phone: 212-581-4700); or British Field Sports Society, 59 Kennington Rd., London SE1 (phone: 928-4742).

CRETE, Greece: Quail and partridge hunting is a special experience in the wild and primitive parts of the island of Dia, across from Heraklion, but a far cry from the busy north shore beaches. This terrain is typical of the savage regions that served partisans so well during the island's German occupation. You will need a guide. The season begins on September 15 and lasts until the end of November. Hare and rabbit until the end of January. For more information: Greek National Tourist Organization in Crete, 1 Xanthoudidou, Herakleion, Crete (phone: 228203); or the Forestry Office, Dassarchio, 22 Iraklion Dedalou St., Herakleion, Crete (phone: 282776).

HIGHLANDS, Scotland: August 12, the "Glorious Twelfth," is the opening day of the 4-month grouse season, a national ceremony of sorts that takes place annually inside the triangle determined by Aberdeen, Perth, and Inverness. Braemar, Ballater, and Aboyne are among the more colorful spots. Hunters in the area also stalk roe, fallow, sika, and red deer at this time of year. The list of Scottish hotels that arrange for both grouse-shooting and deer-hunting expeditions for their guests includes *Raemoir House,* Banchory, Kincardineshire; *Kinloch House,* Tayside, Perthshire; and *Knockie Lodge,* Whitebridge, Inverness-shire. Contact them well in advance, since you may need to write directly to the estates with hunting grounds. See if you can arrange to be there for one of the gatherings of the clans, Scottish ceremonies that also enliven the Highlands. For detailed information: Highlands and Islands Development Board, Bridge House, 27 Bank St., Inverness IV1 1QR, Scotland (phone: 0463-234171).

COTOS OF THE PYRENEES, Spain: Under the administration of its National Institute for the Conservation of Nature, Spain has an extensive network of *cotos* — national hunting reserves. A number of the choices are clustered in the Pyrenees: Alto Pallars, Arán, Los Circos, Fresser, Cadí, Cerdaña, Vall Ferrera. Wild boar are profuse, and the Spanish specialize in tracking these harvest-plunderers; chamois, deer, roebuck, and grouse are also taken in the October to January season. Most big hunting areas have their *Parador Nacional* — a picturesque state-run country hotel. All foreigners planning to hunt in Spain should contact: Administración Turistica Española, Sección de Caza, 25 Calle Velásquez, Madrid, Spain (phone: 435-6641). More information: Federación Española de Caza (National Hunting Federation), 53 Avenida Reina Victoria, Madrid 28006, Spain (phone: 253-3495); or travel agencies that specialize in hunting trips, such as *Cacerias Conde,* 7 Princesa Madrid, Spain (phone: 247-1804);

or *Promoción de Caza y Pesca,* 41 Duque de Sexto, Madrid, Spain (phone: 276-3661).

NOVI SAD, Vojvodina, Yugoslavia: The fertile wooded Vojvodine, north of Belgrade, is the nation's least exploited tourist area — and its richest hunting land. Near Novi Sad and the banks of the Danube, the Odzaci, Karavukovo, Bagremara, and Ristovaca reserves shelter a superabundance of wild hare, pheasant, and partridge. Information: *Lovoturs,* 26 Dr. Salvadora Aljendea, Novi Sad 21000, Yugoslavia (phone: 021-331277); and the Yugoslav National Tourist Office, Rockefeller Center, Suite 280, 630 Fifth Ave., New York, NY 10111 (phone: 212-757-2801).

FISHING HOLES

The best of Europe's fishing is some of the best on the planet. There are swordfish on the Costa Cantábrica in Spain, and carp and pike on Poland's Mazur lakes. The beaches of Brittany in France make for superb surfcasting. Britain lures anglers with the proximity of ancient hotels and quaint inns to its best fishing streams. (The booklet called *BTA Commended Country Hotels,* available from the British Tourist Authority, 40 W. 57th St., New York, NY 10019; phone: 212-581-4700, can provide the details.) Switzerland's fishing centers cater to novices as well as to longtime fly-tiers with special summer fishing courses. The Swiss National Tourist Office, 608 Fifth Ave., New York, NY 10020 (phone: 212-757-5944), can tell you more. Even the cities have their contributions: There's hardly a better way to spend a lazy Sunday than angling in the Belgian canals at Damme, near Bruges.

Here are some of the Old World's most celebrated fishing spots — worth every bit of the traveling you'll have to do to experience them.

MARIAGER FJORD-KATTEGAT, Denmark: Fishing boats leave regularly from the fjord's three main towns — Hobro, Mariager, and Hadsund — to make for the open sea of the Kattegat, where cod, flounder, mackerel, sea trout, and plaice can be hauled out in an abundance as satisfying as the good fellowship aboard the ship. Information: Turistbureauet (Office of Tourism), 26 Adelgade, Hobro, Mariagerfjord DK-9500, Denmark (phone: 525666). Other fine fjords for fishing are Roskildefjord, just west of Copenhagen, and Limfjorden, up north in Himmerland. Information about Roskildefjord: the Office of Tourism, 3 Fondens Bro, Box 278, Roskilde DK-4000, Denmark (phone: 352700); or the Office of Tourism, 3 Østergade, Frederikssund DK-3600, Denmark (phone: 310685). Information about the Limfjorden: the Office of Tourism, 4 Havnen, Nynøbing, Mors DK-7900, Denmark (phone: 720488). For general information: Danish Tourist Board, 655 Third Ave., New York, NY 10017 (phone: 212-949-2333).

ITCHEN and TEST RIVERS, near Nether Wallop, Hampshire, England: For the outsider, topnotch fishing can be hard to find in Izaac Walton's home country: Most of the fishing rights to the best streams are controlled by associations and private citizens. However, there are also many country hotels that own equally productive fishing waters, and these establishments are British institutions. The Test River is a carefully managed, world-famous stream stocked with special fast-growing brown and rainbow trout. Information: Southern Water Authority, Guildbourne House, Worthing, West Sussex BN11 1LD, England (phone: 0903-205252). In the same district, there is exceptional angling on a number of local rivers (practically in the shadow of Winchester Cathedral and Izaak Walton's burial place). The celebrated Itchen produces small, extra-wily wild trout; wild and unspoiled Itchen feeder streams are spring fed and good for large and exceptionally active trophy fish. Other well-known streams in the area include the Avon, the Derwent, the Dove (where Walton fished), the Eden, the Kennet, the Lune, the Ribble, and the Wharfe. They're all clear, fast flowing, and, because of their origins in Britain's chalk hills, highly alkaline; conditions, in other words, are ideal for nurturing big native brown trout that rise freely even when they reach 4 pounds or more. The British Tourist Authority's booklet *Commended Country Hotels,* cited above, provides information on a number of pleasant inns in the area.

CORSICA, France: The fish that teem beneath the transparent blue water surrounding this Mediterranean island are even more varied and abundant than the sunbaked bathers who populate its sandy beaches. For information on lining up a seagoing craft and the necessary equipment for scuba diving and underwater fishing, contact the Fédération Française d'Etudes et de Sports sous-marins, 50 Bd. Général-Graziani, Bastia 20200, France (phone: 95-31-03-32). Inland, trout and salmon fishing in lakes and streams can be arranged from nearby inns and farmhouses. Information: Agence Régionale du Tourisme et des Loisirs, 22 Cours Grandval, BP 19, Ajaccio 20176, France (phone: 95-51-00-22).

LAKE CONSTANCE, Germany: One of the great lakes of Europe, the lovely Bodensee, as this body of water is called in German, is filled with a dozen different kinds of fish, including the prized *forelle* (trout). Ample facilities for boat hire are available both in Switzerland and in Germany (both of which touch the lake's shoreline); picturesque Lindau, a medieval German town on an island connected by bridge to the mainland, is a good place to base yourself. Information: 8990 Verkehrsverein-Lindau, 68 Ludwigstrasse, Bodensee, Germany (phone: 08382-5022).

BALLYNAHINCH RIVER, near Connemara, Ireland: Irish game-fishing waters are among the finest in Europe, and the 3-mile-long Ballynahinch ranks among the nation's best salmon streams. As in the rest of the British Isles, fishing rights are privately held, but guests at the *Ballynahinch Castle,* a cozy, 20-room country hotel that was, in the 17th century, the ancestral home of a family of Connemara chieftains named O'Flaherty, have access to its seven beats. The season for salmon, which average 10 pounds and sometimes exceed 20, runs from January through September. Good-size sea trout are also taken during a late June through September season. The Ballynahinch is part of an extensive complex of lakes, tributaries, and connecting rivers draining into Bertraghboy Bay. Information: Ballynahinch Castle, Ballinafad, County Galway, Ireland (phone: 095-31006); or Bord Failte (Irish Tourist Board), Baggot St. Bridge, Dublin 2, Ireland (phone: 765871).

BLACKWATER RIVER, near Youghal, Ireland: One of Ireland's most famous salmon rivers, rising near the border of Cork and Kerry, the Blackwater takes in 85 miles of long glides and deep pools. Salmon above 20 pounds are sometimes taken in the upper reaches; sea trout are taken lower down, closer to Youghal, where the river empties into the sea. Brown trout, weighing in at an average of about a half pound each, are fairly active on both wet and dry flies on the upper portion. Information: Inland Fisheries Trust, Portmahon House, 77 Strand Rd., Sandymount, Dublin, or Bord Failte (above).

SHANNON RIVER, Ireland: The 240-mile-long Shannon, the longest river in all of Britain and Ireland, drains a fifth of Ireland (about 6,060 square miles); its tributaries are 1,130 miles in length. It is slow moving, punctuated by numerous large lakes, and, for coarse fish (as bream, rudd, pike, perch, tench, and rudd/bream hybrids are collectively known), the Shannon has few equals anywhere; when the fish are biting, a catch of over a hundred pounds (mostly bream) is not unusual. On the Upper Shannon — that is, from the source to Athlone — Carrick-on-Shannon in County Leitrim is one of the best-organized fishing centers, and Strokestown, in County Roscommon, is a favorite destination of specimen rudd hunters. Particularly exciting lakes include Ree, which shelters all varieties of coarse fish; Lough Allen, which offers the best northern pike angling in all of Europe; and Lough Patrick, where, in 1970, two anglers caught over 500 pounds of tench in one short session. On the Lower Shannon, Lough Derg is productive for pike, and the Plassey River — as the Shannon is called where it flows by Limerick City — is a coarse fisherman's dream. The Clare Lakelands, centered on the village of Tulla, are a must for the serious angler looking for a quiet vacation. Information: Bord Failte (above).

TROMS COUNTY, Norway: This is a place for serious fishermen to settle in for a month — or a summer. A hundred different rivers and watercourses, churning across a wild landscape, teem with salmon, sea trout, and sea char. You can fish in the lakes as well or in the saltwater fjords. June to early September is the season. The *International Sea Fishing Festival,* which includes 3 days of competition, takes place every mid-July in Harstad. Information: Harstad Tourist Office, 7C Torvet, Box 447, Harstad 9401, Norway (phone: 826-3235); or the Norwegian Tourist Board, 655 Third Ave., New York, NY 10017 (phone: 212-949-2333). (The book *Angling in Norway,* available from the Norwegian Tourist Board, is detailed and helpful.) The *Fly-spesialisten Reisebyrå,* 1 Kronprinsesse Märthas Pl., N-0160 Oslo, Norway (phone: 413870), specializes in setting up and booking salmon fishing trips and boat rentals.

Wild Europe

The air of the cities is polluted almost beyond hope, and the great monuments are crusted over with the grime of progress. Cement spreads along the seashores and through the countryside like a cancer; crowds throng the museums, the ski slopes, and the beaches; and the seas are, it seems, indelibly stained with oil. But there are still places in Europe where times haven't changed: forests that are still dark and silent; Mediterranean coves that are still deserted; country roads that are still only dirt; high mountain paths where you can walk for hours without meeting another soul — or encountering a chewing gum wrapper. Germany's Wildpark Altenfelden-Mühltal; the plains of the Puszta and the great horse-farming area of Hungary; Italy's National Park of Abruzzo; and Krkonoše, Czechoslovakia's Mountain of the Giants National Park, are only a few examples.

To get away from it all, join the *Iceland Safari,* which spends 7 days in the rough terrain of that wild country, taking in volcanoes, volcanic fissures, hot springs, majestic waterfalls, and more. Information: *Waymark Holidays,* 295 Lillie Road, London SW67LL, England (phone: 01-385-5015).

Or you can go pony trekking in the beautiful countryside around Scotland's Loch Trool and the Forest of Galloway. Information: Dumfries and Galloway Tourist Association, Dashwood Square, Newton Stewart, DG8 6DQ Scotland (phone: 0671-2549).

In Greenland you can go on dogsled expeditions and drive with hunters and dogs across frozen fjords and lakes and through mountain passes to tiny hunting settlements. Information: Ilulissat Tourist Office, Box 128, Ilulissat DK-3952, Denmark (phone: 299-43222); or the Danish Tourist Board, 655 Third Ave., New York, NY 10017 (phone: 212-949-2333).

Or, in France, you can take bicycle tours through the château-dotted Loire Valley. Information: Fédération Française de Cyclotourisme, 8 Rue Jean-Marie-Jégo, Paris 75013, France (phone: 45-80-30-21). Or the Bicyclub de France, 8 Pl. de la Porte de Champerret, Paris 75017, France (phone: 42-27-28-82).

You can even sit around on an empty beach in the altogether: There are scores of places for that, among them the sunny coast of Corsica, near San Nicolao or Porto-Vecchio. For details, contact the Délégation Régionale du Tourisme, 38 Cours Napoléon, 20178 Ajaccio, France (phone: 95-21-55-31); or the Fédération Française de Naturisme, 53 Rue Chaussée d'Antin, 75009 Paris, France (phone: 42-80-05-21).

And that's only the beginning. Here are some more ideas for savoring the wilder side of Europe.

ARDENNES, Belgium: These deep, mysterious forests flanking the River Meuse, the picturesque valleys, and the lacy network of sparkling streams haven't changed all that much since Shakespeare wrote about them as the idyllic Forest of Arden in *As You Like*

It. The manmade attractions are equally unspoiled: Dinant and Durbuy are the quaintest of villages; and the castles at Bouillon, Annevoie, and Spontin look like models for fairy tale illustrations. You can explore underground grottoes at Han-sur-Lesse and Remouchamps or paddle a kayak down the Lesse or the Amblève, flanked by wild high cliffs. Namur is a good base of operations. For information: Fédération du Tourisme de la Province de Namur, 3 Rue Notre-Dame, Namur B-5000, Belgium (phone: 060-312627); or the Belgian National Tourist Office, 745 Fifth Ave., New York, NY 10151 (phone: 212-758-8130).

CAMARGUE, France: A marshy triangle on the southern coast, bounded by the two branches of the Rhone and the sea, the Camargue is the closest thing in Europe to the Wild West: On some 50 *manades,* or ranches, cowboys called *gardians* ride herd on black bulls and wild white horses, who thunder across the swampy plains and salt flats and startle hundreds of pink-winged flamingoes into flight over the Etang de Vaccarès, the largest sanctuary of its kind in Europe. In Arles, the nearest large town, the bulls of the Camargue do bloodless combat in an ancient Roman amphitheater. And a little sea village called Stes.-Maries-de-la-Mer is the destination of a pilgrimage of Gypsies from all over Europe every May 24 and 25. Information: Syndicat d'Initiative d'Arles, 35 Pl. de la République, Arles 13200, France (phone: 90-96-29-35); and Parc de la Camargue, Le Mas du Pont-de-Rousty, Arles 13200, France (phone: 90-97-10-40).

NATIONAL PARK OF THE PYRENEES, France: A mountain range rising as high as the 10,820-foot summit of Mt. Vignemale, the Pyrenees are one of the wildest of Europe's uncharted landscapes; this national park, established in 1967 by the French government, covers a huge area extending from Mt. Lariste to Port Vieux and makes a common boundary on the south with the Spanish National Park of Ordesa. The French park teems with exotic wildlife, including brown bears, ibex, chamois, griffon, and the rare lammergeier, with its huge 9-foot wing span. There are information centers at Arrens, Cauterets, and Arundy, and a well-maintained network of high mountain refuges. Information: Parc National des Pyrénées, BP 300, Tarbes 65013, France (phone: 62-93-30-60).

WALES, Great Britain: The Pembrokeshire Coast National Park, extending from Amroth to Cardigan, takes in a breathtaking 150 miles of rocky cliffs, remote bays, sandy inlets, wild headlands, and, offshore, tranquil islets. You can walk the length of the coastline on a marked footpath. Or, to the north, explore Snowdonia National Park's 1,000 square miles of rugged mountains and moors, limpid lakes, and rolling green countryside speckled with hewn-stone hamlets. You'll want to see the Gower Peninsula, the Mawddach Estuary, and the great monolithic castles of Caernarvon, Caerphilly, Conwy, Harlech, and take one of Wales's eight narrow-gauge steam railways. (Try Llanberis to the summit of Mt. Snowdon.) Go pony trekking in Brecon Beacons National Park. And see if you can llearne just thryye llyttle wyrdds of ancient Welsh. Information: Wales Tourist Board, Brunel House, 2 Fitzaland Road, Cardiff CF2 1UY, Wales (phone: 0222-27281). Ask for the booklets *Wales Walking* (hundreds of different routes) and *Where to Stay in Wales* (farmhouses, country inns, campsites).

IOS, Greece: One of the outermost of the Cyclades island group, Homer's reported burial place, and a pirates' lair, Ios has the dazzling Aegean beauty of its sister islands Mykonos and Paros, but 50 years' less development. Gleaming white churches and chapels and windmills perch on rolling green hills high above secluded, sand-rimmed bays. There's a sleepy harbor village, a fine bathing beach in Milokotos Bay, the remains of a temple of Apollo at Psathi. Life is very simple. Information: Greek National Tourist Organization, 645 Fifth Ave., New York, NY 10022 (phone: 212-421-5777). For hotel reservations: Hellenic Chamber of Hotels, 6 Aristidou St., Athens, Greece (phone: 323-6962).

FINNMARK COUNTY, Norway: The northernmost province of the northernmost country in Europe, Finnmark is well above the Arctic Circle and even shares an odd

100-mile border with the top of Russia; though temperatures rise in summer to a temperate 86F (30C), they plunge in winter to a glacial −60F (−51C). Yet it is a beautiful land, full of peaceful fishing villages, great fjords, vast snowfields that you can cross on sleds, craggy cliffs teeming with wild birds. The Alta may be the best salmon river in the world. Go in midsummer, when the days are warm and the sun never drops below the horizon; or at Easter when, following a picturesque age-old custom, the Lapps who tend the country's 130,000 reindeer drive the animals down to the seacoast. Information: Finnmark Reiselivsrad, Postboks 1223, Alta 9501 (phone: 084-35040).

PUSZCZA BIOLOWIESKA, Poland: One of the last strongholds of the majestic bison, this deep wilderness — the largest forest area in central Europe — also shelters wild boars, stags, lynxes, wolves, elk, and over 200 species of birds. Giant 500-year-old trees still flourish here, and in late September, during the mating season, the deer put on an enthralling spectacle. Culinary highlights of a visit to the area include mushrooms, wild blueberries, and Zubrowka, an aromatic vodka made from a local grass. Information: Orbis, Individual Travel Dept., 142 Marszalkowska, Warsaw, 00061 Poland (phone: 278031) or from the Polish National Tourist Office, 333 N. Michigan Ave., Chicago, IL 60601 (phone: 312-236-9013).

PLITVICE LAKES NATIONAL PARK, Yugoslavia: Just 62 miles (100 km) from Zagreb, in the valley between the wooded mountains of the Mala Kapela and the Plješevica, 16 stunning emerald and turquoise lakes arranged in a series of terraces linked by churning cascades have left immense deposits of tufa and travertine, shaped into marvelous dams and stalactites. The primeval forests around them are fragrant with evergreens, and the sparkling lakes are filled with trout. And in the winter the ice skating can be a mystical experience. Local information is readily available from park attendants or hotel staff members. Or contact Nacionalni Park, 4823 Plitvička Jezera, Yugoslavia (phone: 76314); or the Yugoslav State Tourist Office, Rockefeller Center, Suite 280, 630 Fifth Ave., New York, NY 10111 (phone: 212-757-2801).

For the Mind

Twenty-Five Centuries of History: Europe's Great Museums

 Museum-going is a fine art — one essential to travel enjoyment, but one that few people seem able to master. On the one hand there are the camera-toting tourists like the one in the old *New Yorker* cartoon who accosts a *Louvre* guard: "Quick — where's the *Mona Lisa?* I'm double-parked." Then there are the "serious" tourists in sensible shoes and glasses who plod through the cluttered halls of the *Uffizi,* Baedecker in hand, trying to absorb 600 years of European paintings in an afternoon. Both groups would probably rather be somewhere else.

But museum-going can be a great pleasure if you follow a few simple guidelines. First, make several short visits to a large museum rather than one long one. Stay just an hour and take in no more than a dozen really fine works. (You wouldn't try to skim 70 novels in a morning.)

There is no fatigue like aching, yawny museum fatigue and once it sets in, merely sitting for 3 minutes in front of a Rubens won't cure it. So go when you're fresh — preferably as soon as the museum opens, before the crowds have arrived, or at lunchtime, when the hordes are off refueling.

If possible, know what you want to see before beginning your rounds, so that you don't clutter your senses with bleeding saints and blustery seascapes. At the very least, stop on your way *in* to thumb the catalog and finger the postcards to get an idea of what there is to see and where you'll find it. And when you look at the paintings, don't look at the nameplate first. (You'll find out quickly enough what *you* really like as opposed to what you're *supposed* to like.)

Remember that a very personal experience of a minor museum can be more satisfying than an endless ramble through one of Europe's great warehouses of beauty. There is something essentially deadening about the format in which we are obliged to view the world's greatest art. Break away in any way you can: Take an hour's drive in the country just to see Piero della Francesca's *Madonna del Parto* in the cemetery of tiny Monterchi, 70 miles (112.5 km) southeast of Florence. Don't forget that single altarpiece in the empty village church, the grouping of portraits adorning the fireplace of the ancient mansion — art in the environment for which it was created. And visit a gallery or an auction house occasionally, just to remind yourself that once it was *all* for sale.

KUNSTHISTORISCHES MUSEUM, Vienna, Austria: The heart of the great Habsburg collection, opened to the public by Joseph II, the People's Emperor, survived two world wars intact and appears here today in most of its imperial glory. If you had an hour to devote to just one museum in Europe, you couldn't do better than to spend it in the room that this museum devotes to the work of Pieter Breughel, that dark Flemish Renaissance genius who executed the grotesque *Peasant Wedding,* the icily beautiful *Hunters in the Snow,* and the lunatic *Battle of Carnival and Lent.* Elsewhere, you'll find a roomful of works by Rubens, including the famous portrait of a nude, fur-swathed Helene Fourment, and the Ildefonso altar painting as well as a stunning assortment of Albrecht Dürers and Jan van Eyck's *Cardinal of Santa Croce,* Giorgione's *Three Philosophers,* Titian's *Gypsy Madonna,* plus fine works by Cranach, Velázquez, Rembrandt, Holbein, Van Dyck, and Tintoretto. Open Tuesdays through Sundays from 10 AM to 6 PM,; on Tuesday and Friday evenings parts of the museum are also open until 9 PM, when illumination gives the paintings a special glamour. Closed Mondays. Information: Kunsthistorisches Museum, 1 Maria-Theresien-Platz, Vienna, Austria.

BRITISH MUSEUM, London, England: Trying to knock off this gigantic storehouse of world culture in a single visit is like trying to master nuclear physics while in the barber's chair. The crown jewels of the collection, mainly devoted to archaeology and human history, are the renowned *Elgin Marbles* — the massive sculpture and relief saved from the ruins of the Parthenon and carted off to safe, civil England. Here, too, you'll find the *Rosetta Stone,* the black basalt tablet that provided the key to Egyptian hieroglyphics; the *Royal Gold Cup;* the *Portland Vase;* the *Sutton Hoo Ship Burial.* The collections of Greek, Roman, and Egyptian antiquities are unrivaled anywhere in the world, and one permanent display is devoted entirely to Etruscan civilization. "Man Before Metals" gives you an enthralling look at the art and technology of the Stone Age. The Near and Far Eastern departments are magnificent reminders of the time when Britannia ruled the waves. And at the library's check-out desk, you can ask to inspect one of Shakespeare's first folios. Open Mondays through Saturdays, 10 AM to 5 PM, and on Sundays from 2:30 to 6 PM. Information: British Museum, Great Russell St., London WC1B 3DG, England.

NATIONAL GALLERY, London, England: Started by the British Government in 1824 with the purchase of 38 paintings, the *National Gallery* now houses one of the finest representative collections of European painting from the 13th to the 19th centuries. Among its masterpieces are the *Arnolfini Wedding* of Jan van Eyck; Piero della Francesca's *Baptism of Jesus;* Caravaggio's *Christ at Emmaus;* Botticelli's *Nativity;* Goya's *Dr. Peral;* and a moving, pitiless self-portrait by Rembrandt. Save for a rainy day the very best of British painting, from Hogarth to Turner, though even on your first visit you might catch a glimpse of Constable's *Hadleigh Castle* and Turner's *Fighting Téméraire.* Open weekdays 10 AM to 6 PM and on Sundays from 2 to 6 PM. Information: National Gallery, Trafalgar Sq., London WC2N 5DN, England.

TATE GALLERY, London, England: A gift of Sir Henry Tate, built in 1897 on the site of Millbank Prison, the *Tate* is the national collection of modern painting and sculpture, but also contains British painting of the past. It boasts one of the world's best collections of French Impressionist and post-Impressionist works as well as excellent examples of the sculpture of Rodin, Maillol, Mestrovic, Moore, and Epstein. The British Department is the best place to see the work of William Blake, and the extraordinary Turner collection is in the Clare Gallery. The *Tate* is also very energetic about mounting vast special exhibitions of work on loan from abroad. Open weekdays 10 AM to 6 PM and Sundays 2 to 6 PM. Information: The Tate Gallery, Millbank, London SW1P 4RG, England.

CENTRE GEORGES POMPIDOU, Paris, France: Known as the *Beaubourg* (after the plateau on which it is built), the most arresting thing here is the building itself — a multicolored carnival of tubes, girders, and transparent escalators that looks as though it were built with a giant Erector set. A modern Parisian landmark, this potpourri of ever-changing exhibitions spans world culture, covering everything from an Einstein memorial to the history of the jukebox. Crowded with visitors all day until its closing at 10 PM, it is probably the most successful attempt at museum-making in years. Open weekdays except Tuesdays from noon to 10 PM; weekends from 10 AM to

10 PM. Information: Centre Georges Pompidou, Rue Rambuteau at the corner of Rue St.-Martin, Paris, France (phone: 42-77-12-33).

MUSÉE D'ORSAY, Paris, France: The Impressionist paintings that once crowded intimately into the joyfully informal *Jeu de Paume* museum have found a more spacious and sober home. The brilliant transformation of a vast turn-of-the-century glass and cast-iron train station into a museum has brought the best artistic production of France from 1848 to 1914 under one vaulted, translucent roof. Now Degas, Monet, and Renoir are hung in specially designed spaces within this railroad-cathedral, which they share with 600 fellow painters and sculptors. No detail of light, humidity, or acoustics has been left to chance, and visitors will make this voyage around the art world in perfect comfort and ease. The high point — the Van Goghs on the top floor, glowing under the northern Parisian skylight. Closed Mondays. Information: Musée d'Orsay, Rue de Bellechasse, Paris 75007, France (phone: 45-49-48-14).

LOUVRE, Paris, France: This colossal haystack crammed with needles was initiated by François I in the 16th century with 12 paintings and the casts of a few of his favorite Greek sculptures. Today, a one-way stroll through each of its treasure-laden rooms would cover over 8 miles — and if you never saw the inside of another museum, you could still form a very complete picture of European, Oriental, and ancient art from a study of its collection. You couldn't miss the *Mona Lisa* or the *Venus de Milo* if you were dead set on doing so. But a few delights are easily overlooked in the lavish confusion: van Eyck's *Madonna of Chancellor Rolin;* Albrecht Dürer's *Self-Portrait;* Rigaud's portrait of the narcissistic *Louis XIV;* Ingres's *Turkish Bath;* Frans Hals's *Bohemian;* Memling's *Portrait of an Old Woman;* a small medieval gilded wood statuette of St. Stephen; and the *Handmaiden of the Dead,* a 4,000-year-old Egyptian wood carving of a young girl bearing food and wine for the banquet after death. Open daily 9:45 AM to 6:30 PM, daily except Tuesdays. Information: The Louvre, Palais du Louvre, Paris, France (phone: 42-60-39-26).

DEUTSCHES MUSEUM, Munich, Germany: A change of pace, from the aesthetic to the technical. Unique in Europe, this huge complex on an islet in the Isar River covers the entire history of the development of man's knowledge of the natural sciences and his mastery of technology. Displays include everything from ancient compasses to modern aircraft. Some items are original, others are "faithful to the last detail" reconstructions. There are plenty of hands-on exhibits that can be activated by the spectator, and so children generally go gleefully out of their minds here. But even to diehards who ordinarily prefer Titian to fission, the museum is fascinating and you don't have to be a scientist to enjoy it. Open daily 9 AM to 5 PM. Information: Deutsches Museum, Museuminsel 1, Munich 22 D-8000, Germany (phone: 089-21791).

NATIONAL ARCHAEOLOGICAL MUSEUM, Athens, Greece: The nation's largest museum houses archaeological treasures found all over the country and from every period of ancient Greek history. Without a certain amount of scholarly preparation, you are not likely to be able to distinguish the Neolithic from the Cycladic from the Mycenaean — so just allow yourself to be overwhelmed by this matchless legacy of the most gifted civilization on record. You'll see sculptured bronze shields right from the pages of *The Iliad;* golden mortuary masks; Cycladic idols; Thessalian ceramics; the frescoes recently unearthed on the island of Santorini; and vast quantities of sculpture, including the *Philosopher of Antikythira,* the grave shrine of Aristonautes, the *Poseidon of Artemission,* and the *Dipylon Head.* Open daily except Mondays, 9 AM to 3 PM in winter, 8 AM to 5 PM in summer, Sundays 9:30 AM to 2:30 PM. Information: National Archaeological Museum, 1 Tossitsa St., Athens, Greece.

GALLERIA DEGLI UFFIZI, Florence, Italy: While you are hiking through the glowing rooms of the Uffizi, awash in the golden tides of the Italian Renaissance, just consider that over 90% of Italy's artistic patrimony is stacked in dingy storerooms, hanging in museum wings permanently closed for lack of personnel, and adorning the offices of petty bureaucrats in obscure ministries and consulates out of public view. Consequently, what you see here is the *crema della crema della crema* by Botticelli, Leonardo, Raphael, Piero della Francesca, Giotto, Caravaggio, and virtually every other major Italian artist. Particularly beautiful, and often overlooked, are the 13th- and 14th-century religious paintings on wood panels. Recent hours were from 9 AM to 7 PM, Tuesdays through Saturdays, 9 AM to 1 PM on Sundays; closed on Mondays. But the *Uffizi*'s schedule is frequently shuffled by personnel shortages, labor disputes, and artistic excess. Best to check just before a visit. Information: Galleria degli Uffizi, 6 Loggiato degli Uffizi, Florence, Italy.

VATICAN MUSEUMS, Rome, Italy: The *Vatican Museums* attract not only the usual population of museum-goers, but also pilgrims and Vatican visitors — so crowding can be a problem, and the Sistine Chapel, in particular, often has an aura of the subway in rush hour. (Restoration of the chapel's ceilings and walls will be completed by 1992.) The morning is probably the best time to go: Grab your ticket and dash past the papal robes, old maps, and tomb inscriptions, and you'll leave the school groups and convent delegations far behind. Your goals are the Raphael rooms, the classical statuary (including the *Apollo Belvedere* and the *Laocoön*), the tapestry gallery, and the works of Fra Angelico, Giotto, and Filippo Lippi in the Pinacoteca. This is a difficult museum, and so a catalogue is a good investment. One more word to the weary: Don't combine the museums with a visit to St. Peter's. Open Mondays through Saturdays, and the last Sunday of every month, from 9 AM to 2 PM (but no admittance after 1 PM); and until 5 PM (admission until 4 PM) from July to September. Information: The Vatican Museums, Viale Vaticano, Rome, Italy.

RIJKSMUSEUM, Amsterdam, The Netherlands: The huge red brick building is one of a complex of four museums clustered around Museumplein. (The others are the *Van Gogh Museum,* the *Stedelijk,* and the *Over Holland,* devoted to modern art.) The star attraction at the *Rijksmuseum* is the incomparable Rembrandt collection, which includes *The Night Watch, The Anatomy Lesson, The Jewish Betrothal, The Drapers' Guild,* and a magnificent self-portrait. Here, there are Rembrandts by the roomful. But you'll also find lovely Vermeers, including the famous *Milkmaid,* along with works by Frans Hals, whose *Married Couple* ranks among northern Europe's greatest paintings. There's more — but stick with the Dutch masters on your first visit. Open daily except Mondays, 10 AM to 5 PM and Sundays 1 PM to 5 PM. Information: Rijksmuseum, 42 Stadhouderskade, Amsterdam, Holland. Also visit Rembrandt's house at 4 Jodenbreestraat. Open daily 10 AM to 5 PM and Sundays 1 PM to 5 PM.

PRADO, Madrid, Spain: The heart of the *Prado* is the regal collection assembled by Spain's Bourbon and Habsburg kings. Concentrate first on works by the four great Spanish masters: Velázquez, El Greco, Murillo, and Goya, whose progression from fashionable court painter to embittered madman is documented in breathtaking detail. Then turn to an excellent selection of works by another genius, Hieronymus Bosch, and to the fine Van Dycks, Titians, and Tintorettos — all hanging here as a result of Spain's royal ties with Flanders and Italy. Goya's *Maja Desnuda* is here, as is Velázquez's great *Las Meninas* (which you can view in a mirror, just as it was painted), and a delightful statue of a reclining Hermaphrodite. Thirteen rooms of Flemish masterpieces have opened up. (Picasso's fabled *Guernica* is housed nearby, in the Casón del Buen Retiro.) Open 10 AM to 5 PM Tuesdays through Saturdays, 10 AM to 6 PM in summer. The museum closes at 2 PM on Sundays and is closed on Mondays year-round. Information: The Prado, Paseo del Prado, Madrid, Spain.

HERMITAGE, Leningrad, USSR: For a long time after its founding, the czars made the opulent *Hermitage* the private preserve of themselves and their friends, and it was only with the revolution that the public got a look at the splendid contents — works on the order of Gainsborough's *Duchess of Beaufort;* Renoir's *Girl with a Fan;* Ingres's *Portrait of Count Guriev;* Breughel's *Fair;* Rembrandt's *Old Man in Red;* Titian's

Danaë; Holbein's *Portrait of a Young Man;* and a wonderful, little-known Michelangelo sculpture, the *Crouching Boy.* As you might expect, a great deal of space is allotted to Russian history and culture, and exhibits run the gamut from exquisite antique silver and a map of the Soviet Union in semiprecious stones to "The Heroic Military Past of the Russian People" and turn-of-the-century paintings with fetching titles like *The Dairymaid Spurned* and *The Volunteer Shall Return No More.* The Indian and Oriental art collections are first rate — but unless you are wintering in Leningrad, stick to the magnificent European collection. Open daily from 10:30 AM to 6 PM (summer months: 10 AM to 5 PM); closed on Tuesdays. Information: The Hermitage, 36 Dvortsovaya Naberezhnaya, Leningrad, USSR.

MORE GREAT PAINTINGS

A number of the Continent's finest works of art will be found outside the museums listed above. Here's where you'll find a selection of the standouts.

Cathedral of St. Bavon, Ghent, Belgium – *The Adoration of the Mystical Lamb,* by Jan and Hubert van Eyck.

Musée des Beaux-Arts, Ghent, Belgium – *The Carrying of the Cross,* by Hieronymus Bosch.

Ny Carlsberg Glyptotek, Copenhagen, Denmark – Paul Gauguin's *Vahine No Te Tiare.*

Musée National Marc Chagall, Nice, France – Chagall's *L'Arc-en-ciel.*

Alte Pinakothek, Munich, Germany – Pieter Paul Rubens's *Rubens and Isabella Brant* and Albrecht Dürer's *Portrait of Osvolt Krel.*

Staatsgalerie, Munich, Germany – Edouard Manet's *Lunch in the Studio.*

Pinacoteca Comunale, Borgo San Sepolcro, Italy – Piero della Francesca's *The Resurrection.*

Museo Diocesano, Cortona, Italy – Fra Angelico's *The Annunciation.*

Palazzo Ducale, Mantova, Italy – *La Camera degli Sposi,* by Mantegna.

Cenacolo Vinciano, Milan, Italy – Leonardo da Vinci's *Last Supper.*

Villa dei Misteri, Pompeii, Italy – The frescoes.

Cathedral of Siena, Siena, Italy – Duccio di Boninsegna's *The Maestá.*

Museo Correr, Venice, Italy – *The Courtesans,* by Vittore Carpaccio.

Kunstmuseum, Basel, Switzerland – Holbein's *Portrait of Boniface Amerbach.*

On the Boards: Theater and Opera in Europe

London should be a first — and prolonged — stop on any theatergoer's itinerary; the stages here are some of the liveliest in the world — and there's no language barrier. Yet even on the Continent there are several old, established English-language companies: the *English Theater* (12 Josefsgasse, Vienna, Austria; phone: 421260); the *English Theater of Paris* (55 Rue de Seine; phone: 43-26-63-51); and the *ABC Theater of Oslo,* which performs Scandinavian classics in English during the summer at a variety of sites. The *Café Theater* in Frankfurt (45 Hamburgerallée; phone: 777466) has even sent a play to New York's off-Broadway; and the *English Speaking Theater Amsterdam* plays the *Bellevue,* 90 Leidsekade, in winter months and the *Stadsschouwburg,* 26 Leidseplein, in summer.

Besides which, some theatricals — among Europe's best — are largely nonverbal.

And even when the language barrier does portend problems, you may encounter acting so compelling that you end up forgetting that you're not supposed to understand what's going on. In addition, many of Europe's great companies often perform international classics whose content is familiar. If you don't know the play, it's simple enough to search a city's largest bookstore for an English copy of the plays that are on. (Oddly enough, the simultaneous-translation earphone setups provided by some major theaters seem to create, rather than remove, a barrier between you and the players.)

What about tickets? Before leaving the US, pick up a copy of a local newspaper — the *London Times* or the *Sunday Observer* is the best for London goings-on — and figure out what to see. You can buy tickets in advance for productions of the *Royal Shakespeare Theatre* in Stratford-on-Avon, and for the *Edinburgh Festival,* in the US at *Keith Prowse & Co.,* 234 W. 44th St., New York, NY 10036 (phone: 212-398-1430; 800-223-4446 outside New York), and at *Edwards & Edwards,* One Times Sq. Plaza, New York, NY 10036 (phone: 212-944-0290 or 800-223-6108), both of which can provide tickets for other London theater and cultural events as well. The *London Theatre News* is a monthly newsletter on London theater. They also can provide help with ticket reservations and the like (12 E. 86th St., New York, NY 10028; phone: 212-517-8608). For tickets to performances in other cities, wait until you get there.

BURGTHEATER, Vienna, Austria: Over 200 years old, this is one of Europe's great theaters and most accomplished companies. The repertory has a decidedly classical flavor, and sooner or later, every important play written in German for the last 300 years crosses the stage. The building, at 2 Dr. Karl-Lueger Ring, is an imposing, colonnaded baroque palace, and a première is a glittering Viennese social occasion. The same company performs a somewhat flashier repertory at the *Akademie Theater.* Tickets for both are available from 2 months to 15 days in advance from the Österreichischer Bundestheaterverband, Bestellbüro, 1 Goethegasse, Vienna A-1010, Austria. A week or less in advance, try the central box office, 3 Hanuschgasse, behind the opera house (phone: 51444).

STEIRISCHER HERBST, Graz, Austria: This is a young, electric, eclectic arts festival (whose name translates "Styrian Autumn"); it generally plays from mid-September through early November. You'll encounter a good deal of experimental theater, nonverbal theater, and film; and the performing groups are from all over Europe and America, so language is not a constant problem. The festival is increasingly important as a place to see what's fresh in European theater. Information: Steirischer Herbst, Palais Attems, 17/I Sackstrasse, Graz 8010, Austria (phone: 0316-730070).

LATERNA MAGIKA, Prague, Czechoslovakia: This amalgam of cinema, opera, theater, and circus offers you one of the most fascinating spectacles on the Continent; the name, which translates as "Magic Lantern," attempts to convey the swirling, kaleidoscopic style. Now you know less about it than you did before, so just go — and take children. Information: Laterna Magika, 31 Jungmannova, Prague, Czechoslovakia (phone: 266765). Prague also has a long tradition of mime, and a genius named Fialka, the Marcel Marceau of the Second World, performs regularly at *Na Zabradli.*

NATIONAL THEATRE, London, England: If English-speaking theater is your religion, the *National Theatre* should be your temple. It is, in fact, a complex of three theaters (the *Olivier,* the *Lyttelton,* and the *Cottesloe*) on the South Bank of the Thames. And it is the direct descendant of the nearby *Old Vic,* which was, for decades, London's crown jewel. Gielgud, Richardson, Ashcroft, Plowright, Scofield, Guinness, Finney, and all the other English theater greats have performed here — and the repertory knows no bounds of time, nationality, or style. Information: National Theatre, South Bank, London SE1 9PX, England (phone: 928-2252; or, for recorded ticket information, 928-8126, 24 hours a day).

ROYAL SHAKESPEARE COMPANY, Stratford and London, England: This splendid company, which also picks its stars from the roster of English acting greats, performs in the splashy $280 million *Barbican Arts Centre* and at the *Mermaid Theatre* at Puddle Dock. In Stratford-on-Avon, its home is the *Royal Shakespeare Theatre,* set beautifully alongside the river, as well as the *Swan Theatre* and the tiny 150-seat *The Other Place.* The Stratford season runs from March through January. (Be warned that in midsummer busloads of holidaymakers, fresh from visits to see Anne Hathaway's chamber pot, turn the atmosphere a trifle frantic.) In London, you can generally buy tickets to a production with the same confidence that you'd pick up a Rolls or a Burberry. The company's specialty is breathing life into period pieces so obscure that even the boys at Eton don't have to read them. Information: Royal Shakespeare Theatre, Stratford-on-Avon, Warwickshire CV37 6BB, England (phone: 0789-295623; or, for 24-hour booking information, 0789-69191). In London: Barbican Theatre, 13 Cromwell Tower, Barbican EC2 (phone: 638-8891).

ROYAL COURT, London, England: Once termed experimental and even avant-garde, the *Royal Court* was where John Osborne introduced *Look Back in Anger,* where the Arnold Wesker trilogy was first performed, and where Harold Pinter vented his wrath on the English language. The audience is now very proper British and intermission crowds are indistinguishable from those, say, at the *Royal Ballet.* But the *Royal Court* is still *the* place to watch young England on stage. Information: The Royal Court Theatre, Sloane Sq., London SW1, England (phone: 730-1745).

CHICHESTER FESTIVAL THEATRE, Chichester, England: Launched in 1962, this drama festival offers four plays between May and September, with topflight casts on a par with anything you'd see in London's West End. The theater, a striking hexagonal structure in the middle of a 40-acre parkland, lies just a 1½-hour train ride from Victoria Station. And during the main season, trains don't leave Chichester until the final curtain has fallen. Information: Chichester Festivities, Canon Gate House, South St., Chichester, West Sussex PO19 1PU, England (phone: 0243-785718).

THE HELSINKI FESTIVALS, Helsinki, Finland: More than a decade ago, Finland introduced over 800 summer festivals, produced and presented in various sections of the country. The idea was to attract foreign visitors and to familiarize them with the Finnish people and their achievements and, at the same time, to entertain them with local professional talent and international luminaries. The events range from symphonic concerts and opera performances in a 15th-century castle courtyard to rock, folk, jazz, and pop music; to art exhibitions; to seminars on world problems — cultural fare for everyone, including the small fry. For information, contact *Finland Festivals,* 3A Vuorikatu, 17th floor (phone: 607386).

The *Finland Festival* programs generally start in mid-June and run till mid-August. These are followed by the big *Helsinki Festival,* which stages as many as 100 events between late August and early September. For complete program information, contact *Helsinki Festival,* 28 Unioninkatu (phone: 659688).

COMÉDIE-FRANÇAISE, Paris, France: As much a part of Paris as the *Louvre,* its next-door neighbor, and as French as the Académie Française, the *Comédie-Française* is as totally dedicated as either to the preservation of Gallic language and culture and its productions run to Racine and Corneille, frothy Molière, *Cyrano de Bergerac* done in the grand manner, and even *Waiting for Godot,* now that it's a classic. All the great names of French theater do a turn at the *Comédie,* and even if you know no more French than "La plume de ma tante," go. (Just think of it as a visit to another national monument.) Information: Comédie-Française, 2 Rue de Richelieu, Paris, France (phone: 40-15-00-15).

L'ODÉON, Paris, France: One of France's richly endowed (talent and money) national theaters, the *Odéon*'s style is more streamlined and flashy than some of its conventional cousins. Guest productions from the best French theatrical companies, as well as such glittering foreign attractions as the *Peking Art Theater,* the *Greek*

National Theater performing *Euripides,* and Ingmar Bergman directing Shakespeare. Information: L'Odéon, Pl. de l'Odéon, Paris, France (phone: 43-25-70-32).

MARCEL MARCEAU, Paris, France: Just as the world had only one Edith Piaf and only one Maurice Chevalier, there is only one Marcel Marceau — and if you've never seen him, you're missing a treat. After a long struggle with the forces of anticreation, he has opened his own school of mime, the *Ecole Internationale de Mimodrame,* and, though much of the year sees him gesturing and grimacing his way around the world, he can be found here when he's in Paris. Information: Ecole Internationale de Mimodrame, Rue René-Boulanger 17, Paris, France (phone: 42-09-65-86).

THÉÂTRE RENAUD-BARRAULT, Paris, France: This is the home theater of the reigning king and queen of the French stage — Jean-Louis Barrault and Madeleine Renaud. The repertory is diverse and far-ranging, but there's a good, steady diet of Beckett and Ionesco as well as important new foreign plays. The theater is also a gathering place for stage personalities from all over Europe. Information: Théâtre Renaud-Barrault, Av. Franklin-Roosevelt, Paris, France (phone: 42-56-60-70).

SCHILLER-THEATER, West Berlin, Germany: With one of Europe's richest theatrical traditions, the Berlin stage nurtured half a dozen actors and actresses who later became major stars on Broadway and in Hollywood. The *Schiller,* the prince of German theaters, specializes in lavish, highly styled productions of the classics. Information: Schiller-Theater, 110 Bismarckstrasse, West Berlin, Germany (phone: 319-5236). While you're in town, try to catch a political cabaret, another staple of the German theater scene. Best bets are *Die Stachelschweine* in the Europa-Center (phone: 261-4795) and *Die Wühlmause,* 33 Nürnbergerstrasse (phone: 213-7047). And don't miss the famous *Berliner Ensemble* of Brecht-Weill-Lenya fame; it's well worth crossing The Wall for. Information: Berliner Ensemble, Bertolt Brecht Platz, East Berlin, East Germany (phone: 282-3160).

NATIONAL THEATER OF GREECE, Athens and Epidaurus, Greece: Productions here take you as close as you can get to the mysterious, ritualistic origins of the theater: where the national Greek company performs ancient Greek plays in their original settings. The *Athens Festival* runs throughout the summer in the Odeon of Herod Atticus at the foot of the Acropolis. The *Epidaurus Festival* spans July and August, set in the spectacular theater of Epidaurus, about 90 miles (145 km) southwest of Athens. Information and tickets for both: Greek National Tourist Organization, 2 Spirou Miliou Arcade, Athens, Greece (phone: 322-1459). Tickets are on sale at the Epidaurus amphitheater only on the day of the performance (phone: 0753-21005).

ABBEY THEATRE, Dublin, Ireland: The history of Ireland's national theater goes back into the last century, but its current $2.5-million home (the original "Shabby" having burned in 1951) was built in 1966. The pride of Dublin and the cradle of spirited Irish rhetoric, the *Abbey* is still home to Synge, Yeats, O'Casey, Behan — and the best in modern Irish drama as well. Catch an evening of *Playboy of the Western World* or *Juno and the Paycock,* have a quick whiskey around the corner on O'Connell Street, and, in the space of 3 hours, you can pretty much sense the essence of Ireland. Information: Abbey Theatre, Lower Abbey St., Dublin 1, Ireland (phone: 787-222).

PICCOLO TEATRO, Milan, Italy: Founded just after World War II under the aegis of Giorgio Strehler, the *Piccolo* is Italy's number one company. The original mission was to take theater out of the idle hands of the elite and make it a vital instrument of popular culture — and the spirit still survives, though furs and jewels often clog its modest foyer. The repertory is international and imaginative, the production style original and intense. And there is always talk about keeping the *Piccolo* pure. Along with *La Scala,* this is the city's principal cultural institution. It has finally expanded into new, less piccolo quarters after a decade of debate. Information: Piccolo Teatro, Via Rovello 2, Palazzo del Broletto, Milan 20100, Italy (phone: 869-0631).

EDINBURGH FESTIVAL, Edinburgh, Scotland: Part music and part theater, this mid-August to early September event gets much of its enormous vitality from the Fringe, a ragtag collection of a hundred-odd new productions that arrive in the city every year like a convention of sidewalk artists. Some are scruffy, low-budget, op-pop-punk improvisations. Others — remember *Beyond the Fringe?* — are out-of-town previews for big-time productions. For regular festival information and tickets: Edinburgh International Festival of Music and Drama, 21 Market St., Edinburgh, Scotland (phone: 226-4001). The Fringe has separate quarters: Festival Fringe Society, 170 High St., Edinburgh EH1 1QS, Scotland (phone: 226-5257).

OPERA

Unlike theater, the great opera houses of Europe share a common pool of talent and music. A case in point was *Carmen* (French) at the *Vienna Staatsoper* (Austrian), conducted by Kleiber (German), directed by Zeffirelli (Italian), and sung by Domingo (Spanish) and Obrazova (Russian).

However, operas are generally best heard on their own territory — Wagner in Germany, Verdi in Italy, Bizet in France. Even if the soloists are of mixed nationalities, there is something about most productions that doesn't travel quite as well as you might expect. At any rate, if you are seeing a visiting team, ask what language the performance will be sung in: You might prefer not to hear a Sicilian Brunhilde or a Tyrolean Carmen.

The finely tuned tentacles of the German opera world extend far beyond the city limits of Munich, Berlin, and Frankfurt, and while it's risky to be out of earshot of Avenue de l'Opéra in France, in Germany, a sort of vast, well-managed farm system makes it possible to hear first-rate performances in any one of a dozen provincial centers.

Meanwhile, opera is most fun in Italy (even when questionably performed): Rather than the reverent silence of Teutonic audiences, you'll find zestful participation, and, in the south and the provinces, opera-goers sound catcalls for clinkers and hum along the rest of the time. And — either because of training methods or government subsidies or unpolluted air — the most exciting new voices are turning up in Eastern Europe; and the unknown with the unpronounceable name you may hear in Prague or Warsaw may soon be getting top billing in London or New York.

In general, however, you'll see the best performances at the festivals of *Salzburg, Wiener Festwochen, Bayreuth, Berliner Festwochen, Munich,* and the *Maggio Musicale Fiorentino.* (See *Music Festivals* for descriptions.) From mid-July to late August, try the festival at the *Arena of Verona.* Information: Ente Autonomo Spettacoli Lirici Arena di Verona, 28 Piazza Bra, Verona 37121, Italy (phone: 045-800-5151). And, of course, don't miss these great European opera houses:

The *Staatsoper,* 2 Opernring, Vienna, Austria (phone: 5324-2655). Great for Richard Strauss.

The *Volksoper,* 78 Wahringerstrasse, Vienna, Austria (phone: 5324-2657). Good for Johann Strauss; specializes in Viennese operetta.

English National Opera Company, at the Coliseum, St. Martin's La., London WC2, England (phone: 836-3161). Great opera classics performed in English.

The *Royal Opera House,* Covent Garden, Floral St., London WC2, England (phone: 240-1066, box office; 240-1911, other information).

L'Opéra, Pl. de l'Opéra, Paris, France (phone: 47-42-57-50). For advance bookings, write the Service Location par Correspondance, 8 Rue Scribe, Paris 75009, France.

The *Bayerische Staatsoper,* in the *National Theater,* 2 Max-Joseph-Platz, Munich 2 8000, Germany (phone: 221316).

The *Deutsche Oper,* 10 Richard Wagner Strasse, Berlin 1000, Germany (phone: 341-4449).

La Scala, 2 Via dei Filodrammatici, Milan, Italy (phone: 807041).

San Carlo, Via San Carlo, Naples, Italy (phone: 797-2370).

Teatro La Fenice, 2549 San Fantin, Venice, Italy (phone: 521-0161).

Gran Teatro del Liceu, 65 Rambla Caputxins, Barcelona, Spain (phone: 318-9122; box office, 301-6787).

Bolshoi Opera, Bolshoi Theater, 1 Sverdlov Square, Moscow, USSR.

Europe's Magnificent Music Festivals

 Every summer, Europe bursts into garlands of music festivals, looped in bright tones across the Continent in every direction. Some — like those at Salzburg and Bayreuth — are distinguished old celebrations of musical genius. Others are Ludwig-come-latelies whose thinly disguised purpose is to drum up tourist trade for otherwise quaint but hardly notable old villages. Still, they can make for a pleasant end to a day at the beach, and there will be plenty of last-minute tickets (or space for your blanket on the village green), though the major ones, serious musical pilgrimages, sell out months in advance.

Most of the festivals make inspired use of their home city's finest monuments — ducal palaces, castle courtyards, and Gothic cathedrals — so that concert-going becomes sightseeing. Moreover, music often acquires a new power outside the concert hall. For events not listed here, a good source worth consulting is *Music Festivals in Europe and Britain* by Carol Rabin (Berkshire Traveller Press, Stockbridge, MA 02168; $6.95 plus $2 for postage and handling).

SALZBURG FESTIVAL, Salzburg, Austria: Tickets to concerts of this generally recognized king of European festivals are high — but requests outnumber places by about four to one, and hotel accommodations during the run of the event, between late July and late August, are scarcer still. Still, if you can swing it and if you can afford it, there's nothing else quite like Salzburg. The performers are the best in the world, the audiences are distinguished and reverent, and you can't help but feel as if you are hearing Mozart for the first time. Write for a program in the fall and for tickets by Christmas. Bring dressy clothes: to Austrians, the marriage of Figaro is almost more important than their own. And if you happen to be cruising in the area, without any advance planning, give the festival a try anyway: Tickets for some of the delightful morning chamber concerts are often available. Or the concierge of the *Goldener Hirsch* may slip you one for *Don Giovanni* if you slip him $200; and if somebody dies, he may even let you share a room. Information: Salzburger Festspiele, 140 Postfach, Salzburg 5010, Austria (phone: 0662-842541).

WIENER FESTWOCHEN, Vienna, Austria: Music, as every schoolchild knows, was invented in Vienna; and for 5 weeks every year between early May and early June, the city holds a melomanic orgy to commemorate the event. Bernstein, Levine, and Abbado come to town, with theater groups from all over Europe; and there are new productions at the Staatsoper, premières of new plays, art exhibitions, symposia, colloquia, and plain old songfests. And every one of the city's 23 *Bezirke* (districts) sponsors special district programs. Spring is a nice time to see the city. Information: Wiener Festwochen, 11 Léhargasse, Vienna A-1060, Austria (phone: 586-1676).

FLANDERS FESTIVAL, Brussels, Belgium: The most important collection of musical events in Belgium, this festival is celebrated from spring into October in a number of Belgian towns — Ghent, Bruges, Mechelen, Antwerp, Leuven, and Brussels. Often concerts take place in the towns' most beautiful buildings. Information: Festival van Vlaanderen, 18 Eugeen Flageyplein, Brussels B-1050, Belgium (phone: 648-1484).

PRAGUE SPRING, Prague, Czechoslovakia: This doyen of European festivals has been around since 1945. Conductors and soloists from Eastern Europe are always on the program, along with some fine Russian artists whose performances usually sell out by the time they reach *Carnegie Hall*. Mid-May to early June. Information: International Music Festival "Prague Spring," Dum Umelcu, 12 Alsovo Nabrezi, Prague 1 CS-11001, Czechoslovakia (phone: 231-9307).

BATH FESTIVAL, Bath, England: The weeks between mid-May and early June are beautiful ones in this lovely Georgian town, and the festival offers music to match — a splendid selection of choral works that pays homage to composers like Glück, Monteverdi, and Purcell, and a variety of interesting chamber performances, plus walking tours, film shows, art exhibitions, and garden tours. Information (from January through June): Bath Festival Office, Linley House, 1 Pierrepont Pl., Bath BA1 1JY, England (phone: 0225-63362). Booking in the US through Edwards and Edwards, 1 Times Square, New York, NY 10036 (phone: 212-944-0290).

CHELTENHAM FESTIVAL, Cheltenham, England: Founded just after World War II in this gracious Regency spa, the *Cheltenham Festival* exploits majestic settings like the Pittville Pump Room and the Victorian Town Hall to enhance a musical menu that can run from ancient madrigals to the best in British contemporary. You may also hear the world première of works specially commissioned for the festival. Two weeks in July, with the enchanting Cotswold Hills and Severn Vale a short drive away. Information: Cheltenham Festival Office, Town Hall, Cheltenham, Gloucestershire GL50 1QA, England (phone: 0242-521621).

INTERNATIONAL FESTIVAL OF LYRICAL AND MUSICAL ARTS, Aix-en-Provence, France: This is one of the most attractive towns in the South of France, and the festival, which runs from early July to early August, uses several locations, including two cloisters, the Cathedral of St. Sauveur, the courtyard of the Archbishop's Palace, and the lovely Place des Quatres Dauphins. There is a strong emphasis on what the festival committee calls "the most beautiful instrument" — the human voice — but you'll hear works of all vintages, from early Corelli to late Stockhausen to Negro spirituals. Information: Festival International d'Art Lyrique et de Musique, Palais de l'Ancien Archevêché, Aix-en-Provence 13100, France (phone: 42-23-37-81).

INTERNATIONAL CHAMBER MUSIC FESTIVAL, Divonne-les-Bains, France: Held in a sleepy little village, a 15-minute drive across the border from Geneva, the site of France's most profitable casino, this connoisseur's festival presents chamber music (and only chamber music) of the highest caliber in the jewel-like *Théâtre de Divonne,* whose whimsical decor would enliven even an amateur bassoon recital. At the end of June or the beginning of July, an excursion here can be delightful, so delightful in fact that some particularly faithful patrons come all the way from Paris for a single concert. Information: Syndicat d'Initiative, Rue des Bains BP 23, Divonne-les-Bains 01220, France (phone: 50-20-01-22). (See also *Gambling.*)

FESTIVAL DE STRASBOURG, Strasbourg, France: This 3-week event has been held annually in early June since 1938 and takes place mostly in the *Palais de la Musique et des Congrès,* but some events are also held in the town's majestic cathedral as well as at other venues; succeeding days in one recent year saw performances by pianists Claudio Arrau and Vladimir Ashkenazy, violinist Itzhak Perlman, conductor Leonard Bernstein, singers Pilar Lorengar and Marilyn Horne, and the *Juilliard Quartet.* Between concerts, you can eat yourself under the harpsichord: Strasbourg is generally acknowledged to serve more luscious food than any other town in France (see *The*

Shrines of European Gastronomy). Information: Festival de Strasbourg, 24 Rue de la Mésange, Strasbourg 67081, France (phone: 88-32-43-10).

BAYREUTH FESTIVAL, Bayreuth, Germany: This is the festival that Wagner built. A month-long orgy of Teutonic splendor that occupies the town every year beginning in late July, it features half a dozen Wagner operas presented in the theater that Wagner himself designed for this purpose, just down the road from a museum devoted to him. In their way, the audiences are as devoted as those who worshiped at Woodstock — different god, though, and a different crowd. Information: Bayreuth Festival, Postfach 100262, Bayreuth D-8580, Germany (phone: 921-20221).

BERLINER FESTWOCHEN, Berlin, Germany: Held every September during the crisp Berlin autumn, this eclectic festival offers a wide range of opera, orchestral music, chamber music, theater, mime, dance, and an assortment of circus performances. The roster of conductors who appeared here in one 30-day stretch not long ago — Böhm, Solti, Inbal, Stockhausen, Leinsdorf, Giulini, Abbado, Von Karajan — reads like the list of graduates of Mt. Olympus Conservatory. Information: Berliner Festspiele, Postfach 301648, Berlin 30 D-1000, Germany (phone: 254890).

MUNICH OPERA FESTIVAL, Munich, Germany: In early July, while most of Europe's opera houses sleep, Munich explodes for a melodious month with the music of Wagner, Strauss, Mozart, and, occasionally, the works of hot-blooded Latins like Verdi and Donizetti as well. Performances are held in the monumental *National Theater* and the miraculous *Cuvilliés Theater* (also known as the *Altes Residenztheater*), perhaps the most beautiful auditorium in Europe. Information: Münchner Opernfestspiele, Bayerische Staatsoper, Postfach 745, München 1 D-8000, Germany (phone: 089-21851).

MAGGIO MUSICALE FIORENTINO, Florence, Italy: Italy's answer to Salzburg presents artists just as fine, but programs so much more diverse that it seems a conscious attempt is being made to avoid musical chauvinism; you are as likely to hear Berg and Stravinsky as Rossini and Puccini. Some of the concerts are held in the magical Boboli Gardens — lovely and quintessentially Italian on a June evening. Despite its name, which translates as "Florentine Musical May," the festival continues right through June as well. Information: Maggio Musicale Fiorentino, Teatro Comunale, 15 Via Solferino, Florence 50123, Italy (phone: 27791).

INTERNATIONAL FESTIVAL OF THE TWO WORLDS, Spoleto, Italy: Founded in 1957 by Maestro Gian Carlo Menotti, this celebrated event, which begins in mid-June every year, brings together performers from both sides of the Atlantic for 3 weeks of dance, poetry readings, concerts, drama, opera, and art exhibits; the festival is celebrated for the diversity and high quality of its concerts and for the sizable number of premières of new works on its programs. However, the setting is equally noteworthy. Spoleto, which was the capital for the Dukes of Lombard between the 6th and 8th centuries, is a picturesque place, full of narrow vaulted passages and interesting nooks and crannies, quaint old shops and colorful markets. The final concert is traditionally held in front of the 12th-century cathedral, with the audience sitting on the majestic stairway that overlooks it — in the shadow of handsome palaces and hanging gardens. Menotti himself is still actively involved. Information: Festival dei Due Mondi, 17 Via Margutta, Rome (phone: 361-4009).

EDINBURGH FESTIVAL, Edinburgh, Scotland: Between late August and early September, the *Edinburgh Festival* presents a diverse, jam-packed program of music and theater that includes everything from the *Scottish Chamber Orchestra* playing in the stately 18th-century Hopetoun House to pop-rock multimedia happenings on the steps of the post office to old-fashioned British military tattoos. An assemblage of innovative, low-budget productions known as the Fringe gives the festival its color. The substance derives from the first-rate program of superb operas, concerts, and recitals; and the *Edinburgh Festival* is one of Europe's major musical events. Information:

Edinburgh International Festival of Music and Drama, 21 Market St., Edinburgh EH1 1BW, Scotland (phone: 226-4001).

MENUHIN FESTIVAL, Gstaad, Switzerland: Staged in August in the town of Gstaad-Saanen, among the towering peaks of the Bernese Oberland, this most personal of European music festivals is the work of the master violinist Yehudi Menuhin. The dozen-odd chamber concerts by celebrated virtuosos are held in the ancient church at Saanen. The rehearsals are open to the public, and one of the concerts is given by the top students of London's Menuhin School. Daytimes, you can enjoy spectacular Alpine rambles. Information: Menuhin Festival, Bureau de Renseignements, Gstaad CH-3780, Switzerland (phone: 030-41055).

INTERNATIONAL MUSIC FESTIVAL, Lucerne, Switzerland: Switzerland's major festival, held from mid-August to early September, has brought the likes of Rostropovitch, Richter, Milstein, Pollini, Von Karajan, Fischer-Dieskau, Barenboim, Arrau, and Dorati to this flowered, serene, lakeside town. (There was once a festival that featured appearances by all of them.) A special feature is the intensive program of advanced instrumental courses given by festival performers in collaboration with the Lucerne Conservatory. For program information: Internazionale Musikfestwochen, Luzern, 13 Hirschmattstrasse, Lucerne 6002, Switzerland (phone: 233562). For course information: Sekretariat der Meisterkurse im Konservatorium Luzern, 93 Dreilinden-strasse, Lucerne CH-6006, Switzerland (phone: 367686).

MONTREUX-VEVEY MUSIC FESTIVAL and THE INTERNATIONAL JAZZ FESTI-VAL, Montreux, Switzerland: Montreux has two international festivals a month apart: the blaring, rocking *International Jazz Festival* in July, which attracts everyone from the likes of Herbie Hancock and Dave Brubeck to the Brockville Junior High Half Time Stompers; and, in September, the elegant *Festival de Montreux-Vevey,* featuring some of the world's major musical personalities — Weissenberg, Rostropovich, Milstein, Ashkenazy, and the Soloisti Veneti all took part in the recent fortieth anniversary program in the shadow of the legendary lakeside Château de Chillon. The festival is also the site of the prestigious Clara Haskil Competition. Information: Festival de Jazz, Gd. Rue 42, Montreux CH-1820, Switzerland (phone: 021-963-1212); or the Festival de Musique Montreux-Vevey, 14 Av. des Alpes, Montreux CH-1820, Switzerland (phone: 021-963-1212).

DUBROVNIK SUMMER FESTIVAL, Dubrovnik, Yugoslavia: From mid-July to late August some 100 performances are presented in over 40 different places in this enthralling medieval walled city on the Adriatic. You can enjoy everything from Beethoven symphonies in the courtyard of the Rector's Palace to Bosnian folk dances on the ramparts. Musically, it's not on a par with its Western cousins, but the setting can't be beat. Information: Dubrovnik Summer Festival, 1 Od Sigurate, Dubrovnik, Yugoslavia (phone: 050-27996).

Learning the Language

 Americans, in their splendid isolation, have always had reputations as poor learners of foreign languages, and we walk the world expecting universal mastery of English to have preceded us. If the natives didn't understand, the popular wisdom went, you were supposed to say it again, louder. In the years since World War II, this daydream has been approaching some kind of reality, with English emerging as the international language of trade and tourism. But no matter how many sales managers or desk clerks or headwaiters can answer your questions, there is no substitute for some knowledge of the local language as a way into a foreign culture. Without it, you only skim the surface of the country you visit; you read its dust jacket but never open the book.

The best method to acquire the language skills that will so greatly enhance your travel experience is an academic program in the country whose language you're trying to learn. The sounds and the rhythms of local speech will become a part of your own thought processes; every shop, every market, every street corner, is soon a language lab. Most European countries offer foreigners special courses lasting anywhere from 2 weeks to a full year, in settings as diverse as metropolitan capitals and Alpine castles. Here's *la crème de la crème:*

FRENCH

ALLIANCE FRANÇAISE: Exams at this venerable institution dedicated to the diffusion of French culture are a universal standard of French proficiency. The school is in the heart of the Parisian student quarter, and it has a clientele of all colors and tongues. Information: Alliance Française, 101 Bd. Raspail, Paris Cedex 06 75270, France (phone: 45-44-38-28).

SORBONNE: The University of Paris offers a variety of courses, during both the summer and the academic year, in French language and civilization. The *cours de civilisation française* — a potpourri of grammar, literature, history, and fine arts studies — is a model for courses at a number of other French universities that offer special programs for foreigners. Information: Cour de Civilisation Française, Galerie Richelieu, 47 Rue des Ecoles, Paris 75005, France (phone: 40-46-22-11, ext. 2670).

FRANCE LANGUES: Courses at all levels in French language and civilization, with considerable use of audiovisual methods. Information: France Langues, 2 Rue de Sfax, Paris 75116, France (phone: 45-00-40-15).

EUROCENTRE: An international foundation with head offices in Zurich, twenty schools distributed in seven European countries — and an outpost at Columbia University in New York City. The Paris branch — 16 classrooms, 2 language labs, a film room, and a library, set in the middle of the Latin Quarter — offers a program that blends excursions with course work. Information: Eurocentre, 131 Passage Dauphine, Paris 75006, France (phone: 43-25-81-40). For a complete list of all the Eurocentres, programs, and fees, contact Eurozentren, 247 Seestrasse, Zurich CH-8038, Switzerland (phone: 482-5040).

CHAMBRE DE COMMERCE ET D'INDUSTRIE: The Chamber of Commerce sponsors programs in commercial French, with emphasis on understanding the life of the French business world. For details: Chambre de Commerce et d'Industrie, Direction des Relations Internationales de la Direction de l'Enseignement, 42 Rue du Louvre, Paris 75001, France (phone: 45-08-37-37).

COURS POUR ETUDIANTS ETRANGERS, UNIVERSITÉ DE PROVENCE: A course in French civilization specifically designed for foreign students, under the auspices of the university, in one of the most gracious and charming towns in the south of France. University-age students tend to dominate, and the town is one large, animated campus. Information for both year-round and intensive summer courses: Institut d'Etudes Françaises pour Etudiants Etrangers, 23 Rue Gaston-de-Saporta, Aix-en-Provence 13625, France (phone: 42-23-28-43).

UNIVERSITÉ LIBRE DE BRUXELLES: Courses all year long — designed for everyone from the rank beginner to the college French instructor — with a Belgian accent. Information: Université Libre de Bruxelles, 50 Av. Franklin-Roosevelt, Brussels, Belgium (phone: 642-2030).

GERMAN

GOETHE INSTITUT: Perhaps the most respected school of German language, the institute has some 16 centers in Germany and a number of foreign countries, promoting German culture abroad. Courses, which come in 3-, 4-, and 8-week packages, are intensive and include nearly 24 hours a week of instruction. Special new courses combine sports like sailing, riding, and skiing with language study. For complete information, contact the central office, Goethe Institut, Postfach 201009, 3 Lenbachplatz, Munich 2, 8000 Germany (phone: 599-9200). Or write directly to either of the two big city centers: 38-48 Knesebeckstrasse, Berlin 15 1000, Germany (phone: 881-3051); or 25 Sonnenstrasse, Munich 2 8000, Germany (phone: 592-421).

DEUTSCHER AKADEMISCHER AUSTAUSCHDIENST: This central office handles special courses for foreigners at a variety of German universities. The most desirable university towns are Munich, Hamburg, Augsberg, and Heidelberg (which offers a unique course in German literature, film and theater). Information: DAAD, 50 Kennedyallee, Bonn 2 D-5300, Germany (phone: 8820), or German Academic Exchange Service, 950 Third Ave., 19th Fl., New York, NY 10022 (phone: 212-758-3223).

HUMBOLDT INSTITUT: In the 16th-century castle of Ratzenried, deep in the Allgäu district, at the foot of the German Alps. Beautiful countryside, accommodations at the castle or in nearby private houses. Main courses start on the first Monday of each month, with special sessions available in summer and holiday periods. Information: Humboldt Institut, Schloss Ratzenried, Argenbühl/Allgäu 7989, Germany (phone: 07522-3041).

SALZBURG INTERNATIONAL LANGUAGE CENTER and IFK-INTERNATIONALE FERIENKURSE: Salzburg, Austria, where the courses at these two schools are held, is one of the most charming towns in all of Europe, and so, though you may end up speaking the Austrian dialect, the experience is worth it for the mountains, the music, and the *mohn strudel.* Information: Salzburg International Language Center, 106 Moosstrasse, Salzburg A-5020, Austria (phone: 0662-844485); and IFK-Internationale Ferienkurse, 19 Franz-Josef-strasse, Salzburg A-5020, Austria (phone: 0662-76595).

GREEK

ATHENS CENTRE: In a residential area of Athens, the center offers year-round courses devoted to the intensive study of modern Greek as well as a special Translators' Seminar. Courses provide an insight into aspects of Greek culture, art, and history. The center assists students from abroad in finding accommodations, including summer sublets. Information: The Athens Centre, Greek Language Programs, 48 Archimidous St., Athens 11636, Greece (phone: 701-2268).

HELLENIC-AMERICAN UNION: Popular with Athens' resident American community as well as with locals who come to use the English library and read *The New York Times* on microfilm, the Hellenic-American Union offers courses in modern Greek for students of all proficiencies. Information: The Registrar, Academic Section, Hellenic-American Union, 22 Massalias, Athens, Greece (phone: 362-9886).

ITALIAN

UNIVERSITÀ ITALIANA PER STRANIERI: Founded in 1925 by the Italian government, this "University for Foreigners" is housed in the 18th-century Palazzo Gallenga of Perugia. Well run, with a diverse student body and nominally priced courses in subjects as varied as elementary Italian and Etruscology, it puts much of the country's regular university system to shame. Courses of varying lengths — from 2 weeks to 9 months — are offered throughout the year. Information: Università Italiana per Stranieri, Palazzo Gallenga, Piazza Fortebraccio, Perugia, Italy (phone: 64344).

SOCIETÀ DANTE ALIGHIERI: The Dante is a worldwide organization for the diffusion of Italian culture, with some 400 branches teaching Italian to 50,000 students a year. The Rome branch offers courses in art, music, theater, furniture, and interior decoration; and sponsors films, concerts, lecture series, and assorted excursions. There are four 2-month terms from October to May, plus 2-month-long summer terms in June and July. Fees are quite low and instruction first-rate. Information about instruction in Rome and other Italian cities: Società Dante Alighieri, 27 Piazza Firenze, Rome 00186, Italy (phone: 687-3722).

EUROCENTRO: Eurozentren's sole center in Italy is in a Renaissance *palazzo* in the heart of Florence. In addition to providing first-rate Italian language instruction, the center puts a great deal of emphasis on teaching its students about Italian art and architecture, some of the finest of which can be seen from the school's windows. Information: Eurocentro, 9 Piazza Santo Spirito, Firenze 50125, Italy (phone: 294605).

SPANISH

ESCOLA OFICIAL DE IDIOMES: Because this school is in Barcelona, you will hear a lot of the Catalan dialect in the city's shops and markets rather than the Castilian, which is spoken around Madrid and is the national language. Intensive month-long summer courses are offered as well as two leisurely semesters that begin in October and end in June. Lodging with private families is available. Information: Escola Oficial de Idiomes, Av. de les Drassanes, Barcelona, Spain (phone: 329-3412).

CENTRO DE ESTUDIOS DE CASTELLANO: Founded in 1945, well before the Costa del Sol boom, and situated in a pleasant villa on a suburban street in Málaga, this school limits its classes to eight students each and offers month-long courses at four skill levels throughout the year. Dandy for keeping a winter visit to the sea from descending entirely into frivolity — but the beach is never more than an irregular verb away. Information: Centro de Estudios de Castellano, 110 Av. J. S. Elcano, Málaga 29017, Spain (phone: 290551).

INLINGUA IDIOMAS: Part of a large European chain of effective language schools, Inlingua offers a wide variety of short intensive courses year-round. Housing is available on the school premises as well as with local families. Information: Inlingua Idiomas, 24 Arenal, Madrid 28013, Spain (phone: 248-0225).

COLEGIO DE ESPAÑA: In the noble and lively university town of Salamanca, the Colegio offers Spanish language and literature at every level, with special month-long immersion courses in the summer. Frequent excursions add color to the classroom routine. The university itself also offers excellent courses for foreign students in Spanish language and civilization. Information: Colegio de España, 65 Calle Compañia, Salamanca 37008 (phone: 214788); and Secretaria de la Facultad de Filología, Universidad de Salamanca, Plaza de Anaya, Salamanca 57001 (phone: 216534).

TIPS ON OVERSEAS LANGUAGE PROGRAMS

Whether you're learning French or German, Italian or Spanish, be diligent about exposing yourself to the language you're studying. Read signs religiously, muddle through the newspaper daily, listen to the radio constantly, and eavesdrop on conversations. Stay with good solid lowbrow material — the local tabloid newspaper, not the local *Times*. Follow the latest murder and the hottest rock star romance. Watch the soap operas on television. Go back to comic books. Then hit the movies: Start with dubbed American films — even ones you've seen in English — where your familiarity with the settings, gestures, and lip movements will provide you with clues to the meaning of the lines. Then try out local films: If they're incomprehensible, see them again. And read books on subjects that really interest you; improve your tennis in German, or your love-making in French.

Speak with courage and without fear of error. Be zealous about putting yourself in situations that will demand that you communicate, and don't rely on friends who know the language better to help you do your daily business. Go shopping, talk to the chambermaid about her liver trouble, tell strangers the story of your life. The more you speak, the better you'll do it; 10 minutes in the street is worth an hour at home with chapter 6, exercise 17. Everybody is an expert in his own language, and most people are delighted to give free lessons in grammar or vocabulary while they repair your shoe or show you the way to the zoo.

Finally, remember that *accent* is as much a part of a language as its vocabulary. Listen to sounds and imitate them, and insofar as your ear and your tongue permit, try not to say everything as if you were reading from the Pittsburgh phone book.

Antiquer's Guide to Europe

 Whether you're at Piccadilly Circus, on a dirt road in Andalusia, or in the throbbing heart of downtown Bratislava, sooner or later you'll see a sign that says "Antiques," and sooner or later you'll find yourself pawing over relics of the past as if in search of a gracious way to drain off excess capital. Europe has plenty to entice you — English silver, Persian rugs, fine painting and sculpture, and antique china, not to mention Venetian glass and French and English furniture.

For the most part, you'll do better buying such items in their country of origin — and at auction. Although every once in a while a dealer will underprice an item he doesn't love or understand, it's generally true that most will do the opposite, so that you're likely to pay unnecessarily high prices for Georgian sterling in Italy and Spanish paintings in Scandinavia. Antiques hunting in the auction houses ordinarily saves you about 30% — but only so long as you know the market. If you don't, stick to the shops, and just as auctiongoers are best advised to patronize the first-echelon salerooms and to avoid auction rings and other questionable operations, so should the less than expert buyer stick to reputable dealers, particularly when it comes to high-ticket items. With the booming of the art market, the forgery business has taken on the proportions of an industry. Conscientious dealers will usually guarantee in writing the authenticity of your purchase and will often accept its return, for the original price, if you change your mind. At the same time, a good dealer can advise novices about imperfections.

Ideally, you should buy only the best example you can find of a particular genre, in the best condition: Whether an item is damaged or not is a major factor in determining its market price (and should matter to you if you're buying as a potential investment); and in any case, a stain, a chip, or a warp will probably annoy you in the long run. Helpful antiques dealers can give you some feedback on the matter, can also provide you with the name of a good restorer, and, sometimes, can even arrange for you to pay the trade price for a restoration. Before you buy something that has already been restored, ask the dealer to explain what catchwords like "remodeled," "renewed," and "restyled" actually mean when applied to an item. You don't want to buy a Renaissance Tuscan armoire whose only original part is the keyhole.

You can learn something of what the dealers know at a number of courses that are available throughout the year at *Earnley Concourse,* Chichester, Sussex PO20 7JI, England (phone in Bracklesham Bay: 0243-670392). *Christie's* in London offers a fine arts course that covers the subject in a year. Information: Director, Christie's Education, 63 Old Brompton Rd., London SW7 3JS, England (phone: 581-3933).

To find out where to buy, consult the *Weltkunst* (a world art review), published twice monthly and available at well-stocked newsstands in Germany (or through the magazine's office at 84 Nymphenburgerstrasse, 8000 Munich 19, Germany (phone: 089-126-9900); it contains a good Europe-wide auction calendar. So do the *Antiques Trade Gazette,* available at Metropress Ltd., 17 Whitcomb St., London WC2 H7PL (phone:

930-7192), and *Art and Auction* magazine, 250 W. 57th St., New York, NY 10019 (phone: 212-582-5633). Also see the art and auction page of the weekend edition of the *International Herald Tribune* and the *Guide Emer,* a specialized French publication aimed at the art and antiquity trade available from Emer Publicité, 50 Rue-Quai de l'Hôtel de Ville, Paris 75004 (phone: 42-77-83-44).

Some of the best hunting grounds are in Vienna, London, Paris, Berlin, and Rome; along streets full of antiques shops in other cities; and at a number of antiques fairs that take place all over Europe throughout the year.

ANTIQUES CAPITALS

VIENNA, Austria: Go straight to the Dorotheergasse, a lovely old street off the Graben where antiques shops have proliferated in the shadow of the great *Dorotheum* auction house at #17. The shops flow out into the side streets — the Braünerstrasse, the Spiegelgasse, and the Stallburggasse — and they devote themselves to every imaginable genre of antique. There are generalists who carry furniture, painting, and rugs; and specialists that stock only brocades, or crystal, or music boxes, or clocks and watches, or toy soldiers, and — because this is Vienna — a number that deal exclusively in collectors' instruments, manuscript pages of musical scores, composers' autographed letters, and the like. (Have a look at *Doblinger Musikhaus,* 10 Dorotheergasse.) Also, call at the strongholds of the *Hofstätters,* Vienna's leading antiques dynasty: *Reinhold,* 15 Dorotheergasse, is the sculpture and furniture branch. Arrange also to attend at least one auction at the *Dorotheum,* a major source for dealers, which is always an education even if you never lift a finger. On Saturday, try the less rarefied end of the spectrum: The flea market at Naschmarkt in the 6th district is easily reached from the Stadtbahn's Kettenbrückengasse station. And the city's big annual antiques fair, the *Wiener Kunst Und Antiquitätenmesse,* runs for a week in November in the Hofburg. If you still haven't found anything, you're not really interested in antiques.

LONDON, England: The British Empire is the world's largest antique, but in its heyday the sun never set on the loot that flowed into its prosperous capital. And before that, during the French Revolution, the city was also a safe haven for things of value. Consequently, London has long been the unquestioned center of the antiques trade. Anything can be bought here, and everything has a market value and instant liquidity. The 10-day *Grosvenor House Antiques Fair,* held annually in June, is a sun in the antiques dealer's solar system; you'll find everything from Etruscan heads to Victorian bustles, and every piece has been authenticated by independent experts. The great auction houses, *Christie's* on King Street and *Sotheby's* on Bond Street, are instrumental in setting market prices; they're superb places to develop a feel for the market. Then there are the street markets that blossom and thrive in Camden Passage, Islington, Tuesdays through Saturdays (Wednesdays are best for antiques); at Bermondsey Square and Tower Bridge Road (the New Caledonian), held on Fridays beginning at 5 AM (the best time); and, on Saturdays, on Portobello Road, Westbourne Park, where you'll recognize as sellers the buyers of the previous day's Caledonian. All week long, you can browse in the *Kensington Antique Hypermarket,* 26-40 Kensington High St., the *Chelsea Antique Market,* 253 King's Road or *Gray's Antique Market,* Davies Mews. London's two renowned department stores, *Harrods* and *Fortnum and Mason,* both have excellent antiques departments that stock only the finest quality items. Antiques shops also can be found in quantity along Kensington Church Street, Fulham Road, Bond Street, Mount Street, Jermyn Street, Brompton Road, and King's Road. Buy silver at the *Silver Vaults* under Chancery Lane; porcelain at the *Antique Porcelain Company Ltd.,* 149 New Bond Street; prints at *Colnaghi's,* 14 Old Bond Street, or at *Craddock and Barnard,* 32 Museum Street; books at *E. Joseph,* 1 Vere St.; Oriental rugs at *Alexander Juran,* 74 New Bond Street; and Russian icons at the *Temple Gallery,*

6 Clarendon Cross (phone: 727-3809). *Mallett and Sons,* 40 New Bond St., is a miniature museum. Incidentally, if you've bought — or taken on approval — something you'd like an expert to examine, try the *British Museum* (where you'll never be quoted a value) or *Sotheby's* (where you'll be reminded that the house will be happy to sell it).

PARIS, France: Despite the ravages of the Revolution, you can still do some productive antiques hunting in Paris. The most fruitful market is the giant *Biennale Internationale des Antiquaires,* a marathon fair held in even-numbered years in mid-autumn at the Grand Palais. The rest of the time, visit the venerable *Hôtel Drouot* auction house, both in its quarters at 9 Rue Drouot on the Right Bank and in its brand new venue, the *Théâtre des Champs Elysées* on stylish Avenue Montaigne. In addition, on the site of the old Magasins du Louvre there's an antiques shopping center with 250 shops: *Le Louvre des Antiquaires,* 2 Pl. du Palais Royal; phone: 42-97-27-00 (open daily except Monday, 11 AM to 7 PM). Two other important antiques centers are *Le Village Suisse* at 78 Av. de Suffren and Av. de la Motte-Picquet (open every day except Tuesday and Wednesday; phone: 43-06-26-39) and *La Cour aux Antiquaires* at 54 Rue du Faubourg-St.-Honoré (closed Sundays and Mondays; phone: 47-42-43-99). Saturday, Sunday, and Monday are the days to hit the *Marché aux Puces,* the huge flea market between the Porte de St.-Ouen and the Porte de Clignancourt, where some 3,000 shops, stalls, and blankets display everything from Renoir watercolors to 78 rpm records. The *Porte de Vanves* and the *Porte de Montreuil* markets are also in business on weekends only; you'll find more blankets, fewer shops, and better prices. And if you're in Paris in March or September, don't miss the semiannual *Foire à la Ferraille* at the Parc Floral, Bois de Vincennes, where all the dealers stock up (phone: 42-62-44-44, for information). A number of streets are heavily populated with antiques shops. On the Right Bank, they include the Rue du Faubourg-St.-Honoré, Rue La Boétie, Rue de Miromesnil (especially for armor and toy soldiers), Avenue Victor-Hugo, Rue St.-Honoré, and Rue du Faubourg-St.-Antoine. On the Left Bank, prowl the quai Voltaire, Rue de Grenelle, Boulevard St.-Germain, Rue Bonaparte, Rue de Beaune (scientific instruments), Rue du Bac (dolls, toys), Rue des Saints-Pères, Rue de Seine, and Rue Jacob. In addition, between the two banks, you'll find some pleasant shops in even more pleasant surroundings on the Ile St.-Louis. If you're a stamp fancier, don't miss the open-air stamp market — held on Thursdays, Saturdays, and Sundays at the corner of Avenue Gabriel and Avenue Marigny — or the countless shops along the Rue Drouot and in the arcades of the Palais Royal. Finally, to keep abreast of Parisian auction activities, write for a free copy of *La Gazette de l'Hôtel Drouot,* 99 Rue de Richelieu, Paris 75002.

WEST BERLIN, Germany: Berlin dealers have a long-cultivated and prized reputation for expertise and honesty, and you are likely to have a 30-year guarantee and an item's complete pedigree pressed upon you, even if you're running to catch a plane. And if you ever have any complaints, you can take it to a special court of arbitration established solely to handle antiques matters. The Keithstrasse is virtually one long row of antiques shops with a variety of specialties. Some of the best include *Galerie Eva Lohmaier* (for silver and jewelry), *Hagen Jung* (for porcelain), *Karin Sonnenthal* (for Biedermeier furniture), and *Ruth Schmidt* (for really fine East Asian pieces). The area around Kurfürstendamm and Fasanenstrasse is also productive, as are Eisenacherstrasse, Winterfeldstrasse, Motzstrasse, and Fuggerstrasse. (*Joachim Schröder,* at number 4, has fine silver and furniture). Bleibtreustrasse and Mommsenstrasse are the places to hunt for Jugendstil and Art Deco pieces. The *Berliner Flohmarkt* (flea market) inhabits an old U-Bahn station at Nollendorfplatz, and is open from 11 AM to 7 PM every day except Tuesdays; you'll find a number of shops in the nearby Wilmersdorf and Charlottenburg sections of the city. Another sprawling secondhand market is on

Saturdays and Sundays, 8 AM to 3:30 PM, in the Tiergarten, Strasse des 17 Juni. Among other reputable and well-stocked dealers are the *Galerie Pels-Leusden,* on Fasanenstrasse, in the newly restored Villa Griesbach; *Wilhelm Weick,* on the Eisenacherstrasse (for paintings); *Werner Wormuth,* also on Eisenacherstrasse (for old frames and fine restoration); *Herbert Klewer,* on Viktoria-Luiseplatz (for furniture); and *Seidel und Sohn,* on Eisenacherstrasse (for 18th-century furniture and art). Berlin's giant department store, *Ka-De-We,* also has a first-rate antiques section.

ROME, Italy: The main artery for antiques hunters is the Via del Babuino; for junking, there's the sprawling Sunday morning flea market at Porta Portese; and for items in between there are middlebrow streets like Via dei Coronari (on the pricey side), Via del Governo Vecchio, Via di Panico, and Via Margutta (the site of an annual open-air art show). There is also an annual autumn fair in Via dei Coronari; all the shops are open at night and the strolling is delightful. And all week long throughout the year there is a pleasant collection of stands and stalls in Piazza Borghese. On the aristocratic Via del Babuino, the nobility includes *Di Giorgio, Amedeo di Castro, Apolloni, Olivi, Fallani* (for sculpture), *Luciano Coen* (for rugs), and *Sestieri* at Piazza di Spagna (for paintings). Two other fine Rome shops are *Tanca* on the Salita dei Crescenzi, for antique jewelry and silver; and *Lukacs-Donath* on Via Veneto, for porcelain. It should be noted that Italy's antiques trade is lively in the provinces, as well. The most important events are the sedate *Mostra d'Antiquariato,* held in Florence's Palazzo Strozzi in September and October of odd-numbered years, and Parma's booming *Mercanteinfiera,* a yearly October extravaganza. There are shops of national importance in Florence (*Bartolozzi, Bellini*); Milan (*Longari*); Turin (*Rossi*); and Venice (*Barozzi*). The best auction houses in Rome are *L'Antonina* on Piazza Mignanelli and the branch of *Christie's* at Piazza Navona. *Finarte* is tops in Milan. As a general rule, the antiques market in Italy is less richly international than in other European countries, and you should stick to local creations. Also tread with extreme caution when you inspect classical Roman and Greek pieces: There are enough of them around to fill the Roman Empire six times over.

MORE GREAT STREETS FOR ANTIQUES HUNTING

BRUSSELS, Belgium – Rue Watteau, Rue Lebeau, Rue Ernest-Allard, Chausseé d'Ixelles, and the Place du Grand-Sablon, which has a Saturday- and Sunday-morning antiques market.

COPENHAGEN, Denmark – All the side streets adjacent to Strøget, a half-mile-long pedestrians-only thoroughfare that runs through the city's center.

NICE, France – Village Segurane, at Rue Pierre Gautier, near the harbor.

MUNICH, Germany – The Ottostrasse, near Stachus.

ATHENS, Greece – Pandrossou, Solonos, Kriezotou, and Balaritou streets, and Kolonaki Square.

DUBLIN, Ireland – Grafton Street, Dawson Street, Liffey Street, Bachelor's Walk, and Ormond Quay.

NAPLES, Italy – Via Domenico Morelli and Via Santa Maria di Constantinopoli, near the *Museo Nazionale;* Via Chiaia.

AMSTERDAM, The Netherlands – Nieuwe Spiegelstraat, near the Rijksmuseum. And nearly everywhere in the Hague; there are some 150 antiques shops in the city.

WARSAW, Poland – Nowy Świat, Krakowskie Przedmieście.

MADRID, Spain – Calle del Prado, Plaza de las Cortés, Carrera de San Jerónimo, the new Mercado Puerta de Toledo, and the Rastro, a huge Sunday market.

BERNE, Switzerland – The Kramgasse.

GENEVA, Switzerland – Rue de la Cité, Rue de l'Hôtel de Ville, la Grande Rue.

LAUSANNE, Switzerland – Cheneau de Bourg.

ZURICH, Switzerland – The Schlüsselgasse, Schipfe, Neumarkt, Rindermarkt, and the Oberdorf.

MOSCOW, USSR – The state-run thrift shops, *Komissionyj,* where you'll find everything from a piece of chipped crockery with a picture of a waving cosmonaut to a 17th-century icon of St. Dmitri (though most of the best items have been in London and Paris since 1917). Expect tricky export problems.

ANTIQUES FAIRS

SALZBURGER MESSE, Salzburg, Austria – Generally held in late March or early April in the Residenz, with dealers coming from all over the country.

LA FOIRE DES ANTIQUAIRES DE BELGIQUE, Brussels, Belgium – Held 2 weeks in March at the Palais des Beaux-Arts.

AUER DULT, Munich, Germany – A week-long flea market that takes place three times annually, in April or May, July or August, and October. Mariahilfplatz.

IRISH ANTIQUE DEALERS' FAIR, Dublin, Ireland – Held in August, at about the same time as the chi-chi Royal Dublin Society Horse Show.

ANTIQUES FAIR, Delft, The Netherlands – Held for 2 weeks every autumn in the *Prinsenhof Museum.*

INTERNATIONAL ANTIQUES DEALERS FAIR, Lausanne, Switzerland – A November annual at the Palais de Beaulieu.

SWISS ART AND ANTIQUES FAIR, Basel, Switzerland – An annual exposition generally held in the spring at the Schweitzer Mustermesse.

For the Experience

Quintessential Europe

You've waited in line at the Eiffel Tower, and you've heard Big Ben. You've trekked through the *Louvre* to admire *Mona Lisa*'s greenish complexion (duly noting the permanent traffic jam around it), and you've admired the Colosseum. No one who fancies himself a traveler could tour Europe and omit visits to these great monuments; their grandeur prevails — despite the tourist hordes and 20th-century tarnish. Yet there are scores of other spots in Europe that are not so celebrated and in their way deserve to be: Though not giants like the Eiffel Tower and the Colosseum, these somewhat lesser-knowns do offer an experience that is quintessentially European; here, the foreignness of the Continent and its traditions will come resoundingly home to you.

You will doubtless encounter dozens of these wonders on your own — but to get you started, here is our selection.

DINNER AT THE SACHER AND A PREMIÈRE AT THE STATE OPERA, Vienna, Austria: This is the happiness that money *can* buy — the most gracious, elegant, worldly evening in Europe. The *Sacher* hotel, aptly placed on Philharmonikerstrasse, has been the rendezvous of musicians, artists, and all Vienna since (it seems) the time of the pharaohs; and its own restaurant is among the best on the Continent. In the world of the *Sacher,* everything is just as it has always been — the decor as rich, the service as perfect, the clientele as brilliant, and the Wiener schnitzel, the *palatschinken,* and the *Sachertorte* as delectable as ever. Music is still an Austrian national religion, and the glittering *Staatsoper* is its temple. The frothy *Der Rosenkavalier* is the most Viennese of its productions, and if you can arrange it, *the* opera to hear (Beethoven's *Fidelio* is a close second choice). The black-tie New Year's Eve performance of *Die Fledermaus* is Europe's hardest ticket, though the concierge at the *Sacher* has been known to work even this miracle.

CHRISTCHURCH COLLEGE MEADOW, Oxford, England: A beautiful, manicured English greensward, with the soft, rain-nurtured texture of a hill in the Cotswolds or the lawn at Wimbledon, this meadow was a greenhouse for the British Empire, and 8 centuries of the finest young people of England have strolled through the stone portals of the Great Quadrangle here and listened to the tolling of the evening bells from Tom Tower. Bolingbroke was at Christchurch before he became king; William Penn before he was expelled for "nonconformity;" Gladstone before he was prime minister; Lewis Carroll before he wrote *Alice in Wonderland.* Walk slowly down the High Street. Two debating dons may sweep by you in their flowing black robes. Or there may be a game on Merton Cricket Ground, the players' uniforms a crisp white against the green velvet pitch. Have a pint of bitter and a pork pie at the *Turf Tavern.* Browse in renowned *Blackwell's Book Store.* And you, too, will listen to the bells of Tom Tower.

BOULEVARD ST.-MICHEL, Paris, France: Essentially, this seething, vibrant merry-go-straight has changed very little since Ernest Hemingway and James Joyce and Co. discovered it in the 1920s. You will still find the endless ebb and flow of laughing, arguing students; the Africans and Orientals of every shade, height, and costume; the smells of street-corner crêpes, roasting chestnuts, nougat, and steaming *pommes frites;* the impromptu concerts by guitarists, bongo drummers, solo trumpeters, string quartets, their open instrument cases your invitation to drop in a franc. And there are art movie theaters showing four films in four basements in four different languages — and cafés by the score, their neat rows of seats the orchestra to the stage that is the Boul' Mich'. If you can manage to make the scene for *Bastille Day* — July 14 — by all means do so: The French really do dance in the streets.

OMAHA BEACH, Normandy, France: After the D-day invasion, everything was different. One world ended, another world began. June 6, 1944, has come to be one of those watershed dates, like 1066 and 1775, that divide eras in human history. Here are the pyramids of the 20th century: the German pillboxes on the murderous cliff at Pointe du Hoc (recently dedicated as US soil), the landing craft and giant bulkheads sunk in the sands of Arromanches, the white crosses and stars and silent chapel at St.-Laurent-sur-Mer. Save a gray, blowy late afternoon. You can see it all panoramically, scanning the whole expanse of the coastline that was the site of the greatest mass military operation in history. Or you can find a way down to the beach somewhere along the peninsula, roll up your trousers, and wade through the shallow waters breaking on the sand flats. Whether you're 20 and read about Omaha Beach in a book or 80 and lost a son on these bloodied shoals, a visit here is the most strangely moving experience in all of Europe. In some way, we were all here.

ACROPOLIS OF LINDOS, Rhodes, Greece: Every day, the baking sun and corroding salt reclaim one more tiny particle of this ancient marble memory, a temple to Athena, set 30 miles (48 km) south of the island city of Rhodes, on a soaring promontory 400 feet above the sea. But below, and all around in every direction, the elements of the Greek islands that neither nature nor man has succeeded in eroding endure: the silent, craggy coves; the sweeping blond beaches; the white cottages gleaming against the cloudless sky; the olive groves and vineyards sloping down to the cobalt sea. A fishing boat cuts a momentary ripple in the glassy surface, the waters fold back into the timeless Aegean, and you think of Theseus skin diving and Sophocles grilling sardines. This is a place for dawns, for sunset, for solitude.

ACCADEMIA DELLE BELLE ARTI, Florence, Italy: On the quiet side street of Via Ricasoli, in a pleasant but uninspired building, are three of the greatest works of art of the Renaissance. Most famous, of course, is Michelangelo's stunning *David,* a colossus and a hymn to youth and power in its glorification of the human body. The *Prisoners* — a group of half-finished figures contorted as if to wrench their massive bodies free of the great marble blocks that imprison them — are among Michelangelo's most mature and disturbing works, as dark and yearning as the *David* is sunny and serene. They flank the corridor that leads to the *David.* And in the next room is the splendid *Cassone Adimari,* a 15th-century Tuscan wedding chest delicately embellished with paintings of lavishly robed and coiffed gentlewomen and graceful courtiers. Together, these three masterpieces embody the very spirit of the Renaissance: its boundless optimism and faith in man, its struggle toward freedom from the oppressive past, its festive joy in sheer physical beauty.

GRAND CANAL, Venice, Italy: The best way to come in is by train on the causeway across the lagoon. Walk out of the Santa Lucia Station to the head of the wide steps that lead down to the water. Stand still. And look. The whole lavish length of the Grand Canal is lined with a royal flush of Renaissance palaces that make you feel as though all human endeavor that followed has been more or less superfluous. Take a gondola — a trite, overpriced, touristy gondola — and have your driver pull over at the landing pier of the *Gritti Palace* hotel, and see it all again from the Byzantine windows of your own top-floor suite. If it's your first visit and you don't have a lump in your throat, you have a stone for a heart. Didn't anyone ever say "See Venice and die"?

BULLFIGHT IN SEVILLE, Spain: "Sunday in Andalusia" is the title of this scenario. The morning is cool and quiet, with the southern sun and the heady odor of orange blossoms sliding in through the shutters, but you can feel the heat settling over the city, the excitement building. Follow the crowd: to late morning mass in the Gothic cathedral — one of the largest in Christendom — spectacular with its soaring columns, majestic vaults, rich stone and iron lacework; to the exotic tropical gardens of the Alcázar; to the shade of the riverside for an alfresco lunch of chilled *gazpacho* and *manzanilla;* and finally to the legendary Plaza de la Maestranza bullring. All your senses are assailed by the scene before you: the ocher turf glaring in the late afternoon sun; the tinny blare of the band; the procession's gaudy, spangled costumes; the *bandilleros'* ballet; the coarse, feverish crowd watering its passion with warm wine squirted from bulging skins; the black bull's thundering fury; the arrogant grace of the matador; the swirl of the red *muleta;* the flash of the sword blade. Death, triumph, idle amusement; blood, manhood, music, and sun: an age-old ritual, the core of Spain. At its worst, the *corrida* is a slaughterhouse. At its best, it can be a spectacle of unparalleled glory. Afterward, follow the crowd again: the evening *paseo* — the promenade — on the Sierpes, where all of Seville takes the air, arm in arm. And at night, somewhere in the maze of whitewashed walls and flowered patios in the Barrio de Santa Cruz, heels clack the torrid rhythms of the *flamenco* to the quivering sound of Spanish guitars.

GRINDELWALD, in the Bernese Oberland, Switzerland: At an altitude of 3,500 feet, the village of Grindelwald is the center stage for a great Alpine amphitheater. In the foreground are the sunny plateaus of the Grosse and Kleine Scheidegg and the ice-blue waters of the gleaming Bachsee. In the high distance, in a snowy military row, stand the five great rocky guards: the Wetterhorn, the Schreckhorn, Eiger, Monch, and — at 13,642 feet — the fabled Jungfrau: The rack railway of the Jungfraujoch is Europe's most spectacular transportation experience.

Like so many of the great Swiss and Austrian mountainscapes, this scene shades from the fairyland to the forbidding: from the charming town full of wooden chalets, puffing chimneys, and gaily splurging window boxes, to the craggy peaks and the ominous North Wall of the Eiger, which has taken the lives of so many climbers. If you visit in summer, trudge through the woods to the Bachsee or up the summit of the Faulhorn; from there, it seems that you can see the entire planet. If it's winter, step into your skis and swoop across the great snowfields of the Scheideggs. In any season, when the sun drops behind the peaks and a twilight chill comes over the town, have a steaming glass of *glühwein* and a languid nap under the feathery softness of a Swiss eiderdown.

WHITE NIGHTS OF LENINGRAD, USSR: Once a year, during the last half of June, the sun leaves the horizon over the most beautiful of manmade cities for only a few brief hours, and in place of the night, a mysterious chalky haze hangs over the horizon. The stolid Russians go giddy and sentimental, and in a sort of metropolitan tribal rite that celebrates the return of the White Nights, they flock to Strelka, at the prow of Vassilyevsky Island. The delicate pastel façades of structures put up along the entrancing canals of the Neva in the brilliant heyday of the court of St. Petersburg positively glow in this eerie light; and the great past of Mother Russia comes splendidly alive: the opulence of the czars' Winter Palace, the brooding mystery of Dostoyevsky in the Peter and Paul Fortress, the excitement of the revolution, the romance of Tchaikovsky.

MIDNIGHT SUN IN LAPLAND, Finland: The Midnight Sun occurs between June and July. You must arrive in Rovaniemi, the capital of Lapland, and hope that there are no rains to make the normally magificent sunsets overcast. Otherwise, it is a memorable experience to be able to play golf, tennis, or take a hike after the midnight hour. The Northern Lights, which have been described as "nature's own light show," are often visible during November and December, but are as elusive as shooting stars.

Europe's Most Memorable Hostelries

 Europe is full of fascinating places to get a good night's sleep. In fact, some of the grandest of the world's grand hotels are here; they have the refinement and cachet that you'll find only in establishments that have spent centuries serving royalty and the cream of society. Other hostelries, as quaint as these grandees are luxurious, seem more like country homes; their atmosphere depends on whether you're in Sicily or Slovenia, the Cotswolds or Crete. A number of other lodging places are to be found in what were once spare monasteries or towering castles. The caravansaries we list below, by category, are sure to give you sweet dreams — and plenty of happy memories to look back on when your trip is over.

THE GRANDEST OF THE GRAND HOTELS

Like the great transatlantic liners that were once the centerpiece of European travel, the great hotels of Europe seem destined to disappear, to be gradually replaced by more practical concrete palaces. And when the world has finally been transformed into one gigantic *Holiday Inn,* we will look back longingly on the grand hotels' shimmering chandeliers, their lordly tail-coated concierges, the neat rows of shoes in their corridors awaiting morning massages. Already, these hotels belong more to the past than the present — still extant only by some strange quirk of fate. So enjoy them while you can, these gracious temples of excess, and damn the expense — which is usually monstrous. But don't think of it as just the cost of a hot bath, a night's sleep, a morning's coffee. A stay at a hotel such as Paris's *Ritz* is a concert, a visit to a museum, an evening at the theater, an experience seldom duplicated in the modern world. When you start your day with a turn through those historic revolving doors, you somehow see the whole of the surrounding city from a different, far more glittering perspective.

Some notes on getting the most from your stay: First, opt out of any type of American Plan (AP; full pension, or three meals a day) and Modified American Plan (MAP; half pension, or two meals) in favor of Continental Plan (CP; breakfast only) at urban hotels; apart from the fact that working your way through a capital's hundred best restaurants is a pleasure, many great city hotels serve remarkably ordinary meals. Second, remember that the more princely a hotel, as a rule, the more regal the surcharges applied to telephone calls (300% is not unheard of) — so call collect when you can or telephone from the nearest post office. You can dine out on the difference. Third, remember the story of the irascible New Yorker, a guest at one of the Continent's most fabulous hostelries, who refused to pay the automatic 18% service charge because he said he hadn't had any service. And he won.

Here are some of the world's finest dormitories, on whose crested stationery there will be a good deal to write home about.

SACHER, Vienna, Austria: The quintessential European hotel experience, this rococo monument to good living stands opposite the *Vienna State Opera House* and is a kind of "mission control" for Vienna's rich musical life. The rooms are not all elegant, but the service is uniformly superb, and the concierge is Vienna's prime source of otherwise unavailable opera and concert tickets. Its restaurant serves some of the finest food in Europe; the hotel's clientele has remained unchanged since, it seems, the rise of the Habsburgs. Information: Sacher hotel, 2 Philharmonikerstrasse, Vienna, Austria (phone: 51456).

IMPERIAL, Vienna, Austria: Built more than a century ago as a private palace for the Duke of Württemberg, this establishment manages to be at once majestic and modern, and the impeccable, heel-clicking service that has always been a tradition here is not at all hard to get used to. The *Imperial* was, incidentally, a favorite of such discriminating egoists as Hitler and Wagner. Information: The Imperial, 16 Kartnerring, Vienna A-1015, Austria (phone: 501100).

LA RÉSERVE, Knokke-Heist, Belgium: In the country's finest beach resort, both on the shore of little Lake Victoria and a 2-minute stroll from Knokke's broad, sweeping beach, this is a model vacation hotel: Swimming pool, tennis courts, golf, horseback riding, sailing, and water skiing are on the property, and a large bird sanctuary (to which the hotel's name refers) and a gambling casino are nearby. The food is wonderful, and an extensive art collection adorns the rooms. Information: La Réserve di Knokke-Heist, 160 Elizabethlaan, Knokke-Heist 8300, Belgium (phone: 610606).

CLARIDGE'S, London, England: With India and Australia gone, here is the final bastion of the British Empire. Its supreme, traditional elegance is as much a part of the London experience as the horse guards and the crown jewels. Information: Claridge's, Brook St., London W1A 2JQ, England (phone: 629-8860).

CONNAUGHT, London, England: Another stronghold of 19th-century Britain, luxurious and intimate, that will soon have you feeling like a distinguished guest at Lord Hyphen's townhouse. Small — with a tenaciously faithful clientele — it sometimes seems to be booked several generations in advance. Don't be put off by the hauteur; they've earned it. Information: The Connaught, Carlos Pl., Mayfair, London W1Y 6AL, England (phone: 499-7070).

SAVOY, London, England: This hostelry is to theater what the *Sacher* is to music. The *Savoy* is very near Covent Garden and Waterloo Bridge, and the lobby is often a *Who's Who* of the international entertainment world. The atmosphere is gently Edwardian, but the management is contemporary — and adept at catering to the demands of plutocrats from every part of the planet. The refurbished Thames Suites are London's most elegant address. Information: The Savoy, The Strand, London WC2R OEU, England (phone: 836-4343).

RITZ, London, England: The fellow who was heard to mutter snootily, "Nobody stays at the Ritz anymore," was off-base, especially since the recent renovation restored the old luster and certainly got the bugs out. While the fare offered in the *Ritz* dining room is not quite up to the surroundings, the decor is splendid and the service impeccable. Tea here is as vital a British ritual as the coronation. Information: The Ritz, Piccadilly, London W1, England (phone: 493-8181).

LA RÉSERVE, Beaulieu, France: If thoughts of the French Riviera and Côte d'Azur awaken longings in you, you can get some satisfaction here at this luxurious seaside establishment graced by plenty of sun and surf, plus a sauna and swimming pool — and one of France's most renowned restaurants. The *Monte Carlo Casino* is just minutes away. Information: La Réserve, 5 Bd. Général-Leclerc, Beaulieu-sur-Mer 06310, France (phone: 93-01-00-01).

HÔTEL DU CAP-EDEN ROC, Cap d'Antibes, France: Over a hundred years old, this Riviera landmark stands at the end of the Antibes peninsula in a lovely, semitropical park, looking out over the sea. An immaculately kept private beach, wisteria-rimmed tennis courts, and dinners on the patio of the patrician *Eden Roc* restaurant are highlights. Open from Easter to the end of October. Information: Hôtel du Cap-Eden Roc, Bd. Kennedy, Antibes 06604, France (phone: 93-61-39-01).

NORMANDY, Deauville, France: A great Norman mansion facing the sea in an urbane resort that is often called the Twenty-first Arrondissement of Paris, this hotel is a 5-minute walk from the *Deauville Casino,* which still has Europe's classiest casino clientele, most of whom catch a few hours' sleep at the *Normandy* between wagers. Fine at the height of the August racing season, and fine, too, for a winter weekend, when the rain and wind lash the Norman coast. Information: The Normandy, Rue Jean-Mermoz, Deauville 14800, France (phone: 31-88-09-21).

NÉGRESCO, Nice, France: Something of an anachronism on the heavily trafficked and highly developed Riviera, this beautiful white Belle Epoque cream puff is still one of the shrines of European hotelkeeping. Its charming period rooms give you views over the ultramarine Baie des Anges and the long and lively Promenade des Anglais. Information: The Négresco, 37 Promenade des Anglais, Nice 06007, France (phone: 93-88-39-51).

RITZ, Paris, France: Perhaps the world's most famous hotel, beautifully positioned on Place Vendôme like the national monument it is. A recent 7-year-long overhaul has helped ease it out of French literature and into the 20th century with notable success, and its name is still synonymous with consummate luxury. Two new floors (below street level) have been added to allow construction of a pool and spacious spa, and the rooms and public spaces have been returned to their original elegance and opulence. Information: The Ritz, 15 Pl. Vendôme, Paris 75041, France (phone: 42-60-38-30).

CRILLON, Paris, France: Only the understated gold "C's" on its doors identify this grand example of Louis XV style, wonderfully situated right on Place de la Concorde. This is the only one of Paris's palace hotels still owned by a Frenchman. Once a private mansion, its interior is a regal assembly of 18th-century marble, carved and gilt-covered ornamentation, tapestries, and crystal chandeliers — luxe of the sort usually protected behind velvet cordons, but here eminently approachable. The *Crillon* has 113 large rooms and 30 suites. Those on the square have the best views; those on the courtyards are the quietest. Information: Hôtel de Crillon, 10 Pl. de la Concorde, Paris 75008, France (phone: 42-65-24-24).

GEORGE V, Paris, France: On the avenue of the same name that bisects the Champs-Elysées, this has been a favorite address of American travelers since the days of the Grand Tour. There is a prosperous, worldly air about its bustling halls, a feeling that things of continental importance are going on in the bar or under the sun lamps. The breakfast room serves some of the best warm croissants in town. Information: The George V, 31 Av. George-V, Paris 75008 (phone: 47-23-54-00; 800-223-5672 in the US).

PLAZA-ATHÉNÉE, Paris, France: The most exquisitely French of Paris's major hotels, this one — Paris at its suave and urbane best — has attained such heights that among its regular guests are a few who look down their noses at the *Ritz.* Information: The Plaza-Athénée, 25 Av. Montaigne, Paris 75008, France (phone: 47-23-78-33; 800-223-5672 in the US).

BRENNER'S PARK HOTEL, Baden-Baden, Germany: On the lushly pastoral Lichtentaleralleé, this hotel has a setting like that of a Habsburg summer palace and a wealth of balconies that make the most of it, offering views of particularly lordly trees and a romantic stream. The opulent *Baden-Baden Casino* and the wooded tennis club are an idyllic stroll away, as are all the other pleasures of this playground spa. Information: Brenner's Park Hotel, An der Lichtentaleralleé, Baden-Baden D-7570, Germany (phone: 07221-3530).

VIER JAHRESZEITEN, Hamburg, Germany: That rare combination of urban efficiency and countrified serenity, this fine hotel has a lovely lakefront setting with a view of the waterways that are so characteristic of the city, and all around are flowered promenades, gleaming yachts, and handsome villas. The hotel grill has a friendly fireplace and fine food. Among hotel people, this jewel is known as "the best Swiss hotel outside Switzerland." Information: The Vier Jahreszeiten, 9-14 Neuer Jungfernstieg, Hamburg 36 2000, Germany (phone: 040-34940).

CALA DI VOLPE, Costa Smeralda, Italy: The crown jewel of the complex developed by the Aga Khan on once-remote Sardinia, one of the Mediterranean's most fascinating islands. Rustic in style, like a Sardinian village, but deluxe in its comfort, it is discreetly tucked into a magnificent bright blue bay, just at the water's edge. Tennis, boating, swimming and skin diving, and glamorous nightlife are just outside your door, and it has served as the elegant background for some typical excess in a James Bond film. Open May through September. Information: Cala di Volpe, Costa Smeralda, Porto Cervo 07020, Italy (phone: 0789-96083).

GRITTI PALACE, Venice, Italy: Dramatically situated on the Grand Canal, this Renaissance *palazzo,* a compact version of the Doge's Palace, has a dining terrace that floats on the water in the midst of the gondola traffic. If you just hang out of your window, you will see most of Venice float by in the course of a day. Information: The Gritti Palace, Campo Santa Maria del Giglio, Canal Grande, Venice 30100, Italy (phone: 794611).

DUE TORRI, Verona, Italy: A magnificent living museum fitted out entirely with antiques, this deluxe centuries-old inn is *the* place to be during the opera festival that takes place in the summer at the Arena di Verona. The management and the mood are highly personal, and exquisite good taste has governed the selection of the least important accessory — even the ashtrays are lovely. Information: The Due Torri, 4 Piazza S. Anastasia, Verona 37121, Italy (phone: 045-595044).

HÔTEL DE PARIS, Monte Carlo, Monaco: Across the square from the great *Casino,* this newly refurbished grand symbol of the era when money still bought happiness has been the winter palace for Russian grand dukes and English lords who have been coming to this petit principality for 3-month doses of sun and roulette for over a century. The hotel's elaborately painted and chandeliered dining room is an opera set — as is the whole regal, truly glamorous building. Be sure to sample the world class Provençal food now emerging from the refurbished kitchen. Information: Hôtel de Paris, Pl. du Casino, Monte Carlo 98000, Monaco (phone: 93-50-80-80).

REID'S, Funchal, Portugal: On the island of Madeira, this immensely gracious resort hotel, the perfect place to recover from a difficult year, has something of an old British colonial flavor about it. Set on a promontory above the sea, it's surrounded by a veritable jungle of the flowers and foliage for which the island itself is so famous. The hotel has a private beach, private boats, tennis, two pools, and great charm. Information: Reid's, 139 Estrada Monumental, Funchal, Madeira P-9000, Portugal (phone: 912-3001).

RITZ, Madrid, Spain: A multimillion-dollar refurbishing by Trust House Forte has returned this lavish landmark to the aristocracy of European hotels. Although this white castle is just a Goya's throw from the Prado, its marble terrace and chiaroscuro summer garden may be all you'll ever want to see of Madrid. Information: Ritz hotel, 5 Plaza de la Lealtad, Madrid 28014, Spain (phone: 521-2857).

BÜRGENSTOCK HOTELS, Bürgenstock, Switzerland: This complex of three luxurious hotels (the *Grand,* the *Palace,* the *Park*) is in a 500-acre natural park that sprawls along a massive, wooded ridge some 1,500 feet above Lake Lucerne. Views from the hotel windows seem to take in half of Switzerland; rooms are hung with tapestries and Old Masters and furnished with lovely antiques. Information: The Bürgenstock Estate, Bürgenstock CH-6366, Switzerland (phone: 041-615545).

LE BEAU RIVAGE, Lausanne, Switzerland: A giant, queenly, Victorian manor set on 10 acres of lush private park on the shore of Lac Leman in Lausanne-Ouchy. The constantly tended grounds are like a botanical garden — with tennis courts — and you can come and go by boat to the front door. Information: Beau Rivage, Ouchy, Lausanne 1006 (phone: 021-263831).

PALACE, St.-Moritz, Switzerland: Apprentices from all over the world come to this legend of Swiss hotelkeeping to learn to do things as perfectly as only the Swiss can. Stand on your sun-washed balcony on a crisp February morning, look out on the dazzling snows of the Engadine Valley and its high Alpine backdrop, and you will feel like the King of the Golden Mountain. Information: The Palace, St.-Moritz CH-7500, Switzerland (phone: 082-21101).

DOLDER GRAND, Zurich, Switzerland: A romantic old Gothic fantasy on a forested mountainside 6 minutes by hotel car from downtown Zurich. Golf, tennis, woodland pathways, panoramic views over city and lake, world class cuisine, an ice rink, and an open-air pool with manmade waves are only a few of the delights that will make you want to settle down forever in the hotel's tower suite. Information: The Dolder Grand, Kurhausstrasse 65, Zurich CH-8032, Switzerland (phone: 251-6231).

CASTLE HOTELS

Some of Europe's most fascinating hostelries started their lives as abbeys, baronial mansions, castles and châteaux, monasteries, and palaces. Most national tourist offices can tell you about those within their borders; the book *Castle Hotels of Europe* by Robert P. Long ($7.95) pinpoints hundreds of others in 18 countries on the Continent and in Britain. Also see *Relais & Châteaux,* published by the French organization of the same name, as a guide to a group of castle hotels, restaurants, and inns devoted to maintaining high standards of personalized service and cuisine. Here's our selection of some of the choicest.

SCHLOSS DÜRNSTEIN, Dürnstein, Austria: In northeast Austria, on a rocky plateau above the Danube, this baroque castle has been deftly transformed into a gracious modern hostelry. Formerly the summer residence of the Starhemberg princes, it now features a heated swimming pool, sauna and solarium, and first class Austrian cuisine. Open mid-March to mid-November. Information: Schloss Dürnstein, Dürnstein A-3601, Austria (phone: 02711- 212).

PALAIS SCHWARZENBERG, Vienna, Austria: Small and exclusive, this establishment occupies a wing of a palace still owned by one of Austria's oldest families, in the middle of a 37-acre park close to the center of the city. The hotel is beautifully furnished, partly with antiques, and the atmosphere is perfectly sedate, totally calm. Information: Palais Schwarzenberg, 9 Schwarzenberg Place, Vienna A-1030, Austria (phone: 784515).

CHÂTEAU DE NAMUR, Namur, Belgium: This 31-room château occupies a deep green private park at the summit of La Citadelle above Namur, overlooking the entire Meuse River valley. Swimming in the hotel pool and playing tennis on its courts will keep you busy between excursions to the Ardennes Forest. Information: Château de Namur, Av. de l'Ermitage, Namur 1, Belgium (phone: 081-222546).

STEENSGAARD HERREGARDSPENSION, Millinge, Denmark: This half-timbered manor on the island of Fünen dates from the late 13th century and looks every bit its age, from the armor that surrounds it and the library to the ancient park that surrounds it and the vaulted cellar, now set up for billiards. You can play tennis, take horseback or carriage excursions in the wild countryside, or just enjoy the mile-long private beach. Each of the 14 rooms has a view of the lake or the park. Information: Steensgaard Herregardspension, 4 Steensgard, Millinge, Fünen DK-5642, Denmark (phone: 62-619490).

CLIVEDON, Taplow, Buckinghamshire, England: One of England's great country estates, *Clivedon* stands majestically on 400 wooded acres by the River Thames. Long the property of the legendary Astors — and the meeting place of the fabled "Clivedon Set" — it is now managed by Blakeney Hotels (also the proprietors of the *Fenja* hotel in London), who have preserved and classically redecorated the original rooms of the 17th-century mansion, retaining the works of art that reflect the lives of its previous owners. New garden rooms were being added as we went to press. The incomparable grounds, which once received the attention of as many as 50 gardeners, include a sweeping pasture, dazzling flower borders, hanging woods, exquisite pavilions, temples, sculptures, 2,000-year-old Roman sarcophagi, and an amphitheater where *Rule Britannia* was first performed in 1740. In addition to beautiful walks, guests enjoy boat trips on the Thames, tennis (on both indoor and outdoor courts), swimming squash, fishing, horse racing, polo, golf, and rowing. Details: Clivedon, Taplow, Buckinghamshire (phone: 06286-5069).

EASTWELL MANOR, Ashford, Kent, England: Set in some 3,000 acres of parkland picturesquely speckled with fluffy white sheep, this elegant, rambling stone country house was opened as a hotel just in 1980, but though the present house was rebuilt in 1926, its history can be traced back to the Norman Conquest; over the years it has had 20 owners, and Queen Victoria once made a visit here. The lavish use of space and splendid service reminds guests of an earlier, grander age: one visitor called it "the world's best twenty-room hotel." Though the rooms are absolutely huge, they are so cleverly decorated with sitting areas, soft colors, and pretty fabrics, that they seem positively inviting. An oak-paneled bar lures guests down for drinks before dinner, which is served in a baronial dining room. The menu is French, with an emphasis on nouvelle cuisine; you can order such delicacies as *aspèrges feuilletées au beurre fondu* and *fricassée de fruits de mer.* There is also a short menu of local specialties — among them smoked eel and roast English lamb (which, like the beef, comes from the estate). Information: Eastwell Manor, Eastwell Park, Ashford, Kent TN25 4HR, England (phone: 0233-35751).

CHÂTEAU D'AUDRIEU, Audrieu, France: This magnificent 18th-century country house, preserved over the years by a single family, is set among lovely gardens in a 50-acre park crisscrossed by graveled pathways and scattered with trees that are almost as old as the house itself. The 24 sleeping rooms, which have retained their original paneling despite the ravages of the World War II D-Day battles fought in the area, are furnished with antiques, and the bathrooms are modern. Audrieu is halfway between Caen and Bayeux, a few miles from the historic beaches and just 2 hours' drive from Paris. Information: Château d'Audrieu, Audrieu (Calvados) 14250, France (phone: 31-80-21-52).

CHÂTEAU D'ARTIGNY, Montbazon, France: François Coty, the celebrated French perfumer, spent 2 decades building this opulent, mansard-roofed château on the site of another that had existed there since 1769 — so it isn't the oldest of castles. However, Coty had style and taste, and the château reflects this: The ceilings are almost as ornate as those you've seen at Versailles, and the bathtubs are real marble. There are 32 rooms in the main château; but the establishment's most notable sleeping quarters are on the top floor of the adjacent Pavilion Ariane, accessible via a lovely curved staircase. Information: Château d'Artigny, Montbazon, Route d'Azay-le-Rideau (Indre-et-Loire) 37250, France (phone: 47-26-24-24).

DOMAINE DES HAUTS DE LOIRE, Onzain, France: Here is a Loire Valley château where you can spend the night. Once a hunting pavilion for a French count, this cozy country French establishment, its rooms papered with wonderful toiles and full of giant hand-hewn beams, feels like someone's home; everywhere there are gleaming antique copper pots and pans, often filled with fresh flowers, and the dining room is elegant and airy, so that you can watch the sun set as you wait for supper. Information: Domaine des Hauts de Loire, Onzain (Loir-et-Cher) 41150, France (phone: 54-20-72-57).

SCHLOSSHOTEL KRONBERG, Kronberg, Germany: One of the finest castle hotels in a country that is full of them, this fairy tale structure in the woods about a half-hour from Frankfurt was built in 1888 by the German Empress Friedrich, who was daughter to Queen Victoria and mother to Kaiser Wilhelm II. It has also housed

French army officers, American soldiers and civilians, and assorted European blue-bloods, and, in 1945, was invaded by jewel thieves who made a celebrated haul of heirlooms stored there. Though a relative newcomer on the hotel scene, it is lovely — full of 19th-century furnishings and priceless paintings and tapestries. Information: Schlosshotel Kronberg, 25 Hainstrasse, 6242 Kronberg/Taunus, Germany (phone: 061-737011). If you acquire the *schlosshotel* ("castle hotel") habit, write the Vereinigung der Burg und Schlosshotels, an association of similar establishments, c/o Gast im Schloss, Trendelburg 1 3526, Germany (phone: 05675-1011).

WALD UND SCHLOSSHOTEL FRIEDRICHSRUHE, Öhringen, Germany: One of the best country inns in Germany, this 18th-century baroque castle once served as a hunting lodge for Emperor Johann Friedrich I. Now in two buildings (one, the original castle itself), the 45-room property also boasts a 9-hole golf course, a tennis court, indoor and outdoor swimming pools, and a fine restaurant. Our favorite accommodation is #66, a corner room with a huge mahogany bed and the plushest eiderdown comforter under which we've ever warmed our toes. Number 55, with two beds and an overstuffed sofa, is equally appealing, and in the main building, we favor #35. Freshly squeezed orange juice, mineral water, and a bowl of fresh fruit is placed in the room each morning, and a dish of chocolates is set out before bedtime. It's enough to make one believe that the good life is still alive and well — at least here. Information: Wald und Schlosshotel Friedrichsruhe, Ohringen 7111, Germany (phone: 07941-7078).

DROMOLAND CASTLE, Newmarket-on-Fergus, Ireland: The former seat of the O'Brien clan, this 16th-century conglomeration of turrets and towers — just a short drive from Shannon Airport — is stuffed with huge oil paintings and ornamented by handsome paneling, elaborate stone carvings, and picture windows that give out onto 500 acres of soft greenness; the chandeliered restaurant gleams sumptuously with its silk curtains and upholstery. Riding is a favorite activity, along with tennis, golf (on a 9-hole course), and fishing for trout and salmon. Information: Dromoland Castle, Newmarket-on-Fergus, County Clare, Ireland (phone in Shannon: 061-71144; in the US: 800-346-7007).

VILLA D'ESTE, Lake Como, Italy: To visit Villa d'Este is to fall gently into a life lined with silk: The public rooms at this vast 400-year-old villa seem as fresh and opulent as when the villa was the home of a Renaissance cardinal, awash with antique chairs upholstered in deep blue brocaded silk, polished marble pillars, crystal chandeliers, winged staircases ascending to a balcony, handloomed carpeting, and arched leaded windows that open out to the cliffs and cypresses of the Como countryside. Breakfasts served at the lakeside dining room are a special treat: fresh grapefruit or orange juice (natural or mixed with champagne); freshly baked breads, rolls, brioches, and croissants; strong black coffee; cheeses; and hot baked Parma ham. Days are leisurely, filled with ambling along the marina, sitting in the sun, bathing in a pool built into the lake, and sipping a drink on the terrace. Information: Villa d'Este, Cernobbio, Lake Como 22010, Italy (phone: 031-511471).

CHÂTEAU NEERCANNE, Amsterdam, The Netherlands: Under the same management as the *Kasteel Erenstein,* a 13th-century Renaissance castle, and hotel-restaurant *Winselerhof,* a 16th-century farmhouse. It's possible to arrange a package visit to all three chic hostelries, which are in close proximity to one another and a half-hour ride from the Maastricht airport. The complex has become very popular with business travelers due to its location near Germany, Belgium, and Luxembourg. Full business services and meeting rooms are available. Ideal for a romantic weekend as well. Information: Cannerweg 800 Maastricht, Amsterdam, The Netherlands (phone: 043-251359).

GLENEAGLES, Auchterarder, Scotland: Staying at this immense Regency stone hostelry is a travel experience of a lifetime, akin to seeing the Taj Mahal for the first time. The lofty columned lounge, with its ornate ceilings, plus the cocktail bar, the glittering ballrooms, and the other public rooms are impressive; bedrooms, which range in size from large to cavernous, add to the effect. And there are amenities of all sorts — a swimming pool, tennis and squash courts, playgrounds, billiard rooms, and even facilities for game fishing. However, at this hotel, golf is the king, and on the 700-acre grounds, you'll find not one 18-hole course, but four. As if that's not enough, the four courses at St. Andrews — owned by the townspeople so that anyone can play them — are an easy drive across the meadows of Strathearn. The opulent dining room offers a good choice of classical French as well as Scottish entrées. Information: Gleneagles Hotel, Auchterarder, Tayside, Perthshire PH3 1NF, Scotland (phone: 07646-2231).

INVERLOCHY, Fort William, Scotland: At the foot of the mountain Ben Nevis, this century-old Scottish Highland castle — splendidly Victorian inside, with a magnificently frescoed great central hall — is surrounded outside by 50 acres of woods and a dramatic landscape. You can fish, golf, go riding, play tennis — or just sit around and sip the castle's private-label whisky. Queen Victoria slept here. Information: Inverlochy Castle, Fort William, Inverness-shire PH33 68N, Scotland (phone: 0397-2177).

SON VIDA, Palma de Mallorca, Spain: This spectacular 13th-century castle sits serenely atop a hill overlooking the Bay of Palma, with a breathtaking view of bustling Palma (15 minutes away) and the sea beyond. Tennis courts, a golf course, and riding stables spread out over the 1,400 acres of lavishly landscaped grounds. Information: Son Vida, Palma de Mallorca, Spain (phone: 071-451011).

CHÂTEAU GÜTSCH, Lucerne, Switzerland: A few minutes by private cable car above Lucerne and its gleaming lake, this lovely turn-of-the-century mansion at the edge of the Gütsch woods has a heated swimming pool, public rooms decorated with suits of armor and old Swiss chests, a candlelit dining room in the wine cellar, and rooms fitted out with four-poster beds. The views from this elevation are spectacular — and in some rooms you can enjoy them from the bathtub. Information: Château Gütsch, Kanonenstrasse, Lucerne, CH-6003 Switzerland (phone: 041-220272).

LAKE HOTEL, Llangammarch Wells, Wales: A truly luxurious country house hidden on its own 50 acres. Guests step out of a spectacular flower- and antiques-filled drawing room to enjoy a day of trout fishing, bird or badger watching, a set or two of tennis, or an afternoon in the nearby ultra-Victorian spa town of Llandrindod Wells. All that activity should stimulate a traveler's appetite, which is fine since the property also boasts one of the best dining rooms in Wales. The local lamb and fish are first rate, and the variety of herbed rolls (especially the rosemary) and the Welsh cheeses are very special. Try to book either the Badger or River Suites, each perfectly decorated, with small but well done bathrooms. Information: The Lake Hotel, Llangammarch Wells, Powys, Wales (phone: 05912-202).

COZY INNS AND SMALL HOTELS

If your tastes run toward the rustic, you will be glad to know that Europe can lay claim to a super-abundance of small hotels and inns with the charm and ambience that only years of operation can produce. You can stay at Tuscan villas, half-timbered taverns, Swiss chalets, and Scottish country houses, where the owners take in guests so often that they've come to call their homes inns. These places are decidedly unhomogenized — as quaint as familiar American inns, but far more varied in their styles. A few — the last word in luxurious simplicity — will cost you as much as their five-star urban cousins; at others, a night's lodging is quite reasonably priced.

JAGDSCHLOSS GRAF RECKE, Wald-im-Pinzgau, Austria: This lovely mountain lodge on the edge of the Hohe Tauern National Park makes a fine jumping-off spot for hunting, Alpine touring, and riding excursions in the Oberpinzgau. Information: Jagdschloss Graf Recke, Wald-im-Oberpinzgau 5742, Austria (phone: 06565-6417).

HUBERTUSKROEN, Feldballe, Denmark: A fine example of *kroer,* Danish country inns, this half-timbered building in the middle of a vast estate was built in 1710 on the site of a 13th-century castle and is today an important center of horse breeding and the preparation (for eating) of guinea fowl. Information: Hubertuskroen, Mollerup Gods, Ronde DK-8410, Denmark (phone: 86-371003).

HAMBLETON HALL, Hambleton, Leicester, England: Set on a peninsula jutting into Rutland Water, only 10 miles off the A-1 Motorway, the main northward route from London, this beautifully restored and redecorated old manor house has a dining room that's even better than its superb accommodations. In addition to admiring the scenic vistas over the lake and the surrounding countryside, guests can enjoy fishing, riding, or bicycling on the lake paths. But above all, *Hambleton Hall* provides its visitors with a genuine sense of English country life. Information: Hambleton Hall, Hambleton, Leicester, England (phone: 0572-56991).

HORSTED PLACE, Uckfield, East Sussex, England: A stately Victorian mansion built in 1850 and until recently the home of the late Sir Rupert Neville, treasurer to Prince Philip, it has 17 suites, a heated swimming pool, tennis court, croquet lawn, and 23 acres of magnificent gardens. Furnished with beautiful antiques, the house is bright and cheery with chintz. Afternoon tea is served in the large, many-windowed living room, and an impressive library, complete with fireplace, overlooks the garden. As if all this were not enough to satisfy the most demanding of guests, the dining room dispenses remarkable food — not what is expected in an English hotel, but very French, very fine. Unfortunately, there are only a few tables, so it is limited to registered guests. *Horsted Place* offers the kind of comfortable country elegance that travelers go to England specifically to find. Only 90 minutes south of London, near Glyndebourne. Information: Horsted Place, Uckfield, East Sussex TN22 5TS, England (phone: 0825-75581), or Abercrombie & Kent International, 1420 Kensington Rd., Oak Brook, IL 60521 (phone: 312-954-2922 in Illinois; 800-323-3602 elsewhere.).

LYGON ARMS, Broadway, England: In the heart of the Cotswolds, this fine specimen of a 16th-century English inn has a guest list that includes Charles I and Oliver Cromwell. Information: The Lygon Arms, Broadway, Worcestershire WR12 7DU, England (phone: 0386-852255).

CHEWTON GLEN, New Milton, Hampshire, England: The New Forest, which William the Conqueror claimed as a royal hunting ground in 1079, was already old when this brick mansion went up on 30 acres of peaceful parkland near its fringes. It is now a member of the exclusive Leading Hotels of the World and Relais & Châteaux associations. Rooms are done up with pretty, flowered fabrics that are frequently replaced to keep things looking fresh, and the color TV sets have been equipped to show a feature film every evening. A bottle of sherry is set out to greet arriving guests, and the bathrooms come furnished with fragrant bars of Roger & Gallet soap. The same perfectionism pervades the hotel's elegantly appointed restaurant, the *Marryat Room,* where a young French chef and his staff produce exquisite food. Those who recognize high standards and are irritated by expensive establishments that don't quite measure up will appreciate *Chewton Glen.* Information: Chewton Glen, New Milton, Hampshire BH25 6QS, England (phone: 04252-5341).

GRAVETYE MANOR, near East Grinstead, West Sussex, England: About halfway between London and Brighton, at the end of a meandering country road some 5 miles from East Grinstead, this ivy-covered Elizabethan manor house has become one of rural England's most impressive hostelries since its conversion to a hotel in 1958. Many of the oak-paneled rooms have fireplaces; all have thick carpets, soothing decor, and extras such as a fruit basket, an ice-water thermos, books, a hair dryer, and a special red telephone for emergencies — touches that have earned the hotel membership in the

Relais et Châteaux group. Its restaurant's Michelin star is equally well deserved. Information: Gravetye Manor, East Grinstead, West Sussex RH19 4LJ, England (phone: 0342-810567).

MILLER HOWE, Windermere, Cumbria, England: If you tire of looking at the ever-changing light and shade over Lake Windermere in this lovely, Wordsworth-country hotel, you can play Scrabble, read a book from your private bookshelf, or listen to one of the cassettes on the stereo equipment in your room. There is something very personal about the rooms here, as though this is your own private domain for a day or two. You can wander into the kitchen to watch the friendly cooks prepare the treats that appear on the interesting menu. When you step out from your scented shower, you'll find morning tea waiting for you in pretty floral pots with lemon biscuits to sustain you before a substantial breakfast downstairs. Information: Miller Howe, Windermere, Cumbria LA23 1EY, England (phone: 09662-2536).

OUSTAÙ DE BAUMANIÈRE, Les Baux-de-Provence, France: Famed primarily for its restaurant, one of the very finest in France, the inn is beautifully set on an abandoned quarry in a wild Provençal valley and is elegantly furnished with local antiques; it offers tennis, swimming, and horseback riding to fill your time between the three-star meals. Closed February. Information: Oustaù de Baumanière, Les Baux-de-Provence 13520, France (phone: 90-54-33-07).

BOYER "LES CRAYÈRES," Reims, France: With its move to a stunning 19th-century château, this three-star restaurant has added lodgings that match its food. Set on 19 beautifully landscaped acres, just a stone's throw from the twin Gothic towers of Reims Cathedral, it has 15 sumptuous 2-room suites, some of which open onto terraces overlooking the gardens and all of which are decorated differently, mostly in the style of the Louis Philippe era. *Boyer "Les Crayères"* is a member of the Relais & Châteaux group, and the main attraction is the food. The menu's offerings reflect a finely tuned balance between nouvelle and traditional cuisines, and service is helpful rather than overbearing. In support of the main local industry, the wine list includes more than 60 champagnes. Closed Mondays, Tuesday lunch, and mid-December to mid-January. Information: Boyer "Les Crayères," 64 Bd. Henry-Vasnier, Reims 51100, France (phone: 26-82-80-80).

LE VIEUX LOGIS, Trémolat, France: France's beautiful Dordogne River valley is the setting for this unprepossessing inn, a former farmhouse that has welcomed guests since 1952, but has been in the family of the present owner, Mme. Giraudel-Destord, since it was built. It's a comfortable, enchanting place: The beds are covered with pristine white or bright floral spreads and vast down comforters (a rarity in this area); the cooks are generous with the ebony truffles that are sold in Scarlat, not far away. The proprietors — physicians all — make the raising of geese for foie gras their avocation. Information: Le Vieux Logis, Trémolat 24510, France (phone: 53-22-80-06).

VILLA SAN MICHELE, Fiesole, Italy: Formerly a Renaissance monastery with a façade designed by Michelangelo, this hotel (and Italian National Trust Monument) in the hills above Florence is surrounded by lovely gardens and seems like a gracious Tuscan villa. Information: Villa San Michele, 4 Via di Doccia, Fiesole 50014, Italy (phone: 055-59451).

POUSADA DO INFANTE, Sagres, Portugal: On the western end of the sunny, sandy Algarve coast, this small establishment is a handsome representative of the many official Portuguese inns (*pousadas*). Its 15 rooms must be reserved long in advance. Information: Pousada do Infante, Sagres, Algarve 8650, Portugal (phone: 64222).

PARADOR NACIONAL DE GIL BLAS, Santillana del Mar, Spain: The state-run Spanish *paradors* occupy elegantly restored old convents and castles along the sea, in the mountains, or on the outskirts of ancient villages. The *Gil Blas,* in the region of the beautiful Costa Cantábrica, is typical, with its heavy stone walls and arches, beamed ceilings, tile floors, and gracious rustic furnishings. Information: Parador Nacional de

Gil Blas, Santillana del Mar, Santander, Spain (phone: 042-818000). The central Parador office also handles bookings: Red de Paradores del Estado, 18 Calle Velazquez, Madrid 28001, Spain (phone: 435-9700). For a complete list of all the Spanish *paradors*, write the Spanish National Tourist Office, 665 Fifth Ave., New York, NY 10022 (phone: 212-759-8822).

CHESA GRISCHUNA, Klosters, Switzerland: This establishment in the charming Alpine town of Klosters is as near perfect an Alpine chalet as you'll find: Riotous pink flowerfalls cascade over dark wooden balconies; pine-paneled rooms are warmed with crackling fires; fondue and *glühwein* are standard fare in the cozy dining room; and the eiderdown on your bed is as light as a dollop of whipped cream. Information: Chesa Grischuna, Klosters CH-7250, Switzerland (phone: 083-42222). The Swiss National Tourist Office (608 Fifth Ave., New York, NY 10020; phone: 212-757-5944) has a listing of other Swiss inns and castle hotels.

AND NOW FOR SOMETHING REALLY RUSTIC

The Alps have their hikers' and climbers' huts, but for getting away from it all in the most styleless style, you can't beat:

ARCTIC HOTEL, Narssarssuaq, Denmark: At the southern tip of Greenland, this no-frills establishment occupies an old World War II air base. There are ancient Norse settlements to explore, fjords for boating, the great ice glaciers for hiking adventures — so it doesn't really matter that you won't find a discotheque within 500 miles. Information: The SAS Arctic Hotel, Narssarssuaq, Greenland DK-3923, Denmark (phone: 299-35253; 116502 in Copenhagen; telex: 90336 — often the only way to make contact).

The Shrines of European Gastronomy

In Europe, even ordinary food is very good by stateside standards; and the best attains an excellence only possible where the freshest and most flavorful ingredients are available to culinary artists who, working with the accumulated wisdom of centuries, cook with a religious devotion.

Such are the chefs behind the restaurants we've listed here, the places we prize most among European dining spots. They are not, we must emphasize, the kinds of places where you could eat three meals a day, every day. (That would be a bit like subjecting yourself to three consecutive Wagnerian operas without respite.) Nor are these shrines of European gastronomy meant for grabbing a quick bite on your way to another event; dinners are productions, worth planning for and taking the appropriate time to enjoy.

Reservations should be made several days (and sometimes weeks) in advance whenever possible, and in many cases, writing ahead is the only way to secure a table. But it's also a good idea (where realistic) to pass by the restaurant, choose a table, and look at the menu. Confirmation of your reservation, when you've arrived at your destination, is also wise.

Acquiring at least a rudimentary knowledge of wine also takes a little advance preparation, but is almost a prerequisite for eating in this type of establishment, since wines are as important as the food itself in the composition of your meal. The wine steward (*sommelier*) and the captain will help (so don't be afraid to ask), and afterward will monitor your bites and sips lest some selection falls short of the celestial. (If this happens, don't be bashful about returning it to the kitchen.)

A few more words of advice: Order what appeals to you, and don't be bullied into a rigid menu no matter how zealously it is pressed upon you. Daily specialties are usually good choices, and you should not be frightened off by multicourse epicurean feasts. In fact, these are very small samplings of the many dishes of which the chef is most proud, and can be an unforgettable treat. Prices will, inevitably, be high, but this is a once-in-a-lifetime thing. You should treat it (and enjoy it) as such.

Finally, a note on our choices. Nothing is quite so much fun (or as difficult) as putting together a list of Europe's most appealing restaurants. Actually, little could be more brazen. We could have played it safe by including only those establishments that hold multistar recognition from other appraisers of haute cuisine, but we thought that was misleading at best. It would give short shrift to the enormous variety of cuisines that exist across Europe and to the many world class restaurants that operate across the Continent and that serve meals worth wandering for — but aren't French. So our reach is considerably wider, though we've noted our picks of the best Gallic tables; what follows is a true Europe-wide selection of restaurants that are, quite simply, nonpareil.

ZU DEN DREI HUSAREN (The Three Hussars), Vienna, Austria: This quintessentially Viennese establishment, in the heart of the old city just off the bustling Kärtnerstrasse, offers a whole range of epicurean entrées and a vast selection of hors d'oeuvres. There's not a better place in the world to sample a classic wiener schnitzel. Open for dinner only; closed Sundays and from mid-July to mid-August. Information: Zu den Drei Husaren, 4 Weihburggasse, Vienna, Austria (phone: 512-1092).

SACHER, Vienna, Austria: The venerable hotel restaurant has changed little since its kitchen confected the first *Sachertorte* — a rich, justly celebrated chocolate cake filled with apricot jam and coated with an equally sinful chocolate icing that is always served with a generous dollop of fresh whipped cream. The clicking of heels and the tinkling of crystal blend as naturally as ever into the harmonies of the Vienna Opera across the street, and only the ancient waiters belie the establishment's age. Epic *tafelspitz* (boiled beef) has been served for a century; don't miss it. And for dessert — since you can buy a *Sachertorte* to take out around the corner — have some *palatschinken* — thin pancakes rolled and filled with jam or chocolate and sprinkled with powdered sugar. Information: Hotel Sacher, 4 Philharmonikerstrasse, Vienna, Austria (phone: 523367).

ROMEYER, Brussels, Belgium: Despite its rustic surroundings on the edge of the Soignes Forest about 6 miles (9.6 km) outside the city, this grand lodge offers one of the most cosmopolitan menus you'll find anywhere on the Continent: The restaurant's genial owner and namesake, Belgium's foremost chef, is wont to daub his Ostend oysters with caviar or to shape a mousse of pâté de foie gras like a porcupine and stud it profusely with black truffle "needles." Closed Sunday evenings, Mondays, and February. Information: Romeyer, 109 Chaussée de Groenendael, Hoeilaart 1990, Belgium (phone: 657-0581).

COMME CHEZ SOI, Brussels, Belgium: As an alternative to the very grand country lodge above, we offer this very intimate urban restaurant, distinguished by a kitchen wholeheartedly devoted to modern culinary delights. The talented young chef here considers the "new" in nouvelle cuisine an invitation to experiment, and almost any one of his adventures will provide an evening's repast you will remember long and lovingly. Elegantly decorated and quietly friendly, nothing here will disappoint you. Closed Sundays, Mondays, and July. Information: Comme Chez Soi, 23 Pl. Rouppe, Brussels, Belgium (phone: 512-2921).

CONNAUGHT GRILL, London, England: The *Connaught* is to London what the *Sacher* is to Vienna, and its *Grill* is every bit as well mannered as you'd expect of a place so thoroughly steeped in British tradition. The best dishes on the menu are those on which the Empire was founded: roast beef and Yorkshire pudding, Lancashire hot pot, gooseberry pie. After dinner, you will feel as if the gentlemen should retire to the library with a glass of port and a cigar. Information: The Connaught Hotel, Carlos Pl., London W1, England (phone: 499-7070 or 492-0668).

LE GAVROCHE, London, England: After over 70 years of rating restaurants, the *Guide Michelin* gave its first three-star rating in Britain to this most French of restaurants. It is owned and run by Albert Roux, a former chef for the Rothschild family and once the chef in the royal household. The wine card is exceptionally long and inviting (listing over 400 items, including a 1945 Château Lafite Rothschild for about $1,000, though many modest vintages are available for less than $25). Closed weekends, and late December to early January. Information: Le Gavroche, 43 Upper Brook St., London W1, England (phone: 408-0881).

WATERSIDE INN, Bray-on-Thames, Berkshire, England: Multiple Michelin stars are still not all that common to England. Yet this establishment's claim to being one of the only two honorees is just part of the reason to make a detour to the village of Bray, not far from Windsor and 27 miles (43 km) west of London. Brothers Albert and Michel Roux (French chefs with embassy experience and service for the best private families before they opened London's renowned *Le Gavroche*) chose to open their Thames-side country restaurant in a setting that provides a feast for the eyes before the feast for the palate begins. In spring, enormous red tulips are in bloom all around, flowering cherry trees line the river, and swans circle past as though summoned by a magic wand. In summer, apéritifs are served on the terrace and in two delightful summer houses, and the sight of weeping willows and boats on the water may distract a diner — momentarily — from the extraordinary menu. The Roux brothers are ceaselessly inventive. Among their enduring specialties are *tronconnettes de homard* (chunks of lobster in a white port wine sauce); warm oysters served in a puff pastry case, garnished with bean sprouts, raspberry vinegar butter sauce, and fresh raspberries; a medium-rare roast duckling pierced with cloves and served with a honey-flavored sauce; and a Grand Marnier–infused soufflé laid atop orange sauce and garnished with orange segments. The wine list, which counts no fewer than 400 bin numbers, is first rate, and some of the restaurant's personal touches are charming — for example, *foie gras tartelettes,* gravlax salmon, and haddock quiche served with cocktails. The cost of all this is "rather dear," as the British would say, but less than its equivalent in Paris and well worth it for a memorable occasion. Closed Mondays, Tuesday lunches, Sunday dinners from October through Easter, and from December 26 to February 13. No rooms. Details: Waterside Inn, Ferry Rd., Bray-on-Thames, Berkshire SL6 2AT, England (phone: 0628-2069 or -22941).

BOYER "LES CRAYÈRES," Reims, France: This three-star establishment is now housed in a stunning 19th-century château, set on 19 beautifully landscaped acres, just a stone's throw from the twin Gothic towers of Reims Cathedral. The offerings, which include such dishes as mussel soup with saffron and orange, salmon with lemon and ginger, and standards like foie gras, bass with artichokes, and roast pigeon with garlic and parsley, reflect a finely tuned balance between nouvelle and traditional cuisines. Service is helpful without being overbearing. In support of the main local industry, the wine list includes over 60 champagnes. Closed Mondays, lunch Tuesdays, and mid-December to mid-January. Information: Boyer "Les Crayères," 64 Bd. Henry-Vasnier, Reims 51100, France (phone: 26-82-80-80).

AUBERGE DE L'ILL, Illhaeusern (Alsace), France: There are those who claim that Alsace, not Paris, is France's culinary capital, and this establishment is their strongest piece of evidence. As run by the Haeberlin brothers — Jean-Pierre and Paul (the chef) — and Paul's son, Marc, the restaurant's menu is superbly Alsatian and impeccably prepared: wild hare salad, terrine of crayfish, peach salad with Burgundy. Closed Mondays and Tuesdays, most of February, and the first week in July. Information: Auberge de l'Ill, Rue de Collanges, Illhaeusern, Ribeauvillé 68150, France (phone: 89-71-83-23).

MOULIN DE MOUGINS, Mougins (Côte d'Azur), France: If your vision of the Riviera is dining in distinguished (or at least glamorous) company in a beautiful garden flooded with sunlight in an elegant country setting, what you've experienced is precognition, not hallucination. Just such romantic trances are regularly accomplished hereabouts, often accompanied by the smell of oranges; though far more likely in this case is the wafting aroma of heavenly fish soup, lobster grilled in basil butter, or fowl braised in port. Happy dreams. Closed Mondays, Thursday lunch, and the end of January to mid-March. Information: Moulin de Mougins, 424 Chemin du Moulin, Mougins, France (phone: 93-75-78-24).

ALAIN CHAPEL, Mionnay (Lyons), France: In the flash and sizzle of the new style of cuisine and the chefs perfecting it, don't fail to seek out the unfalteringly fine food at chef Alain Chapel's namesake. The chef himself self-effacing, perhaps because the dishes speak so well for him: lobster with noodles, stuffed calf's ear, a fabulous lobster salad. Closed Mondays, Tuesday afternoons, and January. Information: Alain Chapel, Mionnay 01390, France (phone: 78-91-82-02).

PAUL BOCUSE, Lyons, France: Out of the way though it may be, this city in what Parisians disdainfully label the provinces is home to one of the country's most honored restaurants, and travelers come from all over the world to sample its specialties — *soupe au potiron, loup au four, cassolette d'écrevisses.* In point of fact, the absence of large-scale tourism keeps Bocuse purer than its three-star *confrères* in the capital, which serve so many clients who barely know a *coquille St.-Jacques* from a cheeseburger. Information: Paul Bocuse, 50 Quai Plage, Collonges-au-Mont d'Or 69660, France (phone: 78-22-01-40).

GEORGES BLANC, Vonnas, France: Set on the bank of the river Veyle in the picturesque Beaujolais village of Vonnas, this family-run restaurant-hotel has a history of excellence that goes back four generations. Great-grandmother Blanc, its founder, prepared simple country food. Her daughter developed the cuisine and came to be known all over France as "La Mère Blanc," or "Empress Blanc." Her daughter continued the tradition, and today Georges Blanc — the first male in the line and the first to have formal culinary and hotel schooling — offers an award-winning menu that combines both traditional regional cooking and nouvelle cuisine. There are two menus (two or four courses with cheeses and dessert), outstanding features of which are the braised sweetbreads in spinach, lamb tenderloin with fresh wild mushrooms, and a dessert cart brimming with 15 to 20 pastry selections. There are 23 charming rooms, a swimming pool, and tennis courts for guests who wish to make a real occasion of their dining experience. Closed Wednesdays, Thursdays, and January. Information: Georges Blanc, Vonnas 01540, France (phone: 74-50-00-10).

FRÈRES TROISGROS, Roanne (Lyons), France: More than any other restaurant in France, this splendid house celebrates the land, changing the dishes on its menu season by season to use the area's fresh vegetables, poultry, shrimp, and snails to best advantage. Pierre Troisgros rejoices in the natural flavor of foods delicately enhanced and underscored. A shopping trip with him is something of a lesson in local ecology, wildlife, biology, and topography all rolled into one. Closed Tuesdays, Wednesday afternoons, and most of January. Information: Hôtel des Frères Troisgros, 22 Cours de la République, Roanne 42300, France (phone: 77-71-66-97).

L'AMBROISIE, Paris, France: The only restaurant in all of France to have been promoted to three-star status by Michelin in 1988, this tiny, quietly elegant establishment on the ground floor of a Tudor mansion is the showcase for chef Bernard Paucaud's equally elegant cuisine. The menu is limited to only a few entrées, such as duck with foie gras, skate and sliced green cabbage in sherry vinegar sauce, veal sweetbreads with shallots and parsley on ultra-fresh pasta, lightly battered chicken thighs in a piquant sauce, and oxtail in a savory sauce, but the dishes more than compensate for the limited number of choices with great portions of gustatory pleasure.

Closed Sundays and Monday afternoons, August, February, and holidays. Information: L'Ambroisie, 9 Place des Vosges, Paris (phone: 1-42-78-51-45).

LE TAILLEVENT, Paris, France: Full of tradition, Louis XVI furnishings, 18th-century porcelain dinner service — all in a 19th-century mansion — *Taillevent* offers *cuisine classique* that is currently the best in Paris. Try terrine of truffled sweetbreads, duck in cider, and for dessert, one of chef Claude Deligne's unusual soufflés, like Alsatian pear or cinnamon chocolate. Three stars in the *Guide Michelin.* Closed weekends, part of February, and August. Reserve more than 60 days ahead. Information: Le Taillevent, 15 Rue Lamennais, Paris, France (phone: 45-61-12-90).

GRAND VÉFOUR, Paris, France: At the far end of Palais Royal's serene courtyard, this lovely, lavishly ornamented relic of old Paris is perhaps the most classically French of the great Parisian temples of gastronomy. Specialties of the house include *ballotine de canard* and a fluffy frogs' legs soufflé. Closed Saturday afternoons, Sundays and August. Information: Grand Véfour, 17 Rue de Beaujolais, Paris, France (phone: 42-96-56-27).

JAMIN, Paris, France: Due to the culinary talents of owner-chef Joel Robuchon, *Jamin* is now one of Paris's finest restaurants and has been promoted to three stars by Michelin. Robuchon calls his cuisine "moderne," similar to but not always as light as *la nouvelle.* Closed Saturdays, Sundays, and July. Information: Jamin, 32 Rue de Longchamp, Paris, France (phone: 47-27-12-27).

LASSERRE, Paris, France: A friend once described a meal at *Lasserre* as similar to dining in one of those fabulous Fabergé music boxes, and so it is. The atmosphere in the plush upstairs dining room is very elegant, with waiters in white tie and tails. Service is swift and impeccable, and the cuisine sublime. Some special dishes include crab pâté *au Richard;* terrines of veal, duck, and chicken (served as one dish); eel pâté; frogs' legs in garlic; *rouget en julienne;* and saddle of hare. Write at least a month ahead for reservations, offering a couple of dates; replies are prompt, and this slight effort will ensure a table in the elite center section of the dining room, where the ceiling opens during mid-meal, affording diners a view of the Paris sky. Closed Sundays, Monday lunch, and August. Information: Restaurant Lasserre, 17 Av. Franklin-Roosevelt, Paris, France (phone: 43-59-53-43).

BAMBERGER REITER, West Berlin, Germany: Traditional dark paneling and an old-fashioned homey atmosphere are surprising backdrops for the creative nouvelle Austro-French cuisine served at this dinner-only restaurant. For their more conservative guests, the Austrian owners, the Raneburgers, prepare such classic favorites as pot roast and dumplings; there is also a wide selection of French and German wines. In summer, eating in the front garden is very pleasant. Closed Sundays and Mondays. Information: Bamberger Reiter, 7 Regensburger Strasse, West Berlin, Germany (phone: 244282).

VIER JAHRESZEITEN, Munich, Germany: Everything about it is tastefully discreet, from its half-lit glow to its creamy decor and hushed carpeting. This restaurant in the *Vier Jahreszeiten* hotel offers Bavaria's most elegant and sophisticated cuisine, and when you've had the *Lachsforelle mit Kerbelsahne glaciert* (salmon trout glazed with chervil cream) or the *Kalbsfilet und Morcheln in Blätterteig* (fillet of veal and morels in puff pastry on broccoli cream), you'll forget all about the last time you saw Paris. Information: Restaurant im Hotel Vier Jahreszeiten, 17 Maximilianstrasse, Munich 8000, Germany (phone: 230390).

TAVERNA TA NISSIA, Athens, Greece: One of the best restaurants in all of Greece is in the basement of the *Hilton* hotel. The decor, music, and food are Greek. Notable on the menu are the *kakavia,* a lavish bouillabaisse, and the spit-roasted Olympia lamb. The exotic Greek hors d'oeuvres and salads are also worth making room for. Information: Taverna Ta Nissia, 46 Vassilissis Sofias, Athens, Greece (phone: 722-0201).

HUNGÁRIA, Budapest, Hungary: If the name is unfamiliar to those who knew Budapest in its golden era, that's because the restaurant gained international fame as

Café New York. When it opened in 1894, it was the most famous address in the city, and its destruction during World War II was an international tragedy. The city lovingly restored it to all its former splendor — gilt columns, glittering mirrors, glass globe lights — an outrageous temple of art nouveau spoiled only by a few incongruous Soviet chandeliers. The scene looks like something out of the MGM back lot. Information: Hungária, 9 Lenin Kórút, Budapest, Hungary (phone: 223849).

DANTE, Bologna, Italy: This restaurant is the *crema della crema* of a number of fine ones in a city widely known as the mecca of Italian *bongustaii* (gourmets). On a quiet back street among the ocher porticoes of Bologna, with just a handful of tables in its small dining room. The menu stars exotic delights like *risotto mille e una notte* (1001 Nights rice) and *scaloppa di fegato d'oca al tartufo nero* (black-truffled goose liver cutlet). The perfect complement to them is a bottle of the region's simple, sparkling Lambrusco. Closed for lunch Mondays and Tuesdays in winter; also closed weekends in summer and most of August. Information: Dante, 2/b Via Belvedere, Bologna, Italy (phone: 224464).

ENOTECA PINCHIORRI, Florence, Italy: Michelangelo, Botticelli, and the *Enoteca Pinchiorri* — a perfect Florentine day. The edible art changes with the market's offerings but often exhibits such masterworks as foie gras with pomegranate salad, sole with onion and parsley purée, tiny *gnocchi* (potato dumplings) with basil, and veal with caper and lime sauce. The charming decor of a 15th-century palace and a flawlessly appointed table are all part of the artful setting. An *enoteca* is a type of wine merchant's showroom, which is how Pinchiorri got its start. Closed Sundays, Mondays at lunch, and August. Information: Enoteca Pinchiorri, 87 Via Ghibellina, Firenze 50122, Italy (phone: 242777).

GIANNINO, Milan, Italy: Despite its Lombard location, this is a Tuscan restaurant. The menu now includes exotic international specialties — but the restaurant first made its name in the 19th century with a simple plate of beans, and homegrown delicacies like *olivette di vitello tartufate, panzerotti* (mozzarella in grilled pasta), and *tortelloni al basilico,* which are still the best offerings. Before you leave, make sure you see the spectacular kitchen. Closed Sundays and August. Information: Giannino, 8 Via Amatore Sciesa, Milan, Italy (phone: 551-0585).

RELAIS LE JARDIN, Rome, Italy: Justifiably the darling of the major Italian restaurant guides, this elegant dining room is a bit off the beaten track and, unlike most Roman restaurants, requires reservations. The food is worth the planning, with such unusual dishes as zucchini flowers filled with bean purée, pigeon-stuffed ravioli, and watercress flan with scallops. Closed Sundays. Information: Relais Le Jardin, Hotel Lord Byron, 5 Via Giuseppe de Notaris, Rome, Italy (phone: 360-9541).

TOULÀ, Rome, Italy: Completely unlike the plain, brightly lighted restaurants that are so typical of Rome, this one has a decor that is plush and subtle and a menu that takes you through Venice, Paris, Vienna, and other European capitals. The clientele is aristocratic and well traveled. Closed Saturday lunch, Sundays, and August. Information: Toulà di Roma, 29b Via della Lupa, Rome, Italy (phone: 687-3498).

LONNY'S, Amsterdam, The Netherlands: Straightforward Indonesian cooking in an elegant, authentic, and unpretentious atmosphere. Reasonably priced, as Indonesian cooking was meant to be. Lonny is one of the city's veteran chefs. Take-out available. Open daily for dinner. 48 Rozengracht, Amsterdam, The Netherlands (phone: 238950).

AVIZ, Lisbon, Portugal: You will find Portuguese specialties on the menu of this Lisbon landmark, but the best dishes on the menu include *shashlik au riz,* smoked mallard, and other specialties that had their genesis all over the Continent. The restaurant's management and many of the staff are the legacy of the late, great *Aviz* hotel, once the *Waldorf* of Lisbon. Closed Saturday lunch and Sundays. Information: Aviz, 12-B Rua Serpa-Pinto, Lisbon, Portugal (phone: 328391).

HORCHER, Madrid, Spain: At this legendary establishment transplanted from pre-war Berlin, game and fish are the specialties, but the ever-changing menu usually glitters with fanciful creations like asparagus mousse Cantabrica, pineapple lobster Titus, and crêpes Sir Holten, and no two meals here are ever quite alike. In Madrid, ten in the evening is considered a fine time to start dinner, and the service at *Horcher* is leisurely — so be sure to do enough cocktail-hour snacking to keep body and soul together. Closed Sundays and July. Information: Horcher, 6 Alfonso XII, Madrid, Spain (phone: 232-3596).

ZALACAIN, Madrid, Spain: The coveted third Michelin star that shines on this distinctively Spanish restaurant gives new status to Spain's often-deprecated cuisine. Visitors will find dishes prepared with the unabashedly Spanish flavorings of saffron, green pepper sauce, *escabeche,* and Basque cider served over Mediterranean seafood and broad beans. Though the menu changes with the season, the high quality of the food remains the same. Closed Saturday lunch, Sundays, Easter week, and August. Information: Zalacain, 4 Alvarez de Baena, Madrid, Spain (phone: 261-4840).

OPERAKLLAREN, Stockholm, Sweden: Sunday — the traditional day to eat smorgasbord — is the best time to visit this large, beautifully designed dining palace facing the sea from inside the *Royal Opera House.* This is the particular smorgasbord, piled with seafood from all the waters of the North, that is the pride of Scandinavia. Information: Operakällaren Opera House, Box 1616, Stockholm S-11186 (phone: 111125 or 242700).

GIRARDET, Crissier (just northwest of Lausanne), Switzerland: Merely the best restaurant in the world. Alfred Girardet (known as Fredy) is simply one of the greatest culinary geniuses ever to put saucepan to fire, a master whose art is not wasted in pretensions of any sort, which makes a visit to his informal, comfortable restaurant a special joy. Girardet looks a little like a young, blond Orson Welles, and the only thing more attractive than he is his food. Closed Sundays and Mondays, the first 3 weeks of August, and from Christmas until January 10. Information: Girardet, Hôtel de Ville, 1 Rue d'Yverdon, Crissier, Switzerland (phone: 021-634-0505).

ARAGVI, Moscow, USSR: One of the last oases of even moderate luxury left in the Soviet Union, this bustling Georgian restaurant crowded with commissars, foreign journalists, ballerinas, diplomats, and the like does a booming business in caviar (*ikra* in Russian) and icy vodka. The best dishes are hot and spicy, like *tsiplyata tabaka,* roast chicken pressed between scalding stones, and *shashlik po kharski,* skewered roast Georgian mutton. Sturgeon roasted on a spit is also excellent. Information: Aragvi, 6 Gorky St., Moscow, USSR (phone: 229-3762).

Shopping Spree:
Europe for the Savvy

Shopping and Europe used to go hand in hand. You could buy things in Europe that you couldn't buy at home — or at least at prices far lower than you paid stateside. This is no longer quite so true nowadays, after years of galloping inflation and waltzing currencies. The extraordinary bargains of yore can be hard to find, though the most famous foreign merchandise — the coveted goods that bear the labels of such posh purveyors as Gucci, Louis Vuitton, Burberry, Saint Laurent, and the like — still costs considerably less than its inflated price in US shops.

Duty-free shops are another institution of which a wise shopper should beware: The only connection we have ever been able to see between *duty* and *airports* is that people feel they have a duty to buy something in them. One thing they certainly are is mostly bargain-free.

Furthermore, goods travel a great deal more than they used to, and a lot of the standard items that people used to stalk on the Champs-Elysées are available on Main Street. By the time you've traipsed, lugged, crammed, and declared, you're better off picking up Twining's tea and other such imports at the corner store.

The moral of the story is this: Shop as part of the *experience* of travel. Buy because it brings you into contact with people and places, customs and creation. Shop for things you couldn't find elsewhere, things that will remind you of those people and places when you are back home. Shop for things of very good quality, things you will use often. Then your purchase becomes an expensive snapshot, and the pleasure of the experience lingers.

BEST BUYS

What follows is a list of some of the great shopping experiences of Europe — its finest shops, its special products, small museums of commerce that will interest you even if you're not out to buy. We've indexed them not by place but by item on the theory that you may prefer to look for these purchases when you need them. Similar, more specific shopping lists are part of each individual city chapter in THE CITIES.

Antiques – The *Dorotheergasse* in Vienna; *Sotheby's* and *Christie's* auction houses in London; the giant *Louvre des Antiquaires* on the site of the old Magasins du Louvre in Paris; *Via del Babuino,* Rome.

Birds – *Le Marché aux Oiseaux* — the bird market — held Sundays on Place Louis-Lépine, Paris.

Books – The *Dorotheum* auction house, Vienna; *Blackwell's* in Oxford, England; *Maggs Bros. Ltd.,* 50 Berkeley Sq., London; *Foyle's* and a number of other stores on Charing Cross Rd., London; the *Dom Knigi,* 26 Kalinin Prospekt, Moscow.

Buttons – You'll find 10,000 different designs at *La Boutique à Boutons,* 110 Rue de Rennes, Paris.

Cameras – *Foto-Radio Wegert,* 26-A and 157 Kurfürstendamm, and other branches in West Berlin; the stores of the *Weber* chain in Lucerne (among them *Victoria Ltd.,* Pilatusstrasse, and *Weber Bahnhof,* across from the main railroad station).

China – Augarten porcelain at the *Schloss Augarten* in Vienna; *Bing & Grøndahl,* 4 Amagertorv, Copenhagen; *Rosenthal,* 9 Kaiser, Frankfurt and all over Germany; Delftware from *Focke and Meltzer,* 124 Rokin, Amsterdam; *Richard Ginori,* in major Italian cities; *Vista Alegre* porcelain 18 Largo do Chiado, Lisbon; slightly irregular name-brand china at *Reject China Shop,* 33-35 Beauchamp Pl., SW3, and 134 Regent St., W1, London.

Coats – *House of Burberry,* 18 Haymarket, London; *Loden-Frey,* 7 Maffeistrasse, Munich (for Loden coats); *Roland's* on Piazza di Spagna, Rome.

Copperware – "Dinanderies," hammered copper, from Dinant, Belgium. Villedieu-les-Poëles, a small farm town in Normandy, is wall-to-wall copper; *poëles* — frying pans — have been made there since the 17th century.

Crystal – You'll find Bohemian Moser crystal at 12 Na Příkopě, Prague; Waterford crystal all over Ireland, and Venetian glass at *Pauly,* Ponte dei Consorzi, Venice.

Cutlery – *Henckels,* 11 Rossmarkt, Frankfurt, Kurfürstendamm 33, Berlin, and in all other major German cities.

Diamonds – *Amsterdam Diamond Center,* 1-5 Rokin, Amsterdam.

Eiderdowns – *Fru Lyng,* 47 Akersgaten, Oslo.

Embroidery and Needlework – *Madeira Superbia,* 75-a Av. Duque de Loulé, Lisbon (for Madeiran embroidery); *Casa Bonet,* 3 Puig Dorfila, Palma de Mallorca, Spain.

Enamelware – *David Andersen,* 20 Karl Johansgate, Oslo.

Fabrics – *Galtrucco,* 23 Via del Tritone, Rome.

Food and Liquor – *Fortnum and Mason,* Piccadilly, London; *Harrods,* 87-135 Brompton Rd., Knightsbridge, London, SW1; *Fauchon,* Place de la Madeleine, Paris; *Alois Dallmayr,* 14-15 Dienerstrasse, Munich; *Charlot,* 83 Claudio Coello, Madrid; *Ka De We,* 21-24 Tauentzienstrasse, 6th Fl., Berlin.

Furniture and Furnishings – *Illums Bolighus,* 10 Amagertorv, Copenhagen.

Furs – *Birger Christensen,* 38 Østergade, Copenhagen; *Revillon,* 42 Rue La Boétie, Paris; *Balzani,* 475 Via del Corso, Rome; *Sistovaris and Sons,* 14 Voulis, Athens; *Granlund and Paulsen,* 27 Storgt., Oslo; *GUM* on Red Square, Moscow. (In Russia, a *shapka,* the characteristic fur hat, is your best purchase.)

Gloves – *Perrone,* 92 Piazza di Spagna, Rome.

Guns – *Holland and Holland,* 33 Bruton St., London; *James Purdy and Sons,* 57 S. Audley St., London, W1.

Hats – *James Lock — The Hatters* (since 1759), 6 St. James's St., London; *Bates,* 21a Jermyn St., London SW1.

Haute Couture – The great Paris houses include *Christian Dior,* 30 Av. Montaigne; *Saint Laurent,* 5 Av. Marceau; *Pierre Cardin,* 83 Rue du Faubourg St. Honoré; *Courrèges,* 40 Rue François-I; plus *Givenchy,* at 3 Av. George-V, and *Chanel,* 29 Rue Cambon. For high fashion in Paris at discounted prices, try the following: *Boutique Stock,* 26, 30, and 149 Rue St.-Placide; *Cacharel Stock,* 114 Rue d'Alésia; *Club des 10,* 58 Rue du Faubourg St.-Honoré; *Dorothée Bis Stock,* 74 Rue d'Alésia; *Drôles de Choses pour Drôles de Gens,* 14 Rue des Colonnes-du-Trône; *Halle Bys,* 60 Rue Richelieu; *Le Mouton à Cinq Pattes,* 6, 8, and 10 Rue St.-Placide; *Les Soldes Victor-Hugo,* 111 Av. Victor-Hugo; *Mendès,* 65 Rue Montmartre; *Miss Griffes,* 19 Rue de Penthièvre; *Olivieri Stock,* 115 Av. Victor-Hugo; *Pierre Cardin Stock,* 11 Bd. Sebastopol; *Stéphane,* 130 Bd. St.-Germain; *Stock Griffes,* 17 Rue Vieille du Temple; and *Stock System,* 112 Rue d'Alésia.

Jewelry – *A. E. Köchert,* 15 Neuer Markt, Vienna; *Chaumet,* 82 Av. Louise, Brussels (especially for diamonds); *Asprey & Company,* 165 New Bond St., London; *Cartier,* 7 Pl. Vendôme, and *Van Cleef & Arpels,* 22 Pl. Vendôme, both in Paris; the necklace of shops on the Ponte Vecchio in Florence; *Bulgari,* 10 Via Condotti, Rome; *Nardi,* 69 Piazza San Marco, Venice; *Bonebakker,* 86-90 Rokin, Amsterdam; and various stores in Perth, Scotland, for River Tay pearls.

Kitchenware – The premises of *E. Dehillerin,* 18 Rue Coquillière, Paris, draws the great French chefs. (No matter where you go, it's always nice to bring home the special utensil used for national dishes — a fondue pot and forks from Switzerland; *paelleleros* from Spain; *escargot* sets from France; and *moka express* from Italy.)

Knitwear – *Westaway and Westaway,* 65 Great Russell St., London; *Albertina,* 10 Via Lazio, Rome; *William Schmidt and Co.,* 41 Karl Johansgate, Oslo (for Scandinavian hand-knitted sweaters).

Lace – *Manufacture Belge de Dentelles,* 68 Galerie de la Reine (near the Grand Place), Brussels; many stores in the towns of Bruges and Malines; *Jesurum* at Ponte Canonica, Venice; and, for Dalmatian lace, stores on the islands off the coast of Yugoslavia.

Leather Goods – *Hermès,* 24 Rue du Faubourg-St.-Honoré, Paris; *Ottino,* 60 Via Cerretani, Florence; *Fendi,* 39 Via Borgognona, Rome; *Loewe,* 8 Gran Via or 26 Serrano in Madrid and in other major cities in Spain; and *Gucci,* in Rome, Milan, and Montecatini. Suedes are a good purchase in Yugoslavia: Try *Jugoexport,* 2 Terazije, Belgrade.

Lenses – Contact, telescopic, binocular, or otherwise: *Söhnges,* 7 Briennerstrasse, Munich, as well as in other German cities.

Linen – *Brown Thomas Department Store,* 15 Grafton St., Dublin; *Podarki,* 4 Via Gorky, Moscow.

Maps – *Edward Stanford,* 12 Longacre, London WC2.

Menswear – *Brioni* at 79 Via Barberini and *Carlo Palazzi* at 7 Via Borgognona, both in Rome, sell typically Italian garments — at the former they are more classic, at the latter are flashier. Style at its highest: *Giorgio Armani,* 102 Via del Babuino, Rome; *Valentino,* 13 Via Condotti, Rome. *Charvet,* Paris's answer to Savile Row, 28 Pl. Vendôme, 1er, Paris.

Music – *J. Votruba,* 4 Lerchenfelder Gurtel, or *Doblinger,* 10 Dorotheergasse, both in Vienna; *Ricordi,* 2 Via Montenapoleone, Milan. You'll find Russian records at *Melodye,* 40 Kalinin Prospekt, Moscow — but the sound quality is disappointing. Or get a harmonica from Trossingen, Germany; or a violin from Mittenwald, Germany, or Cremona, Italy — where it all began.

Paintings – Works by contemporary artists will be found in Paris, at galleries along Rue du Faubourg-St.-Honoré, Avenue Matignon, Rue La Boétie (on the Right Bank), and scattered throughout the area around the Rue de Seine, Rue Bonaparte, and Rue des Beaux-Arts (on the Left Bank). Berlin, as vital an art center nowadays as Paris, is liveliest on and around the Kurfürstendamm; a complete directory of galleries is available from *Arbeitsgemeinschaft Berliner Kunstamtsleiter,* 56 Leibnitzstrasse, Berlin, Germany (phone: 882-7020). In Rome do your browsing along the Via Margutta. *Kreisler,* 19 Serrano, and *Kreisler Dos,* 8 Hermosilla, are your best bets in Madrid. The Royal Society of Portrait Painters (17 Carlton House Terrace, London, England; phone: 930-6844) will help you choose an artist to execute your family's portrait.

Perfumes – *Floris,* 89 Jermyn St., and *Penhaligon's,* 41 Wellington St. (both in London); *Catherine,* 6 Rue Castiglione, and *Galéries Lafayette,* in Paris; and throughout the town of Grasse in the south of France, where you can sometimes visit the great perfume factories.

Pewter – Throughout the town of Huy, Belgium; *The Pewter Shop,* 18 Burlington Arcade, London; Nuremberg, Germany; and *N. M. Thune,* 12 Ø. Slottsgate, Oslo.

Pharmaceuticals – The *Boots* chain all over England and *Savory and Moore,* 13 Curzon St. in London; the *Pharmacie Principale,* 11 Rue du Marché, Geneva.

Prints – In London: *Colnaghi,* 14 Old Bond St.; *Craddock and Barnard,* 32 Museum St.; *Weinreb and Douwma,* 93 Great Russell St. (fine maps as well). In Rome: *Ciambrelli,* 143 Via dei Coronari.

Records – Collectors won't want to miss the *Saturn* record store in Cologne, West Germany, reputedly the largest of its kind in the world. Its 3-floor inventory includes jazz, classical, pop, and a comprehensive selection of film soundtracks and Broadway cast albums.

Riding Equipment – *Der Reiter,* 43 Heinestrasse, Vienna.

Rugs – For *flokati* rugs in Athens: *Greco-Floc* at 9 Adrianou and *Karamichos* at 3 Mitropoleos. For Orientals, *Alexander Juran,* 74 New Bond St., London, and *Luciano Coen,* 65 Via Margutta in Rome. Also, the island of Sardinia in Italy and in the souks of Istanbul — if you want to take your chances.

Shoes – Still in Italy, and still *Ferragamo,* 66 and 74 Via Condotti, Rome. Bring gold. *Gucci* has branches in Rome, Milan, and Montecatini; *Tanino Crisci,* 3 Via Montenapoleone, Milan.

Silver – *Georg Jensen,* 40 Østergade, and *Hans Hansen,* 16 Amagertorv, in Copenhagen; *The Silver Vaults,* Chancery La., London; *Armaos,* at 22 Akadimias, and *Argiriou Bros.,* at 103 Kiffissias, in Athens; *Kurt Decker,* at 12 Biblioteksgatan, Stockholm; *Aux Trois Arcades,* 15 Rue Verdaine, Geneva.

Ski Equipment – All along the Maria-Theresienstrasse in Innsbruck; and *Steen and Strøm,* 23 Kongensgate, Oslo.

Sporting Goods – *Lillywhite's,* Piccadilly Circus, London.

Stamps – In London at the stamp auctions held by *Christie's;* in Paris at the outdoor stamp market at the corner of Avenues Gabriel and Marigny (on Thursdays, Saturdays, and Sundays), or at the shops along the Rue Drouot; in Madrid on the Plaza Mayor, every Sunday from 10 AM to 2 PM, or the shops on Calle Felipe III; in Moscow at 16 Dzerzhinsky; and at the *Ufficio Filatelico* of the Republic of San Marino.

Sweets – *Corné Toison d'Or,* 12 Av. de la Toison d'Or, 24-26 Galerie du Roi, and several other branches, Brussels; *Au Duc de Praslin,* 33 Rue Vivienne, Paris; the *Confiserie Sprüngli,* 21 Bahnhofstrasse, Zurich.

Tea – *King's Teagarden,* 217 Kurfürstendamm, Berlin, has 170 different varieties to either take home or drink on the spot. The *Twinings* shop on London's Strand sells a full range of the company's products for the lowest prices available anywhere.

Tobacco – *Dunhill,* 30 Duke St., London. Cigar specialists: *James J. Fox,* 2 Burlington Gardens, London; *Davidoff,* 2 Rue de Rive, Geneva.

Toys – The *Christkindlmarkt* on the Rathausplatz in Vienna, at Christmastime; *Hamley's,* 200 Regent St., London; the city of Nürnberg in Germany (electric trains, Christmas tree ornaments, Steiff animals); port towns like Bremen and Lübeck (for ships in bottles); *Jouets Weber,* 12 Rue Croix d'Or, Geneva (for miniature replicas of trains and cars); *Dom Igrushki,* 8 Kutuzovsky Prospekt, Moscow (for the nesting wooden dolls, *matrioshkas*).

Tweeds – *Irish Cottage Industries,* 44 Dawson St., Dublin; and *Magee* in Donegal.

Umbrellas – And canes, handles, pommels: *Madeleine Gély,* 218 Bd. St.-Germain, Paris; *James Smith and Sons,* Europe's oldest umbrella shop, 53 New Oxford St., London, WC1.

Watches – *Bucherer,* 5 Schwanenplatz, Lucerne, but also sold all over Switzerland; *Patek Philippe,* 41 Rue du Rhône, Geneva; *B&B,* 1 Quai du Mont-Blanc, Geneva, specializes in Ebel timepieces; *Les Ambassadeurs,* 39 Rue du Rhône, Geneva, in Audemars-Piguet. (And don't look for any bargains in classic Swiss watches: The several million handsome phonies ground out every year in Singapore and Taiwan are the only cheapies along the streets of Geneva.) And if you're interested in knowing a little bit more than the time, don't miss Vienna's great *Uhrenmuseum* (translation: the "clock museum").

Wine – The wine auctions at *Sotheby's* and *Christie's* in London; *Fauchon* at Place de la Madeleine in Paris; *Weinhaus Schulmeister,* 9 Langestrasse, Baden-Baden, Germany; *Buccone,* 19 Via Ripetta, Rome; the *Madeira Wine Association* on Av. Arriaga in Funchal, and the wine lodges in Vila Nova de Gaia, across the river from Oporto, Portugal.

Wood Carvings – All through the Tyrol district of Austria; in the town of Spa, Belgium; and in the town of Oberammergau, Germany.

HANDICRAFTS

Some countries now have exposition centers to display their handicrafts; often, the goods must be approved by a design board. For the best in Europe:

Den Permanente, 8 Vesterbrogade, Copenhagen.
Finnish Design Center, 19 Kasarmikatu, Helsinki.
Gobelins looms, 42 Av. des Gobelins, Paris (open Tuesdays, Wednesdays, and Thursdays; tours given at 2 and 3 PM).
National Organization of Hellenic Handicrafts, 3 Mitropoleos, Athens.
Forum, 7 Rosenkrantzgate, Oslo; Norway Designs, 28 Stortingogt, Oslo.
Highland Home Industries, 53 George St., Edinburgh.
Artespaña (Empresa Nacional de Artisania), 14 Hermosilla, 3 Plaza de las Cortés, or 32 Gran Via, Madrid.
Svensk Hemslöjd, 44 Sveavägen, Stockholm.
Schweiz Heimatwerk, Rudolf Brun-Brücke, Zurich.
Craftcentre Cymru, in towns throughout Wales.
Narodna Radinost, throughout Yugoslavia.

DEPARTMENT STORES

Europe's greatest and grandest: *Harrods,* London; *Stockmann,* Helsinki; *Au Printemps,* Paris; *Galéries Lafayette,* Paris; *Kaufhaus des Westens* (Ka De We), West Berlin; *Brown Thomas,* Dublin; *Switzer,* Dublin; *GUM,* Moscow; *NK,* Stockholm; *El Corte Inglés,* Madrid; *De Bijenkorf,* Amsterdam.

SHOPPING STREETS

They vary in size and style — but are all worth a stroll. Take your shopping bag. The *Kärtnerstrasse* and *Graben,* Vienna; *Strøget,* Copenhagen; *Bond Street,* London; *Rue du Faubourg-St.-Honoré,* Paris; the *Kurfürstendamm,* Berlin; the *Ponte Vecchio* and *via Tornabuoni,* Florence; *Via Condotti,* Rome; the *Rialto Bridge* markets, Venice; the flower market along *Singel Canal,* Amsterdam; the *Marktgasse,* Bern; the *Nevsky Prospekt,* Leningrad.

FLEA MARKETS

A country's junk is its life. And its past. And as a result, the myriad flea markets that you find scattered across the Continent are intensely direct experiences of the culture. Some do a thriving trade in semifine antiques; others offer everything from torn inner tubes to inner tubes that are only punctured. Bargain like a Bedouin whether you're in Sicily or Switzerland. Go when it's raining, hang around until closing time, and you'll pay almost fair prices. Here are a few of the liveliest:

Flohmarkt, Vienna – Open Saturday mornings, Naschmarkt in the Sixth District, Vienna.

Marché des Antiquités et du Livre, Brussels – The antiques and book market, as this spot on the Place du Grand Sablon is called. Open all day Saturdays and Sunday mornings.

Marché de la Brocante, Brussels – Place du Jeu de Balle. Open every morning; busiest on Sundays.

Israels Plads, Copenhagen – Open Saturdays from 8 AM to 2 PM, May through September.

Camden Lock, London – Open weekends. Near Chalk Farm.

Camden Passage, London – Open Tuesdays through Saturdays, with open-air market on Wednesdays, Thursdays, and Saturdays all day. Islington.

New Caledonian, London – Open Fridays from 6 AM to 2 PM. Bermondsey Sq. and Tower Bridge Rd.

Petticoat Lane, London – Open Sunday mornings until 2 PM. Middlesex St.

Portobello Road, London – Open Mondays through Saturdays (the best day); mornings only on Thursdays. Near Westbourne Park.

Place de la Banque, Dijon – No town in France is without its *marché aux puces* (literally, "flea market"), and Dijon is no exception. This one is open on Tuesday and Friday mornings.

Villeurbanne, Lyons – Open all day Thursdays and Saturdays, Sunday mornings, and all day the first Sunday of every month, at Chemin de la Feyssine. Also, *Brocante Stalingrad* is open Thursdays and Saturdays and Sunday mornings; 115 Bd. Stalingrad, Villeurbanne.

Boulevard Risso, Nice – Daily except Sundays from 8 AM to 5 PM.

Brocante de la Porte de Montreuil, Paris – Open weekends and Mondays from 7 AM to 7:30 PM; Saturday morning is best. This and the next market on the list are Paris's more rough-and-tumble *marchés.*

Brocante de la Porte de Vanves, Paris – Open weekends all day. Porte de Vanves.

Le Marché aux Puces, Paris – Spread out over a vast area at the Porte de Clignancourt, this market is open all day on weekends as well as on Mondays (which is the best time).

Flohmarkt, West Berlin – In an abandoned subway station at Nollendorfplatz, with the stalls set up in old railway cars. A mandatory beer stop is the famous *Zur Nolle* tavern. Open from 11 AM to 7 PM every day except Tuesday.

Auer Dult, Munich – Held thrice annually in April or May, July or August, and October, for a full week each time on the Mariahilfplatz.

Monastiraki, Athens – Open all day every day, with a special open-air bazaar — *Youssouroum* — on Sunday mornings. Althinas St. and Monastiraki Sq.

Via Pietrapiana, Florence – Open every day during shopping hours.

Piazza Grande, Arezzo – On the first weekend of every month.

Porta Portese, Rome – Off Viale Trastevere on Sunday mornings. Everything from old car parts to mounds of Calabrian country furniture.

Waterlooplein, Amsterdam – Open daily except Sundays, 10 AM to 4 PM. Also the colorful secondhand book market, *Oudemanhuispoort,* in the arcade at the entrance to the university; open daily except Sundays, 10 AM to 4 PM. There's also a flea market every Thursday during the summer in The Hague.

Feira da Ladra, Lisbon – This Thieves' Market is held Tuesdays and Thursdays in Campo da Santa Clara.

Los Encantes, Barcelona – Open Monday, Wednesday, Friday, and Saturday mornings. Near the Plaza de las Glorias. Also try the Thursday all-day antiques market in Plaza de la Catedral.

El Rastro, Madrid – Sunday mornings from 10 AM to 2 PM (but some sections are open mornings all week long). At Plaza Cascorro and Ribera de Curtidores. There's also a stamp market from 10 AM to 2 PM on Sundays at the Plaza Mayor.

Marché aux Puces, Geneva – Held on Wednesday from 7:30 AM to 7 PM and Saturday from 6:30 AM to 5 PM, on the Rondpoint de Plainpalais.

Flohmarkt, Zurich – Saturdays from May to October, 7 AM to 4 PM on the Bürkliplatz. (Also try the *Rosenhof market* in the Niederdorf, open all day Thursdays and Saturdays from May to October.)

Auctions in Europe:
Going, Going, Gone

The auction world has always been something of a private club, where dealers stocked up in order to mark up and amateurs dared not tread. But during the inflation-ridden 1970s, the art market caught the public eye, and auction action became livelier than ever before. (At *Phillips* — London's number three firm — the year-end sales have increased fivefold in a decade.) Many dealers are now so sure of attracting consistently buy-happy crowds that they are also *selling* through the salerooms. So it goes without saying that the days when you could pick up an unnoticed Rembrandt for a song are long gone.

Nonetheless, there are still plenty of reasons to go to auctions: Aside from the fact that auction salerooms are among the best places in the world to learn about art, they are also great theater — high drama at low cost. The bidding has a seductive rhythm, and the tension has a way of catching you up even if you're not faintly interested in the lot on the block. The auctioneer — now more often a sedate gentleman in a business suit than the sort of fast-talking spieler who (as the American satirist Ambrose Bierce once noted) "proclaims with a hammer that he has picked a pocket with his tongue"

— becomes a pied piper, with the bidders winking, blinking, and nodding in time to his music. As any addict will tell you, an auction is stock market, gambling casino, and living theater all rolled into one — the perfect answer to rainy day blues, more fun than watching the ticker tape, less decadent than an afternoon movie.

And though you can no longer expect to make a killing at an auction, there are good values to be found. Sales held when the weather is unspeakably foul may keep down the crowds — and the prices. Similarly, there are sometimes a few bargains at the beginning of a sale, before the bulk of the potential buyers have arrived and before the bidders have warmed up. In addition, prices can be low at the smaller London firms in August, when, because the big houses are closed for holiday, many dealers are on vacation. And in any event, you can usually buy an item on the block for about 30% off its price in a store — providing you know how to go about it.

Seasoned auctiongoers follow some important rules, the most important of which is to visit the exhibition of merchandise that takes place 2, 3, 4 days or more before the sale. ("If you can't be at the sale, you can leave a commission bid with the auctioneer, or even place an order by telephone — but if you can't be at the exhibition, you have no business buying," noted one aficionado.) Only there will you have the chance to examine the lots at close range, to inspect them for nicks, cracks, and other flaws that can affect their value and for signs that what you're paying for is what you're getting. Caveat emptor is the order of the day, and disclaimers are made by the score by nearly every auction house in the business. (One *Christie's* catalogue warned: "Each lot is sold by the Seller thereof, and with all faults and defects therein and with all errors of description, and is to be taken and paid for whether genuine and authentic or not, and no compensation shall be paid for same.") Consequently, it behooves you to make a pest of yourself: Have paintings moved so that you can look at them close up, and objects under lock and key removed from their cases. If you anticipate buying furniture, you'll have to know the dimensions of the empty spaces you intend to fill; take a measuring tape to the exhibition. If you're contemplating a large purchase, get an expert to accompany you.

Reputable houses make every effort to help their customers avoid mistakes, and publish lists of prices they estimate the lots will fetch — and, often, whole illustrated catalogues, full of carefully worded descriptions that can give you a great deal of information about the house's opinion of a lot's age and authenticity. (Here, too, there are disclaimers — that, for instance, the "origin, date, age, attribution, genuineness, provenance, or condition of any lot is a statement of opinion, and is not to be relied upon as a statement or representation of fact." But catalogue descriptions are usually accurate and in some cases are regulated by law.)

An elaborate lexicography prevails, and the catalogue can tell you that a phrase like "style of the 18th dynasty" in a sale of Egyptian statues denotes a fake, whereas a simple "18th dynasty" identifies the real McCoy. "Signed" means that the house believes that the signature on a painting is the artist's own, while "bears signature" indicates only the possibility. "Dated" means that the lot bears a date and that the date may be accurate. Even the typography of the catalogue can help you out. Descriptions that commence with capital letters refer to items that the house considers particularly valuable — but not so valuable as items allotted a whole page. Names of previous owners are also a clue to an item's value: Having belonged to a well-known collector is, for instance, a very fine pedigree indeed.

Once you've digested the catalogue and looked over the goods, you're ready for the auction. Based on your inspection, decide on your top bid (remembering to figure in the house's commission, up to 20%, and Value Added Tax where applicable) and don't allow yourself to be pushed beyond it. (It *can* happen, and often does, that in the excitement of the fray, people bid far out of their price range: Witness the poor Viennese student who, entranced by the bidding, kept raising his hand until he'd bought a Holbein; or the Swiss banker who attended the sale of his jade collection and ended up repurchasing every item from himself.) You will not, however, be held to a bid you regret if you call out promptly "withdrawn" in the appropriate language.

For all of its other troubles, London is still the world's auction capital, and the "market price" of a work of art or antique generally refers to what it (and others of its genre) have fetched in the London salerooms. Everyone knows about *Sotheby's* and *Christie's*, both over 200 years old and not far behind the Changing of the Guard and the red double-deckers as visitor attractions and symbols of the city. But fingers are rising and hammers are falling all over Europe. Here's a selection of the famous houses.

THE DOROTHEUM, Vienna: Founded by the Emperor Joseph I in 1707 as a pawnshop for the poor, the *Dorotheum* was already middle aged when *Sotheby's* and *Christie's* were born, and it's been in the Dorotheergasse, the center of Vienna's antiques district, since 1785. You should see it as a sort of national monument, even if you're not in the market. Besides the repertory of art and antiques auctions that are standard fare at all European auction houses, the *Dorotheum* stages eight major coin auctions a year and, after ignoring the 20th century for years, is rapidly expanding its modern art department. Branches of the *Dorotheum* can now be found in seven other Austrian cities. For details: Dorotheum, 17 Dorotheergasse, Vienna 1, Austria (phone: 515-600).

GALERIE MODERNE, Brussels: This is the aristocrat among the many galleries in this city at the heart of the global art market. You'll find Oriental rugs by the kilometer, small pieces of sculpture, and ornate 18th-century furniture — all of consistently high quality. *Galerie Moderne* has three salerooms; the headquarters is at 3 Rue du Parnasse, Brussels, Belgium (phone: 513-9010). Another Brussels auction house to inspect is *Nova*, with sales of jewelry, stamps, silver, and pianos, 35 Rue du Pepin, Brussels, Belgium (phone: 515-600).

KØBENHAVENS AUKTIONER, Copenhagen: Spread out over approximately 63,-000 square feet, this amalgamation of three old-city firms runs 150 sales a year of everything from heavy-duty machinery and motorboats to paintings and samovars. Items are displayed in the settings in which they'll end up: Machine tools in simulated workshops, Old Masters in elegantly furnished salons. Not on the regular circuit of Continental dealers, Københavens Auktioner attracts just a small number of foreign buyers. Information: Københavens Auktioner, 4 Aebelogade, Copenhagen 2100, Denmark (phone: 31-299000).

ARNE BRUUN RASMUSSEN, Copenhagen: This is strictly a fine arts house, with a large trade in Scandinavian valuables, antique Danish silver and bronze, rare books, rugs, fine wines, and a number of the sort of Russian items that tend to surface in all the Scandinavian salerooms. Ten-day sales take place every month, generally by category. Information: Arne Bruun Rasmussen, 33 Bredgade, Copenhagen DK-1260, Denmark (phone: 136911).

CHRISTIE'S, London: *Christie's* was founded in 1766, so that today an object's whole lineage can often be traced through the records of its appearances in *Christie's* sales; the motherhouse on King Street is a national landmark. Sales take place daily, and the exhibition rooms are a constantly changing museum. There are also branches in a dozen countries. The South Kensington saleroom handles items of recent vintage and generally lower value, such as toys, telescopes, and top hats. In Geneva, sales are generally at the *Hôtel Richemond;* the major emphasis is on more valuable silver, jewelry, clocks. In Rome, not a few sale items come from the hoards of Count X and Princess Y, and there's an air of studied elegance about the salerooms in the glamorous Palazzo Lancellotti on Piazza Navona. For information: contact Christie's at 8 King St., St. James's, London SW1Y 6QT, England (phone: 839-9060); at 85 Old Brompton Rd., South Kensington, London SW7 3JS, England (phone: 581-7611); at 8 Pl. de la Taconnerie, Geneva CH-1204, Switzerland (phone: 282544); at 114 Piazza Navona,

Rome 00186, Italy (phone: 686-4032); or at 57 Cornelis Schuytstraat, Amsterdam, The Netherlands (phone: 020-664-2011).

SOTHEBY PARKE BERNET, London: When the city's oldest auctioneer, *Sotheby's*, merged with another royal auction house, New York's *Parke-Bernet*, in 1972, a sort of multinational corporation of art was born. Although you'll find *Sotheby* sales in many countries, its little white building on Bond Street is a kind of art world nerve center, with a roster of experts in every field that rivals that of the *British Museum;* an important sale of Old Masters, with hundreds of thousands of dollars riding on every twitch, beats an evening at the *National Theatre.* But it also does a thriving trade in lower-priced objects, Victoriana, and collectibles of every sort, from illustrated biscuit tins to yacht fittings. Branch salerooms in London, across Britain, and on the Continent ensure that the sun never sets on a Sotheby auction. Information: Sotheby Parke Bernet, 34-35 New Bond St., London W1A 2AA, England (phone: 493-8080). There is also a *Sotheby's* in Amsterdam, The Netherlands, at 102 Rokin (phone: 020-275656).

PHILLIPS, London: Currently number three and trying harder and harder, it is the only top London house to maintain a full program of sales in the summer months, while its rivals are on holiday. It operates an extensive program of estate sales, often sparsely attended by the general public, so there's a good chance you'll find dealer-level prices. *Phillips* does a large volume in modestly priced lots; its employees are extremely helpful to auction novices. Information: Phillips, 7 Blenheim St., London W1Y 0AS, England (phone: 629-6602).

DROUOT, Paris: This venerable establishment occupies startling steel and glass quarters on the Right Bank street that was named for it and has 16 salerooms on three levels and parking space for 400 cars. Some 60 *commissaires-priseurs* (government-authorized auctioneers) form a kind of cooperative that handles the 600,000-odd lots that are sold here each year. In addition to the whole range of art objects, you can buy thirdhand TV sets, bottles of Château d'Yquem, and even an occasional horse. French auctioneers offer a unique, legal, 30-year guarantee on the authenticity of all purchases. Their Sunday sales are becoming a Parisian institution. For information: Drouot Richelieu, 9 Rue Drouot, Paris 75009, France (phone: 48-00-20-20).

KARL UND FABER, Munich: Once auctioneers of antiquarian books and prints, *Karl und Faber* deals extensively in prints and drawings by the Old Masters, modern paintings and graphics, and top class 19th-century art. There are two principal sale periods annually, in June and November. This is a good place to start a collection of Dürer or Rembrandt etchings. Information: Karl und Faber, 3 Amiraplatz, Munich 2 8000, Germany (phone: 221865).

NEUMEISTER, Munich: This house's sales, which take place about once every 6 weeks, offer particularly good buys in faïence (a kind of crockery) and silver, German furniture, and 19th-century paintings. The catalogues are excellent and detailed and the subscription service efficient enough that you can prepare for the sales well in advance. Information: Neumeister Münchner Kunstauktionshaus, 37 Bärerstrasse, Munich 40 8000 (phone: 283011).

KUNSTHAUS LEMPERTZ, Cologne: A fourth-generation family business, founded in 1845 in one of Germany's richest cities, it specializes in Chinese, Japanese, and Southeast Asian art and also offers medieval work, sculpture, paintings by the Old Masters, and even 20th-century applied arts. New York's *Metropolitan Museum* is a customer at its sales (three in the spring and three in the fall). *Lempertz* maintains a representative, Ernest Werner, 17 E 96th St., New York, NY 10028 (phone: 212-289-5666), to handle relations with its steady US customers. Information: Kunsthaus Lempertz, Neumarkt 3, Cologne 1 D-5000, Germany (phone: 211-236862).

L'ANTONINA, Rome: The auctions at this house on Piazza Mignanelli are also cocktail-hour social events, presided over by superbly suited auctioneers and patronized by suntanned women in fancy jeans and simple mink. When you go, you'll find some good buys (primarily in Italian furniture and religious art) — and plenty of overpriced junk. The salesroom is small; arrive early or you'll be listening from behind a pillar. *L'Antonina* also occasionally auctions the contents of an entire villa, on location. The crowd is smaller, more professional — and the trip to the old estates can be a picturesque excursion into Italy's patrician past. Information: L'Antonina, 23 Piazza Mignianelli, Rome 00187, Italy (phone: 679-4009).

DURAN SUBASTAS DE ARTE, Madrid: Not really in the European big league — but then, Spanish art has a way of staying in Spain. You'll find attractively priced silver and porcelain items, a lot of ivory, and much early Spanish furniture that goes for considerably less than comparable Italian pieces — plus some of the world's most hideous paintings. Monthly sales except August and September. Information: Duran Subastas de Arte, 12 Serrano, Madrid, Spain (phone: 401-3400).

BUKOWSKI, Stockholm: Over 100 years old and highly respected in the trade, Scandinavia's foremost saleroom stages five sales annually — in May and November. They also run four annual sales in Helsinki, spring and autumn. It's not unknown for third-rate French and Italian canvases to be knocked down at vastly inflated figures, but you'll also encounter a good selection of Scandinavian paintings — which rarely drift south of the Baltic Sea. It's a refreshing change of scenery to auction eyes trained in London, Paris, or Rome. Information: Bukowski, 8 Wahrendorffsgatan, Stockholm 11147, Sweden (phone: 102595); or Bukowski, 22 S. Esplanaden, Helsinki 00130, Finland (phone: 640611).

PETER INEICHEN, Zurich: The *Ineichen* salerooms, a Swiss national institution, are a carnival of antique watches and clocks, automatons, weapons, cameras, toys, and various and sundry other things Swiss: miniature Prussian cavalry officers, jeweled poignards, bioscopes, daguerreotypes, nickelodeons, and once, a ballerina clock that chimed the hour by cuckooing *Swan Lake.* Record price for a pocket watch: 650,000 Swiss francs; for a clock: 700,000. That's just in case you're cleaning out your closets. Information: Peter Ineichen, 75 Badenerstrasse, Zurich CH-8004, Switzerland (phone: 242-3944

GALERIE KOLLER, Zurich: As efficient, ethical, and expensive as Switzerland itself, *Koller* stages two 2-week series of auctions annually, one in fall and one in spring, plus a small sale on the first Tuesday of every month. Jewelry — an immense assortment of it — is a consistent highlight. As a sideline, *Koller* also maintains the 12th-century Château de Lucens, a vast living gallery in Lucens, with all furnishings for sale. Commissions charged to both buyer and seller are a hefty 18%. Information: Galerie Koller, 8 Rämistrasse, Zurich CH-8024, Switzerland (phone: 475040).

Spas: Europe's Unique Watering Spots

Long before travelers even dreamed of the pleasures of sea bathing and sun-tanning, spas like *Vichy* and *Badgastein,* blessed with mineral-rich waters thought to have healing powers, were important stops on the Grand Tour — every bit as important as Paris and Rome. Consequently, they all developed such a wide range of facilities over the years — fine hotels, golf courses and tennis courts, racetracks and bridle paths, gambling casinos, and elegant shops — that you can have a splendid spa vacation without taking so much as a sip of the waters that were their original raison d'être.

On the other hand, taking a cure — a favorite pastime of so many historic and fictional folk — is still a possibility, and you'll find baths of every tint and temperature, power showers, steam rooms and saunas, whirlpool baths and sprays, masseuses, mud tubs, paraffin packs, salt and honey rubs, infrared and ultraviolet treatments, facilities for vapor inhalations and gymnastics. And fountains — so that you *can* drink the water. Every resort has its specialty: Some specialize in water cures. (Some waters are good for arthritis, some for ailments of the liver.) Thalassotherapy — practiced at St.-Malo, Pornichet, Quiberon, and Tréboul-Douarnenez, all in Brittany — is a kind of marine approach to thermalism that emphasizes the benefits of salt water and sea air. (Grilled shrimp and oysters on the half shell are the extra added attractions.) Gerovital, a procaine derivative developed by a Romanian doctor named Ana Aslan and used in therapy centers like Constanta, Eforie, Mamaia, and Mangalia along the Romanian Black Sea coast, is claimed to retard the aging process dramatically. True or not, many health insurance plans will cover the cost of a doctor-prescribed spa visit. While there is good deal of controversy about the real medical value of taking the waters, a visit to a spa is usually at least rejuvenating. All the national tourist offices of countries that boast major spas also maintain detailed lists of their countries' facilities, indexed by the ailments that the waters are thought to cure. You can make your arrangements à la carte, or, through your hotel, you can buy a package that will allow you access to most spa facilities throughout your stay. You will, however, generally be required to have a checkup by a local doctor before being submerged, steamed, and pummeled.

Here's a selection of spots at which to sample the spa experience. The tourist offices in all these towns are active and informed, and a note to them should produce ample material on hotels and facilities.

BADGASTEIN, Austria: High in the Alps, some 50 miles (80 km) from Salzburg, this fine old spa was visited by Holy Roman Emperor Frederick III as early as the 15th century and eventually became known as the Spa of Kings. All the patrician elegance of the days of royalty is still very much in evidence, but there are all the facilities of this era as well: three swimming pools, tennis courts, golf courses, pathways for solitary rambles through the lush Alpine countryside. And sooner or later, everyone in *Badgastein* takes the flatcar rail ride through the galleries of the old Bockstein gold mine.

SPA, Belgium: Like a cathedral, the great bathhouse dominates the main square of this town, which lent its name to all of the world's watering spots, and the healthful waters of its mineral springs flow freely from fountains at every turn. The city of Liège is less than an hour away, and the road that takes you there leads past dozens of stately country mansions and lovely forests ribboned with scores of well-marked trails. You can go horseback riding in the woods, or swimming in the tranquil lake. Every August 15, there's the colorful, traditional Battle of Flowers. Long a favorite with the English, *Spa* retains a pleasant Anglo-Saxon air.

MARIENBAD, Czechoslovakia: *Mariánské Lázně,* as this spa is called in Czech, and *Carlsbad* (or *Karlovy Vary*) are the Eastern European spa-dom's two centers, and the grandiose Esplanade, the pastel façades, the palms, and the crystal are all from another, more gracious period that is somehow at odds with the communized monotony of postwar Bohemia. There are beautiful tours in the nearby hills, and you can visit Prince Metternich's superb castle — though you'll have to go to Schloss Nymphenberg near Munich if you want to see where *Last Year at Marienbad* was really filmed. Bookings in Czechoslovakia are necessary well in advance since hotel facilities are limited. The most practical approach is to sign up for one of the comprehensive tours that includes air fare, full room and board, and access to all health facilities, and which can be arranged through Čedok, 10 E. 40th St., New York, NY 10016 (phone: 212-689-9720). Prices are extremely reasonable when compared to those at other major European spas.

EVIAN-LES-BAINS, France: On the south shore of Lac Leman, *Evian* attracts a large number of visitors from nearby Geneva — at least in part for the gambling in its busy casino. But there are also boat excursions and water sports of every sort on the great lake, and the high Alps and Italy are but an easy afternoon away. Like that of its thermal cousin, *Vichy, Evian*'s mineral water has been exported around the world, spreading the fame of the spa. Convalescent vacationers guarantee return trips by gorging on pâté de foie, fondue savoyarde, and mousse au chocolat; most of the dieting is done between meals. Try to stay at the *Royal,* one of France's most luxurious hotels.

BADEN-BADEN, Germany: Since the Romans discovered the springs, which are so hot they are used in the town's central heating systems, this town, equidistant from Stuttgart and Frankfurt, has become so international that it's often called the "summer Paris." And it's still dotted with Russian chapels and villas from the high-living czarist days. The superbly tended Lichtentaler Allée (walkway) is one of the Continent's loveliest strolling places, and the glittering casino is an ancestor of Monte Carlo's. At cocktail hour in the high season, everyone who is anyone — and everyone *is* — gathers in the great frescoed *Trinkhalle* for a glass of warm water.

MONTECATINI, Italy: In the heart of Tuscany, *Montecatini* has a grandeur that makes it look more like a relic of the last days of the Roman Empire than a modern health resort. Its eight separate mineral springs feed into a cluster of buildings amid a vast area of parks and gardens, full of imperial-sized pools, graceful colonnades and portals, and marble statuary and high domes. The *Grand Hotel e La Pace* is a venerable hostelry on the same regal scale as the town. Montecatini is also an art center, with a colony of active galleries and antiques shops; in summer, it plays host to a roster of famous trotting races; and elegant boutiques line its prosperous streets. If that's not enough, Florence is only an hour away.

SATURNIA, Italy: This tiny place in the Tuscan hills, between the Aurelia coast road and the Via Cassia, near a less tiny place named Manciano (Rte. 74), is not really a spa but a warm thermal waterfall with sitting places smoothed and hollowed out of the rocks by 2,000 years of bathers. You can swim and soak here comfortably even on a crisp day in February, as long as you can make it from the car to the springs. If you prefer to soak in style, check into the only hotel, *Terme de Saturnia.*

Wheels of Fortune:
Gambling in Europe

 An old Napoleonic edict forbade roulette within 100 kilometers (62 miles) of Paris. Consequently, the casino of Forge-les-Eaux is exactly 101 kilometers (about 62.5 miles) from the city. Most other European governments still take a similar stance: Gambling is generally not tolerated in cities, where citizens are expected to be hard at work, but is permitted in spas, seaside towns, and other resorts, which are presumed to be frivolous by nature. In London — one exception to the rule — gaming is allowed only in private clubs and only to members of 48 hours' duration.

Restrictions notwithstanding, gambling is booming — and the whole casino scene is changing. Though splendid old dowager queens like Monte Carlo, Deauville, and Baden-Baden have retained their enormous cachet, they are as much national monuments as after-dark hot spots. Elsewhere, dress rules have eased or disappeared. Glossy new casinos are multiplying like rabbits, and slot machines, craps, and junkets are being imported from America.

Casinos are almost but not quite like those in the US, and there are some things to remember:

When you go, be on the safe side, and — despite the new populism — dress with decorum or you may be turned away at the door (albeit with exquisite courtesy).

Take your passport. Most casinos require identification.

Don't be shocked when you're asked to pay an admission fee — it's customary in Europe. The sum may be small and usually includes a few free chips. Or it may be hefty and buy you a whole year's membership in a private club.

Remember that European casinos generally don't open until a discreet midafternoon hour and close at around 3 or 4 AM. Marathon games of Chemin-de-Fer, which can go on around the clock, are the only exceptions. The casinos are, however, open on Sundays and holidays.

If you're new to the games or their foreign terminology, ask at the admission desk for an explanatory booklet. And don't be shy about cross-examining the *chefs de partie* (the floor men). They are there specifically to provide you with every possible assistance in losing your money.

French is still the lingua franca of most Continental roulette wheels. Remember the following: *faites vos jeux* (place your bets); *rien ne va plus* (no more bets); *rouge-noir* (red-black); *pair-impair* (even-odd); *passe-manque* (high-low); *jeton* (chip); *mise* (bet); *en plein* (single number, pays 35 times the *mise*); *à cheval* (two numbers, pays 17 to 1); *transversale* (three numbers, pays 11 to 1); *carré* (four numbers, pays 8 to 1).

With the exception of England, where it's forbidden by law, tipping is usually the croupiers' prime source of income. In roulette, the custom is to leave one of the 35 chips when you hit a number *en plein*. (You will not, however, be expected to tip for smaller wins or for a long period of residence at the table.)

Government regulation of gaming is particularly strict in France and England, less so elsewhere. But avoid semiprivate, semilegal, and uncontrolled clubs, lest you lose your shirt (and bankroll). For most games, the best odds are offered in England — thanks to the British Gaming Board.

Here's where you'll find the best and the brightest of the European casinos:

BADEN-BEI-WIEN, Austria: Vienna is one of the few European capitals that does have a casino. (You'll find it at the *Palais Esterhazy* on the Kärtnerstrasse.) But for the Viennese, who are forbidden to gamble there, a favorite evening's entertainment is the half-hour trip to nearby Baden — which has more space, more atmosphere, and fewer tourists.

LONDON, England: One European capital to offer gambling, London has a number of fine old clubs. *Crockford's,* one of the most distinguished, occupies a beautiful mansion in the middle of Mayfair. Once the private reserve of half the aristocracy of England, it now boasts a membership that is overwhelmingly foreign. The membership fee, about $250 annually, gives you access to one other London casino, the *International Sporting Club.* Unless you can arrange to go as the guest of a member, 48 hours must pass between your application for membership and admission to the club. The same goes for admission to London's major casino, *The Ritz,* in the basement of the *Ritz* hotel (although not owned or operated by the hotel) on Piccadilly. It has an exclusive membership, an elegant atmosphere, and an excellent restaurant. As at many London casinos, there are female croupiers, as deft as they are decorative; they wear richly colored designer gowns and rake in chips and deal blackjack decks with feline grace. Remember, the odds are better for the player in England, and the prohibition on tipping means that you can lose your money more slowly.

CANNES, France: The classiest of the Côte d'Azur casinos and a favorite haunt of vacationing sheiks and oil barons, the *Palm Beach* casino is owned by the great Barrière chain. Its gross receipts always rank among the highest in Europe. Open summer and early fall only.

DEAUVILLE, France: Sometimes known as Paris's 21st Arrondissement, this attractive town on the coast of Normandy has been a playground of European royalty since the 19th century, when Napoleon III's half-brother brought horse racing here and put the place on the map. The casino is a great, glittering wedding cake by the sea, sumptuously decorated, and is host to various social and cultural events during the fashionable summer season, which peaks with the August racing weeks. At that time, formal dress is still required in certain rooms. Stay in the beautiful *Normandy*, owned by the casino, stroll the boardwalk, and spend your winnings on lobster at the seaside *Ciro's*, also a casino property.

DIVONNE-LES-BAINS, France: Just outside wealthy, gambling-free Geneva, in a sleepy little border village, this most profitable of French casinos attracts very big players from the foreign business and numbered-account community, and the sums that change hands on a single spin of the wheel in the handsome, hospitable casino could buy beach houses and thoroughbred race horses. Right beside the gambling tables, there's an excellent restaurant where you can dine until breakfast time.

SEINE-MARITIME, France: Just outside the 100-kilometer roulette-free zone that Napoleon decreed must surround the country's capital, *Forges-Les-Eaux* attracts Parisians who would rather not risk the wheels in that city's various clandestine gaming dives. Try the *Continental* hotel if you're dreading the pre-dawn drive back to Paris.

BADEN-BADEN, Germany: The biggest, oldest, richest, and most beautiful casino in Germany, it has been around for over 200 years. Its rooms are stunning and there is outdoor roulette on a vine-covered patio in summer. The town is one of Europe's most fashionable spas as well, and the Kurhaus next door is the site of countless business congresses and chamber music concerts.

BAD HOMBURG, Germany: A short distance northwest of Frankfurt, this casino occupies a special place in European gaming history: An early venture of the celebrated brothers Blanc, who went on to Monte Carlo 20 years later, it was the setting of that famous novelette of compulsive gambling, *The Gambler*, whose author, the great Russian master Feodor Dostoyevsky, managed to run through a nonfictional fortune of his own.

ATHENS, Greece: Fifteen miles (24 km) north of the city atop Pamitha Mountain, the *Mont Parnes* casino can justly claim a setting more spectacular than any other on the Continent. There's also fine Greek food, a nightclub, and, for those who don't feel like making the return trip to Athens, a hotel. It's more convenient to go by car, but public transportation is available from Syntagma. Some hotels provide a private minibus link.

CAMPIONE D'ITALIA, Italy: The casino (whose name means "sample of Italy") is a delightful 20-minute boat ride across the lake from Lugano in Switzerland. The ferries operate frequently both day and night — to assure the Swiss of plenty of opportunity to sin on someone else's soil. Otherwise the crowd is largely Italian.

VENICE, Italy: In the summer, the *Municipal Casino* is quartered out at the Lido, by the beach. But connoisseurs prefer its winter setting on the Grand Canal, in the majestic *Palazzo Vendramin-Calergi*, where the composer Wagner died. At night in the off-season, the streets of Venice can be quiet and bleak, but the *Palazzo* is always warm, gracious, and animated. There are several first class restaurants and a nightclub.

MONTE CARLO, Monaco: The queen of European casino cities now has three separate gaming establishments: the beautiful old *Palais* on the town's main square, with its fabulous, ornate decor and its sea-view picture windows; the *Monte Carlo Sporting Club*, set on a spectacular manmade promontory by the shore; and the Nevada-style *Loews* in the lobby of the flashy *Loews* hotel — a joint undertaking between the American hotel company and the staid old Société des Bains de Mer, owner of most of Monaco. During the winter, the high rollers crowd the old *salons privés* of the main casino, and in the summer the Rolls and yacht crowd moves down to the *Sporting* complex. The *Loews*, which offers free admission, teems with American junketeers, and the steady din from the neon slots and crap tables is miles away from the hushed elegance of the *salons privés*. Make the rounds of all three for a total picture of the European gambling scene today.

AMSTERDAM, The Netherlands: Holland's newest casino, *The Netherlands,* is in the *Hilton* hotel at 138-140 Apollolaan. Dress is casual, but sneakers are verboten.

ESTORIL, Portugal: This is certainly the gaudiest, flashiest, shiniest casino in Europe. There is a big, slick floor show on double revolving stages and a marvelous seafood restaurant; the clientele is so well groomed and glittering that you can't help but wonder what they all do from 9 to 5. Probably nothing.

PONTEVEDRA, Spain: Gambling has only recently been legalized in Spain, and the *Casino de la Toja* at El Grove is the best of the country's many new gaming houses. On an island near Pontevedra. A glamorous second is the *Casino Castillo de Perelada,* dramatically set in the imposing Perelada castle, near Gerona. The *Casino Gran Madrid* is at Torrelodones, about 17 miles (27 km) outside the capital on the highway to La Coruña.

PORTOROŽ, Yugoslavia: There's plenty of capitalist decadence in this flower-fragrant beach resort on the royal blue Adriatic. Try the *Metropol* hotel for raking in the dinars and for lovely swimming when you've had enough.

Offshore Europe:
Islands of Every Kind

With today's efficient transportation networks, it's getting harder to spot any difference between the center of Majorca and the center of Mykonos. But there are still many landfalls where you can find the solitude and isolation that have always characterized islands — and have, throughout the ages, constituted their main attractions. Herewith a selection of some of our favorites:

BORNHOLM, Denmark: The country's most easterly island is more like a part of Sweden — and, in fact, it takes less time to get to that nation's town of Ystad than it does to the homeland. A cross between a modern Scandinavian summer resort and a medieval Viking shrine, the island is full of attractions: one of Denmark's largest forests, at Almindingen; the spectacular National Trust white dunes at Dueodde; the mysterious grove of monoliths at Gryet; the great coastal cliffs of Helligdommen; plus peaceful old fishing villages like Hasle and Helligpeder, full of half-timbered houses; early medieval round churches like Østerlars near Gudhjem and Nylars near Akirkeby; Viking castles; and herring smokehouses. Rønne, an attractive old merchants' port, is the main town; you can get boats to Copenhagen (7 hours away) as well as Sweden and Germany. While you're there, visit one of the area's ceramic factories and the *Rønne Theater,* the oldest playhouse in Denmark. Clustered off the mother island are some 20 baby islands known as Ertholmene: Christiansø is well worth the 1¼-hour ferry ride it will take you to get there from the beautifully preserved old market town of Svaneke. Information: Bornholm Tourist Office, Havnen, Rønne DK-3700, Denmark (phone: 53-950810), or the North Bornholm Tourist Office, 2 Hammershusvej, Sandvig, Allinge DK-3770, Denmark (phone 53-980001).

FAEROES, Denmark: Forty thousand fiercely independent Faeroese (and twice that number of sheep) inhabit 17 of the rugged islands of this umbrella-shaped archipelago 300 miles from Iceland and 185 miles north of the Shetlands in the middle of the wild North Atlantic. A population of several million wild sea birds of every species — guillemots, gannets, fulmars, oystercatchers, and the tjaldun (the national symbol)

— inhabit the towering shoreline cliffs. One startling island sight is the gathering of the prized guillemot eggs by Faeroese, who dangle by ropes over cliffside nests hundreds of feet above the swirling sea. Another is the *grindadráp,* a midsummer whale-slaughtering expedition, which turns the sea a violent red and ends with an all-night celebration. July 29 is the *Feast of St. Olav,* a gala event that has all the islanders converging on Torshavn for banquets of whale steak, parades, concerts, and contests in ancient island skills. To get there, you can take the 2½-hour flight from Copenhagen to Vagar Airport — 2 hours by road from the capital of Thorshavn. Or go by sea: The romantic voyage lasts 33 hours; *DFDS Danish Seaways* has sailings about once a week from Esbjerg between June and September. And bring your own liquor: The islands went dry a year before American Prohibition and never remoistened. Another sea route is from Scotland via the *P & O Ferry,* Orkney, and Shetland Services, PO Box 5, Jamieson's Quay, Aberdeen AB9 8DL, Scotland (phone: 0224-58922); or *Smyril Line,* PO Box 370, 25 Jonas Broncksgate, FR100 Thorshavn, Faroe Islands (phone: 0298-15900). Information: Danmarks Turistråd, Turistinformationen, 22 Hans Christian Andersen Blvd., Copenhagen V DK-1553,, Denmark (phone: 33-111325).

CORSICA, France: Most people can't remember anything more about Corsica than the fact that it used to belong to Italy (only 7.5 miles north of Sardinia, it is also half as far from the Italian mainland as it is from France) and that Napoleon was born on the island in Ajaccio. "By the fragrance of its soil alone," wrote Napoleon, "I would know Corsica with my eyes closed." Since the French discovered it in force about a decade ago, however, it has become the country's classiest summer resort, and it's jammed in July and August. Yet in other months, and throughout the year when you get away from the main beach centers, Corsica is still a place of savage Mediterranean beauty and startling contrasts: There are deep forests covering more than half the island; 600 miles of coastline to explore; alpine landscapes like those at Monte Rotondo, Conte Cintro, and the little-known Ponte-Leccia; medieval cliff towns like Bonifacio; and a beautiful old port called Bastia. The dialect is a strange amalgam of French and Italian; the bouillabaisse is the fishiest and spiciest in France; and the *paghiella,* a haunting ancient harmony for three male voices, is still sung at all the island's religious festivals and by Corsican shepherds in the fields. Boat crossings from Nice, Toulon, and Marseilles take 5 to 12 hours, and there are frequent 35-minute flights from Paris, Marseilles, and Nice. Information: Centre d'Information, La Maison de la Corse, 12 Rue Godot de Mauroy, Paris 75009 (phone: 47-42-04-34 or Agence Régionale du Tourisme et des Loisirs de Corse, 22 Cours Grandval, BP 19, Ajaccio Cedex 20176 (phone: 95-51-00-22).

MONT-ST.-MICHEL, France: This spectacular granite monument about 2,000 yards off the coast of Normandy was, centuries ago, part of the mainland forest of Scissy. When the forest yielded to the sea, it became an island twice a day with the tides, and the rest of the time guides led visitors across the sodden shoals, between treacherous patches of quicksand. In the 8th century, the bishop of Avranches built a shrine to celebrate a dream vision of the Archangel Michael, and in the 11th century, a Benedictine monastery was carved out of the natural granite. After the revolution, the Mont did a stretch as a state prison, and in 1877 a causeway — all that remains above water during the exceptionally high tides of the spring and fall equinoxes — was built to connect the island to the mainland. The Benedictines are in charge again, and Mont-St.-Michel is one of France's most stunning sights. Walk the single main street, flanked by timbered houses, to the abbey gate; lunch on one of the area's special plump, moist omelettes; and see both the original Romanesque monastery church and La Merveille, the Gothic 13th-century marvel. Rennes, 37 miles (59.5 km) away, is the closest large town. If you're at the Mont during low tide, there's also fine shrimping in the shallows.

ANDROS, Greece: Picking out just one of the magnificent islands of Greece is a little like trying to choose your favorite gold ingot at the Central Bank of Zurich. Lush, verdant Andros seems a fair compromise, situated, as it is, roughly in the middle of the three great island clusters: the Cyclades, the Sporades, and the Dodecanese. More wooded than some of its barren southern cousins and less touristy than crossroads like Rhodes and Mykonos, Andros has all of their magnetic Aegean virtues: a limpid sea and honey-colored beaches (Batsi, Korthion, Gavrio, Kapparia); evocative archaeological remains (ancient Palaeopolis); high mountain slopes (Mt. Petalo); plus pine woods and the fig and lemon groves of the valleys. A grilled *barbounia* (Aegean red mullet), a glass of ouzo, and the lilting music of a *bouzouki* in a *taverna* in the capital town of Andros, built on a promontory and capped with an old Venetian castle, and you will soon be mulling early retirement. Good reading matter for your visit: Thornton Wilder's beautiful novel, *The Woman of Andros.* Daily boats from Rafina and Karistos are available, and there are plenty of possibilities for island-hopping trips to Tinos, Siros, and Naxos. Information: Greek National Tourist Organization, 2 Amerikis St., Athens, Greece (phone: 322-3111); or the Greek National Tourist Organization, 645 Fifth Ave., Olympic Tower, New York, NY 10022 (phone: 212-421-5777).

LIPARI, Italy: Italy's islands are places of summer and sun and sea — and many can be seriously overcrowded, not only by foreign tourists, but also by natives, who seem to prefer vacationing in throngs, and all on the 2 or 3 days around August 15. Altogether different are the Aeolian Isles — a dramatic, volcanic cluster of seven landfalls off the northern coast of Sicily a little more bothersome to get to, and consequently a lot less frequently gotten to. (You may remember an old Roberto Rossellini–Ingrid Bergman film called *Stromboli,* which brought the islands some short-lived notoriety.) Lipari is the center of most activity — now as it once was, long ago, for the ancient Greeks, Romans, and Carthaginians — and the island is rich in archaeological relics, volcanic craters, and thermal springs. You can easily rent a boat to explore the empty coves that scallop the island's rocky shoreline, and regular ferry services are available from Messina, Milazzo, and Naples; during the summer you can hire a super-speedy hydrofoil from Messina, Taormina, Cefalú, or Palermo. Information: Ente Provinciale per il Turismo, Via Calabria, Isolato 301-bis, Messina 98100, Italy (phone: 090-675356); or Azienda Autonoma di Soggiorno e Turismo, 251 Via Vittorio Emanuele, Lipari (Messina) 98050, Italy (phone: 090-981-1580).

CAPRI, Italy: The most famous, most expensive, and most crowded of all the Italian islands, Capri (*Ca*-pri, not Ca-*pree*) is also one of the most beautiful places in the world. To be sure, in July and August the little main square and the Marina Piccola beach are like cans of Mediterranean sardines, so you'd be wise to keep your distance if you're looking for peace and quiet. But Capri can be breathtaking with its sapphire sky and sea, its soft air scented with the heady aroma of the hillside lemon groves, and lush purple explosions of wisteria nearly everywhere you turn. Whenever you go, there's plenty to keep you busy: lazy morning orange juice in one of the Piazzetta cafés, funicular rides from the boat dock, afternoon jaunts down to the marina; rowboat rides around the grottoes; hair-raising minibus trips back up the hairpin road to town; and spooky moonlight rambles to the pagan shrine of the Matromania cave. The Roman Emperor Tiberius built 12 villas here to honor the 12 Olympian deities, and the area around his Villa Jovis — from which he ruled the whole empire for a decade — is a wonderful place to walk for fine views. A wide variety of boats, including the higher-priced, higher-speed hydrofoil, ply the waters between the island and Naples or Sorrento. Information: Ente Provinciale per il Turismo, Via Partenope 10 A, Napoli 80121, Italy (phone: 418988); or the Azienda Autonoma di Soggiorno e Turismo, 1 Piazza Umberto I, Capri 80073, Italy (phone: 081-837-0686).

MADEIRA, Portugal: About 600 miles and an hour's plane ride southwest of Lisbon, this semitropical paradise and former British colony has not been a "discovery" since the inauguration in the mid-1960s of the airport at Funchal, but it is still a flowered and forested place of enormous serenity. The climate is a travel agent's fantasy, and there's year-round sea bathing, exciting skin diving, and fine mountain climbing. You can pluck bananas and nibble the sugarcane that grows in the fertile valleys; then drown any remaining sorrows in the fabled Madeira wine. Funchal, the island's capital, is a gracious, manicured seaside city, where the flowers, the fruit, and the fish from all over the island tend to end up; *Reid's* hotel here is a splendid old relic of another era. You will also find a glittering casino. There is a good deal of ship traffic from Lisbon and points east. The spectacular Funchal fireworks display is one of Europe's great New Year's Eve celebrations. Information: Direcção Regional de Turismo, 18 Av. Arriaga, Funchal (Madeira) 9000, Portugal (phone: 29057).

ARRAN, Scotland, and ARAN, Ireland: Arran is a lovely clump of old Scotland set gently into the Firth of Clyde, about 13 miles from Ardrossan on the mainland; the Aran Islands are three rugged outposts of Ireland strung gently across the mouth of Galway Bay, about 35 miles from the mainland port of Galway. Yet, despite their relative proximity to their home countries, both Arran and the Arans have changed very little over the centuries, and their timeless landscapes and stubborn adherence to age-old traditions set the islands apart from their mainlands in time, if not space. In Brodick, Arran's fair city, you can visit baronial Brodick Castle; watch the Highland Games with the island athletes in their tartan kilts; join the bidding at the annual Highland sheep auction; fish for trout in the icy Goens; or cross moors where red deer roam to the mysterious, prehistoric Standing Stones of Tormore. On the largest of the three Arans, Inishmore, there is Dun Aengus, a cyclopean fort with a circular tower that dates from the first century. The women there still wear red skirts and raw cowhide moccasins called *pampooties;* the men have retained their vests and peaked caps; and Gaelic is spoken in the home. The farming islanders grow potatoes in a homemade soil of sand and seaweed, while the fishing population sets out in wicker-framed, hide-covered *curraghs* (boats) to go lobstering and cockle picking. For information about Arran, write to the Information Center, The Pier, Brodick, Isle of Arran KA27 8AU, Scotland (phone: 0770-2140). For details about the Aran Islands, contact Ireland West Tourism, Áras Fáilte, Galway City, Ireland (phone: 63081); or the Irish Tourist Board, 757 Third Ave., New York, NY 10017 (phone: 212-418-0800).

IBIZA, Spain: A hundred miles from both Alicante and Valencia, Ibiza is the smallest of the three principal Balearic Islands and the least affected by the burgeoning of everything that fuses Spain and the sea. Founded by the Carthaginians in the 7th century BC, you can feel the proximity of Africa in the baking sun, the tropical vegetation, the warm southern winds, the whitewashed Moorish houses, the green palms and pines, and the golden crescents of beach. The 1¼-hour boat trip to Ibiza's satellite, Formentera, is a pleasant way to get away from being away from it all. Boats leave regularly for Barcelona as well as for the two closer ports of Valencia and Alicante. Or you can fly from Barcelona (an hour away) or Valencia (a half-hour distant); the flight is especially pleasant for the view it gives you of the island, looking almost incandescent from on high. Information: Oficina de Información de Turismo, 13 Vara del Rey, Ibiza, Spain (phone: 71-301900).

HVAR, Yugoslavia: An elongated lobster claw of an island off the Dalmatian coast, Hvar has long been a haven for nudists, who control some of the best of the many splendid beaches. It is also known for having the highest percentage of cloudless days per year in the Adriatic, a statistic of which the natives are so proud that they will reimburse you for your room and board on days that it rains for 3 straight hours — and provide full refunds in the event of fog, snow, or subzero temperatures. The city, also called Hvar, is rich in architectural treasures from the palmy days of Venetian rule, and the lovely beaches face even lovelier beaches on tiny splinter islands like Palmižan and Biševo. Split is the closest port, though during the summer, a great variety of boats ply the Adriatic, from Venice on down, and many call in at the busy harbor. Information: Tourist Office, Stari Grad, Hvar 58460, Yugoslavia (phone: 058-74059); or Yugoslav State Tourist Office, Rockefeller Center, Suite 210, 630 Fifth Ave., New York, NY 10020 (phone: 212-757-2801).

Classic Cruises
and Wonderful Waterways

 Whether you're dangling your hand from a dinghy or sitting at the captain's table on a transatlantic liner, being on a boat is something special. People wave and sing and talk to each other, the winds whip your hair, the waves rock you — gently or not — like a baby in a cradle. The pace seems closer to man's own than that of the Concorde.

The flip side is that ship or boat travel takes a relatively long time; that all water looks the same in the deep; that your fellow passengers aren't always congenial; and that the romantic winds can chill you to numbness while the waves make you sick. So it's always a good idea to bring a Windbreaker, a pile of great books, and Dramamine. And if you're the restless type, don't set out on a long voyage until the sea has you hooked.

Here's an assortment of cruises in all styles and lengths that will put you in touch with the delights of putting out to sea:

ATLANTIC CROSSINGS: The days when the Atlantic could be crossed only by boat, when people talked about things like outside cabins and tipping the purser and sitting at the captain's table, and got a lump in their throats on seeing the white cliffs of Dover or the Statue of Liberty are not altogether past. There are still two ways to enjoy all the things that made the *Ile de France* and the *Queen Mary* such legends: The *Queen Elizabeth 2* makes the crossing from Southampton or Cherbourg to New York in 5 days; *Cunard Lines,* which runs her, offers a special package, in conjunction with British Airways, that includes return air fare — just in case you decide the sea voyage is really a *once*-in-a-lifetime experience. Some arrangements also include much-reduced fares for spouses and hotel accommodations in New York or London. Information: Cunard Lines, South Western House, Canute Rd., Southampton SO9 1ZA, England (phone: 0703-34166); or Cunard, 555 Fifth Ave., New York NY 10017 (phone: 212-800-7500). The *Royal Viking Line* occasionally offers a longer New York–Copenhagen run that includes a swing through the Norwegian fjords and stops in Amsterdam, Southampton, and Dublin. Information: Royal Viking Line, 750 Battery St., San Francisco, CA (phone: 415-398-8000 or 800-422-8000).

NORWAY'S NORTH CAPE: This is the kind of scenery that inspired Sibelius's sweeping scores: There are shimmering fjords; angular, towering glaciers; deep evergreen forests; Arctic panoramas palely, eerily illuminated by the midnight sun. A typical cruise starts from Copenhagen or Oslo, takes in the magnificent Romsdalsfjord and Geirangerfjord, crosses the Arctic Circle, and eventually goes as far as Honningsvaag on Norway's North Cape, Europe's northernmost point. Shorter runs leave from Bergen on Norway's western coast for Kirkenes at the top of the cape (which is also accessible by air). Cruises of a variety of durations to the finest, deepest, and steepest fjords are offered by the *Royal Viking Line* (750 Battery St., San Francisco, CA 94111; phone: 415-398-8000 or 800-422-8000); *Det Bergenske Dampskibsselskab* (Passasjeravdelingen, 1 Bradbenken, Bergen 5003, Norway; phone: 317460); *Bennett Travel Bureau* (Karl Johansgate 3, Oslo 1 N-0154, Norway; phone: 209090). More information: Norwegian Tourist Board, 655 Third Ave., New York, NY 10017 (phone: 212-949-2333).

MEDITERRANEAN: A Mediterranean cruise can be nothing more than a 30-minute hydrofoil ride between Naples and Capri — or a languid 14-day odyssey that includes every center of civilization in the ancient world from Alexandria to the Balearic Islands. One typical seven-country, three-continent cruise touches down at Dubrovnik, Kuşadasi, Rhodes, Cyprus, Haifa, Alexandria, and Venice. Another variety takes in the Dalmatian coast, Corfu, Malta, Tunis, Sardinia, Elba, Portofino, and Nice. *Sun, Chandris,* and *Costa* are three good, reliable lines with sleek ships and cheerful, accommodating staff. When you pick a cruise, don't be unduly influenced by mere quantity of ports on the itinerary: Four leisurely and sharply distinct courses usually beat eight hurried appetizers (and anyway, after a while, all handmade rugs, dockside taverns, and burly old seamen look the same). Most cruise space is booked through travel agents, but you can also write directly to the lines: Sun Lines, 1 Rockefeller Plaza, Suite 315, New York, NY 10020 (phone: 397-6400 or 800-445-6400); Chandris Shipping Lines, 95 Akti Miaouli, Piraeus, Greece (phone: 412-6757); and Costa Armatori, 5 Via Gabriele D'Annunzio, Genova (phone: 54831), or their Costa Cruises office in the US, 1 Biscayne Tower, Suite 3190, Miami, FL 33131 (phone: 800-447-6877; in Miami, 305-358-7325).

GREEK ISLANDS: Greek Islands cruises, which come in myriad styles, degrees of luxury (or not), and durations, show you a fascinating section of the marvel-filled Mediterranean. From Piraeus, you can make a quick run out to Aegina and Poros, or you can spend a week drifting out into the Dodecanese. Or you can sail from one wash-white-and-olive-green haven to the next until *you* have become a burly old seaman hawking handmade rugs at a dockside stand. Most cruises come as 3-, 4-, and 7-day packages, the most common ports of call being Santorini, Mykonos, Delos, Crete, Patmos, Rhodes, Kuşadasi, and Lindos. (If you're undecided about the detour Crete requires, remember that the Palace of Knossos is one of the great wonders of the Mediterranean.) Among the best companies are *Med Sun Cruises* (5 Sachtouri St., Piraeus, Greece; phone: 4524726); and *Epirotiki Lines* (87 Akti Miaouli, Piraeus, Greece; phone: 452-6641 in Athens); or in the US at 551 Fifth Ave., New York, NY 10017 (phone: 212-599-1750). *Sun Lines* and *Chandris* are both fine for the islands as well (see above). Alternatively, you can take a toothbrush, a bathing suit, and a copy of the *Odyssey* and do the whole thing on one of the hundreds of local ferries that link all the islands — or even charter your own yacht. You'll never want for bread and wine.

RHINE: The cruise down (or up) the Rhine, once an integral part of every American's Grand Tour, has gone a little out of fashion of late — perhaps when the German mark came so belligerently into ascendency. But if you can afford it, this journey is still an experience of a lifetime. The banks of this *Alter Mann* ("Old Man River") as it cleaves Europe from Rotterdam to Basel are lined with ancient castles and villages that come straight from the fairy tales of the Brothers Grimm. The 160-year-old *KD German Rhine Line* has over a dozen ships, some functioning as waterborne buses and others (like floating hotels) that cover four countries in as many days. Information: KD German Rhine Line, Frankenwerft 15, Cologne 5000, Germany (phone: 0221-20880); Rhine Cruise Agency, D. Neuhold Corp., 170 Hamilton Ave., White Plains, NY 10601 (phone: 914-948-3600).

DANUBE: While it is certainly not blue, this celebrated waterway is long — twice as long as the Rhine — and immeasurably historic: When you've grasped the geography of the Danube and the Rhine, you've acquired the key to understanding much of the movement of European history. Meanwhile, the Danube offers an enormous variety of cruising possibilities. You can nip around Vienna waters for a mere 2½ hours; or you can ride a torpedo for 5 hours to Budapest. You can make a leisurely 4-day trip from Vienna to Passau and back. Or you can go through Yugoslavia and Hungary on the trail of the Habsburg monarchy, a 7-day self-indulgence on a comfortable new ship, MS *Mozart.* Information: DDSG (Donaudampfschiffahrtsgesellschaft!), 265 Handelskai, Vienna 1020 (phone: 217500), or Danube Cruises Austria, 5250 W. Century Blvd., Suite 302, Los Angeles, CA 90045 (phone: 213-641-8001).

CANAL AND RIVER CRUISING BY BOAT OR BARGE: There are two ways to cruise Europe's canals and rivers — by self-skippered boat or by joining a chartered cruise. We'll begin by describing self-skippered boat rentals. It works like this: You get a boat — a simple cabin cruiser. Someone shows you how to work the thing and tells you whom to call if you break down. You buy a pile of groceries, some fishing tackle, and a book of folk songs — and cast off for a floating holiday that will take you along as many of the hundreds of miles of the waterways that crisscross England, Wales, Holland, and France as you choose. There are plenty of places to moor, to walk and bicycle in the countryside (bring your own bike), to buy fresh piles of groceries (including local beer, ale, or wine). If you fear you'll feel as if you're driving at Indy after only an hour of Driver's Ed., hire a skipper to do the piloting. And if you don't feel like cooking, hire a whole crew (or stop in restaurants along the way). It's simple, idyllic, and expensive. And everyone who does it comes back talking about next year. For more information on self-skippered rentals (address of rental firms listed below): British Waterways Board, Melbury House, Melbury Terrace, London NW1 6JX, England (phone: 262-6711), to find out about inland waterways in England, Scotland, and Wales; Inland Waterways Association, 114 Regent's Park Rd., London NW1 8UQ (phone: 586-2510); Anglo-Welsh Waterways Holidays, Canal Basin, Leicester Rd., Market Harborough Leicestershire LE16 7BJ, England (phone: 0858-66910); Frisia, 81 Oude Oppenhuizerweg, Sneek 8606 JC, Holland (phone: 05150-12814).

If self-skippering sounds too intimidating or simply too troublesome, consider joining a charter barge along the canals and small rivers of England, Scotland, the Netherlands, or France. The sailing is handled by captain and crew and the most important person on the entire boat is the cook — ah, the cook. There has been a proliferation of luxury barges and boats in the past 5 years cruising the rivers of England's Cotswolds, across the best "eating" provinces of France, along Holland's wide, interconnecting system of canals. Usually barges are owned by the captain, who intimately knows the area being cruised, and bookings are arranged through larger companies. (Names and addresses of firms offering both self-skippered rentals and charter cruises are listed below.)

Barges are uniformly small — accommodating from 6 to 28 passengers and anywhere from 3 to 8 crew members, not counting dogs that regularly accompany such expeditions — and when not downright luxurious, they are always comfortable. They are also slow, cruising in a week of slow floating the distance a car would cover in a couple of hours of determined driving. They average about 5 miles an hour, but that doesn't account for the many planned and unplanned stops along the way while passengers shop in villages, explore nearby sites, bicycle along the towpath, or help with a lock — all of which happen all the time on any cruise.

And that leisurely pace, really, is the point of the cruise. Passengers see a small section of foreign countryside with an intimacy and warmth simply impossible through any other means of conveyance. Days are leisurely, punctuated by excellent meals (all food — but not drinks and wine — is included in the price of most cruises) cooked from provisions picked up along the way. Passengers can join the cook on shopping forays or spend their time wandering through villages, reading, sketching, biking, visiting nearby historic sites, or making longer half-day or day trips arranged by the captain, with the promise of a fine meal back on board at day's end.

Certainly some of the most luxurious and intimate cruises are those offered by *Continental Waterways* and *Floating Through Europe* (addresses below), but numerous companies have charter cruises through the most inviting waterways of Western Europe. When reading a brochure, keep an eye on itinerary and routes as well as the boat's facilities (most have private cabins but shared bathrooms) and length of the cruise (3 days to a week is standard). The brochure should be specific about the kind of cruise it is (some are specifically "gourmet" fests, with emphasis on food; others make quite a point to visit historic sites along the river or canal or stop at the most beautiful châteaux; some seek out antiques areas for shopping) and give some idea of the activities possible along the route. And most important, the captain and crew should know well the area being cruised, and it should be an area you want to know well, for you will spend the duration of the cruise immersed in a riverside view of provincial life.

Some favorite English itineraries: The River Avon, from Stratford-on-Avon to Tewkesbury, through a string of delicious 16th-century villages, with stops for performances of the *Royal Shakespeare Company* in Stratford and antiquing in nearby Cotswolds' towns; the Thames, from Oxford to Windsor; and the Norfolk Broads, through John Constable country, with more than 200 miles of rivers, lakes, and connecting waterways.

In the Netherlands, cruises generally begin at Rotterdam, that active seaport, and proceed through the country's incredible system of canals to Gouda (home of the famous cheese) and Delft.

Favorite French routes are the canals and rivers of Burgundy, the province prized by lovers of good food and wine, the Canal du Midi in the Mediterranean province of Languedoc, and the canals and rivers of Brittany and Alsace.

These are only a few routes of the dozens offered by the cruise charterers listed below. Whether you do it yourself or join a well-skippered barge, it is the most intimate way to get to know Europe.

Abercrombie and Kent Travel, Sloane Square House, Holbein Place, London SW 1W 8NS, England (phone: 730-9600).

Anglo Welsh Waterways Holidays, The Canal Basin, Market Harborough, Leicester LE16 7BJ, England (phone: 0858-66910).

Bargain Boating, Morgantown Travel Service, 127 High St., Morgantown, WV 26505 (phone: 304-292-8471). Self-skippered, chartered boats and cruisers in England, Holland, France, Ireland, and Scotland.

Blake's Holidays, Wroxham, Norwich NR12 8DH, England (phone: 06053-3226). Chartered boats in England, Scotland, Ireland, Holland, Greece.

Blue Line Cruisers, BP 21, Le Grand Bassin, Castlenaudary 11400, France (phone: 68-23-17-51). Chartered cruises in France.

Emerald Star Line Ltd., 37 Dawson St., Dublin 2, Ireland (phone: 718870). Chartered boats in Ireland.

Europ Yachting, 7 Rue St.-Lazare, Paris 75009, France (phone: 45-26-10-31). Chartered and self-skippered boats in France, Ireland, England, Holland, and Sweden.

Floating Through Europe, 271 Madison Ave., New York, NY 10016 (phone: 212-685-5600). Hotel barge cruises in Belgium, England, France, Germany, and Holland.

Hoseasons Holidays Ltd., Sunway House, Lowestoft, Suffolk NR32 3LT, England (phone: 0502-501010). Self-skippered boats in England, Wales, Scotland, France, Greece, and Ireland.

Quiztour, 19 Rue d'Athenes, Paris 75009 (phone: 45-26-16-59), or *Salt & Pepper Tours,* 7 W. 36th St., Suite 1500, New York, NY 10018-7911 (phone: 212-736-8226). Chartered boats in France.

Skipper Travel, 210 California Ave., Palo Alto, CA 94306 (phone: 415-321-5658). Self-skippered and chartered boats in Ireland, France, Holland, and England.

World Yacht Enterprises, 14 W. 55th St., New York, NY 10019 (phone: 212-246-4811). Private yacht cruises in France, Italy, Spain, Greece, Turkey, and Yugoslavia.

LAKE LUCERNE: The German name of this body of water in central Switzerland — Vierwaldstätter See, or "Lake of the Four Forest Cantons" — refers to the way the lake's angular, bizarrely shaped arms and bays reach into a quartet of the tiny nation's 23 states. Seen from the sky, the lake looks like a missing piece in a jigsaw puzzle. Boats leave from the main landing stage near the railroad station in Lucerne and wander across deep blue green coves, so tiny they look like toys, and friendly open meadows, and up to the edge of some of the most breathtaking landscapes in the Alps. A full-day trip will give you time to stop for lunch and a cable car ride up the Rigi-Kulm that will give you a chance to look down on the lake and the mountains around it. Information: Schiffahrtsgesellschaft des Vierwaldstättersees (SGV), Werftestrasse 5, Lucerne CH-6002, Switzerland (phone: 404540).

CANALS OF VENICE: It's hard to reconcile yourself to doing anything aimed so expressly at the gawking tourist as hiring a gondola. But once you overcome your scruples, you're in for an experience that is poetic, mysterious — and worth every one of the vast number of lire that you are required to spend, particularly at night, when the pale moonlight silvers the city's medieval palaces, the island of San Giorgio Maggiore, and the Giudecca, and turns Venice into a heart-stopping stage that calls to mind Robert Browning's *In a Gondola* and Thomas Mann's *Death in Venice.* Rates — 30% higher after dark — vary little from one gondolier to another; choose one who is pleasant (and perhaps not overly talkative, since twisting around to keep up your end of the conversation can get uncomfortable). Should you opt against the gondola for reasons of price or principle, the *vaporetto* — the Venetian equivalent of a public bus — provides much the same experience at a fraction of the cost. Or take a turn in one of the *traghetti* — gondola ferries — that make 2-minute, 25-cent trips across the Grand Canal at points that are far from a bridge.

DIRECTIONS

Introduction

Fussy as they were, the Victorians were magnificent travelers: extremely thorough, compulsively curious, and driven by intense energy. Their Grand Tour of the Continent often took months, and led from Europe's major cities to the farthest outposts of civilization, wherever interest or curiosity directed.

Rare is the modern traveler who can spend more than 2 or 3 weeks at a time exploring Europe. As frustrating as this limit would seem to our Victorian predecessors, their alarm would be unfounded, for although today's trips are shorter, they are more frequent and aided by fine transportation alternatives. So the days when transatlantic visitors felt they had only one chance to "do" Europe in a lifetime are long over. Two weeks this year, 2 weeks next year, a hard-won month the year after — the North Americans' love affair with Europe intensifies with the frequency of acquaintanceship, not its duration.

Our indefatigable Victorian would be wrong to raise a skeptical eyebrow for another reason. Europe is especially well suited to a series of short visits precisely because of the cultural and historical density that makes it such a daunting prospect taken as a whole. Spend 2 days touring a tiny area in depth or hopscotching the length of the Continent — the time will be equally well spent and the experiences, though very different, equally illuminating.

In the following pages are touring routes through 32 European countries. Organized to cover 3 to 5 days of traveling, they lead you to Europe's areas of greatest scenic and historic interest. From the tiny villages of England's Cotswolds and its great cathedral cities, through France's wine country and the corniches of the Côte d'Azur, across the ancient Roman Via Emilia — used by Roman legions to conquer a continent, through fjords, moors, tors, and lava pours — this is Europe at its most intimate, historic, and dramatic.

Where possible, tours begin at major cities, and though they are most easily negotiated by car, tour operators with local buses cover the same territory, freeing you from the necessity of driving. Entries are not exhaustive or comprehensive; they discuss the highlights of each route and can, in some sense, serve as starting points for longer journeys.

Entries are organized by country; an introduction gives some background and explains the routes that follow. The *Best en Route* section of each route provides hotel and restaurant recommendations along the way (under each city, hotels will come first, in order of expense, followed by restaurants). There is no effort to cover absolutely everything in these selections; our choices are made on the basis of places that offer the most memorable experiences. Since most countries are divided into several routes, it is often possible to string these together to form longer itineraries. But if you are pressed for time, you will find that by following any single itinerary you will see the most notable spots (and attractive accommodations) in the area.

Andorra

A visit to the tiny principality of Andorra, 175 square miles nestled in the Pyrenees, used to be an adventure back in time to feudal Europe. Isolated by dramatic mountains, Andorra offered a picturesque setting that seemed far removed from the pace of the 20th century. In the last 2 decades, however, Andorra has leapt forward 400 years. Now, the quaint mountain villages are being renovated and, although farmers still work the tobacco fields by hand, their sons run computers in banks. As a tax-free enclave and a bargain haven, this is a favorite destination for the Spanish and French for wall-to-wall shopping, 7 days a week. In winter, good ski slopes and inexpensive après-ski amenities attract visitors from northern Europe (whiskey is $4 a bottle). But whatever the season, there is always a line of cars, buses, and trucks hauling visitors and goods to and from the principality on the one main road that wriggles through it from the north (France) to the south (Spain).

The most direct route to Madrid from Andorra, passing through the provinces of Lleida, Zaragoza, and Guadalajara, takes you through 325 miles of diverse topography. The dramatic verticality of the Catalonian Pyrenees is softened by the rolling hills of agricultural Aragón and, finally, flattened by the dry, Central Meseta of Castile. Each region has a distinctive note of architecture, gastronomy, and language, and stops at such towns and villages as Lleida, Zaragoza, Calatayud, the Monasterio de Piedra, and Alcalá de Henares provide a varied itinerary to the capital of Spain from the remote land of Andorra.

The Catalonian region that includes Andorra was reconquered from invading Moors in the year 801 by the son of heroic Charlemagne, Louis I. This prince granted a small tract of his realm to the Spanish Bishop of Seu de Urgel. Successors to the bishop eventually felt their rule challenged by French noblemen and agreed to joint control over the area. The Principality of Andorra was created under the tandem rule of the Count of Foix of France and the Spanish Bishop of Seu de Urgel. Andorrans first waved the country's blue, red, and yellow flag in 1298 and accepted an agreement whereby, in even-numbered years, the Spanish bishop would receive as tribute the equivalent of $12 in addition to six hams, six chickens, and six cheeses. In odd-numbered years, the French prince would be presented with a cash tribute of 960 pesetas.

Celebrating the 700th birthday of the nation in October 1978, Andorrans gathered to pay homage to their two liege lords, France's President Valéry Giscard d'Estaing and Spanish Bishop Joan Martí Alanis. It was the first time that both sovereigns ever met on Andorran soil, and every indication was given that the feudal state would enjoy an updating of tradition in the future. At present, French and Spanish authorities oversee the justice and postal systems (all mail is delivered free within Andorra, and peseta or franc denominations of stamps are issued for mail outside the country). But since 1419 Andorrans have enjoyed free elections of their 24-member Council General and legislative head, the Sindic General, and are therefore proud to have one of the oldest parliaments in Europe. The total independence of the principality is not generally sought by the populace, whose national anthem underscores their present political feelings: "Faithful and free I wish to live, with my Princes as my protectors." Certainly only the unique political arrangement of joint rule provides Andorra with its privileged economic situation today. Originally dominated by a strictly agricultural economy, Andorra is now a model of modernization and growth.

Due to the influx of foreigners eager to establish residency in Andorra and enjoy its tax shelter, the country is attempting to restrict immigration and discourage speculators. In accordance with Andorran tradition, citizenship is only acquired after three generations of permanent residence or by the more expedient method of marriage to an *andorrano,* which is becoming the Catch-22 of the census bureau. At present, therefore, Catalán-speaking mountaineers, shepherds, and farmers share their nationality with savvy French- and Spanish-speaking hoteliers, real estate agents, and department store owners. Andorra is at the crossroads of time, perched in the Pyrénées, isolated from and dependent on the modern commercial world.

One's first impression upon crossing the border into Andorra (a valid passport and the international insurance "green card" for drivers is required) is the monumental traffic jam of cars lined up to leave the country. This situation is evident in the French border town of Pas de la Casa in northeast Andorra (Route 20 from Toulouse), but much more so at the southwestern Spanish border hamlet of Farga de Moles (Route 145 from Lleida). This tie-up is created by the conscientious customs agents of each of the neighboring countries assessing the real value of duty-free purchases made in Andorra. This process is time-consuming since so many ingenious French and Spanish fill every imaginable cranny of their car, luggage, and personal attire with bargain-priced cameras, cosmetics, radios, watches, Scotch, pâté, skis, crystal, jewelry, perfume, and the like, that have not been listed on their customs declaration. In addition, the service stations just within the Andorran border are a mandatory last stop for motorists, since gasoline prices are often one-third less than those of Spain or France.

Once past the entry ordeal, the visitor to Andorra will be impressed by the dramatic landscape, racing rivers, and verdant meadows. The one major highway that crosses the country is excellent, and secondary roads to scenic lakes or hamlets are adequate. It is with a certain nostalgia that the visitor views the peaceful mountain villages and hears distant cowbells. Time should definitely be set aside for serenely experiencing the majesty of the mountains. Agencies in Andorra's capital, such as Andotour (47 Av. Meritxell) and Evisa (11 Pl. Rebes), offer half-day excursions to the most remote forests and peaks of the country. Day trips by private car or reasonably fared minibuses to the ski slopes of Evalira and Pas de la Casa provide exhilarating encounters with nature at its most beautiful.

ANDORRA LA VELLA: Much therapeutic renewal of body and soul is needed after facing the bustle of Andorra la Vella, the nation's capital and the highest in Europe

(3,000 feet). The modern, high-rise buildings almost block out the view of the surrounding peaks, and only the crisp mountain air suggests the splendor beyond the cement constructions. Spending money is the number one pastime, so the visitor should come prepared with American dollars or Spanish or French currencies (almost anything is accepted), comfortable shoes, and a shopping list. All purchases on international name-brand items are bargains (up to 40% off), and many happy hours will be spent window shopping in the throngs of shops lining Andorra la Vella's streets. To recommend one store or another is futile, since most shops have standard prices and stock only the most marketable merchandise. This may prove less fun to the shopping enthusiast who loves to compare and haggle over the price, but it is infinitely more pleasurable to the buyer who knows the cost of the item at home and recognizes a bargain. Shopping hours are amenable even to late sleepers: 9 AM to 8 PM; most stores are open on Sundays.

A visit to the Casa del Vall, the Renaissance meeting house and seat of the Council General, is a cultural parenthesis in this shopping tour. Other adventures of a primarily cultural nature involve contact with the regional cuisine — a marvelous mixture of Spanish and French specialties, seasoned with that special Catalonian flavor. Fine French restaurants include *Molí dels Fanals* (Borda Casadet., Dr. Vilanova) and *1900* (Unió II, Las Escaldes), one of the top 35 in the leading Spanish restaurant guide. For those ready for a big splurge, fine eating and spectacular dining facilities are primarily found in hotels such as the *Andorra Palace* (Prat de la Creu) and *Roca Blanc* (5 Pl. Co-Princeps, Las Escaldes). More modest eateries are abundant throughout the city as well, but most hotels will require that guests take full pension during tourist season; travelers should keep this in mind when checking in.

En Route from Andorra – Directly after leaving Andorra — calculating ample time to get through customs and replenish the gas tank — and heading south down Route 145 to Seu de Urgel, the traveler immediately senses the entry into Spain. The terrain becomes coarser, drier, and the towns less quaint. After passing Seu de Urgel, noted for the bishop and co-prince of Andorra, follow Route 1313 along the Segre River past 77 miles (128 km) of farmland to Lleida. Route 1313 is a poor road, so this drive will take the better part of the morning. The villages passed along the way, however, are interesting and typical of the fertile Valley of Aran in western Catalonia. The medieval parador *Jaime de Urgel* in the town of Balaguer, 5 miles (8 km) west of Route 148, 62 miles (100 km) south of Andorra, is a pleasant place for refreshment before continuing the remaining 16 miles (27 km) along Route 145 through the plains to Lérida.

LLEIDA: The capital of the province, with a population of 120,000, Lleida is built on a hill overlooking the Segre River. At the highest point of the city, the Gothic cathedral of Seu Vieja can be admired and the remains of the ancient Arab fortress of La Zuda explored. The panoramic view of Lleida and the surrounding orchards is spectacular and well worth the drive up the hill. From this vantage point, the strategic importance of Lleida can be appreciated. Indeed, the city's name derives from the Latin word *ilerda,* or "stronghold," so named when the Roman troops of Caesar conquered the original Iberian fortress and, later, the rival army of Pompeii. The invading Moors made "Lareda" the capital of the *taifa,* or feudal realm, until the Christian armies came from the north to reconquer the region. Besieged by invading French troops at various times in its history, Lleida still presents itself as a well-fortressed city.

Due to its strong Catalonian ties, Lleida offers a cultural shock to visitors who think they can speak Spanish. The Catalán accent is more pronounced here than in Barcelona, but the warmth of the people compensates for the language barrier. Enjoy the Catalonian accent in the regional cuisine: the *ensalada catalana, cassolada,* and game dishes. The confection of *turron* and holiday pastries are famous. Recommended is the regional wine, Castelle de Remy. Fine restaurants include *Forn del Nastasi* (10 Salmerón) and *Moli de la Nora,* 4 miles (6.4 km) north on the Seu road at Villanueva de la Barca. Outside the city, on Route NII, the *Condes de Urgel* hotel has fine dining facilities in a picturesque setting.

For further information regarding sights in Lleida, a map of the city and a brochure in English are available at the Office of Tourism (Arc del Pont; phone: 248120).

En Route from Lleida – Drive west on Route NII to Zaragoza, 86 miles (143 km) away. This is a better road, so the trip should not be very tiring. Also, the new six-lane highway from Barcelona can be picked up just outside Lleida, further speeding the mainly uneventful journey past fertile valleys to Zaragoza, a city at the geographic crossroads of the Cantabric and Mediterranean seas and of the Pyrénées and the Central Meseta.

ZARAGOZA: The provincial capital and the largest city of the region of Aragón, with a population of 675,000, Zaragoza has been called the Lady of Four Cultures. The original Iberian city on the banks of the majestic Ebro River was conquered in AD 24 by Roman troops. The plan was to make it a city of peace for legion veterans. The name of the city derives from the Latin name Caesar Augustus, which, when pronounced rapidly, transforms to Zaragoza. The invading Arabs made the city, called Sarakosta by them, a cultural center and the seat of the regional king of Taifa until 1118, when the Christians reconquered Zaragoza for the crown of Aragón. These four cultures blend harmoniously to form the personality of Zaragoza, where Iberian and Roman ruins, Arab palaces, and Christian temples can be seen.

Zaragoza is a modern city today, important for its university and commercial vitality. Still, its main importance is for many visitors spiritual, since it was on a column of a Roman temple in Zaragoza that the Virgin Mary is said to have miraculously appeared to St. James with promises of salvation. The religious devotion to Nuestra Senora del Pilar is most profound in Spain and in Latin America, since the feast day coincides with October 12 celebrations of Hispanic culture. The monumental neo-classic Basilica del Pilar dominates the skyline from the Ebro River and is noted for its sculptured facade and interior frescoes by Goya, a native son. Most of the cultural sights of Zaragoza are within walking distance of the basilica, so it is a very good place to start a city tour.

Remains of Roman walls can be found west of the basilica. Farther west, the church of San Pablo can be seen, noted for its octagonal tower of the Mudéjar style, reflecting the design of Arab architects for Christian temples. A 10-minute walk farther, and not to be missed, is the Aljaferia, the spectacular Arab palace of the 11th century constructed by the Taifa King Abu Chafar Ahmed Almoctadir-bilah. This pleasure retreat is the only example of Taifa architecture still standing and therefore has special artistic interest for those intrigued by Granada's Alhambra and Córdoba's mosque. Under restoration today, the Aljaferia is an unexpected treat for the visitor to Zaragoza. Other sights in Zaragoza are found east of the basilica and include the 16th-century Ayuntamiento, or government house; La Lonja, or market center; and the 14th-century Cathedral of La Seo, with its elaborate plateresque altar and baroque interior. The Office of Tourism, near the old Roman walls, can provide brochures and maps that facilitate sightseeing.

Eating is excellent in Zaragoza, as in all of Aragón, and is characterized by simple but delicious preparation. The abundance of locally grown fruits and vegetables allows for great variety and selection in cooking. Such dishes as eggs *al salmorejo,* chicken *a la chilindrón,* lamb *a la pastora,* or the *ternasco asado* are famed local delicacies, as are the sweets and candied fruits covered with chocolate. The robust table wines of Cariñena are outstanding.

When looking for a place to eat, do not be timid and miss out on the experience of seeing El Tubo, a winding labyrinth of streets in the area directly in front of the basilica. Row upon row of taverns and restaurants serve hearty regional fare in a rustic atmosphere. Since Zaragoza is a university town, there is always singing and guitar music in the air as students converge on their favorite haunt in El Tubo. Recommended restaurants include *El Plato,* one of the taverns in this maze of streets. Elsewhere, good cooking can be found at the *Costa Vasca* (13 Teniente Coronel Valenzuela), *Asador Gayarre* (3 miles/5 km on the road to the airport), *Gurrea* (14 S. Ignacio de Loyola), and *Horno Asador Boyesco* (44 Manuel Lasala). The restaurant and *parilla,* or grill room, of the *Corona de Aragón* hotel offer luxury dining at high prices.

Taking Route NII south out of the city, you drive past 50 miles (80 km) of orchards and vineyards before reaching Calatayud, the second largest city of the province.

CALATAYUD: The ancient Roman city of Bilbilis sat here, at the confluence of the Jalon and Jiloca rivers. Bilbilis flourished in pre-Christian times and is famous for being the home of the philosopher and writer Marcial. The city was renamed Zalat-Ayud by the Arabs, and ruins of the Moorish *ayud,* or castle, can be seen on the hilltop above the city. The many Mudéjar buildings such as the Colegiata de Santa Maria and the churches of San Andrés and San Pedro de los Francos are of artistic interest. Our itinerary takes us just past Calatayud, however, 12 miles (20 km) down Road 202 to the Monasterio de Piedra, founded in the 12th century by monks of the Order of Cister.

MONASTERIO DE PIEDRA: The medieval monastery, today converted into a three-star hotel, is an ideal place to stop and eat or spend the night (see *Best en Route*). In accordance with the original purpose of the monastery, the surroundings of the Monasterio de Piedra lend themselves to the monks' need for solitude and quiet contemplation. Of absolutely breathtaking beauty is the surrounding national park. It seems a wonder, in such an arid region, that the River Piedra could sculpt such spectacular caverns and create such dramatic cascades. The highlights of the park are conveniently indicated by arrows along a mile-long path. The natural beauty at every turn makes this 2-hour walk a delightful afternoon stroll. For those spending the night at the monastery, the evening itself will provide a memorable experience.

En Route from the Monasterio de Piedra – After winding your way back to Route NII, the remaining drive to Madrid includes a varied panorama of rural landscape and the opportunity for several brief stops in interesting towns. Fifty miles (80 km) from Calatayud is the ancient city of Medinaceli, the "city in the sky."

MEDINACELI: A drive to the top of the steep hill upon which the town was founded affords a magnificent view of the area and a chance to get close enough to admire the unique Roman arch that is unexpectedly perched on the edge of a plunging cliff. This 2nd-century construction is one of only two three-tiered arches still in existence (the other one is in Rome) and seems to usher the traveler on toward the heavens — or at least on to the Central Meseta of Castile.

Returning to Route NII for 10 miles (16 km), one can take a short side trip down road C114 for 13 miles (21 km) to medieval Sigüenza.

SIGÜENZA: Built by the Romans on the banks of the Henares River in the 5th century, this picturesque town is best known today for its 12th-century Gothic cathedral. Here is the famous sculpture *El Doncel,* marking the tomb of the poetic and heroic nobleman slain in Granada in 1486, D. Martín Vázquez de Arce.

The remaining 80 miles (128 km) to Madrid, backtracking again to Route NII, bring you past Castilian towns large and small. Thirty-five miles (56 km) from Madrid you'll come to the city of Guadalajara.

GUADALAJARA: Today an industrial center, Guadalajara was at one time a Moorish stronghold, as its name, Valley of Stones, suggests. Later the feudal seat of the powerful Mendoza and Santillana families, it was an important center of Renaissance culture. The only vestige of this noble past, however, is the facade of the Infantado Palace, whose interior was totally destroyed during the Spanish Civil War.

Continuing the journey down Route NII for 14 miles (23 km) to Alcalá de Henares, one last stop can be made before reaching Madrid.

ALCALÁ DE HENARES: The highlights of a visit to Alcalá are the original Universidad Complutense, founded in 1499 by the humanist Cardinal Francisco Jiménez de Cisneros; the house where Cervantes was born; and the Municipal Hall, where an edition of the rare Polyglot Bible is displayed. You can have a medieval meal at the *Hostería del Estudiante,* next to the university, or homemade candied almonds bought through a turntable from the cloistered nuns of the Franciscan Convent of Beaterio de San Diego.

En Route from Alcalá – Back on Route NII, the 21-mile (35-km) drive to Madrid, passing the American Air Force base at Torrejon de Ardoz and the international airport of Barajas, will take approximately half an hour.

BEST EN ROUTE

Hotels in Andorra and the northern provinces of Spain are moderately priced, running from as high as $70 a night, double occupancy, with private baths for expensive establishments, to around $50 in moderate ones, and as low as $30 and under (inexpensive). Restaurants are also inexpensive, costing between $8 and $10 per person for a full-course meal. Most hotels, however, prefer their guests to take full-pension plans. Be sure to make reservations, particularly during the summer, at whichever hotel you intend to stay.

ANDORRA LA VELLA

Andorra Palace – This 130-room hotel offers private baths, a swimming pool, dining room, and cafeteria service. Prat de la Creu (phone: 21072). Expensive.

Andorra Park – A view of the mountains as well as balconies, private baths, dining services, and a swimming pool are found at this 78-room hotel. Roureda Guillemó (phone: 20970). Expensive.

Molí dels Fanals – Restaurant specializing in French cuisine (also a hotel). Borda Casadet., Dr. Vilanova. Expensive.

1900 – Classy French fare, an excellent wine cellar, and pretty rooms on a quiet side street. Unió II, Las Escaldes. Expensive.

Roc Blanc – Since its recent refurbishment, this 240-room hotel is now the most modern in the area. Thermal therapeutic treatments are available. 5 Pl. Co-Princeps, Las Escaldes (phone: 21486). Expensive.

Flora – A bar and breakfast only are available at this 44-room hotel. 23 Antic Carrer Jajor (phone: 21508). Moderate.

Isard-55 – A 51-room hotel with its own dining room. 36 Av. Meritxell (phone: 20092). Moderate.

LLEIDA

Molide la Nora – Found in an old windmill, decorated to look like an old barge inside, this restaurant offers specialties of fish and game in season. 4 miles (6.4 km) north on the Seu road in the village of Villa Nueva de la Barca. Expensive.

Condes de Urgel – This 105-room hotel features private baths, air conditioning, and a dining room. Rte. NII (phone: 202300). Moderate.

Ilerda – A small hotel that also offers dining facilities. Barcelona Hwy. at Km 467 (phone: 21-42-76). Inexpensive.

ZARAGOZA

Asador Gayarre – Fish restaurant in an old, colonial-style house. Salmon (in season) is especially good. 3 miles (5 km) out on the road to the airport. Ctra. Aeropuerto Km 4.3. Expensive.

Corona de Aragón – This 249-room hotel has a rooftop swimming pool and dining room. Via Imperial (phone: 430100). Expensive.

Gran – A 140-room hotel with dining service. 5 Costa (phone: 221901). Expensive.

Costa Vasca – The subtle use of fresh herbs with fish and meat, Basque cooking, and Rioja wines make up the menu here. 13 Teniente Coronel Valenzuela. Moderate.

Goya – A 157-room hotel with private baths and a dining room. 5 Cinco de Marzo (phone: 229331). Moderate.

Gurrea – An international menu is offered in this centrally located restaurant. 14 S. Ignacio de Loyola. Moderate.

Horno Asador Goyesco – Nowadays much more than a grill. Try the imaginative fare, based on local produce. 44 Manuel Lasala. Moderate.

El Plata – This tavern is in the famous El Tubo district, a winding labyrinth of streets in front of the basilica. Inexpensive.

Ramiro – Though it has no dining room, this 105-room hotel does have a bar. 123 Corso (phone: 298200). Inexpensive.

CALATAYUD

Calatayud – Private baths and dining services are provided in this 62-room hotel. Rte. NII, Km 237 (phone: 881323). Moderate.

MONASTERIO DE PIEDRA

Monasterio de Piedra – Housed in a 12th-century monastery for Cistercian monks, this 61-room hotel has a swimming pool, bar, and a dining room. Nueralos, 15 miles (24 km) outside Calatayud (phone: 849011). Moderate.

GUADALAJARA

Pax – This 64-room hotel offers a swimming pool and dining room. Rte. NII, Km 57 (phone: 221800). Moderate.

Austria

Surrounded by West Germany and Czechoslovakia to the north, Hungary to the east, Yugoslavia and Italy to the south, and Switzerland and Liechtenstein to the west, landlocked Austria (covering an area of about 32,375 square miles) is smaller than the state of Maine. Nevertheless, Austria offers more variety than almost any country in Europe. Moody plains with rocky outcroppings are crowned by castles and dense green forests evocative of medieval legends and fairy tales. The beautiful Danube flows for miles through the country's heartland, where robber baron battlements still look down on waters that are no longer blue. In the Salzkammergut Lake Region, ancient glacial waters lap calmly against the shores of little spa towns. There are acres of vineyards in settings more romantic than those in Burgundy or Bordeaux, and of course there are the Alps — some of the most breathtaking and dramatic peaks in the world.

Austria's 7.5 million people are spread out comfortably among city, town, spa, and farm, but the population swells annually by at least a million as tourists flock here to ski, sample the pastries, take the waters, listen to the music, or just generally absorb the splendor of this cultural jewel at the crossroads of Europe. If Vienna, Austria's capital, is the most distinguished city in the German-speaking world, Salzburg is certainly the most elegant; Innsbruck, high in the mountains, combines the best qualities of both and adds its own Alpine flavor; while Graz, to the south, is a medieval gem of an imperial city.

The history of Austria is an incredible mosaic of peoples and religions. Indeed, some of the earliest human relics (dating from the Iron Age) are still being unearthed and studied in the Hallstatt area. Austria (Österreich) means "Eastern Empire" and in AD 788 referred to the eastern reaches of Charlemagne's conquests. The first indigenous monarchy was established by the Babenbergs in 976 at the town of Melk. Much of the country was still independently ruled (Salzburg was in the hands of the prince-archbishops long after this), and it wasn't until the 13th century, after the throne was moved to Vienna, that the Habsburgs came to power and the empire unified and expanded. It grew not only through conflict but through cagey political alliance, and it was during this period that Austria gained its reputation for being more successful in marriage than in war. After repelling the Turks in 1683 (who in retreat left their sacks of coffee outside the walls of Vienna and are therefore credited with the rise of the Viennese coffeehouse), the Empire became, by 1700, the great power of Europe. But though the Habsburgs reigned on, Austria's power was diluted in the 19th century, first by Napoleon and then by the revolution of 1848. The empire never regained its former prominence and was reduced to its present dimensions after World War I. Annexed by Hitler before World War II, Austria was occupied by the Americans, British, French, and Russians after Germany's defeat until 1955, when it once again became an independent state.

Though the political names associated with Austria are sometimes notorious — Charlemagne, Richard the Lion-Hearted, Napoleon, Metternich, and Hitler — the musical names are the ones that spring more happily to mind — Beethoven, Bruckner, Haydn, Mahler, Mozart, Schubert, and the Strausses — and almost every Austrian city boasts a festival in their honor.

Three Austrian routes are outlined below; two start from Vienna and one begins at Salzburg.

The Burgenland route is a 1- or 2-day drive south from Vienna through the quiet towns along the Hungarian border where the food — especially the wild game — is excellent and the wine is fresh. You follow the coast of the Neusiedler See down to the castle of Bernstein and come back north across the face of the Schneeberg, Vienna's Alp, to Baden and then back to the capital.

The trip from Vienna to Salzburg is one of the most picturesque in Europe, taking you through the famous Wachau wine-growing district, along the meandering Danube through Dürnstein (where King Richard the Lion-Hearted was imprisoned), to the historic golden abbey at Melk and on to the city of Linz. Then you head south through the beautiful lakes of the Salzkammergut, skirting the northern Alpine slopes and crisscrossing west to the elegant, three-hilled town of Salzburg.

The route south from Salzburg takes you first to the spa town of Badgastein with its thundering waterfalls and then farther south to the Grossglockner highway — the famous hairpin-turn road around one of the highest peaks in the Alps. From Lienz you head back north to Kitzbühel in the Tyrol and drive west along the Inn River, with mountains rising on both sides all the way up to Innsbruck, an urbane, medieval city where snow-capped peaks are visible from every corner. Through the Arlberg Pass to the Swiss border the Alpine landscape becomes more majestic, and the hillsides are clustered with white, spacious chalets. Our route gradually comes down out of the mountains and to arrive at Bregenz, a neat resort town on Lake Constance at the western tip of the country.

Burgenland

This trip from Vienna into the province of Burgenland and back covers about 230 miles (375 km) and affords a look into the small towns that ring Vienna to the south and hug the Hungarian border to the east. It's a relaxing trip with good food, comfortable lodgings, and an uncrowded itinerary.

Burgenland itself was actually Hungarian until a vote of the citizens after World War I opted for joining with the new Austrian republic. The area boasts superb castles and estates, one of Europe's larger lakes, thousands of acres of prime vineyards, and probably the nation's finest regional cooking. It is difficult to find a really bad restaurant in Burgenland proper. Wild game, duck, and goose dishes, spicy homemade sausages, rich goulashes, and strudels of poppy seed and jam-filled crêpes highlight a cuisine that is at once hearty and still sophisticated enough for the most selective palate. The entire area was under Soviet occupation until Austria was granted its freedom in 1955. For many years people in the region hesitated to make improvements, but this has changed dramatically. Still, the region is not extensively toured, and the farther south from Vienna you get the more of a novelty a North American becomes.

In this section of Austria it is much wiser to follow "town to town" signs rather than highway signs. Many of the towns are so small that a quick stop is enough to absorb their flavor. Some of the highlights of these smaller towns have been lumped together, so, depending on how much time you want to spend, pick your stops in advance. From Vienna you drive east to the plains area of Marchfeld, then south to Rohrau, Haydn's birthplace, and on to the marshy lake country and bird sanctuary surrounding the Neusiedler See. From the lake town of Rust, you abruptly climb westward through low hills to Eisenstadt, the capital of Burgenland, and then south to Bernstein, the southern fulcrum of the trip and suggested evening stopover. Leaving this wooded plains area you reenter Lower Austria and, driving north, encounter the Bucklige Welt ("bumpy world"), a gentle pre-Alpine region of round hills covered with deep forests and orchards. At Puchberg you can climb the Schneeberg — called "our Alp" by the Viennese. Continuing north, the land flattens out as you reach the decorative spa town of Baden, the largest city on the trip and a stone's throw from the Vienna Woods.

VIENNA: For a detailed report on the city and its hotels and restaurants, see *Vienna,* THE CITIES.

En Route from Vienna – Leave Vienna by crossing the main channel of the Danube, noting the signs pointing right, to Grossenzersdorf, where you pick up Route 3 east. You have entered the plains of Marchfeld, an area fought over by the Romans, the Turks (they besieged Vienna from here in 1529), Napoleon (he suffered his first defeat near the village of Aspern), and the Red Army, who sliced through the retreating Nazis here during World War II on their way to liberate Vienna. You go through Orth, 17 miles (27 km) from Vienna, where you can stop at the huge, forbidding, 12th-century castle, now the *Austrian Museum of Fishery and Water Conservation,* and have fish soup and carp (daily except Wednesdays) at the nearby *Uferhaus.* Another 5 watchful miles (8 km) brings you to the tiny hamlet of Eckartsau.

ECKARTSAU: Here is the half-ruined château of Karl I, the last Austrian emperor, to which he fled in 1918 as his empire crumbled around Vienna. For a long time the Austrian government seemed satisfied to let this property crumble, too, but now it is possible to walk through the overgrown baroque gardens and the display rooms of the Imperial Hunting Lodge (1722) and think about the frightened and abandoned royal family hiding here.

En Route from Eckartsau – Make a 19-mile (30-km) deviation northeast on back roads to the little market town of Marchegg, which sits directly on the March (Morava) River, the Czechoslovakian border. There's a castle here from the 13th century (it's since been more comfortably renovated to the spacious Renaissance proportions of the 17th century) that's now a hunting museum. This area offers fine bird hunting (if you've brought your gun this far, you must already know this), and the museum has scenes of various royal hunts, where the harsh outdoor life was softened for the nobles by the chamber orchestras that accompanied them and played as they beat the bushes. Head directly south on Route 49 to the new Danube Bridge in 12.5 miles (20 km).

ROHRAU: On the south side of the river is the village of Bad Deutsch-Altenburg, where there are some Roman ruins (an 8,000-seat amphitheater and a museum); 6.2 miles (10 km) farther south on Route 211 — you have to pick your way carefully — you'll find Joseph Haydn's birthplace, the village of Rohrau, on the Burgenland state line. The house where Haydn was born has been restored, showing off not only the musician's souvenirs but also the simplicity of his family's life. The thatched houses in the white-walled compounds of Burgenland are a counterpoint to the splendor of Vienna and quite simply different from the rest of the country. Rohrau also has a fine château of the Harrach family. When the occupation ended in 1955, the family's painting collection, one of the outstanding private collections in the world, was moved here from Vienna. The *Harrach Collection* is open to the public from April through October, daily except Mondays; its Spanish and Dutch works are particularly fine. Also in the château is a good and surprisingly inexpensive restaurant.

THE NEUSIEDLER SEE: From Rohrau drive southwest on 211 and southeast on 10 to reach the reedy edges of the great Lake of Neusiedl at the village of Winden. This enormous lake, about half the size of Lake Geneva, is a geological freak of nature — it is so shallow that a tall person can literally walk across it. (Every year on the first or second weekend in August an organized walk takes place.) The lake dried up completely in the mid-19th century, filled again, and now has receded a bit. The lake's banks are covered with millions of reeds that give nesting and migratory protection to over 200 species of birds. Symbolic of the region are the cumbersome stork's nests found on top of many cottage chimneys. Used by the Viennese as a prime summer weekend retreat, the Neusiedler See is often filled with hundreds of sailboats.

RUST: As you travel south to the unofficial lake capital of Rust (25 mi/40 km from Rohrau), you cross very old vineyards that grow westward in the low hills surrounding the shore. The wine of the region, notably the unique Blaufränkisch red (with the taste of a particularly robust Burgundy), was highly prized until a 1985 scandal involving the tampering with domestically sold wine. Many of the farmhouses in the region display green boughs on their doors, indicating that you may stop to taste and possibly purchase the vintages. You can also visit a village market and buy a picnic lunch to take along to these alfresco taverns. Two of the most hospitable winemakers are *Just of Rust,* 10. Weinberggasse (phone: 026-85251), which offers white wines, and the *Klosterkeller,* 4 Rathausplatz, in nearby Siegendorf (phone: 026-878252), for red wines. Both are closed Sundays. You won't have to carry your Siegendorf wines home with you because they're distributed in the US by H&S, 30 Somerset St., Belmont, MA 02178 (phone: 617-484-5432).

Rust is a small, quiet town where German is spoken, but Hungarian lurks between the lines. If you're lucky, you'll get to hear gypsy music in the taverns on summer nights and watch costumed, high-booted residents dance to it.

En Route from Rust – Less than 4 miles (6 km) south is the small village of Mörbisch on the Hungarian frontier. There's good swimming and a midsummer music festival on a lakeside stage, where traditional Viennese operettas are performed outdoors on weekends (however, bring some insect repellent).

EISENSTADT: Some 12.5 miles (20 km) west of Rust is Eisenstadt. The road here rises sharply, so you'll see some nice vistas as you arrive. The largest building in town is the hulking Esterhazy Palace, noted not so much for its architecture as for its history. Haydn was a member of Prince Esterhazy's court and, in 1766, was made musical director of the prince's orchestra and chorale. In return, the royal family named a room after Haydn. There are tours of this great hall, where the master nightly conducted his own compositions for the entertainment of his patrons. The rest of the château serves as administrative offices for the provincial government. (You can also see Haydn's house at 21 Haydngasse or his tomb at the Church of the Calvary.)

En Route from Eisenstadt – Drive south for 9.3 miles (15 km) to the large market town of Mattersburg. Turn west for a few miles at Mattersburg and follow signs to the imposing Forchtenstein Castle. This castle, sitting on a towering dolomitic rock, dates from the 13th century, and its vast rooms house good collections of medieval armor, weaponry, and hunting memorabilia. There's also a well almost 500 feet deep, dug by hand by Turkish prisoners of war in the 17th century.

BERNSTEIN: From Mattersburg drive south on Route 331 for 10.5 miles (17 km) through Stoob. Continue south through Oberpullendorf and Lockenhaus, and 12 miles (19 km) from Stoob you'll find Bernstein, the southernmost point on the trip. There's a thriving serpentine jade business here and also the *Almassy* castle hotel. The hill castle in Lockenhaus was built around 1200 by an itinerant Roman archbishop who liked the terrain. This castle is also a museum with a knights hall and a torture chamber. Indeed, one medieval lord of the manor, Graf Uilaky, is rumored to have come home from a 2-week plunder to find his wife's servant at her bedside. He knifed the servant immediately, but chose to brick up his beloved alive behind a handy castle wall. It is said that her ghost occasionally wanders the halls. In July, the castle is one of the sites of the *International Chamber Music Festival,* founded by violinist Gidon Kremer.

THE SCHNEEBERG TOWNS: The next morning, head north 7.5 miles (12 km) to Kirchschlag, pick up Route 55 north, and watch for signs pointing northwest to Neunkirchen. There take Route 26 northwest, a road that runs through one of the finest wooded canyons in all of Europe, to Puchberg (29 mi/46 km from Kirchschlag). At Puchberg you suddenly find yourself in the Alps. The Schneeberg is one of the easternmost mountains, and you can catch a steam-driven, cog-wheel train here to its peak.

Four miles (6 km) east, at Grünbach, you can take a chair lift up to the Hohe Wand, a high plateau nature reserve. From Grünbach continue east another 4 miles (6 km) to Urschendorf and then follow back lanes for about 5.5 miles (9 km) to the famous brewery town of Markt Piesting, where you have a chance to drink as many steins of Piestingerbräu as you can (or want). This famous brew is dark and a little bitter, like stout, and almost impossible to buy elsewhere.

BADEN: From Markt Piesting drive north 21 miles (34 km) through Bad Vöslau and 2.5 miles (4 km) farther to Baden (*Bad* is German for "spa"), the grandfather of all health resorts. The Romans called the town Aquae and used the sulfur thermal springs. Even the city's coat of arms depicts two people in a bathtub. Baden was Soviet occupation headquarters for Austria until 1955, and during this period the city's reputation as a resort suffered. Since the return of capitalism, however, the waters are bubbling again. There are a few historic highlights (Beethoven's house at 10 Rathausgasse; the famous death mask collection at the *Städtisches Rollett-Museum* at 1 Weikersdorfer Platz; and the formal, triangular Hauptplatz with its ornate Trinity column commemorating the plague), but for the most part this is a place for vacationers. For those who can't wait for the waters to cure them there is more instant gratification (or demoralization) available at the *Baden Casino* in the *Spa Center,* where you can play roulette, baccarat, blackjack, or slot machines. There are also facilities for swimming, riding and cycling, saunas, and whatever else you can think of that's healthy. From here it's only 15.5 miles (25 km) back to Vienna; the two cities are connected by a showy old streetcar service, by railroad, and frequent buses.

BEST EN ROUTE

Expect to pay from $85 to $150 or more for a double room with breakfast per night in hotels listed as expensive; $60 to $80 in those listed as moderate; and $35 to $55 in the inexpensive places. Restaurant prices range from $80 to $120 for dinner for two in the expensive category; $50 to $75 in the moderate category; and $30 to $45 in the inexpensive category. Although a 10% tip is included in most menu prices, an extra 5% gratuity is expected if service has been adequate.

GROSSENZERSDORF

Taverne am Sachsengang – This is one of the most remarkable and romantic restaurants in all of Austria. Grossenzersdorf is right outside Vienna, so you might want to include a stop here for lunch — outdoors, over a canal, when weather permits. The wild game is beautifully prepared, and trout or *Fogasch* (a sweet Hungarian fish resembling perch and pike) in *Blätterteig* (pastry dough) are specialties. On the main road (phone: 02249-2297). Expensive.

RUST

Nikolauszeche – Actually in Purbach, on the route from Winden to Rust, this 16th-century Renaissance hotel is the country cousin to Vienna's elegant *Zu den Drei Husaren* but, with local wines and regional cooking, for barely half the price. The cheese dumplings with plums (*topfenknödel mit zwetschkenröster*) is a special dessert. 3 Bodenzeile (phone: 02683-5514). Moderate.

Storchenmühle – The name means "stork's mill," and though it's in the minuscule village of Oslip, just outside Rust, it's one of the most famous places to eat in the Burgenland. *Fogasch* is at its best here. Book your table well in advance (phone: 02684-2127). Moderate.

FORCHTENSTEIN

Reisner – In the village just below the castle sits an unpretentious little inn that might be the best in all of Burgenland. French food critics Henri Gault and Christian Millau found *Reisner's* a few months before we did and gave it a toque, but we're glad to share the discovery. Be sure to reserve ahead and, when you do, someone who speaks German should tell Johann Reisner your likes and dislikes in ingredients. He'll do the rest. Closed Wednesdays and half of January. 141 Hauptstrasse (phone: 02626-3139). Moderate.

BERNSTEIN

Burg Bernstein – A famous old castle on top of a hill, it has only 11 rooms in a quiet setting. All the furniture is antique and the kitchen is excellent. It's closed in winter and still undiscovered (phone: 03354-220). Moderate.

LOCKENHAUS

Burg Lockenhaus – Gidon Kremer's music festival, which runs for 2 weeks every July, has given the castle restaurant in this medieval ruin a new lease on life. On Saturday nights, there is a six-course Robber Baron's Feast (*Raubrittermahl*) that includes wine, schnapps, live music, and a guided tour. Closed in winter. Make reservations (phone: 02616-2321). Moderate.

PUCHBERG

Puchbergerhof – A country hotel filled with folk art and hunting trophies, it has 40 beds and a good kitchen. Just east of the town center. 29 Wr. Neustädter Str. (phone: 02636-2278). Moderate to inexpensive.

Forellenhof – This 145-bed hotel is a little higher up than Puchberg in the Alpine meadows near Losenheim. At the restaurant you can get marvelous mountain trout. 132 Losenheimer Str. (phone: 02636-220511). Inexpensive.

BADEN

Gutenbrunn – In a château, this hotel is one of the city's best. 22 Pelzgasse (phone: 02252-48171). Expensive.

Cholerakapelle – Just west of town, this restaurant in a striking gorge has good *schnitzel* and game. 40a Helenental (phone: 02252-44315). Moderate.

Vienna to Salzburg

A traveler may speed along the Autobahn between Vienna and Salzburg in 3 or 4 easy hours, yet this would be a mistake. The lands between the great Austrian cities offer some of the richest rewards in Europe. Spending 2 days on the route will give you time to experience some of the most beautiful countryside in the world; if you have even more time to spend, it wouldn't be wasted.

Our suggested route meanders north, south, and west, but, including side trips, it is still only about 310 miles (500 km) long. You'll drive through four Austrian *Bundesländer* (provinces): Wien (Vienna) is the capital province; Niederösterreich (Lower Austria) is the stable core of a nation whose boundaries and politics have played musical chairs for 10 centuries; Oberösterreich (Upper Austria) is where the Alps start to rise and the landscape becomes more severe and breathtaking with every kilometer; and Salzburg is another Alpine province bordering Germany on one side and the spa-studded Salzkammergut (Lake Region) on the other. A word here about Upper and Lower Austria: The names are confusing, for Lower Austria is actually northeast of Upper Austria. The logic behind this is the course of the Danube River: From Germany it enters Upper Austria, continues into Lower Austria, and exits into Czechoslovakia and Hungary. (If you're still confused, just accept it and take solace in the fact that if you want to go from Virginia to West Virginia you probably travel north.)

This route offers a mix of history, culture, and physical beauty that is a great source of pride and enjoyment to the Austrian people. It's hard to turn down this opportunity to share it.

VIENNA: For a detailed report on the city and its hotels and restaurants, see *Vienna*, THE CITIES.

En Route from Vienna – Heading northwest from downtown Vienna, you cross the Danube and find yourself climbing into the quietly rolling hills of the Wine Quarter. Austrians like to drink their wine new, and the word for the current year's beverage is Heuriger. It's generally white, not too dry, strong, inexpensive, and good. Once you get over any "young wine" prejudice you may harbor, you'll find yourself stopping at the many *Heurigen* (wine taverns) along the route.

Take S3 northwest from Vienna to Stockerau, then pick up Route 4 and take it as far as Maissau. There, turn north on Route 35, and in about 5 miles (8 km) you'll be in Eggenburg.

EGGENBURG: Like many of the other Lower Austrian towns, this small medieval center used to be a walled fortress. Several of the 14th-century walls are still intact, and so are some of the towers that intersect them. In the Hauptplatz (town square) beside a Trinity column is a late medieval pillory, a squat, primitive reminder of the absolute power of the feudal lords and the circus-like quality of brutal, Gothic justice. Most of the houses are gabled, distorting their actual size and shape; for the church seekers there is Gothic St. Stephan's, with two Romanesque towers. The violence of the Middle Ages and the religious desire to continually redecorate created many churches like this, with different sections from different periods. The Romanesque style predates the Gothic and is usually simpler. (To distinguish between the two, the schoolboy maxim is: "Round arch, Romanesque; pointed arch, Gothic." Don't apply this rule to any later buildings because the romantic styles of the Renaissance took plans and details from every earlier movement and elaborated on them.)

Head west from Eggenburg on Route 303 for 9 miles (14 km) to Horn, the chief town and resort of the Forest District. Continue southwest another 4 miles (6 km) on Route 38 to the great abbey of Altenburg.

ALTENBURG: You've only driven 13 miles (20 km), but you've jumped a century or two into a new architectural style. The Benedictine abbey here was entirely rebuilt between 1650 and 1742, when baroque was the rage and the straight lines of Gothic discipline were softened by a multitude of curves as the vault gave way to the dome. Decoration was not only allowed but encouraged. The architects studied in Italy, but the abundance of bulbous church domes and tower topknots (there's a bulbous belfry here) were taken from more Eastern traditions like the Russian and the Greek. One look at the intricate, hand-carved, gilded woodwork on the church organ is proof that the craftsmen were encouraged to indulge themselves. The abbey library, ornamental staircase, and colorful grotesque baroque frescoes in the crypt are also interesting. It lost some of its collection during the Thirty Years War (1618–48) and even more when the Red Army used it for a barracks during World War II, but the structure itself has been artfully restored.

If you pick up Route 34 south out of Altenburg, you soon meet up with the beautiful Kamp River.

THE KAMP RIVER VALLEY: The trip south through the Kamp River valley is reason enough to travel north from Vienna. In a 30-mile (48-km) stretch you'll see castles and fortresses on either side of a quiet river that flows between flat and wooded banks, neatly planned towns, and occasional low, flat hills. The three towns not to be missed are Rosenburg, Gars, and Langenlois, but travel at your own pace and stop whenever something catches your eye. As you go south you reenter the Wine Quarter, so Heurigen will be popping up frequently.

Rosenburg is a good first stop because its castle is both magnificent and well-preserved (closed Fridays). Many of its rooms are fully furnished with sculpture, paintings, and weaponry, and there is a fine jousting yard.

The next stop on the way south is the pretty market town of Gars, with clean white buildings, small flowered plazas, and a neo-classic archway. We suggest stopping here on the first night out of Vienna because the town has especially good accommodations. Our choice is the *Kamptalhof* (see *Best en Route*); the town is small and the hotel is big, so you won't have any trouble finding it.

Langenlois, 13 miles (20 km) south of Gars, is a larger town, with the most wine growers in Austria. (The best local wine is the dry white called Grüner Veltliner.) The houses are Renaissance, but the *Heimat Museum* deals mostly with earlier subjects, such as prehistory, regional folklore, and, of course, winemaking. From Langenlois it's about 6 miles (9.6 km) to Krems, at the eastern end of the well-known Wachau.

THE WACHAU: You can practice your German pronunciation on this word — the *w* is a soft *v* and the *ch* is hard and guttural. However you pronounce Wachau, though, you'll still find it to be a series of river towns strung together on either side of the Danube. The area is steep and rocky but still manages to produce an abundance of wine, apricots, plums, and peaches. All this farming has kept the land rural and the towns thriving. The vineyard terracing neatly climbs the hillsides, and the hills themselves are topped by ruins of fortified castles. The Wachau has a rich folklore, with every town, castle, or church spinning its own heroic legend like that of the Kuenringer (10th-century lords), who blocked the Danube at its narrowest bend and extracted heavy tolls from all the unsuspecting merchantmen on the river. The aristocratic pirates are gone, but a sense of adventure and the beauty of the river landscape remain. Wander west along the river, stopping at Krems, Dürnstein, and Melk.

The city of Krems started doing business 1,000 years ago. Its business is wine, and a stop at the *Weinbaumuseum* (Dominikanerplatz) is a good idea. Wine is so important to Krems that during the German occupation of World War II, the residents complained that, besides being Nazis, their captors were beer drinkers to boot.

There are some striking Renaissance houses in Krems: One good example is the building at 84 Steiner Landstrasse. The façade is at once Byzantine, Venetian, and German, with golden domed windows, layers of colored friezes, and an ornamentally columned stoa in front of the entrance.

On Route 3, about 4.5 miles (7 km) west of Krems on the north side of the river, is Dürnstein, considered the most beautiful town on the Danube. If time permits you only one stop in the Wachau, this should be it. (The modern road bypasses this small town by tunneling under it, so be on the lookout.) Dürnstein's legend is that Richard the Lion-Hearted was imprisoned here in 1193.

The city is walled and filled with winepresses, ancient houses, and cafés. If Richard didn't enjoy his captivity, it was probably because he never got to sit in one of the cafés and watch the river flow by while sipping some of the strong regional specialty, apricot schnapps. (There are also, of course, gallons of Heuriger wine to be had.) There are tours of the parish church and a former Augustine monastery during the summer, both primarily baroque, but the more secular will appreciate the old wrought-iron signs hanging from the inns along the Hauptstrasse (main street).

Drive west on Route 3 another 19 miles (30 km), cross over to the south side of the Danube, and you'll be in Melk, a historian's paradise. Besides hosting Napoleon between 1805 and 1809 during one of his more successful jaunts, it was also the home of the first Austrian monarchy after 976. At the end of the 11th century, when Leopold III von Babenberg decided to move to Vienna, he presented his castle to the Benedictines, who converted it, after several renovations, into the finest baroque abbey north of Italy. The renovations were a result of various disasters that are recounted during the hour-long tours given in English. As it stands today, this huge, yellow abbey was designed by Jakob Prandtauer and completed by his son-in-law, Franz Munggenast (whose work you have probably already admired in Dürnstein and Altenburg). The interior of the church at Melk seems even grander and more spacious than it is because of its great dome, many windows, colorful frescoes, and statuary. The terrace of Melk's splendid baroque library affords a wondrous view of the Danube.

The town of Melk, though one of the largest in the Wachau, has resisted industrialization and kept its ancient plan intact and functioning. From Melk you can either continue west along the Danube or take E5 (the Autobahn) into Linz.

En Route from Melk – About 55 miles (88 km) west is the ancient town of Enns, believed to be the oldest Roman settlement in Austria. In this century, it marked the dividing points of the American and Soviet zones of postwar occupation in Austria. If you get off the Autobahn here and follow Route 337 and the Enns River north, you'll soon hit its confluence with the Danube, where you'll find a far more dramatic wartime reminder — the small quarry town of Mauthausen.

Until World War II, this town was on few travelers' itineraries. During the war the Nazis built a concentration camp here; the postwar Austrian government declared the campsite a national monument in 1949. Since then, Mauthausen has had many visitors. Outside the camp, memorials have been erected by the various countries of the 200,000 victims exterminated by the Nazis. There's a self-guided, tape-recorded tour (in English) of the camp that takes you through the memorials, the prisoners' huts, the gas chamber, and the notorious Steps of Death that lead into the quarry. This isn't average tourist fare, but most visitors find the trip very moving.

From Mauthausen it's a short jump on Route 3 west to Linz.

LINZ: Linz, a big city that straddles the Danube, is the capital of Upper Austria and a good place to stop. In the Hauptplatz there's a Trinity column that's as much a symbol of this city as the Statue of Liberty is of New York. The column is a baroque totem pole of white marble with cherubs adorning a twisting trunk and a Trinity capped by a golden sun on the top. Linz is also the home of St. Martin's, the oldest church in Austria. It is a simple church of stone with its original beams intact (there's not much in the way of vaulting) and some rare stained glass windows in the apse. The windows here were probably French inspired, for the church was built on Roman foundations by Charlemagne in the 8th century.

Besides preserving St. Martin's, the city has given its name to the Linzer torte, the crown prince of Austrian pastries (the *Sachertorte* is the reigning king). The *Linzertorte* is a far more complex affair, involving varying configurations of almond cake and raspberry jam, with or without *schlag* — whipped cream.

Linz is a modern art center of Austria, and the *Neue Galerie der Stadt Linz* (15 Blütenstrasse) exhibits works by Corinth, Klimt, Kokoschka, Kubin, Liebermann, and Schiele. There's also the *Francisco Carolinum,* the *Provincial Museum of Upper Austria* (14 Museumstrasse), a fortress museum with a large collection of weaponry as well as folk art and musical instruments.

Every September, Linz holds a *Bruckner Festival* to commemorate the symphonies and choral work of Anton Bruckner, a notable native son. Bruckner was actually from St. Florian, a small town 11 miles (18 km) southeast of Linz on Route 1, where he was the organist at the famous St. Florian's Abbey during the 1840s and '50s. He composed his greatest work there and actually wished to be buried under the organ. The pipe housing of the organ is another baroque masterpiece, with gilded angels and cherubs on neo-classic pilasters that run up to a red and gold cross and a ceiling painted with more angels over a fiery orange background. (St. Florian himself was drowned, but is the saint to be invoked in firefighting situations.) The organ appears in many art texts as the prime example of the baroque in Austria. There are tours of the abbey that also take you through the library, the imperial apartments, and the Altdorfer Gallery, with paintings by the Danubian master Albrecht Altdorfer (1480–1538).

If you continue east on Route 1 back to Enns, you can pick up Route 337 south and drive 13 miles (21 km) to Steyr.

STEYR: At the confluence of the Enns and the Steyr rivers, this 1,000-year-old industrial center has a lovely Old Quarter that is a preserved wrought-iron wonder of enduring baroque, largely closed to cars. Besides exploring the Stadtplatz (main square), walk down Grünmarkt to the Neutor (town gate), which looks out at the Enns River.

Just next door to Steyr is the tiny village of Christkindl (Christ Child), where on some Christmas Eves the midnight mass is televised to all of Europe. If you're here in December, a special post office with a special postmark will endorse and endear your mail to all your stamp collecting friends.

Head west out of Steyr on Route 122 through Bad Hall and pick up the Autobahn west at Sattledt. Get off at Steyrermühl and drive south to Gmunden on the Traunsee, 45 miles (72 km) from Steyr and the easternmost lake of the Salzkammergut (Lake Region).

THE SALZKAMMERGUT: Every lake town here is a resort offering swimming, hiking, sailing, and fishing. Though the scenery is beautiful and there are landmarks and architecture to be seen, the accent here is more on vacationing than touring. These are the hills that Julie Andrews sang about, and though the Alpine vistas are special, the lakeside towns are fairly similar, so if you have time pick one and vacation a little. If you don't, drive through them with the windows open to smell the wildflowers and absorb the good health (Salzkammergut means "district of salt mines," and the area is rich in minerals, with mines and health spas).

Gmunden has a mile-long esplanade with picturesque views of Lake Traun and the surrounding mountains. The town has always prospered (both from the salt trade and the upper class vacationers), and the lakeside is cluttered with expansive villas.

There is no lakeside at Bad Ischl, 20 miles (33 km) farther on Route 145, but there are two small rivers, the Traun and the Ischl. Between 1848 and 1914, Emperor Franz Joseph summered here with his entourage, so the town has a formal and imperialistic bearing. Franz Lehár also lived here, and there is operetta in summer. There are tours of the Kaiservilla or you can roam the park on your own and see the garden on foot or from a horse-drawn carriage.

En Route from Bad Ischl – A short detour south on Route 145 brings you to the old mining town of Bad Aussee, now another fashionable resort. Turn west on Route 166 for Obertraun, on Lake Hallstatt. There's a funicular ascent here to the ice caves of Dachstein (the local Alp) that's one of the best in Europe. Follow 166 around the lake to the town of Hallstatt, one of the most ancient places south of Stonehenge. It gives its name to the Hallstatt period (1000–500 BC). The diggings in the area show that it was an Iron Age metropolis. You can go down into a salt mine or up another cable railway to a mountaintop inn. The town itself looks Swiss, with lakeside buildings of yellow stucco, vertical timber siding, and a solitary stone steeple. The return trip north to Bad Ischl makes a loop drive of about 40 miles (65 km).

Route 158 west from Bad Ischl takes you to the base of the Wolfgangsee, where you turn right through Strobl and follow the road until it ends at the village of St. Wolfgang, on the north shore of the lake. Since the road ends so abruptly and the town is such a popular tourist attraction, parking is a major problem, so put your car in one of the two lots at the town entrance and walk. Besides the lake views, hiking paths, and brass band concerts, there's also a Gothic masterpiece in the town church and a long rack-railway ride up the side of the Schafberg (another Alp), from which you can see 13 lakes. The altar in the church is by Michael Pacher and was carved and painted on gilded backgrounds 500 years ago. A paddlewheel boat ride on this loveliest of lakes and a visit to St. Wolfgang's legendary *White Horse Inn* (see *Best en Route*) are highly recommended.

You follow the same road you entered on to Route 158, which you take west through St. Gilgen and on to the Fuschlsee, the smallest lake of the region and the last before you reach Salzburg, 35 miles (56 km) from Bad Ischl.

SALZBURG: For a detailed report on the city and its hotels and restaurants, see *Salzburg*, THE CITIES.

BEST EN ROUTE

Expect to pay $90 to $150 per night for a double room with breakfast in hotels listed as expensive; $60 to $85 in those listed as moderate; and $35 to $55 in the inexpensive places. Restaurant prices range from $40 to $80 for dinner for two in the expensive category; $25 to $40 in the moderate; and $15 to $25 in the inexpensive category. Prices do not include wine. Although a 10% tip is included in most menu prices, an extra 5% gratuity is expected if service has been adequate.

GARS

Kamptalhof – An ideal stopover in this pretty river valley town, this hotel is in a large country house and has 90 beds, splendid grounds, and a fine kitchen. It's open all year and has facilities for swimming, riding, and tennis (phone: 02985-2316). Expensive.

DÜRNSTEIN

Schloss Dürnstein – This 65-room hotel is a fine baroque castle overlooking the Danube. There are swimming and sauna facilities, and the management is especially welcoming. 2 Dürnstein (phone: 02711-212 or 240). Expensive.

Richard Löwenherz – A cozy inn in a former convent that houses a swimming pool, a dreamlike garden, a terrace restaurant on the Danube, and, in every hallway, rustic furnishings worthy of a folkloric museum. Open mid-March to November. 8 Dürnstein (phone: 02711-222). Expensive to moderate.

STEYR

Minichmayr – This newly renovated hotel has 105 beds and a very good restaurant. Steyr is a small ancient town and the hotel is right in the middle (phone: 07252-23410). Moderate.

BAD ISCHL

Post – In the center of town, this fine hotel has 95 beds, a dining room decorated with hunting trophies, and extensive grounds. Its large rooms evoke the old empire days, and consequently it charges empire prices. Closed in winter. (phone: 06132-3441). Expensive.

HALLSTATT

Seehotel Grüner Baum – This is a family operation, and guests often stay for an entire vacation. It has 36 rooms (ask for one facing the lake) and an excellent kitchen. 104 Marktplatz (phone: 06134-263). Moderate.

SAINT WOLFGANG

Romantikhotel im Weissen Rössl (White Horse Inn) – The setting of a famous operetta is alive and well and thriving as a charming 124-bed resort hotel with lakeside eating facilities. Swimming in lake or indoor pool; sauna, gym, boating. 74 Im Stöckl (phone: 06138-2306). Expensive to moderate.

Gasthof Fürberg – Reached by boat from St. Wolfgang or St. Gilgen, and also by car from the latter, this rambling flower-lined inn has a sculpture of a fish over its door and features *Reinanke* and *Saibling,* the fish (distantly related to salmon) of the Wolfgangsee. Closed in winter (phone: 06227-385). Inexpensive.

Salzburg to Innsbruck to the Swiss Border

The trip from Salzburg through Innsbruck to the town of Bregenz on Lake Constance at the Swiss border runs in a relatively straight east-west line, but as routed here with north-south deviations it covers about 415 miles (670 km). The distance can easily be driven in about 2 days, but to enjoy the Alpine scenery and stave off fatigue, take at least 3 or 4. One of the joys of this trip is the combination of fairly short driving distances between stops, unretouched medieval towns, and the natural beauty of the Alps themselves.

This is primarily a trip through the Alps, and the views of craggy, snow-capped peaks rising dramatically around small, chalet-filled villages neatly set in mountain valleys are quite striking and unending. As you drive through the mountains you'll find each new vista more exciting than the last — the Alps are something you don't get used to. It's best to make this drive between June and October; the Alpine winters force road closings and the snows will abridge the route, cutting off some of the more breathtaking, twisting mileage. It's also best to start driving early in the day; as the valleys and lowlands heat up in the morning, the warm air rises and, meeting the cooler air around the mountaintops, shrouds the peaks in clouds by afternoon.

Before leaving the province of Salzburg you leave the city of Salzburg and drive south to Badgastein, Austria's premier spa, with health-giving, naturally hot water, an invigorating atmosphere, and cascading waterfalls in the center of town. From there you come back north a bit and dogleg west to the lakeside resort of Zell am See, the jumping-off point for the spectacular southern loop drive down the winding mountain highway around the Grossglockner, the highest Austrian Alp. This road links the provinces of Salzburg and Carinthia and ends at Lienz, the capital of the East Tyrol. From here you take the Felbertauern route back north, burrowing through the mountains this time instead of going over them. There are no mountain routes in the world that compare with these, and the sharp peaks and blazing glaciers both elate and chill the viewer with a majestic sense of natural history.

Your northern progress stops at Kitzbühel, a medieval town swollen with the ski boom but still picturesque, with tree-lined streets and large old houses. You're in the Tyrol now, and driving west you meet up with the Inn River and follow it, locked between high, green plateaus all the way to Innsbruck. No matter where you're from, Innsbruck is a town you won't want to leave. It combines rangy, Alpine scenery with formal, urban splendor and history — a resort city that hasn't lost its cultured, civilized charm.

From Innsbruck you continue west to the Arlberg region, your second twisting, heady mountain drive that's topped in altitude only by the Grossglockner. During the summer you can deviate south, around and over the peaks via the Silvretta road, and stop for a breather at the flat, man-made Vermunt Lake and Silvretta Dam. At other times of year you travel directly west over the Arlberg Pass or, when driving conditions are very poor, through the highway tunnel (toll) underneath the Arlberg between St. Anton and Langen. Both routes take you to Bludenz in the prosperous Vorarlberg, Austria's westernmost province, where the towns adopt a precise, Swiss mien. You drive on to Feldkirch with its rectangular towers and round turrets and turn north, following the Swiss border to the provincial capital of Bregenz. Here the route ends at the shore of the Bodensee (Lake Constance).

The provinces along this route blend a fierce, local patriotism with a sophisticated European worldliness that articulates itself through expressive folkways (the chalets here aren't just old houses but works of art, with painted and sculpted elevations) and proud, outgoing natives. If you like to ski, you've probably heard of almost every town along this route, but even if you think speeding down mountains is better left to goats, you'll find you won't have a dull moment from start to finish.

SALZBURG: For a detailed report on the city and its hotels and restaurants, see *Salzburg,* THE CITIES.

BADGASTEIN: From Salzburg drive south through Bischofshofen and Lend for 62 miles (100 km) to the elegant spa town of Badgastein. This is more of a spender's park than a town, with a curved strip of imperious shops and hotels that compete with each other for the most space. Badgastein is built into the north slope of the Tauern Range, and the Gasteiner Ache roars down this slope, creating an enormous waterfall in the middle of town. You can park your car and stroll up and down the Kaiser Wilhelm Promenade to see both mountains and town.

The Badgastein waters are world famous, and their therapeutic properties keep the money flowing through this town. The springs supply water that is naturally in the amazing range of 115 to 120F (about 47C). This thermal water is rich in radon, an element that the faithful claim eases (among other things) rheumatic complaints, circulatory problems, gout, and asthma. You can pay for a full cure with a lucky visit to the Badgastein casino; or, just to get your feet wet, there's a large open-air swimming pool fed by the thermal springs opposite the railway station.

THE GROSSGLOCKNER: From Badgastein, return to Lend and head west for 16 miles (26 km) on Route 311 to Zell am See, a resort town built on a flat tongue that extends off a wooded slope onto the Zeller See, a deep glacial ditch filled with blue Alpine water. There's a short cable car ride up the Schmittenhöhe that gives you a foretaste of the Grossglockner highway. This is a good place to stop if you want to get an early morning start for the highway climb south. (In the winter, you skip this loop drive and just head 16 miles (26 km) west on 168 to Mittersill, the return point of this southern deviation.)

The Grossglockner highway begins south of Zell am See at Bruck-an-der-Grossglocknerstrasse. This amazing tollway, completed in 1935, is the prototype for almost all mountain engineering, and if you could only drive a car for 1 day, this is the road you should take. You start out by going down into the dark Fusch Valley, but little by little you start ascending through a series of Grand Prix bends and hairpin turns that force you to take your time and pay homage to the immortal ledges and crags around you. There are car parks and overlooks for patient studiers, but even fanatical non-stoppers won't escape the hundreds of breathtaking panoramas.

You can stop at Edelweiss-Spitze and climb an observation tower to 8,453 feet or just keep driving to the Hochtor Tunnel, the high point of the roadbed at 8,216 feet. There's a cul-du-sac detour west on the Glacier road up to the Franz-Joseph-Höhe that ends in a terrace cut out of stone. Emperor Franz Joseph built a mansion here at the beginning of the Pasterze Glacier, Europe's largest. (In summer, you can walk on the glacier at your own risk.)

Back on the main road, you wind down and bear right for Lienz, the southern turnaround of the loop 56 miles (90 km) from Zell am See.

LIENZ: Lienz is an East Tyrolean town that has begun to crowd up in the summer since 1967, when the Felbertauern Tunnel was finished, opening a western route through the mountains. Now motorists can come through this hub from east and west, entering the Grossglockner road and leaving on the Felbertauern road or vice versa. This newer road has spawned speedy modernization in areas previously cut off from the rest of Austria by the imposing Alpine barrier. This toll road is open all year, and, though no match for its older brother to the east, the sights here are splendid.

En Route from Lienz – Start north from Lienz, again going down into a wooded valley; and then you rise to the resort of Matrei, a thriving ski spot since the road came through. Matrei is also the gateway to the Hohe Tauern National Park, comparable in size and beauty to Yosemite. Beyond Matrei, until very recently, no road at all existed, so that the last stretch of the highway toward Kitzbühel offers a particularly fresh view of virginal forests and once isolated folk life. From here you rise farther, passing deep gorges and hanging glaciers. The tunnel moles its way under a ridge of peaks to emerge on the north mountain slopes; you head downhill into Mittersill, 42 miles (67 km) from Lienz. Cruise through town and push on to Kitzbühel, 17 miles (29 km) up Route 161. You're officially in the Tyrol.

KITZBÜHEL: Kitzbühel's old streets are lined with cafés and pastel houses whose gables extend over the street with arrogant disregard for one-dimensional vertical planes. There are two churches here that are a nice manmade counterpoint to the mountains you just came from (the parish church is Gothic, but its shingled overhanging roof disguises it as yet another chalet).

En Route to Innsbruck – Leave Kitzbühel, driving west on 170 until you hit the Inn River; turn left on the southern bank, taking the local road if you're meandering or the Autobahn if you're in more of a hurry.

Rattenberg is the kind of tiny village you can tell your friends you "discovered" when you get home. The riverside buildings have high, flat, stucco faces that at first glance are reminiscent of the false fronts on movie sets. If you climb up to the fortified stone castle, you can look down and see the sloped roofs that the higher walls conceal. Just above Rattenberg is Alpbach, one of the loveliest resorts in the Tyrol. Spend a night here, and you'll be tempted to stay a week.

INNSBRUCK: Innsbruck is one of Europe's most delightful smaller cities. Particularly vital, it combines light industry, commerce (the main junction since almost prehistory for trade between Germany and Italy, France and Eastern Europe), learning (the university is over 300 years old), and tourism. Perhaps no city has a more dramatic setting, with towering, snow-capped Alps on display from almost every street corner. Stroll down the main shopping street, the Maria-Theresien-Strasse, walking from the Triumphal Arch (to celebrate a successful Habsburg marriage). You'll pass impressive patrician houses, then find yourself in the heart of an arcaded Gothic town with colorful detailing, various bulbous belfries, and intricate wrought-iron signs. The symbol of Innsbruck is the Goldenes Dachl (Little Golden Roof), an ornate Gothic balcony built in 1500 by Maximilian I, who used it to watch parades and concerts. The sculpted crests on the balcony and lower frieze and the heroic wall paintings give the façade an especially regal bearing. The golden roof that covers the balcony consists of over 3,000 gilded copper tiles. In the Hofkirche (Royal Church), known as the Tyrolean Westminster Abbey, 28 larger-than-life statues of ancestors line the tomb of Maximilian, who, alas, isn't buried there.

If you momentarily forget you're in the mountains, hop on a #6 streetcar, and in a little while you'll feel a jerk as the city starts to fall away below you. The trolley has become a cog-wheel train and the conductor has become a tour guide, pointing out peaks and glaciers. The train will take you to the ski spa suburb of Igls (pronounced "eagles"), but the destination isn't as important as the trip. You won't find a better vantage point from which to look at Innsbruck, an Alpine jewel. If you're tired of rides at this point, stay in town and sit in the Hofgarten under the weeping willows where you can listen to concerts on summer evenings.

From Innsbruck you continue west on Route 171 through Landeck into the Arlberg mountain region.

THE ARLBERG: At Landeck you have another seasonal choice: If it's summer, you can take another southern loop up and over the peaks on the Silvretta road; during the winter you must go directly west over the Arlberg Pass or through the Arlberg Tunnel, where you cross an interior border into the last Austrian province of Vorarlberg.

The northern route through the pass takes you by the austere Castle of Wiesberg, past the shimmering, reedlike span of the Trisanna bridge, and up to the posh, treeless slopes of St. Anton, where the Arlberg method of skiing (the art of snowplowing and parallel turning) was developed. As you continue the ascent, you reach the pass at 5,910 feet, just beyond St. Christoph. As the descent begins, the road over the Flexen Pass branches off to the right. Several scenic hairpin turns drop you into Stuben, and a few minutes later you reach Langen. This is also where you emerge if you decide to take the tunnel. From the western end of the tunnel, the route down to Bludenz becomes bleak, passing through a sparsely populated area that's punctuated only by an occasional power station.

The Silvretta route (not much longer than the Arlberg Pass road) is a tollway much more like the Grossglockner and affords the viewer another round of heart-stopping vistas. As you start the climb driving south (you take the left fork at Pians, under the Trisanna bridge), you pass through several neat ski villages with large farmhouse chalets characterized by long balconies, ornate window detailing, and little belfries on the roof peaks. The Silvretta and Vermunt lakes were created by modern dams, and either makes a good rest stop. The Silvretta is at the highest point on this winding road; you can walk across the dam either mulling over man's relationship with his environment or deciding what to have for lunch. On the downhill trip toward Bludenz you pass the ski and cattle town of Schruns, which Hemingway wrote about affectionately in *A Moveable Feast.*

THE VORARLBERG: The Arlberg and Silvretta routes converge at Bludenz, a busy valley town with ancient gates, cobbled plazas, and flowered, marble fountains. Depending on how long you've been driving, you might consider a night's rest here.

From Bludenz it's only 13 miles (21 km) to Feldkirch, a Gothic marketplace equidistant from Paris and Vienna. The Marktplatz is a square in which large houses with high, round-arched entries open onto the street, occasional bulbous belfries break up the roof lines, and wrought-iron signs with almost Art Nouveau spiraling hang from the fronts of the inns. The primitive, stone, 13th-century Schattenburg Castle is here, as are many old town walls, and it doesn't take much imagination to picture Feldkirch as a medieval armed camp. The castle is a museum now, with folk art from the Vorarlberg and the Tyrol well represented. It has an elegantly rustic cellar restaurant that serves a first-rate Schattenburg Schnitzel.

Leaving town head north about 22 miles (36 km) through Dornbirn to Bregenz, the last leg of the journey, along the meadowlands of the Rhine Valley and the Swiss border.

BREGENZ: The Vorarlberg capital is a slick and classy lake resort that is unfortunately bisected by a railroad line separating the preserved upper town from the graceful shorefronts of Lake Constance. On the harbor side of the railway are relaxing walks, manicured gardens, and a lakeside stage, where the *Bregenz Festival* is held every summer. In case of rain, patrons withdraw to the new adjoining indoor festival hall. On the inland side of the tracks in the upper town is the domed St. Martin's tower, quiet squares, and twisting streets that offer sanctuary when the beachfronts crowd up during the season. There's also a last-chance cable railway ride up the richly forested mountain slope of the Pfänder just outside the town. When you reach the peak, you'll find this last aerial view of the lake and the town is another beauty and one that brings back so many of the previous unforgettable vistas this journey offers.

BEST EN ROUTE

Expect to pay $90 to $170 or more per night for a double room with breakfast in hotels listed as expensive; $60 to $85 in those listed as moderate; and $35 to $55 in the inexpensive places. Restaurant prices range from $80 to $120 for dinner for two in the expensive category; $50 to $75 in the moderate; and $30 to $45 in the inexpensive category. Prices do not include wine. Although a 10% tip is included in most menu prices, an extra 5% gratuity is expected if service has been adequate.

ZELL AM SEE

Grandhotel am See – This place is not only on the lake, it's also really grand. Rebuilt according to the original *Grand Hotel* plans, it has a convivial café, a good restaurant, and large bedrooms. You'll feel as if you just stepped off a first class carriage of the *Orient Express*. On Vootsverleih off Espionade (phone: 06542-2387 or 2388). Expensive.

Berghotel Schmittenhöhe – Here's a place for the adventurous — the no sheet-woolen blanket set. It's at the top of the aerial tram with no-frill bedrooms, nourishing hot meals, and vertigo-inducing views (phone: 06542-2489). Inexpensive.

LIENZ

Traube – The bedrooms are comfortable and pretty, but the main attraction here is the restaurant in the cellar, the social center of the entire eastern Tyrol. 14 Hauptplatz (phone: 04852-2551 or 2552). Moderate.

MATREI-IN-OSTTIROL

Rauter – This resort hotel is a longtime favorite of fishermen as well as skiers and other sports-minded people. It has been modernized in a manner that makes it one of the architectural wonders of Austria: Many of the rooms are spacious A-frame chalets *within* the main building. All offer splendid mountain and meadow views. The room rate includes a four-course dinner and a breakfast buffet (phone: 04875-6611). Moderate.

ALPBACH

Böglerhof – Thomas Wolfe discovered this inn in 1936 when it was just a farmhouse that took in guests. He wrote home to mother that the Alpbach Valley had "some of the most beautiful mountains and villages" he'd ever seen. Today the *Böglerhof* is a thriving 110-bed hotel ablaze with geraniums and petunias. The surprisingly good room rate includes a breakfast buffet with fresh breads that are a feast in themselves (phone: 05336-5227 or 5228). Moderate.

INNSBRUCK

Goldener Adler – This inn has actually been in business in the same building for over 600 years. During the 1976 Winter Olympics, television coverage originated from this hotel's romantic *Stube*. It's in the heart of the old town, and if you really want to get into the spirit, request a room with traditional trappings and pretend you're Friar Tuck. 6 Herzog-Friedrichstrasse (phone: 05222-586334). Expensive to moderate.

Weisses Rössl – A comfortable hotel in the heart of town that was recently rebuilt, preserving its 15th-century architecture. Major credit cards. 8 Kiebachgasse (phone: 523057). Moderate.

LECH

Gasthofpost – Lech, just outside St. Anton, is one of the great ski resorts of Europe. This hostelry is an easy pick because of its rich Vorarlberg folk decorations and chic international clientele. There's no pretense here, though, and the management is especially welcoming. Off season the rates are reasonable, but when the skiers hit town the prices go up. 11 Haupstrasse-Nr (phone: 05583-2206). Expensive.

FELDKIRCH

Weisses Kreuz – This solid, well-run country town hotel has an efficient management in the best Swiss tradition. The kitchen is excellent. In the Königshofstrasse in the old quarter (phone: 05522-22209). Moderate.

BREGENZ

Zoll – Since taking over this roadside inn, chef Ernst Huber has made it a shrine to gastronomy that lures pilgrims from nearby Germany and Switzerland as well as from all over Austria. Try the seven-course *Menü,* which features the freshest and most special of regional ingredients, carefully prepared and presented in manageable portions. 118 Arlbergstrasse (phone: 05574-31705). Expensive.

Berghaus Pfänder – Open only from May until late September, this is a mountain restaurant with food as wonderful as the view. Try the *hasenrücken pfänder,* saddle of hare served with *spätzle,* potato croquettes, red cabbage, cranberries, and *Pfifferlinge* mushrooms. Adjacent to the Pfänder cable car station and a charming alpine game preserve (phone: 05574-22184). Moderate.

Weisses Kreuz – The best hotel in town is an ancient, expertly run place that also serves as the town's prime social center. Breakfast only. 5 Römerstrasse (phone: 05574-22488). Moderate.

Belgium

The kingdom of Belgium is a tiny, industrious, and economically mighty nation about the size of Maryland jammed into the North Sea coast between France and the Netherlands. Belgium's 10 million people live on only 11,781 square miles — it's the second most densely populated country in the world — and they make every square meter count, from their ferociously productive factories, to their meticulously cultivated farmlands, to the tight and efficient network of roads, railroads, and inland waterways connecting it all. On a smaller scale, you can see how they make the most of space in the burgeoning flower gardens behind nearly every house. Close as things are, Belgium has forests that support a great variety of wild birds, such as avocets, shrikes, godwits, and grouse, and four-footed animals ranging from wild hamsters to wild boar.

Belgium is a constitutional monarchy, with power distributed among the king, his appointed cabinet, and the bicameral Parliament, consisting of a Senate and House of Representatives. The present king is Baudouin, a direct descendant of Belgium's first king, Leopold I, who took the throne in 1831.

Brussels is the capital, the center of business, industry, and culture; Antwerp is the most cosmopolitan city, one of Europe's greatest ports, a center of the world diamond market and the birthplace of Rubens; Liège is an important university and factory town and a world class maker of firearms; Bruges is famous for its handmade lace and the spectacle of its perfectly preserved medieval Flemish architecture; Ghent is another medieval city — larger, more gracious, and more commercial than Bruges; Ostend is a summer resort on the North Sea.

Julius Caesar found Celts in Belgium when he conquered Gaul in the 1st century BC. The Franks pushed in from Germany in the 3rd century; Belgium's northern people, the Flemish, are descended from the Franks, and the Walloons of the south from the Romanized Celts. The two groups have been squabbling ever since the Frankish invasion. Clovis and Charlemagne put Belgium under the Holy Roman Empire and Christianized it. The empire fell apart after Charlemagne's death in 814, and from the 9th century to World War II, the strategic land that is now Belgium was overrun almost continuously by the Vikings, French, Spanish, English, Austrians, Dutch, and finally the Nazis. National instability strengthened the economic self-reliance and chauvinism of the Belgian cities, which had to fortify themselves as best they could against invaders and to make protective pacts with one ruler to avoid being absorbed by another. In medieval and Renaissance times, Ghent, Bruges, Antwerp, and Ypres grew fat and powerful from the commerce passing through their ports, becoming great centers of art, architecture, and scholarship. The varying condition of Belgium's inland waterways has made their fortunes fluctuate wildly since the Renaissance.

In this century, Belgium was a trampling ground in both world wars and was occupied by Germany both times. During World War II, the Nazis bombed Belgium mercilessly, pilfered machinery, abducted laborers to work in Germany, and imposed general tyranny; the Battle of the Bulge, the German army's last stand before being decimated, took place in Luxembourg province, near the German border. Damage from both wars was so catastrophic that much of the country had to be rebuilt from scratch. Nevertheless, Belgium has recovered better than most countries in Europe, enjoying worldwide trade and the success of her chemical, metalwork, and food-processing industries.

Belgium has three official languages: of its 10 million inhabitants, some 60% speak Flemish, about 40% speak French, and a mere 0.7% speak German (in the southeastern cantons). Dutch is the official language in the northern four provinces, French in the southern four; the central province of Brabant, containing Brussels, is officially bilingual. For centuries, French was the official language of all Belgium, spoken by the wealthy and powerful throughout. However, as Flanders became richer and more industrial and Flemish nationalism acquired more political clout, the Dutch language was accorded more and more official respect; in 1962, Brussels was made officially bilingual as a concession to the northerners. Although political division in Belgium still tends to be along linguistic lines, the matter of Flemish equality is largely settled.

The country is almost entirely Roman Catholic, and about one quarter of the population attends mass regularly. Religious tolerance is written into the constitution, and there are some Jewish and Protestant enclaves. Among the Walloons, there is a strong anti-Church movement; pro- and anticlerical feelings probably rank second, after the language question, as a source of political turmoil.

Belgians are contemptuous of authority, no doubt from centuries of foreign rule. The rights of the individual are considered more important than obligations to society; tax evasion, for example, has been developed to the level of an art. The Flemish in particular are highly independent, living mostly as small farmers and shopkeepers. They have the Teutonic bent for work, order, cleanliness, and conservative rectitude, and they tend to have large families. Walloons are more urbane and Gallic in their outlook, tending more toward radicalism, socialism, big government, and small families — although, like the Flemish, they are very industrious. Family life is a high priority with both groups; parents and grown children often live near each other. Belgians make no major decisions without consulting their families, and they spend most of their social lives with relations and the friends with whom they grew up. Households often do things as a group: Even a shopping trip is a family outing, with the father leading the brood.

In sports, Belgians love cycling best: Bicycles are used not only in races but also for commuting and recreation. Soccer is the most popular organized sport; pigeon racing is also important; and cockfighting, though illegal, still has a following. The annual auto races (held in May, August, and September) at Spa/Francorchamps also draw huge crowds of enthusiasts.

Belgians are perhaps most passionate about good food, both at home and in restaurants. Belgian food, even in an inexpensive bistro, is plentiful, substantial, and good. Butter and rich sauces are used prolifically in pastries, vegetables, and meat dishes; the most popular meat is beef, and dessert is often made with chocolate or whipped cream. (It's not surprising that the nation has a high incidence of obesity, gout, and stomach and intestinal troubles.) Brussels is considered one of the two or three culinary capitals of the world, so prices for a meal in a top restaurant tend to be high. In addition to food, Belgians also take great pride in brewing beer; some brands to try are Orval, Gueuze, Kriek, Trappiste, and Rodenbach.

We've laid out two routes for you to follow through Belgium; they both begin in Brussels, which should be a major stop in its own right (see the city report in THE CITIES). The first route takes you through the Flemish-speaking north, to Antwerp, Ghent, Bruges, and Ypres, hotbeds of the great northern Renaissance in painting and architecture. Evidence of it — the churches, cathedrals, and guildhouses from the 12th to the 17th century — still tower over the narrow streets in many sections of Antwerp; inside are the huge, opulent paintings of the city's most famous son, Peter Paul Rubens. You drive west across the poppy-covered plains of Flanders to sights like the dank and massive forts of 'sGravensteen, in Ghent; Ghent itself has more historic buildings than anyplace else in Belgium. You'll visit the idyllic Princely Béguinage in Bruges; you'll pass on to the white, sandy beaches of Ostend to swim or play tennis, where dikes, fences, dunes, and waterpumps have conspired to hold back the North Sea for 700 years. At Ypres, farther south, is the reconstruction of the great Cloth Hall (a monument to medieval commerce) and the improbable *Festival of the Cat,* a vestige of a prehistoric culture.

The second route, for the nature lover as well as the history buff, goes through the pastoral, French-speaking area of southern Belgium known as the Ardennes. The countryside here is hilly and forested, less populous than the north, and the country's most scenic region. The trek is a long loop through the provinces of Liège, Luxembourg, Namur, and Hainaut, a green country of bluffs, valleys, and ancient armed citadels. The Ardennes is a hunter's paradise: Wild boar abound all year, and deer, pheasant, water birds, and wild sheep all have their season. If you like camping or hiking, allow several days for the wilderness of the Ardennes and the mysterious Belgian Lorraine, with its steep cliffs, dense woods, and lavish wild flowers. As you swing back north, you can witness dramatic folk pageants and tour exquisite country castles such as Annevoie and Beloeil.

Antwerp and Flanders

The western Flemish provinces of Antwerp, West Flanders, and East Flanders were one of the most important medieval and Renaissance art centers in the world. In Antwerp city, Ghent, and Bruges, much of the past is still standing and very much a part of daily life. It is to be expected that thousand-year-old churches are still in use; it's more surprising that many other ancient monuments still function as private houses and government buildings. Northern Belgium makes way for its teeming industries while it holds on to a rare respect for the past and local identity.

Antwerp is a center of publishing, the performing arts, and several industries — notably the diamond trade — and one of the major ports of Europe. Ghent is another industrial and cultural power, with its own port and more than its share of great Flemish art and architecture. Bruges is the preserved and polished medieval jewel of Belgium, having survived 400 years and two world wars with its ancient atmosphere intact. Ypres survived World War I with not much of anything intact and had to be completely rebuilt; it's now a modern city.

The rivers and canals connecting the interior with the ocean at one time made seaports of all the major Flemish cities. The Flanders terrain is so level you can smell the ocean 40 miles inland. The 41-mile shore, which actually sits below sea level, is mostly land reclaimed from the sea over the centuries for farming; the townspeople built dikes and windmills to keep the sea from taking it back. Although resorts and restaurants dot the white sand beaches, the ancient tradition of paying ceremonial homage to the power of the waters in a solemn Blessing of the Sea survives in many of the fishing villages from Knokke-Het-Zoute to the French border.

BRUSSELS: For a detailed report on the city and its hotels and restaurants, see *Brussels,* THE CITIES.

En Route from Brussels – Head north from Brussels, out of Brabant and into the province of Antwerp. Your first stop is the city of Mechelen, the religious capital of Belgium and the seat of the primate. Not only does Mechelen have a grand 49-bell carillon — which peals out concerts regularly — but also a school for *carilloneurs* (bell ringers) to perpetuate the art. Both school and carillon are in the Gothic cathedral of St. Rombout, begun in the 13th century and still not finished: Its great tower was supposed to be 551 feet high but never topped the mere 318 it is now — it's unlikely that anyone will suggest going ahead with those last 233 feet at this point. Inside, the cathedral is sumptuously baroque, with black and white marble and paintings by Van Dyck and other Flemish masters. For Rubens lovers, the church of St. John in Mechelen has his famous *Adoration of the Magi.* Near Mechelen, in Muizen, is a "suburb" of the Antwerp Zoo called Plankendaal Park; it's a special breeding farm and resort for endangered animal species and a beautiful setting in which to see them (open in the warm weather).

Some 10 miles (16 km) to the northeast is the charming, small Flemish town of Lier. Founded in the 8th century, it has produced a number of Belgium's more notable artists. The 13th-century cloisters, or *béguinage,* inside the town is a peaceful miniature of town life. Nearby, the Zimmer Pavilion houses the showpiece of the 1939 World's Fair — an astronomical clock with 93 dials and 14 automata.

ANTWERP: Continue northwest to Antwerp. Founded in the 7th century by missionaries, it is now Belgium's second largest city (pop. 919,000), the third largest seaport in Europe, and a major producer of cars, petrochemicals, and cut diamonds. Seventy percent of the world's diamonds are produced here. The diamond trade goes back to the days of Charles the Bold, Duke of Burgundy, who reigned from 1467 to 1477. According to an old story, a young student invented a method of cutting and polishing stones; Charles entrusted him with three diamonds and was so pleased with the results that he presented one of the stones to the Pope, another to King Louis XI of France, and kept the third for himself. Presumably, the student took the hint and went into business.

Most of the diamond trade today is clustered around the Central Station. *Diamondland* allows visitors to its showroom to watch the craftsmen at work. Tours are at 11 AM and 4 PM daily; closed Sunday. Diamondland is at 33A Appelmansstraat (phone: 03-234-3612).

Antwerp, the birthplace of the painter Peter Paul Rubens, celebrated the 400th anniversary of his birth in 1977. In a way, Rubens personified all that makes Antwerp what it is: art, international affairs, and wealth. He studied in Italy, became a diplomat, traveled widely, and brought an Italian touch to the Flemish painting tradition. His house (9-11 Wapper), open to the public daily from 10 AM to 5 PM, contains his own art and that of his contemporaries — as well as his furniture. Some of the pupils who studied here included Van Dyck, Jordaens, Snyder, and Jean Breughel. Besides painting prolifically, Rubens was a prominent politician, and his house gives you some idea of the private world of a public man in 17th-century Antwerp.

The Cathedral of Our Lady is the largest Gothic church in Belgium and Antwerp's major landmark, containing some of the world's greatest paintings — including Rubens's *Elevation of the Cross, The Descent from the Cross,* and *The Assumption.* It's open weekday afternoons until 5 PM, Saturdays from 12 to 5 PM, and Sundays from 1 to 4 PM.

Near the cathedral is the *Plantin-Moretus Museum* (22 Vrijdagmarkt), site of the Plantin printing shop, famous all over Europe in the 16th century. In the richly furnished interior are Plantin's office and printing room, containing many first editions and engravings. Tapestries, gold-embossed leather bindings, the Biblia Regia, and 13 examples of the Gutenberg Bible are among its treasures.

The Stadhuis (City Hall) built in a grand, far-flung style in 1564, faces the main square near the cathedral (closed Fridays and Tuesday and Saturday mornings). Around it are the headquarters of Antwerp's rich tradesmen's guilds from the same period, furnished with sculpture, paintings, and tapestries.

Rubens is buried in the church of St. James (St. Jacob), a Flamboyant Gothic edifice with a baroque interior. Built in 1491, St. James has an amazing inventory of art by Flemish masters: The marble communion table is by Verbruggen and Kerricx (late 17th century); the carving in the choir stalls is the work of Artus Quellin; there is a *Temptation of Saint Anthony* by Martin de Vos; and one of Rubens's own last works, *The Holy Family,* hangs in the chapel where he is buried.

Antwerp's *Royal Museum of Fine Arts* (L de Waelplaats; closed Mondays) is often called the richest museum in Belgium, a land of museums. There are about 2,500 paintings here, including a staggering collection of Rubens, Frans Hals, Van Dyck, Memling, and Rogier Van der Weyden. Even if you are not a student of art, you will be fascinated at the 800-year history of northern painting displayed here.

As in any seafaring country, *Belgium's Marine Museum* (1 Steenplein), with ancient maps, ships, relics, and instruments, is worth a visit. The museum is in the Steen, a 10th-century fortress and the city's oldest building. For a relaxing cruise of Antwerp's famous harbor, take a *Flandria* sightseeing boat at Steenplein, a short walk from the Grote Markt.

The world-famous Antwerp Zoo is a must. Check out the new Reptile House and the Nocturama, a special darkened habitat for nocturnal animals.

If you are in Antwerp during Lent, make your way to a Goose Race, held on Sundays in several of the surrounding villages; it's just one of the many bizarre and dramatic traditions still thriving in this proudly parochial country. In a Goose Race, competing horsemen thunder along a track trying to snag the head of a dead goose suspended above them. The winner is proclaimed king, and festivities ensue in his honor.

The denizens of Antwerp are great beer lovers, and they know how to create the coziest watering spots (there are about 2,500 of them in town). During your sightseeing rounds, drop in on De Pelgrom, a multi-chambered cellar featuring candlelight and classical music, near the cathedral.

En Route from Antwerp – Go west from Antwerp province into East Flanders (Oost-Vlaanderen), on the road to Ghent. You are entering the historic region of Flanders proper, which starts in the Netherlands and stretches down the North Sea coast into northern France. The poppies grow here, the sheep graze, and everything looks like a familiar landscape — which it is, because it's been painted hundreds of times by the Flemish masters whose works hang in museums all over the world; and centuries of armies have passed this way, leaving memories of the fields of Flanders in our collective consciousness.

If you are here in early September, try to arrive in time to watch the surreal, elephantine grace of the hot-air balloons in the international balloon race held every year in Sint-Niklaas, just west of the Antwerp border.

GHENT: Continue southwest to Ghent (pop. 485,000), the gracious and prosperous capital of East Flanders. Ghent has a long history of civic feistiness that put it in combat with a variety of governments and overlords from Burgundy, Flanders, Spain, and Holland. The city itself spawned an overlord in Charles Quint, the Holy Roman Emperor; King Edward III of England was living in Ghent when his son John was born, best known as John of Gaunt in Shakespeare's *Richard II,* who fathered a long line of English kings.

The center of Ghent is its medieval port, with more historic buildings than any other Belgian city. Surrounding the old quarter are the modern commercial and industrial sections.

The most dramatic introduction to Ghent is by way of 'sGravensteen, the formidable castle of the Counts of Flanders. Built in the 12th century over a 9th-century dungeon, it is a no-nonsense fortress, with walls 6 feet thick. Inside, the cold and damp of centuries hang in the air even in the summer. It has a small museum displaying instruments of torture. Visitors with small children must be on guard here, since there are many high, open walkways and steps.

The most important medieval building in town is the cathedral of St. Bavo, a hybrid of Gothic, Romanesque, and baroque styles. The elaborately carved wood pulpit inside warrants a visit on its own. The four massive bronze candlesticks were ordered by Henry VIII of England for his tomb, but Cromwell got his hands on them after Henry's death and sold them to the Ghent clergy for the cash. In one of the chapels is the Van Eyck *Mystic Lamb,* one of the world's most famous paintings. The history of this painting is a detective thriller in progress, for its origin is still vague. No one knows whether it was painted by both Van Eyck brothers or by only one. Its panels have been cut off, buried, and returned several times. During the religious riots of the 16th century, the panels were hidden in the cathedral tower. They reemerged and were being sent to England as a gift to Queen Elizabeth I when they were intercepted by the family who had originally commissioned them. Two panels were stolen in 1934, and only one returned. Some believe the missing panel, *The Just Judge,* is hidden in the cathedral. The cathedral is open daily until 6 PM from April through September; weekdays until 4 PM; and Sundays until 5 PM from October through March.

Next door is the belfry, the rallying point for the people of Ghent in their many rebellions against their rulers. There is a fine view of the countryside from the tower. The sound and light show here (in English) is a must, as is the unique *Folklore Museum.*

The *Museum of Archaeology,* in the ancient Cistercian Abbey of Byloke, contains a rich assortment of art, glass, porcelain, weapons, and clothing. The *Museum of Fine Arts* has a splendid collection of Flemish primitives as well as Dutch, German, French, English, Italian, and Spanish masters. The neighboring *Museum of Contemporary Art* focuses on post–World War II trends.

Ghent has been noted for its horticulture industry for the last 200 years: It has historically been the center for the growing, breeding, and distribution of new varieties of flowers to all points of the globe. The flowering azalea, native to Korea, was developed in Ghent, and the city's nurseries supply 16 million plants a year — nearly half the world market. Coming in second, at some 80 million tubers a year, is the begonia, developed in Ghent into its present form from a South American flower. Hothouses dot the outskirts of the city. The town of Lochristi, 6 miles (9.6 km) outside Ghent, holds a begonia festival every August, when nurserymen put together floats and pictures using different-colored begonias.

A major event in Ghent is a mammoth flower festival held in the city every 5 years. (The next festival is scheduled for late April of 1990.) Over 450 horticulturists from all over the world will show their best plants in a 9-acre indoor expanse, with a total of 2 million Belgian francs offered in prize money. The first *floralies* (flower festival), in 1809 at the *Frascati Inn*, consisted of 50 potted plants arranged in front of a field of French tricolor flags around a bust of Napoleon.

In the 20th century the crowds are thick — 700,000 strong over the week-long run — peering at the likes of sweet peas and conifer arrangements to be judged by the Belgian Flower Arranging Society, blooming roses and daffodils, and every other conceivable plant presented to the Royal Society of Agriculture and Botany.

En Route from Ghent – Leaving Ghent, make a slight detour southeast to the 13th-century castle of Ooidonck on the River Lys. Ooidonck is decorated with 17th- and 18th-century furniture, china, silver, and crystal (open only afternoons on some religious holidays and Sundays in July, August, and early September). The Lys borders the grounds on two sides, and a long avenue of linden trees links the castle with the Ghent road.

Ten miles (16 km) east of Ghent on Route 345 is the imposing Laarne castle, with its treasures of silver and tapestries. Legend has it that a ghost still stalks the place. Closed Mondays. Entrance fee.

BRUGES: The main road leads directly to Bruges, the capital of West Flanders and the longtime rival of Ghent. Bruges is smaller (pop. 259,000), with a totally different appearance and atmosphere.

The city is virtually a moated museum of the Middle Ages, with stiff-gabled houses perched over cobbled streets and long-necked swans gliding along misty canals. For 200 years, Bruges was the most important commercial center in Western Europe, linking the Baltic and the Mediterranean seas. The riches of the world were piled high on its docks, and no king could equal the splendor of its court. The Counts of Flanders and their merchant princes brought artists and artisans from all over Europe to decorate their palaces, churches, and guildhalls. Their wives were so magnificently gowned that a visiting Queen of France once complained, "I thought that I alone was queen, but here I see hundreds of them around me."

But year after opulent year, the silt rose in the estuary linking Bruges with the North Sea until ships could no longer navigate the narrow, sand-choked waterway, and Bruges became landlocked. This put an end to the city's commercial importance, and Bruges was frozen in time, retaining its medieval atmosphere to this day. The 19th-century English poet Ernest Dowson called Bruges "this autumnal old city — the most medieval town in Europe."

Bruges must be visited on foot. The streets are narrow and twisting; some, like Stoofstraat, are only 3 or 4 feet wide. No skyscraper or high-rise blots the sky; for 7 centuries the highest point has been the 365-foot spire of the church of Notre Dame. For a beautiful view of the city, climb the steps of the belfry at one end of the Grote Market (Main Square). On a clear day you can see Ostend and Zeebrugge and other towns along the coast as well as the maze of canals within Bruges itself. The canals that weave in and around the city give it a melancholy charm; lime trees and willows grow from the banks, and centuries-old buildings of faded brick are reflected in the silent waters. A few places in town offer canal boat tours.

Probably the greatest event in the city's long history took place in 1150, when Thierry d'Alsace, Count of Flanders, rode home from the Second Crusade. According to tradition, he brought with him some drops of Christ's blood, collected on Golgotha by Joseph of Arimathea and given to him by the King of Jerusalem. They are kept in a reliquary in the Basilica of the Holy Blood (around the corner from the town belfry) and every year are carried through the city in procession on Ascension Thursday, a religious holiday in May.

The churches of Bruges are as rich in history as they are in art, some with foundations going back to the 8th and 9th centuries. The dim, dusty-aisled crypt of the basilica, a 12th-century Romanesque chapel, is the oldest unaltered building still standing in Bruges.

The cathedral of St. Salvator was begun more than a thousand years ago. It's hung with Gobelin tapestries, and some of its choir stalls are carved with the crest of one of Europe's oldest orders of chivalry, the Golden Fleece, founded in Bruges by Philip of Burgundy in 1429. It was in this cathedral that his knights assembled to worship.

Only a block away is the church of Notre Dame, where you'll find Michelangelo's marble *Madonna and Child,* the 500-year-old Paradise Porch, and the magnificent mausoleum of Charles the Bold.

Even the former hospital is a museum (closed Wednesdays), for St. John's goes back to the 12th century. One of its 13th-century wards contains six paintings by Hans Memling; other wards have 12th-century frescoes of the Virgin Mary.

Scattered throughout Bruges (and other old cities in Flanders) are "God's houses," a series of compounds built by wealthy families or guilds for the poor and the old. The only requirements for residence are "honesty, good character, and a peaceable nature." There is one in Bruges built by the Meulenaere family in 1613 that has 24 one-story houses, each with its own garden. The community begins and ends each day with prayers for the generations that have lived and died there before them.

At the other extreme is the *Gruuthuse Museum,* the former home of one of the lords of Bruges. Its great hall, reception rooms, and collections of armor, porcelains, lace, coins, and furniture hint at the magnificence of private houses in the city's prime (closed Tuesdays).

Next to it is the *Groeninge Museum,* housing some of the great masterpieces of Flemish art, including paintings by Jan Van Eyck, Hans Memling, Hieronymus Bosch, and Pieter Breughel the Younger (closed Tuesdays).

In all of Bruges there is probably no lovelier place than the Princely Béguinage, one of the convents of the peasant Béguines, who wore a *béguin,* or headdress, tied under the chin. There are *béguinages* throughout Belgium, famous for their manicured gardens. Today they are either maintained as museums or occupied, as in Bruges, by Benedictine nuns who still dress in the 15th-century style of their predecessors. To reach the Princely Béguinage, cross the Bridge of the Vine, which spans the Lake of Love, between the cloister and the main city. Across the lake, sunlight filters through the trees, and the only thing to break the peace is the song of a bird.

The miracle of Bruges is that it still stands, considering all the wars that have raged around it. The port of Zeebrugge, 8 miles (13 km) away, was seized by Germany during World War I and made into a U-boat base. When the British stormed the port, the Germans blew it up. It was rebuilt, destroyed again in World War II, and rebuilt once more.

When the 8th-century chapel of the ironmongers' guild was torn down to make way for a garage a few years ago, a preservation society was created to prevent further desecration. They named it the Marcus Gerards Foundation, after a 16th-century Bruges mapmaker who drew to scale every house and street in town. The foundation researches the history of the old buildings in this monumental city and keeps an eye on how they are maintained.

En Route from Bruges – Ostend and the 41-mile (66-km) stretch of Belgian coast are a short drive west of Bruges. There are resorts, casinos, and nightclubs from nearly one end to the other of this unbroken stretch of fine white sand. July and August are good for swimming, but beaches get very crowded with vacationing Belgians. If you avoid those peak months, you can still have a fine time playing tennis, breathing the sea air, and gambling away your money. At Ostend there is a long boardwalk along the North Sea, and the area is dotted with restaurants specializing in fresh fish, for this is Belgium's main fishing port.

The best areas in which to enjoy the sea away from honky-tonk civilization are in the extreme north and south of the coast. At the Zwin bird sanctuary up by the Dutch border, the sea lavender blooms on the marshes in July and August, where more than 100 species of birds make their home.

At Oostduinkerke, 12 miles (19.2 km) southwest of Ostend, a few fishermen still trawl for shrimp on horseback. Their annual shrimp fishing festival takes place the third weekend in June.

If you are in Ostend just before Lent, you will find yourself caught up in the *Masked Ball of the Dead Rat,* a stupendous carnival that occupies the entire town, but is concentrated in the casino. Candies in the shape of clogs are scattered to the throng at the festival's close. North of Ostend, at Knokke, an international fireworks festival is held every August on 5 nights spread out through the month.

On the final Sunday in May, a solemn procession in the town of Blankenberge culminates in the Blessing of the Sea, when seafaring people make a special peace with their ancient friend and enemy, a ritual that takes place at different times of the year along the coast.

Note: There is now daily jetfoil service from Ostend to Dover (it's a 1½-hour crossing), where trains to London are available. Ferries also operate daily from Ostend and Zeebrugge.

YPRES: Head south to Ypres when you have had your fill of the coast. One of the three great cities of Flanders in the Middle Ages, Ypres was razed in World War I, and a modern city has been built in its place. The 17th-century façades along many streets have been reconstructed, as have the city's two greatest buildings, St. Martin's Cathedral and the towering Cloth Hall — a monument to Ypres's textile industry built in 1214. Unfortunately, no medieval or later buildings survived the bombardment of 1914–18, but the region's red poppy fields, grazing animals, and pastoral countryside are still very much in evidence.

Ypres never fell in World War I, despite the bombardment, but the surrounding battles took over a quarter-million Allied lives. At the Menin Gate, a memorial to the soldiers of the British Commonwealth who died defending Ypres, traffic is stopped every evening for a few minutes while buglers blow a salute on silver bugles. The poem *Flanders Field,* written by John McCrae, one of the soldiers who fought there, best expresses the mood of this place:

> In Flanders Field the poppies blow
> between the crosses row on row
> That mark our place; and in the sky
> the larks, bravely singing, fly
> Scarce heard amid the guns below.

On the second Sunday in May, Ypres holds what is possibly the strangest rite in all of Belgium, *Kattenwoensdag,* or *Festival of the Cats.* Some 2,000 revelers dress up in gaudy costumes portraying cats, witches, and giants and march in procession accompanied by bagpipes. The parade has giant floats dedicated to feline folklore heroes, including Puss in Boots and Cieper, the king of the cats; Cieper has a wife, Minneke Poes, and a kitten-child, Piepertje. The culmination of the festival is when the town jester hurls little wooden cats to the crowd from the top of the town belfry (until 1817, he threw live cats). It is said that the holiday is a vestige of an ancient witch cult.

BEST EN ROUTE

All the major cities and towns you visit in Belgium have comfortable hotels and first-rate restaurants. There are also several good *relais* (inns) in the countryside where you can spend the night or have a splendid lunch or dinner. It's wise to book ahead for a room in a hotel and essential to make a reservation for a meal or room at a *relais*.

Accommodations at an expensive inn will cost about $100 or more per night in a double for two; moderate, about $60; and inexpensive, about $40. A meal at an expensive restaurant will run about $50 or more per person for dinner, including tip, without wine; moderate, about $35; and inexpensive, about $20.

GHENT

St. Jorishof – Built in 1228, this 72-room hotel is believed to be the oldest in northern Europe. It has a Gothic hall with a huge chimney. The interior is hung with the pennants of various clubs and organizations ranging from the medieval guilds to the Rotary Club. Napoleon Bonaparte was a guest. Closed the last 2 weeks in July and during the Christmas season. 2 Botermarkt (phone: 091-242424). Moderate.

BRUGES

De Orangerie – A ravishingly charming 16th-century building turned into a cozy, 18-room hotel overlooking a canal. 10 Kartuizerinnestraat (phone: 050-34-16-49). Expensive.

Duc de Bourgogne – There are only 9 small rooms here, but the restaurant is the best in Bruges. Both the rooms and restaurant are nearly always booked. The dining room extends over a canal, and the area is most impressive at night, when it's floodlit. Near the entrance hall is a medieval version of a small cocktail lounge, where you wait for your table; its walls are hung with tapestries of saints and knights, the chairs and tables are heavy mahogany, and there is a huge fireplace. In the restaurant, order the North Sea fish and, if it's spring or summer, the asparagus. Closed Mondays, Tuesdays for lunch in summer, Sunday evenings in winter, and in July. 12 Huidevettersplein (phone: 050-332038). Expensive.

Pullman – This former *Holiday Inn* (once a 17th-century convent) was recently taken over and upgraded by the Pullman chain. In the heart of Bruges. 2 Boeveriestraat (phone 050-340971). Expensive.

Oud-huis Amsterdam – A handsomely converted townhouse, on a canal, with 17 rooms and a garden. 3 Spiegelrei (phone: 050-34-18-10). Expensive to moderate.

ANTWERP

De Rosier – This work of hostelry genius, inconspicuously off a quiet side street, is one of those rare finds: an impeccably tasteful mansion-hotel (only 10 rooms) graced with antiques, a small indoor pool, and charming garden, run with the greatest discretion and style for its well-heeled clientele. Reservations are very hard to come by, but it's worth the wait. 21-23 Rosier (phone: 03-225-0140). Expensive.

Sir Anthony Van Dijck – A cobblestone passage marks the entrance to an ancient building housing the restaurant. The combination of fine food and a dramatic setting make this worth a stop, especially for lunch. Closed Saturdays. 16 Oude Koornmarkt Vlaaikensgang (phone: 03-231-6170). Expensive.

The Ardennes

South of Brussels is a world so different from Flanders that it's hard to believe they are part of the same country. This is the Ardennes — Shakespeare's Forest of Arden in *As You Like It* — stretching across the south of Belgium. The Ardennes extend into the three provinces of Namur, Liège, and Luxembourg (not to be confused with the Grand Duchy of Luxembourg, a separate country). It is gentle, green, and somehow a bit mysterious compared with the North, a countryside of legends and spirits, abbeys and castles. It is also the place to go if you want to spend your vacation skiing, hunting, hiking, or camping.

You can make a loop through the region by driving southeast of Brussels through Liège, Spa, and Malmédy, south to Bastogne and Arlon, west to Bouillon, north to Namur, west to Mons, and finally north back to Brussels.

BRUSSELS: For a detailed report on the city and its hotels and restaurants, see *Brussels*, THE CITIES.

En Route from Brussels – Heading southeast to Liège, on the left you will pass Catholic University in Louvain, Belgium's oldest university, founded in 1425. Erasmus is one of its distinguished alumni. Architecturally, it ranges from the 15th to the 20th century. The town was badly damaged during the two world wars, but the 15th-century Town Hall and St. Peter's Church are worth visiting. Like Oxford, Louvain has become somewhat commercial and industrial but basically preserves its clerical-academic serenity.

LIÈGE: Seventy miles (112 km) east of Brussels is Liège, Belgium's third largest city (population, 593,000) and a gateway to the Ardennes. Liège has been a prosperous industrial town since coal was discovered here in 1198. Most of the citizens are shopkeepers, artisans, miners, or steelworkers. (Val St.-Lambert crystal and sporting guns are produced here.) But above all, Liège — "the Ardent City" — is a city that loves festivals, art, and music.

The streets of Liège are laid out as fitfully and capriciously as the local temperament, so don't plan your time here too closely. You should enjoy what you find, however. The skyline shows over 100 church spires, and the River Meuse winds its way through every quarter, which means you will often find yourself going over one nice little bridge or another. The city has one of Belgium's most important universities, the University of Liège, so the café life is well catered to.

In the center of Liège is a tiny island, Outre-Meuse (Djus d'la Moûse in the Walloon dialect), reminiscent of the Ile de la Cité in Paris. This "free republic" of garbled cobblestone streets and alleyways is best symbolized by Tchantchès, a beloved marionette character not unlike Punch, and Georges Simenon, the famed creator of Inspector Maigret and probably Liège's best-known native son. He lived here as a child at 25 Rue Pasteur. The tourist office runs tours of Simenon's Liège.

On Mont St. Martin are some particularly fine houses, with winding outdoor stairways and hidden gardens. The Place du Marché and the Place St.-Lambert are the heart of the city. The 11th-century Palace of the Prince Bishops (who ruled Liège until the 18th century) has two great courtyards. Each of the capitals atop the 60 columns of the portico is different from the others. Since the 19th century, the building has been used as the Palace of Justice.

One of Belgium's greatest art treasures is the baptismal font by Reinier van Hoei in the Church of St. Barthélemy, made of tin-coated brass sometime between 1107 and 1118. The Church of St. James is an old abbey with five Renaissance stained glass windows and an exquisite north portal. At the Church of the Holy Cross are a 12th-century enamel reliquary and an 8th-century key of St. Hubert. St. Hubert, the patron saint of hunters, established his bishopric at Liège in the 8th century; he is a very important saint in the Ardennes.

The city has a wide assortment of museums, but be sure to see the *Museum of Walloon Life* (closed Mondays). In a 17th-century convent, it has, among other things, an amazing puppet collection. There's also the *Curtius Museum* (closed Tuesdays), with its unique glass and crystal collection, which displays the history of glassmaking. At the theater on the Rue Féronstrée, marionettes (large, intricate puppets) perform in Liège folklore pageants, religious plays, and sketches based on contemporary gossip. The characters include Tchantchès, biblical characters, and historical figures like Charlemagne and Napoleon. If you understand enough French to try to decipher Liègeois, the local dialect, you will appreciate a real folk art that is still very much alive. Liège is famous for its manufacture of guns, and the *Museum of Weapons* (closed Mondays), with 12,500 pieces, is considered the best firearms collection in the world.

Before leaving, be sure to visit the Citadel; you can climb the 407 steps to the top or drive there. You will get a splendid view of the city and the surrounding countryside. The city's Sunday morning market along the quays even draws shoppers from neighboring Germany. A grand assortment of items is for sale, and it's a great meeting place for residents.

On the Sunday following St. George's Day in the neighboring town of Visé, the guild of crossbowmen, the Ancient Arquebusiers, wearing starched shirtfronts and stovepipe hats, celebrate St. George (the patron of archers) with a mass, procession, and an archery contest.

In the village of Rutten on May 1, the sanguine *Play of St. Evermeire* is performed in an orchard by the townspeople, just as it has been for over 1,000 years; it portrays the story of St. Evermeire and his fellow pilgrims, who were massacred by highwaymen in 699.

And you surely won't want to miss the *Pageant of the Flying Cat* in the town of Verviers on the third Sunday in June. An annual publicity stunt for the town, it commemorates the grand experiment of a chemist named Saroléa in 1641. Saroléa wanted to see if he could get his cat to fly, so he attached pig bladders filled with air to the luckless beast and dropped it off the tower of St. Remacle's Cathedral. Naturally, it plummeted like a stone — although it landed in good enough condition to scamper away and, being a wise cat, never returned. Every year the experiment is repeated (with a toy cat) at the place du Martyr at 5:30 PM, accompanied by a triumphal procession with giant, confetti-belching cat floats. In this technological era the cat does fly successfully, since the bladders are now filled with helium.

En Route from Liège – Drive 24 miles (38 km) southeast to Spa, the site of the thermal spring from which all the spas in the world take their name. During the 18th and early 19th centuries, Spa was a favorite resort for the European nobility and royalty. The oldest spring is named for Peter the Great, who used to make his way from Russia to take the waters. Nowadays Spa is visited more for its grand hotels and wooded environs rather than the curative power of its waters.

Drive southeast to Malmédy, where the countryside is covered with alpine flowers in the summer and meadows and dense pine forests line the road. During the winter, this is a popular ski area. Malmédy, a monastery city founded in the 7th century, is best known today for its pre-Lenten carnival, which includes mass folk dancing and satirical plays in the local dialect. Nearby is the château of Reinhardstein, the ancestral home of the Metternichs and a completely furnished feudal stronghold.

BASTOGNE: Drive southwest, pick up the Liège road, and go directly south to Bastogne, 100 miles (160 km) from Brussels.

This is the site of the Battle of the Bulge, where the Nazis made their last stand as the Allies pushed toward Germany. The Germans launched their counteroffensive on December 16, 1944; the Americans holding Bastogne were hampered by snow and fog, which prevented any air support. On December 22 the Germans demanded an American surrender. The American General Anthony McAuliffe spurned their ultimatum with a single word: "Nuts." The next day the skies cleared, and Allied planes again took to the air; the Third Army, under General George Patton, counterattacked and reached Bastogne on December 26. Early in January, the First Army arrived from the north. By the end of the month, the Germans had been pushed back behind their own frontier, losing 120,000 men.

McAuliffe and his curt reply became part of Belgian folklore. There is a bust of him in town as well as a few derelict tanks scattered there and around the outskirts, mostly bearing the word "Nuts;" there is a *"Nuts" Museum* in town. The Mardasson American war memorial is laid out in the shape of a five-pointed star and inscribed with the names of the home states of the fallen GIs. Across from the Mardasson, also in the shape of a five-pointed star, is the *Bastogne Historical Center,* with the largest collection of Bastogne battle relics in the world as well as a film of the battle in four languages. Some 8,000 American soldiers are buried nearby at the Henri-Chapelle cemetery.

Near the cemetery is a former monastery, the Abbaie Val-Dieu, now a modest but congenial cafeteria-style restaurant. Try the local specialty, *stron d'poye,* a tasty yeast-based spread served with whipped cream cheese on brown bread.

ARLON: Continue south to Arlon, the capital of the province of Luxembourg, where the great Roman road from Rheims intersected the road from the north. While the site of Arlon is the oldest settlement in Belgium, most of the buildings are new. The *Archaeology Museum* has a wealth of Gallo-Roman artifacts; the Church of St. Donat is built on the site of the castle of the counts of Arlon, where Richard the Lion-Hearted set out for the Crusades. The church's terrace commands a sweeping view of the valley of the River Semois and Luxembourg, Germany, and France.

BOUILLON: Swing west to Bouillon, the home of Godfrey of Bouillon, a hero of the First Crusade and first King of Jerusalem. Looking out from his castle, it is easy to understand why whoever held this spot ruled the surrounding countryside: You can see a single figure approaching for miles in every direction. Be sure to see the Hall of Justice inside, with its gallows, and take a walk along the battlements (open daily, March through November; weekends only, January and February).

En Route from Bouillon – Leave some time for hiking in the Ardennes and the Belgian Lorraine as you travel in this entire southeastern region. You can explore the densely wooded plateau country north of the River Semois all the way to Liège and the steep gorges and lush wild flowers of the Belgian Lorraine south of Arlon. Bring some sturdy shoes or boots, a compass, a light jacket or heavy sweater, and perhaps a camera. It's easy to get lost in this rolling landscape, so either stick to the trail markings or know where you are at all times — and beware of marshes after dark. The mountain peaks go to 2,000 feet, and the views are spectacular.

As you drive north, you'll be in the grotto district, where stalactites and stalagmites stretch from floor to ceiling in underground caverns. The most spectacular is the grotto of Han-sur-Lesse, which was sacred to a local prehistoric civilization.

North of Han-sur-Lesse, in the valley of the River Meuse, is the town of Annevoie, the site of one of Belgium's most beautiful castles. The Castle of Annevoie is relatively small and cozy, more like an 18th-century manor house than a fortress. Its gardens are often compared with those of Versailles, but in fact the gardens of Annevoie are prettier and more human. There are fountains, pools, cascades, and canals, one after another, between avenues of trees and flowers. The castle is closed from September until Easter; the gardens are closed from November until April.

Only 10 miles (16 km) to the east is the Spontin château, considered the most remarkable example of medieval military architecture in Belgium. Still inhabited, the château has stylishly furnished drawing rooms, tapestries, masterpieces of art, and an unusual square dungeon. It's in the charming village of Spontin (exit 19 of E411) and is open daily, April through September.

Namur is 20 miles (32 km) north, at the junction of the Sambre and Meuse rivers, a neat little city of 17th-century brick homes. Since the days of Julius Caesar, it has been blasted by one army after another. Louis XIV and William III of Orange fought for it; in both world wars the Germans sacked it and set fire to it. Yet many of its historic treasures have survived. Be sure to visit the House of the Sisters of Notre-Dame (closed Tuesdays), with its magnificent treasury of art and relics. In particular, note the work of Hugo d'Oignies, who embellished his crosses and icons with figures of animals of the region.

Namur also has its own casino. The Citadel, accessible by cable car or on foot, overlooks the Meuse and surrounding countryside.

THE MONS AREA: Mons lies west of Namur along the River Sambre; this region is an essential stop before you make your way back to Brussels.

Shrove Tuesday (before Lent) is celebrated in Belgium's usual splashy and improbable style in the town of Binche, near Mons. In a noisy carnival procession, the revelers, called Gilles, wearing bells, green glasses, and ostrich-plumed hats, perform rhythmic dances while marching and pelt the surging crowd with oranges. The onlookers then join in an increasingly frenzied circle dance with the Gilles. It is said that this pageant somehow portrays the Spanish conquest of the Aztecs in the New World, with the Gilles playing the Indians, hurling gold (oranges) at the Spaniards. However, while the fruit is flying, the anthropology of it probably makes very little difference to the Binchois.

In Jumet, around July 21, an observance honors St. Mary Magdalene and celebrates the town's deliverance from the plague, dating from the epidemic of the 1380s. The procession begins solemnly until the chosen moment, when a messenger announces that the plague has ended because of their prayers to St. Mary; at this point, the entire parade, including the decorous clergy, breaks into a jubilant dance. In Belgian folk rites, the popular conscience exorcises the terrors and deliverances of the last 1,000 years to show the proper respect for fate so disaster will not strike again.

BELOEIL: It is a short drive from Mons to the castle of Beloeil, a fitting culmination of this tour. For at least 10 centuries it has belonged to the family of the Prince of Ligne. The castle is virtually a museum of furniture, tapestry, paintings, sculpture, and porcelain. The family can trace its ancestry to the 7th century; the portraits in the castle are a history of Europe. The treasures of the house include memorabilia from Peter the Great and Catherine II of Russia and a lock of Marie Antoinette's hair. The formal gardens, laid out in the 17th century, feature a lake and tree-lined avenues and cover nearly 300 acres. There, among the flowers of the centuries, you may hope to lose yourself before finding your way home. A Belgium-in-miniature exhibit, displaying the country's major historic sites and monuments on a scale of 1:25, opened at the castle in 1988. Closed from October until April.

BEST EN ROUTE

All the major cities and towns you visit in Belgium have comfortable hotels and first-rate restaurants. There are also several good *relais* (inns) in the countryside where you can spend the night or have a splendid lunch or dinner. It's wise to book ahead for a room in a hotel and essential to make a reservation for a meal or room at a *relais*.

Expensive accommodations will cost about $100 or more per night in a double for two; moderate, about $60; and inexpensive, about $40. A good meal in an expensive place will run $50 or more per person for dinner, including tip, but not wine; moderate, $35; and inexpensive, $20.

GENVAL

Château du Lac – Modeled after a Romanesque abbey but actually built around 1900, this is an ultra-modern hotel-restaurant (38 well-appoined rooms) on the outskirts of Brussels. It overlooks the Lake of Genval and offers a variety of sports. 87 Av. du Lac, Genval (phone: 02-654-1122). Expensive.

DURBUY

Sanglier des Ardennes – The inn-restaurant on this picture-postcard town's main street is noted throughout the country for its fine cuisine. The trout slices on lettuce and the roast pigeon are superb. Closed Thursdays and January. 99 Rue Comte Th. d'Ursel, about 20 miles (32 km) southwest of Spa (phone: 086-211088). Expensive.

LIÈGE

La Commanderie – A command post of the Knights Templar during the Middle Ages, this is now a small inn (14 rooms) with an excellent restaurant. The old stone buildings are in a private park a short drive southwest of Liège. Closed Wednesdays except in summer and January and February. 28 Rue Joseph Pierco, Villers-le-Temple (phone: 085-511701). Accommodations, expensive; restaurant, moderate.

Mamé Vi Cou – This country-style restaurant, with its open fireplace and brick wall decorated with local marionettes, specializes in Liègeois cuisine. The *salade di "Djus d'la"* (bacon, green beans, and potatoes in vinegar), goose scallop, and blood sausage are particularly tasty, especially when washed down with a glass of *peket,* the local liqueur. 9 Rue Wache (phone: 085-23-71-81). Inexpensive.

MALMÉDY

Trôs Marets – Once a private house, this 11-room inn is surrounded by pine forests and has food that lives up to the lush setting. Closed mid-November to mid-December. 1 Rue de Mont (phone: 080-337917). Expensive.

Hôtel des Bains – A comfortable 15-room, lakeside hotel with an elegant restaurant that draws diners from neighboring Germany. Specialties include lobster and game (in season). Before dinner, sip an apéritif in the homey lounge that overlooks gardens and water. Closed Tuesdays and Wednesdays, and all of January. 46 Lac de Robertville, Waimes (phone: 080-679571). Moderate.

EREZÉE

Auberge du Val d'Aisne – Near Erezée, some 6 miles (9.6 km) west of the Liège road. Though the rooms are rustic, the nouvelle cuisine served at this 300-year-old inn is very fine; try the wild mushroom salad and the trout. From the cozy dining room, guests can gaze out over farmlands and a stream. It's worth a stop for the food alone. Closed Tuesdays, Wednesdays, Thursdays except in August, and from mid-December to mid-January and mid-June to mid-July. 15 Rue Franzel, Mormont (phone: 086-489208). Moderate.

BASTOGNE

L'Air Pur – This small hotel, off the road to Namur, has 11 comfortable rooms but no atmosphere inside. Outside, the view of the valley of the Ourthe is dazzling, and the food is excellent. In winter, open weekends only. 1½ miles (2 km) from

Houffalize. 11 Route de Houffalize, La Roche-en-Ardenne (phone: 062-411223 or 411503). Expensive.

L'Auberge du Moulin Hideux – This inn, an old mill that serves some of the best food in Belgium, can be your base for Bastogne, Bouillon, and Annevoie (if you can afford it). There is a little pool by the mill where you can select the trout that will be on your plate for lunch. Even if you don't book one of its cozy bedrooms, try to have a meal; it is worth any inconvenience you may encounter getting here. Extensive wine list. Closed Wednesdays and from mid-November to mid-March. 1 Rue de Dohan, Noirefontaine (phone: 061-467015). Expensive.

Hostellerie du Prieuré de Conques – Between Bastogne and Bouillon on the banks of the Semois, this magnificent 18th-century priory is now a small hotel near the trout-filled Semois River; the chef here will prepare your catch. 176 Rue de Florenville, Herbeumont (phone: 061-411417). Closed Christmas week. Expensive.

Bulgaria

Bordered by Romania, Yugoslavia, Greece, Turkey, and the Black Sea, Bulgaria is 325 miles wide and 250 miles long — slightly larger than Ohio — and one of the countries sharing the Danube River. Though it has a population of about 9 million, Bulgaria is the smallest Eastern European country, with an ancient history that predates even that of Crete.

Bulgaria is the rose capital of the world, exporting more than 95% of the world's supply of rose attar. It is credited with the discovery of yogurt, and its people are among the most long-lived anywhere in the world. In antiquity, the legendary Orpheus sang of Bulgaria's flower-covered meadows, the imposing Balkan and Rhodope massifs, and the deep forests of pine and walnut.

What is now Bulgaria was once the territory of Thracian tribes, whose thousand-year-old civilization eventually succumbed to Roman conquest and, later, to successive waves of Slavic immigration to the Balkans. Following the arrival of the Bulgars in the 7th century, Thracian assimilation into Slavic culture was complete. Today Bulgarians have a strong awareness of their Thracian heritage, as evidenced by the country's intense archaeological activity, yielding dazzling finds for its museums.

By the 9th century, Bulgaria was the cradle of Slav literature. The work of two Byzantine missionaries, the brothers Constantine (later Cyril) and Methodius, who spread the use of the Slavic vernacular in religious practice, found a warm reception in the Bulgarian state, which officially adopted Christianity in 865. The script that Cyril invented to transcribe church texts became the basis for the Cyrillic alphabet, used today by Russians, Ukrainians, Serbs, and Macedonians, in addition to the Bulgarians.

In the 14th century, when its arts and world trading flourished, Bulgaria was the most powerful country in southeastern Europe, largely because of its borders on the Black, Aegean, and Adriatic seas. Bulgaria was the envy of its neighbors, which led to its invasion and conquest by the Ottomans in 1396. Through the next 500 years, the Bulgarians tenaciously managed to hold on to their culture through a network of monasteries where artists and writers were sheltered, producing paintings, books, frescoes, icons, carvings, and musical scores. Today, about half a dozen of these former spiritual and cultural centers, the most famous of which is Rila, attract legions of visitors to their secluded mountain sites. One legacy of Turkish rule is the way Bulgarians shake their heads from side to side to express "yes" and nod for "no" — mannerisms that take some getting used to.

In the 19th century, the small but energetic Bulgarian intelligentsia propelled the development of a "National Revival" of culture and patriotism, which resulted in the April 1876 uprising against Ottoman domination. Although cruelly crushed, it provoked a larger conflict — the Russo-Turkish War of 1877, known in Bulgarian history as the War of Liberation. An independent state was established with strong bonds to Russia; in 1978 Bulgaria celebrated 100 years of independence. An interesting footnote is that the Bulgarian-Russian connection was well established long before the Russian Revolution, so the ties between the two countries are based not so much on ideology (although Bulgaria is a Soviet satellite) as on invocations of "traditional friendship."

The first Bulgarian route starts with the capital, Sofia, on the western plain and climbs through the surrounding pine-forested mountains (with the beautiful Rila Monastery), then runs south and east to Plovdiv and Bachkovo, the historic center of the country. The second route starts in Varna, Bulgaria's main port on the Black Sea, and discusses the new luxury resorts that dot the coastline.

Sofia and the Mountains

This route skirts the country's major ski resorts and takes you into the Rila Mountains, the highest range on the Balkan Peninsula and the fourth highest in Europe. The route ends in the Thracian plains. This 200-mile (322-km) stretch plunges you into the heart of the country's dramatic and cultural past. While the asphalt roads are good (as they are throughout Bulgaria), go slowly to catch the elusive and mysterious notes of ancient history.

SOFIA: In the western part of Bulgaria, Sofia has been the nation's capital only since 1879, but it is one of Eastern Europe's most interesting cities. Nestled in a valley and dominated by the granite slopes of Mt. Vitosha (which is less than a half-hour away and offers good skiing), it is known as the greenest city in Europe because of its 80 beautifully spaced parks. This ancient city, with a population of over a million, clusters most of its hotels, department stores, outdoor markets, memorials, churches, theaters, and opera houses in a downtown area that can be seen on foot, making it an easy and pleasant city to explore on your own. "Ever Growing, Never Old" is the motto of Sofia, inscribed on its coat of arms. The city traces its beginnings to the 5th century BC, when it was settled by the Thracians, who left the country its beautiful gold treasures.

Sofia has gone through several name changes. Called Serdica under the Thracian Serdi, the settlement suffered invasion by the Greeks, Romans, Goths, and Huns, as well as by Byzantium. The Bulgars, who conquered the city in AD 809, called it *Sredets,* meaning "central," and in the 14th century it became known as Sofia, after the 6th-century Church of St. Sophia. Falling to the Ottoman Empire in 1386, Sofia was not liberated until almost 500 years later, when it was made the capital of the newly independent state. These various waves of conquest left their imprint on the city, creating a strange and exciting mix of Byzantine, Roman, Greek, and Turkish architecture, now interspersed among more modern hotels, department stores, and government offices. Sofia is a cosmopolitan city; besides many colleges and libraries, it has theaters, museums, and major art galleries, displaying the fine art of contemporary Bulgarian masters. Bulgaria is also known for its opera singers, and there are two fine opera houses here. Dancing is very close to the Bulgarian heart, and no visit could be complete without a stop at one of the folklore restaurants where you'll find young men and women in their blue and red sequined costumes kicking up their heels.

While English is spoken in the major hotels and restaurants, visitors are confronted with the Cyrillic alphabet, making it a little difficult to know where you are at all times.

A good map of the city will solve any problems. Your first stop should be at *Balkantourist,* 37 Dondukov Blvd. (phone: 88-44-30), or at one of the branches in major hotels; the staff can provide you with maps of the city and country as well as brochures, guides, tours, and even a translation of the Cyrillic alphabet into English, which you will find useful. You can also take a Balkantourist half-day motorcoach tour with a bilingual guide or hire a guide for a walking tour. From then on you'll be completely oriented and able to explore the city on your own. Use the *Sheraton Sofia–Hotel Balkan* as a focal point, even if you don't stay there, because it's in the very center of town at Lenin Square, where Vitosha Boulevard meets Georgi Dimitrov Boulevard as they cross the end of the Largo, the area around the monumental Communist Party headquarters. Looking left from the *Sheraton,* there is the *National Historical Museum* at 2 Vitosha Blvd., with fascinating archaeological treasures and exhibitions of folk art; to the right is the *TSUM* department store, across an underground passage, open in the middle, with a small shopping center and a church — the 14th-century St. Petka Samardjiiska, which can be visited in summer. While digging the underpass, the excavators unearthed Roman ruins that are now an integral part of the new passage, encased in glass. If time permits, make a worthwhile detour to the main outdoor market along Georgi Kirkov Boulevard to admire the produce on view, test the spices, and browse among the handmade woolen goods and ceramic pottery.

Following the example set by Vienna, Budapest, and Prague over the last few years, city planners have rid Vitosha Boulevard of automobile traffic between Lenin Square and the Lyudmila Zhivkova Palace of Culture and have spruced up its shops and snackbars. The lovely folk art stores at #14 have silver jewelry, leather goods, and embroidered blouses (in the left-hand shop) as well as rugs, wooden articles, ceramics, and copper coffee sets (in the right-hand shop).

Immediately behind the *Sheraton* (indeed, partly surrounded by it) is Sofia's most ancient building, the Rotunda of the Church of St. George, built by the Romans in the 4th century, restored much later, and containing three layers of 10th- to 15th-century frescoes.

As you go toward Ruski Boulevard, notice the ocher road tiles that make this street resemble something out of *The Wizard of Oz* as well as the animated traffic police controlling pedestrian and vehicle flow with ballet-like performances.

The Ninth of September Square (on your way) is dominated by the block-long marble mausoleum of Georgi Dimitrov, the international Communist hero (he stood up to the Nazis at the Reichstag Fire Trial) and Bulgarian premier from 1946 to 1949. Watched over by two uniformed soldiers, there is a changing of the guards on the hour here rivaling the one at London's Buckingham Palace. The solemnity of the interior, where visitors file past the preserved corpse, equals that of Lenin's Tomb. Behind the mausoleum are the city gardens, a perfect place to sit and watch the people. On the other side of Ruski Boulevard is the former Royal Palace, now the *National Gallery of Painting and Sculpture* and the *National Ethnographic Museum.*

Continuing down Ruski Boulevard, notice the first of many onion-domed Orthodox churches on the left. Along this street you can buy some of Bulgaria's best leather goods, baskets, and jewelry. Try *Mineralsouvenir* at #10 for marble ashtrays and gold and silver jewelry, the *Shop of the Union of Bulgarian Artists* at #6, and the *Souvenir Shop* at #4. Inexpensive opera and folk music records can be found at the *Maestro Atanassov Record Shop* at #8. At 147 Rakowski St. (turn right off Ruski), works by contemporary Bulgarian artists are for sale.

Ruski Boulevard leads to the modern, 6-story *Grand Hotel Sofia,* which forms a crescent on the Square of the National Assembly and faces a huge equestrian statue of Alexander II (the Russian czar who helped Bulgaria gain its independence from the Turks). Opposite the statue is the Parliament Building. Have a glass of Bulgarian wine or a cup of coffee on the terrace of the *Sofia* and be sure you are well rested before taking in the next — and most glorious — sight in the city: the magnificent neo-Byzantine Alexander Nevsky Memorial Church. Built during 1904–12 as a demonstration of the Bulgarians' gratitude to the Russians for freeing them from Turkish rule, the cathedral, with its gold-leaf dome visible from high in the air, has a museum in its crypt, which contains a remarkable, beautifully displayed collection of icons and church regalia; it is open daily.

If you continue along Ruski Boulevard, on your right is Freedom Park, with a zoo and a number of stadiums. Opposite are the college buildings of Sofia University. As you stroll around, look up often to catch glimpses of Mt. Vitosha's snow-tipped peaks looming over the city.

Sofia is most crowded during its *Music Weeks* (May 24–June 15), when it is filled with competitions, concerts, chamber music, and opera. Also, on the first day of Lent is the *Kukeri Festival,* somewhat similar to Rio's Carnival and definitely worth seeing. For something a little different, see a performance at the *Central Puppet Theater* (14 Gurko St.; phone: 88-54-16).

Boyana and its church make a pleasant half-day excursion. Leave the center on the road to Athens and turn left over the tramlines up a road marked "To Boyana and Kopitoto." The road climbs steadily but easily for about 10 minutes through the Boyana district, where you turn left to visit the famous Boyana Church, hidden in the trees. The church may be entered by only six people at a time because the temperature and humidity have to be strictly controlled to preserve the murals that completely cover the walls and ceiling. Painted by the unknown Boyana Master in 1259, they are among the oldest murals in Bulgaria, depicting real people like King Constantine Assen and Queen Irina. Inquire at *Balkantourist* for hours of operation. Back in the village, go up the hill again to a fork in the road and turn right to get to the *Kopitoto* hotel and restaurant, with wonderful views of Sofia. You can also continue farther to the *Golden Bridges* restaurant (in Bulgarian, *Zlatnite Mostove*), just above a dramatic formation of huge boulders.

Longer excursions can be made to Melnik, a picturesque wine-growing town near the Greek border, or to Koprivshtitsa, a rare gem of preserved folk architecture, where horse-drawn carts still clatter over cobblestones. Tours to most parts of the country can be arranged through *Balkantourist;* perhaps the most unusual one is devoted to Bulgarian yogurt-tasting.

En Route from Sofia – Heading southwest, you'll find the Rila Monastery 75 miles (121 km) from Sofia. Leave early in the day so you can enjoy Rila before proceeding to Plovdiv, which has better accommodations. Leave Sofia on the road for the Greek frontier and Thessaloniki. It's an easy route mostly through open rolling country, with the Rila Mountains beginning to appear on your left. In about 40 miles (65 km) you'll come to Stanke Dimitrov, where you turn left. On your way, you can visit the thermal hot springs of Sapareva Banja before continuing another 16 miles (25 km) and turning left for the monastery.

Here the road starts to wind and climb. The hills are thickly wooded, and the valley falls away below. Driving through these dark pine forests, you cross a bubbling brook, turn a bend, and high up, on the side of the mountain, you see an imposing stone wall over 80 feet high — your first sight of the Rila Monastery.

RILA: Founded in the 9th century by John of Rila, who fled the excesses of court life to found a hermitage, the monastery has always been the cultural shrine of Bulgaria, the defense of its cultural values against the pressures of the Ottomans. Destroyed several times, it was rebuilt in its present form after a devastating fire in 1833. Only Hrelyo's stone tower, built in 1335, remains of the ancient monastery; it dominates the huge inner courtyard of the four-story, eccentrically shaped building.

Behind the imposing gates, the inside courtyard is an amazing scenario of delicate architecture, brightly painted porches, winding staircases, beautiful arches, frescoed walls, and a rectangular courtyard paved with slate. Look for the Chapel of the

Transfiguration, with 14th-century murals, on the top floor of Hrelyo's Tower, and the monastery church in the courtyard, with its lovely wood carvings and murals. The monastery houses a museum containing hundreds of manuals, Bibles written on sheepskin, icons, old weapons, coins, and a crucifix on which are carved 140 scenes with 1,500 figures — each no larger than a grain of rice — representing the life work of one monk. For the practical-minded, there's a vast ancient kitchen (with a flue 62 feet high) that once catered to the brisk pilgrim trade.

To get to Plovdiv, you have to return to Stanke Dimitrov and take a crossroad via Samokov-Borovet to get to the main road to Plovdiv, International Highway 5. A stopover could be made at the Borovets resort in the thickly wooded Rila Mountains, where accommodations include the *Rila* hotel winter sports complex, the new *Yastrebetz* hotel, and the Finnish-designed *Yagoda* bungalow and sauna community.

PLOVDIV: Bulgaria's second largest city, Plovdiv dates from Thracian times. Built on six hills, it is the gateway to the Rhodope Mountains. The *Balkantourist* office in Plovdiv is at 34 Moskva Blvd. (phone: 55-28-07).

By day, Plovdiv is a bustling, modern industrial city with an important annual trade fair; at night, it turns into a stroller's paradise — quiet and tranquil. Divided by the Maritsa River, Plovdiv boasts an old section reached by climbing hundreds of stone steps. At the top you first see the remains of a Roman amphitheater, where chariot races were held. (You'd be well advised to wear sensible shoes up here; after the climb up, you've still got to negotiate the ancient cobblestone streets. Going through the Hissar Kapiya gate, you enter a world of exquisite houses from the 19th-century National Revival period. Their façades are decorated with eaves in the form of waves and bay windows overhanging far into the streets, making the houses look top-heavy. The overhanging bays were a method of extending the house without impinging on pedestrian space in busy thoroughfares.

The *Charshiya* (Crafts Bazaar) on Strâmna Street is a group of five restored houses in which ten workshops sell handmade tufted rugs, embroideries, copper vessels, and carvings. You can also visit the Argir-Koyumdjioglu House (2 Dr. Chomakov St.), now an ethnographic museum with extensive displays of rare Thracian gold treasures. More gold artifacts are exhibited at the *Archaeological Museum* (Sâedinenie Sq.). A nice ending to the tour is a stop at the open-air market for some peaches and cherries, typical native fruits. You can eat these comfortably ensconced on one of the terraces overlooking the city.

BACHKOVO: The Bachkovo Monastery is 18 miles (28 km) from Plovdiv on the old Roman road connecting it to the Aegean coast. This is Bulgarian wine country; you'll find both red and white wines, the best this side of France. The monastery complex is on the right bank of the Chepelarska River. Seen from the road, the monastery looks like an ancient fortress with two courtyards; in the center of each is a cruciform church. Founded in the 11th century, this massive building is decorated with frescoes of exceptional quality. The main Church of the Holy Virgin has rare, silver-clad icons and a wooden iconostasis of the finest workmanship.

ETÛR ETHNOGRAPHIC MUSEUM-PARK: The country's biggest skansen (a recreated historical village) hugs the banks of a mountain stream 5 miles (8 km) south of Gabrovo, roughly halfway between Sofia and the Black Sea coast. Here, on cobblestone streets overhung with balconies full of flowers, dozens of handicrafts and trades are demonstrated, water-powered mills are operated, and folk music is played — a fascinating display of the skills of village artisans and 19th-century rural technology.

BEST EN ROUTE

Bulgaria is one of the most inexpensive places to vacation in Europe, with the exception of the first class city hotels. Double rooms are around $100 per night in the expensive places (a little more expensive during festivals) and about $60 in moderate places, but meals are almost always reasonable. (In the country, you'll get more food and wine than you can handle for $10 to $15.) Make hotel reservations in advance (also book car rentals in advance, and be sure to agree on a fixed price; prices can fluctuate wildly if negotiated inside the country).

SOFIA

Grand Hotel Sofia – This well-located modern hotel has a complex of shops and restaurants and a nightclub. 4 Narodno Sobranie Sq. (phone: 878821). Expensive.

Novotel Evropa – A French-built hotel close to the main railway station. 131 Georgi Dimitrov Blvd. (phone: 31261). Expensive.

Rodina – About a 10-minute walk from the town center, this Swedish-built hotel has a pool, saunas, gym, and solarium. 8 Totleben Blvd. (phone: 5331). Expensive.

Sheraton Sofia–Hotel Balkan – A city landmark that has joined the Sheraton chain and undergone a complete renovation, except for its familiar façade. The new, luxurious *Balkan* has 188 air conditioned rooms, 16 suites, restaurants, snack bars, and a Viennese-style café. The food is superb, service excellent, management American; some people consider it the best urban hotel in the Balkans. In the middle of town. 1 Lenin Sq. (phone: 876541). Expensive.

Vitosha New Otani – This Japanese-owned hotel has a Japanese restaurant, *Sakura*, as well as three other restaurants serving international and Bulgarian dishes. The hotel has a nightclub, casino, pool, gym, 8-lane bowling alley, tennis courts, and 2 saunas. 100 Anton Ivanov Blvd. (phone: 624151). Expensive.

Forum – A handsome new restaurant serving French classics such as onion soup, omelettes, and leg of lamb Robert, also offers a wide selection of Bulgarian wines. 62 Vitosha Blvd. (phone: 521119). Expensive

Bulgaria – Where Bulgarians go for dinner and dancing. *Bulgaria* hotel, 4 Ruski Blvd. (phone: 871977). Moderate.

Rubin – Another local favorite, with an Italian accent and good wines. Lenin Square (phone: 874704). Moderate.

Strandja Tavern – This charming restaurant in the *Museum of Ecclesiastical Art* features the rich local cuisine. 19 Lenin Sq. (phone: 880424). Moderate.

Zheravna – Bulgarian specialties served in a folk art atmosphere. 26 Marshal Tolbuchin Blvd. (phone: 872186). Moderate to inexpensive.

BOYANA

Boyansko Hanche Tavern – Near the historic church, this restaurant has delicious specialties and Bulgarian wines. There's also a folk orchestra and a floor show. In the village of Dragalevtsi; take bus 63 (phone: 563016). Moderate.

RILA

Rila – This plain, clean restaurant serves excellent Bulgarian food. Try Shopska salad with roasted sweet red peppers, cucumbers, small tomatoes, onions, olive oil and vinegar, topped with mounds of feta cheese. Or have some Tarator soup, made of yogurt, walnuts, garlic, dill, and cucumbers. For the main course, try the grilled or roasted beef, lamb, or pork.

PLOVDIV

Novotel Plovdiv – Another member of the French chain with pleasant accommodations, including a sports center, pools, outdoor tennis courts, and saunas. 2 Zlatyu Boyadjiev St. (phone: 55892, 555171). Expensive.

Trimontium – A fine hotel with an Old World atmosphere, first class accommodations, and a garden; at the beginning of the pedestrian zone. 2 Kapitan Raicho St. (phone: 225561). Moderate.

Zlatniya Elen – This folk tavern (formerly the *Bunara*) has good food and Bulgarian dancers. 13 Patriarch Eftimi St. (phone: 226064). Moderate.

BACHKOVO

Bachkovo Monastery – For an atmospheric monastic evening, this is a nice place. There are campsites as well as bungalows. Ask at the monastery or call them for reservations. Inexpensive.

The Bulgarian Black Sea Coast

The Greeks called it Pontos Euxinos — the Hospitable Sea — but the Turks, who feared its storms, renamed it the Black Sea. Whatever its name, the Black Sea coast of Bulgaria — a 235-mile stretch of sandy beach now boasting numerous hotel colonies — is fast becoming known as the Riviera of Eastern Europe. These modern resorts have sprung up relatively recently (most were built in the last 30 years) and today are visited mostly by tourists from Eastern Europe but also from Western Europe, the USSR, and the US.

The major coastal town, however, is anything but recent. Varna, now an industrial center, is an ancient port and Bulgaria's main commercial outlet to the sea. Some 290 miles (469 km) from Sofia, Varna is Bulgaria's summer capital and is only a little more than an hour's drive south from the Romanian border. Varna is a perfect starting point for trips up and down the coast as well as for longer excursions across the sea to Istanbul or inland to the eastern monastery towns of Bulgaria.

Varna's original name was Odessos, and remnants of various past cultures are everywhere. Just outside the town are the remains of a Byzantine basilica, but predating this church is a large thermae built by the Romans that still stands in the middle of the city. Before the Romans, the Greeks were the masters here, having founded the city in 570 BC. Also outside town is the Aladja Rock Monastery, built in the Middle Ages.

Tours to the modern resort towns north and south of Varna should be booked through *Balkantourist* in Sofia (phone: 88-44-30) or in Varna, 3 Musala St. (phone: 225524). For the most part, the hotels are quite similar — modern buildings facing the sea — but the amazing thing about these resorts is that in season, hotel accommodations right on the sea, including three meals a day, cost from $60 to $100 per day for a double room, and various package arrangements are offered. The beach towns are small and generally have uncomplicated layouts. (Unless otherwise noted, the address of a hotel or restaurant is nothing more than the establishment's name.) From Rusalka, north of Varna, to Nessebâr, to the south, the beach towns are all connected by International Highway E87.

RUSALKA: Near the Romanian border, this *Club Méditerranée* holiday village caters to families seeking sun and sports. There are three bays to swim in and 15 tennis courts to play on, and clubs for the kids. For information, contact Club Med offices (in the US, 800-CLUB MED) or travel agencies, or call 19-359-5184.

ALBENA: Albena was named after one of the most attractive female characters in

Bulgarian literature. The town caters to a predominantly younger set, who crowd the many hotels, bars, folk taverns, and 4-mile-long beach. You can play tennis or golf or even brush up on your equestrian skills at the riding school. The town hot spot is the *Starobulgarski Stan* nightclub, with an architectural style that recalls old Bulgarian gypsy tents. On the beach, it offers music and floor shows until 2 AM. The *Balkantourist* office is in the *Bratislava* hotel (phone: 2152, 2930).

ZLATNI PYASÂTSI: Zlatni Pyasâtsi (Golden Sands) is about 8 miles (14 km) from Albena and probably the resort most popular with Americans, having often been compared to Long Beach, California. Again, you'll find an abundance of hotels and bars. The favorite here is a nightclub called the *Kukeri,* which has a wonderful view of the sea and entertainment by the *Kukeri Dancers,* masked men performing stylized pagan routines. For tourist information, phone 855227.

DRUZHBA: This town, whose name means "friendship," is only 6 miles (10 km) from Varna. It's one of the older resorts, better suited to low-key revelers, and is the home of the Swedish-built *Grand Hotel Varna,* the most famous of all the Black Sea hotels, with a complex of restaurants and nightclubs and two sub-floors of spa facilities for exercise, massages, and pearl and mud baths (4 Cervenoarmeiski Blvd.; phone: 86-14-91/8). If the *Grand Hotel Varna* is too expensive, consider stopping at the *Monastery Cellar,* a nightclub that serves a memorable wine called Monastery Whispers.

SLUNCHEV BRYAG: About 60 miles (96 km) down the coast from Druzhba, Slunchev Bryag (Sunny Beach) is a 2½-mile stretch of sandy shores surrounded by a deciduous forest on three sides. This family resort has day care facilities and supervised children's activities, which leave parents free to roam into places like *Khan's Tent Tavern,* another tent nightclub on the beach, or the *Pirate Ship,* a restaurant built like a ship and offering Bulgarian specialties and folk entertainment. Also worth a visit is the nearby city of Burgas and its international music and folklore festival, held every other year during the second half of June. An attractive alternative to the high-rise resort is the Finnish-built *Elenite Holiday Village,* a hillside bungalow complex, including the 100-bed *Emona,* about 6 miles (9.6 km) north of Sunny Beach (phone: 411-32423).

NESSEBÂR: Nessebâr is a vintage fishing village on a peninsula near Slunchev Bryag, where old Greek churches and wooden fishermen's houses along narrow cobblestone streets take you back in time. Nessebâr is an architectural gem and should be included on any Black Sea tour — but just for a visit, not an overnight stay. The *Balkantourist* office is at 18 Jana Laskova (phone: 2855).

SOZOPOL: Another charming collection of 19th-century houses with grapevine-shaded patios along winding lanes. *Balkantourist* is at 2 Chervenoarmeiska (phone 2207), and there are several restaurants, but no major hotel. Stay at one of the three communities making up the *Djuni Holiday Village,* 6 miles (9.6 km) to the south. Like *Elenite, Djuni* was built by the Finns in the mid-1980s (phone: 20442).

Czechoslovakia

At the geographical center of Europe, Czechoslovakia has been a crossroads over which many different peoples have traveled and the sometimes unwilling recipient of their religious, cultural, and political domination. Much that remains of this involved past has been carefully preserved. Indeed, although Czechoslovakia is quite a small country — a little larger than New York State — it contains some 40,000 monuments, 2,500 castles (115 of them open to the public), and 40 preserved towns in which the Gothic, Renaissance, and baroque architecture has been painstakingly protected, down to the cobblestone streets.

The country is composed of three areas: the Bohemian plateau in the west, the Moravian lowlands in the center, and mountainous Slovakia in the east. Each region has many historic sights. The territory of Bohemia and Moravia was the center of European culture in the 14th century, when Charles IV made Prague the capital of the Holy Roman Empire. He initiated a building boom that produced such Gothic wonders as the Charles Bridge in Prague and Karlštejn Castle. In Slovakia, historical monuments go back further, recalling the presence of Roman legions.

Despite its attention to the past, Czechoslovakia is a developed country, with the vast majority of the population of 15.3 million involved in commerce and industry and only 12.5% in agriculture. Czechoslovak companies produce everything from heavy machinery and Škoda cars to bentwood chairs and Bohemian glass. Some 95% of the population is Czech (10 million) and Slovak (5 million), the remainder a mix of Hungarians, Germans, Poles, Ruthenians, and Gypsies. Only 15% of the population lives in cities of more than 100,000 — Prague, the capital and largest city (pop. 1.2 million); Bratislava, the second largest city (pop. 400,000) and the capital of the Slovak Socialist Republic; and Brno, the third largest city (pop. 380,000) and the capital of Moravia. The rest of the population inhabits some 10,000 small towns.

This predominantly small-town culture opens up some appealing possibilities for those interested in folk traditions. If you visit in the spring and the summer, you will encounter (indeed, become part of) the numerous folk festivals in the small towns. While it is true that many of the festivals are organized entertainment events, featuring professional and semi-professional troupes wearing standardized folk costumes, they do attract folk enthusiasts from all over the world. They are a colorful blend of dance and music competitions, Maypole dancing, parades of the king, wine tastings, and open-air markets displaying handsome homemade crafts.

Spring and summer are also the most pleasant times for sightseeing and most sports. Being in the temperate zone, Czechoslovak springs and summers are warm and sunny, with average May temperatures in the high 50s F (15C) and summer temperatures in the high 60s and low 70s F (21C). Though Czechoslovakia is landlocked, it has thousands of ponds and lakes, many developed for swimming, boating, and fishing. A preponderance of these lakes are in southern Bohemia. In northeastern Bohemia stand the Krkonoše (Giant) Mountains, while the High Tatras — the highest mountains in the Carpathian chain — rise in Slovakia. Both regions are winter resort centers popular for downhill and cross-country skiing, tobogganing, and sleigh riding.

Czechoslovakia is a relatively easy country to explore. In the better restaurants and hotels English is understood, but German is the lingua franca for the tourist sector. Advance hotel reservations are necessary even in the off-season (particularly in smaller towns) because the tourist traffic exceeds the population. Make arrangements through your travel agent or through the Czechoslovak National Tourist Office, *Cedok,* 18 Na příkopě, Prague 1 (phone: 212-27111), or in the US at 10 E. 40th St., New York, NY 10157 (phone: 212-689-9720).

The longest of the following three routes links Prague, the nation's capital, with Bratislava, the capital of Slovakia, passing through Bohemia, Moravia, and Slovakia, seeing the most famous spas, castles, and medieval towns. The remaining routes both start from Poprad, a city in eastern Slovakia. One route heads northwest into the High Tatras mountain resorts. The second runs east of Poprad, taking in the medieval towns and lovely landscapes of the Spiš region, where the country folk carry on the rural traditions of their ancestors in settings that have changed little over the generations.

Prague to Bratislava

This 227-mile (365-km) route links Bohemia, Moravia, and Slovakia — Czechoslovakia's three major regions — and takes in the country's capitals as well as its most famous spas, castles, and medieval towns. To follow the route, head northwest out of Prague, circle through Plzeň, south to Tábor, east to Brno, and farther south to Bratislava. You can spend several days touring, for all of the places along the route have reasonable overnight accommodations.

Since you will be passing through the three distinct areas of this country, be alert to subtle changes in traditions and customs. These regional differences will be most obvious at the folk festivals, held during the spring and summer in the small towns. You'll find that the cuisine also differs: In Bohemia, try roast pork, goose, or duck with dumplings accompanied by Pilsner beer. In the lake country of southern Bohemia, keep an eye out for menus offering fresh trout and carp. In Moravia, be sure to sample the local wines.

The highlights of the route include the renowned spa of Karlovy Vary; the Burgher's Brewery in Plzeň, where Pilsner beer has been produced since the Middle Ages; the preserved historic town of Tábor; the formidable Špilberk Castle in Brno; and the capital of Slovakia, Bratislava. (It's possible to take a day-long excursion by bus to either Karlovy Vary or Plzeň. Inquire at *Cedok Tours.* (See *Prague,* THE CITIES, "Sources and Resources.")

PRAGUE: For a complete description of the city and its restaurants and hotels, see *Prague,* THE CITIES.

> **En Route from Prague** – Heading northwest for 2 hours along Route 6, you pass through some of Bohemia's loveliest countryside — deep forests and rich farmlands, where hops are grown. Hillside castles dot the landscape.

KARLOVY VARY: In the narrow valley at the juncture of the Teplá and Ohře rivers lies Karlovy Vary, the most famous of Czechoslovakia's spas. It has 12 developed hot springs, and more than 100 springs in all. Legend has it that Karlovy Vary (Carlsbad in German) was discovered in 1358 by Charles IV — actually by the dog of Charles IV, who stumbled into a hot spring while chasing a stag. Today, the stag is still the symbol of the spa.

The huge spa building is reserved for guests taking the waters, but visitors can stroll along the ornate Colonnade, built in 1871–81, following in the footsteps of kings and queens and such notables as Beethoven, Goethe, and Mozart. The area still retains traces of its once-elegant atmosphere.

While you're visiting the spa, indulge in a few Karlovy Vary rites: Taste the hot bitter waters from a special mug with a long clay straw. Buy a box of *karlovarské oplatky* — delicious large round chocolate and vanilla wafers. Order Becherovka, a liqueur also known jokingly as "the thirteenth spring." Visit the world-famous *Moser Glassworks* and the *Horní Slavkov* and *Stará Role* chinaworks, where you can buy fine Czech crystal and porcelain.

> **En Route from Karlovy Vary** – Stop at the regal Kynžvart, the former summer residence of Count Metternich, the 19th-century Austrian statesman. Constructed in baroque and empire styles, the château contains valuable collections of furniture, art, china, glassware, and arms.

MARIÁNSKÉ LÁZNĚ: Established in 1808, this spa (Marienbad, in German) was a favorite with such notables as Richard Wagner and King Edward VII. It is nicely designed, with parks and colorful façades lining Gottwald Square. Spa yellow, the soft yellow of the exteriors of the major buildings and hotels, can be seen here and at spas throughout the country. Of the 40 springs here, the best known are Křížový, Lesní, and Rudolf. When you're not soaking, you can take advantage of the spa's many other recreational facilities: movies, concerts, a golf course, tennis courts, a pool, cafés, restaurants, and nightclubs. Take a side trip of 10 miles (16 km) east to Teplá to see the 12th-century monastery, with an impressive collection of rare books, manuscripts, and prints.

PLZEŇ: With large factories and a smoky skyline, this city of 174,000 contrasts sharply with the other small Bohemian towns en route. But it is worth a visit to see the Burgher's Brewery, which has produced Pilsner Urquell beer since the Middle Ages. Begin the tour at the *Brewing Museum,* in an old brewing house on Roosevelt Street. It has a fine collection of beer mugs, jugs, pewter tankards, and glasses produced during the last 6 centuries. Also on display is an iron collar — the collar of dishonor — worn by brewers whose beer didn't make the grade. The town's beer stewards will tell you that Pilsner should be drunk from a sparkling clean glass accompanied by sharp cheese, smoked meats, and dark bread. And they're right.

Náměstí Republiky, the square in the center of town, is lined with houses that have Renaissance, baroque, Empire, and neo-Gothic façades. Two particularly lovely Gothic buildings are St. Bartholomew's Church, with its 340-foot tower, and the Abbey Church of the Virgin Mary.

TÁBOR: Set on the River Lužnice, amid the forests and lakes of southern Bohemia, this Gothic town is one of six historical reservations in Czechoslovakia. Tábor was founded in 1420 by the Hussites, an army of anti-Church and -state rebels whose struggle was set off by the death of the Czech religious reformer John Huss (Jan Hus). Huss was burned at the stake as a heretic in 1415, but the Hussite struggle continued for the next 19 years.

Tábor is now a modern, growing town of 22,000, whose historic area is of greatest interest. An equestrian statue of military leader Jan Žižka, who commanded the Hussite forces, stands in the middle of Žižka Square. The most notable building is the Town Hall, which houses a museum documenting the Hussite movement. Underneath the museum are catacombs of tunnels and cellars, built as living quarters and later used to store beer and wine. The narrow, winding streets off Žižka Square, so laid out to confuse attackers, lead to the Old Town. Originally surrounded by ramparts and bulwarks, the Old Town still has remnants of those fortifications, such as the Bechyně Gate and the adjacent Kotnov Tower, once part of a medieval castle that was turned into the town brewery in the 17th century.

If you want to spend some time here, stay at the inexpensive *Jordán* hotel, named for nearby Lake Jordán, where visitors can swim or fish.

BRNO: The capital of Moravia, Brno combines historic and contemporary Czechoslovakia. Here you'll find castles, museums, a baroque outdoor market, fairgrounds, a racetrack, and some of the hottest night spots around.

Špilberk Castle, which dates to 1287, was built as a fortress to resist invaders and later made a prison; it is deeply engraved on the collective conscience of the country. Here, political dissenters were detained and tortured by the ruling Habsburgs. During World War II, Nazi forces reopened the prison, and Špilberk became once again a dungeon and death knell for the hapless. Instruments of torture are on display.

The castle restaurant offers a game menu, Moravian wines, and a view of the city (*Hradní,* phone: 26203, 24170). The park outside the castle has covered benches — a pleasant spot to rest.

The main streets in Brno all converge on Freedom Square (Náměstí Svobody), which is flanked by splendid baroque and Renaissance buildings. From the square you can see Petrov Hill, with the Cathedral of Saints Peter and Paul, a reconstructed Gothic structure built on the site of a Romanesque basilica. The Cathedral on the hill is a welcome refuge from the urban bustle below.

From the cathedral, descend the steps to the outdoor Cabbage Market, sprawled over a steep cobblestone hill; you'll find hundreds of tables attended to by country men and women selling fruits, vegetables, handicrafts, and kitchen utensils. The market sprawls around Parnassas Fountain, which features a baroque sculpture depicting Cerberus, the Watchdog of Hell, and the four continents (its designer, Johann Fisher von Erlach, apparently was unaware of Australia). Among the area's other notable buildings are the old Town Hall and the Gothic Church of St. James, both in the Old Town.

Brno's Exhibition Fairground, down the hill and past the railway station, is the site of events all year, highlighted by the *Consumers' Fair* in April. While here, have lunch at the *Myslivna* (Gamekeeper's Lodge), reached by crossing a wood on the south side of the Svratka River (12 Pisárky; phone: 335911). Try the broiled trout à la Brno.

The city has many first class hotels, the newest and most convenient of which is the *International.* Its bar, *Interclub,* is one of the most popular night spots in the city (phone: 26411).

BRATISLAVA: Rising from the banks of the Danube, this capital of Slovakia was the capital of Hungary from 1541 to 1784, and 17 Hungarian monarchs were crowned here over the centuries. During the thousand years that today's Slovakia was known as Northern Hungary, Bratislava was called "Poszony" in Hungarian and "Pressburg" in German. The city's population was predominantly Hungarian- and German-speaking until the 19th century, when an influx of Slovaks from the countryside began. In 1918, when Slovakia was incorporated into the new nation of Czechoslovakia, Bratislava officially assumed its Slavic name.

Bratislava is a modern city that also boasts some 400 historic buildings, museums, monuments, and castles. BIPS (Bratislavská Informačná a Propagačná Služba), the city tourist office, is in the center at 1 Leningradská (phone: 334-370, 333-715, 334-415). It can provide information, guides, and translators, and it organizes walking tours of the city on summer weekends. The city's most noteworthy sight is the Bratislava Castle, the 13th-century fortress that long guarded the city. Sights in the Old Town that you shouldn't miss are the Gothic-baroque Old Town Hall; the Primatial Palace, with its famous Hall of Mirrors, where Napoleon and Emperor Franz II signed the Peace Treaty of Bratislava in 1805; St. Martin's Cathedral, the scene of many coronations; and *At the Red Crayfish,* a pharmacy museum with a nice collection of apothecary jars. The *Slovak National Museum,* 2 Vajanského nábr. (phone: 336-551-55), has a special exhibition, "The Development of Man," which traces evolution from primitive times to the present.

If you've been eating the Bohemian and Moravian favorites of pork or roast duck with dumplings and sauerkraut, you'll find a marked difference in Slovak cooking. Its generous use of sour cream, paprika, and barbecued meats echo the cuisine of neighboring Hungary. A few places in town that serve regional specialties are the restaurants in Bratislava Castle; the *Klástorná vináren* (wine tavern) — especially its Detva stuffed steak; and the *Bystrica Café,* a revolving glass disk set on a 270-foot tower over the Slovak National Uprising Bridge, which spans the Danube. The *Koliba,* on Kamzík Hill, is one of the many shepherd's hut–style restaurants scattered throughout Slovakia that serve barbecued meat cooked over open pits, mulled wines, and Tatra tea. Gypsy violinists provide entertainment.

If you are visiting during the late spring or summer, you can take a day trip by hydrofoil to Vienna or Budapest.

BEST EN ROUTE

Expect to pay $70 to $110 per night for a double room in hotels in the expensive range; $40 to $60 in the moderate; and around $30, inexpensive. Prices, except at deluxe hotels, include half-board because *Cedok* only accepts bookings on that basis. (Meal vouchers can be used outside the hotel.) A dinner for two will cost $30 and up in the expensive range, between $20 and $30 in the moderate range.

KARLOVY VARY

Grandhotel Moskva – Once favored by Europe's elite, this luxurious, 168-room hotel is in the spa center. Among the facilities are golf, tennis, 6 restaurants including a fine French one, a bar, nightclub, café, and a terrace during the summer. 2 Mírové náměstí (phone: 221215). Expensive.

Centrál – Built in 1910 but recently renovated, this hotel has 70 rooms, all with balconies. Restaurant and wine bar. 17 Leninovo náměstí (phone: 25251). Moderate.

Parkhotel – Right next to the *Grand Moskva,* this old hotel (opened in 1885) has 117 rooms, a French restaurant, and a subdued atmosphere. 2 Mírové náměstí (phone: 22121). Moderate.

MARIÁNSKÉ LÁZNĚ

Golf – A pretty and gracious luxury hotel in a park setting, with swimming pool. As the name suggests, a golf course is at hand (phone: 26516). Expensive.

Esplanade – This 62-room hotel, opened in 1916 and newly renovated, is near the spa center. There is a sauna, fine restaurant, and a café; guests have golf privileges nearby. 19 Washingtonva (phone: 21624). Moderate.

Campanella – This small hotel is convenient to the spa center. Karlovarská 438 (phone: 21624). Inexpensive.

PLZEŇ

Ural – Large and modern, this hotel is on the main square. 33 Náměstí Republiky (phone: 326858). Expensive.

Continental – In the center of town, this hotel was built in 1895. It has 53 rooms and a restaurant and wine bar. 8 Zbrojnická (phone: 36477). Expensive to moderate.

BRNO

Grand – This first class, recently renovated, 114-room hotel has an excellent restaurant serving Moravian specialties and wines. 18-20 Tř. 1 Máje (phone: 26421). Expensive.

International – A deluxe modern hotel with 291 rooms, it has a good view of Špilberk Castle and the Old Town. Among the facilities are 2 restaurants serving international and regional specialties, a bar, café, and a lively nightclub. 16 Husova (phone: 26411). Expensive.

Continental – Favored by business travelers, this modern 228-room hotel has a restaurant, wine bar, and summer garden. 20 Leninova (phone: 75321). Moderate.

Voroněž I & II – A two-building modern hotel next to an excellent, beautifully designed new restaurant that shouldn't be missed, *Moravská Chalupa.* The hotel also has a health club with pool and sauna. 47 and 49 Křížkovského (phone: 336343/9). Moderate.

Slovan – A smaller hotel with a pleasant restaurant. 23 Lidická (phone: 745505). Moderate to inexpensive.

BRATISLAVA

Devín – In the center of town, this deluxe modern hotel has 103 rooms and a restaurant, café, wine bar, and terrace. 4 Riečná (phone: 330851). Expensive.

Forum Hotel Bratislava – The newest luxury hotel in the country has 219 rooms and 11 suites, all with mini-bar and color TV sets. Other features: 3 bars, a Parisian-style café, a nightclub, French and Slovak restaurants, and a fitness center with pool, gym, and solarium. On Mierové nám (phone: 348-111). In the US, Inter-Continental handles reservations (phone: 800-327-0200). Expensive.

Kyjev – This fairly new first class hotel, with 217 rooms, offers the usual amenities — a restaurant, café, wine bar, nightclub, sauna, air conditioned recreation rooms, and shops. 2 Rajská (phone: 56341). Expensive.

Vinárň Vel'ki Františkáni – Spend an entertaining evening at this historic tavern with its vaulted cellar and arcaded courtyard. Liter jugs of Slovak wine, generous helpings of hearty food, and a live gypsy orchestra add to the atmosphere. 7 Diebrovo nám (phone: 333073). Moderate.

The High Tatras

Starting in Poprad, this route takes in the nearby resorts of the High Tatras, the highest mountains of the Carpathian range. In fact, the Tatras are not really that high (Mt. Gerlach, the highest, rises only 8,500 feet), but they soar dramatically from the surrounding plateau and their peaks etch themselves sharply against the skyline. The mountains are popular year-round — in the winter for skiing, tobogganing, and sleighing, and in the summer for hiking, boating, fishing, and swimming. The highlights of the route include the large resort center of Starý Smokovec, the beautiful mountain lake Štrbské Pleso, and the best skiing in the area at Tatranská Lomnica.

POPRAD: The route begins here because the airport accommodates flights from Prague and Bratislava. Although dominated by modern, look-alike housing developments, Poprad has some interesting sights; among them are the 13th-century Gothic Church of St. Egidius, which contains a fresco of a biblical scene with the Tatra Mountains in the background, and the medieval streets of the Old Town, which are lined with baroque and neo-classical buildings.

STARÝ SMOKOVEC: The largest of the resort centers, this is a complex of chalets, restaurants, and hotels at 3,280 feet, with facilities for downhill and cross-country skiing. In the summer, mountaineers can climb Mt. Gerlach or take a side trip to the Studenovodské (Cold Water) Falls. A railway leads up to Mt. Hrebienok, a small village with a toboggan run and a beginner's slope with night lighting.

The most luxurious hotel in Starý Smokovec is the *Grand,* which opened in 1898. Starting from the *Grand,* you can hike for 1 mile into the forest to the *Koliba,* a rustic restaurant in a huge A-frame cabin.

ŠTRBSKÉ PLESO: Štrbské Pleso, or Lake Štrba, is a year-round resort town perched over 4,000 feet high in the Tatras. This spectacular mountain lake covers more than 40 acres. On its shore stands the newest and finest of the hotels, the *Patria;* the rooms naturally offer views of the lake or the mountains (see *Best en Route*).

TATRANSKÁ LOMNICA: The most elegant of the resort centers, this village is set in the second highest park in the Tatras. Restaurants and hotels here are open all year; the favorite is *Grandhotel Praha,* which opened in 1905. It offers sleigh rides in the winter and an excursion on the overhead cable railway to Skalnaté Pleso (Rocky Lake), 5,255 feet high. The downhill skiing on Lomnica Mountain is the best in the Tatras. The *Tatra National Park Museum* has excellent exhibitions documenting the area's past and its natural history.

BEST EN ROUTE

Expect to pay $60 and up per night for a double room with half-board in hotels in the expensive range; $40 to $50 in the moderate; and around $30, inexpensive. A dinner for two will cost $30 and up in the expensive range; between $20 and $30 in the moderate; and $10 and under, inexpensive.

STARÝ SMOKOVEC

Grand – With a spa-yellow exterior, this large alpine chalet is the place to stay. The 103 rooms are first class and the atmosphere is old-fashioned. There are 2 restaurants and a wine bar. 06201 Starý Smokovec (phone: 21546). Expensive.

ŠTRBSKÉ PLESO

Patria – Opened in 1976, this 11-story A-frame lakefront hotel either complements its mountain backdrop or wrecks the scenery, depending on your point of view. It has 151 rooms and 6 suites, all with private baths. Among the facilities are restaurants, a café, bar, snack bar, and nightclub. A new fitness center includes a pool, sauna, gym, and solarium. (phone: 92591). Expensive.

Panorama – Near Štrbské Pleso, this modern, 106-room hotel has a restaurant, café, and game rooms (phone: 92111). Moderate.

TATRANSKÁ LOMNICA

Grandhotel Praha – Opened in 1905 and remodeled in 1973, this classic hotel is the favorite in the area. Its 45 rooms are convenient to ski lifts. There's a restaurant, a wine bar, and sauna. The *Zbojnická Koliba* — a shepherd's hut restaurant where you can have barbecued meat, mulled wine, and tea — is nearby (phone: 967941). Expensive.

Spiš

This route links several small towns in the Spiš region. If you venture off the main roads into some of the remote rural villages, you may get a glimpse of life as it was centuries ago: People farm, weave, and make pottery using the methods of their ancestors. The Czechoslovak government supports a cottage industry to keep its arts and crafts alive, and many of the cottages are here in Eastern Slovakia. The highlights of the route include the lovely Gothic town of Levoča, Spiš Castle, the medieval town of Bardejov, and Hervartov, which has one of the oldest wooden churches in the Carpathians as well as many cottages producing crafts.

POPRAD: This is the starting point for trips to the Spiš towns. For details, see the Poprad section in the *High Tatras* route.

KEŽMAROK: As an alternative, try using this historical town, with its restored Renaissance castle, as a base for touring.

LEVOČA: For centuries one of the most important commercial centers in Hungary, this small Spiš town has a treasury of Gothic architecture. The town is surrounded by ramparts, and the older section has well-preserved buildings dating from the Middle Ages through the 16th and 17th centuries.

Laid out around a central square, the town plan still follows the chessboard pattern of its original design. Town Hall (1615) is outstanding, as are the old burghers' houses with arched Gothic entries. The Thurzo House, #7, epitomizes the local Renaissance style, with characteristic elaborate balconies and loggias. The interior of St. James's Church on the main square has magnificent wooden altars. The celebrated main altar, carved in limewood by Master Paul of Levoča in 1507–17, depicts the Last Supper in fascinating detail.

En route from Levoča – The dramatic hilltop ruins of Spiš Castle are visible from the main highway (E 85) from Poprad and Levoča, and the breathtaking view from the top is worth the trip up.

BARDEJOV: Tracing its history to the 12th century, this town was declared a "historical reserve" because of its notable Gothic and Renaissance architecture.

Bardejov looks medieval, with cobblestone streets, a checkerboard housing pattern, and ramparts begun in 1352. The main architectural monuments line the town square: The Gothic Church of St. Egidius, built in the 14th, 15th, and 16th centuries, has a splendid Gothic altar, intricately hand-carved pews, and shimmering rose windows. Constructed in 1506 at the dawn of the Renaissance in Slovakia, the Town Hall has an interesting transitional blend of Gothic and Renaissance features. Also notable is the Humanistic Gymnasium (1435). On the outskirts of town is Bardejovské Kúpele, a spa with an adjoining skansen of folk architecture.

HERVARTOV: Five miles (8 km) southwest of Bardejov, this village has a beautiful 16th-century wooden church with its original painted ceiling. Ask for the house where the church keys are.

BEST EN ROUTE

If you plan to visit the Spiš region, check with *Cedok* in advance for listings of accommodations. The places we have listed below as moderate cost between $40 and $50 per night for a double room, MAP. The price of an inexpensive hotel will be far less.

POPRAD

Európa – This modest 73-room hotel has 2 restaurants, a café, wine bar, and a nightclub. Wolkrova (phone: 26941). Moderate.

KEŽMAROK

Štart – A friendly place with a ski slope out back. Lesopark (phone: 2916). Moderate to inexpensive.

Denmark

With low, rolling meadows, a countryside speckled with stately castles, charming provincial towns, and remnants of a Viking past, this smallest of the Scandinavian countries has all the enchantment of a Hans Christian Andersen fairy tale and the drama of a Shakespeare play. Once you have seen Denmark, it is not difficult to understand how Andersen, the 19th-century Danish poet, novelist, and author of children's stories, found his inspiration. But it is also here, at Kronborg Castle in Helsingør, that William Shakespeare installed his brooding Hamlet.

Denmark's 16,600 square miles include the large Jutland Peninsula north of West Germany and some 500 islands, about 100 of which are inhabited. Several of the larger islands form stepping-stones across the Baltic Sea from Jutland to Sweden; the easternmost of these is Zealand, where the Danish capital, Copenhagen (København in Danish) is situated. Some of the smaller islands, such as Bornholm and Ærø, have picture-perfect provincial villages with quaint cottages and cobblestone streets. With all its islands, Denmark has 4,600 miles of coastline, although in total size the country is only one-third as large as New York State.

Traditionally an agricultural country, Denmark became more industrialized after World War II — accomplishing this in a more tasteful fashion than almost any other country in Europe. The country is also known for its advanced social planning. Social reforms were carried out in Denmark in the 18th century (serfdom was abolished in 1788), and a system of folk high schools were set up to reeducate Danish farmers. By the latter half of the 19th century, poor peasants were becoming prosperous small farmers. In 1914 and 1915, suffrage was extended to all adult Danes, and the cooperative movement flourished. During this century, further social welfare legislation has provided a wide variety of government services from day-care centers to housing and care for the elderly, though recent economic pressures have weakened these programs.

Denmark's royal family (the House of Glücksborg) represents the oldest continuous monarchy in the world. It is descended from the House of Oldenburg, which was established on the Danish throne in 1448, when Christian I became king. However, Denmark became a constitutional monarchy governed by a bicameral parliament (the Rigsdag) in 1849. In 1953 it was replaced by a single-chamber parliament (the Folketing).

Denmark was first occupied 10,000 years ago by people who followed the receding glaciers north. These inhabitants left numerous dolmens, barrows, and other prehistoric monuments that still fascinate us, and archaeological finds from the Old and New Stone Ages and the Bronze Age are displayed in Danish museums. The country's recorded history dates from the time of the Vikings, about AD 800. These seagoing warriors conquered parts of England and Normandy, invaded the Mediterranean, and visited the coast of North America. From the 8th to the 11th century, they forged Denmark into the most powerful European empire of the era. The dramatic events and heroic figures of the Viking Age were often inscribed on runic stones, some of which may be seen today in forest clearings and along rural roadways.

The Middle Ages was a period of prosperity for Denmark. Beautiful castles with moats were built during this period. (The later Renaissance castles and manors are frequently noted for their beautifully landscaped gardens and grounds.) In 1397, Queen Margrethe I thought the time propitious to unite Sweden and Norway under the Danish crown. The union with Sweden dissolved in 1523, but Norway and Denmark remained united until 1814, a year after the state went bankrupt.

Nonetheless, the 19th century was a golden age for Denmark culturally; there was a flowering of literature and philosophy led by Andersen and the existential philospher, Søren Kierkegaard, and August Bournonville's choreography brought renown to the *Royal Danish Ballet.* Copenhagen blossomed into a culturally energetic and sophisticated capital.

Denmark was neutral in World War I, but although it had signed a nonaggression pact with Hitler, it was occupied by German troops from 1940 to 1945. Most of the Jewish population, as well as Jews fleeing from other countries, were helped to escape from the Nazis by the Danes, who also mounted a strong resistance movement.

In the postwar years, Denmark's bacon, beer and cheeses, modern furniture, porcelain, and, more recently, electronics, textiles, and architectural and engineering skills have won world acclaim. The Danes, proud of their noble history and their country's well-groomed appearance, have also made tourism an important part of the country's modern economy.

Our first Danish route explores Funen (Fyn, in Danish), the island between the mainland of Jutland and the island of Zealand, with stops at Odense, where Hans Christian Andersen was born; Ærø, a small island with cozy old villages; and Langeland, with its Viking burial grounds and small farming villages. Next visit the flat Jutland Peninsula, the country's heartland — an area of crystal fjords, stark moors, dense forests, sandy beaches, and small, medieval towns. The Zealand route from Copenhagen heads north around the large outer island past churches and castles that recall the warrior days of Viking rule.

Funen

This route follows small, well-maintained highways with bridge and ferry connections to various islands in the archipelago, taking you through the charming countryside known as Denmark's Garden. A tour of Funen is an easy 2- or 3-day swing, whether you're circling around from Copenhagen or on your way there from the Jutland Peninsula.

Hans Christian Andersen wrote about his birthplace: "Perhaps Odense will one day become famous and people from many countries will travel to Odense because of me." This was a daring prediction in the mid-19th century, but in fact, the Hans Christian Andersen museums and settings have prompted many people to make a special trip to Odense and the isle of Funen.

Along with literary and historical attractions, Funen and the islands are noted for their unhurried charm and subtle, disarming beauty. Centuries-old inns and museums are scattered throughout a landscape that alternates between gentle, rolling farmland and picturesque harbors, coastline, and beaches. While residents here are slightly less sophisticated than their compatriots in Copenhagen, they are more open to visitors and quite proud of their region.

To reach Odense from Copenhagen, you will have about a 1½-hour drive to the Korsør-Nyborg ferry, a 50-minute ferry ride, and another half-hour's drive from Nyborg to Odense. In peak tourist season, it's advisable to book the ferry in advance. Driving east from Jutland, take E66 or A1 across the island to Odense.

ODENSE: Denmark's third largest city celebrated its 1,000th birthday in 1988. Odense has for centuries been the trade and transportation hub of Funen. Its university, theater, and orchestra also provide a solid cultural base, important for an area far from the nation's capital.

In addition, the white swan and little brown "ugly duckling" decorating most Odense posters and information brochures signify that Hans Christian Andersen still plays a major role in the life of the city. You can visit the storyteller's birthplace at 39-43 Hans Jensensstræde; the museum here has been open since 1908 and contains letters, manuscripts, published editions, and drawings that have illustrated his works. Next door is a delightful, intimate restaurant called, appropriately enough, *Under Lindetraet* (Under the Linden Tree). Andersen buffs will also treasure his childhood home at 3-5 Munkemøllestræde, which no doubt inspired many of his children's stories.

Odense is also the home of delicious almond nougat and marzipan, exported around the world as traditional Christmas confections. These are sold by the loaf for baking or slicing.

To see one of the largest and most complete open-air museums in Denmark, head south from downtown (bus #2) on Sejerskovvej to Funen Village. In a peaceful, wooded setting, a cluster of farms, houses, mills, and brickworks re-create a village typical of the 18th and 19th centuries.

En Route from Odense – The perfect setting for a Danish *Alice in Wonderland,* Egeskov is a 16th-century island fort 1 hour south of Odense, just off A9 on the way to Fåborg or Svendborg. The castle, encircled by a moat edged by gardens in various styles, boasts a maze of hedges from which little Alice would have had trouble escaping (taller visitors can see over the hedges). You can also visit the collection of vintage cars, carriages, and other antique conveyances at the adjoining museum. The castle park is open 9 AM to 5:30 PM daily, May through September. There is a small admission charge. Concerts are held in the Great Hall during the peak season.

The *Faldsled Inn,* outside Fåborg, is more than a hotel; it is a trip back into 19th-century style and splendor. (It is also expensive, but worth an overnight stay.) Fåborg itself is a quiet town with many 18th- and 19th-century homes.

Depending on the direction of your travels, Svendborg can serve as the gateway either to the gardens of Funen or to the southern Danish archipelago. A market town since 1253, Svendborg and its port are still a center of trade. The town makes a good dining spot or resting place for 1 day of the journey. Drive across the bridge to the island of Tåsinge and climb the Bregninge Church tower for a remarkable view of Svendborg, Tåsinge, and the nearby islands.

ÆRØ: Still relatively well protected from modernization, Ærø has, among other things, several fine beaches and the old-fashioned port town of Marstal. Car ferries link "the jewel of the archipelago" to other islands, but the best way to visit is to leave your car in Svendborg and board the ferry as a foot passenger to explore the fairy tale village of Ærøskøbing. As soon as you get off the ferry, the charm of cobblestone streets, narrow lanes, and half-timbered gingerbread houses tells you this Lilliputian town is something special. It is delightfully cozy and compact, and if the store you'd like to visit doesn't seem to be open, you probably just have to fetch the shopkeeper from down the block.

One unusual museum in the village is the home of "Bottle" Peter Jacobsen, the man who reputedly invented the art of building ships in bottles. Before his death in 1960, "Bottle" Peter crafted over 1,700 different bottled ships and 150 scale-model sailing ships. Also in Ærøskøbing are the *Ærø Museum,* in the 1780 Bailiff's House, and the furniture and tile display in Hammerich's House.

TÅSINGE: Elvira Madigan lived and died on this island, also known as Funen's Garden. Although A9 bisects Tåsinge, heading toward Langeland, your best bet is to crisscross it, making frequent stops. Almost in the shadow of the Bregninge Church is the tiny village of Landet and the medieval churchyard where Elvira Madigan and her lover, Count Sixten Sparre, were buried in 1889, when death ended the ill-starred romance of the Swedish officer and the beautiful performer.

Back across A9 the road leads to the seafaring village of Troense, with its small maritime museum and nearby Valdemar's Castle, which was built in 1644, then remodeled in the baroque style in 1754. The manor house is open to visitors, and the compound also includes a naval museum featuring royal barges and other vessels.

After Troense, just continue crisscrossing A9 through the farmland and small towns of Tåsinge at your leisure, stopping whenever the urge hits at a roadside *bageri* (bakery) for one of its fabled pastries.

LANGELAND: This "long island" (54 miles long and 5 miles wide), reached by one bridge and five ferries, offers both historical sites and places for relaxation. Coming from Tåsinge across Langelands Bridge you reach Rudkøbing, the island's capital. A town of half-timbered buildings, winding streets, and carved house doors, it was the birthplace of Denmark's famous physicist H. C. Ørsted, discoverer of electromagnetism.

But in this region of manor houses and castles, it's best to stay outside the city in a place like the *Tranekar Gastgivergaard,* where a typical dinner might be leek soup, roast pheasant, fresh vegetables, and good Danish beer. Less than a mile from the inn is Tranekær Castle. Although rebuilt extensively in 1863, the north wing with its 9-foot-thick walls, is thought to date back to 1160. Part of the castle grounds are open to the public.

Other attractions on Langeland include small farm villages, beaches, and pleasant rolling countryside. For the return trip to Copenhagen, a ferry goes from the fishing village of Spodsbjerg to Tårs, near Nakskov. (On the road back to Copenhagen, a detour at Vordingborg out to the majestic chalk cliffs of Møn is well worth the time.)

BEST EN ROUTE

Expect to pay $100 and up per night for a double room in the places listed as expensive and $60 to $95 in those listed as moderate. Restaurant prices range from $40 and up for a meal for two in places listed as expensive and from $30 to $40 in those listed as moderate. Prices do not include drinks, wine, or tip.

ODENSE

H. C. Andersens – This is a fine example of modern Danish architecture as well as a first-class hotel. 7 Claus Bergsgade (phone: 66-147800). Expensive.

Sara Hotel Grand – Traditional old-style hotel, with furnishings representative of the 18th and 19th centuries. 18 Jernbanegade (phone: 66-117171). Expensive.

Windsor – Simple Scandinavian rooms, with Victorian lobby and restaurant. Vindegade 45 (phone: 66-120652). Moderate.

FALDSLED

Faldsled – Former Royal Charter House with an exquisite garden and a romantic setting. Many rooms have private entrances and courtyards. Superb international cuisine with a French accent (phone: 62-681111). Expensive.

SVENDBORG

Ærø – In the *Ærø* hotel, this restaurant provides good service and warm hospitality; the delicately sautéed fish could hardly be beat in a restaurant costing twice as much. 1 Brogade (phone: 62-210760). Moderate.

LANGELAND

Tranekær Gæstgivergaard – Intimate and homelike; most of the pheasant, wild duck, and other game served at dinner has been shot by a member of the innkeeper's family. Ten of the 15 double rooms have been modernized to make them more comfortable. Very pleasant service. Open year-round. Just around the bend from Tranekær Castle (phone: 62-591204). Moderate.

Jutland

The most direct road from southern Denmark to Skagen, the idyllic resort town on the North Sea, is Highway E3. Following this route, you can reach Skagen in a day or so, but you will be missing most of the special sights of Jutland, the ancient heart of Denmark, the world's oldest kingdom.

A long peninsula separating the North Sea from the Baltic, Jutland (or Jylland, as it is known in Danish) features a topography laced with charming fjords and trimmed with wind-swept moors, beaches, and forests. The only part of Denmark linked to the European continent, it is considerably larger than the 500 or so islands that make up the rest of the country. Thanks to its countryside, its farms and hamlets, and its magnificent, sandy coast, Jutland has been the major vacation spot for the Danes since the days of Hans Christian Andersen.

Andersen himself spent many summers there; and he wrote: "It was so beautiful out in the country. It was summer — the wheat fields were golden, the oats were green, and down among the green meadows, the hay was stacked. There the stork minced about on his red legs, clacking away in Egyptian, which was the language his mother taught him."

In addition to their passionate love for the countryside, the Danes have close ties with their historical tradition, one that has its roots in Jutland. By present dating methods, Jutland was settled about 12,000 years ago by nomadic hunters and fishermen who were following the receding Ice Age. Remains of this culture are scattered in peat bogs and burial mounds all over Jutland and include a wide variety of weapons, tools, and even several remarkably well preserved corpses a few thousand years old, now displayed at local museums.

For the Danes, however, history really begins around the 9th century, when the Danish Vikings, operating from bases in North Jutland, laid waste to England and Scotland, besieged Paris, and plundered towns as far south as Lisbon. King Gorm the Old and Queen Thyra built the Dannevirke Wall in this era, establishing Denmark's southern border, and their son, King Harald Bluetooth, introduced Christianity to the region in about 960. Harald's heirs, Swein Forkbeard and Canute the Great, ruled over an empire consisting of Denmark, England, Norway, and southern Sweden.

With the construction of Roskilde Cathedral and Copenhagen in the 12th century, the focus of Danish culture shifted to Zealand, the large island east of Jutland. Since then, aside from a few bloody Swedish invasions and a fierce border war with the Prussians in 1864, Jutland has been a tranquil repository of agriculture and traditional Danish mores.

The Jutland trip is a winding, 9-day excursion with many stops; it is divided into three sections. Should you need to curtail your vacation, you will invariably be within a short distance of E3 or a ferry to England, Sweden, or Norway.

En Route from Germany – If you are coming from Germany on the Autobahn, you will probably need a break by the time you reach the Danish border town of Frøslev. If so, head east on A8, where, after a 12½-mile (20-km) ride on the northern shores of Flensburger Förde, you will reach Gråsten, the site of Gråsten Castle, dowager Queen Ingrid's summer home. The present baroque palace dates from 1757; the castle church (c. 1700) is open to visitors from April to September — provided, of course, that Queen Ingrid isn't vacationing here with her grandchildren.

If old battlefields are your cup of tea, 3 miles (5 km) east is Dybbøl, where the major battle of the 1864 war with the Prussians was fought. The Prussians took over Schleswig-Holstein, but the Danes' heroic resistance has been memorialized at the Dybbøl Heights, overlooking the old fortifications.

Next to Dybbøl is Sønderborg and the huge Sønderborg Castle, which dates to the 13th century. It was the prison of Danish King Christian II in the 16th century and was burned and looted by the Swedes in the 17th century. The castle, open daily, houses a museum of regional history.

The road north to Åbenrå runs from Augustenborg Fjord to Åbenrå Fjord, and it should give you a feeling for Jutland's symbiotic relationship with the sea. Åbenrå itself has a museum with an intriguing collection of maritime miscellany (33 H. P. Hanssensgade).

Ribe, a fairy tale village, is the next destination, about 50 miles (80 km) northwest on A12. If you are interested in Viking lore, make a detour on Hærvejen, an old Viking road, and see the runic stone at Horslund.

RIBE: First mentioned in 850, Ribe was the site of a church built by St. Ansgar, the man who brought Christianity to Scandinavia. The dominant feature is the cathedral, Ribe Domkirke, built on the site of Ansgar's church and the first thing you see as you approach the town. Built in the first half of the 12th century, it is a striking mixture of Romanesque and Gothic elements and is full of legend and interesting architectural detail. The *Ribe Museum of Antiquities* is also worth a visit, and the town boasts over 100 protected houses from the 16th and 17th centuries. For a bit of local flavor, stop at the charming *Weiss Stue* (c. 1600), near the cathedral, for a meal or a glass of "punch" (warmed aquavit, sweetened with a sugar cube).

The North Sea is just a few minutes away, and its tides are so strong that you may have to resist the temptation to drive across the mud flats of Vadehavet to the island of Mandø. Take the bus instead.

En Route from Ribe – About 15 miles (25 km) north of Ribe on A12 is the city of Esbjerg, the base for Denmark's fishing industry as well as the country's oil capital. Fishmeal plants, a busy international ferry terminal, and waterfront grain silos give Esbjerg a prosaic look, with none of the atmosphere of older Danish towns. (After all, it dates only to 1869.) Do drive down to the docks, however, and take the 20-minute ferry ride to the remarkable little island of Fanø.

FANØ: The ancestors of the 3,300 inhabitants of Fanø bought this island from the Danish Crown in 1741, which explains the preservation of a unique culture on the island. Its lengthy beaches and grassy dunes make it a popular bathing resort, and on the southern spit of the island is the restored old fishing village of Sønderho. Fanø was once a prolific shipbuilding site. Today it has an important navigation school, but perhaps more writers and artists than seafarers make the island their home. Many people live in low houses with thatched roofs. On the first weekend in July, Nordby hosts the *Fanø Fair*. Sønderho's own festival is held the third Sunday in July. On these dates islanders dress in traditional costume and the past comes alive.

En Route from Fanø – Leave the west coast and get acquainted with another kind of scenery by cutting back across Jutland on the road leading northeast to Grindsted. The land changes noticeably as you leave the coast, and you will see some of the rolling farmland for which Denmark is famous.

If you are traveling with children, you might want to take the Vejle road 6 miles (10 km) to Billund and turn them loose on Legoland, a miniature world made from 15 million Lego toy bricks. There is a 40-foot replica of Mt. Rushmore, another of Cape Kennedy, and many activities for youngsters.

Another 19 miles (30 km) takes you to Vejle and the nearby village of Jelling, the ancient Viking capital, where you can see some of Denmark's most famous runic stones and the burial mounds of old King Gorm and Queen Thyra. The *Jelling Kro* is a fine place to sup with the ghosts of the Vikings.

The road north to Horsens via Juelsminde has a spectacular view of the coast and Palsgård Manor House, which is open to tourists.

HORSENS: Founded in the 12th century, this was a Franciscan abbey town during the Middle Ages before becoming a prosperous trading center in the 18th century. The old abbey church still exists, and many of the original decorations and carvings are still intact. The town itself is on a fjord and has many picturesque lanes and lovely 18th-century houses.

Horsens is the end of the first 3-day leg of the tour; you are now entering central Jutland, the second leg. Continuing north on A10, you leave the coast and approach Århus. Here the landscape becomes more wooded, and you may even notice a slight elevation as you pass Yding Skovhøj Hills, the highest point in Denmark at 567 feet.

ÅRHUS: Denmark's second largest city (pop. 250,000), Århus is a major industrial and cultural center, thanks to its harbor and the University of Århus. Among the city's many sights are the 12th-century Århus Cathedral, which contains, among other things, Denmark's biggest church organ; the Old Town, a reconstructed 16th-century village; the *Viking Museum;* and the *Museum of Prehistory,* with an Iron Age collection highlighted by the red-haired mummy of the Graballe man, at the Moesgård Manor

House. If you visit in early September, be sure to catch the *Århus Festival,* the biggest celebration of theater, dance, and music in Scandinavia.

SILKEBORG: Heading due west on A15, you reach the beautiful Lake District and, Silkeborg, in its center. The *Silkeborg Museum,* at Silkeborg Hovedgård, is worth a stop, particularly if you want to see another early Dane, the 2,200-year-old Tollund man. The new *Silkeborg Art Museum* has a memorable modern collection featuring work by native son Asger Jorn. Take a boat trip on the lakes, where you can relax and gaze at slender herons and other waterfowl. One of Denmark's great Resistance heroes, the poet and pastor Kaj Munk, was killed in 1944 by the Nazis at Hørbylund Bakke, 5 miles (8 km) west of Silkeborg.

En Route from Silkeborg – Drive west on A15 to Herning, the center of the Danish textile industry. Here you can get a good buy on a sweater or fabric design, and you can observe 19th-century peasant life and weaving techniques at the *Herning Museum* (Museumsgade). The town has fine modern art collections.

From Herning, A15 winds through the moors and lowlands of the west coast to Ringkøbing, a town economically ruined in the 18th century when accumulated silt deposits on Holmsland Klit cut off Ringkøbing Fjord from the North Sea. To prevent flooding, the Danes have built dikes similar to those in Holland. The area is thus undeveloped. Driving south on Holmsland Klit, you come to Tipperne Bird Sanctuary, the largest in Denmark.

HOLSTEBRO: North of Ringkøbing on A16, Holstebro is Jutland's center for theater and music. A depressed town some 20 years ago, it came into a windfall and spent the money on encouraging the arts. Today it has one of the leading experimental theaters in the world, the *Odin Theater,* at Særkærparken, and a lovely new art museum. Holstebro is a great example of creative city planning.

VIBORG: East on A16 is one of Denmark's oldest towns. Viborg dates to the 8th century, when it was the site of the Viking *ting* and various sacrificial rites, thanks to its placement at a critical crossroads. The Christians who later occupied the area decided to keep it as a religious center and in 1130 built a large cathedral; it was largely destroyed by fire but was restored in the 19th century. Today it is still the largest granite cathedral in all of Europe. It is decorated with a series of lavish frescoes, executed around the start of the 20th century by the painter Joakim Skovgaard. Open daily.

En Route from Viborg – The final leg of the Jutland trip covers the rugged scenery of North Jutland, which is virtually cut off from the rest of the peninsula by the Limfjord, a large body of water that was an important navigation route in Viking times. Here again, deposits of silt have wreaked havoc with maritime commerce, making the passage quite treacherous. Heading northwest toward Nykøbing and Thisted, you will first see the Limfjord at Skive, a small town with an interesting museum collection of Eskimo and prehistoric relics.

About 15 miles (25 km) northwest of Skive, connected by the Sallingsund Bridge, is the Limfjord island of Mors. Its largest town is Nykøbing Mors, the home of the Limfjord oyster industry and Dueholm Abbey, founded in 1377 by the Knights of St. John. Today the abbey houses the museum for the island. It is open daily, with an admission charge.

The best view on Mors is from the cliffs of Hanklit and Salgerhøj, near the Thisted bridge across Vilsund. Thisted itself is the principal town in northwest Jutland, in the Thy area. Nearby, at Hørdum, is a fantastic runic stone depicting Thor's epic struggle with the Midgård serpent.

Following A11 northeast along the northern banks of the Limfjord, you pass the promontory of Feggeklit on the island of Mors. According to the Danish medieval historian Saxo, this was where Hamlet avenged his father's death by killing his treacherous Uncle Fegge. From here, take the north road to Fjerritslev; stop for a swim and a look at the North Sea at Torup Strand.

From Fjerritslev, one can choose either A11 to Ålborg, the next destination, or the southern route via Løgstør. The latter is slower but much more interesting; it passes the Viking town of Aggersborg as well as Løgstør, a fishing hamlet with a good museum on the history and culture of the Limfjord.

ÅLBORG: Denmark's fourth largest city and Jutland's most important town, Ålborg is the center of the tobacco, cement, and — as every good Dane knows — aquavit industries. Like many Danish cities, it has a well-preserved Old Town that must be explored on foot. Be sure to see the Jens Bang's Stenhus, one of the finest Renaissance houses in Denmark, and have a drink in the cavernous *Duus Vinkjaelder* bar, once a wine cellar. The *Ålborg Historical Museum* contains interiors from bourgeois homes of the 17th century (48 Algade), and the *North Jutland Museum of Art* (50 Kong Christians Allé) houses a very modern collection in a marble structure designed by the architect Alvar Aalto. Also of interest are the Ålborg Zoological Garden, Mølleparken, and a smaller replica of Copenhagen's Tivoli called Tivoliland. Well worth a side trip is the annual celebration of the US's independence, held on July 4 at Rebild Hills, 20 miles (32 km) south of Ålborg.

En Route from Ålborg – Nørresundby, a suburb of Ålborg on the northern side of the Limfjord, has the most important Viking burial ground in Scandinavia (Lindholm Høje). There are 682 graves as well as the ruins of a nearby settlement.

From here, A17 runs northwest to Åbybro, where it joins A11 running due north to Løkken and the coast. En route you may want to stop and see the famed church in Jetsmark or detour to swim at the small seaside town of Blokhus. Løkken itself is a popular summer resort, and you can drive the 10 miles (16 km) to Blokhus on the beach. Not far from Løkken is the 12th-century monastery and manor house at Børglum Kloster, open daily from May 15 through September 16; admission charge.

Your route leads next to the commercial center of Hjørring, a 13th-century town, which has a quaint historical museum, Vendsyssels, and St. Catherine's, a fine medieval church.

On the road north to Skagen, you'll see one of the most exotic sights in Denmark. Huge, shifting dunes up to 35 feet high that migrate 25 to 30 feet every year, the Råbjerg Mile is on the northern peninsula of Skagen, the juncture of the Baltic and the North seas.

SKAGEN: This charming little town by the sea became an artists' colony in the 1880s and has been a popular resort ever since. Paintings of people on the strand (the beach) by P.S. Krøer have made Skagen known the world over. Artists' inspiration can be seen in the low, yellow-washed houses and in the town's various museums — the *Skagen Museum,* the *Museum of Old Skagen,* the *Grenen Museum,* and Drachmann's House. The new *Grenen Museum* houses contemporary art. Just west of town is the "church of the dunes," a 13th-century church that was abandoned to the sands in 1795. The history of Skagen's relationship with the sea is reflected in its five lighthouses, only one of which, Grenen, is still in use today. Skagen is the ideal place to end a tour of Jutland, and you may want to stay in one of its quiet little cottages for a while to digest your travels. If you find the area artistically inspiring too, it is possible to study painting. Consult the local tourist board.

BEST EN ROUTE

Expect to pay $75 and up per night for a double room in the places listed as expensive; $50 to $70 in those listed as moderate; and under $50, inexpensive. Restaurant prices range from $40 and up for a dinner for two in the expensive category; $25 to $40 in the moderate category; and $25 and under, inexpensive. Prices do not include drinks, wine, and tip.

RIBE

Dagmar – On the main square of this beautiful little village, this is the best hotel in town, with 50 rooms and full accommodations. 1 Torvet (phone: 75-420033). Moderate.

FANØ

Scan Club – Parents traveling with children may wish to try this beach hotel. All 27 rooms have kitchens, and special weekly rates are offered. Pool, restaurant. Strandvejen, Nordby (phone: 75-163711). Expensive to moderate.

Sønderho Kro – A tiny, elegant, 7-room inn on the southern tip of the island. Full accommodations and a charming restaurant. Sønderho (phone: 75-164009). Moderate.

HORSENS

Snaptun Færgegård – Following the principle of sleeping near the sea, this 50-room inn gives you the chance to be lulled into slumber by the Baltic. Full accommodations. 11 Havnevej, Snaptun (phone: 75-683003 or 75-683511). Moderate.

SILKEBORG

Dania – A nice, respectable, businessman's hotel on the main square of town, with 47 rooms, full accommodations. 5 Torvet (phone: 86-820111). Moderate.

RINGKØBING

Klitten – A fine hotel with restaurant right on the beach. Open from June through August. Søndervig (phone: 97-339100). Moderate.

Strandkroen – Planning an off-season trip? This cozy little inn might be just the thing; 16 rooms, full accommodations. 2 Nordsøvej, Søndervig (phone: 97-339002). Inexpensive.

VIBORG

Missionshotellet – Somehow in this spiritual center it seems appropriate to stay in the inn with an ecclesiastical ring. Also, it's the best in town, with 60 rooms, 10 apartments with bath and kitchen, and full accommodations. 5 Sankt Mathiasqade (phone 86-623700). Moderate.

THISTED

Limfjorden – This hotel, formerly called *Strandhotellet*, has a good view of the Limfjord; 19 rooms and full accommodations. 39 Oddesundvej (phone: 97-924011). Moderate.

ÅLBORG

Hvide Hus – A big-city hotel with all the trimmings, including a swimming pool, sauna, and 199 rooms with full accommodations. 2 Vesterbro (phone: 98-138400). Expensive.

SKAGEN

Skagen – The biggest place in this tiny town, with 83 rooms. Very modern. Gammel Landevej (phone: 98-442233). Expensive.

Important: Skagen and Fanø are very popular in the summer, so be sure to make bookings well in advance.

Zealand

Tours from Copenhagen can be either 1-day loops or extended 2- to 3-day excursions that allow you to take greater advantage of the Zealand countryside and perhaps stay in a charming Danish manor house or traditional hotel.

While Copenhagen is considered one of the most modern and sophisticated cities in Europe, a half-hour's drive transports you to an area of farmland and woods dotted with towns dating back more than 500 years.

Some of the high points of such tours are castles and churches that vividly recreate the time when kings ruled the realm we now call Scandinavia. You can visit a palace still used by the reigning monarch, a church with the tombs of almost all the royalty from the last thousand years, and the ramparts of Kronborg Castle in Helsingør (Elsinore), the scene of Shakespeare's Hamlet.

There is more to enjoy here, however, than colorful history. You can also stop at *Louisiana,* the modern art museum overlooking the sound, drive past a strip of posh shore homes known as the Danish Riviera, and relax on sandy beaches or in old fishing villages.

The most frequently traveled tour bus route is a 1-day loop that heads north from Copenhagen to Louisiana and Helsingør, turns west to castles in Fredensborg and Hillerød, and then returns to Copenhagen. To get the most out of each stop, however, 1½ to 2 full days is recommended.

KLAMPENBORG: Heading north from Copenhagen off the coast road, the first stop is Klampenborg, which, in addition to a bathing beach, has Jægersborg Dyrehave, the royal hunting ground since the end of the 17th century. This is a favorite retreat for Copenhagen residents, where they can stroll among the old oak trees and watch the nearly tame deer. The highlight of the park between mid-April and the end of August is Dyrehavsbakken — or Bakken, as it's commonly known. Scandinavia's and perhaps Europe's oldest amusement park, Bakken is a version of Tivoli, set in the woods. There are enough attractions to merit a full day's visit and bicycles can be rented at the railroad station. Have lunch on the terrace of *Taarbak Kro,* just off the beach.

En Route from Dyrehave – While A3 is the fastest route to Helsingør, the 27-mile (43-km) road that winds along the Øresund coast really doesn't take much more time. Along the way are many elegant homes, fine examples of modern Danish architecture, that make it easy to understand why this stretch is known as the Danish Riviera.

HUMLEBÆK: About 22 miles (35 km) north of Copenhagen, this town is noted for *Louisiana,* a center for modern art. Established in 1958, *Louisiana* stands majestically on the Øresund coast, looking over the sound toward Sweden. Not only does it have an outstanding collection of Danish and foreign art and sculpture, but the museum and gardens themselves are a work of art.

HELSINGØR: Less than a half-hour north of Louisiana, the coast road winds into Helsingør. According to the history books, people were living in the area before AD 1000, and Helsingør had already been named by 1231. But it wasn't until 1574, when Frederik II began the reconstruction of Kronborg Castle, that Helsingør took on strategic and historical importance.

Dating from around 1426, the castle had been completely rebuilt in its present Renaissance style by 1585. Open daily, it houses collections of armor and Renaissance clothing and art. There is a memorial to Shakespeare in the surrounding wall, and the castle itself is well preserved. Also on the Kronborg grounds is the *Mercantile and Maritime Museum,* founded in 1915.

At Helsingør, Denmark and Sweden are less than 2 miles apart. If you haven't taken the Copenhagen hydrofoil to Malmö, it's worth making the 40-minute round trip to Helsingborg and back — if only to say you've been in Sweden.

To see the technological history of Denmark, visit the *Technical Museum,* featuring Denmark's first airplane, railroad train, and trolley. 23 Ndr. Strandvej.

HORNBÆK/GILLELEJE: From Helsingør, the longer tour of North Zealand continues up the coast to the resort towns of Hornbæk and Gilleleje. Both have picturesque fishing harbors and Hornbæk, in particular, a fine beach. Don't be surprised at the amount of nudity on the beaches or at the Danes' apparent nonchalance. The *Strand* in Gilleleje and the *Trouville* in Hornbæk are both well-known hotels that tend to fill up in summer months. Both towns also have campgrounds.

FREDENSBORG: Here is the Fredensborg Palace, the spring and fall home of the reigning monarch. The gardens were designed by the French landscape architect Jardin, who patterned them after those of Versailles. The castle is open only in July (when guided tours are given), but the magnificent grounds are open year-round. Visitors sometimes run into dowager Queen Ingrid taking a stroll. She has apartments in a wing of the palace.

If you opt for the shorter circle route, a good place to stop for a late lunch is the *Store Kro,* next to the palace. The inn has been around for centuries and serves typical Danish fare in traditional settings.

HILLERØD: Continuing west on A6, you come to Hillerød, one of the largest towns in North Zealand. Dominating the town is Frederiksborg Castle, which many people consider the most beautiful Renaissance castle in Europe. Built between 1600 and 1620 by Christian IV, it was reconstructed from the original drawings after fire gutted most of the structure in 1859. Since 1878 the castle has been the *National Historical Museum;* it contains collections of Danish artifacts, costumes, armor, and artwork. Particularly impressive is the chapel, which was untouched by the fire. Adjacent to the edifice is the baroque Castle Park and the Badstuen, a country hunting house for royalty.

ROSKILDE: The focal point of Zealand tours west of Copenhagen is Roskilde, reached via A1. In the center of town is the Roskilde Cathedral, built in the 1170s, the final resting place of nearly all Danish royalty for the last thousand years. The church is a mélange of Romanesque and Gothic architecture, and its interior is rich in frescoes, monuments, sarcophagi, and art objects. On Saturdays in the summer, the Raphaëlis organ dating from 1555 is played at noontime.

By the harbor in Roskilde Fjord is the *Viking Ship Museum.* Inside are five Viking ships, dating from around 1000, which were found in the fjord in 1962. In addition to the well-restored vessels, the museum offers an illuminating film describing the delicate, painstaking procedures used to excavate and restore the Norse relics.

LEJRE: About 7 miles (11 km) southwest of Roskilde is Oldtidsbyen, the Historical-Archaeological Research Center at Lejre. The center is a working village, built to simulate conditions in the Iron Age, 3,000 years ago. The project, supported by the Carlsberg (beer) Foundation, as well as by the Danish government, is a favorite with youngsters. Open daily, May through September. Admission charge.

BEST EN ROUTE

Expect to pay $110 and up per night for a double room in the places listed as expensive. Restaurant prices range from $40 and up for a dinner for two in the expensive category;

$30 to $40 in the moderate category; and $30 and under, inexpensive. Prices do not include drinks, wine, or tip.

KLAMPENBORG

Taarbæk Kro – Offering fine dining right on the beach, this family-run inn features seafood prepared in the French style. Try the *carrelet à la ping,* local fish *meunière,* or, for lunch, the bountiful seafood plate. French and German wines, seating inside or on the terrace, congenial service. 102 Taarbæk Strandvej (phone: 31-631596). Dinner, expensive; lunch, moderate to inexpensive.

HELSINGØR

Marienlyst – Along the coast road just outside Helsingør, the *Marienlyst* is the premier hotel in North Zealand. Sitting by the pool, you can see Kronborg Castle in the distance. Superb international cuisine; 215 rooms and 7 apartments. 2 Ndr. Strandvej (phone: 49-211801). Expensive.

FREDENSBORG

Store Kro – A perfectly situated 49-room hotel on the road between Helsingør and Hillerød, a short walk from Fredensborg Palace. One building dates from 1723, and over the years the hotel has been the scene of receptions and royal weddings. The atmosphere is one of old-fashioned elegance. 1-6 Slotsgade (phone: 42-280047). Expensive.

SØLLERØD

Søllerød Kro – Only 10.5 miles (17 km) north of Copenhagen but surrounded by woods, this is one of the most popular spots for the Danes' Sunday outings. The menu offers both French and national dishes. After a meal, a walk through the woods is recommended. No overnight accommodations. 35 Søllerødvej (phone: 42-80-25-05). Expensive.

Finland

Finland, a country of about 5 million people, is the easternmost Scandinavian landmass. Its southern end juts into the Baltic Sea to create two smaller bodies of water: the Gulf of Bothnia to the west, which forms a natural barrier with Sweden, and the Gulf of Finland to the south, which separates Finland from the Baltic state of Estonia. Finland shares its borders with Norway and Sweden to the west and north and with the USSR to the east.

Finland's neighbors have dominated its history. First part of the Swedish Kingdom, then of the Russian Empire, Finland wasn't officially independent until 1917. This is important because anthropologically Finland is neither Scandinavian nor Russian. The language is Finnish, a Finno-Ugric language; and the people are Magyar-Estonian hybrids who migrated from the southeast.

Finland covers 130,500 square miles (about the size of New England plus New York and New Jersey), one third of which is above the Arctic Circle. The southern two thirds of the country is marbled with over 188,000 lakes dotted with more than 180,000 islands.

Wood-related and metal industries are the main Finnish occupations, but the national pastime is the sauna, and you'll miss something special if you leave Finland without trying one.

Helsinki, the capital, with a half-million people, is on the southern coast. It's a good starting point for any visit to the country. Finland's roads are good, as are the railway, bus, and airline connections. Finnair now serves 22 locations throughout Finland, and the railway offers special holiday tickets for unlimited travel within the country. Car rental is easy and uncomplicated as well. The first route takes you in and out of the beautiful southern lakeland. The waters are cold, clear, and shallow; the land is green and forested. There are also 2- to 5-day guided tours to the Lakelands by bus-boat-plane. The lake networks are vast and trafficked by romantic steamers, modern ferries, and hydrofoils.

The second route takes you into the Arctic wilderness of Lapland, where the people are as much an attraction as the landscape. The fells (mountains raised from early glacial movement) make the land strangely beautiful, even where fir and birch forests end and the tundra begins.

The Lakelands

This long route (703 mi/1,132 km) takes you from Helsinki up, around, and through the beautiful Finnish lakeland. There are ten major towns along the way and many interesting stops that could take a week's meandering, but if you don't have time, you can get a good map and reroute, cutting across some of the larger lakes by ferry.

HELSINKI: For a detailed report on the city and its hotels and restaurants, see *Helsinki,* THE CITIES.

En Route from Helsinki – Leaving the capital for the lakeland, take Route 3 for 65 miles (104 km) to Hämeenlinna. The landscape is luxuriant farmland enriched by clear, blue waters. Before you reach Hämeenlinna, you pass through Riihimäki, where there is the famous *Glass Museum* (23 Tehtaankatu) and a glass works, where you can purchase samples of beautiful Finnish glassware.

HÄMEENLINNA: Having received its royal charter in 1639, this is the oldest inland town in Finland. The city, which grew around the medieval Häme Castle in the northern part of town on Lake Vanajavesi, is a garrison town. Hämeenlinna's *Art Museum* is at 2 Viipurintie, and at 11 Hallituskatu you can visit Sibelius House, where the Finnish composer was born. Hämeenlinna is also a terminal for the Finnish Silverline lake route; you can take a motorship or lake steamer to Tampere or Kangasala.

About 48 miles (77 km) along Route 3 and E79 is the town of Tampere. On the way you might stop for lunch at the Sääksmäki Bridge and eat on the picturesque lakeshore.

TAMPERE: The second largest city in Finland, with 400,000 inhabitants, Tampere was founded 200 years ago on the banks of the Tammer River rapids on the isthmus between two big lakes, Näsijärvi and Pyhäjärvi. There are also some 180 lakes inside the city limits. Tampere is an industrial center known especially for metal, textiles, and footwear, but it is also famous for its theaters and other cultural activities.

Just before the center city, you cross a bridge; down to your right you'll see the charming Koskipuisto (Rapids Park), where you can sit and watch the river flow. Here as well as in Hämeenpuisto (Häme Park), a little farther on, there are summertime folk dances and open-air concerts. There are several impressive churches, not all "15th-century stone" style: the Tampere Cathedral is Gothic and built of Finnish granite, the Kaleva is Finnish modern, and the Eastern Orthodox church of Tampere, with its bulbous towers, is the only neo-Byzantine church in Scandinavia. From Näsinneula, the highest observation tower in Finland, which also boasts a revolving restaurant, you can drink in wide views of both the city and the lakes. Besides an aquarium, a dolphinarium, and a planetarium, Tampere also has one of Finland's best collections of 20th-century art at the *Sara Hildén-Museum;* also visit the *Modern Art Museum* and the unique *Lenin Museum.*

On a northern lake isthmus is Pyynikki Park, with a beautiful ridge of pine trees, calm lake views, and a revolving summer theater. Kauppi Sports Park is the place to jog, swim, or play tennis. *Tampere Hall,* the new congress and concert hall, will open this summer on the edge of Sorsapuisto Park, opposite the university.

JYVÄSKYLÄ: The trip from Tampere is 93 miles (150 km), but you can stop outside town at the industrial island commune of Säynätsalo on Lake Päijänne, where you find one of Alvar Aalto's famous buildings, the Säynätsalo Civic Center. If you're in a hurry, however, don't worry about missing it; the *Aalto Museum,* where you can see most of the Finnish master's buildings, is in Jyväskylä (7 Seminaarinkatu), next to the university, with many other examples of Aalto's work.

Jyväskylä, one of the most popular tourist cities in the country and the capital of Central Finland, was founded in 1837 at the northern end of Lake Päijänne on the site of an ancient marketplace. Its importance as a cultural center is especially obvious in summertime, when various seminars, theater performances, concerts, and exhibitions are staged and well attended. More than anything else, though, this is a city of fine modern architecture, featuring a city theater designed by Aalto as well as the *Laajavuori* hotel with its Sports Center, just north of the center city. The Sports Center is the site of the famous ski jump that earned Olympic medals for Finnish athletes.

For information about lake cruises, sightseeing tours, or other activities, stop at the City Tourist Office (38 Vapaudenkatu; phone: 294083).

TURKU: Only 95 miles (160 km) west of Helsinki and easily reached by bus, train, car, or plane, Turku is Finland's oldest city. Though smaller than Helsinki and Tampere, its historical roots run deeper. Its trade and spiritual heritage once provided an important link that connected medieval Finland to the burgeoning sphere of Western culture.

In 1812, Turku lost its position as the country's capital when Czar Alexander I ordered the seat of government moved to Helsinki. Turku suffered another crushing blow in the fire of 1827, when virtually the entire city was razed. Architect Carl Ludwig Engel created a new master plan for the city in 1828, and today a visit provides a vivid glimpse into its significant past.

On this alternate route from Helsinki, begin with a visit to Turku Castle and Cathedral, two 13th-century monuments. Housed inside the restored castle is a historic museum, which shows medieval artifacts beside modern designs. Farther down the River Aura is the stone cathedral, which was finished in 1300. The *Turku Museum* is worth a visit, but don't skip *Wäinoö Aaltonen Museum,* where works by the renowned Finnish sculptor are displayed in a contemporary building designed by his son (38 Itäinen Rantakatu); it also has a pleasant café.

Nearby is the *Sibelius Museum,* with many orginal scores and unique musical instruments. Concerts are held here regularly (17 Püspankatu).

The Qwensel House, which dates to the 1700s, is a good example of how the old aristocracy lived. Adjoining it is the *Pharmacy Museum,* with mahogany fittings and an original restoration of an apothecary shop, complete with glazed earthenware jars and bottles dating to 1800 (address T/K).

If you want a change from Finnish food, visit *Pizzeria Dennis,* a popular hangout for locals that has inexpensive pasta dishes and plate-size pizzas (17 Linnankatu).

En Route to Kuopio – If it's July and you can't resist strawberries, stop at Suonenjoki, a small town that holds an annual *Strawberry Carnival.* If you have lots of time, you can continue this detour through the towns of Iisvesi, Tervo, and Karttula, where the lake scenery is unmatched.

KUOPIO: This provincial capital is a center of the Savo (province) way of life, humor, and folklore. The city was founded about 200 years ago, and the old traditions are kept alive at the marketplace, where the high-tempered townsfolk meet to barter. You can buy a *kalakukko* (a tasty fish and pork pie), all sorts of vegetables, berries, and regional clothing and souvenirs. If you're not too full to keep exploring, try the *Orthodox Church Museum* (1 Karjalankatu), which has a unique collection of religious icons. The revolving restaurant at Puijo Panorama Tower gives a 360-degree view of the surrounding hills and lakes.

En Route from Kuopio – To get to Joensuu the shortest way, take Route 17, which connects the two provinces and tourist regions of Savo and North Karelia. An alternate route goes south to the city of Varkaus, then northeast along Route 70 to Joensuu.

If you take the longer alternative you can stop at Varkaus, an industrial town at the junction of two extensive lake networks: Kallavesi to the north and Haukivesi to the southeast. The town's business is wood pulp and, except for a large Scandinavian altar fresco in the church, it is best explored by boat. Two-hour sightseeing cruises take you through many idyllic channels and canals, the oldest of which, Taipaleen Kanava, was built in the 1830s.

Farther along this route is the village of Heinävesi, with the only cloisters in Finland, the New Valamo Monastery, with typically Russian cupolas built, oddly enough, out of copper, and the Lintula convent of nuns.

JOENSUU: The main town of North Karelia, Joensuu was founded in 1848 at the mouth of the Pielisjoki River. Its culture is documented at the *Karelia House Museum* (Karjalan Talo) in Ilosaari, where you'll also find a summer theater and restaurant serving regional fish and some of the best pastries in Finland. Again, there's an opportunity to take a lake cruise. Even the most inveterate landlubber shouldn't take the lakeland route without at least one boat trip.

A northern loop trip of about 185 miles (300 km) from Joensuu goes up and around Lake Pielinen. It takes you past the mountains of Koli, the old wooden houses and reconstructed log Bomba Castle at Nurmes, and the Ruunaankoski Rapids near Lieksa. Throughout the trip you might happen upon local bards, founts of indigenous lore who will be glad to sell you the best in regional handicrafts, from unique leather goods to fine linen tablecloths. There's also a variety of wooden souvenirs fashioned from the knot and splint pieces that go unused in the forest industries. There are also many *pradzniks*, religious Russian Orthodox festivals, in summer.

SAVONLINNA: From Joensuu, head southeast toward the Russian frontier on Route 6. You can follow this road all the way to the border, but to get to Savonlinna you cut back west into the lakeland and eastern Savo region. Just outside Savonlinna is the small town of Kerimäki, with the world's largest wooden church. It holds 3,300 people, and during the summer the *Savonlinna Opera Festival* holds concerts here.

Savonlinna itself dates from 1475, when the Olavinlinna Castle was built. The castle was then a border fort manned by united Swedes and Finns on the lookout for czarist armies. The city that surrounds the castle wasn't founded until 1639, and today it is a beautiful lake and spa town. Again, you can take steamer cruises on the lakes from here. The boats leave from slips beside the marketplace and zigzag through the surrounding archipelagos. There are direct boats to and from Kuopio, Joensuu, and Mikkeli. The castle, worth a visit, is the main site of the opera festival, which is always popular. If you're interested, you should book tickets well in advance.

MIKKELI: Mikkeli, 64 miles (104 km) southwest of Savonlinna, is the main city of Savo province and is on the banks of the huge Lake Saimaa. It was the popular headquarters of the national hero Marshal Mannerheim. You can visit his headquarters, now a museum (1-3 Päämajakuja). Then walk north on Porrassalmenkatu to the church museum, where there's a stone sacristy dating from the 1320s. If you crave more lake views, climb the Naisvuori observation tower and admire the various shades of green, blue, and white of the lakes and countryside.

En Route from Mikkeli – There's a choice of two picturesque routes to the town of Imatra, both of which return east toward the Russian border. The first is along Route 434, also called "the panoramic road of Savo," which passes over islands and straits on the shores of Lake Saimaa. The road wanders around hills and meadows with open lake vistas and at one point is punctuated by a short ferry ride.

The second, longer route goes back to Savonlinna (this is the route to take if you've skipped Mikkeli entirely) and takes you through the Punkaharju Ridge, a narrow Ice Age spit that separates Lakes Puruvesi and Pihlajavesi. Just off Punkaharju is Retretti (the Retreat), an amazing new art center with an art gallery and an "acoustic" concert hall in a cave carved belowground.

IMATRA: Imatra is known mainly for the Vuoksi River rapids that roar through the center of town. On selected summer Sundays you can also see the release of the controlled Great Falls. Imatra is another good place to study Alvar Aalto's bold architectural creations, such as the Church of the Three Crosses. The town line is also the national border. As in most of the other lake towns, you can arrive or leave by boat, for Imatra is on the easternmost edge of Lake Saimaa.

LAPPEENRANTA: This city, only 23 miles (37 km) southwest of Imatra, is at the southernmost point of the Saimaa Lake network and has developed into Finland's biggest inland port. There's an involved channel and canal system from here to the Gulf of Finland that gives almost all the lakeland towns access to salt water. The channels, however, flow east through Russian territory before they reach the sea at Viborg. In 1968, Finland worked out a complicated leasing agreement with the USSR that covers boat traffic along the system.

Lappeenranta was founded in 1649, and you can visit the Old Park, surrounded by an 18th-century rampart that encloses a fortress, various museums, and the oldest Orthodox church in Finland, dating from 1785.

En Route from Lappeenranta – About 56 miles (90 km) southwest on the Gulf of Finland is the small military town of Hamina. The entire town was planned and executed as a Renaissance fortress. Much of the 250-year-old wall still stands, enclosing the circular interior where you can see the old Finnish military traditions carried out at the Reserve Officers' Academy. There's also a bulbous Orthodox church dating from 1837.

KOTKA: Only 6 miles (10 km) from Hamina, Kotka lies on the peninsula between the two eastern tributaries of the Kymi River and stretches farther over Kotka Island. The Russians built naval fortifications here that were destroyed when the Russian fleet was overwhelmed by English seapower during the Crimean War. The only building left after the battle was the Orthodox Church of St. Nicolaus, which still stands and houses a collection of valuable icons.

The Finnish town was built in 1878 without Russian aid and is now an industrial center and a major port. You can still get a taste of Imperial Russia if you visit the czar's fishing lodge (now a museum) at the Langinkoski Rapids. If you want more naval history, there's a motorboat to Varissaari Island, where you can review the Battle of Ruotsinsalmi (between the Russians and the Swedes) of 1790. You can examine the cannons and the salvaged ships and plot how you might have guided one fleet or the other more strategically than their admirals did.

PORVOO: Still farther west on the gulf and only 31 miles (50 km) east of Helsinki is Porvoo, the only Finnish city that still has an intact town plan from the 1700s. Porvoo's mercantile heritage goes back to the Middle Ages, when it was established as a trade center in 1346 by King Magnus Eriksson. It's got narrow winding streets, a town hall from 1764 in the middle of a quiet cobbled square, and an A-roofed cathedral built in 1418. The town's layout gives it a more southern European flavor, but the old pastel wooden houses and the brown and white wood detailing of the cathedral façade make it distinctly Scandinavian. Because of its style, Porvoo has always lured the more artistic and poetic Finns. You can visit the house (3 Aleksanterinkatu) where Finland's national poet, Johan Ludvig Runeberg, lived and worked. There's also an honorary residence for Swedish and Finnish poets called the Poet's House; it is easily confused with Runeberg's home but is actually an entirely different building near the cathedral. From this calm town, it's only a little more than a half-hour drive back to Helsinki.

BEST EN ROUTE

A double room in a good hotel in Finland costs $200 and up in those places classified as expensive. There are fancy places for less in the country, but not that much less — even in Lapland (tourism is one of its major industries), therefore a hotel in the moderate category will cost $110 and up; establishments in the inexpensive range will cost about $80 and up, but don't expect to find many of them. A first class meal in Helsinki, especially during the crayfish season, is at least $50 to $70, depending on drinks; again, we consider this expensive. Specialties in the smaller towns are less expensive; reindeer dishes are good, but usually expensive.

HÄMEENLINNA

Rantasipi Aulanko – This fancy hotel is next to a lake in a beautiful national park. There's a restaurant, a nightclub, a pool, and a beach, plus horses, golf, tennis, boats, bicycles, and whatever else you need for outdoor activities (phone: 917-29521). Expensive.

TAMPERE

Ilves – This 18-floor super-hotel in the center of town has 336 rooms, 5 restaurants, and a rooftop sauna with a view of the city. It is connected to a glassed-in mall complex with cinemas, cafés, shops, and a medical center. 1 Hatanpäänvaltatie (phone: 931-121212). Expensive.

Rosendahl – On the stately and beautiful Pyynikki Ridge, this luxurious hotel offers a variety of recreational activities. 13 Pyynikintie (phone: 931-112233). Expensive.

Pirkan Käpyhotelli – Recently opened and centrally located, this hotel is smaller than the others in the area. 6 Käpytie (no phone). Moderate.

KUOPIO

Rivoli – This hotel offers a wide range of services, including sporting facilities, Jacuzzis, winter gardens, and sophisticated dining. 1 Satamakatu (phone: 971-195111). Expensive.

JOENSUU

Kimmel – Here is a large but good hotel, with a nightclub and an excellent restaurant. 1 Itäranta (phone: 973-1771). Expensive.

NURMES

Bomban Talo – A huge, reconstructed Karelian "log castle," it has a good restaurant serving Karelian food. The rooms are in romantic log cottages with bath, phone, and TV sets. 1 Suojärvenkatu (phone: 976-22260). Moderate.

SAVONLINNA

Spa Hotel Casino – This pleasant, 79-room lake resort hotel has a private beach, tennis, boating, and other outdoor sports facilities. Kylpylaitoksentie, PB 60 (phone: 957-22864). Moderate.

MIKKELI

Varsavuori – Modern and comfortable, this hotel has a sauna, pool, and disco, as well as facilities for tennis, boating, skiing, and fishing. Kirkonvarkaus (phone: 955-367111). Moderate.

IMATRA

Imatran Valtionhotelli – An island hotel almost in the midst of the Imatra Rapids, it's actually a stone castle with big rooms and first class cuisine. 2 Torkkelinkatu (phone: 954-63244). Expensive.

LAPPEENRANTA

Lappee – Opened in 1984, this 211-room hotel is well known for its excellent fitness centers, sauna, and pool. 1 Brahenkatu (phone: 9-53-5861). Expensive.

PORVOO

Haikko Manor and Health Spa – This luxurious place has complete spa facilities and a restaurant serving good continental food. About 4 miles (6 km) from the middle of town (phone: 153133). Expensive.

Wanha Laamann – A visit to this restaurant in the heart of the old city is a must. Housed in a 2-story, 18th century complex, with a traditional menu of home cooking (on an open hearth), it will evoke memories of days gone by. 17 Wuorikatu (phone: 915-130455). Moderate.

TURKU

Hamburger Bors – This modern, efficient hotel is opposite the city square in the middle of town. Sauna and pool. 6 Kauppiaskatu (phone: 921-511211). Expensive.

Marina Palace – A luxury hotel on the Aura River, with all the amenities. 32 Linnankatu (phone: 921-336300). Expensive.

JYVÄSKYLÄ

Laajavuori Summer Hotel – Next to the *Sports Center,* which is active year-round. 2 Auvilankujä (phone: 941-251323 or 213269). Expensive.

Jyväaskylä – Centrally located around shops and most of Alvar Aalto's early buildings. Sauna 35 Kauppakatu (phone: 941-630211). Moderate.

Laajari Youth Hostel – A budget alternative for winter sports enthusiasts of all ages. 15 Laajavuorentie (phone: 941-253355). Inexpensive.

Lapland

Lapland is the great remaining wilderness of Finland. Covering the northern third of the country, almost all of it is above the Arctic Circle. This is truly the Land of the Midnight Sun, and in the northernmost town of Utsjoki, at the Norwegian border, there are 70 straight days of uninterrupted daylight that begin in mid-May. The Midnight Sun occurs between June and July. You must arrive in Rovaniemi, the capital of Lapland, and hope that there is no rain to make the normally magificent sunsets overcast. Otherwise, it is a memorable experience to be able to play golf, tennis, or take a hike after midnight. After a 50-day sunset, the sky gets dark at the end of November. The Northern Lights, which have been described as "nature's own light show," are often visible during November and December, but they are as elusive as shooting stars.

The roads across this wilderness run mainly north and south, with rather few connecting east-west arteries. The major routes have hard surfaces (blacktop or concrete) and are plowed regularly through the winter. You'll notice many warning signs for reindeer crossings — pay attention to them. In the dark, surprised reindeer, like deer in America, will often bolt directly into oncoming headlights. If you inadvertly hit a reindeer, you must inform the nearest police unit.

With the exception of its few urban centers, Lapland is a very sparsely populated area, with a density of only about 2 people per square kilometer. That leaves a lot of space for herds of roaming reindeer. You'll find fewer lakes here than in southern and central Finland, but there are many rivers, and between them are vast uninhabited areas. The topography varies greatly: low-lying swamps, river valleys with stands of pine and spruce, and regions of treeless tundra with an occasional scrub of birch on a low fell. (Fells are elevated plains that were left as high ground around gorges formed by retreating glaciers. The Lapp landscape is covered with these gently rounded, baretopped hills.)

Along the northern highways of Finland, many roadside stalls sell authentic Lapp souvenirs. There are about 4,000 Lapps here, and their population is diminishing. Much like the American Indian, they were shunted off to less civilized terrain as the more industrialized Scandinavians, Russians, and Finns came to Finland. The Lapps live off the reindeer, and they use almost every part of the beast for clothing and food. They prize the antlers and make them into sculpture, as whalers do with whalebone. Some 200,000 reindeer wander freely but are owned by 5,800 Lapp families, who depend on them entirely for their living. Reindeer roundups take place from September to January and are colorful events. The Lapps dress in their traditional blue, red, and yellow outfits and their embroidered "caps of the four winds."

The shortest way from Helsinki to Rovaniemi, the capital of Lapland, is Route E4 through Lahti, Jyväskylä, Oulu, and Kemi — almost 520 miles (837 km). And this is before the main Lapland route through Rovaniemi, Sodankylä, Inari, and Utsjoki — another 284 miles (458 km). The thing to do is to take one of the car-sleeper trains. From Helsinki they take 12 hours, but they let you and your car off perfectly rested at the beginning of the route. There are several daily runs, which take about 1¼ hours.

ROVANIEMI: Though people have lived at the confluence of the Kemi and Ounas rivers just south of the Arctic Circle since the Stone Age, the Nazis, on leaving, torched the city and left it looking like a cigarette stub in the Arctic snow. As a result, the "Gateway to Lapland" is an almost entirely new city, planned with meticulous and functional beauty by the Finnish architect Alvar Aalto. Since World War II, the population here has more than tripled. *Santa Claus Workshop* village on the Arctic Circle is worth visiting, no matter what your age. The shops sell handcrafts unique to the region; you can also pet reindeer and sit on Santa's lap. A tourist lodge is on top of Ounasvaara, an Arctic hill overlooking the town that offers a wonderful urban/ Arctic panorama. In town you can visit the *Lapland Provincial Museum* at the Lappia House and see the theater-congress building (11 Hallituskatu), designed by Aalto himself.

Rovaniemi is the administrative capital of Finnish Lapland as well as its most cosmopolitan city; consequently, it's the best place to sample a variety of Lapp delicacies. The dishes are usually based on local fish or game birds such as salmon, whitefish, ptarmigan, grouse, and capercaillie. There's also a wide variety of reindeer concoctions, such as reindeer stew, smoked reindeer, reindeer tongue, cutlets, steaks, and roasts. For dessert, try any of the cloudberry variations, often served over chewy Lapp cheese that has been warmed over a fire; afterward, a liqueur distilled from one of the native berries — bramble- or cranberry — is appropriate.

SODANKYLÄ: After an 80-mile (130-km) drive north through typical Lapland "fell" scenery (the roadbed curves between 1,640-foot hills) you reach the lively village of Sodankylä. Here is the oldest church in Lapland, an unpainted timber church in the middle of town.

Outside town you can stop at smaller villages, all of which are interesting. If it's July, hop south to Porttikoski and the annual lumberjacks' championships. Heading north, you pass between the two big artificial lakes of Lokka and Porttipahta on the way to Tankavaara, where you can actually pan for gold. If you don't want to get your feet wet, go to the *Gold Museum* for the history of the Finnish gold rush.

The scenery grows intensely beautiful as you pass wide fells and long vistas.

INARI: Not as much a town as a borough, Inari is classified as the Finnish city with the largest area. Of its 6,800 people, there are about 1,500 Lapps — or Sami, as they call themselves. Stretching to the northeast is the huge 50-mile-long Lake Inarinjärvi, with cold, exceptionally clear water and 3,000 islands.

At Inari village is the outdoor Sami museum (actually more preserve than museum, it covers almost 2,500 acres), with exhibitions of Sami history and examples of Sami dwellings and towns. In March there's a Lapland "rodeo," with reindeer races, lassoing, and relay skiing races. You can also take several different boat excursions on the lake.

UTSJOKI: As you continue driving north, you suddenly descend from the high fell plateau into the Teno River valley. This area used to be crowded with birch trees, but maggots feasted on them for years before anyone thought about conservation. The experts say it's too late to reforest, and the region is fast giving in to encroaching tundra.

Utsjoki is the only city in Finland where the Lapps outnumber the Finns. It's an outdoorsman's town, so don't expect too much in the way of creature comforts. Also, don't assume that just because it's above the Arctic Circle it's always freezing. During the summer, Utsjoki can be one of the hottest places in Europe. The fishing here is great, but if it's not one of your first loves, Utsjoki won't be either.

Travelers to Lapland need not be concerned with fallout from the Chernobyl disaster. The Finns have tested their food and reindeer products and they declare everything free of radiation.

BEST EN ROUTE

Lapland is a tourist area and therefore commands surprisingly high rates. An expensive room for two runs well over $100 per night, a moderate room will run from $80 to $100, and an expensive meal, between $40 and $60.

ROVANIEMI

Rantasipi Pohjanhovi – This is the city's most famous and traditional hotel. The restaurant is known all over the province and is generally crowded. It probably serves some of the best reindeer dishes in the world. In addition, the hotel offers a wide range of outdoor activities such as reindeer sleigh rides, snowmobiling, and fishing safaris. 2 Pohjanpuisto (phone: 960-313731). Expensive.

Polar – A fine business hotel in the city center. Excellent restaurant serves Lapp and continental delicacies. 23 Valtakatu (phone: 960-23751). Expensive to moderate.

Erämaamaja Karhunpesä – "The Bear's Den" is a charming log hideaway by the lake in the midst of unspoiled wilderness. Sauna; boats for fishing; snowmobiles. Approximately 20 miles (32 km) from Rovaniemi. Bookings should be made through the *Polar* hotel, 23 Valtakatu (phone: 960-23751). Moderate.

Ounasvaara – A family hotel on the top of Ounasvaara Hill, overlooking Rovaniemi. Cozy rooms with private saunas, and a panorama-view restaurant. Five downhill slopes and well-maintained cross-country ski tracks. 96400 Rovaniemi (phone: 960-23371). Moderate.

SODANKYLÄ

Kantakievari Luosto – Approximately 20 miles from Sodankylä, a large lodge built of Lapp timber. Excellent outdoor sporting facilities, and a good variety of programs. Kantakievari Luosto, PB 58, 99601 Sodankylä (phone: 969-313681). Expensive to moderate.

Kantakievari – This 53-room hotel has a restaurant with fine food, a bar, sauna, and pool, and a noteworthy variety of outdoor sports facilities. 15 Unarintie (phone: 909-693-21926). Moderate.

IVALO

Ivalo – A new hotel with modern comforts, an indoor pool, and gastronomic delights in the midst of the wilderness. Some 30 miles (50 km) before arriving at Inari. 34 Ivalontie (phone: 969-721911). Moderate.

UTSJOKI

Utsjoki – By the shores of a famous salmon-fishing river, this offers everything you came this far north to see. The restaurant has fresh salmon and reindeer dishes. 99980 Utsjoki (phone: 969-771121). Moderate.

France

Thomas Jefferson once said, "Every man has two countries — his own and France." The ideals of the French 18th-century Age of Enlightenment were embraced by the American founding fathers; in fact, Rousseau's theory of government by "social contract" formed the basis for the new kind of government boldly proposed in Jefferson's Declaration of Independence. The French inherited their love of reason from the Greeks and the Romans, and for many people, France represents an epitome of human achievement in 2,000 years of Western civilization. Paris is universally beloved as the City of Light, a leader in artistic and intellectual endeavors, and possibly the world's most beautiful city. Most significant, perhaps, has been the French talent for making art out of life. French food, wine, and fashion represent the ultimate in elegance, the perfection of civilized virtues.

To many, Paris is France. Almost 2.5 million of the nation's 53 million people live in the capital; Marseilles, which ranks second, has less than a million people; but neither Marseilles nor any other city can begin to compare with Paris's influence in French politics and culture. France is shaped like a star, with Paris at its heart. All roads and railroads lead to Paris, and anywhere else is regarded as provincial. Like the roads, the French Revolution radiated from Paris, and it is said that when Louis XIV made the mistake of building his palace at Versailles (only 12 mi/19 km outside Paris), he began to lose control over the entire country.

But visitors can hardly be expected to accept such a parochial view of national life. France, of course, is much more than Paris. It is the largest nation in Western Europe and a third larger than California, with an area of 211,208 square miles. To the delight of the French aesthetic sense of symmetry and balance, the country is shaped roughly like a hexagon, three sides bordering on land and three on water. It is a land blessed with great natural beauty and variety: southern sea and northern coast, high mountains and fertile valleys laced with rivers. The jagged Atlantic coastline of Normandy and Brittany forms its western border, and the sun-drenched bays and inlets of the Mediterranean lie to the southeast. The snow-covered Alps, which rise to the dramatic 15,771-foot peak of Mont-Blanc, form the Swiss and Italian borders to the east, and in the south, the high, rugged, olive-treed Pyrenees form a natural border with Spain. The gentle, pine-clad slopes of the Vosges are a continuation of Germany's Black Forest region to the northeast, and the fertile hills and valleys of Champagne and Burgundy are covered with priceless vineyards whose harvest is the source of the world's finest wines.

The French countryside is noted for its long stretches of straight, tree-lined roads, many of which date from Roman times. And although it is an industrial country, France is also a nation of many small privately owned farms. Its rural population comprises 25% of its total population. A visitor can often catch a glimpse of a plow being drawn by horses or oxen. Thus it is not difficult to understand why the French people regard the soil of their country with an attachment that amounts to reverence.

Not only is their land remarkably beautiful, it has been inhabited since prehistoric times. Wall paintings at Lascaux and in other caves in the Dordogne are probably 20,000 to 30,000 years old. When the Celts migrated to the land they called Gaul sometime before the 7th century BC, it was inhabited by Iberians and Ligurians. Greeks colonized the area around Marseilles — which they called Massilia, founding the oldest city in France — and Julius Caesar conquered Gaul for Rome in 57–52 BC. During the 5th century AD, Germanic tribes invaded, especially the Franks, who converted to Christianity under Clovis I and established the kingdom that became known as France.

A unified national spirit was born in France on Christmas Day, 800, when Charlemagne, King of the Franks, was crowned by the Pope in Rome as Holy Roman Emperor. Although Charlemagne's empire was short-lived, it left a lasting impression upon the French consciousness, even though the weakness of successive rulers allowed territorial princes, such as the Dukes of Burgundy and Normandy, to gain great power. In 987, however, the French nobility elected Hugh Capet King of France, and from this point, French national history is generally agreed to begin. Capet helped to centralize the monarchy, led in the Crusades and wars with England, and founded the Capetian dynasty. During the 12th and 13th centuries, trade flourished, craft guilds were established, and towns sprang up. Paris grew in importance as the royal city and as the intellectual center of Europe; the newly founded Sorbonne drew such teachers and philosophers as Abelard, Albertus Magnus, and Thomas Aquinas.

This time of peace was followed by the devastation and bloodshed of the Hundred Years War of 1337–1453 (the period covered by Barbara Tuchman's brilliant history, *A Distant Mirror*). Essentially a dynastic struggle with England, whose Norman kings held vast fiefs in France, this series of wars ended well for France, driving out the English and strengthening the power of the French monarchy. As in the days of Charlemagne, the French throne was once again endowed with a mystic aura, this time with the help of Joan of Arc, whose divine voices encouraged her to lead the French to victory at Orléans in 1429 and to champion Charles VII as King of France.

During the 16th and 17th centuries the Valois and Bourbon kings further increased the royal authority, moving the country toward absolute monarchy. The strong-armed rule of Cardinals Richelieu and Mazarin (1624–61) set the stage for their splendid successor, Louis XIV, whose reign was probably unequaled in the history of Europe for its elaborate and magnificent style. His attitude can be summarized in his famous remark, "L'état c'est moi" ("I am the state"). His was an age of brilliant achievements in art and literature, making France indisputably the intellectual capital of Europe. French became the international language for more than a century afterward. Frederick the Great of Prussia, who lived during the mid-18th century, spoke French, employed the French philosopher Voltaire as a tutor, and was rumored to have said that German was a language fit to be spoken only to horses and dogs.

The very magnificence of the French monarchy helped precipitate its downfall, for it was expensive to maintain and someone had to pay. The major cause of the French Revolution was the system of special privileges that exempted nobles and clergy from the taxes paid by the peasants and the middle class. In 1789, these latter groups rebelled against the monarchy in the person of Louis XVI, guillotined both the king and his queen, Marie Antoinette, and established the short-lived First Republic.

The chaos that followed the revolution resulted in the rise of Napoleon, who proclaimed himself emperor in 1804 and, though a dictator, undertook to spread the ideal of liberty to the world through his conquests. After his fall in 1814, the monarchy was restored. In the 19th century, France alternated between democracy and dictatorship and was characterized by the steady growth of a new French Empire (which disintegrated in the 20th century). A revolution in 1848 established a Second Republic, which was superseded by the dictatorship of Napoleon III, nephew of the emperor. Finally, a Third Republic emerged in 1870 that lasted until 1940, that saddest time in all French history when France capitulated to Nazi Germany. Between 1940 and 1945, the government was led by World War I hero Marshal Philippe Pétain, who, in collaboration with the Nazis, established a puppet government in Vichy in the South of France.

After World War II, the Fourth Republic was created; it collapsed in 1958 under the pressure of a revolution in Algeria. Although the Fifth Republic, engineered by Charles de Gaulle, has been threatened by the great number of political parties in France, it has managed to stand up in the face of such serious threats as the student revolt and general strike of May 1968.

The France of the past can, for the most part, still be seen today. The French preserve their old buildings well, be they the royal châteaux of Blois and Chambord in the Loire Valley or the magnificent cathedrals of Chartres and Reims. The landscapes of France are exciting, from the Pyrenees, the rugged mountains of southern France, and the snow-covered Alps farther north, to the luxuriant vegetation and posh villas of the sun-drenched Riviera on the Mediterranean coast, to the stark, chalk cliffs of Normandy's beaches. If you enjoy wine, you can tour the vineyards of Burgundy, Bordeaux, and Dordogne, and for food, every region of France has a different and highly developed style.

Our ten routes include Paris's weekend vacation land, a 50-mile radius called the Ile-de-France, extending north of the capital to Chantilly, west to Beauvais, and south to Chartres; it contains peaceful forests and valleys, châteaux and cathedrals. Paris itself is treated in detail in *Paris,* THE CITIES. From Paris you can also zigzag west into Normandy in the direction of Cherbourg, passing through green pastures and exploring the cheese industry, fashionable beaches, and busy harbors. Jutting out between the English Channel and the Bay of Biscay, Brittany's peninsula can be toured in a semicircular route from the magnificent shrine at Mont-St.-Michel west to Quimper and back east to the port of Nantes and its château. The Loire Valley, France's most splendid château country, extends east from Angers to Blois and includes some wine country as well. Two celebrated wine routes begin in the city of Bordeaux: The Dordogne lies east toward Rocamadour and Les Eyzies-de-Tayac, including fertile farmlands and prehistoric cave paintings, while Bordeaux runs north toward Pauillac and the fabled wine cellars of Lafite-Rothschild and Mouton-Rothschild.

Two of the most glorious areas in France, Provence and the Riviera, are adjacent to one another and can be seen together. Sunny Provence includes towns unmatched anywhere for their charm and beauty; they are set in the craggy mountains from Avignon southeast to Aix-en-Provence. Just south and west is the Riviera, stretching along the coast from Menton to St.-Tropez, a country beloved by modern painters like Picasso and Matisse for its dramatic cliffs overlooking the clear blue Mediterranean waters, its charming bays and fishing villages, its splendid villas and fashionable beaches.

Burgundy, yet another wine district, opens southward from Auxerre to Bourg-en-Bresse, passing through peaceful hills and valleys and ancient towns. Finally, there are the provinces of Alsace and Lorraine, with their strongly Germanic atmosphere and their beer as well as wine; when you travel east from Nancy to Strasbourg, it often seems that you're in Germany.

The Ile-de-France

The first thing you should know about the "island of France" (Ile-de-France) is that it is not an island. It is, in fact, the region surrounding Paris, and the name "Ile" comes from the rivers that form its boundaries: the Epte, the Aisne, the Marne, the Yonne, and the Eure, with the Seine and the Oise also running through the territory. Don't look for it on a map, though: legally, the region doesn't exist. Its population can't be counted, and neither train nor bus schedule knows it by name.

The Ile-de-France, extending around the city to a radius of roughly 50 miles (80 km), offers something for every visitor. Through this area traveled Charlemagne, St. Louis, Joan of Arc, Louis XIV and all the Kings of France, not to mention Emperor Napoleon, leaving memorials of their passing. The art lover is drawn to the magnificent cathedrals, beautifully preserved medieval abbeys, and sumptuous châteaux — architecture and design unparalleled anywhere else in France. For the nature enthusiast or the weary city dweller, the Ile-de-France has peaceful valleys, forests, and wildlife.

We suggest you make Paris your base for forays into the region. Every site on the route makes a comfortable day trip or can be combined with other stops to fill out a weekend jaunt. To strangers, Paris — the City of Light — can seem rather dark on Sundays and Mondays, when many shops and restaurants are closed. These are ideal days to visit this nearby countryside.

Telephone numbers in the Ile-de-France are dialed as Paris numbers, requiring no additional prefix when dialed from Paris and needing a 1 when dialed from outside Paris or France. Other numbers in this chapter fall outside the official Ile de France boundaries, and may need to be preceded by the prefix 16 when dialing from Paris.

CHANTILLY: Only 25 miles (40 km) from Paris via N16, Chantilly is famous for its château, its parks, and, of course, the racetrack. Five different châteaux have existed on this site in the last 2,000 years, but the present one was built only between 1875 and 1881 at the direction of the duke of Aumale, a son of King Louis-Philippe. The château is small by French standards but exceptionally elegant. Inside is an excellent museum with over 2,000 artworks, including more than 600 oils by French, Flemish, and Italian masters of the 16th to 18th centuries. Also visit the library, with its prodigious collection of rare books; the 18th-century stables; and the chapel, where, to this day, the descendants of the last owner gather for Sunday services. Take time as well to wander through the gardens and the extensive forest which was a favorite hunting ground of the kings and nobles of France for 5 centuries.

En Route from Chantilly – A few miles southwest, taking D118 to D909, you'll come to Royaumont, one of the best-preserved medieval abbeys in France. Royaumont was founded by St. Louis in 1228, and the wealth and beauty that are still apparent attest to the protection lavished on it by successive Kings of France.

St.-Leu-d'Esserent lies 3 miles (4.8 km) northwest of Chantilly via N16 to D44. Its mellow and beautiful 12th-century stone church is renowned for its architectural excellence on a commanding site overlooking the Oise.

Route N924 east leads to the charming town of Senlis, dominated by the Ancienne Cathédrale de Notre-Dame (Pl. Notre Dame), begun in 1153. Of particular interest is the portico, dedicated to the Virgin and the prototype for the porticoes of Chartres, Notre-Dame-de-Paris, and Reims. Also well worth a visit are the ancient church of St.-Pierre (Pl. St.-Pierre), the Château Royal (for its Gallo-Roman walkway), and the hunting museum (*Musée de la Vénerie*) in front of the château. The Gallo-Roman walkway, a defense wall around the chateau's perimeter, provides a good vantage point from which to view the principal monuments.

At Chaalis (7 mi/11.3 km south via N330) are the picturesque ruins of a 13th-century abbey and, in the park, yet another château in addition to a museum that has three rooms devoted to the works of Jean-Jacques Rousseau, who died in nearby Ermenonville in 1778. You can also enjoy the countryside: There are numerous ponds, the famous Mer de Sable (Sea of Sand), and a small zoo at Ermenonville, 2 miles (3.2 km) south on N330.

COMPIÈGNE: On the banks of the Oise, 49 miles (78.4 km) north of Paris via N17, is this village, justly famous for its palace (Pl. du Palais). The palace's exterior is somewhat austere, but the exquisite interior decoration is beautifully preserved.

Compiègne has played a significant role in French history: Most of the Kings of France visited the town at one time or another, and Joan of Arc was taken prisoner here in 1430. In more recent conflicts, the armistices of November 11, 1918, and June 22, 1940, were signed here (the exact site is marked in a clearing — Clairière de l'Armistice — in the woods surrounding the palace). In a sad footnote, from 1941 to 1944, Compiègne served as a deportation center for France's Jewish community en route to concentration camps.

The forest of Compiègne, with nearly 35,000 acres, has majestic avenues, pools (Etangs de St.-Pierre), and picturesque villages, such as Vieux-Moulin and St.-Jean-aux-Bois. Just beyond the forest, via D85, is the splendid 12th-century château-fortress of Pierrefonds, once the property of Napoleon.

BEAUVAIS: About 45 miles (72 km) from Paris via A15 and D927 lies Beauvais. Although the city is in one of the less attractive parts of the Ile-de-France, a visit to the imposing Cathédrale St.-Pierre makes the trip worthwhile.

The cathedral, whose Gothic style is in rather jarring contrast to that of the rest of the city, has had an erratic history, plagued by overambition and underfinancing. The soaring choir section, begun in 1247, was a challenge to architects throughout Europe. Unfortunately, they proved unequal to the challenge, and in 1284 the choir collapsed. In 1500, another generation of bishops decided to continue the work and undertook to finance it by the expedient sale of indulgences. But again the architects literally let

Beauvais down: An experimental cross tower was constructed, but the supporting pillars gave way in 1573. Since then, the cathedral of Beauvais has remained a magnificent — but unfinished — monument.

The vaulted interior of the cathedral appears to rise to dizzying heights. The well-preserved stained glass windows give a luminous light that serves to illuminate the church's magnificent tapestries, attesting to the city's renown as a center of weaving.

Before leaving the city, look also at the Eglise St.-Etienne (Rue de l'Etamine and Rue de l'Infanterie). The stained glass of the choir section is among the most beautiful of the Renaissance.

En Route from Beauvais – Heading south toward Paris, take a detour west on D981 and D181 until you reach the town of Vernon. Nearby you'll find Giverny, the home of impressionist painter Claude Monet from 1883 until his death in 1926. Forty years after Monet died, his home and its gardens were given to the Academy of Beaux-Arts by his son, but they did not open to the public until 1980, after painstaking restoration of the grounds and structures according to Monet's many canvases of the place. Visitors can stroll through the exquisite flower-strewn French gardens and, across the road, the Oriental garden with its familiar Japanese bridge and lily pond, so often painted by Monet. The pink farmhouse and Monet's studio can also be visited. Open daily except Mondays from April to November 1.

From Giverny, take N15 and N13 to St. Germain-en-Laye (from Paris, it's 13 mi/21 km west on N13). This former home of kings is today a favorite weekend retreat for Parisians. Its château was begun in the 12th century, but completely rebuilt in the 16th to bring it up to Renaissance standards. Two floors are occupied by the *Musée des Antiquités Nationales,* with displays of ceramics, glass, and jewelry through the time of Charlemagne. The gardens and terraces are splendid, and the extensive forest surrounding the town offers all manner of recreational activities. The restaurants here include the well-regarded *Cazaudehore,* in the inn *La Forestière* (see *Best en Route*).

Continue west on N13 until you reach the château of Malmaison, bought by Napoleon as a gift to Josephine in 1799 and the place where she settled after her divorce in 1809. It's now a museum with many impressive artworks of the Napoleonic period, some of the house's original furnishings, and documents and mementos of battle tracing the era's history.

Return east on the N13 to N186. Following it south, you pass the most famous palace in all of France: Versailles, the crowning glory of Louis XIV. You will certainly want to stop here — and allow plenty of time; the palace and gardens are immense!

VERSAILLES: The building of this incredibly lavish palace nearly bankrupted the French monarchy. About 6,000 people once lived in the palace, and its vast gardens, designed by the famous royal gardener Le Nôtre in the formal French style, are spread out over 250 acres. A river was diverted to keep the 600 fountains flowing.

There is so much to see in Versailles that you might even want to spend more than 1 day here. On Sundays from May to October you can see the fountains illuminated in a splendid Grandes Eaux Musicales concert several times a day. On alternating Saturday evenings in July, August, and September, the *fête de nuit,* a striking sound and light show, is presented. Check with the Versailles Tourist Office, 7 Rue des Reservoirs (phone: 39-50-36-22), for exact dates and times.

The highlights include the Royal Apartments, the Chapel, and the Hall of Mirrors. Don't miss the gardens and some of the smaller buildings on the grounds, including the Grand Trianon and the Petit Trianon, smaller retreats for kings, queens, and royal mistresses; and Le Hameau, Marie Antoinette's model farm, where she and her companions pretended to be shepherds. New attractions include the recently opened apartments of the Dauphin and the Dauphine, which may be seen Tuesdays through Fridays; on Tuesdays and Fridays, there are guided tours in several languages, including English. Information about Versailles is available from the Versailles Tourist Office (see above).

En Route from Versailles – Just south of Versailles via D91, you enter an area that many Frenchmen consider the prettiest countryside in the Ile-de-France — the Vallée de Chevreuse. Picturesque villages abound: Châteaufort, with its 12th-century fortress; St.-Rémy-lès-Chevreuse; St.-Lambert; Dampierre, the site of a 16th-century château; and Les Vaux de Cernay, one of the loveliest valleys in France. Just south of Les Vaux de Cernay on N306 is Rambouillet, the château that served as a rural retreat for Louis XVI and Napoleon, and is still used today by President François Mitterrand. Originally a medieval fortress, it retains its impressive 14th-century tower. You can tour the château whenever President Mitterrand is away (which is often). From here, take N306 and then N10 straight to Chartres.

CHARTRES: Even though you may think you've seen enough cathedrals for a lifetime, Chartres remains a must. About 50 miles (80 km) southwest of Paris via D988 and N10, Chartres is without doubt the jewel of medieval cathedrals. The Portail Royal, portraying Christ in triumph, is one of the finest examples of French religious art. And Chartres is known above all for its stained glass windows. Dating mostly from the 12th and 13th centuries, with later replacements made from the original designs, they are considered the most beautiful in France, a country where exquisite stained glass has been preserved in remarkable quantity.

The city of Chartres, dotted with ancient gabled houses and charming corners, lives up to the beauty of the cathedral. Walk along the path from the cathedral to the St.-André church, for example, or, behind the bishopric, take the Tertre-St.-Nicholas down to the River Eure with its series of bridges. As you head back toward the cathedral, wander along Rue Chantault, Rue aux Herbes, Rue de la Petite Cordonnerie, and the Place de la Poissonnerie, where curious old houses give one a sense of the medieval city come alive. The museum of Chartres (right behind the cathedral) houses some paintings and sculptures by the Fauvist artist Maurice Vlaminck.

En Route from Chartres – If you reached Chartres via Versailles and have already seen the sights there, you'll find little of interest on the road directly back to Paris. But if you've time for a detour east, you'll enter into the region of Fontainebleau, where there's plenty to see and do (from Chartres take D24 to N837; from Paris take N7 south).

FONTAINEBLEAU: Surrounding the fabulous Renaissance palace is a forest of 50,000 acres, the ancient hunting preserve of the Kings of France. Today, the grounds are open to the public, and picnicking, hiking, or horseback riding among the trees, ravines, and ponds makes a perfect counterpoint to a day of city sightseeing.

The palace itself was transformed from a 12th-century medieval château to a Renaissance palace by Francis I during the early 16th century. Later kings added further alterations and wings, including Napoleon, who lived here during most of his reign. Many people find Fontainebleau more beautiful than Versailles. It's open daily except Tuesdays for a fee, and there's a guided tour through the Throne Room, the Queen's Bedroom, which was redone for Marie-Antoinette, the splendid Royal Apartments with their Gobelin tapestries, the Council Room, and the Red Room, where Napoleon abdicated in 1814.

En Route from Fontainebleau – Just on the edge of the forest lies Barbizon, made famous as an artists and writers colony in the 19th century by the likes of Daumier, Troyon, Musset, and George Sand. You can visit Rousseau's house on the Grand Rue, just behind the Monument aux Morts, and you can stop for a drink at the celebrated *Bas-Bréau,* an elegant second home to many Parisians (see *Best en Route*).

Taking N5 out of Fontainebleau, you'll pass by the ruins of the ancient Abbaye-du-Lys. The next important landmark is Vaux-le-Vicomte, whose 17th-century château and gardens are among the most beautiful in Europe. The château was commissioned by Fouquet, an important government official under Louis XIV. Unfortunately, Fouquet's exquisite taste required greater resources than his personal fortune could accommodate, and access to state funds was all too simple. To build Vaux-le-Vicomte, Fouquet hired the greatest talents of the day: Le Vau as architect, Le Brun as decorator, Le Nôtre as landscape architect. Employing a total of 18,000 laborers, the work was finished 5 years and the equivalent of $10 million later. But Fouquet had committed the fatal error of being grander than his sovereign. In August 1661, he gave a fabulous dinner for Louis XIV. The decoration, the food, and the entertainment were so dazzlingly elegant that they provoked the king's jealous curiosity, and in no time Fouquet's embezzlement was exposed. A few days later, Fouquet was in prison and his property confiscated. But the château had lit a spark in the king's imagination, and Louis XIV employed the same team to build his own dream palace at Versailles, the site of his father's hunting lodge. Many of the splendidly decorated rooms of Vaux-le-Vicomte are open to the public from late March through October.

A 30-mile (48-km) drive along the valley of the Seine (N5) returns you to Paris.

BEST EN ROUTE

Because of their close proximity to Paris, country inns in the Ile-de-France tend to have city prices. Reservations are almost always required. Expect to pay $90 and up per night for a double room in hotels listed as expensive; $50 to $90 in those listed as moderate; and $25 to $50, inexpensive. The restaurants range in price from $90 and up for a dinner for two in the expensive range; $40 to $75 in the moderate range; and below $40, inexpensive.

CHANTILLY

Relais Condé – Small and bright, with a beamed ceiling and huge stone fireplace, this restaurant serves classic cuisine. 42 Av. du Maréchal-Joffre (phone: 44-57-05-75). Moderate.

LYS-CHANTILLY

du Lys – This modest hotel is in a calm, beautiful park. Av. Septième (phone: 44-21-26-19). Moderate.

TOUTEVOIE

Pavillon St.-Hubert – A small hotel in a relaxing setting overlooking a placid pond (phone: 44-57-07-04). Inexpensive.

ST.-JEAN-AUX-BOIS

La Bonne Idée – Fine restaurant in a peaceful setting; 15 rooms available. Royer (phone: 44-42-84-09). Moderate.

BEAUVAIS

L'Esturgeon – Sturgeon are off the menu of this restaurant (they no longer frequent the Seine), but diners can get a good *coulibiac* of salmon, the house specialty. Closed Thursdays and August. 17 miles (26 km) northwest of Paris via N190, at 6 Cours du 14-Juillet, Poissy (phone: 1-39-79-19-94 or 1-39-65-00-04). Expensive.

Mercure Beauvais – Comfortable hotel with modern facilities and outdoor pool. Av. Montaigne, ZAC Quartier St.-Lazare (phone: 44-02-03-36). Moderate.

WARLUIS

Alpes Franco-Suisse – A modest hotel in a wonderful country setting, with modern facilities and swimming. Closed for 1 week in August. Rte. Nationale 1 (phone: 44-89-26-51). Moderate to inexpensive.

ST.-GERMAIN-EN-LAYE

Le Forestière – This charming country inn with lovely gardens is a comfortable place for an overnight stay, but many visit simply for its *Cazaudehore* restaurant, which serves classical cuisine as well as several Basque specialties such as *pipérade* (eggs cooked with peppers, ham, and hot sausage). Closed Mondays. 1 Av. Président-Kennedy (phone: 39-73-36-60). Expensive.

Pavillon Henri IV – An old-fashioned hotel with plush accommodations and a pleasant restaurant (where sauce béarnaise was invented) overlooking the gardens of the château. 21 Rue Thiers (phone: 34-51-62-62). Expensive.

VERSAILLES

Trois Marches – Warm, intimate decor, charming service, and highly original cooking mark this celebrated restaurant. Chef Gérard Vié invents new recipes daily, but his foie gras is famous, as are his oysters and his wild goose. The wines here, especially the Burgundies, are excellent, too. Closed Sundays and Mondays. 3 Rue Colbert (phone: 39-50-13-21). Expensive.

VÉSINET

Les Ibis – In a large park in an attractive residential area, the restaurant offers good food and a warm atmosphere. The rooms are simple but comfortable. Ile du Grand Lac (phone: 1-39-52-17-41)./ Moderate.

ORGEVAL

Auberge Morainvilliurs – Formerly the *Auberge Provençale,* this attractive country inn and restuarant set in private gardens was taken over by new owners in 1988. Take N13 and D198 from St. Germain-en-Laye (phone: 39-75-7-57). Expensive to moderate.

BOUGIVAL

Coq Hardy – This superb restaurant has elegant country decor and a reputation as host to many of France's VIPs. Closed Tuesday evenings and all day Wednesdays. 16 Quai Rennequin-Sualem (Rte. N13) (phone: 1-39-69-01-43). Expensive.

CHARTRES

La Vieille Maison – Elegant dining in an old house near the cathedral. Meals feature the freshest local produce. Closed Sunday evenings and Mondays. 5 Rue au Lait (phone: 37-34-10-67). Expensive.

Grand Monarque – The town's fanciest hotel, which sports a good restaurant serving nouvelle and classic cuisine and a popular bar. The lobby and dining room have recently been redecorated; 11 modern, elegant rooms have been added as well as new meeting rooms and a winter garden. 22 Pl. des Epars (phone: 37-21-00-72). Hotel, moderate; restaurant, expensive.

Le Biniou – An unpretentious Breton *crêperie* that serves up everything on a pancake, using such imaginative ingredients as fried onions, scrambled eggs, and fresh cream for the savory versions and Calvados and apple compote for the sweet ones. Taped music featuring the Breton bagpipe that give the restaurant its name provides the background. Closed Tuesdays and Wednesdays. 7 Rue Serpente (phone: 37-21-53-12). Inexpensive.

Boeuf Couronné – Half of the 26 spotless rooms here look over at the cathedral. There is a bar and outside terraces and a recently renovated restaurant that serves local specialties with a reasonably priced menu. 15 Pl. du Châtelet (phone: 37-21-11-26). Inexpensive.

BARBIZON

Bas-Bréau – An elegant hotel that has welcomed well-heeled Parisians and celebrities since 1867. It has an intimate bar and a truly fine restaurant. A member of the Relais & Châteaux. Closed most of January and February. 22 Rue Grande (phone: 60-66-40-05). Very expensive.

Normandy

Settled by successive waves of Celts, Gauls, and Britons, Normandy was the target of the Roman invasion in 56 BC. In the 9th century AD, the Vikings (north men, hence Normans) sailed from Scandinavia in their longboats — massacring, looting, burning, and taking possession of the land. Finally, in 911, the astute King Charles the Simple (whose name means "honest and straightforward" rather than "feeble-minded") and the Viking leader Rollo agreed to a truce, the terms of which granted to the "Normans on the Seine" the lands they already occupied in exchange for a permanent peace. Thus the duchy of Normandy was founded, and Rollo — later baptized Robert — was its first duke.

The erstwhile pirates proved to be adept both as farmers and as administrators in the rich and fertile valley of the Seine, and a prosperous, civilized state began to flourish within a century. The turbulent Norse blood rose one more time, however, when in 1066 William the Bastard, a direct — if left-handed — descendant of Rollo/Robert was thwarted by the Englishman Harold Godwinson in his claim to the throne of England on the death of Edward the Confessor. William enlisted the Pope to his cause and, by September, was able to set sail for England with 12,000 men in almost 3,000 vessels. The English resistance was fierce, but on October 14, Harold lay dead on the battlefield near Hastings "with an arrow in his eye," and William — now no longer the Bastard but the Conqueror — was crowned King of England in Westminster Abbey on Christmas Day. A remarkable, graphic record of the conquest is preserved in the Bayeux tapestry across from the Bayeux cathedral. Nine hundred years later, an invasion in the opposite direction was accomplished with equal success at the beaches on the coast of Calvados.

The landscape of Normandy is graced by a wealth of historic buildings that reflect the affluence and expansive generosity of the Norman people. Churches, abbeys, castles, and manor houses abound in styles that exemplify the finest of the last 10 centuries of European architecture. The materials for these buildings were delved from the land that supports them: soft, chalky stone in Rouen and the towns bordering the Seine; harder, fine-grained limestone around Caen. The simpler, half-timbered farmhouses and cottages of lower Normandy are typically constructed of whitewashed clay rammed between dark-stained lathes and topped with intricately woven thatch. In the

Suisse Normande, an Alpine character is suggested by shale-covered cottages clustered against the hillsides. Sandstone and granite lend an austere effect to the time-weathered buildings of the Bocage and the Cotentin.

The seaside diversions of the Normandy coast range from the sophisticated glamour of the international resort of Deauville to the long, sandy stretches of Arromanches and Omaha (a name used only since the Allied landing of D-day, June 6, 1944; the three beaches comprising Omaha were formerly called St.-Laurent, Colleville, and Vierville-sur-Mer). The hinterland offers grassy plateaus and undulating valleys threaded with freshwater streams.

The rolling green pastures of Normandy sustain horses ranging in size and temperament from spirited thoroughbreds to the massive Percheron draft-horses. Thousands of acres are given over to raising apples and flax. Most important, goats and sheep are raised for the cheese-making industry, for Normandy is the dairy of France. Norman cheeses such as Camembert and Pont l'Evêque are renowned the world over.

The cream of Normandy — like liquid ivory — complements the fine fish, vegetables, fruit, and game of the region, and for true Normans, of course, cider — *bon bère* — accompanies hearty dinners of regional specialties such as *tripes à la mode de Caen, présalé* lamb from the salt marshes, or duck from Rouen. A pause is customarily taken in the middle of the Norman meal for the *trou Normand* — a quick gulp of the fiery Calvados, applejack distilled from cider and aged for as long as 12 years to achieve a perfect fullness of flavor. An apple tart with cream is a memorable finish to any meal in Normandy.

Since the end of World War II, the Seine Valley and the Caen area have undergone dramatic industrial development. New industries such as motor vehicle assembly and oil refining have drawn workers away from the traditional Norman crafts of tanning and coppersmithing. The old *métiers* still survive on a reduced scale, however, and latter-day planners and developers have preserved — and often restored — the historic monuments and natural features of the landscape.

The arts have enjoyed a long and distinguished tradition in Normandy. The agonies suffered by France during the Hundred Years War inspired Olivier Basselin, a weaver from Les-Vaux-de-Vire, to write songs so spirited and timely that, although the songs themselves eventually passed from common currency, the name by which they were collectively known evolved from its original form to "vaudeville," passing out of the French language into English. Corneille, Flaubert, and Maupassant, among others, were natives of Normandy; Victor Hugo, although not a Norman, is inextricably bound to the province through his moving *Les Contemplations,* in which he mourns the tragic deaths by drowning of his daughter Léopoldine and her husband in the Norman village of Villequier in 1843. The village today is marked by a statue and a museum honoring the author. The luminous skies and delicate tints of the Norman countryside attracted the group of mid-19th-century painters who, in prefiguring the Impressionists, became known as the Barbizon School, after the village in the forest of Fontainebleau. A few years later, the Impressionists — Monet, Renoir, the Englishman Sisley, and others — in turn took their inspiration from the light of Normandy. In the early 20th century, the province was a magnet for some of the finest painters of the period — Valloton, Van Dongen, and Dufy.

Only a half-day's drive from Paris, Normandy has beckoned tourists for generations, and its innkeepers and restaurateurs have maintained a tradition of comfort and hospitality at reasonable prices. The chic terrace cafés of Deauville and other coastal towns are full of Parisian weekenders and vacationers from May to September. Well-organized Syndicats d'Initiative (tourist offices) in the smaller towns will supply all the information you need to enjoy the countryside and its seasonal specialties.

You can drive to Normandy from any point in France, but since most visitors come from Paris, we'll give the quickest route from that direction: Take Autoroute A13 (Autoroute de Normandie) as far as the Chaufour exit, about 48 miles (77 km) from Paris. Then join route N13 for about 6 miles (10 km) to Pacy-sur-Eure; you're in Normandy.

PACY-SUR-EURE: Pacy is the commercial and service center both for residents and for Parisians with country homes in the area. The Gothic church of St.-Aubin, remodeled in the 16th century, is worth a quick visit, and don't miss the well-known restaurant *Mère Corbeau.*

En Route from Pacy-sur-Eure – Autoroute N13 toward Evreux takes you 22 miles (35.2 km) across the flat plateau of St.-André-de-l'Eure, which is strongly reminiscent of the plain of Beauce surrounding Chartres. Wheat and corn are the principal crops in this area of comfortable, conservative farmers.

About 4 miles (6 km) on the right before Evreux you'll see an air force base, built by the US after World War II and turned over to France in 1965. Signs reading Centreville lead you off N13 and into Evreux along the Rue F.-D.-Roosevelt.

EVREUX: The religious and commercial capital of the Eure is a charming, typically Norman town too often neglected by travelers. The town has existed since Gallic times and has survived sacking and pillage by Vandals, Normans, English, and even fellow French. Evreux suffered heavy damage in the 1944 bombings, with the result that today its architecture is a medley of the very new cheek by jowl with ancient Norman half-timbered houses. Rue Chartraine, the main shopping street, is lined with elegant shops offering the products of local craftspeople. The many cafés are an important focus for business discussions and general "catching up" on market days.

If you park in the Cathedral of Notre Dame parking lot, you're in an excellent position to begin a walk at the foot of the Gallo-Roman ramparts along the Iton River, past the elegant 15th-century clock tower. The cathedral itself is a superb example of Gothic construction, with the earliest parts dating from the 12th century. English-language guides are available. In the former Bishop's House not far from the cathedral is a museum with displays of prehistoric and Gallo-Roman archaeology and artifacts of medieval Normandy.

En Route from Evreux – Taking N13 toward Lisieux leads you through the richest cultivated land south of the Seine, dotted here and there with picturesque country churches. At the intersection of N13 and D840, turn right for Neubourg, a pleasant rural town with a lively marketplace. At the market, turn left to enter D137. After about 6 miles (10 km) you come to Champ de Bataille, an imposing 17th-century mansion. A guided tour is well worth the 45 minutes, especially for art lovers, who will admire the fine paintings by Drouais, Van Loo, and Fragonard, among others, as well as sculpture by Canova, Lemoyne, and Pigalle.

Now you are in the heart of the region, the Normandy of legend. Drive carefully, keeping an eye out for the farmers who lead their herds back to the barns for milking in the late afternoon. Continue on D137 toward Brionne, once a medieval stronghold and now a living museum. From Brionne, N138 will take you on one of the most beautiful routes in France to the city of Rouen. Allow time to stop on the way, for every village is a gem. You should be prepared to spend at least a night and half a day in the picturesque and historic city of Rouen.

ROUEN: Though famous as the scene of the disgraceful trial and execution of Joan of Arc, quite independently of "the Maid," Rouen is renowned as a treasury of medieval architecture — the City of 100 Steeples. The capital of upper Normandy, Rouen has kept its ancient character, with houses dating from the 15th century still inhabited on narrow streets. The Syndicat d'Initiative (25 Pl. Cathédrale) can provide detailed tourist information in English. Be sure to see Rouen Cathedral, a fine Gothic structure built in the 11th and 12th centuries. Walk along the renowned Rue du Gros-Horloge (Street of the Great Clock), whose enormous clock is the best-known monument in the city. Two blocks away is the Place du Vieux-Marché (Old Marketplace), where Joan of Arc was burned at the stake in 1431. She is publicly commemorated at the site on the last Sunday of every May.

Small shops in Rouen sell original drawings and paintings and the distinctive blue and white Rouen ceramics.

To reach the coast at Dieppe, take N27 north for 36 miles (58 km) through the Caux Plateau, a rich agricultural region.

DIEPPE: This ancient port has lost only a little of its character to the efficient modern harbor that has turned Dieppe into the largest passenger port in France. Today the traffic through the harbor is likely to consist of fishing vessels or private boats, but in the 16th century the city was a major point of embarkation for explorers, privateers, and merchant ships.

A stroll through old Dieppe is a little like opening a history book tracing ten centuries of development. In the middle of the Fish Market is the ancient Place du Puits Sale (Square of the Salty Well), a major crossroads. The Church of St. James was begun in the 13th century and has portions from the succeeding three centuries, and Dieppe Castle, built for the most part in the 15th century, was constructed around a much earlier tower fortification.

The beach along Maréchal Foch, at the foot of the castle, is extremely popular.

En Route from Dieppe – Travel along D75 and D79 via Fécamp toward Etretat. The road offers breathtaking views of the cliffs of the Côte d'Albâtre (Alabaster Coast). Fécamp is worth a stop for its typical Norman architecture and equally traditional ivory handicrafts. From Fécamp to Etretat, take D11, a pretty drive through the countryside, which alternates between dairy land and high cliffs.

ETRETAT: Etretat is famous for its high cliffs, which inspired many Impressionist painters, including Monet and Boudin. An 11th- and 12th-century church and a reconstructed market add charm and character to the town.

A drive via D910, N810, the Tancaxuitte Bridge, and Autoroute A1 takes you to the famous seaside resort of Deauville.

DEAUVILLE: This beautiful and elegant northern counterpart to St.-Tropez on the Riviera has all the accoutrements of a fashionable resort, complete with casino, lovely sailing harbor, and horse racing. Deauville life is marked by the activity on the boardwalk that runs the length of the beach. (Avoid the restaurants on the promenade, which are overpriced for the quality.) Hotels and restaurants here are very expensive, so we recommend that you spend the night at Honfleur, only 20 minutes away. Trouville is Deauville's twin city and a fishing town, where at sunset you can watch the fishermen bringing in the day's catch. An evening stroll along the harbor is lovely.

En Route from Deauville – The drive from Deauville-Trouville to Honfleur takes you along the Normandy Corniche, with breathtaking views of the sea. Take

N834 through Trouville, past Touques, and into D288. At the David crossroads, bear left onto D279 for Honfleur.

HONFLEUR: Honfleur is a tiny, perfectly preserved old fishing harbor, with many monuments dating as far back as the 13th century. Honfleur was the base for the 17th-century voyages of discovery that led to the settlement of the most important French colonies, including Canada and Louisiana.

A 45-minute drive along A13 takes you to Caen.

CAEN: As the capital of lower Normandy, Caen is the region's agricultural and industrial center. Extensively damaged by World War II, Caen has been rebuilt with the traditional limestone to modern, urban plans.

Few monuments survived the 1944 shellings, but among those undamaged were the twin Abbaye aux Hommes and Abbaye aux Dames — reparation offerings of William the Conqueror and his wife, Queen Matilda. Restorations were carried out in the 17th century to replace areas damaged in the Wars of Religion.

In June 1988, the *Museum of Peace* opened in Caen. Its exhibits emphasize not the military victories but the sufferings of war. (Bd. Montgomery; phone: 31-06-06-44).

A "must" for gourmands is the local specialty: *tripes à la mode de Caen.*

Less than 20 minutes away on N13 lies Bayeux, another town intimately connected with William and his consort.

BAYEUX: This was the first town liberated after D-day. The Gothic cathedral, built in the 11th century, is well worth a visit to see the extraordinary Bayeux tapestry, which presents a blow-by-blow account of the decisive Battle of Hastings. (Recorded English-language tours are available daily except Christmas.)

To reach the historic D-day shore of Arromanches, take a 15-minute drive on D156.

ARROMANCHES: "If we want to land, we must take our harbors with us." With these words, the historic decision was taken to build artificial harbors for the D-day landing. Some parts of the harbor foundation built by the Allies can still be seen. The invasion museum provides an English-language commentary on the events of 1944.

En Route from Arromanches – The American Military Cemetery is about 1½ miles (3 km) beyond Colleville-sur-Mer (Omaha). A memorial fountain stands in front of the monument, surrounded by trees. The site commands an impressive view of the sea.

From the cemetery, take N13 to Cherbourg for the night.

CHERBOURG: When still a naval base, Cherbourg was an important harbor during World War II. The *War and Liberation Museum* illustrates the progress of the war from the Allied landing on D-day right up to the German capitulation in May 1945. Technically speaking, Normandy ends with Cherbourg, although your visit is not complete without seeing the monastery of Mont-St.-Michel, the romantic and beautiful peak that has been a source of dispute between Normandy and Brittany for centuries.

The drive from Cherbourg to Mont-St.-Michel — via D900, D971, and D973 — takes 2½ hours.

MONT-ST.-MICHEL: Atop soaring cliffs that rise from a flat, sandy marsh, the abbey of Mont-St.-Michel dates back to the 8th century, when it is said that the Archangel Michael appeared and commanded that a church be built on the spot. The archangel's footprint — admittedly vague in outline — is still shown to visitors. To tour the abbey, leave your car in one of the official parking lots and enter on foot through the outer gate of the ramparts. Don't miss the Lacework Staircase (Escalier de Dentelle), the superb Gothic buildings (Merveille), and the cloister, which seems suspended between sky and sea. The view from the North Tower is especially dramatic.

BEST EN ROUTE

Expect to pay $100 and up per night for a double room listed as expensive; $40 to $75 in those listed as moderate; and less than $40, inexpensive. Note that hotels in Deauville are very expensive in July and August, often charging closer to $150 for a double room, and in any season, all along the Norman coast, a sea view can add $30 or more to a room's price. The restaurants range in price from $100 and up for a dinner for two in the expensive range; $60 to $100 in the moderate range; and less than $60, inexpensive. Prices do not include wine or tips.

EVREUX

Normandy – Just off the main street and recently restored as a fine example of the best of Norman hospitality. Good restaurant features local specialties. Closed Sundays and in August. 37 Rue E. Feray (phone: 32-33-14-40). Moderate.

ROUEN

Pullman – Part of the modern chain, but it fits astoundingly well into the old quarter, with 125 rooms with all the comforts. Rue de la Croix-de-Fer (phone: 35-98-06-98). Expensive.

Gros Horloge – Old but charming; in the center of vibrant Rouen. Rooms on the Rue du Gros-Horloge offer a unique closeup of the famous clock. 91 Rue Gros-Horloge (phone: 35-70-41-41). Moderate.

La Couronne – With lovely old Norman decor, this is Rouen's most famous restaurant. Duck *à la rouennaise* is the famous dish here, but many regulars prefer other local classics such as *pieds de mouton* (sheep's feet) and *cassolette d'homard* (lobster casserole with fresh vegetables). 31 Pl. du Vieux-Marché (phone: 35-71-40-90). Expensive.

Alcide – The place most recommended for sampling Caen's famous *tripe à la mode,* tripe simmered in Calvados, the region's apple brandy, and served with boiled potatoes and a Calvados chaser. Pl. Courtonne (phone: 31-93-58-29). Moderate to inexpensive.

DIEPPE

Univers – A small and very popular hotel, it has 30 rooms, all furnished with beautiful antiques, and a restaurant on the premises. Be sure to make reservations well in advance. Closed mid-December through mid-January. 10 Bd. Verdun (phone: 35-84-12-55). Moderate.

DEAUVILLE

Altéa – Overlooking the picturesque harbor, with 70 motel-style rooms and 50 studios. Reservations essential, especially in summer. Bd. Eugène-Cornuché (phone: 31-88-62-62). Expensive to moderate.

Trophée – This recent addition to Deauville offers modern rooms (some with balconies), a rooftop sun deck, a pleasant restaurant, and a complete range of services. In the middle of town, just a short walk from the beach. 81 Rue du General-Leclerc (phone: 31-88-45-86). Moderate.

HONFLEUR

Lechat – A comfortable hotel in the heart of the old harbor district. 15 Pl. Ste.-Catherine (phone: 31-89-23-85). Expensive to moderate.

Cheval Blanc – On the quai overlooking the port, this 15th-century inn has attractively refurbished rooms overlooking the water. In winter, the innovative owner offers weekend packages, including painting courses taught by Beaux-Arts instructors. 2 Quai des Passagers (phone: 31-89-13-49). Moderate.

Spinnaker – This increasingly popular spot a little off the main drag is *the* place for gastronomy. Its young chef shows considerable promise. 52 Rue Mirabeau (phone: 31-88-24-40). Moderate.

Ferme de la Grande Cour – In the middle of a beautiful orchard, offering the best cider in the area along with a wide selection of local specialties. Côte de Grâce (phone: 31-89-04-69). Moderate to inexpensive.

BÉNOUVILLE

Manoir d'Hastings – Six miles (9.6 km) north of Caen, this restaurant is in an ivy-covered 17th-century priory with a garden. M. and Mme. Scaviner serve memorable lobsters with herbs, truffles, and foie gras in puff pastry (phone: 31-44-62-43). Expensive.

BAYEUX

Lion d'Or – Particularly pleasant old Norman decor; the cuisine, which has garnered one Michelin star, is among the finest in the province. There are 30 clean, airy rooms upstairs, all with bathrooms. During the summer, half-board is required. Closed mid-December to mid-January. 71 Rue St.-Jean (phone: 31-92-06-90). Moderate.

d'Argouges – An 18th-century mansion is now a simple and very comfortable hotel, a marriage of Old World charm and modern amenities. 21 Rue St.-Patrice (phone: 31-92-88-86). Moderate.

CHERBOURG

Mercure – Formerly a *Sofitel,* this modern, comfortable hotel is now managed by Mercure, another reliable hotel chain. Gare Maritime (phone: 33-44-01-11). Expensive to moderate.

Café du Théâtre – Excellent food in attractive surroundings. Pl. du Général-de-Gaulle (phone: 33-43-01-49). Moderate to inexpensive.

MONT-ST.-MICHEL

Mère Poulard – This serene hotel is a local tradition, as are the omelettes served in its fine restaurant (phone: 33-60-14-01). Expensive.

The Brittany Coast

The natives of France's northwestern peninsula consider their region a country apart, and with good reason. The vast, jagged coastline of Brittany resembles no other in France, and the tranquil interior, still primarily agricultural, seems to be part of another century. First inhabited by a mysterious race whose large, prehistoric megaliths can still be seen, the region was later invaded by the Gauls, the Celts, and finally the Romans. Brittany did not come under French rule until 1532, and even today, the Breton language and folklore are closer to the Celtic-based Welsh and Gaelic than to the French.

Brittany is a land of superstition sometimes verging on the mystical. It is the land that gave birth to the legend of Tristan and Iseult, to the tragic history of Peter Abelard and to the fabulous tales of Chateaubriand. But its traditions are living, as on feast days, when women still wear picturesque, lacy Breton costumes.

The Breton peninsula reaches inland from a rocky, bay-lined coast with numerous excellent natural harbors and several stretches of treacherous rocks. The A11, a new superhighway, has cut the travel time from Paris to Brittany. The route described below begins at St.-Malo and roughly follows the coast.

ST.-MALO AND DINARD: The beaches of the Emerald Coast and St.-Malo, a fortified island, city, and port dating from the 12th century, begin this route. The site is remarkable, and you'll appreciate it most from the ramparts (take the St.-Vincent gateway and then the stairway to the right). From inside the walls you can see the castle and the *St.-Malo Museum,* part of the castle structure. The tomb of the storyteller Chateaubriand lies on nearby Grand Bé Island, which can be reached only at low tide (take the Champs-Vauverts Gate out of town and cross the beach diagonally to the highway).

Across the estuary from St.-Malo is the elegant resort of Dinard, with an atmosphere of opulence topped off by the sparkling white *Casino* (Plage de l'Ecluse). At Moulinet Point you'll have splendid panoramas of the coast. The Grande Plage is a popular beach for swimming and sunbathing.

En Route from St.-Malo and Dinard – From Dinard you can take a boat (or go by car via D766 inland for 18 mi/30 km) to the lovely old town of Dinan, boasting an impressive 14th-century castle overlooking the Rance. To see the old part of town, go along the Rue Ste.-Claire to the Rue de l'Horloge and Rue du Jerzual. (A good place for classic Breton crêpes: *Le Connétable,* 1 Rue Apport; phone: 96-39-06-74.)

The coastal road west (N786) goes to the resorts of St.-Lunaire and St.-Cast, both of which offer fine beaches and seascapes. Taking D13 to N786 and then following the coast on D16 takes you to Fort-la-Latte, a feudal castle begun in the 13th century and finished in the 14th and perched atop the cliffs like some pirate stronghold.

CAP FRÉHEL, LE VAL-ANDRÉ, ST.-BRIEUC: Just a few miles down the coast is Cap Fréhel, its spectacular red, gray, and black cliffs rising to a height of 229 feet above the sea. You can enjoy breathtaking views from the top of the lighthouse.

One of the finest sand beaches in Brittany is just along N786 at Le Val-André, and if you follow N786 to N12 you come to St.-Brieuc, the town that many Bretons consider the beginning of authentic Brittany. A short drive northwest on D6 brings you to Notre-Dame-de-la-Coeur, a lovely village noted for a serenely beautiful 15th-century chapel.

En Route from St.-Brieuc – Follow N786 along the coast for about 45 miles (72 km) to the busy resort of Perros-Guirec. Nearby are the lovely resorts of Ploumanach and Trégastel and the picturesque village of St.-Jean-du-Doigt, whose quaint name is derived from a prized relic — supposedly the finger of St. John the Baptist — which has been kept in the town church since the 15th century.

Along the coast at Carantec and St.-Pol-de-Léon (D786 to D73) and into the northwestern corner, the Coast of Legends, you'll travel windswept shores and be captivated by the typical Breton seascapes. If you find yourself in the area on the Sunday before September 8, drive inland to Le Folgoët (D788 from St.-Pol) for the annual public *pardon* ceremony. These *pardons* are the most characteristic expression of Breton religious fervor, when groups and individuals gather to do public penance, to fulfill a vow, or to seek divine favor. A colorful procession to and from the church is highlighted by the wearing of traditional Breton costumes — for women, a high lace cap of exceptional delicacy — afterward, the whole town takes part in a festival of dancing, feasting, and country games and competitions.

N788 south will also take you to modern Brest (or follow the coast via D27 to D28 and N789). This naval base is also a major urban center. There are numerous historical relics to be seen, and the arsenal and dockyards are worth a visit. A stroll along the 18th-century ramparts is especially interesting. However, it doesn't hold a candle to the smaller towns that lie farther south around the coast — in particular, delightful Locronan, once a center for the manufacture of sailcloth, now noted for well-preserved Renaissance houses built of granite and a marvelous central square (N170 to D7). If you see only one small Breton town, it should be this one.

From here, D7 leads to D9 and the road to Raz Point, where deep, rocky chasms plunge down into the sea. It's a busy place, but the view is nothing short of spectacular.

A brief alternate route: If time prevents your going along the entire northwestern coast, we suggest turning inland at St.-Brieuc. Take N778 south and then follow D778 for a sample of the incredibly peaceful and generally unexplored countryside and a visit to the huge, magnificent castle at Josselin. From there you can reach the southern coast directly via N166 into Vannes. Or take D790 out of St.-Brieuc, then D3 and D15 through the Black Mountains for 84 miles (135 km) into Quimper.

QUIMPER: Thirty miles (48 km) from Raz Point via D784, 42 miles (67 km) south of Brest on N170, and 69 miles (110 km) east of Vannes (N165) is the prosperous old trading city of Quimper. In the fish market, the Breton costume is still often worn; there's a fine Gothic cathedral (Pl. St.-Corentin) with a superb organ, which can be heard on weekends, and a charming old quarter with streets such as the Rue Kéréon, the Rue du Guéodet, and the Rue du Sallé. Quimper is also a center of the manufacture of a distinctive style of blue or yellow pottery. On the fourth Sunday in July, the city hosts the colorful *Great Festival of Cornouaille.*

En Route from Quimper – Following the coast via D783 brings you to Pont-Aven, a flower-filled town with a small museum dedicated to the works of Paul Gauguin, who lived here and founded the Pont-Aven School of Painting. A few miles east along D765 there's a wonderful secluded beach at Kerfany-les-Pins. A short detour north on D16 brings you to Quimperlé, on the Ellé and Isole rivers. The "upper" town is centered around Notre-Dame-de-l'Assomption church (Pl. St.-Michel), and the "lower" town is grouped around the old Abbey of Ste.-Croix (Pl. Hervo). The apse is an excellent example of Romanesque architecture, and the spooky crypt is well worth a visit.

QUIBERON PENINSULA AND BELLE-ILE: Still farther south and east along the coast, turn into D768 to reach the Quiberon Peninsula, whose myriad rocks, caves, and reefs make its stretch of surf-pounded coast one of the most exciting in the province. We suggest walking the Wild Coast (Côte Sauvage) from end to end and stopping at the Bull's Cave (Grottes du Taureau), the Window (Fenêtre), and the Old Woman (Vieille) — all well-marked sights. East and south of the coast are wide beaches and lively fishing ports, and there's a boat to take you to one of the major attractions of the southern coast: Belle-Ile.

The largest of the Breton islands, Belle-Ile is a landscape filled with picturesque whitewashed villages surrounded by farmland. You'll want to see the Apothicairerie Grotto, the Grand Lighthouse, and the boiling surf at Port-Coton. Leaving your car at the port, turn right and you'll come upon stone "needles" (Aiguilles), some of them like pyramids pierced by grottoes. At Port Donnant there's a fine sand beach between soaring cliffs; the setting is splendid but the swimming treacherous.

En Route from Belle-Ile – Regaining D768 north, turn onto D781 east into Carnac, a center for the curious prehistoric megaliths that dot Brittany, presumed to be Druidic, though possibly much older. Of special interest are the Ménec Lines (Alignements de Ménec) 2 miles (3.2 km) outside town along D196. The Lines include more than 1,000 menhirs, as these prehistoric, upright monoliths are known. The spectacle of these stones, set in miles-long rows as straight as a single file of soldiers, is positively eerie.

Taking N781 and D28 north for 8 miles (13 km) brings you into Auray, one of the most enchanting towns in the region. There are wonderful views from Loc Promenade, and the St.-Goustan quarter is charming (access is through the 15th-century Place St.-Sauveur). From Auray, take N165 east for 10 miles (16 km) to Vannes.

VANNES AND THE GULF OF MORBIHAN: The Gulf of Morbihan is the tourist center of southern Brittany. An inland sea dotted with islands — many still privately owned — it is a place of extraordinary sunsets and the almost hallucinatory play of light on water. The best way to see this area is by boat, with excursions leaving from Vannes, Port Navalo, and Auray.

At the head of the gulf, Vannes has a picturesque old quarter enclosed by ramparts and centered around the Cathédrale St.-Pierre (Pl. Henri-IV). From the lower alley of the Promenade de la Garenne you see the most alluring corner of the city, where a stream flows at the foot of city walls built in the 13th century. Vannes makes an agreeable base for your tour of the area. Local cafés and stores can supply all your practical needs, and boat excursions start here for all other points on the gulf.

> **En Route from Vannes** – The short boat trip to Monks' Island (Ile aux Moines) is highly recommended. You can cover the island on foot, exploring the old village where houses are nestled into winding hills overlooking the gulf.
>
> Another stop on the boat tour is Locmariaquer, a village with some of the most important megaliths in Brittany (by car, take N165 west from Vannes and D28 and D781 south). The Great Menhir and the Merchants Table dolmen can be seen if you turn left before the cemetery as you leave town via D781. The island of Gavrinis also has an impressive collection of megaliths and is only a 15-minute boat ride from the colorful fishing village of Larmor-Baden (from Vannes, take D101 and D316).

NANTES: Leaving Vannes by N165 east, turn south at D774 for the chic, bustling resort of La Baule and the busy but unpicturesque seaport of St.-Nazaire. From there, N771 rejoins N165 to lead you into Nantes, once the capital of Brittany and today the major city on the River Loire. At Place de la Duchesse-Anne you can see the 15th-century château, with its low moat and wrought-iron cupola. The beautiful Gothic Cathédrale St.-Pierre et St.-Paul, badly burned in 1972, has been restored and is very much worth seeing (Pl. du Maréchal Foch). At Place Graslin, in the 18th-century section of the city, you can stop for a drink at *La Cigale*, a famous brasserie decked out with Art Nouveau murals and gilt woodwork. Rue Crébillon, toward Place Royale, leads you to the Passage Pommeraye, an interesting mid-19th-century shopping arcade with cast-iron railings and footbridges. And the *Fine Arts Museum* (Rue Clemenceau) is one of the best in France. Don't forget to try some of the food specialties in Nantes — the city is known for its crêpes and the Muscadet wine that is bottled here. From Nantes, Paris is 237 miles (383 km) northeast via N23 and A-11.

A final suggestion: Wherever possible, you should fill out the coastal routes by venturing into the interior of Brittany: towns such as Fougères, a favorite of Victor Hugo and Balzac; Vitré, 18 miles (29 km) south along N178, an enchanting Old World city; Les Rochers, Madame de Sévigné's château, 4 miles (6.4 km) southeast of Vitré; Lampaul-Guimiliau and St.-Thégonnec, the site of elaborately decorated Breton chapels; Tocky Questembert; Kernascléden; Le Faouet; Huelgoat; and hundreds of other towns and villages that make the Breton interior just as entrancing as the fabled coast.

BEST EN ROUTE

Expect to pay $75 and up per night for a double room in hotels listed as expensive; $55 to $75 in those listed as moderate; and under $55, inexpensive. The restaurants range from $80 and up for a dinner for two in the expensive range; $50 to $80 in the moderate range; and $50 and under, inexpensive. Prices do not include drinks, wine, or tip. Note that in summer, it is imperative to reserve hotel rooms and seatings at well-known restaurants far in advance.

ST.-MALO AND DINARD

Elizabeth – A true gem in a town where sparkling exteriors usually conceal run-down guest quarters. 17 rooms; no restaurant. 2 Rue des Cordiers (phone: 99-56-24-98). Expensive.

Central – The premier hotel in St.-Malo, in the old town, it has 46 large, attractively furnished rooms and a formal restaurant. (Restaurant closed January through mid-February.) 6 Grande-Rue (phone: 99-40-87-70). Expensive to moderate.

Duchesse Anne – This polished and gleaming turn-of-the-century restaurant specializes in seafood. Closed Wednesdays and in December and January. 5 Pl. Guy-La-Chambre (phone: 99-40-85-33). Moderate.

Printania – A modest hotel in Dinard with a good view over St.-Malo and the Rance. Closed from November to Easter. 5 Av. Georges-V (phone: 99-46-13-07). Moderate to inexpensive.

DINAN

D'Avaugour – A delight of a hotel with 27 large rooms and an exceedingly good restaurant. 1 Pl. Champs Clos (phone: 96-39-07-49). Expensive.

PLEVEN (NEAR PLANCOET)

Manoir du Vaumadeuc – Sumptuous granite manor house-turned-auberge is one of Brittany's most luxurious hostelries (phone: 96-84-46-17). Expensive.

VAL-ANDRÉ

La Cotriade – Excellent restaurant specializing in the local seafood. Port de Piégu (phone: 96-72-20-26). Expensive.

PONTS-NEUFS

Lorand-Barre – Charmingly decorated in rustic Breton style, it's one of the better-known restaurants in France, 8 miles (13 km) east of St.-Brieuc. Order grilled lobster, sweetbreads in port wine, or delicious crêpes. Closed December to Easter, Sunday evenings, and Mondays. Damour (phone: 96-32-78-71). Expensive.

TREBEURDEN

Ti al-Lannec – This handsome mansion is now an inn with capacious bathrooms, friendly management, very good nouvelle cuisine, and charm to spare. Closed mid-November to mid-March. Allée de Mézo-guen (phone: 96-23-57-26). Expensive to moderate.

QUIMPER

Tour d'Auvergne – A modest hotel with modern facilities and a new restaurant. Closed Christmas week. 13 Rue des Réguaires (phone: 98-95-08-70). Moderate.

PONT-AVEN

Moulin de Rosmadec – An excellent Breton restaurant set in a 15th-century stone mill amid beautiful gardens; 4 modern bedrooms have recently been added next door. Closed Wednesdays, Sunday evenings in low season, the last 2 weeks in October, and the month of February. (phone: 98-06-00-22). Expensive.

Manoir du Menec – This new hotel and leisure center in a gracious 15th-century stone manor northeast of Pont-Aven has cozy individual cottages, each named for a famous painter. Also on the property are 10 deluxe rooms. The restaurant, with ancient stone walls and elegant chandeliers, is in the oldest part of the manor; a heated pool, jacuzzi, sauna, and multi-gym are in the new addition. There are also facilities for small conferences. 29114 Bannalec (phone: 98-39-47-47). Expensive to moderate.

Taupinière – Graced by a beautiful garden and topped with a straw roof, this restaurant lacks nothing in the way of country charm. Specialties include giant crayfish grilled in the fireplace, raw tuna marinated in lime, and anglerfish served in butter and farmer's cider. Closed Monday evenings, Tuesdays, and from mid-September to mid-October. Route de Concerneau, 1½ miles (4 km) from Pont-Aven (phone: 98-06-03-12). Expensive to moderate.

RIEC-SUR-BELON

Chez Mélanie – Though recently taken over by new management, this charming, old-fashioned auberge with original 19th-century art everywhere and much-polished antique mahogany and brass remains unchanged. Closed Tuesdays and from mid-November to mid-December. 2 Pl. de l'Eglise (phone: 98-06-91-05). Moderate.

MOËLAN-SUR-MER

Moulins du Duc – A Relais & Châteaux establishment with a lake, swans, doves, comfortable cottage quarters, a covered swimming pool, a woodsy setting, and an inventive menu. Closed mid-January to March (phone: 98-39-60-73). Expensive.

HENNEBONT

Château de Locguénolé – Elegant rooms, sumptuous food, and manicured, river-view grounds make this stately former castle one of the region's loveliest places to stay. Also a member of the Relais et Chateux. Closed January and Mondays in off-season. Off the D781 (phone: 97-76-29-04). Expensive.

QUIBERON

Sofitel – One of a modern chain, in a pleasant setting, it boasts a very good restaurant. Closed during January (phone: 97-50-20-00). Expensive.

Ker Noyal – A lovely, well-kept, modern hotel with 100 rooms, only a short walk from the beach. Closed from November to March. Rue de St.-Clément (phone: 97-50-08-41). Moderate.

VANNES AND THE GULF OF MORBIHAN

Marébaudière – Set back from the road and quiet, it has 40 handsome rooms. Closed Christmas week and Sunday evenings in the off-season. 4 Rue Aristide-Briand (phone: 97-47-34-29). Moderate.

Richemont – An old-fashioned and charming hotel next door to a restaurant with an elaborate menu. 26 Pl. de la Gare (phone: 97-47-12-95). Moderate.

PEN-LAN POINT (MUZILLAC)

de Rochevilaine – A beautiful old structure spectacularly set overlooking the sea. Closed January and February, Sunday nights and Mondays in the off-season (phone: 97-41-69-27). Expensive to moderate.

QUESTEMBERT

Bretagne – This old stone house wrapped in vines is a Relais & Châteaux establishment, with 6 rooms and an innovative young chef. 13 Rue St.-Michel (phone: 97-26-11-12). Expensive.

NANTES

Domaine d'Orvault – Ten minutes from the center of Nantes, this luxurious Relais & Châteaux member has 30 rooms and is the logical choice for peace and quiet. Chemin des Marais-du-Cens, Orvault (phone: 40-76-84-02). Expensive.

Sofitel – Another in the modern chain dotting France. Ile Beaulieu, Rue Alexandre-Millerand (phone: 40-47-61-03). Expensive to moderate.

Central – A comfortable hotel. 4 Rue Couëdic (phone: 40-20-09-35). Moderate.

Rôtisserie de Palais – Small and unprepossessing but very popular eatery with a fairly substantial menu that changes with the market's offerings. Closed Sundays. 1 Pl. Aristide-Briand (phone: 40-89-20-12). Moderate.

O Cals Tell Nantais – A decidedly "unfancy" restaurant, but with superb food. Closed Sunday evenings and in August. 161 Rue Hauts-Pavés (phone: 40-76-59-54). Moderate to inexpensive.

The Loire Valley

Early in the history of France, the mild climate and natural beauty of the provinces of Orléanais, Touraine, Maine, and Anjou — just southwest of Paris, slightly east of Brittany — attracted the pleasure-loving nobility. First they built feudal fortresses to protect themselves in an age of constant warfare; in more peaceful times — and as the Renaissance flowered in the valley of the Loire — watchtowers were softened with graceful Italianate spires, and windows were pierced in solid walls, the better to enjoy the terrain. Royalty raised pleasure palaces along the banks of the languorous river and its tranquil tributaries. Luxurious mansions and hunting lodges sprang up in the game-filled forests.

More than 7 centuries of architectural splendor are unfolded here, and six castles bring the past to life with *son-et-lumière* spectacles nightly in the summer. As spotlights play across façades, towers, and courtyards, voices re-create the bygone pageantry and intrigue of courtiers and their ladies.

All along the way, travelers will find pleasant wayside inns, frequently in historic residences. It's possible not only to see châteaux, but to sleep and dine in them as well. Don't try to see too many castles in one day: There are 120, plus 20 abbeys and 100 churches — all suffused with the royal "sweetness of life" of which court poets sang. Late spring or fall is the best time to visit, but if you must go in high (summer) season, stay off the main roads and go early everywhere to avoid buses crammed with tourists, for this is one of Europe's classic tourist circuits. The castles for the most part are closed every day between noon and 2 PM.

In the Loire, it is said, the purest French is spoken. The food of the region is superb and is perfectly complemented by the fresh and lively wines. The river and its tributaries are teeming with delicious freshwater fish, most of them familiar to Americans but masquerading on the menu under their French names. It may be useful to know that *alose* is shad; *brême,* bream; *brochet,* pike; *anguille,* eel; *truite,* trout; and *saumon* — well, you can guess that one. A *matelote* is a fish stew; a *friture de la Loire,* a plate of fried river fish; and a *quenelle*, a fish dumpling — usually of pike. Local chefs are fond of serving fish with a white sauce of butter whipped to a froth with a hint of shallots and vinegar (*beurre blanc*). Game is also plentiful: quail, pheasant, and partridge (*caille, faisan, perdrix*) and, of course, venison, called *chevreuil*. The lowly prune is an ingredient favored by Loire cooks. *Pruneaux* (prunes) come from *prunes* (plums), and the orchards are celebrated in the plum tarts of Anjou. The *charcuterie* of Anjou and Touraine is known for *rillons* and *rillettes* (minced and potted pork) as well as for the tripe sausages called *andouilles.*

The wide variety of local white, red, and rosé wines ideally accompany the regional cuisine. The celebrated whites of Vouvray (both still and sparkling), Sancerre, Muscadet, and Pouilly-Fumé are perfect with fish. The fragrant red wines of Bourgueil and Chinon should be sampled here, for they don't travel well. The white dessert wines of Anjou almost rival the more famous Sauternes, and the Champigny of Saumur is a red wine of rare quality. Don't forget the rosés of Anjou — light, dry, delicately perfumed, and wonderfully refreshing on a summer day.

ANGERS: Straddling the Maine River, this pleasant city is famous for fruit and wine and for having given rise to the Plantagenets, who became Kings of England.

High up on a hill, the moated, 17-tower Angers château gives a powerful impression of impregnable strength even in its current half-ruined state. A set of tapestries depicting the Apocalypse is the castle's main attraction. Woven in medieval Paris, the 70 pieces are over 550 feet long and more than 16 feet wide. They are magnificently displayed in a modern gallery in the former Courtyard of the King.

Other things to see in Angers include: the *Logis-Barrault Fine Arts Museum;* the Hôtel Pincé and the *Turpin de Crissé* museum; the former Hôpital St.-Jean, housing ten contemporary tapestries and a small wine museum; the "Doutre" on the right bank, with lovely old houses dating from the 15th to the 18th century; Trinity Church; and the impressive cathedral of St. Maurice, which has three towers and fine stained glass. Each January the city hosts a wine fair lasting 2 weeks and, in June, an arts festival. Summer *son-et-lumière* performances are given at the château.

En Route from Angers – The 66 miles (106 km) between Angers and Tours offer many points of historical and scenic interest as well as several good inns for lunch, dinner, or overnight stays. To reach Saumur, follow D751 through Gennes and Cunault, with its fine church. Along the way you pass scattered dolmens and menhirs, relics of the Celts who lived here in early times.

SAUMUR: This charming town is famous for wine and for its world-renowned cavalry troupe, the Cadre Noir (exhibitions are given the last 2 weeks in July). The château, on a steep promontory, was once splendidly adorned with spires, pinnacles, gilded weathervanes, pointed dormers, and tall chimneys. It is still a majestic structure, with a particularly fascinating museum devoted to the history of the horse. From the watchtower, the view over the blue slate roofs and the church of Notre-Dame-de-Nantilly extends to the vineyard-covered valleys of the Loire and the Thouet. This is rewarding country for antiques hunting. You should not miss a sunset over the Loire viewed from the superb restaurant of *Le Prieuré* (phone: 41-67-90-14) at nearby Chêne-hutte-les-Tuffeaux.

En Route from Saumur – Follow D947 along the Loire to Montsoreau, then turn south on D147 to Fontevrauld and its domed abbey. Here are the tombs of the Plantagenets (Henry II, Eleanor of Aquitaine, Richard the Lion-Hearted, Isabelle of Angoulême) and an extraordinary Romanesque kitchen with 5 immense fireplaces and 20 chimneys, unique in France. Continue east on Routes VO4, D117, D24, and N759 to Chinon, with a stop at La Devinière, the country house where Rabelais spent his childhood.

CHINON: Historic Chinon, overlooking the Vienne River, hasn't changed much since the Middle Ages. Above the town frowns the huge château, dramatically set on a high ridge. The ruins of three fortresses guarded by deep moats jut from the terrain, but only a hearth, now overgrown with ivy, recalls the great hall in which Joan of Arc recognized Charles VII. A steam train transports tourists back and forth to Richelieu, a model of classic 17th-century building.

    En Route from Chinon – North on D7 about 9 miles (14 km) is the Château d'Ussé, said to have inspired Charles Perrault's fairy tale *Sleeping Beauty*. Bell turrets and towers rise delicately from flowering terraces against the rather somber background of the forest of Chinon. The chapel displays Aubusson tapestries depicting the life of Joan of Arc. Your next stop is Azay-le-Rideau; take Routes D7, then D17.

AZAY-LE-RIDEAU: The château here was constructed between 1518 and 1527 by Gilles Berthelot, treasurer under François I, and its fully furnished interior is a fascinating Renaissance museum. Bright white walls, four graceful corner turrets, and a slate roof of blue mirrored in the quiet River Indre form an enchanting backdrop for this fairy tale castle's *son-et-lumière* performance.

    Of interest in Azay are the church of St. Symphorien, with its unusual façade, and the nearby Château Saché, which houses the *Balzac Museum*.

VILLANDRY: North of Azay by about 6 miles (10 km) on Route D7, past poppy fields and rose-covered stone walls, is Villandry, "garden château of the garden of France." The famous triple-tiered gardens cover several acres and are best seen from a balustrade that runs along one side. The handsome Renaissance residence, constructed around the massive square tower of a medieval keep, was built by Jean le Breton, secretary of state to François I.

    En Route from Villandry – Return to D57 and cross the Loire to Langeais, an impressive medieval fortress standing exactly as it was built. This château, where Charles VII married Anne of Brittany, was owned and occupied for many years by a millionaire who furnished it in exact detail to reflect 15th-century life.

    Continue along the Loire on N152 to Tours.

TOURS: The capital of Touraine, in the heart of château country, is a major tourist center, with a charming old quarter, flowering parks and gardens, elegant shops, tree-shaded streets, and lively sidewalk cafés. No less appealing is the city's characteristically superb, refined cooking. In short, Tours offers everything the visitor needs for a taste of the good life typical of the area.

    Among the special attractions of Tours are: St. Gatien Cathedral, as beautiful by night, when fully floodlit, as it is by day; the Basilica of St. Martin; St. Julien Church; and Charlemagne's tower. For a look at the balconies, stairways, and charming little courtyards of the old town, start with Place Plumereau's 15th-century wooden houses, then continue to the Maison de Tristan on Rue Briçonnet, then to Place des Carnes, Rue Paul-Louis Courier, Rue du Change, and the Hôtel Gouin's *Renaissance Museum*. Also of note are the *Musée des Beaux-Arts* and the *Gemmail Museum* on the terraces facing Pont Wilson.

LOCHES: About 25 miles (41 km) south of Tours, via N10 and N143 through the forest of Larçay, is the town of Loches. The château, once notorious as a top-security prison for the enemies of the king, is a fortified acropolis combining several buildings that are totally dissimilar in style and date from several centuries. Four thick walls supported by semicircular buttresses make up the enormous Romanesque keep — really three levels of dungeons — known as the Martelet. In these sinister premises, Louis XI and Louis XII kept such distinguished prisoners as Ludovico il Moro, Duke of Milan, whose paintings and inscriptions can still be seen on the walls. Evoking more pleasant memories are the recumbent statue of Charles VII's beautiful mistress, Agnès Sorel; Anne of Brittany's peaceful oratory; the folklore museum in the gatehouse; and the 11th-century collegiate church of St. Ours, with two curious hollow pyramids roofing the nave. The château and dungeons are closed December and January and Wednesdays off-season. In mid-July, the town stages an old-fashioned "peasants' market," with costumes, artisans selling their wares, and singing and dancing in the streets.

VALENÇAY: Peacocks strut through the gardens of this romantic château, 30 miles (48 km) from Loches via D760 and D960. The castle still remains in the family of Talleyrand, who acquired it in 1803. Luxuriously furnished in Louis XVI, Regency, and First Empire styles, it has the charm of a much-lived-in home. The museum facing the château is devoted to souvenirs of Talleyrand's career and includes a reconstruction of his bedroom. In the surrounding park, deer, flamingoes and llamas roam at liberty.

CHENONCEAUX: The château that many consider the most beautiful in the Loire lies about 34 miles (54 km) from Valençay via D956, then N76. Chenonceaux is certainly the most feminine and graceful of the castles of the Loire, and it is especially interesting because it was fashioned by and associated with some of the most fascinating and accomplished women in France. Thomas Bohier, controller of the Royal Treasury under François I, and his wife, Catherine Briçonnet, built the earlier part between 1513 and 1521. Bohier's official duties kept him away from home for long periods, and the responsibility for the design and construction fell to the capable Catherine. At Bohier's death, the château passed to the Crown in settlement of his debts. To mark the joyful occasion of his accession to the throne in 1547, Henri II presented Chenonceaux as a love token to his mistress, Diane de Poitiers, who commissioned a five-arch bridge to be built to the far bank of the Cher and planted fine gardens. When Henri died in 1559, his widow, the patient Catherine de Médicis, saw her chance for revenge. Catherine forced Diane to vacate Chenonceaux in exchange for the much lesser château of Chaumont. Catherine then added her own touches, which included a magical 2-story, 197-foot gallery. Louise of Lorraine, Catherine's daughter-in-law, inherited the castle, which stood empty after her death until Madame Dupin arrived to enliven it with her famous salons. Madame Dupin's greatest fame, however, is derived from her position as grandmother of George Sand, née Aurore Dupin. The sixth mistress of Chenonceaux was the wealthy Madame Pelouze, who purchased the castle in 1864, then spent her life restoring it to its original grandeur. The property now belongs to the Menier family, chocolate manufacturers.

The château is approached by a long alley of towering trees. Two sphinxes guard the entrance, with Diane's gardens on the left, Catherine de Médicis's on the right. The interior is richly furnished with tapestries, marble statues, and portraits. Allow time for a walk in the gardens and along the river for a splendid view of the castle reflected in the water below its arches in the late afternoon sun.

Within walking distance, in the village, are two good restaurants — *Hôtel du Bon Laboureur* and *Le Gâteau Breton* — (see *Best en Route*) where diners can enjoy dinner before the spectacular *son-et-lumière* performance, which dramatically unfolds the triumphs and defeats of the six chatelaines of Chenonceaux. Return to Tours via N76.

AMBOISE: On the left bank of the Loire, 18 miles (25 km) from Tours via N751, is Amboise. Charles VII was born here, and he died here of injuries sustained when he walked into the stone lintel of a low doorway. Charles was responsible for beautifying Amboise, importing Italian architects, sculptors, decorators, and gardeners to embellish the château. François I came to Amboise as a child and later gathered about him a court of artists and scholars. He was a patron of Leonardo da Vinci, who spent his last years here and was buried in the Gothic chapel of St. Hubert. Clos-Lucé, the brick manor house where he lived, has an interesting exhibit of the models of his inventions. Nightly *son-et-lumière* performances at the château recount one of the more violent episodes in French religious history, the hanging of the Protestant conspirators of Amboise in the castle's courtyard.

The *Town Hall Museum* should be visited for its 14th-century sculpture, Aubusson tapestries, and royal autographs. The *Auberge du Mail* (see *Best en Route*) sets an excellent table.

Cross the river, take a last and best look at the château, and return via the Loire's right bank and Route N152. About 6 miles (9.6 km) from Tours, turn off on the Route du Vouvray through 3,000 acres of vineyards and stop for a sip of still or sparkling white wine at one of the tasting cellars along the way.

Take the quick A10 (Autoroute Aquitaine) 36 miles (58 km) east to Blois.

BLOIS: On the heights above the right bank of the Loire, the city of Blois clusters around the castle. The residence of kings, Blois is steeped in 4 centuries of history, and the castle provides a nutshell review of French architecture — a composite of the styles of several periods, from the massive simplicity of the Middle Ages to the classicism of the 17th century. The highlights are Louis XII's original brick and stone edifice; the François I wing, with its ornate, winding, exterior staircase; and the majestic western wing, a superb example of 17th-century refinement, built by Mansart for Gaston d'Orléans, the scheming brother of Louis XIII. The assassination of the Duc de Guise took place in Henri III's bedroom on the second floor, and the intrigues of Catherine de Médicis are revealed by the 237 secret panels in her study. The Louis XII wing has a museum with 16th-century frescoes, furniture, paintings, and sculpture. Explore the castle's outer façades from the Place du Château; visit St. Louis Cathedral and the Old Quarter, St. Nicholas Church, and the basilica of Notre-Dame. The former Bishop's Palace, now the Town Hall, has gardens and a terrace overlooking the hump-backed bridge across the Loire. On the terrace is a statue of Joan of Arc that is the work of the American sculptor Anna Hyatt Huntington. Stay at either the modern *Novotel* or the simple but comfortable *La Loire* in town or at one of the country inns at nearby Onzain or Ouchamps.

CHAMBORD: Cross the river by N765, then drive upstream on D951 for 11 miles (18 km) to the largest of all the Loire châteaux. Built by François I as a pleasure palace, Chambord is set in a game reserve extending over 13,600 acres enclosed by the longest wall in France — 20 miles around. A striking feature of this extravagant 440-room hunting lodge is the roof — a bristling forest of spires, pinnacles, gables, turrets, and towers, including 365 chimneys. Behind the handsome Renaissance façade are well-maintained royal apartments. The palace has 74 stairways, including the ingenious double staircase, twin spirals constructed so that one person can ascend and another descend without meeting. Don't miss a promenade on the roof terraces, where the king's guests enjoyed a grandstand view of the progress of the royal hunts from a height of 80 feet. Take lunch or tea at the *St. Michel* hotel, next to the château. The first *son-et-lumière* performance was presented here in the spring of 1952, and the spectacle still brings the past to life with stunning effect twice nightly.

CHEVERNY: Continue via D112 and D102 to Cour-Cheverny. Built in 1634 for the counts of Cheverny, the castle is now occupied by a descendant of the original owner. Unlike the royal palaces, this less flamboyant yet handsome house has changed little over the centuries and still retains most of its original furnishings. A long avenue leads to the vast building, Louis XIII in style but already neo-classical. The splendor of the interior decoration and furniture make Cheverny a miniature Versailles, complete to a magnificently ornate king's bedroom. No monarch ever stayed at Cheverny, although the bedroom was kept in readiness in case the king should choose to exercise his right to stay. An outbuilding houses a hunting museum with 2,000 sets of antlers mounted on the walls, and the kennels are home to a pack of 70 hounds. Over 5,000 acres of forest belong to Cheverny; formal hunts are held twice a week from November to April. Non-members may join, but only the master of the hunt has the right to dispatch the quarry with a sword. *Hôtel des Trois Marchands* and the *St.-Hubert* restaurant, close to the château, are fine for lunch (see *Best en Route*). Return to Blois, about 8 miles (13 km) via N765.

CHAUMONT: This final castle to be visited is just over 10 miles (16 km) southwest of Blois on D751. A 10-minute walk up from the village along an avenue lined with venerable old cedars brings you to the château. Chaumont has much of the fortress about it — four wide towers, sentry walls, and a stern drawbridge — but ornamented windows lighten the façades, and the stonework is delicately carved. In the inner courtyard, the three façades opening onto the valley are ornamented by turreted staircases, dormers, and picturesque little bell towers. Catherine de Médicis built an observatory at Chaumont, where, with her resident astrologer, she attempted to divine the future. Here, it is said, she foresaw the violent deaths of all three of her sons. At the beginning of the 19th century, Chaumont provided a haven, if not a home, for Madame de Staël when she was exiled from Paris by Napoleon.

En Route from Blois – Follow N152 east with short stops at Beaugency, known for its wine; Meung, with its tree-lined mall and pleasant riverside rambles; and historic Orléans. Each year this ancient city celebrates the victory of Joan of Arc with processions, bell ringing, and the illumination of the restored Cathédrale de St.-Croix. Few reminders of the Maid of Orléans survived World War II, but there are statues of Joan in Place du Martroi and on the porch of the Hôtel de Ville. Return to Paris, about 72 miles (116 km) via superhighway A10.

BEST EN ROUTE

Expect to pay $85 and up per night for a double room in hotels listed as expensive; $50 to $85 in those listed as moderate; and under $40 in the inexpensive ones. The restaurants range in price from $85 and up for a dinner for two in the expensive range; $45 to $85 in the moderate range; and under $45, inexpensive.

ANGERS

Concorde – Modern convenience in the center of town, with 73 deluxe rooms, a pleasant restaurant, and a brasserie open until 11:30 PM. 18 Bd. Foch (phone: 41-87-37-20). Moderate.

France – Opposite the train station and tourist office, with 61 attractive rooms. Its restaurant, *Plantagenets,* offers fine food and service. 8 Pl. de la Gare (phone: 41-88-49-42). Moderate.

Entr'acte – Popular rustic restaurant near the post office. Specialties: *coquilles St.-Jacques au champagne, saumon du Bourgueil.* Closed Saturdays, Sunday nights, and August. 9 Rue Louis-de-Romain (phone: 41-87-71-82). Moderate.

Logis – Endowed with a Michelin star, it's known for seafood. Closed Saturday nights and Sundays in the summer. 17 Rue St.-Laud (phone: 41-87-44-15). Moderate.

Toussaint – This comfortable restaurant features simple and creative cooking — vegetable cake, *foie gras au Layon,* fresh fruit sherbets. Closed Sunday evenings and Mondays, late February, and 3 weeks in August. 7 Pl. Kennedy (phone: 41-87-46-20). Moderate to inexpensive.

Vert d'Eau – Well-known restaurant with original dishes. Specialties include *poissons de Loire beurre blanc, fricassée de poulet à l'angevine,* and *fraises Marguerite d'Anjou* in season. Closed Sunday evenings, Mondays, and a week in February. 9 Bd. G.-Dumesnil (phone: 41-48-52-86). Moderate to inexpensive.

SAUMUR

Prieuré – Gracious living and dining in an elegant Renaissance manor house in a 60-acre park. Member of Relais & Châteaux. Its 35 rooms, 15 in the château itself, have period furnishings; there's a tennis court, a heated pool, riding, and golf nearby. Closed January 5 to March 5. Reserve well in advance for summer, at least 2 weeks other times of the year. Five miles (8 km) west of Saumur via D751 in Chênehutte-les-Tuffeaux (phone: 41-67-90-14). Expensive.

FONTEVRAUD-L'ABBAYE

Licorne – This small, elegant restaurant with a young, hospitable owner features Loire Valley fish with sorrel sauce, beef with tarragon sauce and homemade carrot-tinted noodles, and a scrumptious chocolate cake. In good weather, ask for a table outside. Closed Sunday nights, Mondays, part of February, and from August 30 to September 7. Allee Ste. Catherine (phone: 41-51-72-49). Moderate.

CHINON

Gargantua – Brick and timber 15th-century mansion with 17 simple but pleasant rooms and an excellent restaurant. Specialties: *poussin braisé en soupière aux écrevisses* and *omelette gargamelle.* Open March to November 5. 73 Rue Haute-St.-Maurice (phone: 47-93-04-71). Moderate.

Château de Marçay – Beautifully restored 15th-century château with 35 charming rooms, 3 suites, and a good restaurant, set in a park with terrace, pool, and a tennis court. Member of Relais & Châteaux. Closed from January to mid-March. About 4 miles (7 km) south of Chinon on Route D116 (phone: 47-93-03-47). Expensive.

Giraudière – This picturesque manor house offers simple charm and 25 rooms, some with kitchenettes. No restaurant, but breakfast is served. Closed from January to mid-March. Three miles (4.8 km) west of Chinon via the road to Bourgueil and the Savigny turnoff (phone: 47-58-40-36). Moderate.

AZAY-LE-RIDEAU

Auberge du XII Siècle – Gothic house serving beautifully prepared dishes. Closed Tuesdays and late January through February. About 4 miles (6 km) from Azay in Saché (phone: 47-26-86-58). Moderate.

Grand Monarque – Peaceful little 30-room inn with a restaurant serving good local specialties and wines. The restaurant is closed from mid-November to mid-March. Pl. de la République (phone: 47-45-40-08). Moderate to inexpensive.

VILLANDRY

Cheval Rouge – A short stroll from the château gardens, this attractive provincial restaurant, which recently has had a very successful facelift, features its own foie gras and smoked salmon, Loire fish, including *sandre* (perch-pike), and good regional wines. There are also 20 rooms in the château. Restaurant serves until 9 PM. Closed Mondays and November to mid-March (phone: 47-50-02-07). Moderate.

LANGEAIS

Hosten – Charming 14-room hostelry with an excellent restaurant. Specialties: *homard cardinal, escalope de saumon à l'oseille, écrevisses au Vouvray, filet à la moëlle.* Reserve in advance. Closed Monday evenings, Tuesdays, December, January, and from June 20 to July 10. 2 Rue Gambetta (phone: 47-96-82-12). Expensive to moderate.

TOURS

Chantepie – Intimate and comfortable hostelry with 28 rooms. No restaurant. Joué les Tours, 4 miles (6 km) from Tours (phone: 47-53-06-09). Expensive.

Jean Bardet – Newly intalled in a grand old mansion in a park near the center of Tours, Bardet (formerly of *Chateauroux*) has quickly established his hotel/restaurant as one of the most outstanding in a region rich with luxurious hostelries. Specialties include fresh steamed salmon with soya, farm rabbit with artichokes, and oven-roasted lobster. 57 Rue Groison (phone: 47-41-41-11). Expensive.

Bordeaux – Old, completely renovated 54-room hotel in the center of town serves classic Touraine cuisine in the good, reasonably priced restaurant. Specialties: *sandre au beurre blanc, coquelet au vin de Chinon.* 3 Pl. Maréchal-Leclerc (phone: 47-05-40-32). Moderate.

Univers – The 92 comfortable rooms have all modern conveniences and a more than acceptable restaurant. Closed Saturdays and February. 5 Bd. Heurteloup (phone: 47-05-37-12). Moderate.

Royal – Pleasant 32-room hotel with modern conveniences and antique furnishings. Bar, but no restaurant. 65 Av. Grammont (phone: 47-64-71-78). Moderate to inexpensive.

Charles Barrier – This venerable chef has garnered top culinary ratings in Tours for decades and continues to merit two stars from Michelin for his refined versions of regional specialties. A *prix fixe* menu offers the pleasure of his elegant dining at a reasonable price. Closed Sunday evenings, Mondays, and July. 101-103 Av. de la Tranchée (phone: 47-54-20-39). Moderate.

Charmilles – A rustic restaurant with a lush garden that faces the Loire, its menu offerings include lobster salad and brill and turbot in béarnaise sauce. Closed Sunday evenings and Mondays in winter. 49 Quai des Maisons, Blanches, St.-Cyr-sur-Loire (phone: 47-54-02-01). Moderate.

Poivrière – Romantically situated in a 15th-century house. The cuisine gives traditional ingredients unconventional twists. There is an inexpensive *prix fixe* menu. Closed Mondays and January. 13 Rue du Change (phone: 47-20-85-41). Moderate.

Rôtisserie Tourangelle – A longtime favorite of residents, this brasserie is noted for good service and a fine menu. Try the smoked breast of duck simmered in local Borgueil wine. Closed from late February to mid-March, Mondays, and Sunday evenings. 23 Rue Commerce (phone: 47-05-71-21). Moderate.

Tuffeaux – Highly regarded, it boasts a special location near the cathedral in Tours's old quarter. Loire Valley fish are especially good here, as are puff pastry desserts. Closed Sundays, and Mondays for lunch. 19 Rue Lavoisier (phone: 47-47-19-89). Moderate.

CHÂTEAUX-HOTELS NEAR TOURS

Domaine de Beauvois – With 39 spacious rooms, pool, tennis, riding, fishing, and a popular dining room. Specialties: *gâteau de légumes, mousseline de brochet de queues d'écrevisses, tarte aux pommes chaude;* Bourgueil and Vouvray wines. Closed from January to mid-March. Luynes, Rte. D49, about 7 miles (12 km) from Tours (phone: 47-55-50-11). Expensive.

Château d'Artigny – A stately château on a plateau above the Indre; it's the most luxurious hotel in the valley, in a 50-acre park with formal gardens, pool, tennis, riding, fishing, and golf nearby. The superb Touraine cuisine in the elegant restaurant is well known, and there's a 40,000-bottle cellar to choose from. Closed from November 27 to January 6. Reserve well ahead. About 1 mile (2 km) southwest by D17 from Montbazon; 7 miles (12 km) from Tours (phone: 47-26-24-24). Expensive.

Domaine de la Tortinière – Beautiful rooms and suites in the Belle Epoque manor house, two-story stable, or cozy stone cottage. Peaceful, beautiful grounds, superb service, and perfect cooking in the Michelin one-star restaurant. Specialties: *saumon fumé, meurettes d'anguilles au Bourgueil, filet aux truffes;* Oisly and Montlouis wines. Open from March 1 to December 20. Reserve well in advance. One mile (1.6 km) north of Montbazon via N10 and D287 (phone: 47-26-00-19). Expensive.

VALENÇAY

Espagne – A former coaching inn with 11 lovely rooms and 6 suites. The restaurant features classic, regional specialties, including *terrine de foies de volailles aux truffes, noisettes d'agneau à l'estragon, delicieuse au chocolat;* Valençay and Chinon wines. Closed January and February, and Sunday evenings and Mondays in the off-season. 8 Rue du Château (phone: 54-00-00-02). Expensive.

CHENONCEAUX

Bon Laboureur et Château – Pretty house covered with ivy and surrounded by a garden where meals are served in summer. Specialties of the restaurant include: *sandre beurre blanc, mousseline de brochet au coulis d'écrevisses, tournedos mariné Vendôme;* Montlouis and Oisly wines. Closed from the end of November to early March, Tuesdays and Wednesdays in fall. 6 Rue Dr.-Bretonneau (phone: 47-23-90-02). Moderate to inexpensive.

Gâteau Breton – Rustic Breton bistro in the heart of the village. The simple home cooking and tasty pastries are more than just good for the price. Closed Tuesdays, Monday evenings, and from mid-November to mid-February. Rue National (phone: 47-23-90-14). Inexpensive.

AMBOISE

Domaine des Hauts de Loire – Gracious 18th-century manor house in a 75-acre park with 8-acre lake; 22 rooms and 6 suites in a separate but equally charming building have antique furnishings and modern bathrooms. Good, elegant dining room, tennis courts. Closed from December to March. Less than 10 miles (16 km) north of Amboise on N152, outside Onzain (phone: 54-20-72-57). Expensive.

Château de Pray – A lovely old château that has 16 guestrooms, a dining room, and a terrace for pleasant summer lunches. Linger over the salmon in sorrel sauce. Closed from January to mid-February. About 2 miles (3.2 km) northeast of Amboise via D751 (phone: 47-57-23-67). Moderate to inexpensive.

Auberge du Mail – This 12-room inn came under new management in 1986. The restaurant, considered the best in Amboise, serves *confit d'oie au Vouvray, saumon poché, célestine de fruits de mer, filet en chevreuil;* Montlouis and Chinon wines. Closed Fridays in the off-season. 32 Quai de Gaulle (phone: 47-57-60-39). Inexpensive.

BLOIS

Novotel – Modern, air conditioned rooms, with restaurant, snack bar, and pool. About 2½ miles (4 km) east of Blois by N152 at La Chaussée St.-Victor (phone: 54-78-33-57). Moderate.

Relais des Landes – A country inn with 18 pretty rooms and good food. Closed from late December to January 8. Ouchamps, about 10 miles (16 km) south of Blois by D751 and D7 (phone: 54-44-03-33). Moderate.

Hostellerie de la Loire – Set on the river with lots of atmosphere, this small hotel has 17 simple but comfortable rooms and a restaurant. Closed from January 15 to February 15. 8 Rue Maréchal-de-Lattre-de-Tassigny (phone: 54-74-26-60). Moderate to inexpensive.

CHAMBORD

Grand St.-Michel – This rambling place with 38 rooms provides a mesmerizing view of Chambord castle across the road. The dining room specializes in game during hunting season, but also has tasty *rillons* (spiced, cubed pork) and poached salmon and trout. The entire place shuts down from mid-November to mid-December (phone: 54-20-31-31). Inexpensive.

COUR-CHEVERNY

St.-Hubert – A pleasant, provincial inn, it is close to the château and is known especially for its fine game (the specialty is *côtelette de chevreuil St.-Hubert*). Closed Tuesday evenings, Wednesdays, and early December to mid-January. Rue National (phone: 54-79-96-60). Moderate to inexpensive.

Trois Marchands – Former coaching inn with sidewalk tables, a courtyard, and good fresh food. Closed mid-January to March and Mondays from October to Easter. Pl. de l'Eglise (phone: 54-79-96-44). Moderate to inexpensive.

Bordeaux

The region of Bordeaux is known to America and most of the world by a litany of wine labels of renowned châteaux — Margaux, Mouton-Rothschild, Haut-Brion — and by famous place names such as Haut-Médoc, St.-Emilion, and Sauternes. To the French, however, Bordeaux simply means the river port itself, known for some of the finest 18th-century architecture outside of Paris as well as for a measured, contented style of living. As for the Bordelais, as they are called, they have been blessed beyond the measure of most people.

Until the middle of the 15th century, Bordeaux — and much of the south-west of France — was a privileged colony of the English, who for the most part let the local burghers have their way. Although the English influence waned after France's victory in the Hundred Years War, the long arm of the Parisian government did not make itself felt in any consistent way until the 18th century, when Louis XV ascended the throne. In the opinion of the king, Bordeaux's commercial and strategic importance made it necessary to assign special governors, called *intendants,* to manage affairs on the spot. It is to this era of the king's *intendants* that Bordeaux owes the soberly elegant façades of its municipal buildings (the Bourse), monuments, and public buildings (the *Grand Théâtre*) as well as of the *hôtels-particuliers,* or townhouses (along Allées Tourny).

The king often used these appointments to rid himself of overly ambitious men in his court. Such was the case of the Duc de Richelieu (1692–1788). A sometime general (he made a poor showing against Frederick II of Prussia in the Seven Years War), professional charmer, and jaded cosmopolite, Riche-lieu found the city of Bordeaux a maze of narrow alleyways and decrepit provincial buildings. He set out at once to change it, broadening streets into boulevards and commissioning a number of buildings, among them Bor-deaux's *Grand Théâtre.* Successive *intendants* continued to reshape and refine the city's image, each trying to outdo his predecessors.

The sum of their legacy in design — beyond the monuments, the Allées Tourny, the Bourse, the Hôtel de Ville, and the numerous fine *hôtels-particu-liers* — is greater than the whole of its elegant parts, for the overriding feeling in Bordeaux is one of order, calm, and refined well-being.

Though not exactly at the gate of the city, vineyards — the world's greatest for their variety and overall excellence — surround Bordeaux on all sides. A half-hour drive northwest puts you in the heart of the Médoc, with its aristo-cratic red wines. A 45-minute drive east is the medieval village of St.-Emilion, whose fine red wines are a fitting complement to the charms and attractions of the town itself. To the south of Bordeaux (actually in its southern suburbs) are found the reds and dry whites of Graves, while still farther south are the fine sweet wines of Sauternes and Barsac. Just a couple of miles southwest of downtown Bordeaux, in Pessac, is Château Haut-Brion, owned by a former US ambassador to France, Douglas Dillon. This famous red wine was the only wine produced outside the Médoc to be classified in 1855.

The bounty to accompany all this drink comes from the farms, forests, and waters surrounding Bordeaux. Between the city and the Atlantic are the Landes, sandy plains, and pine barrens that stretch inland 90 miles or so, the source of excellent duck as well as of foie gras, the liver of fatted duck or goose. The ocean and the rivers provide oysters, mussels, fish, and lampreys — eels that are a local delicacy.

The well-fed Bordelais have any number of beaches at their disposal — from Biarritz, 110 miles (185 km) south, to the tip of the Médoc peninsula — along what they've rather fancifully called the Côte d'Argent. The favorite beaches are Cap Ferret, Le Porge, Carcans, and Montelivet. The last three, on the ocean side of the Médoc, are national parkland and still have many wild, undeveloped stretches.

The best road maps for the region are the *Cartes Touristiques* of the Institut Géographique National (IGN), scaled 1/100,000. For the Médoc, buy map 46; for St.-Emilion, 47; and for Graves and Sauternes, 55. Less detailed but very helpful are the IGN maps scaled 1/250,000. The regional map Bor-deaux-Périgord (110) is also good, as are the Michelin maps.

For a thorough tour of the vineyards, we recommend Alexis Lichine's *Guide to the Wines and Vineyards of France,* a comprehensive review of wine-making throughout the country.

BORDEAUX: This city can be explored by foot, and the best place to start is at the Place de Comédie by the *Grand Théâtre,* whose location and grand scale make it the most impressive monument in the city. On the exterior balcony, twelve columns are surmounted by twelve goddesses and muses of the arts. The view from the theater along the allées Tourny, with its broad promenade lined on either side by elegant shops and town houses, gives a measure of the scale on which the Bordeaux *intendants* worked.

Walk along the Allées Tourny to the Place Tourny; a turn to the left will take you up Boulevard Clemenceau, where the smarter citizens of Bordeaux do much of their shopping for elegant clothes. At Place Gambetta is a small square park surrounded by cafés and pastry shops. Pause here for a cup of coffee at *Le Regent* or for tea and a pastry at the fine *salon de thé* called *Darricau;* or continue through the square to Porte Dijeaux and Rue Bouffard, which leads to the Cathédrale St.-André (built from the 11th to the 15th century) and is a tiny street lined with shops selling antique porcelains, engravings, and prints, silver, furniture, and bibelots.

Rue Ste.-Catherine is a crowded pedestrian walkway and shopping artery that is impossible to avoid; it has a fine bookstore, *Librarie Mallat,* but lacks the delights found elsewhere. More interesting are the small streets that branch off it toward the river leading to old Bordeaux, with its tangle of shops, bistros, and galleries and an open-air market. The recent revitalization here makes this the most exciting area of the city.

The best-known (and purportedly the best) wine stores in Bordeaux are the small, discreet *Badie,* at Pl. Tourny, and *La Vinotheque,* on Cours du XXX Juillet; also of note is *Vignes et Vins de France,* a tiny shop in old Bordeaux at 4 Rue des Bahutiers. The Maison du Vin is Bordeaux's center for wine promotion. The bureau offers adequate maps for the wine regions of Médoc, Graves, Sauternes, St.-Emilion, and Pomerol and has lists of which châteaux receive visitors and when.

Follow the Cour Intendance on the right side of the *Grand Théâtre* down to the quay and turn right, where you'll find the Place de la Bourse on your right. The building now houses the chamber of commerce of Bordeaux and is a magnificent example of 18th-century municipal architecture. The buildings that edge the quays from Place de la Bourse to St. Michael's Church are notable for the faces, called *mascarons,* carved over doorways and in walls, perhaps 200 in all and no two alike.

THE MÉDOC

You don't need to be a wine connoisseur to enjoy a tour of the Bordeaux wine country, especially of the Médoc. Of the hundreds of so-called châteaux in the Médoc, 65 were classified according to excellence in 1855, and these *grands crus classes* continue to demand top dollar today.

The special attraction of the Médoc — apart from its eminence as the source of exquisite, often expensive wine — is the incongruity of the flat, slightly undulating terrain carpeted with green vines. The landscape is dominated by the sky, and the whole vista is seen against the fantastic architecture and gentrified air of the wine châteaux. Some of these estates amount to no more than a good-sized house with a surface cellar (here called a *chai*) where wine is made and stored. Others are grandiose affairs indeed, either built in a style consonant with their times, like Château Margaux (generally Empire) or Château d'Issan (17th century), or built only to express a 19th-century bourgeois conception of a château (Palmer, Lascombes, Cos d'Estournel). (Note that most châteaux are closed at lunchtime; it's always best to call ahead to arrange a visit).

In spite of its fame, the Médoc is not well marked from Bordeaux. From the center of town, follow the signs for Soulac or ask directions to the Barrière du Médoc. This will get you out of town in the right direction. About 2 miles (3.2 km) beyond the turnoff for the Paris Autoroute, the road branches to the right toward Pauillac. This is D2e, the vineyard road, which leads past the greatest of the Médoc châteaux.

CANTENAC: About 9 miles (15 km) from the turnoff, just beyond a church on the left, is the entrance to Château Prieuré-Lichine. Park on the right side of the road opposite the archway and walk into the inner court. Once inside, on your left is a cloister decorated with antique firebacks; follow the gravel walk to the office, where you'll find an English-speaking guide to take you through the *chai.* This 16th-century *chai* is one of the oldest in the Médoc, but it has some of the newest wine-making equipment. Tasting may be enjoyed with the permission of the cellar master, and wines may be purchased. Open daily and during lunch (phone: 56-88-36-28).

Across the road from Prieuré-Lichine is the stone wall and gateway to Château d'Issan. Take a peaceful walk down a long alley of plane trees to the moated, turreted 16th-century château, which is privately owned. Visits to the *chai* can be arranged.

MARGAUX: Another three-quarters of a mile (1.5 km) up D2 from Cantenac will bring you to the turnoff on the right to the renowned Château Margaux. On the way you'll see signs for other prestigious châteaux, including Palmer and Lascombes. Château Margaux was rated a first growth (*cru*) in 1855 with only three others, and this privileged position is evident from the building and the grounds. The Empire château (built around 1802) has sober, classical lines and an imperial-looking stairway. The carefully laid out gardens include ponds where languid swans swim about — a present from Queen Elizabeth II. Although the château is privately owned and not generally open to visitors, a guide is available to take you through the *chai* if you write for an appointment (phone: 56-88-70-28).

ST.-JULIEN: About 10 miles (16 km) beyond Margaux is St.-Julien. Here, Château Beychevelle is the main attraction; take a tour of the *chai* and of the impressive gardens in the rear. Appointments may be made to the château (phone: 56-59-23-00).

The grounds of the stately Château Ducru-Beaucaillou adjoin those of Beychevelle (phone: 56-59-05-20). Not far away is the fabled first growth, Château Latour, which actually straddles the boundary between St.-Julien and the commune of Pauillac. Today, all that remains of the ancient fortress that once stood here is the tower (phone: 56-59-00-51).

PAUILLAC: Pauillac as a wine district takes in more than just the town and includes two of the four first growths: Lafite-Rothschild and Mouton-Rothschild (elevated to first growth in 1973). Mouton "tried harder" during all its years as a second growth, but now, through the efforts of Baron Philippe de Rothschild and his late American wife Pauline, it has become the premier attraction of the Médoc and the second most popular tourist site in the southwest of France (after the shrine of Lourdes). An appointment is necessary, but worth making, to see the *Mouton Wine Museum,* the *chai,* and the cellars. The wine museum contains the Rothschilds' collection of paintings, tapestries, and art objects celebrating the cult of wine and the cultivation of the vine. This *chai* is the most impressive in the Médoc, with ten long neat rows of barrels stretching out for nearly 100 yards. On the far wall, perfectly centered and lit from behind, is the seal of Mouton carved in wood. The château is closed in August and on weekends. Call 56-59-22-22 for tour times.

Continuing up D2, you pass Lafite-Rothschild on your left. Its wine is said to have been the favorite of two royal mistresses, Mme. de Pompadour and Mme. du Barry. To visit the exquisite vaulted *chai,* call 56-59-01-74.

ST.-ESTEPHE: No visit here is complete without a stop at the 19th-century Château Cos d'Estournel, the most exotic of all the Médoc châteaux, with its pagoda towers and massive carved wood doors (phone: 56-59-35-69). Also in St.-Estephe is Château Montrose run by a mother-and-son team (phone: 56-59-30-12).

Continuing north, the flatness of the vineyards gives way to wooded slopes and fields of more conventional farm crops. A salty breeze is a reminder that this last stretch of the Gironde River is the estuary where fresh water meets the Atlantic.

ST.-EMILION AND POMEROL

The wine châteaux of St.-Emilion and Pomerol are more modest than those of the Médoc: The properties are smaller and the châteaux usually no more than houses, so there are few formalities when it comes to visiting.

The two regions border each other on the right bank of the Dordogne. To get there from the center of Bordeaux (a 45-minute drive), follow signs for Périgueux. This will put you on N89 to Libourne. At Libourne take D21e toward Montagne. Two interesting châteaux to visit in Pomerol are Vieux-Château-Certan (follow D21e past Catusseau and take the left-hand fork toward Néac) and Château l'Evangile (take the right-hand fork after Catusseau). To reach St.-Emilion from Pomerol or Libourne, take D17e or D670.

ST.-EMILION: One of the most picturesque wine villages in France, this is a medieval treasure perched on a small limestone plateau overlooking the valley of the Dordogne. In the 12th century, St.-Emilion was a stopping place for the pilgrims who wound their way on foot to the shrine of Santiago da Compostela in Spain. Pilgrims of one sort or another — for wine or for the love of old stones — have been passing through ever since.

Park your car at the Place des Créneaux and walk to the edge of the square for a view over the Dordogne Valley and the houses of the village below. At the nearby Syndicat d'Initiative (Pl. des Créneaux) you can pick up a map of the town with a list of tourist sites and wine châteaux, including visiting times.

St.-Emilion's charm is best appreciated in a leisurely amble through the town, which permits you to take in the sites as well as the peaceful, Old World feeling imparted by the narrow streets and small ocher stone houses with red tile roofs.

L'Eglise Monolithe is a 9th- to 12th-century church hewn into the side of the limestone cliff, the most important monolithic church in France. The Chapelle de la Trinité and the alleged Hermitage de St.-Emilion are part of the church.

Of less historical importance than L'Eglise Monolithe and the Chapelle, but no less compelling for their half-natural, half-manmade strangeness, are the remains of the Couvent des Cordeliers, a 14th- to 15th-century convent and cloister, now an overgrown shell of stone walls and stairways. In an interior court you can buy the locally made sparkling wine by the glass or bottle.

On the northern edge of town is Château Villemaurine. If you have time to visit only one of the almost countless châteaux in St.-Emilion, let this be it. The system of labyrinthine cellars scooped deep into the limestone is among St.-Emilion's (and even Bordeaux's) most dramatic. Philippe Giraud, the owner's son, speaks excellent English and can arrange visits for you (phone: 57-74-46-44). Closed mornings and Mondays.

BEST EN ROUTE

The city of Bordeaux offers a number of first class restaurants and hotels. However, although the Médoc produces some of the greatest wines in the world, it is very poorly served in the matter of food and lodging. There are no hotels to speak of and only one or two restaurants worth the name. With this caution in mind, visitors should visit the Médoc restaurants cited below only for light lunches or suppers. The hotels we have listed as expensive will cost $85 and up for a double room per night; moderate, $45 to $85; and inexpensive, $45. In the restaurants we've mentioned, a meal without wine will cost $90 or more at an expensive place, $50 to $90 at a moderate one, and under $50 at an inexpensive one. Wine can cost as little as $5 a bottle or as much as you're willing to pay.

BORDEAUX

Burdigala – This classic old edifice in the Mériadeck section was recently transformed into an elegant four-star establishment. Its 71 rooms and 7 duplex suites offer modern comforts. 115 Rue Georges-Bonnac (phone: 56-90-16-16). Expensive.

Grand – A hotel since 1850 with a lovely façade that is a perfect counterpoint to the *Grand Théâtre* across the street. The 95 rooms and 3 suites have been modernized and are quiet and comfortable. 2 Pl. de la Comédie (phone: 56-90-93-44). Expensive.

Réserve – In the suburb of Alouette, this is the most pleasant of the Bordeaux hotels and is also blessed with an excellent restaurant, surrounded with gardens and trees. The restaurant alone is worth the trip. 74 Av. Bourgailh, L'Alouette Pessac, about 2 miles (3.2 km) southeast of the airport (phone: 56-07-13-28). Expensive.

Gambetta – Completely renovated and in the center of town. Each of the 33 rooms has a bath or shower and telephone; almost all have a television set. 66 Rue Porte-Dijeaux (phone: 56-51-21-83). Expensive to moderate.

Royal Médoc – A charming hotel with 45 modern, tastefully decorated rooms and a bar. 3-5 Rue de Sèze (phone: 56-81-72-42). Inexpensive.

Vieux Bordeaux – This renovated 18th-century gem has 11 clean, basic rooms. 22 Rue du Cancéra (phone: 56-48-07-27). Inexpensive.

Jean Ramet – Simple, intimate, friendly, and a favorite among the Bordelais. Open weekdays only. Reservations recommended. Near Place de la Bourse, 7-8 Pl. Jean-Jaurès (phone: 56-44-12-51). Expensive.

Bistrot de Bordeaux – Tiny, attractive, and busy, this place has good bistro fare, such as skate salad and duck filet mignon, along with local wines. 10 Rue des Piliers-de-Tutelle (phone: 56-81-35-94). Moderate.

La Ténarèze – An intimate little place on one of Bordeaux's loveliest public squares. Flavorful dishes of southwest France are served at both indoor and outdoor tables. 18 Pl. du Parlement (phone: 56-44-43-29). Moderate.

MARGAUX

Le Relais de Margaux – In a 138-acre park, it has 18 rooms, 4 suites, tennis courts, a pool, and sauna. The restaurant is the best in the Médoc; try the dove or seafood specialties. Vincent Island (phone: 56-88-38-30). Expensive.

Savoie – This inn features straightforward cooking and a wide variety of local wines. When weather permits, dine in the garden. Closed Sundays and holidays. Pl. la Trémoille (phone: 56-88-31-76). Moderate to inexpensive.

LAMARQUE

Relais du Médoc – A simple family-run restaurant, perhaps the best in the Médoc, serving hearty, satisfying lunches and dinners in season, otherwise lunch only; closed Mondays. Just off D2 between Margaux and St.-Julien (phone: 56-58-92-27). Moderate.

PAUILLAC

Relais du Manoir – Modest as it is, this small, 7-room *relais* (a former *bordelle*) is making an honest attempt at refined and imaginative cooking. Good seafood. Less than ½ mile along the quay north of the center of Pauillac (phone: 56-59-05-47). Moderate.

GAILLAN EN MÉDOC

Château Layauga – An 18th-century château that has recently been converted into a small luxury hotel with 7 rooms decorated in Louis XV style. A restaurant serves updated French classics prepared by chef/owner Philipe Gorand. Gaillan en Médoc (phone: 56-41-26-83).

ST.-EMILION

Hostellerie de Plaisance – Lovely little 12-room hotel with a cozy restaurant in the center of town. Pl. du Clocher (phone: 57-24-72-32). Expensive to moderate.

Auberge de la Commanderie – Perched on a hill above Place du Marché, it has the look and feel of a French country house. There are 14 rooms (be sure to reserve in advance) and a very charming restaurant. Rue des Cordeliers (phone: 57-24-70-19). Moderate.

Auberge Saint-Jean – Well worth the 5-mile (8-km) drive south from St.-Emilion, this place is easily one of the best in the entire Bordeaux area. Excellent food prepared with great finesse in a pleasant riverside setting. Closed Sunday nights and Mondays and the last 2 weeks of September. On D670; follow signs for Marmande until you cross the Dordogne at St.-Jean-de-Blaignac; the restaurant is on your left just after the bridge (phone: 57-74-95-50). Expensive.

Logis de la Cadène – This rustic place has 10 tables inside and another 6 outside under an arbor. Basic fare includes *entrecôte* and omelettes. Lunch only. Closed Mondays. Pl. Marché au Bois (phone: 57-24-71-40). Moderate to inexpensive.

The Dordogne

The appeal of the Dordogne is the attraction of extremes: This country of foie gras and truffles prepared with all the country cook's art is the same country whose long-hidden grottoes and secret caves have offered spectacular evidence of man's earliest organized societies — cave drawings, tools, and weapons thousands upon thousands of years old, a glimpse into the prehistory of humankind.

In southwestern France between the Massif Central and the Atlantic seaboard, Dordogne includes the old and historic province of Périgord as well as parts of Limousin, Angoumois, and Saintonge. The entire region is endowed with luxuriant valleys, riverbanks lined with poplars and willows, vineyards, hillsides covered with walnut and fruit orchards, steep peaks crowned with medieval castles, and red-roofed fortified towns (*bastides*) perched above the half-dozen rivers that lace the terrain. Rugged granite and limestone plateaus and rocky outcroppings contrast with the fertile farmland to provide a profusion of natural beauty. The area includes the Périgord Blanc, named for the chalky limestone that imparts a whiteness to the countryside, and the Périgord Noir, which takes its name from the forests of dark oak.

To reap the fullest enjoyment from the Dordogne, equip yourself with a detailed map (Michelin 75 or IGN 47/48) and take your time. Just about every bend in the road (and there are plenty) offers a surprise to delight the eye and the imagination — a fisherman reeling in a trout; a perfect picnic spot; panoramas to photograph or paint; or cool forests inviting you to stroll where prehistoric man once hunted mammoth, bison, and deer.

Lingering over meals will certainly be a highlight of any itinerary. The Périgord's gastronomic glories are world renowned. In addition to the justly famed foie gras, *confit d'oie,* and truffles, the chefs of the Dordogne have almost infinitely subtle ways of preparing game, crayfish, trout, and other lake and river fish. Try *morilles* (morels) and *cèpes* (flap mushrooms); strawberries in season; jams and preserves from the native plums and walnuts. Among the wines to note are robust Cahors; full-bodied white or red Bergerac; Pécharmant, a fruity red wine that goes well with game and poultry; and Monbazillac, the fragrant sweet wine served as an apéritif with foie gras or with desserts.

The logical gateway to the Dordogne is Bordeaux, accessible by a 1-hour flight from Paris or an enjoyable 4-hour ride on one of Europe's fastest trains, which average speeds of 95 mph. Then it's just 145 miles (about 230 km) by car from Bordeaux to Rocamadour, the easternmost point on our itinerary. In between, however, is a good week's worth of wandering on well-maintained country roads with relatively little traffic, except in high season (July and August).

En Route from Bordeaux – For a description of Bordeaux, see the *Bordeaux* route. Leave Bordeaux by Route N89 via Libourne, an ancient stronghold founded by — and named for — Roger de Leybourne, an agent of the 13th-century King of England to whom the region belonged. Proceed along the course of the Isle River to Périgueux (about 75 mi/120 km), the capital of the Dordogne and a good place to make your headquarters for one or two nights.

PÉRIGUEUX: Once two towns separated by a wall, the lower section of Périgueux dates from the Roman era, with the remains of a 3rd-century Gallo-Roman amphitheater and the cylindrical shell of a pagan temple, the Tour de Vésone. The town was devastated in the Vandal invasion of the 4th century, and a new defensive wall was built with stones taken from the ruins. Portions of this fortification may still be seen near the Château Barrière and the Arena.

Two excellent examples of Périgord-Romanesque architecture remain from the Middle Ages: the Church of St.-Etienne-de-la-Cité and the Cathédrale St.-Front. The latter, one of the largest churches in the area, is also one of the most unusual in all of France. The structure is built in the shape of a Greek cross; and the domes and cupolas show Byzantine influence. The bell tower, topped by a lantern-like structure supported by slender columns, is one of the finest Romanesque towers still standing. From the Barris bridge, St.-Front looms huge and white above the upper town, but its impressive interior is well worth a close inspection, and the rooftop gives you a panoramic view of the town.

Browse for souvenirs and food specialties in the shops that line the square near the cathedral, then walk up Rue de la Clarté and Rue Limogeanne to the old quarter, with its fascinating late medieval and Renaissance houses, many with remarkable stairways, gates, and ornate façades. Near the cathedral, at 31 Rue St.-Front, *L'Oison* restaurant serves a classic fish mixed grill in the unique surroundings of an old hosiery workshop. Continue to Cours Tourny and the *Musée du Périgord,* which has a rich collection of more than 14,000 prehistoric artifacts as well as Gallo-Roman mosaics, ceramics, and bronzes. Cours Tourny also has a good restaurant, *Léon.* On the outskirts of town, *Marcel* provides a seductive introduction to the gastronomic specialties of the region. *La Chocolatheque,* at 2 Rue Taillefer, satisfies any sweet tooth with *croquant du Périgord* or *nougatine au cognac.* Pick up additional tourist information at the Syndicat d'Initiative (1 Av. d'Aquitaine; phone: 53-53-10-63) and the Office Départemental du Tourisme (16 Rue du Président-Wilson; phone: 53-53-44-35).

A pleasant half-day excursion (via D710 and D78) can be made of a drive north through the valley of the Dronne River, taking in a visit to the Château de Bourdeilles and the town of Brantôme.

BOURDEILLES: The medieval ramparts of Bourdeilles enclose a double château built on a promontory: The first house is an imposing feudal fortress with a superb octagonal keep; the other is a 16th-century Renaissance palace with sumptuously decorated salons and a comprehensive collection of ancient furniture and tapestries.

BRANTÔME: Brantôme is a delightful little town between two arms of the Dronne. Its fine 18th-century Benedictine abbey is now the Town Hall and houses the Musée Desmoulin, with an absorbing vignette of the town's history. A stroll from the Renaissance Pavillion through the Monks' Garden and along the canalside quays past old houses with flowered balconies and terraces is a peaceful and reflective way to pass an hour or two. Lunch or dinner at the *Chabrol* is highly recommended before the return to Périgueux via D939.

En Route from Périgueux – Start early in the morning heading east on N89 for Brive-la-Gaillarde. En route you will pass the partly restored, late Greek Revival Château de Rastignac. There's a striking similarity between its 18th-century semicircular Ionic peristyle and the southern portico of the White House. South via Routes D65, 67, and 704 is Montignac and the celebrated caves of

Lascaux, unfortunately closed to the public since 1963, when it was found that microorganisms were damaging the beautiful prehistoric frescoes. However, you can now visit a very faithful reproduction of the cave that opened a few years ago near the Lascaux site. At nearby Le Thot, a modern prehistoric art center that shows photographic blowups of the most typical paintings, film projections, and models is open year-round. The terrace provides a good view of the Vézère Valley and the hill of Lascaux.

Head back through Montignac to pick up D704 north and return to N89, following the course of the Vézère River to Terrasson, an active little city at the crossroads of three provinces and the scene of an important truffle and walnut market. From the ramparts of the 15th-century abbey, there's an excellent view over the slate-roofed houses down to the Vézère and the enchanting countryside dotted with poplars beyond. Continue on N89 through the Brive basin's rich plum orchards and vegetable gardens, and try to take time out at the *Château de Castel Novel* (see *Best en Route*), an old mansion in its own park with an excellent restaurant, just north of Brive at Varetz.

At Brive, turn south on N20 to Cressesac, then left on N140 for Martel and Rocamadour. At Réveillon, take D673 through the woods to the hamlet of l'Hospitalet. There's a spectacular vista over the narrow gorge of the Alzou, its rocky wall scaled by the extraordinary little fortified town of Rocamadour, the next stop. But be careful of roaming gaggles of geese along the winding country roads.

ROCAMADOUR: Rocamadour is built in superimposed tiers that are literally hewn out of the steep cliff face. Enter the town by the 13th-century Porte du Figuier near the Gendarmerie and you're on the principal thoroughfare, a narrow cobblestone street lined with souvenir shops. Continue down to the Porte Basse through a picturesque quarter of tiny houses clinging to the cliff, then return to Place de la Caretta and the Great Staircase, which pilgrims have been climbing on their knees each September since the Middle Ages. Some 141 steps up is Place Senhals, with the former clerics' quarters now converted into hotels such as the charming *Ste.-Marie,* with an attractive dining terrace. Near Place Senhals is Rue de la Mercerie, a tiny street lined with 16th-century houses. Climbing another 75 steps leads to Place St.-Amadour and the Basilica of St.-Sauveur with its crypt and chapels; Notre-Dame, with a shrine honoring an ancient miraculous Virgin and child carved out of walnut; and St.-Michel, with two fine exterior frescoes.

Less energetic travelers should take the elevator near the Porte Salmon to the château on the third level and work their way down. From the turrets of the château, built on a promontory and now the home of the caretakers of the shrines, you have an unforgettable view of the sheer drop over the gorge and the town.

From Rocamadour it's just 9 miles (15 km) to the Gouffre de Padirac, a 310-foot-deep gallery and caverns carved out of the limestone by a subterranean river. In an excursion lasting about 1½ hours, you can follow the course of the river for about ½ mile by a succession of narrow footpaths, switching to a boat that glides in and out of vast lakes and chambers and around bizarre rock formations.

En Route from Rocamadour – Route N673 twists and turns for about 13 miles (21 km) to Payrac. Turn left on N20 and head south for 2 miles (3.2 km), then pick up N673 again. At Gourdon turn north on D704 for Sarlat, stopping at the Grottoes of Cougnac. These clearly illuminated, accessible caves have prehistoric wall paintings of red ocher and black pigments that have been remarkably preserved.

SARLAT: Sarlat is a gem of a small, country town — a living museum with narrow, winding streets and ancient houses of gold-colored stone that painstaking restoration has returned to its original beauty. Don't be put off by the rather commercial, modern main street, Rue de la République. Get settled in one of the many pleasant hotels and head straight for the Syndicat d'Initiative (Pl. de la Liberté) for a walking tour map. If you happen to be there on Saturday morning, stop by the colorful street market in the same square.

The cathedral (Pl. du Peyrou) is a good central point for your explorations. Just across the way is one of Sarlat's most handsome Renaissance houses, the Maison de La Boétie, birthplace of the brilliant magistrate, author, and poet Etienne de La Boétie. Continue your visit to the Lanterne des Morts (Lantern of the Dead), the town's oldest and most curious structure; the Rue Montaigne, with a stop at the former coaching inn, now the Galerie Montaigne, displaying the works of local artists and craftsmen; the Présidial, with its splendid gardens, slate roof, and unusual lantern tower; Rue de la Salamandre and its rustic houses; and the Hôtel Plamon, a fascinating private home with three cathedral-like Gothic windows on the second floor. In the western part of town are steep, twisting streets such as Rue des Trois Conils, Rue du Siège, and Rue J.-J. Rousseau.

Sarlat is also the gastronomic capital of Périgord Noir, so stop by one of the inviting food shops for picnic makings or head for a restaurant such as *La Madeleine* (see *Best en Route*) to sample the foie gras that is a specialty of the town.

During the tourist season, guided tours of Sarlat are available. In August the town is host to a famous open-air drama festival, an antiques exhibition, numerous concerts at the cathedral, and important regional fairs.

En Route from Sarlat – The day-long excursion through the Dordogne Valley between Sarlat and St.-Cyprien takes you along 40 miles (64 km) of meandering river, with great rocks towering high above and cliffs crowned with ancient castles and villages in the most romantic settings imaginable.

Take D704 to Carsac; then follow D703 along the right bank of the Dordogne. The highlights include the Château de Montfort, destroyed and rebuilt four times, dominating a narrow loop of the river from its promontory; Dronne, a charming fortified town on the opposite bank with one of the more spectacular views of the valley from its ramparts and precipitous cliffside promenades; La Roque-Gageac, often called France's most beautiful village, especially when the stone houses are reflected by the late afternoon sun in the stream far below; and Beynac, clinging to another bend in the river with a château like an eagle's nest perched 800 feet above. This matchless setting overlooks another loop in the river as well as four more castles: the ruins of Beynac's great rival, feudal Castelnaud; Marqueyssac, with its lofty terraced gardens; Fayrac, the well-restored sentinel castle; and Les Milandes, once owned by the American singer and cabaret star Josephine Baker. Each, of course, has its own dramatic views and is of enough historical interest to merit a brief visit. A late lunch, dinner, or even an overnight stay at Beynac's *Bonnet* or St.-Cyprien's *L'Abbaye* is recommended (see *Best en Route*). Or you can continue to D49, then D706, and Les Eyzies-de-Tayac.

LES EYZIES-DE-TAYAC: This tiny village, hovering under a 600-foot overhanging cliff, is a prehistoric time capsule. Here, in 1868, skeletons dating from more than 30,000 years before were found in the Cro-Magnon Cave by railway workmen. Shortly thereafter, explorations of the nearby caves at Le Moustier and Madeleine uncovered other relics that are landmarks in the chronology of man. Organized tours with commentaries in French, English, and German depart from the Syndicat d'Initiative to the museum and the grottoes of Les Eyzies as well as to other important historical sites Mondays through Saturdays, June to September.

Halfway up the cliff in the center of town is the *National Museum of Prehistory,* in the former castle of the lords of Beynac. There is a good view from the terrace with Dardé's larger-than-life 1930 sculpture of Cro-Magnon man. Inside are eight rooms with a fascinating collection of artifacts, art, skeletons, tools, weapons, and engravings from local excavations.

Within walking distance is the Font de Gaume cave, with over 200 red ocher paintings of animals. This art appears extraordinarily sophisticated to 20th-century eyes. Other nearby sites of interest include the troglodyte Madeleine deposit; Le Moustier; Grand Roc, with a garden of crystalline deposits; Les Combarelles, with more than 300 paintings of animals, including running mammoths; Laugerie; La Mouthe; and the Fish Cave, with a superb salmon figure.

En Route from Les Eyzies – As you head west on D706 and D703, the Vézère curves to Le Bugue, another lovely village with the excellent *Royal Vézère* hotel right on the river (see *Best en Route*); Limeuil, which clings to a hillside above the junction of the Dordogne and the Vézère, each river crossed by an arched stone bridge; and Trémolat, little changed from the Middle Ages, with a view of the sunlit valley and the loop of the river spread out below. From Trémolat to Lalinde, follow D31 along the river, then detour south on N660 for Monpazier, probably the best-preserved fortified town of the region. The great square is surrounded by covered arcades, ancient houses, and arched gateways.

Return to Beaumont and Lalinde, then proceed west on N660 to Bergerac, at the western edge of the Dordogne. This is an active, pleasant little town brimming with flowers. Its old quarter is a maze of twisting streets and Renaissance porches and façades. The elegant silhouette of the Château de Monbazillac dominates a nearby hill, and a tour of its massive round towers and battlements can also include a tasting of the products of the local wine cooperative, which now owns the château. A statue of Edmond Rostand's immortal Cyrano de Bergerac stands at Place de la Myrpe. From Bergerac, it's only about 57 miles (92 km) back to Bordeaux along Route 936, past tobacco fields and vineyards on the rich alluvial plain.

BEST EN ROUTE

Expect to pay $80 and up per night for a double room in hotels listed as expensive; $40 to $80 in those listed as moderate; and less than $40 for an inexpensive one. The restaurants range in price from $80 and up for a dinner for two in the expensive range; $50 to $80 in the moderate range; and under $50 inexpensive. Prices do not include drinks, wine, or tip.

PÉRIGUEUX

Périgord – This member of the Logis de France association features 21 rooms, all with private bath, and a reasonably priced restaurant. 74 Rue Victor-Hugo (phone: 53-53-33-63). Inexpensive.

Oison – Unusual setting in an old hosiery workshop; the fish mixed grill is especially good. 31 Rue St.-Front (phone: 53-09-84-02). Expensive.

BRANTÔME

Moulin de l'Abbaye – A former mill on a gentle bend in the Dronne River, this is one of the most delightful inns in the region. It has 12 elegantly furnished rooms, a wonderful dining room (Chef Rabinel apprenticed with the Troisgros brothers), and a lovely riverside terrace. Closed mid-November to May. Rte. de Bourdeilles (phone: 53-05-80-22). Expensive.

Moulin du Roc – Another old mill that's now a friendly inn with 12 rooms. Its fine restaurant makes it worth a stop just for a meal. Four miles (6 km) northeast of Brantôme via D78, in Champagnac-de-Belair (phone: 53-54-80-36). Expensive.

Chabrol – Refined and comfortable and overlooking the Dronne. The 20 rooms are small but charmingly decorated, and the restaurant serves good regional dishes.

Rue Gambetta (phone: 53-05-70-15). Hotel, moderate; restaurant, expensive to moderate.

VARETZ

Château de Castel Novel – Old mansion in its own park with pool and tennis. Member of the Relais & Châteaux group. It has 28 rooms and an exceptionally fine restaurant serving inventive regional dishes and Cahors and Bergerac wines. Open early May to late October. Reserve in tourist season. Near Varetz, about 7 miles (11 km) northwest of Brive-la-Gaillarde on N901 (phone: 55-85-00-01). Expensive.

ROCAMADOUR

Château de Roumégouse – With 12 rooms and 2 suites in a wooded park with terraces overlooking Le Causse. Member of the Relais & Châteaux group. Riding and tennis nearby; pleasant restaurant. Between Rocamadour and Gramat off N140 (phone: 65-33-63-81). Expensive.

Beau Site et Notre-Dame – In a restored 15th-century house with all modern comforts, 55 rooms, and a restaurant with a terrace that offers a beautiful view. Rue Roland-le-Preux (phone: 65-33-63-08). Moderate.

Ste.-Marie – Small hotel with 22 comfortable rooms and a lovely, flower-lined terrace restaurant overlooking the Alzou Canyon. Pl. des Senhals (phone: 65-33-63-07). Moderate.

SARLAT

Hostellerie de Meysset – Charming, ivy-covered manor house with 20 rooms, 6 suites, and a very agreeable restaurant. One mile (1.6 km) northwest from town on Rte. de Eyzies (phone: 53-59-08-29). Expensive.

Hoirie – In a garden just outside town, this former hunting lodge is now a cozy 15-room inn with lots of local atmosphere and a swimming pool. 1½ miles south of town at La Canéda (phone: 53-59-05-62). Moderate.

Madeleine – Restored, distinguished traditional hostelry; 19 well-kept rooms, 3 suites, and an excellent restaurant with hearty regional food. In high season, guests are required to take breakfast and dinner at the hotel. 1 Pl. Petite-Rigaudie (phone: 53-59-10-41). Moderate.

La Couleuvrine – Actually a restored 12th-century structure, it has 25 rooms with antique furnishings but all the modern amenities. 1 Pl. de la Bouquerie (phone: 53-59-27-80). Inexpensive.

BEYNAC

Bonnet – Delightful small inn nestled in a grove of walnut trees on the banks of the Dordogne, with a wonderful view up to the castle of Beynac. There are 24 rooms, a pleasant staff, and a very popular restaurant. Closed from mid-October to mid-April (phone: 53-29-50-01). Moderate.

ST.-CYPRIEN

Abbaye – Small hostelry of 20 rooms, most with views down to the Dordogne and an excellent restaurant. Open from mid-March to mid-October; closed Wednesdays in September. Rue Entrepot (phone: 53-29-20-48). Moderate.

LES EYZIES-DE-TAYAC

du Centenaire – A sparkling 28-room hotel — more modern than the *Cro-Magnon* but equally worthy of praise — with pool, sauna, and gym. Chef Roland Mazére, who apprenticed with a few of the country's best, takes an up-to-date approach to cooking that's won him two Michelin stars. Closed November to April. Les Eyzies (phone: 53-06-97-18). Hotel, moderate; restaurant, expensive.

Cro-Magnon – Said to be where Cro-Magnon skeletons were found over 115 years ago, this delightful, vine-covered inn provides modern luxury and efficiency without forfeiting charm. There are 20 rooms, a swimming pool, extensive grounds, and a very good restaurant for classic traditional fare and some surprises. Closed mid-October to April. Route de Périgueux (phone: 53-07-20-01). Hotel, moderate; restaurant, expensive to moderate.

LE BUGUE

Royal Vézère – Comfortable, modern, 48-room hotel on the bank of the Vézère with rooftop pool, sunny terrace, and a nightclub. Small, exclusive restaurant with well-prepared regional specialties. Open late April to early October. Pl. Hôtel-de-Ville (phone: 53-06-20-01). Expensive.

TRÉMOLAT

Le Vieux Logis – The epitome of rustic charm in an old house with antique furniture and lovely gardens. With 20 rooms and a good restaurant. Nearby tennis, sailing, fishing, hunting, and riding. Member of the Relais & Châteaux group (phone: 53-22-80-06). Expensive.

BERGERAC

Château Rauly Saulieut – This lovely 19th-century château amid vines, south of Monbazillac, was transformed into a hotel/restaurant in 1988. Its 8 spacious rooms are exquisitely furnished with antiques belonging to the owner, who is also an antiques dealer. More of his items are on sale in a shop at the château. There are also gardens, a pool, a cozy restaurant, and conference rooms. Monbazillac (phone: 53-63-35-31). Expensive.

Le Cyrano – This unpretentious little restaurant serves the classics of the region. There are also 11 rooms, each with private bath. 2 Bd. Montaigne (phone: 53-57-02-76). Moderate.

Bordeaux – Modest, but with 42 adequate rooms and a restaurant. 38 Pl. Gambetta (phone: 53-57-12-83). Moderate to inexpensive.

Provence

As the French who flock here every summer know, one of the most charming regions in the country is Provence, the area along the southern banks of the Rhone River, just north and west of the Riviera. Like the Riviera, Provence is known for its cloudless skies and brilliant southern sunshine. It is also known for its pretty little villages perched high up in the hills or nestled down in the valleys, with their typical red roofs and, in many cases, medieval stone walls intact. Small farms are plentiful here; typical crops are fruits and vegetables. Grapes are cultivated, and thyme, marjoram, and lavender grow wild. Olive groves are everywhere, and rows of tall cypress trees are planted to protect crops from the mistral, the powerful north wind of southern France.

The name "Provence" is derived from the historic fact that the region was once a Roman province; yet its history begins earlier, with the founding of

Marseilles by the Greeks in 600 BC. The Romans invaded in about 125 BC and scattered traces of their stay everywhere. As a result, Provence is the section of France most renowned for its magnificently preserved Roman temples, arches, and amphitheaters. Its star attraction is the amazing 2,000-year-old, three-tier Pont du Gard, between Nímes and Arles, a Roman aqueduct that stands virtually intact.

In addition to Roman remains, Provence is dominated by Avignon, once the papal residence, with its impressive 14th-century Palais des Papes (Papal Palace), a vast stone fortress built during the schism within the papacy known to history as the Babylonian Captivity. The Pont d'Avignon, a bridge made famous in a French children's song, is actually called the Pont St.-Bénézet, and though partly destroyed, it still stretches picturesquely halfway across the Rhone. There's a fascinating side trip from Arles to the strange, marshy land of the Camargue, where bulls are raised for bullfights and wild horses, ducks, and flamingos roam free. At the eastern extreme of the route is Aix-en-Provence, which, except for its festival in July and August, is a quiet old university town adorned with boulevards, fountains, and cafés. Paul Cézanne lived here, and it's one of the loveliest towns in all of France.

Provençal cooking shows the Italian influence in its typical ingredients of garlic, tomatoes, and olive oil. The region produces the outstanding Côtes du Rhone wines such as Châteauneuf-du-Pape, Tavel, and Rasteau.

Avignon, the starting point of the route described below, is a 7-hour drive from Paris along Routes A6 or N7; if you prefer, you can choose the more scenic itinerary along the Loire Valley and through Burgundy. The best maps of the region are the Institut Géographique National's IGN 115 or Michelin nos. 83, 80, 81.

Note: Both Aix-en-Provence and Avignon host 3-week arts festivals in mid-July; both, but especially the one in Aix, are very popular, so make hotel reservations well in advance.

AVIGNON: The walled city of Avignon was the ancient seat of the papacy during the Church's period of schism in the 14th century. Park near the train station (Bd. St.-Roch) and enter the city through the Porte de la République. As you walk straight along the tree-lined Rue de la République, you'll come to the Place de l'Horloge, a good spot to pause at an outdoor café and take in some of the local color. From here it's only a few steps to the Place du Palais, which is dominated by the immense, fortress-like stone walls of the medieval papal residence. Informative English-language tours are given through the vast interior halls of this historic palace.

Coming back out onto the Place du Palais, you'll see a toylike train. Take it. It will carry you up to the Rocher des Doms, a lovely park with a superb view of the Rhone River and its 12th-century bridge, Pont St.-Bénézet. For a better feeling of daily life in Avignon, wander into the pedestrian zone off Place de l'Horloge, browsing, for example, in Rue des Marchands and Rue des Fourbisseurs, then following Rue du Roi-René to the picturesque Rue des Teinturiers, beside a canal and old water wheels. Avignon boasts elegant shopping, particularly for fine (but not cheap) regional antiques. Turn left anywhere off Rue de la République and you'll find many shops. Finally, cross the river to Villeneuve-les-Avignon. It is from this ancient city of cardinals, with Philippe le Bel's tower and the St.-André fort, that you'll get a spectacular view of Avignon at sunset.

En Route from Avignon – Take Route N100 directly west for 15 miles (24 km) to the Pont-du-Gard. This superb Roman aqueduct, some 2,000 years old, is almost completely intact. Standing three tiers high, it is a startling example of Roman engineering.

Doubling back a bit, you can follow N86 for 14 miles (about 22 km) directly into Nîmes, one of the major Roman cities of Provence, dating from the time of Emperor Augustus. Of principal interest are the Roman amphitheater (Pl. des Arènes — still used for bullfights) and Roman temple, the Maison Carrée (Bd. A.-Daudet just beyond Antonin Sq.). For a change of atmosphere, follow the Quai de la Fontaine along the canal to the 18th-century Jardins de la Fontaine. Here are the Temple de Diane and the Tour Magne, a Roman monument built about the end of the 1st century. The gardens offer a good look at the surrounding countryside and in summer are the setting for open-air art exhibitions.

Eleven miles (about 17 km) from Nîmes, via D42, is St.-Gilles, a good coffee stop. This typical Provençal town is known for the superb façade of its church (Pl. de la République), sculpted between 1180 and 1240.

Taking N572 east and N570 north brings you to Tarascon. The medieval château here is exceptionally well preserved, and its terraces, with a splendid view over the Rhone, make it one of the most beautiful feudal structures in France.

From here, taking N99 east, you are only 9 miles (14.5 km) from St.-Rémy-de-Provence, a lovely town with an active weekend open-air market and plenty of tree-shaded streets.

LES ANTIQUES and LES BAUX: Only one-half mile from St.-Rémy, south along Route D5, is Les Antiques, yet another admirably preserved Roman site with a mausoleum — one of the finest Roman structures of its kind to be found today — a municipal arch, and the ruins of Glanum, a thriving city founded 6 centuries before Christ.

Five miles (8 km) farther down D5 is Les-Baux-de-Provence. In the Alpilles Mountains, this village presents an austere and almost lunar landscape of limestone hills. The view from the ancient fortress is breathtaking during the day and quite eerie at night. Understandably, Les Baux's unique beauty is no secret, and nestled into its haunting hills are some of the most fashionable and expensive restaurants and hotels in France. (One such is the three-star *Oustaù de Baumanière*, where you should try the red mullet mousse or the sweetbreads; see *Best en Route.*)

Taking D17 west for 11 miles (17.7 km) brings you to Arles, the next stop.

ARLES: Founded by the Greeks who settled Marseilles, Arles was a major capital during the Roman period, an important religious center during the Middle Ages, and today preserves its past in magnificent architectural ruins and relics. Of special interest are the amphitheater (Rond-Point des Arènes), the "sister" of the one at Nîmes, and the remains of a Roman theater, erected toward the end of the 1st century BC (leaving the amphitheater, take the tiny street right before Rue Porte-de-Laure to reach the theater). At the Place de la République is the city hall (Hôtel de Ville); the *Musée d'Art Paien*, containing antique statues, sarcophagi, and mosaics; and the church of St. Trophime, founded in the reign of Charlemagne, with a magnificent portal and cloisters. Just to the right of the intersection of Rue du Président-Wilson and Rue de la République is the splendid *Musée d'Art Chrétien* (Museum of Christian Art). From its interior, you can descend into a subterranean gallery dating from the 1st century BC. Finally, visit Les Alyscamps (Av. des Alyscamps and Craponne Canal), which was used as a cemetery from Roman times to the end of the Middle Ages.

En Route from Arles – In this case it's more precisely "off the route" — an 82-mile (131-km) detour into the Camargue, a region whose landscape is unique in France: a vast, marshy delta of the two arms of the Rhone, where herds of wild bulls and horses run free and the terrain is dotted with the slender figures of heron stalking fish. In Stes.-Maries-de-la-Mer, the capital of the Camargue, Gypsies from all over Europe gather each May and October to honor their patron saint. From Arles, take N570 south. Come with the Gypsies; May and October are the recommended seasons.

Back in Arles, take N113 to N538 and the turnpike (A7, later becoming A8) for the 45-mile (72-km) trip into Aix-en-Provence.

AIX-EN-PROVENCE: Founded as Aquae Sextius (the Waters of Sextius) by the Roman consul Sextius in 122 BC, this ancient capital of Provence today offers a largely 17th- and 18th-century façade, with elegant private mansions, graceful squares, majestic avenues, and numerous fountains. It is also an intellectual center, having had a famous university since 1409.

The main boulevard — Cours Mirabeau — is bordered by towering, shady plane trees and lined with cafés, shops, and fine, aristocratic-looking town houses. At each end of the Cours are the fountains that recall Aix's origin as a watering place for the Roman legions. This avenue is one of the most pleasant in Provence for strolling, café hopping, and window shopping.

At the Place de l'Hôtel-de-Ville there's a flower market and the remains of the old grain market. Enter the Hôtel de Ville to visit the remarkable 300,000-volume library founded in the 18th century by the Marquis de Méjanes, for whom it is named. Other points of interest can be found at the Place des Martyrs-de-la-Résistance: the *Musée des Tapisseries,* the Cloître St.-Sauveur, and the Cathédrale St.-Sauveur, whose architecture runs the gamut of styles from the 5th to the 16th century. At 34 Rue Célony, the façade of the 17th-century Pavillon de Vendôme offers a fine example of Provençal decorative art. At the Place des Prêcheurs, there's the Eglise Ste.-Marie-Madeleine, containing important paintings, including a large work attributed to Rubens. You'll also want to see Paul Cézanne's studio (*atelier*) on Avenue Paul-Cézanne. The painter was born in Aix in 1839, and his studio has been reconstructed as it was found at his death in 1906.

In July and August, Aix holds an international music festival. This is the high season, action-packed and crowded: Last-minute reservations are risky. Open-air concerts are held in the archbishop's court as well as in the surrounding countryside.

En Route from Aix – Only a few miles outside Aix are several charming restaurants and hotels.

From Aix the route to Marseilles is simple: Just take N8 straight south for 19 miles (30.4 km). For a complete report on Marseilles, see *Marseilles,* THE CITIES.

BEST EN ROUTE

Expect to pay $85 and up per night for a double room in hotels listed as expensive; $50 to $85 in those listed as moderate; and less than $50 in the inexpensive. The restaurants range in price from $80 and up for a dinner for two in the expensive range and $40 to $80 in the moderate range. Prices do not include drinks, wine, and tip.

AVIGNON

Europe – A palace in the 16th century, it is now the best hotel in the city. Aubusson tapestries decorate the high walls in the antique-furnished public rooms, the 50 bedrooms are richly appointed, and it has a pleasant restaurant. 12 Pl. Crillon (phone: 90-82-66-92). Expensive.

Prieuré – The luxury hotel of the area, set in shady grounds with a pool and tennis courts and 36 exquisitely furnished rooms. It boasts a celebrated restaurant that specializes in grilled duck and tournedos with truffles. Closed November through early March. 7 Pl. du Chapitre at Villeneuve-les-Avignon (phone: 90-25-18-20). Expensive.

Hiély – This large, comfortable restaurant is the best in town. The choices are considerable and the value extraordinary. There are fine local wines from the Côtes-du-Rhone. Reservations are essential. Closed Mondays (except in summer), Tuesdays, mid-June through early July, and 2 weeks at Christmas. 5 Rue de la République (phone: 90-86-17-07). Expensive.

ST.-RÉMY-DE-PROVENCE

Hostellerie du Vallon de Valrugues – This establishment, in a beautiful setting, reopened recently after a change of management and extensive renovations, which included the addition of a sauna and golf facilities. Along with a remodeled restaurant headed by an ambitious young chef, there are 24 rooms and 10 apartments. Guests can opt for demi-pension or pension, taking either all or part of their meals at the hotel. Chemin Canto Cigalo (phone: 90-92-04-40). Expensive.

Antiques – Very attractive reception rooms, 27 guestrooms, a park, riding, and swimming. 15 Av. Pasteur (phone: 90-92-03-02). Moderate.

Château de Roussan – A delightful hotel in an 18th-century mansion surrounded by a park. No restaurant. Rte. Tarascon (phone: 90-92-11-63). Moderate.

Canto Cigalo – A modest hotel in quiet surroundings. No restaurant. Closed November through February. Chemin Canto Cigalo (phone: 90-92-14-28). Moderate.

LES BAUX

Oustaù de Baumanière – The jewel of Les Baux, this hotel is elegantly furnished and offers flowered terraces, tennis, swimming, riding, and one of France's top restaurants (it has three Michelin stars). The building looks like a medieval castle and is decorated with antiques. Restaurant specialties include stuffed pigeon, duckling with lime, and *marrons glacés* (glazed chestnuts). Closed mid-January to March; restaurant open daily, except Wednesdays and Thursdays for lunch during the off season. (phone: 90-54-33-07). Very expensive.

Cabro d'Or – A small hotel with a pleasant setting, it offers tennis, swimming, good views, and a fine restaurant. Closed mid-November through mid-December, Tuesdays at lunch, and Mondays mid-October through March. (phone: 90-54-33-21). Expensive.

Mas d'Aigret – A very appealing, modest hotel, with 17 rooms, swimming, a restful setting, and good views. Closed from early January to late February. D27 east (phone: 90-97-33-54). Moderate.

ARLES

Jules César – A former convent, this large, 60-room hotel still features cloisters and interior gardens. Its restaurant, *Lou Marquès,* serves very good regional cuisine. Closed November to December 20. Bd. Lices (phone: 90-93-43-20). Expensive.

d'Arlatan – Amazingly quiet though it's in the center of town. The 46 exquisitely furnished rooms in this half-medieval, half-Renaissance building overlook a garden. 26 Rue du Sauvage (phone: 90-93-56-66). Moderate.

AIX-EN-PROVENCE

Mas d'Entremont – A tiny hotel in a typical Provençal setting with terraces, a park, a fine restaurant featuring seafood and other light dishes. Closed from November to mid-March, Sunday evenings, and Monday lunch, except holidays. Célony, 2 miles (3.2 km) north via N7 (phone: 42-23-45-32). Expensive.

Paul Cézanne – A very comfortable hotel with a beautiful interior. 40 Av. Victor-Hugo (phone: 42-26-34-73). Expensive.

Pigonnet – Framed by the beautiful grounds of the *Pigonnet* hotel, this terrace restaurant looks like a Renoir painting. Try the *noisette d'agneau au basilic* and delight in the refuge from city life provided by the setting. 5 Av. du Pigonnet (phone: 42-59-02-90). Expensive.

Château de Meyrargues – Hotel in a restored 11th-century fortress; good restaurant. The rooms range from the simple to the "master bedroom," where you'll truly feel like a feudal lord. Closed in December and January. Meyrargues, 10 miles (16 km) via N96 (phone: 42-57-50-32). Moderate to inexpensive.

The Riviera

The French Riviera, known in France as the Côte d'Azur, is the privileged Mediterranean coastline stretching from Menton in the east to St.-Tropez in the west and including such world-renowned resorts as Nice, Cannes, and Antibes. It is an area of spectacular beauty, with dazzling white cliffs rising from the sea, gracefully curved bays, and some of the most luxurious and palatial hotels and private villas anywhere in the world. The Riviera includes discreet corners and jet-set haunts, picturesque villages and major cities, but it all is a playground. This is the place for sunning, swimming, gambling, eating, nightclubbing, and, on the cultural side, for seeing some of the finest collections of paintings by modern masters in France (many of the most prominent figures in 20th-century art lived here at one time or another, drawn by the beauty of the terrain and the extraordinary clarity of the light). ·

Although the Riviera has the reputation of being the playground of the rich and famous (which indeed it is), you'll find a remarkably wide spread of prices. After all, this is the vacation paradise of the French themselves (the most demanding of peoples) who ritually crowd down here during the months of July and August. And you can be sure that they have contrived to keep standards high across all price ranges, from simple bistros and camping sites to the renowned gourmet restaurants and luxury hotels. Mind you, "expensive" can really mean just that — up to $400. And don't forget that in France it is usual to pay for the room, not the number of persons. So couples often get a better deal than singles.

Many beaches are rocky or pebbly, but there are plenty of sandy beaches especially between Antibes and St.-Tropez. Some beaches are public and free of charge; others are "private," which usually means they belong to a restaurant or a hotel. But it's worth renting an air mattress and a beach umbrella at one of these for around $10 a day. Topless sunbathing (said to have originated at Tahiti Plage near St.-Tropez) is ubiquitous but hardly the rule. One of the great delights about the Riviera is that everyone does his or her own thing — the French are consummate individualists. So relax. High season is July and August when the inundation of tourists can make it a bit tacky. It's best to visit in May and June or even September and October. The temperatures will be cooler, of course, but still mild, and you'll be able to see something more than wall-to-wall people.

Nice–Côte d'Azur Airport is the busiest in France after Charles de Gaulle and Orly in Paris. It is certainly the most attractive. You come in over the sea to touch down on the edge of a bright white runway and step off the plane to palm trees and a fragrant breeze (called the *mistral* when it really blows). There's a fine restaurant (*Le Ciel d'Azur*) on the second floor of the airport. There are buses to Nice and many towns along the Riviera including Monte Carlo. A taxi to downtown Nice will cost you about $8. There's also helicopter service to Monte Carlo.

You'll have no trouble finding your way around if you take along the IGN map no. 115 (Provence–Côte d'Azur) or Michelin map 195 (Côte d'Azur–Alpes Maritimes). There is sun and sea and scenery wherever you turn, so stop anywhere and enjoy it. That's what the Riviera's all about.

LES CORNICHES: Nice is the usual starting point for the Côte d'Azur. (For a complete report on the city and its hotels and restaurants, see *Nice*, THE CITIES.) But the "real" Riviera begins once you leave the city. You don't have to go far. Between Nice and Menton, a 19-mile (30-km) trip, you'll travel by mountain passes, or *corniches,* that compel you to marvel at dramatic views of both sea and shoreline. From Nice you take N7 to the Grande Corniche. The ascent is quick, and especially magical views can be enjoyed as you pause briefly at Belvédère d'Eze, at La Turbie, at Vistaëro and its medieval château, and at Roquebrune-Cap-Martin. The old towns are enchanting and the landscape, superb. This road also leads to Monaco — where you'll certainly want to spend some time (see *Monaco*, DIRECTIONS) — and terminates in Menton, a city known for its excellent climate, tropical vegetation, and the international chamber music festival held each year in August.

On the return trip, take the lower pass (Corniche Inférieure) to enjoy panoramas that include bird's-eye views of some of the loveliest resorts in the world. At Beaulieu-sur-Mer, as you drive past *La Réserve,* the prestigious hotel and restaurant, you begin to enter the "gold coast" ambience of the Riviera. Stop next at St.-Jean-Cap-Ferrat and visit the Fondation Ephrussi de Rothschild, set among exquisite gardens overlooking the sea. The splendid artworks and furniture date from the 14th to the 19th century. Just a few miles down the coast, the picturesque town of Villefranche is the classic model of a Mediterranean fishing port, with high cliffs that seem to fall into the sea. From here, return to Nice via N559.

En Route from Nice – Between Nice and Cannes, half the fun is definitely getting there. Cagnes-sur-Mer, with its Renoir museum, is 8 miles (about 12 km) west via N7. St.-Paul, while not actually on the coast, is only a few miles inland and well worth the detour (take N7 west and N85 to D2). For lovers of the good life, there's the *Mas d'Artigny* hotel and *La Colombe d'Or,* a second home to some of France's best-known personalities (see *Best en Route*). For art lovers, this onetime home of Georges Braque boasts the *Maeght Foundation,* which houses one of the finest collections of contemporary art in France. Nearby, Vence (3 mi/4.8 km inland via D2) is Chagall's adopted city; it, too, has an impressive art collection at the Galerie les Arts. The jewel-like Chapelle du Rosaire at Vence was designed entirely by Matisse, from the stained glass to the white ceramic walls.

A few miles west back along the coast brings you to Biot, a medieval village perched on a hilltop. Visit the glassworks, where you can buy hand-blown glass and watch it being made. The Fernand Leger Museum is also worth a look. From Biot, the RN7 will take you to Antibes, where the Château-Musée Grimaldi houses a fine collection of the works of Picasso. Antibes, once the home of Monet, is a beautiful port with fortress walls and tiny, winding streets. Just beyond Antibes, you pass through Juan-les-Pins, somewhat gaudy, but a famous resort with good sand beaches.

This is really the heart of luxury sun worship, and elegant private villas line the approach to Cap d'Antibes, one of the most exclusive spots on the Riviera. Take time just to walk around the *Hôtel du Cap d'Antibes* and enjoy a drink on the terrace. It's every glamorous story come to life and epitomizes the Riviera's status as a haven for the rich and famous. Napoleon's *Naval Museum* at Cap d'Antibes is well worth a visit. Follow the coast right around for 6 miles (10 km) to reach Cannes.

CANNES: Unlike some of the earlier stops, Cannes is not quiet and discreet, but it too is the Riviera. The elegant (if sometimes noisy) boulevard de la Croisette, with riotously colorful gardens tracing the line of the Gulf of Napoule, is the key to Cannes. Here are smart boutiques, myriad outdoor cafés, and the *Majestic* and *Carlton* hotels — the headquarters for international stars during the city's annual film festival in the spring. As you follow the boulevard to Pointe de la Croisette you come to the famed (and original) Palm Beach, with your walk enhanced by constant views of the water. Take the boulevard in the opposite direction to get to the port, a harbor for the most extravagant yachts you could hope to see.

Cannes is a chic city, with its café society, nightclubs, and two casinos. But it has more quaint charms as well — for example, the flower market in the Allée de la Liberté or the old city, centered around Place de la Castre. End your visit with a trip to the observatory of Super-Cannes, 3 miles (5 km) outside the city, north on Avenue Isola-Bella. It goes without saying that the panoramas are really sublime from here.

En Route from Cannes – Excursions from Cannes offer some interesting stops for a change of pace. Take D803 to Vallauris, an important center for ceramic art; regular exhibitions are held in the summer. Via N567 and the Esterel–Côte d'Azur Autoroute you arrive at Mougins. This ancient fortified town, once Picasso's home, today houses one of France's finest restaurants, the *Moulin de Mougins* (see *Best en Route*). Seven miles (11.2 km) farther inland is Grasse, the perfume production center of France and a sought-after residential area as well. The perfume factories Molinard (52 Bd. Victor-Hugo) and Fragonard (Bd. Fragonard) are open to the public.

Returning to Cannes, you can take a boat from the port to the nearby islands (Iles de Lérins). The excursion takes half a day, including stops at Ile Ste.-Marguerite, fragrant with eucalyptus and pine forests, and at Ile St.-Honorat, the site of an ancient fortified monastery.

As you wind along the coast westward from Cannes (N559 to N98), the seascapes become vast leading into St.-Tropez, a distance of 45 miles (72 km).

ST.-TROPEZ: Rivaling Cannes as a jet-set favorite, St.-Tropez first became famous when Brigitte Bardot made it her home. Everything you've ever heard about this city is found at the port. You'll see starlets, swingers, spectators, and a whole coterie who'd give anything to be part of the action. The scene is hypnotizing, so settle back to watch with an early-evening Pernod or Blanc Cassis at *Senequier's* in the port. Next day, take a trip out to Môle Jean Réveille or to the Citadelle, built in the 16th and 17th centuries, which offers imposing views. Don't miss the *Musée de l'Annonciade* (Pl. Georges-Grammont), which has an outstanding collection of 20th-century art.

The best beaches at St.-Tropez are a few miles out on the Caps de St.-Tropez, du Pinet, and Camarat. Pampelonne beach is also good, but the most chic is Tahiti Plage (strictly speaking, at Ramatuelle), where you can have a delicious and moderately priced lunch on the terrace overlooking the beach.

A warning: St.-Tropez has experienced a surge of construction — both residential and commercial — in the last several years. It is, of course, one of the "in" fun spots of the Riviera, but in the summer the congestion — both human and automotive — may be more than you care for. If frenzy is not your idea of vacation, you might prefer St.-Tropez in the off-season.

En Route from St.-Tropez – The heart of the Riviera ends at St.-Tropez, and although the region to the west offers fewer restaurants and hotels, the scenery is still dazzling. If you follow N98 to N559, you find high cliffs and expansive seascapes around Cavalaire-sur-Mer; at Lavandou, a long-time favorite of artists, good sand beaches and one of the loveliest fishing ports on the coast await you. From here, it's only 23 miles (37 km) back to St.-Tropez along the coast; but if you have time, take the mountain route (Rte. du Littoral) via the Corniche des Maures. It's twice as long, but the scenery is spectacular. The route ends in St.-Raphaël; from there just follow the coast 45 miles (72 km) east back to Nice.

BEST EN ROUTE

Expect to pay $100 and up per night for a double room in hotels listed as expensive; $60 to $100 in those listed as moderate; and under $60, inexpensive. The restaurants range in price from $80 and up for a dinner for two in the expensive range, $50 in the moderate range, and under $50 in the inexpensive category. Prices do not include drinks, wine, or tip. Service charge and tax are invariably included in the check. In high season, you may need to buy dinner or lunch in order to get a room.

Note: For the entire Riviera, reservations are a must in high season.

ROQUEBRUNE-CAP-MARTIN

Vista Palace – Formerly the *Vistäero* and reopened in 1987 after renovations, this luxurious 68-room hotel set on a cliff has exceptional views of Roquebrune and the coast. A fine restaurant, pool, gardens, and parking complete the amenities. Closed from November to February, though the exact dates vary. About 2 miles (3.2 km) from downtown on the Grande Corniche (phone: 93-35-01-50). Expensive.

BEAULIEU-SUR-MER

Réserve – One of France's top luxury hotels with an internationally known restaurant; heated swimming pool. Right on the sea. Closed mid-November to late December. 5 Bd. du Gén.-Leclerc (phone: 93-01-00-01). Expensive.
Comté de Nice – A comfortable hotel (no restaurant). Open year-round. 25 Bd. Marinoni (phone: 93-01-19-70). Moderate.

ST.-JEAN-CAP-FERRAT

Grand Hôtel du Cap-Ferrat – An extraordinary grand hotel recently renovated. Isolated on the water with an incredible pool, lovely grounds, tennis, superb restaurants, and Old World service and charm. Closed from October through April. Bd. Gén.-de-Gaulle (phone: 93-76-00-21). Expensive.
Voile d'Or – An elegant hotel with a fine restaurant, pool, and superb views of the port. Closed from November through February (phone: 93-01-13-13). Expensive.
Cappa – A top-rate yet reasonably priced seafood restaurant overlooking the port. Closed from November through January. Av. J.-Mermoz (phone: 93-76-03-91). Expensive.

ST.-PAUL-DE-VENCE

La Colombe d'Or – Luxury combining Provençal atmosphere and lush, beautiful gardens. This sumptuous, small hotel is famous for its art collection of works by Miró, Calder, Picasso, and Chagall. Closed mid-November through mid-December (phone: 93-32-80-02). Expensive.
Mas d'Artigny – A stunning luxury hotel with 50 standard rooms that come with balconies, 25 suites with private swimming pools, and a dining room (one Michelin star) that serves fine seafood. Rte. de la Colle and des Hauts de St.-Paul (phone: 93-32-84-54). Expensive.
Hameau – This pleasant hotel has 16 rooms but no restaurant. Closed from mid-November to February. 528 Rte. de la Colle, D7 (phone: 93-32-80-24). Moderate.

Oliviers – Tasty regional food in a pretty garden setting. Rte. D7 (phone: 93-32-80-13). Moderate.

CAP D'ANTIBES

Cap d'Antibes – A truly grand and exclusive luxury hotel with gorgeous grounds and views, swimming, and tennis. Its restaurant, *Pavillon Eden Roc,* serves delicious food. Closed from October to April. Bd. Kennedy (phone: 93-61-39-01 or 93-61-56-63). Very expensive.

Bacon – From a terrace overlooking the sea, diners can enjoy very good bouillabaisse or excellent fresh fish. Closed Sunday nights, Mondays, and mid-November through January. Bd. de Bacon (phone: 93-61-50-02). Expensive.

Gardiole – This simple, quiet hotel among the pines has 20 rooms, some of which face the sea. Chemin de la Garoupe (phone: 93-61-35-03). Moderate.

ANTIBES

Bonne Auberge – Fine Provençal cuisine and attentive service have won this elegant restaurant two Michelin stars. On the right-hand side of N7 coming from Nice. Closed from November 15 through December 15 and on Mondays (phone: 93-33-36-65). Very expensive.

Yacht – A charming pub-restaurant that caters to yacht crews who've put into Port Vauban Harbor, with a grand view of the boats. A few rooms are available in the *Bellevue* hotel (same location as the restaurant). Closed from November through December 15. 15 Av. de la Libération (phone: 93-74-24-00). Moderate.

Mas Djoliba – This small, quiet hotel with 13 rooms has a beautiful park setting right in the center of town. Restaurant closed from November to Easter. 29 Av. de Provence (phone: 93-34-02-48). Moderate to inexpensive.

L'Oursin – This popular but plain little restaurant has the best seafood in the downtown area. Closed Sunday nights, Mondays, and August. Reservations necessary. 16 Rue République (phone: 93-34-13-46). Inexpensive.

CANNES

Carlton – Numero uno in terms of old-fashioned prestige and glamour, and renovation of its 335 rooms has modernized the traditional comforts. The view of the sea is undoubtedly the best in town. 58 Bd. de la Croisette (phone: 93-68-91-68). Expensive.

Gray d'Albion – This modern, comfortable, 174-room hotel has a restaurant that's quite good. 38 Rue des Serbes (phone: 93-68-54-54). Expensive.

Majestic – With the *Carlton,* one of the classic, glamorous hotels of Cannes. Closed November to mid-December. Bd. de la Croisette (phone: 93-68-91-00). Expensive.

Saint-Yves – A quaint, cozy old-fashioned villa in a delightful garden of palm trees, it has 8 rooms, plus 3 apartments. Closed in November. 49 Bd. d'Alsace (phone: 93-38-65-29). Moderate.

MOUGINS

Le Moulin de Mougins – Set in a 16th-century olive oil mill with exotic plants outside the windows and original paintings on the walls, this is one of the most famous restaurants in France. Chef Roger Vergé's specialties include: lobster fricassée, pâté of sole, escalope of fresh salmon, and salade Mikado (with mushrooms, avocado, tomatoes, and truffles). The Réserve wine, a very fine rosé, comes from nearby vineyards, and cold wild strawberry soufflé is delicious. (There are also 3 hotel rooms here that should be booked well in advance.) Closed Mondays and from February to late March. Notre-Dame-de-Vie; southeast 1 mile via D3 (phone: 93-75-78-24). Very expensive.

Amandier de Mougins – Roger Vergé's other restaurant, also in a former olive oil mill, serves simpler and less expensive food. Open year-round. Pl. du Commandant-Lamy (phone: 93-90-00-91). Expensive.

ST.-TROPEZ

Byblos – A grand luxury hotel, decorated in Provençal style with some of the best food in town. Good views are matched by excellent swimming. Closed mid-October to late March. Av. Paul-Signac (phone: 94-97-00-04). Expensive.

Levant – On the road where Colette used to live, this hotel by the sea has 28 rooms, a pool, and a restaurant. Closed mid-October through March. Rte. des Salins (phone: 94-97-33-33). Moderate.

Sube – The most famous of the town's less expensive hotels is set right on the harbor. It has 26 unpretentious rooms. Open year-round. 15 Quai Suffren (phone: 94-97-30-04). Moderate.

Burgundy

Burgundy begins 100 miles (160 km) south of Paris and stretches almost to Lyons. The region has always been a place of passage, a transit zone between northern France and the Mediterranean south and between France and Switzerland. But Burgundy is also important in its own right because of its history, its produce, its art, and its architecture.

The region was conquered by the Romans in 52 BC, when Julius Caesar forced Vercingetorix, the Gallic ruler of the Arverni, to surrender at Alesia. A 5th-century invasion by the Burgundians, who came from the region of the Baltic Sea, gave Burgundy its modern name.

In 534, the Franks conquered the kingdom of Burgundy. The death of the great Frankish king Charlemagne in 814 heralded a 200-year period of chaos and turbulence. The long strife ended when the kingdom, by then reduced to a duchy, passed into the hands of King Robert II of France (known as Robert the Pious), who made his son Robert the first Capetian duke of Burgundy.

Under the Capets, Burgundy became a bastion of Christianity. Monasteries were founded and magnificent churches built. But Burgundy's true golden age came when the Capets were succeeded in 1364 by the Valois — the grand dukes of Burgundy. During their reign, Burgundy spread well beyond its present borders and even beyond those of France to include most of Belgium and Luxembourg and part of Holland. It became a center of art and culture because of the many French and Flemish artists the dukes brought to Dijon, the capital. The dukes of Valois ruled until 1477. After the death of the last duke, Charles the Bold, the duchy was taken by Louis XI of France as part of his kingdom.

Topographically, Burgundy is a land of hills and valleys laced with many streams. One-third of it is forested; in the rest, agriculture is the most important activity. Burgundy's agricultural products are world-famous — the mustard of Dijon, the beef of Charolais cattle, and, of course, the wine. Burgundy also has some industry — steel mills and glass and ceramic manufacturers — concentrated south of Dijon.

The wine country of Burgundy stretches from Dijon to the outskirts of Lyons, a treasure trove of beautiful medieval buildings. Because Burgundy was a center of monastic activity, most of these medieval remains are religious — either churches or abbeys. The predominant architectural style is Romanesque with a Burgundian accent, but there are Gothic structures and some Roman ruins as well.

Burgundy is crossed from north to south by Route A6, a major toll freeway. Most of the other roads have only two lanes but are well paved and maintained. From Paris, take A6 due south to the exit of Auxerre-Nord to enter Burgundy at Auxerre. It's a distance of 104 miles (167 km).

AUXERRE: The gateway to Burgundy was first a Celtic settlement, then a Roman town, and later a religious center in the Middle Ages. The most impressive feature as you approach the town is the view of the Roman ramparts and the silhouettes of church spires above the River Yonne. Inside you get a closer look at the Gothic cathedral and Gaillarde clock tower.

Take N6, then D100 south about 30 miles (48 km) to Vézelay.

VÉZELAY: Once a pilgrimage center and now a Christian shrine, Vézelay began as an abbey in the 9th century. Its church became famous in the 11th century, when a monk associated with the abbey obtained relics reputed to be those of St. Mary Magdalene. Pilgrims flocked to Vézelay, and the town became prosperous. At the beginning of the 12th century, a modest Carolingian church was replaced by the present Romanesque basilica.

At the end of the 13th century, Vézelay declined. When other "relics" of St. Mary Magdalene were found in Provence, the pilgrims dwindled. Huguenots looted Vézelay in 1569, and part of the town was destroyed in the revolution. Not until 1859, after restorations by Viollet-le-Duc (who had achieved fame with his restoration of Notre-Dame de Paris) did Vézelay again become a pilgrimage site — for tourists.

Leave your car at the foot of the village and walk to the basilica, with a superb carving over its main door that represents the apostles' mission after the resurrection of Christ. Once inside, your first impression is one of light and airiness. Next, you notice details, such as the carved capitals on the columns. These figures, representing biblical characters, are very moving for their familiar, human facial expressions. If you want to know who's who, buy an English-language guidebook, on sale in the church.

The village of Vézelay has many shops selling the wares of local artisans. Unusual items include pewter jewelry in religious or zodiac designs and the blue, white, and gilt earthenware from nearby Clamecy.

Vézelay is also a good starting point for the rugged Morvan region just to the south, an area with many fine trout streams. You can get details on the fishing at any of the several charming country inns in the Vézelay region, the *Poste et Lion d'Or* in Vézelay, the *Moulin des Ruats* between Vézelay and Avallon, or the *Poste* in Avallon (see *Best en Route*).

En Route from Vézelay – The 52-mile (83-km) drive east to the Abbey of Fontenay is one of the most interesting on the whole Burgundy route. Take D457 to Avallon, a former walled town. Then follow D954 through the cheese-making town of Epoisses — where you pass a castle with a water-filled moat — to Semur-en-Auxois.

Just before Semur you come to D980, a fork that takes you to Montbard and the Abbey of Fontenay. Pass the abbey for the moment and drive into Semur itself, once a feudal fortified town. It's worth a drive around to see the walls and towers where the townsfolk defied Louis XI's troops in 1478.

Return to D980 and, after driving through the industrial town of Montbard, take D905 and D32 to Fontenay.

FONTENAY: If you want an unspoiled picture of monastic simplicity not crowded by tourists, don't miss Fontenay. At first sight, the abbey looks like a large farm — which is just what a self-contained, self-supporting, 12th-century Cistercian monastery was supposed to be.

Fontenay was founded by Bernard de Clairvaux in 1118. The abbey prospered until the 16th century, at times with as many as 300 monks in residence. With the Wars of Religion, the institution declined and, by the time of the revolution, only three monks remained. They were driven out, and the buildings were sold and turned into a paper mill. In 1906, Fontenay was sold again, and the new owner set out to restore the buildings.

There are guided tours of Fontenay in French; even if you don't understand French, you will understand more of medieval monastic life when you visit, in order, the church with its plain windows and dirt floor; the monks' dormitory; the arched cloister; the chapter house, or meeting hall; the scriptorium, where the monks wrote and illuminated manuscripts; the adjoining *caldarium* — the only heated room other than the kitchen — where the writing monks warmed their fingers to prevent frostbite; the prison, used for minor violators; and the forge.

If you visit Fontenay in the winter, don't go late in the day. There are no lights in the buildings, and late afternoon tours may be canceled because of darkness. There is an admission charge.

Take Route D905 and freeway A8 to Dijon, 52 miles (83.2 km) away.

DIJON: The capital of Burgundy reached the height of its glory under the four Valois Dukes of Burgundy — Philip the Brave, John the Fearless, Philip the Good, and Charles the Bold — who gave it its fine buildings. After Burgundy was annexed by France, Dijon declined for a time, but it revived after 1850 with the coming of the railroad. Today the city is an important industrial and commercial center. It is known especially for its gastronomic specialties: mustard, spice bread, black currant liqueur (*cassis*), and snails. An annual gastronomic fair is held in Dijon during the first 2 weeks in November.

Dijon's main tourist attractions are the former ducal palace and the streets around it. The palace now houses an art museum, with paintings and Burgundian sculptures. The most interesting parts of the palace, however, are the kitchen, with six fireplaces so large you can walk into them, and the guard room, housing the marble and alabaster tombs of Philip the Brave and John the Fearless. The museum charges a small admission fee.

En Route from Dijon – Route N74 leads 23.5 miles (38 km) south to Beaune through famous wine villages: Gevrey-Chambertin, Vougeot, Nuits-St.-Georges. Wherever you see a sign announcing *Dégustation,* you can stop and taste the wines of the region.

BEAUNE: This town is the wine capital of Burgundy, and each year a famous wine auction is held on the third Sunday in November. All proceeds go to the hospital, the Hôtel-Dieu, a marvel of Flemish-Burgundian wooden architecture, founded in 1443 as a general hospital. It remained so until 1971 and is used as a geriatric institution. Parts of the building have been set aside as a museum. Most striking are the main ward — a perfect preservation of a medieval hospital — and an art masterpiece, Rogier van der Weyden's multipaneled painting of the Last Judgment. In medieval times, this vivid depiction of heaven and hell stood in the main ward. There are guided tours for an admission charge.

Wine lovers will want to visit the wine museum and the many cellars around the town's main square. Here you can taste and buy wine and wine accessories, including glasses, corkscrews, serving baskets, and tasting cups.

En Route from Beaune – You have several choices. Wine lovers can continue down N74 through Pommard, Volnay, Meursault, Puligny-Montrachet, and Mercurey, south toward Mâcon. Or you can make a 32-mile (50-km) side trip via D973 to Autun, a former Roman town now best known for its cathedral. However, this cathedral, with a Last Judgment panel over the main door and carved capitals inside, is much like the basilica at Vézelay, so you may just wish to continue down freeway A6 to Mâcon, via Tournus.

TOURNUS: An industrial town, it is worth a stop for its 11th-century Romanesque church. The austere arches and columns and the circular stairway to the bell loft give a special flavor of medieval piety.

You can also get an excellent meal here at *Greuze* (4 Rue A.-Thibaudet) before heading down A6 to Mâcon.

MÂCON: Though this is not a true tourist town, wine lovers may want to visit the *Maison Mâconnaise des Vins,* on N6 at the north end of town, which sells Burgundies at lower cost than in Beaune and offers a good inexpensive meal. Mâcon is a good base for side trips, west via N79 to Cluny and Paray-le-Monial or east on N79 to Bourg-en-Bresse and the church of Brou.

CLUNY: One of the most famous abbeys in France, Cluny was founded in 910 by Duke William the Pious of Aquitaine. In its heyday, from the 11th to the 14th century, the abbey exercised a widespread influence on religious, intellectual, artistic, and political life. Burgundian Romanesque architecture started at Cluny, and its abbey gave the Church three popes. The city enjoyed enormous power and wealth. "Wherever the wind blows, there Cluny's wealth grows," the saying went.

And that, eventually, proved its downfall. The abbots became corrupt, and in 1790, during the Revolution, the abbey was closed. In 1798, the building was sold to a Mâcon dealer, who tore down parts of it for the stone. Fewer than half of the original abbey buildings remain today.

Because of the massive destruction that has taken place, a visit to Cluny may be disappointing. If you take the guided tour, buy a pamphlet in English and study Cluny's history before you begin. Then look for the two buildings that tell the whole story of Cluny's rise and fall: the south transept with its simple lines, all that remains of the great abbey church; and the Gothic chapel of Jean de Bourbon, with its heated side room where the privileged could worship in comfort while the ordinary monks braved the Burgundian winter chill.

PARAY-LE-MONIAL: This town, 43 miles (69 km) west of Mâcon, is dominated by its Romanesque basilica of the Sacred Heart. Founded in 1109 by St. Hugues, founder of the great Cluny church, it is a smaller version of the Cluny building.

Because of the golden limestone used to build it, the basilica appears most impressive on sunny days at sunset. If the weather is poor, you may prefer not to journey out to Paray-le-Monial but turn east to Bourg-en-Bresse.

Go east on N79 from Mâcon for 21 miles (34 km) to D975 and Bourg-en-Bresse.

BOURG-EN-BRESSE: A chicken-raising and furniture-making center, it is noted for its *appellation contrôlée* chickens. Ignore the town itself and go straight to the suburb of Brou and its church, the most beautiful in Burgundy.

Flamboyantly Gothic with a Renaissance cast, the church was completed in 1532. It was a work of love. In 1480, Count Philippe of Bresse was gravely injured in a hunting accident. His wife, Marguerite de Bourbon, vowed that if he recovered, she would turn the priory of Brou into a monastery. The count did recover, but Marguerite died before she could carry out her vow. The count and his son Philibert promised to fulfill it for her, but time passed and they forgot. Then Philibert, married to Marguerite of Austria, died unexpectedly of a chill. Marguerite saw his death as divine punishment and hastened to carry out the lapsed vow as a memorial to her beloved husband. For 400 years the church has stood as a symbol of married love.

Every part of this church — its golden light, its rich ornamentation — delights the eye. Most outstanding are the choir and the chapels. Note the realistic figures in the carved oak choir stalls (one even shows a naughty youth being spanked), the tombs of the two Marguerites and Philibert carved in Italian marble, the sumptuous stained glass windows, the white marble rood screen showing the seven joys of the Virgin.

There are guided tours of the church; the hours vary according to the seasons. The small charge also admits you to an art museum in the former monastery buildings.

Leave Burgundy via N83 for Lyons.

BEST EN ROUTE

Expect to pay $75 and up per night for a double room in hotels listed as expensive; $45 to $75 in those listed as moderate; and $45 and under, inexpensive. The restaurants range in price from $90 and up for a dinner for two in the expensive range; $55 to $90 in the moderate range; and $55 and under, inexpensive. Prices do not include drinks, wine, or tip.

JOIGNY

À la Côte St.-Jacques – In a charming little cobblestone town 17 miles (27 km) north of Auxerre, this is an elegantly decorated restaurant known for its imaginative Burgundian food, which recently garnered a third Michelin star. Their selection of Burgundy wines is one of the finest anywhere. Closed January. 14 Faubourg Paris (phone: 86-62-09-70). Expensive.

VÉZELAY-AVALLON

Espérance – This 22-room hotel provides lovely accommodations, but it's most notable for its restaurant, which has won high praise from many critics, including three stars from Michelin. Closed from early January to early February. St.-Pèresous-Vézelay (phone: 86-33-20-45). Expensive.

Hostellerie de la Poste – An atmospheric inn with 24 rooms and a very fine restaurant. Closed from mid-November to mid-March. 13 Pl. Vauban, Avallon (phone: 86-34-06-12). Expensive.

Poste et Lion d'Or – At the foot of Vézelay village, with a view of rolling hills, 42 rooms, and a good restaurant featuring classic cuisine. Open from mid-March to early November (phone: 86-33-21-23). Expensive to moderate.

Hostellerie du Moulin des Ruats – A charming former mill with a garden on the bank of a stream, where you can eat in pleasant weather. There are 24 rooms and a restaurant. Closed for a month and a half in winter; 2 miles (3.2 km) southwest of Avallon in Vallée du Cousin (phone: 86-34-07-14). Moderate.

DIJON

Hostellerie du Chapeau Rouge – Tastefully decorated, comfortable, and centrally located hotel with a good restaurant serving both regional and nouvelle cuisines; excellent wines. 5 Rue Michelet (phone: 80-30-28-10). Expensive.

BEAUNE

Hostellerie de Levernois – Set in a 10-acre park just 2 miles (3.2 km) outside Beaune, this gracious 12-room hotel/restaurant was recently opened by Jean Crotet, former chef/owner of the highly rated *Cote d'Or* in nearby Nuits-St.-Georges. The rooms, furnished by Mme. Crotet, are spacious and very comfortable, and the inviting, terraced dining room offers the same excellent cuisine for which Chef Crotet has gained two Michelin stars. 21200 Beaune (phone: 80-24-73-58). Expensive.

Poste – Charming older hotel with a garden courtyard; the best restaurant in Beaune. Closed from late December through late March. 1 Bd. Clemenceau (phone: 80-22-08-11). Expensive.

CHAGNY

Lameloise – Nine miles (14 km) south of Beaune, this restaurant is worthy of a detour. At this atmospheric, 15th-century country mansion, which has been rated three Michelin stars, Burgundian cooking is raised to a high art. Prices are pretty high, too, but the gustatory experience is worth it. Closed Wednesdays, Thursdays at lunchtime, and most of January. 36 Pl. d'Armes (phone: 85-87-08-85). Expensive.

TOURNUS

Greuze – Fine Burgundian food and Beaujolais wines are offered at this charming country inn named for Jean-Baptiste Greuze, an 18th-century artist born in Tournus. Chef Jean Ducloux's efforts have earned him two Michelin stars. There are 21 rooms in the nearby *Greuze* hotel, which Ducloux opened in 1986. Closed the first week in December. 1 Rue Thibaudet (phone: 85-51-13-52). Expensive.

MÂCON

Château d'Igé – A remodeled 13th-century fortified castle in a village surrounded by vineyards not far from Cluny; 6 rooms and 6 suites. Closed early November to early February. Igé, 8 miles (14 km) northwest of Mâcon via N79 and D85 (phone: 85-33-33-99). Expensive to moderate.

Altéa – Modern motel with 63 rooms and a good restaurant. 26 Rue Coubertin, less than 1 mile south via N6 (phone: 85-38-28-06). Moderate.

BOURG-EN-BRESSE

Auberge Bressane – Rustic inn specializing in local products, especially Bresse chicken. 166 Bd. de Brou (phone: 74-22-22-68). Expensive.

Le Logis de Brou – Comfortable, old-style hotel with a view of the park; 30 rooms. (Although the hotel has no restaurant, an excellent one, the *Auberge Bressane,* is nearby.) 132 Bd. Brou (phone: 74-22-11-55). Moderate to inexpensive.

Alsace-Lorraine

Since 1870, Alsace and part of Lorraine have spent almost equal time under the German flag and the tricolor. The two provinces are profoundly different from each other, yet their common destiny as "puzzle pieces" on France's northeastern border has caused them to be inextricably linked in people's minds. In Alsace particularly, there is much to make you think you are in Germany. Virtually all Alsatians speak French, but many of them also speak the local German dialect; folk dress appears at festivals celebrating the new wine; houses are frequently decorated with heavy timbered furniture and may even be heated by a ceramic stove in the main room. Indeed, if you had been traveling in Alsace or the Moselle area of Lorraine between 1870 and the end of World War I, you would have been in Germany.

Today, however, the provinces belong wholeheartedly to France even if there is some inevitable ambivalence in culture, language, customs, and accents. Its specialties — *choucroute garnie, kouglof* (*kugelhopf*), quiche Lorraine, Strasbourg sausages, and foie gras — are part of French gastronomic life, as are the magnificent white wines of Alsace and the *vin gris* of Lorraine.

The Place Stanislas and the cathedral of Strasbourg are works of French architecture, and who would deny Joan of Arc — the Maid of Lorraine — her French nationality?

With their turbulent history and strategic border position, Lorraine and Alsace offer a side of France that is very different from the sunny face of Nice or the craggy coast of St.-Malo. Here is a France whose citizens drink beer as often as they drink wine, that celebrates Christmas with decidedly Germanic *gemütlichkeit,* and that enjoys life with a heartiness which, on first acquaintance at least, bears little resemblance to the legendary refinement of French joie de vivre. An evening stroll around the Place Stanislas in Nancy or a stop in *La Petite France* in Strasbourg for a glass of framboise, the fragrant raspberry brandy customarily savored in large balloon glasses, testifies more to the particular charm of Lorraine and Alsace than any words. It is impossible not to be captivated.

Nancy, the starting point of our tour of Alsace-Lorraine, is 190 miles (360 km) east of Paris. For the fastest route from Paris, take A4 east to Metz; then take E12 south to Nancy.

NANCY: An old proverb says: "In Europe there are three magnificent ceremonies: the coronation of an emperor at Frankfurt, the investiture of a king at Reims, and the burial of a duke at Nancy." Founded in the 11th century, Nancy is the capital of Lorraine and was a seat of power during the 17th and 18th centuries. The Dukes of Lorraine wielded international power until François III exchanged his duchy for that of Tuscany. In his place Louis XV installed Stanislas Leczynski, his father-in-law and the dethroned King of Poland, on the throne of Nancy in 1737. This was an astute political move, for on Stanislas's death, Nancy reverted to France.

Stanislas Leczynski is the man responsible for the glory of Nancy. He summoned artists and architects from all over France to celebrate his reign. The result is the Place Stanislas, a magnificent 18th-century square surrounded by seven pavilions decorated with wrought-iron grilles and balconies, all in a harmonious 18th-century style. This square is the center and soul of Nancy. The area around the Place Stanislas is also a part of Stanislas's urban plan. The Place de la Carrière, the Arc de Triomphe, and the Palais de Gouvernement all attest to the duke's refined architectural taste. Behind the Place de la Carrière, La Pépinière is an English garden and zoo. It's also a pleasant spot to while away an hour or two watching the Nancéiens at play.

Other spots of interest are the Musée Historique Lorraine (64 Grande-Rue), which has a wonderfully rich collection relating to the history of Nancy. An archaeological garden displays Celtic, Gallo-Roman, and Frankish artifacts, and there's an almost complete collection of the engravings of Jacques Callot, numerous paintings of Georges de la Tour, a collection of furniture and folk art of the area, Judaica, and a museum of pharmacology.

The *Musée des Beaux-Arts,* in one of the pavilions of the Place Stanislas, is devoted to European painting from the 14th century to modern times. The museum displays works of Delacroix, Manet, Utrillo, Poussin, and Rubens, among others.

Nancy has numerous churches; two are well worth a visit: Eglise des Cordeliers, burial place of the Dukes of Lorraine, and Eglise Notre-Dame-de-Bon-Secours (Av. Strasbourg), where Stanislas Leczynski and his wife, Catherine Opalinska, are buried.

For lovers of Art Nouveau, Nancy offers the *Musée de l'Ecole de Nancy* (Rue du Sergent-Blandan), with objects from the workshop of Emile Gallé. The fluid lines of nature are captured in ceramic, glass, furniture, and other media.

LUNÉVILLE: Leaving Nancy by the southeast route, within 18 miles (30 km) you come to Lunéville — "little Versailles." Built by Léopold, Duke of Lorraine and an admirer of Louis XIV, the palace is a modest replica of the great palace of Versailles. Later, Lunéville became the favorite residence of Stanislas Leczynski, and its corridors resounded with the voices of such notables as Voltaire, Helvetius, and Diderot. There is a museum of documents relating to Lunéville's history. The local museum contains military memorabilia and documents relating to Lunéville's history, but is better known for its collection of Lunéville porcelains.

BACCARAT: Southeast from Lunéville, it's 15 miles (25 km) to Baccarat, a name that has spelled fine crystal to lovers of the very best for more than 2 centuries. A museum displays antique and contemporary crystal works, some dating from the founding of the factory in 1764. Although the factory itself is not open to the public, several shops in town display and sell Baccarat items.

ST. DIÉ: Continuing southwest from Baccarat, you come to St. Dié. It was in the *Cosmographiae Introductio,* printed and published in St. Dié in 1507, that the continent of America was so named for the first time. The town owes its origin and its name to a Benedictine monastery founded in the 7th century by St. Déodat. The Romanesque Eglise Notre-Dame-de-Galilée and the 18th-century Cathédrale St.-Dié, which are united by a 15th-century cloister, are the major points of interest.

    En Route from St. Dié – From St. Dié, at the foot of the Vosges, head through the crest of the Vosges at Col Ste.-Marie and continue through Ste.-Marie-aux-Mines, then east through Fertrupt, winding to the Col du Haut Ribeauvillé and down to Ribeauvillé.

    Ribeauvillé, at the foot of the Vosges, is one of the many wine-growing towns in this area of Alsace. The town is noted for its gewürztraminer and its Riesling. It is also noted for the Pfifferday (Day of the Fifes) festival, held on the last Sunday in August. If you're lucky enough to be in town, you'll see a historic parade, townspeople in regional costume, and folk dances. And you'll be able to drink wine from the "wine fountain" in front of the town hall. *John,* a pastry shop at 58 Grande Rue, sells *kugelhopf* by the slice.

    From Ribeauvillé it's south to Riquewihr, a town that escaped war damage and remains today almost exactly as it was in the 16th century. There are no grand monuments to see in Riquewihr; you see, rather, a lifestyle, an era that has long since passed into history. The half-timbered houses, the old courtyards, the carved stone wells, and the fountains — all join to bring the past to life. If you are in town for the grape harvest in the autumn (usually October, occasionally September), you have the feeling of having stepped into a picture book.

    From Riquewihr, continue south, then west, to Kayserberg. Known mainly as where Albert Schweitzer was born (in 1875), this farm town is also a delightful wine village filled with medieval houses. Sites include the ruins of an ancient castle, elegant 16th-century buildings, the Romanesque Eglise de la Ste.-Croix, and the Schweitzer birthplace (124 Rue du Général-de-Gaulle), now a museum. A grape harvest festival is held here every 5 years.

COLMAR: From Kayserberg head east to Colmar. Unquestionably Alsace's most beautiful city, it is noted for its typically Alsatian character, for the Petite Venise section interlaced by a canal, for the old town with its 16th- and 17th-century houses, for the Eglise St.-Martin with its Gothic choir, and, most of all, for the *Musée d'Unterlinden,* in an old convent that was founded by two widows from a noble family. The 13th-century structure is entered through the cloister. In the chapel is the magnificent Issenheim altarpiece, painted in the 16th century by Mathias Grünewald. This masterwork alone is certainly worth a trip to Colmar, as it symbolizes the mysticism, the passion, and the fervor of the turbulent age from which it sprang. The chapel also has a 24-panel series of the Passion conceived by Martin Schongauer in the late 15th century. The rest of the museum contains diverse displays, including works by Picasso and Léger.

STRASBOURG: The sights are many and varied, but the number one spot for the visitor with only hours to spare is the cathedral, one of the glories of European medieval art and architecture. The original cathedral was begun in 1015 in the Romanesque style, but it burned several times; work on the present cathedral began in the 12th century, this time in pure Gothic. When complete in 1439, the lacy openwork spire made it the tallest building in Christendom. The cathedral has witnessed much of Alsace's turbulent history and has even served the Protestant faith, during the Reformation. Louis XIV and Louis XV worshiped here, and in 1770 Marie-Antoinette was formally greeted here on the way to her wedding to Louis XVI. During the revolution, the spire was saved by being crowned by a huge, red Phrygian cap. The wars of the 19th and 20th centuries damaged the structure, but it survived to present the splendid sight we see today.

Before going inside, note the richly sculptured façade; its complex iconography alone almost sums up medieval religious belief. Stained glass is the marvel of the interior, whether richly colored as in the large rose window or in gray-green *grisaille,* as in St. Catherine's Chapel. Be sure not to miss the Pillar of Angels (Pilier des Anges) and the wonderful 16th-century astronomer's clock, both in the south transept. The latter is an ingenious device that goes into action at 12:31 PM each day — be on hand by 12:15 to catch the taped presentation. Afterward, take a close look at the wood carving of the Maison Kammerzell, the striking half-timbered house on the cathedral square. Now a restaurant, it was built in the 16th century by a rich merchant.

The *Musée de l'Oeuvre Notre-Dame,* to the side of the cathedral, displays original working drawings of the raising of the cathedral as well as originals of many of its statues, which have been replaced by copies. The Château des Rohan, next door, built by a great French family that produced many statesmen and churchmen, is an 18th-century palace where private apartments can be seen, plus a decorative arts museum notable for its collection of ceramics, a fine arts museum, and an archaeological museum. Don't linger, however, because the city also has a historical museum, a museum of modern art, and the thoroughly charming Musée Alsacien of the folk art and traditions in rural Alsace.

The Petite France area is noted for its picturesque views of half-timbered houses reflected in the waters of small canals — this is a must. In the summer, you can take guided tours of old Strasbourg by miniature train; boat trips are also available. Information can be obtained at the Tourist Office (Pl. Gutenberg; phone: 88-32-57-05). But remember that the best way to absorb the feel of a town is by sitting and watching. Find a suitable café, order a cold Alsatian beer, and relax as you savor the other side of France.

BEST EN ROUTE

Expect to pay $120 and up per night for a double room in expensive hotels; $80 to $120 in moderate; and $50 to $80, inexpensive. The restaurants run from about $90 for a dinner for two in the expensive range; $50 to $90 in the moderate range; and under $50, inexpensive.

NANCY

Capucin Gourmand – The city's finest restaurant with some outstanding traditional dishes and some varied light specials. A relatively inexpensive *prix fixe* menu is also available. Closed Sunday evenings, Mondays, and August, and 2 weeks in January. Reservations advised. 31 Rue Gambetta (phone: 83-35-26-98). Expensive.

Grand Hôtel de la Reine – In a renovated landmark 18th-century building on Place Stanislas, this lovely hotel also houses the *Stanislas* restaurant, which has an excellent *prix fixe* menu and a very talented chef. 2 Pl. Stanislas (phone: 83-35-03-01). Expensive.

Altéa Thiers – Its 112 rooms are comfortable and nicely decorated, and it has a fine restaurant and bar. 11 Rue Raymond Poincaré (phone: 83-35-61-01). Expensive to moderate.

Albert Ier Astoria – Quiet and comfortable, with 134 rooms but no restaurant. Close to the train station. 3 Rue de l'Armée-Patton (phone: 83-40-31-24). Moderate.

Gentilhommière – A charming provincial restaurant with very good meat dishes (veal, squab, duck) and excellent sauces. Closed weekends, August, and holidays. 29 Rue des Maréchaux (phone: 83-32-26-44). Moderate.

Excelsior – This Art Nouveau brasserie, classified as a historic monument, was recently taken over and renovated by the Flo Groupe, which owns several lovingly restored classic bistros in Paris. The menu offers a large choice of seafood, fish, and regional items at affordable prices, all amidst beautiful surroundings. 50 Rue Henri-Poincaré (phone: 83-35-24-57). Open daily. Moderate.

RIBEAUVILLÉ

Des Vosges – This clean, modern hotel has 18 rooms and a good restaurant (one Michelin star) with an extensive menu that includes a three-course *prix fixe* meal for a reasonable price. 2 Grande Rue (phone: 89-73-61-39). Expensive to moderate.

Menestrel – Alsace's gently sloping vineyards surround this modern, flower-studded inn, opened in 1989 by a pastry chef and his wife just outside Ribeauvillé. Av. du Général-de-Gaulle (phone: 89-73-80-52). Moderate.

Tour – A picturesque, renovated old winery with 32 pleasant rooms. 1 Rue de la Mairie (phone: 89-73-72-73). Moderate.

Zum Pfiferhüs – An appealing *winstub* in a landmark building with very tasty *choucroute*. Closed Wednesdays, Thursdays, and in February. 14 Grande Rue (phone 89-73-62-28). Inexpensive.

RIQUEWIHR

Auberge de Schoenenbourg – Enjoy Alsatian food with flourishes of nouvelle cuisine while gazing at the vineyard behind the restaurant. The wines served are made from grapes grown here. Closed Thursdays, Wednesday evenings off-season, and from mid-January to mid-February. 2 Rue de la Piscine (phone: 89-47-92-28). Expensive.

KAYSERSBERG

Résidence Chambard – One of the best classic restaurants in Alsace, with a gracious dining room and specialties like foie gras in cabbage leaves. The annex behind the restaurant has a comfortable 20-room hotel. 9 Rue du Général-de-Gaulle (phone: 89-47-10-17). Expensive.

COLMAR

Altea Champ de Mars – Comfortable accommodations and pleasant service. 2 Av. Marne (phone: 89-41-54-54). Moderate.

Hostellerie "Le Maréchal" – At the water's edge in the charming Little Venice quarter, this sprawling collection of half-timbered houses with flower-strewn balconies and crooked stairways has a very individual charm. Rooms are named for composers — Mozart, Wagner, Beethoven — and each is decorated differently. The restaurant, overlooking the water, has tapestry, candlelight, and dark wood. 4-6 Pl. des Six Montagnes-Noires (phone: 89-41-60-32). Expensive.

Maison des Têtes – This simple brasserie is in an extraordinary 17th-century landmark building, where heads of people and mythical animals adorn the façade, imploring guests to enter. Closed from early January to mid-February, Sunday evenings, and Mondays. 19 Rue de Têtes (phone: 89-24-43-43). Expensive to moderate.

Terminus Bristol – Pleasant, reliable hotel near the train station. Its bustling restaurant, *Rendez-vous de Chasse,* offers well-prepared regional dishes as well as local wines that have earned it one Michelin star. 7 Pl. de la Gare (phone: 89-23-59-59). Moderate.

STRASBOURG

Hôtel Cathédrale Dauphin – An old building just in front of the cathedral houses this new hotel. Past the crisply modern lobby, and up a narrow stairway, are tastefully decorated rooms, many of them with fantastic views of the cathedral and square. Guests have access to a nearby health and fitness club. 12 Place de la Cathédrale (phone 88-22-12-12). Expensive.

Sofitel – A modern 163-room hotel with an excellent location, all the comforts of any first class establishment, and a good restaurant. Pl. St.-Pierre-le-Jeune (phone: 88-32-99-30). Expensive.

Des Rohan – Completely modernized, though it looks like a historic landmark. The 36 rooms have private baths and are done in 17th- and 18th-century styles. No restaurant. 17-19 Rue du Maroquin (phone: 88-32-85-11). Expensive to moderate.

Dragon – This appealing addition to the city's hotels in a calm corner of town just slightly off the beaten track is 17th century outside and Bauhaus modern inside. Rooms are in shades of gray with reproduction Mallet Stevens chairs and some views of the cathedral. It's already a favorite with members of the European Parliament. 2 Rue de l'Ecarlate (phone 88-35-79-80). Moderate.

Gutenberg – A small, simple, clean hotel in an old château. About one third of the 50 rooms come with a private bath, and many of them already have an extra bed for a third person or child. 31 Rue des Serruriers (phone: 88-32-17-15). Inexpensive.

Au Crocodile – Unquestionably one of the city's best (three Michelin stars), featuring French cuisine with an Alsatian touch; fish and game specialties are outstanding. Closed Sundays, Mondays, mid-July to early August, and a week at Christmas. 10 Rue de l'Outre (phone: 88-32-13-02). Expensive.

Buerehiesel – A beautiful dining room, very attentive service, wonderful fish and game dishes (in season), and a large list of fine wines. Closed Tuesdays, Wednesdays, 2 weeks in August, and for periods during the winter. 4 Parc de l'Orangerie (phone: 88-61-62-24). Expensive.

Vieille Enseigne – Once a mere *weinstube,* this cozy restaurant with a clublike atmosphere, popular with politicians, has bettered its service and its food over the years, reaching a very high level in both. Closed Saturday lunch and Sundays. 9 Rue des Tonneliers (phone: 88-32-58-50). Expensive to moderate.

Maison des Tanneurs – Bedecked with balconies and flowers at the edge of a canal, this is the place to try *choucroute* (share it). Closed Sundays, Mondays, the first half of July, and late December to late January. 42 Rue du Bain-aux-Plantes (phone: 88-32-79-70). Moderate.

Chez Tante Liesel – It's friendly and cheerful with only nine tables and popular with diners for its family recipes and unexpected treats. Closed Tuesdays, Thursday evenings, Christmas, and New Year's Day. 4 Rue des Dentelles (phone: 88-23-02-16). Inexpensive.

Strissel – Good Alsatian food, wines, and atmosphere make it a local favorite. Convenient to the museums and the cathedral. Closed Sundays, Mondays, a week in February, and most of July. 5 Pl. de la Grande Boucherie (phone: 88-32-14-73). Inexpensive.

East Germany

For the Western tourist, East Germany, or the German Democratic Republic (GDR, or in German, DDR for Deutsche Demokratische Republik), is one of Europe's undiscovered travel lands. Diplomatically isolated from the West until the early 1970s, it became a "concentration camp" country in the popular Western imagination, gray and forbidding behind the barbed wire and mines of its border. The truth, as tourists who are now flocking to the country are finding out, is very different. The barbed wire and the minefields still exist, but the border guards are generally as friendly and helpful as most of their countrymen. Theirs is a land of beautiful, quiet plains, thickly forested mountains, and lingering rural traditions. East Germany also offers Westerners a peek into a Communist state right in the center of Europe. Besides being inquisitive and eager to strike up conversations, its people are now prosperous by Eastern European standards and justly proud of their economic achievements. Most of them are quite content to live in a socialist country.

The modern state of East Germany was created by the cold war aftermath of World War II. In 1945, right in Potsdam, an East German city near Berlin, the victorious Allies divided a bombed and defeated Germany into four zones: American, French, British, and Soviet. As the political split with the USSR grew, the Soviet zone became increasingly isolated from the others. Finally, the unsuccessful Soviet blockade of West Berlin in 1948–49 precipitated the present division of Germany into its two separate states.

Some 3 million of the country's best engineers, doctors, and craftsmen left East Germany during the 12 years after 1949. The GDR has stemmed the debilitating flow of refugees to the West with the building of the much-reviled Berlin Wall in 1961 and has undergone its own "economic miracle." East Germany is now among the top ten industrial countries in the world, and the East Germans enjoy the highest standard of living in Eastern Europe, without the American aid that West Germany received after the war. This is a country that was utterly devastated by a war, in which Dresden (whose war damage was second only to Hiroshima's) lost 80% of its old town center and about 35,000 people on February 13 and 14, 1945.

The GDR is roughly the size of Ohio, covering 41,610 square miles. Its area is half the size, and its population of 17 million people less than one-third that of West Germany. East Berlin is the nation's largest city, with a population of 1.1 million people; Leipzig is second, with 565,000; and Dresden third, with 520,000. Most of the country — bounded by West Germany to the south and west, Czechoslovakia to the south, the Baltic Sea to the north, and Poland to the east — lies in what was once the north German plain, the agricultural section of Germany in former years.

Although East Germany has been transformed into an industrial power, many of its rural attractions still remain. There are the Harz Mountains in the west, the Thuringian Forest in the southwest, and the Erzgebirge (mountains) in the south. The Elbe, one of Europe's major rivers, flows northwest from Czechoslovakia, cutting right across the whole country, past Dresden, Wittenberg, and Magdeburg, and into West Germany; and the Oder River flows along the eastern boundary of the country.

To see the GDR, you can choose one or both of our proposed routes, either singly or in combination. Each one lasts about 3 to 5 days and both originate in Berlin. The first, about 470 miles (752 km) long, follows the western edge of the country from Potsdam, across gently rolling hills to Magdeburg, over the Harz Mountains southward to the foothills of the Thuringian Forest, and then back north to Naumburg. From here you can return to Berlin or branch eastward to Leipzig and the second route (340 mi/544 km) — the better known of the two — which includes the old cultural center of Dresden; Meissen, the town that has manufactured Dresden china since 1705; and the country of the Sorbs, East Germany's largest ethnic minority.

Roads in the GDR are adequate to good on the whole, and, to a Western motorist, delightfully empty. Tractors, recklessly piloted Soviet military vehicles, and slippery cobblestones even on the main routes are the chief dangers, but signposting is thoughtful. Gas stations are, however, few and far between, so it is advisable to take a canister for a reserve supply of gas. A pack of spare parts (light bulbs, fan belt, oil, spark plugs) could be your salvation, and don't forget to fill up wherever you can. Also note that drinking alcohol while driving is forbidden.

The Harz Mountains and the Thuringian Forest

Shaped like a large slanted block, the rugged Harz Mountains in the southwest corner of the GDR are silent witnesses to much of German history. The region, pocked by limestone caves and pierced by tall mountain peaks, is dotted with numerous castles, churches, and fortresses built during the Middle Ages. Our route runs through several cities of import: Potsdam, a residence of Frederick the Great during the 18th century as well as the site of the conference in which Churchill, Stalin, and Truman decided the fate of postwar Germany; Eisenach, birthplace of Johann Sebastian Bach; and Weimar, the home of Goethe and Schiller and namesake of the short-lived republic that fell with the rise of Hitler. Near Weimar is a memorial to Buchenwald, a notorious concentration camp during World War II.

The route begins in East Berlin, then goes to Potsdam, Magdeburg, and the Harz Mountain towns of Quedlinburg and Wernigerode. From Wernigerode it continues southwest to Eisenach, after which it swings eastward to Erfurt and Weimar; this is the area known as the Thuringian Forest, its gentle wooded slopes rounded rather than jagged, peaceful rather than dramatic. After turning northward to Naumburg, you can go on to Leipzig and our second route, or you can return to Berlin.

Maps, brochures, organized tours, and other information are available from the tourist offices in each of the cities and some of the towns. Their headquarters are in East Berlin at the Reisebüro der DDR, 5 Alexanderpl. (phone: 215-4402).

POTSDAM: Most people know Potsdam as the place where the four victorious powers of World War II — Russia, Britain, the US, and France — signed the 1945 agreements that split Germany and Berlin into four zones of occupation. But Potsdam has been known since 1660, when the Princes of Hohenzollern chose it as their country residence and began a palatial building program that ended only in the late 19th century. The 18th century saw the city develop as the military center of Old Prussia, boasting at one time a ratio of 8,000 soldiers to just 17,000 inhabitants. Since World War II, shapeless modern architecture and now-regretted demolition programs have destroyed some of Potsdam's old charm, but the palaces and the parks are still as delightful as ever. Potsdam is also East Germany's Hollywood, producing feature films at its DEFA studios.

The road from Berlin brings you southeast of the town, near the *Interhotel Potsdam*. You might start with a walk round the old town, centering on Klement-Gottwald-Strasse, recently designated a pedestrian precinct with small cafés, shops, and an information bureau at #24. From here it's an easy walk along the Allee nach Sans Souci to Potsdam's main attraction, the Sans Souci Park and Sans Souci Palace (built on Frederick the Great's orders in 1745-47); a picture gallery next door with works by Rubens, Van Dyck, Tintoretto, and others; the ornate Chinese teahouse; statues; shrubberies; and at the end, the New Palace (1769), another creation of Frederick's 46-year reign. Never actually lived in, it was intended to demonstrate the Prussian state's unbroken might after the Seven Years war.

In the northeastern part of town, the Cecilienhof, at Neuer Garten, built during World War I in the style of an English country mansion, is where the 1945 conference took place. The Cecilienhof houses an interesting museum devoted to the conference, which includes the original furniture. Ironically, as if to remind visitors of the consequences of that conference, a stretch of the Berlin Wall, sealing West Berlin from surrounding East Germany, stands just 200 yards away in full view at the bottom of the garden. *Cecilienhof* is also, by the way, an excellent hotel with a mediocre restaurant.

En Route from Potsdam – Route F1, part of the main trans-European artery intended by Hitler to link occupied Paris with Berlin in the 1930s, takes you out of town into the farmland along the Havel River. If you are here in spring, the cherry blossoms on either side of the two-lane highway are breathtaking. Brandenburg, 25 miles (40 km) along the route, was the capital of the Prussian state for centuries, but it declined as Berlin took over the role of administrative center. Another hour's drive along the tree-lined F1 brings you via sleepy villages to Magdeburg, on the Elbe. You are now entering the Harz ("woodland") Mountains, a region of rugged, weather-beaten rocks, medieval churches and castles, rich woodlands, and fertile farm country.

MAGDEBURG: The country's main heavy machineworks, the Ernst Thälmann Engineering Combine (SKET), has its headquarters here, a fitting location since this is where Magdeburg's most famous citizen, former mayor Otto von Guericke (1602–86), proved the power of vacuum and invented the "Magdeburg Hemispheres." Sadly, Magdeburg has had a history of destruction. It burned down almost totally during an attack in 1631, and more than 90% of the rebuilt inner city was razed by Allied bombing in January 1945. Only parts of the city center have been reconstructed as they once were. If you begin with the Old Town Hall (the *Rathaus*), you'll notice the famous

13th-century statue of the *Magdeburg Rider* on his horse facing the building from the square. He's only a copy of the original statue, sculpted in 1240 but now in the city museum on Otto von Guericke Str. A 10-minute walk through what's left of the old town brings you to the mainly 12th-century Cloister of Our Dear Lady, possibly one of the best-restored architectural ensembles in the whole of Germany. Next door is the cathedral, with quaint cloisters around the side entrance; it was first recorded as a place of worship in 955. In the northern transept a group of six wooden figures by Germany's highly regarded 20th-century sculptor, Ernst Barlach, memorializes starkly and impressively the dead of World War I. The Nazis had it removed from the cathedral, but the ensemble was reinstalled in 1957.

En Route from Magdeburg – You can take Route F81 out of Magdeburg, through Egeln and Halberstadt, but for a taste of the small country roads almost completely free of traffic, bear right on the outskirts of the town to head for Wanzleben. You'll pass through typical East German provincial towns, hardly changed since World War II. From Kroppenstedt you go over the top of a small range of hills, a foretaste of things to come. At Halberstadt, drive farther on F79.

QUEDLINBURG: This is East Germany's tourist pride. Hardly hit by the war, it still boasts hundreds of picturesque half-timbered houses, many with the old signs of their former owners. Head for the marketplace, where restorers have done an impressive job on the Renaissance Town Hall and on the colorful wood carvings on the façades of the surrounding 16th-century houses. Looking away from the Town Hall, you'll see the Schlossberg, crowned by a cathedral with its 19th-century towers resting on a medieval body. (Guided tours are given on the half-hour until 3:30 PM.) From the balustrade of the castle (*Schloss*) there's a stunning view of old Quedlinburg with its tiled roofs tilting at all angles. The restaurant in the castle complex serves a respectable lunch, outside if the weather's good, and fine afternoon coffee. It's worth a stop before continuing to drive along the northern base of the Harz Mountains, taking the minor road to Weddersleben and Thale.

En Route from Quedlinburg – After Thale you pass through Blankenburg. Stop briefly at the Regenstein Castle just out of town to the right. It was chiseled out of sandstone and was first used as a fortress in the 5th century.

WERNIGERODE: Nine miles (15 km) farther on is the center of the Harz vacation area. Its colorful and half-timbered 16th-century Town Hall at the crossing of Marktstrasse and Breite Strasse looks like something out of a fairy tale by the Brothers Grimm. There is an unusual feudal museum here, in the medieval castle that overlooks the town; its exhibits include medieval furniture and objects illustrating daily life in the Middle Ages and the history of the Harz region. Wernigerode is also the northern terminal for a narrow-gauge steam railway that links the northern and southern Harz. If you have time, leave the car here and take a trip (it costs only a few pfennigs) up through Drei-Annen-Hohne, and past the Brocken, which at 3,747 feet is the highest peak in the Harz, although inaccessible from the west. It was chosen by Johann Wolfgang von Goethe for the Walpurgisnacht scenes in *Faust*.

En Route from Wernigerode – Take Route F244 toward Elbingerode. On the left toward Rübeland there are some impressive limestone caves worth seeing — if you have the patience to join the long lines. Then head along F81 to Hasselfelde and down through deep leafy gorges along F4 to Nordhausen, southern terminal of the railway from Wernigerode. Nordhausen is the town that produces East Germany's most famous schnapps, Nordhauser Doppelkorn. Most goes for export, so you'll probably find there's none to buy here. Get it at an *Intershop* for Western currency instead.

The Kyffhäuser Mountain 15 miles (24 km) southeast of Nordhausen rises 1,565 feet out of the north Thuringian plain, and is shrouded in legend. One was that Emperor Redbeard, or Barbarossa, would sleep in his underground cave here until the time came to unite the German people. With the proclamation of the united German Reich in 1871, formed by joining the 24 previously independent German states, Kaiser Wilhelm I had a monument erected on the Kyffhäuser mountain peak, representing himself as a glowering and mighty Barbarossa in red sandstone. In good weather, the view from the top of the mountain is breathtaking, extending northward to the Harz and westward into West Germany. The GDR has formally renounced the goal of reunification with West Germany, and making the best of an awkward memorial to an abandoned aim, publications now describe it as evidence of the "aggressive and military nature" of Germany's imperialist past.

Now, you have a choice. You can either go to Eisenach, Erfurt, and Weimar by way of Bad Frankenhausen, Route F85 to Sachsenburg, and Route F86 to Straussfurt — it's 54 miles (87 km) to Eisenach — or, if you wish, you can skip this section and head for Leipzig and the second route.

EISENACH: Now famous as an automobile manufacturing center, Eisenach (pop. 50,000) is better known as the site of the Wartburg, a castle dating from 1067, now a museum. It was the home of the medieval Minnesänger poets immortalized by Richard Wagner in his opera *Tannhäuser.* It also served as Martin Luther's retreat in the 16th century, when he translated the Bible into German, laying the foundations for today's spoken language. The composer Johann Sebastian Bach was also born in Eisenach, and the family home, at 21 Am Frauenplan, houses a fascinating collection of musical instruments and Bach family memorabilia.

En Route from Eisenach – Route F7, with views of the hills on the right, takes you 34 miles (54 km) east to Erfurt. On the way, a half-hour excursion southeast to Arnstadt is very rewarding (head for the Autobahn in Gotha): This is one of the oldest towns in the GDR (first mentioned in 704). Bach was an organist here from 1703 to 1707. Besides a beautifully restored marketplace, Arnstadt also has a 200-year-old doll collection in the Neues Palais (New Castle). From here, Erfurt is a 20-minute drive north.

ERFURT: A provincial capital and major industrial center, Erfurt with its 220,000 inhabitants is the only sizable town in the GDR that was not largely destroyed in World War II. It was liberated by the Americans in April 1945, but was handed over to the Russians under the agreements that divided Germany into occupied zones. Dominating Erfurt are two Catholic churches side by side on the Domberg. The walls of the cathedral and those of St. Severi (both finished by the 15th century) lie just a few feet apart at their closest point. In town, a walk down the Marktstrasse brings you to the Krämerbrücke, a 14th-century ensemble of houses on a bridge over the Gera River. Formerly houses of petty traders, they were restored in the 1960s as delightful little antiques shops, book stalls, and cafés. This is a good place to find that unusual souvenir.

WEIMAR: Thirteen miles (21 km) east of Erfurt on Route F7 lies Weimar, today a town of just 65,000 people but one of the most important centers of German history and culture. Goethe and Schiller both wrote their greatest works here in the 18th and early 19th centuries. In 1919, the first German Republic, also known as the Weimar Republic, proclaimed its constitution in the town's now reconstructed *National Theater;* the Weimar Republic fell during the world economic crisis in the early 1930s, when the extremely nationalistic Nazi party rose to power. The homes of Goethe and Schiller (the former on the Frauenplan and the latter on the Schillerstrasse) are now open as museums. A short walk from Goethe's house past the *Interhotel Elephant* brings you to a park now named after the poet, a place where he used to walk. Across the river is the garden house he used in the summer, now an extension of the main museum.

BUCHENWALD: Before leaving the area, take a detour to Buchenwald, 4 miles (6 km) northwest. Now run as a national memorial, it's the site of one of Hitler's most notorious concentration camps, opened in 1937. Here 56,000 people, including Jews,

Communists, and prisoners of war, died before the surviving inmates were freed by the Americans in April 1945. The contrast between the barbarities once perpetrated here and the humanistic ideals of nearby Weimar is chilling.

En Route from Weimar – Route F7 (we have purposely kept off the Autobahns, as these show you so much less of the countryside than the quieter country roads) takes you toward Jena, but turn left at F87 and head past Apolda to Naumburg.

NAUMBURG: If, after Magdeburg and Erfurt, you can still take some more medieval architecture, the cathedral has to be seen. The town was a major trading and religious center in the Middle Ages. The Cathedral of St. Peter and St. Paul has been beautifully preserved, and its earliest parts date from 1210. Inside are realistic and humorous carved figures of ordinary folk of the time, installed in the late 13th century. Before you leave Naumburg, visit the *Ratskeller* in the town hall (Wilhelm Pieck Pl.), where with any luck you'll find a bottle of excellent and very dry local wine. Try it; it's little known outside the GDR.

En Route from Naumburg – Taking Route F87 again out to the east, you pass through Weissenfels 11 miles (18 km) away, before reaching the main north-south Autobahn. That's the end of this route, and you can return to Berlin, or leave the GDR from the south. But if you've developed a taste for more, take the slightly shorter tour through Leipzig and Dresden, with many attractive tidbits along the way.

BEST EN ROUTE

In East Germany, hotel reservations must be made in advance and prices are generally high; in fact, they are double the rates charged to visitors from Communist countries. Contact Reisebüro der DDR, 5 Alexanderpl., East Berlin (phone: 215-4402). The Consular Section of the East German Embassy (phone: 202-232-3134) can provide a list of US travel agents who work with the Reisebüro.

For a double room in expensive hotels, expect to pay $120 and up; $75 to $115 in the moderate category; under $75 in the inexpensive class. Payment must be made in Western currency or by credit card.

Dinner for two, with drinks and wine, costs about $35 or more at expensive restaurants; between $25 and $30 in the moderate range; and under $25 in inexpensive places. Tips are included in the bill.

POTSDAM

Interhotel Potsdam – This large high-rise hotel, at the entrance to town nearest Berlin, is one of the GDR's most prestigious, with prices to match. It has a sauna, an *Intershop,* dancing, entertainment, a restaurant, and a bar. Lange Brücke (phone: 4631). Expensive.

Cecilienhof – Set in a 20th-century version of an English country house, this historic building was the site of the Potsdam conference in 1945. As a hotel it's smaller and less luxurious than the *Potsdam,* but it has a restaurant, a café, an *Intershop,* and some rooms with baths. Neuer Garten (phone: 2-3141). Expensive to moderate.

Klosterkeller – A comfortable restaurant with decent food. Gutenbergstr. and Friedrich Ebert Str. Inexpensive.

MAGDEBURG

Interhotel International – This big hotel (358 rooms) has baths in all rooms, a restaurant, a café, dancing, and an *Intershop.* Some might consider it modern and characterless, as are most of East Germany's better hotels. 87 Otto von Guericke Str. (phone: 3840). Expensive.

QUEDLINBURG

Schlosskrug – The restaurant is in the castle forecourt, and it serves good lunches and afternoon coffee. 1 Schlossberg (phone: 2838). Expensive to moderate.

EISENACH

Auf der Wartburg – In Wartburg castle, the 30 rooms are in the usual German-modern style, and there is a restaurant. Wartburg (phone: 5111). Expensive.

Stadt Eisenach – This 85-bed hotel has a restaurant and parking. 11-13 Luisenstr. (phone: 3682). Moderate.

Hohe Sonne – Just outside the city, this restaurant is in a lovely rustic area with a view of the Wartburg. Regional Thuringian dishes are its specialty. Open daily. Am Rennsteig (phone: 2903). Inexpensive.

ERFURT

Erfurter Hof – Opposite the railroad station is one of East Germany's best kept and most distinguished hotels, where West Germany's Chancellor Willy Brandt stayed in 1970 on his journey of reconciliation to the GDR. It has all conveniences and an excellent restaurant serving interesting culinary inventions. The rooms in the back are quieter than those facing the station. Bahnhofsvorpl. (phone: 5-1151). Expensive.

Hohe Lilie – An interesting restaurant, it occupies the first two floors of a building that dates from 1540. Spicy Balkan dishes are the house specialty. Closed Mondays. 31 Dompl. (phone: 2-25-78). Inexpensive.

Tourist – Though unpretentious, this hotel is modern and characterless. 158 Yuri Gargarin Ring (phone: 5-1076). Inexpensive.

WEIMAR

Elephant – Centrally located and extensively remodeled, this hotel dates from 1696 but has most of the facilities you could want and some extras, such as horseback riding and dancing. There's a fine restaurant in the basement. Am Markt (phone: 6-1471). Moderate.

Leipzig, Dresden, and Sorb Country

This short but quite interesting route connects Leipzig and Dresden, East Germany's two major cities after Berlin, which were both heavily damaged during the war and have since been restored. Leipzig, long known for its medieval trade fairs, still hosts two important international fairs in November and March. And amazingly enough, you can still eat and drink here in *Auerbachs Keller,* the restaurant and tavern where Goethe had Faust and the Devil meet in *Faust* (see *Best en Route*). Dresden is the place for great art treasures, both in the Zwinger fortress and in the Albertinum, and its restaurants are among the best in East Germany.

You can begin your drive in East Berlin or in Naumburg, where the first route ended. For maps, brochures, and further information, contact the local tourist office. In East Berlin it's Reisebüro der DDR, 5 Alexanderpl. (phone: 215-4402); in Dresden, 22 Ernst Thälmann Str. (phone: 48650); in Leipzig, 1/3 Katharinenstr., (phone: 79210).

LEIPZIG: East Germans call this city of 565,000 people the secret capital of the GDR. It is the country's second most important industrial and commercial center, hosting a week-long trade fair twice a year that attracts exhibitors from up to 60 countries at a time. Leipzig, its name derived from the Slav *Lipsk*, "place of the lime tree," is also home of the East German printing industry, of the second largest GDR university, and of the main sports institute. Bach spent his most creative years, from 1723 to 1750, as choirmaster at the St. Thomas Church here. Leipzig was badly damaged by World War II bombing, but architects have succeeded here better than elsewhere in restoring its former character. The Old Town Hall (16th century) and the Thomaskirche (1494) have been completely restored; the newer Rathaus (19th century), on the edge of the neatly circumscribed old town, was hardly touched. (It has an excellent restaurant in its basement.) Grimmaische Strasse leads to Karl-Marx-Platz, the new university, and the opera, and it's lined with souvenir and book shops. The *Gewandhaus* concert hall has recently been rebuilt.

A short walk back across the market square brings you to the Thomas Church, where the boys' choir, which Bach used to conduct, still gives free concerts of motets every Friday evening and Sunday morning when they are not on tour. Bach lies buried at the eastern end of the church. More than any other East German town, Leipzig abounds in good eating and drinking places. Apart from the main hotels, the *Kaffeebaum,* on the corner of Kleine Fleischergasse and Barfussgässchen, has been serving beer and food for centuries.

Before leaving Leipzig, follow the Strasse des 18 Oktober to the memorial to the Battle of the People (Völkerschlachtdenkmal). You will pass the fairground and a fine Russian Orthodox church erected in 1913. The memorial to the 1813 victory of Russian and German troops over Napoleon's Grande Armée is a monstrous, 300-foot-high edifice completed the same year as the church. The view of Leipzig, and the remarkable acoustics inside, are worth the climb to the top of the monument.

En Route from Leipzig – Route F6 leads to the cathedral, wine, and porcelain town of Meissen, 53 miles (85 km) east, through rolling farming landscapes; later it joins up with the Elbe, one of Europe's greatest rivers, and the GDR's main water artery. Where the Elbe winds between the cliffs of Saxonian Switzerland, between Dresden and the Czech border, visitors might think they are on the Rhine.

MEISSEN: This is the town that gave the world Dresden china, and it is a must on any tourist's itinerary in East Germany. The first porcelain was produced here in 1710, in the 15th-century Albrechtsburg castle that dominates the town. Dresden china was ideally suited to the extravagant rococo style in 18th-century art, and for the first few years the Meissen princes kept their craftsmen virtual prisoners here, lest rivals learn the secret of the "white gold." But it got out, needless to say. Today the factory in the Triebischtal produces china mainly for export, and can be visited during the week.

The town itself, founded in 929 and once the seat of the Saxonian bishops, is one of the best preserved in East Germany. Visit the *Albrechtsburg* castle, now a museum, and the delightful and still privately owned wine house of Vincenz Richter, just off the market square at An der Frauenkirche 12. A good lunch can also be had in the cafés in the courtyard of the Albrechtsburg. Sample the local wines, especially the rare Meissner Domherr.

En Route from Meissen – Rather than go straight along Route F6 to Dresden, take the road north across the river in Meissen and follow the signs to Weinböhla along a small country road. Continue through Auer and in 10 miles (16 km) you come to one of the most beautiful of the country residences built around Dresden by Saxon Prince Frederick Augustus (the Strong) in the 18th century. The Schloss Moritzburg is a museum of baroque porcelain, furniture, and hunting weapons.

Another way to reach Moritzburg is to leave the car in nearby Radebeul and take a narrow-gauge steam railway for five stops.

DRESDEN: One of the high points of any visit to East Germany, this city is alive with cultural tradition and political history. Its many art collections rank among the most valuable in the world, and Dresden is today the GDR's third largest city, with a population of over half a million. To visitors from Britain and America, its name, like that of Hiroshima, is synonymous with the horrors of modern warfare. Up to 35,000 people are believed to have died in the Anglo-American bomber raids on February 13 and 14, 1945, and some 80% of the town center, with its narrow old streets and passageways, was razed to the ground. The Schlosskirche, the *Semper* opera house, and the galleries along the Brühlsche Terrasse have been rebuilt to restore to Dresden the silhouette made famous by the 18th-century painter Canaletto. Behind that waterfront, the rest of the city center has been rebuilt in characterless concrete and glass. By 1990, however, work in progress will have restored old Dresden to its former baroque and rococo splendor.

The city was founded in about 1200, and it remained a trading city until it was chosen by the lavishly spending Saxon princes for their court in the 17th century.

Pragerstrasse, once Dresden's most fashionable street, is now flanked by blocks of flats and shops, but it's pleasantly landscaped with fountains and benches. Past a new cinema and department store, you reach the Old Market (Altmarkt) with the restored Kreuzkirche (Church of the Cross), home of the world-renowned *Kreuzchor* (a boys' choir) on the right. Ahead of you is the new Palace of Culture (1969), and behind that the memorial ruins of the Frauenkirche that once bore one of Europe's most famous cupolas. You are now in the heart of old Dresden, surrounded by car parks and bomb sites that drive home the devastation of that terrible time in 1945. Follow on toward the river and up the steps, and you come to the Albertinum (1559) with its glass dome and exhibitions of state art collections within (closed on Thursdays). There are 19th- and 20th-century German paintings, French Impressionist works, and the famous Green Vault (Grünes Gewölbe) with works of goldsmiths and jewelers from the 15th to the 18th centuries. The Zwinger, a fortress built between 1711 and 1722 at the height of Augustus's reign, was lovingly restored in the postwar years. In magnificent baroque style, with lovely sculptures and chimes of Dresden porcelain, it houses one of the world's most stunning art collections, the *Picture Gallery of Old Masters,* which includes Raphael's *Sistine Madonna* (1513). Also visit its unparalleled collections of china, coins, and hunting weapons.

En Route from Dresden – You can return directly to Berlin via the Autobahn, a distance of about 122 miles (196 km). Or you can spend some time in the Spreewald, a 93-square-mile network of canals, woods, and pastures along the Spree River southeast of the capital. Get off the Autobahn at Lübbenau. Carved wooden road signs tell you the way to the port (*Hafen*) where you can either take a leisurely 3-hour ride in a punt along the slowly flowing canals or hire a canoe if you feel energetic. That's the best way to do it, and try the private boat rental establishment of *Herr Franke* (72 Maxim Gorki Str.), down a small unpaved road before you reach the main harbor. The prices are staggeringly low.

During your excursion, possibly poled along by a Sorb woman in national dress (all the punt owners are private, incidentally, and pool only their passengers in a punting collective), don't miss the waterside cafés along the route. They generally serve good coffee and cakes in the afternoon.

BEST EN ROUTE

In East Germany, hotel reservations must be made in advance and prices are generally high; in fact, they are double the rates charged to visitors from Communist countries. Contact Reisebüro der DDR, 5 Alexanderpl., East Berlin (phone: 215-4402), or Koch Overseas Company, 206-208 E. 86th St., New York, NY 10028 (phone: 212-535-8600).

For a double room in expensive hotels, expect to pay $120 and up; $75 to $115 in the moderate category; under $75 in the inexpensive class. Payment must be made in Western currency or by credit card.

Dinner for two, with drinks and wine, costs about $40 or more at expensive restaurants; between $30 and $35 in the moderate range; and under $30 in inexpensive places. Tips are included in the bill.

LEIPZIG

Merkur – The best hotel in town, it has 4 restaurants, a swimming pool, a sauna, and a nightclub on the 27th floor that offers a breathtaking panorama of the city. And it's away from the downtown area, so it's quiet. *Sakura,* with its Japanese cuisine, is well worth a visit. Gerberstrasse (phone: 7990). Expensive.

Astoria – An excellent hotel, elegantly furnished in traditional late-19th-century style, with all the modern conveniences. It has a good restaurant, a pleasant terrace, a café, and dancing. Like the other big hotels here, it's much used by visiting businesspeople for the trade fairs in March and September. Platz der Republik (phone: 71710). Moderate.

Auerbachs Keller – Goethe made this tavern famous in *Faust,* and the place is decorated with sculptures and paintings inspired by that drama. It's a beautiful restaurant, which serves excellent food, beers, and wines. No reservations. Mädlerpassage (phone: 209131). Moderate.

Kaffebaum – The oldest coffeehouse in Leipzig dates from 1694 and was frequented by many famous people: Goethe, Lessing, Wagner, Liszt, and others. Its original decor includes lovely old wooden tables. The food is basic but good; the beer is good, and the place is very popular. 4 Kleine Fleischergasse (phone: 200452). Moderate.

Stadt Kiew – In the middle of town opposite the Old Town Hall, this popular restaurant specializes in Ukrainian dishes. Markt Peterstr. (phone: 295063). Moderate.

Stadt Leipzig – Opposite the main railway station, this is a first rate hotel by GDR standards. All amenities are available here, including a barber shop and a sauna. The front rooms do tend to be noisy. Richard Wagner Str. (phone: 288814). Moderate.

Stadtpfeiffer – Excellent food in the *Gewandhaus* concert hall complex. Lunch only in July and August. Karl-Marx-Platz (phone: 713-2389). Moderate.

Ratskeller – This is a wonderful student haunt in the basement of the new town hall. Its specialty is a fine potato omelette (*Bauernfrühstück*). Inexpensive.

DRESDEN

Bellevue – The city's second-largest (330 rooms) hotel. Guest rooms have a magnificent view, across the Elbe, of the historic city center. Quiet, pleasant atmosphere. Köpckestr. (phone: 56620). Expensive.

Astoria – A small, comfortable hotel in the city center known for its friendly atmosphere. If you have the chance to book your own lodging, make this your choice, though not every room has a bath. Ernst-Thälmann-Pl. (phone: 47-51-71 or 485-6666). Moderate.

Gewandhaus – The hotel is not open to foreigners, but the fine restaurant is, and it's one of the most pleasant and popular eating places in Dresden. 1 Ringstr. (phone: 496286). Moderate.

Königstein – On Dresden's main shopping street, this large place is less pretentious, less luxurious, and more popular with local and East European tourists. Pragerstr. (phone: 48560). Moderate.

Secundogenitur – Though the place offers only one dish a day, the quality is excellent, and it's in the old baroque city center. Brühlsche Terrasse (phone: 496147). Moderate.

berlausitzer Töpp'l – A rustic eating spot featuring the hearty fare of the Lusatia area, home of the Sorbs. The dishes are reminiscent of Bohemian cuisine. Try the remarkable dark beer, a traditional Lusatian delicacy. Reservations suggested. Str. der Befreiung (phone: 55605). Moderate.

Ratskeller – As in most German towns, the Rathaus (town hall) here has its own restaurant, and like most Ratskellers, it's a good value, unpretentious and noisy. It's great for meeting townsfolk and sampling the atmosphere (phone: 493212). Moderate to inexpensive.

Kügelgen-Haus – Behind the baroque façade is a gastronomic complex consisting of several restaurants and a beer cellar where good food and drink can be found at good prices. The nearby *Meissener Weinkeller* features some very rare East German wines. Reservations suggested. Str. der Befreiung (phone: 52791). Inexpensive.

West Germany

Germany has been the cradle of heroes and monsters — a land of giants such as Bach, Brahms, Beethoven, and Wagner in music; Hegel, Kant, and Heidegger in philosophy; and Goethe, Schiller, and Thomas Mann in literature. Karl Marx and Friedrich Engels were the originators of modern Communist ideology, just as Albert Einstein was the pioneer of modern physics. Paradoxically, it was also in Germany that Hitler came to power, and not long ago, this great people nurtured the cancerous growth of Nazi fascism.

Many people fear a recurrence of the Nazi nightmare in Germany, and sporadic neo-Nazi occurrences fuel this concern. But the fact is that the Green Party — synonymous with peace, anti-nuclear concerns, and environmental awareness — seems much more popular and powerful. The days of leftist terrorism seem largely over as well, and West Germany, its very existence a result of World War II, continues as a government that is steadfastly democratic.

Since the end of World War II, West Germany has accomplished two miracles, one economic and one political. From a country forced into unconditional surrender, devastated by bombings, and suffering from severe food shortages, West Germany has transformed itself — thanks to the Marshall Plan (more than $5 billion worth of US aid) and to the laborious efforts of the German people — into one of the world's wealthiest industrial powers, ranking fourth in the world in steel manufacture and third in the automotive industry. Once characterized by political divisiveness, instability, and a strong tendency toward totalitarianism, West Germany is now firmly committed to the Western European tradition of democracy. In fact, its stability is remarkable, especially when it is compared with France or Italy; between 1949 and 1989, West Germany had only six chancellors.

Though its recently devastated cities and towns have been rebuilt in modern style, for the most part, much of the old Germany is still there for the visitor to see. Many historical buildings were spared the devastation of the bombs; others have been carefully restored. You can still see Neuschwanstein, the unbelievably elaborate castle on Bavaria's Romantic Road, which was created according to the fantasies of King Ludwig II. Cologne Cathedral is one of the world's finest Gothic structures, and the *Dahlem Museum* in Berlin contains some of the world's greatest art treasures. Everywhere in Germany there are sleepy little villages with their characteristic half-timbered houses, places where it is still common for peasants to wear traditional costumes to local markets and festivals.

Bavaria still looks like the setting of a fairy tale by the Brothers Grimm; one medieval walled town after another — Rothenburg, Dinkelsbühl, and Nördlingen — has remained remarkably intact. Germany has always been known for its legends and folk tales: the Pied Piper of Hamelin, Snow White and the Seven Dwarfs, Till Eulenspiegel's pranks, and Baron Münchhausen's adventures. Heroic tales of Siegfried and the Nibelungen haunt the eternally beautiful Rhineland, known for its castles and its magnificent clusters of rock such as the Loreley and the Drachenfels.

The Rhine is celebrated, not only for its great beauty, but as the most important commercial waterway in Europe, highway for the industrial Ruhr; the river passes by such great cities as Düsseldorf, Cologne, and Mainz. It flows in a northwest direction through the western half of West Germany from Switzerland to the Netherlands. On both sides of the Rhine, a truncated West German nation is one of the most densely populated areas in Western Europe. With an area of 95,976 square miles, it is approximately the same size as the United Kingdom. But while Britain has only 56 million people, West Germany has 62 million. Its largest city, West Berlin (pop. 2.2 million), sits 110 miles inside Communist East Germany. Bonn, the capital, is relatively small and uninteresting, with a population of 285,000 and nothing much to recommend it except for the fact that Beethoven was born there. Much larger and more alive are the busy port city of Hamburg (pop. 1.6 million) and Munich, the lively and charming capital of Bavaria (pop. 1.3 million).

In the 500-mile (800-km) stretch from north to south, the terrain of West Germany varies greatly, with coastal lowlands in the north, low mountains in the center, and the higher Bavarian Alps in the south. The center and the south contain vast forests such as the Schwarzwald (Black Forest), with its predominance of fir trees, the Harz with its beeches, and the Spessart with its giant oaks.

A bewildering number of countries, nine in all, border West Germany. To the west are France, Luxembourg, Belgium, and the Netherlands; East Germany and Czechoslovakia lie to the east; Austria and Switzerland to the south; and the North Sea, the Baltic, and Denmark to the north. Its dearth of natural boundaries has been a source of trouble throughout German history, creating a perpetual state of uncertainty, disunity, and divisiveness. To begin with, the land was inhabited as early as the 7th century BC by numerous and distinctly differentiated Germanic tribes such as the Franks, Frisians, Saxons, Thuringians, Franconians, Swabians, and Bavarians — most of whose names survive as regional place names. During the 1st century BC, the Germans expanded at the expense of the Celts, while they were invaded and threatened by the Romans. Eventually, the Franks migrated to France, the Angles and Saxons to Britain, but most of the tribes settled in the area later known as Germany.

The German tribes were gradually converted to Christianity during the 5th through the 9th century. However, with the exception of Charlemagne, Emperor of the Franks, who united a great deal of territory under his sovereignty, localization and feudalism were the rule. The Holy Roman Empire, established by Otto I in 962 and lasting until 1806, was an empire in name only. Claiming descent from ancient Rome and supremacy over Christendom, it was threatened continually both by popes and by local powers, which were often much more powerful. A medieval rival was the Hanseatic League of wealthy trading towns including Hamburg, Lübeck, Bremen, and Brunswick — formally organized in 1348.

While the rest of Europe tended to consolidate into nation-states, Germany remained divided for centuries, both in politics and in religion. The most significant separative force was that of the Reformation, which was begun by Martin Luther (1483-1546), priest and professor of theology at the University of Wittenberg. Luther, a devout ascetic, opposed such excesses of Catholicism as the sale of indulgences (pardons for sins). After studying the Bible, he originated the doctrine of salvation by faith, advocated German control of German religious matters, and was finally excommunicated by the Pope in 1521. His forceful writing and preaching converted many to the Protestant faith, and his uncompromising attitude in matters of doctrine pressed the Lutherans to break with Calvin and Zwingli and resulted in the subdivision of Protestants into sects.

Luther's enormous influence was not confined to matters of religion. His 1534 translation of the Bible was the first major literary work in the German language. Most important, his increasing opposition to the power of the Church spurred all kinds of political conflicts and resulted in a confusion of religious and political issues. Resistance to the church included resistance to the power of the Holy Roman Empire. Ambitious nobles were eager to join the Reformation in order to seize the church lands. The general dissension reached a climax in the Thirty Years War of 1618–48, between the Protestant Union and the Catholic League. Though the war spread to the rest of Europe and had less and less to do with religion, it was fought, for the most part, on German soil. German cities, towns, and countryside were destroyed in its wake.

The 17th and 18th centuries marked the emergence of Prussia and its rivalry with Austria. Power seesawed between the two, with Frederick the Great challenging Austria in the 18th century; the German Confederation emerging under the Austrian leadership of Metternich in 1815; and, at long last, the unification of a Germany dominated by Bismarck's Prussia in 1871. Bismarck's German Empire excluded Austria, and its autocratic government delegated little power to its parliament. A policy of colonial expansion, especially during the reign of Wilhelm II (1888–1918), led to growing conflicts with Britain and France that culminated in World War I.

After that war, the Kaiser was exiled; unfortunately, however, the Weimar Republic was to be weak and short-lived, split by many small political parties. This disunity, together with the worldwide depression of 1929, allowed Adolf Hitler to rise rapidly. His totalitarian Third Reich, which lasted from 1933 to 1945, brought havoc and bloodshed to Germany and to the world. After World War II, in 1945, the victorious Allies met at Yalta and at Potsdam to divide Germany into four zones: British, French, American, and Soviet. The tension between East and West, aggravated by the Soviet blockade of Berlin in 1948–49, resulted in the present division of Germany into East (German Democratic Republic) and West (Federal Republic of Germany) in 1949.

Dividedness, the theme of German history, continues to be that nation's destiny. Oddly enough, the erection of the Berlin Wall in 1961 — concrete monstrosity though it is — has brought about a condition of peace and stability for both Germanys. Relations between the two countries have warmed considerably since Chancellor Willy Brandt, pursuing his open-door policy toward the Eastern powers, signed a treaty with the USSR in 1970 and with East Germany in 1972. West Germans can now visit relatives in East Germany as a matter of course, and foreign visitors to West Berlin can easily obtain day passes to East Berlin. They must, however, cross the border at a special point; most other visitors use "Checkpoint Charlie.".

A visit to West Germany offers many delights, not the least of which are Rhine wines and Munich beer halls; carnivals such as *Fasching* and *Oktoberfest,* both in Munich; and the world-famous ballet in Stuttgart. We have split the extraordinary variety of West German landscapes, cities, and towns into seven routes. There's northern Germany, which extends from Bremen to Schleswig, where a visitor can explore the Hanseatic cities of Hamburg and Lübeck and relax in the lake country of "little Switzerland" or on an ocean beach such as Travemünde on the Baltic Sea. The short, pleasant route from Frankfurt to Heidelberg follows the charming Main River valley through the gentle wooded hills of the historic Odenwald and Spessart areas. Westphalia, land of ham and pumpernickel, castle hotels and wayside inns, can best be seen in a circular route that begins in Dortmund. Castles, vineyards, and dramatic vistas mark the fabled Rhineland, which includes the area from Mainz to Koblenz but can be extended to Cologne and Düsseldorf. Germany's Castle Road meanders along the Neckar River valley, passing more than a dozen castles on the way from Heidelberg to Heilbronn. Rolling hills and thick forests characterize the Black Forest region, which extends from Basel, Switzerland, to the exclusive German spa of Baden-Baden. Last is the Romantic Road from Würzburg on the Main River to Füssen in the Alpine foothills, passing through Bavaria's fabulous walled medieval towns.

Northern Germany

Northern Germany, the area bounded roughly by Bremen, Hamburg, Lübeck, Kiel, and Schleswig, has been virtually undiscovered by modern American tourists. Yet it offers the only ocean beaches in all of the Federal Republic and some of its most historical cities. Relatively flat, the terrain of northern Germany is a pleasant blend of gently rolling hills, sunlit lake country, and fine sandy beaches.

Hamburg, a highly sophisticated city that is rarely on the usual tourist itinerary, is Germany's second largest, with a population of 1.6 million people. Bremen, with over half a million inhabitants, is the oldest German maritime city, having been a market since 965; its 500-year-old medieval section still remains. You can vary your trip to northern Germany by visiting its important ports; exploring its tiny, undiscovered towns such as Stade and Ratzeburg; and enjoying its ocean resorts such as Travemünde. For information and maps about the area, contact the regional tourist office in Oldenburg, just northwest of Bremen: Fremdenverkehrsverband, Nordsee-Niedersachsen-Bremen, 18 Gottorpstr., 2900 Oldenburg (phone: 1-4535).

The dominant force in northern German history was the Hanseatic League, a free association of medieval towns that concentrated on trade. Foremost in the league were the city-states of Bremen, Hamburg, and Lübeck. Since they paid taxes to no larger power, these cities became a powerful force in both domestic and foreign trade. Even today, people from the Hanseatic cities take immense pride in their localities, often identifying themselves as Lübeckers or Hamburgers before saying they are Germans.

Today the Hanseatic League is mere history, although Germans still refer to the direct train line running from Bremen to Hamburg to Lübeck as the Hanseatic Line. This route is convenient, not only for travelers who choose to ride the modern, efficient railways of Germany, but for people who wish to tour northern Germany by car. The tour covers roughly 225 miles (360 km), so you will need at least 3 days.

BREMEN: The natural starting point for any tour of northern Germany, Bremen, along with its sister city of Bremerhaven, is the oldest seaport in Germany. Interestingly enough, it is because of Bremen that Bremerhaven exists at all. In the early 17th century, the merchants of Bremen noticed that their precious port was becoming clogged with mud from the Weser River that flows into it. Dredging operations were not then what they are now, so they simply moved the port downstream to Vegesack. Two hundred years later, Vegesack too became clogged with mud, so the merchants moved on to Bremerhaven, which now ranks as the largest container facility in Europe and Germany's second largest seaport.

The tourist information service in Bremen, in front of the main train station, offers maps, brochures, and information about hotels and pensions (phone: 308000).

Like most European cities, Bremen is best seen on foot. The heart of the city is the old medieval section surrounding the Marktplatz and most of the modern city has grown up around this area. The city used to be enclosed by a great wall, but the land where the wall used to stand is now a ring road that completely encircles the older part of the city.

Bremen's huge market square is worth a visit, if for nothing more than the delicious smell of roasting coffee from the surrounding coffeehouses or the lovely colors and shapes of fresh fruits and vegetables. The old Rathaus, on the market square, is well worth seeing; it houses an excellent restaurant, the *Ratskeller,* with the largest wine list in Germany — more than 600 wines, all of them German.

Other sights in Bremen are the *Focke Museum* (240 Schwachhauser Heerstr.), renowned for its fine collection of historical artifacts from the north, and St. Peter's Cathedral, directly on the market square. The 11th-century cathedral has an unusual cellar called the Bleikeller (lead cellar), where the lead slates for the roof were originally kept. A roofer who fell to his death was once put in the cellar for safekeeping, along with the roofing tiles. Everyone forgot about his body and it was some time before he was discovered, perfectly preserved. Apparently the air in the cellar is so dry that it mummifies anything that is put down there. Several mummified corpses are included in the collection, which is open on weekdays only.

While in Bremen, don't miss the old section of town referred to as the Schnoor, with its narrow 400- and 500-year-old streets, half-timbered houses, and quaint gabled roofs. There are many art galleries and crafts shops that offer some excellent buys on handmade items. Walk on the Rampart Walk (Wallanlagen), with its windmill and lovely green spaces. The *Café Knigge,* a lovely outdoor café with a terrace, is on an old pedestrian street (42 Sögestr.).

For people who have an undeniable urge to set out to sea, there are daily tours of the harbor area by boat, leaving the Martini jetty four times a day.

En Route from Bremen – It is only 75 miles (120 km) to Hamburg, little more than an hour's drive along the speedy German Autobahns. If you have the time, the drive to Hamburg along the secondary highway that more or less parallels the Autobahn (Rte. 75) is well worth the effort, as it weaves through open moors and forests that are so common to this section of Germany. A good overnight stopping place is the little town of Rotenburg; it's just the place for a quiet rest.

STADE: About 25 miles (40 km) north of the Autobahn, on Route 73, lies the town of Stade, which is starting to make a name for itself as a medieval city. Virtually unknown to most tourists, the quiet little town has some beautifully restored buildings, and restoration continues all the time. Be sure to see St. Cosmas Church, the Rathaus, the fish market, and the Bürgermeister Hintze Haus. At one end of the fish market is the restored Swedish warehouse that was built between 1692 and 1705 to serve as a supply depot for the Swedish troops that occupied the region at that time. Today, it serves as a regional museum for Lower Saxony.

HAMBURG: Hamburg is less than an hour's drive from Stade. Germany's largest seaport and second largest city (after Berlin), Hamburg was an independent city-state in the Middle Ages, and even today the city is a state of Germany. Hamburgers have always been extremely proud of their independence, a pride that never showed more clearly than in 1871, when the Kaiser was going to raise a Hamburg merchant to the nobility. The mayor of Hamburg informed the startled Kaiser: "It is impossible to raise a Hamburg citizen." That feeling still lingers today, and the citizens of this great harbor city are never so proud as when they can show off their city to visitors.

Hamburgers are quick to point out that the area the city now occupies has been inhabited continuously over the past 15,000 years, although permanent settlements can be traced back only 6,000 years. The first fortifications were built in 811, and although they were repeatedly pounded by the fierce Viking raiders of the north, the town continued to grow. In 1189, Frederick Barbarossa granted the city a charter as a free city and port, thereby exempting its ships from paying duty. After that, the merchants of the city prospered greatly. During the years of the Hanseatic League, no trading power on earth was the equal of Hamburg.

Despite the heavy bombing raids of World War II that all but flattened the city, it has recovered very well. Its port on the Elbe River is one of Europe's largest and it continues to grow, with a record of 71 million tons traded during 1984. Though less popular with tourists than Munich or Berlin, today's Hamburg is an elegant and sophisticated modern city, with a 300-year-old opera and a renowned vaudeville theater, the *Hansa.*

The tourist office at Bieberhaus near the Central Station at Hachmannpl. (phone: 24-87-00) can provide you with maps: the *Hamburg Guide,* a brochure containing a wealth of tourist information; and a fortnightly program guide, *Where to Go in Hamburg.* For hotel reservations and information, contact the Information Office (Hotelnachweis), also at Central Station, Kirchenallee exit (phone: 248-70230). There is a small fee for this service.

You might want to get an idea of the layout of this large and sprawling city by taking its excellent 2-hour bus tour, which begins at the train station daily.

Some of the sights that should not be missed are Europe's only privately owned zoo and the harbor, an incredible mélange of pleasure boats, oceangoing freighters, coal barges, tugs, and fishing boats. The harbor's 800th anniversary was celebrated in 1989. The fish market, where not only fish is sold, but just about every kind of ware, begins every Sunday at 5 AM near St. Pauli Landungsbrücken. Harbor tours are offered from entrance 2 to the St. Pauli landing by Hadag Ships (phone: 376-80024). The Aussenalster, a particularly wide and lovely branch of the Elbe that looks like a lake, is bordered by long, shaded avenues and green spots and makes a particularly fine place for strolling or boating. During the summer months, a very pleasant 50-minute Alster cruise departs from Jungfernstieg at frequent intervals and affords a lovely view of the city's towers and spires (phone: 341145). Also interesting are Planten en Blomen Gardens, a beautifully arranged park ideal for an afternoon's stroll, and St. Michael's Cathedral, a fine baroque church built in 1762, with a famous tower that offers a panorama of the city.

For those who enjoy museums, Hamburg is just the place. An excellent art museum, the *Hamburg Art Gallery* (1 Glockengiesserwall) has a fine collection of paintings from medieval to modern; the modern section is best, with works by Klee, Munch, and others. There's the *Historical Museum* (Museum für Hamburgische Geschichte, 24 Holstenwall; phone: 349-122360), with an interesting collection relating to the ports and navigation; and the *Decorative Arts and Crafts Museum* (Museum für Kunst und Gewerbe, 1 Steintorpl.; phone: 248-252630), specializing in medieval gold and silver statuary, Renaissance furniture, clocks of northern Germany, and Jugendstil (Art Nouveau) items. The *Helms Museum* (2 Museumsplatz) specializes in prehistory and early history of the Hamburg region. For a more up-to-date impression of this North German countryside and its residents, visit the *Altonaer Museum* (23 Museumstr.). For 20th-century North German art, visit the *Ernst Barlach Haus* (50 Baron-Voght-Str.).

Naturally it is impossible to overlook one of the most famous areas of Hamburg, the Reeperbahn. After dark, this area comes alive with neon lights, loud music, thick crowds, and barkers trying to attract those crowds to their establishments. Here sex shows, porno movies, strip clubs, and bars are the order of the day — or night, as the case may be. Many of these places are clip joints, pure and simple, but some of the better sexy stage shows are pretty safe bets. Among these are those at the *Regina Club,* the *Safari Club,* the *Colibri, Tabu,* and the *Salambo Cabaret.*

One of the best things about Hamburg is its restaurants. Everything is available from haute cuisine to pickled rollmops, in settings that vary from the crystal and china atmosphere of the top restaurants, to the beer and herring atmosphere of the waterfront snack bars (*Imbiss*). Because it's a port city, there are many fine foreign restaurants, the best of which is *Le Canard,* 11 Martinistr. (see *Best en Route*). But Hamburg's specialty is fish, and its most famous specialties are *Aalsuppe* (eel soup) and oysters, raw or baked with Cheshire cheese. You can sample these and many other fine dishes right in the St. Pauli fish market at the Fischerhaus.

RATZEBURG: The distance from Hamburg to Lübeck is only 41 miles (66 km). Still, for the adventurous, the lovely island town of Ratzeburg on Route 208, in the middle of a lake to the south of the E4 Autobahn, makes a lovely place to stay for a weekend, with plenty of swimming, boating, and fishing. Surprisingly enough, the town is only a couple of kilometers from the East German border, yet the easygoing way of life is so pleasant that it is hard to imagine the border, with its ghastly fences, mine fields, and machine guns less than 2.5 miles (4 km) away. By all means see the local church, which has an interesting carved altar and is one of the largest brick churches in northern Germany.

LÜBECK: The capital of the Hanseatic cities during the Middle Ages, Lübeck retains the flavor of a medieval town, complete with towers, and old houses. The huge twin-towered gates at the entrance to the city — the Holstentor — can hardly fail to impress a visitor. These gates were built in 1477 as part of the fortifications, and today the massive towers serve as the symbol of Lübeck; they also house the *Municipal Museum.* Be sure to take a look at the old salt warehouses along one side of the Holstentor.

Like most other German cities, Lübeck has an excellent tourist office, 75 Breite Str. (phone: 12200 or 72339), which can provide information and maps and will help arrange a room for the night in almost any price range for a small fee.

There are four museums in Lübeck, each a minor gem. Besides the *Holstentor,* there is *St. Anne's Museum* (15 St. Annenstr.), an old monastery that now houses local art and handicrafts; the *Behnhaus* (Königstr. at Glockenstr.), a perfectly preserved residence from 1780 that gives an excellent impression of how people lived then; and a museum in the cathedral that contains all the natural history discoveries from the area.

The Rathaus is an unusual brick medieval building in the northern German style, on two sides of the Marktplatz. St. Mary's Church, a French Gothic structure that was built between 1251 and 1350, is known for its famed 17th-century organist, the composer Buxtehude.

The Haus der Schiffergesellschaft (2 Breite Str.), an old sailors' guild house dating from 1535, has an excellent restaurant inside, decorated with marine furniture and artifacts.

One of the products for which Lübeck is most famous is the luscious marzipan candy, made from sugar and crushed almonds. It comes in virtually any shape, and you often see Lübeckers strolling along the streets, happily munching on a marzipan pig, pear, or apple. The best place in Lübeck, probably the best place in the world, to buy marzipan is the *I. G. Niederegger Konditorei and Café,* next to St. Mary's Church. Not only can you have a sinfully sweet piece of marzipan but a delicious cup of coffee to go with it. You can take some marzipan with you or mail it to friends as the perfect gift from Lübeck.

En Route from Lübeck – The drive from Lübeck to Kiel goes through what the Germans call the Holsteinische Schweiz, or little Switzerland, because of its numerous lakes and forests. It is best to take Route 76, which runs north through Plön and Preetz, rather than the faster, but more boring, Route 404 that runs through Bad Segeberg. If you are in the mood for an ocean beach, you can detour to Travemünde, just a few miles northeast of Lübeck, on the Baltic Sea; it's a fashionable resort with a casino. If not, your next stop might be either Plön, which is on the Plönersee, a large, scenic lake, or a bit farther north, Preetz, in the heart of the lovely and peaceful lake country.

KIEL: Kiel attracted a lot of attention when it hosted the sailing event of the 1972 Olympics, but as a center for tourism it leaves a lot to be desired. Most of Kiel was destroyed by the bombing during World War II, and the city has been rebuilt in modern style. It is a clean city, almost spotlessly so, but it has little to offer tourists, except perhaps for its bustling fish market, with an astonishing variety of fish. Besides the market, you will enjoy seeing the Kiel Canal, an outstanding engineering achievement that connects the North Sea and the Baltic and is the busiest canal in the world. Nearby, the Hindenburg Quay (Hindenburgufer), a 2-mile, tree-shaded promenade along the Kiel Förde, offers pleasant views of the harbor.

SCHLESWIG: About 31 miles (50 km) northwest of Kiel is Schleswig, the oldest town in the northern state of Schleswig-Holstein. It was founded by the Vikings and for many years it was a Viking stronghold; from here they plundered and looted the towns to the south, such as Hamburg and Bremen. Schleswig is well worth a visit, as it contains some of the richest Viking artifacts in northern Germany. By all means see the cathedral, built in 1100, with its incredible altarpiece carved elaborately in wood by Bruggeman in 1521.

Schleswig's other big attraction is the Nydam boat, an Anglo-Saxon boat dating from the 4th century, one of the few of its type in the world. The boat is in a building near Gottorf Castle. Built in the 12th century, it is the oldest in Schleswig-Holstein and is well worth a trip all by itself. It houses the *Schleswig-Holstein Museum,* containing fine exhibitions of folklore, art, and handicrafts. Just southeast of town on Route 76 is the open-air *Viking Museum,* at Haddebyer Noor, which contains fascinating artifacts that date from the 8th century AD.

Germans and Scandinavians have enjoyed the beaches, forests, lakes, cities, and towns of northern Germany for many years. Since Americans and other tourists have not yet discovered this area, it is still a place for the more adventurous souls to explore.

BEST EN ROUTE

Hotel prices vary a great deal along this route; costs are generally higher in the larger cities, especially in Hamburg, which is the site of the *Vier Jahreszeiten,* known as one of the world's most outstanding — and expensive — hotels. A double room with breakfast costs about $85 to $140 in the hotels listed as expensive; moderate is $60 to $80; and inexpensive is below $60. In an expensive restaurant, dinner for two without wine will cost $40 to $50; moderate, $25 to $35; and inexpensive, $15 to $20.

BREMEN

Park – Bremen's leading hotel is in an out-of-the-way spot, the lovely Bürgerpark. It has spacious, cheerful public rooms, a heated garden terrace, a fine restaurant, and many rooms with balconies overlooking the pond. Bürgerpark (phone: 340-8555). Very expensive.

Landhaus Louisenthal – A few miles northeast of the city center, in the suburb of Horn, this charming 1835 hotel is noteworthy for its quiet, Old World atmosphere. 105 Leher Heerstr. (phone: 23-20-76). Expensive to moderate.

Übersee – This pleasant, 142-room hotel is near the market square. In addition to the usual amenities, it has a sauna and conference facilities. 27-29 Wachstr. (phone: 36010). Moderate.

Grashoff's Bistro – Don't be misled by the plain (but comfortable) surroundings; the kitchen here is very accomplished. Try the fish dishes, such as crab soup, haddock in mustard sauce, or turbot in baked pike mousse. Centrally located; closed evenings and all day Sundays. Reservations recommended. 80 Contrescarpe (phone: 14740). Expensive.

Ratskeller – Right in the 500-year-old city hall, this place has lots of atmosphere and also serves good food. It's popular with the local people, who meet here to sample its 600 German wines. Closed Mondays. Am Markt (phone: 329-0910). Moderate.

HAMBURG

Vier Jahreszeiten – Considered one of the world's 10 best hotels, this elegant and prestigious place is on Alster Lake in downtown Hamburg. It features conservative patrician furniture, streamlined modern facilities, and the atmosphere of a private home. There's an excellent restaurant, named *Haerlin* after the family that runs the hotel, 2 bars, and a nightclub featuring international bands. 9 Neuer Jungfernstieg (phone: 34940). Very expensive.

Europäischer Hof – Facing the railroad station, this is Hamburg's second largest hotel and a pleasant, traditional establishment. There is a good restaurant (in the breakfast room, you can serve yourself from a marble fountain that spouts six different kinds of juices — and occasionally champagne). 45 Kirchenallee (phone: 24-81-71). Expensive.

Prem – The new management of this traditional establishment has successfully restored the hotel to its former grandeur. Guests can expect friendly service and tasteful decor, as well as excellent cuisine at *La Mer*. The rooms in front face Alster Lake; those in back overlook a charming garden. 9 An der Alster (phone: 241726, hotel; 245454, restaurant). Expensive.

Hafen Hamburg – Originally a seamen's home, this 155-room hostelry has a magnificent harbor view and a maritime motif. Rooms, although simply furnished, offer standard comfort. 9 Seewartenstr. (phone: 311130). Moderate.

Mellingburger Schleuse – An idyllic forest setting enhances this rustic-looking 28-room hotel. A small restaurant is on the premises. 1 Mellingburgredder (phone: 602-4001). Moderate.

City House – A small hotel — 24 rooms — very close to the train station that has been recently renovated. 25 Pulverteich (phone: 280-3850). Inexpensive.

Canard – Both the fine cuisine and the extraordinary selection of wines make this exclusive restaurant well worth a visit. Reservations recommended. Closed Sundays. 11 Martinistr. (phone: 460-4830). Expensive.

Landhaus Scherrer – Its delicious North German cuisine and its lovely view of the Elbe make this another of Hamburg's fine restaurants. Reservations necessary. Closed Sundays. 130 Elbchaussee (phone: 880-1325). Expensive.

Fischerhaus – This place specializes in absolutely perfect fish served in a very plain and unadorned atmosphere. St. Pauli, 14 Fischmarkt (phone: 314053). Moderate.

Harmonie – Because it is in the commercial district, this small restaurant is usually booked for lunch, so try it for dinner. Specialties are lobster soup and scallops in herb sauce. Reservations recommended. Closed Saturday evenings and Sundays. 12 Ost-West-Str. (phone: 327191). Moderate.

RATZEBURG

Seehof Gästehaus Hubertus – This quiet hotel is directly on the lake, and it would be hard to find a more charming place to spend a weekend. Even the restaurant is a bargain. 3 Lüneburger Damm (phone: 2055). Moderate.

LÜBECK

Lysia – The finest hotel in the city is on a canal at the edge of the old town. It has a sauna and an exercise room, a popular dance bar, a restaurant, and 2 conference rooms. Auf der Wallhalbinsel, corner of Holstentorpl. (phone: 15040). Expensive.

Wakenitzblick – This quiet and comfortable hotel, which faces the canal, is reasonably priced. It has parking, a restaurant, and bath and telephone in the rooms. 30 Augustenstr. (phone: 791296). Moderate.

Wullenwever – In a former brewery, this fine new restaurant is, at 400 years of age, one of Lübeck's best. Light, well-prepared cuisine is served courteously amid a country ambience. Reservations recommended. Closed Mondays. 71 Beckergrube (phone: 7-04333). Expensive.

Haus der Schiffergesellschaft – This historic sailors' guild house dates from 1535 and features nautical decor. A broad range of traditional German dishes is served here. Closed Mondays. Reservations recommended. 2 Breite Str. (phone: 7-6776). Moderate.

PREETZ

Drillers – An excellent hotel, beautifully set on a lake, it offers an especially good breakfast. 2 Bismarckpl. (phone: 81241). Inexpensive.

SCHLESWIG

Waldhotel – This hotel is part of the Gottorf Castle. It is quiet, very well maintained, and reasonably priced. The restaurant has a good and fairly inexpensive menu. If peace and quiet are what you seek, then look no further. 1 Stampfmühle (phone: 23288). Moderate to inexpensive.

Frankfurt to Heidelberg

If you drive the 59 miles (94 km) from Frankfurt am Main to Heidelberg on the Autobahn, the trip will take about an hour, but you won't see much more than the backs and sides of huge high-speed trailer trucks. There's a lovely alternate route, however, that wriggles its way south along the Main River valley, through charming old river towns with half-timbered houses, historic churches and abbeys, romantic castles, gentle wooded hills, and fertile green valleys.

Without any side trips, the Main River valley route from Frankfurt to Heidelberg covers about 107 miles (171 km); pleasant detours can add 50% to that distance. You can drive the whole route easily in a single day, but it's far more pleasant to give yourself at least a day and a half.

The areas you'll be driving through are known as the Odenwald and the Spessart. Prehistoric peoples lived along the banks of the Main, but there was no real development until about AD 800, when many monasteries, like the one you can still see in Seligenstadt, were established, and the monks began the region's agricultural development.

Through the centuries, the Odenwald and the Spessart were the territories of various bishoprics. They were shuttled more or less peacefully from one owner to another. During the Thirty Years War (1618–48), these areas, like most of Germany, were the scene of many bloody battles.

Although the Main River is slated to become part of an overall Rhine-Danube international waterway system, its banks are still relatively quiet and peaceful, even in Frankfurt and in the other highly populated industrial areas. The area is not touristy in any way. Tourists in the Main Valley are usually vacationers from Frankfurt and other German cities who are not partial to discos and pizza stands.

Its small towns are unspoiled — like Michelstadt, with its lovely old Marktplatz, or Wertheim, with its red sandstone castle. And Heidelberg may well be the most beautiful city in Germany.

For maps, pamphlets, and information about the Frankfurt area, contact the tourist office in Wiesbaden, Hessischer Landeszentrale für Fremdenverkehr (38 Abraham-Lincoln-Str., 6200 Wiesbaden; phone: 774350); for the Heidelberg vicinity, it's Verkehrsrerein Heidelberg (2 Friedrich-Ebert-Anlage, 6900 Heidelberg 1; phone: 10821).

En Route from Frankfurt – Take Route 43 east toward Mühlheim and Hanau. You might want to stop at Offenbach to see the *German Leather Museum,* containing leather objects from all over the world, or at Hanau, birthplace of the Brothers Grimm and site of an interesting museum of local jewelry called *Goldsmith's House,* a baroque castle, Schloss Philippsruhe, and a monument to the celebrated brothers.

At the intersection of Routes 43 and 45, continue on the unnumbered road toward Hainstadt and Seligenstadt. Park before you reach the center of Seligenstadt, since parking usually is not permitted in the center of small villages in Germany.

SELIGENSTADT: Its principal attraction is a magnificently maintained former Benedictine abbey founded in AD 825 by Einhard, biographer of Charlemagne. However, the town itself is much older. It was a fortified castle on the *limes* — the wall built by the Romans through most of central Germany until the Romans were ejected from their fort by the Alemanni in AD 260.

Guided tours (in German) of the abbey are conducted year-round every day except Mondays. Don't let a German-only tour put you off; you'll understand more than you think you will.

Seligenstadt is a place where you can see the various architectural styles and periods of German history. The abbey itself has undergone many remodelings in a thousand years, and each remodeling has left traces of the style characteristic of the period.

From the abbey, walk toward the Main River. Then turn left and walk toward the ruins of the Kaiserpfalz, known also as the Palatium or the hunting lodge (*Jagdsitz*), built about 1235 for Frederick II, Holy Roman Emperor, who led a fascinating life that included no fewer than three excommunications.

Walk to the Marktplatz along the narrow Palatiumstrasse. All along the way and around the Marktplatz itself you will see some outstanding examples of the famous German *Fachwerkhäuser,* or half-timbered houses.

En Route from Seligenstadt – Leave Seligenstadt on the same road from which you entered, but this time head south toward Stockstadt. You may make a short detour to Aschaffenburg or continue on under the Mainhausen cloverleaf, pick up Route 469 at the Stockstadt Autobahn exchange, and head for Miltenberg.

ASCHAFFENBURG: Chosen by the electors of Mainz as one of their residences, Aschaffenburg has beautiful parks, a large Renaissance castle, and an interesting church. St. Johannisberg Castle, built in 1605–14 for the powerful archbishops of Mainz, is most impressive, shaped like a hollow square. See the palace and walk through its gardens to the Pompeianum, a reproduction of the Castor and Pollux house at Pompeii, built for the capricious Ludwig I of Bavaria. Then walk along the Landingstrasse behind the palace to the Stiftskirche, a 10th-century church that is an interesting mixture of Baroque, Gothic, and Romanesque styles of architecture, but its real attraction is the exceptional church art. There is a Grünewald altarpiece and a Resurrection scene by Lucas Cranach the Elder (1520). To visit the lovely chapel, the altarpiece, and other treasures, look for the sexton. If he's not in the church, try at Stiftgasse 1.

En Route from Aschaffenburg – Leave Aschaffenburg via Löherstrasse, the street directly behind the church, and watch for signs directing you to Schönbusch. This 18th-century park is one of Germany's most charming, with pools, islands, and a country house built for the archbishops in 1780.

Leave Schönbusch Park area on the south side (the one closest to the river) and follow the unnumbered road to its intersection with Route 469. Stay on 469 south for 22 miles (35 km) until you reach Miltenberg.

MILTENBERG: Again, park your car in the first convenient parking lot. Don't try to drive in or through the town center. You can walk from one end of Miltenberg to the other in 15 minutes.

The town showplace is its Marktplatz. It's triangular, relatively small, and surrounded by exceptional half-timbered houses; from the marketplace walk along the main street, the Hauptstrasse, which is also lined with fascinating houses.

The *Riesen* hotel is not as old as Miltenberg, which was little more than a wide spot in the Roman wall until the Thirteenth Legion was ousted by the Germanic tribes in AD 260. The Germans are avid record keepers, and there are files in Mainz, Munich, and Würzburg to prove that the *Riesen* was open and operating in the 12th century. A whole string of Holy Roman Emperors stayed at the *Riesen*, beginning with Frederick Barbarossa who took shelter here in 1158 and 1168, and during the Thirty Years War it housed VIPs from both sides — depending on who was in control at the moment. It's still an ideal overnight stopping place (see *Best en Route*).

The tourist office (Städtisches Verkehrsamt) in the city hall (Rathaus) has an excellent walking guide to Miltenberg (phone: 40-01-190). It's only in German, but so clearly arranged that you can walk in sequence from one spot of interest to the next with no trouble.

En Route from Miltenberg – A worthwhile side trip from Miltenberg is the 18-mile (29-km) jaunt to Wertheim. The road parallels the Main River all the way, or if you want to take a rest from driving, leave your car in Miltenberg and go by boat.

The Main and Tauber rivers meet at Wertheim, and the town is dominated by a castle constructed of red sandstone, which is peculiar to the Odenwald and Spessart areas. A guide is available from the Wertheim tourist office (Fremdenverkehrsgesellschaft) in the city hall (phone: 301230): The Marktplatz is worth seeing, with a Renaissance monument known as the Engelsbrunnen ("Angel's Well") at one end. The church has a number of unusually beautiful, well-preserved tombstones and memorials from the 16th century. You'll have to climb around to see the old castle, but the view of Wertheim and the rivers is worth a little puffing. Don't miss the opportunity to dine at *Schweizer Stuben* (see *Best en Route*), one of Germany's best restaurants.

Pick up Route 469 in Miltenberg again for 5 miles (8 km) to Amorbach.

AMORBACH: You'll notice the red sandstone towers of an abbey church that dominates Amorbach. It was built between 1742 and 1747 on the site of an earlier Romanesque church. The interior of this now-baroque abbey is worth seeing. Its chancel screen is one of the finest in Germany, and it has a justifiably well-known organ; concerts are given here in the high tourist season.

MICHELSTADT: Pick up Route 47, the Nibelungenstrasse, for 15 miles (24 km) to Michelstadt, the heart of Wagner country; this is where all the mythical action of the great operas was set. This is where the Nibelungen, evil guardians of a magic hoard of gold, are supposed to have done their hunting, and somewhat farther south, the great hero Siegfried went on the royal hunt during which Hagen killed him. Whether you are a true believer or not, the gently sloping countryside is lovely.

Michelstadt has what may be the most enchanting Marktplatz in the Odenwald, with a 16th-century fountain, a charming town hall, and many remarkable half-timbered houses. Notice especially the unusual design of the two bay windows in the town hall.

From Michelstadt it's about 42 miles (68 km) to Worms or 38 miles (61 km) to Heidelberg.

WORMS: This city is so packed with history and interest, you will want to take time to see as much as possible. It was destroyed in 436 by Attila the Hun, and in 1521 it was the scene of the famous Imperial Diet that passed judgment on Martin Luther. Worms became a Protestant city in 1525 and, as a result, was subject to heavy reprisals during the Thirty Years War. It was almost totally destroyed by the French in 1689, deprived of its free city status, annexed by France in 1801, and finally awarded to Germany by the Congress of Vienna in 1815. All of this major European history is written on its streets, its buildings, and on every street corner.

The tourist office (Verkehrsverein, 14 Neumarkt; phone: 25045) has a great deal of helpful material and information in English. Look for it just opposite St. Peter's Cathedral, which is itself one of Germany's finest examples of 13th-century Romanesque architecture. The high altar is by Balthasar Neumann, a famous 18th-century master of German baroque architecture.

Worms is one of the oldest centers of Jewish culture in Germany and has the oldest synagogue in the country, founded in the 11th century. The ancient Jewish cemetery, just behind the cathedral, has been in use since the 11th century and is worth a visit. Worms is also the home area of Liebfraumilch wine. Its name came from the Church of Our Lady (Liebfrauenkirche) at the city's northern end.

HEIDELBERG: Beautiful old Heidelberg is surrounded by thickly wooded hills, which rise above its massive ruined castle. Beneath the castle, its old buildings with their red roofs and romantic towers face the peaceful Neckar River and its Old Bridge (Alte Brücke). The oldest university town in Germany, Heidelberg is still best known as an intellectual and cultural center. During the Middle Ages, the city was the political center of the Rhineland Palatinate. Heidelberg and its castle were destroyed by Louis XIV of France in 1689, and to make matters worse, the city was completely demolished by fire in 1693. After these disasters the electors turned their backs on Heidelberg and the town was rebuilt in baroque style.

Stop in at the local tourist office for maps, brochures, and all sorts of useful information (Pavillon am Hauptbahnhof, the central railroad station; phone: 21341).

Both banks of the river afford excellent views of the town. Walk along the right bank, taking Neuenheimer Landstrasse, which runs west from the Old Bridge, and Ziegelhäuser Landstrasse, which runs east; then try the more ambitious Philosophers' Way (Philosophenweg) farther from the river, starting from Bergstrasse in the suburb of Neuenheim and ascending the slopes of the Heiligenberg.

Don't miss the castle, which can be reached on foot, by car, by escalator, or by cable car. See its 17th-century gardens, with their remarkable view from the Scheffel Terrace (named for a Heidelberg poet). You may want to take the guided tour, offered daily at frequent intervals. Be sure to see the Great Vat (Grosses Fass) here, made in the 18th century, with a capacity of 58,000 gallons and a stairway to the top. According to local lore, a dwarf named Perkeo once emptied the whole thing.

Other sights in Heidelberg include the curious Students' Jail (2 Augustinergasse), where unruly students were incarcerated during the 18th and 19th centuries; the *Electoral Palatinate Museum* (Kurpfälzisches Museum; 97 Hauptstr.), in a baroque palace, containing a cast of the jaw of Heidelberg man (50,000 BC) and the great Altarpiece of the Twelve Apostles (Windsheimer Zwölfbotenaltar) by Riemenschneider (1509) among its treasures.

Heidelberg is a small city, well suited to walking and lingering about, especially in the streets of the old quarter and the quays along the river. Fortunately, it came through the Second World War unscathed. From here you can explore the scenic Neckar Valley to the east, its gorge surrounded by high, thickly forested hills.

BEST EN ROUTE

Prices along this route vary; they're significantly higher in the larger cities, so that you'll have to pay more for everything in Frankfurt and Heidelberg. Plan to spend $85 to $140 (more in Heidelberg) for hotels we have classified as expensive; $60 to $80 for moderate; and below $60, inexpensive. A dinner for two without wine will cost $65 to $145 in restaurants listed as expensive; $40 to $60, moderate; and $20 to $35, inexpensive.

SELIGENSTADT

Klosterstuben – Next to the church and the convent garden, this restaurant features excellent German cooking. It also serves a locally brewed beer (becoming increasingly rare in Germany as big breweries take over). Closed Sundays and Mondays. 7 Freihofpl. (phone: 3571). Moderate.

AMORBACH

Schafhof – A romantic 16-room hotel in a former Benedictine monastery. It has an excellent restaurant, noteworthy for its lamb dishes. 2 miles (3.2 km) to the west, Otterbachtal (phone: 8088). Expensive to moderate.

ASCHAFFENBURG

Romantik-Hotel Post – Not far from the Schloss Johannisberg, this hotel is beautifully decorated in the traditional sense of comfort and friendliness. The restaurant offers good continental food with a broad range of choices. 19 Goldbacherstr. (phone: 21333). Moderate.

MILTENBERG

Gasthaus zum Riesen – In operation since the 12th century, this place claims to be Germany's oldest hostel. Based on authenticated guest lists, the owner and restorer, W. Jöst, has furnished a series of bedrooms after the period of some famous visitors — Queen Christina of Sweden, for example. All furnishings are genuine antiques. This is a relatively expensive but a fascinating experience. Reservations are a necessity for the "name" rooms and a good idea at any time. Closed November to March. 97 Hauptstr. (phone: 3644). Moderate.

WERTHEIM

Schweizer Stuben – Follow the signs to this truly excellent restaurant, featuring the finest Swiss-French-German cuisine in comfortable surroundings. It also has 16 rooms. Reservations necessary. Closed Mondays, Sundays, Tuesdays for lunch, and January. 11 Geiselbrunnweg (phone: 3070). Very expensive.

HEIDELBERG

Der Europäische Hof – The leading hotel in Heidelberg consists of three wings, each from a different period. Centrally located facing a park, it's known for its service and for the fine French food in its *Kurfürstenstube* restaurant. There's a terrace for summer dining, a bar with dancing, conference rooms, and public rooms nicely furnished with antiques. Rooms are large and comfortable, and most have refrigerators and TV sets. 1 Friedrich-Ebert-Anlage (phone: 27101). Very expensive.

Hirschgasse – This family-run hotel is opposite the castle in a building that dates from 1472. Tastefully restored, its rooms are modern and comfortable. The hotel, which is known for its romantic flair, has one of the best restaurants in town and a lovely, tree-shaded terrace for breakfast. Closed Sundays. 3 Hirschgasse (phone: 49921). Expensive.

Molkenkur – Nestled in the forest, and perched 300 feet above the castle, this quiet and charming small hotel can be reached either by car or cable car. It has a restaurant with a terrace. Closed in January. Klingenteichstr. (phone: 10894). Moderate to inexpensive.

Simplicissimus – Said to be the best restaurant in town, this pleasant establishment features nouvelle cuisine; its game and fish dishes are excellent. Open evenings only. Closed Tuesdays. Reservations suggested. 16 Ingrimstr. (phone: 13336). Expensive.

Weinstube Schloss Heidelberg – This restaurant, with a terrace right in the castle courtyard, offers a marvelous view of the castle and good food. The tasteful decor is that of a wine tavern, with an ornately paneled ceiling, natural wood tables, and framed engravings. Closed Tuesdays. Schlosshof (phone: 20081). Moderate.

Roter Ochsen – A famous student hangout dating from 1703, this place has students' initials on the walls, oak tables, and mementos of all sorts — like a set from *The Student Prince.* There's piano music in the evening, lots of beer, and typical German cooking. Open evenings only. Closed Sundays. 217 Hauptstr. (phone: 20977). Inexpensive.

Westphalia

Though well liked by Germans and other Europeans, Westphalia, a dreamy area of castles, country inns, half-timbered houses, windmills, forests, hills, and mineral spas, has been little explored by Americans. (The proprietor of the noted *Schütte* hotel-restaurant in Oberkirchen tells us he has never had an American guest.) Perhaps Americans have shunned Westphalia because it contains the great industrial Ruhr Valley; in fact, Dortmund, Westphalia's principal city, is one of the major cities of the Ruhr. However, the well-heeled

Ruhr residents like to have a peaceful, picturesque country area to which they can slip away for a weekend or a business conference.

Westphalia is a region of small, hedged-in farms that form a checkerboard pattern. Strict laws keep the villages small, the forests intact, and the air unpolluted. The castle hotels and wayside inns have turrets and half-timbered exteriors, with baronial interiors and open fireplaces. Yet they also have indoor plumbing, central heating, and 20th-century mattresses. There is none of that run-down look you will find in Europe's more remote and poorer country areas.

In the northern part of Germany, Westphalia extends from the Rhine to the Weser River. For maps and information about the region, contact the tourist office, Landesverkehrsverband Westfalen e.V., Balkenstr., 4600 Dortmund (phone: 571715).

The name Westphalia first appears in connection with a section of the duchy of Saxony in the 10th century. In the later Middle Ages, its major towns of Münster, Paderborn, Bielefeld, and others, were prosperous members of the Hanseatic League (an association of mercantile city-states). The Peace of Westphalia, which was signed in Münster in 1648 to end the Thirty Years War, gave Prussia a foothold in the area, which it maintained — except for the brief Napoleonic reign in 1808–13 — until 1945.

Westphalia is noted for its cuisine, which is the most distinctive in Germany. Lufthansa gets its first class passengers "in the mood for Germany" by serving them a Westphalian snack en route. It starts with an ice-cold *Steinhäger,* a ginlike schnapps drink from the town of Steinhagen near Bielefeld; the drink is poured from a stoneware bottle into one of the deep pewter spoons Westphalians use as shot glasses. Then comes a chaser of cool Westphalian beer from Dortmund, which is second only to Munich as a German brewing city. Finally, there's pumpernickel — also Westphalian in origin — with butter, and justly famous Westphalian ham, eaten on a wooden board just as they do in this region.

You can enjoy the culinary and visual riches of Westphalia by touring the area in a circular route that begins and ends in Dortmund. The round trip is about 400 miles (640 km).

DORTMUND: Like all the cities in the Ruhr, Dortmund was leveled in World War II and rebuilt along coldly modern lines that are rather devoid of character. It is not dirty, however; the whole Ruhr has strict air pollution laws. Have a look at the Westfalenpark, with its German Rosarium (1,500 varieties of roses, half a million plants) and its TV tower topped by a revolving restaurant. Dortmund is best known as a beer-producing center; if you want to visit a brewery, contact the Verband Dortmunder Bierbrauer, 1 Marktstr. (phone: 525532).

Now head east into Westphalia proper, toward the Sauerland, an unspoiled region of woods and lakes to the east and south. The Autobahn gets you out there quickly. Take the Sauerland Line (A 45), following the signs to Siegen and Frankfurt, but leave at Olpe and follow the very scenic Route 55 north.

En Route from Dortmund – At this point you may wish to take a short detour to Attendorn, a place of lakes, a huge stalactite cave, and remarkable rock formations. The cave, called Attahöhle (follow the signs to Tropfsteinhöhle), is open daily for a small fee. Or continue on Route 55 to Lennestadt and then take the scenic Route 236 via the beautiful little village of Oberkirchen to Winterberg (one of the biggest German winter sports areas outside the Alps), and then drive north on Route 480.

OLSBERG: If they are so inclined, summer visitors can get a look at the Old West here at Fort Fun City, an "authentic" Western town, replete with saloon, jail, gambling hall, and a print shop where you can get a wanted poster with your own name on it.

Gevelingen Palace here is the starting point for Gypsy wagons, which you can rent for a tour of the Sauerland on "two horsepower." The wagons come complete with sleeping facilities for seven, blankets, linen, stove, dishes, pots and pans, gas lanterns, and gas heater. You follow a prescribed route and stop each night at a farm where they stable the horses. Continue on Route 480 via Brilon ("the most forested town in Westphalia") to Paderborn. Then take Routes 1 and 239.

DETMOLD: You now are in the middle of the Teutoburg Forest, another popular Westphalian district, which is famous to Germans as the place where the Romans were stopped in their northward march, in an epic battle in AD 9. Germanic tribesmen dealt them a stunning defeat, and the Roman Empire never extended any farther north in continental Europe. A giant statue to the tribal chief Hermann, who led the battle, commands a hill just 4 miles (6 km) outside the city at the village of Heiligenkirchen. It is 175 feet from Hermann's feet to the tip of his upraised sword. Also not to be missed is the bird of prey sanctuary at nearby Bad Berlebeck. The eagles, vultures, and other big birds fly freely at 11 AM and 2:30 PM daily. Detmold also has an open-air museum, the *Lippisches Landsmuseum,* with typically Westphalian farmhouses, which usually combine red brick and half timbering. Continue on Routes 239 and 66.

BIELEFELD: One of Westphalia's larger cities, Bielefeld is coldly modern for the most part, but some fine patrician houses remain and there's also the Sparrenburg Castle (1 Am Sparrenberg), with a network of underground passages below. On the ground level is a museum devoted to playing cards and a good view of the Teutoburg Forest from the tower.

En Route from Bielefeld – From Bielefeld take Route 61 via Herford. On the way to Minden you pass the Porta Westfalica, where the Weser River suddenly emerges spectacularly from between two hills, out of the mountains, and on to the broad North German plain. One of the hills that has a fine view is topped with a monument to Kaiser Wilhelm.

MINDEN: Minden is a good place to board one of the old paddleboats that ply the Weser. See the outstanding Romanesque cathedral with its 11th-century crucifix and a 1480 painting of the Crucifixion by a Westphalian master. There's a bridge where the Mittelland Canal passes over the Weser. Also interesting is the Great Lock (Schachts-chleuse), just north of town; 279 by 33 feet long, it links the Mittelland Canal with the Weser.

En Route from Minden – Proceed along Route 65 to Lübbecke. (Once a year, during a festival in August, a fountain here bubbles with beer instead of water. You can help yourself if you can get near it.) Then take Route 239 to Löhne, and take a short drive west on the Autobahn.

BÜNDE: What is alleged to be the world's only tobacco museum is in this cigar-making town. When you pay your money you get, instead of a ticket, a cigar or a cheap clay pipe, which you can fill at a handy humidor. Displays include the world's largest cigar (5½ feet long, 20 pounds) and a pipe that was obviously highly prized by the Sea Devil, Count Luckner. He dropped it out of a train window and pulled the emergency brake so he could recover it. Continue on the Autobahn to Osnabrück and head south on Routes 51 and 475.

WARENDORF: This is the horse capital of Germany, site of a state-operated stud farm, an important riding school, and the headquarters of the German Olympic Equestrian Committee. There are plenty of rental horses here and lots of riding paths; it is a good place to book a vacation in the saddle. There are big parades here on the last Saturday in September and the first Saturday in October, when horses are led by saddle masters in elegant uniforms. Drive from Warendorf along Routes 64 and 51.

MÜNSTER: Westphalia's historic capital is the site of one of Germany's biggest universities. Every year, on May 15, Münster holds a festival to mark the Peace of Westphalia, negotiated here in 1648 to end the Thirty Years' War. See the Prinzipalmarkt, the oldest and busiest street in town, with its elegant Renaissance houses. If you continue along Bogenstrasse, you'll see the Kiepenkerl, a statue of a peddler with his basket. The low-lying Romanesque cathedral is typically Westphalian, with its astronomic clock in the ambulatory and a Glockenspiel that plays at noon.

The area surrounding Münster is known for its moated medieval castles, particularly the Castle of Vischering, set on an island, with an interesting interior and a prison beneath (closed Tuesdays). Also noteworthy are the castles of Hülshoff and Nordkirchen (the latter is now the university's School of Finance). Farther west is the medieval walled city of Coesfeld.

En Route from Münster – Continue along Route 51 through Dülmen; the estate of the duke of Croy here is the only wild horse sanctuary (with 200 horses) in Europe. The event of the year here is the annual roundup on the last Saturday in May.

Take Route 51 to Recklinghausen and visit the *Icon Museum* (2a Kirchplatz), where icons are exhibited thematically (closed Mondays). In May and June, Recklinghausen is the site of the annual *Ruhr Festival* of music, theater, opera, and art exhibitions.

Next take the Autobahn (Route A43) south to Bochum.

BOCHUM: This is the site of another unique museum, the *Museum of Mining* (*Bergbau Museum;* Wielandstr.). The big attraction is an actual coal mine below the building, with nearly a mile of shafts you can explore. Bochum also has Germany's best-known public observatory and planetarium (corner of Castroper Str. and Hagenstr.). Take Route 1 back to Dortmund.

BEST EN ROUTE

The visitor to Westphalia will delight in the many charming hotels and inns to be found in the smaller towns. Prices here also tend to be lower than they are in the larger, more frequented city areas. A double room with breakfast in an expensive hotel will cost about $70 to 110; moderate is $40 to $65; and inexpensive is below $40. In the expensive restaurants, a dinner for two without wine will cost about $35 to $65; in moderate establishments it will be $20 to $30; inexpensive meals are under $20.

ATTENDORN

Burghotel Schnellenberg – This 13th-century castle in the middle of the woods has a commanding view of the town below. Many of the rooms are in the towers. You can dine in the rustic *Rittersaal Salon,* where game and fish dishes are especially recommended. Recreational opportunities here include tennis, hikes in the woods, and swimming in the Biggesee, 2 miles (3.2 km) away (phone: 6940). Expensive.

OBERKIRCHEN

Schütte – This former 18th-century coach house is in the middle of a Sauerland village of 800 inhabitants. It offers many miles of hiking paths in the surrounding woods, its own swimming pool, and its own stable, where visitors either rent horses or stable their own. Its Westphalian food specialties include ham and *Pfefferpothast,* a very spicy stew. The game dishes are excellent: Try venison with red wine. The typically Westphalian interior is rustic, with an open fireplace. 2 Eggeweg (phone: 820). Expensive to moderate.

PETERSHAGEN

Schloss Petershagen – A moated castle on the Weser River surrounded by meadows and parks houses a small hotel (11 rooms) and an elegant restaurant with international cuisine. The restaurant has deep carpets, rich cloth on the walls, oil paintings, and linen tablecloths. It's not the place for Westphalian specialties, although it does feature fish from the Weser — smoked eel and trout soup. The palace also offers a "knightly banquet" for groups only, with service personnel in medieval costumes and menus offering old recipes. There's a bar in the cellar, and the surrounding park has tennis courts and a heated swimming pool. Originally built in 1306, it doesn't look like the average castle; the tower with the spiral staircase is of recent construction. 5 Schlosstr. (phone: 346). Expensive to moderate.

WARENDORF

Im Engel – Established in 1557, the hotel has been in the hands of the Leve family, the present proprietors, since 1692. It is right in the center of the old city and has the usual rustic interior, with oak furniture, carved beams, pewter, old pictures, and the standard open fireplace. Westphalian specialties include mussel soup; steak garnished with scrambled eggs; turbot served in white Burgundy sauce; and *Schlachtplatte*, literally, "slaughter platter," consisting of Westphalian ham, sausages, and other smoked meats, heaped on a mound of sauerkraut. Facilities include a swimming pool, sauna, and solarium. Closed Saturdays for lunch as well as 2 weeks in July. 37 Brünebrede (phone: 7064). Expensive to moderate.

MÜNSTER

Waldhotel Krautkrämer – About 4 miles (6.4 km) from the center of town, this 70-room hotel has its own lake. It provides a rare combination of comfort, hospitality, sublime surroundings, and one of West Germany's best restaurants. 173 See (phone: 8050). Expensive.

Romantik-Hotel Hof zur Linde – A half-timbered former farmhouse 5 miles (8 km) from downtown, this 30-room hotel has a tranquil location. Excellent restaurant on the premises. 1 Handorfer Werseufer (phone: 325002). Expensive to moderate.

Gasthof Stuhlmacher – This 17th-century restaurant has typical Westphalian decor and cuisine, with ten famous beers on tap. The gabled exterior, right next to the city hall, displays a century-old metal figure of a professor and a worker sitting at a beer barrel, which means that the restaurant catered to all social classes. The interior is elaborately carved in wood and has stained-glass windows, leather seats, and old pictures. Specialties include calf's head stew, homemade *Sülze* (pickled meat in aspic), homemade cheese, and Westphalian ham. Reservations are recommended. 6 Prinzipalmarkt (phone: 44877). Moderate.

Pinkus Müller – At this 19th-century student hangout, tourists, professors, and students sit side by side at long wooden tables on which every inch of surface has been carved with the initials of generations. Each regular customer has his own mug with his name on it, which hangs from a peg on the wall. The decor is German "schmaltz," with stained glass windows, overhead beams with painted mottoes in Low German, an open fireplace, a cannon, and a wooden board (no longer used) on which the names of those delinquent in their accounts were revealed to the public. The customary drink is *Altbier,* a heavy, somewhat sweet beer. You may want to start things off with a schnapps served from a deep spoon. Full meals can be had, but food specialties tend to be snacks that go well with beer, such as *Töttchen,* a small dish of veal and mustard, or a Westphalian stew of various smoked meats and sausages. Closed Sundays. Reservations suggested. 4-10 Kreuzstr. (phone: 45151). Moderate to inexpensive.

The Rhineland

Long before the Autobahn and jetport, before the rail lines stitched the continent into a whole, the Rhine River was Europe's main street and commercial thoroughfare. Fed by melting Alpine snows in Switzerland and sharing frontage with France and the Netherlands, the Rhine is 820 miles long; it is nevertheless the section that flows through Germany that captures the imagination with its castles, vineyards, dangerous whirlpools, and legends of heroes, Rhine maidens, and Loreley. The river flows steadily northward, broad, even-tempered, and unimpeded, in contrast with the tempestuous history of Germany, past and present.

Today as ever, the Rhine is a busy and important shipping route linking dozens of inland ports such as Ludwigshafen and Duisburg to the North Sea and the oceans beyond. However, this majestic river is also part playground, part historical monument, and part natural wonder. Despite the Rhine's more than 800-mile length, "the Rhineland" is a much narrower term, encompassing by common consensus only the 50-mile Rhine gorge between Mainz and Koblenz where the steep banks, striated by vineyards and crowned with castles, create the romantic picture most people associate with this famous river.

History, legend, and magnificent scenery have their attractions, but one cannot forget that the Rhineland is wine land. By most accounts, Germany's best wine district is the Rheingau, extending roughly from Wiesbaden to the mouth of the Lahn River near Kamp, only a few dozen miles downstream. Along this short stretch, a southern exposure ripens noble Riesling grapes to perfection. For the confirmed wine connoisseur, a trip down the Rhine gorge is something of a pilgrimage. For the neophyte sipper, a few well-chosen stopovers here will provide a succinct introduction to the white wines many experts claim are the best in the world. For information about German wine, write to one of these addresses: The German Wine Information Bureau (Lamar Elmore), 79 Madison Ave., New York, NY 10016 (phone: 212-213-0909); or the German Wine Academy, Postfach 1705, D-6500 Mainz, West Germany. And the wine seems to impart an easygoing and fun-loving nature to the people in the surrounding countryside. The traveler can only agree that a relaxed and joyous outlook on life is an excellent one for hoteliers and restaurateurs. In fact, one often finds that Rhinelanders cultivate their guests as attentively as they do their vines.

The Rhine can be explored by car, by rail, or by excursion boat. Multilingual bus tours are also available, and for these, contact the German National Tourist Office (Deutsche Zentrale für Tourismus), 69 Beethoven Str., 6 Frankfurt am Main (phone: 069-75720); or stop at one of the city tourist offices — labeled Verkehrsamt or Verkehrsverein — along the Rhine route. They also provide maps and tourist information. The central tourist office for the region has two branches, one in Bad Godesberg, a suburb of Bonn, and the other in Koblenz: Landesverkehrsverband Rheinland e.V., 69 Rheinallee,

5300 Bonn–Bad Godesberg 1 (phone: 362921); and Fremdenverkehrsverband Rheinland-Pfalz e.V., 103-105 Löhrstr., 5400 Koblenz (phone: 31079).

The above modes of travel can be combined, of course, and the bearer of a Eurailpass can make as many stops as desired along the way to, say, Koblenz, and then use the pass at no extra charge on one of the many Köln-Düsseldorfer (K-D) or Rüdesheim-Bingen river steamers that ply this route, for a pleasant return trip. For information about boat trips, contact *K-D Schiffsagentur* in Köln (Cologne), 15 Frankenwerft (phone: 211864); or in Mainz, *Am Rathaus* (phone: 224511). Rail lines parallel the river on both sides, but the west bank affords the best scenery and most interesting stops. Travelers touring by car have the opportunity to stop and take pictures anywhere or to picnic at rest stops; the auto traveler can easily cross the Rhine at one of several bridges at Koblenz and made a round trip by returning along Route 42 on the east bank. Campgrounds are plentiful along both sides, and at several points car ferries, called *Autofähre,* will transfer you across the river for a nominal fee. The entire route covers about 143 miles (229 km) one way, but you'll want to spend at least 2 or 3 days in this glorious region.

MAINZ: This 2,000-year-old city founded by the Romans is most notable for its favorite son, Johannes Gutenberg, who invented movable type here in 1440. In the *Gutenberg Museum* (5 Liebfrauenpl.) you can see an original Gutenberg Bible and a replica of the famed printer's press, as well as an exhibition of printing through the centuries. Mainz is also the scene of a boisterous carnival, climaxing in the Rosenmontag parade on the last Monday before Ash Wednesday. Mainz Cathedral, though not architecturally impressive, is worth visiting for its art treasures, particularly the medieval sculpture by the Master of Naumburg in its *Diocesan Museum.*

RÜDESHEIM: It's downright touristy — and for good reason. Head straight for the Drosselgasse, a narrow, cobblestone alley lined with restaurants, wine taverns, and souvenir shops. Pick a pub where the oompah band isn't too loud, order yourself a *Römer* (wine goblet with a bottle-green pedestal) of the local product, and get a taste of what the Rhineland is all about. This small city boasts rousing wine festivals in May and August and also has one of Germany's best wine museums, in Brömser Castle (closed Mondays), along Route 42 at the west end of town. For a small fee you can browse through 28 display rooms containing wine presses and various viticultural artifacts showing man's 6,000-year winemaking tradition. A free brochure is available upon request. If you stop here, carry a jacket or sweater with you, for the cellarlike rooms are cool even in summer. To find a room or to collect a handful of brochures describing the sights ahead, contact Rüdesheim's city tourist office, 16 Rheinstr. (phone: 2962), where English-speaking personnel will answer all your questions. Another Rüdesheimer attraction is the curious Siegfried's Mechanical Music Cabinet, a collection of self-playing musical contraptions of the past, housed just off Drosselgasse.

Rüdesheim is a good place to catch a K-D river steamer. The trip to St. Goarshausen and back makes a nice afternoon jaunt, allowing plenty of time for wine sipping and a leisurely meal in the ship's surprisingly good restaurant.

En Route from Rüdesheim – Before crossing to Bingen and the more scenic left bank of the river, you might want to take a 9-mile (14-km) side trip north to Assmannshausen by way of Niederwald Hill. Just north of Rüdesheim along Route 42, you will pass the grim-visaged Amazon that is the Germania Monument, built on Niederwald Hill in the 1870s to commemorate the unification of Germany. You can get there from Rüdesheim by bus or by a chair lift, which carries you up the steep, vine-bearing slopes for spectacular views and picture taking.

On an island in the middle of the river is the Mouse Tower (Mäuseturm) — not to be confused with the Mouse Castle, encountered later — built centuries ago by the wicked archbishop of Mainz as a stronghold for extracting tolls from passing ships. According to legend, the nasty archbishop ordered his henchmen to wipe out a band of beggars who came pleading for handouts. An army of mice rose up to avenge the slain beggars, chased the archbishop into the tower, and gobbled him up alive. One can readily see how the Brothers Grimm found plenty of fairy tale material in Germany! There are short daily boat excursions from Rüdesheim to the village of Assmannshausen via the Mouse Tower.

Assmannshausen is an oddity because it produces only red wine, which comes from the Burgundy-type (Pinot Noir) grape; however, only a local vintner with an exaggerated view of his own product would rank Assmannshausen red anywhere near the noble white Rieslings from the surrounding area.

BINGEN: For the motorist, the left bank of the river affords the best view, so return to Rüdesheim and take the car ferry to Bingen, picking up Route 9 on the other side. In itself, Bingen is not especially interesting. But in common with nearby villages, it shares the typically relaxed Rhineland ambience. After a fine meal with wine, there's no better place in Germany for an evening stroll than through Bingen's narrow brick and cobblestone streets or along the riverfront of one of these delightful Rhineside towns.

En Route from Bingen –

The stretch from Bingen to Koblenz is justly celebrated for its dramatic scenery, romantic castles, and legendary landmarks. The last section on the left bank, between Bacharach and St. Goar, is the narrow, steep road known as the Rheingoldstrasse. Just north of Bingen, several castles on the hills to the left invite you to do a little historical poking around. Especially worthy are Burg Rheinfels, perched on a rock, and Burg Reichenstein, set in a valley — both open to the public. It's useful to know the difference between the German words *Burg* and *Schloss,* both translated as "castle" by most dictionaries. A *Burg* is a fortified medieval structure, today often in ruins. Its military aspect is obvious. A *Schloss,* on the other hand, is more of a palace and is usually lavishly decorated and furnished. Many even offer guest accommodations.

The towns of Bacharach and Oberwesel bid the traveler to stop and explore. There are more castles in the area than one could comfortably see in a week, so don't feel bad about passing up most of them. The Jost family in Bacharach runs a justly famous antique porcelain and glassware shop called *Trödel's* (7 Oberstr.).

On the right, between Bacharach and St. Goar, are the Rhine gorge's two most distinctive landmarks — one might even say trademarks. Die Pfalz is a squat, dome-roofed medieval toll station in the middle of the current between Bacharach and Oberwesel. In the romantic past, Die Pfalz had chains stretched across the river to stop passing ships, and cannons were leveled at stubborn river captains. This fortified structure did a brisk business until an international agreement in 1868 eliminated all such extortion on the Rhine. Try to get a photo of Die Pfalz when an especially colorful river barge is passing in the foreground or background. Seven miles (11 km) downstream from Die Pfalz is the legend-haunted Loreley, a sheer outcropping of rock forever immortalized by the poem of Heinrich Heine. According to the sagas, a blond maiden — a Germanic version of the Sirens — lured sailors from this rock to their deaths with song. As K-D excursion boats pass this point, Schumann strains are played on a sound system, and the German tourists on board suddenly look very reverent indeed — understandably so, because the Loreley is as characteristically German as Old Faithful is American. It's a "must" stop, and today a road runs to the top.

ST. GOAR and ST. GOARSHAUSEN: These twin towns face one another across a broad, lakelike expanse of the Rhine. St. Goar's castle, Burg Rheinfels, is worth a stop.

A few steps beyond St. Goar's tourist office (15 Heer Str.; phone: 383) is the shop of *Doris Mühl,* which offers an incredible array of cuckoo clocks, beer steins, quality glassware, and famous Hummel figurines. Three decades of American GIs have helped this shop thrive, and its English-speaking proprietors gladly welcome Americans.

You can take the car ferry across to St. Goarshausen, which is as delightful as its sister village on the left bank. Travelers with children may find the carnival rides set up near the K-D steamer dock a welcome distraction. St. Goarshausen is the scene of the majestic Rhine in Flames fireworks and spotlight extravaganza on the third Saturday in September. But alas! (for St. Goarshausen-ites): The spectacle is best seen from St. Goar across the river. Just south of St. Goarshausen is the Loreley.

The steep-sided Rhine gorge ends beyond the village of Boppard, a residential valley town with a particularly pleasant promenade aptly, but not too imaginatively, named Rhine Promenade (Rheinallee). At Koblenz the Rhine is joined by the Moselle river, a famous wine river well worth a side trip.

En Route from Koblenz – Though less dramatic than the stretch between Bingen and Koblenz, the area north of Koblenz has many intriguing features. Continuing up the left bank, you may wish to take a look at the abbey of Maria Laach, a Benedictine monastery, with its Romanesque basilica. It's a short detour of 9 miles (14.4 km) west of the river at Andernach. The abbey is most interesting for its location on the Laacher See, the largest of the volcanic lakes in the Eifel plateau, a peaceful, wooded area.

Farther north along the Rhine is the Rheineck, a Burg with a view of the surrounding valley. Still farther, on the slope of a former volcano, is the Rolandsbogen (Roland's arch), the ruins of the castle of the knight Roland, hero of the *Chanson de Roland.*

Southeast of Bonn, on the right bank (there's a car ferry from Bad Godesberg to Königswinter), is the Drachenfels, a romantic, rocky summit with a ruined tower and a panoramic view that includes the Eifel plateau, Bonn, and Cologne. It's in the Seven Mountains (Siebengebirge) range, whose low summits, once crowned with castles, are now crowned with forests; the whole area is a national park. The Drachenfels was named for the legendary dragon slain by Siegfried, the hero who became invincible by bathing in its blood. The area is also known for its wines, the best of which is called Drachenblut ("dragon's blood"). Excursions for Drachenfels (15 minutes by cog railway) leave from Königswinter at frequent intervals.

BONN: The postwar Germans must have wanted the capital of the new Germany in a place where nothing exciting ever happens, for after its spirited street carnival on *Weiberfastnacht* and *Rose Monday* (the dates vary with the calendar), the city goes back into hibernation. Besides the seat of government Bonn has another claim to fame: The composer Ludwig van Beethoven was born and spent his early years in this Rhineside city. The excellently restored Beethoven House (20 Bonngasse) deserves a stop. See also the Alter Zoll, a bastion with a view of the Rhine, and stroll along the promenade on the banks of the river, past the Bundestag, the West German parliament.

COLOGNE (KÖLN): The silhouette of Cologne's great Gothic cathedral dominates the city's skyline; it's one of the world's finest. Begun in 1248, the cathedral was an on-again, off-again project not completed until 1880. Although 90% of the city was leveled by World War II bombing, the cathedral escaped virtually intact. See the 14th-century stained-glass windows, the altarpiece, and the Magi's Shrine. The Cologne tourist office, off the cathedral square (phone: 221-3345), has a good selection of tourist brochures covering the cathedral and other sights. Cologne's Roman beginnings are on display at the *Roman-Germanic Museum* opposite the cathedral, where one may see the striking one-million-piece Dionysus Mosaic, dating from AD 200. Other museums include the modern *Wallraf-Richartz und Ludwig Museum,* between the cathedral and the Rhine, with an excellent collection of old Dutch and Flemish paintings as well as old and modern German works; the modern and contemporary section is outstanding, with a large collection of pop art. The new *Käthe Kollwitz Museum,* Neumarket-Passage (phone: 208-5899), is the first in Germany devoted to this great painter and sculptress.

After a round of sightseeing, you can take a cable car (near the zoo) over the Rhine, enjoy an excellent view of the cathedral, and relax in the Rheinpark. Nearby is the city exposition center, site of Photokina, the world's fair of the photographic industry, held during September in even-numbered years. There's shopping galore along Hohe Strasse and Schildergasse, where every major German department store chain seems to be represented. In the evening, this shopping district blossoms with street vendors and musicians. Other evening entertainment is offered by the pubs of Cologne's modest *Altstadt* (old town), which is nevertheless lively with music. Finally, the carnival here is reputed to be the best in Germany, with events reaching their highest pitch during the weekend before Ash Wednesday.

DÜSSELDORF: The residents have a saying: Düsseldorf is not on the Rhine, it's on the Kö. Certainly, Düsseldorf turns its back on the river and faces instead Königsallee — Kö for short — an elegant, kilometer-long promenade whose fashionable shops are a major center of German haute couture. The Kö is jewelry, furs, fine silverware, art, rare books. But the Kö is also restaurants and friendly open-air cafés where you can sip a drink and see and be seen.

At night the spotlight shifts to Düsseldorf's other center, the lively *Altstadt,* where some 200 pubs and inns jump to the sounds of live music. Nightlife here is rollicking rather than vulgar. But proof that the mellow Rhineland wine villages are far away may be seen in what Düsseldorfers are drinking, for this is beer country, and the local specialty is Altbier or Düsseldorfer Alt, a dark lager brew. The many Yugoslavian, Japanese, Italian, Argentinian, and other ethnic restaurants indicate that this is a city of international business and the business center for the Ruhr region.

Though a very modern city, Düsseldorf has a distinguished history that dates from the 13th century. The city has been known for its prominence in the arts since the 19th century, when Napoleon made it the capital of the grand duchy of Berg; among those who lived here were Heinrich Heine, Robert Schumann, and Felix Mendelssohn. The *Hetjens Museum* (Palais Nesselrode, 4 Schulstr.) has a large collection of ceramics; *Kunstsammlung Nordrhein-Westfalen,* in its beautiful new building at 5 Grabbe Pl., has some fine works of modern art, especially those by Paul Klee; and the *Goethe Museum* (2 Schlob Jägerhot Jacqbistr.) has an extensive collection of the writer's manuscripts and memorabilia. The opera house (Heinrich-Heine-Allee) is also an interesting place, as is Schloss Benrath (104 Benrather Schlossallee).

For maps and further information about Düsseldorf, contact the tourist office (12 Konrad Adenauer Pl.; phone: 350505).

BEST EN ROUTE

The Rhineland is prime tourist country, and has been for over a century. Good hotels abound (little Rüdesheim alone has over 60), though in the wine villages the best were built in an age when guests arrived with servants and steamer trunks. Today they are like faded aristocrats and seem somewhat overpriced by American standards. Hotel restaurants can be excellent, however, and a continental breakfast — often augmented by eggs or sausage — is invariably included in the overnight price. Good double rooms may be found all along the river at prices ranging from $30 to $50 and up. Even at those prices, private bathrooms may not be included, so make sure you get what you want before booking. Our advice is to arrive early and head for the city tourist office, whose personnel can find a room without language problems. In the Rhenish cities, the top hotels meet the highest international standards and command prices to match; here, English is the second language. Below are just a few of the top hotels to choose from. Modest *Gasthäuser* and pensions are plentiful everywhere.

We have classified hotels that charge $85 to $125 for a double room with breakfast as expensive; moderate is $50 to $85; and inexpensive, below $50. A dinner for two without wine will cost $60 to $100 in an expensive restaurant; $35 to $60 is moderate; and $20 to $35, inexpensive.

RÜDESHEIM

Waldhotel Jagdschloss Niederwald – Here's a true *Schloss* hotel high on the Rhine hills, 3 miles (5 km) northwest of Rüdesheim, with an imperial view of the river. The restaurant features wine tasting and game in season — as well it should, for this was part of the former hunting lodge of the Archbishop of Mainz. Closed in the winter (phone: 06722-1004). Expensive to moderate.

ASSMANNSHAUSEN

Krone – Overlooking the Rhine, this 400-year-old inn has a museum in the 2nd-floor lounge, with letters and manuscripts by famous people who have stayed here. The spacious bedrooms have traditional furniture and the public rooms are oak-paneled and full of antiques. The food in the restaurant is outstanding; try especially the turtle soup, fresh salmon, or eels. Closed in the winter. 10 Rheinuferstr. (phone: 06722-2036). Expensive to moderate.

BINGEN

Römerhof – Across the narrow Nahe river in the suburb of Bingerbrück is this charming, tranquil hotel. The view is bewitching, and the site historic. Among the features are a garden and a lovely Rhenish wine tavern. The restaurant is closed Saturdays, and the entire establishment is closed during the winter months. 10 Rupertsberg (phone: 32248). Moderate.

ST. GOAR

Schlosshotel auf Burg Rheinfels – Tucked in the picturesque ruins of a medieval castle, this hotel looks out over St. Goar, the Loreley rock, and the Cat and Mouse castles. It has an open-air terrace with a spectacular view, an indoor pool, a sauna, a museum, a conference room, and a restaurant specializing in venison. 47 Schlossberg (phone: 2071). Expensive to moderate.

Zum Goldenen Löwen – Overlooking the Rhine, this small, moderately priced hotel has a restaurant with an outdoor terrace where the view is excellent. 82 Heerstr. (phone: 1674). Expensive to moderate.

Hauser – With a lovely view of St. Goarshausen across the river, this small, modest hotel has a café and a terrace. 77 Heerstr. (phone: 333). Inexpensive.

BONN

Steigenberger Hotel Venusberg – Bonn's newest hotel, opened in 1989, is on Venusberg Hill. It offers a good view of Bonn and the Rhine Valley. Designed in the style of a French country mansion, this luxurious hostelry has 80 rooms and 6 suites as well as 2 restaurants. 1 An der Casselsruhe (phone: 2880). Very expensive.

COLOGNE (KÖLN)

Excelsior Hotel Ernst – Opposite the cathedral and near the train station, this establishment is everything you would expect from an Old World hotel. Its rooms radiate an aura of luxury, comfort, and charm; the service is very efficient, although not ostentatious. *Hansa-Stube* is its very well regarded restaurant. 1 Trankgasse (phone: 2701). Very expensive.

Altstadt – This small hotel is in the old city near the landing dock for Rhine boats. The owner, Herr Olbrich, once was a steward for the German-American Line. His tastefully decorated rooms are impeccable, and the personal service is outstanding. Rooms have bars and refrigerators. Reserve in advance. Closed most of July. 7 Salzgasse (phone: 234187). Moderate.

Goldener Pflug – This fine restaurant serves exquisite house specialties and has a pleasant setting. Service is first rate. Reservations advised. Closed Sundays and in July. 421 Olpener Str. (phone: 895509). Very expensive.

Weinhaus im Walfisch – Seafood dishes and some of the best German wines are the specialty here. The building predates the last war by more than 300 years, a rarity in hard-hit Cologne. Reservations recommended. Closed Sundays and in July. 13 Salzgasse (phone: 21-95-75). Moderate.

DÜSSELDORF

Breidenbacher Hof – Convenient to both the activities of the downtown area and the Old World charms of the *Altstadt*, this is one of Germany's best addresses. Tradition, luxury, and elegance combine well with very efficient service. Its restaurant, *Grill Royal,* ought not to be missed (closed Sundays). 36 Heinrich-Heine-Allee (phone: 13030). Very expensive.

Zum Schiffchen – Don't miss the jovial atmosphere and hearty food of this beer garden that's a favorite town haunt. Napoleon is said to have dined here, as well as Heinrich Heine, Curd Jürgens, and Arthur Miller. Closed Sundays. 5 Hafenstr. (phone: 132422). Moderate to inexpensive.

The Neckar River Valley

This route along the meandering Neckar River follows Germany's Castle Road (Die Burgenstrasse) from Heidelberg to Heilbronn. More than a dozen castles and strongholds can be found along this road, some of which housed aristocratic families during the Middle Ages. Many of the princely feudal dwellings are in ruins; others are intact and have been restored as museums, hotels, inns, and wine taverns. Zwingenberg Castle, for example, is still inhabited by royalty — by relatives of Britain's Prince Philip — but Hirschhorn and Hornberg castles are now hotels.

One of Germany's wine districts, producing mainly red wines, the scenic Neckar River valley is surrounded by high, forested hills crowned with castles, fortresses, and quaint old towns. Beginning in Heidelberg (see *Frankfurt to Heidelberg*), this 1- or 2-day drive runs 50 miles (80 km) south to the wine-producing town of Heilbronn, where the Castle Road ends. From here it's an additional 32 miles (52 km) through the Swabian Hills to the major industrial and cultural center of Stuttgart, home of the Stuttgart Ballet and Mercedes-Benz. Finally, you can drive yet another 27 miles (43 km) south to see Tübingen, a charming old university town.

Well-marked hiking trails connect towns and castles, and the forested castle areas are generally honeycombed with quiet, scenic trails. Boat trips leave from many locations on the Neckar; passenger and car ferries transport you to interesting sites on the opposite bank. A bicycle lane runs along most of the route. The valley also has health spas and resorts for the recreation-minded. For maps and further information about the region, contact the tourist office in Stuttgart, Landesfremdenverkehrsverband Baden-Württenberg, 23 Bussenstr., 7000 Stuttgart (phone: 481045), or Fremdenverkehrsverband Neckarland-Schwaben, 21 Lohtorstr, 7100 Heilbronn (phone: 629061).

En Route from Heidelberg – Neckargemünd, a 1,000-year-old town by the winding Neckar, features old inns such as *Ritter* (40 Neckarstr.), with open-air terraces overlooking the valley (see *Best en Route*). A church steeple rises over half-timbered houses and the old town hall. Neckargemünd also has the only parachute museum in Western Europe. From here Dilsberg is a short detour of 3 miles (5 km).

Dilsberg, a fortified hamlet high above the Neckar River, resisted Imperial General Tilly and his Bavarian men during the Thirty Years' War. The stout ramparts and lookout towers of this walled city are visible from both banks. If you park your car outside the town walls and enter the town on foot, you can explore the fortress, a mysterious subterranean tunnel, and the castle ruins (Burgruine). The tower (open summers only), with almost 100 stairs, offers a panoramic view of the river. Return by the same route to Neckargemünd, take Route 37 to the north bank, and drive toward Neckarsteinach. You'll spot castle ruins on the ridge as you approach the town, which is 3 miles (5 km) from Neckargemünd.

NECKARSTEINACH: Also known as the Four Castles Corner (Vierburgeneck), this town boasts four medieval citadels built in the 12th and 13th centuries. On the left side of Route 37, shortly before you reach the town, a parking area marks the start of a wooded trail that connects Vorderburg, Mittelburg, Hinterburg, and Schadeck castles. The walk takes about 45 minutes and ends in the town itself, not far from the parking area. On many summer evenings, the town holds the Four Castles Festival, in which the castles are illuminated and fireworks are exploded. Neckarsteinach's center is carefully preserved, so you may also want to stroll around the town. From here follow Route 37 to Hirschhorn, approximately 6 miles (10 km) away.

HIRSCHHORN: This town is dominated by its impressive castle fortress, *Hirschhorn Castle,* which is now a hotel and restaurant. The towered defenses were built in the 13th century, but the castle itself dates from the 16th century. For a small fee you can climb the 121 steps of the tower, which lead to a magnificent view of the sharp Hirschhorn bend in the river. Below the castle, the walled village still holds the remains of a deep moat. Historic Ersheimer Chapel is across the river; from there you can have a good view of the castle. From Hirschhorn continue up the north bank for about 7 miles (11 km) to Eberbach.

EBERBACH: This ancient imperial city has fortress ruins that date from the 11th century. Four powerful towers attest to its medieval beginnings. The old Deutscher Hof, the medieval center of town, is alive with colorful inns, half-timbered houses, and cobbled streets. In the old market square, the town's eventful history is recorded in 14 scenes painted on a front wall of the *Karpfen* hotel. You can see other engraved murals on the oldest inn in the city, the *Gasthaus zum Krabbenstein,* and at the Hay Market (Heumarkt).

After a walk in the old city, stop at the large red and white *Victoria Café* and choose from an immense assortment of confections, candies, and desserts. The town also has a health resort park, large forested reserves, indoor and outdoor swimming pools, tennis courts, and is West Germany's acupuncture center.

ZWINGENBERG: Continue on Route 37 for 7 miles (11 km) to Zwingenberg. Follow signs to the train station (Bahnhof) and park your car. A short distance up the road, a paved path leads to the Zwingenberg Castle, one of the most magnificent of the castles on the Castle Road. The interior of the residence of the Battenbergs, relatives of Britain's Prince Philip, is only open to the public from May 1 to September 30, Tuesdays, Fridays, and Sundays from 2 to 4:15 PM. The fortress has been spared by war and almost untouched by renovation. The lords of Zwingenberg, its first owners in the 13th century, supplemented their income by imposing customs fees on shipping on the Neckar River. Two more castle ruins — Stolzeneck and Minneburg — are on the opposite bank of the river.

NECKARZIMMERN: From Zwingenberg, drive on Route 37 to its junction with Route 27 at Neckarelz, a distance of about 10 miles (16 km). Then follow Route 27 a few miles to Neckarzimmern. Look for the sign for Burg Hornberg and follow the paved road to the left to the *Hotel Schloss Hornberg* (Hornberg Castle, now a hotel).

Overlooking vineyards sloping to the river's bank, this castle was once the home of the Knight of the Iron Fist, Götz von Berlichingen, who wore an artificial hand after losing his right hand in the Bavarian War of 1504. For a small fee, you can explore the castle ruins, visit the museum with its medieval armor and implements, and climb the watchtower (almost 140 wooden steps) for a commanding view of the Neckar Valley. This castle was first mentioned in a document in 1184. Since that time it has changed hands several times; it has been sold, given away, and even pawned during its colorful history.

You may want to pause for a meal or a drink in the castle's former stable, now converted into a restaurant and bar. The windows of the restaurant look out over the valley, and you can sample wines that come from the slopes below.

NECKARMÜHLBACH: From Hornberg drive on Route 27 to Gundelsheim (an interesting historical town with its Castle of Horneck). At Gundelsheim, drive over the bridge across the Neckar and follow the marked road near Neckarmühlbach to Burg Guttenberg (Guttenberg castle), one of the very few medieval German castles that has not been destroyed; it is, in fact, still a residence.

Dating from the 12th century, this castle offers more than just historical and architectural interest. It also houses an extensive collection of live birds of prey, many uncaged, from throughout the world. Here, amidst the stately castle fortifications, stand eagles, vultures, and other predators. The birds entertain visitors during a show in which vultures swoop down over the heads of the audience.

The museum also displays historical remnants, such as a skillfully crafted Madonna, medieval books and documents, instruments of torture, woodcuts, engravings, copper etchings, jewelry, kitchenware, porcelain, and glass. An old spiral stairway takes you to the different floors of the museum and leads to a door marked "zum Turm" (to the tower). If you decide to climb the more than 100 steps to the open tower, you'll be rewarded with a sweeping view of the countryside.

From here, continue on the left side of the river to Bad Wimpfen.

BAD WIMPFEN: This royal city of the Castle Road was the imperial residence of the Hohenstaufens in the 13th century. The Upper Town (Bad Wimpfen am Berg), as the old part of Bad Wimpfen is called, is marked by the towers, spires, and red tile roofs that crown its half-timbered structures.

A short walking tour of the old section takes about an hour and is well worth it. You can see the town hall, market square, the Blue Tower, the picturesque house of Mayor Elsesser, the Steinhaus (Romanesque, from about 1200), the imperial chapel, and the Red Tower, the emperor's refuge in times of danger. A walk down Klostergasse passes half-timbered houses with gardens, the Mansion of the Knights, and the former bath-houses dating from 1543.

En Route from Bad Wimpfen – You can continue on the left bank of the Neckar to Heilbronn or cross the river to Route 27 and drive a short distance to Bad Friedrichshall, a spa town with salt mines. Here you can arrange a tour of the saltworks or visit the local castle-hotel, *Schloss Lehen* (Hauptstr. 2). Then drive along the right bank to Neckarsulm, a town that will interest automobile and motorcycle buffs. You can tour the NSU Automobile Factory weekdays at 10 AM and 2 PM or visit the Zweiradmuseum, in the former castle of the Teutonic Order. This exhibition shows the development of original models of bicycles and motorcycles. Follow either the left or right bank to reach Heilbronn.

HEILBRONN: In the midst of forests and vineyards, this is one of Germany's major wine-producing towns. You can sample the fine wines at the *Heilbronn Harvest,* a traditional wine festival in early September; *Wine Village,* a festival centered around the city hall, also held in September; or at any time in any of Heilbronn's inns such as the *Insel* (see *Best en Route*) at Friedrich Ebert Brücke, on an island in the river.

Formerly a free imperial city, Heilbronn has many interesting buildings. The 1315 Tower of the Church of St. Kilian was Germany's first Renaissance structure. Also in the city's center, you can see the 15th-century city hall with its ornamental clock, made in 1580, and the 14th-century Gothic Käthchenhaus, a patrician dwelling in the market square.

 En Route from Heilbronn – If you have additional time, you may want to continue along the Neckar, taking Route 27 on the right bank, for 32 miles (52 km) to Stuttgart, passing through gently rolling vineyards and small, picturesque medieval towns such as Lauffen, Kirchheim, and Besigheim. You may want to stroll along some of the streets in these old towns.

STUTTGART: A city of more than half a million people, Stuttgart is more than an industrial center. Besides being the headquarters of Mercedes, Stuttgart is home of the highly acclaimed *Stuttgart Ballet* as well as the *State Opera* and a *Philharmonic Orchestra.* Surrounded by the wooded Swabian Hills, Stuttgart has devoted two thirds of its land to green spots, including vineyards that are near the business district and the main railroad station. It is also the capital of the federal state of Baden-Württemberg.

Enjoy the view of Stuttgart and the Swabian Jura from the Television Tower (Fernsehturm) south of the city on Bopser Hill. Built in 1956 from a unique design by Dr. Fritz Leonhardt, the tower has an observation platform and a good restaurant, the *Turmrestaurant.* Then visit the old town where, on the Schillerplatz, you can see Stuttgart's Old Palace, built in both 14th-century Gothic and 16th-century Renaissance styles, with a courtyard surrounded by galleries. It now houses the *Württemberg Regional Museum,* devoted to regional history. Schillerplatz is also the site of a vegetable and flower market on Tuesdays, Thursdays, and Saturdays. Nearby, the ultramodern *Rathaus* is also of interest, with its Glockenspiel that plays folk songs.

The *Stuttgart State Gallery* (Alte Staatsgalerie), 30-32 Konrad-Adenauer-Str., houses a fine collection of paintings from the Middle Ages to the 19th century. The ultramodern *Neue Staatsgalerie* next door displays 20th-century art, including works from the German Expressionist and Bauhaus movements. The most popular museum here, however, is the *Daimler-Benz Museum,* in the Mercedes-Benz plant in the suburb of Untertürkheim. Accessible by bus line 56 from the bus station, or by line 5 from the central train station, it contains displays of cars, car engines, and other motors — racing car, boat, airplane, motorcycle — in addition to the history of the venerable firm, which began in 1900; closed Mondays.

Stuttgart is graced by parks, the most beautiful of which is Killesberg Park, on a hill in the northern part of town. Another park worth a visit is the Cannstatter Wasen, where a popular festival is held every year for 2 weeks at the end of September. Like the *Oktoberfest* in Munich, it is one of West Germany's biggest, most popular festivals. Stuttgart is also known for its modern buildings, particularly the asymmetrical Liederhalle near the town center, designed in 1956 by Adolf Abel and Rolf Gutbrod. The concrete exterior of the Liederhalle, containing three concert halls with excellent acoustics, is enlivened with mosaics, glazed brick, and quartz.

Stuttgart's tourist office is below the main railroad station at Arnulf-Klett-Passage (phone: 222-82-40). There is now direct train service between the main station (Hauptbahnhof) and the Stuttgart airport. On Saturdays at 10 AM, free walking tours leave from Schillerplatz.

TÜBINGEN: From Stuttgart it's 27 miles (43 km) to this lovely old university town. The University of Tübingen, founded in 1477, still uses the town's Renaissance castle, whose terraces, bastions, and gardens offer a fine view of the Neckar and the old town. Nearby is the Marktplatz, which is especially colorful on market days — Mondays, Wednesdays, and Fridays — when you can see peasants in regional dress selling produce.

Don't miss the famous Platanenallee, an avenue of plane trees on a manmade island in the Neckar, a pleasant place both day and night. The Platanenallee may be reached by the Eberhard Bridge. Both the bridge and the island offer excellent views of the town, with its river, its old houses, and its willow trees.

BEST EN ROUTE

On this, Germany's Castle Road, hotels and inns — even those in the castles — are surprisingly reasonable. The most expensive places are in the larger cities such as Stuttgart. A double room with private bath, breakfast, tax, and service included in the price will cost $85 to $150 in hotels listed as expensive; $45 to $80 is moderate; and under $45 is inexpensive. Many of the restaurants along this route are in the hotels and inns. A dinner for two will cost $60 to $100 in an expensive restaurant; $30 to $55 is moderate; and below $30 is inexpensive.

NECKARGEMÜND

Zum Ritter – This charming inn has 41 rooms, a terrace with an extraordinary view, and a good restaurant. 40 Neckarstr. (phone: 7035). Moderate.

HIRSCHHORN

Schloss-Hotel – A hilltop castle hotel with 15 rooms, it overlooks the Neckar River valley and the small town below. Dining facilities include indoor restaurants and an outdoor terrace with an excellent view. Accommodations in the guest house annex are less expensive than those in the castle. Auf Burg Hirschhorn (phone: 1373). Moderate.

NECKARZIMMERN

Götzenburg Hornberg – Another, equally interesting castle-hotel high above the river, this place has 27 rooms and a terrace with a view of the river valley. The restaurant serves regional specialties (don't miss the mushrooms) and wines from the castle vineyards below. The atmosphere is informal (phone: 4064). Expensive to moderate.

NECKARMÜHLBACH

Burgschenke Burg Guttenberg – This fine restaurant, within the castle grounds, offers game dishes such as venison, good desserts, and local wines. The view of the valley is memorable. Closed Mondays. Burg Guttenberg (phone: 06266-228). Moderate.

HEINSHEIM

Schlosshotel Heinsheim – This baroque manor and guest house has its own palace chapel, swimming pool, estate gardens, and vineyard. Indoor and outdoor dining and a classic drawing room provide the final touches. It has excellent service, friendly atmosphere, and good food. In Heinsheim on the left bank, near Bad Wimpfen (phone: 07264-1045). Moderate.

BAD FRIEDRICHSHALL

Schloss Lehen – A quiet, elegant house set back from the road, this hotel is surrounded by greenery and gardens. Built in the 1400s, it offers a homelike atmosphere and a good restaurant. 2 Hauptstr., on the edge of town on the right bank (phone: 4044). Moderate.

HEILBRONN

Insel – In the heart of the city, this 120-room hotel with its own park is actually on a small island in the middle of the Neckar. The modern hotel has a café terrace, a restaurant offering Swabian specialties, and a French restaurant. Most of its rooms have balconies. Friedrich Ebert Brücke (phone: 6300). Expensive.

Wirtshaus am Götzenturm – The idols' tower (*Götzenturm*) in the medieval city wall gave this restaurant its name. Try the fish and the local Württemberg wines. The owner also runs the *Beichtstuhl* wine cellar around the corner. Open evenings only. Closed Sundays. 1 Allerheiligenstr. (phone: 80534). Expensive to moderate.

STUTTGART

Graf Zeppelin – Near the main railroad station, this hotel is the city's largest. It has an indoor swimming pool, sauna, health club, disco, and a pleasant dining room. 7 Arnulf Klett Pl. (phone: 299881). Very expensive.

Alte Post – In a comfortable old tavern, this inn provides regional cuisine and seafood. Among the specialties are medallions of veal, filet of sole in lobster sauce, shrimp cocktail, and fresh oysters when in season. The service matches the high standards of the kitchen. Reservations suggested. Closed Saturdays, Sundays, and Mondays before supper, and early August. 43 Friedrichstr. (phone: 293079). Expensive.

Am Schlossgarten – Completely renovated a few years back, this centrally located property offers above-standard comfort. Two restaurants, one with a terrace view, are next door. 23 Schillerstr. (phone: 20260). Expensive.

Goldener Adler – Regional Swabian dishes — *maultaschen, spätzle,* and fresh mussels — are the specialties of this downtown restaurant. Also, try a bottle of its Württemberg red wine. Closed Mondays. 38 Böheimstr. (phone: 640-1762). Moderate.

TÜBINGEN

Krone – With tasteful traditional furnishings, modern facilities, and an international menu, this 55-room hotel fits well into the atmosphere of the old university town. 1 Uhlandstr. (phone: 1036). Expensive.

The Black Forest

The Black Forest (*Schwarzwald,* in German) lies in southern Germany, bounded roughly by a rectangle made from the cities of Rastatt, Basel, Schaffhausen, and Pforzheim. It is inappropriately named, as the forests are no darker or blacker here than any other forests in Germany; in fact, the whole area receives considerably more sunshine than the overall average for the rest of the country. It is a bright, open land of tree-covered mountains, rolling hills, and intermittent pine and birch forests. There are ski resorts and spas. The ordinary mountain towns are small, rustic, and colorful, often tucked away in valleys of stunning serenity and beauty. Some of the larger cities, such as Baden-Baden and Freiburg, are renowned as cultural centers, but many of the small towns are quaintly provincial in their outlook — in fact, some of the people still wear their regional costumes.

Throughout its history, the Black Forest region has clung tenaciously to its own identity. During the Thirty Years War, the area passed from the hands of the Austrians to the French and then to the Bavarians. The French got it back again for a short time in 1679, then the Austrians returned in 1697, after which the area remained in the Austrian sphere of influence. It became part of the German duchy of Baden and the kingdom of Württemberg in 1815. Now it's part of the state known as Baden-Württemberg. All of this turbulent history has given the Schwarzwalders a strong sense of their own identity; indeed, they revel in their own customs and manners.

There's hardly a section of the Black Forest that is lacking in beauty and charm. If you take the Autobahn from Basel to Baden-Baden, the distance is 102 miles (163 km); our incomparably more scenic byway climbs over the 4,898-foot Feldberg mountain peak and runs along the renowned Schwarzwälder Tälerstrasse (Rte. 294), just to name two of its highlights. The tour could be made in as little as 1 day, but you'll probably prefer to spend 2 or 3.

To hurry through an area like the Schwarzwald is to miss such delights as staying in half-timbered little *Gasthäuser* (hotels) with warm smoky dining rooms where the locals drink their nightly beer and *Kirschwasser,* a fiery local distillation made from cherries. The speedy traveler would also miss such regional specialties as *Schwarzwälder Schinken,* a smoked ham sliced so thin it is transparent; or the luscious taste of fresh mountain trout, cooked in almonds, with heaps of boiled salted potatoes as the perfect side dish. Brochures, maps, and information about the region are available from the tourist office, Fremdenverkehrsverband Schwarzwald e.V., 45 Bertholdstr., 7800 Freiburg (phone: 31317).

En Route from Basel – Starting from the southwest corner of the Black Forest, near the Swiss border town of Basel, it is only a quick 15-minute drive north to Lörrach on Route 317. There are some interesting ruins above Lörrach called Burg Rötteln, and the town museum contains many fine examples of Black Forest handiwork, such as wood carving, clock making, and religious figurines.

Continuing on Route 317, it is a 25-mile (40-km) drive to the village of Todtnau, at an altitude of 2,169 feet. The air here is so clean and pure that Todtnau has been recommended as a resort for people with respiratory ailments. There are not many manmade attractions in the area, but there is still plenty to do. In the winter, the area is renowned for its skiing (both downhill and cross-country) and in the summer, the hikers come out in droves to tramp through the woods and valleys that make up the region surrounding the town. For summer visitors, there is also swimming (both indoor and outdoor pools available), miniature golf, and open-air concerts.

At Todtnau the road splits, with Route 317 continuing east to Titisee via the route over the Feldberg, the highest mountain peak in the Black Forest (4,898 feet). This is a very scenic drive, well worth the time. The Feldberg offers the best skiing in the Black Forest, and during the summer the views from this mountain area are unequaled in the entire region.

As magnificent as the drive over the Feldberg may be, there is an equally attractive way to the city of Freiburg from the turnoff at Todtnau. The road is smaller and narrower, and closed in the winter, but the mountain scenery is superb. This is the Schauinsland Strasse, over the Schauinsland peak, which at 4,212 feet is one of the taller mountains in the Schwarzwald.

FREIBURG: Freiburg is a modern, bustling city of more than 180,000 people, yet it maintains its sense of Old World charm as surely as an aged *Schwarzwälderin* with her round *Bollenhut* on her head. As the Freiburgers say, , it is West Germany's smallest "big town," and where else can you find a modern city that has the cleanest and most sparkling gutters in Europe, with fresh mountain water running through them continuously?

Freiburg was badly damaged during bombing raids in World War II, yet today all of the damage has been repaired, and the famed cathedral, with its 386-foot Gothic tower and spectacular stained glass windows, is the equal of any European church. This is the only Gothic cathedral in Germany that was totally completed during the Middle Ages. (The cathedrals in both Cologne and Ulm were not finished until the 19th century.) Opposite the south side of the cathedral stands the 16th-century *Kaufhaus,* originally erected as a merchants' hall but now used as a festival hall on special occasions. Its shocking color — a cross between blood red and gallbladder yellow — only makes it stand out from the rest of the buildings in the Münsterplatz. Nearby is the Rathausplatz, which contains an unusual Rathaus (town hall), formed by joining two old patrician houses that stood beside each other. Other important sights in the city are the Haus zum Walfisch (Whalehouse) near the Rathaus and the *Augustiner Museum* (Augustinerpl.), which contains medieval and baroque art of the Upper Rhine region.

Freiburg is also known for its cozy little wine taverns, with many of them dispensing wine that has been grown and cultivated within the city limits. For a good local wine, try a Freiburger Schlossberg (though perhaps the best wine in the entire Baden region is made a few miles to the west in the village of Ihringen, where the Doktorgarten and Winklerberg are both considered excellent vineyards).

FURTWANGEN: From Freiburg it is a short drive along Route 31 to the turnoff for Route 500 (north). There are several scenic overlooks along this road, each one of them worth a stop. During the summer, the mountain valleys will be alive with little white and blue flowers, and the tiny villages, many of them nothing more than a handful of houses with barns attached, all seem too perfect to be real.

Furtwangen is worth a stop because of its excellent clock museum (Uhrenmuseum), which is open daily from April through October; closed weekends from November through March. Here, virtually anything that can be made to tell time has been garnered into the museum and displayed. There are cuckoo clocks of every shape, size, and description, from a tiny clock that would fit into the palm of the hand and gives off a cuckoo like a canary with laryngitis to a monstrous old wall-hanger with a cuckoo that still sounds like a canary with laryngitis. There are grandfather clocks, grandmother clocks, and clocks that are simply grand.

TRIBERG: Just before Route 500 winds its way down into Triberg, there is a turnoff with a magnificent view of the surrounding valley. This is also the entrance to the Triberger Waterfall, the highest waterfall in all of Germany at 492 feet. An interesting walk begins at the top of the waterfall and continues down the path beside it to the town of Triberg, a distance of about 3 miles (4.8 km), all on carefully manicured trails with handrails. Sections of the waterfall are beautiful, but don't expect anything on the scale of Niagara or Victoria Falls: It simply is not that kind of waterfall.

Triberg itself is both pretty and interesting. No visitor should miss the *Heimatmuseum,* a collection of local handicrafts and woodcarvings. There is also a fine collection of clocks in the museum, and a room completely decorated with woodcarving

— walls, ceiling, benches, everything. Also in the museum is a collection of old mechanical musical instruments, including player pianos and an old pipe organ that still plays with the loudest racket imaginable. Children of all ages will be entranced by the moving characters in the mechanical band.

NIEDERWASSER: Just outside Triberg, Route 500 intersects Route 33 and continues north. There is an excellent restaurant in the tiny village of Niederwasser, the *Gasthaus Rössle* (see *Best en Route*). Directly across the road from the restaurant is a gift shop selling everything from cuckoo clocks to hand-carved wooden plates, all at prices much lower than at the main tourist centers in Germany. The gift shop accepts major credit cards, a rarity in this part of Germany. Both the restaurant and the gift shop can hardly be missed, as they are the *only* things on the road near Niederwasser.

ALPIRSBACH: At Hausach, Route 500 intersects Route 294, the famous Schwarzwälder Tälerstrasse, which continues on up to Freudenstadt. Along the way, it passes through the charming village of Alpirsbach, with its Benedictine monastery, built in the year 1095.

FREUDENSTADT: Freudenstadt has one of the most elegant new market squares in all of Germany. The original market square was destroyed during the war, but the reconstruction has been well done. Aside from the Marktplatz, there is little to see in Freudenstadt, but it is an excellent town for shopping for such things as clocks and woodcarvings. There are also more than 560 miles of hiking trails leading through the woods and valleys around the town. The small *Ratskeller* is one of Germany's best.

En Route from Freudenstadt – From Freudenstadt, there are two roads to Baden-Baden. One is called the Schwarzwälder Hochstrasse, or the High Road, and the other is the continuation of the Schwarzwälder Tälerstrasse, or the Low Road. Both are beautiful at any time of year, but the Hochstrasse probably has a slight edge in natural scenery; the Tälerstrasse is easier and smoother driving, with fewer curves and hills. The two roads intersect at Baiersbronn, where the magnificent restaurant at *Kur und Sporthotel Traube* is well worth a visit.

BADEN-BADEN: Baden-Baden is internationally famous for its casino and its baths, which have been in operation since Roman times. During the 19th century, this was the most famous spa in Europe and kings and emperors from the world over came here to gamble away their fortunes by night and nurse their hangovers the next day. Though royalty is no more, Baden-Baden remains one of the most exclusive resort towns in all of Europe.

The casino at Baden-Baden is one of the most formal and elegant in all of Europe. By all means stop to admire its crystal chandeliers and oh-so-deep carpets. James Bond would feel right at home here. The castle, the Neues Schloss, is also worth a visit. Be sure to see Lichtentaler Allee, Baden-Baden's lovely and fashionable promenade along the Oos.

Baden-Baden is directly beside the main A5 Autobahn, one of the major north-south arteries in Germany, and from this point the rest of the country can easily be reached in a few hours.

BEST EN ROUTE

Because it is an area of small towns, the Black Forest (except for Baden-Baden) is generally less expensive than many other parts of Germany. A double room with breakfast will cost $80 to $130 in expensive hotels; $50 to $75, moderate; and below $50, inexpensive. A dinner for two without wine runs $50 to $90 in expensive restaurants; $30 to $45, moderate; and below $30, inexpensive.

FREIBURG

Colombi – Near the old city, opposite a park, is Freiburg's top hotel, with fine service, a comfortable and inviting lobby, a good restaurant, and a popular wine tavern. Many rooms have balconies. 16 Rotteckring (phone: 31415). Expensive.

Oberkirchs Weinstuben – This is the place for regional cooking (and comfortable guest rooms in the hotel as well). It's on a little square adjoining the lovely old *Kaufhaus*. The restaurant is an old, dark-paneled place with rustic wooden chairs. Try game dishes here: pheasant, wild boar, deer, and rabbit — all deliciously prepared. Closed Sundays. 22 Münsterpl. (phone: 31011). Expensive to moderate.

Zum Roten Bären – Directly on the Schwabentor, the old gate that still guards the entrance to the city, this is one of the oldest *Gasthäuser* in Germany, founded in 1227. Its charming Old World rooms and its excellent food at moderate prices are hard to beat. 12 Oberlinden (phone: 36913). Expensive to moderate.

Zähringer Burg – Jürgen Kavelmann, one of Freiburg's best chefs, has quickly succeeded in restoring the fine culinary tradition of this restaurant. Don't miss the fish dishes. Closed Sunday evenings and Mondays. Reservations recommended. 19 Reutebachgasse (phone: 54041). Moderate.

FURTWANGEN

Ochsen – This is a quiet place to spend the night, with good simple rooms, inexpensive food, and truly gargantuan portions. Closed Mondays. 1 Unterbregenbach (phone: 2493). Inexpensive.

TRIBERG

Park Hotel Wehrle – In a lovely park, one of the finest hotels in the Black Forest offers good service, a swimming pool, sauna, solarium, and an excellent restaurant known for its trout dishes (20 different ones are listed on the menu). It has comfortable period furniture and lots of atmosphere. Major credit cards. 24 Gartenstr. (860249). Expensive.

NIEDERWASSER

Gasthaus Rössle – In a tiny village, this excellent and reasonably priced restaurant specializes in *Rinderroulade* (small rolls of beef in a tasty brown sauce) and tender veal steaks served with fresh peas and carrots. There are also 6 guestrooms. Closed Wednesdays (phone: 392). Inexpensive.

ALPIRSBACH

Löwen Post – In the marketplace of a charming village, this is a comfortable and pleasant hotel with a good restaurant. Closed Mondays. 12 Marktpl. (phone: 2393). Inexpensive.

FREUDENSTADT

Kurhotel Sonne am Kurpark – This small hotel, in a park opposite the spa center, not only has comfortable accommodations but also boasts one of the Black Forest's best restaurants, featuring regional dishes. 63 Turnhallestr. (phone: 6044). Expensive.

BAIERSBRONN

Schwarzwaldstube – The irresistible combination of excellent food and rustic splendor, as well as a resonably priced French menu, make this one of West Germany's most highly regarded restaurants. Being part of the elegant 200-year-old *Kur und Sporthotel Traube* doesn't hurt, either. Closed Thursdays and Fridays for lunch, and most of July. Reservations recommended. 237 Tonbachstr. (phone: 4920). Expensive.

BADEN-BADEN

Brenners Parkhotel – One of Germany's most luxurious hotels, it's very expensive but worth it. Here kings, celebrities, and Arab sheiks stay. It has everything

— indoor and outdoor pools, gracious service, public areas with river views, music, dancing, miniature golf, and riding. The restaurant, formerly no better than mediocre, has improved somewhat. Solidly booked in season. 4-6 Schillerstr. (phone: 3530). Very expensive.

Pospisil's Restaurant Merkurius – This is what a restaurant ought to be in such mundane surroundings. Try the baby lobster or the leg of lamb: inspired, inspired. Closed Mondays, and for lunch Tuesdays and Saturdays. Reservations suggested. 2 Klosterbergstr., in nearby Varnhalt (phone: 07223-5474). Expensive to moderate.

The Romantic Road

The so-called Romantic Road (Romantische Strasse) runs south through Bavaria, from the imperial city of Würzburg on the Main River to the mountain frontier town of Füssen in the foothills of the snow-clad Bavarian Alps. It is romantic, not for any dramatic scenery on the road itself, which traverses gentle, wooded hills and quiet valleys, but for its glorious medieval towns, some of which are 2,000 years old, and many of which have survived much as they appeared in the Middle Ages.

The wealth of sights along this route almost defies belief. In Würzburg and some of the other towns a visitor can see the incomparable works of Tilman Riemenschneider, Master of Würzburg, a 16th-century Gothic woodcarver and sculptor with a very distinctive style. There's Rothenburg ob der Tauber, Germany's best-preserved medieval city, with its walls, fountains, and gabled patrician houses, and Augsburg, once the richest city in Europe, with elegant avenues, lovely fountains, and mansions of the rich, as well as what is probably the world's oldest extant housing project for the poor, dating from 1519. Also not to be missed are the Wies Church, the rococo masterpiece of Dominikus and Johann Baptist Zimmermann, set in the midst of meadows, and Germany's two most magnificent castles, called the Royal Castles. During the summer, the area has folk festivals, open-air operas, concerts in royal palaces, and traditional centuries-old plays.

This 215-mile (344-km) route begins in Würzburg, taking Route 27 south to Tauberbischofsheim, Route 290 to Bad Mergentheim, and Route 19 to Igersheim. It follows the Tauber River through Weikersheim and Creglingen to Rothenburg, then takes Route 25 through central Bavaria, shifts to Route 2 to Augsburg and Route 17 to Füssen in the Alpine foothills.

Although much of the route follows principal highways, some portions are on small, winding, two-way roads that pass through tiny villages. Look out for signs, because the route is not always clearly marked. In the towns, narrow, cobblestone streets make driving difficult, so you may want to look for a parking area (marked with a large, white *P* on a blue background), and then walk into the old city areas. Since there aren't many gas stations along this route, don't let your gas get too low.

For information and maps of the region, contact the tourist office in Rothenburg: Arbeitsgemeinschaft "Romantische Strasse," Fremdenverkehrsamt, 8803 Rothenburg ob der Tauber (phone: 40492 or 2038).

WÜRZBURG: Set amid the vine-clad hills of the Franconian wine country, this is Germany's outstanding baroque city. Though bombed heavily during World War II, it has been completely restored. Würzburg, which remained staunchly Catholic throughout the Reformation, is known as the "city of the Madonnas," for more than 300 statues of the Virgin stand in front of its houses. The early history of the town was dominated by the prince-bishops who lived there, first in the Marienberg Fortress and later in the Residenz, both of which are still standing. Würzburg is also famous for its art treasures, most of which are the creations of two men: the 16th-century Gothic sculptor Tilman Riemenschneider, known as the Master of Würzburg, and the 18th-century German baroque architect Balthasar Neumann, court architect to the prince-bishops.

The fortress and the palace, on opposite banks of the Main River, are still the major sights in the city. High above the town is the Marienberg Fortress, which now houses the fine *Franconian Museum of the Main* (Mainfränkisches Museum), with its extraordinary sculptures by the Master of Würzburg. Near the fortress is the Käppele, a baroque chapel with rococo decorations and a lovely view of the town, the river, and the fortress. Cross the old bridge (Mainbrücke), dating from the 15th century and decorated with statues of 11 saints, to the Residenz, where you can see the court gardens, the imperial hall (Kaisersaal), the church (Hofkirche), and the grand staircase (Treppenhaus). You might also want to see the Cathedral of St. Kilian, a Romanesque church with sculptures by Riemenschneider, and such secular baroque buildings as Zum Falkenhaus; both are near the Marktplatz on the palace side of the river.

While in this city, stop in one of the restaurants or wine taverns offering Franconian wine and *Mainfischli* (little fish from the Main River).

TAUBERBISCHOFSHEIM: This lovely little town with a 1,200-year history has several focal points: the Palace of the Prince Electors of Mainz, the Manor House and watchman's tower, the double Gothic Chapel of St. Sebastian, and the baroque Church of St. Lioba. Half-timbered buildings and Baroque courtyards lend this valley township the tranquil atmosphere of the past. The town has garnered new fame as a mecca for fencing enthusiasts. From here drive 11 miles (18 km) on Route 290 to Bad Mergentheim.

BAD MERGENTHEIM: This small town is both a spa resort and a historical center. The Order of Teutonic Knights was based in the magnificent Renaissance Mergentheim Palace from 1525 until it was dispossessed by Napoleon in 1809. Founded in 1128, during the Crusades, this religious and military order wielded considerable political power in the surrounding area. You might want to take a look at the palace with its noteworthy baroque church, which was redesigned by Balthasar Neumann during the 18th century.

En Route from Bad Mergentheim – Continue for 9 miles (14 km) to Weikersheim, where the Renaissance castle of the Princes of Hohenlohe is worth a stop for its remarkable 16th- to 18th-century furniture, tapestries, porcelain, and sculptures of emperors and empresses. Continue from Weikersheim about another 9 miles (14 km) to Creglingen and its Church of Our Lord (Herrgottskirche), about a half-mile outside the town on the Blaufelden Road. This little church in the countryside, completed in 1389, contains many art treasures, among them the masterpiece of woodcarver Tilman Riemenschneider (the 16th-century Gothic Master of Würzburg), the altar of the Virgin Mary. It's 14 miles (23 km) from here to Rothenburg. To get in the right mood for this medieval walled town, park outside the walls and walk through a gate into the medieval fortress.

ROTHENBURG: Overlooking the steep, beautiful Tauber River valley, Rothenburg ob der Tauber is the best preserved example of a medieval town in Germany. This former imperial residence has remained intact largely because it failed to recover economically from the Thirty Years War, so it is still a typical 16th-century town, its gabled houses retaining their steep Gothic roofs and oriel windows. Its huge encircling fortress walls and watchtowers are straight out of a fairy tale, and the town inside the walls is intriguingly medieval as well, with its narrow, cobblestone streets and graceful, flowing fountains. Historic inns here display skillfully crafted wrought-iron signs, and horse-drawn carriages still carry visitors through the central area of the city.

According to legend, Rothenburg was saved from destruction during the Thirty Years War by the drinking prowess of its leading citizen. When Tilly, commander of the Imperial Army, threatened to destroy the town, the burgomaster, Nusch, offered him a cup of the best local wine, after which Tilly agreed to spare the town if someone could quaff six pints all at once. Nusch obliged, and this tale is reenacted seven times a day when the clock on the *City Councillors' Tavern* (Ratstrinkstube) strikes 11 AM, noon, and 1, 2, 3, 9, and 10 PM. The doors on each side of the clock open to reveal two figures — a disbelieving General Tilly watching the town mayor empty a more than three-liter bumper of wine in one draught.

The town hall, also in the market square, has two sections, one of which is 14th-century Gothic and the other 16th- and 17th-century Renaissance. You can climb its tower for a spectacular view of the city fortifications, which are shaped like a wine goblet. From the town hall you can walk to the Herrngasse, the widest street in the city, which begins at the market square. The Herrngasse is lined with stately patrician houses, which are decorated with a variety of gables. It's a short walk to the city's oldest and mightiest gate tower, the Burgtor, which leads into the Burggarten, a lovely public garden with a view of the Tauber bend, the curious medieval two-tier bridge called the Topplerschlösschen, and the village of Detwang.

Within the city's walls, countless streets and alleyways beckon you to explore shops, galleries, restaurants, taverns, and museums.

There are festivals here at Whitsuntide (seven Sundays after Easter) and in September, and throughout the year the community sponsors cultural events, concerts, and historical plays. Information about such events is usually posted in the market square, or contact the tourist office, 2 Marktplatz (phone: 40492). There is much to see and do in Rothenburg, so this is a good place to spend at least 1 night.

En Route from Rothenburg – Drive 19 miles (31 km) on Route 25 to Feuchtwangen, where you might want to see the excellent Heimatmuseum, with its fine folklore collection, including Franconian costumes, crafts, and furniture. From here it's 8 miles (13 km) to Dinkelsbühl.

DINKELSBÜHL: Here is yet another beautifully preserved medieval city, complete with walls, towers, and gateways — all mirrored dreamily in the green waters of the town moat.

This is a sleepy 16th-century town, except during a week-long festival in mid-July known as *Children's Treat* (Kinderzeche). The festival celebrates the children of the town, who during the Thirty Years War induced the Swedish invaders to spare Dinkelsbühl. During the summer there is also an outdoor theater, performances by the Dinkelsbühl *Boys' Band,* and a night watchman who makes his rounds.

You might want to wander around the old town, with its unpaved medieval streets lined with 15th- and 16th-century houses, which are decorated with hand-carved signs and with flowers hanging from their balconies. Segringer Strasse and Nördlinger Strasse are particularly interesting, as is the Deutsches Haus on Martin-Luther-Strasse, with its elaborate Renaissance decorations. St. George's Church, in the center of town, is a 15th-century Gothic structure with remarkable carvings and a Romanesque tower. It's about 19 miles (31 km) from here to Nördlingen on Route 25.

NÖRDLINGEN: Known as the living medieval city, this fortified town has retained not only its ancient buildings and city walls, but medieval customs and costumes as well. In the Rübenmarkt in the center of this circular town, the peasants still wear traditional dress on market days. The town is completely encircled by roofed parapet walks that pass the wall's many towers and gates. A watchman still surveys the town, calling out at night from the top of the tower of the late Gothic Church of St. George. The 15th-century church, with its tower of volcanic rock and its lavishly decorated interior, is worth seeing; its lovely painted altarpiece by Friedrich Herlin, however, is in the town museum.

En Route from Nördlingen – It's 11 miles (18 km) to Harburg, where a castle stands guard over a lovely hamlet on the Wörnitz River. The Harburg Castle is worth a stop for the art treasures in its museum — illuminated manuscripts, engravings, Gothic tapestries, and woodcarvings by the incomparable Riemenschneider.

At Donauwörth, yet another medieval town 6 miles (10 km) farther, the Wörnitz River meets the Danube; here our route continues along the Lech River on Route 2 for the 27 miles (43 km) to Augsburg.

AUGSBURG: Historical buildings of every style and epoch grace this, Bavaria's third largest city, the oldest on the Romantic Road. Founded in 15 BC, Augsburg was a Roman provincial capital for 450 years and a free imperial city for 500 years. Two fabulously wealthy families dominated Augsburg during the 15th and 16th centuries, making it a major trading and banking center. The Fuggers, financiers of the Habsburg dynasty, wielded enormous power and influence; the Welsers once owned most of Venezuela.

During and after its Renaissance heyday, Augsburg attracted artists and humanists. Both Holbeins were born here as was the architect Elias Holl, who created the town hall (1620) and other Renaissance buildings. Later, Leopold Mozart, father of the great composer, was born here, and his house still stands as a museum (30 Frauentorstr.; phone: 324-2196). Not far from here, in a side street off Leonhardsberg street, is the house in which the late German playwright Bertolt Brecht was born, in 1898. It, too, is now a museum (phone: 324-2744).

Start at the huge town hall; in front is the impressive Fountain of Augustus, created in 1594. Walk south on the beautiful, wide Maximilianstrasse, the main street, decorated with fountains and lined with mansions built by the wealthy Renaissance burghers. Behind the lovely Hercules Fountain is the very attractive Church of St. Ulrich and St. Afra, built in 1500. Since the 1555 Peace of Augsburg between German Catholics and Protestants, it has contained a Catholic and a Protestant church.

Also worth seeing is the town cathedral, north of the town hall, which has 11th-century bronze doors, the oldest stained glass windows in Germany (12th century), and paintings by Holbein the Elder. The Schaezler Palace (46 Maximilianstr.) contains a magnificently decorated rococo banqueting hall and works by such German masters as Hans Holbein the Elder and Dürer and by non-Germans such as Rembrandt, Rubens, and Veronese. Take a look at the Fuggerei, east of the town center, a housing project for the poor, built by the Fugger family in 1519 and still in operation today; it includes 4 gates, a church, 8 streets, and 66 gabled houses.

For more information about Augsburg, contact the tourist office, Verkehrsverein (7 Bahnhofstr.; phone: 502070).

En Route from Augsburg – Continue on Route 17 for about 24 miles (39 km) to Landsberg where there are many works of the Rococo (18th-century) master architects, the brothers Johann Baptist and Dominikus Zimmermann, including the Rathaus, the Johanniskirche, and the Ursulinenkirche. See the lovely Hauptplatz (main square) with its fountain and the 1425 Bavarian Gate (Bayertor) with its turrets and sculptures.

Continuing toward Füssen on Route 17, don't miss the short detour at Wies to see the marvelous Wies Church, acknowledged as the greatest achievement of Rococo art in Germany, the work of Dominikus and Johann Baptist Zimmermann. Set in the meadows, surrounded by woods, this magnificently ornamented structure was so lovingly built between 1746 and 1754 that Dominikus Zimmermann spent the last 10 years of his life nearby, unwilling to leave his finest creation. The simple exterior stands in marked contrast to the rich interior, with its oval cupola, elaborate woodcarvings, paintings, frescoes, and giltwork — all beautifully lit by many well-placed windows. Time has taken its toll, however, and the church is now undergoing renovation.

SCHWANGAU: Near this small town just 2 miles (3 km) east of Füssen are the two most impressive castles in all Germany, Hohenschwangau and Neuschwanstein, called the Royal Castles (Königsschlösser). Originally a 12th-century castle, Hohenschwangau was restored in 1832-36 by Maximilian II of Bavaria, father of King Ludwig II, "mad king Ludwig," who grew up here, befriended Richard Wagner, and later created the far more extravagant Neuschwanstein in 1886.

Hohenschwangau is in neo-Gothic style, furnished with cherry and maple Biedermeier furniture and decorated with many heavy royal art objects, including a piano on which Wagner played. Neuschwanstein was designed to look like a fairy tale, with its gables, turrets, and pinnacles, perched on a hill overlooking the forests and lakes of the Füssen region. Many of its interiors are made to recall Wagner operas, including an artificial stalactite grotto straight out of *Tannhäuser.* The furnishings are so fabulous as to appear unreal, with tapestries, carvings, chandeliers, gilt, and marble — all on a grand scale. Unfortunately King Ludwig lived here for only 102 days before he committed suicide.

FÜSSEN: This mountain frontier town, once the summer residence of the Augsburg bishops, includes a palace and church high above the River Lech. The majestic wall of Alps behind the town provides a fitting setting for this spa and winter-sports resort. The medieval stone buildings of the town lend a picturesque quality to this, the final stop on the Romantic Road. From here, if you wish, you can cross through mountain passes into the Austrian portion of the Alps.

BEST EN ROUTE

Even though the Romantic Road is very popular with tourists, its hotel and restaurant prices are rather reasonable by West German standards. Rooms with baths are often much more costly then those without. Prices quoted here are for a double room, with bath, breakfast, and service included. On this route, expensive hotels will charge $85 to $140; moderate prices are $40 to $80 and inexpensive is $25 to $35.

A dinner for two will cost $60 to $90 in an expensive restaurant; $30 to $55 in a moderate one; and below $30 in an inexpensive place. Note that many of the restaurants on this route are in the hotels and inns, and are described in the hotel listing.

WÜRZBURG

Rebstock – Once a palace, now a modern hotel with more than 80 rooms, it has a neo-classic façade and is furnished with a harmonious mixture of traditional and modern pieces. It has an attractive terrace, 2 restaurants, and comfortable rooms. Closed Sundays for dinner. 7 Neubaustr. (phone: 30930). Moderate.

Bürgerspital Weinstuben – This traditional wine tavern is a must. The wines are almost impossible to find elsewhere, and Franconian dishes, like *Bratwurst mit Kraut,* are hearty. Closed Tuesdays and mid-July to mid-August. 19 Theaterstr. (phone: 13861). Inexpensive.

ROTHENBURG OB DER TAUBER

Burghotel – A large half-timbered house on the old city wall, this hotel also offers a good view at somewhat less expense than the hotels noted above. It's charmingly set in a small garden with a pool, is attractively decorated, and offers friendly service. 1 Klostergasse (phone: 5037). Expensive.

Eisenhut – A colorful, historical inn, this luxurious 86-room hotel is actually several medieval patrician houses joined together. This is also Rothenburg's top restaurant, with prices to match. Excellent international cuisine and wine can be enjoyed in the richly paneled, galleried dining hall or on the garden terrace overlooking the Tauber River. Try the trout specialties in season. 3-5 Herrngasse (phone: 2041). Expensive.

Goldener Hirsch – In a quaint section of the city, this 80-room hotel is a remake of a 17th-century inn. A comfortable hotel with traditional taste and good service, it features the *Blue Terrace* (Blaue Terrasse) restaurant, with a panoramic view of the river valley. 16 Untere Schmiedgasse (phone: 2051). Expensive.

Baumeisterhaus – Right off the marketplace in a patrician residence built in 1596, this restaurant has a beautiful courtyard, good German food, and reasonable prices. 3 Obere Schmiedgasse (phone: 3404). Moderate.

Ratsstube – Also on the marketplace and very popular, this tavern-style restaurant features such regional dishes as blood sausages with sauerkraut and Bavarian mixed grill. Don't miss the white asparagus dishes in season (May-June). 6 Marktpl. (phone: 5511). Inexpensive.

Zur Höll – A wine tavern — in the town's oldest house (1222) on the town's oldest street — that's well worth a visit, both for its Franconian wines and regional dishes. Open evenings only; closed Tuesdays. 8 Burggasse (phone: 4229). Inexpensive.

BAD MERGENTHEIM

Victoria – This 100-room hotel-spa has bath, massage, and swimming facilities, as well as an excellent restaurant, *Zirbelstuben*. Guests also can dine on the attractive rooftop garden terrace, where there is a heated, glassed-in swimming pool. Rooms have baths and glassed-in balconies. 2 Poststr. (phone: 5930). Expensive.

DINKELSBÜHL

Deutsches Haus – A half-timbered house dating from 1440, this 13-room inn, decorated with richly painted designs and woodcarvings, is elegantly furnished. Its restaurant serves local specialties. 3 Weinmarkststr. (phone: 2346). Moderate.

Goldene Rose – In the heart of town, this pretty, 6-story inn dates from 1450. The 20 rooms are modernized though furnished with antiques, and the hotel offers a homey atmosphere at a reasonable rate. It also has a good restaurant. Closed January and February. 4 Marktpl. (phone: 831). Moderate.

NÖRDLINGEN

Sonne – Next to the town hall and the cathedral, this Old World inn, dating from 1477, has been modernized. It offers 40 comfortable rooms, good service, and a choice of dining rooms. Restaurant closed Fridays. 3 Marktpl. (phone: 5067). Moderate.

AUGSBURG

Drei Mohren – Combining contemporary with traditional decor, this rebuilt 110-room hotel, famous since 1723, was destroyed in an air raid in 1945. Rebuilt in a somewhat overly opulent style, it still offers first class accommodations. Its formal dining room serves international cuisine and features such specialties as venison and filet of sole with white wine sauce. It also has an attractive garden terrace. 40 Maximilianstr. (phone: 510031). Expensive.

Hotel Fischertor – This new restaurant is one of Augsburg's finest. Nouvelle cuisine reigns supreme here. Try the duck with shrimp and avocado cream or the calf's liver with mushrooms. The wines and the service are equally topnotch. Reservations suggested. Closed Sundays and Mondays. 6 Pfärrle (phone: 518662). Expensive.

Gunzenlee – Six miles (10 km) southeast of town, this restaurant has an extensive international menu. The charcoal-grilled meats are one of the best bets. In warm weather you can dine on a pleasant garden terrace. Kissing, 14 Münchner Str. (phone: 08233-6139). Moderate.

Fuggerkeller – Noted not only for its setting — vaulted, cavelike rooms below street level in the former Fugger residence — but also for its fine food and drink. The strong, dark Fugger beer is an experience. Closed Sundays after lunch and in August. 38 Maximilianstr. (phone: 516260). Moderate to inexpensive.

Ratskeller – This town hall restaurant has particularly good, solid German food at reasonable prices. Closed Mondays, Sunday evenings, and in June. 2 Rathauspl. (phone: 154086). Moderate to inexpensive.

HOHENSCHWANGAU

Schlosshotel Lisl und Jägerhaus – Near the two royal castles, this 60-room spot is comfortable and offers a spectacular view. The graciously styled hotel has a terrace and is surrounded by its own gardens. Its dining rooms serve local and international foods. Closed January and February. 1 Neuschwansteinstr. (phone: 8-1006). Expensive to moderate.

FÜSSEN

Hirsch – This 48-bed hotel, centrally located, has a large restaurant. Closed from December to mid-February. 2 Augsburger Tor-Pl. (phone: 6055). Expensive.

Sonne – Also in the center of Füssen, this hotel has 32 comfortable, rustic rooms and a café. 37 Reichenstr. (phone: 6061). Moderate.

Pulverturm – In the idyllic spa center, it serves both continental and regional dishes. You can also dine on the pleasant terrace. Closed in November. 1 Schwedenweg (phone: 6078). Moderate to inexpensive.

Gibraltar

Whether approaching by land or sea, most first time visitors are immediately mesmerized by the Rock of Gibraltar, surely one of the world's most famous natural landmarks. "Gib" stands there, just as strong and steady as it's supposed to, thrusting up defiantly from the Mediterranean like a clenched fist. It's no wonder that this British Crown colony of about 30,000 residents is an anathema to Spain. The reasons for this go back to 1713 and the Treaty of Utrecht, which ended the War of Succession between rival French and Anglo-Dutch pretenders to the Spanish throne. At that time, Bourbon King Philip V gained the crown of Spain but was forced to cede Gibraltar to England. To this day, Spaniards will find every fault with the present British rule of the Rock and insist that Gibraltar must be returned to its rightful owners. The issue over tiny Gibraltar became so bitter that the one point of entry, over an isthmus between La Linea on the Spanish mainland and the Rock itself, was closed for a number of years to all vehicular and pedestrian traffic. And that's quite a controversy when you consider the size of the place — 3 miles long and ¾ mile wide.

On February 4, 1985, Spain reopened its border with Gibraltar, making it vastly easier on travelers who, until then, had to take a ferry or hydrofoil from Málaga or Algeciras to Tangiers, then ferry from the North African port across the Strait of Gibraltar. The crossing took several hours.

Now that the border is open, however, Gibraltar attracts plenty of foreign visitors. All purchases are VAT free, so many people come here just to shop. Others come to bask in the sun: Gibraltar has a mild climate throughout the year, as does the southern Spanish coast. There are yachting marinas, other water facilities, and deep-sea fishing. And, in addition to the historic interest, Gibraltar's very British atmosphere exists in striking contrast to the neighboring Spanish communities and the Moroccan cities across the Strait. However, the Union Jack flies over photographs of the Queen that are emblazoned with the slogan: "Keep the Rock British." Gib is very much a part of the British Empire.

Conflict over who owns the Rock goes back many centuries. In the year 711, the Moorish King Tarik ibn Ziyad landed on the Rock and gave his name to the promontory that was to be the stepping-off point of his invasion of Spain. The pronunciation of Jabal al Tariq (Tarik's Mountain) was modified over the 7 centuries of Moorish rule to become "Gibraltar." Queen Isabel herself personally led Christian troops to capture Gibraltar in 1462 as part of her strategy to weaken the Moors' supply route from nearby Morocco and definitively reconquer all of Spain. The Peñón de Gibraltar, or Rock of Gibraltar, was an integral part of peninsular Spain until the early 18th century, when the Rock was ceded to Britain. During the Great Siege of 1779–83, the Strait of Gibraltar was the battleground of rival European navies. As later proved by the Battle of Trafalgar, the British fleet led by Admiral Nelson was far superior to the Hispano-French armadas, and Gibraltar was retained by the victorious British.

The border was closed in 1969 by Generalissimo Francisco Franco, and the Spanish government issued a strong protest to the UN against the British colonial "occupation" of a territorial possession of Spain. The countries of the NATO Pact repeatedly vetoed attempts to challenge British control over the vitally strategic air and naval bases that are on the Rock of Gibraltar. However, the Brussels Agreement of November 1984 paved the way for the full opening of the frontier in February 1985, allowing people and goods to cross the border. Under this agreement, the British and Spanish governments decided to discuss all differences over Gibraltar, including sovereignty.

THE ROCK OF GIBRALTAR: Surging from the sea to a height of 1,400 feet, the Rock looms up like some familiar life insurance company's advertisement. Originally, the Romans believed the Rock to be one of the two Pillars of Hercules, the entryway to the Mare Nostrum (literally, "Our Sea," or the Mediterranean) and gateway to Western civilization. Beyond the pillars to the west was the Unknown, the end of the world. What was unknown has long since passed into the domain of knowledge, and you can gaze upon it by taking a cable car to the summit of the Rock. The view on a clear day extends north to Granada's Sierra Nevada, south to the glimmering Strait of Gibraltar, and beyond to the Atlas and Rif mountains of Morocco.

Halfway up the hill, the Apes' Den is the home of the only wild simians of Europe. The mystery surrounding the presence of these tailless monkeys on the Rock has given rise to several theories. The one most generally accepted is that the monkeys found subterranean caves in Morocco and followed the passageways 10 miles under the Strait to emerge on Gibraltar. Recent legend has it that as long as the monkeys stay, the Rock will remain British. In any event, by order of Sir Winston Churchill some years ago, the apes were declared a protected species. A word of warning for your own protection: Do not feed the apes — they are fond of human fingers.

At another ridge of the Rock, the ruins of the 14th-century Tower of Homage are a reminder of the original Moorish castle overlooking this strategic strait. You can reach the tower via winding Willis' Road; inexpensive minibus tours of the Rock leave from Gibraltar Town or cars can be rented. When hiring a car, remember that traffic stays to the right. Since blowing your horn is forbidden, it is customary to pound on the side of the car to warn other drivers of your approach or to signal danger.

GIBRALTAR TOWN: The capital has a museum containing intact Moorish baths, several nightclubs, a glamorous new casino, and 2 marinas.

The Week of the Sea sailing competitions lure planeloads of English visitors every summer, as do the July concert festivals. Shoppers always crowd Gibraltar Town's Main Street to take advantage of VAT-free prices on brand-name and luxury items or to barter for Moroccan handicrafts at the Oriental bazaars.

THE GALLERIES: Northeast of town, farther up Queen's Road, are the galleries. Carved out of the Rock by the British during the Great Siege and expanded by Allied engineers during World War II, some sections of the 30 miles of tunnels can be visited today. Labyrinths winding 370 feet deep remain off-limits to civilians.

THE CAVES OF ST. MICHAEL: First explored in 1936, these caves are testimony to the extraordinary geological formation of Gibraltar. Some 1,000 feet above sea level, they feature an underground lake, an amphitheater with wonderfully illuminated stalactites, and an eerie subterranean breeze that could well come from Africa. The sound and light spectacle is thrilling, as is the drive to the caves, up steep Queen's Road, to the southwest of Gibraltar Town.

BEACHES: The best swimming and fishing spots are at Catalán Bay, a village first founded by Italian immigrants on the eastern side of the Rock. Other Mediterranean swimming sites are Eastern Beach and Sandy Bay. On the Bay of Gibraltar, there are 2 rocky beaches — Camp Bay and Little Bay.

EUROPA POINT: Marking the very tip of continental Europe, this is a good spot to view Africa, to the south. The lighthouse, which dates from 1841, is near the Shrine of Our Lady of Europe and guides mariners to safe port. Driving back to Gibraltar Town along Europa Road, stop off at the Alameda Gardens, where there is a monument to General Elliot, the British commander during the Great Siege.

BEST EN ROUTE

Expect to pay about $125 for a double room at either hotel and between $50 and $60 for a meal for two at the *Rock*. The pubs are inexpensive, about $20 for a meal for two.

Holiday Inn – Centrally located and recently remodeled. Facilities include a rooftop swimming pool, sauna, dining room, and coffee shop. Airport transportation is provided and pets are welcome. Major credit cards. Governor's Parade (phone: 70500). Expensive.

Rock – Overlooking the town on the western slopes, with views across the bay. There is a saltwater pool and a playground on the premises. The dining room is quite modern and features international, predominantly European, cuisine. Roast beef with Yorkshire pudding is on the menu. 3 Europa Rd. (phone: 73000). Expensive.

Main Street pubs – Too numerous to list individually, these most British of establishments are the best places to eat in Gibraltar. They have English beer, such as Watney's Red and Guinness, plus a full complement of munchies — Scotch eggs, sausages, and cheese. Inexpensive.

Great Britain

The term Great Britain properly refers, not just to England, but also to Scotland, Wales, and Northern Ireland — the northeastern tip of the island of Ireland that lies to the west of England and Wales, across the Irish Sea. In more recent years the name United Kingdom has become popular, supplanting the Victorian conceit of Great Britain as the heart of an empire that, until World War II, dominated 40% of the planet. Even today, the British influence, from language to such idiosyncratic sports as cricket and rugby, is found worldwide. The British parliamentary system is the midwife, if not the mother, of all modern democracies. The Industrial Revolution was born here.

The semantic change from Great Britain to the United Kingdom reflects the growing nationalist movements England has been forced to accommodate, particularly in Scotland and Wales, where an emphasis on rediscovering, saving, and developing "lost" traditions and language has found a strong resurgence. In Ireland, this changing relationship is one of the underlying causes of the present "troubles" (the British are nothing if not masters of understatement) with Protestant Loyalists (that is, loyal to the British Crown), who are fighting a rear-guard action to maintain control of Northern Ireland when the majority of the population is Catholic.

England, the largest landmass of the four "states" of the United Kingdom, has dominated and controlled the others for centuries. Ireland and Wales were joined to England by the end of the 13th century (which is why, today, the eldest son of the reigning monarch is made Prince of Wales); the English and Scottish thrones were joined at the death of Elizabeth I, in 1603, in the person of James I of England and James VI of Scotland. To a great extent, the history of Great Britain is the history of England, its kings and queens and its parliament. Indeed, the average American is not aware that while the British constitution has never been set down on paper, British Common Law, which goes back to 1066 and William the Conqueror, is England's constitution and has provided a sound basis for the American and other legal systems. Where the US has its Supreme Court as the final arbiter of constitutionality, Great Britain has the House of Lords.

Caught between a reverence for tradition and history that sometimes stifles innovation and the fear that clinging slavishly to its past will turn the country into a "Third World has-been," the UK is painfully discovering that it can no longer compete alone on the world stage. Thus, it became a reluctant member of the European Economic Community (the so-called Common Market) and is now drawing toward a federation of European states that, by 1992, will be the economic equal of the United States and Japan.

It is now clear that Britannia no longer rules the waves, and the British have been adjusting to that hard fact since World War II. Like the Romans, who also once dominated most of the world, the British possess a talent for government. Since 1215, when the nobles forced King John to sign the Magna Carta, rulers have wisely recognized the rights of their subjects. With no written constitution, the complicated British system of Common Law has also long contained safeguards for individual liberties. Above all, the English system is stable, and its revered institutions and traditions have survived the vicissitudes of history with only a single brief civil war. Since revolution just isn't the English way, the people have incorporated changes into their existing institutions by yielding certain rights to the nobles in 1215, to Parliament in 1660, to the middle class in 1832, and to the working class in 1867. Characteristically, the English never abandoned their aristocracy as other European monarchies did; instead, they kept augmenting its ranks by admitting wealthy or accomplished men and women to the peerage.

English people are known for their reserve. Foreigners often have viewed them as silent, cold, morose, melancholy, or just plain snobbish. Many writers, English and foreign, have wondered about the British character. Some have claimed that the British silence stems from a need, as inhabitants of a crowded island, for solitude and peace. Others have claimed they are merely shy. George Santayana, the Spanish-born philosopher, suggested that the Englishman is governed by an "inner atmosphere, the weather in his soul"; similarly, J. B. Priestley, the English novelist and critic, asserted that the English are suspicious of the purely rational and rely upon instinct and intuition more than other Western Europeans do. Their reliance upon intuition might be one clue to the extraordinary wealth and beauty of English literature, which — unlike the stereotypical and probably mythical Englishman — tends to be exuberant and romantic, as the plays of Shakespeare amply testify. The more one examines the English character, however, the more elusive and contradictory it appears; for if the English are traditional and conservative, they are also a nation of eccentrics. If they're gloomy, they are also well known for their marvelous senses of humor, as evidenced by the English comedies that continue to delight audiences of stage and screen.

The British inhabit, in the words of poet William Blake, a "green and pleasant land." Their plentiful rainfall makes for grass that is greener than that of most other countries. Because of the warming effects of the Gulf Stream, roses often bloom until Christmas. Moderation, a keynote of the British character and climate, extends also to the islands' geography. Both are moderate in size, with Great Britain the 8th largest and Ireland the 20th largest island on earth. Compared with other places, Britain has no dramatic geographical features; its mountains and lakes, though lovely, are not unusual in magnitude.

With Northern Ireland, Britain occupies a total of 94,196 square miles, a few miles off the northwestern coast of Europe. The island of Great Britain is not much larger than the state of Arkansas. Most of southern England, except Devon and Cornwall, is lowlands, while the Lake District, Scotland, and Wales are chiefly mountainous. Much of northern England consists of rolling upland scenery. England is divided from Scotland to the north by the Tweed and Liddel rivers and the Cheviot Hills; Wales is a landmass on England's west coast.

The British are a nation of city dwellers; 81% of Britain's 56 million people live in urban areas. London, the capital of England (Edinburgh is the capital of Scotland; Cardiff, of Wales; and Belfast, of Northern Ireland), is by far Britain's largest city, with a population of over 7 million. Birmingham and Manchester, English industrial cities farther north, rank second and third, with 1 million and half a million respectively.

If you have come in search of the "merrie England" of endless villages and farms, you will be disappointed, because relatively little of that remains; nevertheless, mementos of earlier days are everywhere, for the British love history and tradition. Stonehenge and Avebury stand as awesome reminders of a prehistoric Britain, occupied by Bronze Age people even before the Celts arrived in the 5th century BC. Later invaders included the Romans in 55 BC, the Germanic tribes of the Angles, Saxons, and Jutes in the 5th century AD, and, finally, the Normans in 1066.

When the Angles and Saxons invaded, the Celts retreated to Wales, Cornwall, Scotland, and Brittany (France), where they remain to this day. Both Welsh and Gaelic are linguistic outgrowths of a Celtic tongue; English, however, is based upon the Germanic Anglo-Saxon, with the addition of a heavy sprinkling of Norman French. Besides French vocabulary and manners, William the Conqueror brought feudalism to England. Nearly 2 centuries later, in 1215, powerful nobles forced King John to sign the Magna Carta in recognition of their feudal rights.

The next important event in English history was the Hundred Years War, a dynastic struggle with France from 1337 to 1428 punctuated by outbreaks of the Black Death. As England recovered from these disasters, its wool trade prospered and towns grew, along with their new merchant and artisan classes.

The central government expanded under the great Tudor monarchs, particularly Henry VIII and Elizabeth I, who ruled an increasingly strong and prosperous nation from 1485 to 1603. In 1529, Henry VIII broke with the pope, who refused to grant him a divorce, and established the Church of England. Elizabeth was queen during England's golden age, when Sir Francis Drake and Sir John Hawkins (and the weather) defeated the Spanish Armada, and when Christopher Marlowe, William Shakespeare, Ben Jonson, John Donne, and many other great poets and playwrights illumined the English scene.

Although James I united England and Scotland with his ascent to both thrones in 1603, the 17th century brought England to civil war, with the parliamentarians defeating the royalists in 1649, beheading Charles I, and creating the Commonwealth that lasted for 11 years under Oliver Cromwell. The monarchy that was restored in 1660 was different from the earlier one, for this time Parliament had summoned the king; from then on, kings were forced to cooperate with Parliament.

During the 18th century, the British Empire expanded to places as remote as India and North America. Britain became the world's greatest power for 200 years — this despite the loss of the 13 American colonies in 1776.

The Industrial Revolution transformed England late in the 18th century; as a result, the landed aristocracy was joined by a newly powerful middle class that was enfranchised by the Reform Bill of 1832. During the long era of Queen Victoria (1837–1901), Britain led the world in commercial, industrial, and political power. Military and economic rivalry with Germany resulted in World War I. Hitler's rise plunged Britain into World War II, when Britain had to fight Germany alone for an entire year after France fell in 1940 (Russia joined the war effort in 1941). During the heavy night bombings of its cities and the long and lonely Battle of Britain, the nation marshaled truly remarkable courage and strength. The war destroyed large urban areas, including vast chunks of London and Birmingham.

Like the Green Knight in the medieval tale *Sir Gawain and the Green Knight,* who walked off after a duel bearing his chopped-off head under his arm, the British nation has survived and renewed itself. It has transformed its colonial empire into an extensive commercial network, the British Commonwealth of Nations, and it has joined the European Common Market. Since the war it has also nationalized the Bank of England, coal, steel, and the railways, and in 1948 it established a system of socialized medicine. In recent years, however, increasing numbers of nationalized industries have been "privatized" — returned to nongovernmental ownership.

Although Britain today is struggling with the same economic pressures as the rest of the world, it is a wonderful place to visit because, among other things, Britons speak our language — or, rather, we speak theirs. Visitors will notice, however, that their English is different from that heard in America. George Bernard Shaw described the US and Great Britain as two nations separated by a common language. But whether you dream of seeing the changing of the guard at Buckingham Palace, touring the still-rural Shakespeare country, walking through the mountainous Lake District as Wordsworth and Coleridge did, surveying the English moors or the Scottish Highlands, drinking Scotch whisky at its source, watching the sun set in a sleepy Welsh fishing village, or making idle conversation in an authentic Irish pub — these joys and many other surprises await you in Britain.

Any trip to Great Britain should begin in London, one of the great cities of the world. From here you can explore Britain, using any or all of our suggested tour routes. You can see Southeast England by starting near London in Canterbury, proceeding to the coast at Dover, and from there southwest to the resort of Brighton. Traveling farther west, our tour of Southwest England begins at the ancient religious site of Stonehenge and continues west to the rocky peninsula of Devon and Cornwall, past Exeter, the wild and forbidding plain of Dartmoor, and the castle at Tintagel, where the legendary King Arthur is said to have been born. Also to the west is Wales, with its three national parks (Snowdonia, Pembrokeshire, and Brecon Beacons) and its jagged coast sprinkled with charming fishing villages.

Southeast of Wales, the Cotswolds, Shakespeare's country, is one of the prettiest rural districts in England; our circular route, which begins at Bath and ends in Oxford, includes the lovely Cotswolds and Stratford-upon-Avon, Shakespeare's birthplace. Farther north, the Lake District, where the 19th-century Lake Poets — William Wordsworth and Samuel Taylor Coleridge among them — loved to roam, has been preserved as a national park, with lovely mountains, lakes, and fields bounded by dry stone walls.

Crossing England's narrow waist to the opposite coast, our tour of Northeast England begins at York, circling through the Yorkshire moors before heading north along the coast, then branching inland through Durham and Newcastle upon Tyne to Berwick-on-Tweed at the Scottish border. It's easier to explore Scotland in three parts: the Lowlands, or southern section, from Edinburgh to Glasgow and Abbotsford, with their battlefields and sites made famous by Sir Walter Scott; the Highlands, the eastern and central region of magnificent mountains and moors; and finally, Western Scotland, Robert Burns country — a coastal route, a place of resorts, and an ideal departure point for the Hebrides, the rugged islands off Scotland's western coast. The last route goes through Northern Ireland, the ancient province of Ulster, with its uncrowded beaches, bays, cliffs, and castles and its two highest ranges, the Mountains of Mourne in the southeast and the Sperrin Mountains in the north. Though the violence in Northern Ireland is sporadic, coverage of it since the late 1960s has dampened tourism considerably, which means that no crowds will interfere with your pleasure.

Southeast England: Kent, Canterbury, and the Coast

For better or worse, geography conspired to make Kent and East Sussex — the broad foot of land that spills out below London to form the bluff-lined and beach-speckled coast of southeast England — the only welcoming mat England has ever extended to the Continent. It is country suited to landing parties, Kent's rich orchards, hop fields, thatched barns, and high-hedged roads giving way to Sussex's high South Downs, from which one can see for miles in all directions. To the north is the wide estuary of the Thames; to the south, the English Channel; and to the east, where England and France are only some 20 miles apart, the Straits of Dover.

Such an invitation has been hard for European warlords to resist, and for 2,000 years attempts have been made to enter England through the southeast. Some have been successful. The Romans established an administrative center in London, and the Normans conquered all of England after their decisive victory at the town of Battle, near Hastings, in 1066, when William the Conqueror killed King Harold. Others attempts have failed. From August to October 1940, Britain stood virtually alone against the full weight of the Nazi war machine as the Battle of Britain raged over the Weald of Kent. But each of these efforts has left some mark on this extraordinarily rich part of England. Kent, labeled the Garden of England, nurtures as much history as fruit and hops in its fertile countryside.

The major sites along England's southeast coast — as well as Canterbury, Dover, Hastings and Battle, and Brighton — can be visited on day trips from London. Travelers with little time should certainly choose the most appealing destination and make the journey (by car or, even faster, by train). But more rewarding is a perambulation through the countryside, following the coast as a rough guide, and seeing sites great and small along the way. The route outlined below runs clockwise from Canterbury to Brighton.

This route begins south of London at Westerham, near Winston Churchill's home, Chartwell, and tours some of the estates and castles in the area as it moves east to the cathedral city of Canterbury. Here, within the city's ancient walls, are the cathedral and shrine associated with St. Thomas à Becket, who was murdered here in 1170 by four knights after he defied his old friend and former lord, King Henry II.

The historic ports of Sandwich and Deal are a short drive east of Canterbury, and the famed white cliffs of Dover are just to the south. This scalloped shore, across the narrow Straits of Dover from the French coast, has been the target of invading armies from Caesar to Hitler. Along the coast are layers of fortifications, rebuilt and enlarged by successive generations, and castles and seawalls that seem ageless. The narrow channel invited smuggling during more peaceful days, and coastal marshes bred stories of betrayal and death. Read a gentle primer of gothic horror tales before you journey forth — the legends of pre-Roman and Roman blood sacrifices will come alive for you. Perhaps a little inquisitive exploration will lead you to solve the mystery of the skulls in Hythe's church.

Farther south and west, Pevensey Bay was the site of William the Conqueror's landing, and nearby is the town of Battle, where he fought Harold's army. His defeat of King Harold at the Battle of Hastings (October 14, 1066) marked the beginning of a new era for England; it is a date no English schoolchild ever forgets. Farther along the coast is the Royal Pavilion at Brighton, and the trip ends with a visit to the springs at Royal Tunbridge Wells. Its medicinal waters prompted Edward VII to elevate the town to royal status, and its charming atmosphere makes it still popular today. It is just a short drive north from here to London. For more information, contact South East England Tourist Board, 1 Warwick Park, Tunbridge Wells, Kent TN2 5TA (phone: 0892-40766).

LONDON: For a complete description of the city and its hotels and restaurants, see *London,* THE CITIES.

En Route from London – Take Route A21 south through Bromley, continuing as far as the A233 cutoff. Follow A233 south to its junction with A25 near Westerham.

WESTERHAM: *Pitt's Cottage,* a timbered house used as a summer cottage during the late 1700s by William Pitt the Younger, stands on the outskirts of town. Pitt was well regarded as a wartime prime minister and was a motivating force behind two anti-Napoleonic coalitions involving several European nations as well as Russia and England. The cottage has since been converted into a restaurant.

Westerham is the birthplace of General James Wolfe, whose victory over the French troops under the Marquis de Montcalm at Quebec on September 13, 1759, gave England control of Canada. A statue of Wolfe, who was mortally wounded during the decisive battle, stands in the village green not far from his childhood home, now called Québec House. The statue of a more recent war hero, Prime Minister Winston Churchill, shares the town center with Wolfe. Churchill's country home, Chartwell, is about 2 miles (3.2 km) south of town (via Route B2026) on a wooded hillside terraced with a series of gardens. The study where Churchill worked remains as he left it.

En Route from Westerham – Take Route A25 east about 6 miles (10 km) to the village of Sevenoaks. Knole, one of the largest and most magnificent baronial mansions in England, lies just off A25 on A225. The building, referred to by

Virginia Woolf as "a town rather than a house" in her novel *Orlando,* sprawls over 3 acres and includes (according to legend) 7 courtyards corresponding to the days of the week, 52 staircases for the weeks, and 365 rooms — one for each day in the year. The house was begun in 1456 by Archbishop Thomas Bourchier and was held by the Archbishops of Canterbury until turned over to Henry VIII. The estate, named for the grassy knoll on which it stands, was given to the Sackville-West family by Queen Elizabeth I in 1603, the year she died. The house was enlarged, and over the years the estate acquired an incredible art collection, including canvases by Gainsborough, Van Dyck, Reynolds, and others. Today the interior is furnished entirely in the Elizabethan mode, with furnishings virtually untouched since the family was first given the house (open Wednesdays through Saturdays, Sunday and Monday afternoons, and holidays, April through October).

Return to Route A25, traveling east about 2 miles (3.2 km) to the cutoff to Ightham. Ightham Mote is open April through October, Sundays, Mondays, Wednesdays, Thursdays, and Fridays. This stately 14th-century manor house, encircled by a moat, contains a beautiful Tudor chapel. If you find yourself working up a thirst, travel a bit farther to the *Crown Point Inn,* a comfortable paneled pub with its own garden in the tiny village of Seal Chart, outside Plaxtol.

Route A25 becomes M20 and leads directly into Maidstone.

MAIDSTONE: Many historic buildings line the streets of Maidstone, the bustling capital and agricultural center of Kent. Several streets in the High Street area have been closed to vehicular traffic in an effort to preserve these fine examples of early architecture. Near the town's 14th-century Church of All Saints is a tithe barn of the same period, part of the palace of the Archbishop of Canterbury, when it was used as a stable. It's now the home of the *Tyrwhitt Drake Museum,* a fine collection of ornate horse-drawn carriages (open Mondays through Saturdays and Sunday afternoons from Easter through September). The palace itself, which still exists, is open only by special arrangement.

Chillington Manor, an Elizabethan mansion on St. Faith's Street, is now the home of the *Museum and Art Gallery* and contains the memorabilia of essayist William Hazlitt, a native of Maidstone. North of town, on A229, are Allington Castle, an imposing 13th-century castle with a moat, and the Carmelite retreat, Aylesford Priory; both are open daily.

En Route from Maidstone – Readers of Charles Dickens will enjoy a short (8 mi/12.8 km) side trip north to Rochester, which appears so often in his work and, thinly disguised, is the city of Cloisterham in his last story, *The Mystery of Edwin Drood.* Dickens's home at Gad's Hill is not open, but the food, drinks, and atmosphere at the author's favorite inn, *The Leather Bottle* (in Cobham), are ample recompense. You can visit other buildings in Rochester that figure in his work — Eastgate House (now the Dickens Center), the Cathedral, and Guildhall (all open daily).

Rochester Castle, a massive Norman fortress, was erected late in the 11th century and partially rebuilt during the 14th century. The castle is 120 feet high and has walls 12 feet thick. Rochester Cathedral incorporates architectural styles from several periods, from the crypt and tower built in 1082 and the decorative mid-14th-century doorway to the Chapter Room. Open daily, from Easter to September; closed Mondays in winter.

Route A20 continues east-southeast from Maidstone toward Ashford, passing Leeds Castle. This fairy tale fortress stands in the middle of a lake — no mean task in the 1200s, when it was built. It was the home of Lord Culpepper (Governor of Virginia, 1680–83) and later his grandson, Lord Fairfax, and is open daily from April to October; open weekends only November through March.

The remains of a palace of the Archbishops of Canterbury lie within the ancient village of Charing, about 13 miles (21 km) from Maidstone. Stop at the *Swan* hotel for an ample lunch and a tasty brew before continuing south on A20 to Ashford. Pick up A28 eastbound from here to Canterbury, a distance of about 14 miles (22 km) across the meadowy downs that extend through Kent from the outskirts of London to the coast at Dover.

The main road neatly bypasses the delightful village of Chilham, so keep an eye open for the turnoff. The gardens and grounds of Chilham Castle, complete with aviaries and a "pets' corner," are open daily from March to October. Bird-handling demonstrations, with falcons and eagles, are held most afternoons. The castle is the Center of the *British Jousting Association* (jousts are held on most public holidays). The atmosphere of the *White Horse Inn* will confirm the feeling of earlier times; it has often been used in movies because of its virtually unchanged 15th-century appearance inside and out. The food is as enjoyable as the fireplace on a chilly evening, so reservations are advised.

Continuing east on Route A28, a glimpse of the three pinnacled towers of Canterbury Cathedral heralds the ancient city.

CANTERBURY: This approach leads into the heart of Canterbury through the massive West Gate used by countless pilgrims traveling to the shrine of St. Thomas à Becket. It was the murder of Archbishop Thomas à Becket in 1170, and his canonization 2 years later, that elevated the cathedral to its status as a shrine. Following 9 centuries of pilgrims, make your way along the main street and then turn left into the narrow course called Mercery Lane. Straight ahead is Christ Church Gate, leading to the cathedral precincts (or close). Give yourself plenty of time to explore the cathedral treasures — the glowing medieval stained glass windows, the ancient paintings in the crypt, and the elaborate vaulted cloisters; but there is much more to see here.

The Romans built the fortress of Durovernum on this site in AD 43. The remains of the city walls are visible near the Dane John Gardens, and the characteristic mosaic Roman roadway can still be seen at Butchery Lane.

St. Martin's Church, one of the ancient landmarks mentioned in the rhyme in George Orwell's *1984,* is one of the oldest functioning churches in England. Christian services were held here as early as AD 500, and the present building may have evolved from 4th-century Roman villas on the same site. The ruins of St. Augustine's Abbey, established by St. Augustine in AD 602 with the support of King Ethelbert, lie outside the city's East Wall, near the foot of St. Martin's Hill along Longport Street.

There are several inviting inns for food and drink, such as *The Beehive,* at 52 Dover St., and the bow-windowed *Olive Branch* in Burgate.

En Route from Canterbury – Route A257 leads due east from Canterbury to the medieval port of Sandwich, one of the original five Cinque Ports (see *En Route from Deal*). As Sandwich's harbor became clogged with silt in the 16th century, the city lost importance. It gained lasting fame, however, when the fourth Earl of Sandwich invented the world's most popular and enduring meal — the sandwich. According to legend, the earl was loath to leave the gaming tables to eat and asked that a concoction of bread and meat be made for him. The earl — who was infamous for being in charge of the admiralty when Britain lost its North American colony — was a dissolute man, and the story has something of the ring of truth about it. Two inns, the *Bell* and the *King's Arms,* will be glad to provide a sample of this handy bar snack and something with which to wash it down. Richborough Castle, just off Route A257 1.5 miles (2.5 km) north of Sandwich, was established by the Romans around AD 43 and added to by the Saxons during the 3rd century. Open daily, Easter to September. Route A258 leads to Deal, about 6 miles (10 km) south along the coast.

DEAL: Deal was an important shipping center through the early 19th century. Under Henry VIII, three castles were erected here: Deal Castle (open daily), Walmer Castle,

1 mile (1.6 km) south on A258 (open Tuesdays through Sundays), and Sandown Castle (since washed away). There is a good possibility that Caesar's forces landed along this shore when the Romans invaded Britain, and here Henry VIII feared the Pope would launch a Holy War against him as the self-proclaimed head of the Church of England. The coast off Deal, called Goodwin Sands, is a complicated series of sandbanks that are exposed at low tide. Lighthouses and lightships illuminate the area after dark, but maritime accidents persist. The narrow roadstead formed between Goodwin Sands and the coast, not the safest anchorage for shipping, is popularly known as the downs.

En Route from Deal – Traveling south on A258 toward the busy port of Dover, Walmer Castle is only 1 mile (1.6 km) from Deal. The castle has been the residence of the Lord Warden of the Cinque Ports since the mid-1700s. This association of seaports began in the 11th century, when five principal ports (Hastings, Hythe, Dover, Sandwich, and Romney — now New Romney) banded together to provide England with a makeshift navy. Later this was formalized by a charter that granted certain privileges in exchange for the pledge of supplying ships and men for the country's defense. Other ports along this southeast foot of England, the part closest to France, became involved in this arrangement during the dangerous period from the 13th to the 16th century. Following the establishment of the Royal Navy, the importance of the association and the post of Lord Warden declined drastically. Dover is only 7 miles (11 km) farther south on A258.

DOVER: The chalky white cliffs of Dover have been a strategic landmark ever since the early Iron Age, when a settlement was established here. Roman invaders quickly erected a fortress and an octagonal lighthouse, or pharos, that still stands beside a more recent Norman castle. The castle keep surrounds a 240-foot-deep well, and there are rumors that some of the underground passages inside the castle connect with the caves beneath the cliffs once used by smugglers. The ancient Roman roadway called Watling Street begins here and leads to London via Canterbury. On clear days, France is easily visible across the Straits of Dover, 20 miles away, and the view from the battlements of Dover Castle atop the 400-foot bluff overlooking the city and sea is magnificent. Dover is one of the main embarkation points for ferries to France (Calais, Dunkirk, and Boulogne) and Belgium (Ostende and Zeebrugge).

During both world wars, Dover again rose to prominence as a point of departure for troops bound for the Continent and as the goal of planes straggling back from the fighting. The city was pounded by long-range artillery during World War II, and the thick castle walls sheltered the population through the 4-year bombardment.

En Route from Dover – The famous cliffs extend southwest toward Folkestone, neatly trimming the coastline with a tall white chalk sea wall for almost 7 miles. Beyond this point the cliffs fall away, exposing the shore. Stretching westward is a double line of defenses constructed in the early 19th century against the threat of an invasion by Napoleon: a series of 74 small coastal fortresses — circular Martello towers — reinforced by a Royal Military Canal a short distance inland. Additional defenses were erected in 1940 when Hitler massed his forces along the French coast. Take Route A20 southwest along the coast from Dover to Folkestone before picking up Route A259 for the additional 4 miles (6.4 km) to Hythe.

If you're favored with good weather in Folkestone, take a stroll on the Leas — a broad, mile-long, grassy walkway on the crest of the cliffs just west of the harbor. From here the coast of France unfolds in a beautiful panorama 22 miles distant. On the east side of the harbor is the Warren, where a section of the chalk cliff has crumbled and fallen on the beach — a great hunting ground for fossils.

HYTHE: Three Martello towers still guard the former Cinque Port of Hythe, although the harbor has long since silted up and the sea receded. There are also fortifications from other periods, including the ruins of a Roman castrum, Stutfall Castle, near the Royal Military Canal that bisects the city. Lympne Castle, a residence of the

Archdeacons of Canterbury until the mid-1800s, incorporates a square 12th-century Norman tower into its otherwise 14th- and 15th-century construction (open May to September). The castle overlooks Romney Marsh, a sparsely populated, low-lying pasture full of memories of the old smuggling days, when untaxed (and often illegal) cargoes were unloaded here. The fields and marsh grass support a large number of Romney Marsh sheep. A miniature steam railway (open daily Easter to September, and weekends in March and October) runs a 13-mile course from Hythe to New Romney along the fringe of the marsh. The presence of over 1,500 human skulls in the town church has never been explained.

En Route from Hythe – Route A259 parallels both the coast and the railway, passing through Romney Marsh as it travels to New Romney. Dymchurch, half-way between the two closed ports (New Romney lost the use of its harbor in the 13th century), is a popular weekend resort with a 5-mile beach. The small village itself lies in the shelter of a 3-mile fortified seawall built by the Romans to prevent the marshes from flooding. The wall has been continuously improved, and the fortifications were added in 1940. At New Romney the road bears inland, crossing the border of Kent and heading toward the ancient towns of Rye and Winchelsea (21 mi/33.5 km and 24 mi/38.5 km from Hythe, respectively) in neighboring East Sussex.

RYE: The receding sea and centuries of silt buildup have obstructed the port of Rye — like so many of its neighboring ports — limiting traffic to small coastal vessels and fishing boats. The town was razed by the French in 1377 and again in 1448, destroying the most historic buildings, but many of the houses erected during the late 15th century still grace Rye's cobblestone streets. The town retains the atmosphere of that medieval time and a measure of its former bustling activity within its crumbling 14th-century walls.

Both the *Mermaid Inn* (see *Best en Route*), rebuilt during the 15th century and rumored to have been a smugglers' rendezvous, and the timbered *Flushing Inn* (15th century) are excellent haunts for travelers. The works of the great clock (c. 1560) in the 12th-century Church of St. Mary are thought to be among the oldest still functioning in England. Lamb House (West St.) was the residence of novelist Henry James from 1898 until his death in 1916 (open Wednesday and Saturday afternoons, mid-April through October). The 16th-century dramatist John Fletcher's birthplace, a vicarage near Lion and Market streets, is now a tea shop. The de Ypres family purchased the 13th-century tower that bears its name in the early 14th century; it is now a museum (open daily, Easter Sunday to October).

Winchelsea, also added to the Cinque Ports alliance before the changing coastline ruined its harbor, was completely relocated to its present site in 1283 by Edward I. The church, begun soon afterward, is dedicated to St. Thomas à Becket. Parts of William Thackeray's *Denis Duval* are set in the two towns.

En Route from Rye – South of Winchelsea, Route A259 descends toward the shore. At Hastings, 9 miles (14.4 km) from Rye, the road regains the coast. The strategic and psychological importance of this area to England becomes clear when viewed against the historic background of this section of coastline.

Following Edward the Confessor's death in January 1066, Harold ascended to the throne of England, but his claim to the monarchy (through his mother's bloodline) was weak. Duke William of Normandy felt his kinship to Edward (his father had been Edward's cousin), coupled with the oath Harold had sworn in support, justified his claim to the throne.

It was just a few miles west of Hastings, at Pevensey Bay, that William landed his forces on September 28, 1066.

King Harold and his men were busy fighting Tostig in the north and had to march southward from the Battle of Stamford Bridge. He gathered additional support as he traveled but it was not until the morning of October 14 that Harold's army, perhaps 10,000 ax- and spear-carrying foot soldiers, formed a shield wall along a ridge just north of Hastings. William's force was composed of a few thousand archers and several thousand mounted knights and armed men. Norman arrows rained on the defenders, and cavalry charges broke on the wall of spears and shields. In the late afternoon William faked a retreat, drawing many of the inexperienced English militiamen from their positions, and decimated them with his cavalry. King Harold and the remainder of his army were soon slaughtered. On the spot where Harold planted the Royal Standard, where he and his closest followers actually died, William the Conqueror erected Battle Abbey. By Christmas, William was crowned King of England in Westminster Abbey.

HASTINGS (ST. LEONARDS and BATTLE): Although Hastings and adjoining St. Leonards now form a popular resort area, the original Cinque Port city stagnated after the harbor became clogged with silt during the late 12th century. This 600-year sleep kept the Old Town beautifully intact. Narrow streets and age-old houses characterize the east end of town, where Hastings began as a fishing village. Even the tall, skinny sheds used to store the fish nets, built during the 16th century, have survived, as did the 14th-century St. Clement's and the 15th-century All Saints' churches. The *Fisherman's Church* is now a museum, open from late May to late September, weekdays and Sunday afternoons.

The ruins of Hastings Castle, erected around the time of William's invasion, overlook the 3-mile beach area. The magnificent homes in this section of town reflect the resurgence of Hastings as a resort during the late 18th and early 19th centuries. An amusement pier adds to the gaiety of the promenade along the beach, but the most beautiful aspect of the town is natural — the cliffwalks to the east of Hastings and St. Clement's Caves (below the castle), once used by smugglers.

The nearby small town of Battle, which derives its name from the famous Battle of Hastings, includes the abbey founded by William the Conqueror. The battle site, from the ridge where Harold formed his lines to the heights of Senlac and Telham on the far side of the valley, where William's forces gathered, is just southwest of the town. The abbey gatehouse faces Market Square, and the ruins of the abbey church (destroyed around 1540) center on the spot where Harold fell. Those sections of the abbey that survived intact and those added in later years are now used as a school. (The abbey ruins are open Sundays, April through September). The horrors of the clash of forces come vividly to life in the *Battle Museum* in High Street (open daily except Sunday mornings, Easter through September).

En Route from Hastings – Continue southwest along the coast on Route A259 toward the popular seaside resort of Brighton, a distance of about 45 miles (72 km). Since this coastal road may be clogged with traffic during the summer months, it might be a good idea to take the inland route, A27, which veers off from A259 at Pevensey.

BRIGHTON: The flow of travelers and bathers to the shore at Brighton started in the mid-18th century, when a local doctor began recommending the salt water and sea air to several members of England's fashionable elite. It hasn't stopped. By 1783, the Prince of Wales (later George IV) made his home here and ordered the construction of the Royal Pavilion. In 1817, he had the building altered to a more Oriental style; by that time the carnival atmosphere of the resort was well established. Even a partial listing of those who frequented Brighton would sound like a *Who's Who* of English history and literature: Lewis Carroll, Sir Winston Churchill, Conan Doyle, Gladstone, and Herbert Spencer. Aubrey Beardsley was born here, and George Holyoake died here. By 1929, Brighton had tripled in size, sprawling from Hove to Rottingdean (a 7-mile seafront) and several miles inland.

An esplanade stretches the length of the beach, and two amusement piers extend from it at either end. West Pier, badly damaged by storms, is closed; Palace Pier, almost directly in front of the pavilion, is still operating. On the east end of the walk are splendid 19th-century terraces. Maderia Drive leads on to Black Rock, where the Brighton Marina, the largest yachting marina in Europe, opened in 1979. The older section of Brighton forms a permanent bazaar in the area known as the Lanes, bounded by Old Steine Street (near the pavilion) and West Street. The Royal Pavilion and the Royal Stables, now the *Dome Theater,* mark the inland border of this shopping haven. Around the corner on Church Street is the *Museum and Art Gallery* (open daily except Mondays). The Sussex Room at the museum contains a thorough history of the area and a fabulous collection of English ceramics (the Willet Collection). And the Royal Pavilion is itself a living museum of one of the most vivid periods in English taste.

Brighton is not, however, the place for spending your days indoors or even out shopping. Virtually every holiday sport is available here, and if none of the active amusements (sailing, golf, tennis, and such) is to your taste, there are the shows at the *Dome,* the greyhound racing, cricket, and football at Hove, or the horse racing at the *Racecourse.* Then there's the *Sports Arena* and the *Volk's Electric Railroad* from Palace Pier to Black Rock. Many theater productions open here before going to London's West End, and there are some eight movie houses in the area.

En Route from Brighton – Route A23, aided by the M23 motorway, makes a beeline for London, 60 miles (96 km) due north of the beaches. A more entertaining route is A27 northeast from Brighton to Lewes and A26 from there to Royal Tunbridge Wells, the health resort that has been extremely popular since the discovery of the "healing powers" of its mineral waters in 1606. It's about 30 miles (48 km) from Brighton at the junction of A26 and A21. A promenade called the Pantiles, designed as a shopping and visitor area in 1638, is just as popular today. The mineral waters can be sampled from the springs at the far end of the walkway, and the *Duke of York* pub serves those looking for something a little stronger at the tables outside its Victorian building on the promenade. Route A21 leads north toward Westerham and Sevenoaks, about 10 miles (16 km) away.

BEST EN ROUTE

The roads from the coast to London have been lined with inns and guesthouses for centuries, and many of those available to modern travelers are the same ones patronized by kings' messengers (and murderers) 6 centuries ago. The degree of comfort has increased a good deal in the intervening years, however, and you should have no complaints about the quality or range of accommodations available. Expect to pay $100 or more for a double in those places categorized as expensive; between $80 and $100 in the moderate range; and under $80 in any hotel or guesthouse listed as inexpensive. Full English breakfast is usually included in the overnight charge. A meal for two, excluding drinks, wine, or tips, will run about $75 to $85 in places listed as expensive; $60 to $75 in moderate; and under $60 in inexpensive.

WYE

New Flying Horse Inn – It's a 17th-century coaching inn with oak beams, gleaming brasses, 10 rooms, and good food. Upper Bridge St. (phone: 0233-812297). Moderate to inexpensive.

Wife of Bath – Five miles (8 km) south of the tiny town of Chilham is Wye, a village that would escape notice altogether if it weren't for this very fine restaurant with English and French cuisine. Weekly menus change with the season to ensure absolutely fresh food. Reservations are a must. Closed Sundays and Mondays and a week at Christmas. 4 Upper Bridge St. (phone: 0233-812540). Moderate.

CANTERBURY

County – Although this 16th-century hotel has been refurbished in the name of creature comforts, it retains the feel of its older rooms. The original timbers and exposed beams are still there, but certain modern niceties (like private baths in all rooms) have been added. High St. (phone: 0227-66266). Expensive.

DOVER

Dover Moat House – A large, modern, 79-room hotel that's conveniently close to the ferry terminals. Amenities include a restaurant and a heated indoor pool. Townwall St. (phone: 0304-203270). Expensive.

RYE

Mermaid Inn – This beautifully preserved 15th-century inn is one of the most charming old hotels in England. Its walls still conceal the priest holes and secret staircase used to avoid arrest in the old days of pirates and smugglers. Mermaid St. (phone: 0797-223065). Moderate.

HASTINGS

Beauport Park – Set off in a beautiful park area, the stately Georgian hotel has a formal garden to add to the timeless atmosphere. The service is in keeping with that feeling of another age, and the heated outdoor pool is a bonus during the summer. Battle Rd. (phone: 0424-51222). Expensive to moderate.

BRIGHTON

Grand – Right in the center of the seafront, this is an old and very attractive hotel with Victorian architecture at its best in the lobby and landings. Reopened in 1986, the hotel has been lavishly restored following an IRA bombing in 1984. King's Rd. (phone: 0273-21188). Expensive.

Old Ship – On the seafront close to the Lanes, much of its original style and charm remains, especially in the 200-year-old banqueting room used by the Prince Regent. The rooms vary from simple singles to lavish antique-four-poster-bedded delights. King's Rd. (phone: 0273-29001). Expensive.

Ramada Renaissance – A relative newcomer on the seafront, with an imposing atrium overlooking the sea. King's Rd. (phone: 0273-206700). Expensive.

ROYAL TUNBRIDGE WELLS

Calverley – An elegant 18th-century stone mansion set in a delightful garden, overlooking the lower town. There are antiques throughout the hotel, but the chintz coverings detract more from the style than they add to the countrified atmosphere. Crescent Rd. (phone: 0892-26455). Moderate.

Southwest England: Devon and Cornwall

Its atypically warm climate is not all that distinguishes southwest England from the rest of Great Britain, although it is the feature of this thumb of land stuck into the Atlantic that most attracts other Britons. With coasts on the English Channel and the Atlantic Ocean and weather that at its most extreme approaches the subtropical (indefatigable Cornish gardeners have been known to grow palms, much to the consternation of unsuspecting passersby, who find palm trees in England a touch surreal), popular resorts like Torquay and Newquay are full all summer long.

But there is a mysterious quality to Devon and Cornwall born of centuries of relative isolation that is both fascinating and a little frightening. It is this quality — not its reputation for warm weather or seaside frolics — that draws most foreign visitors. For the distinction between rural Somerset and Dorset and Devon's famous moors couldn't be more pronounced. Dartmoor — now a protected national park — is a vast sparse expanse of exposed rock and chalk, eerie and mystical at night, yet beautifully trimmed in a verdant layer of wild grasses and purple heather that glow in the sunlight by day. Across them sweep sudden storms and lashing gales of wind and rain, and from them have come stories of the hounds of hell, dark demons, and druids. The coasts of Cornwall, isolated for centuries, bred generations of sea scavengers as well as culture, language, and customs unlike any others in England.

In Plymouth, Sir Francis Drake busied himself with a game of bowls as the Spanish Armada gathered offshore; from this same port the Pilgrims departed for the New World. Pirates and scavengers alike took delight in hiding among the coves and inlets that line both the north and south coasts of the region, preying on shipping by force and luring their victims to destruction on unmarked rocks and shoals.

From London to the ancient religious site of Stonehenge, the route we offer below bears south into Salisbury and then Dorchester before heading west to Exeter. The district is scattered with Roman ruins, and some of this ancient architecture can still be seen. Farther west, across the wilds of Dartmoor, lies Plymouth, a major port of the British navy since the days of wooden ships. Cornwall's twin peninsulas of Land's End and the Lizard form the southwestern tip of England, and in the bay between these outstretched arms of land is Penzance, a resort and a point of departure for the offshore Isles of Scilly. Nearby is one of England's most spectacular castles, St. Michael's Mount, on a mountain rising 200 feet from the sea.

Returning east along the north coast of Cornwall and then Devon, the route passes the island-fortress of Tintagel, claimed to be the birthplace of King Arthur, and the surfing resort of Bude before ending in the forests and valleys of Exmoor National Park. For more information write to the West Country Tourist Board, Trinity Court, 37 Southernhay East, Exeter EX1 1QS, Devon (phone: 0392-76351).

LONDON: For a detailed report on the city and its hotels and restaurants, see *London,* THE CITIES.

    En Route from London – It's about a 2½- to 3-hour journey to Stonehenge via either the M3 motorway or Route A30, but switch over to A30 at exit 8 of the motorway and follow it until the point where A303 originates and A30 bears south. Take A303 into Amesbury, which marks the eastern entrance to the Salisbury Plain, about 120 miles west of London. This windblown 200-square-mile table of chalk and rock is the bedrock of English history.

STONEHENGE: The best known of almost 80 ancient religious sites in the area, Stonehenge lies 2 miles (3 km) west of town just off Route A303. An earthwork 300 feet in diameter raises the crude formation above the plain and sets it apart from its surroundings. Although the site was used by the Druids for their sun-based festivals beginning around 250 BC, computer evidence supports the theory that these circles served as an astronomical calendar for timing the movements of the moon and stars — and predicting eclipses — around 1500 BC. That anyone could have moved and placed these massive chunks of stone at any time, let alone in 1500 BC, is an incredible act of faith in itself.

The stone monoliths, mined, shaped, and moved to this spot, are arranged in two concentric outer circles with two interior horseshoes. The uprights in the outer circle are 13½ feet tall and linked by fitted capstones; the inner circle is slightly smaller. Many segments of both circles remain intact. The two horseshoes are formed of unconnected trilithons (two uprights supporting a single capstone) in a concentric pattern. The largest of the five still standing is over 20 feet tall and extends 8 feet below ground.

En Route from Stonehenge – Backtrack into Amesbury and stop at the *Antrobus Arms* hotel to discuss the Druids (see *Best en Route*). The present hotel, which evolved from a coaching inn for passengers on the London-Exeter coach, carries its age well. On a cold night its roaring fireplaces (and a whiskey) will chase the chill as well as ever. The abbey at Amesbury was founded by the widow of King Edgar the Peaceful after his death in 975, although parts of the structure date from the 7th century. It was here, according to the tales of King Arthur, that Queen Guinevere took final refuge after the death of Arthur. Route A345 leads directly south to Salisbury, just a few miles away, but there is a much nicer, smaller road running through the Avon Valley, slightly west of the main route.

SALISBURY: The 400-foot spire of Salisbury Cathedral, the tallest in England, dominates the entire plain on which the city is located. Salisbury was established and construction of the cathedral began in 1220, when religious jurisdiction over the area was transferred here from the ancient city of Old Sarum. The remains of Old Sarum — which began as a crude earthwork, grew to a Saxon town, and later became a Norman fortress — lie on a hill north of Salisbury. On the banks of the Avon, the *Rose and Crown* provides comfortable accommodations (see *Best en Route*); and you're bound to feel welcome at one of the three bars at the *Haunch of Venison*.

Take Route A354 southwest from Salisbury to Dorchester, about 40 miles (64 km) distant, across the hills of Dorset Downs. South of Puddletown lies the countryside Thomas Hardy called Egdon Heath in his novels; Salisbury appeared as Melchester.

DORCHESTER: Thomas Hardy transformed this quiet agricultural center where he was born into the city of Casterbridge for his Wessex novels, but Dorchester has withstood much greater alterations throughout its existence. Maiden Castle, a pre-Roman earthwork, is a magnificent ruin left by the native Neolithic Britons. Later, under the Romans, this was a crossroads called Durnovaria, and the nearby Maumbury Rings was the site of an amphitheater. King John later used the town as a hunting center. Today it has an interesting county museum (closed Sundays) that displays finds from the nearby Iron Age fort, Maiden Castle, and a reconstruction of Hardy's study taken from his house at Max Gate; there are also some of his original manuscripts, notebooks, and drawings. In the 17th century, Judge Jeffreys held his Bloody Assizes in Dorchester, consigning some 200 men to the gallows in the wake of the Duke of Monmouth's failed rebellion in 1685. Jeffreys was a notoriously cruel man, and the High West Street building where he roomed is said to be haunted; if you spot the judge, don't speak. The *Royal Oak,* a pub right up the street, should be your next port of call. Hardy's cottage and the fringes of Egdon Heath are accessible from Route A35 about 3 miles (5 km) east of town. The current tenant will open the cottage by appointment, but the gardens are open to the public daily, except Tuesday mornings, from April to October.

En Route from Dorchester – Route A35 leads west, cutting across the hills and farms of beautiful Dorset Downs. Bridport, about 16 miles (26 km) from Dorchester, was Hardy's Port Bredy; it has a good beach on West Bay. The town achieved some notoriety as a major producer of rope and netting, leading to the designation of a hangman's noose as a Bridport dagger. West of Bridport the road divides, and A3052 leads southwest to the resort town of Lyme Regis, on the coast.

LYME REGIS: The steep streets of Lyme Regis lead downhill from the coastal farmlands to the old stone pier known as the Cobb, famously portrayed in *The French Lieutenant's Woman*. It was here that the Duke of Monmouth landed to raise an army among the men of southwest England in his attempt to wrest the crown from James II in 1685. Jane Austen kept a cottage called Wings atop the promenade overlooking the area; she used the setting for Louisa Musgrove's accident in the novel *Persuasion*. The worn chalk cliffs are studded with fossil formations, and an ichthyosaurus was recovered here in 1811 by Mary Anning. The town church contains a magnificent tapestry celebrating the union of Catherine and Henry III in 1509.

Route A3052 continues west through Colyford to the resort area of Sidmouth and goes on to Exeter, a total distance of 32 miles (52 km).

EXETER: The strategic and historic city of Exeter, dominated by beautiful Exeter Cathedral, stands on the banks of the Exe River, guarding the neck of the southwest peninsula containing Devon and Cornwall. It is the county town of Devon. The Romans created a fortified city here, Isca Dumnoniorum, and the crumbling walls that once marked its boundaries can still be seen. Over the years, this site has been besieged, stormed, taken, and sometimes held by and against a long series of attackers. The Saxons called the town Escanestre and founded a monastery in 680. The ruins of Rougemont Castle, erected by William the Conqueror after he seized the town in 1068, testify to the area's military importance.

Exeter Cathedral (High St. near South St.), which evolved from a Norman structure begun in 1112, includes only the massive towers from that period, having been continually rebuilt and altered for almost a century from 1270 until the late 14th century. Intricate construction details, like the vaulted roof and elaborately carved figures on the west façade, contribute to its appeal. The 14th-century Guildhall, decorated inside and out with coats of arms and the insignia of various trade guilds and individuals, may be the oldest municipal building in England.

In its younger days Exeter was a port city, accessible from the English Channel via the navigable Exe River. Several of Queen Elizabeth's favorite sea captains, Sir Francis Drake and Sir Walter Raleigh among them, docked at Exeter and often stepped into *Mol's Coffee House* (now a silver- and goldsmith's shop) in the Cathedral Close. Drake is also thought to have had a few at the *Ship Inn*, which still serves thirsty travelers.

En Route from Exeter – Pick up Route B3212 on the western outskirts of the city, leading into the heart of Dartmoor National Park. The magic of the wild and rugged moors has fascinated English authors, their readers, and travelers for centuries. The bleak windswept hills, capped by high outcroppings of granite called tors, and coarse wild grasses are the home of wild ponies, grazing sheep, literary pilgrims, and even tales of the "hounds of hell," adapted from older legends of the "beast from below" left over from pre-Roman Druidic cults. Ruins of ancient religious sites and bits of Roman construction are scattered about the 300-square-mile area punctuated by tors that reach as high as 2,000 feet. The peaceful air and quietude of the moors make them ideal for an afternoon's tramp or horseback ride, but remember Sherlock Holmes's admonition to Sir Henry Baskerville: "Don't go out upon the moors at night!" Even if the hounds of hell don't get you, the moors are interspersed with spots of soggy marsh and dotted with tiny lakes, and more than one wanderer has been lost here. Also, be wary when setting off on daytime hikes; take along a compass, map, some food, and extra clothing, since Dartmoor can quickly become enshrouded in mist and cold even in summer.

The *Warren House Inn*, about 18 miles (29 km) from Exeter, once quenched the thirsts of tin miners walking home across the moor. The structure dates from the early 18th century but has since been rebuilt. Pause for a bracing Scottish & Newcastle ale before continuing to the intriguing early granite bridge that leads toward Dartmoor Prison. Princetown, the highest town in England and administrative headquarters for the dark-walled prison, is only 6 miles (10 km) beyond the bridge. The prison was established for captured French soldiers in 1809 and was used for American prisoners during the War of 1812. The facility began over a century of service as the Dartmoor Convict Prison in 1850, although sections were destroyed by fire during an insurrection in 1932.

Continue southwest on Route B3212 about 5 miles (8 km) to Yelverton, and take A386 the remaining 8 miles (13 km) into Plymouth.

PLYMOUTH: A principal English seaport for over 500 years, Plymouth dominates the mouths of the Plym and Tamar rivers at Plymouth Sound. This natural harbor, protected by rocky headlands on either side, has been an important military installation since it was fortified during the early 1400s, and many of the famous English privateers used Plymouth as their base for shipping raids. It was here that the outnumbered English fleet awaited the Spanish Armada in 1588.

English naval legends say that Sir Francis Drake was in the middle of a game of bowls on Plymouth Hoe when the Armada was sighted — and calmly finished his game before the battle. A statue of Drake and several other memorials stand on the Hoe's green lawns today, on the southeastern point of the waterfront near the Citadel. The Citadel, part of the fortifications erected under Charles II in the 1660s, is currently in use by the British military, although certain sections may sometimes be toured by arrangement with the commanding officer.

The *Mayflower* colonists set sail from Plymouth's pier at the Mayflower Steps, on the west side of the point near Sutton Pool. Near Barbican Quay, at the foot of Lambhay Street, is the ruin of a gatehouse, part of a 14th-century castle. Large sections of this historic city were damaged by bombs in World War II, but the Barbican area survived in its Elizabethan purity. It is now a lively area full of antiques shops, art galleries, restaurants, and pubs, and the narrow cobblestone streets are overhung by the timber frames of merchant homes. Note the particularly fine Elizabethan house — now called the Armada Experience — on New Street (open daily), beautifully furnished with 16th-century pieces. Other parts of Plymouth have been extensively rebuilt, and, together with the adjoining communities, have grown into a single maritime center. The Royal Dockyards, established by William of Orange at Devonport, a mile west of Plymouth, contributed heavily to this effect. Entrance to the dockyards is restricted.

En Route from Plymouth – The River Tamar marks the boundary between Devon and Cornwall, and Route A38 crosses Plymouth Harbour on the Tamar Suspension Bridge, traveling 30 miles (48 km) west toward the town of Bodmin. Much of the china and raw china clay shipped through the port of Plymouth comes from this area, evidenced by the chalky white piles of mining waste lining the roadways. The route bears north to Liskeard, and then turns west again to Bodmin, skirting the southern fringe of Bodmin Moor. There are some interesting stone formations on this edge of the moor: three odd stone circles known as the Hurlers and a 30-foot mound of granite blocks dubbed "the Cheesewring." If you have some extra time, detour south from Liskeard on B3254 to visit the picturesque fishing ports of Looe, Polperro, and Fowey; then take B3269 into Bodmin.

BODMIN: On the steep western slopes of the rocky tablelands of Bodmin Moor, this agricultural center is a natural touring base for the entire moors area. St. Petroc's Church, rebuilt during the 15th century, is the largest medieval church in Cornwall, and the nearby waters of St. Guron's Well are reputed to have brought about miraculous cures for eye troubles and blindness. If you'd like the mud in your eye to be a little stronger, make your way to the *Hole in the Wall* — through a hole in the wall! The building may have been a debtors' prison during the 18th century. In addition to the stoneworks found in the southern area on the approach to Bodmin and the Roman ruins scattered about, Dozmary Pool (off A30 in the northeast sector) is deep with legends. In the legend of King Arthur, the sword Excalibur was cast into the lake, where it was caught by a single arm extended from beneath the surface. Cornish legends also tell of Jan Tregeagle, who was condemned for his sins to the task of emptying the pool with a leaky shell. Perhaps Tregeagle has escaped his doom, because these days the waters are not deep, and periods of drought dry the lake. The grouping of houses that surround the turnoff to Dozmary Pool is the village of Bolventor, the pirate rendezvous in Daphne du Maurier's *Jamaica Inn.*

Arrange to have tea in *Lanhydrock House,* an impressive estate of woods and gardens covering over 400 acres, about 2.5 miles (4 km) south of Bodmin on Route B3269. Both the gatehouse and the portrait gallery in the north wing are remnants of the original 17th-century construction; other sections of the house were rebuilt in 1881. The elaborate plaster ceiling of the gallery depicts scenes from the Old Testament (open Easter to October; the gardens are open year-round).

En Route from Bodmin – Take Route A30, then A391 south 12 miles (19 km) through Cornwall to St. Austell, an attractive industrial center bounded by both stark moorlands and sandy beaches. Just outside town are the Medacuddle Holy Well and an ancient stone formation called the Stone Chair.

It is 14 miles (22 km) farther on A390, then A39, to the market town of Truro, the administrative center of Cornwall, officially established in 1877. The Georgian edifices along Truro's Lemon and Prince's streets and Trafalgar Row attest to the town's earlier prosperity. Small wonder that when the See of Cornwall was reestablished in 1876, the city was chosen for the first cathedral to be erected since the Reformation. Its bold early Gothic design, added to the site of a 16th-century church, was completed shortly before World War I.

Route A39 leads southwest about 11 miles (18 km) from town to the intersection with A394. A short side trip from here along A39 descends to the port of Falmouth and Pendennis Castle. It's only 13 miles (21 km) west, from the intersection to Helston, at the base of the broad promontory called the Lizard, via A394. Every year in early May, Helston's residents dance through the town's streets in their traditional *Flora* or *Furry* celebration. Popular legends say that this is related to the death of a dragon that dropped a huge rock on the town, but a more likely hypothesis is that it is the remnant of Druidic spring fertility rites.

THE LIZARD: This broad peninsula, varying from 200 to 400 feet above sea level, is the place to go for dramatic views of England's rugged southernmost shore. On the west side of the Lizard is Mullion Cove, where many caves cut into the cliffsides are exposed during low tide — a find for spelunkers and treasure seekers. The colorful cliffs of Kynance Cove lie farther south along the western shore. Lizardtown itself is less than a mile from the lighthouse that marks the southernmost spot in England, Lizard Point. On the eastern shore (off B3293) is the port of Coverack, once a base for smugglers. It is partially protected by the Manacles Rocks, an offshore hazard that has wrecked many a ship.

Penzance, the principal town of the western peninsula known as Land's End, is 13 miles (21 km) west of Helston on A394.

PENZANCE: The fishing and seaport center of England's southwestern extremity, Penzance is well sheltered within Mount's Bay, which splits the tip of Cornwall into the Lizard and Land's End peninsulas. The mild climate here has attracted travelers for centuries, and the city has become a popular resort and shopping center. In bygone days, the town was often sacked by pirates, and it was virtually destroyed by Spanish raiders in 1595. The 1836 Market House (Market Jew St.) is worth seeing, but a far greater rarity in England are the subtropical plants and flowers in Morrab Gardens; only the exceptionally warm climate of this distant area allows these plants to survive in Britain.

Frequent departures from the port by both boat and helicopter shuttle visitors to the Isles of Scilly (pronounced "silly"), an archipelago of over 150 islands and rocky outcroppings about 30 miles southwest of Land's End, near where the Atlantic meets the English Channel. Only five islands are large enough to support populations, but there are several interesting forts and religious sites spread throughout the chain. Star Castle, on St. Mary's, was erected in 1593; Tresco Abbey on Tresco Island has lovely gardens, with between 3,000 and 4,000 varieties of plants (open weekdays, also Sundays in summer), and the *Valhalla Maritime Museum* has some fascinating exhibits; St. Helen's has two ancient ruins: a church and a monastery; and there are numerous other structures on the islands. Legends are the only firm evidence that these islands are the mountaintops of the lands of King Arthur, Lyonnesse, although some of the earlier fortifications could be from that semi-mythical period.

One of the most spectacular visions in all of England is St. Michael's Mount, standing majestically about one-quarter mile off the sandy shore of Marazion, a tiny market town 3 miles (5 km) east of Penzance. In 495, fishermen claimed to have seen a vision of St. Michael appear on the 200-foot mountain that rises from the calm waters of Mount's Bay. In the 11th century the grounds were used for a priory. The castle (open weekdays June through October; Mondays, Wednesdays, and Fridays in November through May; also Thursdays in April and May) can be reached by a causeway during low tide or by ferry from either Penzance or Marazion at highwater periods. (Note that in winter, for obvious reasons, ferry service is irregular.)

En Route from Penzance – A generous coastal esplanade leads south to the picturesque fishing villages of Newlyn (1 mi/1.6 km) and Mousehole (pronounced "mowzal"; 3 mi/5 km), sheltered in the lee of Mount's Bay — perfect material for a beautiful morning's walk. Be sure to stop at the *Ship Inn* for a taste of a local beer, St. Austell, and prevail upon the publican to tell you the story of fisherman Tom Bowcock. Save your evenings for viewing the sunsets from the western tip of Land's End — they're incredible!

About 10 miles (16 km) southwest of Penzance (via either B3315 or an extension of the esplanade, the cliff path) are the sandy beaches of Porthcurno, the cultural hub of Land's End. Here, on a cliff west of the village, is the open-air *Minack Theatre,* which uses its vast panorama of the Atlantic for a backdrop. On the village's east boundary is Logan's Rock, a delicately balanced 65-ton granite boulder that can easily be rocked in place — however, local custom insists that if it falls over, you've got to replace it.

LAND'S END: This immense granite ridge extending into the sea is the westernmost point of England. Once called Penwith in Cornish, the area is privately owned, though open to the public year-round (erratic hours in winter). Avoid the souvenir shops and crowds; slip out onto the point just before dawn or, even better, at dusk for fantastic views of the sun. The Isles of Scilly are easily visible on a clear day, and lighthouses illuminate the most treacherous rocks after dark. Afterward, stop at the *Old Success Inn* overlooking Sennen Cove before heading on.

Inland (toward Zennor, Morvah, and St. Just) are several Stone Age quoits, or dolmens — burial chambers formed by laying a top, or capstone, across stone uprights. Chysauter is the site of an Iron Age village of huts used by Roman and British miners until about AD 100.

The resort of St. Ives, on the north coast of the peninsula, is only 7 miles (11 km) northeast of Penzance. Here the narrow cobblestone streets are lined with the cottages of fishermen. The town, long popular with artists, swells with summertime painters each year. You'll find St. Austell in pubs throughout town as well as national brews.

En Route from Land's End – Traveling northeast from Penzance, Route A30 runs parallel to the coast, gradually bearing inland toward the village of Fraddon, 35 miles (56 km) away. All of the small roads to the left (north) of the highway lead to the coast, and many run along the shoreline before returning to A30. The region is edged with tiny coves and long strands of beach, which can stretch to 4 or 5 miles (6 or 8 km) during low tide. At Fraddon, the *Blue Anchor* deserves a pause for a beer before taking A39 through the attractive countryside of the Vale of Mawgan to Camelford, a trek of some 23 miles (37 km). Then follow B3266 a mile north to B3263, which brings you into Tintagel.

TINTAGEL: Along the craggy slate cliffs of the western Cornish coastline are the ruins of one of the most famous castles in England, Tintagel Castle, reputed to be the birthplace of King Arthur, born to Uther Pendragon and his queen, Igerne. The castle sits on a headland of slate, called Tintagel Head, high above the Atlantic cove. The ancient village of Tintagel, at one time known as Trevena, is on the mainland less than a mile away. The cave in which Merlin is said to have weaved his spells (and perhaps to have been sealed in) is at the foot of the castle's steep cliffs, accessible only at low tide. The castle was built in the 12th century on the ruins of an earlier Celtic monastery. The mainland fortifications were added during the following century to protect the natural rock bridge that once served as the castle entranceway; it has since collapsed and a new bridge built.

En Route from Tintagel – Continuing east on Route B3263 returns you to A39 headed north and east to Bude, an attractive resort about 14 miles (23 km) up the coast. Bude's sandy beaches, though lightly laced with rocky headlands, are famous for both swimming and surfing, and the festive atmosphere of this summer resort has also spawned a golf course and tennis courts.

Route A39 makes it way north about 30 miles (48 km) from Bude to the huge bay (known both as Bideford and Barnstaple Bay) formed at the mouth of the River Taw. The beautiful fishing village of Clovelly, deeply set in a cleft face of the cliffs that line the western curve of the bay, has been fairly inundated by artists and travelers. At one time Bideford, perched on the hills that overlook the mouth of the Torridge River on the west side of the bay, was one of England's busiest seaports, frequented by Sir Walter Raleigh, Sir Francis Drake, and Martin Frobisher. Many fine homes, built by wealthy merchants in the 17th century, still line the town's main street, Bridgeland Street. The town Westward Ho! was named for Charles Kingsley's 1855 novel (3 mi/5 km northwest of Bideford, or take an excursion boat); but, in fact, parts of the book were actually written in Bideford (it's the "little white town" in the book) at the *Royal* hotel. Take a moment to examine the 24-arch bridge in the center of town — it was built in 1460 (and altered slightly in the 1920s). Barnstaple, although no longer the bustling seaport that thrived for 1,000 years, is still a busy market town for the surrounding area. Relieved of the pressures of constant growth, Barnstaple has become a delightful town to visit and a pleasant base for touring the north coast and Exmoor. The *Three Tuns,* more than 500 years old, is an excellent place for meeting people. The downstairs attracts younger drinkers; the upstairs bar tends to be a bit quieter and conservative.

EXMOOR: The twin resorts of Lynton and Lynmouth, both within the boundary of Exmoor National Park, lie another 20 miles (32 km) northeast along A39. Approaching from the lower coastal area of Barnstaple, the rising granite and slate hills of Exmoor are a grand sight. Lynton is the higher of the two resorts, on a cliff almost 500 feet above the sea; Lynmouth lies at the water's edge, where the East and West Lyn rivers join the sea. Coastal walking paths lead both east and west through beautifully wooded rocky high ridges and combes. Inland, the moor's gentle ridges create a maze of valleys and vales.

The Doone Valley, setting for Richard Blackmore's novel *Lorna Doone,* is about 4 miles (6 km) south (inland) from the resort areas. The story is in part an amalgamation of tales about the outlaw band that terrorized the moor for several decades during the 17th century, and Blackmore drew heavily upon both factual events and local legends as well as places in his work.

Route B3223 leads inland from the resorts, through the very heart of Exmoor. Simonbath (9 mi/14 km southeast of Lynmouth) lies just a few miles from the head of the Doone Valley. Time has almost obliterated the ruins at this end of the valley, which are thought to have been occupied by the outlaw band. Route B3223 joins B3224 east of Simonbath and continues to the hunting and fishing center of Exford. Here the staghounds that track Exmoor's famed wild red deer are kenneled, and anglers by the score test their skills against elusive trout. Check with the proprietor of the *Crown* hotel about obtaining a horse for an afternoon ride through the moors, then head off about 4 miles (6 km) northeast to Dunkery Beacon. The beacon is the highest point on the moor, 1,705 feet, and the view extends almost 100 miles in good weather. A healthy trek of about 4 miles (6 km) north across the moors returns you to near the coast at Porlock. This village lies right on A39, about 6 miles (10 km) east of Lynmouth, and somewhere in the intervening stretch may well be the cottage "twixt Porlock and Lynton" where Samuel Taylor Coleridge had the opium vision that resulted in *Kubla Khan.* Some sources claim, however, that the vision occurred in his home at Nether Stowey, about 35 miles (56 km) east of Lynton on A39.

BEST EN ROUTE

Southwest England is amply provided with small inns and historic accommodations, and the traveler so inclined can spend just about every night holed up with the ghosts of his or her choice, though in most cases the accommodations are not going to be modern or splashy. On the other hand, in the major resort areas, every kind of guesthouse, hotel, motel, and rental is available, though reservations are advisable in summer. Expect to pay $115 (or more) a night for a double in the hotels listed as expensive; from $70 to $110 in the moderate range; and under $65 in the inexpensive category. You will find good food at reasonable prices in most places, but for a really excellent dinner for two with wine, expect to pay about $75-$90.

Remember that the value of the dollar does fluctuate, and prices will always vary slightly. The hostelries listed below are merely a selection of our choices for the district; there are any number of acceptable inns lining the roads you will travel.

AMESBURY

Antrobus Arms – This former vicarage has combined modern comfort with its antique style quite nicely. Features include both log fires and central heating, plus a walled garden with a fountain and Cedar of Lebanon tree. Church St. (phone: 0980-23163). Moderate.

SALISBURY

White Hart – A blend of Georgian and modern styles heightens the delightful atmosphere of this well-aged establishment. Three bars to fit your moods, traditional English fare, and a warming fire on chilly days complete this comfortable nest. St. John St. (phone: 0722-27476). Expensive.

Rose and Crown – On the banks of the Avon, this hotel is a happy amalgam of ancient inn and contemporary hotel. There are four-poster beds in the half-timbered old inn and comfortable modern rooms in the annex. Harnham Rd. (phone: 0722-27908). Moderate.

EXETER

Buckerell Lodge Crest – When built in the 13th century, this building served as a hunting lodge. Now it has 54 rooms and wonderful views. Topsham Rd. (phone: 0392-52451). Expensive.

Royal Clarence – This historic building with 63 rooms overlooks the cathedral in the city center. Cathedral Yard (phone: 0392-58464). Moderate.

PENZANCE

Lesceave Cliff – White walls and Mediterranean arches, combined with beach views, belie this hotel's location in England. The staff is exceptionally helpful, and can arrange fishing trips. Praa Sands (phone: 0736-762325). Moderate.

Lamorna Cove – Although the modern additions can't compare with the original granite house or its lovely setting above a tranquil wooded cove, the hotel is a delight. Lots of tasty seafood is served in its restaurant. Lamorna (phone: 0736-731411). Moderate.

ISLES OF SCILLY

Island – On a wonderfully quiet island (no cars!), this hotel combines old and new architectural styles into a beautiful beach resort. The hotel also has a good restaurant, and arranges fishing charters; sailboats are available too. Closed early October to mid-March. Tresco (phone: 0720-22883). Expensive.

ST. IVES

Tregenna Castle – Perched above the old fishing village, this 18th-century home certainly offers the grandest view of the bay available. It is something of a resort, with tennis, golf (18 holes), squash courts, a pool, and more. St. Ives (phone: 0736-795244). Expensive to moderate.

Trecarrell – Less grand, but homey, in a rambling Victorian house that has been nicely refurbished. Carthew Terrace (phone: 0736-795707). Moderate to inexpensive.

BARNSTAPLE

Imperial – In the center of Barnstaple's charming waterfront, the older parts of this hotel are quite beautiful. Taw Vale Parade (phone: 0271-45861). Expensive.

Wales

Like all mountainous countries, Wales has been slow to react to outside change. In part this has been due to poor communications; the roads here rise and fall sharply, twisting and turning around the mountainsides, making contact with the outside world rather difficult. In part, however, it has been due to the character of the Welsh people, who, throughout 5 centuries of Roman occupation, brutal conquest by the Normans, and 700 years of uninterrupted English rule, have managed to hold on to a unique culture, age-old customs, and their own ancient, sonorous language (it is estimated that about one quarter of the population still speaks Welsh). Although technically and for all practical purposes a British principality whose 2.5 million people are governed from Westminster, Wales has retained a distinct identity and an aura of legend and mystery even in the eyes of its English neighbors.

While the scenery here is always marked by its grandeur, it is more diverse than one might imagine. Occupying an 8,000-square-mile landmass that juts west from England into the Irish Sea, Wales is divided informally into three areas — South, Mid, and North Wales — each possessing distinctive topography and points of interest. The route described below covers all three, beginning in the South, at the bustling seaport of Cardiff, and threading its way some 275 miles (440 km) north, first through the grassy mountains and wild moorlands of Brecon Beacons National Park, then west toward the coast. After visiting some of the loveliest seaside resorts and coastal villages of Mid Wales, the route enters the rugged mountain country of the North, passing through the towering beauty of Snowdonia National Park, in the northwest corner of the country. Snowdonia's range is capped by the 3,560-foot peak of Snowdon itself, the highest point in Wales, the summit of which can be reached on the *Snowdon Mountain Railway.* This rack-and-pinion line is one of many still powered by steam engines, all of which operate on extremely narrow-gauge track using small locomotives and carriages, known locally as "the great little trains of Wales."

Wales is renowned for its castles, huge, warlike bastions, many of which were built by Edward I in the 13th century to demonstrate the supremacy of the English Crown over the Welsh. Some of the greatest of these fortresses are along our route in North and South Wales, where they stand, often overlooking the sea, as impressive reminders of the country's turbulent past.

The Wales Tourist Board puts out three excellent publications covering North, South, and Mid Wales. In addition to extensive gazetteers and a regional map, each gives details on activities, nature trails, good beaches, and so forth. For more information, contact the tourist board at Brunel House, 2 Fitzalan Rd., Cardiff CF2 1UY (phone: 0222-499909).

CARDIFF: Connected to London and the rest of the outside world by the M4 motorway, high-speed train service, and its own small airport, Cardiff is an ideal starting point for a tour of Wales. With a population of 277,000, it is the capital and largest city in Wales and one of Britain's most important seaports. Spacious and dignified, the city is also thoroughly cosmopolitan, with large, covered shopping arcades and excellent sports facilities, including that holiest of places for rugby fans, the *National Rugby Stadium.*

Among the city's chief attractions for visitors are its castle and the *National Museum of Wales,* both near the center of town. Cardiff Castle was begun by the Normans in the 11th century on the site of an old Roman camp. A thin layer of brown stone can still be seen running through the castle's surrounding wall, marking the spot where the Roman defenses left off and, centuries later, the Norman work began. The original castle keep stands on a small, moated mound, an example of the Norman motte and bailey. Expanded over the years, the castle was reconstructed in 1865 by the third Marquis of Bute, a young man with a passion for architectural fantasy. Although the ornate Victorian exterior is not to everyone's liking, the castle's interior, with its lavish decorations and rich historical murals, is fascinating. The *National Museum of Wales* (Cathays Park; closed Mondays) displays interesting Welsh archaeological finds, handicrafts, and folk art and is especially noted for its collection of French Impressionist paintings, the centerpiece of which is Renoir's *La Parisienne.*

Two miles (3 km) from the city center, on the banks of the River Taff, is the village-like suburb of Llandaff, home of the 12th-century Llandaff Cathedral, with its striking modern sculpture, *Christ in Majesty,* by Jacob Epstein.

Five miles (8 km) west of Cardiff at the village of St. Fagans is the *Welsh Folk Museum.* This open-air museum is in a woods and garden. Many old houses, mills, farms, and a chapel have been moved from all over Wales and rebuilt on the site to illustrate early Welsh life (open daily April through October, otherwise Mondays through Saturdays). Caerphilly, with its 13th-century castle, is 6 miles (9.6 km) north on A469. A fine white cheese is named after the town, where it is still made).

En Route from Cardiff – Route A470 takes you through Tongwynlais, home of the Victorian extravaganza Castell Coch, another fairy tale edifice built by the young Marquis of Bute. From the outside this castle looks like an ornate French château, and its interior is lavishly fitted.

BRECON: The major center for touring the 519 square miles of Brecon Beacons National Park, Brecon sits at the junction of the rivers Usk and Afon Honddu. It has a massive 13th- and 14th-century fortified priory that stands high above the Afon Honddu on Priory Hill. The town's castle, in the garden of the *Castle of Brecon* hotel, was dismantled by the townsfolk during the 17th-century civil war in an attempt to avoid the bloodshed necessary to defend it.

The *Brecknock Museum,* in the old County Hall in Glamorgan Street (closed Sundays), displays interesting examples of Welsh folk art and local crafts, such as the hand-carved wooden "love spoons" young Welshmen used in bygone days to plight their troth. Just west of the town is the Mountain Center, which has advice and literature for hikers.

En Route from Brecon – Route A40 follows the girth of the Brecon Beacons, three red sandstone peaks, the highest of which looms nearly 3,000 feet high through scenery that is inspiring at any time of year. Often mist rolls downward from the Beacons and the nearby Black Mountains, creating an atmosphere of eerie solitude.

Anglers may want to stop at Llandovery, an important market town well known in the area for its excellent salmon fishing.

CARMARTHEN: Carmarthen is the administrative hub of the southwestern corner of Wales. Its large covered market draws crowds every Wednesday and Saturday, and behind it the cattle market holds sales each Monday, Wednesday, and Thursday.

In Nott Square stands a monument to Dr. Robert Ferrar, Bishop of St. David's, who was burned at the stake on this site in 1555. Also of interest are the *Carmarthen Museum,* in the former Bishop's Palace at Abergwili on the outskirts of the town (open daily except Sundays), and Merlin's Oak, also on the museum grounds. Legend says that when the oak falls, so will the town; to make sure it does not topple, the townspeople have propped it up with concrete.

En Route from Carmarthen – Fans of the poet Dylan Thomas may want to divert onto A4066 at the village of St. Clears for a side trip to Laugharne, where Thomas lived and wrote and where he lies buried in a simple grave in the village churchyard. The Boathouse (open daily to the public from Easter to October) was the poet's residence. Otherwise, take the A477 to Tenby.

TENBY: This ancient walled town stands on a rocky peninsula at the western edge of Carmarthen Bay. With two sandy beaches and a pretty harbor, it makes a delightful base for touring the Pembrokeshire coast. Some 2 ½ miles offshore is Caldey Island, the home of an ancient but still functioning monastery where Cistercian monks make perfume from the island's flowers.

There are many good hotels within the town's 14th-century walls, including the *Imperial* (see *Best en Route*), which actually incorporates parts of the walls in its structure. Local events include golf tournaments (*Tenby Golf Club*'s 18-hole course is at South Beach), *St. Margaret's Fair,* and a lively regatta and carnival, all of which occur in August.

Local pottery and paintings are for sale in the many art shops of Upper Frog Street.

CARDIGAN: Another market town also popular with visitors, Cardigan has a number of cafés and restaurants and a good number of accommodations, mainly in small guesthouses. Its chief attraction is salmon fishing. There are good catches to be had on the Afon Teifi, which flows from here into Cardigan Bay. Some fishermen still use *coracles* — homemade boats of intertwined willow and hazel that look rather like wicker shopping baskets; they have been used for salmon fishing for over a thousand years. Coracle races are held at the Teifiside village of Cilgerran in August.

Three quarters of a mile away, across Cardigan Bridge, is St. Dogmael's, an old Welsh house that was sacked by the Norse and later claimed by the Normans, who turned it into an annex of the Abbey of Tiron in France. The church contains the ancient Sagranus Stone, whose inscriptions in Latin and old Gaelic served as a key to the language of the tribes of the Dark Ages.

En Route from Cardigan – Head north on Route A487 for the 39-mile (63-km) drive along the coastline to Aberystwyth (pronounced "aber-ist-with").

From this road you can reach many of the small coastal villages, including New Quay, which some say is the setting of Dylan Thomas's play *Under Milk Wood* (others claim it's Fishguard). You pass through the popular yachting center of Aberaeron, a 19th-century Georgian town, many of whose buildings are of special architectural or historic interest.

ABERYSTWYTH: A popular seaside resort with both sand and pebble bathing beaches, Aberystwyth is also the seat of the University of Wales and the administrative center for Cardigan Bay. Its lively seafront promenade (now a bit touristy) is lined with hotels and has a pier, bandstand, and the ruins of a castle, which stand sentinel on the headland.

History is carefully preserved at the National Library of Wales (Penglais Hall), which houses some of the earliest Welsh manuscripts; and the past is still very much alive at Alexandra Station, where *British Railways'* last steam-powered service departs for the spectacular falls at Devil's Bridge, high in the Vale of Rheidol, which according to legend was built by the devil himself. Closer to home, the town's cliff railway carries visitors to the peak of Constitution Hill, where they have a splendid view of the bay and the town from the recently built Camera Obscura, the world's largest lens.

Concerts and evening shows are regular summer features along the promenade, and at the *Arts Centre* on the university campus. The *Arts Centre* also holds frequent exhibitions, and the *University Theatre* presents a summer season of plays.

En Route from Aberystwyth – Route A487 skirts the base of the mountains, heading up into the Dovey Valley to Machynlleth, a market town that was made capital of Wales by Owain Glyndwr in the 14th century, during the great Welsh hero's drive to rid the country of English rule. As you drive through town, you pass an immense clock tower, standing like a rocket ready for launching, a gift from the Marquess of Londonderry in 1873. Plas Machynlleth, also in the town, was formerly the Londonderry residence and now houses the local Council.

DOLGELLAU: At the head of the lovely Mawddach Estuary and almost at the foot of the famous Cader Idris Mountain, scenic Dolgellau is an important market town for the many small mountain villages in the vicinity. It makes an ideal base for walks and excursions into the lake and mountain country to the east.

The customs and speech here remain distinctly Welsh, but thanks to its large number of visitors, you should have no trouble being understood. The town itself is quite old and is built largely of the native gray stone. Its bridge, crossing the Afon Wnion, was built in 1638 and is now an officially protected structure. Close to the primary school is an old tollhouse left from the days of turnpikes.

In the Mawddach Valley close to the town you can try your luck panning for gold; gold has been excavated in the surrounding mountains since Roman times, and it is this Welsh gold that was used in some royal family wedding rings, including those of Queen Elizabeth II and the Princess of Wales, in 1981.

HARLECH: Still a small village, Harlech is dominated by its immense gray stone castle, another of the chain of fortifications ordered by Edward I. It was this massive stronghold, the last to yield to the Yorkists in 1468, that provided the inspiration for *Men of Harlech*, one of the best-known traditional Welsh songs. Standing high on a rocky promontory, Harlech Castle (open daily) offers extensive views of land, sea, and mountains. Those with no fear of heights can walk all around the castle on its unfenced, 10-foot-thick walls and climb the 143 steps to the top of its gatehouse. Look toward the sea, half a mile away, and recall that when the castle was built in 1283 it actually stood on the shore. Since that time, however, the sea has receded.

En Route from Harlech – The private village of Portmeirion, near Penrhyndeudraeth, was built by architect Sir Clough Williams-Ellis, who died in 1978. Portmeirion, a strange, pastel dream world built in an Italianate style, became known as the setting for the television series *The Prisoner.*

CAERNARVON: Still mostly enclosed in its 13th-century town walls, Caernarvon is perhaps the best-known Welsh town since the 1969 investiture of Prince Charles as Prince of Wales in its beautiful castle. The castle stands defiantly at the junction of the River Seiont and the Menai Strait, overlooking the Isle of Anglesey. Begun, like Harlech Castle, in 1283, it took 37 years to build, and today it is regarded as a masterpiece of medieval architecture. Inside is the museum of the Royal Welsh Fusiliers, complete with an audiovisual presentation on the town's heritage (open daily).

In addition to being a market center (on Saturdays in Castle Square), Caernarvon also boasts two yacht clubs, tennis, golf, and bowls facilities, and good river and sea fishing. In Castle Square is a statue of Prime Minister David Lloyd George, who was instrumental in securing a future for Caernarfon Castle. He spent his boyhood in the village of Llanystumdwy, near Criccieth.

Near the town is the Roman fort of Segontium, a military center founded in AD 78. A museum here displays the area's archaeological finds. The town of Llanberis, 8 miles (13 km) southeast of Caernarfon is the base station for the *Snowdon Mountain Railway* (April-September). Or follow the spectacular Llanberis Pass, a winding road flanked by steeply rising mountains and the debris of rock slides, to the village of Beddgelert. From the top of the pass, known locally as Pen-y-Pass, you can walk up to the summit of Snowdon.

BEST EN ROUTE

During the peak summer months, the famous *Eisteddfodau* — festivals of music and poetry — are held in towns and villages throughout Wales. If your trip will coincide with any of these, make sure you book hotel reservations well in advance. Note, too, that drinking laws can be idiosyncratic in certain parts of Wales, such as the Lieyn Peninsula and Cardiganshire, where you cannot drink alcoholic beverages on Sundays except as a guest in a hotel. Under the Taste of Wales scheme inaugurated by the Wales Tourist Board, hotels and restaurants are being encouraged to serve traditional Welsh fare. Look for the round Taste of Wales sign, indicating a participating establishment. In the listing below, any establishment charging under $70 per night for a room for two persons are considered inexpensive; $70 to $90, moderate; and more than $90, expensive; prices are slightly higher in Cardiff. You will find good food at reasonable prices in most places, but for a really excellent dinner for two with wine, expect to pay about $65.

CARDIFF

Park – Beautifully appointed 108-room hotel combining the traditional air of a country house with the luxury and comfort of a modern hotel. Two good restaurants. Park Pl., in the center of town. (phone: 0222-383471). Expensive.

Royal – Centrally located, this is one of Cardiff's most dependable hotels, and offers good service, all modern conveniences, a fine restaurant, and an extensive wine list. St. Mary St. (phone: 0222-383321). Expensive.

BRECON

Castle of Brecon (Castle Square) – Pleasant surroundings attached to an old castle overlooking the River Usk. Good restaurant (phone: 0874-4611). Expensive to moderate.

Lansdowne – Recently upgraded, this simple but comfortable Georgian hotel has 12 bedrooms, 4 with bath, and a restaurant. 39 The Watton, Brecon (phone: 0874-3321). Moderate.

CARMARTHEN

Ivy Bush Royal – This historic 80-room hotel has been thoroughly streamlined, offering saunas, and a choice of cocktail lounges. Good restaurant with Welsh cuisine. Spilman St. (phone: 0267-235111). Moderate.

TENBY

Imperial – Immediately above the beach, with fabulous views of St. Catherine's and Caldey islands from most of the rooms. The terrace incorporates part of the medieval town walls. Two restaurants with Welsh cuisine, dinner dances, private tennis court. The Paragon (phone: 0834-3737). Moderate.

Royal Lion – Overlooking Tenby Harbour, this 17th-century coaching inn has been modernized recently and has 36 rooms, 16 with bath. Basically a family hotel, open February until Christmas with a residents' dining room and a seafood restaurant. High St. (phone: 0834-2127). Moderate.

ABERYSTWYTH

Belle Vue Royal – A comfortable hotel overlooking Cardigan Bay, with a restaurant and 42 rooms; there's also free golf for residents on weekdays on an 18-hole golf course nearby. Marine Terrace (phone: 0970-617558). Moderate.

DOLGELLAU

George III – This 300-year-old hotel with restaurant is delightfully situated at the head of the Mawddach estuary. Freshly caught fish is the restaurant's specialty in summer, and in winter, the menu turns to local game. All 13 rooms have views of the estuary and the mountains. Just out of town on the A493 in Penmaenpool (phone: 0341-422525). Moderate.

Golden Lion Royal – The decor here ranges from casual to formal, with 28 comfortable, antique-furnished rooms. Lion St. (phone: 0341-422579). Moderate.

CRICCIETH

Bron Eifion – A country house hotel, conveniently close to Portmeirion and within sight of Cardigan Bay. Lots of Oregon pine paneling distinguishes the interior, as does the caring approach of the Robertson family, who owns it (phone: 0766-522385). Moderate.

HARLECH

Maes-y-Neuadd – Pronounced "Mice-er-Nayeth," this establishment, run by two families, is one of Wales's most charming country-house hotels. The front bedrooms have the best views, overlooking Snowdon and the Troeth Bach estuary. Expect superbly cooked Welsh specialties from the kitchen: lamb in honey, cider, and rosemary; herrings with apple and sage; and Welsh amber pudding. Reservations necessary for non-resident Sunday lunches. At Talsarnau, 3 miles (4.8 km) north of Harlech (phone: 0766-780200). Expensive.

CAERNARVON

Chocolate House – Guests stay in the private studio cottages that hug the pleasant courtyard and dine in — where else? — the *Chocolate House,* which specializes, as its name implies, in chocolate desserts. Open March through October. Plas Treflan, Caeathro (phone: 0286-672542). Moderate.

Royal – A historic coaching inn with 58 rooms that's been updated and made very comfortable. Its good dining room specializes in local produce. North Rd. (phone: 0286-673184). Moderate.

Black Boy Inn – Within the town's medieval walls, this inn dates from the 14th century. Oak beams and inglenooks abound, and the cuisine of its restaurant is simple but good. North Gate St. (phone: 0286-673023). Inexpensive.

The Cotswolds

Less than 100 miles (160 km) west of London is the region known as the Cotswolds. It encompasses about 450 square miles of rolling limestone upland of the Cotswold Hills, punctuated by charming, carefully preserved medieval towns and villages built from the hills' honey-colored stone, which gives the region its character. The Cotswolds themselves stretch northeast in a curving 60-mile arc from Bath to the vicinity of Stratford-upon-Avon. Along their western edge they form a steep ridge of solid limestone, and their crest is the Thames-Severn watershed. But the overall character of the countryside is tranquil and picturesque, like a rich tapestry. Much of this land is a great, sweeping pasture for the famous Cotswold sheep, with their heavy ringlets of fleece that once upon a time brought wealth to the area.

This is the England of the imagination: rolling hills covered by copses of ancient oaks, a landscape scaled to size for country walks and bird-watching. Towns are tied to one another by twisting country lanes that carry a constant commerce of farmers and sheepers, postmen, parsons, and pubgoers. The vista from any hill is as likely to include the square tower of a Norman church as a far field of cropping sheep, and any church is likely to be surrounded by the stone tile roofs of a tiny village, now no longer populated by farm workers but by retired folk, weekenders, and commuters to the larger towns. Village cemeteries are shaded by yews and village streams guarded by weeping willows. Nothing is very far from anything else, but privacy and protective isolation are accentuated by the quiet and country peace that settles over all. Although relatively few ancient customs have survived, village names are remnants of an earlier language and a younger England: Wyck Rissington, Upper and Lower Slaughter, Oddington, Guiting Power, Clapton-on-Hill, Bourton-on-the-Water, Chipping Campden.

The Cotswolds provided a rich agricultural center for the Romans until the 5th century, and the Roman presence is still visible in many places, such as the roads in Cirencester and the baths in Bath. The Romans left, the Danes took over, the Saxons routed the Danes, and the Normans routed the Saxons; and they all left their mark. But when the Cotswold sheep began to pay off, it was the wool merchants of the Middle Ages who built the symbols of the area that have endured — magnificent churches like the 15th-century one at Northleach and the 14th-century one at Cirencester.

The route described below begins in Bath, 115 miles (184 km) west of London, goes north through the heart of the Cotswolds to Stratford, and returns to London by way of Oxford. Starting from London, take the southwesterly Route M3 and the A303 past Stonehenge and swing northwest on A36 to Bath.

An eminently English way to see the Cotswolds is to take to shanks' mare and walk all or part of the 100-mile Cotswold Way, a series of well-marked and easily negotiated paths that follow the crests of the Cotswold hills from Bath to Chipping Campden in the north. Parts of the Way were first used by travelers 3,000 years ago, and later by medieval traders moving from village to village, the same villages that dot its course today. One need not be an accomplished hiker to follow the Way for a distance, and the weak of spirit can take heart in the thought that village and pub are never far apart. The benefits are multiple: Immersed in the countryside, you have a walking-pace view of the villages, buildings, cottages, churches, Roman ruins, Iron Age hill forts, and barrows — Stone Age burial mounds — that dot the region (the barrow at Belas Knap, between Cheltenham and Winchcombe, is one of the most impressive specimens in England).

The Way is maintained by the Gloucestershire County Council, which marks its course with large yellow arrows to make hiking easier. Thornhill Press publishes an excellent guide, *The Cotswold Way,* by Mark Richards, available throughout the area. A detailed guidebook, *The Way of the Cotswolds,* is available from the Heart of England Tourist Board, 2/5 Trinity St., Worcester WR1 2PW (phone: 0905-613132).

BATH: In the southwest corner of the Cotswolds region, Bath is Britain's oldest and most famous spa, where each day over 250,000 gallons of water from the mineral springs gush to the surface at a temperature of 120F (49C). The city's popularity through the ages is reflected in its architectural styles. Many quarters were built and rebuilt to suit the tastes of successive generations who came to "take the waters." But in a tremendous urban planning effort in the 18th century the whole was unified, laid out along classical lines in tier upon tier of Georgian crescents, terraces, and squares up the steep sides of the wooded hills along the winding Somerset Avon. Today it is an elegant Georgian spa that proudly calls itself the best-planned town in England.

According to legend, Bath was founded by the father of Shakespeare's King Lear, who was expelled from court as a leper, became a swineherd, and regained his health by imitating his swine and rolling in the warm mud of the mineral waters. In reality, it was probably the Romans who founded the town when they established an elaborate system of baths here in AD 54 and named the place Aquae Sulis, after a local god.

In the 5th century, after the Romans departed, the town fell into ruin. It was not until the 10th century that the region regained some prominence, when a newly built abbey was chosen for the coronation in 973 of King Edgar as the first King of England. Its fame was short-lived, and it didn't regain its reputation as a spa until the early 17th century, when the ailing Anne of Denmark, the wife of King James I, visited the baths. Kings and queens and their entourages, members of court, country gentry, and notables from all walks of life followed her lead to take the cure or just luxuriate. The baths became so popular that diarist Samuel Pepys wondered how the water could be sanitary with so many bodies jammed in it.

Today's city of elegant squares and exquisite crescent streets is the labor of love of two 18th-century architects, father and son, both named John Wood. They oversaw the rebuilding of the fashionable resort town, built the now-famous Pump Room, with its terrace restaurant, and the Assembly Rooms that today house one of the largest costume collections in the world. (The entire complex, including the Roman baths — which took archaeologists 250 years to uncover — the Pump Room, and the Assembly Rooms, are open daily.) Near the baths is the 15th-century Abbey Church.

But the Royal Crescent is the ultimate expression of Bath, a beautiful scimitar of street with 30 pale amber Georgian stone houses whose 114 Ionic columns, like soldiers on parade, support a continuous cornice the length of the street. It is considered the handsomest street in England. Visitors can see the interior of 1 Royal Crescent, perfectly restored in its Georgian splendor. Landsdown Crescent is another testament to the elegance of the Regency period. At Great Pulteney Street is the *Holburne Museum and Crafts Study Centre* (closed Mondays and January and February), with a superb collection of silver, glass, porcelain, miniatures, and paintings by English masters.

A $15 million development plan has restored three of the city's 18th-century baths and erected a new shopping arcade behind an original façade. The Royal Bath is now a luxury health club, while the Cross Bath is being used for teaching children to swim.

To see Bath as the Georgian era left it, it is best to go by foot, and because Bath is a small city, this is no hardship. Start with a map at the Abbey Church Yard, opposite the Pump Room, site of the tourist office (open daily; phone: 0225-62831). Here you can also get complete information on the city and its environs, including a detailed plan of the baths. Guided tours are available.

About 2 miles (3.2 km) east of the city, on A36, is Claverton Manor, home of the *American Museum in Britain,* which has 18 rooms with period furnishings from the 17th to the 19th century. Open from 2 to 5 PM, daily except Mondays, March to October.

En Route from Bath – Route A46 north takes you immediately into the hills, lifted by an enormous underpinning arm of limestone tilting south and east, where the road winds left and right with the contours of the terrain. It is a particularly beautiful road, lined with hedgerows and trees and many wild flowers in early spring. After about 11 miles (18 km) turn right onto B4040, marked Malmesbury. This narrow road passes close to the village of Badminton, the site of the Duke of Beaufort's stately mansion and the birthplace of the game that bears its name. The 15,000-acre estate of Badminton House is the scene of the renowned horse trials every April; open only to groups by special arrangement. To get to Badminton village, turn left at Acton Turville for about a mile (1.6 km). Ten miles (16 km) farther is Malmesbury.

MALMESBURY: This pleasant little town high above the river Avon is the site of a magnificent Norman abbey with a most unusual history. During the dissolution under King Henry VIII in the 16th century, the building was sold to a clothier for £1,500. The man promptly brought in his weaving machinery and converted it into a factory. It was not until 1823 that a restoration effort was begun. Despite the many years of decay, the restoration was eminently successful, and today the abbey represents the finest example of Norman building remaining in Britain. The richly carved south porch and the musicians' gallery are especially impressive.

The town has two special connections with aviation. The first was at Malmesbury Abbey in the 11th century, when Elmer, a monk, attempted to defy gravity by leaping from the tower wearing a pair of homemade wings. He survived the leap but was lame ever after. And at Kemble, 6 miles (10 km) north of Malmesbury, the Royal Air Force aerobatic team, the *Red Arrows,* practice their aerial formations.

Malmesbury is one of the oldest boroughs in England and a very well planned medieval city; it was already an important town before the Norman invasion. Some medieval remains are still extant, including fragments of walls and ruins of a 12th-century castle that can be seen today at the *Old Bell* hotel. Six bridges lead to the Market Square, at whose center is an impressive octagonal Tudor market cross. There are several lovely 17th- and 18th-century houses built by rich weavers on the adjoining streets. George Washington's ancestors appear to have come from this region, since at least five Washington predecessors are buried in a churchyard in Garsdon, 2 miles (3.2 km) east of Malmesbury.

At Kemble, 8 miles (13 km) after leaving town on A429, the road crosses a frail stream that rises to the surface only a few hundred yards away. This trickle is the mighty River Thames, just starting on its epic journey to London and the sea. Four miles (6 km) farther is the ancient Roman town of Cirencester.

CIRENCESTER: A bustling market town (there is a market on Fridays in Market Place), Cirencester was called Corinium when it was the capital of the Romans' first province in Britain and second in size only to London. Three Roman roads — Akeman Street, Fosse Way, and Ermine Street — radiated from the town, and are still used by traffic today. Mosaic floors, sculpture, and pottery recovered from the digs now form the extensive collection of Roman relics in the *Corinium Museum* on Park Street (open daily from April to September; closed Mondays from October to March). Just outside town, on Quern Hill, are the remains of a Roman amphitheater, just as one would expect in a major provincial capital. Don't miss the magnificent array of medieval stained glass in the 15th-century parish church. A number of events are staged in Cirencester each year, including horse trials, hot-air balloon meetings, polo competitions in May, June, and August, the ancient *Sheep Fair* in September, and a cattle market every Tuesday.

En Route from Cirencester – Take Route A429 out of town. If you have time, travel the more circuitous route to Fossebridge via Barnsley and Bibury. The latter is a most attractive Cotswold village with a trout farm and an interesting folk museum in an old watermill whose moving parts still work. At Fossebridge, 7 miles (11.2 km) north, there is excellent trout fishing. This is also the turnoff for Chedworth Roman Villa, which has some of the best-preserved remains of a Roman house in England. The villa displays mosaic pavements and the hypocaust, or central heating system — an underground fire chamber and a series of tile flues for distributing heat. In season, there is a display of lilies of the valley in the garden, thought to have been originally planted by the Romans (closed Mondays in summer, Wednesdays through Sundays in winter, and all of January and February).

Continuing north on A429 for 5 miles (8 km), you come to the junction with A40 and the town of Northleach. You can stop at this picturesque old coaching town before going 9 miles (14.4 km) farther to Bourton-on-the-Water.

NORTHLEACH: Important in the wool trade in the 15th century, this village of winding streets has changed little. Its proud church with its richly carved south porch is one of the finest built by the medieval wool merchants. Unlike many others in the region, this church miraculously escaped defacement by the Puritans. Also worth visiting are some lovely Tudor almshouses in the village and the Blind House, the windowless 18th-century jail.

BOURTON-ON-THE-WATER: With the River Windrush flowing gently beside the main street, this village is sometimes called the Venice of the Cotswolds. It has a picture-postcard quality: The stream is so clear, the banks are so green, and the tiny 18th-century stone bridges are so picturesque — it all seems like a tableau. A good starting point for a walking tour is the *Old New Inn,* which has a scale model of the village at one-ninth the original size. Don't miss the quaint old house on Sherborn

Street, built in 1650 with dovecotes set right into the wall. Dial House is another old cottage (1698). Most other houses in town date from the 18th century.

Another attraction is Birdland, a bird garden, which contains more than 600 exotic species from all over the world (open daily). Much of the Cotswolds is a bird-watcher's paradise, and the English pursue this favorite pastime with single-minded vigor. A midsummer walk down any wooded lane or along the Cotswold Way is likely to turn up magpies, rooks, or ravens; larks, thrushes, or blue tits; blackbirds, wood pigeons, and the English robin. You might want to take a pair of binoculars and a field guide.

En Route from Bourton-on-the-Water – This is the heart of the Cotswolds, a series of tiny villages signposted along unclassified roads that lead to an England long gone elsewhere. The Rissingtons — Wyck, Little, and Great — are three quiet villages on the western slope of the Windrush Valley. All have the Norman churches so commonly found in Cotswold towns, though Wyck Rissington's is perhaps the oldest, with remnants of an earlier Saxon church incorporated in the structure of its Norman edifice. More imposing — and more than slightly daft — is the tall, straight, comely redwood that rises over the village; visible for miles, the tree was planted by an early visitor to the US.

More famous than the Rissingtons are the Slaughters — Upper and Lower — if fame is the correct word to use for a village of 165 people (in the case of Upper Slaughter), a crystal-clear stream full of watercress and crossed by a ford and a tiny stone bridge alongside. The village center lies behind an old castle mound, and from the byroad to Lower Slaughter, down an avenue of evergreens, you can see the magnificent Upper Slaughter Manor House, with Elizabethan front intact. Opposite the church is the entrance to the *Lords of the Manor* hotel. Lower Slaughter is one of the most renowned villages in England. The footbridge over the gently curving stream has provided a subject for countless artists and photographers. Pick up A436 to Stow-on-the-Wold, now a quiet hill town but once the bustling, prosperous center of the Cotswold wool trade because of its location at the junction of several main roads. The market square is a jumble of old inns and houses, among them the fine St. Edward's Hall, which contains a collection of armor. Continue to Moreton-in-Marsh.

MORETON-IN-MARSH: The town astride the Roman Fosse Way has a medieval stone tower on its main street that was used as a jail; a bell in the tiny tower once sounded curfew. One of the town's most interesting houses is 17th-century Creswyke House; the mulberry tree in its garden is said to have been grown from a cutting of Shakespeare's tree in Stratford. Take A44 west for about 6 miles (9.6 km), then turn right onto B4081 for Chipping Campden.

CHIPPING CAMPDEN: This town was restored carefully by the Campden Trust, a group of people mindful of the past; as a result, it is remarkably well preserved. If you can ignore the traffic — mostly visitors looking for a parking place — the main street looks just as it did hundreds of years ago. And Chipping Campden's many fine old buildings are a delight. The church, though heavily restored by the Victorians, is one of the best in the Cotswolds. Built in the Perpendicular style by the town's wool merchants in the 15th century, it is unusually large and contains several fine brasses. Near the church are almshouses dating to 1612. All along High Street, you'll see many houses built with warm Cotswold stone; also stop at the handsome bow-windowed Grevel House (the former home of a wealthy woolman) on Church Street. Across the way is Woolstapler's Hall, a 14th-century house where wool merchants traded; it's now a museum of the town's history and a tourist information center. The Market Hall, a solid yet graceful structure composed of 14 stone arches built in 1627, was where the area's farmers sold their dairy products. Pick up A46 and proceed south to Broadway.

BROADWAY: Here the diverse elements of Cotswold life come together in perfect harmony. The uniform honey-colored stone buildings lead to the inevitable cricket green; on any afternoon of a match you will hear the distinct Cotswold accent rollicking back and forth from players to spectators in support or friendly raillery. Behind a yew hedge is Abbot's Grange, a 14th-century house with its own chapel. Lording over all is the splendid *Lygon Arms* (see *Best en Route*), a coaching inn visited by Charles I and Cromwell, today one of England's finest hostelries and kitchens. The famous hotel has even brought some industry to Broadway. The workshop set up in 1904 to repair the inn's antique furniture today exports its products worldwide to collectors (the Russell showroom is open alternate Mondays and Fridays). The village has many lovely old buildings, among them the three-gabled Tudor House, the Prior's Manse, and Court Farm, with its garden of rare shrubs, an English passion. If Broadway is an attractive base for Cotswolds' exploration, it is only half the attraction. The other half is Stratford-upon-Avon, only 15 miles (24 km) away.

STRATFORD-UPON-AVON: This illustrious town, forever synonymous with William Shakespeare, is the place of his birth and burial. England carefully guards this image, and the whole town is something of a shrine to Shakespeare's memory, an international center of pilgrimage administered by an official body called the Shakespeare Birthplace Trust. And yet around and beside the thousands of visitors that come to see plays at the *Royal Shakespeare Theatre* and to make the rounds of the Shakespeare sites, Stratford's ancient existence as a very lively market town continues unabated. The town received its first market charter in 1196 — fully 368 years before Shakespeare's birth — and still holds three central markets and one important cattle market a week. As has happened for centuries, once a week Cotswold farmers bring their produce into this charming town filled with half-timbered early-16th-century buildings, set in peaceful countryside of green fields, the gentle Avon, and lovely old halls, castles, and churches.

Stratford is best explored on foot, with a walking map available at the tourist office, Judith Shakespeare House (1 High St; phone: 0789-293127). Inevitably, most of the sites you will want to visit are related to the playwright. So perhaps the best place to start is at his birthplace (Henley St.; open daily), a half-timbered 16th-century building with a lovely garden in back. The house has been furnished in the style of the period and contains memorabilia, including books and manuscripts. Going along Bridge Street, you come to the River Avon and to the lovely 14-arch Clopton Bridge, dating from the 15th century. Spacious riverside gardens lead to the *Royal Shakespeare Theatre*, which in itself draws many visitors. The season runs from April through January, and tickets should be bought as far in advance as possible from the box office (Royal Shakespeare Theatre, Stratford-upon-Avon, Warwickshire CV37 6BB). Adjoining the theater is the picture gallery and exhibition of portraits and relics of famous Shakespearean players (open daily). A pleasant riverside path leads to Holy Trinity Church, where Shakespeare and his family are buried. Nearby is Hall's Croft, once the home of Shakespeare's daughter Susanna and one of Stratford's finest Tudor townhouses. In the center of town and dating from 1596 is Harvard House (High St.), the home of the mother of John Harvard, benefactor of Harvard University. The half-timbered house is now owned by the university. A few yards away is New Place on Chapel Street, all that remains of Shakespeare's last home — the foundation — and in the fine Elizabethan garden is the venerated mulberry tree said to have been grown from a cutting planted by Shakespeare himself. Nash's house next door, which once belonged to the husband of Shakespeare's granddaughter, is now a museum of local history.

Close to Stratford are several other Shakespearean landmarks. Anne Hathaway's Cottage in Shottery, 1 mile (1.6 km) west, is a well-preserved English thatched farmhouse that was the early home of Shakespeare's wife (open daily except Sunday mornings in winter). Mary Arden's House in Wilmcote, north of Shottery, was Shakespeare's mother's home before her marriage. It is one of the outstanding farmsteads in Warwickshire. Most of the 16th-century buildings are made of close-timbered oak beams and native stone, an ideal setting for the museum of rural life they now house. Within the pleasant countryside north of Stratford via A46 is Charlecote Park, where young Will was allegedly caught poaching. The massive Elizabethan mansion, fronted by an avenue of lime trees, is now a museum of historic carriages (open daily except Mondays and Thursdays, March through October). Farm buildings near the picturesque gatehouse have been converted into an attractive restaurant with a walled garden.

From Stratford, take Route A34 to Oxford, 40 miles (64 km) away through rich farmland.

OXFORD: A much-quoted description of Oxford by the 19th-century poet Matthew Arnold — "that sweet city with her dreaming spires" — is still apt today, at least from afar when one first sees the university's towers, domes, and pinnacles rising impressively above the skyline. But it soon becomes clear that today a busy industrial city surrounds the ancient university community. In fact, town preceded gown. Oxford the city was established in about 912, the university 250 years later. Relations between the two were hostile, and after a series of riots the university took virtual control of the town — for 600 years. But peace was eventually made, and now town and gown work closely together to guard the character of the city and keep the historic core of Oxford intact. This core — one of the great living architectural treasures of the world — contains examples of every style of building from Saxon times in less than a square mile.

To do Oxford justice, spend at least one full day, during most of which you will be on foot. The city's charm is in its streets: High Street, with its sweeping curve and magnificent skyline; lovely 17th-century Hollywell Street; and ancient, cobblestone Merton. Peace and quiet here collect in out-of-the-way places: alleyways such as Magpie Lane and Logic Lane off busy High Street; the well-kept college gardens and quadrangles along the banks of the city's two rivers — Thames and Cherwell; the green open spaces in the heart of the city, including Christ Church Meadow, only a few hundred yards from High Street and St. Aldate's. The latter is a good starting point for a walking tour of the historic buildings. A first stop should be the Information Center in St. Aldate's, opposite Town Hall (phone: 0865-726871), which arranges sightseeing tours and provides maps.

More than 600 buildings in the city are considered of outstanding architectural or historic merit. Most belong to the university, and among those you should not miss are Christ Church, established by Henry VIII in 1546, with Tom Tower, which dominates St. Aldate's; Tom Quad, the largest quadrangle in Oxford, and the college chapel, which is Oxford Cathedral; Magdalen College, dating from 1458; Merton, the oldest college, built in 1264, which also has the oldest library and Mob Quad, the oldest complete quadrangle; New College, founded in 1379, which contains parts of the ancient city wall; twin-towered All Souls College, which has a sun dial by Christopher Wren; St. John's College with the Canterbury Quadrangle, a masterpiece of 17th-century architecture; the circular *Sheldonian Theatre,* designed by Wren and completed in 1669, used for university ceremonies; St. Mary the Virgin, the university church dating from the 13th and 14th centuries; and the *Ashmolean Museum,* the first public museum in Britain (closed Mondays and Sunday mornings).

A short 8-mile (12.8-km) drive north of Oxford is Bleinheim Palace, a huge estate with 2,000 acres of parkland, now the home of the 11th Duke of Marlborough.

From Oxford, London is a distance of 57 miles (92 km) away.

BEST EN ROUTE

The Cotswolds are inn country. There is a plethora of coaching or posting inns, converted manor houses, and small historic hostelries. Someone famous has invariably slept in every one of them, and it's often a matter of deciding whether you would rather put your head on a pillow where Cromwell slept before a great battle or rest in a former royal stopover.

The places listed here have a common denominator best described by the word "outstanding," but the outstanding feature may range from the architecture, history, or location of a building to the quality of service, degree of comfort, or price of the establishment. Generally, expect to pay at least $95 per night for a double in those hotels we've listed as expensive; from $75 to $95 in the moderate category; and under $75 in the inexpensive range. The Cotswolds are chockablock with small bed-and-breakfast houses in which a bed and a meal can cost $65 to $75 for two, and though we've restricted the listings below to the more historic and intriguing hostelries, don't overlook these homey, comfortable places while you travel. Expect to pay as much as $80 or more for two for a meal in the expensive restaurants; $55 to $70 in the moderate; under $55, inexpensive.

BATH

Royal Crescent – Forming the impressive center of the famous Royal Crescent, this elegant Georgian hotel occupies an unrivaled location. With commanding views, it is within walking distance of the Assembly Rooms, the Roman baths, the Pump Room, and the abbey. It has 36 super-deluxe rooms and some extra-special apartments. There are magnificent Georgian public rooms, a good restaurant, and on long, lazy hot days, tea is served in the attractive gardens. 15-16 Royal Crescent (phone: 0225-319090). Expensive.

Pratt's – Equally historic, this hotel is in a quiet cul-de-sac of the South Parade near the River Avon and the city center. It has 48 modern, comfortable rooms, all with a private bath. The restaurant serves traditional meals. South Parade (phone: 0225-60441). Moderate.

Hole in the Wall – This restaurant sounds like a cellar but in fact is a beamed and flagstone room, an altogether delightfully civilized place to have dinner. Although the restaurant seats 40 people, reservations are required, especially for Saturday night. Dishes are enticing and there is great variety; the cuisine is mostly French and usually superb. Closed Sundays and 3 weeks at Christmas. 16 George St. (phone: 0225-25242). Expensive.

MALMESBURY

Old Bell – This is a fabulous old inn, a wisteria-clad gabled building, originally the guesthouse of a famous Norman abbey. It still retains a medieval spiral staircase and part of the castle wall. There are 18 rooms, all with central heating. The inn has pretty gardens, a good restaurant, and the charming *Castle Bar.* Abbey Row (phone: 0666-822344). Expensive.

CIRENCESTER

King's Head – Opposite the famous parish church in the attractive marketplace, this 15th-century coaching inn has been completely modernized without losing its charm. Amenities include 70 well-appointed suites and an elegant restaurant offering high-quality, extensive à la carte and table d'hôte menus. Market Pl. (phone: 0285-3322). Expensive to moderate.

Fleece – Dating from the time of Henry VIII, this hotel has an attractive black and white timbered frontage. Inside the downstairs rooms, lounge, and bar have Cotswold stone walls, fine open fireplaces, and low beamed ceilings. A Jacobean staircase leads upstairs to 25 suites, some with teak furniture. The restaurant specializes in nouvelle cuisine. Real ales (try the local brew, the Three B's Ale) are served. The staff is helpful and pleasant. Market Pl. (phone: 0285-68507). Moderate.

UPPER SLAUGHTER

Lords of the Manor – If Upper Slaughter didn't have a beautifully preserved 17th-century manor house and surrounding grounds as a hostelry for visitors, it would be necessary to invent one. Luckily it was done some 300 years ago, and you need only call for reservations. Just outside town (phone: 0451-20243). Expensive.

STOW-ON-THE-WOLD

Fosse Manor – An ivy-covered manor house with 23 spacious rooms and a restaurant serving English country fare. Fosse Way (phone: 0451-30354). Moderate.

King's Arms – So named because King Charles spent a night here in 1645, this 500-year-old inn offers simple lodgings. Market Sq. (phone: 0451-30364). Moderate to inexpensive.

MORETON-IN-MARSH

White Hart Royal – If you stay here, you will have shared a place with royalty — Charles I spent the night in this half-timbered posting inn in 1644. The hotel has 27 rooms and a small timbered dining room. High St. (phone: 0608-50731). Expensive to moderate.

BROADWAY

Lygon Arms – This is one of England's fine old inns. The main building dates from 1530, though parts of it are more than 600 years old. It was frequented by Charles I and Oliver Cromwell, and rooms named after each have been carefully preserved or restored. There is also a well-designed modern extension, and the harmonious relationship of old and new gives the inn a vivid and lively air. There are 64 beautifully appointed rooms (all with bath) with classic antique furnishings. The magnificent Tudor dining room serves expensive meals, but they're worth it. The cuisine has won awards. High St. (phone: 0386-852255). Expensive.

Dormy House – Originally a farmhouse built on an escarpment above Broadway, its ancient beams and exposed stone walls prove its historic pedigree while open fires, wood paneling, and cozy bedrooms bring contemporary warmth. So does the cheery staff under the skipperdom of Harvey Pascoe. Willersey Hill, Broadway (phone: 0386-852711). Moderate.

STRATFORD-UPON-AVON

Moat House International – Behind the somewhat pedestrian façade are all the comforts expected of a major hotel chain. The hotel has 250 rooms, all elegant, many with marvelous views. Guests have free access to an adjacent leisure center. Bridgefoot (phone: 0789-414411). Expensive.

Grosvenor House – On the main Warwick Road, this hostelry is actually several large houses imaginatively linked into one comfortable hotel which features a sauna, fitness center, spa baths, and beauty salon. Close to the center of town. 12 Warwick Rd. (phone: 0789-69213). Moderate.

Payton – A well-maintained little hotel with a homelike atmosphere in a quiet part of town, though only a short walk from the back gate of Shakespeare's birthplace. 6 John St. (phone: 0789-66442). Inexpensive.

OXFORD

Randolph – The best in town, with Victorian-Gothic charm, an efficient staff, and a very good location directly opposite the *Ashmolean Museum*. There are 109 rooms, a restaurant with continental cuisine, a snack shop, and a bar. Cream teas are served every afternoon in the lounge. Beaumont St. (phone: 0865-247481). Expensive.

Studley Priory – A marvelous alternative to an indifferent overnight stay in town is this excellent hotel that was once a 12th-century Benedictine priory, later an Elizabethan manor house. On 13 acres amid rural peace and quiet, it is only 7 miles (11 km) from Oxford. Filmgoers will recognize it as Thomas More's Tudor manor in *A Man for All Seasons.* The 19 rooms provide modern comfort in harmony with period furnishings. There are log fires in the public rooms and good food in the lovely dining room. The easiest approach is from the Headington roundabout on the A40 bypass east of Oxford. Horton-cum-Studley (phone: 0867-35203). Expensive.

The Lake District

The drive from London to Scotland can hit some heavy weather in the western Midlands, where the concentration of heavy-duty industrial cities is particularly high. Stoke-on-Trent, Sheffield, Manchester, Liverpool — these names reverberate with the crash of the steel mill and the roar of the factory. A well-meaning Londoner might urge you to stay steadfastly to the east, ensuring that you encounter the more bucolic pleasures of Cambridge, Lincoln, York, and Northumberland (see the *Northeast England* route). And indeed, so splendid are those towns and the country around them that it would be hard to argue with such advice.

Unless it meant forgoing forever that crumpled, rumpled, well-watered mountain country known as the Lake District, squeezed tarn, mere, beck, and fell into the small county of Cumbria, just an hour or so north of Manchester. Only 30 miles across in any direction, there is a special intensity in the beauty of the Lake District, as if nature were offering a unique reward for the sprawling rigors of the industrial belt. No part of England is so universally loved by Britons — for the purity of its meres, clearwater mountain lakes; its almost vertical fields filled with grazing sheep, each field carefully delineated by painstakingly maintained stone walls; its sharp rocky peaks; and the thousands of tiny lakes (tarns) fed year in and year out by innumerable waterfalls and streams — the becks. What is earth-loving and ancient in the English spirit is drawn irresistibly to the uncompromising beauty of the Lake District.

Small wonder that the Lake District is primarily associated with a group of poets of the late 18th and early 19th centuries who not only celebrated the beauty of the region, but discovered here values to stand against the encroaching horrors of the Industrial Revolution. Chief among these poets was William Wordsworth, who lived here for most of his life, but others are equally well known: Robert Southey, Samuel Taylor Coleridge, and writers John Ruskin and Thomas De Quincey. Much of what you see and do in the region is associated with the Lake Poets.

One of the most surprising things about the Lake District is how small this famous area really is. You can drive right through it in less than an hour and yet spend a month without ever seeing half of what time and nature have created here. Looking at a map, you see that the principal lakes — Derwentwater, Ullswater, Windermere, wild Wastwater, Buttermere, Crummock Water, Tarn Hows, Grasmere, and Rydal Water — radiate from a central mountain mass like the spokes of a wheel. The distances between these postcard-perfect lakes are short, but each of the larger lakes provides a good base for exploring the nearby area. You could easily spend 2 days around each major lake — Derwentwater, Windermere, and Ullswater especially — before moving on, allowing time for some hiking as well as exploring the towns and villages of the district.

The route described below actually begins in the northeastern corner of the Lake District, at the town of Penrith near Ullswater, and cuts a deep V into the heart of the area. From Windermere, in the south-central section of the lakes, there is easy access to the challenging mountain peak of Helvellyn (3,113 feet). The next leg of the trip, north from Windermere to Derwentwater, crosses the paths of the Lake Poets. For the last 37 years of his life Wordsworth lived at Rydal Mount, just a few miles from Ambleside. The home he had occupied previously, Dove Cottage, is a few miles farther north, at Grasmere. Thomas De Quincey, author of *Confessions of an English Opium Eater,* took over the cottage when Wordsworth moved. At the north end of this leg is Derwentwater — perhaps the most beautiful of all the lakes. Robert Southey made his home here, in the town of Keswick, where he frequently was joined by Percy Bysshe Shelley and Coleridge. The twins, Buttermere and Crummock Water, are just a short drive southwest of Keswick, and beyond them, in the northwest corner of the Lake District, is Cockermouth. Wordsworth and his sister Dorothy were both born and raised here, and the family home and nearby fields became part of the joyous imagery of the poetry that introduced this area to readers everywhere. From Cockermouth, the route follows the western boundary of the Lake District, heading south, and numerous small roads lead into the heart of the mountains and the area's best climbing. The route cuts across the base of the Lake District to return you to the main highway and London, north to Scotland, or east to Yorkshire.

LONDON: For a complete description of the city and its hotels and restaurants, see *London,* THE CITIES.

En Route from London – Leave London on either the M4 west (through the Cotswolds) to the M5 and north into the M6, or by taking the M1 north to Rugby and picking up the M6 westbound, later bearing north at Birmingham. Beyond Manchester and Liverpool lie the beautiful Forest of Bowland, and, just beyond, the fringes of the Lake District. Drive along the edge of this mountainous area to Penrith (exit 40), at the northern end of the district.

PENRITH: The charming town of Penrith has withstood time and the onslaught of travelers comfortably. The oldest section of town has grown up around the 13th-century Church of St. Andrew (rebuilt in the early 1700s) and the nearby 16th-century schoolhouse. Several conflicting legends surround the presence of the two stone formations on the church grounds, known as Giant's Grave and Giant's Thumb. One version holds that this is the burial place of an ancient king. The ruins of Penrith Castle are now a town park, but two excellent 16th-century inns are still thriving, the *Gloucester Arms* and the *Two Lions.*

En Route from Penrith – Just outside Penrith on B5320 is the village of Tirril. A few minutes' drive beyond is Pooley Bridge, at the northern end of Ullswater, the second largest of the region's lakes. It is possible to arrange a day's boating or fishing at Pooley Bridge, a fine way to explore this beautiful lake. And keep an eye out for the elusive wild red deer that frequent the southeastern shore of Ullswater. A worthwhile diversion from Pooley Bridge is the secondary road along the southern shore of the lake past the *Sharrow Bay* hotel, which surveys the most scenic views in the district; the road leads ultimately to the peaceful valley of Martindale. Route A592 continues to skirt the northwestern bank of Ullswater, bypassing Gowbarrow Park. This grassy fell comes alive with daffodils each year, and traveling poets can, as Wordsworth did, pause to write about the yellow blooms.

The village of Glenridding, at the head of Ullswater Lake, has a pier to match that of Pooley Bridge, 13 miles (21 km) away by road. (By water, the lake is only 7½ miles long.) Patterdale, which shares the head of the lake, is only a mile farther.

From here the roadway crosses over the Helvellyn mountain range through Kirkstone Pass. There are several good climbing trails through these hills, and some of the most challenging paths lead to the peak of Helvellyn Mount (3,113 feet). But the ascent of Kirkstone Pass (1,489 feet), though fairly steep in some places, certainly holds no difficulties for drivers. At the summit is *Kirkstone Pass Inn,* which has the distinction of being one of the highest taverns in England. On the far side of the pass the road leads down to Troutbeck Valley and the small town of Troutbeck. At the southern end of Troutbeck is the 17th-century Townend House, used as a residence by the family of Yeoman Browne. The interior and furnishings remain intact, as does the timbered barn (open daily except Mondays and Saturdays, April to October).

WINDERMERE AND BOWNESS: The adjoining resort areas of Windermere and Bowness mark the middle of Lake Windermere's east bank. The view of the lake from the town is unimpressive, but if you climb to the peak of Orrest Head (just north of the railroad station) you'll get a far better perspective of the lake and its surrounding mountains. Virtually every recreational activity imaginable — fishing, boating, sailing, golf, tennis, scuba, and even pony trekking — is available in this busy visitor center.

Charles Dickens is known to have spent many hours in the *New Hall Inn* in Bowness, although in his time the inn, founded in 1612, was called the Hole in the Wall. When Dickens visited, the proprietor was Thomas Longmire, a well-known wrestling champion (which may account for the lack of damage inflicted on the pub over the years).

Lake Windermere, the largest of the lakes (10½ miles long), has a much softer aspect than most of the lakes in the region, the happy product of its luxuriantly wooded banks, filled with rhododendrons that burst into flaming color each June. The best way to see it is to take one of the regular cruises that operate between Lake Side in the south and Bowness and Waterhead at the lake's northern end (May through September). There are several small islands in Windermere; on one of them, Belle Isle, is a magnificent 18th-century mansion that is unfortunately not open to the public. Seen from Bowness and other points along the more civilized side of Windermere, the western shore has all the lure of undiscovered territory. Fortunately for intrepid explorers, there is a ferry from Bowness to the far side that deposits travelers on a secondary road leading to the village of Near Sawrey, the site of Hilltop Cottage. This quaint 17th-century house was the home of Beatrix Potter, the author and illustrator whose Peter Rabbit, Squirrel Nutkin, and other characters have been loved by generations of children. A collection of her drawings is on display, and children will be pleased to find the setting of most of her tales right around the house and grounds (open daily, except Mondays, April through October). The road passes a small lake, Esthwaite Water, and continues into Hawkshead, just under 6 miles (9.6 km) from the ferry.

HAWKSHEAD: Far from the resort mood of Windermere, this quiet little village beyond Esthwaite Water offers an introductory course in Lake District life that begins at the 17th-century *Queen's Head Inn,* where you can get a pint of ale to fortify you for a stroll through the stone cottages of the town. Start at the schoolhouse, founded in 1585 by native son Edwin Sandys, Archbishop of York, and attended by Wordsworth between 1778 and 1783. You'll find his name scratched in one of the desks. Wordsworth may have lodged at Ann Tyson's cottage, on a lane off Red Lion Square. Northwest of Hawkshead, a steep byroad leads to Tarn Hows, a small fir-fringed lake high in the hills that has the best views of the surrounding countryside, especially of Coniston Water to the south and the mountain called the Old Man of Coniston, which lords it over the lake. John Ruskin is buried at Coniston Church; his home at Brantwood is open to the public. Take the northbound secondary road out of Hawkshead to nearby Ambleside.

AMBLESIDE: Just less than a mile from the north end of Lake Windermere, Ambleside is an excellent touring base for climbers eager to explore the lakeland's hills and forests. Wordsworth's famed Scafell Pike (3,210 feet) is a considerable hike from Ambleside, but other peaks are more accessible. It is best to obtain detailed maps of trails and to make proper arrangements before starting any trek. The local information center is in Ambleside's old Court House in the Market Square (phone: 05394-32582). A short distance away, up the lane past *The Royal Yachtsman,* is Stockghyll Force, a beautiful waterfall cascading 70 feet to rocks below. St. Mary's Church, erected in 1854 by Sir Gilbert Scott, has a memorial to Wordsworth and a mural of the village's rush-bearing festival, still held yearly on the last Saturday in July. The festival is thought to descend from a Roman harvest ceremony. Just 2 miles (3.2 km) north of Ambleside on A591 is Rydal.

RYDAL: William Wordsworth, with his wife, three children, sister, and sister-in-law, moved to this village in 1813 and lived here until his death in 1850. His home, Rydal Mount, contains a large collection of memorabilia, including several portraits of his family and friends, and his personal library. Wordsworth drew heavily on the surrounding countryside for inspiration and poetic images, and the mute crags and flowered hillsides around his home appear repeatedly in his work. His love of nature is reflected in the 4½-acre garden he grew around Rydal Mount, as attentively cared for today as by the poet.

Just a short distance up the road is Nab Cottage, occupied briefly by Thomas De Quincey (1806) and later by Samuel Taylor Coleridge's eldest son, Hartley. Skirting the north bank of Rydal Water (which, together with the Rothay, links Grasmere and Windermere lakes), the roadway continues to the village of Grasmere.

GRASMERE: Grasmere Lake, just a mile long and half as wide, is almost too perfect for words, complete with an emerald green island in its center. Wordsworth and his sister Dorothy lived on the lake at Dove Cottage from 1799 until 1808. After William married (and fathered three children), he and his family moved to Rydal Mount, turning the cottage over to their friends Thomas De Quincey and his wife, who had been living at Nab Cottage. The *Wordsworth Museum,* across from Dove Cottage, is really a tribute to Wordsworth and his circle. Pages and materials from many area writers, famous and obscure, are displayed along with some interesting relics.

Although August is the most crowded month in which to visit the Lake District, it is also the month of the Grasmere Sports, usually held on the third Thursday of the month. The games feature traditional Lakeland sports, such as fell racing, an all-out dash to the top of the nearest mountain and back, and Cumberland wrestling. Until Cumberland and Westmorland were combined into Cumbria County, competition between these rivals was intense, and the administrative alteration hasn't changed anything; these games have been held every year since 1852. While you're in town, stop in at the Church of St. Oswald (parts of which may be from the 13th century) and, in the yard, at the graves of William Wordsworth, his wife and sister, and Hartley Coleridge.

En Route from Grasmere – Continuing north along the Rothay on A591 toward the wooded shores of Thirlmere, Helvellyn Mount rises to the right. The tiny 17th-century chapel at Wythburn is worth a visit. Its parking lot is the starting point of a climbing trail to the peak of Helvellyn (the parking lot at the north end of Thirlmere is the start of a gentler forest trail). Keswick, 13 miles (21 km) from Grasmere, is just a few miles beyond the north end of the lake. You'll get an excellent view of the area from the crest of Castlerigg, and a road on the right leads to the Castlerigg Stone Circle.

KESWICK: Sheltered by the towering Skiddaw (3,053 feet), this ancient market town sits near the shore of beautiful Derwentwater, 3 miles long and a mile wide, surrounded by a delightful mixture of bare rock, grassy banks, and forested glens and crowned by a wreath of tiny islands. One of these, Floating Island, is no more than a tangled mass of lake weeds riding on a bubble of swamp gas. The other islands, however, are more substantial, and several support beautiful homes; the remains of a 7th-century retreat are on the island of St. Herbert.

Many poets, including Shelley, Southey, Wordsworth, and Coleridge, were drawn here, and the *Keswick Museum and Art Gallery* displays some of their manuscripts, letters, and personal effects (open April to October, closed Sundays). Southey's home, Greta Hall, has become Keswick School; his body lies at the Crosthwaite Churchyard. Southey, Wordsworth, and Coleridge all patronized the bar at the *George* hotel, which claims to be the oldest structure in town. Judging by the crude stone masonry and faded walls, it may well be.

Two of the best points for viewing Derwentwater and its environs are at Castle Head (529 feet), just south of Keswick, and at Friar's Crag, a rocky headland on the lake. John Ruskin was particularly enamored of this spot, and there is a memorial to him here. Southey favored the view from the hill near Greta Bridge.

En Route from Keswick – Drive south along the eastern shore of Derwentwater on B5289 to the incredibly beautiful Borrowdale Valley. Here the Bowder Stone, a huge boulder that tumbled from some nearby height, stands precariously on edge near Castle Crag, a 900-foot-tall rock cone that can be climbed without too much effort in under half an hour. Great Gable, a little farther along the route, is a more challenging target — 2,949 feet of tough climbing. It takes about 3 hours to ascend this monster, but the view is well worth the effort. The entire area from Skiddaw to Windermere, and even the Isle of Man are visible from the crest.

Continue on B5289, crossing over Honister Pass, then dropping through some rough territory until you reach the farm of Gatesgarth. The placid waters of Buttermere come into view as the roadway curves in a giant U, first west and then north. Buttermere's nearby twin, Crummock Water, lies just beyond to the northwest. Scale Force, a lively waterfall with a drop of over 120 feet, is not far from the pretty village of Buttermere. The easiest access is by crossing the stream between the two lakes and following the path on the far side. It will be muddy, so wear boots or hiking shoes. A few miles farther north, B5289 intersects B5292; you can either take B5292 east toward A66, Keswick and Penrith, or extend your trip by heading west toward Cockermouth.

There is no direct road across the mountain barrier in the western half of the Lake District, making it a particularly appealing area for experienced and properly equipped backpackers and hill walkers.

COCKERMOUTH: Strategically placed at the junction of the Cocker and Derwent rivers, Cockermouth is a pre-Roman community, though little remains from its earliest period. Even its 12th-century castle was destroyed during the violence of the mid-1600s. Wordsworth House (open daily except Thursdays from April to October), was built in 1745. This house, in which Dorothy and William grew up, is a fairly simple, countrified example of Georgian architecture that has survived intact. The furnishings used by the Wordsworth family, however, are long gone. William's father is buried in the churchyard. Fletcher Christian of *Mutiny on the Bounty* was born at nearby Moorland Close (1764).

En Route from Cockermouth – Take A5086 south from Cockermouth along the western fringe of the Lake District. Ennerdale Water, perhaps the least visited of the larger lakes, lies about 10 miles (16 km) away, on a secondary roadway to the east. A similar turnoff about 10 miles (16 km) beyond leads to Wastwater, the deepest of the lakes, set among a group of stern and savage-faced mountains. The contrast to gentle Windermere is marked. The village of Wasdale Head, a mile beyond the lake, is an excellent climbing center, but strictly for experts.

Returning to the main road (A5086 becomes A595 near Ennerdale Water), you arrive at Ravenglass, a port at the mouth of the Esk River about 25 miles (40 km) from Cockermouth. The Eskdale Valley can be explored either by road or on the narrow-gauge, steam-powered, 7-mile-long *Ravenglass and Eskdale Railway* (narrow is an understatement; 15 inches make it positively skinny), which runs daily from April to October, with reduced service in winter.

Overlooking the River Esk, just beyond the town, is Muncaster Castle, the seat of the Pennington family for 700 years (open Easter to September, closed Mondays). Farther on, at Broughton, another secondary road (A593) leads up the Duddon Valley toward Coniston Water and Hawkshead. Just east of Broughton, A595 bears south along the coast, and A590 continues east toward A6, the city of Kendal, and the M4 motorway.

BEST EN ROUTE

Travelers to the Lake District have a wide choice of excellent accommodations, varying from some of the best hotels in the country to small (but comfortable) inns and bed-and-breakfast spots. Any number of inns and homes that provide the basics — a warm room and breakfast for a modest price — are hidden among these wooded hills. Expect B&B charges for two to run about $60 to $75. Expect to pay $95 and up per night for a double room in inns listed as expensive; between $75 and $95 for those in the moderate range; and $60 to $75 for those considered inexpensive. The hostelries listed below are a selection of our choices for the area; there are many other inns along the roads you'll be traveling, and the experience of exploring an unknown inn should be all your own. Dinners at the best establishments in the area are about $70 to $95 for two people (moderate).

ULLSWATER

Sharrow Bay Country House – Partners Francis Coulson and Brian Sack have spent 30 years making this one of the most respected and attractive hotels in the area. The dinners at the restaurant are a pleasure. Closed December to early March (phone: 08536-301). Expensive.

Leeming House – Commanding fine views over the lake, it's a gracious country house and restaurant. Closed early December to early March. Watermillock (phone: 08536-622). Expensive.

Old Church – With the Ullswater lapping on their front lawn, owners Kevin and Maureen Whitemore offer an enormous range of sporting activities in the surrounding area, along with good food and comfortable accommodations. Watermillock (phone: 08536-204). Moderate.

WINDERMERE

Belsfield – A magnificent Georgian mansion overlooking Lake Windermere with an interesting blend of period pieces and modern furnishings. A newer wing (in the garden) has been added, making a total of 66 rooms, and there's a jogging trail that winds through 6 acres of grounds. Bowness on Windermere (phone: 09662-2448). Expensive.

Miller Howe – Is it the beautiful view of placid, tree-lined Lake Windermere or the impeccable service that makes this hotel seem such a bastion of calm? In either case, there is hardly a better headquarters for touring the area. Excellent restaurant. Closed mid-December through February. Rayrigg Rd. (phone: 09662-2536). Expensive.

Rothay Manor – This elegant hotel near Ambleside has its own croquet lawn and excellent cuisine. Closed mid-January to early February. Rothay Bridge (phone: 05394-33605). Expensive.

Lowick House – Dorothy Sutcliffe takes a few guests into her beautiful Lakeland farmhouse (and puts whiskey in your porridge if the weather looks grim). Bedrooms are beautifully furnished, and dinners are multi-course feasts. Lowick, near Ulverston (phone: 0229-85227). Moderate.

Quarry Garth – A solid, no-nonsense mansion, typical of scores of private retreats built in the lakes by wealthy industrialists, with just 7 bedrooms, a cozy paneled lounge, and an elegant dining room. Troutbeck (phone: 09662-3761). Moderate.

GRASMERE

Michaels Nook – A charming Victorian country home furnished by the proprietor, Reginald Gifford, with many beautiful antiques. Some of the bathrooms have been "modernized," but the older ones are more fun. There is also a fine restaurant on the premises; reservations are a must (phone: 09665-496). Expensive.

Swan – Immortalized by Wordsworth, this very friendly 41-room hotel is admirably managed and has a good restaurant featuring a number of vegetarian dishes (phone: 09665-551). Expensive to moderate.

KESWICK

Lodore Swiss – On the edge of Derwentwater, with glorious views of the lake and Lodore Falls. Though the building is fairly large and very grand in appearance, it is run by a family (the Englands), and their high standards are readily apparent. Closed November through March (phone: 059684-285). Expensive.

Mary Mount Country House – Also on the shores of Lake Derwentwater, 3 miles (4.8 km) south of Keswick, this comfortable and cozy hotel is set in beautiful woodlands. Closed in December (phone: 059684-223). Expensive to moderate.

Pheasant Inn – This old coaching inn still retains its traditional atmosphere. On Bassenthwaite Lake near Thornthwaite Forest (phone: 07687-72219). Moderate.

Northeast England

Between the Midlands and the border of the Scottish Lowlands, where England narrows to a tight, trim waist of land, lies a section of exceptionally rugged and beautiful geography. The Pennine Chain — a group of hills that reach only 3,000 feet above sea level at their highest — runs straight down the center of this neck of land, dividing east and west as neatly as a surgeon's blade. To the west falls the Lake District and Cumbria (see *The Lake District* route); to the east, stretching across chasms and caves, are the dales and moors of Yorkshire and a long coast on the North Sea.

At England's narrowest point, Roman legions were once posted in an uneasy vigilance against the raids of marauding Pict warriors from the north. In AD 122, goaded past endurance, Emperor Hadrian ordered the construction of an immense wall, to reach from the North Sea at the River Tyne to Solway Firth on the Irish Sea coast, to discourage the savage northerners. The high, parapeted wall, 6 feet high and 8 feet thick, stretched for 73½ miles and was punctuated at every mile by a guard station filled with Roman soldiers — still uneasy. What remains of this magnificent effort are various ruins across Northumberland and many mile stations still standing.

Later, with the coming of the Normans, a network of castles was built across this area. Many of these medieval fortresses are also extant, as obdurate and impregnable as ever, firm against age. Others have crumbled, leaving the history of their passing in broken walls and weary battlements.

It is rather apt that the gateway to this country of rocky moors, forested dales, and sandy resort beaches on the North Sea coast is the ancient city of York, home of York Minster, one of Great Britain's most beautiful cathedrals. As wild as the country is, it has always been a center of British religious experience, and Christianity actually came to Britain through the coastal island of Lindisfarne (Holy Island).

The route described below is circular, leaving York for the journey north through the North York moors to Durham, dominated by Britain's finest Norman cathedral, and then on to Newcastle upon Tyne and along the coastline to Berwick-upon-Tweed on the Scottish border. Here the route turns south again to wander through the central highlands of the Pennines, the moor, and Yorkshire dales on its way back to York. For more information, contact the Northumbria Tourist Board, Aykley Heads, Durham DH1 5UX (phone: 091-3846905), and the Yorkshire and Humberside Tourist Board, 312 Tadcaster Rd., York YO2 2HF (phone: 0904-707961).

LONDON: For a complete description of the city and its hotels and restaurants, see *London,* THE CITIES.

En Route from London – Take the M1 motorway directly north from London to Leeds and pick up A64 going northeast to York. It's a fairly long journey, about 225 miles (360 km) all told, and will take about 4 hours.

YORK: Its very name has the ring of ancient authority about it, and well it should. The Romans established York — then called Eboracum — in AD 71 as a garrison town and the seat of the province. A succession of Roman emperors visited, and it was here, in 306, that Constantine the Great was proclaimed ruler of the known world. Such is the fleeting nature of glory that the Romans abandoned the town only 75 years later, and it slipped quietly from history until the Anglo-Saxons moved 3 centuries later. It was a walled city when King Harold II was in the area in 1066, fighting the Scandinavians, only to be called back to the south of England on the double to meet the forces of William the Conqueror.

The section of the city within the ancient walls is perhaps the best-preserved medieval city in Great Britain, and from its heart rises the largest Gothic cathedral in the country, York Minster. Begun in 1081 on the site of a series of earlier churches, it was not completed until the 15th century. More stunning than its awesome proportions are its stained-glass windows, the largest concentration of stained glass in Great Britain. The giant Great East Window is the size of a tennis court.

The medieval heart of the city is girdled by 3 miles of defensive wall, and the most interesting parts of the city are within them. Just as in the Middle Ages, the quirky, timbered, slightly akimbo buildings in the Shambles — once the butchers' quarter — are devoted to shops, though the butchers have given way to boutiques, galleries, and crafts shops, most with original butcher's block and meat hooks intact. Goodramgate is another medieval shopping area, and Micklegate, the central highway of yore, is lined with much later but very beautiful Georgian homes and buildings. Other required stops are the pillared Assembly Rooms, evoking the elegance of the 18th century, and the medieval timberwork of the Merchant Adventurers' Hall. Then relax at the *Black Swan* in Peasholme Green; in 1417, the Lord Mayor of York lived in the house. Definitely worth seeing are the reconstructed period scenes at the *Castle Museum* (open daily) and *National Railway Museum* (open daily), which houses a history of the railroad.

En Route from York – Take A64 northeast toward the North York Moors National Park, about 40 miles (64 km) away. A roadway about 9 miles (14 km) outside York leads to Castle Howard, a palatial mansion topped by a gilded dome that was used as the setting for the television production of Evelyn Waugh's *Brideshead Revisited* (open daily from Easter through October). Sir John Vanbrugh designed the central structure, erected early in the 18th century. A wing was added in the 1750s. A collection of period clothing is on display; the house is magnificently decorated and furnished. The grounds, including a lake, complete the image of luxuriant living.

Rejoin A64 and continue to the small market town of Malton. Then go north on A169 through Old Malton to Pickering.

PICKERING: This little town is on the fringe of the national park, a vast expanse of rolling hills and valleys that becomes a purple sea abloom with heather during the late summer. Pickering is well suited to the quiet atmosphere of the moor — time has not altered either appreciably. Relax at the *Black Bull Inn,* an ancient stone tollhouse, before exploring the moors. An easy way to view these beautiful valleys and ridges of exposed rock is aboard the Moorsrail, a steam-powered line built in 1836 by George Stephenson that runs between Pickering and Goathland in summer.

En Route from Pickering – Route A169 cuts right through the moorlands to the coast, passing the *Saltersgate Inn* (where peat fires have welcomed travelers for uncounted years) along the road to Whitby. This delightful old port is overlooked from a cliff by the impressive ruins of Whitby Abbey, established in 657 and extensively rebuilt around the 12th century (open daily). Long associated with the sea and sailing ships, the older parts of Whitby still consist of cobbled streets and the red tile cottages used by fishermen and shipwrights. A resort area has grown on the town's West Cliff.

Just a few miles south of Whitby along the coast (off A171), clinging to the cliffs, is the village of Robin Hood's Bay. Here the tall cliffs drop to their lowest point, creating a beautiful setting for the picturesque fishing settlement. Those jumbo globes visible from the road are part of the Ballistic Missile Early Warning Station in the Fylingdale Moor area.

The leading resort town on the Yorkshire coast, Scarborough, lies about 15 miles (24 km) farther south. The clifftop ruins of a 12th-century castle and the Church of St. Mary (also 12th century) separate the two sandy bays that are Scarborough's principal attractions. The shrinking old sector, near the harbor, still preserves its crafts and fish markets and several early homes. The bluff, now the site of a castle ruins, once held an Iron Age lookout-earthwork, a Roman fire beacon, and later a chapel. Beyond is South Bay and a spa with beautiful gardens. This is a residential area, reflected in stately homes and abundant gardens.

Return to Pickering on A170 westbound, skirting the southern fringe of the moors. Having traced a circle northeast of Pickering, continue west on A170 past the town toward Kirkbymoorside and Helmsley.

HELMSLEY: The ruins of a 12th-century castle dominate this small town at the foot of the ridges where the valleys of Pickering and Rye meet. Just 2 miles (3.2 km) away, in the Ryedale Valley, are the magnificent ruins of Rievaulx Abbey, built over a period of almost 200 years in the 12th and 13th centuries. The terrace above the abbey overlooks the ruins themselves and offers a fine view of the pastoral vale. If staying overnight, try the *Black Swan* hotel, (see *Best en Route*) a 400-year-old Georgian and Tudor building with a modern wing.

  En Route from Helmsley – Route A170 goes west, descending to Thirsk in the southwest corner of the moors. From Thirsk, take A19 north toward Middlesbrough and look for signs for A177, which leads northwest to Durham. The whole drive from Helmsley to Durham is about 50 miles (80 km).

DURHAM: Whether it was worship of God or defense against the Scots that was uppermost in the minds of the builders of Durham's magnificent cathedral and equally dramatic castle, the two buildings, facing each other across the Palace Green on a wooded gorge literally hanging over the River Wear, make Durham one of the most dramatically situated cities in Great Britain. When the cathedral was built in the 11th century, the bishop was responsible for the physical as well as the spiritual well-being of his flock, and defense was certainly part of his purpose. The original castle, built about 100 years later at the insistence of William the Conqueror, was replaced by the current keep in the 14th century and the Great Hall added at the same time (the castle is part of Durham University today). The two buildings are breathtaking, with the triple towers of the cathedral visible. Altogether, Durham Cathedral is one of the finest Romanesque churches in Europe. Not to be missed in Durham is the *Gulbénkian Museum of Oriental Art,* on Elvet Hill, with an incredible collection of Eastern art forms spanning many centuries (open weekdays and Sunday afternoons; reduced hours in winter). After a culturally enhancing day of touring, have a beer at the old *Market Tavern.*

  En Route from Durham – Route A167 leaves Durham at a leisurely pace, going north about 15 miles (24 km) toward Newcastle upon Tyne. A few miles before Newcastle lies Washington, once a small mining town. The town's Old Hall, erected early in the 17th century, incorporates parts of an older structure — the 12th-century home of the family of George Washington.

NEWCASTLE UPON TYNE: This lively industrial center of the northeast first became famous as an exporter of coal during the 13th century. Today, Newcastle's steel, petroleum, and shipbuilding industries lead the city's current redevelopment phase. Originally this site was called Pons Aelius, one of the guard stations of Hadrian's Wall. This massive line of fortifications defined the limit of Roman Britain when it was built. To the north was the land of the blue-painted Pict warriors, whom the Romans could not subdue. Outbreaks of violence between these fierce warriors and the area residents continued until the 17th century.

  Robert Curthose, son of William the Conqueror, erected a castle here late in the 11th century. The "new" castle was constructed over a century later, between 1170 and 1250. The *Hancock Museum,* at Barras Bridge, is one of the best natural history museums in England (open daily). The towering spire of St. Nicholas's Cathedral is 194 feet tall and reinforced by flying buttresses. Plan to visit the Beamish open-air "living museum" of the region's past ways of life near Stanley, a short bus ride from the city center. Widely considered one of the most interesting museums in Britain, and named European Museum of the Year in 1987, it is open daily from Easter through mid-September; Tuesdays through Sundays the rest of the year.

  En Route from Newcastle upon Tyne – Take A1 north, traveling between the coast and the forested hills of Northumberland National Park, one of the wildest and least traveled areas in England — a good spot for experienced hikers to get a taste of the country through which Romans and Picts warred. Nearer the roads are fine spots for the more civilized pleasures of a quiet picnic. Some 35 miles (56 km) away is Alnwick, an attractive old town outside the gates of the duke of Northumberland's Alnwick Castle. These stern walls, reinforced between 1310 and 1312, when its towers were erected, mask an interior of truly ducal magnificence (open daily, except Saturdays, May through September). A secondary roadway leads northeast from B1340 to the tiny fishing village of Craster, about 6 miles (10 km) from Alnwick. Treat yourself to a breath of sea air: Park the car and walk 1½ miles (2.5 km) along the coast path to the ruins of Dunstanburgh Castle. This dramatic 14th-century structure, perched on a cliff 100 feet above the sea, was hotly contested during the Wars of the Roses (open daily, Easter through September; closed Mondays in winter).

The popular resort of Seahouses, with an excellent beach area, is only a few miles farther along the coast. Take a boat ride to Inner Farne, a sanctuary for birds (puffins, terns, guillemots, kittiwakes, and others) and gray seals (open May to September).

Bamburgh Castle, one of the largest and most imposing medieval castles in Britain, still stands on a craggy headland overlooking the beach. Built in the early 12th century, the fortress was extensively restored at the beginning of the 20th century (open afternoons, Easter through October).

Continue north along the coast to Beal, where a 3-mile causeway (usable only at low tide) connects the mainland to Holy Island.

LINDISFARNE, or HOLY ISLAND: Here, in the 7th century, St. Aidan established the missionary center from which Christianity spread to the mainland. The ruins of the 11th-century Benedictine priory, including a red sandstone church, and a small castle stand among the picturesque fishermen's cottages on the island today. Lindisfarne is known for the brewing of mead, a potent honey-based liquor. Pick up an extra bottle for yourself before returning to the mainland and the northbound coast road.

BERWICK-UPON-TWEED: The heavily fortified city of Berwick-upon-Tweed shifted between Scotland and England 13 times before being settled in England in 1482. The 16th-century ramparts ringing the old city are in excellent condition and create a massive circular 2-mile promenade. Several well-preserved 18th-century buildings, including the Town Hall and Barracks, are open for inspection. Charles Dickens is said to have read poetry in the 18th-century *King's Arms* hotel, on a rise above the dockyards.

En Route from Berwick-upon-Tweed – Edinburgh is about 60 miles (96 km) northwest along the coast road. If, however, you're returning south, follow the bank of the River Tweed on A698. The ruins of Norham Castle, on the riverbank, are just off the main road 7 miles (11 km) from Berwick (open daily). Continue south on A698 to Cornhill on Tweed, and there pick up A697 southeast to Wooler, at the foot of the Cheviot Hills on the fringe of Northumberland National Park. There you can call for refreshments at the creeper-clad *Tankerville Arms.* The Earl of Tankerville's 14th-century Chillingham Castle is about 5 miles (8 km) east of the village. A unique herd of pure white wild cattle have grazed the castle grounds for 700 years (open April through October; closed Tuesdays).

Return to A697, veering southeast away from the border of the Northumberland Park to the junction with B6341. Take B6341 southwest to Rothbury, deep in the wooded valley of the River Coquet, then continue south until B6342 becomes A6079 leading into Hexham.

HEXHAM: The beautiful priory church typifies the town of Hexham. Little remains of the original structure, but some interesting 12th-century sections are in good shape. There is a 13th-century stone chair used as a frithstool: a sanctuary for whoever sat in it. The present Manor Office is a 14th-century prison, and the 15th-century Moot

Hall was used by the court bailiff. The town is well situated for a detailed look at the Roman wall, it sits just about halfway along its length.

En Route from Hexham – Richmond lies about 70 miles (112 km) southeast of Hexham. From Hexham, forsaking the main highways for a spell, take the hill road (B6306) that climbs up from the Tyne Valley to the village of Blanchland, built around the site of a 12th-century abbey; part of the original church now serves the parish. In the heart of the Pennine Hills, the road makes a switchback on the B6278 to Barnard Castle, an agreeable little town named for its ruined 12th-century castle, from which there is a great view over the River Tees. The town's *Bowes Museum* is a bit of a surprise, since it looks exactly like a French château. John Bowes built it in 1869 in honor of his French wife. Another surprise is its fine collection of paintings, furniture, and porcelain, hardly to be expected on the outskirts of a such small country town. The art collection at Lord Barnard's splendid 14th-century Raby Castle is also quite notable and worth the 6-mile (10-km) drive from the main road. Take B6277, then A66 east to B6274, which leads into Richmond.

RICHMOND: Here the great ruins of Richmond Castle stand precariously above the River Swale, guarding Swaledale and the eastern access to the Yorkshire dales. The original fortress was erected in 1071, and the keep added about 100 years later. The Georgian *Theatre Royal* (1788) has opened to the public after a century of gathering dust; it is one of the oldest theaters in England.

Explorers will find a tour of the dales, a series of beautiful valleys in the Pennine Hills, a delightful activity. They are filled with small villages and warm Yorkshire stone houses. Swaledale, deeper and wilder than most other valleys, is worth following for the village Thwaite at the far end. Here the steep Buttertubs Pass (the buttertubs are circular holes in the limestone) leads over the hills to Hawes, a noted cheese center in pastoral Wensleydale.

En Route from Richmond – Take A6108, then B6270 and a secondary road to Hawes. Stay on the secondary road leading southeast from Hawes toward the villages of Grassington and Burnsall. Visit the ruins of Bolton Abbey just a few miles farther south (open daily).

From here a bona fide main road (A59) goes east to the resort town of Harrogate.

HARROGATE: Now a thriving convention center due to its hotels, parks, and shops, Harrogate had been noted for its mineral waters and clean mountain air (atop a plateau 500 feet above sea level). The 200-acre common, called the Stray, is still the town center. The *Royal Pump Room,* where the public baths were located, is now a museum.

En Route from Harrogate – York is only 23 miles (37 km) east of Harrogate on A59, but be prepared to stop at the old town of Knaresborough. Chief among the local sights is the celebrated Dropping Well, which has petrifying properties — you can leave something here and come back in a few years to find it turned to stone.

BEST EN ROUTE

Some of the nicest places to stay in northeast England are not the larger hotels but the small inns and private homes that offer bed-and-breakfast. In general, they are undistinguished places — roomy, warm, and comfortable — and they provide a basic level of service at a moderate price. Expect to pay $60 and up (including breakfast) for two in establishments classified below as expensive; $45 to $60 in those listed as moderate; and $45 and under at places in the inexpensive category. (Prices in York are slightly higher.)

Please bear in mind that these ranges are expressed in American dollars and that the currency exchange market is far from stable. You will find good food at reasonable prices in most places, but for a really excellent dinner for two with wine, expect to pay about $25 to $30.

YORK

Royal York – A magnificent Victorian structure, this railway hotel has been operating for just over 100 years. Although certain necessary steps toward modernization have been taken, the traditional air remains, especially at teatime in the high-ceilinged lounge. Other features include a fitness room and a putting green in the formal gardens. Station Rd. (phone: 0904-653681). Expensive.

Viking – A large, centrally located modern hotel that stands out because of its excellent service. The interior is quite pleasant, and if you can get a room overlooking the river, it will add immeasurably to your stay. North St. (phone: 0904-59822). Expensive.

Hill – This Georgian establishment is family run, and since it has only 10 rooms, staying here is like staying in a private home — with your own bath or shower, use of a delightful garden, and traditional cuisine. About 2 miles (3.2 km) from the city center. 60 York Rd., Acomb (phone: 0904-790777). Moderate.

Hudson's – A large Victorian hostelry, a few minutes' walk from the city center. All bedrooms have a private bath and a TV set, and good old English dishes are served in the restaurant "below stairs." 60 Bootham (phone: 0904-621267). Moderate.

PICKERING

Forest and Vale – In summer the walled garden is a joy, and in winter curling up by the fireplace in this comfortable Georgian inn is the ultimate expression of quiet and cozy. Malton Rd. (phone: 0751-72722). Moderate to inexpensive.

SCARBOROUGH

Royal – Truly a luxury liner among the resort hotels dotting this small town, this is a picture-perfect example of how the good life should be led. In this aged structure, the idea of ornate decoration comes back to life and blends well with the artwork on display. St. Nicholas St. (phone: 0723-364333). Expensive.

HELMSLEY

Black Swan – As traditional a northern inn as it is possible to find, this hotel was built in the 16th century of local stone, with public rooms of old wood and large fireplaces. Market Pl. (phone: 0439-70466). Expensive.

Feversham Arms – Built of Yorkshire stone with 15 pretty bedrooms, the hotel also has an enjoyable restaurant. 1 High St. (phone: 0439-70766). Moderate.

DURHAM

Royal County – The aviary in the public area must have been added since this inn's days of catering to the horse and carriage set, and it's only one of the many tasteful improvements made over the years. A newer wing of rooms and a sauna have been added. Old Elvet (phone: 09138-66821). Expensive.

NEWCASTLE UPON TYNE

County – An airy Victorian railway hotel, with just enough modernization to make you comfortable, but not so much that the hotel's own personality doesn't show through. The grand central staircase says it all. Neville St. (phone: 091-232-2471). Expensive.

Gosforth Park – One of the very modern, very luxurious establishments in the area, this one is set in a wooded sector close to the racetrack about 4 miles (6.4 km) north of the city. With 178 rooms, there is no shortage of facilities, and the service is excellent. High Gosforth Park (phone: 091-236-4111). Expensive.

BERWICK-UPON-TWEED

King's Arms – This lovely Georgian coaching inn has a walled garden, 2 restaurants one is a coffee shop modeled on an 18th-century stagecoach), and 2 bars (one in the converted stable block). Hide Hill (phone: 0289-307454). Moderate.

BLANCHLAND

Lord Crewe Arms – The medieval atmosphere isn't surprising, since the building includes parts of an 11th-century monastery that once occupied the site of the village. It's haunted, not by a monk, but by the ghost of a pretty girl, one Dorothy Foster, who has apparently been trying to deliver a message for the past 280 years. Near Consett (phone: 043-475251). Moderate.

HARROGATE

Old Swan – A charming building, dating from 1700, that prides itself on old-fashioned comfort and service. The rooms are large, and the manners of the staff belong to the time when graciousness was a way of life rather than a business. Swan Rd. (phone: 0423-500055). Expensive to moderate.

Oliver – One of the most respected restaurants in England. The menu, which consists of four courses, is changed weekly to take advantage of the best fresh produce. The setting is definitely Edwardian, with no detail overlooked, and the service is attended to equally well. Dinner only. 24 King's Rd. (phone: 0423-568600). Expensive.

The Scottish Lowlands: Sir Walter Scott Country

The Scottish Lowlands — the central and southern parts of the country — are, in the international popular imagination, at variance with the Highlands in almost every way. Whereas Highlanders are thought to be romantic, Catholic, Celtic, and volatile, Lowlanders are thought to be practical, Presbyterian, steady, and narrow. There is a grain of truth in this, but only a grain. The Lowlands are nothing if not romantic. They include Scotland's two best-known battle sites, for instance, each of them a mile from Stirling Castle: Stirling Bridge, where William Wallace drove back the English forces in 1297, and Bannockburn, where Robert the Bruce was victorious in the same cause in 1314.

The Scottish Borders, where Sir Walter Scott lived for most of his adult life, are noted for their peaceful rivers and famous ruined abbeys, to say nothing of numerous literary landmarks, including Scott's baronial country house at Abbotsford. The Trossachs, where so much of Scott's writing is set, are known as the Gateway to the Highlands (a title also claimed by Stirling) and are very lovely. Loch Lomond is there. And Glasgow, though inferior to Edinburgh in glamorous topography, is superior in theater and the arts; in recent years it has been transformed into an exceptionally attractive modern city.

An important tip for the unsuspecting motorist: Don't wait for good weather before setting off in your car in the morning — you might be a grandparent by the time it arrives. Pack snacks, bought from your hotel or a local bakery, for everybody (there are tearooms in the palatial *Gleneagles* hotel in Perthshire — see *Best en Route* — but precious few anywhere else). Scottish bakeries sell milk, sandwiches, and stuffed rolls as well as cakes and buttered scones. Try to tour Scotland in April and May or September and October, when crowds are thinner, the air crisper, and colors brighter. If you go in midsummer you will miss the beauteous yellow gorse (spring) and purple heather (autumn).

Your best bet in maps comes in a Scottish Tourist Board kit called *Enjoy Scotland,* which includes a small book listing 1,001 Scottish sights. All are marked on the map, along with golf courses, picnic tables, information centers — everything that legibly fits. The kit costs about $5 from the Scottish Tourist Board's Travel Center on South St. Andrew St. It is also available from the tourist office at Waverly Market, 3 Princes St., Edinburgh; phone: 031-557-1700.

EDINBURGH: For a detailed report on Edinburgh and its hotels and restaurants, see *Edinburgh,* THE CITIES.

    En Route from Edinburgh – Seventeen miles (27 km) west of Edinburgh on the M9 is Linlithgow Palace, on the south shore of Loch Linlithgow. This breathtaking piece of fairy tale architecture was the birthplace of Mary, Queen of Scots in 1542 and is one of Scotland's four royal palaces (the others are Falkland Palace in the kingdom of Fife, Stirling Castle, and Edinburgh's Holyrood House). James I of Scotland built it in the 15th century; later rulers extended it. Adjoining the palace is St. Michael's, one of the finest medieval parish churches in Scotland.

STIRLING: If you want to see into Scotland's soul, stand on the heights of Stirling Castle Rock behind any of the castle cannonades and gaze northeast to the Grampian Mountains, northwest to Stirling Bridge, or south to Bannockburn. Here, for centuries, was Scotland's sole defense against any English invasion of northern cities like Perth (an important medieval Scots town) and the Highlands. Whoever controlled Stirling Castle controlled the only route north across the River Forth. Scots patriot Sir William Wallace (1272–1305) and King Robert Bruce — known to history simply as the Bruce — had to hold the castle against the English to hold Scotland. They succeeded, though after years of intermittent battle, brave Wallace was betrayed to the English and hung, drawn, and quartered in London. Since that time, all kinds of psychological and historical defense mechanisms against the English have become deeply rooted in Scottish hearts.

Once a residence for Stuart kings, the palace section of the castle is intriguing. Mary of Guise, the wife of James V, employed stonemasons from her native France to decorate its façade with Bacchanalian figurines, providing a touch of Renaissance French fancy that is amusingly out of place in such a stern Scottish context. Both Mary, Queen of Scots and King James VI were crowned at Stirling Castle. Surrounding the castle are many impressive buildings from the 16th and 17th centuries as well as the Visitor Centre with a multiscreen show and an imaginative picture gallery (there's a bookshop, crafts shop, and tea garden); open year-round (phone: 0786-62517).

A mile (1.6 km) away, at Bannockburn, is another exhibition on Robert the Bruce, organized by the National Trust for Scotland (open March through October; off the A9, south of Stirling).

DOUNE: The 14th-century castle here is pure picturebook stuff. Owned since the 16th century by the Earls of Moray, one of whom was a half-brother to Mary, Queen of Scots, this stark, towering edifice in a woodland between two streams has survived more or less in its original form, a rarity in Scotland (closed Thursdays and Fridays in winter). And it is so medieval that no one lives in it today. Also at Doune, 2 miles (3.2 km) past the castle on A84, is the present earl's collection of vintage, veteran, and modern cars, the *Doune Motor Museum,* next to Doune Park Gardens, an idyllic 60 acres of woodland walks and flowering shrubs. The castle, museum, and gardens are open from April through October.

TROSSACHS: Scott made this part of Scotland famous with his narrative poem *The Lady of the Lake,* set at Loch Katrine, and with his novel *Rob Roy.* He encouraged his London acquaintances to visit the area until so many came that he complained, "Every London citizen makes Loch Lomond his washpot and throws his shoe over Ben Nevis." Yet today the Trossachs are curiously underdeveloped, which adds to their beauty but makes it difficult to find adequate hotels and restaurants. You will want to drive north on A84 from Callander past Loch Lubnaig to Rob Roy's grave at Balquhidder, a route almost smothered in wild primroses. Turn left onto A821 just north of Callander to tour Lochs Katrine, Achray, and Venachar. Then follow A811 southwest through Killearn to the famous loch itself.

LOCH LOMOND: Loll on the beach on the eastern shore, gazing at purple mountains studded with rivulets and waterfalls. A tourist center at Balloch, on the southern tip of Loch Lomond, will provide plenty of information to inspire you (open May through September; phone: 0389-53533).

GLASGOW: This preeminently industrial city has fallen on hard times since the great days of the "tobacco lords" (merchants involved in trade with America) in the 18th century and the Clydeside shipbuilders in the 19th. Yet nowhere in Scotland is the spirit more indomitable or the humor more pungent, as you'll quickly learn when you talk to Glaswegians. The city is medieval — like so many medieval cities, growing up around a 13th-century cathedral — but little is left of its earliest period. Its most imposing architecture is Victorian, and the buildings around George Square could provide a primer in Victorian excess and excellence. The interior of the city, however, has recently been redesigned to produce an effective and attractive modern landscape. Glasgow Dockland, in particular, has undergone a near-miraculous transformation. After a stroll through George Square, make for the Glasgow University area in Kelvingrove. The art gallery here is studded with the work of French Impressionists and of talented Scots Impressionists who were influenced by them. Treat yourself to a stroll through Kelvingrove Park along the River Kelvin. The *Burrell Collection,* in Pollok Country Park, has become Scotland's most popular tourist attraction, with its 19th-century French paintings and its art objects, ceramics, furniture, and stained glass. It's open year-round, 10 AM to 5 PM, Sundays 2 to 5 PM (phone: 041-649-7151).

At night the excellent *Scottish Opera Company* performs at the *Theatre Royal* (Hope St.; phone: 332-9000, or 248-4567). The *Glasgow Citizens' Theatre Company* (119 Gorbals St.; phone: 429-5561) stages avant-garde productions of traditional plays that make off-Broadway look like a vicar's tea party.

NEW LANARK: The old mills here and the town that is an integral part of them are one of the earliest experiments in progressive labor management. In 1799 the Welsh socialist Robert Owen bought the mills at New Lanark and went about creating a humane work situation. He stopped child labor, instituted a program of health insurance for workers, built clean, livable housing, and opened schools and recreation facilities. In 1829, after disagreements with his partners (one of whom was Jeremy

Bentham), he withdrew, but in the meantime he financed a new utopian experiment in New Harmony, Indiana, that was far less successful (in part, because it was a community of intellectuals committed more to ideology than cooperation).

PEEBLES: This pleasant old wool manufacturing town by the River Tweed is an excellent base for exploring the Borders. Adjoining Peebles on the west is Neidpath Castle, a striking, 13th-century stronghold with walls 11 feet thick.

En Route from Peebles – Seven miles (11 km) east of Peebles on A72 is Traquair House, dating from the 10th century, the oldest continuously inhabited dwelling in Scotland. Twenty-seven Scottish and English monarchs have visited it. Ale is still produced at its 18th-century brewhouse. However, its hours are erratic, so phone 0896-830323 before you visit.

ABBOTSFORD: No visit to Scott country would be complete without a stop at Scott's home on A72, 12 miles (19 km) east of Traquair House. Scott built this ornate mansion between 1817 and 1822, using the most romantic materials he could find. He made a special trip to attend the razing of Edinburgh's 14th-century tollbooth, for instance, known as "the Heart of Midlothian" (also the title of a Scott novel), in order to make off with its front door, which he then had incorporated into the design of his new abode. A guide will take you through from April through October.

Nearby are Melrose and Dryburgh abbeys, two famous border abbeys dear to Scott's heart. Melrose Abbey, founded in 1136, is renowned for its traceried stonework; Dryburgh Abbey, which also dates from the 12th century, houses Scott's tomb. Both are below Abbotsford, on A6091.

BEST EN ROUTE

From May through September it is advisable to book ahead, as accommodations are often hard to find on the spot. Lunches in Scottish hotels are served approximately between noon and 2 PM, dinners approximately between 7 and 9 PM unless otherwise noted. Establishments charging under $60 per night for two occupants are listed as inexpensive; those with rates from $60 to $80 are considered moderate; and those charging $80 and up are listed as expensive. For dinner for two with wine, expect to pay $100 at most restaurants in the area.

STIRLING

Golden Lion – Though now clinging for dear life to its immaculate historic pedigree, this 84-room hotel is nonetheless the best of Stirling's lately rather dubious center-city bets. Robert Burns, the royal family, and a host of film stars have all stayed here. 8 King St. (phone: 75351). Expensive.

CALLANDER

Roman Camp – There are 14 bedrooms and a few very decorative and very alive peacocks trailing across the lawn of this 17th-century hunting lodge. English and Scottish dishes are served in its restaurant. Open March–November. Reservations necessary. Off Main St. (phone: 30003). Expensive.

KILLEARN

Black Bull – Famed for its food as far afield as Glasgow, the cuisine is traditional English and Scottish and perfectly wonderful. Evening meals from 5 PM on (lunches, usual hours). Reservations necessary May through September. Off Main St. (phone: 50215). Expensive.

GLASGOW

Albany – Glasgow's finest business-center-cum-hotel where the visiting pop stars stay in the uneasy company of executives. This is a slick, 251-room, flat-topped box with a big-city image. Inside, it's soft lights, carpets, and chrome. One of the 2 dining rooms is a popular carvery with Scottish traditional cooking. Bothwell St. (phone: 248-2656). Expensive.

Hospitality Inn – A modern, 316-room hotel in the heart of Glasgow, its *Garden Café* serves dinner from 5 to 11 PM for "a taste of Scotland." 36 Cambridge St. (phone: 332-3311). Expensive.

Stakis Grosvenor – This modernized Victorian residence has 95 attractive and comfortable bedrooms. Dinner from 5 PM. Grosvenor Terrace at Great Western Rd. (phone: 041-339-8811). Expensive.

Central – It's comfortable in an old-fashioned way. There are 219 sumptuous bedrooms and *The Malmaison*, a French restaurant that's just about the best in town (closed Sundays). Gordon St. (phone: 221-9680). Expensive to moderate.

PEEBLES

Peebles Hotel Hydro – This palatial estate stands by a lovely waterfall in one of Scotland's most historic areas. English and Scottish traditional cooking. Off A702, on Innerleithen Rd. (phone: 20602). Expensive.

Park – Ideal for fishing, riding, golf, and tennis; its paneled dining room, bar, and lounge look out over landscaped gardens and Cademuir Hills. There are 26 rooms. Innerleithen Rd. (phone: 20451). Moderate.

Scotland's Fabled Golf Courses

If you're a golfer and haven't played in Scotland, you haven't seen where it all began and where it's still mostly "at". Assuming your plane lands at Prestwick, just above the old market town of Ayr, you are already in the heart of Scottish golf country. There are seven championship courses in the Prestwick area, including the course at Prestwick itself, the site of the first-ever Open in 1860. All the courses on the tour outlined below (except Gleneagles and Rosemount) are links courses, which means they consist of tough seaside dunes riddled with furzy clumps and covered by the merest modicum of grass (except, of course, for the bunkers). Americans aren't used to playing on links courses; for a few tips see the *Useful Hints* at the end of this route.

TURNBERRY HOTEL GOLF COURSE: This massive vacationers' paradise, which looks like a landlocked ocean liner, has as its front lawn the world-famous Ailsa Course. If you can afford it, stay at this five-star hotel for 2 or 3 days and use it as a base to make the rounds of the six neighboring championship links (the desk clerk will give you directions).

The 9th hole of the Ailsa, Bruce's Castle, has a tee isolated on a promontory, complete with a picturesque lighthouse, that juts into the Firth of Clyde. You'll need a crack shot over the water to get your ball back on the mainland. The *Turnberry* hotel caters to golfing needs, at a reduced rate for residents. Handicap certificate required. Turnberry Hotel Golf Course, Turnberry, Strathclyde KA26 9LT, Scotland (phone: Turnberry 31000).

ROYAL TROON: Laid out along the beach, with the outgoing nine heading virtually straight down the strand and the closing nine paralleling it only a few yards inland, the only distraction is that the course lies directly below the flight path into Prestwick Airport. Another classic British Open layout, it is one of the few important private clubs in Scotland, though playing privileges are usually made available to visitors who are members of clubs in the US. Women are not permitted on the links. No visitors on Fridays or weekends. Advance booking necessary. Royal Troon Golf Club, Craigend Rd., Troon, Strathclyde, Scotland KA10 6EP (phone: 0292-311555).

PRESTWICK GOLF COURSE: Now considered too old-fashioned for the British Open rota because of its small, whimsical fairways and limited facilities for handling crowds, this tough, historic course, the scene of 24 Opens, is nonetheless full of hidden surprises and is worth playing at least once. This course also gets its share of racket from Prestwick Airport. No visitors on Thursday afternoons or weekends. Prestwick Golf Club, Links Rd., Prestwick KA9 1QG, Ayrshire, Scotland (phone: Prestwick 77404).

THE OLD COURSE, ST. ANDREWS: St. Andrews is Scotland's "home of golf," a shrine to which all serious golfers should eventually make a pilgrimage. The Old Course, famous since golf was played with knives and forks, is on the West Sands at the junction of Golf Place and the Links. It is shaped as God made it, bunkers and all, even where, as on Heathery Hole (the 12th), the bunkers are in the middle of the fairway and not seen from the tee. The Old Course is full of bad kicks and subject to capricious changes in the direction of its high winds. It never plays the same way twice and can damage your ego, yet such is its magic that golfers who begin by hating it invariably end loving it.

Just behind the first tee is the stately, sacrosanct clubhouse headquarters of the *Royal and Ancient Golf Club* (known as the *R & A*). Its members, a kind of board of directors of world golf, gaze at you sardonically from the "Big Room" through a bay window as you tee off. Pay no attention to them. For a real slice of local color, try to get a caddie from the Caddie Master opposite the R & A clubhouse. The true Scottish caddie, now a dying breed, is most often a mature gentleman of modest size with a 10-day growth of beard who is too old to lift a club but too young to forget when he could. He knows each blade of grass on the course by heart, and has seen innumerable Opens. His accent sounds like a pneumatic drill. He'll advise what club you need for every shot, then stand aside implacably while you sklaff into the wee burn. Clubs and carts are also for hire.

It's a good idea to contact the Links Management Committee of St. Andrews 8 weeks before your visit to apply to play on the Old Course. Otherwise you may find you can't get near it. Forms are not issued for Saturdays or Thursday afternoons. Greens are closed Sundays. Handicap certificate required. Write to Links Management Committee of St. Andrews, St. Andrews, Fife, KY16 9JA Scotland (phone: 0334-75757).

En Route from St. Andrews – Take A91 west across Fife, past peaceful Loch Leven, to the Yetts of Muckart (about 37 mi/59.2 km), where you'll join A823. Follow it north 9 miles (14.4 km) into Perthshire to *Gleneagles* hotel. About 5 miles (8 km) beyond the Yetts of Muckart you'll be high above Glen Devon, with a panoramic view southwest across Stirling Plain. Go slowly and enjoy it.

GLENEAGLES: This is Scottish heaven for American golfers, not only because Open championships are played there, but also because the moist, thick turf on its greens is comfortably like the turf at home. *Gleneagles* is also a five-star hotel, even more grand than *Turnberry* (see *Best en Route*) and with almost as many ballrooms as tearooms (plus an Equestrian Centre, of which the queen's son-in-law, Mark, is co-proprietor). It has a system of reduced price equipment-hire and greens fees for hotel residents. Gleneagles Hotel Golf Course, Auchterarder, Perthshire PH3 1NF, Scotland (phone: 07646-3543).

Useful Hints: To play on links courses you need a wedge, a brush-up on your pitch-and-run technique, and a canny way of sizing up the wind, which can change a par three to a par five. Bring a nylon rainsuit that fits over your clothes, wear dark colors if you don't want to be stared at, and take note that women are not allowed in many clubhouse bars. Cut down the number of clubs you carry, and most important of all, speed up your game. Only at *Turnberry* and *Gleneagles* dare you pause to make bets, drink beer, or tell jokes. No four-ball games are allowed at private clubs on weekends. A letter of introduction from your home club secretary must be handed to the secretary of any private club a day in advance. Order lunch in advance in clubhouse dining rooms and wear a shirt and tie.

Listed below, area by area, are suggestions for family outings while the golfers are slamming balls down the fairways.

At St. Andrews:
The West Sands, the town's lovely, long, clean beach.
The *St. Andrews Woollen Mill,* just by the Old Course on the street called the Golf Links. Fair Isle and Shetland knitwear is sold at factory prices. Closed Sundays.
St. Andrews University, the oldest in Scotland (1412). Its buildings dot the town's central shopping area (South St. and district).
Falkland Palace, one of the homes of the Stuart kings, built 1530–40, 15 miles (24 km) west of St. Andrews on A91, then 2 miles (3.2 km) south on A912. Open April through September, weekends only in October.

At Gleneagles:
The town of Auchterarder, a mile away, famed for its antiques shops (the hotel desk clerk will give you directions).

In Ayrshire:
See the *Western Scotland* route, Ayrshire section.

BEST EN ROUTE

Expect to pay $80 and up per night for a double room in any of the fine hotels associated with Scotland's famous golf courses. For restaurants, the ranges are $45 and up for a dinner for two in the expensive category; $25 to $45 in the moderate; and $25 and under in the inexpensive category. Prices do not include wine, drinks, or tip.

PRESTWICK

Carlton – A modern, 39-room hotel near shopping centers and featuring free live entertainment. Dinner from 7 PM. 187 Ayr Rd. (phone: 70292-76811). Expensive.

TURNBERRY

Turnberry – Its restaurant features French fare, in addition to English and Scottish traditional cooking, served in a lavish Edwardian atmosphere in a lovely setting overlooking the sea. On A77, off A719, by Turnberry Lighthouse (phone: 31000). Expensive.

TROON

Marine Highland – Troon's finest hotel has, in addition to its distinguished restaurant, an outstanding health and leisure club. Reservations necessary May through September. Crosbie Rd. (phone: 314444). Expensive.

ST. ANDREWS

Old Course Golf & Country Club – Formerly the *Old Course* hotel, it's been completely converted into a very exclusive golf club with full facilities and newly stylish rooms available to members on a time-sharing plan. No golf on Sundays. Rooms are available to non-members. St. Andrews (phone: 0334-75757). Expensive.
Rusack's – Set beside the 18th hole of the Old Course, this hotel, established in 1887, offers 50 comfortable rooms, off-season golf packages, and full clubhouse facilities. St. Andrews (phone: 74321). Expensive.

St. Andrews Golf – The view here, through bay windows adorned with flower boxes and looking out to sea, is completely delightful. So are the resident owners. English and Scottish traditional cooking. The Scores (phone: 72611). Expensive.

AUCHTERARDER

Gleneagles – Pleasingly palatial, with incomparable service and decor and a menu that is a magnum opus. It's a haven for golfers, with four of the best courses in Scotland; it recently added shooting to the roster of activities. There's also a domed leisure center with a pool, squash court, sauna, and more. Off A823, by Auchterarder (phone: 07646-3543). Expensive.

Scottish Highlands:
Edinburgh to Inverness

The Scottish Highlands, scene of some of the most barbaric events in the history of Britain, are also full of some of the most breathtaking scenery in the world. Highlanders, many of whom are pure Gaels, have the lilting voices and mercurial natures associated with their Irish cousins. Like the peasant Irish, Highlanders were victimized and exploited by an ascendancy class. During the so-called Highland Clearances, which began in the late 18th century, crofters were driven from their homes so that landowners could replace them with sheep, at that time a more lucrative proposition. Those who refused to go had their houses and worldly goods burned. Hundreds of families fled south, jobless and possessionless, at the mercy of fortune, speaking only their native Celtic tongue.

Today 10% of the Scottish population owns 84% of the land, which shows how little things have changed since the 18th century. Great regions of lonely moors and mountains are in the grip of a handful of aristocrats who live in London and come north to hunt, shoot, and fish. You can see them in droves in the spring at 9 AM in the *Station* hotel dining room in Inverness, just off the London train, madly excited by the chill Highland air, dripping with tweeds, and all barking at once for kippers and cream at shy native waitresses.

The Edinburgh-to-Inverness route described here takes you through the eastern and central Highland regions, which are lusher, more prosperous, more forested, and less Gaelic than the western regions. Some west Highland areas (not Gaelic ones) are included in the *Western Scotland* route.

EDINBURGH: For a complete description of the city and its hotels and restaurants, see *Edinburgh,* THE CITIES.

En route from Edinburgh – From the west end of Princes Street, follow Queensferry Road north across the Forth Road Bridge to the two-lane M90 (about 13 mi/22 km). Three miles (5 km) farther is Dunfermline, the capital of Scotland in the early Middle Ages, when Edinburgh was a mere castle.

DUNFERMLINE: Dunfermline Abbey is a royal imperative for tourists. King Robert the Bruce was buried in the abbey choir in 1329 and King Charles I, born in the abbey guesthouse in 1600. An attractive modern brass marks Bruce's grave, now under the roof of the parish church, the Norman nave of which is built over the abbey ruins. Parts of the original 11th-century monastic buildings can still be seen here (Monastery St.; open daily).

The American steel king and millionaire Andrew Carnegie (1835–1919) is a third major personage associated with Dunfermline. He was born here in a damask weaver's cottage that will reopen to the public when repairs currently in progress have been completed (Moodie St.; phone: 0382-724302).

En Route from Dunfermline – Twelve miles (20 km) beyond Dunfermline you might stop for a *coup d'oeil* at the Moors of Kinross and peaceful Loch Leven, on your right. Mary, Queen of Scots was imprisoned in Loch Leven Castle — on the island in the center of the lake — for 11 months in 1567. You can visit the castle by getting off the M90 at the Kinross interchange and taking a ferry from Kinross pier (open daily; April through September).

DUNKELD: Want a taste of paradise? Have a picnic on the Dunkeld Cathedral grounds by the bonnie banks of the River Tay (you can get sandwiches at *Country Kitchen,* Atholl St.). This idyllic spot was the ancient capital of the Picts and Scots from AD 850, and the bones of the great St. Columba of Iona, founder of the Celtic Christian church, were lodged at Dunkeld Cathedral for a time after the Vikings raided Iona in 597. Along with the charming cathedral, you'll love the 40-odd 17th-century row houses, restored by the National Trust for Scotland, that make up the main part of the village.

PITLOCHRY: It seems a veritable Brigadoon with its storybook array of gabled houses and country churches rising sharply up the Tummel River valley brae only to be locked in by giant heather-covered mountains. The town is beautifully situated and consequently a famous resort with many activities, including the *Pitlochry Festival Theatre,* bagpipe and drum pageants, Highland games (mid-September), mountain climbing, pony trekking, organized nature trail hiking (with Scottish National Forest brochures on plants, birds, and animals), golfing, and salmon fishing.

Use Pitlochry as a base for a couple of side trips. A couple of miles north of Pitlochry on B8019 is the entrance to the famed Queen's View above Loch Tummel, where Queen Victoria used to picnic. As you leave Loch Tummel, look to your left for Mt. Schiehallion, the conical peak so perfect in shape that scientists used it to compute the earth's mass. At the village called Kinloch Rannoch, follow the small, unnumbered road around Loch Rannoch's south shore. Here is the beautiful Black Wood of Rannoch, the last piece of medieval forest in Scotland.

South of Pitlochry, cross the River Tay and follow the A827 and then B846 to the turnoff for Glen Lyon (follow the signs for Fortingall). Glen Lyon is the longest glen in Scotland, beloved for its sun-speckled, wooded glades and the plethora of legends associated with it.

En Route from Glen Lyon – At the Bridge of Balgie, over the River Lyon, an unnumbered road runs south to join A827 beside Loch Tay. Take this and turn right at the junction. In 6 miles (9.6 km) you'll be at Killin, famous for its lake view and dazzling waterfall, a typical example of Highland scenery at its finest.

PASS OF KILLIECRANKIE: At this luscious wooded gorge, especially beautiful in autumn, Viscount Claverhouse ("Bonnie Dundee") and his Jacobite army routed the English troops of William III in 1689. The National Trust for Scotland has a Visitor Centre and Battle Display here (open Easter to mid-October).

BLAIR ATHOLL: Nearby is Blair Castle, the family seat of the Dukes of Atholl, head of the Clan Murray. The present duke lives in Blair Castle, where he keeps the last and only legal private army in Britain (about 65 men). Thirty-two rooms of his 700-year-old abode are awash in Chippendales, Limoges, Zoffanys, and Jacobite relics (open, including the attractive tearoom, from April to September).

En Route from Blair Atholl – The A9 runs near Newtonmore, known throughout the Highlands for its shinty team (shinty is a faster, fiercer form of hockey).
You pass the usually bustling shinty field as you enter town.

KINGUSSIE: The ruins of rocky Ruthven Barracks are visible from the main road.
These were maintained by English forces as a defense against Jacobite uprisings between the rebellions of 1715 and 1745. (The fact that there *was* a Jacobite Rebellion
in 1745 may say something about their effectiveness.) Visit Am Fasgadh (the Shelter,
in Gaelic), the Highland folk museum by the river. It has a furnished thatched cottage
that illustrates how bleak life in northern Scotland once was (open weekdays year-
round).

AVIEMORE: Several top-class if rather drearily formal new hotels overlook this
popular ski resort's snow-studded Cairngorm Mountains. Slalom into the sunset above
an incredible view at 11 o'clock at night! The slopes are rough but cheap (information
about prices, opening times, equipment rental, and so forth is available at the Spey
Valley Tourist Organization, Aviemore; phone: 810363).

En Route from Aviemore – Detour off A9 to the town of Carrbridge, nip into
the Landmark Visitor Centre, the first exhibition of its kind in Europe. Ten
thousand years of Highland history are surveyed entertainingly in a triple-screen
audio-visual theater (open daily).

If time isn't pressing, take the B970 along the valley of the River Spey, passing
the Loch Garten Nature Reserve where, in 1959, ospreys (long extinct in Scotland)
returned to nest. From Speybridge, follow the signs on the A939 and the B976 to
Braemar. Here sits Balmoral, the royal family's summer home since 1852. The
estate consists of 11,000 acres beside the delightful River Dee. Only a portion of
the house and grounds are open to the public, and then only when no royalty is
in residence.

INVERNESS: Despite its glamorous site on the Moray Firth, Inverness is the Plain
Jane of Scottish cities. It won't make you wish you were a painter, but it *will* give you
a center from which to strike out in all directions for Scotland's most ethereal parts.
Ideas for day trips are legion at the Inverness, Loch Ness and Nairn Tourist Board,
23 Church St. (phone: 234352). Musts are Culloden Moor, where Bonnie Prince
Charlie's army was decimated in the famous Jacobite uprising of 1745, and Loch Ness,
whose 22-mile length can be scouted for the monster by driving south on A82. The first
recorded sighting of the monster was by St. Columba nearly 1,500 years ago; it continues to be at home to visitors, but with no formal hours.

BEST EN ROUTE

Expect to pay at least $70 in hotels classified as very expensive, $60 and up per night
for a double room in hotels classified as expensive; $45 to $60 in the moderate category;
and under $45 in the inexpensive category. For restaurants, the ranges are $45 and up
for a dinner for two in the expensive category; $25 to $45 in the moderate; and $25
and under in the inexpensive category. Prices do not include wine, drinks, or tip.

DUNFERMLINE

King Malcolm Thistle – Dunfermline's finest is named for the Malcolm who overthrew Macbeth (his wife, Queen Margaret, founded Dunfermline Abbey). Modern
by design, but with English and Scottish traditional cooking. Queensferry Rd.,
Wester Pitcorthie, just south at A823 (phone: 722611). Expensive.

PITLOCHRY

Atholl Palace – This turreted Victorian monster with a glowingly comfortable
interior and sweepingly glorious view was built in 1880 as a health resort alongside

some healing spas. More soothing today is its fine Scottish cooking, including grouse and other game. It's on its own secluded grounds on Atholl Rd.; look for the sign at the turnoff south of Pitlochry on A9 (phone: 2400). Expensive.

Green Park – Its very beautiful setting — on Loch Faskally overlooking the mountains — is much admired by the outdoorsy people who visit this area to fish, hike, or ski. Dinner as well as breakfast comes with the price of the room, which is an advantage only to those who don't mind mediocre food. Clunie Bridge Rd. (phone: 0796-3248). Expensive.

AVIEMORE

Aviemore Post House – Every morning the chef decides what will be on the evening's menu; try requesting your favorite dinner dish at breakfast by getting your waitress to carry a message on a paper napkin. In addition to the main dining room, the hotel has another eatery that's open from 10 AM to 11 PM. On the road to the Cairngorms just past Aviemore Centre; follow the signs from A9 (phone: 810771). Expensive.

Stakis Coylumbridge – Very modern and plush, it has its own ice/roller rink. English and Scottish traditional cooking in the dining room at the usual hours and snacks in the coffee shop from 10 AM to 2 PM. At Coylumbridge, on A951 en route to the Cairngorms from A9 (phone: 810661). Expensive.

BALLATER

Craigendarroch – Half hotel and half time-share, this fomer baronial mansion is set in some of Scotland's most breathtaking highlands, overlooking the river Dee. Guests can use the country club facilities, including a pool, sauna, gym, snooker table and even a dry ski slope. Braemar Rd., Ballater, Royal Deeside (phone: 0338-55858). Expensive.

INVERNESS

Culloden House – *The* place to stay at Inverness, in rural splendor below Culloden Moor. The light, spacious rooms of this beautiful 18th-century palace are full of ornate plasterwork and priceless antique furniture. On Culloden Moor (phone: 790461). Very expensive.

Kingsmills – Ten minutes' walk from downtown, this striking, white, 200-year-old time capsule with its front door in an architraved turret has 70 rooms, private squash courts, and 4 acres of gardens. Culcabock Rd. (phone: 237166). Expensive.

Station – The Victorian decor of this 67-room relic is comfortably plush. Its restaurant serves good traditional English and Scottish fare. Academy St. (phone: 231926). Expensive.

Cummings – In spite of the complete ordinariness of this 38-room rectangle, this place somehow manages to be endearing. Nightly Scottish cabarets here have been wowing audiences from June to September for years. Church St. (phone: 232531). Moderate to inexpensive.

Western Scotland

Ayrshire is famous for its golf courses, its cattle, its golden beaches and quaint Victorian resort towns, its comparatively dry climate, and its view of the Isle of Arran. It is even more famous, however, as the home of Robert Burns, the 18th-century rustic bard who heralded poetry's Romantic Age. Scotland may be the only country in the world to celebrate its national identity by paying homage to a poet. On February 22, when Americans are sedately eating cherry pie in memory of George Washington, the Scots are just beginning to surface after the revels of *Burns Night* (January 25). The festivities include elaborate banquets of Scottish dishes, innumerable toasts, poetry recitals, and piping, singing, and dancing till dawn. This night (together with New Year's Eve) is traditionally a time for the wild side of the Scot, seemingly shrouded the rest of the year in rock-ribbed Presbyterianism, to come out, as it were, for Ayr.

North of Ayrshire is world-famous Inveraray Castle, the seat of the Dukes of Argyll. About 40 miles (64 km) farther up the coast is lovely Oban, a starting place for the Western Isles and a good point of departure for touring the western Highlands.

Assuming you have arrived at Prestwick Airport, take the coast road, A719, 5 miles (8 km) south to Ayr past a succession of Victorian villas that are now small hotels specializing in malt Scotch whiskies.

AYR: This cozy harbor and market town was chartered in the 13th century and is now a popular resort, with a marvelous beach and a nationally famous racecourse. The only architectural relics left in the town are the Tower of St. John, which is believed to date from the 13th century (Citadel Pl. and Eglinton Terr.); the Auld Brig, which Burns praised in his poem *The Twa Brigs* (High St.); 16th-century Loudoun Hall, townhouse of the hereditary sheriffs of Ayrshire (Boat Vennel); and the Auld Kirk, built by Oliver Cromwell in 1654, in which Burns was baptized (off High St., diagonally opposite Newmarket St.). Also on High Street is the famous *Tam O'Shanter Inn,* the traditional starting point of Tam's legendary ride, which now displays Burns relics and memorabilia.

South of the town, off B7024, you might want to spend a happy hour or two at Belleisle Park, which has a zoo, nature trail, gardens, and a championship golf course.

ALLOWAY: Burns's birthplace is a tiny, pastoral village on the River Doon, a leafy haven dominated by the rather incongruous Corinthian columns of the Burns Monument, which makes you feel as though you'd wandered into a painting by Fragonard. The only evidence of time's incursion into Alloway is the Land O'Burns Centre, featuring a visual display, crafts shop, bookstall, cafeteria, and landscaped gardens with picnic tables. Across the street, the humble, whitewashed cottage in which the poet was born in 1759 has been preserved intact. Nearby is the *Burns Museum.* A little farther up the road is the 700-year-old Brig O'Doon, the arched bridge where the witch in Burns's poem *Tam O'Shanter* caught hold of Tam's mare's tail, and Auld Alloway Kirk, the scene of the witches' revels in the poem. If you have a day to spare, you can follow the Burns Heritage Trail, visiting every place Burns ever went, from Ayr to Dumfries in the next county.

En Route from Alloway – On A719, heading south toward Culzean Castle, there's a sign marking the Croy Brae, also known as Electric Brae. As you climb it, shift gear into neutral: you will then coast *uphill!* Coming down the other side, shift into neutral again: Now you are coasting uphill backward! Natives swear it is an optical illusion.

CULZEAN CASTLE: Standing on a cliff overlooking the Firth of Clyde, this breathtaking edifice is Scotland's most-visited castle. Culzean Castle (the name, pronounced "culane," refers to the caves over which the castle is built) was for centuries the seat of the Kennedy family, later the Kennedys of Cassilis. Most of the present structure was designed for the tenth Earl of Cassilis in the late 18th century by the famous

Scottish architect Robert Adam. Adam's achievements here include the much-admired oval staircase and his remarkable drum-shaped drawing rooms (with curved fireplaces) giving onto the sea. The uppermost apartments were given to President Eisenhower to use as his Scottish residence as a token of appreciation after World War II. The castle's portrait of Napoleon was a gift from Josephine, a relation of the Kennedys. The castle opens at noon during April, September, and October, and at 10 AM daily from May through August.

En Route from Culzean Castle – Return to Ayr by A77, past the ruins of Crossraguel Abbey, founded in 1244, whose last abbot was roasted by the Kennedys in the 16th century until he signed away his lands.

Beyond Ayr, traveling north on A78, you come to the sailing towns of Irvine, Saltcoats, and Largs. You can rent boats at the latter (contact the Kilmarnoch Tourist Board; phone: 0563-39090). At Gourock, also a seaside holiday center, hop a ferry for Dunoon, the main town across the firth on the Cowal Peninsula. Ferries run every 20 minutes, but play it safe by booking in advance (phone: 0475-33755).

DUNOON: This burgeoning vacationland has a 4-mile waterside promenade running alongside piers, gardens, amusement arcades, amazing views, and fancy hotels. On summer nights in the gardens there are band concerts, model boat displays, variety shows, flower shows, dances, tournaments, and Highland games. It's a good place to spend a night if you like crowds and gaiety. Holy Loch, with its US submarine base, is just beside it.

INVERARAY: Far more peaceful than Dunoon and more beautiful as well, the hereditary seat of the Dukes of Argyll, chiefs of the powerful Clan Campbell, is ethereal in its isolation by the quiet waters of Loch Fyne. The original village was destroyed in 1644 by the royalist Marquess of Montrose, then rebuilt by the third Duke of Argyll; successive dukes have lavished a great deal of money on preserving its 17th- and 18th-century architecture. The 140-foot bell tower, part of the Episcopal Church of All Saints (the Avenue), houses the world's second heaviest ring of ten bells, which are chimed only during *Inverary Week,* at the end of July. The view from the top of the tower is glorious.

For centuries, the Dukes of Argyll lived in the famous Inveraray Castle nearby. The present castle, which dates from the early 16th century, was replanned and rebuilt from 1743 to 1770. Its unusual mixture of neo-Gothic and Scottish baronial styles and its strange colors and conical towers make it look for all the world like a Disneyland castle. The castle's roof caught fire in 1975, but is now fully restored. The interior contains a wealth of 18th-century ornamentation and architectural curiosities, portraits by Gainsborough and other great artists, and a collection of historical relics that provide virtually a crash course in Highland history. A guided tour is available; open April to mid-October.

En Route from Inveraray – Following A819 north, you'll pass through Glen Aray and along the northeastern shore of Loch Awe. The islands in the loch are the traditional Clan Campbell burying ground. It's romantic to imagine those stark, ancient funerals, in which only the father, brothers, and a lone piper accompanied the dead in a small boat across the waves.

Visible on your left as you skirt the north tip of Loch Awe is the impressive ruin of Kilchurn Castle, a Campbell stronghold since 1440. Six miles (10 km) farther on, on the right, at Cruachan Waterfall, is the Cruachan Underground Visitor Centre. This is a 4-million-kilowatt power station in a vast cavern inside Ben Cruachan, run by the North of Scotland Hydro-Electric Board using water pumped from Loch Awe to a reservoir 1,200 feet up the mountain. Guides and a minibus tour are on hand. Open from late March through late October.

West of Ben Cruachan is the Pass of Brander, where the Clan MacDougall tried unsuccessfully to ambush Robert the Bruce in 1308.

OBAN: Oban was set up as a fish market by a government agency in 1786. Today it is a bustling holiday spot with a picturesque circular harbor, quaint, wedding cake hotels, and a distinctly Highland flavor. Fish auctions are still held on the docks every morning.

As you waft down the town's mile-long esplanade with a couple of glasses of the local whiskies inside you, gaze across the firth to the sun-studded Hebridean islands for a true glimpse of heaven.

There's a variety of good boat trips, including day cruises to the island of Iona, the first Christian settlement in Scotland, famous for its association with St. Columba, who founded a monastery here in 563. Forty-eight Scottish kings lie buried on the island, including Macbeth. Wear a sweater for the boat ride; it's an open craft. For details, contact the Oban, Mull, and District Tourist Board (Argyll Sq.; phone: 63122).

GLENCOE: This ominous, mist-enshrouded glen was the scene of a famous massacre in 1692, when a government force of Campbells wiped out an entire branch of the Clan Macdonald — who had received them as guests — by stabbing them in their beds at daybreak. To learn more details, visit the *Glencoe and North Lorn Folk Museum* (closed Sundays) off A82 just past Ballachulish, Glencoe's only village.

En Route from Glencoe – The small resort town of Fort William is popular and bursting with hotels, but its setting is drab and moorish. The shopping here is quite good, however, and about 5 miles (8 km) beyond the town, on the right, is Ben Nevis, which at 4,406 feet is Britain's highest mountain.

At Loch Oich you can either take A87 west for 50 miles (80 km) to Kyle of Lochalsh or continue up A82 along Loch Ness to Inverness. From Inverness you can follow the Highlands tour route backward to Edinburgh.

If you head west, as you approach Kyle of Lochalsh you pass Loch Duich and, just offshore, Eilean Donan, Scotland's most-photographed castle. Try to be there at sunset, when all is bathed in unearthly light. Then suddenly you come upon the sea and, opposite you, the fabled Isle of Skye, the largest and most famous of the Hebrides, with its dark, jagged Cuillin hills. You may never want to go home.

BEST EN ROUTE

Expect to pay $80 and up per night for a double room in hotels classified as expensive; $60 to $80 in the moderate category; and $45 to $60 in the inexpensive category. For restaurants, the ranges are $50 and up for a dinner for two in the expensive category; $30 to $50 in the moderate; and $30 and under in the inexpensive category. Prices do not include wine, drinks, or tip, and will vary with the dollar, to some extent.

AYR

Marine Court – After a refurbishment, this seaside hotel now has 30 comfortable rooms and a restaurant with a varied menu. 12 Fairfield Rd. (phone: 0292-267461). Expensive to moderate.

Pickwick – One of the best of a seafront string of Victorian villas specializing in pure malt whiskies and Scottish foods. Most of the 15 rooms have baths. 19 Racecourse Rd. (phone: 0292-260111). Moderate.

Belleisle House – Once the property of the Magistrates of Ayr, who evidently saw no reason to stint themselves, this delightful 18-room hotel retains such personal embellishments as engraved fireplaces. (It lends some credence to fellow Ayrshireman Burns's poetic attacks on the divisions between rich and poor, powerful and lowly.) Elegant traditional dishes are served in one of two dining rooms, one a replica of Marie Antoinette's music room, the other modeled after her bedroom.

Inside Belleisle Park grounds on Doonfoot Rd. (phone: 0292-42331). Moderate.

OBAN

Alexandra – Modernized, well-furnished 56-room hotel with magnificent views over the harbor, Oban Bay, and the Firth. Scottish and English cuisine. The Esplanade (phone: 62381). Expensive.

Caledonian – There are excellent sea views from this grand old Victoria Station hotel; Scottish and English food are served in its dining room. Station Sq. (phone: 777210). Expensive.

GLENCOE

Ballachulish – This recently modernized hotel has retained its family atmosphere and is singled out by the knowledgeable for particular praise. It has 28 rooms, baronial lounges, and a restaurant serving a remarkable blend of traditional and international dishes. Through the Pass of Glencoe (on A828 at the Ballachulish Bridge), dominating Loch Linnhe (phone: 08552-606). Moderate.

Kings House – Scotland's oldest licensed inn, this 22-room hotel on Rannoch Moor stands on an old drovers road, along which cattle were once herded to market. A great base for climbers, anglers, skiers, and hikers (phone: 259). Moderate.

KYLE OF LOCHALSH

Lochalsh – A comfortable resort hotel just beside the ferry to the Isle of Skye, with glorious views from most of the 40 rooms. English, Scottish, and French cuisine are served here. Ferry Rd. (phone: 4202). Expensive.

Northern Ireland

Northern Ireland's troubles have given it bad press. This has had two effects: People know Northern Ireland is part of the United Kingdom (it was separated from the rest of Ireland in 1921), and sporadic violence has discouraged visitors. Those who do come, however, find any hostility confined mostly to the two large urban centers of Belfast and Londonderry and directed mainly at members of the police, British army, and paramilitary — all of whom usually maintain low visibility. They also find unspoiled coastline and countryside, empty beaches, uncrowded roads, fine accommodations, and friendly people.

Northern Ireland — virtually synonymous with the ancient province of Ulster and still often so referred to — covers about one-sixth the total area of Ireland. The province is so compact — about 70 miles at its widest by about 100 miles long — that in a short tour of 3 to 4 days you can crisscross its six counties and take in most of their highlights. Among these are several hundred miles of bay-indented coast, with coves, cliffs, castles, and beaches; scores of beautiful inland lakes and hundreds of rivers and streams; two great mountain chains — the fabled Mountains of Mourne, sweeping down to the Irish Sea in the southeast, and the Sperrin Mountains in the northwest.

The tour described below begins in Belfast, the capital of Northern Ireland, and makes a clockwise circle around the province, following the southern part of Ulster's long coastline that encircles County Down. County Down has its share of resorts along the winding shore but is dominated by the Mourne Mountains in the south, where Slieve Donard rises from the sea to 2,796 feet.

County Down is bordered by Armagh to the west, the county whose rich northern fruit-growing area has earned its title as "the garden of Ulster."

County Fermanagh, the farthest west, is "the lakeland of Ulster." The River Erne winds through its center, expanding at Enniskillen into two large lakes, Upper and Lower Erne, both with many islands.

The inland county of Tyrone has a fine variety of scenery — gentle hills, glens, river valleys, moors, and small towns. But the bulk of the land piles up to the 2,000-foot peaks of the Sperrin Mountains.

The county of Londonderry, in the northwestern corner, is an interesting mix: To the south are the Sperrin Mountains (shared with County Tyrone); to the north is the Atlantic coast, fringed with magnificent beaches of surf-washed sands. The county's boundary with County Antrim in the east is the River Bann; in the west the River Foyle borders the Irish Republic.

Antrim is the northeastern corner, its southeastern end buttressed by Belfast. Its magnificent east coast curves around the base of steep headlands, between which the beautiful nine glens of Antrim open to the sea. Almost every bay along the coast is a link in a chain of fine holiday resorts. Near the northernmost point, Torr Head is only 13 miles from Scotland. On the northwestern end of Antrim's coast is the Giant's Causeway, a curious rock formation that's a celebrated natural wonder. The River Bann and Lough Neagh, the largest lake in Ireland and Britain, form the western boundary.

BELFAST: This is a fairly new city that grew rapidly during the 19th-century shipbuilding and linen production boom. Belfast was dubbed "the Athens of the North" during a great cultural blooming in the late 18th and early 19th centuries, when prominent citizens became patrons of learning and art. In the same period the shipbuilding industry grew by leaps and bounds, and new machinery and processes helped Belfast gain a position of supremacy in the linen industry. When the six Ulster counties were separated from the rest of Ireland by an act of the British Parliament in 1920, Belfast became the capital of the province of Northern Ireland.

The port city is on the River Lagan where it joins the sea. Its center is Donegall Square, dominated by the large city hall, a Renaissance building with a tower at each corner and a graceful dome in the center. On the east side stands a sculpture commemorating the 1912 *Titanic* disaster — the largest ship of its time was built here.

Other impressive buildings are St. Anne's Cathedral, the *Ulster Museum and Art Gallery,* the Palm House in the Botanic Gardens, and, on a hill in the suburb of Stormont, Parliament House. One important building damaged during the violence of the 1970s, the ornate Edwardian grand opera house, has been restored and stages all kinds of entertainment. Belfast has three theaters, two universities, more than 300 churches, and excellent shops in the center of town. The port has 7 miles of quays. The shipyards of Harland and Wolff include the largest shipbuilding dock in the world. All can be viewed from the crest of Cave Hill. There are acres of parkland on the outskirts of the city, including Dixon Park, with its 20,000 rose bushes.

Six miles (9.6 km) east of Belfast on Route A2 is the small residential town of Holywood beside Belfast Lough.

HOLYWOOD: Although the town has a good promenade, a golf course, and tennis and yachting facilities, the main reason to stop here is the *Ulster Folk and Transport*

Museum, which spreads over 180 acres and faithfully re-creates 19th-century life — from a blacksmith's forge to a weaver's house. There are farms and craftsmen working at their craft. You can buy their products (open daily; Cultra Manor; phone: 0232-428428).

BANGOR: Ulster's chief yachting center, Bangor is well laid out, with fine promenades, gardens, and recreation grounds. Yacht races go on all the time, setting out from the *Royal Ulster* or the *Ballyholme* clubhouse.

En Route from Bangor – Take A21 south to Newtownards, at the northern end of Strangford Lough, a busy marketing and industrial town. Continue to Comber, where flax yarn for linen is spun. Go south on A22 along Strangford Lough passing Killyleagh, with Ulster's finest residential castle, en route to Downpatrick. St. Patrick is reputed to be buried in the nearby Down Cathedral churchyard in Downpatrick; the gravesite is marked by a huge slab of Mourne granite, and on *St. Patrick's Day,* pilgrims scatter daffodils over the spot. The life of Ireland's patron saint is documented at the nearby *St. Patrick's Heritage Center* (phone: 0396-615218). Halfway between this quiet hilly town and the pretty village of Strangford, 9 miles (14 km) east, lies Saul (signposted), a place with a special meaning for Irish everywhere, for it was here that St. Patrick landed in 432 to begin his Irish mission and build his church. Although the church was destroyed several times, fragments of earlier buildings remain, as well as the little memorial church of St. Patrick (Church of Ireland), built in 1932 to mark the 1,500th anniversary of Patrick's arrival here. The Shrine of St. Patrick, a mile farther west of the prominent hill of Sliabh Padraig, is a place of pilgrimage. A granite figure of the saint stands on the summit.

Continue to Strangford, on the western shore of the strait connecting Strangford Lough with the sea. There is a car ferry every half-hour to the village of Portaferry on the opposite shore (phone: 039686-637). This area is noteworthy for the many castle and monastic ruins around the Lough's indented shore, including Portaferry and Strangford castles, large rectangular structures built by the Anglo-Normans to guard the strait entrance. Portaferry also has Northern Ireland's only aquarium and the Queen's University Marine Biology Station, which is worth a visit for its ecological interest.

From Strangford, take A2 around Dundrum Bay all the way to Newcastle, driving toward the impressive Mourne Mountains looming to the southwest.

NEWCASTLE: This seaside resort is beautifully situated along the sandy beach that fringes Dundrum Bay, with the great bulk of Slieve Donard filling the skyline behind the town.

Two miles (3 km) west, at Bryansford, is scenic Tollymore Forest Park. There are many planned walks here along the Shimna River and on the mountainside. Three miles (5 km) north of Tollymore is another forest park — Castlewellan — with an outstanding arboretum.

Extending southwest for nearly 15 miles are the Mourne Mountains.

En Route from Newcastle – The scenery along the Mourne coastline, Route A2, is superb, particularly at Annalong, a tiny, picturesque fishing harbor with a water-powered corn mill and a visitor center. About 13 miles (21 km) from Newcastle is Kilkeel, the headquarters for a large fishing fleet. The town is a good center for exploring the Mournes and the coast of south Down.

The coast road continues through the charming little resort towns of Rostrevor and Warrenpoint on the edge of Carlingford Lough, where you look across the water to the shores of the Irish Republic and on to the "frontier" town of Newry. This industrial center and port, in a hollow among hills at the head of the Newry River estuary, has been important from ancient times because of its strategic position at the "gap of the north" — the main crossing into Ulster from Dublin and the south. Take A28 into County Armagh and to the town of Armagh, about 20 miles (32 km) northwest.

ARMAGH: This ancient city — once the seat of Ulster kings — has been the ecclesiastical capital of Ireland for over 1,500 years. It was here in 443 that St. Patrick established a cathedral and monastic school, which have been destroyed and rebuilt many times. The Church of Ireland cathedral now occupies the site. The Catholic cathedral stands imposingly on an adjoining hilltop, approached by a long series of steps with terraces. Its inside walls are covered with mosaics, including medallions of the saints of Ireland. Marble is used for everything from altars to pulpit.

The city has an air of quiet dignity. Its well-laid-out streets are dominated by the two cathedrals. At the center of town is the Mall, a pleasant green lined by fine Georgian houses, the excellent *County Museum,* the courthouse, the 17th-century Royal School, and the 18th-century observatory and modern planetarium.

Take Route A28 to Augher and join A4 to Fivemiletown, where you cross into County Fermanagh. Continue to Enniskillen, the center of Northern Ireland's scenic lakeland.

ENNISKILLEN: Between the Upper and Lower Lough Erne, the town is a convenient base for exploring this peaceful countryside on roads along the wooded lakeshores or by boat on the lakes. Abundant fishing and the availability of modern boats for rent have made these lakes very popular. Notable National Trust properties in the area include Castle Coole and Florence Court.

The Marble Arch Caves, 3 miles out on the A4, contain a fascinating underworld of lakes, weirs, waterfalls, and lofty chambers. Well-lit walkways are maintained for visitors. Open daily Easter to October, from 11 AM, but it's wise to call ahead because water levels sometimes rise in the caves (phone: 0365-828855).

En Route from Enniskillen – Take Route A46 to Belleek, the westernmost point of Ulster. This border town, where Northern Ireland meets the Republic, is known for its lovely handmade eggshell-thin pottery. The world's most extensive collection of Belleek lusterware is for sale in the gift shop, and tours are also available (phone: 036565-501).

From Belleek take A47 to Kesh, and A84 into County Tyrone until it joins A32 to Omagh. The Ulster-American Folk Park, 4 miles (6 km) north of Omagh, re-creates bygone rural life in Northern Ireland and illustrates the notable contributions of Ulster men and women to US history, including the ancestors of a dozen US presidents. Open daily, Easter through early September; weekdays in winter (phone: 0662-3292).

LONDONDERRY: This ancient seaport, which stands on a commanding hill overlooking a broad tidal curve of the River Foyle, was founded as a monastic settlement in 546. Although it was never occupied by the Anglo-Normans, it was the scene of many struggles between Irish forces and a succession of invaders. In 1608, with the English in control, the land was granted to the citizens of London (thus, Londonderry). A large colony of Protestants was imported and the walls were fortified. These walls withstood several sieges; the most famous, in 1689, lasted 105 days.

The Old Walls, the city's most prominent feature, are in excellent condition. They are now laid out as a promenade, with many of the old cannons still standing where they once stood, by the four old city gates. Information about guided tours of the city walls can be obtained from the Tourist Information Centre (Foyle St.; closed Sundays; phone: 504-267284).

In Shipquay Place is the Guildhall, an impressive modern Gothic structure with a fine series of stained glass windows illustrating events in the city's history. It was partly destroyed in the disturbances of 1972 but is now mostly restored. Shipquay Street leads to the 17th-century Protestant cathedral. Outside the city walls is the 19th-century Catholic cathedral, on James St. in Bogside.

En Route from Londonderry – Take Route A2 out of the city; you are in for a 74-mile (119-km) treat of the most scenic coast road in Northern Ireland, which leads all the way into Belfast. The road goes east to Limavady, then curves northeast to hug the shore and pass through two noted County Derry resorts: Castlerock and Portstewart. They offer what all resorts on the north coast have in common: excellent beaches, good sea and river fishing, and several fine golf courses. Continue 4 miles (6 km) to Portrush in County Antrim.

PORTRUSH: This resort has an outstanding golf course — the Royal Portrush, the only Irish course ever to host the British Open. There is bus service to the Giant's Causeway, the absolute must-see on this route.

Often called the eighth wonder of the world, and now a UNESCO World Heritage site, the causeway is an intriguing rock formation on the coast near Bushmills. It was formed by cooling lava that burst through the earth's crust in the Cenozoic period as long as 70 million years ago. Here the basaltic lava split into prismatic columns as it cooled. And there they stand, about 40,000 basalt columns packed together in a shape so regular they seem cut by hand.

En Route from Portrush – Continue east to Portballintrae and Old Bushmills, home of the world's oldest licensed whiskey distillery (open to visitors who give advance notice; phone: 026-57-31521.) In July and August, there is occasional open-top bus service to the Giant's Causeway, just north.

Continue past resorts with wide beaches separated by cliffs — white, black, and red — fretted by the sea into strange shapes. Ballycastle is the point of departure for white-cliffed Rathlin Island, the haunt of millions of sea birds. Special trips are available from Easter to September, although visitors can also catch the regular mailboat that leaves from Ballycastle at about 10:30 AM on Mondays, Wednesdays, and Fridays. Six miles (10 km) ahead is Ballyvoy. From here a signposted road goes to Fair Head, the northeastern extremity of Ireland, which rises to 636 feet of sheer cliffs of columnar basalt and offers a fabulous view of Rathlin Island and Scotland. The road goes on to Torr Head, the closest point to the Scottish coast. Rejoin Route A2 near Cushendun and enter the area of the nine glens of Antrim. Continue to Glenariff.

GLENARIFF: Here is the most famous of the Antrim glens. Formed by the Glenariff River at Red Bay, the glen stretches inland for about 5 miles between steep mountains. It has a nature information center.

En Route from Glenariff – The coast road takes you past more glens and beautiful sea views to Larne, the crossing point for car-ferry service from Stranraer and Cairaryan in Scotland, the shortest cross-channel passages between Ireland and Britain. Continue south for 21 miles (34 km) to Belfast.

BEST EN ROUTE

Northern Ireland has an adequate supply of comforatble hotels and restaurants. Hotels and guesthouses are generally clean and fairly inexpensive. The more expensive ones may have a special feature, such as a great view or an unbeatable location. The prices listed here range from expensive — more than $100 per night for a double; to moderate — $65 to $100; to inexpensive — under $65. The range for dinner for two is: more than $60, expensive; $40 to $60, moderate; under $40, inexpensive. All hotels listed have well-respected restaurants.

BELFAST

Culloden – This sumptuous Victorian mansion is set amid gardens and woodlands 6 miles (9.6 km) east of Belfast on the A2 at Cultra, across from the *Ulster Folk Museum.* Once the palace of the Bishops of Down, its Gothic arches and stained glass are still intact. All of the 76 comfortable rooms are furnished with antiques. The elegant restaurant has traditional international cuisine. Cultra (phone: 02317-5223). Expensive.

Dunadry Inn – Once a linen mill, then a paper mill, this charming 64-room hostelry offers good service as well as a bird's-eye view of a bygone era, with converted old mill cottages, the lawn where linen was once laid out to whiten in the sun, and original mill fixtures, including beetling machines, which now adorn the bar. Near Aldergrove Airport, 19 miles (30 km) from downtown Belfast, 2 Islandreagh Dr. in Templepatrick, Co. Antrim (phone: 08494-32474). Expensive.

Europa – In the center of town, this is a modern place with 200 pleasant, well-equipped rooms. There is a coffee shop on the granite and marble ground floor; also a pub bar. A cocktail bar and a more formal restaurant are upstairs. There's live music nightly, except Sundays and Mondays, in the panoramic 12th-floor lounge. Great Victoria St. (phone: 0232-327000). Expensive.

Wellington Park – One of the city's newest hotels, it is in South Belfast, close to Queen's University, the Botanic Gardens, and the *Ulster Museum*. The decor includes a permanent display of contemporary Irish painting and sculpture. 21 Malone Rd. (phone: 0232-381111). Expensive.

CRAWFORDSBURN

Old Inn – This partly thatched attractive village inn, a few miles east of Belfast, dates from 1614. Its 32 bedrooms have many charming Old World features. There is a lovely garden, and very good food is served. 15 Main St. (phone: 0247-853255). Expensive.

NEWCASTLE

Slieve Donard – On the Irish Sea, in the shadow of the magnificent Mourne Mountains, and next to the renowned *Royal County Down Golf Club,* this grand hotel of the railway era has recently been refurbished. All of its 120 rooms have private baths. Downs Rd., (phone: 03967-23681). Expensive.

ENNISKILLEN

Killyhevlin – This stately mansion overlooking Lower Lough Erne, with lawns sloping down to the waterside, provides a very special overnight stay. There are fine views from the 22 spacious rooms; some have balconies. Dublin Rd. (phone: 0365-23481). Expensive.

LONDONDERRY

Everglades – On the River Foyle on the outskirts of town, this upscale hotel has 38 rooms, a dining room, and live piano music. Prehen Rd. (phone: 0504-46722). Expensive.

BLACKHILL, NEAR COLERAINE

Blackheath House – A charming Georgian home with 6 double-occupancy rooms and a fine restaurant, *MacDuff's.* 112 Killeague Rd. (phone: 0265-868433). Expensive.

BALLYGALLY

Ballygally Castle – Northern Ireland's only plantation-era hotel property (built in 1625 but with modern extensions) has some atmospheric turret rooms. This mostly modernized 30-room establishment faces the sea. Antrim Coast Rd. (phone: 0574-83212). Expensive.

CARNLOUGH

Londonderry Arms – Once the property of Sir Winston Churchill, the great-grand-son of the original owner, this 19th-century building is in a seaside village at the mouth of Glencloy, one of the nine glens of Antrim. There are only 14 rooms in this family-run hotel, so make reservations. 20 Harbour Rd. (phone: 0574-85255). Moderate.

Greece

At the southern tip of the Balkan Peninsula, Greece occupies a prominent position on the continent and in European history. Greece covers some 50,944 square miles; the mainland spreads between the Ionian Sea on the west, the Aegean on the east, and the Sea of Crete to the south; more than 3,200 islands lie in the surrounding seas. Because of its island territory (170 of the islands are inhabited), Greece is actually larger than it appears, exceeding neighboring Bulgaria in size.

The sea is a major influence on life in Greece. The Greeks have been seafarers throughout their history, and today their shipping industry, although severely affected by this decade's shipping crisis, is still one of the world's largest. The 9,300-mile coastline is one of the world's longest, and Greece is known for the beauty of its many beaches.

Greece's terrain is quite rugged; some 80% of the land is mountainous. Mt. Olympus, the legendary home of the gods, rises 9,570 feet and is one of the highest peaks in the country. Only 30% of the land is arable. The fertile plains of Thessaly support the country's major crops, wheat and tobacco, though plenty of olives, fruits, and vegetables are grown in Crete and other areas.

Greece has a population of nearly 10 million, 53% of which is urban. Athens is the capital and largest city (pop. 3.26 million in Greater Athens); the other major cities are Thessaloniki (pop. 1 million) and Patras in the Peloponnese (pop. 209,387). Most of the people are Greeks, with Turks and Vlachs — an ancient people speaking a language akin to Romanian — making up the largest ethnic minorities and Slavs, Albanians, and Jews forming smaller groups.

The very cradle of Western civilization, Greece has an extremely rich history. Traces of a Neolithic population in Greece date from 6000 BC, but sometime around 3000 BC a more advanced civilization lived on Crete, which was followed by the development of tribes on the mainland. Some of these tribes banded together to form city-states and eventually developed the more sophisticated social structure of democracy, Greece's greatest contribution to the civilized world. Hellenistic culture reached its apex in the 4th century BC in Athens, where democracy nurtured the works of Plato and Aristotle. Later, in the 3rd century BC, Alexander the Great confederated numerous city-states and conquered new territories, creating a large empire. Greece subsequently became part of the Byzantine Empire (AD 395) and still later (in the 15th century) was conquered by the Ottomans. Not until the early 19th century did most of the country again regain its independence.

The heritage of ancient Greece is the legacy of all contemporary Western nations, but it is a special source of pride to modern Greeks. Numerous vestiges of it remain — Greek, Roman, and Byzantine ruins, from the majestic Acropolis in Athens to the extremely well preserved Theater of Epidaurus on the Peloponnese, where visitors can still see ancient Greek drama as it was performed millennia ago.

In addition to sites of great historical significance, Greece has an extraordinarily beautiful countryside. The Mediterranean landscape dominates the southern mainland, much of the Peloponnese Peninsula, and many of the islands. Rocky hills drop down to long stretches of coast and seas of deep blue and aquamarine. In the north, the vegetation is denser, similar to that found elsewhere on the Continent. The summers are hot, sunny, and dry; winters, cool and damp, and, in the north, snowy. Spring is warm and pleasant, a time when the hills come to life with colorful wildflowers, though Greece in summer reaches its most basic state — sun, rock, and sea. Greece's low prices are another attraction; in fact, prices are considerably lower than in other European countries.

But in many ways, Greece is not European at all. Four centuries of occupation by Turks left a strong Middle Eastern flavor in many aspects of Greek life — from relations between the sexes to food, folklore, and an exasperatingly Byzantine notion of bureaucracy. In planning your stay, bear in mind that many archaeological sites and museums close at 1 or 3 PM, the Greeks generally take a siesta between 3 and 6 PM, so unless you're on a beach or simply like walking, there may be little do during the afternoons.

In addition, air and ferry service between the islands, and guided tours are cut back sharply during the colder, grayer winter months. By contrast, the hotels, beaches, and ruins are packed solid with tourists in summer. To avoid the crowds, travel during the shoulder seasons — spring and fall — is highly recommended, as the weather is still lovely.

The following routes originate in Athens except for the tours of the islands, which are accessible by sea and air from Athens or major island ports. The route through northern Greece heads to Thessaloniki by way of Mt. Olympus and Meteora, then branches off, east to the Turkish border and west to the Yugoslavian border. A short route leads through the Parnassus mountain region to Delphi, once the home of the most celebrated oracle of all time. Island routes focus on Crete, Greece's largest island; the Dodecanese Islands, of which Rhodes is the largest and most popular; the Cyclades, including Mykonos and Delos, which offer everything from varied nightlife to magnificent archaeological sites; the Eastern Aegean islands, of which Lesbos is the most prominent; and Corfu to the west, considered by many to be the most beautiful of all. Another route loops around the Peloponnese Peninsula, taking in 4,000 years of history scattered over 8,000 square miles.

Northern Greece

Northern Greece is markedly different from the rest of the country in both geography and history. Nature seems to have acted more intensely here; the climate is continental rather than Mediterranean, as is the vegetation. The region's history has been turbulent from ancient times through World War

II and the civil war of 1946. Perhaps as a result, the people are less outgoing than other Greeks, though they are still warm and hospitable.

You need time to explore this area. The two suggested routes, from Athens to Thessaloniki and then either west to the Yugoslavian border or east to the Turkish border, take from 3 to 5 days each. To cut the trip shorter, you can fly to Thessaloniki from Athens and rent a car for the rest of your touring. So as not to miss a visit to Meteora, a fascinating monastic community, and the climb up Mt. Olympus, you can also take a plane to Ioannina, then a bus to Meteora. From Meteora, we suggest an overnight side trip to the charming village of Metsovo, which is steeped in Balkan ambience. You can get another plane at Ioannina or rent a car there for the trip to Thessaloniki. To follow the route outlined below, get an early start driving from Athens.

ATHENS: For a complete description of the capital and its hotels and restaurants, see *Athens* in THE CITIES.

   En Route from Athens – Take a break at Kamena Vourla, about 100 miles (160 km) from Athens. You can go for a swim in this attractive resort town or have some refreshments. Between here and Larissa, the route crosses one of the most fertile plains in Greece. Stop at one of the restaurants just before Larissa for lunch. Heading for Meteora, turn west on the road for Trikala for 36 miles (58 km), where a 12-mile (20-km) drive leads to Kalambaka.

METEORA: Rising 1,820 feet high, the 24 formidable rock pillars stand isolated in space. On these precipitous cliffs, 14th-century Byzantine monks built a monastic community that became a sanctuary for the persecuted and the devout. Some centuries later, the community started to deteriorate, and today only 4 of the original 24 monasteries are inhabited, 2 of them by nuns. You can spend the night in Kalambaka. The hotels are small, however, so book ahead during the summer. An excellent, superbly hospitable restaurant — *The Meteora* — is right on the square in Kalambaka (phone: 0432-22316).

   En Route from Meteora – Back on the National Road, you can break for an excellent seafood meal at Platamon. Turn off the road 12 miles (20 km) farther at the village of Plaka to start the ascent to Mt. Olympus, Greece's tallest mountain (9,620 feet) and home of the Olympian gods. A paved road leads to Litohoron, 1,150 feet up the mountain, and on to the chalet at 4,290 feet. From here you can hike to the highest refuge at 6,930 feet. The climb is a rewarding one, especially in spring, when there is still snow but the weather is mild.

METSOVO: This tiny village in the province of Epirus — to which Albania once belonged — is a stunning place that seems more Balkan than Greek. It is carved into a piece of the Pindus mountain range, and its ubiquitous white stucco houses are trimmed, chalet style, with finely carved wooden balustrades and balconies and roofed with red tile or gray slate. Here live the Vlachs, an ancient people of obscure origin who still speak an archaic language resembling Romanian; few residents speak English. Elders dress in richly embroidered costumes. Metsovo, aside from its beauty, is renowned for the quality of its handicrafts: woven goods, filigree jewelry, carved wood, leather, and fur. There is a folklife museum in town, and a 20-minute hike out of town leads to the gorgeous Byzantine frescoes of the former St. Nikolaos monastery. Metsovo is also a ski station; its traditionally decorated hotels are wonderfully cozy in winter. From Kalambaka, head west on Rte. E-87 for about 93 miles (150 km).

THESSALONIKI: Established in 316 BC and named after the stepsister of Alexander the Great, Thessaloniki provides all the amenities of a modern coastal city while preserving its notable past. Touring Greece's second largest city, you'll see numerous Roman remains in the walled-in "acropolis," or high part of the old city, and interesting Byzantine churches, among them the remarkable Church of St. Dimitri, Thessaloniki's first Christian martyr. The *Archaeological Museum* (YMCA Sq.) contains magnificent golden treasures from the tomb of Philip II, father of Alexander the Great. Discovered in 1977, it was the first unlooted tomb found in Macedonia and confirms the theory that Vergina, where it was found (48 mi/77 km from Thessaloniki), was the burial ground of Macedonian kings. Don't miss a visit to the *Byzantine White Tower,* the symbol of this historic city and now a musem housing a small but interesting Byzantine collection. A fascinating and beautiful collection of northern Greek costumes and traditional objects is displayed in the *Folklife/Ethnological Museum.*

For a break in sightseeing, there is shopping at the clothing, book, and folkcraft stores on Tsimiski and Aristotelous streets. Then, have a drink and some seafood at *Tottis'* ouzo bar, on central Aristotelous Square, overlooking the quay. Among the most popular restaurants in town are *Olympos-Naoussa,* where you can have excellent meals in a simple setting, *Krikelas,* where the parade of appetizers leaves little room for the main course, and *Mandragoras,* complete with hanging puppets and imaginative cuisine. Thessaloniki, perhaps because of long (nearly 500 years) Turkish domination, is known for its fine food. So a potluck stop at any of the quayside restaurants in town, or on the winding seaside road north of the city, is likely to produce memorable results.

From Thessaloniki, men can make a fascinating side trip.

MT. ATHOS: The grounds of the 1,000-year-old monastic republic are forbidden "to any woman, any female, to any eunuch, to any smooth visage," according to an edict issued by Emperor Constantine IX in 1060. There aren't many eunuchs around these days, and it's no longer necessary to grow a beard, but females are still excluded.

Mt. Athos, or Aghion Oros (Holy Mountain), the easternmost of the three peninsulas of the Halkidiki, is reached from Thessaloniki by the road to Poligiros, the local capital. At Paleocastron, 35 miles (58 km) from Thessaloniki, the road branches right and left; head left via Arnea, a small village that produces excellent wine and handwoven textiles, and Stagyra, the birthplace of Aristotle. The road leads down the coast along the Bay of Ierissos and on to Ouranoupolis, a lovely seaside town. This is as far as women and cars can go, but there are several good hotels on the beach.

From Ouranoupolis, a short boat ride leads to the port of Daphne; from here a cobbled path ascends through thickets of oleanders to Kariés, capital of the autonomous Mt. Athos community. The imposing monasteries are scattered — sometimes a 5-hour walk from one another — among the lush vegetation of the valley. In the 16th century, Athos accommodated about 40,000 monks in 40 monasteries; today the number has dwindled to 1,500 monks in 20 large monasteries and monastic hermitages. In recent years, however, there's been a reviving interest in monastic life, and those numbers are increasing slightly now. Athos is a living Byzantine museum, and its treasures are priceless.

Visit as many of the monasteries as you care to; hospitality is always extended to the visitor, though it is customary to leave a contribution. A permit from the Foreign Ministry in Athens (phone: 362-6894) or the Ministry of Northern Greece in Thessaloniki (phone: 031-270-092) is needed to enter Mt. Athos; Americans must first obtain clearance from the US Embassy in Athens (phone: 721-2951).

En Route from Mt. Athos – On the way back to Thessaloniki, you can stop off and relax for a few days at one of the lovely beach resorts of Kassandra, the westernmost of the Halkidiki peninsulas. Back in Thessaloniki, there are two alternative routes: west to the Yugoslavian border or east to the Turkish border.

THESSALONIKI TO THE YUGOSLAVIAN BORDER: About 25 miles (40 km) from Thessaloniki en route to Edessa, make a slight detour to see the remarkable ruins of ancient Pella, the birthplace of Alexander the Great. The remains cover an extensive area, including entire streets with buildings that had courtyards surrounded by peristyles. Well-preserved pebble mosaics on the floors depict mythological scenes. The small museum houses many of the finds.

At Edessa, the capital of ancient Macedonia, stop and buy the enormous juicy peaches known as *yarmades*. Some 42 miles (72 km) farther you'll reach Florina, which is only 10 miles (16 km) from Yugoslavia. Vendors in the open-air market speak Serbo-Croatian as a second language. While dining in Florina, try the local specialties made of sweet red peppers.

Take a side trip to Prespes Lake, a resort and wildlife preserve whose shores are skirted by Greece, Yugoslavia, and Albania. You can spend some time on a nicely laid-out beach, have some refreshments at the tourist pavilion, and get a glimpse of the off-limits coast of Albania.

The road to Kastoria passes through spectacular mountain scenery (note: the route can be hazardous in the winter). Once in this lakeside town — the fur center of Greece — you can watch furriers turn scraps into luxurious coats and jackets, which are available at some of Europe's lowest prices. Take a boat ride around the lake and stop at the Monastery of Mavrotissa, with its interesting frescoes.

THESSALONIKI TO THE TURKISH BORDER: If you're traveling through the area from May 20 to 23, take a side trip to the village of Langada, about 12 miles (20 km) from Thessaloniki. Here you can see the *anastenarides* (firewalkers), who dance on burning embers, apparently transported and oblivious to the pain. The tradition originated as a pagan rite but is now a Christian ritual, performed in honor of St. Constantine.

Some 45 miles (75 km) farther, the road climbs high before zigzagging down to Kavala, opening up a sweeping view of the harbor town and the nearby island of Thassos. Kavalla is a large, picturesque town, built around the harbor. Among its highlights are the Roman aqueduct that curves through the center of town and the Byzantine fortifications above the decidedly Oriental eastern section. Mohammed Ali, founder of the Egyptian royal line, was born in an old Turkish building in this area in 1769.

Several waterfront tavernas specialize in fresh fish. If you have time, take a boat to Thassos, a lush green island whose serene beauty is a scenic counterpoint to the oil derricks drilling offshore at Prinos, Greece's only commercially exploited oilfield.

You can take a side trip to Philippi, built by Philip II in 356 BC. The extensive remains of the town lie on both sides of the road.

A good road leads to Xanthi and Komotini. Both towns have a strongly Oriental flavor: Mosques with minarets and black-veiled women wearing Turkish pants attest to the Moslem minority living here since the exchange of citizens between Greece and Turkey in 1923. In Xanthi, stop at the lovely Porto Lagos beach for a swim and some lunch.

En route to Alexandroupolis, you'll probably encounter a few oxcarts. The town is pretty, but not particularly interesting. A short drive leads to the west bank of the Evros River, which separates Greece from Turkey. Soldiers of each nationality guard either side of the bridge.

BEST EN ROUTE

Expect to pay $80 and up per night for a double room in hotels listed as expensive, around $60 in the moderate category, and $30 or so in the inexpensive category. Note that in Thessaloniki, rates rise as much as 20% during September's *International Trade Fair*.

LARISSA

Divani Palace – Each of the 77 rooms is air conditioned and contains telephone and radio. 19 Vassilissis Sophias (phone: 041-252791). Moderate.

KALAMBAKA

Divani – This motel has gardens, a large pool, a restaurant, bar, and 165 air conditioned rooms with telephone and radio. Below the Meteora (phone: 0432-23330). Moderate.

METSOVO

Bitouni – A 24-room hotel, filled with the warm, rich hues of handwoven pillow covers and handsomely carved pine ceilings, it is a study in Greek hospitality. In winter, the owners serve tea before a crackling fire in the hearth. The tiny but adequate rooms look right out onto the town and the mountains beyond it. On the main road heading out of town (phone: 0656-41545). Moderate.

THESSALONÍKI

Electra Palace – A stylish Art Noveau hotel that has plenty of atmosphere, very good views of the city's Aristotelous Square and the well-kept waterfront, and 131 air conditioned rooms. 5a Aristotelous Sq. (phone: 232221). Expensive.

Macedonia Palace – This large hotel on the quay provides luxurious modern accommodations in 287 rooms; those with sea views are in demand. Megalou Alexandrou Ave. (phone: 837521, 837621). Expensive.

Capsis – In the commercial section of town, this 428-room hotel has a friendly atmosphere. 28 Monastiriou (phone: 031-521421, 521321). Moderate.

OURANOUPOLIS

Xenia – A pleasant place to spend the night before taking off for Mt. Athos. Accommodations are in a 42-room hotel or in bungalows. In town (phone: 0377-71202). Moderate.

FLORINA

Lingos – The 40 rooms here are simple and comfortable. In town (phone: 0385-28322). Inexpensive.

KALITHEA

Pallini Beach – A large hotel (495 rooms and bungalows), with its own beach and pool. Facilities include tennis, boating, waterskiing, horseback riding, and a sauna. There are also a seafood restaurant, a cafeteria, and a bar (phone: 0374-22480). Moderate.

KAVALA

Galaxy – This centrally located hotel has 149 rooms. In town (phone: 051-224521, 224811). Inexpensive.

ALEXANDROUPOLIS

Astir – A cozy and comfortable 53-room hotel. On the beach (phone: 0551-2448). Moderate.

Delphi and the Parnassus Region

Even if you're spending only a few days in Greece, the trip to Delphi is a must. Rising from the heart of the mountainous Parnassus region, Delphi is the home of the most celebrated oracle of all times — awe-inspiring in its beauty and austerity. The best time to visit is in the spring or fall, when the wild flowers bloom in colorful variety on the hills and the tourist flow is limited. In the summer, avoid the climb in the early afternoon; the heat and intense sunlight can be exhausting. At all times, Delphi leaves a profound impression on the visitor.

ATHENS: For a complete description of the capital and its hotels and restaurants, see *Athens,* THE CITIES.

En Route from Athens – For a cold drink, stop at the tourist pavilion in Levadia, 70 miles (113 km) from Athens, and sit by the waterfall.

ARAHOVA: Perched over 3,000 feet high on a winding mountain road, this town has cobblestone streets and neat stone houses with pots of aromatic basil and lavender out front. For lunch, have lamb roasted on the spit and the potent local wine, then browse in the shops featuring the splendid multicolored fabrics woven by the townswomen.

You can climb up to the nearby Corycian grotto, dedicated in ancient times to Pan, the god of shepherds, and to the forest nymphs. In ancient times, women from Athens, Boeotia, and Delphi gathered here every 5 years, dressed in animal skins and carrying torches, to dance all night in celebration of the Bacchanalia.

To reach the highest peak of Mt. Parnassus, get set for 3 more hours of climbing. Mountain refuges are available at Kontokedro and Yerondovrahos. In winter, buses take visitors to the Mt. Parnassus ski center, which offers the best skiing in Greece.

DELPHI: The road, winding through olive groves and vineyards, suddenly opens up on the awesome site of the ancient oracle's temple. In this setting, you can understand why the ancient Greeks regarded Delphi as the "navel of the earth." Such is the magnificent isolation of the site, with golden-red cliffs looming around it, the serenity of the sacred valley below, and, in the distance, the Gulf of Itea sparkling in the sunlight. At the center of Delphi stands the sanctuary of Apollo; from here the narrow Sacred Way zigzags past treasury buildings of the ancient Greek city-states to the ruins of the Doric Temple of Apollo. After being purified with water from the nearby Castalian spring, the priestess, dressed in full ceremonial robes, would utter her prophecies.

Above the temple rises the 4th-century BC theater; the high tiers command a panoramic view of the sanctuary and the profoundly secluded landscape. At sunset, when a soft blue light spreads over the glowing pinkish mountains, the feeling that you're alone in the world can be complete — unless a busload of tourists has joined you.

The ruins of the Marmaria (the Marbles), dedicated to the goddess Athena, lie below the main road. Midway between the Marmaria and the sanctuary is the Castalian spring, where you can stop for a drink under the huge plane trees.

The museum on the main road between the village and the sanctuary contains numerous pieces found in the sanctuary and the Marmaria or nearby. The highlight of the collection is a bronze statue known as *The Charioteer,* dating from 478 BC. Among the other displays are the pediments from the Temple of Apollo, several exquisite archaic statues, and recently discovered statuettes of gold and ivory.

BEST EN ROUTE

Expect to pay $50 and up per night for double rooms in the hotels listed below.

DELPHI

Amalia – This large hotel has 185 elegant rooms with air conditioning, a pretty, airy restaurant, a huge lobby with a fireplace (for those who come for the winter skiing), and good views. In town (phone: 0265-82101).

Vouzas – Closer to the ruins, this 58-room hotel has good service and nice views (phone: 0265-8-2232).

Crete

Equidistant from Europe, Asia Minor, and North Africa, Crete has a special location, history, and heritage. Legend has it that Zeus, supreme god of heaven and earth, was born and raised here. The myths of the labyrinth, the minotaur, and the wings of Icarus originated on Crete. And from 3000 to 1400 BC the Minoans flourished here, leaving behind remnants of the first great civilization in Europe. Crete was ruled by Romans, Arabs, Venetians, and Turks at different times until it was finally united with Greece in 1913.

The natural setting of Crete, Greece's largest island and the southernmost point in Europe, is truly magnificent. Rugged mountains rise in the center, east, and west. Between them stretch fertile plains and valleys. At the coasts, the mountains drop down to the sea, forming stretches of sandy beaches and secluded coves.

The best way to see Crete is to rent a car, although regular bus service connects the various towns on the island. Daily air and sea connections link the mainland and other islands with Heraklion and Hania. You can begin your tour in either city; the route outlined here starts in Hania.

To get a full taste of Crete, try the local specialties: cheeses, ranging from the mild manouri to the stronger graviera, a Gruyère-type cheese mellowed in caves; honey from Sfakia usually served over thick yogurt; and figs and pomegranates. Sample *raki,* a sort of home-brewed ouzo, or *tsikoudia,* the gin-based aperitif served in tiny glasses. Cretans down these drinks in one gulp. They're strong stuff, so don't get carried away when they start offering rounds in honor of the foreigner enjoying their favorite drinks. .

HANIA: The capital of Crete, Hania is an interesting mixture of Venetian and Oriental influences. A fruit and vegetable market dominates the center of town, with open stalls and lively scents and colors. Buy *diktamo* here, a rare herb that can be used to brew a delicious tea, considered a panacea by the islanders. After browsing around, have a cold drink at the town square before going down to the charming harbor, with its arched buildings, cobblestone streets, and Venetian lighthouse. After lunch at any of the fish restaurants on the quay, spend the afternoon at the beach and return to the harbor in the evening for a leisurely dinner at a taverna on the quay. Get a good night's rest before starting out the next day for an adventurous all-day hike through the Samarian Gorge.

SAMARIAN GORGE: Reputed to be the longest in Europe, this gorge can take anywhere from 5 to 8 hours to cross. Pack a picnic lunch. Take a bus or drive the 25 miles (40 km) to Omalos. From here you start the descent on a path that zigzags down into the gorge. At this point the hike may seem awesome, but it's actually quite manageable if you're wearing comfortable shoes. The next 11 miles (18 km) are filled with fascinating scenery — mysterious shadows; unusually shaped rocks; and pine, cypress, and fig trees scattered among a myriad of wild flowers. The hike ends at the fishing village of Aghia Roumeli, where you can take a boat across to Chora Sfakion, which claims to produce the tallest and longest-living Greeks. Spend the night here on the shores of southern Crete, where Zorba woke the passions of a young English intellectual, in the famous novel by Nikos Kazantzakis. In the morning, you can take the bus to Hania.

RETHYMNON: Attractive Venetian and Turkish architectural styles predominate in Crete's third largest city. The fortress (1574) is the best-preserved Venetian building on the island. There is a sandy beach in town. If you are visiting Rethymnon on St. George's Day (usually April 23, sometimes later), don't miss the celebration at the mountain village of Asi Ghonia, about an hour's drive away, where flocks of sheep are brought to the churchyard to be blessed; then they're milked and the milk is distributed to visitors. A traditional Cretan *glenti* with songs and dances follows. While here, buy the pungent graviera cheese that is allowed to mellow in the many nearby caves.

En Route from Rethymnon – Before the next few days of sightseeing, you can relax for a day or two in the beach resort of Aghia Pelagia, 12 miles (20 km) before Heraklion.

HERAKLION: Begin your tour of Crete's largest, but certainly not most attractive, city at the Venetian port, where you can walk beside the fortified walls to the 16th-century Venetian castle. Stroll around the marketplace and have a typical Cretan lunch in one of the many tavernas in the area. The *Archaeological Museum* has the world's greatest collection of Minoan treasures, including the famous Disc of Phaistos. Also of interest is the *Historical Museum,* with exhibitions covering the early Christian, Byzantine, Venetian, and Turkish periods.

You can take several interesting side trips from Heraklion. The restored Palace of Knossos, home of the legendary King Minos 4,000 years ago, is a few miles southwest. Plan to arrive early so you can spend a few hours here (guidebooks can be purchased at the entrance).

For a glimpse of village life, drive up to Anoghia in Mt. Idi, 21 miles (35 km) from Heraklion. From here, dedicated climbers can attempt to reach the Idian Cave, where legend says Zeus grew up. Farther up from Anoghia is the village of Axos. Stunning handmade crafts can be purchased in both villages.

Another must in the area is a visit to the Minoan site of Phaistos, 37 miles (62 km) from Heraklion (a guidebook available on the site is recommended). For a relaxing break, drive 6 miles (9.6 km) to Matala to swim in the warm waters of the Libyan Sea and lie on the sandy white beach surrounded by caves — once inhabited by early Christians, since the 1960s by hippies from all over the world.

En Route from Heraklion – On the way to Aghios Nikolaos, stop at Malia with its Minoan palace, narrow winding alleys, and lovely beach. Break for lunch near Malia beach at *Taverna Kalypso,* where the English-speaking chef, Chris, will whip up one of his award-winning specialties using succulent Cretan produce, fresh herbs, and virgin oil from his own olive trees next door.

AGHIOS NIKOLAOS: This chic resort town is a place to sit back, relax, and enjoy the sun and sea. The area has luxury accommodations, and the harbor is packed with tavernas, discos, and souvenir shops.

For a change of pace, visit the village of Critsa, 7 miles (12 km) away, with a superb view of the bay below. Every year, on the last Sunday in August, an old Cretan wedding is performed here, with festivities lasting well into the night.

You can make another side trip to the Diktian Cave, the legendary birthplace of Zeus. The hike entails a drive to the Lasithi Plains, famous for their windmills and hand-woven textiles, and a climb to the cave, starting from the village of Psychro. The cave has stalactites and stalagmites over 200 feet long. If you're up to the arduous 6-hour climb to the summit, start out in the village of Aghios Georgios, 2½ miles (4 km) before Psychro, and hire a guide in the village. The hardships of the climb are rewarded by a spectacular view of the entire island.

En Route from Aghios Nikolaos – The 44-mile (73-km) drive to Sitia passes through whitewashed villages set among orchards and olive groves. Next to the road there's a frightfully sharp drop to the sea. Don't attempt the drive if you've been drinking.

SITIA: This lovely town has many beautiful beaches, the best known of which is Vai (a few miles out of town), a long sandy beach with a dense growth of palm trees. It's a romantic spot to camp out; you can also stay at one of the hotels in town.

IERAPETRA: The largest town in southern Crete, Ierapetra retains an Oriental flavor with Venetian touches here and there. The coast is lined with tavernas, discos, and a few hotels where you can spend the night before crossing Crete at its narrowest point to return to Heraklion or Hania.

BEST EN ROUTE

Expect to pay $80 and up per night for a double room in hotels listed as expensive; around $40 for those in the moderate category; and about $20 for those in the inexpensive range.

HANIA

Kydon – Centrally located, this 113-room hotel has an old-fashioned atmosphere. S. Venizelou Sq. (phone: 0821-26-190). Moderate.

Porto Veneziano – This charming, family-run establishment on the Venetian harbor has 63 rooms (phone: 0831-29311). Moderate.

RETHYMNON

El Greco – Right on the beach, this resort has a pool, tennis, mini-golf, Ping-Pong, a playground for the children, and all water sports. The 307 rooms are in hotel accommodations or bungalows (phone: 0831-71102). Moderate.

AGHIA PELAGIA

Capsis Beach – On a lovely stretch of beach 15 miles (25 km) from Heraklion, this hotel has gardens, three pools, and two sandy beaches. There are 191 hotel rooms and 354 bungalows (phone: 081-233395). Expensive.

HERAKLION

Knossos Beach – Only 7 miles (12 km) from town in Hani Kokkini, this hotel has 106 pleasant rooms and bungalows (phone: 081-280381). Moderate.

Anna-Bella – This pension offers 9 comfortable rooms. In town (081-289728). Inexpensive.

AGHIOS NIKOLAOS

Elounda Beach – Overlooking the sea, this deluxe resort has a pool, tennis, putting green, and water sports facilities. The 297-room hotel and bungalows are set in an attractive wooded area (phone: 084-41412). Expensive.

Minos Beach – This luxurious resort on the beach has 118 bungalows facing the sea, an outdoor pool, and good recreational facilities (phone: 0841-22345). Expensive.

IERAPETRA

Atlantis – A comfortable 69-room hotel that is a good place to spend the night before heading back to Hania or Heraklion. Aghios Andreas (phone: 0842-28555). Inexpensive.

The Dodecanese Islands: Rhodes, Kos, Patmos, and Karpathos

Southeast of the Greek mainland, off the coast of Asia Minor, the 12 islands of the Dodecanese group offer a wide variety of natural attractions and historical ruins. Lying relatively close to one another, the islands have similar histories but diverse personalities. Rhodes is the largest and most popular of the group, with Kos running second in tourist flow and amenities. Two of the less frequented islands — Patmos and Karpathos — are included here for those who want a taste of simple island life. The most rewarding aspect of spending some time on the smaller islands is the genuine warmth and hospitality extended by the islanders.

RHODES: Rhodes has something for everyone: sites of great historic interest, a wealth of natural beauty, accommodations ranging from luxury hotels to simple rooms in village houses, a variety of sports facilities, and a large casino. Because Rhodes is the favorite of sun-worshiping Scandinavians, it can be very congested from June through August. May and September, also hot months, are much more relaxing in Rhodes.

According to Greek mythology, the island sprang out of the sea and was offered as a gift by Zeus to Apollo, the sun god, who named it after his current fling, Rhodos, daughter of Aphrodite. Archaeological evidence indicates that Rhodes was originally settled by the Minoans and Myceneans. The island prospered in the 11th century BC under the Dorians, who founded Ialysos, Kameiros, and Lindos; in 408 BC these three cities united to form the city of Rhodes.

Incorporated into the Byzantine Empire in AD 395, Rhodes was sold by its Genoese masters to the crusading Knights of St. John in 1306. During their 200-year rule, they converted the island into a Christian stronghold; they were finally forced out by the Ottomans, who controlled Rhodes until 1912, when the Italians seized the island. Rhodes was finally reunited with Greece and the other Dodecanese islands in 1947.

The most striking reminders of this diverse history can be found in the town of Rhodes. The Old City has remnants of the Crusaders and the Middle Ages — narrow streets; 13th-, 14th-, and 15th-century buildings adorned with coats of arms; and powerful walls built by the Knights of St. John. Visit the *Archaeological Museum,* housed in the 15th-century Hospital of the Knights, and the massive Palace of the Grand Masters, a 14th-century fortress with underground passages and chambers. The Turkish quarters are nearby, marked by mosques and old Ottoman homes.

Surrounding the Old City is the modern section, a cosmopolitan Greek island capital with fine hotels, a myriad of duty-free shops, and the *Grand* hotel casino. According to legend, the harbor entrance of Mandraki was once straddled by the immense bronze Colossus of Rhodes, one of the Seven Wonders of the World, which towered 126 feet and weighed 300 tons.

You can take side trips to the three Dorian cities from the capital. Little remains of ancient Ialysos, 5 miles (8 km) from Rhodes, but there's a good view from the Acropolis. Kameiros, 20 miles (32 km) from town, has more of interest, including a 3rd-century BC temple and colonnade, a 5th-century cistern, and the agora, or ancient marketplace. Lindos, 21 miles (34 km) from Rhodes, is an attractive old village that can get very busy in summer. The Acropolis (which can be reached on foot or by hired donkey) dominates the ancient city, which was once the center of the cult of the goddess Athena. A 4th-century temple dedicated to her still stands and is currently being restored to its original grandeur. Many 15th-century houses, built when the Knights of St. John converted Lindos to a fortress, line the narrow streets of the town.

Petaloudes (Valley of the Butterflies), 16 miles (26 km) south of Rhodes, is one of the island's most stunning locales. Each spring, thousands of butterflies (actually moths) nestle in the trees of this narrow, thickly wooded valley. If you stir the branches, the creatures fill the air in a bursting reddish-gold cloud.

In Rodini, 2 miles (3 km) south of Rhodes, an annual wine festival is held from mid-July to the end of September. Visitors can sample the local wines to their hearts' content and watch musicians and dancers perform late into the night.

Fine beaches line the shores of the island. Good fishing grounds are found near the villages of Kameiros, Lindos, Kallithea, and Gennadi.

KOS: The birthplace of Hippocrates, the father of medicine, this island has a history similar to that of Rhodes but a quieter atmosphere. The town of Kos is quite attractive, with white, arched houses set in lovely gardens. The coastal road to the port of Mandraki is particularly pleasant for a walk or a bicycle ride. Beaches are excellent all over the island, as are the accommodations.

Historical highlights include the Castle of the Knights of St. John, the ancient agora, the Temple of Dionysus, the Roman baths, the gymnasium, and the town museum, with a statue of Hippocrates. Famous South African doctor Christiaan Barnard recently established an international health center on Kos.

PATMOS: The northernmost of the Dodecanese, Patmos is known primarily for its associations with St. John the Divine, who received the Revelations and dictated them to a disciple in the Sacred Grotto, which lies between the harbor and the capital. The massive, elaborately decorated Monastery of St. John, which has also served as a fortress, is the principal historic site.

Patmos has fine sandy beaches and the white architecture characteristic of many Greek islands. You can do some challenging hiking here, too. Every year on August 15 (feast of the Assumption) there's an all-out celebration with food, music, and dancing.

To really get away from it all, take a caique to the small nearby island of Lipsi, with isolated beaches, good tavernas lining the harbor, and hardly any tourists.

KARPATHOS: Midway between Rhodes and Crete (and accessible from both), Karpathos is a folklorist's paradise. In the densely forested north, people maintain centuries-old traditions. In the village of Olympus (reached by a poor road from the little harbor of Diafani), the women till the fields and do most of the heavy chores. They work in long, dark blue coats worn over bright tops and white breeches, with brightly patterned scarves covering their heads. Bear in mind that this is not a tourist attraction but a way of life.

If you are in Olympus after Easter or in late summer (August 15 and 29 or September 8), you can watch and perhaps participate in a traditional celebration, with plenty of wine, songs, and dances. If a wedding is to take place, the villagers hold an extravagant *glenti,* or feast — 3 days of music, dance, food, wine, and strictly observed customs.

There are several good beaches on the island near the capital, Pigadia. You can take interesting side trips by motorboat to the nearby uninhabited islets of Saris and Armathia.

BEST EN ROUTE

Expect to pay $50 and up per night for a double room in hotels listed as expensive; $35 and up for those in the moderate category; and under $20 for those in the inexpensive range. Most of the bigger — and better — hotels are found on the east coast around Faliraki. Homeowners on the smaller islands rent clean, comfortable rooms at modest prices.

RHODES

Chevaliers Palace – This hotel is a good bet for those who prefer to be in town, as it is within walking distance of the historic town center. Facilities include 188 rooms, a pool, sauna, nightclub, and a fine self-service restaurant. A casino is just across the street, and a beach is nearby. 3 Stratigou Griva (phone: 0241-22781). Expensive.

Rodos Palace – The tallest building on the island, this luxury resort has all the amenities and then some — outdoor and indoor pools, tennis, mini-golf, sauna, restaurants, disco, shops, nightclub, and bowling alley. The 610 air conditioned rooms are fashionably decorated and comfortable; some have gardens or sea views. Ixia, 2½ miles (4 km) from town (phone: 0241-25222). Expensive.

Rodos Bay – Set on a hillside, this modern resort has all recreational facilities. Most of the 330 rooms and bungalows are in the main building — best of all are the maisonettes, split-level bungalows facing the sea with spectacular views. Ixia Trianda (phone: 23661). Moderate.

KOS

Dimitra Beach – Right on the beach, this resort has 134 rooms and bungalows, restaurants, bars, a lounge with dancing, and a snack bar. Aghios Fokas (phone: 0242-28581). Expensive.

PATMOS

Xenia – Simple and comfortable accomodations in a 35-room hotel. In town (phone: 0247-31219). Moderate.

KARPATHOS

Porfyris – This comfortable 22-room hotel is one of the few around. In town (phone: 0245-22294). Inexpensive.

The Cyclades:
Mykonos, Delos, and Santorini

In Greece, a group of islands called Kiklades form a rough circle around the sacred island of Delos, a religious, cultural, and commercial center of the ancient world. Apart from their archaeological interest, each of the 39 islands comprising the group (24 are inhabited) has much to offer the visitor, from the intense nightlife of Mykonos to the isolated beaches of Kimolos, where there are no hotels but plenty of hospitality. The best-known Cycladic islands are described below.

MYKONOS: "Is Greece near Mykonos?" the American tourist is said to have asked his travel agent; though it's probably apocryphal, the question is indicative of the island's fame — and perhaps notoriety.

You name it, and Mykonos is bound to have it: a harbor teeming with luxury yachts and fishing boats; more discotheques, bars, and restaurants than all the other Greek islands put together; narrow cobblestone streets lined with art galleries and chic boutiques; officially designated nude beaches; many windmills; and over 300 churches.

The most outstanding feature of this island is its dazzling brightness; blazing sunlight reflects off the always freshly whitewashed houses and churches. Practically everything is white — even the trunks of the few trees in town are painted white. This brightness makes getting up in the morning a pleasure; it seems a shame to sleep at night. Actually, hardly anyone turns in before the early morning hours, so the popular beaches don't get crowded before noon. These are to the south and are accessible by bus, taxi, or boat. For nude swimming, try Paradise, Super Paradise (preferred by homosexuals), or Helia.

When night falls, Mykonos comes alive with activity to suit every taste. You can watch the colorful international set that frequents the island, have a drink at a bar in Little Venice overlooking the sea, take your time over dinner, then head to one of the current hot spots. Many say Mykonos has the best nightlife in Greece.

If possible, avoid Mykonos in August; the *meltemi,* or north wind, can be annoying, and the island is most crowded then.

DELOS: No one should leave Mykonos without taking the half-hour boat trip to Delos. First settled some 5,000 years ago, Delos became the religious, cultural, and financial center of the Aegean around 1000 BC. It remained prominent until 454 BC, when the island treasury was moved to the Parthenon for safekeeping. In Hellenistic times, Delos revived as a commercial center.

Many of the island's temples and shrines are extremely well preserved. Highlights include the Terrace of the Lions, the Temple of Apollo (according to mythology, the sun god was born here), an agora, sanctuaries, and a museum. Spend the night in the small hostel and take an evening walk in the moonlight. Delos is nearly uninhabited, and the solitude can be deeply moving.

SANTORINI: Known in Greek as Thira, this striking island is of volcanic origin. Some believe that a massive volcanic eruption here in the 16th century BC caused the decline of the Minoan civilization, centered on Crete, to the south. Santorini is often associated with the legendary Atlantis.

Santorini is a crescent-shaped mass of rock with precipitous cliffs up to 1,000 feet high. Donkeys and a special railway wind up the cliff from the harbor, where the cruise ships dock, to the island capital of Fira, with its narrow, cobbled streets and medieval quarter. Ancient Thira was inhabited at various times by Phoenicians, Dorians, Romans, and Byzantines, and some impressive ruins remain. You can swim at one of the island's black (lava) sand beaches just outside Oia, or take a motorboat excursion to the volcano, on an adjacent islet.

BEST EN ROUTE

Expect to pay $80 and up per night for a double room in hotels listed as expensive and about $20 for those in the inexpensive range.

MYKONOS

Petinos – This small 29-room hotel on the beach has a taverna. Plati Yalos (phone: 0289-22127). Inexpensive.

DELOS

Xenia – Since this is the only place on the island to spend the night, you have to be lucky to get one of the few beds available. It's worth a try to experience the solitude after dark. Some camping is also permitted, and there's a very simple restaurant (phone: 0289-22259). Inexpensive.

SANTORINI

Atlantis – On a cliff overlooking the sea, this 2-story whitewashed house has 27 spacious, high-ceilinged rooms. The bar and breakfast terrace have excellent views. In town (phone: 0286-22232). Expensive.

The Islands of the Eastern Aegean: Lesbos, Samos, and Chios

Lush green vegetation in parts, crystal-clear waters in every shade of blue, and small villages clinging to tradition characterize the islands of the northeastern Aegean Sea. The three described here can be reached by air from Athens or by boat from Piraeus, northern Greece, and Rhodes.

LESBOS: In the time of Sappho (600 BC), Lesbos was probably the most advanced city in the world, with its intellectual life at a remarkably high level. It was here that the world's first known great woman poet sang her poems to the young girls she loved; the passion of her descriptions was such that the term "lesbian" has been used to denote love between women ever since. Lesbos was also the birthplace of Aesop, one of the most famous storytellers of all time.

Today Lesbos (also known as Mytilene) preserves little of its ancient glory, but it's a marvelous place for sunning, swimming, hiking, and exploring ancient and Byzantine ruins.

From the island's capital, Mytilene, good roads lead to practically all parts of the island. On the northern tip is Molivos, or Mithimna, reached by a lovely coast road. En route, stop at Thermi to see a recently excavated prehistoric settlement. Swim at the excellent beach in Aghios Stephanos, and have lunch at one of the numerous tavernas. The road passes through extensive olive groves — the island is famous for its olives and olive oil — until reaching Molivos. Set over the beach and fishing harbor, this attractive town seems to grow right out of the surrounding hills. A Genoese castle dominates the town and offers a fine view of the Turkish coast.

SAMOS: Inhabited since 3000 BC, Samos was the birthplace of the great mathematician Pythagoras (6th century BC) and also, according to mythology, of the goddess Hera, sister and wife of Zeus. The landscape is quite striking — golden beaches, blue sea, and mountains in the east and west. About 10% of the island is cultivated with vineyards that produce a very sweet white wine. Flowers bloom everywhere.

Vathi is the capital and tourist center of the island. The *Archaeological Museum* and *Museum of Byzantine Art* both have interesting exhibitions. You can hike up to the monastery of Zoodohos Pighi for a sweeping view of the Turkish coast, only a few miles away, and accessible by boat from Samos.

Samos is a great place for hikes and excursions. Buses link different towns on the island and travel on good roads. You can take a break at any of the beaches or fishing villages along the way, and, in most, you can spend the night in comfortable hotels or in rooms in private houses.

Visit Pithagorio, once the island's capital and now an enchanting fishing village, 10 miles (16 km) south of Vathi. Natives call the town Tigani ("frying pan") because of its shape. Here you can see the remains of an ancient wall, a theater, and an aqueduct that was built through the mountain in the 6th century BC. The view of nearby Asia Minor is superb. Less than a mile away is a monastery constructed deep inside a cave surrounded by a natural cistern. The Heraion, 3 miles (5 km) from Pithagorio, is the site of a temple dedicated to Hera that was considered one of the Seven Wonders of Antiquity.

CHIOS: Chios is fertile and beautiful, and many of its inhabitants are rich: A number of the Golden Greek shipowners come from the island that Homer referred to as "the rocky realm" (according to one legend, the island is his birthplace).

Chios is the original chewing gum producer. For centuries the island's prosperity was based on the cultivation and sale of mastic gum, popular with the courtesans of antiquity for the pleasant aroma it gave their breath. Today, you can buy it wrapped in cellophane or drink it in the form of mastiha — but go easy, it's very potent.

You can take a pleasant walk through the pine trees to the Nea Moni (New Monastery), a fine example of Byzantine architecture. The mastic gum tree area spreads south from the monastery of Aghios Minas. Villages in the area retain a medieval character, with stone houses, narrow arcaded streets, and interesting churches.

While in Chios, take a boat to the five small Oinoussai islands off the northeastern coast. They have good fishing and hunting grounds and sandy beaches. The rich Greek shipowners who were born here return frequently with their families, filling the harbor with luxury yachts. A regular boat service links Chios to the nearby Turkish coast.

BEST EN ROUTE

Expect to pay $$45 per night for a double room in hotels listed as expensive; $30 and up for hotels in the moderate category; and about $20 in the inexpensive range.

LESBOS

Lesbion – On the harbor of Mytilene, this hotel has 38 comfortable rooms. In town (phone: 0251-22038). Moderate.

Lesbos Beach – Outside town, the accommodations consist of 39 furnished apartments. Neapolis (phone: 61531). Moderate.

Sappho – Also on the harbor, this hotel offers 31 standard rooms for modest prices. In town (phone: 28415). Inexpensive.

SAMOS

Doryssa Bay – An attractive hotel with 252 rooms. Pithagorio (phone: 0273-61360). Expensive.

Xenia – This is the most comfortable of the accommodations in town, with 31 rooms. Vathi (phone: 0273-27463). Moderate.

Merope – The attraction here is the lovely view; 80 rooms. In Karlovassi (phone: 0273-32650). Inexpensive.

CHIOS

Chios Chandris – On the port, this branch of the Quality hotel chain is well run. The 156 rooms are nicely appointed. In town (phone: 0271-25761/6). Moderate.

Corfu

Considered by many to be the most beautiful of the Greek islands, Corfu has been praised by Homer in the *Odyssey,* chosen by Shakespeare as the setting for *The Tempest,* and extolled by Henry Miller in *The Colossus of Maroussi,* and by Laurence Durrell in *Prospero's Cell*. Many prominent Greeks frequent Corfu, known locally as Kérkyra.

In the North Ionian Sea, Corfu marks Greece's westernmost point. The semimountainous terrain supports more lush vegetation than any other Greek island. Millions of olive trees grow on the gentle slopes. Orange, lemon, cypress, acacia, and plane trees take root here, and the fragrance of a wide variety of flowers fills the air.

Good roads leading to all parts of the island start from the capital, the town of Corfu on the east coast. You can tour by car, bus, or taxi, or, if you're taken with the island's romantic atmosphere, horse and carriage. For sunning and swimming, you can head to the beaches of the luxury resorts or find isolated beaches and coves all over the island.

Corfu is an entry point into Greece from other places in Europe. The island is accessible by ferry from Brindisi, Ancona, and Otronto, Italy, and from Dubrovnik, Yugoslavia, or by air from most European capitals. Daily flights link Corfu and Athens, and the island can also be reached by ferry from Igoumenitsa in western Greece or Patras on the Peloponnese.

CORFU: The cosmopolitan seaport capital of this island is also called Corfu. It has an interesting architectural style incorporating Byzantine, Venetian, French, Russian, English, and Italian elements, with the medieval section comprising narrow Italianate alleyways, flanked by shuttered tenements with laundry lines flying between them. Even the Greek spoken here is laced with Italian borrowings, such as *nonna* and *pomedor*, from the Italian, *pomodoro*. One of the best introductions to the spirit of the Corfiots is to spend an evening at a taverna or *cafenion* on the Spianada (Esplanade), Greece's largest public square. On summer evenings, open-air concerts are given by earnest local bands.

Corfu is an old town, and you can see the remnants of the civilizations that have played a role in its history. At the tip of Aghios Nikolaos, the northern section of town, is a Venetian fortress, which many historians identify with the Heraion Acropolis, mentioned by Thucydides. Corfu's Town Hall (1663) is a splendid example of Venetian architecture. Mon Repos, the former royal palace, is a neo-classical structure with a Doric portico. Britain's Prince Philip was born here. Other highlights include the *Archaeological Museum* (5 Vraila), with finds from excavations; the *Museum of Asiatic Art* (Kato Platia), with a rich collection of Chinese, Japanese, and Indian art and a very un-Greek, enormous relief carving of the Gorgon; and Kanoni, 2½ miles (4 km) south of town, a semicircular terrace that commands an excellent view of the harbor and provides access to two little islets with monasteries.

The town has excellent facilities for sports and recreational activities. The major resorts have mini-golf, tennis, water skiing, and swimming at their own beaches. There's a public beach at the Mon Repos palace; the most popular beaches on the island are Roda, 22 miles (35 km) north of town, and Glyfada, 10 miles (16 km) west of town. Tennis is available at the *Tennis Club* (Vraila and Romanou) and golf, at the 18-hole course near the village of Vatos. Corfu is also good for other activities — fishing, hiking, and even cricket, an odd relic of British rule, at the Corfu Cricket Green. You can go horseback riding at the stables in Gouvia, 5 miles (8 km) from town right on the Spianada, in Alikes, 3 miles (5 km) from town, or on the west coast, in Paleocastritsa.

In the evenings there is ample entertainment at the hotel clubs and the discos around town. In 1891, Empress Elizabeth of Austria had her summer palace built in Gastouri, 5 miles (8 km) south of town. Named the Achilleion after her favorite hero with the famous heel, today the palace is a casino, scheduled to move to the *Corfu Hilton* in

1990. The structure itself is considered amusing by some and an atrocity by others, but the lovely gardens stretching down to the sea are appreciated by most everyone for evening strolls.

MT. PANTOCRATOR: Rising 3,000 feet in the northern section of the island, Corfu's highest summit commands an excellent view of the surroundings. To the south spreads the city of Corfu and the rest of the island. To the east lies Albania (only a mile away at the closest point). On a clear day, the coast of Italy is visible to the northwest. The monastery on the mountain dates back to 1347.

PALEOCASTRITSA: On a small bay surrounded by hills, this popular resort, 16 miles (26 km) west of Corfu, is popular for its clear water, good fishing, and excellent seafood. Local tavernas specialize in lobster.

PAKI: Less than 8 square miles in area, this islet, 2½ hours by motorboat from Corfu Harbor (boats leave twice daily except on Sundays), is a great place to spend a serene day or two. Covered with dense vegetation, including olive trees and vine plants, the island is unique in its underwater caves and excellent lobsters. You can stay in bungalows on the beach or rent rooms in islanders' houses.

BEST EN ROUTE

Prices for double rooms per night in the hotels listed below start around $40 (considered moderate) and go up to $100 and more (expensive). As on Rhodes, most of the luxury hotels are not actually in town, but shuttle bus service is provided.

Corfu Hilton – This attractive resort has fine facilities — indoor and outdoor pools, tennis, a disco, bowling, several restaurants, bars, and 256 rooms and bungalows. The landscaped beachfront gardens are very pleasant. The hotel provides shuttle service to town and the golf course. Kanoni (phone: 0661-3-6540). Expensive.

Bella Venezia – This is the best, and newest, of the hotels in town, 2 blocks from the Spianade. Price includes breakfast; no credit cards. 4 Zambeli (phone: 0661-46500). Moderate.

Hermones Beach – Sloping down to a private beach, this first class facility has 272 hotel rooms and bungalows. Among the amenities are a pool, restaurants, bars, and a lounge with music. 8½ miles (14 km) from Corfu just before Paleocastritsa (phone: 0661-9-4241). Moderate.

The Peloponnese

Separated from mainland Greece by the Gulf of Corinth, the Peloponnese Peninsula encompasses more than 8,000 square miles of varied and impressive scenery. Much of the peninsula is mountainous, though the different ranges are separated by sweeping, fertile plains, and the low-lying coastal regions give way to some fine beaches. The area is rich in archaeological ruins. Its history has been traced back some 4,000 years through excavations at Mycenae, a great capital of the ancient Hellenic civilization.

The route spans large distances, historically and geographically, and requires about 5 days, though you could easily spend more time. Starting in Athens and heading west to Corinth, the itinerary loops around the peninsula. Among the highlights are Olympia, the site of the first Olympic games; Vassai, with the 5th-century BC Temple of Apollo Epicurus; Mistra, a wonderfully preserved former Byzantine settlement on a mountainside; Mycenae;

and Epidaurus, where you can watch a performance of an ancient drama in a huge open-air amphitheater.

ATHENS: For complete details on the capital and its hotels and restaurants, see *Athens,* THE CITIES.

En Route from Athens – It's best to start out in the morning on the Athens-Patras National Road. Stop at the Corinth Canal, about an hour's drive away, and look at the isthmus that connects the Peloponnese with mainland Greece.

CORINTH: Once the largest city of Greece, Corinth was prosperous to the point of decadence when it was destroyed by the Romans in 146 BC. The area remained uninhabited for the next 100 years until a Roman colony was founded by order of Julius Caesar. Corinth regained its former prominence, though earthquakes and a series of barbarian invasions eventually brought about its decline. The modern town has little of interest. The 6th-century BC Temple of Apollo, in the old town, is the only Greek ruin in ancient Corinth. The museum opposite the temple contains primarily Roman exhibitions. Beyond the old town, the mountain Acrocorinth rises 1,885 feet. Easily reached by car, the summit is topped by an ancient fortress, commanding a spectacular view of the Saronic and Corinthian gulfs. The original Hellenic fortress was later expanded, in succession, by the conquering Franks, Venetians, and Turks.

En Route from Corinth – Head to Patras along either the National Road or the narrower but infinitely more attractive coastal road, which winds its way between a plain of olive trees and the blue waters of the Corinthian Gulf. The largest town along the way is Aegion, designed attractively on three layers above the sea. Stop for a fresh fish lunch here or at one of the smaller villages on the road.

PATRAS: Greece's main western port is a well-laid-out town with arcaded streets and large squares at the harbor. Ancient ruins are scarce, though the history dates back to Mycenaean times. The main sights are the Odeion, built in Roman times; the *Archaeological Museum;* and the Church of St. Andrew, the largest church in the country. From Patras, you can make connections to the Ionian islands (see the *Corfu* route) or Italy. You can spend the night at a hotel in town or, better yet, at Loutra Killini, 50 miles (85 km) southwest, where there are excellent accommodations right on one of the loveliest, whitest beaches in Greece (see *Best en Route*).

OLYMPIA: This fertile valley is the home of the Olympic Games, held in honor of Zeus, their legendary founder. In the first games (776 BC), the gods were pitted against human heroes. Some 200 years later, the games were instituted on a regular, 4-year basis. Events included competitions in wrestling, foot racing, chariot racing, horse racing, the pentathalon, and various artistic contests. The games were discontinued when the Romans conquered Greece. In 1896, they were reinstituted in Athens and since then have been held at 4-year intervals in cities around the world. Athens is vying to host the Golden Olympiad in 1996. Greek leaders have proposed that, from then on, Greece should become the permanent site of the modern Olympics, to avoid the political boycotts and terrorism that have plagued recent games.

The Olympic ideal, combining strong physical development with high intellectual achievement, has been universally adopted. The sacred flame burning at the Altis, symbol of this ideal, has never been extinguished and is still carried to wherever the games are being held.

Some of the best-known Greek myths originated in Olympia. According to legend, Apollo and Herakles were among the first winners. After a questionable victory in a chariot race, Nero introduced a singing contest to display his artistic talents. Statues of the victors were erected in the Altis sanctuary, which contains the ruins of many buildings, including the 5th-century BC Temple of Zeus. The gold and ivory statue of Zeus was destroyed in a fire, but the pediments of the temple are displayed in the

Museum of Olympia. The ruins of the stadium, which could seat 20,000 spectators, are also here.

> **En Route from Olympia** – If you want to do some alpine exploring or just relax amid mountain scenery, take a side trip to Vytina, 60 miles (96 km) west of Olympia. You can stay at a hotel built right on the cliff, with spectacular views of the surrounding area. The food and wine are excellent, and there are good buys in wood carvings made by local craftsmen.

VASSAI: The road ascends to a plateau on which the splendid Temple of Apollo Epicurus sits in awesome solitude. Built in 420 BC by Ictinus, the architect of the Parthenon in Athens, the temple was erected as a token of gratitude after the population was spared decimation by a cholera epidemic. It is made of gray stone indigenous to the area and is unusually designed with elements of three architectural styles — Doric, Ionic, and Corinthian. Before or after the ascent to Vassai, stop at the village of Andritsaina below for a cool drink.

> **En Route from Vassai** – Stop in the seaside town of Kalamata for a meal of fresh fish. There are lovely silk kerchiefs for sale at the monastery in town. Visitors can also witness, at first hand, the devastating effects of the strong earthquake that shook Kalamata literally to pieces in late 1986.

PYLOS: This attractive little town rises from the Bay of Navarino, where, in 1827, the allied fleets of Great Britain, France, and Russia destroyed the Turkish and Egyptian forces to ensure Greek independence. Remains of the sea battle can still be seen from the harbor on a clear day. A memorial to the British sailors stands on the low rock in the center of the harbor.

King Nestor of Pylos, who aided the Achaians in their campaign against Hektor's Trojans, dwelt in a palace above the road south of town. The remains of the palace are quite impressive, particularly the throne room and the monumental entrance on the southeastern side. On a hill, the palace also commands a superb view of the area.

METHONI: Seven miles (11 km) south of Pylos, this small town on the west of the peninsula, along with Coroni on the east of the peninsula (linked by a dirt road), were known as the Eyes of Venice. The towns were the first Venetian foothold on the Greek mainland; the Venetian fortress still stands in Coroni. Nice beaches line the shores, and fishing is good in the area.

SPARTA: The drive to Sparta is delightful, particularly in spring when the wildflowers on Mt. Taygetus are in full bloom. The contemporary town of Sparta is an agricultural center of the Eurotas Valley and a convenient place to spend the night. Little remains of the ancient town, situated north of the modern town, except for the scant ruins of an acropolis and theater. However, ancient Sparta became the greatest military power in Greece after the Spartans defeated the Athenians in the Peloponnesian War. The term "spartan" is still used to denote fierce discipline and endurance.

MISTRA: This deserted medieval town, built as a fortification on the side of a steep hill, has some of the best-preserved examples of Byzantine architecture in Greece. The narrow winding streets are lined with 14th- and 15th-century churches and houses.

For dinner, go to the *Kotopouladiko* in the tiny village of Mistra, below the ruins. Here you can get delicious fried chicken served with salads and bread.

THE MANI: This highland region is the most austere and isolated in the country. Its proud inhabitants live in small villages and in the tall, castle-like houses that have fortified the Mani for centuries. They have always resisted rule by foreign powers, and the many fortified towers seen in the area attest to the Maniots' independent spirit.

At Diros, you can explore caves with impressive stalactites and stalagmites. Have lunch at a taverna on the picturesque quay at Gythion, the port of the Mani.

MONEMVASIA: On a great island-rock connected by a causeway to the mainland, this Byzantine town repulsed numerous attacks thanks to its strategic location and almost impregnable Byzantine and Venetian fortifications. Now the town is an inviting summer retreat, with beautifully restored old houses.

MYCENAE: This ancient city was the center of the Hellenic civilization, and the presumed capital of Agamemnon. Archaeologists maintain that Mycenae was first inhabited around 3000 BC, but its great significance was not discovered until 1874, when Heinrich Schliemann began excavating five of six shaft graves rich with golden treasures, now on display at the *Archaeological Museum* in Athens. The principal points of interest are the six shaft graves, the city walls, a theater, cemetery, and several giant *tholos,* or beehive-shape tombs, with stone-flanked approaches. One of these, originally called the Treasury of Atreus by historians, may actually be the tomb of Agamemnon. But all *tholos* tombs, unlike the shaft graves, were looted, leaving little material to prove this theory.

En Route from Mycenae – Take a short detour to Tyrins, the birthplace of Herakles. The palace and cyclopean walls made of huge stone blocks date from Mycenean times.

NAFPLION: According to legend, this pretty town was created by Palamidi, son of the sea god Poseidon. Set amid orchards on the Bay of Nafplion, the town was the first capital of Greece after the War of Independence. Visit the restored castle of Palamidi (reached by road or a 1,000-step footpath), and the Bourtzi fort, built by the Venetians on an islet in the bay. The nearby beaches of Assini and Tolo are very pleasant, as is a lunch of freshly caught fish at one of the waterfront tavernas.

EPIDAURUS: Once the sanctuary of Asklepios, the god of medicine, this ancient site includes the Doric Temple of Asklepios, the Tholos with its Corinthian columns, notable Greek and Roman baths, and a small museum containing finds from the area.

Spend the evening at the open-air theater, where you can experience a memorable performance of ancient tragedy or comedy. In stunning natural surroundings, the theater, designed by Polycleitus the Younger, is one of the best-preserved structures of ancient Greece. Its seating capacity is 14,000; despite its size, the theater's acoustics are remarkable — even on the last of its 55 tiers you can hear every word uttered onstage. The annual festival of ancient drama lasts from early July to late August. Performances finish at about 11 PM, so you can either spend the night or make the 2-hour drive back to Athens.

BEST EN ROUTE

Expect to pay around $50 per night for a double room in hotels listed as expensive; $25 and up for those in the moderate category; and about $20 for those in the inexpensive range.

PATRAS

Astir – This comfortable 120-room hotel is in the center of town. 16 Aghiou Andreou (phone: 061-277502). Expensive.

Galaxy – Also convenient, this 53-room hotel offers standard accommodations. 9 Aghiou Nikolaou (phone: 061-278815). Moderate.

OLYMPIA

Amalia – Not far from the archaeological site, this extremely pretty, all-white hotel, set amid wooded hillsides, has 147 rooms as well as convention facilities (phone: 22190). Expensive.

Spap – Just outside town; most of the 51 rooms have lovely views of the ancient site and the surrounding area. Above the site (phone: 0624-22514). Expensive.

VYTINA

Xenia – Right on the cliff, this 20-room motel offers a fantastic panorama of mountain scenery. Good food and wine are also available. In town (phone: 0795-21218). Inexpensive.

LOUTRA KILINI

Xenia – This 80-room resort hotel is convenient to the beaches (phone: 0623-96270). Moderate.

SPARTA

Menelaion – These 48 high-ceilinged rooms are decorated with antique furniture. In town (phone: 0731-22161). Moderate.

KALAMATA

Avra – A small pension with 7 comfortable rooms. 10 Santaroza, Paralia (phone: 0721-82759). Inexpensive.

Filoxenia – On a secluded beach, this attractive hotel has 155 rooms and reasonable prices (phone: 0721-23166). Inexpensive.

MYCENAE

Agamemnon – About a mile from the ruins, this 8-room hotel has modest prices. In the village (phone: 0721-66222). Inexpensive.

NAFPLION

Xenia's Palace – Overlooking the Bourtzi fortress, this luxury 54-room hotel offers pleasant accommodations in comfortably furnished, air

Xenia – Many of the rooms in this 58-room hotel have balconies overlooking the bay. The food and service are good. Above town (phone: 0752-28991). Moderate.

EPIDAURUS

Xenia II – This hotel has 24 comfortable cottages near the ancient theater (phone: 0753-22003). Moderate.

Hungary

This small, landlocked country near the geographic center of Europe, with a blend of Eastern and Western traditions, has long appealed to travelers. It is a land of beautiful landscapes, romantic music, decorative folk art, historic monuments, and excellent — if heavy — food.

Despite its size — it is not quite as big as Indiana — and its relative flatness, the country has an extremely colorful and varied landscape. Hungary is bisected by the Danube River (called Duna in Hungarian), which rushes south after carving a sharply angled route through mountains along the country's northwestern border.

To the west of the Danube is Transdanubia, a picturesque area of rolling hills, cultivated vineyards, old towns, and Balaton, Europe's largest warmwater lake. Within the Great Hungarian Plain, east of the Danube, are abundant fruit orchards, fields of waving wheat, sunflowers, and corn, and the prairielike *puszta*. This vast granary is the historic home of Hungary's famous whip-cracking herdsmen on horseback. In addition to the scenic mountains of the Danube Bend in the northwest, there are low, forested mountains along the northeastern frontier, which is also famous for its wine-growing regions. Deer, wild boar, and spiral-horned moufflon roam freely in state game reserves.

Hungary is bordered on the west by Austria, on the north by Czechoslovakia, on the east by the USSR and Romania, and on the south by Yugoslavia. Foggy weather is common in fall, and winters can be bone-chillingly damp; summers are hot and dry.

The fact that Hungary has an extremely homogeneous population today — 96.6% of its 10.6 million people are ethnically Hungarian or, in their language, Magyar — is the result of this century's two European wars. On the losing side in World War I, Hungary was forced to give up vast territories that had been part of its kingdom. Some 600,000 Jews, nearly two thirds of the country's Jewish population, were murdered during World War II.

Adding to Hungary's singularity is its language, which is unlike any other in Europe although, as part of the Finno-Ugric language group, it is distantly related to Finnish and Estonian. The ancestors of today's Magyars were fierce hordes of mounted tribesmen from the Ural Mountains who staged forays deep into Western Europe. Checked by the forces of the Holy Roman Empire in the ninth century, they eventually settled in the general area of what is now Hungary.

Stephen (or István), a descendant of the almost legendary Magyar leader Árpád, became the first King of Hungary in AD 997 and worked strenuously to convert his people from paganism to Catholicism. For his efforts, he received a crown from the Pope and later was canonized. St. Stephen's crown has been a symbol of Hungarian nationhood ever since. (The crown was taken to the US for safekeeping during World War II but was only returned in 1978, some time after tensions between the Church and the Communist government were eased.) About two-thirds of Hungary's population is at least nominally Roman Catholic.

After the Arpád line died out in 1301, various royal houses of Europe struggled for control of Hungary. The coronation of Mátyás Hunyadi (known as Matthias Corvinus) as king in 1458 brought prosperity and national glory to Hungary. This Renaissance king, famous for his dazzling court at Visegrád, restored public finances and reduced the power of masters over serfs. But after his death, central Hungary fell under the yoke of the Turks for some 150 years, while the northern and western sections were drawn into the Austrian Habsburg domain. When the Turks were finally forced to withdraw from the capital of Buda in 1686, the Hungarians were compelled to accept Austrian succession to the Hungarian throne. The Hungarians rose up against Austrian absolutism several times, finally winning the establishment, in 1867, of a dual monarchy in which Austria and Hungary were partners.

After the fall of the Austro-Hungarian Empire in World War I, Hungary was governed by an authoritarian regent, Admiral Horthy, from 1920 to 1944. Its alliance with Nazi Germany was followed by the German occupation, which lasted until the taking of Budapest, after a horrendous 2-month battle, by Soviet troops in 1945. In 1949, the government was taken over by the Hungarian Workers Party (now called Magyar Szocialista Munkáspárt — MSZMP, the Communist party in Hungary), and Hungary has been politically, economically, and militarily aligned with the Soviet Union ever since. In 1956, Soviet forces were called in to help crush an uprising, and 200,000 Hungarians fled into exile. However, starting in the early 1960s the government of János Kádár enacted a number of reforms that took some of the sting out of defeat. Since the end of the "Kádár era" in 1988, the pace of political and economic change has quickened, making a visit to today's Hungary an intellectually heady experience, as well as a pleasure for the senses.

Two sensory pleasures are particularly catered to and may be combined: eating and listening to music. The latter experience can be rewarding in a restaurant, where a gypsy orchestra is often as accomplished as it is in a concert hall.

The Magyar musical heritage comprises classical as well as folk music. It was dramatically expressed in the romantic rhapsodies of Ferenc (Franz) Liszt in the 19th century and in the modern music of the 20th-century masters Béla Bartók and Zoltán Kodály, both of whom devoted years of intensive study to Hungarian folk songs.

The special Hungarian harmony of flavors has made the country's cuisine, based on a superb marriage of meats, spices, and fresh vegetables, internationally appreciated. The special sweet Hungarian paprika is one of the world's most versatile condiments.

This wealth of historical, cultural, and culinary interest, coupled with the fact that Budapest is the brightest and most romantic capital of any Communist country in Europe — indeed, one of the loveliest cities in Europe — has increased tourism to the point where the number of visitors to Hungary each year exceeds the country's population.

For those who would like to see more of the country than its wonderful capital, we have provided three tour routes. If you have only a short time to spend outside Budapest, a visit to the nearby Danube Bend offers an opportunity to enjoy some of the country's most breathtaking scenery while encountering its royal and ecclesiastical past. Our second route, into Transdanubia, is through a softer landscape, also rich in history, to Hungary's busiest center of recreation and relaxation, Lake Balaton. The final route, through the Great Hungarian Plain, allows you to explore the Hungary of peasant folk legend and to see some of Europe's most desirable farmland.

The Danube Bend

As it heads east from its route along the Czechoslovak border, the Danube River makes an elbow bend through the wooded Pilis and Börzsöny hills, divides into two channels that will unite again at Budapest, and gracefully curves south on its long journey to the Black Sea.

This scenic, history-rich area about 31 miles (50 km) north of Budapest is called the Danube Bend and is a favorite place for excursions for residents as well as visitors. Its picturesque environs can be explored leisurely, and most pleasantly, by steamer on the river or by car. The main towns along the route also can be reached by train.

If you drive north, Route 11 follows the general contour of the right bank of the river between Budapest and Esztergom, an early seat of Hungarian kings and an ancient ecclesiastical center. To the west, all along the route, is the Pilis Park Forest, which harbors wild boar and deer. You can make the trip upriver along one bank and downriver along the other, or you may prefer to crisscross the river, visiting key cities on either bank as they appear on the route. For the purposes of description, this route will take the latter course, beginning at Budapest and ending at Esztergom, 40 miles (65 km) away.

BUDAPEST: For a detailed report of the city and its hotels and restaurants, see *Budapest,* THE CITIES.

   En Route from Budapest – The highway leaves the capital on the Buda side of the Danube, which divides into two channels around the huge Szentendre Island just north of the city. The route upriver along the Szentendre channel, to the west of the island, offers the most rewards for tourists and is one of the busiest roads in Hungary on weekends.

SZENTENDRE: This old market town, where the great Hungarian painter Károly Ferenczy worked for the greater part of his life, is filled with interesting churches and art museums. Many artists have settled here in the old merchant houses of the original Serbian and Dalmatian settlers.

The small main square, Marx tér, is lined with lovingly restored, 18th-century Baroque houses. Each summer a theater festival is held in the square. The *Ferenczy Museum* (6 Marx tér) contains works by the Ferenczy family as well as paintings by members of the artists colony established here in 1928. Another museum (1 Vastagh György u.) displays the ceramics of Margit Kovács, and a newly mounted collection of paintings and drawings by Lajos Vajda is on view at 1 Hunyadi János utca. A gallery that sells excellent arts and crafts is now open on Péter-Pál utca.

An open-air skansen, or museum (open from April through October), in the north of town contains original examples of folk architecture, brought here from Hungary's 23 regions. Craftsmen here demonstrate milling, candlestick-making, scone and honey-cake-baking, and so forth, on the first Sunday of each month. There is also a very good restaurant, *Új Étterem,* in the surrounding park. To reach the *Outdoor Village Museum,* follow Szabadság forrás út uphill.

The *Serbian Museum of Ecclesiastical History* (5 Engels út) contains Eastern Orthodox religious art from the 14th through the 18th century, and you can see one of the finest iconostases in Hungary in the Greek Orthodox Belgrade Church on Alkotmány utca. There is an interesting medieval Roman Catholic parish church on Templom Hill, near the main square. This church was rebuilt in 1710, but parts of it date from the 12th century.

Traces of Stone Age men have been found in caves in the vicinity, and the largest Bronze Age cemetery in Central Europe was excavated in nearby Budakalász.

En Route from Szentendre – At Pomáz, an unnumbered road in the direction of Esztergom leads to the popular mountain resort of Dobogókő in the Pilis forest. At Leányfalu, you can stop and hike to the 1,500-foot Red Stone Cliff (Vörös-kő Szikla) for a wonderful panoramic view of the plain and the Danube Bend.

The town of Tahitótfalu spreads along both sides of the channel, and the bridge here is a good place to cross over to the island if you want to stop for some swimming, canoeing, or rowing. The river is quite shallow near the village of Kisoroszi, at the northern tip of the island. It has a good beach and and a ferry can take you back across the channel.

You are now leaving the plain and entering the mountain area, and the two channels of the Danube reunite as the river is forced into a more constricted course.

VISEGRÁD: The setting of this small village among the mountains at the center of the Danube Bend, and the relics of its illustrious past as a royal stronghold during the Middle Ages, make Visegrád an immensely popular tourist center.

During the past few decades, a magnificent summer palace that flowered during the reign of King Matthias Corvinus (1458–90) has been excavated and reconstructed on a hillside on the main street (27 Fő utca). A fine Renaissance fountain of red marble in the ceremonial courtyard bears the king's coat of arms.

You can also see the remains of the citadel (Fellegvár) on Castle Hill and the hexagonal Salamon Tower, a typical 13th-century fortified dwelling with walls 9 feet thick to resist prolonged attacks. On another hill (Sibrik) are the remains of a Roman camp from about the 4th century.

Some of the discoveries of modern excavations and exhibitions of Visegrád's royal past can be seen at the *King Matthias Museum* (*Mátyás Király Múzeum;* 41 Fő utca), in an 18th-century baroque mansion that was once a royal hunting lodge.

En Route from Visegrád – Dömös is at the southernmost point of the bend the Danube makes around the southern foothills of the Börzsöny Mountains. From the slopes of the little town's hills, you get an impressive view of the V-like path of the river. This popular resort is frequently used as a starting point for hiking into the Pilis Mountains.

Pilismarót, near the start of the Danube Bend, has a wonderful 2-mile beach and numerous small bays. The picturesque town across the river, Zebegény, is an artists' colony and popular summer resort that can be reached by ferry.

Up stream from Zebegény is the frontier station of Szob, on the Czechoslovak border. You can visit two baroque castles or enjoy the town's pleasant beach before taking the ferry back to the right bank of the Danube and the last few miles to Esztergom.

ESZTERGOM: The philosopher-emperor Marcus Aurelius is said to have written some of the books of his *Reflections* here when this was an important Roman outpost. But Esztergom is best known as the residence of Magyar kings in the 12th and 13th centuries and the seat of the primate of the Hungarian Catholic church.

The largest cathedral in Hungary (390 feet long) was built here, on Castle Hill (Várhegy), between 1822 and 1856. A Renaissance chapel adjoins the south side of the cathedral, whose treasury includes numerous works of art, including a 13th-century gold cross upon which the Kings of Hungary took their coronation oaths.

The *Castle Museum* next to the cathedral contains fragments of a royal palace that had been destroyed during the Turkish occupation and nearly forgotten until this century, when large-scale excavations were undertaken. The palace was begun in 972 by St. Stephen's father, but its most glorious period came in the late 12th century, during the reign of King Béla III.

The *Christian Museum* (*Keresztény Múzeum;* 2 Berényi Zsigmond u.) contains one of Hungary's most important fine arts collections. It includes excellent examples of Hungarian paintings, minor medieval Italian works, fine Flemish and French tapestries, and a remarkable 15th-century altar.

Esztergom actually sits on a narrow side channel of the Danube, separated from the main stream by a long island connected to the city by bridges.

BEST EN ROUTE

Hotels in the Danube Bend area are relatively simple places, charging about $25 or $35 a night for a double room with breakfast. There are a number of excellent camping sites along the route, including one on Pap Island, near Szentendre, which accommodates up to 500 campers. For restaurants, expect to pay $10 to $12 for a dinner for two without drinks, wine, or tip.

DOBOGÓKŐ

Nimród – A modern hotel with 78 rooms set high in the woods of the Pilis Mountains. The restaurant serves game in season. Reservations are advised. 2 Eötvös sétány (phone: 27644).

VISEGRÁD

Silvanus – Modern, well-designed, this hotel on top of a mountain has a good restaurant, specializing in game, and a bar. Fekete-hegy (phone: 28311).

Fekete Holló – A good private self-service restaurant near the Danube. 12 Rév utca (phone: 26166).

ESZTERGOM

Esztergom – This small hotel overlooking the Danube has its own sports center. Primás Sziget (Primate Island), Nagy-Duna sétány (phone: 8168).

Fürdő – An 89-room hotel near the spa with swimming pools, a restaurant and bar, and central heating. 14 Bajcsy-Zsilinszky út (phone: 292).

Úszófalu Halászcsárda – A good fish restaurant on the island (Esztergom-sziget). Szabad Május sétány (phone: 230).

Volán-Tourist – In the center of town, this small hostelry is run by one of the country's tourist agencies. Some of its rooms have showers. 2 József A. tér (phone: 271).

Lake Balaton

The sandy beaches of Lake Balaton, where water temperatures range from 68F (20C) to 79F (26C) in the summer, attract a solid stream of vacationers, both Hungarian and foreign, from May to September. Since World War II, the Hungarian government has developed the area around Balaton — Central Europe's largest lake — into a mass recreation center; the 122-mile shoreline is virtually one continuous resort.

The southern shore is generally flat, with only an occasional steep hill overlooking the lake, and the water is extremely shallow, making it an ideal beach for families with small children. The north shore is characterized by a chain of long-extinct and now-eroded volcanoes. Gently undulating vineyards cover the basalt hills, producing the grapes for some of the finest wines of Hungary. The area is also known for its effervescent mineral springs.

If you don't like crowds, it is best to visit the lake area in early spring or fall — rates are cheaper then, too. There are good rail connections for most of the larger resort towns, and in summer there are frequent fast trains from Budapest. The following route, beginning and ending in Budapest, explores the various resort areas around the lake.

BUDAPEST: For a detailed report of the city and its hotels and restaurants, see *Budapest,* THE CITIES.

En Route from Budapest – The outskirts of Budapest give way to undulating hills as you travel southwest on Highway 70. The Brunswick Mansion, in a beautiful old park at Martonvásár, about a half-hour from Budapest, is preserved in memory of Ludwig von Beethoven, who composed some of his important works while visiting here in the early 1800s. Concerts of his music are given here during the summer, and there is a *Beethoven Museum.*

Almost one-third of Lake Velence, which begins some 6 miles (9.6 km) beyond Martonvásár, is thick with reeds and dotted with swampy, marshy islets. In spring and autumn its grassy knolls are stopping places for scores of thousands of migrating birds, including rare waterfowl. The 6-mile-long lake is a rapidly developing holiday resort, with good beaches, yachting facilities, hotels, restaurants, and camping sites, particularly along the southern shore near Gárdony and Agárd. The northern shore attracts anglers, hunters, and other sportsmen. It is also possible to drive directly to Székesfehérvár from Budapest on the M7 motorway.

SZÉKESFEHÉRVÁR: Called Alba Regia by the Romans, during the Middle Ages this town was a thriving royal seat where Hungarian kings were crowned and, later, buried. Today, it is an important industrial center in the Meadowland (Mezőföld), where three fourths of the population is engaged in agriculture. Most of the medieval town was destroyed during the Turkish occupation (1543–1688). However, a number of interesting buildings remain in the inner city. The main square of the inner town is Szabadság tér, where you will find the 17th-century baroque Town Hall, the former Zichy Palace, with its attractive rococo and baroque interior, and the Garden of Ruins (Romkert), on the site of the excavations of the former cathedral, where 37 coronations were held.

The *King Stephen (István Király) Museum,* at the corner of Gagarin tér and Népköztársaság, has interesting exhibitions of local archaeology, history, and folklore.

Siófok, the biggest tourist center on Lake Balaton, is about an hour's drive from Székesfehérvár on the M7 motorway — or somewhat longer if you follow Highway 70 through a number of small towns.

SIÓFOK: The shores of Lake Balaton are virtually one long string of beach resorts, but Siófok is the largest town on the southern shore and is continually expanding to take in neighboring communities. It has the most sophisticated tourist operations, some of the best beaches, and crowded facilities from Easter till the season ends.

Although the obvious attraction of Siófok is its long sandy beach, there are a few interesting churches and an excellent riding academy nearby. There is also an open-air theater in Dimitrov Park and many pleasant garden restaurants in which to relax. The

IBUSZ office here can even arrange for you to take a cooking class with a chef from one of the top resort hotels.

There are ferries to the north shore peninsula of Tihany from Szántód Harbor, near Siófok. Inland from the lake, on Highway 65 at Ságvár, are interesting ruins of a fortified Roman camp, dating from the 3rd century.

En Route from Siófok – The shore road winds through numerous resort towns, but at Balatonföldvár a road south leads to Kőröshegy, where many of the original features are retained in a 15th-century, single-naved Gothic church, despite restoration work in the 18th century. The taverns here are good places to sample the regional wine and listen to gypsy music.

After carefully negotiating several dangerous sudden curves through the town of Balatonszemes, the shore road reaches Fonyód, the site of Stone and Bronze Age settlements and now a busy resort area. At Balatonkeresztúr, Highway 7, which has paralleled the lake since Zamárdi, veers south, and Highway 71 serves the north shore.

KESZTHELY: The largest of the lake towns, Keszthely has been a municipality since the early 15th century. Its charming old streets create a pleasant ambience, and there are a number of interesting sights to divert you from the pleasures of the beaches. The Georgikon (Georgikon út) was founded in 1797 and was the first agricultural college established on the European continent. The Helikon Library, in the former palace of Count György Festetics, contains over 52,000 volumes as well as valuable antiquities and art. The *Balaton Museum* (2 Múzeum utca) has interesting historical and ethnographical exhibitions.

Hévíz, the most famous spa in Hungary, with its own freshwater lake (Lake Hévíz, Europe's largest warm-water lake — 82-93F [28-34C]) and indoor and outdoor thermal baths, is a few miles west of here.

En Route from Keszthely – The shore road passes through the Badacsony, a district of basalt terraces where lava from long-extinct volcanoes has created bizarre rock formations. The area also is known for its fruit growing and for the excellence of its vineyards. The ruins of Szigliget Castle, dating from the 13th century, stand on a hill just west of the town of Badacsony.

Beyond Balatonszepezd, a favorite retreat of artists and writers, a mile-long road leads up a hillside to Zánka, where there is a fisherman's lodge in the woods and a 13th-century church that was remodeled in the Baroque style in 1786. Medieval pageants are sometimes held in summer in the 15th-century castle in Nagyvázsony, a town about 10 miles (16 km) farther north.

TIHANY: The small peninsula of Tihany, a series of hills covered with poplar and acacia trees and the scent of lavender, is one of the loveliest spots on Balaton. Its long history as a stronghold can be read in the remains of a 3,000-year-old earthenwork fortification and in Celtic and Roman ruins. A beautiful yellow abbey church with twin spires stands on a hill overlooking the peninsula. The museum here has the richest exhibitions of art and local history on Balaton.

There is excellent fishing in Lake Belső, high on a hill above Balaton — in effect, a lake within a lake; and the villagers' unusual thatch-roofed houses of dark gray volcanic tufa add charm to the landscape. Government institutes have been set up on Tihany to study its wealth of geological and botanical rarities. A new family holiday village occupies the tip of the peninsula (see *Best en Route*). The *Tihany Tourist Center* rents sailboats, among other services.

BALATONFÜRED: The oldest and one of the most renowned health resorts in the area, Balatonfüred is the last large town on Lake Balaton. There are several large, new hotels here, an attractive poplar-lined promenade along the lake, and an inviting central park. There is also a neo-classical Round (Kerek) Church, built in 1846 on Blaha Lujza utca. Yachting races are frequently held here, and the harbor is the busiest on Lake Balaton.

In the main square, Gyógy tér, there is a colonnaded pavilion built over the bubbling waters of a volcanic spring. In all, the town has 11 medicinal springs that for hundreds of years have been attracting those seeking cures, today for heart and nerve disorders in particular.

En Route from Balatonfüred – The shore road can be followed through a dozen or so small communities around the lake back to a connection with the M7 motorway or Highway 70 to return to Budapest. Another alternative is to take Highway 73 north from Balatonfüred into the Bakony hills to Veszprém before heading back to Budapest.

VESZPRÉM: Built on five hills, this picturesque town of cobblestone streets, old gateways, and arches is Bakony's cultural and economic center. It is an old settlement rich in historical monuments. The *Vár (Castle) Museum,* in the Heroes' Gate (Hősök kapuja) near Vörös Hadsereg Square, contains old weapons, armor, and historical documents. The 18th-century baroque Episcopal Palace (12 Tolbuhin út) is next to the early Gothic Gizella Chapel, built in the 13th century.

The *Bakony Museum,* in Lenin Park on Kálvária Hill, has exhibitions that detail the Bakony region's history, customs, and crafts.

BEST EN ROUTE

Lake Balaton is Hungary's most popular resort, so hotel reservations should be made well in advance if you plan to visit during the summer. A double room will cost between $20 and $45 per night, depending on the month and resort chosen. All the hotels listed are open from May to September unless otherwise noted. It is also possible to rent cottages or apartments on the lake, and IBUSZ can arrange for the rental of sailboats that can sleep four at $200 to $400 per week. Restaurants range in price from $25 and up for a dinner for two in the expensive range; around $15 in the moderate; and $10 and under, inexpensive. Prices do not include drink, wine, or tip.

The wines of the Balaton region, particularly the spicy white ones, are justly famous. Among the best are the Badacsony Blue Stalk (*Badacsonyi kéknyelü*), Gray Friar (*Badacsonyi szürkebarát*), and Riesling (*Badacsonyi rizling*). The food specialty is the perch-pike-type fish *fogas.*

SIÓFOK

Balaton – On the lake with a private beach. All rooms have balconies, and the hotel has a nightclub and an espresso bar. 9 Petőfi sétány (phone: 10655). Moderate.

Európa – Lakeshore setting and private beach, pool, sauna, a restaurant and an espresso bar are among this hotel's amenities. 17 Petőfi sétány (phone: 11400). Moderate.

Hungária – Balconied rooms, private beach, restaurant, and bar. 13 Petőfi sétány (phone: 10677). Moderate.

Napfény – Small, family-type hotel near the beach, with balconied rooms. 2 Petőfi sétány (phone: 11408). Inexpensive.

Fogas – Excellent food in a garden setting. 184 Fő u. (phone: 11405). Moderate.

Ménes Csárda – Very good — and very spicy — local specialties are served in this restaurant, actually a restored old stable decorated with antique folk art. In Szántódpuszta, about 6 miles (9.6 km) west of Siófok on the main highway to Balatonföldvár (phone: 31352). Moderate.

KESZTHELY

Helikon – Facing the beach, with its own "island," connected to the hotel by a bridge. Spa facilities, restaurant, bar, tennis courts, and yacht marina. 5 Balatonpart (phone: 11330). Expensive.

Fishermen's Inn (Halász Csárda) – Fish specialties. South of Keszthely on the lakeshore (phone: 12751). Moderate.

Helikon Tavern – Good food and wine and Gypsy music. About 5 miles (8 km) east of town. Moderate.

Hullám – This flower-bedecked small hotel, with a pool and wide-ranging sports activities, consciously tries to evoke the leisurely atmosphere of bygone days (phone: 12644). Moderate.

TIHANY

Club Tihany – Along with 161 Scandinavian-style bungalows, this new 330-room hotel is part of Hungary's first vacation village, which offers families a private beach, pool, boutiques, and all kinds of sports activities. 3 Rév út (phone: 44091). Expensive.

Fogas Csárda – Excellent fish dishes served on a terrace or in one of four dining rooms. Gypsy music. Off Hwy. 71. Expensive to moderate.

Sport – Enjoy excellent food as well as a panoramic lake view. Fürdőtelep (phone: 44016). Expensive to moderate.

BALATONFÜRED

Annabella – Picturesque surroundings on the lakeshore; private beach, restaurant and terrace, nightclub, and pool. Open May to October. 25 Beloiannisz u. (phone: 42222). Expensive.

Marina – On the lake with a private beach; restaurant with Gypsy music, pool, health club, nightclub. Open May to October. 26 Széchenyi út (phone: 40810). Expensive.

The Great Hungarian Plain

The Great Hungarian Plain (Nagy Alföld), east of the Danube, is the heart of Hungary and one of Europe's richest larders. During the past century, the thousands of acres of the drifting sand and needle grass that characterized this seemingly endless flat expanse, called the *puszta,* have been transformed into lush orchards and vineyards, and modern machinery now cultivates the corn and wheat fields.

But the government has taken steps to preserve the heritage of the rural Hungarian peasant, long romanticized by poets and painters: the isolated whitewashed crofts, the special *puszta* gray cattle and horse herds, the traditional arts and crafts. They can still be seen in places such as the National Park of Hortobágy, although like the American prairie the reality of that heritage has vanished completely.

This circular route from Budapest takes you to some of the most important towns of the area of the Great Hungarian Plain, sometimes referred to as Little Cumania, and to some of its art centers. Most of the towns are on main railway lines and can be visited on a train journey through the region. There are also bus connections.

BUDAPEST: For a detailed report on the city and its hotels and restaurants, see *Budapest,* THE CITIES.

En Route from Budapest – About an hour's drive southeast on the E60 motorway, Highway 40 takes you to Cegléd, an old peasant community that was the birthplace of István Tömörkény, one of the great chroniclers of peasant life. The *Lajos Kossuth Museum* (Rákóczi út and Marx K. utca) contains the patriot's death mask. Farther south is Nagykőrös, the center of a rich market-gardening region famous for its Kőrös Morello cherries and other fruit. A splendid morning market is held here. Or, if you are driving directly to Kecskemét on the E75, consider stopping off at Lajosmizse, 13 miles (20 km) before Kecskemét, to visit the *Farmhouse Museum*, or watch the horse shows at the *István Széchenyi Riding Club*, a castle-hotel (see *Best en Route*).

KECSKEMÉT: This is the hometown of Zoltán Kodály, the famous composer of modern music who also collected and wrote about Hungarian folk music. And this sprawling town itself seems to blend two worlds.

Since World War II, Kecskemét has become an important food-processing center, and modern housing estates have replaced many single-story dwellings. But the old peasant architecture can be seen along Bánk Bán and János Hoffman streets. Two examples of Hungarian Art Nouveau that should not be overlooked are the Town Hall on Kossuth Lajos tér and the Ornamented Palace (Cifrapalota) on Szabadság tér. A bit southwest of Kossuth Square, behind the 16-story county council building, is a unique double-gated peasant house with a fine verandah. Beautiful examples of shepherds' cloaks and embroidered clothing of the region are on display at the *József Katona Museum*, 75 Betlenváros. The *Szórakaténusz Toy Workshop and Museum*, (11 Gáspár u) is a must for children.

An artists colony, where many of Hungary's best painters and sculptors of the 20th century have worked, is in a large park on Mártírok út, southeast of the center.

The Kecskemét area is famous for its apricots and apricot brandy, called *barack*, and a grape harvest (Kecskeméti Szüret) is held each September. In odd-numbered years there is a *Kecskemét Folk Music Meeting* of singers and musicians and the International Kodály Seminar for music teachers; an International Creative Camp of Musicians takes place every July. A new event is the March music festival held in conjunction with the *Budapest Spring Festival.*

The Kecskemét riding school, just outside the city on Highway 44, has excellent sport and jump horses selected from the famous stud farms of the *puszta.*

En Route from Kecskemét – Heading south on the E5 motorway you reach Kiskunfélegyháza, an important cultural center of Kiskunság (Little Cumania). The *Kiskun Museum* has a good archaeological collection and an interesting penology display.

A road to the west of town will take you to the Kiskunság National Park and its major section, the Bugacpuszta. The gray cattle and branch-horned *racka* sheep of the region graze here in pastures surrounded by trees, marshes, and sand dunes. The *Shepherd Museum*, a glass-walled, circular building resembling a Mongolian yurt, has displays that detail the old nomadic way of life and animal breeding in the *puszta*. An refurbished old inn nearby provides an ideal setting for sampling Hungarian specialties and regional wines.

Another detour off the E5 motorway, this one to the east just before you reach Szeged, leads to Fehér-tó (Lake Fehér), the home of red heron, ducks, and other fish-eating birds. (Permission to visit the bird sanctuary must be obtained in advance.)

One of the typical sights of the Great Hungarian Plain is storks nesting in the chimneys of farmhouses along the road.

SZEGED: The economic and cultural center of the southern region of the Great Hungarian Plain straddles the Tisza River near the Yugoslav border. The present town was laid out after a devastating flood in the last century, but Szeged has a long, rich history.

It was occupied by the Ottoman Turks for 144 years, until the end of the 17th century, and it was plundered and burned in 1704 in retaliation for its support of the freedom struggle against the ruling House of Habsburg of Austria. During the 1848–49 war of independence from the Habsburgs, Szeged was, for a short time, the capital of the country. During the great Tisza flood of 1879, the town was destroyed once again.

The central town square, Széchenyi tér, has a pleasant promenade of old plane trees and is lined by a number of various public buildings. A few blocks south is the impressive Dóm tér, a square surrounded by arcaded buildings of dark red brick and dominated by the twin-spired Votive Church at its center. The neo-Romanesque church has the second largest organ in Europe (the largest is in Milan's cathedral). Part of the huge square is the site of the Szeged Open-Air Theater, where the Szeged Festival (Szegedi Szabadtéri Játékok) of opera, drama, and ballet is held every year in July and August. Hungary's finest Serbian Orthodox church, known for its outstanding iconostasis, is on the north side of the square.

Szeged is famous for its salami products, beautifully embroidered slippers, and a delicious fish soup, *szegedi halászlé*. In Tápé, an outer district of the town noted for the artistic mats woven by its women, villagers have retained their picturesque folkways and dress. A collection of folk dress and everyday articles can be seen at 4 Vártó utca. A new wildlife park, inhabited by monkeys and crocodiles as well as by animals native to Hungary, was designed with young visitors in mind.

Traditional as well as newer styles of pottery are made in workshops at Hódmezővásárhely, a small town 16 miles (25 km) northeast of Szeged on Highway 47. The *János Tornyai Museum* there has interesting archaeological and ethnographical collections.

En Route from Szeged – About halfway to Baja on Highway 55 you can turn north on Highway 53 to reach Kiskunhalas, home of the famous Halas lace, *halasi csipke.* You can see the lacemakers at work at the Cottage Industry Cooperative, and the Lace House (Csipkeház) has a large exhibition of the fine craft that has won the town a worldwide reputation.

BAJA: This picturesque town on the banks of the Danube and Sugovica rivers has numerous islands with sandy lidos and fine parks, lovely old churches, and an artists colony in a former nobleman's mansion at Arany János utca 1. The folklore and folk art collections of the *István Türr Museum* (Béke tér) are typical of the region.

KALOCSA: This town, 21 miles (34 km) north of Baja on Highway 51, is one of the most important centers of folk art in Hungary. The women of the town are famous for the primitive, ornamental painting with which they decorate the walls of their homes and for the designs they paint on furniture and door panels. The finest examples of their work can be seen at the Népművészetiház (1-3 Tompa Mihály utca), in the same building as the Folk Art Cooperative, where some of these "painting women" work with outsiders interested in learning this folk art.

In quaint little villages nearby, whitewashed houses are often strung with garlands of the red peppers that are grown in the area and used to make fine Hungarian paprika.

Northeast of Kalocsa is Kiskőrös, home of the 19th-century revolutionary poet Sándor Petőfi.

The highway back to Budapest parallels the Danube, passing through Dunapataj, a village near pleasant Szelidi Lake, and through two towns where the poet Petőfi lived and worked — Dunavecse and Szalkszentmárton.

BEST EN ROUTE

First-class hotel accommodations are limited, but prices are relatively low. At the places mentioned, a double room with bath and breakfast will cost about $26 to $30 a night. Meals are also quite inexpensive in the towns of the Great Hungarian Plain.

Dinner for two, with a local wine, will cost between $10 and $12 at most good restaurants.

KECSKEMÉT

Aranyhomok – This 5-story modern hotel on one of Kecskemét's central squares is the best in the area. It has a large restaurant that features excellent goose liver, a coffee shop, and a bar. 3 Széchenyi tér (phone: 20011).

Gerébi Country House and Motel – Situated in a park with a pool, tennis courts, and a riding club, this 18th-century mansion was converted into a hotel with 11 double rooms and 2 suites; there is also a motel with 39 rooms. In Lajosmizse, on Highway 5, 13 miles (21 km) north of Kecskemét. 224 Alsólajos (phone: 20011).

Gúnár – A 34-room hotel, converted from an old inn. 7 Batthyányu (phone: 28106).

Szélmalom Csárda – This restaurant is in a replica of the traditional whitewashed windmills of the Great Hungarian Plain. Just outside town on the E5 motorway, in the direction of Szeged. 167 Városföld (phone: 22166).

SZEGED

Alabárdos – A romantic atmosphere, including Gypsy music, with your food. 13 Oskola utca (phone: 12914).

Hungária – Near a shady park on the bank of the Tisza River, next to the *Szeged National Theater*. All rooms have baths. 2 Komócsin Zoltán tér (phone: 21-211).

International 1st Class Camping Site and Motel – 2 Dorozsmai út (phone: 61255).

Virág Café – Pastries and ice cream in an elegant, old-fashioned setting. Klauzál tér (phone: 11-459).

Iceland

An extended trip to Iceland is a strange blend of culture shock and geological field trip. Though this country might be the world's largest small town (there are only 245,000 people on the whole island, and almost half of them live in Reykjavik), the natives are among the most sophisticated of Europeans, aware of the latest in both fashion and culture. Though Iceland has the oldest republic in the world (founded by Norse wanderers in AD 870), the country is a geological infant, still growing steadily from fissures, lava flows, earthquakes, and volcanoes.

In the North Atlantic between the Denmark Strait to the west and the Norwegian Sea to the east, Iceland is 190 miles from north to south and 300 miles from east to west. Because it's partially ringed by the warm currents of the Gulf Stream, the island is habitable — barely. Its weather is abruptly changeable, and its terrain is unlike any other country on Earth. More than 10% glacier and 10% lava, it's a land of hot and cold. The word "geyser" is Icelandic, and geothermal water is everywhere. Some of this naturally hot water has been harnessed, and one hot spring, Deildartunguhver, has been so pressurized and heated by the earth's interior turbulence that boiling water flows through it at 40 gallons per second. Amazingly, this boiling water flows completely naturally, close to the Arctic Circle, in the Land of the Midnight Sun. There are volcanic eruptions on an average of one every 5 or 6 years, but the Icelanders have started to adapt to even this. (In 1973, when a volcano erupted on the inhabited island of Heimaey, the entire population was evacuated in a matter of hours. Though the eruption lasted from January to May, Icelandic scientists were able to cool and reroute the lava flows with ocean water so that most of the town was saved and the harbor left open.)

The countryside is hauntingly beautiful, with an almost treeless landscape of stark lava fields, awesome glaciers, lakes, mountains, and a fjord-indented coastline. There are rivers in Iceland, but they aren't navigable because of their breakneck currents caused by a combination of rainfall and melting glaciers that also leave the riverbeds strewn with debris. The price of this stark, natural beauty is the need to import almost all raw materials and staples from wood to fruit to fuel. Iceland raises sheep and cattle (also reindeer have been imported and bred); lamb is the staple in the Icelanders' diet. The life here is hard, but the people of Iceland have one of the longest life expectancies in the world.

Outside Reykjavik, the capital, there's not too much in the way of town life. A ring road around the island was completed in 1974, but if you want to travel north, it's best to fly to Akureyri, the northern capital of 13,800 staunch citizens who live on Arctic banks and make wry New Englanders seem like outgoing Texans.

Because of its need to import almost everything, Iceland is generally expensive, but a trip here can be a special experience, one in which you can't help both marveling at the people and becoming keenly aware of the power and life of the earth itself.

REYKJAVIK: Many people stop over here on transatlantic flights, but few have the foresight to stay and explore Iceland's capital and commercial and maritime hub. A good place to start an exploration is the Austurvöllur, the quiet central square at the intersection of Kirkjustraeti and Posthusstraeti. This was the reputed home site of Iceland's first settler, a Norwegian Viking named Ingólfur Arnarson, who arrived in 874. The republic's early history was not all rosy — Iceland was long dominated by both the Norwegians and the Danes. In the 19th century, however, there was a successful independence movement led by Jón Sigurdsson, Iceland's national hero, whose statue stands here in the grassy quadrangle. The city surrounds this square with neat, multistoried buildings topped with red, white, and green roofs, all scrupulously crisp and clean. On the various adjacent edges of the square are the imposing Parliament House, the stone Cathedral of Reykjavik, and the large *Borg* hotel (see *Best en Route*). Also near the square is the Tjörn, the town pond and summer home for many wheeling Arctic terns.

It's an easy city to walk around in, and though the signs are generally incomprehensible, most of the people speak English. The *Thjodminjasafnid* is the national cultural museum (at the corner of Sudurgata and Hringbraut), where you'll also find the national museum of art. Even before the Norse, Irish monks came to Iceland as early as the 8th century. After the establishment of the Althing (the governing body) in 930, art flourished and Icelandic literature — the most sophisticated writings of the Middle Ages — is still preserved in illuminated manuscripts. You'll find a sampling of the precious "saga" manuscripts at the Manuscript Institute of Iceland (Arnagardur), an unassuming modern building. Both these museums are part of the University of Iceland. In nearby Laugardalur you can take a swim and sauna in the city's open-air pool, naturally heated year-round by hot springs.

A circle route from Reykjavik east can, in 1 day, encompass the country's most famous natural and historic attractions: the Geysir hot spring area, the Gullfoss waterfall, and Thingvellir, the site of the ancient parliament. There aren't that many roads, but it's still a good idea to get a clear map and trace your route before you start east from the capital through Hellisheidi to Hveragerdi.

HVERAGERDI: This town is important for its many greenhouses, which Iceland depends on year-round for such warm-weather crops as tomatoes, bananas, and grapes. The greenhouses are heated entirely from the active hot springs of the area. Continue past the towns of Selfoss, Hraungerdi, and Húsatoftir, where you turn north to Flúdir. You can stop at the Skalholt Cathedral here, where there are outdoor concerts on summer Sunday afternoons.

THE GREAT GEYSIR AND THE GULLFOSS: Continue north to two of the most famous natural sights in Iceland. The world "geyser" originated with the Icelandic Great Geysir, a sprouting hot spring that gives its name to similar springs all over the world. The original only rarely performs now, but nearby is another old regular known as Strokkur.

Another 16 miles (26 km) east is the Gullfoss, the Golden Waterfall. Considered to be one of the world's most beautiful, this fall plunges down a series of cascades into a deep gorge of the Hvítá River. Now return west across the Brúará River, past Middalur, to the Laugarvatn Lake area. This is a deep glacial lake and a popular resort area, with hotels, campsites, an indoor swimming pool, and a steambath built directly over the hot springs.

THINGVELLIR: From Laugarvatn, continue west across Lyngdalsheidi to Thingvellir. This Plain of National Assembly, or Althing, was named for the country's first open-air legislative assembly, which was established here in AD 930. The Icelandic Parliament had its roots in these annual 2-week summer confabs, which were attended by tribal chieftains from throughout the country. Thingvellir is starkly and beautifully situated on an immense lava plain intersected by rock fissures and surrounded by a craggy distant horizon. To the northeast is an extinct shield volcano, Skjaldbreidur, at the northern end of Lake Thingvallavatn. Since there are few visible remains of the early meetings, it's best to visit Thingvellir with a knowledgeable guide, but even on your own you can savor the peacefulness here. You can camp at one of the sites in the surrounding national park.

From here travel south to Úlfljótsvatn Lake and the Ljosafoss waterfall via the Thrastalundur woods. You drive alongside the Sogid River, popular with the salmon-fishing set, and head south past Ingólfsfjall Mountain. The secondary road rejoins the main route (just west of Selfoss), which takes you back to Reykjavik.

BEST EN ROUTE

Everything in Iceland is expensive — there's no getting around it. A cup of coffee can cost as much as $1.50, a short cab ride, $3 or $4. The best food and lodgings are in Reykjavik. The ptarmigan (called *rjupa* here) is very good; it's served in a delicious sauce called *rjupusosa*. Expect to pay about $130 for a room for two at hotels and from $20 to $30 for dinner for two at restaurants in Reykjavik. There is no tipping in Iceland. For further information on restaurants, nightlife, galleries, and museums, pick up a copy of *What's On in Reykjavik* at your hotel.

REYKJAVIK

Borg – A traditional, high-ceilinged hotel, it opened in 1930, on the millennial of the founding of the Althing. It's quiet, stylish, and right on Austurvöllur Square. 11 Pósthússtraeti (phone: 11440). Expensive.

Holt – Tucked away on a quiet residential street, this hotel has what many consider the city's best restaurant. 37 Bergstadastraeti (phone: 2-5700). Expensive.

Fógetinn – Reykjavik's oldest house is a popular restaurant serving traditional Icelandic dishes, including lamb, game, and seafood. The atmosphere is warm and rustic, and there is live music nightly. 10 Adalstraeti (phone: 911-6323). Expensive.

Naust – A seafood restaurant in a former fish warehouse — what could be more atmospheric? It has a small dance floor and very good food and is very popular with the residents. 6-8 Vesturgata (phone: 1-7759). Expensive.

Ireland

Whether you come for the salmon and trout that jump onto your line; to share a "jar" at a pub while you listen to traditional music played on pipe and fiddle and old tin whistle; to clamber over craggy mountains or ponder prehistoric monuments; to capture the varied greens of the landscape on canvas or film; to rent a cottage and write a novel; or to visit relatives or make new friends, your welcome in Ireland will be warm.

The Republic of Ireland, across the narrow Irish Sea from England, has few natural resources, but it has two that make it a "little bit of heaven" for travelers: enchanting beauty and charming, friendly people. Since it must import more than it can export, Ireland depends heavily on income from tourism.

It may be the lyricism that first attracts people to this island on the western fringes of Europe — all those songs about the "lilt of Irish laughter" and the way place names roll off the tongue: the Gap of Dunloe, the River Liffey, Galway Bay, Kilkenny and Kildare. The Irish seem born with a love of language, and the poet-philosopher has always been the real king of Ireland, even in ancient times when poets or seers called *fili* preserved Celtic laws and history orally. This is the land that produced the towering artistry of William Butler Yeats, James Joyce, and Samuel Beckett (never mind that the latter two had to leave the country to find full expression). And though Beckett may write in French, there is no doubt he is Irish. Today, Ireland gives special tax breaks to artists and writers.

Although English is the everyday language of most people in the Republic, Irish, a form of Gaelic, is actually the national language. Irish was, in fact, the vernacular outside the cities and larger towns until the early nineteenth century. But with the establishment of a national system of schools, English spread to a point where today there are only pockets of Irish-speaking people. You are more likely to see the Irish language than hear it; public signs frequently are posted in both English and Irish. In Irish-speaking districts near the west coast, signposts are sometimes in Irish only.

Many of the people who believe that the Irish language is an essential part of Irish nationality also work to preserve national games and dances and other riches of Ireland's Celtic past. The best way to hear traditional music and song and to see Irish dancing is to attend one of the frequent sessions held by the more than 200 branches of Comhaltas Ceoltoiri Eireann, the central organization for the promotion of these arts (inquire at any tourist information office). An important 3-day festival of traditional music and song, the *All-Ireland Fleadh,* is held on the last weekend of August each year in a different town.

The Celts came to this island from Central Europe sometime after 600 BC, but it is believed that there were inhabitants here as early as 6000 BC. Ireland has the richest concentration of prehistoric monuments in Western Europe, including numerous megaliths known as dolmens. Most often they are three huge boulders standing upright to support a heavy capstone, and they usually mark an ancient burial site.

The prehistory that has been preserved in Ireland's epic tales, legends, and poetry is a marvelous mixture of myth and fact. There are story cycles dealing with kings — some of them belonging to history, others to legend — like the Fenian cycle, which tells of the deeds of the giant Finn MacCool and his band of warriors, the Fianna. There are stories of the Little People, leprechauns and the like, who, according to folklore, were related to the Tuatha De Danann, an early Irish race with magical powers driven underground by Celtic Milesians, the predecessors of the current Irish, said to come from Spain. It is, perhaps, a measure of how integral fairies and spirits are to the Irish culture to note that this country's greatest poet, William Butler Yeats, once devoted himself to a study of Irish folklore and an extensive classification of the Little People.

When St. Patrick brought Christianity to Ireland in the 5th century, he found an island country of small, separate kingdoms united in language and culture. The development of the church in Ireland along monastic rather than ecclesiastic lines reflects to some extent the development of the country itself. In its early days there were no towns or villages, just simple dwellings with cattle enclosures scattered over the countryside.

Norsemen raided the island repeatedly from the 9th century until their defeat in 1014 at Clontarf, near Dublin, by the High King Brian Boru. The defeat did not promote Irish unity, however, because Boru died soon after, and when his sons initiated wars over the division of his lands, it ultimately gave the Normans, newly arrived in England, an opportunity to land troops in Ireland.

During the next 700 years, the Norman and then Tudor conquests spread over the whole of Ireland. Irish landlords were systematically supplanted by English and Scottish settlers, many of whom were Protestant. Ulster became the stronghold of these settlers, and that northeastern province grew different in character from the rest of the island. With the parliament in the hands of the British-Protestant minority, stiff penal laws were enacted to deprive Catholics and dissenters of civil and religious rights.

Inspired by the American and French Revolutions, followers of Wolf Tone and other leaders challenged the British in 1798, but the uprising was crushed, and in 1801, Ireland became part of the United Kingdom. The great potato famine (1845–48) added to the miseries of the Irish people. During a 5-year period, the population was reduced from 8 million to 4 million, through starvation, disease, and emigration, which many saw as the only hope for a decent life. Such extreme conditions led to the formation of the Irish Republican Brotherhood in 1858 and a renewed sense of Irish nationalism.

In 1914, Parliament passed a Home Rule bill for Ireland (that Protestants in the north opposed), but suspended its implementation on the outbreak of the First World War. Two years later, impatient and distrustful, Patrick Pearse and James Connolly led the Easter Uprising, proclaiming Ireland a Republic. Although the rebels only held out a week, the British aroused the feelings of the whole country by executing 15 of the leaders. At the next general election, 73 of 105 seats in the Irish parliament were won by a militant independence party called Sinn Fein. These Sinn Fein members met in Dublin on January 21, 1919, to issue a declaration confirming the Republic proclaimed in 1916 and to constitute themselves as the National Parliament (Dail).

The attempt by the British to suppress the parliament and the military wing of republicanism, the Irish Republican Army (IRA), led to a guerrilla war for independence, euphemistically referred to as "the Troubles." Britain granted dominion status to the Irish Free State, but Northern Ireland had the option to get out, and the country was partitioned. In 1937, a new constitution declaring Ireland to be a sovereign, independent, democratic state was approved by plebiscite.

The ultimate reunification of Northern Ireland with the Republic is still a major goal of many Irish Catholics. The Irish parliament has outlawed the IRA, but that organization has continued its campaign of violence in England and Northern Ireland, with financial aid from US citizens, since hostilities broke out over demands for just treatment of Catholics in Northern Ireland. Since 1969, thousands of people have been killed and injured in the fighting in Northern Ireland. But although there has been some minor terrorist activity in the Republic, there is little likelihood a visitor will encounter any unpleasantness.

The Republic of Ireland is only a bit larger than the state of West Virginia. At its widest east-west point it is 171 miles across, and at its greatest north-south length it stretches 302 miles. The warm, damp air from the Gulf Stream along its west coast in the Atlantic Ocean combine to keep the weather mild. Temperatures only rarely drop to freezing during the winter, and summer temperatures usually range from 57F (14C) to 61F (16C), but can reach 70F (21C) to 75F (24C) at times. Except for a strip along the east coast, the country receives some rain at least 200 days a year. This climate is responsible for Ireland's remarkable verdant beauty.

Ireland's natural beauty should be explored leisurely. Do it by car if you must, but consider the alternatives. Go on foot along the stone-walled lanes wherever they may lead or take a small map and compass and wander through the hills. There are over 100 centers throughout the country that rent bicycles and provide maps and time estimates for excursions.

The range of accommodations in Ireland is one of the most varied in Europe. There are hotels in castles, in fine old Georgian mansions, in farmhouses, and in old inns. You can also stay in private homes that offer bed and breakfast or rent your own Irish cottage (information is available from the Irish Tourist Board or *Rent an Irish Cottage, Ltd.,* Shannon Airport House, Shannon International Airport, County Clare, Ireland).

The routes we have outlined are designed to afford maximum exposure to the wonders of Ireland. The initial route takes you along the coast from Dublin to Cork through the Wicklow Mountains, the pretty villages and rich farmland of County Wexford and County Waterford, to Blarney Castle and Ireland's second largest city. The second route, from Cork to Killarney, traverses an area of lakes and mountains long celebrated for its beauty by poet and painter alike. It is a fisherman's paradise and a golfer's heaven as well, so it should come as no surprise that it is the area of Ireland most popular with tourists in the summer.

From Killarney to Galway, our third route passes through the rich agricultural area of the Midwest Counties, along the lovely River Shannon and on to the starkly beautiful Cliffs of Moher and the gray rock of the Burren country and then to Galway Bay. From Galway, our fourth route takes in the rugged Aran Islands, then heads north through the austere Connemara Mountains to Sligo and Yeats country. The final route, from Sligo to Donegal, travels through a rugged area dominated by limestone hills — the Ireland of myth and legend.

Southeast Ireland: Dublin to Cork

A scenic 160-mile (256-km) coastal route can take you from Dublin to Cork in 4½ leisurely hours. But to savor the changing moods and character of the Irish scene you must meander. The route you should consider to get a feel for southeast Ireland wanders over more than 250 miles (400 km) in seven counties; it snakes south from Dublin through Wicklow, Wexford, and Waterford, angles north to take in the countryside of Kilkenny, arcs west into legendary Tipperary, and veers south again to Cork and the coast. Ideally, this tour should be spread over 3 days.

It will seem incredible, but a mere half-hour's drive from the city center of Dublin brings you to the splendid isolation of the Wicklow Mountains. Here, great valleys with melodious names like Glenmalure, Glendalough, Imaal, Clara, and Avoca wind through heather-covered hills. Uncrowded roads pass unforgettable sights — a high waterfall, an ancient monastic settlement, a splendid estate.

To the south lies the friendlier, less dramatic landscape of County Wexford; fertile farmland is served by picturesque villages and the historic, narrow-streeted town of Wexford itself. Just to the west is Waterford, a name synonymous with the fine crystal whose renown has tended to overshadow the scenic beauty of the county. Thirty miles (48 km) north of Waterford is ancient Kilkenny, the town dominated by magnificent Kilkenny Castle along the River Nore. The rich pasturelands of Tipperary and the Golden Vale continue into Cork. It is quiet scenery, without the brooding grandeur of the west; rolling hills rise behind ancient towns; Norman castles sit on riverbanks shared with roofless, ruined abbeys.

The suggested stopping points in a 3-day tour are Wexford, Waterford, Kilkenny, or Cashel. If your schedule allows only 2 days for the route, skip Kilkenny.

DUBLIN: For a detailed report on the city and its hotels and restaurants, see *Dublin*, THE CITIES.

En Route from Dublin – The coast road from Dublin leads past two famous resorts: Dun Laoghaire (pronounced "dunleary"), on the south shore of Dublin

Bay, a residential town on a magnificent harbor; and Sandycove, the site of the Martello Tower where James Joyce once lived, today open to the public as a Joyce museum. Continuing to Dalkey and Killiney, one enters George Bernard Shaw territory. Shaw had a cottage on Dalkey Hill that he described as commanding "the most beautiful view in the world." Follow signposts to Bray, which will bring you on to N11. Just before entering that seaside town, swing right, following the Wexford signpost. After 2 miles (3.2 km), another right turn takes you through hills into a wooded hollow where you come upon Enniskerry, one of the prettiest villages in Ireland, renowned for the estate of Powerscourt.

ENNISKERRY: Near the village, signs point the way to Powerscourt, one of Ireland's great estates. Its beautiful Georgian mansion was gutted by fire in 1974, but its substantial skeleton attests to its former grandness. Also remaining are 14,000 acres of resplendent grounds, including gardens with fountains, statuary, and rare shrubberies along the River Dargle; a deer park; and the 400-foot Powerscourt Waterfall, the highest on these islands. The gardens are open from *St. Patrick's Day* to October for a small fee. The Waterfall Gate is open throughout the year.

From Powerscourt, driving through the Wicklow Hills, you come to Roundwood, the highest village in Ireland, and just beyond is Laragh, the gateway to Glendalough.

GLENDALOUGH: This deep glen, set in the Wicklow Mountains between two lakes, is a very special place with a very romantic history. In the 6th century, when St. Kevin came to Wicklow in search of tranquillity, he found it here. But the hermit's sanctity attracted so many disciples that, almost unwittingly, he founded a great monastery that eventually became one of the most renowned centers of learning in Europe. The visitor today sees the remains of many buildings from the 9th through the 13th century, including a perfect example of a Round Tower. There are wonderful nature trails in the valley's forest park.

En Route from Glendalough – Return to Laragh. Following Route T61 to Rathdrum, then T7, you pass through the densely wooded vales of Clara and Avoca. (The latter is the beauty spot where the Avonmore and Avonbeg rivers join to form the River Avoca. Here the poet Thomas Moore wrote his hymn to the vale, "The Meeting of the Waters.")

Heading back to the coast, you come to Arklow, an important fishing port and boatbuilding center. *Gypsy Moth III,* the yacht that took Sir Francis Chichester around the world (now docked at Greenwich, England), was built in an Arklow shipyard.

At Arklow, pick up N11 into County Wexford, through the towns of Gorey and Ferns, to Enniscorthy.

ENNISCORTHY: In a picturesque part of the Slaney Valley, this small town clings to steeply sloping ground along both banks of the river. The object of many attacks throughout history, including seizure of the lands by Oliver Cromwell and his forces in the 17th century, this was the site of a famous rebellion against the British in 1798. The insurgents made their last stand on Vinegar Hill, at the eastern end of the town, and were forever commemorated in the ballad "Boulavogue."

Enniscorthy Castle, dating from the 16th century, is excellently preserved and now devoted to a folk museum. St. Aidan's Cathedral is a fine example of neo-Gothic architecture, made all the more impressive by its commanding site overlooking the River Slaney.

WEXFORD: Also on the River Slaney, along its estuary, is hilly Wexford, settled in 850 by the Vikings, who gave it its name, Waesfjord ("the harbor of the mud flats"). This is where the Anglo-Normans got their first foothold in Ireland. They established a walled town and built Selskar Abbey. Henry II of England spent Lent of 1170 there in penance for the murder of Thomas à Becket. At the Bull Ring, in the center of town, bullfights were staged for the Norman nobles. In 1649, Oliver Cromwell captured Wexford, massacred the townspeople, and destroyed 13 churches. The house where he stayed is now a *Penney's* department store. Other historic Wexford houses, dealt with more fairly by fate, include the birthplace of Sir Robert McClure, the Arctic explorer who discovered the Northwest Passage, and the home of Lady Wilde, mother of Oscar Wilde. A statue to Commodore John Barry, "Father of the American Navy," stands on the quays.

The best way to see the town is on one of the daily walking tours organized by members of the Old Wexford Society. Tours are offered for free, although contributions are always welcome; detailed information is available at the tourist office on Crescent Quay (phone: 053-23111).

In October, Wexford holds the acclaimed *Wexford Opera Festival,* including a program of exhibitions, concerts, recitals, and films.

From Wexford, take Route N25 to New Ross.

NEW ROSS: On a hill overlooking the River Barrow, New Ross is the home of lovely St. Mary's Abbey, a relic of Norman times. Five miles (8 km) east, on L159, is the John Fitzgerald Kennedy Memorial Park, a splendid arboretum commemorating the president, whose ancestors came from nearby Dunganstown. Try the *New Ross Galley* — the restaurant on a boat — where you can combine a good meal with a superb cruise between New Ross and Waterford (see *Best en Route*).

WATERFORD: Route N25 leads to Waterford, another former Viking settlement. Reginald's Tower, a fortification built by Reginald the Dane in 1003, is now a museum. Beautiful 18th-century Christ Church Cathedral is also a tourist attraction (open Monday, Wednesday, and Friday afternoons in the summer). Above all, the city is famous for the crystal that bears its name, and a visit to the Waterford glass factory is a must. The original plant opened in 1783, and the fine glass, exported throughout the world, quickly made its reputation. There was a 100-year hiatus in production when the industry as a whole went into decline, but in 1951 the factory reopened and has since outgrown its buildings several times. Today the company employs 2,000 people and hosts an average of 3,000 visitors a week who watch the master blowers, crystal cutters, and engravers in action (open weekdays; closed the first 2 weeks in August; children under 12 not admitted; phone: 051-73311).

From Waterford take Route N9 to Kilkenny.

KILKENNY: This ancient and historic city is dominated by two beautifully preserved major buildings. The 13th-century Cathedral of St. Canice marks the spot of an even older monastery from which the city grew, and a climb up the Round Tower beside the cathedral offers fine views of the city and surrounding countryside. Dominating the view and everything else in sight is the magnificently preserved Norman palace on the banks of the River Nore, Kilkenny's second treasure. Before the Normans came, the city was the capital of the kingdom of Ossory. In the 14th century, the existing Ossory palace was taken over — and then taken apart — by the Normans, who raised in its place the castle that has stood, defiant of time, ever since. Across the road, in its former stables, is the government-established *Kilkenny Design Workshop,* where artisans create models for industrial and consumer products, developing Irish designs in various media including silver, copper, textiles, and pottery. Visitors are not allowed in the workshops, but splendid showrooms sell products from jewelry to full-fashioned garments. As in Wexford, there are marvelous walking tours of the city. Ask at the tourist office at Shee Alms House, Rose Inn St. (phone: 056-21755).

Take Route N76 going south from Kilkenny and join T37 at Ballymack, continuing to Cashel in County Tipperary.

CASHEL: Dominating the market town that bears its name is the Rock of Cashel — Cashel of the Kings — the history of which spans 16 centuries. From the 4th century, the kings of the province of Munster were crowned on this 300-foot limestone rock and had their palace here. St. Patrick preached Christianity on the site in 450. In the 12th century, King Murtagh O'Brien gave the Rock to the Church and began a period of great ecclesiastical building. Even the now roofless buildings retain their grandeur, but Cormac's Chapel, still roofed, is a gem of 12th-century Hiberno-Romanesque architecture (open daily; small admission charge). The lovely Queen Anne deanery, built for the archbishop in the 18th century, is now a hotel — the *Cashel Palace* — with a fine restaurant (see *Best en Route*). The shop/studio of silversmith Pádraig O Mathúna, near the hotel, is worth visiting. There is excellent trout fishing on the River Suir (permits can be obtained at the tourist office, Town Hall). From Cashel, Route N8 leads south to Cahir.

CAHIR: Cahir Castle, dominating the Suir, is one of the largest and most splendid medieval castles in Ireland. Restored, it is open to the public.

En Route from Cahir – Follow Route N8 out of Cahir to Mitchelstown and N73 to Mallow. To the left rise the Knockmealdown Mountains; on the right are the Galtees. The rich fishing waters of the Blackwater make Mallow a popular angling and hunting center. From Mallow, N20 goes south to Cork city.

CORK: The name Corcaigh means "marshy place," an apt description of its state for centuries after St. Finbarre founded a monastery here in the 6th century where Cork University now stands. (Cork's patron saint is honored in the lovely neo-Gothic Protestant cathedral of St. Finbarre.) It is a city of 120,000 people, the Republic's second largest metropolitan area. Today the city straddles the two branches of the River Lee without getting its feet wet. Cork's excellent shopping center offers many goods. Major department stores are on Patrick Street; one of the best is *Munster Arcade*. Small shops and boutiques abound on Prince and Oliver Plunkett streets. A particularly good crafts shop is *C. MacDonald,* on Winthrop Street, opposite the post office. Walking tour maps are available from the tourist office (Grand Parade). The city also has an active cultural life: a drama festival in March, the *International Choral Festival* in April-May, and the *Cork International Film Festival* in September. There is a good ballet company, operatic society, and theater company. The Cork Literary and Scientific Society is the oldest of its kind in Ireland; its Historical and Archaeological Society is renowned.

Two trips from Cork should not be missed, one to Blarney Castle and the other to Kinsale.

BLARNEY: Route L69 (start off on N20 toward Mallow and Limerick) leads to Blarney, only 6 miles (10 km) away. Few people in the English-speaking world have not heard of the Blarney Stone, which is said to confer the gift of eloquence on all who kiss it. The gift is well earned, however, for the stone juts out just under the battlement, which means you have to lie on your back far above a sheer drop and, with a guide holding your legs, stretch to your utmost to touch lips to stone. The view of the pretty castle park from the tower is better than the kiss. Both castle and park are open daily. Also open to the public is the "new" Blarney Castle House. adjoining the old one. It is the house of the Colthursts, to whom the Blarney connection descended after Cromwell wrested it from the MacCarthys. The small village of Blarney, attractive in its own right, boasts a craft shopping center offering fine products at reasonable prices.

KINSALE: Take the Airport road out of the city to get to Kinsale. With its narrow streets, tall houses, and stormy history, this attractive harbor town 17 miles (27 km) south of Cork is an essential stop for lovers of good food — "the culinary capital of Ireland." There is, for the town's size, an extraordinary range of really top restaurants whose proprietors have banded together in a Good Food Circle, which holds an annual *Gourmet Festival* in September.

BEST EN ROUTE

The southeastern region has some very good hotels and restaurants and a great many that are fair to mediocre. The listings here consider only the best in both accommodations and cuisine.

Expect to pay at least $80 per night for a double in one of the hotels or inns listed as expensive; from $50 to $75 in the moderate range; under $40 in those places listed as inexpensive. Meals at even the best restaurants are reasonable. We have categorized as expensive a meal for two that costs $70; $35 to $60 falls into the moderate range; and you can have quite good meals for as little as $20 to $30 for two in inexpensive spots. Reservations for hotels are a must everywhere during the tourist season and at other times when there are special festivals.

WEXFORD

Talbot – Overlooking Wexford Harbor, this gracious hostelry has had a facelift. There are now 104 rooms, all with private bath and some with hair dryers, 2 restaurants, a leisure center with indoor heated pool, gym, saunas, squash courts, and a solarium. The *Tavern* offers live music from traditional to jazz, and there's a weekly Irish cabaret in the summer. Trinity St. (phone: 053-22566). Expensive.

White's – Originally opened in 1779, it is now also known as the "new" *White's,* with 65 refurbished rooms, all with bath, 2 restaurants, and 2 bars. Both taverns — the *Old Wexford* and the *Shemalier* — are popular for sing-along sessions. George's St. (phone: 053-22311). Expensive.

Killiane Castle – Kathleen Mernagh runs this gracious guesthouse set on 230 acres. In addition to the 8 rooms with shared baths, apartments are available, and there's a 17th-century tower on the grounds. Open March through October. Off the Rosslare Harbour Rd., Drinagh (phone: 053-58885). Inexpensive.

NEW BAWN

Cedar Lodge – In a lovely rural setting among rolling hills, halfway between Wexford and New Ross, this low, modern building has 13 rooms (all suites). Its bar is good for lunchtime snacks, and the restaurant has a very good reputation. Carrigbyrne, near New Ross (phone 051-28386). Expensive.

NEW ROSS

Galley Cruising – This intriguing restaurant on a boat prepares fresh produce with appealing flair, but much of the appeal is the cruise itself — a long munch through the New Ross–Waterford River valleys. Bridge Way (phone: 051-21723). Moderate.

WATERFORD

Ardree – In this modern hotel on a hill on the northern side of the River Suir, all 100 rooms have views that are especially striking at night, when the lights of Waterford are twinkling. Amenities include private baths, air conditioning and central heating, a fine restaurant with panoramic city vistas, golf on an adjoining 18-hole course, and 38 acres of gardens. Ferrybank (phone: 051-32111). Expensive.

Tower – Centrally located on The Mall near historic Reginald's Tower, this 80-room hotel has been tastefully refurbished, with an emphasis on brickwork, mirrors, and flowering plants in the public rooms and eclectic furnishings in the bedrooms. Waterford chandeliers sparkle in the pink-toned dining room, known for its local river trout. The Mall (phone: 051-75801). Expensive.

KILKENNY

Hotel Kilkenny – Ten minutes' walk from the city center, this newly refurbished hotel and leisure complex is built around a gracious house and has 60 suites, a conservatory, indoor swimming pool, Jacuzzi, and sauna. College Road (phone: 056-62000). Expensive.

Newpark – On the north edge of the city, this Victorian country house has been skillfully combined with modern extensions and converted into a comfortable hotel with 60 rooms (each with private bath and phone). Facilities include a first-rate dining room, a noon-to-midnight grillroom, Irish musical entertainment, and twice-weekly discos. The staff is efficient and enthusiastic. Castlecomer Rd. (phone: 056-22122). Moderate.

CASHEL

Cashel Palace – This elegant Queen Anne building, formerly an archbishop's residence, is set amid beautiful formal gardens in the town center. It has 20 rooms with bath. The *Bishops Buttery* features light meals all day, and the *Four Seasons* is a fine dinner spot. Main St. (phone: 062-61411). Expensive.

Chez Hans – An attractive dinner spot, picturesquely set in an old converted church, with pointed windows and doors, right under Cashel's Rock. Chef-proprietor Hans prides himself on what he calls Irish-German cuisine (phone: 062-61177). Expensive.

CAHIR

Kilcoran Lodge – A few miles outside Cahir, on the right side of the Mitchelstown Road, this former shooting lodge is now a charming country hotel on the slope of Galtee Mountain. Recently renovated, it has 22 spacious rooms, all with private bath. The food served in the airy dining room is good (phone: 052-41288). Moderate.

Earl of Glengall – This restaurant serves tasty pub lunches, including Irish stew and steak and kidney pie, at very reasonable prices. Castle St. (phone: 052-41505). Moderate.

MALLOW

Longueville House – This 18-bedroom Georgian mansion overlooks the lovely River Blackwater, where guests may fish. The restaurant features home-grown produce superbly cooked by the owner. Reservations essential (phone: 022-47156). Expensive.

CORK

Arbutus Lodge – Those who want to get as close as possible to what some consider the best restaurant in Cork, and perhaps in Ireland, should head for this elegant mansion overlooking the city and the river. The Georgian decor is enhanced by a collection of modern Irish art. There are 20 small but good rooms, all with bath. Montenotte (phone: 021-501237). Expensive.

Imperial – The dowager of them all, stately in the middle of the South Mall and close to everything, took shape on the drawing board of Thomas Deane. The grande dame is not as starchy as she looks; in fact, all 93 rooms have been renovated with an Art Deco flair and now include private bath. Meals in the very competent French restaurant, *La Duchesse,* are served to the accompaniment of piano music. South Mall (phone: 021-274040). Expensive.

Jurys – On the banks of the River Lee with views of St. Finbarre's Cathedral, this modern establishment has 200 rooms with private baths, a seafood restaurant (*Fastnet*), a sing-along bar, and an atrium-shaped pavilion with indoor-outdoor heated pool, saunas, squash courts, and a gym. Western Rd. (phone: 021-276622). Expensive.

Silver Springs – Another modern hotel on the fringes. Rooms are newly refurbished, all 100 with baths. If you are lucky, yours will have a delightful view of the river with its passing ships. There is a handy coffee shop, a restaurant, and a sports complex. Glanmire Rd. (phone: 021-507533). Expensive.

KINSALE

Acton's – This member of the Trusthouse Forte family has a terrific location facing the harbor, extensive rose gardens, a seafood restaurant, and a nautical tavern. There are 55 rooms, all with private bath. The Waterfront (phone: 021-772135). Expensive.

Blue Haven – In the middle of the village, this small, cozy hotel has 10 individually decorated rooms, 7 with bath. But the star attractions are the dining room's huge platters of local crab, mussels, and lobster and its fish casseroles, veal Cordon Bleu, and duck baked in brandy. The paneled bar, with a wood-burning fireplace, serves seafood soups and sandwiches. Pearce St. (phone: 021-772209). Moderate.

Man Friday – Beautifully situated in its own garden, this friendly restaurant has a rustic decor and a menu ranging from prawns Napoleon and Polynesian chicken to shellfish nouvelle. Scilly (phone: 021-77-22-60). Expensive to moderate.

Vintage – This vine-covered, beamed little restaurant stands in a winding street near the harbor. The cooking is imaginative, with particular emphasis on local produce. Choices include noisettes of lamb, free-range duckling, medallions of monkfish, and wiener schnitzel. Main St. (phone: 021-772502). Expensive to moderate.

Southwest Ireland: Cork to Killarney

Artists and writers have for centuries celebrated the beauty of the Kingdom of Kerry, where the majesty of Ireland's highest mountains contrasts starkly with its romantic glens and the splendor of the rugged coastline gives way to glorious lakes and luxurious forests. It is a landscape of infinite variety and constantly changing colors. Basically, the mountainous southern part of Kerry consists of the three large peninsulas of Beara, Iveragh, and Dingle; the smaller northern part is an area of undulating plain that stretches as far as the Shannon estuary. Along the coast, sandy bays alternate with cliffs and rocky headlands; the inland scenery includes the beautiful lakes of Killarney.

But scenic beauty is by no means Kerry's only attraction. Its many coastal resorts, climbable mountains, excellent fishing waters, good golf courses, and a wealth of ancient monuments make the southwest a paradise for sightseeing or sports-loving travelers.

There are lively, cheerful towns where pub regulars have formed semiformal singing groups, small fishing towns where the lilt of the ancient Irish tongue is on most lips, remote and lovely places where time has stood still.

This route concentrates on Kerry's great peninsulas: Beara, which it shares with Cork; Iveragh, famous for the Ring of Kerry, the complete scenic circuit around the peninsula; and Dingle, the most northerly promontory, which stretches 30 miles west from the low-lying country around Tralee to mountain ranges that turn to wild, deserted hills and lead to magnificent coastal scenery. You should allow 3 days and nights for the tour. If your time is limited, make sure you don't miss the Ring of Kerry, roughly a 110-mile (176-km) round trip from Killarney. To see it leisurely will take most of 1 day.

CORK: For a description of the city, see the previous route.

En Route from Cork – Route T29 takes you along the north bank of the River Lee and passes through the picturesque villages of Dripsey, with its woolen mills, and Coachford.

MACROOM: This thriving market town, worth a quick visit, is set amid a large Irish-speaking district, and on market day Irish can be heard everywhere. The ruined castle, reached via the market square, stands at the center of town.

En Route from Macroom – Go back 1 mile (1.6 km) on the Cork road, T64, and turn left for Inchigeelagh. Past Inchigeelagh the road hugs the north bank of the long and lovely Lough Allua. But the minor road along the south bank is even more beautiful, so that's the one you should take, returning to the T64 at the western end of the lake. Make a right turn 3.7 miles (6 km) beyond Ballingeary, where the sign reads: Gougane Barra.

GOUGANE BARRA: The mountain-encircled lake of Gougane Barra, source of the River Lee, is where St. Finbar, the founder of Cork, had his hermitage in the 6th century. It has a splendid forest park with extensive nature trails.

Return to T64. Continue southwest as the road descends via Keimaneigh Pass and the Ouvane Valley to Ballylickey and Glengarriff.

GLENGARRIFF: The name means "the rough glen" and is only partially true of this lovely village on the Beara Peninsula snuggled into a deeply wooded glen. There is nothing rough about this glen, and sheltered as it is from any harsh winds, the village has a justly famous reputation for mild weather and tropical vegetation. Some of the plants and trees that flourish here are arbutus, eucalyptus, fuchsia, rhododendron, and blue-eyed grass. There is excellent sea and river fishing in and around the town, and bathing is good along the nearby coves, one of which, Poulgorm ("blue pool"), is a picturesque spot with a fine view — just a 2-minute walk from the village post office. There are tennis courts, a golf course, and unlimited terrain for riding and walking.

If time permits, a visit to the lovely Italian Gardens on Garinish Island is recommended. There are plenty of boats and boatmen available for a small charge.

En Route from Glengarriff – If pressed for time, continue directly to Kenmare via N71. Otherwise follow the spectacular Healy Pass road, which is 17 miles (27 km) longer. From Glengarriff this follows L61 along the south coast of mountainous Beara, the least-frequented of the three great southwestern peninsulas. At the foot of the Caha Mountains is Adrigole village. Hungry Hill, from which Daphne du Maurier took the title of her novel, looms to the northwest. At the schoolhouse in Adrigole turn right when you come to the sign: Healy Pass.

HEALY PASS: This road, opened in 1931, was built at the direction of Tim Healy, the first governor-general of the Irish Free State. It climbs to a height of 1,084 feet as it crosses the Caha Mountains, the border between County Cork and County Kerry, and provides magnificent views over Sheep's Head and Mizen Head to the south and Kenmare River and the mountains of the Iveragh Peninsula to the north.

LAURAGH: The Healy Pass road descends to join the scenic sea road, L62, at Lauragh. Not far from Lauragh are the Cloonee Lakes, stocked with salmon and sea and brown trout. Route L62 continues along the coast to Kenmare.

KENMARE: This small town, at the head of the Kenmare River where the Roughty River meets the sea, has the mild climate common to the south coast. It is an excellent center from which to tour both the Beara and Iveragh peninsulas. There is bathing in the sheltered coves west of the town, salmon and brown trout fishing, and boating in the bay. Kenmare is also noted for its lacemaking; a famous point lace is made and exhibited at the convent of the Poor Clare nuns. Other sites of interest include a ring of prehistoric stones, called the Druid's Circle, about one-quarter mile southwest of town, and St. Finan's Holy Well nearby, which is reputed to have healing powers.

Kenmare is the site for the *Fruits de Mer Festival* (usually in September), which features deep-sea fishing, seafood exhibitions and banquets, and a wide range of entertainment.

The most direct road to Killarney is Route T65(N71), over the mountains to Molls Gap, via Ladies View, a lookout point with a panoramic view of the wonderful lakes of Killarney before entering the town. A more circuitous route is the famous Ring of Kerry road that encircles the Iveragh Peninsula by way of Waterville and Cahirciveen, about 100 miles in all. Take N70 from Kenmare.

PARKNASILLA: Renowned for its lush vegetation, this estate is the grounds of the beautiful *Great Southern* hotel (see *Best en Route*), a favorite holiday place of George Bernard Shaw.

SNEEM: This pretty town, where the Dutch royal family has vacationed, lies amid equally pretty scenery at the head of the Sneem River estuary. There is very good fishing here: Brown trout, salmon, and sea trout abound in the river and nearby mountain lakes. You'll want to stop at the *Blue Bull* — a quiet pleasant country pub and restaurant (see *Best en Route*) — if only for a quick drink to see its collection of prints and paintings.

STAIGUE FORT: Beyond Sneem, the Ring of Kerry road winds inland for a few miles through wild scenery, meeting the coast again at Castlecove, a peaceful retreat near a fine sandy beach. Here, make a right turn at a small sign: Staigue Fort. About 1½ miles (2.5 km) north are the imposing ruins of a circular stone fort, one of Ireland's finest archaeological remains, which could date back as far as 1000 BC. Its rough stones are held in place without mortar.

CAHERDANIEL: Back on the coast road, past Westcove, is the village of Caherdaniel, near the shore of Derrynane Bay. In the vicinity is the curious hermitage of St. Crohane, hewn out of solid rock. Nearby is Derrynane House, once the home of Daniel O'Connell, "the Liberator," who gained the emancipation of Irish Catholics in 1829. The house, now restored, contains a museum with O'Connell's personal possessions and furniture. The house is part of Derrynane National Historic Park, with a nature trail through fine scenery. It is open to the public all year.

En Route from Caherdaniel – Route N70 climbs to a height of 700 feet at the Pass of Coomakista and offers a superb view. While the inland mountains rise sharply — to 1,600 feet — on one side, the lonely Skellig Rocks can be seen on the other in the open Atlantic. Skellig Michael bears the remains of a 6th-century monastery; it can be reached on a calm day from Portmagee. On the descent from Coomakista, Ballinskelligs Bay comes into view, with the village of Waterville nestling in its curve.

WATERVILLE: This small, unspoiled village lies between the Atlantic and beautiful Lough Currane on the eastern shore of Ballinskelligs Bay. On the east and south, mountains rise from Lough Currane, reaching 2,000 feet on the east side; in the lake itself float several islands, and in addition to Currane, there are many smaller lakes in the vicinity. With all this water, Waterville is a famous angling center almost by default, and no aquatic pursuit is ignored. There is boating, bathing from the fine sandy beach on the bay shore, and, for resolute landlubbers, golfing on a championship course.

En Route from Waterville – Follow either the coastal Route N70 to Cahirciveen and on to Glenbeigh or take one of the spectacular mountain roads to Glencar and thence to the coast. The latter is recommended. At New Chapel Cross, 1½ miles (2.5 km) outside Waterville, leave N70 for an unclassified road to the Pass of Ballaghisheen. At a point between Bealalaw Bridge and Lough Acoose, a left turn leads to Caragh Lake and descends to rejoin N70 at Caragh

Bridge. A left turn brings you to Glenbeigh after 2 miles (see below). A right turn continues to Killorglin, famous for its *Puck Fair*. (Every August the town holds a 3-day festival during which a goat is enthroned as King Puck to preside over a cattle, sheep, and horse fair. Shops are open day and night. Thousands of people come from all parts of Kerry.) From Killorglin, you may take T67 to Killarney, or continue northward to the Dingle Peninsula. A left turn leads to Glenbeigh.

GLENBEIGH: At the entrance to a semicircle of mountains known as the Glenbeigh Horseshoe, where the Behy River flows into Dingle Bay, the town nestles at the foot of Seefin Mountain (1,621 feet). The scenery here is magnificent, and the circuit of hills from Seefin to Drung Hill (the horseshoe) is one of Kerry's finest mountain walks, with glacial corries and lakes throughout and fabulous trout fishing in innumerable rivers and lakes. Its other glory is nearby Rossbeigh strand, a 3-mile tongue of fine sand and dunes reaching out into Dingle Bay.

En Route from Killorglin – Follow N70 to Castlemaine, where L103 takes you into the Dingle Peninsula, a thriving center of Gaelic language and culture, rich in archaeological remains. This peninsula has been the setting for movies and should be familiar to filmgoers who have seen *Ryan's Daughter*.

INCH: Not far from the head of Dingle Bay, on the south side of the peninsula, lies the sheltered seaside resort of Inch. Its name to the contrary, the village has a 4-mile strip of firm golden sand that provides excellent bathing. The beach is backed by dunes that have yielded evidence of very early habitations.

DINGLE TOWN: The peninsula's chief town lies at the foot of a steep slope on the north side of the harbor and is bounded on three sides by hills. It was the main port of Kerry in the old Spanish trading days, and in the reign of Queen Elizabeth I it was important enough as an outpost to merit a protective wall. It has always been a fishing town; deep-sea fishing facilities are excellent. There is also good bathing and pony trekking into the surrounding hills. It is the gateway to the West Kerry Gaeltacht, the Irish-speaking district, and a good base for extended exploration of this rich area.

En Route from Dingle – The road continues to Ventry, with its delightful beach. To the right of the road beyond Ventry are signs for "beehive huts." These lead to groups of small stone buildings shaped like beehives, constructed without mortar on a corbel principle. They generally served as monks' cells in early Irish monasteries. Since the ancient method of construction is still in use, it is often difficult to distinguish the old from the recent.

The road from Dingle continues to Slea Head at the tip of the peninsula, where the view of the Blasket Islands, the westernmost point in Europe (except for Iceland), is spectacular.

THE BLASKETS: This is a group of seven islands in the Atlantic. The largest, the Great Blasket, is about 4 miles long and three-quarters of a mile wide. Now uninhabited, it used to be known as "the next parish to America" when it had a village settlement. The Blaskets were inhabited from prehistoric times by an Irish-speaking community that gradually thinned out until, in 1953, the last islanders moved to the mainland. Many islanders were exponents of the art of Seanachai, or storytelling. Several books have been written about island life, among them: *Twenty Years A-growing,* by Maurice O'Sullivan; *The Islander,* by Thomas Crohan; and *Peig,* by Peig Sayers — all Blasket islanders. Boats to the Blaskets can be hired in Dunquin, north of Slea Head.

En Route from Slea Head – The road continues through Dunquin and Ballyferriter. About 1.5 miles (2.5 km) northeast is Gallerus Oratory, one of the best-preserved 9th-century buildings in Ireland. Although it is built of unmortared stone, it is completely watertight after more than 1,000 years.

Return to Dingle via Ventry. To get to Tralee, go over the Connor Pass if it's a clear day. Driving this road demands great care; it should be avoided in bad weather. Leave Dingle by the unclassified road marked Connor Pass, climbing northeasterly between Brandon and Slievenea mountains. At the summit (1,500 feet) is a breathtaking view: the bays of Brandon and Tralee to the north, Dingle Bay and Dingle town to the south, and the lakes in the deep valley to the left. The road then winds down along the base of great cliffs and ultimately goes through a valley of boulder-strewn wilderness. Incidentally, Brandon mountain is named for Saint Brandon the Navigator who, according to tradition — and some scholars — reached America from here long before Columbus. In the town of Camp, take adjoining T68 for Tralee.

TRALEE: This friendly, busy trading center is one of the most active towns in southern Ireland. There is salmon and trout fishing in its rivers, excellent deep-sea fishing, a choice of superb beaches, sailing, skin diving, riding, and golf. Throughout the summer, the *Ashe Memorial Theatre* is the scene of *Siamsa* (pronounced "she-amsa"), a folk theater that brings to life, through mime, music, song, and dance, the customs of the Irish countryside. Inquire for details at the tourist office (32 the Mall; phone: 066-21288). The *Irish Ballet Company* also performs here regularly. The greatest attraction of the town, however, is undoubtedly the *Festival of Kerry* at the end of August. This week-long event is described as "the greatest free show on earth." Its highlight is the crowning of the Rose of Tralee, from contestants from all parts of the world. Throughout the festival the town is brilliantly lit; every street is the scene of some outdoor entertainment or sporting event.

KILLARNEY: This is one of the major destinations of most visitors, because of the unrivaled beauty of its location. Three main lakes are in a broad valley stretching south between mountains. Closest to town is the Lower Lake, the largest of the three; the peninsula of Muckross separates it from the Middle Lake, which is connected with the Upper Lake by a narrow strait called the Long Range. The lakes are surrounded by luxuriant woods of oak, arbutus, birch, holly, and mountain ash, among which grow masses of rhododendron as well as ferns, mosses, and other plants. Besides the three main lakes, there is Lough Guitane, 4 miles (6.5 km) southeast, and innumerable small tarns hidden in the folds of mountains and in rockbeds.

Part of Killarney's lake district lies within the 11,000-acre Bourne Vincent Memorial Park, once a private estate and in 1932 presented to the government, which promptly made it a national park. *Muckross House,* a 19th-century manor, is now a folk museum.

South of the town is the Gap of Dunloe, a magnificent gorge that runs for 4 miles between MacGillycuddy's Reeks and the Purple Mountains. Tours through the gap are made on ponies or on foot. In the town and the park, horse-drawn jaunting cars are available. A full day's tour includes a boat ride that, in turn, requires some shooting of rapids to traverse the three lakes.

There are two championship golf courses and a racetrack nearby; salmon and trout fishing on the lakes and nearby rivers; and the highest mountain range in Ireland, the MacGillycuddy's Reeks, offers superb walking and scrambling possibilities to the experienced.

BEST EN ROUTE

The southwest is the most visited area in Ireland. That means that hotels of all degrees from luxurious to plain are plentiful, but rooms are always in demand. Book well in advance, and expect to pay somewhat more than in other parts of Ireland. The good news is that the hotels in the area are excellent (the one exception is Tralee, where neither accommodations nor restaurants warrant a lot of enthusiasm, but where the pubs are simply wonderful) and well versed in dealing with excited and overawed visitors. Many activities associated with the southwest — pony treks and fishing, long hikes in the mountains and deep-sea expeditions — can be arranged through hotels.

There is a wide range of prices in the hotels and restaurants. Certainly there are many lovely bed-and-breakfast houses with extremely reasonable rates, but at the luxurious resorts that are scattered around the route (such as the *Europe* in Killarney), rates can jump to $100 a night for a double in the middle of summer. That's still cheap compared to an international hotel in Stockholm, but for Ireland it's pricey.

In general, expect to pay around $70 per night for a double in those places listed as expensive; from $50 to $70 in the moderate range; and under $45 in the inexpensive. A restaurant listed as expensive will charge as much as $60 for a meal for two; between $25 and $55 in the moderate range; and under 25 for two in the inexpensive category. Prices don't include wine, drinks, or tips.

KENMARE

Park – Widely recognized as one of the country's finest hotels (Ireland's first to win a Michelin star for its dining room), the hotel is on its own palm tree–lined grounds on Kenmare Bay, just at the edge of the village. Guests are greeted like royalty as they sit down to register at an antique stockbroker's desk in the lobby. There are 50 rooms, all with bath, including 6 master suites with four-poster beds and hand-carved armoires. The restaurant, with romantic bay views on long summer days and candlelight in winter, specializes in seafood, especially salmon and shellfish (phone: 064-41200). Expensive.

Kenmare Bay – A pleasant hotel with 68 airy and modern rooms, a lively bar, and a good restaurant. During the *Fruits de Mer Festival,* it can be very crowded. Closed November through March. Sneem Rd. (phone: 064-41300). Moderate.

Purple Heather Bistro – Seafood is the specialty of the house, with meals served in the comfortable bar. Closed from the end of October to March. Henry St. (phone: 064-41016). Moderate.

PARKNASILLA

Great Southern – One of George Bernard Shaw's favorite vacation spots, this beautiful hotel on a lush estate is splendid all around. There are 60 rooms with bath, a private golf course for guests, a heated indoor swimming pool, and fishing or boating on the bay. The cuisine is superb. Closed November through March (phone: 064-45122). Expensive.

SNEEM

Blue Bull – A charming pub made up of three different rooms decorated with fascinating prints of County Kerry scenes and, appropriately, an attention-getting straw blue bull's head. In the summer, a back room becomes a seafood restaurant. Square (phone: 064-45231). Moderate.

WATERVILLE

Waterville Lake – This deluxe resort lies in a setting of unparalleled beauty on the shores of lovely Lough Currane within a stone's throw of the sea, and it makes the most of the panorama. Completely refurbished in 1985, it has 32 rooms, 18 luxurious suites, and a fine restaurant. Other amenities include an 18-hole championship golf course, heated indoor pool, thermal spa pool, sauna, and solarium. Open May through September (phone: 0667-4133). Expensive.

GLENBEIGH

Ard na Sidhe – Elegant, quiet, and beautifully secluded in the forest at Caragh Lake, this was once a private home. Now, there are 20 rooms, all with private bath. To find *Ard na Sidhe,* "hill of the fairies," look for the signs on N70 between Killorglin and Glenbeigh. Open May through August. Killorglin (phone: 066-69105). Moderate.

Towers – This is a popular 22-bedroom family-run hotel; good food is a tradition here, and during the summer season there is Irish entertainment nightly in the bar (phone: 066-68212). Moderate.

TRALEE

Brandon – One of the largest hotels in County Kerry, this is standard modern in style but genial in operation. All 162 rooms have private bath. There's also a dining room, coffee shop, and nightclub with dancing. Princes Street (phone: 066-23333). Expensive to moderate.

Ballygarry House – This recently refurbished country inn with private garden has an Old World look, complete with open fireplaces. All 16 of the individually decorated rooms have a private bath. The restaurant serves mostly continental dishes. 1½ miles (2 km) from town on the Tralee-Killarney road. Leebrook (phone: 066-21233). Moderate.

Tralee Bay – In the lovely seaside town of Castlegregory, 14 miles (22 km) from Tralee, is this small — 13 rooms, 6 with bath — hotel, of modest decor but warm atmosphere. Fermoyle Beach, Castlegregory (phone: 066-39138). Moderate.

Tralee Pubs – *The Abbey Inn,* Bridge St. (phone: 066-22084).
The Bridge Inn, Bridge St. (phone: 066-21827).
The Brogue Inn, Rock St. (phone: 066-22126).
The Oyster Tavern, The Spa, west of Tralee (phone: 066-36102).
The Pig & Whistle, Rock St. (phone: 066-21894).
The Tavern, Boherbue (phone: 066-21161).

KILLARNEY

Dunloe Castle – This is a sister to the *Europe* and is not an old Irish fortress but a modern German-owned château-style hotel near the Gap of Dunloe. All 140 rooms have private baths, and other amenities include an excellent restaurant, a heated indoor pool, sauna, tennis courts, horseback riding, fishing, croquet, putting green, fitness track, tropical gardens, and nightly entertainment. Open April through October. Beaufort (phone: 064-44111). Expensive.

Europe – Like its name, this hotel is more European than Irish. (It is owned by Germans, which may explain it.) With a marvelous location on the shore of one of the Killarney lakes, it has all the amenities of a luxury hotel — a heated indoor pool in a health complex that includes a sauna. The 168 rooms vary in size and degree of luxury, but most have spectacular views and balconies. The *Panorama* restaurant has an international menu with views befitting its name; the *Tyrol* offers faster fare in a skylit alpine setting. Open during March and from May through October. Fossa (phone: 064-31900). Expensive.

Great Southern – The grand old lady of Killarney hotels has 180 comfortable rooms, but some in the modern wing are smallish. The public rooms are very elegant. The ballroom-size dining room is elegant, with a dome and pillars. (phone: 064-31262). Expensive.

Cahernane – This was once the home of the Herberts, the family who owned Killarney. It is 1 mile (1.6 km) outside town, near the famous lakes, with 52 gracious bedrooms, log fires, 2 restaurants, and a fine wine cellar. Muckross Road (phone: 064-33936). Expensive to moderate.

Aghadoe Heights – A modern hotel with 60 rooms that are less than luxurious, but the fine lake views make up for their shortcomings. The *Rooftop* restaurant dispenses exceptionally good local seafood as well as traditional Irish dishes, and the *Abbey Room* provides musical entertainment and dancing every summer evening except Sunday. Amenities for guests include salmon fishing on a private stretch of river and special arrangements at Killarney's golf courses. Closed mid-December to mid-January. Aghadoe (phone: 064-31766). Moderate.

The Midwest Counties:
Limerick and Clare

Limerick is a county of rolling grassland south of the River Shannon estuary. It is a rich agricultural area, particularly in the east, where it is known as the Golden Vale. The majestic Shannon drains the fertile pasturelands, making them ideal for dairy farming. This is countryside with a quiet beauty: Low hill ranges dot the plains; small towns rise here and there, each with its ruined castle or abbey and ancient bridge. Some of Ireland's best fox hunting is in this county, home also of many stud farms.

The huge Shannon estuary separates Limerick from County Clare to the north. Clare provides a stark contrast to the rural beauty of Limerick. Stone is the keynote of the landscape; it predominates everywhere. Along the west coast, spectacular slate and limestone cliffs drop to the incoming Atlantic, forming a coast of spectacular bluffs. To the north this rugged coast rises nearly 700 feet above the sea in the sheer Cliffs of Moher. Inland rises the Burren, an area of bare limestone terraces that shelter many caves and underground streams and a rich profusion of both Arctic and Mediterranean vegetation, which is usually not found in these latitudes.

Limerick is the gateway to the Irish Republic for travelers landing at Shannon International Airport, only 15 miles (24 km) away (in County Clare), 30 minutes by car or bus. Many tourists are routed to the southwest or midwest from Dublin via Limerick. The Dublin to Limerick leg is 123 miles (198 km), a drive of about 3½ hours.

The following route starts at Killarney, going generally north, with some backtracking and detours. It can be done in 2 days with time planned for one of the medieval Shannon castle banquets, which must be booked in advance (phone: 061-61788). The overnight stay could be in Limerick or Ennis.

KILLARNEY: For a description, see the previous route.

En Route from Killarney – You have a choice of two equally pleasant routes: through Listowel, Tarbert, and Askeaton — the Limerick road along the Shannon — or the inland route through Newcastle West and Adare. You can also combine the routes to see the most interesting parts of each. The route that follows is a combination: the estuary road to Askeaton, turning inland at Askeaton to Adare.

Leave Killarney on N22 for Tralee. Continue on N69 through literary Listowel, where a writers' workshop is held for a week every June, with performances of plays by Kerry authors and literary get-togethers. About 11 miles (18 km) north, at Tarbert, you meet the 60-mile-long estuary of the River Shannon. (A car-ferry operates from here to Killimer in County Clare on the north side of the estuary.) Continuing on N69, you enter County Limerick at the dairy town of Glin, the site of beautiful 18th-century Glin Castle, which has a craft shop and tearoom. Askeaton is another picturesque old town with some notable ruins: 15th-century Askeaton Castle straddles the steep banks of the River Deel; a Franciscan friary stands on the banks of the river, and in its Protestant cemetery are the chancel and belfry of St. Mary's Church.

From Askeaton, turn off the main road onto L36, going inland through Rath-keale, a busy market town. On the way out of Askeaton, on the right, are the ruins of the 13th-century Franciscan Friary of St. Mary's.

At Rathkeale, turn east onto N21. About 7 miles (11 km) northeast is the enchanting village of Adare, its thatched cottages and lichened medieval churches surrounded by woods on the River Maigue. The finest of the monastic ruins here is the 15th-century Franciscan friary on the estate of the earl of Dunraven. (The 19th-century manor house and grounds, home of the Earls of Dunraven, has recently been converted to an impressive castle-style hotel (see *Best en Route.*) Among other noteworthy ruins are the 14th-century Adare Castle, 13th-century Trinitarian Abbey (incorporated into the town's Catholic church), and the 14th-century Augustinian priory, now part of the town's Protestant church. Route N21 continues northeast to Limerick, about 11 miles (18 km).

LIMERICK CITY: The fourth largest city in Ireland (pop. 145,000) offers an appropriately engaging introduction to the country for those many, many visitors who begin journeys here after the short half-hour trip in from Shannon Airport. While the city has a reputation for industry, those it is most famous for are all amiably light: traditional Limerick lace, still produced here; wonderfully cured hams and bacon; salmon fishing; and flour milling.

Limerick is a city of wide streets, handsome Georgian houses, and impressive public buildings such as the Custom House and the Town Hall.

This gracious architecture hardly reflects its violent history. It was occupied by the Danes in the 9th century and taken by the Anglo-Normans toward the end of the 12th century. In 1210, King John ordered the building of a strong castle and Shannon Bridge to control the crossing point of the river. In later centuries the city walls were extended for security. In the 17th century the city was torn between revolts by the Irish who seized the city and sieges by the English to bring them to their knees. The Treaty of Limerick in 1691 was to end hostilities and grant political and religious liberty to the Irish and the Catholics, but repeated violations of the treaty forced thousands into exile. The Treaty Stone, on which the pact was signed, stands on Thomond Bridge near King John's Castle; beside the castle is 12th-century St. Mary's Cathedral. This Church of Ireland structure is architecturally interesting; inside is an unusual collection of 15th-century misericords, oak carvings from choir stalls. Remnants of the old city walls, bearing the marks of cannon, can be seen near St. John's Hospital. Also worth a visit is the Limerick lace collection in the Good Shepherd Convent (Clare St.).

Activities include greyhound racing three times weekly at the city track; salmon and trout fishing at Castleconnell, 8 miles (13 km) away, and brown trout and grilse fishing on the River Mulcair, 4 miles (6.5 km) away; horse racing at Greenpark on Lower Killarney Road and Limerick Junction, 21 miles (33 km) out of town; golf at Ballyclough and at Castletroy, 3 miles (5 km) away; and swimming and boating on the River Shannon.

En Route from Limerick – As soon as you leave the city on N18 going west, you are in County Clare. Some 12 miles (20 km) from Limerick you pass Bunratty Castle. This splendidly restored 15th-century castle is open to the public daily, as is Heritage Park on the castle grounds, where visitors can see typical Shannon houses through the ages and watch traditional skills such as candle making, bread baking, and iron forging. Raucous medieval banquets — food and entertainment — are held nightly in the castle. These require reservations through *Shannon Castle Tours* (phone: 061-61788).

Beyond the castle, just before the road turns north, N19 branches off to the left to Shannon Airport. Continuing on N18 to Ennis, another 12 miles (19 km), you pass through Newmarket-on-Fergus.

ENNIS: Friendly, narrow-streeted Ennis is County Clare's capital. It is a progressive business and marketing center, but of greater interest to the visitor are the remains of several abbeys in and around town: Ennis Abbey, built in the 13th century and remodeled through the 15th century, a mixture of architectural styles; Clare Abbey, a 12th-century Augustinian priory; and Killone Abbey, from the same period.

En Route from Ennis – Take Route T70 west through hilly Ennistymon, where the little River Cullenagh falls in cascades through the town center. Here join T69 to get to Lahinch, a resort with a mile-long beach, excellent for bathing and surfing. There is an indoor entertainment center for the unpredictable Irish weather and a challenging golf course, and periwinkles and dilisk are sold in twists of newspapers along the promenade. Route L54 in Lahinch leads to the fishing village of Liscannor and 3 miles (4.8 km) west (a sign indicates the turnoff) are the Cliffs of Moher, one of the outstanding features of County Clare. Rising nearly 700 feet above the sea and extending about 5 miles along the coast, they provide magnificent views — especially from O'Brian's Tower (a short climb from the car park) at their northern end. From here you can see the Aran Islands to the north and, on a clear day, across Galway Bay all the way to Connemara.

LISDOONVARNA: Ireland's only surviving spa is in the hilly Burren country of north Clare, 5 miles (8 km) from the sea. The spa's waters come from sulfur and iron springs that contain iodine and magnesium, beneficial in certain cases of rheumatism and arthritis. The Spa Centre is open from Easter to October. (September is the busiest season for Lisdoonvarna. The end of the harvest brings plenty of aching muscles.) The spa has saunas, sun lounges, mudbaths, and facilities for massage as well as beauty therapy. There is also a café on the premises.

En Route from Lisdoonvarna – Several routes crisscross the Burren (meaning "great rock"), the strange lunar-like region of bare, silvery limestone hills, caves, underground waterways, and "turloughs" (intermittent lakes, sometimes called disappearing lakes because the water is absorbed by the porous limestone, acting like a drain). Though naked and treeless, the Burren is a naturalist's delight because of its rare, low-growing flora, such as Irish orchid and blue spring gentian, scattered over rock and sod. There are about 500 ring forts, or *caher*, where inhabitants of the Burren lived in about 600 BC. The most spectacular of these is Caherdoonerish, 600 feet up on Black Head with 18-foot walls and a view of the Aran Islands.

Just outside Ballyvaughan, you can stop to see the impressive stalactites in Aillwee Cave (open to the public) where there is also a restaurant and a good craft/souvenir shop. At Rinn Point in Ballyvaughan, there is shore fishing for flatfish and mullet, while the bay affords bottom fishing for bass, flounder, and dogfish.

From Ballyvaughan, continue on N67 through Kinvara, and on into County Galway, past *Dun Guaire,* another castle in which medieval banquets are held. At Kilcolgan turn left onto N18 for Galway city.

Beyond Kilcolgan is Clarinbridge, the heart of oyster country and the scene of an oyster festival in September. Route N18 leads to Oranmore, where it becomes N6 into Galway city.

BEST EN ROUTE

Perhaps because County Limerick and County Clare are close to Shannon International Airport, the area offers unusual accommodations along with the somewhat hokey entertainment-cum-restaurant fare offered as medieval castle banquets. Depending on your state of mind, these can be fun, but if you hate crowds, avoid the banquets, particularly the one at *Bunratty Castle; Dun Guaire* is a little more intimate as medieval banquets go, but that's not going very far. Don't make the mistake, however, of writing castles completely off your itinerary. Only 8 miles (12.8 km) from Shannon Airport is *Dromoland Castle,* one of the finest hotels (and arguably the best) in Ireland. The Irish do this sort of thing extremely well (there are about eight of these castle hotels in Ireland) and if you want to spend the money, *Dromoland Castle,* or the newest of the luxury castle group, *Adare Manor Hotel,* are each unique experiences (see *Best En Route* for both).

Price ranges for hotels, including castles, are $150 and up for a double, very expensive; $80 to $100, expensive; $40 to $75, moderate; below $40, inexpensive. For restaurants, expect to pay about $70 for two in the expensive category; $40 to $65, moderate; under $35, inexpensive. Prices don't include wine, drinks, or tips.

ADARE

Adare Manor – The newest of Ireland's truly luxurious hotels, it's in the same tradition as *Ashford Castle* and *Dromoland Castle.* The splendid, ornate, Tudor Revival manor — until recently the private home of the Earls of Dunraven — occupies 840 acres of parkland and gardens near the salmon-filled Maigue River, beside the prettiest village in Ireland. An Equestrian Centre was under construction at press time. There are a total of 29 rooms, including 12 staterooms. Adare (phone: 061-86566). Very expensive.

Dunraven Arms – It's hard to say which is more beautiful, the ivy-covered Old World hotel with its charming garden or its location on Adare's cottage-lined main street. Both are lovely. The hotel has 25 bedrooms, all with bath. It also has a very good restaurant. Main St. (phone: 061-86209). Moderate.

LIMERICK

Dromoland Castle – For true luxury, you must go outside Limerick to Newmarket-on-Fergus, about 16 miles (26 km) (8 mi/13 km from Shannon Airport). This is one of Ireland's castle hotels. Unadulterated luxury prevails in its regally renovated public rooms and 77 guestrooms. It offers 18 holes of golf, riding, tennis, fishing, and shooting within spacious grounds. The dining room is formal, as befits a palace, and its cuisine is excellent. Lodgings are available April through October only. Newmarket-on-Fergus (phone: 061-71144). Very expensive.

Jurys – Just over the bridge from the Limerick city center, overlooking the River Shannon, this modern hotel offers efficient service and 100 well-appointed rooms. There is a new publike bar and coffee shop, but the restaurant, the *Copper Room,* is noteworthy. Small but attractive, it offers excellent French cuisine. Service is efficient and friendly. Open for dinner only. Ennis Rd. (phone: 061-55266). Expensive.

Shannon Shamrock Inn – This Paddy Fitzpatrick hotel has 100 rooms, 10 river suites, a heated indoor pool, a sauna, a French/Irish restaurant, and a bar. It's next to *Bunratty Castle* and *Durty Nelly's* pub. About 10 miles (16 km) from Limerick in Bunratty (phone: 061-361177). Expensive.

Limerick Inn – This modern, comfortable motel has 133 rooms, a commendable Continental restaurant, and above average service. Amenities include a new leisure center with a swimming pool and a gym, plus tennis courts and a putting green. Ennis Rd. (phone: 061-51544). Moderate.

MacCloskeys – Encompassing the former mews and wine cellars of Bunratty House, a restored 1804 mansion, this appealing candlelit restaurant is the creation of Gerry and Marie MacCloskey, who describe their menu as "French with an Irish flair." Specialties include Dover sole, rack of lamb, pheasant, and lobster. Bunratty Folk Park, Bunratty (phone: 061-74082). Expensive.

ENNIS

Old Ground – An ivy-clad, centrally located hotel dating from the 17th century. One of its rooms used to be Town Hall and another one the jail. Recently upgraded, it now has 61 rooms with bath, some with antiques and others more modern in decor. There is a warming fireplace in the lobby and the *Poet's Corner* bar. O'Connell St. (phone: 065-28127). Expensive.

COROFIN

Maryse & Giblin – Beside the lake in its own grounds, this restaurant specializes in French and Italian dishes at modest prices. Open Easter to October (phone: 065-27660). Inexpensive.

LAHINCH

Vaughan's Aberdeen Arms – An oasis of comfort, this hostelry has 48 rooms with bath. The bar serves periwinkles rather than peanuts, and the restaurant offers some very fine seafood. Open April to October (phone: 065-81100). Moderate.

BALLYVAUGHAN

Gregan's Castle – Since the spa of Lisdoonvarna has only mediocre hotels, it is advisable to come to this charming, homey, antiques-filled castle at the foot of Corkscrew Hill, overlooking the Burren country and Galway Bay. There are 16 cozy bedrooms, 12 with bath. Open March through October. The restaurant is excellent (phone: 065-77005). Moderate.

KINVARA

Dun Guaire – This castle serves more intimate, but not less enjoyable, medieval banquets than *Bunratty*. The food is Irish and good; the entertainment, "literary" — featuring recitations from the work of famous Irish writers such as Yeats. Call *Shannon Castle Tours* (phone: 061-61788) for reservations.

KILCOLGAN

Moran's Oyster Cottage – A popular stop that vies with *Raftery's* for the "best oysters" designation. What makes it attractive above and beyond the food is its Old World air and grassy setting on the shores of Galway Bay. People love to sit outside or lounge on the grass in the summer months. The Weir (phone: 091-86113). Moderate.

Paddy Burke's Oyster Inn – The winner of the 1977 National Bar Food competition, this internationally famous oyster tavern offers quality bar food along with its Cordon Bleu fare in the restaurant. It has a warm, relaxed atmosphere. Clarinbridge (phone: 091-96107). Moderate.

Raftery's – In the heart of oyster country, you won't find better oysters and seafood generally than in this country pub with restaurant. And it's less expensive than most of its kind. At the junction of Routes N67 and N18 (phone: 091-86175). Moderate.

The Irish West:
Galway to Mayo to Sligo

Galway is a large county divided into two contrasting regions by the expanse of Lough Corrib. To the west, lying between the lake and the Atlantic, is Connemara — a region of scenic grandeur dominated by the rocky mountain range known as the Twelve Bens. Connemara — with a kaleidoscope of mountain and valley, lake and stream, bog and sea — has inspired many painters. They've painted the sparkle of water in deep valleys, tiny white-washed cottages against purple mountains, great castles on the shores of calm and wooded lakes, fields the size of pocket handkerchiefs, and immense skies. The region east of Lough Corrib is more subdued; it is a fertile limestone plain, partially covered with bogs, that extends to the Galway-Roscommon border and the river Shannon.

The people of Connemara and of the Aran Islands, west of Galway Bay, are an ancient people with ancient ways. They still fish the wild seas in their frail boats called *curraghs,* pasture their sheep on the green and golden mountainsides, and speak mostly Irish, the language of the Celts. Galway city lies south of the lake. It is an important tourist center and the gateway to the scenic areas of the county.

GALWAY CITY: On Galway Bay at the mouth of the River Corrib, Galway is a busy seaport, a thriving city with good hotels and stores and a fine university.

The Magnata mentioned by Ptolemy in the 2nd century AD is thought to have been Galway. The city evolved from a fort built in 1142, then was seized by the Anglo-Normans, who converted it into a walled town by the 13th century, a powerful western stronghold. While they isolated themselves from the native Irish population, the Normans engaged in active trading with the rest of the world. Much of their commerce was with Spain and some intermarriage occurred, which accounts for the dark hair and coloring of many Galway people and the Iberian influence in some of the city's architecture.

Since historic Galway is compact, with narrow streets, it is best seen on foot; walking tour maps, with an interesting path through old Galway clearly laid out, are available at the tourist office; Eyre Sq. (phone: 63081). There are several sights that should not be missed. Lynch's Castle (Shop St.), now a bank, is a fine old mansion, and the 14th-century Church of St. Nicholas (Lombard St.) is supposed to be the last place Christopher Columbus worshiped before sailing for America. Near the fish market is the Spanish Arch leading to Spanish Parade, so named because it was the favorite promenade of Spanish merchants. The Salmon Weir Bridge spanning the River Corrib draws many visitors during the spawning season, when hundreds of salmon can be seen stacked on the riverbed waiting to leap upriver to their spawning grounds in Lough Corrib.

Since Galway is the gateway to Gaelic country, it is only fitting that an authentically Irish — that is, Gaelic — entertainment should flourish here. The folk theater, *Taibhdhearc* (pronounced "tive" — rhyming with "dive" — "yark"), operates year-round on Middle Street (phone: 2024). It puts on special variety shows with music and dancing, called *Seoda,* for visitors three times a week in July and August. Galway's other theatrical company, *Druid,* has won international renown.

Several summer events attract big crowds and fill hotels and guesthouses nearby: the 5-day Galway races in July and August; the week-long Galway oyster festival in September; and an annual ceremony called the Blessing of the Sea at the beginning of the herring season. During festival weeks the town is jammed and accommodations are impossible to find; reservations are a must.

West of the city, on Route L100, close to the shore of Galway Bay, is Salthill, a resort suburb of pastel houses and a long boardwalk with a stunning view. Thirty miles out to sea from Galway are the three Aran islands — Inishmore, the largest with 7,635 acres; Inishmaan; and Inisheer. These rugged and barren chips of land immortalized in Robert Flaherty's film *Man of Aran* offer an interesting side trip. You can reach the islands by boat from Galway in 3 hours or by air in 20 minutes. Flight and boat schedules as well as booking information for both transportation and accommodations for an overnight stay on the islands are available at the tourist office.

On the islands you will be transported back in time to a primitive way of life. The language is Irish, and some of the people still wear homespun clothing. You can watch the islanders create soil from sand and seaweed to grow feed for their livestock and meager produce for themselves; fishermen put out to sea in *curraghs* (boats made of narrow strips of wood and tarred canvas no different from those their ancestors used); and the women spin and weave their own clothing.

If you go for the day, you can tour the island in a jaunting car. If you stay overnight, you can wander the rocky paths in splendid isolation or explore the ancient ruins — forts and churches.

Boats from Galway land at Kilronan, the main town on Inishmore. They sometimes call at the other islands as well, but cannot dock there, so if you want to visit you must disembark into a *curragh* on the high seas for transporation ashore. Another way to get to the smaller islands is to take a *curragh* from Kilronan.

En Route from Galway – North on the main road is Sligo, about 86 miles (137 km) away. Our route, designed to cover as much as possible in 1 day and still see the outstanding sights of Connemara, is roughly twice that distance. Good bases for extended exploration are Cashel, at the head of Bertraghboy Bay on the west coast, and Clifden, farther up the coast on the edge of the Atlantic. Both towns have good hotels.

Leave Galway on N59, going northwest a few miles until you come to Moycullen. On the left side of the road is a Connemara marble factory where you can observe marble being worked — shaped, ground, carved, and polished. Both the plant and a shop that sells finished objects are open daily. Continuing on N59, you are actually parallel to Lough Corrib, but you don't see much of the lake until you get to Oughterard, a lovely trout and salmon angling center.

From Oughterard, N59 curves west through Maam Cross and passes the shores of some of Connemara's lovely lakes — Lough Shindilla, Oorid Lough, beautiful Lough Glendalough at Recess, and Lough Derryclare. This stretch of road has some of the best scenery in Connemara, with the lakes on one side and the Twelve Bens looming majestically ahead. The mountains are conical, with precipitous slopes distinctively colored by lichens and mosses.

Beyond Recess, the first turn to the left is L102, marked Carna. Take this road for about 5 miles (8 km) to an unmarked right turn, which leads to Cashel.

CASHEL: This little angling resort is beautifully situated on the waters of Bertraghboy Bay. Cashel (not to be confused with the town in County Tipperary) is little more than the superb *Cashel House* hotel (see *Best en Route*), where French President Charles de Gaulle vacationed in 1969; a post office, a school, and a couple of shops — and that's it. The village is idyllic for the gardens that thrive in this wooded, sheltered bay amid peace and quiet. There is also ample opportunity for outdoor activities, from freshwater and sea fishing to horseback riding and mountain climbing.

The next stop on our route is less than 5 miles (8 km) west on L102.

ROUNDSTONE: A charming fishing village with whitewashed houses overlooking a tranquil harbor, Roundstone is known for its fine beaches, particularly Dog's Bay, a magnet for naturalists and geologists interested in studying foraminiferans — unusual, large-shelled amoeboid protozoa. Towering over the village is isolated Urrisbeg Mountain, which provides a splendid view of the surrounding lake-dotted countryside and the splendid, irregular coastline.

En Route from Roundstone – Continue around the promontory on coastal Route L102, known as "the brandy and soda road" because of the bracing quality of the air. It passes through Ballyconneely on the remote shores of Ballyconneely

Bay, where there is a good golf course. There are glorious beaches everywhere, including the lovely Coral Strand on the shores of Mannin Bay. Deep-sea fishing can be arranged in many villages along the way.

CLIFDEN: The main town of Connemara, Clifden is an ideal center for exploring the glorious scenery of the region. The busy little town nestles on the edge of the Atlantic against a superb backdrop of mountains. The Connemara Pony Show held here each August attracts buyers from throughout the world.

En Route from Clifden – Route N59 leads north to Moyard and then through Letterfrack (visit the new National Park there) to the romantic Kylemore Pass, a beautiful valley dominated by the 19th-century castellated mansion *Kylemore Abbey,* now a girls' school run by Benedictine nuns; they also manage a pottery and restaurant open to visitors.

Beyond Kylemore, the road follows the southern shore of Killary Harbour, a magnificent fjordlike arm of the sea that runs inland between steep mountains rising like enormous walls. Near the head of Killary Bay is the village of Leenane, another angling resort and an excellent center for mountain climbing.

From Leenane, take Route L100 into County Mayo. Go past the Asleagh Falls, heading west on the north shore of Killary Harbour, where the road turns inland and the landscape alternates between dramatic lakefront and brooding mountains. Gold deposits have been discovered in this remotely beautiful valley; it remains to be seen whether mining activities will be allowed to mar its splendor. At Louisburgh, near the coast, the road becomes Route T39, going east to Westport. Along the way is Ireland's "holy mountain," Croagh Patrick, an isolated conical peak rising 2,510 feet from the shore of Clew Bay and one of the most conspicuous features of western Ireland's landscape. On this mountain, St. Patrick is said to have fasted 40 days during Lent in 441, praying that Ireland would never lose the Christian faith. According to tradition, he summoned all venomous creatures in Ireland to the summit and then cast them out. (To this day there are no snakes in Ireland.) Every year, on the last Sunday in July, thousands of pilgrims — many barefooted — climb the mountain. Throughout the day, masses are celebrated in the little chapel at the top.

WESTPORT: The town is charmingly laid out on an arm of Clew Bay in a hollow surrounded by trees and groves. In recent years, it has become a deep-sea fishing center, and the annual June festival draws many fishermen. The main tourist attraction, however, is Westport House, a beautiful estate less than 2 miles (3 km) miles from town. The fine Georgian mansion overlooking the bay is the home of the Marquess of Sligo (open to the public April through mid-October). The house is a treasure of fine paintings, silver, Waterford glass, and exhibits of historical interest. There is also a small zoo on the grounds.

En Route from Westport – There are a number of routing alternatives from Westport. If you want to base yourself for several days in a fairy tale setting in County Mayo, you must stay at *Ashford Castle* (see *Best en Route*) in Cong, roughly halfway between Galway and Westport, on the north shore of Lake Corrib. The 13th-century fortress, the former home of the Guinness family, is now a luxury hotel with elegant rooms and suites overlooking either the lake, the River Cong, or the landscaped gardens that stretch over several hundred acres. It is a sporting paradise — for hunting, fishing, golf, and tennis.

From Westport to Sligo you have a choice of routes. If you're pressed for time, take N60 east 11 miles (18 km) to Castlebar, a small bustling town in the heart of the limestone plain; continue on N5 to Charlestown and join N17 going northeast until you bump into N4, which will take you into Sligo. This route is roughly 53 miles (85 km).

A more scenic alternative from Castlebar is Route L134 north to Pontoon, a picturesque angling resort between Lough Conn and the smaller Lough Cullen, both of which are full of salmon and trout. Cross the isthmus between the lakes and continue north to Ballina, County Mayo's largest town (pop. 6,000), on the salmon-rich River Moy.

From Ballina, take shore Route T40 into County Sligo through Enniscrone and Easkey. Join the main Sligo road, N4, at Ballisodare.

BEST EN ROUTE

The best accommodations in the northwest can be very good (and very expensive), such as the *Great Southern* hotel in Galway, or *Ashford Castle,* probably the best castle hotel in Ireland. But as you head north there will be fewer and fewer hotels worth noting, and fine restaurants are few and far between. The price range for a double room in the area's hotels is $75 and up, expensive; $35 to $65, moderate; below $35, inexpensive. For a meal for two: $50 and up is considered expensive; $35 to $50, moderate; under $35, inexpensive. Prices don't include wine, drinks, or tip.

GALWAY CITY

Ardilaun House – Once the stately home of an aristocratic scion, the building and grounds still retain a patrician aura. It's hidden among trees and shrubs on Taylor's Hill, the best address in town. Salthill (phone: 091-21433). Expensive.

Great Southern – A superior hotel, with 120 of the most comfortable rooms in Galway. Its elegant foyer is the center of social life in the city, perfect for striking up new friendships. A heated swimming pool and sauna are welcome bonuses. Eyre Sq. (phone: 091-64041). Expensive.

Anno Santo – For those who prefer the quiet life, here is a classy, intimate place with a relaxed atmosphere. Specify private bath. Threadneedle Rd., Salthill (phone: 091-22110). Moderate.

Drimcong House – A lovely old country house now serves as the backdrop for one of Ireland's most accomplished restaurants. Like the decor, the food is elegant yet unpretentious, the service efficient yet unobtrusive. Specialties include wild game, spiced beef, salmon, and oysters. It is a dining experience not to be missed. One mile (1.6 km) past Moycullen village on N59 (phone: 091-85115). Expensive.

OUGHTERARD

Sweeney's Oughterard House – This ivy-clad Georgian house offers Old World charm and comfort in a delightful garden setting. Salmon and trout are specialties on the outstanding menu. At the western end of the little town, on the Clifden road (phone: 091-82207). Expensive.

Currarevagh House – An aristocratic home on Lough Corrib, now a peaceful and relaxing guesthouse. The 15 rooms (only 11 with bath) are old-fashioned but comfortable. Open from April to October. Reservations essential. Four miles (6 km) north of town (phone: 091-82313). Moderate.

CASHEL

Ballynahinch Castle – A glamorous castle hotel in a wonderful setting of lake and mountain. It has 20 rooms (all suites), a good wine cellar, and open fires. At Ballinafad (phone: 095-31006). Expensive.

Cashel House – This Georgian country house, where de Gaulle vacationed, has 30 bright, pleasant bedrooms, 27 with bath. Its dining room fare, cooked by the owner, is so superb that even the French president raved. Closed November through February (phone: 095-31001). Expensive.

CLIFDEN

Abbeyglen – The proprietor sees to it that the hotel is warm and friendly and that the cuisine is of a high standard. There are 42 rooms, 40 with bath, and a heated outdoor swimming pool. Closed December through February. Sky Rd. (phone: 095-21201). Moderate.

Crocknaraw House – Six miles (9.6 km) from Clifden is another country house hotel with a quiet atmosphere, 10 rooms (6 with bath), beautiful grounds, and fine food. Closed November through March. Moyard (phone: 095-41068). Moderate.

Rockglen Manor – Once a shooting lodge, now a small, elegant hotel (30 rooms) with a reputation for fine food (phone: 095-21035). Moderate.

Renvyle House – Elegant and convivial, rambling and gracious, this paneled haven, once the home of writer St. John Gogarty, is perched on the edge of the Atlantic shore. Log fires add extra comfort, and manager Hugh Coyle might even sing to you in the evening. Closed January and February. 10 miles north of town, turn left at Tully Cross (phone: 095-43511). Expensive to moderate.

WESTPORT

Newport House – If you go out of town 7¾ miles (12.5 km) from Westport, there is a delightful, rambling Georgian mansion set in its own wooded estate. It has everything the town hotels don't have: 21 great rooms and delicious cuisine. Newport (phone: 098-41222). Expensive to moderate.

Westport Ryan – A member of the dependable Ryan chain, in a quiet woodland setting, all rooms have color TV sets and telephones. Video films, tennis courts, and other amenities are available. Louisburgh Road (phone: 098-25811). Moderate.

CONG

Ashford Castle – This 13th-century castle is considered by many to be Ireland's finest castle hotel. Beside Lough Corrib in beautiful grounds, it has 77 rooms and suites with views of the lake or the gardens. The rooms are beautifully appointed, as are the public rooms, with their views over the landscaped gardens. It is a fairy tale castle, splendidly run. The superb cuisine often features the day's catch of fish. It is possible to dine at the castle even if you aren't staying there, but reserve well in advance. On Highway 98A just east of Cong (phone: 092-46003). Expensive.

The North: Sligo to Donegal

The northwest is rugged country. County Sligo is a healthy mix of mountain, lake, and coastal scenery. In the western part, the Ox Mountains form a background to the coastal plain, while north of Sligo town the landscape is dominated by steep, flat-topped limestone hills. The low-lying coast is fringed by sandy beaches and low cliffs.

Sligo is extraordinarily rich in archaeological remains and places associated with the heroes and heroines of the ancient Irish epics and sagas. Inextricably linked to this area and its Celtic tradition is the poet William Butler Yeats. His poems, particularly the early ones, create a haunting picture of ancient Ireland, the Ireland of myth and legend, and you won't regret having his cadences and images in your mind's eye when you come to Sligo.

Donegal, the most northerly county in the Republic, extends along much of the northwest coast. Despite patches of tasteless "modernization," it is one of the wildest, loveliest, and most remote parts of Ireland, with distinctive scenery — a bay-indented coast, great areas of blue and purple mountains, deep wooded glens, and many lakes. All kinds of stone, from cave-riddled limestone to mixtures of igneous rocks, make up the foundation of the land and give the scenery its form and color.

SLIGO TOWN: Although Sligo is northwest Ireland's most important town, its population is only 14,000. It is picturesquely situated on the estuary of the Garravogue River on a wooded plain between Lough Gill and the sea. If the lake, with its scattered islands, is not one of Ireland's loveliest, it is most certainly its most famous, immortalized by one of Yeats's best-known poems, "The Lake Isle of Innisfree." The town itself contains some fine buildings, the most notable being the 13th-century Dominican friary, Sligo Abbey. Although the building was sacked in 1641, the ruins — a nave, choir, and central tower — are magnificent. From June to August, guided walking tours of Sligo leave every day at 11 AM from the tourist office (Temple St.; phone: 071-61201).

Sligo is an excellent angling center for game fish. There are fine beaches close to town at Strandhill and Rosses Point. The latter also has a splendid golf course.

A short tour of Yeats country should certainly include a trip along the shore of Lough Gill. Three-hour boat tours leave from Doorly Park (Riverside Quay).

Another site that should not be missed is the archaeologically rich area west of town, bounded by its main natural feature, the Hill of Knocknarea (1,078 feet), on whose summit Ireland's ancient warrior queen Maeve reputedly lies buried beneath an immense cairn. Between Knocknarea and Sligo town is Carrowmore, the "graveyard of the giants," a site containing the greatest concentration of megalithic burial stones in Ireland.

En Route from Sligo – Route N15 goes north through Bundoran and Ballyshannon — wild country scarcely touched by time, where small whitewashed, thatch-roofed cottages huddle together against the fierce Atlantic gales. A few miles from Sligo, the road passes Ben Bulben, known as the "table mountain" for its curious shape. On its slopes, 1,730 feet high, the great warrior and ill-starred lover of Irish myth — Diarmuid — met his death; and at its base is buried Yeats, who celebrated Diarmuid's exploits in poetry. Yeats's grave by the little Protestant church in Drumcliffe lies exactly as he had willed it in his 1938 poem "Under Ben Bulben." The tombstone bears the poem's famous last stanza: "Cast a cold eye/On life, on death/Horseman, pass by!"

Farther along the coast is Bundoran in County Donegal, a popular resort on the south shore of Donegal Bay. Bundoran has a fine bathing beach with a promenade, excellent freshwater and sea fishing, and a championship golf course. It also has one of the best views in the area: the Sligo-Leitrim Mountains to the south, the Donegal hills to the north, and, along the beach, a range of cliffs carved into fantastic shapes by the waves.

A few miles up the coast is the lively hilly town of Ballyshannon, on the banks of the River Erne, reputedly the oldest settlement in Ireland. According to tradition, Parthalon, a Scythian, settled on the islet Inis Saimer in the Erne estuary at Ballyshannon in 1500 BC.

A short detour along L24 from Ballyshannon leads to one of Donegal's most spectacular bathing and surfing beaches, a 3-mile-long strand surrounded by gentle hills at Rossnowlagh. Return to N15 to continue to Donegal town.

DONEGAL TOWN: This thriving market town at the head of Donegal Bay and the mouth of the River Eske is an excellent touring center because of its location where the main roads from Derry, West Donegal, and Sligo converge. *Magees,* which manufactures the celebrated Donegal tweed, is in the town, and its mills are open to the public. Visitors can watch the distinctive technique of close weaving and the use of the plant dyes that produce the tweeds' famous heather tones. The retail store is on the Diamond, the central square; the factory is on Milltown (phone: Donegal 5). The imposing ruin of 16th-century Donegal Castle stands on the bank of the River Eske near the Diamond. South of the town are the remains of the 15th-century Donegal Abbey.

En Route from Donegal – Take Route N56 west to Killybegs, one of Ireland's most important fishing ports on a fine natural harbor. Killybegs is noted also for the greatly valued Donegal carpets. These carpets are hand-knotted in a fine flat weave. They are made to order, often with special patterns, for important public places; the White House, Buckingham Palace, and Dublin Castle all have Donegal carpets in their ceremonial rooms. The craft of hand knotting in pattern goes back to 5th-century Persia. Visitors can watch this old process today in the Killybegs plant, Donegal Carpets Ltd. (phone: Killybegs 21).

From Killybegs, continue on T72A west to Carrick, a good starting place for the ascent of Slieve League (1,972 feet) and for exploring the magnificent cliff scenery of the adjoining coast. In Carrick, make a 2-mile (3.2-km) detour south to Teelin. From here, a mountain track leads over Carrigan Head to the secluded Lough O'Mulligan and the sheer cliffs of Bunglass, which rise out of the water to a height of 1,024 feet. The view from the point, named Amharc Mor ("the great view"), lives up to its name: It is among the most magnificent in Donegal. Experienced climbers can go farther along the cliff edge to One Man's Pass, a narrow ledge with a precipice of more than 1,800 feet on one side, dropping sheer down to the sea, and on the other an almost equally precipitous escarpment falling down to a lonely mountain lake. From there it is not far to the summit of Slieve League, at 1,972 feet the highest maritime cliff in Europe, against whose base the Atlantic hurls powerful crashing waves. The path along the mountaintop is very rough and dangerous.

Retrace your steps from Teelin to Carrick and continue west on T72A to Glencolumbkille.

GLENCOLUMBKILLE: In the heart of the Irish-speaking area of South Donegal, this glen runs into the hills from Glen Bay. Many houses dot its slopes in surroundings at once peaceful and strikingly picturesque. On the north side rises the cliff of Glen Head. The coast has splendid rock scenery and there is a beautiful beach, and it is a popular family vacation spot. Glencolumbkille is rich in monuments dating from pre-Christian times as far back as 5,000 years ago.

Adjacent to the holiday village is a folk village re-creation of cottages representing different periods of Irish life.

En Route from Glencolumbkille – An unclassified road leads to Ardara. This road rises to spectacular Glengesh Pass at 900 feet, then plunges in a steep descent to the valley below. Ardara, in a pretty valley at the mouth of the River Owentocher and Loughros More Bay, is another important center for the manufacture of Donegal homespun tweeds. Route N56 leads north to the Gaelic districts of Dungloe and Gweedore. In Gweedore, make a left turn along L82 until you meet T72, which will take you to Bloody Foreland, the cliff that takes its name from the warm, ruddy color of its rock in the setting sun.

Route T72 curls eastward along the coast to Gortahork, near Ballyness Bay. For the traveler who wants to spend several days in the area, the town of Gortahork, with *McFadden's* hotel and fine restaurant (see *Best en Route*), is a good center for touring the north — to Melmore Head, Horn Head, Fanad Head, and the Inishowen Peninsula with Malin Head, the northernmost point in Ireland. This northland of the Republic consists of spectacular peninsulas ringed by misty, craggy, windswept cliffs rising straight from the water, with dramatic views of the boundless Atlantic Ocean broken by numerous islands and headlands.

An unclassified mountain road will bring you to Glenveagh National Park, which is not to be missed. It has a spectacular lake situated between rugged mountains, with a romantic castle, deer herds, and superb formal gardens which gradually merge with the wild mountainsides. An interesting art gallery is nearby. Open Easter to October.

You can then join the N56 to Letterkenny, the principal town of County Donegal, which overlooks Lough Swilly where the River Swilly empties into the lake. From here there is a selection of routes across the interior of the county to the west coast, all of them passing through superb mountain scenery. Route N56 descends through the twin towns of Stranorlar, where it joins N15, and Balleybofey through the wild and lonely Barnesmore Gap back to Donegal town.

Donegal town is 138 miles (222 km) from Dublin through the inland counties and 176 miles (283 km) from Shannon Airport.

BEST EN ROUTE

Because the north country has spectacular vistas, so do many of the hotels (the vistas are often better than the accommodations themselves). But the north has come a long way, and things are getting better all the time. Still, because hotels and restaurants are rather isolated and some are fairly small, it is necessary to make reservations. Expect to pay $55 and up for a double room in the expensive range; $30 to $45 in the hotels we list as moderate; under $30 in the inexpensive category. For meals, $45 for two is expensive; $15 to $20, moderate; under $15, inexpensive. Prices don't include wine, drinks, or tip.

SLIGO

Ballincar House – Manager Helen O'Brien will make you feel welcome and well cared for in this gracious, small hotel halfway between Sligo town and the Sea at Rosses Point. She is particularly proud of the fish menu, which is based on the day's catch. Rosses Point (phone: 071-45316). Expensive to moderate.

Sligo Park – A reasonably good modern hotel with 60 comfortable rooms, all with phone, TV set, bath, and shower. It's hidden among trees, surrounded by an expanse of green pasture. Pearse Rd. (phone: 071-60291). Moderate.

ROSSNOWLAGH

Sand House – Another spectacular beachside setting marks this hotel. Of its 40 rooms (all with bath), many overlook the sea. The public rooms are elegantly furnished. The entire place exudes a feeling of peaceful rest. The dining room is good, and golf course adjoins the hotel. This is surfing territory, and surfboards are available at the hotel (phone: 072-51777). Moderate.

DONEGAL TOWN

Hyland Central – An outstanding first class hotel, with a welcoming, courteous staff that makes guests feel at home. The tastefully furnished rooms, some of which overlook the River Eske, come with TV set, radio, and phone. The best and most versatile range of cuisine in town — Donegal mountain lamb to Lough Eske salmon and trout — is available at the restaurant. The Diamond (phone: 073-21027). Moderate.

Abbey – A very well run hostelry with 40 rooms, though not all with bath or shower.

Excellent service and fine food. The Diamond (phone: 073-21014). Moderate to inexpensive.

GLENCOLUMBKILLE

Glenbay – An informal, warmhearted place with a fine view over the Atlantic. The dining room has its ups and downs. Overall, however, the food is good. The site is beautiful, about 1½ miles (2.4 km) southwest of Glencolumbkille in Malinmore (phone: 073-30003). Inexpensive.

GORTAHORK

McFaddens – If a hotel can ever be described as sociable, this is it. There are 35 rooms (7 with bath). It has a good reputation for food. Main St., Gortahork (phone: 074-35267). Moderate.

Port-na-Blagh – In another fine location on a cliff overlooking Sheep Haven Bay, this is called a welcoming hotel for its friendliness. It has 58 comfortable rooms, 29 with bath. The seafood is particularly good. Port-na-Blagh (phone: 074-36129). Moderate.

Italy

Italy has played a prime role in forming Western European culture, but paradoxically, the modern nation of Italy, established in 1870, is still in the process of coming into its own. The dual nature of its history is both a burden and a blessing. As Italy experiences the growing pains of a young industrial power, its progress is undermined by political turbulence and strife. And always there is its history to contend with. Not since the glorious age of Rome, when the city was the core of a world empire, has Italy experienced such peace and prosperity. And not since the Renaissance have its artistic and cultural achievements attained such great heights.

This heritage is one of which the Italians are justly proud. The brightest jewels of the Renaissance still glow in Italy — the Foundling Hospital by Brunelleschi in Florence that revolutionized architectural design; the anatomically accurate portrayal of the human form in works by Leonardo da Vinci; Raphael's lifelike Madonnas; and Michelangelo's monumental Sistine Chapel ceilings in Rome.

This rich heritage is one of the major forces unifying the Italian people. Italians take pride in the national treasure of their cultural legacy. This, their common language, and their religion (97% of all Italians are Roman Catholics) are what Italians share, whether they come from Milan, Rome, or Palermo.

Italy's boot-shaped peninsula covers 116,318 miles, stretching from the mainland of southern Europe 745 miles into the seas of the Mediterranean, with 5,280 miles of coast. The country has a confusing maze of borders — France on the northwest, Switzerland and Austria to the north, Yugoslavia to the northeast, the Ligurian Sea to the northwest, the Tyrrhenian Sea to the west, the Ionian Sea to the southeast, and the Adriatic Sea on the east. This country of coasts and water is strung out on a frame of mountains: the highest peaks are in the Alps of the north — Mont Blanc at 15,771 feet and the Matterhorn at 15,205 feet; but along the spine of country run the Apennines, a rocky backbone that goes the entire length of the Peninsula. The climate varies with the topography. Along the seacoast, winters are temperate and summers are hot. In the mountains, summer days are warm, nights cool, and winters cold and snowy.

As the climate varies with topography, so do the economics. The south — rocky, devoted to sheepherding and olive growing — is ravished by poverty. The north, comprising a vast plain drained by the Po River, is far richer, with great industrial centers, such as Milan, Genoa, and Turin, and agricultural areas devoted to rice, wheat, and especially grapes, which find their way into a variety of fine Italian wines.

Italy is the home of some 56 million people, 92% of whom live in its cities. Throughout history, Italians have been urban animals, viewing cities as centers of culture and civilization and settling them with great energy and ingenuity. Even agricultural workers tend to live in cities or towns, preferring to travel long distances to the fields rather than live in them. Some 3 million people live in Rome, the capital and Italy's major cultural and historical center. In Rome is Vatican City, an independent enclave in which the pope is sovereign. Other major cities are Florence, Milan, Turin, Venice, Genoa, Naples, and Palermo, Sicily. Ethnic and linguistic minorities comprise less than 5% of Italy's population. Of these, the major groups live in border regions: Slovenes in Friuli-Venezia Giulia, German speakers in Trentino-Alto Adige, and French speakers in Valle d'Aosta. Some inhabitants of Calabria and Sicily speak Greek and Albanian dialects.

Some of these different groups are actually descended from people who inhabited the country during Italy's long and complicated history. Recorded civilization in Italy dates back to around 2000 BC, when the peninsula was settled by fair, blue-eyed Ligurians, ancestors of the Latins. Around the 9th century BC, the Greeks sailed to Italian shores, and Italy became a setting for the myth of Ulysses and other legends. The Greeks settled southern Italy and Sicily during the 8th century BC, establishing colonies of city-states known as Magna Graecia. The Greek civilization thrived in the 6th and 5th centuries BC, declining in the 4th century BC. While the Greeks were colonizing the south, the Etruscans, a highly artistic civilization from Asia Minor, settled central Italy.

In the 3rd century BC, the Romans conquered Italy and established a great empire from Rome. Julius Caesar reigned during the 1st century BC; his conquest of France — Gaul — made Rome supreme over much of the barbaric as well as the civilized world. Under Caesar, Roman culture flourished, enriched by an infusion of Greek elements. After Caesar's assassination, his nephew Octavian (later known as Augustus) succeeded him and instituted the Pax Romana, 200 years of peace when the Roman Empire was as powerful as it would ever be. At the end of the 2nd century AD, the bishop of Rome gained supremacy as the head of the new Christian religion.

And yet Rome declined in the years following the Pax Romana, and Italy was torn apart by invading groups. For a brief period it was reunited when Charlemagne was named Holy Roman Emperor in 800, but the ensuing century saw the country disintegrate into conflicting groups seeking control of provincial kingdoms. Italy was ravaged by battles between different city-states until Napoleon came to power in the early 19th century.

Despite this internal strife, Italian civilization and culture reached its peak during the Renaissance, in the 15th and 16th centuries. The independent city-states established a delicate balance of power, and rich patrons such as the Medici family of Florence supported the arts. The humanistic secular atmosphere encouraged worldly life and human endeavor. This age spawned some of the greatest artists of Western civilization — Leonardo da Vinci, a genius in many fields, the personification of the Renaissance man (1452–1519); Michelangelo (1475–1564); Raphael (1483–1564); and the architect Brunelleschi (1377–1466).

Napoleon annexed large sections of Italy, including Rome, in the early 19th century. A long tradition of disunity and foreign domination brought about the Risorgimento, the movement for political unity in Italy, that gathered broad support under the popular leader Giuseppe Garibaldi. Italy was finally united under King Victor Emmanuel II in 1870.

The country was ruled as a monarchy and joined the Allies in World War I. Benito Mussolini rose to power during the early 1920s and ushered in one of the darkest periods in Italy's history. Il Duce, a leader of the National Fascist party, promised a vague program of order at home and greater prestige abroad, though what he actually delivered was a totalitarian state controlled by the militia. Mussolini formed an alliance with Hitler and fought against the Allies during World War II. Under his rule, the National Racial Code was implemented, and more than 10,000 Italian Jews were killed in Nazi concentration camps. The Italian Resistance Movement fought Mussolini and the Nazis, but their reprisals took a heavy toll on Italy. Large parts of the country were in ruins, 400,000 people were killed, hundreds of thousands were left homeless, and the economy was sharply disrupted. Mussolini was captured by partisans in 1945 and executed.

The experience of World War II and fascism deeply scarred Italy. Though the country was declared a republic in 1946, during the postwar era Italy has been seriously divided by extreme political differences. Dozens of governments have risen and fallen since the war. The leading parties are the centrist Christian Democrats and the Italian Communist Party. Their diametrical opposition to one another contributes to the rampant factionalization of Italian politics, in which the rising socialists — more akin to the Social Democrats in other countries — have managed to grow progressively as the major parties see their strength being whittled away — all owing to the changing face of Italian society. Neither party has managed to gain a clear majority. In the most recent national election the Christian Democrats won by a slim margin, and currently govern in coalition with other centrist and center-left parties.

From the early 1970s to 1982, terrorist acts aimed at political leaders and wealthy industrialists plagued the country, along with strikes and double-digit inflation. Today, political violence has diminished, but Italy still has many problems. In part, these are caused by the staggering socioeconomic discrepancy between the rich industrial north and the poorer, rural south. Until the past decade, this gap caused great internal migrations from south to north and village to city. At present, the biggest economic problems are widespread unemployment among Italian youth and ongoing inflation, caused by massive government deficits and dependence on dollar-expensive imported raw materials. Though Italy is ranked as the fifth largest industrial power of the non-Communist world, its economy is still underdeveloped in many respects, and promises of vital institutional reform drag on from one government to the next as the country's balance of payments deficit continues to grow. Structural imbalances, an inefficient administrative system, and political fragmentation have made it difficult to proceed with economic and social reforms.

Family ties are particularly strong in Italy. Although divorce was introduced in 1970, so far relatively few Italians have made use of it, although separation, seen as a compromise rather than a means to an end, has now firmly taken hold. It is common for offspring to live at home until they marry, and often married couples unable to find affordable housing will remain with one set of parents. Feminism has made some minor inroads, but the number of women who pursue careers is still lower than in most other Western countries. While children are highly valued, economic considerations, birth control availability, and an extremely liberal abortion law have led to a declining birth rate. Nevertheless, enduring traditions and widespread frustration with a malfunctioning government have strengthened the family as the root of Italian society.

Italians, especially in the North, love opera, and all seem to be passionate soccer fans and avid filmgoers, although the cinema has been dealt a blow by television, where a plethora of channels fight for broadcast space. Neorealism in cinema, which has had a profound influence on contemporary film, was developed in Italy. This movement aimed to portray real life in films by setting them in the streets with amateur casts. Luchino Visconti's *Ossessione,* Vittorio de Sica's *Bicycle Thief,* and Roberto Rossellini's *Open City* exemplify this movement. In the 1960s and '70s, Italian cinema moved away from neorealism. The films of Federico Fellini became increasingly surreal, and Michelangelo Antonioni explored existentialist themes. A younger generation led by Bernardo Bertolucci produced films of social and political comment. In recent years, Italian cinema has been dominated by the genre known as "commedia all'italiana," light comedies with an ironic, bittersweet edge.

The area in which Italian differences shine most brightly is food. The concept that most people carry of Italian food is hopelessly limited. Italy is made up of 20 different regions, each with its own distinct cuisine. The best way to enjoy the delights of Italy's regions is to eat your way through them, sticking to regional specialties and experimenting with new dishes rather than going for a known quantity. In Piedmont, for example, Italy's mountainous northwest corner, the cuisine has been deeply influenced by France and Switzerland. Specialties are exquisite white truffles and *grissini,* crisp breadsticks, as well as the Turin cheese, *fontina,* that is used in a fondue-like dish called *fonduta.* In late summer and early fall a favorite Piedmont dish is the huge, fresh mushroom called *porcini;* for dessert have *zabaione,* the rich whipped pudding made of egg yolks, sugar, and Marsala wine.

Milan, the capital of the Lombardy region, sits on a vast marshy plain north of the Po River better suited to rice and cattle than to wheat and olive trees. Thus rice and butter, rather than pasta and oil, are the basis of Lombardy cuisine. Its most famous dishes are *cotoletta alla milanese,* a thin scaloppine of fine Lombardy veal lightly breaded, and *risotto alla milanese.* A favorite dessert is *panettone,* a brioche-like cake stuffed with fruit. Another good dessert is a pear with Gorgonzola cheese.

Tuscany cuisine centers around finely grilled and spitted meats in such dishes as *bistecca alla fiorentina, capretto* (suckling kid), and *cinghiale* (boar). Rich soups are popular, such as the *zuppa di verdure* (vegetable soup) and *acquacotta* (literally, "cooked water," a mixture of bread, broth, pasta, vegetables, eggs, and cheese so thick that it can be eaten with a fork).

Sicilian cuisine is based on seafood, and tuna, sardines, mullet, octopus, porgy, and salt cod are likely to turn up at any meal. Sicily is the home of *cannelloni,* however, the wonderful squares of noodles rolled into tubes and filled with ricotta cheese and ground meat that are now popular worldwide. And delicious salads, using much eggplant, are ubiquitous. *Caponata* is a cold salad that incorporates onions, olives, celery, and capers; *melanzane alla trapanese* is fried eggplant seasoned with rosemary, tomato puree, and garlic.

Italians eat their main meal in the afternoon around 1 PM. The meal follows a traditional pattern; however, most menus are à la carte, so you can order as much or as little as you want. The opening course is generally antipasto, a mixed platter of cold hors d'oeuvres — cooked vegetables, salami, and prosciutto — or another appetizer. Soup or pasta follows and you can eat pasta in any of its various forms — macaroni (in soup or on a plate), spaghetti, lasagna, or vegetable soup. The entrée consists of meat — veal or chicken are best, or fish in coastal areas — accompanied by a green salad or vegetable. Sauces vary widely but tend toward butter and garlic in the north and tomato bases in the south. Drink Italian wines with the main course. The fruit course follows — peaches, apricots, grapes, or figs, depending on the season; the final course is *dolci,* or sweets, anything from rich Italian pastries to *gelato,* ice cream, or *sorbetto,* refreshing ices. Then try some espresso, strong Italian coffee sometimes served with a touch of anisette. Though Italian cuisine is rich in variety, it is usually hearty and tasty. Wherever you are in Italy, it's hard to go wrong.

In the following pages we outline ten driving routes that cover Italy's major areas of interest, from the Alps along the country's northern border with France and Switzerland, the Italian Riviera, to the islands of Sicily and Sardinia in the Tyrrhenian Sea. The routes are by no means comprehensive, but they offer an introduction to the incredible diversity and the awesome beauty of the Italian countryside and the people. The routes are the Lombardy Lake region from Milan to Sirmione and the Italian-Swiss border to the Po Valley; Emilia, through the Po Valley and western Apennine Mountains from Milan to Ferrara; Piedmont and Val d'Aosta from Entreves to Turin through the foot of the Alps; the Italian Riviera; the Dolomites from Bolzano to Trento, passing through the eastern Alps near the Austrian border; rugged, central Tuscany from Florence to Cortona through the Apennine Mountains; Campania on the southwestern coast around Naples and Paestum; Calabria, the southern toe of Italy's boot; and Sicily and Sardinia.

The Lombardy Lakes

The northwestern border of Italy and Switzerland — rent by the jagged peaks of the Alps and laced together again by a healing series of spectacular, deep lakes — has been a play area since the Romans conquered Gaul and Cicero set up a summer house on Lake Como. The Lombardy lakes were originally formed by the same glaciers that cut the peaks and valleys of the nearby Alps into such fine relief, but Lombardy itself is a great deal larger than just its lake area. Below this stitching of lakes spread 9,000 square miles of gradually flattening land, flowing around Milan from the foothills of the Alps to the green fertile plains of the Po River valley.

Once the center of Roman Gaul, Lombardy suffered a long and turbulent history, during which it was inexorably caught between the forces of northern and southern Europe. Buffeted between one ruling power and another for centuries, it came under the influence of the German Empire, the bishops of Milan, and Venice, France, and Austria. During the Middle Ages, Lombardy was controlled by powerful families, often cultured and worldly and almost always unprincipled and ruthless. As a result the Lombardy heritage includes as much German and French medieval art and architecture as home-grown bloodshed and mayhem.

The dynasties lost their power to Venice in the 15th century, only 100 years before a French invasion swept Lombardy into the Austrian Habsburg empire. It joined the new Italian kingdom in 1860. Much of this history is revealed in the accumulation of architecture around the lakes, from Roman ruins to elegant 18th-century villas. The area's warm climate and fertile soil are responsible for the wide variety of luxuriant Mediterranean flowers, cypress trees, and other flora.

Since Milan is the most central Lombardian city, easily accessible to major highways, it is here that the 5-day route begins. The trip first takes you north toward Lake Maggiore and magnificent views of the distant Alps, along lakeside roads to Lake Lugano and a brief visit to the Swiss town of Lugano. Heading back toward Italian Lombardy again, the route travels down to Lake Como, then cuts across the plains and valleys, past several resort towns, in a southeastern direction. On the last segment of the trip, more time is spent in the cities themselves. Bergamo, the two-tiered city; Brescia, a commercial center; and Garda, site of Italy's largest lake, are some of the stops made on the final portion of the trip.

MILAN: For a detailed report on Milan, and its hotels and restaurants, see *Milan,* THE CITIES.

En Route from Milan – Pass the industrial suburbs of Lainate and Saronno, where the flat plains around the city begin to give way to mountainous terrain. In the Valley of Olona, surrounded by mountain peaks, lies the town of Castiglione Olona. The art treasures of Olona are the work of the medieval Cardinal Branda Castiglione, who embellished his hometown with Renaissance houses for himself and his relatives and his cathedral with a famous series of frescoes by Renaissance artist Masolino de Panicale. See the Castiglione Mansion and its small church in the main square.

VARESE: This is now a center of Italy's shoe industry, but its pleasant hillside surroundings have made it popular as a summer resort as well. From the gardens of the 18th-century Palazzo Comune (City Hall) you get a fine view of the distant Alps, and at nearby Villa Mirabella there is a good museum of prehistoric finds from the lake district.

LAVENO: Commanding an outstanding view of Lake Maggiore, the second largest and what some regard as the most beautiful of the Italian lakes, Laveno is now known primarily for its ceramic industry.

From here take a steamer over to the famous lakeside town and resort of Stresa on the Piedmontese side of the lake, 27 miles (34.5 km) away.

STRESA: On the edge of the Pallanza Bay, Stresa abounds in 18th-century villas and gardens, many of them now luxurious hotels. Among the villas worth noting are Villa Ducale, the Villa Pallavicini, and the Villa Vignola.

En Route from Stresa – Continue north on the lakeside road to Luino, a small industrial town and resort near the mouth of the Tresa River, which runs into the lake. At Ponte Tresa you are on the tip of Lake Lugano, more than half of which is in Italian-speaking Switzerland. Lake Lugano is wilder than Lake Maggiore, with a more exotic beauty. From Ponte Tresa, itself half Swiss, follow the lakeside frontier to Porto Ceresio for the 70-minute ferry ride to Lugano, Switzerland.

LUGANO (Switzerland): Lugano was ceded to the Swiss by Milan in the early 16th century and has remained so despite Italy's attempts to regain it in 1798. Lugano seems modern until you reach the heart of the old city, which is entirely Italian. On Via Cattedrale is the 16th-century cathedral, with some excellent early frescoes and a Renaissance tabernacle. In the old city, right on the lake, is Villa Favorite, one of the finest private art collections in the world, collected by Baron Heinrich Thyssen-Bornemisza, with works from the 16th through the 18th century and some later French Impressionists.

The boat between Lugano and Porto Ceresio stops at Campione d'Italia, a tiny medieval town that, although geographically in Swiss territory, is an enclave answering to Rome. The birthplace of artists and sculptors since the early Middle Ages, it now has one of Italy's four legal casinos.

The road south backtracks to Varese, from which Route 342 leads to Como on beautiful Lake Como.

COMO: Originally settled by the Romans, this ancient city on the southern tip of Lake Como has for centuries been the center of Italian silk manufacturing. Of greater interest to the visitor is the wealth of its architecture, much of which is clustered around the Piazza del Duomo, where the lovely Pretorian palace known as Il Broletto (1215) stands next to the Palazzo del Comune of the same period and the Duomo, begun in Renaissance Gothic style in 1396 and finished by baroque artists in 1750. Along Via Vittorio Emanuele visit the fine Romanesque church of San Fedele.

CERNOBBIO: This lakeside resort, right next to Como, is dominated by the magnificent 16th-century *Villa D'Este,* once the home of the powerful Dukes of Ferrara, now a hotel. The villa stands near a beautiful park on the shores of Lake Como (see *Best en Route*).

En Route from Cernobbio – Before you leave the western end of Lake Como, you can drive around the lake to Varenna or take a steamer directly to Bellagio, leading to the southbound portion of the route. The extra drive of approximately 48 miles (78 km) around the lake is well worth the trip.

GRAVEDONA: This is the principal town on Lake Como's northern shore and one of the three cities that remained independent from the Middle Ages to the late 16th century. In the town center stands the massive square Palazzo Gallio and the small 12th-century church of Santa Maria del Tiglio.

BELLAGIO: The town of Bellagio, sometimes called the Pearl of the Lake, sits at the point where the main part of Lake Como intersects with the leg commonly called Lake Lecco. The narrow streets and ancient buildings make for a lovely, relatively easy walk, full of every sort of diversion. There's a bathing beach beside the Villa Serbelloni, in the middle of town, and the lovely gardens at the Villa Melzi are worth a visit — especially for the marvelous view across the lake toward Tremezzo.

LECCO: The western branch of Lake Como is also known as Lake Lecco, named for this industrial town at its southern tip. Lecco is also the scene of the famous novel *I Promessi Sposi,* by Alessandro Manzoni, whose 18th-century villa still stands in the area.

BERGAMO: The two-tiered city of Bergamo, straddling a hill overlooking the Lombardy plain, is divided into a modern, busy lower center and a silent, medieval upper one. The Lower City, Città Bassa, was almost entirely built in 1924 by the main architect of the Fascist period, Piacentini. Visit the Palazzo dell'Accademia Carrara, with a worthwhile collection of Italian furniture of the 16th and 17th centuries. It also has a good collection of Rubens, Van Dyck, and Clouet.

The Upper City, Città Alta, is reached by a funicular that drops its passengers in Piazza Mercato delle Scarpe, inside the medieval walls of the old city. Bergamo was originally an Etruscan city; then it became a Roman town, a Lombard duchy, and finally part of first the Venetian and then the Austrian dynasties. At the heart of the Città Alta is the Piazza Vecchia amid a breathtaking collection of medieval buildings including the severe 12th-century Palazzo della Ragione and its massive tower. Through the archways of the palace you can see the cathedral square, with the 15th-century Cappella Colleoni, whose façade is a striking composition of colored marbles and delicate carving. The Romanesque basilica Santa Maria Maggiore, to which the chapel is attached, was begun in the 12th century. Also on the square is the small 14th-century baptistry (which was once inside the basilica) and the cathedral, which has a 19th-century façade. Make your way back to Piazza Mercato delle Scarpe, from which Via Rocca leads off to the medieval lookout post, La Rocca, in the middle of a spacious park. From its height you will have a glorious view of the surrounding Bergamasque valleys.

En Route from Bergamo – Cross the industrial Seriana Valley via the tiny sulfur bath resort of Trescore Balneario and the neighboring spa of Gaverina. Stop in the principal resort of Lovere when you reach Lake d'Iseo, one of the smallest and least developed of the Lombardian lakes. The road from Lovere to Sornico is the most scenic along the lake's western bank.

BRESCIA: Badly bombed during World War II, this commercial and industrial city on Lake d'Iseo has been largely restored so that its Renaissance and medieval piazza and buildings are visible once again. Its central Piazza della Vittoria is one of the few comparatively modern constructions. Also visit the original Roman center of the city and the Capitoline Temple, which dates to AD 72 and houses examples of Roman art.

From Brescia take Route 45B through Rezzato and Tormini to Lake Garda.

LAKE GARDA: This is the largest and most spectacular of the Italian lakes. Its northern shores are surrounded by wild mountain scenery while the broader southern part of the lake lies in lower, softer green countryside. Most famous of its lakeside resorts is Gardone Riviera, where the Fascist poet Gabriele D'Annunzio lived and died at the *Vittoriale degli Italiani,* a curious complex of memorials, gardens, and memorabilia, all collected by D'Annunzio himself and left as a museum for future generations.

BEST EN ROUTE

Endearing, gracious, and elegant hotels and inns are found throughout the Lombardy lakes region. Fine restaurants that serve excellent, classic European country cooking are also a hallmark of the area. Expect to pay $100 or more per night for a double room at those hotels we've categorized as expensive; between $65 and $95 at hotels in the moderate category; under $60, inexpensive. Expect to pay $70 or more for a meal for two at expensive restaurants; between $50 and $60 at restaurants in the moderate category; under $50, inexpensive. Prices do not include drinks, wine, or tip.

VARESE

Lago Maggiore – This well-run restaurant serves some of the finest examples of Lombardian cuisine — fillet steaks with cream truffles, roast meat, and game. The selection of wines is excellent. Closed Sundays, Mondays for lunch, and July. 19 Via Carrobbio (phone: 231183). Expensive.

Il Sole – One of the best restaurants in all of Lombardy, it offers a beautiful lakeside view. Another plus is that it has its own beach facilities. Closed Mondays and January. About 14 miles (27 km) north of Varese in Ranco. Piazzo Venezia (phone: 969607). Expensive.

STRESA (PIEDMONT)

Grand Hôtel et des Iles Borromées – This turreted baroque villa is a quintessential luxury hotel. Owned by the CIGA hotel chain, its well-furnished, spacious rooms all have private baths. It has a private beach on Lake Maggiore, an incomparable view, superb gardens, swimming pool, and restaurant. 67 Lungolago Umberto (phone: 30431). Expensive.

L'Emiliano – The culinary repertoire — fillet steaks with truffles, grilled fish, perfectly cooked vegetables, mushrooms in season, and a select choice of wines — is among the best in town. Closed Tuesdays and from mid-November to mid-December. 1 Corso Italia (phone: 31396). Expensive.

Regina Palace – Grand, elegant lakeside hotel with breathtaking gardens, fitness center, tennis, squash, and *Charleston* restaurant for fine dining (phone: 30171). Expensive.

Villa Aminta – Though less extravagant, this has tasteful gardens, a private beach, tennis courts, and a good restaurant. Closed from November through mid-March. 123 Via Nazionale del Sempione (phone: 32444). Expensive to moderate.

Du Park e Villa Pineta – This secluded hotel stands in a lovely garden. Closed October through March. 1 Via Gignous (phone: 30335). Inexpensive.

LUGANO (SWITZERLAND)

Bellevue au Lac – A spacious hotel in a garden setting overlooking Lake Lugano and the surrounding mountains, it has a swimming pool, car park, and a good restaurant. Closed from mid-October to mid-March. 10 Riva Caccia (phone: 543333). Expensive.

De la Paix – This hotel has a heated swimming pool, 3 restaurants, and enviable views of the lakes and mountains. Closed in January. 18 Via Cattori (phone: 542331). Expensive.

Villa Principe Leopoldi – The former residence of royalty, now a charming, sophisticated retreat with tennis, gym, sauna, swimming pool, tearoom, piano bar, and restaurant. All 24 spacious suites are elegantly appointed and have views of Lake Lugano. 5 Via Montalbano (phone: 558855). Expensive.

Bianchi – A traditional and friendly top-quality restaurant in old Lugano. Specialties include cold antipasto, veal dishes, and truffles. 3 Via Pessina (phone: 228479). Expensive to moderate.

CERNOBBIO

Villa d'Este Hotel & Sporting Club – In a magnificent modernized 16th-century villa at a lakeside park, it has a swimming pool, tennis courts, a golf course nearby, and a very good restaurant. Closed Mondays and winters. 40 Via Regina (phone: 511471). Expensive.

Terzo Crotto – This is one of the best restaurants on Lake Como for Northern cuisine — a wide variety of soups, excellent meats, fresh mushrooms, truffles, wild strawberries, and blueberries in their respective seasons. Also a small hotel. Closed Thursdays and November. 21 Via Volta (phone: 512304). Moderate.

COMACINA ISLAND

Locanda dell'Isola Comacina – On the only sizable island in Lake Como, at the end of a winding, narrow path, this place features a menu that hasn't changed in many years. And why should it, when the feast served up includes "Smuggler's Trout" (perfectly grilled fish splashed with olive oil), pressed roast chicken, a huge antipasto (the marinated carrots are especially delicious), and a dessert of home-made vanilla ice cream atop fresh orange slices, doused in banana liqueur. Comacina Island, Lake Como (phone: 55083). Expensive.

MENAGGIO

Grand Hotel Victoria – Delightful Belle Epoque hotel with 50 recently refurbished rooms, many of which overlook the lake. Menaggio (phone: 32003). Expensive.

BERGAMO

Excelsior San Marco – This first class hotel has 150 rooms, all with private bath and air conditioning. There's also an excellent restaurant (closed Sundays). 6 Piazza Repubblica (phone: 232132). Expensive.

La Pergola – A traditionally elegant restaurant in the old part of Bergamo that serves delicious food and has a very good selection of wines. Try the tasty fish ravioli, mushroom soup, and especially the homemade sweets. Closed Sundays and August. 62 Borgo Canale (phone: 223305). Expensive.

La Vendemmia – Exquisitely prepared Bergamasque dishes — smoked goose breast, local salami, and cheese fritters — are served in the garden of this 17th-century house, weather permitting. Closed Mondays. 17 Via Fara (phone: 221141). Expensive.

Taverna del Colleoni – In a 16th-century palace in the old quarter, this place, which was recently taken over by one of Bergamo's great restaurateurs, serves traditional dishes with imaginative variations. *Polenta* (maize pudding) with fried egg and white truffles, fresh mushrooms, truffles, smoked ham, and meat are all delicious. Pasta dishes are light and appetizing. Closed Sundays, Mondays, and August. 7 Piazza Vecchia (phone: 232596). Expensive.

Cappello d'Oro e Del Moro – The restaurant at this unpretentious hotel is excellent. 12 Via Papa Giovanni XXIII (phone: 232503). Moderate.

Emilia

Stretching from the southern end of the flat and fertile Po Valley and the western Apennine Mountains north of Tuscany, Emilia only came into existence as a region in 1860 with the unification of Italy. The name originates from the Roman road, the Via Emilia, which runs in a straight line from Milan to Rimini on the Adriatic coast; it was built by Aemilius Lepidus to connect the Roman Empire with its newly acquired northern European lands. Since that time, the road has been responsible for much of the region's trade development and was an important communication line throughout the various Roman and medieval conflicts that swept through Emilia's cities and countryside. During World War II, it was used by the Allied forces occupying Italy.

Emilia is a small region, but its culture and customs are the product of 20 centuries of densely packed history. Most of its cities — Parma, Bologna, Ferrara — were medieval and Renaissance duchies or principalities and are replete with architectural memorials of long and eventful histories. But it is a rich area to visit for more than its history, for a good part of its cultural distinction is expressed in its cuisine, the richest cooking in Italy. Bologna is known as Bologna the Fat, and for good reason. Emilia is where *tortellini,* those delicious pasta packets filled with meat or cheese, and *tagliatelle,* golden flat egg noodles, are served wrapped in dense *ragù Bolognese,* the traditional meat sauce made with pork, beef, chicken livers, vegetables, butter, and cream. Here is where *mortadella* (the grandfather of American bologna) and salami originated. And here is where Parma, one of Italy's most beautiful cities, inspired delectable Parma ham and world-famous Parmesan cheese.

Although pork is the most popular meat in Emilia, veal is deliciously transformed in Bologna to create *lombatini di vitello* — veal chops wrapped in prosciutto with a cream sauce. The major wines of the region are the frothy Lambrusco and a fruity red called Sangiovese.

It is also a region of geographic contrast — mountainous in the west, where the Apennines shoot down central Italy; flat in the northeast, where a broad expanse of flatlands surrounding the huge Po River cradles some of Italy's best agricultural soil. In the mountains south of Bologna, the Emilian capital, ancient watchtowers still stand atop nearly inaccessible peaks; they were built by medieval warlords to keep constant vigil for enemies approaching in the strife-torn region. These strategic towers were used again by the Allies in the last war.

A logical starting place for a 4-day tour of this region is on the northwestern tip, where the Via Emilia connects Milan to the town of Piacenza. Caught between the Po River and the Apennine foothills, Piacenza is an important trade center. It also offers a first glimpse of the medieval Gothic and Romanesque styles of art and architecture found throughout the cities on this route. Heading south, the other major cities on the route include Parma; Modena, a well-endowed agricultural area as well as an artistic center claiming one of the finest galleries in the country; Bologna, a major hub of commerce and learning, renowned for its ancient university; and Ferrara, a former cultural enclave for artists, writers, and philosophers, now turned toward agriculture and industry.

MILAN: For a detailed report, see *Milan,* THE CITIES.

PIACENZA: The original Roman city is long gone, destroyed by invading barbarian tribes at the dissolution of the Roman Empire, but much of the medieval town that flourished from the 12th century remains, even though Piacenza today is thoroughly modern, caught up in the production of methane gas from the rich fields buried beneath the flatlands of the Po River valley. Wheat, hemp, and maize are traded here in a thriving agricultural market, but the old city, centered around Piazza Cavalli, captures the essence of medieval Emilia as well as any town in the region. Dominated by two statues of medieval rulers belonging to the Farnese family, which held the duchy of Piacenza from the 16th to the 18th century, the piazza is surrounded by the graceful Gothic Palazzo del Comuni, known as Il Gotico, on one side. On the other side stands the 13th-century church of San Francesco, at the beginning of Via Venti Settembre, which ends in front of the Duomo, a rather majestic cathedral in Lombardian-Romanesque style built between the 12th and 13th centuries.

En Route from Piacenza – Travel on the Via Emilia through pleasant green countryside to Salsomaggiore, the second largest spa town in Italy. It has saline waters, which are good for rheumatism, as well as the natural sulfur pools in nearby Tabiano.

PARMA: In the middle of the vast plain south of the Po River, Parma is acclaimed for its architectural beauty and gastronomic delights. It abounds with excellent restaurants, so when exploring, stop in almost any section of town for a satisfying meal. Pork meat cuts in Emilia are generally the most famous in Italy; in Parma, the specialty is prosciutto, which, combined with Parmesan cheese, often garnishes many dishes.

Despite heavy bombing in the last war, Parma still retains much of its splendor as the former capital of the duchy of Farnese. The old center of the town is Piazza Garibaldi, bounded by the governor's palace, clock tower, and the town hall. More spectacular, however, is the group of buildings of the ecclesiastical authorities and their interior frescoes. From the Via del Duomo it is a short walk to Piazza Marconi and the majestic 16th-century church of Madonna dell Steccata, which was damaged by bombs in the last war but admirably restored. Next, visit the *Palazzo della Pilotta,* one of the unfinished buildings begun during the reign of the Dukes of Farnese. It's now a museum, with exhibitions spanning the city's history from prehistoric times to the late Renaissance as well as collections from ancient Egypt and the Far East. Equally interesting is the *National Gallery,* with rooms devoted to Emilian artists, especially the school established in Parma by Correggio, and Italian artists from other regions from the 14th, 15th, and 16th centuries.

MODENA: Originally a Roman colony, this city fell under the control of powerful ducal dynasties in the early Middle Ages, later passing to Austrian dominion. The medieval period proved the strongest influence on Modena's artistic development and today remains the dominant presence in the city's role as a center of art.

For a rich sampling of Gothic and Romanesque design, begin a city tour at the cathedral in the Piazza Grande. Begun in 1099 and finished 3 centuries later, its architecture is mainly early Gothic; inside, frescoes and statues date from the 15th century. Outside the cathedral, notice the tall, graceful Lombardian bell tower known as the Ghirlandina, the city's best-known monument. Going down the Via Emilia, be sure to stop at the *Palazzo dei Musei,* which houses one of Italy's finest art galleries.

BOLOGNA: You would not be a hopeless romantic to see something of the fate of all Italy in the varying fortunes of this city. Built by the Etruscans (who called it Felsina), it was conquered by the Gauls, invaded by the Romans, sacked by northern tribes during the dissolution of the Roman Empire, and finally, in the 12th century, plunged into the interminable internecine warfare of the Guelphs and Ghibillines, who represented no ideology beyond their allegiance to various personalities and vague identification with pro- and antipapal forces. It was not until the Guelphs prevailed in the middle of the 13th century that Bologna came to full flower and the form of the city as it exists today was established — red slate roofs, long arcades, distinctive elliptical domes. During this period the university — the oldest in Europe, founded in 1076 — flourished, and in the 16th century, when the city became associated with several ruling families (of whom the Bentivoglio were the most famous), the city became a center of art, literature, and learning. Today Bologna is a Communist town, the core of the famous industrial Red Belt that crosses Italy from Tuscany through Emilia.

In the center of town is the traffic-free Piazza Maggiore, where three Gothic structures stand within a few steps of one another. The Palazzo Comunale is the most complicated, a group of palaces incorporated into one beautifully proportioned complex. It houses a small but fine municipal art collection of works by some of the finest Renaissance and 18th-century artists. A similar architectural plan, involving seven separate churches of different periods joined together, exists at the church of Santo Stefano complex. This consists of the 11th-century church of the Crucifix, the octagonal church of the Holy Sepulcher (where St. Petronius is buried), and the church of St. Peter and St. Paul. Several other small chapels and churches are housed in this medieval complex as well.

FERRARA: To reach this city, you finally leave the Via Emilia at the Bologna highway junction and head north. Autostrada A15 takes you to new Emilian territory — one of very green countryside dotted with vines and trees. Ferrara itself sits on drained and filled-in marshland. It is now an agricultural and industrial center that once flourished as a commercial and cultural stronghold during the Renaissance. As an independent duchy under the Dukes of Este and their rich courts, it was a haven for some of the most highly talented artists, philosophers, humanists, and writers of the age.

When you arrive, first visit the Castello Estense, a fortress with massive corner towers and a surrounding moat built in the 14th and 15th centuries. Many of the inside rooms are open to the public — some with majestic interiors and frescoed ceilings. The castle chapel and dungeons are open as well. Nearby is the 12th-century Romanesque-Gothic cathedral and marble bell tower facing the 13th-century Palazzo Comunale, which had to be restored in 1924. Along Via Scandiana visit the 14th-century *Palazzo Schifanoia,* which the fabled dukes used for their many amusements. Now a museum, its interior walls have frescoes with scenes from the life of Duke Borso D'Este. A short distance away, in the Via Settembre, stands the unfinished but splendid Renaissance *Palazzo di Ludovico il Moro,* now an archaeological museum full of Etruscan and Roman treasures.

BEST EN ROUTE

In Emilia you'll find some pleasant if not outstanding hotels and some truly splendid restaurants. Expect to pay $100 or more per night for a double room at those hotels categorized as expensive; between $60 and $95 at hotels in the moderate category; under $60, inexpensive. Expect to pay $70 or more for a meal for two at those restaurants we've classified as expensive; between $40 and $60 at restaurants in the moderate category; under $40, inexpensive. Prices do not include drinks or tip.

PARMA

Palace Hotel Maria Luigia – In the town's historic center, this has 90 rooms, elegantly furnished with all modern conveniences. Private parking and a very good *Maxim's* restaurant. 140 Viale Mentana (phone: 281032). Expensive.

Park Hotel Stendhal and Ristorante La Pilotta – This elegant hotel stands in a small square in the old quarter. The restaurant is closed during August and on Sundays. 3 Via Bodoni (phone: 208057). Expensive.

Park Hotel Toscanini and Ristorante al Torrente – Somewhat less fancy, this hotel in the center of town has a very good restaurant (closed Mondays and August). 4 Viale Toscanini (phone: 289141). Expensive.

Angiol d'Or – Here you'll find excellent beef and veal dishes. Closed Sunday evenings, Mondays, mid-January, and late August. 1 Via Scutellari (phone: 282632). Moderate.

La Filoma – The decor is not as lavish as that of the *Angiol d'Or,* but the stuffed veal and *tortelli alla parmigiana* make up for it. Closed weekends. 15 Via Marzo XX (phone: 34269). Moderate to inexpensive.

MODENA

Fini – Roast meat is brought to your table and carved to your liking at this excellent, elegant restaurant. Closed Mondays, Tuesdays, and August. Reservations recommended. Largo San Francesco (phone: 214250). Expensive.

Oreste – Considerably less ornate than the *Fini,* it serves terrific pasta and poultry. Closed on Wednesdays, Sunday nights, and July. 31 Piazza Roma (phone: 243324). Expensive.

Bianca – This simple and homey *trattoria* serves delicious Modenese dishes, and is extremely popular — mainly because Bianca herself has been running its kitchen for over 35 years. Closed Sundays and August. 24 Via Spaccini (phone: 311524). Moderate.

BOLOGNA

Grand Hotel Baglioni – This 17th-century palace-turned-hotel has reopened after extensive restoration. The grand dame of Bologna, it is exquisitely decorated, with impeccable service and the superb *I Carracci* restaurant, one of the city's finest. 8 Via Indepenza (phone: 225445). Expensive.

Roma – In the traffic-free zone, this hotel is centrally located, quiet, and has its own garage. 9 Via d'Azeglio (phone: 274400). Moderate.

Al Pappagallo – This well-known, traditional establishment is known for its fillet steaks cooked in flaky pastry. Closed Sunday evenings, Mondays, and the first 2 weeks in August. 3 Piazza Mercanzia (phone: 232807). Expensive.

Grassilli – Reservations are advisable at this small restaurant where risotto alla chef and filet steaks with bacon and champagne are the specialties. Closed Saturdays, Sunday evenings, Wednesdays, and July. 3 Via del Luzzo (phone: 222961). Expensive.

FERRARA

Astra – A centrally located hotel with first class accommodations and a good restaurant. The restaurant is closed Wednesdays and August. 55 Viale Cavour (phone: 26234). Expensive to moderate.

Ripagrande – In a Renaissance palazzo, this elegant hotel is decorated in a striking blend of antique and modern; the rooms on the upper levels have a lovely view. Good bar and restaurant. 21 Via Ripagrande (phone 34733). Expensive to moderate.

Europa – Although it's on the main street, it has a secluded garden and a parking area. 49 Corso Giovecca (phone: 33460). Inexpensive.

Ferrara – an excellent location provides easy access to city's attractions. 4 Piazza Repubblica (phone: 33015). Inexpensive.

Buca San Domenico – The pizza here is the best in town, but there are also many other good dishes. Closed Mondays and July. 22 Piazza Sacrati (phone: 37006). Moderate.

Grotta Azzurra – A popular place specializing in Northern Italian cuisine. Closed Thursdays, the first 2 weeks of January, and July. 43 Piazza Sacrati (phone: 37320). Moderate.

Vecchia Chitarra – This unpretentious place serves solid Ferrarese cooking. Closed Mondays and Tuesdays. 13 Via Ravenna (phone: 62204). Moderate to inexpensive.

Piedmont and the Val d'Aosta Region

Piedmont, the northwesternmost region of Italy, is one of the shortest routes on our tour of the country. As its name implies, it lies mostly at the foot of the Alps, which surround it on three sides, and borders on France and Switzerland. Its eastern portion is within the outer limits of the great Po River valley.

This route also includes the adjacent region of Val d'Aosta, formed by valleys surrounded by the high peaks of Mont Blanc, the Matterhorn, and Mt.

Rosa in the north and Gran Paradiso in the south. One of Italy's semi-autonomous regions, stretching from Courmayeur to Pont St. Martin, it consists of largely French-speaking mountain villages closely bound by mountain traditions and customs. The mountains surrounding Val d'Aosta are interspersed with medieval castles and sophisticated resorts, many open year-round for skiing.

A tour of both regions begins at Entrèves-Courmayeur, where a modern tunnel connects France and Italy. It continues south through Courmayeur proper and other Val d'Aosta resorts until it enters Piedmont territory. The final portion of the trip is spent in Turin, the capital of Piedmont and an industrial and cultural center.

Piedmont, with access to France, played an important role in Rome's control of its empire, and there are important ruins from the Imperial Age at Aosta (once known as "the Rome of the Alps"), Susa, and Turin. But its richest period was under the dukes of Savoy, from the 16th through the 19th century. The House of Savoy filled Turin with Renaissance, baroque, and rococo palaces and the countryside with castles and hunting lodges such as *Stupinigi* (now a museum of decorative arts) and sanctuaries such as La Superga. In the 19th century, Piedmont was the moving force behind the unification of Italy under the House of Savoy.

In 1861 Turin became the capital of Italy until 1865, when the entire area turned from politics to industrial and resort operations. Today the Turin area has become one of the chief industrial zones of the country, supported by Fiat, Olivetti, and other major corporations, while the mountain areas, particularly the Val d'Aosta, have developed into prosperous resorts for both winter and summer sports.

From Roman times, Val d'Aosta's strategic position — guarding one of the main approaches to Italy from northern Europe — has been its source of power. Hannibal is known to have crossed the Alps here in the 3rd century BC (with elephants in tow), and in 1800 Napoleon I led his army over the Great St. Bernard Pass. Today a tunnel under the same pass assures year-round entry from Switzerland to Italy and the 15 mile (25 km) tunnel under the Mont Blanc range carries very heavy international traffic from France. Both tunnels lead to Aosta, from which Autostrada A5 runs to the north Italian plain. There are several other transalpine passes through this region that are open only in summer, including Little St. Bernard, the Mont Cenis, and Mont Genèvre from France, and the Simplon from Switzerland.

ENTRÈVES: The first in a series of mountain resorts that mark the Piedmont–Val d'Aosta range, Entrèves, which nestles alongside Courmayeur, making the two hardly distinguishable, best serves the area as a base of operations.

You can travel by cable car from Entrèves across four different sections of the Mont Blanc range (the highest in Europe) to Chamonix in France. At its summit of 15,771 feet above sea level, the Mont Blancs open to a sensational panorama of peaks and glaciers — but go only in good weather, otherwise the view is badly obstructed.

Another scenic excursion can be made to the head of the Val Ferret as far as Arnouva. If you are really energetic, hike the mule track to the Pre' de Bar, about one-half mile (1 km), an alpine rise 6,767 feet above sea level with superb views of the surrounding peaks.

COURMAYEUR: This village in the upper Dora Baltea Valley, 3 miles (5 km) from Entrèves, is the largest resort in the Val d'Aosta. Originally a fashionable summer resort, it is now also popular for winter skiing, with 66 hotels and 30 lifts, cable cars and tows, nightclubs, discotheques, and all the usual resort paraphernalia.

AOSTA: The regional capital of Val d'Aosta and the Italian connection for the Great St. Bernard Pass road into Switzerland, Aosta is an ancient town, founded by the Romans in 25 BC. It combines interesting Roman remains (the Arch of Augustus, the Pretorian Gate, sections of the Roman walls and theater), with evidence of a prosperous medieval society. The latter gave rise to the church of Sant' Orso, founded in the 10th century. Its cloister, cathedral, and apse towers were built over a period of three centuries. Aosta is also the starting point for the Gran Paradiso National Park, a nature preserve comprising the Cogne and Valsavarenche valleys.

BREUIL-CERVINIA: Once a summer pasture for cattle from nearby villages, Cervinia is now a completely modern center, with 40 hotels, 21 ski lifts, cable cars and tows, skating rinks, bobsled runs, bowling alleys, swimming pools, and saunas. Towering to the north is the Matterhorn (Il Cervino in Italian) and to the west the Jumeax precipices, making it one of the most beautifully situated resorts in the Val d'Aosta. It is a year-round resort, with winter skiing, summer hiking excursions into near and far mountains (including the Matterhorn and Preithorn), and spectacular views anytime.

The town, however, is not cheap, but within the reasonable to expensive price range, you'll find a wide selection of hotels.

AYAS-CHAMPOLUC: At the foot of the Preithorn and the western peaks of the Monte Rosa massif, this town is a popular winter sports resort, but it's even more pleasant and quiet in the summer. Hotels here are unpretentious and set amid refreshing pine forests or atop mountain slopes.

GRESSONEY VALLEY: Within this valley are a number of year-round resorts, the main ones being Gressoney St. Jean and Gressoney La Trinité. Either one can serve as a starting point for a climb up Monte Rosa, at 15,203 feet the second highest peak in the Alps.

En Route from Gressoney Valley – Beyond Pont St. Martin, the two main southbound highways, A5 and SS26, leave the mountain region of the Val d'Aosta and enter Piedmont proper, marked by the more level area of the north Italian plain. The SS26 highway runs to Chivasso, where it forms a junction with SS11 for Turin. This route is not advisable since it runs through the northern suburbs of Turin, generally congested with very heavy traffic. Instead, take A5, which leads to the city's north end.

TURIN (TORINO): The capital of the Piedmont region, Turin is one of the great industrial centers of Italy, with a population of 1.2 million. Founded by the Romans, it didn't acquire prominence until the 16th century, when the reigning Dukes of Savoy filled Turin with fine baroque palaces and churches. These now stand in the old section of town, the heart of which is the Piazza Castello, a handsome, arcaded square with the former Royal Palace at the north end and the Palazzo Madama on the east. Parts of the Palazzo Madama are Roman, parts medieval, though the elegant façade on the piazza is a baroque addition of the 18th century. On the northeast side of the piazza is the *Opera* (Teatro Regio), also with a baroque façade but with an ultramodern interior, the product of a 1973 restoration. One of the liveliest city streets is the arcaded Via Roma, which leads to the Piazza San Carlo, a cultural and commercial haven that contains the great *Egyptian Museum* and the *Galleria Sabauda,* both in the baroque *Palace of the Academy of Sciences.*

Near the riverbanks in the east is the most peculiar edifice, which has become the emblem of the city. Known as Mole Antonelliana, it was originally a synagogue built in 1863. Its tower ends in a spire 548 feet high and now serves as a lookout point.

Farther east is the Po River, lined with handsome and fashionable residential buildings. Upstream is Valentine Park, laid out in 1830 with an imitation medieval castle and an exhibition village. The park's modern exhibition center is the site of the annual Automobile Show; farther upstream is the *Automobile Museum,* with a good collection of antique cars. On the city's west side is the *Gallery of Modern Art* (Via Magenta), well worth a stop.

Since the traffic problem in Turin is particularly bad and parking is a great problem, it is best to tour the city on foot. Also, it's advisable to take rooms in hotels that have garages or reserved parking lots. But beware: Turin fairly sprawls, and getting around can be confusing and tiring. Arm yourself with a bus map and tickets.

For a gastronomically rewarding excursion on the outskirts of Turin, drive to Alba, a small town in the hilly country known as Le Langhe, the center of one of the great wine-producing regions of Italy.

Since Turin is at the center of a network of highways leading in all directions, it's a convenient starting point for trips throughout Italy and to France. Main roads lead to the Riviera, Genoa, Florence, Rome, Milan, and the Italian lakes.

BEST EN ROUTE

Accommodations in the Piedmont and Val d'Aosta range from elegant to rustic. Expect to pay $85 or more per night for a double room at those hotels classified as expensive; between $60 and $75 for a double room at hotels in the moderate category; under $60, inexpensive. Resort prices can increase by 30% in the ski season. Expect to pay $70 or more for a meal for two at those restaurants categorized as expensive; between $50 and $60 in the moderate category; under $45, inexpensive. Prices do not include drinks, wine, or tip.

ENTRÈVES-COURMAYEUR

Pilier d'Angle – This modest, 12-room hotel (an additional 8 rooms are available nearby) in the middle of the village has a pleasant garden and restaurant (phone: 89129). Moderate to inexpensive.

Portud – Most of the 36 rooms have private baths. Although the view isn't quite as spectacular as that at the *Val Veny,* it is quite pretty. An additional 25 rooms are available nearby. Open summers only. At Portud, 4 miles (6 km) on the Val Veny road (phone: 89960). Moderate to inexpensive.

Astoria – Reasonably priced and centrally located, this hotel has 33 rooms, a garden, a restaurant, and a garage. Closed mid-September to mid-December, May through June. A la Palud N (phone: 89910). Inexpensive.

Val Veny – Beyond the town limits, with a dazzling view of Mont Blanc, this 20-room hotel is open only in the summer. Only 5 of the rooms have private baths. There is a garage. About 2½ miles (4 km) from Entrèves on the Val Veny road, Plan Ponquet (phone: 89904). Inexpensive.

La Clotze – This place serves some of the best Piedmontese cooking around; it also has a fine view of Mont Blanc. Closed Wednesdays and from mid-June to mid-July. About 4 miles (6 km) from Entrèves on the Ferret road at Plampincieux (phone: 89928). Moderate.

Maison de Filippo – A charming, rustic village restaurant, this is a good place for hearty, filling fare. Closed Tuesdays, May, and November. (phone: 89968). Moderate.

COURMAYEUR

Palace Bron – Overlooking the village, it has striking surroundings that help to compensate for its relatively isolated setting (though it does provide transport to and from cable car stations). There are 27 rooms, many with views of the lovely garden and grounds. Closed October to mid-December, and May through June. 37 Via Plan Gorret (phone: 842545). Expensive.

Royal E Golf – Facilities at this classy 80-room hotel include a heated swimming pool, garden, and an excellent restaurant (evenings only, closed Mondays). The hotel is closed in September. In the center of town, at 83 Via Roma (phone: 843621). Expensive.

Cresta et Duc – Open from December through April and from June through September, this is a comfortable 38-room hotel. 7 Via Circonvallazione (phone: 842585). Moderate to inexpensive.

Cadrant Solaire – Huge old stables, converted recently, provide a genuine country feel, while the food is a happy marriage of French cuisine and Italian traditions. Excellent for lunch. Closed Thursdays. 122 Via Roma (phone: 844609). Expensive to moderate.

K2 – Although it's named after the second highest mountain peak in the world (climbed in the 1950s by a Courmayeur citizen), this down-to-earth establishment on the road to Mont Blanc serves well-prepared dishes. Closed Mondays, May, June, and November. Villair (phone: 842475). Moderate.

Vieux Pommier – In the center of town, this restaurant is closed during October and on Mondays. 25 Piazzale Monte Bianco (phone: 842281). Moderate.

AOSTA

Valle d'Aosta – This modern, 100-room hotel has lovely gardens and a garage. Its restaurant, *Grill le Foyer,* is closed Tuesdays and November. 146 Corso Ivrea (phone: 41845). Expensive to moderate.

Rayon de Soleil – A comfortable, 39-room hotel on a broad avenue in the center of town. Its restaurant is closed on Fridays. Viale Gran San Bernardo, Localita Saraillon (phone: 362247). Moderate to inexpensive.

Cavallo Bianco – This former carriage house in the middle of town combines the rustic and the refined to perfection. Try the game (quail or pigeon) or the filet of beef with red wine. Closed Sunday evenings, Monday lunches, and mid-June through mid-July. 15 Via Aubert (phone: 362214). Expensive.

BREUIL-CERVINIA

Cristallo – In addition to 85 well-appointed rooms, there are tennis courts, a covered swimming pool, and a garage. Closed September through November and May through June. In the center of town (phone: 948121). Expensive.

Residence Alto Cielo – This modern 35-room hotel has both indoor and outdoor swimming pools, tennis courts, and a garage. In the center of town (phone: 948759). Expensive to moderate.

Chalet Valdotain – Set amid quiet countryside, with a good view of Lac Bleu, this unpretentious 35-room hotel is closed in May and November. About 1 mile (2 km) from town at Lac Bleu (phone: 949428). Moderate to inexpensive.

Neiges D'Antan – An excellent eatery at the entrance to town. The menu includes delicious fondues. Closed Mondays and July. Frazione Cret. Perreres (phone: 948775). Expensive to moderate.

Grotta – A good restaurant in the center of town. Closed Thursdays. Contrada Montabel (phone: 949492). Moderate.

Pavia – Here is good, plentiful fare in a friendly environment. Closed on Thursdays, mid-May through mid-July, and September 15 through November. In the village (phone: 949010). Moderate.

AYAS-CHAMPOLUC

Anna Maria – In a pine forest, this 20-room charmer is open Christmas through mid-April and mid-June through August. Full board is available. (phone: 307128). Moderate to inexpensive.

Genzianella – Splendidly situated in a mountain valley on the banks of a clear, well-stocked stream, this 20-room hotel offers simple accommodations. Closed in October. Two miles (3.2 km) from Champoluc. St. Jacques (phone: 307156). Inexpensive.

TURIN (TORINO)

All hotels have parking facilities or garages.

Alexandra – The best thing about this modern, 48-room hotel is its site on the Dora River. 14 Lungodora Napoli (phone: 858327). Expensive.

Jolly Ambasciatori – This is the largest hotel in town. Its 197 rooms are air conditioned and it has a restaurant. 104 Corso Vittorio Emanuele (phone: 5752). Expensive.

Jolly Hotel Principi di Piemonte – One of the leading hotels in town, its 105 rooms have air conditioning and it has a good restaurant. 15 Via Gobetti (phone: 532153). Expensive.

Turin Palace – Continental breakfast is included with the price of one of its 125 rooms, but there is no restaurant. Next to the railway station, at 8 Via Sacchi (phone: 515511). Expensive.

Sitea Grand – Recently renovated, this hotel offers excellent service, comfortable rooms, and a central location. 35 Via Carlo Alberto (phone: 557071). Expensive.

President – Centrally located, this 72-room hotel has a lovely terrace and enclosed garden. Service is courteous, and the atmosphere is pleasantly friendly. 67 Via Antonia Cecchi (phone: 859555). Moderate.

Del Cambio – A historical restaurant with classic Victorian design, its cuisine matches the ambience. The house specialties are fondue with truffles, pot roast in Barolo, and mixed boiled meats. Closed Sundays and August. 2 Piazza Carignano (phone: 546690). Expensive.

Vecchia Lanterna – For classic Piedmontese food — risotto with Barolo, agnolotti (a kind of pasta) stuffed with duck, and saddle of venison — make a reservation to dine here. The best in town. Closed Saturdays at noon, Sundays, and August. 21 Corso Re Umberto (phone: 537047). Expensive.

Villa Sassi-El Toulá – Set in an 18th-century villa with a large garden, this luxurious, fashionable restaurant also has 12 rooms with private bath for overnight stays. Closed during August, Sunday evenings, and on Mondays. Across the River Po, 47 Via Traforo del Pino (phone: 890556). Expensive.

Al Gatto Nero – The specialties are Florentine steaks, grilled fish, and meat. There is an excellent wine cellar. Closed Sundays and August. 14 Corso Filippo Turati (phone: 590414). Expensive to moderate.

Montecarlo – The mixed menu here offers classic Italian dishes and nouvelle cuisine concoctions as duck with blueberries. Closed Saturdays lunchtime, Sundays, and August. 37 Via San Francesco da Paola (phone: 541234). Moderate.

Tre Galline – A classic Piedmontese *trattoria* in the city's historic quarter, it enjoys a solid reputation. Closed Sundays, Mondays, and August. 37 Via Bellezia (phone: 546833). Moderate to inexpensive.

Il Blu – A large, lively place, with quick service and a good selection of salads as well as grilled meats and locally produced sausages. Closed Sundays and August. 15 Corso Siccardi (phone: 545550). Inexpensive.

The Italian Riviera

The Italian Riviera stretches in an arc across the northwestern part of the Mediterranean coast of Italy, bordered by France on the west and Tuscany on the east; its apex is just west of Genoa. The Riviera is traversed by two main roads: the Via Aurelia and the Autostrada, both running an average distance of 164 miles (265 km). The Autostrada generally runs a few miles inland from the coast, with exits for the most important towns. Since the coast is mountainous and generally very steep, the views are often spectacular, although sometimes interrupted by tunnels. In fact, take caution when driving in high winds along roads that pass over gulleys, especially when issuing from tunnels. The Via Aurelia runs entirely along the shoreline, passing straight through coastal towns and villages. Although picturesque in spots, the road is narrow and twisting and the traffic usually heavy. The best plan is to take the Autostrada, exiting only at the places you wish to visit.

The warm climate, clear air, and scenic mountain backdrop of the Italian Riviera have made it one of Europe's leading resorts. It is wise, therefore — and during the high summer season essential — to make hotel reservations well in advance. The best seasons for the Riviera are spring (March through June), autumn (mid-September through October), and possibly Christmas week (although it is too cold for swimming). July and August are best avoided because of the crowds, noise, and heavy traffic. Each town has a tourist information office, generally called Azienda di Turismo or Pro Loco, that can provide detailed information on hotels, restaurants, sites, and activities.

There are two border crossing points from France. The Autostrada is reached from Monte Carlo or Menton (an extension from Nice is under construction), with the actual border in the middle of a tunnel. Passport and customs control is on the Italian side of the tunnel. The French shore road runs into the Italian Via Aurelia at Ponte San Ludovico, just outside Menton. Border formalities for tourists are usually perfunctory, but on weekends and during the high season lines can be long. If you travel on the shore road, stop directly after the border crossing to visit the Balzi Rossi caves, where traces of prehistoric human habitation have been discovered. Also explore the Hanbury Gardens of La Mortola, one of the most famous botanical gardens in Europe. From here you can join the Autostrada at the Ventimiglia exit and either stop in the town — set, in part, on a hill with narrow streets and Roman remains — or continue directly to Bordighera.

BORDIGHERA: This is one of the older resort towns of the Riviera, patronized in the late 19th century by the English and by various European royalties. The Italian Riviera was settled not by Latins but by Ligurians, a fair northern race, and like many Ligurian towns, Bordighera consists of an older center on a hill with a newer section along the shore. Between the two are villas, hotels, and beautiful gardens centered along the old Roman road. Bordighera is famed for its palm trees and has held a monopoly for the supply of palms to the Vatican for Palm Sunday since 1586.

Many of the large hotels in town, which in the past catered to dowager duchesses and retired Indian major generals, are now closed or turned into apartment houses, but a few still exist in their original form. Bordighera has 100 hotels, so there is considerable choice.

SAN REMO: This is the largest resort on the Riviera, with a resident population of over 60,000 that is at least quintupled in the summer. It is a noisy, overcrowded, and overbuilt town whose major attraction is the *Municipal Casino,* where you can win a fortune or (more likely) lose your shirt at roulette, baccarat, and other games of chance. You can also get a very fine (but expensive) dinner in the casino restaurant. There are dozens of restaurants, pizzerias, and snack bars in town; for recreation try sailing, water skiing, golf (an 18-hole course can easily be reached by cable car), and shopping.

Several excursions can be made from San Remo. The best is to Monte Bignone, which offers a superb view over the coast and a nearby pine forest. It can be reached by either road or cable car. Another worthwhile trip is to the artists colony at Bussana Vecchia, an old town destroyed by an earthquake in 1887 and abandoned until the 1950s, when it was taken over by a group of artists who settled among the ruins.

En Route from San Remo – Beyond San Remo, for the next 30 miles (48 km) or so, the coast isn't particularly interesting, and it is a good section to cover on the Autostrada until you reach the Andora exit and there rejoin the coastal road, following the signs for Laiguelia and Alassio. (There is a bad section of road around Cape Mele with alternating one-way traffic.)

LAIGUEGLIA: This small resort at the southern end of the Bay of Alassio has a good beach and several hotels. A picturesque old town, it also has many fine old houses and a large baroque church.

ALASSIO: This is one of the oldest resort towns on the Riviera and, despite a good number of unaesthetic modern buildings, it is still quite attractive, with a fine sandy beach over 1½ miles long. The old town along the beach consists of one narrow street (now a pedestrian zone) with shops, taverns, restaurants, and cafés. The town hills rise steeply into the villa district, which has many gardens laid out by the original winter residents, mostly English. The tennis club in town hosts international tournaments, and, at Garlenda (11 mi/18 km distant), an excellent 18-hole golf course, with a country club and bungalows for rent. Good skiing is available at Monesi, about 31 miles (50 km) away, making Alassio a year-round resort. The high season, though, is from April to the end of September.

Alassio is an excellent base from which to explore the churches and ancient monuments of nearby villages. Stop at Moglio, Vegliasco, and Testico, all within a distance of 12 miles (20 km).

ALBENGA: Once an important Roman port, Albenga is now a busy market town for the produce of the hinterland (fruit, particularly peaches, and early vegetables). However, testaments to its interesting history, such as the 5th-century baptistry and fine tower houses, abound. Visit the *Roman Naval Museum,* with the remains of a Roman ship sunk in Albengan waters in the 1st century BC.

From Albenga you can take an interesting excursion inland through the Aroscia Valley past Villanova, an ancient walled town, to Ortovero, a region famous for the red Pigato wine. You can continue on through the pleasant countryside to Ponte di Nava, where you'll find the object of this jaunt, *Beppe's,* a fine restaurant specializing in snails, game, trout, and, in season, raspberries. Before turning back, visit Ormea, a pretty summer resort; Garessio, known for its mineral springs; and, finally, the romantic village of Castelvecchio.

Except for the charming historic section of Finale Ligure, the shore road from Albenga is unattractive, and it is advisable to transfer to the Autostrada as far as Genoa.

GENOA (GENOVA): The greatest port in northern Italy and the main outlet for the "Industrial Triangle" (Turin, Milan, and Genoa), this city (pop. 750,000) rises like an amphitheater from its semicircular port into the hills above the city. Surrounding the harbor is the oldest (medieval) section, with steep and narrow streets and arcades and medieval houses and churches (a total of about 200). Above the port is Renaissance Genoa, consisting of fine palaces built by rich Genoese merchants, once the rivals of the Venetians in cultivating trade with the East. Then, on the higher slopes and in the flat area to the east, is modern Genoa, with wide streets and boulevards, squares and public gardens. Still higher is the Circonvallazione a Monte, a panoramic boulevard winding in and out among the hills, with fine views over the city. The layout of the city is very confusing since it follows no recognizable plan: The visitor would be well advised to buy a city map, available at any newspaper kiosk. Fortunately, the principal sights and monuments are well marked.

The 16th and 17th centuries saw a flurry of artistic activity in this wealthy shipping city. The impetus was provided by a number of Flemish artists — Rubens and Van Dyck, among them — who were invited to come to the city to work for wealthy merchant families, primarily making portraits. To form an image of what the city was like in this grand period, stroll down Via Garibaldi (known as Via Aurea before the last century), lined with 16th-century palaces of elaborate design. The frescoes and gallery of Palazzo Cataldi, the art gallery in Palazzo Bianco (with fine collections of Genoa's adopted Flemish sons), and the antiques in Palazzo Doria Tursi tell reams about the life in Renaissance Genoa.

For one of the best panoramas of the city, take a cable car from Largo della Zecca up to the Righi.

Genoese cuisine features a number of specialties, such as *trenette al pesto* (noodles and a sauce flavored with basil, garlic, and pine nuts); fish *ravioli;* a vegetable pie known as *torta pasqualina* (Easter pie); *cappon magro,* a mixed salad of vegetables and fish with a mayonnaise sauce (very rich); and, of course, fish of all kinds.

En Route from Genoa – From Genoa, continue east on the Autostrada until you reach Camogli, a picturesque small port with tall houses, a favorite residence for sea captains. On the second Sunday in June, a gigantic fish fry is held here.

Continue on the Autostrada to the Rapallo exit, where you get on the shore road leading to Santa Margherita and Portofino on the Tigullo Gulf, one of the most scenic sections of the Riviera. Rapallo itself is grossly overbuilt. It has 65 hotels, a yacht harbor, and a 9-hole golf course. The beaches are barely adequate, but many of the better hotels have swimming pools.

SANTA MARGHERITA LIGURE: This is the best resort in the Tigullo area since it is neither overbuilt nor underdeveloped — perfect for a comfortable stay. The resort has 38 hotels, some situated on the waterfront or overlooking the sea and others above the town, with a view.

PORTOFINO: This is considered by many to be the "pearl" of the Italian Riviera. Originally a small fishing village enclosed in a bay, it has grown into a very exclusive (and expensive) resort, retaining its original atmosphere and charm by very stringent zoning regulations. Take a walk to the lighthouse past the church of San Giorgio for a fine view over the whole bay (total walking time is 1 hour). And don't miss the nearby hamlet of San Fruttuoso, reached by motorboat in 20 minutes.

En Route from Portofino – To get back to the main roads, you must backtrack to Rapallo. Beyond Rapallo, the Autostrada runs almost entirely inland until it reaches the La Spezia exit and continues into Tuscany.

The Via Aurelia follows the coast, past Chiavari and Sestri Levante; then it, too, moves inland, climbing through fine scenery to the Bracco Pass. The coast from here to La Spezia is very steep, rugged, and very beautiful. Unfortunately, except for Monterosso, the other villages of the Cinque Terre, or "Five Lands" — Vernazza, Corniglia, Manarola, and Riomaggiore — the most unspoiled part of the whole Riviera, are difficult or impossible to reach by road. These small fishing and wine-growing towns cling to the rocky coast and are more easily reached by train or from La Spezia on the finished portion of the shore road. (The railroad works its way mostly through tunnels, but each town has a station.)

LERICI: Sailing back from a visit to Leigh Hunt in Pisa, headed for his home in Lerici on the Gulf of Spezi, Percy Bysshe Shelley was capsized and drowned here in 1822; his body, found washed ashore, was burned in a funeral pyre by his wife and companions. This romantic and tragic event has marked this attractive little town ever since, drawing both historians and simple romantics to spend some time here. Lerici acts as a stop on the Riviera route, though short excursions to Tellaro, Monte-marcello, and Bocca di Magra on the estuary of the Magra River are possible from here.

BEST EN ROUTE

Since the Italian Riviera is a resort area, you will find many fine hotels and restaurants, and high seasonal prices. Expect to pay $120 or more per night for a double room at those hotels categorized as expensive; between $55 to $90 at those places in the moderate category; under $55, inexpensive. Expect to pay $75 or more for a meal for two at those restaurants categorized as expensive; between $45 to $70 at a restaurant in the moderate category; under $45, inexpensive. Prices do not include drinks, wine, or tip.

MORTOLA INFERIORE

Eden – In keeping with its name, the 21-room hotel's most gracious feature is its garden. Open from April through mid-November. 68 Corso Montecarlo (phone: 39431). Moderate.

Mortola – Specialties at this international restaurant are scampi with mustard sauce and crêpes Suzette. Closed Monday evenings, Tuesdays, and November through early December,. On SS1 opposite the Hanbury Gardens (phone: 39432). Expensive to moderate.

BORDIGHERA

Grand Hotel del Mare – A 104-room hotel that stands in a park, it is distinguished by its beach. It also has a swimming pool. Closed from mid-November through mid-December. 34 Via Portico della Punta, about 1 mile (1.6 km) from town (phone: 262201). Expensive.

Grand Hotel Cap Ampelio – In a park, this old, established, 104-room hotel has recently been remodeled; there is also a swimming pool and restaurant. Closed in late November for 1 month. 5 Via Virgilio (phone: 264333). Expensive to moderate.

Astoria – This hotel in the villa district has 24 rooms and a garden. 2 Via Tasso (phone: 262906). Inexpensive.

Le Chaudron – This charming restaurant offers very good Italian and French food. Try the spaghetti with lobster and the irresistible homemade desserts. Closed Mondays, January 15 to 30, and July 1 to 15. 2 Piazza Bengasi (phone: 263592). Moderate.

Chez Louis – An eclectic assortment of tasty Italian and French dishes characterizes the culinary repertoire. Closed Tuesdays and November. 30 Corso Italia (phone: 261602). Moderate.

Reserve Tastevin – The menu of this excellent restaurant contains an interesting selection of Mediterranean specialties. Closed Sunday evenings (except in summer), Mondays, and from the second week in November to December 20. 20 Via Arziglia (phone: 261322). Moderate.

Romano – Here, the accent is on pasta and other Italian dishes. Closed Wednesdays. 15 Piazza del Popolo (phone: 265734). Moderate.

SAN REMO

Grand Hotel Londra – Set in a park, this 127-room hotel has a heated swimming pool. Closed October through mid-December. 2 Corso Matuzia (phone: 79961). Expensive.

Méditerranée – Near the yacht harbor, it has 70 rooms, a swimming pool, and fragrant gardens. Closed November through mid-December. 76 Corso Cavallotti (phone: 571000). Expensive.

Royal – Many of the 140 rooms in this classic luxury hotel overlook the beach or surrounding park. There is a heated swimming pool and tennis courts. Closed mid-October to mid-December. 80 Corso Imperatrice (phone: 79991). Expensive.

Astoria–West End – This 120-room hotel is set among spacious gardens near the sea. 8 Corso Matuzia (phone: 70791). Expensive to moderate.

Résidence Principe – If you plan to stay in town for a while, consider booking one of the 52 rooms in this residential hotel, with very pretty gardens, swimming pool, and a lovely view. 96 Via Fratelli Asquasciati (phone: 83565). Moderate.

Villa Maria – This 32-room hotel's most attractive feature is its flower garden. 30 Corso Nuvoloni (phone: 882882). Moderate.

Europa e Della Pace – More than half the 70 rooms in this unpretentious but comfortable hotel have private baths. Many have windows overlooking the sea. 27 Corso Imperatrice (phone: 70605). Moderate to inexpensive.

Casinò – You won't have to gamble on the high quality of food or service here. Ranking epicures rate both as consistently superb. 18 Corso Inglesi in the Municipal Casinò (phone: 79901). Expensive.

Da Giannino – Simplicity and good taste characterize this restaurant; owner and chef Senora Gasperini prepares some very fine fish and squid dishes. Try one of the local Ligurian wines. Closed Monday lunches, Sundays, and the first half of December. 23 Lungomare Trento e Trieste (phone: 504014). Expensive.

Osteria del Marinaro – You will find any number of fish dishes (but only fish) on the menu. Reservations are necessary. Closed Mondays and November. 28 Via Gaudio (phone: 501919). Expensive.

Pesce d'Oro – House specialties are *lasagne al pesto,* fish soup, and grilled scampi. As seating capacity is limited, reservations are necessary. Closed Mondays and mid-February to mid-March. 300 Corso Cavallotti (phone: 576332). Expensive.

U'Nostromû – Here you'll find excellent risotto and well-prepared fish. Closed Wednesdays and November. 2 Piazza Sardi (phone: 501979). Moderate.

LAIGUEGLIA

Laiguelia Residence – This restored old mansion on the shore has 55 rooms. Closed from November through March. 14 Piazza Libertà (phone: 49001). Moderate.

Splendid – Aptly named, this establishment has 50 well-appointed rooms, many of which overlook the beach. There is also a swimming pool. Closed November through March. 4 Via Badarò (phone: 49325). Moderate.

Residence Paradiso – Some of the 32 units at this unpretentious hotel have kitchenettes. 1 Via dei Pini (phone: 49285). Inexpensive.

ALASSIO

Diana Grand – Although some of the 77 rooms have beachside balconies, those at the back of the hotel are noisy. In addition to a private beach, there is a swimming pool, sauna, and restaurant. Closed December and January. 110 Via Garibaldi (phone: 42701). Expensive to moderate.

Grand Hotel Méditerranée – It overlooks the sea of the same name, with its own beach. All 75 rooms have private baths. Closed from October 20 through March. 63 Via Roma (phone: 42564). Moderate.

Regina – Although not a lavish hotel, 31 of its 39 rooms have private baths. Closed October through March. 220 Via Garibaldi (phone: 40215). Moderate.

Lido – This substantial, 52-room hotel is on the beach. Closed October through March. 9 Via Novembre IV (phone: 40158). Moderate to inexpensive.

La Vigna – Be sure to make reservations before heading for this popular terrace restaurant. Closed Wednesdays. 1 Via Lepanto Solva (phone: 43301). Expensive.

Caffè Roma – You can easily while away a few hours at this pleasing café with adjoining snack bar. Closed Mondays. 316 Via Dante (phone: 40188). Moderate.

Excelsior – The restaurant in this small *pensione* is a good place to sample French and Italian cuisine. Closed Wednesdays. 6 Via Robutti (phone: 40454). Moderate.

La Palma – Don't miss the special fish soup and the wonderful *pasta al pesto* served in this superb restaurant. Reservations necessary. Closed Tuesdays and November. 5 Via Cavour (phone: 40514). Moderate.

GENOA (GENOVA)

There are more than 200 hotels, many in each price range, and innumerable restaurants and pizzerias in the Genoa area.

Colombia-Excelsior – A member of the luxury Excelsior chain, this 171-room hotel has a fine restaurant. 40 Via Balbi (phone: 261841). Expensive.

Plaza – As you might expect, this 100-room establishment is in the most fashionable part of town, near the Piazza Corvetto, and has a classy restaurant. 11 Via Martin Piaggio (phone: 893641). Expensive to moderate.

Savoy Majestic – While not as elegant as the former two places, the 116 rooms here are extremely comfortable. The restaurant is also very good. 5 Via Arsenale di Terra (phone: 261641). Expensive to moderate.

Nuevo Astoria – Although this simple hotel near the Brignole railroad station does not have its own restaurant, 60 of its 74 rooms have private baths. 4 Piazza Brignole (phone: 873316 or 873991). Moderate.

Agnello d'Oro – The "Golden Lamb" is a bargain; one of Genoa's better hotels for the price. Rooms are air conditioned with telephones. There is also a restaurant. Closed October through April. 6 Vico Delle Monachette (phone: 262084). Inexpensive.

Fate – Considered by many to be the best in town, especially for fish — often cooked in herbs. Closed Saturday lunchtime and Sundays. 31 Via Ruspoli (phone: 546402). Expensive.

Del Mario – Classic Genoese cooking and a wide choice of good wines. Dinner reservations advised. Closed Saturdays and August 10-25. 33 Via Conservatori del Mare (phone: 298467). Moderate.

Nino – This place serves Ligurian and Piedmontese specialties. Closed Mondays and July. 20 Salita del Fondaco (phone: 205884). Moderate.

Il Rosso – Boisterous and often packed with an after-theater crowd, this restaurant serves great food and is the place to rubberneck. Closed Sundays and January. 44 Via Palestro (phone: 885647). Moderate.

Vittorio Al Mare – This seaside restaurant with a beautiful view specializes in fish and risotto dishes, though the general consensus is that the quality that once distinguished it has diminished. Closed Mondays and August. 1 Belvedere Firpo, at Boccadasse (phone: 312872). Moderate to inexpensive.

CAMOGLI

Cenobio dei Dogi – Its gardens overlook the 88-room hotel's private beach and the bay. It also has a tennis court, swimming pool, and an excellent restaurant (closed on Fridays and from January 7 through February). 34 Via Cuneo (phone: 770041). Expensive.

Da Rosa – A wonderful port restaurant with great views and excellent seafood. Closed Wednesdays and November through Christmas. Largo Casa Bona (phone: 771088). Expensive to moderate.

RAPALLO

Grand Hotel Bristol – Many of the 91 rooms in this modern hotel overlook the gardens, private beach, and heated swimming pool. There is also a restaurant. Closed from November to December 21. 369 Via Aurelia Orientale (phone: 273313). Expensive.

Rapallo Eurotel – This good, 64-room hotel has a garden, swimming pool, and restaurant. 22 Via Aurelia Ponete (phone: 60981). Expensive to moderate.

Riviera – All 20 rooms overlook the sea. There is a good restaurant. Closed from November through mid-December. Piazza Novembre IV (phone: 50248). Moderate to inexpensive.

Da Ardito – This popular restaurant has maintained its high standards for the last 50 years. It serves tasty regional dishes and wonderful local wines. Closed Tuesdays. 9 Via Canale, Dan Pietro di Novello (phone: 51551). Moderate to inexpensive.

Da Monique – Here, too, you'll find imaginative fish and seafood dishes. Closed Tuesdays and from January 20 through February 20. 6 Lungomare Vittorio Veneto (phone: 50541). Moderate to inexpensive.

SANTA MARGHERITA LIGURE

Grand Hotel Miramare – Many of the 79 rooms face the private beach. There is also a garden, heated swimming pool, and a restaurant. 30 Via Milite Ignoto (phone: 287014). Expensive.

Imperial Palace – In a spacious park, this luxury 106-room hotel has a heated swimming pool and a restaurant. 19 Via Pagana (phone: 288991). Expensive.

Laurin – Near the harbor, it has 41 rooms, a swimming pool in a garden, and a restaurant, *La Broche*. Closed from November through Christmas. 3 Corso Marconi (phone: 289971). Expensive to moderate.

Metropole & Santa Margherita – Most of its 48 rooms have private baths. Its garden overlooks a private beach. Closed November through mid-December. 2 Via Pagana (phone: 286134). Moderate.

Vela – This remodeled old villa overlooking the bay has 16 rooms, a garden, and a restaurant. 21 Corso Cuneo (phone: 286039). Moderate to inexpensive.

Da Alfredo – This lively fish restaurant and pizzeria is popular not only with the locals, it's also a favorite of tenor Luciano Pavarotti. Closed Thursdays. 38 Piazza Martiri Liberta (phone: 288140). Moderate.

Bassa Prora – On the waterfront, its specialty is fresh fish and seafood. Closed Monday evenings and mid-September to mid-October. 7 Via Garibaldi (phone: 286586). Moderate.

Paranza – This is another fine fish restaurant. Closed Thursdays and mid-January to mid-February. 46 Via J. Ruffini (phone: 283686). Moderate.

Beppe Achilli – Here you'll find a wide selection of roast meats and fowl. Closed Wednesdays and December. 29 Via Bottaro (phone: 286516). Moderate to inexpensive.

PORTOFINO

Splendido – The most fashionable, exclusive hotel in town has 65 rooms, a heated swimming pool, and tennis courts. Reservations are essential at the restaurant. Closed November through February. On the hillside above the village, 10 Salita Baratta (phone: 269-5151). Expensive.

Nazionale – On the harbor, it has 13 rooms and a restaurant (phone: 269575). Expensive.

Piccolo – Smaller than the *Splendido* and considerably less extravagant, this 26-room hotel has a garden, parking area, and an outdoor restaurant. Closed from November to mid-February. On the hillside above the village, below the *Splendido,* 31 Via Provinciale (phone: 69015). Moderate.

Eden – This economical 9-room hotel in the center of the village also has a restaurant. 21 Vico Dritto (phone: 269091). Inexpensive.

Pitosforo – On the waterfront, it serves some of the best fresh fish and seafood in town. Closed Tuesdays, Wednesday lunchtime, January, and February. On the harbor at Molo Umberto I (phone: 269020). Expensive.

LERICI

Byron – This comfortable, 26-room hotel overlooks the water. 25 Lungomare Biaggini (phone: 967104). Moderate.

Shelley e delle Palme – Most of the 53 rooms overlook the bay. 5 Lungomare Biaggini (phone: 967127). Moderate to inexpensive.

Calata – Lerici's finest fresh fish can be sampled here, on the waterfront. Closed Tuesdays and November. 4 Via Mazzini (phone: 967143). Moderate to inexpensive.

Golfo dei Poeti – Another good seafood restaurant with a nautical atmosphere. Closed Tuesdays. 19 Via Mazzini (phone: 967414). Moderate to inexpensive.

The Italian Dolomites

One of Europe's most beautiful and striking mountain ranges is the Italian Dolomites, part of the eastern Alps, from the central northern region of the Trentino–Alto Adige east to the Veneto region and the Piave River, both only a short distance from the Austrian border. The range continues south to the fringe of the fertile Po Valley. It is the home of some of Italy's most popular ski resorts, including Cortina d'Ampezzo and Val Gardena, site of the 1970 World Cup Ski Championship.

The Dolomites have a fascinating geological history. Their unique formations of pinnacles and sheer rocks are the result of huge prehistoric eruptions from the sea that covered the area millennia ago. Sea fossils are found in the highest peaks, and Stone Age and Iron Age implements have been found in the Alps overlooking Bolzano, indicating that the Dolomites may have been one of the earliest inhabited areas in Europe.

The geologic structure of these mountains — limestone and porphyry — give them their famous rose-pink hue that deepens to an almost fiery red at sunset. Most towns in the Dolomites are a delightful mixture of Roman ruins, medieval fortifications and castles, early medieval buildings decorated with frescoes, and baroque churches. The Dolomites stand at a European crossroads, the meeting point of different peoples, languages, and cultures; and they have become battlegrounds innumerable times, from invasions by Roman legions and Emperor Charlemagne's campaigns to battles between the Austrian Empire and the Italian states. At the end of the ruthless conflicts of World War I, much of the Dolomites were handed over to Italy by Austria, and so Alto Adige — South Tyrol until 1918 — though Italian, is predominatly German-speaking.

The climate is typical of mountainous regions throughout Europe — snow on high ground from November to April, spring rain through June, and hot, sunny weather in the summer — though summer is infamously unpredictable, with sudden rains and fogs likely anytime.

To see as much as possible, one must zigzag through the Dolomites, stopping for cable car climbs or walks through interesting towns. The route described below begins at the Brenner Pass, on the Austrian border, at the Italian town of Bolzano in the eastern Dolomites and follows a very crooked and irregular path until it returns to its starting point. By following it, you will have meandered completely through the eastern portion of the mountains, stopping in such towns as Bressanone, Ortisei, Brunico, Cortina, and San Martino di Castrozza. To cover the western part of the Dolomites, you again begin at Bolzano, but this time travel in the opposite direction, following the twisted southbound route to Trento. Each portion takes a few days, so allow a total of about 6 days. One encouraging factor: The Dolomites have one of the most efficient and dense networks of mountain roads in Europe and offer a wide variety of accommodations at every level.

BOLZANO: An important gateway to northern Europe in ancient times, Bolzano, called Bozen by its German-speaking population, reflects a predominantly Austrian character in its language and culture. It is the traditional capital of the Alto Adige area of the Dolomites.

The old center of Bolzano is entirely Tyrolean (the Alto Adige region was Austrian-controlled South Tyrol until 1918). The 13th-century Gothic cathedral stands in Piazza Walther. Medieval arcades flank Via dei Portici, the narrow main street, along which modern shops have been built. This long street runs into the market square at Piazza delle Erbe, where a lively and colorful fruit market is held each day. Visit the *Civic Museum,* which houses a rare collection of local wooden sculptures and paintings as well as a vast archaeological and ethnographic collection. Then cross the Isarco River for a short walk to the tiny, picturesque village of Gries. Don't miss its charming Gothic parish church.

   En Route from Bolzano – For one of the less frequented, romantic routes to the Dolomites, take the northbound road 508 for 41½ miles (67 km) to Vipiteno. The drive unwinds along the narrow yet lovely green Sarentina Valley, where many medieval castles dominate the scenery. Some are in ruins, others still inhabited, but the renowned Castle Roncolo can be visited Tuesdays through Saturdays, 10 AM to noon and 3 to 5 PM, and well deserves to be seen for its 13th-century frescoes and its dramatic location right on the edge of a gorge.

BRESSANONE: One of the most charming Alto Adige towns, Bressanone claims an eclectic combination of Gothic, Renaissance, and baroque architecture. Its 13th-century cathedral cloister and the tiny chapel with a fresco of St. Christopher are worth a visit, but even if you see nothing else here, you must stop at the *Elefante* (see *Best en Route*), a beautifully preserved 16th-century hotel with original furnishings and one of the best restaurants in the Dolomites.

ORTISEI: At the foot of the grassy slopes of the Alpe di Siusi, Ortisei is a summer and winter resort. It's the chief town of the Val Gardena, one of the most romantic valleys of the Dolomites, carpeted with wild flowers that attract hikers every spring. A 6-minute cable car ride from the town takes you to the upper slopes of this range, opening up to incomparable views of the neighboring Catinaccio (or Rosengartens) and the long, pointed outline of the Sassolungo (Langkopf) Mountain. Back in town, to learn about Val Gardena's folklore and culture, take time to visit the *Ladin Museum.* The artistry of local woodcarvers can be viewed at the *Permanent Exhibition of Groden Handicrafts,* at the Congress Hall (the Tourist Board is also here, phone: 76328).

   En Route from Ortisei – Drive for 6 miles (9.6 km) to Selva di Val Gardena, a skier's and climber's paradise. Travel past the resort of Arabba, then head north through the Val Badia, yet another Dolomite ski valley and one of the few places where the ancient language of Ladino (a derivative of Latin) is still spoken.

BRUNICO: The capital of the Pusteria Valley and almost entirely Austrian in character, Brunico is famous for the spacious and gentle slopes that surround it. It is dominated by the Tyrolean castle of Bishop Bruno of Bressanone, built in 1251, but the area's greatest attraction is a half-hour's walk away — the breathtaking panorama from the Plan di Corones. Guided tours of this lovely town are offered each Wednesday and Friday at 5 PM, from mid-June to September (for information, contact the Tourist Board, phone: 85722).

En Route from Brunico – Follow Route 49 toward the Lake of Misurina, one of the most romantic spots of the Dolomites. Near the lake are the Tre Cime di Lavaredo Mountains, a popular Dolomite climb. Follow Route 48 to Auronzo di Cadore. You are now in the Veneto region, a more sparsely populated area of the Dolomites.

CORTINA D'AMPEZZO: In a sheltered basin surrounded by pine forests and some of the most spectacular Dolomite peaks, Cortina is probably the best-known and best-loved mountain resort in the entire Dolomites. It offers a huge variety of ski runs as well as walking and climbing trails and is well supplied with hotels and restaurants in every category.

SAN MARTINO DI CASTROZZA: This is not merely another popular ski resort. San Martino di Castrozza, surrounded by tall peaks and pine-wooded slopes, is a local scenic wonder. Pale di San Martino, the group of Dolomite pinnacles that dominate the city, are famous for their intense rose-pink glow at sunset. There are many available chalet-style hotels, typical of the region.

En Route from San Martino di Castrozza – Travel north past Predazzo and Moena and on to Vigo di Fassa, the capital of the lovely Fassa Valley and another Ladino-speaking area. To complete the eastern portion of the trip, follow Route 241 back toward Bolzano. It leads into the famous strada delle Dolomiti, the most popular Dolomite road. Make a few short stops along the strada at the Passo di Costalunga, the small Lake of Carezza (Karersee), whose water, for geological reasons, is a deep siena red. The route then descends into the wild, romantic Ega Valley. After passing beneath the main Brenner Pass highway, you are back in Bolzano.

Here again is your starting point, but this time for a trip through the western Dolomites, which lie primarily in the Trentino region. These are marked by local mineral spring waters that course through the lake and mountain areas and by architectural monuments of the medieval and Renaissance ages. You begin this western Dolomite route with Merano.

MERANO: This old-fashioned spa town is typical of South Tyrol's special charm. Its inner core is small, quaint, and Tyrolean while the outer town is marked by massive, somber, 19th-century Austrian hotels.

CLES: This pretty, medieval village in the heart of Val di Non was once the home of the Clesio family, medieval rulers whose ancestral castle dominates the town. A small Renaissance parish church also stands in the village center.

MADONNA DI CAMPIGLIO: Now one of Italy's biggest mountain resorts, Madonna di Campiglio offers countless excursions in summer and winter into the two ranges — Brenta and Adamello. Although mountain climbing in this region is geared to veteran hikers, there are several less challenging trails for beginners.

En Route from Madonna di Campiglio – As you head toward Trento, the road winds through some of the most attractive countryside of the region. You will come upon the spa center of Comano, the romantic lake and castle at Toblino, Lake Santa Massenza (which runs through the tiny spa town of Vigolo Baselga), and the peaceful lakeside village of Terlago.

TRENTO: Only 18½ miles (30 km) south of Bolzano, this city served, for the same strategic reasons as its northern neighbor, as an important Roman town on the Brenner Pass. In the years following Roman rule, Trento fell into relative obscurity, but it once again gained fame in the mid-16th century as the seat of the famous Council of Trent, held by Church authorities to consolidate Church power and curtail abuses in the face of the Protestant Reformation. Trento has always been Italian in character and language, despite its position in Austrian territory until 1918.

Some city highlights include the Via Belenzani, one of Trento's most beautiful streets, lined with Venetian and Renaissance palaces with frescoed exterior walls; the baroque church of San Francisco Saverio; and Trento's most celebrated monument — Il Castello di Buon Consiglio (the Castle of Good Counsel) — the original dwelling place of the bishops of Trentino–Alto Adige, built in the 13th century. Also of special interest is the Duomo (the Cathedral) whose style spans the 12th and 13th centuries, Lombard Romanesque to Gothic.

BEST EN ROUTE

Grand old Tyrolean hotels, inns, and converted castles stand on mountainsides and in the center of town in this part of the country. Expect to pay $70 or more per night for a double room at those places categorized as expensive; between $50 and $65 at hotels in the moderate category; under $45, inexpensive. Hearty country fare and local wines are served in any number of pleasant restaurants. Expect to pay $60 or more for a meal for two at those restaurants categorized as expensive; between $40 and $50 at restaurants in the moderate category; under $35, inexpensive. Prices do not include drinks, wine, or tip.

BOLZANO

Grifone-Greif – There are some beautiful furnishings on the large landings and in the upstairs reading rooms at this traditional Austrian hotel on the central piazza. The restaurant is excellent. 7 Piazza Walther (phone: 977056). Expensive to moderate.

Luna-Mondschein – A somewhat less refined but nonetheless characteristically Tyrolean hotel with a garden and a restaurant specializing in local cuisine. 15 Via Piave (phone: 975642). Expensive to moderate.

Scala-Stiegel – On the edge of the Old Town, this old-fashioned Tyrolean hotel has gardens, a swimming pool, and a restaurant. 11 Via Brennero (phone: 976222). Moderate.

Da Abramo – A fine restaurant housed in a building that was once the Town Hall of Gries; the interior is enlivened by a multitide of flowers and plants. Traditional and Italian dishes are served. Closed Sundays. 16 Piazza Gries (phone: 280141). Moderate.

BRESSANONE

Elefante – In a secluded corner of town with a garden and a heated swimming pool, the inside of this hotel has changed little for the past 400 years except for essential modernizations such as heating. It's filled with genuine 16th-century furnishings. The restaurant, also called *Elefante,* serves local cuisine prepared with great care and the freshest ingredients. Try the house specialty, *piatto Elefante* — a mountainous variety of cold meats served with appropriate sauces. Restaurant is closed Mondays. Hotel is closed mid-November through February. 4 Via Rio Bianco (phone: 22288). Expensive to moderate.

Corona d'Oro – More modest by comparison, this hotel in the old, porticoed center of town has a modern, pleasantly furnished restaurant where simple Tyrolean dishes, wine, and beer are served. 4 Via Fienili (phone: 24154). Moderate.

ORTISEI

Aquila-Adler – This hotel and restaurant have a garden, swimming pool, and garage (phone: 76203). Expensive.

Hell – Don't be deceived by the name. This recently built hotel offers typical Tyrolean comfort in its 27 rooms, international cuisine, hearty breakfasts, a sauna, and a solarium. Via Promenade (phone: 76785). Moderate.

SELVA DI VAL GARDENA (WOLKENSTEIN)

Tyrol – One of Selva's chalet-style hotels has some of the most superb views of the Dolomites. The restaurant is known for good country food and friendly service. Closed from October through mid-December and from mid-April through mid-June (phone: 75270). Expensive to moderate.

Dorfer – This small, relatively isolated hotel has a private garden and a decent restaurant. Closed October through mid-December and May through mid-June (phone: 75204). Moderate to inexpensive.

BRUNICO (BRUNECK)

Royal Hinterhuber – Set on a hill with an impressive, wide-angle view of the surrounding valleys, this hotel has gardens, tennis courts, swimming pool, parking area, and a fine restaurant. Closed mid-October to mid-December and mid-April to mid-May. Nearly 2 miles (3 km) southeast of Brunico (phone: 21221). Expensive to moderate.

Andreas Hofer – Pine walls and typical Tyrolean furniture are the most distinctive decorative features of this modern hotel. Fresh mushrooms in season are the chef's specialty. Closed the first half of December. 1 Via Campo Tures (phone: 85469). Inexpensive.

AURONZO DI CADORE

Al Lago – A pretty little hotel above Santa Caterina Lake, it has quite a good restaurant. Closed from October through May. 14 Via Piave (phone: 9314). Inexpensive.

CORTINA D'AMPEZZO

De la Poste – This luxury, chalet-style hotel has spacious rooms and a well-known restaurant. Closed October 20 to December 20. 14 Piazza Roma (phone: 4271). Expensive.

Capannina – Although not a luxury hotel, it is well situated and has one of the best restaurants in town. The Venetian and Tyrolean cooking is superb, as is the selection of wines. Closed from October through mid-December and mid-April until July. 11 Via della Stadio (phone: 2950, hotel; 2633, restaurant). Expensive to moderate.

Franceschi – In addition to a restaurant, it has tennis courts, a parking area, and a fine garden. Closed from mid-April to mid-June and October to December 20. 86 Via Cesare Battisti (phone: 867041). Expensive to moderate.

Menardi – This little hotel on the northern outskirts of town has a pleasant restaurant and a private garden from which you can see the Dolomites. Closed from October through mid-December and from April until July. 110 Via Majon (phone: 2400). Moderate to inexpensive.

SAN MARTINO DI CASTROZZA

San Martino – Recently modernized and enlarged, this is actually one of the oldest hotels in the area. Most of its rooms have retained their balconies, from which you can see the entire valley. A swimming pool, tennis court, and restaurant round out the facilities. Closed from mid-September through mid-December and mid-April through June (phone: 68011). Moderate to inexpensive.

Rosetta – Not as lavish as the *San Martino,* it, too, maintains an aura of classy tradition and has a garden, parking area, and restaurant. Closed mid-September through mid-December, and mid-April through June. (phone: 68622). Inexpensive.

Birreria Drei Tannen – This lively, elegant little restaurant serves hearty mountain food and local wine at tables set around a fireplace; dinner only. Closed mid-September to mid-December and mid-April through June (phone: 68325). Expensive to moderate.

MERANO

Castel Freiberg – A 14th-century former castle, about 4 miles (7 km) southeast of Merano, with 36 rooms. Facilities include tennis courts, indoor swimming pool, sauna, and solarium (phone: 44196). Expensive.

Andrea – Here you'll find well-prepared Tyrolean cuisine in a friendly atmosphere. Closed Mondays and mid-January to mid-March. 44 Via Galilei (phone: 37400). Expensive to moderate.

MADONNA DI CAMPIGLIO

Golf – This large country hotel has a 9-hole golf course, garden, and parking area. Service is friendly and efficient. The restaurant is excellent. Closed April through June and September through December. Campo Carlo Magno (phone: 410035). Expensive.

Caminetto – The gardens at this comfortable hotel overlook the Dolomites, and the restaurant serves well-cooked Tyrolean meals. Closed from April to mid-July and September through November. 38080 Madonna D'Campiglio (phone: 41242). Moderate.

TRENTO

Villa Madruzzo – This converted 18th-century villa has comfortable rooms and a pretty garden. Nearly 2 miles (3 km) east of town in Cognola. 38050 Cognola (phone: 986220). Moderate to inexpensive.

Chiesa – The menu features appealing local specialties, and the pasta is particularly good. Closed Mondays. 64 Via San Marco (phone: 985577). Moderate.

Birreria Forst – Don't miss the chance to eat in this very popular beer hall. The cuisine is regional as are the wines. Closed Mondays. 38 Via Oss Mazzurana (phone: 35590). Inexpensive.

Tuscany

Extending from the snow-capped Apennines north of Florence to south of the Maremma plains, Tuscany is probably Italy's wealthiest region. Its riches lie in a cultivated diverse land that has prospered since the early Etruscan, Roman, and later medieval periods, with a gastronomical discipline that rivals the finest on the continent. But even more important, Tuscany's art, architecture, and age-old traditions reflect an illustrious history now deeply embedded in its modern culture. Some of its cities and villages number among the oldest in central Italy.

Tuscany derives its name from the Roman Tuscia. Its original inhabitants were the pre-Roman Etruscans, a peaceful, progressive, and artistic people whose origins are obscure, but who spread through an area of Italy between Naples and the northern Po Valley. Eventually overrun by the Romans in 40 BC, the heart of Etruscan civilization — the land between the Tiber and Arno rivers — became a province of the Roman Empire. The Etruscans were wise in agricultural ways, and it's undoubtedly to them that Tuscany owes its reputation as a producer of some of the best wine and food in Europe.

Despite modernization in the past few decades, Tuscany holds fervently to its medieval past. Every year long-standing traditions — such as a 13th-century horse race, the Palio, in Siena; a Saracen jousting tournament in Arezzo; and a medieval football game in Florence — are re-enacted by Tuscans, all of which allow them to remember their roots and relive their past.

The logical starting point for a Tuscan itinerary is Florence, the leading cultural and shopping hub of the region. Slightly west of central Italy, the Tuscan route curves under the cross-country sway of the Apennines. It travels seaward to Pisa, then inland and south to Siena, down toward the marshlands of Maremma, and finally northeast to Arezzo and Cortona, 50 miles (80 km) south of Florence. Between the large cities, it passes through hilltop villages, seafaring towns, and sites of ancient ruins. This is a route on which one could tarry happily for weeks, but properly organized, it can be covered in about 4 or 5 days, hitting the highlights and getting a feel for the area and its people. From Florence (for a complete report on the city, see *Florence,* THE CITIES), the route goes to Lucca, where the tour really begins.

LUCCA: Striking because of its unusual architectural character, Lucca is marked by a mixture of styles that date from the 6th century. The town is surrounded by 16th-century ramparts, and a short walk shows a predominance of Romanesque and Pisan influence. Visit the huge 18th-century Piazza Napoleone at the center of town, the *National Art Gallery* of Lucca, and a cathedral begun in the 6th century, which stands in the stately Piazza di San Martino.

Also a rich architectural center famous for its olive oil, Lucca's market comes alive every morning. Townspeople crowd the vast squares surrounding the church of St. Michele.

PISA: An important Italian port in the early Middle Ages, Pisa was a much-sought-after center of trade until 1405, when it became a Florentine city. Recognizable from afar for its fabled leaning tower, Pisa is a delight of Romanesque architecture. Her builders and stone carvers were among the finest of the Renaissance period.

When you enter Pisa, head for the Piazza del Duomo, where the famous tower stands beside a cathedral and baptistry, richly decorated with carving by the Pisano family. The tower itself was begun by Bonanno Pisano in 1174 and, despite the sinking foundations, was completed in 1350. It's worth climbing up to the top, for the tower affords a panoramic view of the entire city. Visit the nearby Campo Santo, a 12th-century cemetery built by the Crusaders, and its surrounding Gothic galleries.

En Route from Pisa – Turn inland on Route 67, past the industrial town of Pontedera, and veer off at San Miniato Basso to visit the art-filled hilltop town of San Miniato. There, from a castle above the town's 12th-century cathedral, you can look out over the whole Arno Valley. From San Miniato, take a minor road south through unspoiled vineclad Tuscan hills past the villages of Casastrada, Mura, and Il Castagna. Continue for 31 miles (50 km) to San Gimignano, the town of medieval towers. Looking out from the hilltops of this city, it might as well be the 14th century. The lookout posts built for prestige by noblemen during the early medieval wars still offer magnificent views of the surrounding valley Col d'Elsa. Leaving San Gimignano on the main Siena highway (Route 68), turn left and drive through the characteristic wine country of the Chianti Valley to Poggibonsi, a wine trading town. From there, turn south for the last 15½ miles (25 km) to Siena.

SIENA: After Florence, Siena has probably the richest artistic heritage in Tuscany. An important agricultural town, the medieval spirit of Siena is almost entirely preserved. Originally an Etruscan city later taken over by the Romans (who named it Sena Julia), it was a much-contested territory through the medieval wars between the Italian states. After many vicissitudes, including the plague in 1348, Siena became part of the Duchy of Tuscany in 1559.

The city is laid out over three hilltops surrounded by walls. Begin a tour of Siena at the Piazza del Campo, the heart of the city and the scene of the famous Palio, when 10 of the former medieval districts is represented by a horse and bareback rider in a mad race around the piazza. The *Palio,* held on July 2 and August 16 every year, is the highlight of a magnificent festival carried out with color and fervor by the Sienese — not as a staged tourist attraction but as a celebration of their heritage.

In the sloping Piazza del Campo stands the graceful Gothic town hall with its bell tower, accessible to the public. Then make your way to the Piazza del Duomo, where the cathedral dedicated to the Madonna stands on a raised marble platform. Visit the baptistry, which seems to form the crypt of the cathedral, and browse through the *Pinacoteca Nazionale* — the art gallery at Palazzo Buonsignori — for a fundamental knowledge of Sienese art.

Walking along the narrow streets of Via di Città and Via Banchi di Sopra, both of which skirt the Piazza del Campo, you will come to the Chigi-Saracini Palace. Now a music academy, it houses some beautiful Renaissance apartments displaying a gallery of Tuscan paintings, open to the public upon request. Along the same row is the Loggia dei Mercanti, the merchants' center, which once served as the center of commerce. Farther along are the Piazza Salimbeni and its 4 palaces, which were built over a period from the 13th to the 16th century. The palace designs reflect the progression of architectural styles over the years from the medieval to the Renaissance and finally the baroque.

You can spend days in Siena simply wandering through the medieval streets soaking in the atmosphere of the city. Siena is also one of the greatest wine centers in the country. For some of the best Chianti around, buy a bottle at *Cantina Sociale,* and for some excellent cooking, frequent the local *trattorias.* You can stay at hotels converted from Renaissance palaces or at modest but charming hostelries in the outlying country overlooking the Chianti hills.

En Route from Siena – Take the Porta S. Marco and Route 73 for Grosseto, 58 miles (94 km) away. This route is in complete contrast to the gentle, vineclad hills of central Tuscany. Sparsely populated, wild and uncultivated, this is an introduction to the Maremma marshland. Travel past the small villages en route until a vast panorama opens out over the Maremma plains to the sea and the Argentario Peninsula. This gives way beyond Grosseto, the capital of Maremma, to green coastal plains until it reaches the forests and green hills of the national park known as the Uccellina.

UCCELLINA: The home of the original flora and fauna of Maremma, the Uccellina National Park features grasslands and beaches. One example of an Uccellina beach, and generally characteristic of the Tuscan shoreline, is Marina di Alberese, where a long stretch of white sand faces the edge of a pine forest. You can arrange visits to the park through the office some 3 miles (5 km) away in the village of Alberese.

Out of the Maremma region grew an unusual heritage when it became famous in the 18th century as a kind of "Wild West" of Italy. Herds of cattle and wild horses ran free through the plains, and cattle rustlers and bandits abounded.

SATURNIA: A tiny village on a hilltop, it's surrounded by countryside of Etruscan necropolises. In the village lie the remains of a Roman road, the Via Claudia, as well as a reconstructed 12th-century castle. Named Aurinia by the Etruscans, the later name of Saturnia is said to be derived from the Roman god Saturn. In the valley below the village swirl the steaming sulfur springs of the Terme di Saturnia.

En Route from Saturnia – From Saturnia take the road for Sovano and Sorano; these two special villages are perched atop hills of tufo — the soft red earth of Etruria — surrounded by Etruscan tombs. Transfer to the Roman road, the Via Cassia, then turn north for the first time along the route, leaving the Etruscan hills behind and heading back for the fertile green of central Tuscany. Along this final segment of the drive you'll come across many small towns in medieval settings. Follow the turns on the highway that lead to Route 327, and follow it until you reach the town of Arezzo.

AREZZO: The Romans called it Arretium — a town that lies in the middle of olive- and vine-covered hills in a valley where the Chiana and Arno rivers meet. At the center of town is the 14th-century church of St. Francis, which contains a remarkable fresco cycle (look behind the high altar) by Piero della Francesca, a native of Arezzo. Nearby is the sloping Piazza Grande, the focus of urban life for centuries, which is surrounded by buildings in a variety of architectural styles. Note especially the 16th-century Palazzo delle Logge, with its open portico of shops, flanked by Renaissance palaces and medieval homes, as well as the magnificent Pieve di Santa Maria, a Romanesque church that backs onto the square, its tall bell tower of "100 holes" (it actually has 40 mullioned windows) standing alongside. The first weekend of every month, an important antiques fair is held in Piazza Grande, and on the first Sunday in September it is also the scene of the annual Joust of the Saracen — an exciting reenactment of a medieval tournament on horseback.

From the piazza, walk through the old quarter of town to the Ponte Solesta, which spans the Tronto River. Across the bridge is a magnificent view of the town, with its medieval towers and churches.

CORTONA: A visit to Cortona, on the border of Tuscany and Umbria, is like a step back in time to the early Renaissance. Secluded and silent, atop a hill covered with olive trees and vineyards, the walled city of Cortona is characterized by steep, narrow streets that open onto uneven piazzas. Its cathedrals and palaces display collections of paintings and other artwork, and the Palazzo Pretorio (Casali) houses a rich Etruscan museum.

BEST EN ROUTE

In this part of Italy you will find some very pretty hotels and reasonably priced restaurants where regional cuisine is nothing less than a fine art. Expect to pay $70 or more per night for a double room at those hotels categorized as expensive; between $50 and $65 in the moderate category; under $45, inexpensive. Expect to pay $60 or more for a meal for two at those restaurants classified as expensive; between $40 to $55 at restaurants in the moderate category; under $35, inexpensive. Prices do not include drinks, wine, or tip.

LUCCA

Buca di San Antonio – Steeped in history, this place offers some of the best Lucchese cooking in town in a friendly atmosphere. Risotto and game dishes are specialties. Closed Mondays, Sunday evenings, and the last 3 weeks of July. 1-3 Via della Cervia (phone: 55881). Moderate.

PISA

D'Azeglio – One of the better small, first class hotels, it offers inviting decor and good service. 18-B Piazza Vittorio Emanuele (phone: 500310). Expensive.

Arno and Ristorante da Antonio – This hotel and restaurant near the banks of the Arno are within walking distance of the *National Museum*. 6 Piazza della Repubblica (phone: 501820). Inexpensive to moderate.

Buzzino – Here is some of the best Pisan cooking, especially mixed grilled fish and roast veal with herb and mushroom sauce. Chianti wines are plentiful and excellent. Closed Tuesdays and November. 44 Via C. Cammeo (phone: 562141). Expensive.

Sergio – Despite its unpretentious surroundings, this place overlooking the Arno River is probably the best restaurant in town, serving plentiful Pisan food and wine. Closed Monday lunchtime, Sundays, and July 15 to August 16. 1 Lungarno Pacinotti (phone:48245). Expensive.

SAN GIMIGNANO

La Cisterna and Ristorante La Terrazza – In the medieval town square, this 50-room hotel is known for its large, wooden-balconied rooms overlooking the valley that surrounds this quiet hilltop town. The restaurant on the top floor serves excellent Tuscan cuisine. Hotel and restaurant closed from early November to early March; restaurant closed Tuesdays and Wednesday lunchtime. 23 Piazza della Cisterna (phone: 940328). Hotel moderate; restaurant expensive.

SIENA

Park – Set in a beautiful park on the outskirts of town, this elegant 16th-century villa has tennis courts, a heated pool, spacious rooms, and a fine restaurant, *L'Olivo*. It is part of the CIGA hotel chain. 18 Via di Marciano (phone: 44803). Expensive.

Garden – This pleasant, 67-room hotel has lovely gardens, swimming pool, and a restaurant. 2 Via Custoza (phone: 47056). Moderate.

Chiusarelli – At the edge of the old city, this 50-room hotel has a restaurant, a small garden, and a parking area. 9 Viale Curtatone (phone: 288234). Inexpensive.

Grotta di Santa Caterina – You'll find a wide selection of Siena Chianti wines at this characteristically medieval tavern, which is very popular with the Palio crowd. Closed Mondays. 26 Via della Galluzza (phone: 282208). Moderate to inexpensive.

Mariotti–da Mugolone – Hearty home-cooked meals are served in a simple setting. Closed Thursdays and most of July. 8 Via dei Pellegrini (phone: 283235). Inexpensive.

SATURNIA (GROSSETO)

Terme di Saturnia – This large, peaceful, luxurious country hotel has a natural sulfur swimming pool and falls, gym, tennis courts, and a good restaurant offering diet menus. The hotel owns a nearby ranch, with horseback riding and hunting (phone: 601061). Expensive.

CORTONA

San Luca and Ristorante Tonino – Here, the setting is undeniably charming — on the fringe of a medieval town with tranquil, rural surroundings. The restaurant is closed for Monday dinner and Tuesdays. 2 Piazza Garibaldi (phone: 603100). Hotel expensive to moderate; restaurant expensive.

La Fonte dei Frati – In a renovated, centuries-old *casa colonica* (farmhouse) just outside Cortona, this restaurant offers well-prepared simple cuisine indigenous to the area, and rustic but sophisticated ambience. Closed Tuesdays. 234 Case Sparse, Località Camucia (the periphery of Cortona) (phone: 601370). Moderate.

Campania

Campania has long lured enthusiastic visitors with its spectacular natural splendors, its unparalleled wealth of archaeological excavations and historic monuments, and its people, who have cheered the world with their music and their food.

Two picturesque gulfs (Naples and Salerno), three promontories (Phlegrean Fields, the Sorrento Peninsula, and Cilento), a massive volcano (Vesuvius), a forest-covered mountain at the edge of the blue Tyrrhenian Sea (Mt. Faito), and several romantic islands (Capri, Ischia, and Procida) are sufficient reason to tour this region. Add to this plenitude one of the greatest concentrations of archaeological excavations in the world — at Pompeii, Herculaneum, and Paestum, as well as others scattered around the region at other points — unforgettably romantic towns of historical and mythological importance such as Sorrento, Amalfi, Ravello, Positano, and Naples itself, and the region becomes a journey of compulsive interest.

Dominated by the cities of Naples, Amalfi, and Sorrento, the area consists primarily of three sections, each with a splendor of its own. There's the Bay of Naples in the north, a volcanic area with steaming natural hot springs first used by the ancient Romans as thermal spas; a series of three romantic islands off the coast of Naples, including the international resort of Capri; and the Amalfi Coast, the picturesque rocky mountain region winding along the Tyrrhenian Sea from Sorrento to the Gulf of Salerno.

Vesuvius, one of the few volcanoes in Europe still active, stands poised between the northern and southern edges of the Campanian route. Its fiery lava, which buried Pompeii and Herculaneum in AD 79, has not erupted with force since 1944. However, the twin peaks still emit trails of smoke at periodic intervals.

The November 23, 1980, earthquake that devastated vast parts of Campania struck the interior Apennine zone in the southeast, leaving the coast practically untouched. Thus, the islands and the popular Amalfi Coast were spared damage. In Naples, several buildings received dangerous cracks and two collapsed altogether, but the major hotels and restaurants were not damaged. The Pompeii ruins were closed temporarily for repairs but have reopened to tourists. Sorrento suffered some minor damage, and the few hotels that were affected merely used the situation to their advantage and did some repainting and renovating.

The route begins in Naples, the regional capital and the center for fascinating tours to the volcanic region.

NAPLES: For a complete report on the city, see *Naples,* THE CITIES.

    En Route from Naples – While in Naples, take an excursion to the eerie Phlegrean Fields, a steamy volcanic zone of dark, violent beauty about 12½ miles (20 km) from the city. It extends along the Gulf of Pozzuoli on a promontory from Cape Posillipo to Cape Miseno. Visit the semiactive crater of Solfatara near Pozzuoli, then continue to the Lake Avernus crater, regarded by the ancients as the entrance to the Underworld. Continue on to Baia, noted for its ancient Roman baths, and Cape Miseno. The cape has wonderful views of the islands of Ischia and Procida. From Cape Miseno, travel up the outer edges of the promontory to the ruins of Cumae, an 8th-century Greek colony, where Virgil's verses were written in the Cave of the Sibyl. Then drive the 15½ miles (25 km) to Pompeii. If time is a factor, do a combined Pompeiian-Herculaneum day tour. Of the two Roman cities buried in the AD 79 eruption of Vesuvius, the latter is the more interesting. Its patrician villas are more elegant and less thoroughly excavated. If, however, you have time to do the whole thing properly — and it's worth making time — start with the excellent *National Museum* in Naples the day before, where the majority of the Pompeii treasures are exhibited, and at the sites use the guidebooks published by Libreria dello Stato called *Pompeii* and *Herculaneum*.

Take a trip to Vesuvius itself, now a desolate and barren landscape overlooking the Bay of Naples and the rest of Campania.

THE ISLANDS: There is frequent ferryboat and hydrofoil service between the islands of Capri, Ischia, and Procida and the mainland cities as well as helicopter transport from the Naples-Capodichino Airport to Capri and Ischia. Even on a limited schedule, spend at least a day on Capri, and if time is no problem, visit Ischia as well. Procida is the least attractive of the three islands — it's very volcanic, with four craters and black sand.

CAPRI: The gem of the bay, sunny Capri (pronounced *kah*-pree) was a favorite resort for the Phoenicians and ancient Romans as it is today for international jet-setters and day-trippers. It is not, however, a swimmer's paradise; there are few beaches on Capri's dramatic, almost inaccessible coastline. Its villages consist of small public squares, villas and white houses, set amid varied subtropical vegetation. Visit the towns of Capri and Anacapri, the Marina Piccola and Marina Grande, and the famous Blue Grotto sea cave. Also, stop at the ruins of Villa Jovis (one of many resorts built by the Emperor Tiberias) and the Villa San Michele at Anacapri, celebrated by Swedish physician and writer Axel Munthe in *The Story of San Michele*. Spectacular views of the Faraglioni (rock islets) are seen from the Punta Tragara belvedere.

ISCHIA: Twice the size of Capri but half as crowded, Ischia is of volcanic origin (its source, Mt. Epomeo, hasn't erupted in nearly seven centuries, and its slopes now produce the renowned Epomeo wine). Sandy beaches, thermal hot springs, and lush green scenery all contribute to the fast-growing popularity of this Emerald Isle, as it is known. Porto d'Ischia is the charming island harbor town, south of which is Ponte d'Ischia (named for an Aragonese-built bridge), the site of a 15th-century castle. Casamicciola and Lacco Ameno are favorite resorts, and Sant'Angelo is one of the island's several picturesque fishing villages.

AMALFI COAST (COSTA AMALFITANA): Stretching from Sorrento to Salerno along the gulf of that name, the Amalfi Coast is one of the most spectacular drives on any Italian route. On a peninsula, the northern portion around Sorrento has been exploited in recent years, but the southern half of the peninsula remains a romantic paradise — sun-warmed rocks and terraced gardens, lemon and olive groves overlooking sparkling blue bays and coves, flowered promontories and secret beaches. In *The Immoralist* André Gide says that the road from Sorrento to Ravello "was so beautiful that I had no desire . . . to see anything more beautiful on earth."

Although the Amalfi Coast actually begins at Sorrento, a couple of preliminary stops en route make the drive from Naples more interesting. Pick up the Autostrada del Sole (A3) as far as Castellammare di Stabia, less than 31 miles (50 km) from Naples, which was, like Pompeii and Herculaneum, destroyed by Vesuvius in AD 79. Then, take the scenic road (SS145) that curves around the northern coast of the peninsula and stop a short distance farther at Vico Equense. It offers good views of the coast, inexpensive boat service to Capri, and delicious pizzas, sold, like textiles, by the yard — actually, by the meter. Look for a large sign, "Pizza al Metro," towering over some of the town's cliff-hanging white houses.

SORRENTO: Tourists return time and again to Sorrento, a legendary resort amid beautiful gardens. Its clifftop setting is its main attraction, but it features several architectural points of interest, including its Duomo, which has a 13th-century cloister with distinctive pointed arches, reflecting the Moorish influence.

En Route from Sorrento – Be prepared for a treacherous slice of highway that continues clear around the mountains until you reach Positano. To avoid the entire scene, drive back north to Gragnano (famous for its red wine) and take an inland route to Positano.

POSITANO: John Steinbeck once described Positano as "a dream place that isn't quite real." Its white houses and terraced gardens cling gently to slopes that roll into the sea, all around a picturesque port dotted with small fishing boats.

During the 10th century, it was one of the most important mercantile cities in the world, but more recently it has become a refuge for writers and artists, who derive inspiration from its natural and architectural settings. Positano is a particular favorite among the younger set, not only because its vertical architectural plan makes frequent climbing necessary in daily living, but also because its fashions center around original and inexpensive boutique wear designed by local artisans. These items, which are displayed temptingly along narrow cobblestone streets, set the fashion pace for summerwear throughout Italy.

En Route from Positano – The road continues past many fishing villages and Saracen towers — once the haunts of pirates — perched on peaks and reefs above the sea. The cliffside corniche then passes over the great gorges of the Valley of Furore and carves into the rocky walls of the Lattari Mountains east to Amalfi.

AMALFI: A Moorish-looking town with white houses and a curiously Oriental church, Amalfi was originally an important maritime republic loyal to Byzantium. Its greatest period of prosperity was during the 11th century, when the Amalfi Navigation Tables, the oldest maritime code in the world, regulated shipping in the entire Mediterranean. Amalfi's cathedral is worth a stop; its bronze doors were cast in Constantinople in 1066.

RAVELLO: This is by far the most picturesque spot along the Gulf of Salerno. When you arrive in Ravello, first visit the Villa Rufolo, whose gardens so inspired Richard Wagner, then stroll through the gardens of the Villa Cimbrone to the belvedere for a spectacular view of the entire gulf. Ravello's cathedral has a fine set of bronze doors and two famous pulpits.

PAESTUM: This ancient Greek city by the sea is one of the finest archaeological sites in the world, with three temples standing nobly among asphodel, oleander, and aromatic herbs. The Basilica and the so-called Temple of Neptune, side by side, were both probably dedicated to Hera. The latter, dating from the 5th century BC, is one of the most beautiful Doric temples in Italy or Greece and one of the best preserved. A third temple, the Temple of Ceres, was actually dedicated to Athena. Don't miss the museum, particularly the paintings from the Diver's Tomb and the metopes from the sanctuary of Hera Argiva, found nearby.

If returning to Rome by car, pick up the Autostrada via Nola, bypassing Naples, at Salerno.

BEST EN ROUTE

Some of the most truly charming hotels and restaurants in Italy are tucked away in Campania. Expect to pay $90 or more per night for a double room at the hotels categorized as expensive; between $60 to $85 in the moderate category; under $60, inexpensive. Expect to pay $65 or more for a meal for two at those restaurants classified as expensive; between $40 and $60 in the moderate category; under $40, inexpensive. Prices do not include drinks, wine, or tip.

LUCRINO (LAKE AVERNUS)

Ninfea – On a lake that was once part of the Bourbons' hunting reserve, this restaurant is renowned for its fresh fish. Closed Tuesdays and from September 15 to June 15. 1 Via Italia (phone: 866-1326). Expensive to moderate.

CAPRI

Canzone del Mare – This pleasant afternoon restaurant on the beach is a favorite with swimmers and sunbathers, who come for a relaxing meal and a drink before the restaurant closes at dusk. The specialty is fresh fish. Reservations suggested. Closed October to mid-May. Marina Piccola (phone: 837-0104). Expensive.

Luna – The garden terraces at this lovely and comfortable 48-room hotel have a fine offshore view of the Faraglioni. The interior decor is tasteful, service is good, and there is a swimming pool. Closed November through March. 3 Via Matteotti (phone: 837-0433). Expensive.

Punta Tragara – Designed by the master French architect Le Corbusier, it has a splendid view of the Faraglioni. In addition to antique furnishings in the 41 rooms, it has a swimming pool, spa baths, and hydromassages. Closed October 15 through March. 57 Via Tragara (phone: 837-0844). Expensive.

Quisisana e Grand – Recently acquired by German radio-TV magnate Max Grundig, this deluxe, 143-room hotel caters to a well-heeled, well-traveled crowd. It has tennis courts and a swimming pool. Closed January through March. 2 Via Camerelle (phone: 837-0788). Expensive.

Scalinatella – An elegant, small hotel overlooking the sea. Closed November through March 15. 8 Via Tragara (phone: 837-0633). Expensive.

Flora – A 14-room hotel with romantic appeal but no restaurant. Closed November through March. 26 Via Serena (phone: 837-0211). Moderate to inexpensive.

La Capannina – A rather chic restaurant sporting a Michelin star. Specialties are fish and pasta. Try the green *gnocchi* with salmon and the *penne* with eggplant. Closed Wednesdays (except in August), and November through March. 14 Via Delle Botteghe (phone: 837-0732). Expensive.

Da Luigi – Frequented by yachtsmen, since it's accessible by sea. Considered one of the top restaurants on the island. Lunch only. Closed in winter. On the Stradadei Faraglioni (phone: 837-0591). Expensive to moderate.

La Pigna – This well-run restaurant is also frequented by yachtsmen, and owners of neighboring villas. A few minutes' walk from the center of town on the road to Marina Grande. Closed Tuesdays in low season, October, and Easter. 8 Via Roma (phone: 837-0280). Expensive to moderate.

Casina delle Rose – Stick to the local dishes, especially the fish, and avoid the international selections. Closed Tuesdays during spring and fall and from November to mid-March. 30 Via Vittorio Emanuele (phone: 837-0200). Moderate.

Da Gemma – Not far from the piazzetta, this convenient restaurant with a pleasant outdoor terrace is another of Capri's favorite eateries. Reservations advised. Closed Mondays and November. 6 Via Madre Serafina (phone: 837-0461). Moderate.

ISCHIA

Excelsior Belvedere – This extravagantly decorated 67-room Excelsior chain hotel is noted for its excellent service. The building is set among landscaped gardens with a swimming pool and a nearby beach. Closed November to March. 3 Via Emanuele Gianturco (phone: 991020). Expensive.

Grand Hotel Punta Molino – An elegant 88-room hotel overlooking the sea with lovely gardens and a swimming pool. Closed November to late April. Lungomare Telese già Colombo (phone: 991544). Expensive.

Jolly – With 200 comfortable rooms, this hotel at Porto Ischia features thermal spa treatments. There is also a swimming pool and an excellent restaurant. Closed January and February. 42 Via de Luca (phone: 991744). Expensive.

L'Albergo della Regina Isabella e Royal Sporting – A deluxe, super-comfortable

133-room spa, recently acquired by the excellent CIGA chain, it has a swimming pool, private beach, tennis court, and gardens. Closed November through March. 4 Piazza S. Restituta at Lacco Ameno (phone: 994322). Expensive.

Il Moresco – An old Spanish-style building smothered in bougainvillea. It has 63 rooms, a swimming pool, tennis courts, gardens, and a solarium. Closed November through March. 16 Via Emanuele Gianturco at Punta Molino (phone: 981355). Expensive.

Bristol Palace – This 39-room hotel has a restaurant, thermal bath facilities, and gardens. Closed November through March. 10 Via Marone (phone: 992181). Moderate.

Pensione La Villarosa – This charming, family-style, 37-room villa has a splendid garden fragrant with gardenias, and a swimming pool. It is known for friendly, personal service and comfort. Closed November through March. 13 Via Giacinto Gigante (phone: 991316). Inexpensive.

Damiano – The specialty is fish in this modern-looking restaurant with a glass-enclosed terrace. Reservations recommended. Closed October through March. Via Della Vigna, Porto Ischia (phone: 983032). Expensive to moderate.

Gennaro – It has a central location and authentic island decor, and it's known for its fish soups and antipastos. Closed Tuesdays in winter and November to mid-March. 66 Via Porto, Porto Ischia (phone: 992917). Moderate.

Di Massa – The specialties of the house are honest Ischitana dishes — including *coniglio* (fresh fish and rabbit). Closed Tuesdays and winters. 29 Via Seminario, Porto Ischia (phone: 991402). Moderate.

GULF OF NAPLES COAST

Axidie – The 29 balconied rooms have delightful views of the sea. It occupies a former monastery and is furnished with antiques. On the grounds are tennis courts, a swimming pool, and a beach. Marina Aequa, Vico Equense (phone: 879-8181). Expensive to moderate.

Da Gigino – Pizzas are sold by the meter in a spacious, open-air garden in the center of town. 10 Via Nicoteria (phone: 879-8426). Inexpensive.

SORRENTO

Grand Hotel Excelsior Vittoria – This old-fashioned 125-room member of the Excelsior chain is surrounded by orange and lemon groves. The panoramic terraces overlook well-kept grounds with a swimming pool. An elevator whisks you down to the hotel's private beach. 34 Piazza Torquato Tasso (phone: 878-1900). Expensive.

Minerva – Somewhat out of the way, it's worth it because of its lovely position on the sea. With only 50 rooms, this family-style pension has charm and a good restaurant, *La Minervetta.* Closed in winter. 30 Via Capo (phone: 878-1011). Expensive.

Bristol – This pleasant, 130-room hotel has a swimming pool, restaurant, and a terrace with a beautiful view of the gulf. 22 Via Capo (phone: 878-4522). Expensive to moderate.

Imperial Tramontano – This 119-room hotel is in the heart of town, yet surrounded by nice gardens. Many of the rooms overlook the gulf and beach, and there is a swimming pool. Closed January and February. 1 Via Veneto (phone: 878-1940). Expensive to moderate.

Parco dei Principi – A 173-room hotel that was once a Bourbon family villa, it has a stupendous park and a view of the gulf. It, too, has a swimming pool and beach. An excellent hotel, especially for the price. 1 Via Rota (phone: 878-4644). Expensive to moderate.

President – Set high on a bluff amid a pine grove overlooking the bay, this 82-room hotel has a swimming pool and gardens outside Sorrento on Colle Parise. Closed November through March. Via Nastro Verde, Colle Parise (phone: 878-2262). Expensive to moderate.

Bellevue Syrene – A converted 18th-century villa, this 50-room hotel is particularly recommendable. In addition to its charming setting, it has an elevator to a private beach. 5 Piazza della Vittoria (phone: 878-1024). Moderate to inexpensive.

La Tonnarella – This unpretentious 11-room pension on the outskirts of town overlooks the sea, and has a hilltop restaurant in a lemon- and oleander-filled garden. Closed November through March. 31 Via Capo (phone: 878-1153). Inexpensive.

La Favorita o' Parrucchiano – This authentic Sorrentine restaurant serves fresh local cheeses — *trecce, burielli* — vegetables, and fish. Try the very good fish soup. Closed on Wednesdays during winter and spring. 71-73 Corso Italia (phone: 878-1321). Expensive to moderate.

Kursaal – This very popular spot in the center of town turns out good seafood and pizzas. Via Fuorimura (phone: 878-1216). Expensive to moderate.

Antico Francischiello – Cheerful and hospitable, with genuine local cooking. Closed Tuesdays except in summer. 27 Via Villazzano, about 4 miles (6 km) from Sorrento (phone: 877-1171). Moderate.

POSITANO

Poseidon – The 50 rooms in this elegant establishment offer a lovely view of the sea and coastline. There is also a swimming pool. Closed November through late April. 148 Via Paitea (phone: 875014). Expensive.

San Pietro – Built into a cliff next to the sea, this 46-room hotel has an elevator to a private beach, a swimming pool, and tennis courts. Closed January through March. Less than 1 mile (2 km) south of town (phone: 875455). Expensive.

Sirenuse – Author John Steinbeck stayed in one of the 65 rooms of this converted 18th-century villa, now a superb hotel with a good swimming pool and view of the sea. Open year-round. 30 Via Colombo (phone: 875066). Expensive.

Miramare – This 14-room hotel has a distinctive warmth despite its small size. Closed mid-November to mid-March. Viatrara Gencino (phone: 875002). Expensive to moderate.

Palazzo Murat – The 18th-century palace of Gioacchino Murat (a king of Naples and Napoleon's brother-in-law) has been tastefully restored with some period furniture and beamed ceilings. All of the 28 rooms have a certain magic, but especially those overlooking the courtyard filled with purple bougainvillea. Open year-round. 23 Via dei Mulini (phone: 875177). Expensive to moderate.

Casa Albertina – A small and attractive family-run hotel with personal service. All rooms have terraces overlooking the sea. 4 Via della Tavolozza (phone: 875143). Moderate to inexpensive.

La Bougainville – In the center of town, this 14-room hotel is clean and convenient. Closed December through February (phone: 875047). Inexpensive.

Buca di Bacco – This is traditionally Positano's favorite restaurant of the yachting crowd. Try the fish and you might well understand why. Closed mid-October to March 24. Via Marina, opposite the port (phone: 875004). Expensive.

Chez Black – A favorite of bathers taking a lunch break. Try the spaghetti with clams or the mixed fish fry. Closed in winter. 19 Via del Brigantino (phone: 875036). Moderate.

La Cambusa – A very good restaurant that gets better all the time. *La Cambusa* goes so far as to employ its own fishermen, and it also turns out Positano's best spaghetti with zucchini (the town's most characteristic dish) and an excellent fish soup. A lovely veranda overlooks the piazzetta and the beach. Via Amerigo Vespucci (phone: 875432). Moderate.

Da Vincenzo – Less glamorous than some others but a favorite of Positanese. Local cuisine is featured, including lots of fresh vegetables and baked pasta. Up the hill on the Casa Soriano curve, 172-178 Viale Pasitea (phone: 875128) Inexpensive.

AMALFI

Luna Convento – This converted 13th-century convent has 42 rooms, lovely cloisters, and a swimming pool. 19 Via Amendola (phone: 871002). Expensive.

Santa Caterina – This 42-room hotel stands atop a cliff with an elevator leading to a beach. There is also a saltwater swimming pool. 19 Via Nazionale (phone: 871012). Expensive.

Cappuccini Convento – An old monastery converted into a splendid 48-room hotel. High on a cliff, it has sensational views of the coast. Also a solarium and a private beach. 46 Via Annunziatella (phone: 871008). Expensive to moderate.

Belvedere – It's cut into a cliff so that the series of terraces appear to be growing downward. Naturally, it overlooks the sea, with dazzling views from its 36 rooms. There is also a swimming pool. Closed November through March (phone: 831282). Moderate.

Excelsior Grand – This modern, efficient, 85-room member of the Excelsior chain has a beach, swimming pool, and gardens. Closed mid-October to mid-April. Three miles (5 km) outside Amalfi in Pogerola (phone: 871344). Moderate.

Miramalfi – Featuring an elevator to the beach, a swimming pool, and 45 rooms (phone: 871588). Moderate to inexpensive.

Da Gemma – A homey *trattoria* featuring outdoor dining in summer. Seafood specialties include spaghetti with clams and linguine with scampi. Good local wines. Closed Thursdays, January, and February. Via Cavalieri di Malta (phone: 871345). Moderate.

La Caravella – This place serves genuine Southern Italian home-style cooking at bargain prices. What more could you ask for? Closed Tuesdays and November. 12 Via Camera (phone: 871029). Inexpensive.

RAVELLO

Palumbo al Confalone – This utterly romantic 19th-century villa, now a hotel, is built on the ruins of the 12th-century Confalone, perched 1,200 feet above the Amalfi Drive. Its fine restaurant offers specialties like *fusilli al gorgonzola* and *crostini* of mozzarella. Be sure to have lunch in the beautiful garden overlooking the Gulf of Salerno — a special delight. 28 Via San Giovanni del Toro (phone: 857244). Expensive.

Caruso Belvedere – Formerly the 11th-century Palazzo D'Afflitto, it has been transformed into a delightful, 26-room hotel. Its restaurant is deservedly famous. It produces its own wines and a curious house soufflé — half lemon, half chocolate. Not only is the food delicious, the setting is gorgeous. Restaurant closed Tuesdays during winter. 52 Via San Giovanni del Toro (phone: 857111). Moderate.

Parsifal – Not as elegant as the others but nonetheless tasteful, this 20-room hotel is in a section of a 13th-century convent. Closed October through March. 5 Via d'Anna (phone: 857144). Inexpensive.

La Colonna – An attractive restaurant with whitewashed walls and vaulted ceilings. Owner Alfonso Sorrentino makes daily changes to the menu. His wife, Carmela, runs a ceramics shop in the main piazza. Closed Tuesdays. 20 Via Roma (phone: 857411). Moderate to inexpensive.

Compa' Cosimo – Home cooking, Ravello style — fresh fish and vegetables. Specialties include minestrone, bean soup, and pizzas. Closed Mondays in winter. Via Roma (phone: 857156). Moderate to inexpensive.

Calabria

Calabria, the sunny toe in the boot that is Italy, is a strangely beautiful land. It is neither the average tourist's idea of southern Italy (as all sun, song, and smiles) nor is it the strictly dreary picture of a depressed people in a depressed part of the Mezzogiorno forever brooding on their not-insignificant problems. Calabrians have the knack — learned perhaps out of necessity — of living reality rather than worrying about it.

It's a land rich in natural scenery, from the rugged, vineclad slopes of the northern Sila Mountains to the white sandy beaches at the southern tip of the Tyrrhenian Sea. A warm climate produces an abundance of olive, lemon, and orange groves as well as bergamots, figs, and chestnuts that dot the mountains and central plains. But it's more the picturesque towns and the old-fashioned warmth of the Calabrians that set this region of Italy apart.

This is a land of hospitable people who welcome visitors with genuine cordiality, a jug of wine, a home-cooked meal, and a zest for living. Tradition is elemental to the Calabrians and embraces all areas of life. These southern Italians are also a superstitious people, celebrating their many religious feasts with pagan rites and wailing laments reminiscent of ancient Greece — no surprise in an area once known as Magna Graecia.

The region is divided into three provinces named after their capital cities: Cosenza, the inland section in the north; Catanzaro, farther south, near the eastbound Ionian coast; and Reggio di Calabria, at the tip of the toe, separated by only a narrow strait from Sicily.

If you're making your first visit to Calabria, we suggest driving from central Italy. Although you can fly to Lamezia Terme or Reggio di Calabria and rent a car there, the 248-mile (400-km) drive from Salerno (403 mi/650 km from Rome) on the Autostrada del Sole (A3) is unforgettable. You'll wind through some of Italy's most spectacular scenery: through tunnels carved out of the mountains, with views of medieval hill towns, pine forests, and glistening sea below.

The Autostrada (one of the few toll-free *autostrade*) extends into Reggio di Calabria in southern Italy, but there is an alternative in Route 18. You can pick that up by leaving the Autostrada at Lagonegro for Praia a Mare. Remember, though, that in the south of Italy, points of interest are much more widely separated than in the north, and driving is very difficult except for stretches of Route 18, which follow the coast quite closely.

You begin the Calabrian portion of this trip in Praia a Mare, at the northern edge of the region. The route proceeds down the coastline, making several stops along the way at resort beaches and inland medieval towns. The part of the coastline that best captures the essence of Calabria is the Costa Viola (Violet Coast) in the southern province of Reggio. The Costa Viola extends some 31 miles (50 km) from Gioia Tauro to Santa Trada, just north of the provincial capital of Reggio di Calabria. Named for the violet hue that the land and turquoise Tyrrhenian Sea take on at sunset, the Costa Viola consists of a strip of small towns and sandy beaches, the latter interrupted by dramatic cliffs and grottoes. Many of the beaches are accessible only by boat, and the larger ones have only recently been provided access with roads and are indiscriminately dotted with *pensioni* and *trattorie.*

While the towns of this region have been reconstructed in a rather nondescript fashion following the 1908 earthquake, each still has its classic *corso* (main street), which provides the setting for the ritual evening *passeggiata* (promenade) and a favorite *caffè* or bar on the main piazza where townspeople gather to exchange gossip over a coffee, ice cream, or pastry.

From the Costa Viola you drive to Reggio di Calabria, the most modern city of the region, and continue inland toward the eastern coast and the Ionian Sea. There you'll find Italian towns still rich in Greek heritage as well as remnants of medieval architecture.

En Route from Salerno – On the drive south toward Costa Viola from the beginning of Route 18, make your first stop at Paria a Mare or at Diamante, a bit farther along. Either provides a fine introduction to the province of Cosenza, with its wooded plains and beaches, many of which are becoming popular as year-round resorts. H. V. Morton's *A Traveller in Southern Italy* noted: "From Pizzo southward there is an additional clarity in the air, a bluer sea, beautiful clouds . . . one thinks a landscape like this could produce only poets and artists."

Continue right around the cape (Capo Vaticano) past Nicotera (where wonderful terra-cotta masks are made — they ward off evil spirits), returning to Route 18 south. Now you begin the itinerary along the Costa Viola, with the first stop at Gioia Tauro.

GIOIA TAURO: Although this town is not a spectacular entry to the Costa Viola, it does boast some magnificent olive trees on the Plain of Gioia, said to be the oldest and largest in Europe, supposedly dating back to the time of Christ.

PALMI: Beyond the silvery flicker of olive groves along the coastline, the road suddenly opens to the largest of Palmi's sandy beaches, La Tonnara. At the southernmost point of the beach, on a rock jutting out of the sea, stands a solitary ancient olive tree. When the town council declared it Palmi's symbol a few years ago and began fertilizing and doctoring it, *l'olivo* suddenly wilted, demanding to be left once again to its own resources.

Like its symbol, Palmi thrives when left to follow its natural course. Physically lush subtropical plants and uncultivated flora — jasmine, bougainvillea, prickly pears, and of course the bergamots — fill the air with a sweet fragrance; culturally, Palmi's inhabitants continue to follow ancient beliefs and customs. You'll find living proof of the latter at the *Calabrian Folklore Museum,* which has fine collections of old and new masks from Seminara, Greek-style ceramics from the Ionian coast, pastoral art from the Aspromonte, and a number of religious and superstitious objects used to ward off evil spirits.

Before leaving Palmi, don't miss a trip up to the top of Mt. St. Elia, "the balcony over the Tyrrhenian." The magnificient view includes Mt. Etna and Messina in Sicily, the Aeolian islands, and the Calabrian coast as far north as Cape Vatican. And be sure to take a drive to La Marinella, a tiny fishermen's cover, Palmi's bathing beach before the road to La Tonnara was built some 20 years ago. It's not a very comfortable pebble beach, but the area is good for snorkeling.

BAGNARA: South of Palmi, beyond the famous Zibibbo vineyards clinging to rocky terraces that descend toward the sea, you reach the swordfishing center of the Costa

Viola. Activity hasn't changed in this town since the days of the early Greeks. Life centers around the capture, sale, and preparation of swordfish, at least between April and late July or August, when the fish come to spawn from colder Arctic waters. The fishermen harpoon the swordfish by hand as they did in ancient times.

Once ashore, the heavy catch is carried on the heads of the *bagnarote* (women of Bagnara) to the market for sale. Many are also exported to the larger cities and show up in restaurants throughout Italy. (They appear as *pescespada* on the menu.)

Swordfish serves as the main diet staple for the southern Calabrians nearly 4 months a year; it is cooked in so many different ways that no one seems to tire of the meaty morsels. Most often, they are grilled and dowsed with *salmoriglio,* a tasty sauce of garlic, oregano, and olive oil.

SCILLA: As you drive south on the coastal highway with the Aspromonte mountains to the left, the dramatic indented coastline on the right suddenly gives way to the huge rock of Scilla, recalling the myth of Scylla and Charybdis, which inspired poets from Homer to Schiller.

The town named for the rock of Scilla again brings to mind the ancient Greeks and their ancient rituals. This is never more evident than in Scilla's picturesque fishermen's quarters, known as the Chianalea. Here, a narrow cobblestone road lines the houses rooted to the famous rock. Fishermen's wives sit on small chairs outside their doorways when the swordfish aren't running, mending the great nets that provide their livelihood. When walking through the area, stop for lunch in a typical Scillan house, now a restaurant, *Da Glauco.*

Before you even begin to approach Chianalea, you come upon an impressive medieval castle, seemingly sculpted out of the rock of Scilla itself. The foundations date from 493 BC, only it now hosts a youth hostel — one of the best of its kind — and a discotheque. This, as well as the grand terrace of the main town square, is worth a visit. Now a favorite promenade for residents and tourists, the terrace overlooks the rooftops of the old town and the beautiful sandy Sirens Beach.

SANTA TRADA CANNITELLO: The Costa Viola ends with this town, the peninsula's closest point to Sicily and the planned site of a gigantic bridge that will eventually connect the two. The treacherous tidal currents of the Strait of Messina recall the plight of the ancient mariners. In fact, the currents are so strong and the water so cool that swimming between here and Reggio is nothing less than exhilarating, although the calm lukewarm waters between Palmi and Scilla are generally preferable.

VILLA SAN GIOVANNI: From this point there is frequent car ferry and hydrofoil service across the strait to Messina. Similar transport to Messina is also available regularly from Reggio, making a day trip to Taormina, only 31 miles (50 km) from Messina, almost irresistible.

REGGIO DI CALABRIA: A modern city almost entirely rebuilt following the earthquake of 1908, Reggio di Calabria is the gateway to Sicily. Although surrounded by a somewhat unattractive coastal shelf and numerous factories. Reggio has its high points. These include an elegant seaside boardwalk (Lungomare Marina) and the interesting *National Museum,* 26 Piazza de'Nava, housing artifacts from the archaeological excavations in the region — especially of the early Greek and Roman civilizations — and the recovered and restored bronzes of Riace.

GERACE: You'll recognize Gerace well before you arrive, perched high on a sharp rock overlooking Locri. This solemn medieval town has a richness of art treasures unequaled in the region.

LOCRI: Your arrival in Locri itself may be less inspiring, since this flat modern town is more reminiscent of the dry and dreary Far West than of any Greek city you've ever seen. Don't despair. Drive a few miles south to the ruins of the ancient city of Epizephyrii. Take care not to miss the Greek-Roman theater at Portigliola, a fair hike from the *Antiquarium,* or museum, at the entrance to the ruins.

En Route from Locri – Rather than retrace your route across the rugged Aspromonte mountain chain, if it's early enough in the day, you can return to Reggio and the Costa Viola by driving clear around the "toe" on Highway 106 along the Ionian or Jasmine Coast. This will take you past the Bovalino Marina on the slopes of the Aspromonte, Capo Spartivento, and the picturesque locality of Pentidattilo. While this area is particularly enticing for its traditional Indian summer during September and October, the months of June through August are more interesting for the student of folk customs. During this time feasts are celebrated in towns throughout the area, many concluding with elaborate fireworks displays.

BEST EN ROUTE

Hotels have improved a lot in Calabria over the past few years and you won't have much trouble finding comfortable accommodations in the bigger towns, though you won't find extremely luxurious establishments, either. Expect to pay $65 and up for a double room at those hotels categorized as expensive; between $35 and $65 at those in the moderate category; under $35, inexpensive. Expect to pay $50 or more for a meal for two at restaurants in the expensive category; between $30 and $50, moderate; under $30, inexpensive. Restaurants serve generous portions of southern cooking. Prices do not include drinks, wine, or tip.

GIOIA TAURO

Park – Near the Autostrada. Quite comfortable for passing travelers. 21 Via Nazionale (phone: 51159). Moderate.

Euromotel – This simple roadside hotel has adequate accommodations. Rte. 111, about 1 mile (1.6 km) southeast of the city (phone: 52083). Moderate.

Buco – Northern Italian dishes, primarily from Emilia, share the menu with local cuisine. 116 Via Lomoro (phone: 51512). Moderate to inexpensive.

PALMI

Arcobaleno – This small hotel is on the road between Palmi and the Taureana beach and has a restaurant, swimming pool, and tennis courts. Contrada Taureana (phone: 46275). Moderate.

Centro Residenziale Costa Viola – A quiet, countryside summer hotel set among olive groves. The rooms have a lovely sea view. Localita Torre (phone: 22016). Moderate.

Garden – Traditionally considered the town's first hotel because it is the oldest, this is actually undeserving of any accolades that are not contingent on age. 9 Piazza Losardo (phone: 23645). Moderate.

Miami – Although not as sophisticated as its name suggests, it is on a big local beach. Tonnara (phone: 46396). Inexpensive.

Oscar – In the heart of town, this hotel offers a more modern alternative to the *Garden.* Via Roma (phone: 23293). Inexpensive.

La Lampara – Rustic in atmosphere, it serves excellent fish dishes, especially *involtini di pescespada* (swordfish) in season. Closed November and December. Lido Tonnara (phone: 46332). Moderate.

La Marinella – Salvatore's special pasta with tomato sauce, local *pecorino* (sheep's milk cheese), and good fresh fish are your best culinary bets here. Marinella Cove (no phone). Moderate to inexpensive.

Pizzeria La Margherita – Specialities here are *pizza alla pioggia* and homemade whole wheat pasta in anchovy sauce. Open summers only. Across the road from the northern end of the Tonnara beach (no phone). Moderate to inexpensive.

Pinewood Pizzeria (La Pineta) – Pizza is served under pine trees at St. Elia (phone: 22926). Inexpensive.

SCILLA

Sirene – This hotel-restaurant on the beach serves fresh fish alfresco, near the sea. It has only 7 rooms. 57 Via Nazionale (phone: 754019). Inexpensive.

Ulisse – Excellent seafood — the chef used to work at London's *Savoy* — served in elegant surroundings. Closed Mondays. 1 Via Omiccioli (phone: 790190). Moderate.

Alla Pescatora – Run by a former fisherman, it serves fine seafood. Closed Tuesdays and mid-December to March. 32 Via Colombo (phone: 754147). Moderate to inexpensive.

Da Glauco – A typical former house with a magnificent terrace overlooking the fishermen's houses, the port, and the Mediterranean, its special dish is Signora Pontillo's spicy dried tomatoes and pickled eggplant antipasto. At the left end of the Via Chianalea (phone: 46330). Moderate to inexpensive.

VILLA SAN GIOVANNI

Castello Altafiumara – This restored castle by the sea has tennis courts and a swimming pool. Near Villa San Giovanni–Cannitello (phone: 759061). Expensive.

Piccolo – Simply, the best hotel in town. Its restaurant has delicious antipasti, good wine, and homemade sweets and ice cream. Piazza Stazione (phone: 751410). Expensive to moderate.

REGGIO DI CALABRIA

Grand Hotel Excelsior – Another member of the deluxe Excelsior chain, this is *the* hotel in the capital, though some of its rooms and furnishings have seen better days. 66 Via Vittorio Veneto (phone: 25801). Expensive.

Palace Hotel Masoanri's – Slightly less deluxe than its sister hotel, the *Excelsior*, but still very comfortable. 95 Via Vittorio Veneto (phone: 26433). Expensive.

Primavera – A simple but comfortable hotel with 62 rooms. 177 Via Nazionale (phone: 47081). Expensive to moderate.

Baylik – Wonderful fish. Closed Thursdays and mid-July to mid-August. 1 Via Leone (phone: 48624). Expensive.

Bonaccorso – This well-respected restaurant near the station has fine pasta and boiled meat. Closed Mondays and August. 8 Via Cesare Battiste (phone: 96048). Expensive to moderate.

Miramare – Swordfish specialties; game in season. Excellent desserts. Closed Sundays. 1 Via Fata Morgana (phone: 91881). Expensive.

Collina dello Scoiattolo – Classic Calabrian dishes served with art and tradition. Closed Wednesdays. 34 Via Provinciale (phone: 382047). Moderate.

Conti – One of the best restaurants for local antipasto, macaroni, and fish. The carafe wine, Pellaro, is excellent. Closed Mondays, except in summer. 2 Via Giulia (phone: 29043). Moderate.

GERACE

Fagiano Bianco – Unless you are traveling with a group, you may find this lovely cantina closed, but the same food is served at the bar on the main square, where a few tables are set outdoors in fine weather. *Antipasto della casa* and wine are excellent here. Piazza Centrale (no phone). Inexpensive.

LOCRI

Demaco – Modern seafront hotel in the main town with polite management. Restaurant in season; hotel open all year. 28 Via Lungomare (phone: 20247). Moderate.

Faro – If you want to spend some additional time exploring the Greek-Roman theater of Locri, you'll find these accommodations convenient. Portigliola, on Rte. 106 (phone: 361015). Inexpensive.

Rocco Simone – Peasant cooking in this small, welcoming trattoria near the Greek ruins. Piazza Contrada Moschetta (phone: 390005). Inexpensive.

Sicily

The largest island in the Mediterranean (9,925 square miles), Sicily is probably the least "Italian" of Italy's regions. Because of its strategic position between Europe, Africa, and Asia, Sicily has been invaded, conquered, and settled by many people in the last 3,000 years. Each group left traces of its civilization, both in the character of the Sicilians and in the architectural remains of its town churches, temples, and villas.

Originally part of Magna Graecia (Greater Greece), Sicily (and Siracusa, on the southeastern coast, in particular) was a great cultural center until it fell to the Romans and became an exploited colony. With the fall of the Roman Empire, Sicily became open territory, invaded by a succession of armies from barbaric northern tribes and Saracens to Byzantines. Finally, in the 11th and 12th centuries, the Normans brought a period of political peace to the island, and Sicily became an autonomous state whose power extended halfway up the Italian peninsula. Beginning in the 13th century, however, it fell back under foreign rule, to be controlled by France, Spain, and the Bourbon Kings of Naples until the arrival of Garibaldi, who began his campaign for the unification of Italy in Sicily. The island became part of Italy in 1860.

While by nature an agricultural land, Sicily has in the last 20 years or so developed some industry in the form of oil refineries and chemical plants. The island's natural wealth, though, lies in its citrus fruits, olives, and vineyards, with the most fertile land on the slopes of Mt. Etna. Europe's 2 highest active volcano, Mt. Etna at 10,902 feet dominates eastern Sicily.

A common means of access to Sicily is by ferryboat or hydrofoil from the southern tip of the mainland at Reggio di Calabria or Villa San Giovanni across the Strait of Messina. This brings you to the starting point of the Sicilian route at the northeastern end of the island. The route zigzags along coastal roads and inland highways, covering the island in a fragmented, but often-traveled pattern that covers the most interesting towns and villages.

When visiting Sicily, try to arrive in spring or early fall; the climate is closer to that of North Africa than Europe, so it is advisable to avoid the intense heat of July and August.

MESSINA: The main port of Messina, founded by the Greeks in the 8th century BC and occupied by the Carthaginians and then the Romans, was rebuilt after the disastrous earthquake of 1908 and again after the bombardments of World War II.

Perhaps Messina's most unusual feature is a curious mechanical and astronomical clock, the biggest in the world, built in Strasbourg and brought to the town in 1933. Housed in the bell tower of the town's 13th-century Norman cathedral, the mechanism activates various carved figures, and evangelical scenes move into an intricate series of acts at midday that lasts for almost an hour. The clock and cathedral are in the central Piazza del Duomo. Just east of the cathedral is the church of the Annunziata dei Catalani, another Norman construction, and at the end of Viale della Liberta is the *National Museum,* with a choice selection of Renaissance and post-Renaissance art.

TAORMINA: Twenty centuries ago this tiny, well-developed resort town (with only 5,000 full-time residents) was popular with the Greeks and Romans. It gained international fame early in the 20th century, when it was rediscovered by a group of English and German aesthetes. The draw has always been the same: its mild year-round climate and its spectacular position overlooking the bay and the rocky coast below. Best of all, in spite of the quite heavy tourist traffic in the summer, the town has lost none of its historical charm.

The first stop on any tour of Taormina should be the Greek theater, carved out of a natural cavity on the hillside and dominated by the smoking peak of Mt. Etna in the distance. It must be the most dramatic setting for a theater in the world. It is still used for modern productions of Greek tragedy as well as for summer festivals.

In the central Piazza Vittorio Emanuele stands Palazzo Corvaja, the site of Sicily's parliament in the 14th century.

Stroll down the nearby Corso Umberto, the main shopping street, to Piazza IX Aprile, a terrace surrounded by cafés where you can sit and enjoy a local almond wine aperitif and incomparable view of the bay. Farther along is the medieval convent of San Domenico, now one of the most beautifully situated hotels in Taormina. At the end of Corso Umberto I is a tiny funicular station where a cable car takes you down to the beach of Mazzarò in the summer.

In addition to restaurants and hotels, Taormina is also full of nightclubs where Sicilian folklore is reenacted in song and dance by local groups.

CATANIA: Repeatedly destroyed and rebuilt after violent eruptions of Mt. Etna, Catania is a thriving commercial center originally founded as a Greek colony in the 8th century BC. Since the last eruption of Etna to affect Catania was in 1693, the old city center has a 17th- and 18th-century air. In the heart of the city, at the Piazza del Duomo, stands the symbol of Catania — an elephant sculpted out of lava with an obelisk on its back. To the left of this structure is the Chierici Palace; nearby, a small river flows from its underground course along the slopes of Etna.

Catania serves not only as an economic and architectural center but as the starting point for a trip to the top of Mt. Etna. This takes at least half a day (preferably morning) and requires appropriate dress — heavy mountain shoes and some warm clothing. Leave the city along the long, straight main street, Via Etnea, which takes you through a landscape of burned-out craters and lava rocks past a mountain hotel (20 mi/32 km) to a cable car to the top, central crater. There you will see a large sea of magma heaving and bubbling with sulfur fumes. It is advisable to take along a guide from town. *CIT Tours,* (phone: 095-327240 in Catania; 341411 at the airport) conducts tours of the area. Make sure to start your trip back to town at least 2 hours before sunset.

En Route from Catania – Follow Route 114 some 35 miles (58 km) south to Siracusa, passing as you do the bridge over the River Simeto, 5 miles (8 km) from Catania, where English and American troops fought bitterly against the Germans and Italians at the beginning of the Allied advance through Italy in 1943. Several war cemeteries dot the area.

SIRACUSA (SYRACUSE): More than any other Sicilian town, Siracusa shows archaeological evidence of the ancient Greek and Roman civilizations. Although now it has the air of a quiet provincial town, Siracusa was once a major cultural and political center on a par with Rome, Athens, and Carthage. One of the many legends surrounding it involves a Roman attack by sea and an ingenious defense planned by Archimedes, a native of Siracusa. He devised a system of setting fire to the enemy Roman ships by means of reflecting sun rays onto their sails. Siracusa was eventually captured by the

Roman fleet, however, and Archimedes killed. Excavations around both Siracusa and Ortigia, the island site of the city's original settlement, now reveal much of its early Greek and Roman foundations.

Before you explore the city's archaeological remains, visit the new *Archaeological Museum* in Villa Landolina Park. It is one of the most important museums in Italy and necessary for a basic knowledge of Sicily's history and prehistory. In its collection is the magnificent Greek statue, *Venus Anadyomene — Venus from the Sea* — discovered in 1804. The archaeological zone stands behind the present city. Its main highlight is the Greek theater, probably the largest and most complete monument of its type in the ancient world left to us. Sculpted out of rock probably in the 3rd century BC, the theater found frequent use under its main patron at the time, Aeschylus, a prolific playwright. Under his influence, Siracusa saw the birth of Greek drama. The theater is still used today for performances of Greek plays in the late spring of even-numbered years.

Opposite the Greek theater stands the Ara di Ierone II (Hieron II), a huge altar built for public sacrifices. From here it is a short walk to the Roman amphitheater, constructed in the 4th and 3rd centuries BC for the spectacle of Christians fighting lions. Although now planted with cypress and oleander trees, you can still clearly see traces of the original structure.

AGRIGENTO: Its hillside position on the southern coast overlooking the surrounding valley and sea earned for Agrigento the praise of the ancient Greeks and the poet Pindar, who named it "the most beautiful city of mortals." It is the site of the Valley of Temples, a magnificent complex of temples and impressive columns built in the 5th and 6th centuries BC as well as the birthplace of both the ancient philosopher-scientist-priest Empedocles and the modern playwright Luigi Pirandello.

PALERMO: The capital of Sicily and the seat of the regional Sicilian government, Palermo was known by the Greeks as Panormos — all port — for its gulf location, and today it still ranks as the most important seaport on the island.

Architecturally, Palermo is divided into a modern north side and an historic south side. The core of the old quarter is a crossroads known as the Quattro Canti di Città — the Four Corners of the City — bound by a group of baroque buildings built in 1609. Nearby is the Piazza Pretoria and a 16th-century fountain, decorated by statues of pagan gods and nicknamed Piazza della Vergogna — Square of Shame.

Many of the beautiful palaces and churches for which Palermo is often recognized are of Norman design. This is true of the church of the Martorana (Piazza Bellini) and the cathedral along Corso Vittorio Emanuele (a street flanked by baroque palaces). The latter houses five royal tombs.

BEST EN ROUTE

In Sicily you will find a number of luxury hotels, converted historic villas, and many smaller, simpler hotels. Expect to pay around $70 or more for a double room at those hotels categorized as expensive; between $50 and $65 at those in the moderate category; under $45, inexpensive. Fish and seafood are the major ingredients in Sicilian cooking, and you can sample them at quite a few good restaurants. Expect to pay $55 or more for a meal for two at those restaurants categorized as expensive; between $35 and $45 at those in the moderate category; under $30, inexpensive. Prices do not include drinks, wine, or tip.

MESSINA

Jolly Hotel dello Stretto – Part of the well-known, comfortable Italian chain, with views of the Straits. 126 Via Garibaldi (phone: 43401). Expensive to moderate.

Alberto – The most elegant restaurant in town, it serves such delicacies as spaghetti *en papillote.* Closed Sundays and August 5 to September 5. 95 Via Ghibellina (phone: 710711). Expensive.

Pippo Nunnari – A pleasantly rustic place, decorated with antiques, and ideally suited for an introduction to Sicilian cooking. *Pasta alla Norma* (pasta with tomato sauce topped with slices of eggplant), *pescespada* (swordfish), available in May and June, and the Sicilian dessert *pignolata* are served along with robust Sicilian wines. Closed Thursdays and beginning of July. 157 Via Ugo Bassi (phone: 293-8584). Expensive to moderate.

TAORMINA

Grande Albergo Capo Taormina – This large, modern hotel has a private beach, a swimming pool, and a well-run restaurant. Closed December through March. Mazzarò (phone: 24000). Expensive.

San Domenico Palace – A former convent, its spacious rooms, furnished in antiques, were once monastic cells. Low entrances and thick walls help cool the interiors during oppressively hot summers. It has a swimming pool, a private beach, and a restaurant. 5 Piazza San Domenico (phone: 23701). Expensive.

Villa Sant'Andrea – Overlooking a small bay, this recently renovated little hotel has its own private beach, a colorful garden, and a restaurant. Closed January and February. 137 Via Nazionale, Mazzarò (phone: 23125). Expensive.

Timeo – Standing next to the *Greek Theater,* this old villa has been transformed into a tastefully decorated hotel with turn-of-the-century charm. 59 Via Teatro Greco (phone: 23801). Expensive to moderate.

Granduca – Delightful and elegant new restaurant that has quickly become the most popular in town. Il Cavaliere (Sir) Gaetano Li Greggi, Sicily's galloping gourmet, presides over the kitchens. Closed Mondays. 170 Corso Umberto I (phone: 24420). Expensive.

Pescatore – Taormina's best trattoria stands against a hill above the rocky bay. The simple but well-chosen menu mainly features fish. Closed Mondays and November through February. Via Nazionale, Isolabella, Mazzarò (phone: 23460). Expensive to moderate.

CATANIA

Siciliana – This family-style restaurant is Catania's best and has a garden for outdoor dining. The menu includes traditional Sicilian dishes like roast kid and mixed fish grill as well as heady regional wines. Closed Sunday evenings and Mondays. 52-A Viale Marco Polo (phone: 376400). Moderate.

Pagano – A homey, casual restaurant near the courthouse, it serves a wide variety of Sicilian specialties, as well as some innovative local dishes. Closed Sundays and August. 37 Via de Roberto (phone: 322730). Moderate.

SIRACUSA

Grand Hotel Villa Politi – This converted 19th-century villa surrounded by gardens was one of Winston Churchill's favorite vacation spots. Near the archaeological zone, it isn't as grand as it was, but it has a good restaurant, a swimming pool, and tennis courts. 2 Via M. Politi Laudien (phone: 32100). Moderate.

Jonico (a Rutta e Ciauli) – One of the few places in Sicily where the meat is as delicious as the fish. The restaurant's terrace has a great view of the sea and cliffs. Closed Tuesdays, mid-August, and the first half of September. 194 Riveria Dionisio il Grande (phone: 65540). Moderate.

PIAZZA ARMERINA

Jolly – This comfortable, unassuming hotel in the center of town is known for its good restaurant. Via Altacura (phone: 81446). Expensive to moderate.

Selene – Smaller and considerably more modest, the restaurant here is adequate. 30 Viale General Gaeta (phone: 80254). Inexpensive.

AGRIGENTO

Villa Athena – Built at the turn of the century, this charming hotel has a swimming pool, a garden, an excellent restaurant, and a great view over the Valley of Temples. The restaurant, one of the best in Sicily, serves meals where the Arab culinary influence is noticeable. Via dei Templi (phone: 23833 or 56288). Expensive to moderate.

Mosé – Traditional Sicilian cuisine in a pleasant atmosphere. Closed Mondays and August. 6 Contrada San Biagio (phone: 26778). Moderate.

PALERMO

Villa Igiea Grand – This classic Sicilian villa stands on a private beach and has a swimming pool and tennis courts. Both the hotel and its restaurant are renowned for excellent service. 43 Via Belmonte (phone: 543744). Expensive.

Excelsior Palace – A comfortable, recently renovated hotel near the fashionable Via della Libertà. 3 Via Marchese Ugo (phone: 625-6176). Moderate.

Grande Albergo e delle Palme – This large, old-fashioned hotel has an appropriately seductive touch of decadence, which acted even on Wagner, who composed here, and is centrally located. The restaurant, *La Palmetta,* perched atop the roof garden, is excellent. 398 Via Roma (phone: 583933). Moderate.

Charleston – One of Sicily's most famous restaurants because of the consummate excellence of its cuisine. Closed Sundays and from mid-June to late-September. In the summer, *Charleston* has a branch at Mondello Beach (Viale Regina Elena; phone: 450171), which serves excellent fish and wonderful dessert. 30 Piazzale Ungheria (phone: 321366). Expensive.

Gourmand's – One of Palermo's most popular restaurants, it serves and occasionally invents its own classic Sicilian cuisine. Closed Sundays and mid-August. 37/e Via della Libertà (phone: 323431). In summer, the restaurant moves to Via Torre in Mondello (phone: 450049). Expensive.

A'Cuccagna – A lively city restaurant that excells in regional dishes, especially seafood. Closed Mondays and August. 21-A Via Principe di Granatelli (phone: 587267). Expensive to moderate.

Scuderia – Traditional Sicilian dishes are prepared with love and imagination in this modern establishment, one of Palermo's best, located on the outskirts of town near the racetrack. You can dine in the garden. Closed Sunday evenings. 9 Via del Fante (phone: 520323). Expensive to moderate.

N'Grasciata – Good home cooking is found at this typical dockside trattoria off the beaten tourist track. Well known for its seafood. Try the *bottarga* (pressed tuna eggs) by itself or as a sauce for pasta. Closed Sundays. 12 Via Tiro a Segno (phone: 616-1947). Moderate to inexpensive.

Il Dottore del Brodo – This small tavern becomes the gathering place of Sicilian men and women of letters in the evenings. You can get regional soup and pasta dishes according to the season and sometimes grilled fish, meat, and good local wine. Closed Sundays. 5 Vicolo Paterna (phone: 320138). Inexpensive.

Sardinia

Floating in the Tyrrhenian Sea 116 miles from Italy's western coast and 130 miles from Africa's northern coast lies the rugged, sunwashed island of

Sardinia. Originally inhabited in Neolithic times, Sardinia had an early history of invasion by Phoenician and Punic forces who, in addition to warfare, brought the island trade, language, writing, and, of course, art, of which many examples are on exhibit today in the capital city, Cagliari. In the later Roman-Punic wars, Sardinia was conquered by the military forces of the Roman Empire. During the Middle Ages and Renaissance, Sardinia was the object of intense rivalry between various Italian city-states, and its relationship to the rest of Italy was only resolved when it joined the unification in 1860 as a region. Here, on the tiny island of Caprera off Sardinia's northern shore, Giuseppe Garibaldi is buried.

With a population of about 1.5 million, Sardinia is one of the most sparsely populated Italian regions, although it is the second largest island in the Mediterranean. Its people have been firmly planted on their home ground for centuries and are something of a race apart from Italian mainlanders and even the Sicilians, whose island has also been crossed and conquered continuously through the centuries. Sardinians are a hardy, withdrawn, but hospitable people. They believe strongly in an independent economy based on agriculture and fishing, despite the gradual development of industry on the island. For those who live off the land, life is hard even today, and the sight of a lonely shepherd eking out a living on some stony hilltop is still fairly common. Once Sardinia was the main supplier of timber for the Italian mainland; now the land is bare, covered by olive trees, juniper, myrtle, asphodel, and wild roses, the odor of which covers the island in spring.

There are still few roads in Sardinia and not more than half a dozen large towns on its 9,300 square miles. These few towns, though, are invested with a history that makes them well worth visiting. And for those interested in prehistoric ruins, stone dwellings called *nuraghi* abound.

Start your tour of the island in Cagliari, and drive along the western coast past fishing villages, new resorts, and coal mining towns until you reach the unspoiled northern tip of the island at Santa Teresa. Then head back south to Cagliari, but this time along the eastern coast, Costa Smeralda, a sometime haven for jet-setters and Italian business barons. The trip forms a complete loop in approximately 5 days.

CAGLIARI: The city can be reached by the daily car ferry from Civitavecchia, a little over an hour's train journey going north from Rome. Cagliari is to all appearances a modern town and a busy port. It has an old center, however, surrounded by 13th-century walls built by the Pisans. When you enter the medieval core of the town, explore the cathedral and then walk to the Terrazza Umberto I — all that is left of a 16th-century Spanish fortification. The terrace offers a splendid view of the harbor and nearby pine forests. Be certain to visit the Roman amphitheater, Sardinia's largest Roman monument, and the Botanical Gardens, with its display of Mediterranean and tropical plants.

En Route from Cagliari – Before beginning the northward climb up the Sardinian coastline, drive south along the SS 195 for 18 miles (30 km) to Nora. En route you pass Sarroch and Villa St. Pietro, and nearby *nuraghi* colonies. These groups of small, circular stone structures are considered to be the earliest signs of civilization on the island. Nobody has yet determined whether they indicate dwelling places, burial grounds, or fortifications. Nearby is the church of Sant'Efisio, honoring the patron saint of Cagliari. It's enlivened by a colorful traditional religious procession on May 1st.

SAN ANTIOCO: This ancient port, reached by continuing along the SS 195, is now connected by a bridge to the Sardinian mainland. In its old center (where a Genoese dialect is still spoken), visit the *Museum of Ancient Artworks* and the nearby necropolis of Sulcis. Its long sandy beaches and spectacular rocky coastline are an added attraction. From the port of Calasetta (known for its wines) at the north of the island, take the short car-ferry ride to Carloforte on the neighboring island of San Pietro.

SAN PIETRO: Lined with beaches and undulating rock-hewn inlands, Isola San Pietro is the tuna center of Sardinia. Here the killing (called *mattanza*) of huge tuna fish, during May and June is a major event and provides, along with agriculture, one of the island's main sources of income. From San Pietro's Carloforte take the ferry to Portovesme (an hour's crossing) and continue to Iglesias, 18 miles (30 km) inland.

IGLESIAS: This is the capital of the coal mining area and the home of a museum for other mineral specimens found in Sardinian soil. Its architecture reflects a Spanish influence, evident in the town's two Gothic cathedrals. Heading north for 15 miles (18 km), one comes to the Roman temple at Antas.

ORISTANO: Along the Gulf of Oristano and the mouth of the River Tirso, this town survived centuries of foreign invasion. Remains of its original medieval defense walls — the Porta Manna — stand in the central Piazza Roma. In town, visit the *Antiquarium Arborense,* a museum containing archaeological findings from the Neolithic age.

THARROS: Originally a Carthaginian, then a Roman port, this town was probably abandoned around the 11th century. Its ruins reveal something of each age, from Punic waterworks and temples, to Roman baths and houses, to early Paleo-Christian churches and a Jewish temple.

BOSA: On one of the hills surrounding the fishing village of Bosa Marina, this small town at the mouth of the Temo River is dominated by the medieval castle of Serravalle. Primarily Spanish in character, the town's residential section is replete with 16th- and 17th-century façades and wrought-iron balconies. About 1 mile (1.6 km) outside town stands the church of San Pietro Extramuros, the oldest Romanesque church in Sardinia, built in the 11th century.

ALGHERO: Set amid olive and eucalyptus trees, Alghero combines a long stretch of beachland with an old town center clearly Catalan Spanish in character. Many Catalán customs are practiced here to this day.

On your tour, follow the ancient defense walls until you near the town center, then walk toward the stocky round tower, Torre Sulis, for a splendid view of the surrounding coast. It's worth taking a side trip by boat across the bay to Capo Caccia and the Grotte di Nettune, a series of underground caves that have, over the ages, formed crystalline stalactites and stalagmites. Much of the grotto is yet unexplored.

   En Route from Alghero – Travel north (direction Porto Torres) 7 miles (12 km) to the prehistoric (Bronze Age) necropolis of Anghelu Ruiu in the heart of Sardinian wine country (Tenuta dei Pini). From the necropolis, continue north several miles and then east on the SS 291 to Sassari.

SASSARI: This is Sardinia's second capital, founded in the 11th century by coastal inhabitants seeking a more secure dwelling place inland. A relatively independent locality, its citizens are renowned for their courage in resisting the Austrians in World War I.

Sassari's history is best traced by a visit to the *National Museum.* It contains archaeological findings from prehistory to the Middle Ages as well as some fine examples of Sardinian art and craftsmanship. Walk through town past the Fonte Rosello (Spanish fountain) built in 1605 and the remains of the medieval defense walls and towers. Climb the steep slope of Corso Vittorio Emanuele II to the church of Santa

Maria di Bethlehem, with its Romanesque façade and baroque interior. This church houses the concluding ceremonies of Sassari's *Feast of Candlesticks* procession, which is held on August 14 to commemorate the end of an outbreak of the plague in 1580.

CASTELSARDO: Tourist development in Castelsardo hasn't spoiled the loveliness of this former fishing village. The remains of a medieval castle on a high rock overlooking the town still offer an unparalleled view of the Costa Paradiso to the northeast and the Gulf of Asinara to the west, and the old part of the town with its steep winding streets and 16th-century cathedral still stands intact. Castelsardo is also known for craftsmanship, especially basketwork made from the fronds of the dwarf palm trees that abound in the area.

En Route from Castelsardo – Take a leisurely drive north from Castelsardo to Santa Teresa, enjoying the Costa Paradiso, with its red cliffs and fantastic rock formations jutting into a vivid blue sea. The ride is 40 miles (64 km)) on route SS 200.

SANTA TERESA GALLURA: Santa Teresa, on the farthest northern tip of Sardinia, is another small fishing village developed for tourism but still unspoiled. Surrounded by sheltered bays, it's an ideal stopping place. A trip also should be made to the Capo Testa Peninsula, about 3 miles (5 km) outside town, and its amazing rock formations. From there, Corsica appears to be only a stone's throw away.

En Route from Santa Teresa Gallura – As you travel around the northern cap of Sardinia, the coastal road brings you to a pair of islands — Palau and Capo Orso, opposite the archipelago of La Maddalena — that are barren, but beautiful. Accompanied by many other islands surrounding the archipelago, these are rich fishing grounds and renowned tourist spots. One of the most famous islands nearby is Caprera, where Garibaldi is buried. The southbound route along the eastern coast of Sardinia now begins.

COSTA SMERALDA: Called a millionaire's playground, Costa Smeralda (the Emerald Coast), on the northeastern edge of Sardinia, has been transformed by the Aga Khan into one of the most fashionable resorts in Europe. Hotels built in a rustic style border private secluded bays (*Cala di Volpe* is an example; see *Best en Route*), and fishing villages have been transformed into quaint towns with cafés, restaurants, and boutiques. Stop in Porto Cervo and nearby Porto Rotondo, with its terrace overlooking the huge harbors.

For a taste of the local cuisine, it is more advisable, and probably cheaper, to go to Olbia, 11 miles (18 km) south of Porto Rotondo.

OLBIA: One of the main ports that connect Sardinia to Italy, Olbia is easily the prettiest, surrounded by a ragged coastline and picturesque little islands dotted here and there in the gulf.

NUORO: Almost devoid of monuments, churches, or remains that mark its origins, Nuoro is nevertheless worth an overnight stay just to see something of the wild interior of Sardinia. On a hill, it overlooks a vast expanse of woodland and barren mountains, favorite grounds for hunters. It is also the hometown of two of Sardinia's greatest writers — poet Sebastiano Satta and Nobel Prize winner Grazia Deledda, whose house is now preserved as a tiny museum on Via Deledda.

En Route from Nuoro – This final portion of the Sardinian route takes you along southeastern coastal roads and then inland to Cagliari. You pass through a wide, green, and prosperous valley until you reach Oliena, at the bottom of a craggy mountain, the Sopromonte, famous for its vineyards. Continue on to Tortoli and Arbatax, resort towns renowned for their beauty.

Continue south through the coastal plains of Sardinia, past several *nuraghe* excavations, and on to Muravera, an agricultural town, once surrounded by orange groves, now surrounded by a few discretely placed tourist hotels. On route SS 125, turn inland for the last 39½ miles (64 km) to Cagliari, where the road winds through forests and mountain gorges to the Quartu Sant'Elena, a suburb of Cagliari. There, some interesting 15th-century Sardinian paintings are displayed in the parish church. Returning to Cagliari proper, there should be time for a last Sardinian meal before the night ferry leaves for Civitavecchia.

BEST EN ROUTE

Accommodations on Sardinia range from sleek coastal resorts to simpler establishments, but all share a greater or lesser proximity to the sea. On the Costa Smeralda, reservations are necessary. Expect to pay $90 or more per night for a double room at those places categorized as expensive (higher than that on the Costa Smeralda); between $70 and $85 at those in the moderate category; under $65, inexpensive. Expect to pay $50 or more for a meal for two at those restaurants categorized as expensive; between $35 and $45 at restaurants in the moderate category; under $30, inexpensive. Prices do not include drinks or tip.

CAGLIARI

Regina Margherita – This grand old hotel is the only four-star establishment in town. Some of its 100 air conditioned rooms have views of the port; all have private baths. 44 Viale Regina Margherita (phone: 670-0342). Expensive.

Panorama – A modern hotel with 97 air conditioned rooms, swimming pool, and penthouse restaurant (closed Sunday evenings and Mondays). 231 Viale Armando Diaz (phone: 307691). Expensive to moderate.

Italia – Modern and absolutely central, this hotel has 113 rooms and a coffee shop open until reasonably late. Closed August 2 through 23. 31 Via Sardegna (phone: 655772). Moderate.

Dal Corsaro – Fresh and imaginatively cooked lobster, eel, shrimp, and fish are all well worth trying. There are also traditional Sardinian meat dishes and a large selection of robust Sardinian wines. During the summer, the restaurant opens another branch at Poetto. Closed Tuesdays and from December 22 to January 4. 28 Viale Regina Margherita (phone: 664318). Expensive.

Sa Cardiga e Su Schironi – The front of this small, unpretentious restaurant is a grocery store; the back houses a homey restaurant with good local wine and food. Closed Mondays and from late October to late November. On the Pula Road, SS 195, at the Capoterra intersection (phone: 71652). Expensive.

ISOLA SAN PIETRO

Hieracon – Romantics will enjoy this hotel/ristorante with panoramic views of the water and tranquil gardens. All rooms include bathroom, telephone, air conditioning, and heating. True Sardinian ambience, 5 minutes from the ferry. Open year-round. 62 Corso Cavour (phone: 0781-854028). Moderate.

ORISTANO

Mistral – A well-maintained modern hotel near the center, with a reasonably attractive lounge and bar. The hotel's restaurant turns out some of the best food in town, thanks to the eye for detail and service of the German management, and the chef, a Sardinian, tempted back from one of Berlin's top Italian restaurants. Via Martiri di Belfore (phone: 212505). Moderate to inexpensive.

Faro – Considered this town's best restaurant, specialties here include spaghetti with *bottarga* (pressed tuna eggs), *penne* (tubelike pasta) with pecorino cheese, and mixed fish grill. Closed Sundays, Mondays, the first half of January, and the second half of July. 25 Via Bellini (phone: 70002). Expensive to moderate.

Forchetta d'Oro – Fish features prominently on the menu, especially the Sardinian *bottarga.* Its terrace and garden contribute to the restaurant's popularity. Closed Sundays and the last half of August. Via Giovanni XXIII (phone: 70462). Moderate to inexpensive.

Nicolo – The island's Arab connections are celebrated in this jolly trattoria, where *couscous* appears on the menu along with local fare. Closed Fridays except in summer. Via Dante Carloforte (phone: 854048). Moderate to inexpensive.

ALGHERO

Villa Las Tronas – On a promontory overlooking the sea, with its own fine restaurant, this was once a summer residence of the Italian royal family. Only 30 rooms, so book ahead. Hotel open year-round; restaurant closed Wednesdays and from mid-September to mid-May. 1 Lungomare Valencia (phone: 975390). Expensive.

Lepanto – This warm, traditional restaurant (the busiest in town and also claimed to be the best) faces the sea. When available, fresh lobster is the specialty. Caviar is usually on the menu. 135 Via Carlo Alberto (phone: 979116). Expensive to moderate.

Pavone – Great soups, antipastos, risottos, and seafood are served at this small, family-run restaurant. Many think it's the best in town. Closed Wednesdays and January. Reservations suggested. 3-4 Piazza Sulis (phone: 979584). Expensive to moderate.

Del Mare da Uccio – All the local specialties — spaghetti with squid, sea bass, lobster, and crab — are available, as are the best local wines. Closed Tuesdays and November. 8 Via Liverno (phone: 979238). Moderate to inexpensive.

SANTA TERESA GALLURA

Shardana – This secluded hotel and restaurant have a private beach, swimming pool, garden, and tennis courts. Although its isolation is now threatened by encroaching development, its position on the sea is still lovely. Closed from October to late May. Santa Reparata (phone: 754391). Moderate.

Canne al Vento da Brancaccio – The owners of this simple restaurant are also farmers, which accounts for the freshness of the meat and cheese. The wine selection is very good. You can also get an inexpensive room here. Closed Saturdays (except in summer) and from October through November 15. 23 Via Nazionale (phone: 754219). Inexpensive.

Nibbari – In a field between the main road and the rocky Santa Teresa beach, this quiet, comfortable hotel has a good restaurant. Closed October through May. About 1 mile (1.6 km) south of town, Località la Testa (phone: 754453). Inexpensive.

COSTA SMERALDA

Cala di Volpe – Owned by the Aga Kahn, this extravagant hotel has served as a background for James Bond movies and is the jet-set headquarters on Sardinia. The 123 rooms are rustic in decor but luxurious in appointments. Open May through September (phone: 96083). Ultra expensive.

Cervo – A large, elegant hotel with a freshwater swimming pool. Closed November through mid-March. Porto Cervo (phone: 92003). Expensive.

Ginestre – This 64-room hotel has a restaurant and a freshwater swimming pool and is a short walk from a small beach. It's a good choice if you don't care about being directly on the water. Closed October through mid-April. Golfo Pevero (phone: 92030). Expensive.

Mola – Long considered by many to be the best restaurant in the area, it has successfully resisted the moneyed winds of change — everything is still good. Piccolo Pevero (phone: 92436). Moderate.

Lu Stazzu – Here's where to sample Sardinian specialties like *maloreddus* (dumplings with a tomato and sausage sauce) and *porcetto al mirto* (suckling pig roasted on a spit and served on a bed of myrtle leaves). Lu Stazzu Picuccia, on the road from Porto Cervo to Arzachena (phone: 82657). Moderate.

Pomodoro – A chic *pizzeria-ristorante* just behind the *Cervo* hotel. Excellent antipasto and mouth-watering pizzas in an attractive rustic setting indoors or outside under a grape arbor. Open year-round. Porto Cervo (phone: 92207). Moderate to inexpensive.

OLBIA

Gallura – This small, humble dining establishment conceals an excellent kitchen that serves traditional Sardinian dishes. Closed Mondays. Rooms are available, too. Reservations essential. 145 Corso Umberto (phone: 24648). Expensive to moderate.

Tana del Drago – The nearby Golfo degli Aranci keeps this place well supplied with fresh fish. Closed Mondays and November. About 1 mile (2 km) northeast of town in Fruttuosu (phone: 58632). Moderate.

NUORO

Grazia Deledda – The largest hotel in town, it has a fine restaurant where service is good, as is the cooking. 175 Via Lamamora (phone: 31257). Inexpensive.

Fratelli Sacchi – Here you'll find a limited but well-prepared menu. Pasta with asparagus and roast wild boar are house specialties. Rooms are available. Closed Mondays and February. Five miles (8 km) east of town at Monte Ortobene (phone: 31200). Hotel inexpensive; restaurant moderate to inexpensive.

E.S.I.T. – This place offers genuine hospitality and home-cooked food. Monte Ortobene, about 5½ miles (9 km) east of town (phone: 33108). Moderate.

Liechtenstein

Liechtenstein is not the obscure, lunch-stop country it's often made out to be. Almost three times the size of Bermuda, it's a fairy tale land of medieval castles, lush Rhine meadows, ivy-clad chalets, vineyards, and quaint villages clinging to the Alps. Although Liechtenstein borders Switzerland and Austria and is quite close to one of the most popular tourist circuits in Europe, this 62-square-mile principality of 27,700 residents still has the virtue of being off the beaten track of most travelers.

Since 1938, the country has been ruled by Prince Franz Josef II Maria Alois Alfred Karl Johann Heinrich Michael Georg Ignatius Benediktus Gerhardus Majella, the Twelfth Ruling Prince of Liechtenstein, Duke of Troppau, Duke of Jägerndorf, Count of Reitberg, and Knight of the Golden Fleece; he is the longest-reigning ruler in the world (though, since 1984, Crown Prince Adam has substituted for his father). In contrast to the pomp of his name and titles, the prince, one of the wealthiest men in Europe, dresses casually and drives around in his own medium-priced car. He and the royal family live in the 13th-century castle perched about 300 feet above Vaduz, the country's main city. The prince presides over a land that has been continuously inhabited for more than 5,000 years. In the late 1600s, a wealthy Austrian, Prince Liechtenstein, bought out two bankrupt counts with property in the Rhine Valley and created the principality in 1719.

Today, it is an industrial nation producing an array of items from pharmaceuticals to false teeth, yet its factories are virtually impossible to find because they're in low-profile buildings in vineyards, polluting neither the air nor the water. Liechtenstein's people — none of whom is unemployed — enjoy one of the highest standards of living in the world and pay very low taxes. The country is without a military, university, or hospital. Liechtenstein is represented worldwide by the Swiss National Tourist Offices (there are US offices in New York City, Chicago, and San Francisco).

There are several ways to get to the principality: A 5-minute drive or a train ride from Buchs, Switzerland, brings you to the village of Schaan, and it's a half-hour drive from Feldkirch, Austria. Both Buchs and Feldkirch are stops on the Paris-Innsbruck-Vienna express; local trains on the same route stop at three Liechtenstein villages — Schaan, Nendeln, and Schaanwald. A convenient and enjoyable entry route is the hour-long train ride from Zurich on the Zurich-Chur line. The train glides through spectacularly beautiful Swiss countryside along the western shores of the Zurich and Walen lakes to the medieval Swiss town of Sargans. A 15-minute ride by the Swiss Postbus or by taxi takes you from one of the oldest democracies in the world to Vaduz, the capital of monarchal Liechtenstein, one of the last remnants of the Holy Roman Empire.

Vaduz is a convenient base for successive explorations of the northern lowlands, eastern mountain region, and southern Rhine Valley; this 50-mile (80-km) route takes about 2 or 3 days of leisurely travel. If you enter from Switzerland, you won't have any border-crossing headaches because Liechtenstein and Switzerland have the same currency and customs authority. If you enter from Austria, Switzerland's formalities apply. The people of the principality speak the Swiss brand of German.

VADUZ: Most of the highlights in Vaduz (pronounced va-dootz) are in the tiny main street area (the Städtle). Head for the Liechtenstein National Tourist Office (37 Städtle; phone: 21443) and arm yourself with free brochures and guides and a detailed map of the principality (about $1). There are two major attractions in the same building as the tourist office: the *Prince's Art Gallery* and the *Liechtenstein Post Office Museum*. The art gallery is packed with priceless objets d'art, including one of the most impressive Rubens collections in the world. In addition, there are Rembrandts, Botticellis, Pieter Brueghels, and Van Dycks. Many of the paintings are reproduced on Liechtenstein's postage stamps, which can be seen (and purchased) in the *Post Office Museum*. The museum is known to philatelists the world over, as the stamps are among the most decorative and valuable in the world. Right next door is the *National Museum* (43 Stöatle). Get your passport stamped with the impressive crown insignia at the museum's boutique on the first floor. The museum has local artifacts dating from the Iron Age and a vast collection of medieval weapons, sculptures, and paintings.

The boutiques, souvenir shops, and sidewalk cafés in this area are worth a browse. You can find good buys in leather and wooden handicrafts, local wine, art books, chocolates, and domestic liqueurs. Treat yourself to the local grilled game meats, soufflés, and hearty stews served at one of Europe's most celebrated restaurants, in the *Real* hotel, next door to the tourist office. Felix Real, the owner-chef, and his brother, Emil Real, who operates the posh *Park Hotel Sonnenhof* (in a mountainside vineyard half a mile away on Mareestrasse; see *Best en Route*) learned how to cook in their native Italy. They perfected their skills at *Maxim's* of Paris, and have been catering to royalty ever since; they were part of the culinary team at the erstwhile Shah of Iran's multimillion-dollar bash at Persepolis in 1972.

No visit to Vaduz is complete without a trip to the palace, and the most enjoyable way to get there is by taking a leisurely, 20-minute stroll up a wooded footpath from the tourist office. Or take a bus from the Städtle or rent a bicycle (from *Hans Melliger;* 10 Kirchstr.; phone: 21606). Although the castle itself is not open to the public, the terraces and rolling meadows around it are perfect picnic spots, and the elevation provides a panoramic view of Vaduz, the Rhine Valley, and the surrounding Alps. You can drive, cycle, or take the postbus (the Swiss Rail Pass is good on them) from Vaduz north to Schellenberg. It's a half-hour trip.

SCHELLENBERG: Sprawled over wooded hills and lush meadowlands, this community has several archaeological sites dating back to the New Stone Age. In addition, the partially restored ruins of two medieval castles are worth a visit. If you take a walk along the marked Eschnerberg mountain trail, you'll see the historic areas as well as the beautiful woods. The next community to the south — the villages of Mauren and Schaanwald — is virtually in another era.

MAUREN and SCHAANWALD: Bordered by gentle meadows to the south and west and mountains to the east, Mauren and Schaanwald are two villages about a mile apart. Archaeological excavations in Mauren have unearthed the remains of a Roman bath and warehouse dating from the 2nd century. The village has a beautiful parish church and a vicarage erected in 1787. The most popular attraction here, however, is the bird sanctuary–nature path that extends from Mauren east to Schaanwald. From Schaanwald, head west about 3 miles (5 km) to Gamprin-Bendern.

GAMPRIN-BENDERN: The Rhine flows gently past this area of rolling pastures and picture-postcard farmhouses. Here are the remains of a church built around AD 500 and a large building constructed after the Reformation that today serves as a vicarage; the church and vicarage, on a hilltop, can be seen from afar and are favorites with visitors and photographers. It's about a mile southeast to the next area.

ESCHEN and NENDELN: The village of Eschen was first documented in the Carolingian estates registry (c. 831), but excavations reveal that it was inhabited as far back as 5000 BC. Visit the prehistoric settlements of Malanser and Schneller in Eschen and the medieval Holy Cross, St. Sebastian, and Rochus chapels in Nendeln. Then take the road leading up through Eschen to the posh neighborhood of Schönbühl and view the houses of the most desirable residential area in Liechtenstein. From Nendeln drive south along the twisting mountain road, about 4 miles (7 km), to Planken.

PLANKEN: This little village of about 300 people was settled in the 13th century by immigrants — called Walser — from Upper Valais in Switzerland, who populated big areas of the Alps and kept their distinct heritage alive. The dialect used here is drastically different from that of the rest of the Rhine Valley, as are the culture, cuisine, and costumes. It's a beautiful village of meadows and quaint inns. The views of the mountains, villages, and the Rhine Valley are excellent from the road south to Schaan.

SCHAAN: Two miles (3 km) north of Vaduz, this village of trim gardens, flower-decked homes, cafés, and colorful shops features a 12th-century Romanesque church and an imposing 18th-century chapel. Return to Vaduz and head south about 3 miles (5 km) to Triesen, where you can begin exploring the Liechtenstein Alps.

TRIESEN: At the foot of the Alps and on the Rhine, Triesen was once inhabited by Roman nobility as a result of its convenient location. Especially interesting are the Roman section of the village (the Oberdorf) and the Maria and St. Mamerten chapels.

En Route from Triesen – Several hiking paths fan out to the Liechtenstein Alps and south across the Rhine Valley into Switzerland. From Triesen take the excellent road north into the mountains. After twisting and turning for about 4 miles (6 km), the road arrives at the idyllic village that gives the community its name.

TRIESENBERG: The residents of this tiny village (also called Walser) dress in colorful costumes and build their wooden homes in a decorative, regional style that's been in vogue since 1300. An intersting *Folklore Museum* with a slide show tells about the history and life of the Walser community; it's closed Mondays. At its altitude of 3,000 feet, Triesenberg seems nailed to the side of the Alps and commands an excellent view of the misty Rhine Valley below and the Alpine pine forests behind the village. Here you may see chamois and deer darting out of the woods or view the cattle, sporting enormous bells, grazing in the lush meadows.

En Route from Triesenberg – The Rhine and Samina valleys are connected by a 2,800-foot mountain tunnel. Excellent roads and cross-country hiking trails (the distances are usually marked in approximate walking times) zigzag through the Samina. Even if you're pressed for time, instead of proceeding directly east and up to Malbun, give yourself another hour or two and make your way via Masescha, Gaflei, and Steg.

MASESCHA: A quaint hamlet, 4,100 feet high and about 3 miles (5 km) north of Triesenberg, Masescha provides a breathtaking panorama and Theodul's Chapel, a restored medieval monument. If you want to spend some time hiking or mountain climbing, Gaflei, about a mile farther north, is a good bet. One of several mountain paths starting here is the Prince's Climb (Fürstensteig), which follows a high ridge between the Rhine and Samina valleys; originating at 4,900 feet, the path weaves around several peaks up to an altitude of 7,000 feet. Only experienced hikers need attempt it. From Gaflei, there's an excellent road as well as several mountain paths to

Steg, where you can visit the chapel of St. Wendelin, honoring the patron saint of shepherds. From Steg the road meanders southeast along the icy Malbuner Bach about 2 miles (3 km) before reaching Malbun.

MALBUN: At the base of a bowl of mountains, Malbun is rapidly becoming one of the most popular winter ski centers in the eastern Alps. Take the chair lift up to the Soreiserjoch Peak at 6,400 feet — again, for experienced hikers only; a steep ridge road leads from here to the Bettlerjoch, where in summer the *Liechtenstein Alpine Club* (*Pfälzerhütte*) operates a restaurant and provides accommodations at the Bettlerjoch. If you have time, hike from Malbun to the Sareiserjoch border pass into Austria; this adventurous jaunt takes about 2 hours. From Malbun, head back down the road to Triesen and proceed south into Balzers.

BALZERS: Amid rolling meadows, vineyards, and medieval castles, Balzers is dominated by the impressive Gutenberg Castle, built on a prehistoric mound; from 1314 to 1824 it belonged to the Habsburgs. Near the castle and worth visiting are the Mariahilf and St. Peter chapels, the parish church, and the old vicarage. Another attraction here is the Elltal nature preserve and its collection of rare Alpine flora.

BEST EN ROUTE

One good reason for spending time in Liechtenstein is that the prices of its hotels and restaurants are generally more reasonable than those of Switzerland. We've rated hotels charging from $95 to $150 a night for a double room with bath as expensive; from $60 to $95 as moderate; and under $55, inexpensive. Many of Liechtenstein's best restaurants are in the hotels; a meal for two in an expensive restaurant will run $80 to $150; $55 to $80 in the moderate category; inexpensive restaurants run $55 and under. Prices do not include taxes, wine, or tips.

VADUZ

Parkhotel Sonnenhof – Possibly one of the best small hotels in Europe. The cuisine is regional and French and prepared by celebrated chef Emil Real. The dining room is open to hotel guests only. Reservations recommended. Mareestr. (phone: 21192). Very expensive.

Löwen – This historic landmark inn, surrounded by hilly vineyards and with a view of the castle, has 8 rooms. Its moderately priced restaurant features excellent local specialties, such as mountain trout. Reservations requested. 35 Herrengasse (phone: 21408). Expensive.

Landhaus Prasch – In the heart of town, this small hotel serves regional cuisine. Reservations are recommended in summer. Closed November through March. 16 Zollstr. (phone: 24663, 23140). Moderate.

Engel – This small hotel offers French cuisine in its dining room. Open daily. Städtle (phone: 21057, 21186). Moderate to inexpensive.

Real – Hearty and well-prepared regional cooking is featured at this establishment. Städtle (phone: 22222). Expensive to moderate.

Torkel – In the Princely vineyards, this charming, paneled inn has outstanding food, prepared by chef Rolf Berger. A giant, 17th-century winepress (*Torkel*) is also here. Wine tastings can be arranged. Closed Sunday evenings and Mondays. 9 Hintergasse (phone: 24410). Expensive to moderate

SCHELLENBERG

Wirthschaft zum Löwen – A gem of a restaurant and a protected historical monument, found on the most beautiful lookout point of Liechtenstein, surrounded by splendid hiking trails. A "secret," as you find it only by knowing about it: Outside the village, near the Austrian border, it is indicated only by a discreet sign on the building. Simple food with local specialties seldom found anywhere else is offered. Closed Sunday evenings and Thursdays. Im Winkel (phone: 31162). Inexpensive.

ESCHEN-NENDELN

Engel – Lamb and venison are the specialties in this hotel's popular restaurant. Closed Wednesdays. Reservations recommended. 9491 Nendeln (phone: 31260). Moderate.

PLANKEN

Saroya – Small and homey, it's one of the best deals in the principality. Closed Wednesdays. Reservations recommended in summer. 9494 Planken (phone: 31584). Inexpensive.

SCHAANWALD

Waldhof – An unpretentious, pleasant small restaurant, it serves some of the best food in Liechtenstein. Traditional and local dishes are prepared from the freshest of products. Closed Sundays and Mondays. 296 Vorarlbergerstr. (phone: 31388, 33498). Expensive to moderate.

SCHAAN

Dux – There's an excellent restaurant in this hotel serving Swiss, French, and regional cuisine. The house specialty is fondue. Closed August and part of January. 9494 Schaan (phone: 21727). Moderate.

TRIESEN

Meierhof – Fish dishes are the specialty in this hotel's excellent restaurant. Reservations recommended. 9495 Triesen (phone: 21836, 22836). Moderate.

TRIESENBERG

Martha Bühler – The terrace restaurant of this inn offers a fine view. Open daily. Reservations necessary. 9497 Triesenberg (phone: 25777). Moderate to inexpensive.

GAFLEI

Tourotel Gaflei – Swiss, French, and regional fare are served in this large hotel. Open daily. Reservations recommended. 9497 Gaflei (phone: 22091). Moderate.

MALBUN

Alpenhotel Malbun – Here's a good, moderately priced, medium-size hotel that serves both continental and local food. Closed November to mid-December. Reservations recommended. 9497 Malbun (phone: 21181). Moderate.

BALZERS

Engel – THis old inn, in the oldest part of Balzers, is well known for good, simple food, with house specialties. Closed Mondays. 18 Im Höfle (phone: 41201). Inexpensive.

Luxembourg

Bordered by France, Germany, and Belgium, the Grand Duchy of Luxembourg calls itself "the green heart of Europe," for fully one third of the country's 999 square miles is still unspoiled forest. Geographically, there are two regions: in the north, the hilly, picturesque uplands of the Ardennes; in the south, rolling farmlands and woods bordered on the east by the grape-growing valley of the Moselle. Flowers are everywhere. Fields are sprinkled with wild poppies, daisies, clover, and buttercups — the perfect Impressionist landscape. White and purple lilacs outline the roadways, and in early summer the hillsides blaze with yellow gorse bushes. Storybook villages nestle beside peaceful rivers. Castles — some restored and others in ruins — cap the mountaintops.

Luxembourg's hotels and inns are clean and relatively inexpensive, and its restaurants serve a cuisine that combines the subtleties of French cooking with the heartiness of German food. The local white wines are fresh, light, and tart, and they are drunk with both fish and meat (red wines are not produced here).

The nation's history is dense with traces of all the armies that have marched across Europe. Once part of the Roman Empire, the country has been manipulated by dukes and dictators, princes and potentates, knights and nobles. France, Spain, Prussia, Bohemia, and the Netherlands have all had their fingers in its political pie, and for hundreds of years Luxembourg was involved in one alliance, treaty, or confederation after another. Twice in this century the country has been invaded by Germany, but peace and relative prosperity have reigned since the Allies liberated the area in September 1944. Today, Luxembourg is a constitutional monarchy with a bicameral legislature. The upper chamber is appointed by the monarch; the lower house is elected by popular vote. The present ruler is the Grand Duke Jean, who is married to the Princess Josephine Charlotte of Belgium.

With a population of 372,000, Luxembourg is one of the few nations with a declining birth rate, low unemployment, and virtually no poverty; its gross national product is estimated to be the equivalent of $3 billion. Roman Catholicism is the prevalent religion, but the country also has Protestant and Jewish communities.

Iron mining and steel production are the major industries, followed by banking. Agriculture, including the cultivation of grapes, and cattle raising are also important, and a number of major US corporations have subsidiaries in Luxembourg. Tourism is an increasingly valuable revenue producer (Luxembourg hosts 2 million visitors per year); the country's appeal to those who love camping and hiking is on the upswing.

Most international travelers arrive at Luxembourg Airport in Luxembourg City. (For years the city was the European gateway for millions of Americans taking advantage of Icelandair's low transatlantic fares, but vacationers are now urged to stay and see the country.) A valid passport is the only document required for citizens of the US and most other nations. There's a national tourist office in Luxembourg City (Pl. d'Armes; phone: 2-2809, 2-7565), at Findel Airport, at the Air Terminus (near the railway station), and in many other towns.

Using Luxembourg City as a base, you can easily reach any other part of the country within hours, and all of Luxembourg can be covered without strain in a week to 10 days. It's a good idea to spend several nights in smaller towns like Echternach and Vianden to experience the charm of their small inns and hotels and the distinctly medieval atmosphere of the country; in these villages you'll find rebuilt feudal battlements, ancient abbeys, and patrician houses in quiet, verdant settings. You'll find an interesting mixture of Gallo-Roman and Germanic cultural influences as well as three major languages: German, French, and Luxembourgeois (a combination of the other two). It's customary to speak French with waiters. Many people, however, speak English.

LUXEMBOURG CITY: Luxembourg's over-1,000-year-old capital has an exciting location: The oldest part of the city is actually a high plateau whose steep cliffs plunge into the beautifully landscaped valleys of the Alzette River. Some 98 old and modern bridges connect this central plateau to other parts of the city on surrounding hills and plateaus. If you suffer from vertigo or acrophobia, proceed cautiously as you cross the dizzying bridges or the steep precipices.

Winding around the edge of Luxembourg City's central plateau is the celebrated Promenade de la Corniche, a walkway offering breathtaking views of the city. For centuries this area was a fortress of great strategic importance. Although the military fortifications were dismantled from 1867 to 1883, the Casemates — a 13-mile network of underground passages — remain just below the promenade; cut into the solid rock of the plateau, they could shelter thousands of soldiers. Exploring these dark and damp tunnels can be fun for the nimble (enter at Place de la Constitution). As you stroll through the old city, note the Renaissance Grand Ducal Palace, constructed from the 16th to the 18th century (Rue de la Reine), and the Foreign Ministry, built in 1751 (Rue Notre-Dame) adjoining the Cathedral of Notre-Dame (1613-21), with its fine sculptures and crypt. The *National Museum* (Rue de la Boucherie) features interesting archaeological and sculpture exhibitions (closed Mondays). Place d'Armes, in the heart of the city, is a popular public square with outdoor cafés and a bandstand for concerts.

Just 10 minutes east of the city, near Hamm, is the US Military Cemetery. Over 5,000 American Third Army soldiers who died during the Battle of the Bulge are buried here. Later, when General George S. Patton was killed in an automobile accident, he, too, was buried here.

MONDORF-LES-BAINS: Eleven miles (18 km) southeast of Luxembourg City, on the French border, is Luxembourg's famous spa. In an 89-acre public park, it is renowned for its foul-tasting but supposedly curative waters. The warm water has been used to treat rheumatism, liver, and gall bladder problems, and it is a powerful laxative when imbibed. The park has a large, lovely rose garden. The town also boasts a new casino, *Casino 2000,* as well as tennis, boating, fishing and mini-golf.

ECHTERNACH: This medieval village lies along the Sauer River on Luxembourg's eastern border; its name means "the place where horses are brought to drink." Across the river is Germany and the mountains that once held the Siegfried line between France and Germany from 1933 to 1938. (You can still see the bunkers on the hill.)

Heavily damaged during World War II, Echternach has been meticulously restored. The Town Hall, which dates from 1328, is the centerpiece of the charming main square. Nearby, beside the river, is the imposing Benedictine Abbey that was founded in the 7th century by a Northumbrian monk, St. Willibord, whose remains are buried in the crypt of the abbey's basilica. Among the abbey's treasures are its impressive 12th-century frescoes and the brilliant, modern, stained-glass windows. The basilica is the terminus of the famed dancing procession, held every Whittuesday (usually in mid-May). Religious in origin — it is an act of penance, an expression of pious fervor — the event is celebrated by the entire village. Swaying, jumping, and dancing, the crowd moves through the streets as a haunting repetitive tune is played, paying homage to the English saint.

LITTLE SWITZERLAND: Hiking is a top sport throughout Luxembourg, but nowhere is it better — or more beautiful — than in the Moellerdall (Miller's Dale) section of the Ardennes that's also known as Little Switzerland. Just a few minutes north of Echternach, it comes as a complete surprise. After parking your car, you walk through gently rolling fields into a forest, and suddenly you're on a narrow path leading up and down through deep gorges, across bubbling streams, and beside (and through) enormous bolders. The whole area is dense with the kinds of tall straight trees Cézanne loved to paint. Although the area isn't as wild as it looks and the main hiking path is only about 2 miles (3.2 km) long and fairly well defined, you're strongly advised to have either a guide or a very good map of the area. Comfortable clothes and hiking boots are also musts.

VIANDEN: This village on the Our River (an extension of the Sauer) near the German border, a short drive northwest of Echternach and the Little Switzerland area, is one of Europe's more romantic spots. A charming small bridge arches over the river, connecting the two parts of the town, and a formidable castle stands guard high on an overhanging hill. The narrow streets — parts of which date from the 9th century — slope down to the river, where graceful promenades line both banks. Next to the bridge is the little house where French writer Victor Hugo spent part of his exile. In October, a festival celebrating the nut harvest takes place here.

BOURSCHEID AND DELANNOY (CASTLE AT CLERVAUX): Two of Luxembourg's most interesting castles lie just northwest of Vianden; you can stay there and visit both castles in a day's outing, driving out one way and returning another. Bourscheid, an 11th-century walled castle, is perched on a mountaintop overlooking the hills, valleys, and waters of the Ardennes region. The extensive ruins here are restored; open March 1 to September 30. The 11th-century Castle at Clervaux, home of Franklin D. Roosevelt's ancestors, stands in the center of Clervaux, another charming village surrounded by mountains. The castle is open from Whitsun (the eighth Sunday after Easter) to mid-September. Three important permanent exhibitions are housed in the castle: photographer Edward Steichen's "Family of Man" collection, scale models of Luxembourg's medieval castles, and a Battle of the Bulge display. Those particularly interested in the battle can visit the *Battle of the Bulge Museum* in Wiltz, which has numerous monuments and remnants of World War II. Modest entrance fees.

BEST EN ROUTE

This small country has a fairly wide range of hotel prices. The nightly cost of a double room with bath or shower can range from $30 to $100. Accommodations priced from $90 to $100 and up are considered expensive; those from $60 to $90 are termed moderate; and those under $60 are rated inexpensive. Restaurant prices range from $50 and up for a dinner for two in places listed as expensive; around $30 for those in the moderate category; and $12 in the inexpensive category. Prices do not include drinks, wine, or tip. German, French, Chinese, Indian, Thai, Yugoslav, Russian, and Portuguese are among the types of restaurants found here.

LUXEMBOURG CITY

Aérogolf-Sheraton – This ultramodern hotel near the airport — it's totally sound-proof — has fine cuisine. Its top-floor *Cockpit Bar* features excellent light entertainment. Rte. de Trèves, Senningerberg (phone: 34571). Expensive.

Cravat – Luxembourg's most elegant hotel overlooks the Petrusse Valley. 29 Bd. Roosevelt (phone: 21975). Expensive.

Holiday Inn – This 260-room hotel is on the "new plateau" near the European Parliament and European Court of Justice buildings and the Trade Fair Building, overlooking the old part of the city. Handicapped accessible. Rue de Fort Niedergrunewald, Kirchberg (phone: 437761). Expensive.

Ibis – The newest in the chain, opened just last year, is located between the airport and town. Of the 120 rooms, four are specially designed for the handicapped. Conference facitilies, free parking available. Rte. de Trèves, Senningerberg (phone: 438801). Expensive.

Intercontinental Luxembourg – The country's largest is in Europa Park, just minutes from the center of town. A wide range of services are available for both the business and vacation traveler, including a complete health club with indoor pool. Handicapped accessible. 12 Rue Jean Engling, Dommeldange (phone: 43781). Expensive.

Royal – In the heart of the historic old city, this thoroughly modern hotel is complete with swimming pool, sauna, and solarium. Handicapped accessible. 12 Bd. Royal (phone: 41616). Expensive.

Eldorado – This small, modern hotel near the railway station has an excellent restaurant. 7 Pl. de la Gare (phone: 481071/72). Moderate to inexpensive.

Poêle d'Or – Opposite the Grand Ducal Palace, this restaurant serves delicious French food. Start with quail eggs and then have one of the veal dishes. 20 Rue du Marché-aux-Herbes (phone: 460813). Moderate.

EHNEN (near MONDORF-LES-BAINS)

Simmer – This old inn on the Moselle River has long been famous for fine food. Try the pâté, stuffed Luxembourg trout, and Charlotte russe. 117 Rte. du Vin (phone: 76030). Inexpensive.

ECHTERNACH

Bel-Air – A winding road leads you up to this lovely, secluded inn above the river. Surrounded by its own park, the inn has a gracious dining room and a delightful cocktail lounge. 1 Rte. de Berdorf (phone: 729383). Expensive.

Grand – On the Sauer River overlooking the hills of Germany and the old Siegfried Line, is a modern hotel with small but well-designed rooms and large modern bathrooms. Excellent cuisine is served on the enclosed porch facing the river. 27 Rte. de Diekirch (phone: 729672). Moderate.

MONDORF-LES-BAINS

Mondorf – A new, comfortable, 113-room hotel at the famous spa. Each room has a bath, TV set, mini-bar, and balcony. Guests have free access to the spa's sauna, solarium, Turkish bath, and whirlpool bath; there's a small fee for tennis and squash. Mondorf-les-Bains (phone: 670ll). Expensive.

VIANDEN

Heintz – A historic landmark that is a superb small hotel. Once part of the adjoining medieval Trinitarian monastery, it's a delightful place presided over by the warm and expansive Madame Hansen. Each room is individually decorated. And the food is excellent; a typical meal might consist of ham or mushroom quiche, smoked tongue with béarnaise sauce, beans wrapped in bacon, raspberry sherbert with whipped cream, and a carafe of the house wine. 55 Grand'rue (phone: 84155). Inexpensive.

WILTZ

Du Vieux Château – This elegantly decorated restaurant features a terrace and à la carte meals. 1 Grand-Rue (phone: 96018, 958018). Moderate.

Du Commerce – Although this appears to be just an average tavern, the food is memorable. Don't miss the tender, succulent broad beans and the remarkable homemade ice creams. 9 Rue des Tondeurs (phone: 96220, 95670). Inexpensive.

The Maltese Islands

The sun-drenched Maltese Islands — an archipelago comprising the main island of Malta, its smaller sister island of Gozo, the islet of Comino, and two large rocks, Cominotto and Fifla — are near the very center of the Mediterranean some 60 miles south of Sicily. Because of their strategically important location, the islands have always attracted foreign powers; as a result, they possess a wealth of history out of all proportion to their size. From megalithic temples and Roman remains to medieval towns and villages, the foremost of which is the citadel of Mdina; from religious traditions dating to AD 60, when St. Paul is said to have been shipwrecked here, to the enormous artistic achievements of the Knights of St. John of Jerusalem in the 16th, 17th, and 18th centuries, Malta's successive occupants have left behind a rich cultural tapestry set against a backdrop of honey-colored hills and azure sea.

Starting with the Phoenicians, Malta was occupied successively by the Romans, Byzantines, Arabs, Sicilians, and the Knights. Napoleon was here briefly in 1798, and the island passed to British rule in 1800. Nevertheless, the tiny nation, now an independent republic within the British Commonwealth, has remained intensely individualistic. Its 350,000 inhabitants have managed to combine a cosmopolitan attitude with a strong sense of tradition and national pride; along with their own basically Semitic language, nearly all Maltese speak English, Italian, and often French as well. Malta attained its independence from Britain in 1964, and from 1971 to 1987 was governed by pro-Libyan, anti-NATO socialists. The present administration is more pro-West and anxious to encourage investments and develop the country's tourism and industries. Accordingly, a new airport is under construction, and air service and hotel inventory are being expanded. A hydrofoil now runs between Malta and Sicily in just 2½ hours. Overall, some $300 million is being spent on basic infrastructure improvements, focusing on the island's antiquated telecommunications network, roads, and water supply.

Today, Malta is an ideal vacation spot, offering a near-perfect Mediterranean climate, picturesque beaches and lovely harbors, a fascinating variety of architectural and historical treasures, and a genuinely warm and welcoming people. Malta is deluged with package tourists, primarily from Britain, during the peak summer months. Some great bargains are available on all-inclusive tours if you happen to be flying in from London. Given the warm year-round temperatures as well as the lower shoulder season rate, visitors might consider traveling in the spring or fall.

Driving on Malta and Gozo can be a challenge, particularly for Americans. Driving is on the left-hand side and there are no highways, just plenty of good, tarmac roads. Since the total area of Malta and Gozo is barely 119 square miles (Malta itself is only 17 miles long) and the distance between points of interest is very short, you may be tempted to jog rather than drive, but the steep, hilly roads of both islands will soon dispel such notions.

Our route starts out at Malta's capital, Valletta, proceeds inland to the ancient walled city of Mdina, and crosses finally, after several short but interesting detours, to the town of Marfa at the northwest tip of the island, from which point you can take the ferry for a 1- or 2-day visit to Gozo.

VALLETTA: The island's capital was built by Jean de la Valette, Grand Master of the Order of Knights of St. John, after the epic siege by the Turks in 1565. Rising dramatically from the water, in one wide sweep, the city dominates the island's historic Grand Harbor, one of the finest natural ports in Europe and also one of the least polluted; people still swim here. For an excellent introduction to Malta's history, begin a tour of Valletta with *The Malta Experience,* a 40-minute audio-visual presentation given hourly in the Mediterranean Conference Center on Merchants St.

Although Valletta today is a mixture of old and new, the city retains much of its original baroque flavor. You will have no trouble exploring the town on foot; it is only about 1,000 yards long and is built in a regular grid around the main street, now called Republic Street, where many of the better shops are found. Also on Republic Street is the *National Museum of Archaeology* in the 16th-century Auberge de Provence, one of seven palaces built by the Knights of St. John of Jerusalem. Inside, important collections of prehistoric pottery, statuettes, stone tools, and ornaments recovered from Malta's many prehistoric sites are exhibited. Another majestic monument is St. John's Co-Cathedral, historically and artistically one of the most important monuments on the island. Completed around 1577, it was designed by Gerolamo Cassar, chief engineer of the Order, who was also responsible for building much of Valletta itself. Each of the cathedral's chapels was allotted to a national group of the Order and each is notable in its own way. Caravaggio's masterpiece *The Beheading of St. John* hangs in the oratory. The Palace of the Grand Masters, an imposing edifice built around two courtyards off Palace Square, was also designed by Cassar. Many of the State apartments are decorated with friezes depicting episodes from the history of the Order. Running along the back of the building is the Armoury, two halls containing a fine collection of arms and armor. Notice the beautiful marble tombstones — more than 400 of them — covering the cathedral floor. These bear the escutcheons of the Knights, Latin inscriptions, and graphic renderings of the Grim Reaper.

The *National Museum of Fine Arts* (South St.) is in an 18th-century palace; it houses paintings, sculpture, furniture, and objects connected with the Order of St. John. A section of the museum is reserved for works by Maltese artists. Also worth a visit is the *Manoel Theater* (Theatre St.), built as a court theater in 1731 and now one of the oldest in Europe. From the Upper Barrakka Gardens, on the edge of the city, you are rewarded with a magnificent view of Grand Harbor and, across the harbor, the ancient cities of Vittoriosa, Cospicua, and Senglea. The best way to explore the harbor and the Three Cities, as they are called, is in one of Malta's brightly colored *dghajjes* (pronounced "die-yes"), or water taxis, available for hire at the Old Customs House.

As you leave Valletta, and its suburb of Floriana, take a look back at the city's once-formidable 16th-century fortifications. Built to resist attack from non-European invaders, they served most recently to shelter the Maltese population from the determined bombing of Hitler's Luftwaffe.

En Route from Valletta – South of the city in the village of Paola is the Hypogeum, an underground monument built around 2400 BC and consisting of a system of caves, passages, and cubicles cut from the rock. Guided tours are available. Nearby are three well-preserved historic temples that were discovered in 1915; they are believed to be the oldest manmade self-standing buildings in the world.

MDINA: Towering upon a 700-foot plateau, Mdina was once part of the island's capital during the Romans' stay in Malta (218 BC–AD 270). According to tradition, it was here that St. Paul converted the Roman Governor Publius to Christianity and consecrated him the first Bishop of Malta. In 870, the Arab conquerors walled up a small section of the plateau and named it Mdina, the Arab word for a walled city. When Arab rule ended in 1090, Count Roger of Sicily started a building program within the city walls, and between that time and the coming of the Knights of St. John, Mdina was the capital of Malta. Today it is also known as Citta Vecchia, the Old City, and the Silent City; it is the finest and best-preserved city on the island. Historically the home of the Maltese nobility and the archbishopric, it has retained its Maltese flavor and has remained virtually unchanged for centuries. No cars are allowed in the city, so park outside the ramparts.

On entering the city, you soon come to St. Paul's Square, which is dominated by the baroque façade of the Cathedral of St. Peter and St. Paul, built on the site of an older church in 1694. The cathedral museum houses such treasures as the painting of the Madonna and Child attributed to St. Luke, who was shipwrecked in Malta with St. Paul; a flagon by Cellini; engravings by Dürer; and the cross carried to Godfrey of Bouillon in the first crusade to Jerusalem in 1099. The Vilhena Palace, on the right of the square, now houses the *Museum of Natural History*. Follow Villegaignon Street to the city's northern bastion, which offers superb views of the island.

En Route from Mdina – Across the moat from Mdina is the suburb of Rabat, famous for its catacombs and the island's only remaining Roman villa.

To the south lies Verdala Castle, a traditional fortified palace designed by Cassar in 1586 as a summer palace for Grand Master Verdala. The palace grounds, known as the Buskett Gardens, served as hunting grounds in the days of the Knights. Today they are the scene of the Mnarja, the traditional folk festival held June 28-29 and characterized by folk singing, feasting, and dancing. Horse, mule, and bareback donkey races are held near Mdina during the afternoon of June 29.

MOSTA: This is the site of the church of St. Mary, known as the Rotunda. A massive structure built in 1860, it boasts the third largest dome in the world.

En Route from Mosta – The north road leads to St. Paul's Bay, where St. Paul is said to have been shipwrecked. To the northeast stands Mellieha, towering on a high ridge overlooking Ghadira Bay. Here, in a grotto, is the church where St. Luke is supposed to have taken shelter and painted the Madonna.

After skirting the spectacular beach of Ghadira Bay, the road winds up the hills to Cirkewwa, where, twice daily, a ferry carries people, cars, and provisions to the sister island of Gozo.

MARSAXLOKK: This fishing village on the coast, southeast of Valletta — the name means "South Harbor" — is where many of the capital's residents go on Sunday afternoons. Fishermen are out touching up the paint on their colorful boats, while farther along the waterfront, octopus, rockfish, shrimp, and lobster are sold in the fish market. For an excellent seafood lunch, try either *Ruzzu* or *Skuna* restaurants.

En Route from Marsaxlokk – A few miles out of town are the giant, ancient Ghar Dalam caves, housing stalagmites and the bones of countless elephants, hippopotami, and antelopes; evidence of the land bridge that once connected Europe and Africa. Those with an interest in prehistory might also consider stopping at the temples of Tarxien (on the way back to Valletta) and Hagar Qim (southwest of the airport).

GOZO: This is the legendary isle of Calypso, from which Ulysses found it so difficult to tear himself away. The Maltese like to say that a sea divides the islands of Malta and Gozo, although in reality they are only about 4 miles apart. In fact, Gozo does have a character all its own, noticeable the moment you set foot there. The tiny island, only 9 miles long and 4½ miles wide, seems immune to the passage of time; it is sleepy and rural, greener than Malta, a bit more picturesque, and more dominated by its hilltop villages, with their quiet squares.

En Route from Mgarr – It is only a 5-minute ride from the port of Mgarr to the capital, Victoria, but you can make a short detour to visit the village of Xaghra, with its subterranean caves full of stalactites and stalagmites. A short walk brings you to the famous Ggantija Temples, which predate Stonehenge and the Pyramids. Visit Gozo Heritage, a touristy but informative walk-through "experience" of the island's past.

VICTORIA (RABAT): The center of communications for the island, this is nonetheless a quiet, charming town. The Citadel (Gran Castello) was the medieval capital and is built much like Mdina, on a hill overlooking the surrounding countryside. Inside the Citadel is an interesting folklife museum. The town has a modest but graceful cathedral, which, instead of a dome, has a clever perspective painting that simulates one. Victoria's quaint Old Town centers around its main square, It-Tokk. In the early evening it is filled with people strolling, talking, and drinking the good local wine. Also try the peppery local cheese, *gbejniet.*

En Route from Victoria – Just north of the road leading to San Lawrenz is the Basilica of Ta' Pinu, a simple, lovely church that has become a center for pilgrimage. To the west, along the coast, is the Inland Sea and Window, a natural pebbly bathing pool with crystal-clear water and sheer cliffs hanging over it dramatically. Heading north from Victoria, in a few minutes you arrive at Marsalforn, which, in summer, is a popular seaside resort and, in winter, a quiet fishing village. Also on the north coast is Calypso's Cave, with its magnificent view over the red sands of Ramla Bay. The cave itself is not particularly exciting, and there are no traces of the nymph Calypso. A short distance southwest of Victoria lies Xlendi Bay. The small village of Xlendi has the cozy, picturesque charm of many European seaside spots, but it is growing quickly. Hand-knit fisherman sweaters can be purchased here at bargain prices, and the disarmingly simple *St. Patrick's* hotel is right on the water.

COMINO: Only 1 mile square, Comino has one hotel, 14 inhabitants, no cars, and, needless to say, an authentic get-away-from-it-all atmosphere. There are, however, plenty of pigs — survivors of the African swine fever that devastated most of Malta's porcine population in the early 1980s. The boat trip from Malta takes 20 minutes and operates regularly from April to October.

BEST EN ROUTE

Malta is a resort, and a few of the best hotels still have an upper-crust British Empire flavor to them. The government classified lodgings aren't economical by Italian standards (Malta's nearest neighbor), except for hotels offering off-season packages. Among the restaurants, however, the competition is fierce; consequently many good meals are available on romantic seaside terraces or in atmospheric Arabian cafés for reasonable prices. There are restaurants on Malta with Chinese, Mexican, Italian, Viennese, and British menus. The best dishes, though, are local. Much of the meat is shipped frozen from Australia, but the rabbit is fresh and cooked over an open fire in a stew called Stuffat Tal Fenek. The seafood dishes made from fresh Mediterranean catches are also excellent. Many hotel restaurants advertise a per-head flat rate that's usually a good deal.

Expect to pay more than $75 per night for a double room in hotels listed as expensive; about $35 to $50 for those in the moderate category; and $25 or less for those in the inexpensive range. Most room prices include breakfast; half-board is also common. A bounteous Maltese lunch or dinner in an expensive restaurant, including wine, tax, and tip, will cost about $15 per person; about $10 per person in a moderate eatery.

VALLETTA-FLORIANA

Castile – Talk about faded elegance! The rooms are dark and narrow and the fixtures archaic. Nevertheless, this plunky old hotel has a certain charm to it, an unbeatable location right on Castille Square at the entrance to town, a rooftop restaurant with a magnificent harbor view, and a bar that is very popular with the Maltese. Castille Sq. (phone: 623677). Inexpensive.

RABAT-MDINA

Grand Hotel Verdala – There is a pleasant, airy feeling to this place, although its public spaces (with checkered marble floors) are more impressive than the 164 rooms, all of which have balconies. There are 2 swimming pools, a health club, tennis courts, 3 restaurants, and 2 bars. Inguanez St., Rabat (phone: 641700). Moderate.

Palace – If you're staying inland, this might be an interesting choice. It doesn't have much in the way of facilities, but it's air conditioned and it drips with atmosphere. St. Paul's Sq., Mdina (phone: 674002). Moderate.

SLIEMA–ST. JULIANS

Dragonara – There are more hotels in the Sliema area than anywhere else on the island. This is one of the fanciest (200 rooms), in the heart of the resort area, and has it all — private beach, heated swimming pool, color TV sets, private parks. Overall, a very romantic setting. St. Julians (phone: 336421). Expensive.

Holiday Inn – A huge, luxurious resort hotel that incorporates 19th-century military structures. The 182 rooms are spacious, well decorated, and equipped with all the usual appurtenances of this international hotel chain. Facilities include a swimming pool, health club, tennis, beach club, and several restaurants, including a popular pizza parlor. Tinge St., Sliema (phone: 341173). Expensive.

Giannini – A very elegant, sophisticated Italian restaurant with a wonderful view of Manoel Island, overlooking Hastings. 23 Windmill St., St. Michael's Bastions (phone: 227121). Expensive.

Hole in the Wall – A great seafood place that doesn't open until 7 PM and closes all day Sunday. Try the scampi or the dendici. 32 High St., Sliema (phone: 336110). Moderate.

Il-Fortizza – This place is a little too commercial and touristy, but the building is interesting and the food generally good. The specialty is fresh fish in good Italian sauces. Tower Rd., Sliema (phone: 336908). Moderate.

GOZO

Ta' Cenc – The only deluxe hotel on Gozo, it's out of the way but relaxing. Sannat (phone: 556830). Expensive.

Cornucopia – This innovative hotel complex (40 rooms), which opened in 1974 with an addition in 1986, combines elements of Maltese farmhouses, such as pine furniture, with modern conveniences. There are 2 swimming pools and an excellent restaurant. Gnien Imrik, Xaghra (phone: 556486). Moderate.

San Giuliano – A lovely, cheery seafood restaurant looking out over the fishing village at Spinola Bay. For appetizers, don't miss the *busketta* sauce (crushed tomato, garlic, and onion) and *ftira,* a spread made with tuna, tomato paste, olives, white beans, and pickled onions, both of which are served on incomparably delicious Maltese bread. St. Julians (phone: 332000). Expensive.

Monaco

The principality of Monaco, although one of the smallest states in Europe, is, at the same time, one of the most famous because of its wealth and glamour. Today's Monaco is a mixture of old and new, with sleek modern buildings next door to the pastel stucco and tile of traditional French Mediterranean architecture. The emphasis everywhere is on sumptuous elegance. Yachts of the rich and famous fill the port, the shops display the wealth one dreams of — vintage wines, rare jade and ivory, costly jewels, couturier clothes and furs. Tourists, dazzled by the display, may sometimes forget that Monaco, with its rare climate and its turbulent history, has other resources besides manmade riches.

The climate is much like Southern California's: Winters are mild; summers warm, with little rain. The vegetation, too, is like Southern California's, with orange and lemon trees, palms, and live oaks. The water temperature of the Mediterranean is ideal for swimming. The only drawback is the beaches, all rock in their natural state. The few sand beaches here are all manmade, and Monaco's most exclusive stretch of beach is actually just over the border, in France.

Monaco is ruled by the Grimaldi family, one of whose ancestors (Francesco Grimaldi, a Ligurian nobleman immortalized as Malizia, the Cunning One) wrested control of the territory from the Republic of Genoa in 1297. For more than a hundred years, the family fought Genoa to maintain control of its conquest, and once that matter was settled, it still had to contend with other occupying foreign powers — Spain from 1524 to 1641, France from 1641 to 1814. When the Grimaldis regained sovereignty in 1814, Monaco was larger than it is today and included the cities of Roquebrune and Menton, which separate the principality from the Italian border. These two cities grew discontented under the yoke of Monaco and seceded in 1848, reducing the state to its present size.

Modern Monaco, with an area of only 468 acres, is divided into four parts: Monaco (the old city); Monte Carlo (the new city); La Condamine (the port); and Fontvieille (the industrial district, where Monaco brews its own beer). But, in comparison to tourism, industry is of minor importance to Monaco. The tourist business was given a major overhaul by the present ruler, Prince Rainier III, and his American wife, Princess Grace (the former actress Grace Kelly), who died in 1982. Modern hotels and convention centers have been built. Monaco maintains extensive public tennis courts and an 18-hole golf course, and the harbor offers superb sailing and water skiing.

Among special events are the Monte Carlo Rally in January and the famous Grand Prix auto race in late May. The summer months are enlivened by the *International Fireworks Festival* and, in early December, by the *International Circus Festival*. The *Monte Carlo Philharmonic Orchestra* can be heard practically year-round; the *Monte Carlo Opera*'s season is from January through March.

Although Monaco is a sovereign state, with its own postage stamps (favorites with collectors) and car license plates, it is politically bound to France. There are no formalities crossing the border — you may not even realize when you've done it. And French money is the medium of exchange.

Because Monaco is so small, you don't need a car. There is a good internal bus system, which also takes side trips to some interesting neighboring towns. But if you prefer to be independent, you can rent a car from a number of international agencies.

You'll have no language problem in Monaco. English is widely spoken, and lots of English books and magazines are available at newsstands and bookstores.

MONACO

GRAND CASINO: A world-famous landmark. Even if you're not a gambler, you shouldn't miss the casino, where the legend of glamorous Monaco really began. The secession of Menton and Roquebrune reduced the revenues as well as the size of the principality, and when Prince Charles III came to the throne in 1856, he took up his father's idea of opening a gambling casino like the fashionable and successful one at Baden-Baden. A casino was built and struggled along until 1862, when the prince hired an expert manager, François Blanc, who had run the casino in Bad Homburg. Blanc hired boats and carriages to bring people from up and down the coast to Monaco's casino. At the same time, he spurred construction nearby of Monaco's first luxury hotel, the *Hôtel de Paris.* Through Blanc's efforts, the casino became fashionable and by 1869 was bringing in such large sums that the prince was able to abolish all taxes for his citizens. In 1878 Charles Garnier, the architect of the *Paris Opera House,* was commissioned to design the casino building you see today.

Stop for a minute in front of the casino to absorb the drama of the setting: the sea in the background; lush gardens; the building itself, with its copper roof enhanced by a green patina; and always, the coming and going of elegant limousines and sports cars carrying glamorous patrons from all over Europe. When you enter, you can go as far as the American Room and White Salon (slot machines and American-style games) without restriction, though you may have to show a passport to prove you're 21. A passport and an entrance fee are required for the European gaming rooms, such as the Touzet Rooms and Salons Privés. Most rooms open daily at either 10 AM or 3 or 4 PM.

PRINCE'S PALACE: With its crenelated tower sporting a rather incongruous clock and its Louis XIV cannons complete with neat stacks of cannonballs piled like apples in a market, the palace looks like an operetta castle, perfect for a miniature monarchy. At the sentry boxes, the guard changes each day precisely at 11:55 AM. The picture is so quaint you may not wish to risk destroying the illusion by going inside.

You can go inside, however, from July through September. You'll see the Court of Honor, surrounded by mainly 17th-century frescoes, the State Apartments, and the Throne Room. Admission charge.

EXOTIC GARDEN: A cactus garden, but much more, this was a project of Prince Albert I. It clings to the side of a cliff at the western approach to Monaco, more than 300 feet above the sea. The inclination of the cliff provides protection from northern winds and maximum exposure to the winter sun, so the 9,000 species of cacti and succulents from semi-arid climes around the world thrive as well here as in their native habitats. Equally impressive is the view, a sweeping one that embraces the whole principality.

Within the garden, at the base of the cliff, are the Observatory Caves. Although today you're most likely to notice the stalagmites and stalactites, at one time the caves housed prehistoric man, whose bones have been found here. You can take a guided tour of the caves, but note that the climb up and down totals 558 steps. If this seems too much, the nearby *Museum of Prehistoric Anthropology* safeguards what has been found on the site (and elsewhere in the principality and environs). Open daily. A single admission fee covers the garden, caves, and the museum.

OCEANOGRAPHIC MUSEUM: Not only a museum, but a working scientific research institute, this was another brainchild of Prince Albert I, called the "scholar prince" because of his passionate interest in oceanography. Prince Albert wanted a museum to house the results of his scientific expeditions around the world and to promote the science of oceanography. The building on the rock of Monaco, at the edge of a sheer drop, was a bold construction for the time. Pillars had to be built from sea level to support the building, and the rocks below had to be hollowed out to let in sea water for the aquarium. Though the work began in 1899, the inauguration did not take place until 1910.

Start your visit on the lowest level, with the aquarium. It's one of the finest in Europe — not surprising when you learn that the director of the museum is Jacques-Yves Cousteau. On the ground floor are zoological exhibits, skeletons of large marine mammals, and specimens that Prince Albert brought back from his travels. The top floor is perhaps the most interesting. Here are kept Prince Albert's whaleboat, 19th-century brass navigational instruments, and, in complete contrast, ultramodern diving equipment. Open daily. Admission charge.

OUTSKIRTS

LA TURBIE: Take the winding Route de la Turbie from Monaco to the Grand Corniche, and turn west (5 mi/8 km). This is the highest of the three corniches, offering spectacular views of coast and mountains. Built by Napoleon on the site of the ancient Roman Aurelian Way, its highest point is at La Turbie, 1,475 feet above Monaco.

The town is best known for its Roman relic, the Trophy of Augustus. It is worth a visit because there are only two structures of this kind still standing (the other is in Romania). The Trophy was built in 6 BC to commemorate Augustus Caesar's victory over the Gallic tribes of the region. The round pillar originally stood 160 feet high. On the base was engraved a list of the 44 conquered tribes, and above, between Doric columns, were statues of the generals who took part in the campaign. The top was surmounted by a statue of Augustus himself, flanked by two prisoners. A large part of the monument was destroyed by the Lombards in the 6th century, and villagers took much of the fallen stone for their houses. Now it is being restored.

You can climb up on the ruins for some spectacular views and interesting camera shots. If you'd rather, go to the terraces below the Trophy, where you have a panoramic view of Monaco and can see down the coast as far as Bordighera, Italy.

End your visit with the *Trophy Museum.* The display includes a model of the Trophy in its original form as well as interesting photographs of the restoration, much of which was sponsored by an American, Edward Tuck. The Trophy and museum are open daily. Admission charge.

ROQUEBRUNE: Take the Grand Corniche east 4 miles (about 7 km). At the *Vista-ëro,* stop to enjoy the view from this hotel perched right at the edge of a cliff.

The medieval village of Roquebrune is clustered around the oldest castle in France; you should be sure to see it for its very evocative picture of life in the Middle Ages. The village is typical of the medieval architecture all along this coast. The streets are narrow and steep; some are actually stairways, or vaulted passages. The buildings are made of rough stone with red tile roofs. The doors and windows are small to conserve heat in winter and keep the houses cool in summer.

Start from the Place de la République, once the advance defense post for the castle.

Walk along the Rue Raymond-Poincaré to the Place des Deux-Frères, up the Rue Grimaldi, then left into Rue Moncollet. Here you see medieval residences cut right into the rock. Guests of the castle were accommodated here.

The castle itself was built at the end of the 10th century by Conrad I, count of Ventimiglia, for defense against the Saracens. Its ownership was bounced back and forth among Italy, Monaco, and France. It was used as a fortress, a manorial home, and even a prison under the French directorate.

Start your visit in the great Ceremonial Hall. The well in the center was fed by rainwater, a vital detail in this dry countryside. You'll also see the niche for the lords' throne, a 15th-century mullioned window, and, slightly lower, a storeroom. Climb the stairs to the three upper levels. On the first are a small guardroom, the former prison, and the archers' dormitory. On the second are the lords' living quarters, bedrooms, dining room, and kitchen with a primitive bread oven. These rooms have been restored and furnished. From the top level — the artillery platform — there's a glorious view of the red-roofed village, with Monaco and the Mediterranean beyond.

Roquebrune is a pleasant spot for lunch. You can also find some attractive handicrafts by artisans in Roquebrune — colorful pottery, and trays and salad bowls made of olive wood.

You can return to Monaco via Cap Martin. Take the Grande Corniche to the Moyenne Corniche, then go east to D52, where you will cut back west. D52 winds among the magnificent villas of the aristocracy (Empress Eugénie of France once lived here) before joining the Corniche Inférieure, which takes you back to Monaco through Monte Carlo Beach.

EZE-VILLAGE: Take the Moyenne Corniche about 5 miles (8 km) east. It's a better road than the Grand Corniche, but more crowded and less scenic. A cliff-perched town, like Roquebrune, Eze-Village has winding streets, a cactus garden, and a sweeping view of the Mediterranean from the ruins of the castle. It's less historic than Roquebrune, but has two gourmet restaurants. Eze is also a good place to buy locally made copper and enamel jewelry.

BEST EN ROUTE

Expect to pay $100 and up per night for a double room in hotels listed as expensive; $60 and up for those in the moderate category; and under $60 for those in the inexpensive category. Restaurants range in price from $60 and up for a dinner for two in the expensive category; $30 to $60 in the moderate; and less than $30 in the inexpensive category. Prices usually include service charges, but not drinks or wine.

Paris – Like the casino across the square, its contemporary, this is a historic landmark that is *the* address in Monaco. It has 300 luxuriously refurbished rooms as well as the regal Salle Empire dining room and a swank rooftop restaurant (see below) that are among Monaco's best. Pl. du Casino (phone: 93-50-80-80). Expensive.

Hermitage – Opened in 1899, it still looks like a fit setting for a turn-of-the-century grand duke. A winter garden, a restaurant with Belle Epoque decor and food to match, and 200 luxurious rooms. More sedate than the bustling *Hôtel de Paris.* Sq. Beaumarchais (phone: 93-50-67-31). Expensive.

Loews Monte Carlo – An ultramodern polygon right at the edge of the water, with 600-plus rooms, its own American-style casino, swimming pool, disco, nightclub, and several so-so restaurants. Av. des Spélugues (phone: 93-50-65-00). Expensive.

Monte Carlo Beach – One of two Monaco hotels right on a beach. Small (50 renovated rooms) and charming (the terra-cotta-roofed building dates from 1928), it's east of town at the exclusive Monte Carlo Beach Club (phone: 93-78-21-40). Expensive.

Beach Plaza – The other hotel on a private beach, this one is modern, with some 300 air conditioned rooms, swimming pools, and an open-air grill restaurant. 22 Av. Princesse-Grace (phone: 93-30-98-80). Moderate.

Mirabeau – Elegant, yet less expensive than the other Société des Bains de Mer hotels (*Hermitage, Paris, Monte Carlo Beach*). This is in a modern high-rise, with its own pool, restaurants, and 100 rooms. 1 Av. Princesse-Grace (phone: 93-25-45-45). Moderate.

Alexandra – There are 55 rooms with bath or shower in this modest hotel. No restaurant. 35 Bd. Princesse-Charlotte (phone: 93-50-63-13). Inexpensive.

Terminus – These 54 rooms with bath or shower, TV sets, and radio are near the train station. Two restaurants. 9 Av. Prince-Pierre (phone: 93-30-20-70). Inexpensive.

Bec Rouge – Fans of its classic cuisine and elegant air consider it the best in town. The blinis with smoked salmon or caviar are a specialty. Closed January. 11 Av. de Grande-Bretagne (phone: 93-30-74-91). Expensive.

Dominique Le Stanc – Considered topnotch. You'll consume exquisitely refined cuisine while surrounded by a wonderful collection of antique toys. Closed Sundays and Mondays. 18 Bd. des Moulins (phone: 93-50-63-37). Expensive.

Grill – A panoramic location atop the *Paris,* excellent *grillades,* a remarkable wine list, and exquisite raspberry soufflés all conspire to make it memorable. Closed Mondays and most of December. Pl. du Casino (phone: 93-50-80-80). Expensive.

St. Charles – The maritime decor suggests the specialty here: fine seafood. Closed Tuesdays, lunchtime Wednesdays, and from mid-March to mid-April. 33 Av. St.-Charles (phone: 93-50-63-19). Expensive.

Polpetta – This café specializes in Italian and southern French cuisine. Closed for 2 weeks in February. 2 Rue Paradis (phone: 93-50-67-84). Moderate.

Pistou – On the roof of *Loews Monte Carlo* hotel and serving specialties of Provence — lamb with a sauce of vegetables and garlic; local cheeses. Closed early January to mid-February. Av. des Spélugues (phone: 93-50-65-00). Inexpensive.

Nightclubs – Although Monaco's nightlife has traditionally been monopolized by the *Casino of Monte Carlo* (phone: 93-50-69-31), you can also try your luck at the casino in *Loews Monte Carlo* (phone: 93-50-65-00) or at the one in the *Monte Carlo Sporting Club,* open summers only. Then squander your winnings or drown your sorrows at *Jimmy'z* and *Parady'z,* both in the sporting club (phone: 93-30-71-71). In winter, *Jimmy'z* moves to the Pl. du Casino (phone: 93-50-80-80).

ROQUEBRUNE

Roquebrune – This is the place to go for delicious bouillabaisse. Closed November and Wednesdays out-of-season. 100 Corniche Inférieure (phone: 93-35-00-16). Moderate.

Lucioles – There's a delightful view of the sea from an open terrace and a fixed-price menu. Closed Mondays and from November to March. 12 Av. Raymond-Poincaré (phone: 93-35-02-19). Inexpensive.

ÉZE-VILLAGE

Château de la Chèvre d'Or – In a restored medieval manor house overlooking the sea, the cuisine is classic French. Closed Wednesdays and from mid-November to mid-February. On the Moyenne Corniche at Rue Barri (phone: 93-41-12-12). Expensive.

Richard Borsigi – Classic French cuisine, with especially fine sauces. Closed Mondays and 3 weeks in January. Pl. de Gaulle (phone: 93-41-05-23). Expensive.

The Netherlands

The Netherlands is a small country — smaller than most American states — and can be crossed by car in a couple of hours. Packed into this tiny area, however, is an astonishing array of things to see and do. The country's compactness, combined with its excellent freeway system and efficient rail service, is handy for visitors since most points on the recommended tour routes can easily be reached in day trips from Amsterdam.

The unique geography of the Netherlands has shaped the country's history and the character of its people. Named for its unusually low (nether) geographic location — all of western Holland is below sea level — the Netherlands has risen literally from the sea to become an affluent, intriguing nation. During the last Ice Age, a great glacier shaped much of Holland into flat land. As the climate warmed and the glaciers melted, millions of tons of melting ice increased the water level of the North Sea (bordering the Netherlands on the west), causing the sea to inundate these low-lying lands. The land was not flooded evenly, because sand dunes acted as natural breakwaters and this brought about the development of lagoons and swamps. Much of the Netherlands is land reclaimed from the sea by various advanced draining techniques. The Dutch were pioneers of dike building and drainage canals, and their history is a continuous battle with the sea over which they have triumphed. On lands that were once flooded stand the country's greatest cities — Amsterdam, Rotterdam, and The Hague. Perhaps the Dutch people's constant struggle with water — exemplified by the mythical Dutch boy who stuck his finger in the leaking dam and saved his town from flooding — have made them tenacious and successful. What they have accomplished with almost negative natural resources is proof of their success. Well-designed cities with stunning architecture, neat polder fields of the rural landscape, and the enduring works of art of the Netherlands's Golden Age, the 17th century, are among the spoils for the native and the traveler.

Wherever you go, stop first at the local VVV tourist office for information. There are VVVs in practically every town and village, as well as major frontier posts and railway stations. Each one specializes in its own region, though most also carry the standard literature on the rest of the country issued by the National Tourist Office. These brochures, maps, and pamphlets are the best local guides. The Dutch automobile association, ANWB, has the best detailed road maps, and also publishes a large number of specialized touring maps on different themes and regions. You can pick up maps at the ANWB office in The Hague (220 Wassenaarseweg; phone: 010-147147) or in Amsterdam (5 Museumplein; phone: 020-730844). Falk-Verlag also publishes a multilingual road map of the country, available from any newsstand.

As you enter towns and cities, follow the *Centrum* signs to reach the center. *Doorgaand Verkeer* indicates the route for through traffic.

Our first route leads you through Randstad, where the major cities are concentrated. Though the cities are quite close together, they offer remarkable diversity, from the well-preserved old town of Haarlem to the extremely modern-looking Rotterdam. The Northern Netherlands route takes in the typical Dutch polder landscape of the North Holland province, and heads over the immense Enclosing Dike, which contains the North Sea. The Southern Netherlands route passes through the most geographically varied area of the country, through moors and forests, and the hill country of north Brabant and Limburg — the most French of the country's provinces. The last itinerary takes in the eastern region, where medieval castles and fortified towns lie amid forests and purple heathland.

The Randstad:
From Amsterdam to Rotterdam

This region, much of it below sea level, exemplifies Holland's compact diversity. Although the *Randstad* refers to a sort of supercity bounded by Amsterdam, Utrecht, Rotterdam, and The Hague, the greatest distance between any two of these cities is a mere 47 miles (75 km), from Amsterdam to Rotterdam. No four cities, as their inhabitants are quick to point out, could be more different. Nor is it the intention of planners that the four simply expand until they merge in an unbroken mass of concrete. Though this area is the most industrialized and densely populated in the country (60% of Holland's inhabitants live here), villages, farms, and rural and recreational areas are carefully preserved to maintain the variety and livable quality of the megapolis. All the sophisticated attractions of modern urban life can be found here, as well as miles of unbroken flower fields, lush pastures with grazing cows, and small historic towns. The route leaves Amsterdam on the Haarlemmerweg, which becomes the N5 state highway leading to Haarlem, and winds its way south through the bulb fields to Leiden, The Hague, Delft, and Rotterdam.

AMSTERDAM: For a complete report on the city and its hotels and restaurants, see *Amsterdam,* THE CITIES.

HAARLEM: This 900-year-old town has one of the country's best-preserved historic centers. An important city when Amsterdam was only a sleepy fishing village, Haarlem is still remembered for its heroic resistance during Holland's 80-year revolt against Spain, when it was besieged in 1572 for 7 months and finally largely destroyed, along with much of the population.

Haarlem's central square is the medieval Grote Markt, ringed by a number of noteworthy buildings including the 14th-century Stadhuis (town hall), originally a hunting lodge of the counts of Holland; the ornate Renaissance Meat Market, built in 1603 (now a museum); and the Grote Kerk or Church of St. Bavo constructed between 1390 and 1520. The church is also known for its Müller organ, built in 1738. With 68 registers and 5,000 pipes, the organ has lured the likes of Mozart and Handel to Haarlem. Every June, it is the centerpiece of an annual improvisation competition that draws top organists from all over the world. From the beginning of April until mid-October, public concerts are given on Tuesday evenings and Thursday afternoons. Of special interest is the *Frans Hals Museum* (62 Groot Heiligland; phone: 023-319180), originally a home for old men built in 1608. Be sure to visit *Teylers Museum,* said to be the oldest in the country (16 Spaarne; phone: 023-320197). On spring and summer evenings, romantic candlelight concerts are performed in the museum. Haarlem is the starting point of the annual spring flower parade through the bulb district, which takes place on the fourth Saturday in April at 10 AM. It is only a 20-minute train ride from Amsterdam.

En Route from Haarlem – A short detour 6 miles (10 km) west leads to Zandvoort, a popular resort, with its 5½ miles of sandy beaches (including a nudist beach).

Just outside Heemstede you'll find the *Heemstede Cruquius Museum,* 27 and 32 Cruquiusdijk, one of the three original steam-driven pumping stations that drained the immense Haarlem Lake from 1849 to 1852. Today, that lakebed holds the Schiphol international airport, 13 feet below sea level and probably the only airport in the world built on the site of a naval battle. The teahouse next to the museum is a handy place for a break.

At the world's largest flower auction in Aalsmeer some 10 million cut flowers are sold daily (except weekends) in the 75-acre auction hall (Legmeerdijk 313). Tours are available between 8 and 11 AM. Arrive early to see the operation at its blooming best. On the first Saturday in September, Aalsmeer is the starting point of the world's biggest floral parade, which travels to Amsterdam and back. Floats are on view in the auction halls the days before and after the parade.

Nieuw-Vennep is the modern site of the famous Bols Company (7 Lucas Bols-straat). After more than 4 centuries in business, this is the world's oldest distiller of liqueurs.

In April and early May, Holland's vast bulb fields are in brilliant bloom. If you visit at this time, take a minitour by turning south at Hillegom toward Lisse, and follow the signposted flower route. In Lisse, don't miss the Keukenhof (Station-sweg), a spectacular 70-acre garden featuring some 7 million bulbs and 5,000 square yards of greenhouses, open only during the blooming period.

A train/bus/entry ticket package is available from most Dutch railway stations.

LEIDEN: Dating from Roman times, Leiden is one of Holland's oldest towns. For a long time, it was also one of the most important. It is the site of the country's first university, established in 1575 in recognition of the town's heroic role in the revolt against Spain. Part of the university is still housed in the former convent chapel (73 Rapenburg), where it has been since 1581. The lifting of the siege of Leiden in 1574 is celebrated every year on October 3. America's Pilgrim ancestors took refuge here from 1608 to 1620, and you should not miss the chance to visit the Pilgrim Fathers Documents Center (45 Vliet) or the restored St. Pieter's Church, where they worshiped. Also worth a look is the *De Valk Windmill Museum,* 1 Tweede Binnenvestgracht, which is in an 8-story brick windmill dating from 1743 (admission charge; phone: 071-254639). For a light lunch, try some Dutch pancakes, which come in a variety of flavors, at the *Oud Leyden* (51-53 Steenstraat; phone: 071-133144); more elegant dishes are served in the Michelin-starred restaurant next door.

THE HAGUE: This city of half a million, third largest in the Netherlands and the country's political capital and seat of government (Amsterdam is the official capital), provides an excellent capsule illustration of the varied character of the Randstad.

As befits a major world capital housing more than 60 foreign embassies, The Hague is a smart, sophisticated, and cosmopolitan city, known for its beauty, elegance, and stateliness. The city contains three royal palaces — in two of which the royal family reside and hold functions — and retains a distinctively regal air. The daily business of government is carried on in the historic Binnenhof (Inner Court) or Parliament House complex of buildings in the ancient heart of the city, dominated by the magnificent

700-year-old Ridderzaal (Knights' Hall). It was here that the village of Die Haghe grew up around a hunting lodge built by the Count of Holland in the 13th century. Summer offers special treats. The imposing 15th-century church of St. Jacob or Grote Kerk (the Kerkplein) features carillon concerts at noon on Mondays, Wednesdays, and Fridays while the mansion-filled and tree-lined Lange Voorhout is turned into an open-air antiques market every Thursday during the summer. The *Mauritshuis Museum* (8 Korte Vijverberg; phone: 070-469244), a 17th-century palace housing one of the world's best collections of paintings from the Dutch school, is also close by.

An entirely different side of The Hague is presented by the city's lively seafront, Scheveningen, which has long been one of Europe's major resorts and has recently undergone a complete renovation. Features include an attractive promenade and pier, a nudist beach, and one of Holland's major casinos in the landmark *Kurhaus* hotel.

The Hague has more than a score of museums. Principal among these is the *Gemeente (City) Museum* (41 Stadhouderslaan), with its collection of period costumes, paintings, modern art, and rare musical instruments (special concerts are sometimes performed on them). The *Panorama Mesdag* (65b Zeestraat) has the world's largest painting, completed in 1881 and depicting Scheveningen life at the time. The *Gevangenpoort (Prison Gate) Museum* (33 Buitenhof) is a medieval horror chamber with torture rooms and instruments still intact. Other notable museums include the Hague's *Historical Museum* (7 Korte Vijverberg) and the *Museum Scheveningen* (92 Neptunusstraat), illustrating the history of Scheveningen as a fishing village.

The Hague is best known for its unique miniature city, Madurodam, 5 acres of meticulously crafted reproductions of real structures done on a scale of 1:25. Everything works, too, from the 2-mile railway network to the canal locks and harbor fire boats. Nearly 50,000 tiny lights come on at dusk. At 175 Haringkade in the Scheveningse Bosjes woodland park; open from April through September.

Other Hague sights include the Royal Residence at Huis ten Bosch Palace, the home of Queen Beatrix, on the Bezuidenhoutseweg in the Haagse Bos (Hague Woods), and the Peace Palace, Carnegieplein, a gift of the American millionaire and philanthropist Andrew Carnegie and now the site of the International Court of Justice.

With its many woods and parks, The Hague also lays claim to being Holland's greenest city. Worthy of special attention are the 19th-century Japanese Garden, Clingendael Park, open during the blooming season from about mid-May to mid-June, and the world-famous rosarium in the 50-acre Westbroekpark in the Scheveningse Bosjes, with its roses in full glory during August.

The Hague's special combination of city, woodland, seaside, and dunes is reflected in the wide range of recreational facilities available. Greyhounds race at Clingendael on the Rijksstraatweg, and the horses run at Duindigt in Wassenaar (29a Waalsdorperlaan). Nearby Duinrell has a campground, recreational area, and amusement park, where you can even ski on artificial slopes (and snow) in the wintertime. You can swim there year-round and enjoy the thrills of the largest indoor/outdoor waterslide in Europe, or else try the glass-covered surf pool on the Promenade in Scheveningen. In warm weather, there's the North Sea, and for deep-sea fishing or a cruise, try Rederij Jacq. Vrolijk, Doorniksestraat; phone: 70-514021.

Special Hague events include the ceremonial opening of Parliament on the third Tuesday in September, when the Queen sets out in her golden coach, and the week-long annual *North Sea Jazz Festival* in July, which attracts top performers from all over the world. In 1987, a modern concert building, *Dr. Anton Philips Zaal Concert Hall,* was erected. It's divided into two theaters, for dance and music events (phone: 070-60-9810). *Vlaggetjesdag* (Flag Day), celebrated late in May when the colorfully bedecked herring fleet sets out from Scheveningen for the first catch of the new season, is also a special event, but declining herring stocks have made its future somewhat uncertain.

DELFT: This town, dating from 1246 with its architecturally splendid 300-year-old center, is best known outside Holland for the famous pottery that has become synonymous with its name. The Porceleyne Fles (196 Rotterdamseweg) is the only factory that still makes Delftware in the traditional way (others churn out machine-made imitations). You can watch the company's 300 artists painting the entirely handmade Delft Blue.

To the Dutch, Delft is most important for its historical associations. William the Silent of Orange, the country's founding father and precursor of the present royal family, was assassinated here in 1584. Some bullet holes from that attack can still be seen in the walls of the beautiful 15th-century *Prinsenhof Museum* (Agathaplein), William's residence at the time. The museum itself is devoted primarily to the history of Delft and the Netherlands' long struggle for independence from Spain.

Delft is the traditional burial place of the royal family. Tombs are not on public view, but you can visit the mausoleum of William at the New Church, on the Markt, built in 1496. If you have the stamina, climb the tower for a spectacular view of the city.

ROTTERDAM: Holland's second largest city, with a population of about 580,000, Rotterdam once rivaled Amsterdam in beautiful old buildings but was devastated by a Nazi air raid in 1940. The city was rebuilt and is today extremely modern — well designed and attractive. Air and light sometimes seem to have been used as purposefully as glass and steel in its reconstruction. The broad 1¼-mile pedestrian shopping precinct, Lijnbaan, is an attraction in its own right, as is the cubist architecture by the waterfront, which is still referred to as Oudehaven, or Old Harbor. Visit the "white house" building, which was the sole postwar survivor. It's shaped like a pencil. The 600-foot Euromast (20 Parkhaven) is worth a visit for its panoramic restaurant, cafeteria, observation tower, and an airborne ship's bridge manned by retired officers who are happy to explain the instruments.

Don't miss the opportunity to tour the large, modern port complex by boat from Spido at the Willemsplein. Greenery is well provided for by the beautiful Kralingse Bos woodland park, and the *Boymans–van Beuningen Museum* (18-20 Mathenesserlaan) has a fine collection of modern and traditional art. The highly respected *Rotterdam Philharmonic Orchestra* offers the best in classical music at the *Doelen Concert Hall* (50 Schouwburgplein). The *Doelen* also offers a number of special cultural activities, including the *International Poetry Festival* every June.

Rotterdam is not all modern, however. Miraculously spared the Nazi bombs was the historic port of Delfshaven, from which America's founding Pilgrim fathers sailed on the first leg of their voyage to the New World in 1620. A painstaking 20-year project restoring Delfshaven's 110 buildings was completed in 1980, and many of these now belong to artists and practitioners of traditional crafts. Of special interest is the *Guild House* of the Sack Carriers who unloaded the ships (13-15 Voorstraat), where you can buy — at bargain prices — new pewter objects cast in original 17th- and 18th-century molds and watch how they are made. *De Dubbelde Palmboom* historical museum (10-12 Voorhaven) is devoted to old crafts. If you want to see the Pilgrim Fathers' Church, call first or check next door (18 Voorstraat; phone: 010-477-4156). A special commemoration service is held there every Thanksgiving Day.

Close to Rotterdam is Kinderdijk, with Holland's greatest concentration of windmills. On Saturday afternoons July and August, weather permitting, all 19 mills are turning.

Also outside Rotterdam is the town of Gouda; its Cheese Market is held in the 17th-century weigh house in the central Markt on Thursday mornings from 9:30 AM to noon, June 30 to August 31. Nearby is Holland's oldest (1448) and most beautiful town hall, which lures marriage-minded couples from all over the country. On a selected evening in mid-December, the entire square is illuminated by candlelight until the magnificent town Christmas tree, a gift from Norway, is switched on. Carol singing and a concert in the church follow.

BEST EN ROUTE

In the Hague, expect to pay $110 and up for a double room in the expensive range, $70 to $90 in the moderate range, and under $60 in the inexpensive category. In Amsterdam there's a wider variety of good standard accommodations. Rates in most hotels vary according to the time of year and the size of the rooms. In general, Amsterdam hotels are not inexpensive. Expect to pay $150 or more for a double room in those places listed as expensive, $80 to $100 for those we have rated moderate, and under $60 for inexpensive accommodations. Dinner for two should cost from $50 to $75 in expensive restaurants, from $30 to $45 in those listed as moderate, and under $20 in the inexpensive ones. Prices do not include drinks or wine. Indonesian restaurants are particularly of note in The Hague.

THE HAGUE

Kurhaus – Originally opened in 1885, this historic hotel was completely rebuilt and re-opened in 1979. Dominating the seaport resort area of Scheveningen, the hotel has a classical façade that is an exact replica of the original. Inside, there's a luxurious modern hotel, centered around a vaulted dome reception area with old paintings and inlaid mosaics. The most elegant of the Netherlands' casinos is here along with a first class French restaurant and 2 bars. Adjacent to the hotel is an all-weather recreation center with a pool, sauna, and solarium. 1 Kurhausplein (phone: 070-520-052). Expensive.

Park – A 4-star hotel with 3-star prices in the old center of town near the royal palace and the chic shopping district. Rooms have direct dial telephones, cable TV, writing desks, and luxurious marble bathrooms. Rates include buffet breakfast. 350 Molenstraat (phone: 070-624371). Moderate.

Garoeda – An elegant yet unpretentious 2-story restaurant in the center of town, near the American Embassy. Excellent rijstaffel variations. 18a Kneuterdijk (phone: 070-465319). Moderate.

Westbroekpark – This restaurant is in an open glass pavilion in the middle of a beautiful park. You can dine on French specialties while looking at the hundreds of roses growing outside. Try the four-course Golden Rose menu. From June to September, dining is outside in the midst of a blaze of color. Reservations recommended. 35 Kapelweg (phone: 070-546072). Moderate.

Café Schlemmer – A must for a cappuccino or light meal. Its muted colors and distinct furnishings remind one of Schlemmer's paintings from the 1930s. 17 Houtstraat (phone: 070-609000). Inexpensive.

ROTTERDAM

Atlanta – This recently redecorated four-star hotel in the town center, opposite City Hall, offers all modern amenities in a traditional Dutch setting. 4 Aert van Nesstraat (phone: 411-0420). Expensive to moderate.

De Unie – A restaurant done in Art Nouveau style and serving fine Dutch and French fare, with an eclectic clientele. 430 Mauritsweg (phone: 010-4117394). Expensive to moderate.

DELFT

De Prinsenkelder – In a medieval cellar with Gothic arches, old wood, and antique tables, this chic and atmospheric restaurant specializes in French cuisine. Its specialty menus change weekly. Reservations recommended. 11 Schoolstraat (phone: 015-121860). Expensive.

Café de Kerk – A traditional café in the center of town, with tasty soups and sandwiches. 20 Kromstraat. Inexpensive.

The Northern Netherlands

This 155-mile (248-km) route travels through the typical Dutch polder landscape of North Holland province, across the immense Enclosing Dike, which holds back the North Sea, into Friesland, the Netherlands's most unusual province. North Holland is characterized by its flat, rustic meadowlands reclaimed from the sea and sprinkled with church spires and thatch-roofed farmhouses, but it also possesses dreamy fishing villages, as well as the country's most beautiful beaches.

Friesland, particularly the Wadden Islands just off the coast, is a nature-lover's paradise, containing one of Europe's most important bird sanctuaries and wildlife preserves, as well as the country's best facilities for water sports. With its own language, history, and cultural traditions, passionately clung to by the majority of its half-million residents, Friesland gives the impression of being more of a tiny republic than a Dutch province. Its history is in fact older than Holland's; so fierce were the early Frisians that even the Roman legions were unable to subdue them. The Frisians literally built their country with their bare hands, doggedly constructing huge mounds of earth called *terpen* to protect them from the sea. More than 100 million cubic yards of earth (the equivalent of 21 Great Pyramids) were shifted this way. The Frisians, who also have a sense of humor, have made something of a joke out of their legendary pride and stubborn independence by issuing passports. Pick one up at one of the tourist offices. They make intriguing souvenirs and also offer valuable reductions on many attractions.

ZAANDAM: Just outside of town is De Zaanse Schans, a village constructed in 1948 from threatened historic mills and houses that were transported to the site and painstakingly reassembled. It is now a living museum occupied by families, but the windmills — as well as an antique clock museum and an old bakery — are open to the public. In Zaandam (24 Krimp), you can see the cottage where the eccentric Russian Czar, Peter the Great, disguised as a shipyard worker, stayed while on a state visit in 1697. In nearby Koog a/d Zaan (18 Museumlaan) is a windmill museum with models demonstrating how the mills work.

    En Route from Zaandam – The stretch of coastline a few miles west of the route is among the most unspoiled in the country. There is a magnificent 12,500-acre dune reservation with entrances at the villages of Wijk aan Zee, Heemskerk, Castricum, Bakkum, Egmond, and Bergen. The last village is an artists colony.

ALKMAAR: This picturesque town is especially famed for its cheese market on the central Waagplein. On Friday mornings at 10 AM in the spring and summer, a colorful early-17th-century tradition continues as the cheeses are auctioned off and carried to the 14th-century weighing house by members of one of Europe's few surviving medieval guilds.

HOORN: Like others along what was once the Zuider Zee, this historic port town on the shore of Lake Ijssel has adopted tourism and water sports since being cut off from the ocean. Summer is the season for a folklore market that gives demonstrations of traditional crafts, and the historic triangle tour, which includes a trip by steam train to Medemblik, and by boat to Enkhuizen. At the last stop, the *Zuiderzee Museum,* a reconstructed — and inhabited — village of 130 homes and shops depicts the area's turn-of-the-century fishing culture. If hunger calls, the fish restaurants along the quay by the inner harbor offer hearty local dishes that fill your stomach without emptying your purse.

The villages of Marken and Volendam, where the locals still wear traditional costumes (mainly as a draw for tourists), and the little-changed 17th-century cheese town of Edam lie 12½ miles (20 km) south of Hoorn. A rather strange museum in Edam (8 Wowneerstraat) is in a 16th-century house that has a cellar that actually floats; at different times, the house has been occupied by a man famed for his beard, which reached down to his toes and back up to his shoulders; a woman nearly 9 feet tall; and another man who weighed over 500 pounds! Exhibits focus on them and other local curios.

En Route from Hoorn – At Den Oever you may like to make a side trip by heading 16 miles (25 km) to Den Helder, where you can catch a ferry to Texel, the largest and most popular of the Wadden Islands. Although Texel is swamped with campers in the summer, all of the islands are beautiful and undeveloped, and there are small hotels where you can stay — check with the VVV.

Back en route, you cross the Afsluitdijk, a massive 12-mile-long dike separating the North Sea from freshwater Lake Ijssel. Stop at the monument, 4 miles (6 km) from Den Oever, and climb up for a view of the surrounding water. If this dike ever springs a leak, it'll take much more than a boy's finger to plug it up.

A short way up the coast is the seaport town of Harlingen, originally a Norman settlement, now a jumping-off point for the attractive islands of Vlieland and Terschelling. Cars are banned from Vlieland.

Franeker features an unusual working planetarium (3 Eise Eisingastraat) with a model, created by a craftsman in 1781, that demonstrates the solar system as it was known in the 18th century. A short way off the road at the next junction at Dronrijp is Winsum, the center of a uniquely Frisian sport — pole-vaulting over canals. Developed from the practical need of a means of crossing the canal-laced fields, this sport is interesting because most of the contestants end up in the water rather than on the far bank. Championships are held on Saturdays in August.

LEEUWARDEN: Built on three *terpen,* this city is the capital and heart of Friesland. The notorious spy Mata Hari was born here. A statue of her stands on the Korfmakerspijp. The house where she grew up is now occupied by the *Museum of Frisian Literature* (28 Gröte Kerkstraat). The *Fries Museum* (24 Turfmarkt) has English-speaking guides (available by appointment), who provide some insight into the history and culture of this unique province. The *Princessehof Museum* (11 Gröte Kerkstraat) has an excellent ceramics collection, including many one-of-a-kind pieces. From the 16th-century Oldehove Tower (Oldehoofster Kerkhof), you can view the city in the summer. The *Taveerne De Waag,* in the weighing house, built in 1568, is an interesting place to eat.

Another unique form of recreation that is rapidly gaining in popularity with tourists is *wadlopen* — walking through the shallows. The Wadden Sea between the mainland and the islands is so shallow that it is actually possible to walk to three of the islands when the tide is out. Organized treks are an absolute must for bird watchers. They require a day, an experienced guide, suitable clothing and equipment, and some advance planning. Departures are from Holwerd or Wierum on the coast to the north.

For information contact the VVV in Leeuwarden (1 Stationsplein; phone: 058-132224). The hamlet of Hoogebeintum stands on the highest (40 feet) *terp* in the province. To view the 13th-century church, get the key from the minister.

SNEEK: This popular yachting center is the site of a major international regatta in August. In the lake district, Friesland is Holland's prime location for all water sports.

SLOTEN: This walled town with a population of 700 is the smallest in Friesland. Resembling a movie set, this popular center for water sports is worth seeing.

En Route from Sloten – In Wolvega there's a statue of the founding father of New York, Peter Stuyvesant, who was born in the adjoining community of Weststellingwerf.

Zwarlendijkster: Between the villages of Een and Bakkeveen are these preserved fortifications dating from 1593, on which Stuyvesant based New York's defenses. It was this first wall that gave Wall Street its name. The wooded area is an attractive place to walk or bicycle. From here you can easily return to Leeuwarden via Drachten or extend your tour by continuing north to the university city of Groningen, and looping back down to Amsterdam through a few pastoral provinces.

BEST EN ROUTE

Expect to pay $100 and up for a double room in an expensive hotel, $60 to $80 in the moderate range, and about $50 in the inexpensive category. Dinner for two should cost $40 to $50 in the restaurants listed as expensive, $20 to $30 in those listed as moderate, and under $15 in the inexpensive places. Prices do not include drinks or wine.

LEEUWARDEN

Oranje – This completely rebuilt, reasonably priced hotel in the center of town has 78 rooms and a good restaurant specializing in Dutch and international dishes. 4 Stationsweg (phone: 058-126241). Expensive to moderate.

GROUW

Oostergoo – Cozy, simple but comfortable, this 24-room hotel on the lake about 6 miles (10 km) from Leeuwarden has a restaurant serving Dutch food and fish specialties. 1 Nieuwe Kade (phone: 05662-1309). Moderate to inexpensive.

The Southern Netherlands

This 225-mile (360-km) route, bordered by Belgium to the south, passes through the most geographically varied part of the Netherlands, from the estuaries and islands of Zeeland (Sea Land) on the North Sea coast, through the moors and forests of North Brabant, to the hill country — the only hill country in Holland — of Limburg province in the southeastern pocket between Germany and Belgium. These last two, the country's Catholic provinces, are notorious among their sterner Protestant brethren for the annual carnival madness that sweeps the southeast for 3 days in February. The festivities, which include parades, colorful costumes, street music, round-the-clock opening of cafés, and general hysteria, are at their most frenetic in the larger towns, particularly Bergen op Zoom, Den Bosch, Breda, and Maastricht. North Brabant and Limburg are the least Dutch of the country's provinces, with closer cultural, historic, religious, and geographical links to the south. Limburg in particular has a distinctive French flavor.

ROTTERDAM: For a complete description of Rotterdam, see *The Randstad: From Amsterdam to Rotterdam.* Then, head west to the old fortified town of Brielle, the first town to go over to the Protestant cause after being taken by privateers in the service of William the Silent on April 1, 1572. The event is celebrated every year on this date.

STELLENDAM: On the night of January 31, 1953, freak conditions combined to fulfill the worst of Dutch nightmares. Some 300 miles of dikes stretching from Rotterdam southward were overwhelmed by a raging North Sea, resulting in the flooding of 4.5% of the nation's total land area, and the deaths of nearly 2,000 people. The Dutch answer to this disaster was the daring Delta Plan. Completed in 1986, after 31 years of work, this engineering feat closed off the huge estuaries dividing Zeeland, transformed recreation areas, and eliminated more than 400 miles of coastline. Most of the time you travel through Zeeland, you will be driving over water. These roads, linking the formerly isolated province to the rest of the country, were created by the Delta Plan. The Delta Expo, which explains this enormous project with the help of films, mock-ups, a tour of the interior workings of the barrier, and a boat ride, is open daily from March 18 to October, Wednesdays to Saturdays the rest of the year. Burghsluis (phone: 01115-2702).

   En Route from Stellendam – The route passes through a region that has become an important center for water sports, with its beach resorts, campgrounds, dunes, and woods, and its excellent facilities for sailing, fishing, windsurfing, and so on. Zierikzee and Veere are particularly attractive towns. An intriguing place to eat or stay in Veere is *De Campveerse Toren,* originally part of the town fortifications and now a monument. It has also been an inn since 1558 and was selected by William of Orange for his wedding feast, which is the Dutch equivalent of "George Washington slept here."

MIDDELBURG: The completely reconstructed medieval center of this small provincial capital won the title of "model center" during Europe's Architectural Heritage Year, and some of Holland's most interesting old buildings are to be found here. Most famous is the abbey dating from 1120, with its complex of churches, a 1,280-foot tower known as Long John that can be climbed in the summer, a museum depicting Zeeland's history and culture, and a distinctive restaurant done in period decor. If you find the wealth of architectural treasures somewhat overwhelming, visit Miniature Walcheren (Molenwater) where they are all meticulously reproduced on a scale of 1:20. In the summer you can tour the city by horse-drawn tram or attend a Thursday market with residents in regional costume. Surrounded by lovely countryside and coastline, Middelburg is a good place in which to stay over.

   En Route from Middelburg – At the seafront city of Vlissingen, you can lie on the beach and watch an incessant stream of passing ships making their way to and from the major Belgian port of Antwerp. A steam train in Goes makes daily tours of the region in the summer. The old center of Bergen op Zoom, on the Ooster Schelde inlet from the sea, is worth a stop.

BREDA: Principal sights of this historic town, beautifully situated amid moors and woodlands, are the market square and Grote Kerk on the Grote Markt, and nearby Breda Castle, originally dating from 1350. The castle, home of the Royal Military Academy since 1828, is also where the Dutch signed New Amsterdam (later named New York) over to the British in 1667. Two-hour guided tours are given Tuesdays through Fridays in the summer at 2 PM. Breda hosts a popular 1920s-style jazz festival every May, and on Saturdays from April through September there is a curiosities and crafts market on the Havermarkt. The VVV (17 Willemstraat) conducts a historic-mile walking tour of the center in the summer. Holland's newest casino, *Casino Breda,* is open from 2 PM to 2 AM and features French and American roulette, blackjack, slot machines, a bar/restaurant, and a 5-guilder chip with the $4 admission (30 Bijster; phone: 076-227600). Near the E. 37 Highway.

About 12½ miles (20 km) north of Breda lies the unique marshland nature preserve of Biesbosch, a fisherman's and bird watcher's paradise of tangled creeks and waterways. Boat tours of the area are available in summer from *Zilvermeeuw Cruises* (3 Weitjes) in the tiny village of Drimmelen, near Made, site of Europe's largest inland yacht harbor. The *Biesbosch* restaurant has fish specialties and provides an unrivaled view of the watery terrain (open from Easter until mid-October).

TILBURG: This town is a handy jumping-off point for a number of interesting side trips. If you pass town and turn right toward Hilvarenbeck, you will come to the turnoff for the Beekse Bergen amusement and safari park. Also interesting is the crazy-quilt village of Baarle-Nassau, which has two of nearly everything, including mayors. Many of the residents cross the international frontier between Holland and Belgium every time they go from one room of their homes to another. About 7½ miles (12 km) north of Tilburg on the road to Waalwijk is the enchanting fairy-tale park Efteling (at Kaatsheuvel), as well as Europe's biggest amusement park. The *Tilburg Textile Museum* has exhibitions on the history of the textile industry, as well as historical and contemporary textile art (96 Goerkastraat; phone: 013-367475). The Autotron in Roosmalen, near 's-Hertogenbosch, has a fine collection of antique cars.

's-HERTOGENBOSCH: This mouthful, usually known by the more manageable name Den Bosch, is the provincial capital of North Brabant. So taken with the city was the 15th-century painter Hiëronymus Bosch that he adopted it as his last name. His ardor was understandable, as Den Bosch is especially famed for its romantic antique center. Its market square (markets are on Wednesday and Saturday mornings) and the 14th-century St. Janskerk cathedral are among Europe's most beautiful. Even the VVV, housed in a small 13th-century castle (Markt 77), is an attraction in this surprising city.

Weight-watchers can eat in peace at the medieval *Dry Hamerkens* (57 Hinthamerstraat), which features calorie-conscious menus as well as fuller selections. Just outside town in neighboring Vught, on the E9 south, is an impressive restaurant in the 16th-century Maurick Castle, complete with drawbridge.

En Route from 's-Hertogenbosch – Eindhoven is the home of Holland's giant Philips Electronics Company, but also the site of the *Von Abbé Museum,* which is known throughout Europe for its collection and changing exhibitions of 20th-century art (10 Bilderdijklaan; phone: 040-389730).

From here you can drive direct to Maastricht on E9, or take the more leisurely alternative — E3 east to Venlo on the German border, and south from there. This route passes through Limburg's loveliest countryside, dotted with churches and castles. The landscape actually resembles the popular (and largely prewar) picture many people have of Europe. On the way to Venlo detour north via Venray to the village of Overloon, the site of a unique and disturbing war museum (1 Museumpark), which includes a 35-acre park still littered with the battered tanks, field guns, and other weapons left behind after the 3-week Battle of Overloon. Closed weekends.

MAASTRICHT: Dating originally from pre-Roman times, this provincial capital is Holland's oldest city. Maastricht was besieged 21 times; 9 of the 100 castles of Limburg province can be found here, as well as myriad historical monuments. One of Europe's finest restaurants, *Château Neercanne* (see *Best en Route*), is in Holland's only terraced castle. The 40,000-bottle wine cellar is kept at optimal temperature in a grotto beneath the castle. For a lighter touch in haute cuisine, try *Au Coin des Bons Enfants.* Its French owners are particularly well known for their seasonal specialties, including wild game.

The heart of Maastricht is its central square, 't Vrijthof, ringed by numerous cafés and monuments including the 10th-century St. Servaas Church, and *In Den Ouden Vogelstruys*, a café opened in 1312. A good place for a snack, the café is said to be the oldest in Holland. The stone bridge spanning the Maas River, constructed in 1298, is even older.

A unique sight nearby is the 120-mile network of manmade tunnels beneath nearby St. Pietersberg hill, 2 miles (3.2 km) south of the city. Begun by the Romans in search of marl for building stone, the tunnels have also provided a handy refuge during the city's frequent times of trial. Parts of this subterranean realm date from the French occupation of 1794 and include a World War II treasure room, where Rembrandt's immortal *Night Watch* was preserved from the Nazis. Note the signatures of Sir Walter Scott and Napoleon, among countless others, on the tunnel walls. Enter via Châlet Bergrust, 71 Luikerweg.

VALKENBURG: This hill town is a popular vacation spot among the Dutch. Approximately 40 more miles of tunnels lie beneath the ruins of Holland's only hilltop castle. Several entrances lead to a coal-mine museum, a mysterious underground lake, and an exact replica of the Roman catacombs. Aboveground is the province's largest casino at Odapark.

HEERLEN: The *Thermen Museum* (9 Coriovallumstraat), built over an excavated Roman bath in this ancient town, contains many indigenous Roman artifacts.

VAALS: At 1,000 feet, this is the highest point in the Netherlands and the meeting point of Holland, Belgium, and Germany.

BEST EN ROUTE

Expect to pay $100 and up for a double room in the expensive range, $60 to $80 in the moderate range, and about $50 in the inexpensive category. Breakfast is generally included. Dinner for two should cost $40 to $50 in the restaurants listed as expensive, $20 to $30 in those listed as moderate, and under $15 in the inexpensive. Prices do not include drinks or wine.

VEERE

De Campveerse Toren – Close to Middelburg, this historic inn has 19 rooms as well as a restaurant, specializing in fish dishes, that has been catering to tourists for 5 centuries. 2 Kade (phone: 01181-291). Expensive to moderate.

VLISSINGEN

Britannia Watertoren – This pleasant seaside hotel with 35 rooms was recently renovated. Both its restaurants offer local fish specialties and lovely wide-angle views of ships sailing to and from foreign ports of call. 244 Blvd. Evertsen (phone: 01184-13255). Moderate.

WITTEM

Kasteel Wittem – Dating from the 10th century, this 12-room hotel-castle is on its own private grounds. Inside is a Michelin-starred restaurant. 3 Wittemmerallee (phone: 04450-1208). Expensive to moderate.

GULPEN

Kasteel Neubourg – This moated castle, surrounded by woods, features 25 spacious rooms and a French restaurant. Closed in January and February. 1 Rijksweg (phone: 04450-1222). Expensive.

MAASTRICHT

Chateau Neercanne – Under the same management as the *Kasteel Erenstein,* a
13th-century Renaissance castle, and hotel-restaurant *Winselerhof,* a 16th-century
farmhouse. It's possible to arrange a package visit to all three chic hostelries, which
are near one another and a half-hour ride from the Maastricht airport. The
complex has become very popular with business travelers due to its location near
Germany, Belgium, and Luxembourg. Full business services and meeting rooms
are available. Ideal for a romantic weekend as well (phone: 043-251359). Expensive.

Utrecht and the East

Of special interest to nature lovers, this 109-mile (175-km) route passes
through some of Holland's loveliest countryside, from the forests and purple
heathland of the 240-square-mile Veluwe nature preserve with its wild deer
and boar, to the farmlands and great country estates of bordering Achterhoek. With a turbulent history stretching back to Roman times, this area is
rich in castles and fortified towns, and has some of the best-preserved medieval structures in the country.

   En Route from Amsterdam – Take the A1/E35 to Hilversum where you pick
up the A27 to Utrecht. This takes you past Muiden on the former Zuider Zee, a
popular water sports center famous for its 13th-century castle, and moat-ringed
Naarden, a beautifully preserved old fortress town. On the opposite side of Hilversum are the Loosdrecht Lakes, a major center for water sports and recreation.
   UTRECHT: Founded by the Romans in AD 47, this ancient city is the geographic
and historical center of the Dutch nation. Today it has a population of about 234,000
and is Holland's fourth largest city. Worthy of special attention is the medieval city
center and the unique canalside wharves and cellars (now shops and cafés) lining the
Nieuwegracht and Oudegracht. At the heart of the old center is the Domplein, a square
containing one of the country's most magnificent cathedrals. Work on the church was
begun in 1254, and required over 250 years to complete. The 350-foot church tower,
constructed separately and completed in 1382, is the tallest in the Netherlands and
offers rewarding views for the hearty (May–September).
   Utrecht is also the convergence point of the Dutch railway system and there is a
fascinating railway museum in a former station (6 Johan van Oldebarneveltlaan),
exhibiting old steam locomotives and models. The *Music Box Museum* (10 Buurkerk-
hof) has a collection of mechanical music-makers dating from the 18th century, ranging
from singing birds and a violin- and piano-playing monstrosity to musical chairs and
street organs. The *Centraal Museum* (1 Agnietenstraat) contains historical displays,
including an authentic Viking ship. Take a short side trip to the village of Haarzuilens
and the spectacular De Haar Castle, set in an artificial lake amid grounds modeled after
Versailles (3 mi/5 km on E9 toward Amsterdam). The castle is still occupied, but parts
of it are frequently open to the public.
   En Route from Utrecht – A slight detour to Soest on the road leading through
De Bilt and Bilthoven leads past Soestdijk Palace (actually a 17th-century hunting
lodge), home of the former Queen Juliana.
   AMERSFOORT: This town has walls, four city gates, and double moats still ringing
it, as well as a wealth of architectural treasures within its medieval center. In summer,

canal cruises offer a leisurely view of the city, while daylong boat trips up the nearby Vecht River recapture the flavor of Holland's Golden Age. Boats for both trips leave from behind Utrecht's General Post Office, at the Vieburg.

APELDOORN: From here you can tour the wooded Veluwe region by steam train. Trains leave in the summer (daily, except Saturdays) from 13A Stationsplein. The museum at Het Loo Palace (1 Koninklijk Park) was formerly the royal residence and includes many displays on the royal family.

HOGE VELUWE: In the center of this national park in a lovely woodland setting, you'll find the *Rijksmuseum Kröller-Müller,* with its renowned collection of Van Gogh paintings and drawings and modern sculpture garden. During moderate weather, a ride through the woods is memorable. A special exhibit of 250 Van Gogh drawings is featured in 1990, the 100th anniversary of his death. It is a 1½-hour train ride from Amsterdam (via Arnhem or Edam), followed by a short bus or taxi ride — and well worth it. Admission charge; closed Mondays. Otterlo (phone: 083-821241). *De Koperen Kop* is a restaurant in the park, where you can watch the deer being fed. Pick up a park map at the entrance.

ARNHEM: This attractive town had the misfortune to be the scene of Operation Market Garden in 1944, a serious defeat of the British airborne troops, which was portrayed in the film *A Bridge Too Far.* Important mementos of that heroic and desperate battle are the Airborne Cemetery at nearby Oosterbeek and the *Airborne Museum* in Grote Hartensteyn in the same town. The nearby 12th-century *Doorwerth Castle* houses a hunting museum. Immediately north of the city at 89 Schelmseweg is the 100-acre *Openlucht (Open-Air) Museum,* in which actual farms, mills, and homes have been reconstructed to give a complete picture of traditional Dutch country life. There's also a costume museum and a zoo and safari park, where you can drive or take a mini-train through 60 acres of free-roaming lions, giraffes, and other beasts of the wild. A pleasant place for a meal during summer is the farm restaurant *Boerderij Rijzenburg* at nearby Schaarsbergen, also an entrance to the Hoge Veluwe.

ACHTERHOEK: Extending eastward from the Veluwe, this is a protected, rustic region of farms, woodlands, and great country estates. The VVV in Zutphen, 16 miles (26 km) from Arnhem on the A48, has maps for do-it-yourself bike tours through the castle-filled countryside.

BEST EN ROUTE

Expect to pay $110 and up for a double room in the expensive range, $60 to $80 in the moderate range, and about $50 in the inexpensive range. Dinner for two should cost $40 to $50 in the restaurants listed as expensive, $20 to $30 in those listed as moderate, and under $15 in the inexpensive. Prices do not include drinks or wine.

ARNHEM

***Groot Warnsborn* –** Surrounded by forest, this lovely 29-room former manor house is only a few minutes from the center of town. The restaurant features seasonal menus, continental style. 277 Bakenbergseweg (phone: 085-455-751). Expensive.

HEELSUM

***Klein Zwitserland* –** Just west of Arnhem, this 61-room chalet-style hotel also has an indoor pool, a sauna, a solarium, tennis courts, bike rentals, and miniature golf on the premises; horseback riding is available nearby (phone: 08373-19104). Expensive.

***De Kromme Dissel* –** This attractive restaurant is noted for its candlelit, Old World ambience, and has recently earned a Michelin star. Within the Klein Zwitserland complex. 5 Klein Zwitserlandlaan, Heelsum (phone: 08373-19104). Expensive.

Norway

The kingdom of Norway stretches along the western edge of the Scandinavian peninsula, bordering Sweden, Finland, and the Soviet Union to the east. Norway has a 1,700-mile coastline on the North Atlantic, raggedly indented with inlets, fjords, peninsulas, and islands. Because the coast is so well sheltered, and most of the country's land area is so rocky and mountainous, Norwegians have taken to the sea since prehistoric times.

Today's Norway numbers only 4 million people — half of the population of New York City — rattling around over a spacious 149,158 square miles. The country is not particularly urban, and the major cities would be considered large, pleasant villages by most countries' standards. Oslo, the capital and biggest of the towns, has a population of less than half a million; Bergen (pop. 208,400) is an important cultural center, famous for its beautiful fjords; Trondheim (pop. 134,200) is a major center for trade, shipping, and industry; Stavanger (pop. 96,000) is another industrial outpost, handling fish processing, shipbuilding, and pumping Norway's North Sea oil. Other large towns include Kristiansand, Drammen, Skien, Tromsø, Ålesund, and Bodø.

Norway is a constitutional monarchy, ruled by King Olav V and his cabinet, plus a prime minister, *storting* (parliament), and supreme court. The present independent government was installed in 1905, although the apparatus of state has been developing since the early 19th century, heavily inspired by the constitutions and ideals of the American and French revolutions.

Possibly the most important question on the minds of all those who have never been to Norway is: What is a fjord? A fjord is a long, narrow inlet of the sea, with very steep, nearly parallel sides that extend below the surface of the water. A land area with a fjord looks like a macrocosmic cheesecake from which a long, narrow slice has been cut. Norway's Sognefjord runs over 100 miles inland from the North Sea, with walls that plunge 4,000 feet to the ocean floor. The sight from the top of the fjord of tons of ice-blue water roaring and foaming between the rocky walls is one of the most spectacular wonders in nature.

About one quarter of Norway's land area is above the Arctic Circle, yet the climate of Oslo averages only about 12 degrees colder than that of New York. The North Atlantic drift keeps Norway's harbors free of ice.

Rivers like the Glomma and the Rana run through the mountains and valleys and provide much hydroelectric power. In fact, 99% of Norway's electricity is generated by hydropower. One quarter of the country is forested, and the timber industry is big. Fish is exported all over the world; iron, nickel, and aluminum are mined. Community, social, and personal services is the biggest single employer, manufacturing second, employing about one third and one fifth of the working population respectively. About 6% of the work force is in agriculture, about 16% in trade. Norway's merchant fleet, once the pride of the nation, has been reduced considerably in the past few years. Shipping is still important in Norway but is being overshadowed by North Sea oil production. Norwegians are largely responsible for one of today's most glamorous, exciting, and profitable seagoing industries — cruising. Visionary entrepreneurs from Norway have been behind such developments as launching Caribbean cruising, ordering the world's biggest and most luxurious vessels, and marketing cruising to "the masses." Norway is now moving away from the heavy industry of the past into the field of sophisticated technology. Norway's GNP per capita is the seventh largest in the world.

Most Norwegians are of Scandinavian stock — like the Swedes — but in the county of Finnmark in the north live Lapps and Finns. There are two official languages, *bokmål* ("book language"), the language of literature and wealth, a vestige of Danish rule, and *nynorsk,* a language developed by a 19th-century nationalist, based on rural dialects. Both *bokmål* and *nynorsk* are used in the media, but *bokmål* still prevails. In the far north, the Sami dialect is also spoken.

Considering Norway's rough-hewn and beautiful countryside, it isn't too surprising that Norwegians are very outdoors-oriented. Like the Swedes, they have a reputation for having blond hair, robust health, and good looks. They do a lot of walking, as befits a country where distances are great, roads are often rough, and fuel is expensive. The population density is scant, and even cities are laid out with lots of elbow room. Oslo is touted by the city fathers as one of the biggest cities in Europe, since it covers 175 square miles, but it includes vast areas of farmland and forest.

Norwegians get used to snow in winter, and are less likely to burrow inside when the weather is cold than people from warmer climates. The word *ski* is Norwegian, and Norwegians like to joke that they are born with skis on their feet. Both cross-country and downhill skiing are avidly pursued by large numbers of people, and a Nordic specialty is ski-jumping. In the last 50 years, Norway has won more Olympic gold medals in Nordic skiing than any other country. Speed skating also has a long tradition and strong following. Soccer, as in the rest of Europe, is the biggest organized sport. Popular indoor activities include handball, boxing, gymnastics, and ballroom dancing. Lillehammer (pop. 22,000), 110 miles (177 km) north of Oslo, has been selected as the site of the 1994 Winter Olympics. The town draws skiers from all over Europe and has seen more national ski championships than any other Norwegian city. Construction is under way on an Olympic Village that will accommodate 7,500 athletes, and at least one new major hotel is planned. All in all, the Norwegian government has pledged at least $370 million toward the games.

The arts in Norway are encouraged by heavy state subsidies, particularly in film and book publishing. One of the most striking examples of government-sponsored art is the 650-piece sculpture park near Oslo by Gustav Vigeland, built at the city's expense. Norway has produced artists of international renown: painter Edvard Munch, composer Edvard Grieg, and dramatist Henrik Ibsen. It is interesting to note that a brooding, death-obsessed spiritualism pervades the work of the nation's three greatest cultural figures. Some say the stark seasonal contrasts in the land of the midnight sun have a profound effect on the national psyche. On a brighter note, actress Liv Ullmann is also Norwegian, as is the marathon runner Grete Waitz and the pop rock group *A-ha.*

Norwegian folk art is highly practical, using fine handwork in the making of furniture, embroidery, weaving, and silver. The expression *arts and crafts* is based on the Scandinavian concept of *brukskunst;* Norway has several museums devoted to applied art.

The area of Norway was just an agglomeration of small Viking kingdoms until Harald Haarfagre ("fair hair") united them at the end of the 9th century, based on the model of a northern British kingdom he had recently pillaged. Missionaries from Britain brought Christianity to Norway in the 10th and 11th centuries.

Leif Eriksson, a Viking émigré living in Iceland, became the first European to reach America, touching down in Newfoundland in AD 1000. The Vikings established settlements in the northeastern US — some say they got as far south as Massachusetts.

Norway prospered as an independent country until the Black Death of 1349 wiped out half the population. The German Hanseatic League assumed Norway's trade in Bergen and the rest of the country slipped into 400 years of Danish rule. Sweden took over Norway when Denmark was defeated with its ally Napoleon in 1814. During the 19th century, 880,000 Norwegians emigrated elsewhere, mostly to the US. In 1905, the nation finally broke off from the Swedes and set up their own kingdom, appointing Carl, the second son of the King of Denmark, who took the Norwegian name Haakon VII. Haakon's son Olav took the throne at his father's death in 1957.

Norway stayed neutral in World War I, although half her merchant fleet was sunk. The Nazis invaded on April 9, 1940, and occupied Norway until May 1945, bringing with them concentration camps, political executions, and economic disaster. The king and most of the fleet escaped; Norwegian ships were vital to Allied operations in the North Atlantic, and Norwegians at home sabotaged the German occupiers courageously and ruthlessly. The leader of the collaborationist forces in Norway, Vidkun Quisling, whose name has come to be a synonym for *traitor,* was executed at the war's end.

Although Norway joined NATO in 1949, it remains fiercely independent on economic matters. A majority of the population in 1972 voted against joining the European Economic Community (EEC). Since World War II, Norway's wealth of trade, industry, and cheap hydroelectric power have given its citizens one of the highest standards of living in Europe, and with the discovery of large oil and gas deposits off the North Sea coast, the future seemed promising. However, low oil prices and the falling dollar (Norway's oil income is tallied in dollars) have contributed to grave economic problems, which the country is struggling to overcome.

Over 80% of Norway's land area is taken up by mountains and forests. Norway is somewhere you go to see natural beauty, rather than the marvels of civilization: mountains, valleys, fjords, moors, lakes, forests, waterfalls, and, in general, the absence of other people. The weather is often beautiful, just right for as brown a tan as you can get anywhere, but be ready for rain — make good use of clear days.

There are two routes below for exploring Norway. The first begins in Oslo, possibly the least hectic capital city in Europe, and winds down the Oslofjord and up the other side through prime beach and sun country, cuts west through pine-scented forests to the barren Telemark plateau, and finishes in a burst of fjords and flowers in Bergen, on the Atlantic coast. The second route is a 1,000-mile adventure to the point farthest north on the continent of Europe, beginning by road in Trondheim, switching to a coastal steamship from Bodø to Tromsø to take you through the sheer cliffs of the western islands, and finishing again by car to the barren North Cape, far above the Arctic Circle.

Oslo to Bergen

This scenic route begins with the calm and pastoral capital of Norway. Oslo, a city of a mere 450,500 inhabitants and many clapboard houses, farms, and forests, is also the seat of the Norwegian parliament. From here, you'll drive down the Oslofjord, west to the rococo church in Kongsberg, and across Telemark, where you'll find farms, beautiful stave churches, and barren heaths. The last stop is Norway's pride, fjord-bound Bergen, a graceful 11th-century city that has played host to Viking, merchant, and warships, art, and industry in its 1,000-year history.

Another way to travel this route is via the Bergen-Oslo railway. Providing a dramatic 280-mile (451-km) day trip across Norway's rooftop, this classic line spans desolate Hardanger plateau, far above the timber line, 6,000-foot mountains, and the old alpine and cross-country ski resorts of Geilo and Voss. You can make reservations in advance at one of the branches of the Norwegian National Tourist Office in the US. In addition to the ticket price, a seat reservation is purchased separately for a few dollars.

OSLO: For a complete report on the city and its restaurants and hotels, see *Oslo,* THE CITIES.

En Route from Oslo – Along the coast south of Norway's oldest city, Tønsberg, on the Brunlanes Peninsula, are good beaches and quiet coves for swimming and sailing, from Stavern to Nevlunghavn. Historic Tønsberg is worth a visit. Founded by King Bjørn Farmond, the seafaring merchant son of King Harold Haarfagre, the city was mentioned in sagas dating to 872. Norway's largest castle was built here during the Middle Ages and its ruins are among Northern Europe's most impressive. The shoreline twists and turns on itself often, creating many protected beaches along the small towns in the area. The waters are quite warm in July and August. Take Route 8 through Larvik north toward Kongsberg; you'll be driving along the Laagen River through a valley of cornfields and bright red and white farmhouses.

KONGSBERG: Kongsberg, "the king's mountain," was founded by King Christian IV when silver was discovered here in 1624. The city flourished and became the second largest in Norway, but declined as the silver output fell in the 19th century. The last mine was abandoned in 1957. The 18th-century rococo church in Kongsberg is worth seeing; its exterior is unprepossessing brick, with a copper cupola, but inside all is rich and elaborate. The ceiling is covered with paintings and hung with crystal chandeliers;

the pulpit, altar, choir balcony, and organ are carved with great enthusiasm, and painted in golds and blues. There are three tiers in the gallery, and box seats for the king and lesser dignitaries. Kongsberg is a major ski area, with four T-bars, five giant slalom courses (lighted until 9 PM weekdays for night skiing), and touring trails as well as a ski school. Call the Ski Center (03-73-17-55) for information about weather conditions and equipment rentals. The abandoned silver mines are also worth a visit, and the town runs a special little railway into the mines for sightseers. A museum at the entrance to the mines displays silver in a variety of forms.

TELEMARK: West of Notodden begins the county of Telemark, a wild, often barren area of mountains, valleys, and plateaus that stretches all the way to the fjord district. The first inhabitants here were hunters; small, single-family farms followed, in the style of the American prairie. It is thought that skiing was invented here, and today, "Telemark Swing" is used to describe a particular style of skiing. The towns and villages exist mostly in the south and east; this is the prime area for a characteristic feature of rural Norwegian architecture, the *stabbur* or storehouse. In a countryside of individual farms, there was no town warehouse in which to store grain, so a story was added to each house to tuck away surplus for the lean years. Much care was lavished on the building and ornamentation of these houses, from elaborate wall hangings to beautifully carved joists and furniture, intricate 'rose painting' on walls, doorways, clocks, and pottery.

As you proceed west, you'll pass through more valleys, farms, and villages, and by quite a few roadside cafés. Just west of Notodden is Heddal Stave Church, the country's largest stave church. It was built in 1242 and restored in 1954.

At Eidsborg, south of E76, is a fine example of a stave church, nestled on a hill. The outside walls of a stave church are covered with a sheath of hand-carved tiles that overlap each other like the leaves of an artichoke, giving the whole building the look of a single, living plant. Note the elaborate wood carvings on the columns in the doorway and the interior.

The route now cuts through the heart of the Hardangervidda, a nearly uninhabited plateau of lakes and moors, where the elevation is about a mile. Several thousand years ago, a glacier came through here, ripping away everything in its path, leaving the wet, mossy, treeless landscape you see before you. An impressive waterfall, Vøringsfossen, drops 540 feet through a rocky chasm in this plateau. Lakes, boulders, heather, and an awesome bleakness extend left and right until you arrive at the fjords.

LOFTHUS: Turn north onto E47 toward the industrial town of Odda and the Sørfjorden. The road skirting the precipice is both narrow and scenic, burrowing through mountains, and passing over towering waterfalls. The hamlet of Lofthus, which is past Odda on the eastern edge of the fjord, was a favorite retreat of Edvard Grieg. The place has a mystical peacefulness; it is surrounded by snow-capped mountains and the Folgefonn glacier in the distance, and crowded with blossoms in the summertime.

En Route from Lofthus – Continue up to Kinsarvik. About 15 miles (24 km) north is a pretty little gem of a fjord, Eidfjord. Back at Kinsarvik, take the ferry across the mouth of the Sørfjorden to Kvanndal, on the western edge of the great Hardanger Fjord. Drive south along the fjord toward Bergen, as waterfalls spawn rainbows, and mountains rest against each other like the backs of huge sleeping animals. This is one of the most spectacular regions of what is considered by some the most scenic country in the world. Once you arrive in Bergen and find a place to roost, you must, without fail, drive, ferry, and walk through as much of this titanically beautiful region as possible. The best time to go is May and early June, when the fruit trees are in bloom.

BERGEN: Looking like a crowded gingerbread village, Bergen sits in a harbor under Mt. Fløyen, protected and hidden from the North Sea by a peninsula. It is one of

Norway's most worldly, cultural, and physically beautiful cities. The people speak with a distinctive accent that even non-Scandinavians can detect, and their proud and independent spirit can be summed up in the local saying, "I'm not Norwegian; I'm from Bergen."

Vikings used to set out from the coves around Bergen to the lands now known as England, Europe, and Iceland. The city was founded in 1070 by King Olav the Peaceful, who thought it would make a good center for trade with Europe and northern Norway. During the 12th and 13th centuries, it was the country's capital. In 1349 the Black Death came to Norway, destroying over half the native population. Norway's crippled economy enabled the German merchants who had been trading with the city for centuries to gain control of the city's trade. The Germans held on for 200 years, making the port a major trading center of the Hanseatic League and the richest city in Norway. Finally, in 1559, the Danish authorities trained their guns on the Hanseatic buildings and offered the Germans citizenship or oblivion; some left, others became Norwegians. The *Hanseatic Museum* is a reconstructed 16th-century Hansa merchant's house, smelling of cool wood in some rooms and dried cod in others. Norwegian cod was an important item of trade for Catholic Europe, as it often provided Friday's dinner. At the museum you can see the scales the merchants used for weighing goods — one scale for buying, and another for selling. The wharf in the Bryggen section of town is where trade went on. Now, painters, weavers, and artisans have their workshops in the restored medieval wooden houses. Guided tours (in English) are offered in the summer. Tickets are sold at the *Bryggens Museum* (phone: 0531-6710).

Overall, Bergen has an 18th-century grace, with a skyline of close-packed mansard roofs punctuated by church steeples. The best view of the city is from the funicular that goes up Mt. Fløyen (1,050 feet), which operates until midnight. At the summit, paths lead through lakes, flowers, pine, and heather.

In late May and early June is the *Bergen International Festival,* featuring music, drama, opera, ballet, art, and folklore. A lot of the music, understandably, is by local hero Edvard Grieg, and concerts are held every day at *Grieg Hall* in town and in the suburb of Hop at his old residence, Troldhaugen, a pastoral Victorian estate on a lake. World-renowned conductors and soloists are featured. Concerts are also held at Haakonshallen and St. Mary's Church. Plays are performed at *Den Nationale Scene* — Ibsen predominates — and folk plays and dances take place outdoors. Reservations must be made far in advance for a visit during festival time.

Haakonshallen and St. Mary's Church are both worth seeing in their own rights; the 13th-century hall was badly damaged in World War II when a Dutch ship carrying nitroglycerin blew up in the harbor, but the restoration of the massive medieval construction was well done. Bergen's oldest building is St. Mary's Church (Romanesque Mariakirke), built in the early 12th century. It is considered Norway's most beautiful church, with an intricately carved and painted baroque pulpit, donated by the Hansa in the 16th century. The Fantoft Stave Church, built in 1150, is also aesthetically pleasing. Its sharply peaked roofs amd Viking dragons trim are reminiscent of Thai temples.

With the wealth brought in by trade, art was sure to follow, and industrialist Rasmus Meyer's private collection of paintings, drawings, and furniture is probably the best in Norway outside the *Oslo National Gallery.* Meyer lived from 1858 to 1916, and his particular zest was for native Norwegian painters: lots of Munch, of course, plus Nikolai Astrup, Harriet Backer, Gerbard Munthe, and J. C. Dahl.

Only a 10-minute walk from the downtown area, the Bergen Aquarium is open year-round (2 Nordnesparken). During your wanderings, be sure to try some of the local fish dishes and the local beer, Hansa, considered among the world's best. Bergen has one of Norway's most picturesque open-air fish markets, said to be the most photographed in Europe; open daily except Sundays from 8AM to 3 PM.

BEST EN ROUTE

Hotels along this route are rather expensive, around $225 for a double or single room at a luxury, tourist hotel, which provides meals, entertainment, and bars; more moderately priced accommodations are available for $160 and up. We found no inexpensive establishments that met our standards. However, guesthouses, which are smaller and may not have a private bath or shower, cost from $15 to $25 and are scattered throughout villages and towns. All you have to do is ask at a local tourist information center, or flag down a passing Norwegian. If you prefer, you can camp out on one of the many campgrounds in the countryside for $3 to $10 a night; chalets can be rented for $125 to $425 a week, depending on the season (based normally on a minimum occupancy of four), and there are a number of youth hostels, open mostly during the summer, for $10 to $16 a night. Again, tourist information centers in the villages can direct you. The *Royal Norwegian Automobile Club* huts are offered to all *AAA* members: For further information contact KNA, 20 Drammensv. (phone: 561900).

KONGSBERG

Grand – The best hotel in the city; provides small comfortable rooms and good meals in a fine restaurant or an easy-going cafeteria. Facilities include an indoor swimming pool. In the middle of town (phone: 0373-2029). Expensive.

Skikroa – A large eatery popular with the young ski crowd, it offers sandwiches and snacks in an informal setting. By the Kongsberg ski lifts (phone: 0373-1628). Inexpensive.

BERGEN

Neptun – A recently expanded 120-room hotel that has a new floor of luxury suites, a French restaurant, a pub, bar, and café. 8 Walckendorffs Gate (phone: 0532-6000). Expensive.

Norge – Under new management, this classic 348-room luxury hotel has just been enlarged to offer a full range of room categories, from singles and doubles to demi-suites and suites. It has several restaurants, a summer garden café, disco, bars, and an indoor swimming pool. 4 Ole Bulls Plass (phone: 0521-0100). Expensive.

Rosenkrantz – This newly expanded, comfortable hotel has bars and private baths in its 118 rooms. Also a popular nightspot. 7 Rosenkrantzgt (phone: 0531-8080). Expensive.

SAS Royal Bryggen – A 267-room, first class hotel with an executive floor that offers special services and deluxe suites. Restaurant, café, nightclub, and bar, In the Bryggen section of the harborfront (phone: 0531-8000). Expensive.

Suitell Edvard Grieg – This luxury hotel at the airport is the country's first all-suite property. It has 148 suites and 2 restaurants, one more formal than the other, but both featuring Norwegian specialties. There are also 2 large, elegant bars with dancing on Saturday nights to live bands. 50 Sandsliasen (phone: 0522-9901). Expensive.

Admiral – Right next to the scenic harbor, this hotel has been completely remodeled. It has 107 elegant, ultra-modern rooms and 122 suites, many with harbor views. There's also a piano bar and a reasonably priced restaurant serving both seafood and meat dishes. 9 Sundtsgt. (phone: 0532-4730). Moderate.

Bergen Airport – Opened in 1987, convenient to the airport and about 8 miles (13 km) from the city center, its 239 rooms include several suites. Facilities include an indoor swimming pool, squash courts, and a fitness center. A restaurant serves

Norwegian specialties and is open for breakfast, lunch, dinner, and late-night snacks. 3 Kokstad V (phone: 0522-9200). Moderate.

Park Pension – A converted townhouse near the university. In winter it offers rooms with baths at budget prices; in the busy summer season, it opens an annex, where not all rooms have private baths. It's a good buy, but reserve well in advance. 22 Parkveien and (in summer) 35 Harald Harfagres Gate (phone: 0532-0960). Inexpensive.

Bellevue – An old Bergen establishment with an elegant interior and a spectacular view over the fjord. Open for lunch, dinner, and after-theater meals. Downstairs, there's a new, informal grill room, with dancing from 10 PM on. 9 Bellvuebakken (phone: 0531-0240). Expensive to moderate.

Banco Rotto – This spacious new Italian restaurant in a former bank is built in the Italian Renaissance style. A pub and piano bar complete the venue. In the city center, next to the Bank of Bergen (phone: 0532-7520). Moderate.

China Palace – An elegant Chinese restaurant with a plush red and gold decor. Try the jumbo prawns. 2 Strandgt. (phone: 0532-6655). Moderate.

Enhjørningen – This old-fashioned little eatery is near the fish market and specializes in seafood (phone: 0532-7919). Moderate.

Villa Amorini – A family-run restaurant featuring nouvelle and international cuisines. Open for lunch and dinner daily except Sundays. Just a short walk from the *Norge* hotel and *Grieg Concert Hall.* 5 Rasmus Meyers Alle (phone: 0531-0039). Moderate.

Marco Polo Trattoria – Homemade Italian dishes are featured at this intimate, informal restaurant. Open every evening except on Sundays. 45 Kong Oscars Gate (phone: 0531-5913). Inexpensive.

Trondheim to the North Cape

This is a trail for the adventurous. We don't mean that it's physically dangerous, but that it requires an active spirit and a zest for exploration. It's an expedition to the Nordkapp, the northernmost point in Europe. If you drive, you must go in June, July, or August, so the roads will be clear of snow and you can see the midnight sun. If you choose to cruise all the way on a coastal steamer, you can travel year-round, as the coast remains ice-free thanks to the North Atlantic Drift, an extension of the Gulf Stream. During the winter, you may see the spectacular Northern Lights in the night sky. The north of Norway is big, wild, and exotic, but no one can tell you what the beautiful sights are. Here, you write your own guidebook and judge each towering cliff, deep-blue lake, and clump of flowering heather with your own eyes. This is a trip for the young and the young at heart; it's popular with hearty French, German, and Italian adventurers.

Start your trip in a rented car from Trondheim, the capital of the province of Trøndelag, at the threshold of the Arctic. Founded in the 10th century, Trondheim is now a commercial city and the seat of one of Norway's biggest universities. You'll take the Arctic Highway (E6) north from here through lakes and river valleys past Mosjøen and Mo-i-Rana to cross the Arctic Circle into the land of the midnight sun at the top of a barren plateau.

At Bodø, you'll hop on the coastal steamer, which will take you between the sheer cliffs of the Lofoten and Vesterålen islands to Tromsø, the oil boom town, and launching base for many North Pole expeditions. Pick up a car here for the rest of your own expedition: A ferry will carry you across the last strait to Honningsvåg, so you can drive to the North Cape, and look down on all of Europe.

Another way to explore this part of the Norwegian coast is to take the express steamer from Bergen to Kirkenes — 1,500 miles, 6 days one-way or 11 days round-trip. The steamer calls at about 30 fishing villages and towns, including Trondheim, Bodø, Lofoten and Vesterålen, Hammerfest and Honningsvåg. The northeastern terminus, Kirkenes, is on the Russian border, where the Iron Curtain isn't much more than a chain-link fence. The steamers are small and clean, with ample deck space, hearty buffet-style meals, and a bar. Dress is informal; the sea air, invigorating; and the scenery, breathtaking. Tickets may be purchased for any segment of this trip, but reservations for the entire voyage in the peak summer season must be made months in advance. Contact a branch of the Norwegian National Tourist Office in the US, or Bergen Line in New York City.

Norweigan officials are negotiating with the Soviet Union to open a "free border" to Murmansk. This could make it possible to visit Murmansk from Norway without obtaining a visa. Check with the tourist office for more information.

TRONDHEIM: Trondheim is the home of Norway's major technical university and is a big trading town, exporting timber, fish, and farm products. A major shipbuilding and transportation center, it is a pleasant and useful city, but not stunning. Its buildings draw on a tradition of the ordinary from the 19th and 20th centuries: solid stone office buildings and glass and steel cheeseboxes. There are also some old narrow streets of small, pastel wooden houses.

Trondheim's Nidaros Cathedral, built for St. Olav, has attracted pilgrims from all over Europe. It was badly battered during the Reformation, and a lot of the Gothic-Romanesque hybrid that stands now is 20th-century restoration work. Norway's Gustav Vigeland, creator of the mammoth sculpture garden in Oslo's Frogner Park, carved the gargoyles and grotesques for the head tower and north transept. Behind the cathedral is the restored Knight's Hall of the 12th-century Archbishop's Palace. From here, late Viking kings ruled Norway's Christianized colonies in Britain, Iceland, and Greenland.

Be sure to see the *Ringve Museum of Musical History* in a manor house at 60 Lade Allé, in the eastern suburbs. During the tours, the guide plays the well-preserved instruments from time to time: spinets, harpsichords, and pianos, and some vintage string and wind instruments as well. On the walls all around are paintings and photographs of famous composers and musicians.

As you wander along Trondheim's streets, you are likely to pass the second-largest wooden building in Scandinavia — Stiftsgaarden, built in rococo style from 1774 to 1778. It is used as the royal residence when the royal family is in town.

Two of the best features of modern Trondheim are the fish market on the docks and the fruit stands in the Torvet (marketplace). If you visit the city during the summer, take the ferry from downtown Trondheim out to Munkholmen, the small island in the harbor containing the remnants of a Benedictine monastery. During the summer it serves as Trondheim's most popular swimming and outing choice, so pack your swimsuit, camera, and a picnic lunch, or dine at the local restaurant.

En Route from Trondheim – Just north of the city in the Stjørdal Valley, near the village of that name, is the ruin of the fortress of Hegra Festning, built in 1910 as a bulwark against the Swedes (the border is 49 miles to the east). The fort became a symbol of the Norwegian Resistance in World War II when a German force was badly mauled trying to take it in 1940. Peace has taken the fort since then; bushes and flowers are now crowding the barbed wire, gun ports, and blasted walls; the view of the surrounding hills and the valley 1,000 feet below is splendid. Wild strawberries, raspberries, and blueberries grow in the vicinity.

In the village of Hegra, on the other side of the valley, are the Leirfall rock carvings, one of the most prolific sites in Norway, chiseled in 500 BC. They are said to be the religious art of an agricultural civilization, designed to increase fertility; they are symbolic and simple of line, showing stylized ships, and people and animals, some with erect phalluses — as well as circles, dots, swastikas, and footprints. Move on up the highway through the low, wooded Lake Snåsa region; you'll pass near Børgefjell National Park on the right.

About 60 miles (96 km) north of Mo-i-Rana you cross the Arctic Circle in the valley of the great, green Rana River; snow-covered bluffs 4,000 feet high lie to the left and right as you climb to the top of an empty plateau, and into the land of the midnight sun (66°32′N). The line of the Arctic is marked by a stone monument; there is a post office offering Arctic Circle postmarks nearby, and a café with the inevitable souvenir shop.

The countryside following the circle, near Rognan, is some of the most spectacular you will see along this route: The road passes high above the Saltdalsfjord, which is sometimes covered with a light mist, past snow-covered mountains hulking behind.

BODØ: Bodø is the capital of Nordland province; the sun doesn't go down here from June 3 to July 7. It's warm, considering the latitude, sitting at the mouth of the Vestfjorden, sheltered by the Lofoten Islands. Add to this the opportunities that lurk everywhere for fishing, climbing, bird-watching, or just walking around gaping at the scenery, and you can understand why tourists by the droves come here to soak up the midnight sun. Do not miss the famous cathedral, built in 1956: The tall bell tower is separate from the rest of the structure; the main roof is copper, the outer walls concrete, and the inside wonderfully large and airy, with a high ceiling, reddish-brown woodwork, handmade wall hangings, and delicate stained-glass windows at each end of the building. The *Nordlands Museum* (116 Prinsensqt) has exhibitions of tools, fishing industry items, and a terrarium.

Burned and bombed to the ground at the beginning of World War II, Bodø has long since recovered its position as a leading fishing and Arctic communications center. Visitors can try their hand at fishing at Saltstraumen, the world's most powerful maelstrom, 20 miles (32 km) outside town. Millions of gallons of water rush through the narrow passage, guaranteeing catches of cod, halibut, and salmon. No license is required; rent tackle at any Bodø shop. Buses to Saltstraumen depart several times a day from the terminal at 2A Sungt. (phone: 081-21240).

Just south of Bodø is Svartisen, Norway's second largest glacier. On Saturday afternoons in the summer, there are boat tours to this tremendous hulk of ice. Tickets are purchased on board. For more information, contact *Saltens Dampskibsselskab* (phone: 081-21020).

LOFOTEN AND VESTERÅLEN: Now begins the marine portion of your expedition to the Nordkapp; turn in your rented car and claim your bunk on the coastal steamer at Bodø to make the 24-hour passage to Tromsø, threading through the steep cliffs and fishing villages of the Lofoten and Vesterålen islands. The steamer is a functional ship, a cargo and mail vessel that can also take about 200 passengers. It's not the *QE2*, but it's clean, it's only for 24 hours, and you'll get more of the incredible scenery than you could playing chemin de fer on some cushy cruise ship. The islands present a wall of snow-capped mountains and cliffs that rise suddenly from the shore to heights of 2,000 to 3,000 feet. It's particularly dramatic as the steamer slips into a narrow strait between two peaks and seems about to be swallowed in their immense shadows. The ship departs at 3 PM and arrives at Tromsø 24 hours later.

HARSTAD: En route you'll pass through Harstad, a modern town in the heart of Norway's largest island, Hinnøya. Harstad holds the *North Norway Festival,* with historical plays, folkloric programs, and musical performances, each summer around *Midsummer's Day,* June 23. Internationally known artists are always among the performers.

TROMSØ: Disembark at Tromsø and pick up your car. An ancient whaling capital, Tromsø was also base of operations for North Pole explorers and polar bear hunters. Much of its frontier atmosphere has been retained, and it's now something of a boom town. It rather arrogantly refers to itself as "The Paris of the North," a claim made only half in jest. Tromsø has doubled in population to about 49,800 in the past decade, with the advent of a medical school and regional hospital specializing in Arctic ailments. All the establishments in town — restaurants, brewery, pubs, and pizzerias — claim to be the world's northernmost. Worth a look are the local museum devoted to Arctic exploration, the aquarium, and the Arctic Cathedral, whose design is reminiscent of an iceberg. The cable car affords a bird's-eye view of Tromsø and its fjord, where in World War II the German battleship *Tirpitz* was finally sunk by British bombers. On March 2-9, 1990, Tromsø will host the *International Winter Cities Program,* which will highlight positive aspects of communities in cold climes. Business, sports, architecture, and culture will be featured in conferences and exhibitions. Contact the tourist office for more information.

En Route from Tromsø – The last leg in this trek is the shortest, about 280 miles (448 km) over dry plateau, as the Arctic Highway winds around fjords and inlets, and passes a few villages. Lyngen Fjord between Tromsø and Alta is thoroughly alpine, with jagged peaks and hairpin turns. Alta, once little more than an airport and a trading town, is becoming more important as tourism to the North Cape increases. Before turning north, consider a day trip south through Europe's deepest canyon and up across the plateau to Kautokeino, the major center for the nomadic Lapp reindeer herders. The Sami, as they prefer to be called, congregate here to trade and worship, and they have built a church and a hotel in the style of a Sami hut. The town silversmith, whose shop you can visit, makes jewelry in ancient Sami designs. If you plan to spend the night, the modern lodge on the bluff overlooking town is more expensive, but also quieter and more comfortable than the Sami hotel in the valley.

Back in Alta, continue north to Hammerfest. The world's northernmost incorporated town, it was the first Norwegian town to get electric street lights. Stop at the town hall to join the Royal and Ancient Society of Polar Bears, testifying to your northerly adventure. From here you can take an excursion boat directly to the North Cape, or you can drive and ride the ferry up to Honningsvåg, the largest fishing port in Norway.

The first man to reach the North Cape is said to have been a Viking named Ottar, who sailed around it in AD 880, bound for the White Sea. England's King Alfred the Great met Ottar and had his story of the voyage "beyond the known world" set down in writing. The account sits in the *British Museum* today.

Another 21 miles (34 km) will bring you from Honningsvåg to the black cliff that Ottar signed more than 1,100 years ago. Keep your eyes peeled; you are likely to see herds of reindeer grazing beside the road, but their coloring sometimes enables them to blend into the tundra. The *British Museum* probably won't keep your tour diary, but you certainly will; and the Nordkapp post office will also issue you a special certificate testifying that you've been there and mail your postcards to boot. It may be stretching the truth a little to call Nordkapp the most northerly point in Europe, but not much.

The sun shines continuously here from May 14 to July 30; the most beautiful sight, however, is in early August, when the sun dips below the horizon for a few minutes of night, in a spectacular glow of red and purple.

Facilities at the North Cape have recently been upgraded and expanded. In addition to a new café, enlarged souvenir shop, and a video presentation on a giant screen, there is now a tunnel leading down into the cliff itself. The tunnel opens into a grotto with panoramic windows overlooking the sea, historical displays, and exhibits. One ticket provides admission to all the attractions.

BEST EN ROUTE

Most hotels in the Arctic Circle region run between $100 and $225, double or single rooms, which we call expensive. Moderately priced accommodations will run at least $100. We found no inexpensive establishments that met our standards. Nearly all hotels offer private baths and/or showers, plus other amenities found in luxury hotels. Make reservations beforehand: 200,000 visitors a year come to Nordkapp.

TRONDHEIM

Britannia – Above all, well run. Has a kind of medieval-modern air; rooms are large and comfortably furnished. The hotel has its own garden and restaurant — the food is good — and there are fountains and palm trees in the middle of it. 5 Dronningensgt (phone: 0753-0040). Expensive.

Residence – An old, established hotel, recently remodeled, it's near the fish market in the city center. It offers 66 rooms, a restaurant serving Norwegian specialties, plus a café and bar. 26 Munkegt. (phone: 0752-8380). Expensive.

Royal Garden – This large, ultra-modern hotel is Trondheim's newest. Facilities include an elegant restaurant, an indoor swimming pool, and a gymnasium. 73 Kjøpmannsgt. (phone: 0752-1100). Expensive.

Havfruen – An elegant seafood restaurant occupying two levels in an old warehouse. There's a large main dining room downstairs, and a more intimate dining room upstairs. Open all winter for dinner only, from 3 PM; lunch as well in summer from noon. 7 Køppmannsgt. (phone: 0753-2626). Expensive to moderate.

Vertshuset Tavern – A wooden tavern, built in 1739. Mountain-style cooking (smoked ham, diced meat, salami, mutton with garnishes) and also more conventional food. Open April to October. Near the *Folk Museum* at Sverresborg (phone: 0752-0932). Moderate.

BODØ

SAS Royal – This 13-story, 184-room hotel is the largest in the city and offers private baths and showers, a restaurant, pizza cellar, coffee shop, cafeteria, nightclub, bars, and disco. 2 Storgaten (phone: 081-24100). Expensive.

Norrøna – A bed-and-breakfast establishment that has a cozy café facing the main street, a restaurant, and the *Piccadilly Pub,* which also serves light fare. 4B Storgt. (phone: 081-24118). Expensive to moderate.

Bodø – The city's newest hotel has a comfortable atmosphere and such special features as allergy rooms, handicapped rooms, and a bridal suite. The *Skagen Bistro* specializes in fish dishes. 5 Prof. Schyttesgt. (phone: 081-26900). Moderate.

Grand – A 48-room hotel that offers baths and showers, double and single rooms, and a dining room. 3 Storgaten (phone: 081-20000). Moderate.

Normandie – An interesting restaurant with a Viking decor. Specializes in pizza and quiche. 1 Havnegt. (phone: 081-21832). Moderate.

HARSTAD

The two major hotels in town are the *Grand Nordic,* 9 Strand Gate (phone: 082-62170) and the *Viking Nordic,* 2 Fjord Gate (phone: 082-64080). Both are expensive. There are several less expensive hotels, including the *Sentrum Hospits,* 5 Magnus Gate (phone: 082-62938), and its neighbor, the *Høiland Hospits* (phone: 082-64960).

LOFOTEN AND VESTERÅLEN

For the 27-hour steamer trip from Bodø to Tromsø, you must reserve a berth 2 to 3 months in advance in the summer season. A couple can reserve a private cabin, but singles room with strangers, usually of the same sex. Bergen Line, 505 Fifth Ave., New York, NY 10017 (phone: 212-986-2711). Fares vary, and there are discounts for students and senior citizens.

TROMSØ

Grand Nordic – There are 106 rooms, several restaurants, a bar, and many other comforts. A massive expansion and renovation program, scheduled for completion in late 1990, will more than double the number of rooms and add conference facilities for up to 600. 44 Storgaten (phone: 083-85500). Expensive.

SAS Royal – One block from the steamer pier, this large (195 rooms) and convenient hotel has a fine harbor view and several restaurants, including the elegant *Caravel,* which features Norwegian and international dishes. There is also a popular nightclub, *Charly.* 7 Sjøgata (phone: 083-56000). Expensive.

Scandic – A new hotel with 147 rooms (2 of them suites) and a fine view of the fjord. Its restaurant serves international dishes, and there's a nightclub, bar, pool, and sauna. Langes, near the airport (phone: 083-73400). Expensive.

Saga – Simple but good hotel, it has 52 rooms, all with showers. There is also a cafeteria and a typical Norwegian restaurant. Near the harbor. 2 Richard With-splass (phone: 083-81180). Expensive to moderate.

Arktandria – A rustic and cozy new restaurant featuring both seafood and meat dishes; the special is a platter consisting of three kinds of fish and two or three kinds of shellfish. Dinner only, daily from 6 PM except Sundays from 3 PM. 1 Strandtorget (phone: 083-82020). Expensive.

Branko's – This charming, intimate restaurant, owned and operated by Yugoslavian restaurateur Branko and his Norwegian wife, has become a Tromsø favorite; many consider it the best in town. One flight up on the main street, it's open for lunch and dinner. 57 Storgate (phone: 083-82673). Moderate.

Peppermøllen – Here you can sup on fresh, well-prepared fish, reindeer, and grouse. 42 Storgaten (phone: 083-86260). Moderate.

■ **NOTE:** Surprisingly, northerly nightlife is often very exuberant. Hotel nightclubs compete with nearby beer halls, and both should be sampled for a complete picture of life in the North. Unlike their Oslo relatives, citizens up here are quite outgoing, and travelers may find themselves swapping stories with fishermen and petrochemical geologists before the night is through.

ALTA

SAS Alta – The biggest and the best in town, complete with a restaurant, bar, entertainment, disco, sauna, solarium, and jogging track. Centrally located at Løkkeveien (phone: 084-35000). Expensive.

HONNINGSVÅG

SAS Nordkapp – This 386-bed hotel offers private baths and/or showers and 2 restaurants: the *Carolina,* featuring Norwegian specialties, and a grill room for less formal dining. Centrally located on the busy harborfront (phone: 084-72333). Expensive to moderate.

KAUTOKEINO

Kautokeino Tourist – A small (46-room) lodge-style establishment with a large fireplace, restaurant, bar, disco, sauna, and solarium. Ask at the reception desk about seeing reindeer herders at work or taking snowmobile safaris. On the bluff just outside town (phone: 084-56205). Expensive.

Poland

One of the most fascinating things about Poland is that it is both a Roman Catholic and a Communist country. The Polish United Workers' Party (Polska Zjednoczona Patria Robotnicza; PZPR) is economically and militarily aligned with the Soviet Union. Yet, Polish churches overflow with worshipers on Sundays and holy days; as much as 70% of Poland's 37 million people are, at least nominally, Roman Catholic.

Indeed, among the most momentous occasions in recent Polish history were the visits by the first Polish Pope, John Paul II, to his homeland in June 1979 and June 1983. Relations between the church and the government have varied from open conflict to mutual tolerance since the Communists assumed power after World War II. But, seeing a Pope officially welcomed by the government here seemed less an anomaly than it would have in any other Communist country. From almost the very beginning of the country's thousand-year history, Roman Catholicism has been virtually synonymous with Polish nationhood. Today, the church plays a moderating role in Polish society. The birth in 1980 of Solidarnosc (Solidarity), an independent trade union movement, has introduced social, political, and economic opposition to Poland, with the Catholic hierarchy acting as a buffer between the dissidents and the government. The recent recognition of Solidarity and the scheduling of democratic elections suggest the church's effectiveness as negotiator.

The Poles are descended from tribes of western Slavs who were unified in the 10th century by a plains-dwelling tribe, the Polanie, in order to resist increasing invasions from the west by Germanic tribes. In 966, Duke Mieszko I put the new state under the protection of the Holy Roman Empire and accepted Christianity for himself and his people.

Most of Poland lies in the north European plain. It stretches south from the Baltic Sea to the Sudety and Carpathian mountains, which separate it from Czechoslovakia. It is bordered by East Germany on the west; and the Soviet Union on the east. Temperatures are higher than normal for Poland's latitude, but weather conditions vary from region to region. Winters can be severely cold, and there are frequent showers in summer. However, pleasant warm weather continues through October, but often under heavy gray skies.

Prevailing winds and tidal action have resulted in few good harbors along the Baltic coast, but they have created wonderful long sandy beaches that attract tens of thousands of vacationers to the 325-mile seacoast. Below the sand dunes and forests of the coastal belt, there is a stunning postglacial region of thousands of lakes and heavily wooded hills rich in wildlife. Poland has 13 natural parks and some 500 wildlife preserves. The wild European bison is protected here, along with chamois, bear, moose, and the swift, dun-colored tarpan, one of the smallest horses in the world.

The central lowlands are mostly flat and, although they do not have the richest soils, are the most extensively cultivated areas. About 48% of Poland's 37 million people live in rural areas. Poles privately own 80% of the country's arable land, but mechanization has been slow. In general, industrial development has been emphasized at the expense of agriculture. The foothills region paralleling the two mountain ranges along the southwestern border contains most of the country's mineral wealth and its best agricultural land. The upper Silesia region is the most industrial and most heavily populated area of the country.

The mountains themselves are not particularly rugged, except in the High Tatra range of the Carpathian Mountains, and have long been populated by farmers and shepherds. Outdoor activities, the beauty of the scenery, and the charm of local folk art, particularly wood carving, make the mountains an important tourist destination.

The borders of modern Poland are strikingly similar to those of the first Polish state, although the country's history has been one of constant struggle to hold its own against larger, more aggressive neighbors. At one point — from 1795 to 1918 — Poland ceased to exist as an independent state, having been partitioned by Austria, Prussia, and Russia. During that 123-year period, the Roman Catholic faith served as an element of cohesion and unity for the Polish people.

World War II began with the German invasion of Poland on September 1, 1939. After 6 weeks of fierce resistance, the country was conquered and occupied. Poland remained under foreign occupation for 6 years. The devastation and loss of life were among the worst suffered by any of the war's victims. Cracow alone among its cities escaped massive destruction, and 6 million Poles — half of them Jews — were killed in Nazi extermination camps. Today, these camps, such as Auschwitz, are maintained as museums, constant reminders of the war's horrors.

Jews had been welcomed as immigrants early in the 14th century, during the reign of Casimir III (Casimir the Great), one of Poland's greatest rulers, and before World War II, they constituted 10% of the population. Many of the survivors of the war emigrated to Israel following an anti-Semitic campaign in 1968. It is estimated that there are less than 10,000 Jews in Poland today.

After the war, Poland made an extraordinary effort to rebuild its cities and restore monuments and buildings important to its past. In Gdańsk, a whole district of tall, narrow, Gothic houses was reconstructed, reviving the charm and grace of the big port city. The recent completion of the Royal Palace in Warsaw fulfilled a 30-year dream of Poles everywhere, including 7 million Americans of Polish origin. Contributions, both large and small, from many of these Polish Americans helped sustain the restoration work at the palace.

The strong spirit of Polish nationalism can be traced to the fact that the country's population is extremely homogeneous; 98% of the people are ethnically Polish. They are proud of their heritage and their heroes: Nicholaus Copernicus, whose theories about the universe provided the foundation for modern astronomy; Maria Skłodowska-Curie, whose research with her husband led to the discovery of radium; Frederick Chopin, whose mazurkas and polonaises seem to embody the Polish spirit; and, the newest pope of the Roman Catholic Church — the former Karol Cardinal Wojtyla of Cracow. The religious shrine of Our Lady of Częstochowa, Cracow — Poland's second largest and loveliest city — and the breathtaking Tatras draw hundreds of thousands of visitors to southern Poland each year. The route south from Warsaw through heavily industrialized Upper Silesia to the medieval beauty of Cracow and beyond to the serenity of the mountains where centuries-old traditions of farmers and herdsmen are intact offers the traveler a continuum of Polish history. By car, the route from Warsaw to Częstochowa is about 135 miles (216 km), from Częstochowa to Cracow approximately 90 miles (125 km), and from Cracow to Zakopane, some 66 miles (106 km). There are also rail connections.

WARSAW: For a detailed report on the city and its hotels and restaurants, see *Warsaw,* THE CITIES. The capital is the usual point of departure for tours to other parts of Poland.

CZĘSTOCHOWA: The huge monastery complex on top of Jasna Góra Hill has dominated this drab Warta River town since Paulist monks founded it in 1382. The monastery is the focal point of a religious cult devoted to Our Lady of Częstochowa, the so-called *Black Madonna.*

Each year, enormous numbers of pilgrims come to pay homage to the sacred portrait of the madonna, said to have been painted by St. Luke. The portrait, with its darkened paint, hangs over an exquisite altar of wrought silver and ebony wood in a chapel in the monastery church. More than 300,000 people take part in the two pilgrimages each year in August: the *Feast of the Assumption,* August 15, and *St. Mary's Day* for the *Black Madonna,* August 26. Over the centuries, monarchs and others seeking blessings from Our Lady of Częstochowa have donated priceless art, jewelry, and heirlooms to swell the monastery's treasury. Many of the offerings are on permanent exhibition. Only VIPs, by special permission, are allowed to visit the monastery library, which contains some 20,000 valuable documents and records pertaining to Polish history.

Częstochowa itself is one of the chief towns of Poland's largest iron-ore mining region and an important textile industry center. Since World War II, there has been extensive urban and industrial development here.

En Route from Częstochowa – Heading south on E16, you pass some of the region's iron-ore mines before reaching Siewierz, where you can visit the ruins of the medieval castle of the Bishops of Cracow who once ruled here. Katowice, the capital of the Upper Silesia industrial region, is a modern industrial center and home of the renowned *Grand Symphony Orchestra* of the Polish radio. The route continues south to Tychy, once a popular resort center on nearly dry Lake Poprocanskie, then turns east to Oswiecim (Auschwitz), site of the largest Nazi concentration camp of World War II.

Some 4 million people, most of them Jews, were killed at the 3 camps run here from 1940 to 1945. The site of the Auschwitz and Birkenau camps has been made into a national museum. Pictures of the victims, the gas chambers where they died, and the enormous display cases containing their personal belongings — even hair shorn from prisoners and destined to be sold as pillow stuffing — are a chilling reminder of the grisly crimes committed here. A film of Auschwitz and the starving prisoners who were still alive the day the camp was liberated is shown at the museum several times a day.

CRACOW: Cracow (Kraków) is almost everyone's favorite Polish city. Travelers destined for the Tatra resorts to the south almost always stay here longer than they had planned. Unlike Warsaw and other Polish cities, Cracow was untouched by bombs and other massive destruction during World War II. Its medieval charm is still apparent on every tree-shaded street.

Poland's third-largest city, founded in the 9th century, has recently attracted international attention because this is the see Karol Cardinal Wojtyla served before becoming Pope John Paul II, the first Roman Catholic pope from a Communist country.

Wawel Hill, with its fortified castle and cathedral, dominates the skyline, while Rynek Główny, one of the largest town squares in Europe, is the center of city life.

The hill was first fortified to defend a crossing of the Vistula River beneath it. The stately Gothic cathedral was built from 1320 to 1364, and by the time of King Casimir the Great (1333–1370), Wawel was the center of state authority and culture. In the 16th century, King Sigismund the Old had a beautifully proportioned Renaissance palace built as his residence. The north wing was later renovated in accordance with the baroque spirit.

Although the royal court was moved to Warsaw in 1609, Wawel remained the coronation site of Polish kings, and even when Poland was occupied by the Austrians, it was a national treasure that symbolized the country's independence. During World War II, the Nazis had plans to blow up the castle and the cathedral, but a surprise offensive by the Russian army prevented this wanton destruction.

You enter the castle through an arcaded courtyard that is now used for open-air concerts. The castle's 71 rooms are high and airy and richly appointed. Among its treasures is a collection of 136 rare 16th- and 17th-century Flemish tapestries. The Chamber of Deputies has an unusual coffered ceiling that features heads carved and painted in the 16th century to represent members of the royal court. Another chamber is covered entirely in Spanish leather, which has been embossed and hand-painted with fine designs.

The elaborate tomb of St. Stanislaus, Poland's patron saint, stands in the middle of the nave of the adjacent cathedral, and two chapels are particularly noteworthy. These are the Chapel of the Holy Cross, decorated with colorful, 15th-century frescoes, and Sigismund Chapel, in which red marble tombs are set strikingly against white marble walls. An 11th-century crypt, incorporated from an earlier cathedral on this site, is crammed with the tombs of kings, queens, bishops, and Polish national heroes.

Splendid old mansions of noblemen and merchants are clustered on streets at the bottom of Wawel Hill. Grodzka street leads right to the main town square, but along the way there are dozens of narrow passageways between shops that open onto tiny courtyards with workshops and balconied houses.

Most of the buildings in the main square were built between the 14th and 16th centuries. The huge white and brown Cloth Hall (Sukiennice) was built in the 14th century, but was renovated in the Renaissance style in the 16th century. Always a center of commerce, the building now contains dozens of small craft and souvenir shops on the ground floor and houses the *Gallery of Polish Painting,* with a fine collection of 18th- and 19th-century work on the second floor.

St. Mary's Church (Mariacki), opposite the Cloth Hall, is best known for the magnificent altarpiece carved over 500 years ago by Wit Stwosz in late Gothic style. This medieval triptych of life-size figures in gold raiment depicts the assumption of the Virgin Mary. A series of 14th-century stained-glass windows above the triptych take up its themes and colors. The altar opening takes place daily except Sundays at noon.

Diagonally across the square from the church is the old town hall tower, the only reminder of the town hall that was demolished in 1820. The tower houses a branch of the *National Museum,* and its dungeon has been turned into a wine cellar.

The red brick of St. Florian's Gate, the Barbican, and some town walls and towers are all that remain of the medieval fortifications that protected old Cracow. Today the limits of the older parts of the city are marked by a green belt of gardens, known as Planty.

Another important landmark is the Jagiellonian University, founded in 1364 by King Casimir the Great and one of the oldest centers of learning in Europe. A prized possession in its museum is the world globe on which Copernicus first acknowledged America. The country is indicated by the words, "America New Discovery." Today, some 50,000 students study at the university.

Europe's second oldest synagogue, built in the 14th century for exiled Spanish Jews, is on Ul. Szeroka, in the old Jewish quarter. During the war, the Nazis desecrated the synagogue, using it to stable horses. Now a Jewish museum, it is being refurbished by the government.

There were about 60,000 Jews in Cracow before the war; today there are perhaps 2,000. Remu'h Synagogue, nearby (24 Ul. Szeroka), is where they worship. In a cemetery near the synagogues there is a lovely memorial: Pieces of desecrated tombs with Hebrew words and carved decorations have been fashioned into a wall resembling a great stone collage.

Cracow boasts a long and rich theater tradition. The eight repertory theaters here are well known for the quality of their productions. One of the best is *Helena Modrzejewska Stary Theater* (1 Ul. Jagiellonska) and almost every première at its branch, *Kameralny Theater*, is of national interest. The *J. Slowacki Theater* (1 Pl. św. Ducha), which shares the premises with the *Cracow Opera House*, also is highly regarded.

In even-numbered years, the *International Biennale of Graphic Arts* is held here. Works of art by contemporary artists and folk artists are on view and for sale at branches of *Cepelia*, the folk arts and crafts cooperative, and *Desa*, antiques and art shops. Some of the *Cepelia* branches are at 12 Ul. Karmelicka; Sukiennice, 22 Ul. Szewska; 7 Rynek Główny; and 1 Pl. Mariacki. *Desa* branches include the *B Gallery*, 2 Ul. Bracka; the *Modern Art Gallery*, Nowa Huta-Osiedle Kościuszkowskie, pavilion 1A; and the *Contemporary Art Gallery*, 3 Ul. św. Jana.

For general tourist information, check with the Wawel Tourist Information and Advertising Center (8 Ul. Pawia). Excursions can be arranged through various tourist offices, including *Orbis*, the Polish Tourist Office (1 Ul. Puszkina) in the *Orbis-Cracovia* hotel.

ZAKOPANE: This charming town, nestled between the Gubalowka Ridge and the towering Tatras, is an extremely popular, always lively holiday center. In winter, skiing and ski jumping are important added attractions, but all year, it is the beauty of the mountains and valleys and the rich folk culture preserved by the highlanders that draw Poles to Zakopane.

Fir, beech, and spruce grow in the subalpine woods of the Tatras. As you go higher, there are spruce forests and stone pine, dwarf mountain pine, and alpine pastures with little vegetation. Edelweiss and stone pine are among the 260 species of plants here, and the region is a natural habitat for lynx, marmot, chamois, brown bear, various deer, and, sometimes, the golden eagle.

The town itself is a museum of regional folk culture. The wooden gingerbread houses are similar to Norwegian stave churches, but more complicated in design. The lacy look of the carved façades is reminiscent of Victorian valentines. Against the backdrop of pine forests and snow-peaked mountains, these homes seem most idyllic. At the lower end of Ul. Krupówki, near Kościeliska, there are a small mid-19th-century church, several typical highlanders' houses, and a cemetery where nearly every monument is a masterpiece of folk art. The local museum, *Dr. Tytus Chalubinski Tatrzanskie Museum* (10 Ul. Krupówki), includes a reconstruction of a highlander's cottage interior, specimens of plants, birds, and animals native to the Tatras, and a collection of local costumes. *Tea Cottage* (39 Ul. Bulwary Stowackiego) is another museum with typical regional flavor.

Many men of the area still wear white woolen trousers with distinctive black and red embroidery called *parzenica,* and richly embroidered, capelike outer garments, known as *cucha,* to the delight of the tourists. In the outdoor market, country women sell hand-knitted mohair cardigans, the primitive leather moccasins worn by highland people, and special local cheeses.

There are horse carriages available to take you to the surrounding areas, such as the village of Jaszczurówka, where a small wooden church stands as an almost perfect example of elaborate Zakopane architecture, and Harenda which has an 18th-century church built of squared larch trunks.

For a magnificent panorama of the town and the Tatras, you can take a chair lift from near the *Orbis-Kasprowy* hotel to the top of Gubałowka Hill. At Kuźnice, a little more than 2 miles (3 km) south of Zakopane, there is a funicular to Kasprowy Wierch (6,451 feet), the region's most famous ski mountain. There are ski routes down to Zakopane and to Kuźnice.

The Dolina Białego Valley, where the crystal Biały Potok stream flows through steep crags, is just a 15- or 20-minute walk from the center of Zakopane.

Some hotel restaurants serve such regional specialties as braised boar, elk, and rabbit. Nighttime entertainment in Zakopane ranges from folk music and dancing to discotheque.

BEST EN ROUTE

Rooms may be hard to come by at the height of the tourist season and impossible to get at Częstochowa during the August pilgrimage. If you can book one, a double will cost from $55 to $70 a night at an expensive hotel; $40 to $55, at a moderately priced one; and $30 to $40 at an inexpensive hotel.

In Zakopane, non-*Orbis* hotels can arrange accommodations in private homes in the area.

Dinner for two with wine, at an expensive restaurant, will cost $25 to $35; at a moderately priced restaurant, $15 to $25; and at an inexpensive one, as little as $5.

The introduction of private enterprise has allowed Poles to venture into the hotel and restaurant trades, and many new establishments are beginning to flourish in tourist regions. Local tourist offices usually supply their addresses and will assist in making reservations.

CZĘSTOCHOWA

Orbis-Patria – A modern, medium-size hotel on the main avenue to Jasna Góra. It is also one of the best places for food, either in its restaurant or nightclub. 1 Ul. Starucha (phone: 47001 to -09). Expensive.

Motel Orbis – Small motel about 1½ miles (2.4 km) from the monastery. Ul. Wojska Polskiego (phone: 57233). Moderate.

CRACOW (KRAKÓW)

Orbis–Holiday Inn – Although all *Orbis* hotels in Cracow are listed as first class, this one is several shades better than the rest for its decor, restaurant, and general ambience. Totally air conditioned, it has 304 double rooms and 2 suites, as well as a swimming pool. However, it is a 10-minute bus ride or a 5-minute drive to Rynek Główny. 7 Ul. Marsz. Koniewa (phone: 375044). Expensive.

Europejski – A hotel without "Orbis" in its name. 5 Ul. Lubicz (phone: 20911). Moderate.

Krak – The best camping site near Cracow. 99 Ul. Radzikowskiego (phone: 72122). Moderate.

Orbis-Cracovia – Centrally located, with 427 rooms a restaurant, café, and several shops. 1 Ul. Puszkina (phone: 228666). Moderate.

Orbis-Francuski – Built just after the turn of the century, this centrally situated hotel has 56 very good rooms. 13 Ul. Pijarska (phone: 225122 or 225270). Moderate.

Wierzynek – Cracow's attempt at haute cuisine, in a centuries-old home. Market Square, 15 Rynek Główny (phone: 21025). Expensive.

Balaton – Hungarian-style food and a convenient downtown location. 37 Ul. Grodzka. (no phone). Moderate.

Dniepr – Features Russian food; also conveniently downtown. 18 Ul. Stycznia 55. Moderate.

U Wentzla – Another downtown eatery, this one featuring Polish fare, such as *vigos*, a dish of sausage with sauerkraut. 18 Rynek Główny. (no phone). Moderate.

Staropolska – Polish specialties here include several types of wild game. 4 Ul. Sienna. (no phone). Inexpensive.

ZAKOPANE

Orbis-Kasprowy – Beautifully situated on a mountainside, this 288-room hotel is only a 10-minute drive (half-hour walk) from town. Each room has a terrace with a lovely view. Rooms are small, but modern and bright. The restaurant is attractive and serves excellent food. Polana Szymoszkowa (phone: 4011). Expensive.

Gazda – A hotel with a restaurant. 1 Ul. Zaruskiego (phone: 5011). Moderate.

Obrochtowka – This private inn serves regional food (good trout) and has atmosphere. (no phone). Moderate.

Orbis-Giewont – Built in 1910, this hotel has 48 rooms, a restaurant, and a cocktail bar that serves good tap beer. 1 Ul. Kosciuszki (phone: 2011). Moderate.

Gubalowka – A restaurant that is 5 minutes, by funicular, up Gubalowka Hill. (no phone). Moderate.

U Wnuka – This café is in an old inn that has typical regional decor. (no phone). Inexpensive.

The best campground in the Zakopane area is on Ul. Zeromskiego (phone: 2256). Inexpensive.

Portugal

To most people Portugal means either Lisbon — the sophisticated capital city, rich in monuments, museums, and churches — or the Algarve — the famed vacation area, with its congenial mixture of sea, beaches, luxurious hotels, and varied cuisine. However, beyond Lisbon's city limits and away from the southern shore lies a country of ancient towns, walled villages, and captivating scenery.

Portugal's history goes back 3,000 years, to the time when Greek and Phoenician traders established settlements here. Later, Portugal became part of the Roman Empire (the country was then known as Lusitania), and many remains of the Roman occupation survive. Following the decline and fall of Rome, Portugal was subject to invasions by Visigoths from the north and by Moors from the south. By the mid-12th century, Portugal had emerged as a nation with its own culture and language, and by the 15th century it held title to the most extensive empire in the world. Though the empire has disappeared, the past is still very much alive among Portuguese people today. The handicrafts, colorful costumes, festivals and dances, and splendid restoration of historic buildings reflect a cultural heritage almost unchanged in spite of much evidence of modern progress.

Portugal is rectangular, bordered on the north and east by Spain and on the south and west by the Atlantic Ocean. With an area of some 35,553 square miles, Portugal is a relatively small country. Its major cities are Lisbon (pop. 807,167) and Oporto (pop. 327,360). The landscape encompasses a wide variety of contrasts — the lush green valley of the Minho River, the rugged mountains of the Tràs-os-Montes region, the steep-hilled vineyards of the Alto Douro, and the Beira flat coast. In the south the pale gold wheat fields and olive and cork groves of the Alentejo give way to the cosmopolitan resorts of the Algarve, where beaches and imposing cliffs are washed by the warm waves of the Gulf Stream.

The summer's heat is moderated along the coast by sea breezes. Days can be quite hot but the temperature drops in the evening. Winters are mild and snow is seldom seen except in the high mountains. The climate is most pleasant for driving trips in the spring and fall, but travel in the southern region is also comfortable during the winter.

Road development, although fast improving, is still somewhat rudimentary in country areas. A fast toll highway is gradually closing the distance between Lisbon and Oporto and should be completed in the next few years. Away from the coast, a program is under way to widen and improve main roads linking the biggest towns, but much of the network still consists of narrow, poorly surfaced roads. Roadsigns are fairly obvious, but a good road map is a necessity. While driving, watch out for donkeys and oxen. They were on the roads long before the automobile and are still there. Gasoline is expensive, but Portugal is still a bargain in other respects, relative to most European countries. Well-maintained hotels and *pousadas* (government-owned inns in buildings of artistic or historical interest) as well as excellent restaurants are found throughout the country. Accommodations are generally good and plumbing is modern and clean. Tap water is considered safe to drink but most people prefer bottled mineral water. Grapes are grown in many areas and the regional wines are excellent. When dining out, request the house wine if one is available.

Perhaps the most interesting accommodations available are at the many country manor houses that offer bed-and-breakfast. At the moment there are about 150, mainly in the north of the country, and they are invariably fascinating — and comfortable — places to stay. There are three types: *paços,* houses where royalty have stayed; *casas antigas,* houses that have been in the family for more than 300 years; and *quintas,* old farmhouses. Many of the houses belong to aristocrats, and in the evening travelers can often chat with a count or other scion of an old family. The accommodations are always of a high level, but prices are usually moderate. Central booking and information are available through *Turihab,* Ponte de Lima (phone: 058-942333), and *A.C.T.,* Cascais (phone: 286-5132). *Pousadas* can also be booked centrally in Lisbon (phone: 881221).

Two weeks is sufficient to travel around most of Portugal. Our first route originates in Lisbon and heads north through Oporto, the second largest city; from here it loops around the mountainous northern region to Guimarães, the cradle of the Portuguese nation, and Vila Real, home of Mateus wine. The next route starts in Lisbon, circles around the central region taking in the towns of Elvas, Estremoz, and Evora, which are rich in historic sites. The last itinerary focuses on the Algarve, Portugal's southern coast and beach resort area.

The Northern Coastal Region and Western Mountains

This route covers a lot of territory, temporally as well as geographically, starting at the modern capital of Lisbon, traveling through Oporto, industrial center and second largest city, to Guimarães, birthplace of Portugal's first king.

The route from Lisbon to Oporto in the western part of the country along N1 is heavily trafficked. Though the route links Portugal's most densely populated areas, it passes through small towns, forests, farms, woods, olive groves, and a few popular beach resorts on the Atlantic. Many of the highlights of the route are architectural — the extravagant mountaintop castle built by Fernando II between 1846 and 1850 in Sintra; the imposing marble monastery in Mafra built in 1717 for King João V; the walled town of Obidos; and the splendid abbey Mosteiro de Santa Maria, which contains the tombs of two ill-fated lovers of the 14th century. Ranging even farther back you can see the ruins of Conimbriga, the most important Roman settlement on the Iberian Peninsula.

Leaving Oporto, the route heads north, then east and south, circling through the mountainous northern region. The road is a little bumpy, but not unacceptably so. It links small fishing villages, and then travels along the Minho River, Portugal's northernmost natural border with Spain. Highlights along the way are Braga, an ancient city founded by the Romans with monuments from the 12th century through ornate 18th-century baroque styles. Guimarães and Vila Real, home of the famous Mateus wine, are set amidst the deep vales and terraced mountain vineyards of the great port wine producing region.

LISBON: For a detailed report on the capital, its hotels and restaurants, see *Lisbon*, THE CITIES. Depart from Lisbon on N249 in the direction of Queluz and drive 17½ miles (28 km) to Sintra in the verdant hills of the Serra da Sintra. Stop off in Queluz for a look at its 18th-century pink rococo palace, surrounded by formal gardens. Sometimes described as Portugal's Versailles, the palace was built by Pedro III for his "mad queen" Maria. It is now used to house visiting dignitaries, and the former palace kitchen — with its giant spits, marble tables, and walk-in fireplace — is now a charming restaurant.

SINTRA: Nestled on the northern slope of the mountain, the old town is notable for its palaces and elegant mansions with ivy- and lichen-covered walls. Many days of the year, a mist envelopes the peak, giving the town an eerie, fairy tale atmosphere. Sintra so entranced Lord Byron that he remained there to write. For centuries the town was a favored summer residence of Portuguese kings and royal families. The Paço Real on the main square was built by João I in the 14th century on the ruins of a fortress that had been taken from the Moors in 1147 by Portugal's first king, Afonso Henriques. Above the town looms the Castelo dos Mouros (Moorish Castle), a monumental structure dating from between the 7th and 9th centuries. On the mountaintop, reached by a steep ascent, the Palácio da Pena, built by Queen Maria II's consort, Ferdinand Saxe-Coburg-Gotha, with the help of German architect Baron Eschwege from 1840 to 1850, is an extravagant example of the work of a wildly creative imagination, comparable to Ludwig II's castles in Bavaria. The delightful Monserrate Gardens on N375, designed by Francis Cook in the 19th century, display over 3,000 floral and botanical specimens.

On the winding streets, you'll find shops selling antiques and handicrafts. A twice-monthly Sunday antiques market attracts many browsers and buyers to the tiny adjacent village of São Pedro, N9.

En Route from Sintra – Before N247.3 winds into the forest, make a stop at Convento dos Capuchos, a 16th-century monastery with its cells and rooms carved out of rock in the hillside. Make a slight detour to Cabo da Roca for a spectacular view of cliffs, coast, and sea. Its lighthouse marks the westernmost point in Europe. Retrace to Sintra and pick up N9 to Mafra.

MAFRA: The imposing marble Mosteiro rises from the road without preamble. Erected in 1717 for King João V by German architect Fredrich Ludwig, the great edifice contains a monastery, basilica, palace, and once housed a school of sculpture. Its library houses 20,000 volumes of 17th- and 18th-century works on theology, geography, and military theory. The façade alone demands attention with its baroque decorations, columns, statuary, and ornate belfries. You can purchase lovely pale blue and white pottery in the shops facing the monastery or just 3 miles (5 km) away in the town of Sobreiro, where it is made.

En Route from Mafra – At Torres Vedras, 21 miles (34 km) along N9, you'll see distant windmills outlined on the rolling hilltops, vineyards, and apple and pear orchards set out in neat fields. At Bombarral, 16 miles (26 km), take N8 7 miles (11 km) to Óbidos.

ÓBIDOS: This walled town is dominated by the old castle's keep and towers. Taken from the Moors in 1148 by Afonso Henriques, the little city so captivated Queen Isabella in 1228, that her consort, King Dinis, presented it to her. Pass through the double-arched gateway, follow the narrow main street to Igreja de Santa Maria, and park below in the square. Proceed on foot to Igreja de São Tiago where a path on the left leads to the ramparts. On the right is the *Pousada do Castelo,* once the royal palace. The serene dining room inside serves a pleasantly formal lunch. Shops in town offer a wealth of handicrafts: lace, embroidered tablecloths, basketry, fashionable heavy knitted sweaters. Don't miss the octagonal church standing alone in a field below the town. Built by Philip II of Spain, it contains a 14th-century onyx statue of a black virgin which resembles the Black Virgin of Monserrat in Spain.

En Route from Óbidos – Caldas da Rainha, on N8, is a large commercial center noted for its spa dating back to 1485. It was founded by Leonor, the wife of King João II, who believed in the curative power of its waters. The city's hospital and park still bear her name. Traditional regional ceramics are on sale in the town's shops and factories, and an annual ceramics fair draws large crowds.

Veer left at Alfeizerão and head for São Martinho do Porto, a typical beach resort. From the promenade you can see an unusual saltwater lake connected to the ocean through a rift between high coastal cliffs. If you like quiet beaches with good fishing and clean water, try Foz do Arelho Beach on a small, pine-covered peninsula, just 2 miles (3 km) from Caldas.

A short drive north on N242 leads to the famous fishing port of Nazaré, where the beach is lined with brightly painted, high-prowed fishing boats. Nazaré has recently become a rather touristy beach resort, but some customs survive: Men still wear traditional plaid shirts and black caps, and women, black capes. They still dance the *vira* — a spirited folk dance — and cook their tasty fish stew, *caldeirada.* For an excellent view, drive or take a funicular to the Sítio, a section in town perched high above the beach. There is a spectacular view from the belvedere, and on the cliff just below you can see a hoof print. According to legend, it was made by the horse of Portuguese nobleman Dom Fuas Roupinho, who accidentally rode off the cliff while pursuing a deer. He prayed to Our Lady of Nazaré and was saved; in gratitude he built the little Chapel of Memory, which is perched on the cliff. *Mar e Sol* or *Riba Mar* serve good meals along the seaside. Though the shops appear rather touristy, they sell handsome hand-knit fishermen's sweaters at moderate prices.

ALCOBAÇA: Constructed by Cistercian monks in 1178, the Mosteiro de Santa Maria is one of Portugal's most splendid abbeys. The building has been altered and restored, but the interior retains its uplifting spaciousness. The church contains the Flamboyant Gothic styled tombs of Inês de Castro and Dom Pedro, ill-fated lovers of the 14th century. (Inês was murdered by a group of noblemen to prevent King Dom Pedro from marrying her. The enraged king executed them in revenge, after forcing them to pay homage to her dead body dressed in the garb of a queen.) In the cloister you can visit the monks' kitchen with its enormous chimneys and marble tables; a stream of the River Alcoa flows underneath this kitchen. In the Middle Ages the stream provided fresh fish for the royal table. On the Rossio, the sweeping square before the abbey, the distinctive pottery and ceramics of the region are displayed for sale.

BATALHA: A masterpiece of Portuguese Gothic and Manueline (after Manuel I, during whose reign the transition from Gothic to Renaissance styles gave birth to an original artistic form of decoration in Portugal) styles, the town's church is an awesome monument. Embellished with flying buttresses, turrets, and tracery, it was erected between 1402 and 1438 to commemorate the victorious battle of Aljubarrota, which ended Castilian domination of Portugal. The stark, soaring interior of the nave is offset by a richly decorated cloister and lavabo. The small Founder's Chapel contains the tombs of King João I, Queen Philippa of Lancaster, and their children, most notably Prince Henry the Navigator. Guided tours give access to an unfinished section of chapels. The square adjacent to the monastery is lined with small shops and cafés.

FATIMA: A side trip can be made from Batalha to Fatima — a distance of 20 miles (32 km) — the world-famous shrine where the Virgin Mary appeared in 1917 to three shepherd children. The pilgrimages on May 13 and October 13 often bring a million pilgrims from all over the world. The town has several hotels.

LEIRIA: This pleasant town is just 7 miles (11 km) from Batalha on rte. 1. In its center on a volcanic hill stands the Castelo, built in 1135 by Afonso Henriques, from which you have a panoramic view of the picturesque old town and the charming countryside. Leiria is most appealing for an stroll at twilight — when the old streets and houses seem to blend with the modern. A festival held during the last 2 weeks of March features exhibitions and folk dancing. Another worthwhile side trip can be taken to Marinha Grande, 8 miles (13 km) from Leiria. This glassmaking center was founded around 1730, and the glass factory was built by the Stephens brothers, Englishmen who later donated it to the state. You can visit the glass museum and the factories.

En Route from Leiria – The main road to Coimbra, N1, leads through 45 miles (72 km) of farms, olive trees, and pine woods. About 9 miles (14 km) below Coimbra, an archaeological dig has uncovered traces of a Roman town, Conimbriga, inhabited first by Celts in Neolithic times. You can see the remains of what was once the most important Roman settlement on the Iberian Peninsula. Guided tours are available.

COIMBRA: Beginning as a Roman settlement, suffering invasions by barbarians and Moors, taken by Christians in 1064, Coimbra finally came into its own as a cultural and artistic center after the founding of its famed *universidade* in 1290. Climb the steep narrow cobbled way through the old town to the university courtyard for a tour of the ancient buildings. The magnificent Biblioteca is decorated in carved and gilded baroque-styled wood with intricately painted ceilings; it contains an enormous collection of old books. The Ceremonial Hall hung with portraits of the kings of Portugal and the beautiful Manueline ornamented chapel are still in use today. A former episcopal palace nearby holds the *Museu Machado de Castro* (Rua de Borges Carneiro) where one is led from room to room by French-speaking guides determined to explain everything about each of the collections' gold objects, sculptures, paintings, and ceramics. The basement displays ancient relics and marble busts of Romans. Also worth visiting are: the 12th-century cathedral, Sé Velha, with its Flamboyant Gothic altarpiece; the 16th-century Mosteiro de Santa Cruz and its lovely Manueline cloister; a 12th-century Cistercian convent, Mosteiro de Celas; and across the river on N110.2, Convento de Santa Clara-a-Nova. Children will enjoy the nearby Portugal dos Pequenos, a beautifully constructed village with replicas of all the country's famous buildings scaled down to a child's size.

En Route from Coimbra – Follow N1 18 miles (28 km) to Luso, a lovely spa situated in the midst of forested rolling hills. An olympic-size swimming pool in the gardens behind *Grande Hotel das Termas* is open to the public. Admission charge.

BUÇACO: Take the winding road through Buçaco Forest, a park founded in 1628 by Carmelite monks. In the center of the forest a royal hunting lodge, built from 1888 to 1907 by Carlos I, has been transformed into the *Palace* hotel (see *Best en Route*). This incredible structure was designed in a pastiche of Manueline styles and is highly provides an enchanting setting for lunch or dinner. Adjacent to the hotel stands a 17th-century Carmelite monastery, chapel, and cloister open to visitors. The olive tree in the driveway marks the spot where Wellington tied up his horse on the eve of winning a great victory over French invaders in 1810. The well-maintained forest has myriad trails for good hiking.

En Route from Buçaco – Retrace through Luso to Mealhada to pick up N1 north. Along the way you'll see numerous shops carrying copper and brass wares. On the road from Buçaco there are more than a dozen restaurants which specialize in *leitão a bairrada* (suckling pig roasted on a spit) accompanied by a variety of regional vegetables. Also offered is a champagne-like wine called *Espumante* — both white and red — which is delicious when chilled. If you have time turn off at Agueda for a side trip to Aveiro. This coastal fishing village, inhabited since the 11th century, is crisscrossed by lagoons and canals and surrounded by weedy marshes and sand flats. Fishing, seaweed gathering, and ceramic and china manufacturing are the chief industries.

Some 34 miles (54 km) farther up the coast on N109 is the popular resort, Espinho. Featuring a vast swimming pool complex, facilities for all water sports, a fine golf course, clay pigeon shooting, and a casino, Espinho is purely for fun. N109 leads into the superhighway approach to Oporto, the second largest city in Portugal.

OPORTO: Its history dating from the 8th century BC, the region known as Portucale was given to Henri of Burgundy in 1095 as part of the dowry of Princess Teresa. Developed as an important trading center with northern Europe, the area of Portucale eventually gave its name to the entire country after figuring prominently in the struggle for independence. Renamed Oporto, it became the base of the Portuguese shipping fleet, which evolved into a formidable maritime power.

Cross the River Douro via Ponte Dom Luis I; the lodges of Vila Nova da Gaia, storehouses of the world famous port wine, lie below the bridges. Narrow streets, heavy traffic, and many one-way signs contribute to the difficulties the driver may encounter in trying to find the way to the central parking location, Praça do Humberto Delgado. The easiest, most comfortable way to see this tightly built industrial town is to take a Cityrama Bus tour, which will include a stop at the wine center across the Douro. Principal places of interest include the 12th-century catedral, Terreiro da Sé; the Igreja de São Francisco, a Gothic church with a richly decorated interior (Rua Infante Dom Henrique); and the *Museu Soares dos Reis* (Rua de Dom Manuel II), where the exhibits include early paintings, sculpture, pottery, and religious works of art. Many shops display silver, gold, and filigree jewelry, leather goods, and locally made ceramics. Some of the best restaurants are *Portucale, Orfeu, Escondidinho,* and the *Comercial* (see *Best en Route*). With meals, everyone drinks the ultra-dry *vinho verde* wines from the Minho region and the fuller, red table wines from the Douro and Dão regions. For before and after meals, there are various Ports.

En Route from Oporto – The N14 heads north 20 miles (32 km) through vineyards and cornfields to Vila Nova de Famlicão, where you pick up N103 to Barcelos. This attractive town is known for its painted rooster, which has become a popular symbol of Portugal. According to legend, a pilgrim from Galicia, Spain, was staying at the home of a Barcelos judge when the house was robbed. He was unjustly accused of the crime and sentenced to hang. He asked to see the judge who was at dinner and eating a rooster. The pilgrim said to the judge: "May that rooster rise up and crow if I am innocent." It did, and he was set free. Barcelos has a lively Thursday market where you can buy handmade rugs, laces, ceramics, brightly enameled figurines, as well as housewares and blue jeans. The ruined *Ducal Palace* houses an archaeological exhibit and ceramics museum. The 17 miles (27 km) along N14 to Viana do Castelo is a lovely drive. The entire region is known for its good hunting and fishing as well as for its fairs and religious pilgrimages. A list of these activities is available at the Portuguese Tourist Office in town.

VIANA DO CASTELO: This fishing port and holiday resort is nicely situated, with a seascape, river bank, and hillside. One of the most famous festivals in the country, *Festa da Nossa Senhora da Agonia,* is held here each year during the third week of August, when the townspeople don their colorful embroidered costumes to take part in the activities. A former 18th-century palace, the *Museu Municipal,* on the Rua Manuel Espregueira, houses a fine exhibit of tiles, furniture, pottery, and ceramics. The Praça da República has 16th-century buildings and the Igreja da Misericórdia, which are worth a look. Follow the signs for Santa Luzia, up a winding road through pine and eucalyptus, to the Basilica of Santa Luzia for a dazzling view of the entire region.

En Route from Viana do Castelo – Follow Hwy. 203 along the Lima River to Ponte de Lima, a town with a fine Roman and medieval bridge and many 16th- and 17th-century manor houses. Some of these — the Conde de Aurora, for example — are open to the public. For dinner, try lamprey stuffed with rice, a regional specialty.

VALENÇA: In spite of strong fortifications, this town of old stone houses and cobblestone streets was once at the mercy of Spanish invaders. The 13th-century castle at the far end of town has been handsomely reshaped into a modern inn, *Pousada de São Teotónio* (see *Best en Route*). The 17th-century ramparts open on an incomparable view of the Minho Valley and the Spanish mountains beyond. Shops in town carry a good selection of sweaters and embroidered bedspreads.

En Route from Valença – Passing through the gate, turn left down the hill to N101, then it's 11 miles (18 km) to Moncão. This walled town is an attractive base from which to explore the Peneda-Gerês National Park. The National Forest Department can arrange guided excursions through the park, so you can see its many wild horses and boars. Nearby at Bretiandos and Briteiros there are pre-Celtic ruins. A comfortable inn, *Albergaria Atlántico,* has a decent dining room with a nice view. There is also a nice *pousada, Pousada de São Bento,* at Caniçada at one of the entrances to Peneda-Gerês National Park.

The N101 now begins its journey 46 miles (73 km) south to Braga. Take a look at the stately mansion of Brejoeira, before the ascent on the shady mountain road, and stop off in Ponte da Barca to sample its white, dry, "green" wines.

BRAGA: Founded in the 5th century by the Romans, conquered by Visigoths and Moors, this ancient city has developed into a visibly prosperous industrial center. Liberated from the Moors by King Ferdinand of Léon in 1040, Braga came under the influence of the church soon after when the Archepiscopal See was established here. Over the centuries many monuments, churches, and palaces were erected by the bishops; in the 18th century Braga became the center of Baroque art in Portugal. The highly decorated 12th-century Sé Catedral contains a museum of sacred art and the tombs of its founders, Henri of Burgundy and Dona Teresa. Among the buildings of notable architectural design are the Antigo Paço Episcopal church overlooking the Jardim de Santa Barbara, the nearby town hall, and the 13th-century castle and keep. Many of the old buildings are artfully lit in the evenings. A religious festival is held during Holy Week, and the Nativity of St. John is celebrated for 3 days starting on June 23. Every Tuesday there is a market on the edge of town where you can buy handcrafted articles from artisans of the region. *Terraço* is a popular restaurant.

En Route from Braga – Some 3 miles (5 km) from Braga on N103.3, the baroque steps appear which lead to the 18th-century sanctuary of Bom Jesus do Monte. This curious stairway is adorned with chapels and statuary depicting figures from the Passion. Mount the steps as the pilgrims do or reach the top by funicular or motor car for a spectacular view from the church plaza.

Take N101 south to Guimarães.

GUIMARÃES: This attractive, busy town is known as the cradle of the Portuguese nation. Foundations for the village were begun in the 10th century with the construction of a monastery. In 1095 the village was presented to Henri of Burgundy by his father-in-law Alfonso VI, King of León and Castile. The great Castelo, whose keep dates from the 10th century, was the birthplace of Afonso Henriques who became the first King of Portugal. Nearby is the tiny Romanesque church of St. Michael and beyond, the 15th-century palace of the Dukes of Bragança. Visit the Romanesque Igreja Nossa Senhora da Oliveira and its cloister exhibition, *Museu Alberto Sampaio.* Just below the town park lies the Igreja São Francisco whose interior flaunts an ornately carved and gilded baroque altar; old tiles decorate the walls of the chancel. Walk to the old section of town on the Rua Santa Maria, lined with 14th- and 15th-century houses. Hand-embroidered linens are a specialty of this area.

En Route from Guimarães – This 22-mile (35-km) stretch of N101 to Amarante is populated by lacemakers whose wares are spread out at the side of the road. After crossing the Tamega River, turn left onto N15, which wends slowly up into the stern but grand Serra do Marão. Halfway (18 mi/29 km) to Vila Real is the *Pousada de São Gonçalo,* a good place for a lunch break.

VILA REAL–MATEUS: Proceed through Vila Real, following the signs for Murça and Sabrosa on N322 to Mateus, home of the famous wine. At the Mateus Manor, visit the imposing 18th-century baroque residence, so familiar from the label on Mateus bottles. Still owned by the Counts of Vila Real, the manor contains old Portuguese furnishings, family portraits, and cases full of mementos, memorabilia, toys, and personal effects. Access to the chapel and gardens is given but you can only view the vineyards from a distance.

En Route from Vila Real – There are a few alternatives from here. If you have a flexible schedule, the N2 north of Vila Real links notable spa towns — Vidago, with its parks and woodland; and Chaves, an old town with a Roman bridge, 17th-century ramparts, a castle with a 14th-century keep, and a spa.

A longer drive on N15 from Vila Real ambles through a vast mountain region for 86 miles (138 km) to Bragança, whose walled medieval city and towering 12th-century castle keep dominate the lower modern town. Just outside the town is the *Pousada São Bartolomeu,* pleasant for an overnight stay.

If your time is more limited, continue on N2 into the deep vales and terraced mountain vineyards of the great port wine–producing region. Cross the Douro River at Régua, and wind your way through the valley where the grape vines cling to the nearly perpendicular terraced hillsides that drop down to the river to Lamego.

LAMEGO: This is a neatly arranged town of 16th- and 18th-century houses. The Cortes, a representative body of nobles, clergy, and townspeople, met here in 1143 to acknowledge Afonso Henriques as King of Portugal and implement the royal right of succession to the throne. In the *Museu de Lamego,* a former 18th-century bishop's palace, early paintings, tapestries, and 16th- to 18th-century tiles are on display. Several churches of note are the Sé, which dates from the 12th century; the Igreja do Desterro, with fine interior decoration (ask for admission at 148 Calçada do Desterro); and the Santuario Nossa Senhora dos Remédios, a baroque edifice whose impressive staircase is embellished with an unusual arrangement of pinnacles and ornamental tiling. Lamego is also known for its smoked ham and all kinds of sausages.

VISEU: Farther south on N2 is this important agricultural and crafts center. Sixteenth-century residences and 18th-century balconied town houses line the narrow streets of the old section. The cathedral on the Praça da Sé has an interesting cloister and gallery of sacred art. Also worth a look is the *Museu Grão Viseu,* which contains paintings from the 16th-century Viseu school and representative works of old and new Portuguese artists.

En Route from Viseu – The best route to complete the circle to Oporto is N16 west to N1 north at Albergaria-a-Velha and straight on to Oporto (84 mi/134 km). Otherwise you can head south to Tomar along N2, N234, N1, and N110, where you can pick up the central route at its northernmost point.

BEST EN ROUTE

Expect to pay $110 and up for a double room per night in a hotel in the expensive category, $55 to $85 in the moderate, and $30 to $45 in the inexpensive category. A dinner for two people with local wine will cost $40 and up in the expensive range, about $30 in the moderate, and $20 in the inexpensive range. Prices do not include drinks, wine, or tips.

SINTRA–SÃO PEDRO

Palácio dos Seteais – This former 18th-century palace is set in a beautiful park and garden. The 18 rooms are exquisitely furnished and decorated. An elegant dining room serves international and regional cuisine; there is also a bar. 8 Rua Barbosa du Bocage, on N375 (phone: 923-3200). Expensive.

Café Solar dos Mouros – Decorated in Moorish style with beautiful tiles and a fountain, this restaurant is just off the square. 2 R. Consig. Pedroso (phone: 923-1706). Moderate.

Galeria Real – Above an antiques shop, this appealing dining room serves excellent regional and French dishes. Reservations. Rua Tude de Sousa, on N9 (phone: 923-1661). Moderate.

Solar de S. Pedro – Good Portuguese and international fare are served in attractive and comfortable surroundings. Closed Wednesdays. 12 Praça D. Fernando II, S. Pedro de Sintra (phone: 923-1860). Moderate.

ÓBIDOS

Estalagem do Convento – Delightfully converted convent has antique-styled furnishings and 13 rooms. The beamed-ceiling dining room specializes in regional fare. Reservations advised. Rua Dr. João de Ornelas (phone: 95217). Moderate.

Pousada do Castelo – Originally a 16th-century palace, this inn on the ramparts has regional decor, 6 rooms, and a rustically elegant dining room with country and international cuisine; bar. Reservations advised. Paço Real (phone: 95105). Moderate.

SÃO MARTINHO DO PORTO

Parque – This spacious mansion-style hotel has 44 rooms in a garden setting. Only breakfast is served; no restaurant. Av. Marechal Carmona (phone: 98108). Inexpensive.

NAZARÉ

Nazaré – A modern 50-room hotel with bar. Largo Afonso Zuquete (phone: 46311). Inexpensive.

Praia – Another modern hotel (with 40 rooms), it is on a main street near the beach. Breakfast only. 39 Av. Vieira Guimarães (phone: 46423). Inexpensive.

Mar Bravo – It has regional fare and good (but expensive) seafood, plus a panoramic view to recommend it. Praça Sousa Oliveira (phone: 46180). Expensive to moderate.

LEIRIA

Euro-Sol – Nicely landscaped, this attractive, modern, 54-room hilltop hotel has an outdoor pool, an exceptional top-floor dining room, and a bar. Rua D. José Alves Correia da Silva (phone: 24101). Moderate.

Estalagem Claras – Good regional cooking is available at this simple inn. 42 Av. Heróis de Angola (phone: 22373). Inexpensive.

BATALHA

Estalagem do Mestre Afonso Domingues – This sparkling, gracious inn near Batalha's Church — one of Portugal's most renowned monuments — has 21 rooms, air conditioning, and a pleasant dining room. Reservations advised. Batalha (phone: 96260). Inexpensive.

COIMBRA

Astoria – Old-fashioned comfort amid 1930s decor is the advantage of this conveniently located hotel. There's a quiet dining room and a bar. 21 r/c Av. Emidio Navarro. (phone: 22055). Moderate.

Dom Pedro – Good regional and international cuisine is served at this elegantly rustic restaurant. 58 Av. Emidio Navarro (phone: 29108). Moderate.

LUSO

Estalagem do Luso – This lovely guesthouse has 7 artfully furnished rooms and a dining room. Rua Dr. Lúcio Pais Abranches (phone: 93114). Moderate.

Grande Hotel das Termas – Surrounded by gardens and parks, this large resort hotel has 157 rooms, a spacious dining room, and a bar — all newly decorated. Facilities include a huge outdoor pool, spa, tennis, casino, and nightclub. Open from June till mid-October. In town (phone: 93450). Moderate.

BUÇACO

Palace Hotel do Buçaco – Forest, park, and gardens surround this magnificent former royal hunting lodge that features Manueline decorations, fine furniture, 70 luxurious bedrooms, a bar, and a splendid dining room. Floresta do Buçaco (phone: 93101). Expensive.

AVEIRO

Pousada da Ria – This balconied inn overlooking the lagoon and town has 10 comfortable rooms, swimming pool, a dining room with regional cooking, and bar. Torreira-Murtosa (phone: 46132). Inexpensive.

ESPINHO

Praiagolfe – A modern beach hotel with 199 air conditioned rooms, restaurant, bar, nightclub, and a large outdoor pool; golf course adjacent. 6 Rua (phone: 920630). Moderate.

OPORTO

Infante de Sagres – An oasis in the midst of a busy city, this luxury hotel has 84 pleasant rooms, a grand dining room with attentive service, and elaborately decorated lounges. 62 Praça D. Filipa de Lencastre (phone: 28101). Expensive.

Porto Sheraton – Opened in 1986, with 253 rooms and all the customary amenities of the chain. Away from the town center. 1269 Av. Boavista (phone: 668822). Expensive.

Porto Atlántico – This supermodern complex out of the city center has 58 air-conditioned rooms, indoor and outdoor pools, shops, and restaurants. 66 Rua Afonso Lopes Vieira, off E5 (phone: 694941). Moderate.

Tuela – An excellent modern hotel with 43 air conditioned rooms in a reasonably central location. 200 Rua Arquitecto Marques da Silva (phone: 667161). Inexpensive.

Portucale – This first rate restaurant on the 13th floor of the *Albergaria Miradouro* offers splendid views and international and regional cuisine. Reservations. 598 Rua da Alegria (phone: 27861). Expensive.

Orfeu – A modern steak and fish establishment with paneled wood and soft piped-in music. It's favored by fish lovers, particularly cod enthusiasts. Open daily. 928 Rua Júlio Dinis (phone: 64322). Expensive to moderate.

Comercial – This complex has 2 restaurants and a bar. International and regional cuisine is served in the attractive ground-floor restaurant; a good selection is available in *Taverna do Infante* below. 77 Rua Infante Dom Henrique (phone: 22463). Moderate.

Escondidinho – This popular restaurant serves the best regional food in the city. Tiles, marble, and local crafts decorate it inside, while outside it looks like a typical country house — which makes it stand out in the otherwise modern urban street. Closed Sundays. 144 Rua Passos Manuel (phone: 21079). Moderate.

VIANA DO CASTELO

Parque – This modern 120-room hotel overlooking the Lima River has inviting grounds, spacious lounges, a heated pool, a rooftop restaurant with regional and international cuisine, and a bar. Praça da Galiza (phone: 24151). Moderate.

Santa Luzia – High above town, this 42-room hotel surrounded by a park and gardens has an Old World atmosphere and modern amenities — heated pool, tennis courts, excellent restaurant, terrace with a stunning view, and a bar. Monte de Santa Luzia (phone: 22192). Moderate.

VALENÇA

Pousada de São Teotónio – This modern inn at the edge of a walled town has 16 nice rooms, an airy dining room, good food, and a bar. The terrace has a gorgeous view. Valença do Minho (phone: 22252). Inexpensive.

BRAGA

Turismo – Conveniently located on a main street, this modern hotel has a spacious interior, 93 air conditioned rooms, a pool, bar, and shops. Av. da Liberdade (phone: 27091). Moderate.

Do Elevador – A quiet little hotel above the city that provides enchanting night views; 25 rooms. Food is served. Bom Jesus do Monte (phone: 25011). Inexpensive.

Inácio – Tasty regional cooking is served in this popular restaurant, whose ambience is enhanced by stone walls and rough beams. 4 Campo das Hortas (phone: 22335). Moderate.

CANIÇADA

Pousada de São Bento – Stone walls, spectacular views, 10 rooms with rustic decor, a dining room with good, hearty, regional cooking, and an outdoor pool are found at this new inn. Cerdeirinhas-Soengas Caniçada (phone: 57190). Inexpensive.

GUIMARÃES

Pousada de Santa Marinha – A 15th-century royal country palace with 59 rooms, immaculately restored and furnished, on a hill overlooking the town. Banha de Guimarães (phone: 418453). Expensive.

Jordão – Below the Jordão cinema, this spacious, busy restaurant serves a variety of international and regional dishes. 62 Av. Afonso Henriques (phone: 40198). Moderate.

VIDAGO

Vidago Palace – This pleasant 122-room hotel has a tranquil atmosphere, park grounds, pool, tennis, golf course. Breakfast is served. Parque (phone: 97356). Inexpensive.

LAMEGO

Estalagem de Lamego – In a pretty park, this small inn has 7 rooms and a pleasant dining room. On N2 (phone: 62162). Inexpensive.

VISEU

Grão Vasco – Near the old section of town, this modern hotel has 89 rooms, lovely lawns and trees, and a swimming pool. The dining room serves regional and international cuisine; bar. Rua Gaspar Barreiros (phone: 23511). Moderate.

O Cortiço – Probably the most famous restaurant in Portugal, it's noted for robust regional cooking and friendly, lively service. Spread over several nearby addresses, a table in this restaurant is always found even on the busiest nights. 36, 47, 64 Rua Nova (phone: 23853). Moderate.

Central Portugal

This route originates in Lisbon and loops around central Portugal through an area of rolling plains crisscrossed by rivers and known for cork and olive oil production. The bold reds of the stripped tree trunks along the way attest to the wealth of cork growing here. Central Portugal offers much of interest. In Tomar the magnificent Convento de Cristo, a fortified castle and convent, blends styles of architecture from the twelfth through the 17th century. Next, the route swings through Marvão, a medieval village, and through three of Portugal's most engaging towns: Elvas, where a 15th-century aqueduct still carries water to the town; Estremoz, whose artisans are famous for their pottery figurines of people and animals; and Évora, where you can see a Roman temple dating from the 2nd century.

LISBON: For a detailed report on the capital, its hotels and restaurants, see *Lisbon,* THE CITIES. From Lisbon pick up E3, then N3, for the 49-mile (79-km) trip to Santarém.

SANTARÉM: Founded in 10 BC by Iberian King Abidis; taken from the Moors in 1147 by Afonso Henriques, Santarém was once the royal residence. This busy little district capital is now the center of bull breeding for Portugal's bullfighting season. The Igreja de São João de Alporão (Rua Serpa Pinto) serves as an archaeological museum with a diverse assortment of Arabian and Romanesque objects, sculpture, coats of arms, and the Flamboyant Gothic tomb of the Count of Viana. The 14th-century Gothic Igreja da Graça has a particularly attractive interior, but permission for entry must be obtained from the Turismo (the local tourist office), on the Rua Capelo.

En Route from Santarém – Cross the Tagus River on N368 for Alpiarça in order to visit the lovely *Museu Casa dos Patudos,* former residence of José Relvas, statesman and art patron. The collection includes 17th- and 19th-century tapestries and carpets, china, paintings, and furnishings. Follow N118 to N243, recrossing the Tagus to N365. Turn onto N113 for the 35 miles (56 km) to Tomar.

TOMAR: Founded by the Order of the Templars on the River Nabão, this town is crowned by the magnificent Convento de Cristo. The Templars started building the fortified castle and convent in 1160 but construction was not completed until the 17th century. This beautiful monument combines several styles of architecture with the Salamancan entrance, the rotunda modeled after the Holy Sepulcher in Jerusalem, the Italian Renaissance cloister, and the fanciful Manueline window seen from an upper terrace of the Cloister Santa Barbara. Halfway down the hill from the convento, there is a good view from the plaza of the Renaissance Capela de Nossa Senhora da Conceicão. The 15th-century Igreja de São João Baptista (Praça República) has a Manueline belfry and a notable interior. Tomar has a lovely city garden with a lagoon for boating and an old water mill.

En Route from Tomar – The village of Abrantes has a ruined castle-fortress with a splendid view from its belvedere.

CASTELO DE VIDE: This is an appealing spa town of prehistoric origins with whitewashed houses and winding alleys. Because of the supposedly wondrous quality of the waters and the lack of intense heat, it is popular with tourists. The Castelo, rebuilt in 1299 and restored in 1710, provides a marvelous view from its keep. The old Judiaria (Jewish) quarter has many houses with interesting Gothic doorways, and there are numerous charming 17th- and 18th-century buildings.

MARVÃO: Firmly established atop a rough hill sits the medieval village of Marvão, a stronghold fought over during the civil war of 1828–34. Follow signs to Marvão-Beria, wending up the steep incline to the rampart gateway. Either park outside the walls or drive to Pillory Square. Walk to the summit, enter through four gateways, and climb the stairs to the parapets leading to the castle keep. *Pousada de Santa Maria* is a simple friendly inn with a dining room overlooking a panorama of mountains and the Spanish border.

PORTALEGRE: Once a center of tapestry manufacturing and silk production, the 17th- and 18th-century mansions of this attractive town attest to past prosperity. Notable buildings include the cathedral, Largo da Sé, and the tapestry workshops in the old Jesuit monastery (Rua Fernandes).

ELVAS: The great Aqueduto da Amoreira joins the impressive ramparts of this old village and carries water to the inhabitants as it has since the 15th century. Turn into the viaduct gateway and proceed to the mosaic tile, tree-lined Praça da República. Walking around this area, you can see the Igreja de Nossa Senhora da Assuncão with its imposing marble chancel, the tile-faced Igreja Nossa Senhora da Consolação, and the castle in the northwest corner of the ramparts, which dates from Moorish times. The military bastion of Forte de Nossa Senhora da Graça on a hill north of the town and the Forte de Santa Luzia to the south complete the fortifications.

ESTREMOZ: This old hilltop village of red-roofed white houses rises from the plains. The ancient cobbled streets, 13th-century keep, tiled castle chapel, 17th-century walls, and Igreja Santa Maria's collection of primitive paintings are of greatest interest. The village is a fine place for an evening walk.

The artisans of Estremoz, a well-known pottery center since the 16th century, are especially recognized for their unusual pottery figurines depicting people and their animals in scenes of everyday life. You'll also see beautiful objects made of marble from the local quarries.

EVORA: This town is one of the oldest settlements of the Iberian Peninsula. Follow the "centro" signs and park on the Praça do Giraldo or continue on to the *Pousada dos Lóios* and park there. The 2nd-century Templo Romano is one of the few reminders of the Roman past in Portugal. Evora was a center of learning in the 15th century. Its old university — now a public high school — has an *aula magna* (large assembly hall) entirely covered with 17th-century tiles. The Sé (Cathedral) is particularly interesting for its variety of architectural styles and adornments and for the contents of the treasury. This rich collection includes ecclesiastical objects and old illuminated books and manuscripts. The *Museu Regional,* adjacent to the Sé in a former 16th-century episcopal palace, houses ancient sculpture and primitive paintings. The venerated 16th-century Igreja de São Francisco on Praça 28 de Maio, built in the Gothic Manueline style, has a chapel constructed of bones. This oddity was conceived by a Franciscan monk as an incentive for his fellow brothers to meditate on the transitory nature of life. *Cozinha de Sto. Humberto* is a good restaurant.

En Route from Évora – From here you can complete the circle by returning to Lisbon or heading south for the Algarve. If you are returning to Lisbon, go via Setubal to Palmela and Sesimbra for visits to their three castles, for swimming and deep-sea fishing, and for splendid views from the Arrabida Mountains. The entire Arrabida Peninsula once belonged to the dukes of Palmela, but it is now a national park. Its flora is unique in Europe, comparable to Corsica and the Ardennes.

SETUBAL: For centuries an important commercial port, Setubal sits at the mouth of the Sado River, which is noted for its extensive beds of giant oysters. The *Castelo de São Filipe* (see *Best en Route*), built during Spanish domination, sits above the city and is now a fine *pousada.*

Just across the water and easily reached by car ferry or hovercraft is the Troia Peninsula with 20 miles of fine sand beaches for swimming, surfing, and skin diving. A tourist complex with hotels, nightclubs, modern shops, and a golf course bustles, but doesn't intrude upon upon what Hans Christian Andersen once called "a terrestrial paradise". The Troia Peninsula is steeped in history and legend — ruins of a Roman fish factory and chapel have been excavated.

PALMELA: Located 6 miles (10 km) above Setubal in a region famous for its Muscatel wines, Palmela has a royal residence and a 12th-century fortress, recently transformed into a splendid 25-room *pousada.*

SESIMBRA: At the southern foothills of the Arrabida Mountains facing south on a wide bay lies Sesimbra, an old fishing village with the amenities of a modern tourist resort. Unfortunately, unbridled development has destroyed much of the fishing village ambience, and summers are very crowded. There are very good fish restaurants, however, which specialize in grilled red mullet, sea bass, and sardines. If you prefer to catch your own dinner, rent a boat with a professional guide at the docks. The ruins of Sesimbra Castle, overlooking the town, were once a Moorish stronghold.

En Route from Sesimbra – Stop off in Vila Fresca de Azeitão, home of Lancers rosé wines and, more importantly for wine buffs, the home of one of Europe's finest sweet dessert wines — Fonseca's Setubal Muscatel. You can sample both at the Lancers rosé winery and at the company's old wine cellars down the road where Setubal Muscatels are aged.

BEST EN ROUTE

Expect to pay $85 and up per night for a double room in a hotel in the expensive category, $55 to $75 in the moderate, and 40 and under in the inexpensive category. A dinner for two people with local wine will cost $40 and up in the expensive range, about $30 in the moderate, and $20 in the inexpensive range. Prices do not include drinks or tips.

SANTARÉM

Alcaide-Mór – This restaurant has pleasant food and atmosphere at the right price. 26 Rua Luis de Camoes (phone: 23117). Inexpensive.

TOMAR

Pousada de São Pedro – Overlooking Portugal's largest reservoir, this quiet inn has 15 rooms, a dining room with views of the dam and Zêzere River. Castelo do Bode, on N358 (phone: 049-381175). Moderate.

Templários – On landscaped grounds next to a river park, this modern hotel with small town tranquility has 84 air conditioned rooms with balconies, swimming pool, tennis, very good food, and a bar. Reserve odd-numbered rooms for fabulous evening views. 1 Largo Cândido dos Reis (phone: 049-312121). Moderate.

MARVÃO

Pousada de Santa Maria – On a mountainside in an ancient walled town, this inn has 9 small, neat rooms, country decor, and a dining room offering wide views, simple regional cooking, and a bar. Marvão (phone: 93201). Moderate.

ELVAS

Pousada de Santa Luzia – Just off the main road stands this attractive air conditioned inn with 11 rooms and an inviting dining room serving fine regional and international cuisine; bar. Av. de Badajoz, on N4 (phone: 62128). Moderate.

ESTREMOZ

Pousada da Rainha Santa Isabel – In a medieval palace in the old town, this grand luxury hotel has 23 large rooms with spectacular views and canopied beds, a lofty dining room with excellent regional food, a bar, chapel, and an inner patio. Largo Dom Diniz (phone: 068-22618). Expensive.

ÉVORA

Pousada dos Lóios – This elegantly restored convent still has many original details and 28 compact, attractively furnished rooms. The dining room built around the cloister serves regional food prepared according to old convent recipes. There's also a breakfast room and a bar. Largo Conde de Vila Flor (phone: 24051). Expensive.

BEJA

Luís da Rocha – A busy but simple restaurant that serves decent food at modest prices. 63 Rua Capitão João Francisco de Sousa. Inexpensive.

SETÚBAL

Pousada de São Filipe – Built within old castle walls, this rustically furnished inn has 15 rooms, a dining room serving regional specialties, and a bar. Setúbal (phone: 23844). Expensive.

Caranguejus – This bright, modern restaurant specializes in seafood. Closed Mondays. 62A Av. Alexandre Herculano (phone: 29263). Inexpensive.

PALMELA

Pousada de Palmela – In an imposing 12th-century castle that stands on the crest of a high hill, this flagship of the state-owned *pousada* chain has 27 air conditioned rooms, each with a spectacular view of the sea and the countryside. There is a fine restaurant, serving excellent game dishes, and a bar. 2950 Palmela (phone: 01-235-1395). Expensive.

SESIMBRA

Espadarte – A 79-room hotel right on the beach, convenient for fishing. Esplanada Comandante Tenreiro (phone: 223-3189). Moderate.

Do Mar – Built into the side of the hill overlooking the sea, there are 120 rooms with private baths and balconies, a commanding view, plus a swimming pool, bars, a disco, and other comforts. 10 Rua General Humberto Delgado (phone: 065-223-3326). Moderate.

The Algarve

The Algarve has been a favorite holiday area with Europeans for many years. Beach-loving Americans recently have begun vacationing on the southern coast of Portugal. Fine sandy beaches, edged by gigantic sandstone cliffs, offer long stretches of untrammeled shore, as well as tiny hidden coves. Strung along the coast are luxury hotels and attractive first and second class establishments. But the Algarve has not suffered from uninhibited development; in addition to the resort complexes there are small fishing villages and simple residential areas.

The best of many worlds is available in the Algarve, from sophisticated nightlife to seaside solitude. The sports enthusiast will find excellent facilities for tennis, golf, riding, fishing, water skiing, windsurfing, and boating. Shoppers will find a wide selection of fine handcrafted articles — pottery, embroidery, knitwear, and jewelry. Festivals take place throughout the year. There are many excellent restaurants that serve seafood and regional specialties as well as international cuisine.

The best time to visit the Algarve is from the end of January, when the almond trees are in blossom, through the summer until the end of October. But the Algarve is really a year-round resort, as the weather is never very cold by European standards.

The route traced below follows the coast from Vila Real de Santo António in the east to Cabo de São Vincente in the west along N125 for a distance of some 100 miles (160 km). The two-lane road is not a coastal route — in order to reach the beach resorts turn off at the sign for each destination. Although little byways sometimes lead from one beach settlement to another, they are often poorly marked and surfaced.

The most interesting features of the Algarve lie west of Portimão. Here the landscape softens into tree-covered rolling hills with small farms. You pass little painted donkey carts on the road and catch glimpses of the sea. As you approach the turnoff for Sagres, N268, the terrain becomes more rugged. At this spectacular route's end lies the famous school of Henry the Navigator.

PRAIA DE MONTE GORDO: A long flat stretch of beach and several first class hotels make this town a great place to vacation. The early-14th-century ruined castle of the Knights of Christ is an interesting historical site in Castro Marim, west on N125.6.

TAVIRA: This fishing village is built on both shores of the Rio Séqua. A Greek settlement in 380 BC, the town was later conquered by the Goths and Moors. The foundations of the bridge date from Roman times and there is a ruined 13th-century castle. Thanks to a local council that banned construction that might erode the historic quality of the town, expanded tourism hasn't changed the town's character.

OLHÃO: Founded by fishermen in the 18th century, life in this town of cube-shape white houses revolves around its fish market. Fresh produce and local handicrafts are sold in the market.

FARO: The capital of the Algarve was an important Moorish city, taken by Afonso III in 1249 to end Arab domination in Portugal. The old town, surrounded by ancient houses and parts of the defensive walls, has two museums and the Sé (on Largo de Sé), the interior of which is decorated with 17th-century tiles. In the *Ethnological Museum,* an English-speaking guide gives explanations of the historical and folkloric displays. The *Museu Maritimo,* in the old office of the captain of the port on the Doca (marina), exhibits model ships and fishing boats. If possible, take a boat excursion through the Ria Formosa marshlands of Faro, where a guide will point out fiddler crabs, egrets, storks, and other beach denizens. Day trips include bird watching and lunch on Ilha de Faro, an island beach.

LOULÉ: High in the hills above Faro, this little center of handicrafts is a good place to shop for pottery, brassware, copper, basketry, and so on. A market in the center of town (open mornings, except Sunday), has tackier items than in recent years (i.e., Rambo dolls), but unbelievable bargains are still available.

ALMANSIL–VALE DO LOBO: This lovely recreation area surrounds one of the Algarve's most illustrious resort hotels, *Dona Filipa* (see *Best en Route*). There's also a well-designed residential area. *La Réserve* is a good place to dine.

QUARTEIRA: Once a quiet fishing village, this is now a busy, fast-growing resort town with a superb beach.

VILAMOURA: This highly developed vacation and tourist center stretches from the sea to N125. Vilamoura has a large yacht marina and an excellent golf course.

ALBUFEIRA: Called the St.-Tropez of the Algarve, this large resort town has a Moorish ambience that belies its diverse resort activities and sophisticated nightlife. The last town to be taken from the Moors in 1250, there is nothing left here of historical value but it is pleasing to walk around town or watch the return of the fishing boats and explore the caves and grottoes along the beach. There's good shopping for handicrafts and antiques.

ARMAÇÃO DE PERA: This old fishing village lies between sandstone cliffs. You can take boat excursions to the caves and grottoes along the shore.

LAGOA: A typical Algarvean market town, founded in the 15th century on the site of a much earlier Roman settlement. Shopping is the highlight at this crafts center; you can also visit the Lagoa winery. *Toji* is an inviting hilltop restaurant with a spectacular view of the sea.

SILVES: This ancient hill town was once the Moorish capital of the Algarve. All that remains of that time is the impressive, restored castle-fortress. The parapets command a panoramic view, and in the evenings the lighted battlements are a memorable sight. The 13th-century Gothic cathedral, the Sé, contains the remains of a Moorish mosque and tombs presumed to be those of Crusader soldiers.

PORTIMÃO: The largest fishing town on the Algarve has lots of activity, many tourists, and heavy traffic. The approach to the port from the bridge across the Arade River opens up a captivating view of the bay with its boats and quays. The town itself is pleasant for walking and there are many good shops on the Rua Santa Isabel and the Rua do Comércio. Just southeast, before crossing the bridge, is the seaside village of Ferragudo, a small fishing hamlet with a ruined 16th-century castle. There are several luxury hotels along the beach in Praia da Rocha and Praia dos Três Irmãos. For the best in golfing, head to the fine *Penina Golf Hotel* in Penina (see *Best en Route*).

LAGOS: Founded by the Carthaginians in 350 BC, this is the most attractive harbor town in the Algarve. The walls around the old section are traces of Roman occupation. From this port, the caravels of Henry the Navigator embarked on many voyages of exploration and discovery. The 17th-century Forte do Pau da Bandeira still dominates the harbor. The chapel of Igreja de Santo António on Rua General Alberto da Silveira has a baroque interior with much gilded statuary and a painted trompe l'oeil ceiling. Adjacent to the chapel is a museum containing extensive folkloric and archaeological exhibits and sacred art. The Igreja São Sabastião (Rua Conselheiro J. Machado) has some features of artistic merit including a Renaissance door and tiled walls. Shops sell antiques, brass and copperware, and embroidery. For excellent dining try the distinctively decorated *Pousada do Infante* (see *Best en Route*).

Stop off at Ponta da Piedade, a colorful site of caves, beach, and sea, west of town.

En Route from Lagos – The landscape from Lagos to Sagres on N125 becomes grandly severe, supporting a handful of tiny villages ending abruptly at Vila do Bispo. Turn left onto N268 for a few kilometers; you'll come to a right turn leading to the lighthouse overlooking Cabo de São Vicente — allegedly the landing place of the boat containing the martyred body of St. Vincent.

SAGRES: On this windy, solitary headland, Prince Henry established a navigation school in the 15th century, which enabled the Portuguese to maintain naval supremacy for almost 2 centuries. The old school building and residence is now a hostel. From the clifftops, you can do some challenging fishing or watch the boats as they trawl the deep for a rich variety of fish. The area is a very dramatic land's end.

BEST EN ROUTE

Expect to pay $160 and up per night for a double room in a hotel in the expensive category, $65 to $85 in the moderate, and $40 to $50 in the inexpensive category. A dinner for two people with local wine will cost $70 and up in the expensive range, about $30 to $70 in the moderate, and under $30 in the inexpensive range. Prices do not include drinks, wine, or tips. Note that for accomodations in July in August, it is advisable to book well in advance.

MONTE GORDO

Alcazar – An attractive, modern, air conditioned hotel with 95 rooms, a restaurant, bar, and pool. Rua de Ceuta (phone: 42181, 42141). Moderate.

Vasco da Gama – This comfortable beach hotel has 182 rooms and suites, a spacious restaurant, bars, a pool, and tennis. Av. Infante Dom Henrique (phone: 44321). Moderate.

TAVIRA

Eurotel Tavira – In a beautiful setting with a sea view, this hotel is one of the best in the eastern Algarve. It offers 80 rooms, a dining room, and its own pool and sports facilities. Quinta das Oliveiras, 2 miles (3 km) east of town (phone: 081-56218). Moderate.

SÃO BRAZ DE ALPORTEL

Pousada de São Braz – This inn in the hills north of Faro has 21 rooms, a dining room, and bar. São Braz de Alportel (phone: 42305). Moderate.

FARO

Eva – On the marina, this popular modern hotel has 150 air conditioned rooms, a top-floor dining room, rooftop terraced swimming pool, nightclub, and bars. The hotel runs a courtesy bus service to the beach. Av. da República (phone: 24054). Moderate.

Cidade Velha – Discreetly elegant, this restaurant is in the old walled city. Excellent Portuguese and international cooking (phone: 27145). Expensive.

Casa de Lumena – This attractive former family mansion has outdoor patio dining and a varied Portuguese menu. Reservations advised. 27 Praça Alexandre Herculano (phone: 22028). Moderate.

Roque – Popular with the locals for its fresh sea fare and low prices, it is on the Ilha de Faro, a short drive from town on the airport road and then across a long, low bridge. The restaurant faces the beach on the marshland side of the island, with a large outdoor dining area. Closed Wednesdays in winter. Ilha de Faro (phone: 089-817868). Inexpensive.

ALMANSIL–VALE DO LOBO

Dona Filipa – This superbly run and maintained hotel overlooking the beach has 129 attractive air conditioned rooms with large balconies, a terrace with pool, and tennis courts. The dining room has fine continental cuisine and excellent service. A buffet lunch is served in a terrace area. There's a lively bar, an inner patio, and a golf course next to the hotel. Make reservations well in advance. Vale do Lobo (phone: 94141). Expensive.

O Elegante – On the waterfront, this restaurant offers first class Portuguese food. Closed Tuesdays. Reservations. Av. Infante de Sagres (phone: 65339). Expensive.

Isidoro – A spacious dining room done in nautical decor, overlooking the sea, that serves good seafood and regional dishes. Av. Infante de Sagres (phone: 65219). Moderate.

VILAMOURA

Dom Pedro – Close to the beach, this attractive modern hotel has 260 air conditioned rooms with balconies, a swimming pool, tennis, golf course, and a bar. Vilamoura (phone: 35410, 35420, 35430, or 35440). Expensive.

Vilamoura-Boliqueime – This extensive resort complex includes 40 villas, 52 hotel rooms and suites, a restaurant, bars, shops, and a spacious pool. In town (phone: 32321). Moderate.

ALBUFEIRA

Balaia – Surrounded by green lawns on a cliff overlooking the beach, this nicely designed modern hotel has 193 rooms with balconies, 12 family villas, an inviting dining room, a luncheon terrace, bar, a large swimming pool, and boutiques. Praia Maria Luisa (phone: 52681). Expensive.

A Ruína – On the edge of Fishermen's Beach in an old building, this restaurant has very fresh fish and a terrace bar with a marvelous view. Rua Cais Herculano (phone: 089-52094). Moderate.

Borda d'Água – A few kilometers east of Albufeira, this attractive complex of restaurants overlooking the beach serves excellent seafood and continental dishes. Closed Mondays. Reservations recommended. Open June-September. Praia da Oura (phone: 52045). Moderate.

ARMAÇÃO DE PERA

Vilalara – Just a mile west of town, this luxurious resort village has 65 beautifully furnished apartments and villas, appealing indoor and outdoor restaurants, pool, tennis, bar, and private beach. Armação de Pera (phone: 32333). Expensive.

Garbe – This first class, clifftop hotel has 103 rooms and suites, and a dining room and terraced pool overlooking the beach, also a bar and shops. Av. Marginal (phone: 32194 or 32195). Moderate.

PORTIMÃO

Old Tavern – Good English and continental dishes are served in an old Portuguese atmosphere. Closed Saturdays. Reservations advised. 43 Rua Júdice Fialho (phone: 23325). Moderate.

PRAIA DA ROCHA

Algarve – This establishment has a Moorish-inspired modern decor and furnishings, 219 air conditioned rooms and suites, and a giant pool set amid green lawns and gardens. There's also an intimate grill room and bar, and a dining room with a sea view; nightclub and shops. Probably the best first class hotel buy in the Algarve. Av. Tomás Cabreira (phone: 24001). Expensive.

PRAIA DOS TRÊS IRMÃOS

Alvor Praia – In a spectacular beach setting, this hotel has 201 attractive air conditioned rooms and suites. The sparkling split-level dining room has an international menu and an outdoor buffet lunch. There's also a large pool, tennis, fishing, excursion boat, shops, bar, and a nightclub. Praia dos Três Irmãos (phone: 24021). Expensive.

PENINA

Golf da Penina – One of Europe's best golf resorts, the 27-hole championship course was designed by Henry Cotton. Facilities include a driving range, tennis courts, and a huge pool with sun decks and bar. There are 202 air conditioned rooms and suites, nicely decorated lounges, dining room, grill room, and bar with dancing. Penina Portimão (phone: 22051). Expensive.

LAGOS

Lagos – Regular buses take guests to the beach at this first class, 273-room hotel with a fine restaurant. Rua Nova da Aldeia (phone: 62011). Moderate.

Alpendre – This well-staffed first class restaurant has an extensive menu, including local specialties, and an impressive wine list. Closed Wednesdays. Reservations advised. 17 Rua António Barbosa Viana (phone: 082-62705). Moderate.

Lagosteira – Under the same management as *Alpendre*, this eatery specializes in seafood. Closed Tuesdays. Reservations recommended. 26 Rua 1 de Maio (phone: 62486). Moderate.

SAGRES

Pousada do Infante – On the cliffs with an incredible view, this attractive inn has 33 rooms, a dining room with a sea view, and a terrace. In town (phone: 082-64222). Expensive.

Baleeira – A simple, comfortable hotel that is extremely popular because of its prime seaside location; its 120 rooms look out on the sea. There is a saltwater pool, a bar, and a pleasant dining room with smashing views. It also has its own tennis court and bikes for hire. In town (phone: 082-64212). Moderate.

Tasca – This fishermen's restaurant serves good seafood, regional dishes, fresh salads, and has a good wine list. Guests staying at the nearby *Baleeira* receive a 10% discount upon presentation of their check-in card. Closed Saturdays from mid-January to mid-February. In town (phone: 082-64177). Inexpensive.

Romania

Romania is an Eastern European country of some 91,700 square miles bordered by the Soviet Union to the north, the Black Sea to the east, Hungary and Yugoslavia to the west, and Bulgaria to the south. Its population is almost 23 million (Romania has the highest growth rate in Eastern Europe), of which the largest concentration (2.2 million) is in the capital city of Bucharest.

There are three major historic and geographic areas in Romania. Wallachia is on the flat Danube plain in the south. The Danube itself is a natural southern border with Bulgaria, and historically the river brought trade and culture to the valley from the west. Bucharest sprang up here as a major center of government and industry. The Danube flows into the Black Sea and below the river delta there stretches the only Romanian seacoast, primarily a resort area with many beaches. There is a major seaport at Constanţa.

North of the Danube plain the country is fairly mountainous. Transylvania is encompassed by the Carpathian Mountains, crossing the country's center from north to southwest. The area has had a turbulent history of being overrun, from time to time, by various hordes — the Germanic and Magyar from the west and the Ottoman from the south. At present, there is a large Hungarian population (2 million) and remnants of a German minority depleted by postwar emigration.

The northeastern sector of the country is known as Moldavia. It wasn't until 1859 that the principalities of Wallachia and Moldavia were united as a state, and only in 1878 were they free of Ottoman control. As Transylvania still belonged to Hungary, complete unification had to wait until the break-up of the Habsburg Empire at the end of World War I. Romania's inter-war years were stormy. Then, under a Fascist regime, the country entered World War II on the side of Nazi Germany, but in 1944 the government was overthrown and the new leaders pledged allegiance to the Allies. Today, Communist Romania is a Soviet ally, despite its somewhat maverick foreign policy. Romanians claim to be descended from Latin-speaking Daco-Romans, and the Romanian language is a Romance tongue, akin to French and Italian.

The first route in Romania starts with a tour through Bucharest, the spacious and leisurely capital city with parks and lakes, and then takes you north to Braşov, a well-preserved medieval city in Transylvania. The second route is a tour of the famous monasteries of the Bukovina, a small area near the Soviet frontier and the historic seat of the Moldavian monarchy. These folk churches, adorned with dazzling 16th-century wall paintings and nestled in isolated valleys, are not easy to reach. But their unique beauty rewards those who seek them out.

Travel in Romania during the winter months can be very uncomfortable because of lack of food and energy shortages (resulting both in underheated rooms and in the undependable availability of gasoline). The two luxury hotels in the capital, the *Inter-Continental* and the *Bucureşti,* are always well heated and their restaurants are fine at any time of the year, but they are very expensive, partly as a result of the inflated value of the Romanian lei against western currencies.

Bucharest and Braşov:
From Wallachia to Transylvania

This isn't so much a road tour as it is a visit to two urban centers, Bucharest for its own merits and Braşov not only for itself but also as a base for sightseeing. The two cities are separated by about 105 miles (168 km) of good road, which passes through countryside in transition. By the roadside there are endless groups of athletes in fashionable warm-up suits (there's a long list of famous Romanian sports heroes from Nadia Comăneci to Ilie Nastase, and the whole country is very sports conscious), but in the more rural areas you can still see groups of women laundering the week's wash in the streams. There are also cows, water buffalos, herds of geese, and sheep tended by lonely shepherds wrapped down to their ankles in wool cloaks. Handmade clothes with beautiful embroidery can be bought from roadside vendors. Drive carefully, especially at night, because roads are crowded with animals, Gypsy wagons, and people walking to work. Chronic gas shortages lead to endless lines at those pumps that are working, but foreigners (who must buy gas coupons at the border or in hotels) can jump the queue. Take care not to let the tank run low, or you may end up stranded.

Bucharest is a flat and friendly city on the northern Danube plain, but as you drive north to Braşov you ascend the Carpathian Mountains of Transylvania, where the skiing is good and the winter resorts are plentiful.

BUCHAREST: Bucharest is a city of wide streets, spacious parks, and leisurely walks down tree-lined and flowered boulevards. There aren't very big crowds of sightseers anywhere because there aren't any really world-renowned sights to see, but the city does offer a mix of Old World Eastern flavor with that of a modern Communist state. The nightlife in Bucharest isn't very exciting, but there are some nightclubs, an opera, theater, evening shows of the Romanian State Circus, a surviving Yiddish Theater, and lots of old American movies. During the daytime, the city is a bustling combination of stouthearted shoppers — braving the usual shortages — and relaxing lakeside cafés. For a city on the same latitude as Detroit there is an amazing amount of vegetation, and it's all well cared for.

The city as it stands today is only about 500 years old, but the area was a population center since the Stone Age. Originally called the Dímboviţa Citadel, it was renamed Bucharest in 1459 by none other than Vlad the Impaler, more universally known as Dracula, who actually did do much toward unifying his country. There are grand buildings from the days when Bucharest strove to become the Paris of the Balkans, beautiful old Romanian Orthodox churches, and some charming villa districts that survived both the 1977 earthquake and ongoing urban renewal projects.

Impossible to overlook is the brand-new Victory of Socialism Boulevard, which leads to a monumental Civic Center comprising the Communist Party headquarters and other government offices. Be sure to visit the seat of the Romanian Orthodox Patriarchate, the Basilica Patriarhiei, which is rumored to be slated for demolition — like so many other churches and synagogues in the area — to make way for more official buildings.

The nicest walk in town is out to the lakeside Herăstrău Park on the north side site of the extraordinary *Village and Folk Art Museum,* a sprawling collection of representative peasant households from all over the country. From the cafés in the park you can watch small boats and sailing yawls cross the lake against the green backdrop of poplar-lined banks. Several times a year international festivals are held here.

The nicest trip out of town is 9 miles (14 km) through the northwestern parks and forests to the elegant *Mogoşoaia Palace* (1702) of Prince Constantin Brâncoveanu. Now a museum of medieval art and artifacts, the building itself overshadows its contents. A formal structure, it is built on the scale of a Venetian palazzo with ornately arched colonnades, a stately, close-cropped garden, and a quiet reflecting pond.

A starchy dish found here is *mamaligă,* a cornmeal affair that conjures up a crossbreeding of mush and home fries. Try it. It is, after all, the national dish, but it has become almost impossible to find in restaurants. *Brínza* is a white cottage-cheesy item, and *ciorbă* is a national soup that comes in many colors and flavors. The Romanians are most at home with fish dishes, and if you stick to carp and sturgeon you can't go wrong. If you want meat, the *mititei* (skinless sausages blistered over an open fire with a flavor that will keep you alert) are the best bet.

The Romanian wine industry is in a rebuilding phase and the local vintages are noted for having great potential. *Cotnari* is a very good white wine generally served after the main course and it vies with *tuica,* a plum brandy, as the popular evening drink. The Carpaţi-Bucureşti National Tourist Office is at 7 Magheru Bd. (phone: 145160).

BRAŞOV: From Bucharest, drive north on Route 1 (E15) to this early medieval city at the foot of Mt. Tímpa in the Carpathians. The road takes you along the Prahova and Timis river valleys and passes through old Dacian settlements (founded as early as 70 BC) that are now winter ski spas. Braşov is a red-roofed town with winding streets, small squares, and a cable car ride up the mountainside that lets you absorb all the views. When it was known as Kronstadt, Braşov was a prosperous trading center inhabited by Transylvanian Saxons, Protestant merchants who had emigrated from German lands. It's now one of the nation's chief industrial centers, but you wouldn't guess it after a walk through the old town. Behind an imposing Gothic façade, the Black Church houses, unexpectedly, a collection of Oriental rugs, and the *Casa Sfatului,* or *Council Hall* (now a museum of the region) dates from 1420; the large square that surrounds it (23 Piaţa August) has been cleared of parked buses and repaved, making it an inviting pedestrian hub.

The best day trip from Braşov is up into the Carpathian Mountains to the resort town of Poiana Braşov and Bran Castle. Bran is mistakenly touted as Dracula's home base, but in truth Vlad only occasionally vacationed there (generally depending on how much of a lead he had on his pursuers). Still, the hilltop castle is worthy of a visit, with its thick, fortified walls, dramatic peaked towers, and clammy, narrow passageways. Poiana Braşov ("Sunny Glade") is a wonderful stop for summer hikes or winter skiing and skating. The restaurants here feature hot, homemade dishes cooked over open fires.

Sibiu, 89 miles (143 km) west of Braşov, and Cluj-Napoca, double that distance to the northwest, are two other must-see Transylvanian cities. The former has, like Braşov, a German character, and the latter, a Hungarian one. In between are numerous picturesque towns and villages, some of which are known for their fortified medieval churches.

BEST EN ROUTE

Expect to pay anywhere between $90 and $120 per night for a double in hotels we've listed as expensive, between $30 and $75 for those in the moderate category. Meals are a much better deal. Most restaurants charge about $12 for even the most lavish, three-course extravaganza for two; for a restaurant we've listed as moderate, expect to pay between $6 and $8. Be aware, though, that unless you travel in summer, the choice of dishes will be severely limited. Prices do not include drinks, wine, or tips.

BUCHAREST

Athénée Palace – Once grand, now merely atmospheric. There are 2 restaurants (one featuring musical entertainment) and a good take-out pastry shop in the lobby. 1-3 Episcopiei Str. (phone: 140899). Expensive.

Bucureşti – In the center of Bucharest, this deluxe 850-bed hotel is the city's newest. Along with 2 restaurants, it boasts 2 swimming pools, a sauna, and a gym. 63-69 Calea Victoriei (phone: 154580, 154640, or 142401). Expensive.

Inter-Continental Bucharest – This is the kind of centrally located hotel that tries to offer you everything in one place. There are at least *three* of everything here — restaurants, bars, conference halls. There's also a swimming pool and sauna. 4 N. Bălcescu Bd. (phone: 137040 or 140400). Expensive.

Lebăda – A new hotel with conference facilities, tennis courts, and a bowling alley. It's on the site of a recently razed monastery on an island in Lake Pantelimon. Hwy. 3, near the eastern edge of the city (phone: 243000). Expensive.

Hanul Manuc – A former inn (*han*), now a hotel with old-fashioned charm, this city landmark has a popular restaurant with live music. 62 30 Decembrie Str. (phone: 131415). Moderate.

Capşa – This old intellectuals' meeting place has excellent food. If you don't want to try the local specialties you can opt for continental mainstays. The desserts are special. 1 Edgar Quinet Str. (phone: 134482). Expensive to moderate.

Pescăruş – This beautiful terrace restaurant overlooking the lake serves international cuisine. You can eat at your leisure and watch the boats. It's a bit overpriced but still affordable. Herăstrău Park (phone: 16-30-95). Moderate.

BRAŞOV

Carpaţi – The hotel of choice in Braşov. It's very fancy, with big comfortable rooms and a well-supplied restaurant. 9 Gheorghe Gheorghiu-Dej Bd. (phone: 42840). Hotel: expensive; restaurant: moderate.

Cerbul Carpatin – This many-roomed establishment offers well-heeled residents and tourists grilled meat platters, good wine, and a "folklore" floor show as well as music and dancing. 14 Piaţa 23 August (phone: 43981 or 42840). Moderate.

Orient – There's a café on the left (where for a fixed price you get the best cup of coffee in town along with a cold drink and a pastry) and a teahouse on the right. It opened in 1987, but the lovely decor has a turn-of-the-century feel. Don't miss it. Strada Republicii, a main shopping street off Piaţa 23 August (no phone). Moderate.

POIANA BRAŞOV

Sura Dacilor – This restaurant, which looks much older than it is, is surrounded by grassy mountain walks at a Transylvanian ski/summer resort. The pleasing aroma from the kitchen will whet even the most reluctant appetite. In the middle of town (no phone). Moderate.

The Moldavian Monasteries: Bukovina

Bukovina is a small tract of land in the northern Carpathian foothills that gradually rise from the Siret River valley farther north and east. The area, in the northeast corner of Romania, is a Moldavian reservation of beautiful mountain scenery with knobby, green-carpeted hills spotted with dense fir stands. The Moldavians still sport their traditional dress whites, and the almost total lack of English-speaking people (except for tour guides) makes a trip here adventurous. Bukovina is not heavily visited and is not really convenient to any place that is. There's minimal nightlife, few wines of distinction, and travelers are advised to bring along extra canisters of gasoline and food supplies. The five churches and monasteries here, with exterior walls covered by frescoes, are like no other structures in the world.

The buildings are all relatively simple and took months rather than generations to build. They are, however, the epitome of folk architecture, built to an unwieldy and large scale that makes them look from a distance like squat, one-story bungalows. It is only when you approach them that you realize how enormous they are. They have few windows and are covered by peaked-cap roofs that descend steeply and then suddenly bow out, creating wide eaves over thick walls, the outsides of which are covered with artwork. Virtually every façade is bathed in color with frescoes illustrating the Bible, classical philosophy, and local folklore — a historic library of pictograms.

Moldavian history's medieval golden era was overseen by its greatest monarch, Stephen the Great, who, though he never rated a title higher than prince, reigned from 1457 to 1504. Because of the turbulence of the times and the violence of the populace, the length of Stephen's reign was unheard of (and even today ranks with Joe DiMaggio's 56 consecutive, safely hit-in games as a feat of longevity). He was a master tactician who encouraged cultural pursuits, and all the churches were built during his era or shortly thereafter. He is credited with the development of the Moldavian style, which is a blending of rough-hewn, hand building techniques (that were at the same time structurally primitive and colorfully folksy) with the far more sophisticated architectural concepts of the southern Byzantine and the European Gothic. The frescoes on the church walls served the dual purposes of being a showcase for the area's unified cultural expression and a schoolroom, teaching history and religion to a predominantly illiterate constituency. These priceless frescoes have been preserved outside although exposed to the elements since the mid-1500s. Their colors are so rich and true that the blue on the sides of the Voroneț Church has been given a name of its own, Voroneț blue. Though the art world has many times attempted to copy it, this blue has never been accurately duplicated in its total richness.

It's best to plan your tour with the Romanian Tourist Board in Bucharest, where you can arrange to hire an English-speaking guide, if you like, or just get a good road map of the Bukovina and wander on your own.

If you have a lot of time, sufficient gasoline, and extensive food supplies, consider extending your tour of northern Romania westward to the Maramureş region, near the Soviet border. The villages dotting the hilly green countryside are of special interest to ethnographers; here folk art and traditional customs have been preserved as nowhere else in Europe. Only in Maramureş do so many people wear their handmade folk costumes, not only at festivals and on special occasions, but every day. Friendly villagers may invite visitors into their wooden houses for home-distilled spirits and a glimpse of a way of life that has hardly changed for centuries.

SUCEAVA: This town of 50,000 is the major hub of the area and the jumping-off point for any tour of the monasteries. Suceava is 270 miles (432 km) from Bucharest, and you can cover the distance in 1 hour by plane or 6 hours by train (you can also arrange for a car and driver in Bucharest), or you can drive the distance yourself in a day. This was the seat of Moldavian power from 1388 to 1566, and you can still see the vestiges of the medieval citadel — which was often attacked but never conquered, not even by the Ottoman armies commanded by Mohammed II after they overran Constantinople.

There are several interesting churches in town, but since the rest of the route is predominantly architectural, your time here would be better spent browsing the more secular folkwares — mostly spin-offs of the handmade fabrics and local pottery industries — that the Bukovina is famous for. In the 16th-century *Princely Inn* you'll find the *Folk Art Museum,* with a restoration of the interior of an authentic peasant house and exhibitions of national costumes, dolls, masks, wedding regalia, and carpets (5 Ciprian Porumbescu Str.).

The monasteries are spread out over the 56 miles (90 km) or so directly west of Suceava; to stop at all five, you'd better plan on a day out and a day back. If you want to spend less time, make sure to route yourself carefully so that you don't get lost and find night falling in a town where nobody speaks a language you can understand and it takes you an hour to find out that there aren't any hotels in the vicinity. Most important of all, start out with a full tank of gas. Driving northwest out of Suceava on Route 2, turn left at Milişăuţi and you'll soon come to Arbore, the first of the famous churches.

ARBORE: This is the smallest and the simplest of the churches. Though the interior is only dimly lit, the outside walls are covered with frescoes that tell the story of the Genesis and also depict the lives of the saints. The predominant color here is green, and there are five distinct shades of it that mix with reds, blues, and yellows. In the courtyard there are two stone slabs with fifteen even gouges that the artists used for holding and mixing their paints. The best-preserved works are on the western wall and the buttressing. Unlike most primitive wall painting, there is an abundance of detailing here involving the use of perspective, animated figures, and literal facial expressions.

SUCEVIŢA: Continuing west from Arbore, you come to the town of Solca and turn north through Clit to Marginea. From there it's only another 6 miles (9 km) west to Suceviţa. The monastery here is surrounded by thick stone walls and guarded by five imposing towers. There are more frescoes here than at any of the other churches, and they are everywhere, inside and out, except on the northern wall, where the painter fell off his scaffold and died. (Legend has it that the wall was left blank as a tribute to him.) In addition to the religious paintings, there are also portraits of Sophocles, Plato, and

Aristotle along with more Eastern images from the *Arabian Nights.* The village of Sucevița is one of the most picturesque in all of Romania — the houses' verandas have carved wooden pillars, and townspeople dress in national costumes.

MOLDOVIȚA: About 18 miles (29 km) west of Sucevița on Route 17A is the commune of Vatra Moldoviței, in the shadow of Rarău Mountain. Moldovița has another large monastery in the center of the town. The paintings here have a less religious flavor. The most striking series is of the siege of Constantinople, with detailing that outlines the entire city. There's a museum here where you can see engraved and painted furniture, including Prince Petru Rareș's black ornamental throne. The manicured grounds are neatly laid out with flagstone paths that run from fortification to castle to church.

If you continue south you'll come to the town of Cîmpulung Moldovenesc, where you might consider stopping over before returning east to Suceava on the southern half of the route.

VORONEȚ: Driving east along the Moldova River on Route 17, you pass through the towns of Vama, Molidu, and Frasin, stopping at Gura Humorului (18 mi/30 km from Cîmpulung), where you can go north to the Humor Monastery or south to Voroneț. Voroneț is the most famous and the oldest of the monasteries (1488) and was built by Stephen the Great himself. The paintings here began a style that took from the Byzantine art of the south and mixed with it a more Gothic flavor. The building itself is the most elegant of all these structures, more involved and animated, with rows of repeating pilasters capped by round arches, crenelated friezes, and round windows. The famous blue is breathtaking, and the paintings, especially those of the Last Judgment, are simultaneously humane and barbaric, with pretty women, musicians, and people being torn apart by wild beasts.

HUMOR: Less than 4 miles (6 km) north of Gura Humorului, the Humor Monastery is the last of the churches. It was built in 1530 and is unique in that it has a large open veranda, arched on three sides. It's also interesting to note that in one of the frescoes the devil is portrayed as a woman. From here it's only another 22 miles (35 km) back to Suceava on Route 17.

BEST EN ROUTE

Expect to pay anywhere between $20 and $30 per night for a double in the hotels we've listed below. Meals are a much better deal. Most restaurants charge about $12 for even the most lavish, three-course extravaganza for two. Prices do not include drinks, wine, or tips.

SUCEAVA

Arcașul – You might be a little wary of a place that brags about its parking lot, but if you've just driven 8 hours from Bucharest, you'll find the *Arcașul* is just what you want. Besides comfortable rooms with big, soft beds, it's also got a disco/bar and a good restaurant. 4-6 Mihai Viteazul Str. (phone: 10944).

Căprioara – Just outside town in the Adîncata forest is this rustic restaurant. Beautiful surroundings for some good Moldavian fare of strong goulashes and brandy to wash everything down. 5 miles (8 km) from Suceava.

SUCEVIȚA

Sucevița – Close to the monastery, this first class inn has a restaurant that's small but has great food. The people will make you feel as if you are Prince Stephen's long-lost brother-in-law.

The Black Sea Coast

The Romanian coastline on the Black Sea stretches for about 150 miles from the Danube delta at the Soviet border all the way south to the Bulgarian frontier. Roughly 165 miles (266 km) east of Bucharest, this area can be reached by plane in about half an hour or by train or car in about 3 hours. (You ferry across the Danube at the midpoint in the trip.) Sandy beaches and fancy resorts (the most famous is Mamaia) line the coast; the tideless sea assures delightful swimming. And should you tire of toasting yourself on the Black Sea's strands, you can drive into Constanța for a shot of civilization or cruise into the Danube Delta for a whiff of wilderness.

CONSTANȚA: Romania's main port city occupies the site of the ancient citadel, Tomis, founded by Greek merchants during the 6th century BC. The city is a mix of the early Greek, the Roman (Ovid was exiled here, and the square bearing the poet's name features his pensive statue), and the Byzantine. There's also a mosque here with an Arabian mosaic dome and a lighthouse-like minaret). Part of the sand here is flanked by a hedge and tree line that combines with the ornate façades of the older buildings to give this resort a mellow air.

THE DANUBE DELTA: The 2,500-year-old town of Tulcea is 77 miles (123 km) north of Constanța on Route 22, where the Danube trisects and fans into its delta. The Greeks called the city Aegyssus, and the *Danube Delta Museum,* at 32 Progresului Str., chronicles their coming and going. The town is now the main departure point for tourists who want to take river cruises into the delta to see the nature preserve (tours arranged by the Carpați National Tourist Office, *Delta* hotel, 2 Isaccei Str.). The land is wildly beautiful here: marshes crisscrossed by canals and brooks; islands bristling with rushes and reeds; clumps of trees sheltering otters, foxes, wildcats, and boars. During migratory periods, over 300 species of birds nest in the delta.

BEST EN ROUTE

The hotel and restaurants listed below are moderately priced; that is, accommodations will probably run about $30 per night for a double room, dinner for two people, about $12.

CONSTANȚA

Continental – An adequate downtown hotel that offers a private bath, telephone, and TV set in every room and boasts its own wine cellar. 20 Bd. Republicii (phone: 1-5660).

Casa Cu Lei – This hotel's restaurant is an architectural monument, and each of its dining rooms has a different structural design — Brancovan (a particular Romanian style), Venetian, and Spanish. It's worth having a meal here simply for the atmosphere. 1 Dianei Str. (phone: 17416).

Cazino – An ornate restaurant on the seawall (you can't miss it), with huge, round, arched windows, an eating terrace on a promontory stretching out over the water, and fine food.

San Marino

Every year, more than 3 million tourists visit San Marino, the oldest and smallest republic in the world. You might think that this number would overwhelm the country — considering that it has a population of only 22,000 and an area of only 23 square miles — and to a certain extent it does. At high noon on a midsummer day, it is sometimes hard to see San Marino's quaint charm beyond the droves of daytrippers and the gaudy displays of countless souvenir shops vying for their attention. But if that day is a clear one, look again. From any number of points in San Marino, the panorama embraces not only the Apennines to the south, expansive plains and hills to the north, the brilliant blue Adriatic to the east, but also the Yugoslav coast, 156 miles away. No doubt about it, San Marino's mountaintop setting is spectacular, and it is this, along with interesting historical sites and colorful remnants of the republic's long past, that makes a visit worthwhile.

San Marino lies 11 miles from the Adriatic coast of north-central Italy, bordering the regions of Emilia-Romagna to the north and the Marche (Marches) to the south. Most visitors arrive from the coastal town of Rimini, and as you approach from this direction, the republic's distinctive "skyline" comes into view dramatically: Monte Titano (Mt. Titanus), at a height of 2,470 feet, with its three fortified peaks. The territory of San Marino consists of this mountain, with the capital, San Marino city, on top, and the surrounding hills, scattered with eight small villages or "castles" (*castelli*). The climate is temperate, thanks to its altitude and the ever-present "garbino" wind, with summer temperatures that rarely exceed 80F.

According to tradition, San Marino dates back almost 1,700 years, to AD 301 and the arrival of a Christian stonecutter from Dalmatia named Marinus. Fleeing the religious persecution of the Roman Emperor Diocletian, Marinus sought out the secluded safety of Monte Titano, where he built a chapel and began to live a saintly life. Other Christians soon followed him, giving rise to a free community that very early in its history developed the democratic institutions still governing it today.

San Marino's inaccessibility protected it throughout the period of the downfall of the Roman Empire and the subsequent barbarian invasions. Later, when covetous neighbors did cast eyes in its direction, it struggled valiantly to remain independent. Only twice was it unsuccessful, once in the 16th century, when it was occupied by Cesare Borgia, and again in the 18th century, when Cardinal Giulio Alberoni, legate in Romagna, took it upon himself to annex it to the Papal States. In each case, the loss of liberty lasted only a few months.

Along with its freedom, the country prides itself on a long tradition as a place of asylum. The Italian patriot Giuseppe Garibaldi was one of the most famous figures to have found refuge here, in 1849. During World War II, there were 100,000 refugees within the borders. Sadly, the republic was bombed in 1944, despite its proclaimed neutrality.

San Marino does have a small, picturesque, volunteer army. The blue uniforms, blue and white plumed headgear, and old-fashioned muskets and sabers of the militia and the Guardia del Consiglio Grande e Generale (the latter serves as an honor guard to the country's rulers) can be seen on special occasions. Guardsmen of the Guardia di Rocca, however, are on regular duty at the entrance to the government palace, and their green jackets, red trousers, red and white feathered caps, and vintage pistols are no less decorative.

The economy of the country is based on tourism, light industry, some farming, and the sale of postage stamps, which have considerable philatelic value. While the Italian lira is the local currency in common use, the minting of coins, mainly for collectors, is another source of revenue.

San Marino is accessible by bus, car, and even helicopter. The year-round bus service from Rimini leaves frequently from several stops including the Rimini train station and takes about 45 minutes. Buses arrive in San Marino at either Piazzale della Stazione or Piazzale Marino Calcigni, both within easy walking distance of the walls of the historic center. In summer, a helicopter service connects Rimini with Borgo Maggiore, one of San Marino's *castelli*, from where San Marino city is reachable via a cable car ride. The nearest airports are at Miramare di Rimini (9 miles/14.5 km away) and Forlì (38 miles/61 km away). The nearest train station is in Rimini. Travel by car is scenic on the four-lane highway from Rimini, though you can also reach the border along other well-paved but more sinuous routes. The San Marino Tourist Office, in the centrally located Contrada Omagnano (phone: 0549-992101; closed weekends), produces an excellent free guide, with a section in English, covering everything from cable car timetables to advice on how to cope with an overheated engine in traffic jams on the town's steep and narrow streets.

> **En Route from Rimini** – The border is marked by a banner proclaiming, in Italian, "Welcome to the Ancient Land of Liberty." A passport is not needed to enter, and there is no customs control, despite the customs station.
>
> Within minutes you are in Serravalle, the most populous of the *castelli*. Here there is evidence of industrial growth alongside one of the country's oldest and best-kept castles. Since the bestowal of Serravalle to San Marino in 1463, the republic's territory has not grown by a single inch. Not even Napoleon's offer to extend its borders in 1797 was accepted.
>
> Continuing along the winding road, you will see Domagnano, another of the "castles," to the left before arriving at Borgo Maggiore.

BORGO MAGGIORE: A market town established in the 12th century, and worth a stop. Originally known as Mercatale, its weekly open-air market, held on Thursdays, has been taking place since 1244. The porticoed Piazza di Sopra remains practically unchanged. Just off the main square, Piazza Grande, is one of San Marino's most important museums, the *Museo Postale, Filatelico e Numismatico*. It contains examples of all stamps and coins issued by the republic, along with stamps from other countries. Nearby is the *Museo delle Armi da Fuoco* (*Firearms Museum*), whose collection spans the 14th to the 19th century and includes a section dedicated to Garibaldi. Stop also for a look at the ultramodern Santuario della Beata Vergine della Consolazione (Sanctuary of the Blessed Virgin of Consolation), which was built in the 1960s and contrasts sharply with the town's medieval appearance.

En Route from Borgo Maggiore – From Borgo Maggiore you can reach San Marino by foot along the shortcut called the Costa, by car, or by cable car.

SAN MARINO: Proceed along the highway toward San Marino city and leave the car in one of the several parking areas near the historic center. The old city within the walls is entered through the Porta di San Francesco (St. Francis's Gate), begun in the 14th century as the doorway to a convent. Once inside, to the right, you will see the convent and the small Chiesa di San Francesco, both founded in 1361. Though this is the oldest church in the republic, only its façade gives away its age; much of the original character of the interior was lost in 17th- and 18th-century restorations. The cloister next door houses a gallery of changing exhibitions and a museum with some noteworthy old paintings, including one of St. Francis by Guercino.

From the Porta di San Francesco, San Marino's narrow streets must be explored on foot, and the ascent can be quite steep at times. Via Basilicius leads upward to the tiny Piazzetta del Titano, one of the social centers of the town. Not far off the square, on Contrada Omerelli, is the Palazzo Valloni, a structure partly of the 15th and partly of the 18th century. It houses the state archives, with documents dating from 885, as well as the government library. Until recently, it also contained the *Museo Pinacoteca di Stato,* whose collection of paintings and objects of historical and archaeological interest now await a new home. In the meantime, some of the collection is temporarily displayed in the Chiesa di Santa Chiara, farther along on Contrada Omerelli. The street ends with the Porta della Rupe, the gate through which you enter the city if you take the shortcut from Borgo Maggiore.

To continue the ascent, return to Piazzetta del Titano and take the short walk up the hill to Piazza Garibaldi and the government stamp and coin office (Azienda Autonoma di Stato Filatelica e Numismatica). Then turn and follow Contrada del Collegio up to Piazza della Libertà, the largest and most elegant of San Marino's squares. It takes its name from the 19th-century statue of liberty in the middle, but it's also known as the Pianello, since it's one of the few flat spaces within the walls. Off to the left is the mountain shelf and a spectacular view, while directly in front of you, dominating the square, is the Palazzo Pubblico, or government palace.

Although there has been a public building here since the early 14th century, today's Palazzo Pubblico dates only to the end of the 19th century, but it was built in an old-fashioned neo-Gothic style. If you want to arrive for the changing of the guard, stop at the nearby tourist office on Contrada del Collegio for information on the time. (For a fee, this office will also stamp your passport with an unnecessary, but official, San Marino visa.)

San Marino is governed by two Captains Regent chosen twice a year for 6-month terms by the Great and General Council, whose 60 members, in turn, are elected by popular vote and hold office for 5 years. When parliament is in session, your visit to the palace will be limited; otherwise, you will see its most important chamber, the richly decorated Sala del Consiglio, with the double throne of the two rulers at one end beneath a large allegorical painting featuring San Marino at its center. Two other rooms are usually on view, in addition to the atrium and the grand staircase, whose walls are covered with busts and inscriptions, works of art as well as symbols of the republic's past.

Among them is a bust of Abraham Lincoln, who was made an honorary citizen of San Marino in 1861. The Sammarinesi are proud of the thank-you letter, preserved in the state archives, in which he said. "Although your dominion is small, nevertheless your State is one of the most honoured throughout history . . ."

Beyond the Palazzo Pubblico, Contrada del Pianello leads to the cable-car station. En route, it passes the Cava dei Balestrieri, the field on which the *Palio delle Balestre*

Grandi, a crossbow competition complete with Renaissance costumes, is held each year on September 3, in celebration of the Saint's Day of San Marino and the founding of the republic. Don't assume that this colorful event is put on only for tourists — it was mandated by law in the early 17th century, even as crossbows began to be superseded by more modern weapons. Exhibitions are held at other times of the year, but if you miss them, you may still see one of San Marino's crack crossbowmen engaged in target practice.

From here, you can continue the climb by following Contrada Omagnano or by returning to Piazza delle Libertà. Either way, follow signs to the Basilica di San Marino. The mortal remains of the republic's founding saint are buried under the altar of this neo-classic church, which was built in the 19th century to replace an older church that stood on the spot.

From the Basilica, more signs point through the oldest quarter of the city to the first of the three fortified towers that figure on the country's coat of arms. The tower, known as the Rocca or Guaita, dates from the 11th century, although in its overall appearance it is of the 15th century. San Marino is 2,465 feet above sea level at this point. You can climb to the top of the tower and enjoy the cool breezes blowing off the Adriatic as well as a splendid view.

The Rocca is joined by a watch path to the second tower, the Fratta or Cesta, on the hihgest point of Monte Titano (2,470 feet). This tower dates from the 13th century and contains a museum of early arms and armor through which visitors have access to lookouts presenting further magnificent views.

If your legs have held out thus far, you may want to go along the less beaten path to the third tower, the Montale, although it is not open to the public. This narrow, graceful structure was in use from the 13th to the 16th century.

From the Montale tower, a path leads down the slope to the modern Congress Palace. Turn back toward the center along Viale J. F. Kennedy, Via Giacomo Matteotti, and Viale Antonio Onofri and you will see other modern buildings and, just up the hill, tennis facilities, all evidence of the present in this most ancient of states.

San Marino is at its traditional best during its holidays. Besides September 3, celebration of the Saint's Day and the founding of the republic, two choice days to be on hand are the first of April and October, when the elaborate, centuries-old investiture ceremony of the newly elected captains regent takes place.

A note to shoppers. Souvenirs of a very pedestrian nature are the most conspicuous items for sale in San Marino. Nevertheless, there are some legitimate buys. These include stamps and coins, of course, as well as local wines (San Marino produces some excellent wines: Sangiovese, a rich, robust red, and Grilet, a naturally fermented sparkling dry white) and liqueurs. For an idea of craft products available, go to the Mostra dell'Artigianato (Handicraft Exhibition) above the Piazzale Mario Giangi parking area, just off Viale Federico d'Urbino. If you've brought serious spending money, have a look at *G. Arzilli,* 1 Via Donna Felicissima, a large and serious jewelry store, on a par with the best in Italy.

BEST EN ROUTE

Expect to pay $45 or more per night for a double room in hotels rated as expensive; about $35 to $45 in those listed as moderate; and about $30 in inexpensive hotels. A meal for two will cost from $35 to $55 in expensive restaurants and from $25 to $35 in moderate ones. All restaurants serve an economical tourist menu whose fixed price is prominently displayed. Note that most San Marino hotels and restaurants close for a month or two in winter.

Grand Hotel San Marino – Just outside the old city walls, this modern hotel is probably the most comfortable in San Marino. Each of the 54 rooms has a private bath or shower and each of the front rooms has a balcony with a beautiful view of the Apennines. There is a restaurant, the *Arengo,* and a garage. Viale Antonio Onofri (phone: 0549-992400). Expensive.

Bolognese – There are only 5 rooms in this small, family-run hotel, but each is furnished with character, including solid wood antique bedsteads in some cases. The restaurant has a terrace for outdoor dining on warm summer evenings. 28 Via Basilicius (phone: 0549-991163). Moderate.

Excelsior – Not as grand as its name suggests, but nevertheless a clean, comfortable hotel with an award-winning restaurant and parking facilities. Viale J. Istriani (phone: 0549-991163 or 0549-991007). Moderate.

La Grotta – This charming hotel has 14 rooms, all with private bath or shower, and a pleasant restaurant. Contrada Santa Croce, San Marino (phone: 0549-991214). Moderate.

Joli – Just outside the city walls, this small hotel is comfortable and friendly, with the added bonus of a garage to help solve parking problems. 38 Viale Federico D'Urbino, San Marino (phone: 0549-991008). Moderate.

Titano – San Marino's first hotel, it opened in the 1890s, just a few steps from Piazza della Libertà. It has 50 rooms, all with bath or shower and some with a view. The panoramic terrace restaurant is one of the loveliest spots in town. 21 Contrada del Collegio (phone: 0549-991375). Moderate.

Tre Penne – A simple hotel in the higher reaches of the old city. All of the 12 rooms have bath or shower and there is a restaurant. Via Lapicidi Marini (phone: 0549-992437). Moderate.

Diamond – Here are 7 inexpensive rooms for guests and one of the best restaurants in town. The building is quite unusual in that it's been dug out of rock. Open daily from mid-March to mid-October. Contrada del Collegio (phone: 0549-991003). Hotel, inexpensive; restaurant, moderate.

Righi-La Taverna – In summer, the tables right on Piazza della Libertà are filled with tourists feasting on one-dish platters and the grand view of the Palazzo Pubblico. But the local specialties also served at this 2-story restaurant make it very popular with the *sammarinesi* year-round. Open every day in summer; closed Wednesdays in winter and from mid-December through January. Piazza della Libertà (phone: 0549-991196). Expensive.

Buca San Francesco – Straightforward cooking of San Marino and the neighboring Romagna region. Pasta dishes include tagliatelle, tortellini, and green lasagne, while second courses range from *scaloppine al formaggio e funghi* (with cheese and mushrooms) through grilled and mixed roast meats. Open daily from March through October. 3 Piazzetta Placito Feretrano (phone: 0549-991462). Moderate.

Vecchia Stazione – Owned and operated by the Andreani brothers, who also operate the *Joli* hotel next door, this eatery has recently been renovated and is quickly acquiring a reputation for good traditional San Marino cooking. Try *nidi di rondine* (pasta rolls stuffed with ham, cheese, and tomato and baked in a bechamel sauce) and *coniglio porchetta disossato* (oven-roasted rabbit stuffed with fennel). Viale Federico D'Urbino (phone: 0549-991009). Moderate.

The Soviet Union

The Soviet Union is the Communist Revolution and the incredible beauty of Russian churches and religious icons. It is the music of Peter Ilyich Tchaikovsky and Nikolai Rimsky-Korsakov, space exploration, and the art treasures of the *Hermitage*. It is Stalin's purges, vodka and caviar, a *troika* ride across the snow in bitter cold, and the warmth of a family gathering around the samovar. It is a parade of intellectual and religious dissidents, the "Song of the Volga Boatman," the voices of Leo Tolstoy and Fyodor Dostoyevsky, and the Kremlin clock chimes ringing out across Red Square. It is borscht and ballet, balalaikas and bureaucracy.

The Union of Soviet Socialist Republics (USSR) is the world's largest country. It stretches some 6,800 miles from the Baltic Sea in the west to the Bering Strait, which separates it from Alaska, in the east, and extends north-south nearly 3,000 miles. Its 8.65 million square miles represent more than one sixth of the earth's total landmass, covering the eastern half of Europe and the northern third of Asia. Winters can be long and severe, and the short growing season and insufficient rainfall have hindered agricultural development.

This vast country comprises 15 separate (and often contentious) republics, and its 280 million people represent more than 100 ethnic groups — although Russians, Ukrainians, and Byelorussians make up about half the total. Russian is the official language, but the use of local minority languages is encouraged.

The so-called European part of the USSR, ranging from the country's western borders to the Ural Mountains, is the area of densest population and the area most often explored by tourists. We also have included the several southern republics of the Transcaucasus between the Black and Caspian seas, which, though less often visited, offer a most interesting look at a section of the USSR influenced more by the Middle East than Europe.

The tensions between west and east were important in shaping the history of this country, which from the 9th century to 1922 was known as Russia.

The Slavic tribes who lived in the Kiev and Novgorod areas from earliest times were relatively peaceful, but were preyed upon often by Asian and Germanic tribes. In the 9th century, the Viking Varangians were invited by the Novgorod Republic to come and restore order; their reign lasted until the 17th century. Meanwhile, Orthodox religion, adopted from the Byzantine Empire, was introduced in Kievan Russia, and was to remain a dominant theme of Russian life until the Bolshevik Revolution proclaimed official atheism in this century.

The Tatar-Mongol invasions began in the 13th century. Russia was conquered and held in bondage for some 250 years until the State of Muscovy became strong enough, under Ivan IV, also known as Ivan the Terrible, to break the Mongol stranglehold. It was during the Tatar period that the institution of serfdom took hold.

In the 16th century Russian history was dominated by Ivan the Terrible, who built a powerful united state but also imposed a reign of terror. A period of strife and upheaval followed his death. Then Michael Romanov, the first of the dynasty that would rule Russia for over 300 years, was elected Czar. Peter the Great, the first powerful Romanov, came to the throne at the end of the 17th century. He introduced Western customs, culture, and technical achievements that transformed his country from a backward principality to a powerful empire. But neither he nor Catherine the Great, widow of his grandson and the next powerful Russian ruler, dealt with the system of serfdom that enslaved tens of thousands of Russian peasants. Russia's most famous serf rebellion, the Pugachev revolt, occurred during her reign.

In the wake of the French Revolution and the Napoleonic wars, a wave of liberalism spread over Europe, but the czars of Imperial Russia continued to run their country like a private estate. When Czar Alexander I died in 1825, there was an abortive revolution known as the Decembrist uprising, which, although crushed, became a symbol for liberals, radicals, and revolutionaries for the remainder of the century. After Russia was defeated by the French and British in the Crimean War, Czar Alexander II found it practical to issue a proclamation freeing the serfs, but the evils of the system continued. When the czar was killed by a terrorist's bomb in 1881, any gains that had accrued to the peasants were lost and a reactionary attitude set in that would dominate the remaining years of czarist rule.

Still, the 19th century had been an extraordinary one for the arts in Russia. Literature flourished, beginning with Alexander Pushkin, and including Nikolai Gogol, Ivan Turgenev, Dostoyevsky, and Tolstoy. In music, Russia produced Tchaikovsky, Modest Moussorgsky, Alexander Borodin, and Rimsky-Korsakov. Toward the end of the century, there was a flowering of the dramatic arts with the plays of Anton Chekhov and the staging of Konstantin Stanislavsky. And by the early 20th century, Russia had become preeminent in ballet.

At the turn of the century, however, the conditions of the peasants deteriorated further in the wake of a staggering depression and Russia's defeat in the Russo-Japanese War. When a peaceful group of workers and their families tried to petition the czar for relief, the soldiers opened fire on them. This massacre, known as Bloody Sunday, was the first act of violence in the 1905 Revolution, which led to the establishment of a more democratic form of constitutional monarchy. However, Russia's entry into World War I imposed further hardships on the country. In March 1917 (February by the new calendar), a bourgeois democratic revolution brought down the entire structure of czardom, and a provisional government was formed. Then, on November 7, the Bolsheviks, V. I. Lenin's Communist Party, replaced the provisional government with the first Soviet state. A full-scale civil war raged until 1922, when the Red Army emerged victorious and Russia became the Union of Soviet Socialist Republics.

After Lenin died, the Soviet leadership passed to Joseph Stalin, and the country moved into a period of rapid industrialization and brutal collectivization of agriculture. Stalin was a ruthless leader in absolute control of the Communist Party. When he purged the party of those he considered unworthy of membership, they were not merely expelled; they were executed.

Economic development was interrupted by World War II, in which the Soviet Union was allied with Britain, France, and the United States. The people of the Soviet Union suffered extraordinary losses during the war. Huge areas of the country were destroyed, and some 20 million soldiers and civilians were killed. Following the war, Soviet power extended into neighboring countries of Eastern Europe, and by 1946, the Cold War between the Soviet states and the western powers was a fact of life. A so-called Iron Curtain separated the West from the xenophobia of the Communist bloc.

After Stalin's death, his excesses were denounced by Nikita Khrushchev, who, as premier, preached peaceful coexistence with the West. But his tenure also saw the widening of an ideological rift between the USSR and mainland China, which lessened Soviet influence in some parts of the world. Conflicts with the US, especially over Cuba, kept the Cold War simmering. Khrushchev was forced into obscurity in 1964 and was ultimately succeeded by Leonid Brezhnev, who, until the Soviet invasion of Afghanistan, presided over a period of détente with the West as well as domestic economic and political stagnation. At present, with Mikhail Gorbachev representing the first generation of Russian leaders who were not born until after Lenin's death, the Soviet Union appears to be shrugging off some of its old ideological excess baggage. *Glasnost* (openness) and *perestroika* (restructuring) have created a new atmosphere for intellectuals that is reflected in the theater, art world, television, and the press. The effort to change and renew the moribund Soviet economic and political system has still to produce results, but observing the process is stimulating and thought-provoking.

The Soviet Union is different things to different people. In truth, it is neither a workers' paradise nor an authoritarian land of automatons. Where it fits on such a continuum is something for individual assessment. But for the tourist willing to set preconceptions aside for the duration, this huge, important country has much to offer. It has a splendid cultural history and an impressive record of modern technical and scientific achievement.

Traveling in the quiet countryside provides the perfect opportunity to meet and get to know people. A surprisingly high percentage of Soviet citizens speak English, German, or French. For the most part, they are proud of their country and interested in yours. You may learn more about the Soviet Union from such personal encounters than from any other aspect of your trip.

The following routes have been designed to introduce you to some of the interesting places in the European part of the USSR, and to permit you to experience the cultures of several different ethnic groups. The first route, down the mighty Volga River from Kazan to Rostov-on-Don, provides a window on the history of Russia. The second route is actually an exploration of two of the Soviet Union's most important cities — Kiev and Odessa — which introduces you to the Ukrainian culture. For a while we did not recommend this route due to possible danger from the Chernobyl nuclear accident. Now, however — based on radiation readings by a US Dept. of Energy team in Kiev in 1986 and the results of radiometric analyses of food samples by the US Food and Drug Administration — the US State Department has canceled the travel advisory for Kiev imposed after the accident.

For rest and relaxation, we have provided a tour of Black Sea resorts. This route takes you from Yalta in the Crimea along the eastern shore to Sukhumi in Soviet Georgia. Our last tour from Batumi on the Black Sea coast through snow-peaked Caucasus Mountains to Ordzhonikidze will acquaint you with the several nationality groups in Georgia.

The Volga

The Volga is a river the size and strength of Russia itself, a waterway that crosses a continent, a river the Russians call "mother." Tourists who travel its route by steamer come closer to feeling the spirit of the Russians. The timeless atmosphere of quaint rural villages and the old world is juxtaposed with the modern technology of hydroelectric installations and automobile plants. The Volga is a mighty river: 2,300 miles long, from Volgoverkhvoye northwest of Moscow to Astrakhan, a delta city on the Caspian Sea.

Since earliest times, the Volga has carried Finns, Slavs, Turks, Mongols, and Tatars; Jews, Christians, and Moslems, all seeking trade and conquest. In 1552, Ivan the Terrible opened the Volga to the Russians by defeating the Kazan Tatars. The most recent conflict over the Volga came from Hitler and the German army. During the months between August 1942 and February 1943, the Nazis ravaged Stalingrad (now Volgograd) in an unsuccessful attempt to subdue Russia and reach the oil-rich Caspian.

Today, the Volga region hosts thousands of tourists from around the world each year. This river route takes you from Kazan to Ulyanovsk, Togliatti, Volgograd, and Rostov-on-Don, 900 miles (1,440 km) to the south. You can reach Kazan by plane, train, or car. *Intourist* can arrange the Volga River cruise for you. The entire trip from Kazan to Rostov-on-Don takes 11 days, but you may select a shorter itinerary. Cruise boats provide complete accommodations, including meals and lodging.

KAZAN: The capital of the Tatar Autonomous Republic is also the cultural center of the Tatars (or Tartars), one of the many nationalities of the USSR. The city dates from the 15th century. It was the center of a typical medieval Moslem state with many internal conflicts as well as struggles with the Russians. In 1552, Czar Ivan the Terrible and the Russian army captured Kazan. Today, the city is half Russian and half Tatar.

A good place to begin a tour of the city is the Kazan Kremlin (Pervomaiskaya Pl.), which dates from the 15th and 16th centuries. The Kremlin, near where the Kazanka River enters the Volga, is an architectural monument (*kremlin* means "fortress" in old Russian) with marvelous towers and churches. There is an impressive panorama of the Kremlin from the Spassky (Spasskaya) Tower. Across the square from the Spassky Tower is the *Tatar State Museum,* with a good collection of information about the Volga region. Near Lake Kazan there are two imposing 18th-century mosques: Mardzhani, open for services (17 Ul. Nasiri) and Apanayevskaya (29 Ul. Nasiri).

During the 19th century, the University of Kazan (18 Ul. Lenina) was a center of liberal ideas in eastern Russia. V. I. Ulyanov-Lenin was expelled from law school here in 1887 for taking part in student riots. Today there is a statue of Lenin as a student in front of the university. There is also a Lenin Monument in Svodbody Pl., the main square of Kazan.

An important collecting and processing point for Russian furs, Kazan is a major rail junction and one of the largest industrial centers in the Volga basin.

The main shopping street is Ul. Bauman. *Musa Dzhalil Opera and Ballet Theater* is in Svodbody Pl. and the puppet theater is at 21 Ul. Lukovskova. You can relax in Gorky Park on Ul. Ershova or at the zoo and botanical gardens, 112 Ul. Taktasha.

En Route from Kazan – By boat, the trip to Ulyanovsk takes about 12 hours. The boat passes through the Kuybyshev Reservoir and valleys, where, depending on the season, you may see fruit trees in bloom or fields of wheat, sunflowers, or potatoes. Coriander is grown and processed in one of these valleys. Approaching Ulyanovsk, you pass the popular bathing beach on Paltsensky Island, which can be reached by boat from Ulyanovsk.

ULYANOVSK: This small city on a high hill on the Volga-Sviyaga watershed was called Simbirsk until 1924, when it was renamed for its most famous son: Vladimir Ilich Ulyanov, known to the world as V. I. Lenin. Lenin was born here on April 22, 1870.

The *Lenin Museum* (48 Ul. Lenina), which contains mementos of Lenin's youth, is in the house where the family lived in the 1880s before Lenin left to attend the University of Kazan. Nearby a huge Lenin Memorial Complex, including the house in which he was born, his grammar school, and other buildings associated with his life, was opened in 1970 to commemorate the 100th anniversary of his birth. A statue of Lenin as a schoolboy is in front of the railway station.

There are a number of interesting old, low, wooden houses along the narrow streets of the city. The main shopping street is Ul. Goncharov.

En Route from Ulyanovsk – The journey to Volgograd takes about 36 hours by boat and is full of fascinating sights. Shortly after leaving Ulyanovsk, you pass Vinnovskaya Grove, a popular recreation park.

If you made the river journey in the mid-60s and came back today, you would be struck by how much the Volga bears witness to Soviet progress. The former town of Stavropol, south of the Kuibyshev Reservoir and Hydroelectric Plant, has become the new city of Togliatti. This new industrial center was renamed for a former leader of the Italian Communist Party when the Volga Automobile Factory was built and equipped in cooperation with the Italian firm, Fiat. Excursions to Togliatti can be made by hydrofoil from Ulyanovsk. Nearby you can see the Lenin Hydropower Works.

Now the Volga winds around the Zhiguli Mountains. Forests and small settlements of Russian vacation homes, *dachas,* line the banks.

VOLGOGRAD: Historically, this city has been important as a southern outpost to protect Russia from invasions. It was founded in the 16th century as the fortress town of Tsaritsyn to guard the Volga route.

The city made its greatest mark on history during the period in which it was called Stalingrad (1925–61) by handing the German army one of its most significant defeats of World War II. Stalingraders fought the Nazis house to house for a full year until Soviet troops could encircle and defeat them. The Victory Monument to the heroism of Stalingrad's people, on the ancient Mamaev Kurgean hill, is one of the most moving war monuments ever built: Scenes of battle are depicted on the steps leading up from Lenin Prospekt. An eternal flame burns in the circular Hall of Military Glory. Slogans of the street-fighters are carved into the walls, and the names of all the war dead are inscribed on mosaic plaques.

Volgograd stretches along the river for 43 miles. It is the administrative and economic center of the lower Volga region.

There is a planetarium on Ul. Yuri Gagarin, a circus on Ul. Volodarsky, a musical comedy theater on the Central Quay, and a puppet theater at 15 Lenin Prospekt. Shopping is concentrated in the area around the city's center, Fallen Fighters Square (Pavshikh Bortsov Pl.) and the Alleya Geroyev.

En Route from Volgograd – The boat goes west here through the canal connecting the Volga with the River Don.

To reach the Don, your boat passes through a number of locks and the Tsimlyansk Reservoir, which feeds the canal and irrigates the steppe.

ROSTOV-ON-DON (Rostov-na-Dony): If you have come the entire way from Kazan, you may notice the difference in the appearance of this southern city, the gateway to the Caucasus. The area of Rostov-on-Don beyond the central Theater Square (Teatralnyi Pl.) was once the Armenian town of Nakhichevani, and the houses here are typically low, old Armenian dwellings.

Rostov-on-Don became a city in 1797, having grown up around a fortress built to defend Russia from the Turks. Its importance as a port city and trade center was enhanced by the completion of the Volga-Don Canal in 1952. The city now has a population of 1 million.

Shopping and museums are along Ul. Engelsa. There are four theaters, a racecourse, a regional philharmonic orchestra, a bathing beach, a sports stadium, and several parks here.

Some 42 miles (67 km) to the east in the industrial town of Taganrog on the Azov Sea, is the *Chekhov Museum* in the house where the great Russian writer and dramatist was born.

Moscow is about 2 hours by plane from Rostov-on-Don, if you are at the end of your tour. On the other hand, it is a good starting place for a tour of the Black Sea coast. You can also return to Moscow by way of Kiev.

BEST EN ROUTE

Hotel prices throughout the USSR are related to your travel plan, the season, and the class of accommodations you choose, rather than the individual hotels. For Western tourists, lodging is at least as expensive here as in major American cities. Economy options do not usually exist, except for camping.

Restaurants generally open in late morning and close by midnight. Reservations are not usually necessary and prices are relatively low, compared with costs for similar meals in the US.

Private or cooperative cafés and restaurants offer both local and European cuisine. The *Intourist* office in each hotel will provide names and addresses of these establishments.

The cuisine of the Volga region is wholesome and hearty. You might begin your meal with an array of hot and cold appetizers called *zakusky.* Baked fish stuffed with buckwheat groats and *solyanka,* a fish or meat stew made tart with salted cucumbers and olives, are delicious entrées.

KAZAN

Kazan – With *Intourist* office, 9 Ul. Bauman (phone: 20091).
Tatarstan – 86 Ul. Bauman (phone: 24324).
Parus Restaurant – On a houseboat near Lenin Bridge (Lenina Most).
Vostok Restaurant – 13 Ul. Kuybysheva.
Mayak Restaurant – 185 Ul. Dekabristov.

ULYANOVSK

Venets – With *Intourist* office, 15 Ul. Sovietskaya (phone: 94320).
Volga – Ul. Goncharov (phone: 14577).

VOLGOGRAD

Volgograd – Pavshikh Bortsov Pl. (phone: 3772).
Intourist – 14 Ul. Mir (phone: 334553).
Leto Restaurant – Open during the summer in the City Garden.
Mayak Restaurant – On the Volga Embankment.

ROSTOV-ON-DON

Moskovskaya – With *Intourist* office, 62 Ul. Engelsa (phone: 6-5391).
Rostov – 59 Budyonovsky Prospekt (phone: 60198).
Tsentrainy Restaurant – 36 Ul. Engelsa.
Volgodon Restaurant – 31 Ul. Beregovaya.
Teatralny Restaurant – Open in summer; in Oktyabrskoi Revolutsii Park.

Kiev and Odessa

Two of the most important cities in the USSR are in the Ukrainian Soviet Socialist Republic, which lies between Russia, to the east, and the satellite countries of Poland, Czechoslovakia, Hungary, and Bulgaria, to the west. Kiev is the third largest city in the USSR, and Odessa, on the Black Sea, is one of its major ports.

The Ukraine slopes down from the Carpathian Mountains in the west to rolling hills with beautiful oak and beech forests, and broad plains where the soil is rich and black. It is well developed agriculturally as well as industrially, and is sometimes called the breadbasket of the USSR.

Although the sentiment for Ukrainian nationalism has remained strong, Ukrainians have long been considered junior partners in governing the USSR. Leonid Brezhnev, the late general secretary of the Soviet Communist Party, was born here and held important party posts in the Ukraine earlier in his career. Khrushchev, Russian by birth, was a party official here and carried out Stalin's purges in the Ukraine.

Kiev is some 532 miles (851 km) southwest of Moscow. It can be reached by plane, train, or road. Odessa, almost due south of Kiev — about 303 miles (485 km) — is also linked by rail, air, and road, and can be reached by sea. You can sail between Kiev and Odessa on the Dnieper River.

KIEV: The capital and cultural center of the Ukraine is a picturesque city that grew up on a series of wooded hills overlooking the Dnieper. Poplar and chestnut trees along the streets soften the effect of the rather undistinguished buildings built after World War II. Parks and gardens make up nearly 60% of Kiev.

Before the Golden Horde, led by a successor of Ghengis Khan, destroyed the city in 1240, Kiev had been the leading East Slav principality. Christianity had been introduced to Russia through Kiev in the 10th century. After 300 years of repeated invasion by Lithuanians, Crimean Tatars, and Poles, the Ukraine was united with Russia in 1654. Kiev suffered severely during World War II; only one fifth of its prewar population was found alive when Kiev was liberated from the Nazis in 1943.

The oldest monument in the city is the Golden Gate (Zolotye Vorota), built in 1037 as the main entrance to the city at Bolshaya Podvalnaya and Volodimirska streets. St.

Sophia Cathedral (Sofiisky Sobor) with its 13 cupolas and impressive interior frescoes and mosaics is nearby, at 24 Ul. Volodimirska. It is now a state museum.

One of the most fascinating places in Kiev is the Monastery of the Caves (Pechersakaya Lavra; 211 Ul. Sichneve Povstannya), which was founded in 1051 by two monks. This complex of churches, cathedrals, and monuments was built in and around a series of caves on the high right bank of the Dnieper. Mummified bodies of monks can be seen in the tombs of the Nearer Caves, also known as St. Anthony's Caves (Blizhshie Pechory). Just outside the monastery is the church of the Redeemer of the Birchwood (Tserkov Spasa-na-Berestove), where Yuri Dolgorùki, founder of Moscow, and other princes of Kiev are buried.

Pushkin and Gogol are among the Russian writers who lived in Kiev for a time, and Taras Shevchenko, the poet and artist looked upon as the father of the Ukrainian national literature, was born here. You may visit the house in which he was born (8a Ul. Shevchenko); the *Shevchenko Museum* (12 Shevchenko Prospekt) houses his art and literary work. (A memorial park has been established where this great figure of Ukrainian romanticism is buried, about 92 miles/148 km downriver from Kiev near the town of Kanev. The trip can be made by boat.)

To sample the rich Ukrainian culture, visit the *Museum of Ukrainian Art* (29 Ul. Kirova), which includes the work of Ukrainian artists from the 15th to the 19th century and Soviet Ukrainian artists. Examples of handiwork and folk art, such as the intricately painted eggs called *krashenki*, dating from the 16th to the 20th century, are displayed in the *Historical Museum* (2 Ul. Volodimirska).

The controversial World War II monument at Babi Yar, "to the Victims of Fascism," is worth seeing. The ravine where more than 30,000 Jews and other minorities were murdered by the Nazis has been landscaped into a park on the outskirts of Kiev, off Artyomov Street.

Kiev is a wonderful city to explore. The park on Volodimirska provides a marvelous view of the river, and the promenade along the Dnieper is a wonderful place for a summer evening stroll. The city's most popular bathing beach, on Trukhaniv Island in the river, can be reached by a footbridge, Parkovyi Most. There are several theaters, a horse-racing track, a circus, and numerous parks. Kalinin Square, off the Kreshchatik opposite the *Moskva* hotel, is the place to go in the evening for a sample of local nightlife. Young people gather around the square in warm weather to sing, recite poetry, and dance. Shopping is concentrated near Kreshchatik Prospekt, but there also is an interesting outdoor market at 17 Ul. Vorovskov, and a large covered market, Bessarabka, on Shevchenko Prospekt.

Besides the usual forms of public transportation — trams, subway, buses, and trolleys — Kiev has a funicular railway connecting Vladimir's Hill Park (Volodimirska Girka) with the lower town.

ODESSA: Although a settlement and port had flourished here on the north shore of the Black Sea for centuries, Odessa itself is a relatively young city. It was built by order of Catherine the Great after the Russian army captured the entire region from the Turks in 1789. Its favorable location and special privileges granted by the czar enabled the city to quickly become one of the greatest ports in Russia.

The magnificent, wide, granite steps of the Potemkin Staircase, which lead up from the embankment, present an impressive entrance to the city for visitors arriving by sea. The staircase is named for the well-known battleship *Potemkin,* whose sailors mutinied, then stormed up the steps to join Odessa workers in an unsuccessful attempt at revolution in 1905. There are several monuments to the men of the *Potemkin* in the city.

Odessa withstood a 69-day siege by the Nazis during World War II. Later, along with Leningrad, Volgograd, and Sevastopol, Odessa was accorded the title of Hero City by the decree of the Praesidium of the Supreme Soviet. *Intourist* can arrange tours of the catacombs, part of several hundred miles of caves in the area that served as hiding places for World War II partisans (as well as revolutionaries and criminals, at other times).

Primorsky Prospekt, at the top of the Potemkin Staircase, is a main street and popular seaside promenade; the heart of the city is October Revolution Square (Oktyabrskoi Revolutsii Pl.). Poplars, chestnuts, and white acacia trees grow along the avenues.

The façade of the five-domed Assumption (Uspensky) Cathedral (Ul. Sovietskoi Armyiyi) is a combination of Russian and Byzantine styles. The *Opera House* (8 Ul. Lastochkina), one of the country's most beautiful theater buildings, has an Italian Renaissance façade and resembles the Vienna opera house. You can trace the history of the people who have lived along the north coast of the Black Sea through exhibits at the *Archaeological Museum* (Kommunarov Pl.).

For entertainment, there are several theaters, a concert hall, a circus, and a horse-racing track. There are several excellent bathing beaches, including one in Shevchenko Park, and numerous spas along the coast.

From Odessa, many tourists visit the Crimea and the resorts along the eastern coast of the Black Sea.

BEST EN ROUTE

As elsewhere in the Soviet Union, the price of hotel accommodations is related to the season, the class of accommodations you choose, and your travel plan, rather than to individual hotels. For Western tourists, lodging is at least as expensive here as in major American cities. Economy options usually do not exist, except perhaps for camping facilities.

Restaurants open in late morning and usually close by midnight. Reservations are not generally required and prices are relatively low, compared with what similar meals cost in the US.

Private or cooperative cafés and restaurants offer both local specialties and European dishes. The *Intourist* office in your hotel will provide the names and addresses of these establishments.

You must try chicken Kiev in Kiev, though you will find it well prepared in Odessa as well. Beef Stroganoff and various concoctions of ground meat mixtures, called *kotlety,* are good entrées, while *blini* — thin, rolled pancakes with cheese, meat, or vegetable fillings — make good snacks or entrées. The best tortes and sweetcakes in the USSR are baked in the Ukraine.

KIEV

Dnieper – 2 Ul. Kreschchatik (phone: 266569).
Intourist – 26 Ul. Lenina (phone: 245246).
Moskva – 4 Ul. October Revolution (phone: 292804).
Ukraina – 5 Shevchenko Prospekt (phone: 217335).
Abkhazia Restaurant – 42 Ul. Kreschchatik.
Metro Restaurant – 19 Ul. Kreschchatik.
Dynamo Restaurant – 3 Ul. Kirova.
Khata Karasya Restaurant – Ukrainian cuisine. In Svyatoshino on the northwestern outskirts of Kiev.
Kureni Tavern – Ukrainian cuisine. Near the Dnieper.

ODESSA

Odessa Hotel and Restaurant – The best hotel in Odessa. 11 Primorsky Prospekt (phone: 225019).

Krasnaya Hotel and Restaurant – Offers a floor show at night. 15 Ul. Pushkin-skaya (phone: 227220).

Yuzhny Restaurant – 12 Ul. Khalturin.

Ukraina Restaurant – 12 Ul. Karl Marx.

Gamrinus – A beer cellar at the crossing of Deribasovskaya and Zhukova streets.

Georgia

Georgia, from the subtropical climes of its Black Sea coast to the snow-peaked Caucasus Mountains, is one of the most delightful and least explored areas of the USSR. In few other corners of the world are the trade and migration routes of the past better represented by the present than in the Georgian Soviet Socialist Republic.

Mountain and valley communities settled by various nationalities through-out the centuries cling tenaciously to their identities, resisting assimilation. These groups — Imeretians, Abkhazians, Svanetians, Kabards, Ossetians, Daghestanians, and others — speak dozens of different languages and dia-lects, in some cases unintelligible to their nearest neighbors. They are Mos-lem, Christian, and Jew, though their religion now is not emphasized. The predominant language of the region is Georgian; the official language is Russian.

This route takes you from Batumi on the Black Sea — only miles from Turkey — to Tbilisi, the capital of Georgia, and north through the highest points of the Caucasus Mountains to Ordzhonikidze. The route is only about 341 miles (546 km) long, but it leads through rugged mountains, narrow valleys, and over winding roads. The scenery, cuisine, and friendly people will more than compensate for the inconvenience of the terrain.

BATUMI: Magnolias, palms, and other subtropical trees grace this important resort and port city on the Black Sea close to the Turkish border. Situated along one of the best bays of the Black Sea, Batumi's beaches of sand and small pebbles attract sun-worshipers from April to November, despite the intense summertime humidity. Exten-sion of an oil pipeline from Baku in the early part of this century made Batumi part of the oil export trade, increasing its importance as a port.

Batumi's location has led to its occupation at various times by Romans, Greeks, Byzantines, and Turks. For 300 years before it was placed under Russian authority in 1878, Batumi had been dominated by the Turks. During that time, the local population was forced to adopt Islam. The Muslim Georgians are called Ajars and Batumi is the capital of the Ajar (Atchar) Autonomous Republic.

You can still discern the Oriental and Moslem character of the city in parts of the old town, and the Mosque (6 Ul. Chkalov) is open for services. The local museum (4 Ul. Dzhinzaradze) has an interesting exhibition of national costumes; there are also a circus, an aquarium, and several theaters. The *Summer Theater,* built in the Georgian style in 1948, is in Primorsky Park, next to a wide beach. Another pleasant green space is the 45-acre Young Pioneers' Park.

For shopping, there is a market and a department store on Ul. Chavchavadze. The many small cafés throughout the city are good places to sample the mouth-watering, spicy Georgian cuisine.

En Route from Batumi – There's a good beach less than 4 miles (6 km) north of Batumi at Makhindzhauri. The name means "place of the maimed," which refers to the Georgian Christians who were tortured into accepting Islam by the Turks. A little farther along the coast is the Green Cape (Zelyoni Mys) resort; the botanical garden here is said to be the most beautiful in the USSR.

The route inland to Gori passes through a valley where collective farms cultivate tea and tangerines, and bamboo grows beside the road. The valley ends at Dioknisi, where you pass over a low range of mountains to Adigeni. A road to the north takes you to a mineral springs resort, Abastumani. Continuing on the main road, you come to Akhaltsikhe (Ahalcihe), a town famous for an old fortress and its silver filigree. About 37 miles (60 km) farther east is Borzhomi, another warm springs resort. There's a 6th-century monastery here, and numerous spas and vacation homes in the area.

About 24 miles (38 km) to the southeast is a ski resort, Bakuriani, but you'll need to make reservations well in advance if you plan to stop here.

Returning to the main road, you pass through Khashuri (Haøuri) and then Kareli, where you begin to see the high peaks of the Caucasus in the distance.

GORI: This is the town where Stalin was born in 1879, and it's the only place in the Soviet Union that still has a statue of the dictator standing in the town's main square. There are ruins of a 12th-century fortress, Goris-Tsikhe, on a hill overlooking the town, but the town itself dates from the 16th century.

Gori was inhabited by refugee Armenians in the 12th century, and later occupied by Turks, Georgians, and Persians until it was taken by Russia in 1801. An earthquake in 1920 severely damaged the town.

On a hill above the right bank of the River Kura, opposite Gori, there is a 16th-century church dedicated to St. George, the Goris-Dzhavri Monastery. According to legend, it was founded by Queen Tamara in thanksgiving to the saint for rescuing her favorite falcon.

En Route from Gori – The newly resurfaced road along the Kura River east of Gori leads to the ancient cave town of Uplis-Tsikhe (also known as Troglodite Town), which was inhabited before the time of Christ. The town was organized in tiers, and the houses, streets, and markets are distinguishable today. North of the town is the village of Didi Ateni, which has an important Georgian monument: the 7th-century Sioni Church, decorated with 10th-century frescoes.

Heading toward Tbilisi, the capital of Georgia, the scenery begins to change from lush, wooded slopes to barren, almost monotonous cliffs above the raging Kura.

TBILISI: There is a distinctly Mediterranean flavor to this city of olive-skinned Georgians, Azearbaijan peasants, Asian Kurds, and others. Food, drink, and celebration are integral parts of the spirit of Tbilisi and its million inhabitants. On the right bank of the Kura, since ancient times Tbilisi has been a key point on the trade routes from the Caspian to the Black Sea, and from Armenia across the Caucasus to Russia.

The city is bounded on the west by Mt. David (Mtatsminda Mountain), on the east by the Makhat Range, and on the south by the Sololax. It was built on a series of hills in the 5th century on the right bank of the river. This old part of town, or *stary gorod,* is a series of narrow, winding streets where the houses seem to hang from the hills. Recently restored, the Old Town has a number of small cafés and restaurants where traditional gaiety and friendliness enhance the zesty Georgian cooking. Tbilisoba, a folk-art festival, is held here during the last week of October. The Georgian word *tbili* means warm, and the city has long been known for its warm sulphur springs, some of which are still active along the banks of the river. You can visit some of the bathhouses in the old town. The oldest is the Erekle Bath (Ul. Bannaya and Ul. Akhundova).

There are a number of interesting churches in the city and the *Georgian Art Museum*

(1 Ul. Ketskhoveli) has an excellent collection of icons, frescoes, china, and Georgian paintings. The *Georgian State Philharmonic Concert Hall* is at 123 Plekhanov Prospekt. This is the home of the Georgian national dance ensemble, which has won an international reputation, as well as of the *State Symphony Orchestra* and other musical groups. There are a number of other important theaters here, including the *Georgian Puppet Theater* (37 Rustaveli Prospekt).

Several farmers' markets selling fresh produce and, occasionally, crafts of the province dot the city. Rustaveli Prospekt is the main street and the place for shopping. *Tsitsinatella* (23 Rustaveli) is a hard-currency shop, and handicrafts are on sale at *Art Salon* (19 Rustaveli). The city's largest park is atop Mt. David, 1187 feet above the town. You'll find the *Funicular* restaurant on the top floor of a 3-story house in the park.

Average temperatures here in July and August are well above 90F (32C).

MTSETA (MTSKHETA): A short distance north of Tbilisi is the cradle of Georgian culture, the ancient capital of Mtseta on the slopes of the holy Mt. Kartli. According to legend, the Sveti Tskhoveli Cathedral here is built on the spot where the robe that Christ had worn to his crucifixion was rediscovered in AD 328. It supposedly had been brought here by a Jew who had won it when lots were drawn for Christ's garments. The present version of the cathedral is a perfect example of 15th-century Georgian architecture. This is also the city of St. Nina's good works and miracles, and the main church of the Samtavra Convent is dedicated to her. Near the convent is an ancient cemetery that was used from the Iron Age until the 11th century.

En Route from Mtseta – The Georgian Military Highway north through the Caucasus to Ordzhonikidze wanders through some of the most beautiful landscape in the Soviet Union. The highway follows the Aragvi River through the villages of Natakhtari and Zhinvali where you can see the ruins of castles and watchtowers. From Tzilkani, Mt. Kazbek begins to appear intermittently in the distance. After you pass through Ananuri, known for its 16th-century fortress, the road becomes more winding. Pasanauri, at the confluence of the Black Aragvi and the White Aragvi (3,335 feet), is an area of alpine meadows, wild game, and river trout. From Mleti, the road begins a steep ascent via sharp curves around what seem to be perpendicular rock walls. The views are spectacular as you approach Gudauri, where snow is often still deep in June. You reach your highest point at Krestovi Pass (7,700 feet), where avalanches are a problem at certain times of the year.

As you descend toward Ordzhonikidze, you pass through the town of Kazbegi in the shadow of Mt. Kazbek's snowy peak (16,545 feet). The road follows the Terek River down to Gveleti through the Daryal Gorge to Lars and Balta, and finally to Ordzhonikidze (2,345 feet), the capital of the North Ossetian Autonomous Republic.

ORDZHONIKIDZE (ORDŽONIKIDZE): Lime trees and 19th-century houses line the main street — Mir Prospekt — of this strategically located town, north of the snow-covered Caucasus Mountains. The town originally was called Vladikavkaz, which means "mistress of the Caucasus," but was renamed in 1931 in honor of Grigory Ordzhonikidze, a prominent Communist and statesman.

On both sides of the River Terek and protected by rocky cliffs, Ordzhonikidze is especially important because of its position on the Georgian Military Highway, which leads south through the mountains to Tbilisi. At the entrance to the highway, at Tbilisskoye Chaussee, there is a 79-foot granite obelisk in memory of the 17,000 Red Army soldiers who lost their lives in battles with the White Guard during the civil war of 1919.

Exhibitions at the local museums and performances at the *Ossetian Music and Drama Theater* (18 Naberezhnaya) will give you a good picture of Ossetian life.

BEST EN ROUTE

Hotel prices have more relationship to the travel plan or class you opt for and the season than they do with the hotel. Lodging for all Western tourists is at least as expensive in the USSR as in major American cities, and economy options usually do not exist, except in camping. Most restaurants open in late morning and close at 11 PM or midnight. Reservations are usually not necessary for restaurants along the route, and prices are relatively inexpensive.

Addresses and reservations for Old Town restaurants, as well as for cooperative and private cafés, can be provided by the Service Bureau of your hotel.

The most famous Georgian dish is *shasklik:* skewered bits of meat — frequently lamb — marinated in pomegranate juice. A good snack or entrée is the unsweetened pastry filled with meat, cheese, or cabbage, called *pirozhki. Kachapuri* is a delicious cheese-filled pie which varies a bit, according to local traditions within the region. A good baked egg, cheese, and meat dish is called *cheezhi-peezhi.* The favorable climate means that many fresh vegetables are available year-round. When available, caviar from the Caspian Sea and trout from Armenia are prized delicacies.

BATUMI

May Day – 45 Ul. Karl Marx (phone: 97380).
Intourist – 11 Ul. Ninoshvili (phone: 97331).

TBILISI

Iveria – With an *Intourist* office. 6 Ul. Inashvili (phone: 997089).
Intourist Hotel and Restaurant – 7 Rustaveli Prospekt (phone: 832881).
Tbilisi Hotel and Restaurant – 13 Rustaveli Prospekt (phone: 990798).
Aragvi Restaurant – Naberezhnaya.
Daryal Restaurant – 22 Rustaveli Prospekt.

ORDZHONIKIDZE

Intourist – 19 Mira Prospekt (phone: 32552).
Kavkaz – 47 Ul. Vatutin (phone: 34926).
Gorny Orel Restaurant – Typical food and a view of the city, on the slopes of Mt. Lysaya, about 7 miles (11 km) from town.
Terek Restaurant – 32 Mir Prospekt.
Otdykh Restaurant – In Hetagurov Park.

Black Sea Resorts

The seaside towns and holiday resorts along the Black Sea are almost perfect places to strike up acquaintances with Soviet citizens, who vacation here, too. It's easy to begin a casual conversation on the beach or in the relaxed atmosphere of an outdoor café. Actually, vacationers here are an international lot. In addition, many foreigners come to take cures; the area is renowned for its mineral spas.

The resort towns of the Crimea and the eastern coast of the sparkling blue Black Sea are all the more beautiful because the Caucasus Mountains serve as their backdrop. The scenery varies from rocky cliffs to sloping foothills lush with subtropical vegetation, and rare and unusual plants flourish in the marvelous climate.

Cool water temperatures and the high salt content make swimming in the Black Sea an exhilarating experience, and most of the beaches are composed of pebbles and small stones. Nonetheless, many vacationers prefer Black Sea resorts to those of the Mediterranean, which is connected to the Black Sea by the Bosphorus. The climate along the Caucasian coast is similar to that of the French Riviera, which is why some people call this area the Soviet Riviera. Temperatures are a few degrees cooler on the Crimean coast.

A visit to the Black Sea is most enjoyable if made in a leisurely fashion, with stops at various resorts. The entire trip can be done by Black Sea steamer or by car, or in combination with the air service between Adler on the Caucasian coast and Simferopol in the Crimea.

YALTA: All passenger ships sailing to the Crimea and the Caucasus stop at Yalta, a charming resort town that lies in a natural amphitheater formed by mountains as high as 4,500 feet.

Yalta is best known to Westerners as the scene of the 1945 conference attended by US President Franklin D. Roosevelt, British Prime Minister Winston S. Churchill, and Soviet Premier Joseph Stalin during the last stages of World War II. The conference was held at Livadia, the former residence of the czars, a few miles east of Yalta.

One of the special attractions in Yalta is the *Chekhov Museum* (112 Ul. Kirova) in the 2-story white house in which the great writer lived during the last 6 years of his life. It was here that Chekhov wrote two of his most brilliant plays, *The Cherry Orchard* and *The Three Sisters.*

Another favorite tourist stop is the Wine Tasting Hall (1 Ul. Litkins) where talks on Crimean wine production are followed with free samples of the product. The wine-making center of the Crimea is just northeast of the city at Massandra. Beyond Massandra, off the road to Simferopol, is the 80,000-acre Crimean Game Preserve. Guided tours can be arranged through the Intourist office at your hotel. The Nikitsky Botanical Garden, near the seashore east of Yalta, contains the world's largest rose garden with over 1,600 varieties.

Yalta was first mentioned in chronicles in the early 12th century. Once a colony of Genoa, it was under Turkish domination for centuries until it became part of Russia at the end of the 18th century. Another hundred years later, it had become a popular resort. There are scores of sanatoriums along the coast, including dozens in Yalta itself. It is estimated that over a million people vacation in this area each year. The best bathing beach in the Crimea is Golden Beach (Zolotoi Plyazh), southwest of Yalta between Livadia and Miskhor. Alupka, a bit farther to the southwest, is one of the most beautiful resort towns in the Crimea. Its Vorontsov Palace, surrounded by a 100-acre park here, was designed by Edward Blore, one of the architects of Buckingham Palace.

East from Yalta, you can visit Feodosiya, famous in the 13th century as a slave market town, and Kerch, an industrial center and fishing base on the Kerch Straits. There is a railroad from Kerch across the straits to the Caucasian coast. You can also travel to the Caucasian coast from here by boat.

En Route from Yalta – There are car ferries and passenger boats to take visitors from the Crimea to the Greater Sochi coast, and air connections between Simferopol and Adler, the Sochi air terminal. If you prefer, it is possible to drive around the Sea of Azov, from the Crimea to Zhdanov, Rostov-on-Don, and Krasnodar and pick up the coastal route at the port city of Novorossysk.

As you head south, the road passes between bays and beaches to the west and the foothills of the Caucasian Mountains on the east. The first village of note is Gelendzhik, one of the oldest settlements on the Black Sea coast. Burial monuments over 4,000 years old have been found in this area. The coast road gradually climbs to about 2,625 feet, then, after cutting through the Mikhailov Pass, descends to Archipo-Ossipovka at the mouth of the Vulcan River.

Tuapse, an important port that handles crude oil that is piped here from the northern side of the Caucasus, is the last good-sized town before entering Lazarevskoye, the northernmost district of greater Sochi. Ashei, a pleasant little seaside resort just north of the village of Lazarevskoye, is known for its excellent beaches and the nearby mountains which are popular with climbers.

The Memedoo Gorge in the Ashei range near Lazarevskoye has a number of small waterfalls and grottoes.

Dagomys, the northern district of Sochi, is well known as a terminus for hiking routes through the Caucasian State Preserve, and it now has the city's best hotel complex. From a park on the western slopes of Mt. Armyanka, there are stunning views of the Greater Sochi area, the sea, and the mountains.

SOCHI: This is the most important resort in the USSR. Sheltered by mountains, which seem to descend right into the sea, Sochi is favored by a climate similar to that of Nice or San Remo, and is considered the heart of the Soviet Riviera.

Although there was a fortress here in the mid-19th century, the town didn't begin to grow until the area's potential as a health resort, because of its mineral springs, was recognized in 1893. By 1909, the first of the grand spa hotels had been opened; today there are nearly 60 and most of the 250,000 people who live in greater Sochi are employed in some facet of the health or holiday industry. About 2 million people visit greater Sochi each year.

Spectacular panoramas of the town, the sea, and the mountains are available from an observation tower atop Mt. Bolshoi Akhun, about 14 miles (22 km) from the center of Sochi. The viewing platform stands 2,155 feet above sea level, and there is a restaurant nearby. Bus 39 from the Riviera section of the city goes to the mountaintop.

The 25-acre Riviera Park, with its charming outdoor cafés, scores of sports grounds, and an open-air theater, is the center of Sochi life. Kurortny Prospekt, the main street, runs south from the park, paralleling the sea. A 114-foot spire with a star on top, on the roof of the main seaport building, provides an unusual landmark for boats miles at sea.

The public beaches are south of the center of the town.

Some of the sanatoriums that have been built on the hills and cliffs have funicular railways or elevators. One of the most beautiful of these is the Ordzhonikidze Sanatoria, which was built in Italian Renaissance style during the 1930s. The interior was decorated in traditional Russian style by local artists.

In addition to the beautiful mimosas, oleanders, magnolias, and palms that grow along Sochi's streets, there are specimen trees and shrubs from all over the world in the local Dendarium (74 Kurortny Prospekt).

Traces of prehistoric man have been found in some of the caves of the Caucasus. Two, Vorontsovskiye and Kudepstinskiye, are near Sochi, but they should only be visited with an experienced guide.

Other short excursions can be made to the Agur waterfalls near old Matsesta, to the yew and boxtree grove on the eastern side of Mt. Akhun in the Caucasian National Preserve, and to one of the large tea plantations in the area.

En Route from Sochi – About 13 miles (20 km) south of Sochi is the town of Khosta, famous for its health treatment centers and as a hiking station. Then comes Adler, where the central airport for the entire region is located. An extensive drainage system has helped turn Adler, once merely marshland, into a sunny, subtropical garden noted for its health spas and campgrounds.

As you leave the Krasnodar region and enter Abkhazia, an autonomous republic that is part of Soviet Georgia, you may sense differences in the language and culture. The first Abkhazian resort you encounter is Gagra where, thanks to its marvelous climate, roses bloom in winter. The next resort is Pitzunda, with its prehistoric flora reserve. If you leave the coast road, heading northeast, you can visit Lake Ritsa, at 2,860 feet above sea level one of the most beautiful in the Caucasus. The drive, about 38 miles (61 km), takes you through a deep canyon and past forests of spruce, pine, and beech.

Back on the road south, the beaches become more sandy and less pebbly, as you approach Sukhumi. One of the most beautiful beaches on the entire coast is at Gudauta, about 27 miles (43 km) north of Sukhumi.

SUKHUMI: The city seems to be one big park: its avenues lined with lovely laurels, palms, and Himalayan cedars; its gardens rich with eucalyptus, citrus, and banana trees. There is a botanical garden (18 Ul. Chavchavadze) with rare and unusual flowers, and the plants in the 80-acre forest-park on the slopes of Sukhumi Hill have been selected so that the garden is always in bloom.

Sukhumi, which lies between the mouths of the Gumits and Kelasuri rivers, is the capital of Abkhazia. The settlement was built by the Romans in about the 2nd century, and was one of the chief slave markets on the Black Sea under the Turks, before Abkhazia freed itself with the help of Russia. There are a number of interesting ruins, including the 11th-century castle of King Bagrat in the southeastern part of the city. A short distance from the castle ruins is Shrom Cave, a wonderland of stalactites and stalagmites.

Another unusual attraction is the monkey-breeding farm maintained on the slopes of Mt. Trapetsaya under the auspices of the Academy of Sciences of the USSR. The animals, primarily baboons and macaques, are used for scientific research purposes.

Many visitors to the Black Sea resort areas end their trip here, but it is also a starting point for tours of the Georgian Soviet Socialist Republic.

BEST EN ROUTE

The price of your accommodations has less to do with the hotel you choose than with the travel plan or class you select, or whether you visit the Black Sea by cruise ship. Lodging for all Western tourists is at least as expensive in the USSR as in major American cities, and there are not many economy options, other than camping.

Most restaurants open late in the morning and close at 11 PM or midnight. Reservations may be advisable at the better restaurants in the most popular resort areas. Food prices are relatively low. Your hotel Service Bureau will supply the names and addresses of new private and cooperative cafés and restaurants in the resort areas.

Some of the best renditions of Russian, Ukrainian, and Caucasian food are found in Black Sea restaurants. Sample the beef Stroganoff, chicken Kiev, and Caucasian *shashlik* (skewered lamb). The semitropical climate means fruit and fresh vegetables are available year-round. And dairy products such as the feta-like *sulguni* cheese, sour cream or *smetana,* and yogurt, called *matsoni,* are excellent.

YALTA

Oreanda – Less than 100 feet from the shore, along the seaside Promenade. 35/2 Ul. Lenina (phone: 322034).

Tavrida – 13 Ul. Lenina (phone: 321671).

Yalta Hotel and Restaurant – The best hotel in Yalta, with a number of restaurants and bars, a heated swimming pool, and a private beach. Masandra Park, 50 Ul. Draziinski (phone: 350143).

Brigantina Restaurant – 18 Ul. Karl Marx.

Dzalita Restaurant – 8 Ul. Moskovskaya.
Esagnola Bar – On the grounded schooner, opposite the *Oreanda* hotel.
Ukraina Restaurant – 34 Ul. Promenade.

SOCHI

Camellia – 91 Kurortny Prospekt (phone: 990590).
Dagomys – Several hotels, including a 27-floor main hostelry with a variety of
restaurants and bars; tennis, volleyball, and basketball courts; swimming pool and
large private beach. Ul. Leningradskaya (phone: 993846).
Magnolia – 50 Kurortny Prospekt (phone: 993617).
Zemchuzhina Hotel and Restaurant – The city's second-best hotel and restaurant
(its name means "pearl") features a private beach and 2 swimming pools —
one just for children (phone: 994494).
Primorye Restaurant – 10 Ul. Chernomorskaya.
Noviye Sochi Restaurant – Ul. Vinogradnaya.
Akhun Restaurant – On the slopes of Mt. Bolshoi Akhun.

SUKHUMI

Sinop – Tbilisskoye Highway.
Tbilisi – 2 Ul. Dzhghburia (phone: 26027).
Abkhazia Hotel and Restaurant – 2 Ul. Frunze (phone: 25201).
Aragvi Restaurant – 67 Mira Prospekt.
Amra Restaurant – Rustaveli Prospect, by the sea.
Amza Restaurant – Sukhumskaya Gora, on Sukhumi Hill.
Dioscuria Restaurant – Rustaveli Prospect, in the ruined fortress.

Spain

Spain has marvelous beaches, castle-hotels, glorious art, stirring music, sophisticated cities, excellent food, wonderful wines, joyous religious festivals, and the drama of the bullfight. There are items of the highest quality leather and lace for the shopper as well as unique inexpensive souvenirs. There are cultural differences that add special interest to the various regions, and there are churches of astounding beauty.

It is a country whose various layers of civilization can be seen in monuments, architecture, and art: dolmens and cave paintings from prehistoric times; the rounded arches that tell you the Moors were here; Romanesque and Gothic churches from the European Christian period; lavishly ornamented cathedrals from Spain's own golden age; and magnificent paintings by a parade of geniuses from El Greco in the 16th century to Velázquez in the 17th, Goya in the 18th, and Picasso in our own century.

In short, Spain seems almost to have been designed with the tourist in mind. You can explore charming typical villages, virtually unchanged by the passage of time, or head for sophisticated resort areas like the Costa del Sol, which has become more international than Spanish.

With an area of 194,883 square miles, mainland Spain occupies most of the Iberian Peninsula, which lies to the south of France between the Atlantic Ocean and the Mediterranean Sea and is separated from North Africa by the Strait of Gibraltar. (Much smaller Portugal, along the west coast, shares the peninsula.) Spain is the third largest country in Europe (after the USSR and France) and is more mountainous than any other European country except Switzerland. It also has 2,475 miles of coastline, and it is possible to ski in the Sierra Nevada, less than 50 miles from the Costa del Sol. The Balearic Islands in the Mediterranean, and the Canary Islands, just off the coast of Africa and almost 1,000 miles southeast of the peninsula, are worlds apart, yet thoroughly Spanish.

Provinces near the Pyrenees are green and lush, with meadows and fields bordered by trees and hedges. A high (2,000-foot), dry plateau, the *meseta*, dominates central Spain, its brown earth sometimes awash with golden cereal grains; and, to the south, along the Mediterranean, the land supports vineyards and olive groves, as well as lemon and orange trees. Except in the higher reaches of the mountains, temperatures remain relatively high throughout the year in Spain. In the southeast, for instance, temperatures range from 55F (13C) to 60F (15C) in January. The extreme south is the hottest in summer, with thermometers registering above 100F (38C) in some places.

When Phoenicians first came to Spain in the 11th century BC, they found Iberian tribes already living in the eastern parts of the country. It was the Phoenicians who gave the name Hispania to the peninsula, known to them as "Land of Rabbits." Greeks, Celts, Carthaginians, Romans, and Visigoths also invaded the country before the Moors conquered Spain in AD 711 and imposed an Islamic culture. Christianity had spread across Spain as early as the 1st century AD; eventually there ensued a 700-year Christian campaign to reconquer Spain. It was not until the late 15th century that King Ferdinand and Queen Isabella were able to drive the last enclave of Moors from Granada and unite Spain.

Isabella and Ferdinand had instituted the cruel court of the Inquisition to discover and punish converted Jews and later Muslims, who were insincere. Christians also were investigated for heresy. The court lasted until 1834. In the same year as the reconquest of Granada, the Catholic monarchs expelled all Jews who would not convert. Interestingly, the year was 1492, and across the Atlantic Ocean, Christopher Columbus, outfitted by the same monarchs, was opening a new era for Spain, as well as the rest of the world, by discovering America. (The year 1992 will be a commemorative year throughout Spain with the celebration of the 500th Anniversary of the Discovery of America.)

By the 16th century, Spain was a major colonial power. Spanish conquistadores plundered Latin America in search of gold and silver and declared the New World to be part of Spain. Precious minerals were shipped to the homeland by galleons, and Spain's naval prowess became so great that its fleet was known as the Invincible Armada until its defeat, in 1588, by Great Britain. Spain's subsequent military losses in the Thirty Years War, which ended in 1643, further contributed to its decline as a powerful nation.

During the 19th century, Spain suffered a series of internal conflicts, which were, in essence, protests against foreign monarchy. The three Carlist wars, which actually revolved around pretenders to the thrones, finally resulted in the creation of a republic in 1873, but it lasted only a year before the monarchy was restored. At the same time, Spain's Latin American colonies were struggling for autonomy, and Cuban independence at the end of the Spanish-American War in 1898 spelled the end of the Spanish overseas empire.

The bitter division between monarchists and republicans continued well into the 20th century. In 1923, King Alfonso XIII appointed a military dictator, who was so unpopular with the masses that he was forced into exile. The king finally abdicated to avoid a civil war. But when the elections that followed produced a socialist republican majority and the government initiated reforms, it engendered such right-wing opposition that civil war erupted. Francisco Franco, who had led the victorious Nationalist forces, became dictator of Spain. Under his regime, Spain remained neutral in World War II. Political dissent in Spain was suppressed and civil liberties were stifled until Franco's death in 1975, at which time Juan Carlos ascended the throne and undertook a policy of liberalization.

Our seven Spanish routes are northern Spain along the Cantabrian seacoast from the Basque Country west to Santiago de Compostela; Castile, which passes through central Spain's most important historic cities; the Costa del Sol, with Spain's most famous resort towns; the more rugged Costa Brava, along the northern Mediterranean coast to the French border; Andalusia, which has retained more Moorish traditions than any other part of Spain; the Canary Islands, off the northwest coast of Africa; and the Balearic Islands.

Note: If you have always dreamed of castles in Spain, you can now make reservations easily at 86 historic or resort *Paradores de Turismo* through *Marketing Ahead,* 433 Fifth Ave., New York, NY 10016 (phone: 212-686-9213). Information is also available at the Tourist Office of Spain in the US (see *Sources and Resources,* GETTING READY TO GO).

Northern Spain

The north coast of Spain extends from the Basque Mountain range, which abuts the foothills of the Pyrenees, to the country's most westerly reaches on a little ledge above Portugal. This tour begins in the Basque Country, follows the coast to La Coruña, and then turns inland to the south to end in Santiago de Compostela, the spiritual capital of Spain.

The Basque region, which resembles the lower Alpine section of Austria, deserves special attention because the Basque people are very possibly the oldest surviving ethnic group in Europe. (They predate the ancient Iberian tribes of Spain.) The Basques have a strong sense of political and cultural autonomy and, when waxing most poetic, claim direct descent from Adam and Eve via the lost city of Atlantis. Most serious scholarship on the Basques offers no definitive answers as to their ethnic origins, and early Basque history remains something of a mystery.

The Basque language is not believed to be Indo-European in origin; it is something of a linguistic missing link, thought to date from the very beginning of the use of language itself. Non-Latins, the Basques are fair-skinned and live in both Spain and France. Their motto "Four Plus Three Equals One" refers to the four Spanish and three French Basque provinces, and the desire for political independence and autonomy. (After the democratic constitution of 1978, all 52 Spanish provinces were organized into 17 *comunidades autónomas,* of which the Basque Country — País Vasco in Spanish; Euskadi in Basque — is one.)

Our route begins on the Basque part of the coast, due north of Pamplona, at Fuenterrabía, a resort town near the French border and just south of Biarritz. It continues to the charming city of San Sebastián, a major Basque city and a world-renowned summer resort. Following the coast through lovely old Spanish towns like Santillana del Mar, the route includes such natural wonders as the Picos de Europa mountain range, with snow-capped peaks as high as 8,688 feet and the *rías* of northwest Spain, which are inlets similar to the fjords of Norway and the lochs of Scotland. The final stop is Santiago de Compostela, a fascinating historical city that has been a shrine for a thousand years, the destination for pilgrims honoring the Apostle St. James, who is buried there.

FUENTERRABÍA: This popular seaside resort and fishing port has steep streets and tiny houses with flower-bedecked, wrought-iron balconies. Because of its strategic position near the frontier, it was the target of attack by the French for centuries. Each September 8, Fuenterrabía celebrates the *Feast of Our Lady of Guadalupe,* who is said to have saved the town after a 2-month siege by the French in 1638. The town is also noted for its excellent seafood.

PASAJES DE SAN JUAN: This village is best reached via Pasajes de San Pedro; launches cross regularly. Pasajes de San Juan is a tiny town with brightly painted houses squeezed together, rowing clubs, good restaurants, and a central plaza of unparalleled charm. Notice how the freighters and tankers entering the straits dwarf the quayside houses. French author Victor Hugo lived and worked here during his exile in the winter of 1843; his house (59 Calle San Juan) is open to the public.

SAN SEBASTIÁN: On three hills, cut by the Urumea River, and graced with the lovely scallop-shaped bay, the Bahía de la Concha, beautiful San Sebastián with its sandy beaches is one of the major summer resorts of Europe, playground of the wealthy and aristocratic inhabitants of Madrid. It's also a major Basque city and the capital of Guipúzcoa, the smallest province in Spain. Although the Old Town (Parte Vieja) at the foot of Mt. Urgull was destroyed by fire in 1813, it has been rebuilt — narrow streets and all — and is worth exploring, especially at about 8 PM, when the bars and restaurants of its central square, Plaza de la Constitución, are crowded. The balconies around this charming square have numbers because they were ringside seats for bullfights once held here.

The *San Telmo Museum,* on the Calle Coro at the foot of Mt. Urgull, is set in a 16th-century Renaissance monastery, and has interesting Basque memorial crosses, an ethnographic exhibit, and strange old Basque headdresses. You can drive to the top of Mt. Urgull for a fine view of the town and the bay from the public park at the top. The building there is a military museum.

Also be sure to stroll along the Paseo Nuevo, the wide promenade that encircles Mt. Urgull and offers fine vistas of the bay and the sea beyond. For a truly spectacular panorama of the city, the bay, and the sea, drive 3 miles (4.8 km) west along the Concha beach to Mt. Igueldo.

The Basque Country, and particularly San Sebastián, is a place where good eating assumes major importance. The city has a Gastronomic Academy and very exclusive, male-dominated eating societies that sponsor cooking contests, but the flair for good eating spills over into the local restaurants, the most modest of which is likely to serve outstanding food. Seafood is especially good here.

During the summer season San Sebastián holds a 2-week international jazz festival, an international film festival, and a folklore festival called *Basque Week (Semana Grande).* The posh casino is a traditional highlight. For further information, contact the tourist office in San Sebastián, 13 Calle Andia (phone: 426282), or the Tourist Office of Spain in the US.

GUERNICA: Heading west from San Sebastián along the Cantabrian coast road, you reach the town of Guernica, whose wretched decimation during the Spanish Civil War (2,000 died in 3 hours) has been immortalized by Picasso in one of his greatest paintings. (The original canvas, which once hung in New York's *Museum of Modern Art,* was returned to Spain for display in the Casón del Buen Retiro — part of the *Prado* — in Madrid.) The town has been rebuilt in traditional style. A few miles farther west, the beach at Baquio is worth a stop.

BILBAO: The largest city of the autonomous community of the Basque Country, which comprises the provinces of Alava, Vizcaya, and Guipúzcoa, Bilbao is primarily an industrial city. It is lively in the summer during *Semana Grande* and the August bullfights, when you will see some serious animals, feisty matadors, and a spirited festival. Bullfight critics and the matadors themselves stay at the *Ercilla* hotel (see *Best en Route*).

SANTANDER: Proceeding west on the E-50 highway leads to the autonomous region of Cantabria and its capital city, Santander, sometimes called the intellectual and cultural capital of Spain because of its courses at the International Menéndez Pelayo University and the *International Festival of Music and Dance.* It is also a summer magnet for tourists, who come to enjoy the exceptional variety of beaches, including El Sardinero, with its casino. It and several other beaches extend so far out during the spectacularly low tide that they blend into one continuous stretch of sand on which fishing boats tilt on temporary dry dock. The town is divided into an old section — much of which was wiped out during a tragic fire in 1941 — and a new area near the harbor devoted to shops and restaurants.

SANTILLANA DEL MAR: This is a lovely, beautifully preserved medieval Spanish town renowned for its Collegiate Church, which dates from the 12th century; here the relics of St. Juliana (Santillana is a contraction of Santa Juliana) are enshrined. See the Romanesque church with its magnificent sarcophagus honoring the saint and the impressive cloisters, memorable for their capitals, which were carved by a master craftsman during the 12th century. Also noteworthy are the town's old patrician houses, dating from the 15th to the 17th century, particularly the *Villa House,* now an inn, with its semicircular balconies, and the houses along the Calle de las Lindas and the Calle del Río. (The latter street has a stream running down its center.)

En route from Santillana del Mar – Just west of Santillana are the phenomenal Caves of Altamira, the famed 15,000-year-old 'Sistine Chapel of prehistoric stone painting.' The main cave has been reopened to the public on a limited basis. Written permission must be requested 3 months in advance from the Director, *Centro de Investigación y Museo de Altamira,* Santillana del Mar, Santander, Spain (phone: 818102). The adjacent museum and the Cave of the Stalactites are open to the public Mondays through Saturdays from 10 AM to 1 PM and 4 to 6 PM and on Sundays and holidays from 10 AM to 1 PM.

Continue west and you will reach the massive Picos de Europa Cordillera mountain range, where breathtaking gorges have been carved by the mountain streams. These spectacular snow-capped mountains rise between Santander and Oviedo, and their highest peak is 8,688 feet. A good place to stay between Santander and Oviedo is the typically Spanish resort town of Llanes. From here, if you wish, you can catch a glimpse of the mountains, by taking a detour of 11 miles (18 km) to Covadonga, turning south just before the town of Cangas de Onís. Here a shrine was erected in a most dramatic mountain setting, commemorating the reconquest of Spain from the Moors, which began in Covadonga in 722. The road is steep and narrow, but passable.

OVIEDO: Oviedo is the capital of Asturias, a regional entity that was originally a separate kingdom. Known primarily as a mining region, Asturias has a rugged seacoast, a mountainous interior that has been compared to the Swiss Alps, and a natural greenness of exceptional depth and intensity. Salmon and trout, deer and mountain goat populate the Asturian streams and mountains. The coastal villages produce ample seafood. The Oviedo market held daily in the Plaza de Daoiz y Velarde and the Cathedral Square are the main attractions in this small town. Don't miss the matchless 12th-century sculpted columns at the Cámara Santa church, where the gold and silver items in the treasury are also very fine and very old (9th century).

En Route from Oviedo – Continuing along the coast, you enter the region of Galicia in the northwest corner of the Iberian Peninsula. Because of its geographic isolation, Galicia has remained the least developed part of Spain. Its ocean waters are sparkling clean, but there are few tourist accommodations. Life in Galicia is very basic, and its fishermen battle daily with poverty and the dangers of the sea.

An unusual geographic feature here is the *rías* — inlets similar to the sea lochs of Scotland, the fjords of Norway, and the abers of Brittany. The Rías Altas extend along the north coast from Ribadeo to La Coruña and the Rías Bajas continue along the west coast from La Coruña to Pontevedra.

On this route you might want to look for the *cetarias,* seafood pounds, where lobsters and other crustaceans can be bought alive. Nearby open-air restaurants will cook and serve your acquisitions.

The area is also known for the Ribeiros wines; the red is very dark and fruity; the white champagnelike; there's also a light, bubbly cider.

LA CORUÑA: This town, from which Philip II's Armada set sail in 1588 to be defeated by England's Drake and Hawkins, is now called the San Sebastián of Galicia for its lovely beaches. The town itself is also charming, with its medieval walls and its 2nd-century Roman lighthouse, the Hercules Tower, which still functions.

Along the harbor in the park of San Carlos are the 18th-century San Anton and San Carlos forts. The old section of La Coruña, called La Ciudad (the City), has lovely cobbled streets and little squares like the Plaza de Santa Bárbara. The cafés in the old part of town are social centers, and the Plaza de Maria Pita is a good place for eating, drinking, and strolling.

SANTIAGO DE COMPOSTELA: Santiago's only rivals are Rome and Jerusalem, and the shrine here attracts pilgrims from all over the world. Santiago is the contraction for *San Diego,* or St. James. A legend says that St. James the Apostle landed here to proselytize and then died in Judea at the hands of Herod. His body was buried here, lost, and rediscovered by a miracle wrought in the 9th century. It is said that the night sky showered stars upon his grave to reveal its whereabouts to the faithful. The name *compostela* refers to the land (*campo*) of stars (*estrellas*). St. James is still honored by pilgrimages, with very special ones in years when his holy day falls on a Sunday, usually every 5, 6, or 11 years; the next year is 1993. The famous Way of St. James (El Cámino de Santiago), extending from Paris through Pamplona, Burgos, and León to Santiago, and marked with monasteries and churches, is one of the world's oldest tour routes; one early guidebook dates from 1130.

The center of attraction in Santiago is the cathedral, built from the 11th through the 13th century. It can be seen from plazas on all sides, the chief of which is the Plaza de España or del Obradoiro. The magnificent Obradoiro façade is a 1750 baroque creation by Fernando Casas y Novoa. Richly ornate, it is sculpted in a blend of straight and curved lines characteristic of the baroque style. Be sure to see the wonderful 12th-century Romanesque Gate of Glory, the Romanesque Goldsmith's Door, and the 17th-century Holy Door — all inside the cathedral.

Santiago (pop. 93,000) is also the site of one of Spain's earliest universities. The student quarter and the old neighborhood between the cathedral and the university are the most popular strolling and dining areas in town. The summer music school headed by the late Andrés Segovia, the great guitarist, is another attraction.

Explore the Plaza del Obradoiro fronting the cathedral and the Plaza de la Quintana at its east end, and wander along such medieval streets as the Rúa Nueva, Calle del Franco, and Rúa del Villar. On the western side of town is the Paseo de la Herradura, a pleasant promenade along a wooded hill, which offers a fine view of the cathedral and the city.

The annual *Festival of Santiago de Compostela* is celebrated on *St. James's Day,* July 25, with grand processions and much feasting. When the date falls on a Sunday, as it will in 1993, there are special celebrations, so be sure to make hotel reservations in advance. For more information about the city, contact the Tourist Office, 43 Rúa del Villar (phone: 584081) or the Tourist Office of Spain in the US.

BEST EN ROUTE

Expect to pay $100 or more for a double room in those hotels we've categorized as expensive; between $50 and $100 at a hotel in the moderate category; under $50, inexpensive.

Basque gastronomy is a high art, renowned throughout the world. Here, you will find several restaurants of supremely high caliber where every meal is truly unforgettable. Expect to pay $60 or more for a meal for two at those restaurants we've categorized as expensive; between $40 and $60 for a meal for two in the moderate category; under $40, inexpensive. Prices do not include drinks, wine, or tips.

FUENTERRABÍA

Kulluxka-Zeria – A genial place that serves fish and seafood prepared according to Basque recipes. 19-23 Calle San Pedro (phone: 642780). Moderate.

Parador El Emperador – This should be your first stop in Spain as you cross the border from France. Not only is the Basque cooking good, but this former medieval castle cum fortress with real cannonball holes in the façade has an interesting art gallery. Plaza de Armas (phone: 642140). Moderate.

PASAJES DE SAN JUAN

Casa Cámara – Renowned as one of the most important centers of new Basque cooking, the cuisine here features natural ingredients with traditional and innovative recipes. Lobster dishes are the house specialty. 79 Calle San Juan (phone: 356602). Expensive.

Txulotxo – Here you'll find a splendid selection of Basque seafood and fish dishes. Closed Tuesdays and October. 76 Calle San Juan (phone: 356609). Moderate.

SAN SEBASTIÁN

María Cristina – The past splendor of this Belle Epoque hotel has been restored by a thorough refurbishing; it has reopened as part of the CIGA chain. The lounges and spacious rooms, now modernized, are elegant, with original antiques. Paseo República Argentina (phone: 293300). Expensive.

Londres e Inglaterra – Standing on the beach, all wood on the inside, complete with creaking floors and elevators. The four-star, 120-room hotel is an incomparable Old World establishment. 2 Calle Zubieta (phone: 426989). Expensive to moderate.

Arzac – The high priest of the new Basque cuisine, owner-chef Juan Mari Arzak has won Spain's National Gastronomy Prize. His river crabs with truffles and lobster sauce, pastries, apple pudding with strawberry cream, and mousse are considered among the most delectable culinary creations in the country. Closed 2 weeks in June and 3 weeks in November. 21 Calle Alto de Miracruz (phone: 278465). Expensive.

Akelarre – Delicate Basque and French cuisine carefully prepared and served in a lovely setting atop Monte Igueldo. Barrio Igueldo (phone: 212052). Expensive to moderate.

Rekondo – Farm-fresh produce enhances the rich meat and fish dishes. Closed November 1-15. Paseo de Igueldo (phone: 212907). Expensive to moderate.

Aldanondo – This unpretentious chophouse has a distinct rural sporting flavor. 6 Calle Euska-Erria (phone: 422852). Moderate.

Casa Paco – Another bastion of new Basque cooking, it is known for its sea bream, baby eels, and anchovies. 31 Calle de Agosto (phone: 422816). Moderate.

GUETARIA

Kaia and Kaipe – *Kaia,* upstairs, and *Kaipe,* downstairs, serve some of the best seafood on the Basque coast. From the *Kaia,* you can see the port, across the Gulf of Vizcaya, all the way to Biarritz, France. The Txakoli, bottled by Txomin Echaniz for *Kaipe,* is a typical white wine made from sweet-sour grapes grown on the hillsides overlooking the sea. This two-in-one restaurant is on the port. 10 Calle General Arnao (phone: 832414). Expensive to moderate.

GUERNICA

Zimela – This simple restaurant is a good place for a filling meal. 57 Calle Carlos Gangoiti (phone: 685-1012). Moderate to inexpensive.

BILBAO

Ercilla – Crossing the time warp from Old World style to New World comfort, this centrally located hotel is the traditional favorite of matadors and bullfight critics. Its *Bermeo* restaurant is excellent. 37 Calle Ercilla (phone: 443-8800). Expensive.

Carlton – Adequate if hardly luxurious lodging, this is a pleasant alternative to the *Ercilla*, which might well be full during the bullfight season in August. Part of the HUSA chain. 2 Plaza Federico Moyua (phone: 416-2200). Moderate.

Excelsior – Another good choice for comfortable sleeping quarters in Bilbao. 6 Calle Hurtado de Amézaga (phone: 415-3000). Inexpensive.

Guria – Here, diners feast on prized Basque delicacies prepared according to traditional recipes. Codfish and steaks are house specialties. Closed Sundays. 66 Gran Vía López de Haro (phone: 441-0543). Expensive.

Gredos – Though not as lavish as *Guria*, this restaurant offers traditional Basque dishes at reasonable prices. Closed mid-July to mid-August. 50 Calle Alameda de Urquijo (phone: 443-5002). Moderate.

SANTANDER

Real – This large Belle Epoque hotel, an aristocrat atop the city's highest hill, offers true Old World charm plus the modern luxuries of its recent refurbishment. 28 Paseo de Pérez Galdos (phone: 272550). Expensive.

Mar de Castilla – A fine seafood restaurant along the port with a good harbor view. Estación Marítima (phone: 213444). Expensive to moderate.

Casa Valentin – Fish and seafood are served in a more modest setting at reasonable cost. 19 Calle Isabel II (phone: 227049). Inexpensive.

SANTILLANA DEL MAR

Parador Gil Blas – This converted medieval villa provides enchanting accommodations in a remarkably picturesque medieval village, near the prehistoric Altamira caves. Plaza de Ramón Pelayo (phone: 818000). Moderate.

Altamira – Since the *Gil Blas* has a limited number of rooms for guests, this is an alternative in town. It's not nearly as spectacular, but quite charming in its own way. 1 Calle Cantón (phone: 818025). Inexpensive.

COMILLAS

El Capricho – This imaginative *modernista* landmark private villa near the beach was designed by the famed Catalán architect Antoni Gaudí in 1885. After a major refurbishment, it opened in the summer of 1989 as a deluxe restaurant specializing in Cantabrian and international dishes. A separate cafeteria serves more economical fare. On the road between Santillana del Mar and Llanes (phone:). Expensive to moderate.

LLANES

Don Paco – A comfortable Spanish-style resort hotel, modest and quiet, with 42 rooms with baths. Parque de Posada Herrera (phone: 400150). Inexpensive.

Montemar – Similar to the *Don Paco*, this place has a cafeteria and 40 rooms. Calle Jenaro Riestra (phone: 400100). Inexpensive.

OVIEDO

Reconquista – Unquestionably the best place for an overnight stop in Oviedo. 16 Calle Gil de Jaz (phone: 241100). Expensive.

Casa Fermín – Oviedo's most notable restaurant is acclaimed for its venison in season, from October through March, and Asturian codfish. 8 Calle San Francisco (phone: 216452). Expensive to moderate.

Principado – Traditional Asturian cooking. The desserts and pastries here are especially good. In the hotel of the same name. 6 Calle San Francisco (phone: 217792). Moderate to inexpensive.

RIBADEO

Parador de Ribadeo – Built in the 1950s, this well-kept, government-run hostelry overlooks the mouth of the Eo River from a good location near the Santander–La Coruña highway. Its restaurant, which serves Galician dishes — boiled ham with greens, fresh fish, and *empañada* (fish or meat pie) — has a fine reputation. Calle Amadeo Fernández (phone: 110825). Moderate.

LA CORUÑA

Rápido – The best selection of seafood in the city, as well as some Galician dishes, both complemented by Ribeiro and Albariño wines. 7 Calle Estrella (phone: 224221). Expensive.

Fornos – Here you'll find well-prepared regional dishes and a good selection of hearty local wines. 25 Calle Olmos (phone: 221675). Moderate.

VILLALBA

Parador Condes de Villalba – Between Ribadeo and Santiago, this small, 6-room hotel is set in a vine-covered medieval tower and furnished with authentic antiques. Its fine restaurant specializes in *zarzuela,* assorted fish, and *fillaos,* custard-filled crêpes. Calle Valeriano Valdesuso (phone: 510011). Moderate.

SANTIAGO DE COMPOSTELA

Parador de los Reyes Católicos – This immense and magnificently restored monument was originally founded as a royal hospice in 1499 by King Ferdinand and Queen Isabella. Now a deluxe property of the *parador* chain, it is one of the most memorable inns in northern Spain. Plaza de España (phone: 582200). Expensive.

Peregrino – You won't be disappointed at the quality of this elegant old hotel. Calle Rosalía de Castro (phone: 591850). Moderate.

Don Gaiferos – One of the best restaurants in town. Closed Sundays and January. 23 Rúa Nova (phone: 583894). Expensive to moderate.

El Franco – A fine restaurant specializing in Galician cuisine. 28 Avenida del Generalisimo Franco (phone: 581234). Expensive to moderate.

Castile

Although the term *Castile* is used to denote a region embracing 15 provinces (including the autonomous community of Madrid) in the mountainous central plateau, the area is actually divided into two expansive administrative regions (*comunidades autónomas*) — New Castile (Castilla–La Mancha) and Old Castile (Castilla y León). New Castile comprises the provinces of Albacete, Ciudad Real, Cuenca, Guadalajara, and Toledo. Old Castile lies to the north of the Guadarrama and Somosierra ranges of the Cordillera Central and includes the provinces of Avila, Burgos, Segovia, Soria, Palencia, Valladolid, León, Zamora, and Salamanca. In the geographic center of Spain, the *communidad* of Madrid is surrounded by these two regions.

Our itinerary goes from Madrid south to Toledo, then northwest to Avila with a side trip to Salamanca, then northeast to Segovia, Valladolid, and Burgos. From Burgos, you can continue northeast to Pamplona, site of the running of the bulls immortalized by Ernest Hemingway in *The Sun Also Rises.*

MADRID: For a complete report on the capital and its hotels and restaurants, see *Madrid,* THE CITIES. Two small Castilian towns that you might visit as side trips before beginning our tour are Aranjuez and Chinchón, both within about 30 miles (48 km) of Madrid.

Just off route N-IV, Aranjuez is famous for its spring strawberries and asparagus. Its cool shady boulevards and plazas draw many a Madrid family for Sunday promenades. Aranjuez's main sites of interest are the Royal Palace (El Palacio Real), begun by King Philip II; the Sailor's House (Casa de Marinos), which housed the royal boats; the Prince's Garden; and the Farmer's House (Casa del Labrador). This romantic town inspired the haunting, lyrical *Concierto de Aranjuez,* by composer Joaquín Rodrigo. A classical guitar concerto, it has also been interpreted by many jazz artists, Miles Davis among them.

The central plaza of Chinchón is one of the best-known small-town squares in central Spain, and is the site of bullfights during the summer season.

The best way to begin our tour of Castile is to head south from Madrid on the N401 highway for 44 miles (70 km) to Toledo.

TOLEDO: Master artist El Greco's painting *View of Toledo* depicts this 16th-century city standing atop green, windswept hills, under fiercely tormented stormy skies. Whether or not you happen to catch similar climatic forces at work during your visit, you will be inspired anyway by the beauty of Toledo's palaces, private houses, and courtyards, as well as the view of the city itself from the Circunvalación road which runs parallel to the Río Tajo.

A center of Spanish civilization from as far back as the 8th-century Moorish era, Toledo has enough important sites to keep anyone engrossed for a good number of days. Overlooking the city, near the banks of the Río Tajo stands the Alcázar, a fortress that once housed El Cid, the Lord Champion of the 11th century whose valor and heroic exploits were the subject of Spain's first epic poem, *El Poema del Cid,* written in the early 12th century. El Cid was the subject of quite a few poems, tales, and plays through the ages. One of the most famous is the French 17th-century playwright Corneille's neo-classic interpretation of the Spanish hero's life, *Le Cid.* The reconstructed Alcázar is open daily (the original building was destroyed during the Spanish Civil War) and houses the *Museum of the Spanish Civil War.*

The cathedral, at Arco de Palacio, in the center of the city, dates from the 13th century and contains ornate artwork, sanctuaries, chapels, and bell towers, representing literally hundreds of years of devoted, inspired craftsmanship. You can ascend the bell tower, where an 18th-century bell is still in use.

The church of St. Thomas (Iglesia Santo Tomé), at Angel Santo Tomé, houses El Greco's famous painting *The Burial of the Conde de Orgaz.* A few blocks away, on Paseo del Tránsito and the corner of Calle Reyes Católicos, is the 14th-century synagogue El Tránsito (it no longer functions as a Sephardic Jewish house of worship). During the Inquisition, the synagogue became a church, and the Jews who prayed there became Christians. Many of those who failed to convert fled the country. Part of the synagogue houses a museum that is open daily and contains Sephardic religious articles.

The *El Greco House and Museum* (Casa y Museo de el Greco) is the former abode of the 16th-century artist and contains some of his paintings and memorabilia. It is across and up the street from the synagogue.

From Toledo, take N403 northeast to Avila.

AVILA: This city was one of the strongholds of the reconquest of Spain from the Moors by the Christians, a 700-year conflict that finally ended in 1492 when King Ferdinand and Queen Isabella seized Granada and united Spain. Standing at almost 4,000 feet above sea level, the city is famous for its walled battlements. You can get the best view of the walls from the western section of the city, where they overlook the Río Adaja. Guided tours of some sections of the wall and walks along several sentry paths are available, or you can freely roam the parapets. The battlements at Avila are considered to be among the best existing examples of medieval fortifications. The cathedral at the foot of Calle Tostado; the *Deanery Museum* (Casa de los Deanes), containing Flemish and Spanish art; and the Convent of St. Teresa of Avila are the main sites in town.

Not far from Avila stands San Lorenzo del El Escorial, a palace and monastery built by King Philip II in a near-record 21 years. An austere, classical monument, it achieves a rare architectural consistency and contains paintings by Bosch, El Greco, and Velázquez, among others, in addition to its remarkable library and Royal Mausoleum (for complete details on the palace/monastery, see *Extra Special* in *Madrid,* THE CITIES).

En Route from Avila – If you wish to make a side trip to Salamanca, you can simply follow N501 northwest. Salamanca is a university town with a Plaza Mayor that is more elaborate than the one in Madrid. You can walk around the city's major sites in about 3 hours; these include the university, the new and old cathedrals, and the Patio de las Escuelas, a square near the university. Surrounding Salamanca is an agricultural region where bulls are raised and tanned to produce Spanish leather. From Salamanca, you may return to Avila, or take the new highway to Villacastín or San Rafael and follow N-V1 to Segovia.

SEGOVIA: In the city's main square, in 1474, Isabella la Católica was proclaimed Queen of Castile. Other Segovia sites are the Roman aqueduct and 14th-century alcázar (palace) with 19th-century modifications. In the center of town stands a late Gothic cathedral and Romanesque churches. On the road south of Segovia you'll find the stone bridge that Ernest Hemingway described as a steel bridge and used as a setting in his novel *For Whom the Bell Tolls.*

Continue on the N601 highway from Segovia to Valladolid.

VALLADOLID: A university city, Valladolid claims to speak the purest Castilian Spanish. The house of 16th-century author Miguel de Cervantes, who wrote *Don Quixote* and who is known as the father of the modern novel, is near the Plaza Zorrilla, just off Calle Miguel Iscar. The other important sites in town are the cathedral; the 16th-century cloisters of San Gregorio College (Colegio San Gregorio); the *Archaeological Museum* (Museo Arqueológico) containing Roman artifacts; and the university (Universidad de Valladolid).

Take N620 to Burgos.

BURGOS: It was in Burgos, the 10th-century capital of Castile, that Francisco Franco was declared the *caudillo* (military commander) in 1936. The city holds a permanent place in Spanish military history, and none other than El Cid, the 11th-century warrior who became a legend, is buried in the Burgos Cathedral. In fact, the cathedral — with its slender, openwork spires — is the main reason for stopping here. After the cathedrals of Toledo and Seville it is the third largest in the country, dating as far back as the 13th century. Other sections were added in the 14th, 15th, and 16th centuries. Guided tours of the cathedral are conducted daily; it's on Calle Laín Calvo in the center of town.

En Route from Burgos – The wheat fields and lush pine woods that surround Burgos were the inspiration for poet Antonio Machado. After Spain's loss of her last colonial possessions in the Spanish-American War, Machado and a group of writers, called the Generation of '98, turned to celebrate the most characteristically Spanish (really Castilian) countryside. A visit to the town of Soria on N234 will acquaint you with the pastoral landscape. Some fine examples of Romanesque architecture can be seen here, and there are interesting, burnt sienna–colored houses built by successful sheep farmers and a 16th-century cathedral. Northeast of Soria on N111 are the ruins of the city of Numantia, whose citizens, according to legend, committed mass suicide rather than capitulate to the Romans in 133 BC.

Stay on N111 all the way to Pamplona.

PAMPLONA: Not actually in Castile, this city in the province of Navarre is one of the most famous in Spain. In *The Sun Also Rises,* Ernest Hemingway describes the annual *Festival of St. Fermín* (Fiesta de San Fermín), July 6-20, when the bulls are allowed to run through the streets in the early morning hours. The afternoon bullfights are among the most spectacular in the world. The city's main sites are the 14th-century cathedral and the *Navarre Museum* (Museo de Navarra), housing murals and religious sculpture.

BEST EN ROUTE

Decent and frequently even sumptuous accommodations at reasonable prices can be found throughout Castile, especially at one of the numerous government *paradores.* But it's necessary to make reservations months in advance for many of them. Expect to pay between $40 and $50 for a double room in a hotel listed as moderate; under $40 in an inexpensive one.

Castilian restaurants provide gracious, aristocratic atmosphere as well as fine cuisine. Expect to pay $60 or more for a meal for two at those restaurants we've listed as expensive; between $40 and $60 at those restaurants in the moderate category; under $40, inexpensive. Prices do not include drinks, wine, or tips.

TOLEDO

Parador Conde de Orgaz – A low, 2-story hotel commanding a sweeping view of the city, this is generally considered to be one of the most stunning *paradores* in the national chain. The restaurant serves international as well as Castilian cuisine. The rooms have air conditioning. Paseo de los Cigarrales (phone: 221850). Expensive.

Hostal del Cardenal – With unquestionably the best restaurant in town, this small *hostal* is set in a restored 18th-century Toledan palace that once served as a cardinal's residence. It has a lovely garden and 27 charming rooms. 24 Paseo Recaredo (phone: 224900). Expensive to moderate.

Carlos V – If the *Parador* is fully booked, this is a fine alternative in the center of town. Calle Trastamara (phone: 222100). Moderate.

Maravilla – Another good, centrally located hotel. It, too, is definitely worth considering if you can't get a room at *Conde de Orgaz.* 7 Calle Barrio Rey (phone: 223304). Moderate.

Chirón – This restaurant is known for the splendid scenery and surroundings. The building stands across the Puerta de Chambron entryway through the city's walls overlooking the Río Tajo. 1 Paseo Recaredo (phone: 220150). Moderate.

Venta de Aires – A leading restaurant with a tree-filled garden and charming location. 25 Circo Romano (phone: 220545). Moderate.

ARANJUEZ

Casa Pablo – Pleasant Castilian restaurant that serves local asparagus and strawberries in season. 20 Calle Almíbar (phone: 891-1451). Moderate.

CHINCHÓN

Parador de Chinchón – This deluxe member of the *parador* chain was originally a 17th-century monastery. Its restaurant serves fine Castilian dishes, and the cloisters are now glassed in to form a delightful lounge decorated with antique furniture and superb tapestries and overlooking the gardens, fountain, and swimming pool. Travelers often prefer this as a tranquil base from which to visit Madrid, just 28 miles (45 km) away, as well as nearby Aranjuez and Toledo. 1 Avenida Generalisimo (phone: 894-0836). Expensive to moderate.

Mesón Cuevas del Vino – The best restaurant in town is in an old mill. Here — and everywhere else in town — you can sample the potent licorice-flavored liqueur called *chinchón*. 13 Calle Benito Hortelano (phone: 894-0206). Moderate to inexpensive.

ÁVILA

Parador Raimundo de Borgoña – This grand old building was actually an 11th-century palace where Raymond of Burgundy (Raimundo de Borgoña) lived during a military crusade against the Moors. The exterior of the castle is bleached white stone; inside, the rooms have whitewashed walls and tile floors and are artistically furnished. Marqués de Canales y Chozas (phone: 211340). Moderate.

Parador de Gredos – In an old lodge with a new wing added in 1975, it stands in a wooded section of a plateau with excellent views of the Gredos mountain peaks, about an hour from Avila. Inside, the atmosphere is similar to a hunting lodge. Fresh trout is the dining room's specialty. Navarrendonda de la Sierra (phone: 348048). Moderate.

Mesón del Rastro – An old inn that is now a charming restaurant. 1 Plaza del Rastro (phone: 211219). Moderate.

SALAMANCA

Parador de Salamanca – This is a modern *parador* across the river, overlooking the city's Gothic skyline. It offers very good accommodations at exceptionally reasonable cost. Just off the Salamanca-Valladolid road, 2 Calle Teso de la Feria (phone: 228700). Moderate.

SEGOVIA

Parador de Segovia – A new *parador* with a four-star (deluxe) rating. It has a fine view of the city from its hilltop site, only a 5-minute walk from town (phone: 430462). Expensive.

Arcos – Near the colossal Roman aqueduct, this new, built-for-convenience small hotel also serves as a mini-convention center. Its popular restaurant, *La Cocina de Segovia,* features excellent Castilian specialties. 24 Paseo Ezequiel González (phone: 437462). Moderate.

Mesón de Cándido – Segovia's finest restaurant, set in a 15th-century house, specializes in Castilian delicacies — roast suckling pig, lamb roast, veal chops, and a special soup made according to the master chef's recipe. 5 Plaza Azoguejo (phone: 428102). Moderate.

Mesón Duque – This noted restaurant is *Cándido*'s main rival, serving typically Castilian food. 12 Calle Cervantes (phone: 430537). Moderate.

VALLADOLID

Mesón de la Fragua – Of the many restaurants and cafés around Plaza Mayor, this is the best. 10 Paseo Zorrilla (phone: 337102). Moderate.

BURGOS

Landa Palace – This splendid castle-hotel has a very fine restaurant that turns out delicious French dishes along with equally appetizing local specialties. On the Madrid-Irun highway (phone: 206343). Expensive.

SORIA

Parador Antonio Machado – The contemporary hilltop building overlooks the mountains and the Río Duero Valley. The dining room is noted for its Castilian game dishes and rich Rioja wines. Parque del Castillo (phone: 213445). Moderate.

The Costa del Sol

The Costa del Sol is Spain's answer to Acapulco and Rio de Janeiro: miles upon miles of high-rise hotels, condominiums, bungalows, and campsites overlooking the azure Mediterranean. In fact, it is one of Europe's most developed and most popular beach and golf resort areas. Many people look upon the Costa del Sol as an international playground rather than part of Spain. Some argue, incontestably, that the original character of the area — dry, hilly land sprinkled with whitewashed villages — has been changed forever by the resorts that provide accommodations, nightlife, and other recreational opportunities for tourists — about 6 million every year.

The Costa del Sol extends from Almería on the easternmost part of the southern Mediterranean Coast to Algeciras, 236 miles to the west. The center of the coast is the city of Málaga, an important port. Both Algeciras and Málaga have ferries connecting Spain with Tangiers, Morocco, and the Spanish Moroccan port towns of Ceuta and Melilla. In the 84 miles (134 km) between Málaga and Algeciras are the most developed (and crowded) of the Costa del Sol resort towns — Torremolinos, Fuengirola, and Marbella. Along this stretch of road (or beach) you are more likely to hear Swedish, German, French, Arabic, and English spoken than Spanish.

Though not always so named, the Costa del Sol has been attractive to foreign visitors ever since the Phoenicians landed on its shores in about the 6th century BC. They were followed by the Greeks, Romans, and Moors. The Moorish influence, although considerably more visible in the inland villages, can still be seen along the coast. Fortresses and the ruins of guard towers stand on cliffs near the sea. In contrast to the modern, white high-rises that line much of the dry, hilly coast are villages of whitewashed cottages and colorful gardens.

The best time of year to visit is around March and April, before the hordes descend. The temperatures tend to be in the 60s F with clear, sunny skies. In the summer, the mercury climbs into the 80s and 90s F, but because the heat is dry and breezes from the Mediterranean cool the air, few hotels other than expensive ones have air conditioning.

Although you can plan to visit every resort along the Costa del Sol, we recommend that you choose one spot as a base and make 1- or 2-day trips to other towns. The N340 highway runs the entire length of the Costa del Sol and all you need do is follow it.

ALMERÍA: Just beyond the town, the Almería desert contains some of the world's most famous sand dunes. Certainly, they are among the most filmed — *Lawrence of Arabia, The Good, the Bad, and the Ugly,* and *Reds* were made here, to name a few. Residents claim that so many film crews have drifted through town over the years, that they no longer remember the titles of the movies that were (and are) being made. In the 1960s, Almería was known to thousands of young people who were on the road in Europe as the place where you could make a few bucks as an extra in a Western. All you had to do was join the Spanish actors' union, sign on with a film company, and be willing to spend 8 or 9 hours in the sweltering heat dressed as a cowboy or Indian. You can find out which movies are being filmed in the neighborhood by stopping at Almantur, the official tourist board (Carretera de Málaga; phone: 234859), where you can get maps directing you to the film locations in the area.

In town, the main place of interest is the Alcazaba, a Phoenician castle that was converted into a fortress by the Moors. The site of music festivals during the second half of August, the castle stands on a hill. You can't miss it.

The cathedral is another building that has lived through various incarnations. Originally a mosque, it was Christianized in the 16th century; however, architecturally, it has retained something of a Moorish character.

ALMUÑECAR: This town — one of those clean coastal villages that smells of orange blossoms — dates from the Phoenicians, who called it Sexi. But don't get your hopes up. Although the nearby beaches of San Cristóbal, Punta del Mar, La Herradura, and Berenguel can be as sexy as the bodies languishing on them at the moment, Almuñecar itself offers only a Roman aqueduct and a Moorish fortress as sightseeing attractions. As in Almería, the fortress here, too, is called the Alcazaba.

NERJA: Discovered by two youngsters who were poking around the countryside in 1959, the caves for which this little town is world famous were opened to the public in 1960. Since then, visitors have come to wander through the mazes, gazing at the underground waterfalls, crypts, and the stalactites and stalagmites that adorn ceilings and floors, and are lit by multicolored lights. Adjoining the caves is an anthropological museum with prehistoric paintings said to be 20,000 years old. A music and dance festival is held in the caves every year during the first 2 weeks in August.

Apart from its caves, Nerja is known for a natural promontory overlooking the Mediterranean called El Balcón de Europa (the Balcony of Europe). If it sounds like a promising title for a best-seller, perhaps you'll be inspired to start writing after contemplating the stunning seascape.

This is also a good town for festivals. In addition to the music festival in August, there is a procession of boats honoring the Virgin of Carmen on July 16, a series of parades with fireworks honoring San Isidro (St. Isidore) on May 15, and a 4-day bash in honor of Nerja's patron saint, from October 9 through October 12.

En Route from Nerja – Take an interesting side trip to the village of Frigiliana, only 3 miles (5 km) inland from Nerja in the surrounding Almijara mountains. This tiny Andalusian town (pop. 2,160) of winding streets, red tile–roofed cottages, tropical flowers, and enchanting views of the neighboring mountains and valleys may be declared a national monument in order to protect it from possible ravishment by 20th-century developers.

MÁLAGA: The center of the Costa del Sol is known as the place that gave the world sweet Málaga wine. The vineyards that produce the wine grapes cover the hills on the outskirts of town. You can sample Málaga wine at any one of the small *bodegas* (taverns) in the center of town.

In addition to its prized vineyards, Málaga has a few other spots of interest. Overlooking the city, the Gibralfaro Castle spreads along a reddish cliff covered with ivy and cypress trees. The castle dates back to the Phoenician times, and has Moorish modifications that were added in the 8th century. The castle adjoins the alcazaba where the Arab monarchs resided during the 11th century. (It now contains an archaeological museum, which is open daily.) They are both on a hilly park accessible by Calle Mundo Nuevo or Calle Victoria to Ferrandiz.

Málaga's cathedral a 16th-century building with a truncated bell tower, has an ornate interior. The adjoining museum is open daily except Sundays and holidays. The cathedral, not surprisingly, is on the Plaza de la Catedral.

The *Museo de Bellas Artes* (Fine Arts Museum), in an old palace (6 Calle San Agustín), contains an eclectic collection of Roman artifacts, Moorish art, and paintings by El Greco, Murillo, and Picasso, a native son of Málaga. (His birthplace is at 16 Plaza de la Merced.)

To get a feeling for the town, take a carriage ride along the Paseo del Parque, a promenade near the waterfront lined with tropical gardens and sidewalk cafés. Or amble down Calle Marqués de Larios, Málaga's main shopping street. At the Plaza de Toros, at the end of the Paseo del Parque, you can take a guided tour and get a glimpse of what goes on behind the scenes of a bullfight. The most important bullfights of the year take place on Easter Sunday, during the Corpus Christi festivities in June, and during the first week in August. For more information about bullfights and other events, contact the Tourist Information Office, 5 Calle Marqués de Larios (phone: 231445).

Málaga is an excellent jumping-off point for trips to Africa. The ferry and hydrofoil to Tangiers and Ceuta (Spanish Morocco) leave from the Estación Marítima along Muelle Heredia. (Note that the ferry and hydrofoil service operates year-round, except when waters are too turbulent.)

TORREMOLINOS: This is the busiest resort on the Costa del Sol. Not so very long ago, Torremolinos was a quiet little fishing village visited by handfuls of European tourists. You would never know it to look at the place today: White high-rise hotels and apartment complexes, many with tennis courts and swimming pools, line the coast. In town are restaurants, supermarkets, nightclubs, discotheques, and boutiques. Nearby is a golf course, the *Parador Nacional de Golf* (see *Best en Route*), and the 20-acre Tivoli Amusement Park. And of course there is always the Mediterranean.

In the summer, Torremolinos is jam-packed with tourists from all over the world. In November, when the *Benalmádena Film Festival* is held, the town is even more hectic, if that's possible.

BENALMÁDENA COSTA: Although it is difficult to see where Torremolinos ends and Benalmádena Costa begins because the scenery is the same, Benalmádena has a somewhat more subdued atmosphere and a less frenetic nightlife than the super-resort next door. A new casino with a 9-story apartment complex has opened at Torrequebrada outside Benalmádena.

FUENGIROLA: A family resort area of seaside villas and campsites overlooking the sea, Fuengirola is quieter than Torremolinos or Benalmádena. Here you'll find pleasant little beach cafés, bars, and quiet coves as well as wide, white stretches of sand. Overlooking Fuengirola is a 10th-century Moorish castle, Sohail. A few miles north of the coast, in the hills, Lew Hoad, a former Australian tennis star and Wimbledon champion, runs a tennis camp called *Rancho de Tenis.* The 18-hole *Club de Gold de Mijas* is nearby.

MARBELLA: The chic-est of the towns along the Costa del Sol, Marbella is also the most expensive and has retained more of its traditional architecture than any of its neighbors. Many oil sheiks and movie stars have homes here, and the prices in the picturesque little bistros and designer boutiques reflect it. Not far from Marbella are several golf courses: *Golf Río Real/Los Monteros,* designed by Robert Trent Jones; *Golf Nueva Andalucía; Aloha Golf; Golf Guadalmina;* and *Golf Atalaya Park.*

NUEVA ANDALUCÍA: This community is actually a section of Marbella. It has a smashing marina — Puerto José Banús, where hundreds of yachts from all over the world dock. Nueva Andalucía is also the home of the Costa del Sol's first casino at *Club de Playa Torre del Duque,* which offers roulette (European and American), blackjack, baccarat, chemin de fer, and punto y banca. The casino is part of a leisure complex also containing 4 swimming pools, a nightclub, 3 bars, and 3 restaurants.

ESTEPONA: Although developers are starting to build here, Estepona has managed so far to retain its traditional character, with fishermen, goatherds, and farmers living as they have for centuries. Not far from Estepona is the *Club de Golf Sotogrande,* designed by Robert Trent Jones.

ALGECIRAS: Most people don't really get acquainted with this sleepy little port on the southernmost peninsula of Spain. Although it has a few hotels, it is mostly known for its port, from which ferries leave for Tangiers, Morocco, and Ceuta, Spanish Morocco. The people in Algeciras are very friendly and the town market is a fascinating bustling center of peddlers, greengrocers, and butchers.

BEST EN ROUTE

The Costa del Sol has 250,000 hotel beds, ranging from comfortable to elegant. There are apartment houses, hostels, inns, *paradores* (inns owned by the Spanish government), and government-run campsites that cater primarily to families with recreational vehicles or large tents. The biggest bargain here might be renting a villa, condominium, or apartment. Ask a travel agent or write to Sara Burns, Urbanization Los Monteros, Marbella, or José Juan Abrines, Costa del Sol Tourist Promotion Board, PO Box 298, Palacio de Congresos, Torremolinos (Málaga). Expect to pay over $100 for a double room at places listed as expensive; $50 to $100 is moderate; under $50 is inexpensive.

Service, atmosphere, and presentation of food are almost always pleasant on the Costa del Sol. Expect to pay more than $50 for a meal for two at those restaurants listed as expensive; between $25 and $50 at those restaurants in the moderate category; under $25, inexpensive. Prices do not include drinks, wine, or tips.

ALMERÍA

Gran Hotel Almería – There's no shortage of hotels in Almería, but this — clean, modern, with a swimming pool and a fine view of the harbor — is one of the best. In the center of town. 8 Avenida Reina Regente (phone: 238011). Moderate.

NERJA

Parador de Nerja – From its hilltop vantage point, this 2-story resort overlooks the mountains and the Mediterranean. Its swimming pool and tennis courts are in a garden setting, and its restaurant serves international as well as Andalusian cuisine. El Tablazo (phone: 520050). Moderate.

MÁLAGA

Málaga Palacio – A large, traditional establishment with a central location between the park and the cathedral. There are views of the nearby port from the upper rooms, the rooftop pool, and the restaurant. 1 Cortina del Muelle (phone: 215185). Expensive to moderate.

Parador Gibralfaro – With only 12 rooms in its luxuriously appointed interior, this inn is constantly booked. The terrific site — overlooking the sea next to Gibralfaro

Castle — makes the restaurant and bar popular spots. Reservations necessary (phone: 221902). Moderate.

Antonio Martín – This simple restaurant near the harbor serves fresh fish, seafood, and *paella*. It has a view of the harbor. 4 Paseo Marítimo (phone: 222113). Moderate.

Café de París – Hot and cold soups and smoked meats and fish are the specialties of this centrally located restaurant. Vélez Málaga (Malagueta) (phone: 225043). Moderate.

Casa Pedro – Your best bet for a hearty seafood meal served up in an unpretentious spot by the ocean. At El Palo beach, just outside the city. 112 Calle Almería Quitapenas (phone: 290013). Inexpensive.

Marisquería Noelia – This seafood *tasca* can't be beat for the variety and freshness of its catch-of-the-day delicacies, which are on colorful display. Small and unpretentious, it is always crowded with friendly *malagueños* at *tapas* time. In a charming central section of town. 138 Calle La Victoria (phone: 260246). Inexpensive.

TORREMOLINOS

Meliá Torremolinos – This 283-room resort is one of the largest on the Costa del Sol. A member of the Spanish Meliá chain, it offers everything from 2 nightclubs to Sunday morning mass. And it's about 5 minutes' walk from the beach. 109 Avenida Carlota Alessandri (phone: 380500). Moderate.

Parador del Golf – Contemporary in design and on an 18-hole golf course, this is a 40-room newcomer to the *parador* chain. In addition to a beachfront location, it has a swimming pool and a restaurant. Halfway between Málaga and Torremolinos (phone: 381255). Moderate.

Camping Torremolinos – If you're traveling on a budget, but would like to be close to Torremolinos's nightlife and social scene, this is a good alternative to costly hotels. How much you actually have to rough it depends on the kind of RV, camper, or tent you bring; facilities include a swimming pool and showers. It's about a 10-minute walk to the beach. Carretera Torremolinos–Benalmádena (phone: 382602). Inexpensive.

Casa Guaquín – This is a family restaurant in every sense; the owner's family even catches the seafood served. Closed Thursdays and December. 37 Calle Carmen, Playa Carihuela (phone: 384530). Moderate.

Chalana – Continental dishes share the menu with Spanish *paella* and fresh fish. Closed Tuesdays and November through mid-December. Paseo Marítimo (phone: 384956). Moderate.

Cangrejo – Another good place for fish and seafood. 25 Calle Bulto (phone: 380479). Inexpensive.

Hong Kong – Egg roll addicts can get their fix here, Torremolinos-style and Cantonese cooking is generally pretty good. Closed during the first 3 weeks of November. Calle Cauce (phone: 384129). Inexpensive.

Portofino – This terrace that has been built on the beach serves seafood that couldn't taste any fresher if you caught it yourself. Playa Montemar (no phone). Inexpensive.

BENALMADENA-COSTA

Torrequebrada – A new luxury beach resort complex on a 15,000-acre estate, with one of Europe's largest casinos, a complete health spa, nightclub, championship golf course, tennis courts, swimming pools, tropical gardens, 4 restaurants, and views of the Mediterranean and the ancient, white mountainside town of Benalmadena. Carretera de Cádiz, Km 220 (phone: 446000). Expensive.

FUENGIROLA

Casa Zafra – Unmistakably nautical in atmosphere, the inside of this seafood restaurant has been built to resemble a ship. 6 Calle Perla (no phone). Expensive to moderate.

Don Bigote – Another restaurant noteworthy for its decor, this place has a pleasantly rough-hewn Andalusian country air. Spanish cuisine is served. 41 Calle Francisco Cano, Los Boliches (phone: 475094). Moderate.

Langosta – Still another fine seafood establishment. Closed Mondays and December through mid-January. 1 Calle Francisco Cano (phone: 475049). Moderate.

Olla – You can choose from Spanish, Basque, or international dishes at this beachside restaurant with a terrace facing the sea. Closed Mondays. Paseo Marítimo, Los Boliches (phone: 474516). Moderate.

China – For hefty Indonesian meals or old-fashioned Cantonese dishes, this restaurant can't be beat. 27 Calle Ramón y Cajal (phone: 472993). Moderate to inexpensive.

MIJAS

Byblos Andaluz – This sparkling deluxe resort has tennis courts, fabulous swimming pools with poolside bars and buffets, and a complete health spa housing the *Luison Bobet Institute of Thalassotherapy*. The Andalusian-style hotel and villas with patios and fountains overlook 3 Robert Trent Jones par-72 golf courses. Three restaurants serve haute cuisine, regional dishes, and special dietetic meals. Nearby is the picturesque 2,500-year-old town of Mijas. 3 miles (5 km) from Fuenjirola in Urbanización Mijas-Golf (phone: 473050). Expensive.

MARBELLA

Marbella Club – Dazzling and sleek, this newly expanded resort put Marbella on the map. Here you can rub elbows with the jet set — if you're willing to pay for the privilege. Carretera de Cádiz, Km 184 (phone: 771300). Expensive.

Los Monteros – A 171-room complex of 3 buildings spread over the grounds of a former estate, it has 5 swimming pools, 10 tennis courts, a golf club, horseback riding, beachfront, and lots of trees. Urbanización Los Monteros (phone: 771700). Expensive.

Puente Romano – These sun-drenched, palm-studded villas lounge beside the Mediterranean. Each of the 200 airy rooms has a private terrace. Four restaurants, tennis courts, and a *Regine's* discotheque. Carretera Cadiz, km 184 (phone: 770100). Expensive.

NUEVA ANDALUCÍA

Golf Hotel Nueva Andalucía – A sparking white building set among floral gardens, this 21-room hotel is close to 3 Robert Trent Jones golf courses. Equipment can be rented and lessons are available. There is a heated pool, dining room, shopping arcade, and discotheque. Nueva Andalucía (phone: 780300). Expensive to moderate.

ALGECIRAS

Camping Costa Sol – A hilly plot of land given over to tents and campers, its main blessing is its proximity to a stretch of beach offering a fine view of the Rock of Gibraltar. It's about a 20-minute bus ride from town on the Carretera Cádiz-Málaga (phone: 660219). Inexpensive.

Marea Baja – The menu here offers a large variety of fish and seafood entrées, and ice cream crêpes for dessert. Closed Sundays. 2 Calle Trafalgar (phone: 663654). Inexpensive.

The Costa Brava

The Costa Brava (wild coast) forms the twisted, tortuous, rocky northeastern shoreline of Spain. Unquestionably the country's most rugged coast, as well as its shortest, the Costa Brava's granite cliffs rise out of the sea in such jagged forms that they appear to have been chewed out of the earth by a sea monster with serrated teeth. The cliffs shelter a plethora of bays, coves, inlets, vest-pocket beaches, and traditional whitewashed villages.

Technically, the Costa Brava extends from Blanes — an industrial town about 40 miles (64 km) north of Barcelona — to Port-Bou, a fishing village 95 miles (153 km) farther north, perched on the border between Spain and France. Despite its fierce name, the Costa Brava is a popular vacation spot and boasts more hotels and guesthouses than any other single area of Spain.

As recently as the mid-1950s, the Costa Brava attracted primarily painters and poets. The late Surrealist extraordinaire Salvador Dalí was one of the first major artists to settle into a villa at Port Lligat, Cadaqués, near the French border. But in the late 1950s and early 1960s, this relatively unknown coast was besieged by British tourists in search of bargain vacation areas. And before long, many scenic nooks and crannies were being developed into jazzy resorts.

Although its popularity with 20th-century foreign guests is a relatively recent phenomenon, the Costa Brava was first visited by Phoenician sailors around the 11th century BC. Greeks, Romans, Carthaginians, and Moors followed. Along the coast can be seen some of the structures left by these peoples — Phoenician ruins at Rosas, remnants of a Greek edifice at Ampurias, and the Moorish Alcazaba (fortress) at Tossa del Mar, to name but a few.

The Costa Brava is also dotted with structures such as towers, walls, castles, and monasteries that were erected much later — during the Middle Ages, between the 5th and 15th centuries AD, as defenses against the ravages of pirates and privateers who regularly preyed on coastal settlements.

These days, visiting the Costa Brava is immeasurably safer. Especially as far as weather is concerned. Hardly a cloud passes overhead during the dry, hot summers between May and September, when temperatures are generally in the 80s F. Winters, though moist, are mild enough to support miles of umbrella pines, acres of cork trees, and groves of olive and fig trees. In fact, the so-called wild coast is anything but that when it comes to climate — the average annual temperature is a comfortable 60F.

Yet it is precisely this gentleness of climate that accounts for one of the biggest problems you are likely to face when visiting the Costa Brava — overcrowding. Be sure to make reservations well in advance or you might find yourself hopelessly stranded, without any place to sleep.

There is one other thing to keep in mind. Unforgettably dramatic though they are, the roads are dangerous. If you are at all fainthearted on the road, don't attempt to drive here. If you do, do not let your attention wander, even for a moment. Be particularly alert on the single-lane, north-south road between Lloret de Mar and Sant Feliu de Guíxols and between Cadaqués and Port-Bou, where dozens of hairpin turns skirt the seacoast. One saving grace here is the relatively short distances between towns, which means you can get off the road reasonably quickly. In addition, plenty of buses ply the route and any hotel concierge can provide you with an updated schedule.

BLANES: About 40 miles (64 km) north of Barcelona, the southernmost town of the Costa Brava is hardly the most compelling. Blanes's 300-yard-long, relatively flat beach is lined with a strip of aging white apartment buildings and hotels. The permanent population of 16,000 swells considerably during the summer when sailors are drawn to the decent anchorages in the harbor and the yacht club. Tourist information is available at the town hall (phone: 330348).

LLORET DE MAR: While Lloret de Mar is only now being discovered by Americans, it has been a favorite bargain vacation spot with European tourists for many years. The accommodations here are generally quite adequate and inexpensive.

The wide, half-moon-shaped, sandy beach is good for swimming, but it gets very crowded between July and September. Lloret's fine seaside promenade, Paseo de Mosén Jacinto Verdaguer — known as Cinto Verdaguer to Lloretans — is a palm-lined boulevard whose trees cast gentle shadows on the people eating and drinking at its outdoor cafés. But you really have to adore crowds to appreciate it.

On the other hand, about 2 miles (3 km) south is the lovely little beach and bay of Santa Cristina, just off the Blanes-Lloret road, a golden stretch of sand amid greenery and volcanic outcroppings. And in the opposite direction, just another 2 miles (3 km) north of Lloret, is Playa de Canyelles, one of the most beautiful sections of the Catalán coast. The beach is divided in half by El Corquinyoli, a massive rocky ridge. If there's any isolation in the vicinity of Lloret, you may still find it here. For tourist information, contact the town hall (phone: 364735).

TOSSA DE MAR: An 8-mile (13-km) drive from Lloret de Mar along the edge of the sea brings you to one of the most popular resorts on the Costa Brava, the gleaming white town of Tossa de Mar. The old quarter of town (Vila Vella) predates even the Roman civilization. Surrounded by walls constructed later, in the 12th century, it is guarded by a Moorish Alcazaba. (For a very special photograph, try shooting from one of the three ancient towers' arches.)

The town's main beach is exceptionally crowded, but you can find some measure of seclusion on El Codolar behind Vila Vella. If there are still too many people for your liking, try Playa Llorell about 2 miles (3 km) south of town.

We've already mentioned the crush of visitors the Costa Brava area experiences. Beautiful little Tossa de Mar is a case in point: Of the 49 hotels in town, only 17 have more than 100 rooms. So don't expect to be blithely ushered into a room during July and August. You'll have better luck during April, May, September, and October, before and after the height of the season, when the weather still can be relied upon to be pleasant.

Tourist information is available at the town hall (phone: 340100).

SANT FELIU DE GUÍXOLS: This small town stands about 15 miles (24 km) north of Tossa de Mar along one of the meanest stretches of coastal road imaginable. At the edge of a shimmering, sheltered bay, long favored by fishermen, Sant Feliu was the site of a Benedictine monastery in the 11th century. Although the monastery no longer exists, you can still see some of the ruins on the side of the road. Its fine beach, cafés, and bullring make this another very popular resort. Tourist information is available from the town hall (phone: 320380).

S'AGARÓ: If you're traveling on a budget, it's a good idea to stay in San Felíu and spend a day or two visiting the haute monde of the Costa Brava barely 2 miles (3 km) to the north. But if you want a real taste of luxury and you can afford it, head for S'Agaró right away.

With a teeming population of about 200 permanent residents, the village is the summer residence of many Spanish and foreign luminaries. A model of meticulous, strictly enforced city planning codes, S'Agaró's contemporary residential community is the brainchild of architect José Ensesa, who wanted to create the perfect seaside resort. Many visitors to S'Agaró believe he accomplished his task. A walk along the Paseo de Ronda will give you a good idea of the success and extent of the planning — the Paseo is lined with gardens, fountains, statuary, and chalets, ending at lovely Playa Concha. Not bad for a village the size of a postage stamp.

BAGUR: The principal cove in this town is Aiguablava, or blue water, in the local Catalán dialect. Although it is appropriately named, it is nonetheless rivaled by neighboring coves Cala Fornells and Cala de Sa Tuna. Just north of town, Sa Riera is an unusual beach on the open seas. When the winds come from the south, the water is calm and transparent, but when the winds come from the north, the sea boils over the rocks. Sa Riera beach cannot be seen from the road; you must walk down a series of steps through the trees to a concrete balcony built on a granite shelf. From here, another set of steps leads down to the sand and rock outcroppings. For quiet seclusion, few places can compare with Sa Riera.

AMPURIAS: While antiquities of Roman origin are almost commonplace in Spain, Phoenician ruins are a rarity. But here in Ampurias you can visit an archaeological zone containing Phoenician ruins from the 6th century BC as well as those from a later (1st century BC) Roman settlement. The Phoenician community, called Emporion, was uncovered in 1908 and is almost fully excavated. A walk through the restored ruins alone is worth the trip to the Costa Brava, since it gives you an idea of what daily life was like 2,500 years ago. Artifacts from both Phoenician and Roman sites are on display inside the *Archaeological Museum,* where audio tapes provide a full explanation of the rise and fall of both civilizations. It is exceptionally well done and should not be missed.

ROSAS: Known for its sparkling bay and docks where fishermen sell their daily catch from the decks of their boats, Rosas, too, expands well beyond its 8,000 permanent residents during the summer months, when the long beach is practically wall-to-wall people. For a bit more privacy, visit the nearby coves: Canyelles Petites, Canyelles Grosses, Monjoy, and Joncais. Tourist information is available at town hall (phone: 257331).

En Route from Rosas – Although not widely known, in the town of Figueras is the *Dalí Museum,* a converted theater with many works of the late Surrealist painter, as well as his tomb. We're not sure which is more impressive, the gigantic canvases or the 50-foot-high glass ceiling. But it's definitely worth a side trip.

CADAQUÉS: This is undoubtedly a special corner of Spain. Although only several hours' drive from Barcelona, Cadaqués is worlds apart in time and tempo. This little town is pure Catalán, and its austere character reflects the fact that its residents must daily extract their living from the relentless sea. The former home of the Salvador Dalí, the town's most famous resident, is an obvious exception. The painter's estate, formed of adjoining cottages, is marked by gigantic egg-shape ornaments and projects a completely different lifestyle and attitude. Although your first impression of Cadaqués may be of the stark contrast between the dark, brooding mountains and the tiny, pretty white houses, one look at Dalí's whimsical garden will lighten your mood.

Dalí was not the only artist to have made his home here. Since the late 1940s, Cadaqués has been an artists' retreat. Perhaps because of its relative inaccessibility, the town has retained its tranquillity and has not yet been transformed by tourism.

PORT-BOU: Nestled at the foot of the Pyrenees mountains, which meet the Mediterranean in a horseshoe-shape embrace of land and sea, Port-Bou stands on the French border. This busy little fishing village has, in addition to the quiet beach in the cove, two nearby beaches: Cala Tres Plagetas and El Piño.

BEST EN ROUTE

As this is one of the most developed resort areas of Spain, there are all manner of accommodations, from luxury hotels to more modest places. Still, it's wise to make reservations well in advance. Expect to pay $80 or more for a double room at hotels we've classified as expensive; between $40 and $50 at those hotels listed in the moderate category; and under $40, inexpensive.

The Costa Brava has quite a few restaurants that serve well-prepared Mediterranean cuisine in naturally beautiful surroundings. Expect to pay $50 or more for a meal for two at those restaurants we've listed as expensive; between $25 and $50 at those restaurants in the moderate category; under $25, inexpensive. Prices do not include drinks, wine, or tips.

BLANES

Patacano – After three generations of serving fish and seafood, this restaurant has expanded to accommodate its substantial clientele. Closed Mondays in winter. 12 Paseo del Mar (phone: 330002). Moderate.

LLORET DE MAR

Dex – A small hotel on the beach, it has a swimming pool, hairdresser, and bingo. And it is quite reasonably priced. 47-49 Calle Juan Llaverías (phone: 364266). Inexpensive.

Helios Lloret – Centrally located on the beach, this hotel also has a swimming pool. 21 Calle Fernando Agulló (phone: 365108). Inexpensive.

Garbi Park – Yet another beachfront hostelry, but without frills. Urbanización Garbi, 1 Carrer Llaurer (phone: 365482). Inexpensive.

Trull – Near the beach, with a pretty view of the seacoast, this restaurant has a swimming pool. Urbanización Playa Canyelles (phone: 364928). Moderate.

Roca Grossa – This restaurant, which also has a swimming pool, caters to a discriminating international clientele. Closed from mid-October through mid-March. Urbanización Roca Grossa (phone: 365109). Moderate.

TOSSA DE MAR

Gran Hotel Reymar – The largest hotel in town has a great view of the sea, landscaped gardens, beachfront, fishing facilities, swimming pool, and a nightclub. Pets are allowed. There is a doctor on the premises. All rooms are air conditioned. Mar Menuda (phone: 340312). Moderate.

María Angela – Not far from the sea on the main promenade, this simple, pleasant hotel has central heating, an unusual feature for the Costa Brava, and an outdoor café. 17 Paseo del Mar (phone: 340358). Inexpensive.

Castell Vell – Within the ancient walled city, this picturesque little place serves good regional cuisine. Closed from October through March. 1 Plaza Roig y Soler (phone: 341030). Moderate.

Bar Sa Muralla – This old, whitewashed building tucked among the houses close to the wall serves lunch and drinks under colorful umbrellas. Paseo del Mar (no phone). Inexpensive.

SANT FELIU DE GUÍXOLS

Club Náutico – One flight up, it affords a view of the harbor and serves Mediterranean cuisine. Paseo del Mar (phone: 320663). Expensive to moderate.

Eldorado Petit – Under the same ownership as the famed restaurant of the same name in Barcelona, this is an outstanding place to sample fresh fish and seafood. 11 Rambla Vidal (phone: 321818). Expensive to moderate.

Amura – Another good restaurant with an interesting view. Closed from October through March. 1 Plaza San Pedro (phone: 321035). Moderate to inexpensive.

S'AGARÓ

Hostal de la Gavina – Unquestionably one of the most luxurious hotels in the country, with prices to match. Perched on a cliff with 2 beaches below, it has 2 tennis courts lighted for night playing and offers guest privileges at a nearby golf course. The highlight of the white, Spanish mission-style building is its dining room, where evening meals are served by candlelight. Plaza de la Rosaleda (phone: 321100). Expensive.

BAGUR

Cap sa Sal – Yet another cliffside resort that appears to have sprung quite naturally from the gray rock jutting into the blue sea, it has 2 swimming pools, a health club with sauna, tennis courts, motorboats, water skiing, 6 restaurants, and 4 bars. Cala de Aiguafreda (phone: 622100). Expensive.

Parador Costa Brava – The site of this government-run inn is sublime, but its construction must have been an act of sheer courage. It straddles a promontory 150 feet above a sheltered sliver of beach, accessible by weather-beaten granite steps. The water is ideally suited for swimming, snorkeling, and scuba diving. Reservations should be made 6 months in advance for high season. Playa de Aiguablava (phone: 622162). Expensive to moderate.

CADAQUÉS

Rocamar – Although not on the beach, its pretty gardens offer some compensation. So do the swimming pool, tennis courts, and discotheque. The rooms have central heating. Dogs are allowed on the premises. Calle Dr. Bartomeus (phone: 258150). Moderate.

Playa Sol – A quieter establishment with fewer entertainment facilities, this hotel is on a good beach. Playa Pianch (phone: 258100). Moderate.

Campsites – No fewer than 90 government-run campsites cover the coast between Blanes and Port-Bou. That's about one for every mile. Some have swimming pools and recreation rooms. Others occupy choice beachfronts. All of them are jammed during July and August, probably because they are very inexpensive. For information, contact the Tourist Office of Spain in the US.

Galiota – Owner-chef Nuria Riberas and her sister Pepita graciously attend an "artsy" clientele in their small restaurant featuring local seafood dishes and outstanding soufflés. Very crowded during the summer season; in winter, open weekends and holidays only (dogs are allowed). 9 Calle Narciso Monturiol (phone: 258187). Moderate.

PORT-BOU

Ancora – Comfortably decorated with old country furnishings, this place serves French and Spanish cuisine. Closed on Tuesdays and in November. 4 Paseo de la Sardana (phone: 390025). Moderate to inexpensive.

Andalusia

The Andalusian region is, in a very real way, the heart of Spain. Indeed, Andalusia is home to that which most people think of as Spanish: the flamenco, a flamboyant music and dance that's so identified with the Gypsies of Granada and Seville; Spain's many famous matadors — El Cordobés, Manolete, and Lagartijo; the traditional flower-draped, whitewashed cottages clinging precariously to rocky hillsides; and the stunning Moorish palace and garden complex, the Alhambra.

A mountainous region in the southern part of the country, Andalusia comprises eight provinces: Almería, Cádiz, Córdoba, Granada, Huelva, Jaén, Málaga, and Seville. The Sierra Morena, Sierra Nevada, and Sistema Penibética mountain ranges take up large sections of the interior. Much of the land is given over to the cultivation of olives, oranges, sunflowers, and grapes. Andalusia is bordered on the west by the Gulf of Cádiz and on the south and east by the Mediterranean Sea. Andalusia's major cities are Córdoba, Granada, Málaga, and Seville.

The recorded history of the region dates back to the arrival of the Phoenicians between the 11th and 5th centuries BC. Around the same era, the Celts, who migrated south from northern Europe, intermarried with the native Iberian residents; their offspring, the Celtiberians, are the ancestors of today's Spanish. Around the turn of the millennium, the Romans arrived, bringing their culture, politics, and philosophy. They built cities at Itálica (Seville), Córdoba, and Baelo-Claudia, as well as roads, aqueducts, and monuments. The Romans were followed by the Christian Visigoths around the 5th and 6th centuries AD, who were, in turn, vanquished by the Moors in 711. The Moorish era is known as the golden age of Andalusia. During this period, the region was the seat of an independent caliphate that thrived while the rest of the European continent remained in the Dark Ages. The most important Andalusian monuments — the Mezquita of Córdoba, the Giralda of Seville, and the Alhambra of Granada — date from this epoch.

In 1492 the Moslem empire in Spain, already reduced to the kingdom of Granada, was conquered by the Catholic monarchs Ferdinand and Isabella. In the same year, the adventurer Christopher Colombus set off from Palos de la Frontera, an Andalusian port, to discover the New World.

Nowadays, people from the New World travel to discover Andalusia. The best time to visit is in March and April, when the temperatures are in the 60s and 70s F (15 to 21C) and it is not yet crowded. June, July, and August are peak months. It tends to rain in the winter.

Our tour starts in Córdoba, and heads southwest to Seville and Jerez de la Frontera, before winding northeast through the mountains to Ronda and Granada. If you are driving remember that the countryside is very rugged and so are the roads.

CÓRDOBA: Founded by the Romans in 151 BC, it was a city popular with Julius Caesar, Pompey, and Agrippa. Both Senecas were born here. Ruins of Roman walls and a Roman stone bridge reconstructed by the Moors still span the Río Guadalquivir. The former capital of Moorish Spain during the 8th century, it was governed as a separate emirate until the 10th century when the Caliphate of Córdoba was established. During the 10th-century reign of Abderramán III, the city had 500,000 inhabitants and some 300 mosques. It was at that time one of the leading cities in Europe and also one of the leading cities of the Moslem world. Today, the population numbers only 284,737, but in many areas of the town the mystery of the Córdoban past is still very much alive.

While you are in Córdoba, be sure to see La Mezquita, a masterpiece of Moorish–early Spanish architecture that was first a mosque, then a cathedral. During the 8th century, the Moslems shared the mosque with the Christians. After passing through the Patio of the Orange Trees (Patio de los naranjos) you enter a forest of columns — alabaster, jasper, and marble — topped by ocher and tan horseshoe arches. The columns come from as far away as North Africa where they were taken from Roman, Visigoth, and Phoenician ruins. One testimony to the size of the mosque is the fact that the Christians built a full-size cathedral in its center after Córdoba was reconquered in 1236. La Mezquita is open daily (Cardenal Herrero).

Surrounding La Mezquita is the oldest part of the city. Called the Judería, it contains the Jewish quarter to the northwest. On Calle Judíos, there is a 14th-century synagogue with segregated men's and women's sections. Nearby, on Calle Averroes and Calle Judíos, is a patio where flamenco dancers perform during the summer months. Across the street from the synagogue is the Museo Municipal (Municipal Museum), which contains early Córdoban artifacts, and the *Museo Taurino* (Taurino Museum), which has articles that belonged to some of Córdoba's major matadors — Lagartijo, Manolete, El Cordobés, and Guerrita.

Along the banks of the Río Guadalquivir, the Alcázar, a group of splendid Moorish gardens of pools, towers, fountains, and terraces, is open daily. If you are a fan of Don Quixote, be sure to visit Plazuela del Potro, where an inn mentioned in Cervantes's novel is still standing.

About 4 miles (6 km) west of town is the Medina Azahara, the remains of a Moorish city built in the 10th century. It's worth a side trip, especially for the pleasant countryside surroundings.

Although you can shop for souvenirs in the area around La Mezquita, the really worthwhile items are Córdoba embossed leather and filigree silver. There are plenty of little cafés where you can sip coffee and relax.

The Office of Tourist Information is at 13 Calle Hermanos G. Murga (phone: 471235).

Now take the N-IV highway southwest to Seville.

SEVILLE: According to legend, Seville was founded by Hercules the Greek. Although the city shares a similar pattern of earlier history with Córdoba, Seville came into its own after the Christian reconquest of Andalusia in the 13th century. The cathedral contains some of the treasure that Spanish conquistadores brought back from the New World.

The cathedral and Alcázar complex (Av. Queipo de Llano) is the most impressive site in the city. The 15th-century cathedral is the third largest in the world, after St. Peter's and St. Paul's, and the largest Gothic structure in the world. Like the cathedral of Córdoba, it is built on the site of a former mosque adjoining a Patio of the Orange Trees. All that remains of the original mosque is a statuesque 322-foot Moorish tower, La Giralda, which is now the symbol of Seville. After touring the opulent 15th- and 16th-century interior of the cathedral, take the exit called Puerta de los Naranjos, which opens onto the patio. Walk to the Puerta Oriente, across a plaza, and you will find yourself at the Alcázar, the Moorish fortress that was modified by the Christians in the 14th century to resemble the Alhambra in Granada.

After touring the Alcázar, have lunch at the *Hostería del Laurel* (5 Plaza de las Venerables), where none other than Don Juan is supposed to have eaten before or after he went a-wooing. It's still in service and the food is quite good (see *Best en Route*).

After lunch, take a walk through the Barrio de Santa Cruz or down Calle Sierpes, the shopping street reserved for pedestrian traffic. Be sure to spend some time strolling through Parque María Luisa along the banks of the Río Guadalquivir and Av. María

Luisa, and take a boat ride at the Plaza de España. After such a pleasant afternoon, you'll know why Bizet's *Carmen* and Rossini's *Barber of Seville* are set here.

Unlike Córdoba, Seville has maintained its prominence as the spiritual center of Andalusia. In fact, the most exciting times to visit Seville are during *Semana Santa* (Holy Week) and during the *Feria de Sevilla* (spring fair) following Easter. During Easter, many holy images are paraded through the streets; the religious processions are world famous. During the *feria,* the city becomes a nonstop fiesta. Hotel reservations often are made a year in advance.

Speaking of reservations, during 1992 Seville expects millions of visitors at its colossal *Universal Expo-92,* celebrating the 500th anniversary of the discovery of America. Seville played an important role in the discovery and colonization of the New World as a seaport connected to the Atlantic by the Guadalquivir River. The 1,000-acre Island of Cartuja, formed by two branches of the river, will be the site of the fabulous fairgrounds. The Carthusian Monastery of Santa María de las Cuevas, for centuries the only structure on the island (now known for its fine ceramics), will be transformed into Spain's royal and government pavilions.

The E25 highway leads south to Jerez de la Frontera.

JEREZ DE LA FRONTERA: The town that first gave the world sherry is still producing it. Guided tours are conducted through Jerez's wine cellars with wine sampling offered afterward. You can buy sherry on the spot if any particular brand appeals to you. If you imbibe a bit more sherry than you're accustomed to, be sure to spend the night in Jerez before tackling the roads to Ronda, as they twist around cliffs and are difficult to navigate. You can also rent a chauffeured car or take an organized bus tour.

En Route to Granada – Set in the hills of the Serranía de Ronda, one of the oldest cities in Spain, Ronda is divided into two sections by a gorge more than 300 feet deep. South of the gorge is the old Moorish section, with its narrow, curving streets and alleyways. In this part of town is found the Casa del Rey Moro (Palace of the Moorish King); the church of Santa María la Mayor, which was a mosque in an earlier incarnation; and the Moorish baths. The Plaza de Toros is said to be where Pedro Romero started modern bullfighting in the 18th century. The best way to see Ronda is on foot. The splendid views of the surrounding hills and the gorges are truly impressive. Don't expect the Rondeños to welcome you with wide open arms; they are less exuberant than their other Andalusian neighbors. This may have something to do with the fact that the Serranía de Ronda used to be a refuge for bandits and *contrabandistas.*

You can get to Ronda from Jerez by heading east on N342. This road continues to Granada but it is a tortuous, time-consuming route. Scenic, yes; but you'll probably spend so much time praying that you won't enjoy the views. Alternatively, you can take N344 south to Fuengirola and follow the coastal route (N340) through Málaga to Motril, heading north on N323 to Granada. It gets you there without the agony.

GRANADA: To most people, Granada is synonymous with the Alhambra, a lavish fortress-palace-garden complex built on a mountain overlooking the city. Built by the Nasrid royal family (an Islamic group that fought the Christians in the 13th century), the Alhambra is one of the best preserved of all Moorish palaces in the world. It consists of three main areas: the Alcazaba and watch tower, that date from the 9th century; the Alhambra itself; and the Generalife, or summer gardens. Within the Alhambra is the 14th-century palace, which has many spacious courtyards and patios decorated with mosaic arches, fountains, columns, and gardens. A visit to the Alhambra is a dazzling, sensual experience: color, texture, sound, and smell intermingle.

Down the hill from the Alhambra, on Calle San Jerónimo in the cathedral quarter, is the Capilla Real (Royal Chapel), where the Catholic monarchs King Ferdinand and Queen Isabella are buried on the site of their victory over the Moors.

Opposite the Alhambra, the hilly Albaicín neighborhood is an intriguing maze of cottage-lined streets and patio gardens that sprout, like miniature Generalifes, in the middle of each house. The Sacromonte, at the summit of Albaicín, has some Gypsy caves where flamenco dances are performed. Be forewarned that they are overpriced; the shows in town are usually at least as good (if not better) and much less expensive.

For a list of reputable flamenco clubs and information on festivals, contact the Andalusian Tourist Information Office, 19 Calle Pavaneras (phone: 221022).

In winter, from November to May, you can ski at Solynieve ski center at Sierra Nevada, a few miles from Granada. Facilities include a chair lift, 8 ski lifts, and 2 cable cars. For details, see the Tourist Office listed above.

BEST EN ROUTE

Accommodations range from modern hotels to historic *paradores* (government-run inns). Expect to pay $100 or more for a double room at those places we've listed as expensive; between $50 and $100 for a room in the moderate category; under $50, inexpensive.

Andalusian restaurants are known for their pretty flowers, music, and artistic presentation of food that add sparkle to the atmosphere. Expect to pay over $60 for a meal for two at those restaurants we've listed as expensive; between $40 and $60 at those restaurants in the moderate category; under $40, inexpensive. Prices do not include drinks, wine, or tips.

CÓRDOBA

Meliá Córdoba – What this hotel lacks in charm it makes up for in modern amenities and a very convenient location in the center of town. It has a nightclub, bar, dining room, swimming pool, and a shopping arcade. Jardines de la Victoria (phone: 298066). Moderate.

Parador la Arruzafa – On the outskirts of town, this *parador* is not in a historic building but in a fairly ordinary-looking, relatively recent structure. The dining room serves game in winter and gazpacho with almonds in summer. Avenida de la Arruzafa (phone: 275900). Moderate.

Residencial Maimónides – A small hotel right across the street from La Mezquita offers modest accommodations and the most scenic location in town. In the old section. 4 Calle Torrijos (phone: 471500). Moderate to inexpensive.

Caballo Rojo – Córdoba's leading restaurant serves Andalusian gazpacho, tortillas, and Valencian paella. 28 Calle Cardenal Herrero (phone: 475375). Moderate.

El Churrasco – Various styles of steaks are served, with potatoes, rice, and/or eggs. Closed Thursdays and August. 16 Calle Romero, one flight up (phone: 290819). Moderate to inexpensive.

SEVILLE

Alfonso XIII – Seville's most elegant establishment (now part of the CIGA chain), this palatial *gran lujo* hotel was built for the 1929 Expo in neo-Mudejar style, with tiles, grillwork, marble, arches, and columns galore. There is sun and socializing at the garden pool and bar and a grand atmosphere in the lobby, lounges, and restaurant. It's a great place to visit even if you're not staying here. 2 Calle San Fernando (phone: 225580). Expensive.

Sevilla Sol – This deluxe hotel is part of the Sol chain, Spain's biggest. Centrally located near the Plaza de España, it features a swimming pool, physical-fitness center, squash courts, convention facilities, fine restaurants, and the special Club Elite services. 3 Avenida de la Borbolla (phone: 422403). Expensive.

Doña María – Directly across the street from the cathedral in the Barrio de Santa

Cruz, this small, four-star hotel has received good reviews from just about everyone who's crossed its threshold. 19 Calle Don Remondo (phone: 224990). Expensive to moderate.

Inglaterra – Another top contemporary hotel in the center of the city, behind the town hall. Many of its comfortable rooms have large balconies. It's a short walk from here to the cathedral and Calle Sierpes. A good buy for Seville. 7 Plaza Nueva (phone: 224970). Expensive to moderate.

Parador Alcázar del Rey Don Pedro – Originally a 14th-century Moorish fortress, this is a triumph of architectural restoration, with all the modern luxuries, including a restaurant, bar, and swimming pool. In the historic town of Carmona, just 18 miles (29 km) east of Seville, it is well worth the commute (phone: 141010). Moderate.

Dorada – Both the restaurant and the clientele are casually elegant, and the seafood and service are excellent. Closed Sunday evenings and July 15 to August 15. Across the river at 6 Calle Virgen de las Aguas Santas (phone: 455100). The proprietors also operate *La Taberna Dorada,* at José Luis de Casso (phone: 652720), as well as a seafood restaurant in Madrid. Expensive to moderate.

Oriza – One of the fanciest restaurants in town, this is a favorite of the local aristocracy and visiting European epicureans. The Biscayan seafood is excellent, and the unusual decor is highlighted by Eiffel-wrought ironwork. Closed Sundays and August. 41 Calle San Fernando (phone: 227211). Expensive to moderate.

Arenal – This famous cabaret features some of the best and most authentic flamenco performers in Andalusía, in the colorful setting of a 17th-century mansion. Unlike many others, this *tablao* is a favorite of locals and dancers as well as tourists. 7 Calle Rodo (phone: 216492). Moderate.

Burladero – Handsomely decorated with tile ceilings and wood paneling, it's very popular with the Spanish. Start with *angulas de Aguinaga,* baby eels, or gazpacho, then have meat, poultry, game, or *paella.* Service, food, and wine are excellent. 1 Calle Canalejas (phone: 222900). Moderate.

Hostería del Laurel – After touring the Alcázar, have lunch where the infamous Don Juan dined. 5 Plaza de los Venerables (phone: 220295). Moderate.

La Isla – Extraordinary seafood, including fish and shellfish flown in from Galicia. Closed in August. 25 Calle Arfe (phone: 215376). Moderate.

Mesón Don Raimundo – In a former convent with antique furnishings, this restaurant has plenty of atmosphere and good seafood. Closed Sunday nights. 26 Calle Argote de Molina (phone: 223355). Moderate.

Río Grande – Here, wide terraces flank the riverbanks, and the architecture of the building is lovely in its own right. 70 Calle Betis (phone: 273956). Moderate.

JEREZ DE LA FRONTERA

Gaitán – Prepared with savory herbs, the Andalusian stews and soups served here are complemented by delicious original dishes and tempting desserts. Closed Sunday nights, Mondays, and August. 3 Calle Gaitán (phone: 345859). Moderate to inexpensive.

GRANADA

Alhambra Palace – If you can't get a room in the *parador* and still want to stay near the Alhambra, this is a fine alternative. It, too, stands on the Alhambra hill, with great views of the Alhambra and the city. Built in 1910 with design and decor blending with the Moorish-Andalusian architecture of the Alhambra, it has recently been refurbished and 11 deluxe suites have been added. 2 Calle Peña Partida (phone: 221468). Expensive.

Bobadilla – Rambling over 1,500 acres of countryside, this magnificent resort-hotel-ranch complex is midway between Granada, Córdoba, and Seville. The epitome of luxurious Andalusian ambience, it has a Mudejar-style main lobby reminiscent of the Moorish mosque of Córdoba, and no two of its exquisitely decorated rooms are alike. Fountains, patios, and gardens are everywhere, and the central gathering place is a 16th-century-style chapel with a 1,595-pipe organ. A choice of restaurants includes the elegant five-fork *La Finca*. A fitness club, lake-size swimming pool, and conference rooms round out the facilities. Loja (phone 321861). Expensive.

Parador San Francisco – This one tops the list of *paradores*. In a restored 15th-century section of the Alhambra itself, it commands magnificent views of the Generalife, the city, and the Sierra Nevada. Its restaurant features topnotch Andalusian cuisine. Reservations are required at least 8 months in advance, especially for the peak months of May, June, September, and October. Alhambra (phone: 221440). Expensive.

Washington Irving – Named for the American writer whose *Tales of the Alhambra* helped rekindle foreign interest in the place, this hotel is near the Alhambra and offers decent, reasonably priced accommodations. 2 Paseo del Generalife (phone: 227550). Moderate.

Torres Bermejas – One of the best restaurants in town for Andalusian cuisine. Closed Sundays. 5 Plaza Nueva (phone: 223116). Moderate.

Cunini – Granada's most prominent seafood restaurant features fresh catch of the day flown in from the Cantabrian coast. 14 Calle Pescadería (phone: 263701). Moderate to inexpensive.

Colombia – Next door to the Alhambra, meals are served to the accompaniment of flamenco guitarists. Closed Sundays. Calle Antequeruela Baja (phone: 227434). Inexpensive.

The Canary Islands

A cluster of seven major and six minor islands in the South Atlantic, the Canary Island archipelago lies about 65 miles off the northwest coast of Africa. Spread across the 28° north latitude line, just 4° north of the Tropic of Cancer, the Canaries have a springlike climate throughout the year — in the 70s F (21-31C). The major islands are Tenerife, Gran Canaria, Fuerteventura, La Gomera, Hierro, and La Palma, also known as "the green island" because of its comparatively heavy rainfall and the intense green of its forests.

Although legends suggest that the Canary Islands are the remains of the lost continent of Atlantis, history indicates that the first recorded visit occurred during the 1st century AD. According to Roman historian Pliny the Elder, it was Juba II, at that time King of Mauritania, who was the first tourist of note to visit the Canary Islands. In those days, the islands were called Canariae Insulae, which, in the original Latin, means "dog islands." So, when Juba II stepped off the royal barge, he was greeted by a pack of large, snarling dogs. According to Pliny (the only available source), Juba hastily retreated to Mauritania.

It wasn't until the late 15th century that Spain claimed the seven cone-shaped volcanic islands and renamed them Las Canarias after a variety of finch that live in the trees. We don't know what happened to the original Latin dogs for which the islands were named 1,400 years earlier, but we do know that the archipelago became greatly sought after. The two main islands, Gran Canaria and Tenerife, were finally conquered by Kind Ferdinand and Queen Isabella in 1496.

Not much is known about the original inhabitants, the Guanche cave dwellers who were decimated by the Spanish armies, bubonic plague, locust-induced famine, and volcanic eruptions. A tall, blond, light-skinned, blue-eyed people, the Guanche are believed to have been descended from a mixture of Viking, African, Berber, and Phoenician stock. According to archaeologists, who have unearthed ceramic and leather artifacts, the Guanche were monotheistic and mummified their dead.

Today's Canary Islanders are peaceful, friendly, artistic people, who make their living farming, fishing, and producing handicrafts — as well as by working at various jobs in the modern resort developments. Though only recently discovered by American tourists, the Canary Islands have long been popular with vacationing Europeans. The quaint villages of white cottages with red roofs sprinkled throughout the mountainous interior of the volcanic islands make the Canary Island archipelago inviting to travelers who enjoy exploring unusual places and discovering the distinctive character of each island.

GRAN CANARIA

As you fly into Gando International Airport, south of Gran Canaria's capital, Las Palmas, the island looks like Mt. Everest rising from the Sahara. As you descend, the stark, rugged landscape becomes greener and soon you can distinguish banana trees, coffee groves, sugarcane, almond trees, and tomato farms. Each village is actually an oasis.

LAS PALMAS: The capital city of this 592-square-mile island is a duty-free port; Europeans from all over the Continent flock here for the bargains in furs. Two well-known furriers with shops in half a dozen European cities, *Voula Mitsakou* (28 Calle Luis Morote, at the junction of Calle Sagasta and Avenida General Vives) and *Kanellopoulos* (46 Calle Sagasta), charge 30% to 50% less for their sable, ermine, and other skins in Las Palmas than in their other branches. In addition, there are plenty of shops selling Chinese silks, Indian marble, cameras, tape recorders, liquor, shoes, clothing, jewelry, and souvenir items. Bargaining or "negotiation," as it is otherwise called, is highly appropriate, but you have to be good at it to best the Indian, Pakistani, and Lebanese merchants who own most of the stores. It is a good idea to know the range of prices of items you are considering throughout the city before you actually buy. And if you're in the market for a camera, be sure you know the exact model number: It can make a big difference in price.

Las Palmas covers a strip of seafront on the northwest tip of the island. A natural depression in the coastline has provided a sheltered bay for the beach called Playa de las Canteras. The rocky breakwater, shaped rather like an arm, extends almost around the bay and makes it as calm as a lake. Running parallel to the beach, the 2-mile Paseo de las Canteras promenade boasts numerous restaurants: Swedish, Italian, Chinese, Finnish, Mexican, Indian, German, and Spanish, as well as a few of the sit-down or stand-up fast-food variety. In addition, there are many bars, cafés, and bistros.

The rhythm of life in Las Palmas is determined by the sun. Visitors often spend the day lying in the sun from 8 or 9 AM until 4 or 5 PM. Then, in the cool of the evening, they head for the outdoor cafés, shops, restaurants, and bars of the Paseo. Shops remain open until dusk, about 9 PM. If clouds or mist interfere with the sun, people stroll or shop — but only until the sun reappears.

Sometimes people go for a walk in Parque Santa Catalina where Canarian families often come for their evening strolls. It's very pleasant, as local guitarists play impromptu serenades for passersby. To get to the park, walk along Calle Padre Cueto 4 blocks to Castillo, then head right along Castillo for 2 blocks. (By the way, the park, and everywhere else in the Canary Islands, is safe for visiting at night.)

The public market is a good place for taking photographs of people engaged in the ordinary everyday commerce of buying and selling foodstuffs and other provisions. It occupies an entire block at the corner of Calles Néstor de Torre and Galicia. From the Paseo, walk up Calle Thomas Miller, the street with the statue of the dolphin. Take it straight to the market.

Doramas Park (Parque Doramas) contains a zoo, swimming pool, and an unusual model of a Canarian village designed by local painter Néstor de la Torre. The park is easy to get to: Any bus traveling along Calle León y Castillo at Parque Santa Catalina also goes to Parque Doramas. After a visit to the park, the *Bodegón* restaurant is a good place to taste Canarian food (see *Best en Route*). But watch out; first encounters with Canarian food can be explosive. The ubiquitous sauce called *mojo picón* is an *amigo falso* (false friend). Its seemingly benign aroma belies its true nature. *Mojo picón* is not just a hot sauce, it's an incendiary concoction of chili peppers, garlic, oil, vinegar, salt, and pepper. But don't hesitate to order either the *cazuela canaria* or *sancocho de pescado,* a fish casserole and stew, respectively. Try them both — they're delicious.

TEJEDA: About 25 miles (40 km) southwest of Las Palmas along narrow, mountain roads stands the petrified forest, which the Spanish poet Unamuno (1864–1936) called a "petrified storm." It stands about 4,800 feet above sea level amid a bleak, awesome, volcanic landscape. Be sure to take advantage of the sensational lookouts (*miradores*) along the route. Bus excursions and English-speaking taxi drivers also cover this route. The concierge at any hotel will help you arrange transportation.

MASPALOMAS: On the southern edge of Gran Canaria, about 35 miles (56 km) from Gando Airport, lies an ocher strand of beach, Playa del Inglés, that curves around a palm-fringed lagoon, looking like a setting from *The Arabian Nights.* Just 1 mile (1.6 km) to the west of the Maspalomas lighthouse, Playa Pasito Blanco has a deep-water harbor with a marina where deep-sea charters can be hired. There is an 18-hole golf course at *Maspalomas Oasis,* a new resort.

PUERTO RICO: Just 20 miles (32 km) west of Maspalomas, this apartment-condominium complex is great for families and couples who want to spend a month, a summer, or the entire year in a setting complete with marina, beach, swimming pools, restaurants, shopping, nightclubs, and playgrounds. The complex is pretty big, but the design of the community is not overwhelming. You can find out about booking space in Puerto Rico from the Tourist Office in Las Palmas or at the Tourist Office of Spain in the US. (This area is not particularly recommended for singles.)

SAN BARTOLOMÉ DE TIRAJANA: Another day trip from Las Palmas or Maspalomas takes you to this town at the bottom of a huge crater at the foot of the central mountains. At 6,500 feet, the snow-capped Pozo de las Nieves ridge is the highest point on the island. It's a 2-mile hike, straight up, from San Bartolomé to the peaks.

TENERIFE

Only 20 minutes by air from Las Palmas, Tenerife, with 794 square miles, is the largest of the Canary Islands. (It can also be reached by flights from Madrid in a little over 2 hours.) Lusher, with more forest, colorful vegetation, and a somewhat higher rate of rainfall, Tenerife is called the island of "eternal spring." It is also the archipelago's main agricultural center. Most vegetables grown in the Canaries come from Tenerife's soil.

SANTA CRUZ DE TENERIFE: A duty-free port, the capital of Tenerife is more Spanish in character and aesthetically more pleasing than Las Palmas. However, it has no beaches to speak of and is primarily a city of shops. The streets bounded by Calle del Castillo, Calle Valentín Sanz, Calle Emilio Calzadillo, and the ocean form a square within which are literally hundreds of shops selling everything. As in Las Palmas, the Indian, Pakistani, Lebanese, and Spanish shopkeepers are willing to negotiate but they are not about to give anything away. Calle del Castillo is closed to traffic from the Plaza de España to the park at the end of the street. Plaza de España is noteworthy because of its memorial and monument to the men of Tenerife who died in World War II. Due to its height, the monument can be seen from quite a distance, so try to use it as a directional marker as you head into the shopping district, which is almost always jammed with hordes of shoppers.

PLAYA LAS TERESITAS: With barren volcanic cliffs for a backdrop, this beach, about 10 minutes from the center of town along the road to San Andrés, resembles a moonscape. In fact, you would think you were swimming in a moon crater if the moon had water. Only one-quarter of a mile long and about 150 yards wide, the beach is totally protected from the open Atlantic by a stone jetty. You can reach the beach by taking a bus from the Plaza de España.

OROTAVA: One of Tenerife's most compelling sites, Orotava is across the neck of the island from Santa Cruz and overlooks Puerto de la Cruz, 1,000 feet below. This is the best place to shop for indigenous crafts. Be sure to visit the *Artesanía* (Calle San Francisco), one of a national chain of arts and crafts centers established by the Spanish government. It is in an old house with a flower-filled patio. Here you will find the delicate *calado*, drawn-thread embroidery, used for everything from handkerchiefs to tablecloths, manufactured by women working at wooden looms. The women speak English and they are glad to answer questions. In addition to local crafts, ceramics from Seville and leather from Barcelona are also on sale.

The annual *Corpus Christi* festival in June is a celebration of the religious fervor, energy, and artistry of the people of Orotava. Before the festival's procession, the town's squares and streets are covered with carpets of brilliant flowers and colorful sand designs. The largest and most intricate sand carpet is laid on the Plaza del Ayuntamiento, across town from the *Artesanía*. On other streets around town carpets made from hundreds of thousands of flower petals — bougainvillea, dahlias, geraniums, carnations — as well as crushed leaves and pine needles depict a variety of biblical scenes. Although the *Feast of Corpus Christi* is at its most colorful in Orotava, it is celebrated throughout the Canaries, floral carpets and all.

PICOS DEL TEIDE: There are few places on earth where you can explore volcanic craters. Even fewer give you the chance to stand more than 2 miles above sea level and look in all directions, unhindered. El Pico del Teide, a crater more than 40 miles in circumference and more than 6,600 feet above sea level, is one of those rare places. Just beyond the crater stands the highest mountain in Spain, El Teide, at 12,200 feet. Parque Nacional Las Cañadas del Teide has a cable car to the top of the mountain. The 15-minute ride to the summit is breathtaking enough to make even the most avid photographers gaze at the scenery and forget about taking pictures. When there are few clouds, the six other major Canary Islands and the coast of Africa are clearly visible. At dawn, the sun touching the mountains creates splendid shadows that blend with the different shades of lava and ash. The stillness and barrenness is intensely moving.

PUERTO DE LA CRUZ: Considering that Puerto de la Cruz has no beach worthy of its name, it is reasonable to wonder why it is the major tourist center of the Canaries. Put simply, Puerto is pure resort — an enclave of shops, hotels, restaurants, bars, and discos. There is hardly anything else. The town has been given over to strolling, shopping, and eating. To compensate for no beach, clever architects and engineers have built sea-water pools, promenades, man-made lakes, and lounging areas into and around the rocky volcanic outcroppings that extend offshore for hundreds of yards.

The best way to get to know Puerto is on foot. A walk through the most interesting part of town should begin at Plaza de Concejil on Calle Generalisimo Franco. Head right on Calle de Santo Domingo, then left on Calle de San Telmo. San Telmo, the main drag, runs along the waterfront. It's an elegant street with a bevy of fine shops and hotels to match. Follow San Telmo until it becomes Avenida de Colón and runs parallel to Playa de Martiánez. Take it to Calle Agular y Quesada, then back to the Plaza.

Puerto de la Cruz is about a half-hour bus or car ride from the Los Rodeos Airport near Santa Cruz de Tenerife. On the south coast of the island, the Reina Sofía airport is the one most used for Madrid and international flights.

LANZAROTE

An eerie, burnt-out island punctuated by hundreds of extinct volcanoes, Lanzarote is the most physically astonishing of the Canaries. Its scenery is so unusual that people who fly in from Tenerife or Las Palmas always describe the place as unforgettable.

ARRECIFE: The island's capital is actually a fishing town with an airport. Two castles, San Gabriel and San José, stand guard on a hill. Arrecife itself is not particularly interesting, but a drive north to Teguise, the former capital set on top of an extinct volcano, gives you a splendid view of some of the smaller Canaries: La Graciosa, Montaña Clara, Alegranza, Roque del Este, and Roque del Oeste. The highlight of Teguise is Guanapay Castle, perched on top of the cone. Not far from Teguise, the kaleidoscopic Verdes Cave tunnels for miles inside the Corona Volcano labyrinth. Connecting underground is the Jameos del Agua lagoon, a huge grotto with a restaurant-bar-nightclub and a unique pool designed by the island's internationally famed architect César Manrique.

Heading into the interior from Arrecife takes you through the terrace farms of La Gería. Here, farmers spread over their fields a layer of fine volcanic ash, which absorbs the nightly dew and provides moisture for the plants. Out of this bizarre agricultural technique, sumptuous melons, watermelons, figs, onions, tomatoes, and grapes are grown. The grapes are fermented to produce Malvasía wine.

Continuing west farther into the interior of the mountain brings you to Montaña de Fuego, the most stunning of the island's natural attractions. From the top of the mountain, you can see hundreds of extinct volcanoes in the surrounding countryside. The summit is accessible by camel; you ride in chairs slung over either side of the hump. Camel processions leave from Arrecife for the 2-hour trip.

Heading south from Arrecife you will find the Tías resort development, which can accommodate 1,000 visitors in small hotels, cottages, and apartment houses. There is a marina with deep-sea fishing charters available. At the southernmost tip of the island is Playa Blanca, which is, as its name suggests, a white beach.

LA GRACIOSA

To the north of Lanzarote, this tiny, 17-square-mile island has one small mountain, la Montaña de las Agujas. La Graciosa has two fine beaches, Caleta del Sebo and Conchas.

FUERTEVENTURA

Fuerteventura has the longest shoreline of any of the islands, with plenty of spacious, empty beaches. If you really want total seclusion, this is a good spot for it. Playa de Jandía at the southern end of the island and Gran Tarajal have good fishing: Sardines, swordfish, and tuna are quite plentiful and easily caught. The capital, Puerto del Rosario, has an airstrip and not much else.

LA PALMA

Known as "the green island," La Palma covers 281 square miles. Its capital, Santa Cruz de la Palma, slopes along the eastern side of a crater called La Caldera de Taburiente. Approximately 17 miles in circumference, La Caldera is ringed with pine trees and has been declared a national park. You can explore it to a depth of 2,500 feet. The city itself has some 16th-century buildings, including the church of San Salvador and the Ayuntamiento (city hall); a natural history museum containing aboriginal artifacts; and traditional village architecture, featuring ornately hand-carved balconies protruding from the second and third stories of adjoining whitewashed cottages.

At the southernmost tip of the island is the vineyard district of Fuencaliente. To the north of the capital is the verdant forest of Los Tilos where the thick tropical vegetation includes giant ferns.

Although facilities and services for tourists are not as well developed as in Gran Canaria or Tenerife, La Palma does attract good numbers of Europeans who prefer quiet vacations.

LA GOMERA

The craggy seacoast and mountainous terrain of this 146-square-mile island have made transportation difficult. To compensate, the islanders have developed over the centuries a system of communication based on whistling, with which they can "speak" to each other from hilltop to valley.

About 20 miles (32 km) from Tenerife's Playa de los Cristianos (in southern Tenerife), La Gomera is the site of the Church of the Asunción where Columbus and his crews heard mass before setting off for parts unknown. The house in which he lived, called the *Casa de Colón,* is now a museum. The Torre del Conde, an old fortress, has been declared a national historic monument, and the island's Garanjonay National Park is a UNESCO Natural World Heritage Site.

Apart from San Sebastián, the capital, and the whistling Gomera islanders themselves, the island has several banana plantations, orchards, a fishing village called Playa Santiago, and a good, tawny beach on Valle Gran Rey. The island has no airport, but Ferry Gomera makes two trips daily from Tenerife.

HIERRO

The smallest major island of the archipelago (less than 107 square miles), Hierro is called "the island of iron." It is the harshest of all, with black volcanic soil, steep massifs, deep craters, and barren mountains. About 3,500 of the island's 7,000 residents live in the capital, Valverde, the central town of an agricultural area where wine is the major product. In the southern part of Hierro, there is good fishing at La Restinga.

BEST EN ROUTE

With plenty of hotels to choose from, the choices listed below represent those that have some particularly appealing quality — location, service, or aesthetic design. Expect to pay $100 or more for a double room at those places in the expensive category; between $50 and $95 at a hotel in the moderate category; under $50, inexpensive.

Restaurants in the Canary Islands span the culinary spectrum from sleek international dining spots to funky regional places where you can sample local cooking. Expect to pay $60 or more for a meal for two at those places we've categorized as expensive; between $30 and $55 at those restaurants in the moderate category; under $25, inexpensive. Prices do not include drinks, wine, or tips.

GRAN CANARIA

Cristina Sol – Right on the Las Canteras beach, this property is large and luxurious, with swimming pools, fine restaurants, a disco, and lovely gardens. 6 Calle Gomera, Las Palmas (phone: 267600). Expensive.

Iberotel Maspalomas Oasis – The center of the action, this busy, large resort is popular with European tour groups. It has a nightclub, golf course, horseback riding, tennis, health club, shopping arcade, and a number of other facilities. Playa de Maspalomas (phone: 760170). Expensive.

Reina Isabel – Right on the beach at Las Palmas and relatively modern in decor and furnishings, its facilities include a fine restaurant, swimming pool (with adjoining disco), beachfront nightclub, and solarium. It has a very good reputation as a place that appeals to a discriminating clientele. 40 Calle Alfredo L. Jones, Paseo Playa de las Canteras, Las Palmas (phone: 260100). Expensive.

Santa Catalina – Of Las Palmas's more than 100 hotels, this one has the most intriguing atmosphere. An imitation Moorish palace standing in the middle of the flowers of Parque Doramas, it has a large swimming pool, miniature golf, shopping arcade, and fireplaces in the public rooms. It compares favorably with the more modern establishments. Parque Doramas (phone: 243040). Expensive.

Tamarindos – Although far from the fashionable, sophisticated cities of Europe, this hotel rivals the best of them in decor, grounds, and amenities. Its two swimming pools and beach make it a good place for simple lounging in the sun. There is even a full buffet alongside one of the swimming pools, several bars, and a disco. On the hillside across the highway, the huge, white, cast-concrete object with a pole in its center is a sundial — a gift from the Swedish people. And you can set your watch by it. 3 Calle Retama, Playa San Agustín (phone: 762600). Expensive.

Guantánamo – At Mogán, or more specifically on the beach at Playa Tauro, this campsite is about 60 miles (96 km) from Las Palmas. Although it can accommodate 1,500 people, food, beverages, and other supplies are not available on the site. But if you're interested in spending your time on the beaches of the south coast or visiting Cruz de Tejeda, this is your best bet (phone: 241701). Inexpensive.

Temisas – This one is relatively small as campsites go, but then so is the demand. It's built to accommodate about 50 campers. For food, beverages, and other supplies, Aguimes is the closest town (phone: 241701). Inexpensive.

Bogedón – Our favorite place for Canarian food. Try the seafood here; specialties include *cazuela canario* (fish casserole) and *sancocho de pescado* (fish stew). Parque Doramas, Las Palmas (no phone). Moderate.

Nanking – It's a long way from the China Sea to the Mediterranean, but the Cantonese culinary influence has nonetheless weathered the tide. Many people's first choice as the best Chinese restaurant in town, this is certainly one of the most popular. Its air conditioned interior is undoubtedly a factor, along with the food. 11 Calle José F. Roca, Las Palmas (phone: 269870). Moderate.

Pote – Excellent fish, seafood, and lamb as well as Galician specialties and fine ham are found here. Closed Sundays. 41 Calle José María Durán (phone: 278058). Moderate.

San Agustín Beach Club – The best restaurant on the island is resplendent with African decor amid a strikingly contemporary setting. It's renowned for top-notch international cuisine. Closed during May and June. 2 Plaza de los Cocoteros, San Agustín (phone: 760400). Moderate.

Puerto Rico – A decent little eatery that serves local food, particularly fish and seafood. Playa Mogán, Puerto Rico (no phone). Inexpensive.

TENERIFE

Mencey – This charming old yellow building has retained some of its former grandeur despite recent renovations. Set in splendid gardens, its rooms have been refurbished and a new wing with motel-type units has been added. Facilities include 2 swimming pools, tennis courts, bar, and a poolside buffet. 38 Avenida José Naveiras, Santa Cruz (phone: 276700). Expensive.

San Felipe Sol – A convenient, comfortable establishment with a freshwater swimming pool, tennis courts, and a nightclub featuring flamenco dancers. But we think that the service could be spiffier, especially in the huge dining room. 13 Avenida de Colón, Puerto de la Cruz (phone: 383311). Expensive.

Semiramis – Puerto's futuristic centerpiece must be seen to be believed. Imaginative architecture makes it appear to be built from top to bottom, running down a mountain. All rooms overlook the ocean and have refrigerators; some have kitchens. It also has 2 swimming pools, tennis courts, a lounge area with games, and a good dining room. Urbanización La Paz, Puerto de la Cruz (phone: 385551). Expensive.

Parador de las Cañadas del Teide – Ideal for catching the sunrise over the Picos del Teide. In fact, your hosts won't allow you to oversleep. The new wooden inn is modeled after a Swiss chalet with a swimming pool and a lounge with a fireplace. The *parador* is surrounded by nature trails. Reservations required well in advance. Orotava (phone: 332304). Moderate.

Parque San Antonio – If you want to get away from the madding throngs of tourists in Puerto de la Cruz, but wish to be close enough to the center of town to make quick forays, consider this as your first choice for accommodations. Tucked away in a veritable botanic garden all its own, it is merely 5 minutes by bus from the center of town. Carretera de las Arenas, Puerto de la Cruz (phone: 384908). Moderate to inexpensive.

Pescado – The name means "the fish" and that's what you'll find on the menu, prepared in a variety of intriguing ways. Closed Wednesdays and May through September. 3 Avenida Venezuela, Puerto de la Cruz (phone: 382806). Moderate.

Riviera – Snazzy continental dishes are the hallmark of this chic, tastefully decorated restaurant. Closed Sundays and mid-August through mid-September. 155 Rambla Generalisimo Franco, Santa Cruz de Tenerife (phone: 275812). Moderate.

Mesón del Teide – In Las Cañadas National Park, its unparalleled location on the 2,000-foot mountain El Portillo makes this worth the trip, even if you only sip a glass of wine and snack on a sandwich. La Orotava (no phone). Inexpensive.

LANZAROTE

Salinas Sol – Looking like a giant spacecraft newly touched down in a tropical paradise, it offers 310 modern rooms, each with a private terrace facing seaside. Outdoor delights such as tennis, diving, and sailing abound, as do indoor pleasures — restaurants, bars, massage, sauna, cinema, and disco. Costa Teguise (phone: 813040). Expensive.

Arrecife Gran Hotel – Although standing smack in the middle of a village, there is no way this contemporary resort could be considered to be in the center of the action. Its most astounding feature is a restaurant on an island in the middle of a small lake that can only be reached by boat. It also has a pool, cheerful dining room, and lots of flowers. Avenida Mancomunidad (phone: 811254). Moderate.

Castillo de San José – In the bottom of a medieval castle that is now a contemporary art museum, this is one of the most beautiful restaurants on the island. One mile (1.6 km) northeast of Arrecife on the road to Las Caletas (phone: 812321). Moderate.

Casa Salvador – Tucked away in one of the quieter corners of the island, this lovely seafood restaurant stands right on the beach. Playa Blanca de Yaiza (no phone). Moderate to inexpensive.

El Diablo – Another dramatically located restaurant, it stands amid the volcanic mountains of the interior and serves lunch only. Montaña del Fuego, Tinajo (phone: 840057). Inexpensive.

Playa Blanca – There is no menu; excellent seafood dishes depend on the catch of the day. Yaiza (no phone). Inexpensive.

FUERTEVENTURA

Parador de Fuerteventura – Standing on the edge of the ocean, this new, modern *parador* is the most splendid hotel on the island. Puerto del Rosario, Urb. Playa Blanca (phone: 851150). Moderate.

LA PALMA

Parador Santa Cruz de la Palma – This is another sparkling new addition to the national chain. It, too, rates top marks. Avenida Maritima, Santa Cruz de la Palma (phone: 412340). Moderate.

LA GOMERA

Parador Conde de la Gomera – Built in the unique Canarian manorial style, this inn is surrounded by lush tropical gardens. In addition to beautiful ocean views, guests enjoy a swimming pool. It's much in demand, so make reservations early. Calle San Sebastián (phone: 871100). Moderate.

The Balearic Islands

The Balearic Islands lie 90 miles southeast of Barcelona in the Mediterranean Sea. The major section of the archipelago consists of two pair of islands: Mallorca and Minorca (in Spanish, *Menorca*), and Formentera and Ibiza. Many smaller islands of lesser significance complete the archipelagic structure. Of the four major islands, Mallorca (whose name means "the larger") is the largest, best known, and best equipped for tourism. Minorca (whose name means "the smaller") receives fewer foreign visitors and, consequently, has retained its tranquil, seaside communities. Ibiza is home to jet-setters, artists, and pseudo-artists. Formentera is undoubtedly the most secluded of the four islands.

The Balearic Mountains are thick with ancient fig and olive trees while the beaches are shaded by evergreens. The surrounding seas are exceptionally calm and clear despite the prevailing winds.

The Balearic language is a dialect of Catalán, the language of Cataluña, the Barcelona region of mainland Spain. Catalán is a Romance language that resembles Provençal French with some vestiges of colonial Latin as spoken in the Roman Empire.

Remnants of human habitation date from the Bronze Age. In different parts of the islands are large stone pyramids, thought to be Bronze Age tombs, called *talayots*. Later Balearic islanders were mercenaries and seamen in the armies and navies of Rome and Carthage. The Moors reigned from AD 902 until 1229 when the Aragonese reconquest converted the Balearics into a prosperous center of Mediterranean trade. In the 16th century, Spain's attention shifted to the New World and the Balearics fell into the hands of the Turks and the Barbary pirates, whose influence can still be seen in the walls and watchtowers of Mallorca.

During the 18th century, Father Junípero Serra set forth from the Balearics, where he was born, to found the string of missions along the California coast known as El Camino Real, the Mission Trail. In the 19th century, composer Frédéric Chopin and his mistress, author George Sand, chose Mallorca as their island retreat.

Twentieth-century visitors find that May, early June, and September are the best months for a quiet, relaxing visit. The weather is sparkling clear, with temperatures in the 70s and 80s F (21-26 C). July and August are the most intense, active months. The Balearic Islands have a climate temperate enough for year-round water sports: sailing, swimming, diving, and deep-sea fishing for sole, perch, and bream. There is a racetrack in Palma, the capital of Mallorca, and plenty of golf courses and tennis courts.

MALLORCA

PALMA DE MALLORCA: Incredible though it sounds, between June and September, the airport of Palma, the Balearics' and Mallorca's capital, handles more transients than New York's John F. Kennedy Airport. With thousands of hotel rooms and hundreds of restaurants, Palma is one of the world's busiest resort centers.

The Bay of Palma is protected from the wind and weather by the Puig Mayor mountain range which lies to the northwest of the city. Palma Nova and Magaluf beaches are the only two sandy areas to the west of Palma, although there are hotels along the sheer coastline. To the east of the city, although there is less protection, there are miles of excellent beaches and resorts known as the Playas de Palma. With 304,422 residents, the city of Palma contains almost half of the island's population.

Known as the Ciutat de Mallorca after the liberation from the Moors in 1229, the town was colonized by Jews and Genoese and subsequently prospered. James II and his successors were able to build majestic Gothic buildings and Italian-style villas. Mansions were erected in the 15th and 16th centuries by descendants of merchants and landed gentry. The typical Mallorcan casa (with an interior patio framed by marble columns) developed in the 18th century can be seen in many parts of Palma.

The heart of the city is the wide promenade, or *rambla,* known as the Borne (open market).

In the old part of town east of the Borne are shops that specialize in crafts, filigree, embroidery, world-famous pearls, and glasswork. A morning walk might begin at the Ayuntamiento (city hall) at 2 Plaza Cort. Here you'll find the Van Dyck painting *The Martyrdom of San Sebastián* hanging on the first floor. Continue 1 block south to the church of Santa Eulalia (Iglesia Santa Eulalia). Across the street stands the Casa Vivot, one of the best examples of 18th-century Palma town houses with an inner court and paintings by Breughel, Ribera, and others. At Plaza San Francisco, the church of San Francisco contains the tomb of Ramón Llull, famed Doctor Illuminatus, philosopher and humanist of cosmopolitan 13th-century Mallorca. One block south of the Plaza, Casa Palmer is a fine example of 16th-century Gothic and Renaissance architecture. The Moorish Baths, intact from the era of the Caliphate, can be found on Paseo Umjuay. Liberally sprinkled along this route are cafés and saloons for late breakfasts and early aperitifs.

Casa Oleza (2 Calle Morey) is another example of the famous Mallorquín patios or interior courtyards. The Oleza patio is an extraordinarily well balanced composition, which includes an iron-topped well, typical wide arches, and short marble columns supporting a balcony.

To the west of El Borne are the three palaces: Palacios Morell, on Calle San Cayetano; Palacio Sollerich, on the Borne itself, with one of the best patios in the city; and Palacio Montenegro, on the street of the same name.

Other important sights include the cathedral; the Spanish Pueblo (Pueblo Español), which includes exact reproductions of famous houses representing different regions, epochs, and architecture from all parts of Spain; La Almudaina, a Moorish fortress just off Plaza de la Reina; La Lonja, a 15th-century structure built by Guillermo Sagrera to house an exchange; the fishing neighborhood of Puig San Pere; and Bellver Castle, overlooking Palma in Parque Bellver.

For maps and brochures about places of interest, hotels, and restaurants, contact the Tourist Information Office at the airport (phone: 260803) or 10 Avenida Jaime Tercero (phone: 212216) in the center of town.

With 250 miles of coast broken into dazzling coves, inlets, and beaches, Mallorca has much to explore. Because the narrow roads snaking around cliffs with precipitous drops are a legitimate driving hazard, we recommend that you hire a chauffeured car with an English-speaking guide to get to the fishing villages, resorts, and other sites of interest described below. The classic seascapes and mountain scenery deserve to be enjoyed fully, and if you are unused to the surprisingly rugged dips and turns of the roads, chances are you will be too preoccupied with safety to savor the sights. From Palma, there are five distinct touring routes: (1) from Palma north to Valldemosa, Deya, and Sóller; (2) from Palma north to Manacor and the caves; (3) from Palma northeast to Pollença and Formentor; (4) from Palma to the eastern coves; and (5) from Palma to the southwest peninsula.

PALMA TO SÓLLER: The 46-mile (74-km) Valldemosa-Deya-Sóller tour is a relaxed, 1-day trip from Palma. Valldemosa and Deya may be seen in the morning with a late lunch at the Puerto de Sóller. You can stop for coffee in the mountain pass on the road back to Palma.

Valldemosa's main attraction is the Carthusian monastery in which George Sand and Chopin passed the winter of 1838–39. Beyond Valldemosa the road runs along thousand-foot cliffs to San Marroig. The former resident, Archduke Luis Salvador, had a fine view of the Foradada, a famous rock with a doughnut-like perforation.

The village of Deya is surrounded by hills and evergreen forests. Known for its large colony of British artists and bohemians, Deya perches loft-like over the sea. Below the village is a stream outlet, tiny cove, Cala Deya, and beach.

The town of Sóller lies a few miles inland from the port. The road back to Palma over the Alfabia Sierra offers excellent views of the sea and sunset to the west.

PALMA TO THE DRACH CAVES (CUEVAS DEL DRACH): The second recommended route through Manacor, Artá, and the Drach Caves covers 109 miles (175 km), about 3 hours' driving time. Manacor is 30 miles (48 km) from Palma. From the city of Manacor, it is a short distance to Porto Cristo and the caves. Las Cuevas del Drach consist of four chambers of polychromatic pools and stalactite columns spreading over a distance of just over 1 mile. The tour takes 90 minutes and costs about $2. Other caves can be found in Artá and in the city of Manacor. In fact, the Artá caves are said to have inspired Jules Verne to write *Journey to the Center of the Earth.*

Also on this route are found the *talayots,* megalithic stone structures thought to be Bronze Age burial markers. The village of Capdepera is the site of a fortress high over the Mediterranean. Cala Ratjada is a fishing town with small streams and ocean beaches. On the way back to Palma, you can stop at the town of Petra, birthplace of Junípero Serra (1713–1784), the Franciscan monk whose Californian and Mexican missions developed into San Diego, Monterey, and San Francisco.

PALMA TO FORMENTOR: The third route, to Cape Formentor, northernmost point of the island, covers between 109 and 124 miles (175 and 198 km), passing through Pollença and Alcudia, and other points of interest along the way. You can stop at Selva to see the San Lorenzo church; at Campanet to see the caves; and at Alcudia where old Roman ramparts and a Roman theater still stand. Puerto de Pollença is a well-entrenched artists colony with a sheltered bay and fine harbor. Stop in at the museum of the painter Anglada Camerasa, which features the island's most representative artists. Puerto de Pollença has become the home of many Europeans and Americans; you can purchase a cottage for around $30,000 or rent one for anywhere between $200 and $400 a month.

The road from Puerto de Pollença to Formentor passes one genuinely overwhelming vista after another. The best places to stop for a look are Es Colomer Belvedere lookout and the Cape Formentor lighthouse. The golf course in Formentor is made all the more challenging by the constant winds.

PALMA TO EASTERN COVES: The fourth route, which covers the coves or *calas* of the island's east coast, is a 100-mile (160-km) run with stops at Campos, Felanitx, Porto Colom, Cala Mitjana, Cala D'Or, Porto Petro, and Cala Santañyi. For a shorter trip, proceed directly to Santañyi and spend the day visiting only the Calas of Santañyi, Figuera, and Llombarts.

PALMA TO SOUTHWEST PENINSULA: The fifth and last route is a Palma–Palma Nova–Paguera–Andraitx–Estallenchs–Bañalbufar–Esporlas–Palma circuit of 56 miles (90 km). The southwest coast has a fine selection of beaches and the island's most intense concentration of hotels. Santa Ponsa, Cala Fornels, Camp de Mar, Puerto de Andraitx, Estellenchs, and Bañalbufar are the main sites of interest.

MINORCA

Minorca, the second largest Balearic Island, measures 271 square miles, numbers just under 50,000 inhabitants, and is less tourist-oriented than Mallorca. The British occupation of the islands during the 18th century left discernible traces in the architecture: guillotine windows, rocking chairs, folding wing Pembroke-style tables, and stand-up clocks with Queen Anne inlay work. The heath-like countryside, swept by the north wind, is lightly wooded, with wind-bent wild olive trees, low stone walls, and small fields.

Cows and sheep provide the basis for the island's two main industries, shoes and cheese. Mayonnaise owes its name and discovery to Mahón, the island's largest city (pop. 22,926).

Minorca is a place where people go to spend a few weeks or months, as opposed to Mallorca, which caters to shorter-term vacationers. Developments such as Binibeca and Punta Prima near Mahón, and Cabo Dartuch near Ciudadela, Minorca's second largest city, usually offer lodgings for periods of weeks, rather than days.

The spots to visit on the island of Minorca include Ciudadela and Mahón on the western and eastern ends, respectively; Cabo de Caballerias and Fornells to the north; and Cala de Santa Galdana to the south. Mercadal is in the approximate center of the island and was once the site of the island government. Monte Toro, the island's highest point and a religious sanctuary, is 2 miles (3 km) from Mercadal.

Minorca can be reached by air from Palma or Barcelona. The island's airport is at Mahón. Boat service connects Ciudadela to Palma and Alcudia, Mallorca. The Tourist Information Center is in Mahón at 13 Plaza de la Constitución (phone: 363790).

MAHÓN: A gleaming little port that somehow manages to retain an innately unobtrusive air, Minorca's largest city has one of the best sheltered harbors in the Mediterranean with excellent anchorages. The main site of interest is the Finca San Antonio, former residence of British Admiral Nelson. About 1 mile (1.6 km) from town near Trepuco village stand several *talayots.*

CIUDADELA: Minorca's second-largest city is surrounded by exceptionally fine beaches: Cala Santandria, Algañares, Cala Blanca, and Cala Blanes. Boiled lobster with mayonnaise sauce and Mahón cheese with sausages are the tastiest local dishes.

FORNELLS: At first glance this is merely a modest fishing village standing in a grove of evergreens, but its appearance masks its popularity as a resort.

IBIZA

The 209-square-mile island of Ibiza lies 70 miles (112 km) southwest of Palma de Mallorca. Ibiza rose to prominence in the Mediterranean region during the years of Carthaginian hegemony (7th century BC), and to this day, the predominant influence in the island's architecture is North African.

Accessible by air from Barcelona, Madrid, Palma, and Valencia, or by sea from Barcelona, Palma, Valencia, Alicante, and Denia (the closest point), Ibiza attracts a well-heeled, international crowd who tend to stay on the island for months or years at a time.

IBIZA: The island's capital is divided into an upper town (Dalt Vila) and a harbor by an ancient 16th-century wall. Sights in the Dalt Vila include: the Las Tablas Gateway, the cathedral, and the *Archaeological Museum,* containing Punic ruins excavated from Ibizan sites. The town is compact, and you should find these special places easily. From the belfry in the Dalt Vila, there is an excellent view of the town and port. The Tourist Information Office is at 13 Calle Vara de Rey (phone: 301900).

The Marina Quarter explodes into sound and color as you enter from the sedate Dalt Vila. Every afternoon (except Wednesdays), the narrow streets are packed with portable shops where vendors sell nearly everything — shell and silver jewelry, watercolors, leather goods, terra-cotta figurines, and other items — and music blasts from the innumerable indoor-outdoor pubs featuring exotic mixed drinks and even more exotically garbed waiters and waitresses. The streets in this section are lined with boutiques featuring the local fashions for which Ibiza is famous.

Among Ibiza's most popular beaches are Ses Figuretas, Talamanca, and Playa D'En Bossa. Several of Ibiza's beaches have gone "naturalist" (nude), although there is some shedding of bikinis on nearly all of them. About 9 miles (15 km) northwest of Ibiza, the town of San Antonio Abad overlooks the rock island called Isla Conejera. The church of Santa Inés, which has been declared a national monument, sits atop ancient catacombs.

FORMENTERA

Formentera — whose name means "the wheat island," from the Latin "frumentum" — is the smallest of the Balearics, covering 32 square miles. Lying 11 miles south of Ibiza, it is significantly more tranquil than the other three Balearic Islands. With 4,500 year-round inhabitants, it also attracts considerably fewer tourists.

Boat service across the Es Freus channel connects La Sabina, Formentera's harbor, with Ibiza. The tiny capital of the island, San Francisco Javier, has a population of around 1,187 and is a cluster of sparkling white cottages. Topographically, the island consists of a string of beaches with Berberia Cape on the southern end of the island and La Mola Cape, guarded by a lighthouse, on the eastern end. Pine forests and salt flats take up much of the interior.

Although Formentera is a great place for relaxing by the sea or participating in water sports, there is no nightlife to speak of.

BEST EN ROUTE

Hotel prices are comparable to those along the Costa del Sol. You can expect to pay $100 or more for a double room at those places we've listed as expensive; between $50 and $100 for a double room in a hotel we've classified as moderate; under $50, inexpensive.

There are literally dozens of restaurants in Mallorca, the largest and busiest island, but considerably fewer restaurants of note on Minorca, Ibiza, and Formentera. Expect to pay $60 or more for a meal for two at those restaurants we've categorized as expensive; between $40 and $60 at those restaurants in the moderate category; under $40, inexpensive. Prices do not include drinks, wine, or tips.

MALLORCA

Formentor – In a pine grove, its extensive gardens, terraces, swimming pool, anchorage, and overall environment make it the most luxurious of the island's hotels. Its restaurant is also excellent. Playa de Formentor (phone: 531300). Expensive.

Meliá Victoria – On the western side of Palma's bay with stunning views, this hotel, built in the 1920s, has recently been modernized, and the atmosphere is pleasant. 21 Calle Joan Miró, Palma (phone: 232542). Expensive.

Son Vida Sheraton – This converted 18th-century palace, about 4 miles (6 km) from Palma on the road toward Andraitx, stands on a hill with splendid views of the bay, city, and mountains. Activities include swimming, golf, tennis, boating, and horseback riding. Its luxury attracts the international jet set, who enjoy each other's company in the baronial dining room. Castillo de Son Vida, Palma (phone: 451011). Expensive.

Daina – Large enough to be spacious, yet small enough to know you're here, this excellent hotel commands a view of Pollença's Bay. 2 Calle Atilio Boven, Puerto de Pollença (phone: 531250). Moderate to inexpensive.

Caleta – The most elegant of the capital's many restaurants serves continental and Mediterranean food. 19 Calle Federico García Lorca, Palma (phone: 232751). Expensive.

Porto Pi – Outstanding French Basque cuisine. Closed Sundays. 174 Calle Joan Miró, Palma (phone: 400087). Expensive.

Caballito del Mar – Befitting its location near the *lonja* on Paseo Marítimo, this eatery serves superb seafood in generous portions. Closed Sundays. 5 Paseo Sagrera, Palma (no phone). Expensive to moderate.

Becfi – Argentinian *parrillada* (barbecued mixed grill) and lobster are the specialties. Closed Mondays. 9 Avenida Anglada Camarasa, Pollença (phone: 531040). Moderate.

Ca'n Pacienci – Start a meal here with the tomato soup (made with fresh cream) or a pâté, then try the stuffed chicken or one of the traditional Mallorquín dishes. Carretera del Puerto, Pollença (phone: 530787). Moderate.

Casa Sophie – Here the French cuisine is exquisite. Closed Sundays and December. 24 Calle Apuntadores, Palma (phone: 226086). Moderate.

Club Náutico – Fresh seafood and fish are served in a nautical atmosphere. Muelle Viejo, Pollença (phone: 531010). Moderate.

Estación Marítima Stay – This is *the* place for succulent crab creations, other seafood dishes, and the most potent Irish coffee on Mallorca. Malecón del Puerto Pollença (phone: 530013). Moderate.

Jardín Chino – As its name, "Chinese Garden," suggests, this is Palma's finest Chinese restaurant. 2 Plaza Mediterraneo, Palma (phone: 230053). Moderate.

Lonja del Pescado – This restaurant prepares the finest bouillabaisse with fresh lobster on the island. Dique Muelle Viejo Pollença (phone: 530023). Moderate.

Mesón las Tinajas – Nonstop *tapas* from 10:30 AM to 11 PM, and fruit meringue pie as well. 13 Calle Berengario de Toramira (behind *Galerías Preciados*), Palma (phone: 718786). Moderate.

Mi Vaca y Yo – A roadside *tavernita* that serves hearty meals of typical Mallorquín cuisine. Playa de Canyarnel, Capdepera (no phone). Moderate.

Puerto – This notable seafood eatery serves excellent food. Closed Tuesdays. 3 Paseo de Sagrera, Palma (phone: 221104). Moderate.

Tablita – Another little restaurant in a tiny pocket of the island. Cala Ratjada (no phone). Moderate.

Casa Gallega – Although the Balearic Islands are a long way from the northwest corner of mainland Spain, this place specializes in Galician cuisine. 6 Calle Pueyo, Palma (phone: 221141). Moderate to inexpensive.

Petit Celler Carnete – The best restaurant in the center of town. 5 Calle Cetre, Sóller (no phone). Moderate to inexpensive.

Celler Sa Premsa – *Celleres* (cellars) and *tavernitas* (taverns) serve Mallorquín food, primarily combinations of *lechona* (pork), fresh fish, seafood, plenty of squid, and paella. This place is a favorite. 8 Plaza Obispo Berenguer de Palou (phone: 223529). Inexpensive.

Celler El Puerto – A good place for a hefty seafood lunch. 22 Plaza Almirante Oquendo, Pollença (no phone). Inexpensive.

Celler Ca Vostra – This is one of the best *tavernitas* in Pollença. Camino Alcudia, Pollença (phone: 531546). Inexpensive.

MINORCA

Port Mahón – Best hotel in Mahón. Fort de l'Eau, Paseo Marítimo (phone: 362600). Moderate.

Rocamar – For good seafood, especially typical Minorcan *caldereta* (lobster stew), this is a good choice. Cala Fonduco (phone: 365601). Moderate.

D'Es Port – This little café on the docks serves boiled lobster with mayonnaise sauce and Mahón cheese with sausages. Cuidadela (phone: 380003). Moderate.

Greco – Another good place for Mediterranean fare. 49 Calle Doctor Orfila, Mahón (phone: 364367). Moderate to inexpensive.

Casa Diego – Near *D'Es Port,* this place features similar local fare at bargain prices. Ciudadela (no phone). Inexpensive.

Casa Riera – For fresh fish and seafood, this is the best in town. 7 Plaza Generalisimo, Fornells (no phone). Inexpensive.

Chez Gaston – Here you can get continental dishes along with fresh fish and seafood. 13 Conde de Cifuentes (phone: 360044). Inexpensive.

Mare Nostrum – For a generous Minorcan meal, visit this restaurant on the beach. Playa Santandria (no phone). Inexpensive.

Ses Set Voltes – Still another seafood "find" on the beach. Playa Santandria, Ciudadela (no phone). Inexpensive.

IBIZA

Hacienda Na Xamena – One of the most magnificent hotels in all of the Balearics. On the northern part of the island, it commands breathtaking views of the coastline from its clifftop swimming pools, terraces, and luxurious rooms. Superb food is graciously served at the poolside patios and the hotel restaurant. There are tennis courts plus an indoor pool, gym, and sauna, and the charming village and beach cove of San Miguel are a short way down the pine-forested hills. San Miguel (phone: 333046). Expensive.

Pikes – An exclusive, free-wheeling hotel, it has 7 luxury suites and 10 double rooms. The original building, about 600 years old, was an olive and grain mill. Some of the more exotic rooms have sunken tubs and harem-style touches. Other features include 3 restaurants, 2 dining terraces, a video room and film library, a tennis court, and a tile pool. The beach is 10 minutes away. A week's stay is required during summer months. San Antonio (phone: 342222). Expensive.

Torre del Canónigo – Though this 15th-century bishop's mansion has been renovated thoroughly and divided into independent private apartments with modern conveniences, it retains its noble ambience and decor. From its hilltop setting in Ibiza's Dalt Vila, the views are breathtaking; it's easy to recapture the tranquil medieval mood while strolling through the narrow cobblestone streets. Open May through October; reservations are necessary, and there is a minimum stay requirement of 3 to 7 nights, depending on the season. Apartments accommodate from 2 to 4 guests. 8 Calle Obispo Torres (phone: 303884). Moderate.

Mar Blau – A truly fine hotel in relaxed, shady surroundings. Its 15 rooms have windows overlooking the sea. Near the marina, it also has a fine seafood restaurant. Los Molinos (phone: 301284). Inexpensive.

Ses Figueres – One of the smaller Ibiza hotels on the beach, it has splendid views of the bay and offers excellent value. Playa de Talamanca (phone: 301362). Inexpensive.

Campsites – The Spanish government runs three campsites on Ibiza: *San Antonio* and *Cala Bassa* at San Antonio Abad, and *Florida* at Santa Eulalia del Río. For information contact the Tourist Office of Spain in the US (phone: 212-759-8822). Inexpensive.

Masía d'en Sord – In a lovely old Ibizan house with a magnificent garden, it offers grilled meats and international dishes. Closed Saturday lunch and November. Ibiza–San Miguel Hwy. (no phone). Moderate.

FORMENTERA

Sa Volta – Good local food served in a pleasant environment (it's also a small hotel). Es Pujols (phone: 320120). Moderate.

Voramar – A quiet oasis on Es Pujols beach, protected from the wind by Cape Punta Prima, looks across the water to Ibiza. Its restaurant is one of the best on the island for fresh fish and other seafood. Playa Es Pujols (phone: 320121). Inexpensive.

Sweden

The images of Sweden that are universally recognized are a kind of code to this complex Scandinavian culture. Fierce, bearded Vikings; healthy, blond youths; dense silent forests; sparkling blue lakes and crystalline fjords — the fascination of a visit is learning just how these particular images have come to represent Sweden, and in what ways they are a true picture. As always, the truth will prove twice as fascinating as anything you could imagine.

As in any country, history and culture start with geography. Occupying the eastern half of the Scandinavian Peninsula, the country shares borders with Norway to the west and Finland to the northeast. The more populous southern third of the country juts into the Baltic Sea; the northern end creeps over the Arctic Circle. Parts of Sweden are still glacier-bound; several thousand years ago, *all* of Sweden was covered with ice. However, for the most part, Sweden's landscape is now speckled with lakes and carpeted with meadows and forests. Sweden has a temperate climate with warm summers and cold winters. The generally poor soil and rocky terrain have led Swedes to turn to forestry, mining, and steel production for their major industries.

The earliest settlers in Sweden appeared in about the 3rd century BC; these people were mostly farmers and fishermen. Many years later, in the 1st century AD, a seafaring tribe, that turned to plunder and trade, grew very powerful and began to control what is now Sweden. This tribe — the Svea, forefathers of the Vikings — initiated trade, as well as conflict, with parts of Europe and Britain. Sweden was well situated for trade and as it became more lucrative, the Hanseatic League became interested in the country. Soon several German merchants came to live in Visby, a prosperous walled town on the island of Gotland, and in Stockholm, which was then a port and fortress on Lake Mälaren. By the 14th century, the Hansa merchants controlled Sweden; in an effort to resist the Hanseatic influence, Norway, Sweden, and Denmark joined together as the Union of Kalmar. The center of government for this union was in Denmark. Eventually the Swedes began to resent even the Danish rule, and in the 16th century Gustavus Vasa, a Swedish noble, led a rebellion. In 1523, victorious, he was elected king, and thereafter the influence of the Hanseatic League waned.

For several hundred years, until the early 19th century, Swedish kings were constantly at war with their neighbors, including Germany, Denmark, Poland, Finland, and Russia. As a result, Sweden annexed as well as lost many territories in Europe, Scandinavia, and even America (there was a small Swedish colony on the Delaware River from 1638 to 1655). In 1809 Sweden enacted a series of reforms, making the king a ceremonial figurehead and conferring the powers of government on an elected parliament. Later in the 19th century, Sweden declared itself a neutral country, a policy that remained in effect throughout the two world wars.

The Swedish Welfare System was born during the depression of the 1930s and grew up during and after World War II. Basically a system for the redistribution of income, the plan attempts to provide every Swede with a minimum and satisfactory standard of living — food, housing, education, and medical care. The price tag for these humane policies is a staggering 50% to 80% personal income tax.

Sweden is among the world's leaders in the exploration of and experimentation with design. Based on the concept that functional things must also be graceful, Swedish design has influenced or changed the appearance of many everyday items, such as furniture, glassware, ceramics, and textiles.

A strong folkloric heritage provides Sweden with rich cultural texture. In the summer numerous festivals are held, for which men and women don their native costumes and dance around traditional Maypoles — made of detailed wrought iron or wood and decorated with intertwined sprigs of flowers and forest greenery. In the Dalarna region, *spelmanslag* (fiddlers) often entertain at the festivals, playing ancient folk tunes and ballads.

Our tours of Sweden each offer you a taste of new and old Sweden: the Dalarna and Värmland route runs through dense forests and medieval towns; the Gothenburg route takes you north from Sweden's second largest city and maritime capital through the fishing villages and along the dramatic fjords of Sweden's granite coastline; the historic walled city of Visby is the highlight of the Gotland route; and the Lapland route ventures into one of the last unspoiled and uncivilized areas on earth — the Lapp wilderness. *Note:* The numbering of highways in various parts of Sweden was changed in 1985. Therefore use only those maps published *after* 1985.

It is easy to get around on your own, as over 80% of the Swedish people speak and understand English. Foreign television programs are broadcast in their original language with Swedish subtitles.

Dalarna and Värmland

The trip up from Stockholm northwest to Mora and back down to Karlstad covers roughly 520 miles (832 km) and takes you through the Swedish heartland provinces of Dalarna and Värmland. The route meanders through seemingly unending forests that break unexpectedly to reveal breathtaking lake expanses. The roads occasionally rise, resting at overlooks where the landscape unfolds beneath you in long, floating lines. The major towns are clustered around the two great lake districts, Siljan in Dalarna and the Fryken group in Värmland.

The dense Dalarna forests were first cut back for settlement in the sixteenth century, when rich veins of iron ore and copper were discovered and mined under the leadership of King Gustav Wasa. The Dalarna route from Stockholm takes you first to the mining town of Falun and then on to the picturesque Siljan Lake towns of Leksand, Rättvik, and Mora, where you turn south for Värmland. As you travel, you'll notice the landscape changes: the deep forests and weathered wooden sheds of Dalarna give way to Värmland's wide verdant fields and country villas.

Värmland has been home to some of Sweden's "greats": famous writers

Erik Gustaf Geijer and Selma Lagerlöf (a 1909 Nobel laureate in literature), as well as John Ericsson who, after emigrating to New York, changed the concept of sea power with his design for the USS *Monitor,* the first successful ironclad warship. From Mora you can plunge farther west and then south to the Fryken Lake towns of Torsby, Sunne, and Arvika. Or you can follow the Klarälven River directly south through Ransäter to Karlstad, the major city of Värmland on the vast Vänern Lake.

STOCKHOLM: For a detailed report on the city and its hotels and restaurants, see *Stockholm,* THE CITIES. The great city of Stockholm originated as a modest 13th-century Viking fortification built on an island where Lake Mälaren meets the Baltic Sea. As was often the case, the military installation grew into a civilized center of art and commerce, but Stockholm's transition was perhaps more dramatic than that of other cities that developed in this way. Far from the usual random urban sprawl, Stockholm spread over 14 islands into one of the most beautiful and certainly the most ordered city in the world. Stockholm is the home of the Swedish monarch, but the real ruler of the city is design. Streets, buildings, and squares are preserved with religious respect. Trees are judiciously planted along cobbled boulevards, and flower urns are artistically arranged in quiet plazas flanked by pastel-colored three- and four-story buildings capped with elegant and varied entablatures — a stepped arch on one house, a rounded, baroque detail on another, and a rose-windowed gable on a third. The Swedish design concept is evident everywhere and is typified in glassware that developed from involved Venetian decoration into the simpler Scandinavian look of utility with no loss of grace. Utility and grace are carried through from town plan to individual buildings to the furniture inside the buildings and finally to the people themselves.

En Route from Stockholm – Falun is a 3- or 4-hour drive from Stockholm on Routes 70 and 60 and the largest town in Dalarna. The main point of interest here is the Falun Copper Mine that's been in operation since the Vikings forged swords and shields — long before Sweden was even a country. This mine was the Renaissance world's major source of copper, and places like Versailles were roofed with its output. There's a tour of the mine that takes you down an elevator to the winding shafts and cavernous spaces below. While here, note the rock wall autographed by touring royalty and the massive 650-foot timber wall — a marvel of carpentry and probably the tallest wooden edifice in the world. At nearby Sundborn, visit the home of artist Carl Larsson in an idyllic rural setting.

SILJAN LAKE TOWNS: Lake Siljan is a blue glacial lake surrounded by lush evergreen forests and towns that look much as they did in the early Middle Ages.

From Falun, you can either proceed directly to Lake Siljan on Route 80 or double back onto Route 70, where the first lake town you come to is Leksand, a thriving, woodsy resort. On the first Sunday in July there's a boat race here that's a hotly contested national event. The vessels used are called "church boats" and they look like mastless, tiny Viking ships. They widen from a sharp prow and sit low in the water as they glide across the lake, each propelled by 20 oarsmen dressed to the nines in native finery. (The boats don't sit idle the rest of the year, so if you can't get there for the race, you might see them taking worshipers to Rättvik's church for Sunday service from midsummer through the third week in August. Boat races are also held at Siljansnäs, Tällberg, Mora, and Sollerön during late June and early July. In late spring, there's a folk dance festival replete with *spelmän* — fiddlers dressed in the traditional high socks, white shirts, and ornate black vests with red piping. There's also an annual folk miracle play, *Himlaspelet* (*The Road to Heaven*), that's performed outdoors early in July. The new Cultural Center shows folk works painted by wandering peasant artists who went door to door, depicting religious scenes on the residents' ceilings. The biblical heroes in these paintings are invariably clothed in Dalecarlian costume.

If you prefer a thorough and organized view of the lake towns, you can pick up a boat lake tour at Rättvik, only 7½ miles (12 km) from Leksand. If you just want a quick but comprehensive peek at the region, there's an old wooden tower (just outside of town at Vidablick) that you can climb for free. From the top you can reconnoiter at will. Rättvik also has a cultural center with a library and two museums as well as a preserved farm complex called Gammelgård. Many of the wooden structures here were built in the 16th century with incredible care and skill. The tongue and grooving at the corners is so perfectly executed it looks as if the beam ends were machined. The original shingles look more durable than space age plastics and the fences are marvelously designed to adapt to changing terrain.

Mora is the last lake town and the last stop in Dalarna. It's the finishing point of the Wasa Ski Race, the longest cross-country skiing competition in the world, annually attracting more than 10,000 entrants who challenge the grueling 53-mile run. Like the other Siljan towns, Mora celebrates the past in summer festivals and Maypole dancing. The most famous of all Swedish painters, Anders Zorn (1860–1920), lived here and many of his portraits are on display in the *Zorn Museum* along with Scandinavian sculpture, furniture, textiles, and other examples of local crafts. You can also visit the artist's home and studio. There's another lakeside open-air museum that depicts the indigenous rural life of the Middle Ages. Just east of Mora in the town of Nusnäs you can watch craftsmen fashioning the traditional Dala Horse souvenirs that are sold all over the country.

En Route to Karlstad – There are many small destinations in Värmland that take you off the main southern route along the Klarälven River that you pick up at Stöllet. Instead of heading directly south to Karlstad, you can cut back north and take a canoe trip through beautiful scenery at Sysslebäck. The fishing here is great and you can rent tackle along with your canoe. If you head west from Stöllet, you hit Route 234, which you can take south through the Fryken Lake towns of Torsby — a traditional Norwegian/Swedish trading center — and Sunne — the nearest town to the two mansions associated with Selma Lagerlöf, who is perhaps Sweden's most famous author and her home in the town of Mårbacka, just east of Sunne, is now a museum. Ten minutes south of Sunne is the Rottneros Manor, which she used as a model for the Ekeby mansion in her best-known work, *The Saga of Gösta Berling*. Rottneros Manor is now a sculpture park and garden — one of the most beautiful spots in all of Sweden, displaying the works of many prominent Scandinavian artists. As a last stop on this Värmland detour, you might want to continue southwest to Arvika, a small town of 16,000 on the Glafsfjorden Lake where you can take a boat tour of the area or listen to a summer concert at the Ingesund Music College. This lake area is wonderful for hiking and there are more than 125 miles of marked trails across fields, along lakeshores, and through forests.

RANSÄTER: If you drive directly south from Stöllet along the Klarälven River on Route 62, "The Pilgrim's Way," you go through the prosperous and quiet little river town of Ransäter, the home of dramatist Erik Gustaf Geijer. In midsummer, the *Värmlänningarna,* a Swedish *Romeo and Juliet,* is performed outdoors. His home is also open to the public.

The village surrounding the open-air theater is an example of more affluent country habitats, dating back to the time when timber cut from the area started fetching good prices in Great Britain during the end of the Industrial Revolution. The timber was used for props in English coal mines. It was floated down the Klarälven River, and even today tugboats with half-mile-long batches of timber in tow slowly descend the river to Karlstad — the main city of the province — where the timber is processed.

KARLSTAD: This is the capital of the province and the home of the *Värmland Museum,* which has exhibitions of textiles, painting, and crafts as well as historic displays. The museum is centrally located in a manicured park on Sandgrundet. The Marieberg Forest is the town's other large park; here you can see a show at the open-air theater, or dance at one of the music pavilions. Karlstad is a commercial center and the main northern port on the Vänern, the largest lake in Western Europe. The port itself is on the Klarälven River and you can take a tour boat at Residenstorg for a leisurely sail around the city's waterways. Just outside of town in Skutberget and Örsholmsbadet are lakefront open-air baths. If you are of Swedish descent or interested in Swedish emigration to North America, visit the Emigrant Register at 4 Norra Strandgatan (phone: 054-159269).

From Karlstad, you can take an interesting side trip to Filipstad, 25 miles (40 km) to the northeast. Filipstad is the birthplace of John Ericsson and you can visit his home and mausoleum (at different spots to the north and east of town). As we have said, Ericsson migrated to Brooklyn, New York, where he became an ironmonger and builder. At the outbreak of the American Civil War he implemented a visionary plan to combine the new diesel engine with a screw propeller for the design of the Union's ironclad ship, the *Monitor.* This ship soundly defeated the Confederate ironclad entry, the *Merrimack,* winning Ericsson an honored place in naval history. In 1890, the US Navy returned his body to Filipstad where it was entombed and the mausoleum was built. On *Swedish American Day,* at the end of July, there is a mock battle on the lake at Filipstad in his honor.

BEST EN ROUTE

A number of hotels offer special weekend discounts and low summer rates. An expensive hotel can run anywhere from $100 to $150 per night for a double room. The moderate establishments charge $50 to $100, and the inexpensive places go from $25 to $50. It's wise to make reservations in advance or to use one of the "cheque" systems operated by some hotel chains. This can be arranged through any travel agent. If you are traveling on a low budget, try the so-called motoring lodgings offered by 200 hotels. You pay $20 to $26 per bed in a double room; breakfast is extra. For information, contact *Biltur-Logi,* Siljansgården, S-79303 Tällberg, Sweden, or *Cole Travel Service,* 310 W. State St., Geneva, IL 06134. Thirty-nine Best Western hotels offer reduced rates from May 15 through September 15. Contact the national office for more information (phone: 800-528-1234).

MORA

Mora – A small, clean hotel with 92 neat, comfortable rooms. It's easy to find in the center of town at 12 Strandgatan (phone: 0250-11750). Expensive to moderate.

KARLSTAD

Stadshotellet – This stately 140-room hotel is in a large yellow building overlooking the river. You can sit in the nearby café, play tennis or golf nearby, or take a dip in the pool. 22 Kungsgatan (phone: 054-115220). Expensive to moderate.

Gothenburg and the West Coast

The west coast of Sweden, with Gothenburg at its center, is very popular with Scandinavian vacationers but often neglected by international tour operators. This is surprising because the scenic coastal strip combines most of the features the foreign visitor looks for in a typical Scandinavian vacation.

South of Gothenburg is an almost continuous ribbon of sandy beaches and summer resorts, but this trip takes you in the opposite direction — north, toward the Norwegian border. You follow a craggy, granite coastline that breaks up into skerries toward the sea and opens into fjords and lakes toward the land. The whole coast is dotted with tiny isolated fishing villages and peaceful yacht harbors tucked away in rocky coves.

The area attracts many visitors from Scandinavia and northern Europe during the summer months (June through August), yet once away from the busy camping sites and major highways you enter an intimate, peaceful world of great natural beauty that seems untouched by modern industrialization.

Many visitors live the nomadic life in trailer homes or under canvas at the many camp sites. Youth hostels, rented summer chalets, or fishermen's cottages are ideal accommodations for overseas visitors. They're plentiful and reasonably priced.

One interesting aspect of this route is its flexibility. You can head directly up the map to the Norwegian border or meander in and out of the windswept coastal indentations, stopping at any fjord or island that catches your eye. You'll find the drive is at least 200 miles (320 km) long and probably longer if you do a lot of island and fjord hopscotching. You'll also find that the dramatic coastal roadside scenery is as much of an attraction as the stops along the way.

GOTHENBURG: Though this is the principal seaport of Scandinavia and the home of some of Sweden's major industrial concerns, don't make the mistake of hurrying through here without pausing to get acquainted with this friendly unsophisticated city of 700,000. Despite being Sweden's second major city, with a busy downtown commercial area, Gothenburg has a relaxing pace and there are plenty of entertainment spots for the tourist to mix with the native. The Liseberg Amusement Park attracts 3 million visitors annually. Its roller coaster climbs to a height of 150 feet and reaches speeds near 50 mph.

The city was built in the early 17th century by Dutch architects (King Gustav Adolf II granted its first charter in 1621), but has also drawn on the influence of Germans and English over the ensuing centuries. Gothenburg quickly reveals itself to be a garden city with well-kept canals, parks, and botanical gardens like Trädgårdsföreningen and Botaniska Trädgården. Take a Paddan boat canal tour that takes you under 20 bridges to soak in the Dutch influence, and the short boat excursion to lvsborg Fortress to learn about the great naval battles of the 17th century between Swedish and Danish forces.

Kronhuset (Kronhusgatan) is the oldest building in Gothenburg and has a museum recording the history of the city, as well as reconstructions of turn-of-the-century shops. *Sjöfartsmuseet* (Maritime Museum; on Lilla Bommer) displays ship models from Viking times to the present and richly illustrates the maritime traditions of this major port. A Maritime Center with historic ships is under construction near the Nordstan shopping mall.

The main drag in Gothenburg is Kungsportsavenyn, referred to simply as Avenyn (Avenue). It's a wide, tree-lined boulevard with cafés, shops, elegant buildings, and nightclubs. There are restaurants that serve Italian, Scottish, German, and Chinese fare, and even a smattering of American fast-food favorites. The cafés here are the best places in town to sit and watch people go by — during the day, the shoppers and tourists, and during the evening, the local young folk who cruise up and down, finally congregating at the Poseidon Fountain (a work by Carl Milles) in the Götaplatsen, the large square at the end of the avenue. At one side of the fountain is the Stadsbiblioteket (library), where you can check on the progress of your favorite baseball team or get the latest on the US political scene by looking at one of the American newspapers available in the reading room.

The *Gothenburg Art Gallery,* also in the Götaplatsen, has an amazingly good collection of art, including work by Cézanne, Van Gogh, Rodin, and Picasso. There's also work by modern Scandinavian masters like Anders Zorn, Edvard Munch, and Carl Milles.

One place you should not pass up on your visit here is the Feskekörka, or "fish church," next to the fish market in Gothenburg Harbor. The "church," built about 100 years ago, resembles any other normal Lutheran church until you step inside and discover it's actually a fish market, filled with some 20 booths where merchants offer every kind of seafood, from lobsters to herring, fresh and smoked salmon, eels, sole, flounder, crabs, shrimp, and many others. An auction is held at the harbor every morning at 7 AM for the day's fresh catches. There are inexpensive day trips via ferry from Gothenburg to Denmark.

In order to plan your route up the coast in detail, you might want to stop at the Gothenburg Tourist Office (10 Basargatan, in the city center; phone: 031-100740). To start your trip north, you leave town on the main highway, E6, and after a short drive along the Göta River valley, you get off the main road and enter Kungälv, a 1,000-year-old town with a turbulent history.

KUNGÄLV: A merchant town occupied this site as early as the 10th century. Three hundred years later, the location had gained significance strategically as a border stronghold between Norway and Sweden (the present border runs more than 100 miles to the north), and work began on the impregnable Bohus Fortress. This mighty stronghold was subjected to many sieges through the centuries but was never taken by force of arms. The ruined structure still stands proud and impressive, jutting up amid the trees on a now placid island.

Across the river in the old part of the town, around Västra Gatan, are several interesting old wooden buildings, mainly from the 18th century, and an exquisite church dating from 1679, which has a richly adorned baroque interior.

Leaving Kungälv, avoid the main highway and make your way northwest on winding country roads, heading for Tjuvkil and the Instö car ferry across to the island of Koön. From here there is a small passenger-only ferry to Marstrand, a yachting harbor and fashionable summer resort on a small wooded island dominated by the 17th-century Carlsten Fortress.

MARSTRAND: Herring fishing made this island village a prosperous one during the 16th century, but then the lucrative herring shoals moved away and there followed a history of mixed fortunes with periodic devastation by fire and pestilence. Today, the picturesque white-walled timber buildings and crooked alleyways belie this troubled past, never more so than on international regatta days in July or August, when tall-masted yachts swarm the quayside and suntanned visitors stroll the waterfront.

En Route from Marstrand – Make your way back to the mainland and, still keeping to the small country roads, follow the winding coast north until you reach Stenungsund, less than an hour's drive away. Here you sweep to the left and up onto the impressive Tjörn Bridges, spanning three beautiful sounds and linking the mainland with the idyllic islands of Tjörn and neighboring Orust. The Tjörn bridges are a tourist attraction in themselves, offering a splendid vantage point for panoramic views over rocky, heatherclad isles and often a colorful procession of yachts passing through the sound below.

On the seaward fringes of Tjörn Island, there is a fairy tale world of refreshingly unsophisticated fishing communities such as Rönnäng and Skärhamn, where red timber cottages huddle together on rocky headlands or perch precariously on tiny skerries. Rows of stockfish are hung out to dry on large tent-shaped racks, and pleasure boats and round-hulled fishing vessels line the wooden jetties. The area is also rich in Stone Age relics. The northern edge of Tjörn Island is linked by bridge to the neighboring island of Orust, where you can explore more ancient relics and quaint fishing villages, notably the lobster harbor, Mollösund, tucked away on a peninsula in the southwest corner of the island.

Continue to the northwest corner of Orust to Ellös, where a car ferry transports you across to Rågårdsvik on the island of Skaftö. Head north across the island to the attractive seaside resort of Fiskebäckskil where you can stroll at the harbor, enjoy a swim, fish, sail, or try the 9-hole golf course.

From Fiskebäckskil a regular car ferry service takes you to Lysekil.

LYSEKIL: Once the center of the local stone-quarrying industry, this small village of 7,000 is now a popular resort and yacht harbor with many diversions for the summer tourist. By day you can enjoy tennis or swimming, and at night, the area's many restaurants and discos. Boat excursions for sea fishing or general exploration in the surrounding waters are available at the harbor.

At Brastad, some 10 miles (16 km) north, stop to view the remarkable ancient rock carvings, then follow Route 162 again, turning left onto Route 163 at Hallinden. Proceed to a fork in this highway, and turn left toward the coast again in the direction of Åby and Kungshamn.

KUNGSHAMN: Kungshamn and neighboring Smögen are two of the finest and most interesting fishing ports on this coast. Kungshamn has a modern fishing harbor, and if you stay until evening, you can watch the shrimp auction and enjoy a fresh seafood supper. Nearby Smögen can be reached by way of the Smögen Bridge, and is a lovely, picturesque fishing hamlet with quite an international atmosphere in summer. Stroll the long wooden quayside lined with timber boathouses and souvenir shops and admire the elegant pleasure craft and rugged fishing vessels crowding every inch of mooring space. Fishing trips are arranged to go out to the best fishing grounds in the archipelago for whiting, cod, and mackerel.

En Route from Kungshamn – Follow the coast road north past fjords, wide bays, and rocky inlets until you join Route 163 again at Bottne Fjord. Drive north through Hamburgsund and Fjällbacka until you reach Grebbestad. This route shows the rugged, sculptured coastline at its best and all along the way there are places where you can linger awhile for some angling or bathing.

A couple of miles east of Grebbestad lies Tanumshede, the best known of all Sweden's rock carving sites. The strange figures and symbols you see here were carved in the granite rock some 3,000 years ago and are still legible. The most impressive of the carvings is at Fossum and depicts a battle scene.

The route continues north on main Route E6, reaching the Norwegian border at the Svinesund Bridge, some 60 miles (96 km) from Oslo.

BEST EN ROUTE

Expect hotels in Sweden to be priced as high as those in the US. Very expensive hotels, which carry single and double rooms, run anywhere from $100 to $150 a night. More moderate in price are those first class tourist hotels with full accommodations (private baths in most; in some you may have to opt for a bathroom in the corridor); these run $50 to $100 (expensive), single or double room. Other hotels, smaller in size, can run from $40 to $80 (moderate) and $30 to $50 (inexpensive). Reservations are recommended.

There are hotel cheque systems covering all of Sweden. Consult the Swedish Tourist Board, 655 3rd Ave., New York, NY 10017 (phone: 212-949-2333), for details (ask for the free booklet *Hotels in Sweden*). Information on these cheque systems as well as

Swedish summer chalets is available from the Gothenburg Tourist Office, 10 Basargatan, S-411 10 Gothenburg, Sweden (phone: 031-100740).

GOTHENBURG

SAS Park Avenue – A 320-room property offering banquet facilities, bar, restaurant, sauna, and secretarial services (if you need them), among other amenities. 36-38 Kungsportsavenyn (phone: 031-176520). Very expensive.

Sheraton Hotel and Towers – New 343-room establishment opposite Central Station. There is also a swimming pool. 59-65 Södra Hamngatan (phone: 031-101600). Expensive.

Windsor – Smaller, 91-room hotel with a bar and English-style restaurant. 6 Kungsportsavenyn (phone: 031-176540). Expensive.

KUNGÄLV

Fars Hatt – A pleasant hotel in a convenient location. Torget (phone: 0303-10970). Moderate.

MARSTRAND

Alphyddan – Modest 37-room hotel in the center of this small island town. 6 Långgatan (phone: 0303-61030). Moderate.

LYSEKIL

Lysekil – A 50-room hotel with a restaurant and a nightclub. Rosvikstorg (phone: 0523-11860). Moderate.

TANUMSHEDE

Tanums Gestgifveri – This old country inn serves very good food and is an ideal overnight spot for soaking in the historic ambience of this ancient region. Route E6 (phone: 0525-29010). Expensive to moderate.

Gotland

In the time of the Vikings, Gotland was the gateway to Scandinavia. It's Sweden's largest island, off the east coast in the Baltic, and, because of its location, it was historically the guardian of the Scandanavian peninsula. It began as a strategic military base for a succession of Viking kings bent on plundering the lands to the east (now Russia) and later became a trading point and an economic and cultural center. The history of Gotland is still visible all over the island in Stone Age cave dwellings, picture stones, and medieval churches.

After the decline of the Vikings and the development of more civilized methods of international trade, Visby, Gotland's main city, became the center of the Hanseatic League, a Germanic trade association. In the 13th century, the burghers of Visby built an intricate limestone wall modeled on the effective Roman civil defense perimeters. As the town grew prosperous with trade, the people built an affluent city within the wall, out of the marble and the sandstone they found in abundance on their flat, fertile island.

Gotland was civilized long before the Swedish mainland and became one of the wealthiest and most powerful states in Europe, but in 1361 Danish

King Valdemar Atterdag invaded. (Legend has it that the king's lover, the treacherous daughter of Visbian Nils the Goldsmith, opened the city gate and let the Danes in.) In any case, Visby fell and never regained its imperial stature.

Today Gotland is a land of beaches, spas, and sailing, with a beautiful landscape and a warmer climate than the rest of Sweden so that, aside from tourism, farming is the mainstay of the island's economy. Gotland is 78 miles long and 25 miles wide with plenty of room for Gotland sheep — a black-wooled variety — to graze all year round. In the Lojsta Hajd woodland you can also see the wild Gotland Russ ponies, small and temperamental from inbreeding, but unusual looking and still friendly.

Geologically, the most remarkable features of this island are the "marine stacks" or *rauker* — nature's own sculptures of limestone, formed by eroding winds and waters — that give Gotland's lovely sandy beaches a character all their own. The stacks are formed at the stony edges of the slopes leading to the sandy beaches.

You enter Gotland through Visby. In the summer, there are car ferries from Nynäshamn, Oskarshamn, and Västervik on the mainland, and from Grankullavik on the island of Öland. If you bring your own car, make sure to book tickets well in advance as the auto berths are often sold out. Even without a car, advance booking is required since the summer ferries are usually packed with travelers. Flights are available to Visby airport from Stockholm-Arlanda, Norrköping, and Kalmar.

VISBY: This is one of the oldest cities in Sweden and its wall alone would make it worth the trip. The wall is about 2 miles long and is capped by 44 towers with crenelated turrets and long, thin archer's windows. Some towers are also gateways. Inside the walls you can see gleaming whitewashed stone houses with shiny red tile roofs; the city has a sort of southern European look. Eventually, Visby grew too large for its surrounding wall and was forced to build up, around, and over itself. It's now a town of romantic arches and alleyways with clinging vines and bushes growing out of every wall cranny. The red roofs are punctuated by stepped gables, and bicycles are the preferred mode of transportation over the cobbled streets. Visby has been called the city of roses and there are colorful blossoms everywhere. The Almedalen old harbor, lifted by land augmentation over the centuries, has been transformed into a botanic oasis with many varieties of flowers.

There are 100 churches and chapels on Gotland; only 9 of them were built after 1350. Some of them are in ruins, but there's still more stained glass here than anywhere else in Scandinavia. At the church of St. Nicolaus, an outdoor play is put on every summer portraying the life of one of Visby's local saints. A more vivid glimpse into the past, however, is outside the wall at the Galgberget (hanging mound), which was a raised medieval execution area whose stone gallows you can still examine.

Visby is also a tourist town with good restaurants, shops, and comfortable hotels. If you want to rent a bicycle, ask at the tourist office, 9 Strandgatan (phone: 0498-10982). They'll also tell you where you'll find the best sailing, skin diving, and surf.

En Route from Visby – The Väte, a 14th-century stone church, is 18 miles (29 km) south of Visby on Route 142.

From Väte, the route continues along the highway into the Lojsta Hajd woodlands — the home of the Gotland ponies. Half wild, half domestic, the ponies are left to roam around for three years before they are rounded up to be broken in.

Turning east at Fide, you pass the Etelhem Church, go through the village of Hemse, and arrive at Holmhällar fishing village on the southeastern tip of Gotland.

HOLMHÄLLAR: The beaches around Holmhällar are splendid, and here samples of the typical marine stacks can be seen. You'll also find several caves with stalagmites like frozen curtains of stone, formed by millennia of dripping water seeping through the limestone bedrock.

Farther south, the Hoburgen man — a marine stack shaped like a head — marks the island's southernmost point. The view across the Baltic is breathtaking.

En Route from Holmhällar – Returning north to Visby along the coast, stop over at Djupvik fishing village. According to legend, it was here that invading Danes landed. Back in Visby, you can head north on the island, but avoid the uppermost part of Gotland, which is a restricted area.

The Lummelunda caves and the *Lummelunda Geological Museum,* a 20-minute drive north along the coast of Visby, are recommended sites, as is a drive across the island to Slite. Beaches at Slite are excellent, and the Slite Strandbad beach, on a little island off the harbor, is especially enjoyable.

BEST EN ROUTE

Just because you're off the mainland doesn't mean hotel prices will be lower. On the contrary, they're about the same as on previous routes: $75 to $120 (very expensive), $65 to 110 (expensive), $35 to $65 (moderate), and $20 to $35 (inexpensive). Every hotel has double and single rooms, and it's not a bad idea to reserve beforehand, especially during the summer months.

You can also rent private rooms and cottages on the island. Contact *Gotlandsresor AB,* Box 2081, 621 02 Visby (phone: 0498-19010).

VISBY

Visby – An 85-room hotel with 2 restaurants, the *Guldkanten* and *Oskar* (with dancing to live orchestra nightly in summer) and a sauna. 6 Strandgatan (phone: 0498-49687). Expensive to moderate.

Villa Borgen – Pleasant, 18-room hotel, with garden. 11 Adelsgatan (phone: 0498-71170). Moderate.

HEMSE

Hemse – This 20-bed hotel is small but pleasant and has a restaurant. 620 Storgatan, 12 Hemse (phone: 0498-80151). Moderate.

Lapland

For many travelers, Lapland, sprawling across the wild regions of Arctic Scandinavia, has the same sort of fascination usually reserved for remote, isolated destinations like Samarkand, Tibet, and Katmandu.

There is indeed a certain romance about an area still unconquered by man and civilization, a domain of awesome proportions where reindeer roam free and fast-disappearing wildlife such as the bear and golden eagle still hold their own. Man has made but small inroads here: The nomadic Lapps, who are believed to have migrated to Scandinavia from Russia, accepted the hardy lifestyle that Arctic conditions imposed in making this their home, following the migratory reindeer herds. In recent decades, the quest for iron ore and the need for electrical power generated by the mighty rushing rivers has given rise to industrialization in the wilderness. It is the development of modern towns like Kiruna that has made conventional tourism possible in these parts. Of course, along with modernization comes the breaking down of old traditions and it isn't uncommon now to see snowmobiles during reindeer roundups and Lapps wearing blue jeans instead of their ancient colorful outfits fashioned almost entirely of reindeer hides.

When contemplating a vacation trip, bear in mind that the unique rewards of travel in these regions, the joy of experiencing vast tracts of unspoiled nature and of living under the midnight sun, must be paid for in the form of a few discomforts. Your accommodations may be a well-equipped but simple mountain cabin instead of a luxury hotel, and you might suffer a few insect bites if you forget your repellent, but this doesn't mean that you have to be an athlete and outdoorsman to venture this way. Time your visit, however, during the warm summer months of June, July, and August, and possibly even May and September if you do not like cold weather. Winter days are short and temperatures can fall many degrees below freezing, but life goes on here, and the dry cold air means the crisp days can be enjoyed despite the sinking mercury.

The route takes you through a landscape where birch-clad valleys and vast pine forests give way to mountain plateaus, waterfalls, river rapids, and primeval moss-covered fens; where herds of reindeer follow age-old migratory paths, swimming bravely across broad rivers to reach their mountain grazing lands; where the fisherman, naturalist, and amateur photographer have more excitement in one week than friends back home might experience in a lifetime.

The numerous rivers of the region snake down in valleys from the mountainous northwest to spill out finally into the Gulf of Bothnia. Roads tend to follow these river valleys, each ribbonlike highway reaching up into the mountains and, in some cases, winding as far as the Norwegian coast. Each road is a tour route in its own right. They pass fish-rich lakes, vast national parks, snow-capped mountain ranges, and Arctic tundra. Fittingly, each road has a romantic name, like the Blue Road, Way of the Four Winds, the Midnight Sun Road, or the Linné Route.

The following tour route, designed to give you a varied and, as far as possible, complete picture of these northern wilds, traces a winding path northward into the mountains.

For the most part, the roads are modern with hard metal surfaces, but in some of the more remote stretches, you may find yourself driving on well-kept dirt roads.

Our starting point is Luleå, the Baltic port that can be reached by regular air service, railroad, or by main highway E4 from Stockholm, an ideal gateway into the region. At the tourist office here, Nordkalottresor/Norrlands Turistråd (3 Sandviksgatan, phone: 0920-94070), you can collect a useful brochure covering Swedish Lapland. From Luleå, follow Route 97 northwest and you will soon pass the garrison town, Boden. Keen golfers may wish to inquire about the local 9-hole course, one of the world's most northern golf courses and one of the very few where you can tee off by the light of the midnight sun. At Boden turn left and drive southwest on Route 356 heading for lvsbyn some 30 miles (48 km) farther on — a market town on the Pite River deservedly known as the "land of the rapids." At lvsbyn, turn right onto Route 374, traveling northwest to Storforsen, Europe's largest unrestricted waterfall and last untamed giant rapids. See the Pite River crash and rumble its way at breakneck speed down the hillside, falling 252 feet over a stretch of 3 miles. There is a forestry museum here with tar-works and charcoal stacks in operation so you can see what a Swedish lumber camp looked like in days gone by.

Leaving Storforsen, you continue northwest through lake-dotted open moorland, passing over the Arctic Circle (there's little more than a signpost to mark the crossing), and finally reaching the Lapp center of Jokkmokk.

JOKKMOKK: Here at the *Lapp Museum* (Ajtte) you will receive your first insight into the rich and colorful culture of the hardy, nomadic Lapps. The museum displays more than 2,000 Lapp objects, including life-size old storehouses, folk costumes, sleighs, delicately carved wooden utensils, and an array of exquisite silver jewelry. From now on you will become increasingly aware of your presence in the wild domain of the Lapps and their precious reindeer, for you are certain to meet them face to face from time to time during your tour. Since the reindeer herds are nomadic and unpredictable, it is not possible to set dates and places when and where you can see the migration or the summer musters. It's possible to get help and guidance from a friendly Lapp, but don't make the mistake of insulting these taciturn folk by approaching them as some sort of curiosity or tourist attraction. They are a proud people whose labor is honest and whose lifestyle is hard, a nomadic race who are making the difficult transition into 20th-century civilization as their native region, Lapland (an area that cuts across Scandinavian national boundaries), becomes less and less remote. Today, there are only 40,000 Lapps left in Scandinavia, 15,000 of whom live in Sweden.

After you visit the museum, call at the tourist office to collect your Polar Certificate (for a small fee), recognizing your crossing of the Arctic Circle, and then take a look at the Gamla Kyrkan (The Old Church), a small timbered building dating from 1753 (damaged by fire in 1972). Postcards mailed at the post office are canceled with a special Arctic Circle stamp.

The county of Jokkmokk contains the vast, wild, and unforgettably beautiful national parks, Sarek, Padjelanta, and Stora Sjöfallet. These provide a worthwhile detour for the experienced outdoorsman through the last true wilderness in Europe. The 100 glaciers and 20 towering peaks of these wild preserves are the haunt of the osprey, loon, wild goose, and golden eagle. The stepping-off point for hiking expeditions into Sarek and Padjelanta National parks lies about 80 miles (128 km) northwest of Jokkmokk along highway 805 at Kvikkjokk. Here you can pick up the famous King's Trail, a hiking route laid out by the *Swedish Touring Club* and marked by cairns. There are mountain chalets at suitable intervals along the route, but don't attempt this hike unless you know what you're doing. From Kvikkjokk, there are connections by light aircraft to scenic points in the surrounding region as well as aerial sightseeing trips over the mountains.

En Route from Jokkmokk – Take Highway 88 north for about 30 miles (48 km), crossing the Lule River and reaching Porjus, a community developed in conjunction with the hydroelectric project harnessing the Porjus Falls. East of Porjus is the Muddus National Park, an area of virgin pine and spruce forest, untouched swamplands, and undulating granite mountains. Muddus is a nature reserve for bear, elk, marten, and weasel, and the home of many rare migratory birds. Unfortunately, this is also wild country, difficult to penetrate and more for the avid bird-watcher and naturalist than the conventional tourist, although some trails have been laid out with raised wooden duckboards to improve accessibility.

Continue on Highway 97 for about another 30 miles (48 km) and you enter Gällivare, passing Thunder Mountain, which rises some 2,699 feet above sea level.

GÄLLIVARE: This is a flourishing mining community and trading center where you will have much to do: join one of the daily tours to the nearby iron mines at Malmberget; visit the local museum at Vasara with 2,000-year-old skis on display; and view the 18th-century Ettöre Church. A modern building here of considerable interest to the tourist is Björnfällan (The Bear Trap), a 54-square-foot log cabin said to be the largest in the world, built with 80 tons of stone and 230,000 feet of timber, most of which is 400-year-old gray pine. The building acts as a service center for a holiday village of log cabins clustered in the surrounding countryside, and it contains two saunas, a swimming pool, meeting rooms with open fires, shops, and restaurant. From Gällivare, you can book transportation by seaplane or helicopter to mountain fishing camps such as Tjuonajokk, where grayling, char, and salmon trout provide the challenge for the keen angler. Gällivare airport has daily scheduled air service to Stockholm.

En Route from Gällivare – Follow Highway 98 north through moorland and forest, passing scenic lakes and rivers. After some 50 miles (80 km) you reach Svappavaara and, 30 miles (48 km) farther west, Kiruna, a mining town with modern accommodations. Here you can get a wonderful meal of local delicacies such as white grouse (*ptarmigan*) followed by cloudberries and cream for dessert. Kiruna also has tours into the world's biggest underground mine, which extracts up to 30 million tons of iron ore annually.

En route from Kiruna – Continue northwest on the new section of Highway 98 over the mountains to Narvik in Norway. This spectacular scenic route takes you through the truly wild Abisko National Park and along beautiful Torne Lake.

Alternatively, you can drive from Kiruna back to Svappavaara, then east to Vittangi. From here it's 65 miles (104 km) to Karesuando, a church village on the border of Sweden and Finland. The road is through a tundra region of countless lakes and rivers where the subsoil is permanently frozen. From here the lunatic fringe may choose to continue northward via Kautokeino and Alta in Norway all the way up to North Cape, a magnificent precipice that marks the northernmost tip of Europe. Another alternative is to follow Route E78 southeast into Finland. Our less ambitious but nonetheless spectacular route proceeds northwest from Karesuando on Route E78 — the beautiful "Way of the Four Winds," running parallel with the Könkämä River along the Swedish-Finnish border.

Seventy miles (112 km) farther on as you climb steadily into an alpine region, you cross the border into Norway at Siilastupa, finally reaching Skibotn on the Lyngen Fjord. Your first breathtaking glimpse of the awe-inspiring fjord, its sheer rock walls rising nearly vertically, unbroken but for the odd frothy waterfall crashing into the still waters below, tells you have reached the rocky, skerried coastline of northern Norway. Follow the road southwest along the scenic fjord passing Kvesmenes, where you might join a deep-sea fishing trip to the shark waters of the Arctic Ocean. On either side of the Lyngen Fjord rise the ragged peaks of the Lyngen Alps, spewing impressive blue white glaciers right down to the surface of the water. The faces of the glaciers sparkle like diamonds in the sun. Leaving the fjord, follow Route E78 looping northwest onto a large peninsula toward the Arctic fishing port of Tromsø in Norway.

TROMSØ: Your first impression of Tromsø — apart from the obvious beauty of its coastal setting and backdrop of blue mountains — will be the lush green vegetation that contrasts strongly with the Arctic tundra you have recently passed through at similar latitudes. The rich flora and mild climate on this coast are explained by the Gulf Stream that washes warm currents onto these northern shores.

Tromsø is the largest city in northern Norway (see *Norway*) often called the gateway to the Arctic because of the many expeditions that have set out from here. Take the

2½-hour sightseeing tour that leaves from the *SAS Royal* hotel, showing you the best of Tromsø Island, on which most of the city is situated, and the *Town Museum,* which traces the history of the region from the Stone Age through Viking times and up to the present. The museum also has a section devoted to Lappish ethnography. At the end of the tour you are dropped near the cable car ride up to Storsteinen Mountain, where you receive a sweeping panoramic view over the green city, its wide fishing harbor, and the gentle mountains beyond. Here in Tromsø is your chance to enjoy the more conventional tourist pursuits of a shopping spree and an evening out.

Our route ends in Tromsø but there are possibilities to continue south along the coast passing the fishing harbor of Narvik and the wild and beautiful Lofoten Islands.

BEST EN ROUTE

Accommodations are sparse in Lapland, and range from $80 or more for a double room (very expensive), $50 to $75 (expensive), $35 to $45 (moderate), and below $30 (inexpensive). In Lapland, prices usually include three meals. Again, make reservations before you come.

ABISKO

STF Abisko – Scenically located at the start of the King's Trail (Kungsleden). Near the lift, it has 165 rooms and cottages (phone: 0980-40100). Moderate.

BJÖRKLIDEN

Fjället – A comfortable hotel with 66 rooms and well-equipped cottages over looking Lake Torne and Lapp Gate (phone: 0980-40040 or 248360). Moderate.

GÄLLIVARE

Dundret Holiday Village with Björnfällan – First-rate resort made up of log cabins and a service center that includes saunas, a swimming pool, meeting rooms with open fires, shops, and a cafeteria. It also has an impressive view of the surrounding area (phone: 0970-14560). Expensive.

Polar – A 62-room hotel in the center of Gällivare, close to the railroad station. Facilities include a restaurant and a sauna. 9 Per Högströmsgatan (phone: 0970-11190). Moderate.

KIRUNA

Ferrum – This 170-room hotel provides rooms with private baths, dining room and dancing. In town (phone: 0980-18600). Expensive.

Kebne – A 54-room hotel near the railroad station. 4 Magnigatan (phone 0980-12380). Moderate.

TROMSØ

SAS Royal – This 270-room hotel has excellent accommodations, private baths, and a very good restaurant. 7 Sjogata (phone: 083-56000). Very expensive.

Switzerland

Switzerland may be small, but there is probably not one square mile that does not contain something of beauty or interest. The variety of its scenery is enormous and almost everything is within easy reach. Switzerland's people are also incredibly diverse: Four ethnic and linguistic groups — German, French, Italian, Romansh — maintain their characteristics, culture, and independence under the aegis of one central government. Not only do the 26 cantons (states) guard their individual rights fiercely (until 1848 some had even their own money), but so does every community within the cantons. This is why it's possible to pay twice as much in taxes in one village as in another a mile away.

Geographical or historical necessity played less of a part in the formation of the Confederatio Helvetica (Swiss Confederation) than did the will of the people. In prehistoric times most of the territory was inhabited by Celts (the Helvetians were one of the main Celtic tribes). Later it was ruled by the Romans, who brought cultural and economic prosperity, and then it was overrun by Germanic tribes. The latter included the Alemanns, who settled in what is today the German area of the country, and the Burgundians, who settled in the French. In feudal times the territory was part of the Holy German Empire, and was later ruled by princely families or bishops, who often fought each other for supremacy. It was against the Habsburgs that the original three forest cantons (Uri, Schwyz, Unterwalden) rebelled, and they eventually formed an alliance, marking the birth of the nation in 1291. It did not happen as dramatically as the famous legend of William Tell has it, but the spirit of freedom was the same, and Tell and his apple are still revered today. (This story of Swiss nationhood arose in the 15th century and was made world-famous by the German poet Schiller in the 18th century. It tells of a conspiracy, solemnly sworn among representatives of the three cantons, to overthrow the evil Bailiff Gessler, who had subjected the archer Tell to his famous ordeal.) One by one, all the cities and cantons joined or were acquired by the confederation; the last one was Jura in 1979.

The country is now ruled by a federal government, similar to that of the US, which wields executive and legislative power. The executive branch is controlled by a federal council consisting of seven members and headed by a president serving a 1-year term. Since the head of the council is also the country's president, most Swiss don't know who their government's chief executive is for a given year.

You will generally find the Swiss very friendly and helpful. In most hotels, there is always somebody who speaks English. The best times for motoring are June, September, and October, when the high passes are open but the roads aren't clogged with travelers. Despite the changeable weather, any time is good — in recent years, for example, November has been a particularly beautiful month for touring the mountains. Roads are good, but the German Swiss in particular tend to be cautious (and very law-abiding) drivers. Road numbers often exist only on maps and not on road signs. Also, note that a SFr.100 ($60) fine is imposed if you are caught driving on most Swiss autobahns without the special car sticker that is used in lieu of tolls. Rental cars usually have these stickers; if you're driving into Switzerland, they are available for about $20 at border crossings or at service stations.

The best maps are Michelin #427, Switzerland, and the Michelin regional maps. For city maps, ask at the tourist offices. The best quick reference is the green Michelin guidebook *Switzerland;* for statistics and general information, there's a small red paperback, also called *Switzerland,* published yearly by Kümmerly and Frey. The *Swiss Hotel Guide,* available at the tourist offices, is also helpful.

The four itineraries described below take you through the most important regions and cities, giving a good cross section of the country. Three of the four routes originate in Zurich, the largest city and industrial and financial center of Switzerland. The Zurich to Geneva route passes through some of Switzerland's most historic towns, including Murten and Fribourg. The Zurich to Lugano route travels the high Swiss Alps, running through mountain passes famous for their breathtaking scenery. Another routing from Zurich to Lugano, via the Engadine, cuts through the heart of Swiss tourism, with stops at Bad Ragaz and St. Moritz, the famous health spas. The last route, Bern to Montreux, is typical of diverse Switzerland: It connects the Alps with Lake Geneva and en route you will savor subtropical vegetation as well as glacial vistas.

Zurich to Geneva

This itinerary, which stresses culture and cities, is more idyllic and peaceful than the mountain routes. Starting with Zurich, the route goes west along the Rhine to Basel, then proceeds southwest through the country's oldest mountain range, the Jura (where the language changes from German to French), then to the basin of the Biel and Neuchâtel lakes and gentle, pastoral countryside, to its climax, radiant Lake Geneva with its crown of Alps. The trip includes stops in culturally vibrant Basel; charming Neuchâtel; the "museum town" of Murten; historic Fribourg; enchanting Gruyères; and the university town of Lausanne. Any season is good for this 260-mile (416-km) route. Count on doing it in 3 fairly leisurely days; it's possible to do it in 2 by leaving out some museums.

ZURICH: For a complete description of the city and its hotels and restaurants, see *Zurich,* THE CITIES.

   En Route from Zurich – Take the scenic (and actually shorter) Route N7, which passes the airport and proceeds along the Rhine, which is not yet navigable here. Tiny Kaiserstuhl, just off the main road, is worth a short stop, as it has kept its medieval look. Across the old bridge is Germany. After Zurzach, which features a spa with hot springs, the Aare — the largest all-Swiss river — joins the

Rhine in a picturesque confluence at Koblenz. All along the other side of the Rhine loom the Gothic towers of small German towns. Soon after pretty Laufenburg, the road divides; head for Rheinfelden, with its old spa and famous brewery. From here take Route 3 to Augst, site of the impressive ruins of Augusta Raurica, the oldest Roman settlement on the Rhine. Much has been restored, and you can see some of the artifacts found — including silver plates decorated with mythological details — on display at the museum. It's only a few more minutes from here to Basel.

BASEL: Although it's Switzerland's second city (after Zurich) in terms of population and business, Basel is first in culture — a traditional patron of the arts. Of Celtic Roman origin, the city later was ruled by a prince-bishop for over 1,000 years. (This explains the bishop's staff in Basel's coat of arms.) The town joined the Swiss Confederation in 1501, and became Protestant soon after. It has always had major importance as a port (the Rhine is navigable from here on down) and as a road junction, especially after the river's first bridge, the Mittlere Brücke, was built in 1225. It remained the only one to span the Rhine for centuries, and it still stands.

It's easy to get lost in Basel, so park in the center of town and do your exploring on foot. A walk along the Obere Rheinweg, a promenade following the Rhine's right bank, will give you a good overall picture of old Basel; it's also nice to take the ferry across. On the other side of the Rhine is the 12th-century cathedral (Münster), which provides another fine panorama of the town from its twin Gothic towers. Nearby you'll find some interesting patrician town houses. The town hall, on Market Square (still the site of a daily market), is an impressive 16th-century sandstone building that's adorned with frescoes.

And, of course, there are the museums. The *Kunstmuseum* (Fine Arts Museum; St. Albangraben), one of the most remarkable of its kind in the world, features the Amerbach collection. It includes outstanding examples of early German and Flemish art and the largest group of paintings by the Holbein family assembled anywhere. (Amerbach was a friend of the Holbeins.) There are also French Impressionist works and modern abstracts. The *Kirschgarten* (Cherry Orchard Museum; 27 Elizabethenstrasse), in a lovely old patrician mansion, has period furniture, magnificent porcelain, antique watches, and a delightful exhibition of old toys. It also contains a substantial part of the collection of the *Historical Museum;* the latter is in the Gothic Barfüsser church, on Barfüsserplatz.

This Week in Basel, a booklet published by the Tourist Office, provides an excellent suggested walking tour of the old town, complete with a map. While you're here, stop at "three-countries corner," a spot marked by a spire, where the Swiss, German, and French borders all converge, and take in the excellent view of the port and city from the terrace (reachable by elevator) of the Swiss Navigation Companies' silo. And be sure to sample the local cookie specialty, *basler leckerli.* In addition, you can take in a free concert, given in a number of different churches year-round. It's a good idea to visit Basel on the Monday after Ash Wednesday, for that's when the town really comes alive in an annual carnival called *Fasnacht.*

En Route from Basel – Take the road parallel to Route 18 south; just off the road and near Basel's city limits is Arlesheim, with its charming baroque church and famous Silberman organ. On a mountain overlooking this town is the fortress-like Goetheanum, the center of the Anthroposophical Society. The structure was built according to exacting esoteric rules — for example, no right angles. Goethe's scientific theories strongly influenced the movement, and his plays are often performed here.

At Laufen, you enter the pastoral Jura range. The region becomes French-speaking as you drive along the Birs River to Delémont, former summer residence of the prince-bishops of Basel. The lovely baroque palace is the seat of the new

Jura government. Nearby is Courfaivre, with its remarkable modern stained-glass windows created by Fernand Léger in the village church.

Continuing on Route 18, you'll pass through the most unspoiled section of the Jura, the Franches Montagnes; as you ride the high plateau, it's easy to feel on top of the world. Here are lovely natural parks, pastures with grazing horses (this is the major horse-breeding region), low farmhouses, and little inns that serve good local trout and ham. At Le Roselet (off Les Emibois) you can visit a home for old horses. La Chaux de Fonds is the center of Swiss watch manufacturing, and there is a truly fabulous underground watch museum: On view in specially lit sections is the world's most comprehensive collection of timepieces, from sundials to atomic clocks, *Musée International d'Horlogerie* (21 Rue des Musées). A scenic mountain pass road ascends to Vue des Alpes, where there's a lookout point at 4,209 feet. On clear days the panorama of the Bernese Alps and Mont-Blanc is overwhelming. Descending toward Lake Neuchâtel, you come to Valangin, a charming little town with an old castle that's now an interesting regional museum. From here, it's a short ride to Neuchâtel, a honey-colored university town on a peaceful lake.

NEUCHÂTEL: Some claim that the purest French in the world is spoken in this aristocratic city; after the 11th century, it belonged successively — and by inheritance — to the House of Orléans and the King of Prussia. The intellectual and cultural heritage can be felt in a walk through the old town, especially in the 12th-century University Church and the castle. The *Ethnographic Museum* is outstanding for its Egyptian and African collections and thematic display rooms (4 St. Nicolas). The *Museum of Art and History* features ingenious automatons invented in the 18th century (Rue des Beaux-Arts).

En Route from Neuchâtel – Cross the canal connecting the Neuchâtel and Biel lakes north of the city, and head for Murten, on the far side of the lake of the same name.

MURTEN (MORAT): This enchanting town is a museum in itself, having retained most of its medieval ramparts and towers. A historic battle was fought here in the 15th century between the Swiss Confederates and the army of the duke of Burgundy, and it's still commemorated today. A walk around the ramparts provides picturesque views of the old roofs, the lake, and the castle. Main Street (Hauptstrasse) displays a pleasing harmony of design, with its arcaded, geranium-covered houses, fountains, and city gate; a row of restaurants and cafés makes it even more inviting. It's a short drive southeast to Fribourg.

FRIBOURG: You enter one of the most picturesque and interesting cities of the country through an old gate; strangely, it's often bypassed by tourists. Its river, the Sarine, is a true dividing line between the French and German parts of Switzerland. Fribourg is a historical Roman Catholic bastion, and the site of a renowned Catholic university established in 1889. Founded in 1157, the city was ruled by different families until it joined the confederation in 1481. Several major religious orders, such as the Franciscans, Cistercians, and Jesuits, have settled here in the course of centuries.

The Franciscan Church (Église des Cordeliers, Rue de Morat), completed in the 13th century and rebuilt in the 18th century, retains its original chancel and stalls, as well as its splendid St. Anthony altarpiece, painted by two artists whose signatures were red and white carnations. In addition, bridges on the winding Sarine offer marvelous views of the town. The river itself swirls around Fribourg's unusual spurlike rock formations. You should also see the Gothic towers and elaborately decorated interiors of St. Nicholas' Cathedral; the turrets and belfry of the 16th-century town hall; and the excellent collection of sculpture, furniture, and jewelry in the elegant *Museum of Art and History* (all on Rue de Morat).

En Route from Fribourg – Continue along the pretty, manmade Lake Gruyères; for a more scenic route, don't take the freeway or the main road, but the smaller one that goes via Marly and Corbières (stop at the bridge for a good view) through regions of pastoral scenery where folklore is still alive. Then proceed via Broc directly to Gruyères.

GRUYÈRES: This hilltop town, definitely one of the route's highlights, appears to be preserved against time — it could be the setting for medieval fairy tales. Cars are prohibited within the town's walls for a good part of the year, so leave yours in one of the lots on the outskirts. Then take a leisurely stroll down the wide, cobblestone main street that's lined with old houses, observing the house on the left with the gracefully carved 16th-century window frames. Proceed up to the castle, the former abode of the benevolent counts of Gruyères, and view the collection of tapestries, furniture, and medieval war booty housed in the impressive 15th-century edifice. Gruyères is, of course, an excellent place to sample fondue; also try the local heavy cream with berries. In the morning, pay a visit to the cheese factory at the bottom of the hill and watch the product being made. Later, there's an audio-visual show.

En Route from Gruyères – Head north to Bulle, featuring the *Gruèrien Museum,* with its fine collection of regional costumes and furniture. Next, turn south to Châtel St. Denis on the same road, and begin the magnificent descent to Lake Geneva; from here the road to Blonay is more scenic and less direct. The lake begins to come into view here, with the grandiose high Valais Alps providing a beautiful backdrop. Whether you come from the Blonay road or Route 12, you end up near Vevey, a pleasant resort that's the headquarters of the Nestlé Company. The Wine Growers Fraternity displays models of its costumes dating back to the last century in the *Old Vevey Museum.* Although the new freeway to Lausanne is particularly scenic, it's still better to drive there through the vineyards on the specially marked Wine Route (Route de Vignoble) through old villages like Chexbres, Riez, and Grandvaux. On this route, you'll drive along narrow roads, passing old castles (many of which are privately owned), and small pubs and inns that serve regional specialties and their own home-grown white wine. The lake is always in view, and the drive is especially beautiful in late fall when the vineyards turn yellow. Several wine caves are open to visitors. Take the lake road at Lutry and enter Lausanne by way of the port of Ouchy.

LAUSANNE: The route climbs steeply from Ouchy to the old town of this youthful, upbeat university city. Recent excavations of Neolithic skeletons have dated habitation of the area to the Stone Age, and part of the late Roman city of Lousonna has been unearthed slightly west of here. Starting with its consecration in 1275, however, the cathedral has been the center of town and is closely connected with its history.

It is the most beautiful Gothic building in Switzerland with its picturesque towers, sculptured doors, and relief work; a museum containing some of its treasures is in the splended Bishop's Palace next to it. An unusual, fascinating collection of works by mentally deranged artists, donated to the city by the French painter Jean Dubuffet, is nicely exhibited in an 18th-century palace (*Collection d'Art Brut,* Château de Beaulieu, Av. de Bergières). Farther up the hill, in a lovely villa with a park, is the Hermitage Foundation, which stages important art exhibitions every summer (mainly of the Impressionist and later periods). From the center of town, take a funicular down to Ouchy, a bustling port with lovely views of Lake Geneva and the mountains. Stop into one of the cozy pubs here and sample the *raclette* — a melted cheese specialty served with tiny potatoes and pickles.

En Route from Lausanne – A worthwhile, short sidetrip is picturesque Romainmôtier, nestled in a valley some 22 miles (35 km) north of Lausanne via Route 9. Its honeycolored medieval houses are dominated by the oldest and most important Romanesque church in Switzerland (now defunct). While in town, try the outstanding *tartes* of Madame Pittet at *Café Le Môtier* (closed Mondays). Return to Lausanne and take Route 1 toward Geneva; you'll pass through Morges, a pleasant little town with an excellent view of the lake's widest point, as well as the *Vaud Military Museum,* which displays arms and uniforms dating from 1798. Nyon is worth a stop.

NYON: This delightful port, lined with flowers, served Caesar as a base for his Helvetian couriers, and it still bears some traces of Roman times; for example, the god Attis is represented on Caesar's Tower here. The *Roman Museum,* built on the ruins of a recently discovered basilica, is considered the best of its kind in the country. Open daily; closed for lunch. The town's ramparts are also worth seeing.

En Route from Nyon – Before reaching Geneva, you may find a stop at Coppet enjoyable; this town features the château where Germain de Staël, a Swiss novelist, lived after Napoleon's affections for her cooled. It's elegantly furnished in Louis XVI style, and has some fine portrait paintings. The best way to enter Geneva is along the lake. (For more information see *Geneva,* THE CITIES.)

BEST EN ROUTE

Although we haven't listed them, there are many small inns in the Jura region that offer good local food and acceptable lodgings. Accommodations on this route tend to be more costly from mid-June through September, and drop off — sometimes significantly — from November through March. We've assigned an expensive rating to hotel rooms costing $150 and up in high season. Accommodations are moderate if they run from $95 to $130. And we've rated rooms inexpensive if they cost $60 or less. Rates are for a double room with a shower. Restaurant prices range from $100 and up for a dinner for two in places listed as expensive, $55 to $85 in those listed as moderate, and around $40 in the inexpensive category. Prices do not include drinks and wine or coffee; tips are included.

BASEL

Drei Konige (Three Kings) – The oldest luxury hotel in the country, the *Three Kings* boasts a historic guest list — from emperors to authors. It's directly on the Rhine and has excellent rooms and a good restaurant on the terrace. 8 Blumenrain (phone: 255252). Expensive.

Krafft am Rhein – In the Klein (small) Basel section, this hotel has a fine view of the cathedral. 12 Rheingasse (phone: 918877). Moderate.

Bruderholz – In recent years, this elegant restaurant has become one of Switzerland's finest. Outside the center of town, it specializes in French food. 42 Bruderholzallee (phone: 358222). Expensive.

Schloss Bottmingen – This delightful baroque castle has a moat, a lovely garden, and excellent food and service. Closed Sundays and Mondays. 9 Schlossgasse, Bottmingen (phone: 471515). Expensive to moderate.

Confiserie Tea Room Schiesser – Basel's most traditional café overlooks the famous 16th-century town hall and serves excellent pastries and light snacks. Closed Sundays (and Mondays in summer). 19 Marktplatz (phone: 256077). Moderate.

Kunsthalle – The favorite of many artists, this place is lively and has good food. Closed Sundays. 7 Steinenberg (phone: 234233). Moderate.

Zum Goldenen Sternen – In Basel's recently restored, picturesque St. Alban section, Switzerland's oldest pub lacks for nothing in the way of charm. (phone: 231666). Moderate.

NEUCHÂTEL

Beaulac – A modern hotel beautifully situated on the lake harbor. Quais Léopold Robert et du Port (phone: 258822). Moderate.

Maison des Halles – This popular restaurant is in an ancient building in the old town. Place des Halles (phone: 243141). Moderate to inexpensive.

MURTEN

Vieux Manoir – Set right on the lake with its own private beach, this slightly pretentious hotel has pleasant rooms and an excellent restaurant. Closed mid-December through mid-February. 3280 Meyriez-Morat (phone: 711283). Expensive to moderate.

Channes Valaisanne – Serving good, reasonable food in a medieval room that could pass for a small museum. The cellar has vintage wines on exhibit. Closed Tuesdays. 51 Hauptstraat (phone: 712565). Moderate to inexpensive.

GRUYÈRES

Hôstellerie des Chevaliers – This modern, cozy hotel just beyond the medieval ramparts offers wonderful views. The rooms feature rustic or period furnishings and fresh flowers. There is also an excellent restaurant. 1663 Gruyères (phone: 61933). Moderate.

Hôstellerie de St. Georges – The windows of this charming, antiques-furnished, old inn face the open country below. There's a big terrace, and an elegant, cozy Rôtisserie with excellent food. Closed November through March. 1663 Gruyères (phone: 62246). Moderate.

Chalet – This cozy, rustic restaurant is near the castle. It serves fine fondue, *raclette,* and other specialties. 1663 Gruyères (phone: 62154). Moderate.

LAUSANNE

Château d'Ouchy – A romantic hotel in a 12th-century fortress, it is right on the lake. Place du Port (phone: 267451). Expensive to moderate.

Résidence – Combining two charming old villas, every room of *La Résidence* is different. 15 Place du Port (phone: 277711). Expensive to moderate.

Alpha – This cheerful, modern hotel in the heart of Lausanne has a good coffee shop and a cozy cellar restaurant featuring local cheese specialties. Free parking. 34 Rue Petit-Chêne (phone: 230131). Moderate.

Girardet – Managed by chef Fredy Giradet, this restaurant serves the best food in Switzerland — and perhaps in the world! Plan to stop here for a leisurely meal, but be sure to make reservations far in advance — for dinner, 2 months before; for lunch, several weeks before. About 4 miles (6.4 km) from Lausanne. 1 Route d'Yverdon, Crissier (phone: 340505). Expensive.

Grappe d'Or – This is the best place in town for both food and atmosphere; its specialty is meat grilled over a wood fire. Closed Sundays. 3 Cheneau de Bourg (phone: 230760). Expensive.

Goya – Here you can find an inexpensive café as well as a more elegant restaurant; both are intimate and good. 18 Rue de Grand-St.-Jean (phone: 220266). Moderate to inexpensive.

NYON

Clos de Sadex – This 18th-century lakeside manor house is now a charming, relaxed hotel. Du Clos de Sadex, 131 Road du Lausanne (phone: 612831). Expensive to moderate.

COPPET

Du Lac – An enchanting small hotel on the lake, it has rustic yet elegant rooms, an outstanding restaurant, and a garden. 1296 Coppet (phone: 761521). Expensive to moderate.

Zurich to Lugano
via the Four Passes

This, the most scenically spectacular route, with one dramatic highlight after another, takes you zigzagging from north to south through the geographical and historical center of Switzerland, covering eight cantons. The views are often breathtaking: sparkling lakes, snowy peaks, flowery chalets, and pastures with bell-tinkling cows. Although the route is primarily scenic and historical, Lucerne and Lugano offer some points of cultural interest. The Four Passes portion of the trip is possible only in June through October and is closed for the rest of the year; it's advisable to travel here in good weather only. Spend at least 3 days on this 233-mile (373-km) route. You can do it in 2 days if you leave out Lucerne, but even then it would be impossible to absorb everything. It's best to start on the Four Passes circuit in the morning, driving with the sun at your back wherever possible.

En Route from Zurich – You leave Zurich (for more information, see *Zurich,* THE CITIES) on the heavily traveled road to Switzerland's most popular tourist town, Lucerne, then drive along the strangely shaped, highly scenic Lake Lucerne, through the sanctuary of the country, where William Tell shot his legendary apple and the Swiss Confederation started in 1291. In 1991, grand celebrations marking the event's 700th anniversary will take place throughout the region. (It will help you enjoy all the spots of historical interest on this route if you read Schiller's *William Tell* or a synopsis of it.) You gradually ascend on new, excellent roads into the highest Swiss Alps. The route makes a rough circle through three of the mountain passes, proceeding up and down through frequent hairpin curves and great scenery, and then continues south on the fourth, the St. Gotthard Pass road. This was developed in the 13th century after the frightening Schöllenen Gorge was conquered. It has since become a vital artery for tourist trade and military use. By the way, the 6,940-foot-high St. Gotthard Pass is a favorite maneuver area of the Swiss army, and in spring and fall you are bound to see soldiers. Population is scarce and life extremely difficult in these high regions, but you never have to drive too long before you spot an inn, small village, or service station. On the Gotthard Pass you cross the great north-south divide and the scenery soon becomes different; this is also a weather divide and you often pass from clouds into brilliant sunshine. (Strangely, it is seldom the other way around.) The old inn on the pass, *Vecchia Susta,* was restored and opened in 1986 as a museum, with historic documents, vehicles, and a multivision show. Another part of the building still houses an inn. The route continues down the Leventine Valley along the Ticino River, which gave its name to the canton, and passes through vineyards, past campaniles and places with Italian names — it's like a different country, though it has been part of Switzerland since 1803. After Bellinzona, the first sturdy palm trees appear and beautiful Lugano is close by. Although the roads are excellent throughout, they're narrow at certain points; at times, they widen into freeways. There's a great deal of traffic in summer and on weekends, so try to avoid it. And don't rush. A rule of the mountain roads is that the ascending car has the right of way, though on this route roads are wide enough for two.

Take the main road to Lucerne along the pleasant, verdant Sihl Valley. The freeway after Sihlbrugg eliminates a slow and uninteresting stretch between Baar and Zug. (If time permits, a short detour to Zug is worthwhile, for its placid lake and charming old town.) The main road is nothing special, but it gets you to Lucerne in about an hour.

LUCERNE: This most photographed Swiss city is truly beautiful, even in the bad weather, which it often has. Once a modest fishing village, it became famous and rich as the bridgehead of the important Gotthard route, opened in the 13th century. In 1332, it was the first city to join the Swiss Confederation, then consisting of only the three original cantons. Parts of impressive fortifications, like the Musegg tower and wall, are still standing. The Reformation, which swept most of 16th-century Switzerland, never succeeded in Lucerne, which remains today a Roman Catholic bastion. The yearly mid-August *Music Festival* is one of the most important in Europe. Lucerne deserves several days, but if you only have time for the main sights, start with the town symbol: the famous Kapellbrücke, a covered bridge that spans the Reuss River. Along with the flanking Water Tower (Wasserturm), the bridge served as a fortification against attack. The inside partitions of the bridge are graced with 120 paintings, done in the 16th to 18th centuries, which illustrate Lucerne's history. The tower served as a lookout point, a prison, and an archives, and now belongs to the Artillery Club. Other important sights of Lucerne's old town section are the town hall (with its historical museum) on Kornmarkt Square, Weinmarkt Square with its lovely painted houses and Renaissance fountain, and the Spreuerbrücke, a covered bridge which has macabre Death Dance paintings. A walk along the lakeshore quais is also interesting, but another famous Lucerne sight, the Lion Monument (Löwendenkmal, Denkmalstr.), could be left out without much loss. The Glacier Garden (Gletschergarten) next to it is interesting, with its Ice Age glacier potholes and giant stones; there's also a museum containing prehistoric specimens, the first relief map of Switzerland, and some furnishings of old Lucerne. The Cathedral Hofkirche (Leodegarstr.) has an especially atmospheric courtyard, with tombstones in the walls, and the baroque Jesuit Church has been splendidly restored, cheerfully serene in coral and white. The *Swiss Transport Museum* (Verkehrshaus; Lidostr.) is much more interesting than its name indicates: There's a lively exhibition of the development of ships, trains, cars, and planes displaying the oldest specimen of each. The museum also has a marvelous model of the Swiss railway crossing the Gotthard, with 12 trains simultaneously in motion. Also on the premises is the *Hans Erni House,* containing works by the famous Lucerne artist. The *Richard Wagner Museum* is in the southern suburb of Tribschen (in an idyllic villa with a lovely view about 2 mi/3.2 km from Lucerne). The composer lived here for years and wrote some of his major works. Letters, photographs, and Wagner's original scores can be seen at the museum. The villa also houses an interesting collection of old musical instruments from all over the world. (In winter, it's closed Mondays, Wednesdays, and Fridays.)

Shopping is easy and seductive: Watches and clocks, jewelry, handicrafts, embroidery, and souvenirs all can be bought. Most of the shops are around Schwanenplatz or on the way to the cathedral. To find the largest selection of jewelry, pay a visit to *Bucherer* (5 Schwanenpl.). Nearby, there's a good place to shop for embroidery: *Sturzenegger* (7 Schwanenpl). Souvenirs also abound near the Lion Monument.

If you spend an evening in Lucerne, don't miss the night boat; it's garish but fun, and the view of the brightly lit town alone makes the trip worthwhile. You can have a fondue dinner or just wine on board, and dance to live folk music. For the best view of the town, have a drink in the pleasant garden of *Château Gütsch* hotel (Kanonenstr.); the cafés along the Reuss near the Kapellbrücke are also nice stops.

En Route from Lucerne – Drive along Lake Lucerne (also called Vierwaldstättersee, or the Lake of the Four Forest Cantons), with its several distinct branches ("as a handkerchief waving good-bye in four different directions," a poet said), to Meggen. There's an interesting modern church right off the main road. Don't be put off by its exterior: The transparent marble walls inside are wonderful, especially in sunshine. You'll pass Merlischachen and its steep wooden houses with their first floors elevated high above the ground; these houses, accessible only by stairs, are typical of this region. Here also is the Astridchapel, built where Queen Astrid of Belgium had a fatal car accident in 1935. Küssnacht, a little town with an important role in early Swiss history, features the *Engel* hotel, a most remarkable historic building on its main square. Only a mile outside town, on Road 2, is the famous Hohle Gasse; park your car and walk the short sunken road where, according to the legend, William Tell waited to kill Bailiff Gessler. There's a small chapel at the end of the road commemorating his success. Road 2 continues on the shore of Lake Zug to Arth and Goldau, under the slopes of Mount Rigi, with extraordinary views all along, then passes charming little Lauerzer Lake. The *Insel Schwanau* (see *Best en Route*) is a good place to stop for lunch or a drink beneath the ruins of a former fortress. You have to ring the bell on shore for a boat to pick you up. From here, it's only 3 miles (5 km) to Schwyz, which is not on the main road, but worth a short visit. (The fast freeway from Arth bypasses Lauerz. If you want to travel really fast, the freeway from Lucerne, on the alternate lakeside through the long Seelisberg tunnel, takes you directly to Altdorf.)

A more scenic and longer road from Küssnacht to Schwyz follows the sometimes rocky shores of the lake on the "Lucerne Riviera," where flowers blossom early in the season, through the resort areas of Weggis and Vitznau. Vitznau has Europe's oldest rack-and-pinion railway to Mount Rigi. Built by its inventor in 1871, the railway still has over 95% of its original cog racks; the ride up the steep slope is filled with wonderful views. Several lakeshore restaurants along the way specialize in fish. A high, rocky road leads to Gersau, a tiny sovereign republic for 500 years (1390–1800); the lake is deepest here, and has lovely underwater scenery.

If you want to leave Lucerne out of your itinerary, you can proceed directly from Zurich on the freeway to Arth and Schwyz or Brunnen; it's also very scenic.

SCHWYZ: This town provided Switzerland with its name and flag, and its Archive of Federal Charters (off Bahnhofstr.) preserves the original Covenant of Confederation of 1291. The 16th-century town hall, in picturesque Town Hall Square (Rathauspl.) has paintings of historical scenes on its exterior walls. Schwyz, a predominantly Catholic town, supplies the Vatican with some of the Swiss Guard.

BRUNNEN: Many famous guests, including Queen Victoria and Richard Wagner, have visited this old-fashioned resort. It used to be a shelter from the ferocious *föhn* storms, which can whip up the water into 400-foot spouts. Across the lake is Treib, another old storm refuge and a traditional asylum for fugitives. It was the meeting place of the first Confederation of Switzerland; you can still see the first house of parliament, the parlor of a local inn.

En Route from Brunnen – The magnificent Axenstrasse is a road hewn in rock high above the fjordlike Urner Lake (still part of Lake Lucerne), and for 10 miles the view of the steep wild shores across, the deep blue water below, and the Alps ahead is unforgettable. In season, the traffic is quite heavy, but the scenery compensates for everything. Several lookout points between Brunnen and Sisikon provide views of historic Rütli Field, where the representatives of the original cantons took a solemn oath of independence from the Habsburgs, according to Schiller. Each year, on August 1, speeches and celebrations are held here in commemoration of a national holiday. After Sisikon, a tunnel replaces the open mountain road — it's safer for cars, but takes away the view. Leave your car at the south end of the tunnel and walk along the old road, a perfect place to take pictures. The William Tell Chapel (Tellskapelle) commemorates another dramatic event in the Tell legend: Held captive on his enemies' boat, Tell took advantage of a sudden storm and leaped to shore. A short, steep path leads down to the chapel from the roadside parking area. The lake ends at Flüelen and you can continue on the new freeway or drive through Altdorf, the small capital of Uri Canton (one of the original three) and see the statue of William Tell in the main square. Erected in 1895, it has since been made famous by its representation on Swiss postage stamps. Both roads follow the Reuss Valley and slowly start to climb the St. Gotthard massif. If you're interested in trains, drive through Erstfeld; the model in the *Lucerne Transport Museum* is based on the busy railroad station here (see *Lucerne*).

AMSTEG: This is the last village before the big climb starts, and if you haven't stopped yet, the *Stern and Post* hotel is ideal; it has served as a stopover for travelers on stagecoaches and other vehicles for over 150 years (see *Best en Route*).

En Route from Amsteg – The smooth freeway takes you up to Wassen effortlessly. There's a remarkable waterfall, Pfaffensprung, nearby, but you have to park off the old road before Wassen to see it; the cascading waters produce some marvelous rainbows as they hit the rocks. From Wassen, take the old road to Göschenen; this should give you a good idea of how difficult it was to build a road up the Gotthard massif 600 years ago. Göschenen's lively railroad station is found at the north end of the two tunnels that convey trains and cars through the pass. From here, you can get a good view of the Upper Dammastock ice field. Next you pass through the Reuss Valley with its smooth, granite walls culminating in a legendary bottleneck, The Schöllenen Gorge. This defile made the development of a route southward through the Gotthard Pass impossible until the 13th century, when a road was driven through the gorge. The new road diminishes the contemporary traveler's feeling for the eeriness of the place. To recapture some of that awe, park your car near Devil's Bridge (Teufelsbrücke) and take a short walk on the old road. The bridge itself replaced another bridge here, which, according to legend, was built with the aid of the Devil, who asked to be paid with the soul of the first creature to cross it. The result angered the Devil a great deal — the creature turned out to be a goat. The enraged Devil then heaved a huge stone into the valley; one of the large rocks a short distance before the gorge is called the Devil's Stone.

After the gorge, head for Andermatt, a popular ski resort and a true crossroads of the Alps. The Furka and St. Gotthard roads have their junction here. Driving back to Wassen, you get a completely different view of the scenery than you had on the way to Andermatt. At Wassen, take the Susten road going west, unless it is afternoon and the light is against you.

The Susten Road, finished in 1945, was the first Swiss mountain road built especially for motorists. As it starts its steady climb, the route presents an interesting view of the jagged crests of a group of mountains called the Five Fingers. Driving through the upper hairpin bends, you'll see the panorama widen to a final view of the valley. Before you reach the tunnel through the road's crest, you can stop and survey the peaks from a viewing table. Walk to the road's highest point — 7,411 feet — from the large parking lot at the tunnel's west end. The view for the next few miles is the most magnificent the route offers: You'll see an arctic landscape at the foot of the Stein glacier, including a small lake complete with miniature icebergs. You can park at several road bends to enjoy views of the steep descents (from the *Susten Pass* hotel, a short "glacier road" leads even deeper into ice, snow, and rocks). After passing through some fertile valleys, you'll reach Innertkirchen, where you can pick up the Grimsel Road; the ancient *Tännler Inn,* before the junction, is a good place to rest.

The Grimsel Road first passes through pastoral scenery with some huge escarpments. (The avalanches are fierce here in the winter.) Then the views become more and more Dantesque — enormous granite rocks, slabs, and walls polished smooth and shiny by glacier action. Park your car for a view of the spectacular Handegg Waterfall cascading into a narrow gorge. Next, after a small, turquoise lake, you'll see the surrealistic Lake of Grimsel — an elongated reservoir created by two dams. The steep upward bends provide the best view of the lake; at the road's crest there's another small lake where a battle between the Austrians and the French took place in 1799. From here you can turn down to Gletsch, where the Furka Road begins, and catch a first glimpse of the Rhone glacier.

Although Gletsch itself consists of only a few houses, it's a good place to view the constantly receding glacier. Today, the glacier isn't in the basin, but photos of 100 years ago show it reaching the valley. This is where the Rhone, one of the longest rivers of Europe, starts its course. As you climb the Furka, every bend supplies another view of the glacier; the best one is just before the now defunct *Belvedere* hotel. Even though it's disappointingly gray and dirty on the surface because of the heavy flow of traffic, the glacier is still impressive. Stop at the *Belvedere,* which has enough parking space and is the best point from which to view the panorama of the Bernese and Valais Alps. But the main attraction is the ice grotto that's cut into the glacier: Its transparent walls glitter with an unbelievable bluish light as the sun comes through the crevasses. A few miles beyond is the highest point of the Furka Pass, measuring 7,975 feet, with the Galenstock peak hovering above. The road skirts the Alps descending, first gently, then steeply, toward Realp, providing a sweeping view of the barren valley below.

If you don't want to make another stop at Andermatt, turn off at Hospenthal (marked by an old watchtower) to pick up the Gotthard Road. After a few steep turns, the scenery becomes desolate; the road's crest at 6,919 feet has rocks and glacial ponds that are very uninviting. The pass owes its name to a chapel of the patron saint that was built here in about 1300. From here, you can take either the new freeway through the tunnel and viaduct, or the smaller, steeper, somewhat more scenic one through the Tremola, with its view of the Leventine Valley below, to Airolo, a tunnel exit station and tourist resort. Take the freeway from here, as the smaller road (Route 2) is not as scenic.

The Leventine Valley is not very interesting compared to all you have already seen, but the driving's quite fast. Rough stone houses, chestnut trees, and the campaniles of the Ticino River area appear; there are several rushing waterfalls and, a little farther on, vineyards. Giornico has a remarkable Romanesque church, San Nicolao, and charming houses off the main road. You may want to stop at Bellinzona or bypass it and Monte Ceneri on the new but unscenic autobahn.

BELLINZONA: This administrative center of Ticino Canton has guarded the valley for centuries with three old castles. One of them, Castello Montebello, now houses the excellent historical and archaeological *City Museum.* Castello di Sasso Corbaro has a beautiful view and a café.

En Route from Bellinzona – The plain widens and soon Route 2 starts a steep but short climb up Monte Ceneri and offers wonderful glimpses of the Lago Maggiore below. It's about 10 minutes to Lugano from here. For a more scenic approach, take the exit marked "Lugano Süd (south) and Paradiso."

BEST EN ROUTE

Accommodations on this route tend to be more costly from mid-June through September, and drop off — sometimes significantly — from November through March. We've assigned an expensive rating to hotel rooms costing $170 and up in high season. Accommodations are moderate if they run from $100 to $150. And we've rated rooms inexpensive if they cost $80 or less. Rates are for a double room with a shower. Restaurant prices range from $100 and up for a dinner for two in places listed as expensive, $50 to $85 in those listed as moderate, and around $40 in the inexpensive category. Prices do not include drinks and wine or coffee; tips are included.

LUCERNE

Grand Hotel National – Known for its comfortable and luxurious rooms with views of Lake Lucerne, the hotel also has a popular Viennese café with a terrace that's open in summer months. 4 Haldenstr. (phone: 501111). Expensive.

Palace – Lucerne's other high-quality hotel, it also has very comfortable accommodations with lake views. 14 Haldenstr. (phone: 502222). Expensive.

Des Balances – On the Reuss River in Old Town, and furnished with antiques. Weinmarkt (phone: 511851). Expensive to moderate.

Wilden Mann – Owned by the same family for over 100 years, this establishment in an ancient house has small but very charming rooms. Its tavern and elegant restaurant have excellent food. Major credit cards. 30 Bahnofstr. (phone: 231666). Moderate.

Château Gütsch – Featuring a fabulous view from its hillside perch, the hotel has a good restaurant in a rustic setting and serves drinks and snacks in its garden. Since it's a bit difficult to find the place at first, the hotel runs a private cable car from the center of town. Kanonenstr. (phone: 220272). Moderate.

Eden – Gracious, well-located hotel, offering many rooms with balconies, it is an excellent value. Open year-round. 47 Haldenstr. (phone: 513806). Inexpensive.

Pickwick – An informal little hotel on the river in Old Town that has an amusing custom: Each patron gets an apple at night. Breakfast vouchers for a nearby restaurant are supplied on request. (Since it's difficult to find the entrance, ask at the *Pickwick Club.*) 6 Rathausquai (phone: 515927). Inexpensive.

Old Swiss House – This famous restaurant near the Lion Monument has lovely rustic decor and serves Swiss and international cuisine. Major credit cards. 4 Löwenpl. (phone: 516171). Expensive to moderate.

Raben – In a medieval building in Old Town, this is one of Lucerne's best restaurants. It is owned and run by cookbook author Marianne Kaltenbach, who presents delicious, inventive dishes. Major credit cards. Kornmarkt (phone: 515135). Expensive.

Weinhof – A typical Swiss restaurant, small, cozy, and reasonably priced. Closed Saturdays. No credit cards. 12 Weystr. (phone: 511251). Inexpensive.

MERLISCHACHEN

Swiss Chalet – This touristy but very attractive motel-restaurant on the main road serves good snacks. The attached, charming *Schloss* hotel is directly on the lake. Route 2, Merlischachen (phone: 371247). Moderate.

KÜSSNACHT

Gasthof Engel – A splendid example of old local architecture, this hotel was the site of the Helvetian Confederation's sessions from 1423 to 1712. Closed in winter. Küssnacht (phone: 811057). Inexpensive.

VITZNAU

Park – An Art Nouveau castle directly on the lake, with Old World atmosphere and a big park — in good weather, a fairy tale come true. The hotel's spacious rooms have marble baths, and there's also a good restaurant. Closed in winter. Kantonsstr. (phone: 831322). Expensive.

LAUERZERSEE

Insel Schwanau – In a highly romantic setting on a tiny island after which it's named, this restaurant serves good food. You must ring the bell on the lakeshore to be picked up by a boat. Closed in winter. No credit cards. Insel Schwanau (phone: 211757). Moderate.

BRUNNEN

Waldhaus Wolfsprung – This small chalet hotel furnished with brass beds and Persian rugs is in a forest above an Alpine lake and has a private beach. Closed in winter. Axenstr. (phone: 311173). Moderate.

ALTDORF

Goldener Schlüssel – An establishment in a charming historic house in the center of town. 6460 Altdorf (phone: 21002). Inexpensive.

AMSTEG

Stern and Post – A comfortable old stagecoach inn, it features excellent food and paneled, antiques-filled rooms. 6474 Amsteg (phone: 64440). Moderate to inexpensive.

INNERTKIRCHEN

Gasthof Tännler – This hotel is in a lovely old farmhouse. Although the rooms are comfortably appointed, they don't have separate baths. Susten Pass road (phone: 711427). Inexpensive.

Zurich to Lugano
via the Engadine

This 204-mile (325-km) route contains scenery that's dotted with architectural jewels, and takes you through the center of Swiss tourism, the Canton Grisons (Graubünden). Romansh, a language stemming from Illyrian and Latin, is still spoken here; sections of the canton once formed part of ancient Rhaetia, a province of the Roman Empire. The Rhaetians resisted both the Celts (who, in pre-Roman times, occupied all of present Switzerland except Grisons) and the Germanic tribes, who came after the Romans. Rhaetia completely controlled the north-south Alpine crossings before the Gothard Pass was opened. Ruled by feudal lords and bishops, the Rhaetians formed an alliance with three other groups in the fifteenth century. Wars, Habsburg rule, and more wars typify the ensuing history of the area, and the many castles and ruins are vivid signs of this. The canton joined the Swiss Confederation in 1803, but Romansh officially became the country's fourth national language in 1938. Swiss German is also spoken here. Although the passes of the route are open year-round, September is perhaps the best time to take the trip because the special light of the Engadine is most evident then. Spring, when you can see the overwhelming contrast of snowy Grisons with blossoming Ticino, is also a good time to go. Though it's almost as mountainous, this route has scenery that's quite different than that of the central Alps — it's less forbidding, and has more color and variety. Starting again from Zurich in the north, you drive southeast, passing by Lake Walensee, to Chur, the artistic, cultural, and administrative center of the canton; then you climb through spruce-covered mountains to the ancient Roman Julier Pass and descend into the extraordinary Engadine Valley. Here are Switzerland's most famous resorts, including St. Moritz, the queen of them all. From here, the route proceeds down to warmer regions and chestnut groves, dipping briefly into Italy along Lake Como, and turns back into Switzerland's Tessin (Ticino), a cheerful canton that has retained its Lombardian culture since becoming part of Switzerland in 1803.

Although the roads are always excellent, on weekends they're usually crowded. This is a perfect route for seeing the high mountains in winter, as most other crossings are closed, and the skiing is unequaled anywhere. Your car will need winter equipment into late spring. Spend at least 3 days and 2 nights — and preferably more. And don't miss Grison's culinary specialties of *bündnerfleish* (paper-thin slices of air-dried beef that are eaten with the fingers) and rich, delicious nutcake; with a glass of wine, the two make a perfect light meal.

En Route from Zurich – Drive along the highway running adjacent to Lake Zurich; there's a lovely view of the lake and the distant mountains. Traffic gets very heavy at Lake Walensee, but the grand scenery of sheer rocks, waterfalls, and the characteristically jagged peaks make up for it. The lake is treacherous, with sudden storms that take their toll in damages each year. The fortress of Sargans, visible from afar, looms over this important medieval trading route. Soon afterward is Bad Ragaz — the best-known health spa in the country: Its mineral waters have been in use since the 11th century. (In the old days, patients were lowered down with ropes to springs located a little farther on in the Tamina Gorge.) It has elegant hotels, lovely parks, and an 18-hole golf course. Next is Maienfeld, a charming, sleepy little town with beautiful patrician houses. The valley here follows the Rhine, the longest river in Europe, as it flows down the Alps. And the pastures are "Heidi country" — they served as the setting for the famous book.

CHUR: Recent excavations here date the city back to 3000 BC. After the Roman period, Chur was a center of Christianity. Walk the narrow streets of the enchanting old town with its medieval houses, and after crossing under an old gate, climb the steps to the cathedral; there's a famous Gothic triptych inside, as well as a pre-Christian sacrificial stone, near the altar. The splendid baroque Bishop's Palace (Hof), next to the cathedral, is still the bishop's residence. The *Hofkellerei* (see *Best en Route*), a pub in the Bishop's Palace, is a good place for some *bündnerfleish* or other refreshments. The *Rhaetian Museum,* set in a 17th-century mansion on Hofstrasse, has many prehistoric, Roman, and medieval treasures.

En Route from Chur – Leaving Chur, Route 3 climbs steeply, offering a wonderful view of the city and its many spires. The road leads through scented, moss-covered woods to Lenzerheide, a popular resort with one of the most unusual hotels, *Guarda Val;* the hotel's Alpine barns make it worth a stop, even if you don't spend the night (see *Best en Route*). In Lenz (Lantsch), the language changes from German to Romansh and road signs are bilingual. The village itself has an interesting cemetery with ornate iron crosses. This lovely drive through meadows, rounded hillsides, distant chapels, and sweeping views steeply descends toward Tiefencastel, in the Albula Valley. A white church tower marks Tiefencastel, but the real attraction is the Carolingian church of St. Peter of Mistail, built in AD 926. Ask townspeople for directions to the church; they'll also tell you where to get the key if the church is closed. Castle ruins dot the slopes along the road from here, reminders of a turbulent past; you'll pass through Savognin (a resort with three notable baroque churches), to the Marmorera Dam Reservoir, which has flooded two tiny hamlets. Bivio has a jewel of a Catholic church with Renaissance and baroque interiors. The ancient Roman Septimer road branches off from here, and is open only to hikers. The austere Julier Pass, 7,494 feet, used by the Romans, is still the main entrance to the Engadine. Its Latinate name recalls the important role of the Romans in the early Swiss history — two roadside markers are parts of a former Roman temple. From the final steep bends of the now-descending road there's a wonderful panorama of almost the entire Engadine valley. Its clear sky, beautiful lakes, charming architecture, and extraordinary scenery justify its fame. Excursions in the valley are easily taken; Silvaplana is the first village in the Engadine, and a few minutes away is glittering St. Moritz.

ST. MORITZ: The town itself is disappointing, as its urban streets and houses are without charm or character. But the lakeside setting, excellent climate, mineral spas, and jet-set guests have made it famous. The Mauritius Springs have been in use here for about 3,000 years. Don't miss the *Engadine Museum* (on the road to the baths), a delightful reconstruction of local architectural styles, including typical *sgrafitti* (plaster decorations) and a wide-ranging collection of furniture, illustrating the domestic life of farmers, bishops, and lords. The *Segantini Museum* contains works of the Engadine's most famous painter, Giovanni Segantini, an Italian of the late 19th century. Winter is the best time for celebrity watching, and the *Palace* hotel (see *Best en Route*) is a good place to do it — its *King's Club* is a center of nightlife here. For more moderate fare, try the charming *Chesa Veglia* for tea or dinner. Or check out the excellent nutcake at *Café Hanselmann*. In the winter, skiing is superb, snow and sun almost guaranteed; and, at sporting events and on the slopes, you can rub elbows with active and inactive royalty and movie stars who generally have their own homes up here. There are opportunities for dozens of excursions and walks, but there are two things you should do even if you have little time at your disposal: a cable car ride up Muottas Muragl, 8,084 feet, for a spellbinding view of the upper Engadine Valley, and a walk along the Sils Lake on a well-kept footpath. On the latter walk, stop at the Italian-speaking hamlet of Isola for delicious, homemade cheese and a drink. The German philosopher Friedrich Nietzsche spent much time around here, and his house in Sils is now a small museum. A ride up the Corvatsch, 10,840 feet, from Silvaplana takes you to eternal snow and summer skiing. In season, there are many cultural events in St. Moritz, featuring famous artists. Golf, horseback riding, tennis, swimming (in pools, because the lakes are too cold), sailing, and windsurfing are also available.

En Route from St. Moritz – After driving along the Silvaplana and Silser lakes you come to the Maloja Pass, which is not really a pass at all (as it's lower than St. Moritz), but the upcoming sharp drop and curving steep road make it look like one. At the peak of the road, opposite the *Maloja Kulm* hotel, there's a beautiful lookout over the Bergell Valley ahead. This valley has its very own characteristics: It's still alpine but has undeniably southern traits that become more and more pronounced with every turn. Sections of the old Roman road interlace it.

In Vicosoprano, a medieval tower attached to the town hall was a prison and torture chamber used for witch trials in the 16th century. (If it's closed, ask at the office.) A short detour to Soglio is a must: Taking the narrow, winding road through chestnut groves, you reach this spectacular little village on a ledge, with its palaces of the once powerful and still prominent Salis family. The best known of the palaces, the charming *Palazzo Salis* hotel, has a romantic garden (see *Best en Route*). There's also a magnificent view from the little cemetery. At Castasegna, the Alpine vegetation is left behind as you cross into Italy, and vineyards and fruit trees appear, and the architecture becomes distinctly southern. After Chiavenna, take the narrow principal road along the western side of Lake Como toward Como and Lugano; although the road periodically has heavy traffic, the lake is beautiful. At Menaggio take Road 340 right — watch for the tricky turnoff, it's easy to miss — to Lake Lugano (Italians call it Lago di Ceresio). The lake is narrow and finger-shaped here, and there are steep, wooded, roadless slopes on the other side. Near Lugano, between the principal road and the lake, is Gandria, a charming village that's worth a side trip.

GANDRIA: Explore the village by climbing up and down its steps, going under its arches, and walking between its old arcaded houses. It has many boutiques and is a typical artist's village. Sit on the terrace of a café hanging out over the water, and gaze at rows of pastel houses rising directly from the lake. The *Smuggler's Museum,* in an original hideaway on the other side of the lake, is approachable by boat only. Boats usually leave twice a day from Gandria.

En Route from Gandria – At Castagnola the bay opens out and you get the full visual impact of Lugano, one of Switzerland's most picturesque towns.

LUGANO: This cultural center of Ticino is ideal for a spring or fall sojourn. It features a palm tree–lined lakeshore promenade, arcaded streets, sunny piazzas with cafés, and the beautiful old church of Santa Maria degli Angioli with its famous 16th-century frescoes. The main artistic attraction is the *Villa Favorita,* a splendid private art collection of European masters in the owner's residence on Castagnola Road (open weekends only except when there is a special summer exhibition; one has been held for the last 4 years). A 10-minute funicular ride from the Paradiso quarter up Monte San Salvatore provides a fabulous circular panorama of lakes and Alps. You can get an even more sweeping view from Monte Bré on the other side of Lugano. It's possible to drive there via a very narrow, very steep road, but it's easier to take the funicular from Cassarate Road. Boat trips on the lake run frequently and are highly recommended. In the Italian village of Campione, 10 minutes away by boat or car, the casino has recently added craps and blackjack.

BEST EN ROUTE

Accommodations on this route can be costly, especially in famed resorts and health spas like St. Moritz and Bad Ragaz. Hotels that charge $170 to $250 and up for a double room with shower for a night get an expensive rating; extremely elegant resorts, like the *Palace, Suvretta, Kulm,* and *Carlton* hotels in St. Moritz, are considerably more expensive. Accommodations ranging from $100 to $150 are moderate, and those costing below $85 for two for a night in high season are rated inexpensive. Most of these hotels only have half-board plans. Restaurants range in price from $90 and up for a dinner for two in places listed as expensive, $50 to $75 in those listed as moderate, and around $40 in the inexpensive category. Prices do not include drinks, wine or coffee; the tip is included.

BAD RAGAZ

Quellenhof – The most elegant hotel in the spa. 7310 Bad Ragaz (phone: 90111). Expensive.

Tm Schloss Ragaz – A small château with a few charming rooms, plus several modern bungalows. It's in a large park and has a swimming pool. 7310 Bad Ragaz (phone: 92355). Moderate.

CHUR

Hofkellerei – In the Bishop's Palace, this old pub features regional furniture and serves local specialties. 1 Hof (phone: 233230). Moderate to inexpensive.

Stern – This 300-year-old inn serves outstanding cuisine, including Grisons specialties. 11 Reichsgasse (phone: 223555). Moderate to inexpensive.

LENZERHEIDE

Guarda Val – All the modern comforts are provided at this hotel despite its rustic, Alpine, barnlike exterior. Its enchanting restaurant is on a big terrace. Coming down from Chur, turn right as you enter Lenzerheide (phone: 342214). Moderate.

ST. MORITZ

Badrutt's Palace – It looks like a gingerbread castle, on a hillside with lake and mountain views, and draws a jet-set crowd. They come for the luxurious rooms (270 in all), the spacious French restaurant, the renowned wine cellar, the fitness center, and, presumably, for that seductive well-pampered feeling. Via Serias (phone: 21101). Very expensive.

Suvretta House – "What the *Palace* strives for, the *Suvretta* has already achieved," says one guest. This very exclusive hotel attracts old money. A 9-story castle of a building, it is off the beaten track — a self-sustaining resort with its own ski school and private lift, not to mention 2 bowling alleys and an award-winning restaurant. Off Via Suvretta (phone: 21121). Very expensive.

Steffani – This cozy family hotel in the center of town serves Grisons specialties in its restaurant. 7500 St. Moritz (phone: 22101). Moderate.

Chesa Veglia – Owned by the *Palace* hotel, this restaurant-café with a delightful Grisons interior offers excellent food. Dinner only. 7500 St. Moritz (phone: 33596). Expensive.

Café Hanselmann – This popular watering hole serves the best cakes in town. Via Maistra (phone: 33864). Moderate.

SILVAPLANA

Staila – A small hotel in a historic house; a good value. 7513 Silvaplana (phone: 48147). Moderate.

SOGLIO

Palazzo Salis – In one of the old town palaces, this establishment affords a very exclusive atmosphere, even if the comfort isn't always perfect. There's a small garden and a good restaurant. It's closed in winter. In high season, reservations are recommended. 7649 Soglio (phone: 41555). Inexpensive.

LUGANO

Splendide Royal – Featuring Old World elegance, modern comfort, and excellent service, this hotel has rooms with fabulous terraces on the lake. A good value. 7 Riva Caccia (phone: 542001). Expensive.

Villa Principe Leopoldo – This former residence of the Hohenzollern princes overlooks the town and lake. Its luxurious junior suites are furnished in cozy pastels. There is also an excellent restaurant. 5 Via Montalbano (phone: 558855). Expensive.

Antico – A hotel and restaurant featuring a vine-covered dining terrace overlooking the lake. There a a handful of rooms; no private baths. Closed in winter. Gandria (phone: 514871). Inexpensive.

Al Portone – This little restaurant serves outstanding Italian food. Closed Sundays and Mondays for lunch. 3 Via Cassarate (phone: 235995). Expensive to moderate.

Ticino – In an old Tessin palazzo, this eatery has a nice little terrace; the rooms surround a charming inside patio. Closed in winter. No credit cards. 1 Piazza Cioccaro (phone: 227772). Moderate.

Bern to Montreux

Starting in Bern, the capital of Switzerland and one of Europe's loveliest cities, this 184-mile (294-km) route first proceeds east and south to the mountainous Bernese Oberland and then into the unique Valais region, ending up in Montreux, a popular resort on Lake Geneva. Count on 3 days for the tour; the best time to see Valais is in October, when its colors are most beautiful. This route combines scenic, historical, and cultural attractions, and is passable all year round. To climb to the eternal snows of the impressive Jungfrau, however, you have to take a special train.

Although you'll see some lovely pastoral scenery, replete with flowers and clear blue lakes, in the Bernese Oberland, it's the Alpine triumvirate of Eiger, Mönch, and Jungfrau that make the area exceptional. With Interlaken as the jumping-off point, this is one of the world's most famous mountain recreational spots. The upper Rhone Valley, forming part of the canton of Valais, is an altogether different world. Isolated from the rest of the country by the steep mountains, its warm climate and abundant vegetation make it reminiscent of Provence; indeed, the Valais is Switzerland's main wine-growing region. Ruins and castles dot the slopes, and numerous museums and churches bear witness to the canton's historical importance. And the amazing lateral valleys, ascending quickly to more than 6,000 feet, should definitely be explored.

The Bernese and Valais people share a similar history; the region was ruled successively by Celts, Romans, Germanic tribes, and the Holy Roman Empire. Then came the rapid expansion of German-speaking Bern, which eventually dominated more than one third of present Switzerland. The Valais, where the Romans first settled, was later divided between German and French influence and today the eastern part is still German and the western part French. Napoleon temporarily annexed Valais for France and began building the Simplon Pass Road (a passage already used by the Romans), but he did not live to see it in use.

BERN: Built on a peninsula of the winding Aare River, this enchanting capital has kept its character intact. The Duke of Zähringen established the city in 1191 on his thickly wooded hunting ground. It was agreed that the first animal caught on a particular hunt would supply the new city with its name; when the creature turned out to be a bear, the duke dubbed the town Bärn, from which its present name derives, and placed a bear on its coat of arms. In 1353 Bern joined the confederation and later became extremely powerful because of its aggressive expansionist policies. The canton has tenaciously held onto its annexed territories, and Jura was only just recently able to break away. In 1848 it was chosen the seat of the federal government, replacing Zurich.

The arcaded streets of Bern's old town are the city's true main attraction, featuring the Gothic and baroque façades of homes that are often incredibly luxurious inside. (Take a look at the houses on Junkerngasse, for example — it's the city's most prestigious street address.) In 1405, the wooden houses of the old town were completely destroyed by fire; but by the 18th century, they were completely rebuilt in the yellow green sandstone you see here today. Modern Bern simply grew up around the older city, and the aristocratic tradition contrasts nicely with a youthful spirit that also characterizes this university town. Somewhat typically, recently discovered medieval fortifications are structurally integrated with an underground passage in the main railroad station, and explanatory notes have been supplied. All of old Bern's significant sights are within walking distance of each other, and the Tourist Office provides an excellent map of the center of town.

Walk to the Nydegg Bridge for a good view of the irregular group of roofs atop the houses at the bend of the Aare River; as a result of a law quite unusual for the symmetry-minded Swiss, these domiciles could not be built at the same size and height. A few steps across the bridge, you'll find the Bear Pit (Bärengraben), which houses a number of the city's symbolic animals. Across the bridge in the opposite direction, and a short distance down Junkerngasse, the high tower and flying buttresses of the cathedral of St. Vincent (Münster) come into view. The main portal of this impressive Gothic church features several old statues (some of them still painted) depicting aspects of the Last Judgment and dating from the beginning of the 16th century. And if you don't mind climbing the 254 steps to the tower's platform, you'll be rewarded with an excellent panorama of the town and the Bernese Alps. Farther west, you'll find the Clock Tower (Zytglocke), first built in the 12th century and restored in the 16th; at regular intervals during the day, large groups of people cluster to view the mechanical jesters, bears, and kings perform at 4 minutes before the hour in the tower of the astronomical clock.

The dignified, domed Parliament Building is in the Florentine Renaissance style, and one of its regular guided tours can provide some idea of the workings of Swiss government. Every Tuesday and Saturday, there's a lovely flower market in front. Walk along the high Kirchenfeldbrücke for a different view of town around the Parliament Building.

The museums of Bern are worth a separate trip; the *Kunstmuseum* (Fine Arts Museum), for example, has the largest collection of works by Paul Klee, a native of Bern, and a great number of modern French paintings (Hodlerstr.). The *Kunsthalle* houses temporary exhibitions of the latest in international art (Helvetiapl.). The *Bernese Historical Museum* features booty from the Burgundian wars from other expansionist escapades, including arms, standards, tapestries, and manuscripts, as well as beautiful furniture from later periods (Helvetiapl.). Others are the *Natural History Museum* (Bernastr.) with its imaginative display of animals in natural surroundings; the *Swiss Alpine Museum* (Helvetiapl.), which has models of early alpinism and skiing, and reliefs of the Alps; and the *Swiss Postal Museum,* in the same building as the *Alpine Museum,* with one of the largest permanent stamp collections of the world. The National Library has one of the most extensive Bible collections anywhere (Hallwylstr.).

Cellars are as characteristic as arcades in the old town, and they now serve mainly as art galleries, boutiques, theaters, and restaurants. One of the most interesting cellar attractions is the oldest wine tavern of Bern, the *Klötzlikeller* (6 Gerechtigkeitgasse).

Bern's nightlife is surprisingly vibrant, featuring dozens of pubs and nightclubs. It was at the city beach, right under the Parliament windows, that the first topless bathers appeared, igniting a national controversy.

En Route from Bern – The autobahn goes directly to Thun, but if you have time and the weather is good, take the lovely country road via Riggisberg, with its checkerboard fields and wide vistas. On summer afternoons, you can see a most extraordinary private collection of old textiles at the Abegg Foundation in Riggisberg. A short distance east of the freeway, at Kiesen, is an interesting cheese museum with a reconstruction of a workroom and a multilingual audio-visual show. Soon comes Thun, an attractive town on the lake of the same name; its medieval castle has a historical museum containing impressive tapestries, as well as a toy collection. Take the road along the scenic north shore through the resorts of Hilterfingen and Gunten, sometimes passing high over the cold, blue green lake that's one of the country's favorite spots for sailing. Interlaken is highly overrated and not really worth a stop, unless you're interested in the souvenir shops or the especially good pastry served at *Café Schuh;* continue to Grindelwald, a bustling resort village in a glacier with the Alps' Eiger peak hovering above it.

JUNGFRAU (VIRGIN): This is the only one of the three peaks that non–mountain climbers can reach. Count on a minimum of a half-day for the railway climb up to the 11,336-foot Jungfraujoch, the "saddle" of the mountain, and back. In good weather, the high transportation price (around $70 per person) is justifiable, but don't bother taking the trip at all if the visibility is questionable. The train ride itself provides spectacular rocky views, lookout stops, and multilingual explanations. Besides the incredible panoramas to be seen from its terraces, the Jungfraujoch features summer skiing, dogsled riding, and mountain climbing. The Aletsch glacier — the largest in the Alps — can be seen from here. It's also possible to take the train back to Lauterbrunnen, site of a grand waterfall on the other side of the mountain, using circular tickets.

En Route from Grindelwald – Head back to Interlaken and proceed along the south side of Lake Thun (not on the freeway) to picturesque Spiez, which has a lovely view from the railroad station. From here you begin the journey into the Kander Valley, heading south on the main road toward Kandersteg; the route, narrow at first, passes under steep peaks. Then it widens, and weather-beaten, carved wooden houses with large roofs come into view. Stop at Blausee, a small jewel of a lake with extraordinary clear, blue water set in a moss-covered forest; there's a trout hatchery here, and the *Blausee* restaurant, which serves trout specialties. Soon you'll reach Kandersteg, a small resort, where a railway takes cars through the Lötschberg Tunnel in about 15 minutes; from Goppenstein on the other side, a narrow road leads down to Route 9, and the wide, sunny Rhone Valley. (If you're interested in a pilgrimage to the Matterhorn, you can reach Zermatt — closed to autos — via a train from Täsch, which is over an hour's drive south from Goppenstein.) Turning west, you'll soon reach Sierre, the first stop in Valais.

SIERRE: The language changes from German to French within this lovely town, reputed to be the sunniest in Switzerland. In *Château de Villa,* an old castle under huge trees, there's a combination museum and restaurant, serving excellent *raclette* (a Valais cheese specialty) and wine from local vineyards. There is a unique pewter museum in the former *Château Bellevue* hotel.

En Route from Sierre – Proceeding west on Route 9, just before Sion, you'll reach St. Leonard, site of the largest subterranean lake in Europe.

SION: The two peaks that dominate this 2,000-year-old town give it a sense of history. The ruins of a medieval stronghold rest atop the hill called Tourbillon, and a fortresslike church, completed in the 15th century, crowns the Valère peak. The latter structure, Notre Dame de Valère (Our Lady of Valère), is well worth the climb; park your car in the lot between the two hills. An excellent panorama of the lower Valais can be viewed from the terrace. Inside, there are splendid 17th-century stalls with panels that portray scenes from the life of Christ, and the oldest functioning organ in the world (built in 1390). Each year, international organ concerts are held here. The attached museum contains Romanesque furniture that belonged to the bishops of Sion and Valais embroidery and lace. In town, the magnificent Supersaxo mansion, built in 1505, features a wooden ceiling with a huge rose depicting the Nativity. A short distance away is the 17th-century town hall (Hôtel de Ville, Rue de Grand Pont) with its richly ornamented wooden door. Also interesting is the 3,500-piece glass collection on display at the *Archaeological Museum* (Grange à l'Eveque at Majoria).

For an outstanding view of Sion, drive 5 miles (8 km) to Savièse, an ancient-looking mountain village. Sion itself is a good place to start from in exploring the valleys that extend south below the Rhone. These are typified by extreme, rocky landscapes graced with small barns and chalets; two that are particularly interesting are the Hérens and Hérémence valleys.

HÉRENS AND HÉRÉMENCE VALLEYS: Cross the Rhne south from Sion, and take one of the secondary roads that climbs the steep ledge toward Vex, where Dent Blanche, one of the highest peaks in Switzerland, comes into view. From Vex, the road passes high over a stream and later through a tunnel underneath the Pyramids of Euseigne — bizarre, crowned columns formed by the erosion of the rock. The valley narrows and deepens as the road ascends to Evolène, a pleasant mountaineering resort known for its tall, wooden houses filled with flowers. Women of this village still wear local costumes. Head back for Euseigne and drive up from there through the desolate, eerie scenery of the Hérémence Valley. The road ends at the enormous Grand Dixence Dam; a height of 935 feet makes it the tallest dam in the world. Completed in 1966, it's the most formidable construction task yet undertaken by the Swiss. An elevator ascends from the parking lot to water level, and there's a walking path along the top. Return to Sion on the route that passes through the villages of Hérémence and Salins.

En Route from Sion – Take Route 9 until just beyond Ardon, then turn right onto the secondary road through the vineyards; you'll pass through small wine-growing communities like Chamoson, Leyron, and Saillon, which are protected by sunbaked rocky slopes. Saillon features the ruins of an impressive castle as well as picturesque old houses. In this region, you can visit wine caves, and small inns serve local food. At Martigny, called Octodurus by the Romans, the starkly modern Pierre Gianadda Foundation is also interesting. Built over the ruins of a Gallo-Roman temple, it houses a small archeological museum, a collection of vintage cars, and changing exhibitions of modern art. Take Route 9 again, following the Rhone as it turns sharply north. St. Maurice, the capital of Valais under the Romans, is worth a stop. Take a guided tour of the church's treasury, one of the most opulent in the Christian world; among the items on view here are a gold casket decorated with pearls and cameos and a golden ewer that reputedly belonged to Charlemagne. Farther north, near Bex, you can stop for a good meal at *Rôtisserie St. Christoph,* a restaurant and motel in a medieval fortress. Aigle, renowned for white wine, features a 15th-century castle with a *Wine and Salt Museum.* Continue along the freeway for the best view of Montreux.

MONTREUX: Cypresses, fig trees, magnolias, climbing vines, and other Mediterranean forms of vegetation flourish in Montreux, Lake Geneva's most popular resort; its climate is mild all year long. Musical events — including the famous summer jazz festival — enliven the quiet atmosphere here.

Walk through old Montreux — up the hill, with its interesting houses and crooked streets, to the terrace of the church of St. Vincent. From here you can get a good view of the towers of Château Chillon, about 2 miles south. The fortress on Chillon rock was initially constructed in the 9th century to defend the major road to Italy, but its present form dates from the 13th century. Its recurrent use as a prison was made especially famous by Byron's poem "The Prisoner of Chillon."

Montreux also offers other attractive side trips: The spectacular train ride to the Rochers de Naye, for example, shouldn't be missed. The trip affords excellent views of Lake Geneva, the Alps, and the Jura. And for more entertainment, Lausanne is only 20 minutes away.

BEST EN ROUTE

There are some good budget accommodations on this route; a number of hotels charge as little as $55 for a double room with shower for a night. Hotels charging $170 to $200 and up in high season are rated expensive. Those asking $100 to $150 are moderate. We've rated those establishments charging $80 or less as inexpensive. Restaurants range in price from $100 and up for a dinner for two in those places listed as expensive, from $60 to $85 in those listed as moderate, and from $35 to $55 in the inexpensive category. Prices do not include drinks and wine or coffee; the tip is included.

BERN

Bellevue Palace – This is where visiting kings and queens stay. Have a drink on the terrace for the view and atmosphere. 3 Kochergasse (phone: 224581). Expensive.

Schweizerhof – Next to the railroad station, this very comfortable hotel has genuine antique furnishings that have been collected by its owners, the Gauer family, and a fine restaurant (see below). 11 Schweizerhoflaube (phone: 224501). Expensive.

City – A modern, cozy establishment, across from the railroad station. Bubenbergpl. (phone: 225377). Moderate.

Goldener Adler – In the heart of old town, this beautiful old inn provides adequate comfort and a friendly, family atmosphere. 7 Gerechtigkeitsgasse (phone: 221725). Inexpensive.

Schultheiss-Stube – The best restaurant in town is in the *Schweizerhof* hotel; it's cozy and has superb food. 11 Schweizerhoflaube (phone: 224501). Expensive.

Kornhauskeller – Set in a cellar (once a granary) this lively place specializes in *berner platte,* an assortment of boiled meats and sausage served with sauerkraut that's much lighter than it sounds. A brass band entertains at night. Closed Mondays. Kornhauspl. (phone: 221133). Moderate.

Goldener Schlüssel – This small place is popular because of its good food. 72 Rathausgasse (phone: 220216). Moderate to inexpensive.

Klötzlikeller – Over 300 years old, this wine tavern also serves snacks. Closed mornings and Sundays. 62 Gerechtigkeitsgasse (phone: 227456). Inexpensive.

Nightclubs – *Mocambo,* 61 Aarberggasse (phone: 225041), and *Chikito,* 28 Neuengasse (phone: 222680), are the best, offering daily floor shows.

GRINDELWALD

Grand Hotel Regina – One of the best hotels in the Bernese Oberland; it is quite luxurious and serves excellent food. Closed in November. 3818 Grindelwald (phone: 545455). Expensive.

Spinne – This modern hotel has a casual atmosphere. Closed in November. 3818 Grindelwald (phone: 532341). Moderate.

BLAUSEE

Blausee – In a fabulous setting on Blue Lake, this restaurant offers trout specialties. Closed in winter. 3717 Blausee (phone: 711641). Moderate.

SIERRE

Grotte – As its name implies, this small hotel is built into the rocks, on the shore of Lac de Géronde, in the suburb of Chippis. The restaurant here is very popular. Closed in November. Lac de Géronde (phone: 554646). Inexpensive.

Relais du Manoir – This restaurant, run by local wine growers, serves and sells outstanding wines; a few local food specialties, including *raclette,* are also available. It's set in the 16th-century *Château de Villa.* 3960 Sierre (phone: 551896). Moderate.

SION

Caves de Tous Vents – In a 13th-century wine cellar, in the shadow of the Valère church, this restaurant serves excellent Valais specialties (dinner only). *L'Enclos de Valère,* in a lovely garden setting next door, is under the same management and specializes in French cuisine. Both closed Mondays. Rue des Châteaux (phone: *Caves,* 224684; *L'Enclos,* 233230). Expensive to moderate.

Pergola – This small modern hotel is a very good value. Its restaurant specializes in Italian dishes. 116 Rue de Lausanne (phone: 224641). Inexpensive.

BEX

Rôtisserie and Motel St. Christoph – Rustically attractive, the *St. Christoph* serves charcoal-grilled specialties. It's in a small medieval fortress; all rooms have individual terraces and exits to the garden. 1880 Bex-les-Bains (phone: 652977). Hotel, inexpensive; restaurant, expensive to moderate.

MONTREUX

Eden au Lac – Recently renovated, the hotel retains its turn-of-the-century charm. There's a garden right on the lake, where a luncheon buffet is served. Except for the 2 weeks of the jazz festival (usually held July 7-22), it is usually quiet. 11 Rue du Théâtre (phone: 963-5551). Expensive.

Montreux Palace – If you want to splurge, here's a luxury hotel. 100 Grand-Rue (phone: 963-5373). Expensive.

Europe – A typical old "grand hotel," with a lovely lake view, it is a very good value, though it's sometimes overrun with groups. 15 Av. des Alpes (phone: 963-7404). Moderate.

Pont-de-Brent – This little country inn has recently become known as one of the great places to dine in Switzerland. Closed Sundays and Mondays. 1817 Brent (just above Montreux) (phone: 964-5230). Expensive.

Caveau du Museum – You can also dine in this lively discotheque, with its cozy, rustic atmosphere, in the center of old Montreux. Closed Sundays. 40 Rue de la Gare (phone: 963-1662). Moderate.

Vieille Ferme – It's a charming farm, very rustic, slightly out of the center of town, in Montreux-Chailly, and it serves local specialties. Try the *raclette* — accompanied by country music. Closed Mondays (phone: 964-6465). Moderate.

Yugoslavia

The Socialist Federal Republic of Yugoslavia (the southern Slavs) is the remarkable conglomeration of six republics, four to six major languages, and the culture of a dozen different empires from all over world history. Stretched along the Adriatic Sea between Europe and Asia, the area has been ruled and changed for a time by everybody from the ancient Celts to the Ottomans; from the marauding Goths to the stately Austrians; and from Jove to Mohammed to Jesus Christ. Monuments of the different empires are in every part of the country. Its Seven Sights (Dubrovnik, Split, Kotor, Ohrid, the monastery of Sopocani, and the national parks at Plitvice Lakes and Durmitor Mountain) are on UNESCO's official list of the world's natural and cultural heritages.

In Yugoslavia, you'll find that the language, festivals, costume, religion, and cooking style change wherever you go. The land of Yugoslavia is surprisingly varied over its 99,000 square miles. There are the snowy Julian Alps in the north and the warm Adriatic coast in the south, with its 1,000 offshore islands, 66 of them inhabited. Dense forests in several regions still harbor bear, wolves, wild boar, and deer; and the central plains are as low, flat, and lush as medieval Flanders. Hills or mountains cover most of Yugoslavia except for the north central region; rail and road transportation are not very extensive or sophisticated yet. The interior is full of large, clear lakes and warm mineral springs. The biggest river is the Sava (600 miles), which meets the trans-European Danube at Belgrade.

Yugoslavia is governed by its Communist Party, which came to power after resisting German occupation, and liberating the country, in World War II. The state is tolerant of religion, linguistic diversity, and a degree of local autonomy. Despite ties to Stalin during the war, Marshal Tito pulled Yugoslavia away from the USSR's influence in 1948 and forged his own alliances.

Yugoslavians travel freely at home and abroad. The press is less and less subject to censorship, and there is easy access to foreign publications of all kinds in the major cities.

During the 1980s, Yugoslavia has been experiencing deep economic, political, and ethnic crises that included a decline in the standard of living, triple-digit inflation, and the introduction of wide economic reforms. Steps are being implemented, however, to try to encourage private enterprise, foreign investments, and political democratization in order to better integrate the country with the Common Market in Western Europe.

Belgrade is the capital and the center of commerce, industry, and communications. The main cultural and economic centers are Zagreb, Dubrovnik, Ljubljana, Sarajevo, and Skopje. Other large cities include Split, Novi Sad, Rijeka, and Titograd.

About one third of the population works in agriculture, the rest in service and industry. Although the nation is becoming more urban and cosmopolitan, the different ethnic groups in Yugoslavia have a powerful folk tradition, which you will notice wherever you go: Dances, folklore plays, and mystical pageants are celebrated in every region and are taken quite seriously.

Roads in Yugoslavia have improved considerably in recent years. The Adriatic Highway (Jadranska Magistrala) runs along the coast, and is one of the most scenic roads on the Continent. The major route that links the country from the northwest to the southeast is the Autoput Bratstva i Jedinstva (Highway of Brotherhood and Unity). These two routes link up with a number of lateral roads. The Ibarska Magistrala (Ibar Highway), which runs from Belgrade to Skopje in the south, leads through the heart of the ancient Serbian kingdom.

We've laid out three routes for exploring Yugoslavia. The most popular is the coastal route, which begins near Trieste, Italy, and winds south along the Adriatic Sea through the cities of Portoroz, Opatija, Rijeka, Zadar, Split, and Dubrovnik. This coastal area is full of beach resorts, Roman ruins, steep bluffs, cultural festivals, and fine seafood. The second trek begins in Podkoren, in the Julian Alps in northwestern Yugoslavia. Bring your skis. You will drive south through mountains to Ljubljana and Zagreb and on to the capital city of Belgrade. Belgrade has over 30 museums and galleries, hosts symphonies, opera companies, and film festivals, and serves cuisine of every nationality. The third route starts 3 miles from the Greek border and winds north through Macedonia, where you can see Turkish mosques, Byzantine frescoes, and Bohemian folk festivals and stop for fishing and swimming at lakefront resorts. The route continues through Pristina to Belgrade. One can also make a short trip to Sarajevo, site of the 1984 Winter Olympics, and ski the same slopes that brought downhiller Bill Johnson and slalomists Debbie Armstrong and Phil Mahre gold medals for the US ski team.

Trieste to Dubrovnik

Guiding a reader on an auto tour of the Yugoslav Adriatic is different from giving advice on an artistic, historical, or skiing tour. There are no complicated directions; after the first 25 miles (40 km), you'll be going southeast on the Adriatic Highway (Jadranska Magistrala), overlooking the incredibly blue Adriatic Sea — if the water isn't on your right, you took a wrong turn. The areas along the coast are quite diverse, but we're only going to mention a few spots in any detail, since your reasons for driving the coast are probably going to be the same all the way along — sun, rocks, sand, and sea — and you'll know them when you find them. The wonderful thing about this coast is that you'll stumble on what you're looking for everywhere. So, this tour will give you some idea of what you're passing through, tell you about some interesting sights, and give you some broad tactics on where to find your piece of sand.

The most important advice is this: The resort cities are crowded at high season — June, July, and August — so if you want privacy and you don't want to spend too much money, go to the small village beaches (which are as beautiful as any), and stay at pensions or private houses. Then go into town to take your pulse-quickening excitement whenever you're ready for it. If you can travel in May, September, or October, you'll find the tourist population comparatively low, and your lodging costs likewise: Prices drop up to 50% in those months, and the climate is just as fine as at high season.

The northern half of this journey, from Trieste (on the Italian border) to Zadar, goes over a predominantly rocky shoreline, with good pebble beaches. South of Zadar is where the lush Mediterranean vegetation begins, with palm, pine, and hibiscus. Throughout, the beaches are lovely and the weather quite dependably sunny and warm except for a few months in winter, when it sometimes rains. The coastline is among the most jagged in Europe. If you measured its length as the crow flies, it would be 390 miles (628 km); when you follow the contours of all the bays, inlets, and peninsulas, it measures 1,125 miles (1810 km). You will be driving along the coast, following almost every twist, for a total of 530 miles (852 km).

Yugoslavia's Adriatic coast is known for its nudist colonies; this is more or less the center for organized nudism, or "naturism," in southern Europe. Generally speaking, nudism is a very health-oriented, bring-the-kids kind of lifestyle. The philosophy is that clothes give us dirty minds; most nudist camps are notoriously nonsexual. Naturist resorts (marked with FKK signs) are open to anyone, and there are at least 30 well-known ones between Trieste and Ulcinj; some are near large cities, some near small villages, and many on islands. If you don't need a lot of fancy facilities, every seaside village has its own informal nude bathing area.

Over the millennia, sailors, conquerors, and adventurers have left behind their houses, their ships, and their descendants to stay along the Adriatic coast and its islands. However, many of the 1,000 islands off the coast are still inhabited only by seagulls; this applies to many in the Kornati chain off Zadar. Perhaps you'll take some time out to visit a timeless desert island away from your car and your hotel, and listen to the silence.

The route begins in the Slovenian greenery around Trieste at the Lipica horse farm, breeding ground of the proud Lipizzaner horses, and descends to the seaside for a taste of Austro-Hungarian grandeur near the old resorts of Portoroz and Opatija. You will see the Roman amphitheater arena of Pula, still in use, sample two sets of sun-soaked islands, and watch the coast go greener and more lush as you drive south. The pandemonium of Rijeka and Zadar may dizzy you, and Diocletian's palace in Split will certainly awe you; for relief, you can poke along the beach in small Dalmatian villages. The last stop is the cultural and Bohemian capital of the coast, Dubrovnik, where you can, particularly during the summer season, take in the best art, music, and nightlife the twentieth century has to offer, inside the walls of a sixteenth-century town. You may want to take your trip farther down the coast, and there are some suggestions for places to see.

Although hundreds of hotels have been built on the Yugoslav coast since the 1950s, demand for accommodations frequently outruns supply. Since private enterprise is encouraged, one can find bed-and-breakfast establishments in every town, city, and village along the coast. These lodgings can be booked through either the local tourist offices or travel agencies, or just look for the vacancy signs in different languages among any group of houses along the road and bargain with the owners. Speaking and understanding German helps, since Germans form the largest group of foreign visitors. Prices are much lower than in hotels — $10 to $20 per day per person — and you can really get a better feeling for the country and its people.

The culinary specialties are so varied in Yugoslavia — a blend of East and West, of Central Europe and the Mediterranean — that they are sure to satisfy all tastes. Although international cuisine is available in the big hotels, the national dish is *cevapcici* — grilled, sometimes spicy, minced meat — and the national drink is *sljivovica* — rather potent plum brandy. Other local delights are *sarma* (mixed minced meat and rice in sauerkraut), stuffed peppers, *duvec* (baked vegetables and meat), *bosanski lonac* (stewed beef, lamb, vegetables, and spices), *kajmak* (a cheeselike cream from boiled milk), and, for dessert, apple *strudla* (paper-thin pastry stuffed with grated apples, nuts, and sultanas).

TRIESTE: Get on the highway northeast toward Sezana, to cross the border into Yugoslavia just before you reach that town. The approach from Trieste brings you into Yugoslavia's Republic of Slovenia, an area ruled by the German nobility from the time of Charlemagne until World War I. Slovenia was the lush, hilly playground of the Austro-Hungarian Empire, with grand, lakefront resorts.

LIPICA: Off the highway past Sezana is the 4-century-old horse farm at Lipica, the original stud farm of the Lipizzaner horse, founded in 1580 by Archduke Charles of Austria. Lipica supplied the horses for the Austrian cavalry and the famous Spanish riding school of Vienna. All this wouldn't be half so interesting except that they'll let you ride them. For the rest of your days, you'll probably never ride such a thoroughly blue-blooded, beautiful, well-brought-up horse. Instruction is available if you need it, and for spectators there are shows in the indoor riding ring.

En Route from Lipica – Before heading out to the sun and the sea, take a detour to Postojna, 25 miles (37 km) north of Lipica toward Ljubljana. Postojna is renowned for its complex of caves, which are among the largest in Europe. A miniature train takes visitors through concert halls, around underground lakes, and between dazzling and colorful stalactites and stalagmites. Return to Lipica and continue east to Divaca, where you will intersect a highway; turn south toward Kozina and go beyond it about 20 miles (32 km), until you meet up with the road you will follow the rest of this trip, the Adriatic Highway.

Go south to Portoroz, the largest and best-known seaside resort in Slovenia; flowers grow in abundance in this former Old World bastion — Portoroz means "Port of Roses." Sailing and parachuting competitions, cultural events and folklore plays take place here in the summer. In the neighboring town of Seca, there is a permanent outdoor exhibit of stone sculpture called Forma Viva.

Stop at Piran, on a peninsula about 5 minutes outside Portoroz. This is an old Mediterranean town with narrow streets, and small churches with Renaissance and baroque paintings. Piran's city walls are still standing, as is a fragment of a Byzantine wall.

On the way to Pula, the compact stone houses and red roofs of the town of Rovinj are a must-see. This medieval fishing and trading village has been an artists' colony since the 1950s and is one of the most beautiful cities on the Adriatic. The baroque church of St. Euphemia dominates the town and nearby islands.

PULA: From Portoroz, the highway continues down the coast to Pula, a major coastal city built on an ancient Illyrian settlement dating from the 5th century BC. It became a Roman colony; the Roman amphitheater in Pula, which seats 23,000, has lasted better than the one in Rome. Pula's amphitheater is still in use: The annual *Festival of Yugoslav Films* (among other events) is held here. Other Roman buildings include a 1st-century temple to the Emperor Augustus, and the 4th-century Hercules gates. Close to Pula is Medulin, a small seaside village with good beaches.

Another place that should not be overlooked is the Brioni Islands National Park, a short boat ride from Pula. Littered with Greco-Roman and medieval ruins, the islands are famous as the residence of former President Tito and as the meeting place of world leaders. Their exceptional natural and cultural beauties are now accessible to visitors. Lodging on the islands consists of 350 beds in hotels and villas, with another 100 planned in new hotels. Authorities are also planning to open golf and polo grounds (phone: 22455).

En Route from Pula – The road continues through a number of fishing villages. From one of them, Brestova, you can get a car ferry to the resort islands of Cres and Losinj; more on the resort islands below.

OPATIJA: Opatija, at the foot of Mount Ucka, 40 miles (64 km) along the coast, was a popular resort among the Austro-Hungarian nobility. Its streets still have a 19th-century air, with elegant shops, and luxury hotels with formal gardens; they also have casinos. For culture, you can see a play at Opatija's summer theater.

En Route from Opatija – Near Opatija is the medieval village of Volosko. A sand walk stretches along the beach for 6 miles, and goes through the nearby fishing villages of Ika and Icici.

RIJEKA: From Opatija it is 10 miles (16 km) to Rijeka, the largest Yugoslavian port, at which all ship, railway, and bus routes leading to this part of the Adriatic coast converge. It has museums, art galleries, theaters, a library, a university, a Benedictine church, and a Croation fortress from the Middle Ages built by the Frankopans, the former ruling family of Croatia.

En Route from Rijeka – From Rijeka to Split, 240 miles (386 km), the coastal highway affords spectacular views of the sea, Kvarner Bay, and various coves, villages, and islands. Most of the islands visible from the coastal road appear barren, inhospitable, and sun scorched; they are rendered infertile by the strong northerly winds that sweep their flanks year-round, spraying them with tiny drops of salt water. However, the protected sides of the islands, not visible from the mainland, are often rich with vegetation and are usually inhabited. At the entrance of the Bay of Bakar is the town of Kraljevica and its early baroque castle. Nearby is the *Uvala Scott* hotel complex and "vacation village."

Krk is the largest island in Kvarner Bay, and the largest in the Adriatic, with sand and pebble beaches, and lush vegetation. Near the *Uvala Scott,* a new bridge connects Krk with the coast. There are ancient forts and medieval castles as well.

Crikvenica, 9 miles (14 km) from Kraljevica, is a famous seaside resort and medical center that uses thalassotherapy — treating ailments ranging from nervous tension to heart disease with sea water. The small resort of Selce is 2 miles (3 km) from Crikvenica; 4 miles (6 km) farther on is Novi Vinodolski, with a sandy beach.

RAB and LOŠINJ: The island of Rab, in Kvarner Bay between Krk and Pag, is one of the sunniest regions in Europe, with abundant foliage and a mild climate. The main town is Rab, which was an ancient Greek and then a Roman settlement; at times it becomes a crowded bathing resort. Four bell towers rise above the town walls. In the town is a 14th-century palace and the 7th-century church of St. John.

Lošinj is farther out in the bay, beyond the island of Cres, and is extraordinarily green but is also crowded at peak times.

PAG: The island of Pag, famous for its fine (and expensive) sheep's-milk cheese, is just as pretty as the more touristy islands, but more rural, and with fewer hotels and facilities. If you don't mind staying in a pension, you can avoid the crowds here.

ZADAR: Zadar is the southernmost point of the Kvarner Bay area. Besides being an ancient place, settled well before the 1st century — with surviving buildings, gates, and other relics of the Roman Empire — Zadar is the center of 20th-century, bustling, hard-and-fast tourism for the northern half of the coast. There's an airport just north of town, rail service toward the east, and ferry and hydrofoil service leading from Zadar to everywhere. It's not a quiet place. There are lots of high-rise hotels, pleasure boats, and populous beaches. There is also a lot of functional activity on the water: Fishing is done with nets from small boats.

If you feel adventurous, hire a water taxi or a fisherman to take you out to one of the uninhabited Kornati islands, which are set aside as a national park, for the day or the week or longer — making sure to make arrangements for being picked up. You might consider renting a boat yourself in town; you can leave your car with the boat rental people. This could be the most exhilarating part of your trip; it's not often in this life you can rule your own island in the sea. If you have a tent, you can camp out on the sand under the stars for as long as you like. The undisturbed sound of lapping waves is good for the spirit. Come with supplies, though; there's no fresh water anywhere. If you prefer to sightsee with a group, there are regular excursions to the islands from Zadar.

Stop by the town's museums and treasuries — it's had an interesting past — and visit the 9th-century church of St. Donat.

En Route from Zadar – About 40 miles (64 km) south of Zadar is Sibenik, founded in the 10th century at the estuary of the Krka River. Take a boat tour of the port; the view of Sibenik's white-domed medieval and Renaissance palaces from the water is grand. You might also take an excursion to Skradin to see the waterfalls of the Krka.

Primosten is 5 miles (8 km) south of Sibenik, a small peninsula town. Lodging is found mainly in private houses, although a new hotel complex is nearby. There is also a nudist beach.

Do not fail to see Trogir, a "museum town" on an island about 20 miles (32 km) before Split. The animals in the carvings and reliefs of the cathedral of St. Lovro are so vivid they look as if they may drool on you at any moment. There is one ancient Roman relief, the Diety and Petronius, and several medieval buildings, including the cathedral, the Lucic Palace, and the Pamfogna Palace.

SPLIT: Split, on the opposite end of the peninsula from Sibenik, is one of the two or three towns on the Adriatic you shouldn't miss. The present administrative center of the region of Dalmatia, it was founded in the 4th century AD by the Roman emperor Diocletian as his retirement home. The titanic palace and enclosed town he had built make up the old quarter of modern Split. The palace has four gates: gold, silver, iron, and bronze. The chambers are so huge that many of them were made into entire houses in later years; the corridors are now streets in the old town. Symphony concerts, opera, dance performances, and plays take place inside the walls, and the palace basement holds several art and historical galleries.

In the town that grew up outside the walls, there is a 16th-century synagogue and cemetery. Although Split is a big industrial center, there are resort areas along the coast just southeast of the city, with hotels, heated swimming pools, and a good supply of places to go. At the western part of town, just past the *Museum of Ivan Mestrovic Sculptures,* is Marjan, a small pine-tree-covered hill that offers one of the most spectacular views of Split.

You can book an excursion from Split to the inland town of Sinj, where the Alka medieval jousting tournament is held every August, featuring knights on horseback.

En Route from Split – Along the coast from Split to Dubrovnik, 134 miles (214 km), is an area of shimmering blue coves, sandy and pebbled beaches sheltered by pine trees, and balmy offshore islands, all overlooked by the 5,000-foot peaks of the coastal mountains; it is known as the Makarska Riviera, and is the most lush and sunny area on the Adriatic. In this Makarska region are the towns of Brela, Baska Voda, Makarska, Tucepi, and Podgora, and the fishing villages of Drasnice, Igrane, Zivogosce, Drvenik, and Zaostrog. Some 90 km (60 miles) before Dubrovnik, the road forks, one branch leading toward Mostar, with its elegant 16th-century stone bridge over the Neretva River. Halfway to Mostar is Medugorje, a pilgrimage destination where the Virgin Mary is said to visit regularly one of the village girls. The place is to be avoided in July and August, when thousands flock here from all over the world.

SOUTHERN ISLANDS: The islands in this southern end of the coast are the main tourist attractions in Yugoslavia. The most popular ones as well as those less traveled are characterized by a consistently warm, sunny climate, good beaches, thick vegetation, and ancient forts and dwellings.

Brac, a popular island, has extensive pine woods in its hills, good for walking. At Bol is the baroque church Gospa od Kamena and a beautiful sandy beach called Zlatni Rat (Golden Cape).

Hvar is a year-round resort that welcomes many tourists. The main town, also called Hvar, has the oldest theater in Europe, built in 1612; performances are still held there. Hvar's hotel managers are so confident of the weather there, they say that from November through March their guests will pay no rent for any day the temperature goes below freezing, or if it snows or fogs over; they allow 50% off if it rains more than 3 hours, providing guests stay at least 7 days.

Korcula claims Marco Polo as a native son. The town of Korcula has its own cathedral, built between the 13th and 16th centuries, which contains paintings by Tintoretto and Bassani.

Mljet is an out-of-the-way spot, very wild and forested, and is considered the most beautiful of these islands. It has two hotels, lots of private houses with rooms for rent, and a national park. Mljet is definitely for the slightly adventurous.

Solta (near Split) is also off the beaten track, and consequently never gets very crowded. There are lots of boarding houses where you can stay and get to know the islanders.

DUBROVNIK: The city of Dubrovnik, the last stop on your trek, looks like the same powerful, grandiose, and magnificent city it was in the 16th century. Formerly the Free Republic of Dubrovnik, it was a center of art and commerce, and gaudy rival to another city-state on the Adriatic, Venice. Now Dubrovnik, preserved in its medieval splendor, is considered the most beautiful city in Yugoslavia.

Seen from above, the roofs of the city make up a sea of red orange tile, dotted with the white domes of a few particularly grand edifices. The buildings are constructed on a huge scale, with rows of pillars and sweeping arches, imperious towers, gorgeous stonework façades, and momentous fortifications bristling with cannons. And, of course, there are fountains, courtyards, gardens, and bell towers. Particularly awesome buildings are the Rector's Palace, Onoofri's Fountain, the cloisters of Franciscan and Dominican monasteries, and the baroque church of St. Vlaho.

The first thing to do when you get into town is to get a view of the whole place — by walking around the city on top of its thick walls, which will take you about 2 hours (it's best to walk in the late afternoon, when the sun is not so strong). You might want to take a cable car tour as well, to see the bright colors of the landscape from above.

Dubrovnik's summer festival, from mid-July to late August, brings in world class performers of symphonic and chamber music, opera, ballet, drama, and folklore to play in the palaces, gardens, and courtyards. Nightlife in Dubrovnik is either bohemian, cosmopolitan, expensive, or, frequently, all three. The city has several superb restaurants (see *Best en Route*) and a gambling casino. The best entertainment in Dubrovnik, however, is a stroll along Stradun (Main St.), in the Old Town. Regardless of the tourists — or the season — inhabitants of all ages take to the street at sundown to greet friends and exchange gossip.

Dubrovnik's 15th-century synagogue, on Zudioska (Jewish) Street, is the third oldest in Europe. The *Maritime Museum* has artifacts and historical background on the city's 16th-century heyday; there tends to be a museum or gallery on just about every corner.

The island of Lokrum is a particularly good (and popular) bathing spot and park just south and east of the town's mainland. If you feel up to it, you can pick your way through the foliage to the Adriatic side of the island for a more private swim. There is a nudist beach on Lokrum known for its friendly atmosphere.

En Route from Dubrovnik – You may feel like going down the coast from Dubrovnik all the way to the Albanian border. Besides stopping along the way at whatever little beach grabs your fancy, we recommend you visit Cavtat, which has ancient Greek and Roman monuments, and one of the swankiest hotels on the coast (there's also a small population of blacks, descendants of slaves who escaped the wreck of a pirate ship in the 18th century); Herceg-Novi, with its lovely flower gardens; Igalo, Yugoslavia's best-known spa; Budva, founded in the 14th century BC, with Greek and Roman monuments and long, sandy beaches (the spa was partially destroyed by a recent earthquake and has yet to be fully reconstructed); Sveti Stefan, a tiny medieval village on an island connected to the mainland by a causeway, converted entirely into expensive deluxe tourist housing; and Ulcinj, with a long and inviting sandy beach. A worthwhile day trip is a visit to the inland site of the Yugoslav partisans' greatest battle, the Valley of Heroes, and also to the virgin forest of Perucica. On the rugged sides of Sutjeska River Canyon, the visitor is awed by the centuries-old, 100-foot-tall pine trees, which seem to grow out of sheer rock at the most inaccessible and windswept heights.

BEST EN ROUTE

Accommodations for two people in an expensive place will cost $100; moderate, $25 to $60; inexpensive, $15 to $25. Restaurants in the expensive category charge $6 to $15 per person for dinner, including wine; meals that cost less than $6 per person are considered moderate.

PORTOROZ

Bernardin Complex – Comprising the *Bernardin,* the *Grand Emona,* and the *Villas Park.* Splashy, angular, modern hotels, embracing a small marina. 66320 Portoroz (phone: 75271). Expensive to moderate.

Rovinj Park – A modern hotel on the port, the *Rovinj Park,* along with its sister hotel on Crveni Otok (Red Island), offers the best accommodations in town (phone: Rovinj Park, 811077; Crveni Otok, 813055). Moderate.

OPATIJA

Kvarner-Amalia – Turn-of-the-century European restaurant, with banquet halls, chandeliers, and flowered terraces facing the sea. Good continental food and entertainment every night. Park 1, Maja 4, 51410 Opatija (phone: 711211). Moderate.

ISLAND OF KRK

Haludovo – A deluxe hotel built as a Mediterranean fishing village with red tile roofs; constructed originally as a playground by *Penthouse* magazine, now open to the public. Malinska, Krk (phone: 885566). Moderate.

SPLIT

Bellevue – This turn-of-the-century establishment is one of the most charming in Split. Although small (just 86 beds), it's centrally located, overlooking the old port and neo-baroque Prokuratives Square, which is popular with evening strollers (phone: 585655). Moderate.

Lav – The name means "lion," and it's the best hotel complex in the Split area, albeit rather ultramodern and concrete. It's 6 miles (9.6 km) south of Diocletian's palace. 58000 Split (phone: 551444). Moderate.

Marjan – Squarish, glass hotel near the city center, overlooking the old port and Diocletian's Palace (phone: 42866). Moderate.

DUBROVNIK

Babin Kuk Holiday Park – This complex contains 4 ultramodern hotels designed by Edward Durrell Stone, the architect of the *Kennedy Center* in Washington, D.C. Every conceivable facility is available; the *Dubrovnik President* is the most elegant. 50001 Dubrovnik (phone: 20265). Expensive.

Croatia – Tucked into the cliffs overlooking the Adriatic in the tiny town of Cavtat, near Dubrovnik. As good as anything in the city. 50210 Cavtat (phone: 78022). Expensive.

Libertas – Multi-tiered modern structure built into the side of a hill on the beach. It overlooks the city ramparts and the sea; has its own pool, sauna, solarium, restaurant, and nightclub. 1 Lavcevicera, 50000 Dubrovnik (phone: 27445). Expensive.

Argentina – With its villas — Sheherezada and Orsula — this hotel has the best view of the old city and the port. 24 Fran Supila (phone: 23855). Expensive to moderate.

Excelsior – On the water, with a good view of the walled city. An old grand dame of a hotel, popular with Americans. 3 Fran Supila, 50000 Dubrovnik (phone: 23566). Moderate.

Konavski Dvori – At Gruda, 22 miles (35 km) east of the old city. Try the freshwater trout or the lamb on the spit (phone: 79039). Moderate.

Madmaison – A French restaurant in an ancient townhouse inside the walled city. 5 Kolorina (phone: 29443). Moderate.

Orsan – Only a 15-minute drive north from Dubrovnik to find what is probably the best restaurant in Yugoslavia in a converted peasant house made of stone. Famous for seafood. 2 T.Kikerja (phone: 89267). Moderate.

Piccolo Mondo – Specializing in local dishes and good seafood, it's conveniently in the center of the Old City. 18 Prijeko (phone: 26015). Moderate.

SVETI STEFAN

Sveti Stefan – A 16th-century fishing village and pirate stronghold turned deluxe hotel. It completely occupies a small island, connected by a causeway to the mainland. All cars are parked on shore. The cottages' exteriors were preserved intact, and given plush, air conditioned innards. 81315 Sveti Stefan (phone: 41005 or 41333). Expensive.

Milocer – The former residence of the Queen of Montenegro, it has a mansion and 6 villas, its own beautiful pebble beach, and mountains and a pine forest as a backdrop. 81315 Sveti Stefan (phone: 41411). Moderate.

Podkoren to Belgrade

This tour of the heartland begins in the Julian Alps, which are shared by Italy, Austria, and Yugoslavia, in the Yugoslav mountain town of Podkoren. Bring your skis or your hiking clothes, and prepare to take in some heavenly Alpine air. You will visit inland natural beauties such as the Martuljk waterfalls, Lake Bled, and the limestone caves at Postojna. Plan to spend some time at Lake Bled for swimming, rowing, fishing, or skating, depending on the season. As the elevation drops, you'll tour the cultural centers of Ljubljana and Zagreb, where we recommend you see what sports the natives are playing and what concerts they're attending — and also, where they've been going to church for the past 700 years or so. There's an optional side trip to the Plitvice Lakes National Park that would add about 160 miles (256 km) to your total; the Plitvice Lakes form a natural staircase of 16 cascading lakes.

A long drive through a forest full of wild animals such as fox, elk, grouse, and wild boar ensues after Zagreb, followed by the green fertile plains. This grain belt of Slavonija is a good place to meet rural people and get a sense of what it's like to live away from the shrillness of cities; it's exhilarating to get attuned to a place where time does not seem manmade.

Belgrade, the capital, is the end of the journey, the city with the most hustle and bustle in Yugoslavia. Here in the center of Yugoslav industry, commerce, and communication, you can get the best possible sense of what Yugoslavia thinks it's about; everything from industrial fairs to film festivals is held in Belgrade; there are Gypsy street-singers in Skadarlija, the bohemian and theater district; buy a souvenir from a sidewalk craftsman.

PODKOREN: Start at the mountain town of Podkoren, near the Austrian border on Route E94, a main tourist road, and drive south through the blue green Julian Alps at 2,700 feet. If you ski, you can stop at the winter resort at Ratece-Planica, where there are ski slopes, five jumps, and lifts; there are several other resorts in the area: Kranjska Gora (one of Yugoslavia's most developed winter sports centers), Mt. Vitranc, and Gozd Martuljk. If you don't know how to downhill ski, this might be a good time to cross-country ski or learn how — it's not hard to pick up, and there can't be many better spots in the world to begin. Near Gozd Martuljk are the huge Martuljk waterfalls at the foot of Mt. Spik, and the Pericnik waterfall at Mojstrana. There are several hiking trails passing through these Slovenian mountains, one extending all the way from the Baltic Sea in northern Europe to Yugoslavia's Adriatic. The water of the nearby Sava River is a brilliant metallic blue, and the air is Alpine-clear.

BLED: The mountain resort of Bled is 25 miles (40 km) in from Podkoren, sitting on Lake Bled in a valley surrounded by the snow-capped Alps. The 11th-century *Castle of the Bishops of Brixen,* overlooking the lake from a sheer cliff, has been converted into a museum and inn. Lake Bled's waters are restricted to bathing and rowing (no motorboats to break the peace), and skating and curling in the winter. In the area are hunting grounds, fishing spots, tennis courts, riding facilities, and Yugoslavia's only 18-hole golf course.

En Route from Bled – A detour of 19 miles (30 km) to the southeast will bring you to Lake Bohinj, another mountain lake area good for skiing and hiking.

LJUBLJANA: About 55 miles (88 km) down from Podkoren is Ljubljana (pronounced *lyoob*-lyana), the capital of the Republic of Slovenia, and the cosmopolitan and economic center of the state as well. Expositions, concerts, festivals, exhibits, and major sporting events (basketball, hockey, soccer, Ping-Pong) all take place here. Ljubljana's museums are particularly worth a look; the *National Museum* is one of the oldest in Europe. The city is also the center of all official and non-official counter-cultures, with unorthodox happenings taking place all year round. The city's architecture spans the 15th to the 20th century, with many baroque buildings and 30-story modern monoliths.

En Route from Ljubljana – Worth a detour is a visit to the Postojna Caves in Postojna, where in towering chambers of limestone, the dripping water has formed shapes in stalactites and stalagmites, more magnificent and improbable than anything in Minimal Art. Take E70 from Ljubljana, it's just a 40-minute drive.

Highway E94 out of Ljubljana passes through woods, with no intersections. At 39 miles (63 km) south of the city is a turnoff for Novo Mesto, on the Krka River, where you can go swimming or trout fishing. Back on the main highway you will reach the 13th-century castle of *Otocec,* on an island in the Krka. Like many Yugoslav monuments, the castle is now a hotel and restaurant.

The mountains give way to hills and wide river valleys between Ljubljana and the next major Yugoslav city, Zagreb, 93 miles (148 km) away. This region has several spas dedicated to treating a wide range of complaints, from neuralgia to heart disease: Dolenjske Toplice, Smarjeske Toplice, and Cateske Toplice are on or near the main highway. Most spas offer the use of their hotels and hot springs to the healthy as well as the sick.

You will cross the Slovenia-Croatia border on E70 about 16 miles (25 km) from the Croatian capital of Zagreb, Yugoslavia's second largest city and its artistic center.

ZAGREB: Zagreb comprises what is now really three cities: the Upper Town (Gornji Grad), the oldest part of Zagreb, with many buildings from the 13th century; the Lower Town (Donji Grad), built at the turn of the 19th century; and New Zagreb (Novi Zagreb), built since World War II, very stark and square, with wide parking lots. The Upper and Lower towns are protected as national monuments. The oldest parts of the city have recently undergone massive restoration; many turn-of-the-century buildings now have a warm, pastel-colored glow.

Zagreb is an important locale on the world cultural circuit: Major opera companies and symphonies play here, and the *International Festival of Contemporary Music* takes place every other year; *I Solisti di Zagreb* is one of the world's foremost chamber groups; every other year Zagreb hosts the *World Festival of Animated Cartoons;* and every July there is the *International Folklore Festival.*

In 1987, Zagreb was enriched by the opening of a world class museum. Housed in a converted 19th-century high school, the museum's 3,750-piece collection was donated by Ante Topic-Mimara, who died a few months before its opening. On view are Byzantine and Russian icons; paintings by Raphael, Michelangelo, El Greco, Velasquez, Murillo, Goya, Rembrandt, Rubens, Renoir, Manet, Degas, and many others; medieval sculptures; one of the world's most important glass-object collections, with items dating from 3000 BC; and an impressive Far East art collection. All in all, the *Mimara Museum* is a small-scale Balkan *Louvre.*

A permanent exhibition of the so-called Hlebine School of Native Painters is mounted at the *Gallery of Primitive Art.* A visit will give you some idea of this movement. And while you're here, check out any of Zagreb's numerous other museums, galleries, and private collections.

Make sure you see the *Croatian National Theater,* at night, if possible, for its sturdy, majestic exterior and beautiful music box interior: plush red seats, inlaid wooden booths, huge fresco ceiling, and splendid chandelier.

Zagreb's churches are well worth a tour: St. Mark's, a 13th-century church, has medieval coats of arms in mosaic on its tile roof; St. Stephen's Cathedral has intricate stonework towers, over 300 feet high, and thick fortifications.

As Yugoslavia's most culturally sophisticated city, Zagreb has the country's most cosmopolitan nightlife; some streets are cobblestone, and the cafés and restaurants have an Old World Austro-Hungarian style.

In the city environs there are more things to do: In the immediate vicinity are enough woods for walking, hunting, and fishing. Marshal Tito's birthplace in Kumrovec, 28 miles (45 km) away, is done up as a museum dedicated to him — it looks rather Early American, with the exposed cross-beamed ceiling and a rough-hewn rocking cradle in the corner.

At Belec, 22 miles (35 km) from the city, is a baroque church decorated inside with carvings and figurines of diabolical inventiveness, with an altar like a three-dimensional Hieronymus Bosch painting.

En Route from Zagreb – If you have the time, it is worth a side trip to the Plitvice Lakes National Park, 80 miles (128 km) south of Zagreb. Take E70 out of the city, and when the road forks at Karlovac — 30 miles (48 km) on — turn due south (towards Tusilovic); the road signs will direct you as you get near. Plitvice Lakes form a natural staircase of 16 blue green lakes, each cascading down into the next in the middle of a virgin forest. There are hotels near the park and quite a few tourists.

It is 240 miles (384 km) from Zagreb to Belgrade on the main highway, which passes through dense forests, on the Slavonian plains, populated principally by elk, grouse, wild boar, and hunters. The Srem plains follows, the most fertile cropland in Yugoslavia. If you're sick of castles by now, you won't find many here — only sugar beets, green hills, and rustic farm folk who might have stepped out of a painting by Pieter Breughel the Elder.

BELGRADE: Belgrade is the capital of Serbia as well as Yugoslavia's capital and largest city (pop. 1.4 million) and its center of commerce and communication. The Celts were the first to settle it in the 4th century BC, building a fortress on the white rocks overlooking the mouth of the rivers Sava and Danube; Belgrade means "White City." The fort of Kalemegdan now stands on that spot, built on the Celtic foundations, but that is nearly all of Belgrade's tumultuous past that remains — the city has been razed to the ground by invaders 36 times since its founding. The last was during World War II, so most of Belgrade was built since then in a bleak, socialist-modern style, although some sections of 19th-century Mittel European grandeur and Turkish exotica did survive.

As the center of government and industry, Belgrade is the site for various business expositions. At various times of year are the 31lon of Automobiles, the Technical Fair, the Fashion Fair, the Book Fair, and numerous others.

International festivals of film, music, and theater are held in Belgrade as well; the tourism offices in Yugoslavia are always happy to supply details.

Belgrade's *National Museum* has a huge collection, and it is definitely worth a trip to see Yugoslavia's crazy-quilt heritage — Illyrian and Celtic tools, Greek and Roman busts, Bulgarian swords, Byzantine and Serbian icons, Turkish jewelry, and works by Serbian and European painters up to the 20th century. There is a *Museum of Modern Art* as well and an *Ethnographical Museum*. At Mt. Avala, 12 miles (20 km) from town, is a monument to the Unknown Soldier by Yugoslavia's best-known sculptor, Ivan Mestrovic.

Visit the 19th-century Bohemian quarter of the city, Skadarlija, when you go to the theater, for a taste of Old World style. There are cafés, Belgrade's best restaurants, cabarets, Gypsy street-singers, open-air theaters, and folk dancing. In the summer the street is lined with food stands and the stalls of artists and craftsmen.

BEST EN ROUTE

Accommodations for two people in an expensive place will run $50 to $100; moderate, $25 to $50; inexpensive, $15 to $25. The restaurants we've listed below are all in the expensive category, by Yugoslav standards — which means $6 to $15 per person for dinner, including wine.

BLED

Villa Bled – The former Alpine retreat of President Tito is now a small luxury hotel. For big spenders and name-droppers who enjoy luxuriating in the living quarters of world leaders (phone: 77222). Expensive.

Grand Hotel Toplice – A beatifically elegant hotel on Lake Bled in the Julian Alps, with crisp mountain air, damask sofas, Persian rugs, and finely tailored guests. You can go swimming, fishing, or hunting nearby. 20 Cesta Svobode, PO Box 41, 64260 Bled (phone: 77222). Moderate.

Blejski Grad – The oldest tavern in the city, with heavy, rustic wooden furnishings. The cooking is Viennese style.

LJUBLJANA

Holiday Inn – Yes, really. In Europe, *Holiday Inns* are fancy places; this is Yugoslavia's first. In the middle of town, with a full-size swimming pool on the roof (phone: 211434). Expensive to moderate.

ZAGREB

Esplanade – An Art Deco masterpiece, with huge rooms, crystal chandeliers, and black marble walls. Good service, and painstaking 19th-century elegance. Though the *Esplanade* rates an "A" by Yugoslav government standards (it has no swimming pool and is somewhat small), it's still considered the best deluxe hotel in the country. 1 Mihanoviceva (phone: 512222 or 435666). Expensive.

Zagreb Inter-Continental – Glassy and modern, with Yugoslav paintings on the walls, the hotel has big rooms, a swimming pool, and a health club, but service is slow and unfriendly. 1 Krsnjavoga (phone: 443411). Expensive.

Drina – Traditional cooking, with dishes not often found in other Zagreb eating places and generous servings. A specialty is Bosnian pot, three kinds of meat stewed with vegetables in an earthenware dish. 11 Preradoviceva (phone: 422654). Moderate to inexpensive.

Gradski Podrum – The name means "the city cellar," and to enter you descend from the street into a large restaurant that preserves its intimacy by the use of partitions. Continental cooking, elegant atmosphere, and crisp service. Next to *Gradska Kavana,* the town's finest 1920s café — a must!

Opera Rooftop – Despite its pretentious interior, the huge sweeping windows give you nice views of the new and old cities. Try the prune-garnished Dalmatian pot roast or the Bosnian stew served in earthenware pots. At the *Zagreb Inter-Continental.*

BELGRADE

Jugoslavija – A deluxe hotel overlooking the Sava River, with 600 ultra-modern rooms and other facilities. 30 Blvd. E. Kradelja (phone: 600222). Expensive to moderate.

Moskva – Considered by some to be Belgrade's best. In the middle of town; has several duplex suites with a common window lighting both levels. 1 Balkanska Br. (phone: 686255). Expensive to moderate.

Belgrade Inter-Continental – Belgrade's newest deluxe hotel, conveniently next to the Sava Convention Center. M. Popovica, 11000 Belgrade (phone: 138708). Moderate.

Tri Sesira – "The Three Hats," in the Bohemian or Skadarlija section. Spicy Serbian food and mellow Gypsy music. Moderate to inexpensive.

Moskva-Caffee – On the ground floor of the *Moskva* hotel, this café is one of the

best places to enjoy an afternoon drink or strong Turkish coffee and people watch.
1 Balkanska Br. Inexpensive.

PLITVICE LAKES

Lika – Tucked away in the park itself. Homemade bread and brandy, local trout and
cheese, and lamb on the spit.

Bitola to Belgrade

This is a short tour of some of Yugoslavia's most famous art treasures, found
in the churches, mosques, monasteries, and excavated towns of Macedonia and
Serbia. This eastern part of the country was ruled, in order, by the Greeks,
Romans, Byzantines, Serbian medieval kings and Turks. The Greeks and Romans contributed marble statues and tile mosaics; the Byzantines and Serbians
covered the walls of their churches with religious frescoes; and the Turks, forbidden to represent life in art, built magnificent mosques and forts decorated
inside with abstract patterns. If you like art, you should visit here, because you
won't see these objects in the original anywhere else — no museum in New
York or Chicago can ever remove or borrow the frescoes of Sopocani, or the
floor from the Imperial Mosque of Pristina, or the mosaic water nymph from
the bath in the Roman town at Gamzigrad. And besides, these objects are in
their original setting, where the original purpose is a little nearer to the
observer's reach than it could be hanging on a wall in a strange city.

Our tour starts at the ruins of the ancient Greek city of Heraclea near Bitola
and finishes at Belgrade, traversing the works of the Byzantine and Turkish
empires en route. Some of the sites are far-flung; monasteries in particular
tend to be secluded; the beautiful lake and mountain settings should make up
for the inconvenience of reaching some of them. All of the sites are well
known and well marked.

July and August are the peak months for folk festivals; ask the government
Tourist Office for a listing for this region if you are interested.

BITOLA: We begin 3 miles (5 km) from the border of Greece, near the Yugoslav
city of Bitola, in the Republic of Macedonia. About 2 miles (3 km) south of town are
the ruins of the ancient Greek city of Heraclea, which was an important commercial
and strategic center linking Constantinople to the Adriatic coast. Particularly beautiful
are the mosaic tile floor in the foundations of the basilica uncovered there and the
life-size marble statues. At the end of July is a folk festival, *St. Elia's Days,* which
features songs and dances from all over Yugoslavia.

En Route from Bitola – Proceed West on E5S, a main tourist highway, toward
Ohrid. About 15 miles (24 km) along this road, take the left-hand turnoff and head
for the church of St. George in Kurbinovo, near the town of Pretor on the eastern
shore of Lake Prespa. The church itself is rather unassuming, but the frescoes
inside, painted in 1191, are striking — take note particularly of the Assumption
and the Annunciation.

OHRID: Go back up to the main highway and continue to Ohrid, the city on the
shores of Lake Ohrid. The church of St. Sophia in Ohrid is the most famous and

sumptuous medieval monument in Macedonia, built in the 11th and 14th centuries. When the Turks moved in, they covered up the church's dramatic frescoes with mortar — since images of life are forbidden in Islam — but these were carefully uncovered in the 1950s. The Ascension is particularly expressive: note the dour, attentive angels in the friezes, crouching in a background of quiet green and blue. Classical music is played here during the *Ohrid Summer Festival.*

There are brilliantly colored frescoes at another Ohrid monument, the church of St. Clement, including an athletic angel in the Annunciation who is about to touch Mary in midstride, as well as a beautiful wooden statue of St. Clement.

En Route from Ohrid – Take a detour south along Lake Ohrid toward St. Naum's monastery on the Albanian border. The lake will be on your right, and a national park on your left. Take the opportunity to go for a swim in the clear waters and a hike in the park. St. Naum's, when you reach it, is extraordinary for its beautiful setting on the lake, and the state of its preservation. Drive the 19 miles (30 km) back north to the main highway and take it all the way to Skopje.

SKOPJE: Skopje, Macedonia's capital, was badly damaged in an earthquake in 1963, so most of its buildings are modern. Ironically, Skopje was founded in 518 by refugees from the ancient town of Scupi (3 miles from modern Skopje), which had just been destroyed by an earthquake; they named the new settlement after their home.

There is much to see, despite both quakes, in Skopje and its environs. A magnificent medieval footbridge spans the Vardar River, and is still very much in use. The great Mustafa-pasha Mosque and the Daut-pasha bath were built in the 15th century by the Turks.

The church of St. Panteleimon in Nerezi (just south of the city) is the place to see, if you see no other church in Macedonia. The fresco of St. Damian, painted in 1164, is remarkable for its somber dignity in color composition and graceful lines. Experts rank the Lamentation, the Nativity, the Visitation, and the Transfiguration as among the finest in Byzantine art.

Marko's Monastery, properly called the church of St. Demetrius (14th century), is just south of Nerezi, and has frescoes of biblical subjects not conventionally treated in ecclesiastical art. A moving example is Rachel's Tears.

En Route from Skopje – Head north on E27 out of Skopje toward Pristina. Just short of Pristina is the monastery at Gracanica (13th to 14th century); the stones making up the structure are red and yellow, giving the effect of gold. The top of the building has rows of ascending arches and towers, gathering to one pinnacle tower on the roof — it is considered the most beautiful early Serbian building anywhere. The frescoes inside are perfectly preserved, displaying in lively fashion the horrors and glories of this world and the next, sort of an illustrated Dante.

The Roman ruins of Ulpiana, near Gracanica, contain mosaics, tombstones, and a basilica.

PRISTINA: Pristina is the capital of the Province of Kosovo (an autonomous province of Serbia), and is a mixture of old Eastern architecture with ultramodern. The most important monument is the Imperial Mosque, built in 1461 by Sultan Mehmet II; there are also several 19th-century Turkish buildings standing in the town. The collection in the *Museum of Kosovo* tells the Oriental history of the town in detail.

NOVI PAZAR: Go northwest out of Pristina on E27 toward Titova Mitrovica, following the road past that town to Novi Pazar. Novi Pazar is also being built up in modern style, but the Alem-Altum Turkish mosque (16th century) is worth seeing.

The real attraction is 10 miles (16 km) west of the town in the hills at Sopocani. The monastery there was built in 1265 by King Uros I to house his own tomb. The frescoes of Sopocani, with those of Nerezi, are said to be the best in Byzantine art. Using yellow, green, violet, and gold leaf (which has by now peeled away), the artist here painted with great feeling the nobility and tragedy of man. See in particular the Dormition of the Virgin and the saints' portraits.

KRALJEVO: Take the highway north out of Novi Pazar to Kraljevo, to see the restored monastery of Zica, painted bright earthen red, as it was in medieval times. Built from 1208 to 1220, it was here at the seat of the archbishopric of Serbia that the medieval Serbian kings were crowned. The remaining frescoes here are few, but of beautiful quality and color, particularly the *Resurrection,* depicting a robed angel seated at the side of the open tomb. ·

At Visegrad, 100 miles (160 km) east of Kraljevo on the river Drina, you will come upon Yugoslavia's oldest bridge. Built of stone by the Turks in 1571, this graceful, historic span connects Belgrade and Dubrovnik and inspired Yugoslavia's only Nobel Prize winner for literature, Ivo Andric, to write an epic novel about it — *The Bridge on the Drina.*

The Kalenic Monastery near Kraljevo is constructed with graceful and detailed relief in its arches; its architecture is among the best in the Serbian style.

En Route from Kraljevo – Get on the highway east for a final stop before Belgrade. About 22 miles (35 km) after the town of Krusevac, after the highway has turned north and converged with the highway from Nis, take an eastward turnoff (toward Romania) and drive until you get to the town of Zajecar, just shy of the Bulgarian border. Near town are the excavations of the late Roman fortress of Gamzigrad (3rd and 4th centuries). There you will find the palace ruins, a huge Roman bath, and mosaics with a grace, sumptuousness, and eroticism that will refresh you.

Gaze at the splendid city gates of Gamzigrad, which no longer keep anyone in or out; whenever you feel ready, get back on the highway west toward Paracin and the Danube, and turn north to Belgrade and civilization, where the Gamzigrads of the future wait their turn.

BEST EN ROUTE

OHRID

Accommodations for two people in a moderate hotel will cost $30 to $45. The restaurant listed below is in the expensive category, by Yugoslav standards — which means $6 to $15 for dinner, including wine.

Desaret – A new hotel on Lake Ohrid, with a wooden Macedonian-style exterior — which might look Scandinavian to Western eyes (phone: 24040).

Inex Gorica – This modern hotel has the region's best restaurant, which serves Ohrid trout — found only in Lake Ohrid (phone:22020).

Index